D0459166

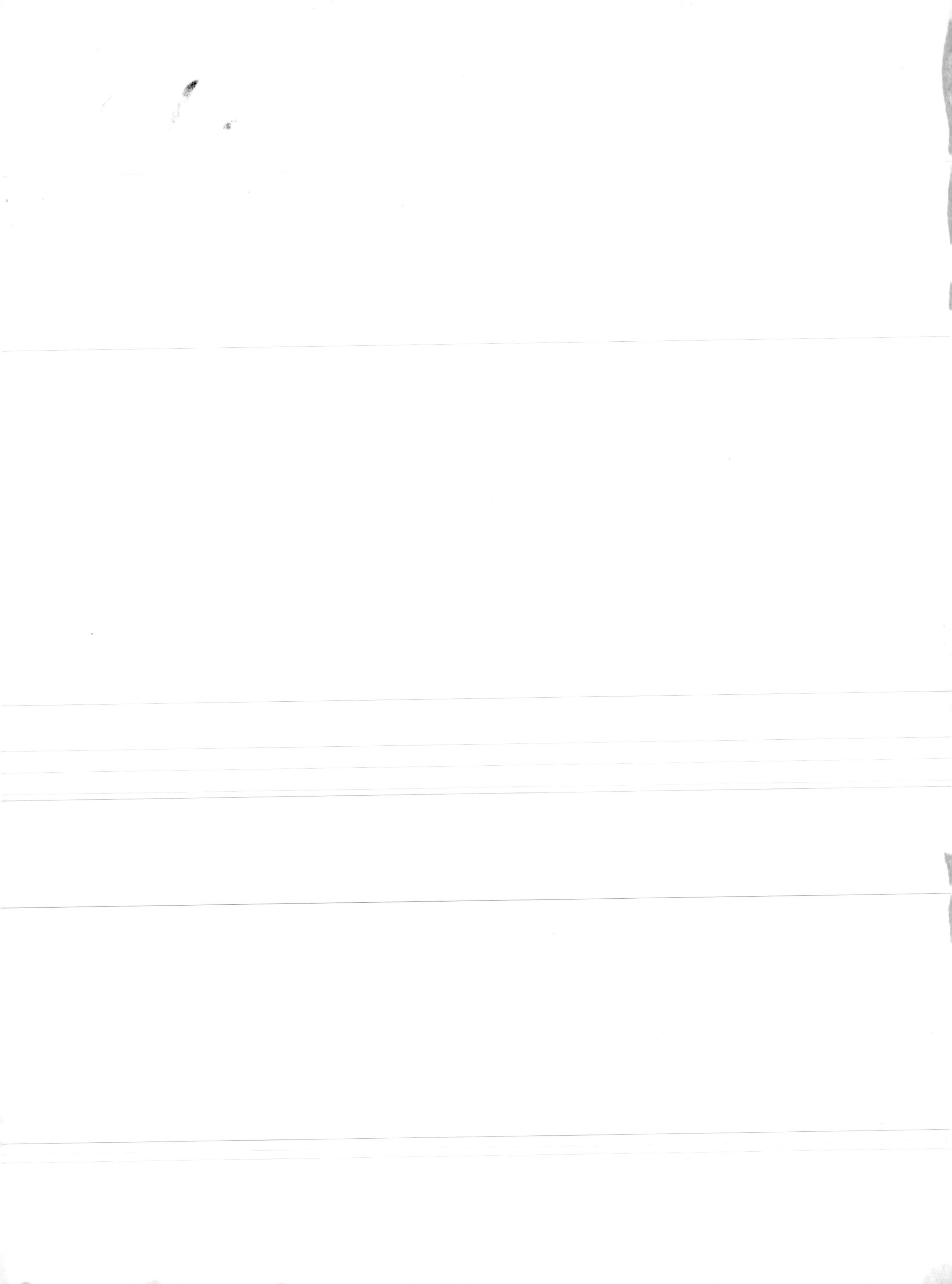

2014
CHASE'S
Calendar of Events

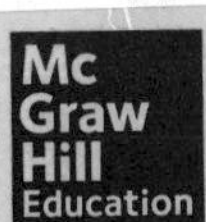

New York Chicago San Francisco Athens London Madrid
Mexico City Milan New Delhi Singapore Sydney Toronto

1 2 3 4 5 6 7 8 9 10 11 12 13 14 15 RHR/RHR 1 0 9 8 7 6 5 4 3

ISBN 978-0-07-182950-2 (book and CD set)
MHID 0-07-182950-4 (book and CD set)

ISBN 978-0-07-183150-5 (book for set)
MHID 0-07-183150-9 (book for set)

e-ISBN 978-0-07-183091-1
e-MHID 0-07-183091-X

ISSN 0740-5286

NOTICE
Events listed herein are not necessarily endorsed by the editors or publisher. Every effort has been made to assure the correctness of all entries, but neither the editors nor the publisher can warrant their accuracy. IT IS IMPERATIVE, IF FINANCIAL PLANS ARE TO BE MADE IN CONNECTION WITH THE DATES OR EVENTS LISTED HEREIN, THAT PRINCIPALS BE CONSULTED FOR FINAL INFORMATION.

About the CD-ROM:
Compatible with PCs running Windows XP and higher
Compatible with MACs OSX 10.7 and higher

This CD-ROM is intended for a single user on a stand-alone computer.
For questions regarding the operation of the CD-ROM please visit
http://www.mhprofessional.com/techsupport/.

This book is printed on acid-free paper.

✦ Contents ✦

✦ Introduction ✦

Welcome to *Chase's Calendar of Events 2014*, the 57th edition of this publication. Within this book are more than 12,500 entries in a range of subject areas—plus exhaustive appendices. All entries are updated and thoroughly fact-checked, making *Chase's* the most respected and comprehensive reference available on holidays, events and anniversaries and special days, weeks and months.

What's New in 2014

2014 ushers in many unique special events and milestone anniversaries—many of which are described more fully in the "Spotlight" section. The United Nations has designated three special-year observances for 2014: International Year of Small Island Developing States, International Year of Family Farming and International Year of Crystallography. In 2014 the people of Scotland will hold a referendum on independence.

2014 is a banner year for sports fans: Games of the XXII Winter Olympiad take place in Sochi, Russia, while the FIFA World Cup takes place in Brazil. Quadrennial and biennial sporting events include the 17th Asian Games, Commonwealth Games, Gay Games 9, Curtis Cup and Ryder Cup.

Anniversaries of note include the 100th and 75th anniversaries of World War I and World War II, respectively. The Panama Canal opened 100 years ago. The Beatles startled the world 50 years ago, while the US saw the passage of the Civil Rights Act of 1964. The 45th anniversary of the moon landing also occurs in 2014.

Among the notable people enjoying a significant birth anniversary are William Shakespeare and Galileo (450), George Washington Carver and Henri de Toulouse-Lautrec (150), Jawaharlal Nehru and Charlie Chaplin (125), Jonas Salk (100), Joe Louis (100), Dylan Thomas (100), Ernest Tubb (100), Sun Ra (100), Joe DiMaggio (100), Sammy Baugh (100) and the creators of Superman: Joe Shuster and Jerry Siegel (both 100). And many, many more!

Types of Entries in *Chase's Calendar of Events*

Astronomical Phenomena

Information about eclipses, equinoxes and solstices, moon phases and other astronomical phenomena is calculated from data prepared by the US Naval Observatory's Nautical Almanac Office and Her Majesty's Nautical Almanac Office. **In *Chase's*, universal time has been converted to eastern time.**

Religious Observances

Principal observances of the Christian, Jewish, Muslim and Baha'i faiths are presented with background information from their respective calendars. We include anticipated dates for Muslim holidays. When known, religious events of China, Japan and India are also listed. There is no single Hindu calendar and different sects define the Hindu lunar month differently. There is no single lunar calendar that serves as a model for all Buddhists, either. Therefore, we are not able to provide the dates of many religious holidays for these faiths.

National and International Observances and Civic Holidays

Chase's features independence days, national days and public holidays from around the world. Technically, there are no national holidays in the United States: holidays proclaimed by the president apply only to federal employees and to the District of Columbia. State governors proclaim holidays for their states. In practice, federal holidays usually are proclaimed by governors as well. Some governors proclaim commemorative days that are unique to their state.

Special Days, Weeks and Months

Whether it's Black History Month, National Police Week or National Grandparents' Day, the annual calendar has myriad special days, weeks and months—and *Chase's* has the most comprehensive listing of them. Until January 1995, Congress had been active in seeing that special observances were commemorated. Members of the Senate and House could introduce legislation for a special observance to commemorate people, events and other activities they thought worthy of national recognition. Because these bills took up a disproportionate amount of time on the part of congressmen and their staffs, Congress decided to discontinue this process in January 1995 when it reviewed and reformed its rules and practices. From time to time Congress does still issue commemorative resolutions, which do not have the force of law. The president of the US has the authority to declare any commemorative event by proclamation, but this is done infrequently. (Some state legislatures and governors proclaim special days, as do mayors of cities.)

So where do all these special days, weeks and months come from? The majority come from national organizations that use their observances for public outreach and to plan specific events. For special months regarding health issues, for example, you can expect to see more information disseminated, special commemorative walks and medical screenings during that month. The *Chase's* editorial staff includes a special day, week or month in the annual reference based on the authority of the organization observing it, how many years it has been observed, the amount of promotion and activities that are a part of it, its uniqueness and a variety of other factors. (We've included a list of 2014 special months in our appendix section.)

Presidential Proclamations

As we noted above, the president has the authority to declare any commemorative event by proclamation. A good number of these will be proclamations for which there has been legislation giving continuing authority for a proclamation to be issued each year. Mother's Day, for example, has been proclaimed since 1914 by public resolution. The White House Clerk's Office initiates the issuing of these proclamations each year, since they are mandated by authorizing legislation. Of course, there will be new ones: Patriot Day (created in the wake of the Sept 11, 2001, terrorist attacks) is a recent example. In *Chase's* we list proclamations that have continuing authority and those that have been issued consistently since 2002 in the main calendar of the book. In our text, ✦ indicates a presidential proclamation. In our appendix, we also offer a complete list of proclamations issued from Jan 1, 2012, to June 30, 2013.

Events and Festivals

Chase's includes national and international special events and festivals—defined again by their uniqueness and their finite brief length of time. Sporting events; book, film, food and other festivals; seasonal celebrations; folkloric events (Groundhog Day, for example); music outings and more make up these types of entries. And these entries are usually sponsored: they have contact information for the general public and all information in the entry comes from the sponsor (see below on sponsored events).

Anniversaries

Anniversaries include historic (creation of states, battles, inventions, publications of note, popular culture events and so on) and biographical (birth or death anniversaries of notable personages) milestones.

Birthdays Today

Living celebrities in politics, the arts, sports and popular culture are included in "Birthdays Today" following each calendar day. If there is a question about the birth day or year, this is noted. **Be aware that the US governors and senators listed are current as of July 2013; November 2013 elections are not reflected.**

Spotlight

The tinted pages starting off *Chase's Calendar of Events* form the "Spotlight" section. In a book as packed as *Chase's*, the reader may need a little help picking out significant anniversaries and events for the current year, and Spotlight is the answer to that need. We cover significant 2014 historical and birth anniversaries as well as major events.

New Style Versus Old Style Dates

Please note: dates for historic events can be assumed to be Gregorian calendar (New Style) dates unless "(OS)" appears after the date. This annotation means that the date in question is an Old Style, or Julian calendar, date. Most of America's founders were born before 1752, when Great Britain and its colonies adopted the Gregorian calendar. As an example of this, we list George Washington's birthday as Feb 22, 1732, the Gregorian or New Style date. However, when he was born Great Britain and its colonies began the year on Mar 25, not Jan 1, so his Julian birthdate was Feb 11, 1731.

About Sponsored Events

Events for which there is individual or organizational sponsorship are listed with the name of the event, inclusive dates of observance, a brief description, estimated attendance figures and the sponsor's name and contact information. We obtain information for these events directly from the sponsors. There is no fee to be listed in *Chase's* and sponsors submit events to be chosen at the discretion of the *Chase's* editors. Neither the editors nor the publisher necessarily endorse these events.

About the CD-ROM

For both Mac and Windows users, this CD-ROM includes all of the January through December birthday and event information for 2014. It provides users a quick way to conduct simple or sophisticated searches—either of a single topic or in combined areas. Search by country, US state, attendance, keyword, type of event and much more. Installation instructions are included on the disk.

Acknowledgments

A book the size of *Chase's* comes about through the care and attention of many organizations and people. The editors and publisher would like to thank the event sponsors; CVBs; chambers of commerce; tourism agencies; nonprofit organizations; publicists; festival organizers; historians; museum directors; librarians; National Park Service employees; embassy staffs; national, state and local government officials and many others who help us put together this reference every year.

We especially wish to thank Bill Chase and his family for their ongoing support of and inspiration for the book. Bill Chase continues to be the champion of the unique passion and pastime of creating holidays and his editorial advice and input are greatly appreciated.

Many talented writers and researchers helped us create *Chase's 2014*. Sandy Whiteley and Johnny Loftus wrote the Spotlight on the Past. Rob Walton penned the histories of the Panama Canal, the "Star-Spangled Banner," George Washington Carver and Joe Louis, Mother's Day, the two World Wars and the Civil Rights Act of 1964. Madeleine Super captured the drama of William Shakespeare and the Storming of the Bastille while Johnny Loftus looked at the phenomenon of Beatlemania in 1964. Sandy Whiteley celebrated the 150th statehood anniversary of Nevada. Loretta Ullrich-Ferguson, Madeleine Super and Johnny Loftus helped us bring scores of famous people to life in Spotlight on People.

We wish to thank James Foster for research, fact checking and writing many new events in the main book, and Charmin White for research and event sponsor outreach. MPS was great to work with as they created our CD-ROM. Steve Straus and Denise Duffy-Fieldman are always there for us. And Patrick Geiger of Interactive Works has been a valuable consultant.

Finally, special thanks to our editorial and production colleagues at McGraw-Hill Professional, a division of McGraw-Hill Education: Handel Low, Joanne Lee, Gigi Grajdura, Julia Anderson Bauer, Tama Harris, Barbara Holton, Arvydas Valiukenas, Lyzette Austen, Leola Grant-Tucker and publisher Christopher Brown.

Holly McGuire, *Editor in Chief*
Kathryn Keil, *Editor*

Spotlight on the Past

1864

150 YEARS AGO

Landmark World Events

Apr The Waikato War, waged by the Maori chief Wiremu Kingi against the colonial government of New Zealand, ended, but other Maori/Colonial conflicts would start again and last until 1872.

May 28 Backed by Napoleon III, Maximilian of Hapsburg landed at Veracruz to take the throne of Mexico. Benito Juárez—forced out of Mexico City in 1863—ran his government-in-exile from present-day Ciudad Juárez and Chihuahua City.

June 30 Great Britain's Parliament passed the "Chimney Sweepers Regulation Act," a tougher piece of legislation (amending an ineffective 1840 one) levying heavy fines to any business employing "climbing boys"—children or teens.

Aug 22 The First Geneva Convention on War (Convention for the Amelioration of the Wounded in Time of War) was ratified by 12 European nations. This multinational conference was instigated by Henri Dunant of the Red Cross after witnessing the suffering and neglect of 40,000 wounded soldiers after the Battle of Solferino in 1859.

Sept 1–9 Charlottetown Conference held at Prince Edward Island debated the unification of Canada. The Dominion of Canada, made up of Ontario, Quebec, Nova Scotia and New Brunswick, would be formed in 1867.

Nov 20 Czar Alexander II of Russia instituted statutes allowing for the creation of *zemstvo*, or local self-government.

▪ Russia succeeded in defeating the people of Circassia to finally force the creation of a Russian province. The Circassians were decimated by resistance, and the surviving population fled their land in the Caucasus region.

Landmark US Events

Jan–Mar Pro-Union governments were restored in Arkansas, Tennessee and Louisiana as areas of these states were captured by Union forces.

Jan 11 Senator John B. Henderson of Missouri proposed a resolution in the Senate abolishing slavery by an amendment to the Constitution. The 13th Amendment would be passed the next year.

Feb President Abraham Lincoln ordered that 500,000 men be drafted in March, to serve for three years or the duration of the war.

Feb 27 Union prisoners of war began arriving at a Confederate camp later to be known as Andersonville.

Mar 9 Ulysses S. Grant was commissioned commander of all Union armies, about 600,000 men in all.

Apr 8 President Lincoln signed a charter authorizing the Columbia Institution (now Gallaudet University) to grant college degrees to deaf students.

Apr 22 By an act of Congress, "In God We Trust" began to be stamped on one- and two-cent US coins.

Apr 27 General Grant issued orders to Sherman to march through Georgia, to Sigel to move through the Shenandoah Valley, to Butler to advance up the James River toward Richmond and to Meade to engage the Army of Northern Virginia under Robert E. Lee. While initially unsuccessful, these orders would lead to the end of the Civil War.

May 4 The House of Representatives passed the Wade-Davis Reconstruction Bill, containing stiff punitive measures against the South. Lincoln killed the bill by using the pocket veto.

May 5–7 Battle of the Wilderness was the first encounter between troops under Robert E. Lee and Ulysses S. Grant. Both sides suffered heavy casualties but the outcome was inconclusive.

May 8–19 Battle of Spotsylvania was the next encounter between Lee and Grant. Lee ordered his troops to fall back during the night.

June 19 The Confederate raider CSS *Alabama* was sunk off the coast of France by the USS *Kearsarge*. Raphael Semmes, the captain of the *Alabama*, had sunk 82 federal merchant ships.

❧ ❧ ❧

June 28 Lincoln signed a bill repealing the fugitive slave acts.

July 30 After failing to defeat Confederate forces at Petersburg, VA—which was just a few miles from Richmond—Grant's troops prepared for a siege of the city. Petersburg and Richmond would not fall until the next year.

Aug 5 At the Battle of Mobile Bay, Union Admiral David Farragut famously said, "Damn the torpedoes! Full speed ahead." With the fall of Mobile, the Confederacy no longer had access to the Gulf of Mexico.

Sept 2 Atlanta, GA, fell to the Union Army led by General William Tecumseh Sherman. It became a virtual military camp.

Oct 19 CSS *Shenandoah* was commissioned by the Confederacy. It would essentially destroy the New England whaling fleet.

Oct 20 Lincoln proclaimed the last Thursday in November to be a day of thanksgiving.

Oct 31 Nevada entered the Union as the 36th state. See "Spotlight on American Anniversaries."

Nov 8 Lincoln was elected to a second term as president, defeating Democratic candidate George B. McClellan. Lincoln won 55 percent of the vote.

Nov 15 Sherman left Atlanta—most of it destroyed by fire—and began his infamous and destructive "March to the Sea" with 60,000 troops.

Nov 29 In the Colorado Territory, US troops killed hundreds (estimates vary between 200 and 500) of Arapaho and Cheyenne men, women and children in the massacre at Sand Creek.

"War Is Cruelty"

On Sept 11, 1864, Atlanta mayor James M. Calhoun wrote occupying Union general William Sherman, begging him to reconsider forcing Atlanta citizens to leave their city. General Sherman's response on Sept 12 has become famous as an explanation of his March to the Sea's tactics:

> We must have peace, not only at Atlanta but in all America. To secure this we must stop the war that now desolates our once happy and favored country. To stop war we must defeat the rebel armies that are arrayed against the laws and Constitution, which all must respect and obey. To defeat these armies we must prepare the way to reach them in their recesses provided with the arms and instruments which enable us to accomplish our purpose. Now, I know the vindictive nature of our enemy, and that we may have many years of military operations from this quarter, and therefore deem it wise and prudent to prepare in time. . . . You cannot qualify war in harsher terms than I will. War is cruelty and you cannot refine it, and those who brought war into our country deserve all the curses and maledictions a people can pour out. . . . You might as well appeal against the thunder-storm as against these terrible hardships of war.

Dec 6 Salmon P. Chase was named Chief Justice of the Supreme Court, replacing the recently deceased Roger Taney.

Dec 16 Union troops defeated Confederate forces at Nashville, effectively knocking the Army of Tennessee out of the war.

Dec 21 The Confederates abandoned Savannah, leaving the city to Sherman, who had now completed his March to the Sea. The March to the Sea left a 50-mile wide, 200-mile long area of destruction, part of Sherman's plan to cripple the Confederacy's ability to make war.

- Swarthmore College was founded.
- University of Denver founded (as The Colorado Seminary).

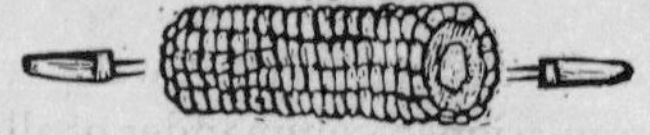

Culture

Literary Arts

Fiction

- *Notes from the Underground*, Fyodor Dostoevsky
- *Our Mutual Friend*, by Charles Dickens, began to be published in installments.
- *Journey to the Center of the Earth*, Jules Verne
- *The Small House at Allington*, by Anthony Trollope, part of his Chronicles of Barsetshire

Nonfiction

- *Fireside Travels*, James Russell Lowell
- *The Maine Woods*, Henry Thoreau (published posthumously)
- *Apologia Pro Vita Sua*, Cardinal John Henry Newman
- *Genius and Madness*, Cesare Lombroso

Poetry

- *Enoch Arden*, Alfred, Lord Tennyson
- *Dramatis Personae*, Robert Browning
- *In War Time*, John Greenleaf Whittier

Journalism

- The first black daily newspaper, *The New Orleans Tribune*, was published.

Theater and Opera

Nov Brothers Junius Brutus Booth, Edwin Booth and John Wilkes Booth staged a benefit performance of *Julius Caesar* at the Winter Garden Theater to raise funds for a statue of Shakespeare in Central Park. Four months later, John Wilkes Booth would assassinate Lincoln.

- *David Garrick*, Thomas William Robertson
- *La Belle Helene*, an opera by Jacques Offenbach, premiered in Paris.

Music

- *Piano Quintet–String Sextet No. 2*, Johannes Brahms
- *Symphony in C minor*, Edvard Grieg
- *Symphony in D Minor*, Anton Bruckner

Popular Songs

- "Sherman's March to the Sea," S.H.M. Byers
- "Beautiful Dreamer," Stephen Foster
- "O Where, O Where Has My Little Dog Gone," Septimus Winner
- "He Leadeth Me," hymn by William B. Bradbury

Art

- *Man with the Broken Nose*, Auguste Rodin
- *Battle of the* Kearsarge *and the* Alabama, Édouard Manet
- *Homage to Delacroix*, Henri Fantin-Latour
- *Symphony in White, No. 2*, James McNeill Whistler
- Yale University Fine Arts Department founded, first in the United States.

Science and Technology

- John Herschel published *General Catalog of Nebulae and Clusters of Stars.*
- Felix Hoppe-Seyler named the colorless part of blood *globin*; hence, *hemoglobin.*

Commerce and New Products

- Northern Pacific Railroad was chartered to build a transcontinental railroad from Lake Superior to the Pacific Ocean, travelling along the northern areas of the Northwest from what is now Duluth and St. Paul, MN, to Tacoma, WA.
- A group of Chicago businessmen founded the Elgin National Watch Company at Elgin, IL.
- Printer R.R. Donnelley was founded.
- Clark Thread Co. was founded at East Newark, NJ. Later merged with Coats to form Coats and Clark.

Sports

Baseball

- The Brooklyn Atlantics won the national championship.

Golf

- Tom Morris Sr. won the British Open.

Horse Racing

- The first run of the Travers Stakes thoroughbred race occurred at Saratoga, NY.

Track

- Track teams from Oxford and Cambridge Universities met in the first intercollegiate track meet. The teams contested eight events.

1864 Deaths

- George Boole, English mathematician, inventor of prototype of Boolean logic
- John Clare, English poet
- George Mifflin Dallas, 11th vice president of the United States
- Stephen Foster, American songwriter of nearly 200 songs, including "Oh, Susanna" and "Camptown Races"
- Nathaniel Hawthorne, author of *The Scarlet Letter* and *The House of Seven Gables*
- J.E.B. Stuart, Confederate Cavalry general
- Roger B. Taney, fifth chief justice of the Supreme Court, most remembered for the Dred Scott decision

1914

100 YEARS AGO

Landmark World Events

June 28 World War I began with the assassination in Sarajevo of Archduke Franz Ferdinand, heir to the throne of the Austro-Hungarian Empire. Within weeks, Germany entered the war on the side of Austria-Hungary, and Russia, France and Great Britain entered on the side of Serbia. The conflict was known as the Great War or the European War until WW II. The United States would not enter the war until 1917. See "Spotlight on World Anniversaries."

July Mohandas Gandhi left South Africa after living there for 21 years. He had worked on behalf of the rights of South Africa's Asian population, using passive resistance for the first time. After six months in England, he sailed to India, arriving there in January 1915.

July 15 Mexico's president Victoriano Huerta, who had overthrown the government of Francisco Madero and had Madero assassinated in 1913, resigned his office and went into exile.

Aug 15 After 10 years of construction, the Panama Canal opened for operation. Building the 48-mile canal cost 5,600 lives during the US phase of the project. The canal cut the sailing distance from the East Coast to the West Coast by 8,000 miles. See "Spotlight on World Anniversaries."

Aug 23 Japan declared war on Germany and Austria-Hungary.

Sept 5–12 At the first Battle of the Marne in France, the Allies halted the German advance on Paris and four years of trench warfare began.

Oct 19–Nov 22 At the First Battle of Ypres in Belgium, the German push to the Channel ports was halted. There was now a static western front that would not move more than 10 miles for the duration of WWI.

Oct 28 Turkey entered the war on the side of Germany.

Dec 18 Britain declared a protectorate over Egypt.

- Russia renamed St. Petersburg, its 211-year-old capital, Petrograd because the original name sounded German.

- The Nobel Peace Prize was not awarded.

- The passenger pigeon became extinct as the last known bird died at the Cincinnati Zoo in the United States.

Landmark US Events

Jan 5 Henry Ford announced that all worthy Ford Motor Company employees would receive a minimum wage of $5 a day.

Apr 20 Miners struggling for recognition of the United Mine Workers Union in Ludlow, CO, were attacked by National Guard troops. Seven adults and 11 children were killed.

Apr 21 US forces occupied Veracruz, Mexico, for six months starting this day after skirmishes between US sailors and Mexican federal soldiers at Tampico earlier in the month. Relations between the two nations were severely strained.

May 8 The Smith-Lever Act passed, creating the system of agricultural extension agents sponsored by state agricultural colleges. It also created the national 4–H program.

May 8 A joint resolution of Congress designated the second Sunday in May as Mother's Day. See "Spotlight on American Anniversaries."

Aug 4 President Woodrow Wilson issued a Proclamation of Neutrality, saying the United States would remain neutral with respect to the war raging in Europe.

Sept 7 The New York Post Office on Eighth Avenue opened, with the inscription from Herodotus over the door: "Neither snow nor rain nor heat nor gloom of night stays these couriers from the swift completion of their appointed rounds."

Sept 17 Veterans of Foreign Wars was created through a merger of American Veterans of Foreign Service (from the Spanish American War) and National Society of the Army of the Philippines.

Sept 26 Federal Trade Commission established.

- Fifty-five African Americans were lynched over the course of 1914.

- Cleveland, OH, set up the world's first red–green traffic lights.

Culture

Literary Arts

- The Nobel Prize for Literature was not awarded.

Fiction

- *Dubliners*, James Joyce
- *Tarzan of the Apes*, Edgar R. Burroughs
- *Penrod*, Booth Tarkington
- *The Titan*, Theodore Dreiser

Nonfiction

- *Our Knowledge of the External World*, Bertrand Russell
- *Drift and Mastery*, Walter Lippmann
- *The Courtship Habits of the Great Crested Grebe*, Julian Huxley

Poetry

- *North of Boston*, Robert Frost
- *The Congo and Other Poems*, Vachel Lindsay
- "Chicago," Carl Sandburg

Children's Literature

- *Tik-Tok of Oz*, L. Frank Baum

Journalism

- *The New Republic* was first published.

Theater and Opera

- *On Trial*, Elmer Rice
- *Pygmalion*, by George Bernard Shaw, opened in London.
- *Le Rossignol*, opera by Igor Stravinsky
- *The Midnight Girl*, operetta by Sigmund Romberg
- *Watch Your Step*, with music by Irving Berlin and with dancers Vernon and Irene Castle doing the Castle Walk
- *Hello, Broadway!*, George M. Cohan
- *The Debutante*, musical comedy by Victor Herbert

Film

- *Making a Living*, Charlie Chaplin's first film
- In *Kid Auto Races at Venice*, Chaplin debuted a new character, the Tramp.
- *Tillie's Punctured Romance*, directed by Mack Sennett (his first feature-length film) and starring Charlie Chaplin, Marie Dressler and the Keystone Kops
- Gloria Swanson, Rudolph Valentino, John and Ethel Barrymore and Oliver Hardy all made their screen debuts in 1914.

Music

- The American Society of Composers, Authors and Publishers (ASCAP) was founded to protect performing rights and distribute fees to members.
- *Piano Trio in A Minor*, Maurice Ravel
- *A London Symphony*, by Ralph Vaughan Williams, premiered in London.

Popular Songs

- "Colonel Bogey March," Kenneth J. Alford
- "Columbia's Pride March," John Philip Sousa
- "By the Beautiful Sea," Harold Atteridge and H. Carroll
- "The Minstrel Parade," Irving Berlin
- "St. Louis Blues," W.C. Handy
- "Chevy Chase Rag," Eubie Blake
- "Soda Fountain Rag," Duke Ellington, his first composition

Art

- *Violin, Mandolin* and *Man with Guitar*, George Braque
- *Gare Montparnasse*, Giorgio de Chirico
- *The Tavern*, Pablo Picasso
- *Backyards, Greenwich Village*, John Sloan
- *Sunset*, John Marin
- *The Spirit of Life*, sculpture by Daniel Chester French

Science and Technology

- Robert Goddard received two patents for rocket design.
- Edward Calvin Kendall isolated thyroxine from the thyroid gland.
- The Nobel Prize in Chemistry was awarded to Theodore W. Richards for his determination of the atomic weights of a large number of elements. He was the first American to win the chemistry Nobel.
- The Nobel Prize in Physics was won by German Max von Laue for his discovery of the diffraction of X-rays by crystals.
- The Nobel Prize in Physiology and Medicine went to Austro-Hungarian Robert Barany for his work on the physiology and pathology of the vestibular apparatus of the ear.

Commerce and New Products

- US auto production reached 500,000 cars, with Ford making 300,000 of them.
- Large Dodge Brothers factory was built at Hamtramck, MI, to build all-steel-bodied cars.
- Gulf Oil distributed the first road maps.
- Precursor of Greyhound Bus Lines founded.
- Monsanto Chemical Co. started making carbolic disinfectant since German and English imports were cut off by the war.
- Clarence Birdseye introduced frozen fish.
- Doublemint Gum introduced by Wrigley.
- Elastic brassiere patented by NY debutante Mary Phelps Jacob.
- Merrill Lynch & Co. founded.
- Booz Allen Hamilton consulting firm founded.

Sports

Auto Racing

- The Indianapolis 500 was won by René Thomas driving a Delage at 82.5 mph.

Baseball

Apr 13 The Federal League opened its first season, challenging the American and National Leagues and accusing them of monopolistic practices. The league lasted only two years.

Apr 22 Babe Ruth made his pitching debut, playing for the minor league Baltimore Orioles. He shut out the Buffalo Bisons, 6–0.

June 9 Pittsburgh Pirates shortstop Honus Wagner got his 3,000th hit. He finished his career in 1917 with 3,420 hits.

July 11 Babe Ruth made his debut in the major leagues, pitching for the Boston Red Sox.

Sept 5 Babe Ruth hit his first home run as a pro, playing for Providence, a minor league affiliate of the Boston Red Sox.

Sept 27 Napoleon Lajoie of the Cleveland Indians made the 3,000th hit of his career. He finished his career with 3,242 hits.

Oct 9–13 The Boston Braves beat the Philadelphia Athletics 4–0 in the World Series.

- Wrigley Field in Chicago opened with the name Weeghman Park.

Basketball

- There was no national collegiate basketball championship, but the Helms Athletic Foundation named Wisconsin, with its 15–0 season, national champions retroactively.

Boxing

June 27 Jack Johnson, 36 years old, retained his world heavyweight title, defeating Frank Moran at the Velodrome d'Hiver in Paris, France. (Neither boxer was able to collect their purses due to the outbreak of WWI.)

Football

- The University of Illinois football team was national collegiate champion.

Golf

- Walter Hagen won the US Open at age 21 and began a great golfing career.
- The US Amateur was won by Francis Ouimet.
- The British Open was won by Harry Vardon.

Hockey

Mar The Stanley Cup was won by the Toronto Blue Shirts, who defeated the Victoria Aristocrats.

Horse Racing

- The Kentucky Derby was won by Old Rosebud.
- The Preakness Stakes was won by Holiday.
- The Belmont Stakes was won by Luke McLuke.

Soccer

Apr 25 Burnley defeated Liverpool 1–0 to take the FA Cup.

- In English league play, the Blackburn Rovers won the league with Aston Villa coming in second.

Tennis

- The Wimbledon men's singles was won by Norman Brooke.
- The Wimbledon women's singles was won by Dorothea Douglass Lambert-Chambers.
- The American men's singles was won by Richard Norris Williams.
- Mary Browne won the American women's singles.

Miscellaneous

Mar 20 The first world's figure skating championships opened in New Haven, CT. Events included men's and women's single, pairs, and waltzing, later known as ice dancing.

July 4 The Harvard University second crew became the first American team to win the top event at the Henley Regatta in England.

1914 Deaths

- John Muir, Scottish-American naturalist, explorer and conservationist
- Pope Pius X
- Jacob Riis, American social reformer
- Richard Warren Sears, founder, with Alvah C. Roebuck, of the huge retail and mail-order firm Sears, Roebuck and Co.
- Adlai E. Stevenson, 23rd vice president of the US and grandfather of Adlai E. Stevenson, candidate for president in 1952 and 1956
- James Sullivan, amateur sports promoter and founder of the Amateur Athletic Union
- John Tenniel, British illustrator and cartoonist
- George Westinghouse, engineer and inventor of the air brake for trains
- Ellen Wilson, first wife of Woodrow Wilson
- Joseph Wilson Swan, British scientist and inventor of the incandescent light bulb

1939

75 YEARS AGO

Landmark World Events

Jan 24 Following the model of previously established offices in Vienna and Prague, the Nazis established the Reich Central Office for Jewish Emigration as part of the Interior Ministry.

Jan 24 In Chile, a massive earthquake—8.3 on the Richter scale—devastated Chillán, killing between 28,000 and 30,000 people.

Jan 26 In the Spanish Civil War, General Francisco Franco's Nationalist forces seized Barcelona.

Jan 30 In a speech to the German parliament (Reichstag), Adolph Hitler openly threatened the Jewish people: "If the international finance-Jewry inside and outside Europe should succeed in plunging the nations into a world war yet again, then the outcome will not be the victory of Jewry, but rather the annihilation of the Jewish race in Europe!"

Feb 6 Amid the turmoil of the country's civil war, the Spanish government fled to France.

Feb 21 The Nazis issued a decree demanding that Jews relinquish their gold and silver.

Mar 2 Italian Cardinal Eugenio Maria Giuseppe Giovanni Pacelli was elected pope; he became Pius XII.

Mar 28 In Spain, Madrid fell to Franco, and the Spanish Civil War was over. The United States recognized Franco's Nationalist government.

Apr 8 Italian troops under Benito Mussolini seized the country of Albania with little resistance. Italy annexed the country.

May 11 At Sutton Hoo in Suffolk, England, archaeologist Basil Brown unearthed a royal Anglo-Saxon ship burial and assorted weapons and precious metals. At 90 feet long and 14 feet wide, the ship was the largest of its kind ever discovered.

May 13 At Hamburg, Jewish refugees boarded an ocean liner en route to Cuba, which turned them away, as did Miami, FL.

May 15 At Ravensbrück, north of Berlin, SS leader Heinrich Himmler completed construction of a women-only concentration camp.

May 22 The foreign ministers of Germany and Italy signed the "Pact of Steel" (*Stahlpakt*), which assured mutual defense and cooperation between the two powers.

Aug 27 The He 178 made its first flight. Developed by German aeronautical engineer Ernst Heinkel, it was the world's first turbojet-powered aircraft.

Sept 1 World War II began with Germany's invasion of Poland. One and a half million troops swarmed into the country, with heavy air support, including incendiaries. See "Spotlight on World Anniversaries."

Sept 3 Its toothless ultimatum to Germany to stand down ignored, Great Britain declared war on Germany, as did France.

Sept 4 Japan declared its neutrality in the European war. (At the time, the Japanese empire was already at war with China; eventually these conflicts would merge.)

Sept 10 Canada declared war on Germany.

Sept 17 The Soviet Union attacked Poland from the east. Vilnius fell a day later.

Sept 17 Off the coast of Ireland, the HMS *Courageous* was torpedoed and sunk by a German U-boat.

Sept 19 German and Soviet army elements linked up at Brest-Litovsk.

Sept 19 At the Battle of Changsha in China, Japanese Imperial forces deployed poison gas against the National Revolutionary Army. The Chinese would eventually retain the city, however, managing to choke off Japan's supply lines.

Sept 27 Decimated by an unprovoked enemy, Polish leaders in Warsaw surrendered to Germany. The Nazis and the Soviets divided Poland into western and eastern zones of control.

Oct 1 Almost immediately after Polish occupation, the Nazis began euthanasia programs, killing off anyone they perceived as somehow less or inadequate, including the old, sick and infirm. Methods of death included lethal injection and carbon monoxide poisoning.

Oct 9 Hitler issued his "Case Yellow" plan, detailing the imminent invasion by Nazi forces of France and the Low Countries.

Oct 12 The Third Reich demarcated occupied Polish areas as the General Government zone, or *Generalgouvernement*. Eventually, forced labor was initiated for Jews within the zone, as was the requirement for all Jews to wear a Star of David patch or armband as ethnic identification.

Nov 30 The Soviet Union invaded Finland. Despite being outnumbered, the Finns began to beat back the Red Army. The Winter War had begun.

Dec 2 In Great Britain, military conscription was increased to include men aged 19–41.

Dec 2 The Olympic Games, to have been held in Finland, were canceled.

Dec 14 The League of Nations expelled the Soviet Union after condemning its attack on Finland.

Dec 15 With the weather worsening and Finnish forces refusing to capitulate—cities were taken and retaken by both sides—the unfinished Mannerheim Line on the Karelian Isthmus in southeast Finland effectively kept the Soviet Army at bay and protected Helsinki from a fall. Fierce Finnish counterattacks inflicted heavy casualties on the Red Army.

Dec 18 At the Battle of Heligoland Bight in the North Sea, three Royal Air Force bomber squadrons attacked Nazi ships in the German bay. While initially successful, a hasty but confident defense mounted by the German air force (Luftwaffe) repelled the RAF and clarified a fact of this new world war: daylight missions came with a significant cost to both personnel and equipment.

▪ No Nobel Peace Prize was awarded in 1939.

Landmark US Events

Jan 4 In his State of the Union address, President Franklin D. Roosevelt (FDR) outlined to Congress how forces at work in the world should be negotiated by the United States: "There comes a time in the affairs of men when they must prepare to defend, not their homes alone, but the tenets of faith and humanity on which their churches, their governments and their very civilization are founded. The defense of religion, of democracy and of good faith among nations is all the same fight. To save one we must now make up our minds to save all."

Jan 12 President Roosevelt asked Congress for an increase in defense spending, at a cost of $525 million over two years.

Feb 13 Justice Louis Brandeis resigned from the Supreme Court. He was succeeded by William O. Douglas.

Mar 3 Begun as a Harvard prank, goldfish swallowing was the hottest trend on US college campuses.

Mar 24 American adventurer Richard Halliburton, attempting to sail a Chinese junk across the Pacific Ocean to the site of the recently opened Golden Gate International Exposition at San Francisco, was never heard from again.

Apr 9 Black American contralto Marian Anderson performed at an open-air concert on the steps of the Lincoln Memorial in Washington, DC, after being shut out of the Daughters of the American Revolution Constitution Hall. The concert was attended by 75,000 people and became an early landmark of the US antidiscrimination movement.

FDR on the European War

In his 14th Fireside Chat, on Sept 3, 1939, President Roosevelt spoke to the American people on the subject of war:

> It is easy for you and for me to shrug our shoulders and to say that conflicts taking place thousands of miles from the continental United States, and, indeed, thousands of miles from the whole American Hemisphere, do not seriously affect the Americas—and that all the United States has to do is to ignore them and go about [our] its own business. Passionately though we may desire detachment, we are forced to realize that every word that comes through the air, every ship that sails the sea, every battle that is fought does affect the American future.

Apr 30 The New York World's Fair opened at Flushing Meadows, New York, NY. Designed to be an inspiration to an American public still reeling from the Great Depression, the fair ran for two years and included the participation of more than 50 nations.

June 7 King George VI and Queen Elizabeth arrived in America for the first-ever visit by the English monarchy. On June 11, President Roosevelt received them at his home in Hyde Park, where they were served hot dogs.

Aug 2 In a letter to President Roosevelt, scientist Albert Einstein described the likely effects of a new weapon, the atomic bomb: "chain reactions, vast amounts of power."

Sept 5 At the outset of war in Europe, America declared its neutrality. Public opinion was against the new conflict, and isolationism was viewed as the better political policy.

Nov 4 The Neutrality Act of 1939 passed Congress, and FDR authorized weapons sales to belligerent and nonbelligerent nations.

Nov 15 At Washington, DC, President Roosevelt laid the cornerstone of the Jefferson Memorial.

Nov 19 At Hyde Park, NY, President Roosevelt laid the cornerstone for the first-ever presidential library.

Culture

Literary Arts

- The Nobel Prize in Literature was awarded to Finnish novelist Frans Eemil Sillanpää.

Fiction

Apr 14 *The Grapes of Wrath* was first published. John Steinbeck's novel of Dust Bowl farmers and the Great Depression won the Pulitzer Prize in 1940.

May 1 *Detective Comics* #27 appeared on newsstands, containing the debut of a new crime fighter, the "Batman," created by Bob Kane and Bill Finger. (The actual release date was some days earlier.)

- *Finnegans Wake*, James Joyce
- *And Then There Were None*, Agatha Christie
- *The Big Sleep*, Raymond Chandler
- *How Green Was My Valley*, Richard Llewellyn
- *Rogue Male*, Geoffery Household
- *Coming Up for Air*, George Orwell
- *The Enchanter*, Vladimir Nabokov
- *Uncle Fred in the Springtime*, P.G. Wodehouse
- *The Day of the Locust*, Nathanael West
- *Pale Horse, Pale Rider*, Katherine Ann Porter
- *All This, and Heaven Too*, Rachel Field
- *The Tree of Liberty*, Elizabeth Page

Nonfiction

- The English translation of Adolf Hitler's *Mein Kampf* (1925) was published.
- *Black Folk, Then and Now*, W.E.B. Du Bois
- *The Coming of the French Revolution*, Georges Lefebvre
- *Country Lawyer*, Bellamy Partridge
- *Wind, Sand and Stars*, Antoine de St. Exupéry
- *A Peculiar Treasure*, Edna Ferber
- *Listen! The Wind*, Anne Morrow Lindbergh

Children's Literature

- *Mike Mulligan and His Steam Shovel*, Virginia Lee Burton
- *By the Shores of Silver Lake*, Laura Ingalls Wilder
- *The Seven Lady Godivas*, Dr. Seuss

Spotlight on the Past

Theater and Opera

- *The Man Who Came to Dinner*, Moss Hart
- *Arsenic and Old Lace*, Joseph Kesselring
- *Too Many Girls*
- *Philadelphia Story*
- *The Time of Your Life*
- *Stars in Your Eyes*

Film

Aug 25 *The Wizard of Oz* was released. Directed by Victor Fleming and starring Judy Garland, the landmark film featured both black-and-white and color sequences. It was nominated for six Academy Awards and won two for best original music score and best song, "Over the Rainbow."

Dec 15 *Gone with the Wind* premiered. The landmark film won eight Academy Awards.

Academy Awards for 1939

(Awarded in 1940)

- Outstanding Production: *Gone with the Wind*
- Best Director: Victor Fleming, *Gone with the Wind*
- Best Actor: Robert Donat, *Goodbye Mr. Chips*
- Best Actress: Vivien Leigh, *Gone with the Wind*
- Best Supporting Actor: Thomas Mitchell, *Stagecoach*
- Best Supporting Actress: Hattie McDaniel, *Gone with the Wind*

Notable Films

- *Mr. Smith Goes to Washington*
- *The Hound of the Baskervilles*
- *Drums Along the Mohawk*
- *Stagecoach*
- *Babes in Arms*
- *The Adventures of Sherlock Holmes*
- *Young Mr. Lincoln*
- *You Can't Cheat an Honest Man*
- *The Three Musketeers*
- *Son of Frankenstein*
- *Oklahoma Kid*
- *Wuthering Heights*

Television

Apr 30 Franklin D. Roosevelt's speech at the New York World's Fair became the first-ever televised appearance of a US president.

Aug 9 New York's experimental TV station W2XBS broadcast tennis—the Eastern Grass Court Championships at Rye, NY—for the first time ever.

Aug 26 A double-header between the Brooklyn Dodgers and Cincinnati Reds became Major League Baseball's first-ever televised games. Red Barber was the broadcaster.

Music

Popular Songs

- "Somewhere Over the Rainbow," sung by Judy Garland, was from *The Wizard of Oz*.
- "Moonlight Serenade," "Tuxedo Junction" and "It's a Blue World," Glenn Miller
- "Strange Fruit," Billie Holiday
- "Three Little Fishies," Kay Kyser
- "Back in the Saddle Again," Gene Autry
- "Your Feets Too Big," Fats Waller
- "Address Unknown," The Ink Spots
- "What's New?," Bing Crosby
- "I Poured My Heart into a Song," Artie Shaw
- "Indian Summer," Tommy Dorsey
- "Well All Right (Tonight's The Night)," Andrews Sisters
- "Beer Barrel Polka," Will Glahe
- "All or Nothing at All," Frank Sinatra
- "Let's Dance," Benny Goodman
- "You Are My Sunshine," Pine Ridge Boys
- "God Bless America," Kate Smith
- "Auld Lang Syne," Guy Lombardo

Art

- In 1939, the Museum of Non-Objective Painting was founded in New York, NY, by philanthropist Solomon R. Guggenheim. He later hired architect Frank Lloyd Wright to design the iconic structure that stands today as the Guggenheim Museum.
- In Racine, WI, Frank Lloyd Wright's iconic Johnson Wax Headquarters was completed.
- Pablo Picasso's 1939 works included *Reclining Woman with Book*, *Seated Woman* and *The Yellow Sweater*.
- Frida Kahlo commemorated her 1939 divorce from Diego Rivera with *The Two Fridas*.
- *Girl in Blue and White*, Diego Rivera
- *Music 1939*, Henri Matisse
- *Midsummer Night's Dream*, Marc Chagall

Science and Technology

Jan 25 Nuclear fission was achieved for the first time in America by a team of scientists working at Columbia University in New York.

■ The Nobel Prize in Chemistry was awarded to Adolf Butenandt (for his work on sex hormones) and Leopold Ruzicka (for his work on polymethylenes and higher terpenes).

■ The Nobel Prize in Physiology or Medicine went to German chemotherapist Gerhard Domagk. (Germany refused to allow him to retrieve his award.)

■ Ernest Lawrence received the Nobel Prize in Physics for his invention of the cyclotron.

Commerce and New Products

Jan 1 The Hewlett-Packard Company was founded in Palo Alto, CA, by Bill Redington Hewlett and Dave Packard.

June 28 Pan Am flew 22 passengers from New York, NY, to Lisbon, Portugal, establishing transatlantic commercial air travel.

Sept 14 Aircraft designer Igor Sikorsky's VS-300 helicopter was successfully test flown.

Oct 15 At New York, NY, Municipal Airport (LaGuardia) was dedicated.

Oct 24 Nylon stockings appeared for the first time anywhere. Nylon had been invented in 1935.

Nov 4 The first-ever air-conditioned vehicle, a Packard, made its debut.

■ Ragnar Frisch and Jan Tinbergen received the Nobel Prize in Economics.

Sports

Auto Racing

■ Wilbur Shaw won the Indianapolis 500.

Baseball

April 20 Ted Williams made his major league debut with the Boston Red Sox, going one for four with a double in a 2–0 loss to the New York Yankees.

May 2 After an ironman streak of 2,130 consecutive games played, New York Yankees first baseman Lou Gehrig asked manager Joe McCarthy to take him out of the lineup for a game against the Detroit Tigers. Gehrig, suffering from amyotrophic lateral sclerosis (ALS), never played again.

June 12 The National Baseball Hall of Fame and Museum was dedicated at Cooperstown, NY.

July 4 After retiring from baseball, Lou Gehrig returned to the Yankees for Lou Gehrig day. In his famous farewell speech, he said, "Today I consider myself the luckiest man on the face of the earth."

Oct 4–8 In the World Series, the New York Yankees swept the Cincinnati Reds, winning all four games.

Basketball

March 27 The Oregon Ducks defeated the Ohio State Buckeyes 46–33 to win the inaugural NCAA men's basketball tournament.

Football

Jan 15 The first NFL pro bowl was held at Wrigley Field. The New York Giants beat the league's All Stars 13–10.

■ The Heisman Trophy went to Nile Kinnick of Iowa.

■ In the NFL championship game, the Green Bay Packers beat the New York Giants 27–0.

Golf

■ Ralph Guldahl won the Masters.

■ Byron Nelson won the US Open.

■ The Open Championship was won by Dick Burton.

■ Henry Picard won the PGA Championship.

Hockey

Apr 6–16 To win the Stanley Cup, the Boston Bruins defeated the Toronto Maple Leafs four games to one.

Horse Racing

■ Johnstown won the Kentucky Derby.

■ Challedon won the Preakness Stakes.

■ Johnstown also won the Belmont Stakes.

Soccer

Apr 29 Portsmouth won the FA Cup in England, defeating Wolverhampton.

■ Everton won the first division of the English soccer league.

Tennis

- Bobby Riggs won the US Open.
- The French Open was won by Don McNeill.
- The Australian Open was won by John Bromwich.
- Bobby Riggs also won Wimbledon.

1939 Deaths

- Norman Bethune, Canadian physician (WWII, Spanish Civil War, Chinese Revolution)
- Heywood Broun, US sportswriter
- Joe Carr, US sports executive
- Joseph Force Crater, US judge (disappeared; declared legally dead)
- Douglas Fairbanks, US actor
- Sigmund Freud, Austrian physician
- Zane Grey, US author (*Riders of the Purple Sage*)
- Sidney Coe Howard, US playwright
- Bob Marshall, US founder of the Wilderness Society
- Charles Horace Mayo, US surgeon
- William James Mayo, US surgeon
- Alphonse Mucha, Czech artist
- James Naismith, Canadian-born athlete and physical education instructor who invented basketball.
- Pope Pius XI, 259th pope of the Roman Catholic Church
- Charles C. Pyle ("Cash and Carry"), US sports promoter
- Arthur Rackham, English artist
- Gertrude "Ma" Rainey, US blues singer
- Jacob Ruppert, US baseball executive
- James Laurie ("Deacon") White, US baseball player
- Ambroise Vollard, French art patron
- William Butler Yeats, Irish poet and dramatist

1964

50 YEARS AGO

Landmark World Events

Jan 5 Pope Paul VI and Patriarch Athenagoras of Jerusalem met in the Holy Land. It was the first meeting in five centuries between a Roman Catholic pontiff and an Eastern Orthodox patriarch.

Jan 9 Rioting broke out in the Panama Canal Zone, causing the deaths of more than 20 Panamanians and four American soldiers; US control of the zone had been an ongoing issue of contention.

Jan 13 The Arab League Summit began in Cairo, Egypt. The immediate effect of the summit was its establishment of a mandate to authorize the formulation of the Palestine Liberation Organization (PLO).

Jan 17 The official PLO charter was issued, establishing Fatah as the organization's military arm and expressing the intent of armed action against Israel.

Mar 31 A bloodless coup occurred in Brazil, resulting in the overthrow of President João Goulart.

Apr 26 Tanganyika, Zanzibar and Pemba united to form Tanzania.

June 12 In South Africa, anti-apartheid leader Nelson Mandela was sentenced to life in prison. He would finally be released in 1990.

June 15 The last French troops departed Algeria.

June 15 The Group of 77 (G-77), an intergovernmental organization within the United Nations, was established to foster growth and cooperation amongst the world's developing countries.

July 6 Malawi gained its independence from Britain.

Aug 12 Charlie Wilson, part of the Great Train Robbery of 1963, escaped from prison in Birmingham, England.

Aug 29 In a period of intense instability, Nguyen Khanh stepped down as president of South Vietnam and Xuan Oanh was named interim prime minister.

Sept 14 Pope Paul VI convened the third session of the Second Ecumenical Council of the Vatican, known as "Vatican II." It lasted until Nov 21.

Sept 25 The Mozambique War for Independence from Portugal began. It would last 10 years.

Oct 3 East Germans began escaping to the west via a 470-foot-long tunnel; 57 people made the trip before the tunnel was discovered. Egon Shultz, an East German border guard, was killed in the resulting melee.

Oct 15 Nikita Krushchev, leader of the Soviet Union, abruptly resigned. While the colorful prime minister cited failing health for his retirement, it was clear to observers that he had been forced out. Krushchev was replaced by Leonid Brezhnev.

Oct 16 The Labor Party's Harold Wilson became prime minister of Great Britain.

Oct 16 China successfully detonated its first atomic bomb, becoming the world's fourth nuclear power.

Oct 24 Northern Rhodesia gained its independence from Britain, changing its name to Zambia.

Nov 2 Faisal bin Abdulaziz Al Saud became king of Saudi Arabia.

Nov 23 The Vatican removed Latin as the official language of the Roman Catholic mass.

■ The Nobel Peace Prize was awarded to Martin Luther King Jr.

Landmark US Events

Jan 3 Republican Senator Barry Goldwater from Arizona announced his candidacy for the presidency of the United States.

Jan 8 President Lyndon Johnson declared a war on poverty in his State of the Union address.

Jan 11 US Surgeon General Luther Terry issued the first major government report to suggest that smoking cigarettes could be harmful to one's health.

Jan 16 President Johnson authorized the transfer of covert operations against North Vietnam from the Central Intelligence Agency to the US military.

Jan 23 With the ratification of the 24th Amendment, poll taxes and other taxes were eliminated from federal voting procedures.

Feb 8 During the congressional debate over the Civil Rights Act of 1964, Representative Martha Griffiths (D-MI) advocated for the prohibition of sex-based discrimination.

Mar 8 Malcolm X officially announced his break from the Nation of Islam, stating his wish to "heighten the political consciousness" of African Americans and increase cooperation with other civil rights leaders. He would be assassinated a year later.

Mar 9 Richard McKenzie and four other Lakota Sioux occupied Alcatraz Island in a protest for Native American rights to the land. The brief action predated a much longer 1969 occupation.

Mar 12 Powerful Teamsters Union boss Jimmy Hoffa was sentenced to eight years in prison for bribery.

Mar 13 Catherine "Kitty" Genovese was stabbed to death in the Kew Gardens neighborhood of Queens, NY. The crime became infamous as it appeared (and was reported in major media outlets) that numerous neighbors did nothing to help her. The case prompted studies of what is now called the bystander effect.

Mar 14 A jury in Dallas sentenced Jack Ruby to death in the murder of Lee Harvey Oswald in 1963.

Mar 26 President Johnson signed a Predelegation of Authority document, authorizing the use of nuclear weapons by military officials if the president could not be reached during a nuclear attack on the United States.

Mar 27 A massive earthquake struck Alaska east of Anchorage, killing 115. At 8.4 on the Richter scale, it was the strongest quake in North American history. A resulting tsunami killed 12 at Crescent City, CA.

Apr 3 A vicious F-5 tornado cut through Wichita Falls, TX, killing seven. The destruction was broadcast live on television.

May 7 Passenger Francisco Gonzales burst into the cockpit of Pacific Air Lines Flight 773 and shot both pilots and then himself. The aircraft crashed soon after, killing all 44 people on board.

May 19 The United States discovered a network of bugging devices in the walls of the American Embassy in Moscow.

May 22 President Johnson delivered his famous "Great Society" speech at the University of Michigan: "We must give every child a place to sit and a teacher to learn from. Poverty must not be a bar to learning, and learning must offer an escape from poverty."

June 19 The Civil Rights Act of 1964 was approved with a vote of 73–27. See "Spotlight on American Anniversaries."

June 20 General William Westmoreland became head of US forces in Vietnam.

June 21 Three civil rights workers disappeared in Mississippi. They had been sent to investigate a church burning.

The Presidential Election of 1964

On Nov 3, 1964, Democratic incumbent Lyndon B. Johnson defeated his Republican challenger, Senator Barry Goldwater of Arizona, in a sweeping victory, garnering more than 60 percent of the popular vote. Johnson had 486 electoral votes and 43,129,566 popular votes. Goldwater had 52 electoral votes and 27,178,188 popular votes. Throughout the campaign, Democrats had framed Goldwater as a warmonger out of touch with regular Americans. For his part, Goldwater refused to budge on his extreme right wing views, which also included the dismantling of the welfare state. After the successes of his term as JFK's replacement—significant expansion of the welfare state, the Civil Rights Act—Johnson was poised to continue that work in a full term, this time with a clear mandate from the American people.

June 28 At Harlem, NY, Malcolm X founded the Organization for Afro American Unity. The OAAU sought to build relations between people of African descent in North America with the people of the African Continent.

July 2 President Johnson signed the Voting Rights Act of 1964 into law, prohibiting discrimination on the basis of race in employment, union membership and voter registration.

July 13 The 28th Republican National Convention opened at The Cow Palace at San Francisco, CA. With party moderates facing off against ultraconservatives and sparring between Barry Goldwater and President Johnson, the convention was chock-full of compelling storylines, all of which became fodder for the increased media presence at the event, itself a function of more effective broadcast technology.

July 14 The United States sent 600 troops to Vietnam.

July 16 Barry Goldwater delivered a speech accepting the Republican nomination for president: "And I pledge that the America I envision in the years ahead will extend its hand in health, in teaching and in cultivation, so that all new nations will be at least encouraged to go our way, so that they will not wander down the dark alleys of tyranny or to the dead-end streets of collectivism. My fellow Republicans, we do no man a service by hiding freedom's light under a bushel of mistaken humility."

July 18 Race riots broke out in Harlem and other predominantly black New York City neighborhoods, fueled by the shooting of 15-year-old James Powell by a white policeman. The riots lasted six days and were followed by violence in Rochester, NY, and other East Coast cities.

July 27 President Johnson sent 5,000 more military advisors to Vietnam.

Aug 2 In the Gulf of Tonkin Incident, two American destroyers were purportedly provoked by North Vietnamese torpedo boats, spurring the government to enact the titular resolution five days later.

Aug 4 The bodies of civil rights workers James Chaney, Andrew Goodman and Michael Schwerner were discovered buried in a muddy dam in Philadelphia, MS.

Aug 5 US planes began to bomb North Vietnam.

Aug 7 Congress approved the "Gulf of Tonkin Resolution," granting President Johnson authority to "take all necessary measures to repel any armed attack against the forces of the United States and prevent further aggression." House of Representatives vote: 414–0; Senate: 88–2.

Aug 20 President Johnson signed a $947.5 million antipoverty bill into law as part of his war on poverty.

Aug 24 At the Democratic National Convention in Atlantic City, NJ, President Johnson accepted the nomination of his party. Hubert Humphrey was nominated as his vice president.

Sept 27 The Warren Commission issued its report on the 1963 assassination of President John F. Kennedy, stating that Lee Harvey Oswald had acted alone.

Oct 20 In Mississippi, a federal jury convicted seven Ku Klux Klan members in the murders of civil rights workers James Chaney, Andrew Goodman and Michael Schwerner.

Oct 27 Ronald Reagan delivered a landmark speech in support of Barry Goldwater, the Republican nominee for President: "You and I are told we must choose between a left or right, but I suggest there is no such thing as a left or right. There is only an up or down. Up to man's age-old dream—the maximum of individual freedom consistent with order—or down to the ant heap of totalitarianism."

Nov 3 Washington, DC, residents cast their first votes for president in the 1964 election, after the 23rd Amendment of 1961.

Nov 18 FBI director J. Edgar Hoover called Martin Luther King Jr. "the most notorious liar in the country," after King had accused the FBI of racial discrimination.

Culture

Literary Arts

- The Nobel Prize in Literature was awarded to John-Paul Sartre, but he declined the prize.

Fiction

- *Little Big Man*, Thomas Berger
- *Herzog*, Saul Bellow
- *Armageddon: A Novel of Berlin*, Leon Uris
- *Last Exit to Brooklyn*, Hubert Selby Jr.
- *Arrow of God*, Chinua Achebe
- *The Penultimate Truth*, Philip K. Dick
- *The Ravishing of Lol Stein*, Marguerite Duras

Nonfiction

- *Reminiscences*, Douglas MacArthur
- *Report of the Warren Commission on the Assassination of President Kennedy*, The Warren Commission
- *Apocalypse Postponed*, Umberto Eco
- *Colonialism and Neocolonialism*, John-Paul Sartre
- *Markings*, Dag Hammarskjold
- *The Negro in the Making of America*, Benjamin Quarles
- *Power at the Pentagon*, Jack Raymond
- *A Moveable Feast*, Ernest Hemingway
- *Why We Can't Wait*, Martin Luther King Jr.
- *A Nation of Immigrants*, John F. Kennedy
- *My Years with General Motors*, Alfred P. Sloan
- *A Very Easy Death*, Simone de Beauvoir

Children's Literature

- *Harriet the Spy*, Louise Fitzhugh
- *Charlie and the Chocolate Factory*, Roald Dahl
- *The Book of Three*, Lloyd Alexander
- *Ribsy*, Beverly Cleary
- *The Giving Tree*, Shel Silverstein
- *Chitty Chitty Bang Bang*, Ian Fleming

Theater and Opera

Jan 16 *Hello, Dolly!* opened on Broadway, beginning a run of more than 2,000 performances.

Jan 23 Arthur Miller's *After The Fall* premiered.

Feb 18 Muriel Resnik's *Any Wednesday* premiered.

Mar 26 *Funny Girl*, starring Barbara Streisand, premiered.

Sept 22 *Fiddler on the Roof* opened on Broadway.

Film

- *The Pink Panther* and *A Shot in the Dark* introduced the world to Peter Sellers's comic creation, Inspector Clouseau, in 1964.

Academy Awards for 1964

(Awarded in 1965)

- Best Picture: *My Fair Lady*, Jack Warner
- Best Director: George Cukor, *My Fair Lady*
- Best Actor: Rex Harrison, *My Fair Lady*
- Best Actress: Julie Andrews, *Mary Poppins*
- Best Supporting Actor: Peter Ustinov, *Topkapi*
- Best Supporting Actress: Lila Kedrova, *Zorba the Greek*

Notable Films

- *A Hard Day's Night*
- *Dr. Strangelove*
- *My Fair Lady*
- *Goldfinger*
- *Mary Poppins*
- *The Carpetbaggers*
- *Sex and the Single Girl*
- *Viva Las Vegas*
- *Kiss Me, Stupid*
- *The Night of the Iguana*
- *Band of Outsiders*
- *Zorba the Greek*
- *The Umbrellas of Cherbourg*
- *Topkapi*
- *Seven Days in May*
- *Pajama Party*
- *Of Human Bondage*
- *A Married Woman*
- *Invitation to a Gunfighter*
- *Becket*
- *Fate Is the Hunter*
- *Bikini Beach*

Spotlight on the Past

Television

Sept 7 "Daisy," a political ad for the Johnson campaign, received its only official airing. The spot was widely thought to align the Barry Goldwater campaign with the threat of nuclear war.

Sept 19 With the introduction of its 1964–1965 TV season, NBC also announced that it was now broadcasting more than half of its shows in color. CBS and ABC continued to broadcast mostly in black and white.

Oct 10 The opening ceremony of the 1964 Summer Olympics was broadcast live via satellite from Tokyo, Japan.

Dec 6 "Rudolph the Red-Nosed Reindeer" premiered.

Notable 1964 TV Premieres

- "Jeopardy!"
- "Another World"
- "Bewitched"
- "The Addams Family"
- "Flipper"
- "Daniel Boone"
- "The Munsters"
- "Gilligan's Island"
- "Gomer Pyle, USMC"
- "The Man from UNCLE"
- "Jonny Quest"
- "Peyton Place"
- "Shindig!"

Music

Jan 1 *Top of the Pops* premiered on the BBC.

Jan 3 A taped appearance from The Beatles aired on the "Jack Paar Show."

Feb 1 Matthew E. Welsh, governor of Indiana, declared The Kingsmen's "Louie Louie" pornographic.

Feb 7 The Beatles arrived at John F. Kennedy Airport at New York, NY, and were greeted by 4,000 fans.

Feb 9 The Beatles' appearance on "The Ed Sullivan Show" launched the British Invasion with 73 million viewers. See "Spotlight on World Anniversaries."

Feb 12 The Beatles played two shows at Carnegie Hall as part of their wildly successful debut US tour.

Mar 14 With the British Invasion raging, *Billboard* announced that The Beatles controlled 60 percent of the US singles market.

Mar 27 Radio Caroline began broadcasting from international waters off the English coast. Catering to pop and rock music fans, pirate radio stations began as a means of circumventing record companies' chokehold on British airwaves.

Apr 4 The Beatles held the top five positions on the Billboard chart with "Can't Buy Me Love," "Twist and Shout," "She Loves You," "I Want to Hold Your Hand," and "Please Please Me."

Apr 11 With 14 entries on the *Billboard* Hot 100, The Beatles surpassed Elvis Presley, who charted nine singles at once in 1956.

June 1 The British Invasion rolled on with The Rolling Stones' arrival at John F. Kennedy Airport at New York, NY, for their first American tour.

July 31 "Gentleman Jim" Reeves, a popular country singer, died in a plane crash in Tennessee.

Oct 28–29 *T.A.M.I. Show* was shot over two days of concerts at Santa Monica, CA. Featuring notables of the day including James Brown, The Rolling Stones, The Supremes, Jan & Dean, Chuck Berry, Smokey Robinson and Marvin Gaye, it has been recognized as a pioneering concert film.

Dec 11 Sam Cooke died in a shooting at the Hacienda Motel at Los Angeles, CA. "A Change Is Gonna Come," one of Cooke's most famous songs, was released Dec 22.

1964 Grammys

- Record of the Year: "Girl from Ipanema," Astrud Gilberto and Stan Getz, artists
- Album of the Year: *Getz/Gilberto*, João Gilberto and Stan Getz, artists
- Song of the Year: "Hello, Dolly!," Louis Armstrong, artist, and Jerry Herman, songwriter
- Best New Artist: The Beatles

Notable Songs

- "A Hard Day's Night," "Can't Buy Me Love," "Twist and Shout," The Beatles
- "The Times They Are A-Changing," Bob Dylan
- "I Get Around," Beach Boys
- "Oh, Pretty Woman," Roy Orbison
- "Everybody Loves Somebody," Dean Martin
- "My Guy," Mary Wells
- "Last Kiss," J. Frank Wilson & the Cavaliers
- "Where Did Our Love Go" and "Baby Love," The Supremes

- "Do Wah Diddy Diddy," Manfred Mann
- "Dancing in the Street," Martha & the Vandellas
- "Under the Boardwalk," The Drifters
- "Glad All Over," Dave Clark Five
- "Rag Doll," Frankie Valli and the Four Seasons
- "It Hurts to Be in Love," Gene Pitney
- "Come a Little Bit Closer," Jay and the Americans
- "Wishin' and Hopin'," Dusty Springfield
- "Walk on By," Dionne Warwick
- "House of the Rising Sun," The Animals
- "My Boy Lollipop," Millie Small
- "The Girl from Ipanema," Stan Getz & Astrud Gilberto
- "Baby I Need Your Loving," Four Tops
- "Leader of the Pack," Shangri-Las
- "The Way You Do the Things You Do," Temptations
- "You Really Got Me," Kinks
- "Chug-a-Lug," Roger Miller
- "Walk Don't Run '64," The Ventures

Notable Albums

- *A Hard Day's Night* and *Beatles for Sale*, The Beatles
- *Getz/Gilberto*, Stan Getz & João Gilberto
- *The Rolling Stones*, The Rolling Stones
- *All Summer Long*, The Beach Boys
- *Where Did Our Love Go*, The Supremes
- *Another Side of Bob Dylan*, Bob Dylan

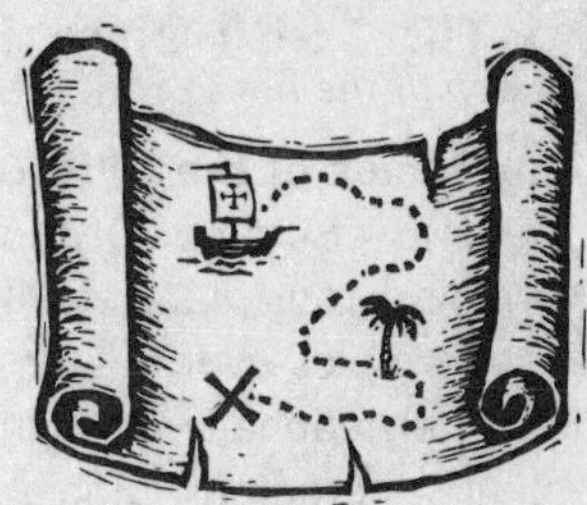

- *Folk Singer*, Muddy Waters
- *Wednesday Morning 3 AM*, Simon & Garfunkel
- *Pain in My Heart*, Otis Redding
- *Presenting the Fabulous Ronettes Featuring Veronica*, The Ronettes
- *Ain't That Good News*, Sam Cooke
- *Coltrane's Sound*, John Coltrane
- *All the News That's Fit to Sing*, Phil Ochs
- *It Might as Well Be Swing*, Frank Sinatra & Count Basie
- *It's My Way!*, Buffy Sainte-Marie
- *Empyrean Isles*, Herbie Hancock
- *Meet the Temptations*, Temptations
- *Make Way for Dionne Warwick*, Dionne Warwick
- *A Girl Called Dusty*, Dusty Springfield
- *Dead Man's Curve/The New Girl in School*, Jan & Dean

Art

- *Three Studies for a Portrait of Lucien Freud*, Francis Bacon
- *Good Morning Darling*, Roy Lichtenstein
- *Woman, Sag Harbor*, Willem de Kooning
- *Brillo Boxes* and *Orange Marilyn*, Andy Warhol
- *Souvenir*, Jasper Johns

Science and Technology

Feb 2 *Ranger 6*, an unmanned spacecraft, crashed as planned on the surface of the moon. It was supposed to begin sending images back to Earth, but the camera system had shorted out along the way, so no images were transmitted.

- Scientist and computer visionary Douglas C. Englebart created the prototype for the computer mouse. It would be demonstrated in 1968.
- Charles Hard Townes, Nicolay Gennadiyevich Basov and Aleksandr Mikhailovich Prokhorov won the Nobel Prize in Physics for their work in quantum electronics.
- The Nobel Prize in Chemistry was awarded to Dorothy Crowfoot Hodgkin.
- The Nobel Prize in Physiology or Medicine was won by Konrad Bloch and Feodor Lynen.

Commerce and New Products

Jan 18 Architect Minoru Yamasaki's plans for the World Trade Center were unveiled.

Feb 1 Hasbro introduced the G.I. Joe action figure. List price: $2.49.

Feb 6 England and France established plans to build a tunnel underneath the English Channel.

Apr 5 Driverless trains debuted in the London Underground metro system.

Apr 7 IBM announced plans for its System/360 series, mainframe computers that customers could upgrade and customize based on software and power requirements.

Apr 17 Ford Motor Company introduced the Mustang at the World's Fair in Flushing Meadows, New York. Suggested retail price: $2,368.

June 24 The Federal Trade Commission announced it would now require tobacco companies to include warning labels on their packaging highlighting the harmful effects of cigarette smoking.

Oct 1 Bullet trains, or Shinkansen, began operation in Japan. The country was first to build dedicated lines for high-speed travel.

Nov 21 The upper level of the Verrazano-Narrows Bridge was completed. At the time it was the longest suspension bridge in the world.

The 1964 Olympics

The Games of the XVIII Olympiad

The 1964 Summer Olympics, known as the Games of the XVIII Olympiad, took place at Tokyo, Japan, Oct 10–24, 1964. It was the first Olympics ever held in Asia, as well as the first to be telecast live internationally through the use of satellite technology. At the opening ceremony, official torch carrier Yoshinori Sakai was chosen because he was born Aug 6, 1945, the day the atomic bomb destroyed Hiroshima, Japan.

The United States led the gold medal count with 36, but the Soviet Union led total medals with 96 to America's 90. Host country Japan finished with 16 gold medals, including that of freestyle wrestler Osamu Watanabe, who retired after the Olympics with a perfect record of 186–0; he never gave up a point. Billy Mills won gold in the 10,000-meter run, marking the only time an American has won the event. US men's swimming won 7 of the 10 available gold medals, while future heavyweight champion of the world Joe Frazier took gold in boxing. Future Dallas Cowboys wide receiver Bob Hayes won gold in the 100 meter with a world-record time of 10.0 seconds. The Soviet Union's Larisa Latynina won two golds, a silver and a bronze in gymnastics, giving her an Olympic-best career total of 18 medals. The Tokyo Olympics saw the first use of fiberglass in the pole vault.

IX Olympic Winter Games

The 1964 Winter Olympics took place at Innsbruck, Austria, Jan 29–Feb 9. While events were at first threatened by a lack of snow, the Austrian army carved ice from the mountain for the bobsled tracks and moved thousands of pounds of snow to ensure ski events.

The Soviet Union led all nations with 25 medal wins, while host nation Austria achieved 12 medals (four gold) and Norway 15 (three gold). The Soviet Union's Klavdiya Boyarskikh took gold in all three cross-country skiing events, while in alpine skiing French sisters Christine and Marielle Goitschel traded victories in slalom and giant slalom. East and West Germany competed in the games as a unified team, while North Korea, Mongolia and India all competed for the first time. Contributing to the Soviets' dominating performance was speed skater Lidiya Skoblikova who won gold in all four speed skating events. Billy Kidd and James Huega became the first American men to medal in Alpine skiing, capturing silver and bronze.

Sports

Auto Racing

- A.J. Foyt won the Indianapolis 500. The race was marred by the fiery and fatal crash of Eddie Sachs.
- Richard Petty was the NASCAR Grand National Champion.

Baseball

Apr 17 The New York Mets played their first-ever game at Shea Stadium.

Apr 23 Despite pitching a no-hitter, Ken Johnson of the Houston Colt .45s lost 1–0 to the Cincinnati Reds after two ninth-inning throwing errors (one by Johnson himself) allowed the Reds to score a run.

May 31 The New York Mets and the San Francisco Giants played the longest doubleheader by game length time. The two games consumed 9 hours, 52 minutes, with the second game lasting 23 innings.

June 4 The Dodgers' Sandy Koufax pitched the third of his four career no-hitters, defeating the Philadelphia Phillies 3–0.

June 21 Jim Bunning of the Philadelphia Phillies pitched a perfect game against the New York Mets, winning 6–0.

July 19 The Cleveland Indians' Luis Tiant pitched a complete game shutout of the New York Yankees, winning 3–0. It was his rookie debut.

Oct 7–15 In the World Series, the St. Louis Cardinals won four games to three over the New York Yankees.

Oct 16 A day after losing the World Series to the St. Louis Cardinals in seven games, the New York Yankees fired manager Yogi Berra.

Boxing

Feb 25 Cassius Clay (later Muhammed Ali) captured the world heavyweight boxing championship by defeating Sonny Liston.

Mar 6 Heavyweight Champion Cassius Clay announced his conversion to the Nation of Islam and his new name, Muhammad Ali.

Basketball

Feb 4 Red Auerbach became the first coach in professional basketball to win 800 games. Auerbach's Boston Celtics bested the St. Louis Hawks 113–101.

Nov 13 St. Louis Hawks forward Bob Pettit reached the 20,000-point mark, a first for an NBA player, in a 123–106 loss to the Cincinnati Royals.

- To win the NCAA Basketball Championship, UCLA beat Duke 98–83.
- In the NBA Finals, the Boston Celtics won four games to the Los Angeles Lakers' one.

Football

Oct 25 Minnesota Vikings defensive end Jim Marshall recovered a fumble and ran it the wrong way—66 yards into his own end zone, where he chucked the ball out of bounds for a San Francisco 49ers' safety. Despite the goof, the Vikings still won 27–22.

Dec 27 The final score of the 1964 National Football League Championship was Cleveland Browns 27, Baltimore Colts 0.

- The Heisman Trophy went to John Huarte of Notre Dame.
- The Associated Press "wire service rankings" champion for the year was the Alabama Crimson Tide.

Golf

- Arnold Palmer won the Masters.
- Ken Venturi was the champion at the US Open.
- The British Open (Open Championship) was won by Tony Lema.
- Bobby Nichols won the PGA Championship.

Hockey

Apr 11–25 To win the Stanley Cup, the Toronto Maple Leafs defeated the Detroit Red Wings four games to three. It was the Leafs' third straight championship and the second time in a row the Wings had lost in the finals.

Horse Racing

- The Kentucky Derby winner was Northern Dancer.
- Northern Dancer also won the Preakness Stakes.
- At the Belmont Stakes, Quadrangle won.

Soccer

May 24 In Lima, Peru, at a soccer match between Peru and Argentina, more than 300 fans died when rioting broke out after a goal was annulled.

May 27 Internazionale defeated Real Madrid to win the European Cup.

- West Ham United defeated Preston North End to take the FA Cup.
- Liverpool won the English first division soccer league.

Tennis

- Roy Emerson won the US Open, the Australian Open and Wimbledon.
- Manuel Santana won the French Open.

1964 Deaths

- Gracie Allen, US comedienne
- Mona Barrie, English actress
- Brendan Behan, Irish playwright and poet
- William Bendix, US actor
- Walter Brown, US sports executive (Basketball Hall of Fame)
- Eddie Cantor, US song and dance man
- Rachel Louise Carson, US scientist, environmentalist and author
- Sam Cooke, US singer
- Stuart Davis, US painter
- Eric Dolphy, US jazz musician
- Eddie Dyer, US baseball player and manager
- Ian Fleming, English journalist and novelist (James Bond series)
- Willie Galimore, US football player
- Gerald Gardner, English founder of Wicca and author

- Ben Hecht, US writer
- Herbert Hoover, 31st president of the United States
- Alan Ladd, US actor
- Gus Lesnevich, US boxer
- Peter Lorre, Hungarian actor
- Douglas MacArthur, US general and supreme commander of Pacific Allied forces in WWII
- Harpo Marx, US comedian (Marx Brothers)
- Mary Pinchot Meyer, US socialite, painter and supposed lover of JFK
- Pierre Monteux, French conductor
- Jawaharlal Nehru, Indian leader and first prime minister after independence
- Sean O'Casey, Irish playwright
- Flannery O'Connor, US novelist and writer
- Steve Owen, US football player, coach and executive
- Cole Porter, US songwriter
- Jim Reeves, US country music singer
- Glenn "Fireball" Roberts, US auto racer (NASCAR)
- Wilbur "Bullet Joe" Rogan, US Baseball Hall of Fame pitcher
- Edith Sitwell, English poet
- Bill Stewart, US hockey coach, referee and baseball umpire
- Buddy Werner, US Olympic skier
- James L. Wilkinson, US baseball executive

1989

25 YEARS AGO

Landmark World Events

Jan 1 With the bombing of Pan Am Flight 103 still raw from late 1988, British prime minister Margaret Thatcher said in a TV interview that she did not necessarily agree with America's vow of retribution. "Revenge can affect innocent people."

Jan 7 After ruling Japan for 62 years, Emperor Hirohito died and Crown Prince Akihito, his only son, succeeded him to the throne later that day. The Heisei era had begun.

Jan 8 A British Midland Boeing 737 crashed on an emergency approach to East Midlands Airport in Leicestershire, England, killing 47.

Jan 10 Cuba began to withdraw its troops from Angola after 13 years there.

Jan 12 Idi Amin was expelled from Zaire and forced to return to Saudi Arabia, where he had been exiled after being deposed as president of Uganda. It was suspected Amin was trying to mount a Ugandan coup from Zaire.

Jan 19 As Israel's minister of defense, Yitzhak Rabin proposed an end to the first intifada (which had begun in 1987) if Israel would allow local elections in Palestinian districts.

Jan 28 Imre Pozsgay, a member of the Hungarian politburo, was first to characterize the 1956 Hungarian Revolution as a popular uprising and not a counterrevolution, helping pave the way for democracy in the country.

Feb Foreign Minister Eduard Shevardnadze participated in three days of high-level talks with Chinese officials, the first Soviet visit there in 30 years.

Feb 3 General Alfredo Stroessner, longtime president of Paraguay, was overthrown in a military coup that killed hundreds.

Feb 8 A US-chartered Boeing 707 crashed into a mountain in the Azores, killing all 144 people aboard.

Feb 11 The presiding bishop of the Episcopal Church, Bishop Edmond L. Browning, consecrated the Reverend Barbara Clementine Harris as the first female Episcopalian bishop.

Feb 14 Offended by Salman Rushdie's book *The Satanic Verses*, Iran's Ayatollah Ruholla Khomeini called on Muslims to kill the British author. Rushdie went into hiding, where he remained until Iran's rescinding of the death sentence in 1998.

Feb 14 Union Carbide settled out of court with Indian authorities for $470 million in damages stemming from the 1984 Bophal gas leak disaster.

Feb 15 The Soviet Union met its goal of a full military withdrawal from Afghanistan, where its troops had spent more than nine years.

Feb 16 Investigators of the Pan Am Flight 103 disaster determined that a bomb in a cassette player had destroyed the aircraft over Lockerbie, Scotland, in December 1988.

Mar 7 Great Britain and Iran suspended their diplomatic ties over the Ayatollah's Rushdie death sentence.

Mar 8 Skirmishes began in Lebanon between Christian forces of government and Syrian armed forces in Lebanon. Rocket attacks and artillery barrages killed hundreds before a ceasefire was reached in 1990.

Mar 13 A blackout swept across the Canadian province of Quebec, the direct effect of the fallout from a massive solar storm on the sun a few days before.

Mar 26 In the Soviet Union's first free elections, Boris Yeltsin was elected to the Congress of People's Deputies of the Soviet Union, signaling the coming end of Communist rule in the country.

Apr 8 The Soviet Union confirmed that the nuclear submarine *Komsomolets* had recently caught fire and sunk in the sea north of Norway. Forty-two submariners died.

Apr 15 In China, former Communist party head Hu Yaobang, who late in life championed reform, died of a heart attack. Thousands mourned him publicly, including 50,000 students who marched into Tiananmen Square with demands of better posthumous treatment of Hu. Violence was imminent.

Apr 15 Ninety-six Liverpool supporters died after thousands of football fans pushed into Hillsborough Stadium in Sheffield, England, for a match between Liverpool and Nottingham Forest and stadium officials stopped monitoring the flow.

Apr 17 The Polish labor union Solidarity was granted legal status and promptly won 99 of the 100 parliamentary seats, ushering in a wave of reformist action against the Polish Communist Party and leading to the formation of a government led by Solidarity.

Apr 27 The crowd of protestors in Tiananmen Square grew to 150,000 students and workers, who cheered and sang in a vibrant call for democracy.

May 3 In Paris, Palestinian Liberation Organization (PLO) leader Yasser Arafat pledged an overturning of previous rhetoric in favor of a peaceful coexistence between Israel and a Palestinian state.

May 7 In Panama's national elections, both dictator Manuel Noriega and his opponent, Guillermo Endara, claimed victory. Noriega refused to recognize any victory but his own, causing unrest in the streets.

May 8 Slobodan Milosevic was elected president of Serbia.

May 10 In Panama, General Manuel Noriega nullified the elections that international observers agreed he had lost by a significant margin.

May 18 Overshadowed by the Tiananmen Square protests was Soviet leader Mikhail Gorbachev's state visit to Beijing, a meeting that softened longstanding Sino-Soviet tensions.

May 20 With millions of people pouring into Beijing and Tiananmen Square to show support for the protesters there, China declared martial law.

June 2 Chinese troops attempting to move into Tiananmen Square were blocked by hundreds of thousands of people in support of the protesters.

June 3 The Ayatollah Ruholla Khomeini, leader of Iran and the Islamic Revolution, died after a battle with cancer.

June 4 In the predawn darkness, troops opened fire on unarmed protesters at Tiananmen Square in Beijing, China, killing hundreds, perhaps thousands. The violence came after nearly a month and a half of student demonstrations for democracy.

June 7 Denmark enacted a law recognizing "registered partnerships" for gay couples.

June 8 In a televised address, Chinese premier Li Peng praised the Chinese military for its role in destroying the prodemocracy protests in Tiananmen Square.

June 17 Continuing its crackdown in the wake of Tiananmen Square, China sentenced eight people to death for destroying military equipment during the protests.

The Berlin Wall Falls

After 28 years as a symbol of the Cold War, the Berlin Wall was opened. East Germany opened checkpoints along its border with West Germany after a troubled month that saw many citizens flee to the West through other countries. Coming amidst the celebration of East Germany's 40-year anniversary, the prodemocracy demonstrations led to the resignation of Erich Honecker, East Germany's head of state and party chief, who had supervised the construction of the wall. He was replaced by Egon Krenz, who promised open political debate and a lessening of restrictions on travel in attempts to stem the flow of East Germans to the West. By opening the Berlin Wall, East Germany began a course that led to the de facto reunification of the two Germanys by summer 1990. On July 1, 1990, the currencies of the two countries became one as East German citizens exchanged their currency for West German marks.

The Berlin Wall was constructed on Aug 13, 1961. Berlin was at the center of a superpower crisis as US President John F. Kennedy increased troop strength in response to the blockade of West Berlin by the Soviets. With Soviet leader Nikita Krushchev's blessing, Honecker started construction of the 27.9-mile wall across the city. Many attempts to scale or breech the wall ensued throughout the years. But on the evening of Nov 9, 1989, citizens of both sides walked freely through the barrier as others danced atop the structure to celebrate the end of a historic era.

June 19 Burma's government renamed the country Myanmar.

June 22 In Angola, a ceasefire was reached between the government and anti-Communist forces, ending 14 years of civil war.

June 30 In Sudan, the elected coalition government was overthrown by a Muslim group that imposed strict sharia law.

July 8 In Argentina, Carlos Saul Menem was elected president, marking the country's first successful transition from one freely elected leader to another.

Aug 3 Hashemi Rafsanjani became president of Iran.

Sept 13 Desmond Tutu led a massive antiapartheid march in South Africa.

Sept 19 A Paris-bound French DC-10 was bombed over the Sahara, killing all 170 people on board. Libyan interests were blamed in the bombing, and the country eventually compensated the families of French and American victims to the tune of millions.

Sept 20 F.W. de Klerk, South Africa's last apartheid president, was sworn into office.

Oct 23 Hungary declared itself an independent republic, effectively ending 33 years of Soviet rule. The declaration continued the domino tumble of Eastern Europe's Communist states.

Nov 9 The Berlin Wall fell, allowing free passage between East and West Germany. The crumbling of the Cold War's lasting symbol in the face of increased social pressure and demonstrations made the wall a symbol for the spirit of democracy as well.

Nov 29 The Communist Party's 41-year chokehold on Czechoslovakia ended with a parliamentary vote giving voice to reform and the rise of the Civic Forum, led by playwright (and eventual president) Vaclav Havel.

Dec 20 In Panama, the United States launched Operation Just Cause, aiming to oust Manuel Noriega and install Guillermo Endara. The action ended on Jan 12, 1990, with 23 US soldiers dead and 320 wounded.

Dec 24 Noriega fled to the Vatican's diplomatic mission in Panama City, where weeks of hounding and loud music playing eventually forced his surrender to US troops.

Dec 25 In Romania, deposed president Nicolae Ceausescu and his wife, Elena, were captured and summarily executed following a popular uprising that saw thousands force their way into the capital. Ceausescu had ruled as a dictator for moe than two decades.

■ The Nobel Peace Prize was awarded to the 14th Dalai Lama.

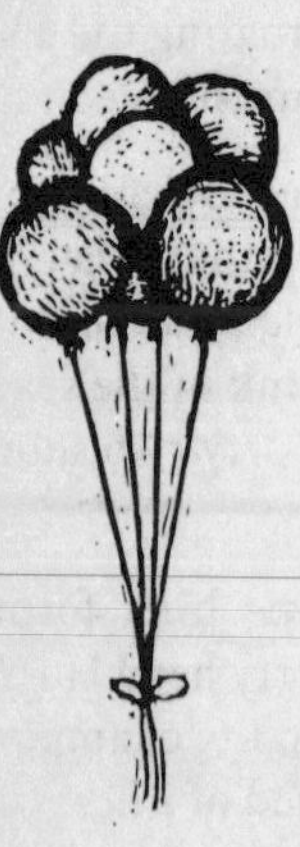

Landmark US Events

Jan 11 President Ronald Reagan gave his farewell address to the American public: "The way I see it, there were two great triumphs, two things that I'm proudest of. One is the economic recovery, in which the people of America created—and filled—19 million new jobs. The other is the recovery of our morale. America is respected again in the world and looked to for leadership."

Jan 12 President-elect George Bush picked former education secretary William Bennett to be the nation's first "drug czar," or director of the Office of National Drug Control Policy.

Jan 17 In Cleveland, Patrick Purdy, a drifter with a criminal record, entered Cleveland Elementary School and shot and killed 5 schoolchildren, wounding 29 others.

Jan 20 George Herbert Walker Bush was sworn in as the 41st president of the United States. Dan Quayle was his vice president. In his inauguration address, Bush stated: "Great nations of the world are moving toward democracy through the door to freedom. Men and women of the world move toward free markets through the door to prosperity. The people of the world agitate for free expression and free thought through the door to the moral and intellectual satisfactions that only liberty allows. We know what works. Freedom works."

Jan 21 David Duke, running as a Republican, successfully ran against a fellow Republican in a run-off to win a seat in the Louisiana House of Representatives. Duke was a former grand wizard of the Ku Klux Klan.

Feb 7 After public outcry, both houses of the US Congress agreed to cancel their recently announced 51 percent pay raise.

Feb 10 Ron Brown became the first African American to head a major political party when he became chairman of the Democratic National Committee.

Feb 17 In an exhibit at the Art Institute of Chicago entitled *What Is the Proper Way to Display a US Flag?*, art student Scott Tyler offered a ledger for opinions mounted over a flag on the floor. Protests from veterans' groups and conservative legislators followed.

Mar 9 John Tower, President Bush's embattled pick for secretary of defense, had his nomination rejected by the US Senate.

Mar 10 A day later, President Bush nominated Richard Cheney for secretary of defense.

Mar 24 The tanker *Exxon Valdez* ran aground on a reef in Prince William Sound in the Gulf of Alaska, spilling 11 million gallons of crude oil into the area's pristine natural habitat.

Mar 29 Junk bond king Michael Milkin was indicted for racketeering at New York, NY.

Mar 31 The FBI announced a criminal investigation into the *Exxon Valdez* oil spill disaster.

Apr 4 Richard M. Daley was elected mayor of Chicago. Daley was the son of legendary Chicago "boss" Mayor Richard J. Daley.

Apr 5 Joseph Hazelwood, captain of the *Exxon Valdez*, surrendered to authorities at Long Island, NY.

Apr 9 Thousands marched on Washington, DC, to demand access to safe, legal abortions.

Apr 19 A jogger was assaulted and raped in Central Park, NY, leading to the arrest and conviction of a group of black and Latino youths, all of whom would later be exonerated when convicted rapist Matias Reyes confessed to the crime. Trisha Melli later revealed herself as the Central Park jogger.

Apr 19 An accidental explosion in the number 2 gun turret on the USS *Iowa* killed 47 sailors.

May 13 President Bush denounced the actions of General Manuel Noriega in Panama and called on the country's military to overthrow their leader.

June 21 The US Supreme Court ruled that burning the American flag as a form of political protest was protected under the First Amendment. President Bush officially criticized the ruling.

June 23 The CDC issued *Guidelines for Prevention of Transmission of Human Immunodeficiency Virus and Hepatitis B Virus to Health-Care and Public Safety Workers.*

June 29 The US House of Representatives voted in favor of increased sanctions against China in the wake of the country's crackdown on the prodemocracy movement.

July 6 The United States destroyed its last series of Pershing missiles, fulfilling the terms of the 1987 Intermediate-Range Nuclear Forces Treaty.

Aug 20 Jose Menendez and his wife, Kitty, were murdered in their Los Angeles home. Eric and

Lyle Menendez, the couple's sons, were tried and convicted for the murders.

Aug 28 A fraud and conspiracy trial opened in Charlotte, NC, concerning former televangelist Jim Bakker, who was eventually convicted of all 24 counts against him.

Sept 7 The US Senate approved the Americans with Disabilities Act, forbidding discrimination in employment, public accommodations, transportation and communications.

Sept 18 Created by the US Congress, the National Commission on AIDS met for the first time. By this time, reported AIDS cases in America had reached 100,000.

Sept 21 Hurricane Hugo made American landfall at Charleston, SC, causing destruction totaling $8 billion.

Oct 17 An earthquake measuring 7.1 on the Richter scale rocked the San Francisco Bay Area, killing 67 and causing billions of dollars in damage. The nation had a front-row seat for some of this destruction, as the quake hit the city just as the 1989 World Series was beginning at Candlestick Park.

Nov 7 David Dinkins became New York City's first black mayor, defeating incumbent Ed Koch.

Nov 30 President Bush left Washington, DC, for a summit with Soviet President Gorbachev to be held aboard ships off Malta in the Mediterranean Sea.

Culture

Literary Arts

- Nobel Prize for Literature: Camilo José Cela

Fiction

- *Billy Bathgate*, E.L. Doctorow
- *Geek Love*, Katherine Dunn
- *The Mambo Kings Play Songs of Love*, Oscar Hijuelos
- *The Joy Luck Club*, Amy Tan
- *The Satanic Verses*, Salman Rushdie
- *A Time to Kill*, John Grisham
- *Clear and Present Danger*, Tom Clancy
- *While My Pretty One Sleeps*, Mary Higgins Clark
- *The Dark Half*, Steven King
- *London Fields*, Martin Amis
- *Foucault's Pendulum*, Umberto Eco
- *A Prayer for Owen Meany*, John Irving
- *The Pillars of the Earth*, Ken Follett
- *The Remains of the Day*, Kazuo Ishiguro
- *The Russia House*, John LeCarre
- *The Temple of My Familiar*, Alice Walker
- *California Gold*, John Jakes
- *Blessings*, Belva Plain
- *Number the Stars*, Lois Lowry
- *Like Water for Chocolate*, Laura Esquivel
- *Sexing the Cherry*, Jeanette Winterson
- *Pyramids*, Terry Pratchett

Nonfiction

- *From Beirut to Jerusalem*, Thomas L. Friedman
- *Barbarian Sentiments: How the American Century Ends*, William Pfaff
- *Mother Country: Britain, the Welfare State and Nuclear Pollution*, Marilynne Robinson
- *Wonderful Life: The Burgess Shale and the Nature of History*, Stephen Jay Gould
- *A Peace to End All Peace: Creating the Modern Middle East 1914–1922*, David Fromkin
- *It's Always Something*, Gilda Radner
- *A Woman Named Jackie*, C. David Heymann
- *The Andy Warhol Diaries*, Andy Warhol and Pat Hackett
- *It Was on Fire When I Lay Down on It*, Robert Fulghum
- *Liar's Poker: Rising Through the Wreckage on Wall Street*, Michael Lewis

Poetry

- *Jimmy Stewart and His Poems*, Jimmy Stewart

Children's Literature

- *The True Story of the Three Little Pigs*, Jon Scieszka and Lane Smith
- *Wayside School Is Falling Down*, Louis Sachar
- *Henry and Mudge Get the Cold Shivers*, Cynthia Rylant

Theater and Opera

Notable 1989 Broadway Openings

- *Hizzoner!*
- *A Few Good Men*
- *City of Angels*
- *Gypsy*
- *Sweeney Todd*

Film

Academy Awards for 1989

(Awarded in 1990)

- Best Picture: *Driving Miss Daisy*
- Best Director: Oliver Stone, *Born on the Fourth of July*
- Best Actor: Daniel Day-Lewis, *My Left Foot*
- Best Actress: Jessica Tandy, *Driving Miss Daisy*
- Best Supporting Actor: Denzel Washington, *Glory*
- Best Supporting Actress: Brenda Fricker, *My Left Foot*

Notable Films

- *Indiana Jones and the Last Crusade*
- *Dead Poets Society*
- *Do the Right Thing*
- *Batman*
- *When Harry Met Sally . . .*
- *Drugstore Cowboy*
- *Crimes and Misdemeanors*
- *The Little Mermaid*
- *Steel Magnolias*
- *Back to the Future Part II*
- *Driving Miss Daisy*
- *Bill & Ted's Excellent Adventure*
- *Lean on Me*
- *Major League*
- *Say Anything . . .*
- *Field of Dreams*
- *Tango & Cash*
- *Lethal Weapon 2*
- *Licence to Kill*
- *Look Who's Talking*
- *Glory*

Television

Jan 9 "The Pat Sajak Show" debuted on CBS late night, featuring the longtime host of "Wheel of Fortune" up against late-night powerhouse Johnny Carson. Sajak's show was cancelled Apr 13, 1990.

Mar 11 "Cops" debuted on Fox. The verité-style documentary show put camera crews in the field with police in departments across the United States, offering an unvarnished eye on the American street.

Mar 23 Dick Clark, the host and centerpiece of the pioneering music television show "American Bandstand" since its debut 33 years before, announced his retirement.

Apr 17 The financial network CNBC debuted.

Apr 23 "Baywatch" had its first appearance. Starring David Hasselhoff and a rotating cast of individuals who looked great in lifeguard gear, it became the most widely viewed TV series in the world with a weekly audience of 1.1 billion.

July 5 "Seinfeld" began on NBC. A critical and commercial hit, the sitcom starring comedian Jerry Seinfeld would run for nine seasons and become a touchstone of contemporary American comedy.

Nov 15 The Comedy Channel, later known as Comedy Central, debuted on American cable.

Dec 17 "The Simpsons" had its first appearance on Fox. Created by Matt Groening and producer James L. Brooks, the family comedy that began life as an animated short airing during Fox's "Tracey Ullman Show" would go on to become the longest-running sitcom in American TV history, animated or otherwise.

Other Notable 1989 Debuts

- "The Arsenio Hall Show" (syndicated)
- "Inside Edition" (syndicated)
- "Coach" (ABC)
- "Quantum Leap" (NBC)
- "Tales from the Crypt" (HBO)
- "America's Funniest Home Videos" (ABC)
- "American Gladiators" (syndicated)
- "Primetime Live" (ABC)
- "Saved by the Bell" (NBC)
- "Doogie Howser, MD" (ABC)

Music

Mar 2 Madonna appeared in a TV advertisement for Pepsi that cross-promoted her album *Like a Prayer*. Later, after her controversial music video for the album's title track came out, Pepsi cancelled the campaign and its sponsorship of Madonna's world tour.

Grammy Awards

- Record of the Year: "Wind Beneath My Wings," Bette Midler, artist; Arif Marden, producer
- Album of the Year: *Nick of Time*, Bonnie Raitt, artist; Don Was, producer
- Song of the Year: "Wind Beneath My Wings," Jeff Silbar and Larry Henley, songwriters
- Best Pop Vocal Performance, Female: *Nick of Time*, Bonnie Raitt, artist
- Best Pop Vocal Performance, Male: "How Am I Supposed to Live Without You," Michael Bolton, artist

Notable Albums

- *Like a Prayer*, Madonna
- *Garth Brooks*, Garth Brooks
- *Flowers in the Dirt*, Paul McCartney
- *In Step*, Stevie Ray Vaughan
- *Bleach*, Nirvana
- *Paul's Boutique*, Beastie Boys
- *Tender Lover*, Babyface
- *Mother's Milk*, Red Hot Chili Peppers
- *Steel Wheels*, Rolling Stones
- *Stone Cold Rhymin'*, Young MC
- *Brave and Crazy*, Melissa Etheridge
- *Storm Front*, Billy Joel
- *Journeyman*, Eric Clapton
- *New York*, Lou Reed
- *Lōc-ed After Dark*, Tone Lōc
- *Skid Row*, Skid Row
- *As Nasty as They Wanna Be*, 2 Live Crew

Popular Songs

- "Wind Beneath My Wings," Bette Midler
- "Paradise City," Guns N' Roses
- "Love Shack," the B-52s
- "Another Day in Paradise," Phil Collins
- "Real Love," Jody Watley
- "Like a Prayer," Madonna
- "Cold Hearted," Paula Abdul
- "Don't Forget My Number," Milli Vanilli
- "Wild Thing" and "Funky Cold Medina," Tone Lōc
- "18 and Life," Skid Row
- "Good Thing," Fine Young Cannibals
- "The End of the Innocence," Don Henley
- "Stand," REM

Science and Technology

Mar English computer scientist Tim Berners-Lee submitted a proposal to his bosses at CERN, the Switzerland-based particle physics research laboratory. Called "Information Management: A Proposal," it specified a list of keywords, including "hypertext," "computer conferencing," "data retrieval," "information management" and "project control." Berners-Lee had collated existing research and his own theories on technology into what would soon become a unified, international data system known as the World Wide Web.

May 4 Space shuttle *Atlantis* was launched with a mission to deploy the *Magellan*, an exploratory spacecraft designed to map the surface of Venus. *Atlantis* landed safely May 8.

July 17 The B-2 Stealth bomber made its first successful flight. Estimated cost per airplane at time of flight: $530 million.

Aug 24 *Voyager 2*, an explorer launched in 1977, reached Neptune. The next day, it began transmitting stunning images of the planet back to Earth.

Sept 4 The US Air Force launched its last Titan 3 rocket, which carried a reconnaissance satellite into space. The Titan debuted in 1964.

Oct 18 Space shuttle *Atlantis* lifted off from Kennedy Space Center with a mission to launch the Galileo spacecraft on its six-year trip to Jupiter.

- The Nobel Prize in Physics went to Norman F. Ramsey, Hans G. Dehmelt and Wolfgang Paul.
- The Nobel Prize in Chemistry was awarded to Sidney Altman and Thomas R. Cech.
- The Nobel Prize in Physiology or Medicine was received by J. Michael Bishop and Harold E. Varmus.

Commerce and New Products

Feb 28 After hundreds of millions of dollars in research and development, the R.J. Reynolds Tobacco Company canceled "Premier," its smokeless cigarette, due to poor sales.

Mar 4 Time, Inc., and Warner Communications announced a massive, $14.9 billion merger, blocking a hostile acquisition attempt by Paramount in the process and forming the multinational media company Time-Warner, Inc.

Sep 18 The first NeXT computer was released. Suggested retail price: $6,500.

- The Nobel Memorial Prize in Economics was awarded to Trygve Haavelmo.

Sports

Auto Racing

■ Emerson Fittipaldi won the Indianapolis 500.

■ Rusty Wallace won the NASCAR Sprint Cup.

Baseball

Feb Pete Rose was questioned by then–Major League Baseball commissioner Peter Ueberroth concerning allegations that he had bet on baseball. Nothing came of it until Ueberroth gave way to new commissioner Bart Giamatti, who reopened the investigation. While Rose maintained his innocence, he also agreed on Aug 24 to permanent ineligibility from the MLB, and a league investigation revealed that he in fact may have bet on Cincinnati Reds games that he was managing.

Oct 14–28 In the World Series, the Oakland Athletics swept the San Francisco Giants, four games to none.

Basketball

Jan 26 Michael Jordan scored his 10,000th point in just five NBA seasons, but his Chicago Bulls still lost 120–108 to the Philadelphia 76ers.

Feb 5 Kareem Abdul-Jabbar hit the 38,000 point mark in the last year of his NBA tenure. He was the first-ever player to reach such a pinnacle.

■ In the NCAA Basketball Championship, Michigan beat Seton Hall 80–79 in overtime.

■ The Detroit Pistons defeated the Los Angeles Lakers four games to none to win the NBA Championship.

Football

Jan 22 In Super Bowl XXIII, the San Francisco 49ers defeated the Cincinnati Bengals 20–16.

Feb 24 Jerry Jones announced his purchase of the Dallas Cowboys and the replacement of Tom Landry, the only head coach in the team's history, with the University of Miami's Jimmy Johnson.

■ Andre Ware of the University of Houston won the Heisman Trophy.

Golf

■ Nick Faldo won the Masters.

■ Curtis Strange won the US Open.

■ The British Open Championship was won by Mark Calcavecchia.

■ Payne Stewart won the PGA Championship.

Hockey

Mar 7 Calgary Flames right winger Lanny McDonald tallied the 1,000th point of his National Hockey League career with a goal in the Flames' 9–5 win over the Winnipeg Jets.

Mar 21 Calgary Flames right winger Lanny McDonald scored the 500th and last goal of his National Hockey League career in a 4–1 Flames win over the New York Islanders. McDonald was the 13th NHL player to reach the milestone.

May 14–25 To win the Stanley Cup, the Calgary Flames defeated the Montreal Canadiens four games to two.

Horse Racing

■ Sunday Silence won both the Kentucky Derby and the Preakness Stakes.

■ Easy Goer won the Belmont Stakes.

Soccer

■ In the European Cup, it was AC Milan over Steaua Bucuresti.

■ Liverpool, mourning the loss of 96 fans the previous month, defeated Everton to take the FA Cup.

■ Manchester United took the English First Division.

Tennis

■ Boris Becker won both the US Open and Wimbledon.

■ Michael Chang was the victor at the French Open.

■ Ivan Lendl won the Australian Open.

1989 Deaths

■ Alvin Ailey, US choreographer and dancer

■ Earl John ("Sparky") Adams, US baseball player

■ James Gilmore (Jim) Backus, US actor

■ Lucille Ball, US film and television pioneer and comedienne

■ George Beadle, US professor of genetics, researcher and college president

■ Samuel Beckett, Irish author, playwright and critic

■ Irving Berlin, US songwriter

■ Earl Henry ("Red") Blaik, US football player and coach

■ Mel Blanc, US voice artist

Spotlight on the Past

- August Adolphus Busch Jr., beer magnate and baseball executive
- George Washington Case, US baseball player
- John Cassavetes, US director and actor
- Graham Chapman, English comedian
- Joseph Edward (Joe) Collins, US baseball player
- John Bertrand ("Jocko") Conlan, US baseball player and umpire
- Salvador Dali, Spanish Surrealist painter
- Bette Davis, US actress
- Murray Monroe Dickson, US baseball player
- Joseph Anthony Foy, US baseball player
- Bibb August Falk, US baseball player, coach and manager
- Sammy Fain, US composer
- Wesley Eugene ("Wes") Fesler, US football player, coach and broadcaster
- Angelo Bartlett (Bart) Giamatti, commissioner of baseball and educator
- Vernon Louis ("Lefty") Gomez, US baseball player
- Andrei Gromyko, Soviet diplomat and statesman
- Hirohito, emperor of Japan
- Abbie Hoffman, US political activist
- William Julius (Judy) Johnson, US baseball player
- Ayatollah Ruhollah Musavi Khomeini, Iranian religious leader
- Sergio Leone, Italian film director
- Mary McCarthy, US novelist, critic and essayist
- Silvana Mangano, Italian actress
- Robert Mapplethorpe, US artist
- Ferdinand Marcos, former ruler of the Philippines
- Billy Martin, US baseball manager and player
- Marvin Middlemark, US inventor ("rabbit ears")
- Donnie Ray Moore, US baseball player
- Laurence Olivier, English actor, director and theater manager
- John Payne, US actor
- Claude Denson Pepper, US representative and senator
- Gilda Radner, US actress and comedienne
- Tim Richmond, US auto racer
- Ray ("Sugar Ray") Robinson, US boxer
- Andrey Sakharov, Soviet physicist, human rights activist and environmentalist
- Truett Banks ("Rip") Sewell, US baseball player
- Georges Simenon, Belgian author
- Thomas Virgil Stallcup, US baseball player
- William Harold (Bill) Terry, US baseball player
- Lee Van Cleef, US actor
- Robert Penn Warren, US poet laureate (1986–88) and author
- Willie ("The Devil") Wells, US baseball player

Spotlight on World Anniversaries

450th Birth Anniversary of William Shakespeare

APR 23, 1564 ✦ 450 YEARS

Almost 400 years after his death, William Shakespeare's drama continues to draw crowds and details about his life continue to fuel the enigma of his life. Shakespeare's exact birthdate is unknown, unsurprising for a playwright whose life is sparsely recorded in official documents. The attributed date is Apr 23, 1564, as it is close to his baptismal date, Apr 26, and coincides with his death date, also Apr 23.

Born and raised at Stratford-upon-Avon, England, Shakespeare presumably attended the Stratford Grammar School. Church documents record that in November 1582, at age 18, he married Anne Hathaway, who was then three months pregnant. By 1594, Shakespeare was an actor, published poet and playwright. Later, he divided his time between London, where he was part-owner in the Globe Theatre beginning in 1599, and Stratford-upon-Avon, where he was a grain merchant. The remaining documents about his life are sundry property records, court documents, tax records and a will. He died at Stratford-upon-Avon on Apr 23, 1616. Because the few known facts about his life are so prosaic and do not explain his genius, speculation about "the real Shakespeare" abounds with an almost cultlike fervor.

The Shakespeare mystique is enhanced by the undocumented "lost years" between 1584 and 1592. By 1585, he had three small children to support, so how did he come to be established in the theater world by 1594—not to mention author of arguably the most brilliant body of literary work in English by 1612? From what wellspring was drawn the power of *Hamlet*, the tragedy of *King Lear* or the comedy of *All's Well that Ends Well*? Considerable ink has been spilled theorizing that the author of these works was actually someone else. The main contenders have been Sir Francis Bacon (with or without Sir Walter Raleigh), Christopher Marlowe and Edward de Vere, 17th Earl of Oxford, the latter being of most interest to 21st-century scholars.

While details of his life are few, the brilliance of Shakespeare's work is unchallenged. His first publication was two narrative poems, *Venus and Adonis* (1593) and *The Rape of Lucrece* (1594), both immediately popular. Shakespeare's 154 sonnets were written between 1593 and 1601 and consider the immortalization of love and beauty by poetry and the ravages of time on youth. While sonnets 1–126 address a "Fair Youth" and sonnets 127–154 were written to a mysterious "Dark Lady," neither person, if real, has ever been satisfactorily identified.

Shakespeare's canon currently includes 38 plays written between 1590 and 1612 and encompasses histories, comedies, tragedies and romances. As was conventional in his day, Shakespeare is known to have collaborated with other playwrights on *The Two Noble Kinsmen* (with John Fletcher), *Pericles Prince of Tyre* (with George Wilkins) and *Timon of Athens* (with Thomas Middleton). Many scholars agree that next up to join the canon will be *The Reign of Edward III*; in 2009 plagiarism software detected Shakespeare's hand in collaboration with Thomas Kyd.

Shakespeare contributed thousands of words to the English language ("fanged," "birth place," "arch-villain," "dewdrop," "still-born") and expanded the dramatic possibilities of blank verse, making it mimic the rhythm of speech even as he elevated speech to poetry. He heightened the psychological realism of his characters, making their struggles endlessly adaptable to theater in different times and places.

Shakespeare discoveries, though rare, continue to make news. In 2009, the Shakespeare Birthplace Trust announced the discovery of the only known Shakespeare portrait made from life, found in the collection of descendants of his patron, the third Earl of Southampton, Henry Wriothesely. In June 2012, archaeologists finally located the foundation of the lost Curtain Theatre in London, where *Henry V* and *Romeo and Juliet* would have first been staged.

The 450th anniversary of Shakespeare's birth will be marked by events around the world. In England, the Shakespeare Birthday Trust will launch the inaugural Shakespeare Week (Mar 17–23), a national celebration and campaign "to bring Shakespeare to life vividly" for more than 3 million children with events in schools and cultural venues around the country. In Washington, DC, the Folger Library plans a conference on "Shakespeare and the Problem of Biography." The New York Shakespeare Exchange is creating Internet videos of all 154 sonnets, performed by 154 different actors in 154 different locations in New York City, which will be available on its own app. The French Shakespeare Society is hosting a week-long conference in Paris, including lectures, roundtables, workshops and performances exploring Shakespeare's influence on French artists since the 1820s.

Did Shakespeare foresee this legacy when he wrote Cassius's lines in *Julius Caesar*: "How many ages hence/Shall this our lofty scene be acted over/In states unborn and accents yet unknown!"?

For information:

Shakespeare Birthplace Trust
The Shakespeare Centre
Henley Street
Stratford-upon-Avon
Warwickshire CV37 6QW
England
E-mail: ShakespeareWeek@shakespeare.org.uk
Web: www.shakespeare.org.uk or www.shakespeareweek.org.uk

Storming of the Bastille

JULY 14, 1789 ✦ 225 YEARS

The storming of the Bastille prison signaled the beginning of the French Revolution and the end of absolute monarchy and the *ancien régime* in France. Originally built in the 14th century as a fortress to defend Paris, the Bastille evolved into a prison for enemies of state—real or imagined. Under Louis XIV, a *lettre de cachet* signed by the king was all that was required to be sent to the Bastille, making it a potent symbol of royal tyranny. Among its famous prisoners were Voltaire, the Man in the Iron Mask and the Marquis de Sade, who left 10 days before its fall. By 1789, the prison was already slated to be closed and housed only seven prisoners: four forgers, two insanity cases and a dissolute aristocrat, sent there by his family.

In June 1789, facing a financial crisis and food shortages, King Louis XVI had convened the Estates-General to raise taxes. As it splintered into warring factions, the Third Estate (the commoners and also France's taxpayers) formed a National Assembly and, on June 20, 1789, made its Tennis Court Oath, pledging to write a new constitution. While Louis XVI accepted the assembly, he also surrounded Paris with troops and dismissed Jacques Necker, his finance minister, who was sympathetic to reform. Many in Paris saw these actions as signs that Louis XVI was planning to reassert his authority by force.

Looking for gunpowder to supply 28,000 muskets taken on July 13 from the Hôtel des Invalides, a mob of around 1,000 approached the Bastille on the morning of July 14 and demanded arms, gunpowder and the release of its prisoners. The Bastille was guarded by only 84 pensioners and 30 Swiss guards, so its governor, the marquis de Launay, began negotiations with the mob. But confusion ensued when part of the crowd in an interior courtyard was fired upon by the Bastille's defenders. The enraged mob escalated its attack, de Launay capitulated and the demolition of the Bastille began. On Aug 26, 1789, the National Assembly adopted the *Declaration of the Rights of Man and of the Citizens*, which defined the principles of liberty that would inspire the French Revolution.

The anniversary of the storming of the Bastille is now a national holiday in France. Bastille Day is often celebrated with military parades, dances, communal meals and fireworks.

World War I Begins

JULY 28, 1914 ✦ 100 YEARS

The summer of 1914 marked the beginning of the 20th century's first global conflict, then called the Great War, initially pitting the Central Powers (Austria-Hungary and Germany) against the Allies or Triple Entente (France, United Kingdom, Russia). The United States would enter the Great War in 1917.

Early in the 20th century, a long, delicate balance of power with shifting alliances had existed among world empires, as well as various arms and technology races. In a volatile atmosphere of rising militarism, fierce competition for colonies, complex diplomatic alliances and increased nationalism, populations were restless and imperial Germany sought an opportunity to implement its expansion plan into France and launch a preventative war against Russia, which was growing stronger. This balance was upset on June 28, 1914, when Archduke Franz Ferdinand of Austria-Hungary was assassinated by a Yugoslavian nationalist, who was trained by the Black Hand, a secret Serbian military society. This ignited the "Powder Keg of Europe" in the Balkan Peninsula and set into motion the events that led to the First World War.

On July 28, the German-backed Austro-Hungarian Empire declared war against Serbia. On July 29, Russia entered the war to defend its neighbor and ally Serbia; on July 30, Austria-Hungary ally Germany officially entered the war and seized the opportunity to implement its expansion plan into France to the West and Russia to the East. The United Kingdom entered the fray on Aug 4, two days after Germany invaded neutral Belgium. Colonies of the Allies—New Zealand and Australia—subsequently captured Samoa and German New Guinea. In August, Japan declared war on Germany, seized German holdings in China and occupied German islands in the Pacific. The world was at war and would remain so until Nov 11, 1918, when German delegates signed an armistice agreement.

International Centenary commemorations begin in 2014. Britain's International War Museum (IWM) leads the First World War Centenary Partnership, a network of more than 500 organizations spanning 24 countries. The United Kingdom's Great War commemorations will involve "somber reflection, proper consideration for the millions who died, and opportunities for a new generation to explore what happened and why." The first of six state occasions will take place on Aug 4 with a commemoration service to include delegations from Germany and all the Commonwealth countries involved in the conflict.

First World War Centenary events include the opening of refurbished First World War Galleries at IWM London and a £1 million grant from the National Heritage Memorial Fund to support HMS *Caroline*, the last surviving warship from the First World War fleet, in Belfast. In Antwerp, the Belgian and Dutch armies will jointly build a temporary pontoon across the River Scheldt, opening Oct 3–5 as a platform for dance and musical performances. A play by *War Horse* author Michael Morpurgo reenacting the famous Christmas Day–truce soccer game between German and British troops will be staged on the battlefield in Ypres, Belgium.

France's First World War Centenary Mission 1914–2014 includes a commemorative program organized around six great national and international events aimed at passing on the memory of the Great War to young people, showcasing cultural and scientific development and encouraging remembrance tourism. Additional WWI commemorative events will take place in 2016 (the Battle of the Somme) and 2018 (Armistice Day).

On Jan 14, 2012, US President Barak Obama signed the World War I Centennial Commission Act, designating American commemorative activities to be coordinated through the National World War I Museum in Kansas City, MO. The museum is home to the 217-foot Liberty Memorial, dedicated as the US national memorial to World War I by President Calvin Coolidge in 1926. The bulk of WWI commemorations in the United States will begin in 2017, 100 years after the US entered the Great War on Apr 6, 1917.

For more information:

United Kingdom: First World War Centenary
Imperial War Museum
Bryony Phillips, Senior Press Officer
IWM London, Lambeth Road
London SE1 6HZ
England
E-mail: bphillips@iwm.org.uk
Web: www.1914.org

France: Pays de Meaux Museum of the Great War
Lyse Hautecoeur, Head of Communication
Musée de la Grande Guerre du Pays de Meaux
Rue Lazare Ponticelli
77100 Meaux
France
E-mail: lyse.hautecoeur@meaux.fr

Web: www.museedelagrande guerre.eu/en

Australia: Anzac Centenary
Department of Veterans' Affairs
Suite M-1-49, Parliament House
Canberra ACT 2600
Australia
E-mail: dvmedia@dva.gov.au
Web: www.anzaccentenary.gov.au

New Zealand: WW100 New Zealand
Jane Keig, Communications Adviser
PO Box 5364
Wellington 6145
New Zealand
E-mail: jane.keig@WW100.govt.nz
Web: ww100.govt.nz

USA: World War I Centennial
National World War I Museum
Denise Rendina, VP of Marketing and Communications
100 W 26th St
Kansas City, MO 64108
E-mail: drendina@theworld war.org
Web: www.theworldwar.org

Panama Canal Opens

AUG 15, 1914 ✦ 100 YEARS

The first ship passed completely through the manmade Panama Canal on Aug 15, 1914. The 50-mile canal created a direct shipping route from the Atlantic to the Pacific Ocean through the Isthmus of Panama in Central America, eliminating roughly 8,000 miles from the only alternate route: around Cape Horn at the southern tip of South America.

Between 1904 and 1914, engineers and workers excavated 211 million cubic yards of earth and rock from hills, dense jungles and swamps; constructed the world's largest dam and manmade lake; and built three sets of double locks, the largest concrete pour in the world at that time. The largest American engineering project up to that date is designated one of the Seven Wonders of the Modern World by the American Society of Civil Engineers.

In the late 1800s, Colombia had sold the rights to build a canal across its province of Panama to a succession of French interests. The French began digging in 1882, but, lacking the technology and tools, the project went bankrupt. During the Spanish-American War in 1898, the US Congress realized the need for a shorter route to get ships from the West Coast to Cuba and agreed to buy the Panamanian rights from the French in 1902. Colombia rejected the treaty in 1903, and a group of Panamanians, fearing the loss of a lucrative economic prospect, revolted and declared their independence from Colombia. The United States hastily signed the Hay–Bunau-Varilla Treaty, recognizing the independent Republic of Panama and in return received the use and control of the 10-mile-wide Panama Canal Zone in perpetuity.

Over the next 10 years, construction of the canal cost $380 million and 5,600 lives. As the water filled the canal during the final three weeks in preparation for the 1914 grand opening ceremonies, Europe entered World War I. The planned cavalcade of 100 US Navy warships was scrapped and instead the steamship SS *Ancon* made the first complete pass through the canal, to little fanfare. It did not make the front page of newspapers.

World War II Begins

SEPT 1, 1939 ✦ 75 YEARS

On Sept 1, 1939, emboldened by the impotence of the League of Nations and the Allied powers' history of appeasement, German forces invaded Poland. On Sept 3, allies Great Britain and France declared war on Germany. Two weeks later, Russia's Red Army joined Germany in the invasion of Poland. The joint September Campaign ended on Oct 6 with western Poland and Danzig being directly annexed by Germany, and portions of eastern Poland absorbed by the Soviet Union. The stage was set for the Second World War in the European Theater.

Although 1939 marked the official beginning of World War II, it was a long time coming. An uneasy peace followed World War I, with the League of Nations established to enforce and mediate the agreements made by the 1919 Treaty of Versailles. But the League proved to be largely toothless. When Japan invaded the Manchurian region of northeast China/Russia in 1931 in an effort to expand access to natural resources, the League formally condemned Japan but took no action. Runaway hunger, depletion of resources and unemployment caused by the Great Depression of 1929 resulted in worldwide dissatisfaction, turning citizens away from global cooperation in favor of self-preservationist nationalism, with current democratic leaders falling out of favor and absolute dictators rising to power in Germany (Adolf Hitler), Russia (Joseph Stalin), Italy (Benito Mussolini) and Spain (Francisco Franco). The social malaise was greatest in Germany, which still owed billions in war reparations mandated by the 1919 Paris Peace Conference, which its people resented. Germany, in accordance with the treaty, had disarmed, but other nations, France in particular, refused to follow suit until an effectual international police system could be established.

Hitler was elected Chancellor of Germany in 1933 on a platform of rearmament and reunification of the Teutonic peoples into a "Greater Germany," and his National Socialist Party withdrew from the League of Nations. Mussolini invaded and conquered Ethiopia for Italy in 1935; the League only offered economic sanctions. During the Spanish Civil War in 1936, Germany and Italy aided Franco's rebel forces while Russia supported Spanish loyalists, with Franco ultimately overthrowing the Spanish government and establishing an absolute dictatorship; the League of Nations remained neutral.

While the Spanish Civil War raged, German troops took Austria in 1938 as part of reunification and closed in on Czechoslovakia. France, Russia and England promised to defend Czechoslovakia, but Hitler claimed he only wanted to reclaim the Sudeten mountain region as his last effort of reunification. France and England signed the Munich Agreement, ceding the Sudetenland region to Germany, but this gesture of appeasement backfired when Hitler took the rest of Czechoslovakia and then the Memel region of Lithuania and demanded the return of Danzig, while Italy occupied Albania. But it wasn't until the invasion of Poland that France and Great Britain declared war.

Before it was over in 1945, more than 100 million people from more than 30 countries would fight in the war, incurring up to 75 million fatalities, making it the most widespread war and deadliest conflict in human history.

Beatlemania

1964 ✦ 50 YEARS

The year 1964 was The Beatles' signature year. The quartet of John Lennon, Paul McCartney, George Harrison and Ringo Starr had become a sensation in England the previous year, sending young pop fans into hysterics on the strength of irresistible early singles like "Twist & Shout" and "Please Please Me." But with the band's arrival at John F. Kennedy Airport in New York City on Feb 7, 1964, their now-legendary performance on the popular "Ed Sullivan Show" two days later and a whirlwind American tour that took them 22,000 miles in 29 days, The Beatles propelled themselves to worldwide stardom, became the biggest deal the still-burgeoning rock scene had yet produced and were catalysts for the eventual British Invasion.

Meet The Beatles!, the quartet's second US album, was released Jan 20, 1964, and hit number one on the Billboard chart Feb 15. It remained there for 11 weeks; in a music industry first, it was supplanted by *The Beatles' Second Album*. The Fab Four were suddenly everywhere, and the world would never be the same.

If their unprecedented chart dominance wasn't enough, The Beatles also became movie stars in 1964. More than just an opportunistic marketing gimmick, *A Hard Day's Night* was a madcap comic spree that showcased the group's quirky sense of humor in addition to the musical segments. *A Hard Day's Night* and its accompanying soundtrack were an immediate hit with Beatlemaniacs everywhere, and the band continued to crank out singles and cause a public relations stir throughout the year, becoming darlings of not only screaming teenage girls, but the media too. From newsreels to television appearances, not to mention concerts across America, The Beatles were a new sensation to the world: fresh-faced kids whose music drew equally from rock and roll and rhythm and blues and added a scintillating layer of innovative songwriting that defined the look and feel of a new pop music form.

The Beatles went on to release "I Feel Fine" in 1964, plus EPs (extended plays) like *Four by The Beatles*, and they closed out the year with the release of *Beatles For Sale*, their fourth studio album. It featured the single "Eight Days a Week," ballads like the Paul McCartney composition "I'll Follow the Sun," and cover songs, too, since the band barely had enough material of their own to keep the world sated. *Beatles For Sale* also featured Lennon's "I'm a Loser," which with its air of maturity illustrated the band's continuing evolution as songwriters. The world had never seen anything like The Beatles before 1964, and there's a good chance no band will ever have that successful of a year again.

Spotlight on American Anniversaries

"The Star-Spangled Banner"

SEPT 14, 1814 ✦ 200 YEARS

The national anthem of the United States started as a poem, hastily scribbled by a lawyer and sung to the tune of a bawdy drinking song.

During the War of 1812, Georgetown lawyer Francis Scott Key was granted permission by President James Madison to negotiate the release of a prominent doctor captured by the British army. In September 1814, accompanied by US Prisoner Exchange Officer John S. Skinner, Key embarked on American vessel the HMS *Minden* to locate the British fleet in Chesapeake Bay. Once aboard Britain's HMS *Tonnant*, they negotiated the release. The Americans, however, were not immediately permitted to return to shore because they had learned of the fleet's impending attack on Baltimore. While detained on the *Minden* at the back of the British fleet, Key witnessed the bombarding of Fort McHenry throughout the day of Sept 13 and all through the night, as British warship *Erebus* provided the "rockets' red glare" and the HMS *Meteor* launched "bombs bursting in air." In the darkness, Key had no idea of the fate of vulnerable Fort McHenry, but at daybreak on Sept 14, the smoke cleared and Key was overjoyed to see the US flag still there.

Emotional and inspired, Key feverishly scrawled a poem he titled "The Defense of Ft. McHenry." The poem was printed in Baltimore newspapers, which suggested it be sung to the tune of a popular drinking song called "To Anacreon in Heaven," composed by British teenager John Stafford Smith in the 1760s.

Key's patriotic lyrics were first published under the title "The Star-Spangled Banner" by a Baltimore music store. It was made the official tune of flag raisings by the secretary of the navy in 1889 and was ordered by President Woodrow Wilson to be played at military occasions in 1916. However, it was not adopted by Congress as the first official national anthem until 1931.

George Washington Carver Birth Anniversary

1864 ✦ 150 YEARS

George Washington Carver, born to slave parents on an unknown date in 1864 on a plantation near Diamond Grove, MO, grew up to become a 20th-century Renaissance man. Dubbed the "Black Leonardo [da Vinci]" by *Time* magazine in 1941, Carver's lifelong accomplishments as a botanist, horticulturist, chemist, inventor and artist serve as an enduring testament to the power of education.

At the end of the Civil War, former slave owners Moses and Susan Carver raised and educated young George as their own on the farm, where he became known as "the plant doctor." He earned his master's degree in botany from Iowa State Agricultural College, then, in 1896 at the invitation of Booker T. Washington, became head of the agricultural department at Tuskegee Institute in Alabama where he remained for 47 years, until his death.

During his tenure, he helped sharecroppers become self-sufficient through farming, particularly by rotating crops. Instead of soil-depleting cotton, he encouraged them to plant nutrient-restoring legumes: first peas, then peanuts and soybeans. Carver took his message to the rural poor through his patented Jesup Wagon, a mobile laboratory and classroom. Faced with sudden surpluses of new crops, he invented hundreds of new uses for peanuts and sweet potatoes including medications, paints, dyes and plastic as well as circulated recipes using these ingredients.

Carver collaborated with Henry Ford to derive an automobile biofuel from soybeans. As a celebrity scientist and an African American role model, he served as advisor to President Theodore Roosevelt and Mahatma Gandhi and joined Benjamin Franklin among the few

Americans invited into the Royal Society of Arts in London. In 1951, the George Washington Carver National Monument was established near Diamond, MO, after a bill passed unanimously in both houses of Congress. It is the first national monument to an African American and the first to a non-president. His life and "birthday" are celebrated on the anniversary of his Jan 5, 1943, death.

Nevada Statehood

OCT 31, 1864 ✦ 150 YEARS

The end of the Mexican-American War in 1848 brought many alterations to the face of the United States. Mexico ceded Nevada and nearby lands to the US, and, in 1850, Nevada was made part of the Utah Territory. Silver was discovered in Nevada in 1859, giving rise to its nickname of the Silver State. The Comstock Lode was the first major discovery of silver ore in the United States, and thousands of people from the East flocked to Nevada as prospectors. As a result of the large population growth, President James Buchanan made Nevada a separate territory in 1861. It became the 36th state in 1864.

Nevada is the most mountainous state in the continental US. The word *nevada* means "snow-covered" in Spanish, and the name refers to the snow-capped Sierra Nevada Mountains on the western side of the state. While much of the state is desert or semiarid, Nevada also shares in a number of natural and manmade wonders. The Hoover Dam on the border of Arizona and Nevada dams the Colorado River, creating Lake Mead. Lake Tahoe is another large lake, bordered by Nevada and California. Nevada contains Great Basin National Park and shares Death Valley National Park with California.

125 Years Old!

125th US statehood anniversaries in 2014:

North Dakota, the Peace Garden State; South Dakota, the Sunshine State; Montana, the Treasure State; Washington, the Evergreen State.

Nevada is also known as the Battle Born State, since it was admitted to the Union during the Civil War. It ranks 7th largest in land area in the nation but only 35th in population. Carson City is its capital, and Las Vegas the largest city. The federal government owns 80 percent of the land.

Nevada's largest industry is tourism, centered on gambling, and 13 of the largest 20 employers in the state are casinos. The second-largest industry is mining; Nevada is the fourth largest producer of gold in the world. Cattle ranching is also important to its economy.

Nevada's Sesquicentennial celebration commenced on Nevada Day 2013 (Oct 31, 2013) and concludes with an expanded Nevada Day celebration on Oct 31, 2014.

For more information:

Nevada 150
PO Box 17025
Reno, NV 89511
Web: www.nevada150.org

Mother's Day: First Official Observance

MAY 10, 1914 ✦ 100 YEARS

During the Civil War, West Virginia Sunday School teacher Ann Jarvis founded nonpartisan Mother's Day Work Clubs to improve sanitation and fight typhoid outbreaks in both Confederate and Union camps. After the war, she established a Mother's Friendship Day to reunite families divided by the Civil War with the intention of expanding it into an annual celebration for mothers.

Upon Jarvis's death in 1905, her daughter, Anna Jarvis, continued her mother's mission by hosting annual Mother's Day services in Andrews Methodist Episcopal Church in Grafton, WV, on the second Sunday in May. In 1908, with the help of Philadelphia, PA, department store magnate John Wanamaker, Anna hosted the first official Mother's Day commemoration, in both Andrews Church and Wanamaker's Auditorium in Philadelphia. By 1909, the celebration spread to New York City, and in 1910, Jarvis started a full-bore campaign to make it a national holiday, even trademarking the terms "Mother's Day" and "second Sunday in May."

On May 8, 1914, Congress passed a law designating the second Sunday in May as Mother's Day; the following day, President Woodrow Wilson issued a proclamation declaring the first national Mother's Day as a day for American citizens to display the flag in honor of those mothers whose sons had died in war. The annual holiday honoring mothers and motherhood caught on quickly, especially with florists and greeting card companies.

Jarvis did not anticipate the commercialization and spent the rest of her days—and the entirety of her family's fortune—fighting it, saying, "A printed card means nothing except that you are too lazy to write to the woman who has done more for you than anyone in the world."

Andrews Church today is the International Mother's Day Shrine and Museum, established to preserve the spirit of motherhood, as exemplified by the lives of Ann and Anna Jarvis, and the institution of Mother's Day they established.

Joe Louis Birth Anniversary

MAY 13, 1914 ✦ 100 YEARS

Joseph Louis Barrow, born May 13, 1914, at Lafayette, AL, was the world heavyweight boxing champion from June 22, 1937, until Mar 1, 1949. Nicknamed "The Brown Bomber," he held the title longer than anyone else in the history of the sport.

While attending a Detroit, MI, vocational school to learn cabinet-making, he became an amateur boxer fighting under the name Joe Louis; by 1934, he held the national Amateur Athletic Union light-heavyweight title, ending his amateur career with 43 knockout victories in 54 matches. As a pro, Louis went undefeated until 1936 when he was knocked out in the 12th round by Germany's Max Schmeling, a favorite of Adolf Hitler. In 1937, Louis knocked out defending champion Jim Braddock for the heavyweight crown, which he kept for the next 12 years.

A 1938 rematch between Louis and Schmeling became one of the major sports events of the 20th century, with Schmeling touted by Hitler as a shining example of his doctrine of Aryan superiority. Before a crowd of 70,000 in Yankee Stadium and broadcast by radio to millions of listeners worldwide, Louis bested Schmeling in two minutes and four seconds.

In 1942, Louis enlisted in the Army and famously stated, "We'll win, 'cause we're on God's side," a phrase that became a wartime recruitment slogan and increased Louis's wide popularity beyond the sports world. Many white Americans embraced an African American man as their representative to the world for the first time. Louis's winning record and his reputation for being a fair fighter and a gracious and generous victor (he donated his purse on several occasions to military relief funds) made him a source of national pride, a hero to international sports fans and an inspiration to African Americans. Louis retired for good in 1951 after Rocky Marciano knocked him out at Madison Square Garden. He died Apr 12, 1981, at Las Vegas, NV.

Civil Rights Act of 1964

JULY 2, 1964 ✦ 50 YEARS

On July 2, 1964, President Lyndon B. Johnson signed into law the Civil Rights Act of 1964. It was the strongest civil rights bill in US history, providing for nondiscrimination in voting, the workplace, public schools, public accommodations and federally funded programs. It ordered businesses that serve the general public, including hotels, restaurants, theaters and stores, to serve everyone regardless of race, color, religion or national origin. The act outlawed discrimination by employers or unions based on the same criteria, with the addition of gender, and established the Equal Employment Opportunity Commission (EEOC) to enforce fair labor practices. It authorized a cutoff of federal funds for any establishment that failed to comply. Most controversially, and most potently, Article III of the act authorized the Attorney General to file lawsuits on behalf of individuals deprived of rights secured by the Constitution or US law, thereby protecting voters and peaceful protestors from police brutality.

In the wake of peaceful civil rights protests and violent retaliation in Birmingham, AL, President John F. Kennedy first called for a civil rights bill during his televised Civil Rights Address of June 11, 1963. The President garnered increasing support among the public and in Congress. Another impetus was the Aug 28, 1963, March on Washington for Jobs and Freedom—the largest civil rights rally ever held and one that featured Martin Luther King Jr.'s "I Have a Dream" speech.

After Kennedy's assassination on Nov 22, 1963, President Johnson kept up Kennedy's momentum, telling Congress the best way to honor the late president would be through passage of the bill. With increased public support, the bill quickly passed the House. But it took some legal maneuvering to navigate it through the Senate, despite the opposition of the "southern bloc" of 18 southern senators—most vocally Strom Thurmond—who filibustered for more than 54 days. With a compromise bill that diluted the government's power to regulate private business, the Senate eventually got 71 supporters and for the first time in history had enough votes to cut off a filibuster on a civil rights bill.

Spotlight on People

The year 2014 brings many significant birth anniversaries, of which a small selection is presented here. See also the main book for many other interesting landmark birth anniversaries.

World History

Galileo Galilei

Birth: Feb 15, 1564 ✦ 450 years

Physicist and astronomer who helped overthrow medieval concepts of the world, born at Pisa, Italy. He proved the theory that all bodies, large and small, descend at equal speed and gathered evidence to support Copernicus's theory that Earth and other planets revolve around the sun. In 1632, Galileo was tried by the Inquisition and found "vehemently suspect of heresy" because his *Dialogue Concerning the Two Chief World Systems* argued in favor of heliocentrism in contradiction to literal readings of scripture. Galileo remained under house arrest until his death in Florence on Jan 8, 1642. The *Dialogue* was finally published in an uncensored form in 1835, and the Catholic Church issued an official apology to Galileo in 2000.

Mikhail Aleksandrovich Bakunin

Birth: May 18, 1814 (OS) ✦ 200 years

Born at Premukhino, Russia, revolutionary agitator Bakunin embodied 19th-century anarchism. Like Karl Marx, he thought religion was an enemy of freedom, although Bakunin advocated completely dismantling the state, arguing that proletariat power was not a lesser evil because a communist state would magnify other states' evil. In 1842, Bakunin wrote, "The passion for destruction is also a creative passion," which became the motto of international anarchism. Involved in various European insurrections, Bakunin espoused liberation of Slav peoples and was exiled to Siberia before escaping to Western Europe where he died at Bern, Switzerland, July 1, 1876.

Grand Duchess Elizabeth Feodorovna/St. Elizabeth Romanova

Birth: Nov 1, 1864 ✦ 150 years

Born at Bessunen, Hesse, Germany, Princess Elizabeth Alexandra Louise was the daughter of Louis IV, Grand Duke of Hesse, and Princess Alice, the daughter of Queen Victoria, and also elder sister of Alexandra, Russia's last czarina. A great beauty, she married the Grand Duke Sergei Alexandrovich of Russia, a son of Emperor Alexander II, in 1884, and converted to Russian Orthodoxy in 1891. After her husband was assassinated by Russian Socialists in 1905, she became a nun and used her wealth to found the Convent of Sts. Mary and Martha, where she cared for the destitute of Moscow. Executed by Bolsheviks on July 18, 1918, she was canonized by the Russian Orthodox Church in 1992.

Adolf Hitler

Birth: Apr 20, 1889 ✦ 125 years

German dictator, born at Braunau am Inn, Austria. Despite a brief time in prison—during which he wrote *Mein Kampf*, published in two volumes in 1925 and 1926—Hitler quickly rose in politics as leader of the Nazis, feeding on German anger over the bleak economy and WWI defeat. He also fanned violent anti-Semitism, which resulted in millions of Jewish deaths in concentration camps. A German plebiscite vested sole executive power in Führer Adolf Hitler Aug 19, 1934. In seeking to increase German power, he started WWII in 1939. Facing certain defeat by the Allied forces, he shot himself Apr 30, 1945, in a Berlin bunker where he had been hiding for more than three months.

Otto Frank

Birth: May 12, 1889 ✦ 125 years

Decorated for bravery as a German officer after WWI, Frank is best remembered as the father of Anne, whose diary he published in hopes of preventing future genocides. Born in Frankfurt, Frank moved his family to Holland in 1933 as anti-Semitism erupted in Nazi Germany. Liberated from Auschwitz in 1945, he was criticized for bowdlerizing the initial publication of Anne's diary. In 1963, he established The Anne Frank Foundation, which undertakes charitable works and social activities in the spirit of Anne Frank. Frank devoted his life to Holocaust education until his death on Aug 19, 1980, at Basel, Switzerland.

Jawaharlal Nehru

Birth: Nov 14, 1889 ✦ 125 years

Born at Allahabad, India, Nehru was an Indian leader who worked for independence and social reform, emphasizing economic welfare. First Indian prime minister after independence in 1947 and architect of India's foreign policy of nonalignment, he was greatly influenced by his friend, Mohandas Gandhi. Nehru left India with no political heir to his leadership when he died May 27, 1964, at New Delhi, although his daughter, Indira Gandhi, later became its third prime minister. After his death, Indians repeated Nehru's own words uttered after Gandhi's assassination: "The light has gone out of our lives and there is darkness everywhere."

American History

Susanna Dickinson

Birth: 1814 ✦ 200 years

Dickinson's place in history is as one of the few witnesses to the Battle of the Alamo during the Texas Revolution. On Mar 6, 1836, the young woman, her 15-month-old baby and a handful of noncombatants walked out of the smoldering Alamo where her husband, Captain Almaron Dickinson, and as many as 250 Texian combatants lay dead before a Mexican army of nearly 2,000. The Mexican president and commander, Antonio López de Santa Anna, allowed Dickinson to leave San Antonio de Béxar with a warning message to Texian revolutionary leader Sam Houston. Dickinson, born in Tennessee, struggled after the Texas Revolution, marrying abusive husbands, before settling down happily in Austin with German carpenter Joseph Hannig. She returned to the Alamo in 1881 and, upon seeing the room where she took shelter during the battle, burst into tears. She died Oct 1, 1883, at Austin, TX.

Frances Elizabeth Caroline Willard

Birth: Sept 28, 1839 ✦ 175 years

One of the best-known, most influential women of the late 19th century for her temperance and suffrage work, Willard was also influential in American education. One of the first female administrators of a major coeducational university when made dean of women for Northwestern University's Women's College, she left education to work with the Women's Christian Temperance Union, of which she was president 1879–98. Born at Churchville, NY, she died at New York, NY, Feb 18, 1898; more than 20,000 people paid their last respects at services in NYC and Chicago.

George Armstrong Custer

Birth: Dec 5, 1839 ✦ 175 years

Born at New Rumley, OH, General Custer was a cavalry officer in the US Civil War whose courage and leadership brought him admiration and fame. He later spent 10 years on the Great Plains fighting in the Indian Wars and leading a successful Black Hills expedition in 1874 to find gold. During a campaign to move the Lakota Sioux onto reservations to make way for the gold rush, Custer attacked an encampment of Sioux and Cheyenne on June 25, 1876. Outnumbered, he and about 215 of his men were quickly killed at the Battle of Little Bighorn. While his wife, Libbie, worked tirelessly after his death promoting his reputation as a military hero, historians dispute whether Custer followed orders or good judgment, and Custer's Last Stand is now considered one of the biggest military fiascoes in US history.

Casey Jones

Birth: Mar 14, 1864 ✦ 150 years

The railroad engineer—real name John Luther Jones—was born near Cayce, KY, the source of his nickname. He died in the crash of the Cannonball Express near Vaughn, MS, Apr 30, 1900, and was memorialized as a hero in Wallace Saunders's eponymous ballad. The ballad presented Jones as a quintessential railroad man, a hero of the industrial age who lost his life at the helm of a machine, in service to a modern system. Railroads represented progress; at the time, Jones represented the future and, later, a romantic symbol of the railroading tradition.

Frances Folsom Cleveland

Birth: July 21, 1864 ✦ 150 years

Born at Buffalo, NY, Frances Cleveland, at age 22, was the youngest first lady of the United States. Her father, Oscar Folsom, was a law partner of Grover Cleveland, who managed Folsom's estate after his untimely death in 1873. Folsom graduated from Wells College in 1885—and was unable to attend the 1885 Cleveland inauguration due to her senior status—then on June 2, 1886, married President Grover Cleveland (27 years older) in the Blue Room of the White House, making her also the first first lady to marry in the White House. The Clevelands had six children, but their daughter Esther was the only one born in the White House. Frances Cleveland was a very popular first lady—reporters followed her, magazines put her on their covers, women copied her hair and dress styles—and she sought to take advantage of her popularity with causes dear to her: charities for Washington, DC–area impoverished girls, Saturday-morning receptions for working women, higher education for women and other causes. After Grover Cleveland's death in 1908, she married art professor Thomas Preston. She died Oct 29, 1947, at Baltimore, MD.

Edward "Butch" O'Hare

Birth: Mar 13, 1914 ✦ 100 years

Born in St. Louis, MO, O'Hare attended the U.S. Naval Academy and later trained as an aviator. He earned the first Congressional Medal of Honor in World War II after shooting down five Japanese planes in an air battle to save the USS *Lexington* aircraft carrier from damage. He did not return from a later mission on Nov 26, 1943, after losing radio contact and was presumed shot down or crashed over the Pacific. In September 1949, O'Hare International Airport in Chicago, IL, was named in his honor.

Literature

Christopher Marlowe

Baptized Feb 26, 1564 ✦ 450 years

One of the great Elizabethan dramatists, born just two months before William Shakespeare, lived a clamorous, controversial and curtailed life. Born at Canterbury, England, to a shoemaker, Marlowe first made a splash on the London theater scene in 1587 with the influential blank verse drama *Tamburlaine The Great*. He wrote for The Admiral's Men stage company and his masterpiece for them was *Doctor Faustus* (premiere date unknown). Marlowe was a poet and translator: his "The Passionate Shepherd to his Love" is one of the most famous Renaissance English poems and prompted many imitations, answers and parodies. Marlowe was arrested several times on various charges—assault, counterfeiting and heresy—but he always seemed to evade imprisonment. There is strong evidence that he was an information gatherer for Sir Francis Walsingham's labyrinthine spy network. On May 30, 1593, Marlowe spent the day in a private home in Deptford with three men who were all Walsingham spies. At the day's conclusion, Marlowe, 29 years old, was dead of a stab wound by Ingram Frizer, who at the inquest (the report of which was only discovered in 1925) claimed self-defense.

Jean-Baptiste Racine

Baptized: Dec 22, 1639 ✦ 375 years

French dramatist and playwright. Working during the reign of Louis XIV, Racine was a contemporary of Molière and ultimately a rival of Corneille. His works include *Andromaque* (1667), *Iphegénie* (1674) and *Phèdre* (1677). He brought to the classical tradition a sublimely refined style, and his plays introduced a new focus—the passions overruling tragic figures—rather than the presentation of a complicated chain of events. He abandoned playwriting in 1677 to become a royal historiographer, writing only two plays after this time, *Athalie* (1691) and *Esther* (1691). Born at La Ferté-Milon, he died Apr 22, 1699, at Paris.

Lady Mary Wortley Montagu

Baptism: May 26, 1689 ✦ 325 years

English author, scholar and "scientific lady" known for her wit and verse, Wortley was born at London, England. Her diaries and letters, including the preeminent *Turkish Embassy Letters*, are considered to be among the most significant literary works of 18th-century England. A proponent of smallpox inoculation, Montagu directed experiments that proved the vaccine's efficacy, although her work was disregarded by the British medical establishment because of her sex. She wrote, "True knowledge consists in knowing things, not words." Died Aug 21, 1762, at London, England.

Samuel Richardson

Birth: Aug 19, 1689 ✦ 325 years

Born at Derbyshire, England, Richardson was an English novelist compared to Shakespeare for his originality, universality and emotional truth. He founded a new school of writing focused on epistolary novels that juxtaposed inner thoughts and states of the individual with the tempo of outer life, coalesced in *Clarissa; or, The History of a Young Lady.* He influenced future writers, including Rousseau, Goethe, James, Eliot, Austen and Wolff. Died July 4, 1761, at London, England. Diderot's elegy proclaimed, "O Richardson! if thou hast not enjoyed in thy lifetime all the reputation which thou merited, how great wilt thou appear to our posterity!"

Ann Ward Radcliffe

Birth: July 9, 1764 ✦ 250 years

English author considered the most original and distinguished Gothic romance novelist, she brought poetry to the genre through her lush scenic descriptions. Works include *The Romance of the Forest* (1791), *The Italian* (1797) and *The Mysteries of Udolpho* (1794), the latter of which was satirized by Jane Austen in *Northanger Abbey.* Radcliffe's shy, reclusive nature added an aura of mystery to her persona, about which there was much speculation. Born at London, England, she died there Feb 7, 1823.

James Fenimore Cooper

Birth: Sept 15, 1789 ✦ 225 years

American novelist, historian and social critic, born at Burlington, NJ, James Fenimore Cooper was one of the earliest American writers to develop a native American literary tradition. His most popular works are the five novels comprising *The Leatherstocking Tales*, featuring the exploits of a unique American fictional character, Natty Bumppo. These novels—*The Deerslayer, The Last of the Mohicans, The Pathfinder, The Pioneers* and *The Prairie*—chronicle Natty Bumppo's continuing flight away from the rapid settlement of America. Other works, including *The Monikins* and *Satanstoe*, reveal Cooper as an astute critic of American life. He died Sept 14, 1851, at Cooperstown, NY, the town founded by his father.

Joaquim Maria Machado de Assis

Birth: June 21, 1839 ✦ 175 years

Considered the greatest of Brazilian authors, Machado was born at Rio de Janeiro to a poor household, and he battled various infirmities, the most serious of which was epilepsy. His entire adult life he worked as a dutiful civil servant in the Ministry of Agriculture. Yet despite this unassuming background, he created an immense body of literature (poetry, short stories, novels, drama, criticism, translations) that has come to be admired the world over for its comic/ironic presentiment of the coming modern age. He was unanimously elected president of the Brazilian Academy of Letters in 1897 and retained that position until his death. His most famous novel is *Epitaph for a Small Winner* (1880, sometimes titled *The Posthumous Memoirs of Bras Cubas*), which is narrated by a dead man: "I hesitated some time, not knowing where to open these memoirs at the beginning or at the end, i.e., whether to start with my birth or with my death." Machado died Sept 29, 1908, in Rio de Janeiro.

Miguel de Unamuno y Jugo

Birth: Sept 29, 1864 ✦ 150 years

Born at Bilbao, Spain, Unamuno was a poet, novelist, essayist and philosophical leader of the "Generation of '98," those intellectuals who saw in Spain's defeat in the Spanish-American War both the end of Spain's colonial empire and the manifestation of its cultural and political decay. Existentialist in nature, Unamuno's writings sought a renewal of Spain's culture and politics and earned him the title "the arouser of Spain." During an anti-Fascist response to General Milan-Astray at a rally, he stated, "Sometimes, to remain silent is to lie." He was placed under house arrest and died on Dec 31, 1936, at Salamanca.

Gabriela Mistral

Birth: Apr 7, 1889 ✦ 125 years

Chilean educator, poet and diplomat (real name Lucila Godoy Alcayaga) born at Vicuña, Chile. Her diplomatic work was extensive: she was Chilean consul in many nations as well as served as a League of Nations and UN representative, notably on the Subcommittee on the Status of Women and promoting UNICEF. Mistral was the first Latin American to be awarded the Nobel Prize for Literature in 1945. Her poetry, notably "Pan-American Manifesto," reflected her belief that national distinctions were unimportant. Called "the spiritual mentor of the Spanish American world in a degree rarely equaled before by any man and never by a woman," she died Jan 10, 1957, at Hempstead, NY.

Anna Akhmatova

Birth: June 23, 1889 ✦ 125 years

Born at Odessa, Russia, Akhmatova was one of the most beloved and renowned Russian poets of the 20th century. Part of the Acmeist literary group devoted to tactile, concrete, material images in poetry, her poems are like photographs or sketches of real life. Her work reflects the historical and spiritual experience of her generation and references many of her poetic predecessors. She wrote, "It could be that poetry itself is one great quotation." Outcast from Soviet literary society for her unwillingness to write about the new socialist order, Akhmatova died Mar 6, 1966, at Moscow, Soviet Union.

Jean Maurice Eugéne Clèment Cocteau

Birth: July 5, 1889 ✦ 125 years

French novelist, poet, director, actor and artist, born at Maisons-Lafitte, near Paris. His notable works include the play *Orpheus* (1926), the novel *The Infernal Machine* (1934) and the films *The Blood of a Poet* (1930) and *Beauty and the Beast* (1946). He called himself "the antipode of Voltaire" and was a key figure in 20th-century French art. His work was experimental and his circle included many of the century's notable artists. Remembered as an avant-garde icon, he influenced several generations of French artists. Cocteau died Oct 11, 1963, at Milly-la-Forêt, near Paris.

Erle Stanley Gardner

Birth: July 17, 1889 ✦ 125 years

Born at Malden, MA, Gardner struggled to support his family during the Depression: he was an attorney by day and a writer of pulp fiction for *Black Mask* magazine by night. He eventually hit on the idea of a hard-hitting, crime-solving attorney named Stark for a successful series of novels. Renamed Perry Mason, the lawyer debuted in *The Case of the Velvet Claws* for William Morrow & Company in 1933. Perry Mason is probably the most famous lawyer in popular culture, featured in 82 novels as well as on TV and film. At the height of this popularity, Mason novels sold 20,000 copies a day. As portrayed on TV (most famously by Raymond Burr, 1957–66), Mason toned down the fisticuffs and became a suave courtroom master. Gardner died at Temecula, CA, Mar 11, 1970.

Conrad Aiken

Birth: Aug 5, 1889 ✦ 125 years

Poet, novelist, short-story writer and critic, born at Savannah, GA, and raised in New England. Winner of the Pulitzer Prize (1930), the National Book Award (1954), the Bollingen Prize (1956) and the National Medal for Literature (1969). He was also a consultant in poetry to the Library of Congress (1950–52)—now termed poet laureate. Aiken died at Savannhah, GA, Aug 17, 1973.

William S. Burroughs

Birth: Feb 5, 1914 ✦ 100 years

One of the most significant writers of the 20th century and renowned Beat author, Burroughs was born at St. Louis, MO. His novels, notably *Naked Lunch* (1959), pushed fiction to the outermost limits and explored previously taboo subjects such as drug use, homosexuality and systems of control, and his books were frequently banned. Much of his work was influenced by personal experience; Burroughs once stated "all fiction is autobiographical and all autobiography is fiction." He died Aug 2, 1997, at Lawrence, KS; his literary works had a lasting impression on many authors, artists, musicians, actors and filmmakers.

Ralph Waldo Ellison

Birth: Mar 1, 1914 ✦ 100 years

American writer and educator, born at Oklahoma City, OK. Author of the acclaimed novel *Invisible Man* (1952), the story of a young black man's struggle for his own identity in the face of rejection from both whites and blacks. Quickly recognized as a classic of 20th-century literature, it won the National Book Award in 1953. While only one of his novels was published, Ellison published collections of his essays, reviews and stories in *Shadow and Act* (1964) and *Going to the Territory* (1986). He died Apr 16, 1994, at New York, NY.

Octavio Paz

Birth: Mar 31, 1914 ✦ 100 years

Poet, diplomat, translator, critic, professor and journal editor, born at Mexico City, Mexico. Paz began writing poetry at age 17. In 1937, he began a series of formative trips: first to Spain in 1937 to attend a congress of anti-Fascist writers, then to the United States on a Guggenheim fellowship, then to France in 1945. During these trips, he met the leading writers and intellectuals of the day. As a Mexican diplomat, he continued his travels—most significantly to India—from 1946 until 1968, when he resigned over the government's violent suppression of student protesters. His seminal prose work is *The Labyrinth of Solitude* (1950), an examination of the Mexican psyche. The prodigious Paz was awarded the Miguel de Cervantes Prize in 1981 and the Nobel Prize in Literature in 1990 "for impassioned writing with wide horizons, characterized by sensuous intelligence and humanistic integrity." He died at Mexico City, Apr 19, 1998.

Bernard Malamud

Birth: Apr 26, 1914 ✦ 100 years

A prominent figure in Jewish-American literature, Malamud's work often illustrates the importance of moral obligation through the use of myth and allegory. Born at Brooklyn, NY, to Russian-Jewish immigrant parents, his writing echoes his family's experiences and reflects a post-Holocaust consciousness in addressing Jewish concerns. His stories also reflect the influence of earlier Jewish literature and American writers like Thoreau, Melville and Hawthorne. Malamud said, "The purpose of a writer is to keep civilization from destroying itself." Winner of a Pulitzer Prize (for *The Fixer*, 1966) and the National Book Award, he died Mar 18, 1986, at New York, NY.

Randall Jarrell

Birth: May 6, 1914 ✦ 100 years

Pulitzer Prize–winning poet and literary critic, born at Nashville, TN. Jarrell served in the US Army during World War II, and the experience greatly influenced his early work, including his most well-known poem, "The Death of the Ball Turret Gunner." Adrienne Rich once stated that "he was the conscience of poetry" and that she and other poets wrote "to the mind of Randall Jarrell." An incisive and sometimes devastating critic, Jarrell influenced the rising appreciation of numerous American poets, including his friend, Robert Lowell, and Marianne Moore. He was struck by a car and died Oct 14, 1965, near Chapel Hill, NC.

Tove Jansson

Birth: Aug 9, 1914 ✦ 100 years

Born at Helsinki, Finland, Finnish artist, cartoonist and novelist Jansson is best known as the creator of Moomintrolls, loosely based on the trolls of Swedish folklore, which began as children's books and later morphed into a syndicated cartoon strip *Moomins*. Her work, which has been translated into more than 30 languages, followed in the tradition of imaginative authors such as J.R.R. Tolkein, Lewis Carroll and Edith Nesbit and created a world in which children's imagination is not hindered by everyday logic and reason. Died June 27, 2001, at Helsinki, Finland.

Julio Cortázar

Birth: Aug 26, 1914 ✦ 100 years

Argentine novelist, short-story writer, translator, born at Brussels, Belgium, most famous for *Hopscotch* (1963), a wildly inventive novel where readers can piece together their own narrative(s). Author of the short story that served as the basis for the 1966 film *Blow-up*. "For me, literature is a form of play," he explained in an interview. "It's a game, but it's a game one can put one's life into. One can do everything for that game." He died Feb 12, 1984, at Paris, France, where he had lived many years in exile from Argentina's military dictatorships.

Nicanor Parra

Birth: Sept 5, 1914 ✦ 100 years

Born at San Fabián de Alico, Chillán, Chile, Parra is a physicist, mathematician and lauded poet—or "Antipoet of Chile" in his own description. Considered Latin America's greatest living poet, his first poetry was published in 1938. *Poems and Antipoems* burst on the literary scene in 1954 to shake up traditional conceptions of poetry, tapping his scientific background. Retired from teaching physics at the University of Chile in Santiago in 1991, Parra continues to create and publish poetry. Having received decades-worth of prestigious awards already, he was awarded the Miguel de Cervantes Prize in 2011.

John Berryman

Birth: Oct 25, 1914 ✦ 100 years

Born at McAlester, OK, Berryman is considered one of the most innovative, important American poets of the 20th century and is best known for bringing idiomatic American English to poetry. His poems, often labeled "confessional," are both brilliant and tormented. Winner of the 1965 Pultizer Prize for *77 Dream Songs* and, later, the National Book Award for the entire *Dream Songs* collection, Berryman died Jan 7, 1972, at Minneapolis, MN, after committing suicide. He once said, "We must travel in the direction of our fear."

Dylan Marlais Thomas

Birth: Oct 27, 1914 ✦ 100 years

Welsh poet, memoirist and playwright, born at Swansea, Wales. Thomas worked as a BBC broadcaster and poetry commentator in the 1940s and 1950s; his sonorous voice made him famous and contributed to the success of his US tours in the early 1950s. As a poet, Thomas was fascinated by the sound and rhythm of language and said poetry is "useful to me for one reason: it is the record of my individual struggle from darkness towards some measure of light." His famous poems include "Do Not Go Gentle into That Good Night" (1951). He died at New York, NY, Nov 9, 1953.

Patrick O'Brian

Birth: Dec 12, 1914 ✦ 100 years

Born Richard Patrick Russ at Chalfont St. Peter, England, O'Brian was a prolific novelist, biographer and translator. His most famous works are the maritime Aubrey-Maturin novels, a 20-volume series set during the Napoleonic wars, which opened with *Master and Commander* (1969). His other works include translations of Henri Charriére's *Papillon* and works by Simone de Beauvoir and a biography of Pablo Picasso. O'Brian died Jan 2, 2000, at Dublin, Ireland.

Journalism

Francis Pharcellus Church

Birth: Feb 22, 1839 ✦ 175 years

Born at Rochester, NY, the longtime journalist (he covered the American Civil War for the *New York Times*) and editor is best known today for writing the most famous editorial in history. As editor of the *New York Sun*, Church responded to the summer 1897 letter of eight-year-old Virginia O'Hanlon, who desperately asked whether Santa Claus existed. On Sept 21, 1897, in the third column of that day's editorials, she received the unsigned response: "Yes, VIRGINIA, there is a Santa Claus. He exists as certainly as love and generosity and devotion exist, and you know that they abound and give to your life its highest beauty and joy. . . . " The *Sun* did not immediately embrace the editorial as a classic—not reprinting it until December 1902, and then not routinely reprinting it until after Church's death in 1906. Church, a member of the prestigious Century Club, died Apr 11, 1906, at New York, NY. After his death, the *New York Sun* revealed that he had been the author of its most famous opinion piece. Church never met O'Hanlon.

Education

Zerna Addis Sharp

Birth: Aug 12, 1889 ✦ 125 years

Educator and originator of the "Dick and Jane" readers used for many years in American schools, Sharp collaborated with illustrator Eleanor B. Campbell and others to create the texts while a reading consultant for Scott Foresman. She selected easy-to-read words, patterning the plots from children's interests, although the books were later criticized for sex-stereotyping because of Dick's apparent dominant status compared to Jane. To this, Sharp replied, "That's all an adult's viewpoint." Born at Hillisburg, IN, she died June 17, 1981, at Frankfort, IN.

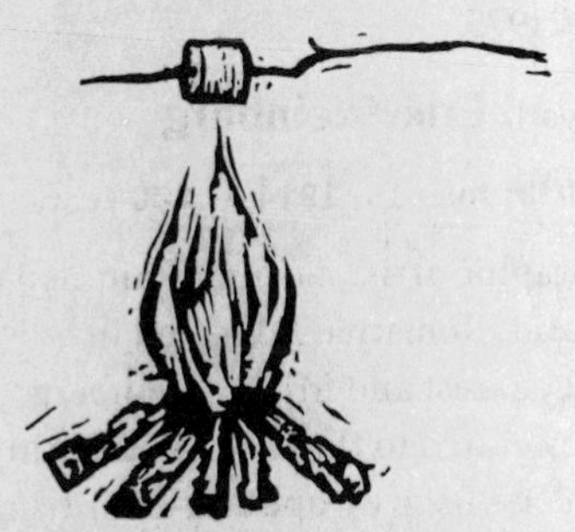

Art

Paul Cézanne

Birth: Jan 19, 1839 ✦ 175 years

Post-Impressionist painter, born at Aix-en-Provence, France. From the Impressionists, Cézanne learned the importance of observation, but he soon dispensed with classical perspective and used planes of color and his distinctive "constructive brushstroke" to create form and depth. Seeking to "treat nature by the cylinder, the sphere, the cone," Cézanne's portraits, still lifes and landscapes are a seminal bridge from the Romantics and Impressionists to the Fauves, Cubists and later modernists. Often working on a painting over several years, he created such masterpieces as *The Bathers* (1875), *The Card Players* (1892), and *Compotier, Pitcher and Fruit* (1892–94). Cézanne died Oct 23, 1906, at Aix, from pneumonia after painting outside in the rain.

Alfred Sisley

Birth: Oct 30, 1839 ✦ 175 years

English by background, but born at Paris, France, Sisley was one of the foremost landscape painters of the Impressionists. Preferring to work in the open air rather than in a studio, he completed more than 900 landscapes. Like other Impressionists, his work was unappreciated at the juried Salon exhibitions and he joined the first Impressionist exhibition in 1874. Never successful in his lifetime, Sisley's most well-known works, such as *Sand Heaps* and *The Bridge at Moret-sur-Loing*, demonstrate his mastery of the subtle interplay of light, color and brushstroke to evoke atmosphere. He died near Fontainbleau, Jan 29, 1899.

Spotlight on People

Alfred Stieglitz

Birth: Jan 1, 1864 ✦ 150 years

Arguably the most important photographer of his time, Steiglitz was also a publisher, art dealer and advocate for the Modernist movement, particularly artist Georgia O'Keeffe, who was his lover and, later, wife. He was convinced photography should be considered a fine art and cofounded the Photo-Secessionist organization, which advocated the Pictoralist style, an approach to photography that emphasizes beauty of subject matter, tonality and composition rather than documentation of reality. Born at Hoboken, NJ, he died July 13, 1946, at New York, NY.

Charles M. Russell

Birth: Mar 19, 1864 ✦ 150 years

Born at St. Louis, MO, Charles Marion Russell moved to Montana at about age 16 and became a horse wrangler and cow herder with his horse Redbird. In the off hours, he sketched the people and country of the Montana Territory. His wife, Nancy, helped and encouraged him to pursue art more avidly, and today Russell is considered one of the greatest western artists. Working in pen and ink, watercolor, oils and bronze, he meticulously recorded the vanishing life of the range and its people, including the Blackfeet tribe, and railed against forces that destroyed the animals of that frontier: "[The Blackfoot] country today is fenced and settled by ranchmen and farmers with nothing but a few deep-worn trails where once walked the buffalo; but I am glad, ... I knew it before nature's enemy the white man invaded and marred its beauty." He died Oct 26, 1926, at Great Falls, MT.

Henri de Toulouse-Lautrec

Birth: Nov 24, 1864 ✦ 150 years

French illustrator, lithographer, post-Impressionist painter. Born at Albi, France, Lautrec, who was deformed at an early age, found in the bohemian demimonde of Paris, especially the nightclubs and brothels of Montmartre, an outsider atmosphere that enticed him both personally and professionally. His drawings and posters in particular evoke the nightlife and habitués of that world. "Ugliness, everywhere and always, has its enchanting side," Lautrec said. "It is fascinating to discover it where no one else had noticed it." He died Sept 9, 1901, at Château Malromé, Gironde, France.

Thomas Hart Benton

Birth: Apr 15, 1889 ✦ 125 years

Born at Neosho, MO, Thomas Hart Benton studied art in Paris and New York. But he left the metropolitan art world in 1935, traveling to Kansas, determined to create work that reacted against European trends and reflected what was felt to be the integrity of the American heartland. He became one of the foremost artists of the populist art movement known as American Regionalism. His works of pastoral life in the Midwest and South were not always flattering to their subjects, but his style became known as a truly American style of painting. He died at Kansas City, MO, Jan 19, 1975.

Saul Erik Steinberg

Birth: June 15, 1914 ✦ 100 years

Graphic artist, born in Ràmnicu Sărat, Romania. Educated in Bucharest and Milan, Steinberg emigrated to the United States in the 1940s to escape anti-Semitism in Italy. *The New Yorker* became Steinberg's bread and butter; for it, he completed more than 90 covers and 1,200 drawings and dinguses. His most famous, oft-imitated cover is a map, *View of the World from 9th Avenue*. Steinberg said of his work, "Drawing makes up its own syntax as it goes along. The line can't be reasoned in the mind. It can only be reasoned on paper." He died May 12, 1999, at New York, NY.

Paul Rand

Birth: Aug 15, 1914 ✦ 100 years

Born Peretz Rosenbaum at New York, NY, Rand showed an early proclivity for art, forbidden in Orthodox Jewish tradition; through persistence, he went on to become the father of modern American graphic design. Seeing the space as a visual unit, he pioneered dynamic equilibrium and played an important role in introducing the visual language of cubism, constructivism, de Stijl and the Bauhaus into American design. He designed iconic logos for IBM, UPS, ABC and Westinghouse, among others, and was an inaugural inductee into the Art Director's Club of New York Hall of Fame. Died Nov 26, 1996, at Norwalk, CT.

Music

Carl Philipp Emanuel Bach

Birth: Mar 8, 1714 ✦ 300 years

Musically the most important and influential of Johann Sebastian Bach's sons, German composer, keyboard performer, and theorist C.P.E. Bach was born at Weimar, Germany. He was a contributor to the Viennese classical style and pioneer of sonata-allegro musical form. The publication of *Essay on the True Art of Playing Keyboard*

Instruments (1753), which remains one of the principal monuments of 18th-century musical thought and practice, made him the most renowned authority of the 18th century on keyboard pedagogy and composition. Influential to Haydn and Beethoven, he died Dec 15, 1788, at Hamburg, Germany.

Modest Petrovich Mussorgsky

Birth: Mar 21, 1839 ✦ 175 years

Romantic composer, born at Karevo, Russia. Mussorgsky was considered a brilliant, if amateur, pianist when he took up composing. A military officer and later a civil servant, he joined The Five, a group of other amatuer Russian composers passionate about creating a Russian music free from European musical conventions. For Mussorgsky, this music would embody "the people . . . sleeping or waking, eating or drinking." Troubled by alcoholism, Mussorgsky did not complete many of his projects, yet enduring works such as *Boris Gudonov* (1874) and *Pictures at an Exhibition* (1874) influenced later composers, including Dmitri Shostakovich and Claude Debussy. He died Mar 28, 1881, at St. Petersburg.

Richard Georg Strauss

Birth: June 11, 1864 ✦ 150 years

German Romantic composer, musician and conductor born at Munich. Some of his best-remembered operas are *Salome* (1905), *Elektra* (1909) and *Der Rosenkavalier* (1911), and his acclaimed symphonic, or tone, poems included *Don Juan* (1889) and *Don Quixote* (1898). He spent the WWII years in Vienna, Austria, and then Switzerland trying to shield his family (especially his Jewish daughter-in-law) from the Nazis. Strauss returned to Germany and died at Garmisch-Partenkirchen after a heart attack Sept 8, 1949, at age 85.

Huddie "Leadbelly" Ledbetter

Birth: Jan 20, 1889 ✦ 125 years

Born on a plantation in Mooringsport, LA, on Jan 20, 1889 (some sources say 1888), Huddie "Leadbelly" Ledbetter learned guitar while working as a farmer and sharecropper. He got his start in the music business as a collaborator with Blind Lemon Jefferson, playing his 12-string at juke joints and dances. In the 1930s, while serving time in Angola Prison, Leadbelly met folklorists and researchers John and Alan Lomax, who first recorded his most famous song, "Goodnight Irene," as well as early versions of the eventual standards "Rock Island Line" and "Midnight Special." Leadbelly worked off and on with the Lomaxes over the next several years and also cut sides for Capitol and the pioneering Folkways label. He died of ALS Dec 6, 1949, at New York, NY, but was still a huge influence on the folk scene of the 1950s and '60s, as well as a creative and cultural touchstone for musicians of the early rock-and-roll era.

Ernest Tubb

Birth: Feb 9, 1914 ✦ 100 years

Country and western singer, born at Crisp, TX. Ernest Tubb was the sixth member to be elected to the Country Music Hall of Fame and the headliner on the first country music show ever to be presented at Carnegie Hall. His first major hit, "Walking the Floor over You," gained him his first appearance at the Grand Ole Opry in 1942, and he attained regular membership in 1943. He died Sept 6, 1984, at Nashville, TN.

Sonny Boy Williamson

Birth: Mar 30, 1914 ✦ 100 years

John Lee Curtis "Sonny Boy" Williamson was born near Jackson, TN. A true innovator, the legendary sides harmonica player Williamson cut for the Bluebird/RCA label between 1937 and 1947 established his distinctive harp sound and became staples of blues musicians for generations, particularly in his adopted hometown of Chicago, IL. His "Good Morning, School Girl" is one of his best-remembered hits and has been covered by many artists. On June 1, 1948, Williamson's popularity was only growing when he was murdered during a robbery on the city's South Side. He was 34. At his grave in Jackson, TN, musicians and fans place harmonicas on his tombstone in tribute to his legacy.

Sun Ra

Birth: May 22, 1914 ✦ 100 years

Born Herman (Sonny) Blount, Sun Ra was a pioneering and innovative jazz musician whose avant-garde performances mixed elements of theater with his surreal composition and performance style. He once said, "I wanted to give God something he's never heard before." His chosen name signified a deep fascination with outer space and ancient Egypt, through which he intended to reawaken African Americans to historical black achievement; his philosophy fit into the era's ongoing black intellectual dialogue about history and civilization. Ra was born at Birmingham, AL, and died there May 30, 1993.

Billy Eckstine

Birth: July 8, 1914 ✦ 100 years

Bandleader and bass-baritone singer Billy Eckstine was born William Clarence Eckstein at Pittsburgh, PA. After performing with the Earl Hines band for almost 20 years, Eckstine formed his own band in 1944. At one time or another, the band's ranks included Charlie Parker, Dizzy Gillespie, Miles Davis, Fats Navarro, Dexter Gordon, Gene Ammons, Art Blakey and vocalist Sarah Vaughan—some of the greatest bebop musicians of all time. Among Eckstine's hits were "Fools Rush In," "Everything I Have Is Yours," "My Foolish Heart," "Blue Moon" and "Body and Soul." Billy Eckstine died Mar 8, 1993, at Pittsburgh, PA.

Entertainment

Léon Gaumont

Birth: May 10, 1864 ✦ 150 years

This early film entrepreneur and inventor was born at Paris, France. Originally a photography businessman, he established the Gaumont Film Production Company in 1895 to capitalize on the growing new entertainment medium. France was at the center of film innovation, production and distribution in the late 19th century and early 20th century, propelled by the work of Gaumont, the Lumière brothers and Charles Pathé. Gaumont's technical work included a camera-projector, an early sound-synchronizing system and an early color process. Gaumont's company produced the first "talkie"—*Eau de Nil* (1928)—in France. The Gaumont Company also comprised studios and a theater chain. Gaumont retired in 1929 and he died Aug 10, 1946, at Sainte-Maxime, Var, France.

Louis Lumière

Birth: Oct 5, 1864 ✦ 150 years

Born at Besançon, France, Louis Lumière with brother Auguste were film pioneers who created the first movie, *Workers Leaving the Lumière Factory* (1895). Lumière,

Superman's Creators and Alter Egos

Joe Shuster

Birth: July 10, 1914 ✦ 100 years

Jerry Siegel

Birth: Oct 17, 1914 ✦ 100 years

Shuster and Siegel, both children of Jewish immigrants, partnered together as teenagers in 1933 to create one of the great icons of American pop culture: Superman. Shuster, the artist, born at Toronto, ON, Canada, and Siegel, the writer, born at Cleveland, OH, collaborated on a number of comic-strip ideas that publishers rejected. Trying out a new idea, that of a villainous "superman," they changed their minds and transformed the villain into a superhero, combining elements from science fiction (in a rocket an alien baby escapes a dying planet) with aspects of their own lives (Superman's alter ego, Clark Kent, for example, owed a lot to Shuster: "I was mild-mannered, wore glasses, was very shy with women."). Superman made his comic book debut in the first issue of *Action Comics* (June 1938) and immediately exploded in popularity. The naive young creators, however, had sold the rights to their character for $130 in 1938. As they saw their creation everywhere yet received no royalties, their relationship with Detective Comics (now DC Comics) soon soured. Shuster and Siegel turned to the courts to gain back creative credit and some revenue—finally succeeding in 1978 in receiving creative credit and a modest annual stipend. Shuster died July 30, 1992, at Los Angeles, CA. Siegel died Jan 28, 1996, also at Los Angeles. Both men have been honored with membership in the Will Eisner Comic Book Hall of Fame and the Jack Kirby Hall of Fame.

George Reeves

Birth: Jan 5, 1914 ✦ 100 years

The boxer turned actor was born George Keefer Brewer at Woodstock, IA. Active in the 1940s in minor Hollywood roles (including a small part in *Gone with the Wind*), Reeves found stardom on the small screen as Superman/Clark Kent in "The Adventures of Superman," which ran 1952–57. Reeves did his own stunts as the "Man of Steel" and was popular with children all over. To his frustration, though, Reeves saw his serious acting career suffer due to being typecast as a cartoon superhero. He died June 16, 1959, of an apparently self-inflicted gunshot wound at his Beverly Hills, CA, home.

considered the father of cinema in France, originally worked in the family's extremely prosperous photography production business in Lyon before diving into the possibilities of moving pictures in 1894. Inspired by Thomas Edison's Kinetoscope, he created (with his brother's assistance) the Cinématographe, which could project and more importantly mechanically *move* a sprocketed strip of film images. This was patented on Feb 13, 1895. On Dec 28, 1895, the brothers projected short films for paying customers—the first time this had ever been done—at Paris's Grand Café. The Lumières directed or produced thousands of short films of both everyday life—a train speeding toward the camera that terrified unsuspecting audiences—and news of the day in what were the first newsreels. The brothers stepped away from film production in 1901 to refocus on their photography business. Louis Lumière spent his later years working on photographic and film innovations, such as an early 3-D system. He died at Bandol, France, on June 6, 1948.

William Surrey Hart

Birth: Dec 6, 1864 ✦ 150 years

American actor and film director best remembered as the first Western movie star and a top box-office leading man in silent movies from 1914 to 1925. One of the rare movie cowboys who had actually worked on a cattle ranch, roles in *Hell's Hinges* (1916) and *The Narrow Trail* (1917) established Hart as the classic cowboy star whether he was playing the outlaw or the hero. Born in 1864 (or 1870) at Newburgh, NY, he closely identified with the Wild West, even serving as a pallbearer at Wyatt Earp's funeral on Jan 16, 1929. Died June 23, 1946, at Newhall, CA.

Victor Lonzo Fleming

Birth: Feb 23, 1889 ✦ 125 years

Film director, born at Pasadena, CA (some sources say 1883). Spanning 30 years, Fleming's career began in silent films working with friend and mentor Douglas Fairbanks. His directorial talents are manifest in two of Hollywood's most popular and enduring movies: *The Wizard of Oz* (1939) and *Gone with the Wind* (1939), for which he won an Academy Award. Handsome and charismatic, he was called "the real Rhett Butler," but his critical legacy was long ignored because his films lacked a defined visual style. He had, nonetheless, what critic David Denby called "the star-making skill that Hollywood has now lost." Died Jan 6, 1949, at Cottonwood, AZ.

Charles Spencer Chaplin

Birth: Apr 16, 1889 ✦ 125 years

The vaudevillean, actor, comedian, director, producer, screenwriter and composer was born at London, England, to itinerant music hall performers. Chaplin made his entertainment debut at age five when he hurriedly replaced his mother when her voice failed on stage. His mother's loss of voice and impending insanity sent Charlie and his brother into grinding poverty and orphanages. But the boys prevailed in traveling shows, and Chaplin succeeded as a dancer and comic. A US tour in the early 1910s resulted in a fortuitous meeting with Mack Sennett of the Keystone film company. Chaplin, working with the Keystone Kops and then on his own, created the "Little Tramp," who became a worldwide sensation. Chaplin, who in 1916 cofounded United Artists Corporation, created full-length comic masterpieces during the 1920s and 1930s, among them *The Kid* (1921), *The Gold Rush* (1925), *City Lights* (1931) and *Modern Times* (1936). Despite fame and success, his personal life was tumultuous, marked by scandal and unfortunate marriages. He married fourth wife Oona O'Neill (daughter of Eugene) in 1943 in what was to be a happy union that perhaps gave comfort to his being hounded out of the United States by the House Un-American Activities Committee in 1952. Chaplin was knighted in 1975 and died Dec 25, 1977, at Vevey, Switzerland.

Charlie Chaplin Explains the Little Tramp

This fellow is many-sided, a tramp, a gentleman, a poet, a dreamer, a lonely fellow, always hopeful of romance and adventure. He would have you believe he is a scientist, a musician, a duke, a polo-player. However, he is not above picking up cigarette-butts or robbing a baby of its candy. And, of course, if the situation warrants it, he will kick a lady in the rear—but only in extreme anger!

William Claude Rains

Birth: Nov 10, 1889 ✦ 125 years

A stage, film and television actor, born at London, England, Rains trained at the Royal Academy of Dramatic Arts and overcame a speech impediment. Exposed to poison gas during WWI, Rains's vocal cords were damaged, giving his deep voice a raspy quality that he used to great effect in *The Invisible Man* (1933), where he is only a voice until the film's final minutes, and as the corrupt Captain Louis Renault in *Casablanca* (1942). Rains's other notable films include *Mr. Smith Goes to Washington* (1939), *The Phantom of the Opera* (1943) and *Notorious* (1946). Died May 30, 1967, at Laconia, NH.

George Simon Kaufman

Birth: Nov 16, 1889 ✦ 125 years

Playwright, director, producer and critic, born at Pittsburgh, PA. Working collaboratively on Broadway and in Hollywood from the 1920s through the 1950s, Kaufman was a theatrical rainmaker; his credits include *The Cocoanuts, Animal Crackers, You Can't Take It with You, The Royal Family, Of Mice and Men* and *Guys and Dolls*. A drama critic for *The New York Times* from 1917 to 1930 and a member of the Algonquin Round Table, his incisive wit and sharp one-liners were legendary: "I saw the play at a disadvantage," he wrote, "the curtain was up." Died June 2, 1961, at New York, NY.

Sir Alec Guinness

Birth: Apr 2, 1914 ✦ 100 years

One of Britain's greatest stage and screen actors, Guinness was born at London, England. He began a professional acting career in 1933. He received an Academy Award for his performance in *The Bridge on the River Kwai* (1957). Other important films included the *Star Wars* trilogy, *Great Expectations, Oliver Twist, The Ladykillers, Lawrence of Arabia, Kind Hearts and Coronets* and *A Passage to India*. On television he originated the role of melancholy spy master George Smiley from the John le Carré novel *Tinker Tailor Soldier Spy*. Knighted in 1959, he died at West Sussex, England, Aug 5, 2000.

Maria Felix

Birth: May 4, 1914 ✦ 100 years

The goddess of Mexico's golden age of cinema (1930s–'50s), Felix was a dominating presence on and off screen; her forceful personality and beauty made her stand apart from her contemporaries. She once said, "People always praised my beauty and intelligence, but I'm just a woman with a man's heart." "La Dona" appeared in more than 45 films and was awarded the first Mexico City Prize for a lifetime of distinguished achievement. Despite iconic status in Mexico, she never made a film in Hollywood because she refused to learn English and despised the denigrating, stereotypical roles available. Born at Alamos, Mexico, she died Apr 8, 2002, at Mexico City, Mexico.

Tyrone Power

Birth: May 5, 1914 ✦ 100 years

American actor, born at Cincinnati, OH, into a theatrical family, who was one of the most popular romantic and swashbuckling leads in Hollywood during the 1930s and 1940s. Power was best known for his roles in *Suez, The Mark of Zorro, Blood and Sand, The Razor's Edge* and *Nightmare Alley*. Died Nov 15, 1958, at Madrid, Spain, during a film shoot.

Frankie Manning

Birth: May 26, 1914 ✦ 100 years

Dancer famed for his innovations and ambassadorship of the Lindy Hop (or the jitterbug). Born at Jacksonville, FL, but living in New York City since three, Manning danced at the Savoy Ballroom in Harlem, New York City, as a teenager, and was lead dancer and chief choreographer of the touring troupe Whitey's Lindy Hoppers, followed by his own post-World War II troupe, the Congaroo Dancers. Appeared in numerous films, including *Hellzapoppin'* (1941). His choreography for the Broadway musical *Black and Blue* earned him a Tony Award in 1989. The recipient of an NEA National Heritage Fellowship Award in 2000, Manning died Apr 27, 2009, at New York, NY.

Robert Earl Wise

Birth: Sept 10, 1914 ✦ 100 years

American film director, born at Winchester, IN. Wise's Hollywood career began in 1933 with a job in RKO Picture's shipping department. He later worked as a sound effects editor but quickly moved on to directing, working proficiently in numerous genres throughout his career. His credits include the horror film *The Body Snatcher* (1945) and a film noir classic, *Born to Kill* (1947), as well as science fiction, melodrama, westerns and two musicals for which he won an Academy Award for Best Director: *West Side Story* (1961) and *The Sound of Music* (1965). A leader in the film industry, Wise served as president of the American Academy of Motion Pictures (1984–87). Died Los Angeles, CA, Sept 14, 2005.

Clayton Moore

Birth: Sept 14, 1914 ✦ 100 years

"Who was that masked man!?" Avid viewers of the successful 1950s' TV series "The Lone Ranger" knew that it was Clayton Moore. Jack Carlton Moore, born at Chicago, IL, was a circus performer before going to Hollywood, where first he was a stuntman. Minor roles in film serials preceded his heroic role on "The Lone Ranger." Moore, who played the West's masked righter-of-wrongs from 1949 to 1952 and 1954 to 1957, embraced the role and was comfortable with being identified as the Lone Ranger long after he retired from acting. With the backing of the public, he won the right to continue wearing the mask when legally challenged by the copyright owners. Inducted to the Hall of Great Western Performers and an honorary inductee to the Stuntman's Hall of Fame, Moore died Dec 28, 1999, at Los Angeles, CA.

Allen Albert Funt

Birth: Sept 16, 1914 ✦ 100 years

Creator, producer and host of the first reality television show, Funt orchestrated elaborate hoaxes, played on unsuspecting passersby and filmed by a hidden camera. With the catchphrase, "Smile, you're on 'Candid Camera,'" Funt would reveal he had captured the subjects "in the art of being themselves." Born at New York, NY, Funt worked with concealed wire recorders in the US Army Signal Corps during WWII. Premiering on radio as "Candid Microphone" in 1948, the show quickly moved to TV as "Candid Camera" and aired, in reruns and with new episodes, later hosted by Funt's son, Peter, until 2004. Funt died Sept 5, 1999, at Pebble Beach, CA.

Jackie Coogan

Birth: Oct 26, 1914 ✦ 100 years

Born John Leslie Coogan at Los Angeles, CA, Coogan became a star after appearing as Charlie Chaplin's companion in *The Kid* (1921), the title becoming a moniker that stuck. Film earnings and merchandise associated with his name earned him considerable income, but it was squandered by his mother and stepfather. Coogan sued them in 1938, and the legal battle resulted in the passage of the protective California Child Actor's Bill, often called the Coogan Act (1939). A glider pilot during WWII, Coogan later returned to film and television, mostly famously as Uncle Fester in "The Addams Family" (1964–66). He died Mar 1, 1984, at Santa Monica, CA.

Norman Lloyd

Birth: Nov 8, 1914 ✦ 100 years

The actor, director and producer was born at Jersey City, NJ. Starting out on the New York stage, he was in the Orson Welles–John Houseman Mercury Theatre company in the 1930s. His most memorable movie appearance is probably in Alfred Hitchcock's thriller *Saboteur* (1942), in which his villain falls from the Statue of Liberty despite the best efforts of hero Robert Cummings. His other collaborations with Hitchcock were in the film *Spellbound* (1945) and as director/producer of the anthology TV series "Alfred Hitchcock Presents." On TV, he appeared in the popular medical drama "St. Elsewhere." He has never retired and still appears on TV and in films.

Science and Technology

Andreas Vesalius

Birth: Dec 31, 1514 ✦ 500 years

Born at Brussels, Belgium, anatomist Vesalius contributed to medicine's inclusion as an empirical science and wrote one of the most important books in medical history, *De Humani Corporis Fabrica* (*On the Fabric of the Human Body*). He broke with medical conventions and dissected cadavers with his students; his subsequent anatomical discoveries overturned the 14-centuries-old Galenic canon and founded modern scientific anatomy. *Fabrica* continues to be renowned for its anatomical accuracy, beauty and aestheticism. He died Oct 15, 1564, in a shipwreck at Zenta, Greece.

Georg Simon Ohm

Birth: Mar 16, 1789 ✦ 225 years

German physicist lauded for his eponymous law, which states the exact relationship of potential and current in electric conduction. Ohm's Law made it possible for scientists to calculate the amount of current, voltage and resistance in circuitry, establishing the science of electrical engineering. He received the Copley Medal in 1841 and was elected to the Royal Society in 1842. Lord Kelvin recognized Ohm's contribution by dubbing the unit of resistance the "ohm" and its reciprocal, the unit of conductance, the "mho." Born at Erlangen, Germany, Ohm died July 7, 1854, at Munich, Germany.

Anders Jonas Angstrom

Birth: Aug 13, 1814 ✦ 200 years

Swedish astronomer born at Logdo, Sweden, Angstrom is noted for founding the science of spectroscopy—the study of light—and in particular, his spectral analyses of the sun and aurora borealis. His studies of the sun's spectra resulted in the discovery of hydrogen in its atmosphere in 1862. Angstrom deduced the principle of spectrum analysis and the angstrom unit of length, which measures one 10-billionth of a meter, was named in his honor. Died June 21, 1874, at Uppsala, Sweden.

Spotlight on People

Carl Ethan Akeley

Birth: May 19, 1864 ✦ 150 years

Born near Claredon, NY, the "father of modern taxidermy" was unhappy with the "upholsterer's method of mounting animals" and spent his life elevating taxidermy to a science. Akeley's research led to many inventions, including shotcrete and a motion picture camera, later used in Hollywood. Akeley survived a leopard attack, charging rhinos and an elephant stampede during his many African expeditions to collect specimens, many of which are still on display in the naturalistic settings he created. Regret over killing a mountain gorilla led him to petition King Albert I of Belgium to create a sanctuary, later Africa's first national park. Akeley died Nov 18, 1926, from a fever near Mt Mkeno, Congo.

Alois Alzheimer

Birth: June 14, 1864 ✦ 150 years

The German psychiatrist and pathologist Alois Alzheimer was born at Markbreit am Mainz, Germany. In 1907, an article by Alzheimer appeared in *Allgemeine Zeitschrift für Psychiatrie*, first describing the disease that was named for him. It was thought of as a kind of presenile dementia, usually beginning between ages 40 and 60. Alzheimer died Dec 19, 1915, at Breslau, Germany.

Calvin Blackman Bridges

Birth: Jan 11, 1889 ✦ 125 years

Born at Schuyler Falls, NY, Bridges joined pioneer geneticist Thomas Hunt Morgan in his research on the fruit fly in Columbia University's legendary "fly room" in 1910. Initially a bottle washer, his work by 1916 helped prove that chromosomes carry genetic information and was published as the first paper in the inaugural issue of *Genetics*. His later work demonstrated a link between chromosome bands and the linear sequence of genes. Bridges died Dec 27, 1938, at Los Angeles, CA.

Igor Ivanovitch Sikorsky

Birth: May 25, 1889 ✦ 125 years

Aeronautical engineer best remembered for his development of the first successful helicopter in 1939, a development he noted which brought people "closer than any other . . . to mankind's dreams of the flying horse and the magic carpet." The first to design and fly a multiengine airplane in 1913, Sikorsky also produced multiengine airplanes and large flying boats, called "Clippers," that made transoceanic air transportation possible. Born at Kiev, Russia, he died Oct 26, 1972, at Easton, CT.

Vladimir Zworykin

Birth: July 30, 1889 ✦ 125 years

Born at Mourom, Russia, American scientist Zworykin held more than 120 patents during his life but is best remembered as the "father of television." His inventions of the iconoscope and kinescope laid the foundation for the picture tube television; he was also active in the field of electron microscopy and invented the electron microscope and infrared vision. In 1967, he was awarded the National Medal of Science by the National Academy of Sciences. When asked to comment on the content of American television in an interview in 1981, Zworykin replied, "Awful." Died July 29, 1982, at Princeton, NJ.

Edwin Powell Hubble

Birth: Nov 20, 1889 ✦ 125 years

American astronomer Edwin Hubble was born at Marshfield, MO. His discovery and development of the concept of an expanding universe has been described as the "most spectacular astronomical discovery" of the 20th century. As a tribute, the Hubble Space Telescope, deployed Apr 25, 1990, from US space shuttle *Discovery*, was named for him. The Hubble Space Telescope, with a 240-centimeter mirror, was to allow astronomers to see farther into space than they had ever seen from telescopes on Earth. Hubble died at San Marino, CA, Sept 28, 1953.

Norman Borlaug

Birth: Mar 25, 1914 ✦ 100 years

Agricultural scientist, plant pathologist and geneticist, born at Saude, IA. Won the 1970 Nobel Prize for Peace for the "Green Revolution" initiated in Mexico, Pakistan and India, where he engineered high-yield, disease-resistant, climate-specific grain hybrids that could theoretically end world hunger. Borlaug established the annual World Food Prize and received the Presidential Medal of Freedom. Died Sept 12, 2009, at Dallas, TX.

James Van Allen

Birth: Sept 7, 1914 ✦ 100 years

American physicist born at Mt Pleasant, IA, Van Allen studied the earth's magnetic field; cosmic rays; and the earth's radiation belts, since named the Van Allen belts. The positions of these belts are now taken into consideration when planning spaceflights in order to plot courses that take spacecrafts through the weakest part of the radiation zones. Awarded the National Medal of

Science in 1987, Van Allen died Aug 9, 2006, at Iowa City, IA.

Jonas Salk

Birth: Oct 28, 1914 ✦ 100 years

Dr. Jonas Salk, developer of the Salk polio vaccine, was born at New York, NY. Salk announced his development of a successful vaccine in 1953, the year after a polio epidemic claimed some 3,300 lives in the United States. Polio deaths were reduced by 95 percent after the introduction of the vaccine. Salk spent the last 10 years of his life doing AIDS research. He died June 23, 1995, at La Jolla, CA.

Business and Commerce

Samuel Colt

Birth: July 19, 1814 ✦ 200 years

Born at Hartford, CT, American inventor and manufacturer Colt is best known for developing the multishot pistol, which he patented in 1836. Before the revolver gained popularity, he was also involved in developing submarine battery and underwater telegraph lines. His company, still currently operational, supplied both the North and South with weaponry during the US Civil War, and at the time of his death on Jan 10, 1862, at Hartford, CT, he was one of the wealthiest men in the United States.

Henri Nestlé

Birth: Aug 10, 1814 ✦ 200 years

Inventor of infant formula and entrepreneur, Nestlé was born Heinrich Nestle at Frankfurt, Germany, but moved to Vevey, Switzerland, where he trained as a pharmacist. In 1867, perhaps spurred on by the high infant mortality among his siblings, he created farine lactée, a substitute breast milk for infants unable to nurse. By the 1870s, he was distributing the formula worldwide. Nestlé sold the Nestlé company in 1875, but the company retained his name, which means "little nest," and only later expanded its business to include chocolate and condensed milk. Died July 7, 1890, at Glion, Switzerland.

Gustavus Swift

Birth: June 24, 1839 ✦ 175 years

American industrialist known for revolutionizing the meatpacking industry. He commissioned the development of the refrigerator car, which allowed the transportation of processed meat for the first time, and his company was one of the first in modern history to implement "vertical integration": it had departments for purchasing, production, shipping, sales and marketing. Swift was also a pioneer in using previously discarded by-products of animal parts for products like glue, fertilizer and soap; this efficiency was the model for the contemptuous fictional Durham Company in Upton Sinclair's *The Jungle* (1906). Born at Sandwich, MA, Swift died Mar 29, 1903, at Chicago, IL.

John Davison Rockefeller

Birth: July 8, 1839 ✦ 175 years

Oil magnate, industrialist and philanthropist, born at Richford, NY. From an austere background, Rockefeller brought his love of discipline and frugality to bear on his business dealings, acquiring his first oil refinery in 1863. By 1870, Rockefeller had created Standard Oil, the world's largest refining operations. He perfected the company's vertical integration, quietly buying out competitors and buying up pipelines, train cars, forests (fuel and barrels) and warehouses. Waste by-products like kerosene and gasoline become profitable side businesses. Standard Oil was declared a monopoly in 1911 and broken into 33 subsidiaries, ironically making Rockefeller richer. At his death, his fortune was $1.4 billion. From the 1880s onward, he made philanthropy his business and once said "the power to make money is a gift from God . . . I believe it is my duty to make money and still more money and to use the money I make for the good of my fellow man. . . ." His gifts were foundational to many institutions, including the University of Chicago, Spelman College and Dension University. The Rockefeller Foundation, originally funded to eradicate hookworm, remains a major humanitarian philanthropy. At his death on May 23, 1937, at Ormond Beach, FL, Rockefeller had given away more than $550 million.

Ransom Olds

Birth: June 3, 1864 ✦ 150 years

American automobile inventor and manufacturer Olds was born at Geneva, OH. Founded the Olds Motor Works, which made Oldsmobile, the first affordable, mass-produced American car. It was also the first automobile produced in quantity with a progressive assembly system and comprised of interchangeable parts. In a marketing innovation, Olds also introduced the policy of insisting that dealers pay cash for cars delivered to them, a practice that became standard and provided much-needed immediate capital for the fledgling automotive industry. Died Aug 26, 1950, at Lansing, MI.

Religion

Thomas Cranmer

Birth: July 2, 1489 ✦ 525 years

English clergyman, reformer and martyr, born at Aslacton, Nottinghamshire, England. Archbishop of Canterbury and spearhead of the English Reformation. One of the principal authors of *The English Book of Common Prayer.* Tried for treason, Cranmer temporarily recanted his Protestantism, but then publicly rejected his recantation at his execution, calling it "the great thing that troubleth my conscience more than any other thing that I ever said or did in my life." Burned at the stake at Oxford, England, Mar 21, 1556.

Philosophy

Max Weber

Birth: Apr 21, 1864 ✦ 150 years

Born at Erfaut, Germany, Weber was a founder of modern sociological thought. His historical and comparative studies of the sociocultural processes of great civilizations, notably *The Protestant Ethic and the Spirit of Capitalism*, are pivotal in sociological history. His focus on the religious roots of modern institutions is often juxtaposed with Karl Marx's economic determinism; *Economy and Society* contains, among other ideas, important theories on religion and law. Weber's ethical themes are foundational in existentialist philosophical thought. He died June 14, 1920, at Munich, Germany.

Ludwig Wittgenstein

Birth: Apr 26, 1889 ✦ 125 years

One of the most influential analytic and linguistic philosophers of the 20th century, born at Vienna, Austria. Wittgenstein had a fundamental influence on logical positivism, linguistic analysis and semantics. He theorized philosophical problems were fundamentally problems of language, and studying "ordinary language," a new field of study his research spawned, would enable one to solve many of these problems. He clarified the distinctions between philosophy and science. "Man has to awaken to wonder—and so perhaps do peoples. Science is a way of sending him to sleep again," he once wrote. Died Apr 29, 1951, at Cambridge, England.

Martin Heidegger

Birth: Sept 26, 1889 ✦ 125 years

Widely regarded as the most original 20th-century philosopher, Heidegger's career focused on answering one fundamental question, the meaning of "being," which he explored in his seminal work *Being and Time* (1927), one of the 20th-century's most influential books. His analysis revitalized the study of philosophy and introduced a number of concepts that strongly influenced Sartre and other existential philosophers. Heidegger rejected the characterization of his work as existentialist, notably in *Letter on Humanism* (1947), arguing that, unlike the existentialists, he was not concerned with man but with being. Born at Messkirch, Germany, Heidegger died May 26, 1976, at Freiburg, Germany.

Exploration

Tenzing Norgay

Birth: May 15, 1914 ✦ 100 years

Sherpa co-conqueror of Mt. Everest, born as Nambyal Wangdi, at Tschechu, Tibet. Raised in Nepal, Tenzing began mountaineering as a porter. Having participated in six previous attempts at scaling Mt Everest, he was the most experienced Everest climber on the British expedition of 1953, and on May 29, he and New Zealander Edmund Hillary were the first two men atop the world's highest mountain. Tenzing later wrote, "At that great moment . . . my mountain did not seem to me a lifeless thing of rock and ice, but warm and friendly and living." Died May 9, 1983, at Darjeeling, India.

Thor Heyerdahl

Birth: Oct 6, 1914 ✦ 100 years

The anthropologist and explorer was born at Larvik, Norway. Seeking to prove the plausibility of South American peoples' having settled Polynesia, he embarked on an epic raft ride with five companions in 1947. The *Kon-Tiki* made the 4,300-mile voyage from Peru to Raroia in 101 days. Heyerdahl's book chronicling the adventure became an international bestseller. He continued his travels (including a solo 1970 trip in a reed boat from North Africa to Barbados) and writing until his death. He died at Italy on Apr 18, 2002.

Sports

William Louis (Bill) Veeck Jr.

Birth: Feb 9, 1914 ✦ 100 years

Baseball Hall of Fame executive, born at Chicago, IL. Veeck was baseball's premier promoter and showman as an owner of several teams. He integrated the American League and sought to provide fans with entertainment in addition to baseball. Inducted into the Hall of Fame in 1991. Died at Chicago, IL, Jan 2, 1986.

Harry Caray

Birth: Mar 1, 1914 ✦ 100 years

Born Harry Christopher Carabina at St. Louis, MO. Caray began his baseball broadcasting career with the St. Louis Cardinals in 1945. He then was the announcer for the Oakland A's, the Chicago White Sox and finally the Chicago Cubs. He became a legend at Wrigley Field with his seventh-inning stretch "Take Me Out to the Ball Game" and his quirky phrase "Holy Cow!" Caray was inducted into the Broadcasters Hall of Fame in 1989. Died at Rancho Mirage, CA, Feb 18, 1998.

Sammy Adrian Baugh

Birth: Mar 17, 1914 ✦ 100 years

Born at Temple, TX, "Slinging Sammy" was one of the top quarterbacks of the 1930s and '40s—first at Texas Christian University, then at the Washington Redskins. Baugh (whose nickname actually referred to his prowess in baseball) was a first-round draft pick (sixth overall) for the Redskins in 1937, and he stayed with the franchise his entire career, until 1952. He was actually a star quarterback, tailback and punter. Uniquely, in 1943, he led the league in passing, punting and pass interceptions. On "Sammy Baugh Day" on Nov 23, 1947, he passed for 355 yards and six touchdowns against the Chicago Cardinals. Baugh's impact on the pro game was making the forward pass (before then little used) an integral part of the offensive toolkit. His number (33) is the only one to be retired by the Redskins. He was inducted (charter member) in the Pro Football Hall of Fame on Sept 7, 1963. Baugh died Dec 17, 2008, at Rotan, TX.

Emmett Littleton Ashford

Birth: Nov 23, 1914 ✦ 100 years

Emmett Littleton Ashford, born at Los Angeles, CA, was the first black to officiate at a Major League Baseball game. Ashford began his pro career calling games in the minors in 1951 and went to the majors in 1966. He was noted for his flamboyant style when calling strikes and outs as well as for his dapper dress, which included cuff links with his uniform. He died Mar 1, 1980, at Marina del Rey, CA.

Joseph Paul (Joe) DiMaggio

Birth: Nov 25, 1914 ✦ 100 years

Baseball Hall of Fame outfielder, born at Martinez, CA. DiMaggio debuted professionally in 1935 with the San Francisco Seals, but he became the legendary "Yankee Clipper" for the New York Yankees beginning in the 1936 season. In 1941, he was on "the streak," getting a hit in 56 consecutive games. "Joltin' Joe" was the American League MVP for three years (1939, 1941, 1947), was batting champion two years (1939 and 1940) and led the league in RBIs in both 1941 and 1948. DiMaggio was part of the Yankees squad for nine World Series Championships. He retired in 1951 and was inducted into the Baseball Hall of Fame in 1955. DiMaggio was married to actress Marilyn Monroe in 1954, but they later divorced. He died at Harbour Island, FL, Mar 8, 1999.

Miscellaneous

George Nissen

Birth: Feb 3, 1914 ✦ 100 years

Nissen is responsible for transforming many a suburban backyard into a personal circus with his invention: the trampoline. A teenage gymnast champion, he was inspired by the nets under circus aerialists and, tinkering in his parents' garage, created what he called a small "bouncing rig" that he could use as a touring acrobat. In 1937, he trademarked the "Trampoline" (borrowing from the Spanish for "diving board"), and after World War II was an indefatigable marketer of the portable jumping station that he also manufactured. He lived to see trampolining become an Olympic event in 2000. Born at Blairstown, IA, Nissen died at San Diego, CA, Apr 7, 2010.

Jack LaLanne

Birth: Sept 26, 1914 ✦ 100 years

The son of French immigrants, born at San Francisco, CA, was to become America's postwar and "Me Generation" fitness guru through his eponymous TV show and wacky stunts. As an awkward teenager, LaLanne decided to improve his life through nutrition and working out. He opened gyms and took his local "The Jack LaLanne Show" TV program national in 1959. By the end of its run in the 1980s, there were 3,000 episodes. LaLanne, who kept a 30-inch waist, popularized the benefits of living heathfully with amazing stunts, such as swimming underwater—with 140 pounds of equipment—for the length of the Golden Gate Bridge or swimming—handcuffed—from Alcatraz Island to Fisherman's Wharf while also towing a 1,000-pound boat (at age 60). LaLanne died Jan 23, 2011, at Morro Bay, CA, at age 96.

Spotlight on 2014 Events

United Nations International Years 2014

JAN 1–DEC 31

International Years are special events declared by the United Nations General Assembly to draw worldwide focus and action to particular causes. The United Nations has declared three International Years for 2014.

The International Year of Small Island Developing States (SIDS) was declared to assist the more than 50 island nations with fragile ecosystems and limited resources, especially to create awareness and devise strategies for adapting to climate change as part of a broader framework of sustainable development. SIDS—among them Bahamas, Barbados, Belize, Cuba, Dominican Republic, Fiji, Haiti, Jamaica, Micronesia, Samoa, Singapore, Suriname, Trinidad and Tobago—are especially vulnerable to the impacts of climate changes because of their size and geographical isolation. SIDS are more susceptible to natural disasters, inundation from rising sea levels, land loss due to coastal erosion and contamination of agricultural land due to saltwater intrusion. For information: United Nations Department of Economic and Social Affairs, Division for Sustainable Development. Web: www.sids2014.org.

The International Year of Family Farming is an initiative launched by the NGO World Rural Forum and supported by more than 360 civil society and farmers' organizations in more than 60 countries. The worldwide celebration aims to raise the profile of farming families, communal units, indigenous groups, cooperatives and fishing families, with a goal of combating poverty and hunger, providing food security and fostering rural development based on the respect for environment and biodiversity. It is the first time in history that civil society is at the origin of an International Year. For information: World Rural Forum. Web: www.familyfarmingcampaign.net.

The International Year of Crystallography 2014 (IYCr2014) commemorates the centennial of X-ray diffraction, which allowed the detailed study of crystalline material, and the 400th anniversary of Kepler's observation in 1611 of the symmetrical form of ice crystals, which began the wider study of the role of symmetry in matter. The major objectives of IYCr2014 are to increase public awareness of the science of crystallography and how it underpins most technological developments, to inspire young people, to illustrate the universality of science, to foster international collaboration between scientists and to involve the large synchrotron and neutron radiation facilities worldwide in the celebrations of IYCr2014, including the SESAME project set up under UNESCO auspices. The Opening Ceremony of IYCr2014 will take place at UNESCO in Place de Fontenoy, Paris, on Jan 20, 2014. For information: The International Union of Crystallography and Unesco. Web: www.iycr2014.org.

Games of the XXII Winter Olympiad

XI Paralympic Winter Games

Sochi, Russian Federation

FEB 7–23; MAR 7–16

The 22nd Winter Olympics and 11th Winter Paralympics take place in Sochi, Russia. This will be the first Winter Olympics held in a subtropical zone: Sochi is a southern city (center of the "Russian Riviera") located on the shores of the Black Sea near Russia's border with Georgia. It is also on track to be the most expensive Winter Olympics ever held.

The Sochi Olympics will feature 15 disciplines of seven winter

sports: biathlon, bobsled (bobsled and skeleton), curling, ice hockey, luge, skating (figure skating, short track speed skating and speed skating) and skiing (alpine, cross-country, Nordic combined, ski jumping, freestyle and snowboard). The XI Paralympic Winter Games follow the Olympic Games from Mar 7 to 16. Athletes compete at the same venues as their Olympic counterparts and in five events: alpine skiing (slalom and giant slalom), biathlon, cross-country skiing, ice sledge hockey and wheelchair curling.

Uniquely, these Olympics are in a very compact area, so athletes, officials, media and an expected 70,000 spectators can circulate to different events in minutes. The so-called "Coastal Cluster" will facilitate this ease of traffic: six venues form a tight circle in the Olympic Park. The gems of this cluster are the Fisht Olympic Stadium and the Bolshoy Ice Dome. The Fisht (named for a nearby mountain in the Caucaus chain) seats 40,000 spectators under a translucent polycarbonate roof that allows views of the spectacular surrounding mountains. The Bolshoy Ice Dome, inspired by a frozen water drop, will convert to a multipurpose entertainment/sports center after the Olympics. All six venues will be used for both the Olympics and the Paralympics, and three are moveable: they can be packed up and transported elsewhere.

The Mountain Cluster is the location for biathlon, ski, bobsled, skiing and snowboarding events. Newly created venues (which will be converted to resorts after the games) include the 2,000-foot-high RusSki Gorki Jumping Center, Sanki Sliding Center, Laura Cross-Country Ski and Biathlon Center, Extreme Park and Rosa Khutor Alpine Resort.

Sochi's climate has created special concerns—most important whether there will be adequate snow. The average high temperature in Sochi in February is 50 degrees. A mild winter in 2013 caused the cancellation of two test sporting events at Sochi, so officials began a stockpiling and storage effort that collected more than 450,000 cubic meters of snow in case of a second mild winter. Organizers have also brought in some 400 snow-making cannons.

The five Winter Olympic mascots were chosen during a live Russian television show using votes from the public. The Hare, the

Other Major 2014 Quadrennial and Biennial Sporting Events

17th Asian Games—Incheon 2014

Incheon, South Korea, Sept 19–Oct 4

The 45 member nations of the Olympic Council of Asia will celebrate the 17th Asian Games. More than 13,000 athletes will participate in 36 events (28 Olympic events) in and around Incheon. Held every four years. See www.incheon2014ag.org.

2014 Commonwealth Games

Glasgow, Scotland, July 23–Aug 3

Held every four years, this will be the 20th Commonwealth Games. Originally called the British Empire Games, the event was first held in 1930 in Canada. About 6,500 athletes from the 71 nations and territories of the Commonwealth compete in 17 different disciplines. See www.glasgow2014.com.

Gay Games 9

Cleveland and Akron, OH, USA, Aug 9–16

International sporting and cultural event first held in 1982 and running every four years. Open to all athletes regardless of sexual orientation, race, gender, religion, ethnic origin, political beliefs, age, physical challenge or health status. Some 10,000 participants from more than 65 nations are expected in 2014. See www.gg9cle.com.

Curtis Cup

St. Louis, MO, USA, June 6–8

Biennial competition (officially named "The Women's International Cup") between teams of women amateur golfers from the United States and the United Kingdom. See www.curtiscup.org.

Ryder Cup 2014

Gleneagles, Scotland, Sept 23–28

Held every two years, this match pits American golfers against a European team. First held in 1927, this will be the 40th match. Europe is the defending champion from 2012. See www.rydercup2014.com.

Polar Bear and the Leopard are the Olympic Winter Games mascots. The Ray of Light and the Snowflake are the Paralympic Winter Games mascots.

For information about the XXII Winter Olympics and XI Winter Olympics, visit www.sochi2014.com.

The 2014 FIFA World Cup—Brazil

JUNE 12–JULY 13

The biggest sporting event in the world—surpassing even the Olympics—is soccer's World Cup. This will be the 20th World Cup, which is sponsored by soccer's world governing body, Fédération Internationale de Football Association (FIFA). Beginning June 12 at Sao Paulo, the monthlong tournament will see 64 total matches played in 12 cities across Brazil (Rio de Janeiro, Brasília, Cuiabá, Curitiba, Porto Alegre, Recife, São Paulo, Belo Horizonte, Fortaleza, Manaus, Natal, Salvador). The title match will be played July 13 in Rio de Janeiro.

This will be the second time that Brazil has hosted the World Cup. Previously, it hosted in 1950—and presented the spectators with what was then the world's biggest soccer stadium, the Maracana. The Uruguayan team was champion that year, disappointing the home favorites, who were runners-up, but Brazil has been the World Cup champion a record five times. Brazil's team will again be favorites in 2014, along with Spain, which is the defending 2010 champion.

And the iconic Maracana stadium will be the centerpiece again, hosting seven games, including the final on July 13. The Maracana's $500 million facelift for 2014 includes modernization and more comfortable features as well as environmentally friendly attributes, most important of which is that the huge stadium will now be powered by solar energy. Its capacity of 88,000 has been reduced to 83,000 for safety concerns (but as many as 150,000 fans have been squeezed inside in the past).

The 2014 FIFA World Cup as a whole will be more environmentally friendly, and another tech-

nology, "goal-line technology," will make its first appearance. At the 2010 World Cup, after field officials failed to see and record an English goal in the game against Germany, FIFA deliberated about adding technology to supplement human refereeing, ultimately making the landmark decision to try new technology that would indicate automatically whether a ball has completely crossed the goal line in 2014.

For more information:

Fédération Internationale de Football Association (FIFA)
FIFA House
FIFA-Strasse 20
PO Box 8044
Zurich, Switzerland
Web: www.fifa.com/worldcup/index.html

✦ January ✦

January 1 — Wednesday

DAY 1 **364 REMAINING**

WEDNESDAY, JANUARY ONE, 2014. Jan 1. First day of the first month of the Gregorian calendar year, Anno Domini 2014, being a Common Year, and (until July 4) 238th year of American independence. 2014 will be year 6727 of the Julian Period, a time frame consisting of 7,991 years that began at noon, universal (Greenwich) time, Jan 1, 4714 BC. Astronomers will note that Julian Day number 2,452,652 begins at noon, universal time (representing the number of days since the beginning of the Julian Period). New Year's Day is a public holiday in the US and in many other countries. Traditionally, it is a time for personal stocktaking, for making resolutions for the coming year and sometimes for recovering from the festivities of New Year's Eve. Financial accounting begins anew for businesses and individuals whose fiscal year is the calendar year. Jan 1 has been observed as the beginning of the year in most English-speaking countries since the British Calendar Act of 1751, prior to which the New Year began Mar 25 (approximating the vernal equinox). Earth begins another orbit of the sun, during which it, and we, will travel some 583,416,000 miles in 365.2422 days. New Year's Day has been called "Everyman's Birthday," and in some countries a year is added to everyone's age on Jan 1 rather than on the anniversary of each person's birth.

ACADIA NATIONAL PARK ESTABLISHED: 95th ANNIVERSARY. Jan 1, 1919. Maine's Sieur de Monts National Monument, authorized in 1916, was established as Lafayette National Park in 1919. The name was changed to Acadia National Park by an act of Congress in 1929.

AUSTRALIA: COMMONWEALTH FORMED: ANNIVERSARY. Jan 1, 1901. On this day the six colonies of Victoria, New South Wales, Queensland, South Australia, Western Australia and Northern Territory were united into one nation. The British Parliament had passed the Commonwealth Constitution Bill in the spring of 1900, and Queen Victoria signed the document Sept 17, 1900.

BE KIND TO FOOD SERVERS MONTH. Jan 1–31. Start the New Year off with a resolution to be kind to your hardworking waiter or waitress. This month's goal is to establish a positive relationship between food servers and the dining public. Has been proclaimed by the State of Tennessee. For info: Sybil Presley, 1056 Linden Ave, #608, Memphis, TN 38104. Phone: (901) 643-1982. E-mail: sybilpresley@bellsouth.net.

BONZA BOTTLER DAY™. Jan 1. (also Feb 2, Mar 3, Apr 4, May 5, June 6, July 7, Aug 8, Sept 9, Oct 10, Nov 11 and Dec 12). To celebrate when the number of the day is the same as the number of the month. Bonza Bottler Day™ is an excuse to have a party at least once a month. Created by the late Elaine Fremont and continued by her family, Bonza Bottler Day is now celebrated not only in the US but also in many other countries. For info: Gail Berger, Bonza Bottler Day, 14 Fernwood Dr, Taylors, SC 29687. Phone: (864) 201-3988. E-mail: bonza@bonzabottlerday.com. Web: www.bonzabottlerday.com.

BOOK BLITZ MONTH. Jan 1–31. Focuses attention on improving authors' relationships with the media in order to create a bestselling book. Free book PR evaluation available. For info: Barbara Gaughen, Media 21, 7456 Evergreen Dr, Santa Barbara, CA 93117. Phone: (805) 968-8567. E-mail: bgaughenmu@aol.com.

CANADA: POLAR BEAR SWIM 2014. Jan 1. English Bay Beach, Vancouver, BC. 94th annual. The Vancouver Polar Bear Swim Club is one of the largest and oldest Polar Bear Clubs in the world. Its initial swim was in 1920 when a small number of hardy swimmers took the plunge into English Bay on New Year's Day. Led by their founder, Peter Pantages, the swim has grown from around 10 swimmers in that year to the record number of 2,246 official entries in 2011. Today, the swim takes place at 2:30 PM on the first day of each new year. Costumes and the Peter Pantages Memorial 100-yard swim race are the highlights of this event. For info: Vancouver Aquatic Centre, 1050 Beach Ave, Vancouver, BC V6E 1T7, Canada. Web: www.vancouver.ca/parks/events/polarbear.

CAPITAL ONE BOWL. Jan 1. Florida Citrus Bowl Stadium, Orlando, FL. 69th annual. Postseason college football game matching the top non-BCS teams from the Big Ten and SEC conferences. Est attendance: 70,000. For info: Florida Citrus Sports, One Citrus Bowl Pl, Orlando, FL 32805. Phone: (407) 423-2476. Fax: (407) 425-8451. Web: www.floridacitrussports.com.

CELEBRATION OF LIFE MONTH. Jan 1–31. As the first month of the year, January signifies a new beginning, a new life, a new happiness in many lives each year. Every community has a new hope to begin a new page in the book of life. Remember always to value the gift of life for all Americans pursuing life, liberty, happiness and justice for all citizens. For info: Judith Natale, Women of Freedom, USA, PO Box 493703, Redding, CA 96049-3703. E-mail: womenoffreedom@aol.com.

CIRCUMCISION OF CHRIST. Jan 1. Holy day in many Christian churches. Celebrates Jesus's submission to Jewish law; on the octave day of Christmas. See also: "Solemnity of Mary, Mother of God" (Jan 1) for Roman Catholic observance since 1969 calendar reorganization.

COMMITMENT DAY. Jan 1. New Year's Day will be one to remember and is no longer about "resolutions." It is about "commitments." In a city near you, thousands of people will set out to do a 5k and end up starting a movement. Men, women, families, coworkers and neighbors are making a commitment to live a healthy lifestyle while helping others do the same. Go ahead, join the movement. Annually, Jan 1. For info: John Sellinger, Commitment Day, 2902 Corporate Pl, Chanhassen, MN 55317. Phone: (240) 888-2952. E-mail: jsellinger@lifetimefitness.com. Web: www.commitmentday.com.

COPYRIGHT REVISION LAW SIGNED: ANNIVERSARY. Jan 1, 1976. The first major revision since 1909 of laws governing intellectual property in the US was signed by President Ford. It took effect two years later on Jan 1, 1978. The act (Public Law 94–553) contains substantial revisions of the principles governing acquisition and duration of copyright and deals with issues that have been raised in recent years concerning photocopying and the use of copyrighted works by public broadcasting and cable television systems.

CUBA: 55th ANNIVERSARY OF THE REVOLUTION. Jan 1. National holiday celebrating the overthrow of the government of Fulgencio Batista in 1959 by the revolutionary forces of Fidel Castro, which had begun a civil war in 1956.

CUBA: LIBERATION DAY. Jan 1. A national holiday that celebrates the end of Spanish rule in 1899. Cuba, the largest island of the West Indies, was a Spanish possession from its discovery by Columbus (Oct 27, 1492) until 1899. Under US military control 1899–1902 and 1906–09; a republican government took over Jan 28, 1909, and controlled the island until overthrown Jan 1, 1959, by Fidel Castro's revolutionary movement.

CZECH-SLOVAK DIVORCE: ANNIVERSARY. Jan 1, 1993. As Dec 31, 1992, gave way to Jan 1, 1993, the 74-year-old state of Czechoslovakia separated into two nations—the Czech Republic and Slovakia. The Slovaks held a celebration through the night in the streets of Bratislava amid fireworks, bell ringing, singing of the new country's national anthem and the raising of the Slovak flag. In the new Czech Republic no official festivities took place, but later in the day the Czechs celebrated with a solemn oath by their parliament. The nation of Czechoslovakia ended peacefully though polls showed that most Slovaks and Czechs would have preferred that it survive. Before the split Czech prime minister Vaclav Klaus and Slovak prime minister Vladimir Meciar reached an agreement on dividing everything from army troops and gold reserves to the art on government building walls.

DIET RESOLUTION WEEK. Jan 1–7. This week emphasizes the importance of watching your weight by focusing on the type—not the amount—of food you put on your plate. Resolve to consume minimally processed, less-refined carbohydrate foods. Slim down permanently with whole grains, legumes, and fresh fruits and vegetables. Eat more but weigh less for life. Delete meat and other animal foods to make minuscule meals and calorie counting obsolete. Start your year off right by eating light with every bite! For info: Vegetarian Awareness Network, PO Box 3545, Washington, DC 20027-0045. Phone: (800) 234-8343.

ELLIS ISLAND OPENED: ANNIVERSARY. Jan 1, 1892. Ellis Island was opened on New Year's Day in 1892. Over the years more than 20 million individuals were processed through the stations. The island was used as a point of deportation as well: in 1932 alone, 20,000 people were deported from Ellis Island. When the US entered WWII in 1941, Ellis Island became a Coast Guard station. It closed Nov 12, 1954, and was declared a national park in 1956. After years of disuse it was restored, and in 1990 it was reopened as a museum.

EMANCIPATION PROCLAMATION TAKES EFFECT: ANNIVERSARY. Jan 1, 1863. Abraham Lincoln, by executive proclamation of Sept 22, 1862, declared that on this date "all persons held as slaves within any state or designated part of a state, the people whereof shall then be in rebellion against the United States, shall be then, thenceforward, and forever, free." Slaves in the four slave states that had not seceded from the Union (Delaware, Maryland, Kentucky and Missouri) were not freed until the passage of the 13th Amendment in 1865. See also: "Thirteenth Amendment to the US Constitution Ratified: Anniversary" (Dec 6).

ENGLAND: THE NEW YEAR'S DAY PARADE AND FESTIVAL. Jan 1. London. 28th annual. The biggest parade of its kind in the world. The event, which attracts huge crowds to the streets of the capital, runs from the Ritz Hotel, Piccadilly, to Piccadilly Circus, lower Regent St, Pall Mall, Trafalgar Square, along Whitehall to Parliament Square. All the pageantry, glitz and razzmatazz remain: dozens of massive marching bands, cheerleaders, mayors of London boroughs, vintage cars, clowns and street performers. The event also includes a spectacular series of orchestral and choral concerts in majestic historic settings. Est attendance: 550,000. For info: The New Year's Day Parade and Festival. Phone: (44) (20) 3275-0190. E-mail: info@londonparade.co.uk. Web: www.londonparade.co.uk.

EURO INTRODUCED: 15th ANNIVERSARY. Jan 1, 1999. The euro, the common currency of members of the European Union, was introduced for use by financial institutions. The value of the currencies of the original 11 nations (Austria, Belgium, Finland, France, Germany, Ireland, Italy, Luxembourg, the Netherlands, Portugal and Spain) was locked in at a permanent conversion rate to the euro. Greece, Slovenia, Estonia, Cyprus, Malta and Slovakia joined the eurozone in subsequent years. On Jan 1, 2002, euro bills and coins began circulating; other currencies were phased out as of Feb 28, 2002.

FIRST BABY BOOMER BORN: ANNIVERSARY. Jan 1, 1946. Kathleen Casey Wilkens, born at one minute after midnight at Philadelphia, PA, was the first of the almost 78 million baby boomers born between 1946 and 1964.

January 2014	S	M	T	W	T	F	S
				1	2	3	4
	5	6	7	8	9	10	11
	12	13	14	15	16	17	18
	19	20	21	22	23	24	25
	26	27	28	29	30	31	

FLIGHT 2014: CENTENNIAL CELEBRATION OF COMMERCIAL AVIATION. Jan 1. St. Petersburg and Tampa, FL. When pioneer aviator Tony Jannus and one paying passenger took off from the St. Petersburg, FL, yacht basin on New Year's Day 1914, they were flying into the annals of aviation history. Aviation historians acknowledge St. Petersburg-Tampa Airboat Line as the world's first airliner. To celebrate this centennial, Kermit Weeks of Fantasy Flight has built an exact reproduction of the original Benoist Airboat airline. Weeks reenacts the first flight today. Other centennial celebrations include First Night (Dec 31, 2013) in St. Petersburg, the St. Petersburg History Museum's exhibits and programs, the Jannus Society's special centennial awards program recognizing contemporary achievement in civil aviation and a Tony Jannus Day held by the International Sun 'n' Fun Expo & International Fly-in. For info: The St. Petersburg Chamber of Commerce. Web: www.stpete.com/general/custom.asp?page=Flight2014.

FORSTER, E.M.: BIRTH ANNIVERSARY. Jan 1, 1879. Edward Morgan Forster, English author born at London, England, is remembered for his six novels: *Where Angels Fear to Tread* (1905), *The Longest Journey* (1907), *A Room with a View* (1908), *Howard's End* (1910), *A Passage to India* (1924) and the posthumously published *Maurice* (1971). He also achieved eminence for his short stories and essays, and he collaborated on the libretto for an opera, Benjamin Britten's *Billy Budd* (1951). Forster died at Coventry, England, June 7, 1970.

GET A LIFE BALANCED MONTH. Jan 1–31. Ever feel like a tumbleweed being blown about with no control because of all the demands put on your time? Overwhelmed by all the choices on your buffet table of life? This month is focused not on New Year's resolutions, but on making better strategic decisions all year long to get your life in balance. Includes the importance of balancing time for self, family and friends. For info: Sheryl Nicholson, 8627 Boysenberry Dr, Tampa, FL 33635. Phone: (727) 678-6707. E-mail: sheryl@sheryl.com.

GET ORGANIZED MONTH. Jan 1–31. Is your New Year's resolution to get more organized? This is an opportunity to streamline your life, create more time, lower your stress and increase your productivity. For info and local chapter events: National Assn of Professional Organizers (NAPO), 15000 Commerce Pkwy, Ste C, Mount Laurel, NJ 08054. Phone: (856) 380-6828. E-mail: napo@napo.net. Web: www.napo.net/gomonth.

GREENBERG, HANK: BIRTH ANNIVERSARY. Jan 1, 1911. Henry Benjamin (Hank) Greenberg, Hall of Fame first baseman and outfielder, born at New York, NY. One of the game's most prodigious sluggers, Greenberg hit 331 home runs and drove in 1,276 runs in only nine full seasons. Baseball's first Jewish superstar, Greenberg entered the army after playing just 19 games in 1941 and did not return to the Detroit Tigers until midway through the 1945 season. His grand slam on that season's last day won the pennant for the Tigers and propelled them toward a World Series triumph. He was inducted into the Hall of Fame in 1956 and died at Beverly Hills, CA, Sept 4, 1986.

HAITI: INDEPENDENCE DAY. Jan 1. A national holiday commemorating the proclamation of independence in 1804. Haiti, occupying the western third of the island Hispaniola (second largest of the West Indies), was a Spanish colony from its discovery by Columbus in 1492 until 1697. Then it was a French colony until the proclamation of independence in 1804.

HANGOVER HANDICAP RUN. Jan 1. Veteran's Park, Klamath Falls, OR. Two-mile fun run at 9 AM New Year's Day. The first-place male and female finishers each take home a beer can trophy. Est attendance: 100. For info: Hangover Handicap, 1800 Fairmount, Klamath Falls, OR 97601. Phone: (541) 882-6922. Fax: (541) 883-6481.

HOOVER, J. EDGAR: BIRTH ANNIVERSARY. Jan 1, 1895. John Edgar Hoover, born at Washington, DC. He led the Palmer Raids and was director of the FBI, 1924–72. During his time as director, Hoover practiced modern investigative techniques, improved FBI agent training and increased FBI funding from Congress. He died May 2, 1972, at Washington, DC.

INTERNATIONAL BRAIN TEASER MONTH. Jan 1–31. Start the year out right and celebrate "thinking fun" all month long! Try to solve the fun and funny hands-on brain teasers, brain twisters and mechanical puzzles at this hands-on museum. Puzzles include rebus, strategy, antique, jumping, mechanicals, matching, disappearing and sliding block puzzles. Good exercise for your gray matter and ageless fun for all, whether you're 5 or 105. The Logic Puzzle Museum includes hands-on time, an exhibit to see, and then a puzzle to make and keep. For info: Logic Puzzle Museum, 533 Milwaukee Ave, Burlington, WI 53105. Phone: (262) 763-3946. E-mail: logicpuzzlemuseum@hotmail.com. Web: www.logicpuzzlemuseum.org.

INTERNATIONAL CHILD-CENTERED DIVORCE AWARENESS MONTH. Jan 1–31. Dedicated to reminding parents about how children are affected by divorce and how to create the most positive outcome during and after divorce. The month is commemorated by divorce professionals and professional associations around the world through free public seminars, webinars, interviews, film showings and complimentary services. Details and free e-book at the website. For info: Rosalind Sedacca. Phone: (561) 385-4205. E-mail: rosalind@childcentereddivorce.com. Web: www.divorcedparentsupport.com/ebook.

INTERNATIONAL CREATIVITY MONTH. Jan 1–31. A month to remind individuals and organizations around the globe to capitalize on the power of creativity. Unleashing creativity and innovation is vital for personal and business success in this age of accelerating change. The first month of the year provides an opportunity to take a fresh approach to problem solving and renew confidence in our creative capabilities. For info: Randall Munson, Pres, Creatively Speaking, 508 Meadow Run Dr SW, Rochester, MN 55902-2337. Phone: (507) 286-1331. Fax: (507) 286-1331. E-mail: Creativity@CreativelySpeaking.com. Web: www.CreativityMonth.com.

INTERNATIONAL NEW YEAR'S RESOLUTIONS MONTH FOR BUSINESSES. Jan 1–31. Set in motion a successful year by focusing on PR and marketing efforts guaranteed to make your cash register ring and your bank statements sing. Resolve to get your business and message in front of your target market. For info: Raleigh R. Pinskey. Phone: (480) 488-4840. E-mail: raleigh@promoteyourself.com. Web: www.promoteyourself.com.

INTERNATIONAL WAYFINDING MONTH. Jan 1–31. Celebrate the spatial and environmental information systems that help you find your way in the built environment. They are what get you to the airport gate, through a parking lot, around a museum! For info: Ann Makowski, Society for Environmental Graphic Design, 1000 Vermont Ave NW, Ste 400, Washington, DC 20005. Phone: (202) 638-5555. Fax: (202) 478-2286. E-mail: ann@segd.org. Web: www.segd.org.

JAPANESE ERA NEW YEAR. Jan 1–3. Celebration of the beginning of the year Heisei 26, the 26th year of Emperor Akihito's reign.

KLIBAN, B(ERNARD): BIRTH ANNIVERSARY. Jan 1, 1935. Cartoonist B. Kliban was born at Norwalk, CT. He was known for his satirical drawings of cats engaged in human pursuits, which appeared in the books *Cat* (1975), *Never Eat Anything Bigger than Your Head & Other Drawings* (1976) and *Whack Your Porcupine* (1977) and on T-shirts, greeting cards, calendars, bedsheets and other merchandise, creating a $50 million industry before his death at San Francisco, CA, Aug 12, 1990.

MOON PHASE: NEW MOON. Jan 1. Moon enters New Moon phase at 6:14 AM, EST.

MUMMERS PARADE. Jan 1. Philadelphia, PA. World-famous New Year's Day parade of 20,000 spectacularly costumed Mummers in a colorful parade that goes on all day. This celebration has taken place since the 1700s. Est attendance: 100,000. For info: Mummers Parade. Web: www.mummers.com.

NATIONAL BE ON-PURPOSE® MONTH. Jan 1–31. An observance to encourage us to start the new year by putting our good intentions into action, personally and professionally, and to trade confusion for clarity as we integrate our lives with more meaning and purpose. For info: Kevin W. McCarthy, CEO, On-Purpose Partners, PO Box 1568, Winter Park, FL 32790-1568. Phone: (407) 657-6000. Fax: (407) 645-1345. E-mail: info@on-purpose.com.

NATIONAL CLEAN UP YOUR COMPUTER MONTH. Jan 1–31. Dedicated to the education of computer users with simple tips and methods to increase the efficiency of their systems. For info: Denise Hall, PO Box 687, Loxley, AL 36551. Phone: (251) 943-3315. Fax: (251) 943-1716. E-mail: denise@specterweb.com. Web: specterweb.com.

NATIONAL ENVIRONMENTAL POLICY ACT: ANNIVERSARY. Jan 1, 1970. The National Environmental Policy Act of 1969 established the Council on Environmental Quality and made it federal government policy to protect the environment.

NATIONAL GLAUCOMA AWARENESS MONTH. Jan 1–31. More than two million Americans aged 40 and older suffer from glaucoma. Nearly half do not know they have the disease—it causes no early symptoms. Prevent Blindness America® will provide valuable information about this "sneak thief of sight." Organizations are encouraged to educate the community through screenings, forums and programs. For info: Prevent Blindness America®, 211 W Wacker Dr, Ste 1700, Chicago, IL 60606. Phone: (800) 331-2020. E-mail: info@preventblindness.org. Web: www.preventblindness.org.

NATIONAL HOT TEA MONTH. Jan 1–31. To celebrate one of nature's most popular, soothing and relaxing beverages; the only beverage in America commonly served hot or iced, anytime, anywhere, for any occasion. For info: The Tea Council of the USA, 362 Fifth Ave, Ste 801, New York, NY 10001. Phone: (212) 986-9415. Fax: (212) 697-8658. E-mail: info@teausa.org. Web: www.teausa.org.

NATIONAL MENTORING MONTH. Jan 1–31. Goals include raising awareness of mentoring in its various forms; recruiting individuals to mentor, especially in programs that have a waiting list of young people; and promoting the rapid growth of mentoring by recruiting organizations to help find mentors for young people. Each January, this monthlong campaign provides nationwide publicity and information about mentoring programs in various communities that need volunteers. The National Mentoring Summit is the culminating event and takes place Jan 30–31 at Arlington, VA. Sponsors: Harvard School of Public Health, MENTOR and the Corporation for National and Community Service (CNCS). For info: MENTOR/National Mentoring Partnership. Web: www.nationalmentoringmonth.org or www.mentoring.org.

NATIONAL PERSONAL SELF-DEFENSE AWARENESS MONTH. Jan 1–31. To educate women and teens about realistic self-defense options that could very well save their lives. Sponsored by the National Self-Defense Institute, Inc, a not-for-profit 501(c)(3) corporation. NSDI/SAFE Program™ seminars and related events nationally emphasize being totally prepared by realizing that awareness + risk reduction = 90 percent of self-defense while the other 10 percent is physical and wake women up to the fact that the key to their own safety lies in themselves. For info: National Self-Defense Institute, Inc, PO Box 398355, Miami Beach, FL 33239-8355. Phone: (305) 868-NSDI. Fax: (305) 867-6634. E-mail: nsdi@att.net. Web: www.nsdi.org.

NATIONAL POVERTY IN AMERICA AWARENESS MONTH. Jan 1–31. To promote public awareness of the continuing existence of poverty and social injustice in America. Individuals are encouraged to support efforts to eradicate poverty by increasing their understanding of the causes and practical solutions and by active participation and support for antipoverty programs. Sponsored by the Catholic Campaign for Human Development, the largest private funder of self-help programs for the poor and disenfranchised in the US regardless of religion, race or ethnic origin. For info: Catholic Campaign for Human Development, US Conference of Catholic Bishops, 3211 Fourth St NE, Washington, DC 20017-1194. Phone: (202) 541-3210. E-mail: jphdmail@usccb.org. Web: www .povertyusa.org.

NATIONAL RADON ACTION MONTH. Jan 1–31. To increase the public's awareness of the effects of radon. For info: Environmental Protection Agency. Radon Hotline: (800) SOS-RADON. Web: www.epa.gov/radon.

NATIONAL SKATING MONTH. Jan 1–31. During this month, US Figure Skating member clubs and Basic Skill Programs reach out to new members in their community by offering the fundamentals of ice-skating from professionally trained instructors across the US. For info: US Figure Skating, 20 First St, Colorado Springs, CO 80906. Phone: (719) 635-5200. Fax: (719) 635-9548. E-mail: info@ usfigureskating.org. Web: www.usfsa.org.

✦NATIONAL SLAVERY AND HUMAN TRAFFICKING PREVENTION MONTH. Jan 1–31. To acknowledge that forms of slavery still exist in the modern era and to recommit American efforts to stop the human traffickers who ply this horrific trade. First proclaimed in 2010 by the Obama administration.

✦NATIONAL STALKING AWARENESS MONTH. Jan 1–31. First proclaimed in 2011 by President Obama to acknowledge stalking as a serious crime and urge those impacted not to be afraid to speak out or ask for help. Also to support victims and survivors and to create communities that are secure and supportive for all Americans.

NATIONAL VOLUNTEER BLOOD DONOR MONTH. Jan 1–31. A time to highlight the importance of giving life through the donation of blood—and to honor past and present donors. For info: US Dept of Health and Human Services. Web: www.organdonor.gov.

NEW YEAR'S DAY. Jan 1. Legal holiday in all states and territories of the US and in most other countries. The world's most widely celebrated holiday.

NEW YEAR'S DISHONOR LIST. Jan 1. Since 1976, America's dishonor list of words banished from the Queen's English. Overworked words and phrases (e.g., *fiscal cliff, spoiler alert, double down, trending, YOLO*). Send nominations via e-mail. For info: Public Relations Office, Lake Superior State University, Sault Ste. Marie, MI 49783. Phone: (906) 635-2315 or (906) 635-2314. Fax: (906) 635-2623. E-mail: banish@lssu.edu. Web: www.lssu.edu/ banished.

OATMEAL MONTH. Jan 1–31. Oatmeal is an affordable, delicious and nutritious way to start the day, and it is also a versatile ingredient for cooking and baking your favorite recipes. When eaten daily as part of a diet low in saturated fat and cholesterol, three grams of soluble fiber from oatmeal may reduce the risk of heart disease. For delicious, sweet and savory recipes and more info: Quaker Oats. Web: www.QuakerOats.com.

OUTBACK BOWL. Jan 1. Raymond James Stadium, Tampa, FL. The Outback Bowl brings together college football teams from the SEC and the Big Ten. In addition, the bowl is highlighted by a variety of special events, sports activities and private functions. Est attendance: 65,000. For info: Tampa Bay Bowl Assn. E-mail: info@ outbackbowl.com. Web: www.outbackbowl.com.

PHILBY, KIM: BIRTH ANNIVERSARY. Jan 1, 1912. Born at Ambala, India, Harold Adrian Russell Philby was the most successful Soviet double agent of the Cold War. Recruited by the KGB while still a student at Cambridge University, Philby first worked as a journalist, but he later joined British Intelligence. Philby held a number of sensitive posts at MI-6, including head of counterespionage and liaison to US intelligence. These posts afforded Philby many opportunities to pass secret information to Moscow and to manipulate British and US intelligence activities. Suspicion mounted against Philby after two of his associates in the intelligence service defected to the USSR. He was dismissed from the service in 1955 and fled to Moscow in 1963. He died May 11, 1988, at Moscow, USSR.

January 2014	S	M	T	W	T	F	S
				1	2	3	4
	5	6	7	8	9	10	11
	12	13	14	15	16	17	18
	19	20	21	22	23	24	25
	26	27	28	29	30	31	

PHILIPPINES: BLACK NAZARENE FIESTA. Jan 1–9. Manila. This traditional nine-day fiesta honors Quiapo district's patron saint. Cultural events, fireworks and parades culminate in a procession with the life-size statue of the Black Nazarene. Procession begins at the historic Quiapo Church.

***PROFILES IN COURAGE* PUBLISHED: ANNIVERSARY.** Jan 1, 1956. Senator John F. Kennedy of Massachusetts published his book to great praise and sales. It won a Pulitzer Prize in 1957.

REVERE, PAUL: BIRTH ANNIVERSARY. Jan 1, 1735. American patriot, silversmith and engraver; maker of false teeth, eyeglasses, picture frames and surgical instruments. Best remembered for his famous ride Apr 18, 1775, celebrated in Longfellow's poem "The Midnight Ride of Paul Revere." Born at Boston, MA; died there May 10, 1818. See also: "Paul Revere's Ride: Anniversary" (Apr 18).

ROSE BOWL GAME. Jan 1. Pasadena, CA. Football conference champions meet in the 100th Rose Bowl game at 1:30 PM, PST. The Tournament of Roses has been an annual New Year's event since 1890; the Rose Bowl football game since 1902. Michigan defeated Stanford 49–0 in what was the first postseason college football game. Called the Rose Bowl since 1923, it is preceded each year by the Tournament of Roses Parade. Presented by Vizio. Est attendance: 93,000. For info: Tournament of Roses, 391 S Orange Grove Blvd, Pasadena, CA 91184. Phone: (626) 449-4100. Fax: (626) 449-9066. Web: www.tournamentofroses.com.

THE ROSE PARADE. Jan 1. Pasadena, CA. 125th annual parade. Rose Parade starting at 8 AM, PST, includes floats, bands and equestrians. 2014 theme is "Dreams Come True." Presented by Honda. Est attendance: 700,000. For info: Pasadena Tournament of Roses Assn, 391 S Orange Grove Blvd, Pasadena, CA 91184. Phone: (626) 449-4100. Fax: (626) 449-9066. E-mail: rosepr@rosemail.org. Web: www.tournamentofroses.com.

ROSS, BETSY: BIRTH ANNIVERSARY. Jan 1, 1752. (Old Style date.) According to legend based largely on her grandson's revelations in 1870, needleworker Betsy Ross created the first Stars and Stripes flag in 1775, under instructions from George Washington. Her sewing and her making of flags were well known, but there is little corroborative evidence of her role in making the first Stars and Stripes. The account is generally accepted, however, in the absence of any documented claims to the contrary. She was born Elizabeth Griscom at Philadelphia, PA, and died there Jan 30, 1836.

RUSSIA: NEW YEAR'S DAY OBSERVANCE. Jan 1–2. National holiday. Modern tradition calls for setting up New Year's trees in homes, halls, clubs, palaces of culture and the hall of the Kremlin Palace. Children's parties with Granddad Frost and his granddaughter, Snow Girl. Games, songs, dancing, special foods, family gatherings and exchange of gifts and New Year's cards.

SAINT BASIL'S DAY. Jan 1. St. Basil's or St. Vasily's feast day observed by Eastern Orthodox churches. Special traditions for the day include serving St. Basil cakes, each of which contains a coin. Feast day observed Jan 14 by those churches using the Julian calendar.

SALINGER, JEROME DAVID (J.D.): 95th BIRTH ANNIVERSARY. Jan 1, 1919. Reclusive author, born at New York City. Wrote 13 short stories mostly for *The New Yorker*. In 1951 he published his only novel, *The Catcher in the Rye*—one of the great books of the 20th century. In 1953 he retreated to Cornish, NH, where he lived in seclusion until his death on Jan 27, 2010.

SELF-HELP GROUP AWARENESS MONTH. Jan 1–31. Hidden community resources are the hundreds of thousands of member-run support groups across the country that exist to help people with almost any illness, disability or addiction, as well as loss of a loved one, parenting situation, caregiver concern, abuse experience or other stressful life situation. Celebrate these groups and their members' stories of recovery from adversity. Learn how to find them and how to form them. For info: Ed Madara, American Self-Help Group Clearinghouse, 375 E Farlan St, Dover, NJ 07801. Phone: (973) 989-1122. Fax: (973) 989-1159. E-mail: emadara@saintclares.org. Web: mentalhelp.net/selfhelp.

SELF-LOVE MONTH. Jan 1–31. Be kinder to yourself in January. Realize that perfection is not reality. Love yourself enough to give yourself the greatest gift of all—yourself—whole and happy on your own. Do something self-loving every day of this month (see the website for the 31 Days of Self-Love Challenge). In-person events in select cities. For info: Daylle Deanna Schwartz, 320 E 52nd St, #10G, New York, NY 10022. Phone: (212) 688-3504. E-mail: daylle@daylle.com. Web: www.howdoiloveme.com.

SHAPE UP US MONTH. Jan 1–31. Shape Up US is a national movement to improve the health of our children. A 501(c)(3) nonprofit corporation dedicated to preventing obesity, Shape Up US contributes to building a healthy future for America's children by improving the health, fitness and overall well-being of youth and their families. During this month especially, we urge awareness, education and action. Programs include the Hip Hop Healthy Heart Program and the Just Clap for Life. January is the perfect time to start living heathfully. For info: Shape Up US, Inc. Phone: (602) 996-6300. E-mail: Jyl@ShapeUpUS.org. Web: www.ShapeUpUS.org.

SILENT RECORD WEEK. Jan 1–7. To commemorate the anniversary of the invention of the silent record in 1960, which was played on Detroit jukeboxes. The following year a Silent Record Concert and Recording Session featured emcee Henry Morgan, Soupy Sales and the 120-piece Hush Symphonic Band. (Originated by the late W.T. Rabe of Sault Ste. Marie, MI.)

SOLEMNITY OF MARY, MOTHER OF GOD. Jan 1. Holy Day of Obligation in the Roman Catholic Church since calendar reorganization of 1969, replacing the Feast of the Circumcision, which had been recognized for more than 14 centuries. See also: "Circumcision of Christ" (Jan 1).

STIEGLITZ, ALFRED: 150th BIRTH ANNIVERSARY. Jan 1, 1864. Arguably the most important photographer of his time, Steiglitz was also a publisher, art dealer and advocate for the Modernist movement, particularly artist Georgia O'Keeffe, who was his lover and, later, wife. He was convinced photography should be considered a fine art and cofounded the Photo-Secessionist organization, which advocated the Pictoralist style, an approach to photography that emphasizes beauty of subject matter, tonality and composition rather than documentation of reality. Born at Hoboken, NJ, he died July 13, 1946, at New York, NY.

STOCK EXCHANGE HOLIDAY (NEW YEAR'S DAY). Jan 1. The holiday schedules for the various exchanges are subject to change if relevant rules, regulations or exchange policies are revised. If you have questions, contact: CME Group (CME, CBOT, NYMEX, KCBT) (www.cmegroup.com), Chicago Board Options Exchange (www.cboe.com), NASDAQ (www.nasdaq.com), NYSE Euronext (www.nyse.com).

SUDAN: INDEPENDENCE DAY. Jan 1. National holiday. Sudan was proclaimed a sovereign independent republic in 1956, ending its status as an Anglo-Egyptian condominium (since 1899).

TAIWAN: FOUNDATION DAYS. Jan 1–2. Public holiday. Commemorates the founding of the Republic of China on Jan 1, 1912.

TEEN DRIVING AWARENESS MONTH. Jan 1–31. Traffic collisions are the leading cause of death among drivers 16 to 25 years of age. The fatality rate for drivers 16 to 25 years old is four times that of drivers age 25 to 69. In their first year as drivers, young adults are almost 10 times more likely to be in a crash than any other driver. The NTSI wants to help change teens' negative driving habits through an understanding of how values, attitude, responsibility and choice, stress and peer pressure all play a part in their driving behavior. For info: National Traffic Safety Institute, 618 E South St, Ste 556, Orlando, FL 32801. Phone: (407) 992-6238. E-mail: asmith@ntsi.com. Web: www.ntsi.com.

TOSTITOS FIESTA BOWL. Jan 1. University of Phoenix Stadium, Glendale, AZ. 43rd annual. Part of the Bowl Championship Series (BCS). The champion of the Big 12 Conference will compete against an at-large BCS team. For info: Fiesta Bowl Office, 7135 E Camelback Rd #190, Scottsdale, AZ 85251. Phone: (480) 350-0900. Web: www.fiestabowl.org.

UNITED KINGDOM: NEW YEAR'S HOLIDAY. Jan 1.

UNITED NATIONS: INTERNATIONAL YEAR OF CRYSTALLOGRAPHY. Jan 1–Dec 31, 2014. In recognition that 2014 provides an opportunity to promote international collaboration as part of the 65th anniversary of the founding of the International Union of Crystallography. Crystallography is present everywhere in our daily lives, in modern drug development, nanotechnology and biotechnology, and underpins the development of all new materials, from toothpaste to aeroplane components. As such, the UN encourages all to promote actions at all levels aimed at increasing public awareness of the importance of crystallography and promoting widespread access to new knowledge and to crystallography activities. (Resolution 66/284 of July 3, 2012.) For info: United Nations, Dept of Public Info, New York, NY 10017. Web: www.un.org.

UNITED NATIONS: INTERNATIONAL YEAR OF FAMILY FARMING. Jan 1–Dec 31, 2014. Recognizing the important contribution that family farming and smallholder farming can play in providing food security and eradicating poverty in the attainment of the internationally agreed development goals, including the Millennium Development Goals, the UN has declared 2014 the International Year of Family Farming (Resolution 66/222 of Dec 22, 2011.) For info: United Nations, Dept of Public Info, New York, NY 10017. Web: www.un.org.

UNITED NATIONS: INTERNATIONAL YEAR OF SMALL ISLAND DEVELOPING STATES. Jan 1–Dec 31, 2014. Facing a future whose only certainty is change, small island developing states are confronted with many problems and difficulties in making progress toward sustainable living and sustainable development. However small island societies have a record of thriving in challenging times. Their long histories are rooted in new and innovative approaches, societal mobilization and technological adaptation. Thus the UN declares this international year. (Resolution 67/206 of Dec 21, 2012.) For info: United Nations, Dept of Public Info, New York, NY, 10017. Web: www.un.org.

WALKER, DOAK: BIRTH ANNIVERSARY. Jan 1, 1927. Ewell Doak Walker, Jr, Hall of Fame and Heisman Trophy running back, born at Dallas, TX. Walker won the Heisman Trophy in 1948 playing for SMU and went on to an outstanding pro career with the Detroit Lions. He was a handsome, humble player during a time when football players could become national heroes. Inducted into the Hall of Fame in 1986. Died at Steamboat Springs, CO, Sept 27, 1998.

WAYNE, "MAD ANTHONY": BIRTH ANNIVERSARY. Jan 1, 1745. (Old Style date.) American Revolutionary War general whose daring, sometimes reckless, conduct earned him the nickname "Mad." His courage and shrewdness as a soldier made him a key figure in capturing Stony Point, NY (1779), preventing Benedict Arnold's "delivery" of West Point to the British and subduing hostile Indians of the Northwest Territory (1794). He was born at Waynesboro, PA, and died at Presque Isle, PA, Dec 15, 1796.

WESTERN PACIFIC HURRICANE SEASON. Jan 1–Dec 31. Most hurricanes occur from June 1 through Oct 1, though the season lasts all year. (Western Pacific: west of the International Date Line.) Info from: US Dept of Commerce, National Oceanic and Atmospheric Administration, Rockville, MD 20852.

WORLDWIDE RISING STAR MONTH. Jan 1–31. A month urging everyone to reach for the stars by designing a personal life plan. It takes place in January because that is the month that people can review the past year and design, revise or redesign their life plans for the current year. Remember to reach for the stars by designing your life plan! For info: Deborah and Peter Kulkkula, 381 Billings Rd, Fitchburg, MA 01420. Phone: (978) 343-4009. E-mail: info@RisingStarMonth.info. Web: www.RisingStarMonth.info.

Z DAY. Jan 1. To give recognition on the first day of the year to all persons and places whose names begin with the letter *Z* and who are always listed or thought of last in any alphabetized list. For info: Tom Zager. E-mail: tom_zager@yahoo.com.

ZAPATISTA REBELLION: 20th ANNIVERSARY. Jan 1, 1994. Declaring war against the government of President Carlos Salinas de Gortari, the Zapatista National Liberation Army seized four towns in the state of Chiapas in southern Mexico in 1994. The rebel group, which took their name from the early 20th-century Mexican revolutionary Emiliano Zapata, issued a declaration stating that they were protesting discrimination against the Indian population of the region and against their severe poverty.

BIRTHDAYS TODAY

Glen "Big Baby" Davis, 28, basketball player, born Baton Rouge, LA, Jan 1, 1986.

Holliday Grainger, 26, actress ("The Borgias," *Jane Eyre*), born Didsbury, Manchester, England, Jan 1, 1988.

Michael Imperioli, 48, actor ("The Sopranos"), born Mount Vernon, NY, Jan 1, 1966.

Helmut Jahn, 74, architect, born Nuremberg, Germany, Jan 1, 1940.

Frank Langella, 74, actor (*Frost/Nixon, The Twelve Chairs, Lolita*), born Bayonne, NJ, Jan 1, 1940.

James McAvoy, 35, actor (*Atonement, Becoming Jane, The Last King of Scotland*), born Glasgow, Scotland, Jan 1, 1979.

Robert Menendez, 60, US Senator (D, New Jersey), born New York, NY, Jan 1, 1954.

Don Novello, 71, actor, comedian ("The Smothers Brothers Show," "Saturday Night Live": Father Guido Sarducci), born Ashtabula, OH, Jan 1, 1943.

January 2014

S	M	T	W	T	F	S
			1	2	3	4
5	6	7	8	9	10	11
12	13	14	15	16	17	18
19	20	21	22	23	24	25
26	27	28	29	30	31	

January 2 — Thursday

DAY 2 **363 REMAINING**

ALLSTATE SUGAR BOWL. Jan 2. Mercedes-Benz Superdome, New Orleans, LA. 80th annual. The Sugar Bowl originated in 1935. Est attendance: 75,000. For info: Allstate Sugar Bowl Office, Louisiana Superdome, 1500 Sugar Bowl Dr, New Orleans, LA 70112. Phone: (504) 828-2440. E-mail: info@sugarbowl.org. Web: www.allstatesugarbowl.org or www.bcsfootball.org.

AMERICAN HISTORICAL ASSOCIATION: ANNUAL MEETING. Jan 2–5. Washington, DC. 128th annual. Approximately 400 sessions will be held covering a wide range of scholarly, professional and pedagogical topics dealing with all areas of history. Theme: "Disagreement, Debate, Discussion." Est attendance: 5,500. For info: American Historical Assn, 400 A St SE, Washington, DC 20003-3889. Phone: (202) 544-2422. Fax: (202) 544-8307. E-mail: aha@historians.org. Web: www.historians.org.

ASIMOV, ISAAC: BIRTH ANNIVERSARY. Jan 2, 1920. Although Isaac Asimov was one of the world's best-known writers of science fiction, his almost 500 books dealt with subjects as diverse as the Bible, works for preschoolers, college course work, mysteries, chemistry, biology, limericks, Shakespeare, Gilbert and Sullivan and modern history. During his prolific career he helped to elevate science fiction from pulp magazines to a more intellectual level. His works include the *Foundation* trilogy, *The Robots of Dawn, Robots and Empire, Nemesis, Murder at the A.B.A.* (in which he himself was a character), *The Gods Themselves* and *I, Robot*, in which he posited the famous Three Laws of Robotics. His *The Clock We Live On* is an accessible explanation of the origins of calendars. Asimov was born near Smolensk, Russia, and died at New York, NY, Apr 6, 1992.

55-MPH SPEED LIMIT: 40th ANNIVERSARY. Jan 2, 1974. President Richard Nixon signed a bill requiring states to limit highway speeds to a maximum of 55 mph. This measure was meant to conserve energy during the crisis precipitated by the embargo imposed by the Arab oil-producing countries. A plan, used by some states, limited sale of gasoline to odd-numbered days for cars whose plates ended in odd numbers and even-numbered days for even-numbered plates. Some states limited purchases to $2–$3 per auto, and lines as long as six miles resulted in some locations. See also: "Arab Oil Embargo Lifted: Anniversary" (Mar 13).

FRANKLIN, JOHN HOPE: BIRTH ANNIVERSARY. Jan 2, 1915. Historian, educator and author Dr. John Hope Franklin was born in the all-black town of Rintiesville, OK. A son of segregation, he received a doctorate from Harvard. Franklin's bestselling 1947 book *From Slavery to Freedom: A History of African-Americans* recast the telling of American history. Franklin was a consultant on 1954's *Brown v Board of Education* Supreme Court case. In 1995, President Bill Clinton awarded him the Medal of Freedom. Franklin died Mar 25, 2009, at Durham, NC.

GEORGIA: RATIFICATION DAY. Jan 2, 1788. By unanimous vote, Georgia became the fourth state to ratify the Constitution.

HAITI: ANCESTORS' DAY. Jan 2. Commemoration of the ancestors. Also known as Hero's Day. Public holiday.

HAPPY MEW YEAR FOR CATS DAY. Jan 2. Felines, ever above mere humans in the great chain of being, have a day unto themselves to celebrate the "mewness" of a new time. Annually, Jan 2. (©2006 by WH.) For info: Thomas & Ruth Roy, Wellcat Holidays, 2418 Long Ln, Lebanon, PA 17046. Phone: (717) 279-0184. E-mail: info@wellcat.com. Web: www.wellcat.com.

JAPAN: KAKIZOME. Jan 2. Traditional Japanese festival gets under way when the first strokes of the year are made on paper with the traditional brushes.

MILLER, ROGER: BIRTH ANNIVERSARY. Jan 2, 1936. Country and western singer, songwriter and musician ("King of the Road"), Roger Miller was born at Fort Worth, TX. Miller won 11 Grammy Awards and a Tony Award (1986 for the score to the Broadway play *Big River*). He died Oct 25, 1992, at Los Angeles, CA.

NATIONAL GEOGRAPHIC BEE, SCHOOL LEVEL. Jan 2–15. (Began Nov 11, 2013. Principals must have registered their schools by Oct 15, 2013.) Nationwide contest involving millions of students at the school level. The Bee is designed to encourage the teaching and study of geography. There are three levels of competition. A student must win a school-level Bee in order to win the right to take a written exam. The written test determines the top 100 students in each state who are eligible to go on to the state level. National Geographic brings each state winner and a teacher from his or her school to Washington for the national-level Bee in May. For info: Natl Geographic Bee, Natl Geographic Society, 1145 17th St NW, Washington, DC 20036. Phone: (202) 828-6659. Web: www.nationalgeographic.com/geobee.

RABI' I: THE MONTH OF THE MIGRATION. Jan 2. Begins on Islamic calendar date Rabi al-Awal 1, 1435. The third month of the Islamic calendar, the month of the migration of the Prophet Muhammad from Mecca to Medina in AD 622, the event that was used as the starting year of the Islamic lunar calendar. Different methods for "anticipating" the visibility of the new moon crescent at Mecca are used by different Muslim groups. US date may vary. Began at sunset the preceding day.

RUSSIA: PASSPORT PRESENTATION. Jan 2. A ceremony for 16-year-olds, who are recognized as citizens of the country. Always on the first working day of the new year.

SCOTLAND: NEW YEAR'S BANK HOLIDAY. Jan 2. Public holiday. The first working day after New Year's Day.

"SOMEDAY WE'LL LAUGH ABOUT THIS" WEEK. Jan 2–8. 37th annual. We've all used the expression, "Someday we'll laugh about this!" Why wait? It usually takes less than seven days for people to violate 90 percent of their New Year's resolutions. This week helps us to remember the art of laughing at ourselves. This week tickles the yoke and joke of perfectionism while encouraging people to strive for excellence at the same time. This week is a great way to start the new year—laughing at the humorous human condition. For info: Dr. Joel Goodman, The Humor Project, Inc, 10 Madison Ave, Saratoga Springs, NY 12866. Phone: (518) 587-8770. E-mail: chase@HumorProject.com. Web: www.HumorProject.com.

SPACE MILESTONE: *LUNA 1* (USSR): 55th ANNIVERSARY. Jan 2, 1959. Launch of robotic moon probe that missed the moon and became the first spacecraft from Earth to orbit the sun.

SPAIN CAPTURES GRANADA: ANNIVERSARY. Jan 2, 1492. Spaniards took the city of Granada from the Moors, ending seven centuries of Muslim rule in Spain.

SWITZERLAND: BERCHTOLDSTAG. Jan 2. Holiday in many cantons. Commemorates the founding of the city of Bern by Duke Berchtold V in the 12th century. Now mainly a children's holiday.

TAFT, HELEN HERRON: BIRTH ANNIVERSARY. Jan 2, 1861. Wife of William Howard Taft, 27th president of the US, born at Cincinnati, OH. Died at Washington, DC, May 22, 1943.

THOMAS, MARTHA CAREY: BIRTH ANNIVERSARY. Jan 2, 1857. The second president of Bryn Mawr College, Martha Carey Thomas gained a reputation for her insistence that the education of women should be as rigorous as that of men. A zealous suffragist, she served as the first president of the National College Women's Equal Suffrage League. Thomas promoted Bryn Mawr's Summer School for Women in Industry (opened in 1921) to provide a liberal education for working women. Born at Baltimore, MD, she died at Philadelphia, PA, Dec 2, 1935.

WOLFE, JAMES: BIRTH ANNIVERSARY. Jan 2, 1727. English general who commanded the British army's victory over Montcalm's French forces on the Plains of Abraham at Quebec City in 1759. As a result, France surrendered Canada to England. Wolfe was born at Westerham, Kent, England. He died at the Plains of Abraham of battle wounds, Sept 13, 1759.

BIRTHDAYS TODAY

Jim Bakker, 75, former television evangelist, born James Orsen at Muskegon, MI, Jan 2, 1939.

Kate Bosworth, 31, actress (*21, Superman Returns, Blue Crush*), born Los Angeles, CA, Jan 2, 1983.

Brian Boucher, 37, hockey player, born Woonsocket, RI, Jan 2, 1977.

Tia Carrere, 47, actress (*Wayne's World, True Lies*), born Honolulu, HI, Jan 2, 1967.

David Cone, 51, former baseball player, born Kansas City, MO, Jan 2, 1963.

Taye Diggs, 42, actor ("Private Practice," *Rent, How Stella Got Her Groove Back*), born Rochester, NY, Jan 2, 1972.

Christopher Durang, 65, playwright, actor, born Montclair, NJ, Jan 2, 1949.

Cuba Gooding, Jr, 46, actor (*Jerry Maguire, As Good as It Gets*), born the Bronx, NY, Jan 2, 1968.

Dennis Hastert, 72, former US congressman, former Speaker of the House (1999–2007), born Aurora, IL, Jan 2, 1942.

Edgar Martinez, 51, former baseball player, born New York, NY, Jan 2, 1963.

Wendy Phillips, 62, actress ("Big Love," "Homefront"), born Brooklyn, NY, Jan 2, 1952.

Dax Shepard, 39, actor, comedian (*Baby Mama, When in Rome*, "Parenthood," "Punk'd"), born Milford, MI, Jan 2, 1975.

Christy Turlington, 45, model, born Walnut Creek, CA, Jan 2, 1969.

January 3 — Friday

DAY 3 **362 REMAINING**

ALASKA: ADMISSION DAY: 55th ANNIVERSARY. Jan 3, 1959. Alaska, which had been purchased from Russia in 1867, became the 49th state. The area of Alaska is nearly one-fifth the size of the rest of the US.

"THE ARSENIO HALL SHOW" TV PREMIERE: 25th ANNIVERSARY. Jan 3, 1989. Arsenio Hall became the first African American to host a successful syndicated late-night talk show. The show attracted a younger audience than that of Johnny Carson's "The Tonight Show" and effectively limited the impact of CBS's 1989 late-night entry, "The Pat Sajak Show." Hall was successful in booking soul and rap music acts that had rarely been seen on other shows. His was also the show on which presidential candidate Bill Clinton appeared, playing the saxophone in dark glasses. Hall was named by *TV Guide* (June 1990) as its first "TV Person of the Year."

AT&T COTTON BOWL CLASSIC. Jan 3. Cowboys Stadium, Arlington, TX. Since 1937. Postseason football game matching a team from the Big 12 against a team from the Southeastern Conference (SEC). Est attendance: 70,000. For info: AT&T Cotton Bowl Classic, One Legends Way, Arlington, TX 76011. E-mail: cso@attcottonbowl.com. Web: www.attcottonbowl.com.

ATTLEE, CLEMENT RICHARD: BIRTH ANNIVERSARY. Jan 3, 1883. English leader of the Labour Party and prime minister (July 1945–October 1951). Born at London, England; died there Oct 8, 1967.

BATTLE OF STONE'S RIVER: ANNIVERSARY. Jan 3, 1863. After three days of fighting near Murfreesboro, TN, General Braxton Bragg withdrew his Confederate troops from the Battle of Stone's River, despite being in relative control of the battlefield on the first day's fighting. Bragg received heavy criticism for his actions at Stone's River. More than 24,000 men were killed in this battle.

COIN, JEWELRY & STAMP EXPO/ARIZONA. Jan 3–5. Holiday Inn, Mesa, AZ. Annual expo. Est attendance: 5,000. For info: Israel Bick, Exec Dir, Intl Stamp & Coin Collectors Society, PO Box 854, Van Nuys, CA 91408. Phone: (818) 997-6496. Fax: (818) 988-4337. E-mail: iibick@sbcglobal.net. Web: www.bickinternational.com.

CONGRESS ASSEMBLES. Jan 3. The Constitution provides that "the Congress shall assemble at least once in every year . . . ," and the 20th Amendment specifies "and such meeting shall begin at noon on the third day of January, unless they shall by law appoint a different day." If Jan 3 happens to fall on a weekend, Congress by resolution will meet on the following Monday or Tuesday.

COOLIDGE, GRACE ANNA GOODHUE: BIRTH ANNIVERSARY. Jan 3, 1879. Wife of Calvin Coolidge, 30th president of the US, born at Burlington, VT. Died at Northampton, MA, July 8, 1957.

DAVIES, MARION: BIRTH ANNIVERSARY. Jan 3, 1897. Born at Brooklyn, NY, Marion Cecilia Douras became Marion Davies and made her first appearance on film in 1917. Her romantic and professional involvement with newspaper magnate William Randolph Hearst ensured the type of publicity that would launch her to stardom. Her films include *When Knighthood Was in Flower, The Patsy* and *Show People*. Davies died at Hollywood, CA, Sept 23, 1961.

DISCOVER ORANGE BOWL. Jan 3. Sun Life Stadium, Miami Gardens, FL. 80th annual. The ACC champion (if available) battles an at-large BCS team. Est attendance: 75,000. For info: Orange Bowl Committee. Phone: (305) 341-4700. Fax: (305) 341-4762. E-mail: info@orangebowl.org. Web: www.orangebowl.org.

DRINKING STRAW PATENTED: ANNIVERSARY. Jan 3, 1888. A drinking straw made out of paraffin-covered paper was patented by Marvin Stone of Washington, DC. It replaced natural rye straws.

LENNON-ONO ALBUM CONFISCATION: 45th ANNIVERSARY. Jan 3, 1969. John Lennon and Yoko Ono posed nude for the cover of their album *Two Virgins*. On this day, a shipment of 30,000 of the albums was confiscated by police at Newark, NJ, as a violation of pornography statutes.

"LOOK UP AND LIVE" TV PREMIERE: 60th ANNIVERSARY. Jan 3, 1954. CBS broadcast this inspirational show on Sunday mornings for 24 years. The Reverend Lawrence McMasters appeared in the early years and Merv Griffin hosted the show in 1955. Pamela Ilott, executive producer, was also director of religious programming for CBS News.

MEMENTO MORI. Jan 3. *Memento, mori*, Latin for "Remember, you die," is also the title of a novel by Muriel Spark. We suggest posting the words at home and at work, not to be morbid, but to remind us to cherish all that we have today . . . for tomorrow may never arrive. (©2006 by WH.) For info: Thomas & Ruth Roy, Wellcat Holidays, 2418 Long Ln, Lebanon, PA 17046. Phone: (717) 279-0184. E-mail: info@wellcat.com. Web: www.wellcat.com.

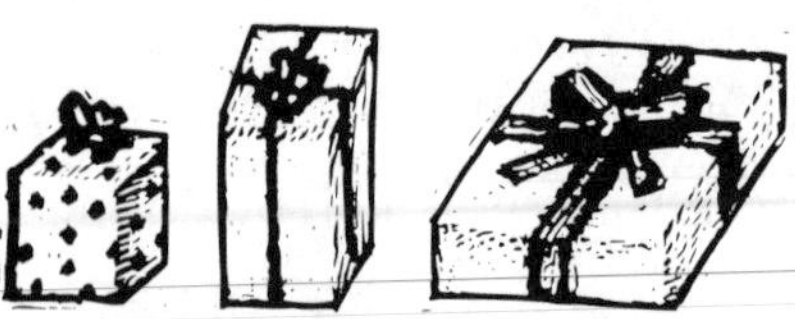

January 2014	S	M	T	W	T	F	S
				1	2	3	4
	5	6	7	8	9	10	11
	12	13	14	15	16	17	18
	19	20	21	22	23	24	25
	26	27	28	29	30	31	

MOTT, LUCRETIA (COFFIN): BIRTH ANNIVERSARY. Jan 3, 1793. American teacher, minister, antislavery leader and (with Elizabeth Cady Stanton) one of the founders of the women's rights movement in the US. Born at Nantucket, MA, she died near Philadelphia, PA, Nov 11, 1880.

"QUEEN FOR A DAY" TV PREMIERE: ANNIVERSARY. Jan 3, 1956. Game show on which prizes were awarded to the contestant who evoked the most sympathy from the studio audience. The show began some 11 years earlier on the radio with Jack Bailey hosting. Five women were chosen from the audience to appear on stage. Each related her story of misfortune and explained what she needed to remedy the situation, and the audience would vote by applause. The lucky winner was then given the royal treatment—crown, scepter and red robe—plus a prize to help with her problem. This soon became the top-rated daytime show. In 1969 the show went into syndication with Dick Curtis as host, but it didn't last long.

RAUH, JOSEPH L., JR: BIRTH ANNIVERSARY. Jan 3, 1911. Political activist Joseph L. Rauh, Jr, was born at Cincinnati, OH. In 1947 he cofounded Americans for Democratic Action (ADA), which supports liberal causes. Rauh helped create the minority civil rights plank at the 1948 Democratic National Convention—a foundation for the federal civil rights legislation in the 1960s. He served on the executive board of the NAACP and was general counsel to the Leadership Conference on Civil Rights. He died Sept 3, 1992, at Washington, DC.

SAINT GENEVIÈVE: FEAST DAY. Jan 3. The patron saint of Paris, St. Geneviève is credited with rallying Parisian resistance to Attila's Huns as they moved west into France in 451. Following her death, a reliquary containing her remains was carried at the head of a parade every Jan 3 and at times of peril and privation in Paris, until the reliquary was melted down during the Revolutionary Terror. She lived from about 422 to about 500.

SPACE MILESTONE: *MARS EXPLORATION ROVER SPIRIT* (US): 10th ANNIVERSARY. Jan 3, 2004. After traveling 302.6 million miles from its June 10, 2003, launch at Cape Canaveral Air Force Station, FL, the *Mars Exploration Rover Spirit* landed at Gusev Crater on Mars. The robotic rover's mission was to examine the soil and environment of the red planet. By Jan 6, *Spirit* had taken the sharpest color photograph of Mars ever achieved. *Spirit's* twin rover, *Opportunity*, landed Jan 24, 2004.

STURGES, JOHN: BIRTH ANNIVERSARY. Jan 3, 1911. Motion picture director John Sturges, born at Oak Park, IL, was known for his action movies. He received an Academy Award nomination in 1955 for *Bad Day at Black Rock*. He also directed *Gunfight at the O.K. Corral* (1956); *The Magnificent Seven* (1960); *The Great Escape* (1963); and his last film, *The Eagle Has Landed* (1977). He died Aug 18, 1992, at San Luis Obispo, CA.

TOLKIEN, J.R.R.: BIRTH ANNIVERSARY. Jan 3, 1892. John Ronald Reuel Tolkien, author of *The Hobbit* (1937) and *The Lord of the Rings*. Though best known for his fantasies, Tolkien was also a serious philologist. Born at Bloemfontein, South Africa, he died at Bournemouth, England, Sept 2, 1973.

WIND CAVE NATIONAL PARK ESTABLISHED: ANNIVERSARY. Jan 3, 1903. President Theodore Roosevelt signed a bill on this date establishing South Dakota's Wind Cave as a national park and preserve. It was the first national park established for the preservation of a cave.

BIRTHDAYS TODAY

Joan Walsh Anglund, 88, author, illustrator of children's books (*Crocus in the Snow, Bedtime Book*), born Hinsdale, IL, Jan 3, 1926.

Dabney Coleman, 82, actor ("Buffalo Bill," *Nine to Five, Tootsie*), born Austin, TX, Jan 3, 1932.

Mel Gibson, 58, actor (*Braveheart, Lethal Weapon*), director (*The Passion of the Christ*), born Peekskill, NY, Jan 3, 1956.

Robert Marvin (Bobby) Hull, 75, Hall of Fame hockey player, born Point Anne, ON, Canada, Jan 3, 1939.

Robert Loggia, 84, actor (*An Officer and a Gentleman, Scarface*), born Staten Island, NY, Jan 3, 1930.

Eli Manning, 33, football player, born New Orleans, LA, Jan 3, 1981.

Danica McKellar, 39, actress ("The Wonder Years," *Sidekicks*), born La Jolla, CA, Jan 3, 1975.

Victoria Principal, 64, actress ("Dallas"), born Fukuoka, Japan, Jan 3, 1950.

Stephen Stills, 69, musician, songwriter, born Dallas, TX, Jan 3, 1945.

January 4 — Saturday

DAY 4 **361 REMAINING**

AMNESTY FOR POLYGAMISTS: ANNIVERSARY. Jan 4, 1893. President Benjamin Harrison issued a proclamation granting full amnesty and pardon to all persons who had since Nov 1, 1890, abstained from unlawful cohabitation in a polygamous marriage. This was intended in the main for a specific group of elderly Mormons who had continued in the practice of contracting serial marriages. Amnesty was based on the condition that those pardoned must obey the law in the future or be "vigorously prosecuted." The practice of polygamy was a factor interfering with attainment of statehood for Utah.

BRAILLE, LOUIS: BIRTH ANNIVERSARY. Jan 4, 1809. The inventor of a widely used touch system of reading and writing for blind people was born at Coupvray, France. Permanently blinded at the age of three by a leatherworking awl in his father's saddle-making shop, Braille developed a system of writing that used, ironically, an awl-like stylus to punch marks in paper that could be felt and interpreted by people who are blind. The system was largely ignored until after Braille died in poverty, suffering from tuberculosis, at Paris, Jan 6, 1852.

COLOMBIA: CARNIVAL OF BLACKS AND WHITES. Jan 4–6. Pasto. Annual multicultural festival of parades, arts, music and costumes—an outgrowth of ancient Indian harvest rituals. During the Jan 5 Carnival of Blacks, partiers dance to African music and streak their bodies with black paint, signifying the day of freedom granted slaves by the Spanish Crown. At the Jan 6 Carnival of Whites, festival-goers throw white talcum powder at one another to symbolize equality and integrate all citizens through a celebration of ethnic and cultural differences. See the official site at www.carnavaldepasto.org.

DIMPLED CHAD DAY. Jan 4. This is a day to commemorate all the dimpled chads of the world, left over from various and sundry contested elections. Chads, roasted in garlic, make an excellent sprinkle topping for salads. (©2006 by WH.) For info: Thomas & Ruth Roy, Wellcat Holidays, 2418 Long Ln, Lebanon, PA 17046. Phone: (717) 279-0184. E-mail: info@wellcat.com. Web: www.wellcat.com.

EARTH AT PERIHELION. Jan 4. At approximately 7 AM, EST, planet Earth will reach perihelion, that point in its orbit when it is closest to the sun (about 91,400,000 miles). Earth's mean distance from the sun (mean radius of its orbit) is reached early in the months of April and October. Note that Earth is closest to the sun during Northern Hemisphere winter. See also: "Earth at Aphelion" (July 3).

ENGLAND: TULLETT PREBON LONDON BOAT SHOW. Jan 4–12. ExCeL, London's Docklands, London. The show promises to be a great day out with a host of features and a wide range of exhibitors. Est attendance: 120,000. For info: British Marine Federation/Natl Boat Shows Ltd. E-mail: info@britishmarine.co.uk. Web: www.londonboatshow.com.

GENERAL TOM THUMB: BIRTH ANNIVERSARY. Jan 4, 1838. Charles Sherwood Stratton, perhaps the most famous little person in history, was born at Bridgeport, CT. He eventually reached a height of three feet, four inches and a weight of 70 pounds. Discovered by P.T. Barnum in 1842, Stratton, as "General Tom Thumb," became an internationally known entertainer and performed before Queen Victoria and other heads of state. On Feb 10, 1863, he married another little person, Lavinia Warren. Stratton died at Middleborough, MA, July 15, 1883.

GRIMM, JACOB: BIRTH ANNIVERSARY. Jan 4, 1785. Librarian, mythologist and philologist, born at Hanau, Germany. Best remembered for *Grimm's Fairy Tales* (in collaboration with his brother Wilhelm). Died at Berlin, Germany, Sept 20, 1863.

MYANMAR: INDEPENDENCE DAY. Jan 4. National Day. The British controlled the country from 1826 until 1948, when it was granted independence. The country's name was changed from Burma to the Union of Myanmar in 1989 to reflect that the population is made up not just of the Burmese but of many other ethnic groups as well.

NEWTON, ISAAC: BIRTH ANNIVERSARY. Jan 4, 1643. Sir Isaac Newton was the chief figure of the scientific revolution of the 17th century, a physicist and mathematician who laid the foundations of calculus, studied the mechanics of planetary motion and discovered the law of gravitation. Born at Woolsthorpe, England, he died at London, England, Mar 31, 1727. Newton was born before Great Britain adopted the Gregorian calendar. His Julian (Old Style) birth date is Dec 25, 1642.

"NIGHT COURT" TV PREMIERE: 30th ANNIVERSARY. Jan 4, 1984. NBC sitcom set in an urban courtroom. The cast included Harry Anderson as Judge Harry T. Stone, John Larroquette as prosecutor Dan Fielding, Richard Moll as court officer Bull Shannon and Selma Diamond as court officer Selma Hacker. Markie Post joined the cast in 1985 as PD Christine Sullivan. Mel Tormé made a few appearances as himself, Harry's idol. The last telecast was July 1, 1992.

NIXON'S REJECTION OF SENATE ORDER: 40th ANNIVERSARY. Jan 4, 1974. President Richard Nixon rejected the Senate Watergate Committee's subpoenas seeking White House tapes and documents.

PATTERSON, FLOYD: BIRTH ANNIVERSARY. Jan 4, 1935. Dominant heavyweight boxer of the 1950s and early '60s, born at Waco, NC. Patterson was the gold middleweight medalist at the 1952 Helsinki Olympics (winning all his matches by knockouts), and in 1956 he became the youngest-ever world heavyweight champion. In 1960 he became the first boxer to regain the title (after he had lost it in 1959). Shy and good natured, Patterson was admired by sportswriters and fans. He died May 11, 2006, at New Paltz, NY.

PENNSYLVANIA FARM SHOW. Jan 4–11. Harrisburg, PA. 98th annual. The largest indoor agricultural event in America: 10,000 competitive events; 300 commercial exhibits; 6,000 animals. Est attendance: 585,000. For info: Pennsylvania Dept of Agriculture, State Farm Products Show Commission, 2300 N Cameron St, Harrisburg, PA 17110. Phone: (717) 787-5373. Fax: (717) 783-8710. E-mail: farmshow@state.pa.us. Web: www.farmshow.state.pa.us.

POP MUSIC CHART INTRODUCED: ANNIVERSARY. Jan 4, 1936. *Billboard* magazine published the first list of bestselling pop records, covering the week that ended Dec 30, 1935. On the list were recordings by the Tommy Dorsey and the Ozzie Nelson orchestras.

RUSH, BENJAMIN: BIRTH ANNIVERSARY. Jan 4, 1746. Physician, patriot and humanitarian of the American Revolution, born on a plantation at Byberry, PA. Rush was a signer of the Declaration of Independence, and his writings on mental illness earned him the title "Father of Psychiatry." His tract *Inquiry* attacked the common wisdom of the time that alcohol was beneficial. He was the first American to call alcoholism a chronic disease. Benjamin Rush died at Philadelphia, PA, Apr 19, 1813.

SETON, ELIZABETH ANN BAYLEY: FEAST DAY. Jan 4. First American-born saint (beatified Mar 17, 1963; canonized Sept 14, 1975). Born at New York, NY, Aug 28, 1774, Seton was the founder of the American Sisters of Charity, the first American order of Roman Catholic nuns. She died at Baltimore, MD, Jan 4, 1821.

TRIVIA DAY. Jan 4. In celebration of those who know all sorts of facts and/or have doctorates in uselessology. For info: Robert L. Birch, Puns Corps, 3108 Dashiell Rd, Falls Church, VA 22042. Phone: (703) 533-3668.

UTAH: ADMISSION DAY: ANNIVERSARY. Jan 4. Utah became the 45th state in 1896.

WORLD HYPNOTISM DAY. Jan 4. A day when hypnotism professionals promote the truth and benefits of hypnotism to the people of the world while removing the myths and misconceptions. Free and low-cost events on and off the Internet. For info: Thomas Nicoli, World Hypnotism Day Committee. Web: www.worldhypnotismday.com.

WORLD'S TALLEST BUILDING: DEDICATION ANNIVERSARY. Jan 4, 2010. On this date, United Arab Emirates (UAE) member Dubai unveiled *Burj Khalifa*—a 2,717-foot tower that, upon opening, became the world's tallest building. Taiwan's *Taipei 101* was the previous record holder at 1,667 feet. Dubbed *Burj Dubai* during its construction, the skyscraper was surprisingly renamed to honor UAE president Sheikh Khalifa bin Zayed who, in 2009, provided Dubai with $25 billion in bailout funds.

BIRTHDAYS TODAY

Dyan Cannon, 77, actress (*Heaven Can Wait, Bob and Carol and Ted and Alice*), born Tacoma, WA, Jan 4, 1937.

Dave Foley, 52, actor ("NewsRadio"), born Toronto, ON, Canada, Jan 4, 1962.

Ann Magnuson, 58, performance artist, actress ("Anything but Love," *Clear and Present Danger*), born Charleston, WV, Jan 4, 1956.

Julia Ormond, 49, actress (*Legends of the Fall, Sabrina*), born Surrey, England, Jan 4, 1965.

Barbara Rush, 87, actress ("Seventh Heaven," "Peyton Place," *Hombre*), born Denver, CO, Jan 4, 1927.

Donald Francis (Don) Shula, 84, Hall of Fame football coach and player, born Painesville, OH, Jan 4, 1930.

Michael Stipe, 54, singer (REM), born Decatur, GA, Jan 4, 1960.

January 5 — Sunday

DAY 5 — **360 REMAINING**

AILEY, ALVIN: BIRTH ANNIVERSARY. Jan 5, 1931. Born at Rogers, TX, Alvin Ailey began his noted career as a choreographer in the late 1950s after a successful career as a dancer. He founded the Alvin Ailey American Dance Theater, drawing from classical ballet, jazz, Afro-Caribbean and modern dance idioms to create the 79 ballets of the company's repertoire. He and his work played a central part in establishing a role for blacks in the world of modern dance. Ailey died Dec 1, 1989, at New York, NY.

"ALL MY CHILDREN" TV PREMIERE: ANNIVERSARY. Jan 5, 1970. This ABC show, created by Agnes Nixon, became TV's top-rated soap opera by the 1978–79 season. Set in Pine Valley, NY, the show originally focused on the Tyler and Martin families. The story included Erica Kane (Susan Lucci), one of daytime TV's most popular characters. The show garnered more than 150 Daytime Emmy Awards, including one for Lucci (in 1999)—she was nominated a record 21 times. Other award-winning or longtime cast members included the late Ruth Warrick as Phoebe Tyler Wallingford, Julia Barr as Brooke English, Michael E. Knight as Tad Martin and David Canary as twin brothers Adam and Stuart Chandler. The show also launched the careers of Kim Delaney, Sarah Michelle Gellar, Eva LaRue and Kelly Ripa. The 10,000th episode aired Nov 12, 2008. ABC cancelled the show in 2011 (the finale aired Sept 23, 2011) but sold rights for an online version.

CARVER, GEORGE WASHINGTON: DEATH ANNIVERSARY. Jan 5, 1943. Black American agricultural scientist, author, inventor and teacher. Born into slavery at Diamond Grove, MO, probably in 1864. His research led to the creation of synthetic products made from peanuts, potatoes and wood. Carver died at Tuskegee, AL. His birthplace became a national monument in 1953.

DAKAR RALLY 2014: ARGENTINA–BOLIVIA–CHILE. Jan 5–18. Held since 1978, when it was the Paris–Dakar Rally, the Dakar Rally, the legendary event of the off-road rally discipline, continues in South America for the sixth time. The 2014 edition starts in Rosario, Argentina, and finishes in Valparaiso, Chile—after a brief visit to Bolivia. Jan 11 is a rest day in Salta, Argentina. Est attendance: 1,000,000. For info: Amaury Sport Organisation, 2 rue Rouget de L'Isle, F92137 Issy les Moulineaux, France. Phone: (33) (141) 33-14-80. Fax: (33) (141) 33-15-39. E-mail: service.presse@dakar.com. Web: www.dakar.com or www.aso.fr.

DECATUR, STEPHEN: BIRTH ANNIVERSARY. Jan 5, 1779. American naval officer (whose father and grandfather, both also named Stephen Decatur, were also seafaring men) born at Sinepuxent, MD. In a toast at a dinner in Norfolk, VA, in 1815, Decatur spoke his most famous words: "Our country! In her intercourse with foreign nations may she always be in the right; but our country, right or wrong." Mortally wounded in a duel with Commodore James Barron, at Bladensburg, MD, on the morning of Mar 22, 1820, Decatur was carried to his home in Washington, DC, where he died a few hours later.

FIVE-DOLLAR-A-DAY MINIMUM WAGE: 100th ANNIVERSARY. Jan 5, 1914. Henry Ford announced that all worthy Ford Motor Company employees would receive a minimum wage of $5 a day. Ford explained the policy as "profit sharing and efficiency engineering." The more cynical attributed it to an attempt to prevent unionization and to obtain a docile workforce that would accept job speedups. To obtain this minimum wage, an employee had to be of "good personal habits." Whether an individual fit these criteria was determined by a new office created by Ford Motor Company—the Sociological Department.

HOME OFFICE SAFETY AND SECURITY WEEK. Jan 5–11. One week each year dedicated to ensuring that the more than 30 million American home offices are safeguarded and protected against break-ins, theft, workplace injury, computer virus and hacking, natural disaster and any other malady that can impact the at-home worker. For info: Jeff Zbar, PO Box 8263, Coral Springs, FL 33075. Phone: (954) 346-4393. E-mail: jeff@chiefhomeofficer.com. Web: www.chiefhomeofficer.com.

January 2014

S	M	T	W	T	F	S
			1	2	3	4
5	6	7	8	9	10	11
12	13	14	15	16	17	18
19	20	21	22	23	24	25
26	27	28	29	30	31	

ITALY: EPIPHANY FAIR. Jan 5. Piazza Navona, Rome, Italy. On the eve of Epiphany a fair of toys, sweets and presents takes place among the beautiful Bernini Fountains.

PICCARD, JEANNETTE RIDLON: BIRTH ANNIVERSARY. Jan 5, 1895. First American woman to qualify as a free-balloon pilot (1934). One of the first women to be ordained as an Episcopal priest (1976). Pilot for record-setting balloon ascent (57,579 feet) into the stratosphere (from Dearborn, MI, Oct 23, 1934) with her husband, Jean Felix Piccard. Identical twin married to identical twin. Born at Chicago, IL, she died at Minneapolis, MN, May 17, 1981. See also: "Piccard, Jean Felix: Birth Anniversary" (Jan 28).

REEVES, GEORGE: 100th BIRTH ANNIVERSARY. Jan 5, 1914. The boxer turned actor was born George Keefer Brewer at Woodstock, IA. Active in the 1940s in minor Hollywood roles (including a small part in *Gone with the Wind*), Reeves found stardom on the small screen as Superman/Clark Kent in "The Adventures of Superman," which ran from 1952 to 1957. Reeves did his own stunts as the "Man of Steel" and was popular with children all over. To his frustration, though, Reeves saw his serious acting career suffer due to being typecast as a cartoon superhero. He died June 16, 1959, of an apparently self-inflicted gunshot wound at his Beverly Hills, CA, home.

ROMAN CATHOLIC/EASTERN ORTHODOX MEETING: 50th ANNIVERSARY. Jan 5, 1964. Pope Paul VI and Patriarch Athenagoras of Jerusalem met in the Holy Land for the first meeting in five centuries between a Roman Catholic pontiff and an Eastern Orthodox patriarch.

RUFFIN, EDMUND: BIRTH ANNIVERSARY. Jan 5, 1794. Born at Prince George County, VA, Edmund Ruffin was an American agriculturist whose discoveries about crop rotation and fertilizer were influential in the early agrarian culture of the US. He published the *Farmer's Register* from 1833 to 1842, a journal that promoted scientific agriculture. A noted politician as well as a farmer, he was an early advocate of Southern secession whose views were widely circulated in pamphlets. As a member of the Palmetto Guards of Charleston, he was given the honor of firing the first shot on Fort Sumter on Apr 12, 1861. According to legend, after the South's defeat he became despondent and, wrapping himself in the Confederate flag, took his own life on June 18, 1865, at Amelia County, VA.

TWELFTH NIGHT. Jan 5. Evening before Epiphany (Jan 6). Twelfth Night marks the end of medieval Christmas festivities. Also called Twelfth Day Eve. See also: "Epiphany or Twelfth Day" (Jan 6).

WILSON, KEMMONS: BIRTH ANNIVERSARY. Jan 5, 1913. The "father of the modern hotel," revolutionized the travel industry by creating the first standardized chain of clean, air-conditioned hotels with swimming pools and ice machines. Born at Osceola, AR, in 1951 Wilson became angered by the conditions and costs of hotels he encountered during what he called "the most miserable vacation trip of my life." From this family vacation, the idea for the Holiday Inn chain was born. Named after the 1942 Bing Crosby film, Holiday Inns were strategically located next to the burgeoning interstate highway system, where growing numbers of post-WWII families could travel from one to the next, knowing there would be no unsavory surprises. Today, there are Holiday Inns in every state and in more than 50 countries worldwide. Wilson died at his home at Memphis, TN, on Feb 12, 2003.

WYOMING INAUGURATES FIRST WOMAN GOVERNOR IN US: ANNIVERSARY. Jan 5, 1925. Nellie Tayloe (Mrs William B.) Ross became the first woman to serve as governor upon her inauguration in Wyoming. She had previously finished out the term of her husband, who had died in office. In 1974 Ella Grasso of Connecticut became the first woman to be elected governor in her own right.

BIRTHDAYS TODAY

Bradley Cooper, 39, actor (*Silver Linings Playbook, The Hangover,* "Alias"), born Philadelphia, PA, Jan 5, 1975.

Warrick Dunn, 39, former football player, born Baton Rouge, LA, Jan 5, 1975.

Robert Duvall, 83, actor (Oscar for *Tender Mercies; Get Low, A Civil Action, The Apostle, Lonesome Dove, The Godfather*), born San Diego, CA, Jan 5, 1931.

Umberto Eco, 82, author (*The Name of the Rose*), born Alessandria, Italy, Jan 5, 1932.

Carrie Ann Inaba, 46, choreographer, television personality ("Dancing with the Stars"), born Honolulu, HI, Jan 5, 1968.

January Jones, 36, actress ("Mad Men"), born Sioux Falls, SD, Jan 5, 1978.

Diane Keaton, 68, actress (*Something's Gotta Give, Looking for Mr Goodbar, Reds*, Oscar for *Annie Hall*), born Diane Hall at Los Angeles, CA, Jan 5, 1946.

Pamela Sue Martin, 60, actress (*The Poseidon Adventure*, "The Nancy Drew Mysteries," "Dynasty"), born Westport, CT, Jan 5, 1954.

Walter Frederick (Fritz) Mondale, 86, 42nd vice president of the US, former senator, born Ceylon, MN, Jan 5, 1928.

Charlie Rose, 72, newscaster, television host, born Henderson, NC, Jan 5, 1942.

January 6 — Monday

DAY 6 **359 REMAINING**

ARMENIAN CHRISTMAS. Jan 6. Christmas is observed in the Armenian Church, the oldest Christian national church.

BCS NATIONAL CHAMPIONSHIP GAME. Jan 6. Rose Bowl Stadium, Pasadena, CA. College football's top two teams in the nation will vie for the national title in the annual BCS National Championship game. For info: BCS National Championship Game. Web: www.bcsfootball.org.

BUSH, GEORGE H.W. AND BARBARA, WEDDING: ANNIVERSARY. Jan 6, 1945. George Herbert Walker Bush was 20 and Barbara Pierce was 19 when they married. They had four sons and two daughters (one of whom died in childhood). Bush served as the 41st president of the US. Their son George W. Bush became the 43rd president of the US.

CARNIVAL SEASON. Jan 6–Mar 4. A secular festival preceding Lent. A time of merrymaking and feasting before the austere days of Lenten fasting and penitence (40 weekdays between Ash Wednesday and Easter Sunday). The word *carnival* probably is derived from the Latin *carnem levare*, meaning "to remove meat." Depending on local custom, the carnival season may start any time between Nov 11 and Shrove Tuesday. Conclusion of the season is much less variable, being the close of Shrove Tuesday in most places. Celebrations vary considerably, but the festival often includes many theatrical aspects (masks, costumes and songs) and has given its name (in the US) to traveling amusement shows that may be seen throughout the year. Observed traditionally in Roman Catholic countries from Epiphany through Shrove Tuesday.

EPIPHANY or TWELFTH DAY. Jan 6. Known also as Old Christmas Day and Twelfthtide. On the 12th day after Christmas, Christians celebrate the visit of the Magi, the first Gentile recognition of Christ. Epiphany of Our Lord, one of the oldest Christian feasts, is observed in Roman Catholic churches in the US on a Sunday between Jan 2 and 8. Theophany of the Eastern Orthodox Church is observed in churches using the Gregorian calendar (Jan 19 in those churches using the Julian calendar). This feast day celebrates the manifestation of the divinity of Jesus at the time of his baptism in the Jordan River by John the Baptist. Note: In centuries past, the day began at sunset. This custom has often led to confusion between Twelfth Night and Twelfth Day.

GIBRAN, KAHLIL: BIRTH ANNIVERSARY. Jan 6, 1883. Lebanese-American poet (*The Prophet*) and artist. Born at Bsherri, Lebanon, he died Oct 10, 1931, at New York, NY.

"HALLMARK HALL OF FAME" TV PREMIERE: ANNIVERSARY. Jan 6, 1952. Carried at different times by ABC, CBS, NBC and PBS, this was a top-quality dramatic anthology series. Originally titled "Hallmark Television Playhouse," the program was sponsored by Hallmark Cards and hosted by Sarah Churchill until 1955. A few of the presentations were *Hamlet*, with Maurice Evans and Ruth Chatterton (Apr 26, 1953); *Moby Dick*, with Victor Jory (May 16, 1954); *Macbeth*, with Maurice Evans, Dame Judith Anderson and House Jameson (Nov 28, 1954); and *Alice in Wonderland*, with Eva LeGallienne, Elsa Lanchester and Reginald Gardiner (Oct 23, 1955). The list goes on with splendid performances by many highly acclaimed actors and actresses.

ITALY: LA BEFANA. Jan 6. Epiphany festival in which the "Befana," a kindly witch, bestows gifts on children—toys and candy for those who have been good, but a lump of coal or a pebble for those who have been naughty. The festival begins on the night of Jan 5 with much noise and merrymaking (when the Befana is supposed to come down the chimneys on her broom, leaving gifts in children's stockings) and continues with joyous fairs, parades and other activities throughout Jan 6.

JAMAICA: MAROON FESTIVAL. Jan 6. Commemorates the 18th-century Treaty of Cudjoe. While Jamaica was a Spanish colony, its native inhabitants (Arawaks) were exterminated. The Spanish then imported African slaves to work their plantations. When the Spanish were driven out (1655), the black slaves fled to the mountains. The "Maroons" (fugitive slaves) were permitted to settle in the north of the island in 1738.

JOAN OF ARC: BIRTH ANNIVERSARY. Jan 6, 1412. Born at the village of Domrémy, in the Meuse River valley of France (probably in 1412), the teenage Jeanne d'Arc heard the voice of God commanding her to take up arms against the English during the Hundred Years War. She led a French army—dressed in men's armor—to try to oust the English from France. After some initial victories, she was captured in 1431 and turned over to a French ecclesiastical court by the British. The court found her guilty of heresy. Joan was burned at the stake May 30, 1431, at age 19, in Rouen, France.

MIX, TOM: BIRTH ANNIVERSARY. Jan 6, 1880. American motion picture actor, especially remembered for cowboy films. Born at Driftwood, PA. Died near Florence, AZ, Oct 12, 1940.

NEW MEXICO: ADMISSION DAY: ANNIVERSARY. Jan 6, 1912. Became 47th state in 1912.

PAN AM CIRCLES EARTH: ANNIVERSARY. Jan 6, 1942. A Pan American Airways plane arrived in New York to complete the first around-the-world trip by a commercial aircraft.

SALOMON, HAYM: DEATH ANNIVERSARY. Jan 6, 1785. American Revolutionary War patriot and financier was born at Lissa, Poland, in 1740 (exact date unknown). Salomon died at Philadelphia, PA.

SANDBURG, CARL: BIRTH ANNIVERSARY. Jan 6, 1878. The bard of the American heartland, Sandburg was poet, biographer of Lincoln, historian and folklorist, born at Galesburg, IL. He was the recipient of two Pulitzer Prizes. In "Chicago" (1916), Sandburg gave that city the nickname it still bears: "City of Big Shoulders." He wrote in 1936, "Sometime they'll give a war and nobody will come." Sandburg died at Flat Rock, NC, July 22, 1967.

SCRUGGS, EARL: 90th BIRTH ANNIVERSARY. Jan 6, 1924. Born at Flint Hill, NC, Earl Scruggs was a legendary bluegrass banjo musician. As a youth, Scruggs developed a trademark three-fingered style and joined the band of the "father of bluegrass," Bill Monroe, in 1945. His innovative syncopation provided the melodic glue in the Blue Grass Boys' sound, and he honed a role for his instrument that eschewed its past as a novelty and revealed its true beauty. "Foggy Mountain Breakdown," his Grammy Award–winning 1949 recording with guitarist Lester Flatt, is now a bluegrass standard as well as the technical mark by which all banjo players are judged. Scruggs also brought bluegrass to a wider audience with "The Ballad of Jed Clampett," the theme song for "The Beverly Hillbillies" (1962–71), a television show on which he regularly appeared. Scruggs died on Mar 28, 2012, at Nashville, TN.

SMITH, JEDEDIAH STRONG: BIRTH ANNIVERSARY. Jan 6, 1799. Mountain man, fur trader and one of the first explorers of the American West, Smith helped develop the Oregon Trail. He was the first American to reach California by land and the first to travel by land from San Diego up the West Coast to the Canadian border. Smith was born at Jericho (now Bainbridge), NY, and was killed by Comanche Indians along the Santa Fe Trail in what is now Kansas on May 27, 1831.

SPACE MILESTONE: *LUNAR EXPLORER* (US). Jan 6, 1998. NASA headed back to the moon for the first time since the *Apollo 17* flight 25 years before. This unmanned probe searched for evidence of frozen water on the moon and found evidence of ice in late 1998.

THOMAS, DANNY: BIRTH ANNIVERSARY. Jan 6, 1912. Comedian Danny Thomas was born Muzyad Yakhoob, later Amos Jacobs, at Deerfield, MI. Thomas began his entertainment career as a radio actor and nightclub comedian and then went on to movies in the late 1940s and early 1950s. His greatest fame came from his television show "Make Room for Daddy" (1953–64) and later as a television producer. He was also a tireless philanthropist who founded St. Jude Children's Research Hospital at Memphis, TN. Thomas died Feb 6, 1991, at Los Angeles, CA.

THREE KINGS DAY PARADE. Jan 6. New York, NY. 37th annual. For more than three decades, El Museo del Barrio has commemorated Three Kings Day with a parade that has been shared by El Barrio and the greater New York City community. The Three Kings Day Parade celebrates the Latino and Latin-American traditions represented by this holiday. Camels, floats, music and much more. Starts at 106th St near Park Ave. For info: El Museo del Barrio, 1230 Fifth Ave, New York, NY 10029. Phone: (212) 660-7138. E-mail: threekings@elmuseo.org. Web: www.elmuseo.org.

THREE KINGS DAY. Jan 6. Major festival of the Christian Church observed in many parts of the world with gifts, feasting, last lighting of Christmas lights and burning of Christmas greens. Twelfth and last day of the Feast of the Nativity. Commemorates the visit of the Three Wise Men (Kings or Magi) to Bethlehem.

"WHEEL OF FORTUNE" TV PREMIERE: ANNIVERSARY. Jan 6, 1975. This quiz show, created by Merv Griffin, is the longest-running syndicated game show in television history. Players spin a wheel and guess letters in a word puzzle, winning money for every correct guess. Originally hosted by Chuck Woolery and originally airing on NBC. Current hosts Pat Sajak and Vanna White took over in 1981, and the show went into syndication in 1983. There are scores of international versions of this show.

January 2014

S	M	T	W	T	F	S
			1	2	3	4
5	6	7	8	9	10	11
12	13	14	15	16	17	18
19	20	21	22	23	24	25
26	27	28	29	30	31	

YOUNG, LORETTA: BIRTH ANNIVERSARY. Jan 6, 1913. Gretchen Michaela Young was born at Salt Lake City, UT. Initially a child extra, Young scooped a role from her unavailable older sister in *Naughty but Nice* (1927) and launched her film career as "Loretta." After a prolific career that saw her navigate from silents to talkies and from ingenue to leading lady, Young won an Oscar as Best Actress in 1947 for *The Farmer's Daughter*. She began a second career on television in 1953, winning three Emmy Awards for her television show, "The Loretta Young Show" (1953–61), becoming one of the first actors to win both an Oscar and Emmy. She died Aug 12, 2000, at Los Angeles, CA.

BIRTHDAYS TODAY

Joey Lauren Adams, 43, actress (*Chasing Amy, Big Daddy*), born Little Rock, AR, Jan 6, 1971.

Gilbert Arenas, 32, basketball player, born Los Angeles, CA, Jan 6, 1982.

Rowan Atkinson, 59, actor ("Mr Bean," "Blackadder"), born Newcastle-upon-Tyne, England, Jan 6, 1955.

E.L. Doctorow, 83, writer (*Ragtime, The March*), born New York, NY, Jan 6, 1931.

Louis Leo (Lou) Holtz, 77, former Notre Dame football coach, born Follansbee, WV, Jan 6, 1937.

Howard M. (Howie) Long, 54, sportscaster, Hall of Fame football player, born Somerville, MA, Jan 6, 1960.

Nancy Lopez, 57, Hall of Fame golfer, born Torrance, CA, Jan 6, 1957.

Eddie Redmayne, 32, actor (*Les Misérables, The Pillars of the Earth, My Week with Marilyn*), born London, England, Jan 6, 1982.

Gabrielle Reece, 44, volleyball player, born La Jolla, CA, Jan 6, 1970.

Norman Reedus, 45, actor (*The Boondock Saints,* "The Walking Dead"), born Hollywood, FL, Jan 6, 1969.

John Singleton, 46, director, screenwriter (*Shaft, Boyz N the Hood*), born Los Angeles, CA, Jan 6, 1968.

Ndamukong Suh, 27, football player, born Portland, OR, Jan 6, 1987.

January 7 — Tuesday

DAY 7 **358 REMAINING**

ADDAMS, CHARLES: BIRTH ANNIVERSARY. Jan 7, 1912. The prolific cartoonist with a macabre sense of humor was born at Westfield, NJ. He became a full-time staff member of *The New Yorker* in 1935 and stayed there for his entire career, producing some 1,300 cartoons. His most famous creation was the ghoulish "Addams Family," who escaped print into television and film. Author of numerous bestselling cartoon collections and the *Charles Addams Mother Goose* (1967), Addams died Sept 29, 1988, at New York, NY. See also: "'The Addams Family' TV Premiere: Anniversary" (Sept 18).

EMPEROR HIROHITO: 25th DEATH ANNIVERSARY. Jan 7, 1989. After ruling Japan for 62 years as its longest-reigning ruler, Emperor Hirohito died at Tokyo of cancer at 6:33 AM on Jan 7, 1989. His only son, Crown Prince Akihito, succeeded him to the throne later that day.

FILLMORE, MILLARD: BIRTH ANNIVERSARY. Jan 7, 1800. 13th president of the US (July 10, 1850–Mar 3, 1853). Fillmore succeeded to the presidency upon the death of Zachary Taylor, but he did not get the hoped-for nomination from his party in 1852. He ran for president in 1856 as candidate of the Know-Nothing Party, whose platform demanded, among other things, that every government employee (federal, state and local) should be a native-born citizen. Fillmore was born at Summerhill, NY, and died at Buffalo, NY, Mar 8, 1874. Now his birthday is often used as an occasion for parties for which there is no other reason.

FIRST BALLOON FLIGHT ACROSS ENGLISH CHANNEL: ANNIVERSARY. Jan 7, 1785. Dr. John Jeffries, a Boston physician, and Jean-Pierre François Blanchard, French aeronaut, crossed the English Channel from Dover, England, to Calais, France, landing in a forest after being forced to throw overboard all ballast, equipment and even most of their clothing to avoid a forced landing in the icy waters of the English Channel. Blanchard's trousers are said to have been the last article thrown overboard.

FIRST US COMMERCIAL BANK: ANNIVERSARY. Jan 7, 1782. The first commercial bank in the US, the Bank of North America, was opened at Philadelphia, PA.

GARDENIA, VINCENT: BIRTH ANNIVERSARY. Jan 7, 1922. Stage, screen and television performer Vincent Gardenia was born Vincent Scognamiglio at Naples, Italy. Gardenia once estimated he had played 500 parts in his lifetime. He received two Oscar nominations, one for playing a baseball manager in *Bang the Drum Slowly* and again for the role of patriarch of a goofy Brooklyn family in *Moonstruck*. He won a Tony for his part in *The Prisoner of Second Avenue* and an Emmy for his portrayal in *Age Old Friends*. Vincent Gardenia died Dec 9, 1992, at Philadelphia, PA.

GERMANY: MUNICH FASCHING CARNIVAL. Jan 7–Mar 4. Munich. From Jan 7 through Shrove Tuesday is Munich's famous carnival season. Costume balls are popular throughout carnival. The high points of the festival occur on Fasching Sunday (Mar 2) and Shrove Tuesday (Mar 4), with great carnival revelry outside at the Viktualienmarkt and on Pedestrian Mall.

HARLEM GLOBETROTTERS PLAY FIRST GAME: ANNIVERSARY. Jan 7, 1927. Basketball promoter Abe Saperstein's "New York Globetrotters" took the floor on this date at Hinckley, IL. Despite the "New York" in their name, the Globetrotters (who included Inman Jackson, Lester Johnson and Walter Wright) hailed from Chicago's South Side. The talented African-American players—unable to play in white professional leagues—barnstormed the nation in serious basketball promotional events. They changed to "Harlem Globetrotters" in the 1930s and added humor to their games in the 1940s.

HURSTON, ZORA NEALE: BIRTH ANNIVERSARY. Jan 7, 1891. One of the most important African-American writers of the 20th century was born at Eatonville, FL, to a preacher and former schoolteacher. Hurston attended Barnard College and then became an integral part of the Harlem Renaissance of the 1920s and 1930s. Hurston published four novels in her lifetime, including the classic *Their Eyes Were Watching God* (1937), as well as important anthropological works, short stories, plays and a moving memoir. She was a trailblazer in collecting regional black folklore. Hurston died at Fort Pierce, FL, on Jan 28, 1960.

I'M NOT GOING TO TAKE IT ANYMORE DAY. Jan 7. A day to fight back and take control of all events that happen in one's life. Stand up for your rights—it's so easy to walk away. For info: Bob O'Brien, Consumer Advocate, 1061 Koelle Blvd, Secaucus, NJ 07094. Phone: (646) 233-6610. E-mail: robtfobrien@aol.com.

INTERNATIONAL CONSUMER ELECTRONICS SHOW. Jan 7–10. Las Vegas, NV. The world's largest annual trade show for consumers and America's largest annual trade show of any kind. Exhibitors are manufacturers, developers and suppliers of consumer technology hardware, content, technology delivery systems and related products and services. Attendees representing more than 115 countries include manufacturers, retailers, content providers and creators, broadband developers, wireless carriers, cable and satellite TV providers, installers, engineers, corporate buyers, government leaders, financial analysts and the media from around the world. Held since 1967. Est attendance: 130,000. For info: Consumer Electronics Assn, 1919 S Eads St, Arlington, VA 22202. Phone: (866) 858-1555. E-mail: press@CE.org. Web: www.cesweb.org.

INTERNATIONAL PROGRAMMERS' DAY. Jan 7. A day to recognize and thank programmers for their contributions to our lives. Programmers are ultimately responsible for many of the conveniences we enjoy such as DVRs, direct deposit, Web surfing, online bill paying, cell phones, etc. Behind most modern-day conveniences, there's a computer programmer! Annually, Jan 7. For info: Dan Loomis. Web: www.internationalprogrammersday.org.

JAPAN: NANAKUSA. Jan 7. Festival dates back to the seventh century and recalls the seven plants served to the emperor that are believed to have great medicinal value—shepherd's purse, chickweed, parsley, cottonweed, radish, hotoke-no-za and aona.

JAPAN: USOKAE (BULLFINCH EXCHANGE FESTIVAL). Jan 7. Dazaifu, Fukuoka Prefecture. "Good Luck" gilded wood bullfinches, mixed among many plain ones, are sought after by the throngs as priests of the Dazaifu Shrine pass them out in the dim light of a small bonfire.

MONTGOLFIER, JACQUES ETIENNE: BIRTH ANNIVERSARY. Jan 7, 1745. Merchant and inventor, born at Vidalon-lez Annonay, Ardèche, France. With his older brother, Joseph Michel, in November 1782, conducted experiments with paper and fabric bags filled with smoke and hot air, which led to the invention of the hot-air balloon and a human's first flight. Died at Serrieres, France, Aug 2, 1799. See also: "First Balloon Flight: Anniversary" (June 5); "Aviation History Month" (Nov 1).

MOON PHASE: FIRST QUARTER. Jan 7. Moon enters First Quarter phase at 10:39 PM, EST.

ONASSIS, ARISTOTLE: BIRTH ANNIVERSARY. Jan 7, 1906. Larger-than-life billionaire Greek shipping magnate who married Jackie Kennedy in 1968. Born in Smyrna (now Izmir), Turkey, Onassis died Mar 15, 1975, near Paris, France.

ORTHODOX CHRISTMAS. Jan 7. Observed by those churches using the Julian calendar.

POL POT OVERTHROWN: 35th ANNIVERSARY. Jan 7, 1979. Pol Pot's Cambodian government fell to combined forces of Cambodian rebels and Vietnamese soldiers.

RUSSIA: CHRISTMAS OBSERVANCE. Jan 7. National holiday.

TRANSATLANTIC PHONING: ANNIVERSARY. Jan 7, 1927. Commercial transatlantic telephone service between New York and London was inaugurated. There were 31 calls made the first day.

BIRTHDAYS TODAY

William Blatty, 86, novelist (*The Exorcist*), screenwriter, born New York, NY, Jan 7, 1928.

Nicolas Cage, 50, actor (*National Treasure, Adaptation, Leaving Las Vegas, Moonstruck*), born Nicolas Coppola at Long Beach, CA, Jan 7, 1964.

David Caruso, 58, actor ("NYPD Blue," "CSI: Miami"), born Forest Hills, NY, Jan 7, 1956.

Nick Clegg, 47, Deputy Prime Minister of Great Britain, born Chalfont St. Giles, England, Jan 7, 1967.

Katie Couric, 57, journalist ("The CBS Evening News," "Today"), born Arlington, VA, Jan 7, 1957.

Dustin Diamond, 37, actor ("Saved by the Bell"), born San Jose, CA, Jan 7, 1977.

Eric Gagne, 38, former baseball player, born Montreal, QC, Canada, Jan 7, 1976.

Erin Gray, 64, actress ("Buck Rogers in the 25th Century," "Silver Spoons"), born Honolulu, HI, Jan 7, 1950 (some sources say 1952).

January 2014

S	M	T	W	T	F	S
			1	2	3	4
5	6	7	8	9	10	11
12	13	14	15	16	17	18
19	20	21	22	23	24	25
26	27	28	29	30	31	

Kenny Loggins, 66, singer, songwriter, born Everett, WA, Jan 7, 1948.

Rand Paul, 51, US Senator (R, Kentucky), born Pittsburgh, PA, Jan 7, 1963.

Jeremy Renner, 43, actor (*The Bourne Legacy, The Hurt Locker, The Town*), born Modesta, CA, Jan 7, 1971.

Paul Revere, 76, singer, pianist (Paul Revere & the Raiders), born Harvard, NE, Jan 7, 1938.

Alfonso Soriano, 36, baseball player, born San Pedro de Macoris, Dominican Republic, Jan 7, 1978.

John R. Thune, 53, US Senator (R, South Dakota), born Pierre, SD, Jan 7, 1961.

Jann Wenner, 67, journalist, publisher, *Rolling Stone* magazine, born New York, NY, Jan 7, 1947.

January 8 — Wednesday

DAY 8 **357 REMAINING**

ARGYLE DAY. Jan 8. 6th annual. Bring some brightness to winter by wearing an argyle print—not just socks: anything with the diagonal diamond pattern. The more argyle, the better! For info: Keely McAleer, 13520 California St, Ste 250, Omaha, NE 68154. Phone: (402) 334-8899. Fax: (403) 334-5599. E-mail: kmcaleer@mheginc.com.

AT&T DIVESTITURE: ANNIVERSARY. Jan 8, 1982. In the most significant antitrust suit since the breakup of Standard Oil in 1911, American Telephone and Telegraph agreed to give up its 22 local Bell System companies ("Baby Bells"). These companies represented 80 percent of AT&T's assets. This ended the corporation's virtual monopoly on US telephone service.

BATTLE OF NEW ORLEANS: ANNIVERSARY. Jan 8, 1815. British forces suffered crushing losses (more than 2,000 casualties) in an attack on New Orleans, LA. Defending US troops were led by General Andrew Jackson, who became a popular hero as a result of the victory. Neither side knew that the War of 1812 had ended two weeks previously with the signing of the Treaty of Ghent, Dec 24, 1814. Battle of New Orleans Day is observed in Louisiana.

BIDDLE, NICHOLAS: BIRTH ANNIVERSARY. Jan 8, 1786. American lawyer, diplomat, statesman and financier who served as president of the Second Bank of the United States. Born at Philadelphia, PA, he died there Feb 27, 1844.

CHOU EN-LAI: DEATH ANNIVERSARY. Jan 8, 1976. Anniversary of the death of Chou En-Lai, premier of the State Council of the People's Republic of China. He was born in 1898 (exact date unknown).

COLLINS, WILLIAM WILKIE: BIRTH ANNIVERSARY. Jan 8, 1824. English novelist, author of *The Moonstone* (one of the first examples of detective fiction), *The Woman in White* and *The Dead Secret*. Born at London, England, he died there Sept 23, 1889.

EARTH'S ROTATION PROVED: ANNIVERSARY. Jan 8, 1851. In his Paris home using a device now known as Foucault's pendulum, physicist Jean Foucault demonstrated that Earth rotates on its axis.

ELVIS PRESLEY'S BIRTHDAY CELEBRATION. Jan 8–11. Graceland, Memphis, TN. Special birthday proclamation on Jan 8 as well as other Elvis birthday events at Graceland. For info: Graceland, 3734 Elvis Presley Blvd, Memphis, TN 38116. Phone: (800) 238-2000 or (901) 332-3322. E-mail: glsales@elvis.com. Web: www.elvis.com.

FERRER, JOSE: BIRTH ANNIVERSARY. Jan 8, 1912. Award-winning actor, producer, writer and director was born at Santurce, Puerto Rico. Nominated three times for an Academy Award, he won Best Actor for his role in *Cyrano de Bergerac*. In addition, Ferrer was awarded Tonys and Critics' Circle prizes during half a century in the entertainment world. He died Jan 26, 1992, at Coral Gables, FL.

GREECE: MIDWIFE'S DAY or WOMEN'S DAY. Jan 8. Midwife's Day or Women's Day is celebrated Jan 8 each year to honor midwives and all women. "On this day women stop their housework and spend their time in cafés, while the men do all the housework chores and look after the children." In some villages, men caught outside "will be stripped . . . and drenched with cold water."

NATIONAL JOYGERM DAY. Jan 8. 33rd annual. A day for men, women and children to grace and lace the world with grins, not grunts; cheers, not jeers; wide-range scope of hope; to answer the call to courage despite delays, denials or disappointment. Pals to one and all. For info: Joygerm Joan E. White, Founder, Joygerms Unlimited, PO Box 555, Syracuse, NY 13206-0555. Phone: (315) 472-2779. E-mail: joygerms@gmail.com.

PRESLEY, ELVIS AARON: BIRTH ANNIVERSARY. Jan 8, 1935. Popular American rock singer, born at Tupelo, MS. Although his middle name was spelled incorrectly as "Aron" on his birth certificate, Elvis had it legally changed to "Aaron," which is how it is spelled on his gravestone. Died at Memphis, TN, Aug 16, 1977.

SAINT GUDULA: FEAST DAY. Jan 8. Virgin, patron saint of the city of Brussels. Died Jan 8, probably in the year 712. Her relics were transferred to the church of St. Michael in Brussels.

SHOW-AND-TELL DAY AT WORK. Jan 8. Students have show-and-tell at school, so adults should get to do the same. (©2006 by WH.) For info: Thomas & Ruth Roy, Wellcat Holidays, 2418 Long Ln, Lebanon, PA 17046. Phone: (717) 279-0184. E-mail: info@wellcat.com. Web: www.wellcat.com.

WAR ON POVERTY: 50th ANNIVERSARY. Jan 8, 1964. President Lyndon Johnson declared a War on Poverty in his State of the Union address. He stressed improved education as one of the cornerstones of the program. The following Aug 20, he signed a $947.5 million antipoverty bill designed to assist more than 30 million citizens.

BIRTHDAYS TODAY

Shirley Bassey, 77, singer, born Cardiff, Wales, Jan 8, 1937.

David Bowie, 67, musician, actor (*The Labyrinth*), born David Robert Jones at London, England, Jan 8, 1947.

Bob Eubanks, 77, game show host ("The Newlywed Game"), born Flint, MI, Jan 8, 1937.

Vladimir Feltsman, 62, pianist, born Moscow, USSR (now Russia), Jan 8, 1952.

Jeff Francoeur, 30, baseball player, born Atlanta, GA, Jan 8, 1984.

Jason Giambi, 43, baseball player, born West Covina, CA, Jan 8, 1971.

Stephen Hawking, 72, physicist, author (*A Brief History of Time*), born Oxford, England, Jan 8, 1942.

Kathleen Noone, 68, actress ("Party of Five," "Sunset Beach"), born Hillsdale, NJ, Jan 8, 1946.

Charles Osgood, 81, journalist, born New York, NY, Jan 8, 1933.

January 9 — Thursday

DAY 9 — **356 REMAINING**

AVIATION IN AMERICA: ANNIVERSARY. Jan 9, 1793. A Frenchman, Jean-Pierre François Blanchard, made the first manned free-balloon flight in America's history at Philadelphia, PA. The event was watched by President George Washington and many other high government officials. The hydrogen-filled balloon rose to a height of about 5,800 feet, traveled some 15 miles and landed 46 minutes later in New Jersey. Reportedly Blanchard had one passenger on the flight—a little black dog.

BEAUVOIR, SIMONE DE: BIRTH ANNIVERSARY. Jan 9, 1908. French feminist and writer. *The Second Sex* lays out her theories of feminism. Born at Paris, France; died there on Apr 15, 1986.

CATT, CARRIE LANE CHAPMAN: BIRTH ANNIVERSARY. Jan 9, 1859. American women's rights leader, founder (in 1919) of National League of Women Voters. Born at Ripon, WI, she died at New Rochelle, NY, Mar 9, 1947.

CHICAGO SKETCH COMEDY FESTIVAL. Jan 9–19. Chicago, IL. 13th annual event that celebrates the best in local and national sketch comedy. Over two weeks audiences can take in more than 100 events, including performances and discussions. This is the world's largest sketch comedy festival, with hundreds of funny people in one convenient location—laughter guaranteed. For info: Jill Valentine, Chicago Sketch Comedy Festival. E-mail: jill@stage773.com. Web: www.chicagosketchfest.com.

CONNECTICUT RATIFIES CONSTITUTION: ANNIVERSARY. Jan 9, 1788. By a vote of 128 to 40, Connecticut became the fifth state to ratify the Constitution.

DENVER, BOB: BIRTH ANNIVERSARY. Jan 9, 1935. Television actor born at New Rochelle, NY. He worked as a mailman and a high school teacher before landing the role—Maynard G. Krebs—that made him famous on "The Many Loves of Dobie Gillis" in 1959. Krebs was one of the first beatniks portrayed on television. When that series ended in 1963, Denver took on the memorable lead character in "Gilligan's Island." That series is one of the most popular in television history. Denver died at Winston-Salem, NC, on Sept 2, 2005.

"IT TAKES A THIEF" TV PREMIERE: ANNIVERSARY. Jan 9, 1968. ABC's adventure series starred Robert Wagner as Alexander Mundy, an unlikely thief who agrees to conduct secret government missions instead of serving out his prison term. Malachi Throne costarred as Noah Bain, chief of the SIA and Mundy's employer. Fred Astaire made cameo appearances as Mundy's father.

NIXON, RICHARD MILHOUS: BIRTH ANNIVERSARY. Jan 9, 1913. Richard Nixon served as 36th vice president of the US (under President Dwight D. Eisenhower) Jan 20, 1953, to Jan 20, 1961. He was the 37th president of the US, serving Jan 20, 1969, to Aug 9, 1974, when he resigned the presidency while under the threat of impeachment. First US president to resign that office. He was born at Yorba Linda, CA, and died at New York, NY, Apr 22, 1994.

PANAMA: MARTYRS' DAY. Jan 9. Public holiday.

PHILIPPINES: FEAST OF THE BLACK NAZARENE. Jan 9. Culmination of a nine-day fiesta. Manila's largest procession takes place in the afternoon of Jan 9, in honor of the Black Nazarene, whose shrine is at the Quiapo Church.

"RAWHIDE" TV PREMIERE: 55th ANNIVERSARY. Jan 9, 1959. CBS western that kept them dogies (cattle) rollin' home from northern Texas to Sedalia, KS, for seven years. The series featured Eric Fleming as trail boss Gil Favor; Clint Eastwood as Rowdy Yates, ramrod and trail boss after Fleming's departure from the show; Jim Murdock as Mushy; Paul Brinegar as the cook, Wishbone; Steve Raines as Quince; Rocky Shahan as Joe Scarlett; Sheb Wooley as scout Pete Nolan; Robert Cabal as Hey Soos; John Ireland as Jed Colby; David Watson as Ian Cabot; and Raymond St. Jacques as Solomon King. Also remembered for its rollicking theme song.

ST. PETERSBURG MASSACRE: ANNIVERSARY. Jan 9, 1905. Guards at St. Petersburg's Winter Palace opened fire on some 150,000 unarmed protesting workers, killing at least 200. This event was the major catalyst for revolution in Russia that year, prompting more strikes and uprisings.

ULTIMATE FISHING SHOW—DETROIT. Jan 9–12. Suburban Collection Showplace, Novi, MI. This event brings together buyers and sellers of boating, fishing and outdoor sporting products. US and Canadian fishing trips, as well as other vacation travel destinations, are featured. Detroit is the largest freshwater fishing market in the nation. Est attendance: 30,000. For info: ShowSpan, Inc, 2121 Celebration Dr NE, Grand Rapids, MI 49525. Phone: (616) 447-2860. Fax: (616) 447-2861. E-mail: events@showspan.com. Web: www.showspan.com.

US LANDING ON LUZON: ANNIVERSARY. Jan 9, 1945. US forces began the final push to retake the Philippines by attacking at the same location where the Japanese had begun their invasion nearly four years earlier. General Douglas MacArthur landed 67,000 troops in the Gulf of Lingayen on the western coast of the big island of Luzon. The Japanese offered little opposition to the landing itself but fought fiercely against Allied advancement, particularly around Clarke Field, the major air base in the islands.

VAN CLEEF, LEE: BIRTH ANNIVERSARY. Jan 9, 1925. Actor Lee Van Cleef was born at Somerville, NJ. He appeared in many westerns and action films including *High Noon* (1952), *The Man Who Shot Liberty Valance* (1962), *The Good, the Bad and the Ugly* (1967) and *Escape from New York* (1981). Van Cleef died on Dec 16, 1989, at Oxnard, CA.

YOUNG, MURAT BERNARD "CHIC": BIRTH ANNIVERSARY. Jan 9, 1901. The comic strip "Blondie" was created by Murat Bernard "Chic" Young in 1930. Originally about a jazz-age flapper who marries a playboy from a socially prominent family, "Blondie" soon changed its direction: two children and a dog were added to the cast, Dagwood became a working stiff, and the strip focused on middle-class family situations and problems. "Blondie" introduced America to the "dagwood," an enormous sandwich made during Dagwood's late-night forays in the refrigerator. Chic Young was born at Chicago, IL, and died at St. Petersburg, FL, Mar 14, 1973.

BIRTHDAYS TODAY

Joan Baez, 73, folksinger, born Staten Island, NY, Jan 9, 1941.

Tyrone Curtis "Muggsy" Bogues, 49, former basketball player, born Baltimore, MD, Jan 9, 1965.

Catherine, Duchess of Cambridge, 32, wife of Prince William, born Catherine Middleton at Reading, Berkshire, England, Jan 9, 1982.

Richard Allen (Dick) Enberg, 79, sportscaster, born Mount Clemens, MI, Jan 9, 1935.

Sergio Garcia, 34, golfer, born Borriol, Spain, Jan 9, 1980.

Crystal Gayle, 63, singer, born Brenda Gayle Webb at Paintsville, KY, Jan 9, 1951.

Mat Hoffman, 42, BMX bike racer, born Oklahoma City, OK, Jan 9, 1972.

Judith Krantz, 86, author (*Dazzle, Scruples*), born Judith Tarcher at New York, NY, Jan 9, 1928.

Dave Matthews, 47, singer, musician (Dave Matthews Band), born Johannesburg, South Africa, Jan 9, 1967.

Joely Richardson, 49, actress (*The Patriot,* "Nip/Tuck"), born London, England, Jan 9, 1965.

J.K. Simmons, 59, actor ("Law & Order," *Spiderman*), born Detroit, MI, Jan 9, 1955.

Byron Bartlett (Bart) Starr, 80, Hall of Fame football player and former coach, born Montgomery, AL, Jan 9, 1934.

Imelda Staunton, 58, actress (*Harry Potter and the Order of the Phoenix, Vera Drake*), born London, England, Jan 9, 1956.

January 2014	S	M	T	W	T	F	S
				1	2	3	4
	5	6	7	8	9	10	11
	12	13	14	15	16	17	18
	19	20	21	22	23	24	25
	26	27	28	29	30	31	

January 10 — Friday

DAY 10 **355 REMAINING**

CHA WINTER CONFERENCE AND TRADE SHOW. Jan 10–14. Anaheim Convention Center, Anaheim, CA. The world's largest trade show for the craft and hobby industry. The CHA show also offers extensive educational programs and workshops. Est attendance: 12,000. For info: Craft & Hobby Assn, 319 E 54th St, Elmwood Park, NJ 07407. Phone: (201) 835-1200. Fax: (201) 797-0657. E-mail: info@craftandhobby.org. Web: www.craftandhobby.org.

***COMMON SENSE* PUBLISHED: ANNIVERSARY.** Jan 10, 1776. More than any other publication, *Common Sense* influenced the authors of the Declaration of Independence. Thomas Paine's 50-page pamphlet sold 150,000 copies within a few months of its first printing.

FIRST UNITED NATIONS GENERAL ASSEMBLY: ANNIVERSARY. Jan 10, 1946. On the 26th anniversary of the establishment of the unsuccessful League of Nations, delegates from 51 nations met at London, England, for the first meeting of the UN General Assembly.

HENRIED, PAUL: BIRTH ANNIVERSARY. Jan 10, 1908. Actor Paul Henried once estimated that he had played in or directed more than 300 films. Though he was a staunch anti-Nazi, his early film parts included a number of German roles, including those in *Goodbye, Mr Chips* and *Night Train.* He eventually moved away from the German stereotype in such films as *Of Human Bondage* and *The Four Horsemen of the Apocalypse* and as Victor Laslo in *Casablanca.* His film career cut short by the anti-Communist blacklist in Hollywood during the 1940s, Henried found a second calling as a director, with more than 80 episodes of TV's "Alfred Hitchcock Presents" to his credit. Born at Trieste, Austria, he died Mar 29, 1992, at Pacific Palisades, CA.

JEFFERS, ROBINSON: BIRTH ANNIVERSARY. Jan 10, 1887. American poet and playwright. Born at Pittsburgh, PA, he died at Carmel, CA, Jan 20, 1962.

LEAGUE OF NATIONS FOUNDING: ANNIVERSARY. Jan 10, 1920. Through the Treaty of Versailles, the League of Nations came into existence. Fifty nations entered into a covenant designed to avoid war. The US never joined the League of Nations, which was dissolved Apr 18, 1946.

"MASTERPIECE THEATRE" TV PREMIERE: ANNIVERSARY. Jan 10, 1971. Television at its best, PBS's long-running anthology series consists of many highly acclaimed original and adapted dramatizations. Many are produced by the BBC. Alistair Cooke, Russell Baker and Laura Linney have hosted the program. The first presentation was "The First Churchills." Other notable programs include "The Six Wives of Henry VIII" and "Elizabeth R" (1972); "Upstairs Downstairs" (1974–77); "I, Claudius" (1978); "The Jewel in the Crown" (1984); "The Buccaneers" (1995); and "White Teeth" (2002). The title of the series is now "Masterpiece."

NATIONAL CUT YOUR ENERGY COSTS DAY. Jan 10. A day to educate people on the ways they can stay warm in the winter and cool in the summer while saving money on their energy bills. By following a few easy steps, home owners and renters can put a reasonable ceiling on their heating and cooling costs and stay comfortable. For info: Tom Peric, Natl Cut Your Energy Costs Day, 2040 Fairfax Ave, Cherry Hill, NJ 08003. Phone: (856) 874-0049. Fax: (856) 874-0052. E-mail: tom@cutyourenergycosts.com. Web: www.cutyourenergycosts.com.

US AND VATICAN REESTABLISH DIPLOMATIC RELATIONS: 30th ANNIVERSARY. Jan 10, 1984. The US and the Vatican established full diplomatic relations after a break of 117 years.

VEGASPEX. Jan 10–12. Las Vegas, NV. Coin, stamp, antique watch, jewelry and collectibles expo. Est attendance: 10,000. For info: Israel Bick, Exec Dir, Intl Coin & Stamp Collectors Society, PO Box 854, Van Nuys, CA 91408. Phone: (818) 997-6496. Fax: (818) 988-4337. E-mail: iibick@sbcglobal.net. Web: www.bickinternational.com.

WOMEN'S SUFFRAGE AMENDMENT INTRODUCED IN CONGRESS: ANNIVERSARY. Jan 10, 1878. Senator A.A. Sargent of California, a close friend of Susan B. Anthony, introduced into the US Senate a women's suffrage amendment known as the Susan B. Anthony Amendment. It wasn't until Aug 26, 1920, 42 years later, that the amendment was signed into law.

BIRTHDAYS TODAY

Pat Benatar, 61, singer, born Patricia Andrejewski at Brooklyn, NY, Jan 10, 1953.

Roy Blunt, 64, US Senator (R, Missouri), born Niangua, MO, Jan 10, 1950.

George Foreman, 65, former boxer, entrepreneur, born Marshall, TX, Jan 10, 1949.

Evan Handler, 53, actor ("Californication," "Sex and the City"), born New York, NY, Jan 10, 1961.

Philip Levine, 86, poet, US poet laureate (2011–12), born Detroit, MI, Jan 10, 1928.

Mark Pryor, 51, US Senator (D, Arkansas), born Fayetteville, AR, Jan 10, 1963.

Rod Stewart, 69, singer, born London, England, Jan 10, 1945.

William Anthony (Bill) Toomey, 75, Olympic decathlete, born Philadelphia, PA, Jan 10, 1939.

January 11 — Saturday

DAY 11 — **354 REMAINING**

BRIDGES, CALVIN BLACKMAN: 125th BIRTH ANNIVERSARY. Jan 11, 1889. Born at Schuyler Falls, NY, Bridges joined pioneer geneticist Thomas Hunt Morgan in his research on the fruit fly in Columbia University's legendary "fly room" in 1910. Bridges started his career as a bottle washer, but his work by 1916 helped prove that chromosomes carry genetic information and was published as the first paper in the inaugural issue of *Genetics*. His later work demonstrated a link between chromosome bands and the linear sequence of genes. Bridges died Dec 27, 1938, at Los Angeles, CA.

CUCKOO DANCING WEEK. Jan 11–17. To honor the memory of Laurel and Hardy, whose theme, "The Dancing Cuckoos," shall be heard throughout the land as their movies are seen and their antics greeted with laughter by old and new fans of these unique masters of comedy. (Originated by the late William T. Rabe of Sault Ste. Marie, MI.)

GREAT FRUITCAKE TOSS. Jan 11. Manitou Springs, CO. What do you do with leftover fruitcake? Toss, hurl, launch competitions. Est attendance: 1,500. For info: Manitou Springs Chamber of Commerce, 354 Manitou Ave, Manitou Springs, CO 80829. Phone: (800) 642-2567. Web: www.manitousprings.org.

HAMILTON, ALEXANDER: BIRTH ANNIVERSARY. Jan 11, 1755. American statesman, an author of *The Federalist* papers, first secretary of the Treasury, born at British West Indies. Engaged in a duel with Aaron Burr the morning of July 11, 1804, at Weehawken, NJ. Mortally wounded there and died July 12, 1804.

HOSTOS, EUGENIO MARIA: 175th BIRTH ANNIVERSARY. Jan 11, 1839. Puerto Rican patriot, scholar and author of more than 50 books. Born at Rio Canas, Puerto Rico, he died at Santo Domingo, Dominican Republic, Aug 11, 1903.

JAMES, WILLIAM: BIRTH ANNIVERSARY. Jan 11, 1842. American psychologist and philosopher of distinguished family that included his brother, novelist Henry James. "There is no worse lie," he wrote in *Varieties of Religious Experience* (1902), "than a truth misunderstood by those who hear it." Born at New York City, he died at Chocorua, NH, Aug 26, 1910.

LEOPOLD, ALDO: BIRTH ANNIVERSARY. Jan 11, 1887. Considered by many to be the father of wildlife ecology, Leopold was a scholar, writer, teacher and philosopher. Born at Burlington, IA, Leopold is best known for his posthumously published book *A Sand County Almanac* (1949), in which he lyrically described putting his ecological theories into practice at a run-down farm in Wisconsin. He died at Madison, WI, on Apr 26, 1948.

MacDONALD, JOHN A.: BIRTH ANNIVERSARY. Jan 11, 1815. Canadian statesman, first prime minister of Canada. Born at Glasgow, Scotland, he died June 6, 1891, at Ottawa. His birth anniversary is observed in Canada.

MOROCCO: INDEPENDENCE DAY. Jan 11. National holiday. Commemorates the date in 1944 when the Independence Party submitted a memo to the Allied authorities asking for independence under a constitutional regime. Morocco gained independence from France in 1956.

NATIONAL WESTERN STOCK SHOW AND RODEO. Jan 11–26. Denver, CO. 108th annual. It's a rodeo and more! See horse shows, Colorado's largest trade show, western art and educational displays and the Super Bowl of livestock shows. Est attendance: 650,000. For info: Natl Western Stock Show and Rodeo, 4655 Humboldt St, Denver, CO 80216. Phone: (303) 297-1166 or (800) 336-6977. Fax: (303) 292-1708. Web: www.nationalwestern.com.

NEPAL: NATIONAL UNITY DAY. Jan 11. Celebration paying homage to King Prithvinarayan Shah (1723–75), founder of the present house of rulers of Nepal and creator of the unified Nepal of today.

PAUL, ALICE: BIRTH ANNIVERSARY. Jan 11, 1885. Women's rights leader and founder of the National Woman's Party in 1913, advocate of an equal rights amendment to the US Constitution. Born at Moorestown, NJ, she died there July 10, 1977.

THEODOSIUS I: BIRTH ANNIVERSARY. Jan 11, 347. Roman emperor known as Theodosius the Great was born at Cauca, Gallaecia, in Spain. In 379 Theodosius was summoned by the emperor Gratian to become emperor of the East. On Feb 28, 380, without consulting religious authorities, he issued the edict that made the Nicene Creed (in which God the Father, the Son and the Holy Spirit are all of the same substance) binding on all subjects. Only those who accepted it would be considered Christians; this was the first recorded use of that designation. Theodosius engaged in a continuing struggle with the West for power. He prohibited pagan worship, but the emperors of the West had strong connections with pagan aristocracy. The two sides came to blows in 394. His final victory in September of that year was seen as a divine victory in which the Christian god had triumphed over the Roman gods. Theodosius died in January 395.

US SURGEON GENERAL DECLARES CIGARETTES HAZARDOUS: 50th ANNIVERSARY. Jan 11, 1964. US Surgeon General Luther Terry issued the first government report saying that smoking may be hazardous to one's health.

WELCOME BACK SNOWBIRDS PANCAKE BREAKFAST. Jan 11. El Centro, CA. Annually, the second Saturday in January. Est attendance: 1,500. For info: El Centro Chamber of Commerce, Box 3006, El Centro, CA 92244. Phone: (760) 352-3681. Fax: (760) 352-3246. E-mail: info@elcentrochamber.com. Web: www.elcentrochamber.com.

BIRTHDAYS TODAY

Mary J. Blige, 43, pop singer, born the Bronx, NY, Jan 11, 1971.

Jean Chretien, 80, 20th prime minister of Canada (1993–2003), born Shawinigan, QC, Canada, Jan 11, 1934.

Ben Daniel Crenshaw, 62, golfer, born Austin, TX, Jan 11, 1952.

Jim Hightower, 71, radio host, author (*Eat Your Heart Out, There's Nothing in the Middle of the Road but Yellow Stripes and Dead Armadillos*), born Denison, TX, Jan 11, 1943.

Naomi Judd, 68, country singer (The Judds), born Ashland, KY, Jan 11, 1946.

Christine Kaufmann, 69, actress (*Taras Bulba, Bagdad Café*), born Lansdorf Graz, Austria, Jan 11, 1945.

Phyllis Logan, 58, actress ("Downton Abbey," *Another Time, Another Place; Secrets and Lies*), born Paisley, Scotland, Jan 11, 1956.

Amanda Peet, 42, actress (*Melinda and Melinda, Something's Gotta Give*), born New York, NY, Jan 11, 1972.

Rod Taylor, 84, actor (*The Birds*, "Masquerade"), born Sydney, Australia, Jan 11, 1930.

Grant Tinker, 88, television executive, born Stamford, CT, Jan 11, 1926.

Stanley Tucci, 54, actor (*The Hunger Games, The Devil Wears Prada, Big Night*), director, born Katonah, NY, Jan 11, 1960.

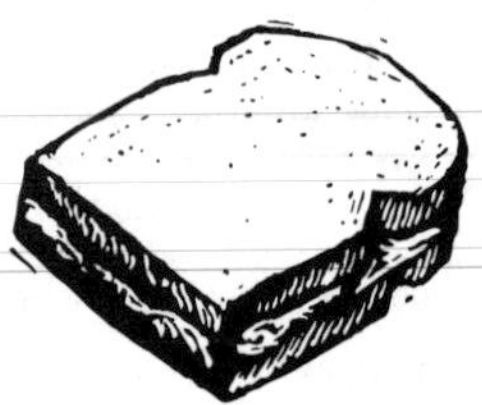

January 12 — Sunday

DAY 12 **353 REMAINING**

"ALL IN THE FAMILY" TV PREMIERE: ANNIVERSARY. Jan 12, 1971. Based on the success of the British comedy "Till Death Us Do Part," Norman Lear created CBS's controversial sitcom "All in the Family." The series was the first of its kind to realistically portray the prevailing issues and taboos of its time with a wickedly humorous bent. From bigotry to birth control, few topics were considered too sacred to discuss on air. Ultraconservative Archie Bunker (played by Carroll O'Connor) held court from his recliner, spewing invective at any who disagreed with him. Jean Stapleton portrayed Archie's dutiful wife, Edith. Sally Struthers and Rob Reiner rounded out the cast as Archie's liberal daughter and son-in-law, Gloria and Mike "Meathead" Stivic. The series had a 12-year run.

January 2014

S	M	T	W	T	F	S
			1	2	3	4
5	6	7	8	9	10	11
12	13	14	15	16	17	18
19	20	21	22	23	24	25
26	27	28	29	30	31	

"BATMAN" TV PREMIERE: ANNIVERSARY. Jan 12, 1966. ABC's crime-fighting show gained a place in Nielsen's top 10 ratings in its first season. The series was based on the DC Comics characters created by Bob Kane in 1939. Adam West starred as millionaire Bruce Wayne and his superhero alter ego, Batman. Burt Ward costarred as Dick Grayson/Robin, the Boy Wonder. An assortment of villains guest-starred each week, including Cesar Romero as the Joker, Eartha Kitt and Julie Newmar as Catwoman, Burgess Meredith as the Penguin and Frank Gorshin as the Riddler. Other stars making memorable appearances included Liberace, Vincent Price, Milton Berle, Tallulah Bankhead and Ethel Merman. The series played up its comic-strip roots with innovative and sharply skewed camera angles, bright bold colors and wild graphics. Although the last telecast was Mar 14, 1968, the show's memorable theme song, composed by Neal Hefti, can be heard today with some 120 episodes in syndication.

BURKE, EDMUND: BIRTH ANNIVERSARY. Jan 12, 1729. British orator, politician and philosopher, born at Dublin, Ireland. "Superstition is the religion of feeble minds," he wrote in 1790, but best remembered is "The only thing necessary for the triumph of evil is for good men to do nothing," not found in his writings but almost universally attributed to Burke. Died at Beaconsfield, England, July 9, 1797.

CONGRESS AUTHORIZED USE OF FORCE AGAINST IRAQ: ANNIVERSARY. Jan 12, 1991. The US Congress passed a resolution authorizing the president of the US to use force to expel Iraq from Kuwait. This was the sixth congressional vote in US history declaring war or authorizing force on another nation.

"DYNASTY" TV PREMIERE: ANNIVERSARY. Jan 12, 1981. The popular ABC prime-time serial focused on the high-flying exploits of the Denver-based Carrington family. The series had a weekly wardrobe budget of $10,000, with many elegant costumes designed by Nolan Miller. In addition to following the juicy story lines, many people tuned in worldwide to view the palatial mansions and lavish sets. John Forsythe played patriarch Blake Carrington, with Linda Evans as his wife, Krystle. Joan Collins played Alexis, Blake's scheming ex-wife and arch business rival.

FARMER, JAMES: BIRTH ANNIVERSARY. Jan 12, 1920. Civil rights leader, born at Marshall, TX. Farmer was one of the founders of CORE, the Congress of Racial Equality, a volunteer organization established in 1942 to improve race relations and eliminate discriminatory practices. Farmer led the nonviolent fight to desegregate buses and terminals in 1961, known as the Freedom Rides. He received the Presidential Medal of Freedom in 1998. Died at Fredericksburg, VA, July 9, 1999.

FIRST ELECTED WOMAN SENATOR: ANNIVERSARY. Jan 12, 1932. Hattie W. Caraway, a Democrat from Arkansas, was the first woman elected to the US Senate. Born in 1878, Caraway was appointed to the Senate on Nov 13, 1931, to fill out the term of her husband, Senator Thaddeus Caraway, who had died a few days earlier. On Jan 12, 1932, she won a special election to fill the remaining months of his term. Subsequently elected to two more terms, she served in the Senate until January 1945. She was an adept and tireless legislator (once introducing 43 bills on the same day) who worked for women's rights (once cosponsoring an equal rights amendment) and supported New Deal policies. She died Dec 21, 1950, at Falls Church, VA. The first woman appointed to the Senate was Mrs W.H. Felton, who in 1922 served for two days. The first woman to be elected to the Senate without having been appointed first was Margaret Chase Smith of Maine, who had served first in the House. She was elected to the Senate in 1948.

GOLDEN GLOBE AWARDS. Jan 12. Beverly Hilton Hotel, Beverly Hills, CA. 71st annual. Sponsored by the Hollywood Foreign Press Association and honoring achievement in film and television. For info: The Hollywood Foreign Press Assn, 646 N Robertson Blvd, West Hollywood, CA 90069. Phone: (310) 657-1731. Fax: (310) 657-5576. E-mail: info@hfpa.org. Web: www.hfpa.org or www.goldenglobes.org.

HAITI EARTHQUAKE: ANNIVERSARY. Jan 12, 2010. An earthquake of magnitude 7.0 struck the impoverished nation of Haiti resulting in more than 200,000 deaths and leaving more than 1 million homeless. The epicenter was only 25 km from the capital, Port-au-Prince, which was reduced to rubble.

HAYES, IRA HAMILTON: BIRTH ANNIVERSARY. Jan 12, 1922. Ira Hayes was one of six US Marines who raised the American flag on Iwo Jima's Mount Suribachi, Feb 23, 1945, following a US assault on the Japanese stronghold. The event was immortalized by AP photographer Joe Rosenthal's famous photo and later by a Marine War Memorial monument at Arlington, VA. Hayes was born on a Pima Indian Reservation at Arizona. He returned home after WWII a much celebrated hero but was unable to cope with fame. He was found dead of "exposure to freezing weather and overconsumption of alcohol" on the Sacaton Indian Reservation at Arizona, Jan 24, 1955.

LONDON, JACK: BIRTH ANNIVERSARY. Jan 12, 1876. American author of more than 50 books: short stories, novels and travel stories of the sea and of the far north, many marked by brutal realism. His most widely known work is *The Call of the Wild*, the great dog story published in 1903. London was born at San Francisco, CA. He died of gastrointestinal uremia on Nov 22, 1916, near Santa Rosa, CA.

MISSION SANTA CLARA DE ASIS: FOUNDING ANNIVERSARY. Jan 12, 1777. California mission built by followers of Father Junipero Serra to educate the Indians. In the 1850s the mission became Santa Clara University, the oldest university in California. The current building, used by the university as its chapel, is a replica of an older building that was destroyed by fire in 1926.

SARGENT, JOHN SINGER: BIRTH ANNIVERSARY. Jan 12, 1856. Born in Florence, Italy, of American parents, Sargent became one of the most famous portrait artists of the late Victorian and Edwardian ages in Britain and the US. His best-known paintings include *Madame X* (1884), *Carnation, Lily, Lily, Rose* (1885–86) and *Ellen Terry as Lady Macbeth* (1889). Sargent died Apr 15, 1925, at London, England.

STEPHEN FOSTER DAY. Jan 12. Stephen Foster Folk Culture Center State Park, White Springs, FL. A musical program and carillon recital in honor of the legendary American composer Stephen Foster. For info: Stephen Foster Day, PO Box G, White Springs, FL 32096. Phone: (877) 635-3655. Fax: (386) 397-4262. E-mail: andrea.thomas@dep.state.fl.us. Web: www.floridastateparks.org.

SWITZERLAND: MEITLISUNNTIG. Jan 12. On Meitlisunntig, the second Sunday in January, the girls of Meisterschwanden and Fahrwangen, in the Seetal district of Aargau, Switzerland, stage a procession in historical uniforms and a military parade before a female General Staff. According to tradition, the custom dates from the Villmergen War of 1712, when the women of both communes gave vital help that led to victory. Popular festival follows the procession.

TANZANIA: ZANZIBAR REVOLUTION DAY. Jan 12. National day. Zanzibar became independent in December 1963, under a sultan; the sultan was overthrown on this day in 1964.

WINTHROP, JOHN: BIRTH ANNIVERSARY. Jan 12, 1588. (Old Style date.) Born at Edwardstone, Suffolk, Puritan John Winthrop is renowned for his leadership in the migration to the Massachusetts Bay Colony and the key role he played in developing its character and its relationship with neighboring colonies and indigenous people. Father of 16 children, most notably son John, who was governor of the Connecticut Colony. Winthrop served 13 annual terms as governor of the Massachusetts Bay Colony from his arrival in 1630 to his death on Mar 26, 1649, at Boston, MA. He kept a detailed journal, which is now considered the foremost historical record of the era.

WOMEN DENIED VOTE: ANNIVERSARY. Jan 12, 1915. The US House of Representatives rejected a proposal to give women the right to vote. Women gained the right to vote in 1920.

BIRTHDAYS TODAY

Kirstie Alley, 59, actress ("Cheers," "Veronica's Closet," *Look Who's Talking*), born Wichita, KS, Jan 12, 1955.

Jeff Bezos, 50, founder, Amazon.com, born Albuquerque, NM, Jan 12, 1964.

HAL, 22, computer in *2001: A Space Odyssey*, by Arthur C. Clarke, "born" Urbana, IL, Jan 12, 1992.

Marian Hossa, 35, hockey player, born Stara Lubovna, Czechoslovakia (now the Czech Republic), Jan 12, 1979.

Rush Limbaugh, 63, talk show host ("The Rush Limbaugh Show"), author, born Cape Girardeau, MO, Jan 12, 1951.

David Mitchell, 45, author (*Cloud Atlas, number9dream*), born Southport, England, Jan 12, 1969.

Oliver Platt, 54, actor ("The Big C," "Huff," "The West Wing," *Dr. Dolittle*), born Windsor, ON, Canada, Jan 12, 1960.

Ray Price, 88, country singer, born Perryville, TX, Jan 12, 1926.

Luise Rainer, 104, actress (Oscars for *The Great Ziegfeld* and *The Good Earth*), born Vienna, Austria, Jan 12, 1910.

Howard Stern, 60, radio and television personality ("The Howard Stern Show"), born Queens, NY, Jan 12, 1954.

Dominique Wilkins, 54, Hall of Fame basketball player, born Paris, France, Jan 12, 1960.

January 13 — Monday

DAY 13 **352 REMAINING**

ALGER, HORATIO, JR: BIRTH ANNIVERSARY. Jan 13, 1834. American clergyman and author of more than 100 popular books for boys (some 20 million copies sold). Honesty, frugality and hard work assured that the heroes of his books would find success, wealth and fame. Born at Revere, MA, he died at Natick, MA, July 18, 1899.

AUSTRALIA: AUSTRALIAN OPEN. Jan 13–26. Melbourne Park, Melbourne. Part of the Grand Slam of tennis tournaments. First held in 1905. For info: Australian Open. Web: www.australianopen.com.

CHASE, SALMON PORTLAND: BIRTH ANNIVERSARY. Jan 13, 1808. American statesman, born at Cornish, NH. US senator, secretary of the Treasury and chief justice of the US. Salmon P. Chase spent much of his life fighting slavery (he was popularly known as "attorney general for runaway Negroes"). He was one of the founders of the Republican Party, and his hopes for becoming candidate for president of the US in 1856 and 1860 were dashed because his unconcealed antislavery views made him unacceptable. Died at New York, NY, May 7, 1873.

CORRIDOR OF DEATH: ANNIVERSARY. Jan 13, 1943. The suffering of the people of Leningrad during the German siege of that city was one of the greatest tragedies of WWII. More than half the population of Russia's second-largest city died during the winter of 1942. On Jan 13, 1943, Soviet troops broke through German lines and opened a 10-mile-wide corridor south of Lake Ladoga. Within a week supplies were arriving in the city by way of this narrow opening. Because fierce German bombardment of the passage continued for another year, the pass came to be called the "Corridor of Death." The siege finally ended Jan 27, 1944, after 880 days.

ENGLAND: PLOUGH MONDAY. Jan 13. Always the Monday after Twelfth Day. Work on the farm is resumed after the festivities of the 12 days of Christmas. On the preceding Sunday ploughs may be blessed in churches. Celebrated with dances and plays.

FULLER, ALFRED CARL: BIRTH ANNIVERSARY. Jan 13, 1885. Founder of the Fuller Brush Company, born at Kings County, NS, Canada. In 1906 the young brush salesman went into business on his own, making brushes at a bench between the furnace and the coal bin in his sister's basement. Died at Hartford, CT, Dec 4, 1973.

HUMANA CHALLENGE. Jan 13–19. La Quinta, CA. 55th annual, formerly known as the Bob Hope Classic. The nation's largest sports event for charity. It features PGA Tour pros, celebrities and amateurs. Est attendance: 110,000. For info: Humana Challenge, 39000 Bob Hope Dr, Rancho Mirage, CA 92270. Phone: (760) 346-8184. Fax: (760) 346-6329. E-mail: info@humanachallenge.com. Web: www.humanachallenge.com.

JAPAN: COMING-OF-AGE DAY. Jan 13. National holiday for youth of the country who reached adulthood during the preceding year. Annually, the second Monday in January.

JOHNNY CASH AT FOLSOM PRISON: ANNIVERSARY. Jan 13, 1968. In a landmark concert, country music star Johnny Cash performed in front of 2,000 inmates at Folsom Prison at Folsom, CA. Backed by the Tennessee Three and accompanied by June Carter, Carl Perkins and the Statler Brothers, Cash performed in the prison cafeteria. The concert was recorded as a live album and was a worldwide hit. Cash's choice to play for prisoners cemented his reputation as a hero to the downtrodden.

MAWLID AL NABI: THE BIRTHDAY OF THE PROPHET MUHAMMAD. Jan 13. Mawlid al Nabi (Birth of the Prophet Muhammad) is observed on Muslim calendar date Rabi al-Awal 12, 1435. Different methods for calculating the visibility of the new moon crescent at Mecca are used by different Muslim groups. US date may vary. Began at sunset the preceding day.

NATIONAL CLEAN-OFF-YOUR-DESK DAY. Jan 13. To provide one day early each year for every desk worker to see the top of the desk and prepare for the following year's paperwork. Annually, the second Monday in January. For info: A.C. Vierow, Box 71, Clio, MI 48420-0071.

NORTH AMERICAN INTERNATIONAL AUTO SHOW. Jan 13–26. Cobo Center, Detroit, MI. 98th annual Detroit show; 26th annual international show. One of the premier auto shows, the NAIAS is a showcase for the world's vehicle introductions. An estimated 70 introductions will take place during the show. Public show is Jan 18–26. Est attendance: 760,000. For info: NAIAS, 1900 W Big Beaver, Ste 100, Troy, MI 48084. Phone: (248) 643-0250. Fax: (248) 637-0784. Web: www.naias.com.

NORWAY: TYVENDEDAGEN. Jan 13. "Twentieth Day" is the traditional end of the Christmas season, marked by festivities. The Christmas tree is taken down and burned.

PEDDLER'S VILLAGE QUILT COMPETITION AND DISPLAY. Jan 13–Apr 6. Peddler's Village, Lahaska, PA. Handmade quilt entries compete for $1,400 in cash prizes in such categories as traditional, Amish, creative, clothing, children's, applique and potluck. A distinguished panel of judges chooses the winners, and quilts are displayed in the Village Gazebo. Open daily to public. Free admission. Est attendance: 250,000. For info: Peddler's Village, Routes 202 and 263, Lahaska, PA 18931. Phone: (215) 794-4000. Fax: (215) 794-4001. E-mail: info@peddlersvillage.com. Web: www.peddlersvillage.com.

RADIO BROADCASTING: ANNIVERSARY. Jan 13, 1910. Radio pioneer and electron tube inventor Lee De Forest arranged the world's first radio broadcast to the public at New York, NY. He succeeded in broadcasting the voice of Enrico Caruso along with other stars of the Metropolitan Opera to several receiving locations in the city where listeners with earphones marveled at wireless music from the air. Though only a few were equipped to listen, it was the first broadcast to reach the public and the beginning of a new era in which wireless radio communication became almost universal. See also: "First Scheduled Radio Broadcast: Anniversary" (Nov 2).

January 2014

S	M	T	W	T	F	S
			1	2	3	4
5	6	7	8	9	10	11
12	13	14	15	16	17	18
19	20	21	22	23	24	25
26	27	28	29	30	31	

RUSSIA: OLD NEW YEAR'S EVE. Jan 13. Although Jan 1 is the official New Year's Day in Russia, some Russians still celebrate on the old Julian date of Jan 13–14. Also celebrated in Belarus and Ukraine.

"THE SOPRANOS" TV PREMIERE: 15th ANNIVERSARY. Jan 13, 1999. The thinking viewer's mob drama, "The Sopranos" featured James Gandolfini as Tony Soprano, whose panic attacks drove him to seek out a psychiatrist (Lorraine Bracco). The HBO drama revolved around Tony's home and crime lives. *TV Guide* named the series one of the greatest TV shows of all time. The final episode aired June 10, 2007.

SWEDEN: ST. KNUT'S DAY. Jan 13. St. Knut's Day (Tjugondag Knut, or "The 20th Day of Knut") marks the end of the Christmas season in Sweden—with parties, song and the dismantling of the yule tree (which traditionally is thrown out the window). Named for Knut (or Canute) IV, also Knut the Holy, former king and patron saint of Denmark. Although St. Knut's feast day is Jan 19, Sweden and Finland have conflated observances of Knut IV with that of his nephew and saint Knut Lavard (feast day is Jan 7).

TOGO: LIBERATION DAY. Jan 13. National holiday. Commemorates 1967 uprising.

VERDON, GWEN: BIRTH ANNIVERSARY. Jan 13, 1926. One of Broadway's premier female dancers and actresses; many of her most successful roles were choreographed by her husband, Bob Fosse. She won Tony Awards for *Can-Can, Damn Yankees, New Girl in Town* and *Redhead*. She also acted in movies, including *Cocoon* and the film adaptation of *Damn Yankees*. Born at Los Angeles, CA, she died Oct 18, 2000, at Woodstock, VT.

BIRTHDAYS TODAY

Trace Adkins, 52, country singer, born Sarepta, LA, Jan 13, 1962.

Kevin Anderson, 54, actor (*Hoffa, Rising Sun*), born Gurnee, IL, Jan 13, 1960.

Orlando Bloom, 37, actor (*Pirates of the Caribbean*, the Lord of the Rings film trilogy), born Canterbury, Kent, England, Jan 13, 1977.

Keith Coogan, 44, actor (*Adventures in Babysitting, Cousins*), born Palm Springs, CA, Jan 13, 1970.

Patrick Dempsey, 48, actor ("Grey's Anatomy," *Enchanted, Sweet Home Alabama*), born Lewiston, ME, Jan 13, 1966.

Nicole Eggert, 42, actress ("Baywatch," "Charles in Charge"), born Glendale, CA, Jan 13, 1972.

Frank Gallo, 81, artist, sculptor, born Toledo, OH, Jan 13, 1933.

Liam Hemsworth, 24, actor (*The Hunger Games, The Last Song*), born Melbourne, Victoria, Australia, Jan 13, 1990.

Nikolai Khabibulin, 41, hockey player, born Sverdlovsk, Russia, Jan 13, 1973.

Julia Louis-Dreyfus, 53, actress ("Seinfeld," "The New Adventures of Old Christine"), born New York, NY, Jan 13, 1961.

Jay McInerney, 59, writer (*Bright Lights, Big City*), born Hartford, CT, Jan 13, 1955.

Penelope Ann Miller, 50, actress (*Adventures in Babysitting, The Freshman, Carlito's Way*), born Los Angeles, CA, Jan 13, 1964.

Richard Moll, 71, actor ("Night Court," *Wicked Stepmother, The Flintstones*), born Pasadena, CA, Jan 13, 1943.

Lorrie Moore, 57, author (*Birds of America, A Gate at the Stairs*), born Glens Falls, NY, Jan 13, 1957.

Joannie Rochette, 28, Olympic figure skater, born Montreal, QC, Canada, Jan 13, 1986.

Frances Sternhagen, 84, actress ("Cheers," *Misery*; stage: *The Good Doctor, The Heiress*), born Washington, DC, Jan 13, 1930.

January 14 — Tuesday

DAY 14 **351 REMAINING**

ARNOLD, BENEDICT: BIRTH ANNIVERSARY. Jan 14, 1741. (Old Style date.) American officer who deserted to the British during the Revolutionary War and whose name has since become synonymous with treachery. Born at Norwich, CT. Died June 14, 1801, at London, England.

FIRST CAESAREAN SECTION: ANNIVERSARY. Jan 14, 1794. Dr. Jesse Bennett, of Edom, VA, performed the first successful caesarean section. The patient was his wife.

MAURY, MATTHEW FONTAINE: BIRTH ANNIVERSARY. Jan 14, 1806. Naval officer, born at Fredericksburg, VA. Maury established oceanography as a branch of science and revolutionized the recording of oceanographic data as a superintendent of the Naval Observatory. Died at Lexington, VA, Feb 1, 1873.

OUTCAULT, RICHARD FELTON: BIRTH ANNIVERSARY. Jan 14, 1863. When Richard Felton Outcault was asked by the *New York World*'s Sunday editor to submit drawings for use with the paper's new color printing process, the "funny papers" were born. Outcault's first color drawing, titled "Origin of a New Species," was published Nov 18, 1894. The first regular colored cartoon, "Hogan's Alley," drawn by Outcault, began appearing with its main character's blustery comments written across his yellow nightshirt—thus making him the "Yellow Kid." The term "yellow journalism" was coined for newspapers featuring the Kid. Outcault's strip "Buster Brown" brought him celebrity and fortune. Outcault was born at Lancaster, OH, and died Sept 25, 1928, at Flushing, NY.

POETRY AT WORK DAY. Jan 14. 2nd annual. Celebrates the power of poetry in the workplace. It also remembers the many poets who led an ordinary life working and writing in tandem. People will be encouraged to embrace their work lives and the potential for poetry to flourish alongside—even inside—work itself. Annually, the second Tuesday in January. For info: Laura Barkat, 21 Belleview Ave, Ossining, NY 10562. Phone/fax: (914) 944-9036. E-mail: llbarkat@yahoo.com. Web: www.tweetspeakpoetry.com.

RATIFICATION DAY. Jan 14, 1784. Anniversary of the act that officially ended the American Revolution and established the US as a sovereign power. On Jan 14, 1784, the Continental Congress, meeting at Annapolis, MD, ratified the Treaty of Paris, thus fulfilling the Declaration of Independence of July 4, 1776.

ROACH, HAL: BIRTH ANNIVERSARY. Jan 14, 1892. American film writer, director and producer Harold Eugene (Hal) Roach was born at Elmira, NY. He pioneered film comedy as chief of his own studio for nearly 40 years. During that time he produced, and sometimes directed and wrote, nearly 1,000 movies. Roach is noted for originating the *Our Gang* comedies in 1922 and for introducing Laurel and Hardy to film audiences. He won Academy Awards for the short films *The Music Box* (1931) and *Bored of Education* (1936). Roach produced the film version of Steinbeck's novel *Of Mice and Men* in 1939. In 1984 he won an honorary Academy Award for career achievement. Roach died Nov 2, 1992, at Los Angeles, CA.

"SANFORD AND SON" TV PREMIERE: ANNIVERSARY. Jan 14, 1972. NBC sitcom that gained immediate popularity depicting an African-American father and son engaged in the junkyard business. Norman Lear and Bud Yorkin developed the comedy series based on the British "Steptoe and Son." Comedian Redd Foxx played Fred Sanford. His son, Lamont, was played by Demond Wilson. Others appearing on the show included Whitman Mayo as Grady, Slappy White as Melvin, LaWanda Page as Aunt Esther and Gregory Sierra as Julio. The last telecast was Sept 2, 1977.

SCHWEITZER, ALBERT: BIRTH ANNIVERSARY. Jan 14, 1875. The Alsatian philosopher, musician, physician and winner of the 1952 Nobel Peace Prize was born at Kayserberg, Upper Alsace, and died at Lambarene, Gabon, Sept 4, 1965.

SPACE MILESTONE: *SOYUZ 4* (USSR): 45th ANNIVERSARY. Jan 14, 1969. First docking of two manned spacecraft (with *Soyuz 5*) and first interchange of spaceship personnel in orbit by means of space walks.

"TODAY" TV PREMIERE: ANNIVERSARY. Jan 14, 1952. NBC program that started the morning news format we know today. Captained by Dave Garroway, the show was segmented with bits and pieces of news, sports, weather, interviews and other features that were repeated so that viewers did not have to stop their morning routine to watch. The segments were brief and to the point. Sylvester Weaver devised this concept to capitalize on television's unusual qualities. What used to take three hours to broadcast live across the country was done in two with videotape on a delayed basis. The addition of chimpanzee J. Fred Muggs in 1953 helped push ratings up. There have been a number of hosts over the years, from John Chancellor and Hugh Downs to Tom Brokaw, Bryant Gumbel and Matt Lauer. Female hosts (originally called "Today Girls") have included Betsy Palmer, Florence Henderson, Barbara Walters, Jane Pauley, Katie Couric and Meredith Viera.

UZBEKISTAN: ARMY DAY. Jan 14. National holiday.

WHIPPLE, WILLIAM: BIRTH ANNIVERSARY. Jan 14, 1730. American patriot and signer of the Declaration of Independence. Born at Kittery, ME, he died at Portsmouth, NH, Nov 10, 1785.

 BIRTHDAYS TODAY

Jason Bateman, 45, actor ("Arrested Development"), born Rye, NY, Jan 14, 1969.

Julian Bond, 74, legislator, civil rights leader, born Nashville, TN, Jan 14, 1940.

Kristin Cavallari, 27, actress ("Laguna Beach: The Real Orange County"), born Chicago, IL, Jan 14, 1987.

Faye Dunaway, 73, actress (Oscar for *Network*; *Bonnie and Clyde, Chinatown*), born Bascom, FL, Jan 14, 1941.

Lawrence Kasdan, 65, filmmaker (*The Bodyguard, The Big Chill, Mumford*), born Miami Beach, FL, Jan 14, 1949.

LL Cool J, 46, actor ("NCIS: Los Angeles," "In the House," *SWAT*), singer, born James Todd Smith at Bay Shore, NY, Jan 14, 1968.

Shannon Lucid, 71, former astronaut, born Shanghai, China, Jan 14, 1943.

Shepard Smith, 50, news anchor, born David Shepard Smith, Jr, at Holly Springs, MS, Jan 14, 1964.

Steven Soderbergh, 51, filmmaker (*Magic Mike, Traffic, Ocean's Eleven, Erin Brockovich*), born Atlanta, GA, Jan 14, 1963.

Holland Taylor, 71, actress ("The Practice," *The Truman Show*), born Philadelphia, PA, Jan 14, 1943.

Nina Totenberg, 70, broadcast journalist, correspondent ("Nightline"), born New York, NY, Jan 14, 1944.

Emily Watson, 47, actress (*Gosford Park, Angela's Ashes, Hilary and Jackie*), born London, England, Jan 14, 1967.

Carl Weathers, 66, actor (*Rocky, Happy Gilmore*), born New Orleans, LA, Jan 14, 1948.

January 15 — Wednesday

DAY 15 **350 REMAINING**

ACE, GOODMAN: BIRTH ANNIVERSARY. Jan 15, 1899. Radio and TV writer, actor, columnist and humorist. With his wife, Jane, created and acted in the popular series of radio programs (1928–45) "Easy Aces." Called "America's greatest wit" by Fred Allen. Born at Kansas City, MO; died at New York, NY, Mar 25, 1982, soon after asking that his tombstone be inscribed "No flowers, please, I'm allergic."

ALPHA KAPPA ALPHA SORORITY FOUNDED: ANNIVERSARY. Jan 15, 1908. Founded at Howard University at Washington, DC, by Ethel Hedgeman Lyle, Alpha Kappa Alpha was the first organization of its type for black women. It was incorporated Jan 29, 1913.

BLACK DAHLIA MURDER: ANNIVERSARY. Jan 15, 1947. On this day, the body of Elizabeth Short was found in an empty lot in Los Angeles, CA. Short, nicknamed the Black Dahlia for her striking looks, had been murdered and mutilated, and her body's discovery sparked a media frenzy. Although dozens of men (and women) confessed to the crime, those confessions were discounted. The murder remains LA's most famous unsolved murder and one that evokes the noirish aura of postwar LA's corruption and crime problems.

BRIDGES, LLOYD: BIRTH ANNIVERSARY. Jan 15, 1913. Film and television actor born at San Leandro, CA. Best known for his successful syndicated television series "Sea Hunt" (1958–61). The show featured filmed underwater sequences, and Bridges, who learned scuba diving for the series, eventually did all his underwater stunts. Died Mar 10, 1998, at Los Angeles, CA.

BRITISH MUSEUM: ANNIVERSARY. Jan 15, 1759. On this date, the British Museum opened its doors at Montague House in London. Incorporated by an act of Parliament in 1753, following the death of British medical doctor and naturalist Sir Hans Sloane, who had bequeathed his personal collection of books, manuscripts, coins, medals and antiquities to Britain. As the national museum of the United Kingdom, the British Museum houses many of the world's most prized treasures. The national library moved to separate facilities in 1997.

FIRST SUPER BOWL: ANNIVERSARY. Jan 15, 1967. The Green Bay Packers won the first NFL–AFL World Championship Game, defeating the Kansas City Chiefs, 35–10, at the Los Angeles Memorial Coliseum. Packers quarterback Bart Starr was named the game's Most Valuable Player. Pro football's title game later became known as the Super Bowl.

"HAPPY DAYS" TV PREMIERE: 40th ANNIVERSARY. Jan 15, 1974. This nostalgic comedy set in Milwaukee in the 1950s starred Ron Howard as teenager Richie Cunningham with Anson Williams and Don Most as his friends "Potsie" Weber and Ralph Malph. Tom Bosley and Marion Ross played Richie's parents, and his sister, Joanie, was played by Erin Moran. The most memorable character was The Fonz—Arthur "Fonzie" Fonzarelli—played by Henry Winkler. "Happy Days" remained on the air until July 12, 1984. "Laverne and Shirley" was a spin-off.

"HILL STREET BLUES" TV PREMIERE: ANNIVERSARY. Jan 15, 1981. Immensely popular NBC police series created by Stephen Bochco and Michael Kozoll that focused more on police officers than crime. The realistic show was highly praised by actual police officers. It won a slew of Emmys and ran for seven seasons. The cast featured Daniel J. Travanti as Captain Frank Furillo, Veronica Hamel as public defender Joyce Davenport and Michael Conrad as Sergeant Phil "Let's be careful out there" Esterhaus. Other cast members included Barbara Bosson, Bruce Weitz, Taurean Blacque, Joe Spano, James B. Sikking, Michael Warren, Betty Thomas, Ed Marinaro and Charles Haid. The last telecast was on May 19, 1987.

ILLINOIS SNOW SCULPTING COMPETITION. Jan 15–18. Rockford, IL. Teams from around the state create enormous works of frozen art, as they compete to represent Illinois in national snow-sculpting competition. In case of inclement weather, event may be postponed. Sponsor: Rockford Park District. Est attendance: 20,000. For info: Rockford Park District, 401 S Main St, Rockford, IL 61101. Phone: (815) 987-8800. Fax: (815) 987-8877. Web: www.snowsculpting.org.

KING, MARTIN LUTHER, JR: 85th BIRTH ANNIVERSARY. Jan 15, 1929. Black civil rights leader, minister, advocate of nonviolence and recipient of the Nobel Peace Prize (1964). Born at Atlanta, GA, he was assassinated at Memphis, TN, Apr 4, 1968. After his death many states and territories observed his birthday as a holiday. In 1983 Congress approved HR 3706, "A bill to amend Title 5, United States Code, to make the birthday of Martin Luther King, Jr, a legal public holiday." Signed by the president on Nov 2, 1983, it became Public Law 98–144. The law sets the third Monday in January for observance of King's birthday. First observance was Jan 20, 1986. See also: "King, Martin Luther, Jr: Birthday Observed" (Jan 20).

LIVINGSTON, PHILIP: BIRTH ANNIVERSARY. Jan 15, 1716. Merchant and signer of the Declaration of Independence, born at Albany, NY. Died at York, PA, June 12, 1778.

MOLIÈRE DAY: BAPTISM ANNIVERSARY. Jan 15, 1622. Most celebrated of French authors and dramatists, Jean Baptiste Poquelin, baptized at Paris, France, Jan 15, 1622, took the stage name Molière when he was about 22 years old. While playing in a performance of his last play, *Le Malade Imaginaire* (about a hypochondriac afraid of death), Molière became ill and died within a few hours at Paris, Feb 17, 1673.

MOON PHASE: FULL MOON. Jan 15. Moon enters Full Moon phase at 11:52 PM, EST.

NATIONAL NO-TILLAGE CONFERENCE. Jan 15–18. Springfield, IL. Attracts innovative farmers interested in reducing tillage to protect the environment and boost profits. Est attendance: 860. For info: Frank Lessiter, Natl No-Tillage Conference, PO Box 624, Brookfield, WI 53008-0624. Phone: (262) 782-4480. Fax: (262) 782-1252. E-mail: info@lesspub.com. Web: www.no-tillfarmer.com.

NATIONAL SOCCER COACHES ASSOCIATION OF AMERICA NATIONAL CONVENTION. Jan 15–19. Philadelphia, PA. The NSCAA is the largest soccer coaches organization in the world. The NSCAA Convention is the largest annual gathering of soccer coaches in the world. The convention features clinics, lectures, exhibits and national awards. Est attendance: 9,000. For info: NSCAA, 800 Ann Ave, Kansas City, KS 66101. Phone: (913) 362-1747. Fax: (913) 362-3439. E-mail: cburt@nscaa.com. Web: www.nscaa.com.

PENTAGON COMPLETED: ANNIVERSARY. Jan 15, 1943. The world's largest office building with 6.5 million square feet of usable space, the Pentagon is located in Virginia across the Potomac River from Washington, DC, and serves as headquarters for the Department of Defense.

QUARTERLY ESTIMATED FEDERAL INCOME TAX PAYERS' DUE DATE. Jan 15. For those individuals whose fiscal year is the calendar year and who make quarterly estimated federal income tax payments, today would be one of the due dates (Jan 15, Apr 15, June 16 and Sept 15, 2014).

January 2014

S	M	T	W	T	F	S
			1	2	3	4
5	6	7	8	9	10	11
12	13	14	15	16	17	18
19	20	21	22	23	24	25
26	27	28	29	30	31	

SIEGMEISTER, ELIE: BIRTH ANNIVERSARY. Jan 15, 1909. American composer Elie Siegmeister was born at New York, NY. He composed eight symphonies and eight operas and a number of concertos, chamber pieces and orchestral works using folk, jazz and street songs to create a contemporary American classical music. He died Mar 10, 1991, at Manhasset, NY.

TELLER, EDWARD: BIRTH ANNIVERSARY. Jan 15, 1908. Born at Budapest, Hungary, Edward Teller was a physicist who worked on the Manhattan Project at Los Alamos, NM, in the 1940s. He promoted the first hydrogen fusion bomb, work that was considered secondary to the atomic bomb research taking place at the same time. He was a vocal critic of Robert Oppenheimer, director of the Manhattan Project, and his comments eventually destroyed Oppenheimer's career. Teller's hydrogen bomb research ultimately proved feasible but was never used in wartime. Throughout his life he remained a profound influence on America's defense and energy policies. He died at Stanford, CA, Sept 9, 2003.

WINGS OVER WILLCOX/BIRDING & NATURE FESTIVAL. Jan 15–19. Willcox, AZ. Tours to the Willcox Playa and Wetlands to see sandhill cranes, hawks, plovers, longspurs and much more. Visit Cochise Lake and see the waders. Workshops on wildlife. Seminars on bird-watching by various experts, a banquet, silent auction and a whole lot more. Est attendance: 800. For info: Willcox Chamber of Commerce. Phone: (800) 200-2272 or (520) 384-2272. Web: www.wingsoverwillcox.com or www.willcoxchamber.com.

WOLF MOON. Jan 15. So called by Native American tribes of New England and the Great Lakes because at this time of winter, the wolves howl in hunger. The January Full Moon.

BIRTHDAYS TODAY

Drew Brees, 35, football player, born Austin, TX, Jan 15, 1979.

Ernest J. Gaines, 81, author (*The Autobiography of Miss Jane Pittman, A Lesson Before Dying*), born Oscar, LA, Jan 15, 1933.

Chad Lowe, 46, actor ("Now and Again," "Life Goes On," *Nobody's Perfect*), born Dayton, OH, Jan 15, 1968.

Andrea Martin, 67, actress (*Wag the Dog, Anastasia*, "SCTV"), born Portland, ME, Jan 15, 1947.

Margaret O'Brien, 77, actress (*Little Women, Meet Me in St. Louis*), born San Diego, CA, Jan 15, 1937.

Pitbull, 33, rapper, record producer, born Armando Christian Pérez at Miami, FL, Jan 15, 1981.

Mario Van Peebles, 57, actor (*Love Kills, Judgment Day*), director, born Mexico City, Mexico, Jan 15, 1957.

January 16 — Thursday

DAY 16 — **349 REMAINING**

APPRECIATE A DRAGON DAY. Jan 16. In school and public libraries everywhere, children will have the opportunity to choose dragons from popular literature and participate in activities to share their enthusiasm for the dragon of their choice. For info: Donita K. Paul, PO Box 25083, Colorado Springs, CO 80936. Phone: (719) 635-3940. E-mail: katepaul@donitakpaul.com. Web: www.donitakpaul.com and www.dragonandturtle.com.

BRITISH AIR RAID ON BERLIN: ANNIVERSARY. Jan 16, 1943. In the first bombing of Germany since the Casablanca Conference, the British Royal Air Force began heavy bombing of Germany by day and night to bring about "the progressive destruction and dislocation of the German military, industrial and economic system, and for the undermining of the morale of the German people." The RAF used their new "target indicator" bombs to mark targets for their bombers.

CIVIL SERVICE CREATED: ANNIVERSARY. Jan 16, 1883. The US Congress passed a bill creating the civil service.

DEAN, DIZZY: BIRTH ANNIVERSARY. Jan 16, 1911. Jay Hanna "Dizzy" Dean, major league pitcher (St. Louis Cardinals) and Hall of Fame member, was born at Lucas, AR. Following his baseball career, Dean established himself as a radio and TV sports announcer and commentator, becoming famous for his innovative delivery. "He slud into third," reported Dizzy, who on another occasion explained that "Me and Paul [baseball player brother Paul "Daffy" Dean] . . . didn't get much education." Died at Reno, NV, July 17, 1974.

EISENHOWER ASSUMES COMMAND: 70th ANNIVERSARY. Jan 16, 1944. General Dwight D. Eisenhower arrived in London to assume command of the Supreme Headquarters Allied Expeditionary Forces in Europe (SHAEF). Having demonstrated his organizational abilities in North Africa as well as his strength as an arbitrator of inter-Allied rivalries, Eisenhower was charged with the most far-reaching push of the war—the invasion of France.

EL SALVADOR: NATIONAL DAY OF PEACE. Jan 16. A peace treaty was signed in Mexico City on this date in 1992 ending the 12-year civil war that had claimed 75,000 lives. On Feb 1, a cease-fire went into effect.

FOSSEY, DIAN: BIRTH ANNIVERSARY. Jan 16, 1932. Born at San Francisco, CA, Fossey went to the Virunga Mountains at Rwanda, Africa, to study the endangered mountain gorillas. Her work, conducted in isolation among the primates, was groundbreaking in terms of increasing science's understanding of the gorillas' social world. Fossey was a vigorous crusader against the poachers who decimate the gorilla population, and she was probably murdered by them: her body was discovered on Dec 26, 1985, at Mount Visoke, Rwanda.

GET TO KNOW YOUR CUSTOMER DAY. Jan 16 (also Apr 17, July 17 and Oct 16). Set aside the third Thursday of each quarter to get to know your customers even better. For example, salespeople might plan to take a customer out to lunch, not to sell, but to learn more about the customer's needs and why the customer likes doing business with them. Executives could get out from behind the desk and go into the field. For info: Shep Hyken, Shepard Presentations, LLC, 711 Old Ballas Rd, Ste 215, St. Louis, MO 63141. Phone: (314) 692-2200. Fax: (314) 692-2222. E-mail: Shep@hyken.com. Web: www.hyken.com or www.GetToKnowYourCustomerDay.com.

GULF WAR BEGINS: ANNIVERSARY. Jan 16, 1991. Allied forces launched a major air offensive against Iraq to begin the Gulf War. The strike was designed to destroy Iraqi air defenses and command, control and communication centers. As Desert Shield became Desert Storm, the world was able to see and hear for the first time an initial engagement of war as CNN broadcasters, stationed at Baghdad, covered the attack live.

JAPAN: HARU-NO-YABUIRI. Jan 16. Employees and servants who have been working over the holidays are given a day off.

MALAWI: JOHN CHILEMBWE DAY. Jan 16. National holiday. Honors a leader for independence who led an uprising against the British in 1915.

MERMAN, ETHEL: BIRTH ANNIVERSARY. Jan 16, 1909. Musical comedy star famous for her belting voice and brassy style. Born Ethel Agnes Zimmerman on Jan 16, 1909 (or 1912—the date changed the older she got, but most sources say 1909), at Queens, NY. Died Feb 15, 1984, at New York, NY.

MICHELIN, ANDRÉ: BIRTH ANNIVERSARY. Jan 16, 1853. French industrialist who, along with his brother Edouard, started the Michelin Tire Company in 1888, manufacturing bicycle tires. They were the first to use demountable pneumatic tires on cars. Born at Paris, France; died there Apr 4, 1931.

MONACO: INTERNATIONAL CIRCUS FESTIVAL OF MONTE CARLO. Jan 16–26. Espace de Fontvielle, Monte Carlo. 38th annual. The best circus acts and performers from five continents compete for the Golden Clown Award at this storied festival. For info: Monte Carlo Festivals, 5, Avenue des Ligures, MC-98000 Monte Carlo, Monaco. Web: www.montecarlofestivals.com.

NATIONAL NOTHING DAY: ANNIVERSARY. Jan 16, 1973. Anniversary of National Nothing Day, an event created by newspaperman Harold Pullman Coffin and first observed "to provide Americans with one national day when they can just sit without celebrating, observing or honoring anything." Since 1975, though many other events have been listed on this day, lighthearted traditional observance of Coffin's idea has continued. Coffin, a native of Reno, NV, died at Capitola, CA, Sept 12, 1981, at the age of 76.

PROHIBITION (EIGHTEENTH) AMENDMENT: 95th ANNIVERSARY. Jan 16, 1919. When Nebraska became the 36th state to ratify the prohibition amendment, the 18th Amendment became part of the US Constitution. One year later, Jan 16, 1920, the 18th Amendment took effect and the sale of alcoholic beverages became illegal in the US, with the Volstead Act providing for enforcement. This was the first time that an amendment to the Constitution dealt with a social issue. The 21st Amendment, repealing the 18th, went into effect Dec 6, 1933.

✦RELIGIOUS FREEDOM DAY. Jan 16. Commemorates the adoption of a religious freedom statute by the Virginia legislature in 1786.

RELIGIOUS FREEDOM DAY. Jan 16, 1786. The legislature of Virginia adopted a religious freedom statute that protected Virginians against any requirement to attend or support any church and against discrimination. This statute, which had been drafted by Thomas Jefferson and introduced by James Madison, later was the model for the First Amendment to the US Constitution.

SERVICE, ROBERT WILLIAM: BIRTH ANNIVERSARY. Jan 16, 1874. Canadian poet, born at Preston, England. Lived in the Canadian northwest for many years and perhaps is best remembered for such ballads as "The Shooting of Dan McGrew" and "The Cremation of Sam McGee" and for such books as *Songs of a Sourdough*, *Rhymes of a Rolling Stone* and *The Spell of the Yukon*. Died at France, Sept 11, 1958.

SUNDANCE FILM FESTIVAL. Jan 16–26. Park City, UT. "The premier US festival for independent filmmakers." More than 120 feature-length films and more than 80 short films screened. Est attendance: 40,000. For info: Sundance Institute, PO Box 684429, Park City, UT 84068. Phone: (435) 658-3456. Fax: (435) 658-3457. E-mail: info@sundance.org. Web: www.sundance.org/festival.

January 2014

S	M	T	W	T	F	S
			1	2	3	4
5	6	7	8	9	10	11
12	13	14	15	16	17	18
19	20	21	22	23	24	25
26	27	28	29	30	31	

TU B'SHVAT. Jan 16. Hebrew calendar date: Shebat 15, 5774. The 15th day of the month of Shebat in the Hebrew calendar year is set aside as Hamishah Asar (New Year of the Trees, or Jewish Arbor Day), a time to show respect and appreciation for trees and plants. Began at sundown on Jan 15.

BIRTHDAYS TODAY

Debbie Allen, 64, dancer, choreographer, singer, actress ("Fame"), born Houston, TX, Jan 16, 1950.

John Carpenter, 66, director (*Halloween, The Thing*), born Carthage, NY, Jan 16, 1948.

David Chokachi, 46, actor ("Baywatch"), born Plymouth, MA, Jan 16, 1968.

Joe Flacco, 29, football player, born Audubon, NJ, Jan 16, 1985.

Anthony Joseph (A.J.) Foyt, Jr, 79, former auto racer, born Houston, TX, Jan 16, 1935.

Marilyn Horne, 80, opera singer, born Bradford, PA, Jan 16, 1934.

William Kennedy, 86, author (*Ironweed, Roscoe*), born Albany, NY, Jan 16, 1928.

James May, 51, television personality ("Top Gear"), born Bristol, England, Jan 16, 1963.

Jack Burns McDowell, 48, former baseball player, born Van Nuys, CA, Jan 16, 1966.

Ronnie Milsap, 70, country singer, born Robinsville, NC, Jan 16, 1944.

Kate Moss, 40, model, designer, born Croyden, Surrey, England, Jan 16, 1974.

Albert Pujols, 34, baseball player, born Santo Domingo, Dominican Republic, Jan 16, 1980.

January 17 — Friday

DAY 17 **348 REMAINING**

ARBOR DAY IN FLORIDA. Jan 17. The third Friday in January is Arbor Day in Florida, a ceremonial day.

ART DECO WEEKEND. Jan 17–19. Miami Beach, FL. 37th annual. Features parade, jazz entertainment, antique furniture expo and plenty of food. This event celebrates the Miami Beach visionaries and includes art deco antiques, vendors and artists, from national and local talent. Est attendance: 300,000. For info: Art Deco Weekend, Miami Design Preservation League, 1001 Ocean Dr, Miami Beach, FL 33139. Phone: (305) 672-2014. Fax: (305) 200-0195. E-mail: info@mdpl.org. Web: www.artdecoweekend.com.

THE BUSINESS OF AMERICA QUOTATION: ANNIVERSARY. Jan 17, 1925. President Calvin Coolidge, in a speech to the American Society of Newspaper Editors, described America in a way that was to define the country in the 20th century and beyond—not just for the prosperous 1920s. "The chief business of the American people," he said, "is business."

CABLE CAR PATENT: ANNIVERSARY. Jan 17, 1871. Andrew Hallikie received a patent for a cable car system that began service in San Francisco in 1873.

CAPONE, AL: BIRTH ANNIVERSARY. Jan 17, 1899. Gangster Alphonse ("Scarface") Capone was born this date at Brooklyn, NY, to immigrants from Naples, Italy. Capone dominated organized crime in Chicago throughout Prohibition. Targeted by the "Untouchables" after 1929's St. Valentine's Day Massacre (which he allegedly ordered), Capone was finally imprisoned on tax evasion charges. He died Jan 25, 1947, at Miami, FL, after suffering from syphilis.

FIRST NUCLEAR-POWERED SUBMARINE VOYAGE: ANNIVERSARY. Jan 17, 1955. At 11 AM, EST, the commanding officer of the world's first nuclear-powered submarine, the *Nautilus*, ordered all lines cast off and sent the historic message: "Under way on nuclear power." Highlights of the *Nautilus*: keel laid by President Harry S Truman June 14, 1952; christened and launched by Mrs Dwight D. Eisenhower Jan 21, 1954; commissioned to the US Navy Sept 30, 1954. It now forms part of the *Nautilus* Memorial Submarine Force Library and Museum at the Naval Submarine Base New London at Groton, CT.

FRANKLIN, BENJAMIN: BIRTH ANNIVERSARY. Jan 17, 1706. "Elder statesman of the American Revolution," oldest signer of both the Declaration of Independence and the Constitution, scientist, diplomat, author, printer, publisher, philosopher, philanthropist and self-made, self-educated man. Author, printer and publisher of *Poor Richard's Almanack* (1733–58). Born at Boston, MA, Franklin died at Philadelphia, PA, Apr 17, 1790. His birthday is commemorated each year by the Poor Richard Club of Philadelphia with graveside observance. In 1728 Franklin wrote a premature epitaph for himself. It first appeared in print in Ames's 1771 almanac: "The Body of BENJAMIN FRANKLIN/Printer/Like a Covering of an old Book/Its contents torn out/And stript of its Lettering and Gilding,/Lies here, Food for Worms;/But the work shall not be lost,/It will (as he believ'd) appear once more/In a New and more beautiful Edition/Corrected and amended/By the Author."

"FRONTLINE" TV PREMIERE: ANNIVERSARY. Jan 17, 1983. PBS hour-long independently produced documentaries. The programs often create controversy, focusing on a variety of political, military and social issues.

"THE GOLDBERGS" TV PREMIERE: 65th ANNIVERSARY. Jan 17, 1949. Originally broadcast by CBS, this show was one of the earliest TV sitcoms. The show centered around a Jewish mother and her family living in the Bronx and later in the suburbs. Gertrude Berg created the hit radio show before she wrote, produced and starred as Molly Goldberg in the television version. Contributing actors and actresses included Philip Loeb, Arlene McQuade, Tom Taylor, Eli Mintz, Menasha Skulnik and Arnold Stang.

HUTCHINS, ROBERT MAYNARD: BIRTH ANNIVERSARY. Jan 17, 1899. American educator, foundation executive and civil liberties activist, born at Brooklyn, NY. He was president and later chancellor of the University of Chicago, where he introduced many educational concepts, including the Great Books program. Died at Santa Barbara, CA, on May 14, 1977.

IKE'S FAREWELL: ANNIVERSARY. Jan 17, 1961. President Dwight D. Eisenhower, in his farewell address to the nation on national radio and television, spoke the sentences that would be the most quoted and remembered of his presidency. In a direct warning, he said, "In the councils of government, we must guard against the acquisition of unwarranted influence, whether sought or unsought, by the military-industrial complex. The potential for the disastrous rise of misplaced power exists and persists."

INTERNATIONAL FETISH DAY. Jan 17. A day belonging to everyone with a fetish. First observed in 2009. Annually, the third Friday in January. For info: International Fetish Day. Web: www.internationalfetishday.com.

JAPAN SUFFERS MAJOR EARTHQUAKE: ANNIVERSARY. Jan 17, 1995. Japan suffered its second most deadly earthquake in the 20th century when a 20-second temblor left 5,500 people dead and more than 21,600 injured. The epicenter was six miles beneath Awaji Island at Osaka Bay. This was just 20 miles west of Kobe, Japan's sixth-largest city and a major port that accounted for 12 percent of the country's exports. Measuring 7.2 on the Richter scale, the quake collapsed or badly damaged more than 30,400 buildings and left 275,000 people homeless.

JUDGMENT DAY. Jan 17. No need to wait 'til it's too late. All you need to do to see how you measure up to the standards of your God is simple: look in the mirror. There's your judgment. (©2006 by WH.) For info: Thomas & Ruth Roy, Wellcat Holidays, 2418 Long Ln, Lebanon, PA 17046. Phone: (717) 279-0184. E-mail: info@wellcat.com. Web: www.wellcat.com.

KID INVENTORS' DAY. Jan 17. Water skis. Earmuffs. The Popsicle. What do these have in common? All were invented by kids! Some 500,000 children and teens invent gadgets and games each year to make our lives easier—and more fun. Celebrate the ingenuity and value of these young brainstormers on the birthday of Benjamin Franklin, who invented the first swim fins at age 12. To learn more about Kid Inventors' Day (KID), or to receive teachers' guides, book lists and links, and information about inventor contests, camps, and clubs for kids, visit www.kidinventorsday.com or contact Lee Wardlaw. E-mail: author@leewardlaw.com.

LEE-JACKSON DAY IN VIRGINIA. Jan 17. Annually, the Friday in January that precedes Martin Luther King Day. To commemorate the January birthdays of Robert E. Lee and Thomas Jonathan "Stonewall" Jackson.

LLOYD GEORGE, DAVID: BIRTH ANNIVERSARY. Jan 17, 1863. Powerful statesman who guided Britain through the tumult of WWI as prime minister (1916–22). After the war, Lloyd George helped shape the Treaty of Versailles at the Paris Peace Conference of 1919. Born at Manchester, England, he died at Llanystumdwy, Caernarvonshire, Wales, Mar 26, 1945.

LOOP ICE CARNIVAL. Jan 17–18. St. Louis, MO. 9th annual. Winter frolics galore: ice slides, ice carving demos, ice sculptures, Friday night Snow Ball, 5k and 10k "Frozen Buns" runs, $1,000 in ice cubes, music, shopping and more. Est attendance: 10,000. For info: Loop Ice Carnival, 6504 Delmar in The Loop, St. Louis, MO 63130. Phone: (314) 727-8000. Web: www.VisitTheLoop.com.

MEXICO: BLESSING OF THE ANIMALS AT THE CATHEDRAL. Jan 17. Church of San Antonio at Mexico City or Xochimilco provides best sights of chickens, cows and household pets gaily decorated with flowers. (Saint's day for San Antonio Abad, patron saint of domestic animals.)

MILWAUKEE BOAT SHOW. Jan 17–26. Wisconsin Expo Center at State Fair Park, Milwaukee, WI. This event brings together buyers and sellers of powerboats, including fishing boats, pontoons and boating accessories, as well as vacation property and travel destinations. Est attendance: 25,000. For info: ShowSpan, Inc, 2121 Celebration Dr NE, Grand Rapids, MI 49525. Phone: (616) 447-2860. Fax: (616) 447-2861. E-mail: events@showspan.com. Web: www.showspan.com.

NATIONAL FRESH-SQUEEZED JUICE WEEK. Jan 17–23. Drinking fresh-squeezed juice is a great, healthy way of living. For info: Bob O'Brien, Consumer Advocate, 1061 Koelle Blvd, Secaucus, NJ 07094. Phone: (646) 233-6610. E-mail: robtfobrien@aol.com.

PALOMARES HYDROGEN BOMB ACCIDENT: ANNIVERSARY. Jan 17, 1966. At 10:16 AM, according to villagers, fire fell from the sky over Palomares, Spain. An American B-52 bomber carrying four hydrogen bombs collided with its refueling plane, spilling the bombs (two of which had "chemical explosions," scattering radioactive plutonium over the area). In a cleanup, American soldiers burned crops, slaughtered animals and removed tons of topsoil (which was sent to South Carolina for burial). More than 19 years later, in November 1985, the Nuclear Energy Board permitted villagers to see their medical reports for the first time.

PGA OF AMERICA FOUNDED: ANNIVERSARY. Jan 17, 1916. Golf great Walter Hagen and some 30 other pro golfers met and formed the Professional Golfers' Association of America and also developed the idea for a national championship. Rodman Wanamaker provided the trophy and the $2,580 purse for the first PGA Championship, which was played Apr 10, 1916, at the Siwanoy course at Bronxville, NY. The winner was British golfer Jim Barnes, who also won the second competition—not held until 1919 because of WWI. In 1921 Walter Hagen became the first American to win, a feat he accomplished four more times—in 1924, '25, '26 and '27.

POLAND: LIBERATION DAY. Jan 17. Celebration of 1945 liberation of the city of Warsaw from Nazi oppression on this day by Soviet troops. Special ceremonies at the Monument to the Unknown Soldier in Warsaw's Victory Square (which had been called Adolf Hitler Platz during the German occupation).

POPEYE DEBUTS: 85th ANNIVERSARY. Jan 17, 1929. In E.C. Segar's newspaper comic strip "Thimble Theatre," a new character, Popeye, appeared on the scene and was an immediate success. Olive Oyl quickly dumped her beau, Ham Gravy, for the colorful sailor. Popeye's signature line was to be "Tha's all I can stands, 'cause I can't stands no more!"

QUEEN LILIUOKALANI DEPOSED: ANNIVERSARY. Jan 17, 1893. Queen Liliuokalani, the last monarch of Hawaii, lost her throne when the monarchy was abolished by the "Committee of Safety," with the foreknowledge of US minister John L. Stevens, who encouraged the revolutionaries. The Queen's supporters were intimidated by the 300 US Marines sent to protect American lives and property. Judge Sanford B. Dole became president of the republic and later was Hawaii's first governor after the US annexed it by joint resolution of Congress on July 7, 1898. Hawaii held incorporated territory status for 60 years. President Dwight D. Eisenhower signed the proclamation making Hawaii the 50th state on Aug 21, 1959.

RUSH, WILLIAM: DEATH ANNIVERSARY. Jan 17, 1833. First American-born sculptor. William Rush's work in wood and clay included busts of many notables, American and European alike; carved wooden female figureheads for ships; the masks of Tragedy and Comedy seen at the Actor's House outside Philadelphia, PA; and the *Spirit of Schuylkill* in Fairmount Park in Philadelphia. In 1805 Rush and others founded the Pennsylvania Academy of the Fine Arts. Rush was born at Philadelphia in 1756.

SAINT ANTHONY'S DAY. Jan 17. Feast day honoring Egyptian hermit who became the first Christian monk and who established communities of hermits; patron saint of domestic animals and patriarch of all monks. Lived about AD 251–354.

SASSOON, VIDAL: BIRTH ANNIVERSARY. Jan 17, 1928. Born into poverty at London, England, this future hairdresser to the stars was raised partly in an orphange and apprenticed to a beauty shop at age 14. He opened his first salon in 1954 and was soon experimenting with geometric styles and angular cuts. He moved to New York in 1965 where his groundbreaking new styles worn by women like Mary Quant, Grace Coddington and Mia Farrow made him into a superstar. His chain of salons and line of affordable hair care products made him a household name among American women. "If you don't look good, we don't look good" was the signature line for his brand. He died at Los Angeles, CA, May 9, 2012.

SOUTHERN CALIFORNIA EARTHQUAKE: 20th ANNIVERSARY. Jan 17, 1994. An earthquake measuring 6.6 on the Richter scale struck the Los Angeles area about 4:20 AM. The epicenter was at Northridge in the San Fernando Valley, about 20 miles northwest of downtown Los Angeles. A death toll of 51 was announced Jan 20. Sixteen of the dead were killed in the collapse of one apartment building. More than 25,000 people were made homeless by the quake and 680,000 lost electric power. Many buildings were destroyed and others made uninhabitable due to structural damage. A section of the Santa Monica Freeway, part of the Simi Valley Freeway and three major overpasses collapsed. Hundreds of aftershocks occurred in the following several weeks. Costs to repair the damages were estimated at $15–30 billion.

SOUTHWESTERN EXPOSITION AND LIVESTOCK SHOW. Jan 17–Feb 8. Fort Worth, TX. Western extravaganza. "World's original indoor rodeo" began in 1918 (45 acres under one roof). Professional rodeo, prize livestock (more than 22,000 head) shows, horse shows, carnival midway, shopping and quality family-oriented entertainment. Est attendance: 1,000,000. For info: Bradford S. Barnes, PO Box 150, Fort Worth, TX 76101-0150. Phone: (817) 877-2400. Fax: (817) 877-2499. Web: www.fwssr.com.

TIP-UP TOWN USA™. Jan 17–19 (also Jan 24–26). Houghton Lake, MI. 64th annual. Michigan's largest winter family festival featuring ice-fishing contests, softball on the ice, polar bear dip, parade, carnival, vendors, fireworks, poker runs and much more. Annually, the last two full weekends of January. Est attendance: 15,000. For info: Chamber of Commerce, 1625 W Houghton Lake Dr, Houghton Lake, MI 48629. Phone: (800) 248-5253. E-mail: hlcc@houghtonlakemichigan.org. Web: www.houghtonlakechamber.net.

BIRTHDAYS TODAY

Muhammad Ali, 72, former heavyweight champion boxer, born Cassius Marcellus Clay, Jr, at Louisville, KY, Jan 17, 1942.

Naveen Andrews, 45, actor ("Lost," *The English Patient*), born London, England, Jan 17, 1969.

Cuauhtémoc Blanco, 41, soccer player, born Mexico City, Mexico, Jan 17, 1973.

Jim Carrey, 52, actor (*I Love You Phillip Morris, Dumb and Dumber, The Truman Show*), comedian ("In Living Color"), born Newmarket, ON, Canada, Jan 17, 1962.

Zooey Deschanel, 34, actress ("The New Girl," *[500] Days of Summer*), born Los Angeles, CA, Jan 17, 1980.

James Earl Jones, 83, actor (*The Great White Hope; Roots: The Next Generations*), born Arktabula, MS, Jan 17, 1931.

Newton Minow, 88, former head of the Federal Communications Commission (1961–63), called television a "vast wasteland," born Milwaukee, WI, Jan 17, 1926.

Michelle Obama, 50, First Lady, wife of Barack Obama, 44th president of the US, born Michelle Robinson at Chicago, IL, Jan 17, 1964.

Maury Povich, 75, talk show host, born Washington, DC, Jan 17, 1939.

Dwyane Wade, 32, basketball player, born Chicago, IL, Jan 17, 1982.

Betty White, 92, actress ("The Mary Tyler Moore Show," "The Golden Girls," "Hot in Cleveland"), animal rights activist, born Oak Park, IL, Jan 17, 1922.

Donald William (Don) Zimmer, 83, baseball executive, former manager and player, born Cincinnati, OH, Jan 17, 1931.

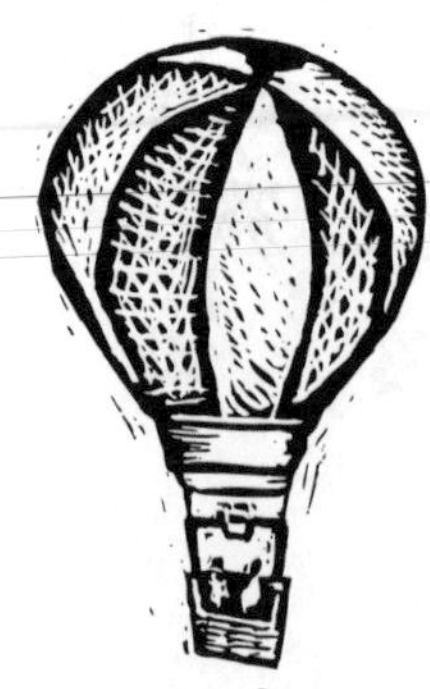

January 2014

S	M	T	W	T	F	S
			1	2	3	4
5	6	7	8	9	10	11
12	13	14	15	16	17	18
19	20	21	22	23	24	25
26	27	28	29	30	31	

January 18 — Saturday

DAY 18 **347 REMAINING**

BALD EAGLE APPRECIATION DAYS. Jan 18–19. River City Mall, Keokuk, IA. Features trained personnel stationed at observation points for viewing the American bald eagle. Indoor activities include a woodcarver's show and Native American activities. Also featuring live eagle demonstrations. Est attendance: 10,000. For info: Keokuk Area Convention and Tourism Bureau, 329 Main St, Keokuk, IA 52632. Phone: (800) 383-1219 or (319) 524-5599. E-mail: info@keokukiowatourism.org. Web: www.keokukiowatourism.org.

EAGLE DAYS. Jan 18. Milford Nature Center/Fish Hatchery, Junction City, KS. Learn more about the magnificent bird that is our national emblem. Meet both a live bald eagle and a golden eagle! Guides with spotting scopes and binoculars will be waiting to show you eagles as they roost and soar around Milford Lake. Sponsors: Kansas Wildlife and Parks; US Army Corps of Engineers. Est attendance: 750. For info: Milford Nature Center, 3415 Hatchery Dr, Junction City, KS 66441. Phone: (785) 238-5323. Fax: (785) 238-5775. Web: www.kdwpt.state.ks.us.

EAGLE DAYS IN SPRINGFIELD. Jan 18–19. Springfield Conservation Nature Center, Springfield, MO. Celebrate the return of bald eagles to Springfield through indoor programs with a live eagle and outdoor viewing opportunities. Est attendance: 2,500. For info: Springfield Conservation Nature Center, 4601 Springfield Nature Center Way, Springfield, MO 65804-4920. Phone: (417) 888-4237. Fax: (417) 888-4241. Web: www.mdc.mo.gov/node/287.

FIRST BLACK US CABINET MEMBER: ANNIVERSARY. Jan 18, 1966. Robert Clifton Weaver was sworn in as secretary of housing and urban development, becoming the first black cabinet member in US history. He was nominated by President Lyndon Johnson. Weaver died at New York, NY, July 17, 1997.

FLOOD, CURT: BIRTH ANNIVERSARY. Jan 18, 1938. Curtis Charles (Curt) Flood, baseball player, born at Houston, TX. Flood was one of baseball's best center fielders in the 1960s, batting .293 over 15 seasons and playing spectacular defense. After the 1969 season, he refused to accept a trade from the St. Louis Cardinals to the Philadelphia Phillies. "I am not a piece of property to be bought and sold irrespective of my wishes," he said in a letter to Commissioner Bowie Kuhn. The resulting lawsuit went to the Supreme Court, where Flood lost. But his stand, taken because he did not want to switch teams, paved the way for the end of baseball's reserve clause and the advent of free agency. Died at Los Angeles, CA, Jan 20, 1997.

GASPARILLA EXTRAVAGANZA AND PIRATE FEST. Jan 18 and Jan 25. Tampa, FL. As any Tampa resident can attest, "Gasparilla" means boats, pirates, parades, merriment and more. On Jan 18, the "Extravaganza" is an alcohol-free family event featuring the Children's Gasparilla Parade and one of the largest fireworks displays in the country. Saturday, Jan 25, The Gasparilla Pirate Fest features 700 citizens, members of Ye Mystic Krewe, reenacting the 1904 invasion of Tampa by a band of pirates. For info: Event Fest, Inc, 1200 W Cass St, Ste 100, Tampa, FL 33606. Phone: (813) 251-3378. Web: www.gasparillapiratefest.com and www.gasparillaextravaganza.com.

GRANT, CARY: BIRTH ANNIVERSARY. Jan 18, 1904. Known as a romantic leading actor, Grant was born at Bristol, England. For more than three decades Grant entertained with his wit, charm, sophistication and personality. His films include *Topper, The Awful Truth, Bringing Up Baby* and *Holiday.* Died at Davenport, IA, Nov 29, 1986.

HARDY, OLIVER: BIRTH ANNIVERSARY. Jan 18, 1892. Born at Atlanta, GA, Hardy teamed up with Stan Laurel in 1926 to form the comedy team of Laurel and Hardy. Among their most popular films: *From Soup to Nuts, Babes in Toyland, Swiss Miss.* Hardy died at Hollywood, CA, Aug 7, 1957.

"THE JEFFERSONS" TV PREMIERE: ANNIVERSARY. Jan 18, 1975. CBS sitcom about an African-American family (formerly neighbors of the Bunkers on "All in the Family") who moved to Manhattan's East Side, thanks to the success of George Jefferson's chain of dry cleaning stores. Having a format similar to "All in the Family," the show featured a black bigot, George Jefferson. Cast included Sherman Hemsley as George Jefferson, Isabel Sanford as Louise Jefferson and Marla Gibbs as maid Florence. The last episode aired July 23, 1985.

KAYE, DANNY: BIRTH ANNIVERSARY. Jan 18, 1913. American entertainer Danny Kaye was born David Daniel Kaminski at Brooklyn, NY. Kaye became a star in films, international stage performances and television. His most notable films are *The Secret Life of Walter Mitty* (1947) and *Hans Christian Andersen* (1952), as well as the classic *White Christmas.* He hosted the television show "The Danny Kaye Show" in the 1960s. In addition, Kaye helped raise millions of dollars for the United Nations International Children's Emergency Fund (UNICEF) and musicians' pension plans. He died Mar 3, 1987, at Los Angeles, CA.

LEWIS AND CLARK EXPEDITION COMMISSIONED: ANNIVERSARY. Jan 18, 1803. Seeking information on what lay west of the young US, President Thomas Jefferson sent a confidential letter to Congress on Jan 18, 1803, requesting funds for an exploratory expedition to be led by Captain Meriwether Lewis and Lieutenant William Clark. After the Louisiana Purchase was signed on Apr 30, 1803, the expedition's mission changed: it became a survey of new American land. The Corps of Discovery set off May 14 from St. Louis and returned with much information about the land, flora and fauna and peoples there on Sept 23, 1806. See also Lewis and Clark anniversaries on May 14, Sept 23 and Nov 16.

PHILIPPINES: ATI-ATIHAN FESTIVAL. Jan 18–19. Kalibo, Aklan. One of the most colorful celebrations in the Philippines, the Ati-Atihan Festival commemorates the peace pact between the Ati of Panay (pygmies) and the Malays, who were early migrants in the islands. The townspeople blacken their bodies with soot, don colorful and bizarre costumes and sing and dance in the streets. The festival also celebrates the Feast Day of Santo Niño (the infant Jesus). Annually, the third weekend in January.

POOH DAY: A.A. MILNE: BIRTH ANNIVERSARY. Jan 18, 1882. Anniversary of the birth of A(lan) A(lexander) Milne, English author, especially remembered for his children's stories: *Winnie the Pooh* and *The House at Pooh Corner.* Also the author of *Mr Pim Passes By, When We Were Very Young* and *Now We Are Six.* Born at London, England; died at Hartfield, England, Jan 31, 1956.

ROGET, PETER MARK: BIRTH ANNIVERSARY. Jan 18, 1779. English physician, best known as author of Roget's *Thesaurus of English Words and Phrases,* first published in 1852. Roget was also the inventor of the "log-log" slide rule. He was born at London and died at West Malvern, Worcestershire, England, Sept 12, 1869.

RUFFIN, DAVIS ELI (DAVID): BIRTH ANNIVERSARY. Jan 18, 1941. American popular singer David Ruffin was born at Meridian, MS. He was one of the original members of the Motown singing group the Temptations, which began in Detroit in the 1960s. Ruffin left the group in 1968 to pursue a solo career. He and the other original members of the Temptations were inducted into the Rock and Roll Hall of Fame in 1989. Ruffin died June 1, 1991, at Philadelphia, PA.

"TED MACK'S ORIGINAL AMATEUR HOUR" TV PREMIERE: ANNIVERSARY. Jan 18, 1948. This immensely popular show, featuring host Ted Mack, introduced amateurs performing their talents on live television. It debuted as a regularly scheduled broadcast on the DuMont network. The show had been a long-running success on radio as "Major Bowes' Original Amateur Hour" until the death of Edward Bowes. Mack became host of the radio show a year later. While a few episodes were televised in 1947, the show did not air weekly until this date. The program ran until 1970 and also continued on radio until 1952.

VERSAILLES PEACE CONFERENCE: 95th ANNIVERSARY. Jan 18, 1919. French president Raymond Poincare formally opened the (WWI) peace conference at Versailles, France. It proceeded under the chairmanship of Georges Clemenceau. In May the conference disposed of Germany's colonies and delivered a treaty to the German delegates on May 7, 1919, fourth anniversary of the sinking of the *Lusitania*. Final treaty-signing ceremonies were completed at the palace at Versailles, June 28, 1919.

WEBSTER, DANIEL: BIRTH ANNIVERSARY. Jan 18, 1782. American statesman and orator who said, on Apr 6, 1830, "The people's government, made for the people, made by the people, and answerable to the people." Born at Salisbury, NH; died at Marshfield, MA, Oct 24, 1852.

WEEK OF CHRISTIAN UNITY. Jan 18–25. From the Conversion of St. Peter (Jan 18) to the Conversion of St. Paul (Jan 25).

BIRTHDAYS TODAY

John Boorman, 81, filmmaker (*Deliverance, Excalibur*), born Shepperton, England, Jan 18, 1933.

Kevin Costner, 59, actor, director (*Field of Dreams, Dances with Wolves, Bull Durham*), born Lynwood, CA, Jan 18, 1955.

Ray Dolby, 81, inventor of the Dolby Sound System for sound recording, born Portland, OR, Jan 18, 1933.

Jane Horrocks, 50, actress (*Little Voice*, "Absolutely Fabulous"), born Lancashire, England, Jan 18, 1964.

Jesse L. Martin, 45, actor ("Law & Order," "Ally McBeal"), born Rocky Mountain, VA, Jan 18, 1969.

Mark Messier, 53, former hockey player, born Edmonton, AB, Canada, Jan 18, 1961.

Martin O'Malley, 51, Governor of Maryland (D), born Bethesda, MD, Jan 18, 1963.

Jason Segel, 34, actor (*Forgetting Sarah Marshall*, "Freaks and Geeks," "How I Met Your Mother"), born Los Angeles, CA, Jan 18, 1980.

January 19 — Sunday

DAY 19 — **346 REMAINING**

AUSTRALIA: SANTOS TOUR DOWN UNDER. Jan 19–26. Adelaide. 15th annual. The world's best cycling teams light up South Australia in the first race of the prestigious UCI ProTour calendar. From beaches to vineyards, through the city of Adelaide and iconic South Australian towns—the six-stage Santos Tour Down Under is a truly world-class event that showcases the speed, skill and spectacle that is professional cycling. For info: Santos Tour Down Under, GPO Box 1972, Adelaide SA 5001, Australia. E-mail: tourdownunder@tourism.sa.com. Web: www.tourdownunder.com.au.

CARLSBAD MARATHON AND HALF MARATHON. Jan 19. Plaza Camino Real, Carlsbad, CA. Race open to runners, walkers, race walkers and the disabled. Postrace festival with refreshments, entertainment, massages and more. Annually, the third Sunday in January. Est attendance: 12,000. For info: Carlsbad Marathon, In Motion, Inc, 6116 Innovation Way, Carlsbad, CA 92009. Phone: (760) 692-2900. E-mail: info@inmotionevents.com. Web: www.carlsbadmarathon.com.

CÉZANNE, PAUL: 175th BIRTH ANNIVERSARY. Jan 19, 1839. Post-Impressionist painter, born at Aix-en-Provence, France. Seeking to "treat nature by the cylinder, the sphere, the cone," Cézanne's portraits, still lifes, and landscapes are a seminal bridge from the Romantics and Impressionists to the Fauves, Cubists and later modernists. He created such masterpieces as *The Bathers* (1875), *The Card Players* (1892), and *Compotier, Pitcher and Fruit* (1892–94). Cézanne died Oct 23, 1906, at Aix, from pneumonia after painting outside in the rain.

CHEVRON HOUSTON MARATHON. Jan 19. Houston, TX. 42nd annual citywide race. The race weekend also features Aramco Houston Half Marathon (Jan 19) and ABB 5k run (Jan 18). Est attendance: 26,000. For info: Houston Marathon Committee, 720 N Post Oak Rd, #200, Houston, TX 77024. Phone: (713) 957-3453. Fax: (713) 957-3406. E-mail: marathon@houstonmarathon.com. Web: www.chevronhoustonmarathon.com.

CLEAN OUT YOUR INBOX WEEK. Jan 19–25. 7th annual. Clean Out Your Inbox Week, observed annually the last business week of January, urges businesses and individuals to cure their e-mail "e-ddictions" and clean out their e-mail inboxes. A new year brings new beginnings—it's a great time to adopt healthy e-mail habits, which make life stress-free and work more productive. People across the country have benefitted from COYIW, which has been recognized by dozens of media outlets from coast to coast. For info: Marsha Egan, InboxDetox.com, 23 Cato Ln, Nantucket, MA 02554. Phone: (610) 777-3795. Fax: (610) 879-2073. E-mail: Marsha@MarshaEgan.com. Web: www.InboxDetox.com/inboxweek.

CONFEDERATE HEROES DAY IN TEXAS. Jan 19. Also called Confederate Memorial Day, observed on anniversary of Robert E. Lee's birthday. Official holiday in Texas.

ETHIOPIA: TIMKET. Jan 19. National holiday. Epiphany in the Ethiopian and Coptic churches. Occurs some years on Jan 20. Also a holiday in Eritrea.

"48 HOURS" TV PREMIERE: ANNIVERSARY. Jan 19, 1988. CBS prime-time newsmagazine program airing each week with first Dan Rather as host and then Leslie Stahl. Recently, the focus has been on crime mysteries.

HEALTHY WEIGHT WEEK. Jan 19–25. 21st annual. People who diet the first week in January and binge the second are ready for better living by the third week: Healthy Weight Week. This is a week to promote healthy lifestyle habits that last a lifetime and prevent weight and eating problems (not cause them, as dieting does); a time to move on to living actively, eating well and feeling good about yourself and others. Annual Healthy Women's Healthy Body Image awards for businesses that honor size diversity are announced the Thursday of this week. For info: Marsha Hudnall, Green Mountain at Fox Run, 262 Fox Ln, Ludlow, VT 05149. E-mail: marsha@fitwoman.com. Web: www.healthyweight.net/hww.htm.

HELMS, EDGAR J.: BIRTH ANNIVERSARY. Jan 19, 1863. Preacher and philanthropist born near Malone, NY. Helms ministered to a parish of poor immigrants in Boston, MA's South End. He developed the philosophy and organization and founded in 1902 the program that eventually became Goodwill Industries. By 1920 there were 15 Goodwills in the US. Helms died Dec 23, 1942, at Boston.

HUNT FOR HAPPINESS WEEK. Jan 19–25. Celebrate the 13th annual Hunt for Happiness Week sponsored by the Secret Society of Happy People. Activities for kids and adults are available.

January 2014

S	M	T	W	T	F	S
			1	2	3	4
5	6	7	8	9	10	11
12	13	14	15	16	17	18
19	20	21	22	23	24	25
26	27	28	29	30	31	

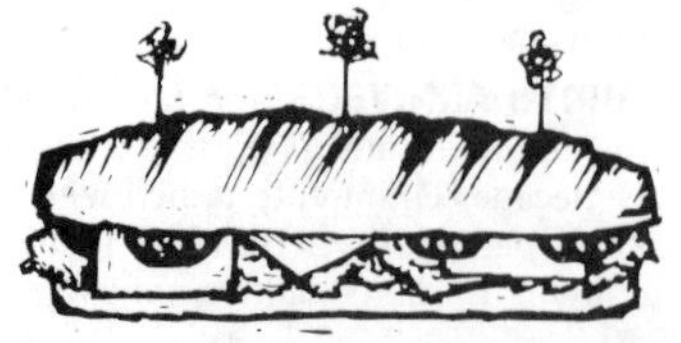

Annually, the third full week in January. For info: Secret Society of Happy People, 425 Busher Dr, Lewisville, TX 75067. Phone: (972) 459-7031. E-mail: pamelagail@sohp.com. Web: www.sohp.com.

JOHNSON, JOHN H.: BIRTH ANNIVERSARY. Jan 19, 1918. Born at Arkansas City, AR, the grandson of a slave, John H. Johnson rose from abject poverty to become one of the most influential black businessmen in America. In 1942 he launched the first of his successful magazines, *Negro Digest*, which reached a circulation of 50,000 within eight months. In 1945 came *Ebony*, followed by *Jet* in 1951. By the time of his death at Chicago, IL, on Aug 8, 2005, Johnson's company was the world's largest African-American owned-and-operated publishing operation. He served the US as goodwill ambassador and received numerous honors, the most important of which was the Presidential Medal of Freedom in 1996 for "building self-respect in the black community."

JOPLIN, JANIS: BIRTH ANNIVERSARY. Jan 19, 1943. Possibly the most highly regarded white female blues singer of all time, Janis Joplin was born at Port Arthur, TX. Joplin's appearance with Big Brother and the Holding Company at the Monterey International Pop Festival in August 1967 launched her to superstar status. Among her recording hits were "Get It While You Can," "Piece of My Heart" and "Ball and Chain." She died of a heroin overdose Oct 4, 1970, at Hollywood, CA, at the age of 27.

LEE, ROBERT E.: BIRTH ANNIVERSARY. Jan 19, 1807. Greatest military leader of the Confederacy, son of Revolutionary War general Henry (Light-Horse Harry) Lee. His surrender Apr 9, 1865, to Union general Ulysses S. Grant brought an end to the Civil War. Born at Westmoreland County, VA, he died at Lexington, VA, Oct 12, 1870. His birthday is observed in Florida, Kentucky, Louisiana, South Carolina and Tennessee. Observed on third Monday in January in Alabama, Arkansas and Mississippi.

NATIONAL HANDWRITING ANALYSIS WEEK. Jan 19–25. To inform the public that handwriting is a form of behavior that can be analyzed for personality traits; that handwriting originates in the brain; that handwriting style, like personality, remains constant over a period of time while reflecting development; and that personality traits can be changed by making changes in one's handwriting. Annually, a week in January to include National Handwriting Day (John Hancock's birthday, Jan 23, 1737 [NS]). For info: American Handwriting Analysis Foundation (AHAF), PO Box 30, Santa Ynez, CA 93460. E-mail: ahafpresident@gmail.com. Web: www.ahafhandwriting.org.

NATIONAL NURSE ANESTHETISTS WEEK. Jan 19–25. Established to provide recognition for the nation's Certified Registered Nurse Anesthetists (CRNAs) and student registered nurse anesthetists. CRNAs administer approximately 32 million anesthetics to patients in the US each year and are the primary providers of anesthesia care in rural America. 13th annual week of recognition. For info: Amer Assn of Nurse Anesthetists, 222 S Prospect Ave, Park Ridge, IL 60068. Phone: (847) 692-7050. Fax: (847) 692-6968. E-mail: info@aana.com. Web: www.aana.com.

POE, EDGAR ALLAN: BIRTH ANNIVERSARY. Jan 19, 1809. American poet and story writer, called "America's most famous man of letters." Born at Boston, MA, he was orphaned in dire poverty in 1811 and was raised by Virginia merchant John Allan. In 1836 he married his 13-year-old cousin, Virginia Clemm. A magazine editor of note, he is best remembered for his poetry (especially "The Raven") and for his tales of suspense. Died at Baltimore, MD, Oct 7, 1849.

TIN CAN PATENT: ANNIVERSARY. Jan 19, 1825. Ezra Daggett and Thomas Kensett obtained a patent for a process for storing food in tin cans.

WAR CRIMES TRIBUNAL APPOINTED (JAPAN): ANNIVERSARY. Jan 19, 1946. An international tribunal for the trial of far-eastern war criminals was appointed by General Douglas MacArthur on Jan 19, 1946. The trial began at Tokyo on May 3, 1946, and ended more than two years later when the judgments were read, Nov 4–12, 1948. Of the 28 defendants, 25 were brought to trial. Seven were sentenced to death by hanging, 16 were sentenced to life imprisonment and 2 were given lesser prison terms. See also: "Tojo Hideki: Execution Anniversary" (Dec 23).

WATT, JAMES: BIRTH ANNIVERSARY. Jan 19, 1736. (Old Style date.) Mechanical engineer and inventor, born at Greenock, Scotland. Watt's tireless efforts to improve the steam engine resulted in a more efficient machine that powered the Industrial Revolution. He died at Heathfield, England, Aug 25, 1819.

WORLD RELIGION DAY. Jan 19. To proclaim the oneness of religion and the belief that world religion will unify the peoples of the earth. Baha'i-sponsored observance established in 1950 by the Baha'is of the US. Annually, the third Sunday in January. For info: Baha'is of the US, Office of Communications, 1233 Central St, Evanston, IL 60201. Phone: (847) 733-3559. Fax: (847) 733-3578. E-mail: ooc@usbnc.org. Web: www.bahai.us.

BIRTHDAYS TODAY

Desi Arnaz, Jr, 61, singer, actor, born Los Angeles, CA, Jan 19, 1953.

Frank Caliendo, 40, comedian ("MadTV," "FrankTV"), born Chicago, IL, Jan 19, 1974.

Michael Crawford, 72, actor, singer (*Phantom of the Opera*), born Salisbury, Wiltshire, England, Jan 19, 1942.

Drea de Matteo, 42, actress ("The Sopranos," "Joey"), born Queens, NY, Jan 19, 1972.

Paula Deen, 67, chef, cookbook author, born Albany, GA, Jan 19, 1947.

Phil Everly, 75, singer, with brother Don (The Everly Brothers), born Chicago, IL, Jan 19, 1939.

Shelley Fabares, 72, actress ("The Donna Reed Show," "Coach"), born Santa Monica, CA, Jan 19, 1942 (some sources say 1944).

Shawn Johnson, 22, Olympic gymnast, born West Des Moines, IA, Jan 19, 1992.

Richard Lester, 82, director (*The Four Musketeers, Superman II, Superman III*), born Philadelphia, PA, Jan 19, 1932.

Robert MacNeil, 83, broadcast journalist, born Montreal, QC, Canada, Jan 19, 1931.

Dolly Parton, 68, singer, actress (*Nine to Five*), born Sevier County, TN, Jan 19, 1946.

William Ragsdale, 53, actor ("Brother's Keeper," "Herman's Head"), born El Dorado, AR, Jan 19, 1961.

Simon Rattle, 59, orchestra conductor, born Liverpool, England, Jan 19, 1955.

Bitsie Tulloch, 33, actress ("Grimm," *The Artist*), born San Diego, CA, Jan 19, 1981.

Jeff Van Gundy, 52, basketball coach, born Inkster, MI, Jan 19, 1962.

Shawn Wayans, 43, actor (*Scary Movie*, "In Living Color"), born New York, NY, Jan 19, 1971.

Fritz Weaver, 88, actor (Tony Award for *Child's Play*; *Holocaust, Marathon Man*), born Philadelphia, PA, Jan 19, 1926.

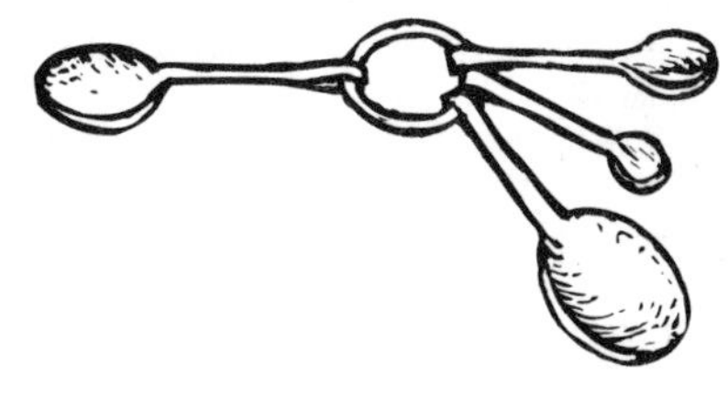

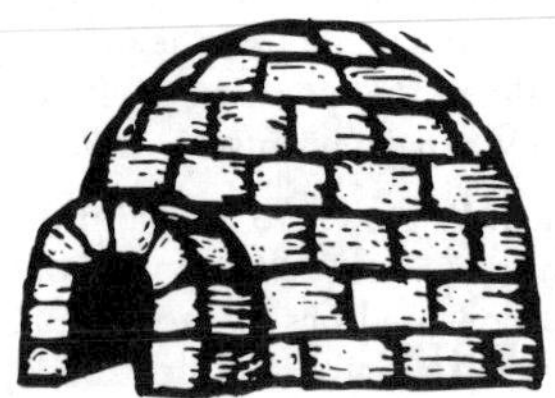

January 20 — Monday

DAY 20 **345 REMAINING**

ADAMSON, JOY: BIRTH ANNIVERSARY. Jan 20, 1910. A conservationist and author who championed the preservation of African wildlife, Adamson was born Friederike Victoria Gessner at Troppau, Silesia, Austria-Hungary or what is now the Czech Republic. In 1939 she moved to Kenya, where she met and married George Adamson, a British game warden. The couple raised Elsa, a lion cub, and eventually released her back into the wild, chronicling the events in a bestselling book, *Born Free* (1960), and two sequels. In 1961 Adamson founded the Elsa Conservation Trust, an international group that financed conservation and education projects. Both Joy and George Adamson met tragic ends: she was murdered by an employee Jan 3, 1980 (Shaba National Reserve, Kenya), and he was killed by animal poachers in 1989.

AQUARIUS, THE WATER CARRIER. Jan 20–Feb 19. In the astronomical/astrological zodiac, which divides the sun's apparent orbit into 12 segments, the period Jan 20–Feb 19 is traditionally identified as the sun sign of Aquarius, the Water Carrier. The ruling planet is Uranus or Saturn.

AUGUSTA FUTURITY. Jan 20–25. Augusta, GA. 35th annual. Brings together the top cutting horses and riders in the world to compete for purse and awards of more than $1 million. Est attendance: 50,000. For info: Augusta Futurity, PO Box 936, Augusta, GA 30903. Phone: (706) 823-3417. E-mail: augusta.futurity@augustafuturity.com. Web: www.augustafuturity.com.

AZERBAIJAN: MARTYRS' DAY. Jan 20. National holiday. Commemorates the Azeris killed by Soviet troops, Jan 20, 1990, as they fought for independence.

BRAZIL: NOSSO SENHOR DO BONFIM FESTIVAL. Jan 20–30. Salvador, Bahia. Our Lord of the Happy Ending Festival is one of Salvador's most colorful religious feasts. Climax comes with people carrying water to pour over church stairs and sidewalks to cleanse them of impurities.

BRAZIL: SAN SEBASTIAN'S DAY. Jan 20. Patron saint of Rio de Janeiro.

BURNS, GEORGE: BIRTH ANNIVERSARY. Jan 20, 1896. Comedian George Burns was born at New York City. He began in vaudeville without much success until he teamed up with Gracie Allen, who became his wife. As Burns and Allen, the two had a long career on radio, in film and with their hit TV show, "The George Burns and Gracie Allen Show." Later he played the roles of God and the Devil in the *Oh, God!* movies. He lived to be 100 and died Mar 9, 1996, at Los Angeles, CA.

FELLINI, FEDERICO: BIRTH ANNIVERSARY. Jan 20, 1920. Director and screenwriter Federico Fellini was born at Rimini, Italy. Four of Fellini's movies won Oscars for best foreign-language film: *La Strada* (1956), *The Nights of Cabiria* (1957), *8½* (1963) and *Amarcord* (1974). He received an honorary Oscar in 1993 in recognition of his cinematic accomplishments. Fellini died Oct 31, 1993, at Rome.

January 2014	S	M	T	W	T	F	S
				1	2	3	4
	5	6	7	8	9	10	11
	12	13	14	15	16	17	18
	19	20	21	22	23	24	25
	26	27	28	29	30	31	

GRAY, HAROLD LINCOLN: BIRTH ANNIVERSARY. Jan 20, 1894. The creator of "Little Orphan Annie" was born at Kankakee, IL. The comic strip featuring the 12-year-old Annie, her dog, Sandy, and her mentor and guardian, Oliver "Daddy" Warbucks, began appearing in the *Chicago Tribune* in 1924. While controversial for its strong conservative views, the strip was highly popular for its stories demonstrating the values of perseverance, independence and courage. Gray created the strip for 44 years until his death May 9, 1968, at La Jolla, CA, at age 74.

GUINEA-BISSAU: NATIONAL HEROES DAY. Jan 20. National holiday.

JOHN MARSHALL APPOINTED CHIEF JUSTICE: ANNIVERSARY. Jan 20, 1801. John Marshall was appointed the fourth chief justice of the US.

KING, MARTIN LUTHER, JR: BIRTHDAY OBSERVED. Jan 20. Public Law 98–144 designates the third Monday in January as an annual legal public holiday observing the birth of Martin Luther King, Jr. First observed in 1986. In New Hampshire, this day is designated Civil Rights Day. See also: "King, Martin Luther, Jr: Birth Anniversary" (Jan 15).

LEDBETTER, HUDDIE "LEAD BELLY": 125th BIRTH ANNIVERSARY. Jan 20, 1889. Born on a plantation in Mooringsport, LA, on Jan 20, 1889 (some sources say 1888), Huddie "Lead Belly" Ledbetter learned guitar while working as a farmer and sharecropper. He got his start in the music business as a collaborator with Blind Lemon Jefferson, playing his 12-string at juke joints and dances. In the 1930s, while serving time in Angola Prison, Lead Belly met folklorists and researchers John and Alan Lomax, who first recorded his most famous song, "Goodnight Irene," as well as early versions of the eventual standards "Rock Island Line" and "Midnight Special." Lead Belly worked off and on with the Lomaxes over the next several years and also cut sides for Capitol and the pioneering Folkways label. He died of ALS Dec 6 1949, at New York, NY.

LEE, RICHARD HENRY: BIRTH ANNIVERSARY. Jan 20, 1732. Signer of the Declaration of Independence. Born at Westmoreland County, VA, he died June 19, 1794, at his birthplace.

LESOTHO: ARMY DAY. Jan 20. Lesotho.

✦MARTIN LUTHER KING, JR, FEDERAL HOLIDAY. Jan 20. Presidential Proclamation has been issued without request each year for the third Monday in January since 1986.

STOCK EXCHANGE HOLIDAY (MARTIN LUTHER KING DAY). Jan 20. The holiday schedules for the various exchanges are subject to change if relevant rules, regulations or exchange policies are revised. For info: CME Group (CME, CBOT, NYMEX, KCBT) (www.cmegroup.com), Chicago Board Options Exchange (www.cboe.com), NASDAQ (www.nasdaq.com), NYSE Euronext (www.nyse.com).

SUGAR AWARENESS WEEK. Jan 20–24. 3rd annual. What effect does sugar have on your mind, body and emotions? During this week, take the five-day challenge of not eating sugar and see what you experience. You can record your results and see others' experiences at our website. Annually, the third work week in January. For info: Rebecca Cooper, Sugar Awareness, 23861 El Toro Rd #711, Lake Forest, CA 92630. Phone: (800) 711-6336. E-mail: rebecca@sugarawareness.com. Web: www.sugarawareness.com.

US HOSTAGES IN IRAN RELEASED: ANNIVERSARY. Jan 20, 1981. The Iran hostage crisis ended with the release of 52 US citizens after 444 days of captivity. The deal was announced minutes after the swearing in of President Ronald Reagan.

US REVOLUTIONARY WAR: CESSATION OF HOSTILITIES: ANNIVERSARY. Jan 20, 1783. The British and US commissioners signed a preliminary "Cessation of Hostilities," which was ratified by England's King George III Feb 14 and led to the treaties of Paris and Versailles, Sept 3, 1783, ending the war.

BIRTHDAYS TODAY

Edwin "Buzz" Aldrin, 84, former astronaut, one of first three men on moon, born Montclair, NJ, Jan 20, 1930.

Tom Baker, 80, actor ("Doctor Who," "Little Britain"), born Liverpool, England, Jan 20, 1934.

James Denton, 51, actor ("The Pretender," "Desperate Housewives"), born Nashville, TN, Jan 20, 1963.

Nikki Haley, 42, Governor of South Carolina (R), born Bamberg, SC, Jan 20, 1972.

Arte Johnson, 80, comedian, actor (Emmy for "Rowan & Martin's Laugh-In"), born Benton Harbor, MI, Jan 20, 1934 (some sources say 1929).

Lorenzo Lamas, 56, actor ("Falcon Crest," "Renegade"), born Los Angeles, CA, Jan 20, 1958.

David Lynch, 68, director ("Twin Peaks," *Blue Velvet*), writer, producer, born Missoula, MT, Jan 20, 1946.

Bill Maher, 58, comedian, television host ("Real Time with Bill Maher"), born New York, NY, Jan 20, 1956.

Geovany Soto, 31, baseball player, born San Juan, Puerto Rico, Jan 20, 1983.

Skeet Ulrich, 44, actor ("Jericho," *Scream*), born New York, NY, Jan 20, 1970 (some sources say 1969).

Rainn Wilson, 46, actor ("The Office," "Six Feet Under," *The Last Mimzy*), born Seattle, WA, Jan 20, 1968.

January 21 — Tuesday

DAY 21 **344 REMAINING**

ALLEN, ETHAN: BIRTH ANNIVERSARY. Jan 21, 1738. Revolutionary War hero and leader of the Vermont "Green Mountain Boys," born at Litchfield, CT. He is best remembered for his capture of British Fort Ticonderoga at Lake Champlain, NY, on May 10, 1775, which was the first major American victory of the Revolutionary War. He was captured by British forces on Sept 25, 1775, while attempting to capture Montreal and was a prisoner of war until 1778 when his release was secured in exchange for a British officer. Upon his return, Allen was an ardent supporter of Vermont's separation from New York for independent statehood, although this goal was not achieved until 1791, two years after his death at Burlington, VT, on Feb 12, 1789.

BALDWIN, ROGER NASH: BIRTH ANNIVERSARY. Jan 21, 1884. Founder of the American Civil Liberties Union, called the "country's unofficial agitator for, and defender of, its civil liberties." Born at Wellesley, MA, he died Aug 26, 1981, at Ridgewood, NJ.

BRECKINRIDGE, JOHN CABELL: BIRTH ANNIVERSARY. Jan 21, 1821. 14th vice president of the US (1857–61), serving under President James Buchanan. Born at Lexington, KY; died there May 17, 1875.

BROWNING, JOHN MOSES: BIRTH ANNIVERSARY. Jan 21, 1855. World-famous gun maker and inventor who was taught gunsmithing by his Mormon pioneer father, Jonathan Browning, was born at Ogden, UT. Starting the J.M. & M.S. Browning Arms Company with his brother, he designed guns for Winchester, Remington, Stevens and Colt arms companies, as well as American and European armies. Browning had more gun patents than any other gunsmith in the world. He is best known for inventing the machine gun in 1890 and the automatic pistol in 1896. He died suddenly Nov 26, 1926, at age 71, while at Belgium on business. The company he founded, known now as Browning Arms Company, is located at Morgan, UT.

DIOR, CHRISTIAN: BIRTH ANNIVERSARY. Jan 21, 1905. Influential French fashion designer who was the world's premier style maker after WWII up until the 1950s. He was also one of the first designers to utilize licensing to help create his own brand. Born at Granville, France, Dior died on Oct 24, 1957, at Montecatini, Italy.

FIRST CONCORDE FLIGHT: ANNIVERSARY. Jan 21, 1976. The supersonic Concorde airplane was put into service by Britain and France. The Concorde ended flights on Oct 24, 2003—bringing an end to supersonic air travel.

JACKSON, THOMAS JONATHAN "STONEWALL": BIRTH ANNIVERSARY. Jan 21, 1824. Confederate general and one of the most famous soldiers of the American Civil War, best known as "Stonewall" Jackson. Born at Clarksburg, VA (now WV). He died of wounds received in battle near Chancellorsville, VA, May 10, 1863.

KIWANIS INTERNATIONAL: ANNIVERSARY. Jan 21, 1915. First Kiwanis Club chartered at Detroit, MI.

MARGARET BRENT DEMANDS A POLITICAL VOICE: ANNIVERSARY. Jan 21, 1648. Margaret Brent made her claim as America's first feminist by demanding a voice and vote for herself in the Maryland colonial assembly. Brent came to America in 1638 and was the first woman to own property in Maryland. At the time of her demands she was serving as secretary to Governor Leonard Calvert. She was ejected from the meetings, but when Calvert died she became his executor and acting governor, presiding over the general assembly.

NATIONAL HUGGING DAY™. Jan 21. Because hugging is something everyone can do and because it is a healthful form of touching, this day should be spent hugging anyone who will accept a hug, especially family and friends. The most "Huggable People" of the year will be announced. Nominations accepted through Jan 10. For info, please send SASE to: Kevin C. Zaborney, 2023 Vickory Rd, Caro, MI 48723. Phone: (989) 673-6696. E-mail: kevin@nationalhuggingday.com. Web: www.nationalhuggingday.com.

RID THE WORLD OF FAD DIETS AND GIMMICKS DAY. Jan 21. The 25th annual Slim Chance Awards for the "worst" weight-loss products of the past year are presented: Worst Product, Worst Claim, Worst Gimmick and Most Outrageous Claim. Diet quackery runs the gamut from diets and supplements that contain dangerous, untested and potent drugs to the merely ridiculous. List of past/current awards, diet quackery information and consumer handouts available on website. For info: William London, Professor, Public Health Dept, California State University, 320 Simpson Tower, 5151 State University Dr, Los Angeles, CA 90032. Phone: (323) 343-5867. E-mail: wlondon@calstatela.edu. Web: www.healthyweight.net/fraud.htm.

SIOUX EMPIRE FARM SHOW. Jan 21–25. Sioux Falls, SD. Winter farm and livestock show featuring all classes of livestock and commercial exhibits. Est attendance: 30,000. For info: Sioux Empire Farm Show, Sioux Falls Area Chamber of Commerce, 200 N Phillips Ave, #102, Sioux Falls, SD 57104. Phone: (605) 373-2016. Fax: (605) 336-6499. E-mail: cchristensen@siouxfalls.com. Web: www.siouxempirefarmshow.org.

STONEWALL JACKSON'S BIRTHDAY CELEBRATION. Jan 21. Stonewall Jackson House, Lexington, VA. Celebrates the birthday of Stonewall Jackson. Annually, on Jan 21. For info: Stonewall Jackson House, 8 E Washington St, Lexington, VA 24450. Phone: (540) 464-7704. E-mail: lynnma@vmi.edu. Web: www.stonewalljackson.org.

WOLFMAN JACK: BIRTH ANNIVERSARY. Jan 21, 1938. Wolfman Jack was born Robert Smith at Brooklyn, NY. He became famous as a disc jockey for radio stations at Mexico in the 1960s. Wolfman Jack was influential as a border radio voice because the Mexican station broadcast at 250,000 watts, five times the legal limit for American stations at the time, and therefore he was heard over a vast part of the US. During his night shift he played blues, hillbilly and other black and white music that wasn't getting a lot of exposure. He later appeared on American radio, in movies and on television as an icon of 1960s radio. Wolfman Jack died July 1, 1995, at Belvidere, NC.

BIRTHDAYS TODAY

Robby Benson, 58, actor ("Search for Tomorrow," *Ode to Billie Joe*), born Robin Segal at Dallas, TX, Jan 21, 1956.

Geena Davis, 57, actress ("Commander in Chief," *Thelma and Louise*, Oscar for *The Accidental Tourist*), born Ware, MA, Jan 21, 1957.

Mac Davis, 72, actor, songwriter ("The Mac Davis Show," *North Dallas Forty*), born Lubbock, TX, Jan 21, 1942.

Plácido Domingo, 73, opera singer, one of the "Three Tenors," born Madrid, Spain, Jan 21, 1941.

Jill Eikenberry, 67, actress ("LA Law"), born New Haven, CT, Jan 21, 1947.

Eric H. Holder, Jr, 63, US Attorney General, born the Bronx, NY, Jan 21, 1951.

Jack William Nicklaus, 74, golfer, born Columbus, OH, Jan 21, 1940.

Billy Ocean, 64, musician, songwriter, born Leslie Charles at Trinidad, West Indies, Jan 21, 1950.

Hakeem Abdul Olajuwon, 51, Hall of Fame basketball player, born Lagos, Nigeria, Jan 21, 1963.

January 22 — Wednesday

DAY 22 **343 REMAINING**

ALLIED LANDING AT ANZIO: 70th ANNIVERSARY. Jan 22, 1944. A predominately American Allied force of 36,000 men was landed at Anzio on Italy's western coast. Commanding officer John P. Lucas failed to take the initiative but instead fortified his original position and thus possibly missed an early opportunity to retake Rome. The Allies entered Rome on June 4, 1944.

ALLIES TAKE NEW GUINEA: ANNIVERSARY. Jan 22, 1943. In the first land victory over the Japanese in WWII, American and Australian soldiers overcame the last pockets of resistance west and south of Sanananda on New Guinea. Three thousand Allies were killed in the battle. The Japanese lost 7,000. Of the 350 prisoners taken, most were Chinese and Korean laborers attached to the Japanese forces. Almost no Japanese allowed themselves to be taken prisoner, preferring to commit hara-kiri.

AMPÈRE, ANDRÉ: BIRTH ANNIVERSARY. Jan 22, 1775. Physicist, student of electrical and magnetic phenomena, founder of the science of electrodynamics. Born at Lyons, France. From his early childhood, tragedy and depression pursued him. His father was executed during the French Revolution. Ampère died at Marseilles, France, June 10, 1836. The epitaph he selected for his tombstone was *tandem felix* ("happy at last"). The ampere, a unit of electrical current, is named for him.

January 2014	S	M	T	W	T	F	S
				1	2	3	4
	5	6	7	8	9	10	11
	12	13	14	15	16	17	18
	19	20	21	22	23	24	25
	26	27	28	29	30	31	

ANSWER YOUR CAT'S QUESTION DAY. Jan 22. If you will stop what you are doing and take a look at your cat, you will observe that the cat is looking at you with a serious question. Meditate upon the question, and then answer it! Annually, Jan 22. (©2006 by WH.) For info: Thomas & Ruth Roy, Wellcat Holidays, 2418 Long Ln, Lebanon, PA 17046. Phone: (717) 279-0184. E-mail: info@wellcat.com. Web: www.wellcat.com.

BACON, FRANCIS: BIRTH ANNIVERSARY. Jan 22, 1561. (Old Style date.) The lawyer, statesman, philosopher and author was born at London, England. Bacon's fame rests on his philosophical works, including the *Advancement of Learning* (1605) and *Novum Organum* (1620). Bacon is considered the father of the scientific method, and he was a hero to scientists later in the century. Bacon died at London, Apr 9, 1626.

BALANCHINE, GEORGE: BIRTH ANNIVERSARY. Jan 22, 1904. Born Georgi Militonovitch Balanchivadze at St. Petersburg, Russia, George Balanchine became one of the leading influences in 20th-century ballet. He choreographed more than 200 ballets including *Concerto Barocco, Apollo, Orpheus, Firebird, Swan Lake, Waltz Academy* and *The Nutcracker*. In 1933 he was invited to the US by Boston philanthropist Lincoln Kirstein to establish a school for American dancers. Together they founded the School of American Ballet in 1934 and then formed several ballet companies, including the New York City Ballet, which was led by Balanchine. Died at New York, NY, Apr 30, 1983.

BYRON, GEORGE GORDON: BIRTH ANNIVERSARY. Jan 22, 1788. Born at London, England, flamboyant Romantic poet Lord Byron was one of the first literary celebrities in the modern sense. His works—*Childe Harold's Pilgrimage, The Corsair, Manfred*—often sold out within days of publication. Described as "Mad, bad and dangerous to know" by Lady Caroline Lamb, Byron died of fever at Missolonghi, Greece, Apr 19, 1824, while fighting for Greek independence.

CANADA: VANCOUVER INTERNATIONAL BOAT SHOW. Jan 22–26. BC Place Stadium and Granville Island Maritime Market and Marina, Vancouver, BC. Sail- and powerboats, sailboards, inflatables, canoes, personal watercraft, marine electronics and accessories, marine services, charters, sailing schools, water skis, sporting goods, travel and resort destinations, fishing equipment and Marine Facts Stage. Est attendance: 38,000. For info: BC Marine Trades Assn. Phone: (604) 678-8820. E-mail: info@bcmta.com. Web: www.vancouverboatshow.ca.

CELEBRATION OF LIFE DAY. Jan 22. A time to celebrate and emphasize the gift and culture of life without prejudice or partiality. A time to honor our children and grandchildren in America. Each child and each life is to be held as a precious gift and should be treated with the highest respect and dignity. For info: Judith Natale, Women of Freedom, USA, PO Box 493703, Redding, CA 96049-3703. E-mail: WomenofFreedom@aol.com.

"EMERGENCY!" TV PREMIERE: ANNIVERSARY. Jan 22, 1972. This NBC program was introduced in midseason up against "All in the Family." It surprised nearly everyone by becoming quite popular. The fast-paced action of the fire department paramedics saving lives by giving victims emergency treatment and then taking them to the hospital demonstrated the steps taken during actual emergency situations. The last episode aired Sept 3, 1977.

GRIFFITH, DAVID (LLEWELYN) WARK: BIRTH ANNIVERSARY. Jan 22, 1875. D.W. Griffith, pioneer producer-director in the American motion picture industry, best remembered for his film *Birth of a Nation* (1915). Born at LaGrange, KY. Died at Hollywood, CA, July 23, 1948.

HOWARD, ROBERT E.: BIRTH ANNIVERSARY. Jan 22, 1906. Born at Peaster, TX, Howard was to become one of the great and prolific pulp fiction writers of the 1920s and 1930s. He is most famous for creating Conan the Barbarian. Committed suicide at Cross Plains, TX, Jan 11, 1936.

"LAUGH-IN" TV PREMIERE: ANNIVERSARY. Jan 22, 1968. Actually the name of this NBC comedy was "Rowan & Martin's Laugh-In." Funny men Dan Rowan and Dick Martin hosted the show, but they seemed staid next to the show's other regulars, most of whom were young unknowns, including Dennis Allen, Chelsea Brown, Judy Carne, Ruth Buzzi, Ann Elder, Richard Dawson, Teresa Graves, Arte Johnson, Goldie Hawn, Alan Sues, Jo Anne Worley and Lily Tomlin. The show moved fast from gag to gag, with heads popping out of bushes or doors in the big wall. The show brought a new energy to comedy as well as new phrases to our vocabulary ("You bet your sweet bippy," "Sock it to me"). The last telecast was May 14, 1973.

PONSELLE, ROSA: BIRTH ANNIVERSARY. Jan 22, 1897. Formerly Rosa Melba Ponzilla, soprano Ponselle was born at Meriden, CT. Her career changed direction from vaudeville to opera when she was discovered by Enrico Caruso at the age of 21. Ponselle made her operatic debut at the Met in Verdi's *La forza del destino*. Her career spanned 19 seasons at the Met and included performances at London and Florence. Ponselle died May 25, 1981, at Baltimore, MD.

QUEEN VICTORIA: DEATH ANNIVERSARY. Jan 22, 1901. Queen Victoria died at age 82 after a reign of 64 years, the longest in British history. She had ruled over the one-quarter of the world that was the British Empire. Born May 24, 1819, at London, she died at Osborne, England.

***ROE v WADE* DECISION: ANNIVERSARY.** Jan 22, 1973. In the case of *Roe v Wade*, the US Supreme Court struck down state laws restricting abortions during the first six months of pregnancy. In the following decades debate has continued to rage between those who believe a woman has a right to choose whether to continue a pregnancy and those who believe that aborting such a pregnancy is murder of an unborn child.

SAINT VINCENT: FEAST DAY. Jan 22. Spanish deacon and martyr who died AD 304. Patron saint of wine growers. Old weather lore says if there is sun on this day, good wine crops may be expected in the ensuing season.

STRINDBERG, AUGUST: BIRTH ANNIVERSARY. Jan 22, 1849. Swedish novelist and dramatist often called Sweden's greatest playwright. Born at Stockholm and died there of cancer on May 14, 1912, at age 63.

UKRAINE: UKRAINIAN DAY. Jan 22. National holiday. Commemorates the proclamation of the Ukrainian National Republic, Jan 22, 1918. Independence was short lived, however; by 1921 Ukraine had become part of the Soviet Union. It gained its independence from the Soviet Union in 1991.

UPJOHN, RICHARD: BIRTH ANNIVERSARY. Jan 22, 1802. American architect and founder of the American Institute of Architects in 1857. A Gothic revivalist, he designed many churches. Among his works were Trinity Chapel, New York, NY; Corn Exchange Bank Building, New York, NY; and Central Congregational Church, Boston, MA. Born at Shaftesbury, England, he died Aug 17, 1878, at Garrison, NY.

VINSON, FRED M.: BIRTH ANNIVERSARY. Jan 22, 1890. The 13th chief justice of the US, born at Louisa, KY. Served in the House of Representatives, appointed director of war mobilization during WWII and secretary of the Treasury under Harry Truman. Nominated by Truman to succeed Harlan F. Stone as chief justice of the US. Died at Washington, DC, Sept 8, 1953.

ZEHNDER'S SNOWFEST (WITH ICE AND SNOW CARVING COMPETITIONS). Jan 22–27. Frankenmuth, MI. Annual festival includes ice carving demonstrations; World Class, State and High School snow sculpting competitions; fireworks; entertainment and food; and many children's activities such as a petting zoo, pony rides, ice miniature golf and more. Est attendance: 130,000. For info: Linda Kelly, Zehnder's of Frankenmuth, 730 S Main St, Frankenmuth, MI 48734. Phone: (800) 863-7999. Fax: (989) 652-3544. Web: www.zehnders.com.

BIRTHDAYS TODAY

Linda Blair, 55, actress (*The Exorcist, Airport*), born Westport, CT, Jan 22, 1959.

Seymour Cassel, 77, actor (*Faces, Dick Tracy, Honeymoon in Vegas*), born Detroit, MI, Jan 22, 1937.

Olivia D'Abo, 47, actress ("The Wonder Years," "The Single Guy"), born London, England, Jan 22, 1967.

Guy Fieri, 46, television personality ("Diners, Drive-Ins and Dives"), restaurant executive, born Columbus, OH, Jan 22, 1968.

Balthazar Getty, 39, actor ("Brothers & Sisters," "Alias," *Lost Highway*), born Los Angeles, CA, Jan 22, 1975.

John Hurt, 74, actor ("And the Band Played On," *The Elephant Man*), born Lincolnshire, England, Jan 22, 1940.

Diane Lane, 49, actress (*Unfaithful, A Walk on the Moon, A Little Romance*), born New York, NY, Jan 22, 1965.

Piper Laurie, 82, actress (*Fighting for My Daughter*, "Twin Peaks"), born Rosetta Jacobs at Detroit, MI, Jan 22, 1932.

Gabriel Macht, 42, actor (*The Spirit*, "Suits"), born New York, NY, Jan 22, 1972.

Christopher Masterson, 34, actor ("Malcolm in the Middle"), born Long Island, NY, Jan 22, 1980.

Greg Oden, 26, basketball player, born Buffalo, NY, Jan 22, 1988.

Steve Perry, 65, singer (Journey), born Hanford, CA, Jan 22, 1949.

Joseph Wambaugh, 77, former police officer, author (*The Onion Field, The Choir Boys*), born East Pittsburgh, PA, Jan 22, 1937.

January 23 — Thursday

DAY 23 **342 REMAINING**

"BARNEY MILLER" TV PREMIERE: ANNIVERSARY. Jan 23, 1975. This ABC sitcom about a New York precinct captain starred Hal Linden as Captain Barney Miller. The 12th Precinct gang included Barbara Barrie as Miller's wife, Abe Vigoda as Detective Phil Fish, Max Gail as Sergeant Stan Wojciehowicz, Gregory Sierra as Sergeant Chano Amenguale, Jack Soo as Sergeant Nick Yemana, Ron Glass as Detective Ron Harris and a host of others. The last episode aired in 1982.

BLACKWELL, ELIZABETH, AWARDED MD: ANNIVERSARY. Jan 23, 1849. Dr. Elizabeth Blackwell became the first woman to receive an MD degree. The native of Bristol, England, was awarded her degree by the Medical Institution of Geneva, NY.

BULGARIA: BABIN DEN. Jan 23. Celebrated throughout Bulgaria as Day of the Midwives or Grandmother's Day. Traditional festivities.

HANCOCK, JOHN: BIRTH ANNIVERSARY. Jan 23, 1737. American patriot and statesman, first signer of the Declaration of Independence. Hancock served as president of the Continental Congress (1775–77) and served as Massachusetts governor for nine terms beginning in 1780. Because of his conspicuous signature on the Declaration, Hancock's name has become part of the American language, referring to any handwritten signature. Born at Braintree, MA, he died at Quincy, MA, Oct 8, 1793. (Some sources cite Hancock's Old Style birth date of Jan 12, 1736/7.)

HEWES, JOSEPH: BIRTH ANNIVERSARY. Jan 23, 1730. Signer of the Declaration of Independence. Born at Princeton, NJ, he died Nov 10, 1779, at Philadelphia, PA.

KOVACS, ERNIE: 95th BIRTH ANNIVERSARY. Jan 23, 1919. Comedian and television pioneer, born at Trenton, NJ. Throughout the '40s and '50s Ernie Kovacs made a name for himself hosting his own shows, including "The Ernie Kovacs Show" and "Ernie In Kovacsland" and a variety of quiz shows. He died in an automobile accident at Los Angeles, CA, Jan 13, 1962.

MANET, ÉDOUARD: BIRTH ANNIVERSARY. Jan 23, 1832. Painter, born at Paris, France. Among his best-known paintings are *Olympia* and *Déjeuner sur l'herbe*. Manet died Apr 30, 1883, at Paris.

NATIONAL HANDWRITING DAY. Jan 23. Popularly observed on birthday of John Hancock to encourage more legible handwriting. (Some sources cite Hancock's Old Style birth date of Jan 12, 1736/7.)

NATIONAL PIE DAY. Jan 23. First observed in 1975 as a day to set aside and celebrate pie! Today is a day to maintain America's pie heritage, pass on the tradition of pie making and promote America's love affair with pie. Annually, Jan 23. For info: American Pie Council, PO Box 368, Lake Forest, IL 60045. Phone: (847) 371-0170. E-mail: piecouncil@aol.com. Web: www.piecouncil.org.

SAINT PAUL WINTER CARNIVAL. Jan 23–Feb 2. St. Paul, MN. One of Minnesota's largest tourist attractions and the nation's oldest and largest winter festival (first celebrated in 1886). The St. Paul Winter Carnival provides the "Coolest Celebration on Earth" with many indoor and outdoor events celebrating the thrills and chills of wintertime fun. Est attendance: 350,000. For info: St. Paul Festival and Heritage Foundation, 429 Landmark Ctr, 75 W 5th St, St. Paul, MN 55102. Phone: (651) 223-4700. Fax: (651) 223-4707. E-mail: info@winter-carnival.com. Web: www.winter-carnival.com.

SNOWPLOW MAILBOX HOCKEY DAY. Jan 23. It's wintertime and time for snowplow drivers everywhere to see how many rural mailboxes they can knock over. Twenty extra points for boosting one into the next township! (©2006 by WH.) For info: Thomas & Ruth Roy, Wellcat Holidays, 2418 Long Ln, Lebanon, PA 17046. Phone: (717) 279-0184. E-mail: info@wellcat.com. Web: www.wellcat.com.

STENDHAL: BIRTH ANNIVERSARY. Jan 23, 1783. French author Marie-Henri Beyle, whose best-known pseudonym was Stendhal. Best remembered are his novels *The Red and the Black* (1831) and *The Charterhouse of Parma* (1839). Born at Grenoble, France, he died at Paris, Mar 23, 1842.

STEWART, POTTER: BIRTH ANNIVERSARY. Jan 23, 1915. Associate justice of the Supreme Court of the US, nominated by President Eisenhower Jan 17, 1959. (Oath of office, May 15, 1959.) Born at Jackson, MI, he retired in July 1981 and died Dec 7, 1985, at Putney, VT, five days after suffering a stroke. Buried at Arlington National Cemetery.

TWENTIETH AMENDMENT TO US CONSTITUTION RATIFIED: ANNIVERSARY. Jan 23, 1933. The 20th Amendment was ratified, fixing the date of the presidential inauguration at the current Jan 20 instead of the previous Mar 4. It also specified that were the president-elect to die before taking office, the vice president–elect would succeed to the presidency. In addition, it set Jan 3 as the official opening date of Congress each year.

TWENTY-FOURTH AMENDMENT TO US CONSTITUTION RATIFIED: 50th ANNIVERSARY. Jan 23, 1964. Poll taxes and other taxes were eliminated as a prerequisite for voting in all federal elections by the 24th Amendment.

USS *PUEBLO* SEIZED BY NORTH KOREA: ANNIVERSARY. Jan 23, 1968. North Korea seized the USS *Pueblo* in the Sea of Japan, claiming the ship was on a spy mission. The crew was held for 11 months. The vessel was confiscated. Accompanying the crew when released—on Dec 22, 1968—was the body of Seaman Duane D. Hodges, the only crewman killed.

WASHINGTON'S BIRTHDAY CELEBRATION™. Jan 23–Feb 24. Laredo, TX. Founded in 1898, Laredo's Washington's Birthday Celebration is the largest celebration of its kind in the US. This monthlong festival includes Jamboozie music street festival, Society of Martha Washington Colonial Pageant and Ball, International Bridge Ceremony, Noche Mexicana, Comedy Jam for George, Washington's Birthday Parade, Jalapeño Festival, Stars & Stripes Air Show, a carnival, fireworks, live concerts and many other fun family events. Est attendance: 400,000. For info: Washington's Birthday Celebration Assn, 1819 E Hillside Rd, Laredo, TX 78041. Phone: (956) 722-0589. Fax: (956) 722-5528. E-mail: wbca@wbcalaredo.org. Web: www.wbcalaredo.org.

WOMEN'S HEALTHY WEIGHT DAY. Jan 23. A day to honor American women of all sizes and confirm that beauty, talent and love cannot be weighed. Winners of the Women's Healthy Weight Awards will be announced—businesses that portray size diversity and reject the national obsession with thinness that is shattering the lives of women, young girls and their families. News releases, awards and consumer handouts available on website. For info: Marsha Hudnall, Green Mountain at Fox Run, 262 Fox Ln, Ludlow, VT 05149. E-mail: marsha@fitwoman.com. Web: www.healthyweight.net/hww.htm.

BIRTHDAYS TODAY

Richard Dean Anderson, 64, actor ("Stargate SG-1," "MacGyver"), born Minneapolis, MN, Jan 23, 1950.

Princess Caroline, 57, born Monte Carlo, Monaco, Jan 23, 1957.

Tom Carper, 67, US Senator (D, Delaware), born Beckley, WV, Jan 23, 1947.

Gil Gerard, 71, actor ("Buck Rogers," "Sidekicks"), born Little Rock, AR, Jan 23, 1943.

Patrick Capper (Pat) Haden, 61, college football executive, former player, born Westbury, NY, Jan 23, 1953.

Mariska Hargitay, 50, actress ("Law & Order: SVU"), born Los Angeles, CA, Jan 23, 1964.

Rutger Hauer, 70, actor (*Blade Runner*), born Breukelen, Netherlands, Jan 23, 1944.

Jeanne Moreau, 86, actress (*Jules and Jim, Viva Maria*), born Paris, France, Jan 23, 1928.

Gail O'Grady, 51, actress ("NYPD Blue"), born Detroit, MI, Jan 23, 1963.

Tito Ortiz, 39, mixed martial artist, born Santa Ana, CA, Jan 23, 1975.

Chita Rivera, 81, singer, actress (*The Kiss of the Spider Woman*), born Conchita del Rivero at Washington, DC, Jan 23, 1933.

Tiffani Thiessen, 40, actress ("Beverly Hills 90210," "Saved by the Bell"), born Long Beach, CA, Jan 23, 1974.

January 2014

S	M	T	W	T	F	S
			1	2	3	4
5	6	7	8	9	10	11
12	13	14	15	16	17	18
19	20	21	22	23	24	25
26	27	28	29	30	31	

January 24 — Friday

DAY 24 **341 REMAINING**

ACHELIS, ELISABETH: BIRTH ANNIVERSARY. Jan 24, 1880. Calendar reform advocate, author of *The World Calendar,* born at Brooklyn, NY. Her proposed calendar made every year the same, with equal quarters, each year beginning on Sunday, Jan 1, and each date falling on the same day of the week every year. Died at New York, NY, Feb 11, 1973.

BELLY LAUGH DAY. Jan 24. Belly Laugh Day is a day to celebrate the great gift of laughter. Smiling and laughing are permitted, encouraged and celebrated. How? Smile, throw your arms in the air and laugh out loud. Join the Belly Laugh Bounce Around the World, as people from Antarctica to Hawaii in kitchens, schools, hospitals, offices, plants and stores stop at 1:24 PM (local time) to bounce a smile and a laugh around the world. For info: Elaine Helle. E-mail: jan24@bellylaughday.com. Web: www.bellylaughday.com.

BELUSHI, JOHN: 65th BIRTH ANNIVERSARY. Jan 24, 1949. Actor, comedian ("Saturday Night Live," *Animal House, The Blues Brothers*), born at Chicago, IL. Died Mar 5, 1982, at Hollywood, CA.

BOLIVIA: ALASITIS FESTIVAL. Jan 24. La Paz. Annual celebration combining both Catholic and ancient Andean beliefs. The principal festivities focus on Ekeko, the god of abundance, to whom the Aymara Indians offer prayers and offerings. Although the festival is ancient, the current date was chosen to acknowledge the 1781 anniversary of a battle between Bolivians and the Spanish colonizers.

BRICKHOUSE, JACK: BIRTH ANNIVERSARY. Jan 24, 1916. Born John Beasley Brickhouse at Peoria, IL. A legend in Chicago broadcasting, Brickhouse was the play-by-play voice for the first baseball game televised by WGN, an exhibition game between the Cubs and the White Sox on Apr 16, 1948. He broadcast Cubs games for 40 years, Chicago Bears games for 24 years and some Chicago Bulls and White Sox games. In 1983 he received the Ford C. Frick Award. Died at Chicago, IL, Aug 6, 1998.

CALIFORNIA GOLD DISCOVERY: ANNIVERSARY. Jan 24, 1848. James W. Marshal, an employee of John Sutter, accidentally discovered gold while building a sawmill near Coloma, CA. Efforts to keep the discovery secret failed, and the gold rush of 1849 was under way.

EAGLES ET CETERA FESTIVAL. Jan 24–26. Bismarck, AR. See bald eagles in the wild and learn about and observe birds of prey. Est attendance: 500. For info: Park Naturalist, DeGray Lake Resort State Park, 2027 State Park Entrance Rd, Bismarck, AR 71929-8194. Phone: (800) 737-8355. Fax: (501) 865-5829. E-mail: degraylakeresort@arkansas.com. Web: www.degray.com.

FDR's "UNCONDITIONAL SURRENDER" STATEMENT: ANNIVERSARY. Jan 24, 1943. At the end of the Casablanca Conference, 1943, Franklin D. Roosevelt and Winston Churchill held a press conference. Roosevelt stated, "Peace can come to the world only by the total elimination of German and Japanese war power. That means the unconditional surrender of Germany, Italy and Japan." This position calling for "unconditional surrender" has subsequently been criticized by some as having prolonged the war.

FIRST CANNED BEER: ANNIVERSARY. Jan 24, 1935. Canned beer went on sale for the first time at Richmond, VA. The American Can Company and the Gottfried Krueger Brewing Company collaborated to package 2,000 cans of Krueger's Finest Beer and Krueger's Cream Ale. It was an immediate success, and by the end of 1935, most major breweries had begun using cans. More than 200 million cans sold that first year.

GOODSON, MARK: BIRTH ANNIVERSARY. Jan 24, 1915. Producer and creator of TV game shows, Mark Goodson was born at Sacramento, CA. His career in entertainment began in radio, where he created his first game show, "Pop the Question." He later teamed with Bill Todman, and that partnership led to "I've Got a Secret," "Password," "The Price Is Right," "What's My Line?" and "Family Feud." He died Dec 18, 1992, at New York, NY.

HEINKEL, ERNST: BIRTH ANNIVERSARY. Jan 24, 1888. Aeronautical engineer, born in Grunbach, Germany. Founder of Heinkel-Flugzeugwerke, which built the military aircraft that powered Germany's early success in WWII. Heinkel built the first jet airplane, the He-178, in 1939. Heinkel died in Stuttgart, West Germany, on Jan 30, 1958.

MOON PHASE: LAST QUARTER. Jan 24. Moon enters Last Quarter phase at 12:20 AM, EST.

NATIONAL COMPLIMENT DAY. Jan 24. This day is set aside to compliment at least five people. Not only are compliments appreciated by the receiver, they lift the spirit of the giver. Compliments provide a quick and easy way to connect positively with those you come in contact with. Giving compliments forges bonds, dispels loneliness and just plain feels good. (Originated by Debby Hoffman and Kathy Chamberlin.)

OREGON TRUFFLE FESTIVAL. Jan 24–26. Eugene, OR. 9th annual. This international event—the first of its kind in the English-speaking world—joins truffle fanciers and truffle experts from all over the world (including Italy, France, New Zealand and Canada) in three days of gourmet celebration, educational seminars, hands (and tongues)-on truffle experiences and technical research seminars. Events include truffle dog demonstrations and in-the-field truffle hunt, cooking demonstrations by James Beard Award–nominated Northwest chefs, truffle farmers market and the spectacular Grand Truffle Dinner prepared by celebrated regional chefs. Est attendance: 500. For info: Oregon Truffle Festival, PO Box 5275, Eugene, OR 97405-0275. Phone: (503) 296-5929. E-mail: info@oregontrufflefestival.com. Web: www.oregontrufflefestival.com.

ROBERTS, ORAL: BIRTH ANNIVERSARY. Jan 24, 1918. Colorful and controversial religious leader who, through the healing ministry and university he founded, attracted millions of followers worldwide. Roberts was among the first to use television to deliver Pentecostal, tent-revival faith healing to the masses. He also staged hundreds of healing "crusades" around the globe. Born Granville Oral Roberts near Ada, OK, to an impoverished preacher's family, he died Dec 15, 2009, at age 91 at Newport Beach, CA.

SPACE MILESTONE: *COSMOS 954* (USSR) FALLS. Jan 24, 1978. Nuclear-equipped reconnaissance satellite launched Sept 18, 1977, fell into Earth's atmosphere and burned over northern Canada. Some radioactive debris reached ground on Jan 24, 1978.

SUGARLOAF CRAFTS FESTIVAL. Jan 24–26. Dulles Expo Center, Chantilly, VA. This show, now in its 16th year, features more than 250 nationally recognized craft designers and fine artists displaying and selling their original creations. Includes craft demonstrations, live music, specialty foods, hourly gift certificate drawings and more. Est attendance: 15,000. For info: Sugarloaf Mountain Works, 19807 Executive Park Circle, Germantown, MD 20874. Phone: (800) 210-9900. Fax: (301) 253-9620. E-mail: sugarloafinfo@sugarloaffest.com. Web: www.sugarloafcrafts.com.

WHARTON, EDITH: BIRTH ANNIVERSARY. Jan 24, 1862. Born at New York, NY, author Edith Wharton in her stories and novels specialized in intense examinations of upper-class Manhattan society at the end of the 19th century. Major novels include *The House of Mirth* (1905) and *The Age of Innocence* (1920), which won a Pulitzer Prize. *Ethan Frome* (1911) departed from the upper-class society milieu to depict a grim New England love triangle and its tragic consequences. Wharton died at Pavillon Colombe, France, Aug 11, 1937.

BIRTHDAYS TODAY

Mischa Barton, 28, actress ("The O.C."), born London, England, Jan 24, 1986.

Neil Diamond, 73, singer, composer, born Coney Island, NY, Jan 24, 1941.

Shaun Donovan, 48, US Secretary of Housing and Urban Development, born New York, NY, Jan 24, 1966.

Ed Helms, 40, actor (*The Hangover*, "The Daily Show," "The Office"), writer, born Atlanta, GA, Jan 24, 1974.

Nastassja Kinski, 54, actress (*Tess, The Hotel New Hampshire*), born Berlin, Germany, Jan 24, 1960.

Matthew Lillard, 44, actor (*Scream, Scooby-Doo*), born Lansing, MI, Jan 24, 1970.

Aaron Neville, 73, singer, songwriter, born New Orleans, LA, Jan 24, 1941.

Michael Ontkean, 68, actor ("Twin Peaks," *Slap Shot*), born Vancouver, BC, Canada, Jan 24, 1946.

Mary Lou Retton, 46, Olympic gymnast, born Fairmont, WV, Jan 24, 1968.

Kristen Schaal, 36, actress ("Bob's Burgers"), comedienne, television personality ("The Daily Show"), born Longmont, CO, Jan 24, 1978.

Yakov Smirnoff, 63, comedian, born Odessa, USSR (now Ukraine), Jan 24, 1951.

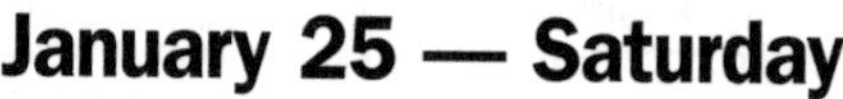

January 25 — Saturday

DAY 25 — **340 REMAINING**

AFRMA FANCY RAT AND MOUSE ANNUAL SHOW. Jan 25. Riverside, CA. Annual show where trophies are awarded to the winners. Rats and mice are emerging as ideal pets: they provide all the pleasure and satisfaction of a warm, cuddly, intelligent and friendly pet companion. The American Fancy Rat and Mouse Association (AFRMA) was founded in 1983 to promote the breeding and exhibition of fancy rats and mice, to educate the public on their positive qualities as companion animals and to provide information on their proper care. Est attendance: 100. For info: AFRMA (CAE), 9230 64th St, Riverside, CA 92509-5924. Phone: (951) 685-2350 or (818) 992-5564. E-mail: afrma@afrma.org. Web: www.afrma.org.

AMHERST RAILWAY SOCIETY RAILROAD HOBBY SHOW. Jan 25–26. West Springfield, MA. Now expanded to four buildings, nearly 8½ acres with dealers, displays, art, manufacturers, more than 40 operating layouts and railroads including Shortline, Tourist, Class 1 and more. Est attendance: 26,000. For info: Amherst Railway Society, PO Box 247, Monson, MA 01057-0247. Phone: (413) 267-4555. E-mail: showoffice@amherstrail.org. Web: www.amherstrail.org or www.railroadhobbyshow.com.

AROUND THE WORLD IN 72 DAYS: ANNIVERSARY. Jan 25, 1890. Newspaper reporter Nellie Bly (pen name used by Elizabeth Cochrane Seaman) set off from Hoboken, NJ, Nov 14, 1889, to attempt to break Jules Verne's imaginary hero Phileas Fogg's record of voyaging around the world in 80 days. She did beat Fogg's record, taking 72 days, 6 hours, 11 minutes and 14 seconds to make the trip, arriving back in New Jersey on Jan 25, 1890.

BOYLE, ROBERT: BIRTH ANNIVERSARY. Jan 25, 1627. Irish physicist, chemist and author who formulated Boyle's law in 1662. Born at Lismore, Ireland, he died at London, England, Dec 30, 1691.

January 2014	S	M	T	W	T	F	S
				1	2	3	4
	5	6	7	8	9	10	11
	12	13	14	15	16	17	18
	19	20	21	22	23	24	25
	26	27	28	29	30	31	

BROOKFIELD ICE HARVEST. Jan 25. Brookfield, VT. Demonstrations of ice harvesting using the original equipment near the Brookfield Floating Bridge, one of only two such bridges remaining in the US today. This 35th annual harvest will feature many special activities. Annually, the last Saturday in January. Est attendance: 1,000. For info: Al Wilder, PO Box 405, Brookfield, VT 05036. Phone/fax: (802) 276-3959.

BURNS, ROBERT: BIRTH ANNIVERSARY. Jan 25, 1759. Farmer, lover of women, father of at least 11 children, freemason, songwriter and beloved poet who wove the folk traditions and dialects of Scotland into lovely lyrics and ballads. Poems and songs include "Tam O'Shanter," "To a Mouse," "Green Grow the Rushes, O" and most of "Auld Lang Syne." "Oh wad some power the giftie gie us/ To see oursels as others see us!" Born at Ayrshire, Scotland, he died at Dumfries, Scotland, July 21, 1796. His birthday is widely celebrated as Burns Night, especially in Scotland, England and Newfoundland.

CHINESE NEW YEAR FESTIVAL AND PARADE. Jan 25–Feb 16. San Francisco, CA. North America's largest Chinese community salutes the Year of the Horse, Lunar Year 4712. Activities include Chinese New Year Flower Market Fair (Jan 25–26); Miss Chinatown USA Pageant (Feb 8) with Coronation Ball (Feb 14); Southwest Airlines Chinese New Year Parade (Feb 15); Chinese Community Street Fair (Feb 15–16). These events showcase the diversity of Chinese culture from Chinese opera and ballet, traditional dance and ancient dynastic costumes to martial arts. Booths feature cooking demonstrations, calligraphy and arts and crafts. Est attendance: 700,000. For info: Chinese New Year Parade Office, 317 W Portal Ave, #27428, San Francisco, CA 94127-1441. Phone: (415) 340-3055. Fax: (415) 340-3056. Web: www.chineseparade.com.

CURTIS, CHARLES: BIRTH ANNIVERSARY. Jan 25, 1860. The 31st vice president of the US (1929–33). Born at Topeka, KS, he died at Washington, DC, Feb 8, 1936.

EGYPTIAN REVOLUTION BEGINS: ANNIVERSARY. Jan 25, 2011. Encouraged by the Tunisian Revolution of December 2010 to January 2011, tens of thousands of protesters took to the streets of Cairo and other Egyptian cities to demand legal and social rights as well as regime change. The "Day of Revolt" on Jan 25 was the spark, catalyzing further protests—both on the streets and in cyberspace through social media—that eventually led to President Hosni Mubarak resigning on Feb 11, 2011, after 30 years in power. On June 30, 2012, Mohamed Morsi was sworn in as new Egyptian president after the first contested elections since before 1981.

FIRST SCHEDULED TRANSCONTINENTAL FLIGHT: 55th ANNIVERSARY. Jan 25, 1959. American Airlines opened the jet age in the US with the first scheduled transcontinental flight—on a Boeing 707 nonstop from California to New York.

FIRST TELEVISED PRESIDENTIAL NEWS CONFERENCE: ANNIVERSARY. Jan 25, 1961. Beginning a tradition that survives to this day, John F. Kennedy held the first televised presidential news conference five days after being inaugurated the 35th president.

FIRST WINTER OLYMPICS: 90th ANNIVERSARY. Jan 25, 1924. The first Winter Olympic Games opened at Chamonix, France, with athletes representing 16 nations. The ski jump, previously unknown, thrilled spectators. The Olympics offered a boost to skiing, which became enormously popular in the next decade.

HOGGETOWNE MEDIEVAL FAIRE. Jan 25–26 (also Jan 31–Feb 2). Alachua County Fairgrounds, Gainesville, FL. 28th annual. Fair features jousting, birds of prey, medieval arts and crafts, food and continuous entertainment on eight stages. Est attendance: 60,000. For info: Linda Piper, City of Gainesville, Dept of Cultural Affairs, PO Box 490 Station 30, Gainesville, FL 32627. Phone: (352) 393-8536. Fax: (352) 334-2249. E-mail: piperLr@cityofgainesville.org. Web: www.gvlculturalaffairs.org.

ICE FEST. Jan 25–26. Ligonier, PA. A weekend of ice-carving demonstrations as blocks of ice are turned into works of art. Est attendance: 5,000. For info: Ligonier Chamber of Commerce, 120 E Main St, Ligonier, PA 15658. Phone: (724) 238-4200. Fax: (724) 238-4610. E-mail: office@ligonierchamber.com.

JAMES, ETTA: BIRTH ANNIVERSARY. Jan 25, 1938. Dynamic singer, born Jamesetta Hawkins at Los Angeles, CA. A vocalist with tremendous power and grace, but with a reckless, raucous streak, too, Etta James was one of the greats of rhythm and blues music. Enduring hits like "At Last" (1961) harnessed her R&B influences to the stately drama of jazz, but James also led a life of itinerant hustle and struggled with addiction, abusive relationships and career missteps. She recorded with legendary labels like Chess, won four Grammys—including one for her 1994 tribute to Billie Holiday—and continued performing into the 21st century. A member of the Rock and Roll Hall of Fame and Blues Hall of Fame, Etta James died on Jan 20, 2012, at Riverside, CA.

KIDFILM® FESTIVAL. Jan 25–26. Angelika Film Center, Dallas, TX. 30th annual. Oldest and best-attended international children's film festival in the world. Fifty shorts and features shown with filmmakers in attendance. Each year, a major figure in media (for all ages) is honored. Est attendance: 24,000. For info: USA Film Festival, 6116 N Central Expressway, Ste 105, Dallas, TX 75206. Phone: (214) 821-6300 or (214) 821-FILM. Fax: (214) 821-6364. E-mail: USAFilmFest@aol.com. Web: www.usafilmfestival.com.

MACINTOSH DEBUTS: 30th ANNIVERSARY. Jan 25, 1984. Apple's Macintosh computer went on sale this day for $2,495. It wasn't until mid-1985, however, that sales began to take off and this computer began to replace the Apple II model.

MAUGHAM, W. SOMERSET: BIRTH ANNIVERSARY. Jan 25, 1874. English short story writer, novelist and playwright, born at Paris, France. Among his best-remembered books: *Of Human Bondage, Cakes and Ale* and *The Razor's Edge.* Died at Cap Ferrat, France, Dec 16, 1965.

MILLS, FLORENCE: BIRTH ANNIVERSARY. Jan 25, 1896. The leading black American singer and dancer of the Jazz Age and the Harlem Renaissance was born Florence Winfree at Washington, DC. She appeared in Langston Hughes's *Shuffle Along* in 1921 and *Plantation Review* on Broadway in 1922, and then at the London Pavilion in *Dover Street to Dixie* in 1923. Offered a spot in the *Ziegfeld Follies*, she turned it down and joined in creating a rival show with an all-black cast. Mills was the first black woman to appear as a headliner at the Palace Theatre. She was so revered for her efforts to create opportunities for black entertainers and to bring the unique culture of blacks to Broadway that more than 150,000 people filled the streets of Harlem to mourn her when she died at New York City, Nov 1, 1927, at age 31.

NATIONAL SEED SWAP DAY. Jan 25. Washington, DC. Bring your extra seeds and swap them with other gardeners. Everyone will leave with a bag full of seeds, new garden friends and expert planting advice. Seed swap categories include natives, edibles, herbs, exotics, annuals, perennials and woodies (trees/shrubs). Learn, network and prepare for next year's seed collecting! If you are outside of the DC area, celebrate seed swapping by setting up an event in your area. Annually, the last Saturday in January. For info: Kathy Jentz, Washington Gardener Magazine, 826 Philadelphia Ave, Silver Spring, MD 20910. Phone: (301) 588-6894. E-mail: wgardenermag@aol.com. Web: www.washingtongardener.com.

ORANGE CITY BLUE SPRING MANATEE FESTIVAL. Jan 25–26. Valentine Park, Orange City, FL. Now in its 29th year, this festival was created to raise awareness of the endangered West Indian manatee. It features more than 90 arts and crafts exhibitors, most of whom honor the manatee in a variety of mediums. Children's games, sand sculpting, family entertainment, animal and environmental exhibits and food vendors round out the event. For info: Orange City Blue Spring Manatee Festival, Inc, PO Box 740862, Orange City, FL 32774. Phone: (386) 775-9224. E-mail: info@themanateefestival.com. Web: www.themanateefestival.com.

"ROBOT" ENTERS WORLD LEXICON: ANNIVERSARY. Jan 25, 1921. On this date, the play *R.U.R.* premiered at the National Theater in Prague, Czechoslovakia. "R.U.R." stood for "Rossum's Universal Robots," and the play concerned artificial human workers who rebel against their human masters. Czech dramatist Karel Capek and his brother, Josef Capek, derived "robot" from the Czech noun *robota*, which means "labor" and "servitude." As the play became a hit worldwide (with an English translation published in 1923), the concept of the robot took hold. Capek's robots were chemically created; today's real and fictional robots are metallic machines.

ROLEX 24 AT DAYTONA. Jan 25–26. Daytona International Speedway, Daytona Beach, FL. 52nd annual running of the most prestigious endurance race in North America. For info: Daytona Intl Speedway, PO Box 2801, Daytona Beach, FL 32120-2801. Phone: (800) PIT-SHOP. Fax: (386) 681-6791. Web: www.daytonainternationalspeedway.com.

A ROOM OF ONE'S OWN DAY. Jan 25. For anyone who knows or longs for the sheer bliss and rightness of having a private place, no matter how humble, to call one's own. (©2006 by WH.) For info: Thomas & Ruth Roy, Wellcat Holidays, 2418 Long Ln, Lebanon, PA 17046. Phone: (717) 279-0184. E-mail: info@wellcat.com. Web: www.wellcat.com.

SAINT DWYNWEN'S DAY. Jan 25. Patron saint of friendship and love in Wales. Dwynwen was a fifth-century saint (died AD 460) who lived in seclusion at Llanddwyn Island. The church (the ruins of which still stand today) there was a medieval pilgrimage site and supposedly featured a magic well. Saint Dwynwen's Day is not officially recognized in the Catholic and Anglican liturgical calendars, but its celebration has become a popular custom in Wales for lovers.

SENIOR BOWL. Jan 25. Ladd-Peebles Stadium, Mobile, AL. 65th annual. All-star football game featuring the nation's top collegiate seniors on teams coached by National Football League coaching staffs. Est attendance: 40,700. For info: Senior Bowl, PO Box 1408, Mobile, AL 36633-1408. Phone: (251) 438-2276. Fax: (251) 432-0409. E-mail: srbowl@seniorbowl.com. Web: www.seniorbowl.com.

STERN, ITZHAK: BIRTH ANNIVERSARY. Jan 25, 1901. An accountant for industrialist Oskar Schindler, Stern advised Schindler to take advantage of the availability of forced labor from the Nazi concentration camps. In collaboration with Schindler and Mietek Pemper, an inmate and assistant to the commandant of Plaszow forced labor camp in Poland, Stern helped to compile lists of Jews who would otherwise be sent to their deaths and to create work histories that would justify their being transferred to Schindler's Krakow plant. In the movie *Schindler's List* the character Itzhak Stern is a composite of Stern and Pemper. Stern, born at Poland, emigrated to Israel after WWII. He died there in 1969. See also: "Pemper, Mietek: Birth Anniversary" (Mar 24).

VISIT YOUR LOCAL QUILT SHOP DAY. Jan 25. An annual celebration for independently owned quilt shops everywhere! Today, retailers and fabric lovers connect in quilt shops with special events and celebrations. For info: Laurie Harsh, Visit Your Local Quilt Shop Day, PO Box 820128, Vancouver, WA 98682. Phone: (360) 892-6500. Fax: (360) 892-6700. E-mail: info@quiltshopday.com. Web: www.quiltshopday.com.

WOOLF, VIRGINIA: BIRTH ANNIVERSARY. Jan 25, 1882. English writer, critic and novelist, author of *Jacob's Room* and *To the Lighthouse.* Born at London, England. After completing her last novel, *Between the Acts,* she collapsed under the strain and drowned herself in the River Ouse near Rodmell, England, on Mar 28, 1941.

BIRTHDAYS TODAY

Vince Carter, 37, basketball player, born Daytona Beach, FL, Jan 25, 1977.

Chris Chelios, 52, former hockey player, born Chicago, IL, Jan 25, 1962.

Dean Jones, 83, actor (*Tea and Sympathy, The Love Bug, Beethoven*), born Decatur, AL, Jan 25, 1931 (some sources say 1935).

Alicia Keys, 33, musician, singer, born Harlem, NY, Jan 25, 1981.

Dinah Manoff, 56, actress ("Soap," "Empty Nest," Tony for *I Ought to Be in Pictures*), born New York, NY, Jan 25, 1958.

Ana Ortiz, 43, actress ("Ugly Betty"), born New York, NY, Jan 25, 1971.

Leigh Taylor-Young, 69, actress ("Peyton Place," "Dallas," *I Love You, Alice B. Toklas*), born Washington, DC, Jan 25, 1945.

Xavi, 34, soccer player, born Xavi Hernández i Creus at Terrassa, Spain, Jan 25, 1980.

January 26 — Sunday

DAY 26 — **339 REMAINING**

AUSTRALIA: AUSTRALIA DAY—FIRST BRITISH SETTLEMENT: ANNIVERSARY. Jan 26, 1788. A shipload of convicts arrived briefly at Botany Bay (which proved to be unsuitable) and then at Port Jackson (later the site of the city of Sydney). Establishment of an Australian prison colony was to relieve crowding of British prisons. Australia Day, formerly known as Foundation Day or Anniversary Day, has been observed since about 1817 and has been a public holiday since 1838.

AUSTRALIA: AUSTRALIA DAY COCKROACH RACES. Jan 26. Brisbane, Queensland. "The greatest gathering of thoroughbred cockroaches in the known universe." Cockroach race enthusiasts celebrate Australia Day at the Story Bridge Hotel, where icky insects (Cocky Balboa, Lord of the Drains or other such) compete. Race includes steeplechase. Also: music, "Miss Cocky" pageant, "Best Dressed" contest and more. Proceeds benefit charity. For info: Story Bridge Hotel, 200 Main St, Kangaroo Point, Brisbane, Queensland 4169 Australia. Phone: (61) (7) 3391-2266. Fax: (61) (7) 3393-0926. Web: www.storybridgehotel.com.au.

CATHOLIC SCHOOLS WEEK. Jan 26–Feb 1. A national celebration focusing on the uniqueness of Catholic schools. Many schools plan special activities celebrating their Catholic heritage. Jointly sponsored by the National Catholic Educational Association and the US Conference of Catholic Bishops. Theme: "Catholic Schools: Communities of Faith, Knowledge and Service." Annually, beginning on the last Sunday in January. For info: Natl Catholic Educational Assn, 1005 N Glebe Rd, Ste 525, Arlington, VA 22201. Phone: (800) 711-6232. E-mail: nceaadmin@ncea.org. Web: www.ncea.org.

January 2014

S	M	T	W	T	F	S
			1	2	3	4
5	6	7	8	9	10	11
12	13	14	15	16	17	18
19	20	21	22	23	24	25
26	27	28	29	30	31	

COLEMAN, BESSIE: BIRTH ANNIVERSARY. Jan 26, 1893. Born at Atlanta, TX, Bessie Coleman would not take no for an answer, especially where it concerned her dreams of flying. Because of her race and gender, she was denied admission to aviation school programs in the US. She therefore worked as a manicurist, earning her way to Paris. There she received an international pilot's license from the Fédération Aéronautique Internationale in 1921. Upon return, "Queen Bess" took part in numerous acrobatic air exhibitions where her stunt flying and "figure eights" won her many admirers. She avidly encouraged others to follow in her footsteps. Coleman, however, perished in a plane crash during a practice session, at Jacksonville, FL, Apr 30, 1926.

DENTAL DRILL PATENT: ANNIVERSARY. Jan 26, 1875. George F. Green, of Kalamazoo, MI, patented the electric dental drill.

DOMINICAN REPUBLIC: NATIONAL HOLIDAY. Jan 26. An official public holiday celebrates the birth anniversary of Juan Pablo Duarte, one of the fathers of the republic.

"THE DUKES OF HAZZARD" TV PREMIERE: 35th ANNIVERSARY. Jan 26, 1979. This comedy/action show ran for seven seasons and featured car chases. Brothers Bo Duke (John Schneider) and Luke Duke (Tom Wopat) were the good guys, fighting crooked law enforcement in their rural Southern community. Other characters included Daisy Duke (Catherine Bach), Uncle Jesse Duke (Denver Pyle), Sheriff Roscoe P. Coltrane (James Best), Deputy Enos Strate (Sonny Shroyer) and Boss Hogg (Sorrell Booke).

FRANKLIN PREFERS TURKEY: ANNIVERSARY. Jan 26, 1784. In a letter to his daughter, Benjamin Franklin expressed his unhappiness over the choice of the eagle as the symbol of America. He preferred the turkey.

THE GRAMMY AWARDS. Jan 26. Staples Center, Los Angeles, CA. 56th annual. Celebrating the best in recording arts and sciences, the Grammys cover more than 100 categories—from classicalw to jazz to pop and rock. Awarded by and to artists and technical professionals. For info: National Academy of Recording Arts & Sciences, 3030 Olympic Blvd, Santa Monica, CA 90404. Phone: (310) 392-3777. Fax: (310) 392-2778. Web: www.grammy.com.

GRANT, JULIA DENT: BIRTH ANNIVERSARY. Jan 26, 1826. Wife of Ulysses Simpson Grant, 18th president of the US. Born at St. Louis, MO; died at Washington, DC, Dec 14, 1902.

INDIA: REPUBLIC DAY. Jan 26. National holiday. Anniversary of Proclamation of the Republic, Basant Panchmi. In 1929 the Indian National Congress resolved to work for establishment of a sovereign republic, a goal that was realized Jan 26, 1950, when India became a democratic republic and its constitution went into effect.

INDIAN EARTHQUAKE: ANNIVERSARY. Jan 26, 2001. An earthquake that struck the state of Gujarat in India left more than 15,000 dead. The quake was estimated to be 7.7 on the Richter scale. India's largest port at Kandla suffered severe damage.

MacARTHUR, DOUGLAS: BIRTH ANNIVERSARY. Jan 26, 1880. US general and supreme commander of Allied forces in Southwest Pacific during WWII. Born at Little Rock, AR, he served as commander of the Rainbow Division's 84th Infantry Brigade in WWI, leading it in the St. Mihiel, Meuse-Argonne and Sedan offensives. Remembered for his "I shall return" prediction when forced out of the Philippines by the Japanese during WWII, a promise he fulfilled. Relieved of Far Eastern command by President Harry Truman on Apr 11, 1951, during the Korean War. MacArthur died at Washington, DC, Apr 5, 1964.

MEAT WEEK. Jan 26–Feb 2. An observance that began in 2005 in the southern US but has spread to every corner of the nation. Meat Week begins the last Sunday in January and continues for eight days straight. Each night, participants dine on BBQ'd meat. Non-meat-eaters also join the celebration by enjoying sides. For info: Chris Cantey and Erni Walker. Phone: (818) 568-1270. E-mail: meat@meatweek.com. Web: www.meatweek.com.

MICHIGAN: ADMISSION DAY: ANNIVERSARY. Jan 26. Became 26th state in 1837.

NEWMAN, PAUL: BIRTH ANNIVERSARY. Jan 26, 1925. Blue-eyed actor, director, race car driver and philanthropist born at Cleveland, OH. Appeared in 65 films, including *Butch Cassidy and the Sundance Kid*, *The Sting*, *Hud* and *Cool Hand Luke*. Received a Best Actor Oscar for *The Color of Money* (1986). Newman was also a successful entrepreneur, establishing Newman's Own, a specialty foods company whose proceeds were donated to charity, in 1982. He died Sept 26, 2008, at Westport, CT.

***PHANTOM OF THE OPERA* BROADWAY PREMIERE: ANNIVERSARY.** Jan 26, 1988. This multiple-award-winning musical, based on the classic Gaston Leroux novel about the tortured soul haunting the Paris Opera House, premiered in London on Oct 9, 1986. Its music and lyrics are by Andrew Lloyd Webber and Charles Hart, with book by Lloyd Webber and Richard Stilgoe. It premiered on Broadway in 1988 and in January 2006 became the longest-running show in Broadway history. On Feb 11, 2012, it reached its 10,000th performance—an unprecedented feat.

ROCKY MOUNTAIN NATIONAL PARK ESTABLISHED: ANNIVERSARY. Jan 26, 1915. Under President Woodrow Wilson, the area covering more than 1,000 square miles in Colorado became a national park.

2014 PRO BOWL. Jan 26. Honolulu, HI. The best football players from the AFC and NFC battle it out. Annually, the Sunday before the Super Bowl. For info: National Football League, 280 Park Ave, New York, NY 10017. Web: www.nfl.com.

VAN HEUSEN, JIMMY: BIRTH ANNIVERSARY. Jan 26, 1913. Jimmy Van Heusen was born Edward Chester Babcock at Syracuse, NY. He was a composer of many popular songs with his lyricist partners Johnny Burke and Sammy Cahn. One of his 76 songs that Frank Sinatra recorded was "My Kind of Town." Van Heusen won four Academy Awards for songs in movies such as *Going My Way* (1944). He was inducted into the Songwriters Hall of Fame when it was founded in 1971. Van Heusen died Feb 7, 1990, at Rancho Mirage, CA.

 BIRTHDAYS TODAY

Anita Baker, 56, singer, born Toledo, OH, Jan 26, 1958.

Father George Harold Clements, 82, Roman Catholic priest, civil rights leader, born Chicago, IL, Jan 26, 1932.

Angela Davis, 70, political activist, born Birmingham, AL, Jan 26, 1944.

Mark Dayton, 67, Governor of Minnesota (D), former US senator, born Minneapolis, MN, Jan 26, 1947.

Ellen DeGeneres, 56, comedienne, actress ("Ellen"), television personality ("The Ellen DeGeneres Show," "American Idol"), born New Orleans, LA, Jan 26, 1958.

Jules Feiffer, 85, cartoonist, writer, born New York, NY, Jan 26, 1929.

Scott Glenn, 72, actor (*The Right Stuff, Silverado*), born Pittsburgh, PA, Jan 26, 1942.

Wayne Gretzky, 53, Hall of Fame hockey player, born Brantford, ON, Canada, Jan 26, 1961.

José Mourinho, 51, soccer manager, born José Mário dos Santos Mourinho Félix at Setúbal, Portugal, Jan 26, 1963.

Andrew Ridgeley, 51, singer, musician (Wham!), born Bushey, England, Jan 26, 1963.

David Strathairn, 64, actor (*Good Night, and Good Luck*; *LA Confidential*), born San Francisco, CA, Jan 26, 1950.

Robert George (Bob) Uecker, 79, sportscaster, former baseball player, actor ("Mr Belvedere"), born Milwaukee, WI, Jan 26, 1935.

Eddie Van Halen, 59, guitarist, born Nijmegen, Netherlands, Jan 26, 1955.

January 27 — Monday

DAY 27 **338 REMAINING**

***APOLLO I*: SPACECRAFT FIRE: ANNIVERSARY.** Jan 27, 1967. Three American astronauts, Virgil I. Grissom, Edward H. White and Roger B. Chaffee, died when fire suddenly broke out at 6:31 PM, EST, in *Apollo I* during a launching simulation test, as it stood on the ground at Cape Kennedy, FL. First launching in the Apollo program had been scheduled for Feb 27, 1967.

ARIZONA MUSICFEST. Jan 27–Mar 6. Carefree/Cave Creek, North Scottsdale, North Phoenix Valley, AZ. Every February, "America's Premier Winter Music Festival" presents top artists of classical, Broadway, jazz and pop in exceptional programs (created especially for Arizona Musicfest) at venues throughout the scenic desert foothills of North Scottsdale and Carefree, Arizona. The Arizona Musicfest Orchestra conducted by Artistic Director Robert Moody is at the heart of the festival. Sixty musicians hand-chosen by Maestro Moody from the nation's finest orchestras perform in a week of sensational concerts. Est attendance: 8,000. For info: Arizona Musicfest, PO Box 5254, Carefree, AZ 85377. Phone: (480) 488-0806. Fax: (480) 488-1401. E-mail: info@azmusicfest.org. Web: www.azmusicfest.org.

AUSCHWITZ LIBERATED: ANNIVERSARY. Jan 27, 1945. The Soviet army liberated about 6,000 prisoners of the Nazi concentration camp Auschwitz. It is estimated that 1.5 million inmates were killed at Auschwitz between 1941 and liberation—95 percent of them were Jewish.

BUBBLE WRAP® APPRECIATION DAY. Jan 27. A day to celebrate the joy that Bubble Wrap® brings to our lives. A day to learn the history and snapping etiquette and to gain a new appreciation of the country's favorite shipping material (invented in 1960). Also, a day to snap and share Bubble Wrap® with coworkers, classmates and loved ones. Annually, the last Monday in January. For info: Sealed Air Corp, 200 Riverfront Blvd, Elmwood Park, NJ 07407. Web: www.sealedair.com. Also for info: High Octane, Spirit 95 Radio WVNI. Phone: (812) 335-9500. Fax: (812) 335-8880. E-mail: spirit95@spirit95fm.com.

DODGSON, CHARLES LUTWIDGE (LEWIS CARROLL): BIRTH ANNIVERSARY. Jan 27, 1832. English mathematician and author, better known by his pseudonym, Lewis Carroll, creator of *Alice's Adventures in Wonderland*, was born at Cheshire, England. *Alice* was written for Alice Liddell, daughter of a friend, and first published in 1865. *Through the Looking-Glass*, an 1871 sequel, and *The Hunting of the Snark* (1876) followed. Dodgson's books for children proved equally enjoyable to adults, and they overshadowed his serious works on mathematics. Dodgson died at Guildford, Surrey, England, Jan 14, 1898.

GERMANY: DAY OF REMEMBRANCE FOR VICTIMS OF NAZISM. Jan 27. Since 1996 commemorated on this day, the date in 1945 that Soviet soldiers liberated the Auschwitz concentration camp in Poland.

GOMPERS, SAMUEL: BIRTH ANNIVERSARY. Jan 27, 1850. Labor leader, first president of the American Federation of Labor, born at London, England. Died Dec 13, 1924, at San Antonio, TX.

KERN, JEROME: BIRTH ANNIVERSARY. Jan 27, 1885. American composer born at New York City; died there Nov 11, 1945. In addition to scores for stage and screen, Kern wrote many memorable songs, including "Ol' Man River," "Smoke Gets in Your Eyes," "I Won't Dance," "The Way You Look Tonight," "All the Things You Are" and "The Last Time I Saw Paris."

"LAVERNE AND SHIRLEY" TV PREMIERE: ANNIVERSARY. Jan 27, 1976. This ABC sitcom was a spin-off of the popular TV show "Happy Days" that was also set during the late '50s in Milwaukee, WI. Penny Marshall (sister of series cocreator Garry Marshall) starred as Laverne DeFazio with Cindy Williams as Shirley Feeney. The two friends worked at a brewery and shared a basement apartment. Also featured in the cast were Phil Foster as Laverne's father, Frank DeFazio; David L. Lander as Andrew "Squiggy" Squiggman; Michael McKean as Lenny Kosnowski; Betty Garrett as landlady Edna Babish; and Eddie Mekka as Carmine Ragusa, Shirley's sometime boyfriend.

LENINGRAD LIBERATED: 70th ANNIVERSARY. Jan 27, 1944. The siege of Leningrad began with German bombing of the city on Sept 4, 1941. The bombing continued for 430 hours. The suffering of the people of Leningrad during the 880-day siege was one of the greatest tragedies of WWII. More than half the population of Russia's second-largest city died during the winter of 1942. The siege finally ended on Jan 27, 1944.

MOZART, WOLFGANG AMADEUS: BIRTH ANNIVERSARY. Jan 27, 1756. One of the world's greatest music makers. Born at Salzburg, Austria, into a gifted musical family, Mozart began performing at age three and composing at age five. Some of the best known of his more than 600 compositions are the operas *Marriage of Figaro, Don Giovanni, Cosi fan tutte* and *The Magic Flute*; his unfinished Requiem Mass; his C major symphony known as the "Jupiter"; and many of his quartets and piano concertos. He died at Vienna, Austria, Dec 5, 1791.

NATIONAL COWBOY POETRY GATHERING. Jan 27–Feb 1. Elko, NV. 30th annual. Soulful poetry and music performed by working cowboys. The event, which includes workshops, jam sessions, western art and buckaroo trappings exhibits, attracts an international audience. For info: Western Folklife Center, 501 Railroad St, Elko, NV 89801. Phone: (775) 738-7508. Fax: (775) 738-2900. E-mail: wfc@westernfolklife.org. Web: www.westernfolklife.org.

NATIONAL GEOGRAPHIC SOCIETY FOUNDED: ANNIVERSARY. Jan 27, 1888. The largest nonprofit scientific and educational institution in the world was incorporated on this date after an initial meeting on Jan 13, 1888, in which a group of 33 geographers, explorers, cartographers, teachers and other professionals met at the Cosmos Club in Washington, DC, to discuss organizing a "a society for the increase and diffusion of geographical knowledge." The first president was Gardiner Greene Hubbard. The first *National Geographic Magazine* was published nine months later in October 1888.

RICKOVER, HYMAN GEORGE: BIRTH ANNIVERSARY. Jan 27, 1900. American naval officer, known as the "Father of the Nuclear Navy." Admiral Rickover directed development of nuclear reactor–powered submarines, the first of which was the *Nautilus*, launched in 1954. Rickover was noted for his blunt remarks: "To increase the efficiency of the Department of Defense," he said, "you must first abolish it." The four-star admiral retired (unwillingly) at the age of 81, after 63 years in the navy. Born in Russia, Rickover died at Arlington, VA, July 9, 1986, and was buried at Arlington National Cemetery.

THOMAS CRAPPER DAY: DEATH ANNIVERSARY. Jan 27, 1910. Born at Thorne, Yorkshire, England, in 1836 (exact date unknown), Crapper is often described as the prime developer of the flush toilet mechanism as it is known today. The flush toilet had been in use for more than 100 years; Crapper perfected it. Founder, London, 1861, of Thomas Crapper & Co, later patentees and manufacturers of sanitary appliances.

UNITED KINGDOM: HOLOCAUST MEMORIAL DAY. Jan 27. Commemorates the day in 1945 that Soviet troops liberated the Auschwitz concentration camp. For info: www.holocaustmemorialday.gov.uk.

UNITED NATIONS: INTERNATIONAL DAY OF COMMEMORATION IN MEMORY OF THE VICTIMS OF THE HOLOCAUST. Jan 27. On Nov 1, 2005, the General Assembly designated Jan 27 as an annual day in memory of the victims of the Holocaust conducted during the Second World War by the Nazi regime (Res 60/7). In doing so, the UN rejected any denial of the Holocaust as a historical event, either in full or part. On Jan 26, 2007, the Assembly condemned without any reservation any denial of the Holocaust and urged all Member States unreservedly to reject any denial of the Holocaust as a historical event, either in full or in part, or any activities to that end (Res 61/255). For info: United Nations, Dept of Public Info, New York, NY, 10017. Web: www.un.org.

January 2014	S	M	T	W	T	F	S
				1	2	3	4
	5	6	7	8	9	10	11
	12	13	14	15	16	17	18
	19	20	21	22	23	24	25
	26	27	28	29	30	31	

VIETNAM PEACE AGREEMENT SIGNED: ANNIVERSARY. Jan 27, 1973. US and North Vietnam, along with South Vietnam and the Viet Cong, signed an "Agreement on ending the war and restoring peace in Vietnam." Signed at Paris, France, to take effect Jan 28 at 8 AM Saigon time, thus ending the US combat role in a war that had involved American personnel stationed in Vietnam since defeated French forces departed under terms of the Geneva Accords in 1954. This was the longest war in US history, with more than one million combat deaths (US: 47,366). However, within weeks of the departure of American troops, the war between North and South Vietnam resumed. For the Vietnamese, the war didn't end until Apr 30, 1975, when Saigon fell to Communist forces.

VON SACHER-MASOCH, LEOPOLD: BIRTH ANNIVERSARY. Jan 27, 1836. Author, born at Lemberg, Austrian Galicia (now Lviv, Ukraine), best known for his 1870 novella *Venus in Furs*, a semi-autobiographical tale of psychosexual perversion and supplication that led the psychiatric field to name the practice of masochism after its author. Von Sacher-Masoch died at Lindheim, Germany, on Mar 9, 1895.

BIRTHDAYS TODAY

Mikhail Baryshnikov, 66, ballet dancer, actor (*White Nights, The Turning Point*), born Riga, USSR (now Latvia), Jan 27, 1948.

(Anthony) Cris Collinsworth, 55, sportscaster, former football player, born Dayton, OH, Jan 27, 1959.

Mairead Corrigan Maguire, 70, pacifist, Nobel Peace Prize winner, born Belfast, Northern Ireland, Jan 27, 1944.

James Cromwell, 72, actor (*The People vs Larry Flynt, Babe, LA Confidential*), born Los Angeles, CA, Jan 27, 1942.

Alan Cumming, 49, actor (*Macbeth*, Tony for *Cabaret*; "The Good Wife," *Spy Kids, Emma*), director, born Perthshire, Scotland, Jan 27, 1965.

Bridget Fonda, 50, actress (*Single White Female, Lake Placid*), born Los Angeles, CA, Jan 27, 1964.

Julie Foudy, 43, sportscaster, former soccer player, born San Diego, CA, Jan 27, 1971.

Keith Olberman, 55, journalist, political commentator, born New York, NY, Jan 27, 1959.

John G. Roberts, Jr, 59, Chief Justice of the US, born Buffalo, NY, Jan 27, 1955.

Mimi Rogers, 58, actress (*The Doors, The Rapture*), born Coral Gables, FL, Jan 27, 1956.

January 28 — Tuesday

DAY 28 **337 REMAINING**

***CHALLENGER* SPACE SHUTTLE EXPLOSION: ANNIVERSARY.** Jan 28, 1986. At 11:39 AM, EST, the space shuttle *Challenger STS-51L* exploded, 74 seconds into its flight and about 10 miles above the earth. Hundreds of millions around the world watched television replays of the horrifying event that killed seven people. The billion-dollar craft was destroyed, all shuttle flights suspended and much of the US manned space flight program temporarily halted. Killed were teacher Christa McAuliffe (who was to have been the first ordinary citizen in space) and six crew members: Francis R. Scobee, Michael J. Smith, Judith A. Resnik, Ellison S. Onizuka, Ronald E. McNair and Gregory B. Jarvis.

"FANTASY ISLAND" TV PREMIERE: ANNIVERSARY. Jan 28, 1978. Ricardo Montalban starred as the prescient guide, Mr Roarke, with Hervé Villechaize as his faithful assistant, Tattoo. Each week, guest stars played characters eager to live out their fantasies in camp splendor. The show's run of 130 episodes, ending on Aug 18, 1984, was produced by Aaron Spelling and Leonard Goldberg. Best remembered is Tattoo's opening line each week: "De plane, de plane!"

GREAT SEAL OF THE US: AUTHORIZATION ANNIVERSARY. Jan 28, 1782. Congress resolved that the secretary of the Congress should "keep the public seal, and cause the same to be affixed to every act, ordinance or paper, which Congress shall direct. . . ." Although the Great Seal did not exist yet, the Congress recognized the need for it. See also: "Great Seal of the US Proposed: Anniversary" (July 4 and Sept 16).

INTERNATIONAL HOOF-CARE SUMMIT. Jan 28–31. Cincinnati, OH. This annual meeting attracts highly innovative professionals interested in learning new ways to provide quality hoof care. Est attendance: 800. For info: Frank Lessiter, International Hoof-Care Summit, PO Box 624, Brookfield, WI 53008-0624. Phone: (262) 782-4480. Fax: (262) 782-1252. E-mail: info@lesspub.com. Web: www.americanfarriers.com.

ISRAELI SIEGE OF SUEZ CITY ENDS: 40th ANNIVERSARY. Jan 28, 1974. The Israeli army lifted its siege of Suez City, freed encircled Egyptian troops and turned over 300,000 square miles of Egyptian territory to the UN, thereby ending the occupation that started during the October 1973 war.

MacKENZIE, ALEXANDER: BIRTH ANNIVERSARY. Jan 28, 1822. The man who became the first Liberal prime minister of Canada (1873–78) was born at Logierait, Perth, Scotland. He died at Toronto, Apr 17, 1892.

MARTÍ, JOSÉ JULIAN: BIRTH ANNIVERSARY. Jan 28, 1853. Cuban author and political activist, born at Havana, Martí was exiled to Spain, where he studied law before coming to the US in 1890. He was killed in battle at Dos Rios, Cuba, May 19, 1895.

PICCARD, AUGUSTE: BIRTH ANNIVERSARY. Jan 28, 1884. Scientist and explorer, born at Basel, Switzerland. Made a record-setting balloon ascent into the stratosphere on May 27, 1931, and also ocean-depth descents and explorations. Twin brother of Jean Felix Piccard. Died at Lausanne, Switzerland, Mar 24, 1962. See also: "Piccard, Jean Felix: Birth Anniversary" (Jan 28).

PICCARD, JEAN FELIX: BIRTH ANNIVERSARY. Jan 28, 1884. Scientist, engineer, explorer, born at Basel, Switzerland. Noted for cosmic-ray research and record-setting balloon ascensions into the stratosphere. Reached 57,579 feet in a sealed gondola piloted by his wife, Jeannette, in 1934. Twin brother of Auguste Piccard. Died at Minneapolis, MN, Jan 28, 1963. See also: "Piccard, Jeannette Ridlon: Birth Anniversary" (Jan 5) and "Piccard, Auguste: Birth Anniversary" (Jan 28).

POLLOCK, JACKSON: BIRTH ANNIVERSARY. Jan 28, 1912. Abstract Expressionist born at Cody, WY. In postwar New York, Pollock placed his canvases on the floor and developed signature "drip" paintings, controversially incorporating the ideas of gravity and chance into the creation process. Pollock was killed in an automobile accident Aug 11, 1956, at East Hampton, NY.

SCOTLAND: UP HELLY AA. Jan 28. Lerwick, Shetland Islands. Norse galley burned in impressive ceremony symbolizing sacrifice to the sun. Old Viking custom. A festival marking the end of Yule. Annually, the last Tuesday in January. For info: Tourist Information Centre, Market Cross, Lerwick, Shetland, Scotland ZE1 0LU. Phone: (44) (1595) 693-434. Fax: (44) (1595) 695-807. E-mail: info@visitshetland.com. Web: www.visitshetland.com.

STANLEY, HENRY MORTON: BIRTH ANNIVERSARY. Jan 28, 1841. Explorer, born at Denbigh, Wales, and leader of the expedition to find the missing missionary-explorer David Livingstone, who had not been heard from for more than two years. Stanley began the search in Africa on Mar 21, 1871, finally finding the explorer at Ujiji, near Lake Tanganyika, on Nov 10, 1871, whereupon he asked the now famous question: "Dr. Livingstone, I presume?" Stanley died at London, England, May 10, 1904.

BIRTHDAYS TODAY

Alan Alda, 78, actor (*Paper Lion, The Four Seasons,* "M*A*S*H"), director, born Alphonso D'Abruzzo at New York, NY, Jan 28, 1936.

John Beck, 71, actor ("Dallas," *Sleeper, The Big Bus*), born Chicago, IL, Jan 28, 1943.

Jessica Ennis, 28, Olympic heptathlete, born Sheffield, England, Jan 28, 1986.

Susan Howard, 71, actress ("Dallas"), born Jeri Lynn Mooney at Marshall, TX, Jan 28, 1943.

Harley Jane Kozak, 57, actress (*When Harry Met Sally . . . , Parenthood*), born Wilkes-Barre, PA, Jan 28, 1957.

Sarah McLachlan, 46, singer, born Halifax, NS, Canada, Jan 28, 1968.

Kathryn Morris, 45, actress (*Mindhunters,* "Cold Case"), born Cincinnati, OH, Jan 28, 1969.

Claes Oldenburg, 85, artist, sculptor, born Stockholm, Sweden, Jan 28, 1929.

Rick Ross, 38, rapper, born William Leonard Roberts II at Coahoma County, MS, Jan 28, 1976.

Nicolas Sarkozy, 59, former president of France, born Paris, France, Jan 28, 1955.

Jeanne Shaheen, 67, US Senator (D, New Hampshire), former governor of New Hampshire, born St. Charles, MO, Jan 28, 1947.

Elijah Wood, 33, actor (the Lord of the Rings film trilogy, *The Ice Storm*), born Cedar Rapids, IA, Jan 28, 1981.

January 29 — Wednesday

DAY 29 **336 REMAINING**

CHEKHOV, ANTON PAVLOVICH: BIRTH ANNIVERSARY. Jan 29, 1860. Russian playwright and short story writer, especially remembered for *The Sea Gull, The Three Sisters* and *The Cherry Orchard.* Born at Taganrog, Russia; died July 15, 1904, at the Black Forest spa at Badenweiler, Germany.

CURMUDGEONS DAY. Jan 29. An annual celebration of the crusty, yet insightful, wags who consistently apply the needle of truth to the balloons of hypocrisy and social norms. Always celebrated on Jan 29, the birthday of W.C. Fields, one of America's most beloved curmudgeons. For info: Michael Montgomery, WBGZ Radio, 227 Market St, Alton, IL 62002. Phone: (618) 465-3535. Fax: (618) 465-3546. E-mail: studio@wbgzradio.com.

FIELDS, W.C.: BIRTH ANNIVERSARY. Jan 29, 1880. Stage and motion picture actor (*My Little Chickadee*), screenwriter and expert juggler. Born Claude William Dukenfield at Philadelphia, PA; died Dec 25, 1946, at Pasadena, CA. He wrote his own epitaph: "On the whole, I'd rather be in Philadelphia."

FREETHINKER'S DAY. Jan 29. Annual celebration of the birth of Thomas Paine. For info: Truth Seeker Co, 239 S Juniper St, Escondido, CA 92025. Phone: (760) 489-5211. E-mail: tseditor@aol.com. Web: www.truthseeker.com.

KANSAS: ADMISSION DAY: ANNIVERSARY. Jan 29. Became the 34th state in 1861.

McKINLEY, WILLIAM: BIRTH ANNIVERSARY. Jan 29, 1843. 25th president of the US (1897–1901), born at Niles, OH. Died in office, at Buffalo, NY, Sept 14, 1901, as the result of a gunshot wound by an anarchist assassin Sept 6, 1901, while he was attending the Pan-American Exposition.

MORMON BATTALION ARRIVAL IN CALIFORNIA: ANNIVERSARY. Jan 29, 1847. The 500 men of the US Mormon Battalion, along with 50 women and children, arrived at San Diego, CA, on this date, having marched 2,000 miles—the longest march in modern military history—since leaving Council Bluffs, IA, on July 16, 1846, to fight in the war against Mexico. In the course of their trek they established the first wagon route from Santa Fe to southern California. Their historic arrival is commemorated each year with a military parade in San Diego's Old Town.

PAINE, THOMAS: BIRTH ANNIVERSARY. Jan 29, 1737. American Revolutionary leader, a corset maker by trade, author of *Common Sense*, *The Age of Reason* and many other influential works, was born at Thetford, England. "These are the times that try men's souls" are the well-known opening words of his inspirational tract *The Crisis.* Paine died at New York, NY, June 8, 1809, but 10 years later his remains were moved to England by William Cobbett for reburial there. Reburial was refused, however, and the location of Paine's bones, said to have been distributed, is unknown.

"THE RAVEN" PUBLISHED: ANNIVERSARY. Jan 29, 1845. One of the most famous poems in American literature was published on this date in New York's *Evening Mirror* newspaper. The author was anonymous, but the poem was such a sensation (it would be reprinted at least 16 times in various periodicals and books that year) that soon the author was revealed as literary critic and author Edgar Allan Poe. Despite the celebrity status Poe enjoyed as a result of "The Raven," it did not relieve his poverty: Poe received $15 for the poem. The classic lines "Once upon a midnight dreary" and "Quoth the Raven, 'Nevermore'" resound in countless anthologies and dramatic readings as well as in parodies.

THE SEEING EYE ESTABLISHED: 85th ANNIVERSARY. Jan 29, 1929. The Seeing Eye, North America's first guide dog school, was incorporated on this date at Nashville, TN. The first Seeing Eye dog was Buddy, a German shepherd. The Seeing Eye was the first program in the US that enabled people with disabilities to be full participants in society. Its mission is to enhance the independence, self-confidence and dignity of people who are blind through the use of Seeing Eye dogs. Since its founding, The Seeing Eye has matched more than 16,000 specially bred dogs with blind people from the US and Canada. In 1931, the school moved to New Jersey, where it continues to breed, raise and train Seeing Eye dogs and instruct blind and visually impaired people in the use and care of their dogs. For info: Michelle Barlak, Public Relations, The Seeing Eye, PO Box 375, Morristown, NJ 07963-0375. Phone: (973) 539-4425. Fax: (973) 539-0922. E-mail: info@seeingeye.org. Web: www.seeingeye.org.

January 2014

S	M	T	W	T	F	S
			1	2	3	4
5	6	7	8	9	10	11
12	13	14	15	16	17	18
19	20	21	22	23	24	25
26	27	28	29	30	31	

SWEDENBORG, EMANUEL: BIRTH ANNIVERSARY. Jan 29, 1688. Born at Stockholm, Sweden, Swedenborg is remembered as a scientist, inventor, writer and religious leader. Swedenborg made plans for machine guns, submarines and airplanes and published Sweden's first scientific journal. His study of human anatomy and his search for the soul led him to begin thinking about religion. His writings interpreting the scriptures formed the basis of the Church of the New Jerusalem, which was established by his devotees soon after his death. He died at London, England, Mar 29, 1772.

US NATIONALS SNOW SCULPTING COMPETITION. Jan 29–Feb 2. Lake Geneva, WI. 19th annual. Snow sculpting competition where each three-person team creates a work of art out of a 7-foot × 9-foot block of snow. Several awards given. Est attendance: 40,000. For info: Lake Geneva Area CVB, 201 Wrigley Dr, Lake Geneva, WI 53147-2004. Phone: (262) 248-4416 or (800) 345-1020. E-mail: info@lakegenevawi.com. Web: www.lakegenevawi.com or www.usnationals.org.

BIRTHDAYS TODAY

Sara Gilbert, 39, actress ("The Big Bang Theory," "Roseanne"), television personality ("The Talk"), born Santa Monica, CA, Jan 29, 1975.

Heather Graham, 44, actress (*The Hangover, From Hell, Boogie Nights*), born Milwaukee, WI, Jan 29, 1970.

Germaine Greer, 75, author (*Daddy We Hardly Knew You, The Female Eunuch*), born Melbourne, Australia, Jan 29, 1939.

Dominik Hasek, 49, former hockey player, born Pardubice, Czechoslovakia (now the Czech Republic), Jan 29, 1965.

Sam Jaeger, 37, actor ("Parenthood," "Eli Stone"), born Perrysburg, OH, Jan 29, 1977.

Ann Jillian, 63, actress ("It's a Living," *The Ann Jillian Story*), born Cambridge, MA, Jan 29, 1951.

Andrew Keegan, 35, actor (*Independence Day*), born Los Angeles, CA, Jan 29, 1979.

Stacey King, 47, sportscaster, former basketball player, born Lawton, OK, Jan 29, 1967.

Adam Lambert, 32, singer, television personality ("American Idol"), born Indianapolis, IN, Jan 29, 1982.

Gregory Efthimios (Greg) Louganis, 54, actor, Olympic diver, born San Diego, CA, Jan 29, 1960.

Bobbie Phillips, 46, actress ("Murder One," *Red Shoe Diaries*), born Charleston, SC, Jan 29, 1968 (some sources say 1972).

Katharine Ross, 71, actress (*The Graduate*), born Los Angeles, CA, Jan 29, 1943.

Tom Selleck, 69, actor ("Blue Bloods," "Magnum, P.I.," *Three Men and a Baby*), born Detroit, MI, Jan 29, 1945.

Nick Turturro, 52, actor ("Blue Bloods," "NYPD Blue"), born Queens, NY, Jan 29, 1962.

Oprah Winfrey, 60, television talk show host ("The Oprah Winfrey Show"), actress (*The Color Purple*), producer (owner of Harpo Studios), born Kosciusko, MS, Jan 29, 1954.

January 30 — Thursday

DAY 30 **335 REMAINING**

ANGOULÊME INTERNATIONAL COMICS FESTIVAL. Jan 30–Feb 2. Angoulême, France. Since 1974, Europe's largest comics show set in the Bordeaux region of France. It attracts fans, critics, publishers, artists, cartoonists, writers and the general public. The highlight of the festival is the presentation of the Grand Prize, a lifetime achievement award given to a master who then becomes the festival's president the following year. Other prizes honor best albums, new talent, heritage comics and more. Annually, the last weekend in January. Est attendance: 200,000. For info: Angouleme: Festival International de la Bande Desinée, 71, rue Hergé, 16000 Angoulême, France. E-mail: info@bdangouleme.com. Web: www.bdangouleme.com.

BEATLES LAST CONCERT: 45th ANNIVERSARY. Jan 30, 1969. On this day the Beatles performed together in public for the last time. The show took place on the roof of their Apple Studios in London, England, but it was interrupted by police after they received complaints from the neighbors about the noise.

BLOODY SUNDAY: ANNIVERSARY. Jan 30, 1972. In Londonderry, Northern Ireland, 14 Roman Catholics were shot dead by British troops during a banned civil rights march. During 1972, the first year of British direct rule, 467 people were killed in the fighting. On June 15, 2010, after a 12-year investigation, the 5,000-page Saville Report was issued that strongly condemned the soldiers who fired and exonerated the victims. As a result, Prime Minister David Cameron issued an apology on behalf of the British government.

CHARLES I: EXECUTION ANNIVERSARY. Jan 30, 1649. English king beheaded by order of Parliament under Oliver Cromwell on this date; considered a martyr by some.

FIRST BRAWL IN THE US HOUSE OF REPRESENTATIVES: ANNIVERSARY. Jan 30, 1798. The first brawl to break out on the floor of the US House of Representatives occurred at Philadelphia, PA. The fight was precipitated by an argument between Matthew Lyon of Vermont and Roger Griswold of Connecticut. Lyon spat in Griswold's face. Although a resolution to expel Lyon was introduced, the measure failed and Lyon maintained his seat.

GANDHI ASSASSINATED: ANNIVERSARY. Jan 30, 1948. Indian religious and political leader, assassinated at New Delhi, India. The assassin was a Hindu extremist, Ram Naturam. See also: "Gandhi, Mohandas Karamchand (Mahatma): Birth Anniversary" (Oct 2).

INANE ANSWERING MESSAGE DAY. Jan 30. Annually, the day set aside to change, shorten, replace or delete those ridiculous and/or annoying answering machine messages that waste the time of anyone who must listen to them. (©2006 by WH.) For info: Thomas & Ruth Roy, Wellcat Holidays, 2418 Long Ln, Lebanon, PA 17046. Phone: (717) 279-0184. E-mail: info@wellcat.com. Web: www.wellcat.com.

JORDAN: KING'S BIRTHDAY. Jan 30. National holiday. Honors King Abdullah II, son of the late King Hussein, who was born Jan 30, 1962, and assumed the throne June 9, 1999.

MARYLAND ADOPTS ARTICLES OF CONFEDERATION: ANNIVERSARY. Jan 30, 1781. Maryland became the last of the 13 original states to adopt the Articles of Confederation.

MOON PHASE: NEW MOON. Jan 30. Moon enters New Moon phase at 4:38 PM, EST.

OSCEOLA: DEATH ANNIVERSARY. Jan 30, 1838. Osceola was a leader during the Second Seminole War (1835–42). During the first two years of the war, he led the fight against removal of the Florida Seminoles to Indian territory. He was captured under a flag of truce in 1837 and imprisoned at Fort Marion in St. Augustine, FL. He was moved to Fort Moultrie at Charleston Harbor, SC, where he died. He was born near present-day Tuskegee, AL, circa 1804.

RAF BOMBS HITLER CELEBRATION: ANNIVERSARY. Jan 30, 1943. British Royal Air Force Mosquito bombers ran a daylight raid on Berlin timed to coincide with a speech being given by Joseph Goebbels in honor of Hitler's 10th year in power.

ROOSEVELT, FRANKLIN DELANO: BIRTH ANNIVERSARY. Jan 30, 1882. 32nd president of the US (Mar 4, 1933–Apr 12, 1945). The only president to serve more than two terms, FDR was elected four times. He supported the Allies in WWII before the US entered the struggle by supplying them with war materials through the Lend-Lease Act; he became deeply involved in broad decision making after the Japanese attack on Pearl Harbor Dec 7, 1941. Born at Hyde Park, NY, he died a few months into his fourth term at Warm Springs, GA, Apr 12, 1945.

SWITZERLAND: ST. MORITZ POLO WORLD CUP ON SNOW. Jan 30–Feb 2. St. Moritz. 30th anniversary. Spectacular winter polo on the frozen lake of St. Moritz 1,800 meters above sea level. Est attendance: 20,000. For info: St. Moritz Polo AG, Via Tinus II, 7500 St. Moritz, Switzerland. Phone: (41) (81) 839-92-92. Fax: (41) (81) 839-92-00. E-mail: info@polostmoritz.com. Web: www.polostmoritz.com.

TET OFFENSIVE BEGINS: ANNIVERSARY. Jan 30, 1968. After calling for a cease-fire during the Tet holiday celebrations, North Vietnam and the National Liberation Front launched a major offensive throughout South Vietnam on that holiday. Attacks erupted in 36 of the 44 provincial capitals and five of the six major cities. In addition, the Viet Cong attacked the US embassy in Saigon, Tan Son Nhut Air Base, the presidential palace and South Vietnamese general staff headquarters. Costing as many as 40,000 battlefield deaths, the offensive was a tactical defeat for the Viet Cong and North Vietnam. The South Vietnamese held their ground, and the US was able to airlift troops into the critical areas and quickly regain control. However, the offensive is credited as a strategic success in that it continued the demoralization of Americans. After Tet, American policy toward Vietnam shifted from winning the war to seeking an honorable way out.

THOMAS, ISAIAH: BIRTH ANNIVERSARY. Jan 30, 1749. American printer, editor, almanac publisher, historian and founder of the American Antiquarian Society. Born at Boston, MA; died Apr 4, 1831, at Worcester, MA.

TUCHMAN, BARBARA W.: BIRTH ANNIVERSARY. Jan 30, 1912. Historian and journalist Barbara Tuchman's most famous works were her Pulitzer Prize–winning books *The Guns of August* (1962) and *Stilwell and the American Experience in China, 1911–45* (1971). Tuchman was known for making history lively. Other well-known books include *The Proud Tower* (1966) and *The First Salute* (1988). Barbara Wertheim Tuchman was born at New York, NY, and died at Greenwich, CT, Feb 6, 1988.

BIRTHDAYS TODAY

Christian Bale, 40, actor (*The Prestige, Batman Begins*, Oscar for *The Fighter*), born Pembrokeshire, West Wales, Jan 30, 1974.

Brett Butler, 56, comedienne, actress ("Grace Under Fire"), born Montgomery, AL, Jan 30, 1958.

Richard (Dick) Cheney, 73, 46th vice president of the US, born Lincoln, NE, Jan 30, 1941.

Phil Collins, 63, musician, singer, songwriter, born Chiswick, England, Jan 30, 1951.

Peter Crouch, 33, soccer player, born Macclesfield, England, Jan 30, 1981.

Charles S. Dutton, 63, actor ("Roc," *Mississippi Masala, Menace II Society*), born Baltimore, MD, Jan 30, 1951.

Gene Hackman, 84, actor (Oscars for *The French Connection* and *Unforgiven*; *The Royal Tenenbaums*), born San Bernardino, CA, Jan 30, 1930.

Johnathan Lee Iverson, 38, circus ringmaster, born New York, NY, Jan 30, 1976.

Davey Johnson, 71, baseball manager and former player, born Orlando, FL, Jan 30, 1943.

Dorothy Malone, 89, actress ("Peyton Place," Oscar for *Written on the Wind*), born Chicago, IL, Jan 30, 1925.

Vanessa Redgrave, 77, actress (Tony for *Long Day's Journey into Night*; Oscar for *Julia*; Emmys for *Playing for Time* and *If These Walls Could Talk 2*), born London, England, Jan 30, 1937.

Jalen Rose, 41, sportscaster, former basketball player, born Detroit, MI, Jan 30, 1973.

Boris Spassky, 77, former chess player, journalist, born Leningrad, USSR (now St. Petersburg, Russia), Jan 30, 1937.

Curtis Strange, 59, golfer, born Norfolk, VA, Jan 30, 1955.

Jody Watley, 55, singer, born Chicago, IL, Jan 30, 1959.

January 31 — Friday

DAY 31 **334 REMAINING**

BLACK HILLS STOCK SHOW AND RODEO. Jan 31–Feb 9. Rapid City, SD. Events include PRCA rodeos, ranch rodeo, timed sheepdog trials, cattle cutting, ranch horse competition, livestock shows and sales, buffalo show and sale, team penning, bucking horse and bull sale, stockman banquet and ball and commercial exhibits. Est attendance: 250,000. For info: Black Hills Stock Show and Rodeo, 800 San Francisco, Rapid City, SD 57701. Phone: (605) 355-3861.

CANADA: WINTERLUDE. Jan 31–Feb 17. Ottawa, ON. Annual celebration of Canadian winter and traditions for the whole family. Skating on Rideau Canal, the world's largest skating rink; snow and ice sculptures; North America's largest snow playground; winter sporting events; performing arts and Taste of Winterlude. Est attendance: 695,000. For info: Winterlude, Natl Capital Commission, 202-40 Elgin St, Ottawa, ON K1P 1C7, Canada. Phone: (613) 239-5000 or (800) 465-1867. E-mail: info@ncc-ccn.ca. Web: www.winterlude.gc.ca.

CHINESE NEW YEAR. Jan 31. Traditional Chinese Lunar Year 4712 begins at sunset on the day of the second New Moon following the winter solstice—the Year of the Horse. Outside China, the date of the New Year may differ by a day. The New Year can begin anytime from Jan 21 through Feb 21. Generally celebrated until the Lantern Festival 15 days later, but merchants usually reopen their stores and places of business on the fifth day of the first lunar month. This holiday is celebrated as Tet in Vietnam. See also: "China: Lantern Festival" (Feb 14).

FIRST SOCIAL SECURITY CHECK ISSUED: ANNIVERSARY. Jan 31, 1940. Ida May Fuller of Ludlow, VT, received the first monthly retirement check—in the amount of $22.54. Fuller had worked for three years under the Social Security program (which had been established by legislation in 1935). The accumulated taxes on her salary over those three years were $24.75. She lived to be 100 years old, collecting $22,888 in Social Security benefits. See also: "Social Security Act: Anniversary" (Aug 14).

FUN AT WORK DAY. Jan 31. Inject some laughter into your workplace by planning a fun and relaxing activity. Do something to encourage enthusiasm and openness and to help build rapport and release tension. When we enjoy our work, we are more productive and creative. Annually, the last Friday of January. For info: Diane C. Decker. Phone: (847) 394-0994. E-mail: dcdecker@msn.com. Web: www.qualitytransitions.com.

January 2014

S	M	T	W	T	F	S
			1	2	3	4
5	6	7	8	9	10	11
12	13	14	15	16	17	18
19	20	21	22	23	24	25
26	27	28	29	30	31	

GOLDWYN, SAMUEL: 40th DEATH ANNIVERSARY. Jan 31, 1974. Motion picture producer and industry pioneer Goldwyn died at Los Angeles, CA. He was born Samuel Goldfish, at Warsaw, Poland, probably in July 1879 (although he always claimed Aug 27, 1882, as his birthday). Famous for his confusing outbursts, Goldwyn is claimed to have said such things as "Anybody who goes to see a psychiatrist ought to have his head examined."

GREY, ZANE: BIRTH ANNIVERSARY. Jan 31, 1872. Zane Grey (original name Pearl Grey), American dentist and prolific author of tales of the Old West, was born at Zanesville, OH. Grey wrote more than 80 books that were translated into many languages and sold more than 10 million copies. The novel *Riders of the Purple Sage* (1912) was the most popular. Grey died Oct 23, 1939, at Altadena, CA.

INSPIRE YOUR HEART WITH THE ARTS DAY. Jan 31. A day to experience art in your life. Food sustains you as a human; art inspires you to be divine. Go to an art museum, browse through an art book at the library, enroll in an art class or commission an artist. Read your favorite poem out loud. Go to a concert or play. Sign up for dance lessons. Today is a day to inspire your heart with the arts! For info: Rev Jayne Howard Feldman, Angel Heights, PO Box 95, Upperco, MD 21155. Phone: (410) 833-6912. E-mail: earthangel4peace@aol.com.

MARSHALL ISLANDS LANDINGS: 70th ANNIVERSARY. Jan 31, 1944. After two months of saturation bombing (the heaviest to precede an attack thus far in the Pacific), the 23rd and 24th Marine Regiments attacked the Marshall Islands. In four days Kwajalein was taken, providing the Allies with a major staging area. The dead numbered 8,122 Japanese and 356 Americans.

MORRIS, ROBERT: BIRTH ANNIVERSARY. Jan 31, 1734. Signer of the Declaration of Independence, the Articles of Confederation and the Constitution. He was one of only two men who signed all three documents. He was born at Liverpool, England, and died May 7, 1806, at Philadelphia, PA.

NATIONAL PRESCHOOL FITNESS DAY. Jan 31. Daycare centers throughout the US. A day promoting healthy lifestyle habits of physical education and healthy eating in preschool children. Annually, the last Friday in January. For info: Michele Silence, Kid-Fit, 40 E Live Oak Ave, Arcadia, CA 91006. Phone: (626) 848-2950. E-mail: michele@kid-fit.com. Web: www.kid-fit.com.

NAURU: NATIONAL HOLIDAY. Jan 31. Republic of Nauru. Commemorates independence in 1968 from a UN trusteeship administered by Australia, New Zealand and the UK.

PROVIDENCE BOAT SHOW. Jan 31–Feb 2. Providence, RI. 21st annual. The boating season starts at this show, featuring power boats, small sailing craft, kayaks, inflatables and more. Seminars, children's section and a special area with a focus on fishing. For info: Newport Exhibition Group, PO Box 698, Newport, RI 02840. Phone: (401) 846-1115. Fax: (401) 848-0455. E-mail: info@newportexhibition.com. Web: www.providenceboatshow.com.

ROBINSON, JACKIE: 95th BIRTH ANNIVERSARY. Jan 31, 1919. Jack Roosevelt Robinson, athlete and business executive, first black to enter professional major league baseball (Brooklyn Dodgers, 1947–56). Voted National League's Most Valuable Player in 1949 and elected to the Baseball Hall of Fame in 1962. Born at Cairo, GA, Robinson died at Stamford, CT, Oct 24, 1972.

SARANAC LAKE WINTER CARNIVAL. Jan 31–Feb 9. Saranac Lake, NY. 117th annual. The oldest winter festival in the eastern US. Come and join the family fun with fireworks, entertainment and much more. The 2014 theme is "Celtic Carnival." For info: The Winter Carnival, Saranac Lake Chamber of Commerce, PO Box 829, Saranac Lake, NY 12983. Phone: (518) 891-1990 or (800) 347-1992. Web: www.saranaclakewintercarnival.com.

SCHUBERT, FRANZ: BIRTH ANNIVERSARY. Jan 31, 1797. Composer, born at Vienna, Austria, and died there of typhus Nov 19, 1828, at age 31. Buried, at his request, near the grave of Beethoven. Schubert last worked on his "Unfinished Symphony" (No. 8) in 1822. On the 100th anniversary of his death in 1928, a $10,000 prize was offered to "finish" the work. The protests were so great that the offer was withdrawn.

SLOVIK, EDDIE D.: EXECUTION: ANNIVERSARY. Jan 31, 1945. Anniversary of execution by firing squad of 24-year-old Private Eddie D. Slovik. Born at Detroit, MI, Feb 18, 1920, Slovik was assigned to Company G, 109th Infantry, 28th Division, US Army. His death sentence, the first for desertion since the Civil War, has been a subject of controversy. First buried in France, Slovik's remains were exhumed in 1987 for reburial beside his wife, Antoinette, who died in 1979, after years of effort to clear Slovik's name and have his body returned to the US.

SPACE MILESTONE: *APOLLO 14* (US). Jan 31, 1971. Launch date of *Apollo 14*. Five days later on Feb 5, astronauts Alan B. Shepard, Jr, and Edgar D. Mitchell landed on the moon (lunar module *Antares*). Command module *Kitty Hawk* was piloted by Stuart A. Roosa. Pacific splashdown on Feb 9.

SPACE MILESTONE: *EXPLORER 1* (US). Jan 31, 1958. The first successful US satellite. Although launched four months later than the Soviet Union's *Sputnik*, *Explorer* reached a higher altitude and detected a zone of intense radiation inside Earth's magnetic field. This was later named the Van Allen radiation belts. More than 65 subsequent *Explorer* satellites were launched through 1984.

SPACE MILESTONE: *LUNA 9* (USSR). Jan 31, 1966. Launch of unmanned mission that accomplished the first soft landing on the moon three days later on Feb 3. Relayed TV photos of the lunar surface.

SPACE MILESTONE: PROJECT MERCURY TEST (US). Jan 31, 1961. A test of Project Mercury spacecraft accomplished the first US recovery of a large animal from space. Ham, the chimpanzee, successfully performed simple tasks in space.

BIRTHDAYS TODAY

Ernest (Ernie) Banks, 83, Hall of Fame baseball player, born Dallas, TX, Jan 31, 1931.

Princess Beatrix of the Netherlands, 76, former queen of the Netherlands, born Sostdijk, Netherlands, Jan 31, 1938.

Carol Channing, 93, actress (Tony Award for *Hello, Dolly!*; *Thoroughly Modern Millie*), born Seattle, WA, Jan 31, 1921.

Portia de Rossi, 41, actress ("Ally McBeal," "Arrested Development"), born Geelong, Victoria, Australia, Jan 31, 1973.

Minnie Driver, 43, actress (*Gross Pointe Blank, Good Will Hunting*), born London, England, Jan 31, 1971.

Philip Glass, 77, composer, born Baltimore, MD, Jan 31, 1937.

John Lydon, 58, singer ("Johnny Rotten," Sex Pistols), composer, born near London, England, Jan 31, 1956.

Kelly Lynch, 55, actress (*Drugstore Cowboy*), born Minneapolis, MN, Jan 31, 1959.

Stuart Margolin, 74, actor, director, writer ("The Rockford Files," *The Big Blue*), born Davenport, IA, Jan 31, 1940.

Marcus Mumford, 27, singer (Mumford & Sons), born Anaheim, CA, Jan 31, 1987.

(Lynn) Nolan Ryan, 67, Hall of Fame baseball player, born Refugio, TX, Jan 31, 1947.

Justin Timberlake, 33, singer, actor (*Alpha Dog, Black Snake Moan*), born Memphis, TN, Jan 31, 1981.

Jessica Walter, 73, actress ("Arrested Development," *Play Misty for Me, The Flamingo Kid*), born Brooklyn, NY, Jan 31, 1941.

Kerry Washington, 37, actress ("Scandal," *Django Unchained, Ray*), born the Bronx, NY, Jan 31, 1977.

✦ February ✦

February 1 — Saturday

DAY 32 **333 REMAINING**

AFRICAN HERITAGE AND HEALTH WEEK. Feb 1–7. Coinciding with Black History Month, African Heritage and Health Week commemorates the foods, flavors and healthy cooking techniques that were core to the well-being of African ancestors from Africa, South America, the Caribbean and the American South. The foods that have sustained cultures are an important part of history. What better time to dedicate a week to African Heritage and Health and learn about the healthy culinary side of history than during Black History Month? Annually, Feb 1–7. For info: Rachel Greenstein, Oldways, 266 Beacon St, Boston, MA 02116. Phone: (617) 421-5500. E-mail: rachel@oldwayspt.org. Web: www.oldwayspt.org/programs/african-heritage-health/african-heritage-health-week.

AMD/LOW VISION AWARENESS MONTH. Feb 1–28. Macular degeneration is a leading cause of vision loss. Low-vision aids can make the most of remaining vision. Information on eye disease warning signs and on low-vision aids will be available. For info: Prevent Blindness America®, 211 W Wacker Dr, Ste 1700, Chicago, IL 60606. Phone: (800) 331-2020. E-mail: info@preventblindness.org. Web: www.preventblindness.org.

AMERICAN DENTAL ASSOCIATION GIVE KIDS A SMILE® PROGRAM. Feb 1. 12th annual. Dental professionals across the nation will provide free dental care to children and adolescents from low-income, underserved families during this special program. Give Kids a Smile (GKAS) is the American Dental Association's major oral health outreach program, launched to encourage parents, health professionals and policy makers to address the year-round need for oral health care for all children. GKAS will provide educational materials, screenings and, where possible, free dental care such as cleanings, x-rays and fillings. Due to the need for signed parental permission, many GKAS events can see only children registered in advance, usually through schools and social service clubs and agencies. For info: American Dental Association, 211 E Chicago Ave, Chicago, IL 60611. Phone: (312) 440-4600. E-mail: gkas@ada.org. Web: givekidsasmile.ada.org.

✦AMERICAN HEART MONTH. Feb 1–28. Presidential Proclamation issued each year for February since 1964. (PL 88–254 of Dec 30, 1963.)

AMERICAN HEART MONTH. Feb 1–28. During this month, the American Heart Association will focus on women with "Go Red for Women," an educational movement about women and cardiovascular disease. Each year cardiovascular diseases claim the lives of nearly 500,000 women. For all of the women you know who have been affected by cardiovascular disease, participate in National Wear Red Day on Friday, Feb 7. For information on American Heart Month and Go Red for Women: American Heart Assn, 7272 Greenville Ave, Dallas, TX 75231. Phone: (800) 242-8721. Fax: (214) 369-3685. Web: www.americanheart.org or www.goredforwomen.org.

BAKE FOR FAMILY FUN MONTH. Feb 1–28. The Home Baking Association has designated February as Bake for Family Fun Month, dedicated to celebrating baking traditions, recipes and providing resources for families to create new baking traditions. For info: Charlene Patton. Phone: (785) 478-3283. Fax: (785) 478-3024. Web: www.homebaking.org.

BEAT THE HEAT MONTH. Feb 1–28. A month encouraging pet owners and veterinarians to spay cats and dogs before the first heat. The goal is to prevent unwanted litters and decrease the number of animals abandoned and euthanized. For info: Marian's Dream, PO Box 150, Trumball, CT 06611. Phone: (203) 450-6112. E-mail: terry@mariansdream.org. Web: www.mariansdream.org.

BLACK MARIA STUDIO: ANNIVERSARY. Feb 1, 1893. The first moving picture studio was built at Thomas Edison's laboratory compound at West Orange, NJ, at a cost of less than $700. The wooden structure of irregular oblong shape was covered with black tar paper. It had a sharply sloping roof hinged at one edge so that half of it could be raised to admit sunlight. Fifty feet in length, it was mounted on a pivot enabling it to be swung around to follow the changing position of the sun. There was a stage draped in black at one end of the room. Though the structure was officially called a Kinetographic Theater, it was nicknamed the "Black Maria" because it resembled the old-fashioned black police wagons, also called "Black Marias," that were common earlier in the century.

CANADA: YUKON QUEST INTERNATIONAL 1,000-MILE SLED DOG RACE. Feb 1–15. Whitehorse, YT, Canada and Fairbanks, AK. Two weeks and 1,000 miles through true northern wilderness in the depths of Arctic winter, between Fairbanks, AK, and Whitehorse, YT. Top mushers from North America and around the world compete. Est attendance: 10,000. For info: Yukon Quest Intl Assn (Canada), #2-1109 First Ave, Whitehorse, YT, Canada Y1A 5G4. Phone: (867) 668-4711. Fax: (867) 668-6674. E-mail: questadmin@polarcom.com. Web: www.yukonquest.com.

CAR INSURANCE FIRST ISSUED: ANNIVERSARY. Feb 1, 1898. Travelers Insurance Company issued the first car insurance against accidents with horses.

CARAWAY, HATTIE WYATT: BIRTH ANNIVERSARY. Feb 1, 1878. Born at Bakersville, TN, Hattie Caraway became a US senator from Arkansas in 1931 when her husband died and she was appointed to fill out his term. The following year, she ran for the seat herself and became the first woman elected to the US Senate. She served 14 years there, becoming an adept and tireless legislator (once introducing 43 bills on the same day) who worked for women's rights (once cosponsoring an equal rights amendment), supported New Deal policies as well as Prohibition and opposed the increasing influence of lobbyists. Caraway died at Falls Church, VA, Dec 21, 1950. See also: "First Elected Woman Senator: Anniversary" (Jan 12).

DECORATING WITH CANDY DAY. Feb 1. Whether it's dipping store-bought cookies, marshmallows, pretzels, or making homemade cake pops and dipping them in chocolate or candy, everyone enjoys the activity and taste of candy-coated sweet treats. It's easy and a fun way to add color, flavor and a professional look to treats. Celebrate this day and share with your friends. Recipes, ideas, projects, inspiration, how-tos and more at the Wilton website. Annually, Feb 1. For info: Wilton, 2240 W 75th St, Woodridge, IL 60517. Phone: (630) 810-2221. E-mail: Vfarrasso@wilton.com. Web: www.wilton.com.

FEBRUARY IS FABULOUS FLORIDA STRAWBERRY MONTH. Feb 1–28. Strawberries in February? You bet your snow boots! Though it's cold and dreary in many parts of the country, February is fabulous in Florida, where strawberry growers are harvesting their winter crop and shipping handpicked fruit to key markets. Strawberries dipped in chocolate or champagne are a Valentine's Day delight. Consider using the ripe, luscious berry in a variety of recipes from salads to shortbread. For info: Florida Strawberry Growers Assn, PO Drawer 2550, Plant City, FL 33564. Phone: (813) 752-6822. Fax: (813) 752-2167. E-mail: info@flastrawberry.com. Web: www.StrawberrySue.com or www.flastrawberry.com.

FESTIVAL OF THE NORTH. Feb 1–28. Ketchikan, AK. A cultural event encompassing performing, visual and literary arts, including an annual Wearable Art Show, ballet performance, quilt show and a variety of arts events. Annually, the month of February. Est attendance: 2,000. For info: Ketchikan Area Arts and Humanities Council, 330 Main St, Ketchikan, AK 99910. Phone: (907) 225-2211. E-mail: info@ketchikanarts.org. Web: www.ketchikanarts.org.

FIRST SESSION OF SUPREME COURT: ANNIVERSARY. Feb 1, 1790. The Supreme Court of the US met for the first time in New York City, with Chief Justice John Jay presiding.

FORD, JOHN: BIRTH ANNIVERSARY. Feb 1, 1895. Film director John Ford was born at Cape Elizabeth, ME, as Sean Aloysius O'Feeney; he changed his name after moving to Hollywood. Ford won his first Academy Award in 1935 for *The Informer.* Among his many other films: *Stagecoach, Young Mr Lincoln, The Grapes of Wrath, How Green Was My Valley, Rio Grande, What Price Glory?* and *Mister Roberts.* During WWII he served as chief of the Field Photographic Branch of the Office of Strategic Services (OSS). Two documentaries made during the war earned him Academy Awards. He died Aug 31, 1973, at Palm Desert, CA.

FREEDOM DAY: ANNIVERSARY. Feb 1, 1865. Anniversary of President Abraham Lincoln's approval of the 13th Amendment to the US Constitution (abolishing slavery): "1. Neither slavery nor involuntary servitude, except as a punishment for crime whereof the party shall have been duly convicted, shall exist within the United States or any place subject to their jurisdiction. 2. Congress shall have power to enforce this article by appropriate legislation." The amendment had been proposed by Congress Jan 31, 1865; ratification was completed Dec 6, 1865.

"FROM AFRICA TO VIRGINIA" MONTH. Feb 1–28. Jamestown Settlement, Williamsburg, VA, and the Yorktown Victory Center, Yorktown, VA. Gallery exhibits and guided tours of the museums' outdoor living-history areas highlight the culture of the first known Africans in Virginia, and the experience of Africans in 17th- and 18th-century Virginia. For info: Jamestown-Yorktown Foundation, PO Box 1607, Williamsburg, VA 23187. Phone: (757) 253-4838 or (888) 593-4682. Fax: (757) 253-5299. Web: www.historyisfun.org.

GABLE, CLARK: BIRTH ANNIVERSARY. Feb 1, 1901. Actor William Clark Gable's first film was *The Painted Desert* in 1931, when talking films were replacing silent films. He won an Academy Award for his role in the comedy *It Happened One Night,* which established him as a romantic screen idol. Other films included *China Seas, Mutiny on the Bounty, Saratoga* and *Gone with the Wind,* for which his casting as Rhett Butler seemed a foregone conclusion due to his popularity as the acknowledged "King of Movies." Gable was born at Cadiz, OH, and died Nov 16, 1960, at Hollywood, CA, shortly after completing his last film, Arthur Miller's *The Misfits,* in which he starred with Marilyn Monroe.

"GENERAL ELECTRIC THEATER" TV PREMIERE: ANNIVERSARY. Feb 1, 1953. CBS's half-hour dramatic anthology series was hosted by Ronald Reagan (in between his movie and political careers). Making their television debuts were Joseph Cotten (1954); Fred MacMurray, James Stewart and Myrna Loy (1955); Bette Davis, Anne Baxter, Tony Curtis and Fred Astaire (1957); Sammy Davis, Jr (1958); and Gene Tierney (1960). Other memorable stars who appeared on the series included Joan Crawford, Harry Belafonte, Rosalind Russell, Ernie Kovacs, the Marx Brothers and Nancy Davis (Reagan), who starred with husband Ronald Reagan in an episode titled "A Turkey for the President" (1958).

G.I. JOE INTRODUCED: 50th ANNIVERSARY. Feb 1, 1964. This toy action figure was introduced by Hasbro and sold for $2.49. It was the first mass-market doll intended for boys and was a great success. The figure's name came from a film, *The Story of G.I. Joe* (1945), that starred Robert Mitchum and Burgess Meredith.

"GOOD TIMES" TV PREMIERE: 40th ANNIVERSARY. Feb 1, 1974. A CBS spin-off of "Maude," which was a spin-off of "All in the Family," "Good Times" featured an African-American family living in the housing projects of Chicago and struggling to improve its lot. The cast featured Esther Rolle and John Amos as Florida and James Evans, Jimmie Walker as son J.J., BernNadette Stanis as daughter Thelma, Ralph Carter as son Michael, Johnny Brown as janitor Mr Bookman, Ja'Net DuBois as neighbor Willona Woods, Janet Jackson as Willona's adopted daughter Penny and Ben Powers as Thelma's husband, Keith Anderson.

GREENSBORO SIT-IN: ANNIVERSARY. Feb 1, 1960. Commercial discrimination against blacks and other minorities provoked a nonviolent protest. At Greensboro, NC, four students from the Agricultural and Technical College (Ezell Blair, Jr; Franklin McCain; Joseph McNeill and David Richmond) sat down at an F.W. Woolworth store lunch counter and ordered coffee. Refused service, they remained all day. In the following days similar sit-ins took place at Woolworth's lunch counter. Before the week was over, they were joined by a few white students. The protest spread rapidly, especially in the South. More than 1,600 people were arrested before the year was over for participating in sit-ins. Civil rights for all became a cause for thousands of students and activists. In response, equal accommodation regardless of race became the rule at lunch counters, hotels and business establishments in thousands of places.

HERBERT, VICTOR: BIRTH ANNIVERSARY. Feb 1, 1859. Born at Dublin, Ireland, Herbert was a cellist, conductor and prolific composer of operettas who dominated the popular American music scene in the late 19th and early 20th centuries. Among his many popular operettas were *Babes in Toyland* (1903) and *Naughty Marietta* (1910). Herbert also helped found the American Society of Composers, Artists and Publishers (ASCAP), which protects artists' intellectual property rights. Herbert died May 26, 1924, at New York, NY.

HUGHES, LANGSTON: BIRTH ANNIVERSARY. Feb 1, 1902. African-American poet and author, born at Joplin, MO. Among his works are the poetry collection *Montage of a Dream Deferred,* plays, a novel, memoirs and short stories. He wrote, "My soul has grown deep like the rivers," and asked, "What happens to a dream deferred?" Hughes died May 22, 1967, at New York, NY.

HULA IN THE COOLA DAY. Feb 1. A day for those longing to escape the winter doldrums to laugh at the cold with a luau party. Put away your winter coats, get out your shorts and flip-flops, play limbo and say, "Aloha!" For info: Aigner/Prensky Marketing Group, 214 Lincoln St, Ste 300, Allston, MA 02134. Phone: (617) 254-9500. Web: www.aignerprenskymarketing.com.

INTERNATIONAL BOOST SELF-ESTEEM MONTH. Feb 1–28. A month to focus on the importance of nurturing and cultivating self-esteem to beat the winter blahs, to boost morale and to inspire yourself and others to seize new challenges. For info: Valla Dana Treuman, MEd, CLYL, 1105 N Lake Howard Dr, Winter Haven, FL 33881. Phone: (863) 875-0759. E-mail: rtreuman@gmail.com.

INTERNATIONAL EXPECT SUCCESS MONTH. Feb 1–28. A month to put the power of confident attitudes and positive living to work for you. Join the movement—touch everyone you meet with this motto: "Expect success—then work like there is no other option." For info: Karla Brandau, 4985 Chartley Circle, Ste 202, Lilburn, GA 30047. Phone: (770) 923-0883. E-mail: karla@karlabrandau.com. Web: www.karlabrandau.com/International-Expect-Success-Month.

"LATE NIGHT WITH DAVID LETTERMAN" TV PREMIERE: ANNIVERSARY. Feb 1, 1982. This is when it all began: stupid pet tricks, stupid human tricks and the legendary top 10 lists. "Late Night" premiered on NBC as a talk/variety show appearing after "The Tonight Show with Johnny Carson." Host David Letterman was known for his irreverent sense of humor and daffy antics. The offbeat show attained cult status among college crowds and insomniacs as many tuned in to see a Velcro-suited Letterman throw himself against a wall. The show also featured bandleader-sidekick

Paul Shaffer, writer Chris Elliott and Calvert DeForest as geezer Larry "Bud" Melman. In 1993 Letterman made a highly publicized exit from NBC and began hosting "The Late Show" on CBS.

LAURA INGALLS WILDER GINGERBREAD SOCIABLE. Feb 1. Pomona, CA. The 48th annual event commemorates the birthday (Feb 7, 1867) of the renowned author of the Little House books. The library has on permanent display the handwritten manuscript of *Little Town on the Prairie* and other Wilder memorabilia. Entertainment includes fiddlers, children's craft activities, apple cider and gingerbread. Annually, the first Saturday in February. Est attendance: 150. For info: Children's Dept, Pomona Public Library, 625 S Garey Ave, Pomona, CA 91766. Phone: (909) 620-2043, ext 2730. Fax: (909) 620-3713. E-mail: library@ci.pomona.ca.us.

LIBRARY LOVERS' MONTH. Feb 1–28. A monthlong celebration of school, public and private libraries of all types. This is a time for everyone, especially library support groups, to recognize the value of libraries and to work to ensure that the nation's libraries will continue to serve. For info: Library Lovers' Month. Web: www.librarysupport.net/librarylovers.

MARFAN SYNDROME AWARENESS MONTH. Feb 1–28. Volunteers across the country distribute educational information about Marfan syndrome and related connective-tissue disorders that can result in life-threatening cardiovascular problems as well as orthopedic and ophthalmologic handicaps. Marfan affects about 200,000 Americans. Annually, the month of February. For info: Cathie Tsuchiya, Natl Marfan Foundation, 22 Manhasset Ave, Port Washington, NY 11050. Phone: (800) 862-7326 or (516) 883-8712. Fax: (516) 883-8040. E-mail: ctsuchiya@marfan.org. Web: www.marfan.org.

✦NATIONAL AFRICAN AMERICAN HISTORY MONTH. Feb 1–28.

NATIONAL BIRD-FEEDING MONTH. Feb 1–28. This national event was created to advance and publicize the wild-bird-feeding and -watching hobby. Each February, the National Bird-Feeding Society promotes a new theme to help celebrate this month. For info: George D. Petrides, Sr, National Bird-Feeding Society, 7370 MacArthur Blvd, Glen Echo, MD 20812. Phone: (866) 945-3247. E-mail: info@birdfeeding.org. Web: www.birdfeeding.org.

NATIONAL BLACK HISTORY MONTH. Feb 1–28. Traditionally the month containing Abraham Lincoln's birthday (Feb 12) and Frederick Douglass's presumed birthday (Feb 14). Observance of a special period to recognize achievements and contributions by African Americans dates from February 1926, when it was launched by Dr. Carter G. Woodson. Variously designated Negro History, Black History, Afro-American History, African-American History, the observance period was initially one week, but since 1976 the entire month of February. 2014 theme: "The Golden Jubilee of the Civil Rights Act." For info: Assn for the Study of African American Life and History, Inc, Howard University, Howard Center, 2225 Georgia Ave, Ste 331, Washington, DC 20059. Phone: (202) 238-5910. Fax: (202) 986-1506. E-mail: info@asalh.net. Web: www.asalh.org.

NATIONAL CHERRY MONTH. Feb 1–28. To publicize the colorful red tart cherry. For info: Cherry Marketing Institute, PO Box 30285, Lansing, MI 48909-7785. E-mail: info@choosecherries.com. Web: www.choosecherries.com.

NATIONAL CONDOM MONTH. Feb 1–28. To educate consumers, patients, students and professionals about the prevention of sexually transmitted diseases, AIDS and teenage pregnancies. National Condom Week is Feb 14–21. For info: Fred S. Mayer, Pharmacists Planning Service, Inc (PPSI), 101 Lucas Valley Rd, Ste 386, San Rafael, CA 94903. Phone: (415) 479-8628. Fax: (415) 479-8608. E-mail: ppsi@aol.com. Web: www.ppsinc.org.

February 2014	S	M	T	W	T	F	S
							1
	2	3	4	5	6	7	8
	9	10	11	12	13	14	15
	16	17	18	19	20	21	22
	23	24	25	26	27	28	

NATIONAL MEND A BROKEN HEART MONTH. Feb 1–28. An annual observance sponsored by the nonprofit My Stuff Bags Foundation, National Mend a Broken Heart Month encourages individuals and groups to support America's children who have been abused, neglected and abandoned by the very people who should love them most. These children must be rescued from their homes, often entering crisis shelters and foster care with no personal belongings. Suggested activities include volunteering or donating funding and new belongings to support America's foster children through local organizations. For info: Diann Neill, My Stuff Bags Foundation, 5347 Sterling Center Dr, Westlake, CA 91361. Phone: (818) 865-3860. Fax: (818) 865-3865. E-mail: dneill@mystuffbags.org. Web: www.mystuffbags.org.

NATIONAL PARENT LEADERSHIP MONTH. Feb 1–28. In order to recognize, honor and celebrate parents for their vital leadership roles in their homes and communities and in state, national and international arenas, Parents Anonymous® Inc has designated the month of February as National Parent Leadership Month. This annual event acknowledges the strengths of parents as leaders and generates awareness about the important roles parents can play in shaping the lives of their families and communities. Founded in 1969, Parents Anonymous® Inc is dedicated to strengthening families by preventing child abuse and neglect all around the world. For info: Parents Anonymous Inc, 250 W First St, Ste 250, Claremont, CA 91711. Phone: (909) 236-5757. E-mail: parentsanonymous@parentsanonymous.org. Web: www.parentsanonymous.org.

NATIONAL PET DENTAL HEALTH MONTH. Feb 1–28. A nationwide effort cosponsored by veterinary dental groups and Hill's Pet Nutrition, Inc, to educate consumers on the importance of good dental care for pets. For info: American Veterinary Medical Assn. Web: www.petdental.com or www.avma.org.

✦NATIONAL TEEN DATING VIOLENCE AWARENESS AND PREVENTION MONTH. Feb 1–28. An alarming number of young people experience physical, sexual or emotional abuse as part of a controlling or violent dating relationship. This poses a threat to the health and well-being of teens across our nation, and it is essential we come together to break the cycle of violence that burdens too many of our sons and daughters. Annually during February, the US recommits to providing critical support and services for victims of dating violence and empowering teens with the tools to cultivate healthy, respectful relationships.

NATIONAL TIME MANAGEMENT MONTH. Feb 1–28. This is the month when those noble plans made in January start to go awry. This observance is dedicated to renewing those best-laid plans; breaking out those new calendars that have yet to be opened; and reevaluating and reprioritizing harried, out-of-balance lives—making specific commitments to balance them. For info: Sylvia Henderson, Springboard Training, PO Box 588, Olney, MD 20830-0588. Phone: (301) 260-1538. E-mail: sylvia@springboardtraining.com.

NATIONAL WOMEN INVENTORS MONTH. Feb 1–28. Chicago, IL. The Women Inventorz Network is the only independent organization for women inventors in the US and Canada; supporting, inspiring and building their brands through connections with each other, the media and retailers! This month we recognize and celebrate women inventors everywhere. The Women Inventor Awards Gala is held during this month. For info: The Women Inventorz Network, 8525-186th St SW, Edmonds, WA 98026. Phone: (425) 672-9794. Fax: (425) 775-1116. E-mail: mknight@womentorz.com.

ORCHID SHOW. Feb 1–Mar 23. Missouri Botanical Garden, St. Louis, MO. Spectacular display of the garden's vast orchid collection. For info: Missouri Botanical Garden, 4344 Shaw Blvd, St. Louis, MO 63110. Phone: (314) 577-5100 or (800) 642-8842. Web: www.mobot.org.

PLANT THE SEEDS OF GREATNESS MONTH. Feb 1–28. Think globally—build for the future—Plant the Seeds of Greatness. If you're unhappy with your present situation, discover how you can remove the barriers and make a change in your life for the better. Use this month to put to use your own unique prosperity consciousness and plant the seeds for your new career, life objectives or goals. Make a difference for yourself, your family, your business or your community. Get outside of your comfort zone and take action on your ideas and dreams. For info: Lorrie Walters Marsiglio, Lorimar Communications, PO Box 284-CC, Wasco, IL 60183-0284. Phone: (630) 584-9368.

RETURN SHOPPING CARTS TO THE SUPERMARKET MONTH. Feb 1–28. A monthlong opportunity to return stolen shopping carts, milk crates, bread trays and ice cream baskets to supermarkets and to avoid the increased food prices that these thefts cause. Annually, the month of February. (Originated by Anthony A. Dinolfo and the Illinois Food Retailers Association.)

ROBINSON CRUSOE DAY. Feb 1, 1709. (Old Style date.) Anniversary of the rescue of Alexander Selkirk, a Scottish sailor who had been put ashore (in September 1704) on the uninhabited island Juan Fernández, at his own request, after a quarrel with his captain. His adventures formed the basis for Daniel Defoe's book *Robinson Crusoe*. A day to be adventurous and self-reliant.

ST. LAURENT, LOUIS STEPHEN: BIRTH ANNIVERSARY. Feb 1, 1882. Canadian lawyer and prime minister, born at Compton, QC, Canada. Died at Quebec City, July 25, 1973.

"THE SECRET STORM" TV PREMIERE: 60th ANNIVERSARY. Feb 1, 1954. "The Secret Storm" lathered up homes for 20 years. The first soap on television, it revolved around the Ames family in fictional Woodbridge and featured a variety of actors and actresses who have moved on to bigger things. Among them are Bibi Besch, Roy Scheider, Diana Muldaur, Nicolas Coster, Robert Loggia, Laurence Luckinbill, Christina Crawford, Diane Ladd, Troy Donahue and Frances Sternhagen.

SIX NATIONS CHAMPIONSHIP (RBS 6 NATIONS). Feb 1–Mar 15. Annual rugby union championship between England, Wales, Scotland, Ireland, France and Italy, with several individual competitions taking place under the umbrella of the tournament (Calcutta Cup, Millennium Trophy, Giuseppe Garibaldi Trophy). Each team plays every other team once, with home field advantage alternating from one year to the next. The Six Nations grew out of the Home International Championship in 1883, with France's membership creating the Five Nations in 1910 and Italy's membership creating the current Six Nations in 2000. For info: Six Nations Rugby Ltd, 1st Floor, Simmonscourt House, Simmonscourt Road, Ballsbridge, Dublin 4, Ireland. Web: www.rbs6nations.com.

SOLO DINERS EAT OUT WEEK. Feb 1–7. Treat yourself to a meal in a restaurant—all by yourself. Settle in at a communal table, nab a stool at a counter or opt for a select table for one. Revel in a meal entirely of hors d'oeuvres or even desserts! Celebrate this all-important lifestyle skill! For info: Marya Alexander, PO Box 2664, Carlsbad, CA 92018. Phone: (760) 720-1011. E-mail: editor@solodining.com. Web: www.solodining.com.

SPACE SHUTTLE *COLUMBIA* DISASTER: ANNIVERSARY. Feb 1, 2003. Minutes before space shuttle *Columbia* was due to land after a successful 16-day scientific mission, it disintegrated 40 miles above the state of Texas, killing its seven-member crew. Commander Rick Husband, pilot William McCool, Michael Anderson, David Brown, Kalpana Chawla (first woman astronaut from India), Laurel Clark and Ilan Ramon (first Israeli astronaut) lost their lives and were mourned worldwide. *Columbia* was the first shuttle to fly in space (1981).

SPAY/NEUTER AWARENESS MONTH. Feb 1–28. Globally, roaming pets and community animals contribute to the problem of street animal overpopulation. Often local authorities and individuals use brutal methods to kill unwanted animals—methods that are not an effective long-term solution to street animal overpopulation. They may also accidentally harm the environment or kill other animals in the community. The message of this month is that by spaying or neutering your pet, by supporting spay/neuter efforts in your community and by informing others of the importance of spay/neuter, you become an important part of the solution! When we spay or neuter pets, feral cats and other street animals, we ensure that those animals' offspring will not add to the millions of already suffering animals. For info: Humane Society International. E-mail: spayday@humanesociety.org. Web: www.worldspayday.org.

SPUNKY OLD BROADS MONTH. Feb 1–28. A monthlong celebration for all women over 50 who are interested in living a regret-free life. For info: Gayle Carson, SOB, 2957 Flamingo Dr, Miami Beach, FL 33140-3916. Phone: (305) 534-8846. Fax: (305) 532-8826. E-mail: Gayle@spunkyoldbroad.com. Web: www.spunkyoldbroad.com.

TAKE YOUR CHILD TO THE LIBRARY DAY. Feb 1. Parents are encouraged to visit the public library with their children to participate in special events and learn about all the wonderful materials and services the library has to offer for families. Annually, the first Saturday in February. For info: Caitlin Augusta, Children's Librarian, Stratford Library Assn, 2203 Main St, Stratford, CT 06615. Phone: (203) 385-4165. Fax: (203) 381-2079. E-mail: caugusta@stratfordlibrary.org.

WINTERFEST FLAGSTAFF. Feb 1–28. Flagstaff, AZ. This festival, now in its 28th year, celebrates the many facets of a Flagstaff winter. Family fun for everyone: concerts, dog sled races, performances, art shows, snow sports, winter workshops, children's events and much more. The fun will go on with or without snow. Est attendance: 20,000. For info: Flagstaff Chamber of Commerce, 101 W Rte 66, Flagstaff, AZ 86001. Phone: (928) 774-4505. Fax: (928) 779-1209. Web: www.flagstaffchamber.com.

WISE HEALTH CARE CONSUMER MONTH. Feb 1–28. Teaching consumers to make better healthcare decisions is a proven way to reduce healthcare costs. For this reason, companies, hospitals and MCOs are offering medical self-care programs for employees, subscribers and patients. Wise Health Care Consumer Marketing packet available. For info: American Institute for Preventive Medicine, 30445 Northwestern Hwy, Ste 350, Farmington Hills, MI 48334. Phone: (248) 539-1800. Fax: (248) 539-1808. E-mail: aipm@healthylife.com. Web: www.healthylife.com/wise.

WOMEN'S HEART WEEK. Feb 1–7. Since 1995. Women's Heart Foundation's nationally recognized program to raise awareness about the number one killer of American women: heart disease. The program introduces fun activities to promote healthier living. View the Women's Heart Week video online at www.womensheart.org. This is a turnkey program for health sites around the country to commemorate using the Seven Focus Days for women's heart wellness and awareness. Suggested activities include a Red Dress luncheon, free screenings and Heart Center tours and presentations. For info: Women's Heart Foundation, PO Box 7827, West Trenton, NJ 08628. Phone: (609) 771-9600. Fax: (609) 771-3778. E-mail: Bonnie@womensheart.org. Web: www.womensheart.org.

WORKING NAKED DAY. Feb 1. Working Naked Day is dedicated to those who are working from home "naked"—stripped of the resources that millions take for granted in the traditional corporate workplace. Annually, Feb 1. For info: Lisa Kanarek, 11700 Preston Rd, Ste 660-120, Dallas, TX 75230. E-mail: lisa@workingnaked.com. Web: www.workingnaked.com.

WORLDWIDE RENAISSANCE OF THE HEART MONTH. Feb 1–28. This month is dedicated to compassionately thinking with your heart as well as your intellect. During this month, you are asked to take a heartfelt look at the way you think. On the first Saturday of this month, the Worldwide Renaissance of the Heart Tea takes place at noon all around the world. This informal tea is dedicated to heartfelt thinking. Remember to give your heart a renaissance! For info: Month Spokesperson Deb Kulkkula, 381 Billings Rd, Fitchburg, MA 01420-1407. Phone: (978) 343-4009. E-mail: RenaissanceLady@RenaissanceoftheHeart.com. Web: www.RenaissanceoftheHeart.com.

YELTSIN, BORIS: BIRTH ANNIVERSARY. Feb 1, 1931. First president of the Russian Federation, born at Butka, Sverdlovsk, Russia. He worked in construction in his youth and rose through the Communist Party ranks to become mayor of Moscow. Estranged from the party for his criticism of Mikhail Gorbachev but popular with the people, he was elected president by the Russian parliament in 1989, and in 1991, after the breakup of the Soviet Union, he was reelected in the first popular election to take place in that nation's history. His work focused on transforming the Russian economy and on establishing a constitution and revising systems of parliament within the Russian government. His administration was fraught with controversy, and he survived two impeachment attempts before he resigned on Dec 31, 1999, appointing Vladimir Putin as his successor. Yeltsin died at Moscow, Apr 23, 2007.

"YOU ARE THERE" TV PREMIERE: ANNIVERSARY. Feb 1, 1953. The program began as an inventive radio show in 1947. News correspondents would comb the annals of history and "interview" the movers and shakers of times past. Walter Cronkite hosted the series on CBS for four seasons. The show's concept was revived for a season in 1971, with Cronkite gearing the program toward children.

YOUTH LEADERSHIP MONTH. Feb 1–28. This month is dedicated to celebrating young people who take on leadership roles in their lives. It is also dedicated to encouraging those who have not yet done so to consider doing so because they can. Programs that focus on youth leadership opportunities and effective leadership skill building are appropriate for this month. For info: Sylvia Henderson, Springboard Training, PO Box 588, Olney, MD 20830-0588. Phone: (301) 260-1538. E-mail: sylvia@springboardtraining.com.

BIRTHDAYS TODAY

Michelle Akers, 48, former soccer player, born Santa Clara, CA, Feb 1, 1966.

Big Boi, 39, singer, musician (Outkast), born Antwan Patton at Savannah, GA, Feb 1, 1975.

Lauren Conrad, 28, television personality ("The Hills," "Laguna Beach"), born Laguna Beach, CA, Feb 1, 1986.

Michael B. Enzi, 70, US Senator (R, Wyoming), born Bremerton, WA, Feb 1, 1944.

Don Everly, 77, singer, musician, with brother Phil (The Everly Brothers), born Brownie, KY, Feb 1, 1937.

Sherilyn Fenn, 49, actress ("Twin Peaks," *Wild at Heart*), born Detroit, MI, Feb 1, 1965.

Michael C. Hall, 43, actor ("Six Feet Under," "Dexter"), born Raleigh, NC, Feb 1, 1971.

Bob Jamieson, 71, broadcast journalist, born Streator, IL, Feb 1, 1943.

Terry Jones, 72, actor, director ("Monty Python's Flying Circus"), born Colwyn Bay, Wales, Feb 1, 1942.

Galway Kinnell, 87, poet, born Providence, RI, Feb 1, 1927.

Garrett Morris, 77, comedian ("Saturday Night Live"), born New Orleans, LA, Feb 1, 1937.

Bill Mumy, 60, actor, born El Centro, CA, Feb 1, 1954.

Lisa Marie Presley, 46, singer, born Memphis, TN, Feb 1, 1968.

Pauly Shore, 44, comedian, actor, born Los Angeles, CA, Feb 1, 1970.

Stuart Whitman, 85, actor ("Cimarron Strip," *The Seekers*), born San Francisco, CA, Feb 1, 1929.

February 2014

S	M	T	W	T	F	S
						1
2	3	4	5	6	7	8
9	10	11	12	13	14	15
16	17	18	19	20	21	22
23	24	25	26	27	28	

February 2 — Sunday

DAY 33 — **332 REMAINING**

BASEBALL HALL OF FAME'S CHARTER MEMBERS: ANNIVERSARY. Feb 2, 1936. The five charter members of the brand-new Baseball Hall of Fame at Cooperstown, NY, were announced. Of 226 ballots cast, Ty Cobb was named on 222, Babe Ruth on 215, Honus Wagner on 215, Christy Mathewson on 205 and Walter Johnson on 189. A total of 170 votes were necessary to be elected to the Hall of Fame.

BENÉT, WILLIAM ROSE: BIRTH ANNIVERSARY. Feb 2, 1886. American poet and critic. Born at Fort Hamilton, NY; died at New York, NY, May 4, 1950.

BONZA BOTTLER DAY™. Feb 2. To celebrate when the number of the day is the same as the number of the month. Bonza Bottler Day™ is an excuse to have a party at least once a month. For more information see Jan 1. For info: Gail Berger, 14 Fernwood Dr, Taylors, SC 29687. Phone: (864) 201-3988. E-mail: bonza@bonzabottlerday.com. Web: www.bonzabottlerday.com.

CANDLEMAS DAY or PRESENTATION OF THE LORD. Feb 2. Observed in the Roman Catholic Church. Commemorates presentation of Jesus in the Temple and the purification of Mary 40 days after his birth. Candles have been blessed since the 11th century. This marks the end of the Christmas liturgical season. Formerly called the Feast of Purification of the Blessed Virgin Mary. Old Scottish couplet proclaims: "If Candlemas is fair and clear/There'll be two winters in the year."

CHILDREN'S AUTHORS & ILLUSTRATORS WEEK. Feb 2–8. To celebrate and recognize authors and illustrators who create books for young people and promote literacy by inspiring enjoyment of quality literature. During this week, members of the Children's Authors Network speak at schools, libraries and children's shelters. Motivate children to read and write: invite authors and illustrators to schools and venues near you! Annually, the first full week in February. For info: Children's Authors Network! (CAN!), 23291 Mobile St, West Hills, CA 91307. Phone: (818) 615-0857. Web: www.childrensauthorsnetwork.com.

ENGLAND: GRIMALDI MEMORIAL SERVICE/CLOWN CHURCH SERVICE. Feb 2. Holy Trinity Church, Dalston, London. Church service (since 1946) celebrating Joseph Grimaldi (1778–1837), England's greatest clown. Also commemorates clowns who have died during the past year. Clowns—in dress and not—attend and entertain afterward. Annually, the first Sunday in February.

FAWCETT, FARRAH: BIRTH ANNIVERSARY. Feb 2, 1947. Actress and '70s pop culture icon, born at Corpus Christi, TX. Almost as famous for her feathered hairstyle as for her acting, she was the star of television's "Charlie's Angels" and later earned several Emmy and Golden Globe nominations for her dramatic roles in made-for-television movies such as *The Burning Bed* and *Small Sacrifices*. Fawcett's 1976 swimsuit poster is the bestselling pinup of all time. She died at Santa Monica, CA, June 25, 2009.

GERMAN SURRENDER AT STALINGRAD: ANNIVERSARY. Feb 2, 1943. Two pockets of starving German soldiers remained in Stalingrad, USSR, on this date. They had received few supplies since Soviet soldiers had encircled the city the previous November. Friedrich Paulus, whom Hitler had promoted to field marshal only the day before, was forced to seek surrender terms, thereby becoming the first German marshal to surrender. Hitler was furious with Paulus, believing he should have preferred suicide to surrender. Approximately 160,000 Germans died in the Stalingrad Battle; 34,000 were evacuated by air. Of the 90,000 captured and sent to Siberia on foot, tens of thousands died on the way. This Allied victory is generally considered the psychological turning point of WWII.

GETZ, STAN: BIRTH ANNIVERSARY. Feb 2, 1927. American jazz saxophonist Stan Getz was born at Philadelphia, PA. He introduced the cool-jazz style, which became a major movement in the 1950s, and the bossa nova (new wave) style of the 1960s. Getz received 11 Grammy Awards and was the first jazz musician to win the Grammy Award for Record of the Year (1965), for "The Girl from Ipanema." Died at Malibu, CA, June 6, 1991.

GROUNDHOG DAY. Feb 2. Old belief that if the sun shines on Candlemas Day, or if the groundhog sees his shadow when he emerges on this day, six weeks of winter will ensue.

GROUNDHOG DAY IN PUNXSUTAWNEY, PENNSYLVANIA. Feb 2. Punxsutawney, PA. Widely observed traditional annual Candlemas Day event at which "Punxsutawney Phil, king of the weather prophets," is the object of a search. Tradition is said to have been established by early German settlers. The official trek (which began in 1887) is followed by a weather prediction for the next six weeks. Phil made his dramatic film debut with Bill Murray in *Groundhog Day*.

HALAS, GEORGE: BIRTH ANNIVERSARY. Feb 2, 1895. George "Papa Bear" Halas, Pro Football Hall of Fame coach and team owner, born at Chicago, IL. After playing football at the University of Illinois and baseball with the New York Yankees, Halas helped to found the National Football League and the Chicago Bears in 1920. As coach of the Bears for 40 years, he compiled a record of 324 wins, 151 losses and 31 ties. Charter member of the Hall of Fame, 1963. Died at Chicago, Oct 31, 1983.

HEDGEHOG DAY. Feb 2. This ancient Roman tradition was the inspiration for Groundhog Day in the US. Romans observed whether a hedgehog emerging from hibernation could see its shadow in the moonlight—if it could, then six more weeks of winter were expected. Later observed as a folk holiday in Europe and the British Isles.

IMBOLC. Feb 2. (Also called Imbolg, Candlemas, Lupercalia, Feast of Pan, Feast of Torches, Feast of Waxing Light, Brigit's Day and Oimelc.) One of the "Greater Sabbats" during the Wiccan year, Imbolc marks the recovery of the Goddess (after giving birth to the Sun, or the God, at Yule) and celebrates the anticipation of spring. Annually, Feb 2.

JOYCE, JAMES: BIRTH ANNIVERSARY. Feb 2, 1882. Irish novelist and poet, author of *Dubliners, A Portrait of the Artist as a Young Man, Ulysses* and *Finnegans Wake*, born at Dublin, Ireland. "A man of genius," he wrote in *Ulysses*, "makes no mistakes. His errors are volitional and are portals of discovery." Of *Finnegans Wake*, Joyce is reported to have replied to an academic whose letter had asked for clues to its meaning, "If I can throw any obscurity on the subject, let me know." Joyce died at the age of 58 of peritonitis Jan 13, 1941, at Zurich, Switzerland, and was buried there.

LUXEMBOURG: CANDLEMAS. Feb 2. Traditional observance of Candlemas. At night children sing a customary song wishing health and prosperity to their neighbors and receive sweets in return. They carry special candles called *Lichtebengel*, symbolizing the coming of spring.

MEXICO: DIA DE LA CANDELARIA. Feb 2. "Day of the Light." All Mexico celebrates. Dances, processions, bullfights.

NEW AMSTERDAM (NEW YORK) INCORPORATED AS CITY: ANNIVERSARY. Feb 2, 1653. The magistrates of the Dutch colony on Manhattan Island signed a municipal charter making New Amsterdam a city. This was the official birth of New York City, as New Amsterdam was renamed in August 1664, when the English took over the colony. New York was named in honor of James, the Duke of York, brother to the English king Charles II.

PUBLICITY FOR PROFIT WEEK. Feb 2–8. Harness the power of free publicity for yourself, your business or your organization. Spend each day this week getting free publicity by doing one task to promote whatever you deem important. For free and easy-to-follow publicity plans, send e-mail request or SASE. Free publicity newsletter also available. For info: Tom Peric, Publicity for Profit, 2040 Fairfax Ave, Cherry Hill, NJ 08003. Phone: (856) 874-0049. Fax: (856) 874-0052. E-mail: tom@thegalileo.com.

RAND, AYN: BIRTH ANNIVERSARY. Feb 2, 1905. Novelist (*The Fountainhead, Atlas Shrugged*), born Alyssa Rosenbaum at St. Petersburg, Russia. Founded the Objectivism school of philosophy. Died Mar 6, 1982, at New York, NY.

***THE RECORD OF A SNEEZE*: ANNIVERSARY.** Feb 2, 1893. One day after Thomas Edison's "Black Maria" studio was completed at West Orange, NJ, a studio cameraman took the first "close-up" in film history. *The Record of a Sneeze*, starring Edison's assistant Fred P. Ott, was also the first motion picture to receive a copyright (1894). See also: "Black Maria Studio: Anniversary" (Feb 1).

SLED DOGS SAVE NOME: ANNIVERSARY. Feb 2, 1925. When a diphtheria outbreak was diagnosed in Nome, AK (population 1,500), on Jan 21, the nearest large amount of antitoxin serum was in Anchorage. Bitter winter temperatures made air delivery impossible, so a heroic dog sled relay was set up. Some 300,000 units of serum were delivered by train to Nenana, AK, and on Jan 27—in temperatures of 40–50 degrees below zero (Fahrenheit)—20 mushers drove scores of dogs on a 674-mile journey to Nome in 127 hours. Togo was the lead dog for the first 350 miles, and Balto was the lead dog on the final 53 miles. The frozen serum arrived at 5:30 AM, and once it was thawed and administered, there were no more diphtheria deaths. Balto became a national hero, and a statue was erected in his honor in New York City's Central Park.

SUPER BOWL XLVIII. Feb 2. MetLife Stadium, East Rutherford, NJ. The battle between the NFC and AFC champions. For info: The National Football League. Web: www.nfl.com.

SWITZERLAND: HOMSTROM. Feb 2. Scuol. Burning of straw men on poles as a symbol of winter's imminent departure. Annually, the first Sunday in February.

TREATY OF GUADALUPE HIDALGO: ANNIVERSARY. Feb 2, 1848. The war between Mexico and the US formally ended with the Treaty of Guadalupe Hidalgo, signed in the village for which it was named. The treaty provided for Mexico's cession to the US of the territory that became the states of California, Nevada and Utah, most of Arizona, and parts of New Mexico, Colorado and Wyoming in exchange for $15 million from the US. In addition, Mexico relinquished all rights to Texas north of the Rio Grande. The Senate ratified the treaty Mar 10, 1848.

WALTON, GEORGE: DEATH ANNIVERSARY. Feb 2, 1804. Signer of the Declaration of Independence. Born at Prince Edward County, VA, 1749 (exact date unknown). Died at Augusta, GA.

"WHAT'S MY LINE?" TV PREMIERE: ANNIVERSARY. Feb 2, 1950. This popular game show premiered on CBS and ran for 17 years in primetime. A panel of four celebrities figured out the professions of the contestants and the identities of the mystery guests by asking yes-or-no questions. The first panel consisted of poet Louis Untermeyer, columnist Dorothy Kilgallen, former New Jersey governor Harold Hoffman and psychiatrist Dr. Richard Hoffman. Yankee Phil Rizzuto was the first mystery guest. John Daly hosted.

BIRTHDAYS TODAY

Christie Brinkley, 61, model, born Monroe, MI, Feb 2, 1953.

John Cornyn, 62, US Senator (R, Texas), born Houston, TX, Feb 2, 1952.

Ina Garten, 66, chef, cookbook author, television personality ("The Barefoot Contessa"), born Brooklyn, NY, Feb 2, 1948.

Bo Hopkins, 72, actor, born Greenwood, SC, Feb 2, 1942.

Zosia Mamet, 26, actress ("Girls," "United States of Tara," "Mad Men"), born Randolph, VT, Feb 2, 1988.

Robert Mandan, 82, actor ("Soap," "Days of Our Lives"), born Clever, MO, Feb 2, 1932.

Graham Nash, 72, musician, singer, born Blackpool, England, Feb 2, 1942.

Liz Smith, 91, journalist, author, born Fort Worth, TX, Feb 2, 1923.

Tom Smothers, 77, comedian, folksinger ("The Smothers Brothers Comedy Hour"), born New York, NY, Feb 2, 1937.

Elaine Stritch, 89, singer, actress (*Company, Elaine Stritch at Liberty*), born Birmingham, MI, Feb 2, 1925.

Michael T. Weiss, 52, actor ("The Pretender"), born Chicago, IL, Feb 2, 1962.

February 3 — Monday

DAY 34 — **331 REMAINING**

BLACKWELL, ELIZABETH: BIRTH ANNIVERSARY. Feb 3, 1821. First woman physician. Born near Bristol, England, she and several other members of her family were active abolitionists, women's suffrage advocates and pioneers in women's medicine. Her family moved to New York State in 1832, and she received a medical doctor's degree at Geneva, NY, in 1849. She established a hospital in New York City with an all-woman staff, where she recruited nurses and trained them for service in the Civil War. Returning to England in 1869, she continued to teach and practice medicine until her death at Hastings, England, May 31, 1910.

CIVIL WAR PEACE TALKS: ANNIVERSARY. Feb 3, 1865. Abraham Lincoln and his secretary of state, William Seward, met to discuss peace with Confederate vice president Alexander Stephens and others at Hampton Roads, VA. The meeting, which took place on board the ship *River Queen*, lasted four hours and produced no positive results. The Confederates sought an armistice first and discussion of reunion later, while Lincoln was insistent that recognition of Federal authority must be the first step toward peace.

"THE DAY THE MUSIC DIED": 55th ANNIVERSARY. Feb 3, 1959. The anniversary of the death of rock-and-roll legend Charles Hardin "Buddy" Holly. "The Day the Music Died," so called in singer Don McLean's song "American Pie," is the date on which Holly was killed in a plane crash in a cornfield near Mason City, IA, along with J.P. Richardson (otherwise known as "The Big Bopper") and Richie Valens. Holly was born Sept 7, 1936, at Lubbock, TX.

DUMP YOUR "SIGNIFICANT JERK" WEEK. Feb 3–9. It's time to take out the garbage and get rid of that "jerk" boyfriend or girlfriend. This year will be the 20th annual call to arms. Annually, the week before Valentine's Day. For info: Marcus P. Meleton, Jr, PO Box 940159, Houston, TX 77094. Phone: (949) 413-3052. E-mail: mm@sharkbaitpress.com.

FIFTEENTH AMENDMENT TO US CONSTITUTION RATIFIED: ANNIVERSARY. Feb 3, 1870. The 15th Amendment granted that the right of citizens to vote shall not be denied on account of race, color or previous condition of servitude.

FOUR CHAPLAINS MEMORIAL DAY: ANNIVERSARY. Feb 3, 1943. Commemorates four chaplains (George Fox, Alexander Goode, Clark Poling, John Washington) who sacrificed their life belts and lives when the SS *Dorchester* was torpedoed off Greenland during WWII.

GREELEY, HORACE: BIRTH ANNIVERSARY. Feb 3, 1811. Newspaper editor, born at Amherst, NH. Founder of the *New York Tribune* and one of the organizers of the Republican Party, Greeley was an outspoken opponent of slavery. Best remembered for his saying, "Go West, young man." Died Nov 29, 1872, at New York City.

INCOME TAX BIRTHDAY: SIXTEENTH AMENDMENT TO US CONSTITUTION RATIFIED. Feb 3, 1913. The 16th Amendment was ratified, granting Congress the authority to levy taxes on income. (Church bells did not ring throughout the land, and no dancing in the streets was reported.)

INTERNATIONAL NETWORKING WEEK®. Feb 3–7. To celebrate the key role that networking plays in the development and success of businesses around the world, recognizing networking as an essential tool for success. Simultaneous events will be held globally, bringing together representatives of government, businesses and the community to network with each other, understand the concept of good networking and listen to talks by networking specialists from around the world. For info: Ivan Misner, PhD, BNI, 545 College Commerce Way, Upland, CA 91786. Phone: (800) 825-8286 or (909) 608-7575. Fax: (909) 608-7676. E-mail: internationalnetworkingweek@bni.com. Web: www.internationalnetworkingweek.com.

JAPAN: BEAN-THROWING FESTIVAL (SETSUBUN). Feb 3. Setsubun marks the last day of winter according to the lunar calendar. Throngs at temple grounds throw beans to drive away imaginary devils.

JOHNSTON, JOSEPH: BIRTH ANNIVERSARY. Feb 3, 1807. Born near Farmville, VA, and died Mar 21, 1891, at Washington, DC. Confederate general in the Civil War whose troops were never directly defeated. Long-standing differences with Jefferson Davis, president of the Confederacy, prevented him from reaching his full potential as a military leader.

LINCOLN, ABRAHAM: OREGON BIRTHDAY OBSERVANCE. Feb 3. Observed annually in Oregon on the first Monday in February. See also: "Lincoln, Abraham: Birth Anniversary" (Feb 12).

February 2014

S	M	T	W	T	F	S
						1
2	3	4	5	6	7	8
9	10	11	12	13	14	15
16	17	18	19	20	21	22
23	24	25	26	27	28	

MICHENER, JAMES: BIRTH ANNIVERSARY. Feb 3, 1907. American author, born at New York, NY. His *Tales of the South Pacific* was the basis for the popular musical *South Pacific*. A prolific author, his works include *Sayonara, Iberia, Hawaii, Centennial* and *Texas*. Died at Austin, TX, Oct 17, 1997.

MOZAMBIQUE: HEROES' DAY. Feb 3. National holiday. Honors all heroic citizens, especially Eduardo Mondlane, leader of the fight for independence, assassinated on Feb 3, 1969.

NAUVOO LEGION CHARTERED: ANNIVERSARY. Feb 3, 1841. Created by Illinois charter and composed of 5,000 Mormon men under the command of Lieutenant General Joseph Smith, the Nauvoo Legion was considered the "largest trained soldiery in the US" except for the US Army.

NISSEN, GEORGE: 100th BIRTH ANNIVERSARY. Feb 3, 1914. Champion teenage gymnast Nissen invented the trampoline, and trademarked the name in 1937. After WWII, he was an indefatigable marketer of the portable jumping station that he also manufactured. He lived to see trampolining become an Olympic event in 2000. Born at Blairstown, IA, Nissen died at San Diego, CA, Apr 7, 2010.

ROCKWELL, NORMAN: BIRTH ANNIVERSARY. Feb 3, 1894. American artist and illustrator especially noted for his realistic and homey magazine cover art for the *Saturday Evening Post*. Born at New York, NY, he died at Stockbridge, MA, Nov 8, 1978.

SPACE MILESTONE: *CHALLENGER STS-10* (US): 30th ANNIVERSARY. Feb 3, 1984. Shuttle *Challenger* launched from Kennedy Space Center, FL, with a crew of five—Vance Brand, Robert Gibson, Ronald McNair, Bruce McCandless and Robert Stewart. On Feb 7 McCandless and Stewart became the first to fly freely in space (propelled by their backpack jets), untethered to any craft. Landed at Cape Canaveral, FL, Feb 11.

STEIN, GERTRUDE: BIRTH ANNIVERSARY. Feb 3, 1874. Avant-garde expatriate American writer, perhaps best remembered for her poetic declaration (in 1913): "Rose is a rose is a rose is a rose." Born at Allegheny, PA; died at Paris, France, July 27, 1946.

VIETNAM: NATIONAL HOLIDAY. Feb 3. National holiday. Anniversary of the founding of the Vietnamese Communist Party, Feb 3, 1930.

WEIL, SIMONE: BIRTH ANNIVERSARY. Feb 3, 1909. French philosopher and social activist whose impact came posthumously with the publication of her many notebooks. Born at Paris, France, Weil died at Ashford, England, on Aug 24, 1943. Her 20 volumes of writings include these thoughts: "What a country calls its vital economic interests are not the things which enable its citizens to live, but the things which enable it to make war. Gasoline is much more likely than wheat to be a cause of international conflict."

BIRTHDAYS TODAY

Robert Bentley, 71, Governor of Alabama (R), born Columbiana, AL, Feb 3, 1943.

Shelley Berman, 88, comedian ("Mary Hartman, Mary Hartman"), born Chicago, IL, Feb 3, 1926.

Thomas Calabro, 55, actor ("Melrose Place"), born Brooklyn, NY, Feb 3, 1959.

Blythe Danner, 71, actress (*Butterflies Are Free, Brighton Beach Memoirs*), born Philadelphia, PA, Feb 3, 1943.

Vlade Divac, 46, former basketball player, born Prijepolje, Yugoslavia (now Serbia), Feb 3, 1968.

Morgan Fairchild, 64, actress ("Dallas," "Falcon Crest," "Flamingo Road"), born Patsy McClenny at Dallas, TX, Feb 3, 1950.

Isla Fisher, 38, actress (*Wedding Crashers, The Lookout*), born Muscat, Oman, Feb 3, 1976.

Keith Gordon, 53, actor (*Dressed to Kill, A Midnight Clear*), director, born New York, NY, Feb 3, 1961.

Robert Allen (Bob) Griese, 69, sportscaster, Hall of Fame football player, born Evansville, IN, Feb 3, 1945.

Nathan Lane, 58, actor (Tonys for *A Funny Thing Happened on the Way to the Forum* and *The Producers*; *The Birdcage*), born Jersey City, NJ, Feb 3, 1956.

Francis Asbury (Fran) Tarkenton, 74, Hall of Fame football player, born Richmond, VA, Feb 3, 1940.

Maura Tierney, 49, actress ("NewsRadio," "ER"), born Boston, MA, Feb 3, 1965.

February 4 — Tuesday

DAY 35 **330 REMAINING**

AFRICAN-AMERICAN COACHES DAY. Feb 4. To provide a day each year to educate the African-American community about the value of working with a personal or business coach and to provide an opportunity for coaches and their clients to acknowledge the results and progress made through the coaching process. Annually, the first Tuesday in February. For info: Monique Belton, PhD, 35 Dix Hills Rd, Huntington, NY 11743. Phone: (631) 549-7314. E-mail: info@drmoniquebelton.com.

ANGOLA: ARMED STRUGGLE DAY. Feb 4. National holiday. Commemorates the beginning of the struggle for independence from Portugal in 1961.

APACHE WARS BEGIN: ANNIVERSARY. Feb 4, 1861. The period of conflict known as the Apache Wars began at Apache Pass, AZ, when army lieutenant George Bascom arrested Apache chief Cochise and other tribe members for raiding a ranch. Bascom killed Cochise's brother, but Cochise escaped and declared war. The wars lasted 25 years under the leadership of Cochise and, later, Geronimo.

FACEBOOK LAUNCHES: 10th ANNIVERSARY. Feb 4, 2004. Mark Zuckerberg and fellow Harvard students Dustin Moskovitz, Chris Hughes and Eduardo Saverin launched "TheFacebook" as a social networking site. Facebook, later dropping the "The," quickly became an Internet sensation, reaching 901 million users by March 2012. The site currently has more than 500 million daily users (80 percent of whom live outside North America) and is offered in 70 languages. On May 18, 2012, Facebook went public, with a volume of 567 million shares trading that day.

FRIEDAN, BETTY: BIRTH ANNIVERSARY. Feb 4, 1921. The cofounder and first president of the National Organization for Women (NOW) was born Bettye Naomi Goldstein at Peoria, IL. She was an outspoken feminist who spent her entire career crusading for women's rights. Her book *The Feminine Mystique* chronicled the frustrations of the 1960s American housewife, to which she referred as "the problem that has no name." The book struck a chord with millions of women and is widely regarded as one of the most influential books of the 20th century. Friedan died at Washington, DC, on Feb 4, 2006, her 85th birthday.

KOŚCIUSZKO, TADEUSZ: BIRTH ANNIVERSARY. Feb 4, 1746. Polish patriot and American Revolutionary War figure. Born at Lithuania, he died at Solothurn, Switzerland, Oct 15, 1817.

LINDBERGH, CHARLES AUGUSTUS: BIRTH ANNIVERSARY. Feb 4, 1902. American aviator Charles "Lucky Lindy" Lindbergh was the first to fly solo and nonstop over the Atlantic Ocean, New York to Paris, May 20–21, 1927. Born at Detroit, MI; died at Kipahulu, Maui, HI, Aug 27, 1974. See also: "Lindbergh Flight: Anniversary" (May 20).

NELSON, BYRON: BIRTH ANNIVERSARY. Feb 4, 1912. "Lord Byron" was the premier golfer of the 1930s and '40s, whose spectacular play in 1945 enshrined him as one of the legendary sportsmen of all time. In 1945 Nelson won 11 consecutive tournaments, with the season's total coming to 18. That single-season victory record has never been equaled. In all, Nelson had 52 PGA victories in a professional career that began in 1932. He retired from full-time play in 1946. Nelson's golf swing is still considered the one to emulate today. Born John Byron Nelson, Jr, near Waxahachie, TX, he died Sept 26, 2006, at Roanoke, TX.

PARKS, ROSA: BIRTH ANNIVERSARY. Feb 4, 1913. Born Rosa Louise McCauley in Tuskegee, AL, Rosa Parks was a seamstress who was active with the NAACP. On a fateful day in Montgomery, AL, in 1955, a time when African Americans were obligated by law to ride in the back of a bus, she refused to give up her seat to a white man during a ride home from work. Parks was subsequently arrested, found guilty of disorderly conduct and fined $14. This simple act sparked the modern civil rights movement, leading to a 381-day boycott of the Montgomery bus system, lawsuits and an eventual Supreme Court decision decreeing segregation to be unconstitutional. A hero to blacks and whites alike, Parks continued work on civil rights until her death on Oct 25, 2005, at Detroit, MI. She was awarded the Presidential Medal of Freedom and the Congressional Gold Medal, and she is the only American woman to lie in state at the US Capitol Rotunda. Many municipalities consider Dec 1, the day of her arrest in 1955, a holiday: Rosa Parks Day.

SRI LANKA: INDEPENDENCE DAY: ANNIVERSARY. Feb 4. Democratic Socialist Republic of Sri Lanka observes National Day. Public holiday. On Feb 4, 1948, Ceylon (as it was then known) obtained independence from Great Britain. The country's name was changed to Sri Lanka in 1972.

USO FOUNDED: ANNIVERSARY. Feb 4, 1941. This civilian agency was founded in 1941 to provide support worldwide for US service people and their families. The United Service Organizations (USO) centers have served as a home away from home for hundreds of thousands of Americans.

BIRTHDAYS TODAY

Gabrielle Anwar, 43, actress (*Scent of a Woman*, "The Tudors," "Burn Notice"), born Laleham, England, Feb 4, 1971.

Clint Black, 52, country singer, songwriter, born Katy, TX, Feb 4, 1962.

David Brenner, 69, comedian, born Philadelphia, PA, Feb 4, 1945.

Gary Conway, 78, actor ("Burke's Law," *I Was a Teenage Frankenstein*), born Boston, MA, Feb 4, 1936.

Alice Cooper, 66, singer, songwriter, born Vincent Damon Furnier at Detroit, MI, Feb 4, 1948.

Rob Corddry, 43, writer, comedian ("The Daily Show"), born Weymouth, MA, Feb 4, 1971.

Oscar De La Hoya, 41, boxer, born Los Angeles, CA, Feb 4, 1973.

Lisa Eichhorn, 62, actress (*The Vanishing, King of the Hill*), born Reading, PA, Feb 4, 1952.

Michael Goorjian, 43, actor ("Party of Five"), born San Francisco, CA, Feb 4, 1971.

J. Danforth (Dan) Quayle, 67, 44th vice president of the US (1989–93), born Indianapolis, IN, Feb 4, 1947.

John Schuck, 74, actor ("McMillan and Wife," *McCabe and Mrs Miller, Dick Tracy*), born Boston, MA, Feb 4, 1940.

Lawrence Taylor, 55, Hall of Fame football player, born Williamsburg, VA, Feb 4, 1959.

February 2014	S	M	T	W	T	F	S
							1
	2	3	4	5	6	7	8
	9	10	11	12	13	14	15
	16	17	18	19	20	21	22
	23	24	25	26	27	28	

February 5 — Wednesday

DAY 36 — **329 REMAINING**

AMERICAN CAMP ASSOCIATION NATIONAL CONFERENCE. Feb 5–8. Orlando, FL. Explore both the meaning and the depth of our experience with children, youth, teens and families. With the strength of our voices and the compelling story of the camp experience, we can make a powerful societal impact. The National Conference will include a wide array of educational programs, keynote addresses and social networking opportunities. For info: American Camp Assn, 5000 State Rd 67 N, Martinsville, IN 46151. Phone: (765) 342-8456. Web: www.ACACamps.org.

BURROUGHS, WILLIAM S.: 100th BIRTH ANNIVERSARY. Feb 5, 1914. Renowned Beat author born at St Louis, MO. His novels, notably *Naked Lunch* (1959), pushed fiction to the outermost limits and explored previously taboo subjects such as drug use, homosexuality and systems of control, and his books were frequently banned. Burroughs once stated "all fiction is autobiographical and all autobiography is fiction." He died Aug 2, 1997, at Lawrence, KS.

CARRADINE, JOHN: BIRTH ANNIVERSARY. Feb 5, 1906. American film actor John Carradine was born Richmond Reed Carradine at Greenwich Village, NY. He appeared in more than 200 films. Frequently observed wandering the streets in a velvet suit and satin cape while reciting Shakespeare, he became known as "the Bard of the Boulevard." Died Nov 27, 1988, at Milan, Italy.

DIGITAL LEARNING DAY. Feb 5. 4th annual. Digital Learning Day is a set of activities in Washington, DC, and across the US that occur all year round but culminate in a national celebration on Feb 5, 2014. This day celebrates teachers and shines a spotlight on successful instructional practice and effective use of technology in classrooms across the country. The inaugural day in 2011 boasted more than 18,000 teachers representing nearly two million students. For info: Alliance for Excellent Education and the Center for Digital Learning. Web: www.digitallearningday.org.

EMPIRE STATE BUILDING RUN UP, POWERED BY MMRF. Feb 5. Empire State Building, New York, NY. 37th annual. One of the premier events in tower racing. This is a race for the adventurous, whether they've been practicing for stair-climbs around the world or they're trying this quirky event for the first time. More than 700 runners face 1,576 steps on their way to the finish. Many run to raise funds for the Multiple Myeloma Research Foundation (MMRF), a leading cancer research foundation. For info: New York Road Runners. Phone: (212) 423-2287. E-mail: mynyrr@nyrr.org. Web: www.nyrr.org.

FAMILY-LEAVE BILL: ANNIVERSARY. Feb 5, 1993. President William Clinton signed legislation requiring companies with 50 or more employees (and all government agencies) to allow employees to take up to 12 weeks of unpaid leave in a 12-month period to deal with the birth or adoption of a child or to care for a relative with a serious health problem. The bill became effective Aug 5, 1993.

JAPAN: SAPPORO SNOW FESTIVAL. Feb 5–11. Sapporo, Hokkaido. 65th annual. Every winter, a large number of splendid snow statues and ice sculptures line Odori Park, the grounds at Community Dome Tsudome and the main street in Susukino. For seven days in February, these statues and sculptures (both large and small) turn Sapporo into a winter dreamland of crystal-like ice and white snow. Est attendance: 2,000,000. For info: Sapporo Snow Festival. Web: www.snowfes.com/english.

LONGEST WAR IN HISTORY ENDS: ANNIVERSARY. Feb 5, 1985. The Third Punic War, between Rome and Carthage, started in the year 149 BC. It culminated in the year 146 BC, when Roman soldiers led by Scipio razed Carthage to the ground. The desolate site was cursed and rebuilding forbidden. On this date, 2,131 years after the war began, Ugo Vetere, mayor of Rome, and Chedli Klibi, mayor of Carthage, met at Tunis to sign a treaty of friendship officially ending the Third Punic War.

MEXICO: CONSTITUTION DAY. Feb 5. National holiday. Present constitution, embracing major social reforms, adopted in 1917.

MOVE HOLLYWOOD & BROADWAY TO LEBANON, PENNSYLVANIA, DAY. Feb 5. There's lots of room, friendly folks and Amish farms. Lebanon is a haven for residents and tourists to serenely indulge in the city's world-famous bologna and the Wertz family homemade candies. (©2006 by WH.) For info: Thomas & Ruth Roy, Wellcat Holidays, 2418 Long Ln, Lebanon, PA 17046. Phone: (717) 279-0184. E-mail: info@wellcat.com. Web: www.wellcat.com.

PEEL, ROBERT: BIRTH ANNIVERSARY. Feb 5, 1788. English Tory statesman, born at Bury, Lancashire, England, who twice served as prime minister (1834–1835; 1841–1846). As chief secretary for Ireland (1812), Peel established the Irish constabulary known as the "Peelers." In June 1829, Greater London's Metropolitan Police were established by an act of Parliament at the request of Peel, then home secretary. London police officers, who first took the streets in September 1829, became affectionately known as "bobbies." As prime minister, he oversaw the repeal of the Corn Laws in 1846 in an effort to address the then-raging Irish potato famine. Sir Robert Peel died July 2, 1850, at London from injuries received in a fall from his horse.

STEVENSON, ADLAI EWING II: BIRTH ANNIVERSARY. Feb 5, 1900. American statesman, governor of Illinois, Democratic candidate for president in 1952 and 1956, US representative to the UN, 1961–65. Born at Los Angeles, CA. Died at London, England, July 14, 1965. Not to be confused with his grandfather, Vice President Adlai Ewing Stevenson. See also: "Stevenson, Adlai Ewing: Birth Anniversary" (Oct 23).

WEATHERMAN'S [WEATHERPERSON'S] DAY. Feb 5. Commemorates the birth of one of America's first weathermen, John Jeffries, a Boston physician who kept detailed records of weather conditions, 1774–1816. Born at Boston, MA, Feb 5, 1744, and died there Sept 16, 1819. See also: "First Balloon Flight Across English Channel: Anniversary" (Jan 7).

WITHERSPOON, JOHN: BIRTH ANNIVERSARY. Feb 5, 1723. Clergyman, signer of the Declaration of Independence and reputed coiner of the word *Americanism* (in 1781). Born near Edinburgh, Scotland. Died at Princeton, NJ, Nov 15, 1794.

BIRTHDAYS TODAY

Henry Louis (Hank) Aaron, 80, Hall of Fame baseball player, baseball executive, 755 career home-run hitter, born Mobile, AL, Feb 5, 1934.

Roberto Alomar, 46, Hall of Fame baseball player, born Ponce, Puerto Rico, Feb 5, 1968.

Bobby Brown, 45, singer, born Roxbury, MA, Feb 5, 1969.

Sara Evans, 43, country singer, born Bookville, MO, Feb 5, 1971.

Christopher Guest, 66, writer, comedian (Emmy for writing *Lily Tomlin*; *Spinal Tap, Best in Show*), born New York, NY, Feb 5, 1948.

Barbara Hershey, 66, actress (*Hannah and Her Sisters*), born Barbara Hertzstein at Los Angeles, CA, Feb 5, 1948.

David Alan Ladd, 67, actor, producer (*A Dog of Flanders, The Day of the Locust*), born Los Angeles, CA, Feb 5, 1947.

Jennifer Jason Leigh, 52, actress (*Miami Blues, Rush, Backdraft*), born Los Angeles, CA, Feb 5, 1962.

Laura Linney, 50, actress (*The Savages, You Can Count on Me, Kinsey*, "John Adams," "The Big C"), born New York, NY, Feb 5, 1964.

Jane Bryant Quinn, 73, financial writer (*Everyone's Money Book*), born Niagara Falls, NY, Feb 5, 1941.

Charlotte Rampling, 68, actress (*Georgy Girl, Farewell My Lovely*), born Sturmer, England, Feb 5, 1946.

Cristiano Ronaldo, 29, soccer player, born Funchal, Portugal, Feb 5, 1985.

David Selby, 73, actor ("Falcon Crest," *Rich and Famous*), born Morgantown, WV, Feb 5, 1941.

Michael Sheen, 45, actor (*Frost/Nixon, The Queen*), born Newport, Gwent, Wales, Feb 5, 1969.

Roger Thomas Staubach, 72, Hall of Fame football player, born Cincinnati, OH, Feb 5, 1942.

Carlos Tévez, 30, soccer player, born Buenos Aires, Argentina, Feb 5, 1984.

Darrell Waltrip, 67, auto racer, born Owensboro, KY, Feb 5, 1947.

February 6 — Thursday

DAY 37 — **328 REMAINING**

ACCESSION OF QUEEN ELIZABETH II: ANNIVERSARY. Feb 6, 1952. Princess Elizabeth Alexandra Mary succeeded to the British throne (becoming Elizabeth II, Queen of the United Kingdom of Great Britain and Northern Ireland and Head of the Commonwealth) upon the death of her father, King George VI, Feb 6, 1952. Her coronation took place June 2, 1953, at Westminster Abbey at London.

BURR, AARON: BIRTH ANNIVERSARY. Feb 6, 1756. Third vice president of the US (Mar 4, 1801–Mar 3, 1805). While vice president, Burr challenged political enemy Alexander Hamilton to a duel and mortally wounded him July 11, 1804, at Weehawken, NJ. Indicted for the challenge and for murder, he returned to Washington to complete his term of office (during which he presided over the impeachment trial of Supreme Court Justice Samuel Chase). In 1807 Burr was arrested, tried for treason (in an alleged scheme to invade Mexico and set up a new nation in the West) and acquitted. Born at Newark, NJ, he died at Staten Island, NY, Sept 14, 1836.

CANADA: CALGARY BOAT AND SPORTSMEN'S SHOW. Feb 6–9. BMO Centre, Stampede Park, Calgary, AB. Sail-, power- and fishing boats; hunting, fishing and camping supplies; resort destinations and outdoor recreation; four-wheel-drive vehicles; family entertainment. Est attendance: 25,000. For info: Canadian Natl Sportsmen's Shows, 5920 Macleod Trail SW, Ste 502, Calgary, AB, T2H 0K2, Canada. Web: www.calgaryboatandsportshow.ca.

CANADA: TORONTO SPORTSMEN'S SHOW. Feb 6–9. Direct Energy Centre, Exhibition Place, Toronto, ON. Fishing manufacturers and retailers, fishing seminars, travel/vacation exhibits, cottages, camping products, boats and marine accessories, wildlife art, pet products, conservation and outdoor organizations, sporting goods and family entertainment. Est attendance: 90,000. For info: Canadian Natl Sportsmen's Shows, 30 Village Centre Pl, Mississauga, ON, L4Z 1V9 Canada. Phone: (905) 361-2677. Fax: (905) 361-2679. E-mail: info@sportshows.ca. Web: www.sportshows.ca.

FLORIDA STATE FAIR. Feb 6–17. Florida State Fairgrounds, Tampa, FL. 110th annual. The fair features the best arts, crafts, competitive exhibits, equestrian shows, livestock, entertainment, midway rides and food found in Florida. Also not to be missed is Cracker Country, a rural-history living museum where cultural and architectural history has been preserved. Est attendance: 500,000. For info: Florida State Fair, PO Box 11766, Tampa, FL 33680. Phone: (813) 621-7821 or (800) 345-FAIR. Web: www.floridastatefair.com.

GERMANY: BERLIN INTERNATIONAL FILM FESTIVAL. Feb 6–16. Potsdamer Platz, Berlin. The 64th festival. One of the premier international film festivals since its inaugural opening in 1951. Includes film competition, children's film festival and other special programs. The awarding of Golden and Silver Bears by the international jury marks the conclusion of the festival. Est attendance: 300,000. For info: Internationale Filmfestspiele Berlin, Potsdamer Strasse 5, 10785 Berlin, Germany. Phone: (49) 30-259-20-0. Fax: (49) 30-259-20-299. E-mail: info@berlinale.de. Web: www.berlinale.de.

LEAKEY, MARY: BIRTH ANNIVERSARY. Feb 6, 1913. Born Mary Douglas Nicol at London, England, archaeologist and paleoanthropologist Mary Leakey made several remarkable discoveries instrumental in the scientific understanding of the pattern of human evolution. For 50 years she worked at various excavation sites in eastern Africa, with the majority of her research taking place at Olduvai Gorge, Tanzania. Her fastidious excavatory techniques resulted in the discovery of the skull of *Proconsul africanus*—a 25-million-year-old common ancestor of both early humans and apes—and a 3.5-million-year-old preserved trail of hominid footprints that conclusively proved human bipedalism at that date. For much of her career Leakey collaborated with her husband Louis Leakey, who interpreted and published much of her research. Leakey died Dec 9, 1996, at Nairobi, Kenya.

MANCHESTER UNITED PLANE CRASH: ANNIVERSARY. Feb 6, 1958. A British European Airways jet crashed on takeoff in Munich, killing 21 people on board, including 8 Manchester United football players: team captain Roger Byrne, Mark Jones, Eddie Colman, Duncan Edwards, Tommy Taylor, Liam Whelan, David Pegg and Geoff Bent. When the survivors arrived later in Manchester, citizens lined the streets for the 12 miles from the airport to the soccer stadium in tribute.

MARLEY, BOB: BIRTH ANNIVERSARY. Feb 6, 1945. With his group, the Wailers, Bob Marley was one of the most popular and influential performers of reggae music. Marley was born at Rhoden Hall in northern Jamaica. Died of cancer at Miami, FL, May 11, 1981.

MASSACHUSETTS RATIFIES CONSTITUTION: ANNIVERSARY. Feb 6, 1788. By a vote of 187 to 168, Massachusetts became the sixth state to ratify the Constitution.

MICHIGAN INTERNATIONAL AUTO SHOW. Feb 6–9. DeVos Place, Grand Rapids, MI. Hundreds of the latest model cars, trucks, vans, SUVs, hybrids and sports cars from all the major manufacturers will be joined by concept cars and preproduction displays. For info: Showspan, 2121 Celebration Dr, Grand Rapids, MI 49525. Phone: (616) 447-2860. Fax: (616) 447-2861. E-mail: events@showspan.com. Web: www.showspan.com.

MOON PHASE: FIRST QUARTER. Feb 6. Moon enters First Quarter phase at 2:22 PM, EST.

NEW ZEALAND: WAITANGI DAY. Feb 6. National Day. Commemorates signing of the Treaty of Waitangi in 1840 (at Waitangi, Chatham Islands, New Zealand). The treaty, between the native Maori and the European peoples, provided for development of New Zealand under the British Crown.

RAVENSCROFT, THURL: 100th BIRTH ANNIVERSARY. Feb 6, 1914. Singer and voice artist known worldwide for his Tony the Tiger cereal commercials ("They're grrrrreat!"). Ravenscroft's distinctive bass was in demand for back-up singing (for Bing Crosby and Elvis Presley, among many), Disney movies (and theme parks) and, most famously, the song "He's a Mean One, Mr Grinch" in the popular TV cartoon "How the Grinch Stole Christmas" (1966). Born at Norfolk, NE, Ravenscroft died May 22, 2005, at Fullerton, CA.

February 2014	S	M	T	W	T	F	S
							1
	2	3	4	5	6	7	8
	9	10	11	12	13	14	15
	16	17	18	19	20	21	22
	23	24	25	26	27	28	

REAGAN, RONALD WILSON: BIRTH ANNIVERSARY. Feb 6, 1911. 40th president of the US (1981–89). Former sportscaster, motion picture actor, governor of California (1967–74); he was the oldest and the first divorced person to become US president. Born at Tampico, IL. Married actress Jane Wyman in 1940 (divorced in 1948); married actress Nancy Davis, Mar 4, 1952. The "Great Communicator" ushered in a decade of conservative policies upon his election in 1980 and was an indefatigable critic of Communist states: he famously challenged Soviet president Mikhail Gorbachev to "tear down this wall!" at the Berlin Wall in 1987. He died at his Los Angeles, CA, home on June 5, 2004.

RUTH, "BABE": BIRTH ANNIVERSARY. Feb 6, 1895. One of baseball's greatest heroes, George Herman "Babe" Ruth was born at Baltimore, MD. The "Sultan of Swat" (who was also a left-handed pitcher) hit 714 home runs in 22 major league seasons of play and played in 10 World Series. Died at New York, NY, Aug 16, 1948.

TRUFFAUT, FRANÇOIS: BIRTH ANNIVERSARY. Feb 6, 1932. Born at Paris, France, Truffaut was the most popular and successful French film director of his time. His films include *The 400 Blows, Jules and Jim, The Last Metro* and *The Story of Adele H.* He died at Paris, Oct 21, 1984.

BIRTHDAYS TODAY

Sarah Brady, 72, handgun control activist, born Alexandria, VA, Feb 6, 1942.

Tom Brokaw, 74, journalist, born Yankton, SD, Feb 6, 1940.

Natalie Cole, 64, singer, born Los Angeles, CA, Feb 6, 1950.

Fabian, 71, singer, actor, born Fabian Forte at Philadelphia, PA, Feb 6, 1943.

Mike Farrell, 75, actor ("M*A*S*H," "Providence"), born St. Paul, MN, Feb 6, 1939.

Zsa Zsa Gabor, 95, actress (*Ninotchka, Special Tonight*), born Budapest, Hungary, Feb 6, 1919.

Gayle Hunnicutt, 71, actress ("Dallas," *The Wild Angels, Marlowe*), born Fort Worth, TX, Feb 6, 1943.

Barry Miller, 56, stage and screen actor (Tony for *Biloxi Blues*; *Saturday Night Fever, The Last Temptation of Christ*), born Los Angeles, CA, Feb 6, 1958.

Kathy Najimy, 57, actress ("Veronica's Closet," *Sister Act*), born San Diego, CA, Feb 6, 1957.

Gigi Perreau, 73, actress (*Bonzo Goes to College, Tammy Tell Me True*), born Los Angeles, CA, Feb 6, 1941.

Rip Torn, 83, actor ("The Larry Sanders Show," *Men in Black*), born Elmore Torn, Jr, at Temple, TX, Feb 6, 1931.

Robert Townsend, 57, actor, director (*The Five Heartbeats, The Mighty Quinn*), born Chicago, IL, Feb 6, 1957.

Michael Tucker, 70, actor ("LA Law"), born Baltimore, MD, Feb 6, 1944.

Mamie Van Doren, 81, actress (*High School Confidential, Three Nuts in Search of a Bolt*), born Rowena, SD, Feb 6, 1933.

February 7 — Friday

DAY 38 **327 REMAINING**

"AMERICA'S MOST WANTED" TV PREMIERE: ANNIVERSARY. Feb 7, 1988. One of the longest-running shows in television history, "America's Most Wanted" asks viewers to help find fugitives from the law by airing dramatic reenactments of crimes and interviewing law enforcement officials for insight. It also highlights cases of missing children. The show has led to more than 1,100 arrests. Popular host John Walsh closes by addressing viewers, "And remember, you can make a difference." The 1,000th episode aired Mar 6, 2010. In summer 2011, FOX canceled the show and moved to a quarterly specials format.

BALLET INTRODUCED TO THE US: ANNIVERSARY. Feb 7, 1827. Renowned French danseuse Mme Francisquy Hutin introduced ballet to the US with a performance of *The Deserter*, staged at the Bowery Theater, New York, NY. A minor scandal erupted when the ladies in the lower boxes left the theater upon viewing the light and scanty attire of Mme Hutin and her troupe.

BLAKE, EUBIE: BIRTH ANNIVERSARY. Feb 7, 1883. James Hubert "Eubie" Blake, American composer and pianist, writer of nearly 1,000 songs (including "I'm Just Wild About Harry" and "Memories of You"). Born at Baltimore, MD. Recipient of the Presidential Medal of Freedom in 1981. Last professional performance was in January 1982. Died at Brooklyn, NY, five days after his 100th birthday, Feb 12, 1983.

BUBBLE GUM DAY. Feb 7. Imagine being able to chew bubble gum at school while helping a worthy cause! Today children around the world will be doing just that. Kids who donate 50 cents or more get to chew gum at school. The money collected is donated to a charity chosen by the school. Don't forget to get your principal's permission! A teacher's guide with related classroom activities is available upon request. If your school or business plans to celebrate and is willing to be interviewed by the media, please notify the organizers in advance so that we can match media requests with local celebrations. Annually, the first Friday in February. For info: Ruth Spiro, PO Box 1023, Deerfield, IL 60015. Web: www.bubblegumday.com.

CANADA: ONTARIO WINTER CARNIVAL BON SOO. Feb 7–16. Sault Ste. Marie, ON. One of Canada's largest winter carnivals features more than 75 festive indoor and hearty outdoor events for all ages during an annual 10-day winter extravaganza that includes winter sports, dances, entertainment, fireworks and winter playground. Est attendance: 75,000. For info: Bon Soo Winter Carnival Inc, 424-C Pim St, Sault Ste. Marie, ON, Canada P6B 2V1. Phone: (705) 759-3000. Fax: (705) 759-6950. E-mail: snow@bonsoo.on.ca. Web: www.bonsoo.on.ca.

CHAPLIN'S "TRAMP" DEBUTS: 100th ANNIVERSARY. Feb 7, 1914. Charlie Chaplin, vaudeville star-turned-comedic actor, debuted a new character in *Kid Auto Races at Venice*, a Keystone Studios short released on this date. The mischievous but romantic "Tramp," sporting a tiny mustache, twirling a cane and wearing a little derby, a tight-fitting jacket, baggy trousers and floppy shoes, was an immediate success with audiences, and soon mass-produced Tramp dolls were selling all over the US and the world.

COIN, JEWELRY & STAMP EXPO. Feb 7–9. Pasadena Convention Center, Pasadena, CA. Est attendance: 5,000. For info: Israel Bick, Exec Dir, Intl Stamp & Coin Collectors Society, PO Box 854, Van Nuys, CA 91408. Phone: (818) 997-6496. Fax: (818) 988-4337. E-mail: iibick@sbcglobal.net. Web: www.bickinternational.com.

CONGENITAL HEART DEFECT AWARENESS WEEK. Feb 7–14. Public relations/media campaign, special events in cities throughout the US. Annually, Feb 7–14. For info: Mona Barmash, Congenital Heart Information Network, PO Box 3397, Margate City, NJ 08402. Phone: (609) 823-4507. E-mail: mb@tchin.org. Web: www.tchin.org.

DICKENS, CHARLES: BIRTH ANNIVERSARY. Feb 7, 1812. English novelist, publisher and social critic, born at Portsmouth, England. Among his most successful books: *Oliver Twist, The Posthumous Papers of the Pickwick Club, A Tale of Two Cities, David Copperfield* and *A Christmas Carol.* Died at Gad's Hill, England, June 9, 1870, and was buried at Westminster Abbey.

ELEVENTH AMENDMENT TO US CONSTITUTION (SOVEREIGNTY OF THE STATES): RATIFICATION ANNIVERSARY. Feb 7, 1795. The 11th Amendment to the Constitution was ratified, curbing the powers of the federal judiciary in relation to the states. The amendment reaffirmed the sovereignty of the states by prohibiting suits against them.

GAMES OF THE XXII WINTER OLYMPIAD. Feb 7–16. Sochi, Russia. More than 2,500 athletes compete in 15 disciplines of 7 winter sports in the 2014 winter Olympics. For info: International Olympic Committee. Web: www.sochi2014.com.

GRENADA: INDEPENDENCE DAY: 40th ANNIVERSARY. Feb 7. National Day. Commemorates independence from Great Britain in 1974.

LEWIS, SINCLAIR: BIRTH ANNIVERSARY. Feb 7, 1885. American novelist and social critic. Recipient of Nobel Prize in Literature (1930). Among his novels: *Main Street, Babbitt* and *It Can't Happen Here.* Born Harry Sinclair Lewis at Sauk Center, MN. Died at Rome, Italy, Jan 10, 1951.

MORE, SIR THOMAS: BIRTH ANNIVERSARY. Feb 7, 1478. Anniversary of the birth of the lawyer, scholar, author, lord chancellor of England, martyr and saint at London, England. Refusing to recognize Henry VIII's divorce from Queen Catherine, the "Man for All Seasons" was found guilty of treason and imprisoned in the Tower of London, Apr 17, 1534. He was beheaded at Tower Hill on July 6, 1535, and his head displayed from Tower Bridge. Canonized in 1935. Memorial observed on June 22.

MURRAY, JAMES AUGUSTUS: BIRTH ANNIVERSARY. Feb 7, 1837. Lexicographer born at Denholm, Roxburghshire, England. Best known as the third editor of the *Oxford English Dictionary*, a post that he took over in 1879. With the goal of compiling a definitive history of the English language from the 12th century on, Murray and his successors sought to define each word and provide an example of how it was used. During his lifetime, Murray, who was primarily self-educated, edited approximately half of the dictionary with the help of several assistants. And after dedicating 40 years to working on the unfinished publication, Murray died on July 26, 1915, at Oxford, Oxfordshire, England, while working on the letter *T.*

NATIONAL WEAR RED DAY. Feb 7. During American Heart Month in February, the American Heart Association will focus on women with "Go Red for Women," a national movement about women and cardiovascular disease. Each year cardiovascular diseases claim the lives of nearly 500,000 women. For all of the women you know who have been affected by cardiovascular disease, participate in Wear Red Day. Annually, the first Friday in February. For info: American Heart Assn, 7272 Greenville Ave, Dallas, TX 75231. Phone: 800-242-8721. Web: www.americanheart.org or www.goredforwomen.org.

SPACE MILESTONE: *STARDUST* (US): 15th ANNIVERSARY. Feb 7, 1999. *Stardust* began its three-billion-mile journey to collect comet dust on this date. The unmanned mission met up with *Comet Wild-2* on Jan 2, 2004, and returned to Earth on Jan 15, 2006, with a 100-pound canister of comet dust samples. This was the first US mission devoted solely to a comet.

WAVE ALL YOUR FINGERS AT YOUR NEIGHBORS DAY. Feb 7. After all the challenges our neighbors and we have faced, it's time to put it all aside for at least one day. Wave "hello" to everybody and mean it. Annually, Feb 7. (©2006 by WH.) For info: Thomas & Ruth Roy, Wellcat Holidays, 2418 Long Ln, Lebanon, PA 17046. Phone: (717) 279-0184. E-mail: info@wellcat.com. Web: www.wellcat.com.

YUMA SQUARE AND ROUND DANCE FESTIVAL. Feb 7–9. Yuma Civic Center, Yuma, AZ. Square and round dance enthusiasts from Southern California and Arizona participate. Est attendance: 2,000. For info: Yuma Civic Center, 1440 W Desert Hills Dr, Yuma, AZ 85365. Phone: (928) 373-5040. Fax: (928) 344-9121. E-mail: ycc@yumaaz.gov. Web: www.yumaaz.gov.

BIRTHDAYS TODAY

Hector Babenco, 68, director (*Ironweed, Kiss of the Spider Woman*), born Buenos Aires, Argentina, Feb 7, 1946.

Oscar Brand, 94, folksinger, born Winnipeg, MB, Canada, Feb 7, 1920.

Garth Brooks, 52, country singer, born Tulsa, OK, Feb 7, 1962.

Miguel Ferrer, 60, actor ("Crossing Jordan," "Twin Peaks," *RoboCop*), born Santa Monica, CA, Feb 7, 1954.

John Hickenlooper, 62, Governor of Colorado (D), born Narberth, PA, Feb 7, 1952.

Juwan Howard, 41, basketball player, born Chicago, IL, Feb 7, 1973.

Eddie Izzard, 52, performer, actor ("The Riches"), born Edward John Izzard at Aden, Yemen, Feb 7, 1962.

Ashton Kutcher, 36, actor ("Two and a Half Men," "That '70s Show," *Jobs, New Year's Eve*), born Cedar Rapids, IA, Feb 7, 1978.

Steve Nash, 40, basketball player, born Johannesburg, South Africa, Feb 7, 1974.

Chris Rock, 48, actor, comedian, born Brooklyn, NY, Feb 7, 1966.

James Spader, 54, actor ("Boston Legal," *Secretary, Stargate*), born Boston, MA, Feb 7, 1960.

Gay Talese, 82, author (*The Kingdom and the Power, Unto the Sons*), born Ocean City, NJ, Feb 7, 1932.

February 8 — Saturday

DAY 39 **326 REMAINING**

ARIZONA RENAISSANCE FESTIVAL. Feb 8–Mar 30. (Saturdays, Sundays and Presidents' Day only.) Gold Canyon, AZ. 26th anniversary season. Enjoy your best day out in history. Find yourself surrounded by medieval merriment with knights, king and queen, maidens and minstrels. Stroll through acres of amusements, shoppes and nonstop revelry as you join our village celebration. The official sister event to the Robin Hood Festival in Sherwood Forest, England. Est attendance: 265,000. For info: Arizona Renaissance Festival, 12601 E Hwy 60, Gold Canyon, AZ 85118. Phone: (520) 463-2600. Web: www.renfestinfo.com.

BOY SCOUTS OF AMERICA FOUNDED: ANNIVERSARY. Feb 8, 1910. The Boy Scouts of America was founded at Washington, DC, by William Boyce, based on the work of Sir Robert Baden-Powell with the British Boy Scout Association.

February 2014	S	M	T	W	T	F	S
							1
	2	3	4	5	6	7	8
	9	10	11	12	13	14	15
	16	17	18	19	20	21	22
	23	24	25	26	27	28	

CORVETTE AND HIGH PERFORMANCE MEET. Feb 8–9 (tentative). Puyallup, WA. 40th annual. Swap meet with 900 booths and new and used car parts and automobilia. Vehicles for sale, Corvette invitational display area. Est attendance: 9,000. For info: Larry Johnson, Show Organizer, PO Box 7753, Olympia, WA 98507. Phone: (360) 786-8844. E-mail: LWJohnson@corvhp.com. Web: www.corvhp.com.

DEAN, JAMES: BIRTH ANNIVERSARY. Feb 8, 1931. American stage, film and television actor who achieved immense popularity during a brief career. Born at Fairmount, IN. Best remembered for his role in *Rebel Without a Cause*. Died in an automobile accident near Cholame, CA, Sept 30, 1955, at age 24.

FARM TOY SHOW AND AUCTION. Feb 8. Sauk Centre, MN. More than 30 vendors display farm toy equipment from 9 AM to 3:30 PM. Est attendance: 800. For info: Sauk Centre Chamber of Commerce, PO Box 222, Sauk Centre, MN 56378. Phone: (320) 352-5201. Fax: (320) 351-5202. E-mail: andrea@saukcentrechamber.com. Web: www.saukcentrechamber.com.

JAMES DEAN BIRTHDAY CELEBRATION. Feb 8–9. Fairmount, IN. The town where James Dean grew up celebrates his birthday with a movie showing, exhibits, refreshments and more. The Fairmount Museum will be open all weekend. For info: Fairmount Historical Museum, Inc, 203 E Washington St, PO Box 92, Fairmount, IN 46928. Phone: (765) 948-4555. Web: www.jamesdeanartifacts.com.

JAPAN: HA-RI-KU-YO (NEEDLE MASS). Feb 8. For Ha-Ri-Ku-Yo, a Needle Mass, observed on Feb 8, women gather their old and broken needles and take them to their temples to offer a prayer of thanks for their hard work. Girls pray to Awashima Myozin (their protecting deity) that their needlework, symbolic of love and marriage, will be good. Girls hope that participation in the Needle Mass will lead to a happy marriage.

LAUGH AND GET RICH DAY. Feb 8. Recognition of laughter's power to add to the bottom line. People who laugh are more effective and tend to remember things better, and laughter helps to lower the turnover rate. For info: Rick Segel, 268 Hamrick Dr, Kissimmee, FL 34759. Phone: (781) 272-9995. Fax: (800) 847-9411. E-mail: rick@ricksegel.com.

LEMMON, JACK: BIRTH ANNIVERSARY. Feb 8, 1925. Stage, screen and television actor, born John Uhler Lemmon III at Boston, MA. Often paired with actor Walter Matthau, he starred in such films as *The Odd Couple, The Fortune Cookie* and *The Front Page*. He was nominated for seven Academy Awards, winning in 1955 for his supporting role in *Mister Roberts* and in 1974 for his leading role in *Save the Tiger*. Other films include *Some Like It Hot, Days of Wine and Roses* and *Grumpy Old Men*. He also starred in television versions of *Inherit the Wind* and *Twelve Angry Men* and won an Emmy in 2000 for the TV movie *Tuesdays with Morrie*. He died at Los Angeles, CA, June 27, 2001.

LOVE MAY MAKE THE WORLD GO 'ROUND, BUT LAUGHTER KEEPS US FROM GETTING DIZZY WEEK. Feb 8–14. 37th annual. This week is dedicated to Victor Borge's notion that "Laughter is the shortest distance between two people" and Joel Goodman's notion that "Seven days without laughter makes one weak." This is a chance to lighten your relationships and to reinforce the connection between "heart" and "hearty laughter." Annually, the week leading up to and including Valentine's Day. For info: Joel Goodman, The HUMOR Project, Inc, 10 Madison Ave, Saratoga Springs, NY 12866. Phone: (518) 587-8770. E-mail: chase@HumorProject.com. Web: www.HumorProject.com.

MARTHA GRIFFITHS SPEAKS OUT AGAINST SEX DISCRIMINATION: 50th ANNIVERSARY. Feb 8, 1964. During the congressional debate over the 1964 Civil Rights Act, Representative Martha Griffiths (D-MI) delivered a memorable speech advocating the prohibition of discrimination based on sex. Her efforts resulted in adding civil rights protection for women to the 1964 Act. She later successfully led the campaign for the Equal Rights Amendment in the House of Representatives.

MARY, QUEEN OF SCOTS: EXECUTION ANNIVERSARY. Feb 8, 1587. Mary Stuart, the queen regent of Scotland, was beheaded at Fotheringhay, England, after being accused of plotting Queen Elizabeth I's death. Mary, the daughter of James V of Scotland by his second wife, Mary of Guise, was born Dec 7 or 8, 1542, at Linlithgow, Scotland, and became queen a week later upon the death of her father, although she did not begin governing until after her mother's death in 1561. Accused of knowingly marrying the alleged murderer of her second husband, Lord Darnley, she was forced to abdicate in favor of her son (James VI) and fled to England for protection, only to find herself a prisoner for the rest of her life—a victim of Elizabethan political intrigue.

OPERA DEBUT IN THE COLONIES: ANNIVERSARY. Feb 8, 1735. The first opera produced in the colonies was performed at the Courtroom, at Charleston, SC. The opera was *Flora; or the Hob in the Well*, written by Colley Cibber.

PORTLAND, OREGON: BIRTHDAY. Feb 8, 1851. The "City of Roses" was incorporated.

REENACTMENT OF COWTOWN'S LAST OLD WEST GUNFIGHT. Feb 8. White Elephant Saloon, Fort Worth, TX. Annual reenactment of Fort Worth's last Old West gunfight, which took place on Feb 8, 1887, between White Elephant Saloon owner Luke Short and former marshal T.I. "Longhaired Jim" Courtright. Annually, Feb 8. Est attendance: 400. For info: Jason Tighe, Dir of Operations, 713 N Main St, Fort Worth, TX 76164. Phone: (817) 624-9712. Fax: (817) 625-9663. E-mail: info@whiteelephantsaloon.com. Web: www.whiteelephantsaloon.com.

SHERMAN, WILLIAM TECUMSEH: BIRTH ANNIVERSARY. Feb 8, 1820. Born at Lancaster, OH, General Sherman is especially remembered for his devastating march through Georgia during the Civil War and his statement "War is hell." Died at New York, NY, Feb 14, 1891.

SLOVENIA: CULTURE DAY. Feb 8. National holiday. Honors France Preseren, Slovenia's national poet, who died Feb 8, 1849.

SPACE MILESTONE: *ARABSAT-1* AND *BRASILSAT-1*. Feb 8, 1985. League of Arab States and Brazilian communications satellites launched into geosynchronous orbit from Kourou, French Guiana, by the European Space Agency.

VERNE, JULES: BIRTH ANNIVERSARY. Feb 8, 1828. French writer, sometimes called "the father of science fiction," born at Nantes, France. Author of *Around the World in Eighty Days, Twenty Thousand Leagues Under the Sea* and many other novels. Died at Amiens, France, Mar 24, 1905.

BIRTHDAYS TODAY

Brooke Adams, 65, actress (*Days of Heaven, Invasion of the Body Snatchers*), born New York, NY, Feb 8, 1949.

Seth Green, 40, actor ("Family Guy," "Greg the Bunny," *Austin Powers*), born Overbrook Park, PA, Feb 8, 1974.

John Grisham, 59, author (*The Firm, The Client*), born Jonesboro, AR, Feb 8, 1955.

Robert Klein, 72, comedian, actor ("Comedy Tonight," *They're Playing Our Song*), born New York, NY, Feb 8, 1942.

Ted Koppel, 74, journalist, born Lancashire, England, Feb 8, 1940.

Alonzo Mourning, 44, former basketball player, born Chesapeake, VA, Feb 8, 1970.

Nick Nolte, 73, actor (*Affliction; The Prince of Tides; Rich Man, Poor Man*), born Omaha, NE, Feb 8, 1941.

Dawn Olivieri, 33, actress ("House of Lies," "The Vampire Diaries," "Heroes"), born Seminole, FL, Feb 8, 1981.

Mary Steenburgen, 61, actress (Oscar for *Melvin and Howard; Elf, Parenthood, Cross Creek*), born Newport, AR, Feb 8, 1953.

John Williams, 82, pianist, conductor (formerly with Boston Pops), composer (scores for *Jaws, Star Wars, Jurassic Park, Schindler's List*), born New York, NY, Feb 8, 1932.

February 9 — Sunday

DAY 40 — **325 REMAINING**

ALLIES RETAKE GUADALCANAL: ANNIVERSARY. Feb 9, 1943. In a major strategic victory of WWII, the American 161st and 132nd Regiments retook Guadalcanal in the Solomon Islands on this date after a six-month-long battle. More than 9,000 Japanese and 2,000 Americans were killed. The fierce resistance by the Japanese was an indication to the Allies of things to come. Guadalcanal put the Allies within striking distance of Rabaul, the major Japanese base in the area.

THE BEATLES APPEAR ON "THE ED SULLIVAN SHOW": 50th ANNIVERSARY. Feb 9, 1964. British pop phenomenon The Beatles began the "British Invasion" of America with their appearance on America's top television variety show. They performed five songs before a screaming studio audience of 728. The estimated viewership for that night's show was 73 million people—making it the most-viewed US TV program in history up to that time. See also: "Beatles Take Over Music Charts" (Apr 4).

BEHAN, BRENDAN: BIRTH ANNIVERSARY. Feb 9, 1923. Playwright (*The Quare Fellow, The Hostage*), poet and author (*Borstal Boy*), born at Dublin, Ireland. Died there Mar 20, 1964.

FREELANCE WRITERS APPRECIATION WEEK. Feb 9–15. Freelance writers do more than query editors and write and submit articles and books (nonfiction and fiction). They provide overworked editors with material, as well as inform and entertain readers. Annually, the second week in February. For info: Dorothy Zjawin, Dir, 61 W Colfax Ave, Roselle Park, NJ 07204.

GYPSY ROSE LEE: 100th BIRTH ANNIVERSARY. Feb 9, 1914. American ecdysiast and author whose real name was Rose Louise Hovick, born at Seattle, WA. Her autobiography, *Gypsy*, was made into a Broadway musical and a motion picture. Died at Los Angeles, CA, Apr 26, 1970.

HARRISON, WILLIAM HENRY: BIRTH ANNIVERSARY. Feb 9, 1773. Ninth president of the US (Mar 4–Apr 4, 1841). His term of office was the shortest in our nation's history—32 days. He was the first president to die in office (of pneumonia contracted during inaugural ceremonies). Born at Berkeley, VA, he died at Washington, DC, Apr 4, 1841. His grandson, Benjamin Harrison, was the 23rd president of the US.

JELL-O® WEEK. Feb 9–15. Celebrated annually the second full week in February. The first Jell-O® Week was officially declared by the Utah legislature in 2001. For info: Hunter Public Relations, 41 Madison Ave, 5th Fl, New York, NY 10010. Phone: (212) 679-6600. Web: www.hunterpr.com.

LEBANON: ST. MARON'S DAY. Feb 9. Holiday of Lebanon's Maronite Christian community. St. Maron was a Syrian hermit of the fourth–fifth centuries.

LOWELL, AMY: BIRTH ANNIVERSARY. Feb 9, 1874. American poet born at Brookline, MA. Died there May 12, 1925.

MAN DAY. Feb 9. A day for celebration by friends, family and associates of the men of the world. Annually, the Sunday before Valentine's Day. (©2002 C. Daniel Rhodes.) For info: C. Daniel Rhodes, 1900 Crossvine Rd, Hoover, AL 35244. Phone: (205) 908-6781. E-mail: rhodan@charter.net.

NATIONAL PANCAKE WEEK. Feb 9–15. Traditional celebration surrounding Shrove, or Pancake, Tuesday to recognize the history and continuing popularity of pancakes. For info: Julie Johnson, Bisquick Baking Mix, General Mills, Inc, #1 General Mills Blvd, Minneapolis, MN 55426. Phone: (763) 764-2865. E-mail: Julie.Johnson2@genmills.com.

READ IN THE BATHTUB DAY. Feb 9. Set aside a day each year to be spent in the bathtub reading a novel. Visit us on Facebook for details! For info: Christine Rogers, Read In the Bathtub Day, PO Box 5364, Sacramento, CA 95817. Phone: (916) 606-5072. E-mail: christine@studioregency.com.

RUSK, (DAVID) DEAN: BIRTH ANNIVERSARY. Feb 9, 1909. US diplomat Dean Rusk was born at Cherokee County, GA. He served as US secretary of state from 1961 to 1969, during which time he supported US involvement in the Vietnam War. He died Dec 20, 1994, at Athens, GA.

TUBB, ERNEST: 100th BIRTH ANNIVERSARY. Feb 9, 1914. Country and western singer, born at Crisp, TX. Ernest Tubb was the sixth member to be elected to the Country Music Hall of Fame and the headliner on the first country music show ever to be presented at Carnegie Hall. His first major hit, "Walking the Floor over You," gained him his first appearance at the Grand Ole Opry in 1942, and he attained regular membership in 1943. He died Sept 6, 1984, at Nashville, TN.

UNION OFFICERS ESCAPE LIBBY PRISON: 150th ANNIVERSARY. Feb 9, 1864. On this date 109 Union officers escaped from Libby Prison at Richmond, VA, in the largest and most dramatic prisoner of war escape of the Civil War. The Libby Prison was the former Libby and Sons candle factory. Forty-eight of the men were recaptured, two drowned and fifty-nine successfully made it back to Federal lines.

VEECK, BILL: 100th BIRTH ANNIVERSARY. Feb 9, 1914. William Louis (Bill) Veeck, Jr, Baseball Hall of Fame executive born at Chicago, IL. Veeck was baseball's premier promoter and showman as an owner of several teams. He integrated the American League and sought to provide fans with entertainment in addition to baseball. Inducted into the Hall of Fame in 1991. Died at Chicago, Jan 2, 1986.

WINTER OCEAN COUNTY BLUEGRASS FESTIVAL. Feb 9. Waretown, NJ. A family-oriented bluegrass festival where no alcoholic beverages or smoking are allowed. Est attendance: 400. For info: Albert Music Hall, PO Box 657, Waretown, NJ 08758. Web: www.alberthall.org.

BIRTHDAYS TODAY

Mia Farrow, 69, actress ("Peyton Place," *Rosemary's Baby, Hannah and Her Sisters*), born Maria de Lourdes Villers at Los Angeles, CA, Feb 9, 1945.

Vladimir Guerrero, 38, baseball player, born Nizao Bani, Dominican Republic, Feb 9, 1976.

Tom Hiddleston, 33, actor (*The Avengers, Midnight in Paris, War Horse*), born London, England, Feb 9, 1981.

Jay Inslee, 63, Governor of Washington (D), born Seattle, WA, Feb 9, 1951.

Carole King, 72, singer, songwriter, born Brooklyn, NY, Feb 9, 1942.

Judith Light, 65, actress ("Ugly Betty," "One Life to Live," "Who's the Boss?"), born Trenton, NJ, Feb 9, 1949.

Roger Mudd, 86, journalist, born Washington, DC, Feb 9, 1928.

Jameer Nelson, 32, basketball player, born Chester, PA, Feb 9, 1982.

Joe Pesci, 71, actor (*Raging Bull, Goodfellas, My Cousin Vinny*), born Newark, NJ, Feb 9, 1943.

Shakira, 37, singer, television personality ("The Voice"), born Shakira Isabelle Mebarak Ripoll at Barranquilla, Colombia, Feb 9, 1977.

Charles Shaughnessy, 59, actor ("Days of Our Lives," "The Nanny"), born London, England, Feb 9, 1955.

Mena Suvari, 35, actress (*American Beauty, Loser*), born Newport, RI, Feb 9, 1979.

Janet Suzman, 75, actress (*Nicholas and Alexandra, A Dry White Season*), born Johannesburg, South Africa, Feb 9, 1939.

Travis Tritt, 51, country singer, born Marietta, GA, Feb 9, 1963.

Alice Walker, 70, author (*The Color Purple*), born Eatonton, GA, Feb 9, 1944.

Ziyi Zhang, 35, actress (*Crouching Tiger, Hidden Dragon; House of Flying Daggers*), born Beijing, China, Feb 9, 1979.

February 2014

S	M	T	W	T	F	S
						1
2	3	4	5	6	7	8
9	10	11	12	13	14	15
16	17	18	19	20	21	22
23	24	25	26	27	28	

February 10 — Monday

DAY 41 **324 REMAINING**

"ALL THE NEWS THAT'S FIT TO PRINT": ANNIVERSARY. Feb 10, 1897. The familiar slogan "All the News That's Fit to Print" has appeared on page one of the *New York Times* since Feb 10, 1897. It had first appeared on the editorial page on Oct 25, 1896. Although in 1896 a $100 prize was offered for a slogan, owner Adolph S. Ochs concluded that his own slogan was best.

ANDERSON, DAME JUDITH: BIRTH ANNIVERSARY. Feb 10, 1898. Film and stage actress Dame Judith Anderson was born Frances Margaret Anderson at Adelaide, Australia. She was nominated for an Academy Award in 1941 for her role in Alfred Hitchcock's film *Rebecca*. In 1960 she was made dame commander of the British Empire by Queen Elizabeth II. She died Jan 3, 1992, at Santa Barbara, CA.

BRECHT, BERTOLT: BIRTH ANNIVERSARY. Feb 10, 1898. German playwright, born at Augsburg, Germany. His plays, such as *Mother Courage*, reflect his Marxist and antimilitary worldview. Also wrote *The Threepenny Opera* in collaboration with composer Kurt Weill. Died at East Berlin, Aug 14, 1956.

***DEATH OF A SALESMAN* PREMIERE: 65th ANNIVERSARY.** Feb 10, 1949. Arthur Miller's postwar dramatic masterpiece opened at Broadway's Morosco Theater on this day. Elia Kazan was the director, and Lee J. Cobb (Willy Loman), Arthur Kennedy (Biff) and Cameron Mitchell (Happy) starred. The play garnered six Tony Awards and was also awarded the 1949 Pulitzer Prize for Drama.

DURANTE, JIMMY: BIRTH ANNIVERSARY. Feb 10, 1893. "The Schnozz," Jimmy Durante, was born at New York City. His break into show biz came when he was 17 and got a regular job playing ragtime at a saloon at Coney Island. Later his friend Eddie Cantor urged him to try comedy. Durante developed a unique comedic style as a short-tempered but lovable personage. His shtick included slamming down his hat and flapping his arms. His clothing, enormous nose, craggy face, gravelly singing voice and mispronunciations were all part of the persona. Durante, whose career spanned six decades, appeared on TV, stage and screen. His television sign-off, "Good night, Mrs Calabash, wherever you are!" became a trademark. Jimmy Durante died at Santa Monica, CA, Jan 29, 1980.

FIRST ACTOR TO PERFORM IN TWO CITIES ON THE SAME DAY: ANNIVERSARY. Feb 10, 1887. Nathaniel Carr Goodwin performed at an 11:30 AM matinee of *Turned Up* at Boston, MA, and then, following the closing curtain, he returned to New York City on the 1 PM train and that evening performed in *The Mascot* at the Bijou Theatre at 8 PM.

FIRST COMPUTER CHESS VICTORY OVER HUMAN: ANNIVERSARY. Feb 10, 1996. IBM's Deep Blue computer defeated world champion Garry Kasparov in 34 moves on this date in Philadelphia, PA—the first such victory by a computer in tournament conditions. Kasparov, however, went on to win the tournament, defeating the computer three times (the other two matches were draws). In May 1997, in a six-game rematch, Deep Blue emerged the overall victor. Deep Blue, an RS/6000 supercomputer, can evaluate 200 million chess positions a second but is not capable of using artificial intelligence to "learn." Kasparov was reigning World Chess Champion from 1985 to 2000.

FIRST WORLD WAR II MEDAL OF HONOR: ANNIVERSARY. Feb 10, 1942. Second Lieutenant Alexander Ramsey "Sandy" Nininger, Jr, was posthumously awarded WWII's first Medal of Honor for heroism at the Battle of Bataan. He had graduated from West Point in 1941 and was on his first assignment after being commissioned.

INTERNATIONAL FLIRTING WEEK. Feb 10–16. Celebrating the ancient art of flirting and recognizing the role it plays in the lives of singles seeking a mate, couples looking to sustain their love and those simply exchanging a playful glance with a stranger, acquaintance, colleague, etc. For info: Robin Gorman Newman, 44 Somerset Dr N, Great Neck, NY 11020. Phone: (516) 773-0911. E-mail: rgnewman@optonline.net. Web: www.lovecoach.com.

LAMB, CHARLES: BIRTH ANNIVERSARY. Feb 10, 1775. Literary critic, poet and essayist, born at London, England. "The greatest pleasure I know," he wrote in 1834, "is to do a good action by stealth, and to have it found out by accident." Died at Edmonton, England, Dec 27, 1834.

LOVE A MENSCH WEEK. Feb 10–16. Mensches are decent, responsible men or women. During this week, singles look to meet a mensch as well as take time to appreciate how mensches enhance our lives. For info: Robin Gorman Newman, 44 Somerset Dr N, Great Neck, NY 11020. Phone: (516) 773-0911. E-mail: rgnewman@optonline.net. Web: www.lovecoach.com.

MALTA: FEAST OF ST. PAUL'S SHIPWRECK. Feb 10. Valletta. Holy day of obligation. Commemorates the shipwreck of St. Paul on the north coast of Malta in AD 60.

"MY FRIEND FLICKA" TV PREMIERE: ANNIVERSARY. Feb 10, 1956. CBS series about a boy and his horse based on the children's book by Mary O'Hara. The series was set in the early 1900s on the Goose Bar Ranch in Montana. Johnny Washbrook starred as Ken McLaughlin; Gene Evans as Ken's father, Rob; Anita Louise as Ken's mother, Nell; Frank Ferguson as Gus, the ranch hand; and Wahama, the beautiful Arabian horse, as Flicka.

PASTERNAK, BORIS LEONIDOVICH: BIRTH ANNIVERSARY. Feb 10, 1890. Russian poet and novelist, born at Moscow, Russia. Best-known work: *Doctor Zhivago*. Died at Moscow, May 30, 1960.

PLIMSOLL DAY (SAMUEL PLIMSOLL BIRTH ANNIVERSARY). Feb 10, 1824. A day to remember Samuel Plimsoll, "the Sailor's Friend," a coal merchant turned reformer and politician, who was elected to the British parliament in 1868. He attacked the practice of overloading heavily insured ships, calling them "coffin ships." His persistence brought about amendment of Britain's Merchant Shipping Act. The Plimsoll Line, named for him, is a line on the side of ships marking maximum load allowed by law. Born at Bristol, England; died at Folkestone, England, June 3, 1898.

RANDOM ACTS OF KINDNESS WEEK. Feb 10–16. This week, annually the second full week of February, raises awareness about kindness and invites people to give and receive kindness daily. Celebrations vary widely. An individual may celebrate kindness by performing anonymous kind acts all week long. An educator may lead a discussion about kindness and involve students in a brief kindness activity. Some celebrations are schoolwide. Some celebrations are community-based rather than school-based. For hundreds of ideas, consult our Kindness Ideas resource, or the Educators and Community sections on our website. For info: Random Acts of Kindness Foundation. Phone: (800) 660-2811. E-mail: info@randomactsofkindness.org. Web: www.randomactsofkindness.org.

TILDEN, BILL: BIRTH ANNIVERSARY. Feb 10, 1893. William Tatem (Bill) Tilden, Jr, tennis player, born at Philadelphia, PA. Generally considered one of the greatest players of all time, Tilden won more tournaments than the record books can count. A nearly flawless player, he was also an egotistical showman on the court with an interest in show business. He turned pro in 1930 and continued to win regularly. Died at Hollywood, CA, June 5, 1953.

TREATY OF PARIS ENDS FRENCH AND INDIAN WAR: ANNIVERSARY. Feb 10, 1763. Known in Europe as the Seven Years' War, this conflict ranged from North America to India, with many European nations involved. In North America, French expansion in the Ohio River Valley in the 1750s led to conflict with Great Britain. Some Indians fought alongside the French; a young George Washington fought for the British. As a result of the signing of the Treaty of Paris, France lost all claims to Canada and had to cede Louisiana to Spain. Fifteen years later, bitterness over the loss of its North American colonies to Britain contributed to France's supporting the colonists in the American Revolution.

TWENTY-FIFTH AMENDMENT TO US CONSTITUTION RATIFIED (PRESIDENTIAL SUCCESSION, DISABILITY): ANNIVERSARY. Feb 10, 1967. Procedures for presidential succession were further clarified by the 25th Amendment, along with provisions for continuity of power in the event of a disability or illness of the president.

WESTMINSTER KENNEL CLUB DOG SHOW. Feb 10–11. Madison Square Garden, New York, NY. 138th annual. First held in 1877, the Westminster Kennel Club Dog Show is America's second-longest continuously held sporting event, behind only the Kentucky Derby. Entry limited to 3,000 dogs. Group and Best in Show competitions televised live on CNBC (Monday) and USA Network (Tuesday). For info: Westminster Kennel Club, 149 Madison Ave, Ste 402, New York, NY 10016. Web: westminsterkennelclub.org.

BIRTHDAYS TODAY

Elizabeth Banks, 40, actress (*The Hunger Games*, "30 Rock," "Scrubs"), born Pittsfield, MA, Feb 10, 1974.

Jim Cramer, 59, financial analyst, television personality ("Mad Money with Jim Cramer"), born Wyndmoor, PA, Feb 10, 1955.

Laura Dern, 47, actress (*Blue Velvet, Rambling Rose*), born Los Angeles, CA, Feb 10, 1967.

Donovan, 68, singer, songwriter, born Donovan P. Leitch at Glasgow, Scotland, Feb 10, 1946.

Leonard Kyle (Lenny) Dykstra, 51, former baseball player, born Santa Ana, CA, Feb 10, 1963.

Roberta Flack, 75, singer, born Black Mountain, NC, Feb 10, 1939.

Justin Gatlin, 32, sprinter, born Brooklyn, NY, Feb 10, 1982.

Frances Moore Lappe, 70, author (*Diet for a Small Planet, Rediscovering America's Values*), born Pendleton, OR, Feb 10, 1944.

Chloe Grace Moretz, 17, actress (*Let Me In, Dark Shadows, Hugo*), born Atlanta, GA, Feb 10, 1997.

Gregory John (Greg) Norman, 59, golfer, born Melbourne, Australia, Feb 10, 1955.

Leontyne Price, 87, opera singer, born Laurel, MS, Feb 10, 1927.

Mark Andrew Spitz, 64, Olympic swimmer, born Modesto, CA, Feb 10, 1950.

Robert Wagner, 84, actor ("It Takes a Thief," "Hart to Hart"), born Detroit, MI, Feb 10, 1930.

February 11 — Tuesday

DAY 42 **323 REMAINING**

BE ELECTRIFIC DAY. Feb 11. A day to honor the birth of Thomas Alva Edison and recognize his electrical inventions, including the lightbulb. It is also the day to discover the electricity in our bodies: when all the electricity is flowing properly in your body and you feel terrific, you are electrific! Annually, Feb 11. For info: Carolyn Finch, Electrific Solutions Inc, 51 Cedar Dr, Danbury, CT 06811. Phone: (203) 791-2756. Fax: (203) 743-5675. E-mail: carolyn@carolynfinch.com.

CAMEROON: YOUTH DAY. Feb 11. Public holiday.

CHILD, LYDIA MARIA: BIRTH ANNIVERSARY. Feb 11, 1802. Writer whose works included *Hobomok*, about early Salem and Plymouth life, and *The Rebels*, which described pre-Revolutionary Boston. In addition, she produced several practical works, including *The Frugal Housewife*, which enjoyed 21 editions, and *The Mother's Book*. In 1833 she and her husband, David Lee Child, published the controversial abolitionist document "An Appeal in Favor of That Class of Americans Called Africans," which called for educating slaves. Their work for abolition continued with the weekly newspaper *The National Anti-Slavery Standard*, which they published at New York City during 1840–44. Born at Medford, MA, Child died Oct 20, 1880, at Wayland, MA.

DUNNE, PHILIP: BIRTH ANNIVERSARY. Feb 11, 1908. American screenwriter and director Philip Dunne was born at New York, NY. In 1947 he joined directors John Huston and William Wyler to found the Committee for the First Amendment, which campaigned against the "blacklisting" in Hollywood of anyone suspected of being a Communist by the House Un-American Activities Committee. He was also a founder of the Screen Writers Guild. Dunne died June 2, 1992, at Malibu, CA.

EDISON, THOMAS ALVA: BIRTH ANNIVERSARY. Feb 11, 1847. American inventive genius and holder of more than 1,200 patents (including the incandescent electric lamp, the phonograph, the electric dynamo and key parts of many now-familiar devices such as the movie camera and the telephone transmitter). Edison said, "Genius is 1 percent inspiration and 99 percent perspiration." His birthday is now widely observed as Inventor's Day. Born at Milan, OH, and died at Menlo Park, NJ, Oct 18, 1931.

FIRST WOMAN EPISCOPAL BISHOP: 25th ANNIVERSARY. Feb 11, 1989. The presiding bishop of the Episcopal Church, Bishop Edmond L. Browning, consecrated the Reverend Barbara Clementine Harris as a bishop of the Episcopal Church.

"THE FRENCH CHEF" TV PREMIERE: ANNIVERSARY. Feb 11, 1963. Beginning on this date, Julia Child demystified French cooking and entertained viewers as "The French Chef" on WGBH-TV, Boston, MA. The show was a great success in syndication on PBS stations, and Child filmed 200 programs—always with her trademark trilling voice and at times slapping around the poultry—signing off with a cheery "Bon appétit!" Child's show, along with her book *Mastering the Art of French Cooking* (1961, authored with Simone Beck and Louisette Bertholle), are credited with awakening Americans to the joy of continental cuisine. See also: "Child, Julia: Birth Anniversary" (Aug 15).

FULLER, MELVILLE WESTON: BIRTH ANNIVERSARY. Feb 11, 1833. Eighth chief justice of the US. Born at Augusta, ME, he died at Sorrento, ME, July 4, 1910.

GET OUT YOUR GUITAR DAY. Feb 11. 2nd annual. Chances are today is a cold, gloomy day—so get out your guitar. If your guitar (or other instrument) has been put away for a while, this is the day to take it out and play it. For info: Arthur Bargar. E-mail: abargar@hotmail.com.

GIBBS, JOSIAH WILLARD: BIRTH ANNIVERSARY. Feb 11, 1839. Chemist and professor of physics at Yale, born at New Haven, CT; he died there, Apr 28, 1903.

IRAN: VICTORY OF ISLAMIC REVOLUTION. Feb 11. National holiday. Commemorates the revolution that overthrew the shah in 1979.

JAPAN: NATIONAL FOUNDATION DAY. Feb 11. Marks the founding of the Japanese nation. In 1872 the government officially set Feb 11, 660 BC, as the date of accession to the throne of the Emperor Jimmu (said to be Japan's first emperor) and designated the day Empire Day, a national holiday. The holiday was abolished after WWII but was revived as National Foundation Day in 1966. Ceremonies are held with Their Imperial Majesties the Emperor and Empress, the prime minister and other dignitaries attending.

MANDELA, NELSON: PRISON RELEASE ANNIVERSARY. Feb 11, 1990. After serving more than 27 years of a life sentence (convicted, with eight others, of sabotage and conspiracy to overthrow the government), South Africa's Nelson Mandela, 71 years old, walked away from the Victor Verster prison farm at Paarl, South Africa, a free man. He had survived the governmental system of apartheid. Mandela greeted a cheering throng of well-wishers, along with hundreds of millions of television viewers worldwide, with demands for an intensification of the struggle for equality for blacks, who make up nearly 75 percent of South Africa's population.

MANKIEWICZ, JOSEPH L.: BIRTH ANNIVERSARY. Feb 11, 1909. Oscar-winning American film writer, director and producer, born at Wilkes-Barre, PA. He coined the famous W.C. Fields phrase "my little chickadee" in his screenplay for the 1932 film *If I Had a Million*. In 1935 he turned to producing and subsequently made *The Philadelphia Story* and *Woman of the Year*. He began directing in 1946, and his stature grew with such films as *The Late George Apley, The Ghost and Mrs Muir, A Letter to Three Wives, All About Eve, Guys and Dolls, Cleopatra* and *Sleuth*. Mankiewicz won four Academy Awards for directing and screenwriting. He died Feb 5, 1993, at Mount Kisco, NY.

NATIONAL SHUT-IN VISITATION DAY. Feb 11. Visit and entertain those unable to leave their homes or residences. Created by the late Monsignor Losito of Reading, PA.

NEW MEXICO: EXTRATERRESTRIAL CULTURE DAY. Feb 11. New Mexico. A day "to celebrate and honor all past, present and future extraterrestrial visitors in ways to enhance relationships among all citizens of the cosmos, known and unknown." Passed as a memorial (not law) by the New Mexico state legislature to

February 2014

S	M	T	W	T	F	S
						1
2	3	4	5	6	7	8
9	10	11	12	13	14	15
16	17	18	19	20	21	22
23	24	25	26	27	28	

acknowledge that ever since the Roswell UFO incident of 1947, New Mexico has been recognized worldwide as a nexus of sightings and unexplained mysteries. Annually, the second Tuesday in February.

PRO SPORTS WIVES DAY. Feb 11. This national day of observance will give polite recognition to nearly a half million active and retired sports wives throughout the country for their public service in the estimated $213 billion professional sports industry. Unknown generally to the public, pro sports wives are the household managers and silent partners who keep their favorite athletes motivated, focused and determined to win and create the feeling of being a winner within us all. Annually, Feb 11. For info: Gena Pitts, PSWA, Inc, 13010 Morris Rd, 6th Fl, Bldg 1, Alpharetta, GA 30004. E-mail: info@prosportswives.com. Web: www.prosportswives.com.

SATISFIED STAYING SINGLE DAY. Feb 11. As Valentine's Day approaches, some single folks would like to point out that they're quite content buying candy and flowers for no one but themselves. Live it up. Shadow dance! (©2006 by WH.) For info: Thomas & Ruth Roy, Wellcat Holidays, 2418 Long Ln, Lebanon, PA 17046. Phone: (717) 279-0184. E-mail: info@wellcat.com. Web: www.wellcat.com.

SHELDON, SIDNEY: BIRTH ANNIVERSARY. Feb 11, 1917. Writer born Sidney Schectel at Chicago, IL. After his college years at Northwestern University, he moved to Hollywood and found work as a screenwriter. B movies led to Broadway musicals, and by the mid-1940s he was one of the most prolific and successful writers of his generation. He earned an Academy Award for *The Bachelor and the Bobby Soxer* in 1947 and a Tony Award for *Redhead* in 1959. He also wrote for television, creating several successful series, including "The Patty Duke Show" and "I Dream of Jeannie." In 1969 he moved to writing novels and shortly became one of the bestselling novelists in history, as titles such as *Rage of Angels, Windmills of the Gods* and *The Other Side of Midnight* were translated into 51 languages, adapted as made-for-TV movies and in all sold more than 300 million copies. He died at Rancho Mirage, CA, Jan 30, 2007.

SPACE MILESTONE: *ENDEAVOUR* MAPPING MISSION (US). Feb 11, 2000. This manned flight spent 11 days in space creating a 3-D map of more than 70 percent of Earth's surface—the most accurate and complete topographic map of Earth ever produced.

SPACE MILESTONE: *OSUMI* (JAPAN). Feb 11, 1970. First Japanese satellite launched. Japan became the fourth nation to send a satellite into space.

VATICAN CITY: 85th INDEPENDENCE ANNIVERSARY. Feb 11, 1929. The Lateran Treaty, signed by Pietro Cardinal Gasparri and Benito Mussolini, guaranteed the independence of the State of Vatican City and recognized the sovereignty of the Holy See over it. Area is about 109 acres.

WHITE SHIRT DAY: ANNIVERSARY. Feb 11, 1937. Anniversary of UAW-GM agreement following 44-day sit-down strike at General Motors' Flint, MI, factories. Blue-collar workers traditionally wear white shirts to work on this day, symbolic of workingman's dignity won. Has been observed by proclamation at Flint.

WORLD AG EXPO. Feb 11–13. Tulare, CA. 47th annual. The largest farm equipment show in North America. Est attendance: 100,000. For info: Intl Agri-Center, PO Box 1475, Tulare, CA 93275-1475. Phone: (800) 999-9186 or (559) 688-1030. Fax: (559) 688-5527. E-mail: info@farmshow.org. Web: www.farmshow.org.

YALTA AGREEMENT SIGNED: ANNIVERSARY. Feb 11, 1945. President Franklin D. Roosevelt, British prime minister Winston Churchill and Soviet leader Joseph Stalin signed an agreement at Yalta, a Soviet city on the Black Sea in the Crimea. The agreement contained plans for new blows at the heart of Germany and for occupying Germany at the end of the war. It also called for a meeting in San Francisco to draft a charter for the United Nations.

BIRTHDAYS TODAY

Jennifer Aniston, 45, actress (*Horrible Bosses, Marley & Me, The Good Girl*, "Friends"), born Sherman Oaks, CA, Feb 11, 1969.

Tammy Baldwin, 52, US Senator (D, Wisconsin), born Madison, WI, Feb 11, 1962.

Paul Bocuse, 88, chef, born Collonges-au-Mont-d'Or, France, Feb 11, 1926.

Brandy, 35, singer, actress ("Cinderella," "Moesha"), born Brandy Norwood at McComb, MS, Feb 11, 1979.

Sheryl Crow, 52, singer, musician, born Kennett, MO, Feb 11, 1962.

Natalie Dormer, 32, actress ("The Tudors"), born Reading, England, Feb 11, 1982.

Taylor Lautner, 22, actor (*Twilight*), born Grand Rapids, MI, Feb 11, 1992.

Damian Lewis, 43, actor ("Homeland," "Band of Brothers"), born St. John's Wood, Westminster, England, Feb 11, 1971.

Tina Louise, 80, actress ("Gilligan's Island," *The Stepford Wives*), born New York, NY, Feb 11, 1934.

Carey Lowell, 53, actress ("Law & Order," *Licence to Kill*), born New York, NY, Feb 11, 1961.

Sergio Mendes, 73, musician, bandleader, born Niteroi, Brazil, Feb 11, 1941.

Sarah Palin, 50, 2008 vice-presidential candidate, former governor of Alaska (R), television personality, born Sandpoint, ID, Feb 11, 1964.

Burt Reynolds, 78, actor (*Hooper, Deliverance, Cannonball Run*, "Evening Shade"), born Waycross, GA, Feb 11, 1936.

February 12 — Wednesday

DAY 43 **322 REMAINING**

ADAMS, LOUISA CATHERINE JOHNSON: BIRTH ANNIVERSARY. Feb 12, 1775. Wife of John Quincy Adams, sixth president of the US. Born at London, England. Died at Washington, DC, May 14, 1852.

BENEKE, "TEX": 100th BIRTH ANNIVERSARY. Feb 12, 1914. Popular big band–era tenor saxophonist and vocalist, born Gordon Beneke at Fort Worth, TX. A member of Glenn Miller's band (Miller dubbed Beneke "Tex"), he was voted most popular sax player in 1941 and 1942 by music journalists. After Miller's WWII death, Beneke became leader of the Glenn Miller Orchestra, then eventually headed his own Tex Beneke and His Orchestra. Best known for vocals (with Miller) for "I've Got a Gal in Kalamazoo" and "Chattanooga Choo Choo"—the latter a million-copy hit. Beneke died at Costa Mesa, CA, May 30, 2000.

BRADLEY, OMAR NELSON: BIRTH ANNIVERSARY. Feb 12, 1893. Appointed major general in February 1943, he was sent to North Africa as field aide to Gen Dwight D. Eisenhower. As successor to Gen George S. Patton as commander of the US 2nd Corps, Bradley stormed Bizerte on May 7, 1943, taking 40,000 prisoners, and took part in the attack on Sicily. Bradley then went to England to participate in the planning of the invasion of Western Europe. He led the US 1st Army in the D-Day invasion of Normandy on June 5–6, 1944, then commanded the 12th Army Group of 1.2 million combat troops, the single largest command ever under one American general. His troops crossed the Rhine in March 1945 and in April met Soviet troops on the Elbe. In 1948, he succeeded

Eisenhower as chief of staff of the Army and in 1949, became the first permanent chairman of the Joint Chiefs of Staff. He retired in 1951. Bradley was born at Clark, MO, and died at New York City on Apr 8, 1981.

DANA, JAMES DWIGHT: BIRTH ANNIVERSARY. Feb 12, 1813. Geologist, naturalist, author, explorer born at New Utica, NY. Made important contributions to the understanding of mountain building, volcanic activity, ocean basins, coral reefs, mineralogy and more. Was the preeminent American geologist of his time, although illness shadowed his career. Among other honors, was awarded the Copley Medal by the Royal Society in 1877. Dana died Apr 14, 1895, at New Haven, CT.

DARWIN, CHARLES ROBERT: BIRTH ANNIVERSARY. Feb 12, 1809. Author and naturalist, born at Shrewsbury, England. Best remembered for his books *On the Origin of Species by Means of Natural Selection, or the Preservation of Favoured Races in the Struggle for Life* and *The Descent of Man, and Selection in Relation to Sex*. Died at Down, Kent, England, Apr 19, 1882.

DARWIN DAY. Feb 12. Darwin Day is an international celebration of science and humanity. Events are coordinated around the world to commemorate the life and work of Charles Darwin and the theory of evolution by natural selection and to recognize the contributions and achievements of science and reason. On a broad scale, the program is an effort to advance science literacy, champion the efforts to humanize science and celebrate the adventurous spirit. Events are held on or near Feb 12, the anniversary of Darwin's birth. For info: American Humanist Assn, 1777 T St NW, Washington, DC 20009. Phone: (202) 238-9088. Fax: (202) 238-9003. E-mail: info@darwinday.org. Web: www.darwinday.org.

***DRACULA* PREMIERE: ANNIVERSARY.** Feb 12, 1931. The horror film classic starring Bela Lugosi premiered on this day at the Roxy Theatre in New York City. It had been slated to premiere on Friday, Feb 13, but director Tod Browning, confessing to a superstitious nature, asked for the opening to be moved up a day. *Dracula* made the Hungarian actor Lugosi a star, but at a price: he was offered only horror film roles the rest of his career.

HARRIS, ROY: BIRTH ANNIVERSARY. Feb 12, 1898. Born at Chandler, OK, Harris was one of the most important composers of the 20th century. He was known for his use of Anglo-American folk tunes. He composed more than 200 works, including 13 symphonies, several ballet scores and much chamber and choral music. His best-known work is his Third Symphony (1939). He died at Santa Monica, CA, Oct 1, 1979.

LEWIS, JOHN LLEWELLYN: BIRTH ANNIVERSARY. Feb 12, 1880. American labor leader, born near Lucas, IA. His parents came to the US from Welsh mining towns, and Lewis left school in the seventh grade to become a miner himself. Became leader of United Mine Workers of America and champion of all miners' causes. Died at Washington, DC, June 11, 1969.

LINCOLN, ABRAHAM: BIRTH ANNIVERSARY. Feb 12, 1809. 16th president of the US (Mar 4, 1861–Apr 15, 1865) and the first to be assassinated (on Good Friday, Apr 14, 1865, at Ford's Theatre at Washington, DC). His presidency encompassed the tragic Civil War. Especially remembered are his Emancipation Proclamation (Jan 1, 1863), his Gettysburg Address (Nov 19, 1863) and his proclamation establishing the last Thursday of November as Thanksgiving Day. Born at Hardin County, KY, he died at Washington, DC, Apr 15, 1865. Lincoln's birthday is observed as part of Presidents' Day in most states but is a legal holiday in Illinois and an optional bank holiday in Iowa, Maryland, Michigan, Pennsylvania, Washington and West Virginia. See also: "Presidents' Day" (Feb 17).

LINCOLN'S BIRTHPLACE CABIN WREATH LAYING. Feb 12. Abraham Lincoln Birthplace National Historical Park, Hodgenville, KY. A wreath is placed at the door of the symbolic "Birthplace Cabin" in commemoration of the birth of Abraham Lincoln. For info: Abraham Lincoln Birthplace NHP, 2995 Lincoln Farm Rd, Hodgenville, KY 42748. Phone: (270) 358-3137. Web: www.nps.gov/abli.

MATHER, COTTON: BIRTH ANNIVERSARY. Feb 12, 1663. Puritan minister, scholar and author born at Boston, MA. With his father, Increase Mather, he led a congregation at Old North Church. A staunch believer in mystical forces, he published *Wonders of the Invisible World* in 1692—a treatise supporting the prosecution of the Salem "witches." The last of a Puritan dynasty, Mather died Feb 13, 1728, at Boston.

MYANMAR: UNION DAY. Feb 12. National holiday. Commemorates the founding of the Union of Burma, Feb 12, 1947. The country changed its name to Union of Myanmar in 1989.

NAACP FOUNDED: ANNIVERSARY. Feb 12, 1909. The National Association for the Advancement of Colored People was founded by W.E.B. Du Bois and Ida Wells-Barnett, among others, to wage a militant campaign against lynching and other forms of racial oppression. Its legal wing brought many lawsuits that successfully challenged segregation in the 1950s and '60s.

OGLETHORPE DAY. Feb 12. General James Edward Oglethorpe (born at London, England, Dec 22, 1696), with some 100 other Englishmen, landed at what is now Savannah, GA, on Feb 12, 1733. Naming the new colony Georgia for England's King George II, Oglethorpe was organizer and first governor of the colony and founder of the city of Savannah. Oglethorpe Day and Georgia Day observed on this date.

PAVLOVA, ANNA: BIRTH ANNIVERSARY. Feb 12, 1881. Russian ballerina Anna Pavlova, thought by some to have been the greatest dancer of all time, was born at St. Petersburg, Russia. After performing with much success with the Ballet Russe and other companies, she formed her own company in 1910 and performed on tour for enthusiastic audiences in nearly every country in the world. Pavlova died at The Hague, Netherlands, Jan 23, 1931.

SAFETYPUP'S® BIRTHDAY. Feb 12. This year Safetypup®, created by the National Child Safety Council, joyously celebrates his birthday by bringing safety awareness/education messages to children and their parents in a positive, nonthreatening manner. Age-appropriate materials available through local law enforcement departments on topics including bike safety, drug abuse prevention, child abduction prevention and farm safety. For info: NCSC, Box 1368, Jackson, MI 49204-1368. Phone: (517) 764-6070. Web: www.nfsc.org.

SENATE ACQUITS CLINTON: 15th ANNIVERSARY. Feb 12, 1999. After President William Clinton was impeached by the US House of Representatives, the Senate began a January trial on the charges of perjury and obstruction of justice. On this date the Senate acquitted Clinton. See also: "Clinton Impeachment Proceedings: Anniversary" (Dec 20).

SIMENON, GEORGES: BIRTH ANNIVERSARY. Feb 12, 1903. Simenon was the bestselling author of the 20th century, selling more than 500 million copies of his novels in more than 50 languages. The prodigious Simenon wrote up to six novels per year, specializing in dark, intellectual crime works. He garnered worldwide acclaim for his Inspector Maigret novels. He also gained worldwide notoriety in 1977 when he claimed to have had sexual relations with at least 10,000 women. Simenon, born at Liège, Belgium, died at Lausanne, France, on Sept 4, 1989.

UTAH WOMEN GIVEN THE VOTE: ANNIVERSARY. Feb 12, 1870. The women in the Utah Territory were granted the right to vote in political elections—50 years before the 19th Amendment was ratified.

February 2014	S	M	T	W	T	F	S
							1
	2	3	4	5	6	7	8
	9	10	11	12	13	14	15
	16	17	18	19	20	21	22
	23	24	25	26	27	28	

BIRTHDAYS TODAY

Maud Adams, 69, actress (*Killer Force, Octopussy*), born Lulea, Sweden, Feb 12, 1945.

Joe Don Baker, 78, actor (*Charlie Varrick, Cool Hand Luke*), born Groesbeck, TX, Feb 12, 1936.

Ehud Barak, 72, former Israeli prime minister, born Mishmar, Hasharon, Israel, Feb 12, 1942.

Judy Blume, 76, author (*Blubber, Superfudge*), born Elizabeth, NJ, Feb 12, 1938.

Josh Brolin, 46, actor (*Milk, No Country for Old Men*), born Los Angeles, CA, Feb 12, 1968.

Cliff De Young, 67, actor (*Blue Collar, F/X*), born Inglewood, CA, Feb 12, 1947.

Joseph Henry (Joe) Garagiola, 88, sportscaster, former baseball player, born St. Louis, MO, Feb 12, 1926.

Robert Griffin III, 24, football player, born Okinawa Prefecture, Japan, Feb 12, 1990.

Arsenio Hall, 59, comedian, actor (*Coming to America*), former television talk show host, born Cleveland, OH, Feb 12, 1955.

Joanna Kerns, 61, actress ("Growing Pains"), former gymnast, born San Francisco, CA, Feb 12, 1953.

Chynna Phillips, 46, singer (Wilson Phillips), born Los Angeles, CA, Feb 12, 1968.

Christina Ricci, 34, actress (*Sleepy Hollow, Ice Storm*), born Santa Monica, CA, Feb 12, 1980.

William Felton (Bill) Russell, 80, Hall of Fame basketball player and former coach, born Monroe, LA, Feb 12, 1934.

Jesse Spencer, 35, actor ("Chicago Fire," "House"), born Melbourne, Victoria, Australia, Feb 12, 1979.

Franco Zeffirelli, 91, stage and film director (*Otello, Romeo and Juliet*), born Florence, Italy, Feb 12, 1923.

February 13 — Thursday

DAY 44 **321 REMAINING**

AMERICAN ASSOCIATION FOR THE ADVANCEMENT OF SCIENCE ANNUAL MEETING. Feb 13–17. Chicago, IL. 180th meeting. Est attendance: 9,000. For info: AAAS, 1200 New York Ave NW, Washington, DC 20005. Phone: (202) 326-6450. E-mail: meetings@aaas.org. Web: www.aaas.org/meetings.

CHURCHILL, RANDOLPH HENRY SPENCER: BIRTH ANNIVERSARY. Feb 13, 1849. English politician and the father of Winston Churchill. Born at Blenheim, Woodstock, Oxfordshire, England, he died at London, Jan 24, 1895.

DRESDEN FIREBOMBING: ANNIVERSARY. Feb 13, 1945. Dresden, Germany. Allied firebombing caused a firestorm that destroyed the city and killed 135,000 people.

EMPLOYEE LEGAL AWARENESS DAY. Feb 13. A day emphasizing the importance of legal education for employees so that large and small businesses reduce their risk of legal problems. For info: Paul Brennan, PO Box 27, Mooloolaba, Queensland 4557, Australia. E-mail: paul.brennan@brennanlaw.com.au.

FIRST MAGAZINE PUBLISHED IN AMERICA: ANNIVERSARY. Feb 13, 1741. (Old Style date.) Andrew Bradford published *The American Magazine* just three days ahead of Benjamin Franklin's *General Magazine*.

GET A DIFFERENT NAME DAY. Feb 13. For the pity of the millions of us who hate our birth names. On this day we may change our names to whatever we wish and have the right to expect colleagues, family and friends to so address us. (©2006 by WH.) For info: Thomas & Ruth Roy, Wellcat Holidays, 2418 Long Ln, Lebanon, PA 17046. Phone: (717) 279-0184. E-mail: info@wellcat.com. Web: www.wellcat.com.

IRWIN EARNS FIRST MEDAL OF HONOR: ANNIVERSARY. Feb 13, 1861. Colonel Bernard Irwin distinguished himself while leading troops in a battle with Chiricahua Apache Indians at Apache Pass, AZ (at the time part of the territory of New Mexico). For those actions Irwin later became the first person awarded the new US Medal of Honor, although he didn't actually receive it until three years later (Jan 24, 1864).

MADLY IN LOVE WITH ME DAY. Feb 13. The international day of self-love, created to inspire people to say "Yes!" to loving, living and being themselves fully and without apology. The day before Valentine's Day people worldwide make a self-love promise—and many host celebrations. For info: Christine Arylo, 2625 Alcatraz Ave #301, Berkeley, CA 94705. E-mail: love@daretoliveyou.com.

MIAMI INTERNATIONAL BOAT SHOW. Feb 13–17. Miami Beach Convention Center, Miami Beach, FL. 72nd annual boat show, the biggest in the US and considered the main event for product introductions. With more than 3,000 boats, this show offers an unparalleled opportunity to view the sport's latest products. Est attendance: 175,000. For info: NMMA, 231 S LaSalle St, Ste 2050, Chicago, IL 60604. Phone: (312) 946-6200. Fax: (312) 946-0388. Web: www.MiamiBoatShow.com.

NATIONAL CONFERENCE ON EDUCATION. Feb 13–15. Nashville, TN. 146th annual conference. The conference is rich with content about the issues and challenges in public education. An opportunity to hear recognized speakers discuss solutions, best practices, challenges and more. For info: American Assn of School Administrators, 1615 Duke St, Alexandria, VA 22314. Phone: (703) 528-0700. Fax: (703) 841-1543. E-mail: info@aasa.org. Web: www.aasa.org.

PIAZZETTA, GIOVANNI BATTISTA: BIRTH ANNIVERSARY. Feb 13, 1682. Prominent 18th-century Venetian painter. Notable among his works are the *Ecstasy of St. Francis* and *Fortune Teller*. Born at Venice, Italy, and died there Apr 28, 1754.

ROBINSON, EDDIE: 95th BIRTH ANNIVERSARY. Feb 13, 1919. One of the winningest coaches in college football history, born at Jackson, LA. As the head coach at Grambling State University in Grambling, LA, he led the Tigers to more than 400 victories during his 56-year tenure (1941–97). Considered a civil rights pioneer for his leadership in an era when doors were not always open for black athletes, he battled segregation and ultimately sent more than 200 players to the NFL. He was elected to the College Football Hall of Fame immediately upon his retirement in 1997 and was diagnosed with Alzheimer's that same year. He died at Ruston, LA, Apr 3, 2007.

SIMPLOT GAMES. Feb 13–15. Holt Arena, Idaho State University, Pocatello, ID. One of the nation's largest indoor high school track-and-field events, featuring 2,000 top high school athletes from the US and Canada. Est attendance: 2,000. For info: Simplot Games, PO Box 912, Pocatello, ID 83204. Phone: (208) 235-5604. Fax: (208) 235-5676. E-mail: info@simplotgames.com. Web: www.simplotgames.com.

TRUMAN, BESS (ELIZABETH) VIRGINIA WALLACE: BIRTH ANNIVERSARY. Feb 13, 1885. Wife of Harry S Truman, 33rd president of the US. Born at Independence, MO, and died there Oct 18, 1982.

WOOD, GRANT: BIRTH ANNIVERSARY. Feb 13, 1892. American artist, especially noted for his powerful realism and satirical paintings of the American scene, born near Anamosa, IA. He was a printer, sculptor, woodworker and high school and college teacher. Among his best-remembered works are *American Gothic, Fall Plowing* and *Stone City.* Died at Iowa City, IA, Feb 12, 1942.

BIRTHDAYS TODAY

Richard Blumenthal, 68, US Senator (D, Connecticut), born Brooklyn, NY, Feb 13, 1946.

Stockard Channing, 70, actress (*Six Degrees of Separation, The House of Blue Leaves,* "The West Wing"), born Susan Stockard at New York, NY, Feb 13, 1944.

Peter Gabriel, 64, singer, songwriter, born London, England, Feb 13, 1950.

Kelly Hu, 47, actress ("Martial Law," "Nash Bridges"), born Honolulu, HI, Feb 13, 1967.

Carol Lynley, 72, actress (*Harlow, Bunny Lake Is Missing*), born New York, NY, Feb 13, 1942.

Randy Moss, 37, football player, born Rand, WV, Feb 13, 1977.

David Naughton, 63, singer, actor (*An American Werewolf in London, Overexposed*), born Hartford, CT, Feb 13, 1951.

Jay Nixon, 58, Governor of Missouri (D), born De Soto, MO, Feb 13, 1956.

Kim Novak, 81, actress (*Bell, Book and Candle*; *Vertigo*), born Marilyn Novak at Chicago, IL, Feb 13, 1933.

George Segal, 80, actor (*A Touch of Class*, "Just Shoot Me"), born Great Neck, NY, Feb 13, 1934.

Jerry Springer, 70, television host ("The Jerry Springer Show"), born London, England, Feb 13, 1944.

Bo Svenson, 73, actor (*North Dallas Forty, Heartbreak Ridge*), born Goteborg, Sweden, Feb 13, 1941.

Peter Tork, 70, singer, actor ("The Monkees"), born Peter Thorkelson at Washington, DC, Feb 13, 1944 (some sources say 1942).

Chuck Yeager, 91, pilot who broke sound barrier, born Myra, WV, Feb 13, 1923.

February 14 — Friday

DAY 45 **320 REMAINING**

ALLEN, MEL: BIRTH ANNIVERSARY. Feb 14, 1913. Born Melvin Allen Israel at Birmingham, AL, he began broadcasting baseball and other sporting events for the CBS radio network in 1936. He became the Yankees' lead announcer after World War II and was nationally famous for two phrases: "How about that!" to describe a fine play and "Going, going, gone," his home run call. After being fired by the Yankees in 1963, Allen attracted a new generation of listeners with his weekly television show "This Week in Baseball." He died at Greenwich, CT, June 16, 1996.

February 2014	S	M	T	W	T	F	S
							1
	2	3	4	5	6	7	8
	9	10	11	12	13	14	15
	16	17	18	19	20	21	22
	23	24	25	26	27	28	

ARIZONA: ADMISSION DAY: ANNIVERSARY. Feb 14. Became 48th state in 1912.

BENNY, JACK: BIRTH ANNIVERSARY. Feb 14, 1894. American comedian. Born Benjamin Kubelsky, Jack Benny entered vaudeville at Waukegan, IL, at age 17, using the violin as a comic stage prop. His radio show first aired in 1932 and continued for 20 years with little change in format. He also had a long-running television show. One of his most well-known comic gimmicks was his purported stinginess. Benny was born at Chicago, IL, and died Dec 26, 1974, at Beverly Hills, CA.

BULGARIA: VITICULTURISTS' DAY (TRIFON ZAREZAN). Feb 14. Celebrated since Thracian times. Festivities are based on the cult of Dionysus, god of merriment and wine.

CHINA: LANTERN FESTIVAL. Feb 14. Traditional Chinese festival falls on the 15th day of the first month of the Chinese lunar calendar year. Lantern processions mark the end of the Chinese New Year holiday season. Also celebrated in Taiwan and Korea. Date in other countries will differ from China's by up to one day. See also: "Chinese New Year" (Jan 31).

ENIAC COMPUTER INTRODUCED: ANNIVERSARY. Feb 14, 1946. J. Presper Eckert and John W. Mauchly demonstrated the Electronic Numerical Integrator and Computer (ENIAC) for the first time at the University of Pennsylvania. This was the first electronic digital computer. It occupied a room the size of a gymnasium and contained nearly 18,000 vacuum tubes. The army commissioned the computer to speed the calculation of firing tables for artillery. By the time the computer was ready, WWII was over. However, ENIAC prepared the way for future generations of computers.

FERRIS WHEEL DAY: GEORGE FERRIS'S BIRTH ANNIVERSARY. Feb 14, 1859. Anniversary of the birth of George Washington Gale Ferris, American engineer and inventor, at Galesburg, IL. Among his many accomplishments as a civil engineer, Ferris is best remembered as the inventor of the Ferris wheel, which he developed for the World's Columbian Exposition at Chicago, IL, in 1893. Built on the Midway Plaisance, the 250-foot-diameter Ferris wheel (with 36 coaches, each capable of carrying 40 passengers) proved one of the greatest attractions of the fair. It was America's answer to the Eiffel Tower of the Paris International Exposition of 1889. Ferris died at Pittsburgh, PA, Nov 22, 1896.

FIRST PRESIDENTIAL PHOTOGRAPH: ANNIVERSARY. Feb 14, 1849. President James Polk became the first US president to be photographed while in office. The photographer was Mathew B. Brady, who would become famous for his photography during the American Civil War.

FRANCE: NICE CARNIVAL. Feb 14–Mar 4. Dates from the 14th century and is celebrated each year during the 19 days ending with Shrove Tuesday. Derived from ancient rites of spring, the carnival offers parades, floats, battles of flowers and confetti and a fireworks display lighting up the entire Baie des Anges. King Carnival is burned on his pyre at the end of the event.

GOLD RUSH DAYS. Feb 14–16. Wickenburg, AZ. 66th annual community-wide celebration of the Old West: rodeo, parade, carnival, gold panning. Named one of the top 100 events in North America by the American Bus Association. Annually, the second full weekend in February. Est attendance: 60,000. For info: Chamber of Commerce, 216 N Frontier St, Wickenburg, AZ 85390. Phone: (928) 684-5479 or (928) 684-0977. Fax: (928) 684-5470. E-mail: events@wickenburgchamber.com. Web: www.wickenburgchamber.com.

GREAT BACKYARD BIRD COUNT. Feb 14–17. 17th annual. Thousands of volunteers nationwide track the number and types of birds that live near their homes. Results help researchers monitor species in trouble. Cosponsored by the National Audubon Society and the Cornell University Lab of Ornithology. For info: National Audubon Society, 225 Varick St, 7th Fl, New York, NY 10014. Phone: (212) 979-3000. E-mail: gbbc@cornell.edu. Web: www.birdsource.org or www.audubon.org.

HANCOCK, WINFIELD SCOTT: BIRTH ANNIVERSARY. Feb 14, 1824. Born at Montgomery, PA; died Feb 9, 1886, at Governor's Island, NY. After his service as a Union general in the Civil War, his command of the military division of Texas and Louisiana won him much favor from the Democratic Party because he allowed local civil authorities to retain their power. He pleased the Democrats so well that they made him their presidential candidate in 1880. He lost to James A. Garfield by a narrow margin.

HINES, GREGORY: BIRTH ANNIVERSARY. Feb 14, 1946. One of the best tap dancers of his generation, Gregory Hines was born at New York, NY. He was a child star, performing regularly at the Apollo Theater in Harlem, NY, by the age of six. As an adult, he turned to acting, working in film, on television and on the Broadway stage. He was nominated for several Tony Awards, winning in 1993 for *Jelly's Last Jam*. His films include *Running Scared* and *The Cotton Club*, and he was nominated for several Emmy Awards for his television dance specials. He died at Los Angeles, CA, Aug 9, 2003.

LEAGUE OF WOMEN VOTERS FORMED: ANNIVERSARY. Feb 14, 1920. While meeting in Chicago, IL, to celebrate the imminent ratification of the 19th Amendment to the Constitution, leaders of the National American Woman Suffrage Association (NAWSA) approved the formation of a new organization—the League of Women Voters. With the vote for women just a few months away, the new organization was created to help American women exercise their new political rights and responsibilities. For info: League of Women Voters. Web: www.lwv.org.

***THE MALTESE FALCON* PUBLISHED: ANNIVERSARY.** Feb 14, 1930. Former Pinkerton agent-turned author Dashiell Hammett's crime novel introducing Sam Spade was published on this day by Alfred A. Knopf in New York, NY. (The novel had been serialized in *Black Mask* magazine in the fall of 1929, but Hammett revised the text.) The novel was a milestone in American literature, offering the model that all "hard-boiled" crime fiction would follow. And in terse tough-guy Sam Spade (who "looked rather pleasantly like a blond satan"), the world found a new pop icon. The notably dark-haired Humphrey Bogart played Spade in the 1941 film version directed by John Huston.

MOON PHASE: FULL MOON. Feb 14. Moon enters Full Moon phase at 6:53 PM, EST.

NATIONAL DATE FESTIVAL. Feb 14–23. Riverside County Fairgrounds, Indio, CA. 68th annual. America's most exotic county fair features Arabian Nights theme, camel and ostrich races, satellite horse wagering, nightly musical pageant, date exhibits and sampling, thousands of competitive exhibits and carnival. Headliner entertainment included with admission. Est attendance: 300,000. For info: Riverside County Fair and National Date Fest, 82-503 Hwy 111, Indio, CA 92201. Phone: (760) 863-8247 or (800) 811-FAIR. Web: www.datefest.org.

NATIONAL DONOR DAY. Feb 14. Valentine's Day is the day of love, and organ donation is the gift of life. Make Feb 14 the day to join thousands of Americans in making the donation decision. National Donor Day was started in 1998 by the Saturn Corporation and its United Auto Workers partners with the support of the US Department of Health and Human Services and many nonprofit health organizations. For info: US Dept of Health and Human Services. Web: www.organdonor.gov.

NATIONAL HAVE-A-HEART DAY. Feb 14. The goal of this celebration of life is to create a new consciousness concerning the impact of our food choices on the environment, world hunger, animal welfare and human health—especially heart health. Vegetarian diets increase longevity and help prevent—and even reverse—heart disease. Total vegetarians live about 15 years longer than nonvegetarians and suffer less than one-tenth the heart disease death rate of nonvegetarians. For info: Vegetarian Awareness Network, PO Box 3545, Washington, DC 20027-0045. Phone: (800) 234-8343.

NCCDP ALZHEIMER'S AND DEMENTIA STAFF EDUCATION WEEK. Feb 14–21. To bring awareness of the importance of staff educators being trained and certified in dementia care, to promote education by means of a face-to-face interactive classroom environment and to provide comprehensive dementia education to all healthcare professionals and line staff. Free tool kit and in-services provided. Annually, Feb 14–21. For info: National Council of Certified Dementia Practitioners (NCCDP), 103 Valley View Trail, Sparta, NJ 07871. Phone: (877) 729-5191. Fax: (973) 860-2244. E-mail: nationalccdp@aol.com. Web: www.nccdp.org.

OREGON: ADMISSION DAY. Feb 14. Became 33rd state in 1859.

PROUT, MARY ANN ("AUNT MARY PROUT"): BIRTH ANNIVERSARY. Feb 14, 1801. It is believed most likely that Mary Prout—social activist, humanitarian, educator—was born free on this date at Baltimore, MD. Prout became a teacher and in 1830 founded a day school. Actively involved in her church, she founded a secret society that became the Independent Order of St. Luke to help with the cost of medical care and burial services for needy blacks, an organization that grew to have 1,500 chapters across the nation by 1900. Prout died at Baltimore in 1884.

RACE RELATIONS DAY. Feb 14. A day designated by some churches to recognize the importance of interracial relations. Formerly was observed on Abraham Lincoln's birthday or on the Sunday preceding it. Since 1970 observance has generally been Feb 14.

REENACTMENT OF THE BATTLE OF OLUSTEE. Feb 14–16. Olustee Battlefield Historic State Park, Olustee, FL. Join us for the 150th anniversary of the largest Civil War battle fought in Florida. Est attendance: 22,000. For info: Elaine McGrath, Special Events Coordinator, Stephen Foster Folk Culture Center State Park, PO Box G, White Springs, FL 32096. Phone: (386) 397-4462. Fax: (386) 397-4262. E-mail: elaine.mcgrath@dep.state.fl.us. Web: www.floridastateparks.org/olustee.

SAINT VALENTINE'S DAY. Feb 14. St. Valentine's Day celebrates the feasts of two Christian martyrs of this name. One, a priest and physician, was beaten and beheaded on the Flaminian Way at Rome, Italy, Feb 14, AD 269, during the reign of Emperor Claudius II. Another Valentine, the bishop of Terni, is said to have been beheaded, also on the Flaminian Way at Rome, Feb 14 (possibly in a later year). Both history and legend are vague and contradictory about details of the Valentines, and some say that Feb 14 was selected for the celebration of Christian martyrs as a diversion from the ancient pagan observance of Lupercalia. An old legend has it that birds choose their mates on Valentine's Day. Now it is one of the most widely observed unofficial holidays. It is an occasion for the exchange of gifts (usually books, flowers or sweets) and greeting cards with affectionate or humorous messages. See also: "Lupercalia" (Feb 15).

SAINT VALENTINE'S DAY MASSACRE: 85th ANNIVERSARY. Feb 14, 1929. Anniversary of gangland executions at Chicago, IL, when gunmen posing as police shot seven members of the George "Bugs" Moran gang.

SALMAN RUSHDIE'S DEATH SENTENCE: 25th ANNIVERSARY. Feb 14, 1989. Iranian leader Ayatollah Ruholla Khomeini, offended by *The Satanic Verses*, called on Muslims to kill the book's British author, Salman Rushdie. On the following day the ayatollah offered a $1 million reward for execution of his sentence. Rushdie, fearful for his life, went into hiding. Worldwide protests against the efforts to abridge academic and literary freedoms, countered by protests of Muslim and other religious fundamentalists, stimulated the sales of *The Satanic Verses*, but Rushdie remained virtually a prisoner, unable to resume a public life. In 1998 the Iranian government rescinded the death sentence.

SHERMAN DESTROYS MERIDIAN: 150th ANNIVERSARY. Feb 14, 1864. After meeting little Confederate resistance, Union General William Tecumseh Sherman marched into Meridian, MS. After taking the town, Sherman's army destroyed it by burning railroad lines, storehouses, depots, arsenals, hospitals, offices and hotels.

SNOW MOON. Feb 14. So called by Native American tribes of New England and the Great Lakes because this time of year sees heavy snowfalls. Also called the Hunger Moon, because of the meager hunting at this time of winter. The February Full Moon.

SPACE MILESTONE: *NEAR* ORBITS ASTEROID. Feb 14, 2000. The robot spacecraft *Near Earth Asteroid Rendezvous* (now called *NEAR Shoemaker*) finished circling the asteroid Eros for the first time on this day. Eros is called a near-Earth asteroid because its orbit crosses that of Earth and poses a potential collision danger. *NEAR* continued orbiting the asteroid for a year, moving closer to the surface to make more precise measurements and transmit thousands of pictures. In October 2000 it passed within three miles of Eros. Though it was never designed for landing, on Feb 12, 2001, *NEAR* touched down on Eros, history's first landing of an object on an asteroid. *NEAR* was launched from Cape Canaveral, FL, Feb 17, 1996.

SPACE MILESTONE: 100th SPACE WALK. Feb 14, 2001. Two astronauts from the space shuttle *Atlantis* took the 100th space walk; the first had been taken by American Edward White in 1965. On their excursion Thomas Jones and Robert Curbeam, Jr, put the finishing touches on the International Space Station's new science lab, *Destiny*. See also: "Space Milestone: *Gemini 4*" (June 3).

WALLET, SKEEZIX: "BIRTHDAY." Feb 14. Comic strip character in "Gasoline Alley," by Frank King. First cartoon character to grow and age with the years of publication. Foundling child of Walt and Phyllis Wallet, discovered on doorstep Feb 14, 1921. Skeezix grew through childhood, marriage and military service in WWII, returning home to parenthood and business after the war. Comic strip began in the *Chicago Tribune*, Aug 23, 1919.

WINGS OVER THE PLATTE SPRING MIGRATION CELEBRATION. Feb 14–Apr 12. Grand Island, NE. Celebrate the arrival of the world's largest concentration of sandhill cranes. Each spring up to 600,000 cranes gather along the Platte River during their northward migration. Seminars, tours, nature hikes, films. Est attendance: 100,000. For info: Grand Island/Hall County CVB, 2424 S Locust St, Ste C, Grand Island, NE 66801. Phone: (800) 658-3178 or (308) 382-4400. Fax: (308) 382-4908. E-mail: info@visitgrandisland.com. Web: www.visitgrandisland.com.

BIRTHDAYS TODAY

Carl Bernstein, 70, journalist, author (*All the President's Men* with Bob Woodward), born Washington, DC, Feb 14, 1944.

Drew Bledsoe, 42, former football player, born Ellensburg, WA, Feb 14, 1972.

Michael Bloomberg, 72, Mayor of New York City (R), born Brighton, MA, Feb 14, 1942.

Enrico Colantoni, 51, actor ("Person of Interest," "Just Shoot Me," "Veronica Mars"), born Toronto, ON, Canada, Feb 14, 1963.

Hugh Downs, 93, broadcaster ("Today," "20/20"), born Akron, OH, Feb 14, 1921.

Renée Fleming, 55, opera singer, born Rochester, NY, Feb 14, 1959.

Zach Galligan, 50, actor (*Gremlins*), born New York, NY, Feb 14, 1964.

Richard Hamilton, 36, basketball player, born Coatesville, PA, Feb 14, 1978.

February 2014

S	M	T	W	T	F	S
						1
2	3	4	5	6	7	8
9	10	11	12	13	14	15
16	17	18	19	20	21	22
23	24	25	26	27	28	

Milan Hejduk, 38, hockey player, born Usti-nad-Labem, Czechoslovakia (now the Czech Republic), Feb 14, 1976.

Florence Henderson, 80, singer, actress ("The Brady Bunch"), born Dale, IN, Feb 14, 1934.

Simon Pegg, 44, actor (*Shaun of the Dead, Hot Fuzz, Star Trek*), born Brockworth, Gloucestershire, England, Feb 14, 1970.

Andrew Prine, 78, actor (*The Miracle Worker, Chisum*), born Jennings, FL, Feb 14, 1936.

Teller, 66, magician (Penn and Teller), born Raymond Joseph Teller at Philadelphia, PA, Feb 14, 1948.

Meg Tilly, 54, actress (*Agnes of God, The Two Jakes*), born Long Beach, CA, Feb 14, 1960.

Jessica Yu, 48, filmmaker, born Los Altos Hills, CA, Feb 14, 1966.

February 15 — Saturday

DAY 46 — **319 REMAINING**

AFGHANISTAN: SOVIET TROOP WITHDRAWAL: 25th ANNIVERSARY. Feb 15, 1989. The USSR's target of withdrawal of all Soviet troops from Afghanistan by this date was essentially met, ending more than nine years of intervention in a civil war.

ARLEN, HAROLD: BIRTH ANNIVERSARY. Feb 15, 1905. American composer and songwriter, born at Buffalo, NY. Arlen wrote many popular songs, including "Over the Rainbow" (for which he won the 1939 Oscar for Best Song), "That Old Black Magic," "Blues in the Night" and "Stormy Weather." Died at New York, NY, Apr 23, 1986.

ASTEROID NEAR MISS: ANNIVERSARY. Feb 15, 2013. In a stunning coincidence, on the same day that a huge meteor exploded over Chelyabinsk, Russia, the asteroid 2012 DA14 passed Earth at a distance of less than 18,000 miles. The asteroid, more than 150 feet across, came so close to Earth that it passed inside the belt of man-made geostationary weather and communications satellites surrounding the planet. The near miss was the closest approach by any object of its size in recorded history.

BARRYMORE, JOHN: BIRTH ANNIVERSARY. Feb 15, 1882. American actor of famous acting family, brother of Ethel and Lionel. Born John Blythe at Philadelphia, PA, and died at Los Angeles, CA, May 29, 1942.

CANADA: MAPLE LEAF FLAG ADOPTED: ANNIVERSARY. Feb 15, 1965. The new Canadian national flag was raised at Ottawa, Canada's capital, on this day. The red-and-white flag with a red maple leaf in the center replaced the Red Ensign flag, which had the British Union Jack in the upper left-hand corner.

CERMAK, ANTON J.: ASSASSINATION ANNIVERSARY. Feb 15, 1933. At Bay Front Park, Miami, FL, an assassin aiming at President-elect Franklin D. Roosevelt had his aim deflected by a spectator. Anton Cermak, mayor of Chicago, IL, born May 9, 1873, at Kladno, Bohemia, Czechoslovakia, was struck and killed instead. Giuseppe (Joe) Zangara, the 32-year-old assassin, who had emigrated from Italy in 1923, was electrocuted at the Raiford, FL, state prison Mar 20, 1933.

CHELYABINSK METEOR EXPLOSION: ANNIVERSARY. Feb 15, 2013. Moving at approximately 40,000 miles per hour, a meteor measuring more than 50 feet in diameter and weighing around 7,000 tons exploded in a massive fireball over Chelyabinsk, Russia. The explosion, captured from dozens of angles in amateur video footage, injured more than 1,500 people and was detected by Comprehensive Nuclear Test Ban monitoring stations from Greenland to Antarctica. At an estimated 450–500 kilotons, it is thought to be the most powerful such event since the Tunguska incident in Siberia in 1908.

CHINESE NEW YEAR PARADE IN SAN FRANCISCO. Feb 15. San Francisco, CA. North America's largest Chinese community salutes the Year of the Horse, Lunar Year 4712. Sponsored by Southwest Airlines. For info: Chinese New Year Parade Office, 317 W Portal Ave, #27428, San Francisco, CA 94127-1441. Phone: (415) 340-3055. Fax: (415) 340-3056. Web: www.chineseparade.com.

CLARK, ABRAHAM: BIRTH ANNIVERSARY. Feb 15, 1726. Signer of the Declaration of Independence, farmer and lawyer. Born at Elizabethtown, NJ, and died there Sept 15, 1794.

LA FIESTA DE LOS VAQUEROS AND TUCSON RODEO. Feb 15–23. Tucson, AZ. 89th annual. Tucson celebrates its Old West heritage with a parade, a PRCA rodeo and other related rodeo events, including an Extreme bull-riding event. Est attendance: 55,000. For info: Tucson Rodeo Committee, Inc, PO Box 11006, Tucson, AZ 85734. Phone: (520) 741-2233 or (800) 964-5662. Fax: (520) 741-7273. E-mail: info@tucsonrodeo.com. Web: www.tucsonrodeo.com.

GALESBURG CHOCOLATE FESTIVAL. Feb 15–16. Galesburg, IL. A chocolate lover's dream! Homemade and commercially made chocolates, tortes, cakes, pies and creams—all you can eat for a small admission fee. Est attendance: 1,500. For info: Galesburg Area CVB, PO Box 60, Galesburg, IL 61402-0060. Phone: (309) 343-2485. Fax: (309) 343-2521. E-mail: visitors@visitgalesburg.com. Web: www.visitgalesburg.com.

GALILEI, GALILEO: 450th BIRTH ANNIVERSARY. Feb 15, 1564. Physicist and astronomer who helped overthrow medieval concepts of the world, born at Pisa, Italy. He proved the theory that all bodies, large and small, descend at equal speed and gathered evidence to support Copernicus's theory that Earth and other planets revolve around the sun. In 1632 Galileo was tried by the Inquisition and found "vehemently suspect of heresy" because his *Dialogue Concerning the Two Chief World Systems* argued in favor of heliocentrism in contradiction to literal readings of scripture. Galileo remained under house arrest until his death in Florence on Jan 8, 1642. The *Dialogue* was finally published in an uncensored form in 1835, and the Catholic Church issued an official apology to Galileo in 2000.

GIES, MIEP: BIRTH ANNIVERSARY. Feb 15, 1909. Dutch woman, born Hermine Santrouschitz at Vienna, Austria-Hungary, who with her husband, Jan Gies, helped hide the Otto Frank family from the Nazis in Amsterdam during WWII. After the Franks were arrested, Gies discovered the now-famous diary of their youngest daughter, Anne. Following the war, Gies returned the diary to Anne's father, who had it published in 1947. Gies died Jan 11, 2010, at the age of 100 at Hoorn, Netherlands.

ICE FISHING DERBY. Feb 15. Fort Peck, MT. 18th annual contest held on Fort Peck Lake. Entry fee of $50 per hole or three holes for $100. Subject to cancellation if no ice. For info: Glasgow Area Chamber of Commerce, PO Box 832, Glasgow, MT 59230. Phone: (406) 228-2222. Fax: (406) 228-2244. E-mail: chamber@nemont.net. Web: www.glasgowchamber.net.

LUPERCALIA. Feb 15. Anniversary of ancient Roman fertility festival. Thought by some to have been established by Romulus and Remus, who, legend says, were suckled by a she-wolf at Lupercal (a cave in Palestine). Goats and dogs were sacrificed. Lupercalia celebration persisted until the fifth century of the Christian era. Possibly a forerunner of Valentine's Day customs.

McCORMICK, CYRUS H.: BIRTH ANNIVERSARY. Feb 15, 1809. Inventor of the reaper, born at Rockbridge County, VA. It is said that Cyrus McCormick's invention of the reaper rates second only to the railroad in the development of the US. Continuing the dream of his father, McCormick constructed a horse-operated reaper, which was demonstrated for the first time in a Virginia wheat field in July 1831. He moved his operation to Chicago, IL, in 1847 in order to be closer to the Midwest's expanding wheat fields. His business prospered despite two decades of constant litigation over patent rights. He died May 13, 1884, at Chicago. In 1902–03, his McCormick Harvesting Machine Company was consolidated with other firms to become the International Harvester Company.

MENENDEZ DE AVILES, PEDRO: BIRTH ANNIVERSARY. Feb 15, 1519. Spanish explorer and naval adventurer. Explored Florida coastal regions for the king of Spain and established a fort at St. Augustine in September 1565. Died Sept 17, 1574, at Santander, Spain.

MONTE CASSINO BOMBED: 70th ANNIVERSARY. Feb 15, 1944. The monastery and abbey at Monte Cassino, Italy, were attacked by 228 heavy and medium American bombers during WWII. The abbey, which was built in AD 529, was destroyed after several hours of bombardment. US commanders reported 200 German soldiers were seen fleeing the fortress during the assault. Benedictine monks were also seen scrambling for cover.

NEW ENGLAND MID-WINTER SURFING CHAMPIONSHIP. Feb 15. Narragansett Town Beach, Narragansett, RI. 46th annual. Competition in all age categories and specialty events with prizes and trophies. Est attendance: 125. For info: Peter Panagiotis, ESA Dir, 31 Othmar St, Narragansett, RI 02882. E-mail: bicsurf@hotmail.com.

REMEMBER THE *MAINE* DAY: ANNIVERSARY. Feb 15, 1898. The American battleship *Maine* was blown up while at anchor in Havana Harbor, at 9:40 PM, on this day in 1898. The ship, under the command of Captain Charles G. Sigsbee, sank quickly, and 260 members of its crew were lost. Inflamed public opinion in the US ignored the lack of evidence to establish responsibility for the explosion. "Remember the *Maine*" became the war cry, and a formal declaration of war against Spain followed on Apr 25, 1898.

SENDLER, IRENA: BIRTH ANNIVERSARY. Feb 15, 1910. Polish social worker who at great personal risk headed a rescue effort to smuggle some 2,500 Jewish children out of the Warsaw Ghetto in WWII. Sendler, a Roman Catholic, recognized early in the war the Nazi threat to Jews and used her bureaucratic contacts to bring medicine and food into the ghetto and then faced the heartbreaking task of separating children from parents in order to save them. Recognized by Yad Vashem in 1965 as Righteous Among the Nations, Sendler died May 12, 2007, in Warsaw, which was also her birthplace.

SERBIA: NATIONAL DAY. Feb 15.

SHACKLETON, ERNEST: BIRTH ANNIVERSARY. Feb 15, 1874. The Antarctic explorer was born at Kilkea, Ireland. His fame rests not on reaching the South Pole (he tried three times), but on his leadership and bravery. During the British Imperial Trans-Arctic expedition of 1914, the icy seas crushed his ship, *Endurance*, but Shackleton protected his men and buoyed their morale for the two years they were marooned. In 1916 he led a six-man team in a lifeboat on a 17-day, 600-mile journey (without sleep) in search of help. Upon arrival at South Georgia Island, he initiated a rescue effort, and three months later all his men were rescued without a death. Shackleton died Jan 5, 1922, at Grytviken, South Georgia Island, while beginning a fourth expedition to the South Pole.

SPANISH WAR MEMORIAL DAY AND *MAINE* MEMORIAL DAY. Feb 15. Massachusetts.

SPRINT UNLIMITED AT DAYTONA. Feb 15. Daytona International Speedway, Daytona Beach, FL. Dash for the cash featuring NASCAR Sprint Cup stars. For info: Daytona International Speedway, PO Box 2801, Daytona Beach, FL 32120-2801. Phone: (800) PIT-SHOP. Web: www.daytonainternationalspeedway.com.

SUSAN B. ANTHONY DAY. Feb 15. Honors one of the first women's rights advocates, working especially for the right to vote. Anthony was born on this day in 1820 at Adams, MA. She died Mar 13, 1906, at Rochester, NY.

SUTTER, JOHN AUGUSTUS: BIRTH ANNIVERSARY. Feb 15, 1803. Born at Kandern, Germany, Sutter established the first Anglo settlement on the site of Sacramento, CA, in 1839. He owned a large tract of land there, which he named New Helvetia. The first great gold strike in the US was on his property, at Sutter's Mill, Jan 24, 1848. His land was soon overrun by gold seekers who, he claimed, slaughtered his cattle and stole or destroyed his property. Sutter was bankrupt by 1852. Died at Washington, DC, June 18, 1880.

TIFFANY, CHARLES LEWIS: BIRTH ANNIVERSARY. Feb 15, 1812. American jeweler whose name became synonymous with high standards of quality. Born at Killingly, CT, and died at New York, NY, Feb 18, 1902. Father of artist Louis Comfort Tiffany. See also: "Tiffany, Louis Comfort: Birth Anniversary" (Feb 18).

WASHINGTON'S BIRTHDAY AT MOUNT VERNON. Feb 15–17. Mount Vernon, VA. George Washington's home is the site of a variety of events in honor of his birthday. Each day of the celebration is kicked off by "George Washington's Surprise Birthday Party" on Mount Vernon's Bowling Green. Visitors can partake of the first president's favorite breakfast on Saturday and Sunday: hoecakes swimming in butter and honey. On Monday, Feb 17, there will be a wreath-laying ceremony at Washington's tomb as well as military demonstrations. Admission is free on Washington's birthday (federal observance). For info: Mount Vernon Ladies' Assn, PO Box 110, Mount Vernon, VA 22121. Phone: (703) 780-2000. E-mail: info@mountvernon.org. Web: www.MountVernon.org.

BIRTHDAYS TODAY

Adolfo, 81, fashion designer, born Adolfo F. Sardina at Havana, Cuba, Feb 15, 1933.

Marisa Berenson, 66, actress (*Cabaret, Barry Lyndon*), model, born New York, NY, Feb 15, 1948.

Claire Bloom, 83, actress (*A Doll's House, The Spy Who Came In from the Cold*), born London, England, Feb 15, 1931.

Susan Brownmiller, 79, author, feminist (*Against Our Will, Femininity*), born Brooklyn, NY, Feb 15, 1935.

Matt Groening, 60, cartoonist ("The Simpsons"), born Portland, OR, Feb 15, 1954.

Jaromir Jagr, 42, hockey player, born Kladno, Czechoslovakia (now the Czech Republic), Feb 15, 1972.

Melissa Manchester, 63, singer, born the Bronx, NY, Feb 15, 1951.

Amber Riley, 28, actress ("Glee"), born Los Angeles, CA, Feb 15, 1986.

Jane Seymour, 63, actress (Emmy for "East of Eden"; "Dr. Quinn: Medicine Woman"), born Hillingdon, England, Feb 15, 1951.

February 2014

S	M	T	W	T	F	S
						1
2	3	4	5	6	7	8
9	10	11	12	13	14	15
16	17	18	19	20	21	22
23	24	25	26	27	28	

February 16 — Sunday

DAY 47 **318 REMAINING**

BERGEN, EDGAR: BIRTH ANNIVERSARY. Feb 16, 1903. Actor, radio entertainer and ventriloquist, voice of Charlie McCarthy, Mortimer Snerd and Effie Klinker. Father of Emmy Award–winning actress Candice Bergen. Born at Chicago, IL; died at Las Vegas, NV, Sept 30, 1978.

BUILD A BETTER TRADE SHOW IMAGE WEEK. Feb 16–22. For companies that exhibit at trade shows, this week is set aside to evaluate and improve exhibit strategies for the upcoming trade show season. "10 Steps to a Better Trade Show Image" tip sheet available. Annually, the third full week in February. For info: Marlys K. Arnold, ImageSpecialist, PO Box 901808, Kansas City, MO 64190-1808. Phone: (816) 746-7888. E-mail: marnold@imagespecialist.com. Web: www.exhibitmarketerscafe.com/free-resources.

DAYTONA 500 QUALIFYING. Feb 16. Daytona International Speedway, Daytona Beach, FL. 56th annual running. Drivers battle to set the Daytona 500 field. Presented by Kroger. For info: Daytona International Speedway, PO Box 2801, Daytona Beach, FL 32120-2801. Phone: (800) PIT-SHOP. Web: www.daytonainternationalspeedway.com.

FLAHERTY, ROBERT JOSEPH: BIRTH ANNIVERSARY. Feb 16, 1884. American filmmaker, explorer and author, called "father of the documentary film." Films include *Nanook of the North, Moana of the South Seas* and *Man of Aran*. Born at Iron Mountain, MI; died at Dunnerston, VT, July 23, 1951.

KENNAN, GEORGE: BIRTH ANNIVERSARY. Feb 16, 1904. US diplomat who coined the phrase "containment policy." Kennan was born at Milwaukee, WI. He served as a diplomat during WWII and was briefly arrested by the Nazis. After the war, he wrote an article for *Foreign Affairs* magazine that had a significant influence on America's Cold War policy. The article, entitled "The Sources of Soviet Conduct" and submitted under the pseudonym "Mr. X," called upon the US and its allies to prevent the territorial spread of communism, either by shows of military force or by economic and technological intervention in at-risk nations. Both the Marshall Plan and the Truman Doctrine were heavily influenced by the ideas expressed in the article. Kennan later had a controversial turn as ambassador to the Soviet Union. He died at Princeton, NJ, at the age of 101, Mar 17, 2005.

LITHUANIA: INDEPENDENCE DAY. Feb 16. National Day. The anniversary of Lithuania's declaration of independence in 1918 is observed as the Baltic state's Independence Day. In 1940 Lithuania became a part of the Soviet Union under an agreement between Joseph Stalin and Adolf Hitler. On Mar 11, 1990, Lithuania declared its independence from the Soviet Union, the first of the Soviet republics to do so. After demanding independence, Lithuania set up a border police force and aided young men in efforts to avoid the Soviet military draft, prompting then Soviet leader Mikhail Gorbachev to send tanks into the capital of Vilnius and impose oil and gas embargoes. In the wake of the failed coup attempt in Moscow, Aug 19, 1991, Lithuanian independence finally was recognized.

NATIONAL ENGINEERS WEEK. Feb 16–22. The 63rd annual observance, cosponsored by more than 140 national engineering societies, federal agencies and major corporations, will feature classroom programs in elementary and secondary schools throughout the US, hands-on activities in science centers and museums, engineering workplace tours, the Future City Competition (www.futurecity.org) and the annual "Introduce a Girl to Engineering Day." Annually, the week that includes George Washington's birthday (observed). For info: Natl Engineers Week Foundation, 1420 King St, Alexandria, VA 22314. Phone: (703) 684-2852. E-mail: info@eweek.org. Web: www.eweek.org.

NBA ALL-STAR GAME. Feb 16. New Orleans Arena, New Orleans, LA. 63rd annual. Est attendance: 100,000. For info: Brian McIntyre, Sr VP, Basketball Communications, Natl Basketball Assn, Olympic Tower, 645 Fifth Ave, New York, NY 10022. Phone: (212) 407-8000. Web: www.nba.com.

SURRENDER OF FORT DONELSON: ANNIVERSARY. Feb 16, 1862. With Confederate troops evacuating Bowling Green, KY, and other points along the Kentucky line, General Ulysses S. Grant's forces encircled Fort Donelson, KY. After hard fighting on land and on the Cumberland River, Grant requested surrender of Fort Donelson, stating that "No terms except unconditional and immediate surrender can be accepted." This earned him the nickname "Unconditional Surrender" Grant. Confederate general Simon Buckner surrendered the fort, in essence giving the Union army control of Tennessee and Kentucky and the Tennessee and Cumberland rivers. Disruption ensued and civilians attempted to flee the area occupied by Federal troops.

WILSON, HENRY: BIRTH ANNIVERSARY. Feb 16, 1812. 18th vice president of the US (1873–75). Born at Farmington, NH; died at Washington, DC, Nov 22, 1875.

BIRTHDAYS TODAY

Jerome Bettis, 42, former football player, born Detroit, MI, Feb 16, 1972.

LeVar Burton, 57, actor, host (*Roots*, "Star Trek: The Next Generation," "Reading Rainbow"), born Landsthul, Germany, Feb 16, 1957.

Christopher Eccleston, 50, actor ("Doctor Who," "Heroes," *Shallow Grave*), born Salford, Lancashire, England, Feb 16, 1964.

Lupe Fiasco, 32, rapper, music executive, born Wasalu Muhammad Jaco at Chicago, IL, Feb 16, 1982.

Richard Ford, 70, author (*Independence Day, The Sportswriter*), born Jackson, MS, Feb 16, 1944.

Ice T, 55, rapper, actor ("Law & Order: SVU," *New Jack City*), born Tracy Morrow at Newark, NJ, Feb 16, 1959.

James Ingram, 58, singer, songwriter, born Akron, OH, Feb 16, 1956.

William Katt, 63, actor ("The Greatest American Hero," *Perry Mason Returns, Carrie*), born Los Angeles, CA, Feb 16, 1951.

Eric Laden, 36, actor ("The Killing," "Mad Men"), born Houston, TX, Feb 16, 1978.

John Patrick McEnroe, Jr, 55, sportscaster, Hall of Fame tennis player, born Wiesbaden, West Germany (now Germany), Feb 16, 1959.

Barry Primus, 76, actor ("Cagney and Lacey," *Absence of Malice, Down and Out in Beverly Hills*), born New York, NY, Feb 16, 1938.

February 17 — Monday

DAY 48 **317 REMAINING**

BARBER, WALTER LANIER "RED": BIRTH ANNIVERSARY. Feb 17, 1908. One of the first broadcasters inducted into the Baseball Hall of Fame, Red Barber was born at Columbus, MS. Barber's first professional play-by-play experience was announcing the Cincinnati Reds' opening day on radio in 1934. That game was also the first major league game he had ever seen. He broadcast baseball's first night game (in Brooklyn) on Aug 26, 1939, the 1947 game in which Jackie Robinson broke the color barrier and Roger Maris's 61st home run in 1961. Red Barber died Oct 22, 1992, at Tallahassee, FL.

CANADA: FAMILY DAY IN ALBERTA. Feb 17. Annually, the third Monday in February.

CHICAGO FLAG EXHIBIT CONTROVERSY: 25th ANNIVERSARY. Feb 17, 1989. An exhibit at the School of the Art Institute of Chicago, titled *What Is the Proper Way to Display a US Flag?*, consisted of a ledger for viewers to write their impressions but required the viewers to stand on a US flag mounted on the floor to reach the ledger. The exhibit by art student Scott Tyler prompted protests from veterans' groups, a failed lawsuit and an introduction of legislation by Senator Bob Dole to make displaying a US flag on the floor or ground a crime. Although that legislation didn't pass, Congress periodically continues to introduce legislation against flag desecration.

CORELLI, ARCANGELO: BIRTH ANNIVERSARY. Feb 17, 1653. Italian composer and virtuoso violinist, born at Fusignano, Italy. From his home in Rome, Corelli made extensive and popular concert tours throughout much of Europe. Died at Rome, Jan 8, 1713.

CRABBE, BUSTER: BIRTH ANNIVERSARY. Feb 17, 1908. Clarence Lindon "Buster" Crabbe, Olympic gold medal swimmer, born at Oakland, CA. Crabbe's first-place finish in the 400-meter freestyle was the only swimming medal won by an American at the 1932 Olympic Games at Los Angeles, CA. After his swimming career was over, he played Tarzan, Flash Gordon and Buck Rogers in the movies. Died at Scottsdale, AZ, Apr 23, 1983.

FORT SUMTER RETURNED TO UNION CONTROL: ANNIVERSARY. Feb 17, 1865. After a siege that lasted almost a year and a half, Fort Sumter in South Carolina returned to Union hands on this date. The site of the first shots fired in the American Civil War on Apr 12, 1861, the fort had become a symbol for both sides. As Union attempts to retake it by shelling diminished the fort's capacity with large bombardments, Southern forces managed to hold out with few casualties.

GEORGE WASHINGTON BIRTHDAY CELEBRATION PARADE. Feb 17. Alexandria, VA. Nation's largest parade honoring George Washington, staged by his hometown. Floats, bands, antique cars, equestrian and military units and bagpipers. Route goes through historic district. Est attendance: 50,000. For info: George Washington Birthday Celebration Committee, 809 Oronoco St, Alexandria, VA 22314. Phone: (703) 549-7662. E-mail: gwbcc@washingtonbirthday.net. Web: www.washingtonbirthday.net.

GERONIMO: DEATH ANNIVERSARY. Feb 17, 1909. American Indian of the Chiricahua (Apache) tribe, born about 1829 in Arizona. He was the leader of a small band of warriors whose devastating raids in Arizona, New Mexico and Mexico caused the US Army to send 5,000 men to recapture him after his first escape. He was confined at Fort Sill, OK, where he died after dictating the story of his life for publication.

LAENNEC, RENE THEOPHILE HYACINTHE: BIRTH ANNIVERSARY. Feb 17, 1781. Famed French physician, author and inventor of the stethoscope, called "the father of chest medicine." He wrote extensively about respiratory and heart ailments. Born at Quimper, France, he died there Aug 13, 1826.

LEAGUE OF UNITED LATIN AMERICAN CITIZENS (LULAC) FOUNDED: 85th ANNIVERSARY. Feb 17, 1929. Delegates from the Corpus Christi Order of the Sons of America, the Knights of America of San Antonio and the League of Latin America Citizens from the Rio Grande Valley met at Obreros Hall, Corpus Christi, TX, to form LULAC. It is now the oldest and largest Hispanic civic organization.

***MADAMA BUTTERFLY* PREMIERE: ANNIVERSARY.** Feb 17, 1904. Giacomo Puccini's *Madama Butterfly* was performed for the first time in Milan, Italy. The sold-out crowd, restive at what they saw as Puccini's lack of originality, responded with boos, moos, groans and heckling to the extent that the performers couldn't hear the orchestra. Rosina Storchio, the soprano portraying Madama Butterfly, began crying on stage. Puccini, enraged at the opera's reception (saying the opera was "daisies thrown to swine"), nevertheless revised the work, and it had a successful performance on May 24.

MALTHUS, THOMAS: BIRTH ANNIVERSARY. Feb 17, 1766. English economist, author and demographer, born near Dorking, England. Malthusian population theories (especially that population growth exceeds growth of production) provoked great controversy when published in 1798. Died near Bath, England, Dec 23, 1834.

McCLURE, SAMUEL SIDNEY: BIRTH ANNIVERSARY. Feb 17, 1857. Irish-American newspaper editor and publisher, founder of newspaper syndicate. Born at County Antrim, Ireland. Died at New York, NY, Mar 21, 1949.

MY WAY DAY. Feb 17. Hundreds of people have their opinions as to who we are. Today is the day we decide who's right. Today we determine our identities all by ourselves. (©2006 by WH.) For info: Thomas & Ruth Roy, Wellcat Holidays, 2418 Long Ln, Lebanon, PA 17046. Phone: (717) 279-0184. E-mail: info@wellcat.com. Web: www.wellcat.com.

NATIONAL PTA FOUNDERS' DAY: ANNIVERSARY. Feb 17, 1897. Founders' Day is a reminder of the substantial role that the PTA has played locally, regionally and nationally in supporting parent involvement and working on behalf of all children and families. It honors the PTA's founders Phoebe Apperson Hearst and Alice McLellan Birney, and the founder of Georgia's Congress of Colored Parents and Teachers, Selena Sloan Butler. For info: National PTA, 1250 N Pitt St, Alexandria, VA 22314. Phone: (800) 307-4782. E-mail: info@pta.org. Web: www.pta.org.

"A PRAIRIE HOME COMPANION" PREMIERE: 35th ANNIVERSARY. Feb 17, 1979. This popular live variety show debuted locally on Minnesota Public Radio in 1974 and was first broadcast nationally on Feb 17, 1979, as part of National Public Radio's Folk Festival USA. It became a regular Saturday-night program in early 1980. Host Garrison Keillor's monologues about the mythical Lake Wobegon and his humorous ads for local businesses such as Bertha's Kitty Boutique, Powdermilk Biscuits and the Chatterbox Cafe were accompanied by various musical groups. Broadcast from the World Theater in St. Paul, MN, the show went off the air in 1986. A series of programs were done for cable TV, and Keillor continues to write works of fiction (*Lake Wobegon Days*). In 1994 "A Prairie Home Companion" went back on the air on Public Radio International.

PRESIDENTS' DAY. Feb 17. Presidents' Day observes the birthdays of George Washington (Feb 22) and Abraham Lincoln (Feb 12). With the adoption of the Monday Holiday Law (which moved the observance of George Washington's birthday from Feb 22 to the third Monday in February), some of the specific significance of the event was lost and added impetus was given to the popular description of that holiday as Presidents' Day. Present usage often regards Presidents' Day as a day to honor all former presidents of the US, though the federal holiday is still Washington's Birthday. Annually, the third Monday in February. See also: "Washington, George: Birthday Observance" below.

PRESIDENTS' DAY: LIVE FROM DELAWARE STREET. Feb 17. Indianapolis, IN. Visit the Benjamin Harrison Presidential Site and listen to the conversations and gossip of the day as you enter each room and speak with family members and household staff, whose roles are re-created by actors. For info: Benjamin Harrison Presidential Site, 1230 N Delaware St, Indianapolis, IN 46202. Phone: (317) 631-1888. Fax: (317) 632-5488. E-mail: events@bhpsite.org. Web: www.bhpsite.org.

STOCK EXCHANGE HOLIDAY (WASHINGTON'S BIRTHDAY). Feb 17. The holiday schedules for the various exchanges are subject to change if relevant rules, regulations or exchange policies are revised. If you have questions, contact: CME Group (CME, CBOT, NYMEX, KCBT) (www.cmegroup.com), Chicago Board Options Exchange (www.cboe.com), NASDAQ (www.nasdaq.com), NYSE Euronext (www.nyse.com).

February 2014

S	M	T	W	T	F	S
						1
2	3	4	5	6	7	8
9	10	11	12	13	14	15
16	17	18	19	20	21	22
23	24	25	26	27	28	

WASHINGTON, GEORGE: BIRTHDAY OBSERVANCE (LEGAL HOLIDAY). Feb 17. Legal public holiday. (Public Law 90–363 sets Washington's birthday observance on the third Monday in February each year—applicable to federal employees and to the District of Columbia.) Observed in all states. See also: "Washington, George: Birth Anniversary" (Feb 22).

BIRTHDAYS TODAY

Vanessa Atler, 32, former gymnast, born Valencia, CA, Feb 17, 1982.

James Nathaniel (Jim) Brown, 78, Hall of Fame football player, activist, actor, born St. Simons Island, GA, Feb 17, 1936.

Ronald DeVoe, 47, singer (Bell Biv DeVoe), born Boston, MA, Feb 17, 1967.

Michelle Forbes, 47, actress ("Homicide: Life on the Street," "Prison Break"), born Austin, TX, Feb 17, 1967.

Brenda Fricker, 69, actress (Oscar for *My Left Foot*; *The Field*), born Dublin, Ireland, Feb 17, 1945.

Joseph Gordon-Levitt, 33, actor (*Inception, [500] Days of Summer*, "3rd Rock from the Sun"), born Los Angeles, CA, Feb 17, 1981.

Paris Hilton, 33, socialite, television personality ("The Simple Life"), born New York, NY, Feb 17, 1981.

Hal Holbrook, 89, actor (*Magnum Force, All the President's Men*), born Harold Rowe, Jr, at Cleveland, OH, Feb 17, 1925.

Barry Humphries, 80, actor, comedian, aka Dame Edna Everidge, born Melbourne, Australia, Feb 17, 1934.

Michael Jordan, 51, Hall of Fame basketball player, basketball executive, born Brooklyn, NY, Feb 17, 1963.

Richard Karn, 55, actor ("Home Improvement"), game show host ("Family Feud"), born Seattle, WA, Feb 17, 1959.

Lou Diamond Phillips, 52, actor (*La Bamba, Stand and Deliver*), born Corpus Christi, TX, Feb 17, 1962.

Denise Richards, 43, actress (*Wild Things, The World Is Not Enough*), born Downers Grove, IL, Feb 17, 1971.

Jason Ritter, 34, actor ("Parenthood," "The Event," "Joan of Arcadia"), born Los Angeles, CA, Feb 17, 1980.

Rene Russo, 60, actress (*The Thomas Crown Affair, Tin Cup, Get Shorty*), born Burbank, CA, Feb 17, 1954.

February 18 — Tuesday

DAY 49 — **316 REMAINING**

ALEICHEM, SHOLEM: BIRTH ANNIVERSARY. Feb 18, 1859. (Old Style date.) Pen name of Russian-born author and humorist Solomon Rabinowitz. The musical *Fiddler on the Roof* drew from Aleichem's short stories about Tevye the Milkman. Affectionately known in the US as "the Jewish Mark Twain." Died at New York, NY, May 13, 1916.

BROWN, HELEN GURLEY: BIRTH ANNIVERSARY. Feb 18, 1922. Longtime editor-in-chief of *Cosmopolitan* magazine and groundbreaking feminist, born at Green Forest, AR. After a successful career in copywriting, she published the book *Sex and the Single Girl* in 1962 and became an outspoken advocate for sexual freedom, breaking the mythology that women had to be "good girls" who saved themselves till marriage. At *Cosmo* she steered women toward careers, dating, beauty, diet and ultimately marriage, telling them that they really could "have it all." She did have it all, married for more than 50 years to film and TV producer David Brown. She died Aug 13, 2012, at New York, NY.

COW MILKED WHILE FLYING IN AN AIRPLANE: ANNIVERSARY. Feb 18, 1930. Elm Farm Ollie became the first cow to fly in an airplane. During the flight, which was attended by reporters, she was milked, and the milk was sealed in paper containers and parachuted over St. Louis, MO.

DAVIS, JEFFERSON: INAUGURATION ANNIVERSARY. Feb 18, 1861. In the years before the Civil War, Senator Jefferson Davis was the acknowledged leader of the Southern bloc and a champion of states' rights, but he had little to do with the secessionist movement until after his home state of Mississippi joined the Confederacy Jan 9, 1861. Davis withdrew from the Senate that same day. He was unanimously chosen as president of the Confederacy's provisional government and was inaugurated at Montgomery, AL, Feb 18. Within the next year he was elected to a six-year term by popular vote and inaugurated a second time Feb 22, 1862, at Richmond, VA.

GAMBIA: INDEPENDENCE DAY. Feb 18, 1965. National holiday. Independence from Britain granted. Referendum in April 1970 established Gambia as a republic within the Commonwealth.

HUGHES, JOHN: BIRTH ANNIVERSARY. Feb 18, 1950. Born at Lansing, MI, this film director and screenwriter created some of the most iconic works of the 1980s and '90s. His "Brat Pack" films, including *Sixteen Candles* (1984) and *The Breakfast Club* (1985), provided hilarious insight into the lives of American teenagers, and his broad comedies *Home Alone* (1990) and *Planes, Trains and Automobiles* (1987) were also huge commercial successes. Hughes died at New York, NY, Aug 11, 2009.

NEPAL: NATIONAL DEMOCRACY DAY. Feb 18. National holiday. Anniversary of the 1952 constitution.

PEABODY, GEORGE: BIRTH ANNIVERSARY. Feb 18, 1795. American merchant and philanthropist, born at South Danvers, MA. He endowed the Peabody Institute at Baltimore, MD, museums at Harvard and Yale and the George Peabody College for Teachers at Nashville, TN. Died at London, England, Nov 4, 1869.

PLUTO DISCOVERY: ANNIVERSARY. Feb 18, 1930. Pluto was discovered by astronomer Clyde Tombaugh at the Lowell Observatory at Flagstaff, AZ. It was given the name of the Roman god of the underworld. It was considered the ninth planet of the solar system until 2006, when astronomers reclassified it as a dwarf planet. See also: "Pluto Demoted: Anniversary" (Aug 24).

SINGLE-TASKING DAY. Feb 18. Multitasking is ineffective—and may cause brain damage! Today, do only one thing at a time without feeling guilty. For info: Theresa Gabriel, 2914 E 38th St, Columbus, NE 68601. Phone: (402) 910-4563. E-mail: tree.gabriel@gmail.com.

TIFFANY, LOUIS COMFORT: BIRTH ANNIVERSARY. Feb 18, 1848. American artist, son of famed jeweler Charles L. Tiffany. Best remembered for his remarkable work with decorative iridescent "favrile" glass. Born at New York, NY; died there Jan 17, 1933. See also: "Tiffany, Charles Lewis: Birth Anniversary" (Feb 15).

WILLKIE, WENDELL LEWIS: BIRTH ANNIVERSARY. Feb 18, 1892. American lawyer, author, public utility executive and politician, born at Elwood, IN. Presidential nominee of the Republican Party in 1940. Remembered for his book, *One World*, published in 1943. Died at New York, NY, Oct 8, 1944.

BIRTHDAYS TODAY

Aldo Ceccato, 80, conductor, born Milan, Italy, Feb 18, 1934.

Matt Dillon, 50, actor (*Crash, There's Something About Mary, Drugstore Cowboy*), born Westchester, NY, Feb 18, 1964.

Dr. Dre, 49, rapper, record producer, born Andre Romelle Young at Compton, CA, Feb 18, 1965.

Milos Forman, 82, film director (Oscars for *Amadeus* and *One Flew Over the Cuckoo's Nest*), born Caslav, Czechoslovakia (now the Czech Republic), Feb 18, 1932.

George Kennedy, 87, actor (Oscar for *Cool Hand Luke*; "The Blue Knight"), born New York, NY, Feb 18, 1927.

Jillian Michaels, 40, personal trainer, television personality ("The Biggest Loser"), born Los Angeles, CA, Feb 18, 1974.

Toni Morrison, 83, Nobel Prize–winning novelist (*Beloved, Jazz, Tar Baby, Sula*), born Lorain, OH, Feb 18, 1931.

Juice Newton, 62, singer, born Judy Cohen at Virginia Beach, VA, Feb 18, 1952.

Yoko Ono, 81, artist, musician, born Tokyo, Japan, Feb 18, 1933.

Molly Ringwald, 46, actress (*Sixteen Candles, The Breakfast Club, Pretty in Pink*), born Roseville, CA, Feb 18, 1968.

Greta Scacchi, 54, actress (*White Mischief, Presumed Innocent*), born Milan, Italy, Feb 18, 1960.

Cybill Shepherd, 64, actress (*The Last Picture Show*, "Moonlighting," "Cybill"), born Memphis, TN, Feb 18, 1950.

John Travolta, 59, actor (*Pulp Fiction, Urban Cowboy, Saturday Night Fever*, "Welcome Back, Kotter"), born Englewood, NJ, Feb 18, 1955.

John William Warner, 87, retired US senator (R, Virginia), born Washington, DC, Feb 18, 1927.

Vanna White, 57, television personality ("Wheel of Fortune"), born Conway, SC, Feb 18, 1957.

February 19 — Wednesday

DAY 50 — **315 REMAINING**

COPERNICUS, NICOLAUS: BIRTH ANNIVERSARY. Feb 19, 1473. Polish astronomer and priest who revolutionized scientific thought with what came to be called the Copernican theory, which placed the sun instead of Earth at the center of our planetary system. Born at Torun, Poland, he died at East Prussia, May 24, 1543.

"EASTENDERS" TV PREMIERE: ANNIVERSARY. Feb 19, 1985. This popular UK soap opera features the residents of Albert Square in the East End of London. More than 30 million viewers tuned in Dec 25, 1986, to make that episode the highest rated in UK soap history. It has won several awards, including BAFTAs.

***THE FEMININE MYSTIQUE* PUBLISHED: ANNIVERSARY.** Feb 19, 1963. Betty Friedan's *The Feminine Mystique* was a call for women to achieve their full potential. The book generated enormous response and revitalized the women's movement in the US.

FIRST BOLLINGEN PRIZE: 65th ANNIVERSARY. Feb 19, 1949. On this date the first Bollingen Prize for poetry was awarded to Ezra Pound for his collection *The Pisan Cantos*. This first award was steeped in controversy because Pound had been charged with treason after making pro-Fascist broadcasts in Italy during WWII.

GARRICK, DAVID: BIRTH ANNIVERSARY. Feb 19, 1717. English actor, theater manager and playwright. Born at Hereford, England; died Jan 20, 1779, at London.

GRAND RAPIDS BOAT SHOW. Feb 19–23. DeVos Place, Grand Rapids, MI. This event brings together buyers and sellers of powerboats ranging from 16 to 50 feet, fishing boats, ski boats, pontoons and motor yachts, boating accessories, docks, dockominiums and vacation properties. Est attendance: 30,000. For info: ShowSpan, Inc, 2121 Celebration Dr NE, Grand Rapids, MI 49525. Phone: (616) 447-2860. Fax: (616) 447-2861. E-mail: events@showspan.com. Web: www.showspan.com.

JAPANESE INTERNMENT: ANNIVERSARY. Feb 19, 1942. As a result of President Franklin Roosevelt's Executive Order 9066, some 110,000 Japanese Americans living in coastal Pacific areas were placed in concentration camps in remote areas of Arizona, Arkansas, inland California, Colorado, Idaho, Utah and Wyoming. The interned Japanese Americans (two-thirds of whom were US citizens) lost an estimated $400 million in property. They were allowed to return to their homes Jan 2, 1945.

KNIGHTS OF PYTHIAS: 150th FOUNDING ANNIVERSARY. Feb 19, 1864. The social and fraternal order of the Knights of Pythias was founded at Washington, DC.

LEARNING DISABILITIES ASSOCIATION OF AMERICA INTERNATIONAL CONFERENCE. Feb 19–22. Anaheim, CA. 51st annual. Est attendance: 1,100. For info: Learning Disabilities Assn of America, 4156 Library Rd, Pittsburgh, PA 15234. Phone: (412) 341-1515. Fax: (412) 344-0224. E-mail: info@ldaamerica.org. Web: www.ldaamerica.org.

LIONEL HAMPTON JAZZ FESTIVAL. Feb 19–22. University of Idaho, Moscow, ID. Each year, college, high school, junior high school and elementary school vocal and instrumental jazz ensembles come from all over the US to participate in student performances and attend concerts and clinics given by the world's greatest jazz artists. For info: Lionel Hampton Jazz Festival. Phone: (208) 885-6765. Fax: (208) 885-6513. E-mail: jazzinfo@uidaho.edu. Web: www.uidaho.edu/jazzfest.

US LANDING ON IWO JIMA: ANNIVERSARY. Feb 19, 1945. Beginning at dawn, the landing of 30,000 American troops took place on the barren 12-square-mile island of Iwo Jima. Initially there was little resistance, but 21,500 Japanese stood ready underground to fight to the last man to protect massive strategic fortifications linked by tunnels. See also: "Iwo Jima Day: Anniversary" (Feb 23).

BIRTHDAYS TODAY

Prince Andrew, 54, Duke of York, born London, England, Feb 19, 1960.

Justine Bateman, 48, actress ("Family Ties," "Men Behaving Badly"), born Rye, NY, Feb 19, 1966.

Lou Christie, 71, singer, born Glen Willard, PA, Feb 19, 1943.

Jeff Daniels, 59, actor ("The Newsroom," *The Purple Rose of Cairo, Something Wild, Dumb and Dumber*), born Chelsea, MI, Feb 19, 1955.

Benicio Del Toro, 47, actor (Oscar for *Traffic*; *Che, 21 Grams, The Usual Suspects*), born Santurce, Puerto Rico, Feb 19, 1967.

Haylie Duff, 29, actress ("7th Heaven," *Napoleon Dynamite*), born Houston, TX, Feb 19, 1985.

Roger Goodell, 55, Commissioner of the National Football League, born Jamestown, NY, Feb 19, 1959.

Jonathan Lethem, 50, author (*Motherless Brooklyn, Fortress of Solitude*), born Brooklyn, NY, Feb 19, 1964.

Hana Mandlikova, 51, Hall of Fame tennis player, born Prague, Czechoslovakia (now the Czech Republic), Feb 19, 1963.

Marta, 28, soccer player, born Marta Vieira da Silva at Dois Riachas, Brazil, Feb 19, 1986.

Stephen Nichols, 63, actor ("Days of Our Lives," "General Hospital"), born Cincinnati, OH, Feb 19, 1951.

Smokey Robinson, 74, singer, songwriter, born William Robinson, Jr, at Detroit, MI, Feb 19, 1940.

Seal, 51, singer, songwriter, born Sealhenry Samuel at London, England, Feb 19, 1963.

Andrew Shue, 47, actor ("Melrose Place"), born South Orange, NJ, Feb 19, 1967.

Amy Tan, 62, author (*The Joy Luck Club*), born Oakland, CA, Feb 19, 1952.

Ray Winstone, 57, actor (*Indiana Jones and the Kingdom of the Crystal Skull, The Departed, Sexy Beast*), born London, England, Feb 19, 1957.

February 2014

S	M	T	W	T	F	S
						1
2	3	4	5	6	7	8
9	10	11	12	13	14	15
16	17	18	19	20	21	22
23	24	25	26	27	28	

February 20 — Thursday

DAY 51 **314 REMAINING**

ADAMS, ANSEL: BIRTH ANNIVERSARY. Feb 20, 1902. American photographer, known for his photographs of Yosemite National Park, born at San Francisco, CA. Adams died at Monterey, CA, Apr 22, 1984.

ALTMAN, ROBERT: BIRTH ANNIVERSARY. Feb 20, 1925. This iconoclastic filmmaker was master of satire, ensemble casts and the long take. His long and lauded career include such classic films as *M*A*S*H* (1970), *McCabe and Mrs Miller* (1971), *Nashville* (1975), *The Player* (1992) and *Gosford Park* (2001). Altman received a Lifetime Achievement Oscar in 2006. Born at Kansas City, MO, Altman died Nov 20, 2006, at Los Angeles, CA.

AMERICAN BIRKEBEINER RACE. Feb 20–22. Cable to Hayward, WI. 41st annual. The largest and most prestigious cross-country ski marathon in North America attracts more than 5,000 participants for the 51k trek. A Nordic festival of related ski events and activities precedes the race (Feb 22). Est attendance: 18,000. For info: American Birkebeiner Ski Foundation, Inc, PO Box 911, Hayward, WI 54843. Phone: (715) 634-5025. Fax: (715) 634-5663. E-mail: birkie@birkie.com. Web: www.birkie.com.

CANADA: MONTREAL HUNTING, FISHING & CAMPING SHOW. Feb 20–23. Place Bonaventure, Montreal, QC. Manufacturers' representatives, distributors and retailers of the outdoors, including camping, fishing, ATVs, hunting, marine (fishing boats, canoes, kayaks, etc), tourism offices, outfitters (lodges), RVs and entertainment. Est attendance: 45,000. For info: Canadian National Sportsmen's Shows, 8150 E Metropolitain Blvd, Ste 330, Anjou, QC, H1K 1A1, Canada. Phone: (514) 866-5409. Fax: (514) 866-4092. Web: www.salonchassepeche.ca.

CANADA: OTTAWA BOAT AND SPORTSMEN'S SHOW. Feb 20–23. CE Centre, Ottawa, ON. Boating, fishing and outdoors information. Products displayed: powerboats, runabouts, inflatables, personal watercraft, fishing tackle, travel information, canoes, kayaks and family entertainment. Est attendance: 25,000. For info: Canadian Natl Sportsmen's Shows, 30 Village Centre Pl, Mississauga, ON, L4Z 1V9, Canada. Phone: (905) 361-2677. Fax: (905) 361-2678. Web: www.ottawaboatandsportshow.ca.

CANADA: YUKON SOURDOUGH RENDEZVOUS. Feb 20–23. Whitehorse, YT. 50th annual. Mad trapper competitions, flour packing, beard-growing contests, old-time fiddle show, sourdough pancake breakfasts, cancan dancers, talent shows and much more. Visitors welcome to participate. Est attendance: 20,000. For info: Yukon Sourdough Rendezvous, Box 31721, Whitehorse, YT Y1A 6L3, Canada. Phone: (867) 667-2148. Fax: (867) 668-6755. E-mail: ysrl@polarcom.com. Web: www.yukonrendezvous.com.

CLOSEST APPROACH OF A COMET TO EARTH: ANNIVERSARY. Feb 20, 1491. An unnamed comet came within 860,000 miles (.0094 AU) of Earth on this date. By comparison, the closest approach that Halley's comet made to Earth was on Apr 10, AD 837, at three million miles.

DOUGLASS, FREDERICK: DEATH ANNIVERSARY. Feb 20, 1895. American journalist, orator and antislavery leader. Born at Tuckahoe, MD, probably in February 1817. Died at Anacostia Heights, DC. His original name before his escape from slavery was Frederick Augustus Washington Bailey.

GEORGIA NATIONAL RODEO. Feb 20–22. Georgia National Fairgrounds & Agricenter, Perry, GA. The rodeo is sanctioned by the Professional Rodeo Cowboys Association (PRCA) and features specialty acts plus cowboys and cowgirls from across the country competing in seven events: saddle bronc riding, bareback riding, tie-down roping, steer wrestling, team roping, bull riding and barrel racing. Points earned at the Georgia National Rodeo qualify riders for the National Finals Rodeo held every December in Las Vegas. Est attendance: 15,000. For info: Georgia National Rodeo, 401 Larry Walker Pkwy, Perry, GA 31069. Phone: (478) 987-3247. Fax: (478) 987-7218. E-mail: mtreptow@gnfa.com. Web: www.gnfa.com.

INTRODUCE A GIRL TO ENGINEERING DAY. Feb 20. 13th annual. During National Engineers Week, the engineering community is asked to mobilize women and men engineers to reach more than one million girls and encourage them to pursue the fields that lead to engineering careers. Website includes links for teachers. For info: Natl Engineers Week Headquarters, 1420 King St, Alexandria, VA 22314. Phone: (703) 684-2852. E-mail: info@eweek.org. Web: www.eweek.org/EngineersWeek/Introduce.aspx.

JEFFERSON, JOSEPH: BIRTH ANNIVERSARY. Feb 20, 1829. Distinguished American actor, born at Philadelphia, PA, into a family of actors. Jefferson made his stage debut at the age of three in Kotzebue's *Pizarro.* After many successes, his search for a character both humorous and pathetic centered on Rip van Winkle, about whom he wrote a short play. Later revised by Dion Boucicault, the play opened with Jefferson in the leading role at London, England, in 1865 and was an immediate success. Rip van Winkle became the signature role for which he was known. Jefferson died at Palm Beach, FL, Apr 23, 1905. He is remembered each year in Chicago, IL, when the Joseph Jefferson (Jeff) Awards are presented to recognize excellence in theatrical productions.

NEWPORT SEAFOOD AND WINE FESTIVAL. Feb 20–23. Newport, OR. Central coastal festival featuring seafood and wines from Oregon, Washington, California and Idaho. Arts and crafts exhibits as well. Annually, the last full weekend in February. Est attendance: 17,000. For info: Greater Newport Chamber of Commerce, 555 SW Coast Hwy, Newport, OR 97365. Phone: (541) 265-8801. Fax: (541) 265-5589. E-mail: info@newportchamber.org. Web: www.newportchamber.org.

NORTHERN HEMISPHERE HOODIE-HOO DAY. Feb 20. At high noon (local time) citizens are asked to go outdoors and yell, "Hoodie-Hoo" to chase away winter and make ready for spring, one month away. (©2006 by WH.) For info: Thomas & Ruth Roy, Wellcat Holidays, 2418 Long Ln, Lebanon, PA 17046. Phone: (717) 279-0184. E-mail: info@wellcat.com. Web: www.wellcat.com.

PISCES, THE FISH. Feb 20–Mar 20. In the astronomical/astrological zodiac, which divides the sun's apparent orbit into 12 segments, the period Feb 20–Mar 20 is traditionally identified as the sun sign of Pisces, the Fish. The ruling planet is Neptune.

PRESCOTT, WILLIAM: BIRTH ANNIVERSARY. Feb 20, 1726. American Revolutionary soldier, born at Groton, MA. Died at Pepperell, MA, Oct 13, 1795. Credited with the order "Don't one of you fire until you see the whites of their eyes," at the Battle of Bunker Hill, June 17, 1775.

SPACE MILESTONE: *FRIENDSHIP 7* (US): FIRST AMERICAN TO ORBIT EARTH. Feb 20, 1962. John Herschel Glenn, Jr, became the first American and the third person to orbit Earth. Aboard the capsule *Friendship 7,* he made three orbits of Earth. Spacecraft was *Mercury-Atlas 6.* In 1998 the 77-year-old Glenn went into space again on the space shuttle *Discovery* to test the effects of aging.

SPACE MILESTONE: *MIR* SPACE STATION (USSR). Feb 20, 1986. A "third-generation" orbiting space station, *Mir* (Peace), was launched without crew from the Baikonur space center at Leninsk, Kazakhstan. Believed to be 40 feet long, weigh 47 tons and have six docking ports. Both Russian and American crews have used the station. After many equipment failures and financial problems, the Russians took *Mir* out of service Mar 23, 2001. See also: "Space Milestone: *Mir* Abandoned (USSR)" (Mar 23).

STOTZ, CARL E.: BIRTH ANNIVERSARY. Feb 20, 1920. Carl E. Stotz shaped the summers of millions of kids as the founder of Little League baseball. Born at Williamsport, PA, he organized the first three-team league there in 1939. Died at Williamsport, June 4, 1992.

UNITED NATIONS: WORLD DAY FOR SOCIAL JUSTICE. Feb 20. Annually, Feb 20, beginning in 2009. Resolution 62/10 of Nov 26, 2007.

BIRTHDAYS TODAY

Charles Barkley, 51, sportscaster, Hall of Fame basketball player, born Leeds, AL, Feb 20, 1963.

Brenda Blethyn, 68, actress (*Secrets and Lies, A River Runs Through It*), born Ramsgate, England, Feb 20, 1946.

Gordon Brown, 63, former prime minister of Great Britain (2007–10), born Glasgow, Scotland, Feb 20, 1951.

Cindy Crawford, 48, model, actress, born DeKalb, IL, Feb 20, 1966.

Sandy Duncan, 68, actress (*Funny Face*, "The Hogan Family," *Peter Pan*), born Henderson, TX, Feb 20, 1946.

Ron Eldard, 51, actor ("Men Behaving Badly," "ER"), born Long Island, NY, Feb 20, 1963.

Philip Anthony (Phil) Esposito, 72, hockey executive, former hockey coach, Hall of Fame hockey player, born Sault Ste. Marie, ON, Canada, Feb 20, 1942.

Stephon Marbury, 37, basketball player, born New York, NY, Feb 20, 1977.

Mitch McConnell, 72, US Senator (R, Kentucky), born Colbert County, AL, Feb 20, 1942.

Jennifer O'Neill, 66, actress (*The Summer of '42*, "Cover-Up"), born Rio de Janeiro, Brazil, Feb 20, 1948.

Sidney Poitier, 87, actor (*In the Heat of the Night*; Oscar for *Lilies of the Field*), born Miami, FL, Feb 20, 1927.

Rihanna, 26, singer, born Robyn Rihanna Fenty at St. Michael, Barbados, Feb 20, 1988.

Buffy Sainte-Marie, 73, folksinger, born Craven, SK, Canada, Feb 20, 1941.

Patty Hearst Shaw, 60, newspaper heiress, kidnap victim, actress (*Cry-Baby*), born San Francisco, CA, Feb 20, 1954.

French Stewart, 50, actor ("3rd Rock from the Sun"), born Albuquerque, NM, Feb 20, 1964.

Peter Strauss, 67, actor (*Rich Man, Poor Man*; *Soldier Blue*), born Croton-on-Hudson, NY, Feb 20, 1947.

Lili Taylor, 47, actress ("Six Feet Under," *I Shot Andy Warhol, Ransom, Mystic Pizza*), born Glencoe, IL, Feb 20, 1967.

Robert William (Bobby) Unser, 80, auto racer, born Albuquerque, NM, Feb 20, 1934.

Gloria Vanderbilt, 90, fashion designer, artist, born New York, NY, Feb 20, 1924.

Justin Verlander, 31, baseball player, born Manakin Sabot, VA, Feb 20, 1983.

Nancy Wilson, 77, singer, born Chillicothe, OH, Feb 20, 1937.

February 21 — Friday

DAY 52 **313 REMAINING**

AUDEN, W.H.: BIRTH ANNIVERSARY. Feb 21, 1907. The Pulitzer Prize–winning Anglo-American poet was born Wystan Hugh Auden at York, England. "Some books," he wrote in *The Dyer's Hand* (1962), "are undeservedly forgotten; none are undeservedly remembered." Died at Vienna, Austria, Sept 28, 1973.

BANGLADESH: MARTYRS DAY. Feb 21. National mourning day in memory of martyrs of the Bengali Language Movement in 1952. Mourners gather at the Azimpur graveyard.

BATTLE OF VERDUN: ANNIVERSARY. Feb 21, 1916. The German High Command launched an offensive on the Western Front at Verdun, France, which became WWI's single longest battle. An estimated one million men were killed, decimating both the German and French armies, before the battle ended on Dec 15, 1916.

BOMBECK, ERMA: BIRTH ANNIVERSARY. Feb 21, 1927. Humorist and writer, born at Dayton, OH. Authored many books, including *The Grass Is Always Greener over the Septic Tank*. Bombeck died at San Francisco, CA, Apr 22, 1996.

CIA AGENT ARRESTED AS SPY: 20th ANNIVERSARY. Feb 21, 1994. Aldrich Hazen Ames and his wife, Maria del Rosario Casas Ames, were arrested on charges they had spied for the Soviet Union beginning in 1985 and had continued to spy for Russia after the Soviet collapse in 1991. Aldrich Ames had worked as a counterintelligence officer for the CIA at its headquarters at Langley, VA. Prosecutors said that the pair had been paid about $2.5 million for their activities and were probably responsible for the deaths of at least 10 CIA agents whom Ames had identified for the Soviets. The government considered this to be one of the most serious spy cases ever uncovered in the US. On Apr 28 Aldrich Ames was sentenced to life in prison. Rosario Ames was sentenced to a 63-month prison term in return for her husband's promise to cooperate with authorities.

LOST DUTCHMAN DAYS. Feb 21–23. Apache Junction, AZ. Arts and crafts show and sale. Three-day rodeo competiton, dance, carnival, parade, business vendors—in celebration of the legend of the Superstition Mountains and the Lost Dutchman Mine. Free musical entertainment. Annually, the last full weekend in February. Est attendance: 30,000. For info: Apache Junction Chamber of Commerce, PO Box 1747, Apache Junction, AZ 85117-1747. Phone: (480) 982-3141. Fax: (480) 982-3234. E-mail: jan@ajchamber.com. Web: www.ajchamber.com or www.lostdutchmandays.org.

MALCOLM X ASSASSINATED: ANNIVERSARY. Feb 21, 1965. Just as he began a speech to his newly formed Organization of Afro-American Unity, black activist leader Malcolm X was gunned down by several men standing among the 400-plus crowd in the Audubon Ballroom at Harlem, New York City. The assassination occurred barely a week after Malcolm X's Queens home was firebombed. Three men were convicted of the murder in 1966 and sentenced to life in prison (two were released in the 1980s and the third won parole in 2010). See also: "Malcolm X: Birth Anniversary" (May 19).

February 2014	S	M	T	W	T	F	S
							1
	2	3	4	5	6	7	8
	9	10	11	12	13	14	15
	16	17	18	19	20	21	22
	23	24	25	26	27	28	

***THE NEW YORKER* PUBLISHED: ANNIVERSARY.** Feb 21, 1925. First issue of the magazine published on this date.

NEXTERA ENERGY RESOURCES 250. Feb 21. Daytona International Speedway, Daytona, FL. NASCAR trucks on the Superspeedway in a 100-lap, 250-mile battle. For info: Daytona International Speedway, PO Box 2801, Daytona Beach, FL 32120-2801. Phone: (800) PIT-SHOP. Web: www.daytonainternationalspeedway.com.

NIXON'S TRIP TO CHINA: ANNIVERSARY. Feb 21, 1972. Richard Nixon became the first US president to visit any country not diplomatically recognized by the US when he went to the People's Republic of China for meetings with Chairman Mao Tse-tung and Premier Chou En-lai. Nixon arrived at Peking on this date and departed China on Feb 28. The "Shanghai Communiqué" was issued Feb 27. See also: "Shanghai Communiqué: Anniversary" (Feb 27).

PALMER, ALICE FREEMAN: BIRTH ANNIVERSARY. Feb 21, 1855. Born at Colesville, NY, Alice Freeman Palmer became president of Wellesley College at the age of 27. Under her leadership the school grew into one of the leading women's colleges. She was also instrumental in bringing the women's school Radcliffe College into its association with Harvard University. One of the organizers of the American Association of University Women, she served as its president for two terms. She was appointed the first dean of women at the University of Chicago when it opened in 1892. Palmer died Dec 6, 1902, at Paris, France.

SANDINO, CESAR AUGUSTO: 80th ASSASSINATION ANNIVERSARY. Feb 21, 1934. Nicaraguan guerrilla leader after whom the Sandinistas are named. Sandino, born in 1893 (exact date unknown), was murdered along with his brother and several aides at Managua on this date. He and his followers had eluded the occupying force of US Marines as well as the Nicaraguan National Guard from 1927 until 1933. Regarded by the US as an outlaw and a bandit, he is revered as a martyred patriot hero by many Nicaraguans. His successful resistance and the resulting widespread anti-US feeling were largely responsible for inauguration of a US counteraction—the Good Neighbor Policy—toward Latin American nations during the administration of President Franklin Roosevelt.

SIMONE, NINA: BIRTH ANNIVERSARY. Feb 21, 1933. The blues and jazz singer was born Eunice Waymon at Tryon, NC. Initially determined to become a concert pianist, Simone instead found a career as a singer of a wide range of musical genres in which she could put her uniquely raw and emotional voice on display. Simone was an ardent supporter of the 1950s and '60s civil rights movement. She died at Carry-le-Rouet, France, on Apr 21, 2003.

TEXAS COWBOY POETRY GATHERING. Feb 21–23. Sul Ross State University, Alpine, TX. 28th annual. Cowboys from Texas and neighboring states gather for poetry readings and music. Est attendance: 2,000. For info: Texas Cowboy Poetry Gathering Committee, PO Box 395, Alpine, TX 79831. E-mail: committee@texascowboypoetry.com. Web: www.cowboy-poetry.org.

UNITED NATIONS: INTERNATIONAL MOTHER LANGUAGE DAY. Feb 21. To help raise awareness among all peoples of the distinct and enduring value of their languages. Annually, on Feb 21. For info: United Nations, Dept of Public Info, New York, NY 10017. Web: www.un.org.

WASHINGTON MONUMENT DEDICATED: ANNIVERSARY. Feb 21, 1885. Monument to the first US president was dedicated at Washington, DC.

BIRTHDAYS TODAY

Christopher Atkins, 53, actor ("Dallas," *The Blue Lagoon*), born Rye, NY, Feb 21, 1961.

William Baldwin, 51, actor ("Dirty Sexy Money," *Born on the Fourth of July, Backdraft*), born Massapequa, NY, Feb 21, 1963.

Corbin Bleu, 25, singer, actor (*High School Musical*), born Brooklyn, NY, Feb 21, 1989.

Mary Chapin Carpenter, 56, singer, musician, born Princeton, NJ, Feb 21, 1958.

Charlotte Church, 28, singer, born Cardiff, Wales, Feb 21, 1986.

Jack Coleman, 56, actor ("Heroes," "Dynasty"), born Easton, PA, Feb 21, 1958.

Tyne Daly, 67, actress ("Judging Amy," Emmy for "Cagney and Lacey"; *Gypsy*), born Madison, WI, Feb 21, 1947.

Christine Ebersole, 61, actress (*Richie Rich, Amadeus*, "Saturday Night Live"), born Chicago, IL, Feb 21, 1953.

David Geffen, 70, record company executive (Geffen Records), born New York, NY, Feb 21, 1944.

Hubert de Givenchy, 87, fashion designer, born Beauvais, France, Feb 21, 1927.

Kelsey Grammer, 59, actor ("Cheers," "Frasier"), born St. Thomas, US Virgin Islands, Feb 21, 1955.

Ashley Greene, 27, actress (*Twilight*), born Jacksonville, FL, Feb 21, 1987.

Jennifer Love Hewitt, 35, actress ("Ghost Whisperer," "Party of Five," "Time of My Life"), born Waco, TX, Feb 21, 1979.

Gary Lockwood, 77, actor (*Splendor in the Grass; 2001: A Space Odyssey*), born Van Nuys, CA, Feb 21, 1937.

Ellen Page, 27, actress (*Juno*; *X-Men: The Last Stand*), born Halifax, NS, Canada, Feb 21, 1987.

William Petersen, 61, actor ("CSI," *Manhunter, To Live and Die in LA*), born Evanston, IL, Feb 21, 1953.

Alan Rickman, 68, actor (the Harry Potter films, *Love Actually, Galaxy Quest*), born Hammersmith, London, England, Feb 21, 1946.

February 22 — Saturday

DAY 53 **312 REMAINING**

ANDERSON, SPARKY: BIRTH ANNIVERSARY. Feb 22, 1934. American baseball manager, born George Lee Anderson at Bridgewater, SD. After an unremarkable playing career, he began managing the Cincinnati Reds in 1970, and with that team won five division titles, three National League Championships and two World Series Championships. After being fired by the Reds, he won another World Series title with Detroit in 1984 and remained with the Tigers until his retirement in 1995. First manager to win a World Series in both the National and American Leagues, Anderson was elected to the Baseball Hall of Fame in 2000. Died Nov 4, 2010, at Thousand Oaks, CA.

BADEN-POWELL, ROBERT: BIRTH ANNIVERSARY. Feb 22, 1857. British army officer who founded the Boy Scouts and Girl Guides. Born at London, England, he died at Kenya, Africa, Jan 8, 1941.

CHURCH, FRANCIS PHARCELLUS: 175th BIRTH ANNIVERSARY. Feb 22, 1839. Born at Rochester, NY, journalist and editor best known for writing the most famous editorial in history. As editor of the *New York Sun*, Church responded to the summer 1897 letter of eight-year-old Virginia O'Hanlon who desperately asked whether Santa Claus existed. On Sept 21, 1897, she saw the unsigned editorial response: "Yes, VIRGINIA, there is a Santa Claus. . . ." Church died Apr 11, 1906, at New York, NY. After his death, the *New York Sun* revealed that he had been the author of its most famous opinion piece.

DRIVE4COPD 300 RACE. Feb 22. Daytona International Speedway, Daytona Beach, FL. 56th annual race. Nationwide Series stars in competition with the stars of the Sprint Cup Series for 120 laps, 300 miles. For info: Daytona International Speedway, PO Box 2801, Daytona Beach, FL 32120-2801. Phone: (800) PIT-SHOP. Web: www.daytonainternationalspeedway.com.

FLORIDA ACQUIRED BY US: ANNIVERSARY. Feb 22, 1819. Secretary of State John Quincy Adams signed the Florida Purchase Treaty, under which Spain ceded Florida to the US. As payment, the US assumed $5 million of claims by US citizens against Spain. Florida became a state in 1845.

***IT HAPPENED ONE NIGHT* FILM RELEASE: 80th ANNIVERSARY.** Feb 22, 1934. Frank Capra's romantic screwball comedy, starring Claudette Colbert as a spoiled runaway heiress and Clark Gable as a cocky reporter on to a good story, was the first film to sweep all the major Academy Awards, winning Best Picture, Best Director, Best Actor, Best Actress and Best Screenplay. (A scene in which Clark Gable leans on a fence munching a carrot inspired the Warner Bros. animation team when they were creating Bugs Bunny.)

KENNEDY, EDWARD: BIRTH ANNIVERSARY. Feb 22, 1932. The youngest brother of the Kennedy political dynasty, this elder statesman of American politics was born at Boston, MA. Elected to his brother John's former seat in the US Senate in 1962, he served almost 47 years representing the state of Massachusetts and was a tireless crusader for liberal causes. For years he battled alcoholism and various family scandals, including responsibility for the death of a young woman in a car accident in 1969. But his reputation as a legislator remained beyond reproach, and he worked with both sides of the political aisle to enact legislative reforms in health care, civil rights, education and voting rights. He was diagnosed with a brain tumor in May 2008 but remained at work on health-care reform until his death at Hyannis Port, MA, Aug 25, 2009.

LOWELL, JAMES RUSSELL: BIRTH ANNIVERSARY. Feb 22, 1819. American essayist, poet and diplomat. Born at Cambridge, MA, he died there Aug 12, 1891.

MILLAY, EDNA ST. VINCENT: BIRTH ANNIVERSARY. Feb 22, 1892. American poet ("My candle burns at both ends . . ."), born at Rockland, ME. She died Oct 19, 1950, at Austerlitz, NY.

MILLS, JOHN: BIRTH ANNIVERSARY. Feb 22, 1908. Popular actor, born at North Elmham, England, who played stalwart, everyman heroes. His career ranged from 1932 to 2004, and his memorable films include *In Which We Serve* (1942), *Great Expectations* (1946), *Tunes of Glory* (1960) and *Ryan's Daughter* (1970)—for which he received a Best Supporting Actor Oscar. Mills was knighted in 1976. He died Apr 23, 2005, at Denham, England.

MIRACLE ON ICE: US HOCKEY TEAM DEFEATS USSR: ANNIVERSARY. Feb 22, 1980. The US Olympic hockey team upset the team from the Soviet Union, 4–3, at the Lake Placid Winter Games to earn a victory often called the "Miracle on Ice." Led by coach Herb Brooks, the Americans went on to defeat Finland two days later and win the gold medal.

MONTGOMERY BOYCOTT ARRESTS: ANNIVERSARY. Feb 22, 1956. On Feb 20 white city leaders of Montgomery, AL, issued an ultimatum to black organizers of the three-month-old Montgomery bus boycott. They said if the boycott ended immediately, there would be "no retaliation whatsoever." If it did not end, it was made clear they would begin arresting black leaders. Two days later, 80 well-known boycotters, including Rosa Parks, Martin Luther King, Jr, and E.D. Nixon, marched to the sheriff's office in the county courthouse, where they gave themselves up for arrest. They were booked, fingerprinted and photographed. The next day the story was carried by newspapers all over the world.

MOON PHASE: LAST QUARTER. Feb 22. Moon enters Last Quarter phase at 12:15 PM, EST.

OPEN THAT BOTTLE NIGHT. Feb 22. 15th annual. A night to finally drink that bottle of wine that you've been saving for a special occasion that never seems to come. Annually, the last Saturday in February. Originated by Dorothy J. Gaiter and John Brecher.

SAINT LUCIA: INDEPENDENCE DAY: 35th ANNIVERSARY. Feb 22. National holiday. Commemorates independence of the island in the West Indies from Britain in 1979.

SCHOPENHAUER, ARTHUR: BIRTH ANNIVERSARY. Feb 22, 1788. German philosopher and author born at Danzig, Prussia (now Gdansk, Poland). Dubbed "the philosopher of pessimism," Schopenhauer was one of the first in his field to suggest that humankind should suppress their natural desires in order to achieve harmony, both cerebrally and universally, in an irrational world. A contemporary of many German Idealists, Schopenhauer's philosophical works directly challenged idealism in favor of rationalism and influenced later scholars such as Nietzsche and Freud, as well as artists Dvorak, Brahms, Borges and Tolstoy, among others. He died at Frankfurt am Main, Germany, Sept 21, 1860.

WADLOW, ROBERT PERSHING: BIRTH ANNIVERSARY. Feb 22, 1918. Tallest man in recorded history, born at Alton, IL. Though only 9 pounds at birth, by age 10 Wadlow already stood more than 6 feet tall and weighed 210 pounds. When Wadlow died at age 22, he was a remarkable 8 feet 11.1 inches tall, 490 pounds. His gentle, friendly manner in the face of constant public attention earned him the name "Gentle Giant." Wadlow died July 15, 1940, at Manistee, MI, of complications resulting from a foot infection.

WASHINGTON, GEORGE: BIRTH ANNIVERSARY. Feb 22, 1732. First president of the US ("first in war, first in peace, and first in the hearts of his countrymen" in the words of Henry "Light-Horse Harry" Lee). Born at Westmoreland County, VA, Feb 22, 1732 (New Style). However, the Julian (Old Style) calendar was still in use in the colonies when he was born, and the year began in March, so the date on the calendar when he was born was Feb 11, 1731. He died at Mount Vernon, VA, Dec 14, 1799. See also: "Washington, George: Birthday Observance (Legal Holiday)" (Feb 17) and "Washington, George: Death Anniversary" (Dec 14).

WOOLWORTH'S FIRST OPENED: ANNIVERSARY. Feb 22, 1879. First chain store, F.W. Woolworth, opened at Utica, NY. In 1997 the closing of the chain was announced.

WORLD SWORD SWALLOWERS DAY. Feb 22. 8th annual. Sword swallowers have been risking their lives for 4,000 years! Today we recognize this ancient art that is still being carried on by a few dozen surviving practitioners. Sword swallowers around the world are encouraged to do what they do best: swallow swords! Events at Ripley's Believe It or Not Odditorium museums worldwide. Annually, the last Saturday in February. For info: Sword Swallowers Assn Intl, 7408 W Augusta Blvd, Yorktown, IN 47396. Phone: (615) 969-2568. E-mail: ssai@swordswallow.org. Web: www.swordswallow.org/wssd.

BIRTHDAYS TODAY

Amy Strum Alcott, 58, golfer, born Kansas City, MO, Feb 22, 1956.

Drew Barrymore, 39, actress (*Charlie's Angels; E.T. The Extra-Terrestrial*), born Los Angeles, CA, Feb 22, 1975.

James Blunt, 37, singer, born Tidworth, Wiltshire, England, Feb 22, 1977.

Michael Te Pei Chang, 42, Hall of Fame tennis player, born Hoboken, NJ, Feb 22, 1972.

February 2014

S	M	T	W	T	F	S
						1
2	3	4	5	6	7	8
9	10	11	12	13	14	15
16	17	18	19	20	21	22
23	24	25	26	27	28	

Jonathan Demme, 70, director (*Silence of the Lambs*), born Centre, MD, Feb 22, 1944.

Paul Dooley, 86, actor (*Slap Shot, Breaking Away, The Player*), born Parkersburg, WV, Feb 22, 1928.

Julius Winfield "Dr. J" Erving, 64, Hall of Fame basketball player, born Roosevelt, NY, Feb 22, 1950.

Kyle MacLachlan, 55, actor ("Twin Peaks," *Blue Velvet, The Flintstones*), born Yakima, WA, Feb 22, 1959.

Miou-Miou, 64, actress (*Entre Nous, La Lectrice*), born Paris, France, Feb 22, 1950.

Rajon Rondo, 28, basketball player, born Louisville, KY, Feb 22, 1986.

Jeri Ryan, 46, actress ("Shark," "Boston Public," "Star Trek: Voyager"), born Munich, Germany, Feb 22, 1968.

Kazuhiro Sasaki, 46, baseball player, born Sendai, Japan, Feb 22, 1968.

Vijay Singh, 51, golfer, born Lautoka, Fiji, Feb 22, 1963.

Julie Walters, 64, actress (*Calendar Girls, Billy Elliot, Educating Rita*), born Birmingham, England, Feb 22, 1950.

February 23 — Sunday

DAY 54 **311 REMAINING**

BRUNEI DARUSSALAM: NATIONAL DAY: 30th INDEPENDENCE ANNIVERSARY. Feb 23. National holiday observed in Brunei Darussalam, located on the island of Borneo. Commemorates independence from Britain, Feb 23, 1984.

CURLING IS COOL DAY. Feb 23. Offer up a worldwide embrace for an Olympic sport the entire family can play! If you don't get it, you ain't cool. (©2006 by WH.) For info: Thomas & Ruth Roy, Wellcat Holidays, 2418 Long Ln, Lebanon, PA 17046. Phone: (717) 279-0184. Fax: (240) 332-4886. E-mail: info@wellcat.com. Web: www.wellcat.com.

DAYTONA 500. Feb 23. Daytona International Speedway, Daytona Beach, FL. 56th annual running of the "Great American Race." Forty-three of the world's top drivers compete in NASCAR's biggest, richest and most prestigious motorsports event. For info: Daytona International Speedway, PO Box 2801, Daytona Beach, FL 32120-2801. Phone: (800) PIT-SHOP. Web: www.daytonainternationalspeedway.com.

DIESEL ENGINE PATENTED: ANNIVERSARY. Feb 23, 1893. Rudolf Diesel received a patent in Germany for the engine that bears his name. The diesel engine burns fuel oil rather than gasoline and is used in trucks and heavy industrial machinery.

Du BOIS, W.E.B.: BIRTH ANNIVERSARY. Feb 23, 1868. William Edward Burghardt Du Bois, American educator and leader of the movement for black equality. Born at Great Barrington, MA, he died at Accra, Ghana, Aug 27, 1963. "The cost of liberty," he wrote in 1909, "is less than the price of repression."

FIRST CLONING OF AN ADULT ANIMAL: ANNIVERSARY. Feb 23, 1997. Researchers in Scotland announced the first cloning of an adult animal, a lamb they named Dolly with a genetic makeup identical to that of her mother. This led to worldwide speculation about the possibility of human cloning. On Mar 4, 1997, President William Clinton imposed a ban on the federal funding of human cloning research.

FLEMING, VICTOR LONZO: 125th BIRTH ANNIVERSARY. Feb 23, 1889. Film director, born at Pasadena, CA (some sources say 1883). His directorial talents are manifest in two of Hollywood's most popular and enduring movies: *The Wizard of Oz* (1939) and *Gone with the Wind* (1939) for which he won an Academy Award. He died Jan 6, 1949, at Cottonwood, AZ.

GROUND WAR AGAINST IRAQ BEGINS: DESERT STORM ANNIVERSARY. Feb 23, 1991. After an air campaign lasting slightly more than a month, allied forces launched the ground offensive against Iraqi forces as part of Desert Storm.

GUYANA: ANNIVERSARY OF REPUBLIC. Feb 23. National holiday. Guyana in South America became a republic within the British Commonwealth, Feb 23, 1970.

HANDEL, GEORGE FREDERICK: BIRTH ANNIVERSARY. Feb 23, 1685. Born at Halle, Saxony, Germany. Handel and Bach, born the same year, were perhaps the greatest masters of Baroque music. Handel's most frequently performed work is the oratorio *Messiah*, which was first heard in 1742. He died at London, England, Apr 14, 1759. See also: "Premiere of Handel's *Messiah*: Anniversary" (Apr 13).

IWO JIMA DAY: ANNIVERSARY. Feb 23, 1945. Anniversary of the day that the US flag was raised on the Pacific island of Iwo Jima by US Marines. Almost 20,000 American soldiers lost their lives before the island was finally taken from the Japanese on Mar 16, 1945.

JAPANESE ATTACK US MAINLAND: ANNIVERSARY. Feb 23, 1942. In the first attack on the US mainland, a Japanese submarine fired 25 shells at an oil refinery at the edge of Ellwood Oil Field, 12 miles west of Santa Barbara, CA. One shell made a direct hit of the rigging, causing minor damage. President Franklin Roosevelt was giving a fireside chat at the time of the attack.

KREWE OF CARROLLTON PARADE. Feb 23. New Orleans, LA. Founded in 1924, the Krewe of Carrollton is the fourth-oldest marching krewe and kicks off the New Orleans carnival season with this popular parade in the Carrollton neighborhood. Annually, two Sundays before Mardi Gras. For info: Krewe of Carrollton. Web: www.kreweofcarrollton.com.

MYSTIC KREWE OF BARKUS PARADE. Feb 23. French Quarter, New Orleans, LA. Popular 15-block walking parade of costumed dogs (and a few cats) held annually two Sundays before Ash Wednesday. The Krewe of Barkus (Barkus is the dog equivalent of Bacchus) is a licensed Mardi Gras Krewe and nonprofit organization. All proceeds of the parade registration fees, merchandise sales and ball profits are donated to worthy animal welfare groups. For info: Mystic Krewe of Barkus. E-mail: info@barkus.org. Web: www.barkus.org.

NATIONAL EATING DISORDERS AWARENESS WEEK. Feb 23–Mar 1. Provides opportunities for eating disorders organizations, mental health professionals, educators, families and concerned individuals around the world to join together to plan events, to provide education on the seriousness of eating disorders and to provide information on how to find help. For info: National Eating Disorders Association, 165 W 46th St, 4th Fl, New York, NY 10036. Phone: (212) 575-6200. E-mail: info@NationalEatingDisorders.org. Web: www.NEDAwareness.org.

ORTHODOX MEATFARE SUNDAY. Feb 23. In preparation for the Great Lent, no meat is eaten after Meatfare Sunday.

PEPYS, SAMUEL: BIRTH ANNIVERSARY. Feb 23, 1633. (Old Style date.) Diarist, born at London, England. Wrote Pepys in his diary (Mar 10, 1666): "The truth is, I do indulge myself a little the more in pleasure, knowing that this is the proper age of my life to do it; and, out of my observation that most men that do thrive in the world do forget to take pleasure during the time that they are getting their estate, but reserve that till they have got one, and then it is too late for them to enjoy it." Died at London, May 26, 1703.

RUSSIA: DEFENDER OF THE FATHERLAND DAY. Feb 23. Commemorates the 1918 birth of the Red Army (when the first drafts took place) and the Red Army's initial combat against invading German troops. Formerly known as Army and Navy Day. Observed with parades and processions. Wreaths are laid at the Tomb of the Unknown Soldier. Also observed on different dates in the former Soviet republics.

SECONDHAND WARDROBE WEEK. Feb 23–Mar 1. A secondhand wardrobe can help people feel great about their appearance, their finances and their impact on the planet. The purpose of this week is to remove the stigma of previously owned clothing through education about the benefits of the secondhand wardrobe. For info: Cheryl Gorn. E-mail: cg@secondhandwardrobe.com. Web: www.secondhandwardrobe.com.

SHIRER, WILLIAM L.: BIRTH ANNIVERSARY. Feb 23, 1904. American journalist and author William L. Shirer was born at Chicago, IL. As the European correspondent from 1927 to 1934 for the *Chicago Tribune* he became a friend of Mohandas K. Gandhi, the leader of India's independence movement. As a result of this he published *Gandhi: A Memoir* in 1980. His best-known book is *The Rise and Fall of the Third Reich* (1960), in which he used his experiences in Europe with the *New York Herald Tribune*, the Universal News Service and CBS Radio. He died Dec 28, 1993, at Boston, MA.

TAYLOR, GEORGE: DEATH ANNIVERSARY. Feb 23, 1781. Signer of the Declaration of Independence. Born 1716 at British Isles (exact date unknown). Died at Easton, PA.

WILLARD, EMMA HART: BIRTH ANNIVERSARY. Feb 23, 1787. Pioneer in higher education for women, born at Berlin, CT. Intent on improving educational opportunities for women, she sent her *Plan for Improving Female Education* to the governor of New York. In it she described her ideal for a girls' school, including the instruction usually offered the girls of her day (music, drawing, penmanship, dancing), as well as adding religious and moral instruction, natural philosophy and domestic science. The New York legislature granted her a charter for the Waterford Academy for Young Ladies. The school later moved to Troy, NY, where it was first named the Troy Female Seminary and later the Emma Willard School. She assisted in the founding of a teachers' training school for girls at Athens, Greece, in 1832. She began the Willard Association for the Mutual Improvement of Female Teachers in 1837, and she authored several textbooks on geography, history and astronomy. Willard died at Troy, Apr 15, 1870.

BIRTHDAYS TODAY

Aziz Ansari, 31, comedian, actor ("Parks and Recreation"), born Columbia, SC, Feb 23, 1983.

Emily Blunt, 31, actress (*The Devil Wears Prada,* "Gideon's Daughter"), born London, England, Feb 23, 1983.

Roberto Martin Antonio (Bobby) Bonilla, 51, former baseball player, born New York, NY, Feb 23, 1963.

Sylvia Chase, 76, newscaster, born Northfield, MN, Feb 23, 1938.

Peter Fonda, 75, actor (*Easy Rider, Ulee's Gold*), born New York, NY, Feb 23, 1939.

Edward Lee "Too Tall" Jones, 63, former football player and boxer, born Jackson, TN, Feb 23, 1951.

Howard Jones, 59, singer, born Southampton, England, Feb 23, 1955.

Kelly Macdonald, 38, actress ("Boardwalk Empire," *No Country for Old Men, Trainspotting*), born Glasgow, Scotland, Feb 23, 1976.

Niecy Nash, 44, comedienne, actress ("Reno 911!"), born Palmdale, CA, Feb 23, 1970.

Patricia Richardson, 63, actress ("Double Trouble," "Home Improvement"), born Bethesda, MD, Feb 23, 1951.

Johnny Winter, 70, singer, musician, born John Dawson III at Beaumont, TX, Feb 23, 1944.

February 24 — Monday

DAY 55 **310 REMAINING**

ESTONIA: INDEPENDENCE DAY. Feb 24. National holiday. Commemorates declaration of independence from Soviet Union in 1918. Independence was brief, however; Estonia was again under Soviet control from 1940 until 1991.

GREGORIAN CALENDAR DAY: ANNIVERSARY. Feb 24, 1582. Pope Gregory XIII, enlisting the expertise of distinguished astronomers and mathematicians, issued a bull correcting the Julian calendar, which was then 10 days in error. The correction was a minor one, changing the rule about leap years. The new calendar named for him, the Gregorian calendar, became effective Oct 4, 1582, in most Catholic countries, in 1752 in Britain and the American colonies, in 1918 in Russia and in 1923 in Greece. It is the most widely used calendar in the world today. See also: "Calendar Adjustment Day: Anniversary" (Sept 2) and "Gregorian Calendar Adjustment: Anniversary" (Oct 4).

GRIMM, WILHELM CARL: BIRTH ANNIVERSARY. Feb 24, 1786. Mythologist and author, born at Hanau, Germany. Best remembered for *Grimm's Fairy Tales,* in collaboration with his brother, Jacob. Died at Berlin, Germany, Dec 16, 1859. See also: "Grimm, Jacob: Birth Anniversary" (Jan 4).

HADASSAH FOUNDED: ANNIVERSARY. Feb 24, 1912. Twelve members of the Daughters of Zion Study Circle met at New York City under the leadership of Henrietta Szold. A constitution was drafted to expand the study group into a national organization called Hadassah (Hebrew for *myrtle* and the biblical name of Queen Esther) to foster Jewish education in America and to create public health nursing and nurses' training in Palestine. Hadassah is now the largest women's volunteer organization in the US, with 1,500 chapters rooted in healthcare delivery, education and vocational training, children's villages and services and land reclamation in Israel.

HOMER, WINSLOW: BIRTH ANNIVERSARY. Feb 24, 1836. Born at Boston, MA, Homer made the transition from commercial illustrator to acclaimed artist while working in a variety of media. "Look at nature, work independently and solve your own problems," was his advice to another artist, but it also served as his motto. Specializing in rural and nautical land- and seascapes, he was noted for the realism of his work, from gentle country life scenes to brutal scenes of nature—a dichotomy that can be observed in two of his famous paintings: *Breezing Up* (1876) and *Gulf Stream* (1899). Somewhat of a recluse in his later years and always struggling financially, Homer died at his home at Prouts Neck, ME, on Sept 29, 1910.

JOBS, STEVE: BIRTH ANNIVERSARY. Feb 24, 1955. CEO, tech innovator, visionary Steve Jobs, the co-creator of Apple, Inc, and 39th on the Forbes Richest People in America list in 2012 when he died of cancer at age 56, was also a college dropout who once searched for enlightenment in rural India. In 1976, Jobs founded Apple with Steve Wozniak in order to sell the Apple I personal computer Wozniak had invented. Next came the Apple II, which Jobs made the first PC housed in consumer-friendly plastic, and in 1984 came the Macintosh, which together with its iconic ad campaign solidified the Apple brand as charismatic, quirky and intuitive, traits that also applied to Jobs himself. A respected leader who was also fired from his own company before returning in 1996—the "Think Different" era—Jobs changed personal computing again with the iPod, iPhone and iPad, devices that forever transformed how society interacts with technology. Born at San Francisco, CA, Jobs died Oct 5, 2011, at Palo Alto, CA.

February 2014	S	M	T	W	T	F	S
							1
	2	3	4	5	6	7	8
	9	10	11	12	13	14	15
	16	17	18	19	20	21	22
	23	24	25	26	27	28	

JOHNSON IMPEACHMENT PROCEEDINGS: ANNIVERSARY. Feb 24, 1867. In a showdown over reconstruction policy following the Civil War, the House of Representatives voted to impeach President Andrew Johnson. During the two years following the end of the war, the Republican-controlled Congress had sought to severely punish the South. Congress passed the Reconstruction Act, which divided the South into five military districts headed by officers who were to take their orders from General Grant, the head of the army, instead of from President Johnson. In addition, Congress passed the Tenure of Office Act, which required Senate approval before Johnson could remove any official whose appointment was originally approved by the Senate. Johnson vetoed this act, but the veto was overridden by Congress. To test the constitutionality of the act, Johnson dismissed Secretary of War Edwin Stanton, triggering the impeachment vote. On Mar 5, 1868, the Senate convened as a court to hear the charges against the president. The Senate vote of 35–19 fell one vote short of the two-thirds majority needed for impeachment.

MEXICO: FLAG DAY. Feb 24. *El Día de la Bandera*. National holiday honoring the Mexican flag, which was created in 1821 after Mexico achieved independence.

NIMITZ, CHESTER: BIRTH ANNIVERSARY. Feb 24, 1885. Commander of all Allied naval, land and air forces in the southwest Pacific during a portion of WWII, Admiral Chester William Nimitz was born at Fredericksburg, TX. During the final assault on Japan in April 1945, Nimitz resumed command of the entire naval operation in the Pacific, which he had shared with General Douglas MacArthur for some time. Nimitz was one of the signers of the Japanese document of surrender Sept 2, 1945, aboard the USS *Missouri* in Tokyo Bay. Nimitz died Feb 20, 1966, at Treasure Island, San Francisco Bay, CA. The USS *Nimitz* was named in his honor.

WAGNER, HONUS: BIRTH ANNIVERSARY. Feb 24, 1874. American baseball great, born John Peter Wagner at Carnegie, PA. Nicknamed "the Flying Dutchman," Wagner was among the first five players elected to the Baseball Hall of Fame in 1936. Died at Carnegie, Dec 6, 1955.

BIRTHDAYS TODAY

Wilson Bethel, 30, actor ("Hart of Dixie," "The Young and the Restless"), born Hillsboro, NH, Feb 24, 1984.

Barry Bostwick, 69, actor (*The Rocky Horror Picture Show*, "Spin City"), born San Mateo, CA, Feb 24, 1945.

Jeff Garcia, 44, football player, born Gilroy, CA, Feb 24, 1970.

Lleyton Hewitt, 33, tennis player, born Adelaide, Australia, Feb 24, 1981.

Steven Hill, 92, actor ("Law & Order"), born Seattle, WA, Feb 24, 1922.

Rupert Holmes, 67, musician, songwriter, born Tenafly, NJ, Feb 24, 1947.

Mark Lane, 87, lawyer, author (*Rush to Judgment, Eyewitness Chicago*), assassination buff, born New York, NY, Feb 24, 1927.

Michel Legrand, 82, composer, conductor, born Paris, France, Feb 24, 1932.

Joseph I. Lieberman, 72, former US senator (I, Connecticut), born Stamford, CT, Feb 24, 1942.

Floyd Mayweather, Jr, 37, boxer, born Las Vegas, NV, Feb 24, 1977.

Eddie Clarence Murray, 58, Hall of Fame baseball player, born Los Angeles, CA, Feb 24, 1956.

Edward James Olmos, 67, actor (*Stand and Deliver*, "Battlestar Galactica"; Emmy for "Miami Vice"), born East Los Angeles, CA, Feb 24, 1947.

Bob Sanders, 33, football player, born Erie, PA, Feb 24, 1981.

Renata Scotto, 78, soprano, born Savona, Italy, Feb 24, 1936.

Helen Shaver, 63, actress (*Desert Hearts, The Color of Money*), born St. Thomas, ON, Canada, Feb 24, 1951.

Abe Vigoda, 93, actor ("Barney Miller," "Fish"), born New York, NY, Feb 24, 1921.

Paula Zahn, 58, television journalist, born Naperville, IL, Feb 24, 1956.

Billy Zane, 48, actor (*Titanic, The Phantom*), born Chicago, IL, Feb 24, 1966.

February 25 — Tuesday

DAY 56 **309 REMAINING**

BACKUS, JIM: BIRTH ANNIVERSARY. Feb 25, 1913. Born James Gilmore Backus at Cleveland, OH. An actor whose career encompassed radio, television and film, Jim Backus is most remembered as the voice behind the nearsighted bumbler Mr Magoo and for his portrayal of Thurston Howell III on the popular TV show "Gilligan's Island." Backus died July 3, 1989, at Santa Monica, CA.

BASCOM, "TEXAS ROSE": BIRTH ANNIVERSARY. Feb 25, 1922. A Cherokee-Choctaw Indian born at Covington County, MS, Rose Flynt married rodeo cowboy Earl Bascom and learned trick roping, becoming known as the greatest female trick roper in the world. She appeared on stage, in movies and on early TV. She toured with the USO during WWII, performing at every military base and military hospital in the US. After the war she entertained servicemen stationed overseas. In 1981 she was inducted into the National Cowgirl Hall of Fame (located at Fort Worth, TX). She died Sept 23, 1993, at St. George, UT.

BURGESS, ANTHONY: BIRTH ANNIVERSARY. Feb 25, 1917. Author (*A Clockwork Orange*). Born at Manchester, England. Died Nov 25, 1993, at London.

CARUSO, ENRICO: BIRTH ANNIVERSARY. Feb 25, 1873. Operatic tenor of legendary voice and fame, born at Naples, Italy. Died there Aug 2, 1921.

CLAY BECOMES HEAVYWEIGHT CHAMP: 50th ANNIVERSARY. Feb 25, 1964. Twenty-two-year-old Cassius Clay (later Muhammad Ali) became world heavyweight boxing champion by defeating Sonny Liston. At the height of his athletic career Ali was well known for both his fighting ability and personal style. His most famous saying was "I am the greatest!" Ali is the only fighter to win the heavyweight fighting title three separate times. He defended that title nine times.

DULLES, JOHN FOSTER: BIRTH ANNIVERSARY. Feb 25, 1888. American statesman born at Washington, DC. In 1953, President Dwight Eisenhower appointed Dulles secretary of state. Dulles was the architect of Eisenhower's Cold War foreign policy that promised "massive retaliatory power" in response to Soviet aggression. He helped create the Southeast Asia Treaty Organization (1954) and the Baghdad Pact Organization (1955) in order to bolster NATO and isolate the USSR. Dulles died May 24, 1959, at Washington, DC.

FENWICK, MILLICENT HAMMOND: BIRTH ANNIVERSARY. Feb 25, 1910. Fashion model, author, member NJ General Assembly and US congresswoman, Millicent Fenwick was born at New York, NY. A champion of liberal causes, Fenwick pointed to her sponsorship of the resolution creating the commission to monitor the 1975 Helsinki accords on human rights as her proudest achievement. She fought for civil rights, peace in Vietnam, aid for the poor, reduction of military programs, gun control and restrictions on capital punishment. Fenwick, the inspiration for Garry Trudeau's "Doonesbury" character Lacey Davenport, died at Bernardsville, NJ, Sept 16, 1992.

FIRST NATIONAL BANK CHARTERED BY CONGRESS: ANNIVERSARY. Feb 25, 1791. The First Bank of the US at Philadelphia, PA, was chartered. Proposed as a national bank by Alexander Hamilton, it lost its charter in 1811. The Second Bank of the US received a charter in 1816, which expired in 1836. Since that time, the US has had no central bank. Central banking functions are carried out by the Federal Reserve System, established in 1913. See also: "Federal Reserve System: Anniversary" (Dec 23).

FREER, CHARLES LANG: BIRTH ANNIVERSARY. Feb 25, 1856. American art collector who built and endowed the Freer Gallery, which was presented to the Smithsonian Institution in 1906. Born at Kingston, NY, he died at New York, NY, Sept 25, 1919.

HARRISON, GEORGE: BIRTH ANNIVERSARY. Feb 25, 1943. Musician and singer born at Liverpool, England, Harrison was the lead guitarist and co-songwriter for The Beatles, alongside John Lennon, Paul McCartney and Ringo Starr. The band is considered to be the most influential rock-and-roll group of all time. Harrison is credited with introducing Eastern musical styles and instrumentation to Western pop. After the breakup of The Beatles, Harrison embarked on a successful solo career, became an independent film producer (*Time Bandits*) and created one of the first charity rock concerts with his Concert for Bangladesh, which brought relief to flood victims of that country. He died at Los Angeles, CA, on Nov 29, 2001.

HEBRON MASSACRE: 20th ANNIVERSARY. Feb 25, 1994. An American-born Jewish settler in Hebron, Israel, Baruch Goldstein, opened fire with an assault rifle in a crowded mosque, part of a complex sacred to both Jews and Muslims because it is believed to contain the tomb of Abraham and his wife, Sarah. Of the more than 400 Muslims gathered for early-morning prayers during the holy month of Ramadan, 29 were killed immediately and 150 were wounded. Others, including Goldstein, were crushed in the panic to flee or during subsequent rioting.

KUWAIT: NATIONAL DAY. Feb 25. National holiday. Commemorates the 1978 accession of King Shaykh Sir 'abdullah Al-Salim al-Sabah.

RENOIR, PIERRE AUGUSTE: BIRTH ANNIVERSARY. Feb 25, 1841. Impressionist painter, born at Limoges, France. Renoir's paintings are known for their joy and sensuousness as well as the light techniques he employed in them. In his later years he was crippled by arthritis and would paint with the brush strapped to his hand. He died at Cagnes-sur-Mer, Provence, France, Dec 17, 1919.

SPACE MILESTONE: *SOYUZ 32* (USSR). Feb 25, 1979. Launched from Baikonur space center in Soviet Central Asia. Cosmonauts Vladimir Lyakhov and Valery Ryumin docked at *Salyut 6* space station Feb 26. Returned to Earth in *Soyuz 34* after what was then a record 175 days in space Aug 19, 1979.

WORLD SPAY DAY. Feb 25. 20th annual. Yearly worldwide campaign of The Humane Society of the United States and Humane Society International, in partnership with the Humane Society Veterinary Medical Association and other organizations. Highlighting the importance of saving animal lives by spaying or neutering. Veterinary clinics, humane societies/shelters, businesses and animal advocates are encouraged to participate. Annually, the last Tuesday in February, with events in honor of World Spay Day taking place throughout the month, which is Spay/Neuter Awareness Month. For info: Spay Day Coordinator, The Humane Society of the United States, 2100 L St NW, Washington, DC 20037. Phone: (301) 258-1486. Fax: (301) 258-3081. E-mail: spayday@humanesociety.org. Web: www.worldspayday.org.

"YOUR SHOW OF SHOWS" TV PREMIERE: ANNIVERSARY. Feb 25, 1950. Sid Caesar and Imogene Coca starred in the NBC 90-minute variety program along with Carl Reiner and Howard Morris. The show included monologues, improvisations, parodies, pantomimes and sketches of varying length. Some of its writers were Mel Tolkin, Lucille Kallen, Mel Brooks, Larry Gelbart, Neil Simon and Woody Allen.

BIRTHDAYS TODAY

Sean Astin, 43, actor (the Lord of the Rings film trilogy, *The Goonies, Rudy, Courage Under Fire*), born Santa Monica, CA, Feb 25, 1971.

Diane Baker, 76, actress (*Silence of the Lambs*), born Hollywood, CA, Feb 25, 1938.

Tom Courtenay, 77, actor (*The Dresser, The Loneliness of the Long Distance Runner, Otley*), born Hull, England, Feb 25, 1937.

Ric Flair, 65, former professional wrestler, born Richard Fliehr at Memphis, TN, Feb 25, 1949.

Karen Grassle, 70, actress ("Little House on the Prairie"), born Berkeley, CA, Feb 25, 1944.

Chelsea Handler, 39, author, television personality ("Chelsea Lately"), born Livingston, NJ, Feb 25, 1975.

Rashida Jones, 38, actress ("The Office," "Parks and Recreation"), born Los Angeles, CA, Feb 25, 1976.

Neil Jordan, 64, director, writer (*The Crying Game, Interview with the Vampire*), born County Sligo, Ireland, Feb 25, 1950.

Tea Leoni, 48, actress (*Jurassic Park III, Deep Impact, Flirting with Disaster*), born New York, NY, Feb 25, 1966.

Joakim Noah, 29, basketball player, born New York, NY, Feb 25, 1985.

Sally Jessy Raphael, 71, talk show host, born Easton, PA, Feb 25, 1943.

Bob Schieffer, 77, television journalist, born Austin, TX, Feb 25, 1937.

Josh Wolff, 37, soccer player, born Stone Mountain, GA, Feb 25, 1977.

February 2014	S	M	T	W	T	F	S
							1
	2	3	4	5	6	7	8
	9	10	11	12	13	14	15
	16	17	18	19	20	21	22
	23	24	25	26	27	28	

February 26 — Wednesday

DAY 57 **308 REMAINING**

ASSOCIATION OF WRITERS AND WRITING PROGRAMS CONFERENCE AND BOOKFAIR. Feb 26–Mar 1. Washington State Convention Center and Sheraton Seattle Hotel, Seattle, WA. Each year, AWP holds its Annual Conference and Bookfair in a different city in North America to celebrate the outstanding authors, teachers, writing programs, literary centers and small press publishers of that region. The conference typically features over 450 readings, lectures, panel discussions and forums, in addition to hundreds of book signings, receptions, dances and informal gatherings. The conference, which attracts more than 10,000 attendees and nearly 600 publishers, is among the largest and most beloved literary gatherings in North America. For info: Assn of Writers and Writing Programs, George Mason University, MSN 1E3, Fairfax, VA 22030. E-mail: conference@awpwriter.org. Web: www.awpwriter.org.

CARNIVAL DE PONCE. Feb 26–Mar 4. Ponce, PR. Carnival, artisans, parade with floats and colorfully dressed people with papier-mâché masks (*vejigantes*). Also featuring kiosks with typical Puerto Rican foods and drinks. First held in 1858. Annually, the week before Ash Wednesday. Est attendance: 100,000. For info: Cultural Development Office, PO Box 331709, Ponce, PR 00733-1709. Phone: (787) 841-8044, ext 2258. E-mail: dcultponce@ponce.pr.gov. Web: www.visitponce.com.

CASH, JOHNNY: BIRTH ANNIVERSARY. Feb 26, 1932. The iconic country music star was born J.R. Cash at Kingsland, AR. His career spanned the 1950s through the year he died, and he recorded more than 1,500 songs, including such hits as "I Walk the Line," "Ring of Fire," "Folsom Prison Blues" and "A Boy Named Sue." He was called "the Man in Black" because he wore a black long-tailed suit in sympathy for those who suffered. The recipient of numerous awards and honors, Cash died at Nashville, TN, on Sept 12, 2003. Cash and Elvis Presley are the only music stars to be inducted into both the Country Music and Rock and Roll halls of fame.

CODY, WILLIAM FREDERIC "BUFFALO BILL": BIRTH ANNIVERSARY. Feb 26, 1846. American frontiersman born at Scott County, IA, who claimed to have killed more than 4,000 buffalo. Subject of many heroic Wild West yarns, Cody became successful as a showman, taking his acts across the US and to Europe. Died Jan 10, 1917, at Denver, CO.

***COMMUNIST MANIFESTO* PUBLISHED: ANNIVERSARY.** Feb 26, 1848. Written by Karl Marx and Friedrich Engels on the eve of the revolutions of 1848, the *Manifesto* provided ideas for Socialist and Communist movements.

DAUMIER, HONORÉ: BIRTH ANNIVERSARY. Feb 26, 1808. French painter and caricaturist famous for his satirical and comic lithographs. Once spent six months in prison for a caricature of Louis Philippe shown as Gargantua consuming the heavy taxes of the citizens. Born at Marseilles, France, he died Feb 11, 1879, at Volmondois, France.

FEDERAL COMMUNICATIONS COMMISSION CREATED: 80th ANNIVERSARY. Feb 26, 1934. President Franklin Roosevelt ordered the creation of a Communications Commission, which became the FCC. It was established by Congress June 19, 1934, to oversee communication by radio, wire or cable. TV and satellite communication later became part of its charge.

FOR PETE'S SAKE DAY. Feb 26. A world wonders: after all these years, who is Pete and why do we do or not do things for his sake? (©2006 by WH.) For info: Thomas & Ruth Roy, Wellcat Holidays, 2418 Long Ln, Lebanon, PA 17046. Phone: (717) 279-0184. E-mail: info@wellcat.com. Web: www.wellcat.com.

GLEASON, JACKIE: BIRTH ANNIVERSARY. Feb 26, 1916. American musician, comedian and actor, Herbert John "Jackie" Gleason was born at Brooklyn, NY. Best known for his role as Ralph Kramden in the long-running television series "The Honeymooners." Died at Fort Lauderdale, FL, June 24, 1987.

GRAND CANYON NATIONAL PARK ESTABLISHED: 95th ANNIVERSARY. Feb 26, 1919. By an act of Congress, Grand Canyon National Park was established. An immense gorge cut through the high plateaus of northwest Arizona by the raging Colorado River and covering 1,218,375 acres, Grand Canyon National Park is considered one of the most spectacular natural phenomena in the world.

GRAND TETON NATIONAL PARK ESTABLISHED: 85th ANNIVERSARY. Feb 26, 1929. Grand Teton, in Wyoming, was established as a national park and preserve by Congress. On Sept 14, 1950, Congress authorized enlarging the park to include areas of Jackson Hole National Monument.

HUGO, VICTOR: BIRTH ANNIVERSARY. Feb 26, 1802. One of the most popular 19th-century authors, born at Besançon, France. His most well-known work is the novel *Les Misérables*, and his most famous character is Quasimodo, the Hunchback of Notre Dame. "An invasion of armies can be resisted," Hugo wrote in 1852, "but not an idea whose time has come." He died at Paris, May 22, 1885, and more than two million people thronged to his state funeral.

INCONVENIENCE YOURSELF™ DAY. Feb 26. Enrich your own life as you focus on ways to show respect to others, the environment and the world you live in. Consider how your everyday actions affect others. Look for opportunities to inconvenience yourself and make a positive impact in the world. Annually, the fourth Wednesday in February. For info: Julie Thompson, 1844 N Nob Hill Rd, #620, Plantation, FL 33322. Phone: (954) 693-4604. Fax: (954) 370-0083. E-mail: julie@InconvenienceYourself.com. Web: www.InconvenienceYourself.com.

KUWAIT: LIBERATION DAY. Feb 26. Public holiday commemorating the liberation of Kuwait from Iraqi occupation by allied forces in 1991. Annually, Feb 26.

MARLOWE, CHRISTOPHER: 450th BIRTH ANNIVERSARY. Feb 26, 1564. Great Elizabethan dramatist and poet, born at Canterbury, England (baptism date used as birth date). Made popular the use of blank verse in drama. Major works include *Doctor Faustus* and *Tamburlaine the Great*. Most famous poem was "The Passionate Shepherd to His Love." Killed in mysterious circumstances (perhaps connected to his working as a spy) on May 30, 1593, at Deptford, London, England.

NATIONAL PERSONAL CHEF DAY. Feb 26. A national day to honor the professional personal chefs who provide delicious, affordable, palate-specific meals from fresh ingredients on a regular basis that may be enjoyed in the comfort of the client's home. For info: American Personal & Private Chef Assn, 4572 Delaware St, San Diego, CA 92116. Phone: (800) 644-8389 or (619) 294-2436. E-mail: info@personalchef.com. Web: www.personalchef.com.

RANDALL, TONY: BIRTH ANNIVERSARY. Feb 26, 1920. Born Leonard Rosenberg at Tulsa, OK, actor Tony Randall had a career that spanned five decades. He was a successful film actor, starring in 1957's *Will Success Spoil Rock Hunter?* and 1959's *Pillow Talk* and performed extensively on the stage. He launched the National Actors Theatre, a company dedicated to performing classic works of theater. He is perhaps best remembered for his role opposite Jack Klugman in television's "The Odd Couple," playing Felix Unger, the tidy, hypochondriac photographer forced by circumstance to share an apartment with slob sportswriter Oscar Madison. The wildly popular series ran from 1970 to 1975. Randall died at New York, NY, May 17, 2004.

STRAUSS, LEVI: BIRTH ANNIVERSARY. Feb 26, 1829. Bavarian immigrant Levi Strauss created the world's first pair of jeans—Levi's 501 jeans—for California's gold miners in 1850. Born at Buttenheim, Bavaria, Germany, he died in 1902, at San Francisco, CA.

UCI TRACK CYCLING WORLD CHAMPIONSHIPS. Feb 26–Mar 2. Cali Veledrome, Cali, Colombia. Sponsored by the International Cycling Union (UCI), a nonprofit organization founded on Apr 14, 1900. For info: International Cycling Union (UCI), Ch de la Mêlée 12, 1860 Aigle, Switzerland. Phone: (41) (24) 468-58-11. Fax: (41) (24) 468-58-12. E-mail: admin@uci.ch or dcu@dcu-cycling.dk. Web: www.uci.ch.

VERCORS, JEAN: BIRTH ANNIVERSARY. Feb 26, 1902. Jean Vercors was the author of the first clandestine novel published during the Nazi occupation of France. Vercors, whose real name was Jean-Marcel de Bruller, was best known for his novel *Silence of the Sea*, which he published with Pierre de Lescure for their publishing house, Les Editions de Minuit, after the Nazis occupied France in 1941. Vercors was born at Paris, France, and died there June 10, 1991.

WORLD TRADE CENTER BOMBING OF 1993: ANNIVERSARY. Feb 26, 1993. A 1,210-pound bomb packed in a van exploded in the underground parking garage of the World Trade Center in New York City, killing six people and injuring more than 1,000 (mostly from smoke inhalation). The powerful blast left a crater 200 feet wide and several stories deep. The cost for damage to the building and disruption of business for the 350 companies with offices in the Center exceeded $591 million. Fifteen people—the fundamentalist Muslim cleric Sheik Omar Abdul Rahman and 14 of his followers—were indicted for the bombing. Rahman was given a life sentence, and the others received prison terms of up to 240 years each.

BIRTHDAYS TODAY

Erykah Badu, 42, singer, born Dallas, TX, Feb 26, 1972.

Michael Bolton, 61, singer, born New Haven, CT, Feb 26, 1953.

Fats Domino, 86, singer, songwriter ("Ain't That a Shame," "Blueberry Hill"), born Antoine Domino at New Orleans, LA, Feb 26, 1928.

Marshall Faulk, 41, sportscaster, Hall of Fame football player, born New Orleans, LA, Feb 26, 1973.

Tim Kaine, 56, US Senator (D, Virginia), former chairman of the Democratic National Committee, former governor of Virginia, born St. Paul, MN, Feb 26, 1958.

February 27 — Thursday

DAY 58 | **307 REMAINING**

AFRICAN BURIAL GROUND NATIONAL MONUMENT ESTABLISHED: ANNIVERSARY. Feb 27, 2006. On this date President George W. Bush signed a proclamation declaring a seven-acre plot at the corners of Duane and Elk streets in Lower Manhattan, New York, to be a national monument. From the 1690s to the 1790s, this land served as a cemetery for both free and enslaved Africans and is believed to be the resting place of more than 15,000 people.

ANDERSON, MARIAN: BIRTH ANNIVERSARY. Feb 27, 1897. Born at Philadelphia, PA (some sources say in 1899 or 1902). Anderson's talent was evident at an early age. Her career stonewalled by the prejudice she encountered in the US, she moved to Europe, where the magnificence of her voice and her versatility as a performer began to establish her as one of the world's finest contraltos. Preventing Anderson's performance at Washington's Constitution Hall in 1939 on the basis of her color, the Daughters of the American Revolution unintentionally secured for her the publicity that would lay the foundation for her success in the States. Her performance was rescheduled, and on Apr 9 (Easter Sunday), 75,000 people showed up to hear her sing from the steps of the Lincoln Memorial. The performance was simultaneously broadcast by radio. In 1955 Anderson became the first African American to perform with the New York Metropolitan Opera. The following year President Dwight Eisenhower named her a delegate to the United Nations. She performed at President John F. Kennedy's inauguration and in 1963 received the Presidential Medal of Freedom. Anderson died Apr 8, 1993, at Portland, OR.

BLACK, HUGO LA FAYETTE: BIRTH ANNIVERSARY. Feb 27, 1886. Born in rural Alabama, Black was a lawyer, New Deal evangelist and US senator before serving on the US Supreme Court 1937–71. Black died on Sept 25, 1971, at Bethesda, MD, only one week after retiring from the bench.

DOMINICAN REPUBLIC: INDEPENDENCE DAY. Feb 27. National Day. Independence gained in 1844 with the withdrawal of Haitians, who had controlled the area for 22 years.

FARRELL, JAMES THOMAS: BIRTH ANNIVERSARY. Feb 27, 1904. American author, novelist and short-story writer, best known for his Studs Lonigan trilogy. Born at Chicago, IL, he died at New York, NY, Aug 22, 1979.

FLORIDA STRAWBERRY FESTIVAL. Feb 27–Mar 9. Plant City, FL. Celebration of winter strawberry harvest. For info: Florida Strawberry Fest, PO Drawer 1869, Plant City, FL 33564-1869. Phone: (813) 752-9194. Fax: (813) 754-4297. Web: www.flstrawberryfestival.com.

HAMILTON, ALICE: BIRTH ANNIVERSARY. Feb 27, 1869. American pathologist Alice Hamilton was born at New York, NY. She contributed to the workmen's compensation laws by reporting on the dangers to workers of industrial toxic substances. She taught at Harvard Medical School from 1919 until 1935. Hamilton died Sept 22, 1970, at Hadlyme, CT.

ITALY: FEAST OF THE INCAPPUCCIATI. Feb 27. Gradoli (near Viterbo). On the Thursday before Ash Wednesday, the members of the Confraternity of Purgatory make the rounds of the town dressed in traditional hooded robes, bearing a banner and walking to the beat of a drum. They stop at every house to collect foodstuffs in the name of the souls in purgatory; the food is then served at the banquet on Ash Wednesday.

KUWAIT LIBERATED AND 100-HOUR WAR ENDS: ANNIVERSARY. Feb 27, 1991. Allied troops entered Kuwait City, Kuwait, four days after launching a ground offensive (Feb 23) against the Iraqi forces who had invaded the country. President George H.W. Bush declared Kuwait to be liberated and ceased all offensive military operations in the Gulf War. The end of military operations at midnight EST came 100 hours after the beginning of the land attack. Feb 26 is commemorated as Liberation Day in Kuwait.

LONGFELLOW, HENRY WADSWORTH: BIRTH ANNIVERSARY. Feb 27, 1807. American poet and writer, born at Portland, ME. He is best remembered for his classic narrative poems, such as *The Song of Hiawatha, Paul Revere's Ride* and *The Wreck of the Hesperus.* Died at Cambridge, MA, Mar 24, 1882.

NATIONAL CHILI DAY. Feb 27. A day to recognize chili as an American staple and to celebrate our love for a great bowl of red—especially in the cold winter months. Annually, the last Thursday in February. For info: Doug Welsh, Hard Times Café, 110 Surrey Ln, Locust Grove, VA 22508. Phone: (703) 608-7725. Fax: (540) 972-4313. E-mail: dougwelsh101@gmail.com.

NATIONAL MONEY SHOW. Feb 27–Mar 2. Atlanta, GA. Numismatic education programs, exhibits and family activities. Buy, sell and trade coins, paper money, medals and tokens. For info: American Numismatic Assn, 818 N Cascade Ave, Colorado Springs, CO 80903. Phone: (800) 367-9723. E-mail: pr@money.org. Web: www.nationalmoneyshow.com.

SARAZEN, GENE: BIRTH ANNIVERSARY. Feb 27, 1902. Gene Sarazen, golfer, born Eugenio Saraceni at Harrison, NY. Sarazen was one of the game's foremost players and in his later years one of its popular goodwill ambassadors. The inventor of the sand wedge, Sarazen was also the first to win the modern grand slam (the Masters, US Open, British Open and PGA), although not in the same year. During the 1935 Masters, he hit one of golf's most famous shots, a four-wood for a double eagle on the par-5 15th hole of the final round. The shot enabled him to tie Craig Wood for the lead and defeat him in a play-off. Sarazen's last shot was the traditional ceremonial tee shot to open the 1999 Masters. Died at Marco Island, FL, May 13, 1999.

SHANGHAI COMMUNIQUÉ: ANNIVERSARY. Feb 27, 1972. On this day President Richard Nixon and Premier Chou En-lai released a joint communiqué (the Shanghai Communiqué) after Nixon's weeklong visit to the People's Republic of China. The two nations agreed to work toward normalizing relations. Stopping short of establishing diplomatic relations, this was the first step in that direction. The two nations entered full diplomatic relations on Jan 1, 1979, during the Carter administration.

TAYLOR, ELIZABETH: BIRTH ANNIVERSARY. Feb 27, 1932. Child star, film actress, international sex symbol and legendary philanthropist, born at London, England, to American parents. Taylor's talent as an actress was apparent early on with roles in several Lassie films, and her breakthrough part was in *National Velvet* (1944) at the age of 12. She became an enormously popular film star, winning Best Actress Oscars for *Who's Afraid of Virginia Woolf?* (1957) and *Butterfield 8* (1960), and earning nominations for three other roles. Her great beauty assured her a permanent place in the public eye, and her multiple romances, affairs, marriages and divorces were fuel for the tabloids for decades. In her later years, she launched very successful perfume and jewelry lines modeled on her great love of diamonds, and was known as a tireless campaigner for AIDS fundraising and research. She struggled with health problems through much of her life, including chronic back pain that could be traced to an injury she received filming *National Velvet.* She died at Los Angeles, CA, Mar 23, 2011.

TERRY, ELLEN: BIRTH ANNIVERSARY. Feb 27, 1847. Popular English actress (Alice) Ellen Terry was born at Coventry, Warwickshire. Terry was best known for her portrayal of Shakespeare's heroines, especially Portia, and as theatrical partner of English actor Henry Irving. Together she and Irving dominated both the British and American theater of their day. She died at Small Hythe, Kent, July 21, 1928.

TWENTY-SECOND AMENDMENT TO US CONSTITUTION (TWO-TERM LIMIT) RATIFICATION: ANNIVERSARY. Feb 27, 1951. After the four successive presidential terms of Franklin Roosevelt, the 22nd Amendment limited the tenure of presidential office to two terms.

BIRTHDAYS TODAY

Adam Baldwin, 52, actor ("Firefly," *My Bodyguard, Full Metal Jacket*), born Chicago, IL, Feb 27, 1962.

Josh Groban, 33, singer, born Los Angeles, CA, Feb 27, 1981.

Alan Guth, 67, physicist, born New Brunswick, NJ, Feb 27, 1947.

Maggie Hassan, 56, Governor of New Hampshire (D), born Boston, MA, Feb 27, 1958.

Howard Hesseman, 74, actor ("WKRP in Cincinnati," "Head of the Class"), born Salem, OR, Feb 27, 1940.

February 2014	S	M	T	W	T	F	S
							1
	2	3	4	5	6	7	8
	9	10	11	12	13	14	15
	16	17	18	19	20	21	22
	23	24	25	26	27	28	

Charlayne Hunter-Gault, 72, broadcast journalist, born Due West, SC, Feb 27, 1942.

Ralph Nader, 80, consumer advocate, lawyer, former presidential candidate, born Winsted, CT, Feb 27, 1934.

Grant Show, 51, actor ("Swingtown," "Melrose Place," "Ryan's Hope"), born Detroit, MI, Feb 27, 1963.

Joanne Woodward, 84, actress (Oscar for *The Three Faces of Eve; Mr and Mrs Bridge*), born Thomasville, GA, Feb 27, 1930.

James Ager Worthy, 53, former basketball player, born Gastonia, NC, Feb 27, 1961.

February 28 — Friday

DAY 59 **306 REMAINING**

ALLILUYEVA, SVETLANA: BIRTH ANNVERSARY. Feb 28, 1926. The only daughter of infamous Soviet Premier Josef Stalin, born at Moscow in the former Soviet Union. She had a distant and strained relationship with her father, and in 1967, leaving her children behind, she sought political asylum in the US during a trip to India. She settled in Arizona with the family of Frank Lloyd Wright, changed her name to Lana Peters, married and had another child. Never happy in the US, in the mid-1980s, desperate to see the children she had left behind, she returned to the USSR, but things went poorly. She returned to the US for good and died at Richland Center, WI, Nov 22, 2011.

BLONDIN, CHARLES: BIRTH ANNIVERSARY. Feb 28, 1824. Daring French acrobat and aerialist (whose real name was Jean François Gravelet), born at St. Omer, France. Especially remembered for his conquest of Niagara Falls on a tightrope. Died Feb 19, 1897, at London, England. See also: "Charles Blondin's Conquest of Niagara Falls: Anniversary" (June 30).

CANIFF, MILTON: BIRTH ANNIVERSARY. Feb 28, 1907. Creator of the comic strips "Terry and the Pirates®" and "Steve Canyon," Milton Caniff was born at Hillsboro, OH. His strips were noted for their fine draftsmanship and action/adventure story lines. Caniff died Apr 3, 1988, at New York City.

FLORAL DESIGN DAY. Feb 28. A day to commemorate floral designing as an art form. Annually, Feb 28. For info: Dr. Stephen Rittner, Rittners School of Floral Design, 345 Marlborough St, Boston, MA 02115. Phone: (617) 267-3824. E-mail: stevrt@tiac.net. Web: www.floralschool.com/floral-design-day.htm.

HECHT, BEN: BIRTH ANNIVERSARY. Feb 28, 1894. In the course of his career Ben Hecht wrote in many genres. His newspaper column, "1,001 Afternoons in Chicago," popularized human interest sketches. His play *The Front Page*, written with Charles MacArthur, was a hit on Broadway (1928) and on film (1931). He was a successful reporter and his first novel, *Eric Dorn*, resulted partly from his time reporting from Berlin after WWI. Hecht wrote or cowrote a number of successful movie scripts, including *Notorious* and *Wuthering Heights*. Born at New York City, he died there Apr 18, 1964.

LYON, MARY: BIRTH ANNIVERSARY. Feb 28, 1797. Mary Lyon, born near Buckland, MA, became a pioneer in the field of higher education for women. She founded Mount Holyoke Seminary (forerunner of Mount Holyoke College) in South Hadley, MA, in 1837 at a time when American women were educated primarily by ministers in classes held in their homes. Mount Holyoke was one of the first permanent women's colleges. Lyon died Mar 5, 1849, at South Hadley.

"M*A*S*H": THE FINAL EPISODE: ANNIVERSARY. Feb 28, 1983. Concluding a run of 255 episodes, this 2½-hour finale was the most-watched television show at that time—77 percent of the viewing public was tuned in. The show premiered in 1972. See also: "'M*A*S*H' TV Premiere: Anniversary" (Sept 17).

MINNELLI, VINCENTE: BIRTH ANNIVERSARY. Feb 28, 1903. Minnelli, director of the classic film musicals *Meet Me in St. Louis* (1944), *Gigi* (1958) and *An American in Paris* (1951), was born at Chicago, IL. He died July 25, 1986, at Beverly Hills, CA.

MONTAIGNE, MICHEL DE: BIRTH ANNIVERSARY. Feb 28, 1533. French essayist and philosopher, born at Perigord, France. "And if you have lived a day," he wrote in Book I of his *Essays*, "you have seen everything. One day is equal to all days. There is no other light, no other night. This sun, this moon, these stars, the way they are arranged, all is the very same your ancestors enjoyed and that will entertain your grandchildren." Died at Montaigne, France, Sept 13, 1592.

NATIONAL TOOTH FAIRY DAY. Feb 28. Why shouldn't the tooth fairy have her own day? Every kid in the country knows about her and every parent is her assistant. Celebrate the hard work she does on the graveyard shift and brush, floss and read books about the tooth fairy in her honor! For info: Katie Davis, PO Box 551, Bedford Hills, NY 10507. Phone: (914) 588-2992. E-mail: katiedavis@katiedavis.com.

NATO PLANES DOWN SERB JETS: 20th ANNIVERSARY. Feb 28, 1994. In the first military action by the North Atlantic Treaty Organization (NATO) in the two-year-old Bosnian civil war and the first combat action by NATO in its 45-year history, UN-designated American fighter planes shot down four of six Bosnian Serb jets operating in a no-fly zone.

PALME, OLOF: ASSASSINATION ANNIVERSARY. Feb 28, 1986. The popular prime minister of Sweden was shot to death as he left a movie theater in Stockholm with his wife. A courageous and dominant figure in Swedish politics, Palme, an aristocrat turned Socialist, had earned international respect. On the day of his death he had signed (with five other world leaders) an appeal to the leaders of the US and the Soviet Union to forgo nuclear testing until the next summit meeting. Born on Jan 30, 1927, Palme was the third European head of government to be assassinated since the beginning of WWII (the others: Prime Minister Armand Calinescu of Romania in 1939 and Prime Minister Luis Carrero Blanco of Spain in 1973).

SAINT OSWALD OF WORCESTER FEAST DAY. Feb 28. Bishop of Worcester, England, from 961 and archbishop of York from 972. Oswald died Feb 29, 992, but Feb 28 is generally celebrated as his feast day.

SIEGEL, "BUGSY": BIRTH ANNIVERSARY. Feb 28, 1906. The gangster Benjamin "Bugsy" Siegel was born in Brooklyn, NY. He was a contemporary of and in cahoots with Meyer Lansky and Lucky Luciano. Siegel moved to Hollywood, CA, in 1937 to lie low after committing a murder. Expanding on his petty gambling operations, Siegel began to construct a hotel and casino called The Flamingo in remote Las Vegas, NV. The hotel, opened in 1946, was initially a failure, until Lansky and Luciano poured more money into the venture. Siegel was shot and died at his girlfriend Virginia Hill's Hollywood home on June 20, 1947; no one was ever convicted of the murder.

TAIWAN: 228 MEMORIAL DAY (PEACE MEMORIAL DAY). Feb 28. A day of remembrance for those killed in a government crackdown following a popular protest that began Feb 27–28, 1947.

TENNIEL, JOHN: BIRTH ANNIVERSARY. Feb 28, 1820. Illustrator and cartoonist, born at London, England. Best remembered for his illustrations for Lewis Carroll's *Alice's Adventures in Wonderland*. Died at London, Feb 25, 1914.

228 INCIDENT: ANNIVERSARY. Feb 28, 1947. On Feb 27, 1947, Chinese agents confiscated the merchandise and life savings of a Taiwanese cigarette vendor because she was violating the state monopoly on tobacco, sparking a riot that left at least one dead. The following day Chinese troops turned machine guns on a peaceful demonstration against the corruption of the Chinese administration of Taiwan. In the ensuing days several cities and towns were taken over by native Taiwanese groups. A week later a large force of Chinese troops arrived to retake control of the island through a campaign of rape and summary public executions. Between 10,000 and 20,000 Taiwanese were killed. Called the "228 Incident" because of the date of the initial massacre, this grim episode in Taiwan's history is commemorated every Feb 28.

USS *PRINCETON* EXPLOSION: ANNIVERSARY. Feb 28, 1844. The newly built "war steamer," USS *Princeton*, cruising on the Potomac River with top government officials as its passengers, fired one of its guns (known, ironically, as the "Peacemaker") to demonstrate the latest in naval armament. The gun exploded, killing Abel P. Upshur, secretary of state; Thomas W. Gilmer, secretary of the navy; David Gardiner, of Gardiners Island, NY; and several others. Many were injured. The president of the US, John Tyler, was on board and narrowly escaped death.

BIRTHDAYS TODAY

Jason Aldean, 37, country singer, born Macon, GA, Feb 28, 1977.

Mario Gabrielle Andretti, 74, former auto racer, born Montona, Trieste, Italy, Feb 28, 1940.

Frank Gehry, 85, architect, born Toronto, ON, Canada, Feb 28, 1929.

Jelena Janković, 29, tennis player, born Belgrade, Yugoslavia (now Serbia), Feb 28, 1985.

Ali Larter, 38, actress ("Heroes," *Final Destination*), born Cherry Hill, NJ, Feb 28, 1976.

Robert Sean Leonard, 45, actor ("House," *The Manhattan Project, Dead Poets Society*), born Westwood, NJ, Feb 28, 1969.

Eric Lindros, 41, hockey player, born London, ON, Canada, Feb 28, 1973.

Bernadette Peters, 70, singer, actress (*Dames at Sea, Annie Get Your Gun*), born Queens, NY, Feb 28, 1944.

Tommy Tune, 75, actor, singer, dancer, director, choreographer (winner of 10 Tony Awards; *My One and Only, Grand Hotel, The Will Rogers Follies, Nine*), born Wichita Falls, TX, Feb 28, 1939.

John Turturro, 57, actor (*O Brother, Where Art Thou?*; *Quiz Show*), born Brooklyn, NY, Feb 28, 1957.

March

March 1 — Saturday

DAY 60 **305 REMAINING**

ALDO LEOPOLD WEEKEND. Mar 1–2. Statewide, Wisconsin. Communities across Wisconsin come together to demonstrate their individual and combined commitment to the "Land Ethic" put forth by renowned environmentalist Aldo Leopold in his famous book, *A Sand County Almanac*. He wrote, "That land is a community is the basic concept of ecology, but that land is to be loved and respected is an extension of ethics." Annually, the first full weekend in March. For info: The Aldo Leopold Foundation, PO Box 77, Baraboo, WI 53913. Phone: (608) 355-0279. Fax: (608) 356-7309. E-mail: jennifer@aldoleopold.org. Web: www.aldoleopold.org.

✦AMERICAN RED CROSS MONTH. Mar 1–31. Presidential Proclamation for Red Cross Month issued each year for March since 1943. Issued as American Red Cross Month since 1987.

THE ARRIVAL OF MARTIN PINZON: ANNIVERSARY. Mar 1, 1493. Martin Alonzo Pinzon (1440–1493), Spanish shipbuilder, navigator and co-owner of the *Niña* and the *Pinta*, accompanied Christopher Columbus on his first voyage, as commander of the *Pinta*. Storms separated the ships on their return voyage, and the *Pinta* first touched land at Bayona, Spain, where Pinzon gave Europe its first news of the discovery of the New World (before Columbus's landing at Palos). Pinzon's brother, Vicente Yanez Pinzon, was commander of the third caravel of the expedition, the *Niña*.

ARTICLES OF CONFEDERATION RATIFIED: ANNIVERSARY. Mar 1, 1781. This compact made among the original 13 states had been adopted by Congress Nov 15, 1777, and submitted to the states for ratification Nov 17, 1777. Maryland was the last state to approve, Feb 27, 1781, but Congress named Mar 1, 1781, as the day of formal ratification. The Articles of Confederation remained the supreme law of the nation until Mar 4, 1789, when the US Constitution went into effect.

"BELIEVE IT OR NOT" TV PREMIERE: 65th ANNIVERSARY. Mar 1, 1949. The series was originally a radio show based on Robert L. Ripley's comic strips describing curiosities. Both the radio program and the NBC TV show were hosted by Robert Ripley until his death in 1949. Robert St. John became Ripley's successor. ABC re-created the show in 1982 with Jack Palance as host.

BOSNIA AND HERZEGOVINA: INDEPENDENCE DAY. Mar 1. Commemorates independence in 1992.

BRADFORD, WILLIAM: BIRTH ANNIVERSARY. Mar 1, 1590. Born at Austerfield, Yorkshire, England, Bradford is best known as a Pilgrim Father and governor of Plymouth Colony. Sailed on the *Mayflower* in 1620. He signed the Mayflower Compact and was elected second governor of the colony after John Carver died; he was subsequently reelected 30 times. Active and vigorous, Bradford was responsible for the financial burdens of the colony until his death at Plymouth, MA, May 9, 1657. His book *Of Plymouth Plantation*, posthumously published in 1856, is a seminal primary source document of the colony's history.

BRAZIL: CARNIVAL. Mar 1–4. Especially in Rio de Janeiro, this carnival is said to be one of the last great folk festivals and the big annual event in the life of Brazilians. Begins on Saturday night before Ash Wednesday and continues through Shrove Tuesday.

CARAY, HARRY: 100th BIRTH ANNIVERSARY. Mar 1, 1914. Born Harry Christopher Carabina at St. Louis, MO (some sources say 1917 or 1920). Caray began his baseball broadcasting career with the St. Louis Cardinals in 1945. He then was the announcer for the Oakland A's, the Chicago White Sox and finally the Chicago Cubs. He became a legend at Wrigley Field with his seventh-inning stretch "Take Me Out to the Ball Game" and his quirky phrase "Holy Cow!" Caray was inducted into the Broadcasters Hall of Fame in 1989. Died at Rancho Mirage, CA, Feb 18, 1998.

CHASE'S DEADLINE APPROACHING. Mar 1. Time to plan ahead. Schedule 2015 celebrations and observances and submit information to *Chase's Calendar of Events 2015* by Apr 15, 2014. Sponsors/information suppliers of events in this book should have received confirmation/revision forms for the 2015 edition by this time. To submit new entries for consideration, go to www.chases.com. Send to: Editor, Chase's Calendar of Events, McGraw-Hill Professional, 303 E Wacker Dr, Suite 2000, Chicago, IL 60601.

CHOPIN, FRÉDÉRIC: BIRTH ANNIVERSARY. Mar 1, 1810. Pianist and influential composer of gorgeous piano works, born at Warsaw, Poland. He died at Paris, France, on Oct 17, 1849, after a 10-year battle with tuberculosis.

COLIC AWARENESS MONTH. Mar 1–31. Established in 2012, a month to broaden awareness of colic, to educate parents about safer soothing techniques for baby and to provide a resource for families. Colic is a condition where otherwise healthy newborn babies cry for more than three hours a day, for three or more days a week, for more than three weeks in a row. For info: Born Free. Phone: (800) 268-6237. Web: www.newbornfree.com/colic-awareness-month.

COLORECTAL CANCER EDUCATION AND AWARENESS MONTH. Mar 1–31. To educate consumers, patients and professionals regarding the need for early diagnosis, education and treatment of colorectal cancer. For info: Fred S. Mayer, RPh, MPH, Pharmacists Planning Service, Inc (PPSI), c/o Pharmacy Council on Colorectal Cancer Education, PO Box 6760, San Rafael, CA 94903. Phone: (415) 479-8628 or (415) 302-7351. Fax: (415) 479-8608. E-mail: ppsi@aol.com. Web: www.ppsinc.org.

CREDIT EDUCATION MONTH. Mar 1–31. Sponsored by Credit Professionals International and the Credit Education Resources Foundation, this event is designed to remind consumers and educators, as well as business and government leaders, of the importance of developing the skills needed to manage their finances efficiently and effectively. For info: Charlotte Rancilio, Credit Professionals Intl, 10726 Manchester Rd, Ste 210, St. Louis, MO 63122. Phone: (314) 821-9393. Fax: (314) 821-7171. E-mail: creditpro@creditprofessionals.org. Web: www.creditprofessionals.org.

ELLISON, RALPH WALDO: 100th BIRTH ANNIVERSARY. Mar 1, 1914. American writer and educator, born at Oklahoma City, OK. Author of the acclaimed novel *Invisible Man* (1952), the story of a young black man's struggle for his own identity in the face of rejection from both whites and blacks. Quickly recognized as a classic of 20th-century literature, it won the National Book Award in 1953. While only one of his novels was published, Ellison published collections of his essays, reviews and stories in *Shadow and Act* (1964) and *Going to the Territory* (1986). He died Apr 16, 1994, at New York City.

EMPLOYEE SPIRIT MONTH. Mar 1–31. This month seeks to inspire the most vital part of any organization: the employees. Motivate your employees this month—create employee spirit. Annually, the month of March. For info and free tips, newsletter and employee morale assessment: Harriet Meyerson, The Confidence Center. Phone: (214) 373-0080. Fax: (469) 854-2957. E-mail: Harriet@ConfidenceCenter.com. Web: www.ConfidenceCenter.com.

EXPANDING GIRLS' HORIZONS IN SCIENCE AND ENGINEERING MONTH. Mar 1–31. Expanding Your Horizons Network is an international nonprofit that encourages middle- and high-school girls to pursue careers in science, technology, engineering and mathematics. During the month of March, the organization promotes increased awareness of girls excelling in these areas. For info: Expanding Your Horizons Network, 5000 MacArthur Blvd, Oakland, CA 94613. Phone: (510) 430-2222. Fax: (510) 430-2090. E-mail: monika@expandingyourhorizons.org. Web: www.expandingyourhorizons.org.

FLORAL CITY STRAWBERRY FESTIVAL. Mar 1–2. Floral City, FL. Arts and crafts festival, children's activities, princess pageants, entertainment, car show and, of course, tons of strawberries! Annually, the first full weekend in March. Est attendance: 28,000. For info: Citrus County Chamber of Commerce, 28 NW US 19, Crystal River, FL 34428. Phone: (352) 795-3149. Web: www.citruscountychamber.com.

FRENCH WEST INDIES: CARNIVAL. Mar 1–5. Martinique. For five days ending on Ash Wednesday, business comes to a halt. Streets spill over with parties and parades. A Carnival Queen is elected. On Dimanche Gras, or Fat Sunday, revelers dressed as red devils parade in the streets. King Carnival is "buried" on Ash Wednesday.

GAINES, WILLIAM M.: BIRTH ANNIVERSARY. Mar 1, 1922. The magazine *Mad*, especially popular in the 1960s and 1970s, was founded and published by William Gaines. Alfred E. Neuman, the loony, freckle-faced mascot of the publication, became a pop-culture hero. The magazine, known for its parodies of movies, comic strips and celebrities as well as its satire of politics and social mores, greatly influenced dozens of humorists. Gaines was born at the Bronx, NY. He died June 3, 1992, at New York City.

HUMORISTS ARE ARTISTS MONTH (HAAM). Mar 1–31. To recognize the important contributions made by various types of humorists to the high art of living. For info: Lone Star Publications of Humor, 8452 Fredericksburg Rd, PMB 103, San Antonio, TX 78229. E-mail: lspubs@aol.com.

ICELAND: BEER DAY. Mar 1. Reykjavik. This event began on Mar 1, 1989, when a 75-year prohibition of beer was lifted. Features celebrations in pubs and restaurants all over Reykjavik.

IDITAROD TRAIL SLED DOG RACE. Mar 1–16. 42nd running of "The Last Great Race on Earth" (first run on Mar 3, 1973). 1,000 miles through Alaskan wilderness from Anchorage to Nome, AK, along the historic Iditarod Trail. More than 60 16-dog teams competing. Finishers' banquet on Sunday, Mar 16. Est attendance: 25,000. For info: Iditarod Trail Committee, PO Box 870800, Wasilla, AK 99687. Phone: (907) 376-5155, ext 108. Fax: (907) 373-6998. Web: www.iditarod.com.

INTERNATIONAL IDEAS MONTH. Mar 1–31. Everybody has ideas! Many people need to be encouraged or motivated or need to build skills in order to communicate and get their ideas out in the open for consideration and/or action. This month is dedicated to all ideas—large, small, great, not-so-great, past and current as well as ideas yet to come. Without constant new ideas, progress and people stagnate. For info: Sylvia Henderson, Springboard Training, PO Box 588, Olney, MD 20830-0588. Phone: (301) 260-1538. E-mail: sylvia@springboardtraining.com.

March 2014	S	M	T	W	T	F	S
							1
	2	3	4	5	6	7	8
	9	10	11	12	13	14	15
	16	17	18	19	20	21	22
	23	24	25	26	27	28	29
	30	31					

INTERNATIONAL LISTENING AWARENESS MONTH. Mar 1–31. Dedicated to learning more about the impact that listening has on all human activity. To promote the study, development and teaching of effective listening in all settings. For info: Nanette Johnson-Curiskis, Intl Listening Assn, PO Box 164, Belle Plaine, MN 56011. Phone: (952) 594-5697. Fax: (952) 856-5100. Web: www.listen.org.

INTERNATIONAL MIRTH MONTH. Mar 1–31. The merry month of March is set aside to encourage more mirthful moments. Its focus is to show people how to use humor to deal with not-so-funny stuff. Mirth Month was founded by Allen Klein, professional speaker and past president of the Association for Applied and Therapeutic Humor (www.aath.org). Free monthly mirth e-mail memo available; request via e-mail. For info: Allen Klein. Phone: (415) 431-1913. Fax: (415) 431-8600. E-mail: humor@allenklein.com. Web: www.allenklein.com.

✦IRISH-AMERICAN HERITAGE MONTH. Mar 1–31. Presidential Proclamation called for by House Joint Resolution 401 (PL 103–379).

JAPAN: OMIZUTORI (WATER-DRAWING FESTIVAL). Mar 1–14. Todaiji, Nara. At midnight, a solemn rite is performed in the flickering light of pine torches. People rush for sparks from the torches, which are believed to have magic power against evil. Most spectacular on the night of Mar 12. The ceremony of drawing water is observed at 2 AM on Mar 13, to the accompaniment of ancient Japanese music.

KLONDIKE DAYS. Mar 1–2. Northland Pines High School and Rocking W Stables, Eagle River, WI. A re-creation of primitive camps used by early buck-skinners, pioneers, trappers and traders. Additional attractions include a two-day horse weight-pull reminiscent of Wisconsin's logging days, a chainsaw carving competition, a Native American cultural presentation featuring a ceremonial dance exhibition, lumberjack competition, craft show, dog weight-pull and much more. Wisconsin's premier multifaceted winter festival. Est attendance: 12,000. For info: Christine Schilling, Exec Dir, Klondike Days, Inc, PO Box 1166, Eagle River, WI 54521. Phone: (800) 359-6315. Web: www.klondikedays.org.

KOKOSCHKA, OSKAR: BIRTH ANNIVERSARY. Mar 1, 1886. Born at Pochlarn, Austria. Avant-garde artist, playwright, teacher and humanitarian whose work evoked violent reaction. After viewing a 1911 exhibition of Kokoschka's work, the Archduke Franz Ferdinand is reported to have declared, "This man deserves to have every bone in his body broken." Kokoschka's work was featured in a 1937 Nazi exhibit of "Degenerate Art." Died at Montreux, Switzerland, Feb 22, 1980.

KOREA: SAMILJOL or INDEPENDENCE MOVEMENT DAY. Mar 1. Koreans observe the anniversary of the independence movement against Japanese colonial rule in 1919.

KREWE OF ENDYMION PARADE. Mar 1. New Orleans, LA. Formed in 1966, the Krewe of Endymion puts on a spectacular carnival parade the Saturday before Mardi Gras. For info: Krewe of Endymion. Web: www.endymion.org.

LAND MINE BAN: 15th ANNIVERSARY. Mar 1, 1999. A United Nations treaty banning land mines took effect on this date. To date 161 nations have signed the treaty; the US, Russia, India and China (among 35 nations) have not. For info: International Committee to Ban Landmines. Web: www.icbl.org.

LINDBERGH KIDNAPPING: ANNIVERSARY. Mar 1, 1932. Twenty-month-old Charles A. Lindbergh, Jr, the son of Charles A. and Anne Morrow Lindbergh, was kidnapped from their home at Hopewell, NJ. Even though the Lindberghs paid a $50,000 ransom, their child's body was found in a wooded area less than five miles from the family home on May 12. Bruno Richard Hauptmann was charged with the murder and kidnapping. He was executed in the electric chair Apr 3, 1936. As a result of the kidnapping and murder, the Crime Control Act was passed on May 18, 1934, authorizing the death penalty for kidnappers who take their victims across state lines.

MALIGNANT HYPERTHERMIA AWARENESS AND TRAINING MONTH. Mar 1–31. To raise awareness of malignant hyperthermia, a reaction to commonly used volatile gaseous anesthesia (enflurane, sevoflurane, isoflurane). Unless the patient receives rapid emergency therapy from medical professionals who have been trained to recognize and treat MH quickly, death can result in minutes. For info: Michael Wesolowski, MHAUS, PO Box 1069, Sherburne, NY 13460. Phone: (607) 674-7901. Fax: (607) 674-7910. E-mail: michael@mhaus.org. Web: www.mhaus.org.

MALTA: CARNIVAL. Mar 1–4. Valletta. Festival dates from 1535 when Knights of St. John of Jerusalem introduced Carnival at Malta. Dancing (featuring the sword dance, or *Il Parata*, and other national dances), bands, decorated trucks and grotesque masks. Annually, the Saturday through Tuesday before Ash Wednesday.

MILLER, GLENN: BIRTH ANNIVERSARY. Mar 1, 1904. American bandleader and composer (Alton) Glenn Miller was born at Clarinda, IA. He enjoyed great popularity preceding and during WWII. His hit recordings included "Moonlight Serenade," "String of Pearls," "Jersey Bounce" and "Sleepy Lagoon." Major Miller, leader of the US Army Air Force band, disappeared Dec 15, 1944, over the English Channel, on a flight to Paris, where he was scheduled to give a show. There were many explanations of his disappearance, but 41 years later, in December 1985, crew members of an aborted RAF bombing said they believed they had seen Miller's plane go down, the victim of bombs being jettisoned by the RAF over the English Channel.

MOON PHASE: NEW MOON. Mar 1. Moon enters New Moon phase at 3:00 AM, EST.

MUSIC IN OUR SCHOOLS MONTH. Mar 1–31. To increase public awareness of the importance of music education as part of a balanced curriculum. Additional information and awareness items are available. For info: Natl Assn for Music Education, 1806 Robert Fulton Dr, Reston, VA 20191. Phone: (800) 336-3768. Web: www.nafme.org.

NATIONAL CAFFEINE AWARENESS MONTH. Mar 1–31. 11th annual. Reduce dependency on caffeine through education. Seminars and other events focus on coffee alternatives and on the harm caffeine causes. For info: The Caffeine Awareness Association, 93 S Jackson St, Ste 46673, Seattle, WA 98104. Phone: (815) 572-8007. E-mail: worthwhilecause@gmail.com. Web: www.caffeineawareness.org.

NATIONAL CHEERLEADING WEEK. Mar 1–7. Various cheer activites conducted on a daily basis throughout the week. Annually, Mar 1–7. For info: Linda Lundy, 59 County Rd 3474, Cleveland, TX 77327. Phone: (877) 68-CHEER or (281) 399-8357. E-mail: linda@cheerintegrity.com. Web: www.ncwinfo.com or www.nationalcheerleadingweek.com.

NATIONAL CLEAN UP YOUR IRS ACT MONTH. Mar 1–31. Special month to focus on resolving problems with IRS. Specialists offer "clean-up" gifts to taxpayers in need of assistance. Sponsored by the American Society of Tax Problem Solvers, a national nonprofit professional organization. For info: Lawrence Lawler, American Society of Tax Problem Solvers, 2250 Wehrle Dr, Ste 3, Williamsville, NY 14221. Phone: (716) 630-1650. Fax: (716) 630-1651. E-mail: larry@astps.org. Web: www.astps.org.

NATIONAL COLORECTAL CANCER AWARENESS MONTH. Mar 1–31. To generate widespread awareness about colorectal cancer and to encourage people to learn more about how to prevent the disease through a healthy lifestyle and regular screening. Observed since 1999, founding partners include the Prevent Cancer Foundation, the American Society for Gastrointestinal Endoscopy, the National Colorectal Cancer Roundtable and The Foundation for Digestive Health and Nutrition. For info: Colon Cancer Alliance, 1025 Vermont Ave NW, Ste 1066, Washington, DC 20005. Web: www.ccalliance.org. Or Centers for Disease Control and Prevention. Web: www.cdc.gov/cancer/colorectal.

NATIONAL CRAFT MONTH. Mar 1–31. Promoting the fun and creativity of crafts and hobbies. For info: Craft & Hobby Association, 319 E 54th St, Elmwood Park, NJ 07407. Phone: (201) 835-1207. Fax: (201) 835-1279. E-mail: cre8time@craftandhobby.org. Web: www.craftandhobby.org or www.cre8time.org.

NATIONAL EYE DONOR MONTH. Mar 1–31. Observed in March since 1983. For info: Eye Bank Assn of America, 1015 18th St NW, Ste 1010, Washington, DC 20036. Phone: (202) 775-4999. Web: www.restoresight.org.

NATIONAL FROZEN FOOD MONTH. Mar 1–31. Promotes national awareness of the convenience, quality and nutritional benefits of frozen foods. Annually, the month of March. For info: Julie Henderson, VP Communications, Natl Frozen & Refrigerated Foods Assn, 4755 Linglestown Rd, Ste 300, Harrisburg, PA 17112. Phone: (717) 657-8601. Fax: (717) 657-9862. E-mail: info@nfraweb.org. Web: www.nfraweb.org.

NATIONAL HORSE PROTECTION DAY. Mar 1. A day to raise awareness through public education about the plight of horses in America—the abuse, neglect, homelessness and slaughter. This day also encourages adoption events around the nation to help unwanted horses find a forever home. For info: Colleen Paige, Animal Miracle Foundation, 4804 NW Bethany Blvd, Ste 12-197, Portland, OR 97229. Phone: (323) 552-9941. E-mail: info@animalmiraclefoundation.org. Web: www.horseprotectionday.com.

NATIONAL KIDNEY MONTH. Mar 1–31. Kidney disease may often be silent for many years until it has reached an advanced stage. The National Kidney Foundation urges everyone to get regular checkups that include tests for blood pressure, blood sugar, urine protein and kidney function. World Kidney Day is Mar 13. For info: Ellie Schlam, National Kidney Foundation, 30 E 33rd St, New York, NY 10016. Phone: (800) 622-9010 or (212) 889-2210. Web: www.kidney.org.

NATIONAL MULTIPLE SCLEROSIS EDUCATION AND AWARENESS MONTH. Mar 1–31. This month focuses on raising awareness of and compassion for those diagnosed with multiple sclerosis. A series of national events takes place, and educational materials and publications are circulated upon request from the Multiple Sclerosis Foundation. For info: Multiple Sclerosis Foundation, 6520 N Andrews Ave, Fort Lauderdale, FL 33309-2130. Phone: (800) 225-6495. Fax: (954) 938-8708. E-mail: admin@msfocus.org. Web: www.msfocus.org.

NATIONAL NUTRITION MONTH®. Mar 1–31. To educate consumers about the importance of good nutrition by providing the latest practical information on how simple it can be to eat healthfully. For info: Academy of Nutrition and Dietetics, 120 S Riverside Plaza, Ste 2000, Chicago, IL 60606-6995. Phone: (312) 899-0040. Fax: (312) 899-4739. E-mail: nnm@eatright.org. Web: www.eatright.org.

NATIONAL PEANUT MONTH. Mar 1–31. This month celebrates one of America's favorite foods! Roasted in the shell for a ballpark snack, ground into peanut butter or tossed in a salad or stir-fry, peanuts find their way into everything from breakfast to dessert. National Peanut Month had its beginnings as National Peanut Week in 1941. It was expanded into a monthlong celebration in 1974. For info: Southern Peanut Growers, 1025 Sugar Pike Way, Canton, GA 30115. Web: www.peanutbutterlovers.com.

NATIONAL PIG DAY. Mar 1. To accord to the pig its rightful, though generally unrecognized, place as one of humankind's most intelligent and useful domesticated animals. Annually, Mar 1. For further information send SASE to: Ellen Stanley, 7006 Miami Ave, Lubbock, TX 79413.

NATIONAL SOCIAL WORK MONTH. Mar 1–31. First commissioned by President Reagan, the National Association of Social Workers and its members spend this month celebrating the accomplish-

ments of social workers and the services they provide to vulnerable populations. For info: Natl Assn of Social Workers, 750 First St NE, Ste 700, Washington, DC 20002-4241. Phone: (202) 408-8600. Fax: (202) 336-8307. E-mail: media@naswdc.org. Web: www.naswdc.org.

NATIONAL UMBRELLA MONTH. Mar 1–31. In honor of one of the most versatile and underrated inventions of the human race, this month is dedicated to the purchase of, use of and conversation about umbrellas. Annually, the month of March. (Originated by Thomas Edward Knibb.)

NATIONAL WOMEN'S HISTORY MONTH. Mar 1–31. A time for reexamining and celebrating the wide range of women's contributions and achievements that are too often overlooked in the telling of US history. 2014 theme: "Celebrating Women of Character, Courage and Commitment." For info: Natl Women's History Project, 1855 Cooper Dr, Santa Rosa, CA 95404. Phone: (707) 636-2888. Fax: (707) 636-2909. E-mail: nwhp@aol.com. Web: www.nwhp.org.

NATIONAL WRITE A LETTER OF APPRECIATION WEEK. Mar 1–7. Send a letter expressing gratitude to others, acknowledging the goodness one finds all around. For info: Mary McManus, 1504 N Richmond Rd, McHenry, IL 60050-1410. Phone: (815) 344-4934. Fax: (815) 344-4934. E-mail: faithhealer@ameritech.net.

NATURAL BRIDGE BATTLE REENACTMENT. Mar 1–2. Tallahassee, FL. 37th annual. Reenactment of the Confederate army's victory at the Natural Bridge site, which kept Tallahassee (the state capital) from falling into Union hands. Annually, the first full weekend in March. Est attendance: 4,500. For info: Natural Bridge Battlefield Historic State Park, 1022 DeSoto Park Dr, Tallahassee, FL 32301. Phone: (850) 922-6007. Web: www.floridastateparks.org/naturalbridge.

NEBRASKA: ADMISSION DAY: ANNIVERSARY. Mar 1. Became 37th state in 1867.

NENANA TRIPOD RAISING FESTIVAL. Mar 1–2. Nenana, AK. Festival centers around the guessing of the exact time of the ice breakup on the Tanana River. Highlights include the Raising of the Tripod, Nenana Banana Eating, sled dog races, arm wrestling, turkey shoot, craft bazaar and much more. Est attendance: 2,500. For info: Nenana Ice Classic, PO Box 272, Nenana, AK 99760. Phone: (907) 832-5446. Fax: (907) 832-5888. E-mail: iceclassic@alaska.net. Web: www.nenanaakiceclassic.com.

OHIO: ADMISSION DAY: ANNIVERSARY. Mar 1. Became 17th state in 1803.

OPTIMISM MONTH. Mar 1–31. To encourage people to boost their optimism. Research proves optimists achieve better health, greater prosperity and more happiness than pessimists. Use this monthlong celebration to practice optimism and turn optimism into a delightful, permanent habit. Free tip sheets available. For info: Dr. Michael Mercer and Dr. Maryann Troiani, The Mercer Group, Inc, 25597 Drake Rd, Barrington, IL 60010. Phone: (847) 382-0690. E-mail: drmercer@mercersystems.com. Web: www.DrMercer.com.

PARAGUAY: NATIONAL HEROES' DAY. Mar 1. National holiday. Honors those who have died for the country, especially Mariscal Francisco Solano López, who died Mar 1, 1870.

PEACE CORPS FOUNDED: ANNIVERSARY. Mar 1, 1961. President John F. Kennedy signed an executive order officially establishing the Peace Corps on this date. The Peace Corps has sent more than 200,000 volunteers to 139 countries to help people help themselves. The volunteers assist in projects such as health, education, water sanitation, agriculture, nutrition and forestry. For info: Peace Corps. Web: www.peacecorps.gov.

March 2014	S	M	T	W	T	F	S
							1
	2	3	4	5	6	7	8
	9	10	11	12	13	14	15
	16	17	18	19	20	21	22
	23	24	25	26	27	28	29
	30	31					

PHILADELPHIA FLOWER SHOW. Mar 1–9. PA Convention Center, Philadelphia, PA. The largest flower show in the US. The premier event of its kind in the world. 2014 theme: "Articulture!" Est attendance: 265,000. For info: Pennsylvania Horticultural Society, 100 N 20th St, 5th Fl, Philadelphia, PA 19103-1495. Phone: (215) 988-8800. Web: www.theflowershow.com.

PLAN A SOLO VACATION DAY. Mar 1. Wanderlust stirring? Tired of waiting for friends' timetables to coincide with yours? Unable to agree with your spouse on the perfect vacation? This is the day to follow the lead of 34.8 million US adults who have taken a vacation by themselves in the past three years. Indulge yourself by spending the day checking out your growing opportunities for solo travel, including tours, cruises and travel clubs that either match roommates or charge little or no supplement. For info: Marya Alexander, Solo Travel Portal, PO Box 2664, Carlsbad, CA 92018. Phone: (760) 720-1011. E-mail: editor@solotravelportal.com. Web: www.solotravelportal.com.

PLAY-THE-RECORDER MONTH. Mar 1–31. American Recorder Society members all over the continent will celebrate the organization's annual Play-the-Recorder Month by performing in public places such as libraries, bookstores, museums and shopping malls. Some will offer workshops on playing the recorder or demonstrations in schools. Founded in 1939, the ARS is the membership organization for all recorder players, from amateurs to leading professionals. Annually, the month of March. For info: American Recorder Society, 10000 Watson Rd, Ste I-L-7, St. Louis, MO 63126. Phone: (314) 966-4082. Fax: (866) 773-1538. E-mail: ars.recorder@americanrecorder.org. Web: www.americanrecorder.org.

POISON PREVENTION AWARENESS MONTH. Mar 1–31. To educate parents, grandparents, schoolchildren and PTAs about accidental poisoning and how to prevent it. PPSI is a nonprofit organization. Annually, the month of March. For info: Fred S. Mayer, RPh, MPH, Pharmacists Planning Service, Inc (PPSI), PO Box 6760, San Rafael, CA 94903. Phone: (415) 479-8628 or (415) 302-7351. Fax: (415) 479-8608. E-mail: ppsi@aol.com. Web: www.ppsinc.org.

RAID ON RICHMOND: 150th ANNIVERSARY. Mar 1, 1864. Believing the Confederate capital of Richmond, VA, to be lightly fortified, President Abraham Lincoln ordered a surprise raid to capture the city and free Union prisoners. Federal troops under General Judson Kilpatrick and Colonel Ulric Dahlgren led the attack on this date but failed when the plan was discovered by Southern forces. In the wake of their retreat, Dahlgren was killed, and two documents were discovered on his body. The incriminating documents contained plans to burn the city and kill Confederate president Jefferson Davis and his cabinet. Confederate general Robert E. Lee complained to the Union commander, George Meade, but a federal investigation was inconclusive.

RED CROSS MONTH. Mar 1–31. To make the public aware of American Red Cross service in the community. There are nearly 600 Red Cross offices nationwide; each local office plans its own activities. For info on activities in your area, contact your local Red Cross. For info: American Red Cross. Web: www.redcross.org.

REFIRED, NOT RETIRED, DAY. Mar 1. This is a day for retirees (or those soon to be retired) to decide that this is the beginning of "Life, Part II," and to commit to making this an exciting adventure. For info: Phyllis May, 1800 Atlantic Blvd, Ste A-312, Key West, FL 33040. Phone: (305) 295-7501. E-mail: pmaykeys@bellsouth.net. Web: www.refiredretired.com.

ROZELLE, PETE: BIRTH ANNIVERSARY. Mar 1, 1926. Alvin Ray ("Pete") Rozelle, commissioner of the National Football League, born at South Gate, CA. Rozelle began his career in the public relations department of the Los Angeles Rams, became general manager and was elected commissioner in 1960. He built the NFL into a sporting power through the use of television. He helped engineer the NFL's merger with the American Football League, created the Super Bowl as America's greatest sports extravaganza, conceived the idea for Monday Night Football and persuaded NFL owners to accept revenue sharing. Died at Rancho Santa Fe, CA, Dec 6, 1996.

SAINT-GAUDENS, AUGUSTUS: BIRTH ANNIVERSARY. Mar 1, 1848. Sculptor, born at Dublin, Ireland. His works include the statue of Lincoln in Lincoln Park, Chicago, and of Admiral Farragut in Madison Square, New York. Saint-Gaudens died at Cornish, NH, Aug 3, 1907.

SALEM WITCH HYSTERIA BEGINS: ANNIVERSARY. Mar 1, 1692. The Massachusetts Bay Colony village of Salem had experienced a strange February in which several teenaged girls exhibited bizarre behavior and attributed their ailments to witches. Three women were then arrested on Feb 29, 1692. One of the accused, Tituba, a West Indian slave, broke down under questioning on Mar 1 and admitted to being a witch. Soon the teenaged girls accused four other residents, and by the end of April, 19 women had been accused of witchcraft and were languishing in jail—including a four-year-old child. Massachusetts governor Sir William Phips, seeking to control the growing terror, ordered trials held. In October, the special court was dissolved after growing protests of the trials' unjust proceedings. By then, 19 people had been hanged, 5 had died in jail, 1 had been tortured to death and more than 150 had been imprisoned. Two dogs were also executed. On Jan 14, 1697, Judge Samuel Sewall publicly apologized and a court-ordered day of atonement began. In 1711, all those accused of witchcraft were pardoned by the colony's legislature. See also: "Salem Witch Trials Begin: Anniversary" (June 2).

SAVE YOUR VISION MONTH. Mar 1–31. To remind Americans of the importance of eye health and regular exams. For info: American Optometric Assn, 243 N Lindbergh Blvd, St. Louis, MO 63141. Phone: (800) 365-2219. Web: www.aoa.org.

SHORE, DINAH: BIRTH ANNIVERSARY. Mar 1, 1917. American radio and television personality Dinah Shore was born Frances Rose Shore at Winchester, TN. In addition to recording many hit songs in the 1930s and 1940s, she was one of the first women to be successful as a television host, beginning in the 1950s with the "Dinah Shore Chevy Show." She received 10 Emmys before she died Feb 24, 1994, at Beverly Hills, CA.

SING WITH YOUR CHILD MONTH. Mar 1–31. This month is a special time to celebrate the joy of families singing, dancing and making music together. Family music-making supports children developmentally and helps form everlasting family bonds. For info: Publicity Manager, 66 Witherspoon St, Princeton, NJ 08542. Phone: (800) 728-2692. Fax: (609) 466-9123. Web: www.musictogether.com/singmonth.

SLAYTON, DONALD "DEKE" K.: 90th BIRTH ANNIVERSARY. Mar 1, 1924. Deke Slayton, longtime chief of flight operations at the Johnson Space Center, was born at Sparta, WI. Slayton was a member of the Mercury Seven, the original group of young military aviators chosen to inaugurate America's sojourn into space. Unfortunately, a heart problem prevented him from participating in any of the Mercury flights. When in 1971 the heart condition mysteriously went away, Slayton flew on the last Apollo mission. The July 1975 flight, involving a docking with a Soviet *Soyuz* spacecraft, symbolized a momentary thaw in relations between the two nations. During his years as chief of flight operations, Slayton directed astronaut training and selected the crews for nearly all missions. He died June 13, 1993, at League City, TX.

SWITZERLAND: CHALANDRA MARZ. Mar 1. Engadine. Springtime traditional event when costumed young people, ringing bells and cracking whips, drive away the demons of winter.

WALES: SAINT DAVID'S DAY. Mar 1. Celebrates patron saint of Wales (Dewi Sant). Welsh tradition calls for the wearing of a leek on this day.

WILL EISNER WEEK. Mar 1–7. An annual celebration promoting graphic novels, literacy, free speech awareness and the legacy of legendary graphic artist and storyteller Will Eisner (1917–2005). Annually, Mar 1–7, which encompasses Eisner's birthday on Mar 6. For info: Will Eisner Studios, Inc. E-mail: info@willeisner.com. Web: www.willeisner.com.

✦WOMEN'S HISTORY MONTH. Mar 1–31.

WORKPLACE EYE WELLNESS MONTH. Mar 1–31. Can you see the dangers at your workplace? Accidents at work are a major cause of preventable blindness. For info: Prevent Blindness America®, 211 W Wacker Dr, Ste 1700, Chicago, IL 60606. Phone: (800) 331-2020. E-mail: info@preventblindness.org. Web: www.preventblindness.org.

WORLD COMPLIMENT DAY. Mar 1. Most positive day in the year! Appreciate with words instead of gifts—brighten everyone's day. Nobody wins commercially, but everyone wins emotionally. First celebration in 2011 was observed by participants from more than 50 nations. Annually, Mar 1. For info: Hans Poortvliet, Baanvak 12, Aalsmeer, Netherlands 1431 LK. E-mail: hans@withcompliments.com. Web: www.worldcomplimentday.com.

YELLOWSTONE NATIONAL PARK ESTABLISHED: ANNIVERSARY. Mar 1, 1872. The first area in the world to be designated a national park, most of Yellowstone is in Wyoming, with small sections in Montana and Idaho. It was established by an act of Congress.

YOUTH ART MONTH. Mar 1–31. Since 1961. To emphasize the value and importance of art and art education in the development of all children and young people. For info: Council for Art Education, Inc, 99 Derby St, Ste 200, Hingham, MA 02043. Phone: (781) 556-1044. Fax: (781) 207-5550. Web: acminet.org.

BIRTHDAYS TODAY

Catherine Bach, 60, actress ("The Dukes of Hazzard"), born Warren, OH, Mar 1, 1954.

Javier Bardem, 45, actor (Oscar for *No Country for Old Men*; *Skyfall, Before Night Falls*), born Las Palmas de Gran Canaria, Canary Islands, Spain, Mar 1, 1969.

Harry Belafonte, 87, singer, born New York, NY, Mar 1, 1927.

Justin Bieber, 20, singer, born Stratford, ON, Canada, Mar 1, 1994.

Robert Conrad, 79, actor ("The Wild Wild West"), born Chicago, IL, Mar 1, 1935.

Roger Daltrey, 70, singer (The Who), born London, England, Mar 1, 1944.

Timothy Daly, 58, actor (*Diner*, "Wings"), born New York, NY, Mar 1, 1956.

George Eads, 47, actor ("CSI"), born Fort Worth, TX, Mar 1, 1967.

Deb Fischer, 63, US Senator (R, Nebraska), born Lincoln, NE, Mar 1, 1951.

Ron Francis, 51, former hockey player, born Sault Ste. Marie, ON, Canada, Mar 1, 1963.

Mark-Paul Gosselaar, 40, actor ("NYPD Blue," "Saved by the Bell"), born Panorama City, CA, Mar 1, 1974.

Yolanda Griffith, 44, former basketball player, born Chicago, IL, Mar 1, 1970.

Ron Howard, 60, director (*Apollo 13*, Oscar for *A Beautiful Mind*), actor, born Duncan, OK, Mar 1, 1954.

Ke$ha, 27, singer, born Kesha Rose Sebert at Los Angeles, CA, Mar 1, 1987.

Alan Thicke, 67, actor ("Growing Pains"), host ("Thicke of the Night"), born Kirkland Lake, ON, Canada, Mar 1, 1947.

Chris Webber, 41, former basketball player, born Detroit, MI, Mar 1, 1973.

Richard Purdy Wilbur, 93, former poet laureate of the US (1987–88), born New York, NY, Mar 1, 1921.

March 2 — Sunday

DAY 61 **304 REMAINING**

ACADEMY AWARDS PRESENTATION. Mar 2. Hollywood and Highland Center, Los Angeles, CA. 86th annual. Honoring film achievements of the previous year. Begins at 5:30 PM, PST. Also televised live by ABC. Nominations announced Jan 16. For info: Academy of Motion Picture Arts and Sciences, 8949 Wilshire Blvd, Beverly Hills, CA 90211-1972. Phone: (310) 247-3000. Web: www.oscars.org.

ARNAZ, DESI: BIRTH ANNIVERSARY. Mar 2, 1917. Born at Santiago, Cuba, as Desidero Alberto Arnaz y Acha III, to a wealthy family. The 1933 revolution sent them (now impoverished) to Miami, FL, and the young Arnaz sought a music career. Arnaz led his own band and introduced the conga line to America. He had several musical hits including "Babalu." He moved into acting, meeting his future wife, Lucille Ball, at RKO. Ball and Arnaz created one of the great TV comedies, "I Love Lucy" (1951–57), and started the innovative Desilu TV production company. Ball and Arnaz divorced in 1960. Arnaz died on Dec 2, 1986, at Del Mar, CA.

BATTLE OF BISMARCK SEA: ANNIVERSARY. Mar 2–4, 1943. Protected by American and Australian fighters, 137 American Flying Fortress and Liberator bombers attacked a Japanese convoy en route from its base at Rabaul to New Guinea on Mar 2, 1943. In the convoy were eight transports carrying 7,000 reinforcements, which were escorted by eight destroyers. All the transports and four of the destroyers were sunk and 3,500 Japanese troops were drowned. Of the 150 Japanese aircraft involved in the fighting, 102 were shot down. The Battle of Bismarck Sea was a major victory for the Allies, ending any efforts by the Japanese to send reinforcements to New Guinea.

BELGIUM: CARNIVAL OF BINCHE. Mar 2–4. Binche. This famous carnival dates back to the 16th century and is on the UNESCO Heritage List. Events include giants parade, children's parade, fireworks, orange tossing and more. Annually, Shrove Sunday to Shrove Tuesday. For more info: Belgium Tourist Office. Web: www.visitbelgium.com/mediaroom/BincheCarnival.htm.

CELEBRATE YOUR NAME WEEK! Mar 2–8. Who would you be if you didn't have a name? Your name identifies you to the world. Celebrate Your Name Week is about honoring your name. It's about making sure your name is a respected part of your personhood. Use this week to connect to your name! See also related events each day this week. Annually, the first full week in March. For info: Jerry Hill. E-mail: celebrateyournameweek@gmail.com. Web: www.namesuniverse.com.

CORAY, MELISSA BURTON: BIRTH ANNIVERSARY. Mar 2, 1828. Coray was born at Mersey, ON, Canada. At the age of 18 she accompanied her Mormon Battalion soldier husband, William Coray, on a 2,000-mile military march on foot from Council Bluffs, IA, to San Diego, CA, then 1,500 more miles across the Sierra Nevada Mountains and the Nevada desert to Salt Lake City, UT, the only woman to make the entire trip. On July 30, 1994, a mountain peak near Carson Pass was named for her, the second peak in California to be named for a woman.

ETHIOPIA: ADWA DAY. Mar 2. Ethiopian forces under Menelik II inflicted a crushing defeat on the invading Italians at Adwa in 1896.

FASCHING SUNDAY. Mar 2. Germany and Austria. The last Sunday before Lent.

GEISEL, THEODOR "DR. SEUSS": BIRTH ANNIVERSARY. Mar 2, 1904. Theodor Seuss Geisel, creator of *The Cat in the Hat* and *How the Grinch Stole Christmas*, was born at Springfield, MA. Known to children and parents as Dr. Seuss, his books have sold more than 200 million copies and have been translated into 20 languages. His career began with *And to Think That I Saw It on Mulberry Street*, which was turned down by 27 publishing houses before being published by Vanguard Press. His books included many messages, from environmental consciousness in *The Lorax* to the dangers of pacifism in *Horton Hatches the Egg* and *Yertle the Turtle*'s thinly veiled references to Hitler as the title character. He was awarded a Pulitzer Prize in 1984 "for his contribution over nearly half a century to the education and enjoyment of America's children and their parents." He died Sept 24, 1991, at La Jolla, CA.

HIGHWAY NUMBERS INTRODUCED: ANNIVERSARY. Mar 2, 1925. A joint board of state and federal highway officials created the first system of interstate highway numbering in the US. Standardized road signs identifying the routes were also introduced. Later the system would be improved with the use of odd and even numbers that distinguish between north-south and east-west routes, respectively.

HOUSTON, SAM: BIRTH ANNIVERSARY. Mar 2, 1793. The American soldier and politician, born at Rockbridge County, VA, is remembered for his role in Texas history. Houston was a congressman (1823–27) and governor (1827–29) of Tennessee. He resigned his office as governor in 1829 and rejoined the Cherokee Indians (with whom he had lived for several years as a teenage runaway), who accepted him as a member of their tribe. Houston went to Texas in 1832 and became commander of the Texan army in the War for Texan Independence, which was secured when Houston routed the much larger Mexican forces led by Santa Anna, Apr 21, 1836, at the Battle of San Jacinto. After Texas's admission to the Union, Houston served as US senator and later as governor of the state. He was deposed in 1861 when he refused to swear allegiance to the Confederacy. Houston, the only person to have been elected governor of two different states, failed to serve his full term of office in either. The city of Houston, TX, was named for him. He died July 26, 1863, at Huntsville, TX.

ITALY: CARNIVAL WEEK. Mar 2–8. Milan. Carnival week is held according to local tradition, with shows and festive events for children on Tuesday and Thursday. Parades of floats, figures in the costume of local folk characters Meneghin and Cecca, parties and more traditional events are held on Saturday. Annually, the Sunday–Saturday of Ash Wednesday week.

JOE CAIN PROCESSION. Mar 2. Mobile, AL. 48th year. Led by Slacabamorinico IV for the 29th time, this event honors the man who in 1867 initiated a more public celebration of Mardi Gras following the War between the States in the midst of Union occupation. Annually, the Sunday before Shrove Tuesday. Est attendance: 100,000. For info: The Rev Wayne Dean, Sr, VP, Joe Cain Society, 1064 Palmetto St, Mobile, AL 36604-3041. Phone: (251) 753-0546. E-mail: joecain50@gmail.com.

***KING KONG* FILM PREMIERE: ANNIVERSARY.** Mar 2, 1933. One of the greatest adventure movies of all time premiered on this date at New York City's Radio City Music Hall and the RKO Roxy. It was to be an immediate hit—the biggest film blockbuster up to that time. Directed by Merian Cooper and Ernest Schoedsack, *King Kong* was a variation of "Beauty and the Beast," with the Beast being the 50-foot ape (actually, an 18-inch model) and Beauty portrayed by actress Fay Wray, who became known as the "Queen of Scream" after this film. Kong climbing the newly completed Empire State Building clutching Wray as biplanes attack him is

March 2014

S	M	T	W	T	F	S
						1
2	3	4	5	6	7	8
9	10	11	12	13	14	15
16	17	18	19	20	21	22
23	24	25	26	27	28	29
30	31					

one of the iconic images of cinema. Technician Willis O'Brien used state-of-the-art, stop-motion photography for the film's special effects.

KREWE OF BACCHUS PARADE. Mar 2. New Orleans, LA. This legendary social club, formed in 1968, throws one of the highlight parades of carnival season. Annually, the Sunday before Mardi Gras. For info: Krewe of Bacchus. Web: www.kreweofbacchus.org.

MOUNT RAINIER NATIONAL PARK ESTABLISHED: ANNIVERSARY. Mar 2, 1899. Located in the Cascade Mountains of Washington State, this is the fourth-oldest national park.

NAMESAKE DAY. Mar 2. Today, ponder your name, and think about why you were given the name you have. Were you named after someone? Explore the history of your name, and have fun discovering whether you have a name twin! You may even be inspired to reach out to a namesake! Annually, the Sunday of Celebrate Your Name Week. For info: Jerry Hill. E-mail: celebrateyournameweek@gmail.com. Web: www.namesuniverse.com.

✦NATIONAL CONSUMER PROTECTION WEEK. Mar 2–8 (tentative).

ORTHODOX CHEESEFARE SUNDAY. Mar 2. The last day for dairy and fish before Clean Monday, which begins Great Lent in the Eastern Orthodox Church.

OTT, MELVIN (MEL): BIRTH ANNIVERSARY. Mar 2, 1909. Baseball Hall of Fame outfielder, born at Gretna, LA. Playing for the New York Giants, Ott hit 511 home runs, a National League record until Willie Mays surpassed it in 1966. Inducted into the Hall of Fame in 1951. Died at New Orleans, LA, Nov 21, 1958.

POPE LEO XIII: BIRTH ANNIVERSARY. Mar 2, 1810. Giocchino Vincenzo Pecci, 256th pope of the Roman Catholic Church, born at Carpineto, Italy. Elected pope Feb 20, 1878. Died July 20, 1903, at Rome, Italy.

POPE PIUS XII: BIRTH ANNIVERSARY. Mar 2, 1876. Eugenio Maria Giovanni Pacelli, 260th pope of the Roman Catholic Church, born at Rome, Italy. Elected pope Mar 2, 1939. Died at Castel Gandolfo, near Rome, Oct 9, 1958.

READ AN E-BOOK WEEK. Mar 2–8. A week set aside to learn about and/or read an electronic book (e-book). For info: Rita Toews, 9 Esker Pl, East St. Paul, MB, Canada, R2E 0K2. Phone: (204) 661-2734. E-mail: r.toews@shaw.ca. Web: www.ebookweek.com.

RETURN THE BORROWED BOOKS WEEK. Mar 2–8. To remind you to make room for those precious old volumes that will be returned to you by cleaning out all that worthless trash that your friends are waiting for. Created by the late Al Kaelin. Annually, the first full week in March. For info: Inter-Global Society for Prevention of Cruelty to Cartoonists, 4626 Richelieu Terrace, Los Angeles, CA 90032. Phone: (323) 222-7944.

RITT, MARTIN: 100th BIRTH ANNIVERSARY. Mar 2, 1914. American film and television director Martin Ritt was born at New York, NY. His best-known films are *Hud* (1963), *Sounder* (1972) and *Norma Rae* (1979). During the 1950s he was blacklisted by McCarthy's anti-Communist crusade. Died Dec 8, 1990, at Santa Monica, CA.

SCHURZ, CARL: BIRTH ANNIVERSARY. Mar 2, 1829. American journalist, political reformer and army officer in Civil War. Born near Cologne, Germany, he died at New York, NY, May 14, 1906.

SHROVETIDE. Mar 2–4. The three days before Ash Wednesday: Shrove Sunday, Monday and Tuesday—a time for confession and festivity before the beginning of Lent.

***THE SOUND OF MUSIC* FILM PREMIERE: ANNIVERSARY.** Mar 2, 1965. The perennially popular family film musical, starring Julie Andrews as Maria Von Trapp, premiered on this date at New York City. Nominated for 10 Academy Awards, the film won 5 Oscars, including awards for Best Picture and Best Director (Robert Wise).

SPACE MILESTONE: *PIONEER 10* (US). Mar 2, 1972. This unmanned probe began a journey on which it passed and photographed Jupiter and its moons, 620 million miles from Earth, in December 1973. It crossed the orbit of Pluto and then in 1983 became the first known Earth object to leave our solar system. On Sept 22, 1987, *Pioneer 10* reached another space milestone at 4:19 PM, when it reached a distance 50 times farther from the sun than the sun is from Earth.

SPACE MILESTONE: *SOYUZ 28* (USSR): ANNIVERSARY. Mar 2, 1978. Cosmonauts Alexi Gubarev and Vladimir Remek linked with *Salyut 6* space station Mar 3, visiting crew of *Soyuz 26*. Returned to Earth Mar 10. Remek, from Czechoslovakia, was the first person in space from a country other than the US or USSR.

TELECOMMUTER APPRECIATION WEEK. Mar 2–8. Sponsored by the American Telecommuting Association, this week is designed to call attention to the benefits of telecommuting: the individual and family as well as the employer and society benefit in a win-win-win situation. For info: American Telecommuting Assn, 827 Second St #104, Santa Monica, CA 90403. Phone: (800) ATA-4-YOU. E-mail: YourATA@YourATA.com.

TEXAS INDEPENDENCE DAY. Mar 2, 1836. Texas adopted Declaration of Independence from Mexico.

TRIAL OF THE TWENTY-ONE: ANNIVERSARY. Mar 2–13, 1938. Third and last of the Moscow show trials that were part of Stalin's Great Purge. Notable for the prominence of the defendants, including the former head of the Communist International, Nikolai Bukharin, the trial convinced many Communist observers of the failure and moral bankruptcy of the Stalin regime. Tortured and coerced with threats to family, the defendants confessed to counterrevolutionary activity and conspiracy to murder Stalin and others. Eighteen of the defendants were sentenced to death and executed on Mar 15. The other three were sent to prison, but all three were killed in a prisoner massacre in September 1941.

 BIRTHDAYS TODAY

Jon Bon Jovi, 52, singer, songwriter, actor, born John Bongiovi at Sayreville, NJ, Mar 2, 1962.

Reggie Bush, 29, football player, born Spring Valley, CA, Mar 2, 1985.

Daniel Craig, 46, actor (*Skyfall, The Girl with the Dragon Tattoo, Casino Royale, Munich*), born Chester, England, Mar 2, 1968.

John Cullum, 84, actor (*Shenandoah, On the Twentieth Century*, "Northern Exposure"), born Knoxville, TN, Mar 2, 1930.

Mikhail Sergeyvich Gorbachev, 83, former Soviet political leader, born Privolnoye, Stavropol, Russia, Mar 2, 1931.

John Irving, 72, author (*The Cider House Rules, The World According to Garp*), born Exeter, NH, Mar 2, 1942.

Henrik Lundqvist, 32, hockey player, born Are, Sweden, Mar 2, 1982.

Chris Martin, 37, singer, songwriter (Coldplay), born Exeter, Devon, England, Mar 2, 1977.

Eddie Money, 65, musician, born Brooklyn, NY, Mar 2, 1949.

Laraine Newman, 62, comedienne ("Saturday Night Live"), born Los Angeles, CA, Mar 2, 1952.

Tom Wolfe, 83, author, journalist (*The Bonfire of the Vanities, The Right Stuff*), born Richmond, VA, Mar 2, 1931.

March 3 — Monday

DAY 62 **303 REMAINING**

AUSTRALIA: EIGHT HOUR DAY or LABOR DAY. Mar 3. Western Australia and Tasmania. Parades and celebrations commemorate trade union efforts during the 19th century to limit working hours. Their slogan: "Eight hours labor, eight hours recreation, eight hours rest!" Annually, the first Monday in March.

BELL, ALEXANDER GRAHAM: BIRTH ANNIVERSARY. Mar 3, 1847. Inventor of the telephone, born at Edinburgh, Scotland, Bell acquired his interest in the transmission of sound from his father, Melville Bell, a teacher of the deaf. Bell's use of visual devices to teach articulation to the deaf contributed to the theory from which he derived the principle of the vibrating membrane used in the telephone. On Mar 10, 1876, Bell spoke the first electrically transmitted sentence to his assistant in the next room: "Mr Watson, come here, I want you." Bell's other accomplishments include a refinement of Edison's phonograph, the first successful phonograph record and the audiometer. He also continued exploring the nature and causes of deafness. He died near Baddeck, NS, Canada, Aug 2, 1922.

BETHUNE, NORMAN: BIRTH ANNIVERSARY. Mar 3, 1890. Canadian physician who worked in the front lines during WWI, the Spanish Civil War and the Chinese Revolution. Bethune was born at Gravenhurst, ON; he died at age 49 at China while treating a soldier of Mao's Eighth Route Army, Nov 11, 1939. He is said to be the only Western man recognized as a hero of the Chinese Revolution.

BONZA BOTTLER DAY™. Mar 3. To celebrate when the number of the day is the same as the number of the month. Bonza Bottler Day™ is an excuse to have a party at least once a month. For more information see Jan 1. For info: Gail Berger, 14 Fernwood Dr, Taylors, SC 29687. Phone: (864) 201-3988. E-mail: bonza@bonzabottlerday.com. Web: www.bonzabottlerday.com.

BULGARIA: LIBERATION DAY. Mar 3. Grateful tribute to the Russian, Romanian and Finnish soldiers and Bulgarian volunteers who, in the Russo-Turkish War, 1877–78, liberated Bulgaria from five centuries of Ottoman rule.

CARNIVAL. Mar 3–4. Period of festivities, feasts, foolishness and gaiety immediately before Lent begins on Ash Wednesday. Ordinarily Carnival includes only Fasching (the Feast of Fools), which is the Monday and Tuesday immediately preceding Ash Wednesday. The period of Carnival may be extended in some areas.

EMANCIPATION OF THE SERFS: ANNIVERSARY. Mar 3, 1861. On this day Czar Alexander II emancipated the serfs of Russia. The 20 million serfs represented one-third of that nation's population.

FASCHING. Mar 3–4. In Germany and Austria, Fasching—also called Fasnacht, Fasnet or Feast of Fools—is a Shrovetide festival with processions of masked figures, both beautiful and grotesque. Always the two days (Rose Monday and Shrove Tuesday) between Fasching Sunday and Ash Wednesday.

FLORIDA: ADMISSION DAY: ANNIVERSARY. Mar 3. Became 27th state in 1845.

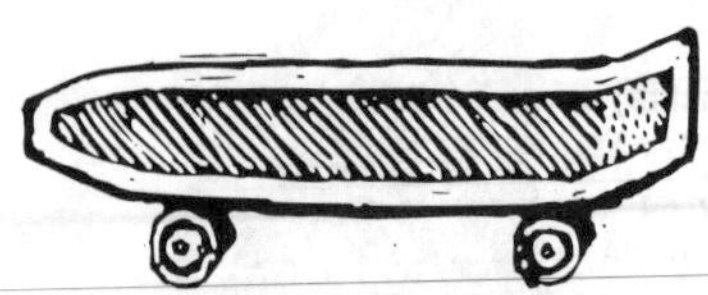

March 2014

S	M	T	W	T	F	S
						1
2	3	4	5	6	7	8
9	10	11	12	13	14	15
16	17	18	19	20	21	22
23	24	25	26	27	28	29
30	31					

FUN FACTS ABOUT NAMES DAY. Mar 3. Celebrate names today by looking up interesting tidbits about names. Get started with fun facts about names on our website. Or maybe you already know the name of Santa's brother? Surprise, entertain, enlighten and amaze others by sharing what you find. Ask others to share the stories of their names. Discuss the exotic names some celebrities give their children. Annually, the Monday of Celebrate Your Name Week. For info: Jerry Hill. E-mail: celebrateyournameweek@gmail.com. Web: www.namesuniverse.com.

GUAM: DISCOVERY DAY or MAGELLAN DAY. Mar 3. Commemorates discovery of Guam in 1521 by Ferdinand Magellan. Annually, the first Monday in March.

HARLOW, JEAN: BIRTH ANNIVERSARY. Mar 3, 1911. Born Harlean Carpenter at Kansas City, MO. Harlow's platinum blond hair, arresting beauty and flair for comedy made her a star in 1930s Hollywood. Following her big break in Howard Hughes's 1930 war epic *Hell's Angels* ("Would you be shocked if I put on something more comfortable?"), Harlow became a superstar at MGM, where she starred in six films with Clark Gable. Harlow's meteoric rise was cut short, however, when she collapsed on the set during the filming of *Saratoga*. She died at Los Angeles, CA, June 7, 1937—she was 26.

ICELAND: BUN DAY. Mar 3. Children invade homes in the morning with colorful sticks and receive gifts of whipped cream buns. On Shrove Monday.

JAPAN: HINAMATSURI (DOLL FESTIVAL). Mar 3. This special festival for girls is observed throughout Japan. Annually, Mar 3.

MALAWI: MARTYR'S DAY. Mar 3. Public holiday in Malawi.

MISSOURI COMPROMISE: ANNIVERSARY. Mar 3, 1820. In February 1819 a bill was introduced into Congress that would admit Missouri to the Union as a state that prohibited slavery. At the time there were 11 free states and 10 slave states. Southern congressmen feared this would upset the balance of power between North and South. As a compromise, on this date Missouri was admitted as a slave state but slavery was forever prohibited in the northern part of the Louisiana Purchase. In 1854 this act was repealed when Kansas and Nebraska were allowed to decide on slave or free status by popular vote.

"MR WIZARD" TV PREMIERE: ANNIVERSARY. Mar 3, 1951. Don Herbert as Mr Wizard explained the mysteries of science while performing experiments in front of wide-eyed children. The series ran on NBC for 14 continuous years. In 1983 Herbert returned to host "Mr Wizard's World" on Nickelodeon.

"MOONLIGHTING" TV PREMIERE: ANNIVERSARY. Mar 3, 1985. Cybill Shepherd and Bruce Willis starred in this ABC comedy-adventure hour about the Blue Moon Detective Agency owned by former model Maddie Hayes (Shepherd), who is partnered with wisecracking detective David Addison (Willis). The two find themselves in a series of madcap adventures. The show featured narrative innovations: having characters directly address the camera, shooting sequences in black and white or going completely off-concept (as in an episode based on Shakespeare's *The Taming of the Shrew*). Last telecast on May 14, 1989.

NATIONAL ANTHEM DAY. Mar 3, 1931. The bill designating "The Star-Spangled Banner" as our national anthem was adopted by the US Senate and went to President Herbert Hoover for signature. The president signed it the same day.

NATIONAL SCHOOL BREAKFAST WEEK. Mar 3–7. Since 1989. To focus on the importance of a nutritious breakfast served in the schools, giving children a good start to their day. Annually, the first full week in March. For info: School Nutrition Association, 120 Waterfront St, Ste 300, National Harbor, MD 20745. Phone: (301) 686-3100. Fax: (301) 686-3115. E-mail: servicecenter@schoolnutrition.org. Web: www.schoolnutrition.org.

NEA'S READ ACROSS AMERICA DAY. Mar 3. Get ready to grab your hat and read with the Cat in the Hat for the 17th annual Read Across America Day. The Seussical celebration will kick off a week of reading across the nation as NEA members gather students, parents and community members together to share their love of reading. Annually, on or near Dr. Seuss's birthday (Mar 2).

For info: Natl Education Assn, 1201 16th St NW, Washington, DC 20036. Phone: (202) 833-4000. E-mail: readacross@nea.org. Web: www.nea.org/readacross.

ORTHODOX GREEN MONDAY. Mar 3. Green, or Clean, Monday is the first Monday of Lent on the Orthodox Christian calendar. Lunch in the fields, with bread, olives and uncooked vegetables and no meat or dairy products.

ORTHODOX LENT. Mar 3–Apr 11. Great Lent, or Easter Lent, observed by Eastern Orthodox churches, lasts 40 days. The first day is known as Clean Monday, which begins the Great Fast, when Orthodox Christians abstain from eating meat, dairy and fish. (Fasting continues on Lazarus Saturday [Apr 12] and a stricter fast is kept during Holy Week [Apr 13–19].)

PULASKI DAY IN ILLINOIS. Mar 3. Celebrates the Polish and American Revolutionary hero Casimir Pulaski (1747–79) on the first Monday in March.

PULLMAN, GEORGE: BIRTH ANNIVERSARY. Mar 3, 1831. Born at Brocton, NY, George Mortimer Pullman was an inventor and industrialist who became famous for his design and production of the "Pullman" railroad sleeping car. His first attempt at improving railroad sleeping accommodations began in 1858, while he was working as a contractor for the Chicago & Alton Railroad at Chicago, IL. His initial model was not adopted, but in 1863 a new design was enthusiastically received. He secured a patent for the folding upper berth design in 1864 and one for the lower berth design in 1865. By 1867 Pullman and his partner organized the Pullman Palace Car Company, which became the greatest railroad car-building organization in the world. In 1881 the town of Pullman, IL, south of Chicago, was formed by Pullman to house his employees. Because rents were not lowered when wages were cut, a strike was initiated against Pullman's company in May 1894. Pullman was eventually forced to give up control of all property in the town not directly required for manufacturing. Pullman died Oct 19, 1897, at Chicago.

RIDGWAY, MATTHEW BUNKER: BIRTH ANNIVERSARY. Mar 3, 1895. American Army officer Matthew Bunker Ridgway was born at Fort Monroe, VA. As major general commanding the newly formed 82nd Airborne Division, he led it in the invasion of Sicily in July 1943 and the invasion of the Italian mainland in 1944. Ridgway replaced MacArthur as commander of the US Eighth Army in Korea in 1951 and succeeded Eisenhower as Supreme Allied Commander of the North Atlantic Treaty Organization in 1952. He became US Army Chief of Staff in 1953. Ridgway died at Fox Chapel, PA, July 26, 1993.

SHROVE MONDAY. Mar 3. The Monday before Ash Wednesday. In Germany and Austria, this is called Rose Monday.

***TIME* MAGAZINE FIRST PUBLISHED: ANNIVERSARY.** Mar 3, 1923. The first issue of *Time* bore this date. The magazine was founded by Henry Luce and Briton Hadden.

TRINIDAD AND TOBAGO: CARNIVAL. Mar 3–4. Port of Spain. This national festival is widely acclaimed as "the mother" of more than 100 carnivals worldwide. The parade of costumed bands and competitions prior to Carnival feature the world's most celebrated calypsonians, steel band players, costume designers and masqueraders. Annually, the two days before Ash Wednesday. For info: Natl Carnival Commission of Trinidad and Tobago. Web: www.ncctt.org.

WATSON, DOC: BIRTH ANNIVERSARY. Mar 3, 1923. Folk guitar virtuoso and prolific songwriter Arthel Lane Watson was born at Deep Gap, NC. Watson lost his sight as an infant but was still raised to work hard on the family property and be self-sufficient. A natural musical talent led him to embrace that career. He possessed a rich baritone, an innovative style of flatpicking, and bluegrass guitar play that mimicked the frenzy of a country fiddle. Watson brought to his songwriting a ranging knowledge of American musical tradition—especially from the Appalachia region. He was a great influence on the thriving folk scene of the 1960s. Awarded a National Medal of Arts in 1997, Watson died at Winston-Salem, NC, on May 29, 2012.

WHAT IF CATS AND DOGS HAD OPPOSABLE THUMBS DAY. Mar 3. We are grateful today that the infinite wisdom of the universe has not allowed cats and dogs to have thumbs. Imagine the cat, able to operate the can opener! Imagine the dog, able to open the refrigerator door! (©2006 by WH.) For info: Thomas & Ruth Roy, Wellcat Holidays, 2418 Long Ln, Lebanon, PA 17046. Phone: (717) 279-0184. E-mail: info@wellcat.com. Web: www.wellcat.com.

WOMAN SUFFRAGE PARADE ATTACKED: ANNIVERSARY. Mar 3, 1913. A parade held by the National American Woman Suffrage Association at Washington, DC, on the day before Woodrow Wilson's inauguration turned into a near riot when people in the crowd began jeering and shoving the marchers. The 5,000 women and their supporters were spit upon, struck in the face and pelted with burning cigar stubs while police looked on and made no effort to intervene. Secretary of War Henry Stimson was forced to send soldiers from Fort Myer to restore order.

WOMEN OF AVIATION WORLDWIDE WEEK. Mar 3–9. The first female pilot license worldwide was issued to Raymonde de Laroche of France on Mar 8, 1910. More than 100 years later, the average percentage of women in all technical aeronautical positions is less than 10 percent (6 percent for pilots). Studies show that the perception that the industry is for males is a key barrier to women's interest in the field. First observed in 2010 and formalized in 2011, Women of Aviation Worldwide Week aims to break down the perception barrier by increasing awareness among the female population of all available opportunities in the industry through female-centric events that celebrate past and present women of aviation while welcoming the next generation of women of aviation with open arms. The City of Frederick, MD, has recognized the week locally in 2012 and 2013. Annually, from the Monday before Mar 8 to the Sunday after Mar 8. Est attendance: 30,000. For info: Women of Aviation Worldwide Week, 1100-1200 W 73rd Ave, Vancouver, BC V6P 6G5, Canada. E-mail: mireilleg@womenofaviationweek.org. Web: www.womenofaviationweek.org.

BIRTHDAYS TODAY

Jessica Biel, 32, actress (*Hitchcock, The Illusionist,* "7th Heaven"), born Ely, MN, Mar 3, 1982.

Julie Bowen, 44, actress ("Modern Family," "Ed"), born Baltimore, MD, Mar 3, 1970.

David Faustino, 40, actor ("Married . . . With Children"), born Los Angeles, CA, Mar 3, 1974.

Ira Glass, 55, radio host ("This American Life"), born Baltimore, MD, Mar 3, 1959.

Santonio Holmes, 30, football player, born Belle Glade, FL, Mar 3, 1984.

Jacqueline (Jackie) Joyner-Kersee, 52, Olympic heptathlete, born East St. Louis, IL, Mar 3, 1962.

Tim Kazurinsky, 64, actor, comedian, writer ("Saturday Night Live"), born Johnstown, PA, Mar 3, 1950.

Brian Leetch, 46, former hockey player, born Corpus Christi, TX, Mar 3, 1968.

Lee Radziwill, 81, sister of the late Jacqueline Kennedy Onassis, born Caroline Lee Bouvier at New York, NY, Mar 3, 1933.

Miranda Richardson, 56, actress (*The Crying Game, Enchanted April*), born Lancashire, England, Mar 3, 1958.

Herschel Walker, 52, former football player, born Wrightsville, GA, Mar 3, 1962.

March 4 — Tuesday

DAY 63 **302 REMAINING**

ADAMS, JOHN QUINCY: RETURN TO CONGRESS: ANNIVERSARY. Mar 4, 1830. On this day John Quincy Adams returned to the House of Representatives to represent the district of Plymouth, MA. He was the first former president to do so and served for eight consecutive terms.

CITY OF CHICAGO INCORPORATED: ANNIVERSARY. Mar 4, 1837. The Illinois state legislature enacted into law a city charter for Chicago on this date. William B. Ogden became the first mayor of this city of 4,170 people. Chicago had been incorporated as a town on Aug 12, 1833. The name "Chicago" was formed from a Native American word, but its meaning is disputed. It probably means "strong" or "great."

CLEVELAND'S SECOND PRESIDENTIAL INAUGURATION: ANNIVERSARY. Mar 4, 1893. Grover Cleveland was inaugurated for a second but nonconsecutive term as president. In 1885 he had become the 22nd president of the US and in 1893 the 24th. Originally a source of some controversy, the Congressional Directory for some time listed him only as the 22nd president. The directory now lists him as both the 22nd and 24th presidents though some historians continue to argue that one person cannot be both. Benjamin Harrison served during the intervening term, defeating Cleveland in electoral votes, though not in the popular vote.

CONGRESS: 225th ANNIVERSARY OF FIRST MEETING UNDER CONSTITUTION. Mar 4, 1789. The first Congress met at New York, NY. A quorum was obtained in the House Apr 1 and in the Senate Apr 5, and the first Congress was formally organized Apr 6. Electoral votes were counted, and George Washington was declared president (69 votes) and John Adams vice president (34 votes).

COURAGEOUS FOLLOWER DAY. Mar 4. We are a country built on the myth of "rugged individualism," in love with the concept of leadership. But all leaders require followers and, in fact, virtually all of us are followers at some times and leaders at others. This day honors the too-often disparaged role of follower. Its purpose is to dispel the myth that followers are passive and to raise awareness that good followership is energetic and at times courageous. In fact, only through active and courageous followership can leaders be counted on to use their power wisely and well. For info: Ira Chaleff. Phone: (540) 631-9026. E-mail: ira.chaleff@exe-coach.com.

"THE DICK CAVETT SHOW" TV PREMIERE: ANNIVERSARY. Mar 4, 1968. Dick Cavett began his television career on ABC with a daytime talk show that subsequently became a late-night program competing with Johnny Carson. Cavett, with his Yale background, had a reputation as an "intellectual" host and was particularly adept at the one-man interview. He has since appeared on the CBS, PBS and USA networks hosting a variety of shows.

March 2014	S	M	T	W	T	F	S
							1
	2	3	4	5	6	7	8
	9	10	11	12	13	14	15
	16	17	18	19	20	21	22
	23	24	25	26	27	28	29
	30	31					

DING LING: DEATH ANNIVERSARY. Mar 4, 1986. Writer and champion of women's rights, born at Hunan Province, China, in 1904. Ding was a prolific author, having written nearly 300 novels as well as plays, short stories and essays. She received the 1951 Stalin Prize for Literature for her novel *The Sun Shines Over the Sanggan River* (1949). She fell from favor in the 1950s, was exiled and in 1970 was imprisoned. After the death of Chairman Mao she was freed, and during her last years she enjoyed renewed attention and favor. Died at age 82 at Beijing, China.

ENGLAND: SHROVETIDE PANCAKE RACE. Mar 4. Olney, Buckinghamshire. The pancake race at Olney has been run since 1445. Competitors must be women over 16 years of age, wearing a traditional housewife's costume, including apron and head covering. With a toss and flip of the pancake on the griddle that each must carry, the women dash from the marketplace to the parish church, where the winner receives a kiss from the ringer of the Pancake Bell. Shriving service follows. Annually, on Shrove Tuesday.

HOT SPRINGS NATIONAL PARK ESTABLISHED: ANNIVERSARY. Mar 4, 1921. To protect the hot springs of Arkansas, the government set aside Hot Springs Reservation on Apr 20, 1832. In 1921 the area became a national park.

HOUSTON LIVESTOCK SHOW AND RODEO™. Mar 4–23. Reliant Park, Houston, TX. First held in 1932. Livestock show with nearly 30,000 entries. Rodeo action and top-name musical entertainment. Est attendance: 2,250,000. For info: Houston Livestock Show and Rodeo, PO Box 20070, Houston, TX 77225-0070. Phone: (832) 667-1000. Fax: (832) 667-1134. E-mail: questions@rodeohouston.com. Web: www.rodeohouston.com.

ICELAND: BURSTING DAY. Mar 4. Feasts with salted mutton and thick pea soup. On Shrove Tuesday.

INTERNATIONAL PANCAKE DAY. Mar 4. Liberal, KS. 65th annual competition between the women of Liberal, KS, and Olney, Buckinghamshire, England. The women, wearing traditional dress, apron and scarf, run a 415-yard S-shaped course, carrying a pancake in a skillet. Other events taking place include a breakfast, parade, Christian artist showcase, talent show, eating and flipping contests and the Miss Liberal scholarship pageant. Annually, on Shrove Tuesday, the day before Ash Wednesday. Est attendance: 5,000. For info: JoAnn Combs, Exec Secy, PO Box 665, Liberal, KS 67905. Phone: (620) 624-6423. Web: www.pancakeday.net.

KREWE OF REX MARDI GRAS PARADE. Mar 4. New Orleans, LA. The Krewe of Rex parade is the main event of New Orleans's Mardi Gras festivities. The parade passes through the Garden District and downtown New Orleans. King Rex presides and is considered the King of New Orleans's Carnival. The Rex motto is "Pro bono publico." Annually, Mardi Gras day.

MARDI GRAS. Mar 4. Last feast before Lent. Although Mardi Gras (Fat Tuesday, literally) is properly limited to Shrove Tuesday, it has come to be popularly applied to the preceding two weeks of celebration. Celebrated especially at New Orleans, LA; Mobile, AL; and certain Mississippi and Florida cities. State holiday in Louisiana. (Observed officially in the Alabama counties of Baldwin and Mobile.)

NATIONAL GRAMMAR DAY. Mar 4. On National Grammar Day, we honor our language and its rules, which help us communicate clearly with each other. In turn, clear communication helps us understand each other—a critical component of peaceful relations. The day is sponsored by The Society for the Promotion of Good Grammar, a rapidly growing worldwide organization with more than 20,000 members. Annually, Mar 4th—both a date and an imperative. For info: Martha Brockenbrough, Society for the Promotion of Good Grammar, 1609 37th Ave, Seattle, WA 98122. Phone: (206) 328-7374. E-mail: martha@marthabee.com. Web: www.nationalgrammarday.com.

NORTH DAKOTA WINTER SHOW. Mar 4–9. Valley City, ND. Six-day agricultural expo featuring world's largest crop show, eight-breed cattle show, three-performance PRCA Rodeos, horse pulls, pickup pull, old-time tractor pull (tractors built prior to 1955), crafts and antique shows, farm toy show and single-performance headliner country concert. Annually, the first week in March. Est attendance: 50,000. For info: ND Winter Show, PO Box 846, Valley City, ND 58072. Phone: (701) 845-1401 or (800) 437-0218. Fax: (701) 845-3914. E-mail: ndws@northdakotawintershow.com. Web: www.northdakotawintershow.com.

OLD INAUGURATION DAY. Mar 4. Anniversary of the date set for beginning the US presidential term of office, 1789–1933. Although the Continental Congress had set the first Wednesday of March 1789 as the date for the new government to convene, a quorum was not present to count the electoral votes until Apr 6. Though George Washington's term of office began on Mar 4, he did not take the oath of office until Apr 30, 1789. All subsequent presidential terms (except successions following the death of an incumbent), until Franklin D. Roosevelt's second term, began Mar 4. The 20th Amendment (ratified Jan 23, 1933) provided that "the terms of the President and Vice President shall end at noon on the 20th day of January . . . and the terms of their successors shall then begin."

PACZKI DAY. Mar 4. Food lovers pick this day to enjoy these round, sugarcoated, fruit-filled Polish pre-Lenten pastries, pronounced "poonch-kee," available in bakeries nationwide. Paczki Day coincides with Shrove Tuesday or Fat Tuesday, the day before Ash Wednesday.

PEACE CORPS DAY. Mar 4. Commemorates the founding of the Peace Corps on Mar 1, 1961, by President John F. Kennedy. Observed on the first Tuesday in March.

PENNSYLVANIA DEEDED TO WILLIAM PENN: ANNIVERSARY. Mar 4, 1681. To satisfy a debt of £16,000, King Charles II of England granted a royal charter, deed and governorship of Pennsylvania to William Penn.

***PEOPLE* MAGAZINE: 40th ANNIVERSARY.** Mar 4, 1974. The popular magazine highlighting celebrities was officially launched with the Mar 4, 1974, issue featuring a cover photo of Mia Farrow.

PERKINS, FRANCES: CABINET APPOINTMENT: ANNIVERSARY. Mar 4, 1933. Frances Perkins became the first woman appointed to the president's cabinet when she was appointed secretary of labor by President Franklin D. Roosevelt.

PULASKI, CASIMIR: BIRTH ANNIVERSARY. Mar 4, 1747. American Revolutionary hero, General Kazimierz (Casimir) Pulaski, born at Winiary, Mazovia, Poland, the son of a count. He was a patriot and military leader in Poland's fight against Russia of 1770–71 and went into exile at the partition of Poland in 1772. He came to America in 1777 to join the Revolution, fighting with General Washington at Brandywine and also serving at Germantown and Valley Forge. He organized the Pulaski Legion to wage guerrilla warfare against the British. Mortally wounded in a heroic charge at the siege of Savannah, GA, he died aboard the warship *Wasp* Oct 11, 1779. In Illinois, Pulaski Day is celebrated as a holiday on the first Monday in March.

ROCKNE, KNUTE: BIRTH ANNIVERSARY. Mar 4, 1888. Football coach, born at Voss, Norway. Rockne played end at the University of Notre Dame and then in 1918 was appointed head coach at his alma mater. Over 13 seasons, Rockne became a living legend, and Notre Dame football rose to a position of unprecedented prominence. His teams won 105 games (and three national championships) against only 12 losses and 5 ties. Rockne died in a plane crash at Bazaar, KS, Mar 31, 1931; he was 43 years old.

SHROVE TUESDAY. Mar 4. Always the day before Ash Wednesday. Sometimes called Pancake Tuesday. This day is a legal holiday in some counties in Florida.

TELEVISION ACADEMY HALL OF FAME: FIRST INDUCTEES ANNOUNCED: 30th ANNIVERSARY. Mar 4, 1984. The Television Academy of Arts and Sciences announced the formation of the Television Academy Hall of Fame at Burbank, CA. The first inductees were Lucille Ball, Milton Berle, Paddy Chayefsky, Norman Lear, Edward R. Murrow, William S. Paley and David Sarnoff.

TOWN MEETING DAY. Mar 4. Vermont. The first Tuesday in March is an official state holiday in Vermont. Nearly every town elects officers, approves budget items and deals with a multitude of other items in a daylong public meeting of the voters.

UNIQUE NAMES DAY. Mar 4. This is the day to salute friends, acquaintances and loved ones who have a unique name. Let's appreciate them for going through life without seeing their names on things such as ready-made key chains, etc. If you or anyone you know has a unique name, discuss it today! Celebrate it! Annually, the Tuesday of Celebrate Your Name Week. For info: Jerry Hill. E-mail: celebrateyournameweek@gmail.com. Web: www.namesuniverse.com.

VERMONT: ADMISSION DAY: ANNIVERSARY. Mar 4. Became 14th state in 1791.

ZULU MARDI GRAS PARADE. Mar 4. New Orleans, LA. The Zulu Social Aid and Pleasure Club, one of New Orleans's oldest social clubs (formally established in 1916), has one of the most anticipated parades of the Mardi Gras season in the city. Annually, Mardi Gras day. For info: Zulu Social Aid and Pleasure Club, Inc, 722 N Broad St, New Orleans, LA 70119. Web: www.kreweofzulu.com.

BIRTHDAYS TODAY

Chaz Bono, 45, author, television personality, born Chastity Sun Bono at Los Angeles, CA, Mar 4, 1969.

Landon Donovan, 32, soccer player, born Redlands, CA, Mar 4, 1982.

Emilio Estefan, 61, musician, born Havana, Cuba, Mar 4, 1953.

Patricia Heaton, 55, actress ("The Middle," "Everybody Loves Raymond"), born Bay Village, OH, Mar 4, 1959.

Kevin Johnson, 48, politician, former basketball player, born Sacramento, CA, Mar 4, 1966.

Patsy Kensit, 46, actress (*The Great Gatsby, Blame It on the Bellboy*), born London, England, Mar 4, 1968.

Kay Lenz, 61, actress (*Rich Man, Poor Man*), born Los Angeles, CA, Mar 4, 1953.

Catherine O'Hara, 60, comedienne, writer ("SCTV Network 90"), actress (*Home Alone*), born Toronto, ON, Canada, Mar 4, 1954.

Rick Perry, 64, Governor of Texas (R), born Haskell, TX, Mar 4, 1950.

Paula Prentiss, 75, actress ("He & She," *What's New Pussycat?*), born Paula Ragusa at San Antonio, TX, Mar 4, 1939.

Steven Weber, 53, actor ("Wings"), born Queens, NY, Mar 4, 1961.

Mary Wilson, 70, singer (original member of the Supremes), born Detroit, MI, Mar 4, 1944.

March 5 — Wednesday

DAY 64 **301 REMAINING**

ASH WEDNESDAY. Mar 5. Marks the beginning of Lent. Forty weekdays and six Sundays (Saturday considered a weekday) remain until Easter Sunday. Named for use of ashes in ceremonial penance.

BLACKSTONE, WILLIAM: BIRTH ANNIVERSARY. Mar 5, 1595. William Blackstone, born at Durham County, England, was the first settler in what is now Boston, MA, and also the first in what is now Rhode Island. Blackstone came to New England with the Captain Robert Gorges expedition in 1623. When the expedition failed and most returned to England, he stayed and settled on what later became Beacon Hill. In 1634 he sold most of his Boston property and moved to the shores of the river that now bears his name. He died there at what is now Cumberland, RI, May 26, 1675.

BOSTON MASSACRE: ANNIVERSARY. Mar 5, 1770. A skirmish between British troops and a crowd at Boston, MA, became widely publicized and contributed to the unpopularity of the British regime in the colonies before the American Revolution. Five men were killed and six more were injured by British troops commanded by Captain Thomas Preston.

CHANNEL ISLANDS NATIONAL PARK ESTABLISHED: ANNIVERSARY. Mar 5, 1980. California's Channel Islands Monument, authorized in 1938 by President Franklin D. Roosevelt, consisted of the islands of Anacapa and Santa Barbara. In 1980 President Jimmy Carter signed a bill establishing the Channel Islands National Park consisting of the islands Anacapa, San Miguel, Santa Barbara, Santa Cruz and Santa Rosa.

CRISPUS ATTUCKS DAY: DEATH ANNIVERSARY. Mar 5, 1770. Honors Crispus Attucks, possibly a runaway slave, who was the first to die in the Boston Massacre.

CULLIGAN, EMMETT J.: BIRTH ANNIVERSARY. Mar 5, 1893. Emmett J. Culligan, founder of the world's largest water treatment organization, was born at Yankton, SD. Culligan first experimented with a water-softening device in the early 1920s—to soften water used to wash his baby's diapers. In 1936 he launched the company from a Northbrook, IL, blacksmith shop. Recipient of the Horatio Alger Award in 1969, Culligan died at San Bernardino, CA, June 3, 1970.

DISCOVER WHAT YOUR NAME MEANS DAY. Mar 5. There are many sources, online and otherwise, for information about names and naming. To discover the (traditional/conventional) meaning of names, possibly yours, consider any of the available sources on the subject. Also try this: Give your name its own meaning that reflects who you are. Make your definition uniquely yours; decide for yourself what your own name means! Annually, the Wednesday of Celebrate Your Name Week. For info: Jerry Hill. E-mail: celebrateyournameweek@gmail.com. Web: www.namesuniverse.com.

GLOBAL MARATHON FOR, BY AND ABOUT WOMEN IN ENGINEERING AND TECHNOLOGY. Mar 5–7. An annual worldwide forum connecting professional women and college students for virtual and in-person conversations about education and careers in engineering and technology. The Marathon has been expanded to three days to accommodate an increase in programming. It is the only event of its kind connecting women in engineering and technology worldwide across a diverse range of disciplines, experience levels, ages, interests, backgrounds, cultures, industries and employers. The marathon is held to coincide with Women's History Month (March) and International Women's Day (Mar 8). For info: Natl Engineers Week Headquarters, 1420 King St, Alexandria, VA 22314. Phone: (703) 684-2852. E-mail: info@eweek.org. Web: www.globalmarathon.net.

HARRISON, REX: BIRTH ANNIVERSARY. Mar 5, 1908. Born Reginald Carey at Huyton, England. Rex Harrison's career as an actor encompassed more than 40 films and scores of plays. He won both a Tony and an Oscar for the role of Henry Higgins in *My Fair Lady*, perhaps his most famous role. Among other films, he appeared in *Dr. Dolittle, Cleopatra, Blithe Spirit* and *Major Barbara*. He claimed he would never retire from acting, and he was appearing in a Broadway revival of Somerset Maugham's *The Circle* three weeks before his death June 2, 1990, at his home at New York, NY.

IRON CURTAIN SPEECH: ANNIVERSARY. Mar 5, 1946. Winston Churchill, speaking at Westminster College, Fulton, MO, established the cold war boundary with these words: "From Stettin in the Baltic to Trieste in the Adriatic an iron curtain has descended across the continent." Though Churchill was not the first to use the phrase *iron curtain*, his speech gave it a new currency and its usage persisted.

ITALY: PURGATORY BANQUET. Mar 5. Gradoli (near Viterbo). On Ash Wednesday, gourmands are on hand for the banquet of penitence for the souls in purgatory, held on the premises of the cooperative winery.

KATYN FOREST MASSACRE ORDERED: ANNIVERSARY. Mar 5, 1940. In a bid to cripple the Polish army and intelligentsia, on this date Stalin ordered the killings of more than 21,000 Polish prisoners, including more than 8,000 officers captured in the Soviet invasion of Poland. In early April the killings began at sites across Russia, with the largest mass graves in Katyn Forest. Soviet and pro-Soviet Polish governments denied the massacre until Mikhail Gorbachev admitted in 1990 that Stalin had ordered the killings.

LENT. Mar 5–Apr 19. Most Christian churches observe a period of fasting and penitence (40 weekdays and six Sundays—Saturday considered a weekday) beginning on Ash Wednesday and ending on the Saturday before Easter.

MERCATOR, GERHARDUS: BIRTH ANNIVERSARY. Mar 5, 1512. Cartographer-geographer Mercator was born at Rupelmonde, Belgium. His Mercator projection for maps provided an accurate ratio of latitude to longitude and is still used today. He also introduced the term *atlas* for a collection of maps. He died at Duisberg, Germany, Dec 2, 1594.

NAIA MEN'S AND WOMEN'S SWIMMING AND DIVING NATIONAL CHAMPIONSHIPS. Mar 5–8. Oklahoma City, OK. Individuals compete for the national championship. 34th annual for women; 58th annual for men. For info: Natl Assn of Intercollegiate Athletics, 1200 Grand Blvd, Kansas City, MO 64106. E-mail: jadams@naia.org. Web: www.naia.org.

NATIONAL COLLEGIATE MEN'S AND WOMEN'S SKIING CHAMPIONSHIPS. Mar 5–8. Site TBD. 61st annual. Est attendance: 1,500. For info: NCAA, PO Box 6222, Indianapolis, IN 46206-6222. Phone: (317) 917-6222. Fax: (317) 917-6826. Web: www.NCAA.com.

SAINT PIRAN'S DAY. Mar 5. Celebrates the birthday of St. Piran, the patron saint of Cornish tinners. Cornish worldwide celebrate this day.

UNITED STATES BANK HOLIDAY: ANNIVERSARY. Mar 5, 1933. On his first full day in office (Sunday, Mar 5, 1933), President Franklin Roosevelt proclaimed a national "Bank Holiday" to help save the nation's faltering banking system. Most banks were able to reopen after the 10-day "holiday" (Mar 4–14), but in the meantime, "scrip" had temporarily replaced money in many American households.

VILLA-LOBOS, HEITOR: BIRTH ANNIVERSARY. Mar 5, 1887. Brazilian composer and musician Heitor Villa-Lobos born at Rio de Janeiro. *Bachianas brasileiras, Amazonas* and *Guitar Concerto* are a few of his works. He once said: "My music is natural, like a waterfall." Villa-Lobos died at Rio de Janeiro on Nov 17, 1959.

BIRTHDAYS TODAY

Kevin Connolly, 40, actor ("Entourage"), born New York, NY, Mar 5, 1974.

Samantha Eggar, 75, actress ("Samantha and the King," *The Collector*), born London, England, Mar 5, 1939.

Penn Jillette, 59, magician, born Greenfield, MA, Mar 5, 1955.

John Kitzhaber, 67, Governor of Oregon (D), born Colfax, WA, Mar 5, 1947.

March 2014

S	M	T	W	T	F	S
						1
2	3	4	5	6	7	8
9	10	11	12	13	14	15
16	17	18	19	20	21	22
23	24	25	26	27	28	29
30	31					

Paul Sand, 70, actor ("St. Elsewhere," Tony for *Story Theatre*), born Paul Sanchez at Los Angeles, CA, Mar 5, 1944.

Dean Stockwell, 78, actor (*The Boy with Green Hair*, "Quantum Leap"), born Los Angeles, CA, Mar 5, 1936.

Marsha Warfield, 60, actress ("Night Court," "Empty Nest"), born Chicago, IL, Mar 5, 1954.

Michael Warren, 68, actor ("Paris," "Hill Street Blues"), born South Bend, IN, Mar 5, 1946.

Fred Williamson, 76, actor ("Julia," "Half Nelson"), former football player, born Gary, IN, Mar 5, 1938.

March 6 — Thursday

DAY 65 **300 REMAINING**

BROWNING, ELIZABETH BARRETT: BIRTH ANNIVERSARY. Mar 6, 1806. English poet, author of *Sonnets from the Portuguese*, wife of poet Robert Browning and subject of the play *The Barretts of Wimpole Street*, was born near Durham, England. She died at Florence, Italy, June 29, 1861.

COSTELLO, LOU: BIRTH ANNIVERSARY. Mar 6, 1906. Born at Paterson, NJ, partner with Bud Abbott in the legendary comedy duo Abbott and Costello. The team formed in 1936 and was popular on radio, TV and film. Films included *Buck Privates* and *Abbott and Costello Meet Frankenstein*. "Who's on First?" was their legendary comedy routine. Costello died Mar 3, 1959, at East Los Angeles, CA.

DRED SCOTT DECISION: ANNIVERSARY. Mar 6, 1857. This was the most famous US Supreme Court decision during the prewar slavery controversy. Dred Scott, a slave, had successfully petitioned for his freedom based on his previous residence in a free state and territory. On this date the Supreme Court overturned Missouri's Supreme Court decision and declared the 1820 Missouri Compromise unconstitutional. Chief Justice Roger Taney wrote that slaves were property, not citizens, and that Congress had no power to restrict slavery in the territories.

EISNER, WILL: BIRTH ANNIVERSARY. Mar 6, 1917. One of the greatest comic book/graphic artists, William Erwin Eisner was born at Brooklyn, NY, to Jewish immigrant parents. In a career spanning eight decades, Eisner created the popular and innovative *Spirit* comic book, started an educational comic book business, taught legions of students graphic narrative techniques and created the first graphic novel, *A Contract with God* (1978). He brought cinematic touches—including German Expressionist style—to comics. The Eisner Awards were created in his honor in 1988 to recognize other bright lights in the field. Eisner died Jan 3, 2005, at Fort Lauderdale, FL.

ENGLAND: CRUFTS DOG SHOW. Mar 6–9. National Exhibition Centre, Birmingham, West Midlands. The World's Greatest Dog Show, where more than 23,000 top pedigree dogs compete to achieve the title of "Best in Show," the most prestigious award in the world of dogs. Held since 1891. Est attendance: 140,000. For info: The Kennel Club, 1-5 Clarges St, London, England W1J 8AB. Phone: (44) (844) 463-3980. Fax: (44) (20) 7518-1028. Web: www.crufts.org.uk.

FALL OF THE ALAMO: ANNIVERSARY. Mar 6, 1836. Anniversary of the fall of the Texan fort, the Alamo. The siege, led by Mexican general Santa Anna, began Feb 23 and reached its climax Mar 6, when the last of the defenders was slain. Texans, under General Sam Houston, rallied with the war cry "Remember the Alamo" and, at the Battle of San Jacinto, Apr 21, defeated and captured Santa Anna, who signed a treaty recognizing Texas's independence.

GHANA: INDEPENDENCE DAY. Mar 6. National holiday. Commemorates independence from Great Britain in 1957.

LARDNER, RING: BIRTH ANNIVERSARY. Mar 6, 1885. Ringgold Wilmer "Ring" Lardner, sportswriter, born at Niles, MI. Lardner wrote about sports for a variety of newspapers, mostly in Chicago, IL. In both his columns and his short stories, he reproduced ballplayers' vernacular speech patterns with great success, thereby laying the groundwork for generations of baseball fiction to come. Lardner abandoned baseball after the Black Sox scandal was exposed. He wrote songs, plays and magazine articles but never the novel that some of his friends thought he should. Taciturn and solemn with a biting sense of humor, Lardner drank and smoked to excess, even after contracting tuberculosis in 1926. Posthumously given the J.G. Taylor Spink Award in 1963 for his baseball writing. Died at East Hampton, NY, Sept 25, 1933.

MICHELANGELO: BIRTH ANNIVERSARY. Mar 6, 1475. Anniversary of the birth, at Caprese, Italy, of Michelangelo di Lodovico Buonarroti Simoni, a prolific Renaissance painter, sculptor, architect and poet who had a profound impact on Western art. Michelangelo's fresco painting on the ceiling of the Sistine Chapel at the Vatican at Rome, Italy, is often considered the pinnacle of his achievement in painting, as well as the highest achievement of the Renaissance. Also among his works were the sculptures *David* and *The Pieta*. Appointed architect of St. Peter's in 1542, a post he held until his death on Feb 18, 1564, at Rome.

NAIA INDOOR TRACK AND FIELD NATIONAL CHAMPIONSHIPS. Mar 6–8. Spire Institute, Geneva, OH. Individuals compete for All-America honors, while teams compete for the national championship. 49th annual competition for men; 34th annual for women. Est attendance: 2,500. For info: Natl Assn Intercollegiate Athletics, 1200 Grand Blvd, Kansas City, MO 64106. E-mail: Dwilke@naia.org. Web: www.naia.org.

NAMETAG DAY. Mar 6. Today's celebration of names stipulates that wherever you are, whatever you're doing, you wear a "Hello, I'm [your name here]" nametag. (Note: This event is not for unsupervised children.) Annually, the Thursday of Celebrate Your Name Week. For info: Jerry Hill. E-mail: celebrateyournameweek@gmail.com. Web: www.namesuniverse.com.

PEALE, ANNA CLAYPOOLE: BIRTH ANNIVERSARY. Mar 6, 1791. American painter of miniatures and a member of the famous Peale family of artists. Born at Philadelphia, PA; died Dec 25, 1878.

UNITED KINGDOM AND IRELAND: WORLD BOOK DAY. Mar 6 (tentative). 17th annual. World Book Day is the biggest annual celebration of books and reading in the UK and Ireland. (Most other countries hold World Book Day on Apr 23.) A main aim of this day is to encourage children to explore the pleasures of books and reading by providing them with the opportunity to have a book of their own. Annually, the first Thursday in March. For info: World Book Day. E-mail: wbd@education.co.uk. Web: www.worldbookday.com

WILLS, BOB: BIRTH ANNIVERSARY. Mar 6, 1905. The Father of Western Swing was born at Kosse, TX. Originally a performer (fiddler) with the Light Crust Doughboys, Wills later formed the popular Texas Playboys. Bob Wills and the Texas Playboys appeared on film and at the Grand Ole Opry and made Western swing popular with such hits as "San Antonio Rose." Wills died May 13, 1975, at Fort Worth, TX.

BIRTHDAYS TODAY

Tom Arnold, 55, actor ("Roseanne," *McHale's Navy, True Lies*), born Ottumwa, IA, Mar 6, 1959.

Connie Britton, 46, actress ("Nashville," "Friday Night Lights," "Spin City"), born Boston, MA, Mar 6, 1968.

Gabriel Garcia Marquez, 86, Nobel Prize–winning author (*A Hundred Years of Solitude, Love in the Time of Cholera*), born Aracaracca, Colombia, Mar 6, 1928.

Dave Gilmour, 70, singer, guitarist (Pink Floyd), born Cambridge, England, Mar 6, 1944.

Alan Greenspan, 88, economist, former chairman of the Federal Reserve Board, born New York, NY, Mar 6, 1926.

D.L. Hughley, 51, comedian, actor ("The Hughleys," *The Original Kings of Comedy*), born Los Angeles, CA, Mar 6, 1963.

Kiri Te Kanawa, 70, opera singer, born Gisborne, New Zealand, Mar 6, 1944.

Ben Murphy, 72, actor ("Alias Smith and Jones," *Yours, Mine and Ours*), born Jonesboro, AR, Mar 6, 1942.

Ryan Nyquist, 35, BMX bike racer, born Los Gatos, CA, Mar 6, 1979.

Shaquille Rashan O'Neal, 42, former basketball player, born Newark, NJ, Mar 6, 1972.

Amy Pietz, 45, actress ("Caroline in the City"), born Oakcreek, WI, Mar 6, 1969.

Rob Reiner, 67, actor ("All in the Family"), director (*When Harry Met Sally, This Is Spinal Tap*), born New York, NY, Mar 6, 1947 (some sources say 1945).

Valentina Tereshkova-Nikolaeva, 77, cosmonaut, born Maslennikovo, USSR (now Russia), Mar 6, 1937.

March 7 — Friday

DAY 66 — **299 REMAINING**

AMERICAN CROSSWORD PUZZLE TOURNAMENT. Mar 7–9. Brooklyn Bridge Marriott Hotel, Brooklyn, NY. Seven hundred solvers from the US and Canada compete on eight puzzles during this 37th annual event. Points are awarded for accuracy and speed. The final puzzle is played on giant white boards for everyone to watch. Prizes are awarded in 22 skill, age and geographic categories, and the grand prize is $5,000. The weekend also includes group word games, guest speakers and appearances by celebrity crossword solvers. Solvers can compete at home for fun, either online or by mail, and receive a ranking in all their solving categories. Est attendance: 1,000. For info: Will Shortz, Director, American Crossword Puzzle Tournament, 55 Great Oak Ln, Pleasantville, NY 10570. Phone: (718) 797-0264. Web: www.crosswordtournament.com.

March 2014	S	M	T	W	T	F	S
							1
	2	3	4	5	6	7	8
	9	10	11	12	13	14	15
	16	17	18	19	20	21	22
	23	24	25	26	27	28	29
	30	31					

BURBANK, LUTHER: BIRTH ANNIVERSARY. Mar 7, 1849. Anniversary of the birth of American naturalist and author, creator and developer of many new varieties of flowers, fruits, vegetables and trees. Burbank's birthday is observed in California as Bird and Arbor Day. Born at Lancaster, MA, he died at Santa Rosa, CA, Apr 11, 1926.

CAMEX. Mar 7–11. Dallas Convention Center, Dallas, TX. The only national conference and trade exhibit designed exclusively for collegiate retailers. College store buyers and suppliers gather at CAMEX to preview products to be seen on college campuses in the coming year. Est attendance: 7,000. For info: Natl Assn of College Stores (NACS), 500 E Lorain St, Oberlin, OH 44074. Phone: (440) 775-7777 or (800) 622-7498. Web: www.camex.org or nacs.org.

CRAFTSMEN'S SPRING CLASSIC ARTS & CRAFTS FESTIVAL. Mar 7–9. South Carolina State Fairgrounds, Columbia, SC. 31st annual. Features work from more than 300 talented artists and craftspeople. All juried exhibitors' work has been handmade by the exhibitors and must be their own original design and creation. See the creative process in action with several exhibitors demonstrating through the weekend. Something for every style, taste and budget with items from the most contemporary to the most traditional. Est attendance: 20,000. For info: Gilmore Enterprises, 3514-A Drawbridge Pkwy, Greensboro, NC 27410-8584. Phone: (336) 282-5550. E-mail: contact@gilmoreshows.com. Web: www.CraftShow.com or www.gilmoreshows.com.

DISTINGUISHED SERVICE MEDAL: ANNIVERSARY. Mar 7, 1918. With US troops fighting in the trenches in France during WWI, President Woodrow Wilson authorized the creation of a new bronze, beribboned medal to be given to US Army personnel who performed "exceptionally meritorious service."

DRESS IN BLUE DAY. Mar 7. Observed on the first Friday in March, the Dress in Blue Day program promotes awareness about colon cancer and encourages people to get their colon checked. Part of National Colorectal Cancer Awareness Month since 2006. For info: Colon Cancer Alliance, 1025 Vermont Ave NW, Ste 1066, Washington, DC 20005. Web: www.ccalliance.org/dressinblueday.

ENGLAND: WORDS BY THE WATER: A FESTIVAL OF WORDS AND IDEAS. Mar 7–16. Lake District. The Theatre by the Lake at Keswick, sitting on the banks of Derwentwater, is the perfect setting for this lively festival. More than 100 speakers and performers participate in lectures, interviews, discussions and readings. For info: Ways with Words, Droridge Farm, Dartington, Totnes, Devon, England TQ9 6JG. Phone: (44) (1803) 867-373. E-mail: admin@wayswithwords.co.uk. Web: www.wayswithwords.co.uk.

HOPKINS, STEPHEN: BIRTH ANNIVERSARY. Mar 7, 1707. Colonial governor (Rhode Island) and signer of the Declaration of Independence. Born at Providence, RI, and died there July 13, 1785.

INTERNATIONAL FESTIVAL OF OWLS. Mar 7–9. Houston, MN. Immerse yourself in owls at this all-owl family event. Kids will delight in the owl face painting, owl crafts and owl storytelling. Adults will enjoy presentations by prominent "owlologists," including a banquet address and the presentation of the World Owl Hall of Fame awards. Live owl presentations with five or more species of owls, hooting contest, owl prowls, medallion hunt, owl merchandise and owl-themed food. Annually, the first full weekend in March. Est attendance: 1,800. For info: Karla Bloem, International Festival of Owls, 215 W Plum St, PO Box 731, Houston, MN 55943. Phone: (507) 896-4668. Fax: (507) 896-5668. E-mail: nature@acegroup.cc. Web: www.festivalofowls.com.

MIDDLE NAME PRIDE DAY. Mar 7. Today's name celebration requires honesty and possibly some courage. Tell three people who don't already know it what your middle name is (even if it's Egbert). Annually, the Friday of Celebrate Your Name Week. For info: Jerry Hill. E-mail: celebrateyournameweek@gmail.com. Web: www.namesuniverse.com.

NAIA WRESTLING NATIONAL CHAMPIONSHIPS. Mar 7–8. Kansas ExpoCentre, Topeka, KS. 57th annual. Individuals compete for All-America honors in 10 weight divisions, while teams compete for the national championship. Est attendance: 10,000. For info: Natl Assn of Intercollegiate Athletics, 1200 Grand Blvd, Kansas City, MO 64106. E-mail: jford@naia.org. Web: www.naia.org.

NATIONAL BE HEARD DAY. Mar 7. There are more than 145 million small businesses in the US, but often, small business owners are less likely to get the media coverage they deserve. National Be Heard Day celebrates and empowers business owners and entrepreneurs who can find their voices, tell their stories and be heard through publicity efforts. For info: Shannon Cherry, 184 Lancaster St, Albany, NY 12210. Phone: (518) 632-6212. E-mail: helper@beheardsolutions.com. Web: beheardday.com.

NATIONAL DAY OF UNPLUGGING. Mar 7–8. 5th annual. National Day of Unplugging is sponsored by Reboot, a nonprofit organization that aims to reinvent the cultures, traditions and rituals of Jewish life. The day is guided by Reboot's Sabbath Manifesto, a project that is encouraging hyperconnected and frequently frantic people to re-embrace the ancient beauty of a day of rest. Reboot encourages people of all backgrounds to recharge their spiritual and personal lives by not using computers, cell phones or any technology for 24 hours—from sundown on Friday, Mar 7, to sundown on Saturday, Mar 8. For info: Reboot, 44 W 28th St, 8th Fl, New York, NY 10001. Web: www.rebooters.net or www.nationaldayofunplugging.com.

XI PARALYMPIC WINTER GAMES. Mar 7–16. Turin, Italy. Some 600 athletes with disabilities and 1,000 officials will take part in these games that feature medal events in alpine skiing (slalom and giant slalom), biathlon, cross-country skiing, ice sledge hockey and wheelchair curling. For info: International Olympic Committee. Web: www.sochi2014.com.

RIO GRANDE VALLEY LIVESTOCK SHOW. Mar 7–16. Mercedes, TX. 75th annual. PRCA rodeo, open cattle show and carnival. For the youth of the four counties in the valley to exhibit their projects. Est attendance: 200,000. For info: Rio Grande Valley Livestock Show Inc, 1000 N Texas, Mercedes, TX 78570. Phone: (956) 565-2456. Fax: (956) 565-3005. E-mail: droe@rgvlivestockshow.com. Web: www.rgvlivestockshow.com.

SHABBAT ACROSS AMERICA/CANADA. Mar 7. More than 400 participating synagogues (Conservative, Orthodox, Reform and Reconstructionist) encourage Jews to observe the Sabbath on this Friday night. Est attendance: 40,000. For info: Natl Jewish Outreach Program, 989 Sixth Ave, 10th Fl, New York, NY 10018. Phone: (888) SHA-BBAT or (646) 871-4444. E-mail: info@njop.org. Web: www.njop.org.

SOUTH BY SOUTHWEST (SXSW). Mar 7–16. Austin, TX. Annual, internationally recognized music, new media and film conference. Hundreds of music, film and interactive events and panels. Est attendance: 45,000. For info: SXSW, PO Box 685289, Austin, TX 78768. Phone: (512) 467-7979. Fax: (512) 637-1535. E-mail: sxsw@sxsw.com. Web: www.sxsw.com.

SUEZ CANAL OPENS: ANNIVERSARY. Mar 7, 1869. This waterway across Egypt connecting the Mediterranean and Red seas was built by the French. In 1956 Egyptian president Nasser nationalized the canal, prompting an invasion by the British, French and Israelis. The Six-Day War in 1967 shut down the canal for eight years.

WORLD DAY OF PRAYER. Mar 7. 127th annual. An ecumenical event that reinforces bonds among peoples of the world as they join in a global circle of prayer. Annually, the first Friday in March. For info: WDP-USA, 475 Riverside Dr, Ste 800, New York, NY 10115. Phone: (212) 870-2466. Web: www.wdp-usa.org.

WORLD'S LARGEST RATTLESNAKE ROUNDUP. Mar 7–9. Sweetwater, TX. 56th annual. With Sweetwater Rifle and Pistol Club Gun Knife and Coin Show. Educational programs about rattlesnakes; flea market; Texas's second-largest cook-off; dances; numerous pounds of live rattlesnakes on display; snake meat available to eat and snake articles for sale. Snake hunts and bus tours available. More than 750 booth spaces are available. Annually, the second weekend in March. Est attendance: 40,000. For info: Sweetwater Chamber of Commerce or Sweetwater Jaycees. Phone: (325) 235-5488 or (800) 658-6757. Fax: (325) 235-1026. Web: www.sweetwatertexas.org or www.rattlesnakeroundup.net.

BIRTHDAYS TODAY

Anthony Armstrong-Jones (Lord Snowdon), 84, photographer, born London, England, Mar 7, 1930.

Bryan Cranston, 58, actor ("Malcolm in the Middle," "Breaking Bad"), born San Fernando Valley, CA, Mar 7, 1956.

Taylor Dayne, 52, singer, born Long Island, NY, Mar 7, 1962.

Michael Eisner, 72, media executive, born Mount Kisco, NY, Mar 7, 1942.

Jenna Fischer, 40, actress ("The Office," *Walk Hard: The Dewey Cox Story*), born Fort Wayne, IN, Mar 7, 1974.

Denyce Graves, 50, opera singer, born Washington, DC, Mar 7, 1964.

Janet Guthrie, 76, former auto racer, born Iowa City, IA, Mar 7, 1938.

Franco Harris, 64, Hall of Fame football player, born Fort Dix, NJ, Mar 7, 1950.

John Heard, 68, actor (*Too Big to Fail, Rambling Rose, The Pelican Brief*), born Washington, DC, Mar 7, 1946.

Jeff Kent, 46, former baseball player, born Bellflower, CA, Mar 7, 1968.

Ivan Lendl, 54, Hall of Fame tennis player, born Ostrava, Czechoslovakia (now the Czech Republic), Mar 7, 1960.

Willard Herman Scott, 80, weatherman ("Today"), friend of centenarians, born Alexandria, VA, Mar 7, 1934.

Nick Searcy, 55, actor ("Justified," *Moneyball*), born Cullowhee, NC, Mar 7, 1959.

Daniel J. Travanti, 74, actor ("Hill Street Blues"), born Kenosha, WI, Mar 7, 1940.

Rachel Weisz, 43, actress (Oscar for *The Constant Gardener*; *Oz the Great and Powerful, The Bourne Legacy, The Deep Blue Sea*), born London, England, Mar 7, 1971.

Peter Wolf, 68, singer (J. Geils Band), born Boston, MA, Mar 7, 1946.

March 8 — Saturday

DAY 67 — **298 REMAINING**

AMERICAN COUNCIL ON EDUCATION ANNUAL MEETING. Mar 8–11. Manchester Grand Hyatt, San Diego, CA. 96th annual meeting. Est attendance: 1,600. For info: American Council on Education, One Dupont Circle NW, Washington, DC 20036. Phone: (202) 939-9300. Fax: (202) 833-5692. E-mail: annualmeeting@acenet.edu. Web: www.acenet.edu.

BACH, CARL PHILIPP EMANUEL: 300th BIRTH ANNIVERSARY. Mar 8, 1714. Musically the most important and influential of Johann Sebastian Bach's sons. German composer, keyboard performer and theorist, C.P.E. Bach was born at Weimar, Germany. A contributor to the Viennese classical style and pioneer of sonata-allegro musical form, the publication of *Essay on the True Art of Playing Keyboard Instruments* (1753), which remains one of the principal monuments of 18th-century musical thought and practice, made him the most renowned authority of the 18th cen-

tury on keyboard pedagogy and composition. Influential to Haydn and Beethoven, he died Dec 15, 1788, at Hamburg, Germany.

BATTLE OF PEA RIDGE: ANNIVERSARY. Mar 8, 1862. Federal troops were surprised by General Earl Van Dorn's Confederate troops at Pea Ridge, AR. Several attempts by the Rebels to rout the Union forces proved unsuccessful. Van Dorn's forces included three regiments of Native American troops. During the next day's fighting, General Samuel Custis's Federal troops continued to hold out as Van Dorn retreated and was ordered to leave the state. The Battle of Pea Ridge was the most significant of the Trans-Mississippi western area.

BEAR TIE BALL. Mar 8 (tentative). Chicago, IL. Bear Necessities Pediatric Cancer Foundation hosts its annual fundraising ball each year in March. The gala is the organization's largest fundraiser, typically raising more than half a million dollars toward the fight against pediatric cancer. Est attendance: 700. For info: Bear Necessities Pediatric Cancer Foundation, 55 W Wacker Dr, Ste 1100, Chicago, IL 60601. Phone: (312) 214-1200. Fax: (312) 214-7797. E-mail: ckrupa@bearnecessities.org. Web: www.bearnecessities.org.

BEAVERS, LOUISE: BIRTH ANNIVERSARY. Mar 8, 1902. The Hollywood career of Louise Beavers spanned 30 years and more than 125 films. Though she was forced to play stereotypical roles, such as those of maids, her authentic talent was always apparent. Her starring role in the film *Imitation of Life* earned her high praise. Beavers was a member of the Black Filmmakers Hall of Fame. She also played the title role in the TV series "Beulah" (1951–53). Born at Cincinnati, OH; died at Los Angeles, CA, Oct 26, 1962.

CAXTON'S *MIRROR OF THE WORLD* TRANSLATION: ANNIVERSARY. Mar 8, 1481. William Caxton, England's first printer, completed the translation from French into English of *Mirror of the World*, a popular account of astronomy and other sciences. In print soon afterward, *Mirror of the World* became the first illustrated book printed in England.

GENEALOGY DAY. Mar 8. Climb into your family tree. Jiggle a few branches. Start piecing together your personal history today via one of the world's fastest-growing hobbies, genealogy, a puzzle waiting to be put together. Annually, the Saturday of Celebrate Your Name Week. For info: Jerry Hill. E-mail: celebrateyournameweek@gmail.com. Web: www.namesuniverse.com.

GRAHAME, KENNETH: BIRTH ANNIVERSARY. Mar 8, 1859. Scottish author, born at Edinburgh. His children's book *The Wind in the Willows* has as its main characters a mole, a rat, a badger and a toad. He died July 6, 1932, at Pangbourne, Berkshire.

HIGHLAND COUNTY MAPLE FESTIVAL. Mar 8–9 (also Mar 15–16). Highland County, VA. 56th annual. Festival welcomes visitors to view the process of syrup making. Large arts and crafts shows and antiques. Est attendance: 50,000. For info: Highland County Chamber of Commerce, PO Box 223, Monterey, VA 24465. Phone: (540) 468-2550. Fax: (540) 468-2551. E-mail: highcc@cfw.com. Web: www.highlandcounty.org.

March 2014	S	M	T	W	T	F	S
							1
	2	3	4	5	6	7	8
	9	10	11	12	13	14	15
	16	17	18	19	20	21	22
	23	24	25	26	27	28	29
	30	31					

INDIANA FLOWER AND PATIO SHOW. Mar 8–16. Indiana State Fairgrounds, Indianapolis, IN. The oldest show of its kind in the Midwest, featuring more than 30 landscaped gardens and products and services for home, yard and patio. Est attendance: 106,000. For info: HSI Show Productions, Box 502797, Indianapolis, IN 46250. Phone: (317) 576-9933. Fax: (317) 576-9955. Web: www.hsishows.com.

INTERNATIONAL FANNY PACK DAY. Mar 8. Over the centuries a form of the fanny pack has been used to carry items for easy access. Today, pay tribute to this fashion essential. Annually, the second Saturday in March. Use this day as a reminder to end hunger locally and give to a food bank—wearing your fanny pack! For info: Nick Yates, International Fanny Pack Day, 6614 W Baron Dr, Boise, ID 83714. Phone: (208) 863-1414. E-mail: yates_nick@hotmail.com.

INTERNATIONAL (WORKING) WOMEN'S DAY. Mar 8. A day to honor women, especially working women. Said to commemorate an 1857 march and demonstration at New York, NY, by female garment and textile workers. Believed to have been first proclaimed for this date at an international conference of women held at Helsinki, Finland, in 1910, "that henceforth Mar 8 should be declared International Women's Day." The 50th anniversary observance, at Peking, China, in 1960, cited Clara Zetkin (1857–1933) as "initiator of Women's Day on Mar 8." This is perhaps the most widely observed holiday of recent origin and is unusual among holidays originating in the US in having been widely adopted and observed in other nations, including socialist countries. In Russia it is a national holiday, and flowers or gifts are presented to women workers.

MOON PHASE: FIRST QUARTER. Mar 8. Moon enters First Quarter phase at 8:27 AM, EST.

NATIONAL PROCRASTINATION WEEK. Mar 8–14. To promote the many benefits of putting off until tomorrow everything that needn't be done today. For info: Les Waas, Pres, Procrastinators' Club of America Inc, PO Box 712, Bryn Athyn, PA 19009. Phone: (215) 947-0500. Fax: (215) 947-9010. E-mail: procrastinators_club_of_america@yahoo.com.

NATIONAL PROOFREADING DAY. Mar 8. Do typos (typographical errors) make you cringe? Strive for 100 percent accuracy in all documents and messages on National Proofreading Day. Grab a red pen or red pencil on Mar 8 to correct misspelled words; misused words; typos; grammatical errors; and missing, overused and misused punctuation marks. For info: Judy Beaver, National Proofreading Day, 26W112 Klein Creek Dr, Winfield, IL 60190. Phone: (630) 917-1015. Fax: (630) 260-5906. E-mail: Judy@NationalProofreadingDay.com. Web: www.NationalProofreadingDay.com.

NORWAY: FINNMARKSLØPET. Mar 8. Alta, Finnmark County. 34th anniversary event. First taking place in 1981, the Finnmarksløpet is the world's northernmost sled dog race. Hosted by Alta Sled Dog Club, the Finnmarksløpet is in fact two races: a 500 km race with up to 8 dogs and a 1,000 km race with a maximum of 14 dogs. Annually, the Saturday of the 10th week of the year. For info: Finnmarksløpet. Web: www.finnmarkslopet.no.

RUSSIA: INTERNATIONAL WOMEN'S DAY. Mar 8. National holiday.

SAINT PIRAN'S DAY CELEBRATION. Mar 8 (tentative). Location available after Jan 1. Celebration in honor of St. Piran, patron saint of Cornwall and Cornish peoples. Held to help preserve history and culture of the Cornish (Celtic). Annually, the Saturday nearest Mar 5. For info: Marjorie Roberts, Greater Kansas City Cornish Society, 24 E 68th St, Kansas City, MO 64113-2414. Phone: (816) 361-1956. E-mail: margeroberts24@gmail.com.

SYRIAN ARAB REPUBLIC: REVOLUTION DAY. Mar 8. Official public holiday commemorating assumption of power by Revolutionary National Council on Mar 8, 1963.

UNITED NATIONS: DAY FOR WOMEN'S RIGHTS AND INTERNATIONAL PEACE. Mar 8. An international day observed by the organizations of the United Nations system. In some years, known as International Women's Day. For info: United Nations, Dept of Public Info, New York, NY 10017. Web: www.un.org.

UNITED STATES INCOME TAX: ANNIVERSARY. Mar 8, 1913. The Internal Revenue Service began to levy and collect income taxes. The 16th Amendment to the Constitution, ratified Feb 3, 1913, gave Congress the authority to tax income. The US had also levied an income tax during the Civil War. See also: "Lincoln Signs Income Tax" (July 1).

VAN BUREN, HANNAH HOES: BIRTH ANNIVERSARY. Mar 8, 1783. Wife of Martin Van Buren, eighth president of the US. Born at Kinderhook, NY, she died at Albany, NY, Feb 5, 1819.

BIRTHDAYS TODAY

Susan Clark, 74, actress ("Webster," *Babe*), born Sarnia, ON, Canada, Mar 8, 1940.

Micky Dolenz, 69, singer, actor ("The Monkees"), director, born Los Angeles, CA, Mar 8, 1945.

Kathy Ireland, 51, model, born Santa Barbara, CA, Mar 8, 1963.

Petra Kvitova, 24, tennis player, born Bílovec, Czechoslovakia (now the Czech Republic), Mar 8, 1990.

Camryn Manheim, 53, actress ("Ghost Whisperer," "The Practice"), born Caldwell, NJ, Mar 8, 1961.

Freddie Prinze, Jr, 38, actor (*Scooby-Doo, She's All That*), born Albuquerque, NM, Mar 8, 1976.

Aidan Quinn, 55, actor ("Elementary," *Eclipse, Desperately Seeking Susan*; stage: *A Streetcar Named Desire*), born Chicago, IL, Mar 8, 1959.

James Edward (Jim) Rice, 61, Hall of Fame baseball player, born Anderson, SC, Mar 8, 1953.

Carole Bayer Sager, 67, singer, songwriter, born New York, NY, Mar 8, 1947.

Raynoma Gordy Singleton, 77, cofounder of Motown Records, born Detroit, MI, Mar 8, 1937.

James Van Der Beek, 37, actor ("Dawson's Creek"), born Cheshire, CT, Mar 8, 1977.

March 9 — Sunday

DAY 68 **297 REMAINING**

BARBIE DEBUTS: 55th ANNIVERSARY. Mar 9, 1959. The popular girls' doll debuted in stores. More than 800 million dolls have been sold.

BATTLE OF HAMPTON ROADS: ANNIVERSARY. Mar 9, 1862. In a Civil War battle that changed the face of naval warfare, two ironclad vessels, the CSS *Virginia* and the USS *Monitor*, engaged in an exchange of fire for two hours. Neither vessel suffered much damage, but injuries forced both commanders to pull back without a clear victory. On the previous day, the heavily armored *Virignia* had succeeded in severely damaging three Union vessels prior to the arrival of the *Monitor*.

BELIZE: BARON BLISS DAY. Mar 9. Official public holiday. Celebrated in honor of Sir Henry Edward Ernest Victor Bliss, a great benefactor of Belize.

CHECK YOUR BATTERIES DAY. Mar 9. A day set aside for checking the batteries in your smoke detector, carbon monoxide detector, HVAC thermostat, audio/visual remote controls and other electronic devices. This could save your life! Annually, the second Sunday in March (with Daylight Saving Time).

DAYLIGHT SAVING TIME BEGINS. Mar 9–Nov 2. Daylight Saving Time begins at 2 AM. The Energy Policy Act of 2005 extended the period of Daylight Saving Time as originally outlined in the Uniform Time Act of 1966 (amended in 1986 by Public Law 99–359). Standard Time in each zone is advanced one hour from 2 AM on the second Sunday in March until 2 AM on the first Sunday in November (except where state legislatures provide exemption). Prior to 1986, Daylight Saving Time began on the last Sunday in April. Many use the popular rule "spring forward, fall back" to remember which way to turn their clocks. See also: "Daylight Saving Time Ends; Standard Time Resumes" (Nov 2).

GAGARIN, YURI ALEXSEYEVICH: 80th BIRTH ANNIVERSARY. Mar 9, 1934. Russian cosmonaut Yuri Gagarin, the first person to travel in space, was born at Gzhatsk, USSR. The 27-year-old Soviet Air Force major made his flight Apr 12, 1961, lasting 108 minutes and orbiting Earth in a rocket-propelled, five-ton space capsule, 187 miles above Earth's surface. Gagarin was killed in an airplane crash near Moscow on Mar 27, 1968. After his death the town in which he was born was renamed Gagarin, and the Gagarin Museum was established in the frame house where he spent his childhood.

GRANT COMMISSIONED COMMANDER OF ALL UNION ARMIES: 150th ANNIVERSARY. Mar 9, 1864. At Washington, DC, Ulysses S. Grant accepted his commission as Lieutenant General, becoming the commander of all the Union armies.

JOE FRANKLIN DAY. Mar 9. A day to honor the king of radio, television and entertainment for all his contributions on the anniversary of his birth. Franklin appeared on late-night television in New York during 1950–93 and continues to entertain people today. For info: Bob O'Brien, "The Answer Man," 1061 Koelle Ave, Secaucus, NJ 07094. Phone: (646) 233-6610. E-mail: robtfobrien@aol.com.

LUXEMBOURG: BÜRGSONNDEG. Mar 9. Young people build a huge bonfire on a hill to celebrate the victorious sun, marking the end of winter. A tradition dating to pre-Christian times. On the Sunday after Ash Wednesday.

MOLOTOV, VYACHESLAV MIKHAILOVICH: BIRTH ANNIVERSARY. Mar 9, 1890. Soviet People's Commissar for Foreign Affairs, Molotov negotiated the German-Soviet nonaggression pact of 1939. An active participant in the Stalinist Great Purge, he signed numerous orders of execution. Molotov's claim that Russian forces were dropping food, and not incendiary bombs, on Finnish forces during the Winter War led the Finns to christen their improvised gasoline bombs "Molotov cocktails." Born Mar 9, 1890 (NS; Feb 25 OS) at Kukarka, Russia, he died Nov 8, 1986, at Moscow, Russia, at the age of 96.

PANIC DAY. Mar 9. Run around all day in a panic, telling others you can't handle it anymore. (©2006 by WH.) For info: Thomas & Ruth Roy, Wellcat Holidays, 2418 Long Ln, Lebanon, PA 17046. Phone: (717) 279-0184. E-mail: info@wellcat.com. Web: www.wellcat.com.

SAINT FRANCES OF ROME: FEAST DAY. Mar 9. Patron of motorists and model for housewives and widows (1384–1440). After 40 years of marriage she was widowed in 1436 and later joined the community of Benedictine Oblates. Canonized in 1608.

TEEN TECH WEEK. Mar 9–15. Sponsored by the Young Adult Library Services Association, Teen Tech Week is a celebration aimed at getting teens to discover the different technologies offered by their libraries, such as DVDs, databases, audiobooks, electronic games and more. For info: Young Adult Library Services Assn (YALSA), American Library Assn, 50 E Huron St, Chicago, IL 60611. Phone: (800) 545-2433, ext. 4390. E-mail: yalsa@ala.org. Web: www.ala.org/teentechweek.

TOKYO BLANKET BOMBING: ANNIVERSARY. Mar 9, 1945. The Japanese capital of Tokyo was bombed by 343 Superfortresses carrying all the incendiary bombs they could hold. Within the targeted areas of the city, population densities were four times greater than those of most American cities, and homes were made primarily of wood and paper. Carried by the wind, the fires leveled 16 square miles. More than a quarter million buildings were destroyed. The death toll was 83,000; 41,000 were injured. For the balance of WWII, American strategic bombing followed this pattern.

VESPUCCI, AMERIGO: BIRTH ANNIVERSARY. Mar 9, 1454. Italian navigator, merchant and explorer for whom the Americas were named. Born at Florence, Italy (some sources cite his birth year as 1451). He participated in at least two expeditions between 1499 and 1502, which took him to the coast of South America, where he discovered the Amazon and Plata rivers. Vespucci's expeditions were of great importance because he believed that he had discovered a new continent, not just a new route to the Orient. Neither Vespucci nor his exploits achieved the fame of Columbus, but the New World was to be named for Amerigo Vespucci by an obscure German geographer and mapmaker, Martin Waldseemuller. Ironically, in his work as an outfitter of ships, Vespucci had been personally acquainted with Christopher Columbus. Vespucci died at Seville, Spain, Feb 22, 1512. See also: "Waldseemuller, Martin: Remembrance Day" (Apr 25).

BIRTHDAYS TODAY

Juliette Binoche, 50, actress (Oscar for *The English Patient*; *Chocolat*), born Paris, France, Mar 9, 1964.

Linda Fiorentino, 54, actress (*Men in Black*), born Philadelphia, PA, Mar 9, 1960.

Mickey Gilley, 78, singer, musician, born Natchez, MS, Mar 9, 1936.

Marty Ingels, 78, actor (*A Guide for the Married Man*), born Brooklyn, NY, Mar 9, 1936.

David Hume Kennerly, 67, photographer, born Rosenburg, OR, Mar 9, 1947.

Emmanuel Lewis, 43, actor ("Webster"), born Brooklyn, NY, Mar 9, 1971.

Terence John (Terry) Mulholland, 51, former baseball player, born St. Paul, MN, Mar 9, 1963.

Jeffrey Osborne, 66, musician, songwriter, born Providence, RI, Mar 9, 1948.

Benito Santiago, 49, former baseball player, born Ponce, Puerto Rico, Mar 9, 1965.

Trish Van Devere, 71, actress (*Where's Poppa?, One Is a Lonely Number*), born Tenafly, NJ, Mar 9, 1943.

Joyce Van Patten, 80, actress (*Monkey Shines*, "The Goodbye Guys"), born Queens, NY, Mar 9, 1934.

March 2014	S	M	T	W	T	F	S
							1
	2	3	4	5	6	7	8
	9	10	11	12	13	14	15
	16	17	18	19	20	21	22
	23	24	25	26	27	28	29
	30	31					

March 10 — Monday

DAY 69 — **296 REMAINING**

BRAIN AWARENESS WEEK. Mar 10–16. Brain Awareness Week is the global campaign to advance public awareness about the progress and benefits of brain research. The Dana Alliance is joined in the campaign by partners in the US and around the world, including medical and research organizations; patient advocacy groups; the National Institutes of Health and other government agencies; service groups; hospitals and universities; K–12 schools and professional organizations. For info: Dana Alliance for Brain Initiatives, 505 Fifth Ave, 6th Fl, New York, NY 10017. Phone: (212) 401-1689. Fax: (212) 593-7623. E-mail: bawinfo@dana.org. Web: www.dana.org/brainweek.

"BUFFY THE VAMPIRE SLAYER" TV PREMIERE: ANNIVERSARY. Mar 10, 1997. The popular WB show mixed B-movie horror with teen drama. Buffy Summers, played by Sarah Michelle Gellar, is a chosen slayer of vampires, but she still has to get through high school. The witty series was a spin-off of the 1992 film of the same name. After changing networks, the series ended in May 2003.

FILL OUR STAPLERS DAY. Mar 10 (also Nov 3). To avoid those annoying empty staplers, the Dull Men's Club has established Fill Our Staplers Day. The day occurs twice a year: the days after the days we change our clocks to and from Daylight Saving Time. For info: Dull Men's Club. E-mail: contactus@dullmensclub.com. Web: www.dullmensclub.com.

FITZGERALD, BARRY: BIRTH ANNIVERSARY. Mar 10, 1888. Actor, born William Joseph Shields, at Dublin, Ireland. He performed with the Abbey Theatre before moving to Hollywood, CA, in 1936. Fitzgerald won a Best Supporting Actor Oscar for his role as Father Fitzgibbon in *Going My Way* (1944)—while also being nominated as Best Actor for the same role. Fitzgerald died Jan 14, 1961, at Dublin.

"THE INCREDIBLE HULK" TV PREMIERE: ANNIVERSARY. Mar 10, 1978. A wonderfully campy action series based on the popular Marvel comic book as well as a modern-day Jekyll and Hyde story. Bill Bixby played the erudite scientist, Dr. David Banner, who accidentally exposed himself to gamma radiation. When provoked, Banner metamorphosed into the shirt-shredding, body-baring, green-skinned, snarling Neanderthal Hulk. The 6'5", 275-pound former Mr Universe, Lou Ferrigno, played the largely nonspeaking part of the Hulk.

JUPITER EFFECT: ANNIVERSARY. Mar 10, 1982. The much-talked-about and sometimes-feared planetary configuration of a semi-alignment of the planets on the same side of the sun occurred on this date without causing any of the disasters or unusual natural phenomena that some had predicted.

LUCE, CLARE BOOTHE: BIRTH ANNIVERSARY. Mar 10, 1903. Playwright and politician Clare Boothe Luce was born at New York City. Luce wrote for and edited *Vogue* and *Vanity Fair*. She also wrote plays, three of which were later adapted into motion pictures—*The Women* (1936), *Kiss the Boys Goodbye* (1938) and *Margin of Error* (1939). She served in the US House of Representatives (1943–47) and as ambassador to Italy (1953–56)—the first woman appointed ambassador to a major country. Luce died Oct 9, 1987, at Washington, DC.

MARIO DAY. Mar 10. A day for all persons named Mario. Using the abbreviation for the month of March, i.e., MAR, with the day, i.e., 10, you get the name spelled out: MAR10. Annually, Mar 10. Created by Mario Fascitelli.

SALVATION ARMY IN THE US: ANNIVERSARY. Mar 10, 1880. Commissioner George Scott Railton and seven women officers landed at New York to officially begin the work of the Salvation Army in the US.

TELEPHONE INVENTION: ANNIVERSARY. Mar 10, 1876. Alexander Graham Bell transmitted the first telephone message to his assistant in the next room: "Mr Watson, come here, I want you," at Cambridge, MA. See also: "Bell, Alexander Graham: Birth Anniversary" (Mar 3).

TUBMAN, HARRIET: DEATH ANNIVERSARY. Mar 10, 1913. American abolitionist, Underground Railroad leader, born a slave at Bucktown, Dorchester County, MD, about 1820 or 1821. She escaped from a Maryland plantation in 1849 and later helped more than 300 slaves reach freedom. Died at Auburn, NY.

UNITED KINGDOM: COMMONWEALTH DAY. Mar 10. Replaces Empire Day observance recognized until 1958. Observed on second Monday in March. Also observed in the British Virgin Islands, Gibraltar and Newfoundland, Canada.

US PAPER MONEY ISSUED: ANNIVERSARY. Mar 10, 1862. After the Legal Tender Act of 1862 passed Feb 25, 1862, the first paper money was issued in the US on this date. The denominations were $5 (Hamilton), $10 (Lincoln) and $20 (Liberty).

BIRTHDAYS TODAY

Joseph (Sepp) Blatter, 78, president of FIFA, born Visp, Switzerland, Mar 10, 1936.

Edie Brickell, 48, singer, born Oak Cliff, TX, Mar 10, 1966.

Kim Campbell, 67, 19th prime minister of Canada (1993), first female prime minister, born Vancouver Island, BC, Canada, Mar 10, 1947.

Prince Edward, 50, third son of Queen Elizabeth II, born London, England, Mar 10, 1964.

Bob Greene, 67, journalist, born Columbus, OH, Mar 10, 1947.

Jasmine Guy, 50, singer, actress ("A Different World"), born Boston, MA, Mar 10, 1964.

Jon Hamm, 43, actor ("Mad Men," "The Division"), born St. Louis, MO, Mar 10, 1971.

Shannon Miller, 37, Olympic gymnast, born Rolla, MO, Mar 10, 1977.

Chuck Norris, 74, actor (*Missing in Action*, "Walker, Texas Ranger"), born Ryan, OK, Mar 10, 1940.

Pam Oliver, 53, sportscaster, born Dallas, TX, Mar 10, 1961.

David Rabe, 74, playwright, born Dubuque, IA, Mar 10, 1940.

Emeli Sandé, 27, singer, born Sunderland, Scotland, Mar 10, 1987.

Sharon Stone, 56, actress (*Basic Instinct, The Specialist, Casino*), born Meadville, PA, Mar 10, 1958.

Timbaland, 43, record producer, born Timothy Zachery Mosley at Norfolk, VA, Mar 10, 1971.

Shannon Tweed, 57, actress ("Pacific Blue," *Detroit Rock City*), born St. John's, NF, Canada, Mar 10, 1957.

Carrie Underwood, 31, singer ("American Idol"), born Muskogee, OK, Mar 10, 1983.

March 11 — Tuesday

DAY 70 **295 REMAINING**

BUREAU OF INDIAN AFFAIRS ESTABLISHED: ANNIVERSARY. Mar 11, 1824. The US War Department created the Bureau of Indian Affairs.

"COPS" TV PREMIERE: 25th ANNIVERSARY. Mar 11, 1989. This long-running, gritty series follows real-life cops in departments across the US as they answer calls, patrol, question suspects and make arrests. The handheld-camera operators wear bulletproof vests as they follow the action. The theme song, "Bad Boys," by Inner Circle, is as famous as the show.

DREAM 2014 DAY. Mar 11. To focus attention on the new millennium—so that all humans, nations and institutions devote this year to unparalleled dreams for a better world and thought, action, inspiration, determination and love to solve the remaining problems and to achieve a peaceful, united human family on Earth. As envisioned by Robert Muller, called the Millennium Man. For info: Barbara Gaughen-Muller, Pres, Gaughen Global Public Relations, 7456 Evergreen Dr, Santa Barbara, CA 93117. Phone: (805) 968-8567.

ENGLAND: CHELTENHAM HORSE RACING FESTIVAL. Mar 11–14. Cheltenham Racecourse, Prestbury, Cheltenham, Gloucestershire. Four days of jump-racing magic, madness and magnificence, played out on a stage framed by the breathtaking vista of the Cotswold Hills. First race on Tuesday is Champion Day, followed by Ladies Day, St. Patrick's Thursday and then the grand finale of Cheltenham Gold Cup Day. Est attendance: 230,000. For info: Cheltenham Racecourse, Prestbury Park, Cheltenham, Gloucestershire, England GL50 4SH. Phone: (44) (1242) 513-014. Fax: (44) (1242) 224-227. Web: www.cheltenham.co.uk.

JAPAN EARTHQUAKE AND TSUNAMI OF 2011: ANNIVERSARY. Mar 11, 2011. With an epicenter near Sendai, Japan, this 9.0 earthquake struck the northeast side of Japan's Honshu island. The earthquake triggered a massive tsunami that caused widespread devastation. The dead and missing were estimated at 24,500. The disaster also caused a level 7 emergency at nuclear power plants at Fukushima when cooling systems failed at three reactors, releasing radiation. This was the worst natural disaster in Japan's recorded history.

JOHNNY APPLESEED DAY (JOHN CHAPMAN DEATH ANNIVERSARY). Mar 11, 1845. Anniversary of the death of John Chapman, better known as Johnny Appleseed, believed to have been born at Leominster, MA, Sept 26, 1774. The planter of orchards and friend of wild animals was regarded by the Indians as a great medicine man. He died at Allen County, IN. See also: "Appleseed, Johnny: Birth Anniversary" (Sept 26).

LITHUANIA: RESTITUTION OF INDEPENDENCE DAY. Mar 11. National holiday. Commemorates independence from the Soviet Union in 1990. Lithuania had initially declared its independence in 1918 but lost it to the Soviet Union in 1940.

MADRID TRAIN BOMBINGS: 10th ANNIVERSARY. Mar 11, 2004. Ten terrorist bombs exploded on four commuter trains in Spain's busy capital on this date, killing 191 people and injuring 1,800. It was the worst loss of life by violence in Europe since WWII. Nations around the world expressed their sorrow, and demonstrations against terrorism were held in Brussels, Paris, Helsinki, Geneva, Berlin and Stockholm. Spain observed a three-minute period of silence at noon on Mar 15 in order to remember the wounded and slain. Several European countries arrested suspects in the case, and seven militants considered major suspects blew themselves up at Madrid to avoid capture on Apr 3. The terrorists responsible were believed to be allied with Al Qaeda.

NAPNAP ANNUAL CONFERENCE. Mar 11–14. Hynes Convention Center, Boston, MA. The National Association of Pediatric Nurse Practitioners, an association of more than 7,000 pediatric nurse practitioners and specialty nurses in advanced practice providing primary health care to infants, children, adolescents and young adults, holds its 35th annual conference. For info: NAPNAP, 5 Hanover Sq, Ste 1401, New York, NY 10004. Phone: (917) 746-8300. Fax: (212) 785-1713. E-mail: info@napnap.org. Web: www.napnap.org.

ORGANIZE YOUR HOME OFFICE DAY. Mar 11. One day each year for the more than 34 million home office households to find files, purge papers and tackle to-do lists. Annually, the second Tuesday in March. For info: Lisa Kanarek, HomeOfficeLife.com, 11700 Preston Rd, Ste 660-120, Dallas, TX 75230. E-mail: lisa@homeofficelife.com. Web: www.homeofficelife.com.

PAINE, ROBERT TREAT: BIRTH ANNIVERSARY. Mar 11, 1731. Jurist and signer of the Declaration of Independence. Born at Boston, MA; died there May 11, 1814.

PANDEMIC OF 1918 HITS US: ANNIVERSARY. Mar 11, 1918. The first cases of the "Spanish" influenza were reported in the US when 107 soldiers became sick at Fort Riley, KS. By the end of 1920 nearly 25 percent of the US population had been infected. As many as 500,000 civilians died from the virus, exceeding the number of US troops killed abroad in WWI. Worldwide, more than 1 percent of the global population, or 22 million people, had died by 1920 because of the virus. The origin of the virus was never determined absolutely, though it was probably somewhere in Asia. The name "Spanish" influenza came from the relatively high number of cases in that country early in the epidemic. Due to the panic, cancellation of public events was common, and many public service workers wore masks on the job. Emergency tent hospitals were set up in some locations due to overcrowding.

TASSO, TORQUATO: BIRTH ANNIVERSARY. Mar 11, 1544. Poet of the late Renaissance, born at Sorrento, Italy. His violent outbursts and acute sensitivity to criticism led to his imprisonment for seven years, during which the "misunderstood genius" continued his literary creativity. Died at Rome, Italy, Apr 25, 1595.

TURKEY VULTURES RETURN TO THE LIVING SIGN. Mar 11–17. Entire Canisteo Valley, Canisteo, NY. Traditionally turkey vultures return on St. Pat's Day to their roosting sites in and around the world-famous living sign, as mentioned in "Ripley's Believe It or Not." The sign spells out "Canisteo" using 250 trees on a ridge above Greenwood Street. For info: Bill Berry, 6950 Lain Rd, Hornell, NY 14843-9419. Phone: (607) 661-5500. E-mail: thepaperwolf@gmail.com.

WELK, LAWRENCE: BIRTH ANNIVERSARY. Mar 11, 1903. Bandleader Lawrence Welk was born at Strasburg, ND. He learned to play the accordion and at 17 formed his first band. After playing all over the Midwest, he moved to Los Angeles, CA, where in 1955 his show began its nationwide television broadcast of "Champagne Music." The longest-running prime-time program in TV history, "The Lawrence Welk Show" played each Saturday on ABC from 1955 until 1971 when it was dropped because sponsors thought its audience was too old. Welk kept the show on a network of more than 250 independent stations for 11 more years, and it still can be seen in reruns. Welk's entertainment empire included the purchase of royalty rights to songs, among them the entire collection of songs by Jerome Kern. Welk died at Santa Monica, CA, May 17, 1992.

WILSON, HAROLD: BIRTH ANNIVERSARY. Mar 11, 1916. British statesman and twice prime minister (1964–70 and 1974–76), leader of the Labour Party. Born at Huddersfield, Yorkshire. He died May 24, 1995, at London.

BIRTHDAYS TODAY

John Barrowman, 47, actor ("Arrow," "Torchwood," "Doctor Who"), born Glasgow, Scotland, Mar 11, 1967.

Elton Brand, 35, basketball player, born Peekskill, NY, Mar 11, 1979.

Curtis Brown, Jr, 58, astronaut, born Elizabethtown, NC, Mar 11, 1956.

Sam Donaldson, 80, journalist, born El Paso, TX, Mar 11, 1934.

Didier Drogba, 36, soccer player, born Abidjan, Ivory Coast, Mar 11, 1978.

Terrence Howard, 45, actor (*Iron Man, Hustle & Flow, Get Rich or Die Tryin'*), born Chicago, IL, Mar 11, 1969.

Alex Kingston, 51, actress ("ER"), born London, England, Mar 11, 1963.

Bobby McFerrin, 64, jazz musician, singer, songwriter, conductor, born New York, NY, Mar 11, 1950.

Matt Mead, 52, Governor of Wyoming (R), born Teton County, WY, Mar 11, 1962.

Rupert Murdoch, 83, media executive, born Melbourne, Australia, Mar 11, 1931.

Antonin Scalia, 78, Associate Justice of the US, born Trenton, NJ, Mar 11, 1936.

Jerry Zucker, 64, writer, (*Naked Gun* movies with brother David), producer (*Airplane!*), born Milwaukee, WI, Mar 11, 1950.

March 2014	S	M	T	W	T	F	S
							1
	2	3	4	5	6	7	8
	9	10	11	12	13	14	15
	16	17	18	19	20	21	22
	23	24	25	26	27	28	29
	30	31					

March 12 — Wednesday

DAY 71 **294 REMAINING**

ATATÜRK, MUSTAFA KEMAL: BIRTH ANNIVERSARY. Mar 12, 1881. The founder of modern Turkey was born at Salonika, Greece (then part of the Ottoman Empire). After a distinguished army career, he led the Turkish revolution after WWI and was elected Turkey's first president. He died at Istanbul, Nov 10, 1938.

AUSTRIA INVADED BY NAZI GERMANY: ANNIVERSARY. Mar 12, 1938. As a test of its own war readiness and of the response of the other major powers, Germany occupied Austria. A year later Germany invaded Czechoslovakia and, in September 1939, Poland, beginning WWII.

BERMUDA COLONIZED BY ENGLISH: ANNIVERSARY. Mar 12, 1609. The ship of Admiral Sir George Somers, taking settlers to Virginia, was wrecked on the reefs of Bermuda. The islands had been discovered in the early 1500s but were uninhabited until 1609.

BOYCOTT, CHARLES CUNNINGHAM: BIRTH ANNIVERSARY. Mar 12, 1832. Charles Cunningham Boycott, born at Norfolk, England, has been immortalized by having his name become part of the English language. In County Mayo, Ireland, the Tenants' "Land League" in 1880 asked Boycott, an estate agent, to reduce rents (because of poor harvest and dire economic conditions). Boycott responded by serving eviction notices on the tenants, who retaliated by refusing to have any dealings with him. Charles Stewart Parnell, then president of the National Land League and agrarian agitator, retaliated against Boycott by formulating and implementing the method of economic and social ostracism that came to be called a "boycott." Boycott died at Suffolk, England, June 19, 1897.

CHURCH OF ENGLAND ORDAINS WOMEN PRIESTS: 20th ANNIVERSARY. Mar 12, 1994. The Church of England for the first time ordained 32 women at Bristol Cathedral. About 700 male members of the clergy and unknown thousands of members indicated they would leave the Church of England and join the Roman Catholic Church. The Catholic Church responded to the ordination by saying that it "constitutes a profound obstacle to every hope of reunion between the Catholic Church and the Anglican Communion." This day's ordinations were not the first. Earlier that year about 1,380 women priests were ordained in churches of the Anglican Communion outside of Great Britain.

FDR'S FIRST FIRESIDE CHAT: ANNIVERSARY. Mar 12, 1933. President Franklin Delano Roosevelt made the first of his Sunday-evening "fireside chats" to the American people. Speaking by radio from the White House, he reported rather informally on the economic problems of the nation and on his actions to deal with them.

GABON: NATIONAL DAY. Mar 12. Observes founding of Gabonese Democratic Party on Mar 12, 1968.

GIRL SCOUTS OF THE USA FOUNDING: ANNIVERSARY. Mar 12, 1912. Juliette Low founded the Girl Scouts of the USA at Savannah, GA.

GREAT BLIZZARD OF '88: ANNIVERSARY. Mar 12, 1888. One of the most devastating blizzards to hit the northeastern US began in the early hours of Monday, Mar 12, 1888. A snowfall of 40–50 inches, accompanied by gale-force winds, left drifts as high as 30–40 feet. More than 400 persons died in the storm (200 at New York City alone). Some survivors of the storm, "The Blizzard Men of 1888," held annual meetings at New York City as late as 1941 to recount personal recollections of the event.

KEROUAC, JACK: BIRTH ANNIVERSARY. Mar 12, 1922. American poet and novelist Jack (Jean-Louis) Kerouac, leader and spokesman for the Beat movement, was born at Lowell, MA. Kerouac is best known for his novel *On the Road*, published in 1957, which celebrates the Beat ideal of nonconformity. Kerouac published *The Dharma Bums* in 1958, followed by *The Subterraneans* the same year, *Doctor Sax* and its sequel *Maggie Cassidy* in 1959, *Lonesome Traveler* in 1960, *Big Sur* in 1962 and *Desolation Angels* in 1965. Kerouac died at St. Petersburg, FL, at age 47, Oct 21, 1969. A previously unpublished part of *On the Road* called *Visions of Cody* was published posthumously in 1972.

LESOTHO: MOSHOESHOE'S DAY. Mar 12. National holiday. Commemorates the great leader Chief Moshoeshoe I, who unified the Basotho people, beginning in 1820.

MAURITIUS: INDEPENDENCE DAY. Mar 12. National holiday commemorates attainment of independent nationhood (within the British Commonwealth) on Mar 12, 1968.

NEWCOMB, SIMON: BIRTH ANNIVERSARY. Mar 12, 1835. Astronomer, born at Wallace, NS, Canada. Newcomb investigated the orbits of Uranus, Neptune and the inner planets and devised planetary tables that were used universally by observatories. Died at Washington, DC, July 11, 1909.

PIERCE, JANE MEANS APPLETON: BIRTH ANNIVERSARY. Mar 12, 1806. Wife of Franklin Pierce, 14th president of the US. Born at Hampton, NH. Died at Concord, NH, Dec 2, 1863.

REGISTERED DIETITIAN DAY. Mar 12. This day commemorates the dedication of RDs as advocates for advancing the nutritional status of Americans and people around the world. For info: Academy of Nutrition and Dietetics, 120 S Riverside Plaza, Ste 2000, Chicago, IL 60606. Phone: (312) 899-4854. Fax: (312) 899-4739. E-mail: sdenny@eatright.org. Web: www.eatright.org.

SCHIRRA, WALLY: BIRTH ANNIVERSARY. Mar 12, 1923. One of the original seven *Mercury* astronauts, born Walter Marty Schirra, Jr, at Hackensack, NJ. A US Navy pilot during WWII and the Korean conflict, Schirra entered the US space program in 1959. He was the only man to fly all three of the first manned space missions (*Mercury, Gemini* and *Apollo*), logging a total of 295 hours, 15 minutes in space. He won an Emmy Award for the footage he sent back from *Apollo 7*, the first televised pictures from space, and later worked with Walter Cronkite on broadcasts of other NASA missions. He died at La Jolla, CA, May 3, 2007.

SPACE MILESTONE: *SOYUZ T-4* (USSR). Mar 12, 1981. Launched this day. Two cosmonauts (V. Kovalyonok and V. Savinykh) docked at *Salyut 6* space station (in orbit since Sept 29, 1977) on Mar 13. Returned to Earth May 26, after 75 days in space.

SPAIN: FIESTA DE LAS FALLAS. Mar 12–19. Valencia. This festival of burning effigies and fireworks has been celebrated for more than 150 years.

SUN YAT-SEN: DEATH ANNIVERSARY. Mar 12, 1925. The heroic leader of China's 1911 revolution is remembered on the anniversary of his death at Peking, China. Observed as Arbor Day in Taiwan.

BIRTHDAYS TODAY

Edward Albee, 86, playwright, born Washington, DC, Mar 12, 1928.

Rob Cohen, 65, producer (*Bird on a Wire*), director (*Dragonheart*), born Cornwall-on-Hudson, NY, Mar 12, 1949.

David Daniels, 48, opera singer, born Spartanburg, GA, Mar 12, 1966.

Aaron Eckhart, 46, actor (*Thank You for Smoking, The Black Dahlia*), born Cupertino, CA, Mar 12, 1968.

Barbara Feldon, 73, actress ("Get Smart," *Smile*), born Pittsburgh, PA, Mar 12, 1941.

Marlon Jackson, 57, singer (Jackson 5), born Gary, IN, Mar 12, 1957.

Al Jarreau, 74, singer, songwriter, born Milwaukee, WI, Mar 12, 1940.

Liza Minnelli, 68, singer, actress (Oscar for *Cabaret*; *The Sterile Cuckoo, Arthur*), born Los Angeles, CA, Mar 12, 1946.

Raul Mondesi, 43, former baseball player, born San Cristobal, Dominican Republic, Mar 12, 1971.

Dale Murphy, 58, former baseball player, born Portland, OR, Mar 12, 1956.

Mitt Romney, 67, 2012 presidential candidate, former governor of Massachusetts (R), born Detroit, MI, Mar 12, 1947.

Darryl Strawberry, 52, former baseball player, born Los Angeles, CA, Mar 12, 1962.

James Taylor, 66, singer, musician, born Boston, MA, Mar 12, 1948.

Andrew Young, 82, civil rights leader, born New Orleans, LA, Mar 12, 1932.

March 13 — Thursday

DAY 72 | **293 REMAINING**

ANNENBERG, WALTER: BIRTH ANNIVERSARY. Mar 13, 1908. Publisher, philanthropist and ambassador, Walter Annenberg was born at Milwaukee, WI. He inherited the *Philadelphia Inquirer* from his father and built the newspaper into the cornerstone of a publishing empire that included newspapers, magazines and radio and television stations. He founded many enduring publications, including *Seventeen* (1944) and *TV Guide* (1953). He served as US ambassador to the United Kingdom during 1969–76. As a philanthropist, Annenberg gave billions to charities. He died at Wynnewood, PA, on Oct 1, 2002.

ARAB OIL EMBARGO LIFTED: 40th ANNIVERSARY. Mar 13, 1974. The oil-producing Arab countries agreed to lift their five-month embargo on petroleum sales to the US. During the embargo, prices went up 300 percent and a ban was imposed on Sunday gasoline sales. The embargo was in retaliation for US support of Israel during the October 1973 Middle East War.

CLARENCE DARROW DEATH COMMEMORATION. Mar 13. Jackson Park, Chicago, IL. Annually, on the anniversary of his death, a wreath is tossed from the Jackson Park Clarence Darrow Bridge, named in honor of the famed lawyer and civil libertarian, at 10 AM. At 11 AM a discussion follows in the Columbian Room of the Museum of Science and Industry, Chicago. For info: Clarence Darrow Death Commemoration. E-mail: editor@windycitymediagroup.com.

DEAF HISTORY MONTH. Mar 13–Apr 15. Observance of three of the most important anniversaries for deaf Americans: Mar 13, 1988, the victory of the Deaf President Now movement at Gallaudet University; Apr 8, 1864, charter signed by President Abraham Lincoln authorizing the Board of Directors of the Columbia Institution (now Gallaudet University) to grant college degrees to deaf students; Apr 15, 1817, establishment of the first permanent public school for the deaf in the Western Hemisphere, later known as the American School for the Deaf in Hartford, CT. For info: Library for Deaf Action, 2930 Craiglawn Rd, Silver Spring, MD 20904-1816. E-mail: ahagemeyer@gmail.com. Web: www.folda.net.

DELMONICO, LORENZO: BIRTH ANNIVERSARY. Mar 13, 1813. Famed restaurateur and gastronomic authority born at Marengo, Switzerland. Immigrating to New York in 1831, he joined his uncle in the family's small wine, confectionary and catering business and quickly became a junior partner before assuming complete ownership in 1842. The opening of the first of several Delmonico restaurants in New York, NY, revolutionized American eating habits and the standard American diet by turning the preparation and eating of food into an art form. The restaurants specialized in native foods, much of which was grown on the Delmonicos' privately owned 200-acre farm in Brooklyn. Nicknamed "Lorenzo the Great," Delmonico was the preeminent American epicure of his era and a noted philanthropist until his death at Sharon Springs, NY, on Sept 3, 1881.

EARMUFFS PATENTED: ANNIVERSARY. Mar 13, 1887. Chester Greenwood of Maine received a patent for earmuffs.

FILLMORE, ABIGAIL POWERS: BIRTH ANNIVERSARY. Mar 13, 1798. First wife of Millard Fillmore, 13th president of the US. Born at Stillwater, NY. It is said that the White House was without any books until Abigail Fillmore, formerly a teacher, made a room on the second floor into a library. Within a year, Congress appropriated $250 for the president to spend on books for the White House. Died at Washington, DC, Mar 30, 1853.

GENOVESE MURDER: 50th ANNIVERSARY. Mar 13, 1964. Catherine "Kitty" Genovese was stabbed to death in the Kew Gardens neighborhood of Queens, NY. The crime became infamous as it appeared (and was reported in major media outlets) that numerous neighbors did nothing to help her when they heard her screams. The case prompted studies of what is now called the bystander effect, which describes a phenomenon where the greater number of bystanders present to a crime or crisis, the less likely one or any of them will offer aid.

GOOD SAMARITAN INVOLVEMENT DAY. Mar 13. A day to emphasize the importance of unselfish aid to those who need it. Recognized on the anniversary of the killing of Catherine (Kitty) Genovese, Mar 13, 1964, in Kew Gardens, Queens, NY.

HOLY SEE: NATIONAL HOLIDAY. Mar 13. The State of Vatican City and the Holy See observe Mar 13 as a national holiday (on the anniversary of the coronation day of the current pope).

HUBBARD, L. RON: BIRTH ANNIVERSARY. Mar 13, 1911. Lafayette Ronald Hubbard, science fiction writer, recluse and founder of the Church of Scientology, was born at Tilden, NE. His best-known book was *Dianetics: The Modern Science of Mental Health.* Died at San Luis Obispo County, CA, Jan 24, 1986.

LOWELL, PERCIVAL: BIRTH ANNIVERSARY. Mar 13, 1855. American astronomer, founder of the Lowell Observatory at Flagstaff, AZ. Born at Boston, MA, he died at Flagstaff, Nov 12, 1916. Lowell was initiator of the search that resulted (25 years after the search began and 14 years after his death) in discovery of Pluto. The discovery was announced on Lowell's birthday, Mar 13, 1930, by the Lowell Observatory.

MATTEL INTRODUCES THE KEN DOLL: ANNIVERSARY. Mar 13, 1961. On this date the popular Barbie doll, introduced by Mattel in 1959, got a boyfriend: Ken Carson.

NATIONAL OPEN AN UMBRELLA INDOORS DAY. Mar 13. The purpose of this day is for people to open umbrellas indoors and note whether they have any bad luck. Annually, Mar 13. (Originated by Thomas Edward Knibb.)

March 2014	S	M	T	W	T	F	S
							1
	2	3	4	5	6	7	8
	9	10	11	12	13	14	15
	16	17	18	19	20	21	22
	23	24	25	26	27	28	29
	30	31					

NATIONAL WEEK OF THE OCEAN FESTIVAL SEA-SON. Mar 13–June 8. Fort Lauderdale, FL. 35th annual. This multiweek celebration includes school marine fair, marine flea market, waterway cleanup, a plywood regatta, Mother Ocean Day and marine awards. Est attendance: 50,000. For info: Cynthia Hancock, Pres, Natl Week of the Ocean, Inc, PO Box 179, Fort Lauderdale, FL 33302. Phone: (954) 462-5573. Web: www.national-week-of-the-ocean.org.

O'HARE, EDWARD "BUTCH": 100th BIRTH ANNIVERSARY. Mar 13, 1914. Born at St. Louis, MO, O'Hare attended the US Naval Academy and later trained as an aviator. He earned the first Congressional Medal of Honor in World War II after shooting down five Japanese planes in an air battle to save the USS *Lexington* aircraft carrier from damage. He did not return from a later mission on Nov 26, 1943, after losing radio contact and was presumed shot down or crashed over the Pacific. In September 1949 O'Hare International Airport at Chicago, IL, was named in his honor.

OPERATION FLASH: ANNIVERSARY. Mar 13, 1943. Disillusioned German officers planned to take the life of Adolf Hitler on this date. Hitler was to stop at Smolensk on his way to his headquarters, and an officer who was not involved in the plot had been commissioned to deliver a package to Hitler's plane, which he was told contained two bottles of liquor for a friend in Rastenburg. A bomb in the package was timed to go off over Minsk, but it reached Rastenburg without detonating. The package was later recovered and a defective detonator was found. See also: "Gersdorff Hitler Assassination Attempt: Anniversary" (Mar 21).

PLANET URANUS DISCOVERY: ANNIVERSARY. Mar 13, 1781. German-born English astronomer Sir William Herschel discovered the seventh planet from the sun, Uranus.

POPE FRANCIS: ELECTION ANNIVERSARY. Mar 13, 2013. Argentine cardinal and Archbishop of Buenos Aires Jorge Mario Bergoglio was elected 266th pope of the Roman Catholic Church by a papal conclave after the resignation of Pope Benedict XVI. Pope Francis is the first pope chosen from the Americas, the first from the Southern Hemisphere and the first Jesuit. He was born Dec 17, 1936, at Buenos Aires, Argentina.

PRIESTLY, JOSEPH: BIRTH ANNIVERSARY. Mar 13, 1733. (Old Style date.) English clergyman and scientist, discoverer of oxygen, born at Fieldhead, England. He and his family narrowly escaped an angry mob attacking their home because of his religious and political views. They moved to the US in 1794. Died at Northumberland, PA, Feb 6, 1804.

SAINT AUBIN, HELEN "CALLAGHAN" CANDAELE: 85th BIRTH ANNIVERSARY. Mar 13, 1929. Helen Candaele Saint Aubin, known as Helen Callaghan during her baseball days, was born at Vancouver, BC, Canada. Saint Aubin and her sister, Margaret Maxwell, were recruited for the All-American Girls Professional Baseball League, which flourished in the 1940s when many major league players were off fighting WWII. She first played at age 15 for the Minneapolis Millerettes, an expansion team that moved to Indiana and became the Fort Wayne Daisies. For the 1945 season the left-handed outfielder led the league with a .299 average and 24 extra-base hits. In 1946 she stole 114 bases in 111 games. Her son Kelly Candaele's documentary on the women's baseball league inspired the film *A League of Their Own*. Saint Aubin, known as the "Ted Williams of women's baseball," died Dec 8, 1992, at Santa Barbara, CA.

SMART & SEXY DAY. Mar 13. This event was created to instill women with the knowledge and confidence they need to achieve self-sufficiency through employment. The focus of the day is to provide knowledge and confidence through workforce training, professional image classes and the personal support required to local low-income women, enabling them to take action to secure employment that will change their lives and the lives of their families. Annually, Mar 13. For info: Carrie H. Veurink, Managing Partner, The Women's Alliance, 1425 K St NW, Ste 350, Washington, DC 20005. Phone: (925) 849-7500. E-mail: cveurink@thewomensalliance.org. Web: www.thewomensalliance.org.

TA'ANIT ESTHER (FAST OF ESTHER). Mar 13. Hebrew calendar date: Adar 11, 5774. Commemorates Queen Esther's fast, in the sixth century BC, to save the Jews of ancient Persia. Began at sundown Mar 12. Ordinarily observed Adar 13, the Fast of Esther is observed on the previous Thursday (Adar 11) when Adar 13 falls on a Sabbath—as it does in 2014.

WORLD KIDNEY DAY. Mar 13. The purpose of this day is to raise awareness about the importance of our kidneys—amazing organs that play a crucial role in keeping us alive and well—and to spread the message that kidney disease is common, harmful and treatable. Observed since 2006—now in 100 countries. Annually, the second Thursday in March. For info: World Kidney Day. E-mail: info@worldkidneyday.org. Web: www.worldkidneyday.org.

BIRTHDAYS TODAY

Thomas Andrew (Andy) Bean, 61, golfer, born Lafayette, GA, Mar 13, 1953.

Caron Butler, 34, basketball player, born Racine, WI, Mar 13, 1980.

Charo, 63, singer, actress ("Chico and the Man"), born Maria Martinez at Murcia, Spain, Mar 13, 1951.

Adam Clayton, 54, musician (U2), born Dublin, Ireland, Mar 13, 1960.

Dana Delany, 58, actress ("Body of Proof," "Desperate Houewives," "China Beach"), born New York, NY, Mar 13, 1956.

Glenne Headly, 57, actress (*The Purple Rose of Cairo, Dick Tracy, Mortal Thoughts*), born New London, CT, Mar 13, 1957 (some sources say 1955).

Emile Hirsch, 29, actor (*Speed Racer, Into the Wild, Alpha Dog*), born Palms, CA, Mar 13, 1985.

John Hoeven, 57, US Senator (R, North Dakota), born Bismarck, ND, Mar 13, 1957.

William H. Macy, 64, actor (*Door to Door, Fargo, Pleasantville, Boogie Nights*, "ER"), born Miami, FL, Mar 13, 1950.

Neil Sedaka, 75, singer, songwriter, born Brooklyn, NY, Mar 13, 1939.

March 14 — Friday

DAY 73 — **292 REMAINING**

CRAFTSMEN'S SPRING CLASSIC ARTS & CRAFTS FESTIVAL. Mar 14–16. Richmond Raceway Complex, Richmond, VA. 30th annual. Features work from more than 350 talented artists and craftspeople. All juried exhibitors' work has been handmade by the exhibitors and must be their own original design and creation. See the creative process in action with several exhibitors demonstrating throughout the weekend. Something for every style, taste and budget with items from the most contemporary to the most traditional. Est attendance: 20,000. For info: Gilmore Enterprises, Inc, 3514-A Drawbridge Pkwy, Greensboro, NC 27410-8584. Phone: (336) 282-5550. E-mail: contact@gilmoreshows.com. Web: www.CraftShow.com or www.gilmoreshows.com.

EINSTEIN, ALBERT: BIRTH ANNIVERSARY. Mar 14, 1879. Theoretical physicist best known for his theory of relativity. Born at Ulm, Germany, he won the Nobel Prize in 1921. Died at Princeton, NJ, Apr 18, 1955.

FOOTE, HORTON: BIRTH ANNIVERSARY. Mar 14, 1916. American writer who wrote more than 60 films and plays. Foote's screenplays for *To Kill a Mockingbird* and *Tender Mercies* both won Academy Awards. His play *The Young Man from Atlanta* also earned him the Pulitzer Prize. Born at Wharton, Texas, Foote died Mar 4, 2009, at Hartford, CT.

JONES, CASEY: 150th BIRTH ANNIVERSARY. Mar 14, 1864. The railroad engineer—real name John Luther Jones—was born near Cayce, KY, the source of his nickname. He died in the crash of the Cannonball Express near Vaughn, MS, Apr 30, 1900, and was memorialized as a hero in Wallace Saunders's eponymous ballad.

MARSHALL, THOMAS RILEY: BIRTH ANNIVERSARY. Mar 14, 1854. 28th vice president of the US (1913–21). Born at North Manchester, IN, he died at Washington, DC, June 1, 1925.

MOTH-ER DAY. Mar 14. A day set aside to honor moth collectors and specialists. Celebrated in museums or libraries with moth collections. For info: Bob Birch, Puns Corps Grand Punscorpion, 3108 Dashiell Rd, Falls Church, VA 22042. Phone: (703) 533-3668.

NCAA DIVISION I MEN'S & WOMEN'S INDOOR TRACK AND FIELD CHAMPIONSHIPS. Mar 14–15. Albuquerque Convention Center, Albuquerque, NM. Annually, the second weekend in March. Est attendance: 7,000. For info: NCAA, PO Box 6222, Indianapolis, IN 46206-6222. Phone: (317) 917-6222. Fax: (317) 917-6826. Web: www.NCAA.com.

NCAA DIVISION I RIFLE CHAMPIONSHIPS. Mar 14–15. Site TBD. 16th annual. For info: NCAA, PO Box 6222, Indianapolis, IN 46206-6222. Web: www.NCAA.com.

NETHERLANDS: THE EUROPEAN FINE ART FAIR (MAASTRICHT 2014). Mar 14–23. MECC, Maastricht. Old Master paintings, antiques, textile arts, modern paintings and sculptures, antiquities, books and prints. Est attendance: 75,000. For info: The European Fine Art Foundation, Broekwal 64, 5268 HD Helvoirt, The Netherlands. Phone: (31) (411) 64-50-90. Fax: (31) (411) 64-50-91. E-mail: info@tefaf.com. Web: www.tefaf.com.

PI DAY. Mar 14. A day to celebrate pi—the ratio of a circle's circumference to its diameter. Since that mathematical constant is about 3.14, Mar 14 became the day to observe it.

SEOUL RECAPTURED BY UN FORCES: ANNIVERSARY. Mar 14, 1951. Seoul, Korea, which had fallen to Chinese forces in January 1951, was retaken by United Nations troops during the Korean War.

TAYLOR, LUCY HOBBS: BIRTH ANNIVERSARY. Mar 14, 1833. Lucy Beaman Hobbs, first woman in America to receive a degree in dentistry (Ohio College of Dental Surgery, 1866) and to be admitted to membership in a state dental association. Born at Franklin County, NY. In 1867 she married James M. Taylor, who also became a dentist (after she instructed him in the essentials). Active women's rights advocate. Died at Lawrence, KS, Oct 3, 1910.

"10 MOST WANTED" LIST DEBUTS: ANNIVERSARY. Mar 14, 1950. The Federal Bureau of Investigation instituted the "10 Most Wanted Fugitives" list in an effort to publicize particularly dangerous criminals who were at large. From 1950 to 2013, 498 fugitives have appeared on the list; 469 have been located or apprehended. Generally, the only way to get off the list is to die or be captured. In the summer of 2011, the two top fugitives exited the list: terrorist Osama Bin Laden was killed in a raid in May and gangster James "Whitey" Bulger was arrested in June.

BIRTHDAYS TODAY

Frank Borman, 86, former astronaut, airline executive, born Gary, IN, Mar 14, 1928.

Michael Caine, 81, actor (Oscars for *The Cider House Rules* and *Hannah and Her Sisters*), born Maurice Micklewhite at London, England, Mar 14, 1933.

Tom Coburn, 66, US Senator (R, Oklahoma), born Casper, WY, Mar 14, 1948.

Billy Crystal, 67, actor (*Analyze This, When Harry Met Sally, City Slickers*, "Soap"), born Long Beach, NY, Mar 14, 1947.

Rick Dees, 63, disc jockey, comedian, born Jacksonville, FL, Mar 14, 1951.

Bobby Jenks, 33, baseball player, born Mission Hills, CA, Mar 14, 1981.

Quincy Jones, 81, composer, producer, born Chicago, IL, Mar 14, 1933.

Grace Park, 40, actress ("Battlestar Galactica," "Hawaii Five-0"), born Los Angeles, CA, Mar 14, 1974.

Tamara Tunie, 55, actress ("24," "Law & Order: SVU," "As the World Turns"), born McKeesport, PA, Mar 14, 1959.

Rita Tushingham, 72, actress (*Dr. Zhivago, A Taste of Honey*), born Liverpool, England, Mar 14, 1942.

March 15 — Saturday

DAY 74 **291 REMAINING**

BELARUS: CONSTITUTION DAY. Mar 15. National holiday. Commemorates the adoption of the constitution on Mar 15, 1994.

BRUTUS DAY. Mar 15. No matter where you work, you must admit there's as much intrigue, plotting and backstabbing as was found in ancient Rome or is found today inside the Washington Beltway. (©2006 by WH.) For info: Thomas & Ruth Roy, Wellcat Holidays, 2418 Long Ln, Lebanon, PA 17046. Phone: (717) 279-0184. E-mail: info@wellcat.com. Web: www.wellcat.com.

"EIGHT IS ENOUGH" TV PREMIERE: ANNIVERSARY. Mar 15, 1977. This one-hour comedy-drama was set in Sacramento, CA, and starred Dick Van Patten as Tom Bradford, a columnist for a local paper and a widower with eight children. Diana Hyland played his wife, Joan; she died from cancer after filming five shows. The children were played by Grant Goodeve, Lani O'Grady, Laurie Walters, Susan Richardson, Dianne Kay, Connie Needham, Willie Aames and Adam Rich. In the fall of 1977 Betty Buckley joined the cast as tutor Abby Abbott, who later married Tom. Most of the cast was reunited for Tom's 50th birthday on "Eight Is Enough: A Family Reunion," shown on Oct 18, 1987.

***THE GODFATHER* FILM PREMIERE: ANNIVERSARY.** Mar 15, 1972. Francis Ford Coppola directed what many consider the greatest American film—perhaps challenged only by the sequel released two years later. Based on the Mario Puzo novel that traced the fortunes of the Corleone crime family, *The Godfather* was nominated for 11 Oscars, picking up 3, for Best Picture, Best Adapted Screenplay and Best Actor (Marlon Brando in a legendary performance). Costars Al Pacino, James Caan and Robert Duvall were all nominated for Best Supporting Actor. *The Godfather: Part II*, which premiered in New York City on Dec 12, 1974, was also nominated for 11 Oscars and won 6, including Best Picture. A third film was released on Dec 25, 1990.

March 2014	S	M	T	W	T	F	S
							1
	2	3	4	5	6	7	8
	9	10	11	12	13	14	15
	16	17	18	19	20	21	22
	23	24	25	26	27	28	29
	30	31					

HUNGARY: ANNIVERSARY OF THE 1848 REVOLUTION. Mar 15. National Day. Commemorates when the country briefly attained autonomy from Austria.

IDES OF MARCH. Mar 15. In the Roman calendar the days of the month were not numbered sequentially. Instead, each month had three division days: kalends, nones and ides. Days were numbered from these divisions: e.g., IV Nones or III Ides. The ides occurred on the 15th of the month (or on the 13th in months that had fewer than 31 days). Julius Caesar was assassinated on this day in 44 BC. This system was used in Europe well into the Renaissance. When Shakespeare wrote "Beware the ides of March" in *Julius Caesar*, his audience knew what he meant.

JACKSON, ANDREW: BIRTH ANNIVERSARY. Mar 15, 1767. The seventh president of the US (Mar 4, 1829–Mar 3, 1837) was born in a log cabin at Waxhaw, SC. Jackson was the first president since George Washington who had not attended college. He was a military hero in the War of 1812. His presidency reflected his democratic and egalitarian values. Died at Nashville, TN, June 8, 1845. His birthday is observed as a holiday in Tennessee.

LIBERIA: J.J. ROBERTS DAY. Mar 15. National holiday. Commemorates the birth in 1809 of the country's first president.

MAINE: ADMISSION DAY: ANNIVERSARY. Mar 15. Became 23rd state in 1820. Prior to this date, Maine had been part of Massachusetts.

MILITARY THROUGH THE AGES. Mar 15–16. Jamestown Settlement, Williamsburg, VA. Centuries of military history unfold as reenactors depicting soldiers and military encounters throughout history demonstrate camp life, military tactics and weaponry. For info: Tracy Perkins, Jamestown-Yorktown Foundation, PO Box 1607, Williamsburg, VA 23187. Phone: (757) 253-4838 or (888) 593-4682. Fax: (757) 253-5299. Web: www.historyisfun.org.

NATIONAL QUILTING DAY. Mar 15. 23rd annual celebration. Sponsored by the National Quilting Association since 1992, this day is a grassroots effort to unite quilters and quilt lovers everywhere, not only in this country, but also around the world. Individuals, groups of quilters, shop owners, publishers and the entire quiltmaking community are invited to join NQA in recognizing and promoting the tradition of quilt making. Annually, the third Saturday in March. For info: The Natl Quilting Assn, Inc, PO Box 12190, Columbus, OH 43212-0190. Phone: (614) 488-8520. E-mail: nqa@nqaquilts.org. Web: www.nqaquilts.org.

NORWAY: BIRKEBEINERRENNET. Mar 15. Rena and Lillehammer. Since 1932, ski marathon of 54 km between the cities of Rena and Lillehammer in which competitors carry a backpack weighing 3.5 kg. The race and the backpack commemorate an epic journey in Norwegian history: On Christmas Day in 1205, in the midst of a power struggle for the Norwegian throne, two birkebeiners (warriors who wore birch-bark leg coverings) smuggled infant prince Hakon Hakonsson by ski over mountainous terrain to safety away from a rival faction. The baby survived to become King Hakon Hakonsson IV, and he ended the civil war. For info: Birkebeinerrennet, Fabrikkveien 2, 2450 Rena, Norway. Phone: (47) (41) 77-29-00. Fax: (47) (62) 44-07-35. E-mail: info@birkebeiner.no. Web: www.birkebeiner.no.

SAINT PATRICK'S DAY PARADE. Mar 15. Downtown Hornell, NY. 27th annual. It's a "come as you are" line of march, open to anyone, with no entry fee, no judges, no prizes. Hornell's parade is designed as purely a fun affair, especially for those people who've always wanted to be in a parade but never had the opportunity. It's larger and longer every year, with more and more "would-be Irish" strolling down Main Street. Est attendance: 5,000. For info: Wolf Berry, 6950 Lain Rd, Hornell, NY 14843-9419. Phone: (607) 661-5500. E-mail: thepaperwolf@gmail.com.

SAINT PATRICK'S DAY PARADE: "THE WEARIN' OF THE GREEN." Mar 15. Baton Rouge, LA. 29th annual parade includes floats, precision marching bands and bagpipers. Largest St. Patrick's Day celebration in the region rolls through historic Hundred Oaks area in the heart of the city starting at 10 AM. Est attendance: 135,000. For info: Parade Group, LLC, 6906 Moniteau Ct, Baton Rouge, LA 70809. Phone: (225) 925-8295. E-mail: bririshparade@gmail.com. Web: www.paradegroup.com.

SAVE THE FLORIDA PANTHER DAY. Mar 15. Florida. A ceremonial holiday on the third Saturday in March.

"THREE'S COMPANY" TV PREMIERE: ANNIVERSARY. Mar 15, 1977. This half-hour comedy featured two girls and a guy sharing an apartment. In order for the landlord to go along with the living arrangements, Jack Tripper, played by John Ritter, had to pretend he was gay. Cast included Joyce DeWitt, Suzanne Somers, Norman Fell, Audra Lindley, Richard Kline, Don Knotts and Priscilla Barnes. The last telecast aired on Sept 18, 1984.

TRUE CONFESSIONS DAY. Mar 15. Confession is good for the soul. Go into work today and tell all. If you plan to stay home, make an appointment with your mirror. (©2006 by WH.) For info: Thomas & Ruth Roy, Wellcat Holidays, 2418 Long Ln, Lebanon, PA 17046. Phone: (717) 279-0184. E-mail: info@wellcat.com. Web: www.wellcat.com.

VAN BROCKLIN, NORM: BIRTH ANNIVERSARY. Mar 15, 1926. Norman Van Brocklin, Pro Football Hall of Fame quarterback and coach, born at Eagle Butte, SD. Van Brocklin played college football at Oregon and then signed with the Los Angeles Rams. He helped the Rams win their only NFL title in 1951. After finishing his playing career with the Philadelphia Eagles, he coached the Minnesota Vikings and the Atlanta Falcons. Inducted into the Pro Football Hall of Fame in 1979. Died at Social Circle, GA, May 2, 1983.

WASHINGTON'S ADDRESS TO CONTINENTAL ARMY OFFICERS: ANNIVERSARY. Mar 15, 1783. George Washington addressed a meeting at Newburgh, NY, of Continental army officers who were dissatisfied and rebellious for want of back pay, food, clothing and pensions. General Washington called for patience, opening his speech with the words "I have grown gray in your service. . . ." Congress later acted to satisfy most of the demands.

WILD AZALEA FESTIVAL. Mar 15. White Springs, FL. 14th annual. Celebrate the blooming of Florida's wild azaleas with music and dance by Florida entertainers, arts and crafts and regional foods. Annually, the third Saturday in March. For info: Elaine McGrath, Stephen Foster Folk Culture Center State Park, PO Box G, White Springs, FL 32096. Phone: (877) 635-3655. Fax: (386) 397-4262. E-mail: elaine.mcgrath@dep.state.fl.us. Web: www.floridastateparks.org/stephenfoster.

"THE WONDER YEARS" TV PREMIERE: ANNIVERSARY. Mar 15, 1988. A coming-of-age tale set in suburbia in the 1960s and 1970s. This drama/comedy starred Fred Savage as Kevin Arnold; Josh Saviano as his best friend, Paul; and Danica McKellar as his girlfriend, Winnie. Kevin's dad was played by Dan Lauria, his homemaker mom by Alley Mills, his hippie sister by Olivia d'Abo and his bully brother by Jason Hervey. Narrator Daniel Stern was the voice of the grown-up Kevin. The last episode ran Sept 1, 1993, but it remains popular in syndication.

BIRTHDAYS TODAY

Harold Baines, 55, former baseball player, born St. Michael's, MD, Mar 15, 1959.

Alan Bean, 82, former astronaut, born Wheeler, TX, Mar 15, 1932.

Mary Carillo, 57, sportscaster, former tennis player, born Queens, NY, Mar 15, 1957.

Fabio, 53, model, born Fabio Lanzoni at Milan, Italy, Mar 15, 1961.

Ruth Bader Ginsburg, 81, Associate Justice of the US, born Brooklyn, NY, Mar 15, 1933.

Judd Hirsch, 79, actor (Emmy for "Taxi"; "Numb3rs," *Ordinary People*), born New York, NY, Mar 15, 1935.

Eva Longoria, 39, actress ("Desperate Housewives," "The Young and the Restless"), born Corpus Christi, TX, Mar 15, 1975.

Mike Love, 73, singer, musician (The Beach Boys), born Los Angeles, CA, Mar 15, 1941.

Kellan Lutz, 29, actor (*Twilight*, "90210"), born Dickinson, ND, Mar 15, 1985.

Mark McGrath, 46, singer (Sugar Ray), born Newport Beach, CA, Mar 15, 1968.

Bret Michaels, 51, musician, television personality ("Rock of Love," "Celebrity Apprentice"), born Butler, PA, Mar 15, 1963.

Park Overall, 57, actress ("Empty Nest," *Mississippi Burning*), born Nashville, TN, Mar 15, 1957.

Kim Raver, 45, actress ("Grey's Anatomy," "Third Watch," "24"), born New York, NY, Mar 15, 1969.

Dee Snider, 59, singer (Twisted Sister), composer, born Massapequa, NY, Mar 15, 1955.

Sly Stone, 70, singer, musician (Sly & the Family Stone), born Sylvester Stewart at Dallas, TX, Mar 15, 1944.

Earl Ray Tomblin, 62, Governor of West Virginia (D), born Logan County, WV, Mar 15, 1952.

Craig Wasson, 60, actor ("Phyllis," *Body Double, Malcolm X*), born Ontario, OR, Mar 15, 1954.

March 16 — Sunday

DAY 75 **290 REMAINING**

BLACK PRESS DAY: ANNIVERSARY OF THE FIRST BLACK NEWSPAPER. Mar 16, 1827. Anniversary of the founding of the first black newspaper in the US, *Freedom's Journal*, on Varick Street at New York, NY.

BONHEUR, ROSA: BIRTH ANNIVERSARY. Mar 16, 1822. French painter and sculptor best known for her paintings of animals, Rosa (Marie-Rosalie) Bonheur was born at Bordeaux. With the income from the sale of her art she purchased the castle of By near Fontainebleau at Melun, France, where she died May 25, 1899. Bonheur's *The Horse Fair*, which she painted in 1853, was purchased by the American millionaire Cornelius Vanderbilt for $53,600, a record price at the time. In 1865 Bonheur was awarded the Grand Cross of the Légion d'Honneur, the first woman so honored. An early Bohemian and feminist, Bonheur defied female convention of the day by dressing in pants and smoking cigarettes.

CLYMER, GEORGE: 275th BIRTH ANNIVERSARY. Mar 16, 1739. Signer of the Declaration of Independence and of the US Constitution. Born at Philadelphia, PA, and died there Jan 24, 1813.

CURLEW DAY. Mar 16. Traditional arrival date for the long-billed curlew at the Umatilla (Oregon) National Wildlife Refuge. More than 500 of the long-billed curlews have been reported at this location during their nesting season.

FREEDOM OF INFORMATION DAY. Mar 16. The American Library Association supports free and open access to government information created at taxpayer expense. On or near the birthday of James

Madison (Mar 16), ALA urges libraries and librarians to join in celebrating the public's "right to know" by sponsoring activities to educate their communities about the importance of promoting and protecting freedom of information. Sponsored by the Freedom Forum and the American Library Association. For info: American Library Assn. E-mail: alawash@alawash.org. Web: www.ala.org.

GODDARD DAY. Mar 16, 1926. Commemorates first liquid-fuel-powered rocket flight launched by Robert Hutchings Goddard (1882–1945) at Auburn, MA.

"THE GUMBY SHOW" TV PREMIERE: ANNIVERSARY. Mar 16, 1957. This kids' show was a spin-off from "Howdy Doody," where the character of Gumby was first introduced in 1956. Gumby and his horse, Pokey, were clay figures whose adventures were filmed using the process of "claymation." "The Gumby Show," created by Art Clokey, was first hosted by Bobby Nicholson and later by Pinky Lee. It was syndicated in 1966 and again in 1988.

LIPS APPRECIATION DAY. Mar 16. Where would all those lovely teeth we paid a bundle for be without a lovely frame? Do something nice for your lips today. Buy a lip balm. Better yet, kiss somebody! (©2006 by WH.) For info: Thomas & Ruth Roy, Wellcat Holidays, 2418 Long Ln, Lebanon, PA 17046. Phone: (717) 279-0184. E-mail: info@wellcat.com. Web: www.wellcat.com.

MADISON, JAMES: BIRTH ANNIVERSARY. Mar 16, 1751. Fourth president of the US (Mar 4, 1809–Mar 3, 1817), born at Port Conway, VA. He was president when British forces invaded Washington, DC, requiring Madison and other high officials to flee while the British burned the Capitol, the president's residence and most other public buildings (Aug 24–25, 1814). Died at Montpelier, VA, June 28, 1836.

MARDI GRAS INDIANS SUPER SUNDAY. Mar 16. New Orleans, LA. In a tradition dating back to the 19th century, the Crescent City's Mardi Gras Indian tribes don their colorful and weighty (up to 150 pounds) costumes on the third Sunday in March (or the Sunday closest to St. Joseph's Day, Mar 19). This is the only time other than Mardi Gras that the tribes don their costumes. The 50 tribes engage in neighborhood processions and "strut their stuff." St. Joseph is patron saint of fathers and laborers and his feast day is an important observance in New Orleans.

MOON PHASE: FULL MOON. Mar 16. Moon enters Full Moon phase at 1:08 PM, EDT.

MY LAI MASSACRE: ANNIVERSARY. Mar 16, 1968. Most-publicized atrocity of the Vietnam War. According to findings of US Army's investigating team, approximately 300 noncombatant Vietnamese villagers (at My Lai and Mykhe, near the South China Sea) were killed by infantrymen of the American Division.

NATIONAL ANIMAL POISON PREVENTION WEEK. Mar 16–22. In conjunction with National Poison Prevention Week, the ASPCA sponsors this important week to educate Americans about common household products, plants and foods that can be dangerous or even deadly to pets. For info: Media & Communications Dept, ASPCA, 520 8th Ave, 7th Fl, New York, NY 10018. Phone: (212) 876-7700, ext 4655. E-mail: press@aspca.org. Web: www.aspca.org.

✦NATIONAL POISON PREVENTION WEEK. Mar 16–22. Presidential Proclamation issued each year for the third week in March since 1962 (PL 87–319 of Sept 26, 1961).

NATIONAL POISON PREVENTION WEEK. Mar 16–22. To aid in encouraging the American people to learn of the dangers of unintentional poisoning and to take preventive measures against it. Annually, the third full week in March. For info: Poison Prevention Week Council. Web: www.poisonprevention.org.

NIXON, THELMA CATHERINE PATRICIA (PAT) RYAN: BIRTH ANNIVERSARY. Mar 16, 1912. Wife of Richard Milhous Nixon, 37th president of the US. Born at Ely, NV, she died at Park Ridge, NJ, June 22, 1993.

OHM, GEORG SIMON: 225th BIRTH ANNIVERSARY. Mar 16, 1789. German physicist lauded for his eponymous law, which states the exact relationship of potential and current in electric conduction. Ohm's law made it possible for scientists to calculate the amount of current, voltage and resistance in circuitry, establishing the science of electrical engineering. Lord Kelvin recognized Ohm's contribution by dubbing the unit of resistance the "ohm" and its reciprocal, the unit of conductance, the "mho." Born at Erlangen, Germany, Ohm died July 7, 1854, at Munich, Germany.

PURIM. Mar 16. Hebrew calendar date: Adar 14, 5774. Feasts, gifts, charity and the reading of the Book of Esther mark this joyous commemoration of Queen Esther's intervention, in the sixth century BC, to save the Jews of ancient Persia. Haman's plot to exterminate the Jews was thwarted, and he was hanged on the very day he had set for execution of the Jews. Began at sundown Mar 15.

SPACE MILESTONE: *GEMINI 8* (US). Mar 16, 1966. Launched on this day, *Gemini 8* executed the first docking of orbiting spacecraft when it connected with *Agena*. A malfunction caused a scare when the craft began to spin uncontrollably and pilot Neil Armstrong immediately disengaged, but the craft did eventually land safely.

TERMITE AWARENESS WEEK. Mar 16–22. Termites feed on the cellulose found in wood and paper products and cause more than $5 billion in property damage every year. With termite season upon us, home owners should be on the lookout for swarmers (winged termites), which serve as a warning that a colony may have already settled inside. The National Pest Management Association (NPMA) launched this week to spread awareness, promote public vigilance and provide essential prevention advice. For info: National Pest Management Assn, 10460 North St, Fairfax, VA 22030. Phone: (703) 352-6762. Fax: (703) 352-3031. E-mail: NPMATeam@vaultcommunications.com. Web: www.pestworld.org.

US MILITARY ACADEMY FOUNDED: ANNIVERSARY. Mar 16, 1802. President Thomas Jefferson signed legislation establishing the US Military Academy to train officers for the army. The college is located at West Point, NY, on the site of the oldest continuously occupied military post in America. Women were admitted to West Point in 1976. The academy's motto is "Duty, Honor, Country." For info: www.usma.edu.

WORM MOON. Mar 16. So called by Native American tribes of New England and the Great Lakes because at this time of year there are signs of earthworms as the ground thaws in preparation for spring. The March Full Moon.

BIRTHDAYS TODAY

Bernardo Bertolucci, 73, filmmaker (Oscar for *The Last Emperor*; *Last Tango in Paris*), born Parma, Italy, Mar 16, 1941.

Erik Estrada, 65, actor ("CHiPs," *Honey Boy*), born New York, NY, Mar 16, 1949.

Judah Friedlander, 45, actor ("30 Rock," *American Splendor*), born Gaithersburg, MD, Mar 16, 1969.

Victor Garber, 65, actor (*Argo*, *Godspell*, "Alias"), born London, ON, Canada, Mar 16, 1949.

Lauren Graham, 47, actress ("Parenthood," "Gilmore Girls"), born Honolulu, HI, Mar 16, 1967.

March 2014	S	M	T	W	T	F	S
							1
	2	3	4	5	6	7	8
	9	10	11	12	13	14	15
	16	17	18	19	20	21	22
	23	24	25	26	27	28	29
	30	31					

Todd Heap, 34, football player, born Mesa, AZ, Mar 16, 1980.

Alice Hoffman, 62, writer (*Practical Magic, Aquamarine*), born New York, NY, Mar 16, 1952.

Isabelle Huppert, 59, actress (*Violette, The Piano Teacher*), born Paris, France, Mar 16, 1955.

Jerry Lewis, 88, comedian, actor (*The Family Jewels, The Nutty Professor, The Bellboy*), director, philanthropist, born Newark, NJ, Mar 16, 1926.

Kate Nelligan, 63, actress (*Eye of the Needle, Frankie and Johnny, The Prince of Tides*), born London, ON, Canada, Mar 16, 1951.

Alan Tudyk, 43, actor ("Firefly," "Dollhouse," *Abraham Lincoln: Vampire Hunter*), born El Paso, TX. Mar 16, 1971.

Chuck Woolery, 72, game show host ("Love Connection," "Scrabble"), born Ashland, KY, Mar 16, 1942.

March 17 — Monday

DAY 76 **289 REMAINING**

ACT HAPPY WEEK. Mar 17–23. Method acting techniques are prescribed by physicians to release chemicals in the body that aid health, wealth and friendship. During this week, select your own Act Happy Day and celebrate! Annually, the week beginning with the third Monday in March. For info: Dale L. Anderson, MD, 2982 W Owasso Blvd, St Paul, MN 55113. Phone: (651) 484-5162. E-mail: dr@acthappy.com.

AUSTRALIA: CANBERRA DAY. Mar 17. Australian Capital Territory. Public holiday the third Monday in March.

BAUGH, SAMMY ADRIAN: 100th BIRTH ANNIVERSARY. Mar 17, 1914. Born at Temple, TX, "Slinging Sammy" was one of the top quarterbacks of the 1930s and '40s. Baugh (whose nickname actually referred to his prowess in baseball) was a first-round draft pick (sixth overall) for the Washington Redskins in 1937, and he stayed with the franchise his entire career—until 1952. He was actually a star quarterback, tailback and punter. Uniquely, in 1943, he led the league in passing, punting and pass interceptions. Baugh's impact on the pro game was making the forward pass (before then little used) an integral part of the offensive tool kit. He was inducted (charter member) into the Pro Football Hall of Fame on Sept 7, 1963. Baugh died Dec 17, 2008, at Rotan, TX.

BRIDGER, JIM: BIRTH ANNIVERSARY. Mar 17, 1804. American fur trader, frontiersman and scout, born at Richmond, VA, and died July 17, 1881, near Kansas City, MO. Believed to be the first white man to visit (in 1824) the Great Salt Lake, he also established Fort Bridger in southwestern Wyoming as a fur-trading post and as a way station for pioneers heading west on the Oregon Trail. Bridger National Forest in western Wyoming is named for him.

CAMP FIRE: ANNIVERSARY. Mar 17, 1910. To commemorate the anniversary of the founding of Camp Fire and the service given to children and youth across the nation. Founded in 1910 as Camp Fire Girls. For info: Camp Fire, 1100 Walnut St, Ste 1900, Kansas City, MO 64106-2197. Phone: (816) 285-2010. Fax: (816) 285-9444. E-mail: info@campfire.org. Web: www.campfire.org.

CAMP FIRE BIRTHDAY WEEK. Mar 17–23. A week to celebrate the anniversary of Camp Fire (founded Mar 17, 1910, as Camp Fire Girls). For info: Camp Fire, 1100 Walnut St, Ste 1900, Kansas City, MO 64106-2197. Phone: (816) 285-2010. Fax: (816) 285-9444. E-mail: info@campfire.org. Web: www.campfire.org.

COLE, NAT "KING" (NATHANIEL ADAMS COLE): 95th BIRTH ANNIVERSARY. Mar 17, 1919. Nat King Cole was born at Montgomery, AL, and began his musical career at an early age, playing the piano at age four. He was the first black entertainer to host a national television show. His many songs included "The Christmas Song," "Nature Boy," "Mona Lisa," "Ramblin' Rose" and "Unforgettable." Although he was dogged by racial discrimination throughout his career, including the cancellation of his television show because opposition from Southern white viewers decreased advertising revenue, Cole was criticized by prominent black newspapers for not joining other black entertainers in the civil rights struggle. Cole contributed more than $50,000 to civil rights organizations in response to the criticism. Nat King Cole died Feb 25, 1965, at Santa Monica, CA.

CORBETT-FITZSIMMONS TITLE FIGHT: ANNIVERSARY. Mar 17, 1897. In one of boxing's greatest fights—and the first heavyweight title fight to be filmed—"Gentleman Jim" Corbett lost the world title to "Ruby Robert" Fitzsimmons at Carson City, NV. Fitzsimmons, seemingly a long shot at 34 years of age, hung on for 13 rounds before landing the "solar plexus punch" that felled Corbett. Western legends in attendance were Bat Masterson (overseeing security) and Wyatt Earp.

EVACUATION DAY: ANNIVERSARY. Mar 17, 1776. A public holiday at Boston and Suffolk County, MA, celebrates the anniversary of the evacuation from Boston of British troops.

FEMALE RELIEF SOCIETY OF NAUVOO ORGANIZED: ANNIVERSARY. Mar 17, 1842. Twenty Mormon women formally initiated this organization at Nauvoo, IL, which is now known as the Relief Society and has grown to more than five and a half million members.

HOWARD, SHEMP: BIRTH ANNIVERSARY. Mar 17, 1895. A member of the original Three Stooges (with Moe Howard and Larry Fine), Howard was born Samuel Horwitz at Brooklyn, NY. He teamed with brother Moe as comic relief with vaudeville entertainer Ted Healy in the early 1920s. In 1925 Larry Fine joined them to create the Three Stooges. Shemp left the trio in 1932—little brother Curly replaced him—and had roles in many films. Upon Curly's retirement in 1946, Shemp rejoined the Stooges until his death on Nov 23, 1955, at Hollywood, CA.

INDIA: HOLI. Mar 17–18. In this spring festival, people run through the streets throwing brightly hued powders and colored water at each other. This is observed by Indians without regard to caste. Huge bonfires are built on the eve of Holi. Because there is no one universally accepted Hindu calendar, this holiday may be celebrated on a different date in some parts of India, but it usually falls in March.

IRELAND: NATIONAL DAY. Mar 17. St. Patrick's Day is observed in the Republic of Ireland as a legal national holiday.

JONES, BOBBY: BIRTH ANNIVERSARY. Mar 17, 1902. Golfing great Robert Tyre Jones, Jr, first golfer to win the grand slam (the four major British and American tournaments in one year). Born at Atlanta, GA, he died there Dec 18, 1971.

NORTHERN IRELAND: SAINT PATRICK'S DAY HOLIDAY. Mar 17. National holiday.

NUREYEV, RUDOLF HAMETOVICH: BIRTH ANNIVERSARY. Mar 17, 1938. Rudolf Nureyev, one of the most charismatic ballet stars of the 20th century, was born on a train in southeastern Siberia. Nureyev's defection from the Soviet Union on June 17, 1961, while on tour with the Kirov Ballet, made headlines worldwide. The dancer was known for his ability to combine passion with a high level of perfectionism. His long partnership with Dame Margot Fonteyn of the Royal Ballet was legendary, and he performed frequently with the Martha Graham Dance Company. Nureyev also choreographed and restaged many classics and served as the Paris Opera Ballet's artistic director. He died Jan 6, 1993, at Levallois, France, a suburb of Paris.

PARKER, GEORGE: 250th DEATH ANNIVERSARY. Mar 17, 1764. George Parker, the second Earl of Macclesfield, was born in 1697 (exact date unknown). The eminent English astronomer was president of the Royal Society from 1752 until his death. He was one of the principal authors of the Bill for Regulating the Commencement of the Year (British Calendar Act of 1751), which was introduced in parliament by Lord Chesterfield. That act caused the adoption, in 1752, of the "New Style" Gregorian calendar, which is still in use today. Parker died at Shirburn Castle, England.

RUSTIN, BAYARD: BIRTH ANNIVERSARY. Mar 17, 1910. Black pacifist and civil rights leader, Bayard Rustin was an organizer of and participant in many of the great social protest marches—for jobs, freedom and nuclear disarmament. He was arrested and imprisoned more than 20 times for his civil rights and pacifist activities. Born at West Chester, PA, Rustin died at New York, NY, Aug 24, 1987.

SAINT PATRICK'S DAY. Mar 17. Commemorates the patron saint of Ireland, Bishop Patrick (AD 387–493?), who, about AD 432, left his home in the Severn Valley, England, and introduced Christianity into Ireland. Feast day in the Roman Catholic Church. A national holiday in Ireland and Northern Ireland.

SAINT PATRICK'S DAY PARADE. Mar 17. New York, NY. One of New York City's greatest traditions, held for the first time on Mar 17, 1762. Today it is the largest parade in the world, featuring up to 250,000 marchers. The parade is held in honor of the patron saint of Ireland and the Archdiocese of New York and is reviewed each year from the steps of Saint Patrick's Cathedral by the current Archbishop of New York. For the past 150 years, members of the National Guard's 69th Regiment have proudly led the way up Fifth Avenue, followed by members of various Irish societies of the city, the 32 Irish County Societies, various schools, colleges, Emerald societies and Irish-language and nationalist societies. The parade remains true to its roots as a traditional marchers' parade by not allowing floats, automobiles and other commercial aspects to participate. Annually, Mar 17, except when the 17th falls on a Sunday—in that case it is celebrated the day before, Mar 16, because of religious observances. Est attendance: 2,000,000. For info: St. Patrick's Day Parade and Celebration Committee, PO Box 295, Woodlawn Station, Bronx, NY 10470. Phone: (718) 231-4400. Fax: (718) 231-4401. Web: www.nycstpatricksparade.org.

SOUTH AFRICAN WHITES VOTE TO END MINORITY RULE: ANNIVERSARY. Mar 17, 1992. A referendum proposing ending white minority rule through negotiations was supported by a whites-only ballot. The vote of 1,924,186 (68.6 percent) whites in support of President F.W. de Klerk's reform policies was greater than expected.

SPACE MILESTONE: *VANGUARD 1* (US). Mar 17, 1958. Established "pear shape" of Earth. At only three pounds it was the first solar-powered satellite.

TANEY, ROGER B.: BIRTH ANNIVERSARY. Mar 17, 1777. Fifth chief justice of the US, born at Calvert County, MD. Served as attorney general under President Andrew Jackson. Nominated as secretary of the treasury, he became the first presidential nominee to be rejected by the Senate. His rejection centered on his strong stance against the Bank of the United States as a central bank and his role in urging President Jackson to veto the congressional bill extending its charter. A year later, he was nominated to the Supreme Court as an associate justice by Jackson, but his nomination was stalled until the death of Chief Justice John Marshall July 6, 1835. Taney was nominated to fill Marshall's place on the bench and, after much resistance, he was sworn in as chief justice in March 1836. His tenure on the Supreme Court is most remembered for the Dred Scott decision. He died at Washington, DC, Oct 12, 1864.

UNITED KINGDOM: SHAKESPEARE WEEK. Mar 17–23. A national celebration of the 450th anniversary of William Shakespeare's birth. This inaugural week seeks to bring Shakespeare to life vividly for the nation's children and will be celebrated in schools, theaters, historic sites, museums, galleries, cinemas and libraries all over the UK. Every child will be given the chance to be inspired by Shakespeare's stories, language and heritage. For info: Shakespeare Birthplace Trust. E-mail: ShakespeareWeek@shakespeare.org.uk. Web: www.shakespeare.org.uk or www.shakespeareweek.org.uk.

WELLDERLY WEEK. Mar 17–23. Celebration and recognition of senior citizens who never act their age. During this week, select your own Wellderly Day and celebrate in style. Annually, the week that begins on the third Monday in March. For info: Dale L. Anderson, MD, 2982 W Owasso Blvd, St. Paul, MN 55113. Phone: (651) 484-5162. E-mail: dr@acthappy.com.

WORLD FOLK TALES AND FABLES WEEK. Mar 17–23. To encourage children and adults to explore the cultural background and lessons learned from folktales, fables, myths and legends from around the world. For info: Anneke Forzani, Language Lizard, PO Box 421, Basking Ridge, NJ 07920. Phone: (888) 554-9273. Fax: (908) 613-3639. E-mail: info@LanguageLizard.com. Web: www.LanguageLizard.com.

BIRTHDAYS TODAY

Daniel Ray (Danny) Ainge, 55, basketball coach, former basketball and baseball player, born Eugene, OR, Mar 17, 1959.

Lesley-Anne Down, 60, actress ("Upstairs, Downstairs," *The Pink Panther Strikes Again*), born London, England, Mar 17, 1954.

Patrick Duffy, 65, actor ("Step by Step," "Dallas"), born Townsend, MT, Mar 17, 1949.

Paul Horn, 84, composer, musician, born New York, NY, Mar 17, 1930.

Kyle Korver, 33, basketball player, born Lakewood, CA, Mar 17, 1981.

Vicki Lewis, 54, actress ("NewsRadio," *Godzilla*), born Cincinnati, OH, Mar 17, 1960.

Rob Lowe, 50, actor ("Brothers & Sisters," "The West Wing," *St. Elmo's Fire*), born Charlottesville, VA, Mar 17, 1964.

Kurt Russell, 63, actor (*Backdraft*, *Elvis*), born Springfield, MA, Mar 17, 1951.

Gary Sinise, 59, actor (*Forrest Gump*, *Apollo 13*, "CSI: New York"), director (*True West*, *Buried Child*), born Chicago, IL, Mar 17, 1955.

Natalie Zea, 39, actress ("Passions," "The Following," "Dirty Sexy Money," "Justified"), born Harris County, TX, Mar 17, 1975.

March 2014	S	M	T	W	T	F	S
							1
	2	3	4	5	6	7	8
	9	10	11	12	13	14	15
	16	17	18	19	20	21	22
	23	24	25	26	27	28	29
	30	31					

March 18 — Tuesday

DAY 77 — **288 REMAINING**

ARUBA: FLAG DAY. Mar 18. Aruba national holiday. Display of flags, national music and folkloric events.

AWKWARD MOMENTS DAY. Mar 18. Celebrate the humor in life's uncomfortable situations. Recognize those moments that make us feel unsure and embarrassed; then harness the power of humor, laughter and fun to cope with them. For info: Rick Segel, Rick Segel and Associates, 268 Hamrick Dr, Kissimmee, FL 34759. Phone: (781) 272-9995. Fax: (800) 847-9411. E-mail: rick@ricksegel.com.

CALHOUN, JOHN CALDWELL: BIRTH ANNIVERSARY. Mar 18, 1782. American statesman and first vice president of the US to resign that office (Dec 28, 1832). Born at Abbeville District, SC, died at Washington, DC, Mar 31, 1850.

CLEVELAND, GROVER: BIRTH ANNIVERSARY. Mar 18, 1837. The 22nd and 24th president of the US was born Stephen Grover Cleveland at Caldwell, NJ. Terms of office as president: Mar 4, 1885–Mar 3, 1889, and Mar 4, 1893–Mar 3, 1897. He ran for president for the intervening term and received a plurality of votes cast but failed to win electoral college victory. Only president to serve two nonconsecutive terms. Also the only president to be married in the White House. He married 21-year-old Frances Folsom, his ward. Their daughter, Esther, was the first child of a president to be born in the White House. Died at Princeton, NJ, June 24, 1908.

FIRST ELECTRIC RAZOR MARKETED: ANNIVERSARY. Mar 18, 1931. The first electric razor was marketed by Schick, Inc.

FORGIVE MOM AND DAD DAY. Mar 18. Is there a parent alive who has not made mistakes? It's time to let Mom and Dad down off the wedding cake and into the world of mere humans. Besides, you're an alleged grown-up now, and it's time to stop living your life as a reaction to what used to be. (©2006 by WH.) For info: Thomas & Ruth Roy, Wellcat Holidays, 2418 Long Ln, Lebanon, PA 17046. Phone: (717) 279-0184. E-mail: info@wellcat.com. Web: www.wellcat.com.

JOHNSON, WILLIAM H.: BIRTH ANNIVERSARY. Mar 18, 1901. African-American artist born at Florence, SC, he died Apr 13, 1970, at Islip, NY. Johnson spent many years in Europe painting expressionist works. He was strongly influenced by the vivid styles and brushstrokes of Henry O. Tanner, Vincent van Gogh, Paul Gauguin, Edvard Munch and Otto Dix. He left Europe when Hitler began destroying art that had primitivist or African themes. Back in the US, Johnson developed a new, flatter style and delved into subjects of his own experience as well as historical African-American figures and events. *Going to Church* (1940–41) and *Mom and Dad* (1944) are examples of his later work.

NATIONAL BIODIESEL DAY. Mar 18. Birthday of Rudolph Diesel, who invented the diesel engine and unveiled it at the World Fair in 1900. Diesel originally designed the engine to run on peanut oil and was a big believer in the role plant oils could play in fueling America. Biodiesel is a cleaner-burning, petroleum-free alternative to diesel that can be made from any fat or vegetable oil. This day honors the man whose vision comes full circle as biodiesel becomes an increasingly popular fuel. For info: National Biodiesel Board, PO Box 104898, Jefferson City, MO 65110-4898. Phone: (573) 635-3893. Fax: (573) 635-7913. E-mail: info@biodiesel.org. Web: www.biodiesel.org.

NJCAA DIVISION II MEN'S BASKETBALL NATIONAL FINALS. Mar 18–22. Danville, IL. Junior College Division II national men's basketball finals tournament. Est attendance: 8,000. For info: Danville Area CVB, 100 W Main St, #146, Danville, IL 61832. Phone: (800) 383-4386. Fax: (217) 442-2137. E-mail: info@danvilleareainfo.com.

PLIMPTON, GEORGE: BIRTH ANNIVERSARY. Mar 18, 1927. Born at New York, NY, writer and editor George Plimpton called himself a "participatory" journalist, going to great lengths to research his narratives. After training with the 1963 Detroit Lions, he wrote *Paper Lion* based on his experiences; the book is widely considered one of the best pieces of sports writing ever published. He also founded *The Paris Review*, a highly regarded literary quarterly that published the first works of such writers as Philip Roth and Jack Kerouac. The American Academy of Arts and Letters called him a "central figure in American letters" when they inducted him in 2002. He died at New York, NY, Sept 25, 2003.

SPACE MILESTONE: *VOSKHOD 2* (USSR). Mar 18, 1965. Colonel Aleksey Leonov stepped out of the capsule for 20 minutes in a special space suit, the first man to leave a spaceship. It was two months prior to the first US space walk. See also: "Space Milestone: *Gemini 4* (US)" (June 3).

UPDIKE, JOHN: BIRTH ANNIVERSARY. Mar 18, 1932. Pulitzer Prize–winning writer who authored more than 50 books, as well as hundreds of short stories, essays and poems. Updike often wrote of mundane life in Middle America and is best known for his novels about Harry "Rabbit" Angstrom. Born at Reading, PA, Updike died Jan 27, 2009, at Danvers, MA.

BIRTHDAYS TODAY

Bonnie Blair, 50, Olympic speed skater, born Cornwall, NY, Mar 18, 1964.

Irene Cara, 55, singer ("Fame," "The Dream"), actress (*Ain't Misbehavin'*), born the Bronx, NY, Mar 18, 1959.

Dane Cook, 42, comedian, actor (*Good Luck Chuck*), born Boston, MA, Mar 18, 1972.

Frederik Willem de Klerk, 78, former president of South Africa, born Johannesburg, South Africa, Mar 18, 1936.

Kevin Dobson, 70, actor ("Kojak," "Knots Landing"), born New York, NY, Mar 18, 1944.

Brad Dourif, 64, actor (*One Flew Over the Cuckoo's Nest, Blue Velvet, Jungle Fever*), born Huntington, WV, Mar 18, 1950.

John Kander, 87, composer (Tonys [with lyricist Fred Ebb] for *Cabaret, Woman of the Year, Kiss of the Spider Woman*; *Chicago*), born Kansas City, MO, Mar 18, 1927.

Shashi Kapoor, 76, actor (*Heat and Dust, Sammy and Rosie Get Laid*), born Calcutta, India, Mar 18, 1938.

Queen Latifah, 44, singer, actress (*Bringing Down the House, Chicago*), born Dana Owens at East Orange, NJ, Mar 18, 1970.

Adam Levine, 35, singer (Maroon 5), television personality ("The Voice"), born Los Angeles, CA, Mar 18, 1979.

Charley Pride, 76, singer, former minor league baseball player, born Sledge, MS, Mar 18, 1938.

Vanessa Williams, 51, singer, actress ("Ugly Betty," *Bye Bye Birdie, Kiss of the Spider Woman*), born New York, NY, Mar 18, 1963.

Alexei Yagudin, 34, figure skater, born Leningrad, Russia, Mar 18, 1980.

March 19 — Wednesday

DAY 78 — **287 REMAINING**

BRYAN, WILLIAM JENNINGS: BIRTH ANNIVERSARY. Mar 19, 1860. American political leader, member of Congress, Democratic presidential nominee (1896), "free silver" advocate, assisted in prosecution at Scopes trial, known as "the Silver-Tongued Orator." Born at Salem, IL, he died at Dayton, TN, July 26, 1925.

EARP, WYATT: BIRTH ANNIVERSARY. Mar 19, 1848. Born at Monmouth, IL, and died Jan 13, 1929, at Los Angeles, CA. A legendary figure of the Old West, Earp worked as a railroad hand, saloon keeper, gambler, lawman, gunslinger, miner and real estate investor at various times. Best known for the gunfight at the OK Corral Oct 26, 1881, at Tombstone, AZ.

IRAN: NATIONAL DAY OF OIL. Mar 19. National holiday. Commemorates the nationalization of Iran's oil fields in 1963.

LIVINGSTONE, DAVID: BIRTH ANNIVERSARY. Mar 19, 1813. Physician, missionary and explorer born at Blantyre, Scotland. From 1841 until his death, Livingstone was in Africa, evangelizing, seeking to end slavery and making important geographic observations of the African interior. During a search for the origins of the Nile (1866 to 1871), an ailing Livingstone lost touch with the

Western world, occasioning the famous search by journalist Henry M. Stanley. Stanley found him at Ujiji, near Lake Tanganyika in Africa, on Nov 10, 1871. Dr. Livingstone died at Chitambo (now Zambia), May 1, 1873.

McKEAN, THOMAS: BIRTH ANNIVERSARY. Mar 19, 1734. Signer of the Declaration of Independence and governor of Pennsylvania. Born at Chester County, PA, he died June 24, 1817.

NAIA DIVISION I MEN'S BASKETBALL NATIONAL CHAMPIONSHIP. Mar 19–25. Municipal Auditorium, Kansas City, MO. 77th annual tournament. Sponsored by Buffalo Funds. Est attendance: 40,000. For info: Natl Assn of Intercollegiate Athletics, 1200 Grand Blvd, Kansas City, MO 64106. E-mail: cmuehlbach@naia.org. Web: www.naia.org or www.naiahoops.com.

NAIA DIVISION I WOMEN'S BASKETBALL NATIONAL CHAMPIONSHIP. Mar 19–25. Frankfort, KY. 34th annual. 32-team field competes for the national championship. Est attendance: 38,000. For info: Natl Assn of Intercollegiate Athletics, 1200 Grand Blvd, Kansas City, MO 64106. E-mail: jadams@naia.org. Web: www.naia.org.

OPERATION IRAQI FREEDOM: ANNIVERSARY. Mar 19, 2003. At 9:30 PM, EST, two hours past a deadline for Iraqi dictator Saddam Hussein to step down from power, US and British forces began air strikes against his regime. A ground campaign (adding Australian forces) followed quickly, and by Apr 9, Baghdad was under the control of allied forces. Hussein was captured by US forces on Dec 13, 2003. On June 28, 2004, Iraq regained its sovereignty. On Dec 15, 2005, 70 percent of Iraq's registered voters turned out for parliamentary elections—one of the freest elections on record in the Arab world. Sectarian and terrorist violence prevented the withdrawal of US and other national combat troops until Aug 18, 2010.

ROGERS, EDITH NOURSE: BIRTH ANNIVERSARY. Mar 19, 1881. Edith Nourse Rogers was a YMCA and Red Cross volunteer in France during WWI. In 1925 she was elected to the US Congress to fill the vacancy left by the death of her husband. An able legislator, she was reelected to the House of Representatives 17 times and became the first woman to have her name attached to major legislation. She was a major force in the legislation creating the Women's Army Auxiliary Corps (May 14, 1942) during WWII. Rogers was born at Saco, ME, and died Sept 10, 1960, at Boston, MA.

RUSSELL, CHARLES M.: 150th BIRTH ANNIVERSARY. Mar 19, 1864. Born at St. Louis, MO, Charles Marion Russell moved to Montana at age 16 and became a horse wrangler and cow herder with his horse Redbird. In the off hours, he sketched the people and country of the Montana Territory. His wife Nancy helped and encouraged him to pursue art more avidly, and today Russell is considered one of the greatest western artists. He died Oct 26, 1926, at Great Falls, MT.

RYDER, ALBERT PINKHAM: BIRTH ANNIVERSARY. Mar 19, 1847. Painter Albert Pinkham Ryder was born at New Bedford, MA, where he gained a great love for the sea, the subject of many of his works. Ryder was a misanthrope and recluse. He dedicated himself to his painting, working slowly and piling layer after layer of paint on his canvases until he achieved the look he was after. In his lifetime Ryder created only 150 paintings. Three of his best-known works are *The Race Track*, *Toilers of the Sea* and *Siegfried and the Rhine Maidens*. Ryder died Mar 28, 1917, at Elmhurst, NY. Because of his method of painting, many of his works have deteriorated since their creation.

SAINT JOSEPH'S DAY. Mar 19. Feast day of Joseph, husband of the Virgin Mary and foster father of Jesus. Patron of the Catholic Church, fathers and carpenters.

March 2014	S	M	T	W	T	F	S
							1
	2	3	4	5	6	7	8
	9	10	11	12	13	14	15
	16	17	18	19	20	21	22
	23	24	25	26	27	28	29
	30	31					

SIRICA, JOHN JOSEPH: BIRTH ANNIVERSARY. Mar 19, 1904. John Sirica, "the Watergate Judge," was born at Waterbury, CT. During two years of trials and hearings, Sirica relentlessly pushed for the names of those responsible for the June 17, 1972, burglary of the Democratic National Committee headquarters in Washington's Watergate Complex. His unwavering search for the truth ultimately resulted in the toppling of the Nixon administration. Judge John Sirica died Aug 15, 1992, at Washington, DC.

SWALLOWS RETURN TO SAN JUAN CAPISTRANO. Mar 19. Traditional date (St. Joseph's Day), since 1776, for swallows to return to the old mission of San Juan Capistrano, CA. See also: "Saint John of Capistrano: Death Anniversary" (Oct 23).

TAIWAN: BIRTHDAY OF KUAN YIN, GODDESS OF MERCY. Mar 19. A Buddhist deity, Kuan Yin is also the patron goddess of Taiwan. Nineteenth day of Second Moon of the lunar calendar, celebrated at Taipei's Lungshan (Dragon Mountain) and other temples.

TENNESSEE WILLIAMS/NEW ORLEANS LITERARY FESTIVAL. Mar 19–23. French Quarter, New Orleans, LA. Founded in 1986, the festival celebrates the region's rich cultural heritage as well as the special bond between Williams (born Mar 26, 1911) and the adopted city he called his "spiritual home." Events include theater, food and music events; celebrity interviews; a scholars' conference; a poetry slam, writing marathon and breakfast book club; French Quarter literary walking tours; a book fair; short fiction, poetry and one-act play competitions; and special evening events and parties. The riotous closing ceremony is the "Stanley and Stella Shouting Contest," a playful homage to the bellowing mates in *A Streetcar Named Desire*. Est attendance: 10,000. For info: Tennessee Williams / New Orleans Literary Festival, 938 Lafayette St, Ste 514, New Orleans, LA 70113. Phone: (504) 581-1144 or (800) 990-FEST. E-mail: info@tennesseewilliams.net. Web: www.tennesseewilliams.net.

US STANDARD TIME ACT: ANNIVERSARY. Mar 19, 1918. Anniversary of passage by Congress of the Standard Time Act, which authorized the Interstate Commerce Commission to establish standard time zones for the US. The act also established "daylight saving time," to save fuel and to promote other economies in a country at war. Daylight saving time first went into operation on Easter Sunday, Mar 31, 1918. The Uniform Time Act of 1966, as amended in 1986 and again in 2005, now governs standard time in the US. See also: "Daylight Saving Time Begins" (Mar 9).

WARREN, EARL: BIRTH ANNIVERSARY. Mar 19, 1891. American jurist, 14th chief justice of the US. Born at Los Angeles, CA; died at Washington, DC, July 9, 1974.

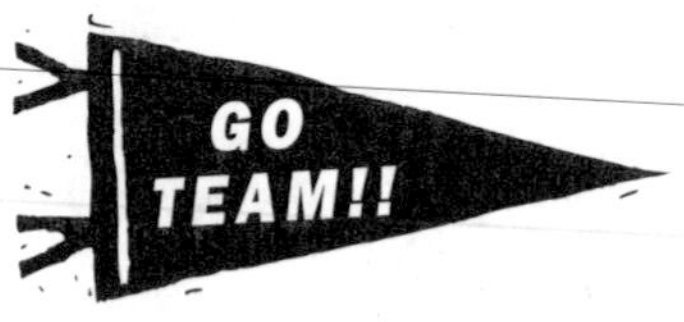

BIRTHDAYS TODAY

Ursula Andress, 78, actress (*Dr. No, What's New Pussycat?*), born Bern, Switzerland, Mar 19, 1936.

Michael Bergin, 45, actor ("Baywatch"), born Naugatuck, CT, Mar 19, 1969.

Glenn Close, 67, actress (*The Big Chill, Fatal Attraction*, Emmy for "Damages," Tonys for *Sunset Boulevard, Death and the Maiden, The Real Thing*), born Greenwich, CT, Mar 19, 1947.

Ornette Coleman, 84, composer, saxophonist, born Fort Worth, TX, Mar 19, 1930.

Philip Roth, 81, author (*The Great American Novel, Portnoy's Complaint*), born Newark, NJ, Mar 19, 1933.

Brent Scowcroft, 89, business executive, consultant, born Ogden, UT, Mar 19, 1925.

Renee Taylor, 79, actress ("The Nanny," *The Producers, A New Leaf*), born New York, NY, Mar 19, 1935.

Hedo Turkoglu, 35, basketball player, born Hiyadet Turkoglu at Istanbul, Turkey, Mar 19, 1979.

Bruce Willis, 59, actor (*Sin City, The Sixth Sense, Die Hard*), born Idar-Oberstein, West Germany (now Germany), Mar 19, 1955.

March 20 — Thursday

DAY 79 **286 REMAINING**

ABSOLUTELY INCREDIBLE KID DAY. Mar 20. 18th annual. Camp Fire, one of the nation's leading youth development organizations, sponsors this day of appreciation for America's youth. Celebrate by writing letters of love and encouragement to the absolutely incredible children in your life. Annually, the third Thursday in March. For info: Camp Fire, 1100 Walnut St, Ste 1900, Kansas City, MO 64106-2197. Phone: (816) 285-2010. Fax: (816) 285-9444. E-mail: info@campfire.org. Web: www.campfire.org.

CANADA: QUEBEC CITY HUNTING, FISHING, CAMPING AND BOAT SHOW. Mar 20–23. Centre de foires d'ExpoCite, Quebec City. Major manufacturers, distributors and retailers of the outdoors, including camping, fishing and hunting, marine (fishing boats, canoes, kayaks and other craft), tourism offices, outfitters (lodges) and entertainment. Est attendance: 38,000. For info: Canadian National Sportsmen's Shows, 8150 Metropolitan Blvd E, Ste 330, Anjou, Montreal, QC, Canada H1K 1A1. Phone: (514) 866-5409 or (418) 622-8118. Fax: (514) 866-4092. Web: www.salonchassepeche.ca.

FESTIVAL OF HOUSES AND GARDENS. Mar 20–Apr 19. Charleston, SC. Held annually since 1947. Provides a rare opportunity to explore the private dwellings and gardens of historic downtown Charleston. Est attendance: 15,000. For info: Historic Charleston Foundation, 40 E Bay St, Charleston, SC 29401. Phone: (843) 722-3405. E-mail: hcf@historiccharleston.org. Web: www.historiccharleston.org/festival.

GREAT AMERICAN MEATOUT. Mar 20. Since 1985, Meatout has become the world's largest annual grassroots diet education campaign. Promotes a meat-free diet to improve health, protect the environment and save animals. "Kick the Meat Habit" for at least Mar 20—when spring begins. A thousand events in all 50 US states and two dozen other countries throughout March. Free Vegetarian Starter Kits with recipes available to all. For info: Meatout, 10101 Ashburton Ln, Bethesda, MD 20817. Phone: (888) FARM-USA. E-mail: info@farmusa.org. Web: www.meatout.org.

IBSEN, HENRIK: BIRTH ANNIVERSARY. Mar 20, 1828. Norwegian playwright born at Skien, Norway. Among his best-remembered plays are *Peer Gynt, The Pillars of Society, The Wild Duck, An Enemy of the People* and *Hedda Gabler*. Died at Oslo, Norway, May 23, 1906.

JAPAN: VERNAL EQUINOX DAY. Mar 20. National holiday in Japan. (When the vernal equinox falls on a Sunday, it is observed on the following Monday.)

KISS YOUR FIANCÉ DAY. Mar 20. A day for brides and grooms around the world to forget wedding planning and all the stress and kiss your fiancé! Annually, Mar 20. For info: Tracee Wright, Weddings Done Wright, 2560 Rte 22, #304, Scotch Plains, NJ 07076. Phone: (732) 980-6224. E-mail: kiss@kissyourfianceday.com. Web: www.kissyourfianceday.com.

NATIONAL CHERRY BLOSSOM FESTIVAL. Mar 20–Apr 13. Various sites in Washington, DC. Celebrating the 102 years of cherry blossoms in our nation's capital. In the midst of thousands of beautiful cherry blossom trees—a gift from Tokyo in 1912—festivities include cultural performances by local and international artists, tours, sporting events, art exhibits and other events celebrating spring. Highlights include Family Days and the Opening Ceremony, a spectacular Fireworks Festival and the National Cherry Blossom Festival Parade and Sakura Matsuri—Japanese Street Festival. For info: National Cherry Blossom Festival, 1250 H St NW, Ste 1000, Washington, DC 20005. Phone: (877) 44-BLOOM. Web: www.nationalcherryblossomfestival.org.

NCAA DIVISION I FENCING CHAMPIONSHIP. Mar 20–23. Site TBD. For info: NCAA, PO Box 6222, Indianapolis, IN 46206-6222. Phone: (317) 917-6222. Web: www.NCAA.com.

NCAA DIVISION I WOMEN'S SWIMMING AND DIVING CHAMPIONSHIPS. Mar 20–22. University of Minnesota Aquatic Center, Minneapolis, MN. Est attendance: 3,000. For info: NCAA, 700 W Washington St, PO Box 6222, Indianapolis, IN 46206-6222. Phone: (317) 917-6222. Fax: (317) 917-6888. Web: www.ncaa.com.

NCAA DIVISION I WRESTLING CHAMPIONSHIPS. Mar 20–22. Chesapeake Energy Arena, Oklahoma City, OK. 86th annual. For info: NCAA, PO Box 6222, Indianapolis, IN 46206-6222. Phone: (317) 917-6222. Web: www.NCAA.com.

NERVE GAS ATTACK ON JAPANESE SUBWAY: ANNIVERSARY. Mar 20, 1995. Twelve people were killed and 5,000 injured in a nerve gas attack on the Tokyo subway system during rush hour. Suspected in the attack was the Japanese religious sect Aum Shinrikyo, founded and led by Shoko Asahara (real name Chizuo Matsumoto). The group, which professes belief in a hybrid of Buddhist-Hindu teachings, predicts an apocalypse. In a raid conducted against the sect's main compound in Kamikuishiki on Mar 25, police seized literature that predicted 90 percent of the people in the world would be killed by poison gas. Also seized were two tons of chemicals for making sarin, the poison used in the Mar 20 attack. This cache was reported to contain enough material to kill five million people. In a second raid, Asahara was arrested.

OSTARA. Mar 20. (Also called Alban Eilir.) One of the "Lesser Sabbats" during the Wiccan year, Ostara is a fire and fertility festival that marks the beginning of spring. Annually, on the spring equinox.

PROPOSAL DAY!®. Mar 20 (also Sept 22). A holiday for those who seek marriage. Single adults who are ready to marry are encouraged to propose marriage to their true love on the days of the vernal equinox and the autumnal equinox. Thousands of men and women are married today as a result of a marriage proposal made on a "Proposal Day!"®—including the creator of the holiday. For info: John Michael O'Loughlin, 3124 Chisolm Trail, Irving, TX 75062. Phone: (972) 258-4996. E-mail: lldjohn@aol.com. Web: www.proposalday.com.

ROGERS, FRED: BIRTH ANNIVERSARY. Mar 20, 1928. Born Fred McFeely Rogers at Latrobe, PA, Rogers began producing television for children in 1953. His first program, "The Children's Hour," was the precursor to "Mister Rogers' Neighborhood," which premiered in Canada in 1966 and the US in 1968. The show ran on public television until Rogers's death, and he became known worldwide for his dedication to the well-being of children and for his demonstrations of the importance of kindness, compassion and learning. He authored a number of books for parents and children, wrote more than 200 songs and won dozens of awards, including Emmys, Peabodys and the Presidential Medal of Freedom. He died Feb 27, 2003, at his home in Pittsburgh, PA.

SKINNER, B.F.: BIRTH ANNIVERSARY. Mar 20, 1904. American psychologist Burrhus Frederic Skinner was born at Susquehanna, PA. He was a pioneer in behaviorism and is best known for developing the "Skinner box" (an enclosed experimental environment). He died Aug 18, 1990, at Cambridge, MA.

SNOWMAN BURNING. Mar 20. Reading of poetry heralding the end of winter and the arrival of spring, followed by sacrifice in effigy, toasts and cheers. Annually, on or near the first day of spring. Est attendance: 300. For info: Public Relations Office, Lake Superior State University, Sault Ste. Marie, MI 49783. Phone: (906) 635-2315 or (906) 635-2314. Fax: (906) 635-2623. Web: www.lssu.edu/snowman.

SPRING. Mar 20–June 21. In the Northern Hemisphere, spring begins today with the vernal equinox, at 12:57 PM, EDT. Note that in the Southern Hemisphere today is the beginning of autumn. Sun rises due east and sets due west everywhere on Earth (except near poles), and the daylight length (interval between sunrise and sunset) is virtually the same everywhere today: 12 hours, 8 minutes.

TAYLOR, FREDERICK WINSLOW: BIRTH ANNIVERSARY. Mar 20, 1856. Vilified and praised, Frederick Winslow Taylor changed the face of business forever as the "Father of Scientific Management." Born at Philadelphia, PA, Taylor was a chief engineer at Philadelphia's Midvale Steel Company, when he introduced time-and-motion studies in 1881, which helped companies find efficiencies in worker movement and drive out time wasting on the assembly lines. Henry Ford, in particular, put Taylor's theories to work. Taylor died at Philadelphia, Mar 21, 1915.

TUNISIA: INDEPENDENCE DAY. Mar 20. Commemorates treaty in 1956 by which France recognized Tunisian autonomy.

ULTIMATE SPORT SHOW—GRAND RAPIDS. Mar 20–23. DeVos Place, Grand Rapids, MI. This event brings together buyers and sellers of hunting and fishing-boat equipment and accessories, as well as other outdoor sporting goods. US and Canadian hunting and fishing trips and other vacation travel destinations are featured. All aspects of fishing, including tackle boats, seminars, demonstrations and displays, are emphasized. Est attendance: 35,000. For info: ShowSpan, Inc, 2121 Celebration Dr NE, Grand Rapids, MI 49525. Phone: (616) 447-2860. Fax: (616) 447-2861. E-mail: events@showspan.com. Web: www.showspan.com.

WON'T YOU BE MY NEIGHBOR DAY. Mar 20. An annual day celebrating Fred Rogers (born today in 1928) and his legacy of neighborliness on his birthday. Neighbors everywhere are encouraged to wear a favorite sweater and promote neighborliness in their neighborhood. For info: The Fred Rogers Company. Web: www.fci.org/neighbor.

BIRTHDAYS TODAY

Holly Hunter, 56, actress (Oscar for *The Piano*; "Saving Grace," *Broadcast News, Raising Arizona*), born Conyers, GA, Mar 20, 1958.

William Hurt, 64, actor (*Too Big to Fail, The Accidental Tourist, Broadcast News*), born Washington, DC, Mar 20, 1950.

Spike Lee, 57, director, producer, writer, actor (*She's Gotta Have It, Do the Right Thing, Malcolm X*), born Atlanta, GA, Mar 20, 1957.

Hal Linden, 83, actor ("Barney Miller," "Blacke's Magic"), born Harold Lipshitz at the Bronx, NY, Mar 20, 1931.

Brian Mulroney, 75, 18th prime minister of Canada (1984–93), born Baie Comeau, QC, Canada, Mar 20, 1939.

Robert Gordon (Bobby) Orr, 66, Hall of Fame hockey player, born Parry Sound, ON, Canada, Mar 20, 1948.

Carl Reiner, 92, actor ("The Dick Van Dyke Show," "Your Show of Shows"), writer, director, born the Bronx, NY, Mar 20, 1922.

Patrick James (Pat) Riley, 69, basketball coach and former player, born Schenectady, NY, Mar 20, 1945.

Theresa Russell, 57, actress (*Straight Time, Black Widow*), born San Diego, CA, Mar 20, 1957.

David Thewlis, 51, actor (*War Horse, Besieged*, Harry Potter films), born Blackpool, Lancashire, England, Mar 20, 1963.

Fernando Torres, 30, soccer player, born Fuenlabrada, Spain, Mar 20, 1984.

Louis (Louie) Vito, 26, Olympic snowboarder, born Columbus, OH, Mar 20, 1988.

Paul Junger Witt, 71, producer (*Three Kings*, "Everything's Relative"), director, born New York, NY, Mar 20, 1943.

March 21 — Friday

DAY 80 **285 REMAINING**

ARIES, THE RAM. Mar 21–Apr 19. In the astronomical/astrological zodiac, which divides the sun's apparent orbit into 12 segments, the period Mar 21–Apr 19 is traditionally identified as the sun sign of Aries, the Ram. The ruling planet is Mars.

BABE DIDRIKSON PITCHES FOR ATHLETICS: 80th ANNIVERSARY. Mar 21, 1934. Mildred ("Babe") Didrikson, perhaps the greatest woman athlete of all time, pitched one inning of baseball for the Philadelphia Athletics in an exhibition game against the Brooklyn Dodgers. Didrikson hit the first batter she faced and walked the next. The third hit into a triple play.

BACH, JOHANN SEBASTIAN: BIRTH ANNIVERSARY. Mar 21, 1685. Organist and composer, one of the most influential composers in musical history. Born at Eisenach, Germany, he died at Leipzig, Germany, July 28, 1750.

BURKE, SOLOMON: BIRTH ANNIVERSARY. Mar 21, 1940. American musician and singer, born at Philadelphia, PA, widely considered to be one of the greatest soul singers of all time. Burke's hits include 1962's "Cry to Me" and 1964's "Everybody Needs Somebody to Love." He was a flamboyant showman, performing from a throne in keeping with his self-styled King of Rock and Soul persona. Burke's personal life was outsized as well: he weighed more than 400 pounds at the time of his death and he fathered at least 21 children. He died at an airport in Amsterdam, Netherlands, on Oct 10, 2010.

CHARLESTON ANTIQUES SHOW. Mar 21–23. Memminger Auditorium, Charleston, SC. A world-class antiques show featuring a roster of 30 dealers exhibiting museum-quality objects in every category with a concentration on period furnishings and decorative pieces. (Preview Party is Mar 20.) Est attendance: 3,000. For info: Historic Charleston Foundation, 40 E Bay St, Charleston, SC 29401. Phone: (843) 722-3405. E-mail: hcf@historiccharleston.org. Web: www.historiccharleston.org/AntiquesShow.

CRANE WATCH FESTIVAL. Mar 21–30. Kearney, NE. "World's Largest Concentration of Cranes." Each spring some 650,000 sandhill cranes (80 percent of the world's population of this species) gather on the Platte River "staging area" during their northward migration. For info: Crane Watch Festival. Phone: (800) 652-9435. Web: www.visitkearney.org.

March 2014	S	M	T	W	T	F	S
							1
	2	3	4	5	6	7	8
	9	10	11	12	13	14	15
	16	17	18	19	20	21	22
	23	24	25	26	27	28	29
	30	31					

FIRST ROUND-THE-WORLD BALLOON FLIGHT: 15th ANNIVERSARY. Mar 21, 1999. Swiss psychiatrist Bertrand Piccard and British copilot Brian Jones landed in the Egyptian desert on this date, having flown 29,056 miles nonstop around the world in a hot-air balloon. Leaving from Chateau d'Oex in the Swiss Alps on Mar 1, the trip took 19 days, 21 hours and 55 minutes. Piccard is the grandson of balloonist Auguste Piccard, who was the first to ascend into the stratosphere in a balloon. See also: "First Solo Round-the-World Balloon Flight: Anniversary" (July 2) and "Piccard, Auguste: Birth Anniversary" (Jan 28).

GALLO, JULIO: BIRTH ANNIVERSARY. Mar 21, 1910. American vintner Julio Gallo was born at Oakland, CA. He is best known for his role in the Ernest and Julio Gallo Winery, of Modesto, CA, which at one time claimed about 26 percent of the US wine industry. He died May 2, 1993, near Tracy, CA.

GERSDORFF HITLER ASSASSINATION ATTEMPT: ANNIVERSARY. Mar 21, 1943. In a suicide/assassination attempt planned for this date, Major General Baron von Gersdorff was to carry a bomb in the pocket of his greatcoat to the "Heroes Memorial Day" annual dedication to the dead of the First World War. Hitler was to attend this event to inspect some weaponry taken from captured Russian soldiers. The bomb was to go off within 10 minutes of Hitler's arrival at the event, as he was not expected to be there for very long. The conspirators were unable to locate the necessary short time fuse and the attempt had to be called off. This was the second serious plan to assassinate Hitler in 1943.

INTERNATIONAL CHERRY BLOSSOM FESTIVAL. Mar 21–30. Macon, GA. 32nd annual Cherry Blossom Festival features concerts, exhibits, parades, children's events, hot-air balloons, fireworks, food, fun and family entertainment. More than 300,000 Yoshino cherry trees. Est attendance: 700,000. For info: Macon Cherry Blossom Fest, 794 Cherry St, Macon, GA 31201. Phone: (478) 330-7050. Fax: (478) 751-7408. Web: www.cherryblossom.com.

IRANIAN NEW YEAR: NORUZ. Mar 21. National celebration for all Iranians, this is the traditional Persian New Year. (In Iran, spring comes Mar 20 or 21.) It is a celebration of nature's rebirth. Every household spreads a special cover with symbols for the seven good angels on it. These symbols are sprouts, wheat germ, apples, hyacinth, fruit of the jujube, garlic and sumac heralding life, rebirth, health, happiness, prosperity, joy and beauty. A fishbowl is also customary, representing the end of the astrological year, and wild rue is burned to drive away evil and bring about a happy New Year. This pre-Islamic holiday, a legacy of Zoroastrianism, is also celebrated as Navruz, Nau-Roz or Noo Roz in Afghanistan, Albania, Azerbaijan, Kazakhstan, Kyrgyzstan, Tajikistan, Turkmenistan and Uzbekistan. For info: Mahvash Tafreshi, Librarian, Farmingdale Public Library, 116 Merritts Rd, Farmingdale, NY 11735. Phone: (516) 249-9090. Fax: (516) 694-9697, or Yassaman Djalali, Librarian, West Valley Branch Library, 1243 San Tomas Aquino Rd, San Jose, CA 95117. Phone: (408) 244-4766.

JUAREZ, BENITO: BIRTH ANNIVERSARY. Mar 21, 1806. A full-blooded Zapotec Indian, Benito Pablo Juarez was born at Oaxaca, Mexico, and grew up to become that country's president. He learned Spanish at age 12. Juarez became judge of the civil court in Oaxaca in 1842, a member of congress in 1846 and governor in 1847. In 1858, following a rebellion against the constitution, the presidency was passed to Juarez. He died at Mexico City, July 18, 1872. A symbol of liberation and of Mexican resistance to foreign intervention, his birthday is a public holiday in Mexico.

LESOTHO: NATIONAL TREE PLANTING DAY. Mar 21. Lesotho.

LEWIS, FRANCIS: BIRTH ANNIVERSARY. Mar 21, 1713. Signer of the Declaration of Independence, born at Wales. Died Dec 31, 1802, at Long Island, NY.

LUNSFORD, BASCOM LAMAR: BIRTH ANNIVERSARY. Mar 21, 1882. Songwriter and folklorist who authored the song "Mountain Dew," Lunsford started the first folk music festival in 1928 at Asheville, NC. This event, which led to the formation of the National Clogging and Hoedown Council, is held to this day. He was known as the "father of clogging dance" and the "king of folk music." He recorded some 320 folk songs, tunes and stories for the Library of Congress. Born at Mars Hill, NC, Lunsford died Sept 4, 1973, at South Turkey Creek, NC.

MEMORY DAY. Mar 21. To encourage awareness of the traditional memory system using pattern t,d = 1; n = 2; m = 3; r = 4; l = 5; j,ch = 6; k,q,g-hard = 7; f,v = 8; b,p = 9. Study historic examples of the use of the memory system in the writings of Milton, Thomas Gray, Longfellow, Lincoln and others. For info: Robert L. Birch, Coord, Puns Corps, 3108 Dashiell Rd, Falls Church, VA 22042. Phone: (703) 533-3668.

MUSSORGSKY, MODEST: 175th BIRTH ANNIVERSARY. Mar 21, 1839. Romantic composer, born at Karevo, Russia. A military officer, and later a civil servant, he joined The Five, a group of other amateur Russian composers passionate about creating a Russian music free from European musical conventions. Best-known works are *Boris Gudonov* (1874) and *Pictures at an Exhibition* (1874). He died Mar 28, 1881, at St. Petersburg, Russia.

NAMIBIA: INDEPENDENCE DAY. Mar 21. National Day. Commemorates independence from South Africa in 1990.

NATIONAL PUPPY DAY. Mar 21. To celebrate the puppies in our lives and rescue the ones who need a good home. The goal is to have 10,000 puppies adopted across the US on National Puppy Day! For info: Colleen Paige, Animal Miracle Foundation, 4804 NW Bethany Blvd, Ste 12-197, Portland, OR 97229. Phone: (323) 552-9941. Web: www.nationalpuppyday.com.

NAW-RUZ. Mar 21. Baha'i New Year's Day, which falls on the spring equinox. One of the nine days of the year when Baha'is suspend work. Naw-Ruz is an ancient Persian festival celebrating the "new day" and for Baha'is it marks the end of the annual 19-Day Fast. For info: Baha'is of the US, Office of Communications, 1233 Central St, Evanston, IL 60201. Phone: (847) 733-3559. Fax: (847) 733-3578. E-mail: ooc@usbnc.org. Web: www.bahai.us.

NCAA DIVISION I WOMEN'S ICE HOCKEY CHAMPIONSHIP. Mar 21 and 23. TD Bank Sports Center, Hamden, CT. For info: NCAA, PO Box 6222, Indianapolis, IN 46206-6222. Web: www.NCAA.com.

PITTSBURGH ARTS & CRAFTS SPRING FEVER FESTIVAL. Mar 21–23. Monroeville, PA. Approximately 175 booths, including pottery, flowers, jewelry, quilts, furniture, tole and decorative painting, toys and much more. Find that perfect gift. Est attendance: 7,000. For info: Debbie & Dave Stoner, Family Festivals Assn, PO Box 166, Irwin, PA 15642. Phone: (724) 863-4577. E-mail: info@familyfestivals.com. Web: www.familyfestivals.com.

POCAHONTAS (REBECCA ROLFE): DEATH ANNIVERSARY. Mar 21, 1617. Pocahontas, daughter of Powhatan, born about 1595, near Jamestown, VA, leader of the Indian union of Algonkin nations, helped to foster goodwill between the colonists of the Jamestown settlement and her people. Pocahontas converted to Christianity, was baptized with the name Rebecca and married John Rolfe Apr 5, 1614. In 1616 she accompanied Rolfe on a trip to his native England, where she was regarded as an overseas "ambassador." Pocahontas's stay in England drew so much attention to the Virginia Company's Jamestown settlement that lotteries were held to help support the colony. Shortly before she was scheduled to return to Jamestown, Pocahontas died at Gravesend, Kent, England, of either smallpox or pneumonia.

SCHMECKFEST. Mar 21–22 (also Mar 28–29). Freeman, SD. 56th annual. Sausage and sauerkraut, kuchen and pluma moos. These are just a few of the dishes served at this German "festival of tasting" where visitors can also watch cooking and craft demonstrations and an evening musical. Est attendance: 5,000. For info: Schmeckfest. E-mail: schmeckfest@gmail.com. Web: www.freemansd.com.

SECOND BATTLE OF SOMME: ANNIVERSARY. Mar 21–Apr 4, 1918. General Erich Ludendorff launched the Michael offensive, the biggest German offensive of 1918, on Mar 21 with a five-hour artillery barrage. The Central Powers' objective was to drive a wedge between the British and French forces and drive the British to the sea. Although they did not accomplish this objective, in the south they captured Montdidier and advanced to a depth of 40 miles. They managed to create a bulge in the front south of Somme and end what had effectively been a stalemate. The Allies lost nearly 230,000 men and the Germans lost almost as many.

SELMA CIVIL RIGHTS MARCH: ANNIVERSARY. Mar 21, 1965. More than 3,000 civil rights demonstrators led by Dr. Martin Luther King, Jr, began a four-day march from Selma, AL, to Montgomery, AL, to demand federal protection of voting rights. There were violent attempts by local police, using fire hoses and dogs, to suppress the march. A march two weeks before on Mar 7, 1965, was called "Bloody Sunday" because of the use of nightsticks, chains and electric cattle prods against the marchers by the police.

SOUTH AFRICA: HUMAN RIGHTS DAY. Mar 21. National holiday. Commemorates the Mar 21, 1960, massacre at Sharpeville and all those who lost their lives in the struggle for equal rights as citizens of South Africa.

STRANG, JAMES JESSE (KING STRANG): BIRTH ANNIVERSARY. Mar 21, 1813. Perhaps America's only crowned king was born at Scipio, NY, and christened Jesse James Strang (which he later changed to James Jesse Strang). He was crowned king of Mormons at Beaver Island, MI, July 8, 1850, and ruled his kingdom until his death. Elected to the Michigan legislature in 1852 and 1854. Wounded by assassins June 16, 1856, at Beaver Island, and died June 19, 1856, at Voree, WI.

SUGARLOAF CRAFTS FESTIVAL. Mar 21–23. Garden State Exhibit Center, Somerset, NJ. This show, now in its 21st year, features 250 nationally recognized craft designers and fine artists displaying and selling their original creations. Includes craft demonstrations, live music, specialty foods, children's entertainment, hourly gift certificate drawings and more! Est attendance: 16,000. For info: Sugarloaf Mountain Works, 19807 Executive Park Circle, Germantown, MD 20874. Phone: (800) 210-9900. Fax: (301) 253-9620. E-mail: sugarloafinfo@sugarloaffest.com. Web: www.SugarloafCrafts.com.

UNITED NATIONS: INTERNATIONAL DAY FOR THE ELIMINATION OF RACIAL DISCRIMINATION. Mar 21. Initiated by the United Nations General Assembly in 1966 to be observed annually Mar 21, the anniversary of the killing of 69 African demonstrators at Sharpeville, South Africa, in 1960, as a day to remember "the victims of Sharpeville and those countless others in different parts of the world who have fallen victim to racial injustice" and to promote efforts to eradicate racial discrimination worldwide. For info: United Nations, Dept of Public Info, New York, NY 10017. Web: www.un.org.

UNITED NATIONS: WEEK OF SOLIDARITY WITH THE PEOPLES STRUGGLING AGAINST RACISM AND RACIAL DISCRIMINATION. Mar 21–27. Annual observance initiated by the UN General Assembly as part of its program of the Decade for Action to Combat Racism and Racial Discrimination. For info: United Nations, Dept of Public Info, New York, NY 10017. Web: www.un.org.

WORLD DOWN SYNDROME DAY. Mar 21. 9th annual. A global awareness day (officially observed by the United Nations since 2012) raising awareness of what Down syndrome is, what it means to have Down syndrome and how people with Down syndrome play a vital role in our lives and communities. Join the cause to create a single global voice for advocating for the rights, inclusion and well-being of people with Down syndrome. Annually, Mar 21. For info: Down Syndrome International. E-mail: contact@ds-int.org. Web: www.worlddownsyndromeday.org.

BIRTHDAYS TODAY

Matthew Broderick, 52, actor (*Godzilla, Inspector Gadget, Election*; stage: *The Producers*), born New York, NY, Mar 21, 1962.

Peter Brook, 89, theater director, born London, England, Mar 21, 1925.

Timothy Dalton, 68, actor (James Bond movies, *Cleopatra, Centennial*), born Colwyn Bay, Wales, Mar 21, 1946.

Kevin Federline, 36, dancer, born Fresno City, CA, Mar 21, 1978.

Al Freeman, Jr, 80, actor (*A Patch of Blue*; *Roots: The Next Generations*), born San Antonio, TX, Mar 21, 1934.

Rosie O'Donnell, 52, actress (*A League of Their Own*), television personality ("The Rosie O'Donnell Show"), born Commack, NY, Mar 21, 1962.

Gary Oldman, 56, actor (Harry Potter films, *Tinker Tailor Soldier Spy, Sid and Nancy, JFK*), director, born South London, England, Mar 21, 1958.

Adrian Peterson, 29, football player, born Palestine, TX, Mar 21, 1985.

Ronaldinho, 34, soccer player, born Ronaldo de Assis Moreira at Porto Alegre, Brazil, Mar 21, 1980.

March 22 — Saturday

DAY 81 **284 REMAINING**

AS YOUNG AS YOU FEEL DAY. Mar 22. Now more than ever you are as young as you feel. So stop acting your chronological age and get out there and start feeling peppy! (©2006 by WH.) For info: Thomas & Ruth Roy, Wellcat Holidays, 2418 Long Ln, Lebanon, PA 17046. Phone: (717) 279-0184. E-mail: info@wellcat.com. Web: www.wellcat.com.

EQUAL RIGHTS AMENDMENT SENT TO STATES FOR RATIFICATION: ANNIVERSARY. Mar 22, 1972. The Senate passed the 27th Amendment, prohibiting discrimination on the basis of sex, sending it to the states for ratification. Hawaii led the way as the first state to ratify and by the end of the year, 22 states had ratified it. On Oct 6, 1978, the deadline for ratification was extended to June 30, 1982, by Congress. The amendment still lacked three of the required 38 states for ratification. This was the first extension granted since Congress set seven years as the limit for ratification. The amendment failed to achieve ratification as the deadline came and passed and no additional states ratified the measure.

March 2014	S	M	T	W	T	F	S
							1
	2	3	4	5	6	7	8
	9	10	11	12	13	14	15
	16	17	18	19	20	21	22
	23	24	25	26	27	28	29
	30	31					

INDIA: NEW YEAR'S DAY. Mar 22. This is the first day of the New Year on the Saka calendar adopted by India after independence from Great Britain. The Saka calendar is a solar calendar with the same leap year schedule as the Gregorian calendar. In common years, the New Year is Mar 22; in leap years, the New Year falls on Mar 21.

INTERNATIONAL DAY OF THE SEAL: ANNIVERSARY. Mar 22. In 1982 Congress declared an International Day of the Seal to draw attention to the cruelty of seal hunts and the virtual inevitability of these creatures' extinction. Zoos and aquariums around the world observe this day with special programs and activities; contact your local affiliate for a schedule of activities.

L'AMOUR, LOUIS: BIRTH ANNIVERSARY. Mar 22, 1908. Popular author Louis Dearborn LaMoore was born at Jamestown, ND. He began writing stories in the 1930s, initially selling them to pulp magazines. Despite an interruption by military service during WWII, L'Amour was a quite successful writer of adventure stories, Westerns and scripts for television and film. He eventually authored 116 Western novels that sold 20 million copies in 20 different languages. He was the first novelist to be awarded the Congressional Medal of Freedom (1983) and was also given the Presidential Medal of Freedom (1984). L'Amour died June 10, 1988, at Los Angeles, CA.

LASER PATENTED: ANNIVERSARY. Mar 22, 1960. The first patent for a laser (light amplification by stimulated emission of radiation) granted to Arthur Schawlow and Charles Townes.

MARX, CHICO: BIRTH ANNIVERSARY. Mar 22, 1887. Known for his sly wisecracks and put-on Italian accent, Chico Marx—born Leonard Marx in New York City—was the oldest of the five Marx brothers. The brothers, in various combinations, performed first as a singing group and later as a comedy act featuring music. After honing their act on the vaudeville circuit, they mounted three successful shows on Broadway, two of which were made into movies, *The Cocoanuts* and *Animal Crackers*. After the team disbanded in 1941, Chico led his own big band before settling into semiretirement until his death at age 74, Oct 11, 1961, at Hollywood, CA.

NATIONAL GOOF-OFF DAY. Mar 22. A day of relaxation and a time to be oneself; a day for some good-humored fun and some good-natured silliness. Everyone needs one special day each year to goof off. Annually, Mar 22. For info: Monica A. Dufour, 5408 N State Rd, Davison, MI 48423. Phone: (810) 654-0226. E-mail: monduf22@netzero.com.

NEUHARTH, AL: 90th BIRTH ANNIVERSARY. Mar 22, 1924. Flamboyant, innovative media executive who transformed the American media landscape first as chief executive of the Gannett Company and then as the founder of *USA Today*. Neuharth grew Gannett from a regional news group into the nation's largest newspaper chain. *USA Today*, founded in 1982 and the only major daily established in the US after WWII, brought color, lifestyle coverage, shorter articles and other innovations to media. *USA Today* was embraced by the public and forced other journals to make changes. Born at Eureka, SD, Neuharth died Apr 19, 2013, at Cocoa Beach, FL.

PUERTO RICO: EMANCIPATION DAY. Mar 22. Holiday commemorates the end of slavery on Mar 22, 1873.

TUSKEGEE AIRMEN ACTIVATED: ANNIVERSARY. Mar 22, 1941. This pioneering and highly decorated WWII African-American aviator unit gained their name during training at the US Army airfield near Tuskegee, AL, and at the Tuskegee Institute. They were activated as the 99th Pursuit Squadron and later formed the 332nd Fighter Group (with the 100th, 301st and 302nd squadrons); 992 black pilots emerged from training to fly P-39, P-40, P-47 and P-51 aircraft in more than 15,000 sorties in North Africa, Sicily and Europe. On escort missions, they were the only unit that never lost a US bomber. They shot down 111 enemy planes and destroyed 273 planes on the ground. Lieutenant Colonel Benjamin O. Davis, Jr—later the US Air Force's first black general—was their commander. When President Harry Truman integrated the US military, the all-black group was deactivated. See also: "Davis, Benjamin O., Jr: Birth Anniversary" (Dec 18).

UNITED NATIONS: WORLD WATER DAY. Mar 22. The General Assembly declared this observance (Res 47/193) to promote public awareness of how water resource development contributes to economic productivity and social well-being. Annually, on Mar 22.

BIRTHDAYS TODAY

George Benson, 71, singer, guitarist, born Pittsburgh, PA, Mar 22, 1943.

Robert Quinlan (Bob) Costas, 62, sportscaster, born New York, NY, Mar 22, 1952.

Bruno Ganz, 73, actor (*The American Friend, Wings of Desire*), born Zurich, Switzerland, Mar 22, 1941.

Orrin Grant Hatch, 80, US Senator (R, Utah), born Pittsburgh, PA, Mar 22, 1934.

Andrew Lloyd Webber, 66, composer (*Cats, The Phantom of the Opera*), born London, England, Mar 22, 1948.

Matthew Modine, 55, actor (*Full Metal Jacket*, "And the Band Played On"), born Loma Linda, CA, Mar 22, 1959.

James Patterson, 67, author (*Kiss the Girls, Along Came a Spider*), born Newburgh, NY, Mar 22, 1947.

Cristen Powell, 35, race car driver, born Portland, OR, Mar 22, 1979.

Pat Robertson, 84, television evangelist, born Lexington, VA, Mar 22, 1930.

William Shatner, 83, actor ("Star Trek," "Boston Legal"), author (*Tek* novels), born Montreal, QC, Canada, Mar 22, 1931.

Stephen Sondheim, 84, composer (*A Little Night Music*), born New York, NY, Mar 22, 1930.

Elvis Stojko, 42, former figure skater, born Newmarket, ON, Canada, Mar 22, 1972.

M. Emmet Walsh, 79, actor (*Serpico, Blood Simple, Raising Arizona*), born Ogdensburg, NY, Mar 22, 1935.

Reese Witherspoon, 38, actress (Oscar for *Walk the Line*; *Vanity Fair, Legally Blonde, Election*), born Nashville, TN, Mar 22, 1976.

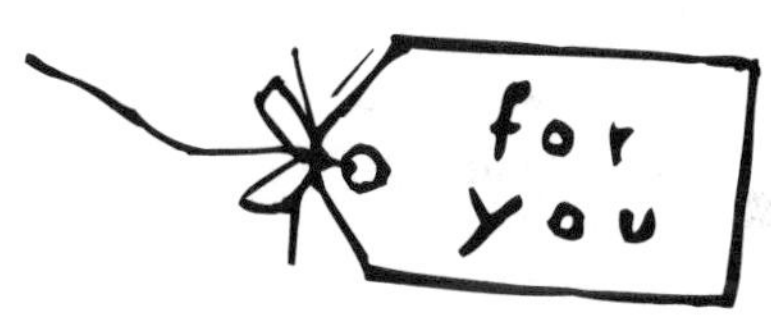

March 23 — Sunday

DAY 82 **283 REMAINING**

BATTLE OF KERNSTOWN: ANNIVERSARY. Mar 23, 1862. As General George McClellan began the Peninsular campaign to move on the Confederate capital of Richmond, VA, Confederate general Stonewall Jackson engaged a larger force of Union troops at Kernstown in the northern Shenandoah Valley of Virginia on Mar 23, 1862. Although he ultimately was forced to retreat, the Battle of Kernstown provided a diversion central to the South's military strategy. Fearing an attack on Washington, DC, Northern troops were kept around Washington as part of its defense, leaving fewer troops available for the Peninsular campaign.

"BIG BERTHA" PARIS GUN: ANNIVERSARY. Mar 23, 1918. Germany initiated use of a terrifying new weapon—the Paris Gun—so-called because it was first used against that city. The great gun, with a 25-foot carriage, was first used in combat when it was fired from a wooded location near Laon, France, on Mar 23, 1918. It took 176 seconds for a shell to reach the city from a distance of 75 miles. On that first day 15 shots killed 16 individuals. Ridiculing the designers and manufacturers of the weapon, Parisians nicknamed it "Big Bertha" after the wife of the head of the munitions corporation. On Good Friday, Mar 29, a shell from the armament struck the church of Saint Gervais, which was crowded with worshipers. The casualty toll was 88 dead and 68 injured.

"THE BOLD AND THE BEAUTIFUL" TV PREMIERE: ANNIVERSARY. Mar 23, 1987. A continuing daytime serial created by William Bell and Lee Phillip Bell to be "young and hip." It is set in the fashion industry of Los Angeles, CA, with two central families, the Logans and the Forresters. The cast has included, as the Forresters: John McCook, Susan Flannery, Clayton Norcross, Jeff Trachta, Ronn Moss, Teri Ann Linn and Colleen Dion and as the Logans: Robert Pine, Judith Baldwin, Nancy Burnette, Nancy Sloan, Carrie Mitchum, Ethan Wayne, Brian Patrick Clarke, Katherine Kelly Lang and Lesley Woods.

CLARK, BARNEY: DEATH ANNIVERSARY. Mar 23, 1983. Barney Clark died after living almost 112 days with an artificial heart. The heart, made of polyurethane plastic and aluminum, was implanted in Clark at the University of Utah Medical Center, Salt Lake City, Dec 2, 1982. Clark was the first person ever to receive a permanent artificial heart. Born at Provo, UT, Jan 21, 1921, Clark was 62 when he died.

COLFAX, SCHUYLER: BIRTH ANNIVERSARY. Mar 23, 1823. 17th vice president of the US (1869–73). Born at New York, NY. Died Jan 13, 1885, at Mankato, MN.

CRAWFORD, JOAN: BIRTH ANNIVERSARY. Mar 23, 1905 (some sources say 1904 or 1907). Actress, born Lucille Fay LeSueur at San Antonio, TX. Crawford became a Hollywood star with her performance in *Our Dancing Daughters*. She won an Oscar in 1945 for her role in *Mildred Pierce*. Events of Crawford's life are chronicled in *Mommie Dearest*. Other films include *The Women, Whatever Happened to Baby Jane?* and *Twelve Miles Out*. She died at New York, NY, May 10, 1977.

DICK CLARK RETIRES FROM "AMERICAN BANDSTAND": 25th ANNIVERSARY. Mar 23, 1989. After 33 years, 59-year-old Dick Clark retired from hosting the television program "American Bandstand."

KUROSAWA, AKIRA: BIRTH ANNIVERSARY. Mar 23, 1910. Acclaimed filmmaker (*Rashomon, The Seven Samurai, Kagemusha, Ran*), born at Tokyo, Japan. The ambassador of Japanese cinema to the West, Kurosawa is considered one of the greatest film directors of all time. Died at Tokyo, Sept 6, 1998.

LIBERTY DAY: ANNIVERSARY. Mar 23, 1775. Anniversary of Patrick Henry's speech for arming the Virginia militia at St. John's Church, Richmond, VA. "I know not what course others may take, but as for me, give me liberty or give me death."

MOON PHASE: LAST QUARTER. Mar 23. Moon enters Last Quarter phase at 9:46 PM, EDT.

NATIONAL PROTOCOL OFFICERS WEEK. Mar 23–29. Recognizes protocol officers—the trusted advisers who plan and orchestrate international VIP visits, meetings, ceremonies and special events for the military, government, academia and business world. This week acknowledges those who influence worldwide diplomacy by understanding and embracing customs such as forms of address, flag etiquette, titles and more. Annually, the last week in March. For info: The Protocol School of Washington, PO Box 676, Columbia, SC 29202. Phone: (877) 766-3757. E-mail: info@psow.edu. Web: www.psow.edu.

NEAR MISS DAY: 25th ANNIVERSARY. Mar 23, 1989. A mountain-sized asteroid passed within 500,000 miles of Earth, a very close call according to NASA. Impact would have equaled the strength of 40,000 hydrogen bombs, created a crater the size of the District of Columbia and devastated everything for 100 miles in all directions.

NEW ZEALAND: OTAGO AND SOUTHLAND PROVINCIAL ANNIVERSARY. Mar 23. In addition to the statutory public holidays of New Zealand, there is in each provincial district a holiday for the provincial anniversary. This day is observed in Otago and Southland.

"OK" FIRST APPEARANCE IN PRINT: 175th ANNIVERSARY. Mar 23, 1839. *The Boston Morning Post* printed the first known "ok" on this day in 1839. It derived from a jovial misspelling of "all correct": "oll korrect." Etymologist Allen Read doggedly tracked down the word's origin in the 1960s. "OK" is now used in most languages.

PAKISTAN: REPUBLIC DAY. Mar 23, 1940. National holiday. In 1940 the All-India-Muslim League adopted a resolution calling for a Muslim homeland. On the same day in 1956 Pakistan declared itself a republic.

RALLY FOR DECENCY: 45th ANNIVERSARY. Mar 23, 1969. Anita Bryant, Jackie Gleason and Kate Smith rallied with 30,000 others in Miami, FL, on this day in reaction to Jim Morrison's arrest for indecent exposure.

SPACE MILESTONE: *MIR* ABANDONED (USSR). Mar 23, 2001. The 140-ton *Mir* space station, launched in 1986, was brought down into the South Pacific near Fiji, about 1,800 miles east of New Zealand, just before 1 AM, EST. Two-thirds of the station burned up during its controlled descent. *Mir*'s core component had been aloft for more than 15 years and orbited Earth 86,330 times. Nearly 100 people, seven of them American, had spent some time on *Mir*. See also: "Space Milestone: *Mir* Space Station (USSR)" (Feb 20).

UNITED NATIONS: WORLD METEOROLOGICAL DAY. Mar 23. An international day observed by meteorological services throughout the world and by the organizations of the UN system. Annually, on Mar 23. For info: United Nations, Dept of Public Info, New York, NY 10017. Web: www.un.org.

BIRTHDAYS TODAY

Louie Anderson, 61, comedian, actor ("Life with Louie"), born Minneapolis, MN, Mar 23, 1953.

Dr. Roger Bannister, 85, distance runner, broke the four-minute-mile record in 1954, born Harrow, Middlesex, England, Mar 23, 1929.

Mo Farah, 31, Olympic runner, born Mogadishu, Somalia, Mar 23, 1983.

Richard Grieco, 49, actor (*Ultimate Deception, Blackheart*), born Watertown, NY, Mar 23, 1965.

Perez Hilton, 36, gossip columnist, blogger, born Mario Lavandeira at Miami, FL, Mar 23, 1978.

Chaka Khan, 61, singer, born Yvette Marie Stevens at Chicago, IL, Mar 23, 1953.

Jason Kidd, 41, basketball player, born San Francisco, CA, Mar 23, 1973.

Moses Eugene Malone, 60, Hall of Fame basketball player, born Petersburg, VA, Mar 23, 1954.

Amanda Plummer, 57, actress (Tony for *Agnes of God*; *The Fisher King*), born New York, NY, Mar 23, 1957.

Keri Russell, 38, actress (*Waitress, Mission: Impossible III*, "Felicity"), born Fountain Valley, CA, Mar 23, 1976.

March 2014	S	M	T	W	T	F	S
							1
	2	3	4	5	6	7	8
	9	10	11	12	13	14	15
	16	17	18	19	20	21	22
	23	24	25	26	27	28	29
	30	31					

March 24 — Monday

DAY 83 **282 REMAINING**

ARGENTINA: NATIONAL DAY OF MEMORY FOR TRUTH AND JUSTICE. Mar 24. Public holiday since 2002 commemorating victims of the military coup d'état of 1976.

BARBERA, JOE: BIRTH ANNIVERSARY. Mar 24, 1911. Joseph Roland Barbera, born at New York, NY, was one-half of one of the world's most prolific and beloved animation teams: Hanna-Barbera. Working with Bill Hanna, Barbera created the Tom and Jerry theatrical shorts for MGM that garnered seven Oscars. Moving to television, Hanna-Barbera produced some 100 cartoon series, including the groundbreaking sitcom-style shows "The Flintstones" and "The Jetsons." Barbera continued working in animation almost to his death, creating a Tom and Jerry short in 2005. He died at Los Angeles, CA, on Dec 18, 2006.

***EXXON VALDEZ* OIL SPILL: 25th ANNIVERSARY.** Mar 24, 1989. The tanker *Exxon Valdez* ran aground at Alaska's Prince William Sound, leaking 11 million gallons of oil into one of nature's richest habitats.

HEIGHT, DOROTHY: BIRTH ANNIVERSARY. Mar 24, 1912. African-American civil rights leader and champion of education and women's causes, born at Richmond, VA. She was an active member of the National Council of Negro Women, serving as its president for 40 years, and was a consultant to several governmental offices and presidential administrations on education and civil rights issues. Height died at Washington, DC, Apr 20, 2010.

HOUDINI, HARRY: BIRTH ANNIVERSARY. Mar 24, 1874. Magician and escape artist. Born Erik Weisz at Budapest, Hungary, died at Detroit, MI, Oct 31, 1926. Lecturer, athlete, author, expert on the history of magic, exposer of fraudulent mediums and motion picture actor. He was best known for his ability to escape from locked restraints (handcuffs, straitjackets, coffins, boxes and milk cans). The anniversary of his death (Halloween) has been the occasion for meetings of magicians and attempts at communication by mediums.

"LETTER FROM AMERICA" RADIO PREMIERE: ANNIVERSARY. Mar 24, 1946. Acclaimed news correspondent and broadcaster Alistair Cooke began his weekly observations on American life on this date, with a story about British war brides traveling to America on the *Queen Mary*. Broadcast from Radio 4 and the BBC World Service, "Letter from America" would become the world's longest continuously running radio talk program. Cooke created 2,869 "letters." His last broadcast was Feb 20, 2004, and the BBC announced his retirement on Mar 2, 2004.

MELLON, ANDREW W.: BIRTH ANNIVERSARY. Mar 24, 1855. American financier, industrialist, government official (secretary of the treasury) and art and book collector, born at Pittsburgh, PA. Died Aug 26, 1937, at Southampton, NY.

MORRIS, WILLIAM: BIRTH ANNIVERSARY. Mar 24, 1834. English poet, artist and social reformer. Born at Walthamstow, England; died at Hammersmith, London, Oct 3, 1896.

PEMPER, MIETEK: BIRTH ANNIVERSARY. Mar 23, 1920. In his position as personal typist to Amon Goeth, commandant of the Plaszow forced labor camp in Poland, Pemper learned that all labor camp inmates not engaged in work on the war effort would be liquidated. He persuaded industrialist Oskar Schindler to convert his enamel works to the production of grenade parts. He then falsified records to suggest that certain Plaszow inmates had essential manufacturing skills and compiled lists of inmates to be transferred to Schindler's factory. These, along with names compiled by Itzhak Stern, later became known as "Schindler's list." The scheme saved the lives of 1,200 people. Born at Krakow, Poland, Pemper died at Augsburg, Germany, on June 7, 2011. See also: "Stern, Itzhak: Birth Anniversary" (Jan 25).

PHILIPPINE INDEPENDENCE. Mar 24, 1934. President Franklin Roosevelt signed a bill granting independence to the Philippines. The bill, which took effect July 4, 1946, brought to a close almost half a century of US control of the islands.

POWELL, JOHN WESLEY: BIRTH ANNIVERSARY. Mar 24, 1834. American geologist, explorer, ethnologist. He is best known for his explorations of the Grand Canyon by boat on the Colorado River. Born at Mount Morris, NY, he died at Haven, ME, Sept 23, 1902.

PRESLEY INDUCTED INTO THE ARMY: ANNIVERSARY. Mar 24, 1958. Teenagers across the US mourned as rock idol Elvis Presley was inducted into the US Army on this date at Memphis, TN. Presley completed basic training and then was posted overseas to Germany. He left active service on Mar 5, 1960.

RHODE ISLAND VOTERS REJECT CONSTITUTION: ANNIVERSARY. Mar 24, 1788. In a popular referendum, Rhode Island rejected the new Constitution by a vote of 2,708 to 237. The state later ratified the Constitution (May 29, 1790) and the Bill of Rights (June 7, 1790).

SAINT GABRIEL: FEAST DAY. Mar 24. Saint Gabriel the Archangel, patron saint of postal, telephone and telegraph workers.

STRATTON, DOROTHY CONSTANCE: BIRTH ANNIVERSARY. Mar 24, 1899. Dorothy Constance Stratton, born at Brookfield, MO, was instrumental during WWII in organizing the SPARS, the women's branch of the US Coast Guard (authorized Nov 23, 1942). Under Lieutenant Commander Stratton's command some 10,000 women were trained for supportive noncombat roles in the Coast Guard. SPARS was dissolved in 1946 after the war ended. Stratton worked with many women's organizations, including the Girl Scouts as national executive director in the '50s. Stratton died at age 107 on Sept 17, 2006, at West Lafayette, IN.

WESTON, EDWARD: BIRTH ANNIVERSARY. Mar 24, 1886. One of the greatest photographers of the 20th century, Weston was born at Highland Park, IL. Weston's work gradually changed from a self-described pictorial style to one that was more realistic yet abstract. He created a great body of work that included nudes, barren landscapes (especially in California and Mexico) and natural still lifes. Weston died on Jan 1, 1958, at Carmel, CA.

WORLD TUBERCULOSIS DAY. Mar 24. Designed to promote awareness about the serious health consequences of tuberculosis throughout the world. Observed on the anniversary of Dr. Robert Koch's 1882 announcement that he had discovered the bacillus that causes TB. Sponsored by the World Health Organization, the International Union Against Tuberculosis and Lung Disease and other international health agencies. For info: Stop TB Partnership. Web: www.stoptb.org.

ZARAGOZA, IGNACIO SEGUÍN: BIRTH ANNIVERSARY. Mar 24, 1829. Born at Bahía del Espíritu Santo, Coahuila and Texas, Mexico (now Goliad, TX), General Ignacio Zaragoza was the hero of the daylong Battle of Puebla on May 5, 1862. He led the Mexican army to victory over invading French forces under the command of General Charles Latrille Laurencez. The French lost about 500–1,000 personnel (estimates have varied); the Mexican army lost fewer than 100. Zaragoza, acclaimed as a hero, tragically succumbed to typhoid fever at Puebla on Sept 8. A grateful President Benito Juarez honored Zaragoza with a state funeral and on Sept 11 declared Cinco de Mayo a national holiday that has been celebrated since.

BIRTHDAYS TODAY

Chris Bosh, 30, basketball player, born Dallas, TX, Mar 24, 1984.

Lara Flynn Boyle, 44, actress ("Twin Peaks," "The Practice," *Dead Poets Society*), born Davenport, IA, Mar 24, 1970.

Jessica Chastain, 37, actress (*Zero Dark Thirty, The Help, The Tree of Life*), born Sacramento, CA, Mar 24, 1977.

R. Lee Ermey, 70, actor (*Full Metal Jacket, Mississippi Burning*), born Emporia, KS, Mar 24, 1944.

Lawrence Ferlinghetti, 95, Beat poet, author (*Coney Island of the Mind*), born Yonkers, NY, Mar 24, 1919.

Byron Janis, 86, pianist, born McKeesport, PA, Mar 24, 1928.

Star Jones, 52, television personality, born Badin, NC, Mar 24, 1962.

Bob Mackie, 74, costume and fashion designer, born Monterey Park, CA, Mar 24, 1940.

Peyton Manning, 38, football player, born New Orleans, LA, Mar 24, 1976.

Jim Parsons, 41, actor (Emmy for "The Big Bang Theory"), born Houston, TX, Mar 24, 1973.

Donna Pescow, 60, actress (*Saturday Night Fever*, "Angie"), born Brooklyn, NY, Mar 24, 1954.

Annabella Sciorra, 50, actress (*The Hand That Rocks the Cradle, Jungle Fever*), born Wethersfield, CT, Mar 24, 1964.

Peter Shumlin, 58, Governor of Vermont (D), born Brattleboro, VT, Mar 24, 1956.

March 25 — Tuesday

DAY 84 **281 REMAINING**

AMERICAN DIABETES ASSOCIATION ALERT DAY. Mar 25. A one-day "wake-up call" to raise awareness about the seriousness of diabetes and its risk factors. The centerpiece of the alert is the diabetes risk test, which is distributed and promoted through national and local media. Annually, the fourth Tuesday in March. For info: 800-DIABETES (342-2383) or www.diabetes.org/alert.

BARTOK, BELA: BIRTH ANNIVERSARY. Mar 25, 1881. Hungarian composer, born at Nagyszentmiklos (now in Romania). Died at New York, NY, Sept 26, 1945.

BED-IN FOR PEACE: 45th ANNIVERSARY. Mar 25–31, 1969. After their Mar 20 wedding, John Lennon (of The Beatles) and Yoko Ono celebrated their honeymoon with a "happening": a bed-in for peace at their hotel room. In Room 902 of the Hilton Hotel in Amsterdam, pajama-clad Lennon and Ono received the world's print, radio and TV media while sitting up in bed: singing and talking for seven days encouraging the world to choose peace. The couple held another bed-in May 26–June 2 in Montreal, during which "Give Peace a Chance" was recorded.

BORGLUM, GUTZON: BIRTH ANNIVERSARY. Mar 25, 1867. American sculptor who created the huge sculpture of four American presidents (Washington, Jefferson, Lincoln and Theodore Roosevelt) at Mount Rushmore National Memorial in the Black Hills of South Dakota. Born John Gutzon de la Mothe Borglum at Bear Lake, ID, the son of Mormon pioneers, he worked the last 14 years of his life on the Mount Rushmore sculpture. He died at Chicago, IL, Mar 6, 1941.

March 2014	S	M	T	W	T	F	S
							1
	2	3	4	5	6	7	8
	9	10	11	12	13	14	15
	16	17	18	19	20	21	22
	23	24	25	26	27	28	29
	30	31					

BORLAUG, NORMAN: 100th BIRTH ANNIVERSARY. Mar 25, 1914. Agricultural scientist, plant pathologist and geneticist, born at Saude, IA. Won 1970 Nobel Prize for Peace for the "Green Revolution" initiated in Mexico, Pakistan and India, where he engineered high-yield, disease-resistant, climate-specific grain hybrids that could theoretically end world hunger. Borlaug established the annual World Food Prize and received the Presidential Medal of Freedom. Died Sept 12, 2009, at Dallas, TX.

"CAGNEY & LACEY" TV PREMIERE: ANNIVERSARY. Mar 25, 1982. "Cagney & Lacey" broke new ground as the first TV crime show in which the central characters were both female. The series was based on a made-for-TV movie that aired Oct 8, 1981, starring Loretta Swit and Tyne Daly. When the show became a weekly series, Meg Foster played Swit's character, Chris Cagney, but after one season she was replaced by Sharon Gless. Daly and Gless together won six Emmys for their roles. The last telecast aired on Aug 25, 1988.

COSELL, HOWARD: BIRTH ANNIVERSARY. Mar 25, 1918. Howard Cosell, broadcaster, born at New York, NY. After earning a law degree, Cosell began his broadcasting career as the host of "Howard Cosell Speaking of Sports." He achieved national prominence and a great deal of notoriety for his support of Muhammad Ali's stand against the Vietnam War and then as cohost of ABC's "Monday Night Football." Died at New York, Apr 23, 1994.

FEAST OF THE ANNUNCIATION. Mar 25. Celebrated in the Roman Catholic Church in commemoration of the message of the Angel Gabriel to Mary that she was to be the mother of Christ.

GREECE: INDEPENDENCE DAY. Mar 25. National holiday. Celebrates the beginning of the Greek revolt for independence from the Ottoman Empire, Mar 25, 1821 (OS). Greece attained independence in 1829.

✦GREEK INDEPENDENCE DAY: A NATIONAL DAY OF CELEBRATION OF GREEK AND AMERICAN DEMOCRACY. Mar 25.

LEAN, SIR DAVID: BIRTH ANNIVERSARY. Mar 25, 1908. British film director Sir David Lean was born at London. He directed 16 films and won two Best Director Academy Awards. His films include *Bridge on the River Kwai* (1957), *Lawrence of Arabia* (1962) and *Dr. Zhivago* (1965). He died Apr 16, 1991, at London.

MARYLAND DAY. Mar 25. Commemorates arrival of Lord Baltimore's first settlers at Maryland in 1634.

NATIONAL MEDAL OF HONOR DAY. Mar 25. Annual day honoring the heroic recipients of the Medal of Honor, the highest award that can be given by the president, in the name of Congress, to members of the armed forces who have distinguished themselves beyond the call of duty. Created by Congressional resolution (PL 101-564) in 1991.

NATO FORCES ATTACK YUGOSLAVIA: 15th ANNIVERSARY. Mar 25, 1999. After many weeks of unsuccessful negotiations with Serb leader Slobodan Milosevic over the treatment of ethnic Albanians by Serb forces in the Kosovo Province of Yugoslavia, NATO forces began bombing Serbia and Kosovo. In response, the Serb army forced hundreds of thousands of ethnic Albanians to flee Kosovo for neighboring Albania, Macedonia and Montenegro. On June 10, 1999, NATO and Yugoslav officials signed an agreement providing for withdrawal of Serb troops from Kosovo, the end of Allied air strikes and the return of Kosovo refugees.

OLD NEW YEAR'S DAY. Mar 25. In Great Britain and its North American colonies this was the beginning of the new year up through 1751, when with the adoption of the Gregorian calendar the beginning of the year was changed to Jan 1.

PECAN DAY. Mar 25, 1775. Anniversary of the planting by George Washington of pecan trees (some of which still survive) at Mount Vernon, VA. The trees were a gift to Washington from Thomas Jefferson, who had planted a few pecan trees from the southern US at Monticello, VA. The pecan, native to southern North America, is sometimes called "America's own nut." First cultivated by Native Americans, it has been transplanted to other continents but has failed to achieve wide use or popularity outside the US.

ROME EXECUTIONS: 70th ANNIVERSARY. Mar 25, 1944. Nazis occupying Rome during WWII executed 300 Italian priests, Jews and women, including two 14-year-old boys. The executions were in retaliation for the deaths of 33 German soldiers who had been killed by Italian partisans. Hitler demanded 50 Italian lives for each German life that had been taken, but German officials in Italy lowered the number.

SLAVE TRADE ABOLISHED BY ENGLAND: ANNIVERSARY. Mar 25, 1807. The English parliament abolished the slave trade after a long campaign against it.

TOLKIEN READING DAY. Mar 25. A day dedicated to reading the works of J.R.R. Tolkien, including *The Hobbit* and *The Lord of the Rings.* Celebrated on the fictional anniversary of the downfall of Sauron, the shape-shifting antagonist in the *Rings.* The event exists to encourage the use of Tolkien's works in education and to get schoolteachers and library staff to participate in reading Tolkien to their classes and in their libraries. Public readings are performed and online communities have discussions and debates. For info: Ian Collier, Publicity Officer, The Tolkien Society, 22 Oaklands Rd, Wolverhampton, UK WV3 0DS. E-mail: publicity@tolkiensociety.org. Web: www.tolkiensociety.org.

TOSCANINI, ARTURO: BIRTH ANNIVERSARY. Mar 25, 1867. Italian opera and symphony conductor Arturo Toscanini was born at Parma, Italy. He had an all-encompassing repertoire but was famous primarily for the operas of Verdi and the symphonies of Beethoven. Toscanini died at New York City, Jan 16, 1957.

TRIANGLE SHIRTWAIST FIRE: ANNIVERSARY. Mar 25, 1911. At about 4:45 PM, fire broke out at the Triangle Shirtwaist Company at New York, NY, minutes before the seamstresses were to go home. Some workers were fatally burned while others leaped to their deaths from the windows of the 10-story building. The fire lasted only 18 minutes but left 146 workers dead, most of them young immigrant women. Some of the deaths were a direct result of workers being trapped on the ninth floor by a locked door. Labor law forbade locking factory doors while employees were at work, and owners of the company were indicted on charges of first- and second-degree manslaughter. The tragic fire became a turning point in labor history, bringing about reforms in health and safety laws.

UNITED NATIONS: INTERNATIONAL DAY OF REMEMBRANCE FOR THE VICTIMS OF SLAVERY AND THE TRANSATLANTIC SLAVE TRADE. Mar 25. Recognizing how little is known about the 400-year-long transatlantic slave trade and its lasting consequences, felt throughout the world, the General Assembly has designated Mar 25 as an annual day of remembrance (Res 62/122, Dec 17, 2007). For info: United Nations, Dept of Public Info, New York, NY, 10017. Web: www.un.org.

BIRTHDAYS TODAY

Bonnie Bedelia, 66, actress ("Parenthood," "The Division," *Die Hard*), born New York, NY, Mar 25, 1948.

Anita Bryant, 74, singer ("The George Gobel Show"), former Miss America, born Barnsdall, OK, Mar 25, 1940.

Marcia Cross, 52, actress ("Melrose Place," "Everwood," "Desperate Housewives"), born Marlborough, MA, Mar 25, 1962.

Eileen Ford, 92, model agency executive, born New York, NY, Mar 25, 1922.

Aretha Franklin, 72, singer ("Respect," "Think"), born Memphis, TN, Mar 25, 1942.

Paul Michael Glaser, 71, actor ("Starsky and Hutch"), director (*Butterflies Are Free*), born Cambridge, MA, Mar 25, 1943.

Tom Glavine, 48, former baseball player, born Concord, MA, Mar 25, 1966.

Cammi Granato, 43, former hockey player, born Maywood, IL, Mar 25, 1971.

Mary Gross, 61, comedienne, actress ("Saturday Night Live"), born Chicago, IL, Mar 25, 1953.

Elton John, 67, musician, singer, songwriter, born Reginald Kenneth Dwight at Pinner, England, Mar 25, 1947.

Avery Johnson, 49, basketball coach and former player, born New Orleans, LA, Mar 25, 1965.

James Lovell, 86, former astronaut, born Cleveland, OH, Mar 25, 1928.

Katharine McPhee, 30, actress ("Smash"), singer, television personality ("American Idol"), born Los Angeles, CA, Mar 25, 1984.

Lee Pace, 35, actor ("Pushing Daisies," "Wonderfalls"), born Chickasha, OK, Mar 25, 1979.

Sarah Jessica Parker, 49, actress (*Sex and the City, Honeymoon in Vegas*, "Sex and the City"), born Nelsonville, OH, Mar 25, 1965.

Danica Patrick, 32, race car driver, born Beloit, WI, Mar 25, 1982.

Gloria Steinem, 79, feminist (original publisher of *Ms* magazine), journalist, author, born Toledo, OH, Mar 25, 1935.

John Stockwell, 53, actor, writer, director (*Top Gun, Under Cover*), born Galveston, TX, Mar 25, 1961.

Sheryl Swoopes, 43, basketball player, US Olympic basketball team member (1996, 2000, 2004), born Brownfield, TX, Mar 25, 1971.

March 26 — Wednesday

DAY 85 — **280 REMAINING**

BANGLADESH: INDEPENDENCE DAY. Mar 26. Commemorates East Pakistan's independence in 1971 as the state of Bangladesh. Celebrated with parades, youth festivals and symposia.

BOWDITCH, NATHANIEL: BIRTH ANNIVERSARY. Mar 26, 1773. American mathematician and astronomer, author of the *New American Practical Navigator.* Born at Salem, MA, he died at Boston, MA, Mar 16, 1838.

CAMP DAVID ACCORD SIGNED: 35th ANNIVERSARY. Mar 26, 1979. Israeli prime minister Menachem Begin and Egyptian president Anwar Sadat signed the Camp David peace treaty, ending 30 years of war between their two countries. The agreement was fostered by President Jimmy Carter.

DELANO, JANE: BIRTH ANNIVERSARY. Mar 26, 1862. Jane Arminda Delano, dedicated American nurse and teacher, superintendent of the US Army Nurse Corps, chair of the American Red Cross Nursing Service and recipient (posthumously) of the Distinguished Service Medal of the US, was born near Townsend, NY. While on an official visit to review Red Cross activities, she died Apr 15, 1919, in an army hospital at Savenay, France. Her last words: "What about my work? I must get back to my work." Originally buried at Loire, France, her remains were reinterred at Arlington National Cemetery in 1920.

FROST, ROBERT LEE: BIRTH ANNIVERSARY. Mar 26, 1874. American poet who tried his hand at farming, teaching, shoemaking and editing before winning acclaim as a poet. Pulitzer Prize winner. Born at San Francisco, CA, he died at Boston, MA, Jan 29, 1963.

LEGAL ASSISTANTS DAY. Mar 26. A day recognizing the many contributions made to the legal profession by legal assistants. For info: Claudia Evart, PO Box 85, New York, NY 10163. Phone: (646) 544-4780. E-mail: paralegalcaevart@earthlink.net.

MAKE UP YOUR OWN HOLIDAY DAY. Mar 26. This day is a day you may name for whatever you wish. Reach for the stars! Make up a holiday! Annually, Mar 26. (©2006 by WH.) For info: Thomas & Ruth Roy, Wellcat Holidays, 2418 Long Ln, Lebanon, PA 17046. Phone: (717) 279-0184. E-mail: info@wellcat.com. Web: www.wellcat.com.

PRINCE JONAH KUHIO KALANIANOLE DAY. Mar 26. Hawaii. Commemorates the man who, as Hawaii's delegate to the US Congress, introduced the first bill for statehood in 1919. Not until 1959 did Hawaii become a state.

SOVIET COSMONAUT RETURNS TO NEW COUNTRY: ANNIVERSARY. Mar 26, 1992. After spending 313 days in space in the Soviet *Mir* space station, cosmonaut Serge Krikalev returned to Earth and to what was for him a new country. He left Earth May 18, 1991, a citizen of the Soviet Union, but during his stay aboard the space station, the Soviet Union crumbled and became the Commonwealth of Independent States. Originally scheduled for October 1991, Krikalev's return was delayed by five months due to his country's disintegration and the ensuing monetary problems.

WILLIAMS, TENNESSEE: BIRTH ANNIVERSARY. Mar 26, 1911. Tennessee Williams was born at Columbus, MS. He was one of America's most prolific playwrights, producing such works as *The Glass Menagerie; A Streetcar Named Desire* and *Cat on a Hot Tin Roof,* both of which won Pulitzer Prizes; *Night of the Iguana; Summer and Smoke; The Rose Tattoo* and *Sweet Bird of Youth.* Williams died at New York, NY, Feb 25, 1983.

"THE YOUNG AND THE RESTLESS" TV PREMIERE: ANNIVERSARY. Mar 26, 1973. This daytime serial is generally thought of as TV's most artistic soap and has won numerous Emmys for outstanding daytime drama series. Its original storylines revolved around the Brooks and Foster families, but by the early '80s most of them were gone and the Abbott and Williams families were highlighted. The serial's very large and changing cast has included now-famous actors David Hasselhoff, Tom Selleck, Wings Hauser, Deidre Hall and Michael Damian. In 1980 "Y&R" expanded from a half-hour to an hour. Its theme music is well known as "Nadia's Theme," as it was played during Nadia Comaneci's routine at the 1976 Olympics.

BIRTHDAYS TODAY

Marcus Allen, 54, former football player, sportscaster, born San Diego, CA, Mar 26, 1960.

Alan Arkin, 80, actor (*Argo, Catch-22, Little Miss Sunshine*), director (*Little Murders*), born New York, NY, Mar 26, 1934.

Pierre Boulez, 89, composer, conductor, born Montbrison, France, Mar 26, 1925.

James Caan, 74, actor (*Elf, Misery, Thief, The Godfather*), born New York, NY, Mar 26, 1940.

Lincoln Chafee, 61, Governor of Rhode Island (I), born Providence, RI, Mar 26, 1953.

Kenny Chesney, 46, country singer, born Knoxville, TN, Mar 26, 1968.

Leeza Gibbons, 57, television personality, born Hartsville, SC, Mar 26, 1957.

Jennifer Grey, 54, actress (*Dirty Dancing*), born New York, NY, Mar 26, 1960.

Erica Jong, 72, author, poet (*Fear of Flying, Becoming Light*), born New York, NY, Mar 26, 1942.

Catherine Keener, 54, actress (*Capote, The 40-Year-Old Virgin, Being John Malkovich*), born Miami, FL, Mar 26, 1960.

T.R. Knight, 41, actor ("Grey's Anatomy"), born Minneapolis, MN, Mar 26, 1973.

Keira Knightley, 29, actress (*Atonement, Pride and Prejudice, Pirates of the Caribbean*), born Teddington, Middlesex, England, Mar 26, 1985.

March 2014	S	M	T	W	T	F	S
							1
	2	3	4	5	6	7	8
	9	10	11	12	13	14	15
	16	17	18	19	20	21	22
	23	24	25	26	27	28	29
	30	31					

Vicki Lawrence, 65, singer, actress ("The Carol Burnett Show," "Mama's Family"), born Inglewood, CA, Mar 26, 1949.

Josh Lucas, 42, actor (*Sweet Home Alabama, American Psycho*), born Little Rock, AR, Mar 26, 1972.

Leslie Mann, 42, actress (*Knocked Up, Big Daddy*), born San Francisco, CA, Mar 26, 1972.

Leonard Nimoy, 83, actor ("Star Trek"), director (*Three Men and a Baby*), writer, born Boston, MA, Mar 26, 1931.

Sandra Day O'Connor, 84, former Associate Justice of the US, born El Paso, TX, Mar 26, 1930.

Nancy Pelosi, 74, Congresswoman (D, California), former Speaker of the US House of Representatives, born Baltimore, MD, Mar 26, 1940.

Diana Ross, 70, singer, actress (*Lady Sings the Blues, The Wiz*), born Detroit, MI, Mar 26, 1944.

Martin Short, 64, comedian, actor (*Martin Short: Fame Becomes Me*, "Primetime Glick"), born Hamilton, ON, Canada, Mar 26, 1950.

John Stockton, 52, Hall of Fame basketball player, born Spokane, WA, Mar 26, 1962.

Steven Tyler, 66, singer (Aerosmith), television personality ("American Idol"), born Steven Victor Tallarico at Yonkers, NY, Mar 26, 1948.

Bob Woodward, 71, journalist, author (*All the President's Men* with Carl Bernstein, *Plan of Attack*), born Geneva, IL, Mar 26, 1943.

March 27 — Thursday

DAY 86 **279 REMAINING**

CANARY ISLANDS PLANE DISASTER: ANNIVERSARY. Mar 27, 1977. The worst accident in the history of civil aviation. Two Boeing 747s collided on the ground; 570 people lost their lives—249 on the KLM Airlines plane and 321 on the Pan Am plane.

CELEBRATE EXCHANGE: NATIONAL EXCHANGE CLUB BIRTHDAY. Mar 27, 1911. Anniversary of the day when the first Exchange Club was founded at Detroit, MI, by Charles A. Berkey. Since 1911, Exchange clubs have been working to improve their communities through service projects, by promoting patriotism and pride of country and through their national project, Child Abuse Prevention. Celebrated annually by 25,000 Exchangites at 800 clubs in the US and Puerto Rico. For info: The Natl Exchange Club, 3050 Central Ave, Toledo, OH 43606-1700. Phone: (800) 924-2643. Fax: (419) 535-1989. E-mail: info@nationalexhangeclub.org. Web: www.nationalexchangeclub.org.

CURRIER, NATHANIEL: BIRTH ANNIVERSARY. Mar 27, 1813. Lithographer born at Roxbury, MA. With James Merritt Ives, established the immensely popular and successful Currier & Ives printing firm, which produced millions of prints from an inventory of 7,500 scenes. Very few American parlors were without a Currier & Ives print in the mid-19th century. Currier died Nov 20, 1888, at Amesbury, MA. The printing firm survived until 1907—although its images remain popular today.

EARTHQUAKE STRIKES ALASKA: ANNIVERSARY. Mar 27, 1964. The strongest earthquake in North American history (8.4 on the Richter scale) struck Alaska, east of Anchorage; 117 people were killed. This was the world's second-worst earthquake of the 20th century in terms of magnitude.

FDA APPROVES VIAGRA: ANNIVERSARY. Mar 27, 1998. The US Food and Drug Administration approved the drug Viagra for treatment of male impotence on this date. It had been patented in 1996.

FUNKY WINKERBEAN: ANNIVERSARY. Mar 27, 1972. Anniversary of the nationally syndicated comic strip. For info: Tom Batiuk, Creator, 2750 Substation Rd, Medina, OH 44256. Phone: (330) 722-8755.

HILL, PATTY SMITH: BIRTH ANNIVERSARY. Mar 27, 1868. Patty Smith Hill, schoolteacher, author and education specialist, was born at Anchorage (suburb of Louisville), KY. She was author of the lyrics of the song "Good Morning to All," which later became known as "Happy Birthday to You." Her older sister, Mildred J. Hill, composed the melody for the song, which was first published in 1893 as a classroom greeting in the book *Song Stories for the Sunday School*. A stanza beginning "Happy Birthday to You" was added in 1924, and the song became arguably the most frequently sung song in the world. Hill died at New York, NY, May 25, 1946. See also: "Happy Birthday to 'Happy Birthday to You'" (June 27).

LUXEMBOURG: OSWEILER. Mar 27. Blessing of horses, tractors and cars.

MIES VAN DER ROHE, LUDWIG: BIRTH ANNIVERSARY. Mar 27, 1886. Born Maria Ludwig Michael Mies at Aachen, Germany, Mies van der Rohe was recognized by peers, critics, casual observers and the scope of history as one of the most influential architects of the 20th century. His profound, simple and resolutely powerful works represented a shift in style, technique and appreciation for material structure that defined the look and feel of the modern industrial era. From 1938 to 1958, he served as chairman of the school of architecture at Illinois Institute of Technology in Chicago; the campus contains 20 of his buildings. Mies van der Rohe died at Chicago, IL, Aug 17, 1969.

MYANMAR: RESISTANCE DAY. Mar 27. National holiday. Commemorates the day in 1945 when Burma officially joined the Allies in WWII. Also called Armed Forces Day.

NCAA DIVISION I MEN'S SWIMMING AND DIVING CHAMPIONSHIPS. Mar 27–29. Site TBD. For info: NCAA, 700 W Washington St, PO Box 6222, Indianapolis, IN 46206-6222. Phone: (317) 917-6222. Fax: (317) 917-6888. Web: www.ncaa.org.

NORTH SEA OIL RIG DISASTER: ANNIVERSARY. Mar 27, 1980. The Alexander L. Keilland Oil Rig capsized during a heavy storm in the Norwegian sector of the North Sea. The pentagon-type, French-built oil rig had about 200 persons aboard, and 123 lives were lost.

QUIRKY COUNTRY MUSIC SONG TITLES DAY. Mar 27. We love those old country music quirky song titles, and it's time to create some new ones. How about "Put Me Out at the Curb Darlin', 'Cause the Recycling Truck's A-comin', and You Done Throwed Me Out," for starters? (©2006 by WH.) For info: Thomas & Ruth Roy, Wellcat Holidays, 2418 Long Ln, Lebanon, PA 17046. Phone: (717) 279-0184. E-mail: info@wellcat.com. Web: www.wellcat.com.

RÖNTGEN, WILHELM KONRAD: BIRTH ANNIVERSARY. Mar 27, 1845. German scientist who discovered x-rays (1895) and won a Nobel Prize in 1901. Born at Lennep, Prussia, he died at Munich, Germany, Feb 10, 1923.

ROSTROPOVICH, MSTISLAV: BIRTH ANNIVERSARY. Mar 27, 1927. Russian composer and conductor, perhaps the finest cellist of the 20th century. Born at Baku, USSR (now Azerbaijan), to parents who were also musicians, he studied under Shostokovich and Prokofiev and was performing all over the world by the early 1950s. Fiercely dedicated to human rights and freedom of speech and expression, he was forced to flee the Soviet Union in the early 1970s when the government attempted to interfere with his travels due to his support of dissident writer Alexander Solzhenitsyn. Rostropovich became an American citizen and was named the musical director of the US National Symphony Orchestra in 1977, a job he held until 1994. He is also remembered for his impromptu performance at the Berlin Wall in 1989, and his trip to Moscow in 1991 to support the new Russian government. He died at Moscow, Russia, Apr 27, 2007.

ROYCE, HENRY: BIRTH ANNIVERSARY. Mar 27, 1863. Industrialist and pioneering automotive manufacturer born at Alwalton, Huntingtonshire, England. In 1906 his successful engineering business, Royce Ltd, merged with C.S. Rolls's company to form Rolls-Royce Ltd. Royce's insistence on perfection and attention to detail, as well as his refusal to reduce the quality of his product to make his prices more competitive, made the company's automobile and airplane engines legendary. Awarded the Order of the British Empire (1918) and created a baronetcy (1930), Royce died at West Wittering, Sussex, England, on Apr 22, 1933.

THE SAVANNAH TOUR OF HOMES AND GARDENS. Mar 27–30. Savannah, GA. 79th annual. Residents of Savannah open their homes to visitors to view 18th- and 19th-century architecture. Enjoy special events as well! The beauty of spring makes this tour of homes and gardens even more breathtaking. Est attendance: 4,000. For info: The Savannah Tour of Homes and Gardens, PO Box 10585, Savannah, GA 31412. Phone: (912) 234-8054. Fax: (912) 234-2123. E-mail: tourinfo@savannahtourofhomes.org. Web: www.savannahtourofhomes.org.

SCHULBERG, BUDD: 100th BIRTH ANNIVERSARY. Mar 27, 1914. Best known for writing the Academy Award–winning film *On the Waterfront* (1954) and the novel *What Makes Sammy Run* (1941). Questioned in 1951 by the House Un-American Activities Committee and later, Schulberg, discussing the role of the writer, said, "It's the writer's responsibility to stand up against . . . power. The writers are really almost the only ones, except for very honest politicians, who can make any dent on [the] system. I tried to do that. And that's affected me my whole life." Born at New York, NY, he died Aug 5, 2009, at Westhampton, NY.

***SINGIN' IN THE RAIN* FILM PREMIERE: ANNIVERSARY.** Mar 27, 1952. MGM's joyous, comic film musical premiered on this date at New York, NY. Starring Gene Kelly, Debbie Reynolds and Donald O'Connor and featuring the songs "Singin' in the Rain," "Good Morning" and "Make 'Em Laugh," *Singin' in the Rain* depicted a Hollywood romance at the time the talkies arrived. Directed by Kelly and Stanley Donen and written by Betty Comden and Adolph Green, the film was nominated for only two Oscars, yet is now regarded as one of the greatest movie musicals.

SMITH, THORNE: BIRTH ANNIVERSARY. Mar 27, 1892. Perhaps the most critically neglected popular author of the 20th century, Smith was born James Thorne Smith, Jr, at Annapolis, MD, was educated at Dartmouth and died at Sarasota, FL, June 21, 1934. Author of numerous humorous supernatural fantasy novels, including *Rain in the Doorway*, *The Stray Lamb* and *Topper*, he was the master of the pointless conversation. The "Thorne Smith" touch has inspired several motion pictures and television series, including "Bewitched." For info: George H. Scheetz, Exec Secy, The Thorne Smith Society, 406 Wolcott Ln, Batavia, IL 60510-2838.

SPACE MILESTONE: *VENERA 8* (USSR). Mar 27, 1972. Launched on this date, this unmanned probe made a soft landing on Venus July 22 and sent back radio transmissions of surface data.

STEICHEN, EDWARD: BIRTH ANNIVERSARY. Mar 27, 1879. Celebrated American photographer. Born at Luxembourg, Germany, and died Mar 25, 1973, at West Redding, CT.

SWANSON, GLORIA: BIRTH ANNIVERSARY. Mar 27, 1899. American film actress (*Sunset Boulevard*) and businesswoman. Born Gloria May Josephine Svensson at Chicago, IL. Author of an autobiography, *Swanson on Swanson*, published in 1980. Died at New York, NY, Apr 4, 1983.

VAUGHAN, SARAH: 90th BIRTH ANNIVERSARY. Mar 27, 1924. Legendary jazz singer, born at Newark, NJ, renowned for her melodic improvising, wide vocal range and extraordinary technique. She began her career by winning an amateur contest at New York's Apollo Theater in 1943. She was hired by Earl Hines to accompany his band as his relief pianist as well as singer. She was given the nickname "The Divine One" by Chicago disc jockey Dave Garroway, a moniker that would remain with her the rest of her life. Died at Los Angeles, CA, Apr 3, 1990.

BIRTHDAYS TODAY

Mariah Carey, 44, singer, born Long Island, NY, Mar 27, 1970.

Randall Cunningham, 51, former football player, born Santa Barbara, CA, Mar 27, 1963.

Fergie, 39, singer, musician (The Black-Eyed Peas), born Stacy Ferguson at Hacienda Heights, CA, Mar 27, 1975.

Nathan Fillion, 43, actor ("Castle," "Firefly," *Serenity*), born Edmonton, AB, Canada, Mar 27, 1971.

Kimbra, 24, musician, born Kimbra Johnson at Hamilton, New Zealand, Mar 27, 1990.

Austin Pendleton, 74, actor (*Mr and Mrs Bridge, Guarding Tess*), born Warren, OH, Mar 27, 1940.

Quentin Tarantino, 51, director (*Reservoir Dogs, Kill Bill*), screenwriter (Oscars for *Django Unchained* and *Pulp Fiction*), born Knoxville, TN, Mar 27, 1963.

William Caleb (Cale) Yarborough, 74, former auto racer, born Timmonsville, SC, Mar 27, 1940.

Michael York, 72, actor (*Cabaret, The Three Musketeers*), born Fulmer, England, Mar 27, 1942.

March 28 — Friday

DAY 87 | **278 REMAINING**

BARTHOLOMEW, FREDDIE: 90th BIRTH ANNIVERSARY. Mar 28, 1924. Child star of the 1930s, Freddie Bartholomew was born Frederick Llewellyn at Great Britain. He appeared in 24 films and became the second-highest-paid child star after Shirley Temple. He died Jan 23, 1992, at Sarasota, FL.

BATTLE OF LA GLORIETTA PASS: ANNIVERSARY. Mar 28, 1862. At Pigeon's Ranch, a stagecoach stop on the Santa Fe Trail (about 19 miles southeast of Santa Fe, NM), Confederate forces briefly prevailed over Union troops in what some have called the most important battle of the Civil War in the Southwest. It was feared that if Union troops failed to hold here, the Confederate forces would proceed to Fort Union and on to control the rich gold fields of Colorado and California.

March 2014	S	M	T	W	T	F	S
							1
	2	3	4	5	6	7	8
	9	10	11	12	13	14	15
	16	17	18	19	20	21	22
	23	24	25	26	27	28	29
	30	31					

COLTS SNEAK OUT OF BALTIMORE: 30th ANNIVERSARY. Mar 28, 1984. With little or no warning, the Baltimore Colts loaded moving vans in the dead of night and left for Indianapolis. Baltimore was left without an NFL team until 1996 when the Cleveland Browns moved there and were renamed the Ravens.

CRAFTSMEN'S SPRING CLASSIC ARTS & CRAFTS FESTIVAL. Mar 28–30. Dulles Expo and Convention Center, Chantilly, VA. 18th annual. Features work from more than 350 talented artists and craftspeople. All juried exhibitors' work has been handmade by the exhibitors and must be their own original design and creation. See the creative process in action with several exhibitors demonstrating throughout the weekend. Something for every style, taste and budget with items from the most contemporary to the most traditional. Est attendance: 20,000. For info: Gilmore Enterprises, Inc, 3514-A Drawbridge Pkwy, Greensboro, NC 27410-8584. Phone: (336) 282-5550. E-mail: contact@gilmoreshows.com. Web: www.CraftShow.com or www.gilmoreshows.com.

CZECH REPUBLIC: TEACHERS' DAY. Mar 28. Celebrates birth on this day of Jan Amos Komensky (Comenius), Moravian educational reformer (1592–1671).

DAYTONA SPRING TURKEY RUN. Mar 28–30. Daytona International Speedway, Daytona Beach, FL. 25th annual. See more than 1,300 classic, vintage, muscle and race cars and trucks for show and sale. Massive swap meet with more than 400 vendors of auto parts and accessories. Handcrafted arts and fashion bazaar. Est attendance: 25,000. For info: Daytona Beach Car Shows, PO Box 1958, Daytona Beach, FL 32115-1958. Phone: (386) 255-7355. E-mail: kim@daytonabeachcarshows.com. Web: www.daytonabeachcarshows.com.

EMERALD CITY COMICCON. Mar 28–30. Washington State Convention Center, Seattle, WA. The largest comic book and pop culture convention in the Pacific Northwest! Est attendance: 64,000. For info: Emerald City Comiccon, 19009 33rd Ave W, Ste 305, Lynnwood, WA 98036. E-mail: info@emeraldcitycomiccon.com. Web: www.emeraldcitycomiccon.com.

"GREATEST SHOW ON EARTH" FORMED: ANNIVERSARY. Mar 28, 1881. P.T. Barnum and James A. Bailey merged their circuses to form the "Greatest Show on Earth."

INTERNATIONAL LISTENING ASSOCIATION ANNUAL CONVENTION. Mar 28–29. Minneapolis, MN. Convention dedicated to learning more about the impact that listening has on all human activity. To promote the study, development and teaching of effective listening in all settings. For info: International Listening Assn, PO Box 164, Belle Plaine, MN 56011. Phone: (952) 594-5697. Fax: (952) 856-5100. E-mail: info@listen.org. Web: www.listen.org.

LAZAR, IRVING "SWIFTY": BIRTH ANNIVERSARY. Mar 28, 1907. Hollywood talent agent whose clients included Ernest Hemingway, Lillian Hellman, Cole Porter, Richard Nixon and Humphrey Bogart (who nicknamed him "Swifty" after Lazar met Bogart's challenge to make him five film deals in one day in 1955). He died Dec 30, 1993, at Beverly Hills, CA.

LIBYA: BRITISH BASES EVACUATION DAY. Mar 28. National holiday. Commemorates the closing of British bases on this day in 1970.

PALMETTO SPORTSMEN'S CLASSIC. Mar 28–30. South Carolina State Fairgrounds, Columbia, SC. 30th annual. Largest family-oriented wildlife show in the Carolinas with information on natural resources education and conservation, hunting, fishing and outdoor recreation. You will find activities for kids and adults throughout the show. Rain or shine. Est attendance: 40,000. For info: Palmetto Sportsmen's Classic, 1000 Assembly St, Columbia, SC 29201. Phone: (803) 734-4008. E-mail: psc@dnr.sc.gov. Web: www.dnr.sc.gov/psc.

SAINT JOHN NEPOMUCENE NEUMANN: BIRTH ANNIVERSARY. Mar 28, 1811. The first male saint from the US was born at Prachitiz, Bohemia (now the Czech Republic). After seminary school, he immigrated to the US, arriving at Manhattan, NY, in 1836. Neumann took a post in a rural area, walking miles from farm to farm to meet settlers from many countries. His facility with languages (he spoke 12 fluently) allowed him to minister to a

wide variety of people. He joined an order called the Redemptionists at Pittsburgh, PA, in 1840 and became bishop of Philadelphia in 1852 (affectionately known as the "Little Bishop"). During his tenure, a cathedral was begun, 50 churches were built, almost 100 schools were opened and the number of parochial students grew from 500 to 9,000. He died at Philadelphia, PA, on Jan 5, 1860. Beatified on Oct 13, 1963, Neumann was canonized on June 19, 1977.

SPACE MILESTONE: *NOAA 8* (US). Mar 28, 1983. Search and Rescue Satellite (SARSAT) launched from Vandenburg Air Force Base, CA, to aid in locating ships and aircraft in distress. *Kosmos 1383*, launched July 1, 1982, by the USSR, in a cooperative rescue effort, is credited with saving more than 20 lives.

THREE MILE ISLAND NUCLEAR POWER PLANT ACCIDENT: 35th ANNIVERSARY. Mar 28, 1979. A series of accidents, beginning at 4 AM, EST, at Three Mile Island on the Susquehanna River about 10 miles southeast of Harrisburg, PA, was responsible for extensive reevaluation of the safety of existing nuclear power-generating operations. Equipment and other failures reportedly brought Three Mile Island close to a meltdown of the uranium core, threatening extensive radiation contamination.

BIRTHDAYS TODAY

Conchata Ferrell, 71, actress ("Two and a Half Men"), born Charleston, WV, Mar 28, 1943.

Kate Gosselin, 39, television personality ("Jon & Kate Plus 8"), author, born Wernersville, PA, Mar 28, 1975.

Ken Howard, 70, actor ("Crossing Jordan," "The White Shadow"), born El Centro, CA, Mar 28, 1944.

Lady Gaga, 28, musician, born Stefani Germanotta at Yonkers, NY, Mar 28, 1986.

Reba McEntire, 60, singer, actress ("Reba"), born Chockie, OK, Mar 28, 1954.

Byron Scott, 53, basketball coach and former player, born Ogden, UT, Mar 28, 1961.

Jerry Sloan, 72, former basketball coach and player, born McLeansboro, IL, Mar 28, 1942.

Julia Stiles, 33, actress (*The Prince & Me, The Bourne Identity, Save the Last Dance, O*), born New York, NY, Mar 28, 1981.

Keith Tkachuk, 42, hockey player, born Melrose, MA, Mar 28, 1972.

Vince Vaughn, 44, actor (*Wedding Crashers, Old School, Swingers*), born Minneapolis, MN, Mar 28, 1970.

Dianne Wiest, 66, actress (Oscars for *Hannah and Her Sisters* and *Bullets Over Broadway*; "Law & Order"), born Kansas City, MO, Mar 28, 1948.

March 29 — Saturday

DAY 88 — **277 REMAINING**

BAILEY, PEARL MAE: BIRTH ANNIVERSARY. Mar 29, 1918. American singer and Broadway musical star Pearl Bailey was born at Newport News, VA. She began her career in vaudeville and won a special Tony Award in 1968 and the Presidential Medal of Freedom in 1988. Bailey died Aug 17, 1990, at Philadelphia, PA.

CANADA: BRITISH NORTH AMERICA ACT: ANNIVERSARY. Mar 29, 1867. This act of the British parliament established the Dominion of Canada, uniting Ontario, Quebec, Nova Scotia and New Brunswick. The remaining colonies in Canada were still ruled directly by Great Britain until Manitoba joined the Dominion in 1870, British Columbia in 1871, Prince Edward Island in 1873, Alberta and Saskatchewan in 1905 and Newfoundland in 1949. Union was proclaimed July 1, 1867. See also: "Canada: Canada Day" (July 1).

CENTRAL AFRICAN REPUBLIC: BOGANDA DAY. Mar 29. National holiday. Commemorates the death of Barthelemy Boganda, the first president, in 1959.

COMMITTEE ON ASSASSINATIONS REPORT: 35th ANNIVERSARY. Mar 29, 1979. The House Select Committee on Assassinations released on this day the final report on its investigation into the assassinations of President John F. Kennedy, Martin Luther King, Jr, and Robert Kennedy. Based on available evidence, the committee concluded that President Kennedy was assassinated as a result of a conspiracy, although no trail of a conspiracy could be established. It also concluded that on the basis of scientific acoustical evidence two gunmen fired at the president, although no second gunman could be identified. (Note: In December 1980, the FBI released a report discounting the two-gunmen theory, stating that the distinguishable sounds of two separate guns were not proven scientifically.) In addition the committee concluded that the possibility of conspiracy did exist in the cases of Dr. King and Robert Kennedy, although no specific individuals or organizations could be pinpointed as being involved. See also: "Warren Commission Report: Anniversary" (Sept 27).

DOW JONES TOPS 10,000: 15th ANNIVERSARY. Mar 29, 1999. The Dow Jones Index of 30 major industrial stocks topped the 10,000 mark for the first time.

EARTH HOUR. Mar 29. This event reaches more than one billion people in 4,000 cities around the world, inviting communities, businesses and governments to switch off lights for one hour at 8:30 PM, local time—sending a powerful global message that we care enough about climate change to take action. For info: World Wildlife Fund, 1250 24th St NW, Washington, DC 20037-1193. Web: www.worldwildlife.org or www.earthhour.org.

ENGLAND: HEAD OF THE RIVER RACE. Mar 29. Mortlake to Putney, River Thames, London. Processional race for 400 eight-oared crews, starting at 10-second intervals. Est attendance: 7,000. For info: Dr. A. Ruddle, 59 Berkeley Ct, Weybridge, Surrey, KT13 9HY UK. Phone: (44) (1932) 220-401. E-mail: secretary@horr.co.uk. Web: www.horr.co.uk.

HOOVER, LOU HENRY: BIRTH ANNIVERSARY. Mar 29, 1875. Wife of Herbert Clark Hoover, 31st president of the US. Born at Waterloo, IA, she died at Palo Alto, CA, Jan 7, 1944.

KNIGHTS OF COLUMBUS FOUNDER'S DAY. Mar 29. The first Knights of Columbus charter was granted in 1882 by the state of Connecticut. This Catholic and family fraternal service organization has grown into a volunteer force of Knights and family members totaling nearly 1.8 million who annually donate tens of millions of dollars and volunteer hours to countless charitable projects. For info: Knights of Columbus, 1 Columbus Plaza, New Haven, CT 06510. E-mail: info@kofc.org. Web: www.kofc.org.

MADAGASCAR: COMMEMORATION DAY. Mar 29. Memorial Day for those who died in the 1947 rebellion against the French.

MCCARTHY, EUGENE: BIRTH ANNIVERSARY. Mar 29, 1916. Born at Watkins, MN, the longtime congressman and senator from Minnesota is best remembered for his campaign for the 1968 Democratic presidential nomination. McCarthy ran on a strong antiwar platform, garnering support from those opposed to American involvement in the Vietnam conflict, but ultimately lost the nomination to Hubert Humphrey. McCarthy never held public office again, despite four more tries at the presidency, and died at Washington, DC, Dec 10, 2005.

"MUTT AND JEFF" DEBUT: ANNIVERSARY. Mar 29, 1908. "Mutt and Jeff," the first comic strip to appear daily with the same protagonists, debuted on this date in William Randolph Hearst's *San Francisco Examiner.*

NATIONAL KITE MONTH. Mar 29–May 3. Celebrates kiting with more than 600 events throughout the country, including kite festivals, kite-making classes for kids and adults, kite-making classes in schools, kite displays in museums and public libraries and "fun flys" at local parks and beaches. For info: Mel Hickman, American Kitefliers Assn, PO Box 22365, Portland, OR 97269. Phone: (609) 755-5483. E-mail: Admin@NationalKiteMonth.org. Web: www.NationalKiteMonth.org.

NATIONAL MOM AND POP BUSINESS OWNERS DAY. Mar 29. A day recognizing those very special husband-and-wife business owner teams that work and commune together. Take this day to strike a balance between business and love. For info: Rick and Margie Segel, 268 Hamrick Dr, Kissimmee, FL 34759. Phone: (781) 272-9995. Fax: (800) 847-9411. E-mail: rick@ricksegel.com.

NIAGARA FALLS RUNS DRY: ANNIVERSARY. Mar 29, 1848. A massive assemblage of ice blocks formed upstream of Niagara Falls late on Mar 29, 1848, and by midnight had stopped water flow over the falls (which are actually three falls: the American, the Horseshoe [or Canadian] and the Bridal Veil). The ice jam held until Apr 1, when the waters of Lake Erie punched through and things got back to normal. Until that happened, hundreds of the curious swarmed into the now-waterless gorge to hunt for geologic souvenirs while thousands of spectators watched from above. Although the American Falls had stopped flowing before, this 1848 stoppage was the first and only time the entire falls was affected.

QUINLAN, KAREN ANN: 60th BIRTH ANNIVERSARY. Mar 29, 1954. Born at Scranton, PA, Karen Ann Quinlan became the center of a legal, medical and ethical controversy over the right to die. She became irreversibly comatose on Apr 14, 1975. A petition filed by her adoptive parents in New Jersey's Superior Court, Sept 12, 1975, sought permission to discontinue use of a respirator, allowing her to die "with grace and dignity." In 1976 the petition was upheld by New Jersey's Supreme Court. Quinlan lived nearly a decade without the respirator, until June 11, 1985. Her plight brought into focus the ethical dilemmas of advancing medical technology—the need for a new understanding of life and death; the right to die; and the role of judges, doctors and hospital committees in deciding when not to prolong life.

TAIWAN: YOUTH DAY. Mar 29.

TEXAS LOVE THE CHILDREN DAY. Mar 29. A day recognizing every child's right and need to be loved. Promoting the hope that one day all children will live in loving, safe environments and will be given proper health care and equal learning opportunities. Precedes the start of National Child Abuse Prevention Month (April). Think SHELL: Safety, Health, Education, Laughter, Love. For info: Patty Murphy, 1204 Briarwood Blvd, Arlington, TX 76013. Phone: (817) 980-9591. E-mail: MURPH0@swbell.net.

TWENTY-THIRD AMENDMENT TO US CONSTITUTION RATIFIED: ANNIVERSARY. Mar 29, 1961. District of Columbia residents were given the right to vote in presidential elections under the 23rd Amendment.

TYLER, JOHN: BIRTH ANNIVERSARY. Mar 29, 1790. Tenth president of the US (Apr 6, 1841–Mar 3, 1845). Born at Charles City County, VA, Tyler succeeded to the presidency upon the death of William Henry Harrison. Tyler's first wife died while he was president, and he remarried before the end of his term in office, becoming the first president to marry while in office. Fifteen children were born of the two marriages. In 1861 he was elected to the Congress of the Confederate States but died at Richmond, VA, Jan 18, 1862, before being seated. His death received no official tribute from the US government.

WALTON, SAM: BIRTH ANNIVERSARY. Mar 29, 1918. Founder of Wal-Mart discount stores, born at Kingfisher, OK. One of the wealthiest men in America, he died at Little Rock, AR, Apr 5, 1992.

YOUNG, DENTON TRUE (CY): BIRTH ANNIVERSARY. Mar 29, 1867. Baseball Hall of Fame pitcher, born at Gilmore, OH. Young is baseball's all-time winningest pitcher, having accumulated 511 victories in his 22-year career. The Cy Young Award is given each year in his honor to Major League Baseball's best pitchers. Inducted into the Hall of Fame in 1937. Died at Peoli, OH, Nov 4, 1955.

YO-YO AND SKILL TOY CONVENTION. Mar 29–30. Spinning Top and Yo-Yo Museum, Burlington, WI. 19th annual. Featuring a preconvention exhibition (Mar 15–28) of more than 1,000 yo-yos, plus videos, demonstration of classic yo-yo tricks and an I Spy hunt. Another highlight is GizmoTime with science and action toys for families, and the weekend features old-fashioned yo-yo contests, juggling, a hula hoop contest, paddleball marathon and the Worldwide Yo-Yo Contests with prizes and awesome yo-yo shows. See Walk-the-Dog, Rock-the-Baby, Boingy-Boingy and more! All events are for both participants and spectators, and the contests are nationally recognized standards. For info: Spinning Top and Yo-Yo Museum, 533 Milwaukee Ave, Burlington, WI 53105. Phone: (262) 763-3946. E-mail: thetopmuseum@hotmail.com. Web: www.topmuseum.org.

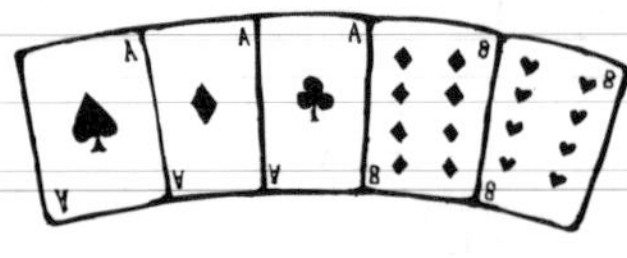

BIRTHDAYS TODAY

Earl Christian Campbell, 59, Hall of Fame football player, born Tyler, TX, Mar 29, 1955.

Jennifer Capriati, 38, Hall of Fame tennis player, born New York, NY, Mar 29, 1976.

Bud Cort, 66, actor (*Harold and Maude, Brewster McCloud*), born New Rochelle, NY, Mar 29, 1948 (some sources say 1950).

Michel Hazanavicius, 47, director (*The Artist; OSS 117: Cairo, Nest of Spies*), born Paris, France, Mar 29, 1967.

Megan Hilty, 33, actress ("Smash"), born Bellevue, WA, March 29, 1981.

Eric Idle, 71, actor ("Monty Python's Flying Circus," "Suddenly Susan"), author, born Durham, England, Mar 29, 1943.

Christopher Lambert, 57, actor (*Greystoke: The Legend of Tarzan, Lord of the Apes*), born New York, NY, Mar 29, 1957.

Lucy Lawless, 46, actress ("Xena"), born Mount Albert, Auckland, New Zealand, Mar 29, 1968.

Elle Macpherson, 50, model, actress (*Sirens*), born Sydney, Australia, Mar 29, 1964.

John Major, 71, former British prime minister (1990–97), born Brixton, England, Mar 29, 1943.

John McLaughlin, 87, editor, columnist, television personality ("The McLaughlin Group"), born Providence, RI, Mar 29, 1927.

Kurt Thomas, 58, Olympic gymnast, born Miami, FL, Mar 29, 1956.

March 2014

S	M	T	W	T	F	S
						1
2	3	4	5	6	7	8
9	10	11	12	13	14	15
16	17	18	19	20	21	22
23	24	25	26	27	28	29
30	31					

March 30 — Sunday

DAY 89 **276 REMAINING**

ANESTHETIC FIRST USED IN SURGERY: ANNIVERSARY. Mar 30, 1842. Dr. Crawford W. Long, having seen the use of nitrous oxide and sulfuric ether at "laughing gas" parties, observed that individuals under their influence felt no pain. On this date, he removed a tumor from the neck of a man who was under the influence of ether.

DOCTORS' DAY. Mar 30. Traditional annual observance since 1933 to honor America's physicians on the anniversary of the occasion when Dr. Crawford W. Long became the first acclaimed physician to use ether as an anesthetic agent in a surgical technique, Mar 30, 1842. The red carnation has been designated the official flower of Doctors' Day.

ENGLAND: MOTHERING SUNDAY. Mar 30. Fourth Sunday of Lent, formerly occasion for attending services at Mother Church, family gatherings and visits to parents. Now popularly known as Mother's Day and a time for visiting and taking gifts to mothers.

EUROPEAN UNION: DAYLIGHT SAVING TIME (SUMMER TIME) BEGINS. Mar 30. All members of the European Union observe daylight saving (summer) time from the last Sunday in March until the last Sunday in October. See also: "European Union: Daylight Saving Time (Summer Time) Ends" (Oct 26).

GOYA, FRANCISCO JOSE de: BIRTH ANNIVERSARY. Mar 30, 1746. Spanish painter and etcher. It is estimated that he executed more than 1,800 paintings, drawings and lithographs during his lifetime. Born at Aragon, Spain; died at Bordeaux, France, Apr 16, 1828.

GRASS IS ALWAYS BROWNER ON THE OTHER SIDE OF THE FENCE DAY. Mar 30. A day to honor all of those who did not jump ship, did not quit the same old job or did not leave the same old relationship because things appeared to look better somewhere else. (©2006 by WH.) For info: Thomas & Ruth Roy, Wellcat Holidays, 2418 Long Ln, Lebanon, PA 17046. Phone: (717) 279-0184. E-mail: wellcat@comcast.net. Web: www.wellcat.com.

"JEOPARDY!" TV PREMIERE: 50th ANNIVERSARY. Mar 30, 1964. The "thinking person's" game show, "Jeopardy!" has a reputation as an intelligent and classy program. Art Fleming was the original host of the show, in which three contestants won cash by giving the correct questions to answers in six different categories. Contestants go through two rounds and "final jeopardy," where they can wager up to all their earnings on one question. The series returned in 1984 with Alex Trebek as the popular host.

LUXEMBOURG: BRETZELSONNDEG. Mar 30. The fourth Sunday in Lent is an occasion for boys to give pretzel-shaped cakes to sweethearts, who may respond, on Easter Sunday, with a gift of a decorated egg or sweet.

MOON PHASE: NEW MOON. Mar 30. Moon enters New Moon phase at 2:45 PM, EDT.

NATIONAL WEEK OF THE OCEAN. Mar 30–Apr 5. 31st annual. A week focusing on humanity's interdependence with the ocean, asking each of us to appreciate, protect and make wise use of the ocean. For info: Natl Week of the Ocean, Inc, PO Box 179, Fort Lauderdale, FL 33302. Phone: (954) 462-5573. Web: www.national-week-of-the-ocean.org.

O'CASEY, SEAN: BIRTH ANNIVERSARY. Mar 30, 1880. Irish playwright (*Juno and the Paycock*). Born at Dublin, Ireland, he died at Torquay, England, Sept 18, 1964.

PENCIL PATENTED: ANNIVERSARY. Mar 30, 1858. First pencil with the eraser top was patented by Hyman Lipman.

REAGAN, RONALD: ASSASSINATION ATTEMPT: ANNIVERSARY. Mar 30, 1981. President Ronald Reagan was shot in the chest by a 25-year-old gunman at Washington, DC. Three other persons were wounded. John W. Hinckley, Jr, the accused attacker, was arrested at the scene. On June 21, 1982, a federal jury in the District of Columbia found Hinckley not guilty by reason of insanity, and

he was committed to St. Elizabeth's Hospital at Washington, DC, for an indefinite time.

ROOT CANAL AWARENESS WEEK. Mar 30–Apr 5. 8th annual. To calm the fears of Americans across the country and to educate the public about misconceptions of root canal treatment and the true benefits of the procedure, the American Association of Endodontists (AAE) has established this week. AAE hopes to teach patients that root canals are virtually painless and can have important implications for overall health. Endodontists, the root canal specialists, perform 25 root canals per week on average and root canal treatment saves more than 16 million natural teeth each year, making the procedure more hero than villain. For info: Meredith Friedman, Public Relations Coordinator, American Assn of Endodontists, 211 E Chicago Ave, Ste 1100, Chicago, IL 60611. Phone: (800) 872-3636 or (312) 266-7255. Web: www.aae.org.

TRINIDAD AND TOBAGO: SPIRITUAL/SHOUTER BAPTIST LIBERATION DAY. Mar 30. Public holiday. Celebrates the 1951 repeal of the Shouter Prohibition Ordinance of 1917.

UNITED KINGDOM: SUMMER TIME. Mar 30–Oct 26. "Summer Time" (one hour in advance of Standard Time), similar to daylight saving time, is observed from the last Sunday in March until the last Sunday in October.

VAN GOGH, VINCENT: BIRTH ANNIVERSARY. Mar 30, 1853. Dutch Postimpressionist painter, especially known for his bold and powerful use of color. Born at Groot Zundert, Holland, he died at Auvers-sur-Oise, France, July 29, 1890.

WILLIAMSON, SONNY BOY: 100th BIRTH ANNIVERSARY. Mar 30, 1914. Legendary and influential harmonica player, born John Lee Curtis "Sonny Boy" Williamson near Jackson, TN. Helped make the harmonica a blues staple. "Good Morning, School Girl" is one of his best remembered hits. Murdered during a robbery on June 1, 1948, at Chicago, IL.

BIRTHDAYS TODAY

John Astin, 84, actor ("The Addams Family"; stage: *The Three Penny Opera*), director, born Baltimore, MD, Mar 30, 1930.

Warren Beatty, 76, actor (*Bonnie and Clyde*), director (*Reds, Dick Tracy*), producer, born Richmond, VA, Mar 30, 1938.

Tracy Chapman, 50, singer, born Cleveland, OH, Mar 30, 1964.

Eric Clapton, 69, singer, songwriter, guitarist, born Ripley, England, Mar 30, 1945.

Robbie Coltrane, 64, actor (*GoldenEye*, Harry Potter films, "Cracker"), born Anthony Robert McMillan at Rutherglen, Scotland, Mar 30, 1950.

Celine Dion, 46, singer, born Charlemagne, QC, Canada, Mar 30, 1968.

Jason Dohring, 32, actor ("Veronica Mars," *Black Cadillac*), born Dayton, OH, Mar 30, 1982.

Richard Dysart, 85, actor ("LA Law"), born Augusta, ME, Mar 30, 1929.

M.C. Hammer, 51, rapper, born Stanley Kirk Burrell at Oakland, CA, Mar 30, 1963.

Norah Jones, 35, singer, born New York, NY, Mar 30, 1979.

Peter Marshall, 87, television host, actor, born Pierre La Cock at Huntington, WV, Mar 30, 1927.

Paul Reiser, 57, actor (*Diner*, "Mad About You"), born New York, NY, Mar 30, 1957.

March 31 — Monday

DAY 90 **275 REMAINING**

BUNSEN BURNER DAY: BIRTH ANNIVERSARY OF ROBERT BUNSEN. Mar 31. A day to honor the inventor of the Bunsen burner, Robert Wilhelm Eberhard von Bunsen, who provided chemists and chemistry students with one of their most indispensable instruments. The Bunsen burner allows the user to regulate the proportions of flammable gas and air to create the most efficient flame. Bunsen was born at Gottingen, Germany, on Mar 31, 1811, and was a professor of chemistry at the universities at Kassel, Marburg, Breslau and Heidelberg. He died at Heidelberg, Germany, Aug 16, 1899.

CHAVEZ, CESAR ESTRADA: BIRTH ANNIVERSARY. Mar 31, 1927. Labor leader who organized migrant farm workers in support of better working conditions. Chavez initiated the National Farm Workers Association in 1962, attracting attention to the migrant farm workers' plight by organizing boycotts of products including grapes and lettuce. He was born at Yuma, AZ, and died Apr 23, 1993, at San Luis, AZ. His birthday is a holiday in California.

CHESNUT, MARY BOYKIN MILLER: BIRTH ANNIVERSARY. Mar 31, 1823. Born at Pleasant Hill, SC, and died Nov 22, 1886, at Camden, SC. During the Civil War, Chesnut accompanied her husband, a Confederate staff officer, on military missions. She kept a journal of her experiences and observations, which was published posthumously as *A Diary from Dixie*, a perceptive portrait of Confederate military and political leaders and an insightful view of Southern life during the Civil War.

DALAI LAMA FLEES TIBET: 55th ANNIVERSARY. Mar 31, 1959. The Dalai Lama fled Chinese suppression and was granted political asylum in India. In 1950 Tibet had been invaded by China, and in 1951 an agreement was signed under which Tibet became a "national autonomous region" of China. Tibetans suffered under China's persecution of Buddhism, and after years of scattered protest a full-scale revolt broke out in 1959. The Dalai Lama fled, and with the beginning of the Chinese Cultural Revolution the Chinese took brutal repressive measures against the Tibetans, with the practice of religion banned and thousands of monasteries destroyed. The ban was lifted in 1976 with the end of the Cultural Revolution. The Dalai Lama received the Nobel Peace Prize in 1989 for his commitment to the nonviolent liberation of his country.

DESCARTES, RENE: BIRTH ANNIVERSARY. Mar 31, 1596. French philosopher and mathematician, known as the "father of modern philosophy," born at La Haye, Touraine, France. Cartesian philosophical precepts are often remembered because of his famous proposition "I think, therefore I am" (*Cogito, ergo sum* . . .). Died of pneumonia at Stockholm, Sweden, Feb 11, 1650.

EIFFEL TOWER: 125th ANNIVERSARY. Mar 31, 1889. Built for the Paris Exhibition of 1889, the tower was named for its architect, Alexandre Gustave Eiffel, and is one of the world's best-known landmarks.

March 2014	S	M	T	W	T	F	S
							1
	2	3	4	5	6	7	8
	9	10	11	12	13	14	15
	16	17	18	19	20	21	22
	23	24	25	26	27	28	29
	30	31					

FITZGERALD, EDWARD: BIRTH ANNIVERSARY. Mar 31, 1809. English author, born at Bredfield, England, perhaps best known for his translation of Omar Khayyam's *Rubaiyat*. Died at Merton, Norfolk, June 14, 1883.

GOGOL, NIKOLAI VASILEVICH: BIRTH ANNIVERSARY. Mar 31, 1809. Russian author of plays, novels and short stories. Born at Sorochinsk, Russia, he died at Moscow, Russia, Mar 4, 1852. Gogol's most famous work is the novel *Dead Souls*.

HAYDN, FRANZ JOSEPH: BIRTH ANNIVERSARY. Mar 31, 1732. "Father of the symphony," born at Rohrau, Austria-Hungary. Composed about 120 symphonies, more than a hundred works for chamber groups, a dozen operas and hundreds of other musical works. Died at Vienna, Austria, May 31, 1809.

JOHNSON, JOHN (JACK) ARTHUR: BIRTH ANNIVERSARY. Mar 31, 1878. In 1908 Jack Johnson became the first black to win the heavyweight boxing championship when he defeated Tommy Burns at Sydney, Australia. Unable to accept a black man's triumph, the boxing world tried to find a white challenger. Jim Jeffries, former heavyweight title holder, was badgered out of retirement. On July 4, 1910, at Reno, NV, the "battle of the century" proved to be a farce when Johnson handily defeated Jeffries. Race riots swept the US, and plans to exhibit the film of the fight were canceled. Johnson was born at Galveston, TX, and died in an automobile accident June 10, 1946, at Raleigh, NC. He was inducted into the Boxing Hall of Fame in 1990.

KRAFT NABISCO CHAMPIONSHIP. Mar 31–Apr 6. Mission Hills Country Club, Rancho Mirage, CA. The first major of the year on the LPGA tour. Held since 1972, this tournament is often called the Master's of women's professional golf. For info: Kraft Nabisco Championship. E-mail: knc@kraft.com. Web: www.kncgolf.com.

MARVELL, ANDREW: BIRTH ANNIVERSARY. Mar 31, 1621. English poet. Born at Winestead, Yorkshire, England. From his poem "To His Coy Mistress": "Had we but world enough and time/this coyness, lady, were no crime. . . . But at my back I always hear/time's winged chariot drawing near. . . ." Died at London, England, Aug 18, 1678.

NATIONAL "SHE'S FUNNY THAT WAY" DAY. Mar 31. On this day individuals will pay tribute to the humorous nature of women, by listing the top five ways in which women in our lives make us laugh. For info: Brenda Meridith, 50 Hall Rd, Winchendon, MA 01475. Phone: (978) 297-1820. Fax: (978) 297-2519. E-mail: BMeridith@leominster.mec.edu.

***OKLAHOMA!* BROADWAY PREMIERE: ANNIVERSARY.** Mar 31, 1943. Rodgers and Hammerstein's landmark musical (their first collaboration) opened at the St. James Theatre on this date in 1943. (It had its world premiere under the title *Away We Go* at the Shubert Theatre in New Haven, CT, on Mar 11, 1943.) *Oklahoma!* is considered significant because it was the first musical in which songs, music, characterization and story were integrated into an emotional whole. It changed musicals forever. It was also the first musical to run more than 2,000 performances and to have a cast album recorded. Agnes de Mille was the choreographer. It received a special Pulitzer Prize for drama on May 2, 1944. In May 1953, "Oklahoma!" became that state's official song.

PAZ, OCTAVIO: 100th BIRTH ANNIVERSARY. Mar 31, 1914. Poet, diplomat, translator, critic, professor and journal editor born at Mexico City, Mexico. His seminal prose work is *The Labyrinth of Solitude* (1950), an examination of the Mexican psyche. The prodigious Paz was awarded the Miguel de Cervantes Prize in 1981 and the Nobel Prize in Literature in 1990 "for impassioned writing with wide horizons, characterized by sensuous intelligence and humanistic integrity." He died at Mexico City, Apr 19, 1998.

PEARSE, RICHARD: ANNIVERSARY OF MONOPLANE FLIGHT. Mar 31, 1903. Richard Pearse, a farmer and inventor, flew a monoplane of his own design several hundred yards along a road near Temuka, New Zealand, and then landed it on top of a 12-foot-high hedge. Pearse had built the craft, which consisted of a steerable tricycle undercarriage and an internal combustion engine. A Pearse commemorative medal was issued on Sept 19, 1971, by the Museum of Transport and Technology, Auckland, New Zealand.

SEWARD'S DAY: ANNIVERSARY OF THE ACQUISITION OF ALASKA. Mar 31. Observed in Alaska near the anniversary of its acquisition from Russia in 1867. The treaty of purchase was signed between the Russians and the Americans Mar 30, 1867, and ratified by the Senate May 28, 1867. The territory was formally transferred Oct 18, 1867. Annually, the last Monday in March.

SOVIET GEORGIA VOTES FOR INDEPENDENCE: ANNIVERSARY. Mar 31, 1991. On this date the Soviet Republic of Georgia voted to declare its independence from the Soviet Union. Georgia followed the Baltic states of Lithuania, Estonia and Latvia by becoming the fourth republic to reject Mikhail Gorbachev's new vision of the Soviet Union as espoused in a new Union Treaty. Totals revealed that 98.9 percent of those voting favored independence from Moscow. Hours after the election, troops were dispatched from Moscow to Georgia under a state of emergency.

SUBARU CHERRY BLOSSOM FESTIVAL OF GREATER PHILADELPHIA. Mar 31–Apr 25 (tentative). Philadelphia, PA. Welcome to the world of the cherry blossoms (*sakura*). A program of the Japan America Society of Greater Philadelphia, this festival is an initiative to encourage a better understanding of the cultural, social and educational customs of Japan and the United States. For hundreds of years, Japan has been celebrating the beauty of the elegant pink cherry blossom with picnics under the trees accompanied by traditional music and dance. Set under the blossoming canopy of Philadelphia's cherry trees, the festival is a chance to experience a centuries-old tradition that celebrates the fleeting splendor of spring like no other. Sakura Sunday is the festival's major event. Benefits the JASGP Community Tree Planting Project. Est attendance: 50,000. For info: Japan America Society of Greater Philadelphia, 200 S Broad St, Ste 700, Philadelphia, PA 19102. Phone: (215) 790-3810. Fax: (215) 790-3805. Web: www.subarucherryblossom.org.

US VIRGIN ISLANDS: TRANSFER DAY. Mar 31. Commemorates transfer resulting from purchase of the Virgin Islands by the US from Denmark, Mar 31, 1917, for $25 million.

BIRTHDAYS TODAY

Herb Alpert, 79, musician (Tijuana Brass), born Los Angeles, CA, Mar 31, 1935.

Mark Begich, 52, US Senator (D, Alaska), born Anchorage, AK, Mar 31, 1962.

Pavel Bure, 43, former hockey player, born Moscow, USSR (now Russia), Mar 31, 1971.

Richard Chamberlain, 79, actor ("Dr. Kildare," *Shogun*), born Los Angeles, CA, Mar 31, 1935.

William Daniels, 87, actor (Emmy for "St. Elsewhere"; "Boy Meets World"), born Brooklyn, NY, Mar 31, 1927.

Al Gore, 66, 45th vice president of the US (1993–2001), environmental activist, author, documentary filmmaker (*An Inconvenient Truth*), born Albert Gore, Jr, at Washington, DC, Mar 31, 1948.

Gordon (Gordie) Howe, 86, Hall of Fame hockey player, born Floral, SK, Canada, Mar 31, 1928.

John Jakes, 82, author (*North and South*, the Kent Family Chronicles), born Chicago, IL, Mar 31, 1932.

James Earl (Jimmy) Johnson, 76, Hall of Fame football player, born Dallas, TX, Mar 31, 1938.

Shirley Jones, 80, actress (Oscar for *Elmer Gantry*; *The Music Man, Oklahoma!*, "The Partridge Family"), born Smithton, PA, Mar 31, 1934.

Gabe Kaplan, 68, actor ("Welcome Back, Kotter"), born Brooklyn, NY, Mar 31, 1946.

Angus King, Jr, 70, US Senator (I, Maine), former governor of Maine (I), born Alexandria, VA, Mar 31, 1944.

Patrick J. Leahy, 74, US Senator (D, Vermont), born Montpelier, VT, Mar 31, 1940.

Edward Francis (Ed) Marinaro, 64, actor ("Hill Street Blues," "Sisters"), former football player, born New York, NY, Mar 31, 1950.

Marc McClure, 57, actor (*Freaky Friday, Back to the Future*), born San Mateo, CA, Mar 31, 1957.

Ewan McGregor, 43, actor (*The Ghost Writer, Moulin Rouge, Trainspotting, Star Wars* films), born Crieff, Scotland, Mar 31, 1971.

Rhea Perlman, 66, actress ("Cheers," *Carpool*), born Brooklyn, NY, Mar 31, 1948.

Steve Smith, 45, former basketball player, born Highland Park, MI, Mar 31, 1969.

Christopher Walken, 71, actor (*Hairspray, Catch Me If You Can, The Deer Hunter*), born Queens, NY, Mar 31, 1943.

April

April 1 — Tuesday

DAY 91 **274 REMAINING**

ALCOHOL AWARENESS MONTH. Apr 1–30. Since 1987, a month to help raise awareness among community prevention leaders and citizens about the problem of underage drinking. Concentrates on community grassroots activities. For info: Public Info Dept, Natl Council on Alcoholism and Drug Dependence, Inc, 217 Broadway, Ste 712, New York, NY 10007. Phone: (212) 269-7797. Fax: (212) 269-7510. E-mail: national@ncadd.org. Web: www.ncadd.org.

APAWS INTERNATIONAL POOPER-SCOOPER WEEK. Apr 1–7. The Association of Professional Animal Waste Specialists (aPaws), founded in February 2002, has established April 1–7 as a special week of educating pet owners on the importance of cleaning up after their dogs. With the week in full swing, pet owners should be aware of the problems concerning dog waste. The American Pet association estimates that this country's 71 million pet dogs produce over 4.4 billion pounds of waste per year. That's enough to cover 900 football fields with 12 inches of dog waste! For info: aPaws, PO Box 2325, Santa Clarita, CA 91386-2325. E-mail: info@apaws.org. Web: www.apaws.org.

APRIL FOOLS' or ALL FOOLS' DAY. Apr 1. April Fools' Day seems to have begun in France in 1564. Apr 1 used to be New Year's Day, but the New Year was changed to Jan 1 that year. People who insisted on celebrating the "old" New Year became known as April fools, and it became common to play jokes and tricks on them. The general concept of a feast of fools is, however, an ancient one. The Romans had such a day, and medieval monasteries also had days when the abbot or bishop was replaced for a day by a common monk, who would order his superiors to do the most menial or ridiculous tasks. According to Brady's *Clavis Calendaria* (1812): "The joke of the day is to deceive persons by sending them upon frivolous and nonsensical errands; to pretend they are wanted when they are not, or, in fact, any way to betray them into some supposed ludicrous situation, so as to enable you to call them 'An April Fool.'"

AZALEA FESTIVAL. Apr 1–30. Honor Heights Park, Muskogee, OK. One of the oldest and most celebrated public parks in the southwest: 132 acres of 625 varieties of azaleas. Ranked in the top 100 events by the American Bus Association. Many related events take place during the month, including entertainment, arts and crafts, carriage rides and more. Annually in April since 1967. Est attendance: 500,000. For info: Muskogee Chamber of Commerce, PO Box 797, Muskogee, OK 74402. Phone: (918) 682-2401. E-mail: info@muskogeechamber.org. Web: www.muskogeechamber.org.

BATTLE OF OKINAWA BEGINS: ANNIVERSARY. Apr 1, 1945. On Easter Sunday, the US 10th Army began operation *Iceberg*, the invasion of the Ryukyu Islands of Okinawa. Ground troops numbering 180,000 plus 368,000 men in support services made a total of 548,000 troops involved—the biggest amphibious operation of the Pacific war.

BRIDGE OVER THE NEPONSET: ANNIVERSARY. Apr 1, 1634. The first bridge built in the US spanned the Neponset River between Milton and Dorchester, MA. The authority to build the bridge and an adjoining mill was issued to Israel Stoughton on this date by the Massachusetts General Court.

BULGARIA: SAINT LASARUS'S DAY. Apr 1. Ancient Slavic holiday of young girls, in honor of the goddess of spring and love.

CANADA: NUNAVUT INDEPENDENCE: 15th ANNIVERSARY. Apr 1, 1999. Nunavut became Canada's third independent territory. This self-governing territory with an Inuit majority was created from the eastern half of the Northwest Territories.

✦CANCER CONTROL MONTH. Apr 1–30.

CAR CARE MONTHS. Apr 1–30 (also Oct 1–31). A nationwide effort to focus motorists' attention on the importance of vehicle maintenance and care. Annually, the months of April and October. For info: Car Care Council, 7101 Wisconsin Ave, Ste 1300, Bethesda, MD 20814. Phone: (240) 333-1088. Fax: (301) 654-3299. E-mail: info@carcare.org. Web: www.carcare.org.

CHANEY, LON: BIRTH ANNIVERSARY. Apr 1, 1883. The "Man of a Thousand Faces" was born Leonidas Chaney at Colorado Springs, CO. One of the biggest box office stars of the silent era, Chaney was a master of disguise and makeup (he kept his transformation tools and methods a closely guarded secret) who specialized in playing tortured, tragic and often menacing characters. He is best known for his gripping portrayals of Quasimodo in *The Hunchback of Notre Dame* (1923) and of the Phantom in *The Phantom of the Opera* (1925). He died of cancer on Aug 26, 1930, at Hollywood, CA—only one month after his first sound film was released. His impact on films was such that all Hollywood studios observed a moment of silence in his honor to commemorate his death.

CHILD ABUSE PREVENTION MONTH. Apr 1–30. In 1979 the National Exchange Club adopted the prevention of child abuse as its national project and established the National Exchange Club Foundation. The Foundation is a chartered nonprofit corporation in Ohio. The Foundation has established Exchange Club Child Abuse Prevention Centers throughout the US. More than 690,000 families have received services from the Exchange Club Child Abuse Prevention network. For info: The Natl Exchange Club Foundation, 3050 Central Ave, Toledo, OH 43606-1700. Phone: (419) 535-3232 or (800) 924-2643. Fax: (419) 535-1989. E-mail: cap@nationalexchangeclub.org. Web: www.preventchildabuse.com.

CIGARETTE ADVERTISING BANNED: ANNIVERSARY. Apr 1, 1970. Radio and television ads for cigarettes were banned by legislation signed by President Richard Nixon on this date. The ban went into effect Jan 1, 1971.

COMMUNITY SPIRIT DAYS. Apr 1–30. Any town may observe this period by doing a special project to help those in need or by having a ceremony to present that community's Spirit of America Foundation Tributes for outstanding volunteerism. For info: Spirit of America Foundation, PO Box 5637, Augusta, ME 04332.

CONFEDERATE HISTORY MONTH. Apr 1–30. A month to learn more about the role men and women of the Confederate States of America played in the history of the US. Traditionally observed in the month of April in the South. Proclaimed by the states of Mississippi and Georgia, as well as by various municipalities. For info: The Sons of Confederate Veterans. Web: confederateheritagemonth.com.

COUPLE APPRECIATION MONTH. Apr 1–30. To show thanks for each other's love and emotional support. Do something special to reinforce and celebrate your relationship. Annually, the month of April. For info: Donald Etkes, PhD, 112 Harvard Ave, #148, Claremont, CA 91711. Phone: (310) 405-9814. E-mail: drdonetkes@aol.com.

DEFEAT AT FIVE FORKS: ANNIVERSARY. Apr 1, 1865. After withdrawing to Five Forks, VA, Confederate troops under George Pickett were defeated and cut off by Union troops. This defeat, according to many military historians, sealed the immediate fate of Robert E. Lee's armies at Petersburg and Richmond. On Apr 2, Lee informed Confederate president Jefferson Davis that he would have to evacuate Richmond. Davis and his cabinet fled by train to Danville, VA.

DEFEAT DIABETES MONTH. Apr 1–30. A month focused on preventing diabetes and/or its complications. See the website for activities, dietary advice and health information. For info: Defeat Diabetes Foundation, 150 153rd Ave, Ste 300, Madeira Beach, FL 33708. Phone: (415) 391-5050 or (415) 671-2991. E-mail: dswidorski@DefeatDiabetes.org. Web: www.DefeatDiabetes.org.

DISTRACTED DRIVING AWARENESS MONTH. Apr 1–30. Since 2010, Distracted Driving Awareness Month informs people on the dangers of cell phone use while driving and furthers understanding of cognitive distraction to the brain. The National Safety Council saves lives by preventing injuries and deaths at work, in homes and communities and on the road through leadership, research, education and advocacy. For info: National Safety Council, Communications Department, 1121 Spring Lake Dr, Itasca, IL 60143. Phone: (800) 621-7615. E-mail: media@nsc.org. Web: www.nsc.org/DDmonth.

"THE DOCTORS" TV PREMIERE: ANNIVERSARY. Apr 1, 1963. "The Doctors" premiered on NBC on the same day as ABC's long-running soap "General Hospital," providing viewers with a double dose of medical drama. The show was set at Hope Memorial Hospital and began as an anthology series that was subsequently transformed into a serial in 1964. "The Doctors" ran for 19 years. Ellen Burstyn, Anna Stuart, Nancy Pinkerton, Jonathan Hogan, Julia Duffy and Alec Baldwin are some of its famous alums.

EMOTIONAL OVEREATING AWARENESS MONTH. Apr 1–30. Millions overeat in an attempt to numb feelings with food. The challenge this month is to experience your feelings without anesthetizing yourself with sugars, fat and salt. Try to recognize these urges to eat for emotional reasons and deal with them in more appropriate and satisfying ways. Use the month of April to pay attention to your emotional appetite! For info: Dr. Denise Lamothe, PO Box 1013, Exeter, NH 03833. Phone: (603) 493-6043. E-mail: Denise@DeniseLamothe.com.

FRESH FLORIDA TOMATO MONTH. Apr 1–30. To publicize the Florida tomato as a versatile, nutritious, flavorful food. For info: Florida Tomato Committee, 800 Trafalgar Ct, Ste 300, Maitland, FL 32751. Phone: (407) 660-1949. Fax: (407) 660-1656. E-mail: samantha@floridatomatoes.org. Web: www.floridatomatoes.org.

"GENERAL HOSPITAL" TV PREMIERE: ANNIVERSARY. Apr 1, 1963. "General Hospital," ABC's longest-running soap, revolves around the denizens of fictional Port Charles, NY. "GH" was created by Doris and Frank Hursley. John Beradino, who was with the show from the beginning until his death in May 1996, played the role of Dr. Steve Hardy, upstanding director of medicine and pillar of the community. In the '80s, story lines became unusual with plots involving international espionage, mob activity and aliens. The wedding of supercouple Luke and Laura (Anthony Geary and Genie Francis) was a ratings topper. By the '90s, stories moved away from high-powered action to more conventional romance. Many actors received their big break on the show, including Demi Moore, Janine Turner, Jack Wagner, Richard Dean Anderson, Rick Springfield, John Stamos, Emma Samms, Mark Hamill, Finola Hughes, Ricky Martin and Tia Carrere.

GRANGE MONTH. Apr 1–30. State and local recognition for Grange's contribution to rural/urban America. Celebrated at National Headquarters at Washington, DC, and in all states with local, county and state Granges. Begun in 1867, the National Grange is the oldest US rural community-service, family-oriented organization with a special interest in agriculture. Annually, the month of April. For info: The Natl Grange of the Patrons of Husbandry, 1616 H St NW, Washington, DC 20006. Phone: (202) 628-3507 or (888) 4-GRANGE. Fax: (202) 347-1091. E-mail: info@nationalgrange.org. Web: www.nationalgrange.org.

HARVEY, WILLIAM: BIRTH ANNIVERSARY. Apr 1, 1578. (Old Style date.) Physician, born at Folkestone, England. The first to discover the mechanics of the circulation of the blood. Died at Roehampton, England, June 3, 1657 (OS).

HOLY HUMOR MONTH. Apr 1–30. To recognize the healing power of Christian joy, humor and celebration; to celebrate "Holy Humor Sunday," the Sunday after Easter (Apr 27) and to be "Fools for Christ" on April Fools' Day (Apr 1). Churches and prayer groups nationwide participate. For info: Cal Samra, The Joyful Noiseletter, PO Box 895, Portage, MI 49081-0895. Phone: (269) 324-0990. E-mail: joyfulnz@aol.com. Web: www.joyfulnoiseletter.com.

HOME IMPROVEMENT TIME. Apr 1–Sept 30. To explain the investment advantages of spending disposable income for home improvement to create better family living and an improved community environment. Editorial package includes approximately 50 camera-ready stories and photos free to editors. Also available on website. (May is a promotion focal point.) For info: Carole Stewart, Home Improvement Time, PO Box 247, Oakdale, PA 15071-0247. Phone: (412) 787-2881. Fax: (412) 787-3233. E-mail: carole.stewart@homeimprovementtime.com. Web: homeimprovementtime.com.

INFORMED WOMAN MONTH. Apr 1–30. You owe it to yourself to feel happy and fulfilled. To have confidence that you're in charge of your life and you're guiding it in the right direction. You can have whatever you want, but you need to determine what you need to know, where to go and whom to contact. Discover how to enjoy better living today and learn how to become a more informed and aware individual for the future. Ideas and tips for the month available for $2.50. For info: Lorrie Marsiglio, PO Box 284-CC, Wasco, IL 60183-0284. Phone: (630) 584-9368.

INTERNATIONAL CUSTOMER LOYALTY MONTH. Apr 1–30. We highlight this month to honor and generate customer loyalty! Even though building customer loyalty should be a year-round thing, not just a month, take this month to strategize on how you can improve on relationships with your customers through better service, higher quality, etc. For info: Shep Hyken, Shepard Presentations, LLC, 711 Old Ballas Rd, #215, St. Louis, MO 63141. Phone: (314) 696-2200. E-mail: Shep@hyken.com. Web: www.CustomerLoyaltyMonth.com.

INTERNATIONAL TWIT AWARD MONTH. Apr 1–30. Any famous name (celebrity with the worst sense of humor) is eligible to be designated most Tiresome Wit (TWIT) of 2013. For info: Lauren Barnett, Lone Star Publications of Humor, 8452 Fredericksburg Rd, #103, San Antonio, TX 78229. E-mail: lspubs@aol.com.

IRAN: ISLAMIC REPUBLIC DAY. Apr 1. National holiday. Commemorates the approval of the new constitution of the Islamic Republic of Iran in 1979.

JAZZ APPRECIATION MONTH. Apr 1–30. Every April, Jazz Appreciation Month (JAM) highlights the glories of jazz as both a historical and a living treasure. Here is one special month to draw greater public attention to the extraordinary heritage and history of jazz and its importance to American culture. Musicians, concert halls, schools, colleges, museums, libraries and public broadcasters are encouraged to offer special programs during this month. The Smithsonian Institution's National Museum of American History (which operates the world's most comprehensive set of jazz programs) leads this initiative in concert with a distinguished roster of federal agencies, nongovernmental organizations and broadcasting networks. For info: The Smithsonian Institution, National Museum of American History, PO Box 37012 MRC 616, Washington, DC 20013. Phone: (202) 633-3604. E-mail: jazz@si.edu. Web: www.smithsonianjazz.org.

LAUGH AT WORK WEEK. Apr 1–7. Laughter and humor are vital to a healthy, productive workplace. Benefits of laughing at work include improved productivity, teamwork, communication, stress relief, job satisfaction and employee retention. This week, which begins on April Fools' Day, focuses on the very serious business of humor. For info: Randall Munson, Creatively Speaking, 508 Meadow Run Dr SW, Rochester, MN 55902-2337. Phone: (507) 286-1331. Fax: (507) 286-1331. E-mail: humor@CreativelySpeaking.com. Web: www.LaughAtWorkWeek.com.

LIBRARY SNAPSHOT DAY. Apr 1–30. The American Library Association encourages all libraries to choose a day during the month of April and record what happens in that single day in their libraries. How many books are checked out? How many people receive help finding a job? Doing their taxes? Doing their homework? This initiative provides an easy means to collect statistics, photos and stories that will enable library advocates to prove the value of their libraries to decision makers and increase public awareness. The ALA provides free wiki software to help libraries publish their statistics for their community. For info: American Library Assn, Public Info Office, 50 E Huron St, Chicago, IL 60611. Phone: (312) 280-5044. Fax: (312) 280-5274. E-mail: pio@ala.org. Web: www.ala.org.

MEDICATION SAFETY WEEK. Apr 1–7. Starting on April Fools' Day, this week serves to raise awareness about medication safety and improving health communication. When it comes to taking medications and supplements—don't be fooled. A free "Medication Safety" presentation for community education is available to partnering health organizations upon request. Observed since 1999. For info: Women's Heart Foundation, PO Box 7827, West Trenton, NJ 08628. Phone: (609) 771-9600. Fax: (609) 771-3778. Web: www.womensheart.org.

MONTH OF THE YOUNG CHILD®. Apr 1–30. Michigan. Since 1985, a month to promote awareness of the importance of young children and their specific needs in today's society. Many communities celebrate with special events for children and families. For info: Michigan Assn for Education of Young Children, 839 Centennial Way, Ste 200, Lansing, MI 48917-9277. Phone: (800) 336-6424. Fax: (517) 351-0157. E-mail: moyc@miaeyc.org. Web: www.miaeyc.org.

MYLESDAY. Apr 1. A day to celebrate the life and works of Irish writer Brian O'Nolan (also known as Flann O'Brien and Myles na gCopaleen). The author of *At Swim-Two-Birds* and countless satiric newspaper columns was born Oct 5, 1911, and died Apr 1, 1966. First observed at the Palace Bar, Dublin, Ireland, in 2011, the year of his birth centennial. See "O'Brien, Flann: Birth Anniversary" (Oct 5).

April 2014	S	M	T	W	T	F	S
			1	2	3	4	5
	6	7	8	9	10	11	12
	13	14	15	16	17	18	19
	20	21	22	23	24	25	26
	27	28	29	30			

NATIONAL AFRICAN-AMERICAN WOMEN'S FITNESS MONTH. Apr 1–30. A national event designed to encourage health awareness through physical activity for African-American women. The event will increase awareness of the health risks associated with a sedentary lifestyle and promote the benefits of an active lifestyle. For info: Sheila Madison, Natl African-American Women's Fitness Month, PO Box 2733, Washington, DC 20013-2733. Phone: (281) 750-2767. E-mail: info@sheilamadison.com. Web: www.sheilamadison.com.

NATIONAL AUTISM AWARENESS MONTH. Apr 1–30. In order to highlight the growing need for concern and awareness about autism, the Autism Society has been celebrating National Autism Awareness Month since the 1970s. This month creates a special opportunity for people to educate themselves and others about autism and issues within the autism community. For info: Autism Society, 4340 East-West Hwy, Ste 350, Bethesda, MD 20814. Web: www.autism-society.org.

NATIONAL CARD AND LETTER WRITING MONTH. Apr 1–May 11. An annual effort to promote literacy and celebrate the art of letter writing. The writing, sending and receiving of letters, postcards and greeting cards is a tradition that has preserved our nation's history and changed lives. Unlike other forms of communications, card and letter writing is timeless, personal and immediately tangible. Postmasters and managers of customer service at post offices across the country are encouraging card and letter writing by hosting friendly competitions among local youth or by supporting activities at local libraries or schools. Annually, from Apr 1 until Mother's Day.

✦NATIONAL CHILD ABUSE PREVENTION MONTH. Apr 1–30.

NATIONAL CHILD ABUSE PREVENTION MONTH. Apr 1–30. A time to recognize that we each can play a part in promoting the social and emotional well-being of children and families in communities. For info: Administration for Children and Families, US Department of Health and Human Services. Web: www.childwelfare.gov/preventing/preventionmonth.

NATIONAL DECORATING MONTH. Apr 1–30. This month is dedicated to learning more about the many aspects of home decor while promoting the fun and creativity of DIY decorating. For info: Donna Babylon, PO Box 1603, Westminster, MD 21158. Phone: (410) 876-3121. Fax: (410) 848-3293. E-mail: natldecmonth@aol.com.

✦NATIONAL DONATE LIFE MONTH. Apr 1–30.

NATIONAL FUN AT WORK DAY. Apr 1. Today and every day the workplace should be spiced with fun, laughter and a playful attitude. Morale will increase, productivity will soar and the bottom line will improve. Annually, Apr 1 (or the following Thursday, if April 1 falls on a weekend). For info: Matt Weinstein, Playfair, 5883 Lucas Valley Rd, Nicasio, CA 94946. Phone: (415) 662-9899. E-mail: playfair1@aol.com. Web: www.playfair.com.

NATIONAL FUN DAY. Apr 1. A day to laugh and reminisce about the good old days when Apr 1 meant an exploding pen, a hand buzzer, a nice stick of pepper gum or maybe some fake doggie poo. Play a prank on a friend, family member or coworker to keep the spirit of April Fools' alive. For info: Aigner/Prensky Marketing Group, 214 Lincoln St, Ste 300, Allston, MA 02134. Phone: (617) 254-9500. Web: www.aignerprenskymarketing.com.

NATIONAL HUMOR MONTH. Apr 1–30. 38th anniversary. A month urging everyone to focus on appreciating, embracing, endorsing and experiencing the joy of humor in all its forms. Free materials and project ideas available. For info: Steve Wilson, Director, World Laughter Tour, 1159 S Creekway Ct, Columbus, OH 43230. Phone: 800-NOW-LAFF. E-mail: info@worldlaughtertour.com. Web: www.humormonth.com.

NATIONAL KNUCKLES DOWN MONTH. Apr 1–30. To recognize and revive the American tradition of playing and collecting marbles and keep it rolling along. Please send SASE with inquiries. For info: Cathy C. Runyan-Svacina, The Marble Lady, 7812 NW Hampton Rd, Kansas City, MO 64152. Phone: (816) 587-8687. E-mail: themarblelady@aol.com. Web: www.themarblelady.com.

NATIONAL LANDSCAPE ARCHITECTURE MONTH. Apr 1–30. Discover what landscape architects do to promote healthy living through design. Many architects will have site tours, exhibits, school visits and community projects this month. Annually, during April, as Apr 26 is the birth anniversary of Frederick Law Olmsted. Olmsted is widely regarded as the founder of the profession of landscape architecture. For info: ASLA, 636 Eye St NW, Washington, DC 20001. Phone: (202) 898-2444. E-mail: pstamper@asla.org. Web: www.asla.org.

NATIONAL OCCUPATIONAL THERAPY MONTH. Apr 1–30. To recognize the services and accomplishments of occupational therapy practitioners and promote awareness of the benefits of occupational therapy. For info: The American Occupational Therapy Assn, Inc, PO Box 31220, Bethesda, MD 20814-1220. Phone: (301) 652-6611 or (800) 377-8555 (TDD). Fax: (301) 652-7711. Web: www.aota.org.

NATIONAL PECAN MONTH. Apr 1–30. A celebration of the great taste, health benefits and versatility of pecans. This delicious tree nut native to North America adds unmistakable flavor, crunch and texture to just about any meal or snack. Pecans have proven cholesterol-lowering properties and contain more than 19 important vitamins and minerals. Almost 90 percent of the fats in pecans are of the heart-healthy, unsaturated variety. For info: Natl Pecan Shellers Assn, 1100 Johnson Ferry Rd, Ste 300, Atlanta, GA 30342. Phone: (404) 252-3663. Fax: (404) 252-0774. E-mail: info@ilovepecans.org. Web: www.ilovepecans.org.

NATIONAL PEST MANAGEMENT MONTH. Apr 1–30. For more than 30 years, April has been celebrated as National Pest Management Month, recognizing the professional pest management industry for its role in protecting public health and property from significant pest threats. For info: National Pest Management Assn, 10460 North St, Fairfax, VA 22030. Phone: (703) 352-6762. Fax: (703) 352-3031. E-mail: NPMATeam@vaultcommunications.com. Web: www.pestworld.org.

NATIONAL POETRY MONTH. Apr 1–30. Annual observance to pay tribute to the great legacy and ongoing achievement of American poets and the vital place of poetry in American culture. In a proclamation issued in honor of the first observance, President Bill Clinton called it "a welcome opportunity to celebrate not only the unsurpassed body of literature produced by our poets in the past, but also the vitality and diversity of voices reflected in the works of today's American poets. . . . Their creativity and wealth of language enrich our culture and inspire a new generation of Americans to learn the power of reading and writing at its best." Spearheaded by the Academy of American Poets, this is the largest and most extensive celebration of poetry in American history. For info: Academy of American Poets, 75 Maiden Ln, Ste 901, New York, NY 10038. Phone: (212) 274-0343. Fax: (212) 274-9427. E-mail: npm@poets.org. Web: www.poets.org.

NATIONAL REBUILDING MONTH. Apr 1–30. Hundreds of thousands of volunteers come together to rehabilitate the homes of low-income, elderly or disabled people and nonprofit facilities. For info: Rebuilding Together, 1899 L St NW, Ste 1000, Washington, DC 20036. Phone: (202) 483-9083 or (800) 4-REHAB-9. Web: www.rebuildingtogether.org.

✦NATIONAL SEXUAL ASSAULT AWARENESS AND PREVENTION MONTH. Apr 1–30. Created by President Barack Obama in 2009 to urge Americans to respond to sexual assault by establishing policies at work and school, by engaging in discussions with family and friends and by making the prevention of sexual assault a priority in their communities.

NATIONAL SEXUALLY TRANSMITTED DISEASES (STDs) EDUCATION AND AWARENESS MONTH. Apr 1–30. To educate consumers, patients, students and professionals about the prevention of sexually transmitted diseases. For info: Fred S. Mayer, RPh, MPH, Pharmacists Planning Service, Inc (PPSI), PO Box 6760, San Rafael, CA 94903. Phone: (415) 479-8628 or (415) 302-7351. E-mail: ppsi@aol.com. Web: www.ppsinc.org.

NATIONAL SEXUAL ASSAULT AWARENESS AND PREVENTION MONTH. Apr 1–30. Every two and a half minutes, somewhere in America, another person is sexually assaulted. During this month, efforts are focused on raising awareness of sexual assault, promoting legislative efforts to address sexual violence, lauding efforts of more than 10,000 volunteers across the US who assist in crisis services and related areas, promoting resources for victims such as the National Sexual Assault Hotline (800-656-HOPE) and, above all, demonstrating solidarity with victims of sexual assault. Celebrated nationally by state sexual assault coalitions, local rape crisis centers and other similar organizations. Passed by House/Senate; signed by president. For info: National Sexual Violence Resource Center, 123 N Enola Dr, Enola, PA 17025. Phone: (877) 739-3895. Fax: (717) 909-0714. E-mail: resources@nsvrc.org. Web: www.nsvrc.org.

NATIONAL SOYFOODS MONTH. Apr 1–30. A key time to provide up-to-date, exciting information on new soy products, soy and health research, soyfood sales and the soyfoods industry to retailers, consumers and members of the press. For info: Soyfoods Assn of North America, 1050 17th St NW, Ste 600, Washington, DC 20036. Phone: (202) 659-3520. Fax: (202) 659-3522. E-mail: info@soyfoods.org. Web: www.soyfoods.org.

NATIONAL YOUTH SPORTS SAFETY MONTH. Apr 1–30. Bringing public attention to the prevalent problem of injuries in youth sports. This event promotes safety in sports activities and is supported by more than 60 national sports and medical organizations.

PET FIRST AID AWARENESS MONTH. Apr 1–30. Sponsored by Pet Tech, Inc, the first international training center for pet CPR, first aid and care. To help pet owners everywhere in understanding the importance of knowing the skills and techniques of CPR and first aid and care for their pets. For info: Pet Tech, Inc, PO Box 2285, Carlsbad, CA 92018. Phone: (760) 930-0309. E-mail: PFAAM@PetTech.net. Web: www.PetTech.net.

PHARMACISTS' WAR ON DIABETES. Apr 1–30. To educate consumers, patients and health care professionals about prevention of diabetes, especially focusing on "Know Your Numbers for Diabetes" and screening along with awareness and interest in the diabetes epidemic. For info: Fred S. Mayer, RPh, MPH, Pharmacists Planning Service, Inc (PPSI), c/o the Pharmacy Council on Diabetes Education (PCDE), PO Box 6760, San Rafael, CA 94903. Phone: (415) 479-8628 or (415) 302-7351. E-mail: ppsi@aol.com. Web: www.ppsinc.org.

PREVENTION OF ANIMAL CRUELTY MONTH. Apr 1–30. Sponsored by the ASPCA, this crucial month is designed to educate Americans about animal cruelty and to urge them to report instances of violence toward animals. For info: Media & Communications Dept, ASPCA, 520 8th Ave, 7th Fl, New York, NY 10018. Phone: (212) 876-7700, ext 4655. E-mail: press@aspca.org. Web: www.aspca.org.

RAM, JAGJIVAN: BIRTH ANNIVERSARY. Apr 1, 1908. Indian political leader and coworker with Mohandas K. Gandhi and Jawaharlal Nehru in the fight for Indian independence. Born into a family of "untouchables" at the village of Chandwa, Bihar, India, Ram was one of the first of that class to attend school and university. Known as the champion and spokesman for India's 100 million untouchables, he overcame most of the handicaps of caste. He served in a number of ministerial cabinet posts and twice was a candidate for prime minister. Ram died at New Delhi, India, July 6, 1986.

READING IS FUNNY DAY. Apr 1. April Fools' Day is a great time to share riddles with children. Besides showing them that reading can be both fun and funny, riddles improve vocabulary, comprehension and oral reading; enhance deductive and inductive thinking skills; and develop a sense of humor. See the website for ideas of how to celebrate! For info: Dee Anderson, Reading Is Funny Day, 1023 25th St, Apt 1, Moline, IL 61265. Phone: (309) 793-5975. E-mail: hm38th@hotmail.com. Web: www.ala.org/editions/extras/Anderson09577.

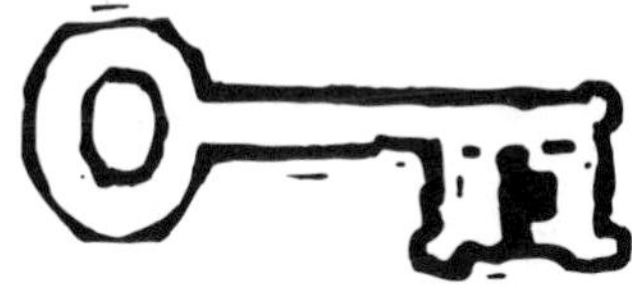

ROBERT THE HERMIT: DEATH ANNIVERSARY. Apr 1, 1832. One of the most famous hermits in American history died in his hermitage at Seekonk, MA. Robert was a bonded slave, the son of an African mother and probably an Anglo-Saxon father. After obtaining his freedom, he was swindled out of it and shipped to a foreign slave market, then later escaped to America. He was separated from his first wife by force and rejected by his second wife after a long sea voyage, before withdrawing from society.

ROSACEA AWARENESS MONTH. Apr 1–30. Rosacea Awareness Month has been designated by the National Rosacea Society to raise awareness and understanding of this increasingly common disease. Rosacea is a facial skin condition that can cause permanent physical and psychological damage if it is not diagnosed and treated. For info: Natl Rosacea Society, 196 James St, Barrington, IL 60010. Phone: (847) 382-8971 or (888) NO-BLUSH. Fax: (847) 382-5567. E-mail: rosaceas@aol.com. Web: www.rosacea.org.

SCHOOL LIBRARY MONTH. Apr 1–30. Celebrates the work of school librarians in our nation's elementary and secondary schools. For info: American Assn of School Librarians, American Library Assn, 50 E Huron St, Chicago, IL 60611. Phone: (800) 545-2433, ext 4382. E-mail: aasl@ala.org. Web: www.ala.org/aasl.

SKAGIT VALLEY TULIP FESTIVAL. Apr 1–30. Skagit County, La Conner, Mount Vernon and Burlington, WA. To celebrate and share the spectacular beauty of more than 1,000 acres of blooming daffodils and tulips that herald the arrival of spring in the Skagit Valley of Washington State. Est attendance: 350,000. For info: Cindy Verge, SVTF Exec Dir, PO Box 1784, Mount Vernon, WA 98273. Phone: (360) 428-5959. Fax: (360) 428-6753. E-mail: info@tulipfestival.org. Web: www.tulipfestival.org.

SORRY CHARLIE DAY. Apr 1. To honor Charlie the Tuna, who has been rejected for decades and still keeps his spunk. A day to recognize anyone who has been rejected and lived through it. Join the "Sorry Charlie, No-Fan-Club-for-You Club" by sending in your best rejection story. Please send SASE with inquiries. For info: Cathy Runyan-Svacina, 7812 NW Hampton Rd, Kansas City, MO 64152. Phone: (816) 520-9919. Fax: (816) 587-8687. Web: www.themarblelady.com.

STRAW HAT MONTH. Apr 1–30. A month of celebration during which the felt hat is put aside in favor of the straw or fabric hat by both men and women. Local businesses and the media are encouraged to plan hat-related activities. Widely observed in the fashion industry. Originally sponsored by the Headwear Information Bureau.

STRESS AWARENESS MONTH. Apr 1–30. To promote public awareness of what stress is, what causes it to occur and what can be done about it. A monthlong focus on the dangers of stress, successful coping strategies and the myths about stress that are prevalent in our society. For info: Morton C. Orman, MD, Dir, The Health Resource Network, 908 Cold Bottom Rd, Sparks, MD 21152. Web: www.stressawarenessmonth.com.

TESTICULAR CANCER AWARENESS WEEK. Apr 1–7. This public awareness and education program was conceived in 1997 to create a better public understanding of the dangers of undetected testicular cancer in young men aged 15–34. The campaign is designed to promote the importance of early detection, which saves hundreds of young men's lives each year. Make a monthly self-exam a habit for health. Information is made available to high school and college health centers to ensure correct diagnosis. For info: Gordon Clay, PO Box 12-CH, Brookings, OR 97415-0001. Web: www.tcaw.org.

April 2014	S	M	T	W	T	F	S
			1	2	3	4	5
	6	7	8	9	10	11	12
	13	14	15	16	17	18	19
	20	21	22	23	24	25	26
	27	28	29	30			

US AIR FORCE ACADEMY ESTABLISHED: 60th ANNIVERSARY. Apr 1, 1954. President Dwight Eisenhower signed the bill this day that created the US Air Force Academy to train officers for the US Air Force. Construction on the Colorado Springs, CO, academy began July 11, 1955, and ended in 1958. The academy was accredited in 1959. Women were admitted in 1976. For info: www.usafa.edu.

US HOUSE OF REPRESENTATIVES ACHIEVES A QUORUM: 225th ANNIVERSARY. Apr 1, 1789. First session of Congress was held Mar 4, 1789, but not enough representatives arrived to achieve a quorum until Apr 1.

WOMEN'S EYE HEALTH AND SAFETY MONTH. Apr 1–30. Women often manage family health concerns. Do you know how to protect your sight? Hormonal changes, age and smoking can endanger sight. Information on women's and family eye-health issues will be provided. For info: Prevent Blindness America®, 211 W Wacker Dr, Ste 1700, Chicago, IL 60606. Phone: (800) 331-2020. E-mail: info@preventblindness.org. Web: www.preventblindness.org.

WORKPLACE CONFLICT AWARENESS MONTH. Apr 1–30. At today's harried pace, workplace conflict is increasing. Many of us try to avoid this conflict, but instead we take it home with us. This month was created to make people aware that trying to avoid conflict is futile; we must learn to deal with it and manage it. For info: Richard Brenner, Chaco Canyon Consulting, 700 Huron Ave, Ste 11J, Cambridge, MA 02138. Phone: (617) 491-6289. Fax: (617) 395-2628. E-mail: rbrenner@ChacoCanyon.com.

WORLD HABITAT AWARENESS MONTH. Apr 1–30. A worldwide observance in recognition of the need to protect the habitat of all Earth's creatures, to make a conscious effort to preserve nature's ecosystems. Annually, the entire month of April. For info: PALS Foundation, PO Box 3631, San Luis Obispo, CA 93403. Phone: (805) 544-0984. Web: www.PALS.R8.org.

WORLDWIDE BEREAVED SPOUSES AWARENESS MONTH. Apr 1–30. A month to promote support for bereaved spouses. Often people don't know what to say to or do for grieving spouses. So sometimes they turn away and do nothing. We encourage people to turn back and begin to reach out to bereaved spouses by listening to them without advising them; offering a shoulder to cry on; and hugging them when appropriate and needed. Remember to reach out to the bereaved so they won't have to grieve alone! For info: Peter and Deb Kulkkula, Coordinators, Bereavement Awareness, 381 Billings Rd, Fitchburg, MA 01420-1407. Phone: (978) 343-4009. E-mail: help@bereavementawareness.com. Web: www.bereavementawareness.com.

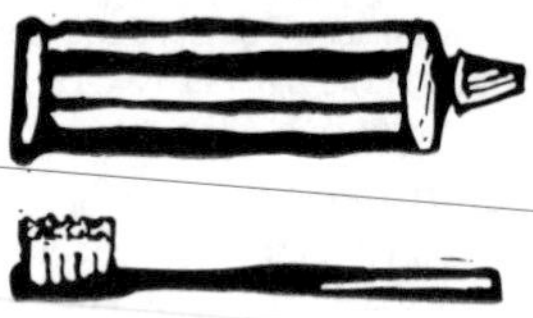

BIRTHDAYS TODAY

Samuel A. Alito, Jr, 64, Associate Justice of the US, born Trenton, NJ, Apr 1, 1950.

Asa Butterfield, 17, actor (*Hugo, The Boy in the Striped Pajamas*), born Islington, London, England, Apr 1, 1997.

David Eisenhower, 67, author (*Eisenhower at War*), lawyer, born West Point, NY, Apr 1, 1947.

Jon Gosselin, 37, television personality ("Jon & Kate Plus 8"), born Wyomissing, PA, Apr 1, 1977.

Ali MacGraw, 75, actress (*Goodbye, Columbus*; *Love Story*), born Pound Ridge, NY, Apr 1, 1939.

Rachel Maddow, 41, political commentator, born Castro Valley, CA, Apr 1, 1973.

Dan Mintz, 33, actor, writer ("Bob's Burgers," "Crank Yankers"), born Anchorage, AK, Apr 1, 1981.

Randy Orton, 34, professional wrestler, born Knoxville, TN, Apr 1, 1980.

Annette O'Toole, 61, actress (*Smile, 48 Hrs*), born Houston, TX, Apr 1, 1953.

Jane Powell, 85, actress (*Seven Brides for Seven Brothers*), born Suzanne Burce at Portland, OR, Apr 1, 1929.

Debbie Reynolds, 82, actress (*Singin' in the Rain, Mother*), born El Paso, TX, Apr 1, 1932.

Libby Riddles, 58, first woman to win the 1,135-mile Iditarod Alaskan dogsled race, born Madison, WI, Apr 1, 1956.

Daniel Joseph "Rusty" Staub, 70, former baseball player, born New Orleans, LA, Apr 1, 1944.

April 2 — Wednesday

DAY 92 **273 REMAINING**

ANDERSEN, HANS CHRISTIAN: BIRTH ANNIVERSARY. Apr 2, 1805. Author chiefly remembered for his more than 150 fairy tales, many of which are regarded as classics of children's literature. Andersen was born at Odense, Denmark, and died at Copenhagen, Denmark, Aug 4, 1875.

ARGENTINA: MALVINAS DAY. Apr 2. Public holiday. Full name is Day of the War Veterans and the Fallen in the Malvinas Islands. Commemorates the Argentine dead and wounded as a result of the attempt to regain the Falkland Islands in 1982. Observed since 2001.

"AS THE WORLD TURNS" TV PREMIERE: ANNIVERSARY. Apr 2, 1956. One of the longest-running soaps to air on television, "ATWT" premiered on CBS. The series was set in midwestern Oakdale and revolved around the Hughes family and their neighbors. Irma Phillips was the show's creator and head writer. Some of its famous former cast members were Meg Ryan, Julianne Moore, Steven Weber and Swoosie Kurtz. The final episode aired on Sept 17, 2010.

BARTHOLDI, FREDERIC AUGUSTE: BIRTH ANNIVERSARY. Apr 2, 1834. French sculptor who created *Liberty Enlightening the World* (better known as the Statue of Liberty), which stands at New York Harbor. Also remembered for the *Lion of Belfort* at Belfort, France. Born at Colman, at Alsace, France. Died at Paris, Oct 4, 1904.

CASANOVA, GIOVANNI GIACOMO GIROLAMO: BIRTH ANNIVERSARY. Apr 2, 1725. Celebrated Italian writer-librarian and, by his own account, philanderer, adventurer, rogue, seminarian, soldier and spy, born at Venice, Italy. As the Chevalier de Seingalt, he died at Dux, Bohemia, June 4, 1798, while serving as librarian and working on his lively and frank *History of My Life*, a brilliant picture of 18th-century life.

"DALLAS" TV PREMIERE: ANNIVERSARY. Apr 2, 1978. Oil tycoons battled for money, power and prestige in this prime-time CBS drama that ran for nearly 13 years. The Ewings and Barneses were Texas's modern-day Hatfields and McCoys. Larry Hagman starred as the devious, scheming womanizer J.R. Ewing. When J.R. was shot in the 1980 season-ending cliffhanger, the revelation of the mystery shooter was the single most-watched episode of its time (it was Kristin, J.R.'s sister-in-law, played by Mary Crosby). Cast members included Jim Davis, Barbara Bel Geddes, Donna Reed, Ted Shackelford, Joan Van Ark, Patrick Duffy, Linda Gray, Charlene Tilton, David Wayne, Keenan Wynn, Ken Kercheval, Victoria Principal and Steve Kanaly. A spin-off show was "Knots Landing." "Dallas" was revived in 2012 with many of the original cast as well as a new generation of troublemakers.

EBSEN, BUDDY: BIRTH ANNIVERSARY. Apr 2, 1908. Born Christian Rudolph Ebsen, Jr, at Belleville, IL. Buddy Ebsen started his career as a vaudeville "song-and-dance" man, then was popular throughout the 1930s on film as well. He almost played the Tin Man in *The Wizard of Oz* (1939) but had a serious allergic reaction to the makeup and was forced to stop filming. In the 1950s, he played Davy Crockett's sidekick on television and in film. He played Jed Clampett in "The Beverly Hillbillies" (1962–71) and starred as "Barnaby Jones" (1973–80). He died at Torrance, CA, July 6, 2003.

"THE EDGE OF NIGHT" TV PREMIERE: ANNIVERSARY. Apr 2, 1956. "The Edge of Night" premiered on CBS along with "As the World Turns." Though the plots initially revolved around crime and courtroom drama, the serial's format soon developed along more conventional soap story lines of romance. The soap shifted to ABC in 1975 but was canceled in 1984. Larry Hagman, Dixie Carter, Lori Loughlin, Willie Aames and Amanda Blake were some of the show's most prominent players.

FALKLAND ISLANDS WAR: ANNIVERSARY. Apr 2–June 15, 1982. Argentina, claiming sovereignty over the nearby Falkland Islands (called the Malvinas by Argentina), invaded and occupied the British Crown colony on Apr 2, 1982. British forces defeated the Argentinians on June 15, 1982. About 250 British and 600 Argentine lives were lost in the conflict. In 1986 three military officers, including General Leopoldo Galtieri (who was president of Argentina at the time of the invasion), were convicted and sentenced for the military crime of negligence. Commemorative ceremonies are observed as Malvinas Day in Argentina.

FIRST WHITE HOUSE EASTER EGG ROLL: ANNIVERSARY. Apr 2, 1877. The first White House Easter Egg Roll took place during the administration of Rutherford B. Hayes. The traditional event was discontinued by President Franklin D. Roosevelt in 1942 and reinstated Apr 6, 1953, by President Dwight D. Eisenhower.

GUINNESS, SIR ALEC: 100th BIRTH ANNIVERSARY. Apr 2, 1914. One of Britain's greatest stage and screen actors, born at London, England. He received an Academy Award for his performance in *The Bridge on the River Kwai* (1957). Other important films include the *Star Wars* initial trilogy, *Great Expectations, Oliver Twist, The Ladykillers, Kind Hearts and Coronets* and *A Passage to India.* Knighted in 1959, he died at West Sussex, England, Aug 5, 2000.

INTERNATIONAL CHILDREN'S BOOK DAY. Apr 2. Observes Hans Christian Andersen's birthday and commemorates the international aspects of children's literature. Sponsor: Intl Board on Books for Young People, Nonnenweg 12, Postfach, CH-4003 Basel, Switzerland. Web: www.ibby.org. For info: USBBY, National Louis University, 5202 Old Orchard Rd, Ste 300, Skokie, IL 60077. Phone: (224) 233-2030. E-mail: secretariat@usbby.org. Web: www.usbby.org/icbd.html.

NATIONAL DAY OF HOPE. Apr 2. During National Child Abuse Prevention Month, this day asks all Americans to keep victims of abuse and neglect in their thoughts and prayers, to seek to break the cycle of child abuse and neglect, and to give victimized children hope for the future. This is also a day when the faith community, nonprofit organizations and volunteers across America should recommit themselves and mobilize their resources to assist abused and neglected children. Observed since 2000. Annually, the first Wednesday in April. For info: Natl Day of Hope, Childhelp, 15757 N 78th St, Scottsdale, AZ 85260. Phone: (480) 922-8212. Fax: (480) 922-7061. Web: www.childhelp.org.

NATIONAL FERRET DAY. Apr 2. A day to educate the public to respect this lively and intelligent companion animal—the domesticated ferret. This day is also a time to focus on such ferret issues as welfare, care, nutrition and responsible ownership. Annually, Apr 2 (in the United States). For info: American Ferret Association, PO Box 554, Frederick, MD 21705-0554. Phone: (888) FER-

RET-1. Fax: (240) 358-0673. E-mail: afa@ferret.org. Web: www.ferret.org/nationalferretday.

NATIONAL LOVE YOUR PRODUCE MANAGER DAY. Apr 2. A day honoring the exemplary customer service in US supermarket produce departments. Frieda's encourages supermarket executives to recognize their produce staff and shoppers to say "hello" to their local produce managers. The supermarket produce manager plays a key role in making a variety of unique fruits and veggies available to US consumers. In 1962, a produce manager was instrumental to the introduction of kiwifruit to America, when he fulfilled a customer's request using Frieda's. Frieda's launched the first appreciation day in 2012. Annually, Apr 2. For info: Frieda's, 4465 Corporate Center Dr, Los Alamitos, CA 90720. Phone: (714) 826-6100. Fax: (714) 816-0273. E-mail: news.bureau@friedas.com. Web: www.friedas.com/SchnucksLYPM.

NICKELODEON DEBUT: 35th ANNIVERSARY. Apr 2, 1979. Nickelodeon, the cable TV channel for kids owned by MTV Networks, debuted on this date.

PARAPROFESSIONAL APPRECIATION DAY. Apr 2. This holiday honors the contributions of paraprofessionals, especially in education. Annually, the first Wednesday in April. For info: Valerie Pennington, Upper Elementary School, 1100 Cox School Rd, Odessa, MO 64076. Phone: (816) 633-5396. E-mail: vpennington@odessa.k12.mo.us.

PASCUA FLORIDA DAY. Apr 2. A legal holiday in Florida, designated as State Day. When it falls on a Saturday or Sunday, the governor may declare either the preceding Friday or the following Monday as State Day. Florida also observes Pascua Florida Week during Mar 27–Apr 2. Commemorates the sighting of Florida by Ponce de Leon in 1513. He named the land Pascua Florida because of its discovery at Easter, the "Feast of the Flowers."

PONCE DE LEON DISCOVERS FLORIDA: ANNIVERSARY. Apr 2, 1513. Juan Ponce de Leon discovered Florida, landing at the site that became the city of St. Augustine. He claimed the land for the king of Spain.

POPE JOHN PAUL II: DEATH ANNIVERSARY. Apr 2, 2005. Karol Wojtyla, 264th pope of the Roman Catholic Church, elected Oct 16, 1978, died at Vatican City.

RECONCILIATION DAY. Apr 2. Columnist Ann Landers wrote, "Since 1989, I have suggested that April 2 be set aside to write that letter or make that phone call and mend a broken relationship. Life is too short to hold grudges. To forgive can be enormously life-enhancing."

***2001: A SPACE ODYSSEY* PREMIERE: ANNIVERSARY.** Apr 2, 1968. Directed by Stanley Kubrick, this influential film has elicited many different interpretations. Sci-fi novelist Arthur C. Clarke based the screenplay on his 1968 book, which was prescient in several ways. Writing before men had landed on the moon, Clarke describes an expedition launched to Jupiter to track a mysterious signal emanating from the moon. Clarke gave the world's population as six billion (achieved in 1999) and described a space station. During flight, a character reads the news on his electronic news pad. The film starred Keir Dullea, William Sylvester, Gary Lockwood, Daniel Richter and HAL 9000, the creepy computer that had human emotions. The theme music was Richard Strauss's *Also Sprach Zarathustra*.

UNITED NATIONS: WORLD AUTISM AWARENESS DAY. Apr 2. Deeply concerned by the prevalence and high rate of autism in children in all regions of the world, the General Assembly designated Apr 2 as World Autism Awareness Day on Dec 18, 2007 (Resolution 62/139). Autism affects children in all regions, irrespective of gender, race or socioeconomic status. It poses challenges to long-term health care, education, training and intervention programs, and it has a tremendous impact on children, families, communities and societies. For info: United Nations, Dept of Public Info, New York, NY, 10017. Web: www.un.org.

US MINT: ANNIVERSARY. Apr 2, 1792. The first US Mint was established at Philadelphia, PA, as authorized by an act of Congress.

WHITE, CHARLES: BIRTH ANNIVERSARY. Apr 2, 1918. Renowned African-American artist, born at Chicago, IL; died Oct 3, 1979. Charles White began his professional career by painting murals for the WPA during the Depression. He was influenced by Mexican muralists Diego Rivera and David Alfaro Siqueiros. Among his most notable creations are *J'Accuse* (1966), a series of charcoal drawings depicting a variety of African Americans from all ages and walks of life; the *Wanted* posters (c. 1969), a series of paintings based on old runaway slave posters and *Homage to Langston Hughes* (1971).

WHOLE GRAIN SAMPLING DAY. Apr 2. Whole grains are certainly healthy—but some people may not realize how delicious they can be. On Whole Grain Sampling Day, you'll find opportunities to try delicious whole grains everywhere you go. Supermarkets, restaurants and schools will be offering special tastes of whole grains, and you'll find special deals on social media. It's all coordinated by the nonprofit Oldways and its Whole Grains Council, with creative and original events across the US. Annually, the first Wednesday in April. For info: Oldways, 266 Beacon St, Boston, MA 02116. Phone: (617) 421-5500. E-mail: rachel@oldwayspt.org. Web: www.oldwayspt.org or www.wholegrainscouncil.org.

ZOLA, ÉMILE: BIRTH ANNIVERSARY. Apr 2, 1840. Prolific French novelist of the naturalist school, remembered especially for his role in the Dreyfus case (resulting in retrial and vindication of Alfred Dreyfus). Émile Edouard Charles Antoine Zola was born at Paris, France. Defective venting of a stove flue in his bedroom (which some believed to be the work of political enemies) resulted in his death from carbon monoxide poisoning at Paris, Sept 28, 1902.

BIRTHDAYS TODAY

Michael Fassbender, 37, actor (*Prometheus, X-Men: First Class, Jane Eyre*), born Heidelberg, Germany, Apr 2, 1977.

Emmylou Harris, 67, singer, born Birmingham, AL, Apr 2, 1947.

Linda Hunt, 69, actress ("NCIS: Los Angeles," "The Practice"; Oscar for *The Year of Living Dangerously*), born Morristown, NJ, Apr 2, 1945.

Bethany Joy Lenz, 33, actress, musician ("One Tree Hill," "Guiding Light"), born Hollywood, FL, Apr 2, 1981.

Christopher Meloni, 53, actor ("True Blood," "Law & Order: SVU," "Oz"), born Washington, DC, Apr 2, 1961.

Camille Paglia, 67, literature professor and literary and cultural critic, born Endicott, NY, Apr 2, 1947.

Pamela Reed, 61, actress (*The Right Stuff, Bob Roberts*), born Tacoma, WA, Apr 2, 1953 (some sources say 1949).

Leon Russell, 73, musician, born Lawton, OK, Apr 2, 1941.

April 2014	S	M	T	W	T	F	S
			1	2	3	4	5
	6	7	8	9	10	11	12
	13	14	15	16	17	18	19
	20	21	22	23	24	25	26
	27	28	29	30			

April 3 — Thursday

DAY 93 **272 REMAINING**

BIRMINGHAM RESISTANCE: ANNIVERSARY. Apr 3, 1962. In retaliation against a black boycott of downtown stores, the Birmingham, AL, city commission voted not to pay the city's $45,000 share of a $100,000 county program that supplied surplus food to the needy. More than 90 percent of the recipients of aid were black. When the NAACP protested the commission's decision, Birmingham mayor Arthur J. Hanes dismissed the complaint as a "typical reaction from New York Socialist radicals."

BLACKS RULED ELIGIBLE TO VOTE: 70th ANNIVERSARY. Apr 3, 1944. The US Supreme Court, in an 8–1 ruling, declared that blacks could not be barred from voting in the Texas Democratic primaries. The high court repudiated the contention that political parties are private associations and held that discrimination against blacks violated the 15th Amendment.

BOSTON PUBLIC LIBRARY: ANNIVERSARY. Apr 3, 1848. The Massachusetts legislature passed legislation enabling Boston to levy a tax for a public library. This created the funding model for all public libraries in the US. The Boston Public Library opened its doors in 1854.

BRANDO, MARLON: 90th BIRTH ANNIVERSARY. Apr 3, 1924. Born at Omaha, NE, Marlon Brando was perhaps the most influential film actor of his generation. Using the Method style of acting as taught by Stella Adler, his powerful performances in *A Streetcar Named Desire* (1951) and *Viva Zapata!* (1952) established his presence as a star, and *On the Waterfront* (1953) earned him an Academy Award. Later films included *Last Tango in Paris* (1972) and *Apocalypse Now* (1979), but he is perhaps best remembered for his role as Vito Corleone from *The Godfather* (1972), for which he won his second Oscar. Somewhat of a recluse later in his life, he died July 1, 2004, at Los Angeles, CA.

BURROUGHS, JOHN: BIRTH ANNIVERSARY. Apr 3, 1837. American naturalist and author, born at Roxbury, NY. "Time does not become sacred to us until we have lived it," he wrote in 1877. Died en route from California to New York, Mar 29, 1921.

ENGLAND: GRAND NATIONAL. Apr 3–5. Aintree Racecourse, Liverpool. Often called the world's greatest steeplechase, the John Smith's Grand National is one of the most famous steeplechases in the world. It is a unique test of horsemanship for the rider and also a test of great significance for a horse. The course is nearly two and a quarter miles in length and has 16 unique fences. First held in 1839. For info: Grand National, Aintree Racecourse, Ormskirk Rd, Aintree, Liverpool L9 5AS, England. Web: www.aintree.co.uk.

FALL OF RICHMOND: ANNIVERSARY. Apr 3, 1865. After the withdrawal of Robert E. Lee's troops, the Confederate capital of Richmond and nearby Petersburg surrendered to Union forces on this day. Richmond had survived four years of continuous threats from the North. On Apr 4, the city was toured by President Abraham Lincoln.

GRAHAM, CALVIN "BABY VET": BIRTH ANNIVERSARY. Apr 3, 1930. The man who became known as WWII's "baby vet," Calvin Graham was born at Canton, TX, and enlisted in the navy at the age of 12. As a gunner on the USS *South Dakota*, he was struck by shrapnel during the battle of Guadalcanal in 1942 but still helped pull fellow crew members to safety. The navy gave Graham a dishonorable discharge, revoked his disability benefits and stripped him of his decorations, including a Purple Heart and Bronze Star, after discovering his age. Eventually, through congressional efforts, he was granted an honorable discharge and won back all but the Purple Heart. His benefits were restored in 1988. Graham died Nov 6, 1992, at Fort Worth, TX.

GUINEA: ANNIVERSARY OF THE SECOND REPUBLIC. Apr 3. National holiday. Commemorates the establishment of the Second Republic in 1984.

HOWARD, LESLIE: BIRTH ANNIVERSARY. Apr 3, 1893. Romantic actor of Hollywood's Golden Age who became a casualty of WWII. During the return trip from a British government–sponsored tour of Spain, a plane transporting Leslie Howard was shot down by German raiders. Howard's most-remembered film role is that of Ashley Wilkes in *Gone with the Wind*. Born at London, England; died at sea June 1, 1943.

INAUGURATION OF PONY EXPRESS: ANNIVERSARY. Apr 3, 1860. The Pony Express began when the first rider left St. Joseph, MO, heading west. The following day another rider headed east from Sacramento, CA. For $5 an ounce, letters were delivered within 10 days. There were 190 way stations between 10 and 15 miles apart, and each rider had a "run" of between 75 and 100 miles. The Pony Express lasted less than two years, ceasing operation in October 1861, when the overland telegraph was completed.

IRVING, WASHINGTON: BIRTH ANNIVERSARY. Apr 3, 1783. American author, attorney and onetime US minister to Spain, Irving was born at New York, NY. Creator of *Rip van Winkle* and *The Legend of Sleepy Hollow*, he was also the author of many historical and biographical works, including *A History of the Life and Voyages of Christopher Columbus* and the *Life of Washington*. Died at Tarrytown, NY, Nov 28, 1859.

ISLE ROYALE NATIONAL PARK ESTABLISHED: ANNIVERSARY. Apr 3, 1940. Isle Royale is the largest of a group of more than 200 islands that make up this national park preserve. To preserve upper Michigan's flora and fauna, Congress authorized a national park in 1931 and it was established in 1940.

LUCE, HENRY: BIRTH ANNIVERSARY. Apr 3, 1898. American editor and publisher, born to missionary parents at Penglai, China. He built his publishing empire with *Time, Fortune, Life* and *Sports Illustrated*. Luce also was involved in broadcasting. Died at Phoenix, AZ, Feb 28, 1967.

MARSHALL PLAN: ANNIVERSARY. Apr 3, 1948. Suggested by Secretary of State George C. Marshall in a speech at Harvard, June 5, 1947, the legislation for the European Recovery Program, popularly known as the Marshall Plan, was signed by President Truman on Apr 3, 1948. After distributing more than $12 billion, the program ended in 1952.

MIAEYC EARLY CHILDHOOD CONFERENCE. Apr 3–5. Amway Grand Plaza Hotel and DeVos Place, Grand Rapids, MI. This three-day conference sponsored by the Michigan Association for the Education of the Young Child (MiAEYC) focuses on issues affecting children from birth to age eight. Invited are educators, students, advocates and parents; participants can attend one, two or all three days. Each day includes a keynote address, two full-day focus sessions and 75+ workshops. For info: MiAEYC, 839 Centennial Way, Ste 200, Lansing, MI 48917-9277. Phone: (800) 336-6424. Fax: (517) 351-0157. E-mail: MiAEYC@MiAEYC.org. Web: www.MiAEYC.org.

MULE DAY. Apr 3–6. Columbia, TN. Started in 1934 as Breeders Day when mules were brought into town to be sold and traded. Today this homecoming is celebrated with arts and crafts, a flea market, a knife show, a huge parade and several mule shows. Est attendance: 40,000. For info: Mule Day, PO Box 66, Columbia, TN 38402. Phone: (931) 381-9557. E-mail: info@muleday.com. Web: www.muleday.com.

RAND, SALLY: BIRTH ANNIVERSARY. Apr 3, 1904. American actress, ecdysiast and inventor of the fan dance, which gained fame at the 1933 Chicago World's Fair. Born Helen Gould Beck at Hickory County, MO. Died at Glendora, CA, Aug 31, 1979.

SWITZERLAND: NAFELS PILGRIMAGE. Apr 3. Canton Glarus. Commemoration of the Battle of Nafels, fought on Apr 9, 1388. Observed annually on first Thursday in April, with processions, prayers, sermon and a reading out of the names of those killed in the battle.

TWEED DAY: BIRTH ANNIVERSARY OF WILLIAM TWEED. Apr 3, 1823. Day to consider the cost of political corruption. Birthday of William March Tweed, New York City political boss, whose "Tweed Ring" is said to have stolen $30 million to $200 million from the city. Born at New York, NY, Apr 3, 1823, he died in his cell at New York's Ludlow Street Jail, Apr 12, 1878. Cartoonist Thomas Nast deserves much credit for Tweed's arrests and convictions.

WEED OUT HATE: SOW THE SEEDS OF PEACE DAY. Apr 3. Decades after Dr. Martin Luther King, Jr, gave his prophetic "I've Been to the Mountaintop" speech on Apr 3, 1968, much of his "Promised Land" vision has come to fruition. Unfortunately, there are still persistent weed seeds of hate that remain embedded in our society. Just as weeds compete for nutrients and water that cultivated garden plants require, our inner weed seeds—the germs of hate—prevent our children from experiencing the deepest root-connections to nature. Removing weeds from our yards and gardens can serve as a paradigm for eradicating the inner bullying instincts that many of our children harbor and too often suppress. Freed from this negativity, spirits will bloom, enabling children everywhere to sow the seeds of peace. Planting sunflowers on this day is a marvelous symbolic gesture for participating in the completion of Dr. King's great dream. For info: Marc Daniels, Weed Out Hate, 4001 Lavender Ln, Springfield, IL 62711. Phone: (217) 726-5938. Fax: (217) 726-5953. E-mail: marc@weedouthate.org. Web: www.weedouthate.org.

WOMAN PRESIDES OVER US SUPREME COURT: ANNIVERSARY. Apr 3, 1995. Supreme Court Justice Sandra Day O'Connor became the first woman to preside over the US high court when she sat in for Chief Justice William H. Rehnquist and second-in-seniority Justice John Paul Stevens when both were out of town.

BIRTHDAYS TODAY

Alec Baldwin, 56, actor ("30 Rock," *The Cooler, The Hunt for Red October*), born Massapequa, NY, Apr 3, 1958.

Jamie Bamber, 41, actor ("Battlestar Galactica"), born Hammersmith, London, England, Apr 3, 1973.

Amanda Bynes, 28, actress (*Big Fat Liar*, "What I Like About You"), born Thousand Oaks, CA, Apr 3, 1986.

Doris Day, 90, singer, actress ("Young at Heart," *The Man Who Knew Too Much, Pillow Talk*, "The Doris Day Show"), born Doris Von Kappelhoff at Cincinnati, OH, Apr 3, 1924.

Max Frankel, 84, journalist, born Gera, Germany, Apr 3, 1930.

Jennie Garth, 42, actress ("Beverly Hills 90210"), born Champaign, IL, Apr 3, 1972.

Jane Goodall (Baroness Van Lawick-Goodall), 80, anthropologist known for study of chimpanzees, born London, England, Apr 3, 1934.

Leona Lewis, 29, singer, born Islington, London, England, Apr 3, 1985.

Jonathan Lynn, 71, writer, actor, director (*Into the Night, Nuns on the Run, My Cousin Vinny*), born Bath, England, Apr 3, 1943.

Marsha Mason, 72, actress (*The Goodbye Girl, Cinderella Liberty*), born St. Louis, MO, Apr 3, 1942.

Eddie Murphy, 53, comedian ("Saturday Night Live"), actor (*Dreamgirls, Trading Places, Beverly Hills Cop*), born Brooklyn, NY, Apr 3, 1961.

Wayne Newton, 72, singer, born Norfolk, VA, Apr 3, 1942.

Tony Orlando, 70, singer (Tony Orlando and Dawn), born Michael Orlando Cassivitis at New York, NY, Apr 3, 1944.

April 2014

S	M	T	W	T	F	S
		1	2	3	4	5
6	7	8	9	10	11	12
13	14	15	16	17	18	19
20	21	22	23	24	25	26
27	28	29	30			

Bernie Parent, 69, Hall of Fame hockey player, born Montreal, QC, Canada, Apr 3, 1945.

David Hyde Pierce, 55, actor (Tony for *Curtains*; Emmys for "Frasier"), born Albany, NY, Apr 3, 1959.

Adam Scott, 41, actor ("Party Down," "Parks and Recreation"), born Santa Cruz, CA, Apr 3, 1973.

Cobie Smulders, 32, actress ("How I Met Your Mother," "The L Word"), born Vancouver, BC, Canada, Apr 3, 1982.

Picabo Street, 43, Olympic skier, born Triumph, ID, Apr 3, 1971.

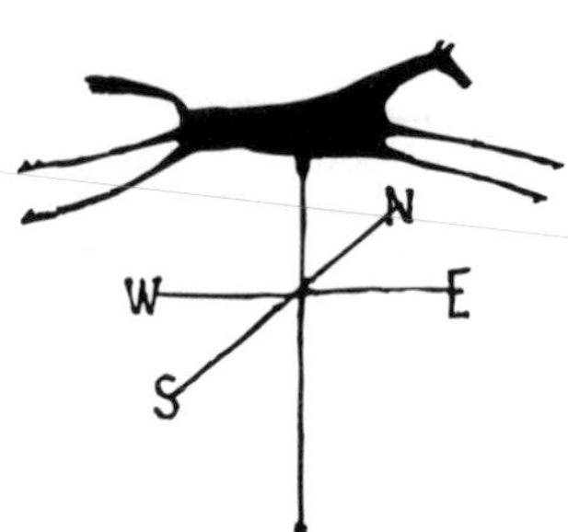

April 4 — Friday

DAY 94 **271 REMAINING**

BEATLES TAKE OVER MUSIC CHARTS: 50th ANNIVERSARY. Apr 4, 1964. On this date the Beatles held the top five positions of the Billboard Hot 100 chart: "Can't Buy Me Love" was number one, followed by (in order) "Twist and Shout," "She Loves You," "I Want to Hold Your Hand" and "Please, Please Me." The Beatles had made their first US appearance barely two months before. In the same week, they held the top six places on the Australian music chart.

BONZA BOTTLER DAY™. Apr 4. To celebrate when the number of the day is the same as the number of the month. Bonza Bottler Day™ is an excuse to have a party at least once a month. For more information see Jan 1. For info: Gail Berger, 14 Fernwood Dr, Taylors, SC 29687. Phone: (864) 201-3988. E-mail: bonza@bonzabottlerday.com. Web: www.bonzabottlerday.com.

CRAFTSMEN'S SPRING CLASSIC ARTS & CRAFTS FESTIVAL. Apr 4–6. Greensboro Coliseum Complex Special Events Center, Greensboro, NC. 32nd annual. Features work from more than 275 talented artists and craftspeople. All juried exhibitors' work has been handmade by the exhibitors and must be their own original design and creation. See the creative process in action with several exhibitors demonstrating throughout the weekend. Est attendance: 25,000. For info: Gilmore Enterprises, Inc, 3514-A Drawbridge Pkwy, Greensboro, NC 27410. Phone: (336) 282-5550. E-mail: Contact@GilmoreShows.com. Web: www.CraftShow.com or www.gilmoreshows.com.

DIX, DOROTHEA LYNDE: BIRTH ANNIVERSARY. Apr 4, 1802. American social reformer and author, born at Hampden, ME. Left home at age 10, was teaching at age 14 and founded a home for girls at Boston, MA, while still in her teens. In spite of frail health, she was a vigorous crusader for humane conditions in insane asylums, jails and almshouses and for the establishment of state-supported institutions to serve those needs. Named superintendent of women nurses during the Civil War. Died at Trenton, NJ, July 17, 1887.

DURAS, MARGUERITE: 100th BIRTH ANNIVERSARY. Apr 4, 1914. Novelist, playwright, screenwriter and filmmaker Duras was one of France's most prolific, popular writers after WWII. Best-known works are her screenplay for *Hiroshima, Mon Amour* (1959) and her novel *The Lover* (1984). Duras said, "Even when my books are completely invented, even when I think they have come from elsewhere, they are always personal." Born Marguerite Donnadieu at Saigon, Vietnam, she died Mar 3, 1996, at Paris, France.

FLAG ACT OF 1818: ANNIVERSARY. Apr 4, 1818. Congress approved the first flag of the US.

GIAMATTI, ANGELO BARTLETT: BIRTH ANNIVERSARY. Apr 4, 1938. Baseball commissioner and former president of Yale University. Born at Boston, MA, Giamatti was the youngest person to be named president of Yale, at the age of 39, in 1978. He became the president of Major League Baseball's National League in 1986 and served in that capacity until he was appointed Commissioner of Baseball Apr 1, 1989. An accomplished author, he moved freely between the worlds of literature and baseball, often linking the two in the many articles he wrote. One week prior to his death, he suspended Pete Rose for life for betting on baseball games. Giamatti died at Martha's Vineyard, MA, Sept 1, 1989.

HATE WEEK. Apr 4–10. Recognizes the day on which the fictional character Winston Smith started his secret diary and wrote the words "DOWN WITH BIG BROTHER," Wednesday, Apr 4, 1984. From George Orwell's dystopian novel, *1984*, portraying the end of human privacy and the destruction of the individual in a totalitarian state (first published in 1949). "Hates" varied from the daily two-minute concentrated hate to the grand culmination observed during Hate Week.

KING, MARTIN LUTHER, JR: ASSASSINATION: ANNIVERSARY. Apr 4, 1968. The Reverend Dr. Martin Luther King, Jr, was shot at Memphis, TN. James Earl Ray was serving a 99-year sentence for the crime at the time of his death in 1998. See also: "King, Martin Luther, Jr: Birth Anniversary" (Jan 15).

***LADY BE GOOD* LOST: ANNIVERSARY.** Apr 4, 1943. The nine-man crew of the WWII American Liberator bomber *Lady Be Good* bailed out 200 miles off course over the Sahara Desert and disappeared. They were returning to their base in Libya after a raid over southern Italy. On Nov 9, 1958, 15 years after the plane went down and more than 13 years after the war had ended, a pilot flying across the Sahara south of Tobruck sighted wreckage of an aircraft in the sand. Eight skeletons and a diary describing the final days of the crew were recovered near the wreckage. The radio, guns and ammunition in the plane were in working order.

MEDIEVAL FAIR. Apr 4–6. Reaves Park, Norman, OK. Arts and crafts and living-history fair. The Middle Ages come alive with dancers, music, theater, jousting, knights in combat and a human chess match. Feasts and follies include games and food "fit for a king." Meet such characters as King Arthur, Sir Lancelot and Merlin. Admission is free. Est attendance: 325,000. For info: Ann Marie Eckart, 1700 Asp Ave, Room 222, Norman, OK 73072-6400. Phone: (405) 325-8610. Fax: (405) 325-0860. Web: www.medievalfair.org.

✦NATIONAL D.A.R.E. DAY. Apr 4. The Drug Abuse Resistance Education (D.A.R.E.) Program, founded in 1983 by the Los Angeles Police Department and the Los Angeles Unified School District, helps give children in grades K–12 the skills they need to avoid involvement in drugs, gangs and violence. Nearly 75 percent of American school districts offer D.A.R.E. training.

NATIONAL GEOGRAPHIC BEE, STATE LEVEL. Apr 4. Site is different in each state—many are in the state capital. Winners of school-level competitions who scored in the top 100 in their state on a written test compete in the State Geographic Bees. The winner of each state bee will go to Washington, DC, for the national level in May. For info: Natl Geographic Bee, Natl Geographic Society, 1145 17th St NW, Washington, DC 20036. Phone: (202) 828-6659. Web: www.nationalgeographic.com/geobee.

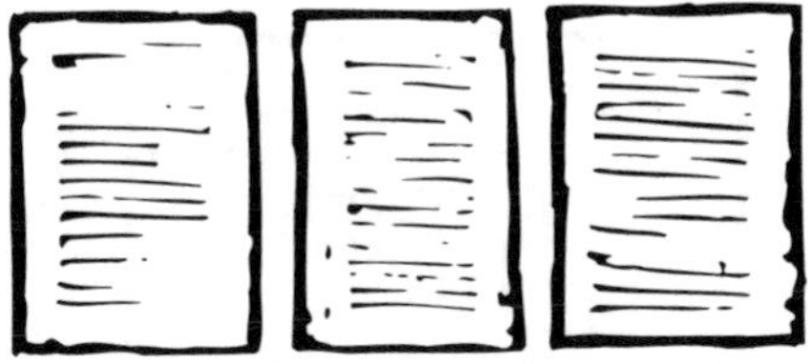

NORTH ATLANTIC TREATY RATIFIED: 65th ANNIVERSARY. Apr 4, 1949. The North Atlantic Treaty Organization was created by this treaty, which was signed by 12 nations, including the US. (Other countries joined later.) The NATO member nations are united for common defense. The treaty went into effect Apr 24, 1949, and the first session of the North Atlantic Council was held Sept 17, 1949.

PERKINS, ANTHONY: BIRTH ANNIVERSARY. Apr 4, 1932. American actor Anthony Perkins was born at New York, NY. Best known for his movie role as homicidal innkeeper Norman Bates in the film *Psycho* (1960), Perkins appeared in many Broadway plays in addition to his numerous film roles. He received an Oscar nomination for his supporting role in *Friendly Persuasion* (1956). Perkins died Sept 12, 1992, at Hollywood, CA.

POTEET STRAWBERRY FESTIVAL. Apr 4–6. Poteet, TX. One of the oldest and largest festivals in Texas, established to promote Poteet's crop—strawberries. Great food and family entertainment. Est attendance: 100,000. For info: Festival Coord, Poteet Strawberry Festival Assn, PO Box 227, Poteet, TX 78065. Phone: (830) 742-8144 or (888) 742-8144. Fax: (830) 742-3608. E-mail: annaskurka@sbcglobal.net. Web: www.strawberryfestival.com.

SALTER ELECTED FIRST WOMAN MAYOR IN US: ANNIVERSARY. Apr 4, 1887. The first woman elected mayor in the US was Susanna Medora Salter, who was elected mayor of Argonia, KS. Her name had been submitted for election without her knowledge by the Women's Christian Temperance Union, and she did not know she was a candidate until she went to the polls to vote. She received a two-thirds majority vote and served one year for the salary of $1.

SENEGAL: INDEPENDENCE DAY. Apr 4. National holiday. Commemorates independence from France in 1960.

SMOTHERS BROTHERS FIRED: 45th ANNIVERSARY. Apr 4, 1969. CBS canceled the brothers' popular comedy series on this date. The hour-long show strongly influenced television humor during the two years it aired. Tom and Dick, however, frequently found themselves at odds with the censors over material that would be considered tame today. Guests and cast members frequently knocked the Vietnam War and the Nixon Administration. Acts featuring antiwar protestors such as Harry Belafonte were often cut.

SPACE MILESTONE: *CHALLENGER STS-6* (US): ANNIVERSARY. Apr 4, 1983. Shuttle *Challenger* launched from Kennedy Space Center, FL, with four astronauts (Paul Weitz, Karol Bobko, Storey Musgrave and Donald Peterson). Four-hour space walk by Musgrave and Peterson. Landed at Edwards Air Force Base, CA, Apr 9.

SPEAKER, TRIS: BIRTH ANNIVERSARY. Apr 4, 1888. Tristram E. Speaker, Baseball Hall of Fame outfielder, was born at Hubbard City, TX. Known as "the Gray Eagle," Speaker was one of the greatest center fielders of all time. He started his career with the Boston Red Sox, where he was part of the Hooper-Speaker-Lewis outfield, and then achieved stardom in a second city, playing for the Cleveland Indians. Inducted into the Hall of Fame in 1937, he died at Lake Whitney, TX, Dec 8, 1958.

STUDENT GOVERNMENT DAY IN MASSACHUSETTS. Apr 4. Annually, the first Friday in April.

SUGARLOAF CRAFTS FESTIVAL. Apr 4–6. Montgomery County Fairgrounds, Gaithersburg, MD. This show, now in its 39th year, features more than 250 nationally recognized craft designers and fine artists displaying and selling their original creations. Craft demonstrations, live music, hourly gift certificate drawings, specialty foods and more! Est attendance: 15,000. For info: Sugarloaf Mountain Works, Inc, 19807 Executive Park Circle, Germantown, MD 20874. Phone: (800) 210-9900. Fax: (310) 253-9620. E-mail: sugarloafinfo@sugarloaffest.com. Web: www.sugarloafcrafts.com.

SWAYZE, JOHN CAMERON: BIRTH ANNIVERSARY. Apr 4, 1906. Pioneering television journalist whose catchphrase was "hopscotching the world for news." Swayze was one of the first reporters to do on-air interviews and report on breaking news stories. Born at Wichita, KS, he died at Sarasota, FL, Aug 15, 1995.

TAIWAN: CHILDREN'S DAY. Apr 4. Public holiday the day before Tomb-Sweeping Day. Reinstated holiday starting in 2011.

UNITED NATIONS: INTERNATIONAL DAY FOR MINE AWARENESS AND ASSISTANCE IN MINE ACTION. Apr 4. Calling for continued efforts by member states, with the assistance of the United Nations and relevant organizations, to foster the establishment and development of national mine-action capacities in countries where mines and explosive remnants of war constitute a serious threat to the safety, health and lives of the civilian population, or an impediment to social and economic development at the national and local levels. UN Resolution 60/97 of Dec 8, 2005. For info: United Nations, Dept of Public Info, New York, NY 10017. Web: www.un.org.

VITAMIN C ISOLATED: ANNIVERSARY. Apr 4, 1932. Vitamin C was first isolated by C.C. King at the University of Pittsburgh.

WATERS, MUDDY: BIRTH ANNIVERSARY. Apr 4, 1915. Born McKinley Morganfield at Rolling Fork, MS, American blues guitarist and singer Muddy Waters played a significant part in developing the modern rhythm and blues that came to be known as Chicago, or urban, blues. It was predominantly from this music that later forms such as rock and roll and soul sprang. Muddy Waters died at Westmont, IL, Apr 30, 1983.

YALE, LINUS: BIRTH ANNIVERSARY. Apr 4, 1821. The American portrait painter and inventor of the lock that is named for him was born at Salisbury, NY. He was creator of the Yale Infallible Bank Lock and developer of the cylinder lock. Yale died at New York, NY, Dec 25, 1868.

YAMAMOTO, ISOROKU: BIRTH ANNIVERSARY. Apr 4, 1884. Considered Japan's greatest naval strategist, Admiral Isoroku Yamamoto, who planned the attack on Pearl Harbor, was born at Nagaoka, Honshu. Yamamoto also devised the complex attack on Midway Island, which ended in defeat for the Japanese because the Allies had the key to the Imperial fleet code and were prepared for the June 4, 1942, attack. The US intercepted reports of Yamamoto's proposed 1943 tour of the Western Solomons and shot down his plane Apr 18, while he was touring Japanese installations in the area.

BIRTHDAYS TODAY

Maya Angelou, 86, poet, author (*I Know Why the Caged Bird Sings*), born St. Louis, MO, Apr 4, 1928.

David Blaine, 41, magician, born Brooklyn, NY, Apr 4, 1973.

Robert Downey, Jr, 49, actor (*Iron Man, Zodiac, Chaplin, Natural Born Killers*), born New York, NY, Apr 4, 1965.

Kitty Kelley, 72, author (*Jackie Oh!, Nancy Reagan*), born Hartford, CT, Apr 4, 1942.

Christine Lahti, 64, actress (Emmys for "Chicago Hope"; *Swing Shift*), director (Oscar for "Lieberman in Love"), born Birmingham, MI, Apr 4, 1950.

Nancy McKeon, 48, actress ("The Facts of Life," "The Division"), born Westbury, NY, Apr 4, 1966.

Dave Mirra, 42, BMX bike racer, born Syracuse, NY, Apr 4, 1972.

Craig T. Nelson, 68, actor ("Parenthood," "Coach," "The District," *The Family Stone, Poltergeist*), born Spokane, WA, Apr 4, 1946.

Michael Parks, 76, actor ("Then Came Bronson," "Twin Peaks," *The Happening*), born Corona, CA, Apr 4, 1938.

Barry Pepper, 44, actor (*The Kennedys, True Grit, Saving Private Ryan*), born Campbell River, BC, Canada, Apr 4, 1970.

Scott Rolen, 39, baseball player, born Evansville, IN, Apr 4, 1975.

Jill Scott, 42, musician, actress ("The No. 1 Ladies' Detective Agency"), born Philadelphia, PA, Apr 4, 1972.

April 2014

S	M	T	W	T	F	S
		1	2	3	4	5
6	7	8	9	10	11	12
13	14	15	16	17	18	19
20	21	22	23	24	25	26
27	28	29	30			

April 5 — Saturday

DAY 95 **270 REMAINING**

CANADA: ELMIRA MAPLE SYRUP FESTIVAL. Apr 5. Elmira, ON. 50th anniversary. Tours of maple bush by hay wagon, sugaring-off shanty in operation, Pennsylvania Dutch cuisine and other varieties of food, handcrafted goods, arts and crafts, antiques and much more. Fun for the whole family! Est attendance: 70,000. For info: Elmira Maple Syrup Festival, 24 Church St W, PO Box 158, Elmira, ON, Canada N3B 2Z6. Phone: (519) 669-6000. Fax: (519) 669-9348. Web: www.elmiramaplesyrup.com.

CHINA: QING MING FESTIVAL OR TOMB-SWEEPING DAY. Apr 5. This Confucian festival was traditionally celebrated on the fourth or fifth day of the third month but is now on fixed dates (Apr 4 or 5) in China. It is observed by the maintenance of ancestral graves, the presentation of food, wine and flowers as offerings and the burning of paper money at gravesides to help ancestors in the afterworld. People also picnic and gather for family meals. Also observed in Taiwan on Apr 5.

DAVIS, BETTE: BIRTH ANNIVERSARY. Apr 5, 1908. American actress Bette Davis was born Ruth Elizabeth Davis at Lowell, MA. In addition to acting in more than 80 films, earning 10 Academy Award nominations and winning the Academy Award twice, for Best Actress in *Dangerous* (1935) and *Jezebel* (1938), Davis claimed to have nicknamed the Academy Award "Oscar" after her first husband, Harmon Oscar Nelson, Jr. She died Oct 6, 1989, at Neuilly-sur-Seine, France.

"FIRESIDE THEATRE" TV PREMIERE: 65th ANNIVERSARY. Apr 5, 1949. Gene Raymond and later Jane Wyman hosted this NBC anthology program consisting of 15- and 30-minute dramas. One of its most acclaimed presentations was "The Reign of Amelika Jo" on Oct 12, 1954. It was set in the South Pacific during WWII and had a mostly black and Asian cast.

FIRST US CHAMBER OF COMMERCE FOUNDED: ANNIVERSARY. Apr 5, 1768. The first chamber of commerce in the US was founded at New York City.

HELEN KELLER'S MIRACLE: ANNIVERSARY. Apr 5, 1887. Anne Sullivan went to Tuscumbia, AL, in March 1887 to teach the "unteachable" deaf and blind Helen Keller. Although Keller was resistant, Sullivan was determined, and after only one month she succeeded in reaching her: she placed Keller's hand under a gushing water pump and used sign language to spell "w-a-t-e-r" into her palm. Helen grasped the meaning—spelling the word back into Sullivan's palm—and excitedly learned 30 more words that day. Keller's life changed at that breakthrough moment, as she recalled later: "As the cool stream gushed over one hand . . . I felt a misty consciousness as of something forgotten, a thrill of returning thought, and somehow the mystery of language was revealed to me." Keller would go on to become the first deaf and blind person to graduate from college, write books and crusade for the disabled. See also: "Keller, Helen: Birth Anniversary" (June 27).

HISTORIC PENDLETON SPRING JUBILEE. Apr 5–6. Pendleton, SC. 37th annual. Come and join the fun in historic Pendleton with fine arts, food, live entertainment and much more. Annually, the first full weekend in April. Est attendance: 20,000. For info: Historic Pendleton Spring Jubilee, PO Box 565, Pendleton, SC 29670. Phone: (864) 646-3782 or (800) 862-1795. Fax: (864) 646-7768. E-mail: brooke@pendletondistrict.org. Web: www.pendletondistrict.org/jubilee.

INTERNATIONAL HOME FURNISHINGS MARKET (SPRING). Apr 5–10. High Point and Thomasville, NC. The largest wholesale home furnishings market in the world. (Not open to the general public.) Est attendance: 82,000. For info: High Point Market Authority, 164 S Main St, Ste 700, High Point, NC 27260. Phone: (336) 869-1000 or (800) 874-6492. Fax: (336) 869-6999. Web: www.highpointmarket.org.

LISTER, JOSEPH: BIRTH ANNIVERSARY. Apr 5, 1827. English physician who was the founder of aseptic surgery, born at Upton, Essex, England. Died at Walmer, England, Feb 10, 1912.

"MARRIED . . . WITH CHILDREN" TV PREMIERE: ANNIVERSARY. Apr 5, 1987. This raunchy FOX TV show premiered as the antidote to Cosby-style family shows. Ed O'Neill starred as boorish, luckless shoe salesman Al Bundy; Katey Sagal portrayed Al's big-haired, spandex-clad, sex-starved wife, Peggy; Christina Applegate played their airheaded bombshell daughter, Kelly; and David Faustino played their hormone-driven son, Bud. The last episode aired Apr 20, 1997.

MONEY SMART WEEK®. Apr 5–12. The American Library Association has partnered with the Federal Reserve Bank of Chicago to create this national initiative to promote personal financial literacy. Libraries of all types can partner with community groups, financial institutions, government agencies, educational organizations and other financial experts to help consumers learn to better manage their personal finances. The ALA and the Federal Reserve Bank of Chicago have launched a special section of the Money Smart Week website devoted to libraries, with information on how to participate, as well as tool kits, resources and examples of programming for public, academic, school and special libraries. For info: American Library Assn, 50 E Huron St, Chicago, IL 60611. Phone: (312) 280-5044. E-mail: pio@ala.org. Web: www.moneysmartweek.org/ala.

NAB 2014/NATIONAL BROADCASTERS CONVENTION. Apr 5–10. Las Vegas Convention Center, Las Vegas, NV. World's largest convention of radio, television and other types of multimedia. The awards for the National Broadcasting Hall of Fame are also presented at the convention. For info: Natl Assn of Broadcasters, 1771 N St NW, Washington, DC 20036-2891. Phone: (202) 429-5300. E-mail: nab@nab.org. Web: www.nabshow.com.

NATIONAL DEEP DISH PIZZA DAY. Apr 5. To celebrate Chicago deep dish pizza—originated by Uno's—and the efforts by Uno Chicago Grill to bring deep dish pizza to the entire United States. The original restaurant, which opened in 1943, began serving deep dish as a way to make sure hungry families could get a "real meal" when it came to pizza. Up to that point, pizza was hardly more than a snack. Annually celebrated on the anniversary of the day (Apr 5, 1979) that the first restaurant outside Chicago opened (in Boston, MA). For info: Uno Restaurants, 100 Charles Park Rd, West Roxbury, MA 02132. Phone: (617) 323-9200. Web: www.unos.com.

NATIONAL LOVE OUR CHILDREN DAY. Apr 5. This day is celebrated annually across the US to honor children and strengthen families and raise awareness for efforts to protect children. Please e-mail for event details. For info: Ross Ellis, Love Our Children USA, 220 E 57th St, 9th Fl, Ste G, New York, NY 10022. Phone: (888) 347-KIDS. E-mail: info@loveourchildrenusa.org. Web: www.loveourchildrenusa.org.

NCAA DIVISION I MEN'S BASKETBALL CHAMPIONSHIP (FINAL FOUR). Apr 5 and 7. Cowboys Stadium, Arlington, TX. 76th annual. For info: NCAA, 700 W Washington St, PO Box 6222, Indianapolis, IN 46206-6222. Phone: (317) 917-6222. Fax: (317) 917-6827. Web: www.NCAAsports.com/finalfour.

PECK, GREGORY: BIRTH ANNIVERSARY. Apr 5, 1916. Born Eldred Gregory Peck at La Jolla, CA, Gregory Peck was one of Hollywood's most popular and likable leading men. Nominated five times for Best Actor, he finally won the Oscar for his role as Atticus Finch in 1962's *To Kill a Mockingbird*. Other popular films included *Roman Holiday, Gentlemen's Agreement* and Alfred Hitchcock's *Spellbound*. He also founded the La Jolla Playhouse with Dorothy McGuire and Mel Ferrer in 1947 and appeared there throughout his career. He died at his home in La Jolla on June 11, 2003.

RESNIK, JUDITH A.: 65th BIRTH ANNIVERSARY. Apr 5, 1949. Dr. Judith A. Resnik, the second American woman in space (1984), was born at Akron, OH. The 36-year-old electrical engineer was mission specialist on space shuttle *Challenger*. She perished with all others aboard when *Challenger* exploded Jan 28, 1986. See also: "*Challenger* Space Shuttle Explosion: Anniversary" (Jan 28).

SCOTLAND: EDINBURGH INTERNATIONAL SCIENCE FESTIVAL. Apr 5–20. Edinburgh. A massive public celebration of science and technology, with more than 120 events at 15 venues. Includes workshops, talks, tours and exhibitions. Est attendance: 70,000. For info: Media Officer, Edinburgh Intl Science Festival, Ste 1, Mitchell House, 5 Mitchell St, Edinburgh, Scotland EH6 7BD. Phone: (44) 131-553-0320. Fax: (44) 131-553-1455. E-mail: laurabain@scifest.co.uk. Web: www.sciencefestival.co.uk.

"SECRET AGENT" TV PREMIERE: ANNIVERSARY. Apr 5, 1961. Before Patrick McGoohan became the star of "The Prisoner," he played the role of intelligence agent John Drake on this CBS adventure series. Produced in England by ATV, it also aired there as "Danger Man."

SFC SPRING ARTS FESTIVAL. Apr 5–6. Gainesville, FL. Artists and craftspeople from all areas of the US display their work. Also, Kids Art Jungle—a complete art fest for kids. Est attendance: 130,000. For info: Santa Fe College, Spring Arts Festival, 3000 NW 83rd St, Gainesville, FL 32606. Phone: (352) 395-5355. Fax: (352) 336-2715. E-mail: kathryn.lehman@sfcollege.edu.

SPRING SWING CITY ELECTRA-QUANAH-WIDE GARAGE SALE. Apr 5. Electra, TX. More than 50 miles of garage sales throughout the Electra area. Chamber of commerce will provide free coffee and maps at 7 AM; sales start at 8 AM. The chamber of commerce office will close at 8 AM so that we too may enjoy all of the bargains. Est attendance: 500. For info: Sherry Strange, Electra Chamber of Commerce, 112 W Cleveland, Electra, TX 76360. Phone: (940) 495-3577. E-mail: electracoc@electratel.net. Web: www.electratexas.org.

SWITZERLAND: LUCERNE FESTIVAL AT EASTER. Apr 5–13. Lucerne. Sacred and concert music at truly unique sites: in the beautiful churches and at the concert hall of the KKL Lucerne. For the period of this festival, the Bavarian Radio Symphony is orchestra-in-residence. For info: Lucerne Festival, PO Box CH-6002, Lucerne, Switzerland. Phone: (41) 41-226-4400. Fax: (41) 41-226-4460. E-mail: info@lucernefestival.ch. Web: www.lucernefestival.ch.

TAIWAN: NATIONAL TOMB-SWEEPING DAY. Apr 5. National holiday since 1972. According to Chinese custom, the tombs of ancestors are swept "clear and bright" and rites honoring ancestors are held. Tomb-Sweeping Day is observed Apr 5, which is also the anniversary of the death of Chiang Kai-shek.

TANGIBLE KARMA™ DAY. Apr 5. Tangible Karma™ Day celebrates occasions when giving (your time, your love, your talents, your "extras") feels as good as receiving. Groups and individuals set aside one hour of this day to purposefully become aware of the needs of those they are in contact with and actively do something to help fulfill those needs. Annually, the first Saturday in April. For info: Tangible Karma, 202 E Dean Ave, Madison, WI 53716. Phone: (773) 844-2022. E-mail: info@tangiblekarma.com. Web: www.tangiblekarma.com.

TRACY, SPENCER: BIRTH ANNIVERSARY. Apr 5, 1900. Born at Milwaukee, WI, Spencer Tracy was one of the most respected actors in film history. He won Academy Awards for Best Actor for 1937's *Captains Courageous* and 1938's *Boys Town* and was nominated seven other times. In 1942, he met actress Katharine Hepburn, and they shared a relationship that lasted until his death, although they never married. Together, they starred in nine films, including *Adam's Rib* in 1949 and *Guess Who's Coming to Dinner* in 1967. Tracy died June 10, 1967, at Hollywood Hills, CA.

WASHINGTON, BOOKER TALIAFERRO: BIRTH ANNIVERSARY. Apr 5, 1856. Black educator and leader born at Franklin County, VA. "No race can prosper," he wrote in *Up from Slavery*, "till it learns that there is as much dignity in tilling a field as in writing a poem." Died at Tuskegee, AL, Nov 14, 1915.

BIRTHDAYS TODAY

Roger Corman, 88, filmmaker, born Detroit, MI, Apr 5, 1926.

Max Gail, 71, actor ("Barney Miller," *Pearl*), born Grosse Point, MI, Apr 5, 1943.

Michael Moriarty, 72, actor (*The Last Detail, Bang the Drum Slowly*, "Law & Order"), born Detroit, MI, Apr 5, 1942.

Mitch Pileggi, 62, actor ("The X-Files"), born Portland, OR, Apr 5, 1952.

Colin Luther Powell, 77, former US secretary of state, general, former chairman of the US Joint Chiefs of Staff, born New York, NY, Apr 5, 1937.

April 6 — Sunday

DAY 96 — **269 REMAINING**

"BARNEY & FRIENDS" TV PREMIERE: ANNIVERSARY. Apr 6, 1992. Although most adults find it hopelessly saccharine, this PBS program is hugely popular with preschoolers. Purple dinosaur Barney; his pals, dinosaurs Baby Bop and B.J.; and a multiethnic group of children sing, play games and learn simple lessons about getting along with one another.

BAT APPRECIATION WEEK. Apr 6–12. A time to raise awareness and appreciation of these important and greatly misunderstood creatures. During this week there are bat conservation, education and celebration events around the world. For info: Bat Conservation International, 500 Capital of TX Hwy N, Bldg 1, Austin, TX 78746. Web: www.batcon.org.

BATTLE OF SHILOH: ANNIVERSARY. Apr 6, 1862. General Ulysess S. Grant's Union forces at Shiloh, or Pittsburgh Landing, TN, were attacked by a large force under General Albert Sidney Johnston on this date. After heavy fighting, the first day of the battle ended without a conclusive victory for either side. Grant was reinforced before the Confederates on the second day, and Confederate general P.T. Beauregard, in command after Johnston's death the previous day, ordered a retreat back to Corinth, MS, leaving the Federal troops in a stronger position in Tennessee than before the battle. Losses on both sides totaled more than 23,000.

BRIGHAM YOUNG'S LAST MARRIAGE: ANNIVERSARY. Apr 6, 1868. Brigham Young, Mormon Church leader, married his 27th, and last, wife on this day.

CHURCH OF JESUS CHRIST OF LATTER-DAY SAINTS: ANNIVERSARY. Apr 6, 1830. Under the leadership of Joseph Smith, Jr, The Church of Jesus Christ of Latter-day Saints was founded with six members in a log cabin at Fayette, NY.

CONSIDER CHRISTIANITY WEEK. Apr 6–12. A week to encourage Christians to examine the evidence and reasons for their faith and for non-Christians to take another look at the faith that has played such an important role in shaping the history and culture in which we live. Annually, beginning two Sundays before Easter. For info: Hanna Hushbeck, PR, Aletheia, 3675 N 108th Ave, Wausau, WI 54401. Phone: (715) 675-7361. E-mail: hanna@consider.org. Web: www.consider.org.

DROWSY DRIVER AWARENESS DAY. Apr 6. Annual memorial for people who have died in collisions related to drowsy driving. This is an official state-recognized "day" in the state of California. Annually, on Apr 6. For info: Phil Konstantin, PO Box 17515, San Diego, CA 92177-7515. E-mail: chpofficerphil@yahoo.com. Web: www.drowsydriverawarenessday.com.

ENGLAND: CARE SUNDAY. Apr 6. The fifth Sunday of Lent, also known as Carling Sunday and Passion Sunday. First day of Passiontide, remembering the sorrow and passion of Christ.

FIRST MODERN OLYMPICS: ANNIVERSARY. Apr 6, 1896. The first modern Olympics formally opened at Athens, Greece, after a 1,500-year hiatus. Thirteen nations participated, represented by 235 male athletes.

FIRST TONY AWARDS PRESENTED: ANNIVERSARY. Apr 6, 1947. The American Theatre Wing bestowed the first annual Tony Awards for distinguished service to the theater.

GANDHI MAKES SALT: ANNIVERSARY. Apr 6, 1930. Mohandas Gandhi, frustrated by British indifference to Indian civil rights demands, planned a symbolic, peaceful protest by conducting a 241-mile march from Sabarmati Ashram to the coast at Dandi. Leaving on Mar 12, Gandhi and his followers arrived at Dandi on Apr 5, and on Apr 6, he made salt by boiling seawater—a violation of the salt law, which granted royal monopoly in its manufacture and levied heavy taxes on its purchasers. His peaceful act and the two-mile-long procession that accompanied it gained worldwide headlines. Besides Gandhi, thousands of Indians were arrested as they, too, made salt in protest.

GREECE: DUMB WEEK. Apr 6–12. The week preceding Holy Week on the Orthodox calendar is known as Dumb Week, as no services are held in churches throughout this period except on Friday, eve of the Saturday of Lazarus.

LALIQUE, RENÉ: BIRTH ANNIVERSARY. Apr 6, 1860. Born at Ay, France, Lalique was a goldsmith, jeweler, glass artist and interior designer known for his Art Nouveau and Art Deco works. He died on May 5, 1945, at Paris.

April 2014

S	M	T	W	T	F	S
		1	2	3	4	5
6	7	8	9	10	11	12
13	14	15	16	17	18	19
20	21	22	23	24	25	26
27	28	29	30			

MULLIGAN, GERRY: BIRTH ANNIVERSARY. Apr 6, 1927. American jazz saxophonist Gerry Mulligan was born at New York, NY. He performed with many great jazz musicians, including Miles Davis, Dave Brubeck, Chet Baker and Duke Ellington, and is credited with helping create the cool-jazz movement with Miles Davis. Mulligan died Jan 20, 1996, at Darien, CT.

✦NATIONAL VOLUNTEER WEEK. Apr 6–13.

NATIONAL VOLUNTEER WEEK. Apr 6–13. National Volunteer Week has become the official time to recognize and celebrate the efforts of volunteers at the local, state and national levels. It began in 1974 when President Richard Nixon signed an executive order establishing the week as an annual celebration of volunteering. Every president since has signed a proclamation promoting National Volunteer Week, as have governors, mayors and other elected officials. For info: Points of Light Institute, 600 Means St NW, Ste 210, Atlanta, GA 30318. Phone: (404) 979-2900. Fax: (404) 979-2901. Web: www.pointsoflight.org.

NATIONAL WINDOW SAFETY WEEK. April 6–12. Designed to increase awareness of the importance of windows in home safety plans, including their use as emergency escape routes. This week will also address issues of children falling out of windows. For info: Natl Safety Council, 1121 Spring Lake Dr, Itasca, IL 60143-3201. Phone: (800) 621-7615. E-mail: media@nsc.org. Web: www.nsc.org.

NCAA DIVISION I WOMEN'S BASKETBALL CHAMPIONSHIP (WOMEN'S FINAL FOUR). Apr 6 and 8. Bridgestone Arena, Nashville, TN. 33rd annual. Est attendance: 30,000. For info: NCAA, PO Box 6222, Indianapolis, IN 46206-6222. Phone: (317) 917-6222. Web: www.NCAAsports.com.

NORTH POLE DISCOVERED: ANNIVERSARY. Apr 6, 1909. Robert E. Peary reached the North Pole after several failed attempts. The team consisted of Peary, leader of the expedition; Matthew A. Henson, a black man who had served with Peary since 1886 as ship's cook, carpenter and blacksmith, and then as Peary's coexplorer and valuable assistant; and four Eskimo guides—Coquesh, Ootah, Eginwah and Seegloo. They sailed July 17, 1908, on the ship *Roosevelt*, wintering on Ellesmere Island. After a grueling trek with dwindling food supplies, Henson and two of the Eskimos were first to reach the Pole. An exhausted Peary arrived 45 minutes later and confirmed their location. Dr. Frederick A. Cook, surgeon on an earlier expedition with Peary, claimed to have reached the Pole first, but that could not be substantiated and the National Geographic Society credited the Peary expedition.

PASSION WEEK. Apr 6–12. The week beginning on the fifth Sunday in Lent; the week before Holy Week.

PASSIONTIDE. Apr 6–19. The last two weeks of Lent (Passion Week and Holy Week), beginning with the fifth Sunday of Lent (Passion Sunday) and continuing through the day before Easter (Holy Saturday or Easter Even).

RAPHAEL: BIRTH ANNIVERSARY. Apr 6, 1483. Raffaello Santi (Sanzio), Italian painter and architect. Probably born Apr 6, 1483, at Urbino, Italy. Died on his birthday, at Rome, Italy, Apr 6, 1520.

SCHNEIDERMAN, ROSE: BIRTH ANNIVERSARY. Apr 6, 1882. A pioneer in the battle to increase wages and improve working conditions for women, Rose Schneiderman was born at Saven, Poland, and her family immigrated to the US six years later. At age 16 she began factory work in New York City's garment district and quickly became a union organizer. Opposed to the open-shop policy, which permitted nonunion members to work in a unionized shop, Schneiderman organized a 1913 strike of 25,000 women shirtwaist makers. She worked as an organizer for the International Ladies Garment Workers Union (ILGWU) and for the Women's Trade Union League (WTUL), serving as president for more than 20 years. During the Great Depression President Roosevelt appointed her to his Labor Advisory Board—the only woman member. Died Aug 11, 1972, at New York, NY.

SCOTTSBORO TRIAL: ANNIVERSARY. Apr 6, 1931. In what became a cause célèbre, nine black youths went on trial at Scottsboro, AL, accused of raping two white women on a freight train. All were convicted in a hasty trial but by 1950 were free by parole, appeal or escape.

TARTAN DAY. Apr 6. Groups and societies throughout North America take the anniversary of the Declaration of Arbroath (1320) as the day to celebrate their Scottish roots.

TEFLON INVENTED: ANNIVERSARY. Apr 6, 1938. Polytetraflouroethylene resin was invented by Roy J. Plunkett while he was employed by E.I. Du Pont de Nemours & Co. Commonly known as Teflon, it revolutionized the cookware industry. This substance or something similar coated three-quarters of the pots and pans in America at the time of Plunkett's death in 1994.

THAILAND: CHAKRI DAY. Apr 6. Commemorates the foundation of the present dynasty by King Rama I (1782–1809), who also established Bangkok as the country's capital.

THOMAS, LOWELL: BIRTH ANNIVERSARY. Apr 6, 1892. World traveler, reporter, editor and radio newscaster, whose broadcasts spanned more than half a century, 1925–76. His radio sign-off, "So long until tomorrow," was known to millions of listeners, and he is said to have been the first to broadcast from a ship, an airplane, a submarine and a coal mine. Born at Woodington, OH, he died at Pawling, NY, Aug 29, 1981.

TRAGEDY IN RWANDA: 20th ANNIVERSARY. Apr 6, 1994. A plane carrying the presidents of Rwanda and Burundi was shot down near Kigali, the Rwandan capital, exacerbating a brutal ethnic war that led to the massacre of hundreds of thousands. Presidents Juvenal Habyarimana of Rwanda and Cyprien Ntaryamira of Burundi were returning from a summit in Tanzania where they discussed ways of ending the killing in their countries sparked by ethnic rivalries between the Hutu and Tutsi tribes. Following the attack on the two leaders, Rwanda descended into chaos as the two tribes began killing each other in a genocidal battle for power, leading to a mass exodus of civilians caught in the maelstrom.

US ENTERS WORLD WAR I: ANNIVERSARY. Apr 6, 1917. Congress approved a declaration of war against Germany and the US entered WWI, which had begun in 1914. The first US "doughboys" landed in France June 27, 1917.

US SENATE ACHIEVES A QUORUM: 225th ANNIVERSARY. Apr 6, 1789. The US Senate was formally organized after achieving a quorum.

WEEK OF THE YOUNG CHILD. Apr 6–12. To focus on young children and the importance of quality early childhood education. For info: Natl Assn for the Education of Young Children, 1313 L St NW, Ste 500, Washington, DC 20005. Phone: (800) 424-2460. Fax: (202) 328-1846. E-mail: naeyc@naeyc.org. Web: www.naeyc.org/woyc.

BIRTHDAYS TODAY

Michele Bachmann, 58, US Congresswoman (R, Minnesota), born Waterloo, IA, Apr 6, 1956.

Bert Blyleven, 63, Hall of Fame baseball player, born Rik Aalbert Blijleven at Zeist, Netherlands, Apr 6, 1951.

Bret Boone, 45, baseball player, born El Cajon, CA, Apr 6, 1969.

Zach Braff, 39, actor ("Scrubs," *Garden State*), born South Orange, NJ, Apr 6, 1975.

Candace Cameron Bure, 38, actress ("Full House"), born Canoga Park, CA, Apr 6, 1976.

Merle Haggard, 77, singer, songwriter, born Bakersfield, CA, Apr 6, 1937.

Marilu Henner, 62, actress ("Taxi," "Evening Shade"), born Chicago, IL, Apr 6, 1952.

Olaf Kolzig, 44, former hockey player, born Johannesburg, South Africa, Apr 6, 1970.

Barry Levinson, 72, director, producer, writer, actor ("The Carol Burnett Show," *Rain Man, Avalon, Bugsy*), born Baltimore, MD, Apr 6, 1942.

Andre Previn, 85, composer, conductor, born Berlin, Germany, Apr 6, 1929.

John Ratzenberger, 67, actor ("Cheers," *Toy Story* films), born Bridgeport, CT, Apr 6, 1947.

Paul Rudd, 45, actor (*I Love You, Man; Anchorman; Clueless*), born Passaic, NJ, Apr 6, 1969.

Roy Thinnes, 76, actor ("The Invaders," "The Outer Limits"), born Chicago, IL, Apr 6, 1938.

James Watson, 86, discoverer (with Francis Crick) of the structure of DNA, born Chicago, IL, Apr 6, 1928.

Billy Dee Williams, 77, actor (*Brian's Song, Lady Sings the Blues, Return of the Jedi*), born New York, NY, Apr 6, 1937.

April 7 — Monday

DAY 97 — **268 REMAINING**

BATTLE OF LYS RIVER: ANNIVERSARY. Apr 7, 1918. Having failed to break through Allied lines at the Somme in March, General Erich Ludendorff made another attempt by attacking Flanders along the Lys River. On the hot, misty, sticky mornings of Apr 7 and 8, 1918, the Germans released mustard gas. On Apr 9 the Central Powers began a high-explosive bombardment along the 12-mile front from LaBasse to Armentieres. The British managed to avoid a break in their line, and finally General Ferdinand Foch sent nine French divisions to take over a portion of it. On Apr 30, realizing that "further attacks promised no success," Ludendorff ended the offensive. As a result of this battle the British were unable to initiate an offensive for three months. The Allies suffered 240,000 casualties while the German losses exceeded 348,000.

CAMP, WALTER: BIRTH ANNIVERSARY. Apr 7, 1859. Walter Chauncey Camp, college athlete, coach and administrator, was born at New Britain, CT. Camp played football and several other sports at Yale, but he gained prominence for helping to reshape the rules of rugby football into American football. Among his innovations were reducing the number of players on a side from 15 to 11, introducing the scrimmage, giving one team definite possession of the ball and proposing the downs system. He served as a volunteer coach at Yale and became a national figure as a promoter of football. He selected an All-American team member from 1889 until his death. Died at New York, NY, Mar 14, 1925.

April 2014

S	M	T	W	T	F	S
		1	2	3	4	5
6	7	8	9	10	11	12
13	14	15	16	17	18	19
20	21	22	23	24	25	26
27	28	29	30			

CHANNING, WILLIAM ELLERY: BIRTH ANNIVERSARY. Apr 7, 1780. Well-known abolitionist and leader of the Unitarian movement in the US, born at Newport, RI. He stood for religious liberalism and influenced such people as Longfellow, Bryant, Emerson, Lowell and Holmes. Died at Bennington, VT, Oct 2, 1842.

EXPLORE YOUR CAREER OPTIONS WEEK. Apr 7–11. Maybe you're aspiring to a new career or merely interested in more opportunities in your present career. Get a fresh start by taking stock of all available options. For info: Dorothy Zjawin, Dir, 61 W Colfax Ave, Roselle Park, NJ 07204.

FAIRCHILD, DAVID GRANDISON: BIRTH ANNIVERSARY. Apr 7, 1869. American botanist, government official and explorer, born at East Lansing, MI. Noted for scientific studies on importation of tropical plant species such as avocados and mangoes. Died at Miami, FL, Aug 6, 1954.

HOLIDAY, BILLIE: BIRTH ANNIVERSARY. Apr 7, 1915. Billie Holiday (born Eleanora Fagan, nicknamed "Lady Day") is considered by many jazz critics to have been the greatest jazz singer ever recorded. In her 26-year career, despite having received no formal training, she demonstrated a unique style with sophisticated and dramatic phrasing. Among her best-known songs are "Lover Man," "God Bless the Child," "Don't Explain" and "Strange Fruit." Holiday was born at Philadelphia, PA. She died at New York, NY, July 17, 1959.

INTERNATIONAL BEAVER DAY. Apr 7. Dolgeville, NY, and other sites worldwide. This day celebrates the species that restores the most valuable terrestrial ecosystem—wetlands. Beavers: Wetlands & Wildlife, an educational nonprofit organization, created this event to highlight the animal that acts as our life-support system by restoring wetlands, which absorb carbon dioxide and help moderate the droughts and major floods that are increasing with global warming. Beaver exhibits, talks and hikes to ponds will be held, and free beaver materials distributed. Annually, Apr 7 (with other events throughout April). For info: Beavers: Wetlands & Wildlife, 146 Van Dyke Rd, Dolgeville, NY 13329. Phone: (518) 568-2077. Fax: (518) 568-6046. E-mail: castor@frontiernet.net. Web: www.BeaversWW.org.

INTERNATIONAL SNAILPAPERS DAY. Apr 7. A day to celebrate hard-copy media. Pick up a print newspaper today and read it! Annually, Apr 7. For info: Danny Bloom, PO Box 1000, Chiayi City, Taiwan, Republic of China. E-mail: danbloom@gmail.com.

KING, WILLIAM RUFUS DEVANE: BIRTH ANNIVERSARY. Apr 7, 1786. The 13th vice president of the US died on Apr 18, 1853, the 46th day after taking the oath of office, of tuberculosis, at Cahaba, AL. The oath of office had been administered to King at Havana, Cuba, as authorized by a special act of Congress (the only presidential or vice presidential oath to be administered outside the US). Born on this day at Sampson County, NY, King was the only vice president who had served in both the House of Representatives and the Senate. King's term as vice president was Mar 4–Apr 18, 1853.

MALINOWSKI, BRONISLAW: BIRTH ANNIVERSARY. Apr 7, 1884. Leading British anthropologist, author and teacher, born at Krakow, Poland. His pioneering anthropological fieldwork in Melanesia inspired his colleagues and students. In 1939 he became a visiting professor at Yale University. Died at New Haven, CT, May 16, 1942.

THE MASTERS TOURNAMENT. Apr 7–13. Augusta National Golf Club, Augusta, GA. Prestigious golf tournament, first held Mar 22, 1934, created by Bobby Jones and Clifford Roberts. Champions don the fabled green jacket that members of Augusta began wearing in 1937. Sam Snead was the first Masters champion to be given the green jacket. For info: Augusta National Golf Club. Web: www.masters.com or www.augusta.com.

McGRAW, JOHN: BIRTH ANNIVERSARY. Apr 7, 1873. John Joseph McGraw, Baseball Hall of Fame third baseman and manager, born at Truxton, NY. Generally regarded as the best manager ever or close to it, McGraw ran the New York Giants with an iron hand from 1902 to 1932. A scrappy ballplayer with the Baltimore Orioles in the 1890s, McGraw demanded and got total effort from his players. Inducted into the Hall of Fame in 1937. Died at New Rochelle, NY, Feb 25, 1934.

METRIC SYSTEM: ANNIVERSARY. Apr 7, 1795. The metric system was adopted in France, where it had been developed.

MISTRAL, GABRIELA: 125th BIRTH ANNIVERSARY. Apr 7, 1889. Chilean educator, poet and diplomat born Lucila Godoy Alcayaga at Vicuna, Chile. Diplomatic work was extensive: was Chilean consul in many nations, served as a League of Nations and UN representative, notably on the Subcommittee on the Status of Women and promoting UNICEF. Mistral was the first Latin American to be awarded the Nobel Prize in Literature in 1945. Called "the spiritual mentor of the Spanish American world in a degree rarely equaled before by any man and never by a woman," she died Jan 10, 1957, at Hempstead, NY.

MOON PHASE: FIRST QUARTER. Apr 7. Moon enters First Quarter phase at 4:31 AM, EDT.

NATIONAL BEER DAY. Apr 7. When the Cullen-Harrison Act went into effect at 12:01 AM on Apr 7, 1933, thirsty customers could buy a beer that was 3.2 percent alcohol by weight instead of the "near beer" they had suffered with all through Prohibition. The public lined up on "New Beer's Eve" (Apr 6) at breweries in 20 states and Washington, DC, and purchased 1.5 million barrels. Apr 7 has remained an unofficial holiday celebrating beer in the US.

NEW YORK SLAVE REVOLT: ANNIVERSARY. Apr 7, 1712. Nine whites were killed in a slave revolt in New York City. Planned by 27 slaves, the rebellion was begun by setting fire to an outhouse; as whites came to put the fire out, they were shot. The state militia was called out to capture the rebels, and the city of New York responded to the event by strengthening its slave codes. Twenty-one blacks were executed as participants, and six alleged participants committed suicide. New York outlawed slavery in 1799, though the last slaves were not freed until 1827.

NO HOUSEWORK DAY. Apr 7. No trash. No dishes. No making of beds or washing of laundry. And no guilt. Give it a rest. (©2006 by WH.) For info: Thomas & Ruth Roy, Wellcat Holidays, 2418 Long Ln, Lebanon, PA 17046. Phone: (717) 279-0184. E-mail: info@wellcat.com. Web: www.wellcat.com.

RWANDA: GENOCIDE REMEMBRANCE DAY. Apr 7. National holiday. Commemorates massacres of 1994.

SHANKAR, RAVI: BIRTH ANNIVERSARY. Apr 7, 1920. Sitar player and composer who introduced Indian music to the Western world, born at Varanasi, India. He began performing music and dance as a child and was soon recognized and trained by the head musician of the Maihar court. A key figure in the movement to bring world music to the attention of mass audiences, he toured extensively and taught around the world—influencing such musicians as George Harrison, John Coltrane and Philip Glass. Shankar also used his music to bring attention to the plight of the poor around the world, especially in Bangladesh. He died at Long Beach, CA, Dec 12, 2012.

SPACE MILESTONE: *MARS ODYSSEY* (US). Apr 7, 2001. *Odyssey* was launched on this day and successfully entered Mars's orbit on Oct 23, 2001. The one-way trip was 286 million miles. The 2½-year mission monitored space radiation, sought out underground water and identified minerals on the Red Planet.

UNITED NATIONS: WORLD HEALTH DAY. Apr 7. A UN observance commemorating the establishment of the World Health Organization in 1948. For info: United Nations, Dept of Public Info, New York, NY 10017. Web: www.un.org.

WINCHELL, WALTER: BIRTH ANNIVERSARY. Apr 7, 1897. Journalist, broadcaster, reporter and gossip columnist Walter Winchell was born at New York, NY, and died at Los Angeles, CA, Feb 20, 1972. He was admired for his way with turning a phrase. His show business columns were voraciously read by millions of Americans between 1924 and 1963.

WORDSWORTH, WILLIAM: BIRTH ANNIVERSARY. Apr 7, 1770. English Lake Poet and philosopher, born at Cumberland, England. "Poetry," he said, "is the spontaneous overflow of powerful feelings: it takes its origin from emotion recollected in tranquility." Wordsworth died Apr 23, 1850, at Rydal Mount, Westmorland, England.

WORLD HEALTH ORGANIZATION: ANNIVERSARY. Apr 7, 1948. This agency of the UN was founded to coordinate international health systems. It is headquartered at Geneva, Switzerland. Among its achievements is the elimination of smallpox.

BIRTHDAYS TODAY

Jerry Brown, 76, Governor of California (D), born San Francisco, CA, Apr 7, 1938.

Hodding Carter III, 79, television and newspaper journalist, born New Orleans, LA, Apr 7, 1935.

Jackie Chan, 60, actor (*The Forbidden Kingdom, Rush Hour, Shanghai Noon*), born Hong Kong, Apr 7, 1954.

Francis Ford Coppola, 75, filmmaker (*Godfather* films, *Apocalypse Now*), born Detroit, MI, Apr 7, 1939.

Russell Crowe, 50, actor (Oscar for *Gladiator*; *Cinderella Man, LA Confidential, A Beautiful Mind*), born Auckland, New Zealand, Apr 7, 1964.

Anthony Drew (Tony) Dorsett, 60, Hall of Fame football player, born Rochester, PA, Apr 7, 1954.

Daniel Ellsberg, 83, author (released the "Pentagon Papers" to the *New York Times*), born Chicago, IL, Apr 7, 1931.

David Frost, 75, entertainer ("That Was the Week That Was"), interviewer, born Tenterden, England, Apr 7, 1939.

James Garner, 86, actor (*Space Cowboys*, "Maverick," "The Rockford Files"), born James Baumgardner at Norman, OK, Apr 7, 1928.

John Oates, 66, singer (Hall & Oates), born New York, NY, Apr 7, 1948.

Wayne Rogers, 81, actor ("M*A*S*H," "House Calls"), born Birmingham, AL, Apr 7, 1933.

Gerhard Schroeder, 70, former chancellor of Germany, born Mossenberg, Germany, Apr 7, 1944.

April 8 — Tuesday

DAY 98 — **267 REMAINING**

ASSOCIATION OF AMERICAN GEOGRAPHERS ANNUAL MEETING. Apr 8–12. Tampa, FL. 110th annual national meeting of members with workshops, paper and poster sessions and field trips. Est attendance: 7,000. For info: Assn of American Geographers, 1710 16th St NW, Washington, DC 20009-3198. Phone: (202) 234-1450. E-mail: gaia@aag.org. Web: www.aag.org.

CHILDREN'S DAY IN FLORIDA. Apr 8. A legal holiday in Florida commemorated on the second Tuesday in April.

CRAFT BREWERS CONFERENCE & BREWEXPO AMERICA®. Apr 8–11. Denver, CO. This conference (sponsored by the Brewers Association) is the number-one environment in North America for professional brewers, brewery owners and brewery marketing directors for concentrated, affordable brewing education and idea sharing to improve brewery quality and performance. This is the only industry event that serves both brewpubs and breweries. BrewExpo America allows exhibitors and buyers to develop profitable business relationships and helps them encounter the latest and the best that industry vendors have to offer. Est attendance: 4,000. For info: Brewers Association, 736 Pearl St, Boulder, CO 80302. Phone: (303) 447-0816. Fax: (303) 447-2825. E-mail: info@brewersassociation.org. Web: www.CraftBrewersConference.com.

ENGLAND: LONDON BOOK FAIR. Apr 8–10. Earls Court, London. One of the world's most important publishing events. Est attendance: 23,000. For info: London Book Fair, Oriel House, 26 The Quadrant, Richmond, England TW9 1DL. Web: www.londonbookfair.co.uk.

FEDERAL GOVERNMENT SEIZURE OF STEEL MILLS: ANNIVERSARY. Apr 8, 1952. On this date President Harry S Truman seized control of the nation's steel mills by presidential order in an attempt to prevent a shutdown by strikers. On Apr 29, a US district court declared the seizure unconstitutional and workers immediately walked out. Production dropped from 300,000 tons a day to less than 20,000. After 53 days the strike ended July 24, with steelworkers receiving a 16-cent hourly wage raise plus a 5.4-cent hourly increase in fringe benefits.

FISCUS, KATHY: 65th DEATH ANNIVERSARY. Apr 8, 1949. While playing, three-year-old Kathy Fiscus of San Marino, CA, fell into an abandoned well pipe 14 inches wide and 120 feet deep. Rescue workers toiled for two days while national attention was focused on the tragedy. Her body was recovered Apr 10, 1949. An alarmed nation suddenly became attentive to other abandoned wells and similar hazards, and "Kathy Fiscus laws" were enacted in a number of places requiring new safety measures to prevent recurrence of such an accident.

FORD, BETTY: BIRTH ANNIVERSARY. Apr 8, 1918. Former First Lady, wife of Gerald Ford, 38th president of the US, born Elizabeth Ann Bloomer at Chicago, IL. She spoke openly on policy issues, was a strong advocate for women's rights and endorsed legalized abortion. Ford used her 1974 mastectomy as an opportunity to educate women on breast cancer, and after her own struggles with alcohol and prescription drugs, opened an addiction-treatment clinic to help others. The Betty Ford Center opened in 1982 and is still one of the premier treatment facilities in the US. She and President Ford were married for 58 years until his death in 2006, and she died at Rancho Mirage, CA, July 8, 2011.

HENIE, SONJA: BIRTH ANNIVERSARY. Apr 8, 1912. Sonja Henie, Olympic gold medal figure skater, born at Oslo, Norway. Henie competed in the 1924 Winter Olympics when she was just 11 but finished last in ladies' singles. She won gold medals at the Winter Games of 1928, 1932 and 1936. She became a professional skater and an actress (*Sun Valley Serenade*). Died Oct 13, 1969.

HOME RUN RECORD SET BY HANK AARON: 40th ANNIVERSARY. Apr 8, 1974. Henry ("Hammerin' Hank") Aaron hit the 715th home run of his career, breaking the record set by Babe Ruth in 1935. Playing for the Atlanta Braves, Aaron broke the record at Atlanta in a game against the Los Angeles Dodgers. He finished his career in 1976 with a total of 755 home runs. At the time of his retirement, Aaron also ranked first in RBIs, second in at bats and runs scored and third in base hits. On Aug 7, 2007, Barry Bonds of the San Francisco Giants hit his 756th home run to break Aaron's record.

HUNTER, "CATFISH": BIRTH ANNIVERSARY. Apr 8, 1946. James Augustus ("Catfish") Hunter, Baseball Hall of Fame pitcher, born at Hertford, NC. Died Sept 9, 1999, at Hertford.

INTERNATIONAL ROMA DAY. Apr 8. A day to celebrate Roma culture and history and the contributions of Roma to our societies. Also a day to acknowledge historical and systemic discrimination against this population, one of the largest minority groups in Europe (at 10 to 12 million Roma). Originally declared on Apr 8, 1971, at the Fourth Romani World Congress.

April 2014

S	M	T	W	T	F	S
		1	2	3	4	5
6	7	8	9	10	11	12
13	14	15	16	17	18	19
20	21	22	23	24	25	26
27	28	29	30			

JAPAN: FLOWER FESTIVAL (HANA MATSURI). Apr 8. Commemorates Buddha's birthday. Ceremonies in all temples.

KNIGHT, O. RAYMOND: BIRTH ANNIVERSARY. Apr 8, 1872. The "Father of Canadian Rodeo," O. Raymond Knight was born at Payson, UT. His father, the Utah mining magnate Jesse Knight, founded the town of Raymond, AB, Canada, in 1901. In 1902 O. Raymond Knight produced Canada's first rodeo, the "Raymond Stampede." He also built rodeo's first grandstand and first chute in 1903. O. Raymond Knight died Feb 7, 1947.

McRAE, CARMEN: BIRTH ANNIVERSARY. Apr 8, 1920. After winning an amateur contest at Harlem's legendary Apollo Theatre in her hometown of New York City, McRae went on to become a noted jazz singer, singing with the Earl Hines, Mercer Ellington and Benny Carter bands, among others, and recording more than 20 albums. She died Nov 10, 1994, at Beverly Hills, CA.

MORRIS, LEWIS: BIRTH ANNIVERSARY. Apr 8, 1726. Signer of the Declaration of Independence, born at Westchester County, NY. Died Jan 22, 1798, at Morrisania Manor at NY.

NATIONAL BE KIND TO LAWYERS DAY. Apr 8. Lawyers are perhaps the most reviled and ridiculed profession in the world today, and yet people flock to lawyers the moment they need help writing a will, running a business or avoiding jail time. This is the one day out of the year to give an ounce or two of respect to the men and women who daily tip the scales of justice. Whether you take your favorite attorney out to lunch or simply refrain from telling lawyer jokes for 24 hours, this is the day to give a little love to the attorneys in your life. Annually, the second Tuesday in April. For info: Steve Hughes, 412 Luther Ct, St. Louis, MO 63122. Phone: (314) 821-8700. E-mail: info@hityourstride.com. Web: www.BeKindToLawyers.com.

POLL TAX OUTLAWED: ANNIVERSARY. Apr 8, 1966. In the last of a series of moves to abolish poll taxes, a three-judge federal court at Jackson, MS, outlawed Mississippi's $2 poll tax as a voting requirement for state and local elections.

SCOTTSDALE CULINARY FESTIVAL™. Apr 8–13. Scottsdale, AZ. 36th annual. Six fun days of food, wine and music. With events ranging from luxurious dinners and chic cocktail parties to casual feasting favorites, this festival has something to offer every palate. All event proceeds fund art and art education programs for youth in the community. Est attendance: 40,000. For info: Scottsdale Culinary Festival, 7309 E Evans, Scottsdale, AZ 85260. Phone: (480) 945-7193. E-mail: info@scottsdaleculinaryfestival.org. Web: www.scottsdaleculinaryfestival.org.

SEVENTEENTH AMENDMENT TO US CONSTITUTION RATIFIED: ANNIVERSARY. Apr 8, 1913. Prior to the 17th Amendment, members of the Senate were elected by each state's respective legislature. The advent and popularity of primary elections during the last decade of the 19th century and the early 20th century and a string of senatorial scandals, most notably a scandal involving William Lorimer, an Illinois political boss in 1909, forced the Senate to end its resistance to a constitutional amendment requiring direct popular election of senators.

VOYAGEURS NATIONAL PARK ESTABLISHED: ANNIVERSARY. Apr 8, 1975. Minnesota's Voyageurs land was preserved by Congress on Jan 8, 1971. Four years later, it became the 36th US national park.

WILLIAMS, WILLIAM: BIRTH ANNIVERSARY. Apr 8, 1731. Signer of the Declaration of Independence, born at Lebanon, CT. Died there Aug 2, 1811.

BIRTHDAYS TODAY

Kofi Annan, 76, former UN secretary-general (1997–2006), born Kumasi, Ghana, Apr 8, 1938.

Patricia Arquette, 46, actress ("Medium," *Lost Highway, Flirting with Disaster*), born Chicago, IL, Apr 8, 1968.

William D. Chase, 92, librarian and chronicler of contemporary civilization as cofounder and coeditor of *Chase's Annual Events*, born Lakeview, MI, Apr 8, 1922.

Shecky Greene, 89, comedian, actor, born Chicago, IL, Apr 8, 1925.

John J. Havlicek, 74, Hall of Fame basketball player, born Lansing, OH, Apr 8, 1940.

Seymour Hersh, 77, journalist, born Chicago, IL, Apr 8, 1937.

Ron Johnson, 59, US Senator (R, Wisconsin), born Mankato, MN, Apr 8, 1955.

Barbara Kingsolver, 59, author (*The Bean Trees, The Poisonwood Bible, The Lacuna*), born Annapolis, MD, Apr 8, 1955.

Julian Lennon, 51, musician, singer, son of John Lennon, born Liverpool, England, Apr 8, 1963.

Stuart Pankin, 68, actor ("Not Necessarily the News," *Irreconcilable Differences, Arachnophobia*), born Philadelphia, PA, Apr 8, 1946.

Katee Sackhoff, 34, actress ("Battlestar Galactica," "The Bionic Woman"), born Portland, OR, Apr 8, 1980.

John Schneider, 54, actor ("Smallville," "The Dukes of Hazzard"), singer, born Mount Kisco, NY, Apr 8, 1960.

Robin Wright, 48, actress (*House of Cards, White Oleander, The Princess Bride*), born Dallas, TX, Apr 8, 1966.

April 9 — Wednesday

DAY 99 — **266 REMAINING**

AFRICAN METHODIST EPISCOPAL CHURCH ORGANIZED: ANNIVERSARY. Apr 9, 1816. The first all-black US religious denomination, the AME Church was organized at Philadelphia, PA, with Richard Allen, a former slave who had bought his freedom, as the first bishop.

CIVIL RIGHTS BILL OF 1866: ANNIVERSARY. Apr 9, 1866. The Civil Rights Bill of 1866, passed by Congress over the veto of President Andrew Johnson, granted blacks the rights and privileges of American citizenship and formed the basis for the 14th Amendment to the US Constitution.

CIVIL WAR ENDING: ANNIVERSARY. Apr 9, 1865. At 1:30 PM General Robert E. Lee, commander of the Army of Northern Virginia, surrendered to General Ulysses S. Grant, commander in chief of the Union Army, ending four years of civil war. The meeting took place in the house of Wilmer McLean at the village of Appomattox Court House, VA. Confederate soldiers were permitted to keep their horses and go free to their homes, while Confederate officers were allowed to retain their swords and sidearms as well. Grant wrote the terms of surrender. Formal surrender took place at the courthouse on Apr 12. Death toll for the Civil War is estimated at 500,000 men.

DENMARK: OBSERVATION OF NAZI OCCUPATION. Apr 9. Flag-flying day to observe the anniversary of the 1940 Nazi invasion and occupation of the country.

ECKERT, J(OHN) PRESPER, JR: 95th BIRTH ANNIVERSARY. Apr 9, 1919. Coinventor with John W. Mauchly of ENIAC (Electronic Numerical Integrator and Computer), which was first demonstrated at the Moore School of Electrical Engineering at the University of Pennsylvania at Philadelphia Feb 14, 1946. This is generally considered the birth of the computer age. Originally designed to process artillery calculations for the army, ENIAC was also used in the Manhattan Project. Eckert and Mauchly formed Electronic Control Company, which later became Unisys Corporation. Eckert was born at Philadelphia and died at Bryn Mawr, PA, June 3, 1995.

JENKINS'S EAR DAY: ANNIVERSARY. Apr 9, 1731. Spanish *guardacosta* boarded and plundered the British ship *Rebecca* off Jamaica, and among other outrages, they cut off the ear of English master mariner Robert Jenkins. Little notice was taken until seven years later, when Jenkins exhibited the detached ear and described the atrocity to a committee of the House of Commons. In consequence, Britain declared war on Spain in October 1739, a war that lasted until 1743 and is still known as the "War of Jenkins's Ear." Nothing else is known of him.

JUMBO THE ELEPHANT ARRIVES IN AMERICA: ANNIVERSARY. Apr 9, 1882. The most famous elephant in history was captured as a calf near Lake Chad, Africa, in 1861. He was a tremendously popular part of the London Zoo from 1865 to 1882. At London, he gained the name Jumbo (from a West African word for elephant). In 1882, American circus impresario P.T. Barnum bought the 11½-foot-tall and seven-ton animal for $10,000. Jumbo arrived at Manhattan, NY, on Easter Sunday. In an amazing spectacle, Jumbo paraded up Broadway in a crate pulled by 16 horses. Jumbo was just as popular in the US as he was in Britain, and his name entered the English language to describe anything oversized.

KING, FRANK: BIRTH ANNIVERSARY. Apr 9, 1883. Influential comic strip artist who created "Gasoline Alley" in 1919. Originally about men's interest in autos, "Gasoline Alley" had a notable jump in popularity in 1921 when its main character, Walt, adopted a foundling called Skeezix. Devoid of melodrama, this strip sympathetically described the day-to-day lives of Walt, Skeezix and their friends and family, and it was the first American cartoon in which the characters actually aged. Frank King was born at Cashton, WI, and died at Winter Park, FL, June 24, 1969.

MARIAN ANDERSON EASTER CONCERT: 75th ANNIVERSARY. Apr 9, 1939. On this Easter Sunday, black American contralto Marian Anderson sang an open-air concert from the steps of the Lincoln Memorial at Washington, DC, to an audience of 75,000, after having been denied use of the Daughters of the American Revolution (DAR) Constitution Hall. The event became an American antidiscrimination cause célèbre and led First Lady Eleanor Roosevelt to resign from the DAR.

MUYBRIDGE, EADWEARD: BIRTH ANNIVERSARY. Apr 9, 1830. English photographer famed for his studies of animals in motion. Born Edward James Muggeridge, at Kingston-on-Thames, England. Died there May 8, 1904.

✦NATIONAL FORMER PRISONER OF WAR RECOGNITION DAY. Apr 9.

PHILIPPINES: ARAW NG KAGITINGAN. Apr 9. Day of Valor. National observance to commemorate the fall of Bataan in 1942. The infamous "Death March" is reenacted at the Mount Samat Shrine, the Dambana ng Kagitingan.

ROBESON, PAUL BUSTILL: BIRTH ANNIVERSARY. Apr 9, 1898. Paul Robeson, born at Princeton, NJ, was an All-American football player at Rutgers University and received his law degree from Columbia University in 1923. After being seen by Eugene O'Neill in an amateur stage production, he was offered a part in O'Neill's play *The Emperor Jones*. His performance in that play with the Provincetown Players established him as an actor. Without ever having taken a voice lesson, he also became a popular singer. His stage credits include *Show Boat, Porgy and Bess, The Hairy Ape* and *Othello*, which enjoyed the longest Broadway run of a Shakespeare play. In 1950 he was denied a passport by the US for refusing to sign an affidavit stating whether he was or ever had been a member of the Communist Party. The action was overturned by the Supreme Court in 1958. His film credits include *Emperor Jones, Show Boat, King Solomon's Mines* and *Song of Freedom*. Robeson died at Philadelphia, PA, Jan 23, 1976.

SPACE MILESTONE: *SOYUZ 35* (USSR). Apr 9, 1980. Two cosmonauts (Valery Ryumin and Leonid Popov) were launched from Baikonur space center at Kazakhstan, USSR. Docked at *Salyut 6* Apr 10. Ryumin and Popov returned to Earth Oct 11, 1980, after setting a new space endurance record of 185 days.

TEXAS PANHANDLE TORNADO: ANNIVERSARY. Apr 9, 1947. A monster tornado clearing a 1.5-mile-long path struck through at least 12 towns in Texas, Oklahoma and Kansas, killing 169 people and causing more than $15 million in damage. The tornado traveled 221 miles across the three states.

TUNISIA: MARTYRS' DAY. Apr 9.

WINSTON CHURCHILL DAY. Apr 9. Anniversary of enactment of legislation in 1963 that made the late British statesman an honorary citizen of the US.

BIRTHDAYS TODAY

Hugh Hefner, 88, founder of *Playboy*, born Chicago, IL, Apr 9, 1926.

Taylor Kitsch, 33, actor (*John Carter, Savages*, "Friday Night Lights"), born Kelowna, BC, Canada, Apr 9, 1981.

Paul Krassner, 82, editor, journalist, born Brooklyn, NY, Apr 9, 1932.

Michael Learned, 75, actress ("The Waltons"), born Washington, DC, Apr 9, 1939.

Tom Lehrer, 86, songwriter, pianist, mathematician, born New York, NY, Apr 9, 1928.

Leighton Meester, 28, actress ("Gossip Girl," *Country Strong*), born Marco Island, FL, Apr 9, 1986.

Cynthia Nixon, 48, actress ("Sex and the City," *Amadeus*), born New York, NY, Apr 9, 1966.

Keshia Knight Pulliam, 35, actress ("The Cosby Show"), born Newark, NJ, Apr 9, 1979.

Dennis Quaid, 60, actor (*Far from Heaven, The Rookie, Traffic*), born Houston, TX, Apr 9, 1954.

Kristen Stewart, 24, actress (*Twilight Saga* films, *Snow White and the Huntsman, On the Road*), born Los Angeles, CA, Apr 9, 1990.

Jacques Villeneuve, 43, race car driver, born St. Jean d'Iberville, QC, Canada, Apr 9, 1971.

April 2014	S	M	T	W	T	F	S
			1	2	3	4	5
	6	7	8	9	10	11	12
	13	14	15	16	17	18	19
	20	21	22	23	24	25	26
	27	28	29	30			

April 10 — Thursday

DAY 100 **265 REMAINING**

BATAAN DEATH MARCH: ANNIVERSARY. Apr 10, 1942. On this morning American and Filipino prisoners were herded together by Japanese soldiers on Mariveles Airfield at Bataan (in the Philippine islands) and began the Death March to Camp O'Donnell, near Cabanatuan. During the six-day march they were given only one bowl of rice. More than 5,200 Americans and many more Filipinos lost their lives in the course of the march.

THE BEATLES BREAK UP: ANNIVERSARY. Apr 10, 1970. In a press release accompanying promotional copies of his new solo album, Paul McCartney announced that he had no plans for working with the Beatles because of "personal differences, business differences, musical differences." He stated that he didn't know if the break was temporary or permanent, but the years-long tension in the group coupled with the musicians' solo work brought about the end of the band that year. McCartney sued to dissolve the Beatles on Dec 31, 1970, and the group was formally dissolved four years later.

BOOTH, WILLIAM: BIRTH ANNIVERSARY. Apr 10, 1829. General William Booth, founder of the movement that became known, in 1878, as the Salvation Army, was born at Nottingham, England. Apprenticed to a pawnbroker at the age of 13, Booth experienced firsthand the misery of poverty. He broke with conventional church religion and established a quasi-military religious organization with military uniforms and ranks. Recruiting from the poor, from converted criminals and from many other social outcasts, his organization grew rapidly and its influence spread from England to the US and to other countries. At revivals in slum areas the itinerant evangelist offered help for the poor, homes for the homeless, sobriety for alcoholics, rescue homes for women and girls, training centers and legal aid. Booth died at London, England, Aug 20, 1912. See also: "Salvation Army Founder's Day" (Apr 10).

BRAHMS *REQUIEM* PREMIERE: ANNIVERSARY. Apr 10, 1868. Composer Johannes Brahms fortified his reputation as one of the leading figures in 19th-century German Romantic music with the success of his *Requiem*, which premiered at Bremen Cathedral on this date. The choral piece, at turns both melancholy and exuberant, is one of the more recognized and often-sung funerary works in the musical canon.

COMMODORE PERRY DAY. Apr 10, 1794. Birth anniversary of Matthew Calbraith Perry, commodore in the US Navy, negotiator of first treaty between US and Japan (Mar 31, 1854). Born at South Kingston, RI. Died Mar 4, 1858, at New York, NY.

CONNORS, CHUCK (KEVIN JOSEPH): BIRTH ANNIVERSARY. Apr 10, 1921. "The Rifleman" of television fame, Chuck Connors played that title role from 1958 to 1963. His portrayal of a slave owner in the miniseries *Roots* won him an Emmy nomination. Connors acted in more than 45 films and appeared on many TV series and specials. He played professional basketball and baseball before becoming an actor. Born at Brooklyn, NY; died Nov 10, 1992, at Los Angeles, CA.

FIRST PGA CHAMPIONSHIP: ANNIVERSARY. Apr 10, 1916. The then-recently formed Professional Golfers' Association of America held its first championship at Siwanoy golf course at Bronxville, NY. The trophy and the lion's share of the $2,580 purse were won by British golfer Jim Barnes.

FRENCH QUARTER FESTIVAL. Apr 10–13. New Orleans, LA. This festival focuses on all that makes the Quarter special—art, antiques, food, music, shopping, lifestyles and the people. Free concerts on 18 stages featuring 800 local musicians, historic patio tours, parade, children's and other family activities. Est attendance: 450,000. For info: French Quarter Festivals, Inc, 400 N Peters St, #205, New Orleans, LA 70130. Phone: (504) 522-5730 or (800) 673-5725. Fax: (504) 522-5711. E-mail: info@fqfi.org. Web: www.fqfi.org.

GOOD FRIDAY PEACE AGREEMENT IN NORTHERN IRELAND: ANNIVERSARY. Apr 10, 1998. Protestant and Catholic factions reached a power-sharing agreement on Good Friday, 1998. It was endorsed by referenda in Northern Ireland and the Republic of Ireland on May 22, 1998. As a result, a provincial government was established in Northern Ireland to replace direct rule by Britain. The Northern Ireland Assembly met for the first time June 5, 2000.

GROTIUS, HUGO: BIRTH ANNIVERSARY. Apr 10, 1583. (Old Style date.) Anniversary of the birth of Hugo Grotius, the Dutch theologian, attorney, scholar and statesman whose beliefs profoundly influenced American thinking, especially with regard to the conscience of humanity. Born at Delft, Holland, he died at Rostock, Germany, Aug 28, 1645 (OS).

NATIONAL SIBLINGS DAY. Apr 10. A commemorative day to honor, appreciate and celebrate all brothers and sisters, and, in cases of deceased siblings, holding them in memory. Recognizing the bond between siblings for the special gift it is. Founded by Claudia Evart of New York City through her nonprofit charity, Siblings Day Foundation, to honor the memories of her sister Lisette and brother Alan; they both died from accidents early in their lives. Since 1998, 75 governors have signed proclamations in 44 states recognizing this day. Presidents Clinton (2000) and Bush (2008) have also issued presidential messages acknowledging this day. Annually, Apr 10. For info: Claudia Evart, Siblings Day Foundation, 30 Park Ave #2P, New York, NY 10016. E-mail: siblingsday@earthlink.net. Web: www.siblingsday.org.

NCAA DIVISION I MEN'S ICE HOCKEY CHAMPIONSHIP (FROZEN FOUR). Apr 10 and 12. Wells Fargo Center, Philadelphia, PA. 67th annual. For info: NCAA, PO Box 6222, Indianapolis, IN 46206-6222. Web: www.NCAA.com.

ODESSA RETAKEN: 70th ANNIVERSARY. Apr 10, 1944. The Red Army retook the Ukrainian city of Odessa, a port on the northwest coast of the Black Sea that had been in the hands of the Nazis since October 1941.

PERKINS, FRANCES: BIRTH ANNIVERSARY. Apr 10, 1880. First woman member of a US presidential cabinet. Born at Boston, MA, she was married in 1915 to Paul Caldwell Wilson but used her maiden name in public life. She was appointed secretary of labor by President Franklin D. Roosevelt in 1933, a post in which she served until 1945. Died at New York, NY, May 14, 1965.

PULITZER, JOSEPH: BIRTH ANNIVERSARY. Apr 10, 1847. American journalist and newspaper publisher, founder of the Pulitzer Prizes, born at Budapest, Hungary. Died at Charleston, SC, Oct 29, 1911. Pulitzer Prizes awarded annually since 1917.

SAFETY PIN PATENTED: ANNIVERSARY. Apr 10, 1849. Walter Hunt of New York patented the first safety pin.

SALVATION ARMY FOUNDER'S DAY. Apr 10, 1829. Birth anniversary of William Booth, a Methodist minister who began an evangelical ministry in the East End of London, England, in 1865 and established mission stations to feed and house the poor. In 1878 he changed the name of the organization to the Salvation Army. Booth was born at Nottingham, England; he died at London, Aug 20, 1912. See also: "Booth, William: Birth Anniversary" (Apr 10).

SPRING FAIR. Apr 10–13. Washington State Fair Events Center, Puyallup, WA. First held in 1990, this fair celebrates spring, including exhibits, animals, flowers, rides, demonstrations, gardening, KidZone, lots of entertainment, food and much more. Est attendance: 110,000. For info: Spring Fair, 110 9th Ave SW, Puyallup, WA 98371. Phone: (253) 845-1771. Fax: (253) 841-5390. E-mail: info@thefair.com. Web: www.thefair.com.

WOODWARD, ROBERT BURNS: BIRTH ANNIVERSARY. Apr 10, 1917. Nobel Prize–winning (1965) Harvard University science professor whose special field of study was molecular structure of complex organic compounds. Called "one of the most outstanding scientific minds of the century." Born at Boston, MA, he died at Cambridge, MA, July 8, 1979.

BIRTHDAYS TODAY

Kenneth "Babyface" Edmonds, 57, singer, songwriter, born Indianapolis, IN, Apr 10, 1957.

Dolores Huerta, 84, cofounder, with Cesar Chavez, of the United Farm Workers of America labor union, born Dawson, NM, Apr 10, 1930.

Chyler Leigh, 32, actress ("Grey's Anatomy," "The Practice"), born Charlotte, NC, Apr 10, 1982.

Peter MacNicol, 60, actor ("Numb3rs," "Ally McBeal," *Ghostbusters II*), born Dallas, TX, Apr 10, 1954.

John Madden, 78, sportscaster, Hall of Fame football coach, video game namesake, born Austin, MN, Apr 10, 1936.

Haley Joel Osment, 26, actor (*The Sixth Sense, Bogus*), born Los Angeles, CA, Apr 10, 1988.

Michael Pitt, 33, actor ("Boardwalk Empire," *Last Days*), born West Orange, NJ, Apr 10, 1981.

Steven Seagal, 63, actor, producer (*Hard to Kill, On Deadly Ground*), born Lansing, MI, Apr 10, 1951.

Omar Sharif, 82, actor (*Lawrence of Arabia, Dr. Zhivago*), born Michael Shalhoub at Alexandria, Egypt, Apr 10, 1932.

Paul Theroux, 73, author (*The Mosquito Coast, Millroy the Magician*), born Medford, MS, Apr 10, 1941.

Max Von Sydow, 85, actor (*The Seventh Seal, The Emigrants*), born Lund, Sweden, Apr 10, 1929.

April 11 — Friday

DAY 101 **264 REMAINING**

BARBERSHOP QUARTET DAY. Apr 11. Commemorates the gathering of 26 persons at Tulsa, OK, Apr 11, 1938, and the founding there of the Society for the Preservation and Encouragement of Barbershop Quartet Singing in America.

BLISS, LIZZIE "LILLIE": 150th BIRTH ANNIVERSARY. Apr 11, 1864. Lizzie "Lillie" Bliss was born at Boston, MA. She was one of the three founders (all women) of the Museum of Modern Art at New York City in 1929. She died Mar 12, 1931, at New York City.

BOLIN, JANE MATILDA: BIRTH ANNIVERSARY. Apr 11, 1908. Jane Matilda Bolin, born at Poughkeepsie, NY, was the first black woman to graduate from the Yale School of Law (1931) and went on to become the first black woman judge in the US. She served as assistant corporation counsel for the city of New York before being appointed to the city's Domestic Relations Court and the Family Court of the State of New York. Bolin died Jan 8, 2007, at New York, NY.

CIVIL RIGHTS ACT OF 1968: ANNIVERSARY. Apr 11, 1968. Exactly one week after the assassination of Martin Luther King, Jr, the Civil Rights Act of 1968 (protecting civil rights workers, expanding the rights of Native Americans and providing antidiscrimination measures in housing) was signed into law by President Lyndon B. Johnson, who said: "[T]he proudest moments of my presidency have been times such as this when I have signed into law the promises of a century."

COACHELLA VALLEY MUSIC AND ARTS FESTIVAL. Apr 11–13 (and Apr 18–20). Empire Polo Grounds, Indio, CA. Since 1999, annual music and arts festival held in the California Desert. Features established and emerging artists on multiple stages—and usually a major band reunion. Rain or shine. Camping available; carpooling encouraged. Est attendance: 200,000. For info: Coachella. E-mail: info@coachella.com. Web: www.coachella.com.

COIN, JEWELRY & STAMP EXPO. Apr 11–13. Hotel Pennsylvania, New York, NY. Annual expo. Est attendance: 10,000. For info: Israel Bick, Exec Dir, Intl Stamp & Coin Collectors Society, PO Box 854, Van Nuys, CA 91408. Phone: (818) 997-6496. Fax: (818) 988-4337. E-mail: iibick@sbcglobal.net. Web: www.bickinternational.com.

COSTA RICA: JUAN SANTAMARÍA DAY. Apr 11. National holiday. Commemorates the 1856 Battle of Rivas.

✦EDUCATION AND SHARING DAY. Apr 11. Proclaimed annually each year on the Jewish calendar date of 11 Nissan, in honor of Rabbi Menachem Mendel Schneerson, an advocate for youth around the world.

GLOBAL YOUTH SERVICE DAY. Apr 11–13. An annual campaign that celebrates and mobilizes the millions of children and youth who improve their communities each day of the year through service and service-learning. Established in 1988, GYSD is the largest service event in the world and is now celebrated in more than 100 countries. On GYSD, children and youth address the world's most critical issues in partnership with families, schools, community and faith-based organizations, businesses and government. For info: Youth Service America. Web: www.GYSD.org.

HAROLD WASHINGTON ELECTED FIRST BLACK MAYOR OF CHICAGO: ANNIVERSARY. Apr 11, 1983. Harold Washington defeated Bernard Epton and became the first black mayor of Chicago, IL. Of the city's 1.6 million voters, a record 82 percent voted. Washington won 51 percent of the votes, which split along racial lines. He was reelected in April 1987 but died suddenly seven months later at his office, Nov 25, 1987.

HUGHES, CHARLES EVANS: BIRTH ANNIVERSARY. Apr 11, 1862. Prominent American conservative, born at Glens Falls, NY, who served his country in a variety of roles. Hughes was governor of New York (1907–10), associate justice of the US (1910–16), US secretary of state (1921–25) and 11th chief justice of the US (1930–41). He also was the 1916 Republican candidate for president who was defeated by Woodrow Wilson. Hughes died at Osterville, MA, Aug 27, 1948.

INTERNATIONAL "LOUIE LOUIE" DAY. Apr 11. A day to celebrate what has been called the greatest party song of all time. "Louie Louie" has been recorded more times than any other rock song in history and was very nearly declared the official state song of Washington. Annually, Apr 11, the birthday of composer Richard Berry in 1935, who first released the song as a B-side in 1957. Created by the Louie Louie Advocacy and Music Appreciation Society (LLAMAS).

JULIAN, PERCY: BIRTH ANNIVERSARY. Apr 11, 1899. Percy Julian, producer of a synthetic progesterone using soybeans, was born at Montgomery, AL. He also developed a cheaper method of producing cortisone, as well as a drug to treat glaucoma and a chemical foam to fight petroleum fires. Julian died Apr 19, 1975, at Waukegan, IL.

April 2014	S	M	T	W	T	F	S
			1	2	3	4	5
	6	7	8	9	10	11	12
	13	14	15	16	17	18	19
	20	21	22	23	24	25	26
	27	28	29	30			

KENTUCKY DERBY FESTIVAL. Apr 11–May 2. Louisville, KY. Civic celebration since 1956 as Louisville warms up for the Kentucky Derby. About 70 events, two-thirds of which are free to the public. Est attendance: 1,500,000. For info: Kentucky Derby Festival, Inc, 1001 S Third St, Louisville, KY 40203. Phone: (502) 584-FEST. Fax: (502) 589-4674. E-mail: info@kdf.org. Web: www.kdf.org.

LIBERATION OF BUCHENWALD CONCENTRATION CAMP: ANNIVERSARY. Apr 11, 1945. Buchenwald, north of Weimar, Germany, was entered by Allied troops. It was the first of the Nazi concentration camps to be liberated. It had been established in 1937, and about 56,000 people died there.

MAIN STREET BBQ & BLUESFEST. Apr 11–12. Washington, MO. A professional barbeque cooking competition, featuring 50 professional cookers. People's Choice tasting, live blues music and a full food court. For info: Downtown Washington Inc, 123 Lafayette St, PO Box 144, Washington, MO 63090. Phone: (636) 239-1743. Fax: (636) 239-4832. E-mail: events@downtownwashmo.org. Web: www.downtownwashmo.org.

MENNONITE RELIEF SALE. Apr 11–12. Kansas State Fair Grounds, Hutchinson, KS. More than 70 Mennonite, Brethren in Christ and Amish congregations in Kansas sponsor this annual festival and benefit auction for the worldwide hunger-relief and community-aid programs of the Mennonite Central Committee. Auctions of quilts, furniture, tools and crafts. Free admission and parking, great food and lots more. No vendors. Est attendance: 30,000. For info: Matthew Voth, 447 120th, Newton, KS 67114. Phone: (620) 367-2917. Web: www.kansas.mccsale.org.

MESSICK, DALE: BIRTH ANNIVERSARY. Apr 11, 1906. Dalia (Dale) Messick, born at South Bend, IN, was the creator of the intrepid, glamorous globe-trotting reporter Brenda Starr in the comic strip of the same name that debuted in June 1940. Messick, one of the first women to break into comics, retired from the strip in the 1980s and died at Sonoma County, CA, on Apr 5, 2005.

NATIONAL TEACH CHILDREN TO SAVE DAY. Apr 11. Since 1997, an annual day when more than 100,000 banker volunteers across America teach children of all ages the importance of saving and making fiscal fitness a lifetime habit. For info: American Bankers Assn Education Foundation, 1120 Connecticut Ave NW, Washington, DC 20036. Phone: (202) 663-5453. Fax: (202) 663-7578. Web: www.aba.com/abaef or www.teachchildrentosave.com.

NCAA DIVISION I MEN'S GYMNASTICS CHAMPIONSHIP. Apr 11–12. Crisler Center, Ann Arbor, MI. For info: NCAA, PO Box 6222, Indianapolis, IN 46206-6222. Web: www.NCAA.com.

OZARK MOUNTAIN UFO CONFERENCE. Apr 11–13. Best Western Inn of the Ozarks, Eureka Springs, AR. 26th annual meeting of researchers from various states and foreign countries to inform the public of the latest news concerning UFOs. Speakers include authors of books on the subject and people who have investigated UFO cases; program includes audiovisual presentations of UFO evidence. Est attendance: 600. For info: Ozark Mountain UFO Conference. E-mail: info@ozarkufoconference.com. Web: www.ozarkufoconference.com.

SPACE MILESTONE: *APOLLO 13* LAUNCHED (US). Apr 11, 1970. Fifty-six hours into flight, astronauts James Lovell (commander), Fred Haise and John Swigert were endangered when an oxygen tank ruptured. The planned moon landing was canceled, and details of the accident were made public. The entire world shared concern for the crew, who splashed down successfully in the Pacific Apr 17.

SPELMAN COLLEGE ESTABLISHED: ANNIVERSARY. Apr 11, 1881. Spelman College, with funding from the Rockefeller family, opened its doors for the first time with the purpose of educating young African-American women. The institution, located at Atlanta, GA, was dubbed "the Radcliffe for Negro women."

UGANDA: LIBERATION DAY. Apr 11. Republic of Uganda celebrates anniversary of overthrow of Idi Amin's dictatorship in 1979.

BIRTHDAYS TODAY

Tony Brown, 81, television journalist, born Charleston, WV, Apr 11, 1933.

Steve Bullock, 48, Governor of Montana (D), born Missoula, MT, Apr 11, 1966.

Jeremy Clarkson, 54, television personality ("Top Gear"), born Doncaster, South Yorkshire, England, Apr 11, 1960.

Ellen Goodman, 66, Pulitzer Prize–winning columnist, born Newton, MA, Apr 11, 1948.

Joel Grey, 82, actor (Oscar for *Cabaret*; *The Seven-Per-Cent Solution*), born Joe Katz at Cleveland, OH, Apr 11, 1932.

Tricia Helfer, 40, actress ("Battlestar Galactica"), born Donalda, AB, Canada, Apr 11, 1974.

Bill Irwin, 64, actor, choreographer (*The Regard of Flight*), born Santa Monica, CA, Apr 11, 1950.

Ethel Kennedy, 86, widow of Robert Kennedy, born Greenwich, CT, Apr 11, 1928.

Louise Lasser, 75, actress ("Mary Hartman, Mary Hartman"), born New York, NY, Apr 11, 1939.

Peter Riegert, 67, actor (*Local Hero, Crossing Delancey*), born New York, NY, Apr 11, 1947.

Bret William Saberhagen, 50, former baseball player, born Chicago Heights, IL, Apr 11, 1964.

Meshach Taylor, 67, actor ("Dave's World," "Designing Women"), born Boston, MA, Apr 11, 1947.

April 12 — Saturday

DAY 102 | **263 REMAINING**

ATTACK ON FORT SUMTER: ANNIVERSARY. Apr 12, 1861. After months of escalating tension, Major Robert Anderson refused to evacuate Fort Sumter at Charleston, SC. Confederate troops under the command of General P.T. Beauregard opened fire on the harbor fort at 4:30 AM and continued until Major Anderson surrendered on Apr 13. No lives were lost despite the firing of some 40,000 shells in the first major engagement of the American Civil War.

THE BIG WIND: 80th ANNIVERSARY. Apr 12, 1934. The highest-velocity natural wind ever recorded occurred in the morning at the Mount Washington, NH, observatory. Three weather observers, Wendell Stephenson, Alexander McKenzie and Salvatore Pagliuca, observed and recorded the phenomenon in which gusts reached 231 mph—"the strongest natural wind ever recorded on the earth's surface." The 50th anniversary was observed at the site in 1984, with the three original observers participating in the ceremony.

CLAY, HENRY: BIRTH ANNIVERSARY. Apr 12, 1777. Statesman, born at Hanover County, VA. Served as the Speaker of the House of Representatives and later became the leader of the new Whig Party. He was defeated for the presidency three times. Clay died at Washington, DC, June 29, 1852.

CYPRUS: THE PROCESSION OF ICON OF SAINT LAZARUS. Apr 12. Larnaca. The tomb of Lazarus (the man raised from the dead by Christ) resides in the Ayios Lazaros Church—built by Emperor Leo VI in the ninth century. Eight days before the Orthodox Easter Sunday, his icon is taken through the streets of Larnaca.

FDR COMMEMORATIVE CEREMONY. Apr 12. Little White House, Warm Springs, GA. Annual ceremony honoring Franklin Delano Roosevelt on the anniversary of his death in Warm Springs. Keynote speaker and Marine color guard highlight this impressive ceremony. Est attendance: 1,000. For info: Little White House, 401 Little White House Rd, Warm Springs, GA 31830. Phone: (706) 655-5870.

HALIFAX INDEPENDENCE DAY: ANNIVERSARY. Apr 12, 1776. North Carolina. Anniversary of the resolution adopted by the Provincial Congress of North Carolina at Halifax, NC, authorizing the delegates from North Carolina to the Continental Congress to vote for a Declaration of Independence.

HALL, LYMAN: BIRTH ANNIVERSARY. Apr 12, 1724. Signer of the Declaration of Independence. Born at Wallingford, CT, he died at Burke County, GA, Oct 19, 1790.

JOHN WILKES BOOTH ESCAPE ROUTE TOUR. Apr 12, 19, 26 and May 3. (Also Sept 6, 13, 20, 27.) Clinton, MD. A 12-hour bus tour over the route used by Lincoln's assassin. Bookings begin no earlier than Jan 15, 2014. For info: Laurie Verge, Dir, Surratt House Museum, 9118 Brandywine Rd, Clinton, MD 20735. Phone: (301) 868-1121. Fax: (301) 868-8177. Web: www.surratt.org.

LAZARUS SATURDAY. Apr 12. Orthodox celebration of Christ raising Lazarus from the dead. Only time the resurrection liturgy is used on a day other than Sunday. Occurs eight days before Pascha.

MASSACRE AT FORT PILLOW: 150th ANNIVERSARY. Apr 12, 1864. After surrounding Fort Pillow, TN, Confederate general Nathan Bedford Forrest attacked the stronghold on this date. The ensuing Confederate victory led to many casualties, many of them black Union soldiers. Although Forrest claimed that the large number of casualties was a result of the fort's refusal to surrender, most believe that Forrest's men massacred the defenseless troops after the fort was surrendered. The action inflamed Northern sentiments and is considered one of the most controversial events of the Civil War.

NATIONAL D.E.A.R. DAY—NATIONAL DROP EVERYTHING AND READ DAY. Apr 12. A special reading celebration to remind and encourage families to make reading together on a daily basis a family priority. Annually, Apr 12, the birthday of author Beverly Cleary. For info: American Library Assn. Web: www.ala.org.

NATIONAL LICORICE DAY. Apr 12. Celebrating black licorice, including its history, health benefits and world renown as a delightful confection. Throughout the entire month of April (which is also National Licorice Month), Licorice International offers tours and free samples to the public. For info: Elizabeth Erlandson, Licorice International, 803 Q St, Ste 300, Lincoln, NE 68508. Phone: (402) 488-2230. E-mail: licoricenews@licoriceinternational.com. Web: www.licoriceinternational.com or www.ilovelicorice.com.

POLIO VACCINE: ANNIVERSARY. Apr 12, 1955. Anniversary of announcement that the polio vaccine developed by American physician Dr. Jonas E. Salk was "safe, potent and effective." Incidence of the dreaded infantile paralysis, or poliomyelitis, declined by 95 percent following introduction of preventive vaccines. The first mass innoculations of children with the Salk vaccine had begun in Pittsburgh, PA, Feb 23, 1954.

ROOSEVELT, FRANKLIN DELANO: DEATH ANNIVERSARY. Apr 12, 1945. With the end of WWII only months away, the nation and the world were stunned by the sudden death of the president shortly into his fourth term of office. Roosevelt, 32nd president of the US (Mar 4, 1933–Apr 12, 1945), was the only president to serve more than two terms—he was elected to four consecutive terms. He died at Warm Springs, GA.

SPACE MILESTONE: *COLUMBIA STS-1* (US) FIRST SHUTTLE FLIGHT. Apr 12, 1981. First flight of shuttle *Columbia.* Two astronauts (John Young and Robert Crippen), on first manned US space mission since *Apollo-Soyuz* in July 1976, spent 54 hours in space (36 orbits of Earth) before landing at Edwards Air Force Base, CA, Apr 14.

SPACE MILESTONE: *VOSTOK I*, FIRST MAN IN SPACE. Apr 12, 1961. Yuri Gagarin became the first man in space when he made a 108-minute voyage, orbiting Earth in a 10,395-pound vehicle, *Vostok I*, launched by the USSR.

TRUANCY LAW: ANNIVERSARY. Apr 12, 1853. The first truancy law was enacted at New York. A $50 fine was charged against parents whose children between the ages of 5 and 15 were absent from school.

"21 JUMP STREET" TV PREMIERE: ANNIVERSARY. Apr 12, 1987. Youthful big-city cops busted crime in the local schools and colleges in this FOX police drama. Starred Johnny Depp as Tom Hanson, Holly Robinson Peete as Judy Hoffs, Dustin Nguyen as H.T. Loki, Peter DeLuise as Doug Penhall, Frederic Forrest as Captain Jenko, Steven Williams as Captain Adam Fuller and Richard Grieco as Dennis Booker. It was one of the FOX network's early hits.

UNITED NATIONS: INTERNATIONAL DAY OF HUMAN SPACE FLIGHT. Apr 12. Marking the anniversary of the flight of Russian cosmonaut Yuri Gagarin on Apr 12, 1961, this day reaffirms the important contribution of space science and technology in achieving sustainable development goals. The General Assembly has designated Apr 12 each year as the International Day of Human Space Flight (Res 65/271 of Apr 7, 2010). For info: United Nations, Dept of Public Info, New York, NY 10017. Web: www.un.org.

WALK ON YOUR WILD SIDE DAY. Apr 12. Time's wasting, friends. It's high time you went out and did some things no one expects you to do. Be unpredictable for once. Go to work dressed like a gorilla, get a master's degree—do something "they" said you'd never ever do. (©2006 by WH.) For info: Thomas & Ruth Roy, Wellcat Holidays, 2418 Long Ln, Lebanon, PA 17046. Phone: (717) 279-0184. E-mail: info@wellcat.com. Web: www.wellcat.com.

"YOUR HIT PARADE" RADIO PREMIERE: ANNIVERSARY. Apr 12, 1935. This program debuted on radio in 1935 with its countdown of the week's top songs. In 1950 it became a TV program. See also: "Your Hit Parade TV Premiere: Anniversary" (Oct 7).

April 2014	S	M	T	W	T	F	S
			1	2	3	4	5
	6	7	8	9	10	11	12
	13	14	15	16	17	18	19
	20	21	22	23	24	25	26
	27	28	29	30			

BIRTHDAYS TODAY

David Cassidy, 64, singer, actor ("The Partridge Family"), born New York, NY, Apr 12, 1950.

Tom Clancy, 67, author (*The Hunt for Red October, Red Storm Rising*), born Baltimore, MD, Apr 12, 1947.

Beverly Cleary, 98, author (the Ramona Quimby series; Newbery Medal for *Dear Mr Henshaw*), born McMinnville, OR, Apr 12, 1916.

Claire Danes, 35, actress ("Homeland," *Temple Grandin, Shopgirl, The Hours*), born New York, NY, Apr 12, 1979.

Shannen Doherty, 43, actress ("Beverly Hills 90210," "Charmed," *Heathers*), born Memphis, TN, Apr 12, 1971.

Andy Garcia, 58, actor (*Ocean's Eleven, The Untouchables*), born Havana, Cuba, Apr 12, 1956.

Herbie Hancock, 74, musician, born Chicago, IL, Apr 12, 1940.

Dan Lauria, 67, actor ("The Wonder Years," *Stakeout*), born Brooklyn, NY, Apr 12, 1947.

David Letterman, 67, comedian, television talk show host ("Late Show with David Letterman"), born Indianapolis, IN, Apr 12, 1947.

Sarah Jane Morris, 37, actress ("Brothers & Sisters," "Felicity"), born Memphis, TN, Apr 12, 1977.

Ed O'Neill, 68, actor ("Modern Family," "Married . . . With Children," *Wayne's World*), born Youngstown, OH, Apr 12, 1946.

Saoirse Ronan, 20, actress (*Atonement, The Lovely Bones*), born New York, NY, Apr 12, 1994.

April 13 — Sunday

DAY 103 **262 REMAINING**

BECKETT, SAMUEL: BIRTH ANNIVERSARY. Apr 13, 1906. Author, critic and playwright, born at Foxrock, County Dublin, Ireland. Beckett is best remembered for his plays, including *Waiting for Godot, Endgame, Krapp's Last Tape* and *Happy Days.* Beckett settled at Paris, France, in 1937 and served with an underground resistance group during the early years of WWII. In the years following the war, he wrote the challenging novels *Molloy, Malone Dies* and *The Unnamable* and two plays, *Eleutheria* and *Waiting for Godot. Waiting for Godot* received an acclaimed production at Paris in January 1953, and with it Beckett achieved worldwide renown. Awarded the Nobel Prize for Literature in 1969, he died Dec 22, 1989, at Paris.

BUTTS, ALFRED M.: BIRTH ANNIVERSARY. Apr 13, 1899. Alfred Butts was a jobless architect in the Depression when he invented the board game Scrabble. The game was just a fad for Butts's friends until a Macy's executive saw the game being played at a resort in 1952, and the world's largest store began carrying it. Manufacturing of the game was turned over to Selchow & Righter when 35 workers were producing 6,000 sets a week. Butts received three cents per set for years. He said, "One-third went to taxes. I gave one-third away, and the other third enabled me to have an enjoyable life." Butts was born at Poughkeepsie, NY. He died Apr 4, 1993, at Rhinebeck, NY.

CASSIDY, BUTCH: BIRTH ANNIVERSARY. Apr 13, 1866. Notorious outlaw who robbed banks and trains throughout the American West during the late 1800s. Born Robert LeRoy Parker at Beaver, UT, Cassidy formed "the Wild Bunch"—a gang that teamed him with Harry Longabaugh ("the Sundance Kid"). Under pressure from Pinkerton agents, Cassidy and Sundance fled to South America in the early 1900s. Details of Cassidy's death are uncertain, but many believe he was killed in San Vicente, Bolivia, in 1909, while attempting to rob a mine station.

CIMARRON TERRITORY CELEBRATION AND WORLD COW CHIP-THROWING® CHAMPIONSHIP CONTEST. Apr 13–20. Beaver, OK. 45th annual. A highly specialized international organic sporting event that draws dung flingers from around the world. Also featuring a craft fair, carnival, chili cook-off, chuck wagon feed, food vendors and a parade. Est attendance: 2,000. For info: Beaver County Chamber of Commerce, PO Box 81, Beaver, OK 73932-0878. Phone: (580) 625-4726. E-mail: bvrchamber@ptsi.net. Web: www.beaverchamber.com.

DR. PEPPER DALLAS CUP XXXV. Apr 13–20. Pizza Hut Park, Frisco, TX. 35th annual. International invitation-only boys' (under 13 to under 19) soccer competition, sanctioned by the USSF and FIFA. In past years, 180 teams from more than 13 countries have been represented. Many of the world's premier teams participate. Annually, from Palm Sunday to Easter Sunday. Est attendance: 120,000. For info: Dallas Cup, 12700 Park Central Dr, Ste 507, Dallas, TX 75251-1500. Phone: (214) 221-3636. Fax: (214) 221-4636. Web: www.dallascup.com.

ENGLAND: VIRGIN LONDON MARATHON. Apr 13. London. Held since 1981 and awarded a road race Gold Label by the International Association of Athletics Federations, the London Marathon hosts more than 46,000 participants in 26 miles from Greenwich to The Mall. For info: Virgin London Marathon. Phone: (44) (20) 7902-0200. Web: www.virginlondonmarathon.com or www.worldmarathonmajors.com.

FAWKES, GUY: BIRTH ANNIVERSARY. Apr 13, 1570. Englishman who, along with a small group of fellow Catholics, conspired to blow up England's Houses of Parliament and kill its Protestant members—including King James I—on Nov 5, 1605. The "Gunpowder Plot" was foiled the night before, and Nov 5 is commemorated as a day of delivery each year with bonfires, fireworks and burning of life-size Fawkes effigies (called "guys"—origin of the English word). Born to a wealthy Protestant family in York, England, Fawkes converted to Catholicism later in life. He was executed Jan 31, 1606, at London. See also: "England: Guy Fawkes Day" (Nov 5).

FIRST BASEBALL STRIKE ENDS: ANNIVERSARY. Apr 13, 1972. Major league baseball players and owners agreed on a settlement in which owners added $500,000 to the players' pension fund. This ended the first baseball strike, which had begun Apr 5 when the season opener was canceled.

HOLY WEEK. Apr 13–19. Christian observance dating from the fourth century, known also as Great Week. The seven days beginning on the sixth and final Sunday in Lent (Palm Sunday), consisting of Palm Sunday, Monday of Holy Week, Tuesday of Holy Week, Spy Wednesday (or Wednesday of Holy Week), Maundy Thursday, Good Friday and Holy Saturday (or Great Sabbath or Easter Even). A time of solemn devotion to and memorializing of the suffering (passion), death and burial of Christ. Formerly a time of strict fasting.

JEFFERSON, THOMAS: BIRTH ANNIVERSARY. Apr 13, 1743. Third president of the US (Mar 4, 1801–Mar 3, 1809), second vice president (1797–1801), born at Albermarle County, VA. Jefferson, who died at Charlottesville, VA, July 4, 1826, wrote his own epitaph: "Here was buried Thomas Jefferson, author of the Declaration of American Independence, of the statute of Virginia for religious freedom, and father of the University of Virginia." A holiday in Alabama and Oklahoma. See also: "Adams, John, and Jefferson, Thomas: Death Anniversary" (July 4).

MEXICO: PASSION PLAY IN IZTAPALAPA (SEMANA SANTA EN IZTAPALAPA). Apr 13–19. Iztapalapa, Mexico City. One of the largest and most amazing religious passion plays in the world, where the small community of Iztapalapa has acted out the Way of the Cross since 1843 (the original *Semana Santa*, or Holy Week, play was given in gratitude after a devastating cholera epidemic finally dissipated). A cast of thousands—none of whom are professional actors—performs. Annually, from Palm Sunday to Good Saturday. For info: COSSIAC (Comité Organizador de Semana Santa en Iztapalapa AC). Web: www.iztapalapa.gob.mx. Est attendance: 1,000,000.

NATIONAL LIBRARY WEEK. Apr 13–19. National Library Week is a time to celebrate the contributions of our nation's libraries and librarians and to promote library use and support. All types of libraries—school, public, academic and special—participate. For info: American Library Assn, Public Info Office, 50 E Huron St, Chicago, IL 60611. Phone: (312) 280-5041. Fax: (312) 280-5274. E-mail: pio@ala.org. Web: www.ala.org/nlw.

ORTHODOX HOLY WEEK. Apr 13–19.

ORTHODOX PALM SUNDAY. Apr 13. Celebration of Christ's entry into Jerusalem, when his way was covered with palms by the multitudes. Beginning of Holy Week in the Orthodox Church.

PALM SUNDAY. Apr 13. Commemorates Christ's last entry into Jerusalem, when his way was covered with palms by the multitudes. Beginning of Holy (or Great) Week in Western Christian churches.

✦PAN AMERICAN WEEK. Apr 13–19. Presidential Proclamation customarily issued as "Pan American Day and Pan American Week." Always issued for the week including Apr 14 (except from 1946 through 1948, 1955 through 1977 and 1979).

PHILIPPINES: HOLY WEEK. Apr 13–19. National observance. Flagellants in the streets, *cenaculos* (passion plays) and other colorful and solemn rituals mark the country's observance of Holy Week.

PREMIERE OF HANDEL'S *MESSIAH*: ANNIVERSARY. Apr 13, 1742. In a charity performance at the New Musick Hall on Fishamble Street, Dublin, Ireland, George Frederick Handel sat at the harpsichord and conducted the first concert of his masterpiece, *Messiah*. This sacred oratorio became Handel's most popular work and has been performed every year since 1742. Newspapers of the day anticipated the popularity of the first performance and asked ladies not to wear hoops under their skirts and gentlemen not to wear swords so that 700 people could fit into a hall designed for 600. Some years later, King George II stood up in admiration of the Hallelujah Chorus, starting a tradition still followed by audiences to this day.

***SILENT SPRING* PUBLISHED: ANNIVERSARY.** Apr 13, 1962. Rachel Carson's *Silent Spring* warned humankind that for the first time in history every person is subjected to contact with dangerous chemicals from conception until death. Carson painted a vivid picture of how chemicals—used in many ways but particularly in pesticides—have upset the balance of nature, undermining the survival of countless species. This enormously popular and influential book was a soft-spoken battle cry to protect our natural surroundings. Its publication signaled the beginning of the environmental movement.

SRI LANKA: SINHALA AND TAMIL NEW YEAR. Apr 13–14. This New Year festival includes traditional games, the wearing of new clothes in auspicious colors and special foods. Public holiday.

THAILAND: SONGKRAN FESTIVAL. Apr 13–15. Public holiday. Thai New Year festival (also known as the "Water Festival"). To welcome the new year, the image of Buddha is bathed with holy or fragrant water and lustral water is sprinkled on celebrants. Joyous event, especially observed at Buddhist temples.

✦THOMAS JEFFERSON DAY. Apr 13. Honoring the birth of the US's third president. Presidential Proclamation 2276, of Mar 21, 1938, covers all succeeding years. (Pub Res No. 60 of Aug 16, 1937.)

WELTY, EUDORA: BIRTH ANNIVERSARY. Apr 13, 1909. Great novelist and short-story writer whose characters lived in the rural South. Her short stories are considered the zenith of the art. Wrote *The Ponder Heart* (1954), among other works. Lived her entire life in Jackson, MS, and died there July 23, 2001.

BIRTHDAYS TODAY

Peabo Bryson, 63, singer, born Greenville, SC, Apr 13, 1951.

Jack Casady, 70, musician, born Washington, DC, Apr 13, 1944.

Robert Casey, 54, US Senator (D, Pennsylvania), born Scranton, PA, Apr 13, 1960.

Bill Conti, 72, composer (Oscar for *The Right Stuff*), born Providence, RI, Apr 13, 1942.

Baron Davis, 35, basketball player, born Los Angeles, CA, Apr 13, 1979.

Tony Dow, 69, actor ("Leave It to Beaver"), born Hollywood, CA, Apr 13, 1945.

Sergei Gonchar, 40, hockey player, born Chelyabinsk, Russia, Apr 13, 1974.

Al Green, 68, singer, born Forrest City, AR, Apr 13, 1946.

Garry Kasparov, 51, International Grandmaster chess player, born Baku, Azerbaijan, Apr 13, 1963.

Davis Love III, 50, golfer, born Charlotte, NC, Apr 13, 1964.

Ron Perlman, 64, actor (*Hellboy*, "Sons of Anarchy," "Beauty and the Beast"), born New York, NY, Apr 13, 1950.

Saundra Santiago, 57, actress ("Miami Vice"), born the Bronx, NY, Apr 13, 1957.

Rick Schroder, 44, actor ("Silver Spoons," "NYPD Blue," *The Champ*), born Staten Island, NY, Apr 13, 1970.

Paul Sorvino, 75, actor ("Law & Order"), born Brooklyn, NY, Apr 13, 1939.

Lyle Waggoner, 79, actor ("The Carol Burnett Show," "Wonder Woman"), born Kansas City, KS, Apr 13, 1935.

Max M. Weinberg, 63, musician (E Street Band), bandleader ("Late Night with Conan O'Brien"), born South Orange, NJ, Apr 13, 1951.

April 2014

S	M	T	W	T	F	S
		1	2	3	4	5
6	7	8	9	10	11	12
13	14	15	16	17	18	19
20	21	22	23	24	25	26
27	28	29	30			

April 14 — Monday

DAY 104 **261 REMAINING**

CAMPBELL BECOMES FIRST AMERICAN AIR ACE: ANNIVERSARY. Apr 14, 1918. Lieutenant Douglas Campbell became the first American pilot to achieve the designation of ace when he shot down his fifth German aircraft.

CHILDREN WITH ALOPECIA DAY. Apr 14. If you are a child (or have a child) who is losing hair because of the autoimmune hair-loss disease alopecia areata, today is your day to stand up and be proud of not having hair while still being you! For info: Jeffery Woytovich, The Children's Alopecia Project, PO Box 6036, Wyomissing, PA 19610. Phone: (610) 741-5552. E-mail: info@childrensalopeciaproject.org. Web: www.childrensalopeciaproject.org.

FIRST AMERICAN ABOLITION SOCIETY FOUNDED: ANNIVERSARY. Apr 14, 1775. The first abolition organization formed in the US was The Society for the Relief of Free Negroes Unlawfully Held in Bondage, founded at Philadelphia, PA.

FIRST DICTIONARY OF AMERICAN ENGLISH PUBLISHED: ANNIVERSARY. Apr 14, 1828. Noah Webster published his *American Dictionary of the English Language.*

GIELGUD, SIR JOHN: BIRTH ANNIVERSARY. Apr 14, 1904. Director and actor, born at London, England. A legend of the stage, he played the role of Hamlet more than 500 times. He made his professional film debut in *Who Is the Man?* in 1924. Other film credits include *Arthur, Murder on the Orient Express* and *Plenty.* He won the Tony Award for Best Director in 1961 for *Big Fish Little Fish.* He died at Buckinghamshire, England, May 21, 2000.

***GRAPES OF WRATH* PUBLISHED: 75th ANNIVERSARY.** Apr 14, 1939. John Steinbeck's novel of the Great Depression, *Grapes of Wrath*, won the 1940 Pulitzer Prize. It chronicled the mass migration to California of dispossessed farmers from the Dust Bowl region of the Great Plains.

HONDURAS: DIA DE LAS AMERICAS. Apr 14. Pan-American Day, a national holiday.

HUYGENS, CHRISTIAAN: BIRTH ANNIVERSARY. Apr 14, 1629. Scientist, born at The Hague, Netherlands. He discovered the rings of Saturn and formulated the wave theory, or pulse theory, of light. In 1656 he invented the pendulum clock. He died at The Hague, June 8, 1695.

INDIA: VAISAKHI. Apr 14. Sikh holiday (also known as Khalsa Day) that commemorates the founding of the brotherhood of the Khalsa in 1699. This harvest festival is regarded as the Sikh New Year.

INTERNATIONAL MOMENT OF LAUGHTER DAY. Apr 14. Laughter is a potent and powerful way to deal with the difficulties of modern living. Since the physical, emotional and spiritual benefits of laughter are widely accepted, this day is set aside for everyone to take the necessary time to experience the power of laughter. For info: Izzy Gesell, Head Honcho of Wide Angle Humor, PO Box 962, Northampton, MA 01061. Phone: (413) 586-2634. E-mail: izzy@izzyg.com. Web: www.izzyg.com.

LINCOLN, ABRAHAM: ASSASSINATION ANNIVERSARY. Apr 14, 1865. President Abraham Lincoln was shot while watching a performance of *Our American Cousin* at Ford's Theatre, Washington, DC. He died the following day. The assassin was John Wilkes Booth, a young actor.

✦PAN-AMERICAN DAY. Apr 14. Presidential Proclamation 1912, of May 28, 1930, covers every Apr 14 (required by Governing Board of Pan-American Union). Proclamation issued each year since 1948. Commemorates the first International Conference of American States in 1890.

PAN-AMERICAN DAY IN FLORIDA. Apr 14. A ceremonial day in Florida that is observed in the public schools as a day honoring the republics of Latin America. When Apr 14 does not fall on a school day, the governor may designate the preceding Friday or the following Monday as Pan-American Day.

PASSOVER BEGINS AT SUNDOWN. Apr 14. See "Pesach" (Apr 15).

PATHOLOGISTS' ASSISTANT DAY. Apr 14. A pathologists' assistant is an intensively trained allied healthcare professional who provides surgical and autopsy pathology services under the direction and supervision of a pathologist. This day honors these professionals. Annually, on Apr 14 (the day the AAPA's Articles of Incorporation were recevied and filed in 1972). For info: American Assn of Pathologists' Assistants, 2345 Rice St, Ste 220, St. Paul, MN 55113. Phone: (800) 532-AAPA or (651) 697-9264. Fax: (651) 317-8048. E-mail: info@pathassist.org. Web: www.pathassist.org.

PRESIDENT TAFT OPENS BASEBALL SEASON: ANNIVERSARY. Apr 14, 1910. President William Howard Taft began a sports tradition by throwing out the first baseball of the season at an American League game between Washington and Philadelphia. Washington won, 3–0.

SULLIVAN, ANNE: BIRTH ANNIVERSARY. Apr 14, 1866. Anne Sullivan, born at Feeding Hills, MA, became well known for "working miracles" with Helen Keller, who was blind and deaf. Nearly blind herself, Sullivan used a manual alphabet communicated by the sense of touch to teach Keller to read, write and speak and then to help her go on to higher education. Anne Sullivan died Oct 20, 1936, at Forest Hills, NY.

TOYNBEE, ARNOLD JOSEPH: 125th BIRTH ANNIVERSARY. Apr 14, 1889. English historian, author of the monumental *Study of History*. Born at London, England; died at York, England, Oct 22, 1975.

UNDERGRADUATE RESEARCH WEEK. Apr 14–18. Annual week celebrating the achievements of students and faculty participating in collaborative research. Sponsored by The Council on Undergraduate Research (CUR), a not-for-profit organization whose mission is to support and promote high-quality student-faculty collaborative research and creative inquiry. All academic institutions are invited to submit their related events for posting with CUR and to participate in CUR sponsored webinars, receptions and research presentations. For info: The Council on Undergraduate Research, 734 15th St NW, Ste 550, Washington, DC 20005. Phone: (202) 783-4810. Fax: (202) 783-4811. E-mail: robin@cur.org. Web: www.cur.org.

VAN CLIBURN CONQUERS MOSCOW: ANNIVERSARY. Apr 14, 1958. Young Texan pianist Van Cliburn won the first International Tchaikovsky Competition in Moscow, USSR (now Russia)—sparking a music frenzy that brought a brief thaw to the Cold War. Embraced by Muscovites, Cliburn was also treated to a ticker tape parade in New York City (the only musician so honored). His subsequent recording of Tchaikovsky's Piano Concerto No. 1 was the first classical music album to go platinum.

BIRTHDAYS TODAY

Abigail Breslin, 18, actress (*Little Miss Sunshine, Signs*), born New York, NY, Apr 14, 1996.

Adrien Brody, 41, actor (Oscar for *The Pianist*; *The Darjeeling Limited, King Kong*), born New York, NY, Apr 14, 1973.

Peter Capaldi, 56, actor ("The Thick of It," "Doctor Who"), born Glasgow, Scotland, Apr 14, 1958.

Robert Carlyle, 53, actor ("Once Upon a Time," *Angela's Ashes, The Full Monty*), born Glasgow, Scotland, Apr 14, 1961.

Julie Christie, 74, actress (*Dr. Zhivago, Shampoo, Away from Her*), born Chukua, India, Apr 14, 1940.

Cynthia Cooper, 51, former basketball player, born Chicago, IL, Apr 14, 1963.

Brad Garrett, 54, comedian, actor ("Everybody Loves Raymond"), born Woodland Hills, CA, Apr 14, 1960.

Sarah Michelle Gellar, 37, actress (*Scooby-Doo*, "Buffy the Vampire Slayer"), born New York, NY, Apr 14, 1977.

Anthony Michael Hall, 46, actor, comedian ("The Dead Zone," *Sixteen Candles, The Breakfast Club*), born Boston, MA, Apr 14, 1968.

David Christopher Justice, 48, former baseball player, born Cincinnati, OH, Apr 14, 1966.

Loretta Lynn, 79, singer/songwriter, born Butcher's Hollow, KY, Apr 14, 1935.

Greg Maddux, 48, former baseball player, born San Angelo, TX, Apr 14, 1966.

Pete Rose, 73, former baseball manager and player, born Cincinnati, OH, Apr 14, 1941.

Emma Thompson, 55, actress (Oscar for *Howards End*; *Wit, Sense and Sensibility*), screenwriter (Oscar for *Sense and Sensibility*), born London, England, Apr 14, 1959.

April 15 — Tuesday

DAY 105 **260 REMAINING**

ASTRONOMERS FIND NEW SOLAR SYSTEM: 15th ANNIVERSARY. Apr 15, 1999. Astronomers from San Francisco State University working at an observatory in Arizona announced the discovery of the first multiplanet system ever found orbiting around a star other than our own. Three planets orbit the star Upsilon Andromedae, which can be seen with the naked eye. This suggests that the Milky Way probably teems with similar planetary systems.

BENTON, THOMAS HART: 125th BIRTH ANNIVERSARY. Apr 15, 1889. Born at Neosho, MO, Thomas Hart Benton studied art in Paris and New York. But he left the metropolitan art world in 1935, traveling to Kansas, determined to create work that reacted against European trends and reflected what was felt to be the integrity of the American heartland. He became one of the foremost artists of the populist art movement known as American Regionalism. He died at Kansas City, MO, Jan 19, 1975.

BOSTON MARATHON BOMBINGS: ANNIVERSARY. Apr 15, 2013. At 2:49 PM in the midst of the running of the Boston Marathon, Boston, MA, two pressure-cooker bombs exploded in short succession near the finish line killing three people and wounding more than 260. As the city of Boston faced an unprecedented manhunt, during the late evening of Apr 18 and into Apr 19, authorities accosted the bombers, two brothers of Chechen ethnicity from Russia. The brothers had murdered a police officer on Apr 18. The manhunt left one bomber dead, the other arrested, and 16 police officers wounded.

CHINA: CANTON SPRING TRADE FAIR. Apr 15–May 15. The Guangzhou (Canton) Spring Trade Fair is held on the same dates each year.

EIGHTY-NINER DAYS CELEBRATION. Apr 15–19. Guthrie, OK. 85th annual. Celebrating the first Oklahoma land run on Apr 22, 1889, this historically restored town features Old West gunfights, chuck wagon feed, professional rodeo and Oklahoma's largest parade of bands, floats and roundup clubs from across the state. Est attendance: 32,000. For info: 89 Days, American Legion Lebron Post #58, 123 N 1st St, Guthrie, OK 73044. E-mail: lebronpost58@gmail.com. Web: www.89erdays.com or www.guthrieok.com.

FDA APPROVES BOTOX: ANNIVERSARY. Apr 15, 2002. The US Food and Drug Administration approved the cosmetic use of Botox (an injected preparation of purified botulism) on this date.

FIRST McDONALD'S OPENS: ANNIVERSARY. Apr 15, 1955. The first franchised McDonald's was opened at Des Plaines, IL, by Ray Kroc, who had gotten the idea from a hamburger joint at San

Bernardino, CA, run by the McDonald brothers. On opening day a hamburger was 15 cents. The Big Mac was introduced in 1968 for 49 cents and the Quarter Pounder in 1971 for 53 cents. By the 21st century, there were more than 31,000 McDonald's in 119 countries.

FIRST SCHOOL FOR DEAF FOUNDED: ANNIVERSARY. Apr 15, 1817. Thomas Hopkins Gallaudet and Laurent Clerc founded the first US public school for the deaf, the Connecticut Asylum for the Education and Instruction of Deaf and Dumb Persons (now the American School for the Deaf), at Hartford, CT.

HILLSBOROUGH TRAGEDY: ANNIVERSARY. Apr 15, 1989. During a soccer match between Liverpool and Nottingham Forest at Hillsborough Stadium, Sheffield, England, 96 Liverpool supporters died after thousands pushed their way into the stadium, crushing many against metal barriers that separated fans from the field. Some 800 people were also injured. Following the Hillsborough tragedy, many stadiums removed these metal barriers, and seats were required for all spectators. Later reports found that stadium security made what proved to be fatal mistakes regarding crowd control and also that local police and municipal officials colluded to blame the victims for the tragedy.

"IN LIVING COLOR" TV PREMIERE: ANNIVERSARY. Apr 15, 1990. FOX's sketch comedy series, created by Keenen Ivory Wayans, was modeled after "Saturday Night Live." The show featured Wayans, his brothers Damon, Marlon and Shawn and his sister Kim. Between skits, the Fly Girls would entertain the studio audience with hip-hop dance. The dance segments of the show helped launch the careers of celebrities including Rosie Perez, Carrie Ann Inaba and Jennifer Lopez, and many comedians including David Alan Grier, Jamie Foxx, Kim Coles and Jim Carrey also began their careers on the show. Some of the most popular recurring characters were Homey, the embittered clown, the flammable Fire Marshall Bill and the effeminate movie critics of "Men on Film."

INCOME TAX PAY DAY. Apr 15. A day all Americans need to know—the day by which taxpayers are supposed to make their accounting of the previous year and pay their share of the cost of government. The US Internal Revenue Service provides free forms.

JAMES, HENRY: BIRTH ANNIVERSARY. Apr 15, 1843. Novelist and critic, born at New York, NY. Among his best-known works are *The Portrait of a Lady, Washington Square* and *The Ambassadors.* James died Feb 28, 1916, at London, England.

KIM IL SUNG: BIRTH ANNIVERSARY. Apr 15, 1912. President Kim Il Sung, first leader of North Korea, was born at Man'gyandae, Korea. A Stalinist-styled dictator, Kim created a godlike personality cult surrounding himself and his son and heir Kim Jong Il. Kim died July 8, 1994—just a few weeks before a historic summit with the president of South Korea was to occur at Pyongyang, North Korea. Kim's death came at a crucial time in world politics: North Korea and the US had recently cooled rhetoric regarding North Korea's nuclear program and had begun further talks just hours prior to the announcement of Kim's death. The North-South Summit and the US–North Korean talks were postponed.

LIBERATION OF BELSEN CONCENTRATION CAMP: ANNIVERSARY. Apr 15, 1945. British troops reached the concentration camp at Belsen, Germany. They counted approximately 35,000 corpses there.

LONGYEAR, JOHN MUNROE: BIRTH ANNIVERSARY. Apr 15, 1850. American capitalist, landowner, philanthropist and onetime mayor of Marquette, MI. Disapproving of a railway route through Marquette, he had his home, a stone castle-like showplace, torn down in 1903 and moved, stone by stone and stick by stick, in more than 190 freight cars and reerected at Brookline, MA. Born at Lansing, MI, he died May 28, 1922.

April 2014	S	M	T	W	T	F	S
			1	2	3	4	5
	6	7	8	9	10	11	12
	13	14	15	16	17	18	19
	20	21	22	23	24	25	26
	27	28	29	30			

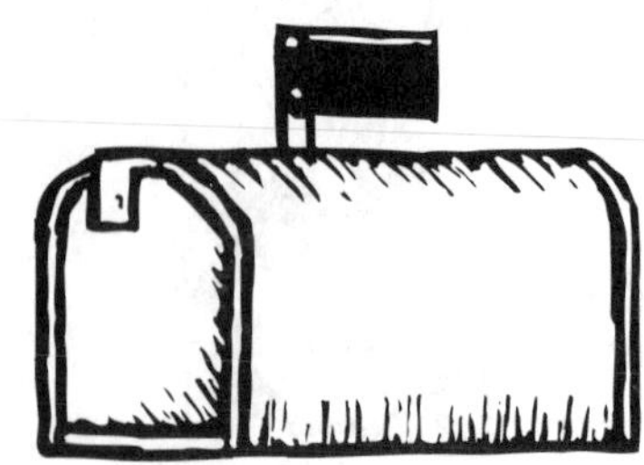

LUNAR ECLIPSE. Apr 15. Total eclipse of the moon. Visible in Australia, the Pacific and the Americas.

MOON PHASE: FULL MOON. Apr 15. Moon enters Full Moon phase at 3:42 AM, EDT.

✦NATIONAL EQUAL PAY DAY. Apr 15 (tentative). This day symbolizes the day when an average American woman's earnings finally match what an average American man earned in the past year. From reshaping attitudes to developing more comprehensive community-wide efforts, the White House is taking steps to eliminate the barriers women face in the workforce.

NATIONAL LIBRARY WORKERS DAY. Apr 15. First celebrated in 2004, this day is designated to honor and recognize all library workers, including librarians, support staff and others who make library service possible every day. Annually, on the Tuesday of National Library Week. For info: American Library Assn, Public Info Office, 50 E Huron St, Chicago, IL 60611. Phone: (312) 280-5044. Fax: (312) 280-5274. E-mail: pio@ala.org. Web: www.ala.org.

NATIONAL TAKE A WILD GUESS DAY. Apr 15. The day honoring guesses, hunches, inspirations, speculations and other forms of "intuitive intelligence." For info: Jim Barber, 1101 Marcano Blvd, Fort Lauderdale, FL 33322. Phone: (954) 476-9252. E-mail: wildguessday@thebarbershop.com. Web: www.thebarbershop.com/wildguessday.

NATIONAL THAT SUCKS DAY. Apr 15. Income tax pay day, quarterly estimated federal income tax payers' due date and the anniversary of the sinking of the *Titanic* all fall on Apr 15. These events and more support a designation for a National That Sucks Day. Visit our website's history of things that suck. Annually, Apr 15. For info: Bruce Novotny, PO Box 1270, Bandon, OR 97411. Phone: (541) 347-5468. Fax: (541) 347-4252. E-mail: novovet@kcnet.com. Web: www.thatsucks.net.

PEALE, CHARLES WILLSON: BIRTH ANNIVERSARY. Apr 15, 1741. (Old Style date.) American portrait painter (best known for his many portraits of colonial and American Revolutionary War figures), born at Queen Anne County, MD. His children Raphaelle, Rembrandt, Titian and Rubens and his niece Sarah were also artists. Died at Philadelphia, PA, Feb 22, 1827.

PESACH or PASSOVER. Apr 15–22. Hebrew calendar dates: Nisan 15–22, 5774. The first day of Passover begins an eight-day celebration of the delivery of the Jews from slavery in Egypt. Unleavened bread (matzo) is eaten at this time. Began at sundown Apr 14.

PINK MOON. Apr 15. So called by Native American tribes of New England and the Great Lakes because at this time of the season wildflowers—especially the pink ground phlox—herald the newly arrived spring. The April Full Moon.

QUARTERLY ESTIMATED FEDERAL INCOME TAX PAYERS' DUE DATE. Apr 15. For those individuals whose fiscal year is the calendar year and who make quarterly estimated federal income tax payments, today is one of the due dates (Jan 15, Apr 15, June 16 and Sept 15, 2014).

ROBINSON BREAKS BASEBALL COLOR LINE: ANNIVERSARY. Apr 15, 1947. Jackie Robinson became the first African American to play in the major leagues in the 20th century when he made his debut for the Brooklyn Dodgers against the Boston Braves. Robinson went 0-for-3 but scored the deciding run as the Dodgers prevailed, 5–3. He was later voted 1947's Rookie of the Year.

SIMMS, HILDA: BIRTH ANNIVERSARY. Apr 15, 1920. American stage and film actress, born Hilda Moses at Minneapolis, MN. She joined the American Negro Theater at Harlem, NY, in 1943 and was given the title role in *Anna Lucasta*. When the production moved to Broadway in 1944, it became the first all-black production to be performed on Broadway without a racial theme. Simms was the creative arts director of New York State's human rights division, through which she was instrumental in bringing discrimination against black actors to public attention during the 1960s. She died at Buffalo, NY, Feb 6, 1994.

SINKING OF THE *TITANIC*: ANNIVERSARY. Apr 15, 1912. The "unsinkable" luxury liner *Titanic* on its maiden voyage from Southampton, England, to New York, NY, struck an iceberg just before midnight Apr 14, and sank at 2:27 AM, Apr 15. The *Titanic* had 2,224 persons aboard. Of these, more than 1,500 were lost. About 700 people were rescued from the icy waters off Newfoundland by the liner *Carpathia*, which reached the scene about two hours after the *Titanic* went down. See also: "*Titanic* Discovered: Anniversary" (Sept 1).

SMITH, BESSIE: BIRTH ANNIVERSARY. Apr 15, 1894. The "Empress of the Blues," Bessie Smith, was born at Chattanooga, TN (year varies as late as 1900). She was assisted in her efforts to break into show business by Ma Rainey, the first great blues singer. Her first recording was made in February 1923. Smith died of injuries she sustained in an automobile accident at Clarksdale, MS, Sept 26, 1937.

WASHINGTON, HAROLD: BIRTH ANNIVERSARY. Apr 15, 1922. Illinois legislator and mayor of Chicago (1983–87). Born at Chicago, IL, and died there Nov 25, 1987. Harold Washington was one of the first African Americans to head a major US city. He was instrumental in tearing down Chicago's famed Democratic machine, a holdover from the many decades of domination by the Richard J. Daley administration.

BIRTHDAYS TODAY

Evelyn Ashford, 57, Olympic track athlete, born Shreveport, LA, Apr 15, 1957.

Linda Bloodworth-Thomason, 67, producer, writer ("Designing Women," "Evening Shade"), born Poplar Bluff, MO, Apr 15, 1947.

Roy Clark, 81, singer, guitarist, television personality ("Hee Haw"), born Meherrin, VA, Apr 15, 1933.

Heloise Cruse Evans, 63, newspaper columnist ("Hints from Heloise"), born Waco, TX, Apr 15, 1951.

Ilya Kovalchuck, 31, hockey player, born Tver, Russia, Apr 15, 1983.

Madeleine Martin, 21, actress ("Californication"), born New York, NY, Apr 15, 1993.

Seth Rogen, 32, actor (*Knocked Up, Pineapple Express*), born Vancouver, BC, Canada, Apr 15, 1982.

Jason Sehorn, 43, former football player, born Mount Shasta, CA, Apr 15, 1971.

Emma Watson, 24, actress (Harry Potter films, *The Bling Ring*), born Paris, France, Apr 15, 1990.

Amy Wright, 64, actress (*Breaking Away, Wise Blood, The Accidental Tourist*), born Chicago, IL, Apr 15, 1950.

April 16 — Wednesday

DAY 106 **259 REMAINING**

AMIS, KINGSLEY: BIRTH ANNIVERSARY. Apr 16, 1922. Author (*The Old Devils, Lucky Jim*), poet, critic, editor, born at London, England, and died there Oct 22, 1995.

CHAPLIN, CHARLES SPENCER: 125th BIRTH ANNIVERSARY. Apr 16, 1889. Actor, comedian, director, producer, screenwriter and composer born at London, England. He suffered through extreme poverty as a child but escaped the workhouses as a touring music hall dancer and comic. He joined Mack Sennett's Keystone film company and with Keystone and on his own created funny and poignant film masterpieces beginning in 1914—many featuring his "Little Tramp." The derby-hatted Little Tramp—a bit of a dreamer and a bit of a scamp—was a worldwide sensation. Chaplin was knighted in 1975 and died Dec 25, 1977, at Vevey, Switzerland. See also: "Chaplin's 'Tramp' Debuts: Anniversary" (Feb 7).

DENMARK: QUEEN MARGRETHE II'S BIRTHDAY. Apr 16. Thousands of children gather to cheer the queen (born 1940) at Amalienborg Palace, and the Royal Guard wears scarlet gala uniforms.

DIEGO, JOSÉ de: BIRTH ANNIVERSARY. Apr 16, 1866. Puerto Rican patriot and political leader José de Diego was born at Aguadilla, PR. His birthday is a holiday in Puerto Rico. He died July 16, 1918, at New York, NY.

FRANKLIN, JOHN: BIRTH ANNIVERSARY. Apr 16, 1786. Born at Spilsby, Lincolnshire, England, John Franklin was a British naval officer, administrator and explorer. His four Arctic expeditions to map the Northwest Passage solidified his name in history. Three were successes; the fourth was a disaster. Setting sail from England in May 1845, Franklin's outfit was locked in thick ice off the Canadian archipelago by the autumn of 1846. The entire party died there, detached from civilization and suffering from a host of horrible ailments, including hypothermia, starvation and lead poisoning. Franklin himself died June 11, 1847, near King William Island, Canada.

MANCINI, HENRY: 90th BIRTH ANNIVERSARY. Apr 16, 1924. Born at Cleveland, OH, Mancini made his mark in Hollywood composing film scores and songs. He won 20 Grammy Awards and four Oscars (song "Moon River" and score for *Breakfast at Tiffany's*; song "Days of Wine and Roses" for the same-titled film; score for *Victor/Victoria*). He also composed *The Pink Panther*, "Peter Gunn" and "Mr Lucky" themes. Died June 14, 1994, at Beverly Hills, CA.

NATIONAL BOOKMOBILE DAY. Apr 16. An annual celebration of the contributions of our nation's bookmobiles and the dedicated professionals who make quality bookmobile outreach possible in their communities. First celebrated in 2010 by the American Library Association Office for Literacy and Outreach Services (OLOS), the Association of Bookmobile and Outreach Service (ABOS), and the Association for Rural and Small Libraries (ARSL). Annually, the Wednesday of National Library Week. For info: American Library Assn, Public Info Office, 50 E Huron St, Chicago, IL 60611. Phone: (312) 280-5044. Fax: (312) 280-5274. E-mail: pio@ala.org. Web: www.ala.org.

NATIONAL STRESS AWARENESS DAY. Apr 16. To focus public awareness on one of the leading health problems in the world today. Health-related organizations throughout the country are encouraged to sponsor stress education programs and events. Annually, the first workday after income taxes are due. For info: Morton C. Orman, MD, Dir, The Health Resource Network, 908 Cold Bottom Rd, Sparks, MD 21152. Web: www.stressawarenessmonth.com.

NATURAL BRIDGES NATIONAL MONUMENT: ANNIVERSARY. Apr 16, 1908. Utah. Natural Bridges National Monument was established on this date.

SAVE THE ELEPHANT DAY. Apr 16. Although its founder, renowned elephant and environmental conservationist Sangduen "Lek" Chailert, rescued her first elephant in 1996, the 250-acre parcel of land now known as Elephant Nature Park in Thailand (outside Chiang Mai) relocated to its current plot of land on Apr 16, 2003. Today, Save Elephant Foundation's Elephant Nature Park is a refuge for more than 30 Asian elephants, providing a natural, safe haven for these endangered animals. Save the Elephant Day, observed each year on the anniversary of ENP's move to the new land, is a day for people around the world to take some time and raise awareness about the plight of the Asian elephant—and to learn what they can do to help save them. Join us in our mission to protect Asian elephants and help us spread the word to save them! For info: Save Elephant Foundation, 1 Ratmakka Rd, Phrasing, Muang, Chiang Mai, 50200 Thailand. E-mail: info@saveelephant.org. Web: www.saveelephant.org/save_elephant_day.html.

SLAVERY ABOLISHED IN DISTRICT OF COLUMBIA: ANNIVERSARY. Apr 16, 1862. Congress abolished slavery in the District of Columbia. One million dollars was appropriated to compensate owners of freed slaves, and $100,000 was set aside to pay district slaves who wished to emigrate to Haiti, Liberia or any other country outside the US.

SLOANE, HANS: BIRTH ANNIVERSARY. Apr 16, 1660. British medical doctor and naturalist whose personal collection became the nucleus of the British Museum, born at County Down, Ireland. Upon his death at Chelsea, England, Jan 11, 1753, his collections of books, manuscripts, medals and antiquities were bequeathed to Britain and accepted by an act of Parliament that incorporated the British Museum. It was opened to the public at London, England, Jan 15, 1759. It is the national museum of the United Kingdom.

SPACE MILESTONE: *APOLLO 16* (US). Apr 16, 1972. Astronauts John W. Young, Charles M. Duke, Jr, and Thomas K. Mattingly II (command module pilot) began an 11-day mission that included a 71-hour exploration of the moon (Apr 20–23). Landing module named *Orion*. Splashdown in Pacific Ocean within a mile of target, Apr 27.

SYNGE, JOHN MILLINGTON: BIRTH ANNIVERSARY. Apr 16, 1871. Irish dramatist and poet, most of whose plays were written in the brief span of six years before his death at age 37 of lymphatic sarcoma. His best-known work is *The Playboy of the Western World* (1907), which caused protests and rioting at early performances. Synge (pronounced "Sing") was born near Dublin, Ireland, and died there Mar 24, 1909.

TEXAS CITY DISASTER: ANNIVERSARY. Apr 16–17, 1947. The worst industrial disaster in US history. The French-owned *Grandcamp*, docked at the oil and port town of Texas City, TX, and carrying a load of ammonium nitrate, was discovered to have a smoldering fire in the hold. At 9:12 AM, as onlookers gathered and a small firefighting team attempted to extinguish the blaze, the ship exploded with tremendous force, immediately killing everyone at the dock area. The resulting fires destroyed the nearby Monsanto Chemical Company and spread through oil pipelines into the city. At 1 AM, another ship, the *High Flyer*, exploded. The city was left defenseless due to the deaths of almost the entire fire department. There were 576 known casualties, but most estimate that at least 100 more died in the conflagrations. Thousands were injured. The fires burned for a week. The disaster prompted new regulations on handling chemicals. With thousands of lawsuits, the US Congress passed a special act to settle claims in 1956.

USTINOV, PETER: BIRTH ANNIVERSARY. Apr 16, 1921. British actor and playwright born at London, England, Peter Ustinov wrote his first play at age 19. He performed on stage, television and the screen, winning two Oscars (for 1961's *Spartacus* and 1965's *Topkapi*) and several Emmys. He wrote dozens of plays, screenplays and novels and also directed several films, including the highly regarded 1962 version of *Billy Budd*. He played Agatha Christie's detective Hercule Poirot in several screen adaptations. He was knighted by Queen Elizabeth II and dedicated many years to fund-raising for UNICEF. He died at Geneva, Switzerland, Mar 28, 2004.

VIRGINIA TECH SHOOTINGS: ANNIVERSARY. Apr 16, 2007. In the worst shooting in US history, a disturbed college student shot and killed 32 people on the Virginia Tech University campus at Blacksburg, VA.

WRIGHT, WILBUR: BIRTH ANNIVERSARY. Apr 16, 1867. Aviation pioneer, born at Millville, IN. Died at Dayton, OH, May 30, 1912. See also: "Wright Brothers First Powered Flight" (Dec 17).

BIRTHDAYS TODAY

Kareem Abdul-Jabbar, 67, Hall of Fame basketball player, born Lewis Ferdinand Alcindor, Jr, at New York, NY, Apr 16, 1947.

Akon, 41, singer, born Aliaune Damala Budara Akon Thiam at St. Louis, MO, April 16, 1973.

Ellen Barkin, 59, actress (*Tender Mercies, Diner*), born New York, NY, Apr 16, 1955.

Benedict XVI, Pope Emeritus, 87, retired; born Joseph Ratzinger at Marktl Am Inn, Germany, Apr 16, 1927.

Jon Cryer, 49, actor ("Two and a Half Men," *Pretty in Pink, Hot Shots!*), born New York, NY, Apr 16, 1965.

Luol Deng, 29, basketball player, born Wow, Sudan, Apr 16, 1985.

Lukas Haas, 38, actor (*Witness, Rambling Rose*), born West Hollywood, CA, Apr 16, 1976.

Martin Lawrence, 49, comedian, actor (*Wild Hogs, Bad Boys, Big Momma's House*), born Frankfurt-am-Main, Germany, Apr 16, 1965.

Freddie Ljungberg, 37, former soccer player, born Vittsjo, Sweden, Apr 16, 1977.

Jay O. Sanders, 61, actor ("Crime Story," *Tucker: A Man and His Dream*), born Austin, TX, Apr 16, 1953.

Bobby Vinton, 79, singer, born Canonsburg, PA, Apr 16, 1935.

April 17 — Thursday

DAY 107 **258 REMAINING**

AMERICAN SAMOA: FLAG DAY. Apr 17. National holiday commemorating first raising of American flag in what was formerly Eastern Samoa in 1900. Public holiday with singing, dancing, costumes and parades.

ANSON, CAP: BIRTH ANNIVERSARY. Apr 17, 1852. Adrian Constantine ("Cap") Anson, Baseball Hall of Fame player and manager, born at Marshalltown, IA. Anson played professional baseball from 1871 through 1897 and is considered one of the game's greatest first basemen. As a manager, he piloted the Chicago White Stockings (today's Cubs) to five National League pennants and a .575 winning percentage. Inducted into the Hall of Fame in 1939. Died at Chicago, IL, Apr 18, 1922.

BAY OF PIGS INVASION LAUNCHED: ANNIVERSARY. Apr 17, 1961. More than 1,500 Cuban exiles invaded Cuba in an ill-fated attempt to overthrow Fidel Castro.

April 2014

S	M	T	W	T	F	S
		1	2	3	4	5
6	7	8	9	10	11	12
13	14	15	16	17	18	19
20	21	22	23	24	25	26
27	28	29	30			

BLAH BLAH BLAH DAY. Apr 17. Today's the day to do any of the following, or whatever. Stop smoking, take out the trash, empty the cat litter, lose weight, pick up your clothes, put dirty dishes in the sink, get a job or quit your job. Annually, Apr 17. (©2006 by WH.) For info: Thomas & Ruth Roy, Wellcat Holidays, 2418 Long Ln, Lebanon, PA 17046. Phone: (717) 279-0184. E-mail: info@wellcat.com. Web: www.wellcat.com.

CAMBODIA FALLS TO THE KHMER ROUGE: ANNIVERSARY. Apr 17, 1975. Cambodia fell when its capital, Phnom Penh, was captured by the Khmer Rouge. The Pol Pot regime inaugurated "Year One," and the wholesale slaughter of intellectuals, political enemies and peasants began. As many as two million Cambodians perished. See also: "Pol Pot Overthrown: Anniversary" (Jan 7).

CHASE, SAMUEL: BIRTH ANNIVERSARY. Apr 17, 1741. Signer of the Declaration of Independence. Born at Somerset County, MD, he died June 19, 1811.

ELLIS ISLAND FAMILY HISTORY DAY. Apr 17. By official proclamation of our nation's governors, Apr 17 has been designated as "Ellis Island Family History Day." Sponsored by The Statue of Liberty–Ellis Island Foundation, Inc, this annual day recognizes the achievements and contributions made to America by Ellis Island immigrants and their descendants. Historically, Apr 17 marks the day in 1907 when more immigrants were processed through the island than on any other day in its colorful history: 11,747 people. In addition, the Foundation has established the "Ellis Island Family Heritage Awards," which are given annually to a select number of Ellis Island immigrants or their descendants who have made a significant contribution to the American experience. For info: Elizabeth Oravetz, Statue of Liberty–Ellis Island Foundation, Inc, 17 Battery Pl, Ste 210, New York, NY 10004. Phone: (212) 561-4500. Fax: (212) 779-1990. E-mail: eoravetz@ellisisland.org. Web: www.ellisisland.org.

FIESTA SAN ANTONIO. Apr 17–27. San Antonio, TX. Eleven days of culture, heritage, beauty and remembrance. Parades, carnivals, sports, fireworks, music, ethnic feasts, art exhibits, dances—more than 100 events. This colorful fiesta originated in 1891 with the Battle of Flowers parade honoring the memory of Texas heroes who fought against General Santa Anna for Texan independence at the Alamo and San Jacinto. Est attendance: 3,500,000. For info: Fiesta San Antonio Commission, Inc, 2611 Broadway, San Antonio, TX 78215-1022. Phone: (210) 227-5191 or (877) 723-4378. Fax: (210) 227-1139. Web: www.fiesta-sa.org.

HOLDEN, WILLIAM: BIRTH ANNIVERSARY. Apr 17, 1918. William Holden's first starring role was in *Golden Boy.* The actor, born at O'Fallon, IL, won an Oscar for his role in *Stalag 17* in 1953. He was found dead at Los Angeles, CA, Nov 16, 1981.

ITALY: PROCESSION OF THE ADDOLORATA AND PROCESSION OF THE MYSTERIES. Apr 17–18. Taranto. Procession of the Addolorata is held on Holy Thursday, and the Procession of the Mysteries takes place on Good Friday. Both processions have in common the very slow pace of the participants and their unusual costumes.

MAUNDY THURSDAY or HOLY THURSDAY. Apr 17. The Thursday before Easter, originally "dies mandate," celebrates Christ's injunction to love one another, "Mandatus novum do vobis. . . ." ("A new commandment I give to you. . . .")

MORGAN, JOHN PIERPONT: BIRTH ANNIVERSARY. Apr 17, 1837. American financier and corporation director, born at Hartford, CT. Morgan died Mar 31, 1913, at Rome, Italy, leaving an estate valued at more than $70 million.

NATIONAL HAIKU POETRY DAY. Apr 17. A celebration of the genre of haiku, whose origins date back a millennium in Japan; and more specifically of English-language haiku, which has now been written for more than a century. This day is observed in the heart of National Poetry Month, under the auspices of The Haiku Foundation. The Foundation encourages public events, readings, exhibitions and competitions on this day and culminates the celebration with the announcement of winners from its annual HaikuNow! Contest. For info: The Haiku Foundation. E-mail: haikupoetryday@thehaikufoundation.org. Web: www.thehaikufoundation.org.

NATIONAL HIGH FIVE DAY. Apr 17. 13th annual. National High Five Day is devoted to celebration of the high five and occurs annually on the third Thursday in April. Each year, there are numerous parties, newspaper articles, television appearances and radio interviews. For info: National High Five Day. Web: www.nationalhighfiveday.com.

NEEDHAM, THERESA: BIRTH ANNIVERSARY. Apr 17, 1912. Owner of Chicago's legendary South Side blues bar Theresa's Lounge, Theresa Needham was born at Meridian, MS. Especially memorable at the bar were "Blue Monday" all-day jams at which the city's top blues performers locked horns in musical battles. Needham, who was bartender, bouncer and talent agent, came to be known as "the Godmother of Chicago Blues." Died at Chicago, IL, Oct 16, 1992.

NETHERLANDS AND SCILLY ISLES PEACE: ANNIVERSARY. Apr 17, 1986. The 335-year "state of war" that had existed between the Netherlands and the Scilly Isles came to an end on this date when Dutch ambassador Jonkheer Huydecoper flew to the Scilly Isles to deliver a proclamation terminating the war that had started in 1651. Though hostilities had ceased three centuries earlier, a standing joke in the islands was that no one had bothered to declare an end to the war.

NOTHING LIKE A DAME DAY. Apr 17. A day to pay homage to dames and their unique blend of wit, wisdom, strength and style. Nothing Like a Dame Day celebrates the dames who've gone before and urges you to cultivate the "dame" that lies within. Annually, Apr 17. For info: Dixie Laite, 25 W 54th St, Ste 2DE, New York, NY 10019. E-mail: dixie@dixielaite.com.

PHILIPPINES: MORIONE'S FESTIVAL. Apr 17–20. Marinduque Island. Provincewide masquerade, Lenten plays and celebrations. Annually, Holy Thursday through Easter Sunday.

REASONER, HARRY: BIRTH ANNIVERSARY. Apr 17, 1923. American television journalist Harry Reasoner was born at Dakota City, IA. In 1956 Reasoner joined CBS News, where he anchored the "CBS Sunday News" (1963–70) and was one of the two original anchors, along with Mike Wallace, of the newsmagazine show "60 Minutes." He was coanchor of the "ABC Evening News" from 1970 until 1978, when he returned to CBS and "60 Minutes." He died Aug 6, 1991, at Norwalk, CT.

SOLIDARITY GRANTED LEGAL STATUS: 25th ANNIVERSARY. Apr 17, 1989. After nearly a decade of struggle and suppression, the Polish labor union Solidarity was granted legal status, clearing the way for the downfall of the Polish Communist Party. Solidarity and the Polish people surprised the government by winning 99 of the 100 parliamentary seats in the election. General Wojciech Jaruzelski was elected president on July 19 and nominated Czelaw Kiszczak prime minister, enraging the Lech Walesa–led Solidarity. On Aug 7 Walesa swayed the traditional allies of the Communist Party—the United Peasant and Democratic parties—to switch sides. Kiszczak resigned as prime minister a week later after failing to form a government, forcing Jaruzelski to accept the principle of a government led by Solidarity.

STEIGER, ROD: BIRTH ANNIVERSARY. Apr 17, 1925. The magnetic character actor was born at Westhampton, NY. In a 50-year career, Steiger played a wide range of roles for some of the best directors of the day. He won a Best Actor Oscar for *In the Heat of the Night* and was also nominated for *On the Waterfront* and *The Pawnbroker*. He died at Los Angeles, CA, July 9, 2002.

SUPPORT TEEN LITERATURE DAY. Apr 17. To raise awareness among the general public that young adult literature is a vibrant, growing genre with much to offer today's teens. Annually, the Thursday of National Library Week. For info: American Library Assn, Public Info Office, 50 E Huron St, Chicago, IL 60611. Phone: (312) 280-5044. Fax: (312) 280-5274. E-mail: pio@ala.org. Web: www.ala.org.

SYRIAN ARAB REPUBLIC: INDEPENDENCE DAY. Apr 17. Official holiday. Proclaimed independence from League of Nations mandate under French administration in 1946.

VERRAZANO DAY: ANNIVERSARY. Apr 17, 1524. Celebrates discovery of New York harbor by Giovanni Verrazano, Florentine navigator, 1485–1527.

WILDER, THORNTON: BIRTH ANNIVERSARY. Apr 17, 1897. Pulitzer Prize–winning American playwright (*Our Town*) and novelist, born at Madison, WI. Died at Hamden, CT, Dec 7, 1975.

BIRTHDAYS TODAY

Sean Bean, 56, actor ("Game of Thrones"; *The Lord of the Rings: Fellowship of the Ring*; *Stormy Monday*; *Patriot Games*), born Sheffield, Yorkshire, England, Apr 17, 1958.

Victoria Adams Beckham, 39, designer, singer (Posh Spice of Spice Girls), born Hertfordshire, England, Apr 17, 1975.

Norman Julius "Boomer" Esiason, 53, sportscaster, former football player, born West Islip, NY, Apr 17, 1961.

Jennifer Garner, 42, actress (*Juno, 13 Going on 30,* "Alias," "Felicity"), born Houston, TX, Apr 17, 1972.

Olivia Hussey, 63, actress (*Romeo and Juliet*), born Buenos Aires, Argentina, Apr 17, 1951.

Rooney Mara, 29, actress (*The Social Network*, *The Girl with the Dragon Tattoo* [US]), born Bedford, NY, Apr 17, 1985.

Cynthia Ozick, 86, feminist, writer, born New York, NY, Apr 17, 1928.

Liz Phair, 47, rock singer/songwriter, born New Haven, CT, Apr 17, 1967.

Lela Rochon, 48, actress (*Waiting to Exhale, Boomerang*), born Los Angeles, CA, Apr 17, 1966.

April 2014	S	M	T	W	T	F	S
			1	2	3	4	5
	6	7	8	9	10	11	12
	13	14	15	16	17	18	19
	20	21	22	23	24	25	26
	27	28	29	30			

April 18 — Friday

DAY 108 — **257 REMAINING**

AFRMA DISPLAY AT AMERICA'S FAMILY PET EXPO. Apr 18–20 (tentative). Costa Mesa, CA. Rats and mice are emerging as ideal pets: they provide all the pleasure and satisfaction of a warm, cuddly, intelligent and friendly pet companion. The American Fancy Rat and Mouse Association (AFRMA) was founded in 1983 to promote the breeding and exhibition of fancy rats and mice, to educate the public on their positive qualities as companion animals and to provide information on their proper care. For info: AFRMA (CAE), 9230 64th St, Riverside, CA 92509-5924. Phone: (951) 685-2350 or (818) 992-5564. E-mail: afrma@afrma.org. Web: www.afrma.org.

CANADA: CONSTITUTION ACT OF 1982: ANNIVERSARY. Apr 18, 1982. Replacing the British North America Act of 1867, the Canadian Constitution Act of 1982 provided Canada with a new set of fundamental laws and civil rights. Signed by Queen Elizabeth II, at Parliament Hill, Ottawa, Canada, on Apr 17, it went into effect at 12:01 AM, Sunday, Apr 18, 1982.

CHINCOTEAGUE ISLAND EASTER DECOY SHOW. Apr 18–19. Chincoteague Island, VA. One hundred local and national carvers and artists exhibit their work. Awards are given in various carving categories, art and photography. Special awards are given for best carving display and best art display. There is also a Children's Choice Award given for a favorite artist. The Curtis Merritt Award of Excellence is awarded to the exhibitor who displays excellence as an individual as well as an artist and/or carver. This award is voted on by the exhibitors. There are hand-carved and/or painted wooden Easter eggs designed by various exhibitors, which will be offered in a silent auction. Annually, Easter weekend. Est attendance: 2,000. For info: Chincoteague Chamber of Commerce, 6733 Maddox Blvd, Chincoteague Island, VA 23336. Phone: (757) 336-6161. Fax: (757) 336-1242. E-mail: chincochamber@verizon.net. Web: www.chincoteaguechamber.com or www.chincoteaguedecoyshow.com.

CLEANING FOR A REASON WEEK. Apr 18–24. Established by the Cleaning for a Reason Foundation in 2009 to raise awareness that there is an organization that works to provide free residential cleaning to women who are undergoing treatment for cancer. Activities will be held nationwide to let women know that there is a foundation that allows them to focus on their health while we focus on their home. For info: Cleaning for a Reason Foundation. Web: www.cleaningforareason.org.

CONSUMER AWARENESS WEEK. Apr 18–23. Consumer advocate Bob O'Brien kicks off a weeklong event aimed at advising and helping consumers regarding their rights. For info: Bob O'Brien, Consumer Advocate, 1061 Koelle Blvd, Secaucus, NJ 07094. Phone: (646) 233-6610. E-mail: robtfobrien@aol.com.

CRAWFORD, SAMUEL EARL "WAHOO SAM": BIRTH ANNIVERSARY. Apr 18, 1880. Major league baseball player with the Detroit Tigers, born at Wahoo, NE. Wahoo Sam played pro ball for 20 years, racking up a career batting average of .309. His record of 309 career triples still stands. He was inducted into the Baseball Hall of Fame in 1957. Crawford died June 15, 1968, at Hollywood, CA.

DARROW, CLARENCE SEWARD: BIRTH ANNIVERSARY. Apr 18, 1857. American attorney often associated with unpopular causes, from the Pullman strike in 1894 to the Scottsboro case in 1932, born at Kinsman, OH. At the Scopes trial, July 13, 1925, Darrow said: "I do not consider it an insult, but rather a compliment, to be called an agnostic. I do not pretend to know where many ignorant men are sure—that is all that agnosticism means." Darrow died at Chicago, IL, Mar 13, 1938.

ENGLAND: BRITISH AND WORLD MARBLES CHAMPIONSHIP. Apr 18. Greyhound Public House, Tinsley Green, West Sussex. Since 1932, more than 100 competitors have vied for team and individual titles in the marbles tournament. Annually, on Good Friday. For info: British Marbles Board of Control. E-mail: admin@britishmarbles.org.uk. Web: www.britishmarbles.org.uk or www.greyhoundmarbles.com.

ENGLAND: DEVIZES TO WESTMINSTER INTERNATIONAL CANOE RACE. Apr 18–21. 66th year. Starts from Wharf Car Park, Wharf St, Devizes, Wiltshire. Canoes race along 125 miles of the Kennet and Avon canals and the River Thames, ending at County Hall Steps, Westminster Bridge Rd, London. Annually, Good Friday to Easter Monday. Est attendance: 6,000. For info: DW Organisation Ltd, Wokingham Waterside Centre, Thames Valley Park Dr, Earley, Reading, England RG6 9PQ. Phone: (44) (020) 7620-0298. Web: www.dwrace.org.uk.

GOOD FRIDAY. Apr 18. Oldest Christian celebration—commemorates the crucifixion. Possible corruption of "God's Friday." Observed in some manner by most Christian sects. Public holiday in many nations. In the US, a public or part holiday in Connecticut, Delaware, Hawaii, Indiana, Kentucky, Louisiana, New Jersey, North Carolina, North Dakota, Pennsylvania, Tennessee and Texas.

THE HOUSE THAT RUTH BUILT: ANNIVERSARY. Apr 18, 1923. More than 74,000 fans attended Opening Day festivities as the New York Yankees inaugurated their new stadium. Babe Ruth christened it with a game-winning three-run homer into the right-field bleachers. In his coverage of the game for the *New York Evening Telegram*, sportswriter Fred Lieb described Yankee Stadium as "The House That Ruth Built," and the name stuck. The stadium hosted its last game on Sept 21, 2008, when the Yankees played the Baltimore Orioles, and was demolished in 2010. The Yankees opened the 2009 season with a new stadium built across the street from the old, also called "Yankee Stadium."

INTERNATIONAL AMATEUR RADIO DAY. Apr 18. Annual, international day recognizing the services and accomplishments of amateur radio operators in wireless technology, emergencies and education. Sponsored by the ARRL, the national association for amateur radio. For info: Allen Pitts, ARRL, 225 Main St, Newington, CT 06111. Phone: (860) 594-0328. Fax: (860) 594-0259. E-mail: apitts@arrl.org. Web: www.arrl.org.

JAPAN BOMBED: ANNIVERSARY. Apr 18, 1942. For the first time during WWII, the mainland of Japan was bombed. Brigade General James Doolittle led a squadron of B-25s from the US carrier *Hornet*. Cities bombed included Tokyo, Yokohama, Kobe and Nagoya. Doolittle said they flew so low that "one of our party observed a ball game in progress." Although the bombers did little damage, the psychological victory was enormous.

NATIONAL ADULT AUTISM AWARENESS DAY. Apr 18. This day recognizes the challenges faced by those aging with autism, including higher education, independent living and career development. Annually, Apr 18. For info: Luciana Randall, Autism Connection of PA, 35 Wilson St #100, Pittsburgh, PA 15223. Phone: (412) 781-4116 or (800) 827-9385. E-mail: support@autismofpa.org. Web: www.autismofpa.org.

NATIONAL COLLEGIATE WOMEN'S GYMNASTICS. Apr 18–20. BJCC Arena, Birmingham, AL. 33rd annual. For info: NCAA, PO Box 6222, Indianapolis, IN 46206-6222. Phone: (317) 917-6222. Fax: (317) 917-6837. Web: www.NCAA.com.

PAUL REVERE'S RIDE: ANNIVERSARY. Apr 18, 1775. The "Midnight Ride" of Paul Revere and William Dawes started at about 10 PM to warn American patriots between Boston, MA, and Concord, MA, of the approaching British.

PET OWNERS INDEPENDENCE DAY. Apr 18. Dog and cat owners take the day off from work and the pets go to work in their place, since most pets are jobless, sleep all day and do not even take out the trash. (©2006 by WH.) For info: Thomas & Ruth Roy, Wellcat Holidays, 2418 Long Ln, Lebanon, PA 17046. Phone: (717) 279-0184. E-mail: info@wellcat.com. Web: www.wellcat.com.

POLICE OFFICERS WHO GAVE THEIR LIVES IN THE LINE OF DUTY WEEK. Apr 18–23. A week of events remembering all police officers nationwide who gave their lives to protect others. In addition, lectures on how famous crimes were solved. For info: Bob O'Brien, Consumer Advocate, 1061 Koelle Blvd, Secaucus, NJ 07094. Phone: (646) 233-6610. E-mail: robtfobrien@aol.com.

"REAL PEOPLE" TV PREMIERE: 35th ANNIVERSARY. Apr 18, 1979. Real people do the darnedest things—from making paintings out of lint to making houses out of aluminum cans. NBC developed the program to spotlight the achievements, funny inventions and extraordinary stunts of ordinary Americans. Hosts of the show included Fred Willard, Sarah Purcell, John Barbour, Skip Stephenson, Byron Allen and Peter Billingsley. The show aired until 1984.

SAN FRANCISCO 1906 EARTHQUAKE: ANNIVERSARY. Apr 18, 1906. Business section of San Francisco, some 10,000 acres, destroyed by earthquake. First quake at 5:13 AM, followed by fire. Nearly 4,000 lives lost.

STOCK EXCHANGE HOLIDAY (GOOD FRIDAY). Apr 18. The holiday schedules for the various exchanges are subject to change if relevant rules, regulations or exchange policies are revised. If you have questions, contact: CME Group (CME, CBOT, NYMEX, KCBT) (www.cmegroup.com), Chicago Board Options Exchange (www.cboe.com), NASDAQ (www.nasdaq.com), NYSE Euronext (www.nyse.com).

"THIRD WORLD" DAY: ANNIVERSARY. Apr 18, 1955. Anniversary of the first use of the phrase "third world," which was by Indonesia's President Sukarno in his opening speech at the Bandung Conference. Representatives of nearly 30 African and Asian countries (2,000 attendees) heard Sukarno praise the American war of independence, "the first successful anticolonial war in history." More than half the world's population, he said, was represented at this "first intercontinental conference of the so-called colored peoples, in the history of mankind." The phrase and the idea of a "third world" rapidly gained currency, generally signifying the aggregate of nonaligned peoples and nations—the nonwhite and underdeveloped portion of the world.

***TITAN 34-D* ROCKET FAILURE: ANNIVERSARY.** Apr 18, 1986. Launched from Vandenburg Air Force Base, CA, the $65 million *Titan* exploded when it was only a few hundred feet into flight, destroying the $500 million *KH-11* reconnaissance satellite payload. Poisonous fumes were released by the explosion, causing concern for the safety of people in nearby communities.

UNITED KINGDOM: GOOD FRIDAY BANK HOLIDAY. Apr 18. Bank and public holiday in England, Wales, Scotland and Northern Ireland.

ZIMBABWE: INDEPENDENCE DAY. Apr 18. National holiday commemorates the recognition by Great Britain of Zimbabwean independence on this day in 1980. Prior to this, the country had been the British colony of Southern Rhodesia.

BIRTHDAYS TODAY

America Ferrera, 30, actress ("Ugly Betty," *The Sisterhood of the Traveling Pants*), born Los Angeles, CA, Apr 18, 1984.

Barbara Hale, 93, actress ("Perry Mason"), born DeKalb, IL, Apr 18, 1921.

Melissa Joan Hart, 38, actress ("Sabrina the Teenage Witch"), born Long Island, NY, Apr 18, 1976.

Robert Hooks, 77, actor, director, producer (*Star Trek III: The Search for Spock*; stage: *Day of Absence*), born Washington, DC, Apr 18, 1937.

John James, 58, actor ("Search for Tomorrow," "Dynasty"), born Minneapolis, MN, Apr 18, 1956.

Jane Leeves, 53, actress ("Murphy Brown," "Frasier," "Hot in Cleveland"), born East Grinstead, England, Apr 18, 1961.

Dorothy Lyman, 67, actress ("All My Children," "Mama's Family"), director, born Minneapolis, MN, Apr 18, 1947.

Eric McCormack, 51, actor ("Lonesome Dove," "Will & Grace"), born Toronto, ON, Canada, Apr 18, 1963.

Hayley Mills, 68, actress (*Pollyana, The Parent Trap, The Moon Spinners*), born London, England, Apr 18, 1946.

Rick Moranis, 60, actor, writer (*Ghostbusters; Honey, I Shrunk the Kids*), born Toronto, ON, Canada, Apr 18, 1954.

Conan O'Brien, 51, television talk show host, born Brookline, MA, Apr 18, 1963.

John Pankow, 60, actor ("Episodes," "Mad About You"), born St. Louis, MO, Apr 18, 1954.

Eric Roberts, 58, actor (*Runaway Train, Star 80*), born Biloxi, MS, Apr 18, 1956.

Eli Roth, 42, actor (*Inglourious Basterds, Death Proof*), director, born Boston, MA, Apr 18, 1972.

David Tennant, 43, actor ("Doctor Who," *Harry Potter and the Goblet of Fire*), born Bathgate, West Lothian, Scotland, Apr 18, 1971.

James Woods, 67, actor (*Holocaust, The Onion Field*), born Vernal, UT, Apr 18, 1947.

April 19 — Saturday

DAY 109 **256 REMAINING**

BATTLE OF LEXINGTON AND CONCORD: ANNIVERSARY. Apr 19, 1775. Massachusetts. Start of the American Revolution as the British fired the "shot heard 'round the world."

BRANCH DAVIDIAN FIRE AT WACO: ANNIVERSARY. Apr 19, 1993. After a 51-day standoff between the Branch Davidians and law-enforcement groups, the compound of the religious cult burned to the ground with 86 of its members inside, near Waco, TX, after federal agents began battering the compound with armored vehicles. Nine people escaped, but the 86 who perished included 17 children and the cult's leader, David Koresh.

EASTER BEACH RUN. Apr 19. Daytona Beach, FL. The 47th annual beach run on "the world's most famous beach" includes a four-mile and two-mile run for various age divisions, a two-mile fun health walk and several different kids' runs. Annually, Easter Saturday. Est attendance: 1,200. For info: Easter Beach Run, Daytona Beach Leisure Services Dept, 301 S Ridgewood Dr, Daytona Beach, FL 32114. Phone: (386) 671-8337. Fax: (386) 671-3299. E-mail: TerryV@codb.us. Web: www.easterbeachrun.org.

EASTER EVEN. Apr 19. The Saturday before Easter. Last day of Holy Week and of Lent.

April 2014	S	M	T	W	T	F	S
			1	2	3	4	5
	6	7	8	9	10	11	12
	13	14	15	16	17	18	19
	20	21	22	23	24	25	26
	27	28	29	30			

EXPLOSION ON THE USS *IOWA*: 25th ANNIVERSARY. Apr 19, 1989. In one of the worst naval disasters since the war in Vietnam, a freak explosion rocked the battleship USS *Iowa*, killing 47 sailors. The explosion occurred in the number 2 gun turret as the *Iowa* was participating in gunnery exercises about 300 miles northeast of Puerto Rico.

GARFIELD, LUCRETIA RUDOLPH: BIRTH ANNIVERSARY. Apr 19, 1832. Wife of James Abram Garfield, 20th president of the US, born at Hiram, OH. Died at Pasadena, CA, Mar 14, 1918.

GEORGIA RENAISSANCE SPRING FESTIVAL. Apr 19–June 8. (Weekends and Memorial Day.) Atlanta, GA. A rollicking rendition of a 16th-century English faire. Jousting knights, jugglers, Shakespearean parodies and more than 100 shows daily. Feast like a king and shop like royalty. Saturdays, Sundays and Memorial Day. Est attendance: 200,000. For info: Sarah Petermann, Georgia Renaissance Festival, PO Box 986, Fairburn, GA 30213. Phone: (770) 964-8575. Fax: (770) 964-1477. E-mail: info@garenfest.com. Web: www.garenfest.com.

JOHN PARKER DAY. Apr 19. Remembering John Parker's order, at Lexington Green, MA, Apr 19, 1775: "Stand your ground. Don't fire unless fired upon; but if they mean to have a war, let it begin here." Parker, Revolutionary soldier, captain of minutemen, was born at Lexington, MA, July 13, 1729. He died Sept 17, 1775.

MOORE, DUDLEY: BIRTH ANNIVERSARY. April 19, 1935. British comedian, actor and classically trained pianist, born at Dagenham, near London, England. Initially pursuing a career as a concert and jazz pianist, Moore was invited by Peter Cook to join the comedy revue *Beyond the Fringe*. Moore was best known for his movies *10* and *Arthur*, for which he was nominated for an Oscar. Moore died at New Jersey on Mar 27, 2002.

NATIONAL AUCTIONEERS DAY. Apr 19. Recognizes the auction profession and its contribution to American commerce. Annually, the third Saturday in April. For info: Natl Auctioneers Assn, 8880 Ballentine St, Overland Park, KS 66214. Phone: (913) 541-8084. Fax: (913) 894-5281. E-mail: info@auctioneers.org. Web: www.auctioneers.org.

NATIONAL HANGING OUT DAY. Apr 19. Project Laundry List joins hundreds of organizations from around the country to educate communities about energy consumption. National Hanging Out Day was created to demonstrate how it is possible to save money and energy by using a clothesline. Annually, Apr 19. For info: Project Laundry List, Inc, PO Box 719, Hanover, NH 03755. Phone: (603) 941-4500. E-mail: info@laundrylist.org. Web: www.laundrylist.org.

NATIONAL PAPERBOARD PACKAGING WEEK. Apr 19–25. The Paperboard Packaging Council (PPC) sponsors this week to raise awareness of the environmental benefits of paperboard packaging. As part of this campaign, PPC publicizes municipal paperboard recycling programs to increase recycling rates nationwide. A program for schoolchildren demonstrates how paperboard packaging can be recycled and reused in planting saplings. Annually, the week in April, Saturday through Friday, that includes Earth Day (Apr 22). Held in conjunction with TICCIT Week ("Trees into Cartons, Cartons into Trees"). For info: PPC, 1350 Main St, Ste 1508, Springfield, MA 01103-1628. Phone: (413) 686-9191. Fax: (413) 747-7777. Web: www.ppcnet.org.

✦NATIONAL PARK WEEK. Apr 19–27 (tentative).

NESS, ELIOT: BIRTH ANNIVERSARY. Apr 19, 1903. The legendary Prohibition Era lawman was born at Chicago, IL. He gained lasting fame as the leader of the "Untouchables": young, dedicated federal agents handpicked by Ness who could not be bribed by the mobsters they were targeting. Ness especially went after Chicago gangster Al Capone's bootlegging business, which was finally brought down in 1931. After stints in other federal and municipal agencies, Ness died May 7, 1957, at Coudersport, PA—just before publication of his memoirs, *The Untouchables*, which went on to inspire a TV series and later a film.

NETHERLANDS–US DIPLOMATIC RELATIONS: ANNIVERSARY. Apr 19, 1782. Anniversary of establishment of America's oldest continuously peaceful diplomatic relations. On this date, the States General of the Netherlands United Provinces admitted John Adams (later to become second president of the US) as minister plenipotentiary of the young American republic. This was the second diplomatic recognition of the US as an independent nation. Within six months Adams had succeeded in bringing about the signing of the first Treaty of Amity and Commerce between the two countries (Oct 8, 1782).

NICARAGUA: CIVIL WAR TRUCE: ANNIVERSARY. Apr 19, 1990. The Contra guerrillas, the leftist Sandinistas and the incoming Chamorro government agreed to a truce, ending a nine-year civil war.

OKLAHOMA CITY BOMBING: ANNIVERSARY. Apr 19, 1995. A car bomb exploded outside the Alfred P. Murrah Federal Building at Oklahoma City, OK, at 9:02 AM, killing 168 people, 19 of them children at a day-care center; a nurse died of head injuries sustained while helping in rescue efforts. The bomb, estimated to have weighed 5,000 pounds, had been placed in a rented truck. The blast ripped off the north face of the nine-story building, leaving a 20-foot-wide crater and debris two stories high. Structurally unsound and increasingly dangerous, the bombed building was razed May 23. Timothy J. McVeigh, a decorated Gulf War army vet who is alleged to have been angered by the Bureau of Alcohol, Tobacco and Firearms (ATF) attack on the Branch Davidian compound at Waco, TX, exactly two years before, was convicted of the bombing and was executed June 11, 2001. The ATF had offices in the federal building. Terry L. Nichols, an army buddy of McVeigh's, was convicted of murder and conspiracy charges and was sentenced to life in prison.

PATRIOTS' DAY IN FLORIDA. Apr 19. A ceremonial day to commemorate the first blood shed in the American Revolution at Lexington and Concord in 1775.

POPE BENEDICT XVI: ELECTION ANNIVERSARY. Apr 19, 2005. German cardinal Joseph Ratzinger was elected 265th pope of the Roman Catholic Church by a papal conclave of 115 cardinals after the death of Pope John Paul II. He resigned from the papacy on Feb 28, 2013.

RECORD STORE DAY. Apr 19. 7th annual. Hundreds of independently owned music stores across the country will celebrate Record Store Day. On this day, all of these stores will simultaneously link and act as one with the purpose of celebrating the culture and unique place that they occupy both in their local communities and nationally. Check your local record store for special events—including artist appearances. Annually, the third Saturday in April. For info: Record Store Day. E-mail: information@recordstoreday.com. Web: www.recordstoreday.com.

RICARDO, DAVID: BIRTH ANNIVERSARY. Apr 19, 1772. Economist David Ricardo, whose writings greatly influenced later economic theory, was born at London, England. He is recognized as the man who first systematized economics. In his best-known work, *Principles of Political Economy and Taxation* (1817), he discussed wages and rent and the economic relationships among landlords, workers and owners of capital. In 1819 Ricardo purchased his own seat in the House of Commons and became a member of Parliament. He died Sept 11, 1823, at Gatcombe Park, Gloucestershire, England.

SHERMAN, ROGER: BIRTH ANNIVERSARY. Apr 19, 1721. (Old Style date.) American statesman, member of the Continental Congress (1774–81 and 1783–84), signer of the Declaration of Independence and of the Constitution, born at Newton, MA. He also calculated astronomical and calendar information for an almanac. Sherman died at New Haven, CT, July 23, 1793.

SIERRA LEONE: NATIONAL HOLIDAY. Apr 19. Sierra Leone became a republic in 1971.

SPACE MILESTONE: *SALYUT* (USSR). Apr 19, 1971. The Soviet Union launched *Salyut*, the first manned orbiting space laboratory. It was replaced in 1986 by *Mir*, a manned space station and laboratory.

SWAZILAND: KING'S BIRTHDAY. Apr 19. National holiday. Commemorates the birth of King Mswati III, born Apr 19, 1968.

URUGUAY: LANDING OF THE 33 PATRIOTS DAY. Apr 19. National holiday. Commemorates the arrival in 1825 of Juan Lavelleja, an anticolonial leader, and his 33 fighters. This landing marked the first stage in the fight for independence from Brazil in 1828.

WARSAW GHETTO REVOLT: ANNIVERSARY. Apr 19, 1943. A prolonged revolt began at Warsaw, Poland, when German troops tried to resume deportation of Jewish residents of the Warsaw Ghetto to the Treblinka concentration camp. With only 17 rifles and handmade grenades, for almost a month 1,200 Jewish fighters resisted 2,100 German troops who were armed with machine guns. When the uprising ended on May 16, 300 Germans and 7,000 Jews had died and the Warsaw Ghetto lay in ruins.

BIRTHDAYS TODAY

Hayden Christensen, 33, actor (*Shattered Glass, Star Wars* films), born Vancouver, BC, Canada, Apr 19, 1981.

Tim Curry, 68, actor (*The Rocky Horror Picture Show*; stage: *Spamalot, Amadeus, My Favorite Year*), born Cheshire, England, Apr 19, 1946.

Elinor Donahue, 77, actress ("Father Knows Best," "The Andy Griffith Show"), born Tacoma, WA, Apr 19, 1937.

James Franco, 36, actor (*Oz the Great and Powerful, Rise of the Planet of the Apes, 127 Hours*), born Palo Alto, CA, Apr 19, 1978.

Kate Hudson, 35, actress (*Fool's Gold*; *Almost Famous*; *You, Me and Dupree*), born Los Angeles, CA, Apr 19, 1979.

Ashley Judd, 46, actress (*High Crimes, Double Jeopardy, Kiss the Girls*), born Los Angeles, CA, Apr 19, 1968.

Hugh O'Brian, 84, actor ("The Life and Legend of Wyatt Earp," *Broken Lance, Ten Little Indians*), born Rochester, NY, Apr 19, 1930.

Tony Plana, 60, actor ("Ugly Betty," "Resurrection Boulevard"), born Havana, Cuba, Apr 19, 1954.

Alan Price, 72, singer, songwriter, born Fairfield, England, Apr 19, 1942.

Maria Sharapova, 27, tennis player, born Nyagan, Russia, Apr 19, 1987.

Al Unser, Jr, 52, race car driver, born Albuquerque, NM, Apr 19, 1962.

April 20 — Sunday

DAY 110 **255 REMAINING**

ADMINISTRATIVE PROFESSIONALS WEEK. Apr 20–26. Acknowledgment of the contributions of all administrative professionals and their vital roles in business, industry, education and government. Annually, the last full week (Sunday–Saturday) in April. Administrative Professionals Day is observed on Wednesday of this week (Apr 23 in 2014). For info: Intl Assn of Administrative Professionals, 10502 N Ambassador Dr, Ste 100, Kansas City, MO 64153-1291. Phone: (816) 891-6600, ext 2222. Fax: (816) 891-9118. E-mail: ray.weikal@iaap-hq.org. Web: www.iaap-hq.org.

BEDBUG AWARENESS WEEK. Apr 20–26. Bedbugs continue to plague Americans as they infest hotels, schools, college dorms, residences and other places where people gather. A 2013 survey conducted by the NPMA and the University of Kentucky found that nearly 100 percent of pest professionals had encountered bedbugs in the past year; a number that has steadily risen over a 10-year period. In an effort to encourage public education about this resilient pest, NPMA launched "Bedbug Awareness Week" as a part of National Pest Management Month to spread awareness, promote public vigilance and provide essential prevention advice. For info: National Pest Management Assn, 10460 North St, Fairfax, VA 22030. Phone: (703) 352-6762. Fax: (703) 352-3031. E-mail: NPMATeam@vaultcommunications.com. Web: www.pestworld.org.

COLUMBINE HIGH SCHOOL KILLINGS: 15th ANNIVERSARY. Apr 20, 1999. At this high school at Littleton, CO, students Eric Harris and Dylan Klebold killed 12 other students, a teacher and then themselves.

***DEEPWATER HORIZON* OIL RIG EXPLOSION: ANNIVERSARY.** Apr 20, 2010. On this day, an oil rig run by British Petroleum (BP) exploded in the Gulf of Mexico about 50 miles off the Louisiana coast, resulting in the largest offshore oil spill in US history. The fire and explosions on the platform—perhaps caused by escaping methane gas—killed 11 workers and injured 17. The rig eventually sank, and the damage to the drilling equipment resulted in an unrelenting flow of oil from the well directly into the gulf. Several attempts to staunch the flow were unsuccessful, primarily because of the difficulty in working at such depths (approximately 5,000 feet below sea level). At the height of the disaster, the well was pouring as much as 60,000 barrels of oil per day into the Gulf of Mexico, and the damage to marine wildlife and the surrounding coastal areas is immeasurable.

EASTER SUNDAY. Apr 20. Commemorates the Resurrection of Christ. Most joyous festival of the Christian year. The date of Easter, a movable feast, is derived from the lunar calendar: the first Sunday following the first ecclesiastical full moon on or after Mar 21—always between Mar 22 and Apr 25. The Council of Nicaea (AD 325) prescribed that Easter be celebrated on the Sunday after Passover, as that feast's date had been established in Jesus's time. After 1582, when Pope Gregory XIII introduced the Gregorian calendar, Orthodox Christians continued to use the Julian calendar, so Easter can sometimes be as much as five weeks apart in the Western and Eastern churches—though in 2014 it falls on the same date for both. Easter in 2015 will be Apr 5; in 2016 it will be Mar 27; in 2017 it will be Apr 16. Many other dates in the Christian year are derived from the date of Easter. See also: "Orthodox Easter Sunday or Pascha" (Apr 20).

FRENCH, DANIEL CHESTER: BIRTH ANNIVERSARY. Apr 20, 1850. American sculptor, born at Exeter, NH. One of the most important artists of the 19th and early 20th centuries as a sculptor of public monuments, French is best known for his 1875 *Minute Man* statue at Concord, MA, and his 1922 statue of the seated Abraham Lincoln in the Lincoln Memorial at Washington, DC. French died at Stockbridge, MA, Oct 7, 1931. His home and studio at Stockbridge were donated to the National Trust for Historic Preservation and are open to the public. For info: Chesterwood, PO Box 827, Stockbridge, MA 01262-0827.

April 2014	S	M	T	W	T	F	S
			1	2	3	4	5
	6	7	8	9	10	11	12
	13	14	15	16	17	18	19
	20	21	22	23	24	25	26
	27	28	29	30			

HAMPTON, LIONEL: BIRTH ANNIVERSARY. Apr 20, 1908. The jazz great was born at Louisville, KY. Hampton started out on piano and drums, but Louis Armstrong urged him to take up the vibraphone in 1930. Hampton went on to make that his signature instrument. He recorded and played with Armstrong, Benny Goodman, Dizzy Gillespie, Benny Carter and other legends before becoming a bandleader himself. He played almost up until his death on Aug 31, 2002, at New York, NY.

HITLER, ADOLF: 125th BIRTH ANNIVERSARY. Apr 20, 1889. German dictator, born at Braunau am Inn, Austria. Despite a brief time in prison—during which he wrote *Mein Kampf* (published in 1925 and 1926)—Hitler quickly rose in politics as leader of the Nazis, feeding on German anger over the economy and WWI defeat. He also fanned violent anti-Semitism, which later resulted in millions of Jewish deaths in concentration camps. A German plebiscite vested sole executive power in Führer Adolf Hitler Aug 19, 1934. In seeking to increase German power, he started WWII in 1939. Facing certain defeat by the Allied forces, he shot himself Apr 30, 1945, in a Berlin bunker where he had been hiding for more than three months.

ITALY: EXPLOSION OF THE CART. Apr 20. Florence. At noon on Easter Sunday in Piazza del Duomo a cart full of fireworks is exploded, perpetuating a ceremony of ancient origin and recalling the fire that was kindled during the *Gloria* at Easter mass and then distributed to all of Florence's households. The tradition is held to date back to the time of the First Crusade, when the valorous Pazzino dei Pazzi was awarded some pieces of flint from the Holy Sepulcher. After his return to Florence the holy fire was kindled with these flints, now preserved in the church of Santi Apostoli.

LLOYD, HAROLD: BIRTH ANNIVERSARY. Apr 20, 1893. A comic genius of early American film, Harold Lloyd frequently played the boy-next-door whose distinguishing feature was his round horn spectacles. This character thrilled audiences in "daredevil" comedy featuring dangerous stunts (Lloyd never used a double). Lloyd's hits included *Safety Last* (1923), where he dangled from a building's clock face, *The Freshman* (1925) and *Speedy* (1928). The biggest box-office star of the 1920s, Lloyd survived with lesser success in the talkie 1930s. He was given an honorary Oscar in 1953 for being a "master comedian and good citizen." Born at Burchard, NE, Lloyd died on Mar 8, 1971, at Hollywood, CA.

LUDLOW MINE INCIDENT: 100th ANNIVERSARY. Apr 20, 1914. Miners struggling for recognition of their United Mine Workers Union were attacked at Ludlow, CO, by National Guard troops. The guardsmen were paid by the mining company. A tent colony was destroyed, five men and one boy were killed by machine-gun fire, and 11 children and two women were burned to death.

MERRIE MONARCH FESTIVAL WITH WORLD'S LARGEST HULA COMPETITION. Apr 20–26. Hilo, HI. Cultural event honoring King David Kalakaua. Festival culminates with the world's largest hula competition. Hawaii's finest hula schools compete in ancient and modern divisions. Annually, beginning on Easter Sunday. Est attendance: 6,000. For info: Merrie Monarch Office, 865 Piilani St, Hilo, HI 96720. Phone: (808) 935-9168. Web: www.merriemonarch.com.

NATIONAL COIN WEEK. Apr 20–26. 92nd annual. Discover the world of money and the hobby of coin collecting. Annually, the third full week of April, Sunday through Saturday. For info: American Numismatic Assn, 818 N Cascade Ave, Colorado Springs, CO 80903. Phone: (800) 367-9723. E-mail: pr@money.org. Web: www.money.org.

✦NATIONAL CRIME VICTIMS' RIGHTS WEEK. Apr 20–26 (tentative). Date varies—a week in April.

NATIONAL KARAOKE WEEK. Apr 20–26. Karaoke has grown by leaps and bounds in the US. Though it was once thought to be a fad, more and more people are recognizing the benefits of karaoke—increased self-esteem, confidence and stress release. For info: Visual Perspectives, 5306 Mirror Lakes Blvd, Boynton Beach, FL 33472. E-mail: shirai2@comcast.net.

ORTHODOX EASTER SUNDAY OR PASCHA. Apr 20. Observed by Eastern Orthodox churches on this date. Normally Easter falls on different Sundays in the Eastern and Western churches, but not in 2014.

PUENTE, TITO: BIRTH ANNIVERSARY. Apr 20, 1923. The King of the Mambo—or "El Rey"—was born Ernesto Antonio Puente, Jr, at Spanish Harlem, New York City, to Puerto Rican parents. The legendary Puente had a career that spanned more than six decades, starting in 1937. He popularized the timbal but played many other percussion instruments and was also a composer, arranger and bandleader. His album *Dance Mania* (1958) was an international bestseller, and he released more than 100 albums. His song "Oye Como Va" was covered by Carlos Santana and has become a classic. Puente won five Grammys, was inducted into the Jazz and Hispanic halls of fame and received a Smithsonian Lifetime Achievement Award. President Jimmy Carter pronounced him "the Goodwill Ambassador of Latin American Music." Puente died on May 31, 2000, at New York, NY.

SKY AWARENESS WEEK. Apr 20–26. A celebration of the sky and an opportunity to appreciate its natural beauty, to understand sky and weather processes and to work together to protect the sky as a natural resource. Events are held at schools, nature centers and other settings all across the US. For info: Barbara G. Levine and H. Michael Mogil, How The Weatherworks, 7765 Preserve Ln, Ste 5, Naples, FL 34119. Phone: (239) 591-2468. Web: www.weatherworks.com.

SMITH, HOLLAND: BIRTH ANNIVERSARY. Apr 20, 1882. Considered the father of amphibious warfare, Holland "Howling Mad" Smith was born at Hatchechubie, AL. Smith developed techniques for amphibious assaults that involved coordination of land, sea and air forces. During WWII he led troops in assaults in the Marshall and Mariana Islands and also directed forces at Guam, Iwo Jima and Okinawa. Smith died Jan 12, 1967, at San Diego, CA.

TAURUS, THE BULL. Apr 20–May 20. In the astronomical/astrological zodiac that divides the sun's apparent orbit into 12 segments, the period Apr 20–May 20 is traditionally identified as the sun sign of Taurus, the Bull. The ruling planet is Venus.

TED WILLIAMS'S DEBUT: 75th ANNIVERSARY. Apr 20, 1939. Ted Williams made his major-league debut for the Boston Red Sox, getting one double in four at bats, as the Sox lost to the New York Yankees, 2–0.

BIRTHDAYS TODAY

Felix Baumgartner, 45, skydiver, daredevil, BASE jumper, born Salzburg, Austria, Apr 20, 1969.

Carmen Electra, 41, actress ("Baywatch," "Singled Out"), born Cincinnati, OH, Apr 20, 1973.

Crispin Glover, 50, actor (*Willard, Back to the Future, The People vs Larry Flynt*), born New York, NY, Apr 20, 1964.

Danny Granger, 31, basketball player, born New Orleans, LA, Apr 20, 1983.

Jessica Lange, 65, actress (Oscars for *Tootsie* and *Blue Skies*; *Frances, Sweet Dreams*), born Cloquet, MN, Apr 20, 1949.

Joey Lawrence, 38, actor ("Blossom," "Brotherly Love"), born Strawbridge, PA, Apr 20, 1976.

David Leland, 67, actor (*Time Bandits*), writer, director (*Mona Lisa, Wish You Were Here*), born Cambridge, England, Apr 20, 1947.

Don Mattingly, 53, former baseball player, born Evansville, IN, Apr 20, 1961.

Shemar Moore, 44, actor ("Criminal Minds"), host ("Soul Train"), born Oakland, CA, Apr 20, 1970.

Ryan O'Neal, 73, actor ("Peyton Place," *Love Story, Paper Moon*), born Los Angeles, CA, Apr 20, 1941.

Pat Roberts, 78, US Senator (R, Kansas), born Topeka, KS, Apr 20, 1936.

Steve Spurrier, 69, football coach and former player, born Miami Beach, FL, Apr 20, 1945.

John Paul Stevens, 94, former associate justice of the US, born Chicago, IL, Apr 20, 1920.

April 21 — Monday

DAY 111 — **254 REMAINING**

AGGIE MUSTER. Apr 21. Texas A&M University, College Station, TX, and around the world. A ceremony where current and former students (Aggies) of Texas A&M University gather together to recall their days at the university and to honor fellow Aggies who have died in the past year. During the ceremony, a Roll Call for the Absent is read and a comrade answers "here" for the deceased. The school's most sacred and time-honored tradition. First held in 1883, but in 1903 the Muster date was moved to Apr 21—San Jacinto Day. Celebrated on the school campus and at more than 400 locations around the world. Annually, Apr 21. Est attendance: 100,000. For info: The Association of Former Students, 505 George Bush Dr, College Station, TX 77840-2918. E-mail: aggienetwork@aggienetwork.com. Web: www.aggienetwork.com.

BOSTON MARATHON—118th RUNNING. Apr 21. Boston, MA. The marathon begins in the rural New England town of Hopkinton, winds through eight cities and towns and finishes near downtown Boston. Always the third Monday in April. 27,000 participants. Athletes qualify by meeting time standards that correspond to age. Est attendance: 500,000. For info: Boston Athletic Assn, Boston Marathon, One Ash St, Hopkinton, MA 01748. Phone: (617) 236-1652. E-mail: info@baa.org. Web: www.baa.org.

BRASÍLIA INAUGURATED: ANNIVERSARY. Apr 21, 1960. At 9:30 AM, Brazil's new federal capital, Brasília, was inaugurated. The futuristic-looking city, located on the country's central plain and featuring the bold architecture of Oscar Niemeyer and others, was built in four years under the master plan of Lúcio Costa, who won a national contest to create a plan. The former capital was Rio de Janeiro.

BRAZIL: TIRADENTES DAY. Apr 21. National holiday commemorating execution of national hero, dentist José da Silva Xavier, nicknamed Tiradentes (tooth-puller), a conspirator in revolt against the Portuguese in 1789.

BRONTË, CHARLOTTE: BIRTH ANNIVERSARY. Apr 21, 1816. English novelist, born at Hartshead, Yorkshire, England. "Conventionality," she wrote in the preface to *Jane Eyre*, "is not morality. Self-righteousness is not religion. To attack the first is not to assail the last." She died Mar 31, 1855, at Haworth, Yorkshire.

CANADA: NEWFOUNDLAND: SAINT GEORGE'S DAY. Apr 21. Holiday observed at Newfoundland on Monday nearest feast day (Apr 23) of Saint George.

DYNGUS DAY USA. Apr 21. Dyngus Day celebrates the end of Lent and the joy of Easter. "Dyngus" comes from a medieval Polish word for "worthy, proper." Over the decades, the day has become a wonderful way to celebrate Polish-American culture, heritage and traditions. With the largest concentration of festival locations, live polka music and authentic traditions, Buffalo, NY, is the "Dyngus Day Capital of the World!" Many parties begin during the mid-morning with a large buffet of traditional Easter foods (kielbasa, ham, fresh breads, eggs). The most important tradition of Dyngus Day is the exchange of pussy willow branches and water as a playful form of flirting. Men and women tap each other with the pussy willows and squirt each other with water to attract attention. Annually, the Monday after Easter. For info: Dyngus Day USA, PO Box 828, Buffalo, NY 14215. Phone: (716) 894-2400. E-mail: DyngusDay@aol.com. Web: www.DyngusDay.com.

EASTER MONDAY. Apr 21. Holiday or bank holiday in many places, including England, Northern Ireland, Wales and Canada.

ENGLAND: HALLATON BOTTLE KICKING. Apr 21. Hallaton, Leicestershire. Ancient custom dating back at least 600 years. Annually, Easter Monday.

FESTIVAL OF RIDVAN. Apr 21–May 2. Annual Baha'i festival commemorating the 12 days (Apr 21–May 2, 1863) when Baha'u'llah, the prophet-founder of the Baha'i Faith, resided in a garden called Ridvan (Paradise) in Baghdad, at which time he publicly proclaimed his mission as God's messenger for this age. The first, ninth (Apr 29) and twelfth days are celebrated as holy days and are three of the nine days of the year when Baha'is suspend work. For info: Baha'is of the US, Office of Communications, 1233 Central St, Evanston, IL 60201. Phone: (847) 733-3559. Fax: (847) 733-3578. E-mail: ooc@usbnc.org. Web: www.bahai.us.

FIBROID AWARENESS WEEK. Apr 21–25. An observance promoted by the Fibroid Treatment Collective to increase visibility for the diagnosis and treatment of fibroids, which affect upwards of 50 percent of all women. Annually, the fourth week in April (Monday through Friday). For info: Fibroid Treatment Collective, 450 N Roxbury Dr, #275, Beverly Hills, CA 90210. Phone: (866) 362-3463. Fax: (310) 208-2621. E-mail: info@fibroids.com. Web: www.fibroids.com.

FROEBEL, FRIEDRICH: BIRTH ANNIVERSARY. Apr 21, 1782. German educator and author Friedrich Froebel, who believed that play is an important part of a child's education, was born at Oberwiessbach, Thuringia. Froebel invented the kindergarten, founding the first one at Blankenburg, Germany, in 1837. Froebel also invented a series of toys that he intended to stimulate learning. (The American architect Frank Lloyd Wright as a child received these toys [maplewood blocks] from his mother and spoke throughout his life of their value.) Froebel's ideas about the role of directed play, toys and music in children's education had a profound influence in England and the US, where the nursery school became a further extension of his ideas. Froebel died at Marienthal, Germany, June 21, 1852.

INDONESIA: KARTINI DAY. Apr 21. Honors the birth in 1879 of Raden Adjeng Kartini, pioneer in the emancipation of the women of Indonesia.

ITALY: BIRTHDAY OF ROME. Apr 21. Celebration of the founding of Rome, traditionally thought to be in 753 BC.

KINDERGARTEN DAY. Apr 21. A day to recognize the importance of play, games and "creative self-activity" in children's education and to note the history of the kindergarten. Observed on the anniversary of the birth of Friedrich Froebel, in 1782, who established the first kindergarten in 1837. German immigrants brought Froebel's ideas to the US in the 1840s. The first kindergarten in a public school in the US was started in 1873, at St. Louis, MO.

LUXEMBOURG: EMAISHEN. Apr 21. Luxembourg (city). Popular traditional market and festival at the "Marche-aux-Poissons." Young lovers present each other with earthenware articles, sold only on this day. Annually, Easter Monday.

MUIR, JOHN: BIRTH ANNIVERSARY. Apr 21, 1838. Scottish-American naturalist, explorer, conservationist and author for whom the 550-acre Muir Woods National Monument (near San Francisco, CA) is named. Muir, born at Dunbar, Scotland, emigrated to the US in 1849, eventually settling out west, where he was instrumental in the creation of numerous national parks, including Yosemite, Sequoia, Mount Rainier and Grand Canyon. His writings and his work in the Sierra Club (founded in 1892) created public support for his belief that national parks should be federally protected and their resources left untapped. Muir died at Los Angeles, CA, Dec 24, 1914.

NATIONAL BULLDOGS ARE BEAUTIFUL DAY. Apr 21. In addition to recognizing the beauty in our portly pets, National Bulldogs Are Beautiful Day celebrates people's differences whether they're big, small, short, tall, skinny or stout or have names like Stinky or Lulu. For info: Jackie Valent, 3250 Pleasant View Ct, Brookfield, WI 53045. Phone: (414) 232-8271. E-mail: stinkythebulldog@sbcglobal.net.

NATIONAL PLAYGROUND SAFETY WEEK. Apr 21–25. An opportunity for families, community parks, schools and child-care facilities to focus on preventing public playground–related injuries. Sponsored by the National Program for Playground Safety (NPPS), this event helps educate the public about the more than 200,000 children (that's one child every 2½ minutes) that require emergency room treatment for playground-related injuries each year. For info: Natl Program for Playground Safety, HPC105, University of Northern Iowa, Cedar Falls, IA 50614-0618. Phone: (800) 554-PLAY. Fax: (319) 273-7308. Web: www.playgroundsafety.org.

PATRIOTS' DAY IN MASSACHUSETTS AND MAINE. Apr 21. Commemorates battles of Lexington and Concord, 1775. Annually, the third Monday in April.

QUINN, ANTHONY: BIRTH ANNIVERSARY. Apr 21, 1915. Actor, sculptor and painter, Anthony Rudolf Oaxaca Quinn was born at Chihuahua, Mexico, and moved to the US as a child. He became a US citizen in 1947. He won Academy Awards for Best Supporting Actor in 1952 for *Viva Zapata!* and in 1956 for *Lust for Life*. His best-remembered role is that of the title character in *Zorba the Greek*, for which he was nominated for Best Actor in 1964. He died at Boston, MA, on June 3, 2001.

RED BARON SHOT DOWN: ANNIVERSARY. Apr 21, 1918. German flying ace Baron Manfred von Richtofen was shot down and killed during the Battle of the Somme. The "Red Baron," so named for the color of his Fokker triplane, was credited with 80 kills in less than two years. Royal Flying Corps pilots recovered his body, and the Allies buried him with full military honors. Asked about his fighting philosophy, he was quoted as saying, "I am a hunter. My brother Lothar is a butcher. When I have shot down an Englishman, my hunting passion is satisfied for a quarter of an hour."

SAN JACINTO DAY. Apr 21. Texas. Commemorates Battle of San Jacinto in 1836, in which Texas won independence from Mexico. A 570-foot monument, dedicated on the 101st anniversary of the battle, marks the site on the banks of the San Jacinto River, about 20 miles from present-day Houston, TX, where General Sam Houston's Texans decisively defeated the Mexican forces led by Santa Anna in the final battle between Texas and Mexico.

SOUTH AFRICA: FAMILY DAY. Apr 21. National holiday. Annually, Easter Monday.

SPACE MILESTONE: *COPERNICUS, OAO 4* (US). Apr 21, 1972. Launch of Orbiting Astronomical Observer, named in honor of the Polish astronomer.

SWITZERLAND: EGG RACES. Apr 21. Rural northwest Swiss Easter Monday custom. Race among competitors carrying large numbers of eggs while running to neighboring villages.

April 2014

S	M	T	W	T	F	S
		1	2	3	4	5
6	7	8	9	10	11	12
13	14	15	16	17	18	19
20	21	22	23	24	25	26
27	28	29	30			

UNITED KINGDOM: EASTER MONDAY BANK HOLIDAY. Apr 21. Bank and public holiday in England, Wales and Northern Ireland. (Scotland not included.)

WEBER, MAX: 150th BIRTH ANNIVERSARY. Apr 21, 1864. Born at Erfaut, Germany, Weber was a founder of modern sociological thought. His historical and comparative studies of the sociocultural processes of great civilizations, notably *The Protestant Ethic and the Spirit of Capitalism*, are pivotal in sociological history. Weber's ethical themes are foundational in existentialist philosophical thought. He died June 14, 1920, at Munich, Germany.

WHITE HOUSE EASTER EGG ROLL. Apr 21. Traditionally held at executive mansion's south lawn on Easter Monday. Custom said to have started at Capitol grounds about 1810. Transferred to White House lawn in 1870s.

BIRTHDAYS TODAY

Ed Belfour, 49, former hockey player, born Carman, MB, Canada, Apr 21, 1965.

Tony Danza, 63, actor ("Taxi," "Who's the Boss?"), born Brooklyn, NY, Apr 21, 1951.

Queen Elizabeth II, 88, Queen of the United Kingdom, born London, England, Apr 21, 1926.

Charles Grodin, 79, actor (*Midnight Run, Beethoven*), director, talk show host ("The Charles Grodin Show"), born Pittsburgh, PA, Apr 21, 1935.

Patti LuPone, 65, singer, stage and screen actress (Tonys for *Gypsy, Sweeney Todd* and *Evita*), born Northport, NY, Apr 21, 1949.

Andie MacDowell, 56, actress (*Harrison's Flowers, Four Weddings and a Funeral, Groundhog Day*), born Gaffney, SC, Apr 21, 1958.

Elaine May, 82, actress, writer, director (*A New Leaf*), born Philadelphia, PA, Apr 21, 1932.

Iggy Pop, 67, singer, born James Newell Osterberg, Jr, at Ann Arbor, MI, Apr 21, 1947.

Tony Romo, 34, football player, born San Diego, CA, Apr 21, 1980.

April 22 — Tuesday

DAY 112 — **253 REMAINING**

BABE RUTH'S PITCHING DEBUT: 100th ANNIVERSARY. Apr 22, 1914. Babe Ruth made his professional pitching debut, playing for the Baltimore Orioles in his hometown. Allowing just six hits and contributing two singles himself, Ruth shut out the Buffalo Bisons, 6–0.

BRAZIL: DISCOVERY OF BRAZIL DAY. Apr 22. Commemorates discovery by Pedro Alvarez Cabral in 1500.

CHEMISTS CELEBRATE EARTH DAY. Apr 22. An environmental awareness campaign designed to enhance public awareness of important contributions made through chemistry in preserving our planet and improving our environment. The American Chemical Society provides contests, resources, products and various other activities to engage local communities in the national celebration. For info: Alvin Collins, Member Communities, American Chemical Society, 1155 16th St NW, Washington, DC 20036. Phone: (800) 227-5558. E-mail: outreach@acs.org. Web: www.acs.org/earthday.

COINS STAMPED "IN GOD WE TRUST": 150th ANNIVERSARY. Apr 22, 1864. By act of Congress, the phrase "In God We Trust" began to be stamped on all US coins.

✦**EARTH DAY.** Apr 22. To encourage all citizens to help protect our environment and contribute to a healthy, sustainable world.

EARTH DAY. Apr 22. Earth Day, first observed Apr 22, 1970, with the message "New Energy for a New Era" and attention to accelerating the transition to renewable energy worldwide. Note: Earth Day activities are held by many groups on various dates, often on the weekends before and after Apr 22. Search for events online. For info: Earth Day Network, 1616 P St NW, Ste 340, Washington, DC 20036. Phone: (202) 518-0044. Fax: (202) 518-8794. Web: www.earthday.net.

FIRST SOLO TRIP TO NORTH POLE: 20th ANNIVERSARY. Apr 22, 1994. Norwegian explorer Borge Ousland became the first person to make the trip to the North Pole alone. The trip took 52 days, during which he pulled a 265-pound sled. Departing from Cape Atkticheskiy at Siberia Mar 2, he averaged about 18½ miles per day over the 630-mile journey. Ousland had traveled to the Pole on skis with Erling Kagge in 1990.

LENIN, NIKOLAI: BIRTH ANNIVERSARY. Apr 22, 1870. Russian Socialist and revolutionary leader (real name: Vladimir Ilyich Ulyanov), ideological follower of Karl Marx, born at Simbirst, on the Volga, Russia. Leader of the Great October Socialist Revolution of 1917. Died at Gorky, near Moscow, Jan 21, 1924. His embalmed body, in a glass coffin at the Lenin Mausoleum, has been viewed by millions of visitors to Moscow's Red Square.

MOON PHASE: LAST QUARTER. Apr 22. Moon enters Last Quarter phase at 3:52 AM, EDT.

NATIONAL CATHOLIC EDUCATIONAL ASSOCIATION CONVENTION AND EXPO. Apr 22–24. David L. Lawrence Convention Center, Pittsburgh, PA. This meeting is for NCEA members and anyone else working in, or interested in, the welfare of Catholic and faith-based education. Annually, the week after Easter Sunday. Est attendance: 7,000. For info: Daniel Baczkowski, Dir of Events, Natl Catholic Educational Assn, 1005 N Glebe Rd, Ste 525, Arlington, VA 22201. Phone: (571) 257-0010. Fax: (703) 243-0025. Web: www.ncea.org.

NATIONAL JELLY BEAN DAY. Apr 22. A day to celebrate the colorful candy that has been around since Biblical times. For info: National Confectioners Association, 1101 30th St NW, Ste 200, Washington, DC 20007. Phone: (202) 534-1440. E-mail: info@CandyUSA.org. Web: www.CandyUSA.org.

OKLAHOMA LAND RUSH: 125th ANNIVERSARY. Apr 22, 1889. At noon a gunshot signaled the start of the Oklahoma land rush as thousands of settlers rushed into the territory to claim land. Under pressure from cattlemen, the federal government opened 1,900,000 acres of central Oklahoma that had been bought from the Creek and Seminole tribes.

UNITED NATIONS: INTERNATIONAL MOTHER EARTH DAY. Apr 22. Acknowledging that Earth and its ecosystems are our home, and convinced that to achieve a just balance among the economic, social and environmental needs of present and future generations, it is necessary to promote harmony with nature and Earth, the UN General Assembly has proclaimed Apr 22 to be celebrated annually as International Mother Earth Day. (Resolution 63/278 of Apr 22, 2009.) For info: United Nations, Dept of Public Info, New York, NY 10017. Web: www.un.org.

BIRTHDAYS TODAY

Byron Allen, 53, comedian, television host ("The Byron Allen Show," "Real People"), actor (*Case Closed*), born Detroit, MI, Apr 22, 1961.

Glen Campbell, 79, singer, guitarist, born Billstown, AR, Apr 22, 1935.

Francis Capra, 31, actor ("Veronica Mars," *A Bronx Tale*), born New York, NY, Apr 22, 1983.

Peter Frampton, 64, singer, guitarist, born Beckenham, England, Apr 22, 1950.

Amber Heard, 28, actress (*Pineapple Express, The Informers*), born Austin, TX, Apr 22, 1986.

Kaká, 32, soccer player, born Ricardo Izecson dos Santos Leite at Brasilia, Brazil, Apr 22, 1982.

Eric Mabius, 43, actor ("Ugly Betty," "The L Word"), born Harrisburg, PA, Apr 22, 1971.

Chris Makepeace, 50, actor (*My Bodyguard*), born Montreal, QC, Canada, Apr 22, 1964.

Jack Nicholson, 78, actor (Oscars for *One Flew Over the Cuckoo's Nest, Terms of Endearment* and *As Good as It Gets*), born Neptune, NJ, Apr 22, 1936.

Charlotte Rae, 88, actress ("Diff'rent Strokes," "The Facts of Life"), born Milwaukee, WI, Apr 22, 1926.

Sherri Shepard, 47, actress, television personality ("30 Rock," "The View"), born Chicago, IL, Apr 22, 1967.

Ryan Stiles, 55, actor ("The Drew Carey Show," "Whose Line Is It Anyway?"), born Seattle, WA, Apr 22, 1959.

John Waters, 68, filmmaker (*Pink Flamingos*), born Baltimore, MD, Apr 22, 1946.

April 23 — Wednesday

DAY 113 **252 REMAINING**

ADMINISTRATIVE PROFESSIONALS DAY. Apr 23. Annually, the Wednesday of Administrative Professionals Week. For info: Intl Assn of Administrative Professionals, 10502 N Ambassador Dr, Kansas City, MO 64153-1291. Phone: (816) 891-6600, ext 2222. E-mail: ray.weikal@iaap-hq.org. Web: www.iaap-hq.org.

AMERICAN QUILTER'S SOCIETY QUILT SHOW. Apr 23–26. Paducah, KY. 30th annual. More than 400 quilts are exhibited, with $100,000 awarded in prizes. Lectures, workshops and quilt auction. Est attendance: 35,000. For info: American Quilter's Society, PO Box 3290, Paducah, KY 42002. Phone: (270) 898-7903. Fax: (270) 898-1173. Web: www.americanquilter.com.

"BAYWATCH" TV PREMIERE: 25th ANNIVERSARY. Apr 23, 1989. Set on a California beach, this program starred David Hasselhoff and a changing cast of nubile young men and women as lifeguards. Later the program was moved to Hawaii; the last episode was made in 2001. The most widely viewed TV series in the world, the program aired in 142 countries with an estimated weekly audience of 1.1 billion.

April 2014	S	M	T	W	T	F	S
			1	2	3	4	5
	6	7	8	9	10	11	12
	13	14	15	16	17	18	19
	20	21	22	23	24	25	26
	27	28	29	30			

BERMUDA: PEPPERCORN CEREMONY. Apr 23. St. George. Commemorates the payment of one peppercorn in 1816 to the governor of Bermuda for rental of Old State House by the Masonic Lodge.

BUCHANAN, JAMES: BIRTH ANNIVERSARY. Apr 23, 1791. 15th president of the US, born at Cove Gap, PA. Buchanan was the only president who never married. He served one term in office, Mar 4, 1857–Mar 3, 1861, and died at Lancaster, PA, June 1, 1868.

CERVANTES SAAVEDRA, MIGUEL DE: DEATH ANNIVERSARY. Apr 23, 1616. Spanish poet, playwright and novelist, died at Madrid, Spain. The exact date of his birth at Alcala de Henares is unknown, but he was baptized Oct 9, 1547. As soldier and tax collector, Cervantes traveled widely. He spent more than five years in prisons in Spain, Italy and North Africa. His greatest creation was Don Quixote, the immortal Knight of La Mancha whose profession was chivalry. Riding his nag, Rozinante, and accompanied by Squire Sancho Panza, Don Quixote tilts at windmills of the mind in the world's best-known novel. Nearly a thousand editions of *Don Quixote* (a bestseller since its first appearance in 1605) have been published, and it has been translated into more languages than any other book except the Bible.

DOUGLAS, STEPHEN A.: BIRTH ANNIVERSARY. Apr 23, 1813. Famous for his oratorical skills, American politician Stephen A. Douglas was born at Brandon, VT. Upon adulthood, he moved to the Illinois frontier where he rose to prominence in the Democratic Party while serving in various elected positions in both the Illinois and US legislatures. Douglas's US Senate reelection campaign of 1858 is renowned for its seven debates with Abraham Lincoln. Despite winning the Senate contest, Douglas was soundly defeated by Abraham Lincoln two years later in the 1860 presidential race, due in large part to the disaffection of Southern Democrats. Following Lincoln's inauguration Douglas argued vigorously against secession. He died June 3, 1861, at Chicago, IL.

EDISON AWARDS. Apr 23–24. New York, NY. The Edison Awards™ are among the most prestigious accolades honoring excellence in new product and service development, marketing, human-centered design and innovation. Unique to the world of award programs, the Edison Awards™ are focused on the innovators as much as the innovations. Award winners represent "game changing" products, services and excellence and leadership in innovation around four criteria: Concept, Value, Delivery and Impact. An Edison Award represents significant value to the award winner and to the cause of innovation. Annually, the last Wednesday and Thursday in April. Est attendance: 450. For info: Edison Awards, 8117 W 124th St, Palos Park, IL 60464. Phone: (312) 810-9413. E-mail: mhensler@edisonawards.com. Web: www.edisonawards.com.

FIRST MOVIE THEATER OPENS: ANNIVERSARY. Apr 23, 1896. The first movie was shown at Koster and Bials Music Hall at New York City. Up until this time, people saw films individually by looking into a kinetoscope, a boxlike "peep show." This was the first time in the US that an audience sat in a theater and watched a movie together. See also: "First Cinema Anniversary" (Dec 28).

FIRST PUBLIC SCHOOL IN AMERICA: ANNIVERSARY. Apr 23, 1635. (New Style date.) The Boston Latin School opened—America's oldest public school.

PEARSON, LESTER B.: BIRTH ANNIVERSARY. Apr 23, 1897. 14th prime minister of Canada, born at Toronto, Canada. He was Canada's chief delegate at the San Francisco conference where the UN charter was drawn up and later served as president of the General Assembly. He wrote the proposal that resulted in the formation of the North Atlantic Treaty Organization (NATO). He was awarded the Nobel Peace Prize. Died at Rockcliffe, Canada, Dec 27, 1972.

PHYSICISTS DISCOVER TOP QUARK: 20th ANNIVERSARY. Apr 23, 1994. Physicists at the Department of Energy's Fermi National Accelerator Laboratory found evidence for the existence of the subatomic particle called the top quark, the last undiscovered quark of the six predicted to exist by current scientific theory. The discovery provides strong support for the quark theory of the structure of matter. Quarks are subatomic particles that make up protons and neutrons found in the nuclei of atoms. The five other quark types that had already been proven to exist are the up quark, down quark, strange quark, charm quark and bottom quark. Further experimentation over many months confirmed the discovery, and it was publicly announced Mar 2, 1995.

PLANCK, MAX: BIRTH ANNIVERSARY. Apr 23, 1858. Formulator of the quantum theory, which revolutionized physics, born at Kiel, Germany. Einstein's application of quantum theory to light led to the theories of relativity. Planck died at Göttingen, Germany, Oct 3, 1947.

POLK COUNTY RAMP TRAMP FESTIVAL. Apr 23–26. Polk County 4-H Camp, Camp McCroy, near Benton, TN. A tribute to the ramp, a wild leek that grows only in the Appalachian Mountains. Bluegrass music and feast of the ramps. Est attendance: 1,200. For info: Polk County Ramp Tramp Festival, Box 189, Benton, TN 37307. Phone: (423) 338-4503. Web: www.ramptrampfestival.com.

ROGER EBERT'S FILM FESTIVAL (EBERTFEST). Apr 23–27. Virginia Theatre, Champaign, IL. Spring film festival founded by the late Roger Ebert, University of Illinois journalism graduate and Pulitzer Prize–winning film critic. The festival presents 12 films representing a cross section of important cinematic works. Each film is introduced, then a panel—often composed of the films' producers, writers, actors or directors as well as scholars—discusses it on stage afterward. For general audiences, distributors and international critics. Sponsored by the College of Media, University of Illinois. For info: Mary Susan Britt, University of Illinois, College of Media, 119 Gregory Hall, 810 S Wright St, Urbana, IL 61801. Phone: (217) 244-0552. Fax: (217) 333-0411. E-mail: marsue@illinois.edu. Web: www.ebertfest.com.

SAINT GEORGE: FEAST DAY. Apr 23. Martyr and patron saint of England, who died Apr 23, AD 303. Hero of the St. George and the Dragon legend. The story says that his faith helped him slay a vicious dragon that demanded daily sacrifice after the king's daughter became the intended victim.

SHAKESPEARE, WILLIAM: 450th BIRTH ANNIVERSARY. Apr 23. Author of at least 38 plays and 154 sonnets, the dramatist, actor, poet and theater manager Shakespeare created the most influential and lasting body of work in the English language, an extraordinary exploration of human nature. Shakespeare contributed thousands of words to the English language and expanded the dramatic possibilities of blank verse, making it mimic the rhythm of speech even as he elevated speech to poetry. He was born at Stratford-on-Avon, England, Apr 23, 1564, was baptized there three days later and died there on his birthday, Apr 23, 1616.

SPAIN: BOOK DAY AND LOVER'S DAY. Apr 23. Barcelona. Saint George's Day and the anniversary of the death of Spanish writer Miguel de Cervantes have been observed with special ceremonies in the Palacio de la Disputacion and throughout the city since 1714. Book stands are set up in the plazas and on street corners. This is Spain's equivalent of Valentine's Day. Women give books to men; men give roses to women.

TUCSON INTERNATIONAL MARIACHI CONFERENCE. Apr 23–26. Casino del Sol, Tucson, AZ. An exciting festival that showcases the best in *baile folklórico* and mariachi. Events are open to the public: the Participant Showcase, the Espectacular Concert, the Mariachi Mass and the Fiesta de Garibaldi. The conference also includes workshops giving students of all ages the opportunity to study the music and dance of Mexico and learn from the masters. Est attendance: 50,000. For info: La Frontera Tucson Intl Mariachi Conference, 504 W 29th St, Tucson, AZ 85713. Phone: (520) 838-5593. Fax: (520) 792-0654. E-mail: TIMC@lafrontera.org. Web: www.tucsonmariachi.org.

TURKEY: NATIONAL SOVEREIGNTY AND CHILDREN'S DAY. Apr 23. Commemorates Grand National Assembly's inauguration in 1923.

UNITED NATIONS: WORLD BOOK AND COPYRIGHT DAY. Apr 23. By celebrating this day throughout the world, UNESCO seeks to promote reading, publishing and the protection of intellectual property through copyright. It was a natural choice for UNESCO's General Conference to pay a worldwide tribute to books and authors on Apr 23, because on this date and in the same year of 1616, Cervantes, Shakespeare and Inca Garcilaso de la Vega all died. It is also the date of birth or death of other prominent authors such as Maurice Druon, Halldor Laxness, Josep Pla, Manuel Mejía Vallejo and William Wordsworth. Observed throughout the United Nations system. For info: United Nations, Dept of Public Info, New York, NY 10017. Web: www.un.org.

USA FILM FESTIVAL. Apr 23–27 (tentative). Angelika Film Center, Dallas, TX. 44th annual. Major showcase of new studio and independent films (features and shorts), filmmaker discussions with audience, Master Screen Artist, Great Director and other tributes and retrospectives. Festival is noncompetitive except for Annual National Short Film and Video Competition with cash awards in multiple categories. Est attendance: 15,000. For info: USA Film Festival, 6116 N Central Expressway, Ste 105, Dallas, TX 75206. Phone: (214) 821-6300 or (214) 821-FILM. Fax: (214) 821-6364. E-mail: USAFilmFest@aol.com. Web: www.usafilmfestival.com.

WOODS, GRANVILLE T.: BIRTH ANNIVERSARY. Apr 23, 1856. Granville T. Woods was born at Columbus, OH. He invented the Synchronous Multiplex Railway Telegraph, which allowed communication between dispatchers and trains while the trains were in motion, which decreased the number of train accidents. In addition, Woods is credited with several other electrical inventions. Died Jan 30, 1910, at New York, NY.

WORLD BOOK NIGHT. Apr 23. This night is a celebration of books and reading—World Book and Copyright Day—when passionate volunteers around the world hand out books within their communities to those who don't regularly read. In 2012, World Book Night was celebrated in the US, the UK, Ireland and Germany and saw more than 80,000 people gift more than 2.5 million books. World Book Night was first celebrated in the UK and Ireland in 2011; in 2012, it was also celebrated in the USA and Germany. For info: World Book Night. Web: www.worldbooknight.org.

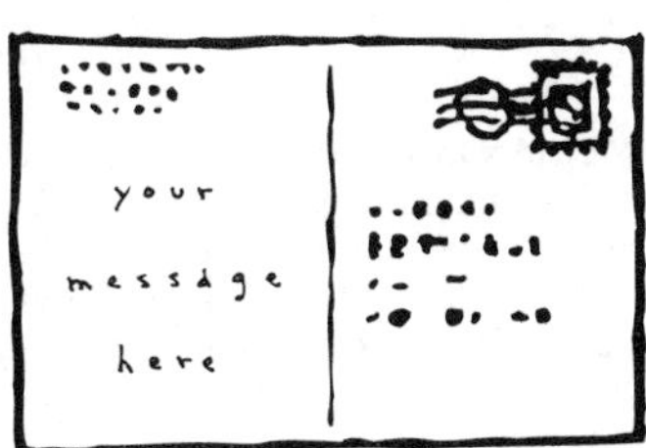

BIRTHDAYS TODAY

Valerie Bertinelli, 54, actress ("One Day at a Time," "Hot in Cleveland"), born Wilmington, DE, Apr 23, 1960.

David Birney, 74, actor ("Love Is a Many Splendored Thing," "Bridget Loves Bernie"), born Washington, DC, Apr 23, 1940.

Shirley Temple Black, 86, former ambassador to Ghana, child actress (*Heidi, Curly Top, Little Miss Marker*), television hostess ("Shirley Temple's Storybook" and "Shirley Temple Theatre"), born Santa Monica, CA, Apr 23, 1928.

John Cena, 37, professional wrestler, born West Newbury, MA, Apr 23, 1977.

Judy Davis, 59, actress ("Life with Judy Garland," *Husbands and Wives, A Passage to India, My Brilliant Career*), born Perth, Australia, Apr 23, 1955.

Joyce Dewitt, 65, actress ("Three's Company"), born Wheeling, WV, Apr 23, 1949.

Jan Hooks, 57, actress ("Saturday Night Live," "Designing Women"), born Atlanta, GA, Apr 23, 1957.

Andruw Jones, 37, baseball player, born Wellemstad, Curacao, Netherlands Antilles, Apr 23, 1977.

Melina Kanakaredes, 47, actress ("CSI: New York," "Providence," "Guiding Light"), born Akron, OH, Apr 23, 1967.

Jaime King, 35, actress (*Sin City, Pearl Harbor,* "Hart of Dixie"), born Omaha, NE, Apr 23, 1979.

George Lopez, 53, comedian, actor (*Beverly Hills Chihuahua,* "George Lopez"), born Mission Hills, CA, Apr 23, 1961.

Lee Majors, 74, actor ("The Six Million Dollar Man," "The Fall Guy"), born Wyandotte, MI, Apr 23, 1940.

Bernadette Devlin McAliskey, 67, political activist, born Cookstown, Northern Ireland, Apr 23, 1947.

Michael Moore, 60, author (*Dude, Where's My Country?*), filmmaker (Oscar for *Bowling for Columbine*; *Sicko, Fahrenheit 9/11*), born Flint, MI, Apr 23, 1954.

Dev Patel, 24, actor (*Slumdog Millionaire*), born Harrow, England, Apr 23, 1990.

Kal Penn, 37, actor (*The Namesake, Harold & Kumar Go to White Castle,* "House"), born Montclair, NJ, Apr 23, 1977.

April 24 — Thursday

DAY 114 **251 REMAINING**

ARMENIA: ARMENIAN MARTYRS DAY. Apr 24. Commemorates the massacre of Armenians under the Ottoman Turks in 1915. Deportations from Turkey began. Also called Armenian Genocide Memorial Day. Adolf Hitler, in a speech at Obersalzberg, Aug 22, 1939, is reported to have said, "Who today remembers the Armenian extermination?" in an apparent justification of the Nazis' use of genocide.

BASCOM, GEORGE N.: BIRTH ANNIVERSARY. Apr 24, 1836. Born at Owingsville, KY, West Point graduate Lieutenant George N. Bascom was the catalyst for one phase of the Apache Wars that ravaged the American West. Bascom was assigned to search out Apache chief Cochise, believed to be responsible for an 1861 raid on an Arizona ranch. He arrested Cochise and his family at Apache Pass, but the chief escaped. In the ensuing chaos, Bascom's men shot and killed Cochise's brother and two nephews. Cochise, in retaliation, launched a reign of terror. Bascom responded in kind until he became a casualty of the Civil War battle at Fort Craig, Valverde, NM, Feb 21, 1862.

April 2014

S	M	T	W	T	F	S
		1	2	3	4	5
6	7	8	9	10	11	12
13	14	15	16	17	18	19
20	21	22	23	24	25	26
27	28	29	30			

BOB WILLS DAY. Apr 24–26. Turkey, TX. 43rd annual. Celebration of the creator of western swing, with music, fiddlers contest, parade and barbecue lunch. Appearances by his former band, the Texas Playboys. Annually, the last Saturday in April, with festivities preceding on Thursday and Friday. Est attendance: 10,000. For info: City of Turkey. Web: www.turkeytexas.net.

CARTWRIGHT, EDMUND: BIRTH ANNIVERSARY. Apr 24, 1743. English cleric and inventor (developed the power loom and other weaving inventions) born at Nottinghamshire, England. He died at Hastings, Sussex, England, Oct 30, 1823.

DOGWOOD FESTIVAL. Apr 24–27. Camdenton, MO. This annual rite of spring features music, carnival, food, parade, arts and crafts, art exhibitions and more. For info: Camdenton Area Chamber of Commerce, PO Box 1375, Camdenton, MO 65020. Phone: (573) 346-2227 or (800) 769-1004. Fax: (573) 346-3496. E-mail: info@CamdentonChamber.com. Web: www.CamdentonChamber.com/DogwoodFestival.

ENGLAND: HARROGATE SPRING FLOWER SHOW. Apr 24–27. Great Yorkshire Showground, Harrogate, North Yorkshire. Beautiful show gardens, more than 100 plant nurseries, Britain's biggest exhibition of floral art, spectacular spring blooms. Est attendance: 60,000. For info: Martin Fish, Show Dir, North of England Horticultural Society, Regional Agricultural Centre, Great Yorkshire Showground, Harrogate, North Yorkshire, England HG2 8NZ. Phone: (44) (1423) 546-158. E-mail: info@flowershow.org.uk. Web: www.flowershow.org.uk.

FIDDLER'S FROLICS. Apr 24–27. Knights of Columbus Hall, Hallettsville, TX. First held in 1971, competition to determine the Texas state champion fiddler and inductees to the Texas Fiddlers Hall of Fame. Includes jam sessions, dances, concerts. Up to $25,000 in prize money awarded during the weekend. There's also the Gone To Texas contest, with competitors from all over the US and world. Est attendance: 15,000. For info: Kenneth Henneke, PO Box 46, Hallettsville, TX 77964. Phone: (361) 798-5934 or (361) 798-2311. Fax: (361) 798-4365. E-mail: kchall2006@sbcglobal.net. Web: www.kchall.com.

ICELAND: "FIRST DAY OF SUMMER." Apr 24. A national public holiday, *Sumardagurinn fyrsti*, with general festivities, processions and much street dancing, especially at Reykjavik, greets the coming of summer. Flags are flown. Annually, the Thursday between Apr 19 and 25.

IRELAND: EASTER RISING: ANNIVERSARY. Apr 24, 1916. Irish nationalists seized key buildings in Dublin and proclaimed an Irish republic. The rebellion collapsed, however, and it wasn't until 1922 that the Irish Free State, the predecessor of the Republic of Ireland, was established.

LIBRARY OF CONGRESS: ANNIVERSARY. Apr 24, 1800. Congress approved an act providing "for the purchase of such books as may be necessary for the use of Congress . . . and for fitting up a suitable apartment for containing them." Thus began one of the world's greatest libraries.

NATIONAL SCOOP THE POOP WEEK. Apr 24–30. Between the snowy storms of winter and the backyard barbecues of summer, now is the perfect time for dog owners to catch up on all those "canine calling cards" that have accumulated during the cold months. Besides creating a nasty mess in your yard, it's a health hazard, it pollutes the groundwater and it annoys the neighbors. It doesn't go away by itself, so get it cleaned up this week. And remind your dog-owning friends! Your family, neighbors and dog will love you for it. For info: Matthew Osborn, PO Box 28412, Columbus, OH 43228. E-mail: matthew@pooper-scooper.com. Web: www.pooper-scooper.com.

SANDBURG DAYS—FESTIVAL FOR THE MIND. Apr 24–26. Galesburg, IL. A festival for the mind! Annual celebration of the life and legacy of Galesburg-born, two-time Pulitzer Prize–winning poet and Lincoln biographer—Carl Sandburg. Includes three days of literary, historical, sporting and children's events. For info: Carl Sandburg College, 2400 Tom L. Wilson Blvd, Galesburg, IL 61401. Phone: (309) 341-5221. Web: www.sandlburg.edu/festival.

SPACE MILESTONE: *CHINA 1* (PEOPLE'S REPUBLIC OF CHINA). Apr 24, 1970. China became the fifth nation to orbit a satellite with the launch of its own rocket. The satellite broadcast the Chinese song "Tang Fang Hung" ("The East Is Red") and telemetric signals.

TAKE OUR DAUGHTERS AND SONS TO WORK® DAY. Apr 24. 21st annual. A national public education campaign sponsored by the Take Our Daughters and Sons to Work Foundation in which children aged 8–18 go to work with adult hosts—parents, grandparents, cousins, aunts, uncles and friends. More than 36 million youths and adults participate at more than 3 million workplaces across the country. Annually, the fourth Thursday in April. For info: Take Our Daughters and Sons to Work Foundation, 209 E Fearing St, Ste 1, Elizabeth City, NC 27909. Phone: (800) 676-7780. Fax: (252) 331-1728. E-mail: todastw@mindspring.com. Web: www.DaughtersandSonstoWork.org.

THOMAS, ROBERT BAILEY: BIRTH ANNIVERSARY. Apr 24, 1766. Founder and editor of *The Farmer's Almanac* (first issue for 1793), born at Grafton, MA. Thomas died May 19, 1846, while working on the 1847 edition.

TROLLOPE, ANTHONY: BIRTH ANNIVERSARY. Apr 24, 1815. English novelist (*Barchester Towers*), born at London, England, and died there Dec 6, 1882. "Of the needs a book has," he wrote in his autobiography, "the chief need is that it be readable."

US ATTEMPT TO FREE IRAN HOSTAGES: ANNIVERSARY. Apr 24, 1980. US Marines attempted to stage a surprise raid to free citizens held at the US embassy in Tehran, Iran, but their helicopters collided at the desert staging area. Eight were killed and five were wounded. No further military rescues were attempted, and the hostages were later released in January 1981 after 444 days of captivity.

WARREN, ROBERT PENN: BIRTH ANNIVERSARY. Apr 24, 1905. American poet, novelist, essayist and critic. America's first official poet laureate, 1986–88, Robert Penn Warren was born at Guthrie, KY. Warren was awarded the Pulitzer Prize for his novel *All the King's Men* (1947), as well as for his poetry in 1958 and 1979. He died of cancer Sept 15, 1989, at Stratton, VT.

WASHINGTON STATE APPLE BLOSSOM FESTIVAL. Apr 24–May 4. Wenatchee, WA. 95th annual. To showcase the greater Wenatchee Valley and its people and heritage by producing an ongoing community celebration. Parades, arts and crafts, food concessions, entertainment in the park, theatrical productions, Youth Day and carnival. More than 40 events. Annually, the last weekend in April through the first weekend in May. Est attendance: 100,000. For info: Washington State Apple Blossom Festival, Box 2836, Wenatchee, WA 98807. Phone: (509) 662-3616. Fax: (509) 665-0347. E-mail: festival@appleblossom.org. Web: www.appleblossom.org.

BIRTHDAYS TODAY

Eric Balfour, 37, actor (*Rescue Me, No One Would Tell*), musician, born Los Angeles, CA, Apr 24, 1977.

Eric Bogosian, 61, actor, playwright (*Talk Radio*), performance artist, born Boston, MA, Apr 24, 1953.

Cedric the Entertainer, 50, comedian, actor (*Street Kings, Barbershop, Be Cool*), born Cedric Kyles at Jefferson City, MO, Apr 24, 1964.

Kelly Clarkson, 32, singer, born Fort Worth, TX, Apr 24, 1982.

Richard M. Daley, 72, former mayor of Chicago, born Chicago, IL, Apr 24, 1942.

Sue Grafton, 74, author (*L Is for Lawless, M Is for Malice*), born Louisville, KY, Apr 24, 1940.

Djimon Hounsou, 50, actor (*Blood Diamond, In America*), born Cotonou, Benin, Apr 24, 1964.

Chipper Jones, 42, former baseball player, born DeLand, FL, Apr 24, 1972.

Stanley J. Kauffmann, 98, critic, born New York, NY, Apr 24, 1916.

Shirley MacLaine, 80, author, actress (Oscar for *Terms of Endearment*; *The Turning Point, Being There*), born Richmond, VA, Apr 24, 1934.

Michael O'Keefe, 59, actor (*The Great Santini, Caddyshack*; stage: *Mass Appeal*), born Larchmont, NY, Apr 24, 1955.

Barbra Streisand, 72, singer, actress (Oscar for *Funny Girl*; *The Way We Were, Yentl*), director (*The Prince of Tides*), born Brooklyn, NY, Apr 24, 1942.

April 25 — Friday

DAY 115 — **250 REMAINING**

ABORTION FIRST LEGALIZED: ANNIVERSARY. Apr 25, 1967. The first law legalizing abortion in the US was signed by Colorado governor John Arthur Love. The law allowed therapeutic abortions in cases in which a three-doctor panel unanimously agreed.

ANZAC DAY. Apr 25. Australia, New Zealand and Samoa. Memorial day and veterans' observance, especially to mark WWI ANZAC (Australia and New Zealand Army Corps) landing at Gallipoli, Turkey, in 1915.

ARBOR DAY FESTIVAL. Apr 25–27. Nebraska City, NE. Celebrate Arbor Day, the tree planters' holiday, in the hometown of J. Sterling Morton, the founder of Arbor Day. Citywide events include the community tree planting, commemorative tree planting and reception, tree-planting demonstrations and Arbor Day Farm Tree Adventure. Also featured: 5k/10k run and walk, parade, children's festival, chili cook-off and a variety of live music venues. Est attendance: 15,000. For info: Nebraska City Tourism and Commerce, 806 1st Ave, Nebraska City, NE 68410. Phone: (402) 873-6654. Fax: (402) 873-6701. E-mail: tourism@nebraskacity.com. Web: www.nebraskacity.com.

ARBOR DAY IN ARIZONA. Apr 25. The last Friday in April is proclaimed as Arbor Day in Arizona. It is not a legal holiday.

BATTLE OF GALLIPOLI: ANNIVERSARY. Apr 25, 1915–January 1916. During WWI the Gallipoli Expedition, or the Dardanelles Campaign, combined Allied naval and military forces tried to capture the Gallipoli peninsula in Turkey in order to effect an open route to Russia via the Black Sea. One French and four British divisions were forced back by a strong Turkish-German defense after almost nine months of fighting. The Australian and New Zealand Army Corps (ANZAC) took much of the brunt of the battle.

BRENNAN, WILLIAM: BIRTH ANNIVERSARY. Apr 25, 1906. US Supreme Court Associate Justice William J. Brennan was appointed to the Supreme Court in 1956 by President Dwight Eisenhower. His liberal leanings and judicial activism raised the ire of many conservatives. He was responsible for many landmark decisions, including the decision requiring the Little Rock, AR, schools to desegregate. His legacy also includes major decisions upholding affirmative action, a losing battle to declare the death penalty unconstitutional, decisions broadening free speech and free press guarantees, expansion of the due process guarantees under the 14th Amendment, and protection of flag burning as a form of expression. Brennan was born at Newark, NJ; he died at Arlington, VA, July 25, 1997.

CHICAGO COMIC & ENTERTAINMENT EXPO (C2E2). Apr 25–27. McCormick Place, Chicago, IL. A convention spanning the latest and greatest from the worlds of comics, movies, television, toys, anime, manga and video games. From a show floor packed with hundreds of exhibitors, to panels and autograph sessions giving fans a chance to interact with their favorite creators, to screening rooms featuring sneak peeks at films and television shows months before they hit either the big or small screen. For info: C2E2. E-mail: inquiry@c2e2.com. Web: www.c2e2.com.

***COSMOGRAPHIAE INTRODUCTIO* PUBLISHED: ANNIVERSARY.** Apr 25, 1507. Little is known about the obscure scholar now called "the godfather of America," the German geographer and mapmaker Martin Waldseemuller, who gave America its name. In a book titled *Cosmographiae Introductio*, published Apr 25, 1507, Waldseemuller wrote: "Inasmuch as both Europe and Asia received their names from women, I see no reason why any one should justly object to calling this part Amerige, i.e., the land of Amerigo, or America, after Amerigo, its discoverer, a man of great ability." Believing it was the Italian navigator and merchant Amerigo Vespucci who had discovered the new continent, Waldseemuller sought to honor Vespucci by placing his name on his map of the world, published in 1507. First applied only to the South American continent, it soon was used for both the American continents. Waldseemuller did not learn about the voyage of Christopher Columbus until several years later. Of the thousand copies of his map that were printed, only one is known to have survived. Waldseemuller probably was born at Radolfzell, Germany, about 1470. He died at St. Die, France, about 1517–20. See also: "Vespucci, Amerigo: Birth Anniversary" (Mar 9).

EGYPT: SINAI DAY. Apr 25. National holiday celebrating the return of Sinai to Egypt in 1982 after the peace treaty between Egypt and Israel.

FARRAGUT CAPTURES NEW ORLEANS: ANNIVERSARY. Apr 25, 1862. Union forces under the command of Flag Officer David Farragut seized the city of New Orleans, LA, resulting in the surrender of several Confederate forts along the Mississippi in subsequent days. This action removed any Confederate resistance to Northern action on the Mississippi River as far north as New Orleans. General Benjamin Butler arrived on Apr 27 and took command of the management of the captured city.

FIRST LICENSE PLATES: ANNIVERSARY. Apr 25, 1901. New York began requiring license plates on automobiles, the first state to do so.

FITZGERALD, ELLA: BIRTH ANNIVERSARY. Apr 25, 1917. "First Lady of Song," born at Newport News, VA. Jazz singer known for her treatments of Rogers and Hart, Gershwin, Irving Berlin, Cole Porter and Duke Ellington. Fitzgerald died at Beverly Hills, CA, June 15, 1996.

April 2014

S	M	T	W	T	F	S
		1	2	3	4	5
6	7	8	9	10	11	12
13	14	15	16	17	18	19
20	21	22	23	24	25	26
27	28	29	30			

INTERSTATE MULLET TOSS. Apr 25–27. Pensacola, FL, and Orange Beach, AL. 30th annual. Intrepid fish flingers compete to see who can throw a dead, one-pound mullet the farthest, starting from a 10-foot-diameter circle in Alabama, into the state of Florida. A contribution for each fish flung goes to Local Youth Charities. Shuttles run between both states to the competition area. Annually, the last full weekend in April. For info: Flora-Bama, 17401 Perdido Key Dr, Pensacola, FL 32507. Phone: (850) 492-0611. Web: www.florabama.com.

ITALY: LIBERATION DAY. Apr 25. National holiday. Commemorates the liberation of Italy from German troops in 1945.

LEIBER, JERRY: BIRTH ANNIVERSARY. Apr 25, 1933. An influential lyricist, songwriter and record producer, Jerry Leiber and his longtime composing partner Mike Stoller wrote such iconic songs of the early rock 'n' roll era as "Hound Dog," "Jailhouse Rock," "Yakety Yak" and "Stand by Me." Born at Baltimore, MD, Leiber met Stoller as a high schooler in Los Angeles, where the two combined Leiber's ear for street-smart lyrics with Stoller's love of rhythm and blues, a formula that would prove successful for the next three decades. Leiber died Aug 22, 2011, at Los Angeles, CA.

LLOYD, POP: BIRTH ANNIVERSARY. Apr 25, 1884. John Henry "Pop" Lloyd, Baseball Hall of Fame shortstop, born at Palatka, FL. Lloyd was often compared to Honus Wagner and considered one of the best shortstops ever. He played with and managed black teams and made quite a career in Cuba, where the fans nicknamed him "Cuchara" (scoop or shovel) for his big hands. Inducted into the Hall of Fame in 1977. Died at Atlantic City, NJ, Mar 19, 1965.

✦MALARIA AWARENESS DAY. Apr 25. To promote awareness of this devastating disease, and to promote initiatives to combat the spread of the disease across Africa and around the world. Annually, Apr 25.

MARCONI, GUGLIELMO: BIRTH ANNIVERSARY. Apr 25, 1874. Inventor of wireless telegraphy (1895), born at Bologna, Italy. Died at Rome, Italy, July 20, 1937.

MURROW, EDWARD R.: BIRTH ANNIVERSARY. Apr 25, 1908. Among the greatest journalists in American history, Edward R. Murrow was born at Greensboro, NC. He was a European war correspondent for CBS during WWII and rose to prominence with his dramatic and vivid radio broadcasts. After the war, CBS moved him to television, where he was the trusted host of "See It Now," a newsmagazine show spotlighting hot-button issues of the day. He died at Pawling, NY, Apr 27, 1965.

NATIONAL ARBOR DAY. Apr 25. Since 1872, a day to honor and plant trees. Observed the last Friday in April (although some states have different dates), which is generally a good planting date throughout the country. First observance of Arbor Day was in Nebraska, Apr 10, 1872, where it is still a state holiday. For info: Arbor Day Foundation, 100 Arbor Ave, Nebraska City, NE 68410. Phone: (888) 448-7337. Web: www.arborday.org/arborday.

NATIONAL DREAM HOTLINE®. Apr 25–27. Now in its 26th year, the National Dream Hotline® is sponsored by the School of Metaphysics as an educational service to people throughout the world. Faculty and staff of the College and Schools of Metaphysics throughout the Midwest offer the benefits of decades of research into the significance and meaning of dreams by manning the hotline phones from 6 PM CDT, Friday until midnight Sunday. Annually, the last weekend in April. For info: School of Metaphysics, World Headquarters, 163 Moon Valley Rd, Windyville, MO 65783. Phone: (417) 345-8411. Fax: (417) 345-6668. E-mail: som@som.org. Web: www.som.org or www.dreamschool.org.

NATIONAL HAIRBALL AWARENESS DAY. Apr 25. A day to recognize and take steps to eliminate hairballs in cats. Hairballs are more than an inconvenience for cat owners: they cause great discomfort and irritation in our cat companions. Take steps now to stop this injustice of nature for our feline friends. Annually, the last Friday in April. For info: Dr. Blake Hawley, Hill's Pet Nutrition, Building 5, Croxley Green Business Park, Hatters Ln, Watford, Herts WD18 8YL, United Kingdom. E-mail: blake_hawley@HillsPet.com. Web: www.HillsPet.co.uk.

NATIONAL PIE CHAMPIONSHIPS. Apr 25–27. Celebration, FL. This is the official national pie championships for pie makers competing in the junior, amateur, professional and commercial divisions. Sponsored annually by Crisco and the American Pie Council. For info: American Pie Council, PO Box 368, Lake Forest, IL 60045. Phone: (847) 371-0170. E-mail: piecouncil@aol.com. Web: www.piecouncil.org.

NEW ORLEANS JAZZ & HERITAGE FESTIVAL. Apr 25–May 4. New Orleans, LA. A two-weekend festival with hundreds of musicians playing. Evening concerts, outdoor daytime activities, Louisiana specialty foods and handmade crafts. Est attendance: 500,000. For info: New Orleans Jazz & Heritage Festival, 336 Camp St, Ste 250, New Orleans, LA 70130. Phone: (504) 410-4100. Web: www.nojazzfest.com.

PORTUGAL: LIBERTY DAY. Apr 25. Public holiday. Anniversary of the 1974 revolution.

SPACE MILESTONE: HUBBLE SPACE TELESCOPE DEPLOYED (US). Apr 25, 1990. Deployed by *Discovery*, the telescope is the largest on-orbit observatory to date and is capable of imaging objects up to 14 billion light-years away. The resolution of images was expected to be seven to ten times greater than images from Earth-based telescopes, since the Hubble Space Telescope is not hampered by Earth's atmospheric distortion. Launched Apr 12, 1990, from Kennedy Space Center, FL. Unfortunately, the telescope's lenses were defective, so the anticipated high quality of imaging was not possible. In 1993, however, the world watched as a shuttle crew successfully retrieved the Hubble from orbit, executed the needed repair and replacement work and released it into orbit once more. Further repairs were completed in 1997, 1999, 2002 and 2009, and the telescope remains functional today.

SUGARLOAF CRAFTS FESTIVAL. Apr 25–27. Maryland State Fairgrounds, Timonium, MD. This show, now in its 36th year, features more than 250 nationally recognized craft designers and fine artists displaying and selling their original creations. Includes craft demonstrations, live music, specialty food, hourly gift certificate drawings and more. Est attendance: 16,000. For info: Sugarloaf Mountain Works, Inc, 19807 Executive Park Circle, Germantown, MD 20874. Phone: (800) 210-9900. Fax: (310) 253-9620. E-mail: sugarloafinfo@sugarloaffest.com. Web: www.sugarloafcrafts.com.

SWAZILAND: NATIONAL FLAG DAY. Apr 25. National holiday.

THEODORE ROOSEVELT NATIONAL PARK ESTABLISHED: ANNIVERSARY. Apr 25, 1947. Located in North Dakota, the Theodore Roosevelt National Park includes two sections of the Badlands on the Missouri River as well as Theodore Roosevelt's Elkhorn Ranch.

WARD WORLD CHAMPIONSHIP WILDFOWL CARVING COMPETITION AND ART FESTIVAL. Apr 25–27. Roland E. Powell Convention Center, Ocean City, MD. 44th annual. Life-size, miniature, interpretive wildfowl carving and sculpture competitions. Festival includes vendors selling carvings, folk art, paintings, home decorating items and art supplies. Est attendance: 6,000. For info: Special Events Coord, Ward Museum of Wildfowl Art, 909 S Schumaker Dr, Salisbury, MD 21804. Phone: (410) 742-4988. Fax: (410) 742-3107. E-mail: wardevents@salisbury.edu. Web: www.wardmuseum.org.

WORLD MALARIA DAY. Apr 25. A day to provide education and understanding of malaria as a global scourge that is preventable and a disease that is curable. Annually, April 25. For info: The Malaria Community. Web: www.worldmalariaday.org.

WORLD WAR II: EAST MEETS WEST: ANNIVERSARY. Apr 25, 1945. US Army lieutenant Albert Kotzebue encountered a single Soviet soldier near the German village of Lechwitz, 75 miles south of Berlin. Patrols of US general Leonard Gerow's 5th Corps saluted the advance guard of Marshall Ivan Konev's Soviet 58th Guards Division. Soldiers of both nations embraced and exchanged toasts. The Allied armies of East and West had finally met.

BIRTHDAYS TODAY

Hank Azaria, 50, actor ("Huff," *The Birdcage*, many voices on "The Simpsons"), born Forest Hills, NY, Apr 25, 1964.

Emily Bergl, 39, actress ("Men in Trees"), born Milton Keynes, Buckinghamshire, England, Apr 25, 1975.

Johan Cruyff, 67, soccer executive and former player, born Amsterdam, Netherlands, Apr 25, 1947.

Jeffrey DeMunn, 67, actor ("The Walking Dead," *Citizen X, The Green Mile*), born Buffalo, NY, Apr 25, 1947.

Tim Duncan, 38, basketball player, born St. Croix, Virgin Islands, Apr 25, 1976.

Jason Lee, 44, actor ("My Name Is Earl," *Almost Famous, Chasing Amy*), born Orange, CA, Apr 25, 1970.

Meadow George "Meadowlark" Lemon III, 82, Hall of Fame basketball player, born Lexington, SC, Apr 25, 1932.

Paul Mazursky, 84, director (*Harry and Tonto, An Unmarried Woman, Scenes from a Mall*), born Brooklyn, NY, Apr 25, 1930.

Al Pacino, 74, actor (Oscar for *Scent of a Woman*; *Dog Day Afternoon, Godfather* movies), born New York, NY, Apr 25, 1940.

Talia Shire, 68, actress (*Godfather* films, *Rocky* films), born Jamaica, NY, Apr 25, 1946.

Gina Torres, 45, actress ("Suits," "Firefly"), born New York, NY, Apr 25, 1969.

Renee Zellweger, 45, actress (Oscar for *Cold Mountain*; *Miss Potter, Chicago, Bridget Jones's Diary*), born Katy, TX, Apr 25, 1969.

April 26 — Saturday

DAY 116 **249 REMAINING**

AUDUBON, JOHN JAMES: BIRTH ANNIVERSARY. Apr 26, 1785. American artist and naturalist, best known for his *Birds of America*, born at Haiti. Died Jan 27, 1851, at New York, NY.

CALIFORNIA POPPY FESTIVAL. Apr 26–27. Lancaster, CA. Celebrating the golden poppy as the state flower of California, the California Poppy Festival features unique homemade crafts, a variety of musical entertainers, delicious food booths, cultural demonstrations and exotic animals. Visitors can stop by the Wildflower Information Center to get maps of the best poppy fields. Both kids and adults will enjoy the carnival, crafts and live music. Est attendance: 55,000. For info: City of Lancaster, 44933 N Fern Ave, Lancaster, CA 93534. Phone: (661) 723-6077. Fax: (661) 723-5913. Web: www.poppyfestival.com.

CHERNOBYL NUCLEAR REACTOR DISASTER: ANNIVERSARY. Apr 26, 1986. At 1:23 AM, local time, an explosion occurred at the Chernobyl atomic power station at Pripyat in the Ukraine. The resulting fire burned for days, sending radioactive material into the atmosphere. More than 100,000 persons were evacuated from a 300-square-mile area around the plant. Three months later 31 people were reported to have died and thousands exposed to dangerous levels of radiation. Estimates projected an additional 1,000 cancer cases in nations downwind of the radioactive discharge. The plant was encased in a concrete tomb in an effort to prevent the still-hot reactor from overheating again and to minimize further release of radiation.

"CHINA BEACH" TV PREMIERE: ANNIVERSARY. Apr 26, 1988. The stories of "China Beach" revolved around the lives of the women serving at a Da Nang armed forces hospital during the Vietnam War. The theme and background music of the series evoked plenty of nostalgia from the turbulent era. The ABC drama was created by William Broyles, Jr, and John Sacret Young. The cast featured Dana Delany, Michael Boatman, Nancy Giles, Jeff Kober, Robert Picardo, Concetta Tomei, Brian Wimmer, Marg Helgenberger, Chloe Webb, Nan Woods, Megan Gallagher, Ned Vaughn and Ricki Lake.

CIVIL WAR REENACTMENT. Apr 26–27. Rand Park, Keokuk, IA. Battle reenactment, military ball, historic encampment, ladies' style show and Civil War memorial service. Est attendance: 12,000. For info: Keokuk Area Convention and Tourism Bureau, 329 Main, Keokuk, IA 52632. Phone: (800) 383-1219 or (319) 524-5599. E-mail: info@keokukiowatourism.org. Web: www.keokukiowatourism.org.

CONFEDERATE MEMORIAL DAY IN FLORIDA AND GEORGIA. Apr 26. Observed on the anniversary of Confederate general Joseph E. Johnston's surrender to General William T. Sherman at Durham, NC, in 1865. Other Southern states observe this day on different dates.

FAUSET, JESSIE REDMON: BIRTH ANNIVERSARY. Apr 26, 1882. African-American poet, editor and novelist, born at Fredericksville, NJ, and died in 1961. Fauset, as literary editor of *Crisis* (a publication of the NAACP), was a patron to so many writers of the Harlem Renaissance that her efforts prompted Langston Hughes to dub her the "midwife of the so-called New Negro Literature." Along with W.E.B. DuBois, Fauset also published and edited the children's magazine *The Brownie Book*. Her novels about the African-American middle-class experience dealt with issues of identity, autonomy and struggles for fulfillment. Her most recognized works include *The Chinaberry Tree* (1931) and *Comedy, American Style* (1933).

FOXFIELD RACES. Apr 26 (also Sept 28). Charlottesville, VA. Steeplechase horse racing, held annually on the last Saturday in April and the last Sunday in September. Est attendance: 20,000. For info: W. Patrick Butterfield, Racing Mgr, Foxfield Racing Assn, PO Box 5187, Charlottesville, VA 22905. Phone: (434) 293-9501. Fax: (434) 293-8169. E-mail: wpbutterfield@foxfieldraces.com.

GREAT AMERICAN PIE FESTIVAL. Apr 26–27. Celebration, FL. 13th annual festival celebrating all things pie! PieCasso arts and crafts, pie-eating contests, celebrity pie making demos, music, games and other festival activities. The Never Ending Pie buffet is a festival highlight featuring 87,000 slices of pie. Cosponsored by Crisco. Est attendance: 35,000. For info: American Pie Council, PO Box 368, Lake Forest, IL 60045. Phone: (847) 371-0170. E-mail: piecouncil@aol.com. Web: www.piecouncil.org.

GUERNICA MASSACRE: ANNIVERSARY. Apr 26, 1937. Late in the afternoon, the ancient Basque town of Guernica, in northern Spain, was attacked without warning by German-made airplanes. Three hours of intensive bombing left the town in flames, and citizens who fled to the fields and ditches around Guernica were machine-gunned from the air. This atrocity inspired Pablo Picasso's mural *Guernica*. Responsibility for the bombing was never officially established, but the suffering and anger of the victims and their survivors are still evident at anniversary demonstrations. Intervention by Nazi Germany in the Spanish Civil War has been described as practice for WWII.

☆ ☆ ☆

April 2014	S	M	T	W	T	F	S
			1	2	3	4	5
	6	7	8	9	10	11	12
	13	14	15	16	17	18	19
	20	21	22	23	24	25	26
	27	28	29	30			

HERB FESTIVAL. Apr 26. Mattoon, IL. Fresh herbs, everlasting plants, scented geraniums and lots of perennials. Annually, the last Saturday in April. Est attendance: 7,000. For info: The Picket Fence, 901 Broadway Ave, Mattoon, IL 61938. Phone: (217) 258-6364.

HESS, RUDOLF: BIRTH ANNIVERSARY. Apr 26, 1894. One of the most bizarre figures of WWII Germany, Walter Richard Rudolf Hess was born at Alexandria, Egypt. He was a close friend, confidant and personal secretary to Adolf Hitler, who had dictated much of *Mein Kampf* to Hess while both were prisoners at Landsberg Prison. Third in command in Nazi Germany, Hess surprised the world on May 10, 1941, by flying alone to Scotland and parachuting from his plane on what he called a "mission of humanity": offering peace to Britain if it would join Germany in attacking the Soviet Union. He was immediately taken prisoner of war. At the Nuremberg Trials (1946), after questions about his sanity, he was convicted and sentenced to life imprisonment at Spandau Allied War Crimes Prison at Berlin, Germany. Outliving all other prisoners there, he was the only inmate from 1955 until he succeeded (in his fourth attempt) in committing suicide. He died at West Berlin, Germany, Aug 17, 1987.

HISTORIC GARDEN WEEK IN VIRGINIA. Apr 26–May 3. This annual statewide event, celebrating its 81st anniversary, is billed as "America's Largest Open House." Showcases more than 250 of Virginia's finest homes, gardens, plantations and landmark properties on more than 30 separate tours on different days of the week. A 200-page guidebook is available March 2014. Please mail a contribution of $10 to cover postage and handling. Est attendance: 30,000. For info: Historic Garden Week, Garden Club of Virginia, 12 E Franklin St, Richmond, VA 23219. Phone: (804) 644-7776. Fax: (804) 644-7778. E-mail: gdnweek@verizon.net. Web: www.VAGardenweek.org.

HUG AN AUSTRALIAN DAY. Apr 26. To show our great appreciation for all the love and support the Aussies have given us over the years. (©2006 by WH.) For info: Thomas & Ruth Roy, Wellcat Holidays, 2418 Long Ln, Lebanon, PA 17046. Phone: (717) 279-0184. E-mail: info@wellcat.com. Web: www.wellcat.com.

JUST PRAY NO! WORLDWIDE WEEKEND OF PRAYER AND FASTING. Apr 26–27. 24th annual. Churches throughout the world participate. Concerts of prayer, fasting, street rallies and marches to gain media attention. Bible studies and sermons concerning alcoholism and drug abuse and revival meetings aimed at those bound by addiction. For info: Just Pray No, Ltd, 1875 Sunset Point Rd, #704, Clearwater, FL 33765. E-mail: justprayno@aol.com. Web: www.justprayno.org.

LOOS, ANITA: BIRTH ANNIVERSARY. Apr 26, 1893. American author and playwright, born at Sisson, CA. She is best remembered for her book *Gentlemen Prefer Blondes*, published in 1925. Loos, a brunette, died at New York, NY, Aug 18, 1981.

MALAMUD, BERNARD: 100th BIRTH ANNIVERSARY. Apr 26, 1914. Pulitzer Prize–winning novelist, born to Russian-Jewish immigrant parents at Brooklyn, NY. Works include *The Natural* (1952) and *The Fixer* (1966). Also a two-time recipient of the National Book Award, he died Mar 18, 1986, at New York, NY.

MONTGOMERY WARD SEIZED: 70th ANNIVERSARY. Apr 26, 1944. Montgomery Ward chairman Sewell Avery was physically removed from his office when federal troops seized Ward's Chicago offices after the company refused to obey President Franklin D. Roosevelt's order to recognize a CIO union. Government control ended May 9, shortly before the National Labor Relations Board announced the United Mail Order Warehouse and Retail Employees Union had won an election to represent the company's workers.

NATIONAL DANCE DAY. Apr 26. As a prelude to International Dance Day, participants across America organize events in every community to celebrate the spirit and diversity of dance of all kinds. For info: Sharon King, 480 Park Ave, New York, NY 10022. Phone: (212) 750-9857. E-mail: info@nationaldanceday.org. Web: www.nationaldanceday.org.

NATIONAL GO BIRDING DAY. Apr 26. The day celebrating birding as a national pastime. Participants are encouraged to put up bird feeders and houses, take a trip to go birding, learn about their local bird species. Annually, the last Saturday in April. For info: Nancy Millar, McAllen CVB, PO Box 790, McAllen, TX 78505-0790. Phone: (956) 682-2871. Fax: (956) 631-8571. E-mail: nmillar@mcallencvb.com. Web: www.mcallencvb.com.

NATIONAL HELP A HORSE DAY. Apr 26. Horses have been central to the ASPCA's work since its founding, with the first successful arrest for the mistreatment of a horse on Apr 26, 1866, when ASPCA founder Henry Bergh stopped a cart driver from beating his horse. Today, the ASPCA continues to assist domesticated and wild horses through legislation, advocacy, rescue and targeted grants. Many Americans have never had the opportunity to interact with an equine, but while these noble animals may be out of sight for some, they should never be far from our thoughts. Horses are extremely intelligent, sensitive animals and a true American icon. Not everyone is aware of the challenges facing racehorses once their careers on the track are over, nor are many aware of the inhumane practice of horse slaughter. Be a voice for horses on National Help A Horse Day. Annually, Apr 26. For info: ASPCA, Media and Communications Dept, 520 8th Ave, 7th Fl, New York, NY 10018. Phone: (212) 876-7700. E-mail: press@aspca.org. Web: www.aspca.org.

NETHERLANDS: KING'S DAY (OBSERVED). Apr 26. National holiday celebrating the birth of King Willem-Alexander, born Apr 27, 1967. When Apr 27 falls on a Sunday, as it does in 2014, the day is observed on Apr 26. The holiday was formerly observed on Apr 30 (in honor of Queen Juliana [1909–2004] and Queen Beatrix [1938–]). The whole country parties as young and old participate in free markets, theater, music, games and *Oranjegekte* ("orange fever").

OLMSTED, FREDERICK LAW: BIRTH ANNIVERSARY. Apr 26, 1822. Known as "the father of landscape architecture in America," Olmsted participated in the designing of Yosemite National Park, New York City's Central Park and parks for Boston, MA; Hartford, CT; and Louisville, KY. Born at Hartford, CT; died at Waverly, MA, Aug 28, 1903. Olmsted's home and studio, Fairsted Estate, outside of Boston, is now preserved as a National Historic Site and is open to the public: 99 Warren St, Brookline, MA 02146.

RAINEY, MA (GERTRUDE BRIDGET): BIRTH ANNIVERSARY. Apr 26, 1886. Known as "the Mother of the Blues," Gertrude "Ma" Rainey was born at Columbus, GA. She made her stage debut at the Columbus Opera House in 1900 in a talent show called "The Bunch of Blackberries." After touring together as "Rainey and Rainey, the Assassinators of the Blues," she and her husband eventually separated, and she toured on her own. She made her first recording in 1923 and her last on Dec 28, 1928, after being told that the rural Southern blues she sang had gone out of style. She died Dec 22, 1939, at Columbus, GA.

REDBUD TRAIL RENDEZVOUS. Apr 26–27. Rochester, IN. Reenactment of a pre-1840 gathering to trade furs on the Tippecanoe River, featuring tepee and wigwam villages, traditional music and crafts, pioneer and Indian dances and foods cooked over wood fires. Seven Years' War field day; Hoosier Ladies Aside demonstrate riding sidesaddle. Museum, round barn and Living History Village at north end of grounds. For frontier fun, follow the redbuds blooming along the Tippecanoe River. Est attendance: 2,000. For info: Fulton County Historical Society, 37 E 375 N, Rochester, IN 46975. Phone: (574) 223-4436. Web: www.fultoncountyhistory.org.

RICHTER SCALE DAY. Apr 26. A day to recognize the importance of Charles Francis Richter's research and his work in development of the earthquake magnitude scale that is known as the Richter scale. Richter, an American author, physicist and seismologist, was born Apr 26, 1900, near Hamilton, OH. An Earthquake Awareness Week was observed in recognition of his work. Richter died at Pasadena, CA, Sept 30, 1985.

ROLFE, LILIAN: 100th BIRTH ANNIVERSARY. Apr 26, 1914. Born at Paris, France, to British parents, Rolfe was a WWII secret agent (Special Operations Executive) who transmitted details on Nazi troop movements to the Allies and assisted the French Resistance in occupied France. She was arrested July 31, 1944, and tortured for months before being executed at Ravensbrück (a women's concentration camp), Germany, on Feb 5, 1945. Awarded the Croix de Guerre among many posthumous honors.

SIRK, DOUGLAS: BIRTH ANNIVERSARY. Apr 26, 1900. Film director Douglas Sirk was born Detlef Sierck at Hamburg, Germany. His films include *Magnificent Obsession* (1954), *Written on the Wind* (1956) and *Imitation of Life* (1959). He died Jan 14, 1987, at Lugano, Switzerland.

SOUTH AFRICAN MULTIRACIAL ELECTIONS: 20th ANNIVERSARY. Apr 26–29, 1994. For the first time in the history of South Africa, the nation's approximately 18 million blacks voted in multiparty elections. This event marked the definitive end of apartheid, the system of racial separation that had kept blacks and other minorities out of the political process. The election resulted in Nelson Mandela of the African National Congress being elected president and F.W. de Klerk (incumbent president) of the National Party vice president.

SOUTHERN MARYLAND CELTIC FESTIVAL & HIGHLAND GATHERING. Apr 26. Jefferson Patterson Park and Museum, St. Leonard, MD. 36th annual. Scottish fiddling championship, bagpipe competition, Scottish heptathlon, Highland dancing competition, Celtic marketplace and crafts, parade of clans and nations, Celtic harp competition, Celtic music, demonstrations and Celtic foods. Annually, the last Saturday in April. Est attendance: 8,000. For info: Celtic Society of Southern Maryland, PO Box 209, Prince Frederick, MD 20678. Phone: (443) 975-0972 . E-mail: Festival@cssm.org. Web: www.cssm.org.

TANZANIA: UNION DAY. Apr 26. Celebrates union between mainland Tanzania (formerly Tanganyika) and the islands of Zanzibar and Pemba, in 1964.

WITTGENSTEIN, LUDWIG: 125th BIRTH ANNIVERSARY. Apr 26, 1889. One of the most influential analytic and linguistic philosophers of the 20th century, born at Vienna, Austria. Wittgenstein had a fundamental influence on logical positivism, linguistic analysis and semantics. He theorized that philosophical problems were fundamentally problems of language, and studying "ordinary language" would enable one to solve many of these problems. Died Apr 29, 1951, at Cambridge, England.

WORLD HEALING DAY. Apr 26. A day to focus human consciousness on personal and global healing, inspired by research from the Global Consciousness Project, which evolved from preliminary research at Princeton University on how human consciousness affects the physical world. This day is globally observed in hundreds of cities in more than 70 nations. There are also many allied events under the umbrella event of World Healing Day, including World Healing Meditation Day, World Art Day, World Tai Chi Day, World Yoga Day, World Qigong Day, World Sufi Dance Day, World Native Aboriginal Sacred Dance Day and several others. Annually, the last Saturday in April. For info: World Healing Day. E-mail: admin@worldhealingday.org. Web: www.worldhealingday.org.

WORLD TAI CHI AND QIGONG DAY. Apr 26. World Tai Chi and Qigong Day (also spelled T'ai Chi and Ch'i Kung) is an annual event held the last Saturday in April each year to promote the related disciplines of tai chi and qigong in 70 countries since 1999. The mission of this multinational effort is ongoing: to expose people to the growing body of medical research related to traditional Chinese medicine and direct them to teachers in their hometowns. For info: Bill Douglas, World Tai Chi and Qigong Day, 10100 Roe Ave, Overland Park, KS 66207. Phone: (913) 648-2256. E-mail: billdouglas@worldtaichiday.org. Web: www.worldtaichiday.org.

WORLD VETERINARY DAY. Apr 26. World Veterinary Day was instigated by the World Veterinary Association (WVA) in 2000 to be celebrated annually on the last Saturday of April. Apart from their well-known role as animal doctors, veterinarians create prevention and control programs against infectious diseases, including those transmissible to humans. Much more than that, be it for food security, poverty alleviation, prevention and management of risks at the animal-human interface, animal welfare, scientific research or political commitment, veterinarians operate in all sectors of the society. For info: OIE Organisation Mondiale de la Santé Animale, 12, rue de Prony, 75017 Paris, France. E-mail: oie@oie.int. Web: www.oie.int.

BIRTHDAYS TODAY

Carol Burnett, 78, actress ("The Carol Burnett Show," *The Four Seasons*), born San Antonio, TX, Apr 26, 1936.

Joan Chen, 53, actress ("Twin Peaks," "Golden Gate"), born Shanghai, China, Apr 26, 1961.

Joe Crede, 36, baseball player, born Jefferson City, MO, Apr 26, 1978.

Michael Damian, 52, actor ("The Young and the Restless"; stage: *Joseph and the Amazing Technicolor Dreamcoat*), born San Diego, CA, Apr 26, 1962.

Duane Eddy, 76, musician, born Corning, NY, Apr 26, 1938.

Giancarlo Esposito, 56, actor ("Revolution," *Do the Right Thing, Twilight*), born Copenhagen, Denmark, Apr 26, 1958.

Kosuke Fukudome, 37, baseball player, born Osaki, Japan, Apr 26, 1977.

April 2014	S	M	T	W	T	F	S
			1	2	3	4	5
	6	7	8	9	10	11	12
	13	14	15	16	17	18	19
	20	21	22	23	24	25	26
	27	28	29	30			

Kevin James, 49, actor ("The King of Queens"), born Stony Brook, NY, Apr 26, 1965.

Jemima Kirke, 29, actress (*Tiny Furniture*, "Girls"), born London, England, Apr 26, 1985.

Jet Li, 51, actor (*The Forbidden Kingdom, Hero, Kiss of the Dragon*), former martial arts champion, born Li Lian Jie at Beijing, China, Apr 26, 1963.

Boyd Matson, 67, television journalist ("National Geographic Explorer"), born Oklahoma City, OK, Apr 26, 1947.

Bobby Rydell, 72, singer, born Philadelphia, PA, Apr 26, 1942.

Natasha Trethewey, 48, Poet Laureate of the US (2012–), born Gulfport, MS, Apr 26, 1966.

Tom Welling, 37, actor ("Smallville"), born New York, NY, Apr 26, 1977.

Gary Wright, 71, musician, born Englewood, NJ, Apr 26, 1943.

April 27 — Sunday

DAY 117 **248 REMAINING**

BABE RUTH DAY: ANNIVERSARY. Apr 27, 1947. Babe Ruth Day was celebrated in every ballpark in organized baseball in the US as well as Japan. Mortally ill with throat cancer, Ruth appeared at Yankee Stadium to thank his former club for the honor.

CALIFORNIA MILLE. Apr 27–May 1. San Francisco, CA, and environs. 24th running. The quiet back roads of California and Nevada resonate with the seductive four-cylinder sound of mid-'50s Alfa Giulietta Sprints, the big blower blast from a '30s Bentley and some 65 historic race cars when the California Mille begins in San Francisco. The California Mille, a salute to Italy's most famous open road race, the Mille Miglia (Thousand Mile), brings together cars that could have qualified for the Italian event that ran from 1927 to 1957—cars from three foreign countries and sixteen US states. The event kicks off with the largest free car show in America on Mason St, San Francisco. For info: Amici americani della Mille Miglia, 154 Mitchell Blvd, San Rafael, CA 94903. Phone: (415) 479-9950. Fax: (415) 479-9911. E-mail: info@californiamille.com. Web: www.californiamille.com.

DENNIS, SANDY: BIRTH ANNIVERSARY. Apr 27, 1937. American actress Sandy Dennis was born Sandra Dale Dennis at Hastings, NE. In addition to two Tony Awards, she won an Academy Award for her supporting role in *Who's Afraid of Virginia Woolf* (1966). She died Mar 2, 1992, at Westport, CT.

GIBBON, EDWARD: BIRTH ANNIVERSARY. Apr 27, 1737. (Old Style date.) English historian and author. His *History of the Decline and Fall of the Roman Empire* remains a model of historical writing. From his description of the Roman emperor Gordianus II: "Twenty-two acknowledged concubines, and a library of sixty-two thousand volumes, attested the variety of his inclinations; and from the productions which he left behind him, it appears that the former as well as the latter were designed for use rather than for ostentation." Born at Putney, Surrey, England, Gibbon died at London, Jan 6, 1794.

GRANT, ULYSSES SIMPSON: BIRTH ANNIVERSARY. Apr 27, 1822. 18th president of the US (Mar 4, 1869–Mar 3, 1877), born Hiram Ulysses Grant at Point Pleasant, OH. He graduated from the US Military Academy in 1843. President Lincoln promoted Grant to lieutenant general in command of all the Union armies Mar 9, 1864. On Apr 9, 1865, Grant received General Robert E. Lee's surrender, at Appomattox Court House, VA, which he announced to the secretary of war as follows: "General Lee surrendered the Army of Northern Virginia this afternoon on terms proposed by myself. The accompanying additional correspondence will show the conditions fully." Nicknamed "Unconditional Surrender Grant," he died at Mount McGregor, NY, July 23, 1885, just four days after completing his memoirs. He was buried at Riverside Park, New York, NY, where Grant's Tomb was dedicated in 1897.

HELENA RAILROAD FAIR. Apr 27. Civic Center, Helena, MT. 34th annual. Largest railroad hobby event in Montana features a mix of scale and tin-plate trains; railroad memorabilia and collectibles; real-life train watching at the MRL Helena depot. Annually, the last Sunday in April. Est attendance: 2,500. For info: Helena Railroad Fair, PO Box 4914, Helena, MT 59604-4914. Phone: (406) 443-1578 or (406) 227-0158. E-mail: rrfair@mt.net.

KING, CORETTA SCOTT: BIRTH ANNIVERSARY. Apr 27, 1927. The wife of Dr. Martin Luther King, Jr, was born on a farm near Heiberger, AL. She picked cotton as a child but was able to go to college, where she met and married the young minister-turned-civil-rights-activist. She worked by his side, establishing Freedom Concerts and other social-change movements, while also raising the couple's four children. After King's 1968 assassination, she took on his mission, founding the Martin Luther King Jr Center for Nonviolent Social Change in Atlanta (now just called The King Center), and also spearheading the efforts to have a national holiday established in her late husband's honor. The American Library Association established a prestigious children's literature award for African-American writers and illustrators in her name in 1970, and in her later years she was a tireless advocate for gay and lesbian rights. She died at Rosarito, Mexico, Jan 30, 2006.

LANTZ, WALTER: BIRTH ANNIVERSARY. Apr 27, 1900. Originator of Universal Studios' animated opening sequence for their first major musical film, *The King of Jazz.* Walter Lantz is best remembered as the creator of Woody Woodpecker, the bird with the wacky laugh and the taunting ways. Lantz received a Lifetime Achievement Academy Award for his animation in 1979. He was born at New Rochelle, NY, and died Mar 22, 1994, at Burbank, CA.

MAGELLAN, FERDINAND: DEATH ANNIVERSARY. Apr 27, 1521. Portuguese explorer Ferdinand Magellan was probably born near Oporto, Portugal, about 1480, but neither the place nor the date is certain. Usually thought of as the first man to circumnavigate the earth, he died before completing the voyage; thus, his coleader, Basque navigator Juan Sebastian de Elcano, became the world's first circumnavigator. The westward, round-the-world expedition began Sept 20, 1519, with five ships and about 250 men. Magellan was killed by natives of the Philippine island of Mactan.

MATANZAS MULE DAY. Apr 27, 1898. In one of the first naval actions of the Spanish-American War, US naval forces bombarded the Cuban village of Matanzas. It was widely reported that the only casualty of the bombardment was one mule. The "Matanzas Mule" became instantly famous and remains a footnote in the history of the Spanish-American War.

MORSE, SAMUEL FINLEY BREESE: BIRTH ANNIVERSARY. Apr 27, 1791. The American artist and inventor, after whom the Morse code is named, was born at Charlestown, MA, and died at New York, NY, Apr 2, 1872. Graduating from Yale University in 1810, he went to the Royal Academy of London to study painting. After returning to America, he achieved success as a portraitist. Morse conceived the idea of an electromagnetic telegraph while on shipboard, returning from art instruction in Europe in 1832, and he proceeded to develop his idea. With financial assistance approved by Congress, the first telegraph line in the US was constructed, between Washington, DC, and Baltimore, MD. The first message tapped out by Morse from the Supreme Court Chamber at the US Capitol building on May 24, 1844, was "What hath God wrought?"

MOST TORNADOES IN A DAY (US): ANNIVERSARY. Apr 27–28, 2011. The 24-hour period from 8 AM, Apr 27, to 8 AM, Apr 28, saw more tornadoes in a day—226—than in any other period in US history. Striking in the southeast US, this was part of a larger outbreak from Apr 25–28, called the "2011 Super Outbreak," that was one of the most deadly systems of extreme weather that the US has ever seen. In Alabama, 50 tornadoes struck. 334 people died during this 24-hour period.

MOTHER, FATHER DEAF DAY. Apr 27. A day to honor deaf parents and recognize the gifts of culture and language they give to their hearing children. Annually, the last Sunday of April. For info: Children of Deaf Adults International Inc. Web: www.coda-international.org.

NATIONAL SPORTING GOODS ASSOCIATION MANAGEMENT CONFERENCE. Apr 27–30. Palm Springs, CA. 50th annual Management Conference and 16th annual Team Dealer Summit. The premier educational and networking event for the sporting goods industry. Attracts leading retailers, dealers, manufacturers, agents, media and industry organizations. Est attendance: 400. For info: Natl Sporting Goods Assn, 1601 Feehanville Dr, Ste 300, Mount Prospect, IL 60056-6035. Phone: (800) 815-5422. Fax: (847) 391-9827. E-mail: info@nsga.org. Web: www.nsga.org.

PRESERVATION WEEK. Apr 27–May 3. Some 630 million items in collecting institutions require immediate attention and care, with no budget or staff allocated. Some 2.6 billion items are not protected by an emergency plan. As natural disasters of recent years have taught us, these resources are in jeopardy should a disaster strike. Personal, family, and community collections are equally at risk. The ALA encourages libraries and other institutions to use this week to connect our communities through events, activities and resources that highlight what we can do, individually and together, to preserve our personal and shared collections. For info: American Library Assn, Public Info Office, 50 E Huron St, Chicago, IL 60611. Phone: (312) 280-5044. Fax: (312) 280-5274. E-mail: pio@ala.org. Web: www.ala.org.

ST. LOUIS EARTH DAY FESTIVAL. Apr 27. St. Louis, MO. An educational event with hundreds of exhibitors related to environmental issues and their solutions. Est attendance: 30,000. For info: St. Louis Earth Day. Phone: (314) 282-7533. E-mail: info@stlouisearthday.org. Web: www.stlouisearthday.org.

SIERRA LEONE: INDEPENDENCE DAY. Apr 27. National Day. Commemorates independence from Britain in 1961.

SLOVENIA: INSURRECTION DAY. Apr 27. National holiday. Commemorates the founding of the Liberation Front in 1941 to resist Slovenia's occupation by the Axis powers.

SOUTH AFRICA: FREEDOM DAY. Apr 27. National holiday. Commemorates the day in 1994 when, for the first time, all South Africans had the opportunity to vote.

***SULTANA* STEAMSHIP EXPLOSION: ANNIVERSARY.** Apr 27, 1865. Early in the morning on this day, America's worst steamship disaster occurred. The *Sultana*, heavily overloaded with an estimated 2,300 passengers, exploded in the Mississippi River, just north of Memphis, TN, en route to Cairo, IL. Most of the passengers were Union soldiers who had been prisoners of war and were eagerly returning to their homes. Although there was never an accurate accounting of the dead, estimates range from 1,450 to nearly 2,000. Cause of the explosion was not determined, but the little-known event is unparalleled in US history.

SWITZERLAND: LANDSGEMEINDE. Apr 27. In one of the last examples of direct democracy, the citizens of Switzerland's smallest canton, Appenzell Inner Rhoden, gather annually on the last Sunday in April to vote. Uniquely, they don't cast secret ballots but raise their arms in full view of their neighbors. About 2,000 to 3,000 voters of 18 years and older come to the square of the canton capital, Appenzell, after attending a morning church service. Once affairs of the canton are voted on, festivities begin. As part of the tradition, which dates back to the 14th century, men wear swords.

TOGO: INDEPENDENCE DAY. Apr 27. National holiday. In 1960 Togo gained its independence from French administration under a UN trusteeship.

WOLLSTONECRAFT, MARY: BIRTH ANNIVERSARY. Apr 27, 1759. Writer and advocate of equality for women, Mary Wollstonecraft was born at London, England. Rebelling against her father, she left home at age 18 and served as a lady's companion, opened a school and worked as a governess. Beginning with *Thoughts on the Education of Daughters* in 1787, Wollstonecraft attracted notice as a writer in favor of women's rights. Her *A Vindication of the Rights of Woman* (1792) argued that women should be given an education that would allow them to gain economic independence. She died at London on Sept 10, 1797, 11 days after giving birth to her second daughter (Mary Wollstonecraft Shelley, the author of *Frankenstein*).

BIRTHDAYS TODAY

Anouk Aimee, 80, actress (*A Man and a Woman, 8½, La Dolce Vita*), born Paris, France, Apr 27, 1934.

Sheena Easton, 55, singer, born Sheena Shirley Orr at Bellshill, Scotland, Apr 27, 1959.

Casey Kasem, 82, radio and television personality ("America's Top 40"), born Detroit, MI, Apr 27, 1932.

King Willem-Alexander, 47, King of the Netherlands, born Utrecht, Netherlands, Apr 27, 1967.

April 28 — Monday

DAY 118 **247 REMAINING**

BARRYMORE, LIONEL: BIRTH ANNIVERSARY. Apr 28, 1878. Famed actor of the celebrated acting family, Lionel Barrymore was born Lionel Blythe, at Philadelphia, PA. Brother of actors Ethel and John Barrymore, he was a prolific actor who was not slowed down by partial paralysis sustained in 1938. Barrymore won a Best Actor Oscar for *A Free Soul* (1931) and appeared in *You Can't Take It With You, Young Dr. Kildare, It's a Wonderful Life* and *Key Largo*, among many others. He died at Van Nuys, CA, Nov 15, 1954.

BIOLOGICAL CLOCK GENE DISCOVERED: 20th ANNIVERSARY. Apr 28, 1994. Northwestern University announced that the so-called biological clock, that gene governing the daily cycle of waking and sleeping called the circadian rhythm, had been found in mice. Never before pinpointed in a mammal, the biological clock gene was found on mouse chromosome 5.

CANADA: NATIONAL DAY OF MOURNING. Apr 28. A national day of mourning for workers killed or injured on the job in Canada. The Canadian Labour Congress first officially recognized the day in 1986. Pointing to the nearly one million workplace injuries each year in Canada, the CLC has called for stricter health and safety regulations and for annual recognition of this day throughout Canada. Federal legislation (Bill D-223) first recognized this day in 1991.

April 2014	S	M	T	W	T	F	S
			1	2	3	4	5
	6	7	8	9	10	11	12
	13	14	15	16	17	18	19
	20	21	22	23	24	25	26
	27	28	29	30			

CONFEDERATE MEMORIAL DAY IN ALABAMA. Apr 28. On the fourth Monday in April. Other Southern states observe Confederate Memorial Day on different dates.

CONFEDERATE MEMORIAL DAY IN MISSISSIPPI. Apr 28. Annually, on the last Monday in April. Observed on other dates in some states.

GIBBS, MIFFLIN WISTER: BIRTH ANNIVERSARY. Apr 28, 1828. Mifflin Wister Gibbs was born at Philadelphia, PA. In 1873 he became the first black man to be elected a judge in the US, winning an election for city judge at Little Rock, AR.

HOMER, LOUISE DILWORTH: BIRTH ANNIVERSARY. Apr 28, 1871. The mesmerizing Louise Dilworth Homer was one of the most formidable contraltos of her time. Her plum roles in *Aïda, Tristan und Isolde, Hänsel und Gretel* and *Samson et Dalilah* (with the legendary Caruso) brought her tremendous acclaim. She was born at Sewickley, PA, and died at Winter Park, FL, May 6, 1947.

HUSSEIN, SADDAM: BIRTH ANNIVERSARY. Apr 28, 1937. Military dictator Saddam Hussein Abd al-Majid al-Tikriti was born at Al-Awja, Iraq. A member of the Baath Party, which took control of the Iraqi government in 1968, he became president of Iraq in 1979 and served in that role until he was overthrown in a US-led multinational military action in 2003. During his tenure he was considered a major threat to Western interests and waged wars against Iran and Kuwait, and he was tried by an Iraqi Special Tribunal in 2006 for crimes against humanity. He was executed Dec 30, 2006, at Kadhimiya, Iraq.

ISRAEL: HOLOCAUST DAY (YOM HASHOAH). Apr 28. Hebrew calendar date: Nisan 27, 5774. A day established by Israel's Knesset as a memorial to the Jewish dead of WWII. Anniversary in Jewish calendar of Nisan 27, 5705 (corresponding to Apr 10, 1945, in the Gregorian calendar), the day on which Allied troops liberated the first Nazi concentration camp, Buchenwald, north of Weimar, Germany, where about 56,000 prisoners, many of them Jewish, perished. Began at sundown Apr 27. (When Nisan 27 falls on a Sunday, Holocaust Day is observed on a Monday.)

JAMES MONROE BIRTHDAY CELEBRATION. Apr 28. Ash Lawn–Highland, home of President James Monroe, Charlottesville, VA. For info: Ash Lawn-Highland, 2050 James Monroe Pkwy, Charlottesville, VA 22902. Phone: (434) 293-8000. Fax: (434) 979-9181. E-mail: info@al-h.us. Web: www.ashlawnhighland.org.

MARYLAND CONSTITUTION RATIFICATION: ANNIVERSARY. Apr 28, 1788. Maryland became the seventh state to ratify the Constitution, by a vote of 63 to 11.

MONROE, JAMES: BIRTH ANNIVERSARY. Apr 28, 1758. The fifth president of the US was born at Westmoreland County, VA, and served two terms in that office (Mar 4, 1817–Mar 3, 1825). Monrovia, the capital city of Liberia, is named after him, as is the Monroe Doctrine, which he enunciated at Washington, DC, Dec 2, 1823. The last of three presidents to die on US Independence Day, Monroe died at New York, NY, July 4, 1831.

MUSSOLINI EXECUTED: ANNIVERSARY. Apr 28, 1945. Italian partisans shot Benito Mussolini near the lakeside village of Dongo. Leaders of the Fascist Party, several of his friends and his mistress Clara Petacci also were executed. The 23-year-long Fascist rule of Italy was ended.

MUTINY ON THE *BOUNTY*: 225th ANNIVERSARY. Apr 28, 1789. The most famous of all naval mutinies occurred on board HMS *Bounty*. Captain of the *Bounty* was Lieutenant William Bligh, an able seaman and a mean-tempered disciplinarian. The ship, with a load of breadfruit tree plants from Tahiti, was bound for Jamaica. Fletcher Christian, leader of the mutiny, put Bligh and 18 of his loyal followers adrift in a 23-foot open boat. Miraculously Bligh and all of his supporters survived a 47-day voyage of more than 3,600 miles, before landing on the island of Timor, June 14, 1789. In the meantime, Christian had put all of the remaining crew (excepting 8 men and himself) ashore at Tahiti, where he picked up 18 Tahitians (6 men and 12 women) and set sail again. Landing at Pitcairn Island in 1790 (probably uninhabited at the time), they burned the *Bounty* and remained undiscovered for 18 years, when an American whaler, the *Topaz*, called at the island (1808) and found only one member of the mutinous crew surviving. However, the little colony had thrived and, when counted by the British in 1856, numbered 194 persons.

SCHINDLER, OSKAR: BIRTH ANNIVERSARY. Apr 28, 1908. German industrialist Oskar Schindler was born Apr 28, 1908, at Svitavy, Moravia, Austria-Hungary (now Zwittau, Czech Republic). For his role in saving over 1,200 Jews during WWII, Schindler was declared a "Righteous Gentile" by Israel in 1962. Although financial opportunism initiated Schindler's employment of Polish Jews in his enamel factory, by 1944 he embraced his part in saving many of them from execution. Despised by many of his countrymen for his actions during and following WWII, he died Oct 9, 1974, at Frankfurt am Main, Germany. He was buried in Jerusalem, Israel—more than 500 *Schindlerjuden* were in attendance at his funeral. Schindler was later immortalized in the 1982 novel *Schindler's Ark* and 1993 film *Schindler's List*.

SPACE MILESTONE: FIRST TOURIST IN SPACE. Apr 28, 2001. Millionaire US businessman Dennis Tito reportedly paid the Russian space agency $20 million to accompany *Soyuz TM* to the International Space Station. The rocket with Tito and two Russian cosmonauts was launched this day from the Baikonur launch site in Kazakhstan and arrived at the ISS on Apr 30, 2001. The crew returned to Earth in a week. NASA initially objected to the inclusion of the 60-year-old tycoon on the mission but dropped its opposition.

WORKERS MEMORIAL DAY. Apr 28. First proclaimed in 1989 to commemorate the founding of the Occupational Safety and Health Administration (OSHA) on Apr 28, 1970 (signed into law in 1971). In some places this holiday is observed on the fourth Friday in April.

BIRTHDAYS TODAY

Jessica Alba, 33, actress (*Good Luck Chuck, Fantastic Four, Into the Blue, Sin City,* "Dark Angel"), born Pomona, CA, Apr 28, 1981.

Ann-Margret, 73, actress (*Carnal Knowledge, Tommy, Grumpy Old Men*), born Ann-Margaret Olsson at Stockholm, Sweden, Apr 28, 1941.

Penelope Cruz, 40, actress (Oscar for *Vicky Cristina Barcelona*; *Nine, Volver, Bandidas*), born Madrid, Spain, Apr 28, 1974.

John Daly, 48, golfer, born Carmichael, CA, Apr 28, 1966.

Jorge Garcia, 41, actor ("Lost," "Becker"), born Omaha, NE, Apr 28, 1973.

Paul Guilfoyle, 65, actor ("CSI"), born Boston, MA, Apr 28, 1949.

Elena Kagan, 54, Associate Justice of the US, born New York, NY, Apr 28, 1960.

Barry Larkin, 50, former baseball player, born Cincinnati, OH, Apr 28, 1964.

Harper Lee, 88, author (*To Kill a Mockingbird*), born Nelle Harper Lee at Monroeville, AL, Apr 28, 1926.

Jay Leno, 64, television talk show host ("The Tonight Show"), comedian, born New Rochelle, NY, Apr 28, 1950.

Nicklas Lidstrom, 44, former hockey player, born Vasteras, Sweden, Apr 28, 1970.

Mary McDonnell, 62, actress ("Battlestar Galactica," *Independence Day, Dances with Wolves*), born Wilkes-Barre, PA, Apr 28, 1952.

Ian Rankin, 54, author (*Black and Blue, The Hanging Garden*), born Cardenden, Fife, Scotland, Apr 28, 1960.

Marcia Strassman, 66, actress ("Welcome Back, Kotter"; *Honey, I Shrunk the Kids*), born New York, NY, Apr 28, 1948.

Jenna Ushkowitz, 28, actress ("Glee"), born Seoul, South Korea, Apr 28, 1986.

Bradley Wiggins, 34, cyclist, born Ghent, Belgium, Apr 28, 1980.

April 29 — Tuesday

DAY 119 **246 REMAINING**

EARNHARDT, DALE: BIRTH ANNIVERSARY. Apr 29, 1952. Stock car racer, born at Kannapolis, NC. Dale Earnhardt was one of NASCAR's most popular personalities, winning the Winston Cup seven times. He was killed while driving in the Daytona 500 at Daytona Beach, FL, Feb 18, 2001.

ELLINGTON, "DUKE" (EDWARD KENNEDY): BIRTH ANNIVERSARY. Apr 29, 1899. Duke Ellington, one of the most influential individuals in jazz history, was born at Washington, DC. Ellington's professional career began when he was 17, and by 1923 he was leading a small group of musicians at the Kentucky Club at New York City that became the core of his big band. Ellington is credited with being one of the founders of big band jazz. He used his band as an instrument for composition and orchestration to create big band pieces, film scores, operas, ballets, Broadway shows and religious music. Ellington was responsible for more than 1,000 musical pieces. He drew together instruments from different sections of the orchestra to develop unique and haunting sounds such as that of his famous "Mood Indigo." Ellington died May 24, 1974, at New York City.

ELLSWORTH, OLIVER: BIRTH ANNIVERSARY. Apr 29, 1745. (Old Style date.) Third chief justice of the US, born at Windsor, CT. Died there, Nov 26, 1807.

***HAIR* BROADWAY OPENING: ANNIVERSARY.** Apr 29, 1968. The controversial rock musical *Hair*, produced by Michael Butler, opened at the Biltmore Theatre at New York City, after playing off-Broadway. For those who opposed the Vietnam War and the "Establishment," this was a defining piece of work—as evidenced by some of its songs, such as "Aquarius," "Hair" and "Let the Sunshine In."

HEARST, WILLIAM RANDOLPH: BIRTH ANNIVERSARY. Apr 29, 1863. Media magnate of the late 19th and early 20th centuries, who, starting with the *San Francisco Examiner* in 1887 and the *New York Morning Journal* in 1895, built an empire consisting of 28 dailies, 18 magazines, radio stations and other outlets. The Hearst brand of journalism—stoked by vicious competition with other chains—tended to be sensational and truculent. It was dubbed "yellow journalism" by detractors. The film classic *Citizen Kane* was loosely based on his life. Born at San Francisco, CA, Hearst died at Beverly Hills, CA, Aug 14, 1951.

HIROHITO MICHI-NO-MIYA, EMPEROR: BIRTH ANNIVERSARY. Apr 29, 1901. Former emperor of Japan, born at Tokyo. Hirohito's death, Jan 7, 1989, ended the reign of the world's longest-ruling monarch. He became the 124th in a line of monarchs when he ascended to the Chrysanthemum Throne in 1926. Hirohito presided over perhaps the most eventful period in the 2,500 years of recorded Japanese history, including the attempted military conquest of Asia; the attack on the US that brought that country into WWII, leading to Japan's ultimate defeat after the US dropped atomic bombs on Hiroshima and Nagasaki; and the amazing economic restoration following the war, which led Japan to a preeminent position of economic strength.

JAPAN: GOLDEN WEEK HOLIDAYS. Apr 29–May 5. National holidays. This period includes Showa Day (Apr 29), Constitution Memorial Day (May 3), Greenery Day (May 4) and Children's Day (May 5).

JAPAN: SHOWA DAY. Apr 29. Formerly celebrated as Greenery Day until 2007. Honors Emperor Hirohito (1901–89) and is observed on his birthday. "Showa" refers to Japan's postwar era. Part of the Golden Week Holidays.

LIBERATION OF DACHAU: ANNIVERSARY. Apr 29, 1945. The Charlie Battery of the 522nd Field Artillery Battalion liberated the concentration camp at Dachau, Germany. The 522nd, part of the legendary 442nd (Go for Broke) regimental combat team, was made up of nisei—second-generation Japanese Americans. Dachau was the first concentration camp opened in Germany, and more than 200,000 prisoners were housed there throughout the course of WWII. An estimated 35,000 people lost their lives in the camp, and more than 32,000 were liberated when the Americans arrived beginning on this date.

LOS ANGELES RIOTS: ANNIVERSARY. Apr 29, 1992. A jury in Simi Valley, CA, failed to convict four Los Angeles police officers accused in the videotaped beating of Rodney King, providing the spark that set off rioting, looting and burning at South Central Los Angeles, CA, and other areas across the country. The anger unleashed during and after the violence was attributed to widespread racism, lack of job opportunities and the resulting hopelessness of inner-city poverty.

MOON PHASE: NEW MOON. Apr 29. Moon enters New Moon phase at 2:14 AM, EDT.

'PEACE' ROSE INTRODUCED TO WORLD: ANNIVERSARY. Apr 29, 1945. The 20th century's most popular rose was publicly released by the Pacific Rose Society at Pasadena, CA, just as Berlin, Germany, was falling to the Allies. The history of 'Peace' is interwoven with events of WWII, and for many the hybrid tea rose has symbolized the hope that grew out of terrible conflict. French rose grower Frances Meilland bred the cream and pink rose (then called 'Mme A. Meilland') in the late 1930s and knew he had something extraordinary. A seedling was smuggled out of France in an American diplomatic pouch on one of the last planes to leave that country before Nazi occupation. American rose company Conrad-Pyle carefully cultivated it. To note Germany's surrender, 'Peace' blooms were presented to all delegates during the first United Nations Conference that May of 1945.

SAINT CATHERINE OF SIENA: FEAST DAY. Apr 29, 1347. St. Catherine of Siena was born at Tuscany, Italy. Patron saint of Italy. She died Apr 29, 1380, at Rome, Italy.

SOLAR ECLIPSE. Apr 29. Annular eclipse of the sun. Visible in Australia, Antarctica and the southern Indian Ocean.

TAIWAN: CHENG CHENG KUNG LANDING DAY. Apr 29. Commemorates landing in Taiwan in 1661 of Ming Dynasty loyalist Cheng Cheng Kung (Koxinga), who ousted Dutch colonists who had occupied Taiwan for 37 years. Main ceremonies held at Tainan, in south Taiwan, where the Dutch had their headquarters and where Cheng is buried.

ZIPPER PATENTED: ANNIVERSARY. Apr 29, 1913. Gideon Sundbach of Hoboken, NJ, received a patent for the zipper.

April 2014	S	M	T	W	T	F	S
			1	2	3	4	5
	6	7	8	9	10	11	12
	13	14	15	16	17	18	19
	20	21	22	23	24	25	26
	27	28	29	30			

BIRTHDAYS TODAY

Andre Agassi, 44, former tennis player, born Las Vegas, NV, Apr 29, 1970.

Daniel Day-Lewis, 57, actor (Oscars for *Lincoln, There Will Be Blood* and *My Left Foot*), born London, England, Apr 29, 1957.

Nora Dunn, 62, actress (*Three Kings*, "Saturday Night Live"), born Chicago, IL, Apr 29, 1952.

Robert Gottlieb, 83, editor, born New York, NY, Apr 29, 1931.

Rod McKuen, 81, poet, singer, born San Francisco, CA, Apr 29, 1933.

Zubin Mehta, 78, conductor, born Bombay (now Mumbai), India, Apr 29, 1936.

Kate Mulgrew, 59, actress ("Star Trek: Voyager," "Ryan's Hope"), born Dubuque, IA, Apr 29, 1955.

Michelle Pfeiffer, 56, actress (*What Lies Beneath, Batman Returns, Dangerous Liaisons*), born Santa Ana, CA, Apr 29, 1958.

Eve Plumb, 56, actress ("The Brady Bunch," "Fudge"), born Burbank, CA, Apr 29, 1958.

Jerry Seinfeld, 60, comedian, actor ("Seinfeld"), born Brooklyn, NY, Apr 29, 1954.

Debbie Stabenow, 64, US Senator (D, Michigan), born Clare, MI, Apr 29, 1950.

Uma Thurman, 44, actress (*Kill Bill* films, *Gattaca, Pulp Fiction*), born Boston, MA, Apr 29, 1970.

Jonathan Toews, 26, hockey player, born Winnipeg, MB, Canada, Apr 29, 1988.

Carnie Wilson, 46, singer, born Bel Air, CA, Apr 29, 1968.

April 30 — Wednesday

DAY 120 **245 REMAINING**

BELTANE. Apr 30. (Also called Bealtaine, May Eve, Walpurgis Night, Cyntefyn, Roodmass and Cethsamhain.) One of the "Greater Sabbats" during the Wiccan year, Beltane celebrates the union or marriage of the Goddess and God. In Scotland Beltane was one of the quarter days, or terms when rents were due and debts settled. On the eve of Beltane, two fires were built close together and cattle were driven between them to ward off disease prior to putting the stock out to pasture for the new season. Annually, on Apr 30.

BUGS BUNNY'S DEBUT: ANNIVERSARY. Apr 30, 1938. Warner Bros.' "wascally wabbit" first appeared on screen in the theatrical short "Porky's Hare Hunt," directed by Ben "Bugs" Hardaway and released on this date. Chuck Jones and Tex Avery further developed him into the character we know now—in such cartoons as "A Wild Hare" (1940), in which Bugs asks, "What's up, Doc?" for the first time and first kisses perennial foe Elmer Fudd. The rabbit's noisy carrot munching was based on Clark Gable's carrot chewing in the film *It Happened One Night* (1934).

CAMBODIA INVADED BY US: ANNIVERSARY. Apr 30, 1970. President Richard Nixon announced the US was sending troops into Cambodia in an attempt to destroy the "sanctuaries" from which men and materiel were infiltrated into South Vietnam. This sparked widespread protests on the home front, including a march on Washington and the closure of many American colleges and universities. See also: "Kent State Students' Memorial Day: Anniversary" (May 4).

CHARLIE PARKER FIRST RECORDED: ANNIVERSARY. Apr 30, 1941. The first commercially recorded work of Charlie (Bird) Parker, alto saxophonist and originator of the bebop style of modern jazz, was cut this date at Decca Records. During the recording session, picking up from the last two bars of "Swingmatism," Parker took off into a flowing improvisation that included "Hootie Blues," an example of a Parker blues chorus complete with a characteristic riff figure.

DÍA DE LOS NIÑOS/DÍA DE LOS LIBROS. Apr 30. A celebration of children, families and reading, held annually on Apr 30, emphasizing the importance of advocating literacy for every child regardless of linguistic and cultural background. Originally proclaimed by the National Association to Promote Library and Information Services to Latinos and the Spanish Speaking (REFORMA) as an enhancement of Children's Day, which began in 1925. In 1996, nationally acclaimed children's book author Pat Mora proposed linking the celebration of childhood and children with literacy, to found this unique day. Est attendance: 15,000. For info: American Library Assn, Association for Library Service to Children (ALSC), 50 E Huron St, Chicago, IL 60611. Phone: (312) 280-5044. E-mail: dia@ala.org. Web: www.dia.ala.org.

FIRST NORTH AMERICAN THEATRICAL PERFORMANCE: ANNIVERSARY. Apr 30, 1598. On the banks of the Rio Grande, near present-day El Paso, TX, the first North American theatrical performance took place. The play was a Spanish commedia featuring an expedition of soldiers. On July 10 of the same year, the same group produced *Moros y Los Cristianos* (*Moors and Christians*), an anonymous play.

FIRST PRESIDENTIAL TELECAST: 75th ANNIVERSARY. Apr 30, 1939. Franklin D. Roosevelt became the first president to appear on television when he was televised at the New York World's Fair. However, the appearance was only beamed to 200 TV sets in a 40-mile radius. See also: "First Scheduled Television Broadcast: Anniversary" (July 1).

HARRISON, MARY SCOTT LORD DIMMICK: BIRTH ANNIVERSARY. Apr 30, 1858. Second wife of Benjamin Harrison, 23rd president of the US, born at Honesdale, PA. Died at New York, NY, Jan 5, 1948.

INTERNATIONAL JAZZ DAY. Apr 30. In November 2011, the United Nations Educational, Scientific and Cultural Organization (UNESCO) officially designated Apr 30 as International Jazz Day in order to highlight jazz and its diplomatic role of uniting people in all corners of the globe. This special day brings together communities, schools, artists, historians, academics and jazz enthusiasts worldwide to celebrate and learn about jazz and its roots, future and impact; raise awareness of the need for intercultural dialogue and mutual understanding; and reinforce international cooperation and communication. UNESCO and United Nations missions, US embassies and government outposts around the world hosted special events for the first annual International Jazz Day on Apr 30, 2012. More than one billion people around the world were reached through 2013 International Jazz Day programs and media coverage. Cosponsored by the Thelonius Monk Institute of Jazz. For info: UNESCO and Thelonious Monk Institute of Jazz, 5225 Wisconsin Ave NW, Ste 605, Washington, DC 20015. Web: www.jazzday.com or www.monkinstitute.org.

LILLY, WILLIAM: BIRTH ANNIVERSARY. Apr 30, 1602. (Old Style date.) English astrologer, author and almanac compiler, born at Diseworth, Leicestershire, England. His almanacs were among the most popular in Britain from 1644 until his death, June 9, 1681 (OS), at Hersham, Surrey, England.

LOUISIANA: ADMISSION DAY: ANNIVERSARY. Apr 30. Became 18th state in 1812.

LOUISIANA PURCHASE DAY: ANNIVERSARY. Apr 30, 1803. One of the greatest real estate deals in history was completed in 1803, when more than 820,000 square miles of the Louisiana Territory was turned over to the US by France, for $15 million. This almost doubled the size of the US, extending its western border to the Rocky Mountains.

MUHAMMAD ALI STRIPPED OF TITLE: ANNIVERSARY. Apr 30, 1967. Muhammad Ali was stripped of his world heavyweight boxing championship when he refused to be inducted into military service. Said Ali, "I have searched my conscience, and I find I cannot be true to my belief in my religion by accepting such a call." He had claimed exemption as a minister of the Black Muslim religion. He was convicted of violating the Selective Service Act, but the Supreme Court reversed this decision in 1971.

NATIONAL ANIMAL ADVOCACY DAY. Apr 30. The ASPCA's Government Relations department works closely with lawmakers and citizen advocates to secure the strongest possible protections for animals through the passage of humane legislation and regulations. We encourage all animal advocates to get involved in the legislative process and make a real difference for the animals in their community. Help the ASPCA enact meaningful protections for animals at the federal, state and local level by celebrating National Animal Advocacy Day and being an effective voice for animals in the lawmaking process. Annually, Apr 30. For info: ASPCA, Media and Communications Dept, 520 8th Ave, 7th Fl, New York, NY 10470. Phone: (212) 876-7700. E-mail: press@aspca.org. Web: www.aspca.org.

NATIONAL HONESTY DAY (WITH HONEST ABE AWARDS). Apr 30. To celebrate honesty and those who are honest and honorable in their dealings with others. Nominations accepted for most honest people and companies. Winners to be acknowledged with "Honest Abe" awards and given "Abies" on National Honesty Day. Also presented are dishonorable mentions for notables who have been less than honest. Schools, religious organizations and the media are encouraged to make honesty a subject of discussion on or near this day. Annually, Apr 30. For info: M. Hirsh Goldberg, 3103 Szold Dr, Baltimore, MD 21208. Phone: (410) 486-4150. E-mail: mhgoldberg@comcast.net.

ORGANIZATION OF AMERICAN STATES FOUNDED: ANNIVERSARY. Apr 30, 1948. The OAS regional alliance was founded by 21 nations of the Americas at Bogotá, Colombia. Its purpose is to further economic development and integration among nations of the Western Hemisphere, to promote representative democracy and to help overcome poverty. The Pan-American Union, with offices at Washington, DC, serves as the General Secretariat for the OAS.

RANSOM, JOHN CROWE: BIRTH ANNIVERSARY. Apr 30, 1888. Influential and award-winning poet, professor and critic, born at Pulaski, TN. Part of the 1920–30s "New Criticism" movement, which gained its name from his book *The New Criticism*, published in 1941. Founded and edited *The Kenyon Review*. His *Selected Poems* received the National Book Award. Ransom died July 3, 1974, at Gambler, OH.

SMITH, MICHAEL J.: BIRTH ANNIVERSARY. Apr 30, 1945. Forty-year-old pilot of the space shuttle *Challenger* on Jan 28, 1986. It was to have been Commander Smith's first space flight. Born at Beaufort, NC, Smith perished with all others on board when *Challenger* exploded. See also: "*Challenger* Space Shuttle Explosion: Anniversary" (Jan 28).

SOUTH VIETNAM FALLS TO VIETCONG: ANNIVERSARY. Apr 30, 1975. The president of South Vietnam announced the country's unconditional surrender to the Vietcong. Communist troops moved into Saigon, and 1,000 Americans in the city were hastily evacuated. Thousands of South Vietnamese also tried to flee. The surrender announcement came 21 years after the 1954 Geneva agreements divided Vietnam into North and South. The last American troops had left South Vietnam in March 1973.

SPANK OUT DAY USA. Apr 30. A day on which all caretakers of children—parents, teachers and day-care workers—are asked not to use corporal punishment as discipline and to become acquainted with positive, effective disciplinary alternatives. For info: Deb Sendek, The Center for Effective Discipline, 327 Groveport Rd, Canal Winchester, OH 43110. Phone: (614) 834-7946. E-mail: info@stophitting.org. Web: www.stophitting.org.

SUNFEST. Apr 30–May 4. West Palm Beach, FL. Florida's largest music, art and waterfront festival features some of the best acts in jazz, rock, blues and more. Includes a juried art show, fireworks, water and youth park activities and fabulous foods. Annually, the long weekend that includes the first Sunday in May. Est attendance: 275,000. For info: SunFest of Palm Beach County, Inc, 525 Clematis St, West Palm Beach, FL 33401. Phone: (561) 659-5980. Fax: (561) 659-3567. E-mail: info@sunfest.com. Web: www.sunfest.com.

SWEDEN: FEAST OF VALBORG. Apr 30. An evening celebration in which Sweden "sings in the spring" by listening to traditional hymns to the spring, often around community bonfires. Also known as Walpurgis Night, the Feast of Valborg occurs annually Apr 30.

VIETNAM: LIBERATION DAY. Apr 30. National holiday. Commemorates the fall of Saigon to the Communists in 1975, ending the Vietnam War.

WALPURGIS NIGHT. Apr 30. The eve of May Day, which is the feast day of St. Walpurgis, the protectress against the magic arts. According to German legend, witches gather this night and celebrate their sabbath on the highest peak in the Harz Mountains. Celebrated particularly by university students in northern Europe.

WASHINGTON, GEORGE: 225th PRESIDENTIAL INAUGURATION ANNIVERSARY. Apr 30, 1789. George Washington was inaugurated as the first president of the US under the new Constitution at New York, NY. Robert R. Livingston administered the oath of office to Washington on the balcony of Federal Hall, at the corner of Wall and Broad streets.

WILSON, ELLIS: BIRTH ANNIVERSARY. Apr 30, 1899. African-American artist born at Mayfield, KY, and died at New York, NY, Jan 1, 1977. Wilson painted realistic portrayals of African Americans at work and at play. In 1944 he was awarded a Guggenheim fellowship. He visited South Carolina, painting city scenes and fishing towns. In the 1950s, Wilson took a revelatory trip to Haiti, which changed the way he painted. Unable to note any facial features on the Haitians he painted from a distance, Wilson began painting flat, stylized silhouettes. *Haitian Funeral Procession* remains Wilson's most popular and accessible painting.

BIRTHDAYS TODAY

Dianna Agron, 28, actress ("Glee," "Heroes"), born Savannah, GA, Apr 30, 1986.

Jane Campion, 60, director (*The Piano*), born Wellington, New Zealand, Apr 30, 1954.

Kirsten Dunst, 32, actress (*Spider-Man* films, *Marie Antoinette, The Cat's Meow*), born Point Pleasant, NJ, Apr 30, 1982.

Johnny Galecki, 39, actor ("The Big Bang Theory," "Roseanne," *Suicide Kings*), born Bree, Belgium, Apr 30, 1975.

Stephen Harper, 55, 22nd Prime Minister of Canada (2006–), born Toronto, ON, Canada, Apr 30, 1959.

Perry King, 66, actor (*Slaughterhouse Five, The Lords of Flatbush, Switch*), born Alliance, OH, Apr 30, 1948.

Cloris Leachman, 84, actress ("Raising Hope," "Phyllis," Oscar for *The Last Picture Show*), born Des Moines, IA, Apr 30, 1930.

Kunal Nayyar, 33, actor ("The Big Bang Theory"), born London, England, Apr 30, 1981.

Willie Nelson, 81, singer, actor (*Honeysuckle Rose*), born Abbott, TX, Apr 30, 1933.

Adrian Pasdar, 49, actor ("Heroes," "Judging Amy"), born Pittsfield, MA, Apr 30, 1965.

Isiah Thomas, 53, basketball coach and Hall of Fame player, born Chicago, IL, Apr 30, 1961.

Burt Young, 74, writer, actor (*Chinatown, Rocky, Once Upon a Time in America*), born New York, NY, Apr 30, 1940.

✦ May ✦

May 1 — Thursday

DAY 121 **244 REMAINING**

ADDISON, JOSEPH: BIRTH ANNIVERSARY. May 1, 1672. (Old Style date.) English essayist born at Milston, Wiltshire, England. Died at London, June 17, 1719 (OS). "We are," he wrote in *The Spectator*, "always doing something for Posterity, but I would fain see Posterity do something for us."

AMTRAK: ANNIVERSARY. May 1, 1971. Amtrak, the national rail service that combined the operations of 18 passenger railroads, went into service.

ARTHRITIS AWARENESS MONTH. May 1–31. This observance seeks to focus attention on the large and growing problem of arthritis in the US. As the nation's most common cause of disability, arthritis affects 50 million Americans and nearly 300,000 children. By 2030 an estimated 67 million people in the US will be affected by arthritis. The prevalence of arthritis continues to rise even though the condition can often be prevented by staying active through physical activities such as walking. During May, the Arthritis Foundation hosts Arthritis Walks around the country designed to educate Americans about the health benefits of walking, while raising critical funds to fight arthritis. For info: Arthritis Foundation, PO Box 7669, Atlanta, GA 30357-0669. Phone: (800) 283-7800. Web: www.arthritis.org.

✦ASIAN AMERICAN AND PACIFIC ISLANDER HERITAGE MONTH. May 1–31. Presidential Proclamation issued honoring Asian/Pacific Americans each year since 1979. Public Law 102-450 of Oct 28, 1992, designated the observance for the month of May each year.

BATMAN DEBUTS: 75th ANNIVERSARY. May 1, 1939. In the May issues of *Detective Comics* #27, which appeared on newsstands on this day or a few days earlier, a new crime fighter, the "Batman," debuted, created by Bob Kane (collaborating with Bill Finger). The caped hero was an immediate success. See also: "Superman Debuts: Anniversary" (June 1).

BELGIUM: PLAY OF SAINT EVERMAAR. May 1. Annual performance (for more than 1,000 years) of a mystery play, in its original form, by the village inhabitants.

BETTER HEARING AND SPEECH MONTH. May 1–31. A nationwide public information campaign held each May to inform the 41 million Americans with hearing and speech problems that help is available. Annually, the month of May. For info: American Speech-Language-Hearing Assn, 2200 Research Blvd, Rockville, MD 20850-3289. Phone: (800) 638-8255. E-mail: bhsm@asha.org. Web: www.asha.org.

***CITIZEN KANE* FILM PREMIERE: ANNIVERSARY.** May 1, 1941. Orson Welles's directorial masterpiece premiered at New York City's RKO Palace. The premiere had been delayed almost three months due to studio jitters about what media magnate William Randolph Hearst's reaction would be—since the film was a thinly disguised version of his life. The film's multiple points of view, deep-focus photography and witty script made it a favorite with critics at the time: John O'Hara in *Newsweek* said, "Your faithful bystander reports that he has just seen a picture which he thinks must be the best picture he ever saw." Nominated for nine Academy Awards, *Citizen Kane* won for Best Original Screenplay by Herman J. Mankiewicz and Welles. The film did not perform well commercially (due in part to Hearst's influence) but is now regarded as the greatest American film.

CLARK, MARK: BIRTH ANNIVERSARY. May 1, 1896. US general who served in both world wars, Mark Clark was born at Madison Barracks, NY. In November 1942 he commanded the US forces taking part in the invasion of North Africa, and in January 1943 he became commander of the US Fifth Army, which invaded Italy in September 1943, taking Rome in June 1944. After the Germans capitulated in Italy, Clark was appointed commander of US occupation forces in Austria. He died at Charleston, SC, Apr 17, 1984.

COLUMBIAN EXPOSITION OPENING: ANNIVERSARY. May 1, 1893. At 12:08 PM President Grover Cleveland, in the presence of nearly a quarter of a million people, placed his finger on a golden key opening the Columbian Exposition at Chicago, IL. Amid the unfurling of thousands of flags, sounding of trumpets and booming of cannons, the key activated an electromagnetic valve, steam rushed into great cylinders, and an immense pump began its enormous burden of pumping 15 million gallons of water a day to provide the 685-acre fair and its visitors with an ample water supply.

EXECUTIVE COACHING DAY. May 1. Workers deserve the best leaders they can get. Sports stars have skill and strength coaches, great actors have speech and movement coaches, politicians have media coaches. Why don't more corporate and union executives who are responsible for effectively leading thousands of employees and members utilize the power of coaching? This is a day to applaud all organizational leaders who take their profession seriously enough to improve their skills through coaching. A day to raise the awareness of those who do not use coaching to improve their capacity to effectively lead their organizations. For info: Ira Chaleff, Pres, Executive Coaching & Consulting Associates, PO Box 663, Front Royal, VA 22630. Phone: (540) 631-9026. E-mail: ira.chaleff@exe-coach.com.

FIBROMYALGIA EDUCATION AND AWARENESS MONTH. May 1–31. To promote education and awareness of the dangers of fibromyalgia, which is also known as fibromyalgia syndrome, fibrositis or chronic muscle pain syndrome. Fibromyalgia affects more than 12 million American women. For info: Fred S. Mayer, RPh, MPH, Pharmacists Planning Services, Inc (PPSI), PO Box 6760, San Rafael, CA 94903. Phone: (415) 479-8628 or (415) 302-7351. Fax: (415) 479-8608. E-mail: ppsi@aol.com. Web: www.ppsinc.org.

FIRST SKYSCRAPER: ANNIVERSARY. May 1, 1884. Construction was begun on the Home Insurance Company building on this date in Chicago, IL. The 10-story building was completed in 1885. Designed by William Le Baron Jenney, it had a steel frame that carried the weight of the building. The walls provided no support but hung like curtains on the metal frame. This method of construction revolutionized American architecture and allowed architects to build taller and taller buildings. The Home Insurance Building was demolished in 1931.

FORD, GLENN: BIRTH ANNIVERSARY. May 1, 1916. Born at Sainte-Christine, QC, Canada, Ford was a popular Hollywood actor who appeared in more than 100 films. Important films include *Gilda* with Rita Hayworth, *Blackboard Jungle* with Sidney Poitier, *3:10 to Yuma* and *The Rounders*. He won a Golden Globe Award in 1962 for his leading role in Frank Capra's *Pocketful of Miracles*. He died at Hollywood, CA, Aug 30, 2006.

GARDENING FOR WILDLIFE MONTH. May 1–31. Be it an apartment balcony or a 20-acre farm, any space can accommodate a garden that attracts beautiful wildlife and helps restore habitat in commercial and residential areas. By providing food, water, cover and a place for wildlife to raise their young you not only help wildlife, but your property can also qualify to become an official Certified Wildlife Habitat. During May, the National Wildlife Federation sponsors this month to inspire and assist anyone who is passionate about wildlife to make a difference right in their own backyard. For info: National Wildlife Federation. Web: www.nwf.org.

GEORGE MALLORY FOUND ON EVEREST: 15th ANNIVERSARY. May 1, 1999. On June 8, 1924, British mountaineers George Mallory and Andrew Irvine began their final ascent of Mount Everest in Nepal—Mallory hoping to become the first human to reach the top. But both men disappeared in a snowstorm and were never seen again. On this date in 1999, Conrad Anker of the Mallory and Irvine Research Expedition (an endeavor sponsored by the BBC) found the remains of a frozen, mummified body wearing antique clothing that bore labels of "G.L. Mallory." The evidence—broken bones and contusions—indicated Mallory died in a fall, but unknown is whether Mallory (and Irvine) died on the way up the summit or on the way down. After a simple Anglican service, the expedition team covered Mallory with rocks and scree. Irvine has never been found.

GET CAUGHT READING MONTH. May 1–31. Launched in 1999, this month is a nationwide campaign to remind people of all ages how much fun it is to read. Because of research indicating that early language experience actually stimulates a child's brain to grow and that reading to children gives them a huge advantage when they start school, we hope to encourage people of all ages to enjoy books and magazines and to share that pleasure with the young children in their lives. For info: Assn of American Publishers, 71 Fifth Ave, 2nd Fl, New York, NY 10003-3004. Phone: (212) 255-0200. Web: www.publishers.org or www.getcaughtreading.org.

GIFTS FROM THE GARDEN MONTH. May 1–31. May is the month to celebrate the many ways gardens and gardening benefit people. From flowers and fitness to color and conversation, many treasures are growing in your own backyard. For info: C.L. Fornari, PO Box 355, Osterville, MA 02655. Phone: (508) 428-5895. E-mail: clfornari@yahoo.com. Web: www.gardenlady.com.

GLOBAL CIVILITY AWARENESS MONTH. May 1–31. Champion civility with 31 days of considerate conduct by practicing the behaviors and communication that encourage respect and impact campuses, corporations and communities worldwide. Inspire civility because civility counts. For info: Image Impact International, 474 W 238th St, #6I, Riverdale, NY 10463. Phone: (718) 530-3500. Web: www.imageimpact.org.

GO FETCH! NATIONAL FOOD DRIVE FOR HOMELESS ANIMALS. May 1–31. An annual, monthlong national food drive to raise awareness about starving and malnourished stray animals. These animals may live on the streets, be abused or neglected, be feral or be homeless pets living with their homeless families in shelters. For info: Go Fetch!, PALS Foundation, PO Box 3631, San Luis Obispo, CA 93403. Phone: (805) 544-0984. Web: www.gofetch.r8.org.

GREAT BRITAIN FORMED: ANNIVERSARY. May 1, 1707. (Old Style date.) A union between England and Scotland resulted in the formation of Great Britain. (Wales had been part of England since the 1500s.) Today's United Kingdom consists of Great Britain and Northern Ireland.

HAITIAN HERITAGE MONTH. May 1–31. Boston, MA. A series of events is organized throughout May in the Boston Haitian-American community featuring exhibits, flag raisings, concerts, games, parades and presentations. The events are organized to honor Haitian general Toussaint Louverture, to remember the consensus reached by black and mulatto officers to fight for Haitian independence in 1803 and to celebrate the Haitian flag created that same year. The flag-raising ceremony will take place on May 16, and the Haitian-American Unity Day Parade will take place on May 18. For info: Haitian-Americans United, Inc, 1464 Blue Hill Ave, PO Box 260440, Mattapan, MA 02126. Phone: (617) 298-2976. E-mail: unity@hauinc.org. Web: www.hauinc.org or www.haitianheritagemonth.net.

★ ★ ★

May 2014	S	M	T	W	T	F	S
					1	2	3
	4	5	6	7	8	9	10
	11	12	13	14	15	16	17
	18	19	20	21	22	23	24
	25	26	27	28	29	30	31

HEAL THE CHILDREN MONTH. May 1–31. To encourage survivors of childhood abuse and neglect to speak out. By revealing their painful experiences, they can inspire others to prevent children from suffering the same ordeals. Annually, the month of May. For info: Donald Etkes, PhD, 112 Harvard Ave, #148, Claremont, CA 91711. Phone: (310) 405-9814. E-mail: drdonetkes@aol.com. Web: www.AbuseHealing.com.

HEALTHY VISION MONTH. May 1–31. May is Healthy Vision Month, and through Eye Smart, the American Academy of Ophthalmology wants to remind the public how important it is to protect your vision. Diseases or injuries that can rob a person of vision can strike at any time. For info: American Academy of Ophthalmology, PO Box 7424, San Francisco, CA 94120-7424. Phone: (415) 447-0258. Fax: (415) 561-8533. E-mail: eyemd@aao.org. Web: www.geteyesmart.org.

HOME SCHOOLING AWARENESS MONTH. May 1–31. Promoted since 2010 to bring awareness to the general population and to parents of school-age children about the benefits of homeschooling. See the website for support, inspiration and resources. For info: Jane Andrews, 381 Billings Rd, Fitchburg, MA 01420-1407. Phone: (978) 343-4009. E-mail: info@HomeSchoolingAwarenessMonth.com. Web: www.HomeSchoolingAwarenessMonth.com.

HUNTINGTON'S DISEASE AWARENESS MONTH. May 1–31. Sponsored by the Huntington's Disease Society of America, a month spotlighting this devastating, hereditary, degenerative brain disorder for which there is, at present, no cure. For info: Huntington's Disease Society of America, 505 Eighth Ave, Ste 902, New York, NY 10018. Phone: (212) 242-1968 or (800) 345-4372. Fax: (212) 239-3430. E-mail: hdsainfo@hdsa.org. Web: www.hdsa.org.

INTERNATIONAL MEDITERRANEAN DIET MONTH. May 1–31. Traditional diets from the lands surrounding the Mediterranean Sea abound in olive oil, vegetables, fish, whole grains and other healthy foods. Decades of scientific research have shown that the "Med Diet" is one of the world's healthiest ways to eat. During International Mediterranean Diet Month, Oldways and the Mediterranean Foods Alliance offer education and promotions to consumers, retailers and health professionals to celebrate a way of eating that is both delicious and healthy. For info: Cynthia Harriman, Oldways, 266 Beacon St, Boston, MA 02116. Phone: (617) 421-5500. Fax: (617) 421-5511. E-mail: cynthia@oldwayspt.org. Web: www.oldwayspt.org.

INTERNATIONAL VICTORIOUS WOMAN MONTH. May 1–31. Celebrating every woman who has shaped her challenges into victories. Events during this month include the International Victorious Woman Contest and the Victorious Woman Project's annual celebration, the Girlfriend Gala (May 21, 2014). For info: Annmarie Kelly, Victorious Woman Project. E-mail: info@victoriouswoman.com. Web: www.victoriouswoman.com.

ITALY: FESTIVAL OF SAINT EFISIO. May 1–4. Cagliari. Said to be one of the biggest and most colorful processions in the world. Several thousand pilgrims on foot, in carts and on horseback wearing costumes dating from the 17th century accompany the statue of the saint through the streets.

✦JEWISH AMERICAN HERITAGE MONTH. May 1–31. Formerly celebrated as Jewish Heritage Week.

JONES, MARY HARRIS (MOTHER JONES): BIRTH ANNIVERSARY. May 1, 1830. Irish-born American labor leader. After the death of her husband and four children (during the Memphis yellow fever epidemic of 1867) and loss of her belongings in the Chicago Fire in 1871, Jones devoted her energies and her life to organizing and advancing the cause of labor. It seemed she was present wherever there were labor troubles. She gave her last speech on her 100th birthday. Born at Cork, Ireland, she died Nov 30, 1930, at Silver Spring, MD.

KANSAS BARBED WIRE SWAP/SELL AND FESTIVAL. May 1–3. La Crosse, KS. Barbed Wire Collectors Association show and meeting. Est attendance: 200. For info: Kansas Barbed Wire Collectors Assn, PO Box 578, La Crosse, KS 67548. Phone: (785) 222-9900. E-mail: barbedwire@rushcounty.org. Web: www.rushcounty.org/barbedwiremuseum.

KEEP KIDS ALIVE—DRIVE 25® DAY. May 1. 8th annual. Keep Kids Alive—Drive 25® Day is a call to action on the part of citizens in communities of all sizes across the US to commit to safe driving behaviors on neighborhood streets. Communities develop activities to educate and engage citizens in the effort through neighborhoods, schools, businesses and civic organizations. In many communities law enforcement and public officials take the lead. Annually, May 1. For info: Tom Everson, Keep Kids Alive—Drive 25, 12418 C St, Omaha, NE 68144. Phone: (402) 334-1391. E-mail: Tom@kkad25.org. Web: www.KeepKidsAliveDrive25.org.

LABOR DAY. May 1. In 140 countries, May 1 is observed as a workers' holiday. When it falls on a Saturday or Sunday, the following Monday is observed as a holiday. Bermuda, Canada and the US are the only countries that observe Labor Day in September. The Bahamas observe Labor Day in June.

LATINO BOOKS MONTH. May 1–31. In its ongoing efforts to promote books by and for Latinos, the Association of American Publishers (AAP) has designated May as Latino Books Month. During the monthlong celebration, booksellers, librarians and others in the book industry will encourage people in their communities to read books by and for Latinos, in both English and Spanish. Launched in 2004. For info: Assn of American Publishers, 71 Fifth Ave, 2nd Fl, New York, NY 10003-3004. Phone: (212) 255-0200. Web: www.publishers.org.

✦LAW DAY, USA. May 1. Presidential Proclamation issued each year for May 1 since 1958 at request. (Public Law 87–20 of Apr 7, 1961.)

LAW ENFORCEMENT APPRECIATION MONTH IN FLORIDA. May 1–31. Law Enforcement Appreciation Day is May 15 in Florida, a ceremonial day.

LEI DAY. May 1. Hawaii. On this special day—the Hawaiian version of May Day—leis are made, worn, given, displayed and entered in lei-making contests. One of the most popular Lei Day celebrations takes place at Honolulu at Kapiolani Park at Waikiki. Includes the state's largest lei contest, the crowning of the Lei Day Queen, Hawaiian music, hula and flowers galore.

✦LOYALTY DAY. May 1. Presidential Proclamation issued annually for May 1 since 1959 at request. (Public Law 85–529 of July 18, 1958.) An earlier proclamation was issued in 1955.

MARSHALL ISLANDS, REPUBLIC OF THE: CONSTITUTION DAY. May 1. National holiday.

MAY DAY. May 1. The first day of May has been observed as a holiday since ancient times. Spring festivals, maypoles and maying are still common, but the political importance of May Day has grown since the 1880s, when it became a workers' day in the US. Now widely observed in countries as a workers' holiday or as Labor Day. (Bermuda, Canada and the US observe Labor Day in September.) In most European countries, when May Day falls on Saturday or Sunday, the Monday following is observed as a holiday, with bank and store closings, parades and other festivities.

MELANOMA/SKIN CANCER DETECTION AND PREVENTION MONTH. May 1–31. A month to focus on skin cancer. Current estimates are that one in five Americans will develop skin cancer. You can prevent and detect skin cancer with (1) prevention: seek shade, cover up and wear sunscreen; (2) detection: look for new or changing spots on your skin; and (3) awareness: see a dermatologist if you spot anything changing, itching or bleeding. For info: American Academy of Dermatology, PO Box 4014, Schaumburg, IL 60168-4014. Phone: (866) 503-7546. Web: www.aad.org.

MOTHER GOOSE DAY. May 1. To reappreciate the old nursery rhymes. Motto: "Either alone or in sharing, read childhood nursery favorites and feel the warmth of Mother Goose's embrace." Website has ideas for celebrating, including recipes. Annually, May 1. For info: Gloria T. Delamar, Founder, Mother Goose Society. E-mail: mothergoosesociety@delamar.org. Web: www.delamar.org/mothergoosesociety.html.

MOTORCYCLE SAFETY MONTH. May 1–31. This month is dedicated to encouraging safe motorcycle-riding practices. Learn safe riding practices through state and local motorcycle-safety courses and continue improving skills through advanced riding courses. Set a safe environment this month to prepare for a safe riding season. For info: Sylvia Henderson, Springboard Training, PO Box 588, Olney, MD 20830-0588. Phone: (301) 260-1538. E-mail: sylvia@springboardtraining.com.

NATIONAL ALLERGY/ASTHMA AWARENESS MONTH. May 1–31. For info: Fred S. Mayer, RPh, MPH, Pharmacists Planning Service, Inc (PPSI), c/o Allergy Council of America (ACA), PO Box 6760, San Rafael, CA 94903. Phone: (415) 479-8628 or (415) 302-7351. Fax: (415) 479-8608. E-mail: ppsi@aol.com. Web: www.ppsinc.org.

NATIONAL BARBECUE MONTH. May 1–31. To encourage people to start enjoying barbecuing early in the season when daylight saving time lengthens the day. Annually, the month of May. For info: Hearth, Patio & Barbecue Assn, 1901 N Moore St, Ste 600, Arlington, VA 22209. Phone: (703) 522-0086. Fax: (703) 522-0548. Web: www.hpba.org.

NATIONAL BIKE MONTH. May 1–31. 58th annual celebration of bicycling for fun, fitness and transportation. Local activities sponsored by bicycling organizations, environmental groups, PTAs, police departments, health organizations and civic groups. About 5 million participants nationwide. Annually, the month of May. For info: League of American Bicyclists, 1612 K St NW, Ste 510, Washington, DC 20006. Phone: (202) 822-1333. Fax: (202) 822-1334. E-mail: bikeleague@bikeleague.org. Web: www.bikeleague.org/bikemonth.

NATIONAL BUBBA DAY. May 1. Comedian T. Bubba Bechtol has created a holiday for Bubbas everywhere. Annually, May 1 (formerly June 2). For info: T. Bubba Bechtol, 339 Panferio Dr, Pensacola Beach, FL 32561. Phone: (850) 932-3162. E-mail: tbubba@tbubba.com. Web: www.tbubba.com.

✦NATIONAL DAY OF PRAYER. May 1. Presidential Proclamation always issued for the first Thursday in May since 1981. (Public Law 100–307 of May 5, 1988.) Beginning in 1957, a day in October was designated, except in 1972 and 1975–77.

NATIONAL DAY OF REASON. May 1. A day to celebrate reason and to raise public awareness about the persistent threat to religious liberty posed by government intrusion into the private sphere of worship. This day also exists to inspire the secular community to be visible and active on this day to set the right example for how to effect positive change. Local organizations might use "Day of Reason" to label their events, or they might choose labels such as Day of Action, Day of Service or Rational Day of Care. The important message is to provide a positive, useful, constitutional alternative to the exclusionary National Day of Prayer. Annually, the first Thursday in May. For info: American Humanist Assn, 1777 T St NW, Washington, DC 20009-7125. Phone: (202) 238-9088 or (800) 837-3792. Fax: (202) 238-9003. Web: www.NationalDayOfReason.org.

NATIONAL FOSTER CARE MONTH. May 1–31. A time to renew our commitment to ensuring a bright future for the more than 400,000 children and youth in foster care and celebrate all those who make a meaningful difference in their lives. For info: Children's Bureau, Administration for Children and Families, US Department of Health and Human Services. Web: www.childwelfare.gov/fostercaremonth.

NATIONAL GOOD CAR-KEEPING MONTH. May 1–31. To promote increased safety and value through good car maintenance. For info: Sander Allen, Good Car-Keeping Institute, 990 N Lake Shore Dr, Ste 11-A, Chicago, IL 60611.

NATIONAL HAMBURGER MONTH. May 1–31. Sponsored by White Castle, the original fast-food hamburger chain (founded in 1921), to pay tribute to one of America's favorite foods. With or without condiments, on or off a bun or bread, hamburgers have grown in popularity since the early 1920s and are now an American meal mainstay. For info: White Castle Management Co, Marketing Dept, 555 W Goodale St, Columbus, OH 43215-1158. Phone: (614) 228-5781. Fax: (614) 228-8841. Web: www.whitecastle.com.

NATIONAL HEPATITIS AWARENESS MONTH. May 1–31. A month to raise awareness of and increase research on viral hepatitis, while also promoting prevention through schools, health departments, churches, community organizations and other groups. For info: Hepatitis Foundation Intl, 504 Blick Dr, Silver Spring, MD 20904. Phone: (800) 891-0707. E-mail: info@HepatitisFoundation.org. Web: www.HepatitisFoundation.org.

NATIONAL MEDITATION MONTH. May 1–31. A monthlong campaign to educate the public about the physical, emotional and mental benefits of meditation. Sponsored by The Deep Calm, an organization committed to creating awareness about meditation and its link to inner peace and peace in the world. Annually, in May. For info: Elesa Commerse, The Deep Calm, 4258 W High Bridge Ln, Ste 100, Chicago, IL 60646-6041. Phone: (773) 777-7754. E-mail: info@thedeepcalm.com. Web: www.thedeepcalm.com.

NATIONAL MENTAL HEALTH MONTH. May 1–31. Mental Health Month was created more than 60 years ago by Mental Health America to raise awareness about mental health conditions and the importance of mental wellness and promoting good mental health for all. One in four American adults lives with a diagnosable, treatable mental health condition. For info: Mental Health America, 2000 N Beauregard St, 6th Fl, Alexandria, VA 22311. Phone: (800) 969-6642 or (703) 684-7722. Web: www.mentalhealthamerica.net/go/may.

NATIONAL MILITARY APPRECIATION MONTH. May 1–31. 16th annual. This month honors, remembers, recognizes and appreciates all military personnel—those men and women who have served throughout our history and all who now serve in uniform and their families as well as those Americans who have given their lives in defense of the freedoms we all enjoy today. For info: Duncan Munro, MSgt USAF (Ret), Natl Events Coordinator, Natl Military Appreciation Month, PO Box 123, Bena, VA 23018-0123. E-mail: nmam@nmam.org. Web: www.nmam.org.

NATIONAL MOVING MONTH. May 1–31. Recognizing America's mobile roots and kicking off the busiest moving season of the year. Each year more than 43 million Americans pack up their belongings and relocate to new homes and communities. More than half of these moves take place between May and September. During National Moving Month, moving experts will be educating Americans on how to plan a successful move, pack efficiently and handle the uncertainties and questions that children may have.

May 2014	S	M	T	W	T	F	S
					1	2	3
	4	5	6	7	8	9	10
	11	12	13	14	15	16	17
	18	19	20	21	22	23	24
	25	26	27	28	29	30	31

NATIONAL OSTEOPOROSIS MONTH. May 1–31. Osteoporosis is not a natural part of aging. Find out what you can do to prevent, diagnose and treat it by joining the NOF family. For info: Natl Osteoporosis Foundation, 1150 17th St NW, Ste 850, Washington, DC 20036. Phone: (800) 231-4222. E-mail: info@nof.org. Web: www.nof.org.

NATIONAL PHOTO MONTH. May 1–31. This monthlong celebration of the memories market is the perfect opportunity to capture special moments. Visit your local photo retailer for prints or other photo memorabilia. Annually, every May. For info: Photo Marketing Association International, 2282 Springport Rd, Ste F, Jackson, MI 49202. Phone: (517) 788-8100 or (800) 762-9287. Fax: (517) 788-8371. Web: www.pmai.org.

NATIONAL PHYSICAL FITNESS AND SPORTS MONTH. May 1–31. Encourages individuals and organizations to promote fitness activities and programs. Popularly known as "May Month," it was established by the President's Council on Physical Fitness and Sports in 1983. For info: President's Council on Fitness, Sports and Nutrition, 1101 Wootton Pkwy, Ste 560, Rockville, MD 20852. Phone: (240) 276-9567. Fax: (240) 276-9860. Web: www.fitness.gov or www.presidentschallenge.org.

NATIONAL PRESERVATION MONTH. May 1–31. To draw public attention to historic preservation, including neighborhoods, districts, landmark buildings, open space and maritime heritage. For info: Natl Trust for Historic Preservation, 1785 Massachusetts Ave NW, Washington, DC 20036-2117. Phone: (202) 588-6000. Fax: (202) 588-6038. E-mail: info@savingplaces.org. Web: www.preservationnation.org.

NATIONAL SALAD MONTH. May 1–31. This year marks the 21st anniversary of National Salad Month. Celebrate healthy eating and good nutrition with salads and salad dressing. For info: Jacqueline Petty, The Association for Dressings and Sauces, 1100 Johnson Ferry Rd NE, Ste 300, Atlanta, GA 30342. Phone: (404) 252-3663. Fax: (404) 252-0774. E-mail: jpetty@kellencompany.com. Web: www.dressings-sauces.org or www.saladaday.org.

NATIONAL SALSA MONTH. May 1–31. Recognizing salsa as America's favorite way to add flavor to all kinds of food, such as eggs, burgers, chicken, tacos, chips, potatoes, rice and much more. Celebrates more than 65 years of picante sauce, a salsa created in 1947, and celebrates Cinco de Mayo, a major Mexican holiday now recognized across North America. For info: Pace Foods, c/o Dublin & Assoc, 3015 San Pedro, San Antonio, TX 78212. Phone: (210) 227-0221. Web: www.pacefoods.com.

NATIONAL STROKE AWARENESS MONTH. May 1–31. A time to educate the nation and spread awareness about stroke prevention, symptom recognition and recovery. For info: Natl Stroke Assn, 9707 E Easter Ln, Ste B, Centennial, CO 80112. Phone: (800) 787-6537. E-mail: info@stroke.org. Web: www.stroke.org.

NATIONAL SWEET VIDALIA® ONION MONTH. May 1–31. America's favorite sweet onions come into season each year at about this time and are available fresh in the market through Labor Day. These hand-planted, hand-harvested sweeties are low in pyruvate, the chemical that makes onions hot and causes cooks to tear up when cutting. Vidalia onions grow only in a 20-county area in southeast Georgia. In fact, the Georgia Department of Agriculture has registered the name *Vidalia* as it pertains to onions. The temperate climate and unique soil ensure the onions will have a mild and sweet taste—folks have even been known to bite into a Vidalia onion as if it were an apple. Vidalia onions were a favorite of James Beard, the father of American cuisine. For info and recipes: Vidalia Onion Committee, PO Box 1609, Vidalia, GA 30475. Phone: (912) 537-1918. E-mail: info@vidaliaonion.org. Web: www.vidaliaonion.org.

NATIONAL VINEGAR MONTH. May 1–31. Celebrate the season of cleaning and cooking with one of the home's most versatile products. For info: Jacqueline Petty, The Vinegar Institute, 1100 Johnson Ferry Rd NE, Ste 300, Atlanta, GA 30342. Phone: (404) 252-3663. Fax: (404) 252-0774. E-mail: jpetty@kellencompany.com. Web: www.versatilevinegar.org.

NCAA DIVISION I MEN'S VOLLEYBALL CHAMPIONSHIP. May 1 and 3. Joseph J. Gentile Arena, Loyola University, Chicago, IL. For info: NCAA, PO Box 6222, Indianapolis, IN 46206-6222. Web: www.NCAA.com.

NEW HOME OWNER'S DAY. May 1. You have faced all the challenges—now take the time as a new home owner to stand back and reflect on your new home and savor the feeling. For info: Dorothy Zjawin, 61 W Colfax Ave, Roselle Park, NJ 07204.

✦OLDER AMERICANS MONTH. May 1–31. Presidential Proclamation; from 1963 through 1973 this was called "Senior Citizens Month." In May 1974 it became Older Americans Month. In 1980 the title included Senior Citizens Day, which was observed May 8, 1980. Issued annually since 1963.

PAAR, JACK: BIRTH ANNIVERSARY. May 1, 1918. Radio personality, actor and humorist Jack Paar began hosting the "The Tonight Show" on NBC in 1957. With his catchphrase "I kid you not," he revolutionized late-night television, changing the format of traditional late shows from variety hours to talk shows and charming his audience and celebrity guests with a witty interviewing style. Paar introduced dozens of new stars to the American public, including Bill Cosby, Woody Allen, Carol Burnett and the Smothers Brothers. He left the show in 1962, handing it over to Johnny Carson, and retired from show business a few years later. Born at Canton, OH, he died at Greenwich, CT, Jan 27, 2004.

PHILIPPINES: FEAST OF OUR LADY OF PEACE AND GOOD VOYAGE. May 1–31. Pilgrimage to the shrine of Nuestra Sra de la Paz y Buen Viaje at Antipolo, Rizal.

PHILIPPINES: SANTACRUZAN. May 1–31. Maytime pageant-procession that recalls the quest of Queen Helena and Prince Constantine for the Holy Cross.

REACT MONTH. May 1–31. Highlights the two-way safety radio efforts of volunteer REACT Teams worldwide. REACT communications specialists receive emergency radio calls from travelers, boaters and others and relay them to authorities. REACTers also teach correct emergency radio use to the public. (This includes cell phone emergencies, since cells are really two-way radios.) REACT Teams provide two-way safety radio communications for local events, parades, walkathons, etc, on request. Teams also offer speakers on radio safety to community groups. REACT welcomes new members eager to serve their communities with two-way radio. For info: REACT Intl, PO Box 21064, Glendale, CA 91221. Phone: (301) 316-2900 or (866) 732-2899. Fax: (800) 608-9755. E-mail: REACT.HQ@REACTintl.org. Web: www.REACTintl.org.

RUSSIA: INTERNATIONAL LABOR DAY. May 1–2. Public holiday in Russian Federation. Official May Day demonstrations of working people.

SCHOOL PRINCIPALS' DAY. May 1. A day of recognition for all elementary, middle and high school principals for their leadership and dedication to providing the best education possible for their students. Annually, May 1. For info: Janet M. Dellaria, PO Box 39, Trout Creek, MI 49967. Phone: (906) 852-3539.

SMITH, KATE: BIRTH ANNIVERSARY. May 1, 1909. One of America's most popular singers. Kate Smith, who never took a formal music lesson, recorded more songs than any other performer (more than 3,000), made more than 15,000 radio broadcasts and received more than 25 million fan letters. On Nov 11, 1938, she introduced a new song during her regular radio broadcast, written especially for her by Irving Berlin: "God Bless America." It soon became the unofficial national anthem. Born Kathryn Elizabeth Smith at Greenville, VA, she began her radio career May 1, 1931, with "When the Moon Comes over the Mountain," a song identified with her throughout her career. She died at Raleigh, NC, June 17, 1986.

SOCIAL SECURITY EDUCATION MONTH. May 1–31. People are aware of Social Security but do not understand how the program works. More than 90 percent of all Social Security recipients leave money on the table as they are not aware that options exist. Social Security many times is a joint lifetime benefit. Recipients must understand their benefit options. This is a month to get educated—for the public and professional advisers. For info: Marc Kiner, Social Security Education Month, 50 E-Business Way, Ste 170, Sharonville, OH 45241. Phone: (513) 351-5707. Fax: (513) 842-2770. E-mail: mkiner@mypremierplan.com. Web: www.socialsecurityeducationmonth.com.

SOWERBY, LEO: BIRTH ANNIVERSARY. May 1, 1895. Pulitzer Prize–winning composer of more than 550 compositions, born at Grand Rapids, MI, and died July 7, 1968, at Port Clinton, OH.

SPIRITUAL LITERACY MONTH. May 1–31. Promoting respect for and among the world's religions and spiritual traditions by encouraging people to read the "book of the world" for sacred meaning. Practice Circles are set up in libraries, community centers, houses of worship, homes and online. (Formerly observed in December.) For info: Mary Ann Brussat, Spiritual Literacy Project, 15 W 24th St, New York, NY 10010. Phone: (212) 691-5240. E-mail: brussat@spiritualrx.com.

STRIKE OUT STROKES MONTH. May 1–31. Dedicated to the prevention of strokes. Factors resulting from heredity or natural processes can't be changed, but with proper medical treatment, early detection and healthful lifestyle adjustments, some risk factors can be eliminated. For info: Fred S. Mayer, RPh, MPH, c/o Pharmacists Planning Service, Inc (PPSI), PO Box 6760, San Rafael, CA 94903. Phone: (415) 479-8628 or (415) 302-7351. Fax: (415) 479-8608. E-mail: ppsi@aol.com. Web: www.ppsinc.org.

TEEN CEO MONTH. May 1–31. A month to celebrate the young entrepreneur and business leader. Sponsored by the youngest CEO to ever ring the NASDAQ stock market bell (on Oct 16, 2008). For info: Leanna Archer, PO Box 1194, Central Islip, NY 11722. Phone: (631) 885-4136. Fax: (631) 439-1760. E-mail: Leanna@leannashair.com. Web: www.leannashair.com.

TENNIS MONTH. May 1–31. A month to promote the benefits of playing tennis, sponsored by the United States Tennis Association. Established in 1881, the USTA is the national governing body for the sport of tennis and is the largest tennis organization in the world, with 17 geographic sections, more than 740,000 individual members and 7,000 organizational members, thousands of volunteers and a professional staff dedicated to growing the game. For info: United States Tennis Assn, 70 W Red Oak Ln, White Plains, NY 10604. Phone: (914) 696-7000. Web: www.usta.com or www.tennismonth.com.

ULTRAVIOLET AWARENESS MONTH. May 1–31. Exposure to UV rays can burn delicate eye tissue and raise the risk of developing cataracts and cancers of the eye. Protecting your eyes from UV dangers by choosing the right sunglasses is the message of this month. For info: Prevent Blindness America®, 211 W Wacker Dr, Ste 1700, Chicago, IL 60606. Phone: (800) 331-2020. E-mail: info@preventblindness.org. Web: www.preventblindness.org.

U-2 INCIDENT: ANNIVERSARY. May 1, 1960. On the eve of a summit meeting between US president Dwight D. Eisenhower and Soviet premier Nikita Khrushchev, a U-2 espionage plane flying at about 60,000 feet was shot down over Sverdlovsk, in central USSR. The pilot, CIA agent Francis Gary Powers, survived the crash, as did large parts of the aircraft, a suicide kit and sophisticated surveillance equipment. The sensational event, which US officials described as a weather reconnaissance flight gone astray, resulted in cancellation of the summit meeting. Powers was tried, convicted and sentenced to 10 years in prison by a Moscow court. In 1962 he was returned to the US in exchange for an imprisoned Soviet spy. He died in a helicopter crash in 1977. See also: "Powers, Francis Gary: Birth Anniversary" (Aug 17).

WILLIAMS, ARCHIE: BIRTH ANNIVERSARY. May 1, 1915. Archie Williams, along with Jesse Owens and others, debunked Hitler's theory of the superiority of Aryan athletes at the 1936 Berlin Olympics. As a black member of the US team, Williams won a gold medal by running the 400-meter in 46.5 seconds (0.4 second slower than his own record of earlier that year). Williams, who was born at Oakland, CA, earned a degree in mechanical engineering from the University of California–Berkeley in 1939 but had to dig ditches for a time because companies weren't hiring black engineers. He became an airplane pilot and for 22 years trained Tuskegee Institute pilots, including the black air corps of WWII. When asked during a 1981 interview about his treatment by the Nazis during the 1936 Olympics, he replied, "Well, over there at least we didn't have to ride in the back of the bus." Archie Williams died June 24, 1993, at Fairfax, CA.

WOMEN'S HEALTH CARE MONTH. May 1–31. To initiate a public education campaign devoted to increasing awareness of the many health concerns unique to women. Focus will be on the prevention of the major causes of death and poor health among women—heart disease, cancer, arthritis, osteoporosis and bone fractures—as well as on depression and alcoholism in women. Annually, the month of May. For info: Fred S. Mayer, RPh, MPH, Pharmacists Planning Service, Inc (PPSI), PO Box 6760, San Rafael, CA 94903. Phone: (415) 479-8628 or (415) 302-7351. Fax: (415) 479-8608. E-mail: ppsi@aol.com. Web: www.ppsinc.org.

YOUNG ACHIEVERS/LEADERS OF TOMORROW MONTH. May 1–31. International Leadership Network's Young Achievers/Leaders of Tomorrow Program recognizes and encourages positive achievement, behavior, leadership and service. Community and national recognition events honor student leaders in grades 5–11. Annually, the month of May. For info: Tom Eichhorst, 1750 S Brentwood Blvd, Ste 502, St. Louis, MO 63144. Phone: (314) 961-5978. E-mail: ilnleadnet@aol.com. Web: www.ilnleadnet.com.

BIRTHDAYS TODAY

Wes Anderson, 45, director, screenwriter (*Moonrise Kingdom, Fantastic Mr Fox, The Royal Tenenbaums, Rushmore*), born Houston, TX, May 1, 1969.

Charles (Chuck) Bednarik, 89, Hall of Fame football player, born Bethlehem, PA, May 1, 1925.

Steve Cauthen, 54, former jockey, born Walton, KY, May 1, 1960.

Emilia Clarke, 27, actress ("Game of Thrones"), born London, England, May 1, 1987.

Judy Collins, 75, singer, born Seattle, WA, May 1, 1939.

Rita Coolidge, 69, singer, born Nashville, TN, May 1, 1945.

Sonny James, 85, singer, born Jimmy Loden at Hackleburg, AL, May 1, 1929.

Curtis Martin, 41, former football player, born Pittsburgh, PA, May 1, 1973.

May 2014

S	M	T	W	T	F	S
				1	2	3
4	5	6	7	8	9	10
11	12	13	14	15	16	17
18	19	20	21	22	23	24
25	26	27	28	29	30	31

Bobbie Ann Mason, 74, writer (*In Country, The Girl in the Blue Beret*), born Mayfield, KY, May 1, 1940.

Tim McGraw, 47, country singer, born Delhi, LA, May 1, 1967.

Shahar Peer, 27, tennis player, born Jerusalem, Israel, May 1, 1987.

Charlie Schlatter, 48, actor ("Diagnosis Murder"), born Englewood, NJ, May 1, 1966.

Paul Teutul, Sr, 65, motorcycle designer, television personality ("American Chopper"), born Yonkers, NY, May 1, 1949.

May 2 — Friday

DAY 122 **243 REMAINING**

BERLIN SURRENDERS: ANNIVERSARY. May 2, 1945. At 6:45 AM, Soviet marshal Georgi Zhukov accepted the surrender of Berlin, the German capital. The victory came at a terrible cost for the Red Army, with 304,887 men killed, wounded or missing—10 percent of its soldiers. About 125,000 Berliners died in the siege, many by suicide.

COIN, JEWELRY & STAMP EXPO. May 2–4. Radisson Hotel, Anaheim, CA. Est attendance: 4,000. For info: Israel Bick, Exec Dir, Intl Stamp & Coin Collectors Society, PO Box 854, Van Nuys, CA 91408. Phone: (818) 997-6496. Fax: (818) 988-4337. E-mail: iibick@sbcglobal.net. Web: www.bickinternational.com.

DANDELION MAY FEST. May 2–3. Dover, OH. Old-fashioned festival includes finals in a nationwide dandelion recipe contest, cooking demonstrations, live entertainment and food booths featuring dishes made from dandelions, such as dandelion coffee ice cream, dandelion pizza, dandelion bread and dandelion gravy. Also, dandelion wine and jelly tasting, family entertainment and 5k fun run. Festival highlight is 21st Great Dandelion Cook-Off; for entry forms for cook-off call (800) 843-9463. Est attendance: 15,000. For info: Anita Davis, Coord, Der Marktplatz-Breitenbach Wine Cellars, 5934 Old Rte 39 NW, Dover, OH 44622. Phone: (330) 343-3603. Fax: (330) 343-8290. E-mail: info@breitenbachwine.com. Web: www.dandelionfestival.com.

GEHRIG'S STREAK ENDS: 75th ANNIVERSARY. May 2, 1939. New York Yankees first baseman Lou Gehrig asked manager Joe McCarthy to take him out of the lineup for the game against the Detroit Tigers. By his sitting out, Gehrig's record streak of consecutive games played, begun May 25, 1925, stopped at 2,130. The slugger complained of fatigue, but he was really suffering from ALS, amyotrophic lateral sclerosis, a condition later known as Lou Gehrig's disease. Gehrig never played again.

ISLE OF EIGHT FLAGS SHRIMP FESTIVAL PRESENTED BY PUBLIX. May 2–4. Fernandina Beach, FL, on beautiful Amelia Island. Florida commemorates Fernandina's role as the birthplace of the modern shrimping industry. Festival includes juried fine arts and crafts show, entertainment, antiques, pirates, Kids Fun Zone and lots of food and shrimp. Est attendance: 135,000. For info: Isle of Eight Flags Shrimp Festival, PO Box 6146, Fernandina Beach, FL 32035. Phone: (866) 4-AMELIA (toll-free). E-mail: 4info@shrimpfestival.com. Web: www.shrimpfestival.com.

KING JAMES BIBLE PUBLISHED: ANNIVERSARY. May 2, 1611. King James I had appointed a committee of learned men to produce a new translation of the Bible in English. This version, popularly called the King James Version, is known in England as the Authorized Version.

LEONARDO DA VINCI: DEATH ANNIVERSARY. May 2, 1519. Italian artist, scientist and inventor. Painter of the famed *Last Supper*, perhaps the first painting of the High Renaissance, and of the *Mona Lisa*. Inventor of the first parachute. Born at Vinci, Italy, in 1452 (exact date unknown), he died at Amboise, France.

MAY DAY FAIRIE FESTIVAL. May 2–4. Spoutwood Farm, Glen Rock, PA. 23rd annual. A celebration of spring, featuring nature spirits of all kinds. Entertaining and educational. Annually, the first full weekend in May. Est attendance: 15,000. For info: Rob Wood, Spoutwood Farm, 4255 Pierceville Rd, Glen Rock, PA 17327. Phone: (717) 235-6610. E-mail: events@spoutwood.org. Web: www.spoutwood.org.

ORANGEBURG FESTIVAL OF ROSES. May 2–4. Edisto Memorial Gardens, Orangeburg, SC. 43rd annual. This annual event celebrates the blooming of Orangeburg's beautiful roses and the beginning of a yearlong opportunity to enjoy the natural setting of the Edisto Memorial Gardens along the banks of the Edisto River, the longest black-water river in the world. Annually, the first weekend in May. Est attendance: 35,000. For info: Orangeburg County Chamber of Commerce, PO Box 328, Orangeburg, SC 29116-0328. Phone: (803) 534-6821 or (800) 545-6153. Fax: (803) 531-9435. E-mail: chamber@orangeburgsc.net. Web: www.festivalofroses.com.

OSAMA BIN LADEN KILLED: ANNIVERSARY. May 2, 2011. US Navy SEAL Team Six raided a large compound in Abbottabad, Pakistan, and killed Al-Qaeda terrorist leader Osama Bin Laden. Bin Laden's body was buried at sea in accordance with Islamic rites later that day. Bin Laden was born Mar 10, 1957, at Riyadh, Saudi Arabia. Bin Laden was the world's most-wanted terrorist.

POSITIVE POWER OF HUMOR AND CREATIVITY CONFERENCE. May 2–4. Saratoga Springs, NY. 57th annual. Participants from all continents laugh while they learn practical and powerful ideas at the longest-running humor conference in the world. Past conferences have featured Steve Allen, Sid Caeser, Victor Borge, Al Roker, Elmo and The Smothers Brothers. Est attendance: 500. For info: The Humor Project, 10 Madison Ave, Saratoga Springs, NY 12866. Phone: (518) 587-8770. E-mail: chase@HumorProject.com. Web: www.HumorProject.com.

RAY, SATYAJIT: BIRTH ANNIVERSARY. May 2, 1921. Film director Satyajit Ray was born at Calcutta, India. Possibly India's best-known film director, he made more than 30 films and won numerous international awards, including an Academy Award for lifetime achievement. His films include the trilogy *Pather Panchali* (1956), *Aparajito* (1956) and *The World of Apu* (1959). Ray died Apr 23, 1992, at Calcutta.

ROBERT'S RULES DAY: ROBERT, HENRY: BIRTH ANNIVERSARY. May 2, 1837. Anniversary of the birth of Henry M. Robert (US Army general), author of *Robert's Rules of Order*, a standard parliamentary guide. Born at Robertville, SC. Died at Hornell, NY, May 11, 1923.

SPOCK, BENJAMIN: BIRTH ANNIVERSARY. May 2, 1903. Pediatrician and author, born at New Haven, CT. His book on child rearing, *Common Sense Book of Baby and Child Care* (later called *Baby and Child Care*), has sold more than 30 million copies. In 1955 he became professor of child development at Western Reserve University at Cleveland, OH. He resigned from this position in 1967 to devote his time to the pacifist movement. Spock died at San Diego, CA, Mar 15, 1998.

TOAD SUCK DAZE. May 2–4. Downtown Conway, AR. 33rd annual. Festival features toad-jumping contests, concerts, parade, carnival, softball tournament, 5k and 10k runs, arts and crafts and more. Annually, the first weekend in May. Est attendance: 160,000. For info: Conway Area Chamber of Commerce, 900 Oak St, Conway, AR 72032. Phone: (501) 327-7788. Fax: (501) 327-7790. E-mail: toadsuck@conwayarkansas.org. Web: www.toadsuck.org.

BIRTHDAYS TODAY

Christine Baranski, 62, actress (Tonys for *The Real Thing* and *Rumors*; *Mame*, "The Good Wife"), born Buffalo, NY, May 2, 1952.

David Beckham, 39, former soccer player, born Leytonstone, London, England, May 2, 1975.

Elizabeth Berridge, 52, actress (*Amadeus*, "The John Larroquette Show"), born Westchester, NY, May 2, 1962.

Theodore Bikel, 90, singer, actor (*Man on the Run, My Fair Lady*), born Vienna, Austria, May 2, 1924.

Larry Gatlin, 65, singer, songwriter, born Odessa, TX, May 2, 1949.

Lesley Gore, 68, singer, born Tenafly, NJ, May 2, 1946.

Sarah Hughes, 29, Olympic figure skater, born Manhasset, NY, May 2, 1985.

Bianca Jagger, 69, actress, political activist, born Managua, Nicaragua, May 2, 1945.

David Suchet, 68, actor ("The Way We Live Now," "Hercule Poirot Mysteries"), born London, England, May 2, 1946.

Jenna Von Oy, 37, actress ("Blossom"), born Newtown, CT, May 2, 1977.

May 3 — Saturday

DAY 123 **242 REMAINING**

APPLE BLOSSOM FESTIVAL. May 3–4. South Mountain Fairgrounds, Gettysburg, PA. 59th annual event, always held the first weekend in May. Est attendance: 20,000. For info: Adams County Fruit Growers Assn, 33 Musselman Ave, Biglerville, PA 17307. Phone: (717) 677-7444. E-mail: acfga@comcast.net. Web: www.appleblossomfestival.info.

BARK IN THE PARK. May 3. Lincoln Park, Chicago, IL. In recognition of Be Kind to Animals Week, thousands of paws and feet will hit the ground walking for this 5k event to raise funds for the animals. Entrance fee. Est attendance: 3,500. For info: The Anti-Cruelty Society, 157 W Grand Ave, Chicago, IL 60654. Phone: (312) 329-8726. E-mail: events@anticruelty.org. Web: www.barkinthepark.org.

BROWN, JAMES: BIRTH ANNIVERSARY. May 3, 1933. Singer and songwriter born at Barnwell, SC. Brown began singing gospel while in reform school. He quickly moved into pop music and by the early 1960s was a hugely successful performer. Transcending musical genres, he called himself the "Godfather of Soul" but was equally prominent in rock, gospel and rhythm and blues. He was a spectacular dancer and showman, known for outlandish costumes and energy-filled performances. The "hardest working man in show business" died Dec 25, 2006, at Atlanta, GA.

"CBS EVENING NEWS" TV PREMIERE: ANNIVERSARY. May 3, 1948. The news program began as a 15-minute telecast with Douglas Edwards as anchor. Walter Cronkite succeeded him in 1962 and expanded the show to 30 minutes; Eric Sevareid served as commentator. Dan Rather anchored the newscasts upon Cronkite's retirement from 1981 to 2005. Katie Couric assumed the anchor seat in 2006; Scott Pelley came to the helm in 2011.

CHINCOTEAGUE SEAFOOD FESTIVAL. May 3. Chincoteague Island, VA. This all-you-can-eat festival promotes the seafood industry on Virginia's Eastern Shore. Here, there's fresh local seafood. Renowned festival cooks, volunteers and professionals prepare exciting offerings and signature dishes from local restaurants as well as old and new Eastern Shore favorites. Little neck clams, a longtime festival staple, are available along with fish, clams and oysters prepared in a variety of ways. Annually, the first Saturday in May. Est attendance: 2,700. For info: Chincoteague Chamber of Commerce, 6733 Maddox Blvd, Chincoteague, VA 23336. Phone: (757) 336-6161. Fax: (757) 336-1242. E-mail: chincochamber@verizon.net. Web: www.chincoteaguechamber.com.

COTTON PICKIN' FAIR. May 3–4 (also Oct 4–5). Gay, GA. Skilled artisans feature art, antiques and crafts in a 1910-era family farmstead. The Peach Packing Shed, Cotton Gin and Warehouse, 1891 Farmhouse and a number of smaller buildings create a unique backdrop for a great day of family fun in the country. Includes a wonderful variety of Southern food plus live entertainment on six stages. A Southeast Tourism Society "Top Twenty Event" and designated a "Producer of Distinction" by the Georgia Tourism Foundation. Biannually: the first weekends of May and October. Est attendance: 35,000. For info: Cotton Pickin' Fair, 18830 Georgia Hwy 85, Gay, GA 30218. Phone: (706) 538-6814. E-mail: info@cpfair.org. Web: www.cpfair.org.

CROSBY, HARRY LILLIS "BING": BIRTH ANNIVERSARY. May 3, 1903. Bing Crosby, born at Tacoma, WA, was the bestselling artist, most popular radio star and biggest box office draw in his day—even beyond the emergence of rock in the mid-1950s. His "White Christmas" was one of the bestselling single records of the 20th century. He appeared in numerous comedic and dramatic film roles. He earned an Oscar for his performance in *Going My Way* (1944) and was also known for his *Road* films with Bob Hope. Crosby died on Oct 14, 1977, directly after shooting an 85 on 18 holes at La Moraleja Golf Course in Madrid, Spain.

DOW JONES TOPS 11,000: 15th ANNIVERSARY. May 3, 1999. The Dow Jones Index of 30 major industrial stocks topped the 11,000 mark for the first time.

ENGLAND: CLUN GREEN MAN FESTIVAL. May 3–5. Clun, Shropshire. A traditional springtime festival full of live music, drama, color and medieval malarkey. Concludes on Monday with the famous "Battle on the Bridge," when the Clun Green Man battles the Frost Queen to bring in spring. The Green Man then enters Clun Castle accompanied by the May Queen and a procession of maypole dancers, morris dancers and entertainers. The procession is followed by a traditional May Fair in the grounds of Clun Castle (courtesy of English Heritage), with local craft stalls, demonstrating artisans, food stalls, tea tent and beer tent. Annually, the first May bank holiday weekend of the year. For info: Clun Green Man Festival, The White Horse Inn, The Square, Clun, England. E-mail: info@clungreenman.org.uk. Web: www.clungreenman.org.uk.

May 2014	S	M	T	W	T	F	S
					1	2	3
	4	5	6	7	8	9	10
	11	12	13	14	15	16	17
	18	19	20	21	22	23	24
	25	26	27	28	29	30	31

FREE COMIC BOOK DAY. May 3. Each year, independent comic book stores give out free comic books to children. Some 2,000 stores in all 50 states and around the world give more than 3 million comic books out. Annually, the first Saturday in May. For info: Diamond Comic Distributors, 1966 Greenspring Dr, Ste 300, Timonium, MD 21093. Phone: (800) 45-COMIC. E-mail: press@diamondcomics.com or fans@diamondcomics.com. Web: www.freecomicbookday.com.

GALVESTON HISTORIC HOMES TOUR. May 3–4 (also May 10–11). Galveston Island, TX. 40th annual. Discover Galveston Island's great treasures of Victorian and post-Victorian architecture as privately owned homes are opened to the public for tours. Annually, the first two full weekends in May. Est attendance: 5,000. For info: Galveston Historical Foundation, 502 20th St, Galveston, TX 77550. Phone/fax: (409) 765-6831. E-mail: foundation@galvestonhistory.org. Web: www.galvestonhistory.org.

GARDEN MEDITATION DAY. May 3. Let go of your concerns and center your full attention on the garden for even a few minutes today. Focusing on weeding, tilling the soil or cleaning up the garden is a relaxing way to direct your concentration to just one thing. Annually, May 3. For info: C.L. Fornari, PO Box 355, Osterville, MA 02655. Phone: (508) 428-5895. E-mail: clfornari@yahoo.com. Web: www.gardenlady.com.

HOLLAND TULIP TIME FESTIVAL. May 3–10. Holland, MI. 85th annual. Named Readers Digest's "Best Small Town Festival." Visitors from all over the world come to see millions of tulips planted in parks, gardens and lanes throughout the Holland community. Celebrate Dutch culture and join us for tulips, parades, street scrubbing, carnival, Klompen Dancers, Dutch Marktplaats, concerts, theater shows, art and craft fair, fireworks, kids events, trolley tours and so much more! Est attendance: 500,000. For info: Holland Tulip Time Festival, Inc, 74 W 8th St, Holland, MI 49423. Phone: (616) 396-4221 or (800) 822-2770. Fax: (616) 396-4545. E-mail: tulip@tuliptime.com. Web: www.tuliptime.com.

INGE, WILLIAM: BIRTH ANNIVERSARY. May 3, 1913. Award-winning American playwright, much of whose work was turned into successful Hollywood films. Best known for *Come Back, Little Sheba* (1950), *Picnic* (1953) and *Bus Stop* (1955). Inge received a Pulitzer Prize for *Picnic* and an Oscar for his original screenplay of *Splendor in the Grass* (1960). Born at Independence, KS, Inge committed suicide at Hollywood, CA, on June 10, 1973.

JAPAN: CONSTITUTION MEMORIAL DAY. May 3. National holiday commemorating adoption of the constitution in 1947. Part of the Golden Week Holidays.

JOIN HANDS DAY. May 3. A national day of volunteering that brings youths and adults together to improve their own communities. Sponsored by America's Fraternal Benefit Societies. Annually, the first Saturday in May. For info: Join Hands Day, 1301 W 22nd St, Ste 700, Oak Brook, IL 60523. Phone: (630) 522-6322, ext 113. Fax: (630) 522-6326. E-mail: actioncenter@joinhandsday.org. Web: www.joinhandsday.org.

KENT STATE COMMEMORATION. May 3–4. Kent State University, Kent, OH. 44th annual commemoration remembering the victims of the May 4, 1970, shootings at Kent State during an antiwar rally. Candlelight vigil and march begin at 10:30 PM on May 3 and continue through the night until the afternoon of May 4. May 4 ceremony includes ringing the Victory Bell at 12:24 PM, the time of the shootings. For info: May 4 Task Force, Center for Student Life, Kent State University, Kent, OH 44242. E-mail: may4taskforce@yahoo.com. Web: www.m4tf.org.

KENTUCKY DERBY. May 3. Churchill Downs, Louisville, KY. The 140th running of America's premier Thoroughbred horse race, inaugurated in 1875. First jewel in the Triple Crown, traditionally followed by the Preakness (second Saturday after the Derby) and the Belmont Stakes (fifth Saturday after the Derby). Annually, the first Saturday in May. Est attendance: 150,000. For info: Churchill Downs, 700 Central Ave, Louisville, KY 40208. Phone: (502) 636-4400. Web: kentuckyderby.com.

LOWCOUNTRY SHRIMP FESTIVAL. May 3. McClellanville, SC. 38th annual. Seafood, arts, crafts, civic display, entertainment and blessing of the fleet. Annually, the first Saturday in May. Est attendance: 15,000. For info: The Archibald Rutledge Academy, 1011 Old Cemetery Rd, McClellanville, SC 29458. Phone: (843) 887-3323. Web: www.lowcountryshrimpfestival.com.

LUMPY RUG DAY. May 3. To encourage the custom of teasing bigots and trigots for shoving unwelcome facts under the rug. When many cans of worms have been shoved under the rug, the defenders of the status quo obtain a new rug high enough to cover the unwanted facts. For info: Robert L. Birch, Puns Corps, 3108 Dashiell Rd, Falls Church, VA 22042. Phone: (703) 533-3668.

MACHIAVELLI, NICCOLO: BIRTH ANNIVERSARY. May 3, 1469. Italian writer and statesman, born at Florence, Italy. Author of *The Prince*, a book of advice for a ruler that prescribes strong, absolute government. Died at Florence, June 22, 1527.

MEIR, GOLDA: BIRTH ANNIVERSARY. May 3, 1898. Born Goldie Mabovitch at Kiev, Russia, Meir was prime minister of Israel 1969–74. She died at Jerusalem, Dec 8, 1978.

MEXICO: DAY OF THE HOLY CROSS. May 3. Celebrated especially by construction workers and miners, a festive day during which anyone who is building must give a party for the workers. A flower-decorated cross is placed on every piece of new construction in the country.

NATIONAL PUBLIC RADIO FIRST BROADCAST: ANNIVERSARY. May 3, 1971. National noncommercial radio network, financed by the Corporation for Public Broadcasting, began programming.

NATIONAL TWO DIFFERENT COLORED SHOES DAY. May 3. A day to recognize and celebrate the uniqueness and diversity of humanity. The simple and lighthearted act of purposely wearing two different colored shoes demonstrates the courage to take a risk and step outside of one's daily routine. Annually, May 3. For info: Arlene Kaiser, EdD, 3424 Spring Creek Ln, Milpitas, CA 95035. Phone: (408) 946-4444. E-mail: drarlenekaiser@mac.com. Web: www.NTDCSD.com.

PARANORMAL DAY. May 3. A day for all paranormal enthusiasts to get together and share their unique experiences with each other. Seminars, radio broadcasts and readings will take place worldwide. For info: Bob O'Brien, Consumer Advocate, 1061 Koelle Blvd, Seacaucus, NJ 07094. Phone: (646) 233-6610. E-mail: robtfobrien@aol.com.

PEDDLER'S VILLAGE STRAWBERRY FESTIVAL. May 3–4. Lahaska, PA. Strawberries served up in various forms—dipped in chocolate, in assorted pastries and shortcake, in jams, in fritters and fresh and unadorned. Craftspeople gather to show their wares and demonstrate their skills. Live entertainment and pie-eating contests add to the festivities of this traditional spring celebration. Free admission. Est attendance: 18,000. For info: Peddler's Village, Rtes 202 and 263, Lahaska, PA 18931. Phone: (215) 794-4000. Fax: (215) 794-4001. E-mail: info@peddlersvillage.com. Web: www.peddlersvillage.com.

POLAND: CONSTITUTION DAY (SWIETO TRZECIEGO MAJA). May 3. National Day. Celebrates ratification of Poland's first constitution, 1791.

ROBINSON, SUGAR RAY: BIRTH ANNIVERSARY. May 3, 1921. Ray "Sugar Ray" Robinson, boxer, born Walker Smith, Jr, at Detroit, MI. Generally considered "pound for pound the greatest boxer of all time," Robinson was a welterweight and middleweight champion who won 175 professional fights and lost only 19. A smooth and precise boxer, he fought until he was 45, dabbled in show business and established the Sugar Ray Robinson Youth Foundation to counter juvenile delinquency. Died at Los Angeles, CA, Apr 12, 1989.

SIEGE OF YORKTOWN OUSTS REBELS: ANNIVERSARY. May 3, 1862. After nearly a month's siege, General Joseph Johnston's outnumbered Confederate forces evacuated Yorktown, VA, and moved back to Richmond. General McClellan's Army of the Potomac occupied Yorktown the following day. With the capture of Yorktown, President Abraham Lincoln left Washington, DC, for Fort Monroe, VA, to observe the ongoing Peninsula Campaign.

UNITED NATIONS: WORLD PRESS FREEDOM DAY. May 3. A day to recognize that a free, pluralistic and independent press is an essential component of any democratic society and to promote press freedom in the world. For info: United Nations, Dept of Public Info, New York, NY 10017. Web: www.un.org.

VIRGINIA GOLD CUP. May 3. Great Meadow, The Plains, VA. 89th annual. Race day features six steeplechase races, Jack Russell Terrier races and hat and tailgate competitions. The $75,000 Virginia Gold Cup race is run over a challenging four-mile post-and-rail course of 23 fences. Annually, the first Saturday in May. Est attendance: 50,000. For info: Virginia Gold Cup Assn, PO Box 840, Warrenton, VA 20188. Phone: (540) 347-2612. Fax: (540) 349-1829. E-mail: info@vagoldcup.com. Web: www.vagoldcup.com.

VIRGINIA STATE CHAMPIONSHIP CHILI COOK-OFF. May 3. Railside Plaza, Roanoke, VA. Live entertainment, pepper-eating contest, children's festival area, vendors and the best chili samples from across the eastern US and the commonwealth of Virginia. All compete for the state title. Annually, the first Saturday in May. Est attendance: 8,000. For info: Emily Phillips, Greenvale School, 627 Westwood Blvd, Roanoke, VA 24017. Phone: (540) 632-8208. Fax: (540) 344-0876. E-mail: ephillips@greenvale-school.org.

BIRTHDAYS TODAY

Joseph Addai, 31, football player, born Houston, TX, May 3, 1983.

Greg Gumbel, 68, television personality, sportscaster, born New Orleans, LA, May 3, 1946.

Christina Hendricks, 39, actress ("Mad Men"), born Knoxville, TN, May 3, 1975.

Dulé Hill, 40, actor ("The West Wing," "Psych"), born Orange, NJ, May 3, 1974.

Engelbert Humperdinck, 78, singer, born Gerry Dorsey at Madras, India, May 3, 1936.

C.L. (Butch) Otter, 72, Governor of Idaho (R), born Caldwell, ID, May 3, 1942.

Jim Risch, 73, US Senator (R, Idaho), born Milwaukee, WI, May 3, 1941.

Pete Seeger, 95, folksinger, songwriter, born New York, NY, May 3, 1919.

Frankie Valli, 77, singer, born Newark, NJ, May 3, 1937.

David Vitter, 53, US Senator (R, Louisiana), born New Orleans, LA, May 3, 1961.

Ron Wyden, 65, US Senator (D, Oregon), born Wichita, KS, May 3, 1949.

May 4 — Sunday

DAY 124 **241 REMAINING**

"ANOTHER WORLD" TV PREMIERE: 50th ANNIVERSARY. May 4, 1964. Created by Irna Phillips and sponsored by P&G, this soap was set in fictional Bay City. It was the first soap to air for a full hour and the first to beget two spin-offs ("Somerset" and "Texas"). Charles Durning, Ted Shackelford, Eric Roberts, Ray Liotta, Kyra Sedgwick, Faith Ford, Morgan Freeman, Jackée Harry, Victoria Wyndham and Valarie Pettiford are some of its well-known alums. The show was canceled in 1999, and the last episode aired June 25, 1999.

BE KIND TO ANIMALS WEEK®. May 4–10. Observed since 1915. To promote kindness and humane care toward animals. Features "Be Kind to Animals Kid Contest" with grand prize. Annually, the first full week of May, beginning on Sunday. For info: American Humane Assn. E-mail: info@americanhumane.org. Web: www.americanhumane.org.

CHINA: YOUTH DAY. May 4. Annual public holiday recalls the demonstration on May 4, 1919, by thousands of patriotic students in Beijing's Tiananmen Square to protest imperialist aggression in China.

CURAÇAO: MEMORIAL DAY. May 4. Victims of WWII are honored on this day. Military ceremonies at the War Monument. Not an official public holiday.

DISCOVERY OF JAMAICA BY CHRISTOPHER COLUMBUS: ANNIVERSARY. May 4, 1494. Christopher Columbus discovered Jamaica. The Arawak Indians were its first inhabitants.

FELIX, MARIA: 100th BIRTH ANNIVERSARY. May 4, 1914. The goddess of Mexico's golden age of cinema (1930s–50s), "La Dona" appeared in more than 45 films and was awarded the first Mexico City Prize for a lifetime of distinguished achievement. Born at Alamos, Mexico, Felix died Apr 8, 2002, at Mexico City, Mexico.

FIRST WOMAN BRITISH PRIME MINISTER: 35th ANNIVERSARY. May 4, 1979. With the Conservative Party victory in the British election of May 3, 1979, Margaret Thatcher accepted Queen Elizabeth's appointment as prime minister on May 4. She thus became the first woman prime minister in 700 years of English parliamentary history. Thatcher, dubbed the "Iron Maiden" by a Soviet journalist for her toughness, held the office until forced to resign on Nov 22, 1990.

FREEDOM RIDERS: ANNIVERSARY. May 4, 1961. Militant students joined James Farmer of the Congress of Racial Equality (CORE) to conduct "freedom rides" on public transportation from Washington, DC, across the Deep South to New Orleans. The trips were intended to test Supreme Court decisions and Interstate Commerce Commission regulations prohibiting discrimination in interstate travel. In several places riders were brutally beaten by local people and policemen. On May 14 members of the Ku Klux Klan attacked the Freedom Riders in Birmingham, AL, while local police watched. In Mississippi, Freedom Riders were jailed. They never made it to New Orleans. The rides were patterned after a similar challenge to segregation, the 1947 Journey of Reconciliation, which tested the US Supreme Court's June 3, 1946, ban against segregation in interstate bus travel.

GOODWILL INDUSTRIES WEEK. May 4–10. To celebrate and recognize Goodwill Industries' job training and community-based services, including free tax preparation and youth mentoring, that help people find jobs, earn paychecks and strengthen their families and communities. Goodwill® provides opportunities for people with disabilities, those who lack education or job experience and others who face challenges to finding employment. Each year, Goodwill celebrates Goodwill Industries Week by hosting a Virtual Career Fair to connect employers with qualified job seekers. Annually, the first full week of May. For info: Goodwill Industries International, Public Relations Department. Phone: (301) 530-6500. E-mail: newsroom@goodwill.org. Web: www.goodwill.org.

HAYMARKET SQUARE RIOT: ANNIVERSARY. May 4, 1886. Labor union unrest at Chicago, IL, led to violence when a crowd of unemployed men tried to enter the McCormick Reaper Works, where a strike was under way. Although no one was killed, anarchist groups called a mass meeting in Haymarket Square to avenge the "massacre." When the police advanced on the demonstrators, a bomb was thrown and several policemen were killed. Four leaders of the demonstration were hanged, and another committed suicide in jail. Three others were given jail terms. The case aroused considerable controversy around the world. See also: "Haymarket Pardon: Anniversary" (June 26).

HEPBURN, AUDREY: 85th BIRTH ANNIVERSARY. May 4, 1929. Audrey Hepburn, whose first major movie role in *Roman Holiday* (1953) won her an Academy Award as Best Actress, was born Edda Van Heemstra Hepburn-Rusten near Brussels, Belgium. She made 26 movies during her career and received four additional Oscar nominations. During the latter years of her life, Hepburn served as spokesperson for the United Nations Children's Fund, traveling worldwide raising money for the organization. Audrey Hepburn died Jan 20, 1993, at Tolochenaz, Switzerland.

HOME AND GARDEN FESTIVAL. May 4. Chestnut Hill, PA. Lively street festival in charming urban village. Garden-related merchandise and handcrafts, live entertainment, food court and children's activities. Annually, the first Sunday in May. Est attendance: 25,000. For info: Peggy Miller, Chestnut Hill Visitors Center, 8426 Germantown Ave, Philadelphia, PA 19118. Phone: (215) 247-6696. E-mail: inquiry@chestnuthillpa.com. Web: www.chestnuthillpa.com.

INTERNATIONAL RESPECT FOR CHICKENS DAY. May 4. Launched in 2005, International Respect for Chickens Day (IRCD) is a project of United Poultry Concerns, a nonprofit organization that promotes the compassionate and respectful treatment of domestic fowl. IRCD is a day to celebrate chickens throughout the world by encouraging people to do an "action" for chickens on May 4, showing the world that chickens matter. Ideas include arranging a library display/video presentation, an IRCD school celebration, letters to the editor, radio talk show participation, a local mall exhibit, etc. UPC supplies posters, brochures, videos and event ideas. For info: United Poultry Concerns, PO Box 150, Machipongo, VA 23405. Phone: (757) 678-7875. Fax: (757) 678-5070. E-mail: karen@upc-online.org. Web: www.upc-online.org.

JAPAN: GREENERY DAY. May 4. National holiday. Celebrates nature. Formerly observed on Apr 29, but moved to May 4 in 2007.

KENT STATE STUDENTS' MEMORIAL DAY: ANNIVERSARY. May 4, 1970. Four students (Allison Krause, 19; Sandra Lee Scheuer, 20; Jeffrey Glenn Miller, 20; and William K. Schroeder, 19) were killed by the National Guard during demonstrations against the Vietnam War at Kent (Ohio) State University.

MANN, HORACE: BIRTH ANNIVERSARY. May 4, 1796. American educator, author and public servant, known as the "father of public education in the US," was born at Franklin, MA. Founder of Westfield (MA) State College, president of Antioch College and editor of the influential *Common School Journal.* Mann died at Yellow Springs, OH, Aug 2, 1859.

May 2014	S	M	T	W	T	F	S
					1	2	3
	4	5	6	7	8	9	10
	11	12	13	14	15	16	17
	18	19	20	21	22	23	24
	25	26	27	28	29	30	31

MOTORCYCLE MASS AND BLESSING OF THE BIKES. May 4. Paterson, NJ. 44th annual. Since 1969 a blessing of motorcycles, their riders and friends. Annually, the first Sunday in May. For info: Cathedral of St. John the Baptist, 381 Grand St, Paterson, NJ 07505. Est attendance: 2,000.

NATIONAL ANXIETY AND DEPRESSION AWARENESS WEEK. May 4–10. Educational programs and screenings for anxiety and depressive disorders. For info: Freedom from Fear, 308 Seaview Ave, Staten Island, NY 10305. Phone: (718) 351-1717, ext 19, for screening locations. Fax: (718) 980-5022. E-mail: help@freedomfromfear.org. Web: freedomfromfear.org.

NATIONAL FAMILY WEEK. May 4–10. Traditionally the first Sunday and the first full week in May are observed as National Family Week in many Christian churches.

NATIONAL HUG HOLIDAY WEEK. May 4–10. Huggers of all ages are invited to make a difference one hug at a time! The Hugs 4 Health movement needs your help to increase hugs, friendship and volunteer support for elderly people living in senior care and residential communities. Send SASE for a "Hugger's Package." For info: Hugs 4 Health, PO Box 896, Seal Beach, CA 90740-0896. Web: www.hugs4health.org.

NATIONAL INFERTILITY SURVIVAL DAY®. May 4. Beat the Mother's Day blues the week *before* Mother's Day. Here is the chance for infertile women and those who love them to celebrate themselves, too! Infertility survivors also are encouraged to reach out to those struggling to find resolution to their challenges, through friendship, fundraising and other supportive and creative endeavors. National Infertility Survival Day® is for those who want to use their experiences to attain positive outcomes for themselves and others. Annually, the first Sunday in May. For info: Beverly Barna. E-mail: infertilitysucks@aol.com. Web: www.infertilitysurvivalday.com.

NATIONAL PET WEEK. May 4–10. To promote responsible pet ownership and public awareness of veterinary medical service for animal health and care. Annually, the first full week in May. For info: The American Veterinary Medical Assn, 1931 N Meacham Rd, Ste 100, Schaumburg, IL 60173-4360. Phone: (800) 248-2862. Web: www.petweek.org.

PETITE AND PROUD DAY. May 4. A day for petite women (those 5'4" and under) to embrace and celebrate their small stature in a big way! Annually, May 4. For info: Elizabeth Bates, PO Box 892, Marquette, MI 49855. Phone: (619) 333-6383. E-mail: elizabeth@thepetiteshop.com.

QUINCY PRESERVES SPRING TOUR. May 4. Quincy, IL. Walking tour of historic homes. Each year the tour features a different neighborhood. Homes range in size from grand mansions to quaint cottages. Annually, the first Sunday in May. Est attendance: 1,000. For info: Quincy Preserves, PO Box 1012, Quincy, IL 62306-1012. Phone: (217) 228-8696.

RHODE ISLAND: INDEPENDENCE DAY. May 4. Rhode Island abandoned allegiance to Great Britain in 1776.

SPACE MILESTONE: *ATLANTIS* (US): 25th ANNIVERSARY. May 4, 1989. First American planetary expedition in 11 years. Space shuttle *Atlantis* was launched, its major objective to deploy the *Magellan* spacecraft on its way to Venus to map the planet's surface. The shuttle was on its 65th orbit when it landed May 8, mission accomplished.

STAR WARS DAY. May 4. A day celebrated worldwide by fans of the *Star Wars* series. Fans greet each other by saying "May the 4th be with you," have lightsaber fights and indulge in other fun connected to the sci-fi world created by George Lucas.

TD BANK FIVE BORO BIKE TOUR. May 4. New York, NY. The largest recreational cycling event in America. Share a truly unique adventure with 32,000 cyclists and experience 42 car-free miles through the five boroughs of New York City. Venture with fellow cyclists onto the Madison Ave, Third Ave, Queensboro, Pulaski and majestic Verrazano-Narrows bridges—what better way is there to see the sights of New York City? Preregistration required. Annually, the first Sunday in May. Est attendance: 32,000. For info: Bike New York, 475 Riverside Dr, 13th Fl, New York, NY 10115. Phone: (212) 870-2080. Fax: (212) 870-2099. E-mail: info@BikeNewYork.org. Web: www.BikeNewYork.org.

TYLER, JULIA GARDINER: BIRTH ANNIVERSARY. May 4, 1820. Second wife of John Tyler, 10th president of the US, born at Gardiners Island, NY. Died at Richmond, VA, July 10, 1889.

WADE-DAVIS RECONSTRUCTION BILL PASSES THE HOUSE: 150th ANNIVERSARY. May 4, 1864. Over the objections of President Abraham Lincoln, the House of Representatives on this date passed the Wade-Davis Reconstruction Bill, containing stiff punitive measures against the South that if put into law would have destroyed Lincoln's more moderate reconstruction aims. The bill was also adamantly opposed by radical Republicans led by Thaddeus Stevens, for whom it was insufficiently severe in its treatment of the Southern rebels. Lincoln eventually killed the bill by using the pocket veto.

BIRTHDAYS TODAY

Erin Andrews, 36, sportscaster, born Lewiston, ME, May 4, 1978.

Francesc (Cesc) Fabregas, 27, soccer player, born Vilessoc de Mar, Spain, May 4, 1987.

Ben Grieve, 38, baseball player, born Arlington, TX, May 4, 1976.

David Guterson, 58, author (*Snow Falling on Cedars*), born Seattle, WA, May 4, 1956.

Jackie Jackson, 63, singer (Jackson 5), born Sigmund Esco Jackson at Gary, IN, May 4, 1951.

Richard Jenkins, 67, actor (*The Visitor*, "Six Feet Under"), born DeKalb, IL, May 4, 1947.

Rory McIlroy, 25, golfer, born Hollywood, Northern Ireland, May 4, 1989.

Roberta Peters, 84, opera singer, born the Bronx, NY, May 4, 1930.

Dawn Staley, 44, former basketball player, born Philadelphia, PA, May 4, 1970.

Randy Travis, 55, country musician, born Marshville, NC, May 4, 1959.

George F. Will, 73, editor, columnist, baseball executive, born Champaign, IL, May 4, 1941.

Pia Zadora, 58, actress, singer, dancer, born Hoboken, NJ, May 4, 1956.

May 5 — Monday

DAY 125 | **240 REMAINING**

AMERICAN MEDICAL ASSOCIATION FOUNDED: ANNIVERSARY. May 5, 1847. The American Medical Association was organized at a meeting at Philadelphia, PA, attended by 250 delegates. This was the first national medical convention in the US.

BATTLE OF PUEBLA: ANNIVERSARY. May 5, 1862. Mexican troops under General Ignacio Zaragoza, outnumbered three to one, defeated invading French forces of Napoleon III at the city of Puebla. This day is commemorated as a national holiday in Mexico.

BATTLE OF THE WILDERNESS: 150th ANNIVERSARY. May 5, 1864. The Battle of the Wilderness was the first major encounter between opposing troops under Robert E. Lee and Ulysses S. Grant. So named for the area of dense forest and underbrush of northern Virginia where it occurred. The engagement was especially fierce, with opposing armies often fighting at point-blank range as the battle lines became obscured in the smoke-filled forest. Both sides suffered heavy casualties totaling more than 28,000, and after the fighting had ceased on the second day, more than 200 wounded Federal troops were trapped and killed by the flames of fires started by the battle.

BEARD, JAMES: BIRTH ANNIVERSARY. May 5, 1903. The "father of American cooking" was born at Portland, OR. In a long and busy culinary career, he penned more than 20 classic cookbooks, appeared on television's first cooking show in 1946 and was an enthusiastic ambassador for American regional cooking. He died Jan 21, 1985. His Greenwich Village brownstone is America's only culinary historic landmark and serves as the headquarters of the James Beard Foundation.

BLY, NELLIE: BIRTH ANNIVERSARY. May 5, 1867. Born at Cochran's Mills, PA. "Nellie Bly" was the pseudonym used by pioneering American journalist Elizabeth Cochrane Seaman. Like her namesake in a Stephen Foster song, Nellie Bly was a social reformer and human rights advocate. As a journalist, she is best known for her exposé of conditions in what were then popularly called "insane asylums," where she posed as an "inmate." As an adventurer, she is best known for her 1889–90 around-the-world tour in 72 days, in which she bettered the time of Jules Verne's fictional character Phileas Fogg by eight days. She died at New York, NY, Jan 27, 1922.

BONZA BOTTLER DAY™. May 5. To celebrate when the number of the day is the same as the number of the month. Bonza Bottler Day™ is an excuse to have a party at least once a month. For more information see Jan 1. For info: Gail Berger, 14 Fernwood Dr, Taylors, SC 29687. Phone: (864) 201-3988. E-mail: bonza@bonzabottlerday.com. Web: www.bonzabottlerday.com.

CARTOONISTS DAY. May 5. To honor all cartoonists in the industry: animation, magazines, comic strips, etc. For info: Polly Keener, 400 W Fairlawn Blvd, Akron, OH 44313. Phone: (330) 836-4448. E-mail: pollytoon@aol.com or hamsteralley@aol.com.

DENMARK: OBSERVATION OF 1945 LIBERATION. May 5. Flag-flying day to commemorate the 1945 liberation of Denmark from the Nazi occupation.

ETHIOPIA: PATRIOTS VICTORY DAY. May 5. National holiday. Commemorates the 1941 liberation of Addis Ababa by British and Ethiopian forces.

IRELAND: MAY DAY BANK HOLIDAY. May 5. Bank holiday in the Republic of Ireland the first Monday in May.

ISRAEL: REMEMBRANCE DAY (YOM HA'ZIKKARON). May 5. Honors the more than 20,000 soldiers killed in battle since the start of the nation's war for independence in 1947. Hebrew calendar date Iyar 4, 5774. Began at sundown May 4. (When Iyar 4 falls on a Sunday, Remembrance Day is observed on the Monday after.)

JAPAN: CHILDREN'S DAY. May 5. National holiday. Observed on the fifth day of the fifth month each year.

JOHNSON, AMY: FLIGHT ANNIVERSARY. May 5, 1930. Yorkshire-born Amy Johnson began the first successful solo flight by a woman from England to Australia. Leaving Croydon Airport in a de Havilland Tiger Moth named *Jason*, she flew 9,960 miles to Port Darwin, Australia, arriving May 28. The song "Amy, Wonderful Amy" celebrated the fame of this "wonder girl of the air," who became a legend in her own lifetime. Serving as an air ferry pilot during WWII, she was lost over the Thames Estuary in 1941.

MARX, KARL: BIRTH ANNIVERSARY. May 5, 1818. German socialist, founder and father of modern communism, author of *Das Kapital* and (with Friedrich Engels) the *Communist Manifesto*. Born at Treves, Germany, he died at London, England, Mar 14, 1883, at age 64.

May 2014	S	M	T	W	T	F	S
					1	2	3
	4	5	6	7	8	9	10
	11	12	13	14	15	16	17
	18	19	20	21	22	23	24
	25	26	27	28	29	30	31

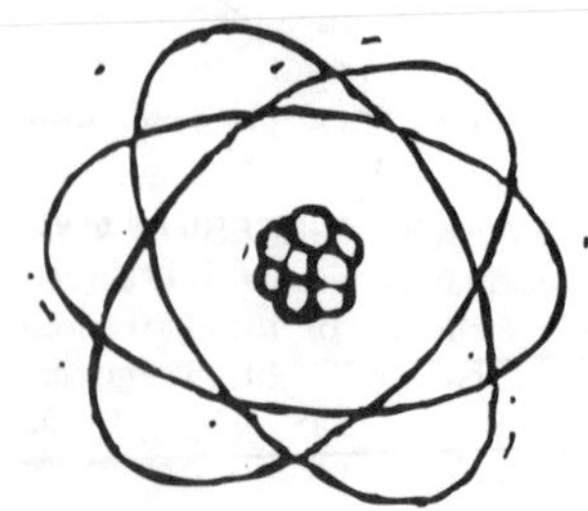

MELANOMA MONDAY. May 5. Also known as National Skin Self-Examination Day. People are encouraged to examine their skin for skin cancer. Annually, the first Monday in May. For info: American Academy of Dermatology, PO Box 4014, Schaumburg, IL 60168-4014. Phone: (866) 503-SKIN (7546). Web: www.aad.org or www.melanomamonday.org.

MEXICO: CINCO DE MAYO. May 5. Mexican national holiday recognizing the anniversary of the Battle of Puebla in 1862. Anniversary is observed by Mexicans everywhere with parades, festivals, dances and speeches.

NATIONAL WILDFLOWER WEEK. May 5–11. A week "to encourage the observation, cultivation and study of native wildflowers." Remarkable photos will be on display at the center in cooperation with *Texas Highways* magazine. Annually, the first full week in May. For info: Lady Bird Johnson Wildflower Center, 4801 La Crosse Ave, Austin, TX 78739-1702. Phone: (512) 232-0100. E-mail: brodriguez@wildflower.org. Web: www.wildflower.org.

NETHERLANDS: LIBERATION DAY. May 5. Marks liberation of the Netherlands from Nazi Germany in 1945.

POWER, TYRONE: 100th BIRTH ANNIVERSARY. May 5, 1914. American actor, born at Cincinnati, OH, into a theatrical family, who was one of the most popular romantic and swashbuckling leads in Hollywood during the 1930s and '40s. Best known for his roles in *Suez, The Mark of Zorro, Blood and Sand, The Razor's Edge* and *Nightmare Alley*. Tyrone Power died Nov 15, 1958, at Madrid, Spain, during a film shoot.

PTA TEACHER APPRECIATION WEEK. May 5–9. PTAs across the country conduct activities to strengthen respect and support for teachers and the teaching profession. Founded in 1984. Annually, the first full week of May. For info: Natl PTA. E-mail: info@pta.org. Web: www.pta.org.

SØREN KIERKEGAARD: BIRTH ANNIVERSARY. May 5, 1813. Philosopher and Christian apologist was born at Copenhagen, Denmark. Kierkegaard's philosophy was a major influence on both existentialism and modern theology. A central idea is his "leap of faith"—taking the risk to believe in the face of doubt. His major works include *Fear and Trembling* (1843), *Either/Or: A Fragment of Life* (1843), *Stages on Life's Way* (1845) and *Sickness Unto Death* (1849). These works deal with the subjectivity of truth and the despair and suffering inherent in life. He also crafted polemics against the conventional institutions of the time, especially the protestant Church of Denmark. Kierkegaard died in Copenhagen on Nov 11, 1855.

SOUTH KOREA: CHILDREN'S DAY. May 5. A time for families to take their children on excursions. Parks and children's centers throughout the country are packed with excited and colorfully dressed children. A national holiday since 1975.

SPACE MILESTONE: *FREEDOM 7* (US). May 5, 1961. First US astronaut in space, second man in space, Alan Shepard, Jr, projected 115 miles into space in suborbital flight reaching a speed of more than 5,000 mph. This was the first piloted *Mercury* mission.

SPRING ASTRONOMY WEEK. May 5–11. To take astronomy to the people. Spring Astronomy Week is observed during the calendar week in which Spring Astronomy Day falls. See also: "Spring Astronomy Day" (May 10). Similar events also take place in the fall. For info: The Astronomical League. Web: www.astroleague.org.

STOCK MARKET CRASH OF 1893: ANNIVERSARY. May 5, 1893. Wall Street stock prices took a sudden drop. By the end of the year, 600 banks had closed. The Philadelphia and Reading, the Erie, the Northern Pacific, the Union Pacific and the Atchison, Topeka and Santa Fe railroads had gone into receivership; 15,000 other businesses went into bankruptcy. Other than the Great Depression of the 1930s, this was the worst economic crisis in US history; 15–20 percent of the workforce was unemployed.

"STOP THE MUSIC" TV PREMIERE: 65th ANNIVERSARY. May 5, 1949. ABC's prime-time musical-game show hosted by Bert Parks. Featured the singing talents of Kay Armen, Jimmy Blaine, Betty Ann Grove, Estelle Loring, Jaye P. Morgan and June Valli, and the dancing numbers of Sonja and Courtney Van Horne. Harry Salter conducted the band.

THAILAND: CORONATION DAY. May 5. National holiday. Commemorates the crowning of the current king in 1946.

UNITED KINGDOM: MAY DAY BANK HOLIDAY. May 5. Bank and public holiday in England, Wales, Scotland and Northern Ireland. Annually, the first Monday in May.

UPDATE YOUR REFERENCES WEEK. May 5–11. A reminder to all job seekers to update their references annually because people are always moving or changing jobs. Additionally, it reminds former supervisors, etc, of who you are. Keeping an updated list of references means job seekers can be ready when the opportunity presents itself. For info: Laura DeCarlo, Career Directors International, 1665 Clover Circle, Melbourne, FL 32935. Phone: (321) 752-0442. E-mail: info@careerdirectors.com.

BIRTHDAYS TODAY

Adele, 26, singer, born Adele Laurie Blue Adkins at Tottenham, England, May 5, 1988.

Chris Brown, 25, singer, born Tappahannock, VA, May 5, 1989.

Pat Carroll, 87, actress (Emmy for "Caesar's Hour"; "The Ted Knight Show"), born Shreveport, LA, May 5, 1927.

Henry Cavill, 31, actor (*Man of Steel*, "The Tudors"), born Jersey, Channel Islands, May 5, 1983.

Richard E. Grant, 57, actor (*Henry and June, LA Story, The Age of Innocence*), born Mbabane, Swaziland, May 5, 1957.

Lance Henriksen, 71, actor (*Dog Day Afternoon, The Terminator, Near Dark*), born New York, NY, May 5, 1943 (some sources say 1940).

Paul Konerko, 38, baseball player, born Providence, RI, May 5, 1976.

Jean-Pierre Leaud, 70, actor (*The 400 Blows, Stolen Kisses, Bed and Board*), born Paris, France, May 5, 1944.

Michael Murphy, 76, actor (*Nashville, Manhattan, Salvador*), born Los Angeles, CA, May 5, 1938.

Ziggy Palffy, 42, hockey player, born Skalica, Czechoslovakia (now Slovakia), May 5, 1972.

Michael Palin, 71, actor, comedian ("Monty Python's Flying Circus," *Life of Brian*), author, born Sheffield, Yorkshire, England, May 5, 1943.

Tina Yothers, 41, singer, actress ("Family Ties"), born Whittier, CA, May 5, 1973.

May 6 — Tuesday

DAY 126 **239 REMAINING**

BABE RUTH'S FIRST MAJOR LEAGUE HOME RUN: ANNIVERSARY. May 6, 1915. George Herman "Babe" Ruth of the Boston Red Sox hit his first major league home run in a game against the New York Yankees in New York.

BANNISTER BREAKS FOUR-MINUTE MILE: 60th ANNIVERSARY. May 6, 1954. Running for the British Amateur Athletic Association in a meet at Oxford University, Roger Bannister broke the four-minute barrier with a time of 3:59.4. Four minutes for a mile at the time was considered not only a physical barrier but also a psychological one.

CHINA: BIRTHDAY OF LORD BUDDHA. May 6. Religious observances are held in Buddhist temples, and Buddha's statue is bathed. Annually, eighth day of fourth lunar month. Date in other countries will differ from China's.

FREUD, SIGMUND: BIRTH ANNIVERSARY. May 6, 1856. Austrian physician, born at Freiberg, Moravia. Founder of psychoanalysis. Freud died at London, England, Sept 23, 1939.

***HINDENBURG* DISASTER: ANNIVERSARY.** May 6, 1937. At 7:20 PM, the dirigible *Hindenburg* exploded as it approached the mooring mast at Lakehurst, NJ, after a transatlantic voyage. Of its 97 passengers and crew, 36 died in the accident, which ended the dream of mass transportation via dirigible.

ISRAEL: INDEPENDENCE DAY (YOM HA'ATZMA'UT). May 6. Celebrates proclamation of independence from British mandatory rule by Palestinian Jews and establishment of the state of Israel and the provisional government May 14, 1948 (Hebrew calendar date: Iyar 5, 5708). Dates in the Hebrew calendar vary from their Gregorian equivalents from year to year. Hebrew calendar date Iyar 5, 5774. Began at sundown May 5. (Because Remembrance Day moved to Monday, May 5, Independence Day is observed on Tuesday, May 6, in 2014.)

JARRELL, RANDELL: 100th BIRTH ANNIVERSARY. May 6, 1914. Poet, author and incisive literary critic, born at Nashville, TN. Jarrell served in the US Army during World War II and the experience greatly influenced his early work, including his most well-known poem, "The Death of the Ball Turret Gunner." He was struck by a car and died Oct 14, 1965, near Chapel Hill, NC.

JOSEPH BRACKETT DAY. May 6. Day honoring the Shaker religious leader, born May 6, 1797, at Cumberland, ME. In 1848 he composed the popular Shaker song "Simple Gifts" (also known as "'Tis the Gift to Be Simple") while at the Shaker community in Alfred, ME. This Shaker dance song became known worldwide after Aaron Copland used it in his score for the ballet *Appalachian Spring* in 1944. Elder Joseph Brackett died at New Gloucester, ME, July 4, 1882. For info: PineTree Productions, 235 Prospect St, Stoughton, MA 02072. E-mail: pinetreemusic@aol.com. Web: www.americanmusicpreservation.com/JosephBrackettSimpleGifts.htm.

MACKINAC ISLAND LILAC FESTIVAL. May 6–18. Mackinac Island, MI. 65th annual. The lilac festival—celebrating the island's thousands of lilac blooms—is the first and largest Mackinac summer event. There are art shows, wine tastings, a lilac symposium and a Grand Parade rich with horse-drawn floats. Favorite festival events include The Feast of Epona Blessing of the Animals, Taste of Mackinac and the Mackinac Island Dog and Pony Show. Est attendance: 30,000. For info: Mackinac Island Tourism Bureau, PO Box 451, Mackinac Island, MI 49757. Phone: (906) 847-3783. Fax: (906) 847-3571. Web: www.mackinacislandlilacfestival.org.

MOON PHASE: FIRST QUARTER. May 6. Moon enters First Quarter phase at 11:15 PM, EDT.

NATIONAL NURSES WEEK. May 6–12. A week to honor the outstanding efforts of nurses everywhere to strengthen the health of the nation. Annually, beginning May 6, National Nurses Day, and ending May 12, Florence Nightingale's birthday. Call or write for a free catalog. For info: American Nurses Assn, 8515 Georgia Ave, Ste 400, Silver Spring, MD 20910. Phone: (800) 244-4ANA. Fax: (301) 628-5001. Web: www.nursingworld.org.

NATIONAL TEACHER DAY. May 6. To pay tribute to American educators, sponsored by the National Education Association, Teacher Day falls during the National PTA's Teacher Appreciation Week. Local communities and organizations are encouraged to use this opportunity to honor those who influence and inspire the next generation through their work. Annually, the Tuesday of the first full week in May. For info: Natl Education Assn, 1201 16th St NW, Washington, DC 20036-3290. Phone: (202) 833-4000. Web: www.nea.org.

NO DIET DAY. May 6. A day to stop dieting and/or stop hazardous weight-loss attempts. No Diet Day celebrates a paradigm shift to the diet-free healthy-living approach to health and well-being, to acceptance and respect for oneself and others. Discover the top 10 reasons not to diet and the risks of weight loss on website. For info: Francie M. Berg, Healthy Weight Network, 402 S 14th St, Hettinger, ND 58639. E-mail: fmberg@healthyweight.net (please put "Berg-No Diet Day" in subject line). Web: www.healthyweight.net.

NO HOMEWORK DAY. May 6. Millions of kids, all of them overloaded with homework, get a much-needed night off tonight. Give 'em a break, teachers! These young folks are working harder than Mom 'n' Dad. (©2006 by WH.) For info: Thomas & Ruth Roy, Wellcat Holidays, 2418 Long Ln, Lebanon, PA 17046. Phone: (717) 279-0184. E-mail: info@wellcat.com. Web: www.wellcat.com.

PEARY, ROBERT E.: BIRTH ANNIVERSARY. May 6, 1856. Born at Cresson, PA. Peary served as a cartographic draftsman in the US Coast and Geodetic Survey for two years and then joined the US Navy's Corps of Civil Engineers in 1881. He first worked as an explorer in tropical climates as he served as subchief of the Inter-Ocean Canal Survey in Nicaragua. After reading about the inland ice of Greenland, Peary became attracted to the Arctic. He organized and led eight Arctic expeditions and is credited with the verification of Greenland's island formation, proving that the polar ice cap extended beyond 82° north latitude, and the discovery of the Melville meteorite on Melville Bay, in addition to his famous discovery of the North Pole, Apr 6, 1909. Peary died Feb 20, 1920, at Washington, DC.

PENN, JOHN: BIRTH ANNIVERSARY. May 6, 1740. Signer of the Declaration of Independence, born at Caroline County, VA. Died Sept 14, 1788.

PRIMARY DAY: LIVE FROM DELAWARE STREET. May 6. Indianapolis, IN. Visit the Benjamin Harrison Presidential Site and listen to the conversations and gossip of the day as you enter each room and meet and speak with all the family members and household staff, whose roles are re-created by exceptional actors. For info: Benjamin Harrison Presidential Site, 1230 N Delaware St, Indianapolis, IN 46202. Phone: (317) 631-1888. Fax: (317) 632-5488. E-mail: events@bhpsite.org. Web: www.bhpsite.org.

SACK OF ROME: ANNIVERSARY. May 6, 1527. The Renaissance ended with the Sack of Rome, which began on this date. As part of a series of wars between the Hapsburg Empire and the French monarchy, German troops killed some 4,000 inhabitants of Rome and looted works of art and libraries. Pope Clement VII, who supported the French, was imprisoned at the Castel St. Angelo. Nearly a year passed before order could be restored in the city.

★ ★ ★

May 2014	S	M	T	W	T	F	S
					1	2	3
	4	5	6	7	8	9	10
	11	12	13	14	15	16	17
	18	19	20	21	22	23	24
	25	26	27	28	29	30	31

STOVER, RUSSELL: BIRTH ANNIVERSARY. May 6, 1888. Entrepreneur, born in a sod house at Alton, KS, who became the founder of a candy company whose products can now be found in more than 20 countries around the world. Stover and his wife, Clara, launched their candy business from their home in Denver, CO, in 1923, with Clara as the sole production team and Russell the sales force. The venture was practically an overnight success with the Stovers opening their first factory the following year. At the time of his death at Kansas City, MO, on May 11, 1954, Russell Stover Candies was selling 11 million pounds of candy each year.

TAGORE, RABINDRANATH: BIRTH ANNIVERSARY. May 6, 1861. Hindu poet, mystic and musical composer born at Calcutta, India. A prolific author, he wrote some 50 volumes of poetry besides his other work. He received the Nobel Prize in Literature in 1913. Died at Calcutta, Aug 7, 1941. His birthday is observed in Bangladesh on the 25th day of the Bengali month of Baishakha (second week of May), when the poet laureate is honored with songs, dances and discussions of his works.

VALENTINO, RUDOLPH: BIRTH ANNIVERSARY. May 6, 1895. Rodolpho Alfonzo Rafaello Pietro Filiberto Guglieimi Di Valentina D'Antonguolla, whose professional name was Rudolph Valentino, was born at Castellaneta, Italy. Popular cinema actor. For years press reports claimed that "at least one weeping veiled woman in black brought flowers to his tomb" (at Hollywood Memorial Park) every year on the anniversary of his death at New York, NY, Aug 23, 1926.

WELLES, ORSON: BIRTH ANNIVERSARY. May 6, 1915. Actor and director born at Kenosha, WI. *Citizen Kane*, which he directed and in which he played the title role, is one of the most influential films ever made. Other films in which he had a role include *The Third Man* and *The Magnificent Ambersons*. Welles died at Los Angeles, CA, Oct 10, 1985.

WORLD ASTHMA DAY. May 6. This day is organized by the Global Initiative for Asthma (GINA) in collaboration with healthcare groups and asthma educators to raise awareness about asthma and improve asthma care throughout the world. The first day, in 1998, was celebrated in more than 35 countries in conjunction with the first World Asthma Meeting held in Barcelona, Spain. Participation has increased with each World Asthma Day held since then, and the day has become one of the world's most important asthma awareness and education events. Annually, the first Tuesday in May. For info: Global Initiative for Asthma. Web: www.ginasthma.org.

BIRTHDAYS TODAY

Tom Bergeron, 59, television personality and host ("Hollywood Squares," "America's Funniest Home Videos," "Dancing with the Stars"), born Haverhill, MA, May 6, 1955.

Tony Blair, 61, former British prime minister (1997–2007), born Edinburgh, Scotland, May 6, 1953.

Martin Brodeur, 42, hockey player, born Montreal, QC, Canada, May 6, 1972.

George Clooney, 53, actor (Oscar for *Syriana*; *The Descendants, Ocean's Eleven, Michael Clayton*), born Lexington, KY, May 6, 1961.

Alan Dale, 67, actor ("Ugly Betty"), born Dunedin, South Island, New Zealand, May 6, 1947.

Roma Downey, 50, actress ("Touched by an Angel"), born Derry, Northern Ireland, May 6, 1964.

Leslie Hope, 49, actress ("24," *Talk Radio*), born Halifax, NS, Canada, May 6, 1965.

Ben Masters, 67, actor (*All That Jazz, Making Mr Right*), born Corvallis, OR, May 6, 1947.

Willie Mays, 83, Hall of Fame baseball player, born Westfield, AL, May 6, 1931.

Chris Paul, 29, basketball player, born Winston-Salem, NC, May 6, 1985.

Bob Seger, 69, singer, musician, born Ann Arbor, MI, May 6, 1945.

Richard C. Shelby, 80, US Senator (R, Alabama), born Birmingham, AL, May 6, 1934.

Gabourey Sidibe, 31, actress (*Precious: Based on the Novel "Push" by Sapphire*, "The Big C"), born Brooklyn, NY, May 6, 1983.

Lynn Whitfield, 61, actress (*Stepmom, Eve's Bayou*), born Baton Rouge, LA, May 6, 1953.

May 7 — Wednesday

DAY 127 **238 REMAINING**

BEAUFORT SCALE DAY (FRANCIS BEAUFORT BIRTH ANNIVERSARY). May 7, 1774. A day to honor the British naval officer, Sir Francis Beaufort, who in 1806 devised a scale of wind force from 0 (calm) to 12 (hurricane) that was based on observation, not requiring any special instruments. The scale was adopted for international use in 1874 and has since been enlarged and refined. Beaufort was born at Flower Hill, Meath, Ireland, and died at Brighton, England, Dec 17, 1857.

BEETHOVEN'S NINTH SYMPHONY PREMIERE: ANNIVERSARY. May 7, 1824. Beethoven's Ninth Symphony in D Minor was performed for the first time at Vienna, Austria. Known as the *Choral* because of his use of voices in symphonic form for the first time, the Ninth was his musical interpretation of Schiller's *Ode to Joy*. Beethoven was completely deaf when he composed it, and it was said a soloist had to tug on his sleeve when the performance was over to get him to turn around and see the enthusiastic response he could not hear.

BONNIE BLUE NATIONAL HORSE SHOW. May 7–10. Virginia Horse Center, Lexington, VA. Major all-breed event, "A"-rated show of the American Horse Show Association. For info: Virginia Horse Center, 487 Maury River Rd, Lexington, VA 24450. Phone: (540) 464-2950. Fax: (540) 464-2999. E-mail: dwork@horsecenter.org. Web: www.horsecenter.org.

BRAHMS, JOHANNES: BIRTH ANNIVERSARY. May 7, 1833. Regarded as one of the greatest composers of 19th-century music, Johannes Brahms was born at Hamburg, Germany. His works were firmly rooted in traditional classical principles and truly Romantic in spirit. When Brahms was 17, his talent was discovered and promoted by the Hungarian violinist Eduard Remenyi, who took him on a national concert tour. During this tour Brahms met composer Robert Schumann and his wife, Clara Schumann, who was also a composer and the most brilliant concert pianist of her day. The endorsement and support of the Schumanns quickly established his musical reputation. After Schumann's death in 1856, Brahms became devoted to Clara, supporting her and her children. Brahms completed his most important work, *Ein Deutsches Requiem* (*The German Requiem*), after his mother's death in 1865. It is considered one of the best examples of 19th-century choral music and was presented with much success throughout Germany. Brahms died at Vienna, Austria, Apr 3, 1897.

BROWNING, ROBERT: BIRTH ANNIVERSARY. May 7, 1812. English poet and husband of poet Elizabeth Barrett Browning, born at Camberwell, near London. Known for his dramatic monologues. Died at Venice, Italy, Dec 12, 1889.

COOPER, GARY: BIRTH ANNIVERSARY. May 7, 1901. Frank James Cooper was born at Helena, MT. He changed his name to Gary at the start of his movie career. He is best known by baseball fans for his portrayal of Lou Gehrig in *The Pride of the Yankees*. Other films include *Wings, The Virginian, The Plainsman, Beau Geste, Sergeant York* (for which he won his first Academy Award), *High Noon* (winning his second Oscar for Best Actor), *The Court Martial of Billy Mitchell* and *Friendly Persuasion*. He died May 13, 1961, at Hollywood, CA.

DIEN BIEN PHU FALLS: 60th ANNIVERSARY. May 7, 1954. Vietnam's victory over France at Dien Bien Phu ended the Indochina War.

DOW JONES TOPS 15,000: ANNIVERSARY. May 5, 2013. The Dow Jones Index of major industrial stocks closed above 15,000 for the first time. On May 3, 2013, it had briefly surpassed 15,000 before closing at 14,974.

EL SALVADOR: DAY OF THE SOLDIER. May 7. National holiday. Anniversary of the founding of the country's armed forces in 1824.

ENGLAND: MITSUBISHI MOTORS BADMINTON HORSE TRIALS. May 7–11. Badminton, Gloucestershire. Famous international horse trials consisting of show jumping, cross-country and dressage. Est attendance: 180,000. For info: Box Office, Badminton Horse Trials, Badminton, Glos, England GL9 1DF. Phone: (44) (1454) 21-8375. Fax: (44) (1454) 21-8596. E-mail: info@badminton-horse.co.uk. Web: www.badminton-horse.co.uk.

FIRST PRESIDENTIAL INAUGURAL BALL: 125th ANNIVERSARY. May 7, 1789. Celebrating the inauguration of George Washington, the first Presidential Inaugural Ball was held at New York, NY.

GERMANY: 825th HAMBURG HARBOR BIRTHDAY. May 7, 1189. "Hafengeburtstag" celebrates establishment of Hamburg as a free city.

GERMANY'S FIRST SURRENDER: ANNIVERSARY. May 7, 1945. Russian, American, British and French ranking officers crowded into a second-floor recreation room of a small red-brick schoolhouse (which served as General Dwight Eisenhower's headquarters) at Reims, Germany. Representing Germany, Field Marshal Alfred Jodl signed an unconditional surrender of all German fighting forces. After a signing that took almost 40 minutes, Jodl was ushered into Eisenhower's presence. The American general asked the German if he fully understood what he had signed and informed Jodl that he would be held personally responsible for any deviation from the terms of the surrender, including the requirement that German commanders sign a formal surrender to the USSR at a time and place determined by that government.

GREAT AMERICAN GRUMP OUT. May 7. We are asking America to go 24 hours without being grumpy, crabby or rude. Can *you* meet the challenge? Schoolchildren, parents, businesses and the community will be involved in promoting peace, harmony and lighthearted humor on this day. For info: Janice Hathy, Smile Mania, 1300 N River Rd, C-15, Venice, FL 34293. Phone: (941) 492-2166. E-mail: janlsmile@aol.com. Web: www.smilemania.com.

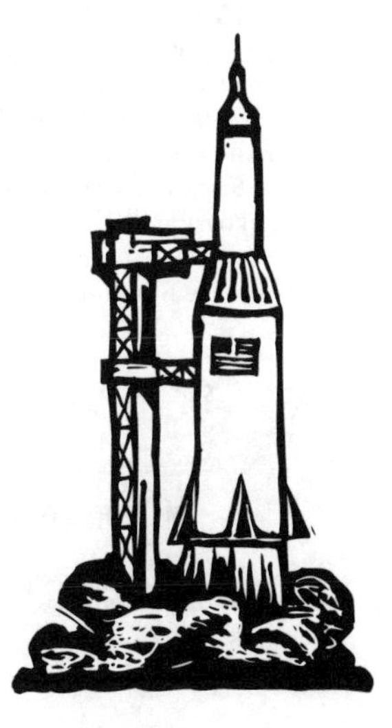

HUME, DAVID: BIRTH ANNIVERSARY. May 7, 1711. Scottish Enlightenment philosopher born at Edinburgh (Old Style date, Apr 26, 1711). Hume's ideas present the culmination of the philosophical movement of empiricism. Hume addressed such questions as the limits of knowledge. He rejected metaphysical questions and stated that we should be skeptical of all conclusions reached by the use of reason. A prolific author, Hume wrote the six-volume *History of England* (1754–62), as well as other essays and historical work. Today, his *A Treatise of Human Nature* is seen as his most important work. Hume died on Aug 25, 1776, at Edinburgh.

"KRAFT TELEVISION THEATRE" TV PREMIERE: ANNIVERSARY. May 7, 1947. Live theatrical programs appearing on both the NBC and ABC networks. The show was a gold mine for discovering new talent. Among the playwrights getting their big breaks were Rod Serling, Paddy Chayefsky and Tad Mosel. Some of the show's most notable plays were "The Easy Mark" (1951) with Jack Lemmon, "Double in Ivory" (1953) with Lee Remick, "To Live in Peace" (1953) with Anne Bancroft, "The Missing Years" (1954) with Anthony Perkins and Mary Astor and "A Profile in Courage" (1956) with James Whitmore. The last play was based on a book by Senator John F. Kennedy, who appeared on the program to introduce the drama.

***LUSITANIA* SINKING: ANNIVERSARY.** May 7, 1915. British passenger liner *Lusitania*, on its return trip from New York to Liverpool, carrying nearly 2,000 passengers, was torpedoed by a German submarine off the coast of Ireland, sinking within minutes; 1,198 lives were lost. US president Woodrow Wilson sent a note of protest to Berlin on May 13, but Germany, which had issued a warning in advance, pointed to *Lusitania*'s cargo of ammunition for Britain. The US maintained its neutrality for the time being.

MacLEISH, ARCHIBALD: BIRTH ANNIVERSARY. May 7, 1892. American poet and librarian of Congress (1939–44), born at Glencoe, IL. MacLeish, who was also a playwright, Pulitzer Prize winner, editor, lawyer, professor and farmer, died at Boston, MA, Apr 20, 1982.

NATIONAL SCHOOL NURSE DAY. May 7. Established to foster a better understanding of the role of school nurses in the educational setting. Annually, the Wednesday of National Nurses Week (May 6–12). For info: NASN, 1100 Wayne Ave, Ste 925, Silver Spring, MD 20910. Phone: (866) 627-6767. E-mail: nasn@nasn.org. Web: www.nasn.org.

"STRIKE IT RICH" TV PREMIERE: ANNIVERSARY. May 7, 1951. The downtrodden and the poverty-stricken showed up on this game show to tell their sob stories. Whoever received the most votes from the studio audience was declared the winner. The losers were able to receive help from sympathetic viewers through a telephone "heart line." The show got in trouble with the New York City Welfare Department in 1954 when 55 of the show's hopeful contestants remained in New York and went on welfare.

TCHAIKOVSKY, PETER ILICH: BIRTH ANNIVERSARY. May 7, 1840. (New Style date.) One of the outstanding composers of all time, Peter Ilich Tchaikovsky was born at Vatkinsk, Russia. Among his famous works are the symphony *Pathétique*; the opera *Eugene Onegin*; and the ballets *Swan Lake*, *Sleeping Beauty* and *The Nutcracker*. He was the first to turn the ballet into a sustained dramatic expression. Tchaikovsky died of cholera during an epidemic at St. Petersburg, Nov 6, 1893—nine days after conducting his *Pathétique* symphony for the first time.

☆ ☆ ☆

May 2014

S	M	T	W	T	F	S
				1	2	3
4	5	6	7	8	9	10
11	12	13	14	15	16	17
18	19	20	21	22	23	24
25	26	27	28	29	30	31

TWENTY-SEVENTH AMENDMENT RATIFIED: ANNIVERSARY. May 7, 1992. The 27th Amendment to the Constitution was ratified, prohibiting Congress from giving itself midterm pay raises.

UNITAS, JOHNNY: BIRTH ANNIVERSARY. May 7, 1933. Born at Pittsburgh, PA, Johnny Unitas played football for the University of Louisville. After college, he went to work as a construction worker but continued to play football (for $6 per game) for the Bloomfield Rams, a semipro team that played on dirt, not grass. Based on a fan's letter, the Baltimore Colts gave him a conditional contract, and soon he was a star. He played 17 seasons for the Colts, was the MVP three times, went to 10 Pro Bowls and led his team to three NFL championships. He was inducted into the Pro Football Hall of Fame in 1979 and has often been called the greatest quarterback ever to play the game. He died at Baltimore, MD, Sept 11, 2002.

BIRTHDAYS TODAY

Amy Heckerling, 60, filmmaker (*Fast Times at Ridgemont High*, *Look Who's Talking*), born New York, NY, May 7, 1954.

Gary R. Herbert, 67, Governor of Utah (R), born American Fork, UT, May 7, 1947.

Shawn Marion, 36, basketball player, born Waukegan, IL, May 7, 1978.

Peter Reckell, 59, actor ("Days of Our Lives"), born Elkhart, IN, May 7, 1955.

May 8 — Thursday

DAY 128 **237 REMAINING**

BATTLE OF THE CORAL SEA: ANNIVERSARY. May 8, 1942. Beginning on this date, the Battle of the Coral Sea impeded Japanese expansion and introduced a new form of naval warfare. None of the surface vessels exchanged fire—the entire battle was waged by aircraft. The US lost a carrier, destroyer and tanker. The Japanese lost seven warships, including a carrier.

CZECH REPUBLIC: LIBERATION DAY. May 8. Commemorates the liberation of Czechoslovakia from the Germans in 1945.

DUNANT, JEAN-HENRI: BIRTH ANNIVERSARY. May 8, 1828. Author and philanthropist, founder of the Red Cross, born at Geneva, Switzerland. His book *Un Souvenir de Solferino* (1862) is both a firsthand recounting of one of the bloodiest battles of the 19th century and a proposal to establish relief aid to wartime wounded. The conference that resulted as a response to its call to action had two significant results: the founding of the Red Cross and the implementation of the international treaty known as the Geneva Convention. Dunant was awarded the first Nobel Peace Prize in 1901. Died at Heiden, Switzerland, Oct 30, 1910.

ENGLAND: HELSTON FURRY DANCE. May 8. Helston, Cornwall. The world-famous Helston Furry Dance is held each year on May 8 (except when the 8th is a Sunday or Monday, in which case it is held on the preceding Saturday). Dancing around the streets begins early in the morning and continues throughout the day. The dance leaves Guildhall at the stroke of noon and winds its way into and out of many of the larger buildings.

FRANCE: VICTORY DAY. May 8. Commemorates the surrender of Germany to Allied forces and the cessation of hostilities in 1945.

GERMANY'S SECOND SURRENDER: ANNIVERSARY. May 8, 1945. Stalin refused to recognize the document of unconditional surrender signed at Reims the previous day, so a second signing was held near Berlin. The event was turned into an elaborate formal ceremony by the Soviets, who had lost some 20 million lives during the war. As in the Reims document, the end of hostilities was set for 12:01 AM local time on May 9.

GOTTSCHALK, LOUIS MOREAU: BIRTH ANNIVERSARY. May 8, 1829. American pianist of international fame who toured the US during the Civil War. Gottschalk composed for the piano, combining American and Creole folk themes and rhythms in his work. Born at New Orleans, LA, he died Dec 18, 1869, at Rio de Janeiro, Brazil.

HIDALGO Y COSTILLA, MIGUEL: BIRTH ANNIVERSARY. May 8, 1753. Father of Mexican Independence and Catholic priest, born at Corralejo, New Spain (now Mexico). Famously, on Sept 16, 1810, he rang the church bell at Dolores calling for the people to fight for independence from Spain. Defeated at the Battle of Calderón Bridge on Jan 17, 1811, Hidalgo tried to lead his depleted revolutionary forces to the US but was captured. He was executed on July 30, 1811, at Chihuahua.

JOHNSON, ROBERT: BIRTH ANNIVERSARY. May 8, 1911. Born at Hazelhurst, MS, and murdered at age 27, Aug 16, 1938, at Greenwood, MS (poisoned by a jealous husband), Johnson was a master blues guitarist, singer and songwriter of broad influence. He developed a unique guitar style of such skill that it was said he acquired his ability by selling his soul to the devil. Johnson's only two recording sessions captured the classics "Sweet Home Chicago," "Cross Road Blues," "Me and the Devil Blues" and others. Johnson was inducted into the Blues Hall of Fame in 1980 and the Rock and Roll Hall of Fame in 1986.

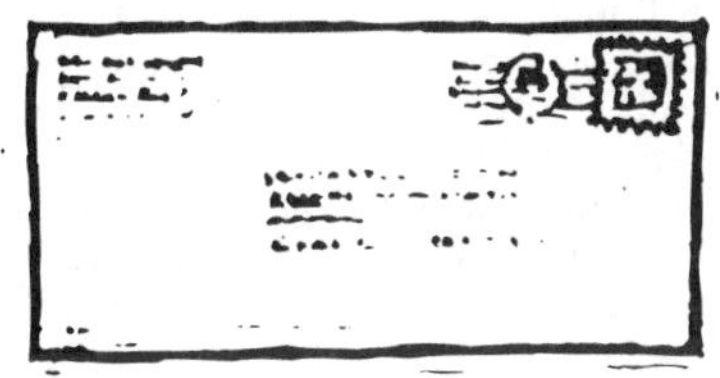

LAVOISIER, ANTOINE-LAURENT: EXECUTION ANNIVERSARY. May 8, 1794. French chemist and the "father of modern chemistry." Especially noted for having first explained the real nature of combustion and for showing that matter is not destroyed in chemical reactions. Born at Paris, France, Aug 26, 1743, Lavoisier was guillotined at the Place de la Révolution for his former position as a tax collector. The Revolutionary Tribunal is reported to have responded to a plea to spare his life with the statement: "We need no more scientists in France."

LISTON, SONNY: BIRTH ANNIVERSARY. May 8, 1932. Charles "Sonny" Liston, boxer born at St. Francis County, AR. Liston rose above a record of criminal activity to defeat Floyd Patterson for the heavyweight title on Sept 25, 1962. He defeated Patterson in a rematch but then lost the title to Cassius Clay, who later changed his name to Muhammad Ali. In a rematch Ali knocked Liston out with a punch few observers saw. Died at Las Vegas, NV, Dec 30, 1970.

MARTIN Z. MOLLUSK DAY. May 8. Moorlyn Terrace Beach, Ocean City, NJ. If Martin Z. Mollusk, a hermit crab, sees his shadow at 11 AM, EST, summer comes a week early in Ocean City—if he doesn't, summer begins on time. For info: Mark Soifer, City Hall, 9th St and Asbury Ave, Ocean City, NJ 08226. Phone: (609) 525-9300 or (609) 364-4010. Fax: (609) 525-0301. E-mail: msoifer@hotmail.com.

MOUNT PELÉE ERUPTION: ANNIVERSARY. May 8, 1902. In the worst volcanic disaster of the 20th century, Mount Pelée erupted on the tiny French Caribbean island of Martinique. In minutes a cloud of ashes, gases and rocks destroyed the thriving port city of Saint-Pierre, killing all but one of its 30,000 inhabitants.

NO SOCKS DAY. May 8. If we give up wearing socks for one day, it will mean a little less laundry, thereby contributing to the betterment of the environment. Besides, we will all feel a bit freer, at least for one day. Annually, May 8. (©2006 by WH.) For info: Thomas & Ruth Roy, Wellcat Holidays, 2418 Long Ln, Lebanon, PA 17046. Phone: (717) 279-0184. E-mail: info@wellcat.com. Web: www.wellcat.com.

OUIMET, FRANCIS DESALES: BIRTH ANNIVERSARY. May 8, 1893. American amateur golfer who is credited with establishing the popularity of golf in the US. Born at Brookline, MA, he began his golfing career as a caddy. In 1913, at age 20, he generated national enthusiasm for the game when he became the first American and first amateur to win the US Open Golf Championship. He won the US Amateur Championship in 1914 and 1931 and was a member of the US Walker Cup team from its first tournament in 1922 until 1949, serving as its nonplaying captain for six of those years. In 1951 he became the first American to be elected captain of the Royal and Ancient Golf Club of St. Andrews, Scotland. Ouimet died at Newton, MA, Sept 2, 1967.

SLOVAKIA: LIBERATION DAY. May 8. Commemorates the liberation of Czechoslovakia from the Germans in 1945.

SORENSEN, THEODORE (TED): BIRTH ANNIVERSARY. May 8, 1928. Political strategist and trusted adviser to President John F. Kennedy, born at Lincoln, NE. As a researcher and speechwriter for Kennedy beginning in the early 1950s, Sorensen collaborated on the then-senator's Pulitzer Prize–winning *Profiles in Courage* (1956). His writing was considered the stuff of genius, and included Kennedy's famous "Ask not what your country can do for you . . . " inaugural address in 1961 and a 1962 letter to Nikita Khrushchev that may well have prevented nuclear conflict. After Kennedy's death, Sorensen practiced law and remained prominent in Democratic politics. He died at New York, NY, Oct 31, 2010.

TRUMAN, HARRY S: BIRTH ANNIVERSARY. May 8, 1884. The 33rd president of the US, succeeded to that office upon the death of Franklin D. Roosevelt, Apr 12, 1945, and served until Jan 20, 1953. Born at Lamar, MO, Truman was the last of the nine US presidents who did not attend college. Affectionately nicknamed "Give 'em Hell Harry" by admirers. Truman died at Kansas City, MO, Dec 26, 1972. His birthday is a holiday in Missouri.

UNITED NATIONS: TIME OF REMEMBRANCE AND RECONCILIATION FOR THOSE WHO LOST THEIR LIVES DURING THE SECOND WORLD WAR. May 8–9. By its Resolution 59/26 of Nov 22, 2004, the General Assembly declared these days as a time of remembrance and reconciliation and invited member states, United Nations bodies, nongovernmental organizations and individuals to observe annually either one or both of those days in an appropriate manner to pay tribute to all those who lost their lives in WWII. For info: United Nations, Dept of Public Info, New York, NY 10017. Web: www.un.org.

V-E DAY: ANNIVERSARY. May 8, 1945. Victory in Europe Day commemorates unconditional surrender of Germany to Allied forces. The surrender document was signed by German representatives at General Dwight D. Eisenhower's headquarters at Reims to become effective, and hostilities to end, at one minute past midnight May 9, 1945, which was 9:01 PM, EDT, on May 8 in the US. President Harry S Truman on May 8 declared May 9, 1945, to be "V-E Day," but it later came to be observed on May 8. A separate German surrender to the USSR was signed at Karlshorst, near Berlin, May 8. See also: "Russia: Victory Day" (May 9).

WORLD RED CROSS RED CRESCENT DAY. May 8. A day for commemorating the 1828 birth of Jean-Henri Dunant, the Swiss founder of the International Red Cross Movement in 1863, and for recognizing the humanitarian work of the Red Cross and Red Crescent around the world. For info: International Committee of the Red Cross. Web: www.icrc.org or www.redcross.org.

BIRTHDAYS TODAY

Stephen Amell, 33, actor (*Justice for Natalee Holloway,* "Arrow," "Hung"), born Toronto, ON, Canada, May 8, 1981.

David Attenborough, 88, author, naturalist (*Life on Earth, Trials of Life*), born London, England, May 8, 1926.

Joe Bonamassa, 37, guitarist, born New Hartford, NY, May 8, 1977.

Bill Cowher, 57, sportscaster, former football coach and player, born Pittsburgh, PA, May 8, 1957.

Melissa Gilbert, 50, actress ("Little House on the Prairie," *The Miracle Worker*), born Los Angeles, CA, May 8, 1964.

Enrique Iglesias, 39, singer, born Madrid, Spain, May 8, 1975.

David Keith, 60, actor (*The Great Santini, An Officer and a Gentleman*), director, born Knoxville, TN, May 8, 1954.

Bobby Labonte, 50, race car driver, born Corpus Christi, TX, May 8, 1964.

Ronald Mandel (Ronnie) Lott, 55, Hall of Fame football player, born Albuquerque, NM, May 8, 1959.

Janet McTeer, 53, actress (*Albert Nobbs, Tumbleweeds*), born Newcastle, Tyne and Wear, England, May 8, 1961.

Thomas Pynchon, 77, author (*Vineland, V, Gravity's Rainbow*), born Glen Cove, NY, May 8, 1937.

Don Rickles, 88, comedian, actor (*Blazing Saddles*, "The Dean Martin Show"), born New York, NY, May 8, 1926.

Toni Tennille, 71, singer (Captain & Tennille), born Montgomery, AL, May 8, 1943.

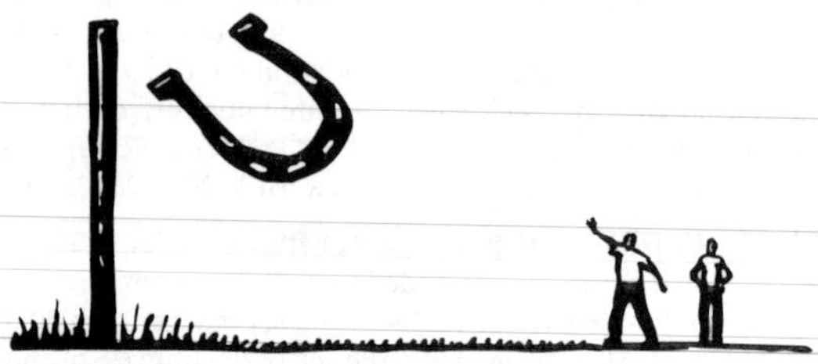

May 9 — Friday

DAY 129 — **236 REMAINING**

BARRIE, JAMES M.: BIRTH ANNIVERSARY. May 9, 1860. Playwright and author, born at Kirriemuir, Angus, Scotland. Barrie is best known for his play *Peter Pan, or the Boy Who Would Not Grow Up*, which was first performed in 1904 and published in 1928. Barrie died June 19, 1937, at London, England.

BLUEBERRY HILL OPEN DART TOURNAMENT. May 9–11. St. Louis, MO. 42nd annual. America's oldest and largest pub dart tournament open to everyone. Est attendance: 450. For info: Joe Edwards, Blueberry Hill, 6504 Delmar in The Loop, St. Louis, MO 63130. Phone: (314) 727-4444. Web: www.BlueberryHill.com.

BOYD, BELLE: BIRTH ANNIVERSARY. May 9, 1843. The notorious Confederate spy who later became an actress and lecturer was born at Martinsburg, VA. Author of the book *Belle Boyd in Camp and Prison*, she died June 11, 1900, at Kilbourne, WI.

May 2014	S	M	T	W	T	F	S
					1	2	3
	4	5	6	7	8	9	10
	11	12	13	14	15	16	17
	18	19	20	21	22	23	24
	25	26	27	28	29	30	31

BRITISH CAPTURE ENIGMA MACHINE: ANNIVERSARY. May 9, 1941. During WWII, when a German U-110 submarine attacked a British convoy, two British vessels, the *Bulldog* and *Aubretia*, were able to retaliate so quickly with depth charges that the submarine was disabled and unable to dive. With the submarine captured, British sailors investigated the radio room and discovered the typewriter-like Enigma, a ciphering machine that enabled safe German communication, and documents of tables that helped explain how it worked. The U-110's capture was kept secret, and British cryptographers used this break to begin unraveling German code during the war.

BROWN, JOHN: BIRTH ANNIVERSARY. May 9, 1800. Abolitionist leader born at Torrington, CT, and hanged Dec 2, 1859, at Charles Town, WV. Leader of attack on Harpers Ferry, VA, Oct 16, 1859, which was intended to give impetus to the movement for escape and freedom for slaves. His aim was frustrated and in fact resulted in increased polarization and sectional animosity. Legendary martyr of the abolitionist movement.

ELECTRA GOAT BBQ COOK-OFF. May 9–10. Electra Goat Grounds, Electra, TX. Goat brisket, pork ribs, chicken cook-off, live band, Jackpot Steak & Beans Competition, children's games and crafts. Friday night dance and salsa contest. Est attendance: 2,000. For info: Sherry Strange, Electra Chamber of Commerce, 112 W Cleveland, Electra, TX 76360. Phone: (940) 495-3577. E-mail: electracoc@electratel.net. Web: www.electratexas.org.

EUROPEAN UNION: ANNIVERSARY OBSERVANCE. May 9, 1950. Member countries of the European Union commemorate the announcement by French statesman Robert Schuman of the "Schuman Plan" for establishing a single authority for production of coal, iron and steel in France and Germany. The European Coal and Steel Community was founded in 1952. This organization was a forerunner of the European Economic Community, founded in 1958, which later became the European Union. At the European Summit at Milan in 1985, this day was proclaimed the Day of Europe.

FINTASTIC FRIDAY: GIVING SHARKS A VOICE! May 9. Kids nationwide will join WhaleTimes, Inc and the Shark Research Institute to raise their voices to help save unsung ocean heroes—sharks. This collaborative effort of two nonprofit organizations will raise awareness of the worldwide plight of sharks and get students involved in an important conservation issue. People kill as many as 100 million sharks a year for fins, liver or meat. Populations are declining at catastrophic rates. It is time to correct and update the image of sharks. Annually, the second Friday in May. For info: Ruth Musgrave, WhaleTimes, Inc, PO Box 2702, Tualatin, OR 97062. E-mail: seamail@whaletimes.org. Web: www.whaletimes.org.

GONZALES, PANCHO: BIRTH ANNIVERSARY. May 9, 1928. Richard Alonzo "Pancho" Gonzales, tennis player born at Los Angeles, CA. A self-taught player, Gonzales won the 1948 US National Singles Championship and repeated in 1949. He turned pro and won the world championship from 1954 through 1962. Gonzales was an aggressive, temperamental player who rarely trained. Died at Las Vegas, NV, July 3, 1995.

HUNTER FREES THE SLAVES: ANNIVERSARY. May 9, 1862. At Hilton Head, SC, General David Hunter, commander of the Department of the South, issued orders freeing slaves in South Carolina, Florida and Georgia. Not having congressional or presidential approval, the orders were countermanded by President Abraham Lincoln on May 19.

JOSEY'S WORLD CHAMPION JUNIOR BARREL RACE. May 9–11. Josey's Ranch, Marshall, TX. Youth barrel-racing competition. Est attendance: 4,000. For info: Geraldine Mauthe, Marshall CVB, PO Box 1437, Marshall, TX 75671-1437. Phone: (903) 702-7777. Fax: (903) 702-7780. E-mail: cvb@visitmarshalltexas.org. Web: www.visitmarshalltexas.org.

LILAC FESTIVAL. May 9–18. Highland Park, Rochester, NY. Developed by renowned park designer Frederick Law Olmsted, Highland Park is the site of the Lilac Festival, the largest celebration of its kind in North America. In addition to the spectacle of more than 500 varieties of lilacs in bloom, the festival provides free admission, free entertainment, free children's entertainment, a parade, a 10k race, two juried art shows, a senior citizens' day and free music concerts. Est attendance: 400,000. For info: Lilac Festival. Phone: (585) 473-4482. E-mail: info@rochesterevents.com. Web: www.lilacfestival.com.

MARSTON, WILLIAM MOULTON: BIRTH ANNIVERSARY. May 9, 1893. Born at Cliftondale, MA, psychologist and author William Marston's legacy continues to have a profound impact on contemporary criminal science and popular culture. While an undergraduate at Harvard he created the Marston Deception Test—now known as the lie detector—and was its most ardent advocate. Marston was also a prolific writer, penning many academic and popular texts, although his most well-known work, the Wonder Woman comic book series, which depicted the first female superhero, was written under the pseudonym Charles Moulton. Ahead of his time, Marston foresaw the increasing empowerment of women in the future, famously writing, "I fully believe I am hitting a great movement now under way, the growth in power of women." He died of cancer May 2, 1947, at Rye, NY.

✦MILITARY SPOUSE APPRECIATION DAY. May 9. First proclaimed by President Ronald Reagan in 1984 to recognize and honor the contributions and sacrifices of military spouses. Annually, the Friday before Mother's Day.

MILITARY SPOUSE APPRECIATION DAY. May 9. Observed on US military posts worldwide, this day celebrates the strength and patriotism of the spouses of members of the military. Annually on the Friday before Mother's Day, events are commonly sponsored to recognize the husbands and wives of men and women in uniform for their support, contributions and sacrifices.

NATIONAL MOSCATO DAY. May 9. 3rd annual. A day celebrating the popular wine that has taken the country by a storm. Both wine aficionados and novices alike are invited to toast with Moscato to celebrate its approachable, sweeter taste profile and the many ways in which it is currently being enjoyed. Sponsored by Gallo Family Vineyards, who first started this day in 2012. For info: Alexandra Conway on behalf of Gallo Family Vineyards. E-mail (for media): aconway@hunterpr.com. Web: www.gallofamily.com.

NATIONAL SPECIALLY-ABLED PETS DAY. May 9. Celebrated on May 9 annually, with events around the nation, this day helps educate the public about caring for disabled pets, features disabled animals looking for a home and encourages animal lovers to consider choosing a disabled pet when looking to bring home a new furry family member. For info: Animal Miracle Foundation, 4804 NW Bethany Blvd, Ste 12-197, Portland, OR 97229. Phone: (323) 552-9941. E-mail: info@animalmiraclefoundation.org. Web: www.disabledpetsday.com.

NCAA DIVISION I WOMEN'S WATER POLO CHAMPIONSHIP. May 9–11. Uytengsu Aquatic Center, Los Angeles, CA. Est attendance: 32,000. For info: NCAA, PO Box 6222, Indianapolis, IN 46206-6222. Web: www.NCAA.com.

RENO, NEVADA: ANNIVERSARY. May 9, 1868. First known as Fullers Crossing, and then Lakes Crossing, on this date it officially became Reno, known today as "the Biggest Little City in the World." Its six-week residency requirement for divorce became law on May 1, 1931.

RUSSIA: VICTORY DAY. May 9. National holiday observed annually to commemorate the 1945 Allied forces' defeat of Nazi Germany in WWII and to honor the 20 million Soviet people who died in that war. Hostilities ceased and the German surrender became effective at one minute after midnight on May 9, 1945. See also: "V-E Day: Anniversary" (May 8).

SAVOR: AN AMERICAN CRAFT BEER AND FOOD EXPERIENCE. May 9–10. National Building Museum, Washington, DC. First held in 2008, this is the premier beer and food pairing event in the US. Attendees enjoy beers from 76 small and independent American breweries, hailing from 31 different states and representing all regions of the country. Along with tasting some of the finest craft beers, attendees also enjoy a diverse array of food pairings. For info: Brewers Association. E-mail: info@brewersassociation.org. Web: www.brewersassociation.org or www.savorcraftbeer.com.

SNOW, HANK: 100th BIRTH ANNIVERSARY. May 9, 1914. Country Hall of Fame singer born at Brooklyn, Nova Scotia, Canada. Snow, whose career spanned six decades, was most popular in the 1950s. His first hit among many was 1950's "I'm Moving On"—it stayed on top of the charts for 21 weeks. Snow, a regular at the Grand Ole Opry, was instrumental in getting Elvis Presley on the bill there in 1954. Snow died Dec 20, 1999, at Madison, TN.

UZBEKISTAN: DAY OF MEMORY AND HONOR. May 9. Honors Uzbek citizens killed in WWII. Formerly Victory Day when Uzbekistan was part of the Soviet Union.

"VAST WASTELAND" SPEECH: ANNIVERSARY. May 9, 1961. Speaking before the bigwigs of network TV at the annual convention of the National Association of Broadcasters, Newton Minow, the new chairman of the Federal Communications Commission, exhorted those executives to sit through an entire day of their own programming. He suggested that they "will observe a vast wasteland." Further, he urged them to try for "imagination in programming, not sterility; creativity, not imitation; experimentation, not conformity; excellence, not mediocrity."

WALLACE, MIKE: BIRTH ANNIVERSARY. May 9, 1918. Over more than 60 years as a journalist and broadcaster, Mike Wallace was known for his tireless work ethic and strident interviewing style, firing probing questions at his subjects in a relentless quest for the real story. Born Myron Leon Wallace to Russian immigrants at Brookline, MA, Wallace got his start as a radio announcer, game show host and pitchman, but by 1960 had developed his hard-hitting style. ABC even promoted him as "the Terrible Torquemada of the TV Inquisition." He brought that tenacity to "60 Minutes" when it debuted in 1968, helping to shape the style and substance of the long-running CBS newsmagazine, and in the process became a star in his own right. Wallace was arrested at the 1968 Democratic Convention; conducted legendary interviews with the Ayatollah Khomeini, Jack Kevorkian and Mahmoud Ahmadinejad; won 21 Emmys; and stayed active on "60 Minutes" until 2008. He died Apr 7, 2012, at New Canaan, CT.

BIRTHDAYS TODAY

Candice Bergen, 68, actress (*Starting Over*, "Murphy Brown," "Boston Legal"), born Beverly Hills, CA, May 9, 1946.

James L. Brooks, 74, director, producer, screenwriter (Oscar for *Terms of Endearment*; *As Good as It Gets*, "Taxi," "The Mary Tyler Moore Show"), born Brooklyn, NY, May 9, 1940.

Rosario Dawson, 35, actress (*He Got Game, Sin City*), born New York, NY, May 9, 1979.

Albert Finney, 78, actor (*The Bourne Ultimatum, Erin Brockovich, The Dresser, Tom Jones*), born Salford, England, May 9, 1936.

Tony Gwynn, 54, Hall of Fame baseball player, born Los Angeles, CA, May 9, 1960.

Glenda Jackson, 77, actress (Oscars for *Women in Love* and *A Touch of Class*), born Cheshire, England, May 9, 1937.

Billy Joel, 65, singer, composer ("It's Still Rock and Roll to Me," "Just the Way You Are"), born Hicksville, NY, May 9, 1949.

Charles Simic, 76, former US poet laureate (2007–8), born Belgrade, Yugoslavia (now Serbia), May 9, 1938.

Steve Yzerman, 49, hockey player, born Cranbrook, BC, Canada, May 9, 1965.

May 10 — Saturday

DAY 130 **235 REMAINING**

ALBANY TULIP FESTIVAL. May 10–11. Washington Park, Albany, NY. 66th annual. A celebration of spring, the Tulip Festival features thousands of tulips abloom throughout the city and honors Albany's Dutch heritage. Events include crowning of a Tulip Queen, arts and crafts vendors, food vendors, entertainment on three stages and children's activities. Est attendance: 80,000. For info: City of Albany Office of Special Events, City Hall, Room 402, 24 Eagle St, Albany, NY 12207. Phone: (518) 434-2032. Fax: (518) 426-0759. E-mail: specialevents@ci.albany.ny. Web: www.albanyevents.org.

ASTAIRE, FRED: BIRTH ANNIVERSARY. May 10, 1899. Actor, dancer and choreographer, born at Omaha, NE. Astaire began dancing with his sister, Adele, and in the mid-1930s began dancing with Ginger Rogers. After Astaire's first Hollywood screen test, a producer noted of him: "Can't act. Slightly bald. Can dance a little." Despite this, Astaire starred in more than 40 films, including *Holiday Inn, The Gay Divorcée, Silk Stockings* and *Easter Parade.* Died at Los Angeles, CA, June 22, 1987.

ASTOR PLACE RIOT: ANNIVERSARY. May 10, 1849. A riot erupted outside the Astor Place Opera House at New York, NY, where the British actor William Charles Macready was performing. Led by the American actor Edwin Forrest, angry crowds revolted against dress requirements for admission and against Macready's public statements on the vulgarity of American life. On May 8 Macready's performance of *Macbeth* was stopped by Forrest's followers. Two days later, a mob led by Ned Buntline shattered the windows of the theater during a performance. Troops were summoned and ordered to fire, killing 22 and wounding 26.

BARTH, KARL: BIRTH ANNIVERSARY. May 10, 1886. The most influential Protestant theologian of the 20th century, Barth was born at Basel, Switzerland. Among his scores of works are *The Epistle to the Romans* (1918) and the 13-volume *Church Dogmatics* (1932–67). In 1934, Barth lost his teaching position at the University of Bonn when he did not sign the oath of allegiance to German chancellor Adolf Hitler. He explained afterward that he refused "to begin a commentary on the Sermon on the Mount with 'Heil Hitler.'" He died on Dec 10, 1968, at Basel, Switzerland.

BOOTH, JOHN WILKES: BIRTH ANNIVERSARY. May 10, 1838. Born near Bel Air, MD, into a famous theatrical family, Booth was himself a well-known actor when he assassinated President Abraham Lincoln. Fanatically opposed to abolition, Booth was present at the hanging of the abolitionist John Brown in 1859. During the Civil War, he outspokenly supported the South and denounced Lincoln, whom he regarded as a tyrant. As leader of a small group of conspirators, on the evening of Apr 14, 1865, Booth entered the presidential box at Ford Theatre in Washington, DC, and shot the president in the back of the head. Shouting "Sic semper tyrannis!" he jumped to the stage, injuring his leg, and escaped on horseback. Tracked to a farm near Port Royal, VA, Booth was shot evading capture on Apr 26, 1865, and died from his wounds.

	S	M	T	W	T	F	S
May					1	2	3
2014	4	5	6	7	8	9	10
	11	12	13	14	15	16	17
	18	19	20	21	22	23	24
	25	26	27	28	29	30	31

CARTER, MAYBELLE: BIRTH ANNIVERSARY. May 10, 1909. The guitar/banjo-playing cofounder of the singing Carter Family was born at Nickelsville, VA. The Carter Family were the first country music stars in America, reigning from 1927 to the 1950s and combining the influences of folk, bluegrass, rural country and gospel. Their hits include "Wabash Cannonball" and "Will the Circle Be Unbroken." Carter died Oct 23, 1978, at Nashville, TN.

CONFEDERATE MEMORIAL DAY IN NORTH AND SOUTH CAROLINA. May 10. Observed on the anniversary of the capture of Jefferson Davis by Union troops in 1865. Other Southern states observe Confederate Memorial Day on different dates.

GAUMONT, LÉON: 150th BIRTH ANNIVERSARY. May 10, 1864. Important early film entrepreneur and inventor born at Paris, France. He established the Gaumont Film Production Company in 1895 to capitalize on the growing new entertainment medium. Gaumont's technical work included a camera-projector, an early sound-synchronizing system and an early color process. Gaumont's company produced France's first "talkie"—*Eau de Nil* (1928). The Gaumont Company also comprised studios and a theater chain. Gaumont retired in 1929, and he died Aug 10, 1946, at Sainte-Maxime, Var, France.

GOLDEN SPIKE DRIVING: ANNIVERSARY. May 10, 1869. Anniversary of the meeting of Union Pacific and Central Pacific railways at Promontory Point, UT. On that day a golden spike was driven by Leland Stanford, president of the Central Pacific, to celebrate the linkage. The golden spike was promptly removed for preservation. Long called the final link in the ocean-to-ocean railroad, this event cannot be accurately described as completing the transcontinental railroad, but it did complete continuous rail tracks between Omaha and Sacramento. See also: "Transcontinental US Railway Completion: Anniversary" (Aug 15).

HOUSTON ART CAR PARADE. May 10. Houston, TX. 28th annual. The world's oldest and largest art car parade, featuring mobile masterpieces from the surreal to the sublime. Associated events are the Art Car Ball and Sneak Peek. Est attendance: 250,000. For info: Orange Show Foundation, 2402 Munger St, Houston, TX 77023. Phone: (713) 926-6368. Fax: (713) 926-1506. Web: www.orangeshow.org.

INTERNATIONAL MIGRATORY BIRD CELEBRATION. May 10. Chincoteague, VA. Walks, talks, workshops, boat tours, children's activities and an art celebration, all conducted outdoors with the birds. Annually, Mother's Day weekend. Est attendance: 10,000. For info: Chincoteague Chamber of Commerce, 6733 Maddox Blvd, Chincoteague, VA 23336. Phone: (757) 336-6161. Fax: (757) 336-1242. E-mail: chincochamber@verizon.net. Web: www.chincoteaguechamber.com.

INTERNATIONAL MIGRATORY BIRD DAY. May 10. To educate the public about migratory birds and the preservation of their habitats in the US and Central America. Annually, the second Saturday in May.

ITALY: GIRO D'ITALIA. May 10–June 1. 97th edition. In 2014, the legendary Giro spends its first days in Northern Ireland and Ireland, starting in Belfast (preceeded by festivities beginning May 7), before moving to Armagh and Dublin. One of world cycling's three Grand Tours, the Giro d'Italia was organized in 1909 as a way to boost circulation of *La Gazzetta dello Sport*, a Milan-based daily newspaper covering sports. Modeled on the Tour de France, the Giro is held annually over the last three weeks of May on a course that changes from year to year. The race is broadcast in 165 countries with an estimated global viewing audience of 775 million. Est attendance: 12,500,000. For info: RCS Sport SpA or Union Cycliste Internationale. Web: www.gazzetta.it.

JAMESTOWN DAY. May 10. Jamestown Settlement and Historic Jamestowne, Williamsburg, VA. Maritime demonstrations, military drills, archaeology and programs on English and Powhatan Indian contact, exploration and discovery mark the anniversary of the 1607 founding of Jamestown, America's first permanent English colony. Separate admission. For info: Jamestown-Yorktown Foundation, PO Box 1607, Williamsburg, VA 23187. Phone: (757) 253-4838 or (888) 593-4682. Fax: (757) 253-5299. Web: www.historyisfun.org.

LETTER CARRIERS "STAMP OUT HUNGER" FOOD DRIVE. May 10. Every year since 1993, on the second Saturday in May, letter carriers in more than 10,000 cities and towns across the 50 states, the District of Columbia, Puerto Rico, the Virgin Islands and Guam collect nonperishable food items left by mailboxes and in post offices from their postal customers. The National Association of Letter Carriers "Stamp Out Hunger" Food Drive is the largest one-day food drive in the nation. In 2012, the food drive gathered more than 70 million pounds of food. The US Postal Service, Campbell Soup Company and Valpak are major sponsors among many others. For info: Natl Assn of Letter Carriers, 100 Indiana Ave NW, Washington, DC 20001-2144. Phone: (202) 662-2489. E-mail: vonbergen@nalc.org. Web: www.nalc.org.

MANDELA INAUGURATION: 20th ANNIVERSARY. May 10, 1994. In a dramatic and historic exchange of power, former political prisoner Nelson Mandela was inaugurated as president of South Africa. Long the focal point of apartheid foes' attempts to end the enforced policy of discrimination in South Africa, Mandela handily won the first free election in South Africa despite many attempts by various political factions to either stop the electoral process or alter the outcome.

MICRONESIA, FEDERATED STATES OF: CONSTITUTION DAY. May 10. Proclamation of the Federated States of Micronesia in 1979. National holiday.

MOTHER OCEAN DAY. May 10. To celebrate the wonder, vastness and beauty of the ocean. Casting of roses into the sea from the beach and from the water. Annually, on the day before Mother's Day. For info: Cynthia Hancock, Pres, Natl Week of the Ocean, Inc, PO Box 179, Fort Lauderdale, FL 33302. Phone: (954) 462-5573. Web: www.national-week-of-the-ocean.org.

MOTHER'S DAY ANNUAL RHODODENDRON SHOW. May 10–11. Crystal Springs Rhododendron Gardens, Portland, OR. Spectacular display of rhododendron and azalea blooms and plant sale. Est attendance: 6,000. For info: Kathy Van Veen, American Rhododendron Society, Portland Chapter, PO Box 86424, Portland, OR 97286. Phone: (503) 777-1734. Fax: (503) 777-2048.

NATIONAL BABYSITTERS DAY. May 10. To give babysitters across the nation appreciation and special recognition for their quality child care. Annually, the Saturday before Mother's Day. For info: Barbara Baldwin, RN, Safety Whys, PO Box 1177, Helotes, TX 78023-1177. Phone: (210) 695-9838. E-mail: bbaldwin@satx.rr.com. Web: www.safetywhys.com.

NATIONAL TRAIN DAY. May 10. 7th annual. On May 10, 1869, at Promontory Summit, UT, the "golden spike" was driven into the final tie that joined 1,776 miles of the Central Pacific and Union Pacific railways, ceremonially creating the nation's first transcontinental railroad. And America was transformed. Now, there has never been a better time to take the train. Trains are a more energy-efficient mode of travel than either autos or airplanes. Riding the rails is a perfect way to reduce your carbon footprint. Not to mention meet interesting people and see breathtaking scenery. National Train Day celebrates the way trains connect people and places—with events from coast to coast. Annually, the Saturday closest to May 10. For info: National Train Day. E-mail: info@nationaltrainday.com. Web: www.nationaltrainday.com.

NETHERLANDS: NATIONAL WINDMILL DAY. May 10. About 1,170 windmills survive, and some 300 are used occasionally and have been designated national monuments by the government. As many windmills as possible are in operation on National Windmill Day for the benefit of tourists. Annually, the second Saturday in May.

ROSS, GEORGE: BIRTH ANNIVERSARY. May 10, 1730. Signer of the Declaration of Independence. Born at New Castle, DE, he died July 14, 1779, at Philadelphia, PA.

SEVEN DAYS IN MAY SHOW AND SALE. May 10–11 (also May 17–18; 24–26). Chapel Hill, NC. Unique architectural antiques, featuring an extensive collection of period wrought-iron artifacts (especially iron gates, garden art and home embellishments). For info: Gaines Steer, The Last Unicorn, 536 Edwards Ridge Rd, Chapel Hill, NC 27517. Phone: (919) 968-8440. E-mail: info@thelastunicorn.com. Web: www.thelastunicorn.com.

SINGAPORE: VESAK DAY. May 10. Public holiday. Monks commemorate their Lord Buddha's entry into nirvana by chanting holy sutras and freeing captive birds.

SPRING ASTRONOMY DAY. May 10. To take astronomy to the people. International Spring Astronomy Day is observed on a Saturday near the first quarter moon between mid-April and mid-May. Cosponsored by 14 astronomical organizations. See also: "Spring Astronomy Week" (May 5–11). For info: Gary E. Tomlinson, Coord, Astronomy Day Headquarters, 30 Stargazer Ln, Comstock Park, MI 49321. Phone: (616) 784-9518. E-mail: gtomlins@sbcglobal.net. Web: www.astroleague.org.

STAY UP ALL NIGHT NIGHT. May 10. A night when people are encouraged to stay awake through the night, reliving the excitement of staying up late as a child. It's a chance to catch up on chores, do some cleaning, watch films, read, cook, drink or chat with friends. There is something incredibly satisfying in staying up to see the sun rise—and everyone should do it at least once a year. Annually, the second Saturday in May. For info: George Mahood. E-mail: george@georgemahood.com. Web: www.georgemahood.com/stayupallnight.

STEINER, MAX: BIRTH ANNIVERSARY. May 10, 1888. Composer, born Maximilian Raoul Steiner at Vienna, Austria-Hungary. A musical prodigy who studied under Gustav Mahler as well as a conductor, he went to Hollywood in 1929 and became one of the top film composers of the 20th century. Nominated 20 times for an Academy Award, he received the Oscar three times—for *The Informer; Now, Voyager* and *Since You Went Away.* Other famous scores include those for *King Kong, Gone with the Wind, Casablanca* and *The Treasure of the Sierra Madre.* Steiner died Dec 28, 1971, at Los Angeles, CA.

WORLD FAIR TRADE DAY. May 10. A day to promote Fair Trade as an alternative economic model. "Fair Trade" means that trading partnerships are based on reciprocal benefits and mutual respect; prices paid to producers reflect the work they do; workers have the right to organize; national health, safety and wage laws are enforced; and products are environmentally sustainable and conserve natural resources. Celebrated worldwide in 70 countries with a variety of events from live music to symposia. Annually, the second Saturday in May. For info: World Fair Trade Organization, Prijssestraat 24, 4101 CR Culemborg, The Netherlands. Phone: (31) (345) 53-59-14. Fax: (31) (847) 47-44-01. E-mail: info@wfto.com. Web: www.wfto.com.

WORLD LUPUS DAY. May 10. An international call to action has been issued by more than 100 lupus organizations based in countries around the world. Goal is to call attention to the confusing characteristics of this potentially fatal autoimmune disease that mimics other, less serious illnesses. In addition, observing World Lupus Day offers lupus patients the comfort of knowing their condition is recognized and being addressed on a global level. For info: Dir of Communications, Lupus Foundation of America, 2000 L St NW, Ste 410, Washington, DC 20036. Phone: (202) 349-1155. Fax: (202) 349-1156. E-mail: info@lupus.org. Web: www.lupus.org or www.worldlupusday.org.

BIRTHDAYS TODAY

Bono, 54, singer (U2), humanitarian activist, born Paul Hewson at Dublin, Ireland, May 10, 1960.

Barbara Taylor Bradford, 81, author (*A Woman of Substance, Hold the Dream*), born Upper Armley, Leeds, Yorkshire, England, May 10, 1933.

T. Berry Brazelton, 96, pediatrician, author, born Waco, TX, May 10, 1918.

Jason Brooks, 48, actor ("Days of Our Lives"), born Colorado Springs, CO, May 10, 1966.

Missy Franklin, 19, Olympic swimmer, born Pasadena, CA, May 10, 1995.

Dean Heller, 54, US Senator (R, Nevada), born Castro Valley, CA, May 10, 1960.

Dave Mason, 68, singer, musician, songwriter, born Worcester, England, May 10, 1946.

Gary Owens, 78, actor ("Rowan & Martin's Laugh-In," "The Gong Show"), born Mitchell, SD, May 10, 1936.

Ara Raoul Parseghian, 91, former football coach and sportscaster, born Akron, OH, May 10, 1923.

Kenan Thompson, 36, comedian, actor ("All That," "Saturday Night Live," *Good Burger*), born Atlanta, GA, May 10, 1978.

May 11 — Sunday

DAY 131 **234 REMAINING**

BATTLE OF HAMBURGER HILL: 45th ANNIVERSARY. May 11, 1969. Beginning of one of the most infamous battles that signified the growing frustration with America's involvement in the Vietnam War. Attempting to seize Dong Ap Bia mountain, American troops repeatedly scaled the hill over a 10-day period, often engaging in bloody hand-to-hand combat with the North Vietnamese. After finally securing the objective, American military decision makers chose to abandon it, and the North Vietnamese retook it shortly thereafter. The heavy casualties in the struggle to take the hill inspired the name "Hamburger Hill."

BATTLE OF YELLOW TAVERN: 150th ANNIVERSARY. May 11, 1864. Attempting to head off Union General Phil Sheridan's cavalry advance on Richmond, Confederate General J.E.B. Stuart's Confederate cavalry encountered the Federals at Yellow Tavern, VA. Stuart was mortally wounded in the battle and died the following day. The loss of one of its most colorful and effective cavalry leaders was a great blow to the South. The battle delayed the Federal advance long enough for the Confederates to strengthen the defenses at Richmond, and Sheridan was forced to change his plans.

May 2014	S	M	T	W	T	F	S
					1	2	3
	4	5	6	7	8	9	10
	11	12	13	14	15	16	17
	18	19	20	21	22	23	24
	25	26	27	28	29	30	31

BERLIN, IRVING: BIRTH ANNIVERSARY. May 11, 1888. Songwriter born Israel Isidore Baline at Tyumen, Russia. Irving Berlin moved to New York, NY, with his family when he was four years old. After the death of his father, he began singing in saloons and on street corners in order to help his family and worked as a singing waiter as a teenager. Berlin became one of America's most prolific songwriters, authoring such songs as "Alexander's Ragtime Band," "White Christmas," "God Bless America," "There's No Business like Show Business," "Doin' What Comes Naturally," "Puttin' on the Ritz," "Blue Skies" and "Oh! How I Hate to Get Up in the Morning," among others. He could neither read nor write musical notation. Berlin died Sept 22, 1989, at New York.

BUNKER, CHANG AND ENG: BIRTH ANNIVERSARY. May 11, 1811. Conjoined twins born in Meklong, Siam (now Thailand), Chang and Eng found worldwide fame as the Siamese Twins, their rare condition and flair for showmanship wowing royalty and regular folk alike. The twins settled on a plantation in Wilkesboro, NC; bought slaves; were naturalized as American citizens; and in 1843 married a pair of local sisters. The couples eventually had 21 children between them. Chang and Eng died hours apart at Wilkesboro, Jan 17, 1874. They were never separated.

DALI, SALVADOR: BIRTH ANNIVERSARY. May 11, 1904. A leading painter in the surrealist movement, Salvador Dali was equally well known for his baffling antics and attempts to shock his audiences. The largest collection of his works resides in the Salvador Dali Museum at St. Petersburg, FL. Born at Figueras, Spain, Dali died there Jan 23, 1989.

EAT WHAT YOU WANT DAY. May 11. Here's a day you may actually enjoy yourself. Ignore all those on-again, off-again warnings. (©2006 by WH.) For info: Thomas & Ruth Roy, Wellcat Holidays, 2418 Long Ln, Lebanon, PA 17046. Phone: (717) 279-0184. E-mail: info@wellcat.com. Web: www.wellcat.com.

FAIRBANKS, CHARLES WARREN: BIRTH ANNIVERSARY. May 11, 1852. 26th vice president of the US (1905–09), born at Unionville Center, OH. Died at Indianapolis, IN, June 4, 1918.

GLACIER NATIONAL PARK ESTABLISHED: ANNIVERSARY. May 11, 1910. Located in northwest Montana on the Canadian border. In 1932 Glacier National Park and Waterton Lakes National Park in Alberta were joined together by the governments of the US and Canada as Waterton-Glacier International Peace Park.

GRAHAM, MARTHA: BIRTH ANNIVERSARY. May 11, 1894. Martha Graham was born at Allegheny, PA, and became one of the giants of the modern dance movement in the US. She began her dance career at the comparatively late age of 22 and joined the Greenwich Village Follies in 1923. Her new ideas began to surface in the late '20s and '30s, and by the mid-1930s she was incorporating the rituals of the southwestern American Indians in her work. She is credited with bringing a new psychological depth to modern dance by exploring primal emotions and ancient rituals in her work. She performed until the age of 75 and premiered in her 180th ballet, *The Maple Leaf Rag*, in the fall of 1990. Died Apr 1, 1991, at New York, NY.

HART, JOHN: DEATH ANNIVERSARY. May 11, 1779. Signer of the Declaration of Independence, farmer and legislator, born about 1711 (exact date unknown), at Stonington, CT; died at Hopewell, NJ.

JAPAN: CORMORANT FISHING FESTIVAL. May 11–Oct 15. Cormorant fishing on the Nagara River, Gifu. This ancient method of catching ayu, a troutlike fish, with trained cormorants, takes place nightly under the light of blazing torches.

MINNESOTA: ADMISSION DAY: ANNIVERSARY. May 11. Became 32nd state in 1858.

✦MOTHER'S DAY. May 11. Presidential Proclamation always issued for the second Sunday in May. (Pub Res No. 2 of May 8, 1914.)

MOTHER'S DAY: 100th ANNIVERSARY. May 11. Observed first in 1907 at the request of Anna Jarvis of Philadelphia, PA, who asked her church to hold a service in memory of all mothers on the anniversary of her mother's death. In 1909, two years after her mother's death, Jarvis and friends began a letter-writing campaign to create a Mother's Day observance. Congress passed legislation in 1914 designating the second Sunday in May as Mother's Day. Some say the predecessor of Mother's Day was the ancient spring festival dedicated to mother goddesses: Rhea (Greek) and Cybele (Roman).

MOTHER'S DAY AT THE WALL. May 11. Washington, DC. Annual observance at the Vietnam Veterans Memorial since 2000 honoring the mothers of those who died in combat. Area schoolchildren offer cards.

NATIONAL NURSING HOME WEEK. May 11–17. A community outreach program designed to familiarize the public with nursing facilities and the services they provide. Activities are conducted locally by individual nursing facilities. Annually, Mother's Day through the following Saturday. For info: American Health Care Assn, 1201 L St NW, Washington, DC 20005. Phone: (202) 842-4444. Fax: (202) 842-3860. E-mail: tburke@ahca.org. Web: www.ahca.org.

NATIONAL POLICE WEEK. May 11–17. See also: "Peace Officer Memorial Day" (May 15). For info: American Police Hall of Fame and Museum, 6350 Horizon Dr, Titusville, FL 32780. Phone: (321) 264-0911. E-mail: policeinfo@aphf.org. Web: www.aphf.org.

NATIONAL RETURN TO WORK WEEK. May 11–17. Annually 4.1 million employees are injured; 2.1 million employees lose at least seven days from work. Annually there are 80 million lost workdays due to occupational injury or illness. This week will focus on implementing proactive return-to-work programs that will get injured, ill or disabled employees back to work successfully. Annually, the second full week in May. For info: Margaret Spence, PO Box 211835, West Palm Beach, FL 33421. Phone: (561) 795-3036. E-mail: mspence@nationalreturntoworkweek.org. Web: www.nationalreturntoworkweek.org.

✦NATIONAL TRANSPORTATION WEEK. May 11–17. Presidential Proclamation issued for week including third Friday in May since 1960. (PL 86–475 of May 20, 1960, first requested; PL 87–449 of May 14, 1962, requested an annual proclamation.)

✦POLICE WEEK. May 11–17. Presidential Proclamation 3537 of May 4, 1963, covers all succeeding years. (Public Law 87–726 of Oct 1, 1962.) Since 1962, the week including May 15.

PREPARE TOMORROW'S PARENTS MONTH. May 11–June 15. To celebrate mothers and fathers, do at least one activity between Mother's Day and Father's Day to help prepare a child or teen to become a better parent in the future. To get ideas for parenting-preparation activities for this month and year-round, visit the website, which posts easy, fun steps to take at home as well as classroom-ready learning experiences for teachers, parents and youth organization leaders. For info: Prepare Tomorrow's Parents, 454 NE 3rd St, Boca Raton, FL 33432. Phone: (561) 241-9139. E-mail: info@preparetomorrowsparents.org. Web: www.preparetomorrowsparents.org.

SALUTE TO 35+ MOMS WEEK. May 11–17. Motherhood is challenging at any age, and if you become a mom when you're 35 or older, it can be quite an adjustment. This week is dedicated to moms with more life experience than baby experience. Now, and throughout the year, it is empowering to connect with peers and share the joys and trials and tribulations that child rearing may encompass when you parent later in life. For info: Robin Gorman Newman, 44 Somerset Dr N, Great Neck, NY 11020. Phone: (516) 773-0911. E-mail: rgnewman@optonline.net. Web: www.motherhoodlater.com.

SUTTON HOO SHIP BURIAL DISCOVERED: 75th ANNIVERSARY. May 11, 1939. On this date in a large mound at Sutton Hoo in rural Suffolk, England, archaeologist Basil Brown discovered an undisturbed royal Anglo-Saxon ship burial. The ship—the largest ever found—was 90 feet long and 14 feet wide (the wood had rotted away, leaving only an outline and rivets). Also discovered were gold, bronze, silver and gemmed artifacts and weapons. The buried ship is believed to be that of King Raedwald of East Anglia, who ruled in the early AD 600s.

***VIRGINIA* DESTROYED: ANNIVERSARY.** May 11, 1862. After a standoff with the Union ironclad *Monitor* on Mar 9, the Confederate ironclad *Virginia* was destroyed by the Confederate navy on May 11. In the wake of advancing Union troops in the Peninsular Campaign, the South was forced to destroy the valuable vessel to prevent its capture by Union forces. See also: "Battle of Hampton Roads: Anniversary" (Mar 9).

BIRTHDAYS TODAY

Louis Farrakhan, 81, Nation of Islam leader, born New York, NY, May 11, 1933.

Bernard Fox, 87, actor ("Bewitched," *Titanic*), born Portalbot, South Wales, May 11, 1927.

Boyd Gaines, 61, actor (Tonys for *Gypsy, Contact, She Loves Me, The Heidi Chronicles*), born Atlanta, GA, May 11, 1953.

Jonathan Jackson, 32, actor ("Nashville," "General Hospital"), born Orlando, FL, May 11, 1982.

Robert Jarvik, 68, physician, inventor of artificial heart, born Midland, MI, May 11, 1946.

Matt Leinart, 31, football player, born Santa Ana, CA, May 11, 1983.

Cam Newton, 25, football player, born Atlanta, GA, May 11, 1989.

Mort Sahl, 87, comic actor (*Don't Make Waves; Doctor, You've Got to Be Kidding*), born Montreal, QC, Canada, May 11, 1927.

May 12 — Monday

DAY 132 **233 REMAINING**

BATTLE OF SPOTSYLVANIA: 150th ANNIVERSARY. May 12, 1864. After the Battle of the Wilderness, Grant and Lee next engaged at the Battle of Spotsylvania (VA). Lee had positioned his troops in breastworks along a horseshoe formation, utilizing the natural features of the landscape. During Grant's attack on this strong defensive position, both sides suffered losses of more than 12,000 in what became known as "the Bloody Angle." Lee was forced to use every available man in order to protect the position and so ordered his troops to pull back during the night.

CHILDREN'S BOOK WEEK. May 12–18. An annual event, established in 1919 and sponsored by The Children's Book Council, to encourage the enjoyment of reading for young people. For info: The Children's Book Council, Inc, 54 W 39th St, 14th Fl, New York, NY 10018. Phone: (212) 966-1990. Fax: (212) 966-2073. E-mail: cbc.info@cbcbooks.org. Web: www.cbcbooks.org or www.bookweekonline.com.

DONIZETTI'S *L'ELISIR D'AMORE* PREMIERE: ANNIVERSARY. May 12, 1832. Italian composer Gaetano Donizetti's famed comic opera *L'Elisir d'amore* (*The Elixir of Love*) premiered on this date. With a libretto written by Felice Romani, the opera is about a poor peasant's attempts to woo a wealthy and spirited girl. It remains among Donizetti's best-known works.

FRANK, OTTO: 125th BIRTH ANNIVERSARY. May 12, 1889. Decorated for bravery as a German officer after WWI, Frank is best remembered as the father of Anne, whose diary he published in 1947 in hope of preventing future genocides. Born in Frankfurt, Germany, Frank moved his family to Holland in 1933 as anti-Semitism erupted in his homeland. His wife and two daughters died in concentration camps, but Frank was liberated from Auschwitz in 1945. In 1963, he established The Anne Frank Foundation, which undertakes charitable works and social activities in the spirit of Anne Frank. Frank devoted his life to Holocaust education until his death on Aug 19, 1980, at Basel, Switzerland.

GEORGE VI'S CORONATION: ANNIVERSARY. May 12, 1937. George VI was crowned at Westminster Abbey at London, England, following the abdication of his brother, Edward VIII. Born Dec 14, 1895, King George died Feb 6, 1952. He was succeeded by his daughter Elizabeth, the current reigning monarch.

HEPBURN, KATHARINE: BIRTH ANNIVERSARY. May 12, 1907. American actress Katharine Houghton Hepburn was born at Hartford, CT. Nominated for 12 Oscars over the course of her career, she won four times: for 1933's *Morning Glory,* 1967's *Guess Who's Coming to Dinner,* 1968's *The Lion in Winter* and 1981's *On Golden Pond.* She is best remembered for her on- and offscreen pairing with Spencer Tracy. Together, they made nine films, including *Adam's Rib* and *Woman of the Year,* and enjoyed a 27-year personal relationship. There is often confusion regarding her date of birth: in her 1991 autobiography, *Me: Stories of My Life,* she confirmed the May date and admitted often giving out a late brother's birth date as her own. She died at Old Saybrook, CT, June 29, 2003.

LEAR, EDWARD: BIRTH ANNIVERSARY. May 12, 1812. English artist and author, best remembered for his light verse and limericks. Lear published *A Book of Nonsense* in 1846. His most famous poem, "The Owl and the Pussycat," appeared in 1867. Lear was born at Highgate, England, and died at San Remo, Italy, Jan 29, 1888. See also: "Limerick Day" (below).

LIMERICK DAY. May 12. Observed on the birthday of one of its champions, Edward Lear. The limerick, which dates from the early 18th century, has been described as the "only fixed verse form indigenous to the English language." It gained its greatest popularity following the publication of Edward Lear's *Book of Nonsense* (and its sequels). Example: There was a young poet named Lear/ Who said, it is just as I fear/Five lines are enough/For this kind of stuff/Make a limerick each day of the year. See also: "Lear, Edward: Birth Anniversary" (above).

NATIONAL ETIQUETTE WEEK. May 12–16. National Etiquette Week is the national recognition of etiquette and protocol in all areas of American life—business, social, dining, travel, technology, wedding and international protocol. The week will raise awareness of all people to act with courtesy, civility, kindness, respect and manners as well as rally people to act with good manners in their everyday lives. Annually, the workweek beginning with the second Monday in May. For info: Cindy Haygood, Two S Main St, Town Center North, Watkinsville, GA 30677. Phone: (888) 769-5150. Fax: (706) 310-0003. E-mail: cindyh@etiquetteleadership.com.

NATIONAL STUTTERING AWARENESS WEEK. May 12–18. Annually, the second full week of May, Monday to Sunday. For info: Jane Fraser, President, Stuttering Foundation of America, PO Box 11749, Memphis, TN 38111-0749. Phone: (800) 992-9392 or (901) 761-0343. E-mail: info@stutteringhelp.org. Web: www.stutteringhelp.org or www.tartamudez.org in Spanish.

NATIVE AMERICAN RIGHTS RECOGNIZED: ANNIVERSARY. May 12, 1879. When the US tried to forcibly remove the Poncas from their homeland in Nebraska to an Oklahoma reservation, their chief, Standing Bear, brought suit to prevent it. The US claimed that Standing Bear could not bring suit because as a Native American he had no legal standing in US law. In *Standing Bear v George Crook* at US District Court, Judge J. Dundy ruled on this day that "an Indian is a PERSON within the meaning of the laws of the United States." This landmark decision was appealed by the US to the Supreme Court, which dismissed it. Standing Bear was not forced to move his tribe, but other Native Americans were unable to use the decision to their advantage in other disputes with the US.

May 2014	S	M	T	W	T	F	S
					1	2	3
	4	5	6	7	8	9	10
	11	12	13	14	15	16	17
	18	19	20	21	22	23	24
	25	26	27	28	29	30	31

NIGHTINGALE, FLORENCE: BIRTH ANNIVERSARY. May 12, 1820. English nurse and public health activist who, through her unselfish devotion to nursing, contributed perhaps more than any other single person to the development of modern nursing procedures and the dignity of nursing as a profession. Founder of the Nightingale training school for nurses. Author of *Notes on Nursing.* Born at Florence, Italy. Died at London, England, Aug 13, 1910.

ODOMETER INVENTED: ANNIVERSARY. May 12, 1847. Anniversary of the invention of the odometer by Mormon pioneer William Clayton while crossing the plains in a covered wagon. Previous to this, mileage was calculated by counting the revolutions of a rag tied to a spoke of a wagon wheel.

PORTUGAL: PILGRIMAGE TO FATIMA. May 12–13. Commemorates first appearance of the Virgin of the Rosary to little shepherd children May 13, 1917. Pilgrims come to Cova da Iria—religious center, candlelit procession, mass of the sick—for annual observance.

SMITH, HOWARD K.: 100th BIRTH ANNIVERSARY. May 12, 1914. Born at Ferriday, LA, Smith was an acclaimed and opinionated war correspondent, broadcast journalist, anchor and author who was one of the "Murrow's Boys" (those who worked closely with Edward R. Murrow—especially during WWII). Smith had long stints at CBS and ABC. He also moderated the first televised US presidential debate between Richard Nixon and John F. Kennedy in 1960. Smith died Feb 15, 2002, at Bethesda, MD.

WORK AT HOME MOMS WEEK. May 12–18. The challenge of motherhood and working at home can be a balancing act. All women who do it every day: you are applauded this week and always. For info: Robin Gorman Newman, 44 Somerset Dr N, Great Neck, NY 11020. Phone: (516) 773-0911. E-mail: rgnewman@optonline.net. Web: www.motherhoodlater.com.

BIRTHDAYS TODAY

MacKenzie Astin, 41, actor (*The Last Days of Disco*), born Los Angeles, CA, May 12, 1973.

Burt Bacharach, 85, composer, born Kansas City, MO, May 12, 1929.

Stephen Baldwin, 48, actor (*The Usual Suspects*), born Massapequa, NY, May 12, 1966.

Lawrence Peter "Yogi" Berra, 89, Hall of Fame baseball player, former baseball coach and manager, born St. Louis, MO, May 12, 1925.

Jason Biggs, 36, actor (*American Pie, Loser*), born Pompton Plains, NJ, May 12, 1978.

Clare Bowen, 25, actress (*Dead Man's Burden,* "Nashville"), born Australia, May 12, 1989.

Bruce Boxleitner, 63, actor (*How the West Was Won,* "Scarecrow and Mrs King"), born Elgin, IL, May 12, 1951.

Cheryl Burke, 30, professional dancer, television personality ("Dancing with the Stars"), born San Francisco, CA, May 12, 1984.

Gabriel Byrne, 64, actor ("In Treatment," *The Usual Suspects*), born Dublin, Ireland, May 12, 1950.

Christian Campbell, 42, actor ("Malibu Shores," *Cold Hearts*), born Toronto, ON, Canada, May 12, 1972.

Lindsay Crouse, 66, actress (*House of Games, The Verdict, Places in the Heart*), born New York, NY, May 12, 1948.

Emilio Estevez, 52, actor (*The Breakfast Club, Repo Man*), born New York, NY, May 12, 1962.

Kim Fields, 45, actress ("The Facts of Life," "Living Single"), born Los Angeles, CA, May 12, 1969.

Kim Greist, 56, actress (*Brazil, Throw Momma from the Train*), born Stamford, CT, May 12, 1958.

Tony Hawk, 45, skateboarder, born Carlsbad, CA, May 12, 1969.

Dave Heineman, 66, Governor of Nebraska (R), born Falls City, NE, May 12, 1948.

Jamie Luner, 43, actress ("Melrose Place," "Profiler"), born Los Angeles, CA, May 12, 1971.

Millie Perkins, 76, actress ("Knots Landing," *The Diary of Anne Frank, Wall Street*), born Passaic, NJ, May 12, 1938.

Ving Rhames, 53, actor ("Kojak," "Don King: Only in America," *Mission: Impossible* films, *Pulp Fiction*), born New York, NY, May 12, 1961.

Frank Stella, 78, artist (*Empress of India*), born Malden, MA, May 12, 1936.

Emily VanCamp, 28, actress ("Brothers & Sisters," "Everwood"), born Port Perry, ON, Canada, May 12, 1986.

Steve Winwood, 66, musician, singer, born Birmingham, England, May 12, 1948.

May 13 — Tuesday

DAY 133 **232 REMAINING**

ATTEMPTED ASSASSINATION OF POPE JOHN PAUL II: ANNIVERSARY. May 13, 1981. Pope John Paul II was shot twice at close range while riding in an open automobile at St. Peter's Square at Rome, Italy. Two other persons also were wounded. An escaped terrorist, Mehmet Ali Agca (already under sentence of death for the murder of a Turkish journalist), was arrested immediately and was convicted July 22, 1981, of attempted murder of the pope. After convalescence Pope John Paul II was pronounced recovered by his doctors Aug 14, 1981. In 2000 Agca was released from prison and extradited to Turkey.

BRIMFIELD ANTIQUES AND COLLECTIBLES FAIR. May 13–18 (also July 8–13 and Sept 2–7). Brimfield, MA. 55th annual. The classic antique event of the year, with three shows in May, July and September. The fair is located within a one-mile stretch on both sides of Route 20. There are 21 fields—each approximately three to five acres. Each show brings into this lovely, little New England town about 6,000 dealers and 333,000 collectors from all over the world. Est attendance: 1,000,000. For info: Deb Kulkkula, Brimfield Antiques and Collectibles Fair, 381 Billings Rd, Fitchburg, MA 01420-1407. Phone: (978) 343-4009. E-mail: Deb@DebKulkkula.com. Web: www.brimfield.com or www.brimfieldshow.com.

EVANS, GIL: BIRTH ANNIVERSARY. May 13, 1912. A true jazz innovator, Gil Evans was a pianist, composer and arranger who started out in big bands but went on to help shape the sound of modal and free jazz, particularly with his work as an arranger and bandleader for Miles Davis (*Miles Ahead, Porgy and Bess, Sketches of Spain*). Evans worked steadily throughout the 1970s and '80s, as well, releasing music under his own name and collaborating with artists as varied as Astrud Gilberto and Sting. Born at Toronto, Canada, Evans died at Cuernavaca, Mexico, on Mar 20, 1988.

LOUIS, JOE: 100th BIRTH ANNIVERSARY. May 13, 1914. World heavyweight boxing champion, 1937–49, nicknamed the "Brown Bomber," Joseph Louis Barrow was born near Lafayette, AL. He died Apr 12, 1981, at Las Vegas, NV. Buried at Arlington National Cemetery. (Louis's burial there, by presidential waiver, was the 39th exception ever to the eligibility rules for burial in Arlington National Cemetery.)

MEXICAN WAR DECLARED: ANNIVERSARY. May 13, 1846. Although fighting had begun days earlier, Congress officially declared war on Mexico on this date. The struggle cost the lives of 11,300 American soldiers and resulted in the annexation by the US of land that became parts of Oklahoma, New Mexico, Arizona, Nevada, California, Utah and Colorado. The war ended in 1848. See also: "Treaty of Guadalupe Hidalgo: Anniversary" (Feb 2).

NAIA MEN'S AND WOMEN'S TENNIS NATIONAL CHAMPIONSHIPS. May 13–16. Mobile, AL. 63rd annual for men, 34th annual for women. Team format single-elimination tournament involving 24 teams (each gender). Est attendance: 500. For info: Natl Assn of Intercollegiate Athletics, 1200 Grand Blvd, Kansas City, MO 64106. E-mail: jadams@naia.org. Web: www.naia.org.

NAIA MEN'S GOLF NATIONAL CHAMPIONSHIP. May 13–16. Salem, OR. 63rd annual. Est attendance: 500. For info: Natl Assn of Intercollegiate Athletics, 1200 Grand Blvd, Kansas City, MO 64106. E-mail: kgillette@naia.org. Web: www.naia.org.

PHILADELPHIA POLICE BOMBING: ANNIVERSARY. May 13, 1985. During the siege of the radical group MOVE at Philadelphia, PA, police in a helicopter reportedly dropped a bomb containing the powerful military plastic explosive C-4 on the building in which the group was housed. The bomb and the resulting fire left 11 persons dead (including four children) and destroyed 61 homes.

SAINT LAWRENCE SEAWAY ACT: 60th ANNIVERSARY. May 13, 1954. President Dwight D. Eisenhower signed legislation authorizing US-Canadian construction of a waterway that would make it possible for oceangoing ships to reach the Great Lakes.

SPACE MILESTONE: *ENDEAVOUR* (US). May 13, 1992. Three astronauts from the shuttle *Endeavour* simultaneously walked in space for the first time.

SULLIVAN, ARTHUR: BIRTH ANNIVERSARY. May 13, 1842. English composer best known for light operas (with Sir William Gilbert), born at London, England. Died there Nov 22, 1900.

WELLS, MARY: BIRTH ANNIVERSARY. May 13, 1943. Motown's first big star, Mary Wells was born at Detroit, MI. She was known for such hits as "You Beat Me to the Punch," "Two Lovers" and her signature song, "My Guy." She was one of a group of black artists of the '60s who helped end musical segregation by having their work played on white radio stations. Mary Wells died July 26, 1992, at Los Angeles, CA.

BIRTHDAYS TODAY

Franklyn Ajaye, 65, actor ("Deadwood," *Car Wash*), born Brooklyn, NY, May 13, 1949.

Frances Barber, 57, actress (*Sammy and Rosie Get Laid, We Think the World of You*), born Wolverhampton, England, May 13, 1957.

Mike Bibby, 36, basketball player, born Cherry Hill, NJ, May 13, 1978.

Stephen Colbert, 50, writer, comedian ("The Daily Show," "The Colbert Report"), born Charlestown, SC, May 13, 1964.

Lena Dunham, 28, writer, actress (*Tiny Furniture*, "Girls"), born New York, NY, May 13, 1986.

John Kasich, 62, Governor of Ohio (R), born McKees Rocks, PA, May 13, 1952.

Harvey Keitel, 75, actor (*Mean Streets, Blue Collar, Bugsy, The Piano*), born Brooklyn, NY, May 13, 1939.

Robert Pattinson, 28, actor (*Twilight Saga* films, *Water for Elephants, Harry Potter and the Goblet of Fire*), born London, England, May 13, 1986.

Julianne Phillips, 52, actress (*Allie & Me*, "Sisters"), born Lake Oswego, OR, May 13, 1962.

Tim Pigott-Smith, 68, actor ("The Jewel in the Crown," *Remains of the Day*), born Rugby, England, May 13, 1946.

Dennis Rodman, 53, Hall of Fame basketball player, born Trenton, NJ, May 13, 1961.

Darius Rucker, 46, singer (Hootie and the Blowfish), born Charleston, SC, May 13, 1968.

Bobby Valentine, 64, baseball manager, former player and broadcaster, born Stamford, CT, May 13, 1950.

Stevie Wonder, 64, singer, musician, born Steveland Morris Hardaway at Saginaw, MI, May 13, 1950.

May 14 — Wednesday

DAY 134 **231 REMAINING**

BIRTHDAY OF THE BUDDHA: BIRTH ANNIVERSARY. May 14. Among Buddhist holidays, this day is the most important, as it commemorates the birthday of the Buddha. It is also known as the Day of Vesak. The founder of Buddhism had the given name Siddhartha, the family name Gautama and the clan name Shaka. He is commonly called the Buddha, meaning in Sanskrit "the enlightened one." He is thought to have lived in India from circa 563 BC to 483 BC. Some countries celebrate this holiday on the lunar calendar, so the date changes from year to year, but it always occurs in either April or May. This day is a holiday in India, Indonesia, Korea, Singapore and Thailand. This is also a holiday in China, but the date differs on the Chinese calendar.

CANNES FILM FESTIVAL. May 14–25 (tentative). Cannes, France. 67th annual. Premier international film festival, with hundreds of screenings (in competition and out), critical panels, director spotlights, Cannes Market for film distribution and numerous other cultural and artistic activities. Palme d'Or, Caméra d'Or, Grand Prix and other awards presented on the last day of the festival. The festival was first held in September 1946, and there have been only three cancellations since then, in 1948, 1950 and 1968. For info: Assoc Française du Festival Intl du Film, 3, rue Amelie, F-75007 Paris, France. Phone: (33) 0-53-59-61-00. E-mail: festival@festival-cannes.fr. Web: www.festival-cannes.com.

CARLSBAD CAVERNS NATIONAL PARK ESTABLISHED: ANNIVERSARY. May 14, 1930. Located in southwestern New Mexico, Carlsbad Caverns was proclaimed a national monument Oct 25, 1923, and was later established as a national park and preserve.

CRUISIN' DOWNTOWN 2014. May 14 (also June 11, July 9, Aug 13 and Sept 10). Toms River, NJ. Enjoy classic automobiles and motorcycles along Washington St. Live entertainment, crafters and food. Est attendance: 2,500. For info: Downtown Toms River, 218 Main St, Toms River, NJ 08753. Phone: (732) 341-8738. Fax: (732) 341-8748. E-mail: info@downtowntomsriver.com. Web: www.downtowntomsriver.com.

DONATE A DAY'S WAGES TO CHARITY DAY. May 14. 13th annual. All working people are asked to donate the money they make on May 14, 2014, to charity. If unable to afford the donation, they are then asked to take the day off of work and donate their time to charity. Annually, the second Wednesday in May. For info: E-mail: donatetocharity@yahoo.com.

ENGLAND: ROYAL WINDSOR HORSE SHOW. May 14–18. Home Park, Private Windsor, Berkshire. Major annual show jumping and showing event with royal pageantry and color. Est attendance: 65,000. For info: Penelope Henderson, Sec'y, Royal Windsor Horse Show, The Royal Mews, Windsor Castle, Windsor, Berkshire, England SL4 1NG. E-mail: info@rwhs.co.uk. Web: www.rwhs.co.uk.

May 2014	S	M	T	W	T	F	S
					1	2	3
	4	5	6	7	8	9	10
	11	12	13	14	15	16	17
	18	19	20	21	22	23	24
	25	26	27	28	29	30	31

"ERNIE KOVACS" TV PREMIERE: ANNIVERSARY. May 14, 1951. Comedian Ernie Kovacs first hosted "It's Time for Ernie," a 15-minute afternoon program on NBC, in May 1951 before replacing "Kukla, Fran and Ollie" with "Ernie in Kovacsland." "The Ernie Kovacs Show" debuted on Dec 30, 1952. Kovacs also appeared on a variety of daytime and prime-time series and was a fill-in for Steve Allen on the "The Tonight Show." His early shows featured his wife, Edie Adams.

FAHRENHEIT, GABRIEL DANIEL: BIRTH ANNIVERSARY. May 14, 1686. German physicist born at Danzig, Prussia (now Gdansk, Poland). Fahrenheit introduced the use of mercury in thermometers and markedly improved their accuracy. He devised the Fahrenheit temperature scale (based on 32° for the freezing/melting point of water/ice) that is still used in the US (the Celsius scale is used more universally). He died at Amsterdam, The Netherlands, on Sept 16, 1736.

FLOWER MOON. May 14. So called by Native American tribes of New England and the Great Lakes because by this time of the year, flowers are everywhere. The May Full Moon.

GAINSBOROUGH, THOMAS: BAPTISM ANNIVERSARY. May 14, 1727. (Old Style date.) English landscape and portrait painter. Among his most remembered works: *The Blue Boy*, *The Watering Place* and *The Market Cart*. Born at Sudbury, Suffolk, England, he was baptized on May 14, 1727 (OS), and he died at London, Aug 2, 1788.

JAMESTOWN, VIRGINIA: FOUNDING ANNIVERSARY. May 14, 1607. (Old Style date.) The first permanent English settlement in what is now the US took place at Jamestown, VA (named for England's King James I), on this date. Captains John Smith and Christopher Newport were among the leaders of the group of royally chartered Virginia Company settlers who had traveled from Plymouth, England, in three small ships: *Susan Constant*, *Godspeed* and *Discovery*.

LEWIS AND CLARK EXPEDITION SETS OUT: ANNIVERSARY. May 14, 1804. Charged by President Thomas Jefferson with finding a route to the Pacific, Captain Meriwether Lewis and Lieutenant William Clark left St. Louis, MO, with a 33-member group skilled in botany, zoology, outdoor survival and other scientific skills. They arrived at the Pacific coast of Oregon in November 1805 and returned to St. Louis on Sept 23, 1806.

MOON PHASE: FULL MOON. May 14. Moon enters Full Moon phase at 3:16 PM, EDT.

NATIONAL NIGHTSHIFT WORKERS DAY. May 14. To honor those workers who reverse their natural circadian rhythm to keep business running 24 hours a day. Annually, the second Wednesday of May. For info: Velcea Kae, 3 Chester Rd, Springfield, VT 05156.

NATIONAL RECEPTIONISTS DAY. May 14. This is a day of recognition for the frontline personnel in business, the Directors of First Impressions. You only get one chance to make a good first impression, and that is their job. Receptionists may have other titles: front-desk personnel, operator or customer service representative. The National Receptionists Association inaugurated this day of recognition to include anyone responsible for creating or maintaining a favorable image for the company. According to the Bureau of Labor Statistics, there are more than a million receptionists in the US. Annually, the second Wednesday in May. For info: Jennifer Alexander, Natl Receptionists Association. Phone: (203) 273-1179. Fax: (800) 827-0465. E-mail: jennifer@nationalreceptionists.com. Web: www.nationalreceptionists.com.

NATIONAL THIRD SHIFT WORKERS DAY. May 14. To show appreciation for and to honor those often-forgotten workers who toil through the night to keep countless companies and businesses running smoothly. Annually, the second Wednesday in May. For info: Jeff Corbett, PO Box 2, Statesville, NC 28687.

NORWAY: MIDNIGHT SUN AT NORTH CAPE. May 14–July 30. North Cape. First day of the season with around-the-clock sunshine. At North Cape the sun never dips below the horizon from May 14 to July 30, but the night is bright long before and after these dates.

OWEN, ROBERT: BIRTH ANNIVERSARY. May 14, 1771. English progressive owner of spinning works, philanthropist, utopian socialist, founder of New Harmony, IN, born at Newtown, Wales. Died there Nov 17, 1858.

PHILIPPINES: CARABAO FESTIVAL. May 14–15. Pulilan, Bulacan; Nueva Ecija; Angono, Rizal. Parade of farmers to honor their patron saint, San Isidro, with hundreds of "dressed-up" *carabaos* (water buffalo) participating.

SMALLPOX VACCINE DISCOVERED: ANNIVERSARY. May 14, 1796. In the 18th century smallpox was a widespread and often fatal disease. Edward Jenner, a physician in rural England, heard reports of dairy farmers who apparently became immune to smallpox as a result of exposure to cowpox, a related but milder disease. After two decades of studying the phenomenon, Jenner injected cowpox into a healthy eight-year-old boy, who subsequently developed cowpox. Six weeks later, Jenner inoculated the boy with smallpox. He remained healthy. Jenner called this new procedure *vaccination*, from *vaccinia*, another term for cowpox. Within 18 months, 12,000 people in England had been vaccinated and the number of smallpox deaths dropped by two-thirds.

SPACE MILESTONE: *SKYLAB* (US). May 14, 1973. The US launched *Skylab*, its first manned orbiting laboratory.

"THE STARS AND STRIPES FOREVER" DAY. May 14, 1897. Anniversary of the first public performance of John Philip Sousa's march "The Stars and Stripes Forever," at Philadelphia, PA. The occasion was the unveiling of a statue of George Washington, and President William McKinley was present.

UNDERGROUND AMERICA DAY. May 14. 38th anniversary. Underground America Day is one man's (the late Malcolm Wells's) attempt to get others to think of designing and building structures underground. Wells published illustrations and humorous suggestions for celebrating Underground America Day. Annually, May 14. For info: Karen North Wells, 673 Satucket Rd, Brewster, MA 02631. Web: www.malcolmwells.com.

WAAC: ANNIVERSARY. May 14, 1942. During WWII women became eligible to enlist for noncombat duties in the Women's Auxiliary Army Corps (WAAC) by an act of Congress. Women also served through Women Accepted for Voluntary Emergency Service (WAVES), Women's Auxiliary Ferrying Squadron (WAFS) and Coast Guard or Semper Paratus Always Ready Service (SPARS), the Women's Reserve of the Marine Corps.

BIRTHDAYS TODAY

Cate Blanchett, 45, actress (Oscar for *The Aviator*; *I'm Not There, Elizabeth, Babel*), born Melbourne, Australia, May 14, 1969.

David Byrne, 62, singer, composer, born Dumbarton, Scotland, May 14, 1952.

Meg Foster, 66, actress ("Cagney & Lacey," *The Emerald Forest, They Live*), born Reading, PA, May 14, 1948.

Roy Halladay, 37, baseball player, born Denver, CO, May 14, 1977.

Suzy Kolber, 50, sportscaster, born Philadelphia, PA, May 14, 1964.

George Lucas, 70, filmmaker (*Star Wars* films), born Modesto, CA, May 14, 1944.

Jose Dennis Martinez, 59, former baseball player, born Granada, Nicaragua, May 14, 1955.

Patrice Munsel, 89, opera singer, born Spokane, WA, May 14, 1925.

Atanasio (Tony) Perez, 72, Hall of Fame baseball player, born Camaguey, Cuba, May 14, 1942.

Tim Roth, 53, actor (*The Incredible Hulk, Planet of the Apes, Rob Roy, Pulp Fiction*), born London, England, May 14, 1961.

Amber Tamblyn, 31, actress (*The Sisterhood of the Traveling Pants*, "Joan of Arcadia"), born Santa Monica, CA, May 14, 1983.

Ronan Tynan, 54, opera singer (The Irish Tenors), born Dublin, Ireland, May 14, 1960.

Robert Zemeckis, 62, director (Oscar for *Forrest Gump*; *Flight, Cast Away, Back to the Future*), screenwriter, born Chicago, IL, May 14, 1952.

Mark Zuckerberg, 30, computer programmer, founder of Facebook, born White Plains, NY, May 14, 1984.

May 15 — Thursday

DAY 135 **230 REMAINING**

ASPENCASH MOTORCYCLE RALLY. May 15–18. Ruidoso, NM. $10,000 cash poker run, trade show, poker run pin. Est attendance: 12,000. For info: Golden Aspen Rally Assn, PO Box 1467, Ruidoso, NM 88355. Phone: (575) 973-4977. E-mail: info@motorcyclerally.com. Web: www.motorcyclerally.com.

AVEDON, RICHARD: BIRTH ANNIVERSARY. May 15, 1923. Influential photographer born at New York, NY. Avedon began his career with the merchant marines, taking personnel identification photos and images of shipwrecks. Later, he worked for *Harper's Bazaar* and *Vogue*, where his artistic style of shooting fashion models against famous backgrounds revolutionized that industry's approach to fashion layouts. He was known for taking memorable, while not necessarily flattering, portraits and was honored with retrospectives and exhibits at many museums. He received the National Medal for the Arts in 2003 and died at New York, Oct 1, 2004.

BAUM, LYMAN FRANK: BIRTH ANNIVERSARY. May 15, 1856. The American newspaperman who wrote the Wizard of Oz stories was born at Chittenango, NY. Although *The Wonderful Wizard of Oz* is the most famous, Baum also wrote many other books for children, including more than a dozen about Oz. He died at Hollywood, CA, May 6, 1919.

COTTEN, JOSEPH: BIRTH ANNIVERSARY. May 15, 1905. Stage and screen star Joseph Cotten was born at Petersburg, VA. Among Cotten's movie credits are *Citizen Kane, The Magnificent Ambersons* and *The Third Man*. Among his most noted performances on Broadway were *The Philadelphia Story* and *Once More with Feeling*. Joseph Cotten died Feb 6, 1994, at Los Angeles, CA.

CURIE, PIERRE: BIRTH ANNIVERSARY. May 15, 1859. Born at Paris, France, Curie was one of the founders of modern physics. His research had already brought important results (in heat waves, crystals, magnetism, symmetry) and the formulation of Curie's law before he married Marie Sklowdowska in 1895. Together, the Curies discovered polonium and radium while conducting research in radioactivity. With Henri Becquerel, the Curies were awarded the Nobel Prize for Physics in 1903. Tragically, Pierre Curie was struck by a dray in Paris and died Apr 19, 1906.

EASTERN PACIFIC HURRICANE SEASON. May 15–Nov 30. Eastern Pacific defined as coast to 140° west longitude. Info from: US Dept of Commerce, Natl Oceanic and Atmospheric Admin, Rockville, MD 20852.

FIRST FLIGHT ATTENDANT: ANNIVERSARY. May 15, 1930. Ellen Church became the first airline stewardess (today's flight attendant), flying on a United Airlines flight from San Francisco, CA, to Cheyenne, WY.

GEORGE WALLACE SHOT: ANNIVERSARY. May 15, 1972. George Wallace, a former governor of Alabama and a symbol of segregation, was shot by Arthur Bremer while Wallace was at Laurel, MD, campaigning for the US presidency. For the remainder of his life (until he died in 1998), Wallace was paralyzed from the waist down. On Aug 4, 1972, Bremer was sentenced to 67 years in prison for the shooting.

HYPEREMESIS GRAVIDARUM AWARENESS DAY. May 15. To raise awareness about the debilitating pregnancy disease known as hyperemesis gravidarum. Women around the world are struggling to survive through their pregnancies. Their bodies are debilitated due to the lack of hydration and food intake they cannot receive. Women are left to suffer in silence as they waste away trying to maintain their lives and the lives of their unborn children. For info: H.E.R. Foundation, 932 Edwards Ferry Rd, Ste 23, Leesburg, VA 20176. Phone: (703) 399-1272. E-mail: annmarie@helpher.org. Web: www.helpher.org or www.hyperemesis.org.

JAPAN: AOI MATSURI (HOLLYHOCK FESTIVAL). May 15. Kyoto. The festival features a pageant reproducing imperial processions of ancient times that paid homage to the shrine of Shimogamo and Kamigamo.

MEXICO: SAN ISIDRO DAY. May 15. Day of San Isidro Labrador celebrated widely in farming regions to honor St. Isidore, the Plowman. Livestock gaily decorated with flowers. Celebrations usually begin about May 13 and continue for about a week.

MILES CITY BUCKING HORSE SALE. May 15–18. Miles City, MT. Miles City is real "Lonesome Dove" country, and its annual bucking horse sale is where rodeo stock operators from around the nation and Canada head to purchase their bucking horses for the coming rodeo season. A festive event, the sale not only involves cowboys trying to ride some of the wildest horses in the country but also includes Western artists displaying and creating works in a weekend art show, a Western trade show featuring practical and gift items, a Saturday-morning parade and Miles City's Western attractions such as the Range Riders Museum. (Miles City is the community featured in the novel and two television miniseries about "Lonesome Dove.") Est attendance: 10,000. For info: Bucking Horse Sale Office, PO Box 1027, Miles City, MT 59301. Phone: (406) 874-BUCK. Web: www.buckinghorsesale.com.

NCAA DIVISION I MEN'S AND WOMEN'S TENNIS CHAMPIONSHIPS. May 15–26. Site TBD. 77th annual for men and 32nd annual for women. For info: Natl Collegiate Athletic Assn, PO Box 6222, Indianapolis, IN 46206-6222. Phone: (317) 917-6222. Web: www.NCAA.com.

NORGAY, TENZING: 100th BIRTH ANNIVERSARY. May 15, 1914. Sherpa co-conqueror of Mount Everest, born as Nambyal Wangdi, at Tschechu, Tibet. Raised in Nepal, Tenzing began mountaineering as a porter. Having participated in six previous attempts at scaling Mount Everest, he was the most experienced Everest climber on the British expedition of 1953, and on May 29, he and New Zealander Edmund Hillary were the first two men atop the world's highest mountain. Died May 9, 1983, at Darjeeling, India.

NYLON STOCKINGS: ANNIVERSARY. May 15, 1940. Nylon hose went on sale at stores throughout the country. Competing producers bought their nylon yarn from E.I. du Pont de Nemours and Company (later DuPont). W.H. Carothers, of DuPont, developed nylon, called "Polymer 66," in 1935. It was the first totally manmade fiber and over time was substituted for other materials and came to have widespread application.

PARAGUAY: INDEPENDENCE DAY. May 15. Commemorates independence from Spain, attained in 1811.

✦PEACE OFFICER MEMORIAL DAY. May 15. Presidential Proclamation 3537, of May 4, 1963, covers all succeeding years. (PL 87–726 of Oct 1, 1962.) May 15 of each year since 1963; however, first issued in 1962 for May 14.

PEACE OFFICER MEMORIAL DAY. May 15. An event honored by some 21,000 police departments nationwide. The memorial ceremonies are in the American Police Hall of Fame and Museum, Titusville, FL. See also: "National Police Week" (May 11–17). Sponsor: National Association of Chiefs of Police. For info: American Police Hall of Fame and Museum, 6350 Horizon Dr, Titusville, FL 32780. Phone: (321) 264-0911. E-mail: policeinfo@aphf.org. Web: www.aphf.org.

PORTER, KATHERINE ANNE: BIRTH ANNIVERSARY. May 15, 1890. American prose writer Katherine Anne Porter was born at Indian Creek, TX. Her one long novel, *Ship of Fools* (1962), is considered by some to be one of the greatest allegorical works in English. She won the Pulitzer Prize and the National Book Award in 1966 for *Collected Stories*. Died Sept 18, 1980, at Silver Spring, MD.

SCHNITZLER, ARTHUR: BIRTH ANNIVERSARY. May 15, 1862. Austrian playwright, novelist and medical doctor, Arthur Schnitzler was born at Vienna. Noted for his psychoanalytic examination of Viennese society. Died at Vienna, Oct 21, 1931.

SPACE MILESTONE: *FAITH 7* (US). May 15, 1963. Launched with Major Gordon Leroy Cooper and orbited Earth 22 times.

UNITED NATIONS: INTERNATIONAL DAY OF FAMILIES. May 15. The General Assembly (Resolution 47/237) on Sept 20, 1993, voted this as an annual observance beginning in 1994. For info: United Nations, Dept of Public Info, New York, NY 10017. Web: www.un.org.

WILSON, ELLEN LOUISE AXSON: BIRTH ANNIVERSARY. May 15, 1860. First wife of Woodrow Wilson, 28th president of the US. Born at Savannah, GA; died at Washington, DC, Aug 6, 1914.

BIRTHDAYS TODAY

Anna Maria Alberghetti, 78, singer, actress (*Cinderfella, Carnival*), born Pesaro, Italy, May 15, 1936.

Madeleine Albright, 77, former US secretary of state (Clinton administration), born Prague, Czechoslovakia (now the Czech Republic), May 15, 1937.

George Brett, 61, Hall of Fame baseball player, executive, born Glen Dale, WV, May 15, 1953.

David Charvet, 42, actor ("Melrose Place," "Baywatch"), born Lyon, France, May 15, 1972.

David Cronenberg, 71, filmmaker (*Eastern Promises, A History of Violence, The Fly*), born Toronto, ON, Canada, May 15, 1943.

Dwayne De Rosario, 36, soccer player, born Scarborough, ON, Canada, May 15, 1978.

Brian Eno, 66, avant-garde musician, born Woodbridge, England, May 15, 1948.

Giselle Fernandez, 53, television host, actress, born Mexico City, Mexico, May 15, 1961.

Lee Horsley, 59, actor ("Nero Wolfe," "Matt Houston"), born Muleshoe, TN, May 15, 1955.

Jasper Johns, 84, artist, born Augusta, GA, May 15, 1930.

Lainie Kazan, 72, singer, actress (*My Big Fat Greek Wedding, My Favorite Year, Beaches*), born New York, NY, May 15, 1942.

David Krumholtz, 36, actor ("Numb3rs"), born New York, NY, May 15, 1978.

Trini Lopez, 77, singer, actor (*Marriage on the Rocks, The Dirty Dozen*), born Dallas, TX, May 15, 1937.

Justin Morneau, 33, baseball player, born New Westminster, BC, Canada, May 15, 1981.

Andy Murray, 27, tennis player, born Dunblane, Scotland, May 15, 1987.

Chazz Palminteri, 63, actor (*Bullets Over Broadway*), playwright, screenwriter (*A Bronx Tale*), born the Bronx, NY, May 15, 1951.

May 2014

S	M	T	W	T	F	S
				1	2	3
4	5	6	7	8	9	10
11	12	13	14	15	16	17
18	19	20	21	22	23	24
25	26	27	28	29	30	31

Dan Patrick, 58, sportscaster, radio personality, born Zanesville, OH, May 15, 1956.

Kathleen Sebelius, 66, US Secretary of Health and Human Services, former governor of Kansas (D), born Cincinnati, OH, May 15, 1948.

Jamie-Lynn Sigler, 33, actress ("The Sopranos"), born Jericho, NY, May 15, 1981.

Emmitt Smith, 45, Hall of Fame football player, born Pensacola, FL, May 15, 1969.

John Smoltz, 47, broadcaster, former baseball player, born Warren, MI, May 15, 1967.

Sam Trammell, 43, actor ("True Blood"), born New Orleans, LA, May 15, 1971.

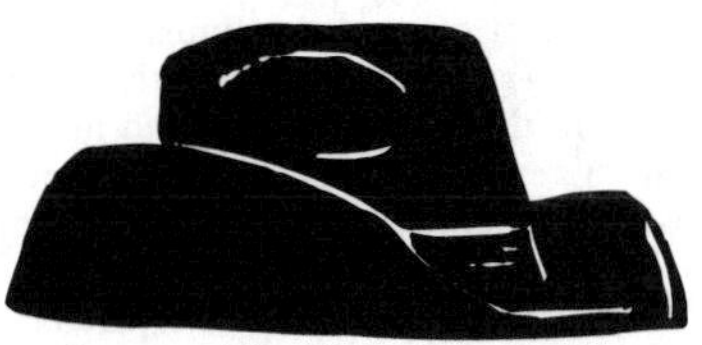

May 16 — Friday

DAY 136 **229 REMAINING**

ART FAIR AND WINEFEST. May 16–18. Washington, MO. The largest Missouri wine tasting of state wines as well as a juried art show featuring 60 Midwestern artists. Art fair is free. Admission to the wine pavilion includes a commemorative wineglass. Est attendance: 20,000. For info: Downtown Washington, Inc, PO Box 144, Washington, MO 63090. Phone: (636) 239-1743. Fax: (636) 239-4832. E-mail: events@downtownwashmo.org. Web: www.downtownwashmo.org.

BATTLE OF DREWRY'S BLUFF: 150th ANNIVERSARY. May 16, 1864. In a dense fog General Benjamin Butler's Union forces were attacked at Drewry's Bluff, VA. Butler, after landing at the Bermuda Hundred on the Virginia peninsula, had been slowly moving on the Confederate city of Petersburg, outside Richmond. His troops were defeated by Confederate forces under P.T. Beauregard, and Butler was forced to withdraw to the Bermuda Hundred. Although this was another in a long line of bumbling exploits by Butler, Lincoln was reluctant to remove him from command because of Butler's political influence in the North.

BIOGRAPHERS DAY. May 16. Anniversary of the meeting, at London, England, May 16, 1763, of James Boswell and Samuel Johnson, beginning history's most famous biographer-biographee relationship. Boswell's *Journal of a Tour to the Hebrides* (1785) and his *Life of Samuel Johnson* (1791) are regarded as models of biographical writing. Thus this day is recommended as one on which to start reading or writing a biography.

COIN, JEWELRY & STAMP EXPO. May 16–18. Pasadena Convention Center, Pasadena, CA. Annual expo. Est attendance: 5,000. For info: Israel Bick, Exec Dir, Intl Stamp & Coin Collectors Society, Box 854, Van Nuys, CA 91408. Phone: (818) 997-6496. Fax: (818) 988-4337. E-mail: iibick@sbcglobal.net. Web: www.bickinternational.com.

DENMARK: COMMON PRAYER DAY. May 16. Public holiday. The fourth Friday after Easter, known as "Store Bededag," is a day for prayer and festivity.

FIRST ACADEMY AWARDS: 85th ANNIVERSARY. May 16, 1929. About 270 people attended a dinner at the Hollywood Roosevelt Hotel at which the first Academy Awards were given in 12 categories. The silent film *Wings* won Best Picture. A committee of only 20 members selected the winners that year. By the third year the entire membership of the Academy voted. The Academy Awards were first televised in 1953.

FIRST WOMAN TO CLIMB MOUNT EVEREST: ANNIVERSARY. May 16, 1975. Japanese climber Junko Tabei, leading an all-woman expedition to Mount Everest, became the first woman to reach the summit on this date in 1975. Taking the South-East Ridge route, Tabei was delayed by an avalanche before her last leg up the mountain. "Even after reaching the peak," she later recalled, "instead of shouting with excitement, I was simply happy that I didn't have to go any higher!"

FISHING HAS NO BOUNDARIES—HAYWARD EVENT. May 16–17. Lake Chippewa Campgrounds, Hayward, WI. 27th annual three-day fishing experience for disabled persons. Any disability, age, sex, race, etc, eligible. Fishing with experienced guides on one of the best fishing waters in Wisconsin, attended by 150 participants and 350 volunteers. Est attendance: 2,000. For info: Fishing Has No Boundaries, PO Box 375, Hayward, WI 54843. Phone: (715) 634-3185. Fax: (715) 634-1305. E-mail: hayfhnb@cheqnet.net. Web: www.haywardFHNB.org.

FONDA, HENRY: BIRTH ANNIVERSARY. May 16, 1905. American stage, TV and screen actor (*The Grapes of Wrath, Mister Roberts*), Academy Award winner, born Henry Jaynes Fonda at Grand Island, NE. Began his acting career at the Omaha (NE) Playhouse. Fonda died at Los Angeles, CA, Aug 12, 1982.

GWINNETT, BUTTON: DEATH ANNIVERSARY. May 16, 1777. Signer of the Declaration of Independence, born at Down Hatherley, Gloucestershire, England, about 1735 (exact date unknown). Died following a duel at St. Catherines Island, off of Savannah, GA.

HERMAN, WOODY: BIRTH ANNIVERSARY. May 16, 1913. The legendary jazz clarinetist, saxophonist, singer and bandleader was born at Milwaukee, WI. After cutting his teeth playing with bands led by others in Chicago, IL, Herman formed his first band in 1936. For the next 50 years he continued to form and front talented ensembles that played in a variety of jazz styles—from blues and improvisation to bop and jazz-rock. Herman died Oct 29, 1987, at Los Angeles, CA.

INTERNATIONAL VIRTUAL ASSISTANTS DAY. May 16. This day acknowledges the dedication, experience, expertise and determination of virtual professionals and exemplifies their integrity and commitment to provide superior administrative and other business support services—virtually. This day is celebrated during the Online International Virtual Assistants Convention and sponsored by the Alliance for Virtual Businesses, a consortium of international virtual assistant organizations. Annually, the third Friday in May. For info: Alliance for Virtual Businesses. Phone: (410) 521-7001. Fax: (410) 521-9742. E-mail: info@oivac.com. Web: www.oivac.com.

LIBERACE: 95th BIRTH ANNIVERSARY. May 16, 1919. Wladziu Valentino Liberace, concert pianist who began with a piano, a candelabra, a brother named George and a huge engaging smile, threw in extravagant clothes and jewels and became a Las Vegas headliner and the winner of two Emmy Awards, six gold albums and two stars on the Hollywood Walk of Fame. Liberace was born at West Allis, WI; he died Feb 4, 1987, at Palm Springs, CA.

MAGNOLIA BLOSSOM FESTIVAL. May 16–17. Magnolia, AR. 26th annual. Events include parade, arts and crafts, entertainment and activities for all. World Championship Steak Cook-Off served under fragrant magnolia trees. Est attendance: 15,000. For info: Magnolia-Columbia County Chamber of Commerce, 211 W Main St, PO Box 866, Magnolia, AR 71754-0866. Phone: (870) 234-4352. E-mail: ea@ccalliance.us. Web: www.blossomfestival.org.

MAIFEST. May 16–18. MainStrasse Village, Covington, KY. MainStrasse celebrates the German tradition of welcoming the first spring wines and the beginning of the festival season. Artist and crafts exhibits, food and drink, live music and entertainment. Est attendance: 125,000. For info: Donna Kremer, Administrative Coord, MainStrasse Village, 406 W 6th St, Ste 201, Covington, KY 41011. Phone: (859) 491-0458. Fax: (859) 655-7932. E-mail: dkremer@mainstrasse.org. Web: www.mainstrasse.org.

MARTIN, BILLY: BIRTH ANNIVERSARY. May 16, 1928. Baseball player and manager born at Berkeley, CA. Billy Martin's baseball career included managerial stints with five major league teams: the New York Yankees, Minnesota Twins, Detroit Tigers, Texas Rangers and Oakland Athletics. After a successful playing career, he compiled a record of 1,258 victories to 1,018 losses in his 16 seasons as a manager. His combative style both on and off the field kept him in the headlines, and he will long be remembered for his on-again, off-again relationship with Yankees owner George Steinbrenner, for whom he managed the Yankees five different times. Martin died in an auto accident near Fenton, NY, Dec 25, 1989.

MORTON, LEVI PARSONS: BIRTH ANNIVERSARY. May 16, 1824. 22nd vice president of the US (1889–93), born at Shoreham, VT. Died at Rhinebeck, NY, May 16, 1920.

NATIONAL BIKE TO WORK DAY. May 16. At the state or local level, Bike to Work events are conducted by small and large businesses, city governments, bicycle clubs and environmental groups. Annually, the third Friday in May. Est attendance: 2,000,000. For info: League of American Bicyclists, 1612 K St NW, Ste 510, Washington, DC 20006. Phone: (202) 822-1333. Fax: (202) 822-1334. E-mail: bikeleague@bikeleague.org. Web: www.bikeleague.org/bikemonth.

✦NATIONAL DEFENSE TRANSPORTATION DAY. May 16. Presidential Proclamation customarily issued as "National Defense Transportation Day and National Transportation Week." Issued each year for the third Friday in May since 1957. (PL 85-32 of May 16, 1957.)

NATIONAL PIZZA PARTY DAY. May 16. As the school year winds down, students and parents should celebrate with pizza parties! Local promotions will support the day within classrooms and at home. Annually, the third Friday in May. For info: Garlic Jim's Famous Gourmet Pizza, 3922 148th St SE, Ste 107, Mill Creek, WA 98012. Phone: (425) 948-7603. Fax: (425) 948-7945. E-mail: ross@garlicjims.com. Web: www.garlicjims.com.

PEABODY, ELIZABETH PALMER: BIRTH ANNIVERSARY. May 16, 1804. Born at Billerica, MA, Peabody was an innovative educator, author and publisher. She opened her first school at Lancaster, MA, when only 16. In 1839 Peabody opened a bookstore that quickly became the intellectuals' hangout. With her own printing press Peabody became the first woman publisher in Boston, MA, and possibly the US. She published three of her brother-in-law Nathaniel Hawthorne's books. For two years she published and wrote for *The Dial*, the literary magazine and voice of the transcendental movement. Peabody's enduring accomplishment was the establishment of the first kindergarten in the US, in 1860 at Boston. She created a magazine, *Kindergarten Messenger*, in 1873. Died Jan 3, 1894, at Jamaica Plain, MA.

May 2014	S	M	T	W	T	F	S
					1	2	3
	4	5	6	7	8	9	10
	11	12	13	14	15	16	17
	18	19	20	21	22	23	24
	25	26	27	28	29	30	31

RAF BOMBS RUHR DAMS: ANNIVERSARY. May 16–17, 1943. Over these two days Royal Air Force Lancasters attacked three dams in the German Ruhr Valley. They dropped 4.5-ton bombs designed specifically for this mission. The Mohne and the Eder (the largest dam in Europe at the time) were both damaged. These two dams provided drinking water for 4 million people and supplied 75 percent of the electrical power for industry. Widespread flooding and many deaths resulted.

REY, MARGARET: BIRTH ANNIVERSARY. May 16, 1906. Children's author, born at Hamburg, Germany. Together with her illustrator husband, H.A. Rey, she produced the Curious George series. Rey died at Cambridge, MA, Dec 21, 1996.

RICH, ADRIENNE: 85th BIRTH ANNIVERSARY. May 16, 1929. Born at Baltimore, MD, Adrienne Rich was one of the preeminent poets and feminist theorists of her era. She famously wrote, "The most notable fact our culture imprints on women is the sense of our limits. The most important thing one woman can do for another is to illuminate and expand her sense of actual possibilities." Rich's extensive body of work critiques many social systems—most prominently, patriarchy—and exhibits her progression as a poet, migrating from more formal and structured form earlier in her career to a looser, more personal and intimate form later. Distinguished works include *Of Woman Born: Motherhood as Experience and Institution* (1976) and *Diving into the Wreck: Poems 1971–1972* (1973) for which she received the National Book Award. Rich died Mar 27, 2012, at Santa Cruz, CA.

SEWARD, WILLIAM HENRY: BIRTH ANNIVERSARY. May 16, 1801. American statesman, secretary of state under Lincoln and Andrew Johnson. Seward negotiated the purchase of Alaska from Russia for $7,200,000. At the time some felt the price was too high and referred to the purchase as "Seward's Folly." Seward was governor of New York, 1839–43, and a member of the US Senate, 1848–60. On the evening of Lincoln's assassination, Apr 14, 1865, Seward was stabbed in the throat by Lewis Posell, a fellow conspirator of John Wilkes Booth. Seward recovered and maintained his cabinet position under President Andrew Johnson until 1869. Born at Florida, NY, he died at Auburn, NY, Oct 10, 1872.

TEACHER'S DAY IN FLORIDA. May 16. A ceremonial day observed on the third Friday in May.

TERKEL, STUDS: BIRTH ANNIVERSARY. May 16, 1912. The Chicago-based radio interviewer-turned-oral historian was born Louis Terkel on this date at New York City. Terkel was a self-described "guerrilla journalist" who authored dozens of books, including the Pulitzer Prize–winning *The Good War: An Oral History of World War II* (1984), as well as the similarly structured *Working* (1974). Good interviewing was, Terkel said, listening with respect. He died Oct 31, 2008, at Chicago, IL.

BIRTHDAYS TODAY

David Boreanaz, 43, actor ("Bones," "Angel," "Buffy the Vampire Slayer"), born Philadelphia, PA, May 16, 1971.

Pierce Brosnan, 61, actor (*The Ghost Writer, The Thomas Crown Affair,* "Remington Steele," James Bond films), born County Meath, Ireland, May 16, 1953.

Daniel R. Coats, 71, US Senator (R, Indiana), born Jackson, MI, May 16, 1943.

Jean-Sebastien Giguere, 37, hockey player, born Montreal, QC, Canada, May 16, 1977.

Tracey Gold, 45, actress ("Growing Pains"), born New York, NY, May 16, 1969.

Janet Jackson, 48, singer, born Gary, IN, May 16, 1966.

Olga Korbut, 59, Olympic gymnast, born Grodno, USSR (now Belarus), May 16, 1955.

John Scott (Jack) Morris, 59, former baseball player, born St. Paul, MN, May 16, 1955.

Matt Ryan, 29, football player, born Exton, PA, May 16, 1985.

Gabriela Sabatini, 44, Hall of Fame tennis player, born Buenos Aires, Argentina, May 16, 1970.

Joan (Benoit) Samuelson, 57, Olympic runner, born Cape Elizabeth, ME, May 16, 1957.

Bill Smitrovich, 67, actor ("Crime Story," *Splash, Manhunter*), born Bridgeport, CT, May 16, 1947.

Tori Spelling, 41, television personality ("Tori & Dean"), actress ("Beverly Hills 90210"), author, born Beverly Hills, CA, May 16, 1973.

Jim Sturgess, 33, actor (*Across the Universe, 21*), born London, England, May 16, 1981.

Mare Winningham, 55, actress (*Mildred Pierce, St. Elmo's Fire*), born Phoenix, AZ, May 16, 1959.

May 17 — Saturday

DAY 137 **228 REMAINING**

✦ARMED FORCES DAY. May 17. Presidential Proclamation 5983, of May 17, 1989, covers the third Saturday in May in all succeeding years. Originally proclaimed as "Army Day" for Apr 6, beginning in 1936 (S.Con.Res. 30 of Apr 2, 1936). S.Con.Res. 5 of Mar 16, 1937, requested annual Apr 6 issuance, which was done through 1949. Always the third Saturday in May since 1950. Traditionally issued once by each administration.

BELL, JAMES "COOL PAPA": BIRTH ANNIVERSARY. May 17, 1903. Negro League baseball player James "Cool Papa" Bell was born at Starkville, MS. He played 25 seasons from 1922 to 1946 (one year before Jackie Robinson broke the "color barrier" in major league baseball) with a career average of .338. Regarded as the fastest man ever to play the game—he could round the bases in 13 seconds—he was inducted into the Baseball Hall of Fame in 1974. Bell died Mar 7, 1991, at St. Louis, MO.

***BROWN v BOARD OF EDUCATION* DECISION: 60th ANNIVERSARY.** May 17, 1954. The US Supreme Court ruled unanimously that segregation of public schools "solely on the basis of race" denied black children "equal educational opportunity" even though "physical facilities and other 'tangible' factors may have been equal. Separate educational facilities are inherently unequal." The case was argued before the Court by Thurgood Marshall, who would go on to become the first black appointed to the Supreme Court.

CALIFORNIA ARTICHOKE FESTIVAL. May 17–18. Castroville, CA. 55th annual. Annually, in the Artichoke Capital of the World. Events include wine tasting, chef demos, agro-art contest, vintage car show and 5k and 10k runs. Annually, the third weekend in May. Est attendance: 32,000. For info: Castroville Artichoke Festivals, Inc, PO Box 1041, Castroville, CA 95012. Phone: (831) 633-2465. Fax: (831) 633-0485. E-mail: info@artichoke-festival.org. Web: www.artichoke-festival.org.

ENGLAND: FA CUP. May 17. Wembley Stadium, London, England. Established in 1871, the oldest cup competition in the world. Teams in the leagues of England's Football Association compete in single-elimination games leading up to this cup final. For info: Football Association. Web: www.thefa.com/TheFACup.

FIRST KENTUCKY DERBY: ANNIVERSARY. May 17, 1875. The first running of the Kentucky Derby took place at Churchill Downs, Louisville, KY. Jockey Oliver Lewis rode the horse Aristides to a winning time of 2:37.25.

FIRST US SAME-SEX MARRIAGES: 10th ANNIVERSARY. May 17, 2004. Massachusetts became the first US state to sanction gay marriage on this date. Hundreds of gay and lesbian couples received licenses and were married.

FISHING HAS NO BOUNDARIES. May 17–18. Freeman Lake, Monticello, IN. A two-day event for people with disabilities to experience fishing on the lake. Any disability, sex, age, race, etc, eligible. For info: Fishing Has No Boundaries, PO Box 325, Battle Ground, IN 47920. Phone: (765) 567-2567. E-mail: smlinder2000@yahoo.com.

GETTYSBURG OUTDOOR ANTIQUE SHOW. May 17 (and Sept 27). Gettysburg, PA. Features 150 dealers in antiques with exhibits and displays. Est attendance: 25,000. For info: Gettysburg Area Retail Merchants Association, PO Box 4070, Gettysburg, PA 17325. Phone: (717) 253-5750. E-mail: gettysburgantiqueshow@comcast.net. Web: gettysburgretailmerchants.com.

JENNER, EDWARD: BIRTH ANNIVERSARY. May 17, 1749. English physician, born at Berkeley, England. He was the first to establish a scientific basis for vaccination with his work on smallpox. Jenner died at Berkeley, Jan 26, 1823.

LEWIS AND CLARK HERITAGE DAYS. May 17–18. St. Charles, MO. Authentic reenactment of Lewis and Clark's 1804 encampment prior to embarking on the exploration of the Louisiana Purchase. Activities include a parade with fife and drum corps, church service, 19th-century crafts, music, food and demonstrations. Est attendance: 25,000. For info: Greater St. Charles CVB, 230 S Main St, St. Charles, MO 63301-2855. Phone: (800) 366-2427 or (636) 946-7776. E-mail: cgarrett@historicstcharles.com. Web: www.lewisandclark.net.

MOREL MUSHROOM FESTIVAL. May 17–18. Muscoda, WI. Wisconsin's "Morel Mushroom Capital" celebrates the end of the morel mushroom's two-week peak season. The 32nd annual celebration includes the buying and selling of morels, food vendors, softball tournament, arts and crafts, antique tractor pull, flea market and many fun activities for the whole family. Saturday evening is the annual Fireman's Steak Feed followed by music and fireworks; Sunday brings a large parade. Annually, the weekend after Mother's Day. Est attendance: 3,000. For info: Village of Muscoda, Morel Mushroom Fest, PO Box 206, Muscoda, WI 53573-0206. Phone: (608) 739-3182. Fax: (608) 739-3183. E-mail: cljohnson@wppienergy.org. Web: www.muscoda.com.

NATIONAL LEARN TO SWIM DAY. May 17. 3rd annual. A nationwide campaign designed to raise awareness about the importance of teaching children to swim. It takes place annually on the Saturday the week before the unofficial start of summer: Memorial Day weekend. Families nationwide are invited to participate by attending a local event, teaching their children to swim with at-home instruction, visiting a community pool as a family or enrolling children in swim lessons at a local facility. For info: SwimWays Corp, 5816 Ward Court, Virginia Beach, VA 23455. E-mail: mjones@swimways.com. Web: www.teachmetoswim.com.

✦NATIONAL SAFE BOATING WEEK. May 17–23. Presidential Proclamation during May since 1995. From 1958 through 1977, issued for a week including July 4 (PL 85–445 of June 4, 1958). From 1981 through 1994, issued for the first week in June (PL 96–376 of Oct 3, 1980). From 1995, issued for a seven-day period ending on the Friday before Memorial Day. Not issued 1978–80.

NATIONAL SAFE BOATING WEEK. May 17–23. Brings boating safety to the public's attention, decreases the number of boating fatalities and makes the waterways safer for all boaters. Sponsors: National Safe Boating Council and US Coast Guard. For info: Natl Safe Boating Council. E-mail: outreach@safeboatingcouncil.org. Web: www.safeboatingcouncil.org.

NEW YORK STOCK EXCHANGE ESTABLISHED: ANNIVERSARY. May 17, 1792. Some two dozen merchants and brokers agreed to establish what is now known as the New York Stock Exchange. In fair weather they operated under a buttonwood tree on Wall St, at New York, NY. In bad weather they moved to the shelter of a coffeehouse to conduct their business.

NORWAY: CONSTITUTION DAY OR INDEPENDENCE DAY. May 17. National holiday. Constitution signed and Norway separated from Denmark in 1814. Parades and children's festivities.

O. HENRY MUSEUM PUN-OFF (WORLD CHAMPIONSHIP). May 17. The O. Henry Museum, Austin, TX. Pundits and punographers match wits for a wordy cause in two separate pun-filled competitions (Punniest of Show and High Lies & Low Puns). Sponsors: The City of Austin Parks and Recreation Dept and Punsters United Nearly Yearly (PUNY). Annually, the third Saturday in May. Est attendance: 2,000. For info: Quinn Argall, O. Henry Museum, 409 E Fifth St, Austin, TX 78701. Phone: (512) 472-1903. Fax: (512) 974-3833. E-mail: quinn.argall@austintexas.gov. Web: www.ohenrymuseum.org.

O'SULLIVAN, MAUREEN: BIRTH ANNIVERSARY. May 17, 1911. This MGM star was born at Boyle, Ireland, and was discovered at Dublin in 1930 when a visiting Hollywood film director spotted her. Although she had a long (1930–88) and varied film career, O'Sullivan's lasting fame comes from the many Tarzan films she made as Jane Parker opposite Johnny Weissmuller and Cheetah (a costar she was not fond of). Her first film in the Tarzan series was *Tarzan the Ape Man* (1932) and her last was *Tarzan's New York Adventure* (1942). O'Sullivan died on June 23, 1998, at Scottsdale, AZ.

OUACHITA RIVER BIG BASS FISHING TOURNAMENT. May 17–18. Lazarre Park, West Monroe, LA. Join family and friends at this fun event for fishing enthusiasts across the South! The Kids' Fishing Tournament is in partnership with Louisiana Wildlife and Fisheries at Forsythe Point Recreation Area. Annually, the third weekend in May. For info: Ronald McDonald House Charities of Northeast Louisiana, 200 S Third St, Monroe, LA 71202. Phone: (318) 387-7933. E-mail: rmh@bayou.com. Web: www.bayou.com/rmh.

PREAKNESS STAKES. May 17. Pimlico Race Course, Baltimore, MD. The Preakness Stakes, the middle jewel in Thoroughbred racing's Triple Crown, was inaugurated in 1873. Annually, the third Saturday in May—two Saturdays after the Kentucky Derby—and followed, three Saturdays later, by the Belmont Stakes. Est attendance: 120,000. For info: Maryland Jockey Club, Pimlico Race Course, Baltimore, MD 21215. Phone: (410) 542-9400. Web: www.preakness.com.

May 2014	S	M	T	W	T	F	S
					1	2	3
	4	5	6	7	8	9	10
	11	12	13	14	15	16	17
	18	19	20	21	22	23	24
	25	26	27	28	29	30	31

SANTA CRUZ BEACH BOARDWALK GIANT DIPPER: 90th ANNIVERSARY. May 17, 1924. The Giant Dipper roller coaster opened at Santa Cruz Beach Boardwalk at Santa Cruz, CA, and quickly became the park's most popular ride. The Dipper was built by Arthur Looff, the son of master carousel-horse carver Charles I.D. Looff. In June 1987 the Giant Dipper and the Looff carousel were designated National Historic Landmarks by the US National Park Service.

UNITED NATIONS: WORLD TELECOMMUNICATION AND INFORMATION SOCIETY DAY. May 17. On Mar 27, 2006, the UN General Assembly proclaimed this annual day to help raise awareness of the possibilities that the Internet and other information and communication technology can bring to societies and economies, as well as of ways to bridge the digital divide (Resolution 60/252). For info: United Nations, Dept of Public Info, New York, NY 10017. Web: www.un.org.

USS *STARK* ATTACKED: ANNIVERSARY. May 17, 1987. The US Navy's guided missile frigate *Stark*, sailing off the Iranian coast in the Persian Gulf, was struck and set afire by two Exocet sea-skimming missiles fired from an Iraqi warplane at 2:10 PM, EDT. Also struck was a Cypriot flag tanker. At least 28 American naval personnel were killed. Only hours earlier a Soviet oil tanker in the Gulf had struck a mine.

WISCONSIN DELLS AUTOMOTION. May 17–18. Noah's Ark Waterpark, Wisconsin Dells, WI. With signs of spring popping up all around, come take in the warmer weather at this showcase of more than 1,000 classic cars! Show features great live music, fire truck displays, fabulous food and a whole "trunkload" of other nifty family activities. Est attendance: 20,000. For info: Wisconsin Dells Visitor & Convention Bureau, Box 390, Wisconsin Dells, WI 53965. Phone: (800) 223-3557. E-mail: info@wisdells.com. Web: www.wisdells.com/automotion.

WRIGHT PLUS. May 17. Oak Park, IL. 40th annual. The Frank Lloyd Wright Preservation Trust's annual house walk will be "All Wright," featuring rare interior tours of eight privately owned homes and three public buildings, all designed by Frank Lloyd Wright. In 2014, the Preservation Trust celebrates the 125th anniversary of Wright's Home and Studio. Tickets available Oct 1, 2013. For info: Frank Lloyd Wright Preservation Trust, 209 S LaSalle St, Chicago, IL 60604. Phone: (312) 994-4000. E-mail: info@gowright.org. Web: www.gowright.org.

BIRTHDAYS TODAY

Craig Ferguson, 52, comedian, actor ("The Drew Carey Show"), television talk show host ("The Late Late Show with Craig Ferguson"), author, born Glasgow, Scotland, May 17, 1962.

Mia Hamm, 42, Hall of Fame soccer player, born Selma, AL, May 17, 1972.

Christian Lacroix, 64, fashion designer, born Arles, France, May 17, 1950.

Ray Charles (Sugar Ray) Leonard, 58, former boxer, born Washington, DC, May 17, 1956.

Tony Parker, 32, basketball player, born Bruges, Belgium, May 17, 1982.

Bill Paxton, 59, actor ("Big Love," *A Simple Plan, One False Move, Twister*), born Fort Worth, TX, May 17, 1955.

Sendhil Ramamurthy, 40, actor ("Heroes"), born Chicago, IL, May 17, 1974.

Nikki Reed, 26, actress (*Thirteen, Twilight*), born Los Angeles, CA, May 17, 1988.

Trent Reznor, 49, singer (Nine Inch Nails), born Mercer, PA, May 17, 1965.

Bob Saget, 58, actor ("Full House"), host ("America's Funniest Home Videos"), born Philadelphia, PA, May 17, 1956.

Debra Winger, 59, actress (*Terms of Endearment, Shadowlands*), born Columbus, OH, May 17, 1955.

May 18 — Sunday

DAY 138 **227 REMAINING**

ALLIES CAPTURE MONTE CASSINO: 70th ANNIVERSARY. May 18, 1944. Between Oct 12, 1943, and Jan 17, 1944, there were five Allied attempts to take the German position at the Benedictine abbey at Monte Cassino. Although the abbey had been reduced to rubble, it served as a bunker for the Germans. In the spring of 1944 Marshal Alphonse Pierre Juin devised an operation that crossed the mountainous regions behind the fortresslike structure, using Moroccan troops of the French Expeditionary Force. Specially trained for mountain operations, they climbed 4,850 feet to locate a pass. On May 15, 1944, they attacked the Germans from behind. On May 18 Polish troops attached to this force took Monte Cassino.

BAKUNIN, MIKHAIL ALEKSANDROVICH: 200th BIRTH ANNIVERSARY. May 18, 1814. Revolutionary agitator born at Premukhino, Russia. Bakunin advocated completely dismantling the state and in 1842 wrote, "The passion for destruction is also a creative passion," which became the motto of international anarchism. Involved in various European insurrections, Bakunin espoused liberation of Slav peoples and was exiled to Siberia before escaping to Western Europe where he died at Bern, Switzerland, July 1, 1876.

BAY TO BREAKERS. May 18. San Francisco, CA. Established in 1912, the Bay to Breakers is the largest footrace in the world, attracting 70,000 runners each year, from world-class athletes to fun runners. Includes a post-race festival with music, food and beverages. Sponsored by Zazzle. Annually, the third Sunday in May. Est attendance: 150,000. For info: Bay to Breakers, 600 Townsend St, Ste 410, San Francisco, CA 94103. E-mail: info@baytobreakers.com. Web: www.baytobreakers.com.

CAPRA, FRANK: BIRTH ANNIVERSARY. May 18, 1897. Academy Award–winning director whose movies were suffused with affectionate portrayals of the common man and the strengths and foibles of American democracy. Capra was born at Palermo, Sicily. He bluffed his way into silent movies in 1922 and, despite total ignorance of moviemaking, directed and produced a profitable one-reeler. He was the first to win three directorial Oscars—for *It Happened One Night* (1934), *Mr Deeds Goes to Town* (1936) and *You Can't Take It with You* (1938). The Motion Picture Academy voted the first and third of these as Best Picture. Capra said his favorite of the films he made was *It's a Wonderful Life* (1946). He died at La Quinta, CA, Sept 3, 1991.

FONTEYN, MARGOT: 95th BIRTH ANNIVERSARY. May 18, 1919. Born Margaret Hookman at Reigate, Surrey, England, Dame Margot Fonteyn thrilled ballet audiences for 45 years. She emerged from the Sadler's Wells company during the 1930s and 1940s as a solo artist and followed those successes by partnering with Soviet exile Rudolph Nureyev in the 1960s. She died Feb 21, 1991, at Panama City, Panama.

HAITI: FLAG AND UNIVERSITY DAY. May 18. Public holiday.

INTERNATIONAL MUSEUM DAY. May 18. To pay tribute to museums of the world. "Museums are an important means of cultural exchange, enrichment of cultures and development of mutual understanding and peace among people." Observed annually on May 18 since 1977. Sponsor: International Council of Museums (ICOM), Paris, France. For info: ICOM. Web: icom.museum/imd.html.

INTERNATIONAL NEW FRIENDS, OLD FRIENDS WEEK. May 18–24. A week to celebrate and make time for old friends and new friends and remember how vital friends are for our emotional and physical health and well-being and even professional or career success. *Friendshifts®* is the word coined by author and sociologist Jan Yager to denote the way our ideas about friendships as well as who our friends are may change as we go through different stages of life. But at every stage, friendship is crucial for children, teenagers, young adults, singles, couples, new mothers, the middle-aged and especially those who are older, retired or widowed. For info: Jan Yager, PhD, 1127 High Ridge Rd, #110, Stamford, CT 06905. E-mail: jyager@aol.com.

LAG B'OMER. May 18. Hebrew calendar date: Iyar 18, 5774. Literally, the 33rd day of the Omer (harvest time), the 33rd day after the beginning of Passover. Traditionally a joyous day for weddings, picnics and outdoor activities. Began at sundown May 17.

MOUNT SAINT HELENS ERUPTION: ANNIVERSARY. May 18, 1980. A major eruption of Mount Saint Helens volcano, in southwestern Washington, blew steam and ash more than 11 miles into the sky. First major eruption of Mount Saint Helens since 1857, though on Mar 26, 1980, there had been a warning eruption of smaller magnitude.

NATIONAL STATIONERY SHOW. May 18–21. Jacob K. Javits Center, New York, NY. 67th annual. The National Stationery Show is the world's most comprehensive collection of stationery and related lifestyle products. With more than 800 exhibiting companies featuring more than 10,000 lines, the show brings all sides of the diverse business community together: manufacturers (the exhibitors), buyers, sales reps, designers, licensors, distributors, trade/consumer press and manufacturing suppliers (the exhibitors in The Supply Side division). Est attendance: 12,000. For info: National Stationery Show, GLM, 1133 Westchester Ave, Ste N136, White Plains, NY 10604. Web: www.nationalstationeryshow.com.

NEIGHBOR DAY. May 18. A "Day of Special Observance" in Rhode Island, declared by the General Assembly, and also by resolution of the US Senate in 2008 (S. Res. 650). Annually, the Sunday before Memorial Day weekend. For info: Mary Jane DiMaio, Town of Westerly Coordinator, 101 Shore Rd, Westerly, RI 02891. E-mail: mjdimaio1@cox.net. Web: www.neighbordayworldwide.com.

POPE JOHN PAUL II: BIRTH ANNIVERSARY. May 18, 1920. Karol Wojtyla, 264th pope of the Roman Catholic Church, born at Wadowice, Poland. Elected pope Oct 16, 1978, he was the first non-Italian to be elected pope in 456 years and the first Polish pope. His theology was conservative and traditional, and he was known for his worldwide travels to bring the message of the Catholic Church to people around the world. He survived an assassination attempt in 1981 and died at Vatican City on Apr 2, 2005. He was beatified May 1, 2011.

PORTLAND PUG CRAWL. May 18. MacTarnahan's Taproom, Portland, OR. 14th annual. The pug crawl is expected to be one the largest gathering of pugs in the world, attracting an estimated 500 four-legged friends and more than 1,000 people. The highlight of the day is the Parade of Pugs, where almost 100 costumed pugs walk the runway competing for first place. Admission proceeds benefit the animals at the Oregon Humane Society, the largest and oldest humane society in the Northwest. For info: Oregon Humane Society, PO Box 11364, Portland, OR 97211-0364. Web: www.oregonhumane.org.

PORTLAND ROSE FESTIVAL. May 18–June 15 (weekends and Memorial Day). Portland, OR. Annual celebration includes more than 50 events and features four parades, dragon boat races, a CityFair with amusement rides and Navy fleet visits. Est attendance: 2,000,000. For info: Portland Rose Festival Foundation, 1020 SW Naito Pkwy, Portland, OR 97204. Phone: (503) 227-2681. Fax: (503) 227-6603. E-mail: info@rosefestival.org. Web: www.rosefestival.org.

SPACE MILESTONE: *APOLLO 10* (US): 45th ANNIVERSARY. May 18, 1969. Launched with astronauts Colonel Thomas Stafford and Commander Eugene Cernan, who brought lunar module "Snoopy" within nine miles of the moon's surface on May 22. *Apollo 10* circled the moon 31 times and returned to Earth May 26.

TURKMENISTAN: REVIVAL AND UNITY DAY. May 18. National holiday. Commemorates the 1992 adoption of the constitution.

TURNER, BIG JOE: BIRTH ANNIVERSARY. May 18, 1911. The "boss of the blues" and "grandfather of rock and roll" was born Joseph Vernon Turner, Jr, at Kansas City, MO. After a lengthy career singing blues, swing and jazz, Turner helped usher in the rock and roll era with his 1954 hit "Shake, Rattle and Roll" (later covered with cleaner lyrics by Bill Haley and His Comets). Turner died Nov 24, 1985, at Inglewood, CA. He was inducted into the Blues Hall of Fame in 1983 and the Rock and Roll Hall of Fame in 1987.

UNION'S FIRST OFFENSIVE ENGAGEMENT OF CIVIL WAR: ANNIVERSARY. May 18, 1861. Union troops engaged Confederate batteries at Sewall's Point, VA, in the North's first offensive action of the Civil War.

URUGUAY: BATTLE OF LAS PIEDRAS DAY. May 18. National holiday. Commemorates battle fought for independence from Spain in 1811.

VISIT YOUR RELATIVES DAY. May 18. A day to renew family ties and joys by visiting often-thought-of-seldom-seen relatives. Annually, May 18. For info: A.C. Vierow, Box 71, Clio, MI 48420-0071.

WILLSON, MEREDITH: BIRTH ANNIVERSARY. May 18, 1902. American musician, playwright and composer best known for *The Music Man.* Born at Mason City, IA, Willson received Oscar nominations for *The Little Foxes* and *The Great Dictator.* Many of his songs, including "It's Beginning to Look a Lot like Christmas," "Seventy-Six Trombones" and "Till There Was You" have become standards. Willson died at Santa Monica, CA, June 15, 1984.

WOMAN INDUCTED INTO NATIONAL INVENTORS HALL OF FAME: ANNIVERSARY. May 18, 1991. Gertrude Belle Elion, corecipient of the 1988 Nobel Prize in Medicine, became the first woman inducted as a member of the National Inventors Hall of Fame. Elion's research led to the development of leukemia-fighting drugs and the immunosuppressant Imuran, which is used in kidney transplants.

✦WORLD TRADE WEEK. May 18–24. Presidential Proclamation has been issued each year since 1948 for the third week of May with three exceptions: 1949, 1955 and 1966.

XTERRA OAK MOUNTAIN MUD RUNS. May 18. Oak Mountain State Park, Pelham, AL. The XTERRA Trail Run Series boasts more than 80 events across the country with runs ranging from 5k to 50k. These extreme, off-road trail runs give runners the chance to prove their skills against a variety of terrain. From calf-burning hills to slippery, mud-covered paths, athletes face the ultimate test of endurance. This race features off-road 5k and 10k mud runs and half-marathon and full-marathon trial runs. For info: Emily McIlvaine, XTERRA/TEAM Unlimited, 720 Iwilei Road #290, Honolulu, HI 96817. Phone: 877-XTERRA-1. E-mail: emily@xterraplanet.com. Web: www.xterraplanet.com.

BIRTHDAYS TODAY

Chow Yun-Fat, 59, actor (*Crouching Tiger, Hidden Dragon*; *Anna and the King*; *Bulletproof Monk*), born Lamma Island, Hong Kong, May 18, 1955.

Tina Fey, 44, writer, comedienne ("30 Rock," *Baby Mama, Mean Girls,* "Saturday Night Live"), born Upper Darby, PA, May 18, 1970.

Brad Friedel, 43, soccer player, born Lakewood, OH, May 18, 1971.

Dwayne Hickman, 80, actor ("The Many Loves of Dobie Gillis"), born Los Angeles, CA, May 18, 1934.

Reginald Martinez (Reggie) Jackson, 68, Hall of Fame baseball player, born Wyncote, PA, May 18, 1946.

Jari Kurri, 54, Hall of Fame hockey player, born Helsinki, Finland, May 18, 1960.

Yannick Noah, 54, Hall of Fame tennis player, born Sedan, France, May 18, 1960.

Brooks Robinson, 77, Hall of Fame baseball player, born Little Rock, AR, May 18, 1937.

James Stephens, 63, actor ("The Paper Chase"), born Mount Kisco, NY, May 18, 1951.

George Strait, 62, country singer, musician, born Poteet, TX, May 18, 1952.

Tom Udall, 66, US Senator (D, New Mexico), born Tucson, AZ, May 18, 1948.

Vince Young, 31, football player, born Houston, TX, May 18, 1983.

May 2014	S	M	T	W	T	F	S
					1	2	3
	4	5	6	7	8	9	10
	11	12	13	14	15	16	17
	18	19	20	21	22	23	24
	25	26	27	28	29	30	31

May 19 — Monday

DAY 139 **226 REMAINING**

AKELEY, CARL: 150th BIRTH ANNIVERSARY. May 19, 1864. Born near Claredon, NY, the "father of modern taxidermy" was unhappy with the "upholsterer's method of mounting animals" and spent his life elevating taxidermy to a science. Akeley's research led to many inventions and innovations that benefited museums worldwide. Akeley survived a leopard attack, charging rhinos and an elephant stampede during his many African expeditions to collect specimens, many of which are still on display in the naturalistic settings he created. Regret over killing a mountain gorilla led him to petition King Albert I of Belgium to create a sanctuary, later Africa's first national park. Akeley died Nov 18, 1926, from a fever near Mt. Mkeno, Congo.

BOLEYN, ANNE: EXECUTION ANNIVERSARY. May 19, 1536. Born around 1501, Anne Boleyn captured the eye of England's King Henry VIII in 1527. Her demand that he make her a wife, not a mistress, caused the married Henry's break with the Catholic Church (which didn't allow divorce), which in turn led to decades of religious turmoil in England. Henry had his marriage to Catherine of Aragon annulled and wed Boleyn in 1533. Boleyn's inability to bear a male heir (although her daughter with Henry was the future Queen Elizabeth I) and court intrigue caused her arrest on charges of adultery. She was executed by sword at the Tower of London. The morning of her execution she said, "I heard say the executioner was very good, and I have a little neck."

BOYS' CLUBS FOUNDED: ANNIVERSARY. May 19, 1906. The Federated Boys' Clubs, which later became the Boys' and Girls' Clubs of America, was founded.

CANADA: VICTORIA DAY. May 19. Commemorates the birth of Queen Victoria May 24, 1819. Observed annually on the Monday preceding May 25.

DARK DAY IN NEW ENGLAND: ANNIVERSARY. May 19, 1780. At midday near-total darkness unaccountably descended on much of New England. Candles were lit, fowls went to roost and many fearful persons believed that doomsday had arrived. At New Haven, CT, Colonel Abraham Davenport opposed adjournment of the town council in these words: "I am against adjournment. The day of judgment is either approaching or it is not. If it is not, there is no cause for an adjournment. If it is, I choose to be found doing my duty. I wish therefore that candles may be brought." No scientifically verifiable cause for this widespread phenomenon was ever discovered.

FINLAND: OULU INTERNATIONAL CHILDREN'S THEATRE FESTIVAL. May 19–24. Oulu. The oldest and largest annual international theater festival for children and young people in Finland. A weeklong theater feast presenting some 80 performances centering on traditional and contemporary children's theater and including pantomime, dance and puppet theater and many international guest performances, seminars, exhibits and clubs. Est attendance: 10,000. For info: Oulun kaupunginteatteri. Web: teatteri.ouka.fi/festival/en/home.

HANSBERRY, LORRAINE: BIRTH ANNIVERSARY. May 19, 1930. American playwright Lorraine Hansberry was born at Chicago, IL. For her now classic play *A Raisin in the Sun*, she became the youngest American and first black to win the Best Play Award from the New York Critics' Circle. The play, titled after the Langston Hughes poem, deals with issues such as racism, cultural pride and self-respect and was the first stage production written by a black woman to appear on Broadway (1959). *To Be Young, Gifted, and Black*, a book of excerpts from her journals, letters, speeches and plays, was published posthumously in 1969. Lorraine Hansberry died of cancer Jan 12, 1965, at New York, NY.

HO CHI MINH: BIRTH ANNIVERSARY. May 19, 1890. Vietnamese leader and first president of the Democratic Republic of Vietnam, born at Kim Lien, a central Vietnamese village (Nghe An Province), probably May 19, 1890. His original name was Nguyen That Thanh. Died at Hanoi, Vietnam, Sept 3, 1969. The anniversary of his birth is a national holiday in Vietnam, as is the anniversary of his death.

MALCOLM X: BIRTH ANNIVERSARY. May 19, 1925. Black nationalist and civil rights activist Malcolm X was born Malcolm Little at Omaha, NE. While serving a prison term, he resolved to transform his life. On his release in 1952 he changed his name to Malcolm X and worked for the Nation of Islam until he was suspended by Black Muslim leader Elijah Muhammad Dec 4, 1963. Malcolm X later made the pilgrimage to Mecca and became an orthodox Muslim. He was assassinated as he spoke to a meeting at the Audubon Ballroom at New York, NY, Feb 21, 1965.

NATIONAL BACKYARD GAMES WEEK. May 19–26. Observance to celebrate the unofficial start of summer by fostering social interaction and family togetherness through backyard games. Get outside and be both physically and mentally stimulated, playing classic games of the past while discovering and creating new ways to be active and interact with friends and neighbors. For info: Beth Muehlenkamp, Patch Products, 1400 E Inman Pkwy, Beloit, WI 53511. Phone: (608) 362-6896. Fax: (608) 362-8178. E-mail: bethm@patchproducts.com. Web: www.patchproducts.com.

NATIONAL GEOGRAPHIC BEE: NATIONAL FINALS. May 19–21. National Geographic Society Headquarters, Washington, DC. The first-place winner from each state-level competition (that took place on Apr 4) advances to the national level. The finals are televised on the National Geographic Channel and public television stations. Contestants compete for scholarships and prizes totaling more than $50,000. For info: Natl Geographic Bee, Natl Geographic Society, 1145 17th St NW, Washington, DC 20036. Phone: (202) 828-6659. Web: www.nationalgeographic.com/geographicbee.

SCOBEE, FRANCIS R.: 75th BIRTH ANNIVERSARY. May 19, 1939. Commander of the ill-fated space shuttle *Challenger*, 46-year-old pilot Francis R. Scobee had been in the astronaut program since 1978 and had been pilot of the *Challenger* in 1984. Born at Cle Elum, WA, Scobee perished with all others on board when the *Challenger* exploded on Jan 28, 1986. See also: "*Challenger* Space Shuttle Explosion: Anniversary" (Jan 28).

SIMPLON TUNNEL OPENING: ANNIVERSARY. May 19, 1906. Tunnel from Brig, Switzerland, to Iselle, Italy, officially opened on this day. Construction started in 1898.

SPACE MILESTONE: *MARS 2* AND *MARS 3* (USSR). May 19 and 28, 1971. Entered Martian orbits on Nov 27 and Dec 2, respectively. *Mars 3* sent down a TV-equipped capsule that soft-landed and transmitted pictures for 20 seconds.

TURKEY: YOUTH AND SPORTS DAY. May 19. Public holiday commemorating the beginning of a national movement for independence in 1919, led by Mustafa Kemal Ataturk.

BIRTHDAYS TODAY

James Fox, 75, actor (*A Passage to India, The Russia House, Patriot Games*), born London, England, May 19, 1939.

Kevin Garnett, 38, basketball player, born Mauldin, SC, May 19, 1976.

David Hartman, 77, actor, broadcaster (Emmy for "Good Morning America"), born Pawtucket, RI, May 19, 1937.

Grace Jones, 62, model, singer, actress (*A View to a Kill*), born Spanishtown, Jamaica, May 19, 1952.

William (Bill) Laimbeer, Jr, 57, former basketball player and coach, born Boston, MA, May 19, 1957.

Jim Lehrer, 80, journalist, political analyst, former anchor ("PBS NewsHour"), author (*Viva Max!*), born Wichita, KS, May 19, 1934.

Eric Lloyd, 28, actor ("Jesse," *Dunston Checks In*), born Glendale, CA, May 19, 1986.

Archie Manning, 65, former football player, born Drew, MS, May 19, 1949.

Pete Townshend, 69, musician (The Who), born London, England, May 19, 1945.

May 20 — Tuesday

DAY 140 **225 REMAINING**

AMELIA EARHART ATLANTIC CROSSING: ANNIVERSARY. May 20, 1932. Leaving Harbor Grace, Newfoundland, Canada, at 7 PM, Amelia Earhart landed near Londonderry, Ireland. The 2,026-mile flight took 13 hours and 30 minutes. She was the first woman to fly solo across the Atlantic.

BALZAC, HONORÉ DE: BIRTH ANNIVERSARY. May 20, 1799. French author of a huge cycle of stories and novels known as *The Human Comedy*, born at Tours, France. "It is easier," Balzac wrote in 1829, "to be a lover than a husband for the simple reason that it is more difficult to be witty every day than to say pretty things from time to time." Died at Paris, Aug 18, 1850.

CAMEROON: NATIONAL HOLIDAY. May 20. Republic of Cameroon. Commemorates adoption of constitution in 1972.

COUNCIL OF NICAEA I: ANNIVERSARY. May 20–Aug 25, 325. First ecumenical council of Christian Church, called by Constantine I, first Christian emperor of Roman Empire. Nearly 300 bishops are said to have attended this first of 21 ecumenical councils (latest, Vatican II, began Sept 11, 1962), which was held at Nicaea, in Asia Minor (today's Turkey). The council condemned Arianism (which denied the divinity of Christ), formulated the Nicene Creed and fixed the day of Easter—always on a Sunday.

EAST TIMOR: INDEPENDENCE ANNIVERSARY. May 20, 2002. East Timor became fully independent from Indonesia on this day. Indonesia had controlled the tiny nation since 1975. It had previously been a colony of Portugal for 450 years.

ELIZA DOOLITTLE DAY. May 20. To honor Miss Doolittle (heroine of George Bernard Shaw's *Pygmalion*) for demonstrating the importance and the advantage of speaking one's native language properly. For info: Doolittle Day Committee, 2460 Devonshire Rd, Ann Arbor, MI 48104-2706.

HERZL, THEODOR: BIRTH ANNIVERSARY. May 20, 1860. Founder of the modern Zionist movement, born at Budapest, Hungary. Herzl died at Edlach, Austria, July 3, 1904.

HEWLETT, WILLIAM: BIRTH ANNIVERSARY. May 20, 1913. Born at Ann Arbor, MI, engineer and businessman William Hewlett started the Hewlett-Packard Company with cofounder David Packard in 1939. Hewlett served the company in various capacities as president, CEO, chairman and vice-chairman of the board, and director emeritus. The recipient of numerous honorary degrees, he was awarded the prestigious National Medal of Science in 1983. Packard died Jan 12, 2001, at Palo Alto, CA, one of the richest people in the world with an estate valued at more than $9 billion.

HOMESTEAD ACT: ANNIVERSARY. May 20, 1862. President Abraham Lincoln signed the Homestead Act opening millions of acres of government-owned land in the West to settlers, or "homesteaders," who had to reside on the land and cultivate it for five years.

LINDBERGH FLIGHT: ANNIVERSARY. May 20–21, 1927. Anniversary of the first solo transatlantic flight. Captain Charles Augustus Lindbergh, 25-year-old aviator, departed from rainy, muddy Roosevelt Field, Long Island, NY, alone at 7:52 AM, May 20, 1927, in a Ryan monoplane named *Spirit of St. Louis.* He landed at Le Bourget airfield, Paris, France, at 10:24 PM, Paris time (5:24 PM, NY time), May 21, winning a $25,000 prize offered by Raymond Orteig for the first nonstop flight between New York City and Paris (3,600 miles). The "flying fool," as he had been dubbed by some doubters, became "Lucky Lindy," an instant world hero. See also: "Lindbergh, Charles Augustus: Birth Anniversary" (Feb 4).

MADISON, DOLLY (DOROTHEA) DANDRIDGE PAYNE TODD: BIRTH ANNIVERSARY. May 20, 1768. Wife of James Madison, 4th president of the US, born at Guilford County, NC. Died at Washington, DC, July 12, 1849.

MECKLENBURG DAY. May 20. North Carolina. Commemorates claimed signing of a declaration of independence from England by citizens of Mecklenburg County on this day, 1775.

NAIA WOMEN'S GOLF NATIONAL CHAMPIONSHIPS. May 20–23. Wilderness Creek Golf Club, Lincoln, NE. 20th annual. Est attendance: 400. For info: Natl Assn of Intercollegiate Athletics, 1200 Grand Blvd, Kansas City, MO 64106. E-mail: eolson@naia.org. Web: www.naia.org.

NCAA DIVISION I WOMEN'S GOLF CHAMPIONSHIPS. May 20–23. Tulsa Country Club, Tulsa, OK. For info: NCAA, PO Box 6222, Indianapolis, IN 46206-6222. Phone: (317) 917-6222. Web: www.NCAA.com.

ROUSSEAU, HENRI JULIEN FELIX: BIRTH ANNIVERSARY. May 20, 1844. Henri Rousseau, nicknamed "Le Douanier" because of his onetime post as customs tollkeeper, was a celebrated French painter born at Laval, Mayenne, France. Painted deceptively "primitive" pictures of exotic foliage, flowers and fruit of the jungle, with stilted human and animal figures. Died at Hospital Necker, Paris, Sept 4, 1910.

SPACE MILESTONE: *PIONEER VENUS I* (US): ANNIVERSARY. May 20, 1978. Launched this date, became first Venus orbiter the following Dec 4.

STEWART, JIMMY: BIRTH ANNIVERSARY. May 20, 1908. Film actor born James Stewart at Indiana, PA. Best known for his everyman roles and work with directors Frank Capra and Alfred Hitchcock. Starred in *Mr Smith Goes to Washington, It's a Wonderful Life, Rear Window* and many classic Westerns. Stewart won a Best Actor Oscar for *The Philadelphia Story.* He died July 2, 1997, at Beverly Hills, CA.

WEIGHTS AND MEASURES DAY. May 20. Anniversary of international treaty, signed May 20, 1875, providing for the establishment of an International Bureau of Weights and Measures. The bureau was founded on international territory at Sèvres, France.

BIRTHDAYS TODAY

Iker Casillas, 33, soccer player, born Madrid, Spain, May 20, 1981.

Cher, 68, singer, actress (Oscar for *Moonstruck*; *Mask, Silkwood*), born Cherilyn Sarkisian at El Centro, CA, May 20, 1946.

Joe Cocker, 70, singer, born Sheffield, England, May 20, 1944.

Michael Crapo, 63, US Senator (R, Idaho), born Idaho Falls, ID, May 20, 1951.

Matt Czuchry, 33, actor ("The Good Wife"), born Manchester, NH, May 20, 1977.

Chris Froome, 29, cyclist, born Nairobi, Kenya, May 20, 1985.

Tony Goldwyn, 54, actor ("Scandal," *Ghost, Kiss the Girls*), born Los Angeles, CA, May 20, 1960.

Stan Mikita, 74, Hall of Fame hockey player, born Sokolce, Czechoslovakia (now Slovakia), May 20, 1940.

Timothy Olyphant, 46, actor ("Justified," "Damages"), born Honolulu, HI, May 20, 1968.

Tahmoh Penikett, 39, actor ("Battlestar Galactica," "Dollhouse"), born Whitehorse, YT, Canada, May 20, 1975.

Bronson Pinchot, 55, actor ("Perfect Strangers," "Step by Step"), born New York, NY, May 20, 1959.

Ronald Prescott Reagan, 56, television host, commentator, born Los Angeles, CA, May 20, 1958.

Anthony Zerbe, 78, actor ("Harry-O," *Cool Hand Luke, Papillon*), born Long Beach, CA, May 20, 1936.

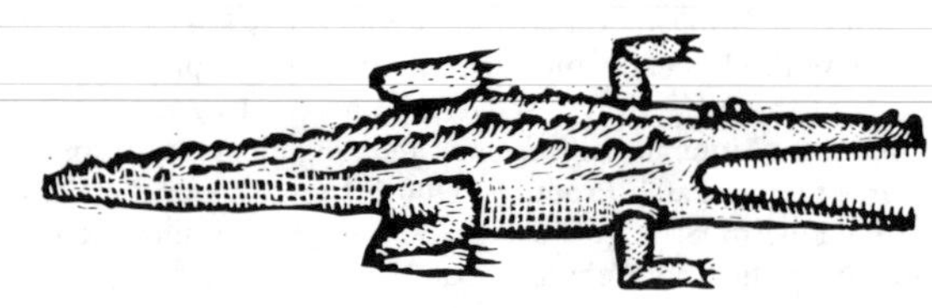

May 21 — Wednesday

DAY 141 | **224 REMAINING**

AMERICAN RED CROSS FOUNDED: ANNIVERSARY. May 21, 1881. Commemorates the founding of the American Red Cross by Clara Barton, its first president. The Red Cross had been founded in Switzerland in 1864 by representatives from 16 European nations. It is a not-for-profit organization governed and directed by volunteers and provides disaster relief at home and abroad. Its 1.1 million volunteers are involved in community services such as collecting and distributing donated blood and blood products, teaching health and safety classes and acting as a medium for emergency communication between Americans and their armed forces.

BURR, RAYMOND WILLIAM STACY: BIRTH ANNIVERSARY. May 21, 1917. Stage, film and TV actor best known for the role of Perry Mason in the long-running series of the same name. His films include *Rear Window* and *Godzilla,* and he was also the star of TV's "Ironside." Born at New Westminster, BC, Canada, Burr died near Healdsburg, CA, Sept 12, 1993.

May 2014

S	M	T	W	T	F	S
				1	2	3
4	5	6	7	8	9	10
11	12	13	14	15	16	17
18	19	20	21	22	23	24
25	26	27	28	29	30	31

CHILE: BATTLE OF IQUIQUE DAY. May 21. Commemorates a naval battle in 1879, part of the War of the Pacific with Peru and Bolivia.

CURTISS, GLENN HAMMOND: BIRTH ANNIVERSARY. May 21, 1878. American inventor and aviator, born at Hammondsport, NY. The aviation pioneer died at Buffalo, NY, July 23, 1930.

DÜRER, ALBRECHT: BIRTH ANNIVERSARY. May 21, 1471. German painter and engraver, one of the foremost artists of the Renaissance, was born at Nuremberg, Germany, and died there Apr 6, 1528.

FLEET WEEK NEW YORK 2014. May 21–28. New York, NY. 30th annual. Held nearly every year since 1984, Fleet Week New York is the city's celebration of the sea services. Fleet Week New York provides an opportunity for the citizens of New York City and the surrounding tri-state area to meet sailors, marines and coast guardsmen, as well as see, firsthand, the latest capabilities of today's maritime services. More than 6,000 service men and women from the US and foreign nations will arrive aboard the ships. For info: Navy Region Mid-Atlantc. Web: www.fleetweeknewyork.com.

FRY, ELIZABETH GURNEY: BIRTH ANNIVERSARY. May 21, 1780. English reformer who dedicated her life to improving the condition of poor people and especially of women in prison, born at Earlham, Norfolk, England. Died at Ramsgate, Oct 12, 1845.

GEMINI, THE TWINS. May 21–June 20. In the astronomical/astrological zodiac, which divides the sun's apparent orbit into 12 segments, the period May 21–June 20 is traditionally identified as the sun sign of Gemini, the Twins. The ruling planet is Mercury.

HAMMER, ARMAND: BIRTH ANNIVERSARY. May 21, 1898. American industrialist Armand Hammer was born at New York, NY. He built the Occidental Petroleum Company into a $20 billion conglomerate after he invested $100,000 in it in 1956 and it was awarded two oil concessions in Libya. He was a trained physician who was sympathetic to the Soviet people and gave away millions of dollars through philanthropy to cancer research. Hammer died Dec 10, 1990, at Los Angeles, CA.

HUMMEL, SISTER MARIA INNOCENTIA: BIRTH ANNIVERSARY. May 21, 1909. Born at Massing, Bavaria, Sister Maria Innocentia Hummel attended Munich's Academy of Fine Arts. She entered Siessen Convent, run by the Sisters of the Third Order of St. Francis, and began teaching art to kindergarten children. In 1934 Franz Goebel obtained an exclusive license to translate her drawings into three-dimensional figurines. The first M.I. Hummel figurines were displayed at the Leipzig Trade Fair in 1935; they made their first appearance in the American market in May 1935. She died Nov 6, 1946, at Siessen, Germany. Many M.I. Hummel Clubs across the country commemorate her birth date with special events and fund-raisers for local charities.

"I NEED A PATCH FOR THAT" DAY. May 21. They have patches for nicotine and they have patches for heart patients. How about a patch for runny noses or bad hair? (©2006 by WH.) For info: Thomas & Ruth Roy, Wellcat Holidays, 2418 Long Ln, Lebanon, PA 17046. Phone: (717) 279-0184. E-mail: info@wellcat.com. Web: www.wellcat.com.

MOON PHASE: LAST QUARTER. May 21. Moon enters Last Quarter phase at 8:59 AM, EDT.

NATIONAL WAITSTAFF DAY. May 21. A day for restaurant managers and patrons to recognize and to express their appreciation for the many fine and dedicated waitresses and waiters. For info: Gaylord F. Ward, Promotion Dir, 1505 E Bristol Rd, Burton, MI 48529-2214.

POPE, ALEXANDER: BIRTH ANNIVERSARY. May 21, 1688. Poet, critic, satirist born at London, England. "A man," Pope wrote in 1727, "should never be ashamed to own he has been in the wrong, which is but saying, in other words, that he is wiser today than he was yesterday." *The Rape of the Lock* (1712) firmly established Pope as the foremost poet of the time and remains his most popular work. Died at Twickenham, May 30, 1744.

RAJIV GANDHI ASSASSINATED: ANNIVERSARY. May 21, 1991. Former Indian prime minister Rajiv Gandhi was assassinated in the midst of a reelection campaign. He was killed when a bomb, hidden in a bouquet of flowers given by admirers, exploded as he approached a dais to begin a campaign rally. He had served as prime minister between 1984 and 1989 after succeeding his mother, Indira Gandhi, who was assassinated in 1984.

SAKHAROV, ANDREY DMITRIYEVICH: BIRTH ANNIVERSARY. May 21, 1921. Soviet physicist, human rights activist and environmentalist Andrey Sakharov was born at Moscow, Russia. A collaborator in producing the first Soviet atomic bomb and later the hydrogen bomb, Sakharov denounced shortcomings of his country's government and was exiled to Gorky, Russia, 1980–86. He was a formulator of the reform and restructuring concept known as *perestroika* and of *glasnost* (freedom). He was named to the Soviet Congress of People's Deputies eight months before his death at Moscow on Dec 14, 1989. As a physicist, he was a developer of destructive weapons; as a humanitarian, he was courageous as a dissident against militarism and an advocate of human rights.

UNITED NATIONS: WORLD DAY FOR CULTURAL DIVERSITY FOR DIALOGUE AND DEVELOPMENT. May 21. Recognizing the need to enhance the potential of culture as a means of achieving prosperity, sustainable development and global peaceful coexistence, the General Assembly, on Dec 20, 2002, proclaimed May 21 to serve as this day. The Assembly acknowledged the close link between protecting cultural diversity and the larger framework of the dialogue among civilizations. For info: United Nations, Dept of Public Info, New York, NY 10017. Web: www.un.org.

BIRTHDAYS TODAY

Bobby Cox, 73, baseball manager, former executive and player, born Tulsa, OK, May 21, 1941.

Janet Dailey, 70, romance novelist, born Storm Lake, IA, May 21, 1944.

Lisa Edelstein, 47, actress ("House," "Felicity"), born Boston, MA, May 21, 1967.

Al Franken, 63, US Senator (D, Minnesota), comedian, actor, writer (*Rush Limbaugh Is a Big Fat Idiot and Other Observations*), born New York, NY, May 21, 1951.

Gotye, 34, musician, born Wouter De Backer at Bruges, Belgium, May 21, 1980.

Josh Hamilton, 33, baseball player, born Raleigh, NC, May 21, 1981.

Heinz Holliger, 75, oboist, composer, conductor, born Langenthal, Switzerland, May 21, 1939.

Ian McEwan, 66, author (*On Chesil Beach, Atonement, Amsterdam*), born Aldershot, Hampstead, England, May 21, 1948.

Sarah Ramos, 23, actress ("Parenthood," "American Dreams"), born Los Angeles, CA, May 21, 1991.

Judge Reinhold, 57, actor (*Beverly Hills Cop*), born Wilmington, DE, May 21, 1957.

Leo Sayer, 66, singer, songwriter, born Shoreham, England, May 21, 1948.

Mr T, 62, actor (*Rocky III*, "The A-Team"), born Lawrence Tureaud at Chicago, IL, May 21, 1952.

May 22 — Thursday

DAY 142 **223 REMAINING**

BEST, GEORGE: BIRTH ANNIVERSARY. May 22, 1946. Mercurial soccer star of the 1960s and '70s. Beginning his professional career at 17, Best played mainly for Manchester United, for which he scored 178 goals in 466 appearances. His playboy lifestyle off the field was as famous as his quicksilver brilliance on it. Born at Belfast, Northern Ireland, Best died at London, England, on Nov 22, 2005. More than 100,000 mourners lined the streets of Belfast for his funeral procession, and at British soccer matches a minute of silence (or applause) was observed in his honor.

CANADIAN IMMIGRANTS' DAY. May 22. A day to celebrate and recognize the contributions made by legal immigrants to Canada and to discuss Canadian immigration law and policy. For info: Sergio R. Karas, BA, LLB, Barrister and Solicitor, Karas & Assoc, 65 Queen St W, Ste 1505, Toronto, ON, Canada M5H 2M5. Phone: (416) 506-1800. Fax: (416) 506-1305. E-mail: karas@karas.ca. Web: www.karas.ca.

CASSATT, MARY: BIRTH ANNIVERSARY. May 22, 1844. Leading American artist of the Impressionist school, Mary Cassatt was born May 22, 1844 (some sources give 1845), at Allegheny City, PA (now part of Pittsburgh). She settled in Paris, France, in 1874, where she was influenced by Degas and the Impressionists. She was later instrumental in their works becoming well known in the US. The majority of her paintings and pastels were based on the theme of mother and child. After 1900 her eyesight began to fail, and by 1914 she was no longer able to paint. Cassatt died at Chateau de Beaufresne near Paris, June 14, 1926.

CRATER LAKE NATIONAL PARK ESTABLISHED: ANNIVERSARY. May 22, 1902. One of the world's deepest lakes, Crater Lake was first discovered in 1853. In 1885 William Gladstone Steele saw the Oregon lake and made it his personal goal to establish the lake and surrounding areas as a national park. His goal was attained 17 years later.

DOYLE, SIR ARTHUR CONAN: BIRTH ANNIVERSARY. May 22, 1859. British physician Sir Arthur Conan Doyle is best remembered as a mystery author and the creator of Sherlock Holmes and Dr. Watson. Doyle was born at Edinburgh, Scotland. He was deeply interested in and lectured on the subject of spiritualism. Died at Crowborough, Sussex, England, July 7, 1930.

HARVEY MILK DAY. May 22. 5th annual. Day celebrating the life story, message and legacy of civil rights leader Harvey Milk (1930–78). Annually, May 22. For info: Harvey Milk Foundation. Web: www.harveymilkday.co.

HERRINFESTA ITALIANA. May 22–26. Herrin Civic Center, Herrin, IL. Authentic Italian food, concerts, bocce tournament, Midwest Pasta Sauce Contest, road races, grape stomp and more. Est attendance: 55,000. For info: Herrinfesta Italiana, PO Box 2005, Herrin, IL 62948. Phone: (800) ITF-ESTA. Web: www.herrinfesta.com.

JOHNNY CARSON'S FINAL SHOW: ANNIVERSARY. May 22, 1992. After almost 30 years as host of the "The Tonight Show," Johnny Carson hosted his last show. Carson became host of the late-night talk show, which began as a local New York program hosted by Steve Allen, on Oct 1, 1962. Over the years Carson occasionally made headlines with such extravaganzas as the marriage of Tiny Tim and Miss Vicki. Carson received Emmys for his work four years in a row, 1976–79. Ed McMahon, his sidekick of 30 years, and Doc Severinsen, longtime bandleader, left the show with Carson. Jay Leno, the show's exclusive guest host, became the new regular host.

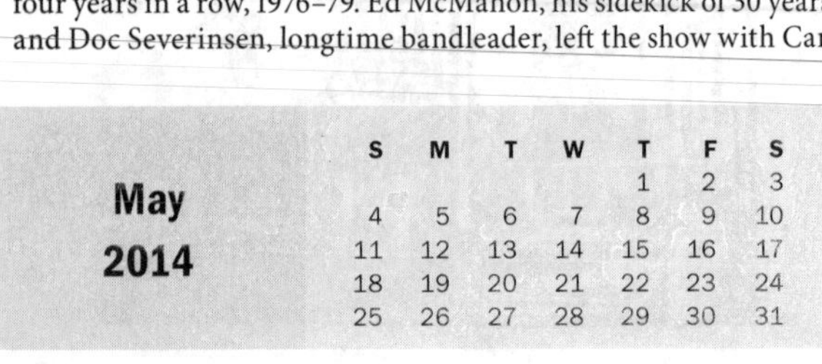

May 2014

S	M	T	W	T	F	S
				1	2	3
4	5	6	7	8	9	10
11	12	13	14	15	16	17
18	19	20	21	22	23	24
25	26	27	28	29	30	31

JOPLIN, MISSOURI, TORNADO: ANNIVERSARY. May 22, 2011. Beginning about 5:40 PM in the evening an EF-5 tornado, with wind speeds in excess of 200 miles per hour, struck the southern end of Joplin, MO, a city of about 50,000 residents. The storm resulted in the deaths of 161 people, injured more than 1,100 people and caused an estimated $2.8 billion in damage. The unusually large and slow-moving twister destroyed about a third of the city, including hundreds of homes, a high school and a hospital.

KODIAK CRAB FESTIVAL. May 22–26. Kodiak, AK. 56th annual. A celebration of spring on the Emerald Isle. Delectable food, exciting midway rides, carnival booths and entertaining events, such as parades, running and bicycle races, survival suit race, bed races, a blessing of the fleet ceremony and memorial services. Annually, Memorial Day weekend. Est attendance: 15,000. For info: Kodiak Crab Festival, 100 E Marine Way, Ste 300, Kodiak, AK 99615. Phone: (907) 486-5557. Fax: (907) 486-7605. Web: www.kodiak.org/crabfest.

MEMORY DAYS. May 22–24. Grayson, KY. Parade, art show and live shows. Est attendance: 10,000. For info: Robert L. Caummisar, Chamber of Commerce, 301 W Main St, Grayson, KY 41143. Phone: (606) 474-9522. Fax: (606) 474-4422. E-mail: barrister9@yahoo.com.

"MISTER ROGERS' NEIGHBORHOOD" TV PREMIERE: ANNIVERSARY. May 22, 1967. Presbyterian minister Fred Rogers hosted this long-running PBS children's program. Puppets and human characters interacted in the Neighborhood of Make-Believe. Rogers voiced many of the puppets and educated young viewers on a variety of important subjects. The last episodes of the program were made in 2001. Almost 1,000 episodes were produced over the show's history. Rogers died in 2003. See also: "Rogers, Fred: Birth Anniversary" (Mar 20).

MONACO: GRAND PRIX DE MONACO. May 22–25. Monte Carlo. 72nd edition. One of the premier sporting events in the world. Thrilling Formula 1 race: 77 laps through the streets of Monte Carlo, held since Apr 14, 1929. For info: Automobile Club de Monaco, 23 blvd Albert 1er, BP 464, Monaco. Web: www.acm.mc.

MUDBUG MADNESS. May 22–25. Riverfront, Shreveport, LA. The state's delectable crustacean, the crawfish, and Cajun heritage are celebrated during this four-day festival. Est attendance: 100,000. For info: DSU, 401 Edwards, Ste 205, Shreveport, LA 71101. Phone: (318) 222-7403. E-mail: mbacon@downtownshreveport.com. Web: www.mudbugmadness.com.

NAIA OUTDOOR TRACK AND FIELD NATIONAL CHAMPIONSHIPS. May 22–24. Site TBD. 63rd annual men's and 34th annual women's competition. Est attendance: 2,500. For info: Natl Assn of Intercollegiate Athletics, 1200 Grand Blvd, Kansas City, MO 64106. E-mail: DWilke@naia.org. Web: www.naia.org.

✦**NATIONAL MARITIME DAY.** May 22. Presidential Proclamation issued for May 22 since 1933. (Pub Res No. 7 of May 20, 1933.)

NATIONAL MARITIME DAY. May 22. Anniversary of departure for first steamship crossing of Atlantic from Savannah, GA, to Liverpool, England, by steamship *Savannah* in 1819.

NIXON FIRST AMERICAN PRESIDENT TO VISIT MOSCOW: ANNIVERSARY. May 22, 1972. President Richard Nixon became the first American president to visit Moscow. Four days later on May 26, Nixon and Soviet leader Leonid Brezhnev signed a treaty on antiballistic missile systems and an interim agreement on limitation of strategic missiles.

OLIVIER, LAURENCE: BIRTH ANNIVERSARY. May 22, 1907. Actor, director and theater manager, born at Dorking, England. Thought by many to be the most influential actor of the 20th century. Olivier's theatrical and film career shaped the art forms in which he participated. Honored with nine Academy Award nominations, three Oscars and five Emmy Awards, his repertoire included most of the prime Shakespearean roles and roles in such films as *Rebecca, Pride and Prejudice, Marathon Man* and *Wuthering Heights.* Olivier was an innovative theater manager with London's Old Vic company and the National Theatre of Great Britain. The National Theatre's largest auditorium and Britain's equivalent of Broadway's Tony Awards carry his name. He was knighted in 1947 and made a peer of the throne in 1970. Olivier died at Ashurst, England, July 11, 1989.

RA, SUN: 100th BIRTH ANNIVERSARY. May 22, 1914. Born Herman (Sonny) Blount, Sun Ra was a pioneering and innovative jazz musician whose avant-garde performances mixed elements of theater with his surreal composition and performance style. He once said, "I wanted to give God something he's never heard before." Ra was born at Birmingham, AL, and died there May 30, 1993.

SENIOR PGA CHAMPIONSHIP. May 22–25. Harbor Shores, Benton Harbor, MI. 75th competition for the oldest major championship in senior golf. Conducted by the Professional Golfers' Association of America. Presented by KitchenAid. For info: PGA of America, 100 Ave of the Champions, Palm Beach Gardens, FL 33418. Phone: (561) 624-8400. Fax: (561) 624-8448. Web: www.pga.com.

SPACE MILESTONE: SPACEX *DRAGON* LAUNCHES. May 22, 2012. In the first commercial mission to the International Space Station, this free-flying, reusable spacecraft delivered food, clothing, computer equipment and supplies for science experiments, and returned with trash, scientific research and samples. A Falcon 9 rocket launched the capsule into space from Cape Canaveral, FL, and it splashed down May 31, 2012, in the Pacific Ocean off the coast of Baja California, Mexico. The *Dragon* is owned by SpaceX, a private American transportation company.

SRI LANKA: NATIONAL HEROES DAY. May 22. Commemorates the struggle of the leaders of the National Independence Movement to liberate the country from colonial rule in 1971. Public holiday.

STRONGEST EARTHQUAKE OF THE 20th CENTURY: ANNIVERSARY. May 22, 1960. An earthquake of magnitude 9.5 struck southern Chile, killing 2,000 people and leaving 2 million homeless. The earthquake also caused damage in Hawaii, Japan and the Philippines. While 20th-century earthquakes in Mexico City, Japan and Turkey resulted in far more deaths, this earthquake in Chile was of the greatest magnitude.

SUMNER ATTACKED IN THE SENATE: ANNIVERSARY. May 22, 1856. Two days after he decried the "Crime Against Kansas," US senator Charles Sumner of Massachusetts was attacked with a walking cane by South Carolina congressman Preston Brooks in the Senate Chamber (the Senate was not in session). Abolitionist Sumner needed three years to recuperate.

TRUMAN DOCTRINE: ANNIVERSARY. May 22, 1947. Congress approved the Truman Doctrine on this day. In order to contain communism after WWII, it provided for US aid to Greece and Turkey. A corollary of this doctrine was the Marshall Plan, which began sending aid to war-torn European countries in 1948.

UNITED NATIONS: INTERNATIONAL DAY FOR BIOLOGICAL DIVERSITY. May 22. On Dec 19, 1994, the General Assembly proclaimed this observance for Dec 29, the date of entry into force of the Convention on Biological Diversity (Resolution 49/119). In 2000 the date was changed to May 22. This day is an opportunity to strengthen people's commitment and actions for the conservation of the world's biological diversity. For info: United Nations, Dept of Public Info, New York, NY 10017. Web: www.un.org.

WAGNER, RICHARD: BIRTH ANNIVERSARY. May 22, 1813. German composer born at Leipzig who made revolutionary changes in the structure of opera. Best known for his Ring Cycle (*Der Ring des Nibelungen*). Died at Italy, Feb 13, 1883.

WALES: HAY FESTIVAL. May 22–June 1. Hay-on-Wye, Powys. Largest annual festival of literature takes place in the beautiful market town of Hay-on-Wye in the Black Mountains on the Welsh border. Est attendance: 100,000. For info: The Hay Festival, Drill Hall, 25 Lion St, Hay-on-Wye, Wales, United Kingdom HR3 5AD. Phone: (44) (1497) 822-620. Fax: (44) (1497) 821-066. E-mail: admin@hayfestival.org. Web: www.hayfestival.org.

WORLD GOTH DAY. May 22. A day on which the goth scene gets to celebrate its own being and make its presence known to the rest of the world. First observed in the UK in 2009. Annually, May 22. For info: World Goth Day. Web: www.worldgothday.com.

YEMEN: NATIONAL DAY. May 22. Public holiday. Commemorates the reunification of Yemen in 1990.

 BIRTHDAYS TODAY

Charles Aznavour, 90, singer, songwriter, actor (*Shoot the Piano Player, Candy, The Tin Drum*), born Paris, France, May 22, 1924.

Richard Benjamin, 76, actor (*Goodbye Columbus, Diary of a Mad Housewife*, "He & She"), born New York, NY, May 22, 1938.

Naomi Campbell, 44, model, born London, England, May 22, 1970.

Frank Converse, 76, actor ("Movin' On," *Hurry Sundown*), born St. Louis, MO, May 22, 1938.

Novak Djokovic, 27, tennis player, born Belgrade, Yugoslavia (now Serbia), May 22, 1987.

Ginnifer Goodwin, 36, actress ("Big Love," "Once Upon a Time"), born Memphis, TN, May 22, 1978.

Thomas Edward (Tommy) John, 71, former baseball player, born Terre Haute, IN, May 22, 1943.

A.J. Langer, 40, actress ("My So-Called Life," "Brooklyn South"), born Columbus, OH, May 22, 1974.

Lisa Murkowski, 57, US Senator (R, Alaska), born Ketchikan, AK, May 22, 1957.

Peter Nero, 80, conductor, composer, pianist, born Brooklyn, NY, May 22, 1934.

Garry Wills, 80, author (*John Wayne's America, Lincoln at Gettysburg*), born Atlanta, GA, May 22, 1934.

May 23 — Friday

DAY 143 **222 REMAINING**

BONNIE AND CLYDE: 80th DEATH ANNIVERSARY. May 23, 1934. The two-year crime spree of Bonnie Parker and Clyde Barrow, bank robbers accused of at least 12 murders, came to an end when a law enforcement posse led by Frank Hamer opened fire on the couple in an ambush at Gibsland, LA. The couple had operated in Texas, Oklahoma, Missouri, Louisiana and other states, and had sent ballads to local newspapers chronicling their exploits, making them two of the most notorious—and romanticized—of many Depression-era gangsters. Some 20,000 people lined up to see the body of Clyde Barrow put on display in a mortuary in downtown Dallas, TX.

BROOKINGS-HARBOR AZALEA FESTIVAL. May 23–26. Brookings, OR. 75th festival. Parade, street fair, art shows, seafood, 10k run, bonsai exhibit, regional quilt show, crafts fair, Coast Guard demonstration, live music. Annually, Memorial Day weekend. Est attendance: 12,000. For info: Brookings-Harbor Chamber of Commerce, PO Box 940, Brookings, OR 97415. Phone: (800) 535-9469. Fax: (541) 469-4094. E-mail: chamber@brookingsor.com. Web: www.brookingsharborchamber.com.

CLOONEY, ROSEMARY: BIRTH ANNIVERSARY. May 23, 1928. The beloved pop and jazz singer was born at Maysville, KY. She became popular in the 1950s for singing the novelty song "Come-on-a-My House" and pop standards. She also starred in the holiday film *White Christmas* (1954). She died June 29, 2002, at Beverly Hills, CA.

COIN, JEWELRY & STAMP EXPO. May 23–25. Wilshire Ebell Convention Complex, Los Angeles, CA. Est attendance: 4,000. For info: Israel Bick, Exec Dir, Intl Stamp & Coin Collectors Society, PO Box 854, Van Nuys, CA 91408. Phone: (818) 997-6496. Fax: (818) 988-4337. E-mail: iibick@sbcglobal.net. Web: www.bickinternational.com.

DECLARATION OF THE BAB. May 23. Baha'i commemoration of May 23, 1844, when the Bab, the prophet-herald of the Baha'i Faith, announced in Shiraz, Persia, that he was the herald of a new messenger of God. One of the nine days of the year when Baha'is suspend work. For info: Baha'is of the US, Office of Communications, 1233 Central St, Evanston, IL 60201. Phone: (847) 733-3559. Fax: (847) 733-3578. E-mail: ooc@usbnc.org. Web: www.bahai.us.

FAIRBANKS, DOUGLAS ELTON: BIRTH ANNIVERSARY. May 23, 1883. Douglas Fairbanks was born at Denver, CO. He made his professional debut as an actor at Richmond, VA, Sept 10, 1900, in *The Duke's Jester.* His theatrical career shifted to Hollywood, and he became a movie idol, appearing in such films as *The Mark of Zorro, The Three Musketeers, Robin Hood, The Thief of Bagdad, The Black Pirate* and *The Gaucho.* He married "America's Sweetheart," Mary Pickford, in 1918, and in 1919 they joined with D.W. Griffith and Charlie Chaplin to form the production company United Artists. He died at Santa Monica, CA, Dec 12, 1939.

May 2014	S	M	T	W	T	F	S
					1	2	3
	4	5	6	7	8	9	10
	11	12	13	14	15	16	17
	18	19	20	21	22	23	24
	25	26	27	28	29	30	31

FIRST BLACK RECEIVES CONGRESSIONAL MEDAL OF HONOR: ANNIVERSARY. May 23, 1900. Sergeant William H. Carney, of the 54th Massachusetts Colored Infantry, was the first black to win the Congressional Medal of Honor. He was cited for his efforts, although wounded twice, during the Battle of Fort Wagner, SC, June 18, 1863.

FLORIDA FOLK FESTIVAL. May 23–25. Stephen Foster Folk Culture Center State Park, White Springs, FL. To celebrate Florida's folk heritage with music, song, dance and stories. Est attendance: 20,000. For info: Stephen Foster Folk Culture Center State Park, PO Box G, White Springs, FL 32096. Phone: (877) 6FL-FOLK.

FULLER, MARGARET: BIRTH ANNIVERSARY. May 23, 1810. Journalist and author Sarah Margaret Fuller, born at Cambridgeport, MA, began reading Virgil at age six. Her conversational powers won her the admiration of students at Harvard University, and she was befriended by Ralph Waldo Emerson. She shared editorial duties with Emerson on the transcendentalist quarterly *The Dial* and was hired by Horace Greeley as literary critic for the *New York Tribune.* Her book *Women in the Nineteenth Century,* the first feminist statement by an American writer, brought her international acclaim. In 1846, as a foreign correspondent for the *Tribune,* she became caught up in the Italian revolutionary movement and secretly married a young Roman nobleman, the Marquis Giovanni Angelo Ossoli. En route to the US, Fuller and her husband and child died July 19, 1850, when their ship was wrecked off Fire Island near New York, NY.

INTERNATIONAL WORLD TURTLE DAY. May 23. An observance sponsored by American Tortoise Rescue to help people celebrate and protect turtles and tortoises, as well as their habitats around the world. For info: Susan Tellem, American Tortoise Rescue, 30765 Pacific Coast Hwy #243, Malibu, CA 90265. E-mail: info@tortoise.com. Web: www.tortoise.com.

MANSFIELD, ARABELLA: BIRTH ANNIVERSARY. May 23, 1846. Arabella Mansfield, born Belle Aurelia Babb near Burlington, IA, was the first woman admitted to the legal profession in the US. In 1869 while teaching at Iowa Wesleyan College, Mansfield was certified as an attorney and admitted to the Iowa bar. According to the examiners, "she gave the very best rebuke possible to the imputation that ladies cannot qualify for the practice of law." Mansfield never did practice law, however, continuing her career as an educator. She joined the faculty of DePauw University, at Greencastle, IN, where she became dean of the schools of art and music. One of the first woman college professors and administrators in the US, Mansfield was also instrumental in the founding of the Iowa Woman Suffrage Society in 1870. She died Aug 2, 1911, at Aurora, IL.

MESMER, FRANZ ANTON: BIRTH ANNIVERSARY. May 23, 1734. German physician after whom mesmerism was named. Magnetism and hypnotism were used by him in treating disease. Born at Iznang, Swabia, Germany. Died Mar 5, 1815, at Meersburg, Swabia.

MOROCCO: NATIONAL DAY. May 23. National holiday. Commemorates referendum on the majority of the king in 1980.

NAIA BASEBALL WORLD SERIES. May 23–30. Lewiston, ID. 58th annual AVISTA-NAIA World Series. Est attendance: 40,000. For info: Natl Assn of Intercollegiate Athletics, 1200 Grand Blvd, Kansas City, MO 64106. E-mail: jford@naia.org. Web: www.naia.org.

NAIA SOFTBALL NATIONAL CHAMPIONSHIP. May 23–29. South Commons Softball Complex, Columbus, GA. 34th annual. Est attendance: 2,000. For info: Natl Assn of Intercollegiate Athletics, 1200 Grand Blvd, Kansas City, MO 64106. E-mail: dgreen@naia.org. Web: www.naia.org.

NATIONAL POLKA FESTIVAL. May 23–25. Ennis, TX. 48th annual. A Czech-heritage festival for the entire family in a small-city atmosphere. Kicks off Friday evening with the King and Queen Dance Contest, where everyone is encouraged to wear traditional Czech *kroj* (costumes). Saturday morning features a colorful parade twisting through historic downtown Ennis with polka bands, floats, the Shriners, motorcycles, horseback riders, clowns and more. Other events: Polkafest Run, horseshoe tourney and more. Experience "a little bit of the Czech Lands" and enjoy a weekend of polka dancing, Czech foods and 13 sensational live polka bands.

Annually, Memorial Day weekend. For info: Ennis CVB, PO Box 1237, Ennis, TX 75120. Phone: (972) 878-4748. E-mail: ennis4u@swbell.net. Web: www.nationalpolkafestival.com.

NCAA DIVISION I WOMEN'S LACROSSE CHAMPIONSHIP. May 23 and 25. Johnny Unitas Stadium, Towson, MD. Est attendance: 8,000. For info: NCAA, 700 W Washington St, Indianapolis, IN 46206-6222. Phone: (317) 917-6222. Web: www.NCAAsports.com.

NEW YORK PUBLIC LIBRARY: ANNIVERSARY. May 23, 1895. New York's then-governor Samuel J. Tilden was the driving force that resulted in the combining of the private Astor and Lenox libraries with a $2 million endowment and 15,000 volumes from the Tilden Trust to become the New York Public Library. The main branch of the library opened to the public on this day in 1911.

NORTHWEST FOLKLIFE FESTIVAL. May 23–26. Seattle Center, Seattle, WA. 43rd annual. Ethnic and traditional arts event celebrating world cultures in the Northwest region. Includes music, dance, food, crafts, visual arts exhibits, children's programs, demonstrations and more. More than 6,000 performers. Annually, Friday through Monday of Memorial Day weekend. Est attendance: 275,000. For info: Northwest Folklife, 305 Harrison St, Seattle, WA 98109-4623. Phone: (206) 684-7300. Fax: (206) 684-7190. E-mail: folklife@nwfolklife.org. Web: www.nwfolklife.org.

RITZVILLE WESTERN ART SHOW. May 23–25. Ritzville, WA. Centrally located in the heart of historic downtown Ritzville, the show celebrates art that captures the spirit of the West, rural living, Native American life, wildlife and agriculture. The art show is free to the general public and features live entertainment, youth activities, "Legends of the Old West" gun reenactments, dutch oven cook-off and more. Annually, Memorial Day weekend. Est attendance: 2,200. For info: Ritzville Western Art Show, PO Box 432, Ritzville, WA 99169. Phone: (509) 660-0654. E-mail: info@ritzvillewesternart.com. Web: www.ritzvillewesternart.com.

RIVERFEST. May 23–25. Riverfront Park, Little Rock, and North Shore Riverwalk, North Little Rock, AR. 36th annual outdoor festival of the visual and performing arts with 100 acts on five stages, food vendors, visual artists, kid stuff. Est attendance: 250,000. For info: Riverfest, 500 President Clinton Ave, Ste 217, Little Rock, AR 72201. Phone: (501) 255-FEST. Fax: (501) 255-3379. E-mail: director@riverfestarkansas.com. Web: www.riverfestarkansas.com.

SACRAMENTO MUSIC FESTIVAL. May 23–26. Sacramento, CA. More than 70 bands perform American traditional jazz and related music in approximately 23 venues around Sacramento. Annually, Memorial Day weekend. Est attendance: 70,000. For info: Sacramento Music Festival, 106 K St, #1, Sacramento, CA 95814. Phone: (916) 372-5277. Fax: (916) 372-3479. E-mail: info@sacjazz.com. Web: www.sacmusicfest.com.

SHAKER MUSEUM OPENING DAY. May 23. Sabbathday Lake Shaker Village, New Gloucester, ME. The 84th season of the Shaker Museum opens with tours, exhibits and special events. Open through Columbus Day (closed on Sundays). For info: Sabbathday Lake Shaker Village, Rte 26, New Gloucester, ME 04260. Phone: (207) 926-4597. E-mail: usshakers@aol.com. Web: www.shaker.lib.me.us.

SLOVO, JOE: BIRTH ANNIVERSARY. May 23, 1926. South African Communist Party leader Joe Slovo was a longtime friend and ally of Nelson Mandela's. The first white to become a member of the African National Congress (ANC) Executive Committee, he lived in exile from 1963 to 1990, serving as head of the military arm of the ANC during that period. Born at Obelai, Lithuania, he died Jan 6, 1995, at Johannesburg, South Africa.

SOUTH CAROLINA CONSTITUTION RATIFICATION: ANNIVERSARY. May 23, 1788. By a vote of 149 to 73, South Carolina became the eighth state to ratify the Constitution.

SPOLETO FESTIVAL USA. May 23–June 8. Charleston, SC. Comprehensive arts festival with a mix of more than 150 performances of opera, dance, theater, chamber and symphonic music, jazz and visual arts set in one of America's most beautiful and historic cities. For info: Spoleto Festival USA, 14 George St, Charleston, SC 29401. Phone: (843) 579-3100. Web: www.spoletousa.org.

SUPREME COURT UPHOLDS BAN ON ABORTION COUNSELING: ANNIVERSARY. May 23, 1991. In the case *Rust v Sullivan*, the Supreme Court, in a 5–4 ruling, upheld federal regulations that barred federally funded family planning clinics from providing any information about abortion.

SWEDEN: LINNAEUS DAY. May 23, 1707. Stenbrohult. Commemorates birth of Carolus Linnaeus (Carl von Linne), Swedish naturalist, born May 23, 1707 (OS), and died at Uppsala, Sweden, Jan 10, 1778.

TAPPAN, LEWIS: BIRTH ANNIVERSARY. May 23, 1788. Abolitionist and merchant born at Northampton, MA. Best known for his vigorous participation in the US antislavery movement. Helped found the American Anti-Slavery Society (1833) and led the efforts to aid the Mendi people who revolted against their captors on the slave ship *Amistad*. Tappan also created the first credit rating service in the US in 1841. The Mercantile Service's success enabled Tappan to retire a wealthy man and to focus on abolition and philanthropy. (In 1858, the Mercantile Service was bought by Graham Dun and evolved into Dun & Bradstreet.) Tappan died June 21, 1873, at Brooklyn, NY.

WORLD CHAMPIONSHIP OLD-TIME PIANO PLAYING CONTEST. May 23–26. Hotel Père Marquette, Peoria, IL. Competition and festival of ragtime, honky-tonk and old-time music. Includes Old-Time Orchestry, workshops and dealers rooms. Annually, Memorial Day weekend. Sponsor: Old-Time Music Preservation Association (OMPA) Inc. Est attendance: 1,000. For info: World Championship Old-Time Piano Playing Contest, 108 E Garwood, Champaign, IL 61820. E-mail: eballard@illinois.edu. Web: oldtimepiano.com.

BIRTHDAYS TODAY

Mitch Albom, 56, journalist, author (*Tuesdays with Morrie, The Five People You Meet in Heaven*), born Passaic, NJ, May 23, 1958.

Barbara Barrie, 83, actress ("Suddenly Susan"; *One Potato, Two Potato; Breaking Away*), born Chicago, IL, May 23, 1931.

H. Jon Benjamin, 48, actor ("Bob's Burgers," "Archer," "Family Guy"), born Worcester, MA, May 23, 1966.

Brian Campbell, 35, hockey player, born Strathroy, ON, Canada, May 23, 1979.

Drew Carey, 53, actor ("The Drew Carey Show"), host ("The Price Is Right"), born Cleveland, OH, May 23, 1961 (some sources say 1958).

Joan Collins, 81, actress ("Dynasty"), born London, England, May 23, 1933.

"Marvelous" Marvin Hagler, 60, former boxer, born Newark, NJ, May 23, 1954.

Jewel, 40, singer, born Jewel Kilcher at Payson, UT, May 23, 1974.

Charles Kimbrough, 78, actor ("Murphy Brown"), born St. Paul, MN, May 23, 1936.

May 24 — Saturday

DAY 144 **221 REMAINING**

ALMA HIGHLAND FESTIVAL AND GAMES. May 24–25. Alma College, Alma, MI. 47th annual. Old-world pageantry honoring Scottish traditions—Highland dancing, piping, drumming, athletic competitions, clan tents and grand parade. Annually, Memorial Day weekend. Est attendance: 15,000. For info: Alma Highland Festival, 110 W Superior St, PO Box 516, Alma, MI 48801. Phone: (989) 463-8979. Fax: (989) 463-6588. E-mail: highland@almahighlandfestival.com. Web: www.almahighlandfestival.com.

ANTI-SALOON LEAGUE FOUNDED: ANNIVERSARY. May 24, 1893. The Anti-Saloon League was founded by Howard H. Russell at Oberlin, OH. Efforts in that state were so successful that the Anti-Saloon League of America was organized in 1895. The league's permanent home became Otterbein College at Westerville, OH, in 1909.

BASEBALL FIRST PLAYED UNDER LIGHTS: ANNIVERSARY. May 24, 1935. The Cincinnati Reds defeated the Philadelphia Phillies by a score of 2–1, as more than 20,000 fans enjoyed the first night baseball game in the major leagues. The game was played at Crosley Field, Cincinnati, OH.

BELIZE: COMMONWEALTH DAY. May 24. Public holiday.

BROOKLYN BRIDGE OPENED: ANNIVERSARY. May 24, 1883. Nearly 14 years in construction, the $16 million Brooklyn Bridge over the East River opened. Designed by John A. Roebling, the steel suspension bridge has a span of 1,595 feet.

BROTHER'S DAY. May 24. Celebration of brotherhood for biological brothers, fraternity brothers and brothers bonded by union affiliation or lifetime experiences. Annually, May 24. (©2001 C. Daniel Rhodes.) For info: C. Daniel Rhodes, 1900 Crossvine Rd, Hoover, AL 35244. Phone: (205) 908-6781. E-mail: rhodan@charter.net.

BULGARIA: CULTURE DAY. May 24. National holiday festively celebrated by schoolchildren, students and people of science and art.

ECUADOR: BATTLE OF PICHINCHA. May 24. National holiday. Commemorates battle in 1822 that marked the final defeat of Spain in Ecuador.

ERITREA: INDEPENDENCE DAY. May 24. National Day. Gained independence from Ethiopia in 1993 after 30-year civil war.

INTERNATIONAL TIARA DAY. May 24. A day when all women embrace and celebrate their powers of leadership. Real or virtual tiara-wearing is optional. For info: Lynanne White, Miss American Rose Pageants, 25767 Norval Ln, Poulsbo, WA 98730. E-mail: miss@americanrose.com. Web: www.internationaltiaraday.com.

May 2014	S	M	T	W	T	F	S
					1	2	3
	4	5	6	7	8	9	10
	11	12	13	14	15	16	17
	18	19	20	21	22	23	24
	25	26	27	28	29	30	31

JULIA PIERPONT DAY. May 24. Julia Pierpont is recognized by many historians for having originated "Decoration Day" in May 1866, which is now the US federal holiday Memorial Day. This day pays tribute to Pierpont by readying veterans' graves for Memorial Day. It was proclaimed in West Virginia in 2005. For info: Dr. Doreen Larson, President, Pierpont Community and Technical College, 200 Locust Ave, Fairmont, WV 26554. Phone: (304) 367-4692. E-mail: doreen.larson@pierpont.edu.

LEUTZE, EMANUEL: BIRTH ANNIVERSARY. May 24, 1816. Obscure itinerant painter, born at Württemberg, Germany, came to the US when he was nine years old, began painting by age 15. Painted some of the most famous of American scenes, such as *Washington Crossing the Delaware, Washington Rallying the Troops at Monmouth* and *Columbus Before the Queen*. Died July 18, 1868, at Washington, DC.

LOBSTER DAYS. May 24–26. Mystic Seaport, Mystic, CT. A New England lobster bake on the banks of the Mystic River over the Memorial Day weekend, put on by the Rotary Club of Mystic. Est attendance: 10,000. For info: Mystic Seaport, 75 Greenmanville Ave, PO Box 6000, Mystic, CT 06355-0990. Phone: (860) 572-0711 or (888) 973-2767. Web: www.mysticseaport.org.

MISSOURI RIVER IRISH FEST. May 24–25. Frontier Park, St. Charles, MO. 10th annual. Free Irish festival featuring traditional and Celtic rock bands, Irish dancers, Irish vendors, cultural exhibits, athletic competitions, children's village, Sunday church service and more. Est attendance: 60,000. For info: Greater St. Charles CVB, 230 S Main St, St. Charles, MO 63301. Phone: (800) 366-2427 or (636) 946-7776. Web: www.moriveririshfest.com.

MORSE OPENS FIRST US TELEGRAPH LINE: ANNIVERSARY. May 24, 1844. The first US telegraph line was formally opened between Baltimore, MD, and Washington, DC. Samuel F.B. Morse sent the first officially telegraphed words—"What hath God wrought?"—from the Capitol building to Baltimore. Earlier messages had been sent along the historic line during testing, and one, sent May 1 from a meeting in Baltimore, contained the news that Henry Clay had been nominated for president by the Whig Party. This message reached Washington one hour prior to a train carrying the same news.

NCAA DIVISION I MEN'S LACROSSE CHAMPIONSHIP. May 24 and 26. M&T Bank Stadium, Baltimore, MD. For info: NCAA, PO Box 6222, Indianapolis, IN 46206-6222. Web: www.NCAA.com.

NEWHOUSE, SAMUEL I.: BIRTH ANNIVERSARY. May 24, 1895. Multimillionaire businessman who built a family publishing and communications empire. Born to immigrant parents in a New York City tenement, Newhouse became "America's most profitable publisher." He accumulated 31 newspapers, seven magazines, six television stations, five radio stations and 20 cable television systems. He died at New York, NY, Aug 29, 1979.

PALMER, LILLI: 100th BIRTH ANNIVERSARY. May 24, 1914. Stage, screen and television actress Lilli Palmer was born Lillie Marie Peiser at Poznan, Poland. She also painted and was the author of several novels and an autobiography titled *Change Lobsters—and Dance*. She died at Los Angeles, CA, Jan 27, 1986.

SPACE MILESTONE: *AURORA 7* MERCURY SPACE CAPSULE (US). May 24, 1962. With this launch Scott Carpenter became the second American to orbit Earth, circling it three times.

TASTE OF CINCINNATI. May 24–26. Cincinnati, OH. 35th annual. Cincinnati is famous for its fine food, from elegant five-star dining to five-way chili. This popular eating extravaganza presents a taste of the most delicious culinary delights available. Annually, Memorial Day weekend. Est attendance: 500,000. For info: Cincinnati USA Regional Chamber, 441 Vine St, Ste 300, Cincinnati, OH 45202. Phone: (513) 579-3100. Fax: (513) 579-3101. E-mail: info@cincinnatichamber.com. Web: www.tasteofcincinnati.com.

TIVOLI FEST. May 24–25. Elk Horn, IA. Annual Danish celebration with parade, folk dancers, foods from Denmark, historical tours, arts and crafts for sale and more. Annually, Memorial Day weekend. Sponsor: Better Elk Horn Club. Est attendance: 5,000. For info: Danish Windmill. E-mail: info@danishwindmill.com. Web: www.danishwindmill.com.

UTICA SERTOMA ICE CREAM FESTIVAL. May 24–26. Utica, OH. Saluting "America's favorite dessert," ice cream, with a weekend of fun and entertainment: parade, queen contest, arts and crafts, antique gas engines, sheepherding with border collies and plenty of delicious ice cream. Est attendance: 30,000. For info: Utica Ice Cream Festival, 515 N Main St, Utica, OH 43080. Phone: (740) 892-4272. Web: www.velveticecream.com or www.uticaoldfashionedicecreamfestival.com.

BIRTHDAYS TODAY

DaMarcus Beasley, 32, soccer player, born Fort Wayne, IN, May 24, 1982.

Jim Broadbent, 65, actor (*Moulin Rouge, Topsy-Turvy*, Oscar for *Iris*), born Lincoln, Lincolnshire, England, May 24, 1949.

Gary Burghoff, 71, actor (Emmy for "M*A*S*H"), born Bristol, CT, May 24, 1943.

Tommy Chong, 76, actor (*Up in Smoke, The Corsican Brothers*), born Edmonton, AB, Canada, May 24, 1938.

Eric Close, 47, actor ("Nashville," "Without a Trace"), born Staten Island, NY, May 24, 1967.

Bob Dylan, 73, composer, singer, born Robert Zimmerman at Duluth, MN, May 24, 1941.

Alyson Hannigan, 40, actress ("How I Met Your Mother," "Buffy the Vampire Slayer," *American Pie*), born Washington, DC, May 24, 1974.

Patti LaBelle, 70, singer, born Patricia Louise Holte at Philadelphia, PA, May 24, 1944.

Tracy McGrady, 35, basketball player, born Bartow, FL, May 24, 1979.

Alfred Molina, 61, actor (*An Education, Frida, Chocolat*), born London, England, May 24, 1953.

Frank Oz, 70, director, puppeteer, born Hereford, England, May 24, 1944.

Priscilla Beaulieu Presley, 69, actress ("Dallas," *Naked Gun* films), born Brooklyn, NY, May 24, 1945.

Kristin Scott Thomas, 54, actress (*Gosford Park, The English Patient, The Horse Whisperer*), born Cornwall, England, May 24, 1960.

May 25 — Sunday

DAY 145 | **220 REMAINING**

AFRICAN FREEDOM DAY. May 25. Public holiday in Chad, Zambia and some other African nations. Members of the Organization for African Unity (formed May 25, 1963) commemorate their independence from colonial rule. Sports contests, political rallies and tribal dances.

AMERICAN FLIGHT CRASHES AT O'HARE: 35th ANNIVERSARY. May 25, 1979. An American Airlines DC-10 lost an engine upon takeoff at Chicago O'Hare Airport and crashed seconds later, killing all 272 aboard and three people on the ground.

ANDERSONVILLE MEMORIAL DAY CEREMONIES. May 25. Andersonville, GA. Each year the Andersonville National Historic Site hosts a series of activities to commemorate Memorial Day and to pay tribute to our country's men and women who paid for our freedom with their lives. Saturday morning, volunteers, including scout and youth groups from across the state, place flags throughout Andersonville National Cemetery. During the weekend volunteer Cemetery Wardens also assist with maintaining the gravesite flags and interacting with visitors to the cemetery. The focal point of all these activities is the Sunday afternoon Memorial Day ceremony, which takes place at the National Cemetery rostrum. The service traditionally includes a musical program, speaker and the placement of memorial wreaths. Annually, the Sunday of Memorial Day weekend (with activities all during the weekend). For info: Park Ranger, Andersonville National Historic Site. Phone: (229) 924-0343. Web: www.nps.gov/ande.

ARGENTINA: REVOLUTION DAY. May 25. National holiday. Commemoration of revolt against Spanish rule in 1810.

CARVER, RAYMOND: BIRTH ANNIVERSARY. May 25, 1938. American poet and short-story writer who chronicled the lives of America's working poor. Born at Clatskanie, OR, he died Aug 2, 1988, at his home at Port Angeles, WA, soon after finishing a book of poetry titled *A New Path to the Waterfall*.

CONSTITUTIONAL CONVENTION: ANNIVERSARY. May 25, 1787. At Philadelphia, PA, delegates from seven states, forming a quorum, opened the Constitutional Convention, which had been proposed by the Annapolis Convention Sept 11–14, 1786. Among those who were in attendance: George Washington, Benjamin Franklin, James Madison, Alexander Hamilton and Elbridge Gerry. See also: "1786 Annapolis Convention: Anniversary" (Sept 11).

DAVID, HAL: BIRTH ANNIVERSARY. May 25, 1921. Together with composer Burt Bacharach, lyricist Hal David produced a sophisticated string of songs that not only have become standards but also pop music legends. Romance, sensuality and a profound intimacy were hallmarks of David's lyrical style, on display in such classics as "Walk on By," "What the World Needs Now Is Love" and the Carpenters' "Close to You." The pair won a 1970 Best Song Oscar for "Raindrops Keep Falling on My Head." In the 1970s David and Bacharach's partnership dissolved into acrimony, but by then their pop music legacy was set in stone. Born at New York, NY, David died Sept 1, 2012, at Los Angeles, CA.

DAVIS, MILES: BIRTH ANNIVERSARY. May 25, 1926. Jazz trumpeter Miles Davis was born at Alton, IL. He was influenced by the bebop music style of Charlie Parker and Dizzy Gillespie and ended up leaving the Juilliard School of Music to join Parker's quintet in 1945. He experimented with different styles throughout his career, exploring new voicings in jazz with arranger Gil Evans and musicians John Coltrane and Red Garland, delving into modal music with Tony Williams and Wayne Shorter and moving into a fusion sound in the '60s. His career was beset with bouts of drug addiction, but in the 1970s his return to the music scene found him creating a sound that melded his bebop origins, modal chord progressions and driving rock rhythms. He died Sept 28, 1991, at Santa Monica, CA.

DOWIE, JOHN ALEXANDER: BIRTH ANNIVERSARY. May 25, 1847. The evangelist and claimant of the title "Elijah the Restorer" was born at Edinburgh, Scotland. He established the Christian Catholic Church at Zion, IL, where some 5,000 followers created a unique community without pharmacies, physicians, theaters or dance halls and where smoking, drinking and the eating of pork were prohibited. Dowie's ostentatiously expensive personal lifestyle and his unsuccessful attempt to convert New York City were partially responsible for the falling away of his followers. He was expelled from the Church in 1906 and died at Chicago, IL, Mar 9, 1907.

EMERSON, RALPH WALDO: BIRTH ANNIVERSARY. May 25, 1803. American author and philosopher born at Boston, MA, and died there Apr 27, 1882. It was Emerson who wrote (in his essay "Self-Reliance," 1841), "A foolish consistency is the hobgoblin of little minds, adored by little statesmen and philosophers and divines. With consistency a great soul has simply nothing to do."

FRANCE: FRENCH OPEN TENNIS TOURNAMENT. May 25–June 8. Roland-Garros Stadium, Paris. Storied clay-court international tournament—part of the Grand Slam of Tennis—played annually since 1925. (Qualifying begins earlier, May 20–24.) For info: Fédération Française de Tennis, 2 avenue Gordon Bennett, 75016 Paris, France. E-mail: fft@fft.fr. Web: www.fft.fr or www.rolandgarros.com.

GREATEST DAY IN TRACK AND FIELD: JESSE OWENS'S REMARKABLE RECORDS: ANNIVERSARY. May 25, 1935. During the Big Ten Championships at the University of Michigan at Ann Arbor, Jesse Owens, representing Ohio State University, broke three world records and tied a fourth in the space of 45 minutes—from 3:15 PM to 4:00 PM. The "Buckeye Bullet" (who was suffering from an injured back) set records in the running broad jump, the 220-yard dash and the 220-yard hurdles and tied the record for the 100-yard dash. See also: "Owens, Jesse: Birth Anniversary" (Sept 12).

INDIANAPOLIS 500-MILE RACE. May 25. Indianapolis, IN. Recognized as the world's largest single-day sporting event. First race was in 1911. Annually, the Sunday of Memorial Day weekend. For info: Indianapolis Motor Speedway. Web: www.indy500.com.

ISRA AL MI'RAJ: ASCENT OF THE PROPHET MUHAMMAD. May 25. Islamic calendar date: evening after Rajab 26, 1435. Commemorates the journey of the Prophet Muhammad from Mecca to Jerusalem, his ascension into the Seven Heavens and his return on the same night. Muslims believe that on that night Muhammad prayed together with Abraham, Moses and Jesus in the area of the Al-Aqsa Mosque in Jerusalem. The rock from which he is believed to have ascended to heaven to speak with God is the one inside the Dome of the Rock. Different methods for "anticipating" the visibility of the new moon crescent at Mecca are used by different Muslim groups. US date may vary.

ITALY: PALIO DEI BALESTRIERI (PALIO OF THE ARCHERS). May 25. Gubbio. The last Sunday in May is set aside for a crossbow contest that has been held since medieval times between the neighboring towns of Gubbio and Sansepolcro. Participants wear medieval costumes and bear medieval arms. Sansepolcro hosts the second part of the contest on the second Sunday of September. The colorful event is accompanied by a parade.

JORDAN: INDEPENDENCE DAY. May 25. National holiday. Commemorates treaty in 1946, proclaiming independence from Britain and establishing a monarchy.

MURRAY, PHILIP: BIRTH ANNIVERSARY. May 25, 1886. The American labor leader and founder of the Congress of Industrial Organizations, also active in and a leader of the United Mine Workers, was born near Blantyre, Scotland. Murray died at San Francisco, CA, Nov 9, 1952.

NATIONAL MISSING CHILDREN'S DAY. May 25. To promote awareness of the problem of missing children, to offer a forum for change and to offer safety information for children in school and the community. Annually, May 25. For info: Child Find of America, Inc, PO Box 277, New Paltz, NY 12561-0277. Phone: (845) 883-6060 or (800) I-AM-LOST. E-mail: information@childfindofamerica.org. Web: www.childfindofamerica.org.

NATIONAL TAP DANCE DAY. May 25. To celebrate this unique American art form that represents a fusion of African and European cultures and to transmit tap to succeeding generations through documentation and archival and performance support. Held on the anniversary of the birth of Bill "Bojangles" Robinson to honor his outstanding contribution to the art of tap dancing on stage and in films through the unification of diverse stylistic and racial elements.

May 2014	S	M	T	W	T	F	S
					1	2	3
	4	5	6	7	8	9	10
	11	12	13	14	15	16	17
	18	19	20	21	22	23	24
	25	26	27	28	29	30	31

POETRY DAY IN FLORIDA. May 25. In 1947 the legislature decreed this day to be "Poetry Day in all of the public schools of Florida."

ROBINSON, BILL "BOJANGLES": BIRTH ANNIVERSARY. May 25, 1878. Born at Richmond, VA, the grandson of a slave, Robinson is considered one of the greatest tap dancers. He is best known for a routine in which he tap-danced up and down a staircase. He appeared in several films with Shirley Temple and starred in *Stormy Weather.* Died at New York, NY, Nov 25, 1949.

ROGATION SUNDAY. May 25. The fifth Sunday after Easter is the beginning of Rogationtide (Rogation Sunday and the following three days before Ascension Day). Rogation Day rituals date from the fifth century.

RURAL LIFE SUNDAY OR SOIL STEWARDSHIP SUNDAY. May 25. Rural Life Sunday emphasizes the concept that Earth belongs to God, who has granted humanity the use of it, along with the responsibility of caring for it wisely. At the suggestion of the International Association of Agricultural Missions, Rural Life Sunday was first observed in 1929. The day is observed annually by churches of many Christian denominations and includes pulpit exchanges by rural and urban pastors. Under the auspices of the National Association of Soil and Water Conservation Districts, the week beginning with Rural Life Sunday is now widely observed as Soil Stewardship Week, with the Sunday itself alternatively termed Soil Stewardship Sunday. Traditionally, Rural Life Sunday is Rogation Sunday, the Sunday preceding Ascension Day.

SIKORSKY, IGOR: 125th BIRTH ANNIVERSARY. May 25, 1889. Aeronautical engineer best remembered for his development of the first successful helicopter in 1939. The first to design and fly a multiengine airplane in 1913, Sikorsky also produced multiengine airplanes and large flying boats, called "Clippers," that made transoceanic air transportation possible. Born at Kiev, Russia (now Ukraine), he died Oct 26, 1972, at Easton, CT.

SILLS, BEVERLY: 85th BIRTH ANNIVERSARY. May 25, 1929. The acclaimed coloratura soprano was born Belle Silverman at Brooklyn, NY. Signature roles were the title roles in *Lucia di Lammermoor* and *Anna Bolena*, as well as Queen Elizabeth I in *Roberto Devereux*. She was a dedicated ambassador of opera in America and was instrumental in making it accessible both as a singer and later as a television personality and opera executive. She died July 2, 2007, at New York, NY.

SOLZHENITSYN GOES HOME: 20th ANNIVERSARY. May 25, 1994. After 20 years living in exile, mostly in the US, Russian author Aleksandr Solzhenitsyn returned to his homeland. The author had been expelled from the Soviet Union in 1974 after his three-volume work exposing the Soviet prison camp system, *The Gulag Archipelago*, was published in the West. After the collapse of the Soviet Union late in 1991, he announced his intention to go back.

SPACE MILESTONE: *SKYLAB 2* (US). May 25, 1973. Joseph P. Kerwin, Paul J. Weitz and Charles (Pete) Conrad, Jr, spent 28 days in experimentation on this space station, which had been launched May 14. Pacific splashdown occurred June 22.

***STAR WARS* RELEASED: ANNIVERSARY.** May 25, 1977. "May the Force be with you" entered the modern lexicon as a new kind of science fiction film opened at 32 theaters. George Lucas's space epic, starring Mark Hamill as Luke Skywalker, Harrison Ford as Han Solo and Carrie Fisher as Princess Leia, featured stunning special effects and was a smash hit worldwide. It went on to win six Academy Awards out of ten nominations—plus an additional special Academy Award for sound effects. The film was part of a larger saga and in later years was retitled *Star Wars—Episode IV: A New Hope* as prequels were released.

TITO (JOSIP BROZ): BIRTH ANNIVERSARY. May 25, 1892. Josip Broz, Yugoslavian soldier and political leader, born near Zagreb, Yugoslavia. Died May 4, 1980, at Ljubljana, Yugoslavia (now Slovenia), and was interred in the garden of his home at Belgrade. Tito, a Croat, had managed to keep the many nationalities and religions that made up Yugoslavia in one state, but in the early 1990s the nation broke up as Croats, Serbs and others went to war against each other.

TOWEL DAY. May 25. In honor of Douglas Adams, the author of *Hitchhiker's Guide to the Galaxy*, carry a towel on this day and make sure that it is conspicuous. Wrap it around your head, use it as a weapon or sleep on it beneath the stars. For info: Towel Day. E-mail: info@towelday.org. Web: www.towelday.org.

TUNNEY, JAMES JOSEPH (GENE): BIRTH ANNIVERSARY. May 25, 1898. Heavyweight boxing champion, business executive. The famous "long count" occurred in the seventh round of the Jack Dempsey–Gene Tunney world championship fight, Sept 22, 1927, at Soldier Field, Chicago, IL. Tunney was born at New York, NY, and died Nov 7, 1978, at Greenwich, CT.

UNITED NATIONS: WEEK OF SOLIDARITY WITH THE PEOPLES OF NON-SELF-GOVERNING TERRITORIES. May 25–31. On Dec 6, 1999 (Resolution 54/91), the General Assembly requested the Special Committee on Decolonization to observe this week beginning on May 25, Africa Liberation Day. For info: United Nations, Dept of Public Info, New York, NY 10017. Web: www.un.org.

BIRTHDAYS TODAY

Jessi Colter, 67, singer, songwriter, born Miriam Johnson at Phoenix, AZ, May 25, 1947.

Tom T. Hall, 78, singer, songwriter, born Olive Hill, KY, May 25, 1936.

Anne Heche, 45, actress ("Men in Trees," *Wag the Dog, Volcano*), born Aurora, OH, May 25, 1969.

Justin Henry, 43, actor (*Kramer vs Kramer, Sixteen Candles*), born Rye, NY, May 25, 1971.

Lauryn Hill, 39, singer, actress (*Sister Act 2*), born South Orange, NJ, May 25, 1975.

K.C. Jones, 82, Hall of Fame basketball player, former coach, born Tyler, TX, May 25, 1932.

Jamie Kennedy, 44, actor ("JKX: The Jamie Kennedy Experiment," *Malibu's Most Wanted*), born Upper Darby, PA, May 25, 1970.

Amy Klobuchar, 54, US Senator (D, Minnesota), born Plymouth, MN, May 25, 1960.

Sir Ian McKellen, 75, actor (Tony for *Amadeus*; the Lord of the Rings film trilogy, *Gods and Monsters*), born Burnley, England, May 25, 1939.

Mike Myers, 51, comedian, actor ("Saturday Night Live," *Wayne's World, Austin Powers: International Man of Mystery* and sequels), born Scarsborough, ON, Canada, May 25, 1963.

Aly Raisman, 20, Olympic gymnast, born Needham, MA, May 25, 1994.

Connie Sellecca, 59, actress ("Hotel," *While My Pretty One Sleeps*), born the Bronx, NY, May 25, 1955.

Ethan Suplee, 38, actor ("My Name Is Earl," "Boy Meets World," *Art School Confidential*), born New York, NY, May 25, 1976.

Leslie Uggams, 71, actress (Tony for *Hallelujah, Baby!*; "Sing Along with Mitch," *Roots*), singer, born New York, NY, May 25, 1943.

Brian Urlacher, 36, former football player, born Lovington, NM, May 25, 1978.

Karen Valentine, 67, actress ("Room 222"), born Sebastopol, CA, May 25, 1947.

May 26 — Monday

DAY 146 — **219 REMAINING**

AUSTRALIA: SORRY DAY. May 26. A day to express sorrow for the forced removal of aboriginal children from their families.

BOLDER BOULDER 10K. May 26. Boulder, CO. 36th annual. A 10k race of walkers, joggers and world-class runners through the streets of Boulder. Presented by Crocs. Annually, on Memorial Day. Est attendance: 50,000. For info: Bolder Boulder, 5500 Central Ave, Ste 110, Boulder, CO 80301. Phone: (303) 444-7223. E-mail: race@bolderboulder.com. Web: www.bolderboulder.com.

DUNKIRK EVACUATED: ANNIVERSARY. May 26, 1940. The British Expeditionary Force had become trapped by advancing German armies near this port on the northern coast of France. On this date the evacuation of 200,000 British and 140,000 French and Belgian soldiers began. Sailing on every kind of transport available, including fishing boats and recreational craft, these men were safely brought across the English Channel by June 2.

ENGLAND: GLOUCESTERSHIRE CHEESE ROLLING. May 26. Cooper's Hill, near Gloucester, Stroud and Cheltenham in the Cotswolds. Ancient tradition dating to pre-Roman times. Held continuously for the last 200 years, an event in which contestants race down a steep 300-yard hill after a seven-to-nine-pound wheel of double Gloucester cheese. The races (four in total, with 10–15 participants) begin at noon, with a top-hatted master of ceremonies beginning the countdown: "One to be ready, two to be steady, three to prepare and four to be off!" Spectators lining the hill chant, "Roll that cheese!" The unusual festival is marked by many injuries of racers and spectators. The winner gets the cheese. Annually, the last Monday in May—the second May bank holiday. Est attendance: 4,000.

FEAST OF SAINT AUGUSTINE OF CANTERBURY. May 26. Pope Gregory sent Augustine to convert the pagan English. Augustine became the first archbishop of Canterbury. He died May 26, AD 604.

GEORGIA: INDEPENDENCE DAY. May 26. National Day. Commemorates declaration of independence from Russia in 1918. Was absorbed by the Soviet Union in 1922 (until 1991).

GOULD, JAY: BIRTH ANNIVERSARY. May 26, 1836. American financier, seen by some as a robber baron, born at Roxbury, NY. In 1867, he joined the board of the Erie Railroad and made millions manipulating Erie stock. In 1869, he conspired to control the price of gold by buying up all the gold in New York City, causing the Black Friday Panic of Sept 24, in which thousands of investors sustained losses and Gould made a fortune. He began developing railroads in the West in 1872; by 1880, he controlled more than 8,000 miles of railroad track. He also gained control of the Western Union Telegraph Co and several elevated railroads in New York City. Gould died on Dec 2, 1892, at New York City.

HELM, LEVON: BIRTH ANNIVERSARY. May 26, 1940. Born at Marvell, AR, Levon Helm grew up listening to Grand Ole Opry radio shows and early rock and roll, sounds that informed his long career as a drummer, bandleader and respected singer-songwriter. Helm formed The Band in the late 1950s, and played drums with the roots rock outfit on legendary albums such as *Songs from Big Pink* and *The Last Waltz* (1978). As a bandleader he issued a string of solo records in the 1980s and '90s, and continued to work steadily; the folky *Dirt Farmer* (2007) was a late critical favorite. Helm died of cancer Apr 19, 2012, at New York City.

JOLSON, AL: BIRTH ANNIVERSARY. May 26, 1886. "You ain't heard nothin' yet" was the famous catchphrase of the world's first full-length talkie, *The Jazz Singer* (1927). It starred the legendary entertainer Al Jolson, who by that time already had decades of showbiz experience behind him. Born Asa Yoelson at St. Petersburg, Russia, Jolson first appeared in front of an audience as a child singing in the synagogue where his father was cantor. But he yearned for a show business career, quickly becoming a star in minstrel-type shows in vaudeville and then on Broadway. He was also a successful recording star before moving on to film, where he made several melodramatic shorts and features. Jolson died at San Francisco, CA, on Oct 23, 1950.

LEE, PEGGY: BIRTH ANNIVERSARY. May 26, 1920. Singer, songwriter and actress Peggy Lee was born Norma Deloris Egstrom at Jamestown, ND. She got her start singing on a Fargo, ND, radio station and was soon hired by Benny Goodman to sing with his band. Known for her simple, jazzy style as well as her sex appeal. Her biggest hits were "Fever" (1958) and "Is That All There Is?" (1969). She is perhaps best remembered for the songs that she cowrote and performed in Disney's *Lady and the Tramp.* She continued to perform until the 1990s, when poor health forced her to retire. She died Jan 21, 2002, at Los Angeles, CA.

MANNING, FRANKIE: 100th BIRTH ANNIVERSARY. May 26, 1914. Dancer famed for his innovations and ambassadorship of the Lindy hop (or the jitterbug). Born at Jacksonville, FL, but living in New York City since three, Manning danced at the Savoy Ballroom in Harlem, NYC, as a teenager; then was lead dancer and chief choreographer of the touring troupe Whitey's Lindy Hoppers, followed by his own post-World War II troupe, the Congaroo Dancers. Appeared in numerous films, including *Hellzapoppin'*. His choreography for the Broadway musical *Black and Blue* earned him a Tony Award in 1989. The recipient of an NEA National Heritage Fellowship Award in 2000, Manning died Apr 27, 2009, at New York, NY.

MEMORIAL DAY. May 26. Legal public holiday. (PL 90–363 sets Memorial Day on the last Monday in May. Applicable to federal employees and District of Columbia.) Also known as Decoration Day because of the tradition of decorating the graves of servicepeople. An occasion for honoring those who have died in battle. (Observance dates from Civil War years in US: first documented observance at Waterloo, NY, May 5, 1866.)

MEMORIAL DAY PARADE AND CEREMONIES. May 26. Gettysburg, PA. The parade starts at 2 PM at Lefever St and concludes at the Soldiers' National Cemetery. The ceremony begins at 3 PM at the rostrum in the Soldiers' National Cemetery. Keynote speaker is Governor Tom Corbett. Est attendance: 5,000. For info: Gettysburg CVB, 571 W Middle St, Gettysburg, PA 17325. Phone: (717) 334-6274. Fax: (717) 334-1166. E-mail: info@gettysburg.travel. Web: www.gettysburg.travel.

MONTAGU, LADY MARY WORTLEY: 325th BAPTISM ANNIVERSARY. May 26, 1689. English author, scholar and "scientific lady" known for her wit and verse, Wortley was born at London, England. Her diaries and letters, including the preeminent *Turkish Embassy Letters*, are considered to be among the most significant literary works of 18th-century England. A proponent of smallpox inoculation, Montagu directed experiments that proved the vaccine's efficacy, although her work was disregarded by the British medical establishment because of her sex. She wrote, "True knowledge consists in knowing things, not words." Died Aug 21, 1762, at London, England.

MORLEY, ROBERT: BIRTH ANNIVERSARY. May 26, 1908. British actor Robert Morley was born at Semley, England. Among his best-known film credits are *Major Barbara* (1939) and *The African Queen* (1951). He died June 3, 1992, at Reading, England.

✦PRAYER FOR PEACE, MEMORIAL DAY. May 26. Presidential Proclamation issued each year since 1948. PL 81–512 of May 11, 1950, asks the president to proclaim annually this day as a day of prayer for permanent peace. PL90–363 of June 28, 1968, requires that beginning in 1971 it will be observed the last Monday in May. Often titled "Prayer for Peace Memorial Day," and traditionally requests the flying of the flag at half-staff "for the customary forenoon period."

May 2014

S	M	T	W	T	F	S
				1	2	3
4	5	6	7	8	9	10
11	12	13	14	15	16	17
18	19	20	21	22	23	24
25	26	27	28	29	30	31

RIDE, SALLY KRISTEN: BIRTH ANNIVERSARY. May 26, 1951. Dr. Sally Ride, one of the first women in the US astronaut corps and the first American woman in space, was born at Encino, CA. Her flight aboard the space shuttle *Challenger* was launched from Cape Canaveral, FL, June 18, 1983, and landed at Edwards Air Force Base, CA, June 24. The six-day flight was termed "nearly a perfect mission." She died July 23, 2012, at La Jolla, CA.

SILVERHEELS, JAY: BIRTH ANNIVERSARY. May 26, 1912. Best known as Tonto, the faithful companion of the Lone Ranger on the long-running television series, Jay Silverheels was born Harold Smith at the Six Nations Indian Reserve, a Mohawk reservation at Brantford, ON, Canada. He excelled at athletics as a young man and found work as an itinerant boxer and lacrosse player before landing in Hollywood, where he was a stuntman and bit player in films before landing the defining role of his career as Tonto in 1949. Silverheels died of a stroke at Calabasas, CA, on Mar 5, 1980.

SPACE MILESTONE: *PHOENIX* LANDS ON MARS (US). May 26, 2008. NASA's *Phoenix* spacecraft landed successfully on the northern plains of Mars. Designed to be stationary, *Phoenix* analyzed soil and permafrost samples and transmitted photographs back to Earth.

STOCK EXCHANGE HOLIDAY (MEMORIAL DAY). May 26. The holiday schedules for the various exchanges are subject to change if relevant rules, regulations or exchange policies are revised. For info: CME Group (CME, CBOT, NYMEX, KCBT) (www.cmegroup.com), Chicago Board Options Exchange (www.cboe.com), NASDAQ (www.nasdaq.com), NYSE Euronext (www.nyse.com).

SWITZERLAND: PACING THE BOUNDS. May 26. Liestal. Citizens set off at 8 AM and march along boundaries to the beating of drums and firing of pistols and muskets. Occasion for fetes. Annually, the Monday before Ascension Day.

TOUR OF SOMERVILLE. May 26. Somerville, NJ. 71st running. The oldest continuously run major bicycle race in America. Attracts more than 500 top amateur cyclists for four events. Annually, on Memorial Day. Est attendance: 40,000. For info: Middle Earth, PO Box 8045, Bridgewater, NJ 08807. Phone: (908) 725-7223. Fax: (908) 722-5411. E-mail: office@middleearthnj.org. Web: www.tourofsomerville.org.

UNITED KINGDOM: SPRING BANK HOLIDAY. May 26. Bank and public holiday in England, Wales, Scotland and Northern Ireland. Observed on the last Monday in May.

VIETNAM AND US RESUME RELATIONS: 20th ANNIVERSARY. May 26, 1994. Nearly 20 years after the end of the Vietnam War, the US and Vietnam agreed to resume diplomatic relations. In the early 1990s Vietnam had become one of the fastest-growing economies in Asia after giving up Communist controls and allowing economic reform. Earlier in 1994 President William Clinton had lifted the American embargo that hindered Americans from doing business in Vietnam.

WAYNE, JOHN: BIRTH ANNIVERSARY. May 26, 1907. American motion picture actor, born Marion Michael Morrison, at Winterset, IA. The quintessential Western actor for five decades. Among his films are *Stagecoach* (1939), *Red River* (1948), *The Searchers* (1956) and *True Grit* (1969), for which he won a Best Actor Oscar. He died at Los Angeles, CA, June 11, 1979. "Talk low, talk slow and don't say too much" was his advice on acting.

WORLD LINDY HOP DAY. May 26. World Lindy Hop Day welcomes people from all walks of life, of all ages and from around the world to experience this exuberant African-American social dance. Originating at the Savoy Ballroom at Harlem, New York City, in the 1920s and 1930s, the Lindy hop (aka swing dancing or jitterbug) is usually danced to the big band jazz of the era. Lindy hop features creative and exhilarating movements that allow partners to connect in a way that uplifts the spirit, promotes human connection and develops generosity. It allows dancers to meet in a positive environment that supports the building of bridges on personal, community and global levels. Annually, May 26—the birth anniversary of Frankie Manning (1914–2009), one of the most important ambassadors and innovators of the Lindy hop. 2014 marks his 100th birth anniversary. For info: Frankie Manning Foundation, 92 Willowdale Ave, 2nd Fl, Montclair, NJ 07042. Phone: (718) 662-8729. E-mail: info@frankiemanningfoundation.org. Web: www.worldlindyhopday.com.

BIRTHDAYS TODAY

Helena Bonham Carter, 48, actress (Harry Potter films, *The King's Speech, Sweeney Todd, A Room with a View*), born London, England, May 26, 1966.

Genie Francis, 52, actress ("General Hospital"), born Englewood, NJ, May 26, 1962.

Pam Grier, 65, actress (*Jackie Brown, Ghosts of Mars, Foxy Brown*), born Winston-Salem, NC, May 26, 1949.

Kay Hagan, 61, US Senator (R, North Carolina), born Shelby, NC, May 26, 1953.

Lenny Kravitz, 50, actor, singer, musician, songwriter, born New York, NY, May 26, 1964.

Brent Musburger, 75, sportscaster, born Portland, OR, May 26, 1939.

Stevie Nicks, 66, singer (Fleetwood Mac), songwriter, born Phoenix, AZ, May 26, 1948.

Philip Michael Thomas, 65, actor ("Miami Vice," *Hair*), born Los Angeles, CA, May 26, 1949.

Hank Williams, Jr, 65, singer, born Shreveport, LA, May 26, 1949.

May 27 — Tuesday

DAY 147 **218 REMAINING**

BENNETT, ARNOLD: BIRTH ANNIVERSARY. May 27, 1867. English novelist, playwright and critic Enoch Arnold Bennett was born at Hanley, in the pottery-manufacturing district of North Staffordshire, England. Best known of his novels is *The Old Wives' Tale* (1908). His *Journals* from 1896 until near the time of his death in 1931 provide insight into Bennett's thought. "The price of justice," Bennett wrote, "is eternal publicity." He contracted typhoid fever in France and died at London, England, May 27, 1931.

BLOOMER, AMELIA JENKS: BIRTH ANNIVERSARY. May 27, 1818. American social reformer and women's rights advocate, born at Homer, NY. Her name is remembered especially because of her work for more sensible dress for women and her recommendation of a costume that had been introduced about 1849 by Elizabeth Smith Miller but came to be known as the "Bloomer Costume" or "bloomers." Amelia Bloomer died at Council Bluffs, IA, Dec 30, 1894.

CARSON, RACHEL LOUISE: BIRTH ANNIVERSARY. May 27, 1907. American scientist and author, born at Springdale, PA. Author of *Silent Spring* (1962), a book that provoked widespread controversy over the use of pesticides. Died Apr 14, 1964, at Silver Spring, MD.

CELLOPHANE TAPE PATENTED: ANNIVERSARY. May 27, 1930. Richard Gurley Drew received a patent for his adhesive tape, later manufactured by 3M as Scotch tape.

DUNCAN, ISADORA: BIRTH ANNIVERSARY. May 27, 1878. American-born interpretive dancer who revolutionized the entire concept of dance. Barefooted, freedom-loving, liberated woman and rebel against tradition, she experienced worldwide professional success and profound personal tragedy (her two children drowned, her marriage failed and she met a bizarre death when the long scarf she was wearing caught in a wheel of the open car in which she was riding, strangling her). Born at San Francisco, CA; died at Nice, France, Sept 14, 1927.

FIRST FLIGHT INTO THE STRATOSPHERE: ANNIVERSARY. May 27, 1931. In a balloon launched from Augsburg, Germany, Paul Kipfer and Auguste Piccard became the first to reach the stratosphere. In a pressurized cabin they rose almost 10 miles during their flight.

FIRST RUNNING OF PREAKNESS: ANNIVERSARY. May 27, 1873. The first running of the Preakness Stakes at Pimlico, MD, was won by Survivor with a time of 2:43. The winning jockey was G. Barbee.

GOLDEN GATE BRIDGE OPENED: ANNIVERSARY. May 27, 1937. Some 200,000 people crossed San Francisco's Golden Gate Bridge on its opening day.

HAMMETT, DASHIELL: BIRTH ANNIVERSARY. May 27, 1894. The man who brought realism to the genre of mystery writing, Samuel Dashiell Hammett was born at St. Marys County, MD. His first two novels, *Red Harvest* (1929) and *The Dain Curse* (1929), were based on his eight years spent as a Pinkerton detective. Hammett is recognized as the founder of the "hard-boiled" school of detective fiction. Three of his novels have been made into films: *The Maltese Falcon* (1930), considered by many to be his finest work; *The Thin Man* (1932), which provided the basis for a series of five movies starring William Powell and Myrna Loy; and *The Glass Key* (1931). Hammett was called to testify but refused to name members of an alleged subversive organization during House Un-American Activities Committee hearings. He died Jan 10, 1961, at New York City.

HICKOK, WILD BILL: BIRTH ANNIVERSARY. May 27, 1837. Born at Troy Grove, IL, and died Aug 2, 1876, at Deadwood, SD. American frontiersman, legendary marksman, lawman, army scout and gambler. Hickok's end came when he was shot dead at a poker table by a drunk in the Number Ten saloon.

HUMPHREY, HUBERT HORATIO: BIRTH ANNIVERSARY. May 27, 1911. The 38th vice president of the US (1965–69) was born at Wallace, SD. As mayor of Minneapolis, MN (1945–48), Humphrey successfully led the fight for a strong party stand on civil rights at the 1948 Democratic National Convention. He was elected to the US Senate in 1948, the first Democratic senator to come from Minnesota since the Civil War. He served five terms; in 1961 he was the Senate Democratic whip. In 1964 he was elected vice president under Lyndon Johnson. As the Democratic nominee for president he was narrowly defeated by Richard Nixon in 1968. Humphrey died on Jan 13, 1978, at Waverly, MN.

NCAA DIVISION I MEN'S GOLF CHAMPIONSHIPS. May 27–June 1. Prairie Dunes Country Club, Hutchinson, KS. 76th annual. For info: NCAA, PO Box 6222, Indianapolis, IN 46206-6222. Phone: (317) 917-6222. Web: www.NCAA.com.

PRICE, VINCENT: BIRTH ANNIVERSARY. May 27, 1911. This silken-voiced actor—best known for his portrayal of sinister villains in horror films—was born at St. Louis, MO. After graduating from Yale, Price first sought theater work but was successful in film, especially in Roger Corman's series of Edgar Allan Poe adaptations in the 1960s. A noted art historian, Price was also an epicure who authored several cookbooks. In his later years, he was a host of the PBS anthology series "Mystery!" and had a moving part in Tim Burton's *Edward Scissorhands* (1990). Price died at Los Angeles, CA, on Oct 25, 1993.

RMS *QUEEN MARY* MAIDEN VOYAGE: ANNIVERSARY. May 27, 1936. Anniversary of the maiden voyage from Southampton, England, to New York Harbor. In 1967 the ship sailed to Long Beach, CA, where it is permanently berthed and used as a hotel.

ST. PETERSBURG FOUNDED: ANNIVERSARY. May 27, 1703. Czar Peter the Great founded the city of St. Petersburg on the banks of the Neva River by laying the first stone of the Peter and Paul Fortress. It became the capital of Russia in 1712. See also: "St. Petersburg Name Restored: Anniversary" (Sept 6).

SNEAD, SAM: BIRTH ANNIVERSARY. May 27, 1912. The winningest US Tour golfer of the 20th century was born at Hot Springs, VA. He turned pro in 1934 and went on to become the only golfer to win tournaments in six different decades. He won 84 US Tour events and 182 tournaments in total. Snead always wore a snappy straw hat and was a favorite on the Tour. He was one of the founders of the US Senior Tour. Snead died at Hot Springs, on May 23, 2002.

BIRTHDAYS TODAY

Jeff Bagwell, 46, former baseball player, born Boston, MA, May 27, 1968.

John Barth, 84, author (*Last Voyage of Somebody the Sailor, Letters*), born Cambridge, MD, May 27, 1930.

André Benjamin, 39, singer, musician (André 3000, Outkast), actor, born Atlanta, GA, May 27, 1975.

Todd Bridges, 49, actor ("Diff'rent Strokes"), born San Francisco, CA, May 27, 1965.

Pat Cash, 49, former tennis player, born Melbourne, Australia, May 27, 1965.

Chris Colfer, 24, actor ("Glee"), born Fresno, CA, May 27, 1990.

Joseph Fiennes, 44, actor (*Shakespeare in Love*), born Salisbury, England, May 27, 1970.

Peri Gilpin, 53, actress ("Frasier"), born Waco, TX, May 27, 1961.

Louis Gossett, Jr, 78, actor (Emmy for *Roots*; Oscar for *An Officer and a Gentleman*), born Brooklyn, NY, May 27, 1936.

Henry Kissinger, 91, former US secretary of state, author, born Fuerth, Germany, May 27, 1923.

Christopher Lee, 92, actor (the Lord of the Rings films, *Dracula, The Mummy*), born London, England, May 27, 1922.

Ramsey Lewis, 79, jazz musician, born Chicago, IL, May 27, 1935.

Jack McBrayer, 41, actor ("30 Rock"), born Macon, GA, May 27, 1973.

Lee Meriwether, 79, actress ("Barnaby Jones," "Batman"), former Miss America (1955), born Los Angeles, CA, May 27, 1935.

Jamie Oliver, 39, chef, television personality ("The Naked Chef"), born Clavering, Essex, England, May 27, 1975.

Richard Schiff, 59, actor ("The West Wing"), born Bethesda, MD, May 27, 1955.

Frank Thomas, 46, former baseball player, born Columbus, GA, May 27, 1968.

Bruce Weitz, 71, actor ("Hill Street Blues"), born Norwalk, CT, May 27, 1943.

Herman Wouk, 99, writer (*Marjorie Morningstar, The Winds of War*), born New York, NY, May 27, 1915.

May 2014

S	M	T	W	T	F	S
				1	2	3
4	5	6	7	8	9	10
11	12	13	14	15	16	17
18	19	20	21	22	23	24
25	26	27	28	29	30	31

May 28 — Wednesday

DAY 148 **217 REMAINING**

AGASSIZ, LOUIS: BIRTH ANNIVERSARY. May 28, 1807. Professor of zoology and geology at Harvard, born at Motier, Switzerland. He was a major influence in spawning American interest in natural history and helped to establish the Harvard Museum of Comparative Zoology. "The eye of the trilobite," Agassiz wrote in 1870, "tells us that the sun shone on the old beach where he lived; for there is nothing in nature without a purpose, and when so complicated an organ was made to receive the light, there must have been light to enter it." Died at Cambridge, MA, Dec 14, 1873.

AMNESTY INTERNATIONAL FOUNDED: ANNIVERSARY. May 28, 1961. This Nobel Prize–winning human rights organization was founded by London lawyer Peter Benenson after he read about two Portuguese students arrested simply for drinking a toast to freedom. He realized that people around the world were at risk daily for peacefully expressing their views. AI currently has more than 3 million members in every corner of the world. Its mission is to undertake research and action focused on preventing and ending grave abuses of the rights of physical and mental integrity, freedom of conscience and expression and freedom from discrimination, within the context of its work to promote all human rights. For info: Amnesty International Secretariat, 1 Easton St, 5 Penn Plaza, London WC1X 0DW, England. Web: www.amnesty.org.

AZERBAIJAN: DAY OF THE REPUBLIC. May 28. Public holiday. Commemorates the declaration of the Azerbaijan Democratic Republic in 1918.

CANADA: ANNAPOLIS VALLEY APPLE BLOSSOM FESTIVAL. May 28–June 2. Windsor to Digby, NS. Annual festival with barbecues, sports events, art show, Princess Tea, coronation ceremonies, concerts, fireworks, children's parade, Grand Street Parade and "Family Fun Day at Scotian Gold." Annually, since 1933. Est attendance: 125,000. For info: Annapolis Valley Apple Blossom Festival, 217 Belcher St, Kentville, NS, B4N 1E2 Canada. Phone: (902) 678-8322. Fax: (902) 678-3710. E-mail: info@appleblossom.com. Web: www.appleblossom.com.

DIONNE QUINTUPLETS: 80th BIRTHDAY. May 28, 1934. Five daughters (Marie, Cecile, Yvonne, Emilie and Annette) were born to Oliva and Elzire Dionne, near Callander, ON, Canada. They were the first quints known to have lived for more than a few hours after birth. Emilie died in 1954, Marie in 1970, Yvonne in 2001. The other two sisters are still living.

END OF THE PARIS COMMUNE: ANNIVERSARY. May 28, 1871. On Mar 18, 1871, a revolt of the Parisian workers' parties against the policies of the national government erupted. It ended just over two months later in a hail of buildings in flames, frustrated social foment in the streets and harsh reprisals from Versailles. In the violence that followed, 147 members of the Commune were murdered, their bodies dumped in a trench along a wall beside Père Lachaise Cemetery. May 28 is a date still considered sacred by the French left.

ETHIOPIA: NATIONAL DAY. May 28. National holiday. Commemorates the downfall of the Dergue, the military government that ruled Ethiopia from 1974 to 1991.

FISCHER-DIESKAU, DIETRICH: BIRTH ANNIVERSARY. May 28, 1925. Born at Berlin, Germany, preeminent baritone Fischer-Dieskau was perhaps the world's most recorded classical singer. He made hundreds of recordings that set the standard for lieder (German art song) performance and also recorded a wider-ranging repertoire than any other singer, performing selections from Bach to Wagner to Stravinsky to Schumann, among others. After an abrupt retirement from performing in 1992, Fischer-Dieskau continued to teach and conduct for many years thereafter until his death on May 18, 2012, at Berg, Bavaria.

FLEMING, IAN: BIRTH ANNIVERSARY. May 28, 1908. English journalist, novelist, creator of the James Bond series, beginning with *Casino Royale* in 1953. Fleming also penned the children's classic *Chitty Chitty Bang Bang.* Born at London, died Aug 12, 1964, at Sandwich, England.

GUILLOTIN, JOSEPH IGNACE: BIRTH ANNIVERSARY. May 28, 1738. French physician and member of the Constituent Assembly who urged the use of a machine that was sometimes called the Maiden for the execution of death sentences—a less painful, more certain way of dispatching those sentenced to death. The guillotine was first used on Apr 25, 1792, for the execution of a highwayman, Nicolas Jacques Pelletier. Other machines for decapitation had been in use in other countries since the Middle Ages. Guillotin was born at Saintes, France, and died at Paris, Mar 26, 1814.

ISRAEL: JERUSALEM DAY (YOM YERUSHALAYIM). May 28. Hebrew calendar date: Iyar 28, 5774. Commemorates the liberation of the old city, June 7, 1967. Began at sundown May 27.

MOON PHASE: NEW MOON. May 28. Moon enters New Moon phase at 2:40 PM, EDT.

NATIONAL SENIOR HEALTH AND FITNESS DAY. May 28. More than 1,000 local events held on the same day in all 50 states. 21st annual event to promote the value of fitness and exercise for older adults. During this day—as part of Older Americans Month activities—seniors across the country are involved in locally organized health-promotion activities. Call the toll-free number for further info and how to participate. Annually, the last Wednesday in May. Est attendance: 100,000. For info: Patricia Henze, Executive Director, Mature Market Resource Center, 328 W Lincoln Ave, Libertyville, IL 60048. Phone: (800) 828-8225. Fax: (847) 816-8662. E-mail: info@fitnessday.com. Web: www.fitnessday.com.

NEPAL: REPUBLIC DAY. May 28. Public holiday. Commemorates the anniversary of Nepal becoming a democratic republic in 2008 after years of being a monarchy.

PITT, WILLIAM: BIRTH ANNIVERSARY. May 28, 1759. British prime minister from 1783 to 1801 and from 1804 to 1806, Pitt was influenced by Adam Smith's economic theories and reduced England's large national debt caused by the American Revolution. Born at Hayes, Kent, England, he died Jan 23, 1806, at Putney. He was the son of William Pitt, first earl of Chatham, for whom the city of Pittsburgh was named.

SAINT BERNARD OF MONTJOUX: FEAST DAY. May 28. Patron saint of mountain climbers, founder of Alpine hospices of the Great and Little St. Bernard, died at age 85, probably on May 28, 1081.

SIERRA CLUB FOUNDED: ANNIVERSARY. May 28, 1892. Founded by famed naturalist John Muir, the Sierra Club promotes conservation of the natural environment by influencing public policy. It has been especially important in the founding and protection of our national parks. For info: Sierra Club, 85 Second St, 2nd Fl, San Francisco, CA 94105-3441. Phone: (415) 977-5500. Fax: (415) 977-5797. E-mail: information@sierraclub.org. Web: www.sierra club.org.

SLUGS RETURN FROM CAPISTRANO DAY. May 28. It's a little-known secret that slimy slugs spend their winters in lovely Capistrano and return to our patios and gardens on this date. Bare feet are not a good idea now through first frost. (©2006 by WH.) For info: Thomas & Ruth Roy, Wellcat Holidays, 2418 Long Ln, Lebanon, PA 17046. Phone: (717) 279-0184. E-mail: info@wellcat .com. Web: www.wellcat.com.

THORPE, JAMES FRANCIS (JIM): BIRTH ANNIVERSARY. May 28, 1888. Olympic gold medal track athlete, baseball player and football player, born at Prague, OK. Thorpe, a Native American, won the pentathlon and the decathlon at the 1912 Olympic Games but later lost his medals when Olympic officials declared that an earlier stint as a minor-league baseball player besmirched his amateur standing. He later played professional baseball and football and was acclaimed the greatest male athlete of the first half of the 20th century. Died at Lomita, CA, Mar 28, 1953. (Thorpe's medals were returned to his family many years after his death when the earlier decision was reversed.)

"ZOO PARADE" TV PREMIERE: ANNIVERSARY. May 28, 1950. NBC's half-hour program on animals and animal behavior was hosted by Marlin Perkins and Jim Hurlbut. Initially, it was broadcast from Lincoln Park Zoo in Chicago, IL, but after 1955 the show was broadcast from other locales throughout the country. A successor program, "Mutual of Omaha's Wild Kingdom," was shot almost entirely in the wild and ran into the 1980s.

BIRTHDAYS TODAY

Carroll Baker, 83, actress (*Baby Doll, Harlow*), born Johnstown, PA, May 28, 1931.

Kirk Gibson, 57, baseball manager, former player, born Pontiac, MI, May 28, 1957.

Rudolph Giuliani, 70, former mayor of New York City, born Brooklyn, NY, May 28, 1944.

Elisabeth Hasselbeck, 37, television personality ("The View," "Survivor"), born Cranston, RI, May 28, 1977.

Jake Johnson, 36, actor ("New Girl"), born Evanston, IL, May 28, 1978.

Gladys Knight, 70, singer, born Atlanta, GA, May 28, 1944.

Sondra Locke, 67, actress (*The Heart Is a Lonely Hunter, Bronco Billy*), director (*Ratboy*), born Shelbyville, TN, May 28, 1947.

Christa Miller, 50, actress ("The Drew Carey Show," "Scrubs"), born New York, NY, May 28, 1964.

Carey Mulligan, 29, actress (*The Great Gatsby, An Education, Drive, Never Let Me Go*), born Greater London, England, May 28, 1985.

Marco Rubio, 43, US Senator (R, Florida), born Miami, FL, May 28, 1971.

May 29 — Thursday

DAY 149 **216 REMAINING**

AMNESTY ISSUED FOR SOUTHERN REBELS: ANNIVERSARY. May 29, 1865. President Andrew Johnson issued a proclamation giving a general amnesty to all who participated in the rebellion against the US. High-ranking members of the Confederate government and military and those who owned more than $20,000 worth of property were excepted and had to apply individually to the president for a pardon. Once an oath of allegiance was taken, all former property rights, except those in slaves, were returned to the former owners.

ASCENSION OF BAHA'U'LLAH: ANNIVERSARY. May 29, 1892. Baha'i observance of the anniversary of the death in exile of Baha'u'llah (the prophet-founder of the Baha'i Faith). One of the nine days of the year when Baha'is suspend work. For info: Baha'is of the US, Office of Communications, 1233 Central St, Evanston, IL 60201. Phone: (847) 733-3559. Fax: (847) 733-3578. E-mail: ooc@ usbnc.org. Web: www.bahai.us.

ASCENSION DAY. May 29. Commemorates Christ's ascension into heaven. Observed since AD 68. Ascension Day is the 40th day after the Resurrection, counting Easter as the first day.

BELGIUM: PROCESSION OF THE HOLY BLOOD. May 29. Religious historical procession. Recalls adventurous crusaders, including Count Thierry of Alsace, who carried back relics of the Holy Blood. Always on Ascension Day.

BOOKEXPO AMERICA TRADE EXHIBIT. May 29–31. Jacob K. Javits Center, New York, NY. Publishers display fall titles for booksellers and all interested in reaching the retail bookseller. Book-related items also on display. Consumers welcomed on Saturday, May 31; register as a Power Reader. For info: BookExpo America, 383 Main Ave, Norwalk, CT 06851-1543. Phone: (800) 840-5614. Web: www.bookexpoamerica.com.

CHARLES II: RESTORATION ANNIVERSARY. May 29, 1660. Restoration of Charles II to English throne. Also his birthday (May 29, 1630). English monarchy restored after Commonwealth period under Oliver Cromwell.

CHESTERTON, GILBERT KEITH: BIRTH ANNIVERSARY. May 29, 1874. English author and critic born at London, England. Died June 14, 1936, at Beaconsfield, Buckinghamshire, England.

CONSTANTINOPLE FALLS TO THE TURKS: ANNIVERSARY. May 29, 1453. The city of Constantinople was captured by the Turks, who later renamed it Istanbul. This conquest marked the end of the Byzantine Empire; the city became the capital of the Ottoman Empire.

HENRY, PATRICK: BIRTH ANNIVERSARY. May 29, 1736. American Revolutionary leader and orator, born at Studley, VA, and died near Brookneal, VA, June 6, 1799. Especially remembered for his speech (Mar 23, 1775) for arming the Virginia militia, at St. Johns Church, Richmond, VA, when he declared: "I know not what course others may take, but as for me, give me liberty or give me death."

HOPE, BOB: BIRTH ANNIVERSARY. May 29, 1903. The comedic actor was born Leslie Townes Hope at Eltham, England. Hope had a long career in vaudeville, stage, radio, film and TV. His first film appearance was in *The Big Broadcast of 1938* (in which he sang his signature song, "Thanks for the Memory"). Hope went on to appear in more than 75 films—most memorably with crooner Bing Crosby in their series of *Road* movies. He received five honorary Oscars (among them the Jean Hersholt Humanitarian Award) and numerous other honors. Hope tirelessly entertained US troops during every war from WWII to the Gulf War. President Lyndon Johnson presented him with the Medal of Freedom, and he was knighted in 1998. Hope died July 27, 2003, at Toluca Lake, CA.

KENNEDY, JOHN FITZGERALD: BIRTH ANNIVERSARY. May 29, 1917. 35th president of the US (1961–63), born at Brookline, MA. Assassinated while riding in an open automobile at Dallas, TX, Nov 22, 1963. (Accused assassin Lee Harvey Oswald was killed at the Dallas police station by a gunman, Jack Ruby, two days later.) Kennedy was the youngest man ever elected to the presidency, the first Roman Catholic and the first president to have served in the US Navy. He was the fourth US president to be killed by an assassin and the second to be buried at Arlington National Cemetery (first was William Howard Taft).

MOSCOW COMMUNIQUÉ: ANNIVERSARY. May 29, 1972. President Richard Nixon and Soviet Party leader Leonid Brezhnev released a joint communiqué after Nixon's weeklong visit to Moscow. During the visit the two men acknowledged their major differences on the Vietnam War and signed a treaty on antiballistic missile systems, as well as an interim agreement on limitation of strategic missiles and an agreement for a joint space flight in 1975. This was the first visit ever to Moscow by a US president (May 22–30, 1972).

MOUNT EVEREST SUMMIT REACHED: ANNIVERSARY. May 29, 1953. New Zealand explorer Sir Edmund Hillary and Tensing Norgay, a Sherpa guide, became the first team to reach the summit of Mount Everest, the world's highest mountain.

May 2013	S	M	T	W	T	F	S
				1	2	3	4
	5	6	7	8	9	10	11
	12	13	14	15	16	17	18
	19	20	21	22	23	24	25
	26	27	28	29	30	31	

NCAA DIVISION I SOFTBALL CHAMPIONSHIP (WOMEN'S COLLEGE WORLD SERIES). May 29–June 4. ASA Hall of Fame Stadium, Oklahoma City, OK. 33rd annual. For info: NCAA, PO Box 6222, Indianapolis, IN 46206-6222. Phone: (317) 917-6222. Fax: (317) 917-6210. Web: www.NCAA.com.

ORTHODOX ASCENSION DAY. May 29. Observed by Eastern Orthodox churches.

RHODE ISLAND: RATIFICATION DAY. May 29. The last of the 13 original states to ratify the Constitution in 1790.

***THE RITE OF SPRING* PREMIERE AND RIOT: ANNIVERSARY.** May 29, 1913. In the most notorious world premiere in any of the arts, Igor Stravinsky's *The Rite of Spring* received a rough reception at the Théatre des Champs-Elysées at Paris, France, on this date. Performed by Sergey Diaghilev's Ballets Russes and choreographed by the legendary Vaslav Nijinsky, the ballet and music presented scenes from pagan Russia. The audience began to boo at Stravinsky's challenging and dissonant music, and before long fistfights between different camps of music lovers broke out. The police were called to restore order. Despite its inauspicious beginning, *The Rite of Spring* is now regarded as a masterpiece.

SOCCER TRAGEDY: ANNIVERSARY. May 29, 1985. A riot at Heysel stadium at Brussels, Belgium, killed 39 people. Fans attending the European Cup Final, between Liverpool and Juventus of Turin, clashed before the match started. Some 400 people were injured in the riot. The incident was televised and viewed by millions throughout Europe. More than two years later, Sept 2, 1987, the British government announced that 26 British soccer fans (identified from television tapes) would be extradited to Belgium for trial. Hooliganism at soccer matches became the target of increased security measures for England's professional teams following the 1985 tragedy.

SOJOURNER TRUTH'S "AIN'T I A WOMAN" SPEECH: ANNIVERSARY. May 29, 1851. During the Women's Rights Convention held at Akron, OH, from May 28 to May 29, 1851, former slave Sojourner Truth delivered an impassioned speech that is now titled after its common refrain: "I have ploughed, and planted, and gathered into barns, and no man could head me! And ain't I a woman? I could work as much and eat as much as a man—when I could get it—and bear the lash as well! And ain't I a woman? And when I cried out with my mother's grief, none but Jesus heard me. And ain't I a woman?"

SPENGLER, OSWALD: BIRTH ANNIVERSARY. May 29, 1880. German historian, author of *The Decline of the West*, born at Blankenburg-am-Harz, Germany. Died at Munich, Germany, on May 8, 1936.

UNITED NATIONS: INTERNATIONAL DAY OF UNITED NATIONS PEACEKEEPERS. May 29. The Assembly has designated May 29 of each year as a day to pay tribute to all the men and women who have served in United Nations peacekeeping operations for their high level of professionalism, dedication and courage, and to honor the memory of those who have lost their lives in the cause of peace (Resolution 57/129, Dec 11, 2002). The Assembly invited all member states, organizations of the United Nations system, nongovernmental organizations and individuals to observe the day in an appropriate manner. For info: United Nations, Dept of Public Info, New York, NY 10017. Web: www.un.org.

VIRGINIA PLAN PROPOSED: ANNIVERSARY. May 29, 1787. Just five days after the Constitutional Convention met at Philadelphia, PA, the "Virginia Plan" was proposed. It called for establishment of a new governmental organization consisting of a legislature with two houses, an executive branch (chosen by the legislature) and a judicial branch.

WISCONSIN: ADMISSION DAY: ANNIVERSARY. May 29. Became 30th state in 1848.

 **BIRTHDAYS TODAY**

Carmelo Anthony, 30, basketball player, born New York, NY, May 29, 1984.

Annette Bening, 56, actress (*American Beauty, The Grifters, The Kids Are All Right*), born Topeka, KS, May 29, 1958.

Kevin Conway, 72, actor (*When You Comin' Back, Red Ryder?*; *Of Mice and Men*; *Other People's Money*), born New York, NY, May 29, 1942.

Eric Davis, 52, former baseball player, born Los Angeles, CA, May 29, 1962.

Paul Ehrlich, 82, population biologist, born Philadelphia, PA, May 29, 1932.

Melissa Etheridge, 53, singer, guitarist, born Leavenworth, KS, May 29, 1961.

Rupert Everett, 55, actor (*An Ideal Husband, My Best Friend's Wedding*), born Norfolk, England, May 29, 1959.

Anthony Geary, 66, actor ("General Hospital"), born Coalville, UT, May 29, 1948.

Jerry Moran, 60, US Senator (R, Kansas), born Great Bend, KS, May 29, 1954.

Adrian Paul, 55, actor ("Highlander"), born London, England, May 29, 1959.

Alfred (Al) Unser, Sr, 75, former auto racer, born Albuquerque, NM, May 29, 1939.

Francis Thomas (Fay) Vincent, Jr, 76, former commissioner of baseball, born Waterbury, CT, May 29, 1938.

Lisa Whelchel, 51, actress ("The Facts of Life"), born Fort Worth, TX, May 29, 1963.

May 30 — Friday

DAY 150 **215 REMAINING**

BATTLE OF THE ALEUTIAN ISLANDS: ANNIVERSARY. May 30, 1943. The islands of Kiska and Attu in the Aleutian Islands off the coast of Alaska were retaken by the US 7th Infantry Division. The battle (Operation Landgrab) began when an American force of 11,000 landed on Attu May 12. In three weeks of fighting, US casualties numbered 552 killed and 1,140 wounded. Only 28 wounded Japanese were taken prisoner. Japan's dead amounted to 2,352, of whom 500 committed suicide.

BLANC, MEL: BIRTH ANNIVERSARY. May 30, 1908. The greatest voice artist in history, Mel Blanc was born at San Francisco, CA. He performed more than 400 voices in his career, but he is best remembered for "Looney Tunes" and "Merrie Melodies," in which he performed the voices of Bugs Bunny, Elmer Fudd, Porky Pig, Sylvester, Tweetie Pie and Road Runner. He died on June 10, 1989, at Los Angeles, CA.

CULLEN, COUNTEE: BIRTH ANNIVERSARY. May 30, 1903. One of the leading poets of the Harlem Renaissance (*Color*, 1925). He died at New York City, Jan 9, 1946.

ENGLAND: ENGLISH RIVIERA DANCE FESTIVAL. May 30–June 6. Torquay, Devon. Demonstrations by world champions and participatory events including modern, ballroom, disco and Latin American dance styles. Est attendance: 2,000. For info: Philip Wylie, 73 Hoylake Crescent, Ickenham, Middlesex, England UB10 8JQ. Phone: (44) (1895) 632-143. E-mail: info@holidayanddance.co.uk Web: www.holidayanddance.co.uk.

FABERGÉ, CARL: BIRTH ANNIVERSARY. May 30, 1846. Goldsmith, designer and jeweler Peter Carl Fabergé was born on this date at St. Petersburg, Russia. He made the House of Fabergé an internationally known name with fantastical bejeweled decorative objects. His workshop began creating the famous imperial Easter eggs for czars Alexander III and Nicholas II in 1885. After the Russian Revolution, the Bolsheviks shut down the House of Fabergé, and the family fled the country. Fabergé died at Lausanne, France, on Sept 24, 1920. (His birth date was May 18 on the Old Style [Julian] calendar.)

FIRST AMERICAN DAILY NEWSPAPER PUBLISHED: ANNIVERSARY. May 30, 1783. *The Pennsylvania Evening Post* became the first daily newspaper published in the US. The paper was published at Philadelphia, PA, by Benjamin Towne.

GOODMAN, BENNY: BIRTH ANNIVERSARY. May 30, 1909. Jazz clarinetist and bandleader, born Benjamin David Goodman at Chicago, IL. The "King of Swing" reigned in popularity, especially in the 1930s and 1940s. His band was the first to play jazz at New York's Carnegie Hall. He died June 13, 1986, at New York, NY.

HUG YOUR CAT DAY. May 30. Cats act as if they don't want or need attention—but they do. Apricat, the pampered star of her own book series, has created a special day for humans to hug their cats without fear of scratches or hisses. For info: Marisa D'Vari, PO Box 2347, New York, NY 10163.

INDIANAPOLIS 500: ANNIVERSARY. May 30, 1911. Ray Harroun won the first Indy 500, averaging 74.6 mph. The race was created by Carl Fisher, who in 1909 replaced the stone surface of his 2.5-mile racetrack with a brick one—hence the nickname "The Brickyard."

LINCOLN MEMORIAL DEDICATION: ANNIVERSARY. May 30, 1922. The memorial is made of marble from Colorado and Tennessee and limestone from Indiana. It stands in West Potomac Park at Washington, DC. The memorial was designed by architect Henry Bacon, and its cornerstone was laid in 1915. A skylight lets light into the interior where the compelling statue *Seated Lincoln*, by sculptor Daniel Chester French, is situated.

LOOMIS DAY. May 30. To honor Mahlon Loomis, a Washington, DC, dentist who received a US patent on wireless telegraphy in 1872 (before Marconi was born). Titled "An Improvement in Telegraphing," the patent described how to do without wires; this patent was backed up by experiment on the Massanutten Mountains of Virginia. For info: Robert L. Birch, Puns Corps, 3108 Dashiell Rd, Falls Church, VA 22042. Phone: (703) 533-3668.

MEMORIAL DAY (TRADITIONAL). May 30. This day honors the tradition of making memorial tributes to the dead, especially remembering those who have died in battle. Observed as a legal public holiday on the last Monday in May.

NCAA DIVISION I ROWING CHAMPIONSHIP. May 30–June 1. Eagle Creek Park, Indianapolis, IN. For info: NCAA, PO Box 6222, Indianapolis, IN 46206-6222. Web: www.NCAA.com.

THE ORIGINAL SOUTH DAKOTA BBQ CHAMPIONSHIPS. May 30–31. South Dakota State Fairgrounds, Huron, SD. These championships are a Kansas City BBQ Society sanctioned event with a prize purse of $10,000. Est attendance: 2,000. For info: Original SD BBQ Championships, 890 3rd St SW, Huron, SD 57350. Phone: (605) 353-7354. Fax: (605) 353-7348. E-mail: candi.hettinger@state.sd.us. Web: www.sdbbqchampionships.com.

PETER I: BIRTH ANNIVERSARY. May 30, 1672. Peter I (Peter the Great), Czar and Emperor of all the Russias. His primary aim was to make Russia a major power equal to its size and potential, and the way he saw to do this was through education and technology. He established printing presses and published translations of foreign books, particularly scientific and technical material. The Russian alphabet was simplified, and Arabic numerals were introduced. Peter encouraged trade with foreign countries, mercantilism within Russia and the entrepreneurial skills of resident foreigners; he allowed industrialists to own serfs, a right previously limited to landholders. He completely overhauled the government, the Russian Orthodox Church, the military system and the structure of taxes, ultimately increasing the power of the monarchy at the expense of the nobility and the national church. Upon his death, Jan 28, 1725, he was succeeded by his wife, Catherine.

RIPKEN STREAK BEGINS: ANNIVERSARY. May 30, 1982. Baltimore Oriole Cal Ripken took the baseball field on this date and began a consecutive-games-played streak that lasted for 2,130 games—a major league record. His streak ended Sept 6, 1995.

ROUTE 66 SUMMERFEST. May 30–June 1. Rolla, MO. Annual citywide celebration including car shows, crafts, entertainment and food. Annually, the weekend after Memorial Day. Est attendance: 4,000. For info: Summerfest Chairman. Phone: (573) 341-5488. E-mail: cse@fidmail.com. Web: www.route66summerfest.com.

SAINT JOAN OF ARC: FEAST DAY. May 30. French heroine and martyr, known as the "Maid of Orleans," led the French against the English invading army. Captured, found guilty of heresy and burned at the stake in 1431 (at age 19). Innocence declared in 1456. Canonized in 1920.

SPACE MILESTONE: *MARINER 9* (US). May 30, 1971. Unmanned spacecraft was launched, entering Martian orbit the following Nov 13. The craft relayed temperature and gravitational-field information and sent back spectacular photographs of both the surface of Mars and its two moons. First spacecraft to orbit another planet.

TRINIDAD AND TOBAGO: INDIAN ARRIVAL DAY. May 30. Public holiday. Commemorates the 1845 arrival of the first Indian laborers to Trinidad.

WHEEL JAM. May 30–June 1. South Dakota State Fairgrounds, Huron, SD. Cars, motorcycles, semis—and live music! Wheel Jam has a whole slug of activities over the course of the weekend—from the Wheel Jam Parade to the Dynamic Engine Brake Competition. Annually, the first full weekend in June. Est attendance: 6,000. For info: Wheel Jam, 890 3rd St SW, Huron, SD 57350. Phone: (605) 353-7354. Web: www.wheeljam.com.

	S	M	T	W	T	F	S
May 2014					1	2	3
	4	5	6	7	8	9	10
	11	12	13	14	15	16	17
	18	19	20	21	22	23	24
	25	26	27	28	29	30	31

WORLD TRADE CENTER RECOVERY AND CLEANUP ENDS: ANNIVERSARY. May 30, 2002. New York, NY. A solemn and mostly silent ceremony marked the symbolic end of recovery operations at Ground Zero, the former site of the World Trade Center, after the Sept 11, 2001, terrorist attacks. The last standing steel girder was cut down on May 28. An honor guard carried an empty stretcher draped with an American flag to represent those victims who were not recovered from the ruins. Members of the NYFD and NYPD and city, state and federal workers, as well as family members and Ground Zero recovery teams, participated in the ceremony.

BIRTHDAYS TODAY

Blake Bashoff, 33, actor (*Bushwhacked, Big Bully*), born Philadelphia, PA, May 30, 1981.

Keir Dullea, 78, actor (*David and Lisa, 2001: A Space Odyssey*), born Cleveland, OH, May 30, 1936.

Steven Gerrard, 34, soccer player, born Liverpool, England, May 30, 1980.

Jared Gilmore, 14, actor ("Once Upon a Time," "Mad Men"), born San Diego, CA, May 30, 2000.

Cee Lo Green, 40, singer, rapper, record producer, born Thomas DeCarlo Callaway at Atlanta, GA, May 30, 1974.

Wynonna Judd, 50, singer, born Ashland, KY, May 30, 1964.

Ted McGinley, 56, actor ("Married . . . with Children," *Revenge of the Nerds*), born Newport Beach, CA, May 30, 1958.

Colm Meaney, 61, actor ("Star Trek: Deep Space Nine," *Layer Cake, The Snapper*), born Dublin, Ireland, May 30, 1953.

Trey Parker, 42, director, creator ("South Park"), born Auburn, AL, May 30, 1972.

Michael J. Pollard, 75, actor (*Bonnie and Clyde*), born Passaic, NJ, May 30, 1939.

Manny Ramirez, 42, baseball player, born Santo Domingo, Dominican Republic, May 30, 1972.

Gale Sayers, 71, Hall of Fame football player, born Wichita, KS, May 30, 1943.

Stephen Tobolowsky, 63, actor ("Deadwood," *The Grifters, Groundhog Day*), born Dallas, TX, May 30, 1951.

Clint Walker, 87, actor (*The Dirty Dozen*, "Cheyenne"), born Hartford, IL, May 30, 1927.

May 31 — Saturday

DAY 151 **214 REMAINING**

AMECHE, DON: BIRTH ANNIVERSARY. May 31, 1908. Film, stage, radio and TV actor. Born Dominic Felix Amici at Kenosha, WI, and died Dec 6, 1993, at Scottsdale, AZ.

BATTLE OF SEVEN PINES: ANNIVERSARY. May 31, 1862. Confederate General Joseph Johnston's troops defeated McClellan's Army of the Potomac at the Battle of Seven Pines (or Fair Oaks, VA). Although the Confederates scored a major battlefield victory and McClellan's forces withdrew the next day, the effect of the battle did little to ease the pressure on the besieged Confederate capital of Richmond. During the battle Johnston was wounded, and Robert E. Lee was named commander of the Army of Northern Virginia.

COPYRIGHT LAW PASSED: ANNIVERSARY. May 31, 1790. President George Washington signed the first US copyright law. It gave protection for 14 years to books written by US citizens. In 1891 the law was extended to cover books by foreign authors as well.

FAIRMOUNT ACADEMY 1800s FESTIVAL. May 31. Fairmount, MD. Rain date the following Saturday. Restored school, spelling bees, square dancing, quilt show, folk arts and crafts, music and plenty of good food. Annually, the last Saturday in May. Est attendance: 2,500. For info: Nevette Muir, Fairmount Academy Festival Assn, PO Box 134, Upper Fairmount, MD 21867. Phone: (410) 651-0351 or (410) 651-3945.

HARRIS, PATRICIA ROBERTS: 90th BIRTH ANNIVERSARY. May 31, 1924. Born at Mattoon, IL. The first African-American woman to serve in an ambassadorial post, the first African American to hold a cabinet position (Secretary of Housing and Urban Development) and the first woman to serve as dean of a law school. Died Mar 23, 1985, at Washington, DC.

JOHNSTOWN FLOOD: 125th ANNIVERSARY. May 31, 1889. Heavy rains caused the Connemaugh River Dam to burst. At nearby Johnstown, PA, the resulting flood killed more than 2,300 people and destroyed the homes of thousands more. Nearly 800 unidentified drowning victims were buried in a common grave at Johnstown's Grandview Cemetery. So devastating was the flood and so widespread the sorrow for its victims that "Johnstown Flood" entered the language as a phrase to describe a disastrous event. The valley city of Johnstown, in the Allegheny Mountains, has been damaged repeatedly by floods. Floods in 1936 (25 deaths) and 1977 (85 deaths) were the next most destructive.

PEALE, NORMAN VINCENT: BIRTH ANNIVERSARY. May 31, 1898. American religious leader Norman Vincent Peale was born at Bowersville, OH. He is best known for his book *The Power of Positive Thinking* (1952), which combines religion and psychology. He was a minister at the Marble Collegiate Church at New York, NY. He died Dec 24, 1993, at Pawling, NY.

POPE PIUS XI: BIRTH ANNIVERSARY. May 31, 1857. Ambrogio Damiano Achille Ratti, 259th pope of the Roman Catholic Church, born at Desio, Italy. Elected pope Feb 6, 1922. Died Feb 10, 1939, at Rome, Italy.

PRINCE RAINIER OF MONACO: BIRTH ANNIVERSARY. May 31, 1923. Born Prince Rainier Louis Henri Maxence Bertrand in the small principality of Monaco, he ascended the throne in 1949. In 1956 he married Hollywood actress Grace Kelly and Monaco soon became the glamour destination for the rich and famous. By changing tax shelter laws and encouraging the casino industry, Rainier changed the destiny of his country, bringing it back from the brink of bankruptcy to become one of the wealthiest nations in Europe. He was Europe's longest-reigning monarch when he died at Monaco on Apr 6, 2005.

"SEINFELD" TV PREMIERE: ANNIVERSARY. May 31, 1990. "Seinfeld"—the show about nothing—premiered on NBC to wide acclaim. The show revolved around the everyday lives of its four main leads, whose story lines intertwined for some surprising plot twists. Some of the programs concerned relationships, valet parking, annoying dogs and waiting for Chinese food. The cast featured Jerry Seinfeld as himself; Michael Richards as his neighbor, Cosmo Kramer; Julia Louis-Dreyfus as his ex-girlfriend, Elaine Benes; and Jason Alexander as his best friend, George Costanza. The series ended with the May 14, 1998, episode.

"SURVIVOR" TV PREMIERE: ANNIVERSARY. May 31, 2000. On this immensely popular reality show, 16 people were sequestered on a deserted island in Malaysia for 39 days. They competed for the right to remain on the island, with the final survivor winning $1 million. Hosted by Jeff Probst, the show drew a total audience of 51 million people. The show has consistently ranked at the top of the Nielsen ratings.

UNITED NATIONS: WORLD NO-TOBACCO DAY. May 31.

WHAT YOU THINK UPON GROWS DAY. May 31. A day to remind people of the power of positive thinking. For info: Stephanie West Allen, 1376 S Wyandot St, Denver, CO 80223. Phone: (303) 935-8866. E-mail: stephanie@westallen.com.

WHITMAN, WALT: BIRTH ANNIVERSARY. May 31, 1819. Poet and journalist, born at West Hills, Long Island, NY. Whitman's best-known work, *Leaves of Grass* (1855), is a classic of American poetry. His poems celebrated all of modern life, including subjects that were considered taboo at the time. Died Mar 26, 1892, at Camden, NJ.

BIRTHDAYS TODAY

Tom Berenger, 64, actor (*Born on the Fourth of July, Major League, Gettysburg*), born Chicago, IL, May 31, 1950.

Clint Eastwood, 84, actor, director (Oscars for *Unforgiven* and *Million Dollar Baby*), born San Francisco, CA, May 31, 1930.

Chris Elliott, 54, writer, comedian, actor ("Get a Life"), born New York, NY, May 31, 1960.

Colin Farrell, 38, actor (*Total Recall, In Bruges, Minority Report, Tigerland*), born Castleknock, Dublin, Ireland, May 31, 1976.

Sharon Gless, 71, actress ("Burn Notice," Emmy for "Cagney & Lacey"), born Los Angeles, CA, May 31, 1943.

Gregory Harrison, 64, actor ("Logan's Run," "Trapper John, MD"), born Avalon, Catalina Island, CA, May 31, 1950.

Phil Keoghan, 47, television personality, host ("The Amazing Race"), born Christchurch, New Zealand, May 31, 1967.

Kenny Lofton, 47, baseball player, born East Chicago, IN, May 31, 1967.

Roma Maffia, 56, actress ("Chicago Hope," "Nip/Tuck"), born New York, NY, May 31, 1958.

Joseph William (Joe) Namath, 71, Hall of Fame football player, former sportscaster, actor, born Beaver Falls, PA, May 31, 1943.

Archie Panjabi, 42, actress (Emmy for "The Good Wife"; *Bend It like Beckham*), born London, England, May 31, 1972.

Kyle Secor, 56, actor ("Homicide: Life on the Street"), born Tacoma, WA, May 31, 1958.

Brooke Shields, 49, actress (*Pretty Baby, The Blue Lagoon*, "Suddenly Susan"), born New York, NY, May 31, 1965.

Lea Thompson, 53, actress ("Caroline in the City," *Back to the Future, Howard the Duck*), born Rochester, MN, May 31, 1961.

Terry Waite, 75, Church of England special envoy, former hostage in Lebanon (1987–91), born Bollington, Cheshire, England, May 31, 1939.

Peter Yarrow, 76, composer, singer (Peter, Paul and Mary), born New York, NY, May 31, 1938.

✦ June ✦

June 1 — Sunday

DAY 152 **213 REMAINING**

ADOPT-A-SHELTER-CAT MONTH. June 1–30. To promote the adoption of cats from local shelters, the ASPCA sponsors this important observance. "Make Pet Adoption Your First Option®" is a message the organization promotes throughout the year in an effort to end the euthanasia of all adoptable animals. For info: Media & Communications Dept, ASPCA, 520 8th Ave, 7th Fl, New York, NY 10018. Phone: (212) 876-7700, ext 4655. E-mail: press@aspca.org. Web: www.aspca.org.

✦AFRICAN-AMERICAN MUSIC APPRECIATION MONTH. June 1–30. Proclaimed annually since 2009 to honor the rich musical traditions of African-American musicians and their gifts to our country and our world, and to celebrate the legacy of African-American music and its enduring power to bring life to the narrative of our nation. (Proclaimed by some previous administrations as Black History Month.)

ATLANTIC, CARIBBEAN AND GULF HURRICANE SEASON. June 1–Nov 30. For info: US Dept of Commerce, Natl Oceanic and Atmospheric Admin, Rockville, MD 20852.

AUDIOBOOK APPRECIATION MONTH. June 1–30. To encourage new listeners to learn more about the fascinating history and current status of audiobooks in the United States. Audiobooks are one of the fastest-growing areas of the publishing industry. For info: Stephanie Frost, Executive Director, Audio Publishers Association, 191 Clarksville Rd, Princeton Junction, NJ 08550. Phone: (609) 269-2388. E-mail: sfrost@audiopub.org. Web: www.audiopub.org.

BLACK SINGLE PARENTS' WEEK. June 1–7. This week honors all the black single parents who have successfully raised their sons and daughters despite poor schools, crime and drug-infested neighborhoods to be responsible, self-sufficient (and sometimes famous) citizens. For info: Will Barnes, Exec Dir, The Black Single Parents' Network, 7732 S Cottage Grove, #431, Chicago, IL 60619. Phone: (773) 933-1061. Fax: (773) 933-1059. E-mail: wwillbar@gmail.com.

CANCER FROM THE SUN MONTH. June 1–30. To promote education and awareness of the dangers of skin cancer from too much exposure to the sun. For info: Fred S. Mayer, RPh, MPH, Pharmacists Planning Service, Inc (PPSI), PO Box 6760, San Rafael, CA 94903. Phone: (415) 479-8628 or (415) 302-7351. Fax: (415) 479-8608. E-mail: ppsi@aol.com. Web: www.ppsinc.org.

✦CARIBBEAN-AMERICAN HERITAGE MONTH. June 1–30. To pay tribute to the diverse cultures and immeasurable contributions of all Americans who trace their heritage to the Caribbean.

CATARACT AWARENESS MONTH. June 1–30. Cataracts are the leading cause of blindness in the world. There are close to 22.3 million Americans age 40 and older with cataracts. More than half of all Americans will have cataracts by age 80. Prevent Blindness America® offers tips about prevention and information about surgery. (Formerly observed in August.) For info: Prevent Blindness America®, 211 W Wacker Dr, Ste 1700, Chicago, IL 60606. Phone: (800) 331-2020. E-mail: info@preventblindness.org. Web: www.preventblindness.org.

CELEBRATION OF THE ARTS. June 1. Hurless Barton Park, Yorba Linda, CA. A fine arts and music festival for all ages. More than 100 exhibitors, art demonstrations and hands-on activities. Continuous entertainment on four stages includes dance, drama, bands and choirs. Free event. Annually, the first Sunday in June. Est attendance: 3,000. For info: Yorba Linda Arts Alliance, PO Box 1037, Yorba Linda, CA 92885. Phone: (714) 996-1960. E-mail: info@artsyl.org. Web: www.artsyl.org.

CENTRAL PACIFIC HURRICANE SEASON. June 1–Oct 31. Central Pacific is defined as 140° west longitude to the International Date Line (180° west longitude). For info: Natl Dept of Commerce, Natl Oceanic and Atmospheric Admin, Rockville, MD 20852.

CHILD VISION AWARENESS MONTH. June 1–30. To better educate and counsel the public on children's vision problems and detection of eye diseases in infants and children, to increase the number of school-aged children who have an eye exam by an eye doctor and to increase the number of children with learning disabilities who have a developmental vision exam to rule out vision problems. For info: Fred S. Mayer, RPh, MPH, Pharmacists Planning Service, Inc (PPSI), PO Box 6760, San Rafael, CA 94903. Phone: (415) 479-8628 or (415) 302-7351. Fax: (415) 479-8608. E-mail: ppsi@aol.com. Web: www.ppsinc.org.

CHILDREN'S AWARENESS MONTH. June 1–30. A monthlong celebration of America's children in our everyday lives and communities. We choose to remember our children and grandchildren during the month of June by celebrating the gift of children. For info: Judith Natale, CEO & Founder, NCAC America-USA, PO Box 493703, Redding, CA 96049-3703. E-mail: childaware@aol.com.

CHINA: INTERNATIONAL CHILDREN'S DAY. June 1. Shanghai.

CNN DEBUT: ANNIVERSARY. June 1, 1980. The Cable News Network, TV's first all-news service, went on the air.

DAIRY ALTERNATIVES MONTH. June 1–30. This event encourages you to eliminate dairy products from your diet and explore alternative foods made from beans, nuts or grains. Why not try soy, rice or almond milk on your cereal? For info: VEGANET, PO Box 321, Knoxville, TN 37901-0321. Phone: (800) 234-8343.

EFFECTIVE COMMUNICATIONS MONTH. June 1–30. The most important cog in the wheel of interpersonal relationships is communication. Active listening, verbal language, paralanguage, body language and written communication skills are the essence of how humans relate to each other personally and professionally. This month is dedicated to learning how to communicate more effectively. For info: Sylvia Henderson, Springboard Training, PO Box 588, Olney, MD 20830-0588. Phone: (301) 260-1538. E-mail: sylvia@springboardtraining.com.

ENTREPRENEURS "DO IT YOURSELF" MARKETING MONTH. June 1–30. Are you looking for better results from your marketing efforts? Would you like to become a new resource the media calls? Remember, your success is a matter of choice, not chance. Discover and apply creative and effective problem-solving marketing ideas that will help you gain the competitive edge. Act now and remove the barriers that are stopping you from achieving your goals. For info: Lorrie Walters Marsiglio, Lorimar Communications, PO Box 284-CC, Wasco, IL 60183-0284. Phone: (630) 584-9368.

FIREWORKS SAFETY MONTHS. June 1–July 31. Activities during this period will alert parents and children about the dangers of playing with fireworks. Prevent Blindness America® will offer suggestions for safer ways to celebrate the Fourth of July. For info: Prevent Blindness America®, 211 W Wacker Dr, Ste 1700, Chicago, IL 60606. Phone: (800) 331-2020. E-mail: info@preventblindness.org. Web: www.preventblindness.org.

GAY AND LESBIAN PRIDE MONTH. June 1–30. Observed this month because on June 28, 1969, the clientele of a gay bar at New York City rioted after the club was raided by the police. President Clinton issued presidential proclamations for this month, but President Bush did not declare it during his administration. President Obama resumed proclaiming this month as Lesbian, Gay, Bisexual and Transgender Pride Month in 2009. See also: "Stonewall Riot: Anniversary" (June 28).

GENERAL MOTORS CORPORATION BANKRUPTCY: 5th ANNIVERSARY. June 1, 2009. The one-hundred-year-old automaker filed for Chapter 11 bankruptcy protection on this date. In response the US federal government invested $57 billion in the company, making the US Treasury GM's majority shareholder, owning a 60 percent stake. The reorganized GM, now General Motors Company, exited bankruptcy July 10, 2009, eliminating 13 US plants, 2,000 dealerships and 20,000 jobs.

GEORGIA BLUEBERRY MONTH. June 1–30. A month heralding the Georgia blueberry harvest and recognizing that Georgia has the longest blueberry season in the US: from late April through the end of July. For info: Marcia Crowley, Georgia Agricultural Commodity Commission for Blueberries (GACCB), Commodities Promotion Division, Georgia Dept of Agriculture, 328 Agriculture Building, Capitol Sq, Atlanta, GA 30334. Phone: (404) 656-3678. Fax: (404) 656-9380. Web: www.georgiablueberry.org.

✦GREAT OUTDOORS MONTH. June 1–30. To celebrate the rich blessings of our nation's natural beauty and to renew our commitment to protecting the environment and keeping our country's open spaces beautiful and accessible to our citizens.

HEIMLICH MANEUVER INTRODUCED: 40th ANNIVERSARY. June 1, 1974. The June issue of the journal *Emergency Medicine* published an article by Dr. Henry Heimlich outlining a better method for aiding choking victims. Instead of the prevailing method of backslaps (which merely pushed foreign objects farther into the airways), Dr. Heimlich advocated "subdiaphragmatic pressure" to force objects out. Three months later, the method was dubbed "the Heimlich Maneuver" by the *Journal of the American Medical Association.*

INTERNATIONAL CHILDHOOD CANCER AWARENESS MONTH. June 1–30. Optimist Clubs worldwide plan and hold special events that benefit patients, families and caregivers associated with pediatric oncology. Events range from picnics to fund-raisers. For info: Optimist International, Programs Dept, 4494 Lindell Blvd, St. Louis, MO 63108. Phone: (800) 500-8130. Fax: (314) 371-6006. Web: www.optimist.org.

INTERNATIONAL MEN'S MONTH. June 1–30. This program was initiated in 1996 to increase media and local community awareness of the many unique issues that impact men's lives and that are of concern to the people who love them. In an effort to promote positive changes in male roles and relationships, a different issue is addressed each day of the month during June, and information and resources on that issue are provided on the website. For info: Gordon Clay, PO Box 12-CH, Brookings, OR 97415-0001. E-mail: menstuff@aol.com. Web: www.menstuff.org.

INTERNATIONAL SURF MUSIC MONTH. June 1–30. 6th annual. Surf instrumental music, born in the US in the 1960s, reflects the freedom and joy of surf culture. This month celebrates that music and the bands the world over that inject local flavors into it. Concerts take place around the world. For info: Sandy Rosado, NESMA, 653 Browns Rd, Storrs Mansfield, CT 06268. E-mail: sandy9thwave@yahoo.com. Web: www.nesmasurf.org.

ITALY: GIOCO DEL PONTE. June 1. Pisa. The first Sunday in June is set aside for the Battle of the Bridge, a medieval parade and a contest for possession of the bridge.

ITALY: WEDDING OF THE SEA. June 1. Venice. The feast of the Ascension is the occasion of the ceremony recalling the "Wedding of the Sea," performed by Venice's doge, who cast his ring into the sea from the ceremonial ship known as the *Bucintoro* to symbolize eternal dominion. Annually, on the Sunday following Ascension.

JAPAN: DAY OF THE RICE GOD. June 1. Chiyoda. Annual rice-transplanting festival observed on first Sunday in June. Centuries-old rural folk ritual revived in 1930s and celebrated with colorful costumes, parades, music, dancing and prayers to the Shinto rice god Wbai-sama.

JUNE DAIRY MONTH. June 1–30. Observed since 1937. Promotes national awareness of the quality and nutritional benefits of refrigerated dairy foods. For info: Julie Henderson, Natl Frozen & Refrigerated Foods Assn, 4755 Linglestown Rd, Ste 300, Harrisburg, PA 17112. Phone: (717) 657-8601. Fax: (717) 657-9862. E-mail: info@nfraweb.org. Web: www.nfraweb.org.

JUNE IS PERENNIAL GARDENING MONTH. June 1–30. June is the perfect month to celebrate the versatility and beauty of perennial garden plants. We'll offer some good gardening tips on how to keep your perennial garden beautiful all season long and highlight many individual perennials that bloom for the month of June. For info: Steven Still, 3383 Schrirtzinger Rd, Hilliard, OH 43026. Phone: (614) 771-8431. E-mail: ppa@perennialplant.org. Web: www.perennialplant.org.

KENTUCKY: ADMISSION DAY: ANNIVERSARY. June 1. Became 15th state in 1792.

KENYA: MADARAKA DAY. June 1. Madaraka Day (Self-Rule Day) is observed as a national public holiday. Commemorates attainment of self-government in 1963.

✦LESBIAN, GAY, BISEXUAL AND TRANSGENDER PRIDE MONTH. June 1–30. This month, the White House recognizes the immeasurable contributions of LGBT Americans and renews the commitment to the struggle for equal rights for LGBT Americans and to ending prejudice and injustice wherever it exists.

LITTLE, CLEAVON: 75th BIRTH ANNIVERSARY. June 1, 1939. Best known for his role as the black sheriff who cleaned up a town of bumbling redneck toughs in the movie *Blazing Saddles*, Cleavon Little was born at Chickasha, OK. Little won a Tony Award for the 1970 musical *Purlie* and an Emmy in 1989 for a guest appearance on the television series "Dear John." Died Oct 22, 1992, near Sherman Oaks, CA.

MARQUETTE, JACQUES: BIRTH ANNIVERSARY. June 1, 1637. Father Jacques Marquette (Père Marquette) was a Jesuit missionary-explorer of the Great Lakes region. Born at Laon, France; died at Ludington, MI, May 18, 1675.

MEN'S HEALTH EDUCATION AND AWARNESS MONTH. June 1–30. A month to keep informed about health concerns for men and to learn how to prevent heart disease, prostate cancer, COPD, osteoporosis, ED, BPH, HIV, STDs and other diseases. For info: Fred S. Mayer, RPh, MPH, Pharmacists Planning Service, Inc (PPSI), PO Box 6760, San Rafael, CA 94903. Phone: (415) 479-8628 or (415) 302-7351. Fax: (415) 479-8608. E-mail: ppsi@aol.com. Web: www.ppsinc.org.

MIGRAINE AWARENESS MONTH. June 1–30. To educate the public on the personal and societal costs of migraines while providing resources for the 30 million migraine patients and their families. Nine out of ten migraine sufferers report they can't "function normally" during days a migraine strikes, and nearly three in ten require bed rest. Every day approximately 430,000 people are unable to work due to migraines, equaling about 157 million workdays lost annually. For info: National Headache Foundation, 820 N Orleans, Ste 411, Chicago, IL 60610-3132. Phone: (312) 274-2652. Fax: (312) 640-9049. E-mail: info@headaches.org. Web: www.headaches.org.

MONROE, MARILYN: BIRTH ANNIVERSARY. June 1, 1926. American actress and sex symbol of the '50s, born at Los Angeles as Norma Jean Mortensen or Baker. She had an unstable childhood in a series of orphanages and foster homes. Her film career came to epitomize Hollywood glamour. In 1954 she wed New York Yankee legend "Jolting Joe" DiMaggio, but the marriage didn't last. Monroe remained fragile and insecure, tormented by the pressures of Hollywood life. Her death from a drug overdose Aug 5, 1962, at Los Angeles, CA, shocked the world. Among her films: *The Seven Year Itch, Bus Stop, Some Like It Hot, Gentlemen Prefer Blondes* and *The Misfits*.

NATIONAL ACCORDION AWARENESS MONTH. June 1–30. To increase public awareness of this multicultural instrument and its influence and popularity in today's music. For info: Tom Torriglia, All Things Accordion, PO Box 475136, San Francisco, CA 94147-5136. Phone: (415) 440-0800. E-mail: tom@ladyofspain.com. Web: www.ladyofspain.com.

NATIONAL APHASIA AWARENESS MONTH. June 1–30. More than one million Americans have acquired aphasia, a language-processing disorder that impairs a person's ability to speak or understand speech. The mission of the National Aphasia Association (NAA) is to reduce the social and emotional consequences of aphasia by raising awareness of and giving a voice to people who cannot use their own. Annually, the month of June. For info: National Aphasia Assn, 350 Seventh Ave, Ste 902, New York, NY 10001. Phone: (800) 922-4622. E-mail: naa@aphasia.org. Web: www.aphasia.org.

NATIONAL BATHROOM READING MONTH. June 1–30. Since 1988, the Bathroom Readers' Institute has led the movement to stand up for those who sit down and read in the bathroom. National Bathroom Reading Month celebrates the 66 percent of Americans who proudly admit to this time-honored pastime. For info: Bathroom Readers' Institute, PO Box 1117, Ashland, OR 97520. Phone: (888) 488-4642, ext 100. Fax: (541) 482-6159. E-mail: mail@bathroomreader.com. Web: www.bathroomreader.com.

NATIONAL BUSINESS ETIQUETTE WEEK. June 1–7. 8th annual. A week to recognize the need for proper business etiquette/business intelligence necessary to compete in the growing global marketplace. Review everything from how to network to the proper handshake to how to remember names. Check the proper forms of address in business as well as government, military and academic areas. Annually, the first full week in June. For info: The Protocol School of Washington, PO Box 676, Columbia, SC 29202. Phone: (877) 766-3757. E-mail: info@psow.edu. Web: www.psow.edu.

NATIONAL CANCER SURVIVORS DAY. June 1. The 27th annual celebration of life. Hundreds of communities nationwide honor survivors who are living with and beyond cancer. Annually, the first Sunday in June. For info: Natl Cancer Survivors Day Foundation, PO Box 682285, Franklin, TN 37068-2285. Phone: (615) 794-3006. Fax: (615) 794-0179. E-mail: info@ncsd.org. Web: www.ncsd.org.

NATIONAL CARIBBEAN-AMERICAN HERITAGE MONTH. June 1–30. Since the 16th century, the destinies of the peoples of the Caribbean and the American continent have been inextricably linked. Through the commemoration of this month, we hope to ensure that America is reminded that its greatness lies in its diversity. Caribbean immigrants from founding father Alexander Hamilton to journalist Malcolm Gladwell have shaped the American dream. For info: Institute of Caribbean Studies, 1629 K St NW, Ste 300, Washington, DC 20006. Phone: (202) 638-0460. E-mail: ics@icsdc.org. Web: www.caribbeanamericanmonth.org.

June 2014	S	M	T	W	T	F	S
	1	2	3	4	5	6	7
	8	9	10	11	12	13	14
	15	16	17	18	19	20	21
	22	23	24	25	26	27	28
	29	30					

NATIONAL GLBT BOOK MONTH. June 1–30. Created to increase the recognition of gay, lesbian, bisexual and transgender writing. Begun in 1992 by the Publishing Triangle, June was selected in honor of the anniversary of the 1969 Stonewall Riot in New York City. It was this brave resistance to police harassment that kick-started the gay pride movement in the US. Libraries, bookstores, publishers and bibliophiles everywhere are invited to form a chorus line and celebrate with the community. Annually, the month of June. For info: Gay Lesbian Bisexual Transgender Roundtable, c/o American Library Association, Office for Literacy and Outreach Services, 50 E Huron St, Chicago, IL 60611. Web: www.ala.org/glbtrt.

NATIONAL ICED TEA MONTH. June 1–30. To celebrate one of the most widely consumed beverages in the world and one of nature's most perfect beverages, and to encourage Americans to refresh themselves with this all-natural, low-calorie, refreshing thirst-quencher. For info: The Tea Council of the USA, 362 Fifth Ave, Ste 801, New York, NY 10001. Phone: (212) 986-6998. Fax: (212) 697-8658. E-mail: info@teausa.org. Web: www.teausa.org.

NATIONAL RIVERS MONTH. June 1–30. Commemorated by local groups in many states.

NATIONAL SAFETY MONTH. June 1–30. National Safety Month promotes safety of US residents at work, at home, on the road and in our communities. The National Safety Council saves lives by preventing injuries and deaths through leadership, research, education and advocacy. For info: Natl Safety Council, 1121 Spring Lake Dr, Itasca, IL 60143-3201. Phone: (800) 621-7615. Web: www.nsc.org.

NATIONAL SOUL FOOD MONTH. June 1–30. A month to recognize, educate and celebrate the heritage and history of the foods and foodways of African Americans and peoples from the African diaspora. The culinary contributions of this group have had an indelible impact on the American menu and on mainstream American life and culture. For info: Culinary Historians of Chicago. E-mail: chc2001@att.net. Web: www.culinaryhistorians.org.

PHARMACISTS DECLARE WAR ON ALCOHOLISM. June 1–30. To encourage pharmacists, healthcare professionals and consumers to better educate and counsel the public on alcoholism and other substance abuse illnesses. By promoting alcohol abuse awareness and education to healthcare professionals and the general public, PPSI strives to break the stereotype surrounding alcoholism that keeps millions of Americans from receiving proper treatment. For info: Fred S. Mayer, RPh, MPH, Pharmacists Planning Service, Inc (PPSI), PO Box 6760, San Rafael, CA 94903. Phone: (415) 479-8628 or (415) 302-7351. Fax: (415) 479-8608. E-mail: ppsi@aol.com. Web: www.ppsinc.org.

"THE PRISONER" TV PREMIERE: ANNIVERSARY. June 1, 1968. "The Prisoner" was one of the most imaginative shows on TV, regarded by some as the finest dramatic series in TV history. Patrick McGoohan, who produced and starred in the series, also wrote and directed some episodes. In the series, McGoohan found himself in a self-contained community known as "the village" where he was referred to not by name but as Number 6. Number 6 realized he was a prisoner and spent most of the series trying to escape or learn the identity of the leader, Number 1.

REBUILD YOUR LIFE MONTH. June 1–30. This is an opportunity for adults neglected and/or abused as children to celebrate their self-worth and discover inner power. They can learn to heal their lives and emotional pain by helping others. For info send SASE: Donald Etkes, PhD, 112 Harvard Ave, #148, Claremont, CA 91711. Phone: (310) 405-9814. E-mail: drdonetkes@aol.com.

SAMOA: INDEPENDENCE DAY. June 1. National holiday. Commemorates independence from New Zealand in 1962. The former Western Samoa changed its name in 1997.

SAY SOMETHING NICE DAY. June 1. This is a day to say thank you to those who make our lives better just by being a part of them. A day to recognize those who contribute to our lives in specific ways. And a day to apologize for words spoken in frustration, anger or disappointment. One day is one day, but perhaps we can stretch it to two, and then just maybe if we encourage one another, we might change the world! This day has been declared by Mayor Summey of North Charleston, the SC Baptist Convention, the Charleston-Atlantic Presbytery and Mayor Riley of Charleston. For info: Mitch Carnell, 2444 Birkenhead Dr, Charleston, SC 29414. Phone: (843) 556-2310. E-mail: mitch@mitchcarnell.net. Web: www.mitchcarnell.net or www.fbcharleston.org.

***SGT PEPPER'S LONELY HEARTS CLUB BAND* RELEASED: ANNIVERSARY.** June 1, 1967. After 700 hours of studio work, The Beatles released what many consider one of the greatest rock albums of the 20th century. No singles were released, but the album included such popular tracks as "Lucy in the Sky with Diamonds," "With a Little Help from My Friends," "When I'm Sixty-Four" and "A Day in the Life."

SKYSCRAPER MONTH. June 1–30. Skyscraper month celebrates the evolution of the high-rise building and the oldest commercial real estate association, the Building Owners and Managers Association (BOMA) International. BOMA will observe this month at its annual conference June 22–24, at the Gaylord Palms Resort and Convention Center, Kissimmee, FL. For info: BOMA International, 1101 15th St NW, Ste 800, Washington, DC 20005. Phone: (202) 326-6300. Fax: (202) 326-6377. Web: www.boma.org or www.everybuildingconference.org.

SPORTS AMERICA KIDS MONTH. June 1–30. To encourage the health and well-being of all America's children. Physical fitness and healthy thinking, through the efforts of teamwork with individual self-esteem, can help America's children to appreciate the gift of life and the value of respecting the lives of others. A time for adults and kids to embrace the wonderful outdoors and the benefits of healthy living with physical fitness. For info: Judith Natale, NCAC America-USA, PO Box 493703, Redding, CA 96049-3703. E-mail: childaware@aol.com.

STUDENT SAFETY MONTH. June 1–30. To heighten the awareness of safety and of making sound decisions following graduations, parties, senior proms and other special events. Encourages young people everywhere not to drink and drive and to use good judgment while celebrating throughout the month. For info: Carole Copeland Thomas, 6 Azel Rd, Lakeville, MA 02347. Phone: (508) 947-5755. Fax: (508) 947-3903. E-mail: TellCarole@mac.com. Web: www.TellCarole.com.

SUPERMAN DEBUTS: ANNIVERSARY. June 1, 1938. Ohio teenagers Joe Shuster and Jerry Siegel wowed the comic book world with a new kind of pulp hero: Superman. Superman, a refugee with super powers from the planet Krypton, appeared in the June issue of *Action Comics* #1. Now a pop culture icon, Superman was then a smash hit who ushered in many more fantastical superheroes. (The comic book's actual release date was earlier, either Apr 18 or May 3.) See also: "Batman Debuts: Anniversary" (May 1).

TENNESSEE: ADMISSION DAY: ANNIVERSARY. June 1. Became 16th state in 1796. Observed as a holiday in Tennessee.

YOUNG, BRIGHAM: BIRTH ANNIVERSARY. June 1, 1801. Mormon church leader born at Whittingham, VT. Known as "the American Moses," having led thousands of religious followers across 1,000 miles of wilderness to settle more than 300 towns in the West. He died at Salt Lake City, UT, Aug 29, 1877, and was survived by 17 wives and 47 children. Utah observes, as a state holiday, the anniversary of his entrance into the Salt Lake Valley, July 24, 1847.

BIRTHDAYS TODAY

Rene Auberjonois, 74, actor (*M*A*S*H*, "Boston Legal," "Benson"; Tony for *Coco*), born New York, NY, June 1, 1940.

James Hadley Billington, 85, Librarian of Congress, born Bryn Mawr, PA, June 1, 1929.

Lisa Hartman Black, 58, actress ("Tabitha," "Knots Landing"), born Houston, TX, June 1, 1956.

Pat Boone, 80, singer, actor (*State Fair*), author, born Jacksonville, FL, June 1, 1934.

Sarah Wayne Callies, 37, actress ("The Walking Dead," "Prison Break"), born La Grange, IL, June 1, 1977.

Mark Curry, 50, comedian, actor ("Hangin' with Mr Cooper"), born Oakland, CA, June 1, 1964.

Morgan Freeman, 77, stage and film actor (Oscar for *Million Dollar Baby*; *The Shawshank Redemption, Driving Miss Daisy*), born Memphis, TN, June 1, 1937.

Justine Henin, 32, former tennis player, born Liege, Belgium, June 1, 1982.

Javier "Chicharito" Hernández, 26, soccer player, born Guadalajara, Mexico, on June 1, 1988.

Heidi Klum, 41, fashion model, television personality ("Project Runway"), born Bergisch-Gladbach, Germany, June 1, 1973.

Alexi Lalas, 44, soccer executive and former player, born Detroit, MI, June 1, 1970.

Alanis Morissette, 40, singer, born Ottawa, ON, Canada, June 1, 1974.

Jonathan Pryce, 67, actor (*Glengarry Glen Ross*; stage: *Miss Saigon*, Tony for *Hamlet*), born Holywell, North Wales, June 1, 1947.

Frederica von Stade, 69, opera singer, born Somerville, NJ, June 1, 1945.

Ron Wood, 67, musician (Rolling Stones), born London, England, June 1, 1947.

Carlos Zambrano, 33, baseball player, born Puerto Cabello, Venezuela, June 1, 1981.

June 2 — Monday

DAY 153 **212 REMAINING**

BELGIUM: PROCESSION OF THE GOLDEN CHARIOT. June 2. Mons. Horse-drawn coach carrying a reliquary of St. Waudru circles the town of Mons. Procession commemorates delivery of Mons from the plague in 1349. In the town square, in the afternoon, St. George fights the dragon.

BHUTAN: CORONATION DAY. June 2. National holiday. Commemorates the crowning of the fourth king in 1974.

BULGARIA: HRISTO BOTEV DAY. June 2. Poet and national hero Hristo Botev fell fighting Turks, 1876.

CHINA: DRAGON BOAT FESTIVAL. June 2. An important Chinese observance, the Dragon Boat Festival commemorates a hero of ancient China, poet Qu Yuan, who drowned himself in protest against injustice and corruption. It is said that rice dumplings were cast into the water to lure fish away from the body of the martyr, and this is remembered by the eating of *zhong zi*, glutinous rice dumplings filled with meat and wrapped in bamboo leaves. Dragon boat races are held on rivers. The Dragon Boat Festival is observed in many countries by their Chinese populations (date will differ from China's). Also called Fifth Month Festival or Summer Festival. Annually, the fifth day of the fifth lunar month.

HAMLISCH, MARVIN: 70th BIRTH ANNIVERSARY. June 2, 1944. Composer and conductor of film and Broadway scores, born at New York, NY. A child prodigy accepted to Julliard at age seven, Hamlisch composed his first hit song before he turned 21. Famous film scores include *The Sting* (1973) and *The Way We Were* (1973), and his best-known Broadway work includes *A Chorus Line* (1975) and *They're Playing Our Song* (1979). Winner of multiple Emmy, Grammy, Oscar and Tony awards, as well as the 1976 Pulitzer Prize for Drama for *A Chorus Line*, he died at Los Angeles, CA, Aug 6, 2012.

ITALY: REPUBLIC DAY. June 2. National holiday. Commemorates 1946 referendum in which republic status was selected instead of return to monarchy.

KOREA: TANO DAY. June 2. Fifth day of fifth lunar month. Summer food offered at the household shrine of the ancestors. Also known as Swing Day, since girls, dressed in their prettiest clothes, often compete in swinging matches. The Tano Festival usually lasts from the third through eighth day of the fifth lunar month.

MAINE LAW: ANNIVERSARY. June 2, 1851. America's first statewide statute prohibiting the sale of alcoholic beverages was enacted in the state of Maine. The following Independence Day the mayor of Bangor showed his support of the new law by smashing 10 kegs of confiscated booze.

MARQUIS DE SADE: BIRTH ANNIVERSARY. June 2, 1740. Donatien-Alphonse-François, Comte de Sade, was born at Paris, France. French military man, governor-general and author, who spent much of his life in prison because of his acts of cruelty and violence, outrageous behavior and debauchery. The word *sadism* was created from his name to describe gratification in inflicting pain. He died near Paris, at the Charenton lunatic asylum, Dec 2, 1814.

NATIONAL LEAVE THE OFFICE EARLIER DAY. June 2. Employees commit to working productively all day so they can get their work done, leave the office earlier and get home to their families. For info: Laura Stack, The Productivity Pro, 9948 Cottoncreek Dr, Highlands Ranch, CO 80130. Phone: (303) 471-7401. Fax: (303) 471-4702. E-mail: Laura@TheProductivityPro.com. Web: www.TheProductivityPro.com.

NATIONAL THANK GOD IT'S MONDAY! DAY. June 2. Besides holidays, such as Presidents' Day, being celebrated on Mondays, people everywhere start new jobs, have birthdays, celebrate promotions and begin vacations on Mondays. A day in recognition of this first day of the week. For info: Dorothy Zjawin, 61 W Colfax Ave, Roselle Park, NJ 07204.

SAINT ERASMUS DAY. June 2. Feast day of Erasmus, also known as Elmo, bishop of Formiae, Campagna, Italy, who was martyred around AD 303. Patron saint of sailors. The blue light seen around ship masts that marks atmospheric electricity is popularly called St. Elmo's fire from the ancient belief that it signifies the saint's protection of sailors during storms.

SAINT PIUS X: BIRTH ANNIVERSARY. June 2, 1835. Giuseppe Melchiorre Sarto, 257th pope of the Roman Catholic Church, born at Riese, Italy. Elected pope Aug 4, 1903. Died Aug 20, 1914, at Rome. Canonized May 29, 1954.

SALEM WITCH TRIALS BEGIN: ANNIVERSARY. June 2, 1692. As the village of Salem was gripped by terror of witches, Massachusetts Bay Colony Governor Sir William Phips ordered a special court created on May 27, 1692, to expedite judgment of the more than 150 people accused of witchcraft. Unpopular resident Bridget Bishop, originally accused in April, was the first of the jailed brought to trial on June 2. At her April examination her accusers—teenaged girls—had collapsed in fits as she appeared, but Bishop adamantly denied the charges: "I am no witch—I know not what a witch is." She was convicted June 2 and hanged June 10. See also: "Salem Witch Hysteria Begins: Anniversary" (Mar 1).

UNITED KINGDOM: CORONATION DAY. June 2. Commemorates the crowning of Queen Elizabeth II in 1953.

WASHINGTON, MARTHA DANDRIDGE CUSTIS: BIRTH ANNIVERSARY. June 2, 1731. Wife of George Washington, first president of the US, born at New Kent County, VA. Died at Mount Vernon, VA, May 22, 1802.

WEISSMULLER, JOHNNY: BIRTH ANNIVERSARY. June 2, 1904. Peter John (Johnny) Weissmuller, actor and Olympic gold medal swimmer, born at Windber, PA. Weissmuller won three gold medals at the 1924 Olympics and two more at the 1928 games. He set 24 world records and in 1950 was voted the best swimmer of the first half of the 20th century. After retiring from amateur competition, he appeared as Tarzan in a dozen movies and as "Jungle Jim" in the movies and on television. Died at Acapulco, Mexico, Jan 20, 1984.

YELL "FUDGE" AT THE COBRAS IN NORTH AMERICA DAY. June 2. Anywhere north of the Panama Canal. In order to keep poisonous cobra snakes out of North America, all citizens are asked to go outdoors at noon, local time, and yell "Fudge." Fudge makes cobras gag and the mere mention of it makes them skedaddle. Annually, June 2. (©2006 by WH.) For info: Thomas & Ruth Roy, Wellcat Holidays, 2418 Long Ln, Lebanon, PA 17046. Phone: (717) 279-0184. E-mail: info@wellcat.com. Web: www.wellcat.com.

BIRTHDAYS TODAY

Morena Baccarin, 35, actress ("Homeland," "V," "Firefly"), born Rio de Janeiro, Brazil, June 2, 1979.

Diana Canova, 61, actress ("Soap," "I'm a Big Girl Now"), born West Palm Beach, FL, June 2, 1953.

Dana Carvey, 59, comedian, actor (*Wayne's World*, "Saturday Night Live"), born Missoula, MT, June 2, 1955.

Dominic Cooper, 36, actor (*Abraham Lincoln: Vampire Hunter, The Devil's Double, An Education, The History Boys*), born Greenwich, England, June 2, 1978.

Nikolay Davydenko, 33, tennis player, born Severodonezk, Ukraine, June 2, 1981.

Gary Grimes, 59, actor (*Summer of '42, Class of '44*), born San Francisco, CA, June 2, 1955.

Charles Haid, 71, actor ("Hill Street Blues," "Delvecchio"), producer, born San Francisco, CA, June 2, 1943.

Dennis Haysbert, 60, actor ("24," *Waiting to Exhale, Major League*), born San Mateo, CA, June 2, 1954.

Stacy Keach, Jr, 73, actor (*Conduct Unbecoming*, "Mickey Spillane's Mike Hammer"), born Savannah, GA, June 2, 1941.

Sally Kellerman, 78, actress (*M*A*S*H, Back to School*), born Long Beach, CA, June 2, 1936.

Justin Long, 36, actor (*Dodgeball, Live Free or Die Hard*, "Ed"), born Fairfield, CT, June 2, 1978.

Jerry Mathers, 66, actor ("Leave It to Beaver"), born Sioux City, IA, June 2, 1948.

Wentworth Miller, 42, actor ("Prison Break," *The Human Stain*), born Chipping Norton, Oxfordshire, England, June 2, 1972.

Zachary Quinto, 37, actor (*Star Trek*, "Heroes," "24"), born Pittsburgh, PA, June 2, 1977.

Charlie Watts, 73, musician (Rolling Stones), born Islington, England, June 2, 1941.

June 2014	S	M	T	W	T	F	S
	1	2	3	4	5	6	7
	8	9	10	11	12	13	14
	15	16	17	18	19	20	21
	22	23	24	25	26	27	28
	29	30					

June 3 — Tuesday

DAY 154 **211 REMAINING**

BAKER, JOSEPHINE: BIRTH ANNIVERSARY. June 3, 1906. The sensation of 1920s Paris, Baker was born into poverty at St. Louis, MO. She began working as a dancer at age 16 and went to Paris in 1925, where her semi-nude "danse sauvage" became a hit. She was the first American-born woman to be awarded the Croix de Guerre and the Legion of Honor for her Red Cross work during WWII. Baker performed up until her death on Apr 12, 1975, at Paris, France.

BATTLE OF COLD HARBOR: 150th ANNIVERSARY. June 3, 1864. Although Confederate General Robert E. Lee had placed his troops behind considerable breastworks, Union General Ulysses S. Grant launched an all-out attack on the Southern army in Virginia. More than 7,000 Union troops were killed within one-half hour of battle on the first attack. After a second unsuccessful attack, Grant's orders for a third assault were all but ignored. Battlefield tradition held that the first commander who sought a truce in order to tend to the wounded was the loser. Grant refused to admit defeat by seeking such a truce, and the wounded were left on the ground for three days following the battle. As a consequence, all but two of the thousands of wounded men died either from their wounds, hunger, thirst or exposure.

BRINKER, NORMAN: BIRTH ANNIVERSARY. June 3, 1931. Restaurant entrepreneur, born at Denver, CO. Lauded as "the most influential person in the restaurant industry" by *Nation's Restaurant News.* Innovator of casual-dining concept of full-service for middle-class customers. Mainstreamed the salad bar. Created Steak & Ale (1966), conceived Bennigan's (1978) and grew Chili's from 28 restaurants to 1,000-location chain from 1984–2001 under Brinker International, which also includes Maggiano's Little Italy and On the Border Mexican Grill. Initial funder and board member of the Susan G. Komen Breast Cancer Foundation, created by wife and named for her sister in 1982. Died June 9, 2009, at Colorado Springs, CO.

CHIMBORAZO DAY. June 3. To bring the shape of Earth into focus by publicizing the fact that Mount Chimborazo, Ecuador, near the equator, pokes farther out into space than any other mountain on Earth, including Mount Everest. (The distance from sea level at the equator to the center of Earth is 13 miles greater than the radius to sea level at the North Pole. This means that New Orleans is about six miles farther from the center of Earth than is Lake Itasca at the headwaters of the Mississippi, so the Mississippi flows uphill.) For info: Robert L. Birch, Puns Corps, 3108 Dashiell Rd, Falls Church, VA 22042. Phone: (703) 533-3668.

CONFEDERATE MEMORIAL DAY IN KENTUCKY, LOUISIANA AND TENNESSEE. June 3. Ceremonial holiday on the birthday of Jefferson Davis. Also observed as Jefferson Davis Day in Kentucky and Confederate Decoration Day in Tennessee.

CURTIS, TONY: BIRTH ANNIVERSARY. June 3, 1925. Film star from Hollywood's Golden Age, born Bernard Schwartz at the Bronx, NY. He was a master of both dramatic and comedic roles, garnering acclaim for such films as *The Defiant Ones* (1958), *Some Like It Hot* (1959) and *The Boston Strangler* (1968). He died at Henderson, NV, Sept 29, 2010.

DAVIS, JEFFERSON: BIRTH ANNIVERSARY. June 3, 1808. American statesman, US senator, only president of the Confederate States of America. Imprisoned May 10, 1865–May 13, 1867, but never brought to trial, deprived of rights of citizenship after the Civil War. Davis was born at Todd County, KY, and died at New Orleans, LA, Dec 6, 1889. His citizenship was restored, posthumously, Oct 17, 1978, when President Carter signed an Amnesty Bill. This bill, he said, "officially completes the long process of reconciliation that has reunited our people following the tragic conflict between the states." Davis's birth anniversary is observed in Florida, Kentucky and South Carolina on this day; in Alabama on the first Monday in June and in Mississippi on the last Monday in May. Davis's birth anniversary is observed as Confederate Decoration Day in Tennessee.

DEWHURST, COLLEEN: 90th BIRTH ANNIVERSARY. June 3, 1924. Colleen Dewhurst was born at Quebec, Canada. Her 40-year career as an actress spanned stage, screen and television. After making her Broadway debut in Eugene O'Neill's *Desire Under the Elms* in 1952, she became the actress most associated with O'Neill's works in the latter part of the 20th century, also performing in *Long Day's Journey into Night; Mourning Becomes Electra; Ah, Wilderness!* and *A Moon for the Misbegotten*, for which she won her second Tony Award. At the time of her death, she was president of Actor's Equity Association, the union for professional actors. She won three Emmy Awards. She died Aug 22, 1991, at South Salem, NY.

DREW, CHARLES RICHARD: BIRTH ANNIVERSARY. June 3, 1904. African-American physician who discovered how to store blood plasma and who organized the blood bank system in the US and UK during WWII. Born at Washington, DC, he was killed in an automobile accident near Burlington, NC, Apr 1, 1950.

DUKE OF WINDSOR MARRIAGE: ANNIVERSARY. June 3, 1937. The Duke of Windsor who, as King Edward VIII, had abdicated the British throne on Dec 11, 1936, was married to Mrs Wallis Warfield Simpson of Baltimore, MD, at Monts, France. The couple made their home in France after their marriage and had little contact with the royal family. The Duke died at Paris on May 28, 1972, and was buried near Windsor Castle in England. The Duchess died Apr 24, 1986.

FIRST WOMAN RABBI IN US: ANNIVERSARY. June 3, 1972. Sally Jan Priesand was ordained the first woman rabbi in the US. She became assistant rabbi at the Stephen Wise Free Synagogue, New York City, Aug 1, 1972.

GINSBERG, ALLEN: BIRTH ANNIVERSARY. June 3, 1926. Poet of the Beat Generation, social activist, born Newark, NJ. Best known for "Howl" (published 1956) and "Kaddish" (published 1961). The sexual content of "Howl" caused the book to be impounded and Ginsberg to be charged with obscenity until a judge ruled that the work was not without "redeeming social importance." Recipient of the National Book Award, the Robert Frost Medal and the American Book Award, Ginsberg died Apr 5, 1997, at New York, NY.

HOBART, GARRET AUGUSTUS: BIRTH ANNIVERSARY. June 3, 1844. 24th vice president of the US (1897–99), born at Long Branch, NJ. Died at Paterson, NJ, Nov 21, 1899.

IRELAND: BANK HOLIDAY. June 3. National holiday in the Republic of Ireland.

JACK JOUETT'S RIDE: ANNIVERSARY. June 3, 1781. Jack Jouett made a heroic 45-mile ride on horseback during the night of June 3–4, 1781, to warn Virginia Governor Thomas Jefferson and the Virginia legislature that the British were coming. Jouett rode from a tavern in Louisa County to Charlottesville, VA, in about 6½ hours, arriving at Jefferson's home at dawn on June 4. Lieutenant Colonel Tarleton's British forces raided Charlottesville, but Jouett's warning gave the Americans time to escape. Jouett was born at Albemarle County, VA, Dec 7, 1754, and died at Bath, KY, in 1822 (exact date unknown).

KHOMEINI, AYATOLLAH RUHOLLA: 25th DEATH ANNIVERSARY. June 3, 1989. The Ayatollah Ruholla Khomeini, leader of the Islamic Revolution, lifelong foe of the Shah of Iran, was arrested in 1963 after giving a speech accusing the Shah of seeking to destroy Islam. He was exiled to Turkey in 1964, following which he spent 13 years in Iraq and Paris, where he gained exposure to the world press for his cause. On Jan 16, 1979, the Shah of Iran left the country for a supposed vacation, setting the stage for Khomeini's triumphant return on Jan 31. The monarchy fell on Feb 11, 1979. Khomeini proceeded to reorganize the government based on Islamic principles. On Nov 11, 1979, a group of students loyal to Khomeini occupied the American Embassy in Tehran after the Shah was given admittance to the US for medical treatment, placing the Ayatollah at the center of a diplomatic crisis that consumed the presidency of Jimmy Carter. Khomeini focused attention on the US as the "Great Satan" and blamed many of his country's problems on imperialistic intervention. The anniversary of his death is a national holiday in Iran.

"MIGHTY CASEY HAS STRUCK OUT": ANNIVERSARY. June 3, 1888. The famous comic baseball ballad "Casey at the Bat" was printed in the Sunday *San Francisco Examiner.* Appearing anonymously, it was written by Ernest L. Thayer. Recitation of "Casey at the Bat" became part of the repertoire of actor William DeWolf Hopper. The recitation took 5 minutes and 40 seconds. Hopper claimed to have recited it more than 10,000 times, the first being at Wallack's Theater at New York, NY, in 1888. See also: "Thayer, Ernest Lawrence: Birth Anniversary" (Aug 14).

MISSION SAN CARLOS BORROMEO DE CARMELO: FOUNDING ANNIVERSARY. June 3, 1770. California mission to the Indians founded on this date.

OLDS, RANSOM: 150th BIRTH ANNIVERSARY. June 3, 1864. American automobile inventor and manufacturer Olds was born at Geneva, OH. Founded the Olds Motor Works, which made Oldsmobile, the first affordable, mass-produced American car. It was also the first automobile produced in quantity with a progressive assembly system and comprised of interchangeable parts. In a marketing innovation, Olds also introduced the policy of insisting that dealers pay cash for cars delivered to them, a practice that became standard and provided much-needed immediate capital for the fledgling automotive industry. Died Aug 26, 1950, at Lansing, MI.

SHAVUOT BEGINS AT SUNDOWN. June 3. Jewish Pentecost. See also: "Shavuot" (June 4).

SPACE MILESTONE: *GEMINI 4* (US). June 3, 1965. James McDivitt and Edward White made 66 orbits of Earth. White took the first space walk by an American and maneuvered 20 minutes outside the capsule.

ZOOT SUIT RIOTS: ANNIVERSARY. June 3–8, 1943. In Los Angeles, CA, simmering racial unease exploded as 200 white sailors stormed into East LA and began beating Hispanics in response to an earlier altercation between a few sailors and some street kids. The sailors targeted Zoot Suiters—youths outfitted in the defiant, exaggerated suit of their community (long jackets, wide trousers and ankle-length watch chains). The rioting grew as police either stood by or arrested the victims. The media, antagonistic to the Hispanic community, spurred on the violence with sensational headlines. Finally, military brass declared Los Angeles off-limits to its personnel and the LA City Council banned zoot suits. There were no deaths, but the injuries and mayhem were such that a special state committee was convened and First Lady Eleanor Roosevelt wrote in her newspaper column that the riots were symptomatic of a problem with deep roots.

June 2014

S	M	T	W	T	F	S
1	2	3	4	5	6	7
8	9	10	11	12	13	14
15	16	17	18	19	20	21
22	23	24	25	26	27	28
29	30					

BIRTHDAYS TODAY

Chuck Barris, 85, television producer ("The Dating Game," "The Gong Show"), born Philadelphia, PA, June 3, 1929.

Raúl Castro, 83, President of Cuba, born Holguín, Cuba, June 3, 1931.

Anderson Cooper, 47, journalist, television personality ("Anderson Cooper 360," "The Mole"), born New York, NY, June 3, 1967.

Jan-Michael Gambill, 37, tennis player, born Spokane, WA, June 3, 1977.

Charles Hart, 53, lyricist, composer, born London, England, June 3, 1961.

Hale S. Irwin, 69, golfer, born Joplin, MO, June 3, 1945.

Larry McMurtry, 78, author (*Terms of Endearment, Lonesome Dove, The Last Picture Show*), screenwriter (Oscar for *Brokeback Mountain*), born Wichita Falls, TX, June 3, 1936.

Rafael Nadal, 28, tennis player, born Manacor, Spain, June 3, 1986.

James Purefoy, 50, actor ("The Following," *Rome*), born Taunton, Somerset, England, June 3, 1964.

Scott Valentine, 56, actor ("Family Ties"), born Saratoga Springs, NY, June 3, 1958.

Deniece Williams, 63, singer, born Gary, IN, June 3, 1951.

Penelope Wilton, 68, actress ("Downton Abbey," "Doctor Who," *Shaun of the Dead*), born Scarborough, North Yorkshire, England, June 3, 1946.

June 4 — Wednesday

DAY 155 | **210 REMAINING**

BATTLE OF MIDWAY: ANNIVERSARY. June 4–6, 1942. A Japanese task force attempted to capture Midway Island in the Central Pacific, but American bombers from Midway and from two nearby aircraft carriers sent the Japanese into retreat. The Japanese lost four carriers, two large cruisers and three destroyers. Midway was one of the most decisive naval battles of WWII. Japan never regained its margin in carrier strength, and the Central Pacific was made safe for American troops.

"CAVALCADE OF STARS" TV PREMIERE: 65th ANNIVERSARY. June 4, 1949. Although the Dumont network was not very successful, it was around long enough to launch this popular show. The one-hour variety show was hosted by Jack Carter (1949–50), Jackie Gleason (1950–52) and Larry Storch (in the summer of 1952). It also served as a showcase for the soon-to-be-immortal "The Honeymooners" with Gleason and Pert Kelton starring as the Kramdens.

CHINA: TIANANMEN SQUARE MASSACRE: 25th ANNIVERSARY. June 4, 1989. After almost a month and a half of student demonstrations for democracy, the Chinese government ordered its troops to open fire on the unarmed protestors at Tiananmen Square in Beijing. Under the cover of darkness, early June 4, troops opened fire on the assembled crowds and armored personnel carriers rolled into the square crushing many of the students as they lay sleeping in their tents. Although the government claimed that few died in the attack, estimates range from several hundred to several thousand casualties. In the following months thousands of demonstrators were rounded up and jailed.

FENDER, FREDDY: BIRTH ANNIVERSARY. June 4, 1937. Born Baldemar Huerta at San Benito, TX, to migrant farm workers, Fender was a Grammy-winning balladeer who worked in country, R&B and Tex-Mex music styles—singing in both Spanish and English. In the 1970s, Fender had several number-one country hits, including "Before the Next Teardrop Falls" and "Wasted Days and Wasted Nights." He died Oct 14, 2006, at Corpus Christi, TX.

FINLAND: FLAG DAY. June 4. Finland's armed forces honor the June 4, 1867, birth anniversary of Carl Gustaf Mannerheim.

FIRST FREE FLIGHT BY A WOMAN: ANNIVERSARY. June 4, 1784. Marie Thible, of Lyons, France, accompanied by a pilot (Monsieur Fleurant), became the first woman in history to fly in a free balloon. She drifted across Lyons in a balloon named *Le Gustave* (for King Gustav III of Sweden, who was watching the ascent). The balloon reached a height of 8,500 feet in a flight that lasted about 45 minutes. The event occurred one day short of a year after the first flight in history by a man. See also: "First Balloon Flight: Anniversary" (June 5).

GEORGE III: BIRTH ANNIVERSARY. June 4, 1738. As King of Great Britain and Ireland from 1760 to 1820, George III was also elector and, later, king of Hanover. His reign was uneven, marked by political instability and popularity that wavered. He alienated Parliament and populace when he lost the American colonies in a costly war but was embraced as the embodiment of England during its war with France in 1793. Often called "The Mad King," George III suffered from periods of insanity, possibly from porphyria. After 1811 he was permanently insane. Born at London, England, he died Jan 29, 1820, at Windsor.

PULITZER PRIZES FIRST AWARDED: ANNIVERSARY. June 4, 1917. The first Pulitzer Prizes were awarded on this date: for biography, *Julia Ward Howe* by Laura E. Richards and Maude H. Elliott assisted by Florence H. Hall and for history, *With Americans of Past and Present Days* by Jean Jules Jusserand, the French ambassador to the US. Prizes were also awarded for journalistic achievement.

ROME LIBERATED: 70th ANNIVERSARY. June 4, 1944. The US 9th Army, commanded by General Mark Clark, entered the southern suburbs of Rome as the last of the German rear guard retreated from Mussolini's former capital. Fearful of a last-ditch effort by the Germans to hold the city, the populace remained behind closed doors as Clark's forces entered the Eternal City.

SHAVUOT or FEAST OF WEEKS. June 4–5. Jewish Pentecost holy days. Hebrew dates, Sivan 6–7, 5774. Celebrates giving of Torah (the Law) to Moses on Mount Sinai. Began at sundown June 3.

TONGA: EMANCIPATION DAY. June 4. National holiday. Commemorates independence from Britain in 1970.

UNITED NATIONS: INTERNATIONAL DAY OF INNOCENT CHILDREN VICTIMS OF AGGRESSION. June 4. On Aug 19, 1982, the General Assembly decided to commemorate June 4 of each year as a day to call attention to the urgent need to protect the rights of children. It reminds people that throughout the world there are many children suffering from different forms of abuse. For info: United Nations, Dept of Public Info, New York, NY 10017. Web: www.un.org.

BIRTHDAYS TODAY

Cecilia Bartoli, 48, opera singer, born Rome, Italy, June 4, 1966.

Russell Brand, 39, comedian, actor (*Forgetting Sarah Marshall, Bedtime Stories*), born Grays, Essex, England, June 4, 1975.

James Callis, 43, actor ("Battlestar Galactica," *Bridget Jones's Diary*), born London, England, June 4, 1971.

Keith David, 58, actor (*Platoon, Barbershop,* "Jazz"), born New York, NY, June 4, 1956.

Eldra DeBarge, 53, musician, born Grand Rapids, MI, June 4, 1961.

Bruce Dern, 78, actor (*Coming Home, The 'Burbs*), born Chicago, IL, June 4, 1936.

Bettina Gregory, 68, journalist, born New York, NY, June 4, 1946.

Andrea Jaeger, 49, former tennis player, born Chicago, IL, June 4, 1965.

Angelina Jolie, 39, actress (Oscar for *Girl, Interrupted*; *The Tourist, Mr & Mrs Smith, Lara Croft: Tomb Raider*), director, born Los Angeles, CA, June 4, 1975.

Mike Lee, 43, US Senator (R, Utah), born Mesa, AZ, June 4, 1971.

Evan Lysacek, 29, Olympic figure skater, born Chicago, IL, June 4, 1985.

Michelle Phillips, 69, singer (The Mamas and the Papas), actress ("Knots Landing"), born Long Beach, CA, June 4, 1945.

Parker Stevenson, 61, actor ("Falcon Crest," "Baywatch," *Lifeguard*), born Philadelphia, PA, June 4, 1953.

Dr. Ruth Westheimer, 85, television and radio host for shows on sexual relationships, born Frankfurt, Germany, June 4, 1929.

Scott Wolf, 46, actor ("Party of Five," *The Evening Star*), born Boston, MA, June 4, 1968.

Noah Wyle, 43, actor ("Falling Skies," "ER," *A Few Good Men*), born Hollywood, CA, June 4, 1971.

June 5 — Thursday

DAY 156 **209 REMAINING**

AIDS FIRST NOTED: ANNIVERSARY. June 5, 1981. The Centers for Disease Control first described a new illness striking gay men in a newsletter on June 5, 1981. On July 27, 1982, the CDC adopted Acquired Immune Deficiency Syndrome as the official name for the new disease. The virus that causes AIDS was identified in 1983 and in May 1985 was named Human Immunodeficiency Virus (HIV) by the International Committee on the Taxonomy of Viruses. The first person killed by this disease in the developed world died in 1959. More than 617,000 Americans have died of AIDS. Worldwide, more than 30 million people have died of AIDS. About 34 million people worldwide are living with HIV/AIDS.

AMERICAN BAHA'I COMMUNITY: ANNIVERSARY. June 5, 1894. The first formal classes on the Baha'i were held at Chicago, IL.

APPLE II COMPUTER RELEASED: ANNIVERSARY. June 5, 1977. The Apple II computer, with 4K of memory, went on sale for $1,298. Its predecessor, the Apple I, was sold largely to electronic hobbyists the previous year. Apple released the Macintosh computer Jan 24, 1984.

BOYD, WILLIAM: BIRTH ANNIVERSARY. June 5, 1895. Born at Hendrysburg, OH, Boyd went to Hollywood in 1919 and got a job as a film extra. In 1935 he got the role of Hopalong Cassidy in a series of popular Westerns. He made 66 of these films between 1935 and 1948. Some of them were edited and shown on television; Boyd then made some episodes especially for TV. Died at Hollywood, CA, Sept 12, 1972. See also: "'Hopalong Cassidy' TV Premiere: Anniversary" (June 24).

CANADA: WINNIPEG INTERNATIONAL CHILDREN'S FESTIVAL. June 5–8. The Forks, Winnipeg, MB. 32nd annual. Festival features song, dance, theater, mime, puppetry and music by local, national and international artists. Est attendance: 20,000. For info: Winnipeg Intl Children's Fest, 201-One Forks Market Rd, Winnipeg, MB R3C 4L9, Canada. E-mail: kidsfest@kidsfest.ca. Web: www.kidsfest.ca.

CURWOOD FESTIVAL. June 5–8. Owosso, MI. Homecoming celebration commemorating James Oliver Curwood, Owosso-born author and conservationist (June 12, 1878–Aug 13, 1927). The Curwood castle was built for a writing studio. Open to the public, the festival has 40 events, including parades, races and music. Annually, the Thursday through Sunday of the first full weekend in June. Est attendance: 40,000. For info: Curwood Festival,

PO Box 461, Owosso, MI 48867. Phone: (989) 723-2161. Fax: (989) 729-6098. E-mail: curwoodfestival@michonline.net. Web: www.curwoodfestival.com.

DENMARK: CONSTITUTION DAY. June 5. National holiday. Commemorates Denmark becoming a constitutional monarchy in 1849 and the new constitution adopted in 1953.

FIRST BALLOON FLIGHT: ANNIVERSARY. June 5, 1783. The first public demonstration of a hot-air balloon flight took place at Annonay, France, where brothers Joseph and Jacques Montgolfier succeeded in launching the 33-foot-diameter *globe aerostatique* that they had invented. The unmanned balloon rose an estimated 1,500 feet and traveled, wind-borne, about 7,500 feet before landing after a 10-minute flight—the first sustained flight of any object achieved by man.

GREAT AMERICAN BRASS BAND FESTIVAL. June 5–8. Centre College Campus, Danville, KY. Brass bands and ensembles from throughout the country in concert Thursday through Sunday. Free to the public. Est attendance: 40,000. For info: Great American Brass Band Festival, PO Box 429, Danville, KY 40423. Phone: (859) 319-8426. E-mail: info@gabbf.org. Web: www.gabbf.org.

IRAN: FIFTEENTH OF KHORDAD. June 5. National holiday. Commemorates the deaths of Islamic clerics in a clash with the shah's forces in 1963.

KENNEDY, ROBERT F.: ASSASSINATION ANNIVERSARY. June 5, 1968. Senator Kennedy was shot while campaigning for the Democratic presidential nomination at Los Angeles, CA; he died the following day. Sirhan Sirhan was convicted of his murder.

KEYNES, JOHN MAYNARD: BIRTH ANNIVERSARY. June 5, 1883. British economist born at Cambridge, England. Author of *Treatise on Money* and *The General Theory of Employment, Interest and Money* that focused on "expansionist" economic policy. Died at Firle, England, Apr 21, 1946.

MOON PHASE: FIRST QUARTER. June 5. Moon enters First Quarter phase at 4:39 PM, EDT.

SCARRY, RICHARD McCLURE: 95th BIRTH ANNIVERSARY. June 5, 1919. Author and illustrator of children's books born at Boston, MA. Two widely known books of the more than 250 authored by Scarry are *Richard Scarry's Best Word Book Ever* (1965) and *Richard Scarry's Please & Thank You* (1973). The pages are crowded with small animal characters that live like humans. More than 100 million copies of his books have sold worldwide. Died Apr 30, 1994, at Gstaad, Switzerland.

SMITH, ADAM: BIRTH ANNIVERSARY. June 5, 1723. (Old Style date.) Scottish economist and philosopher, author of *An Enquiry into the Nature and Causes of the Wealth of Nations* (1776), born at Kirkaldy, Fifeshire, Scotland. Died at Edinburgh, Scotland, July 17, 1790. "Consumption," he wrote, "is the sole end and purpose of production; and the interest of the producer ought to be attended to only so far as it may be necessary for promoting that of the consumer."

UNITED NATIONS: WORLD ENVIRONMENT DAY. June 5. Observed annually June 5, the anniversary of the opening of the UN Conference on the Human Environment held in Stockholm in 1972, which led to establishment of UN Environment Programme, based in Nairobi. The General Assembly has urged marking the day with activities reaffirming concern for the preservation and enhancement of the environment. For info: United Nations, Dept of Public Info, New York, NY 10017. Web: www.un.org.

June 2014

S	M	T	W	T	F	S
1	2	3	4	5	6	7
8	9	10	11	12	13	14
15	16	17	18	19	20	21
22	23	24	25	26	27	28
29	30					

BIRTHDAYS TODAY

Chad Allen, 40, actor ("Dr. Quinn: Medicine Woman"), born Cerritos, CA, June 5, 1974.

Jill Biden, 63, Second Lady, wife of US Vice President Joseph R. Biden, Jr, born Hammonton, NJ, June 5, 1951.

Margaret Drabble, 75, author (*The Gates of Ivory*), born Sheffield, Yorkshire, England, June 5, 1939.

Ken Follett, 65, author (*The Pillars of the Earth, The Eye of the Needle*), born Cardiff, Wales, June 5, 1949.

Brian McKnight, 45, singer, born Buffalo, NY, June 5, 1969.

Bill Moyers, 80, journalist ("Bill Moyers' Journal"), born Hugo, OK, June 5, 1934.

Mark Wahlberg, 43, actor (*The Fighter, The Departed, Boogie Nights*), former rapper, born Dorchester, MA, June 5, 1971.

June 6 — Friday

DAY 157 **208 REMAINING**

BAHAMAS: LABOR DAY. June 6. Public holiday. First Friday in June celebrated with parades, displays and picnics.

BONZA BOTTLER DAY™. June 6. To celebrate when the number of the day is the same as the number of the month. Bonza Bottler Day™ is an excuse to have a party at least once a month. For more information see Jan 1. For info: Gail Berger, 14 Fernwood Dr, Taylors, SC 29687. Phone: (864) 201-3988. E-mail: bonza@bonzabottlerday.com. Web: www.bonzabottlerday.com.

BUFFALO DAYS CELEBRATION (WITH BUFFALO CHIP THROWING). June 6–8. Luverne, MN. Parade, Arts in the Park, cruise-in, parade and unique buffalo chip throwing contest. Annually, the first weekend in June. Est attendance: 5,000. For info: Luverne Area Chamber, 213 E Luverne St, Luverne, MN 56156. Phone: (507) 283-4061. Fax: (507) 283-4061. E-mail: luvernechamber@co.rock.mn.us. Web: www.luvernechamber.com.

COIN, JEWELRY & STAMP EXPO. June 6–8. Radisson Hotel, Sherman Oaks, CA. Est attendance: 5,000. For info: Israel Bick, Exec Dir, Intl Stamp & Coin Collectors Society, PO Box 854, Van Nuys, CA 91408. Phone: (818) 997-6496. Fax: (818) 988-4337. E-mail: iibick@sbcglobal.net. Web: www.bickinternational.com.

CURTIS CUP. June 6–8. St. Louis Country Club, St. Louis, MO. 39th edition. Biennial competition (officially named "The Women's International Cup") between teams of women amateur golfers from the US and the UK and Ireland. Named after British golfing sisters Harriot and Margaret Curtis. Contested in even-numbered years since 1932 (except during WWII). Sponsored by the USGA and Ladies' Golf Union. For info: USGA. E-mail: usga@usga.org. Web: www.usga.org or www.curtiscup.org.

D-DAY: 70th ANNIVERSARY. June 6, 1944. In the early morning hours Allied forces landed in Normandy on the north coast of France. In an operation that took months of planning, a fleet of 2,727 ships of every description converged from British ports from Wales to the North Sea. Operation *Overlord* involved 2,000,000 tons of war materials, including more than 50,000 tanks, armored cars, jeeps, trucks and half-tracks. The US alone sent 1,700,000 fighting men. The Germans believed the invasion would not take place under the adverse weather conditions of this early June day. But as the sun came up, the village of Saint Mère Eglise was liberated by American parachutists, and by nightfall the landing of 155,000 Allies attested to the success of D-Day. The long-awaited second front had at last materialized.

ENGLAND: INVESTEC DERBY FESTIVAL. June 6–7. Epsom Downs, Surrey. Ladies' Day is June 6 and Derby Day is June 7. The Derby dates back to 1780 and is still ranked the greatest flat race in the world. With winnings of 1.25 million pounds, the Investec Derby has one of the biggest prizes in UK racing, matched only by the prestige that victory brings. It remains the race that everyone wants to win, as horses and riders push themselves to the limit around the unique and challenging course. Annually, the first weekend in June. For info: Epsom Downs Racecourse. Web: www.epsomdowns.co.uk.

FARMINGTON COUNTRY DAYS. June 6–8. Farmington, MO. Three-day event featuring amusement rides, family entertainment, Nashville country concerts, craft show, parade and lots more fun for the whole family. Est attendance: 30,000. For info: Farmington Chamber of Commerce, PO Box 191, Farmington, MO 63640. Phone: (573) 756-3615. Fax: (573) 756-1003. E-mail: info@farmingtoncountrydays.com. Web: www.farmingtoncountrydays.com.

FIRST DRIVE-IN MOVIE OPENS: ANNIVERSARY. June 6, 1933. Richard M. Hollingshead, Jr, opened America's first drive-in movie theater in Camden, NJ, on this date. At the height of their popularity in 1958, there were more than 4,000 drive-ins across America. Today there are fewer than 600 open.

GREAT WISCONSIN CHEESE FESTIVAL. June 6–8. Little Chute, WI. Festival features cheese breakfast, parade, cheese tasting, cheese-carving demo and cheesecake contest. Est attendance: 10,000. For info: Great Wisconsin Cheese Festival, 1940 Buchanan St, Little Chute, WI 54140-1414. Phone: (920) 788-7390. Fax: (920) 788-7820. Web: www.littlechutewi.org/cheesefest.

HALE, NATHAN: BIRTH ANNIVERSARY. June 6, 1755. American patriot Nathan Hale was born at Coventry, CT. During the battles for New York in the American Revolution, he volunteered to seek military intelligence behind enemy lines and was captured on the night of Sept 21, 1776. In an audience before General William Howe, Hale admitted he was an American officer and was ordered hanged the following morning. Although some question them, his dying words, "I only regret that I have but one life to lose for my country," have become a symbol of American patriotism. He was hanged Sept 22, 1776, at Manhattan, NY.

HARVARD MILK DAYS™ FESTIVAL. June 6–8. Harvard, IL. This salute to the dairy farmer includes a parade, evening entertainment, horse show, business expo, milk-drinking contest, antique farm tractor display, flea market, carnival, fireworks, 2-mile milk run, 2-mile milk walk, 10k milk run, kids dash, junior dairy cattle show, talent show and wee farm. Est attendance: 100,000. For info: Harvard Milk Days, Inc, PO Box 325, Harvard, IL 60033-0325. Phone: (815) 943-4614. Fax: (815) 943-7404. E-mail: info@milkdays.com. Web: www.milkdays.com.

KHACHATURIAN, ARAM (ILICH): BIRTH ANNIVERSARY. June 6, 1903. Armenian musician and composer, noted for compositions based on folk music and legend, born at Tbilisi, Georgia, USSR. Died at Moscow, May 1, 1978.

KOREA: MEMORIAL DAY. June 6. Nation pays tribute to the war dead, and memorial services are held at the National Cemetery in Seoul. Legally recognized Korean holiday.

NATIONAL DONUT DAY. June 6. Founded in 1938 by the Salvation Army for fundraising during the Great Depression, National Donut Day is now an annual tradition. During WWI, doughnuts were served to doughboys by the Salvation Army. Later, symbolic paper "donuts" were given to charitable contributors. This day now celebrates the doughnut itself. Annually, the first Friday in June. For info: National Donut Day. Web: donutdayusa.com.

NATIONAL YO-YO DAY. June 6. A celebration of yo-yos and yo-yo playing held on the birth anniversary of Donald F. Duncan (1892–1971), the entrepreneur (founder of the Duncan Toys Company) who was the great popularizer of the toy. A day to practice the sleeper, walk the dog, skin the cat, rock the baby or around the world. Created by Daniel Volk, a former yo-yo demonstrator, in 1990.

PROPOSITION 13: ANNIVERSARY. June 6, 1978. California voters (65 percent of them) supported a primary election ballot initiative to cut property taxes 57 percent. Regarded as a possible omen of things to come across the country—a taxpayers' revolt against high taxes and government spending.

PUSHKIN, ALEXANDER: BIRTH ANNIVERSARY. June 6, 1799. Nobleman, poet and author born at Moscow, Russia. During periods of exile created some of his greatest work, notably his "novel in verse" *Eugene Onegin*. Other well-known works include *Boris Godunov, Queen of Spades, Tales of Belkin* and *The Bronze Horseman*. Goaded into a duel by an admirer of his wife on Jan 27, 1837, Pushkin died of his injury on Jan 29, 1837, at St. Petersburg. His birthday is widely observed in Russia.

SCOTT, ROBERT FALCON: BIRTH ANNIVERSARY. June 6, 1868. British naval officer and polar explorer, born at Devonport, England. Led the ill-starred expedition to the South Pole that arrived on Jan 18, 1912—one month after Norwegian Roald Amundsen's team became the first humans to set foot on the South Pole. Scott and four team members died on the return journey and their bodies were found November 1912. Scott's diary, with a final entry of Mar 29, 1912, had a message to the public: "Had we lived, I should have had a tale to tell of the hardihood, endurance, and courage of my companions which would have stirred the heart of every Englishman. These rough notes and our dead bodies must tell the tale."

SECURITIES AND EXCHANGE COMMISSION CREATED: 80th ANNIVERSARY. June 6, 1934. President Franklin D. Roosevelt signed the Securities Exchange Act that established the SEC. Wall Street had operated almost unfettered since the end of the 18th century. However, the stock market crash of 1929 necessitated regulation of the exchanges. The SEC is composed of five members appointed by the president of the US.

"SEX AND THE CITY" TV PREMIERE: ANNIVERSARY. June 6, 1998. HBO's modern comedy of manners focused on four fashionable women navigating the perilous waters of New York City's dating scene. Starred Sarah Jessica Parker (Carrie Bradshaw), Kristin Davis (Charlotte York), Kim Cattrall (Samantha Jones) and Cynthia Nixon (Miranda Hobbes). More than 10 million viewers tuned in to watch the 94th and final episode on Feb 22, 2004.

SITKA SUMMER MUSIC FESTIVAL. June 6–July 5. Sitka, AK. Sitka hosts a highly acclaimed chamber music festival that attracts performers and spectators from around the world. Est attendance: 5,000. For info: Sitka Summer Music Festival, PO Box 3333, Anchorage, AK 99835. Phone: (907) 277-4852. E-mail: director@sitkamusicfestival.org. Web: www.sitkamusicfestival.org.

SPACE MILESTONE: *SOYUZ 11* (USSR). June 6, 1971. Launched with cosmonauts G.T. Dobrovolsky, V.N. Volkov and V.I. Patsayev, who died during the return landing June 30, 1971, after a 24-day space flight. *Soyuz 11* had docked at *Salyut* orbital space station June 7–29; the cosmonauts entered the space station for the first time and conducted scientific experiments. First humans to die in space.

SUMMER FARM TOY SHOW. June 6–7. National Farm Toy Museum and Beckman High School, Dyersville, IA. 30th annual. This two-day show attracts farm toy dealers and collectors from all over the country who buy, sell and trade in farm toys. Thousands of farm toy collectibles and farm machinery memorabilia can be found for purchase. Annual show events include a 50-mile tractor ride and colorful tractor parade through downtown. Est attendance: 5,000. For info: National Farm Toy Museum, 1110 16th Ave Ct SE, Dyersville, IA 52040. Phone: (563) 875-2727. E-mail: farmtoys@dyersville.com. Web: www.nationalfarmtoymuseum.com.

SURRENDER OF MEMPHIS: ANNIVERSARY. June 6, 1862. Confederate gunboats engaged a Union flotilla near Memphis, TN. As crowds of spectators watched from the riverbanks, the outgunned Confederates were defeated. The city of Memphis surrendered shortly before noon of that day, effectively opening up the Mississippi region.

SUSAN B. ANTHONY FINED FOR VOTING: ANNIVERSARY. June 6, 1872. Seeking to test for women the citizenship and voting rights extended to black males under the 14th and 15th Amendments, Susan B. Anthony led a group of women who registered and voted at a Rochester, NY, election. She was arrested, tried and sentenced to pay a fine. She refused to do so and was allowed to go free by a judge who feared she would appeal to a higher court.

SWEDEN: NATIONAL DAY. June 6. Public holiday since 2005. Commemorates two key dates in Swedish sovereignty—both falling on June 6: the day Gustavus I (Gustavus Vasa) ascended the throne of Sweden in 1523 and the day in 1809 when Sweden adopted a new constitution—one that established civil rights and liberties. Originally observed as Flag Day beginning in 1916, then changed to National Day in 1983.

***TECUMSEH!*: THE EPIC OUTDOOR DRAMA.** June 6–Aug 30 (excluding Sundays). Chillicothe, OH. Witness the spectacular reenactment of the life and death of the great Shawnee leader Tecumseh, held in the large, tiered amphitheater nestled in the hardwood forest of Sugarloaf Mountain. Take a backstage tour, visit the Prehistoric Museum and dine in the open-air Tecumseh Restaurant Terrace. Est attendance: 50,000. For info: Tecumseh!, PO Box 73, Chillicothe, OH 45601-0073. Phone toll-free: (866) 775-0700. Fax: (740) 775-4349. E-mail: tecumseh@bright.net. Web: www.tecumsehdrama.com.

June 2014

S	M	T	W	T	F	S
1	2	3	4	5	6	7
8	9	10	11	12	13	14
15	16	17	18	19	20	21
22	23	24	25	26	27	28
29	30					

TEXAS FOLKLIFE FESTIVAL. June 6–8. San Antonio, TX. Provides an entertaining and historic understanding of the crafts, art, food, music, history and heritage of the more than 40 different cultures and ethnic groups that settled and developed the state of Texas. Est attendance: 50,000. For info: Texas Folklife Festival, Institute of Texan Cultures, 801 E Cesar E. Chavez Blvd, San Antonio, TX 78205-3296. Phone: (210) 458-2224. Fax: (210) 458-2113. Web: www.texasfolklifefestival.org.

"20/20" TV PREMIERE: ANNIVERSARY. June 6, 1978. An hourly newsmagazine developed by ABC to compete with CBS's "60 Minutes." Its original hosts, Harold Hayes and Robert Hughes, were cut after the first show and replaced by Hugh Downs. Barbara Walters became coanchor in 1984. The show consisted of investigative and background reports. Contributors to the show have included Tom Jarriel, Sylvia Chase, Geraldo Rivera, Thomas Hoving, John Stossel, Lynn Sherr and Stone Phillips.

BIRTHDAYS TODAY

Sandra Bernhard, 59, actress (*The King of Comedy*), performer ("I'm Still Here . . . Damn It!"), born Flint, MI, June 6, 1955.

Gary U.S. Bonds, 75, singer, songwriter, born Gary Anderson at Jacksonville, FL, June 6, 1939.

Bjorn Borg, 58, Hall of Fame tennis player, born Sodertalje, Sweden, June 6, 1956.

Marian Wright Edelman, 75, president of the Children's Defense Fund, civil rights activist, born Bennettsville, SC, June 6, 1939.

Harvey Fierstein, 60, actor/playwright (Tonys for *Hairspray, La Cage aux Folles* and *Torch Song Trilogy*), born Brooklyn, NY, June 6, 1954.

Kenny G, 58, saxophone player, born Kenny Gorelick at Seattle, WA, June 6, 1956.

Paul Giamatti, 47, actor ("John Adams," *Sideways, American Splendor*), born New York, NY, June 6, 1967.

Amanda Pays, 55, actress ("Max Headroom," *Exposure*), born Berkshire, England, June 6, 1959.

Billie Whitelaw, 82, actress (*The Krays, The Dressmaker, The Omen, Happy Days, Rockabye*), born Coventry, England, June 6, 1932.

June 7 — Saturday

DAY 158 **207 REMAINING**

APGAR, VIRGINIA: BIRTH ANNIVERSARY. June 7, 1909. Dr. Apgar developed the simple assessment method that permits doctors and nurses to evaluate newborns while they are still in the delivery room to identify those in need of immediate medical care. The Apgar score was first published in 1953, and the Perinatal Section of the American Academy of Pediatrics is named for Dr. Apgar. Born at Westfield, NJ, Apgar died Aug 7, 1974, at New York, NY.

BELMONT STAKES. June 7. Belmont Park, NY. 146th annual. Final race of the "Triple Crown" was inaugurated in 1867. Traditionally run on the fifth Saturday after Kentucky Derby (third Saturday after Preakness). Est attendance: 60,000. For info: Press Office, New York Racing Assn, PO Box 90, Jamaica, NY 11417. Phone: (718) 641-4700. Web: www.nyra.com.

BOONE DAY. June 7. Each year on June 7, the Kentucky Historical Society celebrates the anniversary of the day in 1767 when Daniel Boone, America's most famous frontiersman, reportedly first sighted the land that would become Kentucky. The June 7 date is taken from the book *The Discovery, Settlement and Present State of Kentucky*, by John Filson, published in 1784, with an appendix titled "The Adventures of Colonel Daniel Boone." The information in the appendix supposedly originated with Boone, although Filson is the actual author. The work is not considered completely reliable by historians.

BRADDOCK, JAMES: BIRTH ANNIVERSARY. June 7, 1906. James Walter Braddock, boxer, born at New York, NY. Braddock rose from the ranks of undistinguished fighters to win three key bouts in 1934 and 1935 that propelled him to a match for the heavyweight title. He upset the defending champion, Max Baer, on June 13, 1935, remained inactive for two years and then lost his first title defense to Joe Louis. Died at North Bergen, NJ, Nov 29, 1974.

BRUMMELL, GEORGE BRYAN "BEAU": BIRTH ANNIVERSARY. June 7, 1778. Born at London, England, Beau Brummell was, early in his life, a popular English men's fashion leader, the "arbiter elegantarium" of taste in dress. His extravagance and lack of tact (it was he who reportedly said—indicating the Prince of Wales, later George IV—"Who's your fat friend?") led him from wealth and popularity to poverty and disrepute. Once imprisoned for debt, he became careless of dress and personal appearance. He died in a charitable asylum at Caen, France, Mar 30, 1840.

CAPITOL HILL PEOPLE'S FAIR. June 7–8. Civic Center Park, Denver, CO. More than 500 arts and crafts and other exhibit booths and live entertainment featuring local talent on six stages. Est attendance: 250,000. For info: Capitol Hill United Neighborhoods, 1290 Williams St, Ste 102, Denver, CO 80218-2657. Phone: (303) 830-1651. Fax: (303) 830-1782. E-mail: andreafurness@chundenver.org. Web: www.chundenver.org.

DENMARK: EEL FESTIVAL. June 7–8. Jyllinge (near Roskilde). Festival celebrated since 1968. Every restaurant and pub in town serves delicious fried eel. Other entertainments include theater, sports, tattoo bands, sailing competitions, flea markets and fireworks. Annually, the first weekend in June.

DO-DAH PARADE. June 7 (tentative). Kalamazoo, MI. "Salute to Silliness"—the official parody of anything and everything. Since 1981 offbeat entries have included a precision grill team (complete with spatulas) and a herbie curbie brigade. Sponsored by Downtown Kalamazoo, Inc, and WKFR Radio. Est attendance: 40,000. For info: Downtown Kalamazoo, Inc, 141 E Michigan Ave, Ste 501, Kalamazoo, MI 49007. Phone: (269) 344-0795. Fax: (269) 344-0898. E-mail: dki@dki.org. Web: www.downtownkalamazoo.org.

GAUGUIN, (EUGENE HENRI) PAUL: BIRTH ANNIVERSARY. June 7, 1848. French painter born at Paris, France. Formerly a stockbroker, he became a painter in his middle age and three years later renounced his life at Paris to move to Tahiti. He is remembered best for his broad, flat tones and bold colors. Gauguin died May 8, 1903, at Atoana on the island of Hiva Oa in the Marquesas.

HORSERADISH FESTIVAL. June 7–8. Collinsville, IL. Join in the fun at the horseradish capital of the world. "Root Derby" (build a race car out of a horseradish root and win prizes), races, food, great bands and more. For info: Collinsville Chamber of Commerce, 221 W Main St, Collinsville, IL 62234. Phone: (618) 344-2884. E-mail: director@discovercollinsville.com.

INTERNATIONAL CLOTHESLINE WEEK. June 7–14. The public is encouraged to save energy by hanging clothes to dry instead of using their electric dryers. Annually, the week beginning the first Saturday in June, Saturday to Saturday. For info: Gary Drisdelle. E-mail: gdrisdelle@rogers.com. Web: www.hangtodry.com.

MALAYSIA: HEAD OF STATE'S OFFICIAL BIRTHDAY. June 7. National holiday. The first Saturday in June.

MALTA: NATIONAL DAY. June 7. National day, or (in Maltese) Sette Giugno.

MARITIME GIG FESTIVAL. June 7–8. Gig Harbor, WA. This annual family event begins with the parade route that follows the edge of the beautiful harbor with the marina and view of majestic Mount Rainier. The event is jam-packed with family entertainment, family fun run, crafts and games for children, foods of every description, open markets, live music, arts and fine crafts. Annually, the first Saturday and Sunday in June. Est attendance: 20,000. For info: Gig Harbor Chamber of Commerce, PO Box 102, Gig Harbor, WA 98335. Phone: (253) 851-6865 or (800) 359-8804. E-mail: info@gigharborchamber.com. Web: www.maritimegig.com.

MARTIN, DEAN: BIRTH ANNIVERSARY. June 7, 1917. Actor/singer Dean Martin was born Dino Paul Crocetti, at Steubenville, OH. Martin's career was barely moving in 1946, when he met Jerry Lewis. Together they formed an unforgettable comedy act that carried them to dizzying heights of success. When the team broke up, Martin found continued success as a singer as well as a Hollywood film star. He died Dec 25, 1995, at Beverly Hills, CA.

NATIONAL TRAILS DAY. June 7. National Trails Day celebrates trails and the volunteers who maintain them. The first Saturday of every June, hundreds of trail organizations, agencies and businesses across the country host thousands of outdoor events, including new trail dedications, workshops, educational exhibits, equestrian and mountain bike rides, boat paddling, trail maintenance projects and, as always, hikes on backcountry trails on America's lands. For info: American Hiking Society, 1422 Fenwick Ln, Silver Spring, MD 20910. Phone: (800) 972-8608. Web: www.americanhiking.org.

PEDDLER'S VILLAGE FINE ART & CONTEMPORARY CRAFTS SHOW. June 7–8. Lahaska, PA. Juried competition of paintings, prints, photography and more created by fine artists, plus contemporary crafts. Hands-on art activities for children. Shops offer various art-related events. Live music, face painting and balloons. Free admission. Est attendance: 12,000. For info: Peddler's Village, Routes 202 and 263, Lahaska, PA 18931. Phone: (215) 794-4000. Fax: (215) 794-4001. E-mail: info@peddlersvillage.com. Web: www.peddlersvillage.com.

SOUTH DAKOTA OUTDOOR EXPO. June 7–8. South Dakota State Fairgrounds, Huron, SD. The SD Outdoor Expo is a statewide event with a hands-on educational focus. Its purpose is to introduce thousands of families and children to outdoor activities. Through interactive exhibits and activities, it teaches an understanding and appreciation for conservation and outdoor recreation and its importance of preserving our outdoor recreation heritage. Annually, the weekend before Father's Day. Est attendance: 5,000. For info: Candi Hettinger, South Dakota Outdoor Expo, 890 3rd St SW, Huron, SD 57350. Phone: (605) 353-7354. Fax: (605) 353-7348. Web: www.sdoutdoorexpo.com.

STRAWBERRY FESTIVAL. June 7. Vaile Mansion, Independence, MO. Outdoor Victorian-type festival featuring strawberry treats, crafts, antiques, children's activities, carriage rides, flea market and entertainment. Annually, first Saturday in June. Est attendance: 900. For info: Cori Day, Tourism Dir, 111 E Maple, Independence, MO 64050. Phone: (816) 325-7111. Fax: (816) 325-7932. Web: www.visitindependence.com.

SUPREME COURT STRIKES DOWN CONNECTICUT LAW BANNING CONTRACEPTION: ANNIVERSARY. June 7, 1965. In *Griswold v Connecticut*, the Supreme Court guaranteed the right to privacy, including the freedom from government intrusion into matters of birth control.

TANDY, JESSICA: BIRTH ANNIVERSARY. June 7, 1909. Born at London, England, Tandy was an acclaimed stage actress who often collaborated with her husband, Hume Cronyn. She originated the role of Blanche DuBois in Tennessee Williams's *A Streetcar Named Desire* (1947) and was awarded a Tony. Her other Tony Awards came for her work in *The Gin Game* (1977) and *Foxfire* (1982). Also a frequent film actress, she won an Academy Award for her leading role in *Driving Miss Daisy* (1989). She continued to work up until her death on Sept 11, 1994, at Easton, CT.

TURTLE RACES. June 7. Knights of Columbus, Danville, IL. 50th annual. More than 100 turtles compete in races throughout the day. Concessions available. Food and fun. Proceeds help people in the area with disabilities. Annually, the first Saturday in June. Est attendance: 1,000. For info: Michael Puhr, President, Turtle Club, 512 W Woodlawn, Danville, IL 61832. Phone: (217) 443-6034 or (217) 260-1983. E-mail: michaelpuhr@sbcglobal.net.

VCR INTRODUCED: ANNIVERSARY. June 7, 1975. The Sony Corporation released its videocassette recorder, the Betamax, which sold for $995. Eventually, another VCR format, VHS, proved more successful and Sony stopped making the Betamax.

XTERRA RICHMOND TRAIL RUNS. June 7. Richmond, VA. The XTERRA Trail Run Series boasts more than 80 events across the country with runs ranging from 5k to 50k. These extreme, off-road trail runs give runners the chance to prove their skills against a variety of terrain. From calf-burning hills to slippery, mud-covered paths, athletes face the ultimate test of endurance. Includes an off-road, half-marathon distance trail run and an off-road, 10k adventure run. For info: Emily McIlvaine, XTERRA/TEAM Unlimited, 720 Iwilei Road #290, Honolulu, HI 96817. Phone: 877-XTERRA-1. E-mail: emily@xterraplanet.com. Web: www.xterraplanet.com.

BIRTHDAYS TODAY

Roberto Alagna, 51, opera singer, born Clichy-sous-Bois, Seine-Saint-Denis, France, June 7, 1963.

Michael Cera, 26, actor (*Superbad, Juno,* "Arrested Development"), born Brompton, ON, Canada, June 7, 1988.

Louise Erdrich, 60, author (*Love Medicine, The Beet Queen*), born Little Falls, MN, June 7, 1954.

Bear Grylls, 40, television personality ("Man vs Wild"), author, born Isle of Wight, England, June 7, 1974.

Bill Hader, 36, comedian, actor ("Saturday Night Live," *Adventureland*), born Tulsa, OK, June 7, 1978.

Allen Iverson, 39, basketball player, born Hampton, VA, June 7, 1975.

Jenny Jones, 68, talk show host, born London, ON, Canada, June 7, 1946.

Tom Jones, 74, singer, born Thomas Woodward at Pontypridd, Wales, June 7, 1940.

Anna Kournikova, 33, tennis player, born Moscow, Russia, June 7, 1981.

Bill Kreutzmann, Jr, 68, drummer, singer, cofounder of The Grateful Dead, born Palo Alto, CA, June 7, 1946.

Mike Modano, 44, former hockey player, born Livonia, MI, June 7, 1970.

Liam Neeson, 62, actor (*Taken, Kinsey, Ethan Frome, Schindler's List*), born Ballymena, Northern Ireland, June 7, 1952.

Orhan Pamuk, 62, author, born Istanbul, Turkey, June 7, 1952.

Mike Pence, 55, Governor of Indiana (R), born Columbus, IN, June 7, 1959.

Prince, 56, musician, singer, born Prince Rogers Nelson at Minneapolis, MN, June 7, 1958.

John Napier Turner, 85, 17th prime minister of Canada (1984), born Richmond, Surrey, England, June 7, 1929.

June 2014	S	M	T	W	T	F	S
	1	2	3	4	5	6	7
	8	9	10	11	12	13	14
	15	16	17	18	19	20	21
	22	23	24	25	26	27	28
	29	30					

June 8 — Sunday

DAY 159 **206 REMAINING**

AMERICAN HEROINE REWARDED: ANNIVERSARY. June 8, 1697. On Mar 16, 1697, in an attack on Haverhill, MA, Indians captured Hannah Duston and killed her baby, also killing or capturing 39 others. After being taken to an Indian camp, she escaped on Apr 29 after killing 10 Indians with a tomahawk and scalping them as proof of her deed. On June 8 her husband was awarded, on her behalf, the sum of 25 pounds for her heroic efforts, the first public award to a woman in America.

ATTACK ON THE USS *LIBERTY*: ANNIVERSARY. June 8, 1967. At 2 PM local time, the unescorted US intelligence ship USS *Liberty*, sailing in international waters off the Egyptian coast, was attacked without warning by Israeli jet planes and three Israeli torpedo boats. It was strafed and hit repeatedly by rockets, cannon, napalm and finally a torpedo. Out of a crew of 294 Americans, there were 34 dead and 171 wounded. Israel apologized, claiming mistaken identity, but surviving crew members charged that it was a deliberate attack by Israel and cover-up by US authorities.

BELGIUM: MILITARY MUSIC FESTIVAL. June 8. Tournai. Traditional cultural observance. Annually, the second Sunday in June.

BILL OF RIGHTS PROPOSED: 225th ANNIVERSARY. June 8, 1789. The Bill of Rights, which led to the first 10 amendments to the US Constitution, was first proposed by James Madison.

CHILDREN'S DAY IN MASSACHUSETTS. June 8. Annually, the second Sunday in June. The governor proclaims this day each year.

CHILDREN'S SUNDAY. June 8. Traditionally the second Sunday in June is observed as Children's Sunday in many Christian churches.

COCHISE: DEATH ANNIVERSARY. June 8, 1874. Born around 1810 in northern Mexico (now Arizona), Cochise was a fierce and courageous leader of the Chiricachua Apache. As a chief, Cochise maintained a delicate peace with Mexican and American authorities, but in 1861, American military murdered his brother and Cochise launched the Apache Wars, which lasted until 1872. He died near his stronghold in southeastern Arizona.

CRICK, FRANCIS: BIRTH ANNIVERSARY. June 8, 1916. Discoverer with James Watson of the structure of DNA in 1953. Born at Northampton, England, Crick died at San Diego, CA, July 28, 2004.

HOMESTEAD DAYS®. June 8–15. Beatrice, NE. This community-wide celebration recognizes the importance of the Homestead Act of 1862 to the settlement of Nebraska. Entertainment, parades and special museum exhibits. Est attendance: 30,000. For info: Homestead Days, Beatrice Area Chamber of Commerce, 218 N 5th St, Beatrice, NE 68310. Phone: (402) 223-2338 or (800) 755-7745. E-mail: info@beatricechamber.com. Web: www.beatricechamber.com.

ICELAND: LAKI VOLCANO ERUPTION: ANNIVERSARY. June 8, 1783. One of the most violent and important volcanic eruptions of recorded history began on this date. Laki, or Skafta, volcano in southern Iceland continued erupting for eight months, expelling an estimated 4½ cubic miles of lava, ultimately causing a famine and the deaths of nearly 10,000 persons. Acid rain reached Western Europe, and other climatic and atmospheric changes were worldwide. English naturalist Gilbert White described some of the "horrible phenomena" of the summer of 1783, including the "peculiar haze, or smokey fog . . . Unlike anything known within the memory of man." The effects of this volcanic eruption and its possible long-term consequences are still being studied by scientists. See also: "White, Gilbert: Birth Anniversary" (July 18).

McKINLEY, IDA SAXTON: BIRTH ANNIVERSARY. June 8, 1847. Wife of William McKinley, 25th president of the US, born at Canton, OH. Died at Canton, OH, May 26, 1907.

✦NATIONAL FLAG WEEK. June 8–14. Presidential Proclamation issued each year since 1966 for the week including June 14 (PL 89–443 of June 9, 1966). In addition, the president often calls upon the American people to participate in public ceremonies in which the Pledge of Allegiance is recited.

ORTHODOX PENTECOST. June 8. Observed by Eastern Orthodox churches.

PENTECOST. June 8. The Christian feast of Pentecost commemorates the descent of the Holy Spirit unto the Apostles, 50 days after Easter. Observed on the seventh Sunday after Easter. Recognized since the third century. See also: "Whitsunday" (below).

RACE UNITY DAY. June 8. Baha'i-sponsored observance promoting racial harmony and understanding and the essential unity of humanity. Annually, the second Sunday in June. Established in 1957 by the Baha'is of the US. For info: Baha'is of the US, Office of Communications, 1233 Central St, Evanston, IL 60201. Phone: (847) 733-3487. Fax: (847) 733-3578. E-mail: ooc@usbnc.org. Web: www.bahai.us.

SPACE MILESTONE: *VENERA 9* AND *10* (USSR). June 8 and 14, 1975. Launched on these dates, unmanned exploration vehicles landed on Venus Oct 22 and 25, respectively. Sent first pictures ever transmitted from Venus, atmospheric analysis and other data.

UNITED NATIONS: WORLD OCEANS DAY. June 8. The UN General Assembly has designated June 8 annually as World Oceans Day (Resolution 63/111 of Dec 8, 2008). The Assembly noted that ecosystem approaches to ocean management should be focused on managing human activities in order to maintain and, where needed, restore ecosystem health. The aim would be to sustain goods and environmental services, provide social and economic benefits for food security, sustain livelihoods in support of international development goals and conserve marine biodiversity. For info: United Nations, Dept of Public Info, New York, NY 10017. Web: www.un.org.

UPSY DAISY DAY. June 8. A day to remind people to get up gloriously, gratefully and gleefully each morning. For info: Stephanie West Allen, 1376 S Wyandot St, Denver, CO 80223. Phone: (303) 935-8866. E-mail: stephanie@westallen.com.

WHITE, BYRON RAYMOND: BIRTH ANNIVERSARY. June 8, 1917. One of the longest-serving justices of the Supreme Court of the US, Byron White was born at Fort Collins, CO. He was a football star in college (College Football Hall of Fame) and in the National Football League, as well as an academic standout: he was a Rhodes Scholar among other honors. A graduate of Yale Law School, White was a successful lawyer and director of the Justice Department before being nominated by President Kennedy for the highest court on Apr 3, 1962. White took the oath of office Apr 16, 1962, and served 31 years before retiring in 1993. He died on April 15, 2002, at Denver, CO.

WHITSUNDAY. June 8. Whitsunday, the seventh Sunday after Easter, is a popular time for baptism. "White Sunday" is named for the white garments formerly worn by the candidates for baptism and occurs at the Christian feast of Pentecost. See also: "Pentecost" (above).

WORLD OCEANS DAY. June 8. World Oceans Day was first proposed in 1992 by Canada at the Earth Summit in Rio de Janeiro, Brazil. Officially designated by the United Nations in 2008, this day is recognized by an increasing number of countries as an annual opportunity to celebrate our world ocean and our personal connection to the sea. The Ocean Project, working closely with the World Ocean Network, helps to coordinate events and activities with aquariums, zoos, museums, conservation organizations, universities, schools and businesses. Annually, June 8. For info: The Ocean Project, PO Box 2506, Providence, RI 02906. Phone: (401) 709-4071. E-mail: aisakower@theoceanproject.org. Web: www.worldoceansday.org.

WRIGHT, FRANK LLOYD: BIRTH ANNIVERSARY. June 8, 1867. American architect born at Richland Center, WI. In his autobiography Wright wrote: "No house should ever be *on* any hill or on anything. It should be *of* the hill, belonging to it, so hill and house could live together each the happier for the other." Wright died at Phoenix, AZ, Apr 9, 1959.

WYTHE, GEORGE: DEATH ANNIVERSARY. June 8, 1806. Signer of the Declaration of Independence. Born at Elizabeth County, VA, about 1726 (exact date unknown). Died at Richmond, VA.

BIRTHDAYS TODAY

Scott Adams, 57, cartoonist ("Dilbert"), born Windham, NY, June 8, 1957.

Kathy Baker, 64, actress ("Picket Fences," *The Right Stuff*), born Midland, TX, June 8, 1950.

Tim Berners-Lee, 59, inventor of the World Wide Web, born London, England, June 8, 1955.

Barbara Pierce Bush, 89, former first lady, wife of George H.W. Bush, 41st president of the US, born Rye, NY, June 8, 1925.

Bernie Casey, 75, former football player, actor (*I'm Gonna Git You Sucka!*), born Wyco, WV, June 8, 1939.

Kim Clijsters, 31, tennis player, born Bilzen, Belgium, June 8, 1983.

James Darren, 78, singer, actor (*Gidget*), born Philadelphia, PA, June 8, 1936.

Lindsay Davenport, 38, former tennis player, sportscaster, born Palos Verdes, CA, June 8, 1976.

Griffin Dunne, 59, actor (*After Hours, An American Werewolf in London*), director, producer, born New York, NY, June 8, 1955.

Gabrielle Giffords, 44, former US congresswoman (R, Arizona), born Tucson, AZ, June 8, 1970.

Julianna Margulies, 48, actress ("The Good Wife," "ER"), born Spring Valley, NY, June 8, 1966.

Sara Paretsky, 67, author (*Killing Orders, Burn Marks*), born Ames, IA, June 8, 1947.

Joan Rivers, 77, comedienne, television personality ("Fashion Police"), born New York, NY, June 8, 1937.

Boz Scaggs, 70, singer, musician, songwriter (*Silk Degrees, Middle Man*), born Dallas, TX, June 8, 1944.

Nancy Sinatra, 74, singer, born Jersey City, NJ, June 8, 1940.

Jerry Stiller, 85, comedian, actor (*Hairspray*, "Seinfeld," "The King of Queens"), born Brooklyn, NY, June 8, 1929.

Keenen Ivory Wayans, 56, actor ("In Living Color"), born New York, NY, June 8, 1958.

Andrew Weil, MD, 72, physician and writer on natural healing, born Philadelphia, PA, June 8, 1942.

Kanye West, 37, singer, producer, born Atlanta, GA, June 8, 1977.

June 9 — Monday

DAY 160 **205 REMAINING**

CUMMINGS, ROBERT: BIRTH ANNIVERSARY. June 9, 1908. American actor Robert Cummings was born Charles Clarence Robert Orville Cummings at Joplin, MO. His best-known role was in the film *Dial M for Murder* (1954). He won an Emmy for his role in the television version of *Twelve Angry Men* (1954) and starred in the popular comedy "The Bob Cummings Show" (1955–59). He died Dec 2, 1990, at Woodland Hills, CA.

DONALD DUCK: 80th BIRTHDAY. June 9, 1934. Donald Duck made his screen debut on this date with the release of "The Wise Little Hen," a short film in the Disney series of "Silly Symphonies."

ENGLAND: DICING FOR BIBLES. June 9. An old Whitmonday ceremony at All Saints Church, St. Ives, Huntingdonshire. A bequest (in 1675) with the intent of providing Bibles for poor children of the parish required winning them at a dice game played in the church. In recent years the dicing has been moved from the altar to a "more suitable" place. Six Bibles are given on Whitmonday each year.

HONG KONG: LEASE SIGNING ANNIVERSARY. June 9, 1898. Hong Kong, consisting of about 400 square miles (islands and mainland) with more than five million persons, was administered as a British Crown Colony after a 99-year lease was signed on June 9, 1898. In 1997 Hong Kong's sovereignty reverted to the People's Republic of China.

JORDAN: ACCESSION DAY. June 9. National holiday. Commemorates the accession to the throne of King Abdullah II in 1999, following the death of his father, King Hussein.

KUTNER, LUIS: BIRTH ANNIVERSARY. June 9, 1908. Human rights attorney Luis Kutner was born at Chicago, IL. Responsible for the release of many unjustly confined prisoners, he came to be known as "The Springman." He helped free Hungarian Cardinal Josef Mindszenty, poet Ezra Pound and former Congo president Moise Tshombe. He was the author of the living will and founded the World Habeas Corpus. Kutner was nominated nine times for the Nobel Peace Prize. He died Mar 1, 1993, at Chicago, IL.

LOLOMA, CHARLES: BIRTH ANNIVERSARY. June 9, 1921. Charles Loloma was a major influence on modern Native American art and was famous for changing the look of American Indian jewelry. A painter, sculptor and potter, he was best known for his jewelry, which broke tradition with previous Indian styles using materials such as coral, fossilized ivory, pearls and diamonds. Loloma was born at Hotevilla on the Hopi Indian Reservation and died June 9, 1991, at Scottsdale, AZ.

MCNAMARA, ROBERT: BIRTH ANNIVERSARY. June 9, 1916. Former US Secretary of Defense (1961–68) and chief architect of the Vietnam War, McNamara's handling of the conflict in Vietnam made him a much-maligned public figure. Born at San Francisco, CA, McNamara graduated from the Harvard Business School and was president of the Ford Motor Co before serving under presidents Kennedy and Johnson. Years later, in the Oscar-winning documentary *The Fog of War* (2003) and elsewhere, McNamara publicly acknowledged his failures in judgment and execution with regard to Vietnam. He died July 6, 2009, at Washington, DC.

June 2014	S	M	T	W	T	F	S
	1	2	3	4	5	6	7
	8	9	10	11	12	13	14
	15	16	17	18	19	20	21
	22	23	24	25	26	27	28
	29	30					

NATIONAL AUTOMOTIVE SERVICE PROFESSIONALS WEEK. June 9–15. Sponsored by the National Institute for Automotive Service Excellence (ASE), which was incorporated on June 12, 1972. ASE was founded to improve the quality of automotive service through voluntary testing and certification of service professionals. The goal of this week is to recognize automotive service professionals nationwide for their contribution to keeping America's cars and trucks running. The nonprofit organization also serves as an information source for professionals and consumers about automotive repair and related topics. For info: Tony Molla, 101 Blue Seal Dr, Leesburg, VA 20175. Phone: (703) 669-6600. Fax: (703) 669-6127. E-mail: tmolla@ase.com. Web: www.ase.com.

PAUL, LES: BIRTH ANNIVERSARY. June 9, 1915. Legendary American musician, born at Waukesha, WI, who designed one of the first solid-body electric guitars. Though best known for the guitars that bear his name, Paul also made groundbreaking contributions in guitar effects and recording techniques (such as multitrack recording). A performer into his 90s, Paul died Aug 13, 2009, at the age of 94 at White Plains, NY.

PAYNE, JOHN HOWARD: BIRTH ANNIVERSARY. June 9, 1791. American author, actor and diplomat, born at New York, NY, and died at Tunis, Apr 9, 1852. Author of opera libretto (*Clari, or The Maid of Milan*) that contained the song "Home, Sweet Home."

PORTER, COLE: BIRTH ANNIVERSARY. June 9, 1891. Cole Porter published his first song, "The Bobolink Waltz," at the age of 10. His career as a composer and lyricist for Broadway was launched in 1928 when five of his songs were used in the musical play *Let's Do It.* His prolific contributions to the Broadway stage include *Fifty Million Frenchmen, Wake Up and Dream, The Gay Divorcée, Anything Goes, Leave It to Me, Du Barry Was a Lady, Something for the Boys, Kiss Me Kate, Can Can* and *Silk Stockings.* Porter was born at Peru, IN, and died at Santa Monica, CA, Oct 15, 1964.

QUEEN'S OFFICIAL BIRTHDAY. June 9. A holiday in Australia (except for Western Australia), Belize, Cayman Islands, Fiji and Papua New Guinea on the second Monday in June. (In New Zealand and Tuvalu it is commemorated on the first Monday in June.) Celebrating Queen Elizabeth II's "official" birthday, not the day she was actually born (which is Apr 21).

STEPHENSON, GEORGE: BIRTH ANNIVERSARY. June 9, 1781. English inventor, developer of the steam locomotive, born near Newcastle, England. Died near Chesterfield, England, Aug 12, 1848.

THAYER, SYLVANUS: BIRTH ANNIVERSARY. June 9, 1785. A military engineer and educator, born at Braintree, MA. He was appointed superintendent of West Point at 32 and became known as the "Father of the Military Academy." Thayer died at Braintree, MA, Sept 7, 1872.

WHITMONDAY. June 9. The day after Whitsunday is observed as a public holiday in some countries.

BIRTHDAYS TODAY

Tedy Bruschi, 41, sportscaster, former football player, born San Francisco, CA, June 9, 1973.

Patricia Cornwell, 58, author (*All That Remains, Postmortem*), born Miami, FL, June 9, 1956.

Johnny Depp, 51, actor (*Pirates of the Caribbean* films, *The Lone Ranger, Alice in Wonderland, Sweeney Todd, Edward Scissorhands*), born Owensboro, KY, June 9, 1963.

Michael J. Fox, 53, actor ("Family Ties," "Spin City," *Back to the Future* films), born Edmonton, AB, Canada, June 9, 1961.

Marvin Kalb, 84, educator, journalist, born New York, NY, June 9, 1930.

Miroslav Klose, 36, soccer player, born Opole, Poland, June 9, 1978.

Jackie Mason, 80, comedian ("Chicken Soup," *The World According to Me*), born Yacov Moshe Maza at Sheboygan, WI, June 9, 1934.

Dave Parker, 63, former baseball player, born Calhoun, MS, June 9, 1951.

Natalie Portman, 33, actress (Oscar for *Black Swan*; *Thor, Closer*), born Natalie Hershlag at Jerusalem, Israel, June 9, 1981.

Ashley Postell, 28, former gymnast, born Cheverly, MD, June 9, 1986.

Gloria Reuben, 50, actress ("ER"), born Toronto, ON, Canada, June 9, 1964.

Peja Stojakovic, 37, basketball player, born Predrag Stojakovic at Belgrade, Yugoslavia (now Serbia), June 9, 1977.

Dick Vitale, 75, sportscaster, born East Rutherford, NJ, June 9, 1939.

Mae Whitman, 26, actress ("Arrested Development," "Parenthood," *One Fine Day*), born Los Angeles, CA, June 9, 1988.

June 10 — Tuesday

DAY 161 **204 REMAINING**

ALCOHOLICS ANONYMOUS FOUNDED: ANNIVERSARY. June 10, 1935. On this day at Akron, OH, Dr. Robert Smith completed his first day of permanent sobriety. "Doctor Bob" and William G. Wilson are considered to have founded Alcoholics Anonymous on that day.

BALLPOINT PEN PATENTED: ANNIVERSARY. June 10, 1943. Hungarian Laszlo Biro patented the ballpoint pen, which he had been developing since the 1930s. He was living in Argentina, where he had gone to escape the Nazis. In many languages, the word for ballpoint pen is *biro*.

BELLOW, SAUL: BIRTH ANNIVERSARY. June 10, 1915. Born at Lachine, Canada, Bellow would become one of America's great postwar authors, examining the urban antiheroes at war with the society they live in. His novels include *The Adventures of Augie March* (1953), *Herzog* (1964) and *Mr Sammler's Planet* (1970). Garnered numerous National Book Awards as well as a Pulitzer. Winner of the Nobel Prize for Literature in 1976. Died at Brookline, MA, Apr 5, 2005.

BURLINGTON STEAMBOAT DAYS/AMERICAN MUSIC FESTIVAL. June 10–15. Mississippi Riverfront at Port of Burlington, IA. 52nd annual. Weeklong event offers community and visitors a chance to enjoy top-name entertainment and a carnival setting. Est attendance: 100,000. For info: Steamboat Days, PO Box 271, Burlington, IA 52601. Phone: (319) 754-4334. Fax: (319) 752-1299. E-mail: stephanie@steamboatdays.com. Web: www.steamboatdays.com.

CONGO (BRAZZAVILLE): DAY OF NATIONAL RECONCILIATION. June 10. National holiday. Commemorates official conference in 1991.

CZECHOSLOVAKIA: RAPE OF LIDICE: ANNIVERSARY. June 10, 1942. Nazi German troops executed, by shooting, all male inhabitants of the Czechoslovakian village of Lidice (total population about 500 persons), burned every house and deported the women and children to Germany for "reeducation." (In New Jersey, June 10 is observed as Lidice Memorial Day.)

FIRST MINT IN AMERICA: ANNIVERSARY. June 10, 1652. In defiance of English colonial law, John Hull, a silversmith, established the first mint in America. The first coin issued was the Pine Tree Shilling, designed by Hull.

GARLAND, JUDY: BIRTH ANNIVERSARY. June 10, 1922. American actress and singer born Frances Gumm at Grand Rapids, MN. While Garland played in many films and toured widely as a singer, she is probably most remembered for her portrayal of Dorothy Gale in the now-classic *The Wizard of Oz*. Died June 22, 1969, at London, England.

GERMANY: WALDCHESTAG (FOREST DAY). June 10. Frankfurt. For centuries Frankfurters have spent the Tuesday after Whitsunday in their city forest (Am Oberforsthaus). See also: "Whitsunday" (June 8).

JORDAN: GREAT ARAB REVOLT AND ARMY DAY. June 10. National holiday. Commemorates the beginning of the Great Arab Revolt in 1916.

McDANIEL, HATTIE: BIRTH ANNIVERSARY. June 10, 1895. Hattie McDaniel was the first African American to win an Academy Award, winning it in 1940 for her role in the 1939 film *Gone with the Wind*. Her career spanned radio and vaudeville in addition to her screen roles in *Judge Priest, The Little Colonel, Showboat* and *Saratoga*, among others. She was born at Wichita, KS (some sources say 1889 or 1892), and died Oct 26, 1952, at Los Angeles, CA.

MUSEUM MILE FESTIVAL. June 10. New York, NY. 36th annual. On the second Tuesday in June each year, ten of the country's finest museums—all ones that call Fifth Avenue home—collectively open their doors from 6 PM to 9 PM for free to visitors for a mile-long block party and visual art celebration. Festivities begin at the steps of the landmark National Academy Museum building at 5:45 PM. Participating museums: National Academy Museum, Museum of the City of New York, Metropolitan Museum of Art, Museum for African Art, El Museo del Barrio New York, The Jewish Museum, Cooper-Hewitt, Guggenheim, Neue Galerie and Goethe Institute. Twenty-three car-free blocks, family activities, art in the street, live music. Rain or shine. For info: Museum Mile Festival, Culture Partners. E-mail: robin@museummilefestival.org. Web: www.museummilefestival.org.

PETIT JEAN ANTIQUE AUTO SHOW AND SWAP MEET. June 10–14. Petit Jean Mountain, Morrilton, AR. 56th annual show and meet with more than 125 antique and classic cars competing for awards, from turn-of-the-century to 25-year-old models. More than 1,500 vendor spaces filled with antique cars, parts and related items. Also, arts and crafts. Est attendance: 85,000. For info: Alan Hoelzeman, Museum of Automobiles, 8 Jones Ln, Morrilton, AR 72110. Phone: (501) 727-5427. E-mail: info@motaa.com. Web: www.motaa.com.

PORTUGAL: DAY OF PORTUGAL. June 10. National holiday. Anniversary of the death in 1580 of Portugal's national poet, Luis Vas de Camoes (Camoens), born in 1524 (exact date unknown) at either Lisbon or Coimbra. Died at Lisbon, Portugal.

SENDAK, MAURICE: BIRTH ANNIVERSARY. June 10, 1928. Author and illustrator born at Brooklyn, NY. In a career spanning more than half a century, Sendak wrote and illustrated many notable children's books, including *In the Night Kitchen, Kenny's Window*, and his most famous work, *Where the Wild Things Are*. Widely regarded as the first picture book artist to deal openly with the children's emotions, Sendak received numerous awards for his work, notably the Caldecott Medal (1964), the Hans Christian Andersen Award (1970) and the Laura Ingalls Wilder Medal (1983). He died May 8, 2012, at Danbury, CT.

BIRTHDAYS TODAY

F. Lee Bailey, 81, lawyer, born Waltham, MA, June 10, 1933.

John Edwards, 61, former US senator (D, North Carolina), born Seneca, SC, June 10, 1953.

Linda Evangelista, 49, model, born St. Catharines, ON, Canada, June 10, 1965.

Jeff Greenfield, 71, author, journalist, born New York, NY, June 10, 1943.

Nat Hentoff, 89, music critic, journalist, born Boston, MA, June 10, 1925.

Elizabeth Hurley, 49, model, actress (*Austin Powers: International Man of Mystery*), born Basingstoke, England, June 10, 1965.

Bobby Jindal, 43, Governor of Louisiana (R), born Piyush Jindal at Baton Rouge, LA, June 10, 1971.

Tara Lipinski, 32, Olympic figure skater, born Philadelphia, PA, June 10, 1982.

Doug McKeon, 48, actor (*On Golden Pond*), born Pomptain Plains, NJ, June 10, 1966.

Prince Philip, 93, Duke of Edinburgh, husband of Queen Elizabeth II, born Corfu, Greece, June 10, 1921.

Leelee Sobieski, 32, actress (*Joan of Arc, A Soldier's Daughter Never Cries*), born New York, NY, June 10, 1982.

Jeanne Tripplehorn, 51, actress ("Big Love," *The Firm, Waterworld*), born Tulsa, OK, June 10, 1963.

Kate Upton, 22, model, born St. Joseph, MI, June 10, 1992.

June 11 — Wednesday

DAY 162 — **203 REMAINING**

"AMERICAN IDOL" TV PREMIERE: ANNIVERSARY. June 11, 2002. FOX's phenomenally successful talent show was based on a British program. Talented singers compete for a major label record deal while being judged by a panel of highly critical music experts: initially, Simon Cowell, Paula Abdul and Randy Jackson; later, by several other entertainment stars. The audience participates by phoning in votes for favorites. Ryan Seacrest hosts. The first "American Idol" was Kelly Clarkson, who has gone on to chart-topping success and Grammys.

CONSTABLE, JOHN: BIRTH ANNIVERSARY. June 11, 1776. English landscape painter. Born at East Bergholt, Suffolk, England, he died at London, Mar 31, 1837.

COUSTEAU, JACQUES: BIRTH ANNIVERSARY. June 11, 1910. French undersea explorer, writer and filmmaker born at St. Andre-de-Cubzac, France. He invented the Aqua-Lung™, which allowed him and his colleagues to produce more than 80 documentary films about undersea life, two of which won Oscars. This scientist and explorer was awarded the French Legion of Honor for his work in the Resistance in WWII. He died June 25, 1997, at Paris.

GETTYSBURG FESTIVAL. June 11–14 (tentative). Gettysburg, PA. A nonprofit cultural arts festival showcasing American art, culture and cuisine. This annual festival has more than 100 events, more than half of which are free and open to the public. The festival offers events that appeal to all ages by presenting more than 800 world-class artists and performers, along with unique educational opportunities, against the historic backdrop of Gettysburg, PA. Est attendance: 25,000. For info: Gettysburg Festival, Inc, 113 Carlisle St, Gettysburg, PA 17325. Phone: (717) 334-0853. E-mail: info@gettysburgfestival.org. Web: www.gettysburgfestival.org.

ICE CREAM DAYS. June 11–14. Le Mars, IA. Art in the park, parade, Tristate Cruisers show, children's activities, outdoor movie, 3-on-3 basketball tournament, band concert, fishing derby, rib rally fest, bike ride and food from the "Ice Cream Capital of the World," home of Wells's Blue Bunny. Est attendance: 10,000. For info: Sue Butcher, Operations Mgr, Le Mars Area Chamber of Commerce, 50 Central Ave SE, Le Mars, IA 51031. Phone: (712) 546-8821. Fax: (712) 546-7218. E-mail: info@lemarschamber.org. Web: www.lemarsiowa.com.

JONSON, BEN: BIRTH ANNIVERSARY. June 11, 1572. (Old Style date.) English playwright and poet. "Talking and eloquence," he wrote, "are not the same: to speak and to speak well, are two things." Born at London, England, he died there Aug 6, 1637 (OS). The epitaph written on his tombstone in Westminster Abbey: "O rare Ben Jonson."

KING KAMEHAMEHA I DAY. June 11. Designated state holiday in Hawaii honors memory of Hawaiian monarch (1737–1819). Governor appoints state commission to plan annual celebration.

LIBYA: EVACUATION DAY. June 11. National day. Commemorates the closing of US base in 1970.

LOMBARDI, VINCE: BIRTH ANNIVERSARY. June 11, 1913. Vincent Thomas Lombardi, Pro Football Hall of Fame coach, born at New York, NY. Lombardi played football for Fordham's famed "Seven Blocks of Granite" line in the mid-1930s, became a teacher and began to coach high school football. He became offensive line coach at West Point in 1949 and moved to the New York Giants in 1954. Five years later, he was named head coach of the Green Bay Packers. His Packers won five NFL titles and two Super Bowls in nine years, and Lombardi was generally regarded as the greatest coach and the finest motivator in pro football history. He retired in 1968 but was lured back to coach the Washington Redskins a year later. Inducted into the Pro Football Hall of Fame posthumously in 1971. Died at Washington, DC, Sept 3, 1970.

MOUNT PINATUBO ERUPTS IN PHILIPPINES: ANNIVERSARY. June 11, 1991. Long-dormant volcano Mount Pinatubo erupted with a violent explosion, spewing ash and gases that could be seen for more than 60 miles. The surrounding areas were covered with ash and mud created by rainstorms. US military bases Clark and Subic Bay were also damaged. On July 6, 1992, Ellsworth Dutton of the National Oceanic and Atmospheric Administration's Climate Monitoring and Diagnostics Laboratory announced that a layer of sulfuric acid droplets released into Earth's atmosphere by the eruption had cooled the planet's average temperature by about 1°F. The greatest difference was noted in the Northern Hemisphere with a drop of 1.5°. Although the temperature drop was temporary, the climate trend made determining the effect of greenhouse warming on Earth more difficult.

NCAA DIVISION I MEN'S & WOMEN'S OUTDOOR TRACK & FIELD CHAMPIONSHIPS. June 11–14. Hayward Field, Eugene, OR. Est attendance: 20,000. For info: NCAA, PO Box 6222, Indianapolis, IN 46206-6222. Phone: (317) 917-6222. Fax: (317) 917-6826. Web: www.NCAA.com.

June 2014	S	M	T	W	T	F	S
	1	2	3	4	5	6	7
	8	9	10	11	12	13	14
	15	16	17	18	19	20	21
	22	23	24	25	26	27	28
	29	30					

ORIGINS GAME FAIR. June 11–15. Greater Columbus Convention Center, Columbus, OH. 40th annual. Enjoy board games, card games, role-playing, miniatures, classic games and more. More than 170 vendors in the exhibit hall, art show featuring fantasy artists from around the world. Informative seminars on world history, game development and games in education. With more than 4,300 events, it's one of North America's largest game conventions. Special programs for parents and other non-gaming family members. Kids nine and under are free with paid adult admission. Est attendance: 14,000. For info: Game Manufacturers Assn, 240 N Fifth St, Ste 340, Columbus, OH 43215. Phone: (614) 255-4500. Fax: (614) 255-4499. E-mail: pr@gama.org. Web: www.originsgames.com.

RANKIN, JEANNETTE: BIRTH ANNIVERSARY. June 11, 1880. First woman elected to the US Congress, a reformer, feminist and pacifist, was born at Missoula, MT. She was the only member of Congress to vote against a declaration of war against Japan in December 1941. Died May 18, 1973, at Carmel, CA.

RED ARMY DEPARTS BERLIN: 20th ANNIVERSARY. June 11, 1994. After 49 years, the Russian military occupation of the region once called East Germany ended. At one time there had been 337,800 Soviet troops stationed in Germany. The departure was celebrated with a parade in Wuensdorf south of Berlin, which was the Soviet Union's military headquarters in the former German Democratic Republic.

"SPACE ODDITY" SONG RELEASE: 45th ANNIVERSARY. June 11, 1969. This single recorded by David Bowie was released to coincide with *Apollo 11*'s trip to the moon, during which Neil Armstrong and Edwin Aldrin, Jr, landed and walked on the surface of the moon.

STRAUSS, RICHARD GEORG: 150th BIRTH ANNIVERSARY. June 11, 1864. German romantic composer, musician and conductor born at Munich. Some of his best-remembered operas are *Salome* (1905), *Elektra* (1909) and *Der Rosenkavalier* (1911), and his acclaimed symphonic, or tone, poems included *Don Juan* (1889) and *Don Quixote* (1898). Strauss died at Garmisch-Partenkirchen, Germany, on Sept 8, 1949.

STYRON, WILLIAM: BIRTH ANNIVERSARY. June 11, 1925. Winner of both the National Book Award and the Pulitzer Prize for Literature, Styron was born at Newport News, VA. His acclaimed 1967 novel, *The Confessions of Nat Turner*, a fictionalized memoir of the leader of an 1831 slave rebellion, drew upon his knowledge of Virginia. *Sophie's Choice* (1979) chronicled the life of a non-Jewish Nazi victim. He also chronicled his own struggles with debilitating depression in *Darkness Visible* (1990). Styron died at Martha's Vineyard, MA, Nov 1, 2006.

BIRTHDAYS TODAY

Adrienne Barbeau, 69, actress ("Maude"), born Sacramento, CA, June 11, 1945.

Peter Bergman, 61, actor ("All My Children," "The Young & the Restless"), born Guantanamo Bay, Cuba, June 11, 1953.

Dennis Daugaard, 61, Governor of South Dakota (R), born Garretson, SD, June 6, 1953.

Peter Dinklage, 45, actor ("Game of Thrones," *The Station Agent*), born Morristown, NJ, June 11, 1969.

Joshua Jackson, 36, actor ("Fringe," "Dawson's Creek," *Scream 2*), born Vancouver, BC, Canada, June 11, 1978.

Hugh Laurie, 55, actor ("House," "Jeeves & Wooster"), born Oxford, Oxfordshire, England, June 11, 1959.

Joseph C. (Joe) Montana, Jr, 58, Hall of Fame football player, born New Eagle, PA, June 11, 1956.

Jackie Stewart, 75, former auto racer, born Dunbartonshire, Scotland, June 11, 1939.

Gene Wilder, 75, actor (*The Producers, Willy Wonka & the Chocolate Factory, Blazing Saddles, Young Frankenstein*), director, born Milwaukee, WI, June 11, 1939 (some sources say 1935 or 1933).

June 12 — Thursday

DAY 163 **202 REMAINING**

BASEBALL'S FIRST PERFECT GAME: ANNIVERSARY. June 12, 1880. Lee Richmond of the Worcester Ruby Legs (National League) pitched baseball's first perfect game (not allowing a single opposing player to reach first base), 1–0, against the Cleveland Indians.

BIG BEND NATIONAL PARK ESTABLISHED: 70th ANNIVERSARY. June 12, 1944. Area on the "big bend" of the Rio Grande in western Texas along the Mexican border was established as a national park (authorized June 20, 1935). For info: Big Bend Natl Park, PO Box 129, Big Bend Natl Park, TX 79834.

BONNAROO MUSIC AND ARTS FESTIVAL. June 12–15 (tentative). Manchester, TN. 12th annual. An escape into excitement, music, art, discoveries, trees, fresh air, green grass. Bonnaroo is a four-day, multi-stage camping festival held on a beautiful 700-acre farm. Bonnaroo brings together some of the best performers in rock and roll, along with dozens of artists in jazz, Americana, hip-hop and electronica. The festival's 100-acre entertainment village buzzes around the clock with attractions and activities including a classic arcade, on-site cinema, silent disco, comedy club, theater performers, a beer festival and a music technology area. Annually, the second weekend in June. Est attendance: 80,000. For info: Bonnaroo Music and Arts Festival. E-mail: info@bonnaroo.com. Web: www.bonnaroo.com.

BUSH, GEORGE HERBERT WALKER: 90th BIRTHDAY. June 12, 1924. 41st president of the US (1989–93), 43rd vice president of US (1981–89), born at Milton, MA.

FIFA WORLD CUP BRAZIL. June 12–July 13. Brazil. The 20th FIFA World Cup, the world's largest sporting event, will be played in 12 cities in Brazil. The opening match will be played in São Paulo, while the July 13 title match will take place at the iconic Maracana Stadium in Rio de Janeiro. Thirty-two national soccer teams representing all regions of the world compete in eight groups of four. For info: FIFA, PO Box 85, Zurich 8030, Switzerland. Web: www.fifa.com/worldcup.

FINLAND: KUOPIO DANCE FESTIVAL. June 12–18. Kuopio. 45th annual. Come and experience sunlit summer nights, thousands of lakes and exotic dance art at the Kuopio Dance Festival. This major dance event will feature both familiar and new artists from Finland and abroad. The festival arranges high quality international dance performances, dance courses and workshops. The festival expects annually as many as 700 participants to enroll in these courses, 10,000 visitors in the main performances and an audience of tens of thousands in the program free of charge. Est attendance: 45,000. For info: Kuopio Dance Festival, Torikatu 18, FIN-70110 Kuopio, Finland. E-mail: press@kuopiodancefestival.fi. Web: www.kuopiodancefestival.fi.

FIRST MAN-POWERED FLIGHT ACROSS ENGLISH CHANNEL: 35th ANNIVERSARY. June 12, 1979. Bryan Allen, 26-year-old Californian, pedaled the 70-pound *Gossamer Albatross* 22 miles across the English Channel, from Folkestone, England, to Cape Gris-Nez, France, in 2 hours, 49 minutes, winning (with the craft's designer, Paul MacCready of Pasadena, CA) the £100,000 prize offered by British industrialist Henry Kremer for the first man-powered flight across the English Channel.

FORT UNION TRADING POST RENDEZVOUS. June 12–15. 25 miles southwest of Williston, ND. Re-creation of the fur trade era. Fur trade fair, music, blacksmith and craft demonstrations and Trader's Row. Sponsor: National Park Service, Fort Union Trading Post National Historic Site. Est attendance: 4,000. For info: Fort Union Trading Post NHS, 15550 Hwy 1804, Williston, ND 58801. Phone: (701) 572-9083. Fax: (701) 572-7321. Web: www.nps.gov/fous.

FRANK, ANNE: 85th BIRTH ANNIVERSARY. June 12, 1929. Born at Frankfurt, Germany. Anne Frank's family moved to Amsterdam to escape the Nazis, but after Holland was invaded by Germany, they had to go into hiding. In 1942 Anne began to keep a diary. She died at Bergen-Belsen concentration camp in 1945. After the war, her father published her diary, on which a stage play and movie were later based. See also: "Diary of Anne Frank: The Last Entry: Anniversary" (Aug 1).

***LOVING v VIRGINIA*: ANNIVERSARY.** June 12, 1967. The US Supreme Court decision in *Loving v Virginia* swept away all 16 remaining state laws prohibiting interracial marriages.

NATIONAL BASEBALL HALL OF FAME DEDICATED: 75th ANNIVERSARY. June 12, 1939. The National Baseball Hall of Fame and Museum was dedicated at Cooperstown, NY. More than 200 individuals have been honored for their contributions to the game of baseball by induction into the hall. The first players chosen for membership (1936) were Ty Cobb, Honus Wagner, Babe Ruth, Christy Mathewson and Walter Johnson. Relics and memorabilia from the history of baseball are housed at this shrine of America's national sport.

NATIONAL JERKY DAY. June 12. First observed in 2012, National Jerky Day celebrates the rich history, immense popularity and nutritional benefits of dried meat snacks. In the US, the practice of drying meat dates back centuries: Native Americans and early European settlers needed to store food for long periods of time; explorers of the West sought highly portable, satiating foods that required no refrigeration. Today, there are hundreds of different jerky offerings. Meat snacks are the fourth-largest-grossing sector within the overall salty-snack category. Quality beef jerky is actually very lean and is naturally high in protein and low in fat, making it a better snack choice. Sponsored by the Wisconsin Beef Council. For info: Shannon Dickey, National Jerky Day, Carmichael Lynch, 110 N Fifth St, 10th Fl, Minneapolis, MN 55403. Phone: (612) 334-6000. Fax: (612) 375-8501. E-mail: nationaljerkyday@clynch.com.

NATIONAL NURSING ASSISTANTS DAY AND WEEK. June 12–19. 37th annual. Recognizes those nursing assistants who provide care to all ill, elderly and long-term residents in nursing homes and other long-term nursing care centers. Begins on Career Nurse Assistants' Day, June 12, 2014. For info: Natl Network of Career Nursing Assistants, 3577 Easton Rd, Norton, OH 44203. Phone: (330) 825-9342. Fax: (330) 825-9378. E-mail: cnajeni@aol.com. Web: www.cna-network.org.

PARAGUAY: PEACE WITH BOLIVIA DAY. June 12. Commemorates the end of the Chaco War in 1935.

PHILIPPINES: INDEPENDENCE DAY. June 12. National holiday. Declared independence from Spain in 1898.

RUSSIA: RUSSIA DAY. June 12. National holiday. Commemorates the date—June 12, 1990—when the First Congress of People's Deputies of the Russian Federation adopted the Declaration of State Sovereignty of the Russian Soviet Federative Socialist Republic.

June 2014	S	M	T	W	T	F	S
	1	2	3	4	5	6	7
	8	9	10	11	12	13	14
	15	16	17	18	19	20	21
	22	23	24	25	26	27	28
	29	30					

SPACE MILESTONE: *VENERA 4* (USSR). June 12, 1967. Launched on this date, this instrumental capsule landed on Venus by parachute on Oct 18 and reported a temperature of 536°F.

SUPERMAN CELEBRATION. June 12–15. Metropolis, IL. 36th annual. Weekend full of "super" activities. See 15-foot Superman statue, live entertainment, celebrity appearances, super museum, costume contest, road race, carnival, Supertrek bicycle ride, super car show, washer pitch tournament, weight lifting, children's games and food fair. Est attendance: 50,000. For info: Metropolis Area Chamber of Commerce, 607 Market St, Metropolis, IL 62960. Phone: (618) 524-2714. Fax: (618) 524-4780. E-mail: office@metropolischamber.com. Web: www.supermancelebration.net.

"TEAR DOWN THIS WALL" SPEECH: ANNIVERSARY. June 12, 1987. US President Ronald Reagan, standing at the Brandenburg Gate and the Berlin Wall, gave one of the most powerful speeches of his career when he challenged Soviet President Mikhail Gorbachev to give liberalization in the Eastern Bloc more than lip service: "General Secretary Gorbachev, if you seek peace, if you seek prosperity for the Soviet Union and Eastern Europe, if you seek liberalization: Come here to this gate! Mr Gorbachev, open this gate! Mr Gorbachev, tear down this wall!" The speech was audible to East Berliners, but East German police made a gathering crowd at the wall disperse. The State Department had sought to make the speech more conciliatory, but Reagan and his speechwriter, Peter Robinson, refused. The wall was finally opened in 1989. See also: "Berlin Wall Opened: Anniversary" (Nov 9).

US OPEN (GOLF) CHAMPIONSHIP. June 12–15. Pinehurst Resort, Pinehurst, NC. Since 1895, golf's greatest players have competed at this major world championship. For info: USGA, Golf House, Championship Dept, PO Box 708, Far Hills, NJ 07931. Phone: (908) 234-2300. Fax: (908) 234-9687. E-mail: usga@usga.org. Web: www.usga.org.

BIRTHDAYS TODAY

Marv Albert, 71, sportscaster, born Marvin Philip Aufrichtig at New York, NY, June 12, 1943.

Timothy Busfield, 57, actor ("thirtysomething," *Field of Dreams*), born Lansing, MI, June 12, 1957.

George Herbert Walker Bush, 90, 41st president of the US (1989–93), born Milton, MA, June 12, 1924.

Chick Corea, 73, musician, born Chelsea, MA, June 12, 1941.

Vic Damone, 86, singer ("On the Street Where You Live"), born Vito Farinola at New York, NY, June 12, 1928.

Rick Hoffman, 44, actor ("Suits," "The Bernie Mac Show," *Battleship*), born New York, NY, June 12, 1970.

Hideki Matsui, 40, baseball player, born Ishikawa, Japan, June 12, 1974.

Jim Nabors, 82, actor ("The Andy Griffith Show," "Gomer Pyle, U.S.M.C."), singer, born Sylacauga, AL, June 12, 1932.

Frances O'Connor, 45, actress (*The Importance of Being Earnest*, *Mansfield Park*), born Oxford, England, June 12, 1969.

David Rockefeller, 99, banker, born New York, NY, June 12, 1915.

June 13 — Friday

DAY 164 **201 REMAINING**

AVON HERITAGE DUCT TAPE FESTIVAL. June 13–15. Veterans Memorial Park, Avon, OH. 11th annual. This three-day event celebrates duct tape, its enthusiasts and its wacky and fun uses. The festival also honors the history and heritage of the city that is proclaimed the Duct Tape Capital of the World. From sculptures and fashion to games and a parade, everything at the festival revolves around duct tape. A perfect celebration for Father's Day weekend, also includes a Duct Tape Parade on Saturday, and all the classic fair food, rides and live entertainment that make festivals such a great time. Est attendance: 40,000. For info: Avon Heritage Duct Tape Committee, 3701 Veterans Memorial Pkwy, Avon, OH 44011. Phone: (866) 818-1116. E-mail: avonducttapefestival@hotmail.com. Web: www.ducttapefestival.com.

BANANA SPLIT FESTIVAL. June 13–14. JW Denver Williams Memorial Park, Wilmington, OH. 20th annual. A festival celebrating Wilmington as the birthplace of the banana split. Enjoy live concerts, crafters, vendors, great food, games, kids' activities and a make-your-own banana split booth. Est attendance: 5,000. For info: Clinton County CVB, 13 N South St, Wilmington, OH 45177. Phone: (877) 428-4748. Fax: (937) 382-1738. E-mail: info@clintoncountyohio.com. Web: www.clintoncountyohio.com.

BLAME SOMEONE ELSE DAY. June 13. To share the responsibility and the guilt for the mess we're in. Blame someone else! Annually, the first Friday the 13th of the year. For info: A.C. Vierow, Box 71, Clio, MI 48420-0071.

BLUES ON THE FOX. June 13–14. Aurora, IL. A celebration of the historical blues recordings done in Aurora, Blues on the Fox brings famous blues musicians from around the country. Annually, Father's Day weekend. For info: Blues on the Fox, RiverEdge Park, 360 N Broadway, Aurora, IL 60505. Phone: (630) 896-6666. E-mail: info@RiverEdgeAurora.com. Web: www.RiverEdgeAurora.com.

"THE CLOSER" TV PREMIERE: ANNIVERSARY. June 13, 2005. This original cable (TNT) series features Kyra Sedgwick as Deputy Police Chief Brenda Leigh Johnson, a former Atlanta detective brought to Los Angeles to head a special LAPD homicide unit. The premiere telecast set a record for an ad-supported cable original series, and Sedgwick won a Golden Globe for her performance.

CRAWFORDSVILLE STRAWBERRY FESTIVAL. June 13–15. Crawfordsville, IN. Festival at historic Lane Place includes three days of arts and crafts, food, music and children's activities. Great music, classic car show (Sunday), softball and tennis tournaments, antique tractor exhibits and 4k run. All city museums open. Est attendance: 20,000. For info: Montgomery County CVB, 218 E Pike St, Crawfordsville, IN 47933. Phone: (800) 866-3973. Fax: (765) 362-5215. E-mail: request@crawfordsville.org. Web: www.thestrawberryfestival.com.

EVERS, MEDGAR ASSASSINATED: ANNIVERSARY. June 13, 1963. Civil rights leader Medgar Wiley Evers was active in seeking integration of schools and voter registration. He was assassinated by Byron de la Beckwith. The public outrage following his death was one of the factors that led President John F. Kennedy to propose a comprehensive civil rights law.

FIRST ROLLER COASTER OPENS: ANNIVERSARY. June 13, 1884. The world's first roller coaster opened on this day in 1884 at Coney Island, Brooklyn, NY. Built and later patented by LaMarcus Thompson, the "Gravity Pleasure Switchback Railway" boasted two parallel 600-foot tracks that descended from 50 feet. The cars traveled at six miles per hour. Riders paid five cents each for their rides. The roller coaster was a sensation, and soon amusement parks all over the US and the world featured them.

FRIDAY THE THIRTEENTH. June 13. Variously believed to be a lucky or an unlucky day. Every year has at least one Friday the 13th, but never more than three; this is the only Friday the 13th in 2014. Fear of the number 13 is known as triskaidekaphobia. Fear of Friday the 13th is known as paraskavedekatriaphobia.

GERMANY: BACHFEST LEIPZIG. June 13–22. Leipzig. Since 1904, the festival has been held in Leipzig, where Johann Sebastian Bach lived in his later years and composed some of his best-known works. Est attendance: 75,000. For info: Bach-Archiv Leipzig, PO Box 101349, 04013 Leipzig, Germany. E-mail: bachfest@bachfest-leipzig.de. Web: www.bachfest-leipzig.de.

GRANGE, RED: BIRTH ANNIVERSARY. June 13, 1903. Harold Edward ("Red") Grange, Pro Football Hall of Fame halfback and broadcaster, born at Forksville, PA. Perhaps the most famous football player of all time, Grange had a spectacular college career at the University of Illinois, being named an All-American in 1923, 1924 and 1925. When Illinois dedicated its Memorial Stadium on Oct 18, 1924, Grange scored four touchdowns against Michigan in the game's first 12 minutes. Known as the "Galloping Ghost," Grange joined the Chicago Bears in 1925 for what amounted to a barnstorming tour, the start of a professional career dictated by Grange and his manager, Charles C. ("Cash and Carry") Pyle. He retired in 1934 following a knee injury, having put pro football on the sports map. Grange entered business and did announcing work on radio and television. In retirement, he lived quietly and humbly. Inducted into the Hall of Fame as a charter member in 1963. Died at Lake Wales, FL, Jan 28, 1991.

HUCK FINN'S JUBILEE. June 13–15. Cucamonga-Cuasti Regional Park, Ontario, CA. A Huck Finn celebration for families, camping enthusiasts and vacation travelers, with three days of live music, camping, classic cars, mountain-man villages, vittles, crafts from the 1800s and more. Annually, on Father's Day weekend. Est attendance: 15,000. For info: Huck Finn's Jubilee. Phone: (951) 780-8810. E-mail: huckfinn@huckfinn.com. Web: www.huckfinn.com.

KIAMICHI OWA-CHITO FESTIVAL OF THE FOREST. June 13–14. Beavers Bend State Park, Broken Bow, OK. A festival to acquaint the people of Oklahoma and the world with the beauty, heritage, culture, industry and progress in Kiamichi Country. The spirit and heritage of the forest comes to life in the contests of men and women who make their life from the woods. Contests include double buck sawing, pole felling, ax throwing, jack-n-jill crosscut, as well as other forestry events. A "Bull of the Woods" winner is selected from the field each year. Recent additions to the festival are Choctaw cultural demonstrations, dominos, concerts in the park, bluegrass night, jam sessions (bring your instrument and a seat) and BMX United Free Style Stunt Team. Est attendance: 30,000. For info: Broken Bow Chamber of Commerce, 113 W Martin Luther King Dr, Broken Bow, OK 74728. Phone: (580) 584-3393. Fax: (580) 584-7698. E-mail: bchamber@pine-net.com. Web: www.brokenbowchamber.com.

MAINSTRASSE VILLAGE "ORIGINAL" GOETTAFEST. June 13–15. MainStrasse Village, Covington, KY. A celebration of goetta, a favorite regional food. Arts and crafts, great entertainment, plenty of goetta and other favorite festival food make this a fun-filled weekend for the entire family. Est attendance: 25,000. For info: Donna Kremer, MainStrasse Village, 406 West 6th St, Ste 201, Covington, KY 41011. Phone: (859) 491-0458. Fax: (859) 655-7932. E-mail: dkremer@mainstrasse.org. Web: www.mainstrasse.org.

***MIRANDA* DECISION: ANNIVERSARY.** June 13, 1966. The US Supreme Court rendered a 5–4 decision in the case of *Miranda v Arizona*, holding that the Fifth Amendment of the Constitution "required warnings before valid statements could be taken by police." The decision has been described as "providing basic legal protections to persons who might otherwise not be aware of their rights." Ernesto Miranda, the 23-year-old whose name became nationally known, was retried after the Miranda Decision, convicted and sent back to prison. Miranda was stabbed to death in a card game dispute at Phoenix, AZ, in 1976. A suspect in the killing was released by police after he had been read his "Miranda rights." Police procedures now routinely require the reading of a prisoner's constitutional ("Miranda") rights before questioning.

MISSION SAN LUIS REY DE FRANCIA: FOUNDING ANNIVERSARY. June 13, 1798. California mission to the Indians founded on this date. Abandoned by 1846; restoration begun in 1892.

MOON PHASE: FULL MOON. June 13. Moon enters Full Moon phase at 12:11 AM, EDT.

NATIONAL HERMIT WEEK. June 13–20. This week take an adventure in solitude. Discover yourself by journeying within or going off-the-grid. Celebrate the contributions of others who have indulged their need to hermit. Whether you seek inner peace, spiritual release or a moment's peace, this eight-day week is just for you. Annually, June 13–20. Observed since 1996. For info: Eleece Jel, PhD, The Hermit Project, PO Box 2628, Spotsylvania, VA 22553. Phone: (540) 841-4980. E-mail: seh2@nyu.edu. Web: www.nationalhermitweek.org.

PRAIRIE VILLA RENDEZVOUS. June 13–15. Prairie du Chien, WI. Rendezvous with history and learn about life during the fur trading days and experience the fur trader lifestyle firsthand. Many participants come from around the country to display furs, others demonstrate the cumbersome process of loading a rifle with gunpowder and some prepare Indian fry bread and buffalo burgers. Demonstrations on a variety of subjects including basket weaving and beadworking. With more than 400 lodges and teepees, this is one of the largest Midwest trading rendezvous. Annually, on Father's Day weekend. Est attendance: 15,000. For info: Prairie du Chien Area Chamber of Commerce, PO Box 326, Prairie du Chien, WI 53821. Phone: (800) 732-1673. E-mail: info@prairieduchien.org. Web: www.prairieduchien.org.

SAINT ANTHONY OF PADUA: FEAST DAY: DEATH ANNIVERSARY. June 13. Born at Lisbon, Portugal, Aug 15, 1195, St. Anthony is patron of the illiterate and the poor. Died at Padua, June 13, 1231. Public holiday, Lisbon.

SCOTT, WINFIELD: BIRTH ANNIVERSARY. June 13, 1786. Through five wars and more than 50 years as an officer, Winfield Scott was the early US Army's most enduring influence. A hero of both the War of 1812 and the Mexican-American War (1846–48), he also led the Cherokee nation out of Georgia on the infamous Trail of Tears. As brilliant a tactician as he was an infamous clotheshorse, Scott developed the Anaconda Plan that the Union employed in its defeat of the Confederacy. Scott retired from active duty in 1861, when he was removed as lieutenant general of the US forces by Abraham Lincoln. The Whig Party chose Scott as their presidential nominee in 1848 and 1852, but he was never elected to office. Born at Petersburg, VA, he died at West Point, NY, on May 29, 1866.

June 2014	S	M	T	W	T	F	S
	1	2	3	4	5	6	7
	8	9	10	11	12	13	14
	15	16	17	18	19	20	21
	22	23	24	25	26	27	28
	29	30					

SHOW-ME STATE GAMES. June 13–15 (tentative; also July 18–20 and July 25–27). Columbia, MO. An Olympic-style athletic festival for Missouri citizens. This statewide multisport program is designed to inspire Missourians of every age and skill level to develop their physical and competitive abilities to the height of their potential through participation in fitness activities. Est attendance: 65,000. For info: Show-Me State Games, 1105 Carrie Francke Dr, Room 01, Columbia, MO 65211. Phone: (573) 882-2101. Fax: (573) 884-4004. E-mail: PeurrungE@missouri.edu. Web: www.smsg.org.

STRAWBERRY MOON. June 13. So called by Native American tribes of New England and the Great Lakes because at this time of the year the strawberry ripened. The June Full Moon.

WINDSURFING REGATTA/UNVARNISHED MUSIC FESTIVAL. June 13–15. Worthington, MN. Windsurfing on Lake Okabena. Regatta, surfing instruction, swap meet. Traditional music. At sunset, "unvarnished and unamplified" music on the beach. Beer garden and food vendors. Est attendance: 8,000. For info: Worthington Conv & Visitors Bureau, 1121 Third Ave, Worthington, MN 56187. Phone: (800) 279-2919 or (507) 372-2919. Fax: (507) 372-2827. E-mail: wcofc@frontiernet.net.

WORK@HOME FATHER'S DAY. June 13. One day each year to honor and celebrate those fathers who have elected to work from home—either as home-based entrepreneurs or teleworkers—to improve family interaction and professional satisfaction. Annually, the Friday before Father's Day. For info: Jeff Zbar, PO Box 8263, Coral Springs, FL 33075. Phone: (954) 346-4393. E-mail: jeff@chiefhomeofficer.com. Web: www.chiefhomeofficer.com.

YEATS, WILLIAM BUTLER: BIRTH ANNIVERSARY. June 13, 1865. Nobel Prize–winning Irish poet and dramatist, born at Dublin, Ireland. He once wrote: "If an author interprets a poem of his own, he limits its suggestibility." Yeats died at France, Jan 28, 1939. After WWII his body was returned, as he had wished, for reburial in a churchyard at Drumcliff, Ireland.

BIRTHDAYS TODAY

Tim Allen, 61, comedian, actor ("Home Improvement," *Galaxy Quest*), born Denver, CO, June 13, 1953.

Ban Ki-Moon, 70, UN Secretary-General, born Eumseong, Korea (now South Korea), June 13, 1944.

Christo, 79, conceptual artist (*Running Fence, Valley Curtain*), born Christo Javacheff at Babrovo, Bulgaria, June 13, 1935.

Kat Dennings, 28, actress ("Two Broke Girls," *Nick and Norah's Infinite Playlist*), born Bryn Mawr, PA, June 13, 1986.

Chris Evans, 33, actor (*The Avengers, Captain America: The First Avenger*), born Boston, MA, June 13, 1981.

Malcolm McDowell, 71, actor (*A Clockwork Orange, O Lucky Man!*), born Leeds, England, June 13, 1943.

Ashley Olsen, 28, fashion designer, actress ("Full House," "Two of a Kind"), born Los Angeles, CA, June 13, 1986.

Mary-Kate Olsen, 28, fashion designer, actress ("Weeds," "Full House," "Two of a Kind"), born Los Angeles, CA, June 13, 1986.

Ally Sheedy, 52, actress (*St. Elmo's Fire, The Breakfast Club*), born New York, NY, June 13, 1962.

Stellan Skarsgard, 63, actor (*The Avengers, The Girl with the Dragon Tattoo* [US]), born Gothenburg, Sweden, June 13, 1951.

Richard Thomas, 63, actor ("The Waltons," *Roots: The Next Generations*), born New York, NY, June 13, 1951.

June 14 — Saturday

DAY 165 **200 REMAINING**

ALZHEIMER, ALOIS: 150th BIRTH ANNIVERSARY. June 14, 1864. The German psychiatrist and pathologist Alois Alzheimer was born at Markbreit am Mainz, Germany. In 1907 an article by Alzheimer appeared in *Allgemeine Zeitschrift für Psychiatrie* first describing the disease that was named for him. It was thought of as a kind of presenile dementia, usually beginning at age 40–60. Alzheimer died Dec 19, 1915, at Breslau, Germany.

BARTLETT, JOHN: BIRTH ANNIVERSARY. June 14, 1820. American editor and compiler (*Bartlett's Familiar Quotations* [1855]) was born at Plymouth, MA. Though he had little formal education, he created one of the most-used reference works of the English language. No quotation of his own is among the more than 25,000 listed today, but in the preface to the first edition he wrote that the object of this work "originally made without any view of publication" was to show "the obligation our language owes to various authors for numerous phrases and familiar quotations which have become 'household words.'" Bartlett died at Cambridge, MA, Dec 3, 1905.

BIG MAC SHORELINE SPRING SCENIC BIKE TOUR. June 14–15. Mackinaw City, MI. Bike tours of 25-, 50-, 75- and 100-mile routes along the Lake Michigan shoreline past sparkling water and windswept dunes, through the renowned "Tunnel of Trees," over rolling hills and through quaint resort towns. The weekend concludes with a Sunday morning bike ride across the Mighty Mackinac Bridge. For info: Mackinaw Chamber of Commerce, PO Box 856, Mackinaw City, MI 49701. Phone: (231) 436-5574. Fax: (231) 436-7989. E-mail: info@mackinawchamber.com. Web: www.mackinawchamber.com.

BOURKE-WHITE, MARGARET: BIRTH ANNIVERSARY. June 14, 1904. Margaret Bourke was born at New York City. One of the original photojournalists, she developed her personal style while photographing the Krupp Iron Works in Germany and the Soviet Union during the first Five-Year Plan. Bourke-White was one of the four original staff photographers for *Life* magazine in 1936. The first woman attached to the US armed forces during WWII, she covered the Italian campaign, siege of Moscow and American soldiers' crossing of the Rhine into Germany, and she shocked the world with her photographs of the concentration camps. Bourke-White photographed Mahatma Gandhi and covered the migration of millions of people after the Indian subcontinent was divided into Hindu India and Muslim Pakistan. She served as a war correspondent during the Korean War. Among her several books, the most famous was her collaboration with her second husband, novelist Erskine Caldwell, a study of rural poverty in the American South called *You Have Seen Their Faces.* She died Aug 27, 1971, at Stamford, CT.

BUZZARD DAY FESTIVAL. June 14. Makoshika State Park, Glendive, MT. Festival activities include 5k and 10k runs, a pancake breakfast, kids' fun fest, nature walks, FOLF (frisbee golf) tournament and lots more. Est attendance: 600. For info: Makoshika State Park, 1301 Snyder Ave, PO Box 1242, Glendive, MT 59330. Phone: (406) 377-6256. Fax: (406) 377-8043. E-mail: makoshika@mt.gov. Web: www.makoshika.org.

CAMBRIDGE POTTERY FESTIVAL AND US POTTERY GAMES. June 14–15. Cambridge, WI. An all-clay event. A nationally recognized art fair featuring potters from all over the US. Professional potters compete in timed events in the US Pottery Games and auction off pottery for scholarships. The hands-on learning center lets you try your hand at wheel-throwing. Lots of food, fun and raku firing by the local clay guild. Est attendance: 5,000. For info: Cambridge Pottery Festival and US Pottery Games, 1688 Hammen Dr, Cambridge, WI 53523. Web: www.cambridgepotteryfestival.org.

ENGLAND: TROOPING THE COLOUR—THE QUEEN'S OFFICIAL BIRTHDAY PARADE. June 14 or 21. Horse Guards Parade, Whitehall, London. Colorful ceremony with music and pageantry during which Her Majesty The Queen takes the salute from her Household Division. Observance dates from 1805 in the reign of King George III. Starts at 11 AM. When requesting info, send SASE. Trooping the Colour is always the second or third Saturday in June; The Queen's real birthday is Apr 21. Est attendance: 6,500. For info: The Ticket Office, HQ Household Division, Horse Guards, Whitehall, London, England SW1A 2AX. Phone: (44) (020) 7414-2479. Web: www.royal.gov.uk.

FAMILY HISTORY DAY. June 14. Every summer, family reunions are so busy with games and activities that most of us forget the true purpose: to share the folklore, legends and myths that bind us together. Each participant should share at least one good recollection (fact or fiction). Don't forget the hot dogs and lemonade. (©2006 by WH.) For info: Thomas & Ruth Roy, Wellcat Holidays, 2418 Long Ln, Lebanon, PA 17046. Phone: (717) 279-0184. E-mail: info@wellcat.com. Web: www.wellcat.com.

FIRST NONSTOP TRANSATLANTIC FLIGHT: 95th ANNIVERSARY. June 14–15, 1919. Captain John Alcock and Lieutenant Arthur W. Brown flew a Vickers Vimy bomber 1,900 miles nonstop from St. Johns, Newfoundland, to Clifden, County Galway, Ireland. In spite of their crash landing in an Irish peat bog, their flight inspired public interest in aviation. See also: "Lindbergh Flight: Anniversary" (May 20).

FIRST US BREACH OF PROMISE SUIT: ANNIVERSARY. June 14, 1623. The first breach of promise suit in the US was filed in the Virginia Council of State, at Charles City, VA. Reverend Greville Pooley brought suit against Cicely Jordan, who had jilted him in favor of another man. (Jordan won the suit.)

✦FLAG DAY. June 14. Presidential Proclamation issued each year for June 14. Proclamation 1335, of May 30, 1916, covers all succeeding years. Has been issued annually since 1941 (PL 81–203 of Aug 3, 1949). Customarily issued as "Flag Day and National Flag Week," as in 1986; the president usually mentions "a time to honor America," Flag Day to Independence Day (89 Stat. 211). See also: "National Flag Day USA: Pause for the Pledge" (below).

FLAG DAY: ANNIVERSARY OF THE STARS AND STRIPES. June 14, 1777. John Adams introduced the following resolution before the Continental Congress, meeting at Philadelphia, PA: "Resolved, That the flag of the thirteen United States shall be thirteen stripes, alternate red and white; that the union be thirteen stars, white on a blue field, representing a new constellation." Legal holiday in Pennsylvania.

"THE GONG SHOW" TV PREMIERE: ANNIVERSARY. June 14, 1976. This popular show featured a panel of three celebrities judging amateur and professional acts, from the ordinary to the unusual. At any time, a judge could bang a gong to end the act; this was often done with gusto. Completed acts were then rated and the winner received a cash prize. Chuck Barris created (along with Chris Bearde) and hosted the show for all seasons and in syndication with the exception of one syndicated season hosted by Gary Owens. Celebrities who frequently appeared were Jaye P. Morgan, Rex Reed, Arte Johnson, Phyllis Diller and Jamie Farr.

HERITAGE DAYS FESTIVAL. June 14–15. Cumberland, MD. 46th annual. Held in historic downtown Cumberland, the festival showcases more than 150 arts and crafts booths. Also, music, entertainment, children's activities, carnivals, tours of historic homes and buildings and historic reenactments. Annually, the second weekend in June. Est attendance: 15,000. For info: Heritage Days Festival, PO Box 984, Cumberland, MD 21501-0984. Phone:

(301) 722-0037. E-mail: info@heritagedaysfestival.com. Web: www.heritagedaysfestival.com.

IVES, BURL: BIRTH ANNIVERSARY. June 14, 1909. American singer and actor Burl Icle Ivanhoe Ives was born at Hunt, IL. He helped to reintroduce Anglo-American folk music in the '40s and '50s. Ives won an Academy Award for his supporting role in *The Big Country* (1958), and he is well known for his role as Big Daddy in both the film and Broadway productions of *Cat on a Hot Tin Roof.* He died Apr 14, 1995, at Anacortes, WA.

JAPAN: RICE PLANTING FESTIVAL. June 14. Osaka. Ceremonial transplanting of rice seedlings in paddy field at Sumiyashi Shrine, Osaka.

MALAWI: FREEDOM DAY. June 14. National holiday. Commemorates free elections in 1994.

MUNICH FOUNDED: ANNIVERSARY. June 14, 1158. Traditional date of the founding of Munich (or, "Home of the Monks"), when a marketplace was founded on the banks of the Isar River by Benedictine monks with the blessing of Henry the Lion, Duke of Bavaria.

NATIONAL FLAG DAY USA: PAUSE FOR THE PLEDGE. June 14. Held simultaneously across the country at 7 PM, EDT. PL 99–54 recognizes the Pause for the Pledge as part of National Flag Day ceremonies. The concept of the Pause for the Pledge of Allegiance was conceived as a way for all citizens to share a patriotic moment. National ceremony at Fort McHenry National Monument and Historic Shrine.

NCAA DIVISION I MEN'S COLLEGE WORLD SERIES. June 14–25. TD Ameritrade Park Omaha, Omaha, NE. For info: NCAA, PO Box 6222, Indianapolis, IN 46206-6222. Phone: (317) 917-6222. Web: www.NCAA.com.

OIL BOWL FOOTBALL CLASSIC. June 14. Memorial Stadium, Wichita Falls, TX. 77th annual. High school all-stars battle head to head for football bragging rights and to raise funds for Shriners Hospital for Children. Annually, the second Saturday in June. Est attendance: 3,500. For info: Wichita Falls CVB, 1000 5th St, Wichita Falls, TX 76301. Phone: (940) 716-5500. Fax: (940) 716-5509. E-mail: info@wichitafalls.org. Web: www.wichitafalls.org.

SPACE MILESTONE: *MARINER 5* (US). June 14, 1967. Launched on this date, interplanetary probe established that 72.5–87.5 percent of Venus's atmosphere is carbon dioxide on Oct 18 flyby of the planet.

STOWE, HARRIET BEECHER: BIRTH ANNIVERSARY. June 14, 1811. American writer Harriet Beecher Stowe, daughter of the Reverend Lyman Beecher and sister of Henry Ward Beecher. Author of *Uncle Tom's Cabin* (1850), an antislavery novel that provoked a storm of protest and notoriety. It sold 300,000 copies in its first year alone. The reaction to *Uncle Tom's Cabin* and its profound political impact are without parallel in American literature. It is said that during the Civil War, when Harriet Beecher Stowe was introduced to President Abraham Lincoln, his words to her were, "So you're the little woman who wrote the book that made this great war." Stowe was born at Litchfield, CT, and died at Hartford, CT, July 1, 1896.

UNIVAC COMPUTER: ANNIVERSARY. June 14, 1951. Univac 1, the world's first commercial computer, designed for the US Bureau of the Census, was unveiled, demonstrated and dedicated at Philadelphia, PA. Though this milestone of the computer age was the first commercial electronic computer, it had been preceded by ENIAC (Electronic Numeric Integrator and Computer). Univac was completed under the supervision of J. Presper Eckert, Jr, and John W. Mauchly at the University of Pennsylvania in 1946.

US ARMY ESTABLISHED BY CONGRESS: ANNIVERSARY. June 14, 1775. Anniversary of Resolution of the Continental Congress establishing the army as the first US military service.

WARREN G. HARDING BECOMES FIRST PRESIDENT TO BROADCAST ON RADIO: ANNIVERSARY. June 14, 1922. Warren G. Harding became the first president to broadcast a message over the radio. The event was the dedication of the Francis Scott Key Memorial at Baltimore, MD. The first official government message was broadcast Dec 6, 1923.

WORLD BLOOD DONOR DAY. June 14. This day seeks to raise awareness of the need for safe blood and blood products and to thank voluntary unpaid blood donors for their life-saving gifts of blood. Give the gift of life: donate blood. Annually, June 14. For info: World Health Organization. Web: www.who.int/campaigns.

WORLD JUGGLING DAY. June 14. Juggling clubs all over the world hold local festivals to demonstrate, teach and celebrate their art. Annually, the Saturday on or closest to June 15. For info: Intl Jugglers' Assn, PO Box 580005, Kissimmee, FL 34758. E-mail: wjd@juggle.org. Web: www.juggle.org.

BIRTHDAYS TODAY

Yasmine Bleeth, 46, actress ("Baywatch," "Nash Bridges"), born New York, NY, June 14, 1968.

Boy George, 53, singer (Culture Club), born George Alan O'Dowd at London, England, June 14, 1961.

Diablo Cody, 36, screenwriter (*Juno,* "United States of Tara"), born Chicago, IL, June 14, 1978.

Marla Gibbs, 68, actress ("227," "The Jeffersons"), born Chicago, IL, June 14, 1946 (some sources say 1931 or 1941).

Stephanie Maria (Steffi) Graf, 45, Hall of Fame tennis player, born Bruhl, West Germany (now Germany), June 14, 1969.

Eric Arthur Heiden, 56, Olympic speed skater, born Madison, WI, June 14, 1958.

Traylor Howard, 48, actress ("Monk," "Two Guys and a Girl"), born Orlando, FL, June 14, 1966.

Kevin McHale, 26, actor ("Glee," "Zoey 101"), born Plano, TX, June 14, 1988.

Eddie Mekka, 62, actor ("Laverne and Shirley"), born Worcester, MA, June 14, 1952.

Will Patton, 60, actor ("The Agency," *Remember the Titans, Armageddon, No Way Out*), born Charleston, SC, June 14, 1954.

Patricia (Pat) Summitt, 62, former college basketball coach, former player, born Clarksville, TN, June 14, 1952.

Donald Trump, 68, real estate mogul, television personality ("The Apprentice"), born New York, NY, June 14, 1946.

June 2014

S	M	T	W	T	F	S
1	2	3	4	5	6	7
8	9	10	11	12	13	14
15	16	17	18	19	20	21
22	23	24	25	26	27	28
29	30					

June 15 — Sunday

DAY 166 **199 REMAINING**

ANDROPOV, YURY VLADIMIROVICH: 100th BIRTH ANNIVERSARY. June 15, 1914. Leader of the Soviet Union (as General Secretary of the Central Committee) from November 1982 to February 1984. Previously, Andropov was KGB head from 1967 to 1982—the longest serving head in that organization's history. Political dissidents were dealt with harshly during Andropov's time at the KGB, and he was the architect of the "extreme measures" used by the USSR in destroying the Prague Spring movement in Czechoslovakia in 1968. Born at Nagutskoye, Russia, Andropov died Feb 9, 1984, at Moscow, USSR.

ARKANSAS: ADMISSION DAY: ANNIVERSARY. June 15. Became 25th state in 1836.

✦FATHER'S DAY. June 15. Presidential Proclamation issued for third Sunday in June in 1966 and annually since 1971 (PL 92–278 of Apr 24, 1972).

FATHER'S DAY. June 15. Recognition of the third Sunday in June as Father's Day occurred first at the request of Mrs John B. Dodd of Spokane, WA, on June 19, 1910. It was proclaimed for that date by the mayor of Spokane and recognized by the governor of Washington. The idea was publicly supported by President Calvin Coolidge in 1924, but not presidentially proclaimed until 1966. It was assured of annual recognition by PL 92–278 of April 1972. Also celebrated on this day in Britain.

FIRST FATAL AVIATION ACCIDENT: ANNIVERSARY. June 15, 1785. Two French aeronauts, Jean François Pilatre de Rozier and P.A. de Romain, attempting to cross the English Channel from France to England in a balloon, were killed when their balloon caught fire and crashed to the ground—the first fatal accident in aviation history. Pilatre de Rozier was the first man to fly.

GREAT SMOKY MOUNTAINS NATIONAL PARK ESTABLISHED: 80th ANNIVERSARY. June 15, 1934. Area along southern section of Tennessee–North Carolina boundary was authorized May 22, 1926; established for administration and protection only Feb 6, 1930; and finally established for full development as a national park in 1934. For further park info: Great Smoky Mountains Natl Park, Gatlinburg, TN 37738.

GRIEG, EDVARD: BIRTH ANNIVERSARY. June 15, 1843. Pianist, composer, conductor and teacher, the first Scandinavian to compose nationalistic music. Born at Bergen, Norway, and died there Sept 4, 1907.

"HEE HAW" TV PREMIERE: 45th ANNIVERSARY. June 15, 1969. "Hee Haw" has been described as a country-western version of "Laugh-In," composed of fast-paced sketches, silly jokes and songs. Though critics didn't like it, it had popular appeal and did well as a syndicated show. It was cohosted by Buck Owens and Roy Clark, alternating with guest hosts. Regular performers included Louis M. "Grandpa" Jones, Junior Samples, Jeannine Riley, Lulu Roman, David "Stringbean" Akeman, Sheb Wooley, Marianne Gordon, Minnie Pearl and Gordie Tapp.

HUSBAND CAREGIVER DAY. June 15. Coinciding with Father's Day, today we will honor husbands who give health care to their wives or children. For info: Richard Boyd, MD, 1111 W Spruce St, #30, Yakima, WA 98902. Phone: (509) 575-1922. Fax: (509) 248-2501. E-mail: rboyd@richardboydmd.com.

JACKSON, RACHEL DONELSON ROBARDS: BIRTH ANNIVERSARY. June 15, 1767. Wife of Andrew Jackson, 7th president of the US, born at Halifax County, NC. Died at Nashville, TN, Dec 22, 1828.

MAGNA CARTA DAY: ANNIVERSARY. June 15. Anniversary of King John's sealing, in 1215, of the Magna Carta "in the meadow called Ronimed between Windsor and Staines on the fifteenth day of June in the seventeenth year of our reign." This document is regarded as the first charter of English liberties and one of the most important documents in the history of political and human freedom. Four original copies of the 1215 charter survive.

"MY LITTLE MARGIE" TV PREMIERE: ANNIVERSARY. June 15, 1952. "My Little Margie" was a half-hour sitcom about a "womanizing widower and his meddlesome daughter." Margie was played by Gale Storm and Charles Farrell played her father, Vern Albright.

NATIVE AMERICAN CITIZENSHIP DAY. June 15. Commemorates the day in 1924 when the US Congress passed legislation recognizing the citizenship of Native Americans.

NATURE PHOTOGRAPHY DAY. June 15. A day to promote the art and science of nature photography as a medium of communication, inspiration, nature appreciation and environmental protection. Annually, June 15. For info: North American Nature Photography Association, 6382 Charleston Rd, Alma, IL 62807. Phone: (618) 547-7616. Fax: (618) 547-7438. E-mail: info@nanpa.org. Web: www.nanpa.org.

NORWAY: CELEBRATION OF EDVARD GRIEG'S BIRTH ANNIVERSARY. June 15. Special celebrations at Lofthus on the Hardanger fjord where Grieg's cabin still stands.

ORTHODOX FESTIVAL OF ALL SAINTS. June 15. Observed by Eastern Orthodox churches on the Sunday following Orthodox Pentecost (June 8 in 2014). Marks the end of the 18-week Triodion cycle.

STEINBERG, SAUL: 100th BIRTH ANNIVERSARY. June 15, 1914. Artist, born at Ràmnicu Sarat, Romania, who emigrated to the US in the 1940s to escape anti-Semitism in Italy. Most famous for his work for the *New Yorker* magazine, for which he completed 90 covers and 1,200 drawings. Steinberg said of his work, "drawing makes up its own syntax as it goes along. The line can't be reasoned in the mind. It can only be reasoned on paper." He died May 12, 1999, at New York, NY.

TRINITY SUNDAY. June 15. Christian Holy Day on the Sunday after Pentecost commemorates the Holy Trinity, the three divine persons—Father, Son and Holy Spirit—in one God. See also: "Pentecost" (June 8).

TWELFTH AMENDMENT TO US CONSTITUTION RATIFIED: ANNIVERSARY. June 15, 1804. The 12th Amendment to the Constitution was ratified. It changed the method of electing the president and vice president after a tie in the electoral college during the election of 1800. Rather than each elector voting for two candidates with the candidate receiving the most votes elected president and the second-place candidate elected vice president, each elector was now required to designate his or her choice for president and vice president, respectively.

US LANDING ON SAIPAN: 70th ANNIVERSARY. June 15, 1944. In a continued effort to penetrate the Japanese inner defenses, US amphibious forces invaded the Mariana Islands. A huge fleet of 800 ships from Guadalcanal and Hawaii carried the 2nd and 4th Marine Divisions, consisting of 162,000 men. By the end of the day 20,000 of these men had established a 5½-mile-long beachhead on the island of Saipan. Though the American forces suffered heavy losses during an overnight counterattack, on the morning of June 16 the Marines still held the area they had taken the day before.

BIRTHDAYS TODAY

Jim Belushi, 60, actor ("Saturday Night Live," "According to Jim"), born Chicago, IL, June 15, 1954.

Wade Boggs, 56, Hall of Fame baseball player, born Omaha, NE, June 15, 1958.

Simon Callow, 65, actor (*A Room with a View, Howards End*), author, born London, England, June 15, 1949.

Courteney Cox, 50, actress ("Friends," "Cougar Town," *Scream*), born Birmingham, AL, June 15, 1964.

Julie Hagerty, 59, actress (*Airplane!, Lost in America, Reversal of Fortune*), born Cincinnati, OH, June 15, 1955.

Neil Patrick Harris, 41, actor ("Doogie Howser, MD," "How I Met Your Mother"), born Albuquerque, NM, June 15, 1973.

Mike Holmgren, 66, football executive, former coach, born San Francisco, CA, June 15, 1948.

Helen Hunt, 51, actress (*Then She Found Me, Cast Away*, Oscar for *As Good as It Gets*; "Mad About You"), born Los Angeles, CA, June 15, 1963.

Justin Leonard, 42, golfer, born Dallas, TX, June 15, 1972.

Bob McDonnell, 60, Governor of Virginia (R), born Philadelphia, PA, June 15, 1954.

Nicola Pagett, 69, actress ("Upstairs, Downstairs"; *There's a Girl in My Soup*), born Cairo, Egypt, June 15, 1945.

Leah Remini, 44, actress ("The King of Queens," "Saved by the Bell"), born Brooklyn, NY, June 15, 1970.

Anna Torv, 36, actress ("Fringe"), born Melbourne, Australia, June 15, 1978.

June 16 — Monday

DAY 167 **198 REMAINING**

BLOOMSDAY: ANNIVERSARY. June 16, 1904. Anniversary of events in Dublin recorded in James Joyce's *Ulysses*, whose central character is Leopold Bloom.

GRIFFIN, JOHN HOWARD: BIRTH ANNIVERSARY. June 16, 1920. American author and photographer deeply concerned about racial problems in the US. To better understand blacks in the American South, Griffin blackened his skin by the use of chemicals and ultraviolet light, keeping a journal as he traveled through the South, resulting in his best-known book, *Black Like Me*. Born at Dallas, TX. Died at Fort Worth, TX, Sept 9, 1980.

HOUSE DIVIDED SPEECH: ANNIVERSARY. June 16, 1858. Political newcomer Abraham Lincoln, beginning his campaign for the Illinois US senate seat, addressed the Republican State Convention at Springfield, IL, and made a controversial speech that has come to be known as the House Divided speech. Attacking the Kansas-Nebraska Act of 1854, Lincoln said, "A house divided against itself cannot stand. I believe this government cannot endure, permanently, half slave and half free. I do not expect the Union to be dissolved; I do not expect the house to fall; but I do expect it will cease to be divided. It will become all one thing, or all the other."

June 2014	S	M	T	W	T	F	S
	1	2	3	4	5	6	7
	8	9	10	11	12	13	14
	15	16	17	18	19	20	21
	22	23	24	25	26	27	28
	29	30					

LADIES' DAY INITIATED IN BASEBALL: ANNIVERSARY. June 16, 1883. The New York Giants hosted the first Ladies' Day baseball game. Both escorted and unescorted ladies were admitted to the game free.

LAUREL, STAN: BIRTH ANNIVERSARY. June 16, 1890. Worked with Oliver Hardy as the comedy team of Laurel & Hardy for more than 30 years. Born at Ulverston, England, Laurel died Feb 23, 1965, at Santa Monica, CA.

MEET A MATE WEEK. June 16–22. To inspire singles seeking a mate to take advantage of summer by pursuing warm-weather meeting opportunities. Options include singles travel, sports activities, New Blood parties and volunteer work. For info: Robin Gorman Newman, 44 Somerset Dr N, Great Neck, NY 11020. Phone: (516) 773-0911. Fax: (516) 773-0173. E-mail: rgnewman@optonline.com. Web: www.lovecoach.com/events.html.

NATIONAL OLD-TIME FIDDLERS' CONTEST® AND FESTIVAL. June 16–21. Weiser, ID. For more than 60 years, the largest event in the world dedicated to perpetuate old-time fiddling. Annually, the third full week in June. Est attendance: 50,000. For info: National Old-Time Fiddlers' Contest, PO Box 447, Weiser, ID 83672. Phone: (208) 414-0255. E-mail: admin@fiddlecontest.com. Web: www.fiddlecontest.com.

***PSYCHO* FILM PREMIERE: ANNIVERSARY.** June 16, 1960. Millions of filmgoers (and star Janet Leigh) avoided the shower after this thriller's debut in 1960. Alfred Hitchcock's shocker, punctuated by shrieking violins and sudden knife attacks, juxtaposed the old-time horror of the dark gothic mansion with a new locus of fear: the isolated postwar roadside motel. *Psycho* led the way to the "slasher" films of the 1970s and later. Anthony Perkins starred as motel proprietor and bird lover Norman Bates.

QUARTERLY ESTIMATED FEDERAL INCOME TAX PAYERS' DUE DATE. June 16. For those individuals whose fiscal year is the calendar year and who make quarterly estimated federal income tax payments, today is one of the due dates (Jan 15, Apr 15, June 16 and Sept 15, 2014).

SOUTH AFRICA: YOUTH DAY. June 16. National holiday. Commemorates a student uprising in Soweto against "Bantu Education" and the enforced teaching of Afrikaans in 1976.

SPACE MILESTONE: *VOSTOK 6* (USSR): FIRST WOMAN IN SPACE. June 16, 1963. Valentina Tereshkova, 26, former cotton-mill worker, born on a collective farm near Yaroslavl, USSR, became the first woman in space when her spacecraft, *Vostok 6*, took off from the Tyuratam launch site. She manually controlled *Vostok 6* during the 70.8-hour flight through 48 orbits of Earth and landed by parachute (separate from her cabin) June 19, 1963. In November 1963 she married cosmonaut Andrian Nikolayev, who had piloted *Vostok 3* through 64 Earth orbits, Aug 11–15, 1962. Their child, Yelena (1964), was the first born to space-traveler parents.

US VIRGIN ISLANDS: ORGANIC ACT DAY. June 16. Commemorates the enactment by the US Congress, July 22, 1954, of the Revised Organic Act, under which the government of the Virgin Islands is organized. Observed annually on the third Monday in June.

BIRTHDAYS TODAY

Sonia Braga, 64, actress ("American Family," *Kiss of the Spider Woman*), born Maringá, Paraná, Brazil, June 16, 1950.

John Cho, 42, actor (*Star Trek, Harold & Kumar Go to White Castle*), born Seoul, South Korea, June 16, 1972.

Roberto Duran, 63, former boxer, born Chorillo, Panama, June 16, 1951.

Abby Elliott, 27, comedian, actress ("Saturday Night Live"), born Wilton, CT, June 16, 1987.

Cobi Jones, 44, former soccer player, born Westlake Village, CA, June 16, 1970.

Laurie Metcalf, 59, actress (Emmy for "Roseanne"; "The Norm Show"), born Edwardsville, IL, June 16, 1955.

Phil Mickelson, 44, golfer, born San Diego, CA, June 16, 1970.

Joyce Carol Oates, 76, writer (*The Gravedigger's Daughter, Blonde, What I Lived For, Black Water*), born Lockport, NY, June 16, 1938.

Joan Van Ark, 71, actress ("Knots Landing"), born New York, NY, June 16, 1943.

Kerry Wood, 37, former baseball player, born Irving, TX, June 16, 1977.

June 17 — Tuesday

DAY 168 **197 REMAINING**

BELLAMY, RALPH: BIRTH ANNIVERSARY. June 17, 1904. American actor Ralph Rexford Bellamy was born at Chicago, IL. He appeared in more than 100 films and was best known for his stage and film portrayals of President Franklin D. Roosevelt. He was a founder of the Screen Actors' Guild and president of Actors' Equity. Bellamy was awarded an honorary Academy Award in 1987. He died Nov 29, 1991, at Los Angeles, CA.

BUNKER HILL DAY. June 17. Suffolk County, MA. Legal holiday in the county in commemoration of the Battle of Bunker Hill that took place in 1775.

ENGLAND: ROYAL ASCOT. June 17–21. Ascot, Berkshire. There are few sporting venues that can match the rich heritage and history of Ascot Racecourse. Since 1711, Royal Ascot has established itself as a national institution and the centerpiece of the British social calendar as well as being the ultimate stage for the best racehorses in the world. There are a total of 18 "Group" races over the five days. Est attendance: 300,000. For info: Enquiry Office, Ascot Racecourse, Ascot, Berkshire SL5 7JX, England. Web: www.ascot.co.uk.

FAIN, SAMMY: BIRTH ANNIVERSARY. June 17, 1902. American composer Sammy Fain was born Samuel Feinberg at New York, NY. He won an Academy Award for his song "Secret Love" from *Calamity Jane* (1953) and for "Love Is a Many-Splendored Thing" from the film of the same name (1955). He died Dec 6, 1989, at Los Angeles, CA.

HERSEY, JOHN: 100th BIRTH ANNIVERSARY. June 17, 1914. American novelist, born at Tientsin, China, who wrote *A Bell for Adano*, which won the Pulitzer Prize in 1945. *The Wall* and *Hiroshima* are both based on fact and set in Poland and Japan, respectively, during WWII. Died at Key West, FL, Mar 24, 1993.

HOOPER, WILLIAM: BIRTH ANNIVERSARY. June 17, 1742. Signer of the Declaration of Independence, born at Boston, MA. Died Oct 14, 1790, at Hillsboro, NC.

ICELAND: INDEPENDENCE DAY: 70th ANNIVERSARY. June 17. National holiday. Anniversary of founding of republic and independence from Denmark in 1944 is major festival, especially in Reykjavik. Parades, competitions and street dancing.

MIDNIGHT SUN FESTIVAL. June 17–22. Nome, AK. A celebration of the summer solstice, which is when Nome experiences the midnight sun with more than 22 hours of direct sunlight. The festival usually includes a parade, raft race, folk fest and barbecue. Annually, on the weekend closest to the summer solstice. For info: Nome CVB, PO Box 240, Nome, AK 99762. Phone: (907) 443-6555. Fax: (907) 443-5832. Web: www.visitnomealaska.com.

SOUTH AFRICA REPEALS LAST APARTHEID LAW: ANNIVERSARY. June 17, 1991. The Parliament of South Africa repealed the Population Registration Act, removing the law that was the foundation of apartheid. The law, first enacted in 1950, required the classification by race of all South Africans at birth. It established four compulsory racial categories: white, mixed race, Asian and black. Although this marked the removal of the last of the apartheid laws, blacks in South Africa still could not vote.

STRAVINSKY, IGOR FYODOROVICH: BIRTH ANNIVERSARY. June 17, 1882. Russian composer and author, born at Oranienbaum (near Leningrad). Among his best-known music: the ballets *The Firebird, Petrushka* and *The Rite of Spring*; the choral work *Symphony of Psalms*; and *Abraham and Isaac, A Sacred Ballet.* Died at New York, NY, Apr 6, 1971.

UNITED NATIONS: WORLD DAY TO COMBAT DESERTIFICATION AND DROUGHT. June 17. Proclaimed by the General Assembly Dec 19, 1994 (Res 49/115). States were invited to promote public awareness of the need for international cooperation to combat desertification and the effects of drought and the implementation of the UN Convention to Combat Desertification. For info: United Nations, Dept of Public Info, New York, NY 10017. Web: www.un.org.

WATERGATE ARRESTS: ANNIVERSARY. June 17, 1972. Anniversary of arrests at Democratic Party Headquarters (in Watergate complex, Washington, DC) that led to revelations of political espionage, threats of imminent impeachment of the president and, on Aug 9, 1974, the resignation of President Richard M. Nixon.

WESLEY, JOHN: BIRTH ANNIVERSARY. June 17, 1703. Born at Epworth, England. Wesley, along with his younger brother, Charles, was the founder of Methodism. John Wesley died Mar 2, 1791.

BIRTHDAYS TODAY

Thomas Haden Church, 54, actor (*Sideways*, "Wings"), born Thomas McMillen at El Paso, TX, June 17, 1960.

Tom Corbett, 65, Governor of Pennsylvania (R), born Philadelphia, PA, June 17, 1949.

Will Forte, 44, comedian, actor ("Saturday Night Live," *MacGruber*), born Alameda County, CA, June 17, 1970.

Tommy R. Franks, 69, retired general, US Army, born Wynnewood, OK, June 17, 1945.

Newt Gingrich, 71, politician, born Harrisburg, PA, June 17, 1943.

Dan Jansen, 49, Olympic speed skater, sportscaster, born West Allis, WI, June 17, 1965.

Greg Kinnear, 51, actor (*Little Miss Sunshine, The Matador, As Good as It Gets*), born Logansport, IN, June 17, 1963.

Mark Linn-Baker, 61, actor ("Perfect Strangers," *My Favorite Year*), born St. Louis, MO, June 17, 1953.

Barry Manilow, 68, singer, songwriter, born Brooklyn, NY, June 17, 1946.

Joe Piscopo, 63, comedian ("Saturday Night Live"), born Passaic, NJ, June 17, 1951.

Venus Williams, 34, tennis player, born Lynwood, CA, June 17, 1980.

June 18 — Wednesday

DAY 169 **196 REMAINING**

BATTLE OF WATERLOO: ANNIVERSARY. June 18, 1815. Date of the decisive defeat of Napoleon by a combined Anglo-Allied and Prussian army led by generals Wellington and Blucher, near Waterloo in central Belgium.

CAHN, SAMMY: BIRTH ANNIVERSARY. June 18, 1913. Tin Pan Alley legend Sammy Cahn was born Samuel Cohen at New York City. He was nominated for 26 Academy Awards and won four times for "Three Coins in the Fountain" (1954), "All the Way" (1957), "High Hopes" (1959) and "Call Me Irresponsible" (1963). In the late 1940s he began working with composer Jimmy Van Heusen, and the two in essence were the personal songwriting team for Frank Sinatra. Cahn wrote the greatest number of Sinatra hits, including "Love and Marriage," "The Second Time Around" and "The Tender Trap." Died Jan 15, 1993, at Los Angeles, CA.

EGYPT: EVACUATION DAY. June 18. Public holiday celebrating the anniversary of the withdrawal of the British Army from the Suez Canal area of Egypt in 1954.

FOLGER, HENRY CLAY, JR: BIRTH ANNIVERSARY. June 18, 1857. American businessman and industrialist who developed one of the finest collections of Shakespeareana in the world and bequeathed it (The Folger Shakespeare Library, Washington, DC) to the American people. Born at New York, NY. Died June 11, 1930, at Brooklyn, NY.

INTERNATIONAL SUSHI DAY. June 18. Celebrate one of the original "fast foods"! Not only is sushi delicious, it's also an art form meant to be appreciated and worthy of celebration. Once a means of preserving fish in Southeast Asia, sushi has now become a popular dish and experience enjoyed by people of all ages at restaurants around the world. Everyone from sushi connoisseurs to sushi novices are invited to dine on their favorite sushi items or perhaps try something new! For info: RA Sushi Bar Restaurant. Phone: (480) 222-0191. Fax: (480) 998-1424. E-mail: Office@RAsushi.com. Web: www.RAsushi.com.

KYSER, KAY: BIRTH ANNIVERSARY. June 18, 1906. American bandleader whose radio show, "Kay Kyser's Kollege of Musical Knowledge," enjoyed immense popularity in the swing era. He was born James King Kern Kyser at Rocky Mount, NC. A shrewd showman and performer, he said he never learned to read music or play an instrument. Among his hit recordings were "Three Little Fishes" and "Praise the Lord and Pass the Ammunition," a WWII favorite. Kyser retired from show business in 1951 and died at Chapel Hill, NC, July 23, 1985.

LITTLE BIGHORN DAYS. June 18–23. Hardin, MT. To celebrate the history of the Old West. This annual celebration commemorates the anniversary of Custer's Last Stand. Activities include Custer's Last Stand reenactment, historical book fair, quilt show, arts and crafts, cowboy breakfast, street dance, parade, Grand Ball and Grand March. Est attendance: 4,000. For info: Hardin Area Chamber of Commerce, PO Box 446, Hardin, MT 59034. Phone: (406) 665-1672 or (406) 665-3577. E-mail: info@thehardinchamber.org. Web: www.custerlaststand.org.

MALLORY, GEORGE LEIGH: BIRTH ANNIVERSARY. June 18, 1886. English explorer and mountain climber born at Mobberley, Cheshire, England. Last seen climbing through the mists toward the summit of the highest mountain in the world, Mount Everest, on the morning of June 8, 1924. Best remembered for his answer when asked why he wanted to climb Mount Everest: "Because it is there." In 1999 Mallory's body was found by an expedition to Mount Everest, 75 years after his death at age 37.

MISS TENNESSEE PAGEANT. June 18–21. Carl Perkins Civic Center, Jackson, TN. Part of the Miss America Organization. For info: Miss Tennessee Pageant, PO Box 938, Jackson, TN 38302. Phone: (731) 425-8590. Fax: (731) 668-2758. E-mail: MissTNED@bellsouth.net. Web: www.misstennessee.org.

SEYCHELLES: CONSTITUTION DAY. June 18. National holiday commemorating adoption of constitution in 1993.

SPACE MILESTONE: FIRST AMERICAN WOMAN IN SPACE. June 18, 1983. Dr. Sally Ride, 32-year-old physicist and pilot, functioned as a "mission specialist" and became the first American woman in space when she began a six-day mission aboard the space shuttle *Challenger*. The "near-perfect" mission was launched from Cape Canaveral, FL, and landed June 24, 1983, at Edwards Air Force Base, CA. See also: "Space Milestone: *Vostok 6* (USSR): First Woman in Space" (June 16).

WAR OF 1812: DECLARATION ANNIVERSARY. June 18, 1812. After much debate in Congress between "hawks" such as Henry Clay and John Calhoun and "doves" such as John Randolph, Congress issued a declaration of war on Great Britain. The action was prompted primarily by Britain's violation of America's rights on the high seas and British incitement of Indian warfare on the frontier. War was seen by some as a way to acquire Florida and Canada. The hostilities ended with the signing of the Treaty of Ghent on Dec 24, 1814, at Ghent, Belgium.

BIRTHDAYS TODAY

Lou Brock, 75, Hall of Fame baseball player, born El Dorado, AR, June 18, 1939.

Eddie Cibrian, 41, actor ("Third Watch"), born Burbank, CA, June 18, 1973.

David Giuntoli, 34, actor ("Grimm"), born Milwaukee, WI, June 18, 1980.

Willa Holland, 23, model, actress (*Tiger Eyes*, "Arrow," "The O.C."), born Los Angeles, CA, June 18, 1991.

Carol Kane, 62, actress (*Hester Street, The Princess Bride*, "Taxi"), born Cleveland, OH, June 18, 1952.

Donald Keene, 92, literary critic, translator, educator, born New York, NY, June 18, 1922.

Richard Madden, 28, actor ("Game of Thrones," *Birdsong*), born Elderslie, Scotland, June 18, 1986.

Paul McCartney, 72, singer, songwriter (The Beatles, Wings), born Liverpool, England, June 18, 1942.

Richard Powers, 57, author (*The Echo Maker, Galatea 2.2*), born Evanston, IL, June 18, 1957.

John D. Rockefeller IV, 77, US Senator (D, West Virginia), born New York, NY, June 18, 1937.

Isabella Rossellini, 62, model, actress (*Blue Velvet, Cousins*), born Rome, Italy, June 18, 1952.

Blake Shelton, 38, country singer, television personality ("The Voice"), born Ada, OK, June 18, 1976.

June 2014

S	M	T	W	T	F	S
1	2	3	4	5	6	7
8	9	10	11	12	13	14
15	16	17	18	19	20	21
22	23	24	25	26	27	28
29	30					

June 19 — Thursday

DAY 170 **195 REMAINING**

BASCOM, EARL W.: BIRTH ANNIVERSARY. June 19, 1906. Rodeo showman and pioneer, Earl W. Bascom was born at Vernal, UT. During his career he developed the first side-delivery rodeo chute (1916), the first hornless bronc saddle (1922) and the first one-handed bareback rigging (1924). He produced the first rodeo in Mississippi and also produced the first rodeo performed at night under electric lights (1935). Bascom died Aug 28, 1995, at Victorville, CA.

BATTLE OF PHILIPPINE SEA: 70th ANNIVERSARY. June 19–20, 1944. Determined to prevent any further advancement by the Allies in Japan's area of inner defense, Vice Admiral Jisaburo Ozawa ordered the imperial fleet to the Mariana Islands. Admiral Raymond Spruance, possibly the US's greatest and most successful naval commander, ordered a strike force against the Japanese fleet in the Philippine Sea. A furious battle developed in the skies between US carrier-borne aircraft and Japanese aircraft from their carriers and land bases on the Marianas. The Japanese lost three aircraft carriers (*Shokaku, Taiho* and *Hiyo*), two destroyers and one tanker. Three carriers, one battleship, three cruisers, one destroyer and three tankers were seriously damaged. The Japanese lost at least 400 aircraft, the Americans 130.

CORPUS CHRISTI. June 19. Roman Catholic festival celebrated in honor of the Eucharist. A solemnity observed on the Thursday following Trinity Sunday since 1246. In the US Corpus Christi is celebrated on the Sunday following Trinity Sunday. See also: "Corpus Christi (US Observance)" (June 22).

CZECH DAYS. June 19–21. Tabor, SD. 66th annual. Czechs dress in their festive costumes and gather with people from all parts of the world in this gala celebration. Fine Czech foods, dancing, music and entertainment. Est attendance: 15,000. For info: Tabor Area Chamber of Commerce, Inc, PO Box 21, Tabor, SD 57063. Phone: (605) 463-2478. E-mail: taborczechdays@yahoo.com. Web: www.taborczechdays.com.

EMANCIPATION DAY IN TEXAS. June 19, 1865. In honor of the emancipation of the slaves in Texas. See also: "Juneteenth" (below).

FIRST RUNNING OF THE BELMONT STAKES: ANNIVERSARY. June 19, 1867. The first running of the Belmont Stakes took place at Jerome Park, NY. The team of jockey J. Gilpatrick and his horse, Ruthless, finished in a time of 3:05. The Belmont Stakes continued at Jerome Park until 1889; moved to Morris Park, NY, 1890–1905; and in 1906 settled at Belmont Park, NY, where it has continued to the present day. The Belmont Stakes is the oldest event of horse racing's Triple Crown.

FORTAS, ABE: BIRTH ANNIVERSARY. June 19, 1910. Abe Fortas was born at Memphis, TN. He was appointed to the Supreme Court by President Lyndon Johnson in 1965. Prior to his appointment he was known as a civil libertarian, having argued cases for government employees and other individuals accused by Senator Joe McCarthy of having Communist affiliations. He argued the 1963 landmark Supreme Court case of *Gideon v Wainwright*, which established the right of indigent defendants to free legal aid in criminal prosecutions. In 1968 he was nominated by Johnson to succeed Chief Justice Earl Warren, but his nomination was withdrawn after much conservative opposition in the Senate. In 1969 Fortas became the first Supreme Court Justice to be forced to resign after revelations about questionable financial dealings were made public. He died Apr 5, 1982, at Washington, DC.

GARFIELD: BIRTHDAY. June 19, 1978. America's favorite lasagna-loving cat celebrates his birthday. "Garfield," a modern classic comic strip created by Jim Davis, first appeared in 1978 and has brought laughter to millions. For info: www.garfield.com.

GEHRIG, LOU: BIRTH ANNIVERSARY. June 19, 1903. Baseball great Henry Louis Gehrig (lifetime batting average of .341), who played in seven World Series, was born at New York, NY, and died there June 2, 1941, from the degenerative muscle disease amyotrophic lateral sclerosis (ALS), which has become known as Lou Gehrig's disease.

HOWARD, MOE: BIRTH ANNIVERSARY. June 19, 1897. The head stooge in the Three Stooges, Moe Howard was born Moses Horwitz at Bensonhurst, NY. He died May 4, 1975, at Hollywood, CA. Howard began his show business career at age 12 by running errands at Vitagraph studios. He worked with Ted Healy in various comedy and singing acts, and together they teamed with Shemp Howard and Larry Fine in the mid-1920s for an early Stooges act. In 1930 the Stooges made their film debut in *Soup to Nuts.* Although the members of the Three Stooges changed over the years, Moe Howard was one of the constants. Howard appeared in four feature films without the other Stooges, including *Doctor Death, Seeker of Souls.*

HUBBARD, ELBERT: BIRTH ANNIVERSARY. June 19, 1856. Born at Bloomington, IL, Elbert Green Hubbard, American author and craftsman, founded the Roycroft Press at East Aurora, NY. Best known of his writings are *A Message to Garcia* and a series of essays titled *Little Journeys.* He also became famous for his furniture designs. Hubbard lost his life with the sinking of the *Lusitania*, May 7, 1915.

JUNETEENTH. June 19. Celebrated in Texas to commemorate the day in 1865 when Union General Granger proclaimed the slaves of Texas free. Also proclaimed as Emancipation Day by the Florida legislature. Juneteenth has become an occasion for commemoration by African Americans in many parts of the US.

MOON PHASE: LAST QUARTER. June 19. Moon enters Last Quarter phase at 2:39 PM, EDT.

PASCAL, BLAISE: BIRTH ANNIVERSARY. June 19, 1623. French philosopher, physicist and mathematician born at Clermont-Ferrand and died at Paris, Aug 19, 1662. It was Pascal who said, "Had Cleopatra's nose been shorter, the whole history of the world would have been different." And, in his *Provincial Letters*, he wrote, "I have made this letter longer than usual because I lack the time to make it short."

RECESS AT WORK DAY. June 19. Seeking engaged, productive, happier and healthier employees? Take a break from the norm this month—it's time for recess. Take an hour for some teambuilding. Play some games. Engage in a creativity or innovation exercise. Work on improving employee morale. Just make sure you make it fun. Annually, the third Thursday in June—or, better, commit to engage employees throughout the year on the third Thursday of each month. For info: Rich DiGirolamo, PO Box 584, Marion, CT 06444. Phone: (203) 879-5970. E-mail: rich@RichDiGirolamo.com. Web: www.recessatworkday.com.

ROSENBERG EXECUTION: ANNIVERSARY. June 19, 1953. Anniversary of the electrocution of the only married couple ever executed together in the US. Julius (35) and Ethel (37) Rosenberg were executed for espionage at Sing Sing Prison, Ossining, NY. Time for the execution was advanced several hours to avoid conflict with the Jewish sabbath. Their conviction has been a subject of controversy over the years.

SHAKESPEARE ON THE GREEN. June 19–July 6. Elmwood Park, University of Nebraska, Omaha, NE. Nonprofit professional productions of the works of William Shakespeare in a beautiful outdoor setting offered free to the families of the Great Plains region. One of the largest donation-driven festivals across the country. Includes music, singing and juggling; preshow seminars and workshops; picnic area and concessions. Est attendance: 25,000.

For info: Nebraska Shakespeare, Dept of Fine Arts, Creighton University, Omaha, NE 68178. Phone: (402) 280-2391. Fax: (402) 280-2320. E-mail: info@nebraskashakespeare.com. Web: www.nebraskashakespeare.com.

SPACE MILESTONE: *ARIANE* (ESA). June 19, 1981. Launched from Kourou, French Guiana, by the European Space Administration, *Ariane* carried two satellites into orbit: *Meteostat 2*, an ESA weather satellite, and *Apple*, a geostationary communications satellite for India, to be stationed over Sumatra.

STOVER FAIR. June 19–21. Stover, MO. 103rd annual. Fun and entertainment for the entire family. Food, rides, vendors, classic car show and much more. No admission fees. All stage entertainment at no cost. For info: Stover Fair, PO Box 250, Stover, MO 65078. Phone: (660) 668-2326. E-mail: stoverfair@yahoo.com or rmfischer@wildblue.net.

URUGUAY: ARTIGAS DAY. June 19. National holiday. Commemorates the birth in 1764 of General José Gervasio Artigas, the father of Uruguayan independence.

US WOMEN'S OPEN CHAMPIONSHIP. June 19–22. Pinehurst Resort, Pinehurst, NC. For info: USGA, Golf House, Championship Dept, PO Box 708, Far Hills, NJ 07931-0708. Phone: (908) 234-2300. Fax: (908) 234-9687. E-mail: usga@usga.org. Web: www.usga.org.

"WAR IS HELL": ANNIVERSARY. June 19, 1879. Addressing the graduating class at Michigan Military Academy, General William Tecumseh Sherman uttered his famous words on war—more than a decade after the Civil War had ended. He said, "War is at best barbarism. . . . Its glory is all moonshine. It is only those who have neither fired a shot nor heard the shrieks and groans of the wounded who cry aloud for blood, more vengeance, more desolation. War is hell."

WORLD SAUNTERING DAY. June 19. A day to revive the lost art of Victorian sauntering and to discourage jogging, lollygagging, sashaying, fast walking and trotting. (Originated by the late W.T. Rabe of Sault Ste Marie, MI.)

BIRTHDAYS TODAY

Paula Abdul, 52, singer, dancer, choreographer, television personality ("American Idol"), born Los Angeles, CA, June 19, 1962.

Aung San Suu Kyi, 69, Nobel Peace Prize recipient, born Rangoon, Burma (now Myanmar), June 19, 1945.

Hugh Dancy, 39, actor (*Elizabeth I, Ella Enchanted*, "Hannibal," "The Big C"), born Stoke-on-Trent, Staffordshire, England, June 19, 1975.

Jean Dujardin, 42, actor (Oscar for *The Artist*), born Rueil-Malmaison, France, June 19, 1972.

Andy Lauer, 49, actor ("Caroline in the City," *I'll Be Home for Christmas*), born Santa Monica, CA, June 19, 1965.

Brian McBride, 42, former soccer player, born Arlington Heights, IL, June 19, 1972.

Poppy Montgomery, 42, actress ("Without a Trace"), born Sydney, Australia, June 19, 1972.

Dirk Nowitzki, 36, basketball player, born Wurzburg, West Germany (now Germany), June 19, 1978.

Phylicia Rashad, 66, actress ("The Cosby Show"), born Houston, TX, June 19, 1948.

Gena Rowlands, 84, actress ("Peyton Place," *A Woman Under the Influence*), born Cambria, WI, June 19, 1930 (some sources say 1934 or 1936).

June 2014	S	M	T	W	T	F	S
	1	2	3	4	5	6	7
	8	9	10	11	12	13	14
	15	16	17	18	19	20	21
	22	23	24	25	26	27	28
	29	30					

Salman Rushdie, 67, author (*The Satanic Verses, Midnight's Children*), born Bombay (now Mumbai), India, June 19, 1947.

Zoe Saldana, 36, actress (*Avatar, Star Trek*), born Passaic, NJ, June 19, 1978.

Kathleen Turner, 60, actress (*Body Heat, Peggy Sue Got Married, Romancing the Stone*), born Springfield, MO, June 19, 1954.

Ann Wilson, 63, musician (Heart), born San Diego, CA, June 19, 1951.

June 20 — Friday

DAY 171 **194 REMAINING**

ANTIQUES ON THE BAY. June 20–21. St. Ignace, MI. 18th annual show for antique and classic original vehicles 25 years or older. Special tours and awards plus auto world celebrities. For info: Nostalgia Productions, Inc, 268 Hillcrest Blvd, St. Ignace, MI 49781. Phone: (906) 643-8087. Fax: (906) 643-9784. E-mail: ereavie@nostalgia-prod.com. Web: www.nostalgia-prod.com or www.stignacecarshow.com.

ARGENTINA: FLAG DAY. June 20. National holiday. Commemorates the death in 1820 of Manuel Belgrano, the designer of the Argentine flag.

CHESNUTT, CHARLES W.: BIRTH ANNIVERSARY. June 20, 1858. Born at Cleveland, OH, Chesnutt was considered by many as the first important black novelist. His collections of short stories included *The Conjure Woman* (1899) and *The Wife of His Youth and Other Stories of the Color Line* (1899). *The Colonel's Dream* (1905) dealt with the struggles of the freed slave. His work has been compared to later writers such as William Faulkner, Richard Wright and James Baldwin. He died Nov 15, 1932, at Cleveland.

CLARKSON CZECH FESTIVAL. June 20–22. Main St, Clarkson, NE. Czech food, entertainment, music, polkas, cooking, demonstrations, carnival and arts and crafts. Annually, the third full weekend in June. Sponsor: Clarkson Commercial Club. Est attendance: 10,000. For info: Robert Brabec, 515 Elm St, Clarkson, NE 68629. Phone: (402) 892-3331 or (402) 892-3561. Fax: (402) 892-3318. E-mail: cphtvh@yahoo.com.

DALESBURG MIDSUMMER FESTIVAL. June 20. Dalesburg Lutheran Church, rural Vermillion, SD. Celebration of Scandinavian and rural heritage. Programs, dances to raise the Midsummer Pole, a supper, children's activities and more. Est attendance: 600. For info: Ronald Johnson, Midsummer Committee, Dalesburg Midsummer Festival, 30595 University Rd, Vermillion, SD 57069-6507. Phone: (605) 253-2575. Web: www.dalesburg.org.

DELMARVA CHICKEN FESTIVAL. June 20–21. Queen Anne's County 4-H Park, Centreville, MD. 65th annual. A family event focusing on chicken, the leading agricultural enterprise on the Delmarva Peninsula. Food, entertainment and children's activities are featured. Est attendance: 25,000. For info: Delmarva Poultry Industry, Inc. Phone: (800) 878-2449. E-mail: dpi@dpichicken.com. Web: www.dpichicken.com.

"THE ED SULLIVAN SHOW" ("TOAST OF THE TOWN") TV PREMIERE: ANNIVERSARY. June 20, 1948. "The Ed Sullivan Show" was officially titled "Toast of the Town" until 1955. It was the longest-running variety show (through 1971) and the most popular for decades. Sullivan, the host, signed all types of acts, both well-known and new, trying to have something to please everyone. Thousands of performers appeared, many making their television debut, such as Irving Berlin, Victor Borge, Hedy Lamarr, Walt Disney, Fred Astaire and Jane Powell. Two acts attracted the largest audience of the time: Elvis Presley and The Beatles.

FIRST BALLOON HONEYMOON: ANNIVERSARY. June 20, 1909. Roger Burnham and Eleanor Waring took the first balloon honeymoon, ascending at 12:40 PM in the balloon *Pittsfield*. They began their trip at Woods Hole, Cape Cod, MA, and landed at 4:30 PM in an orchard at Holbrook, MA.

FIRST DOCTOR OF SCIENCE DEGREE EARNED BY A WOMAN: ANNIVERSARY. June 20, 1895. Caroline Willard Baldwin became the first woman to earn a doctor of science degree, at Cornell University, Ithaca, NY.

FULTON COUNTY HISTORICAL POWER SHOW. June 20–22. Rochester, IN. This show features a different tractor each year. Power show includes antique tractors, hit 'n' miss engines, equipment and antique trucks. Also features vendors of swap parts, crafts, food, trading post in the Round Barn, horse pulling and toy show. Contests held for exhibitors. Admission fee. Annually, the third weekend in June. Est attendance: 2,000. For info: Fulton County Historical Power Assn, c/o Fulton County Historical Society, 37 E 375 N, Rochester, IN 46975. Phone: (574) 223-4436. E-mail: melinda@rtcol.com. Web: www.fultoncountyhistory.org.

HELLMAN, LILLIAN: BIRTH ANNIVERSARY. June 20, 1905. One of the 20th century's important playwrights, author of such works as *The Children's Hour* (1934), *The Little Foxes* (1939) and *Toys in the Attic* (1960). One of many artists blacklisted by Hollywood in the 1950s. Hellman was the companion for 30 years of novelist Dashiell Hammett. Born at New Orleans, LA, Hellman died June 30, 1984, at Martha's Vineyard, MA.

***JAWS* FILM RELEASE: ANNIVERSARY.** June 20, 1975. With its tagline "Don't go in the water" and its ominous cello music, the Steven Spielberg–directed thriller shocked audiences on this date. Adapted from a Peter Benchley bestseller, *Jaws* showed a great white shark preying on the beachgoers of a New England town. It won three Oscars—best editing, best sound and best original score (by John Williams)—and was a blockbuster success.

LIZZIE BORDEN VERDICT: ANNIVERSARY. June 20, 1893. Spectators at her trial cheered when the "not guilty" verdict was read by the jury foreman in the murder trial of Lizzy Borden on this date. Elizabeth Borden had been accused of and tried for the hacking deaths of her father and stepmother in their Fall River, MA, home, Aug 4, 1892.

MURPHY, AUDIE: 90th BIRTH ANNIVERSARY. June 20, 1924. Born at Kingston, TX, Murphy was the most decorated soldier in WWII. He later became an actor in Western and war movies. He died May 28, 1971, in a plane crash near Roanoke, VA.

NATIONAL PRODUCTIVITY DAY. June 20. Every company defines productivity in its own unique way. The purpose of National Productivity Day, sponsored by Steel Horse™ Coffee from Mars Drinks, is to celebrate, share and honor best practices of the most innovative, forward-thinking and productive companies and fuel productivity in offices everywhere. Events include a motivational morning podcast, productivity tips on the hour, free webinar, naming of America's Most Productive Company and more. Annually, June 20. For info: Linda Parry, Natl Productivity Day. Phone: (914) 251-1500. E-mail: lparry@msco.com. Web: www.fuelingproductivity.com.

OLD TIME MUSIC OZARK HERITAGE FESTIVAL. June 20–21. Historic Court Square, West Plains, MO. Celebrate the unique culture of the Ozark Highlands. Old-time music performances (with headliners), artisans in action, exhibits and activities. Jig dance competition, mule jumping competition, cooking and old-time gospel stage, Brush Arbor, Civil War reenactments and workshops. For info: Ozark Heritage Welcome Center, 2999 Porter Wagoner Blvd, West Plains, MO 65775. Phone: (888) 256-8835. Fax: (417) 255-1038. E-mail: tourism@westplains.net. Web: www.oldtimemusic.org.

ROCHESTERFEST. June 20–29. Rochester, MN. This community festival includes children's and seniors' events, gigantic street parade, street vendors with exotic foods, country night, street dance and breakfast on the farm. Est attendance: 150,000. For info: Carole Brown, Exec Dir, Box 007, Rochester, MN 55903. Phone: (507) 285-8769. Fax: (507) 285-8718. Web: www.rochesterfest.com.

SPANISH-AMERICAN WAR SURRENDER OF GUAM TO US: ANNIVERSARY. June 20, 1898. Not knowing that a war was in progress and having no ammunition on the island, the Spanish commander of Guam surrendered to Captain Glass of the USS *Charleston*.

TAKE YOUR DOG TO WORK DAY®. June 20. A day to celebrate the great companions dogs make and to encourage adoptions from animal shelters. Annually, the first Friday after Father's Day. For info: Pet Sitters Intl, 201 E King St, King, NC 27021. Phone: (336) 983-9222. Fax: (336) 983-5266. E-mail: takeyourdog@petsit.com. Web: www.takeyourdog.com.

UNITED NATIONS: WORLD REFUGEE DAY. June 20. A day to bring attention to the situation of refugees—their rights, as well as their suffering. First observed on June 20, 2001, the 50th anniversary of the 1951 Convention on the Status of Refugees. Date chosen to coincide with Africa Refugee Day. For info: United Nations, Dept of Public Info, New York, NY 10017. Web: www.un.org.

WEST VIRGINIA: ADMISSION DAY: ANNIVERSARY. June 20, 1863. Became 35th state in 1863. Observed as a holiday in West Virginia. The state of West Virginia is a product of the Civil War. Originally part of Virginia, West Virginia became a separate state when Virginia seceded from the Union.

WOMAN RUNS THE HOUSE: ANNIVERSARY. June 20, 1921. Alice Robertson of Oklahoma became the first woman to preside in the US House of Representatives. Robertson presided for half an hour.

BIRTHDAYS TODAY

Danny Aiello, Jr, 81, actor (*The Last Don, Hudson Hawke, Do the Right Thing*), born New York, NY, June 20, 1933.

Olympia Dukakis, 83, actress, (Oscar for *Moonstruck*; *Steel Magnolias*), theatrical director, born Lowell, MA, June 20, 1931.

John Goodman, 62, actor ("Roseanne," *The Big Lebowski; O Brother, Where Art Thou?*), born Afton, MO, June 20, 1952.

Nicole Kidman, 47, actress (Oscar for *The Hours*; *Cold Mountain, Moulin Rouge, Rabbit Hole*), born Honolulu, HI, June 20, 1967.

Frank Lampard, 36, soccer player, born Romford, England, June 20, 1978.

Martin Landau, 83, actor (*Tucker: The Man and His Dream; Crimes and Misdemeanors*; Oscar for *Ed Wood*), born Brooklyn, NY, June 20, 1931.

Michael Landon, Jr, 50, actor ("Bonanza: The Return," "Bonanza: The Ghosts"), born Encino, CA, June 20, 1964.

Cyndi Lauper, 61, singer, born Brooklyn, NY, June 20, 1953.

John Mahoney, 74, actor ("Frasier"), born Manchester, England, June 20, 1940.

Anne Murray, 69, singer, born Springhill, NS, Canada, June 20, 1945.

Lionel Richie, 65, singer, songwriter, born Tuskegee, AL, June 20, 1949.

Robert Rodriguez, 46, director, screenwriter (*Sin City, Spy Kids, Desperado*), born San Antonio, TX, June 20, 1968.

James Tolkan, 83, actor (*Serpico, Back to the Future, Dick Tracy*), born Calumet, MI, June 20, 1931.

Bob Vila, 68, handyman, television personality ("This Old House"), born Miami, FL, June 20, 1946.

Abby Wambach, 34, soccer player, born Pittsford, NY, June 20, 1980.

Andre Watts, 68, pianist, born Nuremburg, Germany, June 20, 1946.

Brian Wilson, 72, singer (The Beach Boys), songwriter, born Hawthorne, CA, June 20, 1942.

June 21 — Saturday

DAY 172 **193 REMAINING**

ANNE AND SAMANTHA DAY. June 21 (also Dec 21). Celebrated worldwide, this twice-yearly holiday is meant for reflection on Anne Frank's and Samantha Smith's contributions to our world and to promote them as subjects worthy to be honored on official American postage stamps, as well as the stamps of all nations. Annually, on the solstice each June and December. For info: John O'Loughlin, 3124 Chisholm Trail, Irving, TX 75062. Phone: (972) 258-4996. E-mail: lldjohn@aol.com. Web: www.anneandsamantha.com.

BATTLE OF OKINAWA ENDS: ANNIVERSARY. June 21, 1945. With American grenades exploding in the background, inside the Japanese command cave at Mabuni the battle for Okinawa was ended when Major General Isamu Cho and Lieutenant General Mitsuru Ushijima killed themselves in the ceremonial rite of hara-kiri. In the long battle that had begun Apr 1, the American death toll reached enormous proportions by Pacific battle standards—7,613 died on land and 4,907 in the air or from kamikaze attacks. A total of 36 US warships were sunk. More than 70,000 Japanese and 80,000 civilian Okinawans died in the course of the battle.

BAYMEN'S SEAFOOD AND MUSIC FESTIVAL. June 21–22. Tuckerton Seaport, Tuckerton, NJ. Stroll the Tuckerton Seaport and sample delicious Jersey fresh clams, crabs and shrimp from the finest seafood purveyors. After you satisfy your appetite, move your feet to the beat of live, toe-tapping entertainment. Bring the family and beach chairs and plan to spend the whole day. Est attendance: 1,600. For info: Renee Kennedy, Tuckerton Seaport, 120 W Main St, PO Box 52, Tuckerton, NJ 08087. Phone: (609) 296-8868. Fax: (609) 296-5810. E-mail: info@tuckertonseaport.org. Web: www.tuckertonseaport.org.

BELGIUM: NAPOLEON BIVOUACS. June 21–22 (tentative). Waterloo. 16th annual. More than 1,200 "combatants" bivouac and fight in a reenactment of Napoleon's battle against Allied forces led by the Duke of Wellington. Equipment, meals, weaponry and first aid are all in the Napoleonic style. Annually, the Saturday and Sunday closest to the battle's date of June 18. For more info: Maison du Tourisme de Waterloo. Web: www.waterloo-tourisme.be.

BHUTTO, BENAZIR: BIRTH ANNIVERSARY. June 21, 1953. The first woman democratically elected to lead a Muslim nation, born at Karachi, Sindh, Pakistan. She served as that nation's prime minister 1988–90 and 1993–96, and she accomplished much national reform, especially on women's issues. However, during both of her terms, she was ejected from office under charges of corruption in Pakistan's turbulent and often violent political climate. She was assassinated by a suicide bomber as she tried to mount her third campaign for prime minister, Dec 27, 2007, at Rawalpindi, Punjab, Pakistan.

CANCER, THE CRAB. June 21–July 22. In the astronomical/astrological zodiac, which divides the sun's apparent orbit into 12 segments, the period June 21–July 22 is traditionally identified as the sun sign of Cancer, the Crab. The ruling planet is the moon.

DENMARK: VIKINGESPIL (VIKING PLAYS). June 21–July 6 (tentative). Frederikssund. Famous, long-running cultural festival featuring outdoor theater based on Viking legends and mythology. Also features an authentic reimagining of a Viking market with plenty of mead. Begins the Saturday on or after the summer solstice. For info: Vikingespil Frederikssund. Web: www.vikingespil.dk.

FRANCE: 24 HOURS OF LE MANS. June 21–22 (tentative). Le Mans. 82nd annual. Organized on a regular basis since 1923, it is the biggest sporting challenge for car manufacturers because it is based on "being the best over 24 hours." More than 55 teams compete in this storied road test. Est attendance: 250,000. For info: Automobile Club de l'Ouest, Circuit des 24 Heures, 72019 Le Mans, France. Web: www.lemans.org.

GO SKATEBOARDING DAY. June 21. This day, held on June 21 annually since 2003, is the official holiday of skateboarding. Founded by the International Association of Skateboard Companies (IASC), this day gives passionate skateboarders as well as those who are simply inspired by skateboarding the opportunity to drop everything and get on a skateboard. A cooperative of decentralized events that take place around the globe. In the years since the first observance, this day continues to grow, but the mission remains the same: Have fun, go skateboarding! For info: International Association of Skateboard Companies, 22431 Antonio Pkwy, Ste B160-412, Rancho Santa Margarita, CA 92688. Phone: (949) 455-1112. Fax: (949) 455-1712. E-mail: info@skateboardiasc.org. Web: www.skateboardiasc.org or goskateboardingday.org.

GREENLAND: NATIONAL DAY. June 21. National holiday.

HIRSCHFELD, AL: BIRTH ANNIVERSARY. June 21, 1903. Caricature artist known for his inimitable sketches of Broadway and Hollywood stars, Al Hirschfeld was born at St. Louis, MO. His first cartoon appeared in 1926 in the now-defunct *New York Herald Tribune*. Later moving to the *New York Times*, his drawings appeared on the drama page for seven decades. He was known for hiding "Nina" (his daughter's name) somewhere in every caricature that he created after 1945. His art is found in many museums, including the Metropolitan Museum of Art in New York City. He died Jan 20, 2003, at New York, NY.

HURRICANE AGNES: ANNIVERSARY. June 21–26, 1972. Hurricane Agnes hit the eastern seaboard wreaking havoc across seven Atlantic Coast states. Casualties included 118 lives and 116,000 homes, leaving more than 200,000 homeless after Agnes dumped 28.1 trillion gallons of water over 5,000 square miles.

LONG BEACH BAYOU AND BLUES FESTIVAL. June 21–22. Rainbow Lagoon, Long Beach, CA. 28th annual. Celebrate Cajun/Creole cultures with food; live nonstop Cajun, Zydeco and blues music; arts and crafts; and a Mardi Gras parade. Est attendance: 10,000. For info: Benoit Entertainment Group, LLC, 879 W 190th St, Ste 400, Gardena, CA 90248. Phone: (310) 217-4196. Web: www.longbeachbayoufest.com.

LONGEST DAM RACE. June 21. Fort Peck, MT. The run crosses Fort Peck Dam. The 5k is flat. Both distances finish running downhill grade from the top of the dam. Included in the events is a 10-mile novice bike race. There are also a 5k run/walk and a 1-mile run/walk. Annually, the third weekend in June. Est attendance: 400. For info: Glasgow Chamber of Commerce and Agriculture, Box 832, Glasgow, MT 59230. Phone: (406) 228-2222. Fax: (406) 228-2244. E-mail: chamber@nemont.net. Web: www.glasgowchamber.net.

June 2014	S	M	T	W	T	F	S
	1	2	3	4	5	6	7
	8	9	10	11	12	13	14
	15	16	17	18	19	20	21
	22	23	24	25	26	27	28
	29	30					

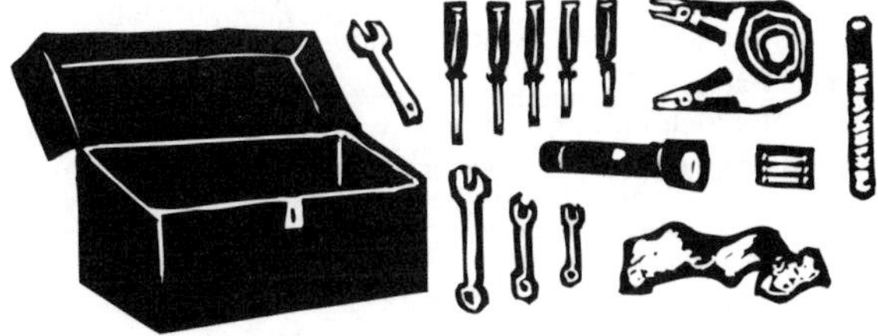

MACHADO DE ASSIS, JOAQUIM MARIA: 175th BIRTH ANNIVERSARY. June 21, 1839. Considered the greatest of Brazilian authors, Machado is best known for his novel *The Posthumous Memoirs of Bras Cubas* (1880). A civil servant in the Ministry of Agriculture all his adult life, he nevertheless created an immense and acclaimed body of literature and served as president of the Brazilian Academy of Letters from 1897 until his death. Born at Rio de Janeiro, he died there on Sept 29, 1908.

MATHER, INCREASE: 375th BIRTH ANNIVERSARY. June 21, 1639. Puritan minister, author, college administrator (Harvard) and influential colonial citizen, born at Dorchester, Massachusetts Bay Colony. Father of Cotton Mather. Author of *Case of Conscience Concerning Evil Spirits Personating Men* (1693), in which he expressed concern over the Salem witch trials. Mather died Aug 23, 1723, at Boston.

MCCARTHY, MARY: BIRTH ANNIVERSARY. June 21, 1912. Acerbic novelist, critic and essayist born at Seattle, WA. The list of her 28 published fiction and nonfiction books include *Memories of a Catholic Girlhood, The Group, Birds of America, The Mask of State* and *How I Grew.* She died Oct 25, 1989, at New York, NY.

MIDNIGHT SUN BASEBALL GAME. June 21. Fairbanks, AK. To celebrate the summer solstice. Game is played without artificial lights at 10:35 PM. Est attendance: 4,000. For info: Alaska Goldpanners, Box 71154, Fairbanks, AK 99707. Phone: (907) 451-0095. Web: www.goldpanners.com.

MIDSUMMER. June 21. One of the "Lesser Sabbats" during the Wiccan year, celebrating the peak of the Sun God in his annual cycle. Annually, on the summer solstice.

MIDSUMMER DAY/EVE CELEBRATIONS. June 21. Celebrate the beginning of summer with maypoles, music, dancing and bonfires. Observed mainly in northern Europe, including Finland, Latvia and Sweden. Day of observance is sometimes St. John's Day (June 24), with celebration on St. John's Eve (June 23) as well, or June 19. Time approximates the summer solstice. See also: "Summer" (June 21).

NATIONAL DAYLIGHT APPRECIATION DAY. June 21. Sponsored by Solatube International but serving as a public service, this special day celebrates daylight as the best-quality illumination for a greener planet. This is a reminder to home and business owners to find a way to bring daylight indoors on the summer solstice, the longest day of the year. For info: Beth McRae, Solatube International, 2210 Oak Ridge Way, Vista, CA 92081. Phone: (888) 765-2882. E-mail: info@solatube.com.

NEW HAMPSHIRE RATIFIES CONSTITUTION: ANNIVERSARY. June 21, 1788. By a vote of 57 to 47, New Hampshire became the ninth state to ratify the Constitution. With this ratification, the Constitution became effective for all ratifying states; approval of nine states was required for the Constitution to go into effect.

NORSKEDALEN'S MIDSUMMER FEST. June 21. Norskedalen Nature and Heritage Center, Coon Valley, WI. Celebrate the summer solstice in Scandinavian style. Pioneer crafts and demonstrations, children's activities, entertainment, food, raffle, nature hikes, animal presentations and horse-drawn wagon rides. Also woodcarving show and competition, open-air museum and artisans demonstrating and selling their works. Est attendance: 1,500. For info: Norskedalen Nature and Heritage Center, Inc, PO Box 235, Coon Valley, WI 54623. Phone: (608) 452-3424. Fax: (608) 452-3157. E-mail: info@norskedalen.org. Web: www.norskedalen.org.

POLAR BEAR SWIM. June 21. Nome, AK. Held annually since 1975. At 2 PM on the red sand beaches, more than 100 intrepid swimmers have plunged into the frigid Bering Sea on this day. The swim may be rescheduled if the ocean ice hasn't sufficiently broken up. For info: Leo B. Rasmussen, Nome Rotary Club, PO Box 2, Nome, AK 99762. Phone: (907) 443-2798. E-mail: leaknome@alaska.com.

QUAD CITY AIR SHOW. June 21–22 (tentative). Davenport Municipal Airport, Davenport, IA. 28th annual. Largest aviation fun-filled weekend in the area featuring the very best of civilian and military aviation. Sat and Sun: gates open at 8 AM, and flying starts at 9 AM with the WWII Dawn Patrol. Action continues nonstop both in the sky and on the ground. For info: Quad Cities Air Show. Phone: (563) 285-7469. Web: www.quadcityairshow.com or www.visitquadcities.com.

SARTRE, JEAN-PAUL: BIRTH ANNIVERSARY. June 21, 1905. French philosopher, "father of existentialism," born at Paris, France. In 1964 Sartre rejected the Nobel Prize for Literature when it was awarded to him. He died at Paris, Apr 15, 1980. In *Being and Nothingness*, he wrote: "Man can will nothing unless he has first understood that he must count on no one but himself; that he is alone, abandoned on earth in the midst of his infinite responsibilities, without help, with no other aim than the one he sets for himself, with no other destiny than the one he forges for himself on this earth."

SEAFAIR. June 21–Aug 17. Seattle, WA. The Northwest's largest summer festival. More than 35 events in all, highlighted by the Milk Carton Derby, Triathlon Torchlight Run and Torchlight Parade and Air Show. Also dozens of community parades and events. Seafair Weekend is the first weekend in August. Est attendance: 2,000,000. For info: Seafair, 2200 6th Ave, Ste 400, Seattle, WA 98121. Phone: (206) 728-0123. Fax: (206) 728-9506. E-mail: info@seafair.com. Web: www.seafair.com.

SPACE MILESTONE: FIRST MANNED PRIVATE SPACEFLIGHT: 10th ANNIVERSARY. June 21, 2004. Michael Melvill, flying the privately financed *SpaceShipOne*, flew 62 miles in altitude on this date, leaving Earth's atmosphere. The spacecraft was designed by Burt Rutan and was financed by Paul Allen, philanthropist and Microsoft cofounder. *SpaceShipOne* made the flight from Mojave Airport at Mojave, CA.

SPIRIT OF THE WOODS FOLK FESTIVAL. June 21. Dickson Township Park, Brethren, MI. A one-day free outdoor festival of folk music, dance and handicrafts. Family friendly, this event features two stages, children's activities and good food. Annually, the third Saturday in June since 1978. For info: Spirit of the Woods Music Assn, 11171 Kerry Rd, Brethren, MI 49619. Phone: (231) 477-5381. E-mail: spiritmusic@jackpine.com. Web: www.spiritofthewoods.org.

SUMMER. June 21–Sept 22. In the Northern Hemisphere summer begins today with the summer solstice, at 6:51 AM, EDT. Note that in the Southern Hemisphere today is the beginning of winter. Anywhere between the equator and the Arctic Circle, the sun rises and sets farthest north on the horizon for the year and length of daylight is maximum (12 hours, 8 minutes at equator, increasing to 24 hours at the Arctic Circle).

TANNER, HENRY OSSAWA: BIRTH ANNIVERSARY. June 21, 1859. Tanner was one of the first black artists to have works exhibited in galleries in the US. He was born at Pittsburgh, PA, and died May 25, 1937, at Paris, France.

TOMPKINS, DANIEL D.: BIRTH ANNIVERSARY. June 21, 1774. 6th vice president of the US (1817–25), born at Fox Meadows, NY. Died at Staten Island, NY, June 11, 1825.

WORLD HUMANIST DAY. June 21. World Humanist Day is celebrated annually on June 21 as a way to spread information—and combat misinformation—about the positive aspects of humanism as a philosophical life stance and means to effect change in the world. For info: American Humanist Assn, 1777 T St NW, Washington, DC 20009. Phone: (202) 238-9088. Fax: (202) 238-9003. Web: www.secularseasons.org/June/world_humanist.html.

WORLD MUSIC DAY/FÊTE DE LA MUSIQUE. June 21. Originated in 1982 by composer Maurice Fleuret within the auspices of France's Department of Culture, World Music Day celebrates music on the summer solstice by encouraging free outdoor concerts—by anyone, amateur or professional. The day has been embraced by more than 100 nations around the world. Annually, on June 21.

BIRTHDAYS TODAY

Kris Allen, 29, singer, television personality ("American Idol"), born Jacksonville, AR, June 21, 1985.

Meredith Baxter, 67, actress ("Bridget Loves Bernie," "Family," "Family Ties"), born Los Angeles, CA, June 21, 1947.

Berkeley Breathed, 57, author, cartoonist ("Bloom County"), born Encino, CA, June 21, 1957.

Thomas Doane (Tom) Chambers, 55, former basketball player, born Ogden, UT, June 21, 1959.

Sammi Davis-Voss, 50, actress ("Homefront," *Hope and Glory*), born Kidderminster, Worcestershire, England, June 21, 1964.

Joe Flaherty, 74, writer, actor ("SCTV," "SCTV Network 90"), born Pittsburgh, PA, June 21, 1940.

Michael Gross, 67, actor ("Family Ties"), born Chicago, IL, June 21, 1947.

Mariette Hartley, 73, actress ("Peyton Place"), born New York, NY, June 21, 1941.

Richard Jefferson, 34, basketball player, born Los Angeles, CA, June 21, 1980.

Bernie Kopell, 81, actor ("Get Smart," "The Love Boat," "When Things Were Rotten"), born New York, NY, June 21, 1933.

Juliette Lewis, 41, singer, actress (*Kalifornia*, *Natural Born Killers*), born Los Angeles, CA, June 21, 1973.

Nils Lofgren, 63, musician, singer, songwriter, born Chicago, IL, June 21, 1951.

Chris Pratt, 35, actor ("Parks and Recreation," "Everwood"), born Virginia, MN, June 21, 1979.

Doug Savant, 50, actor ("Melrose Place," "Desperate Housewives"), born Burbank, CA, June 21, 1964.

Rick Sutcliffe, 58, sportscaster, former baseball player, born Independence, MO, June 21, 1956.

Lana Wachowski, 49, filmmaker with brother Andy Wachowski (*The Matrix*), born Larry Wachowski at Chicago, IL, June 21, 1965.

Benjamin Walker, 32, actor (*Abraham Lincoln: Vampire Hunter; Flags of Our Fathers*), born Cartersville, GA, June 21, 1982.

Prince William (William Arthur Philip Louis), 32, son of Prince Charles and Princess Diana, born London, England, June 21, 1982.

June 2014	S	M	T	W	T	F	S
	1	2	3	4	5	6	7
	8	9	10	11	12	13	14
	15	16	17	18	19	20	21
	22	23	24	25	26	27	28
	29	30					

June 22 — Sunday

DAY 173 **192 REMAINING**

BLASS, BILL: BIRTH ANNIVERSARY. June 22, 1922. Born at Fort Wayne, IN, William Ralph Blass moved to New York at 17 to study fashion design. After service in WWII, he returned to New York and went to work for Anne Klein. By 1970 he had his own company and put American fashion on the map—favoring a sporty yet classy silhouette. His client list soon included Jacqueline Kennedy, Barbra Streisand and Gloria Vanderbilt, and he became one of the most successful fashion designers in history. He was known as a philanthropist in his later years and died soon after retirement at New Preston, CT, June 12, 2002.

BRADLEY, ED: BIRTH ANNIVERSARY. June 22, 1941. Television journalist Edward Rudolph Bradley, Jr, was born at Philadelphia, PA. His career began with battlefield reporting as he covered the fall of Saigon, and he was the first African-American television correspondent to cover the White House. He spent his entire career with CBS and worked on the venerable "60 Minutes" for 26 years. Highly respected for his journalistic integrity, he earned 19 Emmy Awards and four George Peabody Awards in the course of his career. He died at New York, NY, Nov 7, 2006.

BUTLER, OCTAVIA: BIRTH ANNIVERSARY. June 22, 1947. African-American science fiction author, born at Pasadena, CA. Significant works include *The Parable of the Sower* and the Patternist series, featuring *Wild Seed* and *Clay's Ark*. Winner of multiple Hugo and Nebula awards, in 1995, she became the first science fiction writer to be awarded a MacArthur Foundation fellowship, and in 2000 she received a PEN Award for lifetime achievement. She died Feb 24, 2006, at Seattle, WA.

CARPENTER ANT AWARENESS WEEK. June 22–28. Wood-destroying organisms cost Americans $5 billion in property damage annually. This week focuses attention on the identification, biology and habits of carpenter ants and provides consumers with information on the elimination of these costly pests. Annually, the last full week of June. For info: Christine Venuti, Consumer Marketing Mgr, or Jerry Batzner, Pres, Batzner Pest Management, Inc, 16948 W Victor Rd, New Berlin, WI 53151. Phone: (262) 797-4160. Fax: (262) 797-4166. E-mail: JerryB@batzner.com.

***CHESAPEAKE-LEOPARD* AFFAIR: ANNIVERSARY.** June 22, 1807. One of the events leading to the War of 1812 occurred about 40 miles east of Chesapeake Bay. The US frigate *Chesapeake* was fired upon and boarded by the crew of the British man-of-war *Leopard*. The *Chesapeake*'s commander, James Barron, was court-martialed and convicted of not being prepared for action. Later Barron killed one of the judges (Stephen Decatur) in a duel fought at Bladensburg, MD, Mar 22, 1820.

CIRCUS TRAIN WRECK: ANNIVERSARY. June 22, 1918. A Michigan Central Railroad troop train, after several days shuttling soldiers to New York from Chicago, was deadheading back to the Midwest when it struck the rear of the Hagenbeck-Wallace Circus train. The circus train had stopped to have its brake box overhauled at Ivanhoe, IN. Fifty-three circus performers were killed. Of the circus animals not killed outright, many that were crippled and maimed had to be destroyed by police officers. The performers, of whom only three could be identified, were buried in a mass grave. The engineer, A.K. Sargent, who was accused of falling asleep at the throttle, was tried and acquitted.

CORPUS CHRISTI (US OBSERVANCE). June 22. A movable Roman Catholic celebration commemorating the institution of the Holy Eucharist. The solemnity has been observed around the world on the Thursday following Trinity Sunday since 1246, except in the US, where it is observed on the Sunday following Trinity Sunday.

CROATIA: ANTIFASCIST STRUGGLE DAY. June 22. National holiday. Commemorates uprising against Fascist invaders in 1941.

HUXLEY, JULIAN: BIRTH ANNIVERSARY. June 22, 1887. Evolutionary biologist, scholar and educator; brother of author Aldous Huxley. He segued easily from his early work as an ornithologist to establishing the biology department at Rice University, Houston, TX; later, he was a professor of zoology at King's College London, and an author (with H.G. Wells) of the multivolume study of biology *The Science of Life*. Huxley was the first director of UNESCO, a cofounder of the World Wildlife Fund, and coined the phrase "evolutionary synthesis" to describe the discipline of evolution. He died at London, England (his birthplace), on Feb 14, 1975.

JOE LOUIS v MAX SCHMELING FIGHT: ANNIVERSARY. June 22, 1938. Exactly one year after he won the World Heavyweight Championship by knocking out James J. Braddock (June 22, 1937), Joe Louis met Germany's Max Schmeling, at New York City's Yankee Stadium. Louis knocked out Schmeling in the first round. He retained his title until his retirement in 1949.

LEVITT PAVILION PERFORMING ARTS/MUSIC FESTIVAL. June 22–Aug 31. Levitt Pavilion, Westport, CT. 41st annual. Performing arts/music festival conducts more than 50 nights of high-quality entertainment offered free to the general public. In addition, a few special concerts are presented with a nominal admission charged to underwrite the free nights of the festival. Est attendance: 60,000. For info: Freda Welsh, Exec Dir, Levitt Pavilion, 260 S Compo Rd, Westport, CT 06880. Phone: (203) 226-7600. Fax: (203) 226-2330. E-mail: levitt@westportct.gov. Web: www.levittpavilion.com.

LIGHTNING SAFETY AWARENESS WEEK. June 22–28. 14th annual. "When Thunder Roars, Go Indoors!" The NOAA's National Weather Service hosts this annual lightning safety campaign to educate people about the danger of lightning and to reduce the number of deaths caused by lightning each year. The National Weather Service offers toolkits, online information, expert help and more. Annually, the last full week in June. For info: NOAA, National Weather Service. Web: www.lightningsafety.noaa.gov.

LINDBERGH, ANNE MORROW: BIRTH ANNIVERSARY. June 22, 1906. American author and aviator, born at Englewood, NJ. Wife of aviator Charles A. Lindbergh, she served as his copilot and navigator when he broke the transatlantic speed record in 1930. A prolific author and poet, in *Gift from the Sea* she wrote: "By and large, mothers and housewives are the only workers who do not have regular time off. They are the great vacationless class." She died Feb 7, 2001, at Passumpsic, VT.

MALTA: MNARJA. June 22–23. Buskett Gardens. A folk-cum-harvest festival. An all-night traditional Maltese "festa" with folk music, dancing and impromptu Maltese folksinging (ghana). This festival originated in the Middle Ages, and the word *Mnarja* is derived from *luminarja* because the countryside and the bastions around Mdina, Malta's ancient capital, used to be illuminated by "Fjakkoli" (torches made of sand mixed with oil and animal fat) on the eve of and on the feast day itself.

MARADONA'S "HAND OF GOD" GOAL: ANNIVERSARY. June 22, 1986. Argentine superstar Diego Maradona scored one of the most controversial goals in soccer history when, in a World Cup win over England, he used his fist to punch the ball into England's net. Though obvious to many, the official missed the illegal act and allowed the goal. After the game, Maradona said the goal was scored, "A little with the head of Maradona, and a little with the hand of God."

NATIONAL MOSQUITO CONTROL AWARENESS WEEK. June 22–28. The American Mosquito Control Association's "Mosquito Week" educates the general public about the significance of mosquitoes in their daily lives and the important service provided by mosquito control workers throughout the United States and worldwide. Annually, the week that includes June 26. For info: American Mosquito Control Assn, 1500 Commerce Pkwy, Ste C, Mount Laurel, NJ 08054. Phone: (856) 439-9222. Fax: (856) 439-0525. E-mail: amca@mosquito.org. Web: www.mosquito.org.

PAPP, JOSEPH: BIRTH ANNIVERSARY. June 22, 1921. Born Yosl Papirofsky at Brooklyn, NY, Joe Papp became one of the leading figures in American theater. At the helm of the New York Public Theatre, Papp produced a wide range of works from the classical to that of the newest American dramatists, including *Hair, Two Gentlemen of Verona, The Pirates of Penzance, The Mystery of Edwin Drood, That Championship Season* and *A Chorus Line*. He began in 1954 with the Shakespeare Theatre Workshop, taking touring productions around the city on a flatbed truck. When the truck broke down in Central Park, Papp turned his touring company into Shakespeare-in-the-Park. Producing and directing more than 400 productions, Papp garnered three Pulitzer Prizes, six New York Critics Circle Awards and 28 Tonys. He died Oct 31, 1991, at New York, NY.

SINGING ON THE MOUNTAIN. June 22. Grandfather Mountain, Linville, NC. 90th annual sing. Modern and traditional gospel music featuring top groups and nationally known speakers. Annually, the fourth Sunday in June. Free admission. Est attendance: 5,000. For info: Grandfather Mountain, PO Box 129, Linville, NC 28646. Phone: (800) 468-7325. Web: www.grandfather.com.

SOVIET UNION INVADED: ANNIVERSARY. June 22, 1941. German troops invaded the Soviet Union, beginning a conflict that left 27 million Soviet citizens dead. Ceremonies are held this day in Russia, Belarus and Ukraine, the areas of the former Soviet Union that bore the brunt of the initial invasion.

STUPID GUY THING DAY. June 22. Women are always talking about it, so here's the day to commemorate it! Women everywhere are to make a list of "stupid guy things" and pass it on! (©2006 by WH.) For info: Thomas & Ruth Roy, Wellcat Holidays, 2418 Long Ln, Lebanon, PA 17046. Phone: (717) 279-0184. E-mail: info@wellcat.com. Web: www.wellcat.com.

SWITZERLAND: MORAT BATTLE ANNIVERSARY. June 22, 1476. The little, walled town of Morat played a decisive part in Swiss history. There, the Confederates were victorious over Charles the Bold of Burgundy, laying the basis for French-speaking areas to become Swiss. Now an annual children's festival.

US DEPARTMENT OF JUSTICE: ANNIVERSARY. June 22, 1870. Established by an act of Congress, the Department of Justice is headed by the attorney general. Prior to 1870, the attorney general (whose office had been created Sept 24, 1789) had been a member of the president's cabinet but had not been the head of a department.

VANCOUVER, GEORGE: BIRTH ANNIVERSARY. June 22, 1757. English navigator, explorer and author for whom Vancouver Island and the cities of Vancouver (British Columbia and Washington) are named. Born at Norfolk, England, he joined the navy at the age of 13. He surveyed the coasts of Australia, New Zealand and western North America and sailed with Captain James Cook to the Arctic in 1780. Vancouver died at Petersham, Surrey, England, May 10, 1798, just as he was correcting the final pages of his *Journal*, which was published at London later that year.

WILDER, BILLY: BIRTH ANNIVERSARY. June 22, 1906. One of the greatest directors of Hollywood's Golden Age was born Samuel Wilder at Sucha Beskidzka in the Austro-Hungarian Empire. After a short career in Berlin, Wilder fled Germany in 1933 and eventually landed in Hollywood, where he directed and cowrote some of the 20th century's foremost films. His classics include the film noir works *Double Indemnity* and *Sunset Boulevard*, the searing dramas *Stalag 17* and *The Lost Weekend* and the comic gem *Some Like It Hot*. He received six Oscars (out of 21 nominations), and Best Film Oscars went to *The Lost Weekend* and *The Apartment*. Wilder died at Los Angeles, CA, on Mar 27, 2002.

BIRTHDAYS TODAY

Darrell Armstrong, 46, basketball coach and former player, born Gastonia, NC, June 22, 1968.

Klaus Maria Brandauer, 70, actor (*Out of Africa, White Fang*), born Altausse, Austria, June 22, 1944.

Amy Brenneman, 50, actress ("Private Practice," "Judging Amy"), born Glastonbury, CT, June 22, 1964.

Dan Brown, 50, author (*The Da Vinci Code, Angels & Demons*), born Exeter, NH, June 22, 1964.

Randy Couture, 51, mixed martial artist, born Everett, WA, June 22, 1963.

Carson Daly, 41, host ("MTV Live," "Last Call with Carson Daly"), born Santa Monica, CA, June 22, 1973.

Clyde Drexler, 52, basketball coach and Hall of Fame player, born Houston, TX, June 22, 1962.

Dianne Feinstein, 81, US Senator (D, California), born San Francisco, CA, June 22, 1933.

Kris Kristofferson, 78, singer, actor (*Alice Doesn't Live Here Anymore, A Star Is Born*), born Brownsville, TX, June 22, 1936.

Michael Lerner, 73, actor (*The Candidate, Eight Men Out, Barton Fink*), born Brooklyn, NY, June 22, 1941.

Tracy Pollan, 54, actress ("Family Ties," *Bright Lights, Big City*), born New York, NY, June 22, 1960.

Todd Rundgren, 66, singer, producer, born Upper Darby, PA, June 22, 1948.

Meryl Streep, 65, actress (*Doubt, The Devil Wears Prada*; Oscars for *Kramer vs Kramer* and *Sophie's Choice*), born Summit, NJ, June 22, 1949.

Kurt Wagner, 43, former football player, born Burlington, IA, June 22, 1971.

Lindsay Wagner, 65, actress ("The Bionic Woman," *The Paper Chase*), born Los Angeles, CA, June 22, 1949.

Elizabeth Warren, 65, US Senator (D, Massachusetts), born Oklahoma City, OK, June 22, 1949.

June 2014	S	M	T	W	T	F	S
	1	2	3	4	5	6	7
	8	9	10	11	12	13	14
	15	16	17	18	19	20	21
	22	23	24	25	26	27	28
	29	30					

June 23 — Monday

DAY 174 **191 REMAINING**

AKHMATOVA, ANNA: 125th BIRTH ANNIVERSARY. June 23, 1889. Born at Odessa, Russia, Akhmatova was one of the most beloved and renowned Russian poets of the 20th century. Part of the Acmeist literary group devoted to tactile, concrete, material images in poetry, her poems are like photographs or sketches of real-life. Her work reflects the historical and spiritual experience of her generation and references many of her poetic predecessors. She wrote, "It could be that poetry itself is one great quotation." Outcast from Soviet literary society for her unwillingness to write about the new socialist order, Akhmatova died Mar 6, 1966, at Moscow, Soviet Union.

BABY BOOMERS RECOGNITION DAY. June 23. Baby boomers will never forget The Beatles, the Vietnam War and other sixties events. However, many of them have accomplished a great deal, becoming successful in business, education, medicine and other fields. This special day commemorates their contributions. For info: Dorothy Zjawin, 61 W Colfax Ave, Roselle Park, NJ 07204. Phone: (908) 241-6241.

"THE BREAKFAST CLUB" RADIO PREMIERE: ANNIVERSARY. June 23, 1933. "The Breakfast Club with Don McNeil," which hit radio airwaves on this date, had a 35-year run. It was carried by 400 affiliates, and tickets became as sought-after as those for a taping of "The Tonight Show" are today. The hour-long show included celebrities such as Fran Allison of "Kukla, Fran and Ollie" fame. Its popularity, however, stemmed mainly from regular features such as "Memory Time," when McNeil read poems and letters from listeners. During WWII, "Prayer Time" was started. McNeil's "Call to Breakfast," which was announced every 15 minutes, invited listeners to get up and march around the breakfast table. McNeil died in 1996.

CANADA: NEWFOUNDLAND DISCOVERY DAY. June 23. Commemorates the discovery of Newfoundland by John Cabot, June 24, 1497. Commemorated on the Monday nearest June 24.

CASH, JUNE CARTER: 85th BIRTH ANNIVERSARY. June 23, 1929. Grammy-winning country-western star born Valerie June Carter at Maces Springs, VA. As a member of the Carter Family, a group that included her mother, sisters and various cousins, she toured as a performer from childhood. She met Johnny Cash on the road in 1961. She cowrote his hit song "Ring of Fire," and they began recording together. They married in 1968 and won two Grammys for their duets. She died May 15, 2004, at Nashville, TN.

DENMARK: MIDSUMMER EVE. June 23. Celebrated all over the country with bonfires and merrymaking.

ENGLAND: LAWN TENNIS CHAMPIONSHIPS AT WIMBLEDON. June 23–July 6. Wimbledon, London. World-famous men's and women's singles and doubles championships for the most coveted titles in tennis. Tickets are allocated via public ballot. Send SASE for details between Aug 1 and Dec 15, 2013. For info: All England Lawn Tennis and Croquet Club, Church Road, Wimbledon, London, England SW19 5AE. Phone: (44) (20) 8944-1066. Fax: (44) (20) 8947-8752. Web: www.wimbledon.org.

ESTONIA: VICTORY DAY. June 23. National holiday. Commemorates victory against Germany in 1919.

FIRST TYPEWRITER: ANNIVERSARY. June 23, 1868. First US typewriter was patented by Luther Sholes.

FOSSE, ROBERT LOUIS (BOB): BIRTH ANNIVERSARY. June 23, 1927. Bob Fosse was born at Chicago, IL. The son of a vaudeville singer, he began his show business career at the age of 13. He was the only director in history to win an Oscar, an Emmy and a Tony for his work. As a choreographer he was known for his unique dance style that focused on explosive angularity of the human body in its movement. His body of work includes the plays *Pippin, Sweet Charity, Pajama Game, Chicago* and *Damn Yankees* and the films *Cabaret, Lenny* and *All That Jazz*. Fosse died Sept 23, 1987, at Washington, DC.

KINSEY, ALFRED: BIRTH ANNIVERSARY. June 23, 1894. Born at Hoboken, NJ, Kinsey was a professor of zoology who moved into the study of human sexual behavior in the 1940s at Indiana University's Institute for Sex Research (later renamed after him). Kinsey published two controversial books based on his research: *Sexual Behavior in the Human Male* (1948) and *Sexual Behavior in the Human Female* (1953). Kinsey died Aug 25, 1956, at Bloomington, IN.

LAST FORMAL SURRENDER OF CONFEDERATE TROOPS: ANNIVERSARY. June 23, 1865. The last formal surrender of Confederate troops took place in the Oklahoma Territory. Cherokee leader and Confederate Brigadier General Waite surrendered his command of a battalion formed by Indians.

LET IT GO DAY. June 23. Whatever it is that's bugging you, drop it! It's only eating away at you and providing nothing positive. (©2006 by WH.) For info: Thomas & Ruth Roy, Wellcat Holidays, 2418 Long Ln, Lebanon, PA 17046-1708. Phone: (717) 279-0184. E-mail: info@wellcat.com. Web: www.wellcat.com.

LUXEMBOURG: NATIONAL HOLIDAY. June 23. Official birthday of His Royal Highness Grand Duke Jean in 1921. Also, Luxembourg's independence is celebrated June 23.

RUDOLPH, WILMA: BIRTH ANNIVERSARY. June 23, 1940. Olympic gold medal sprinter, born at Bethlehem, TN. She won the 100-, 200- and 400-meter relays at the 1960 Rome games, thus becoming the first woman to win three gold medals at the same Olympics. She overcame polio as a child and went on to Tennessee State University to become an athlete. Rudolph won the Sullivan Award in 1961. Died at Brentwood, TN, Nov 12, 1994.

SWEDEN: MIDSUMMER. June 23–24. Celebrated throughout Sweden with Maypole dancing, games and folk music.

TURING, ALAN: BIRTH ANNIVERSARY. June 23, 1912. British mathematician, logician and cryptographer, recognized as the father of modern computer science and artificial intelligence. Born at London, England, Alan Mathison Turing conceived in 1936 the "Turing Machine," an abstract information-processing mathematical model that foreshadowed digital computers. During WWII, he was a member of the top-secret code-breaking team at England's Bletchley Park. The decoding team saved incalculable Allied lives. Turing was made a member of the Order of the British Empire for his wartime service. In 1945, Turing designed the Automatic Computing Engine—what would have been the first digital computer had it been built. In the 1950s, Turing devised the "Turing Test" that would determine the success of an artificial intelligence machine (of whether it was thinking). Turing was stripped of his government security clearance after being convicted in 1952 for "gross indecency"—Turing was openly gay and homosexuality was a crime in England. He committed suicide June 7, 1954, at Wilmslow, England.

UNITED KINGDOM: NATIONAL INSECT WEEK. June 23–29. Diversity isn't just about wildlife in exotic locations. Get involved in National Insect Week and you'll discover that insect diversity is just as relevant and fascinating to explore in your garden or local countryside as it is in the savannas, deserts, wetlands and rain forests of the tropics. Lots of events all over the UK for all ages: beastie hunts, pond surveys, bug-house building, special exhibits, photo competition and more. For info: Royal Entomological Society. E-mail: info@nationalinsectweek.co.uk or (for media) lizzie@cicada-comms.com. Web: www.nationalinsectweek.co.uk or www.royensoc.co.uk.

UNITED NATIONS: PUBLIC SERVICE DAY. June 23. The General Assembly designated June 23 of each year as United Nations Public Service Day (Resolution 57/277). It encouraged member states to organize special events on that day to highlight the contribution of public service in the development process. For info: United Nations, Dept of Public Info, New York, NY 10017. Web: www.un.org.

BIRTHDAYS TODAY

Bryan Brown, 67, actor (*A Town Like Alice, Breaker Morant, F/X*), born Sydney, Australia, June 23, 1947.

Randy Jackson, 58, musician, television personality ("American Idol"), born Baton Rouge, LA, June 23, 1956.

James Levine, 71, pianist, conductor (Metropolitan Opera of New York City), born Cincinnati, OH, June 23, 1943.

Frances McDormand, 57, actress (Oscar for *Fargo*; *Mississippi Burning, Almost Famous*), born Chicago, IL, June 23, 1957.

Chellsie Memmel, 26, Olympic gymnast, born West Allis, WI, June 23, 1988.

Ted Shackelford, 68, actor ("Knots Landing," "Dallas"), born Oklahoma City, OK, June 23, 1946.

Bridget Sloan, 22, Olympic gymnast, born Cincinnati, OH, June 23, 1992.

Clarence Thomas, 66, Associate Justice of the US, born Pinpoint, GA, June 23, 1948.

LaDanian Tomlinson, 35, football player, born Waco, TX, June 23, 1979.

Louis Van Amstel, 42, professional dancer, television personality ("Dancing with the Stars"), born Amsterdam, Netherlands, June 23, 1972.

Zinedine Zidane, 42, former soccer player, born Marseille, France, June 23, 1972.

June 24 — Tuesday

DAY 175 **190 REMAINING**

BATTLE OF BANNOCKBURN: 700th ANNIVERSARY. June 24, 1314. Decisive battle for Scottish independence in which a smaller force of Scots (mainly pike men) under Robert the Bruce defeated the English (with 3,000 horsemen) under King Edward II. The battle took place by the strategically important Stirling Castle at the Bannock Burn stream and the River Forth. The battle began June 23 and ended June 24 in a rout—the worst English defeat since the Battle of Hastings.

BEECHER, HENRY WARD: BIRTH ANNIVERSARY. June 24, 1813. Famous clergyman and orator, brother of Harriet Beecher Stowe, born at Litchfield, CT. From the pulpit at Plymouth Church, Beecher advocated for many controversial issues of his era, including temperance, women's suffrage, Darwinian evolution, and—most notably—abolition. Beecher's tactics in support of abolition were often sensational and contentious, as was the case when he raised money to provide rifles—widely dubbed "Beecher's Bibles"—to antislavery settlers in Kansas in 1856. In the 1870s Beecher was the subject of one of the biggest scandals of the century—the Beecher-Tilton Affair—when he was accused of adultery by a parishioner and sued in civil court. The trial resulted in a hung jury, and although Beecher was exonerated by two ecclesiastical courts, public opinion about his innocence was divided. Died Mar 8, 1887, at Brooklyn, NY. His dying words were, "Now comes the mystery."

BERLIN AIRLIFT: ANNIVERSARY. June 24, 1948. In the early days of the Cold War the Soviet Union challenged the West's right of access to Berlin. The Soviets created a blockade, and an airlift to supply some 2,250,000 people resulted. The airlift lasted a total of 321 days and brought into Berlin 1,592,787 tons of supplies. Joseph Stalin finally backed down and the blockade ended May 12, 1949.

CANADA: ST. JEAN-BAPTISTE DAY. June 24. Public holiday in Quebec.

CELEBRATION OF THE SENSES. June 24. Treat yourself to a stimulation of the five senses—taste, touch, scent, sight and sound—and you may experience the elevation known to many mystics as the elusive sixth sense. (©2006 by WH.) For info: Thomas & Ruth Roy, Wellcat Holidays, 2418 Long Ln, Lebanon, PA 17046. Phone: (717) 279-0184. E-mail: info@wellcat.com. Web: www.wellcat.com.

CHINA: MACAU DAY. June 24. Celebrates defeat of the Dutch invasion forces of 1622 and pays homage to patron saint of Macau, Saint John the Baptist. Macau is a former Portuguese colony that is now part of China.

DEMPSEY, JACK: BIRTH ANNIVERSARY. June 24, 1895. William Harrison Dempsey, known as "The Manassa Mauler," was world heavyweight boxing champion from 1919 to 1926. Following his boxing career Dempsey became a successful New York restaurant operator. Born at Manassa, CO, Dempsey died May 31, 1983, at New York, NY.

"HOPALONG CASSIDY" TV PREMIERE: 65th ANNIVERSARY. June 24, 1949. A Western series starring William Boyd in the title role as a hero who wore black and rode a white horse. The original episodes were segments edited from 66 movie features of Hopalong Cassidy and his sidekick, Red Connors (Edgar Buchanan). The films were so popular that Boyd produced episodes especially for TV.

ITALY: CALCIO FIORENTINO. June 24–28. Florence. Revival of a 16th-century football match in medieval costumes.

LATVIA: JOHN'S DAY (MIDSUMMER NIGHT DAY). June 24. The festival of Jani, which commemorates the summer solstice and the name day of (Janis) John, is one of Latvia's most ancient as well as joyous rituals. This festival is traditionally celebrated in the countryside, as it emphasizes fertility and the beginning of summer. Festivities begin June 23.

NATIONAL COLUMNISTS' DAY. June 24. Newspaper columnists, who bring you joy all year long, deserve to be celebrated by their readers at least once a year. Now you can send your favorite columnists, local or nationally syndicated, your own wishes for a Happy Columnists' Day and make them feel wonderful. Annually, the fourth Tuesday in June. For info: Jim Six, Columnist, *South Jersey Times*, 309 S Broad St, Woodbury, NJ 08096. Phone: (856) 845-3300. Fax: (856) 845-5480. E-mail: jimsix@southjerseymedia.com.

ONIZUKA, ELLISON S.: BIRTH ANNIVERSARY. June 24, 1946. Lieutenant Colonel Ellison S. Onizuka, 39-year-old aerospace engineer, mission specialist aboard the space shuttle *Challenger* when it exploded Jan 28, 1986 (killing all aboard). Onizuka was born at Kealakekua, Kona, HI. See also: "*Challenger* Space Shuttle Explosion Anniversary" (Jan 28).

PERU: COUNTRYMAN'S DAY. June 24. Half-day public holiday.

SAINT JOHN THE BAPTIST DAY. June 24. Celebrates the birth of the saint.

SWIFT, GUSTAVUS: 175th BIRTH ANNIVERSARY. June 24, 1839. American industrialist known for revolutionizing the meatpacking industry. He commissioned the development of the refrigerator car, which allowed the transportation of processed meat for the first time, and his company was one of the first in modern history to implement "vertical integration": it had departments for purchasing, production, shipping, sales and marketing. Swift was also a pioneer in using by-products of animal parts previously discarded for products like glue, fertilizer and soap; this efficiency was the model for the contemptuous fictional Durham Company in Upton Sinclair's *The Jungle*. Born at Sandwich, MA, Swift died Mar 29, 1903, at Chicago, IL.

THORNTON, MATTHEW: DEATH ANNIVERSARY. June 24, 1803. Signer of the Declaration of Independence. Born at Ireland about 1714, he died at Newburyport, MA.

VENEZUELA: BATTLE OF CARABOBO DAY. June 24. National holiday. Commemorates a victory in 1821 that assured Venezuelan independence from Spain.

WESTERN DAYS. June 24–28. Elgin, TX. Events include a parade, horseshoe contest, volleyball tournament, Miss Western Days contest, live music, arts and crafts and carnival. Est attendance: 20,000. For info: Gena Carter, Elgin Chamber of Commerce, PO Box 408, Elgin, TX 78621. Phone: (512) 285-4515. Web: www.elgintxchamber.com.

WINDJAMMER DAYS. June 24–25. Boothbay Harbor, ME. The premier maritime event along the coast of Maine. Parades, concerts, waterfront food, interactive children's activities, live music, fireworks, windjammers sailing into harbor under full sail and much more. Fun for the whole family. Est attendance: 20,000. For info: Boothbay Harbor Region Chamber of Commerce, PO Box 356, Boothbay Harbor, ME 04538. Phone: (207) 633-2353. Fax: (207) 633-7448. E-mail: seamaine@boothbayharbor.com. Web: www.boothbayharbor.com.

BIRTHDAYS TODAY

Nancy Allen, 64, actress (*Carrie, Blow Out, Robocop*), born New York, NY, June 24, 1950.

Mick Fleetwood, 72, musician (Fleetwood Mac), born Cornwall, England, June 24, 1942.

Phyllis George, 65, former sportscaster, former Miss America, born Denton, TX, June 24, 1949.

Juli Inkster, 54, golfer, born Santa Cruz, CA, June 24, 1960.

Mindy Kaling, 35, actress ("The Office," "The Mindy Project"), author (*Is Everyone Hanging Out Without Me?*), born Vera Mindy Chokalingam at Cambridge, MA, June 24, 1979.

Michele Lee, 72, actress ("Knots Landing"), born Los Angeles, CA, June 24, 1942.

Lionel Messi, 27, soccer player, born Rosario, Argentina, June 24, 1987.

Predrag (Preki) Radosavljevic, 51, soccer coach and former player, born Belgrade, Yugoslavia (now Serbia), June 24, 1963.

Sherry Stringfield, 47, actress ("NYPD Blue," "ER"), born Colorado Springs, CO, June 24, 1967.

Lotte Verbeek, 32, actress ("The Borgias"), born Venlo, Limburg, Netherlands, June 24, 1982.

Peter Weller, 67, actor (*Robocop, Naked Lunch*), born Stevens Point, WI, June 24, 1947.

June 2014

S	M	T	W	T	F	S
1	2	3	4	5	6	7
8	9	10	11	12	13	14
15	16	17	18	19	20	21
22	23	24	25	26	27	28
29	30					

June 25 — Wednesday

DAY 176 **189 REMAINING**

ARNOLD, HENRY H. "HAP": BIRTH ANNIVERSARY. June 25, 1886. US general and commander of the Army Air Force in all theaters throughout WWII, Arnold was born at Gladwyne, PA. Although no funds were made available, as early as 1938 Arnold was persuading the US aviation industry to step up manufacturing of airplanes. Production grew from 6,000 to 262,000 per year from 1940 to 1944. He supervised pilot training and by 1944 Air Force personnel strength had grown to two million from a prewar high of 21,000. Made a full general in 1944, he became the US Air Force's first five-star general when the Air Force was made a separate military branch equal to the Army and Navy. Arnold died Jan 15, 1950, at Sonoma, CA.

BATTLE OF LITTLE BIGHORN: ANNIVERSARY. June 25, 1876. Lieutenant Colonel George Armstrong Custer, leading military forces of more than 200 men, attacked an encampment of Sioux Indians led by Chiefs Sitting Bull and Crazy Horse near Little Bighorn River, MT. Custer and all men in his immediate command were killed in the brief battle (about two hours) of Little Bighorn. One horse, named Comanche, is said to have been the only survivor among Custer's forces.

BHUTAN: NATIONAL DAY. June 25. National holiday observed.

CANADA'S FIRST WOMAN PRIME MINISTER: ANNIVERSARY. June 25, 1993. After winning the June 13 election to the leadership of the ruling Progressive-Conservative Party, Kim Campbell became Canada's 19th prime minister and its first woman prime minister. However, in the general election held Oct 25, 1993, the Liberal Party routed the Progressive-Conservatives in the worst defeat for a governing political party in Canada's 126-year history, reducing the former government's seats in the House of Commons from 154 to 2. Campbell was among those who lost their seats.

CBS SENDS FIRST COLOR TV BROADCAST OVER THE AIR: ANNIVERSARY. June 25, 1951. Columbia Broadcast System broadcast the first color television program. The four-hour program was carried by stations at New York City, Baltimore, Philadelphia, Boston and Washington, DC, although no color sets were owned by the public. At the time CBS itself owned fewer than 40 color receivers.

CENTRAL CHINA FLOOD: ANNIVERSARY. June 25, 1991. The Huai River flooded its banks and ravaged major portions of the central Chinese province of Anhui. The poor agricultural region was devastated and approximately 3,000 people were killed. The Anhui region sustained enormous damages when the government ordered dikes broken and sluice gates opened in the rural area to prevent flooding of economically important rivers farther downstream.

CIVIL WAR IN YUGOSLAVIA: ANNIVERSARY. June 25, 1991. In an Eastern Europe freed from the iron rule of communism and the USSR, separatist and nationalist tensions suppressed for decades rose to a violent boiling point. The republics of Croatia and Slovenia declared their independence, sparking a fractious and bitter war that spread throughout what was formerly Yugoslavia. Ethnic rivalries between Serbians and Croatians began the military conflicts that spread to Slovenia, and in 1992 fighting began in Bosnia-Herzegovina between Serbians and ethnic Muslims. Although the new republics were recognized by the UN and sanctions passed to stop the fighting, it raged on through 1995 despite the efforts of UN peacekeeping forces.

ENGLAND: GLASTONBURY FESTIVAL. June 25–29. Vale of Avalon, Glastonbury. The world's largest greenfield music and performing arts festival. The 1,000-acre festival offers music, theater, circus, cabaret, markets, children's activities and more. Annually, the Wednesday through Sunday after the summer solstice. For info: Glastonbury Festival. E-mail: office@glastonburyfestivals.co.uk. Web: www.glastonburyfestivals.co.uk.

GILLARS, MILDRED "AXIS SALLY" E.: DEATH ANNIVERSARY. June 25, 1988. Mildred E. Gillars received the nickname "Axis Sally" during WWII when she broadcast Nazi propaganda to US troops in Europe. An American citizen, born about 1900 at Portland, ME, she was arrested after the war, tried and convicted of treason. She was sentenced to 10 to 30 years in prison and fined $10,000. She was released after 12 years and later taught music in a convent school at Columbus, OH. She died June 25, 1988, at Columbus, OH.

HELEN KELLER FESTIVAL. June 25–29. Tuscumbia, AL. Commemorates the remarkable life of Helen Keller with stage shows for all ages, arts and crafts fair, free musical entertainment, races, historic tours of Helen Keller's birthplace and other beautiful homes and much more. *The Miracle Worker* is performed evenings during the festival and for five weekends following. Est attendance: 105,000. For info: Helen Keller Festival. E-mail: info@helenkellerfestival.com. Web: www.helenkellerfestival.com.

KOREAN WAR BEGAN: ANNIVERSARY. June 25, 1950. Forces from northern Korea invaded southern Korea, beginning a civil war. US ground forces entered the conflict June 30. An armistice was signed at Panmunjom July 27, 1953, formally dividing the country in two—North Korea and South Korea.

LUMET, SIDNEY: 90th BIRTH ANNIVERSARY. June 25, 1924. Acclaimed film director, born at Philadelphia, PA. Lumet's remarkable list of films directed include *Long Day's Journey into Night, Fail-Safe* and *Serpico*. He was Oscar-nominated as best director for *12 Angry Men, Dog Day Afternoon, Network* and *The Verdict*, although he never took home the prize. Lumet was awarded an honorary Lifetime Achievement Academy Award in 2005. Died Apr 9, 2011, at New York, NY.

MISS OREGON SCHOLARSHIP PAGEANT. June 25–28. Seaside Civic and Convention Center, Seaside, OR. Part of the Miss America Organization. The Miss Oregon Scholarship Program is a not-for-profit corporation established solely to provide contestants with the opportunity to enhance their professional and educational goals and to achieve those pursuits with the assistance of monetary grants and awards. For info: Miss Oregon Scholarship Pageant, 217 Broadway, Seaside, OR 97138. E-mail: miss-or@seasurf.net. Web: www.missoregon.org.

MONTSERRAT: VOLCANO ERUPTS: ANNIVERSARY. June 25, 1997. After lying dormant for 400 years, the Soufriere Hills volcano began to come to life in July 1995. It finally erupted, wiping out the capital city of Plymouth and two-thirds of the rest of this lush Caribbean island on June 25, 1997. Two-thirds of the population relocated to other islands or to Great Britain.

MOZAMBIQUE: INDEPENDENCE DAY. June 25. National holiday. Commemorates independence from Portugal in 1975.

O'NEILL, ROSE CECIL: BIRTH ANNIVERSARY. June 25, 1874. Rose O'Neill was born at Wilkes-Barre, PA. Her career included work as an illustrator, author and doll designer, the latter gaining her commercial success with the Kewpie Doll. In 1910 *The Ladies Home Journal* devoted a full page to her Kewpie Doll designs, which were a marketing phenomenon for three decades. Died at Springfield, MO, Apr 6, 1944.

ORWELL, GEORGE: BIRTH ANNIVERSARY. June 25, 1903. English satirist, author of *Animal Farm, 1984* and other works, born at Motihari, Bengal. George Orwell was the pseudonym of Eric Arthur Blair. Died at London, England, Jan 21, 1950.

REVERE, ANNE: BIRTH ANNIVERSARY. June 25, 1903. American actress Anne Revere was born at New York, NY. She won an Academy Award for her supporting role in *National Velvet* (1944) but was barred from films for 20 years after she refused to testify before the House Committee on Un-American Activities in the 1950s. In 1960 she won a Tony Award for her role in *Toys in the Attic*. Revere died Dec 18, 1990, at Locust Valley, NY.

SEVEN DAYS CAMPAIGN: ANNIVERSARY. June 25–July 1, 1862. In an effort to prevent an attack on Richmond, VA, Confederate General Robert E. Lee launched a series of engagements that became known as the Seven Days Campaign. Battles at Oak Grove, Gaine's Mills, Garnett's Farm, Golding's Farm, Savage's Station, White Oak Swamp and, finally, Malvern Hill left more than 35,000 casualties on both sides. Despite losing the final assault at Malvern Hill, the Confederates succeeded in preventing the Union army from taking Richmond.

SLOVENIA: NATIONAL DAY. June 25. Public holiday. Commemorates independence from the former Yugoslavia in 1991.

SMITHSONIAN FOLKLIFE FESTIVAL. June 25–29 and July 2–6 (tentative). National Mall, Washington, DC. Initiated in 1967, the festival has become a national and international model of a research-based presentation of contemporary living cultural traditions. Over the years, it has brought more than 23,000 musicians, artists, performers, craftspeople, workers, cooks, storytellers and others to demonstrate the skills, knowledge and aesthetics that embody the creative vitality of community-based traditions. It has featured exemplary tradition bearers from more than 90 nations, every region of the United States, scores of ethnic communities, more than 100 Native American groups and some 70 different occupations. Annually, the two weeks overlapping the Fourth of July holiday. Est attendance: 1,000,000. For info: Center for Folklife and Cultural Heritage, Smithsonian Institution, PO Box 37012, MRC 520, Washington, DC 20013-7012. Phone: (202) 633-6440. Fax: (202) 633-6474. E-mail: folklife-info@si.edu. Web: www.folklife.si.edu.

SUMMERFEST. June 25–29 (and July 1–6). Milwaukee, WI. First held in 1968, Summerfest is the world's largest music festival. For 11 days, more than 800 bands play across the 11 stages featured on the permanent 75-acre festival site. On any given day, attendees can enjoy national, alternative, rock, country, R&B, pop, reggae headliners and more. Est attendance: 1,000,000. For info: Milwaukee World Festival, Inc, 200 N Harbor Dr, Milwaukee, WI 53202. Phone: (414) 273-2680. Web: www.summerfest.com.

SUPREME COURT ABORTION NOTIFICATION RULING: ANNIVERSARY. June 25, 1990. The Supreme Court ruled, in a 5–4 decision, that it was unconstitutional for a state to require, without providing other options, that a minor notify both her parents before obtaining an abortion.

SUPREME COURT BANS SCHOOL PRAYER: ANNIVERSARY. June 25, 1962. The Supreme Court ruled, 6–3, that a prayer read aloud in public schools violated the First Amendment's separation of church and state. The court again struck down a law pertaining to the First Amendment when it disallowed an Alabama law that permitted a daily one-minute period of silent meditation or prayer in public schools June 1, 1985.

SUPREME COURT UPHOLDS RIGHT TO DIE: ANNIVERSARY. June 25, 1990. In the case *Cruzan v Missouri*, the Supreme Court, in a 5–4 ruling, upheld the constitutional right of a person whose wishes are clearly known to refuse life-sustaining medical treatment.

TWO YUGOSLAV REPUBLICS DECLARE INDEPENDENCE: ANNIVERSARY. June 25, 1991. The republics of Slovenia and Croatia formally declared independence from Yugoslavia. The two northwestern republics did not, however, secede outright.

VIRGINIA: RATIFICATION DAY. June 25. 10th state to ratify the Constitution in 1788.

BIRTHDAYS TODAY

Anthony Bourdain, 58, author (*Kitchen Confidential*), television personality ("Anthony Bourdain: No Reservations"), born New York, NY, June 25, 1956.

Linda Cardellini, 39, actress (*Scooby-Doo, Legally Blonde*), born Redmond City, CA, June 25, 1975.

Carlos Delgado, 42, baseball player, born Mayaguez, Puerto Rico, June 25, 1972.

Ricky Gervais, 53, actor, comedian ("The Office" [UK], "Extras"), born Reading, Berkshire, England, June 25, 1961.

John Benjamin Hickey, 51, actor ("The Big C"; stage: *The Normal Heart*), born Plano, TX, June 25, 1963.

June Lockhart, 89, actress ("Lassie," "Lost in Space"), born New York, NY, June 25, 1925.

George Michael, 51, singer (Wham!), born Radlett, England, June 25, 1963.

Dikembe Mutombo, 48, former basketball player, humanitarian, born Kinshasa, Zaire, June 25, 1966.

Willis Reed, Jr, 72, Hall of Fame basketball player, basketball executive and former coach, born Hico, LA, June 25, 1942.

Carly Simon, 69, singer, songwriter, born New York, NY, June 25, 1945.

Sonia Sotomayor, 60, Associate Justice of the US, born the Bronx, NY, June 25, 1954.

Billy Wagner, 43, baseball player, born Tannersville, VA, June 25, 1971.

Jimmie Walker, 66, actor, comedian ("Good Times," "B.A.D. Cats"), born New York, NY, June 25, 1948.

June 26 — Thursday

DAY 177 **188 REMAINING**

AMERICAN LIBRARY ASSOCIATION ANNUAL CONFERENCE. June 26–July 1. Las Vegas, NV. The American Library Association (ALA), the oldest and largest library association in the world, holds its annual conference each summer. Its attendees include librarians, educators, writers, publishers, friends of libraries, trustees and special guests. More than 2,000 meetings, discussion groups, tours, special events and awards ceremonies are spread throughout the weeklong conference. Est attendance: 25,000. For info: Public Information Office, American Library Assn, 50 E Huron St, Chicago, IL 60611. Phone: (312) 280-5041 or (800) 545-2433. Fax: (312) 280-5274. E-mail: pio@ala.org. Web: www.ala.org.

BAR CODE INTRODUCED: 40th ANNIVERSARY. June 26, 1974. A committee formed in 1970 by US grocers and food manufacturers recommended in 1973 a Universal Product Code (i.e., a bar code) for supermarket items that would allow electronic scanning of prices. On this day in 1974 a pack of Wrigley's gum was swiped across the first checkout scanner at a supermarket in Troy, OH. Today bar codes are used to keep track of everything from freight cars to cattle.

June 2014	S	M	T	W	T	F	S
	1	2	3	4	5	6	7
	8	9	10	11	12	13	14
	15	16	17	18	19	20	21
	22	23	24	25	26	27	28
	29	30					

BORDEN, SIR ROBERT LAIRD: BIRTH ANNIVERSARY. June 26, 1854. Canadian statesman and prime minister, born at Grand Pre, Nova Scotia. Died at Ottawa, June 10, 1937.

BUCK, PEARL SYDENSTRICKER: BIRTH ANNIVERSARY. June 26, 1892. American author (*The Good Earth*), noted humanitarian and authority on China. Nobel Prize winner. Born at Hillsboro, WV. Died Mar 6, 1973, at Danby, VT.

CANADA: NATIONAL CANOE DAY. June 26. In 2007, the canoe was named one of the Seven Wonders of Canada via a CBC Radio feature in which more than one million votes were cast. In celebration of this, the Canadian Canoe Museum founded this day with the aim of increasing participation in paddlesports in Canada, engaging new paddlers and reaching across generational and cultural divides to introduce the canoe to those who haven't had the opportunity to experience this great national heritage. National Canoe Day has grown to become a truly countrywide event, with participants paddling across the country, from the midnight sun of the north to the urban rivers of the south. National Canoe Day has also been celebrated internationally by groups in the US and UK. Annually, June 26. For info: Canadian Canoe Museum, 910 Monaghan Rd, Peterborough, ON K9J 5K4, Canada. Phone: (705) 748-9153. Fax: (705) 748-0616. Web: www.nationalcanoeday.net or www.canoemuseum.ca.

CN TOWER OPENED: ANNIVERSARY. June 26, 1976. Birthday of the world's second-tallest building and freestanding structure, the CN Tower, 1,815 feet, 5 inches high, at Toronto, Ontario, Canada. It was the world's tallest building until the Burj Khalifa in Dubai (dedicated in 2010).

DOUBLEDAY, ABNER: BIRTH ANNIVERSARY. June 26, 1819. Abner Doubleday served in the US Army during the Mexican War and the Seminole War in Florida prior to his service in the American Civil War. His service found him at the battles of Second Bull Run, Antietam and Fredericksburg, and as a major general he commanded a division at Gettysburg. A commission set up by sporting goods manufacturer Albert Spalding to investigate the origins of baseball credited Doubleday with inventing the game in 1839. Subsequent research has debunked the commission's finding. Doubleday was born at Ballston Spa, NY, and died at Mendham, NJ, Jan 26, 1893.

FEDERAL CREDIT UNION ACT: 80th ANNIVERSARY. June 26, 1934. Commemorates signing by President Franklin Delano Roosevelt of the Federal Credit Union Act, thus enabling the formation of credit unions anywhere in the US.

"GUIDING LIGHT" TV PREMIERE: ANNIVERSARY. June 26, 1952. "Guiding Light," previously on radio, holds the title of longest-lasting daytime show and longest-lasting series. Set in the fictional Midwestern town of Springfield, this soap ended on Sept 18, 2009, after a 72-year run.

***HARRY POTTER AND THE PHILOSOPHER'S STONE* PUBLISHED: ANNIVERSARY.** June 26, 1997. Bloomsbury published this acclaimed children's fantasy book by Joanne (J.K.) Rowling in the United Kingdom with an initial hardcover print run of 500 copies. The first book in a seven-title series, it became a smash hit almost overnight. The seventh title, *Harry Potter and the Deathly Hallows*, was published July 21, 2007. The books—which became a blockbuster film series—have been translated into 69 languages and have sold more than 450 million copies.

HAYMARKET PARDON: ANNIVERSARY. June 26, 1893. Illinois Governor John Peter Altgeld pardoned Samuel Fielden, Michael Schwab and Oscar Neebe, three of the anarchists who had been convicted in the violence connected with the Haymarket Riot on May 4, 1886. At a protest meeting at Haymarket Square an unknown individual threw a bomb that caused the death of several policemen. Eight anarchists were tried and convicted of the bombing. Of those, one committed suicide the day before he was to be hanged; three were hanged; and Fielden, Schwab and Neebe were imprisoned. In 1893 the newly elected Altgeld, at the urging of Clarence Darrow, reviewed the transcripts of the trial of these men and concluded that they had been railroaded. The pardon was widely criticized. It was an act of political suicide for Altgeld.

HUMAN GENOME MAPPED: ANNIVERSARY. June 26, 2000. Biologists J. Craig Venter and Francis S. Collins announced that their research groups had mapped the human genome, a strand of DNA with three billion parts that spell out our genetic code.

MADAGASCAR: INDEPENDENCE DAY. June 26. National holiday. Commemorates independence from France in 1960.

MIDDLETON, ARTHUR: BIRTH ANNIVERSARY. June 26, 1742. American Revolutionary leader and signer of the Declaration of Independence, born near Charleston, SC. Died at Goose Creek, SC, Jan 1, 1787.

MISS VIRGINIA PAGEANT. June 26–28. Roanoke Civic Center Auditorium, Roanoke, VA. Scholarship pageant held since 1953. Miss Virginia then appears in the Miss America pageant. Est attendance: 3,000. For info: Miss Virginia Pageant, 220 Bremble Dr, Moneta, VA 24121. Phone: (540) 721-2877. Web: www.missva.com.

NATIONAL HANDSHAKE DAY. June 26. Get a grip on a professional handshake today! The handshake is an important part of corporate America and can make or break a business deal, interview or other encounter. Take this day to perfect your own handshake and put it into practice. Annually, the last Thursday in June. For info: Miryam S. Roddy, BRODY Professional Development, 115 West Ave, Ste 114, Jenkintown, PA 19046. Phone: (215) 886-1688. E-mail: mroddy@BrodyPro.com.

NORTH AMERICAN ORGANIC BREWERS FESTIVAL. June 26–29. Overlook Park, Portland, OR. Designed to raise awareness about organic beer and sustainable living, the NAOBF serves up four-dozen organic beers and ciders from around the nation. There's also live local music, organic food, sustainability-oriented vendors and nonprofits, a soda garden with complimentary Crater Lake Root Beer for minors and designated drivers and a children's area. The NAOBF is a family-friendly event, and minors are welcome with parents. Annually, the last weekend in June. Est attendance: 15,000. For info: North American Organic Brewers Festival. Phone: (503) 314-7583. E-mail: chris@naobf.org. Web: www.naobf.org.

PIZARRO, FRANCESCO: DEATH ANNIVERSARY. June 26, 1541. Spanish conqueror of Peru, born at Extremadura, Spain, circa 1471. Pizarro died at Lima, Peru.

SAINT IGNACE AUTO SHOW. June 26–28. St. Ignace, MI. 39th anniversary. Parade, cruise night and swap meet. Entries from 25 states and Canada. Est attendance: 80,000. For info: Edward K. Reavie, 268 Hillcrest Blvd, St. Ignace, MI 49781. Phone: (906) 643-8087. Fax: (906) 643-9784. E-mail: ereavie@nostalgia-prod.com. Web: www.nostalgia-prod.com or www.stignacecarshow.com.

SAINT LAWRENCE SEAWAY DEDICATION: 55th ANNIVERSARY. June 26, 1959. President Dwight D. Eisenhower and Queen Elizabeth II jointly dedicated the St. Lawrence Seaway in formal ceremonies held at St. Lambert, QC, Canada. A project undertaken jointly by Canada and the US, the waterway (which provides access between the Atlantic Ocean and the Great Lakes) had been opened to traffic Apr 25, 1959.

SUPREME COURT STRIKES DOWN DEFENSE OF MARRIAGE ACT: ANNIVERSARY. June 26, 2013. In *United States v Windsor*, by a vote of five to four, the US Supreme Court struck down the federal Defense of Marriage Act, ruling that same-sex couples were entitled to federal benefits.

UNITED NATIONS CHARTER SIGNED: ANNIVERSARY. June 26, 1945. The UN Charter was signed at San Francisco by representatives of 50 nations.

UNITED NATIONS: INTERNATIONAL DAY AGAINST DRUG ABUSE AND ILLICIT TRAFFICKING. June 26. Following a recommendation of the 1987 International Conference on Drug Abuse and Illicit Trafficking, the General Assembly (Resolution 42/112) expressed its determination to strengthen action and cooperation for an international society free of drug abuse and proclaimed June 26 as an annual observance to raise public awareness. For info: UN, Dept of Public Info, Public Inquiries Unit, RM GA-57, New York, NY 10017. Phone: (212) 963-4475. E-mail: inquiries@un.org.

UNITED NATIONS: INTERNATIONAL DAY IN SUPPORT OF VICTIMS OF TORTURE. June 26. For info: United Nations, Dept of Public Info, New York, NY 10017. Web: www.un.org.

WATERMELON THUMP (WITH WORLD CHAMPION SEED-SPITTING CONTEST). June 26–29. Luling, TX. 61st annual. Features World Champion Seed-Spitting Contest, dance and concert each night, giant parade on Saturday, free live entertainment in the Beer Garden and Spitway, champion melon auction, arts and crafts exhibit and sales, food, games and rides. Annually, the last weekend in June (Thursday–Sunday). Est attendance: 45,000. For info: Luling Watermelon Thump Assn, PO Box 710, Luling, TX 78648. Phone: (830) 875-3214. Fax: (830) 875-2082. E-mail: jamie@watermelonthump.com. Web: www.watermelonthump.com.

ZAHARIAS, MILDRED "BABE" DIDRIKSON: BIRTH ANNIVERSARY. June 26, 1911. Born Mildred Ella Didrikson at Port Arthur, TX, the great athlete was nicknamed "Babe" after legendary baseball player Babe Ruth. She was named to the women's All-America basketball team when she was 16. At the 1932 Olympic Games, she won two gold medals and also set world records in the javelin throw and the 80-meter high hurdles; only a technicality prevented her from obtaining the gold in the high jump. Didrikson married professional wrestler George Zaharias in 1938, six years after she began playing golf casually. In 1946 Babe won the US Women's Amateur tournament, and in 1947 she won 17 straight golf championships and became the first American winner of the British Ladies' Amateur tournament. Turning professional in 1948, she won the US Women's Open in 1950 and 1954, the same year she won the All-American Open. Babe also excelled in softball, baseball, swimming, figure skating, billiards—even football. In a 1950 Associated Press poll she was named the woman athlete of the first half of the 20th century. She died of cancer on Sept 27, 1956, at Galveston, TX.

BIRTHDAYS TODAY

Claudio Abbado, 81, conductor, born Milan, Italy, June 26, 1933.

Neil Abercrombie, 76, Governor of Hawaii (D), born Buffalo, NY, June 26, 1938.

Paul Thomas Anderson, 44, director, screenwriter (*Punch-Drunk Love, Magnolia, Boogie Nights*), born Studio City, CA, June 26, 1970.

Sean P. Hayes, 44, actor ("Will & Grace"), born Glen Ellyn, IL, June 26, 1970.

Chris Isaak, 58, singer, musician, actor ("The Chris Isaak Show"), born Stockton, CA, June 26, 1956.

Derek Jeter, 40, baseball player, born Pequannock, NJ, June 26, 1974.

Greg LeMond, 53, former cyclist, born Lakewood, CA, June 26, 1961.

Chris O'Donnell, 44, actor ("NCIS: Los Angeles," *Batman Forever, Scent of a Woman*), born Winnetka, IL, June 26, 1970.

Nick Offerman, 44, actor ("Parks and Recreation," "Children's Hospital"), born Joliet, IL, June 26, 1970.

Chad Pennington, 38, football player, born Knoxville, TN, June 26, 1976.

Aubrey Plaza, 30, actress ("Parks and Recreation," *Scott Pilgrim vs the World*), born Wilmington, DE, June 26, 1984.

Jason Schwartzman, 34, actor (*The Darjeeling Limited, Rushmore*), born Los Angeles, CA, June 26, 1980.

Shannon Sharpe, 46, sportscaster, Hall of Fame football player, born Chicago, IL, June 26, 1968.

Gretchen Wilson, 41, country singer, born Granite City, IL, June 26, 1973.

Charlotte Zolotow, 99, author (*The Moon Was the Best, Peter and the Pigeons*), born Norfolk, VA, June 26, 1915.

June 2014	S	M	T	W	T	F	S
	1	2	3	4	5	6	7
	8	9	10	11	12	13	14
	15	16	17	18	19	20	21
	22	23	24	25	26	27	28
	29	30					

June 27 — Friday

DAY 178 **187 REMAINING**

"CAPTAIN VIDEO AND HIS VIDEO RANGERS" TV PREMIERE: 65th ANNIVERSARY. June 27, 1949. "Captain Video" was the first of several TV space shows. The show was set in the 22nd century and starred Richard Coogan as Captain Video, a human who led a squad of agents (the Video Rangers) fighting villains from their own and other worlds. Al Hodge later replaced Coogan. Also featured were Ernest Borgnine, Jack Klugman and Tony Randall as guest villains.

COIN, JEWELRY & STAMP EXPO. June 27–29. Elks Lodge, Pasadena, CA. Est attendance: 4,000. For info: Israel Bick, Exec Dir, Intl Stamp & Coin Collectors Society, Box 854, Van Nuys, CA 91408. Phone: (818) 997-6496. Fax: (818) 988-4337. E-mail: iibick@sbcglobal.net. Web: www.bickinternational.com.

"DARK SHADOWS" TV PREMIERE: ANNIVERSARY. June 27, 1966. This soap opera was completely different from all others because it featured vampires as main characters and had a dark, Gothic feel to it. The show focused on the Collins family living at Collinsport, ME, particularly Barnabas Collins (Jonathan Frid), a 200-year-old vampire. Other cast members included David Selby, Kate Jackson, Lara Parker and Jerry Lacy. Action shifted between the 1800s and the 1960s. This show was very popular with teenagers and was remade as a short-lived series in 1991.

DECIDE TO BE MARRIED DAY. June 27. To focus attention on the joy of couples deciding to get married. Based on the poem "Decide to Be Married": "It's in the deciding to be united in love, to express your joyful oneness to every person you meet, and in every action you take and together a perfect marriage you'll make." For info: Barbara Gaughen-Muller, Pres, Gaughen Global Public Relations, 7456 Evergreen Dr, Santa Barbara, CA 93117. Phone: (805) 968-8567. E-mail: Barbara@rain.org.

DJIBOUTI: INDEPENDENCE DAY. June 27. National day. Commemorates independence from France in 1977.

GRANTSVILLE DAYS. June 27–29. Grantsville Park, Grantsville, MD. Three-day annual homecoming weekend. Free entertainment Friday 6:45 PM–Sunday 6 PM. Lion's chicken BBQ, local noncommercial food booths, children's games, truck- and tractor-pulling contests, parade (Friday) and fireworks (Friday and Saturday nights). Annually, the last weekend in June. Est attendance: 20,000. For info: Grantsville Lions Club, PO Box 450, Grantsville, MD 21536. Fax: (301) 895-3623. E-mail: gbeachy@verizon.net. Web: www.grantsvilledays.net.

HAPPY BIRTHDAY TO "HAPPY BIRTHDAY TO YOU." June 27, 1859. The melody of probably the most often sung song in the world, "Happy Birthday to You," was composed by Mildred J. Hill, a schoolteacher born at Louisville, KY, on this date. Her younger sister, Patty Smith Hill, was the author of the lyrics, which were first published in 1893 as "Good Morning to All," a classroom greeting published in the book *Song Stories for the Sunday School*. The lyrics were amended in 1924 to include a stanza beginning "Happy Birthday to You." Now it is sung somewhere in the world every minute of the day. Although the authors are believed to have earned very little from the song, reportedly it later generated about $1 million a year for its copyright owner. Mildred Hill died at Chicago, IL, June 5, 1916, without knowing that her melody would become the world's most popular song. See also: "Hill, Patty Smith: Birth Anniversary" (Mar 27).

HEARN, LAFCADIO: BIRTH ANNIVERSARY. June 27, 1850. Author, born on the Greek island of Santa Maura. Hearn, who had been a newspaper reporter at Cincinnati, OH, and at New Orleans, LA, went to Japan in 1890 as a magazine writer. Deeply attracted to the country and to the Japanese people, he stayed there as a writer and teacher until his death at Okubo, Japan, Sept 26, 1904. Though his writings are little remembered in America, he remains a popular figure in Japan, where his books are still used, especially in language classes. His home at Matsue is a tourist shrine.

INDUSTRIAL WORKERS OF THE WORLD FOUNDED: ANNIVERSARY. June 27, 1905. With the slogan "One Big Union for All," 43 labor groups merged together to found the IWW at Chicago, IL. Eventually known as the Wobblies, the IWW had a tremendous impact on US labor history.

KEESHAN, BOB: BIRTH ANNIVERSARY. June 27, 1927. Beloved by generations of American children as Captain Kangaroo, Robert J. Keeshan was born at Lynbrook, NJ. He made his acting debut at age 21 as the original Clarabell, the ever-silent clown, sidekick to Buffalo Bob Smith on "The Howdy Doody Show." He was eventually fired from the show, but his future as a children's entertainer was secure. On Oct 3, 1955, "Captain Kangaroo" premiered on CBS, and it remained on the air for 38 years. Captain Kangaroo was joined by characters Mr Green Jeans, Grandfather Clock, Bunny Rabbit and Mr Moose. His gentle, patient wisdom entertained and educated millions of children over the years. Keeshan died in Vermont on Jan 23, 2004.

KELLER, HELEN: BIRTH ANNIVERSARY. June 27, 1880. Born at Tuscumbia, AL, Helen Keller was left deaf and blind by a disease she contracted at 18 months of age. With the help of her teacher, Anne Sullivan, Keller graduated from college and had a career as an author and lecturer. She died June 1, 1968, at Westport, CT.

LOUISIANA PEACH FESTIVAL. June 27–28. Ruston, LA. The 64th annual Louisiana Peach Festival features rodeo, parade, concerts, cooking contests, sporting events, arts and crafts and more. Annually, the fourth weekend in June. Est attendance: 20,000. For info: Ruston-Lincoln Chamber of Commerce, 2111 N Trenton St, Ruston, LA 71270. Phone: (800) 392-9032. E-mail: peach@rustonlincoln.org. Web: www.louisianapeachfestival.org.

MOON PHASE: NEW MOON. June 27. Moon enters New Moon phase at 4:08 AM, EDT.

NATIONAL HIV TESTING DAY. June 27. A nationwide campaign encouraging education, voluntary HIV testing and counseling to people at risk for HIV. For info: Natl Assn of People with AIDS, 8401 Colesville Rd, Ste 505, Silver Spring, MD 20910. Phone: (240) 247-0880. Fax: (240) 247-0574. E-mail: info@napwa.org. Web: www.napwa.org.

NED KELLY'S LAST STAND: ANNIVERSARY. June 27–29, 1880. Australian folk hero and outlaw Ned Kelly, escaping with his gang from pursuing law officers, made a last stand at Glenrowan—rounding up the townspeople and holing up in a hotel. There he and his mates constructed 90-pound iron body armor. The armor hampered more than it helped, and Kelly's gang—including his brother Dan—were all killed. Kelly was captured and hanged on Nov 11, 1880, at Melbourne. The Kelly Gang in their grim armor offered an antihero image that Australians have embraced in film and art.

NEWPORT FLOWER SHOW. June 27–29. Rosecliff, Newport, RI. New England's premier summertime flower and horticulture show includes judged flower arrangements, horticultural exhibits brimming with plants and flowers, demonstrations, lectures and a spectacular garden marketplace in the elegant reception rooms and on the expansive oceanfront lawn of Rosecliff, a Gilded Age mansion. For info: The Preservation Society of Newport County, 424 Bellevue Ave, Newport, RI 02840. Phone: (401) 847-1000. Fax: (401) 841-1361. E-mail: events@newportmansions.org. Web: www.newportflowershow.org.

OREGON BACH FESTIVAL. June 27–July 13. Hult Center for the Performing Arts and the University of Oregon, Eugene, OR (with concerts in Eugene, Portland and other Oregon cities). Artistic director and conductor Matthew Halls leads an international gathering of musicians in choral-orchestral masterworks, intimate concerts and chamber music, informal free concerts and family events, adult education programs and master classes for conductors and composers. Emphasis is on J.S. Bach and his influence on succeeding generations of composers. Est attendance: 40,000. For info: George Evano, Oregon Bach Festival, 1257 University of Oregon, Eugene, OR 97403. Phone: (800) 457-1486 or (541) 346-5666. Fax: (541) 346-5669. E-mail: bachfest@uoregon.edu. Web: www.oregonbachfestival.com.

PARNELL, CHARLES STEWART: BIRTH ANNIVERSARY. June 27, 1846. Irish nationalist leader and home-rule advocate born at Avondale, County Wicklow, Ireland. Politically ruined as a result of an affair with Katherine O'Shea, the estranged wife of a member of Parliament. O'Shea was divorced by her husband (who named Parnell correspondent), and on June 25, 1891, she married Parnell. Less than a month later Parnell was defeated in a by-election. He made his last public speech Sept 27, 1891, and died in the arms of his wife, at Brighton, Oct 6, 1891. Reportedly he was given "a magnificent funeral" by the city of Dublin, where he was buried. The anniversary of Parnell's death is observed by some as Ivy Day when a sprig of ivy is worn on the lapel to remember him. See also: "Ireland: Ivy Day" (Oct 6).

PERRY, ANTOINETTE: BIRTH ANNIVERSARY. June 27, 1888. Esteemed actress, producer and director born at Denver, CO. She starred in numerous theater productions before a stroke in 1927 ended her onstage career. She then became a successful stage director. Perry died June 16, 1946, at New York, NY. In 1947 the American Theater Wing established the annual Antoinette Perry Awards—the Tony Awards—for outstanding accomplishments in theater.

SMITH, JOSEPH, JR, AND HYRUM SMITH: DEATH ANNIVERSARY. June 27, 1844. The founding prophet of The Church of Jesus Christ of Latter-day Saints and his brother Hyrum were shot to death by an armed mob in Carthage, IL. At the time, Joseph Smith was the presidential candidate of the National Reform Party, the first US presidential candidate to be assassinated. Joseph Smith was born at Sharon, VT, Dec 23, 1805; Hyrum Smith was born at Tunbridge, VT, Feb 9, 1800.

SMITHSON, JAMES: DEATH ANNIVERSARY. June 27, 1829. Scientist and founder of the Smithsonian Institution, James Smithson was born at Paris, France, in 1765 (exact date unknown) and died at Genoa, Italy. His will, dated Oct 23, 1826, bequeathed his great wealth to a nation he had never visited, to found "at Washington under the name of the Smithsonian Institution, establishment for the increase and diffusion of knowledge among men." In spite of opposition, the Congress approved, on Aug 10, 1846, an act to establish the Smithsonian Institution. Most of Smithson's personal documents, books and collections were destroyed by fire in 1865. Smithson's remains were removed from Italy to Washington, DC, in 1904.

SOUTH ST. PAUL KAPOSIA DAYS. June 27–29. South St. Paul, MN. Family-oriented city festival including parades, pageant, children's activities, athletic competitions, craft and flea markets, musical entertainment and fireworks. Annually, the last full weekend in June. For info: South St. Paul Kaposia Days, PO Box 144, South St. Paul, MN 55075. Phone: (651) 451-2266. Fax: (651) 451-0846. E-mail: carol@riverheights.com. Web: www.kaposiadays.org.

THURGOOD MARSHALL RESIGNS FROM SUPREME COURT: ANNIVERSARY. June 27, 1991. Signaling an end to the era of a liberal Supreme Court, Associate Justice Thurgood Marshall announced his resignation from the US Supreme Court on this date. Marshall was a pioneering civil rights lawyer who helped lead the fight to end racial segregation and served as US Solicitor General prior to his appointment to the high court by President Lyndon Johnson in 1967 as the first African American ever to sit on the Supreme Court. Marshall's 24-year tenure on the bench was marked by his strong liberal voice championing the rights of criminal defendants and defending abortion rights, his opposition to the death penalty and his commitment to civil rights. On July 1, 1991, President George Bush selected Clarence Thomas, a conservative black jurist, to succeed Marshall. See also: "Marshall, Thurgood: Birth Anniversary" (July 2).

WATER SKI DAYS. June 27–29. Lake City, MN. Hot summer fun! Festival features water ski show, grand parade (Sunday), antique car and tractor show, arts and crafts show, carnival, food vendors and more. Live entertainment all three nights at the beer tent. Annually, the last full weekend in June. Est attendance: 20,000. For info: Lake City Chamber of Commerce, 101 W Center St, Lake City, MN 55041. Phone: (651) 345-4123. E-mail: chamberevents@lakecity.org. Web: www.lakecity.org.

BIRTHDAYS TODAY

J.J. Abrams, 48, television executive ("Lost"), film director (*Star Trek, Mission: Impossible III*), born New York, NY, June 27, 1966.

Isabelle Adjani, 59, actress (*The Story of Adele H., Camille Claudel*), born Paris, France, June 27, 1955.

Kelly Ayotte, 46, US Senator (R, New Hampshire), born Nashua, NH, June 27, 1968.

Julia Duffy, 63, actress ("Newhart," "Designing Women"), born St. Paul, MN, June 27, 1951.

Shirley-Anne Field, 76, actress (*Alfie, My Beautiful Laundrette, Getting It Right*), born London, England, June 27, 1938.

Norma Kamali, 69, fashion designer, born New York, NY, June 27, 1945.

Svetlana Kuznetsova, 29, tennis player, born Leningrad, USSR (now St. Petersburg, Russia), June 27, 1985.

Tobey Maguire, 39, actor (*Spider-Man, Seabiscuit, The Cider House Rules*), born Santa Monica, CA, June 27, 1975.

Jason Patric, 48, actor (*Speed 2, Sleepers*), born Queens, NY, June 27, 1966.

H. Ross Perot, 84, philanthropist, businessman, former presidential candidate, born Texarkana, TX, June 27, 1930.

Chuck Connors Person, 50, former basketball player, born Brantley, AL, June 27, 1964.

Chandler Riggs, 15, actor ("The Walking Dead"), born Atlanta, GA, June 27, 1999.

Ed Westwick, 27, actor ("Gossip Girl," *Son of Rambow*), born Stevenage, Hertfordshire, England, June 27, 1987.

June 2014	S	M	T	W	T	F	S
	1	2	3	4	5	6	7
	8	9	10	11	12	13	14
	15	16	17	18	19	20	21
	22	23	24	25	26	27	28
	29	30					

June 28 — Saturday

DAY 179 **186 REMAINING**

"AMOS 'N' ANDY" TV PREMIERE: ANNIVERSARY. June 28, 1951. This show was based on the popular radio show about black characters played by white dialecticians Freeman Gosden and Charles Correll. In fact, it was the first dramatic series with an all-black cast. The cast included Tim Moore, Spencer Williams, Alvin Childress, Ernestine Wade, Amanda Randolph, Johnny Lee, Nick O'Demus and Jester Hairston. The series was widely syndicated until pressure from civil rights groups, who claimed the show was stereotypical and prejudicial, caused CBS to withdraw it from syndication.

ARRL FIELD DAY. June 28–29. Weekend-long amateur radio event in which thousands of "hams" set up radio stations in remote and unusual places as they practice emergency operations such as were used in Hurricane Katrina. Sponsored by the ARRL, the national association for amateur radio. Annually, the fourth full weekend in June. Est attendance: 100,000. For info: Sean Kutzko, Media Relations Manager, ARRL, 225 Main St, Newington, CT 06111. Phone: (860) 594-0232. Fax: (860) 594-0259. E-mail: fdinfo@arrl.org. Web: www.arrl.org/fieldday.

BISCAYNE NATIONAL PARK ESTABLISHED: ANNIVERSARY. June 28, 1980. Including the coral reefs and waters of Biscayne Bay and the area of the Atlantic Ocean that surrounds the northernmost Florida Keys, Biscayne National Monument was authorized Oct 18, 1968. It became a national park in 1980.

COLORADO BREWERS' FESTIVAL. June 28–29. Fort Collins, CO. The kegs will be tapped once again for the annual festival in Downtown Fort Collins, Colorado. Every year more than 30 Colorado breweries, including local favorites Odells and New Belgium, come celebrate Colorado's rich brewing history and feature their best native beers. Annually, the fourth weekend of June. Est attendance: 30,000. For info: Downtown Fort Collins Business Assn, 19 Old Town Square #230, Fort Collins, CO 80524. Phone: (970) 484-6500. E-mail: info@downtownfortcollins.com. Web: www.downtownfortcollins.com.

COMECON AND WARSAW PACT DISBAND: ANNIVERSARY. June 28, 1991. The last vestiges of the Cold War–era Soviet bloc, the Council for Mutual Economic Assistance (COMECON) and the Warsaw Pact, formally disbanded on June 28 and July 1, 1991, respectively.

CYPRUS: SAINT PAUL'S FEAST. June 28–29. Kato Paphos, Cyprus. Religious festivities at Kato Paphos at which the archbishop officiates. Procession of the icon of Saint Paul through the streets.

GALESBURG RAILROAD DAYS. June 28–29. Galesburg, IL. Annual festival celebrating the city's railroad heritage that dates back to 1854. Carnival, concerts, street fair, railroad exhibits and displays, 5k and 10k runs. Hobby train show with more than 200 exhibitions and tables. Includes more than 40 events. Est attendance: 15,000. For info: Galesburg Area CVB, 2163 E Main St, Galesburg, IL 61401. Phone: (309) 343-2485. Fax: (309) 343-2521. E-mail: visitors@visitgalesburg.com. Web: www.visitgalesburg.com.

GREAT AMERICAN BACKYARD CAMPOUT. June 28. 10th annual. The National Wildlife Federation encourages people of all ages to get outside and camp. Participants register their campsites online and receive exclusive information regarding activities, recipes, wildlife and more. More than 40,000 campers have participated in past events. Annually, the fourth Saturday in June. For info: National Wildlife Federation, 11100 Wildlife Center Dr, Reston, VA 20190. Phone: (800) 822-9919. E-mail: campout@nwf.org. Web: www.backyardcampout.org.

LADIES OF COUNTRY MUSIC SHOW. June 28. Waretown, NJ. Featuring Albert Music Hall's ladies of country and bluegrass. No alcoholic beverages or smoking allowed. For info: Albert Music Hall, PO Box 657, Waretown, NJ 08758. Web: www.alberthall.org.

MAASS, CLARA: BIRTH ANNIVERSARY. June 28, 1876. Commemorates the birth in 1876 of Clara Louise Maass, the heroic nurse who gave her life in the yellow fever experiments of 1901. Maass died at Havana, Cuba, Aug 24, 1901.

MAYER, MARIA GOEPPERT: BIRTH ANNIVERSARY. June 28, 1906. German-American physicist Maria Goeppert Mayer was born at Kattowitz, Germany. A participant in the Manhattan Project, she worked on the separation of uranium isotopes for the atomic bomb. Mayer became the first American woman to win the Nobel Prize when she shared the 1963 prize for physics with J. Hans Daniel Jensen and Eugene P. Wigner for their explanation of the atomic nucleus, known as the nuclear shell theory. Mayer died Feb 20, 1972, at San Diego, CA.

MONDAY HOLIDAY LAW: ANNIVERSARY. June 28, 1968. President Lyndon B. Johnson approved PL 90-363, which amended section 6103(a) of Title 5, United States Code, establishing Monday observance of Washington's Birthday, Memorial Day, Labor Day, Columbus Day and Veterans Day. The new holiday law took effect Jan 1, 1971. Veterans Day observance subsequently reverted to its former observance date, Nov 11. See individual holidays for further details.

PURPLEHULL PEA FESTIVAL AND WORLD CHAMPIONSHIP ROTARY TILLER RACE. June 28. Emerson, AR. 25th annual festival. World Cup purplehull pea–shelling competition, rotary tiller race, concessions, arts, crafts, entertainment, children's games, the Great Purplehull Peas and Cornbread Cook-off, Queen's pageant (various ages) and more. Est attendance: 5,000. For info: Bill Dailey, Pea-R Guy, Purplehull Pea Fest, PO Box 1, Emerson, AR 71740. Phone: (501) 416-4657. E-mail: purplehull@juno.com. Web: www.purplehull.com.

RADNER, GILDA: BIRTH ANNIVERSARY. June 28, 1946. Actress, comedienne ("Saturday Night Live," *Hanky Panky*), born at Detroit, MI. Died May 20, 1989, at Los Angeles, CA.

RAMADAN: THE ISLAMIC MONTH OF FASTING. June 28–July 27. Begins on Islamic lunar calendar date Ramadan 1, 1435. Ramadan, the ninth month of the Islamic calendar, is holy because it was during this month that the Holy Qur'an (Koran) was revealed. All adults of sound body and mind fast from dawn (before sunrise) until sunset to achieve spiritual and physical purification and self-discipline, abstaining from food, drink and intimate relations. It is a time for feeling a common bond with people who are poor and needy, a time of piety and prayer. Different methods for "anticipating" the visibility of the new moon crescent at Mecca are used by different Muslim groups. US date may vary. Began at sunset the preceding day.

RED WINE AND BLUES FESTIVAL. June 28. Tuckerton, NJ. Team up with the Tuckerton Seaport for a perfect afternoon of wine tasting from New Jersey's finest wineries plus live blues entertainment, food, crafts and more. For info: Renee Kennedy, Tuckerton Seaport, 120 W Main St, PO Box 52, Tuckerton, NJ 08087. Phone: (609) 296-8868. Fax: (609) 296-5810. E-mail: info@tuckertonseaport.org. Web: www.tuckertonseaport.org.

ROUSSEAU, JEAN-JACQUES: BIRTH ANNIVERSARY. June 28, 1712. Philosopher, born at Geneva, Switzerland. Died July 2, 1778, at Ermenonville, France. "Man is born free," he wrote in *The Social Contract*, "and everywhere he is in chains."

RUBENS, PETER PAUL: BIRTH ANNIVERSARY. June 28, 1577. Flemish painter and diplomat born at Siegen, Westphalia. Died of gout at Antwerp, Belgium, May 30, 1640.

SIEGE OF VICKSBURG: ANNIVERSARY. June 28, 1862. The siege of the Confederate city of Vicksburg, MS, began in earnest when Admiral David Farragut succeeded in taking a fleet past the Mississippi River stronghold on this date. The siege continued for over a year.

STONEWALL RIOT: 45th ANNIVERSARY. June 28, 1969. Early in the morning of June 28, 1969, the clientele of a gay bar, the Stonewall Inn at New York City, rioted after the club was raided by police. The riot was followed by several days of demonstrations. This event is now recognized as the start of the gay liberation movement.

TREATY OF VERSAILLES: 95th ANNIVERSARY. June 28, 1919. The signing of the Treaty of Versailles at Versailles, France, formally ended WWI.

BIRTHDAYS TODAY

Kathy Bates, 66, actress (Oscar for *Misery*; *Failure to Launch, Fried Green Tomatoes*), born Memphis, TN, June 28, 1948.

Donald Edward (Don) Baylor, 65, baseball manager, former player, born Austin, TX, June 28, 1949.

Danielle Brisebois, 45, actress ("All in the Family," "Knots Landing"), born Brooklyn, NY, June 28, 1969.

Mel Brooks, 86, actor, director (*The Producers, Blazing Saddles*), born Melvyn Kaminsky at New York, NY, June 28, 1928.

John Cusack, 48, actor (*High Fidelity, Say Anything, The Grifters, Bullets Over Broadway*), born Chicago, IL, June 28, 1966.

Bruce Davison, 68, actor (*Ulzana's Raid, Longtime Companion, Six Degrees of Separation*), born Philadelphia, PA, June 28, 1946.

John Elway, 54, football executive and former player, born Port Angeles, WA, June 28, 1960.

Mark Grace, 50, sportscaster, former baseball player, born Winston-Salem, NC, June 28, 1964.

Thomas Hampson, 59, opera singer, born Elkhart, IN, June 28, 1955.

Alice Krige, 60, actress (*Chariots of Fire, Barfly*), born Upington, South Africa, June 28, 1954.

Carl Levin, 80, US Senator (D, Michigan), born Detroit, MI, June 28, 1934.

Mary Stuart Masterson, 48, actress (*Fried Green Tomatoes, Benny & Joon*), born New York, NY, June 28, 1966.

June 29 — Sunday

DAY 180 **185 REMAINING**

AMERICA'S KIDS DAY. June 29. A day set aside to reach out and teach children in America the value of life, liberty and the pursuit of happiness. A time to help kids learn about the great nation that they live in; adults can help them learn by demonstrating what it means to be an American. Annually, the last Sunday in June. For info: Judith Natale, NCAC America-USA, PO Box 493703, Redding, CA 96049-3703. E-mail: childaware@aol.com.

CANADA: ROYAL NOVA SCOTIA INTERNATIONAL TATTOO. June 29–July 6. Halifax, NS. The Tattoo combines more than 2,000 international military and civilian performers in bands, singing, dancing, marching, gymnastics and comedy. Includes Canada Day Parade (July 1). Est attendance: 60,000. For info: Royal Nova Scotia Intl Tattoo, 1586 Queen St, Halifax, NS B3J 2J1, Canada. Phone: (902) 420-1114 or (800) 563-1114. Fax: (902) 423-6629. E-mail: info@nstattoo.ca. Web: www.nstattoo.ca.

DEATH PENALTY BANNED: ANNIVERSARY. June 29, 1972. In a decision that spared the lives of 600 individuals then sitting on death row, the US Supreme Court, in a 5–4 vote, found capital punishment a violation of the Eighth Amendment, which prohibits "cruel and unusual punishment." Later overruling themselves, the court determined on July 2, 1976, that the death penalty was not cruel and unusual punishment and on Oct 4, 1976, lifted the ban on the death penalty in murder cases. On Jan 15, 1977, Gary Gilmore became the first individual executed in the US in more than 10 years.

GAY AND LESBIAN PRIDE PARADE. June 29. Chicago, IL. Chicago's 45th annual parade begins at 12 PM. Est attendance: 850,000. For info: Gay and Lesbian Pride Parade, 3712 N Broadway, PMB #544, Chicago, IL 60613. Phone: (773) 348-8243. E-mail: pridechgo@aol.com. Web: www.chicagopridecalendar.org.

GOETHALS, GEORGE WASHINGTON: BIRTH ANNIVERSARY. June 29, 1858. American engineer and army officer, chief engineer of the Panama Canal and first civil governor of the Canal Zone, born at Brooklyn, NY. Died at New York, NY, Jan 21, 1928.

HERRMANN, BERNARD: BIRTH ANNIVERSARY. June 29, 1911. Herrmann was a pioneering film composer, working with such directors as Alfred Hitchcock, Orson Welles and Martin Scorsese. He introduced the theremin in his score for *The Day the Earth Stood Still* (1951). Other notable credits include Hitchcock's *Psycho* (1960), Welles's *Citizen Kane* (1941), Scorsese's *Taxi Driver* (1976) and the TV shows "The Twilight Zone" and "Lost in Space." Born at New York City, Herrmann died on Dec 24, 1975, at Hollywood, CA.

INDEPENDENCE SUNDAY IN IOWA. June 29. Sunday preceding July 4, by proclamation of the governor.

★ ★ ★

June 2014

S	M	T	W	T	F	S
1	2	3	4	5	6	7
8	9	10	11	12	13	14
15	16	17	18	19	20	21
22	23	24	25	26	27	28
29	30					

INTERSTATE HIGHWAY SYSTEM BORN: ANNIVERSARY. June 29, 1956. President Dwight Eisenhower signed a bill providing $33.5 billion for highway construction. It was the biggest public works program in history.

LATHROP, JULIA C.: BIRTH ANNIVERSARY. June 29, 1858. A pioneer in the battle to establish child-labor laws, Julia C. Lathrop was the first woman member of the Illinois State Board of Charities and in 1900 was instrumental in establishing the first juvenile court in the US. In 1912 President Taft named Lathrop chief of the newly created Children's Bureau, then part of the US Dept of Commerce and Labor. In 1925 she became a member of the Child Welfare Committee of the League of Nations. Born at Rockford, IL, she died there Apr 15, 1932.

LOG CABIN DAY. June 29. Commemorates log cabins with tours, open houses and special festivities throughout the state of Michigan. Est attendance: 3,000. For info: Virginia Handy, Sec/Treas, Log Cabin Society of Michigan, 3503 Rock Edwards Dr, Sodus, MI 49126. Phone: (269) 925-3836. E-mail: logcabinsociety@att.net. Web: www.qtm.net/logcabincrafts.

MAYO, WILLIAM JAMES: BIRTH ANNIVERSARY. June 29, 1861. American surgeon, one of the Mayo brothers, establishers of the Mayo Foundation, born at LeSueur, MN. Died July 28, 1939, at Rochester, MN.

PUNXSUTAWNEY GROUNDHOG FESTIVAL. June 29–July 5. Punxsutawney, PA. Provides residents and visitors a festive week of free entertainment. Music, crafts, food, entertainers and contests. No admission charge. Est attendance: 16,000. For info: Roger Steele, Groundhog Festival Committee, PO Box 1001, Punxsutawney, PA 15767. Phone: (814) 938-2947. Web: www.groundhogfestival.com.

SAINT PETER AND PAUL DAY. June 29. Feast day for Saint Peter and Saint Paul. Commemorates dual martyrdom of Christian apostles Peter (by crucifixion) and Paul (by beheading) during persecution by Roman Emperor Nero. Observed since third century.

SAINT PETER'S DAY. June 29. Antakya, Turkey. Peter first preached Christianity at this place. Ceremonies at Saint Peter's Grotto, early Christian cave near Antakya.

SEYCHELLES: INDEPENDENCE DAY. June 29. National holiday. Gained independence from Great Britain in 1976.

SPACE MILESTONE: *ATLANTIS* (US) AND *MIR* (USSR) DOCK. June 29, 1995. An American space shuttle docked with a Russian space station for the first time, resulting in the biggest craft ever assembled in space. The cooperation involved in this linkup was to serve as a stepping-stone to building the International Space Station.

VANDERZEE, JAMES: BIRTH ANNIVERSARY. June 29, 1886. This pioneering African-American photographer, born at Lenox, MA, set up a portrait studio at Harlem, NY, in 1916, just as that black community was exploding culturally, politically and materially. VanDerZee was the semiofficial photographer of the Harlem Renaissance (1920s to WWII), capturing such luminaries as poet Countee Cullen and Jamaican leader Marcus Garvey, but also dancers, soldiers, street preachers and prosperous middle-class residents. He died May 15, 1983, at Washington, DC.

BIRTHDAYS TODAY

Gary Busey, 70, actor (*Under Siege*, *The Buddy Holly Story*), musician, born Goose Creek, TX, June 29, 1944.

Theo Fleury, 46, former hockey player, born Oxbow, SK, Canada, June 29, 1968.

Fred Grandy, 66, former congressman (R, Iowa), actor ("The Love Boat"), born Sioux City, IA, June 29, 1948.

Joe Johnson, 33, basketball player, born Little Rock, AR, June 29, 1981.

Sharon Lawrence, 52, actress ("Fired Up," "NYPD Blue"), born Charlotte, NC, June 29, 1962.

June 30 — Monday

DAY 181 **184 REMAINING**

BRITAIN CEDES CLAIM TO HONG KONG: ANNIVERSARY. June 30, 1997. The crested flag of the British Crown Colony was officially lowered at midnight and replaced by a new flag (marked by the bauhinia flower) representing China's sovereignty and the official transfer of power. Though Britain owned Hong Kong in perpetuity, the land areas surrounding the city were leased from China and the lease expired July 1, 1997. Rather than renegotiate a new lease, Britain ceded its claim to Hong Kong.

CHARLES BLONDIN'S CONQUEST OF NIAGARA FALLS: ANNIVERSARY. June 30, 1859. Charles Blondin, a French acrobat and aerialist (whose real name was Jean François Gravelet), in view of a crowd estimated at more than 25,000, walked across Niagara Falls on a tightrope. The walk required only about five minutes. On separate occasions he crossed blindfolded, pushing a wheelbarrow, carrying a man on his back and even on stilts. Blondin was born Feb 28, 1824, at St. Omer, France, and died at London, England, Feb 19, 1897.

CONGO (DEMOCRATIC REPUBLIC OF THE): INDEPENDENCE DAY. June 30. National holiday. Democratic Republic of the Congo was previously known as Zaire. Commemorates independence from Belgium in 1960.

***GONE WITH THE WIND* PUBLISHED: ANNIVERSARY.** June 30, 1936. Margaret Mitchell's epic novel of the Civil War South was published on this date. It would be awarded the Pulitzer Prize and National Book Award as best novel of 1936. It has been a bestseller since publication, and 40 countries have published translations. See also: "*Gone with the Wind* Film Premiere: Anniversary" (Dec 15).

GUATEMALA: ARMED FORCES DAY. June 30. Public holiday.

HORNE, LENA: BIRTH ANNIVERSARY. June 30, 1917. Born at Brooklyn, NY, Horne began singing with the chorus line at the Cotton Club in Harlem at age 16. A career on Broadway and in Hollywood followed in rapid succession and she soon became the symbol for African-American actors and singers trying to break the color barrier. She found success with both black and white audiences, although she did face her share of racial prejudice throughout her lifetime. Best remembered for her nightclub and Broadway performances of torch songs, jazz standards and classics like her signature "Stormy Weather," she died at New York, NY, on May 9, 2010.

LEAP SECOND ADJUSTMENT TIME. June 30. This day is one of the times that has been favored for the addition or subtraction of a second from our clock time to coordinate atomic and astronomical time. The determination to adjust is made by the International Earth Rotation Service of the International Bureau of Weights and Measures, at Paris, France. See also: "Note about Leap Seconds" in appendices.

MILOSZ, CZESLAW: BIRTH ANNIVERSARY. June 30, 1911. The great Polish-American poet, author and teacher was born at Szetejnie, Lithuania (then part of Russia). He lived in Warsaw during WWII and participated in the Polish Resistance. Milosz was a diplomat after the war but defected to France in 1951. In 1960, he moved to the US as a teacher of Slavic languages and literature at the University of California at Berkeley, eventually becoming a US citizen. He was awarded the Nobel Prize in Literature in 1980. Milosz died on Aug 14, 2004, at Krakow, Poland.

MONROE, ELIZABETH KORTRIGHT: BIRTH ANNIVERSARY. June 30, 1768. Wife of James Monroe, fifth president of the US, born at New York, NY. Died at their Oak Hill estate at Loudoun County, VA, Sept 23, 1830.

NOW FOUNDED: ANNIVERSARY. June 30, 1966. The National Organization for Women was founded at Washington, DC, by people attending the Third National Conference on the Commission on the Status of Women. NOW's purpose is to take action to bring women into full partnership in the mainstream of American society, exercising all privileges and responsibilities in equal partnership with men. For info: Natl Organization for Women, 1100 H St NW, Ste 300, Washington, DC 20005. Phone: (202) 628-8NOW. Fax: (202) 785-8576. E-mail: now@now.org. Web: www.now.org.

SIBERIAN EXPLOSION: ANNIVERSARY. June 30, 1908. Early in the morning, a spectacular explosion occurred over central Siberia. The seismic shock, firestorm, ensuing "black rain" and illumination that was reportedly visible for hundreds of miles led to speculation that a meteorite was the cause. Said to have been the most powerful explosion in history.

SUDAN: REVOLUTION DAY. June 30. National holiday. Commemorates a bloodless coup in 1989.

WHEELER, WILLIAM ALMON: BIRTH ANNIVERSARY. June 30, 1819. 19th vice president of the US (1877–81), born at Malone, NY. Died there June 4, 1887.

 BIRTHDAYS TODAY

Fantasia Barrino, 30, singer ("American Idol"), born High Point, NC, June 30, 1984.

Vincent D'Onofrio, 55, actor ("Law & Order: Criminal Intent," *Men in Black*), born Brooklyn, NY, June 30, 1959.

Nancy Dussault, 78, actress ("Too Close for Comfort," "The Ted Knight Show"), born Pensacola, FL, June 30, 1936.

Rupert Graves, 51, actor (*A Room with a View, Maurice*), born Weston-Super-Mare, England, June 30, 1963.

David Alan Grier, 59, actor (*A Soldier's Story, I'm Gonna Git You Sucka!*), born Detroit, MI, June 30, 1955.

Monica Potter, 43, actress (*Along Came a Spider,* "Parenthood," "Boston Legal"), born Cleveland, OH, June 30, 1971.

Patricia Schroeder, 74, former president of the Association of American Publishers, former congresswoman (D, Colorado), born Portland, OR, June 30, 1940.

Michael Gerard (Mike) Tyson, 48, former heavyweight champion boxer, born New York, NY, June 30, 1966.

✦ July ✦

July 1 — Tuesday

DAY 182 **183 REMAINING**

ALOPECIA MONTH FOR WOMEN, INTERNATIONAL. July 1–31. A month to raise awareness about alopecia areata and the nearly five million Americans at risk for this autoimmune hair-loss disease. Bald Girls Do Lunch sponsors social events and rallies for women who cannot grow hair normally by fostering camaraderie, public awareness and self-acceptance. For info: Thea Chassin, Bald Girls Do Lunch Inc, PO Box 9122, Scarborough, NY 10510. Phone: (800) 578-5332. E-mail: info@BaldGirlsDoLunch.org. Web: www.BaldGirlsDoLunch.org.

ARAFAT RETURNS TO PALESTINE: 20th ANNIVERSARY. July 1, 1994. Yasser Arafat, head of the Palestine Liberation Organization (PLO), returned to Palestine for the first time in 33 years. Israel's control of Palestine had prevented his visiting the region because he was a sworn enemy of the State of Israel and was regarded by Israelis as a terrorist. An agreement between Israel and the PLO, signed in September 1993, made possible Arafat's return. He went first to Gaza City in the Gaza Strip, where he was welcomed by a crowd estimated at 200,000. Three days later he flew by helicopter to the city of Jericho. Both areas were granted Palestinian rule by the treaty.

ARTOWN. July 1–31. Reno, NV. More than 500 arts-related events including dance, plays, concerts, fine arts exhibits and demonstrations, hands-on programs for children and film. For info: Artown, Jones Vargas Center, 528 W First St, Reno, NV 89503. Phone: (775) 322-1538. Fax: (775) 322-8777. E-mail: office@renoisartown.com. Web: www.renoisartown.com.

BATTLE OF GETTYSBURG: ANNIVERSARY. July 1–3, 1863. After the Southern success at Chancellorsville, VA, Confederate general Robert E. Lee led his forces on an invasion of the North, initially targeting Harrisburg, PA. As Union forces moved to counter the invasion, the battle lines were eventually formed at Gettysburg, PA, in one of the Civil War's most crucial battles. On the climactic third day of the battle (July 3), Lee ordered an attack on the center of the Union line, later to be known as Pickett's Charge. The 15,000 rebels were repulsed, ending the Battle of Gettysburg. After the defeat, Lee's forces retreated back to Virginia, listing more than one-third of the troops as casualties in the failed invasion. Union general George Meade initially failed to pursue the retreating rebels, allowing Lee's army to escape across the rain-swollen Potomac River. With more than 50,000 casualties, this was the worst battle of the Civil War.

BIOTERRORISM/DISASTER EDUCATION AND AWARENESS MONTH. July 1–31. To educate consumers, healthcare professionals, nonprofit organizations and healthcare facilities about being prepared for natural disasters, emergency care, bioterrorism and acts of God. For info: Fred S. Mayer, RPh, MPH, Pharmacists Planning Service, Inc (PPSI), PO Box 6760, San Rafael, CA 94903. Phone: (415) 479-8628 or (415) 302-7351. Fax: (415) 479-8608. E-mail: ppsi@aol.com. Web: www.ppsinc.org.

BLERIOT, LOUIS: BIRTH ANNIVERSARY. July 1, 1872. Louis Bleriot, aviation pioneer and first man to fly an airplane across the English Channel (July 25, 1909), was born at Cambrai, France. He died at Paris, France, Aug 2, 1936.

BOTSWANA: SIR SERETSE KHAMA DAY. July 1. National holiday. Commemorates the birth in 1921 of the first president of Botswana.

BUREAU OF INTERNAL REVENUE ESTABLISHED: ANNIVERSARY. July 1, 1862. The Bureau of Internal Revenue was established by an act of Congress.

BURUNDI: INDEPENDENCE DAY. July 1. National holiday. Anniversary of establishment of independence from Belgian administration in 1962. Had been part of Ruanda-Urundi.

CANADA: CANADA DAY. July 1. Canada's National Day, formerly known as Dominion Day. Observed on following day when July 1 is a Sunday. Commemorates the confederation of Upper and Lower Canada and some of the Maritime Provinces into the Dominion of Canada in 1867.

CANADA: CANADA DAY CELEBRATION. July 1. Ottawa, ON. Annual event celebrating Canada's anniversary. The heart of the capital comes alive with shows, street performers, concerts, games and activities for the whole family. In the evening a spectacular show featuring top Canadian performers is staged on Parliament Hill and culminates with a fireworks display. Est attendance: 350,000. For info: Natl Capital Commission, 202-40 Elgin St, Ottawa, ON, K1P 1C7, Canada. Phone: (800) 465-1867 or (613) 239-5000. E-mail: info@ncc-ccn.ca. Web: www.canadaday.gc.ca.

CANADA: MINERAL-COLLECTING FIELD TRIPS. July 1–Aug 30. Bancroft, ON. Geologist-led, mineral-collecting field trips visit nearby rock dumps, abandoned mines and collecting sites. Participants are educated about mineral identification, collecting techniques and earth sciences. Annually, every Tuesday, Thursday and Saturday in July and August. Est attendance: 1,000. For info: Bancroft and District Chamber of Commerce, PO Box 539, Bancroft, ON, Canada K0L 1C0. Phone: (613) 332-1513. Fax: (613) 332-2119. E-mail: chamber@bancroftdistrict.com. Web: www.bancroftdistrict.com.

CANADA: YUKON GOLD PANNING CHAMPIONSHIPS. July 1. Dawson City, YT. Yukon residents compete for the honor of Territorial Champion Gold Panner. Dawson visitors can join in and compete for the Cheechako Award. Annually, July 1, Canada Day. Est attendance: 200. For info: Klondike Visitors Assn, PO Box 389C, Dawson City, YT, Y0B 1G0, Canada. Phone: (867) 993-5575. Fax: (867) 993-6415. E-mail: kva@dawson.net. Web: www.dawsoncity.ca.

CELL PHONE COURTESY MONTH. July 1–31. There are more than 325 million cell phone users in the US. This month is dedicated to encouraging the increasingly unmindful corps of cell phone users to be more respectful of their surroundings and those around them. Annually, the month of July. For info: Jacqueline Whitmore, Etiquette Expert, PO Box 3073, Palm Beach, FL 33480. Phone: (561) 586-9026. E-mail: info@etiquetteexpert.com. Web: www.etiquetteexpert.com.

CHINA: HALF-YEAR DAY. July 1. National holiday in China. Midyear Day in Thailand.

CLEVELAND'S SECRET SURGERY: ANNIVERSARY. July 1, 1893. President Grover Cleveland boarded the yacht *Oneida* for surgery to be performed in secret on a cancerous growth in his mouth. As this was during the 1893 depression, secrecy was thought desirable to avoid further panic by the public. The whole left side of Cleveland's jaw was removed as well as a small portion of his soft palate. A second, less extensive operation was performed July 17. He was later fitted with a prosthesis of vulcanized rubber that he wore until his death on June 24, 1908. A single leak of the secret was plugged by Cleveland's secretary of war, Daniel Lamont, the only member of the administration to know about the surgery. The illness did not become public knowledge until an article appeared Sept 22, 1917, in the *Saturday Evening Post*, written by William W. Keen, who assisted in the surgery.

COURT TV DEBUT: ANNIVERSARY. July 1, 1991. The continuing evolution of entertainment brought on by the advent of cable television added another twist on July 1, 1991, with the debut of Court TV. Trials are broadcast in their entirety, with occasional commentary from the channel's anchor desk and switching between several trials in progress. Trials with immense popular interest, such as the Jeffrey Dahmer and O.J. Simpson trials, are broadcast along with lower-profile cases. In 2008 the name of the American network was changed to truTV, although Canada still uses the original branding. More reality-based programming has been added to the lineup of trials and criminal justice shows.

DIANA, PRINCESS OF WALES: BIRTH ANNIVERSARY. July 1, 1961. Former wife of Charles, Prince of Wales, and mother of Prince William and Prince Harry. Born Lady Diana Spencer at Sandringham, England, she died in an automobile accident at Paris, France, Aug 31, 1997.

DIXON, WILLIE: BIRTH ANNIVERSARY. July 1, 1915. Blues legend Willie Dixon was born at Vicksburg, MI. He moved to Chicago, IL, in 1936 and began his career as a musician with the Big Three Trio. With the advent of instrument amplification Dixon migrated away from his acoustic upright bass into producing and songwriting with Chess Studios, where he became one of the primary architects of the classic Chicago sound in the 1950s. His songs were performed by Elvis Presley, the Everly Brothers, the Rolling Stones, Led Zeppelin, the Doors, Cream, the Yardbirds, Aerosmith, Jimi Hendrix and the Allman Brothers, among others. Dixon died Jan 29, 1992, at Burbank, CA.

DORSEY, THOMAS A.: BIRTH ANNIVERSARY. July 1, 1899. Thomas A. Dorsey, the father of gospel music, was born at Villa Rica, GA. Originally a blues composer, Dorsey eventually combined blues and sacred music to develop gospel music. It was Dorsey's composition "Take My Hand, Precious Lord" that the Reverend Dr. Martin Luther King, Jr, had asked to have performed just moments before his assassination. Dorsey, who composed more than 1,000 gospel songs and hundreds of blues songs in his lifetime, died Jan 23, 1993, at Chicago, IL.

EASTPORT FOURTH OF JULY AND "OLD HOME WEEK" CELEBRATION. July 1–4. Eastport, ME. Event features a craft fair, theater, music, dance, parades, contests, games, fireworks display and public entertainment July 3–4, US naval ship in port and a variety of contests. Eastport, the easternmost city in the US, is bounded by the Atlantic Ocean on the Bay of Fundy and surrounded by Canadian islands. Canada Day, July 1, is celebrated every year. Est attendance: 10,000. For info: Eastport Fourth of July Committee Inc, PO Box 187, Eastport, ME 04631. Phone: (207) 853-2501. E-mail: contact@eastport4th.com. Web: www.eastport4th.com.

FIRST PHOTOGRAPHS USED IN A NEWSPAPER REPORT: ANNIVERSARY. July 1, 1848. The first instance of photojournalism occurred during the Paris Riots of 1848, when an enterprising French photographer known only as Thibault scrambled to a rooftop to chronicle the events. Taken on June 25 and 26, the two resulting daguerreotypes show first a deserted street, the rue St. Maur, with barricades, and then the same street with insurgents and the military in combat. Wood engravings were made of the daguerreotypes, and on July 1, 1848, the images appeared in the weekly newspaper *L'Illustration Journal Universel*. More than 3,000 Parisians lost their lives during the June revolt.

FIRST SCHEDULED TELEVISION BROADCAST: ANNIVERSARY. July 1, 1941. The National Broadcasting Company (NBC) began broadcasting from the Empire State Building on this day. The Federal Communications Commission had granted the first commercial TV licenses to 10 stations on May 2, 1941.

FIRST US POSTAGE STAMPS ISSUED: ANNIVERSARY. July 1, 1847. The first US postage stamps were issued by the US Postal Service, a 5-cent stamp picturing Benjamin Franklin and a 10-cent stamp honoring George Washington. Stamps had been issued by private postal services in the US prior to this date.

FIRST US ZOO: ANNIVERSARY. July 1, 1874. The Philadelphia Zoological Society, the first US zoo, opened. Three thousand visitors traveled by foot, horse and carriage and steamboat to visit the exhibits. Price of admission was 25 cents for adults and 10 cents for children. There were 1,000 animals in the zoo on opening day.

GHANA: REPUBLIC DAY. July 1. National holiday. Commemorates the inauguration of the republic in 1960.

GRAND TETON MUSIC FESTIVAL. July 1–Aug 16. Walk Festival Hall, Teton Village, WY. 53rd annual. A seven-week summer celebration of classical music in the spectacular setting of Jackson Hole, WY. The festival features the world's finest artists in orchestral and chamber music concerts under the direction of Music Director Donald Runnicles. Est attendance: 25,000. For info: Grand Teton Music Festival, 4015 W Lake Creek Dr, #1, Wilson, WY 83014. Phone: (307) 733-1128. Fax: (307) 739-9043. E-mail: gtmf@gtmf.org. Web: www.gtmf.org.

HERBAL/PRESCRIPTION INTERACTION AWARENESS MONTH. July 1–31. To educate health professionals, patients and consumers on dietary supplements, herbs and nutritionals along with mixing those products with prescription drugs. For info: Fred S. Mayer, RPh, MPH, Pharmacists Planning Service, Inc (PPSI), PO Box 6760, San Rafael, CA 94903. Phone: (415) 479-8628 or (415) 302-7351. Fax: (415) 479-8608. E-mail: ppsi@aol.com. Web: www.ppsinc.org.

INTERNATIONAL BLONDIE AND DEBORAH HARRY MONTH. July 1–31. Each July, this special month celebrates the Rock and Roll Hall of Fame band Blondie and its lead singer, Deborah Harry, and their contributions to popular music. For info: Allan Metz, 937 S Alex Ave, Springfield, MO 65802. E-mail: ametz@drury.edu.

INTERNATIONAL ZINE MONTH. July 1–31. An annual celebration of zines, self-publishing and small press culture that happens in the month of July. Observe International Zine Month by creating your own zine, participating in the 24-hour zine project, attending zine readings or events or supporting zine libraries and alternative presses. For info: International Zine Month, Portland Button Works, 1322 N Killingsworth, Portland, OR 97217. E-mail: brainscanzine@gmail.com. Web: internationalzinemonth.wordpress.com.

LAUDER, ESTÉE: BIRTH ANNIVERSARY. July 1, 1908 (some sources say 1906). The cosmetics magnate was born Josephine Esther Mentzer at Corona, Queens, NY. In high school she took an interest in the work of her uncle, John Schotz, a Hungarian-born chemist who made beauty products for women. She began a business at her kitchen table in 1946 that has gone on to become one of the world's largest, most successful cosmetics companies. The introduction of her breakthrough formula for the bath oil Youth Dew in the 1950s led the way to a company currently worth more than $10 billion. At the time of her death on Apr 24, 2004, at New York, NY, Lauder was among the 500 richest women in the world.

"THE LIBERACE SHOW" TV PREMIERE: ANNIVERSARY. July 1, 1952. A pianist known for his outrageous style and a candelabra on his piano, Liberace hosted popular shows in the '50s and '60s. The first premiered on KLAC-TV in Los Angeles, CA, and went national in 1953. That did so well that he began a half-hour syndicated series that featured his brother George as violinist and orchestra leader. After a brief leave, he returned to TV in 1958 with a half-hour show. Liberace also hosted a British series and a summer series produced in London, England.

LINCOLN SIGNS INCOME TAX BILL: ANNIVERSARY. July 1, 1862. President Abraham Lincoln signed into law a bill levying a 3 percent income tax on annual incomes of $600–$10,000 and 5 percent on incomes of more than $10,000. The revenues were to help pay for the Civil War. This tax law actually went into effect, unlike an earlier law passed Aug 5, 1861, making it the first income tax levied by the US. It was rescinded in 1872.

"MAMA" TV PREMIERE: 65th ANNIVERSARY. July 1, 1949. One of TV's first popular sitcoms, "Mama" told the story of a Norwegian family living in San Francisco, CA, in 1917. The show aired live through 1956; after it was canceled, a second, filmed version lasted only 13 weeks. Cast members included Peggy Wood, Judson Laire, Rosemary Rice, Dick Van Patten, Iris Mann, Robin Morgan, Ruth Gates, Malcolm Keen, Carl Frank, Alice Frost, Patty McCormack and Kevin Coughlin. Toni Campbell replaced Robin Morgan in the revival.

MAMMOTH CAVE NATIONAL PARK ESTABLISHED: ANNIVERSARY. July 1, 1941. Area of central Kentucky, originally authorized May 25, 1926, was established as a national park. For info: Mammoth Cave Natl Park, Mammoth Cave, KY 42259.

MEDICARE: ANNIVERSARY. July 1, 1968. Medicare, the US health insurance program for senior citizens, went into effect. The legislation authorizing the program had been signed by President Lyndon Johnson July 30, 1965. Former president Harry Truman received the first Medicare card.

MORRILL LAND GRANT ACT PASSED: ANNIVERSARY. July 1, 1862. This federal legislation led to the creation of the land grant universities and agricultural experiment stations in each state.

NATIONAL BLUEBERRIES MONTH. July 1–31. To make the public aware that this is the peak month for fresh blueberries. For info: US Highbush Blueberry Council. Web: www.blueberry.org.

NATIONAL "DOGHOUSE REPAIRS" MONTH. July 1–31. Celebrate "Doghouse Repairs" Month by staying out of trouble with those you love and care about by doing something extra special. For info: Heidi Richards Mooney, PO Box 550856, Fort Lauderdale, FL 33355-0856. Phone: (954) 625-6606. E-mail: heidi@successandthensome.com.

NATIONAL EDUCATION ASSOCIATION MEETING. July 1–6. Denver, CO. Representative Assembly. For info: Natl Education Assn, 1201 16th St NW, Washington, DC 20036-3290. Phone: (202) 833-4000. Web: www.nea.org.

NATIONAL GRILLING MONTH. July 1–31. The sizzle, the smoke and the mouthwatering aromas that come from a grill can be yours if you take the time out this month and enjoy the fun and ease of cooking on a grill—indoor or out!

NATIONAL GSA EMPLOYEE RECOGNITION DAY. July 1. The General Services Administration was established on July 1, 1949, to streamline the administrative work of the federal government. Today, through its two largest offices—the Public Buildings Service and the Federal Acquisition Service—and various staff offices, the GSA provides workspace to more than one million federal civilian workers, oversees the preservation of more than 480 historic buildings and facilitates the purchase of high-quality, low-cost goods and services from quality commercial vendors. Annually, July 1. For info: Richard Baker, 400 15th St SW, Auburn, WA 98001. Phone: (253) 931-7299. E-mail: richard.e.baker@gsa.gov. Web: www.gsa.gov.

NATIONAL HORSERADISH MONTH. July 1–31. What 3,000-year-old plant has been used as a bitter herb for Passover seders and a flavorful accompaniment for beef, chicken and seafood? If you guessed horseradish, you're right. This month, celebrate the healthful and hot horseradish, which has been praised for its numerous food uses for centuries. For info: Horseradish Information Council, 1100 Johnson Ferry Rd NE, Ste 300, Atlanta, GA 30342. Phone: (404) 252-3663. Fax: (404) 252-0774. E-mail: jpetty@kellencompany.com. Web: www.horseradish.org.

★ ★ ★

July 2014	S	M	T	W	T	F	S
			1	2	3	4	5
	6	7	8	9	10	11	12
	13	14	15	16	17	18	19
	20	21	22	23	24	25	26
	27	28	29	30	31		

NATIONAL HOT DOG MONTH. July 1–31. Celebrates one of America's favorite and most patriotic foods with fun facts and new recipes. More than 20 billion hot dogs per year are consumed in the US. For info: Natl Hot Dog and Sausage Council, 1150 Connecticut Ave NW, 12th Fl, Washington, DC 20036. Phone: (202) 587-4200. Fax: (202) 587-4300. Web: www.hot-dog.org.

NATIONAL ICE CREAM MONTH. July 1–31. First designated by President Ronald Reagan in 1984, this month celebrates ice cream as a fun and nutritious food that is enjoyed by a full 90 percent of the nation's population. For info: Intl Dairy Foods Assn, 1250 H Street NW, Ste 900, Washington, DC 20005. Phone: (202) 737-4332. Fax: (202) 331-7820. Web: www.idfa.org.

NATIONAL MAKE A DIFFERENCE TO CHILDREN MONTH. July 1–31. To remind us of the many ways adults can make a positive difference to children. Create opportunities for kids during this midsummer month when most children are not in school by doing three things: 1. Commit to do one special thing with a child in July—make some kind of positive difference for that child. 2. Support an organization that focuses on children—there are many to choose from. 3. Communicate with your elected leaders to make children a priority in policy and budget issues they address. For info: Kim Ratz, 3665 Woody Ln, Minnetonka, MN 55305. Phone: (952) 938-4472. E-mail: kimratz@aol.com. Web: www.kimratz.com/madtc.html.

NATIONAL PARK AND RECREATION MONTH. July 1–31. Since 1985, America has celebrated July as the nation's official Park and Recreation Month. During this month, people everywhere should be talking about what they love about parks and recreation and why parks and recreation are so vital in our lives. For info: Natl Recreation and Park Assn, 22377 Belmont Ridge Rd, Ashburn, VA 20148. Phone: (800) 626-6772. E-mail: july@nrpa.org. Web: www.nrpa.org.

NATIONAL UNASSISTED HOMEBIRTH WEEK. July 1–7. Conferences and activities to create awareness and encouragement for couples who intentionally seek to give birth without a midwife or doctor. For info: Lynn M. Griesemer, 4103 Plaza Ln, Fairfax, VA 22033. Phone: (703) 263-2468. E-mail: greeze@juno.com. Web: www.unassistedhomebirth.com.

RWANDA: INDEPENDENCE DAY. July 1. National holiday. Commemorates independence from Belgium in 1962.

SAND, GEORGE: BIRTH ANNIVERSARY. July 1, 1804. The French novelist, author of more than 100 volumes, whose real name was Amandine Aurore Lucile (Dupin) Dudevant, was born at Paris, France. Died at Nohant, France, June 8, 1876. She is better remembered for having been a liberated woman during a romantic epoch than for her literary works.

SECOND HALF OF THE NEW YEAR DAY. July 1. How are you doing on your New Year's resolutions? July 1 is your midyear checkpoint. Celebrate accomplishments, look at what you did not complete and why, or set new goals. This is a day to help people stay on track and achieve healthier, happier and more successful lives. For info: Cindy Kubica, 414 Parish Pl, Franklin, TN 37067. Phone: (615) 771-3800. E-mail: cindy@cindykubica.com.

SMART IRRIGATION MONTH. July 1–31. Most home owners over-irrigate their lawns by 30 percent—not only wasting water but also washing nutrients into rivers and streams and away from the root zone where the plants can use them. Evaluate your irrigation system this month. For smart irrigation, consider adding a "smart" controller (one that uses weather, plant and soil data to determine when to water) or a rain-sensor shutoff device. To find out where your system might be wasting water, seek an irrigation system audit by a qualified irrigation auditor. For info: The Irrigation Assn, 6540 Arlington Blvd, Falls Church, VA 22042. Phone: (703) 536-7080. Fax: (703) 536-7019. E-mail: info@irrigation.org. Web: www.smartirrigationmonth.org.

SOMALIA DEMOCRATIC REPUBLIC: NATIONAL DAY. July 1. Anniversary of the merger of newly independent British Somaliland and Italian Somaliland on July 1, 1960.

SPACE MILESTONE: *CASSINI-HUYGENS* REACHES SATURN: 10th ANNIVERSARY. July 1, 2004. Launched on Oct 15, 1997, the *Cassini-Huygens* spacecraft, a joint venture of NASA, the European Space Agency (ESA) and the Italian Space Agency (ISA), reached Saturn on this date and maneuvered into orbit. The ESA's *Huygens* probe touched down on Saturn's moon Titan on Jan 14, 2005. The purpose of the multibillion-dollar NASA/ESA/ISA mission is to explore the Saturnian system.

SPACE MILESTONE: *KOSMOS 1383* (USSR). July 1, 1982. First search-and-rescue satellite—equipped to hear distress calls from aircraft and ships—launched in cooperative project with the US and France.

SURINAME: LIBERATION DAY. July 1. National holiday. Commemorates the 1863 abolition of slavery in Dutch territory.

TEN THOUSAND CRESTONIANS. July 1–4. Downtown and McKinley Park, Creston, IA. Parade, fireworks, flea market, talent show, historical village, carnival and food. All to celebrate US founding. Est attendance: 10,000. For info: Creston Chamber of Commerce, PO Box 471, Creston, IA 50801. Phone: (641) 782-7021. E-mail: chamber@crestoniowachamber.com. Web: www.crestoniowachamber.com.

TWENTY-SIXTH AMENDMENT RATIFIED: ANNIVERSARY. July 1, 1971. The 26th Amendment to the Constitution granted the right to vote in all federal, state and local elections to all persons 18 years or older. On the date of ratification the US gained an additional 11 million voters. Up until this time, the minimum voting age was set by the states; in most states it was 21.

WOMEN'S MOTORCYCLE MONTH. July 1–31. This month is dedicated to honoring women who ride, co-ride or wish they could ride motorcycles or their derivatives (sidecar rigs, trikes, etc). For info: Sylvia Henderson, Springboard Training, PO Box 588, Olney, MD 20830-0588. Phone: (301) 260-1538. E-mail: sylvia@springboardtraining.com.

WORLDWIDE BEREAVED PARENTS AWARENESS MONTH. July 1–31. This month seeks to promote support for bereaved parents. Often people don't know what to say to or do for grieving parents. This observance encourages people to reach out to bereaved parents and their families by listening to them without advising them, giving them a shoulder to cry on and giving them a hug when appropriate and needed. Basically, this month seeks to inspire people to "be there" for the bereaved individuals. Remember to reach out to the bereaved. For info: Peter and Deb Kulkkula, Coordinators, Bereaved Parents Awareness Month, 381 Billings Rd, Fitchburg, MA 01420-1407. Phone: (978) 343-4009. E-mail: info@bereavedparentsawarenessmonth.info. Web: www.bereavedparentsawarenessmonth.info.

ZAMBIA: UNITY DAY. July 1. Memorial day for Zambians who died in the struggle for independence. Political rallies stressing solidarity throughout country. Annually, the first Tuesday in July.

ZIP CODES INAUGURATED: ANNIVERSARY. July 1, 1963. The US Postal Service introduced the five-digit zip code on this day.

BIRTHDAYS TODAY

Pamela Anderson, 47, model, actress ("V.I.P.," "Baywatch"), born Ladysmith, BC, Canada, July 1, 1967.

Dan Aykroyd, 62, actor (*Ghostbusters, Trading Places, The Blues Brothers*), born Ottawa, ON, Canada, July 1, 1952.

Andre Braugher, 52, actor ("Homicide: Life on the Street," "Thief," *City of Angels*), born Chicago, IL, July 1, 1962.

Genevieve Bujold, 72, actress (*Choose Me, Trouble in Mind, Dead Ringers*), born Montreal, QC, Canada, July 1, 1942.

Hilarie Burton, 32, actress ("One Tree Hill"), host (MTV's "TRL"), born Sterling, VA, July 1, 1982.

Leslie Caron, 83, actress (*Gigi, Lili, An American in Paris*), dancer, born Paris, France, July 1, 1931.

Olivia de Havilland, 98, actress (Oscars for *To Each His Own* and *The Heiress*; *Gone with the Wind*), born Tokyo, Japan, July 1, 1916.

Missy Elliott, 43, singer, born Portsmouth, VA, July 1, 1971.

Jamie Farr, 80, actor ("M*A*S*H," *The Blackboard Jungle*), born Jameel Farah at Toledo, OH, July 1, 1934.

Debbie Harry, 69, singer (Blondie), born Miami, FL, July 1, 1945.

Jarome Iginla, 37, hockey player, born Edmonton, AB, Canada, July 1, 1977.

Frederick Carlton (Carl) Lewis, 53, Olympic track athlete, born Birmingham, AL, July 1, 1961.

Jean Marsh, 80, actress ("Upstairs, Downstairs"), writer, born Stoke Newington, England, July 1, 1934.

Alan Ruck, 58, actor ("Spin City," *Ferris Bueller's Day Off*), born Cleveland, OH, July 1, 1956.

Twyla Tharp, 73, dancer, choreographer (Tony for *Movin' Out*), born Portland, IN, July 1, 1941.

Liv Tyler, 37, actress (Lord of the Rings film trilogy, *Armageddon*), born Portland, ME, July 1, 1977.

July 2 — Wednesday

DAY 183 **182 REMAINING**

AMELIA EARHART DISAPPEARS: ANNIVERSARY. July 2, 1937. In 1937 aviatrix Amelia Earhart planned an around-the-world trip via the equatorial route that would be the longest ever made. Having completed 22,000 miles of her journey, Earhart, accompanied by navigator Fred Noonan, took off on this date from Lae, New Guinea, for the final 7,000 miles over the Pacific. About 800 miles into their flight to tiny Howland Island, radio contact was lost with her craft. Despite a massive search by the US Navy and US Coast Guard, Earhart, Noonan and their plane were never found.

"THE ANDY WILLIAMS SHOW" TV PREMIERE: ANNIVERSARY. July 2, 1957. Singer Andy Williams hosted many variety shows, including "The Andy Williams–June Valli Show," "The Chevy Showroom" and "The Andy Williams Show." His shows featured Dick Van Dyke, the Bob Hamilton Trio, the New Christy Minstrels, the Osmond Brothers, Charlie Callas, Irwin Corey and Janos Prohaska. In 1976 Williams hosted "Andy," a syndicated show.

CANADA: THE NORTH AMERICAN TOURNAMENT. July 2–6 (tentative). Spruce Meadows, Calgary, AB. Strong contingents from North America and Europe compete in this show-jumping tournament. The weekend features the ATCO POWER Queen Elizabeth II Cup and the Sun Life Financial Reach for the Sun. The tournament also features a tribute to our Canadian military with exhibits for all to experience. Live entertainment Friday through Sunday on the Plaza. Est attendance: 100,000. For info: Spruce Meadows, 18011 Spruce Meadows Way SW, Calgary, AB, T2J 5G5, Canada. Phone: (403) 974-4200. Web: www.sprucemeadows.com.

CIVIL RIGHTS ACT OF 1964: 50th ANNIVERSARY. July 2, 1964. President Lyndon Johnson signed the Civil Rights Act of 1964 into law, prohibiting discrimination on the basis of race in pub-

lic accommodations, in publicly owned or operated facilities, in employment and union membership and in the registration of voters. The bill included Title VI, which allowed for the cutoff of federal funding in areas where discrimination persisted.

CONSTITUTION OF THE US TAKES EFFECT: ANNIVERSARY. July 2, 1788. Cyrus Griffin of Virginia, the president of the Congress, announced that the Constitution had been ratified by the required nine states (the ninth being New Hampshire June 21, 1788), and a committee was appointed to make preparations for the change of government.

CRANMER, THOMAS: 525th BIRTH ANNIVERSARY. July 2, 1489. English clergyman, reformer and martyr, born at Aslacton, Nottinghamshire, England. Archbishop of Canterbury and spearhead of the English Reformation. One of the principal authors of *The English Book of Common Prayer.* Tried for treason, Cranmer temporarily recanted his Protestantism but then publicly rejected his recantation at his execution, calling it "the great thing that troubleth my conscience more than any other thing that I ever said or did in my life." Burned at the stake at Oxford, England, Mar 21, 1556.

DECLARATION OF INDEPENDENCE RESOLUTION: ANNIVERSARY. July 2, 1776. Anniversary of adoption by the Continental Congress, Philadelphia, PA, of a resolution introduced June 7, 1776, by Richard Henry Lee of Virginia: "Resolved, That these United Colonies are, and of right ought to be, free and independent States, that they are absolved from all allegiance to the British Crown, and that all political connection between them and the State of Great Britain is, and ought to be, totally dissolved. That it is expedient forthwith to take the most effectual measures for forming foreign Alliances. That a plan of confederation be prepared and transmitted to the respective Colonies for their consideration and approbation." This resolution prepared the way for adoption, July 4, 1776, of the Declaration of Independence. See also: "Declaration of Independence Approval and Signing: Anniversary" (July 4).

DENMARK: AALBORG AND REBILD FESTIVAL (AMERICAN INDEPENDENCE DAY CELEBRATION). July 2–4. Aalborg and Rebild. Since 1912. This celebration of the American Independence Day, at the Rebild National Park, south of Aalborg, Denmark, is described as "the largest single gathering for this occasion in the world." Guest speakers and Danish and American entertainment. Est attendance: 10,000. For info: Visit Aalborg. E-mail: info@visitaalborg.com. Web: www.visitaalborg.com/go/july4 or www.rebildfesten.dk.

ENGLAND: HENLEY ROYAL REGATTA. July 2–6. Henley-on-Thames, Oxfordshire. International rowing event that is one of the big social events of the year. Annually since 1839. Est attendance: 330,000. For info: The Secretary, Henley Royal Regatta, Regatta Headquarters, Henley-on-Thames, Oxfordshire, England RG9 2LY. Phone: (44) (1491) 57-2153. Fax: (44) (1491) 57-5509. Web: www.hrr.co.uk.

July 2014

S	M	T	W	T	F	S
		1	2	3	4	5
6	7	8	9	10	11	12
13	14	15	16	17	18	19
20	21	22	23	24	25	26
27	28	29	30	31		

FIRST SOLO ROUND-THE-WORLD BALLOON FLIGHT: ANNIVERSARY. July 2, 2002. In his sixth attempt, Steve Fossett became the first person to circumnavigate the world nonstop and in a nonmotorized craft. In his "Spirit of Freedom" balloon, Fossett traveled 19,400 miles. He began his odyssey on June 18, 2002, at Northam, Australia, and arrived at his starting longitude (117° east) on July 2. (The first balloon flight around the world was accomplished by a two-man team in 1999. See also: "First Round-the-World Balloon Flight: Anniversary" [Mar 21].)

GARFIELD, JAMES ABRAM: ASSASSINATION ANNIVERSARY. July 2, 1881. President James A. Garfield was shot as he entered the railway station at Washington, DC. He died Sept 19, 1881, never having recovered from the wound. The assassin, Charles J. Guiteau, was hanged June 30, 1882.

GLUCK, CHRISTOPH: 300th BIRTH ANNIVERSARY. July 2, 1714. Influential opera composer, who, with librettist Rainiere de' Calzabigi, created a series of "reform operas," most notably *Orfeo ed Euridice* (1761) and *Alceste* (1767), that were hybrids of Italian and French operatic traditions. Born at Erasbach, Bavaria, Germany, Gluck died Nov 15, 1787, at Vienna, Austria.

HALFWAY POINT OF 2014. July 2. At noon, July 2, 2014, 182½ days of the year will have elapsed and 182½ will remain before Jan 1, 2015.

ITALY: PALIO. July 2 (also Aug 16). Siena. Colorful medieval horse race, competing for the banner (Palio).

LACOSTE, RENÉ: BIRTH ANNIVERSARY. July 2, 1904. Jean René Lacoste, tennis player and clothier, born at Paris, France. Lacoste, known as the Crocodile, was one of the four great French tennis players in the 1920s known as the Four Musketeers. He won Wimbledon and the US championship twice each, won the French Open three times and was ranked number one in the world in 1926–27. He designed the first shirt specifically for tennis, a loose-fitting cotton polo shirt that soon became the standard. He adorned the Lacoste shirt with a small crocodile, the first apparel logo. Died at St. Jean-de-Luz, France, Oct 12, 1996.

"THE LAWRENCE WELK SHOW" TV PREMIERE: ANNIVERSARY. July 2, 1955. This musical series, hosted by accordionist and bandleader Lawrence Welk, lasted for almost three decades. In its early years it was known as "The Dodge Dancing Party." Regulars included the Lennon Sisters, Alice Lon, Norma Zimmer, Tanya Falan, Arthur Duncan, Joe Feeney, Guy Hovis, Jim Roberts, Ralna English, Larry Hooper, Jerry Burke and Bobby Burgess. During 1956–59 this show was on concurrently with either "Lawrence Welk's Top Tunes and New Talent" or "The Plymouth Show Starring Lawrence Welk (Lawrence Welk's Little Band)."

MADE IN THE USA DAY. July 2. A day to encourage US manufacturing and the purchase of made-in-the-USA products. Annually, on July 2—the date in 1776 when the American colonies voted for independence. For info: Joel D. Joseph, Chairman, Made in the USA Foundation, 11950 San Vicente Blvd, Ste 220, Los Angeles, CA 90049. Phone: (310) MADE-USA. Web: www.madeusafdn.org.

MARSHALL, THURGOOD: BIRTH ANNIVERSARY. July 2, 1908. Thurgood Marshall, the first African American on the US Supreme Court, was born at Baltimore, MD. For more than 20 years, he served as director-counsel of the NAACP Legal Defense and Educational Fund. He experienced his greatest legal victory May 17, 1954, when the Supreme Court decision on *Brown v Board of Education* declared an end to the "separate but equal" system of racial segregation in public schools in 21 states. Marshall argued 32 cases before the Supreme Court, winning 29 of them, before becoming a member of the high court himself. Nominated by President Lyndon Johnson, he began his 24-year career on the high court Oct 2, 1967, becoming a voice of dissent in an increasingly conservative court. Marshall announced his retirement June 27, 1991, and he died Jan 24, 1993, at Washington, DC.

RIVERFEST. July 2–5. Riverside Park, LaCrosse, WI. 32nd annual Riverfest—the city's premier summer event! River activities, four stages to provide continuous entertainment, a children's area with games, face painting, food pavilion featuring 16 different vendors, beverage tent and an arts and crafts area. July 4 features a fireworks display. Est attendance: 40,000. For info: Riverfest, Inc, PO

Box 1745, LaCrosse, WI 54602. Phone: (608) 782-6000. Fax: (608) 784-1580. E-mail: riverfest@centurytel.net. Web: www.riverfestlacrosse.com.

SAINT LOUIS RACE RIOTS: ANNIVERSARY. July 2, 1917. Between 20 and 75 blacks were killed in a race riot in St. Louis, MO; hundreds more were injured. To protest this violence against blacks, W.E.B. DuBois and James Weldon Johnson of the NAACP led a silent march down Fifth Avenue at New York City.

VESEY, DENMARK: DEATH ANNIVERSARY. July 2, 1822. Planner of what would have been the biggest slave revolt in US history, Denmark Vesey was executed at Charleston, SC. He was born around 1767, probably in the West Indies, where he was sold at about age 14 to Joseph Vesey, captain of a slave ship. He purchased his freedom in 1800. In 1818 Vesey and others began to plot an uprising; he held secret meetings, collected disguises and firearms and chose a date in June 1822. But authorities were warned, and police and the military were out in full force. Over the next two months 130 blacks were taken into custody; 35, including Vesey, were hanged and 31 were exiled. As a result of the plot, Southern legislatures passed more rigorous slave codes.

BIRTHDAYS TODAY

José Canseco, Jr, 50, former baseball player, born Havana, Cuba, July 2, 1964.

Sean Casey, 40, former baseball player, born Willingsboro, NJ, July 2, 1974.

Vicente Fox Quesada, 72, former president of Mexico, born Mexico City, Mexico, July 2, 1942.

Polly Holliday, 77, actress ("Alice," "Home Improvement"), born Jasper, AL, July 2, 1937.

Lindsay Lohan, 28, actress (*Freaky Friday, Mean Girls*), born New York, NY, July 2, 1986.

Jimmy McNichol, 53, actor ("The Fitzpatricks," "California Fever"), born Los Angeles, CA, July 2, 1961.

Richard Petty, 77, former race car driver, born Level Cross, NC, July 2, 1937.

Joe Thornton, 35, hockey player, born London, ON, Canada, July 2, 1979.

Ashley Tisdale, 29, actress, singer ("The Suite Life of Zach and Cody," *High School Musical*), born West Deal, NJ, July 2, 1985.

Johnny Weir, 30, Olympic figure skater, born Coatesville, PA, July 2, 1984.

July 3 — Thursday

DAY 184 **181 REMAINING**

AIR-CONDITIONING APPRECIATION DAYS. July 3–Aug 15. Northern Hemisphere. During Dog Days, the hottest time of the year in the Northern Hemisphere, to acknowledge the contribution of air-conditioning to a better way of life. Annually, July 3–Aug 15. (Originated by John C. Nash.)

BELARUS: INDEPENDENCE DAY. July 3. National holiday. Commemorates liberation of Minsk in 1944.

BELGIUM: OMMEGANG PAGEANT. July 3. Brussels. Splendid historic festival of medieval pageantry at the illuminated Grand-Palace in Brussels. The annual event (first Thursday in July) re-creates an entertainment given in honor of Charles V and his court. For info: Ommegang Pageant. Web: www.ommegang.be.

BENNETT, RICHARD BEDFORD: BIRTH ANNIVERSARY. July 3, 1870. Former Canadian prime minister, born at Hopewell Hill, NB, Canada. Died at Mickelham, England, June 26, 1947.

CANADA: RBC BLUESFEST. July 3–13. Le Breton Flats, Ottawa, ON. 21st annual. Enjoy a spectacular explosion of blues, gospel, roots, world and popular music in the heart of Canada's national capital. The festival takes place on multiple stages with more than 250 performances. Est attendance: 300,000. For info: Allison Shalla, RBC Royal Bank Bluesfest, 265 Catherine St, Ottawa, ON, K1R 7S5 Canada. Phone: (613) 247-1188. Fax: (613) 247-2220. E-mail: info@ottawabluesfest.ca. Web: www.ottawabluesfest.ca.

COMPLIMENT-YOUR-MIRROR DAY. July 3. Participation consists of complimenting your mirror on having such a wonderful owner and keeping track of whether other mirrors you meet during the day smile at you. For info: Bob Birch, Grand Punscorpion, Puns Corps, 3108 Dashiell Rd, Falls Church, VA 22042. Phone: (703) 533-3668.

COPLEY, JOHN SINGLETON: BIRTH ANNIVERSARY. July 3, 1738. Born to Irish immigrants in Boston, MA, perhaps on July 3, 1738, Copley was the most important American painter of the 18th century. After rapid early success in Boston as an in-demand portrait painter (among his subjects was Paul Revere), Copley moved to London, England, in 1774 and traveled in Europe to study further. Copley's best-known painting is *Watson and the Shark* (1782), depicting a youth saved from the jaws of the approaching predator in the Bay of Havana, Cuba. Copley died at London on Sept 9, 1815.

DOG DAYS. July 3–Aug 11. Hottest days of the year in Northern Hemisphere. Usually about 40 days, but variously reckoned at 30–54 days. Popularly believed to be an evil time "when the sea boiled, wine turned sour, dogs grew mad, and all creatures became languid, causing to man burning fevers, hysterics and phrensies" (from Brady's *Clavis Calendarium*, 1813). Originally the days when Sirius, the Dog Star, rose just before or at about the same time as sunrise (no longer true owing to precession of the equinoxes). Ancients sacrificed a brown dog at the beginning of Dog Days to appease the rage of Sirius, believing that star was the cause of the hot, sultry weather.

EARTH AT APHELION. July 3. At approximately 8 PM, EDT, planet Earth will reach aphelion, that point in its orbit when it is farthest from the sun (about 94,510,000 miles). Earth's mean distance from the sun (mean radius of its orbit) is reached early in the months of April and October. Note that Earth is farthest from the sun during Northern Hemisphere summer. See also: "Earth at Perihelion" (Jan 4).

ENNIS RODEO AND PARADE. July 3–4. Ennis, MT. Billed as the fastest two-day rodeo in Montana, this is a nonstop rodeo of excitement. Parade with clowns, bucking broncos and everything imaginable. Annually, July 3–4. Est attendance: 4,000. For info: Ennis Rodeo Club, PO Box 236, Ennis, MT 59729. Phone: (406) 682-4700.

FISHER, M.F.K.: BIRTH ANNIVERSARY. July 3, 1908. The prolific author Mary Frances Kennedy Fisher was born at Albion, MI. With the publication of her first book, *Serve It Forth* (1937), she essentially invented a new genre: essays about food. Her other titles include *The Gastronomical Me* (1943) and *With Bold Knife and Fork* (1969). Fisher died at Glen Ellen, CA, June 22, 1992.

HUNTINGTON, SAMUEL: BIRTH ANNIVERSARY. July 3, 1731. President of the Continental Congress, governor of Connecticut, signer of the Declaration of Independence, born at Windham, CT, and died at Norwich, CT, Jan 5, 1796.

IDAHO: ADMISSION DAY: ANNIVERSARY. July 3. Became 43rd state in 1890.

IRAN AIR FLIGHT 655 DISASTER: ANNIVERSARY. July 3, 1988. At 10:54 AM in the Persian Gulf, the US Navy warship *Vincennes* fired two surface-to-air missiles at Iran Air Flight 655, which destroyed the airbus, killing all 290 passengers aboard. The *Vincennes,* boasting the world's most sophisticated radar-detection equipment, reportedly misread radio signals of the airbus, mistaking it for a hostile F-14 fighter plane. A self-conducted military inquiry blamed human failure—stress on the tense crew rather than equipment malfunction—for the disaster. In the summer of 1992 the public learned that the ship had been in Iranian waters at the time in the course of an operation aimed at preventing Iranian boats from laying mines.

LEXINGTON'S FOURTH OF JULY BALLOON RALLY. July 3–5. Virginia Military Institute, Lexington, VA. Enjoy craft and food vendors, live entertainment, balloon glows, tethered balloon rides and actual balloon flights! For info: Sunrise Rotary Club, PO Box 63, Lexington, VA 24450. E-mail: info@sunriserotarylexva.org. Web: www.sunriserotarylexva.org/balloon.htm.

"MR PEEPERS" TV PREMIERE: ANNIVERSARY. July 3, 1952. This sitcom was broadcast live and focused on mild-mannered junior high school science teacher Robinson J. Peepers (Wally Cox). The cast also included Tony Randall, Georgann Johnson, Marion Lorne, Reta Shaw, Jack Warden and Ernest Truex. This half-hour series was a summer replacement, but it earned such positive reviews that it was brought back as a regular series. In 1954 *TV Guide* wrote that "'Mr Peepers' . . . comes close to being the perfect TV show."

MORRISON, JIM: DEATH ANNIVERSARY. July 3, 1971. Jim Morrison, charismatic lead singer for the rock group The Doors, was found dead in his bathtub on this date at Paris, France. The probable cause of death was heart failure. Morrison was buried at Paris's famous Cimetière du Père-Lachaise, and his grave quickly became a shrine. See also: "Morrison, Jim: Birth Anniversary" (Dec 8).

MOUNT RUSHMORE INDEPENDENCE DAY CELEBRATION. July 3–4. Mount Rushmore National Memorial, SD. For info: Mount Rushmore Natl Memorial, 13000 Hwy 244, Bldg 31, Ste 1, Keystone, SD 57751. Phone: (605) 574-2523. Fax: (605) 574-2307. Web: www.nps.gov/moru.

QUÉBEC FOUNDED: ANNIVERSARY. July 3, 1608. French explorer Samuel de Champlain founded a settlement called Québec, from the Algonquin word *kébec,* meaning "where the river narrows." Québec City is thus one of the oldest settlements of European origin in North America.

RAID ON ENTEBBE: ANNIVERSARY. July 3, 1976. An Israeli commando unit staged a raid on the Entebbe airport in Uganda and rescued 103 hostages on a hijacked Air France airliner. Three of the hostages, seven hijackers and 20 Ugandan soldiers were killed in the raid. The plane had been en route from Tel Aviv to Paris when it was taken over by the pro-Palestinian guerrillas.

STAY OUT OF THE SUN DAY. July 3. For health's sake, give your skin a break today. (©2006 by WH.) For info: Thomas & Ruth Roy, Wellcat Holidays, 2418 Long Ln, Lebanon, PA 17046. Phone: (717) 279-0184. E-mail: info@wellcat.com. Web: www.wellcat.com.

US VIRGIN ISLANDS: DANISH WEST INDIES EMANCIPATION DAY. July 3, 1848. Commemorates freeing of slaves in the Danish West Indies. Ceremony at Frederiksted, St. Croix, where actual proclamation was first read by Governor-General Peter Von Scholten.

❀ ❀ ❀

July 2014	S	M	T	W	T	F	S
			1	2	3	4	5
	6	7	8	9	10	11	12
	13	14	15	16	17	18	19
	20	21	22	23	24	25	26
	27	28	29	30	31		

VICKSBURG SURRENDERS: ANNIVERSARY. July 3, 1863. After weeks of immediate siege at the end of a yearlong campaign, Vicksburg, MS, surrendered to General Ulysses S. Grant. Formal surrender was consummated on July 4, and on July 8 the besieged city of Port Hudson also surrendered, giving the Union complete control of the Mississippi River. This move cut off the western Confederacy from the rest of the South.

WASHINGTON TAKES COMMAND OF THE CONTINENTAL ARMY: ANNIVERSARY. July 3, 1775. George Washington took command of the Continental Army at Cambridge, MA.

WESTMORELAND ARTS AND HERITAGE FESTIVAL. July 3–6. Twin Lakes Park, Greensburg, PA. 40th annual festival celebrating four decades of arts and humanities. Multicultural celebration including food booths, children's area, crafts, fine art exhibition and continuous entertainment on four stages. Est attendance: 150,000. For info: WAHF, 252 Twin Lakes Rd, Latrobe, PA 15650. Phone: (724) 834-7474. E-mail: info@artsandheritage.com. Web: www.artsandheritage.com.

BIRTHDAYS TODAY

Lamar Alexander, 74, US Senator (R, Tennessee), born Maryville, TN, July 3, 1940.

Moises Alou, 48, former baseball player, born Atlanta, GA, July 3, 1966.

Julian Assange, 43, journalist, publisher (www.WikiLeaks.ch), born Townsville, Queensland, Australia, July 3, 1971.

Dave Barry, 67, humorist, author, born Brooklyn, NY, July 3, 1947.

Betty Buckley, 67, actress (*Cats, Sunset Boulevard,* "Eight Is Enough"), born Fort Worth, TX, July 3, 1947.

Tom Cruise, 52, actor (*Mission: Impossible* films, *Collateral, Jerry Maguire, Top Gun*), born Thomas Cruise Mapother IV at Syracuse, NY, July 3, 1962.

Pete Fountain, 84, jazz musician, born New Orleans, LA, July 3, 1930.

Thomas Gibson, 52, actor ("Criminal Minds," "Dharma & Greg"), born Charleston, SC, July 3, 1962.

Teemu Selanne, 44, hockey player, born Helsinki, Finland, July 3, 1970.

Kurtwood Smith, 72, actor ("That '70s Show," *Robocop*), born New Lisbon, WI, July 3, 1942.

Tom Stoppard, 77, playwright (Tonys for *The Coast of Utopia, The Real Thing, Travesties* and *Rosencrantz and Guildenstern Are Dead*), screenwriter (Oscar for *Shakespeare in Love*), born Thomas Straussler at Zlin, Czechoslovakia (now Czech Republic), July 3, 1937.

Montel Williams, 58, talk show host ("The Montel Williams Show"), born Baltimore, MD, July 3, 1956.

July 4 — Friday

DAY 185 **180 REMAINING**

ADAMS, JOHN, AND JEFFERSON, THOMAS: DEATH ANNIVERSARY. July 4, 1826. Former US presidents John Adams and Thomas Jefferson died on the same day, July 4, 1826, the 50th anniversary of adoption of the Declaration of Independence. Adams had once written to Jefferson (1813): "You and I ought not to die before we have explained ourselves to each other." They thus began a spirited correspondence until their deaths. Adams's last words: "Thomas Jefferson still survives." Jefferson's last words: "This is the Fourth?"

"AMERICA THE BEAUTIFUL" PUBLISHED: ANNIVERSARY. July 4, 1895. The poem "America the Beautiful" by Katherine Lee Bates, a Wellesley College professor, was first published in the *Congregationalist*, a church publication.

"AMERICAN TOP 40" RADIO PREMIERE: ANNIVERSARY. July 4, 1970. Casey Kasem's hit-parade music countdown radio program, "American Top 40," was first broadcast on seven AM stations in the US on July 4, 1970. It is now heard in hundreds of markets around the world. For info: Pete Battistini, 6576 Lake Forest Dr, Avon, IN 46123. Phone: (317) 839-1421. E-mail: at40@aol.com. Web: www.at40book.com.

ANVIL MOUNTAIN RUN. July 4. Nome, AK. 36th annual. At 8 AM the 17k run up 1,134-foot Anvil Mountain and return to the city of Nome starts the day's activities. Record time: 1 hour, 11 minutes, 23 seconds. Annually, July 4. Est attendance: 1,500. For info: Rasmussen's Music Mart, PO Box 2, Nome, AK 99762-0002. Phone: (907) 443-2798. E-mail: leaknome@alaska.com.

BOOM BOX PARADE. July 4. Willimantic, CT. Connecticut's unique people's parade. Anyone can march, enter a float or watch; only requirement: bring a radio. No "real" bands allowed. (Marching music broadcast on WILI-AM radio and played by "boom boxes" along the parade route.) Begins at 11 AM. Est attendance: 10,000. For info: Grand Marshall Wayne Norman, WILI-AM, 720 Main St, Willimantic, CT 06226. Phone: (860) 456-1111. Fax: (860) 456-9501. E-mail: wayne@wili.com. Web: www.wili.com/am.

BRISTOL FOURTH OF JULY CELEBRATION. July 4. Bristol, RI. The nation's oldest continuous Fourth of July parade and celebration. Features floats, bands, veteran and patriotic organizations and military units. Patriotic exercises, a tradition dating to 1785, are held prior to the parade. Annually, July 4 except when July 4 is a Sunday, then the parade is held Monday, July 5. Est attendance: 100,000. For info: Bristol Fourth of July Celebration, PO Box 561, Bristol, RI 02809. E-mail: admin@july4thbristolri.com. Web: www.july4thbristolri.com.

CALITHUMPIAN PARADE. July 4. Biwabik, MN. Funny parade, clowns and bands; Biwabik's population of 1,000 jumps to more than 15,000 for a day. Annually, on the Fourth of July. Est attendance: 15,000. For info: 4th of July, Biwabik Area Civic Assn, Box 449, Biwabik, MN 55708. Phone: (218) 865-4183.

CANADA: CALGARY STAMPEDE. July 4–13. Calgary, AB. "The Greatest Outdoor Show on Earth." Since 1912. The Calgary Stampede is made up of sights, sounds, tastes and feelings that create a lifetime of memories. More than a century of tradition is distilled into 10 days of music, food, excitement, education, friendship and community. Includes the world's richest tournament-style rodeo, Rangeland Derby, Grandstand Show, Stampede Parade, Heavy Horse Show, World Championship Blacksmith's Competition, North American Sheep Shearing Challenge, carnival, food and much more. Est attendance: 1,218,000. For info: Calgary Exhibition and Stampede, PO Box 1060, Station M, Calgary, AB, T2P 2K8, Canada. Phone: (403) 261-0101 or (800) 661-1260. E-mail: info@calgarystampede.com. Web: www.calgarystampede.com.

CANADA: MUSIC AND BEYOND FESTIVAL. July 4–14. Ottawa, ON. Widely considered one of Canada's major classical music festivals and one of North America's most innovative arts festivals, Music and Beyond presents classical music in all formations including orchestras, choirs, bands, wind ensembles, instrumental and vocal recitals, and small ensembles. The festival pursues links with music and other art forms and cultural disciplines including visual art, drama, literature and many more. Est attendance: 40,000. For info: Julian Armour, Music and Beyond Festival, PO Box 20585 RPO Rideau East, Ottawa, ON, Canada K1N 1A3. Phone: (613) 241-0777. E-mail: julian.armour@sympatico.ca. Web: www.musicandbeyond.ca.

CELEBRATION ON THE CANE: AN OLD-FASHIONED FOURTH OF JULY. July 4. Natchitoches, LA. Featuring hot dogs, apple pie, lemonade and a variety of traditional Fourth of July fare. Musical entertainment and fireworks over the scenic Cane River Lake. Est attendance: 10,000. For info: Natchitoches CVB. Phone: (318) 352-8072 or (800) 259-1714. Fax: (318) 352-2415. Web: www.natchitoches.net.

COOLIDGE, CALVIN: BIRTH ANNIVERSARY. July 4, 1872. The 30th president of the US was born John Calvin Coolidge at Plymouth, VT. He succeeded to the presidency Aug 3, 1923, following the death of Warren G. Harding. Coolidge was elected president once, in 1924, but did "not choose to run for president in 1928." Nicknamed Silent Cal, he is reported to have said, "If you don't say anything, you won't be called on to repeat it." Coolidge died at Northampton, MA, Jan 5, 1933.

DECLARATION OF INDEPENDENCE APPROVAL AND SIGNING: ANNIVERSARY. July 4, 1776. The Declaration of Independence was approved by the Continental Congress: "Signed by Order and in Behalf of the Congress, John Hancock, President, Attest, Charles Thomson, Secretary." The official signing occurred Aug 2, 1776. The manuscript journals of the Congress for that date state: "The declaration of independence being engrossed and compared at the table was signed by the members."

ENGLAND: THE TELEGRAPH WAYS WITH WORDS FESTIVAL OF WORDS AND IDEAS. July 4–14. Dartington Hall, Dartington, Devon. The United Kingdom's most stylish literature festival. Some 150 writers participate in lectures, seminars, interviews, discussions and readings. On-site bar, restaurant. Bookshop and craft stalls. Est attendance: 15,000. For info: Ways with Words, Droridge Farm, Dartington, Totnes, Devon, England TQ9 6JG. Phone: (44) (1803) 867-373. E-mail: admin@wayswithwords.co.uk. Web: www.wayswithwords.co.uk.

FIREWORKS CELEBRATION. July 4. Demopolis, AL. Each year the Demopolis Area Chamber of Commerce presents a spectacular array of fireworks in celebration of Independence Day. The fireworks celebration is held at the Demopolis City Landing and begins at 9 PM. Event also includes a children's patriotic parade. Est attendance: 10,000. For info: Demopolis Area Chamber of Commerce, Box 667, Demopolis, AL 36732. Phone: (334) 289-0270. Fax: (334) 289-0216. E-mail: demopchamber@yahoo.com. Web: www.demopolischamber.com.

FOSTER, STEPHEN: BIRTH ANNIVERSARY. July 4, 1826. Stephen Collins Foster, one of America's most famous and best-loved songwriters, was born at Lawrenceville, PA. Among his nearly 200 songs: "Oh! Susanna," "Camptown Races," "Old Folks at Home" ("Swanee River"), "Jeanie with the Light Brown Hair," "Old Black Joe" and "Beautiful Dreamer." Foster died in poverty at Bellevue Hospital at New York, NY, Jan 13, 1864.

GOLDBERG, RUBE: BIRTH ANNIVERSARY. July 4, 1883. The cartoonist with an engineering degree who put his education to work inventing elaborate machines with involved steps to accomplish ludicrously simple tasks. He is best remembered for the creative inventions of his cartoon character Lucifer Gorgonzola Butts. Born at San Francisco, CA, Goldberg died Dec 7, 1970, at New York City.

THE GREAT INTERNATIONAL CHICKEN WING SOCIETY COOK-OFF. July 4–6. Reno, NV. 13th annual. Festival where bars, restaurants and individuals compete to make the best chicken wings. Est attendance: 60,000. For info: Willie Davison, Great Intl Chicken Wing Society, PO Box 190, Sparks, NV 89431. Phone: (775) 358-8376. E-mail: mrdavison@aol.com.

GREAT SEAL OF THE US PROPOSED: ANNIVERSARY. July 4, 1776. The Continental Congress, meeting at Philadelphia, PA, after voting to adopt the Declaration of Independence, went on to approve the following: "Resolved, that Dr. Franklin, Mr J. Adams and Mr Jefferson, be a committee, to bring in a device for a seal for the United States of America," thus beginning the history of the Great Seal of the US on the first day of independence. The seal wasn't designed and used until 1782.

HAWTHORNE, NATHANIEL: BIRTH ANNIVERSARY. July 4, 1804. Novelist and short-story writer, born at Salem, MA. Works include *The Scarlet Letter*, *The House of the Seven Gables* and *The Blithedale Romance*. Hawthorne died at Plymouth, NH, May 19, 1864.

ICE CREAM SOCIAL. July 4. Benjamin Harrison Presidential Site, Indianapolis, IN. Independence Day celebration. Music, lawn games and living history. Est attendance: 500. For info: Benjamin Harrison Presidential Site, 1230 N Delaware St, Indianapolis, IN 46202. Phone: (317) 631-1888. Fax: (317) 632-5488. E-mail: events@bhpsite.org. Web: www.bhpsite.org.

INDEPENDENCE DAY CELEBRATION. July 4. Mystic Seaport, Mystic, CT. Visitors can participate in a re-creation of an 1870s Fourth of July with costumed staff. There are patriotic ceremonies and a children's parade. Kids' old-fashioned spelling bee and 19th-century games on the Green. Est attendance: 3,500. For info: Mystic Seaport, 75 Greenmanville Ave, Box 6000, Mystic, CT 06355. Phone: (860) 572-0711 or (888) 973-2767. Web: www.mysticseaport.org.

INDEPENDENCE DAY: THE FOURTH OF JULY. July 4, 1776. The US commemorates adoption of the Declaration of Independence by the Continental Congress. The nation's birthday. Legal holiday in all states and territories.

INDEPENDENCE-FROM-MEAT DAY. July 4. Don't be a slave to tradition. Declare your freedom from flesh foods. Your fiery Fourth will be fantastic with a good-for-you vegetarian barbecue. Why not fix a freedom feast featuring veggie burgers and veggie dogs for your family and friends? It will be fun for you and your animal friends too! For info: Vegetarian Awareness Network, PO Box 3545, Washington, DC 20027-0045. Phone: (800) 234-8343.

July 2014	S	M	T	W	T	F	S
			1	2	3	4	5
	6	7	8	9	10	11	12
	13	14	15	16	17	18	19
	20	21	22	23	24	25	26
	27	28	29	30	31		

INDIVISIBLE DAY. July 4. This day recognizes the necessity for the separation of church and state. For info: American Humanist Assn, 1777 T St NW, Washington, DC 20009. Phone: (202) 238-9088. Fax: (202) 238-9003. Web: www.secularseasons.org/July/indivisible_day.html.

JACK JOHNSON v JIM JEFFRIES: ANNIVERSARY. July 4, 1910. Boxers Johnson, heavyweight champion of the world, and Jeffries, "the Great White Hope," met in Reno, NV, in what was billed as "the Battle of the Century." More than 20,000 people (whites mostly) were on hand to see Johnson—a 10-to-4 underdog going into the bout—dominate Jeffries from start to finish. Jeffries's brawling style was no match for Johnson, who smiled and talked to spectators ringside as he landed and slipped punches round after round. Finally, in the 15th round, Jeffries's corner threw in the towel before Johnson could knock the former champion out. Afterward, spontaneous celebrations by blacks were marred by white attackers and devolved into race riots in 50 cities in 25 states, leaving 25 dead and hundreds injured.

JULY FOURTH CELEBRATION AND ANVIL SHOOT. July 4. Museum of Appalachia, Norris, TN. An old-fashioned celebration highlighted by the "shooting" of an anvil; also musicians, patriotic ceremonies and demonstrations of old-time activities including sassafras tea brewing, spinning, rail splitting and more! For info: Museum of Appalachia, 2819 Andersonville Hwy, Clinton, TN 37716. Phone: (865) 494-7680. E-mail: museum@museumofappalachia.org. Web: www.museumofappalachia.org.

KOKO THE GORILLA: BIRTHDAY. July 4, 1971. Koko, a lowland gorilla (full name: Hanabi-Ko, or "Fireworks Child" in Japanese), was born this day at the San Francisco Zoo. She is probably the most famous gorilla in the world due to her participation in the longest continuous experiment to teach language to animals. She was taught sign language beginning when she was about a year old, and she currently has a vocabulary of 1,000 signs.

LANDERS, ANN: BIRTH ANNIVERSARY. July 4, 1918. Born Esther Pauline Friedman at Sioux City, IA, the advice columnist was beloved worldwide. In 1955 she won a contest to be the new "Ann Landers" columnist for the *Chicago Sun-Times*. For 47 years, with spunky yet compassionate replies that were a refreshing change from prior columnists' styles, she helped everyday people overcome their problems. A trademark admonishment was "40 lashes with a wet noodle." (Her twin sister, Pauline Friedman, followed in her footsteps with a "Dear Abby" column.) By 2002 her column was carried in more than 1,200 newspapers worldwide and had a readership of 30 million. She died June 22, 2002, at Chicago, IL.

LAURA INGALLS WILDER PAGEANT. July 4–6 (also July 11–13 and 18–20). De Smet, SD. An outdoor pageant on the natural prairie stage depicting scenes historically based on Laura Ingalls Wilder's life and books. Est attendance: 10,000. For info: The Laura Ingalls Wilder Pageant, PO Box 154, De Smet, SD 57231. Phone: (800) 880-3383. Web: www.desmetpageant.org.

LIBERTY CELEBRATION. July 4–6. Yorktown Victory Center, Yorktown, VA. Tactical drills, military exercises and role-playing demonstrations salute the anniversary of America's independence. Visitors can see in museum galleries a rare broadside printing of the Declaration of Independence dating to July 1776. For info: Jamestown-Yorktown Foundation, PO Box 1607, Williamsburg, VA 23187. Phone: (757) 253-4838 or (888) 593-4682. Fax: (757) 253-5299. Web: www.historyisfun.org.

LOU GEHRIG DAY: 75th ANNIVERSARY. July 4, 1939. After retiring from baseball, Lou Gehrig returned to the New York Yankees for Lou Gehrig Day. In his famous farewell speech he said, "Today I consider myself the luckiest man on the face of the earth."

MACKINAW CITY'S FOURTH OF JULY FIREWORKS. July 4. Mackinaw City, MI. Starting at 1:30 PM on the marina lawn, fun and games for all ages. One of the largest fireworks displays in the North is shot off over the harbor at dusk. For info: Mackinaw City Chamber of Commerce, PO Box 856, Mackinaw City, MI 49701. Phone: (231) 436-5574 or (888) 455-8100. Web: www.mackinawchamber.com.

OLD VERMONT FOURTH. July 4. Woodstock, VT. A traditional Fourth of July with patriotic speeches and debates, the making of "1890" flags, a spelling bee for adults, ice cream making, sack race and more. Est attendance: 750. For info: Billings Farm and Museum, Rte 12 N, Woodstock, VT 05091. GPS address: 69 Old River Rd, Woodstock, VT 05091. Phone: (802) 457-2355. Fax: (802) 457-4663. E-mail: info@billingsfarm.org. Web: www.billingsfarm.org.

PEACHTREE ROAD RACE. July 4. Atlanta, GA. 45th annual. The largest 10k run in the world. 55,000-runner limit; advance registration only. Online registration begins in March; see website for details. Est attendance: 150,000. For info: Atlanta Track Club, 3097 E Shadowlawn Ave, Atlanta, GA 30305. Phone: (404) 231-9064, ext 10. E-mail: atc@atlantatrackclub.org. Web: www.atlantatrackclub.org or www.peachtreeroadrace.org

PHILIPPINES: FIL-AMERICAN FRIENDSHIP DAY. July 4. Formerly National Independence Day, when the Philippines were a colony of the US, now celebrated as Fil-American Friendship Day.

SMITHVILLE FIDDLERS' JAMBOREE AND CRAFTS FESTIVAL. July 4–5. Smithville, TN. 32 categories of old-time bluegrass including clogging, buck dancing, old-time fiddle band, five-string banjo, dulcimer, dobro, flat-top guitar and fiddle-off to decide the Grand Champion Fiddler. Annually, the Friday and Saturday nearest July 4. Est attendance: 100,000. For info: Smithville Fiddlers' Jamboree, PO Box 83, Smithville, TN 37166. Phone: (615) 597-8500. Web: www.smithvillejamboree.com.

SPACE MILESTONE: *DEEP IMPACT* SMASHES INTO TEMPEL 1 (US). July 4, 2005. After a six-month journey and 83 million miles, the *Deep Impact* spacecraft smashed—as planned—into the comet Tempel 1. The purpose of the 820-pound, barrel-shaped craft's mission is to give scientists more information about comets.

SPACE MILESTONE: *MARS PATHFINDER* (US). July 4, 1997. Unmanned spacecraft landed on Mars after a seven-month flight. Carried *Sojourner*, a roving robotic explorer that sent back photographs of the landscape. One of its missions was to find if life ever existed on Mars. See also: "Space Milestone: *Mars Global Surveyor* (US)" (Sept 11).

SPIRIT OF FREEDOM CELEBRATION. July 4. Florence, AL. Celebrate America's birthday on the banks of the beautiful Tennessee River at McFarland Park. Enjoy sunning, swimming, bicycling, golfing and live music. Largest fireworks show in the Southeast. Playground, picnic tables and campground available. Annually, on July 4. Est attendance: 60,000. For info: Florence/Lauderdale Tourism, One Hightower Pl, Florence, AL 35630. Phone: (256) 740-4141. Fax: (256) 740-4142. E-mail: Debbie@VisitFlorenceAl.com. Web: www.VisitFlorenceAl.com.

STAR-SPANGLED FOURTH OF JULY CELEBRATION. July 4. Hollywood, FL. Family event featuring evening of popular music at the Hollywood Beach Theatre and a spectacular fireworks display offshore Hollywood Beach. Est attendance: 100,000. For info: Marketing, City of Hollywood, Dept of Parks, Recreation & Cultural Arts, 1405 S 28th Ave, Hollywood, FL 33020. Phone: (954) 921-3404.

STEINBRENNER, GEORGE: BIRTH ANNIVERSARY. July 4, 1930. Baseball executive and longtime owner of the New York Yankees. Nicknamed "the Boss," George Michael Steinbrenner III was born at Rocky River, OH, and died at Tampa, FL, July 13, 2010.

STOCK EXCHANGE HOLIDAY (INDEPENDENCE DAY). July 4. Also early closures on July 3. The holiday schedules for the various exchanges are subject to change if relevant rules, regulations or exchange policies are revised. If you have questions, contact: CME Group (CME, CBOT, NYMEX, KCBT) (www.cmegroup.com), Chicago Board Options Exchange (www.cboe.com), NASDAQ (www.nasdaq.com), NYSE Euronext (www.nyse.com).

TUSKEGEE INSTITUTE OPENING: ANNIVERSARY. July 4, 1881. Booker T. Washington's famed agricultural-industrial institution was built from the ground up by dedicated students seeking academic and vocational training. The institute started in a shanty before Washington purchased an abandoned plantation at Tuskegee, AL. The students built the dormitories, classrooms and chapel from bricks out of their own kiln.

VAN BUREN, ABIGAIL: BIRTH ANNIVERSARY. July 4, 1918. Influential advice columnist ("Dear Abby") born Pauline Esther Friedman at Sioux City, IA. She was a housewife (married name Phillips) who had never held a job when, in 1955, she approached the *San Francisco Chronicle* and declared that she could write better advice than the current columnist. A few sample responses later and a career was born. Van Buren engaged in a personal and professional rivalry with her identical twin sister, Ann Landers, then an already established advice columnist for the *Chicago Sun-Times*. The columns quickly entered the realm of pop culture and journalism history as they ran in competing papers for decades. Van Buren was known for her outspoken, snappy answers and quick wit. Her daughter Jeanne Phillips began to assist with the column in 1987 and took over in an official capacity in 2000 as her mother battled Alzheimer's. Van Buren died at Minneapolis, MN, Jan 16, 2013.

BIRTHDAYS TODAY

Signy Coleman, 54, actress ("The Young and the Restless"), born Bolinas, CA, July 4, 1960.

Horace Grant, 49, former basketball player, born Augusta, GA, July 4, 1965.

Gina Lollobrigida, 86, actress (*Belles de Nuit*; *Bread, Love and Dreams*), born Auviaco, Italy, July 4, 1928.

Becki Newton, 36, actress ("Ugly Betty"), born New Haven, CT, July 4, 1978.

Geraldo Rivera, 71, journalist, talk show host ("Geraldo," *Exposing Myself*), born New York, NY, July 4, 1943.

Eva Marie Saint, 90, actress (Oscar for *On the Waterfront*; *North by Northwest*, *Exodus*), born Newark, NJ, July 4, 1924.

Pamela Howard (Pam) Shriver, 52, sportscaster, Hall of Fame tennis player, born Baltimore, MD, July 4, 1962.

Neil Simon, 87, playwright (*The Odd Couple*, *Barefoot in the Park*), born New York, NY, July 4, 1927.

Mike "The Situation" Sorrentino, 32, television personality ("Jersey Shore"), born New Brighton, NY, July 4, 1982.

July 5 — Saturday

DAY 186 — **179 REMAINING**

ALGERIA: INDEPENDENCE DAY. July 5. National holiday. Commemorates the day in 1962 when Algeria gained independence from France.

BARNUM, PHINEAS TAYLOR: BIRTH ANNIVERSARY. July 5, 1810. Promoter of the bizarre and unusual. Barnum's American Museum opened in 1842, promoting unusual acts including the Feejee Mermaid, Chang and Eng (the original Siamese twins) and General Tom Thumb. In 1850 he began his promotion of Jenny Lind, "the Swedish Nightingale," and parlayed her singing talents into a major financial success. Barnum also cultivated a keen interest in politics. A founder of the newspaper *Herald of Freedom*, he wrote outspoken editorials that resulted not only in lawsuits but also in at least one jail sentence. In 1852 he declined the Democratic nomination for governor of Connecticut but did go on to serve two terms in the Connecticut legislature beginning in 1865.

He was defeated in a bid for US Congress in 1866 but served as mayor of Bridgeport, CT, from 1875 to 1876. In 1871 "The Greatest Show on Earth" opened at Brooklyn, NY; Barnum merged with his rival J.A. Bailey in 1881 to form the Barnum and Bailey Circus. P.T. Barnum was born at Bethel, CT, and died at Bridgeport, CT, Apr 7, 1891.

BIKINI DEBUT: ANNIVERSARY. July 5, 1946. The skimpy two-piece bathing suit created by Louis Reard debuted at a fashion show in Paris, France. It was named after an atoll in the Pacific where the hydrogen bomb was first tested.

CALLAS'S LAST PERFORMANCE: ANNIVERSARY. July 5, 1965. Opera's preeminent soprano, Maria Callas, appeared on the operatic stage for the last time as Tosca at the Royal Opera House at Covent Garden, London, England. Months of health problems had forced Callas to cancel all but one scheduled performance in London—which was a charity gala with the royal family in attendance—and it turned out to be her last. Marshaling her strength, Callas delivered a performance that thrilled the audience, who asked for close to 15 curtain calls at the opera's conclusion.

CANADA: ABBOTSFORD BERRY BEAT FESTIVAL. July 5–6. Abbotsford, BC. 33rd annual. Sample the best berries in North America at the Berry Capital of Canada. Race berries through obstacle courses, judge them in baking competitions, also pie-eating contests, art, games, music, entertainment, specialty food stands and, of course, enjoy shopping at boutique stores and restaurants. Annually, the weekend after Canada Day. Est attendance: 30,000. For info: Abbotsford Downtown Business Assn, 2615-A Montrose Ave, Abbotsford, BC, V2S 3T5, Canada. Phone: (604) 850-6547. Fax: (604) 859-6507. E-mail: executive@downtownabbotsford.com. Web: www.downtownabbotsford.com.

CAPE VERDE: NATIONAL DAY. July 5. Public holiday. Commemorates independence from Portugal in 1975.

COCTEAU, JEAN: 125th BIRTH ANNIVERSARY. July 5, 1889. French novelist, poet, director, actor and artist, born at Maisons-Lafitte, near Paris, France. His notable works include the play *Orpheus* (1926), the novel *The Infernal Machine* (1934) and the films *The Blood of a Poet* (1930) and *Beauty and the Beast* (1946). Remembered as an avant-garde icon, Cocteau influenced several generations of French artists. He died Oct 11, 1963, at Milly-la-Forêt, near Paris.

July 2014	S	M	T	W	T	F	S
			1	2	3	4	5
	6	7	8	9	10	11	12
	13	14	15	16	17	18	19
	20	21	22	23	24	25	26
	27	28	29	30	31		

FARRAGUT, DAVID: BIRTH ANNIVERSARY. July 5, 1801. Born near Knoxville, TN, and died Aug 14, 1870, at Portsmouth, NH. Admiral in the American Civil War who was famous for his naval victories. At Mobile Bay, AL, in a disastrous attack on his entire fleet by the Confederates' Fort Morgan, Farragut proclaimed the famous cry, "Damn the torpedoes—full speed ahead!" They escaped the attack, and Mobile Bay surrendered.

INTERNATIONAL CHERRY PIT SPITTING CHAMPIONSHIP. July 5. Tree-Mendus Fruit Farm, Eau Claire, MI. 41st annual. A nutritious sport—is there a better way to dispose of the pits once you have eaten the cherry? Entrants eat a cherry and then spit the pit as far as possible on a blacktop surface. The entrant who spits the pit the farthest including the roll is the champ. Youth through adult categories. Annually, the first Saturday in July. Est attendance: 300. For info: Tree-Mendus Fruit Farm, 9351 E Eureka Rd, Eau Claire, MI 49111. Phone: (269) 782-7101. Fax: (269) 782-7166. E-mail: contactus@treemendus-fruit.com. Web: www.treemendus-fruit.com.

MOON PHASE: FIRST QUARTER. July 5. Moon enters First Quarter phase at 7:59 AM, EDT.

NATIONAL LABOR RELATIONS ACT (THE WAGNER ACT): ANNIVERSARY. July 5, 1935. This bill guaranteed workers the right to organize and bargain collectively with their employers. It also prohibited the formation of company unions. An enforcement agency, the National Labor Relations Board, was created by the act.

OLIVER NORTH ROLE IN IRAN-CONTRA SCANDAL: 25th ANNIVERSARY. July 5, 1989. Retired Marine Lieutenant Colonel Oliver North was sentenced on this date for his role in the Iran-Contra scandal after being convicted in May of falsifying and destroying documents, accepting an illegal gratuity and aiding and abetting in the obstruction of Congress. North became the focal point of an investigation surrounding allegations that the US sold weapons to Iran in order to secure the release of American hostages and funneled the proceeds from the sales to aid the Contras in Nicaragua. As a member of the National Security Council staff, North became a key operator in antiterrorism, hostage rescues and efforts to overthrow the Sandinista government. On July 20, 1990, a federal appeals court overturned his conviction on the destruction-of-documents charge and suspended the other charges. At issue was whether parts of North's Congressional testimony had been used in the trial resulting in his conviction. On May 28, 1991, the Supreme Court let the appeals court ruling stand. On Sept 16, 1991, all charges against North were dropped.

RAFFLES, STAMFORD: BIRTH ANNIVERSARY. July 5, 1781. Sir Stamford Raffles, English colonial official, founder of Singapore, where he is supposed to have landed Jan 29, 1819, was born at sea, off Jamaica. He discovered with Joseph Arnold an East Indian fungus that is named after them, *Rafflesia Arnoldi*. Raffles died near London, England, on his birthday, July 5, 1826.

RHODES, CECIL JOHN: BIRTH ANNIVERSARY. July 5, 1853. English-born South African millionaire politician. Said to have controlled at one time 90 percent of the world's diamond production. His will founded the Rhodes Scholarships at Oxford University for superior scholastic achievers. Rhodesia (now Zimbabwe) was named for him. Born at Bishop's Stortford, Hertfordshire, England, Rhodes died Mar 26, 1902, at Cape Town, South Africa.

SLOVAKIA: SAINT CYRIL AND METHODIUS DAY. July 5. This day is dedicated to the Greek priests and scholars from Thessaloniki, who were invited by Prince Rastislav of Great Moravia to introduce Christianity and the first Slavic alphabet to the pagan people of the kingdom in AD 863.

STAFFORDSHIRE HOARD DISCOVERED: 5th ANNIVERSARY. July 5, 2009. The most valuable treasure ever discovered in the United Kingdom, the Staffordshire Hoard, was found by metal-detector hobbyist Terry Herbert near Lichfield, England. The Anglo-Saxon hoard, probably warriors' loot, dates to the seventh century and includes 1,500 pieces of gold and silver sword hilts, shield bosses, helmets, crosses and more.

TOUR DE FRANCE. July 5–27. 101st edition. One of the great sporting events in the world. Cycling's best compete for more than 3,500 kilometers in 21 stages in the country of France. Stages are flat-terrain races, mountain races and time trials. For 2014, the Grand Dèpart takes place in Leeds, England, and continues through Yorkshire for two stages. The third stage takes riders from Cambridge to London, ending at the Mall and Buckingham Palace. As in every year since the race's beginning in 1903, the last stage will arrive in Paris at the Champs Elysees. Est attendance: 5,000,000. For info: Amaury Sport Organisation, 253 Quai de la Bataille de Stalingrad, 92137 Issy-les-Moulineaux cedex, France. Web: www.letour.fr.

UNITED NATIONS: INTERNATIONAL DAY OF COOPERATIVES. July 5. On Dec 16, 1992, the General Assembly proclaimed this observance for the first Saturday in July 1995 (Resolution 47/60). On Dec 23, 1994, recognizing that cooperatives were becoming an indispensable factor of economic and social development, the Assembly invited governments, international organizations, specialized agencies and national and international cooperative organizations to observe this day annually (Resolution 49/155). For info: United Nations, Dept of Public Info, New York, NY 10017. Web: www.un.org.

VENEZUELA: INDEPENDENCE DAY. July 5. National holiday. Commemorates proclamation of independence from Spain in 1811. Independence was not achieved until 1821.

WEST QUODDY HEAD LIGHT KEEPERS ASSOCIATION ANNIVERSARY CELEBRATION. July 5. Quoddy Head State Park, Lubec, ME. Live entertainment, local food vendors, raffle, museum, art gallery and special lighthouse tower climbing (supervised by the US Coast Guard). Annually, the Saturday after July 4. Est attendance: 300. For info: West Quoddy Head Light Keepers Assn & Visitor Center, 973 S Lubec Rd, Lubec, ME 04652. Phone: (207) 733-2180. E-mail: info@westquoddy.com. Web: www.westquoddy.com.

ZETKIN, CLARA: BIRTH ANNIVERSARY. July 5, 1857. Women's rights advocate, born at Wiederau, Germany. Zetkin has been credited with being the initiator of International Women's Day, which has been observed on Mar 8 at least since 1910. She died at Arkhangelskoe, Russia, June 20, 1933. See also: "International (Working) Women's Day" (Mar 8).

BIRTHDAYS TODAY

François Arnaud, 29, actor ("The Borgias"), born Montreal, QC, Canada, July 5, 1985.

Edie Falco, 51, actress ("The Sopranos," "Nurse Jackie"), born Brooklyn, NY, July 5, 1963.

Eliot Feld, 72, choreographer, dancer, born Brooklyn, NY, July 5, 1942.

Richard Michael "Goose" Gossage, 63, Hall of Fame baseball player, born Colorado Springs, CO, July 5, 1951.

Chris Gratton, 39, hockey player, born Brantford, ON, Canada, July 5, 1975.

Katherine Helmond, 80, actress (stage: *The House of Blue Leaves*; "Soap," "Who's the Boss?"), born Galveston, TX, July 5, 1934.

Shirley Knight, 78, stage and screen actress (Tony for *Kennedy's Children*; *Sweet Bird of Youth, Petulia*), born Goessel, KS, July 5, 1936.

Huey Lewis, 64, singer (Huey Lewis and the News), born Hugh Anthony Cregg III at New York, NY, July 5, 1950.

Amélie Mauresmo, 35, former tennis player, born Saint-Germain-en-Laye, France, July 5, 1979.

Robbie Robertson, 70, singer, musician, born Toronto, ON, Canada, July 5, 1944.

Gary Shteyngart, 42, author (*Russian Debutante's Handbook, Super Sad True Love Story*), born Igor Semyonovich Shteyngart at Leningrad, USSR (now Russia), July 5, 1972.

Janos Starker, 90, musician, born Budapest, Hungary, July 5, 1924.

Roger Wicker, 63, US Senator (R, Mississippi), born Pontotoc, MS, July 5, 1951.

July 6 — Sunday

DAY 187 **178 REMAINING**

BE NICE TO NEW JERSEY WEEK. July 6–12. A time to recognize the assets of the state most maligned by American comedians. Annually, the first full week in July. For info: Lauren Barnett, Lone Star Publications of Humor, 8452 Fredericksburg Rd, PMB 103, San Antonio, TX 78229. E-mail: lspubs@aol.com.

BUSH, GEORGE W.: BIRTHDAY. July 6, 1946. 43rd president of the US (2001–2009). Born at New Haven, CT.

COMOROS: INDEPENDENCE DAY. July 6. Federal and Islamic Republic of Comoros commemorates declaration of independence from France in 1975.

CZECH REPUBLIC: COMMEMORATION DAY OF BURNING OF JOHN HUS. July 6. National holiday. In honor of Bohemian religious reformer John Hus, who was condemned as a heretic and burned at the stake July 6, 1415.

DUCKTONA 500. July 6. River Park, Sheboygan Falls, WI. Plastic duck race along with dunk tank, car show, craft show, live music, games for children, pancake breakfast, burgers, brats and beverages. Annually, the first Sunday in July. Est attendance: 7,000. For info: Shirl Breunig, Sheboygan Falls Chamber Main St Office, 504 Broadway, Sheboygan Falls, WI 53085. Phone: (920) 467-6206. E-mail: chambermnst@sheboyganfalls.org. Web: www.sheboyganfalls.org.

FIRST AIRSHIP CROSSING OF ATLANTIC: 95th ANNIVERSARY. July 6, 1919. The first airship crossing of the Atlantic was completed as a British dirigible landed at New York's Roosevelt Field.

FIRST SUCCESSFUL ANTIRABIES INOCULATION: ANNIVERSARY. July 6, 1885. Louis Pasteur gave the first successful antirabies inoculation to a boy who had been bitten by an infected dog.

GRIFFIN, MERV: BIRTH ANNIVERSARY. July 6, 1925. Born at San Mateo, CA, Mervyn Edward Griffin, Jr, began his career as a nightclub singer who happened by chance to land a film role that would launch a legendary career. He moved from film to television in 1958, working as a game show host, and in 1962 was given his own daytime talk show at NBC. "The Merv Griffin Show" ran for more than 21 years in syndication and won 11 Emmy Awards. He created and produced two of the most successful game shows in television history, "Jeopardy!" and "Wheel of Fortune," and also composed the iconic "Jeopardy!" theme music. He was a real estate mogul and at the time of his death was worth an estimated $1.6 billion. He died at Los Angeles, CA, Aug 12, 2007.

JONES, JOHN PAUL: BIRTH ANNIVERSARY. July 6, 1747. (Old Style date.) American naval officer born at Kirkbean, Scotland. Remembered for his victory in the battle of his ship, the *Bonhomme Richard*, with the British frigate *Serapis*, Sept 23, 1779. When Jones was queried: "Do you ask for quarter?" he made his famous reply: "I have not yet begun to fight!" Jones was victorious, but the *Bonhomme Richard*, badly damaged, sank two days later. Jones died at Paris, France, July 18, 1792.

KAHLO, FRIDA: BIRTH ANNIVERSARY. July 6, 1907. The great surrealist painter was born Magdalena Carmen Frida Kahlo Calderón at Coyoacán, Mexico. In 1925 she endured severe injuries in a bus accident that would plague her for the rest of her life (and become artistic subject matter). She turned to art at about this time, encouraged by the master muralist Diego Rivera, whom she married in 1929 (and 1941). She is known almost as much for her tumultuous life (she had an affair with Soviet exile Leon Trotsky and was active in leftist politics) as for her vibrant art works filled with symbols and the flora and fauna of her beloved Mexico. She was one of the first women painters to sell a work to the Louvre. She died at her Casa Azul family home in Coyoacán on July 13, 1954.

LEIGH, JANET: BIRTH ANNIVERSARY. July 6, 1927. Born Jeanette Helen Morrison at Merced, CA, Leigh was signed to a contract by MGM while still a teenager. She starred in *Touch of Evil* with Orson Welles (1958), *The Manchurian Candidate* with Frank Sinatra (1962) and *Bye Bye Birdie* (1963) with Dick Van Dyke. She is best remembered for the scene where she was attacked in the shower by Norman Bates, in Alfred Hitchcock's 1960 classic, *Psycho*. She died Oct 3, 2004, at Los Angeles, CA.

LENNON MEETS McCARTNEY: ANNIVERSARY. July 6, 1957. On this day in Liverpool, England, 15-year-old Paul McCartney watched a band called the Quarrymen led by the almost 17-year-old John Lennon. The two teens met later that day and before long created one of the most popular rock groups of the 20th century—The Beatles.

LITHUANIA: DAY OF STATEHOOD. July 6. National holiday. Commemorates the 1252 crowning of Mindaugas, who united Lithuania.

LUXEMBOURG: ETTELBRUCK REMEMBRANCE DAY. July 6. In honor of US general George Patton, Jr, liberator of the Grand-Duchy of Luxembourg in 1945, who is buried at the American Military Cemetery at Hamm, Germany, among 5,100 soldiers of his famous Third Army.

MAJOR LEAGUE BASEBALL HOLDS FIRST ALL-STAR GAME: ANNIVERSARY. July 6, 1933. The first midsummer All-Star Game was held at Comiskey Park, Chicago, IL. Babe Ruth led the American League with a home run, as they defeated the National League, 4–2. Prior to the summer of 1933, All-Star contests consisted of pre- and postseason exhibitions that often found teams made up of a few stars playing beside journeymen and even minor leaguers.

MALAWI: REPUBLIC DAY. July 6. National holiday. Commemorates attainment of independence from Britain in 1964. Malawi was formerly known as Nyasaland.

"NAME THAT TUNE" TV PREMIERE: ANNIVERSARY. July 6, 1953. "Name That Tune" was a musical identification show that appeared in different formats in the '50s and the '70s. Red Benson was the host of the NBC series, and Bill Cullen (and later George De Witt) was the CBS host. Two contestants listened while an orchestra played a musical selection, and the first contestant who could identify it raced across the stage to ring a bell. The winner of the round then tried to identify a number of tunes within a specific time period. In 1974 new network and syndicated versions appeared.

NATIONAL FARRIER'S WEEK. July 6–12. A salute from horse owners to the men and women who keep their horses shod and equine feet and legs in top-notch condition. Annually, the second week in July. For info: Frank Lessiter, *American Farriers Journal*, PO Box 624, Brookfield, WI 53008-0624. Phone: (262) 782-4480. Fax: (262) 782-1252. E-mail: info@lesspub.com.

"THE QUIZ KIDS" TV PREMIERE: 65th ANNIVERSARY. July 6, 1949. This show began on radio and continued on TV with the original host, Joe Kelly, and later with Clifton Fadiman. The format was a panel of five child prodigies who answered questions sent in by viewers. Four were regulars, staying for weeks or months, while the fifth was a "guest child." The ages of the panelists varied from 6 to 16.

REPUBLICAN PARTY FORMED: ANNIVERSARY. July 6, 1854. The Republican Party originated at a convention at Ripon, WI, on Feb 28, 1854. A state convention meeting in Michigan formally adopted the name Republican on July 6.

SPACE MILESTONE: *SOYUZ 21* (USSR). July 6, 1976. Launched this date. Two cosmonauts, Colonel B. Volynov and Lieutenant Colonel V. Zholobov, traveled to *Salyut 5* space station (launched June 22, 1976) to study Earth's surface and conduct zoological-botanical experiments. Their stay was 48 days. Return landing on Aug 24.

TAKE YOUR WEBMASTER TO LUNCH DAY. July 6. Keep the person running your website happy by making sure he or she is well fed. It makes your webmaster feel loved and gives him or her the energy to fix all the typos that you have on your site. (©2006 by WH.) For info: Thomas & Ruth Roy, Wellcat Holidays, 2418 Long Ln, Lebanon, PA 17046. Phone: (717) 279-0184. E-mail: info@wellcat.com. Web: www.wellcat.com.

BIRTHDAYS TODAY

Allyce Beasley, 60, actress ("Moonlighting"), born Brooklyn, NY, July 6, 1954.

Ned Beatty, 77, actor ("Homicide: Life on the Street," *Hear My Song, Deliverance*), born Louisville, KY, July 6, 1937.

George W. Bush, 68, 43rd president of the US, former governor of Texas (R), born New Haven, CT, July 6, 1946.

Dalai Lama, 79, Tibet's spiritual leader and Nobel Peace Prize winner, born Taktser, China, July 6, 1935.

Pau Gasol, 34, basketball player, born Barcelona, Spain, July 6, 1980.

Grant Goodeve, 62, actor ("Eight Is Enough," "Dynasty"), born New Haven, CT, July 6, 1952.

Kevin Hart, 34, comedian, actor (*Laugh at My Pain, Think Like a Man*), born Philadelphia, PA, July 6, 1980.

Hilary Mantel, 62, author (*Wolf Hall, Beyond Black*), born Glossop, Derbyshire, England, July 6, 1952.

Nancy Davis Reagan, 93, former first lady, wife of Ronald Reagan, 40th president of the US, born New York, NY, July 6, 1921.

Della Reese, 82, singer, actress ("Touched by an Angel"), born Deloreese Patricia Early at Detroit, MI, July 6, 1932.

Geoffrey Rush, 63, actor (*Pirates of the Caribbean, The King's Speech*; Oscar for *Shine*), born Toowoomba, Queensland, Australia, July 6, 1951.

Sylvester Stallone, 68, actor (*Rocky* and *Rambo* films), director, born New York, NY, July 6, 1946.

Burt Ward, 69, actor ("Batman"), born Los Angeles, CA, July 6, 1945.

July 2014

S	M	T	W	T	F	S
		1	2	3	4	5
6	7	8	9	10	11	12
13	14	15	16	17	18	19
20	21	22	23	24	25	26
27	28	29	30	31		

July 7 — Monday

DAY 188 **177 REMAINING**

BONZA BOTTLER DAY™. July 7. To celebrate when the number of the day is the same as the number of the month. Bonza Bottler Day™ is an excuse to have a party at least once a month. For more information see Jan 1. For info: Gail Berger, 14 Fernwood Dr, Taylors, SC 29687. Phone: (864) 201-3988. E-mail: bonza@bonza bottlerday.com. Web: www.bonzabottlerday.com.

CARIBBEAN DAY OR CARICOM DAY. July 7. The anniversary of the treaty establishing the Caribbean Community (also called the Treaty of Chaguaramas), signed by the prime ministers of Barbados, Guyana, Jamaica and Trinidad and Tobago July 4, 1973. Observed as a public holiday in Guyana and St. Vincent. Annually, the first Monday in July.

CHAGALL, MARC: BIRTH ANNIVERSARY. July 7, 1887. Born at Vitebsk, Russian Empire (in what is now Belarus), Chagall was one of the most important artists of the 20th century, blending a modern sense of the abstract, surreal or magical with a very personal and emotive style. He was an accomplished master in many media, including painting, etching, engraving, set design and stained glass. Chagall died Mar 28, 1985, at Saint-Paul, Alpes-Maritimes, France.

FATHER-DAUGHTER TAKE A WALK TOGETHER DAY. July 7. A special time in the summer for fathers and daughters of all ages to spend time together in the beautiful weather. Annually, July 7. For info: Janet Dellaria, PO Box 39, Trout Creek, MI 49967. Phone: (906) 852-3539.

HAWAII ANNEXED BY US: ANNIVERSARY. July 7, 1898. President William McKinley signed a resolution annexing Hawaii. No change in government took place until 1900, when Congress passed an act making Hawaii an "incorporated" territory of the US. This act remained in effect until Hawaii became a state in 1959.

ISLE OF MAN: TYNWALD DAY. July 7. For more than 1,000 years, the people of the Isle of Man have gathered at Tynwald Hill at St. John's to hear new laws read out, to present petitions and to swear in the island's four coroners. Tynwald (a word of Norse extraction) is the name of the Manx parliament, which is the world's oldest continually held parliament. Held annually on July 5, unless that date falls on a weekend, in which case the event occurs on the following Monday.

JAPAN: TANABATA (STAR FESTIVAL). July 7. As an offering to the stars, children set up bamboo branches to which colorful strips of paper bearing poems are tied.

KUNSTLER, WILLIAM: 95th BIRTH ANNIVERSARY. July 7, 1919. Radical attorney, defense lawyer for the Chicago Seven, born at New York, NY. Died Sept 4, 1995, at New York, NY.

LINCOLN ASSASSINATION CONSPIRATORS HANGING: ANNIVERSARY. July 7, 1865. Four persons convicted of complicity with John Wilkes Booth in the assassination of President Abraham Lincoln on Apr 14, 1865, were hanged at Washington, DC. The four: Mary E. Surratt, Lewis Payne, David E. Harold and George A. Atzerodt. Mary Surratt became the first woman executed for a crime in the US. Her conviction was and is a subject of controversy, as the only crime she appeared to have committed was to own the boardinghouse where John Wilkes Booth planned the assassination.

LONDON TERRORIST BOMBINGS: ANNIVERSARY. July 7, 2005. In the most violent attack on London, England, since WWII, terrorists exploded four bombs in quick succession on three subway cars and one bus, killing more than 50 people and injuring 700. A splinter group of Al Qaeda claimed responsibility.

MENOTTI, GIAN CARLO: BIRTH ANNIVERSARY. July 7, 1911. Composer, born at Cadegliano-Viconago, Italy, who wrote his first opera at age 11. He won two Pulitzer Prizes—for popular operas *The Consul* (1950) and *The Saint of Bleecker Street* (1955). His *Amahl and the Night Visitors* is a Christmas favorite. He died at Monte Carlo, Monaco, on Feb 1, 2007.

MOTHER FRANCES XAVIER CABRINI CANONIZED: ANNIVERSARY. July 7, 1946. Pope Pius XII presided over the canonization ceremonies for Mother Frances Xavier Cabrini as she became the first American to be canonized. She was the founder of the Missionary Sisters of the Sacred Heart of Jesus, and her principal shrine is at Mother Cabrini High School, New York, NY. Cabrini was born at Lombardy, Italy, July 15, 1850, and died at Chicago, IL, Dec 22, 1917. Her feast day is celebrated on Dec 22.

NUDE RECREATION WEEK. July 7–13. Looking for a way to relax this summer? Why not go barefoot all over? Give nude recreation a try this week by attending special events at a clothing-optional beach, campground or resort near you. For info: The Naturist Society, 627 Bay Shore Dr, Ste 200, Oshkosh, WI 54901. Phone: (800) 886-7230. Fax: (920) 426-5184. E-mail: naturist@naturistsociety .com. Web: www.naturistsociety.com.

PAIGE, LEROY ROBERT (SATCHEL): BIRTH ANNIVERSARY. July 7, 1906. Baseball Hall of Fame pitcher born at Mobile, AL. Paige was the greatest attraction in the Negro Leagues and was also, at age 42, the first black pitcher in the American League. Inducted into the Hall of Fame in 1971. Died at Kansas City, MO, June 8, 1982.

"RYAN'S HOPE" TV PREMIERE: ANNIVERSARY. July 7, 1975. This ABC soap ran until 1989 and was set mostly at the fictional Ryan's Tavern or Riverside Hospital at New York City. The show depicted the lives of the ardently Irish Ryan family. The original cast included Faith Catlin, Justin Deas, Bernard Barrow, Helen Gallagher, Michael Hawkins, Ilene Kristen, Malcom Groome and Kate Mulgrew. Marg Helgenberger, Nell Carter, Yasmine Bleeth, Gloria DeHaven, Corbin Bernsen and Grant Show were among the show's other regulars.

SOLOMON ISLANDS: INDEPENDENCE DAY. July 7. National holiday. Commemorates independence from Britain in 1978.

SPAIN: RUNNING OF THE BULLS. July 7–14. Pamplona. Event made famous by Hemingway in his novel *The Sun Also Rises*, in which young men dressed in white with red scarves run through the streets of Pamplona chased by bulls from the bullring. Part of the festival of San Fermin.

SWITZERLAND: SEMPACH BATTLE COMMEMORATION. July 7. On the morning of the first Monday after July 4, the Lucerne government, military and student delegations and historical groups make their way in solemn procession to the battlefield of 1386. Commemorative address, battle report and solemn service in the chapel. Also an evening procession.

TANZANIA: SABA SABA DAY. July 7. Tanzania's mainland ruling party, TANU, was formed on this day in 1954. Saba Saba means "Seven-Seven."

TELL THE TRUTH DAY. July 7. Today every American is challenged to go one whole day without telling a lie or saying anything misleading or dishonest. Annually, July 7. For info: Kepa Freeman, Art for Growth, 9506 Silver Fox Turn, Clinton, MD 20735. Phone: (301) 537-0205. E-mail: director@artforgrowth.org.

ZAMBIA: HEROES DAY. July 7. First Monday in July is a Zambian national holiday—a memorial day for Zambians who died in the struggle for independence. Political rallies stress solidarity. See also: "Zambia: Unity Day" (July 1).

BIRTHDAYS TODAY

Bérénice Bejo, 38, actress (*The Artist*), born Buenos Aires, Argentina, July 7, 1976.

Billy Campbell, 55, actor ("The 4400," "Once and Again," *The Rocketeer*), born Charlottesville, VA, July 7, 1959.

Pierre Cardin, 92, fashion designer, born Venice, Italy, July 7, 1922.

Shelley Duvall, 65, actress (*Popeye, Nashville, Roxanne*), born Houston, TX, July 7, 1949.

Jorja Fox, 46, actress ("CSI," "ER"), born New York, NY, July 7, 1968.

Michelle Kwan, 34, Olympic figure skater, born Torrance, CA, July 7, 1980.

Lisa Leslie, 42, former basketball player, born Inglewood, CA, July 7, 1972.

Joe Sakic, 45, former hockey player, born Burnaby, BC, Canada, July 7, 1969.

Ralph Lee Sampson, 54, former basketball player, born Harrisonburg, VA, July 7, 1960.

Doc Severinsen, 87, composer, conductor, musician (former bandleader on "The Tonight Show"), born Arlington, OR, July 7, 1927.

Ringo Starr, 74, singer, musician (The Beatles), born Richard Starkey at Liverpool, England, July 7, 1940.

July 8 — Tuesday

DAY 189 **176 REMAINING**

ASPINWALL CROSSES US ON HORSEBACK: ANNIVERSARY. July 8, 1911. Nan Jane Aspinwall rode into New York City carrying a letter to Mayor William Jay Gaynor from San Francisco mayor Patrick Henry McCarthy, becoming the first woman to cross the US on horseback. She began her trip in San Francisco, CA, on Sept 1, 1910, and covered 4,500 miles in 301 days.

DE SILHOUETTE, ÉTIENNE: BIRTH ANNIVERSARY. July 8, 1709. Born at Limoges, France, de Silhouette was briefly the French controller general of finances in 1759 under Louis XV. De Silhouette drew public scorn for his severe economic measures, and "silhouette" was coined to describe a figure reduced to its simplest form. The word evolved to describe black profile cutouts. He died Jan 20, 1767.

DECLARATION OF INDEPENDENCE FIRST PUBLIC READING: ANNIVERSARY. July 8, 1776. Colonel John Nixon read the Declaration of Independence to the assembled residents at Philadelphia's Independence Square in Pennsylvania.

ECKSTINE, BILLY: 100th BIRTH ANNIVERSARY. July 8, 1914. Bandleader and bass-baritone singer Billy Eckstine was born William Clarence Eckstein at Pittsburgh, PA. After performing with the Earl Hines band for almost 20 years, Eckstine formed his own band in 1944. At one time or another the band's ranks included Charlie Parker, Dizzy Gillespie, Miles Davis, Fats Navarro, Dexter Gordon, Gene Ammons, Art Blakey and vocalist Sarah Vaughan—some of the greatest bebop musicians of all time. Among Eckstine's hits were "Fools Rush In," "Everything I Have Is Yours," "My Foolish Heart," "Blue Moon" and "Body and Soul." Billy Eckstine died Mar 8, 1993, at Pittsburgh.

JOHNSON, PHILLIP: BIRTH ANNIVERSARY. July 8, 1906. Postmodern architect who promoted the International Style. He was director of the Department of Architecture of New York's Museum of Modern Art, worked with Mies van der Rohe on the Seagram Building at New York City and designed his own "Glass House" at New Canaan, CT. Born at Cleveland, OH, and died Jan 25, 2005, in his home at New Canaan.

JORDAN, LOUIS: BIRTH ANNIVERSARY. July 8, 1908. "The King of the Jukebox" was born at Brinkley, AR. The bandleader-vocalist-saxophonist performed from the mid-1920s through the 1950s. A pioneer in American jazz, he was one of the most successful and influential African-American musicians of his era. *Rolling Stone* magazine proclaimed Jordan number 59 on its list of the "100 Greatest Artists of All Time." He died Feb 4, 1975, at Los Angeles, CA.

MOULIN, JEAN: DEATH ANNIVERSARY. July 8, 1943. Jean Moulin, a Free French representative, born at Beziers, France, June 20, 1899, parachuted into occupied France on Jan 1, 1942, with the task of uniting the underground resistance. Moulin had with him (in the false bottom of a matchbox) a personal message of admiration for the resistance from General Charles de Gaulle. On May 27, 1943, the underground agreed to the creation of a National Resistance Council with Moulin as president. A month later he was arrested at Lyon by the Gestapo. He was tortured for 11 days but betrayed no one. Moulin died on a train while being transferred by the Nazis to a concentration camp.

OLIVE BRANCH PETITION: ANNIVERSARY. July 8, 1775. Representatives of New Hampshire, Massachusetts Bay, Rhode Island, Providence, Connecticut, New York, New Jersey, Pennsylvania, Delaware, Maryland, Virginia, North Carolina and South Carolina signed a petition from the Congress to King George III, a final attempt by moderates in the Second Continental Congress to avoid a complete break with England.

ROCKEFELLER, JOHN D.: 175th BIRTH ANNIVERSARY. July 8, 1839. Oil magnate, industrialist and philanthropist, born at Richford, NY. From an austere background, Rockefeller brought his love of discipline and frugality to bear on his business dealings, acquiring his first oil refinery in 1863. By 1870 Rockefeller had created Standard Oil, the world's largest refining operations. He perfected the company's vertical integration, quietly buying out competitors and buying up pipelines, train cars, forests (fuel and barrels) and warehouses. Waste by-products like kerosene and gasoline become profitable side businesses. Standard Oil was declared a monopoly in 1911 and broken into 33 subsidiaries, ironically making Rockefeller richer. At his death, his fortune was $1.4 billion. From the 1880s onward he made philanthropy his business. His gifts were foundational to many institutions, including the University of Chicago, Spelman College and Denison University. The Rockefeller Foundation, originally funded to eradicate hookworm, remains a major humanitarian philanthropy. At his death on May 23, 1937, at Ormond Beach, FL, Rockefeller had given away more than $550 million.

ROCKEFELLER, NELSON ALDRICH: BIRTH ANNIVERSARY. July 8, 1908. Born at Bar Harbor, ME. Governor of New York (1958–73). Nominated as vice president by President Gerald R. Ford, Aug 20, 1974, under provisions of the 25th Amendment. Sworn in Dec 19, 1974, after confirmation by the Senate and served until Jan 20, 1977. Died at New York, NY, Jan 26, 1979. Rockefeller was the second person to become vice president without having been elected (Ford was the first).

July 2014	S	M	T	W	T	F	S
			1	2	3	4	5
	6	7	8	9	10	11	12
	13	14	15	16	17	18	19
	20	21	22	23	24	25	26
	27	28	29	30	31		

SCUD DAY (SAVOR THE COMIC, UNPLUG THE DRAMA). July 8. A day to remind people of the benefits of spending more time in the Comic Zone and less in the Drama Zone. For info: Stephanie West Allen, 1376 S Wyandot St, Denver, CO 80223. Phone: (303) 935-8866. E-mail: stephanie@westallen.com.

SPACE MILESTONE: LAST MISSION OF THE SPACE SHUTTLE PROGRAM. July 8, 2011. Space shuttle *Atlantis* took off from Kennedy Space Center, FL, for the 135th and last mission of the space shuttle program. *Atlantis* was carrying supplies for the International Space Station, and its 12-day mission included an investigation into robotically refueling spacecraft. The first flight of a space shuttle was Apr 12, 1981. Robert L. Crippen, commander on the first flight, was among the attendees for the final launch. The shuttle returned safely to Kennedy Space Center on July 21, 2011.

WALES: LLANGOLLEN INTERNATIONAL MUSICAL EISTEDDFOD. July 8–13. Llangollen, Denbighshire, North Wales. 68th annual. Thousands of singers and folk dancers from more than 50 countries take part in this annual international music festival. Friendly rivalry among amateur groups performing amid the Welsh rivers and mountains. Est attendance: 80,000. For info: Llangollen Intl Musical Eisteddfod, Llangollen, North Wales, United Kingdom LL20 8SW. Phone: (44) (1978) 862-001. Fax: (44) (1978) 862-002. E-mail: info@international-eisteddfod.co.uk. Web: www.international-eisteddfod.co.uk.

ZEPPELIN, FERDINAND: BIRTH ANNIVERSARY. July 8, 1838. Born at Konstanz, Baden, Germany, into a noble family, Ferdinand Adolf August Heinrich, Count von Zeppelin, invented the rigid airship (or dirigible) that now bears his name. A military officer, he journeyed to the US during the American Civil War as an observer for the Union army. In that capacity in 1863, he took his first balloon flight at St. Paul, MN—a flight that inspired his postmilitary career as airship innovator. The zeppelin is a cylindrical, framed balloon held aloft by internal gas cells. On July 2, 1900, at Lake Konstanz, Germany, Zeppelin's craft became the first to make a human-directed flight—the cigar-shaped frame held a motor-controlled gondola, propellers and steering controls. By WWI, more than 100 such zeppelins were being used for military purposes. Zeppelin himself died at Charlottenburg near Berlin on Mar 8, 1917, before he could see transcontinental flight achieved.

***ZIEGFELD FOLLIES OF 1907*: ANNIVERSARY.** July 8, 1907. Theater impresario Florenz Ziegfeld staged the first of his extravagant musical revues in New York City. The show's slogan was "Glorifying the American Girl." The last *Follies* closed in 1957.

BIRTHDAYS TODAY

Kevin Bacon, 56, actor ("The Following," *Mystic River, Apollo 13, Footloose*), born Philadelphia, PA, July 8, 1958.

Sophia Bush, 32, actress ("One Tree Hill," *The Hitcher*), born Pasadena, CA, July 8, 1982.

Raffi Cavoukian, 66, children's singer and songwriter, born Cairo, Egypt, July 8, 1948.

Billy Crudup, 46, actor (Tony for *The Coast of Utopia: Voyage*; *Stage Beauty, Big Fish, Almost Famous*), born Manhasset, NY, July 8, 1968.

Kim Darby, 66, actress (*Rich Man, Poor Man*; *True Grit*), born Los Angeles, CA, July 8, 1948.

Cynthia Gregory, 68, former ballerina, choreographer, teacher, born Los Angeles, CA, July 8, 1946.

Beck Hansen, 44, rock singer, songwriter, born Beck David Campbell at Los Angeles, CA, July 8, 1970.

Anjelica Huston, 63, actress (Oscar for *Prizzi's Honor*; *The Royal Tenenbaums, The Addams Family*), born Los Angeles, CA, July 8, 1951.

Toby Keith, 53, country singer, born Clinton, OK, July 8, 1961.

Steve Lawrence, 79, singer, born Sidney Liebowitz at New York, NY, July 8, 1935.

Jeffrey Tambor, 70, actor ("Arrested Development," "The Larry Sanders Show"), born San Francisco, CA, July 8, 1944.

Milo Ventimiglia, 37, actor ("Heroes," "Gilmore Girls"), born Anaheim, CA, July 8, 1977.

Alyce Faye Wattleton, 71, former executive director of Planned Parenthood Federation, born St. Louis, MO, July 8, 1943.

Michael Weatherly, 46, actor, ("NCIS"), born New York, NY, July 8, 1968.

July 9 — Wednesday

DAY 190 — **175 REMAINING**

ARGENTINA: INDEPENDENCE DAY. July 9. Anniversary of establishment of independent republic, with the declaration of independence from Spain in 1816.

EDWARDS, VINCE: BIRTH ANNIVERSARY. July 9, 1928. As Dr. Ben Casey on the 1961 television show "Ben Casey," Edwards displayed a muscular, brooding charm that made him an overnight sex symbol. Medical school enrollment increased while he was on the air. Born at Brooklyn, NY, he died at Los Angeles, CA, Mar 11, 1996.

FIRST OPEN-HEART SURGERY: ANNIVERSARY. July 9, 1893. In Provident Hospital on the South Side of Chicago, IL, black surgeon Dr. Daniel Hale Williams performed the first successful open-heart surgery.

FOURTEENTH AMENDMENT TO US CONSTITUTION RATIFIED: ANNIVERSARY. July 9, 1868. The 14th Amendment defined US citizenship and provided that no state shall have the right to abridge the rights of any citizen without due process and equal protection under the law. Coming three years after the Civil War, the 14th Amendment also included provisions for barring individuals who assisted in any rebellion or insurrection against the US from holding public office, and releasing federal and state governments from any financial liability incurred in the assistance of rebellion or insurrection against the US.

GERMAN ARMY GROUP CENTER CUT OFF IN BALTIC: 70th ANNIVERSARY. July 9, 1944. German Army Group Center was taken by surprise when the Soviets began an offensive between the Baltic Sea and the Carpathian Mountains. The Germans had expected an attack farther south, where the Red Army had already penetrated deep into Poland. When Hitler refused to allow a German retreat, the Soviets easily broke through the German lines, and the Reich's forces were isolated in the Baltic states. Within a week Army Group Center was virtually annihilated, with a loss of 200,000 men.

HIGHEST TSUNAMI IN RECORDED HISTORY: ANNIVERSARY. July 9, 1958. An earthquake registering 8.3 on the Richter scale caused a massive landslide at the head of Lituya Bay, AK, which in turn created a tsunami of 1,700 feet—higher than the Willis Tower in Chicago, IL (which is 1,450 feet). A 300-foot wave immediately followed, scouring bare about four to five square miles of land on both sides of the bay. Of three boats anchored at this remote spot, one was sunk, with the loss of two lives; miraculously, the other two boats with their passengers survived the powerful waves.

HOWE, ELIAS: BIRTH ANNIVERSARY. July 9, 1819. American inventor of the sewing machine. Born at Spencer, MA, he died Oct 3, 1867, at Brooklyn, NY.

MARTYRDOM OF THE BAB. July 9. Baha'i observance of the anniversary of the execution by a firing squad, July 9, 1850, at Tabriz, Persia, of the 30-year-old Siyyid Ali Muhammed, the Bab (prophet-herald of the Baha'i Faith). One of the nine days of the year when Baha'is suspend work. For info: Baha'is of the US, Office of Communications, 1233 Central St, Evanston, IL 60201. Phone: (847) 733-3559. Fax: (847) 733-3578. E-mail: ooc@usbnc.org. Web: www.bahai.us.

MOROCCO: YOUTH DAY. July 9. National holiday. On the birthday in 1929 of King Hassan II.

RADCLIFFE, ANN WARD: 250th BIRTH ANNIVERSARY. July 9, 1764. English author considered the most original and distinguished Gothic romance novelist, she brought poetry to the genre through her lush scenic descriptions. Among her works are *The Romance of the Forest* (1791), *The Mysteries of Udolpho* (1794) and *The Italian* (1797). She was born at London, England, and died there Feb 7, 1823.

RESPIGHI, OTTORINO: BIRTH ANNIVERSARY. July 9, 1879. Italian composer (*The Fountains of Rome*), born at Bologna, Italy. He died at Rome, Apr 18, 1936.

RUSSELL-EINSTEIN MANIFESTO: ANNIVERSARY. July 9, 1955. Philosopher Bertrand Russell released this plea, signed by 11 prominent scientists, three months after Albert Einstein's death. Einstein had agreed to put his name to it in his final days. The manifesto urged nations to find peaceful ways to settle differences and to renounce the use of nuclear weapons, which only promised "universal death."

SOUTH SUDAN DECLARES INDEPENDENCE: ANNIVERSARY. July 9, 2011. After almost 50 years of civil war resulting in millions of casualites, South Sudan broke away from Sudan and declared its independence.

BIRTHDAYS TODAY

Brian Dennehy, 76, actor (Tony for *Long Day's Journey into Night*), born Bridgeport, CT, July 9, 1938.

Margaret Gillis, 61, dancer, choreographer, born Montreal, QC, Canada, July 9, 1953.

Lindsey Graham, 59, US Senator (R, South Carolina), born Pickens County, SC, July 9, 1955.

Tom Hanks, 58, actor (*Saving Private Ryan, Cast Away*; Oscars for *Philadelphia* and *Forrest Gump*), born Concord, CA, July 9, 1956.

David Hockney, 77, artist, born Bradford, England, July 9, 1937.

Mathilde Krim, 88, geneticist, philanthropist, born Como, Italy, July 9, 1926.

Courtney Love, 49, singer, actress (*The People vs Larry Flynt*), born San Francisco, CA, July 9, 1965.

Kelly McGillis, 57, actress (*Witness, Top Gun, The Accused*), born Newport Beach, CA, July 9, 1957.

Richard Roundtree, 72, actor (*Shaft, Q, Roots*), born New Rochelle, NY, July 9, 1942 (some sources say 1939).

Fred Savage, 38, actor ("The Wonder Years," "Working," *The Princess Bride*), born Highland Park, IL, July 9, 1976.

Orenthal James (O.J.) Simpson, 67, former sportscaster and actor, Hall of Fame football player, born San Francisco, CA, July 9, 1947.

Jimmy Smits, 59, actor (*Glitz*, "LA Law," "NYPD Blue"), born New York, NY, July 9, 1955.

John Tesh, 62, television host ("Entertainment Tonight"), composer, born Garden City, NY, July 9, 1952.

Jack White, 39, singer, guitarist (The White Stripes, The Raconteurs, The Dead Weather), producer, born John Anthony Gillis at Detroit, MI, July 9, 1975.

July 2014	S	M	T	W	T	F	S
			1	2	3	4	5
	6	7	8	9	10	11	12
	13	14	15	16	17	18	19
	20	21	22	23	24	25	26
	27	28	29	30	31		

July 10 — Thursday

DAY 191 **174 REMAINING**

ALLIED INVASION OF SICILY: ANNIVERSARY. July 10, 1943. Operation Husky, the Allied infantry attack on Italy, began on the island of Sicily. The British entry into Syracuse was the first Allied success in Europe in WWII. General Dwight D. Eisenhower, the Allied commander in chief, described the invasion as "the first page in the liberation of the European Continent."

ASHE, ARTHUR: BIRTH ANNIVERSARY. July 10, 1943. Born at Richmond, VA, Arthur Ashe became a legend for his list of firsts as a black tennis player. Chosen for the US Davis Cup team in 1963, he became captain in 1980. He won the US men's singles championship and US Open in 1968 and in 1975 the men's singles at Wimbledon. Ashe won a total of 33 career titles. In 1985 he was inducted into the International Tennis Hall of Fame. He helped create inner-city tennis programs for youths and wrote the three-volume *A Hard Road to Glory: A History of the African-American Athlete*. Ashe announced Apr 8, 1992, that he had contracted HIV, probably through a transfusion during bypass surgery in 1983. In September 1992 he began a $5 million fund-raising effort on behalf of the Arthur Ashe Foundation for the Defeat of AIDS and campaigned for public awareness regarding the AIDS epidemic. He died at New York, NY, Feb 6, 1993, from pneumonia.

BAHAMAS: INDEPENDENCE DAY. July 10. Public holiday. At 12:01 AM in 1973 the Bahamas gained their independence after 250 years as a British Crown colony.

"BASEBALL'S SAD LEXICON" PUBLISHED: ANNIVERSARY. July 10, 1910. Journalist Franklin P. Adams created the second best-known baseball poem (after "Casey at the Bat") for the *New York Evening Mail*. Adams extolled the double-play trio of Chicago Cubs Joe Tinker (shortstop), Johnny Evers (second base) and Frank Chance (first base): "These are the saddest of possible words/'Tinker to Evers to Chance.'/Trio of bear cubs, and fleeter than birds,/Tinker and Evers and Chance./Ruthlessly pricking our gonfalon bubble,/Making a Giant hit into a double—/Words that are heavy with nothing but trouble:/'Tinker to Evers to Chance.'" See also: "Mighty Casey Has Struck Out: Anniversary" (June 3) and "Tinker to Evers to Chance: First Double Play Anniversary" (Sept 15).

BETHUNE, MARY McLEOD: BIRTH ANNIVERSARY. July 10, 1875. Mary Jane McLeod Bethune was born at Mayesville, SC, the first in her family to be born free. Bethune became a teacher and in 1904 founded her own school in Florida, the Daytona Normal and Industrial School for Negro Girls. In 1931 the school merged with a local men's college, Cookman Institute, and was renamed Bethune-Cookman College. An adviser on minority affairs under President Franklin D. Roosevelt, she directed the Division of Negro Affairs of the National Youth Administration. She died May 18, 1955, at Daytona Beach, FL.

BORIS YELTSIN INAUGURATED AS RUSSIAN PRESIDENT: ANNIVERSARY. July 10, 1991. Boris Yeltsin took the oath of office as the first popularly elected president in Russia's 1,000-year history. He defeated the Communist Party candidate resoundingly, establishing himself as a powerful political counterpoint to Mikhail Gorbachev, the president of the Soviet Union, of which Russia was the largest republic. Yeltsin had been dismissed from the Politburo in 1987 and resigned from the Communist Party in 1989. His popularity forced Gorbachev to make concessions to the republics in the new union treaty forming the Confederation of Independent States. Suffering from poor health, Yeltsin resigned as president at the end of 1999.

BRINKLEY, DAVID: BIRTH ANNIVERSARY. July 10, 1920. Born at Wilmington, NC, David Brinkley was one of the most recognizable faces in American broadcast journalism for more than 50 years. He was NBC's first White House correspondent, and his outstanding coverage of the 1956 Democratic and Republican national conventions landed him the anchor job on NBC's nightly TV newscast, paired with Chet Huntley until 1970. In 1981 Brinkley moved to ABC, creating a Sunday-morning interview show called "This Week with David Brinkley." He died on June 12, 2003, at Houston, TX.

CALVIN, JOHN: BIRTH ANNIVERSARY. July 10, 1509. Theologian, born at Noyon, France. Reformer and founder of Presbyterianism. Calvin died at Geneva, Switzerland, May 27, 1564.

CLERIHEW DAY. July 10. A day recognized in remembrance of Edmund Clerihew Bentley, journalist and author of the celebrated detective thriller *Trent's Last Case* (1912), but perhaps best known for his invention of a popular humorous verse form, the clerihew, consisting of two rhymed couplets of unequal length: "Edmund's middle name was Clerihew/A name possessed by very few,/But verses by Mr Bentley/Succeeded eminently." Bentley was born at London, England, July 10, 1875, and died there, Mar 30, 1956.

DALLAS, GEORGE MIFFLIN: BIRTH ANNIVERSARY. July 10, 1792. 11th vice president of the US (1845–49), born at Philadelphia, PA. Died there, Dec 31, 1864.

DINOSAUR ROUNDUP RODEO. July 10–12. Vernal, UT. 63rd annual presentation of one of the top PRCA rodeos, fun for the entire family. Est attendance: 12,000. For info: Vernal Rodeo, PO Box 1501, Vernal, UT 84078. Phone: (435) 790-1307. E-mail: vernalrodeo@gmail.com. Web: www.vernalrodeo.com.

DON'T STEP ON A BEE DAY. July 10. Wellcat Holidays reminds kids and grown-ups that now is the time of year when going barefoot can mean getting stung by a bee. If you get stung, tell Mom. (©2006 by WH.) For info: Michael Roy, Wellcat Holidays, 2418 Long Ln, Lebanon, PA 17046. Phone: (717) 279-0184. E-mail: info@wellcat.com. Web: www.wellcat.com.

GILBERT, JOHN: BIRTH ANNIVERSARY. July 10, 1897. Silent film star John Gilbert was born John Pringle at Logan, UT. In 1916 he had his billed screen debut in *Bullets and Brown Eyes*. In the early 1920s Gilbert had leading roles in several films, such as *The Merry Widow* and *The Big Parade*. Although he was a popular leading man, he was unable to succeed when sound came to movies, and MGM released him from his contract in 1934. He died Jan 9, 1936, at Los Angeles, CA.

GWYNNE, FREDERICK HUBBARD: BIRTH ANNIVERSARY. July 10, 1926. Stage, screen and TV actor, best known for the TV roles Herman Munster in "The Munsters" and Officer Muldoon in "Car 54, Where Are You?" Gwynne was born at New York, NY, and died at Taneytown, MD, July 2, 1993.

HODAG COUNTRY FESTIVAL. July 10–13. Hodag "50" Track, Rhinelander, WI. 37th annual country music festival, one of the oldest open-air festivals in the Midwest. Annually, the second full weekend in July. Est attendance: 70,000. For info: Hodag Country Festival, PO Box 1184, Rhinelander, WI 54501-1184. Phone: (715) 369-1300. Fax: (715) 362-3919. E-mail: hcf@hodag.com. Web: www.hodag.com.

HOT DOG NIGHT. July 10. Luverne, MN. 52nd annual. More than 10,000 hot dogs are served free of charge, and free drink is also provided. Various demonstrations including wiener dog races. Est attendance: 5,000. For info: Luverne Area Chamber, 213 E Luverne St, Luverne, MN 56156. Phone: (507) 283-4061. Fax: (507) 283-4061. E-mail: luvernechamber@co.rock.mn.us. Web: www.luvernechamber.com.

MARION COUNTY FAIR. July 10–13. Oregon State Fairgrounds, Salem, OR. Exceptional food and entertainment, carnival, talent show, car show, commercial exhibits, 4-H/FFA exhibits, open-class exhibits, dog flyball tournament and Rescue Row animal rescue. Est attendance: 27,000. For info: Marion County Fair, PO Box 14500, Salem, OR 97309. Phone: (503) 585-9998. Fax: (503) 373-4460. E-mail: marioncountyfair@co.marion.or.us. Web: www.mcfair.net.

MONTANA GOVERNOR'S CUP WALLEYE TOURNAMENT. July 10–12. Fort Peck, MT. Two-person team event, limited to 150 teams. $15,000 awarded in day money (based on a full field). There is a 100 percent payback of $300 entry fee. Kids' fishing event also. Est attendance: 1,000. For info: Glasgow Area Chamber of Commerce and Agriculture, Box 832, Glasgow, MT 59230. Phone: (406) 228-2222. Fax: (406) 228-2244. E-mail: chamber@nemont.net. Web: www.mtgovcup.com.

***NEWS OF THE WORLD* CEASES PUBLICATION: ANNIVERSARY.** July 10, 2011. Once the bestselling newspaper in English, the *News of the World* was closed by its parent company, News International, in an attempt to quell a scandal over journalistic ethics. The 168-year-old tabloid had been the subject of police and government inquiries into allegations that reporters accessed the voice-mail boxes of celebrities, royals and other public figures. Several of the paper's reporters and editors had already been arrested when it came to light that reporters had accessed and deleted some of the contents of the voice mail of a 13-year-old murder victim. At the time the paper ceased publication, its circulation was 2.6 million.

OREGON TRAIL DAYS. July 10–13. Gering, NE. Oldest continuing celebration in state of Nebraska commemorating Oregon Trail. Parade, barbecues, street dances, International Food Fair, concert, Nebraska State CASI Chili Cookoff, musical entertainment, quilt show and an art show highlight the annual celebration. Annually, the second full weekend in July. Est attendance: 30,000. For info: Oregon Trail Days, PO Box 334, Gering, NE 69341. Phone: (308) 436-4457. E-mail: info@oregontraildays.com. Web: www.oregontraildays.com.

PROUST, MARCEL: BIRTH ANNIVERSARY. July 10, 1871. Famed author, born at Auteuil, France. He gained an international reputation for his 13-volume masterpiece, *A la Recherche du Temps Perdu* (*Remembrance of Things Past*). "Happiness," he wrote in *The Past Recaptured*, "is beneficial for the body but it is grief that develops the powers of the mind." Proust died Nov 19, 1922, at Paris, France.

SHRIVER, EUNICE KENNEDY: BIRTH ANNIVERSARY. July 10, 1921. Philanthropist, born at Brookline, MA. Sister of President John F. Kennedy; mother of journalist Maria Shriver. Eponym of National Institute of Child Health and Human Development (1961). As advocate of mentally disabled, founded Special Olympics in 1968. Received Presidential Medal of Freedom in 1984. Died Aug 11, 2009, at Hyannis, MA.

SHUSTER, JOE: 100th BIRTH ANNIVERSARY. July 10, 1914. Shuster, born at Toronto, ON, Canada, but raised in Cleveland, OH, teamed with friend Jerry Siegel to create the comic book superhero Superman, who debuted in *Action Comics* in June 1938. Shuster, the artist of the team, based a bit of Superman's alter ego, Clark Kent, on himself: "I was mild-mannered, wore glasses, was very shy with women." Despite Superman's runaway success, Siegel and Shuster never profited greatly, having sold the rights to their character in 1938 (although later legal action ensured a modest stipend and creative credit). Shuster died July 30, 1992, at Los Angeles, CA.

SPACE MILESTONE: *TELSTAR* (US). July 10, 1962. First privately owned satellite (American Telephone and Telegraph Company) and first satellite to relay live TV pictures across the Atlantic was launched.

US LIFTS SANCTIONS AGAINST SOUTH AFRICA: ANNIVERSARY. July 10, 1991. President George H.W. Bush lifted US trade and investment sanctions against South Africa. The sanctions had been imposed through the Comprehensive Anti-Apartheid Act of 1986, which Congress had passed to punish South Africa for policies of racial separation.

US SENIOR OPEN (GOLF) CHAMPIONSHIP. July 10–13. Oak Tree National Golf Club, Edmond, OK. For info: USGA, Golf House, Championship Dept, PO Box 708, Far Hills, NJ 07931. Phone: (908) 234-2300. Fax: (908) 234-9687. E-mail: usga@usga.org. Web: www.usga.org.

WHISTLER, JAMES ABBOTT McNEILL: BIRTH ANNIVERSARY. July 10, 1834. American painter especially known for *Arrangement in Grey and Black: The Artist's Mother* (1871, also known as *Whistler's Mother*), born at Lowell, MA. Died at London, England, July 17, 1903. When a woman declared that a landscape reminded her of Whistler's paintings, he reportedly said, "Yes, madam, Nature is creeping up."

WILD HORSE STAMPEDE. July 10–12. Wolf Point, MT. The "Granddaddy" of all Montana rodeos features a wild-horse race, three rodeos, two parades and Native American culture. This is the oldest PRCA rodeo in Montana. Annually, the second weekend in July (Thursday to Saturday). Est attendance: 12,000. For info: Wolf Point Chamber of Commerce, 218 Third Ave S, Ste B, Wolf Point, MT 59201. Phone: (406) 653-2200. E-mail: wpchmber@nemont.net. Web: www.wolfpointchamber.org.

WYOMING: ADMISSION DAY: ANNIVERSARY. July 10. Became 44th state in 1890.

BIRTHDAYS TODAY

Andre Dawson, 60, Hall of Fame baseball player, born Miami, FL, July 10, 1954.

David Norman Dinkins, 87, former and first black mayor of New York City (D), born Trenton, NJ, July 10, 1927.

Ron Glass, 69, actor ("Firefly," "Barney Miller"), born Evansville, IN, July 10, 1945.

Adrian Grenier, 38, actor ("Entourage"), born Brooklyn, NY, July 10, 1976.

Arlo Guthrie, 67, singer, born Brooklyn, NY, July 10, 1947.

Jerry Herman, 81, composer, lyricist, born New York, NY, July 10, 1933.

Sue Lyon, 68, actress (*Lolita, The Flim-Flam Man*), born Davenport, IA, July 10, 1946.

Alice Munro, 83, author (*Dance of the Happy Shades, Dear Life*), born Wingham, ON, Canada, July 10, 1931.

Lawrence Pressman, 75, actor ("Doogie Howser, MD," *The Hanoi Hilton*), born Cynthiana, KY, July 10, 1939.

Karen Russell, 33, author (*Swamplandia!*), born Miami, FL, July 10, 1981.

Jessica Simpson, 34, singer, actress (*The Dukes of Hazzard*), born Abilene, TX, July 10, 1980.

Sofía Vergara, 42, actress ("Modern Family," *Medea Goes to Jail*), born Barranquilla, Colombia, July 10, 1972.

Virginia Wade, 69, Hall of Fame tennis player, born Bournemouth, England, July 10, 1945.

July 11 — Friday

DAY 192 — **173 REMAINING**

ADAMS, JOHN QUINCY: BIRTH ANNIVERSARY. July 11, 1767. The sixth president of the US and the son of the second president, John Quincy Adams was born at Braintree, MA. After his single term as president, he served 17 years as a member of Congress from Plymouth, MA. He died Feb 23, 1848, at the House of Representatives (in the same room in which he had taken the presidential oath of office on Mar 4, 1825). John Quincy Adams was the only US president whose father had also been president until George W. Bush became president in January 2001.

BABE RUTH'S DEBUT IN THE MAJORS: 100th ANNIVERSARY. July 11, 1914. Babe Ruth made his debut in major league baseball when he took the mound in Fenway Park for the Boston Red Sox against the Cleveland Indians. Ruth was relieved for the last two innings but was the winning pitcher in a 4–3 game.

BLISSFEST. July 11–13. Harbor Springs, MI. Folk and roots music, three stages, four workshop areas, camping, kids' area and activities. Music styles from jazz to blues to bluegrass. Est attendance: 4,500. For info: Blissfest, 914 Grove St, Petoskey, MI 49770. Phone: (231) 348-7047. Web: www.blissfest.org.

BOWDLER'S DAY. July 11. A day to remember the prudish medical doctor, Thomas Bowdler, born near Bath, England, on July 11, 1754. He gave up the practice of medicine and undertook the cleansing of the works of Shakespeare by removing all the words and expressions he considered to be indecent or impious. His *Family Shakespeare*, in 10 volumes, omitted all those words that "cannot with propriety be read aloud in a family." He also "purified" Edward Gibbon's *History of the Decline and Fall of the Roman Empire* and selections from the Old Testament. His name became synonymous with self-righteous expurgation, and the word *bowdlerize* has become part of the English language. Bowdler died at Rhyddings, in South Wales, Feb 24, 1825.

BURR-HAMILTON DUEL: ANNIVERSARY. July 11, 1804. US vice president Aaron Burr shot and mortally wounded former secretary of the treasury (and primary author of *The Federalist* papers) Alexander Hamilton in a duel at Weehawken, NJ, on this date. Hamilton had insulted Burr and refused to make a public apology. Hamilton died the next day. Although Burr returned to Washington, DC, to execute his duties as vice president, the duel ended his political career.

CALIFORNIA STATE FAIR. July 11–27 (tentative). Sacramento, CA. Top-name entertainment, fireworks, live stage shows, California counties exhibits, livestock nursery, culinary delights, carnival rides and award-winning wines and microbrews. For info: California State Fair, PO Box 15649, Sacramento, CA 95852. Phone: (916) 263-FAIR. Web: www.bigfun.org.

COMPASSIONATE FRIENDS NATIONAL CONFERENCE. July 11–13. Hyatt Regency O'Hare, Chicago, IL. 37th annual. Compassionate Friends from around the country gather to provide and receive friendship, understanding and hope after suffering the excruciating loss of a child, sibling or grandchild. Events include keynote speakers, workshops, memorial candle lighting and more. The Compassionate Friends Walk to Remember is July 13. Est attendance: 1,500. For info: The Compassionate Friends, 900 Jorie Blvd, Ste 78, Oak Brook, IL 60522. Phone: (877) 969-0010. E-mail: wayne@compassionatefriends.org. Web: www.compassionatefriends.org.

July 2014	S	M	T	W	T	F	S
			1	2	3	4	5
	6	7	8	9	10	11	12
	13	14	15	16	17	18	19
	20	21	22	23	24	25	26
	27	28	29	30	31		

DAY OF THE FIVE BILLION: ANNIVERSARY. July 11, 1987. An eight-pound baby boy, Matej Gaspar, born at 1:35 AM, EST, at Zagreb, Yugoslavia, was proclaimed the five billionth inhabitant of Earth. The United Nations Fund for Population Activities, hoping to draw attention to population growth, proclaimed July 11 as "Day of the Five Billion," noting that 150 babies are born each minute. See also: "Day of the Six Billion: Anniversary" (Oct 12).

MONGOLIA: NAADAM NATIONAL HOLIDAY. July 11. Public holiday. Commemorates overthrow of the feudal monarch in 1921.

NAPALM USED: ANNIVERSARY. July 11, 1945. The US dropped several thousand pounds of the recently developed weapon napalm on Japanese forces still holed up on Luzon in the Philippines during WWII. Napalm, which was later used heavily as a defoliant in Vietnam, was a thickener consisting of a mixture of aluminum soaps used to jell gasoline.

"THE NEWLYWED GAME" TV PREMIERE: ANNIVERSARY. July 11, 1966. Four newly married couples compete for prizes on this game show created by the inimitable Chuck Barris. The winners are the husband and wife who best predict each other's responses. Bob Eubanks served as host for three incarnations of the show.

NEWPORT MUSIC FESTIVAL. July 11–27. Newport, RI. Three, four and even five concerts held daily in Newport's fabled mansions featuring unique chamber music programs, American debuts, world-class artists and special events. Est attendance: 27,000. For info: The Newport Music Festival, PO Box 3300, Newport, RI 02840-0992. Phone: (401) 846-1133 or (401) 849-0700. Fax: (401) 849-1857. E-mail: staff@newportmusic.org. Web: www.newportmusic.org.

NIAGARA MOVEMENT FOUNDED: ANNIVERSARY. July 11, 1905. Led by W.E.B. Du Bois, 29 black intellectuals and activists founded the Niagara Movement at Niagara Falls, ON, Canada. The name of their movement alluded both to the location of their founding and to the "mighty current" of protest they hoped to undam. The movement disbanded in 1910, and the NAACP took over its goals.

SLOW PITCH SOFTBALL TOURNAMENT. July 11–13. Elm Park, Williamsport, PA. 41st annual charitable tournament with 36 teams. Benefits Williamsport Lions Club charities. Sponsor: Yuengling Mid-State Beverage Co. Est attendance: 7,500. For info: Don Phillips, 532 Sylvan Dr, South Williamsport, PA 17702. Phone: (570) 322-3331 or (570) 777-0165. E-mail: dphillips28@verizon.net.

SMITH, JAMES: DEATH ANNIVERSARY. July 11, 1806. Signer of the Declaration of Independence, born at Ireland about 1719 (exact date unknown). Died at York, PA.

SPACE MILESTONE: *SKYLAB* (US) FALLS TO EARTH: 35th ANNIVERSARY. July 11, 1979. The 82-ton spacecraft launched May 14, 1973, reentered Earth's atmosphere. Expectation was that 20–25 tons probably would survive to hit Earth, including one piece of about 5,000 pounds. This forecast generated intense international public interest in where it would fall. The chance that some person would be hit by a piece of *Skylab* was calculated at one in 152. Targets were drawn and *Skylab* parties were held, but *Skylab* broke up and fell to Earth in a shower of pieces over the Indian Ocean and Australia, with no known casualties.

THREE RIVERS FESTIVAL. July 11–19. Fort Wayne, IN. A citywide extravaganza of more than 100 events including a parade, food, juried art show, concerts, raft race and water wars, bed race, International Village, amusement rides, children's events and fireworks. Est attendance: 400,000. For info: Three Rivers Festival, 102 Three Rivers N, Fort Wayne, IN 46802. Phone: (260) 426-5556. Fax: (260) 420-8611. Web: www.threeriversfestival.org.

***TO KILL A MOCKINGBIRD* PUBLISHED: ANNIVERSARY.** July 11, 1960. Harper Lee's evocative novel of tomboy Scout Finch coming of age in a Depression-era Alabama town was published this day by J.B. Lippincott. A bestseller almost immediately, it earned Lee a Pulitzer Prize on May 1, 1961. Librarians voted it the best novel of the 20th century.

UNITED NATIONS: WORLD POPULATION DAY. July 11. In June 1989 the Governing Council of the United Nations Development Programme recommended that July 11 be observed by the international community as World Population Day. An outgrowth of the Day of the Five Billion (July 11, 1987), this day seeks to focus public attention on the urgency and importance of population issues, particularly in the context of overall development plans and programs and the need to create solutions to these problems. For info: United Nations, Dept of Public Info, Public Inquiries Unit, RM GA-57, New York, NY 10017. Phone: (212) 963-4475. E-mail: inquiries@un.org.

WANAMAKER, JOHN: BIRTH ANNIVERSARY. July 11, 1838. Entrepreneur best known for creating a new kind of retail establishment in Philadelphia, PA, by combining specialty shops underneath one roof to form a department store—indeed, what would become one of the largest in the nation. Wanamaker cofounded a clothing firm with Nathan Brown in 1861, which led to his department store creation, John Wanamaker and Company, in 1869. From 1889 to 1893 he also held the position of US postmaster general. Born July 11, 1838, at Philadelphia, Wanamaker died there on Dec 12, 1922.

WAYNE CHICKEN SHOW. July 11–13. Wayne, NE. 34th annual. To allow humankind to pay tribute to chickenkind (without laying the proverbial egg). National Cluck-Off, Hard-Boiled Egg Eating Contest, parade, fly-in, car show, street dance, food and craft vendors, games, contests and musical entertainment. Est attendance: 10,000. For info: Wayne Area Chamber of Commerce, 108 W Third St, Wayne, NE 68787. Phone: (402) 375-2240. E-mail: info@wayneworks.org. Web: www.chickenshow.com.

WHITE, E.B.: BIRTH ANNIVERSARY. July 11, 1899. Versatile author of books for adults and children (*Charlotte's Web, Stuart Little*) and editor at the *New Yorker.* Born at Mount Vernon, NY, White died at North Brooklyn, ME, Oct 1, 1985.

WORLDFUTURE 2014. July 11–13. Hilton Orlando Bonnet Creek, Orlando, FL. The World Future Society's meetings are unique, excitement-packed events. Since the First General Assembly in 1971, the Society has brought together futurists from around the world to share ideas and vital information about the trends and events that will affect the world tomorrow. Society meetings provide an opportunity for people from many different fields to examine significant issues and discuss common problems. Each meeting has a rich variety of sessions and speakers, allowing registrants to sample a true cross-section of futures thinking. Past Society conferences have focused on topics ranging from energy, communications and the global economy to crisis management and conflict resolution, work and careers and education. For info: World Future Society, 7910 Woodmont Ave, Ste 450, Bethesda, MD 20814. Phone: (800) 989-8274 or (301) 656-8274. Fax: (301) 951-0394. E-mail: info@wfs.org. Web: www.wfs.org.

BIRTHDAYS TODAY

Giorgio Armani, 78, fashion designer, born Romagna, Italy, July 11, 1936.

Harold Bloom, 84, literary critic, born New York, NY, July 11, 1930.

Justin Chambers, 44, actor ("Grey's Anatomy," *The Wedding Planner*), born Springfield, OH, July 11, 1970.

Greg Grunberg, 48, actor ("Heroes," "Alias," "Felicity"), born Los Angeles, CA, July 11, 1966.

John Henson, 47, television talk show host ("Talk Soup"), born Stamford, CT, July 11, 1967.

Tab Hunter, 83, actor (*Damn Yankees*, "The Tab Hunter Show"), born Arthur Gelien at New York, NY, July 11, 1931.

Jacoby Jones, 30, football player, born New Orleans, LA, July 11, 1984.

Stephen Lang, 62, actor (*Avatar, Public Enemies, Tombstone*), born Queens, NY, July 11, 1952.

Al MacInnis, 51, hockey executive and former player, born Inverness, NS, Canada, July 11, 1963.

Bonnie Pointer, 63, singer (Pointer Sisters), born East Oakland, CA, July 11, 1951.

Ed Markey, 68, US senator (D, Massachusetts), born Malden, MA, July 11, 1946.

Michael Rosenbaum, 42, actor ("Smallville," *Sweet November*), born Oceanside, NJ, July 11, 1972.

Richie Sambora, 54, musician (Bon Jovi), born Amboy, NJ, July 11, 1960.

Leon Spinks, 61, former boxer, born St. Louis, MO, July 11, 1953.

Beverly Todd, 68, actress, director, producer (*Baby Boom, Clara's Heart*), born Chicago, IL, July 11, 1946.

Suzanne Vega, 55, singer, born Santa Monica, CA, July 11, 1959.

Sela Ward, 58, actress ("CSI: New York," "Sisters," "Once and Again"), born Meridian, MS, July 11, 1956.

Caroline Wozniacki, 24, tennis player, born Odenske, Denmark, July 11, 1990.

July 12 — Saturday

DAY 193 — **172 REMAINING**

BALD IS IN. July 12. Annual celebration of the bald look for women, men and children with medical hair loss due to alopecia. Bald Is In inspires people of all ages and both sexes to choose bald and feel beautiful. This day of awareness affirms that being bald is not only just OK—bald is in! Annually, the second Saturday in July. For info: Thea Chassin, Bald Girls Do Lunch, PO Box 9122, Scarborough, NY 10510. Phone: (800) 578-5332. E-mail: info@baldgirlsdolunch.org. Web: www.baldgirlsdolunch.org.

BATTLE OF KURSK: ANNIVERSARY. July 12, 1943. The largest tank battle in history took place during WWII outside the small village of Prohorovka, Russia. Nine hundred Russian tanks attacked an equal number of German Panther and Porsche tanks. Though the German equipment was larger, that advantage was lost in a close-range battle where the tanks lacked maneuverability. When Hitler ordered a cease-fire, 300 German tanks remained strewn over the field.

BERLE, MILTON: BIRTH ANNIVERSARY. July 12, 1908. His nickname was "Mr Television," but Milton Berle had a long career as a vaudeville, film, radio and theater comedian as well. He was born Mendel Berlinger at Harlem, NY. He was popular before becoming the host of NBC's "Texaco Star Theater" in 1948, but that variety show made him a huge national star. Dressing in drag, rattling off corny jokes and drawing the day's biggest stars, "Uncle Miltie" made the show a television event until its end in 1953. He was one of the first seven inductees into the Academy of Television Arts and Sciences' TV Hall of Fame. Berle died Mar 27, 2002, at Los Angeles, CA.

July 2014	S	M	T	W	T	F	S
			1	2	3	4	5
	6	7	8	9	10	11	12
	13	14	15	16	17	18	19
	20	21	22	23	24	25	26
	27	28	29	30	31		

BUCK MOON. July 12. So called by Native American tribes of New England and the Great Lakes because at this time of year the new antlers of buck deer begin to appear. Also called Thunder Moon, for summer thunderstorms. The July Full Moon.

CANADA: HARRISON FESTIVAL OF THE ARTS. July 12–20. Harrison Hot Springs, BC. A celebration of world music, dance, theater and visual art including a large outdoor art market. Various venues throughout the village. Variety of activities for the entire family. Est attendance: 12,000. For info: Mel Dunster, General Mgr, Harrison Festival, Box 399, Harrison Hot Springs, BC, V0M 1K0, Canada. Phone: (604) 796-3664. Fax: (604) 796-3694. E-mail: info@harrisonfestival.com. Web: www.harrisonfestival.com.

CARVER DAY. July 12. George Washington Carver National Monument, Diamond, MO. 71st annual. A celebration of the man that features ranger-led programs interpreting the life of Carver. Guest speakers, music groups, storytellers, junior ranger station and exhibits. Annually, the second Saturday in July. For info: George Washington Carver National Monument, 5646 Carver Rd, Diamond, MO 64840. Phone: (417) 325-4151. Fax: (417) 325-4231. E-mail: GWCA_interpretation@nps.gov. Web: www.nps.gov/gwca.

CIRCUS CITY FESTIVAL. July 12–19. Peru, IN. Youth amateur circus performed by children 7 to 21 years of age helping to preserve the circus heritage of Miami County, IN. Circus parade, July 19, 10 AM. Annually, beginning the Saturday before and ending the Saturday after the third Wednesday in July. Est attendance: 75,000. For info: Circus City Festival Inc, 154 N Broadway, Peru, IN 46970. Phone: (765) 472-3918. Fax: (765) 472-2826. Web: www.perucircus.com.

CLIBURN, VAN: 80th BIRTH ANNIVERSARY. July 12, 1934. Internationally acclaimed pianist whose musical genius briefly thawed the Cold War after he won the first Tchaikovsky Competition in 1958. Born Harvey Lavan Cliburn, Jr, at Shreveport, LA, Cliburn was taught piano by his mother as a child and made his concert debut in 1947. He thrilled Muscovites with his interpretation of the romantics at the Tchaikovsky Competition, and surprised competition officials asked Soviet premier Nikita Khrushchev's permission before awarding an American first prize. Cliburn subsequently embarked on a successful concert career and founded the Van Cliburn International Piano Competition to aid young pianists. He died Feb 27, 2013, at Fort Worth, TX, his longtime home. See also: "Van Cliburn Conquers Moscow: Anniversary" (Apr 14).

CORN HILL ARTS FESTIVAL. July 12–13. Corn Hill neighborhood, Rochester, NY. Fine arts and crafts show organized by neighborhood residents for more than 45 years. Great food and live musical entertainment on four stages. All proceeds are reinvested in neighborhood projects. Est attendance: 200,000. For info: Corn Hill Arts Festival, 133 S Fitzhugh St, Rochester, NY 14608-2204. Phone: (585) 262-3142. Fax: (585) 546-4788. E-mail: chna@cornhill.org. Web: www.cornhillartsfestival.com.

DeRITA, JOE: BIRTH ANNIVERSARY. July 12, 1909. American comedian Curly Joe DeRita was the last surviving member of the Three Stooges comedy team. He joined the team in 1959 after Joe Besser left. He appeared in *Have Rocket, Will Travel* (1959), *Snow White and the Three Stooges* (1961) and *The Outlaw Is Coming* (1965). Born at Philadelphia, PA, DeRita died July 3, 1993, at Los Angeles, CA.

"EVENING AT POPS" TV PREMIERE: ANNIVERSARY. July 12, 1970. PBS's popular concert series premiered with conductor Arthur Fiedler heading the Boston Pops Orchestra. Conductor/composer John Williams took over the post upon Fiedler's death in 1979; Keith Lockhart is the current conductor.

"FAMILY FEUD" TV PREMIERE: ANNIVERSARY. July 12, 1976. From the production team of Mark Goodson and Bill Todman, this game show sets two families against each other to accumulate the greater number of points. The contestants have to predict the most common answers to a given survey question. Richard Dawson (TV's famous kissing host), the late Ray Combs, Louie Anderson, Richard Karn and John O'Hurley have been hosts.

FULLER, BUCKMINSTER: BIRTH ANNIVERSARY. July 12, 1895. Architect, inventor, engineer and philosopher, born Richard Buckminster Fuller at Milton, MA. His geodesic dome was one of the most important structural innovations of the 20th century. He died July 1, 1983, at Los Angeles, CA.

HAMMERSTEIN, OSCAR: BIRTH ANNIVERSARY. July 12, 1895. Master of the "musical play" form, Oscar Hammerstein II was a titan of the theater. Born Oscar Greeley Clendenning Hammerstein at New York, NY, the lyricist, playwright and producer worked with such collaborators as Jerome Kern and—most famously—Richard Rodgers. The partnerships produced *Oklahoma!, Show Boat, Carousel, The King and I, South Pacific* and *The Sound of Music*, among other well-known shows. Many of Hammerstein's songs have settled permanently into the repertoires of vocalists everywhere. The recipient of two Academy Awards, the Pulitzer Prize for Drama and eight Tony Awards, Hammerstein died Aug 23, 1960, at Doylestown, PA. Following his death, lights at Times Square, New York City, and the West End of London, England, were dimmed in his honor.

JONES WINS FIRST GRAND SLAM OF GOLF: ANNIVERSARY. July 12, 1930. Bobby Jones won the US Open Championship by two strokes over Macdonald Smith at the Interlachen Country Club at Hopkins, MN. Having already won the British Open, the British Amateur and the US Amateur, Jones became the only golfer to win the Grand Slam (the four major tournaments in one calendar year)—a usage that had to be invented by sportswriters, since no one had achieved that feat before.

KIRIBATI: INDEPENDENCE DAY: 35th ANNIVERSARY. July 12. Republic of Kiribati attained independence from Britain in 1979. Formerly known as the Gilbert Islands.

MOON PHASE: FULL MOON. July 12. Moon enters Full Moon phase at 7:25 AM, EDT.

NIGHT OF NIGHTS. July 12. Annual event held by the Maritime Radio Historical Society (MRHS) to commemorate the history of maritime radio and the closing of commercial Morse operations in the US on July 12, 1999. These on-the-air events are intended to honor the men and women who followed the radiotelegraph trade on ships and at coast stations around the world and made it one of honor and skill. For Night of Nights, stations KPH, KSM and KFS return to the air. Other stations including WLO, KLB, NMC and NOJ often join in. Calls from ships at sea make the event seem as if the golden age of maritime radio has returned. The transmitters are located in Bolinas, CA, at the transmitting station established in 1913 by the American Marconi Co. The original KPH transmitters, receivers and antennas are used to activate frequencies in all the commercial maritime HF bands and on MF as well. For info: MRHS, PO Box 392, Point Reyes Station, CA 94956. E-mail: info@radiomarine.org. Web: www.radiomarine.org.

"NORTHERN EXPOSURE" TV PREMIERE: ANNIVERSARY. July 12, 1990. In CBS's comedy-drama Dr. Joel Fleischman (Rob Morrow) was forced to practice medicine in remote Cicely, AK, to pay off his student loans. He gradually accepted his lot with the help of the town's quirky citizens, who needed him because he was the only doctor in town. The show's cast included Janine Turner as bush pilot Maggie O'Connell and John Corbett as DJ Chris Stevens. The last episode aired in 1995.

SÃO TOMÉ AND PRÍNCIPE: INDEPENDENCE DAY. July 12. National holiday observed. Gained independence from Portugal in 1975.

SODBUSTER DAYS. July 12–13. Fort Ransom State Park, Fort Ransom, ND. Remember the way things were done in rural North Dakota during the early 1920s with shelling corn by hand, rope weaving, horse-drawn plowing and haying. Ladies' demonstrations, kids' games, live music. Located along the Sheyenne River Valley National Scenic Byway. Est attendance: 3,000. For info: Fort Ransom State Park, 5981 Walt Hjelle Pkwy, Fort Ransom, ND 58033-9712. Phone: (701) 973-4331. Fax: (701) 973-4151. E-mail: frsp@nd.gov. Web: www.parkrec.nd.gov.

SPACE MILESTONE: *PHOBOS 2* (USSR): ANNIVERSARY. July 12, 1988. Sent back the first close-up photos of Phobos, one of two small moons of Mars. Launched from Soviet space probe in central Asia on this date.

STONE HOUSE DAY. July 12. Hurley, NY. Tour eight privately owned, 225- to 325-year-old stone houses, six within a 150-yard radius. Annually, the second Saturday in July. Est attendance: 750. For info: Stone House Day, PO Box 328, Hurley, NY 12443. Phone: (845) 331-4121. Fax: (845) 331-4153. E-mail: info@StoneHouseDay.org. Web: www.StoneHouseDay.org.

THOREAU, HENRY DAVID: BIRTH ANNIVERSARY. July 12, 1817. American author and philosopher, born at Concord, MA. Died there May 6, 1862. In *Walden* he wrote, "I frequently tramped eight or ten miles through the deepest snow to keep an appointment with a beechtree, or a yellow birch, or an old acquaintance among the pines."

TURNER'S FRONTIER ADDRESS: ANNIVERSARY. July 12, 1893. Historian Frederick Jackson Turner delivered his paper "The Significance of the Frontier in American History" at a meeting of the American Historical Association at Chicago, IL, during the Columbian Exposition. Stating that the frontier was a spawning ground for many of the social and intellectual traits that made Americans different from Europeans, Turner saw the end of the frontier as a major break in the psychology of the nation. Turner's formalization of this idea came in part from his reading the *Extra Census Bulletin No 2: Distribution of Population According to Density: 1890*, which said, "Up to and including 1890 the country had a frontier of settlement, but at present the unsettled area has been so broken into by isolated bodies of settlement that there can hardly be said to be a frontier line."

WEDGWOOD, JOSIAH: BIRTH ANNIVERSARY. July 12, 1730. Famed pottery designer and manufacturer, born at Burslem, Staffordshire, England. Died at Etruria, Staffordshire, Jan 3, 1795.

BIRTHDAYS TODAY

Lisa Nicole Carson, 45, actress ("ER," "Ally McBeal"), born Brooklyn, NY, July 12, 1969.

Bill Cosby, 76, comedian, actor (Emmys for "I Spy" and "The Cosby Show"), born Philadelphia, PA, July 12, 1938.

Anna Friel, 38, actress ("Pushing Daisies," *Our Mutual Friend*), born Rochdale, Lancashire, England, July 12, 1976.

Mel Harris, 57, actress ("Something So Right," "thirtysomething"), born Bethlehem, PA, July 12, 1957.

Cheryl Ladd, 62, actress ("Charlie's Angels"), born Huron, SD, July 12, 1952.

Brock Lesner, 37, mixed martial artist, born Webster, SD, July 12, 1977.

Christine McVie, 71, singer, musician (Fleetwood Mac), born Birmingham, England, July 12, 1943.

Denise Nicholas, 69, actress ("Room 222," "In the Heat of the Night," *Let's Do It Again*), born Detroit, MI, July 12, 1945.

Jamey Sheridan, 63, actor ("Law & Order: Criminal Intent," *The House on Carroll Street*), born Pasadena, CA, July 12, 1951.

Richard Simmons, 66, television personality, weight-loss guru, author, born New Orleans, LA, July 12, 1948.

Erik Per Sullivan, 23, actor ("Malcolm in the Middle," *The Cider House Rules*), born Worcester, MA, July 12, 1991.

Rolonda Watts, 55, talk show host ("Rolonda"), born Winston-Salem, NC, July 12, 1959.

Jordyn Wieber, 19, Olympic gymnast, born Dewitt, MI, July 12, 1995.

Kristi Tsuya Yamaguchi, 43, Olympic figure skater, born Hayward, CA, July 12, 1971.

July 13 — Sunday

DAY 194 — **171 REMAINING**

BATTLE OF MURFREESBORO: ANNIVERSARY. July 13, 1862. Confederate forces under General Nathan Bedford Forrest defeated Northern forces under General Thomas Crittenden at Murfreesboro, TN. Nearly all of Crittenden's men were captured, and the North lost a large amount of military equipment and supplies.

EMBRACE YOUR GEEKNESS DAY. July 13. Into dungeon games, comic books and vampire dress-up? Spend endless hours going strange places on the Internet? You're a geek, and this is the day to roar! (©2006 by WH.) For info: Thomas & Ruth Roy, Wellcat Holidays, 2418 Long Ln, Lebanon, PA 17046. Phone: (717) 279-0184. E-mail: info@wellcat.com. Web: www.wellcat.com.

ENGLAND: THE OPEN CHAMPIONSHIP (BRITISH OPEN). July 13–20. Royal Liverpool Golf Club, Hoylake. One of the sporting world's greatest events, first held at Prestwick Golf Club, Scotland, Oct 17, 1860. Since 1873 the prize has been The Golf Champion Trophy, but it's affectionately known as The Claret Jug. Final rounds, July 17–20. Est attendance: 170,000. For info: Ticket Office, Business Affairs Dept, The R&A, St. Andrews, Fife, Scotland KY16 9JD. Phone: (44) (1334) 460-010. E-mail: tickets@randa.org. Web: www.theopen.com.

FAIRBANKS SUMMER ARTS FESTIVAL. July 13–27. University of Alaska, Fairbanks, AK. A unique study-performance festival involving workshops and master classes in visual and performing arts with more than 120 prestigious guest artists. Performance opportunities in orchestra, jazz band, jazz, choral groups, dance, opera theater, creative writing, healing arts and culinary arts. Est attendance: 1,200. For info: Fairbanks Summer Arts Festival, Box 82510, Fairbanks, AK 99708. Phone: (907) 474-8869. E-mail: festival@alaska.net. Web: www.fsaf.org.

FIFA WORLD CUP FINAL. July 13. Maracana Stadium, Rio de Janeiro, Brazil. After one month of competition among 32 teams, the final 2 national soccer teams battle for the cup today. For info: FIFA, PO Box 85, Zurich 8030, Switzerland. Web: www.fifa.com/worldcup.

FORREST, NATHAN BEDFORD: BIRTH ANNIVERSARY. July 13, 1821. Confederate cavalry commander whose birthday is observed in schools in Tennessee, Forrest was also one of the founders of the short-lived original Ku Klux Klan. Forrest was born at Bedford County, TN, and died Oct 29, 1877, at Memphis, TN.

FRANCE: NIGHT WATCH (LA RETRAITE AUX FLAMBEAUX). July 13. Celebration on the eve of Bastille Day with parades and fireworks.

GRUNTLED WORKERS DAY. July 13. There's so much news about disgruntled workers that today's the day for gruntled workers to unite! Drive to a fast-food restaurant and say, "Thanks. Your service is fast. Have a nice day." (©2006 by WH.) For info: Thomas & Ruth Roy, Wellcat Holidays, 2418 Long Ln, Lebanon, PA 17046. Phone: (717) 279-0184. E-mail: info@wellcat.com. Web: www.wellcat.com.

JAPAN: BON FESTIVAL (FEAST OF LANTERNS). July 13–15. Religious rites throughout Japan in memory of the dead, who, according to Buddhist belief, revisit Earth during this period. Lanterns are lighted for the souls. Spectacular bonfires in the shape of the character *dai* are burned on hillsides on the last day of the Bon (or O-Bon) Festival, bidding farewell to the spirits of the dead. (Some regions celebrate during mid-August.)

"LIVE AID" CONCERTS: ANNIVERSARY. July 13, 1985. Concerts at Philadelphia, PA, and London, England (Kennedy and Wembley stadiums), were seen by 162,000 attendees and an estimated 1.5 billion television viewers. Organized to raise funds for African famine relief; the musicians performed without a fee, and nearly $100 million was pledged toward aid to the hungry.

NORTHWEST ORDINANCE: ANNIVERSARY. July 13, 1787. The Northwest Ordinance, providing for government of the territory north of the Ohio River, became law. The ordinance guaranteed freedom of worship and the right to trial by jury, and it prohibited slavery.

July 2014

S	M	T	W	T	F	S
		1	2	3	4	5
6	7	8	9	10	11	12
13	14	15	16	17	18	19
20	21	22	23	24	25	26
27	28	29	30	31		

REPUBLIC OF MONTENEGRO: NATIONAL DAY. July 13.

SPORTS CLICHÉ WEEK. July 13–19. This week honors the use of sports clichés by fans, athletes, sports announcers and sportswriters. Annually, the week of the Major League Baseball All-Star game. For info: Don Powell, PhD, 30445 Northwestern Hwy, Ste 350, Farmington Hills, MI 48334. Phone: (248) 539-1800, ext 235. Fax: (248) 539-1808. E-mail: dpowell@healthylife.com.

WORLD CUP INAUGURATED: ANNIVERSARY. July 13, 1930. The first World Cup soccer competition was held at Montevideo, Uruguay, with 14 countries participating. On July 30 Uruguay defeated Argentina by a score of 4–2 to take the cup.

 BIRTHDAYS TODAY

Cameron Crowe, 57, director, screenwriter (*Fast Times at Ridgemont High, Jerry Maguire,* Oscar for *Almost Famous*), born Palm Springs, CA, July 13, 1957.

Harrison Ford, 72, actor (*Witness, The Fugitive,* the first *Star Wars* trilogy, the *Indiana Jones* films), born Chicago, IL, July 13, 1942.

Robert Forster, 73, actor ("Banyon," *Diamond Men, Jackie Brown*), born Rochester, NY, July 13, 1941.

Jane Hamilton, 57, author (*A Map of the World, The Book of Ruth*), born Oak Park, IL, July 13, 1957.

Louise Mandrell, 60, country singer, born Corpus Christi, TX, July 13, 1954.

Cheech Marin, 68, writer, actor (Cheech and Chong films, "Nash Bridges"), born Los Angeles, CA, July 13, 1946.

Roger McGuinn, 72, musician (The Byrds), born James Joseph McGuinn at Chicago, IL, July 13, 1942.

Erno Rubik, 70, inventor of the Rubik's Cube, born in a hospital air raid shelter, Budapest, Hungary, July 13, 1944.

Wole Soyinka, 80, Nobel Prize–winning author (*The Lion and the Jewel, The Strong Breed*), born Abeokuta, Nigeria, July 13, 1934.

Michael Spinks, 58, former boxer, born St. Louis, MO, July 13, 1956.

Patrick Stewart, 74, actor ("Star Trek: The Next Generation," *X-Men* films, *A Christmas Carol, Excalibur*), born Mirfield, England, July 13, 1940.

David Storey, 81, author, playwright (*The Performance of Small Firms*), born Wakefield, England, July 13, 1933.

Anthony Jerome "Spud" Webb, 51, former basketball player, born Dallas, TX, July 13, 1963.

July 14 — Monday

DAY 195 **170 REMAINING**

BASCOM, FLORENCE: BIRTH ANNIVERSARY. July 14, 1862. After receiving her third bachelor's degree from the University of Wisconsin in 1884 and a master's degree in 1887, Florence Bascom entered Johns Hopkins University and received a doctorate in 1893. She taught at Ohio State and became a professor at Bryn Mawr College. She also was the first woman appointed a geologist with the US Geological Survey, was associate editor of *American Geologist* (1890–1905) and became the first woman elected a Fellow of the Geological Society of America. Born at Williamstown, MA; died at Northampton, MA, June 18, 1945.

BERGMAN, INGMAR: BIRTH ANNIVERSARY. July 14, 1918. One of the most influential filmmakers of the 20th century, Bergman directed such classics as *Fanny and Alexander, Wild Strawberries* and *Cries and Whispers.* He wrote or directed 62 films and more than 170 stage plays, mainly in his native Sweden, but was renowned all over the world and was nominated for nine Academy Awards. Born at Uppsala, Sweden, he died July 30, 2007, at Faro, Sweden.

CHANCELLOR, JOHN: BIRTH ANNIVERSARY. July 14, 1927. Television broadcast journalist John Chancellor was born at Chicago, IL. He rose through the ranks at the *Chicago Sun-Times*, from copyboy to feature writer. Chancellor spent more than four decades with the NBC network, beginning in 1950. During that time he took a two-year respite from journalism to serve President Lyndon Johnson as director of the Voice of America. Chancellor retired in 1993, but his distinctive, familiar voice was still heard, such as when he narrated a PBS documentary in 1996. He died July 12, 1996, at Princeton, NJ.

CHILDREN'S PARTY AT GREEN ANIMALS. July 14. Green Animals Topiary Garden, Portsmouth, RI. Annual party for children and adults at Green Animals, a delightful topiary garden and children's toy museum. Party includes pony rides, games, clowns, refreshments, hot dogs, hamburgers and more. Annually, July 14. Est attendance: 1,500. For info: The Preservation Society of Newport County, 424 Bellevue Ave, Newport, RI 02840. Phone: (401) 847-1000. Web: www.NewportMansions.org.

EDWARDS, DOUGLAS: BIRTH ANNIVERSARY. July 14, 1917. American television journalist Douglas Edwards was born at Ada, OK. He began his career in radio, but in 1947 he became the first major announcer to move to television. He was anchor for CBS's first nightly news program, "Douglas Edwards with the News" (1948–62), where he gave memorable on-scene coverage of such events as the sinking of the *Andrea Doria* in 1956. Edwards worked for CBS until his retirement, two years before he died on Oct 13, 1990, at Sarasota, FL.

ENGLAND: BIRMINGHAM RIOT: ANNIVERSARY. July 14, 1791. Following a dinner celebrating the second anniversary of the fall of the Bastille, an angry mob rioted at Birmingham, England. The main target of their wrath was the home of scientist (discoverer of oxygen) Joseph Priestley, who was unpopular because of his religious views and his approval of the American and French revolutionary causes. The mob ruled Birmingham for three days, burning Priestley's home and laboratory as well as the homes of his friends. Priestley, in disguise, and his family narrowly escaped with their lives. They lived for a time at London before moving in 1794 to America. See also: "Priestley, Joseph: Birth Anniversary" (Mar 13).

ENGLAND: FARNBOROUGH INTERNATIONAL AIRSHOW. July 14–20. Farnborough Airfield, Farnborough. Held since 1948, this is the world's largest and most important air show—open to the trade for one week and to the public for two days. Some 1,300 exhibiting companies from 35 countries attend the show. Over the decades dozens of new aircraft have made their debut at Farnborough, including the Comet, Concorde and Airbus A380. Est attendance: 270,000. For info: Farnborough Intl Airshow, ShowCentre, ETPS Rd, Farnborough, Hampshire, England GU14 6FD. Phone: (44) (1252) 532-800. Fax: (44) (1252) 376-015. E-mail: enquiries@farnborough.com. Web: www.farnborough.com.

FORD, GERALD RUDOLPH: BIRTH ANNIVERSARY. July 14, 1913. 38th president of the US (1974–77). Born Leslie King at Omaha, NE, Ford became 41st vice president of the US on Dec 6, 1973, by appointment, following the resignation of Spiro T. Agnew from that office on Oct 10, 1973. Ford became president on Aug 9, 1974, following the resignation from that office on that day of Richard M. Nixon. He was the first nonelected vice president and president of the US. He died at Rancho Mirage, CA, Dec 26, 2006.

FRANCE: BASTILLE DAY OR FÊTE NATIONALE. July 14. Public holiday commemorating the fall of the Bastille prison at the beginning of the French Revolution, July 14, 1789. Also celebrated or observed in many other countries.

GUTHRIE, WOODROW WILSON "WOODY": BIRTH ANNIVERSARY. July 14, 1912. American folksinger, songwriter ("This Land Is Your Land," "Union Maid," "Hard Traveling"), born at Okemah, OK. Traveled the country by freight train, singing and listening. Died Oct 3, 1967, at New York, NY.

HANNA, WILLIAM: BIRTH ANNIVERSARY. July 14, 1910. Born at Melrose, NM, William Hanna was the cocreator of such popular animated characters as Tom and Jerry, Yogi Bear, Snagglepuss and Magilla Gorilla. With partner Joe Barbera, he won seven Academy Awards for his Tom and Jerry cartoon shorts, and eight other works were nominated. The Hanna-Barbera team created the first animated TV sitcom for adults, *The Flintstones* (1960), and such favorites as *The Jetsons* and *Scooby-Doo, Where Are You!* Hanna died at Los Angeles, CA, on Mar 22, 2001.

INTERNATIONAL TOWN CRIERS DAY. July 14. A day recognizing the ancient and honorable art and tradition of town crying and the significant contribution town criers make to promoting their respective towns and cities. Annually, the second Monday in July. For info: Doug Turvey, Official Town Crier, Township of Zorra and Town of Ingersoll, 784119 Rd 78, RR #5, Embro, ON, Canada N0J 1J0. Phone: (519) 475-4937. E-mail: zoringtowncrier@xplornet.com.

MISSION SAN ANTONIO DE PADUA: FOUNDING ANNIVERSARY. July 14. California. Mission to the Indians founded July 14, 1771.

MURRAY, KEN: BIRTH ANNIVERSARY. July 14, 1903. American comedian Ken Murray was born at New York, NY. He began in vaudeville and then moved to films and television. He died Oct 12, 1988, at Beverly Hills, CA.

NORTHERN IRELAND: ORANGEMEN'S DAY. July 14. National holiday commemorates Battle of Boyne, July 1 (OS), 1690, in which the forces of King William III of England, Prince of Orange, defeated those of James II, at Boyne River in Ireland. Ordinarily observed on July 12, but if that date falls on a weekend, as it does in 2014, the holiday is celebrated on the following Monday.

SARTO, ANDREA DEL: BIRTH ANNIVERSARY. July 14, 1486. The celebrated painter was born near Florence, Italy. "Sarto," a nickname referring to his father's trade as a tailor, was the name he chose during his lifetime, though the real surname was probably either Vanucchi or di Francesco. He was one of the most renowned artists of his time, and his paintings hang in the major galleries of the world. He died at Florence on Jan 22, 1531.

US AMATEUR PUBLIC LINKS (GOLF) CHAMPIONSHIP. July 14–19. Sand Creek Station Golf Course, Newton, KS. For info: USGA, Golf House, Championship Dept, PO Box 708, Far Hills, NJ 07931. Phone: (908) 234-2300. Fax: (908) 234-9687. E-mail: usga@usga.org. Web: www.usga.org.

US WOMEN'S AMATEUR PUBLIC LINKS (GOLF) CHAMPIONSHIP. July 14–19. The Home Course, Dupont, WA. For info: USGA, Golf House, Championship Dept, PO Box 708, Far Hills, NJ 07931. Phone: (908) 234-2300. Fax: (908) 234-9687. E-mail: usga@usga.org. Web: www.usga.org.

BIRTHDAYS TODAY

Polly Bergen, 84, actress ("To Tell the Truth," *The Winds of War*), singer, born Knoxville, TN, July 14, 1930.

Matthew Fox, 48, actor ("Lost," "Party of Five"), born Crowheart, WY, July 14, 1966.

Missy Gold, 44, actress ("Benson"), born Great Falls, MT, July 14, 1970.

Roosevelt (Rosey) Grier, 82, actor, former football player, born Cuthbert, GA, July 14, 1932.

Jackie Earle Haley, 53, actor (*Breaking Away, The Bad News Bears, Little Children*), born Northridge, CA, July 14, 1961.

Jane Lynch, 54, actress ("Glee," "The Cleveland Show," *The 40-Year-Old Virgin*), born Dolton, IL, July 14, 1960.

Susana Martinez, 55, Governor of New Mexico (R), born El Paso, TX, July 14, 1959.

Scott Porter, 35, actor ("Hart of Dixie," "Friday Night Lights"), born Omaha, NE, July 14, 1979.

Joel Silver, 62, producer (*Lethal Weapon, Die Hard*), born South Orange, NJ, July 14, 1952.

Harry Dean Stanton, 88, actor (*Repo Man*; *Paris, Texas*; *Wild at Heart*), born West Irvine, KY, July 14, 1926.

Steve Stone, 67, sportscaster, former baseball player, born Euclid, OH, July 14, 1947.

Robin Ventura, 47, former baseball player, born Santa Maria, CA, July 14, 1967.

July 15 — Tuesday

DAY 196 **169 REMAINING**

ALPENFEST. July 15–19. Gaylord, MI. 50th annual. Swiss-inspired festival that has something for the whole family. Annual traditions include "The World's Largest Coffee Break," Lampion Parade, Burning of the Boogg and a Grand Parade. Free food and entertainment daily, 75 arts and crafts booths, free kids' games, contests and a carnival. Est attendance: 50,000. For info: Alpenfest, PO Box 513, Gaylord, MI 49734. Phone: (800) 345-8621. Fax: (989) 732-7990. E-mail: events@gaylordchamber.com. Web: www.gaylordchamber.com or www.gaylordalpenfest.com.

BATTLE OF GRUNWALD: ANNIVERSARY. July 15, 1410. (Also known as the Battle of Tannenberg.) Poland and Lithuania joined forces to halt the aggressive advance of the Knights of the Teutonic Order, and they emerged victorious after a 10-hour battle near the villages of Tannenberg and Grunwald in Poland. The political and military power of the Teutonic Knights was severly diminished after this defeat.

BATTLE OF THE MARNE: ANNIVERSARY. July 15, 1918. General Erich Ludendorff launched Germany's fifth, and last, offensive to break through the Chateau-Thierry salient in WWI. This all-out effort involved three armies branching out from Reims, France, to cross the Marne River. The Germans were successful

July 2014

S	M	T	W	T	F	S
		1	2	3	4	5
6	7	8	9	10	11	12
13	14	15	16	17	18	19
20	21	22	23	24	25	26
27	28	29	30	31		

in crossing the Marne near Chateau-Thierry before American, British and Italian divisions stopped their progress. On July 18 General Ferdinand Foch, commander in chief of the Allied troops, launched a massive counteroffensive that resulted in a German retreat that continued for four months until Germany sued for peace in November.

CANADA: SAINT SWITHUN'S SOCIETY ANNUAL CELEBRATION. July 15. Toronto, ON. Goals include the promotion of feelings of goodwill, the encouragement of the celebration of St. Swithun's Day (July 15) and the patterning of members' lives after the example of our patron. Affiliated with the Friends of Winchester Cathedral. The society publishes "The Water Spout" newsletter, free upon request. Est attendance: 100. For info: Norman A. McMullen, KStG, President, St. Swithun's Society, 427 Lynett Crescent, Richmond Hill, ON, Canada L4C 2V6. Phone: (905) 883-0984. E-mail: nmcmullen@rogers.com.

DERRIDA, JACQUES: BIRTH ANNIVERSARY. July 15, 1930. Influential French philosopher; proponent of deconstruction. Born at El Biar, Algeria, Derrida died Oct 8, 2004, at Paris, France.

FAST OF TAMMUZ. July 15. Shiva Asar B'Tammuz begins at first light of day and commemorates the first-century Roman siege that breached the walls of Jerusalem. Begins a three-week time of mourning. Hebrew calendar date: Tammuz 17, 5774.

MAJOR LEAGUE BASEBALL ALL-STAR GAME. July 15 (tentative). Target Field, Minneapolis, MN. 85th annual All-Star game. For info: Major League Baseball. E-mail: fanfeedback@website.mlb.com or tickets@website.mlb.com. Web: www.mlb.com.

MAXWELL, GAVIN: 100th BIRTH ANNIVERSARY. July 15, 1914. Author and naturalist born at Mochrum, Wigtown, Scotland. His best-known work is *Ring of Bright Water* (1960), a memoir about living with rambunctious otters that was later adapted into a popular film. Maxwell died Sept 6, 1969, at Inverness, Scotland.

MOORE, CLEMENT CLARKE: BIRTH ANNIVERSARY. July 15, 1779. American author and teacher, best remembered for his popular verse "A Visit from Saint Nicholas" ("'Twas the Night Before Christmas"), which was first published anonymously and without Moore's knowledge in a newspaper, Dec 23, 1823. Moore was born at New York, NY, and died at Newport, RI, July 10, 1863. (In recent years Moore's authorship of the poem has been challenged, with Henry Livingston, Jr, offered as the creator.)

"ONE LIFE TO LIVE" TV PREMIERE: ANNIVERSARY. July 15, 1968. Set in a fictional Pennsylvania town, this Agnes Nixon drama originally depicted the class and ethnic struggles of the town's denizens, and the initial cast featured many Jewish, Polish and African-American characters. The show departed from interethnic storytelling in the 1980s for more fantastic adventures set in heaven, the Old West and a futuristic mountain silo called Eternia. After that phase, the show returned to its strengths of traditional storytelling by featuring Latino and African-American actors as integral characters. Award-winning actress Erika Slezak heads the cast as the venerable Viki Lord Riley Buchanan Carpenter, the town's matron with five alternate personalities. Among those who have appeared on "OLTL" are Tom Berenger, Judith Light, Tommy Lee Jones, Laurence Fishburne, Jameson Parker, Phylicia Rashad, Christine Ebersole, Richard Grieco, Blair Underwood, Joe Lando, Audrey Landers, Christian Slater and Yasmine Bleeth. Although canceled in 2011—with the final episode airing Jan 13, 2012—the show returned in a new incarnation as a Web series in 2013.

REMBRANDT: BIRTH ANNIVERSARY. July 15, 1606. Dutch painter and etcher, born Rembrandt Harmenszoon van Rijn at Leiden, Netherlands. One of the undisputed giants of Western art. Known for *The Night Watch* and many portraits and self-portraits. He died at Amsterdam, Netherlands, Oct 4, 1669.

SAINT FRANCES XAVIER CABRINI: BIRTH ANNIVERSARY. July 15, 1850. First American saint, founder of schools, orphanages, convents and hospitals, born at Lombardy, Italy. Died of malaria at Chicago, IL, Dec 22, 1917. Canonized July 7, 1946.

SAINT SWITHIN'S DAY. July 15. Swithin (or Swithun), bishop of Winchester (AD 852–862), died July 2, 862. Little is known of his life, but his relics were transferred into Winchester Cathedral July 15, 971, a day on which there was a heavy rainfall. According to old English belief, it will rain for 40 days thereafter when it rains on this day. "St. Swithin's Day, if thou dost rain, for 40 days it will remain; St. Swithin's Day, if thou be fair, for 40 days, will rain nea mair."

SNAKE RIVER STAMPEDE. July 15–19. Nampa, ID. In its 99th year, this is one of the top 15 professional rodeo events in the nation, featuring the world's top cowboys and cowgirls in action. Events include bareback bronc riding, saddle bronc riding, bull riding, calf roping, team roping, steer wrestling and barrel racing. Est attendance: 45,000. For info: Jimmie Hurley, Snake River Stampede, 16114 Idaho Center Blvd, Ste 4, Nampa, ID 83687. Phone: (208) 466-8497. Fax: (208) 465-4438. E-mail: sstampede@earthlink.net. Web: www.snakeriverstampede.com.

BIRTHDAYS TODAY

Willie Aames, 54, actor ("Eight Is Enough," "Charles in Charge"), born Newport Beach, CA, July 15, 1960.

Kim Alexis, 54, model, born Lockport, NY, July 15, 1960.

Julian Bream, 81, musician (classical guitar, lute), born London, England, July 15, 1933.

Jonathan Cheechoo, 34, hockey player, born Moose Factory, ON, Canada, July 15, 1980.

Lolita Davidovich, 53, actress (*Indictment, Cobb*), born London, ON, Canada, July 15, 1961.

Brian Austin Green, 41, actor ("Beverly Hills 90210"), singer, born Van Nuys, CA, July 15, 1973.

Arianna Huffington, 64, author, journalist ("The Huffington Post"), born Athens, Greece, July 15, 1950.

Irene Jacob, 48, actress (*Red, Othello*), born Paris, France, July 15, 1966.

Ken Kercheval, 79, actor ("Dallas," "Search for Tomorrow"), born Wolcottville, IN, July 15, 1935.

Terry O'Quinn, 62, actor ("Lost," "The West Wing," "Alias"), born Newberry, MI, July 15, 1952.

Lana Parilla, 37, actress ("Once Upon a Time," "Swingtown"), born Brooklyn, NY, July 15, 1977.

Linda Ronstadt, 68, singer, songwriter, born Tucson, AZ, July 15, 1946.

Richard Russo, 65, author (*Empire Falls, Straight Man, Nobody's Fool*), born Johnstown, NY, July 15, 1949.

Adam Savage, 47, television personality, host ("MythBusters"), born New York, NY, July 15, 1967.

Jesse Ventura, 63, former professional wrestler, former governor of Minnesota (I), born Minneapolis, MN, July 15, 1951.

Jan-Michael Vincent, 70, actor ("The Winds of War," "Airwolf"), born Denver, CO, July 15, 1944.

Forest Whitaker, 53, actor (Oscar for *The Last King of Scotland*; "The Shield," *Bird, The Crying Game*), director (*Waiting to Exhale*), born Longview, TX, July 15, 1961.

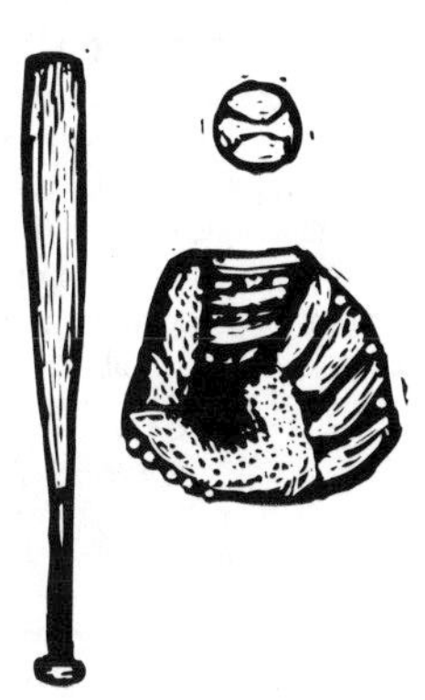

July 16 — Wednesday

DAY 197 **168 REMAINING**

AMUNDSEN, ROALD: BIRTH ANNIVERSARY. July 16, 1872. Norwegian explorer born near Oslo, Norway, Roald Amundsen was the first man to sail from the Atlantic Ocean to the Pacific Ocean via the Northwest Passage (1903–05). He discovered the South Pole (Dec 14, 1911) and flew over the North Pole in a dirigible in 1926. He flew, with five companions, from Norway on June 18, 1928, in a daring effort to rescue survivors of an Italian Arctic expedition. No trace of the rescue party or the airplane was ever located. See also: "South Pole Discovery: Anniversary" (Dec 14).

ANN ARBOR SUMMER ART FAIR®. July 16–19. Ann Arbor, MI. Juried art fair with more than 300 of the nation's finest artists and contemporary craftspeople. Free family art activity area and performance areas. Annually, beginning the third Wednesday in July. Est attendance: 600,000. For info: The Guild of Artists and Artisans, 118 N Fourth Ave, Ann Arbor, MI 48104-1402. Phone: (734) 662-3382. E-mail: info@theguild.org. Web: www.theguild.org.

ATOMIC BOMB TESTED: ANNIVERSARY. July 16, 1945. In the New Mexican desert at Alamogordo Air Base, 125 miles southeast of Albuquerque, the experimental atomic bomb was set off at 5:30 AM. Dubbed "Fat Boy" by its creator, the plutonium bomb vaporized the steel scaffolding holding it as the immense fireball rose 8,000 feet in a fraction of a second—ultimately creating a mushroom cloud to a height of 41,000 feet. At ground zero the bomb emitted heat three times the temperature of the interior of the sun. All plant and animal life for a mile around ceased to exist. When informed by President Truman at Potsdam, Germany, of the successful experiment, Winston Churchill responded, "It's the Second Coming in wrath!"

BOLIVIA: LA PAZ DAY. July 16. Founding of city, now capital of Bolivia, on this day, 1548.

COMET CRASHES INTO JUPITER: 20th ANNIVERSARY. July 16, 1994. The first fragment of the comet Shoemaker-Levy crashed into the planet Jupiter, beginning a series of spectacular collisions, each unleashing more energy than the combined effect of an explosion of all our world's nuclear arsenal. Video imagery from earthbound telescopes as well as the Hubble telescope provided vivid records of the explosions and their aftereffects. In 1993 the comet had shattered into a series of about a dozen large chunks that resembled "pearls on a string" after its orbit brought it within the gravitational effects of our solar system's largest planet.

DISTRICT OF COLUMBIA ESTABLISHING LEGISLATION: ANNIVERSARY. July 16, 1790. George Washington signed legislation that selected the District of Columbia as the permanent capital of the US. Boundaries of the district were established in 1792. Plans called for the government to remain housed at Philadelphia, PA, until 1800, when the new national capital would be ready for occupancy.

EARTHQUAKE JOLTS PHILIPPINES: ANNIVERSARY. July 16, 1990. An earthquake measuring 7.7 on the Richter scale struck the Philippines, killing an estimated 1,621 persons and leaving approximately 1,000 missing. The quake struck in an area north of Manila, and heavy damage was reported at Cabanatuan, at Baguio and on Luzon island. The quake was the worst in the Philippines in 14 years.

EDDY, MARY BAKER: BIRTH ANNIVERSARY. July 16, 1821. Founder of Christian Science; born near Concord, NH, she died at Chestnut Hill, MA, Dec 3, 1910.

FAIRFEST. July 16–20. Adams County Fairgrounds, Hastings, NE. Annual county fair featuring midway; open-class competitions in culinary arts, needlework, floral culture, woodworking and the visual arts; Adams County 4-H competition; livestock show; strolling acts and live entertainment. Est attendance: 65,000. For info: Sandy Himmelberg, Gen Mgr, 947 S Baltimore, Hastings, NE 68901. Phone: (402) 462-3247. Fax: (402) 462-4731. Web: www.adamscountyfairgrounds.com.

FOLKMOOT USA: THE NORTH CAROLINA INTERNATIONAL FOLK FESTIVAL. July 16–27. Waynesville, NC. 31st annual. A festival of international folk dance featuring groups from 12 countries. Est attendance: 75,000. For info: Folkmoot USA, PO Box 658, Waynesville, NC 28786. Phone: (828) 452-2997 or (877) FOLK-USA. Fax: (828) 452-5762. Web: www.folkmootusa.org.

MISSION SAN DIEGO DE ALCALA: FOUNDING ANNIVERSARY. July 16, 1769. First of 21 California missions to the Indians.

NATIONAL BABY FOOD FESTIVAL. July 16–19. Fremont, MI. 24th annual. Baby yourself at this festival in the hometown of Gerber Products. Adults face off in the baby-food-eating contest and tots crawl in races. Two entertainment stages, two parades and arts and crafts show round out the fun. Est attendance: 100,000. For info: Natl Baby Food Festival, 7 E Main St, Fremont, MI 49412. Phone: (231) 924-0770. E-mail: nbff@fremontcommerce.com. Web: www.babyfoodfest.com.

RAFLE DU VÉLODROME D'HIVER: ANNIVERSARY. July 16, 1942. In the largest roundup of Jews in occupied France to date, nearly 13,000 Jews, mainly foreign-born, were arrested and held at the Vélodrome d'Hiver, an indoor cycling track. After five days, men, women and children were separated for transport to a holding camp and then to Auschwitz. The raids were conducted by French police, with the help of volunteers from the PPF, France's largest Fascist party. French president Jacques Chirac admitted and apologized for French complicity in the deportations on July 16, 1995.

REYNOLDS, JOSHUA: BIRTH ANNIVERSARY. July 16, 1723. (Old Style date.) English portrait painter whose paintings of 18th-century English notables are among the best of the time. Born at Plympton, Devon, England, Sir Joshua died at London, Feb 23, 1792, at age 68. "He who resolves never to ransack any mind but his own," Reynolds told students of the Royal Academy in 1774, "will be soon reduced, from mere barrenness, to the poorest of all imitations; he will be obliged to imitate himself, and to repeat what he has before often repeated."

ROGERS, GINGER: BIRTH ANNIVERSARY. July 16, 1911. Born Virginia Katherine McMath at Independence, MO, Ginger Rogers won a Charleston contest when she was 15, a feat that began a six-decade career in vaudeville, Broadway and film. She became a star of the silver screen as Fred Astaire's dance partner in 10 romantic musicals, including *Top Hat* (1935) and *Swing Time* (1936). Rogers was a versatile actress who appeared in 70 films, winning an Oscar for her performance in *Kitty Foyle* (1940). She died on Apr 25, 1995, at Rancho Mirage, CA.

July 2014

S	M	T	W	T	F	S
		1	2	3	4	5
6	7	8	9	10	11	12
13	14	15	16	17	18	19
20	21	22	23	24	25	26
27	28	29	30	31		

SPACE MILESTONE: *APOLLO 11* (US): MAN SENT TO THE MOON: 45th ANNIVERSARY. July 16, 1969. This launch resulted in man's first moon landing, the first landing on any extraterrestrial body. See also: "Space Milestone: Moon Day" (July 20).

STANWYCK, BARBARA: BIRTH ANNIVERSARY. July 16, 1907. Actress Barbara Stanwyck was born Ruby Stevens at the Flatbush section of Brooklyn, NY. At the age of 18 she won a leading role in the Broadway melodrama *Noose*, appearing for the first time as Barbara Stanwyck. She appeared in 82 films including *Stella Dallas, Double Indemnity* and *The Lady Eve* and in the television series "The Big Valley." In 1944 the government listed her as the nation's highest-paid woman, earning $400,000 per year. Stanwyck died at Santa Monica, CA, Jan 21, 1990.

WELLS, IDA B.: BIRTH ANNIVERSARY. July 16, 1862. African-American journalist and antilynching crusader Ida B. Wells was born the daughter of slaves at Holly Springs, MS, and grew up as Jim Crow and lynching were becoming prevalent. Wells argued that lynchings occurred not to defend white women but because of whites' fear of economic competition from blacks. She traveled extensively, founding antilynching societies and black women's clubs. Wells's *Red Record* (1895) was one of the first published accounts of lynchings in the South. She died Mar 25, 1931, at Chicago, IL.

BIRTHDAYS TODAY

Gareth Bale, 25, soccer player, born Cardiff, Wales, July 16, 1989.

Ruben Blades, 66, singer, actor (*Crossover Dreams, The Milagro Beanfield War*), born Panama City, Panama, July 16, 1948.

Phoebe Cates, 51, actress (*Fast Times at Ridgemont High, Gremlins*), born New York, NY, July 16, 1963.

Stewart Copeland, 62, composer, musician (The Police), born Alexandria, VA, July 16, 1952.

Corey Feldman, 43, actor (*Stand by Me, The Lost Boys*), born Reseda, CA, July 16, 1971.

Will Ferrell, 47, comedian, actor (*Semi-Pro, Blades of Glory, Stranger than Fiction, Anchorman*), born Irvine, CA, July 16, 1967.

Michael Flatley, 56, dancer (*Lord of the Dance, Feet of Flames*), born Chicago, IL, July 16, 1958.

Mark Indelicato, 20, actor ("Ugly Betty"), born Philadelphia, PA, July 16, 1994.

Jayma Mays, 35, actress ("Glee," "Heroes," "Ugly Betty"), born Grundy, VA, July 16, 1979.

Bess Myerson, 90, former Miss America (1945), former government official, born New York, NY, July 16, 1924.

Barry Sanders, 46, former football player, born Wichita, KS, July 16, 1968.

Pinchas Zukerman, 66, violinist, born Tel Aviv, Israel, July 16, 1948.

July 17 — Thursday

DAY 198 — **167 REMAINING**

ABBOTT, BERENICE: BIRTH ANNIVERSARY. July 17, 1898. Berenice Abbott was born at Springfield, OH, and went on to become a pioneer of American photography. She is best remembered for her black-and-white photographs of New York City in the 1930s, many of which appeared in the book *Changing New York*. After publishing this collection, she began photographing scientific experiments that illustrated the laws and processes of physics. She died at Monson, ME, Dec 11, 1991.

ASTOR, JOHN JACOB: BIRTH ANNIVERSARY. July 17, 1763. Founder of what is considered the first American business monopoly—the American Fur Company (1808)—Astor broke into the fur trade in 1786 by starting a fur-goods store in New York City. He made considerable transactions in Canada and the Great Lakes region as well as China, through special permission from the British East India Company. Astor was born near Waldorf, Germany, the son of a poor butcher, but by the time he died Mar 29, 1848, at New York, NY, he was the wealthiest person in the United States and had established an Astor dynasty.

COMIC-CON INTERNATIONAL. July 17–20 (tentative). San Diego Convention Center, San Diego, CA. One of the largest showcases of comic art, artists, products and more. Some 9,000 exhibitors. Est attendance: 114,000. For info: Comic-Con International, PO Box 128458, San Diego, CA 92112. Phone: (619) 491-2475. Fax: (619) 414-1022. E-mail: cci-info@comic-con.org. Web: www.comic-con.org/cci.

CZAR NICHOLAS II AND FAMILY EXECUTED: ANNIVERSARY. July 17, 1918. Russian czar Nicholas II; his wife, Alexandra; son and heir, Alexis; and daughters, Anastasia, Tatiana, Olga and Marie, were executed by firing squad on this date. The murder of the last of the 300-year-old Romanov dynasty occurred at Yekaterinburg, in the Ural Mountains of Siberia, where Nicholas had been imprisoned since his abdication in 1917. Local Soviet officials, concerned about advancing promonarchist forces, executed the royal family rather than have them serve as a rallying point for the White Russians. In 1992 two of nine skeletons dug up the previous summer from a pit at Yekaterinburg were identified as the remains of the czar and czarina.

DELAWARE STATE FAIR. July 17–26. Harrington, DE. 95th annual fair will feature major concert and motor events, acres of carnival rides, livestock shows, petting zoos, commercial and competitive events, exotic food and free attractions throughout the grounds. Est attendance: 300,000. For info: Delaware State Fair, PO Box 28, Harrington, DE 19952. Phone: (302) 398-3269. Fax: (302) 398-5030. E-mail: info@thestatefair.net. Web: www.delawarestatefair.com.

DISNEYLAND OPENED: ANNIVERSARY. July 17, 1955. Disneyland, America's first theme park, opened at Anaheim, CA.

GARDNER, ERLE STANLEY: 125th BIRTH ANNIVERSARY. July 17, 1889. American author of detective fiction, born at Malden, MA. Best remembered for his smash-hit series featuring lawyer-detective Perry Mason, who debuted in *The Case of the Velvet Claws* in 1933. Perry Mason is probably the most famous lawyer in popular culture: he has been featured in 82 novels as well as on TV and film. At the height of their popularity, Mason novels sold 20,000 copies a day. Gardner died at Temecula, CA, Mar 11, 1970.

GERRY, ELBRIDGE: BIRTH ANNIVERSARY. July 17, 1744. The fifth vice president of the US (1813–14), born at Marblehead, MA. Died at Washington, DC, Nov 23, 1814. His name became part of the language (gerrymander) after he signed a redistricting bill favoring his party while governor of Massachusetts in 1812.

HEMINGWAY LOOK-ALIKE CONTEST. July 17–20. Key West, FL. 34th annual. One of many events in Key West celebrating the birthday of Ernest Hemingway and honoring his work as author and sportsman. Preliminary rounds are Thursday and Friday. The Final is Saturday when Papa 2014 is announced. Judging is handled by former Look-Alike winners. Contestants arrive in "Hemingway Garb": safari outfits, khakis and even excruciatingly hot wool fisherman's turtleneck sweaters. Some bring their own cheering squad. Others try to bribe the judges. The event wraps up Sunday with the 28th annual Arm Wrestling Contest and birthday cake for Papa Hemingway. Annually, the weekend nearest to or including Hemingway's birthday (July 21). For info: Sloppy Joe's, 201 Duval St, Key West, FL 33040. Phone: (305) 296-2388, ext 121. E-mail: info@sloppyjoes.com. Web: www.sloppyjoes.com.

KANSAS CITY HOTEL DISASTER: ANNIVERSARY. July 17, 1981. Anniversary of the collapse of aerial walkways at the Hyatt Regency Hotel at Kansas City, MO. About 1,500 people were attending the popular weekly tea dance when, at about 7 PM, two concrete and steel skywalks that were suspended from the ceiling of the hotel's atrium broke loose and fell on guests in the crowded lobby, killing 114 people. In 1986 a state board revoked the licenses of two engineers convicted of gross negligence for their part in designing the hotel.

KOREA: CONSTITUTION DAY. July 17. Legal national holiday. Commemorates the proclamation of the constitution of the Republic of Korea in 1948. Ceremonies at Seoul's capitol plaza and all major cities.

MINIMUM LEGAL DRINKING AGE AT 21: 30th ANNIVERSARY. July 17, 1984. Mothers Against Drunk Driving (MADD) helped pass the 21 Minimum Legal Drinking Age (MLDA) law because it makes sense and saves lives. President Ronald Reagan signed MLDA federal legislation making it illegal for anyone under 21 to purchase or publicly possess alcohol. An estimated 1,000 lives are saved each year as a result. For info: MADD. Phone: 877-ASK-MADD. Web: www.madd.org.

"POORMAN'S PARADISE" GOLD PANNER CONTEST. July 17. Nome, AK. 115th anniversary. Open to all ages. Contestants pan a coffee can of beach material to free three small gold nuggets. All contestants are timed to determine the fastest gold panner. Trophies for first, second and third place overall; first place 12 years and younger; first place women. Held on Anvil City Square. Est attendance: 500. For info: Rasmussen's Music Mart, PO Box 2, Nome, AK 99762. Phone: (907) 443-2798 or (907) 443-2919. E-mail: leaknome@alaska.com. Or Gold Prospector's Assn of America, 43445 Business Park Dr, Ste 113, Temecula, CA 92590. Phone: (800) 551-9707.

PUERTO RICO: MUÑOZ-RIVERA DAY. July 17. Public holiday on the anniversary of the birth of Luis Muñoz-Rivera. The Puerto Rican patriot, poet and journalist was born at Barranquitas, Puerto Rico, in 1859. He died at Santurce, a suburb of San Juan, Puerto Rico, Nov 15, 1916.

SPACE MILESTONE: *APOLLO-SOYUZ* TEST PROJECT (US, USSR). July 17, 1975. After three years of planning, negotiation and preparation, the first US-USSR joint space project reached fruition with the linkup in space of *Apollo 18* (crew: T. Stafford, V. Brand, D. Slayton; landed in Pacific Ocean July 24, during 136th orbit) and *Soyuz 19* (crew: A.A. Leonov, V.N. Kubasov; landed July 21, after 96 orbits). *Apollo 18* and *Soyuz 19* were linked for 47 hours (July 17–19) while joint experiments and transfer of personnel and materials back and forth between crafts took place. Launch date was July 15, 1975.

SPACE MILESTONE: *SOYUZ T-12* (USSR): 30th ANNIVERSARY. July 17, 1984. Cosmonaut Svetlana Savitskaya became the first woman to walk in space (July 25) and the first woman to make more than one space voyage. Docked at *Salyut 7* July 18 and returned to Earth July 29.

	S	M	T	W	T	F	S
July 2014			1	2	3	4	5
	6	7	8	9	10	11	12
	13	14	15	16	17	18	19
	20	21	22	23	24	25	26
	27	28	29	30	31		

SPANISH CIVIL WAR BEGINS: ANNIVERSARY. July 17, 1936. General Francisco Franco led an uprising of army troops based in North Africa against the elected government of the Spanish Republic. Spain was quickly divided into a Nationalist and a Republican zone. Franco's Nationalists drew support from Fascist Italy and Nazi Germany. On Apr 1, 1939, the Nationalists won a complete victory when they entered Madrid. Franco ruled as dictator in Spain until his death in 1975.

STEALTH BOMBER FLIGHT: 25th ANNIVERSARY. July 17, 1989. The B-2 Stealth bomber airplane was flown successfully over the desert near Palmdale, CA, for almost two hours. A decade of work and $22 billion reportedly were spent on the project prior to the first flight. Designed to penetrate Soviet radar, the B-2 Stealth bomber was said to be capable of delivering up to 25 tons of nuclear or other bombs. Average cost of each of the 132 bombers requested by the US Air Force was estimated to be $530 million. On this first test flight the plane flew at speeds of up to 180 knots (200 mph) and was put through several types of turns. Higher speeds and retraction of the landing gear were left for subsequent test flights.

VIRGINIA LAKE FESTIVAL. July 17–19. Clarksville, VA. Fun-filled three days with tethered hot-air balloon rides for children on Thursday; opening ceremonies on Friday; arts and crafts show, live entertainment for children and adults and fireworks on Saturday. Annually, the third full weekend in July. Est attendance: 100,000. For info: Clarksville Lake Country Chamber of Commerce, PO Box 1017, Clarksville, VA 23927. Phone: (434) 374-2436 or (800) 557-5582. E-mail: director@kerrlake.com. Web: www.clarksvilleva.com.

"WRONG WAY" CORRIGAN DAY: ANNIVERSARY. July 17, 1938. Douglas Groce Corrigan, an unemployed airplane mechanic, left Brooklyn, NY's Floyd Bennett Field, ostensibly headed for Los Angeles, CA, in a 1929 Curtiss Robin monoplane. He landed 28 hours, 13 minutes later at Baldonnell Airport in Dublin, Ireland, after a 3,150-mile nonstop flight without radio or special navigation equipment and in violation of American and Irish flight regulations. Born at Galveston, TX, Jan 22, 1907, Corrigan received a hero's welcome home; he was nicknamed "Wrong Way" Corrigan because he claimed he accidentally followed the wrong end of his compass needle. Died at Santa Ana, CA, Dec 9, 1995.

BIRTHDAYS TODAY

Lucie Arnaz, 63, actress ("Here's Lucy," "The Lucie Arnaz Show," *Lost in Yonkers*), born Los Angeles, CA, July 17, 1951.

Luke Bryan, 38, country singer, born Leesburg, GA, July 17, 1976.

Diahann Carroll, 79, singer, actress ("Julia," "Dynasty"), born Carol Diahann Johnson at New York, NY, July 17, 1935.

David Hasselhoff, 62, actor ("Knight Rider," "Baywatch"), born Baltimore, MD, July 17, 1952.

Jason Jennings, 36, baseball player, born Dallas, TX, July 17, 1978.

Aaron Lansky, 59, founder of the National Yiddish Book Center, born New Bedford, MA, July 17, 1955.

Donald Sutherland, 79, actor (*Space Cowboys, M*A*S*H, Klute*), born St. John, NB, Canada, July 17, 1935.

Dawn Upshaw, 54, opera singer, born Nashville, TN, July 17, 1960.

Alex Winter, 49, actor (*Bill & Ted's Excellent Adventure*), born London, England, July 17, 1965.

July 18 — Friday

DAY 199 **166 REMAINING**

BIG SKY STATE GAMES. July 18–20. Billings, MT. An Olympic-style festival for Montana citizens. This statewide multisport program is designed to inspire people of all ages and skill levels to develop their physical and competitive abilities to the height of their potential through participation in fitness activities. There are 10,000 participants. Est attendance: 30,000. For info: Big Sky State Games, Box 7136, Billings, MT 59103-7136. Phone: (406) 254-7426. Fax: (406) 254-7439. E-mail: info@bigskygames.org. Web: www.bigskygames.org.

CHICAGO GOLF CLUB: ANNIVERSARY. July 18, 1893. The first 18-hole golf course in America, laid out by Charles Blair MacDonald, was incorporated at Wheaton, IL. MacDonald was the architect of many of the early US courses, which he attempted to model on the best in Scotland and England. It was his belief that at each tee a golfer should face a hazard at the average distance of his or her shot.

EVANS, CHICK: BIRTH ANNIVERSARY. July 18, 1890. Charles (Chick) Evans, Jr, golfer born at Indianapolis, IN. Evans competed as an amateur against the best professionals in the early 20th century, winning the US Open in 1916. In the 1920s he established the Chick Evans Caddie Foundation, later called the Evans Scholarship Fund, which has helped send more than 4,000 people to college. Died at Chicago, IL, Nov 6, 1979.

FIRST PERFECT SCORE IN OLYMPIC HISTORY: ANNIVERSARY. July 18, 1976. At the Montreal Olympics, Romanian gymnast Nadia Comaneci scored the first "10" in Olympic history with her flawless performance of the compulsory exercise on the uneven bars. The scoreboard displayed a "1.00" because it couldn't go up to "10." Comaneci had seven total perfect scores and won five medals, including the gold for all-around performance. Four months previous to the Olympics, Comaneci had earned the first perfect score in international gymnastics competition history.

GEORGIA MOUNTAIN FAIR. July 18–26. Georgia Mountain Fairgrounds, Hiawassee, GA. Authentic mountain demonstrations including corn milling, board splitting and soap and hominy making in our Pioneer Village with one-room school, log cabin, barn, old store, corncrib and more. Nashville talent, clogging, midway, arts and crafts and much more. (The Georgia Mountain Fall Festival is Oct 10–18.) Est attendance: 60,000. For info: Georgia Mountain Fair, PO Box 444, Hiawassee, GA 30546. Phone: (706) 896-4191. Fax: (706) 896-4209. E-mail: gamtfair@windstream.net. Web: www.georgiamountainfairgrounds.com.

THE GREAT WELLSVILLE BALLOON RALLY. July 18–20. Wellsville, NY. 39th annual. The Great Wellsville Balloon Rally is a great community and western New York State event that boasts four free mass hot-air balloon launches. More than 40 hot-air balloons launch, weather permitting, at 6 PM Friday and Saturday and 6 AM Saturday and Sunday. The weekend's festivities include a huge Wellsville Main Street Merchant Sidewalk Sale, free music, delicious food, fireworks and afterglow. Est attendance: 50,000. For info: Wellsville Balloon Committee, PO Box 1206, Wellsville, NY 14895. Phone: (585) 593-5080. Web: www.wellsvilleballoonrally.com.

HAYAKAWA, SAMUEL ICHIYE: BIRTH ANNIVERSARY. July 18, 1906. S.I. Hayakawa was born at Vancouver, BC, Canada, and came to the US in 1927. An academic, in 1968 he was appointed acting president of San Francisco State College. During student demonstrations on his first day in office, he climbed atop a sound truck and disconnected the wires, silencing the demonstrators. His actions gained him enormous popularity among conservatives, and he was promoted to permanent president by Governor Ronald Reagan. As his popularity grew, he switched from the Democratic to the Republican Party and in 1976 was elected to the US Senate. He led the successful California initiative to declare English the state's official language in 1986. Hayakawa wrote nine textbooks on language and semantics. He died Feb 27, 1992, at Greenbrae, CA.

ITALY: STRESA FESTIVAL. July 18–20 (tentative). Also July 24–27 and Aug 23–Sept 5. Stresa. 53rd annual. International festival includes concerts by symphonic orchestras, chamber music and recitals. Since 2006 the Stresa Music Academy has organized master classes given by important musicians during the festival period, followed by a couple of concerts held by the best students. For info: Settimane Musicali di Stresa del Lago Maggiore, Via Carducci, 38, 28838 Stresa (VB), Italy. Phone: (39) (0323) 31095. Fax: (39) (0323) 33006. E-mail: info@stresafestival.eu. Web: www.stresafestival.eu.

MANDELA DAY. July 18. First observed in 2009, this day is a celebration of Nelson Mandela's life and a global call to action for people to recognize their individual ability to make an imprint and change the world around them. The hope is to inspire people from every corner of the earth to embrace the values of Nelson Mandela as they seek to improve their lives through service to their communities. Annually, on Nelson Mandela's birthday, July 18. For info: 46664 Campaign. E-mail: info@mandeladay.com. Web: www.mandeladay.com.

MANDELA, NELSON: BIRTHDAY. July 18, 1918. Former South African president Nelson Rolihlahla Mandela was born the son of a Tembu tribal chieftain at Qunu, near Umtata, in the Transkei territory of South Africa. Giving up his hereditary rights, Mandela chose to become a lawyer and earned his degree at the University of South Africa. He joined the African National Congress (ANC) in 1944, eventually becoming deputy national president in 1952. His activities in the struggle against apartheid resulted in his conviction for sabotage in 1964. During his 28 years in jail, Mandela remained a symbol of hope to South Africa's nonwhite majority, the demand for his release a rallying cry for civil rights activists. That release finally came Feb 11, 1990, as millions watched via satellite television. In 1994 Mandela was elected president of South Africa in the first all-race election there. See also: "Mandela, Nelson: Prison Release Anniversary" (Feb 11).

MOON PHASE: LAST QUARTER. July 18. Moon enters Last Quarter phase at 10:08 PM, EDT.

NATCHITOCHES–NORTHWESTERN STATE UNIVERSITY FOLK FESTIVAL AND THE LOUISIANA STATE FIDDLE CHAMPIONSHIP. July 18–19. Prather Coliseum, Northwestern State University, Natchitoches, LA. The festival is a "purist" folk festival in that only folk artists who are reviving a traditional Louisiana folk art or still working a Louisiana tradition are invited. Music, food, crafts and narrative sessions. A four-time winner of the Top Twenty Events in the Southeast, as determined by the Southeast Tourism Society. Est attendance: 5,000. For info: Shane Rasmussen, Louisiana Folklife Center, Natchitoches/NSU Folk Festival, NSU PO Box 3663, Natchitoches, LA 71497. Phone: (318) 357-4332 or (800) 259-1714. Fax: (318) 357-4331. E-mail: folklife@nsula.edu. Web: www.nsula.edu/folklife.

NORTH DAKOTA STATE FAIR. July 18–26. Minot, ND. The North Dakota State Fair features the best in big-name entertainment, farm and home exhibits, displays, midway and rodeo. Est attendance: 250,000. For info: North Dakota State Fair, Box 1796, Minot, ND 58702. Phone: (701) 857-7620. Fax: (701) 857-7622. E-mail: ndsf@minot.com. Web: www.ndstatefair.com.

ODETS, CLIFFORD: BIRTH ANNIVERSARY. July 18, 1906. Clifford Odets began his writing career as a poet before turning to acting. He helped found the Group Theatre in 1931. In 1935 he returned to writing with works for the Group Theatre such as

Waiting for Lefty, Awake and Sing! and *Golden Boy.* His proletarian views helped make him a popular playwright during the Depression years. Odets was born at Philadelphia, PA, and died at Los Angeles, CA, Aug 15, 1963.

PRESIDENTIAL SUCCESSION ACT: ANNIVERSARY. July 18, 1947. President Harry S Truman signed an executive order determining the line of succession should the president be temporarily incapacitated or die in office. The Speaker of the House and president pro tem of the Senate are next in succession after the vice president. This line of succession became the 25th Amendment to the Constitution, which was ratified Feb 10, 1967.

QUISLING, VIDKUN: BIRTH ANNIVERSARY. July 18, 1887. Born at Fyresdal, Norway, Vidkun Quisling was military attaché and minister of defense for Norway. He left the government in 1933 to form the fascist National Union Party. After personally urging Hitler to invade his home country (April 1940), Quisling served first as head of the Norwegian puppet state and then as "minister president" of the occupying government, in which capacity Quisling facilitated the deportation of nearly a thousand Jews to concentration camps. Following Norway's liberation Quisling was convicted of treason and executed on Oct 24, 1945, at Oslo, Norway. The name Quisling has come to mean "traitor" or "collaborator" in a number of languages, including English, due to Quisling's collaboration with the Nazis.

RESTLESS LEG SYNDROME (RLS) EDUCATION AND AWARENESS WEEK. July 18–25. More than 12 million Americans have severe leg pains called restless leg syndrome (RLS), and this education and awareness week, sponsored by the Pharmacy Council on Women's Health, is a means to educate and to call attention to various treatments and diagnoses to assist patients with this problem. For info: Fred S. Mayer, RPh, MPH, Pharmacists Planning Service, Inc (PPSI), PO Box 6760, San Rafael, CA 94903. Phone: (415) 479-8628 or (415) 302-7351. Fax: (415) 479-8608. E-mail: ppsi@aol.com. Web: www.ppsinc.org.

RUTLEDGE, JOHN: DEATH ANNIVERSARY. July 18, 1800. American statesman, associate justice on the Supreme Court, born at Charleston, SC, in September 1739. Nominated second chief justice of the US to succeed John Jay and served as acting chief justice until his confirmation was denied because of his opposition to the Jay Treaty. He died at Charleston, SC.

SHERWOOD ROBIN HOOD FESTIVAL. July 18–19. Sherwood, OR. Renaissance group; knighting ceremony; kids and family area; parade; world's only archery contest between Sherwood and Nottingham, England; castle contest; teen dance; music; food and crafts vendors and much more! Est attendance: 20,000. For info: Robin Hood Festival Assn, PO Box 496, Sherwood, OR 97140. Phone: (503) 625-4233. E-mail: webster@robinhoodfestival.org. Web: www.robinhoodfestival.org.

SKELTON, RED: BIRTH ANNIVERSARY. July 18, 1913. Pantomimist, radio and television comedian, vaudeville performer and artist, born Richard Bernard Skelton at Vincennes, IN, who appeared in nearly 30 movies and whose own eponymous television show ran for 20 years on CBS (1951–71). Best known for his pratfalls, one-liners and comic characterizations (Freddie the Freeloader, Clem Kaddiddlehopper, Sheriff Deadeye, the Mean Widdle Kid). He died Sept 17, 1997, at Rancho Mirage, CA.

SPACE MILESTONE: *ROHINI 1* (INDIA). July 18, 1980. First successful launch from India, orbited 77-pound satellite.

THACKERAY, WILLIAM MAKEPEACE: BIRTH ANNIVERSARY. July 18, 1811. Author, best remembered for his novels *Vanity Fair* (1848) and *Pendennis* (1850). In his time, Thackeray was second only to Charles Dickens in the hearts of British book lovers. Born at Calcutta, India, he died at London, England, Dec 23, 1863.

July 2014	S	M	T	W	T	F	S
			1	2	3	4	5
	6	7	8	9	10	11	12
	13	14	15	16	17	18	19
	20	21	22	23	24	25	26
	27	28	29	30	31		

THOMPSON, HUNTER S.: 75th BIRTH ANNIVERSARY. July 18, 1939. Journalist and author born at Louisville, KY, Thompson was one of the first practitioners of "New," or "Gonzo," journalism, a style that featured first-person accounts and scathing criticism of contemporary American society. His most famous work, "Fear and Loathing in Las Vegas," published in *Rolling Stone* magazine in 1972, featured an alter-ego character in search of the American Dream via use of hallucinogenic drugs. Other works include *Hell's Angels, The Great Shark Hunt* and *The Proud Highway.* Long hailed as a hero of counterculture, Thompson committed suicide at his home in Woody Creek, CO, Feb 21, 2005.

UNITED NATIONS: NELSON MANDELA INTERNATIONAL DAY. July 18. Recognizing Nelson Rolihlahla Mandela's leading role in Africa's struggle for liberation and unity, his dedication to the service of humanity as a humanitarian and his contribution to the struggle for democracy internationally and in promoting a culture of peace worldwide, the General Assembly has designated July 18 (his birthday) each year as Nelson Mandela International Day (Resolution 64/13 of Nov 10, 2009). For info: United Nations, Dept of Public Info, New York, NY 10017. Web: www.un.org.

URUGUAY: CONSTITUTION DAY. July 18. National holiday. Commemorates the country's first constitution in 1830.

W.C. HANDY MUSIC FESTIVAL. July 18–27. Florence, AL. A week-long street-strutting, toe-tapping and hand-clapping celebration of the musical heritage of Florence native W.C. Handy ("the father of the blues"). Great jazz and blues music can be heard throughout the Shoals at restaurants, theaters, malls, parks and other locations. The week includes more than 100 events perfect for the jazz and blues enthusiast as well as the whole family. Est attendance: 150,000. For info: Visit Florence, One Hightower Pl, Florence, AL 35630. Phone: (256) 740-4141. Fax: (256) 740-4142. E-mail: debbie@visitflorenceal.com. Web: www.visitflorenceal.com.

WHITE, GILBERT: BIRTH ANNIVERSARY. July 18, 1720. Born at Selborne, Hampshire, England, Gilbert White has been called the father of British naturalists. His book *The Natural History of Selborne*, published in 1788, enjoyed immediate success and is said never to have been out of print. White died near his birthplace, June 26, 1793. His home survives as a museum.

YARMOUTH CLAM FESTIVAL. July 18–20. Yarmouth, ME. 49th annual. Family-oriented festival featuring clams and more. Annually, starts the third Friday in July. Est attendance: 120,000. For info: Yarmouth Chamber of Commerce, 162 Main St, Yarmouth, ME 04096. Phone: (207) 846-3984. Fax: (207) 846-5419. E-mail: info@clamfestival.com. Web: www.clamfestival.com.

BIRTHDAYS TODAY

Kristen Bell, 34, actress (*You Again, Forgetting Sarah Marshall*, "Veronica Mars," "House of Lies"), born Detroit, MI, July 18, 1980.

James Brolin, 73, actor (Emmy for "Marcus Welby, MD"; "Hotel"), born Los Angeles, CA, July 18, 1941.

Richard Totten (Dick) Button, 85, sportscaster, Olympic figure skater, born Englewood, NJ, July 18, 1929.

Chace Crawford, 29, actor ("Gossip Girl"), born Lubbock, TX, July 18, 1985.

Vin Diesel, 47, actor (*XXX, The Fast and the Furious, Pitch Black*), born Mark Vincent at New York, NY, July 18, 1967.

Dion DiMucci, 75, singer (Dion and the Belmonts), born the Bronx, NY, July 18, 1939.

Nick Faldo, 57, golfer, born Welwyn Garden City, England, July 18, 1957.

Steve Forbes, 67, publisher, chairman, Forbes Newspapers, born Morristown, NJ, July 18, 1947.

John Glenn, 93, astronaut, first American to orbit Earth, former US senator (D, Ohio), born Cambridge, OH, July 18, 1921.

Anfernee "Penny" Hardaway, 42, former basketball player, born Memphis, TN, July 18, 1972.

Margo Martindale, 63, actress ("Justified," "Dexter," "Mercy"), born Jacksonville, TX, July 18, 1951.

Elizabeth McGovern, 53, actress ("Downton Abbey," *Racing with the Moon*), born Evanston, IL, July 18, 1961.

Calvin Peete, 71, former golfer, born Detroit, MI, July 18, 1943.

Martha Reeves, 73, singer (Martha and the Vandellas), born Detroit, MI, July 18, 1941.

Ricky Skaggs, 60, musician (bluegrass guitar), singer, born Cordell, KY, July 18, 1954.

Joe Torre, 74, baseball executive, former manager and player, born New York, NY, July 18, 1940.

Mark Udall, 64, US Senator (D, Colorado), born Tucson, AZ, July 18, 1950.

Yevgeny Yevtushenko, 81, poet, born Zima, USSR (now Russia), July 18, 1933.

July 19 — Saturday

DAY 200 **165 REMAINING**

ATTACK ON FORT WAGNER: ANNIVERSARY. July 19, 1863. In a second attempt to capture Fort Wagner, outside Charleston, SC, Federal troops were repulsed after losing 1,515 men as opposed to Southern losses of only 174. The attack was led by the 54th Massachusetts Colored Infantry, commanded by Colonel Robert Gould Shaw, who was killed in the action. This was the first use of black troops in the war. The film *Glory* was based on the Massachusetts 54th, and this was the attack featured in the film. Fort Wagner was never taken by the Union.

BANNACK DAYS. July 19–20. Bannack, MT. Montana's first territorial capital, now a well-preserved ghost town, comes to life with a celebration of Montana's mining and pioneer history. Wagon rides, Main Street gunfights, old-time dancing, lots of music and fun are provided during this two-day celebration along Grasshopper Creek each year. Bannack State Park allows visitors to explore the old town and imagine what life was like in the mid-1800s. It is open year-round to the public. Five dollars per vehicle. Est attendance: 5,000. For info: Montana Fish, Wildlife and Parks, 4200 Bannack Rd, Dillon, MT 59725. Phone: (406) 834-3413. E-mail: bannack@smtel.com.

CELEBRATION OF THE HORSE. July 19–20. Houston, TX. In honor of the human/equine bond and how horses affect people on an individual basis. Annually, the third weekend in July. For info: Tim Raisbeck, Charlotte's Saddlery, 11623A Katy Freeway, Houston, TX 77079. Phone: (281) 596-8225. Fax: (281) 596-8258. E-mail: csadd@charlottes-saddlery.com. Web: www.charlottes-saddlery.com.

COLT, SAMUEL: 200th BIRTH ANNIVERSARY. July 19, 1814. Born at Hartford, CT, inventor and manufacturer Colt is best known for developing the multishot pistol, which he patented in 1836. Before the revolver gained popularity, he was also involved in developing a submarine battery and underwater telegraph lines. His company, still currently operational, supplied both the North and South with weaponry during the US Civil War, and at the time of his death on Jan 10, 1862, at Hartford, he was one of the wealthiest men in the US.

COLTON COUNTRY DAY. July 19. Colton, NY. Annual flea market, live entertainment, museum exhibits. Fireworks at dusk. Sponsor: Colton Historical Society. Est attendance: 1,500. For info: Dennis Eickhoff, Town Historian, PO Box 95, Colton, NY 13625. Phone: (315) 262-2800. Fax: (315) 262-2182. E-mail: collib@ncls.org.

DEGAS, EDGAR: BIRTH ANNIVERSARY. July 19, 1834. The French Impressionist painter, especially noted for his paintings of dancers in motion, was born at Paris, France, and died there Sept 26, 1917.

ELVIS PRESLEY'S FIRST SINGLE RELEASED: 60th ANNIVERSARY. July 19, 1954. "That's All Right (Mama)" backed by "Blue Moon of Kentucky" was released on this date by Sun Records of Memphis, TN. It was 19-year-old Elvis Presley's first professional record. Presley recorded it with guitarist Scotty Moore and bassist Bill Black. Memphis DJ Dewey Phillips previewed the single on July 7—literally two days after it was recorded—on his radio show and his listeners went crazy, demanding that Phillips play it again and again. See also: "Elvis Presley's First Concert Appearance: Anniversary" (July 30).

FIRST UNASSISTED TRIPLE PLAY: ANNIVERSARY. July 19, 1909. Cleveland Blues shortstop Neal Ball recorded the first unassisted triple play in American League history in a game against the Boston Pilgrims. Ball caught a line drive hit by Amby McConnell, stepped on second base to double off Heine Wagner and tagged Jake Stahl before Stahl could get back to first base. Ball also hit a home run as Cleveland won, 6–1.

FIRST WOMAN VICE-PRESIDENTIAL CANDIDATE: 30th ANNIVERSARY. July 19, 1984. Congresswoman Geraldine Ferraro was nominated to run with presidential candidate Walter Mondale on the Democratic ticket. They were defeated by the Republican ticket headed by Ronald Reagan.

LINKLETTER, ART: BIRTH ANNIVERSARY. July 19, 1912. Television and radio personality born Gordon Arthur Kelly at Moose Jaw, SK, Canada. He is remembered for his mainly unscripted programs "People Are Funny" and "House Party," in which audience volunteers would become the butt of the joke by way of live pranks and mischievous setups. A particular segment in which he asked young children seemingly innocuous questions became his legacy. "Kids Say the Darndest Things!" also became a series of books and spawned several TV specials. Died May 26, 2010, at Los Angeles, CA.

***THE LORD OF THE RINGS*: FIRST PART PUBLISHED: 60th ANNIVERSARY.** July 19, 1954. *The Fellowship of the Ring*, the first part of J.R.R. Tolkien's epic *The Lord of the Rings*, was published on this date in London, England, by George Allen and Unwin. The publishers chose to publish the novel in three parts because it was so long. *The Two Towers* was published on Nov 11, 1954, and *The Return of the King* was published on Oct 20, 1955.

MAYO, CHARLES HORACE: BIRTH ANNIVERSARY. July 19, 1865. American surgeon, one of the Mayo brothers, founders of the Mayo Clinic and Mayo Foundation, born at Rochester, MN. Died at Chicago, IL, May 26, 1939.

McGOVERN, GEORGE: BIRTH ANNIVERSARY. July 19, 1922. US politician and WWII hero, born at Mitchell, SD. McGovern began his career in public service in 1956. Representing South Dakota in both houses of Congress, he was a voice in support of civil rights and social issues throughout the 1960s—as well as a vocal opponent of American involvement in the Vietnam War. The Democratic presidential candidate in 1972, McGovern and his party were targeted by the operatives of the Nixon administration in the form of illegal information gathering and wiretapping—the Watergate scandal. He lost the election to Richard Nixon in a crushing defeat, and later he returned to the Senate. His work with UN hunger causes earned him the Presidential Medal of Freedom in 2000. McGovern died at Sioux Falls, SD, Oct 21, 2012.

MERRIAM, EVE: BIRTH ANNIVERSARY. July 19, 1916. A poet, playwright and author of more than 50 books for both adults and children. Merriam's works, which often focused on feminism, include *It Doesn't Always Have to Rhyme, After Nora Slammed the Door: The Women's Unfinished Revolution, Mommies at Work* and a book of poems attacked by authorities as glamorizing crime, *The Urban Mother Goose.* She also wrote the first documentary on women's rights for network TV, *We the Women.* Born at Philadelphia, PA, she died at New York, NY, Apr 11, 1992.

NATIONAL WOODIE WAGON DAY. July 19. The "woodie wagon," made famous in the 1940s and '50s, romanticized the American outing. From Route 66 to the surfer lifestyle, the woodie wagon was there. This national day will be celebrated in individual cities and towns across the US and will pay homage to this great American symbol of freedom and the casual lifestyle. Annually, the third Saturday in July. For info: Historic Preservations, Inc, PO Box 49241, Denver, CO 80249. Phone: (303) 949-5964. E-mail: gregoryaraymer@yahoo.com.

NICARAGUA: NATIONAL LIBERATION DAY. July 19. Following the National Day of Joy (July 17—anniversary of date in 1979 when dictator Anastasio Somoza Debayle fled Nicaragua) is the annual July 19 observance of National Liberation Day, anniversary of day the National Liberation Army claimed victory over the Somoza dictatorship.

SAINT VINCENT DE PAUL: OLD FEAST DAY. July 19. A day remembering the founder of the Vincentian Congregation and the Sisters of Charity, born at Pouy, France, Apr 24, 1581. He died Sept 27, 1660, at Paris, France. His feast day was formerly observed on July 19 but is now observed on the anniversary of his death, Sept 27.

TOSS AWAY THE "COULD HAVES" AND "SHOULD HAVES" DAY. July 19. On this day people write down their "could haves" and "should haves" on a piece of paper and then throw that list into the trash. Then they make this resolution: "From this day forward, I choose not to live in the past—the past is history that I can't change. I can do something about the present—I choose to live in the present." Annually, the third Saturday in July. For info: Martha Ross-Rodgers, 2442 Annie Circle, Chesapeake, VA 23323. Phone: (757) 543-9290. E-mail: MRossrodge@aol.com. Web: www.jirehpublishers.com.

WOMEN'S RIGHTS CONVENTION AT SENECA FALLS: ANNIVERSARY. July 19, 1848. A convention concerning the rights of women, called by Lucretia Mott and Elizabeth Cady Stanton, was held at Seneca Falls, NY, July 19–20, 1848. The issues discussed included voting, property rights and divorce. The convention drafted a "Declaration of Sentiments" that paraphrased the Declaration of Independence, addressing man instead of King George, and called for women's "immediate admission to all the rights and privileges which belong to them as citizens of the United States." This convention was the beginning of an organized women's rights movement in the US. The most controversial issue was Stanton's demand for women's right to vote.

YALOW, ROSALYN: BIRTH ANNIVERSARY. July 19, 1921. Medical physicist born at New York City. Along with Andrew V. Schally and Roger Guillemin, in 1977 Yalow was awarded the Nobel Prize in Physiology or Medicine. Through her research on medical applications of radioactive isotopes, Yalow developed RIA, a sensitive and simple technique used to measure minute concentrations of hormones and other substances in blood or other body fluids. First applied to the study of insulin concentration in the blood of people with diabetes, RIA was soon used in hundreds of other applications. She died May 30, 2011, at the Bronx, NY.

BIRTHDAYS TODAY

Benedict Cumberbatch, 38, actor ("Sherlock," *Star Trek Into Darkness, Tinker Tailor Soldier Spy*), born London, England, July 19, 1976.

Anthony Edwards, 52, actor ("ER," *Fast Times at Ridgemont High, Top Gun*), born Santa Barbara, CA, July 19, 1962.

Topher Grace, 36, actor (*Spider-Man 3, In Good Company, Traffic,* "That '70s Show"), born New York, NY, July 19, 1978.

Clea Lewis, 49, actress ("Ellen," *The Rich Man's Wife*), born Cleveland Heights, OH, July 19, 1965.

Ilie Nastase, 68, Hall of Fame tennis player, born Bucharest, Romania, July 19, 1946.

Campbell Scott, 52, actor (*Roger Dodger, Singles*), born Westchester County, NY, July 19, 1962.

July 20 — Sunday

DAY 201 **164 REMAINING**

"THE ARTHUR MURRAY PARTY" TV PREMIERE: ANNIVERSARY. July 20, 1950. This ballroom dancing show appeared on all four networks (ABC, DuMont, CBS and NBC) and was hosted by Kathryn Murray, wife of famed dance school founder Arthur Murray.

ATTEMPT ON HITLER'S LIFE: 70th ANNIVERSARY. July 20, 1944. During the daily staff meeting at German headquarters at Rastenburg, an attempt was made to assassinate Adolf Hitler. Count Claus Schenk von Stauffenberg, chosen from a group of German military and civil servants involved in the plot, left a briefcase containing a bomb only six feet from Hitler under the staff table in the briefing room. Four people were killed in the blast, but Hitler's life was saved, probably because Colonel Heinz Brandt (who was among those killed) had found the briefcase in his way and moved it farther from the German dictator.

AURORA THEATER SHOOTING: ANNIVERSARY. July 20, 2012. James Holmes, whose psychiatrist only weeks before had warned police that he was experiencing homicidal thoughts, bought a ticket for a midnight showing of *The Dark Knight Rises* at the Century 16 multiplex theater in Aurora, CO. Shortly after the movie began, Holmes propped open an emergency exit, walked to his car and returned heavily armed and wearing body armor. Standing at the front of the theater, he began discharging tear gas and a variety of weapons into the panicked crowd, killing 12 and wounding 58. It was the fourth and largest of the seven mass shootings in the US in 2012.

July 2014

S	M	T	W	T	F	S
		1	2	3	4	5
6	7	8	9	10	11	12
13	14	15	16	17	18	19
20	21	22	23	24	25	26
27	28	29	30	31		

✦CAPTIVE NATIONS WEEK. July 20–26. Presidential proclamation issued each year since 1959 for the third week in July. (Public Law 86–90 of July 17, 1959.)

CODMAN ESTATE ANTIQUE AUTO SHOW. July 20. Codman Estate, Lincoln, MA. A fun-filled day of viewing antique and classic cars, trucks, motorcycles and fire engines. Not a contest or a race but a day of appreciation; an opportunity for antique car enthusiasts to see and be seen. Live music, clown, children's crafts and a tour of the historic house museum. For info: Historic New England. E-mail: festivals@HistoricNewEngland.org. Web: www.HistoricNewEngland.org.

COLOMBIA: INDEPENDENCE DAY. July 20. National holiday. Commemorates the beginning of the independence movement with an uprising against Spanish officials in 1810 at Bogotá. Colombia gained independence from Spain in 1819 when Simon Bolívar decisively defeated the Spanish.

CONCOURS d'ELEGANCE. July 20. Forest Grove, OR. Set among the beauty of the Pacific University campus, this is one of the premier car shows on the West Coast, with 300-plus beautifully restored vintage autos. A great family event. Annually, the third Sunday in July. Est attendance: 6,000. For info: Forest Grove Rotary Club, PO Box 387, Forest Grove, OR 97116. Phone: (503) 357-2300. Web: www.forestgroveconcours.org.

GENEVA ACCORDS: 60th ANNIVERSARY. July 20, 1954. An agreement covering cessation of hostilities in Vietnam, signed at Geneva, Switzerland, on behalf of the commanders in chief of French forces at Vietnam and the People's Army of Vietnam. A further declaration of the Geneva Conference was released July 21, 1954. Partition, foreign troop withdrawal and elections for a unified government within two years were among provisions.

HILLARY, SIR EDMUND PERCIVAL: 95th BIRTH ANNIVERSARY. July 20, 1919. Explorer, mountaineer, born at Auckland, New Zealand. With Tenzing Norgay, a Sherpa guide, became first to ascend summit of highest mountain in the world, Mount Everest (29,028 feet), at 11:30 AM, May 29, 1953. "We climbed because nobody climbed it before," he said. Hillary, who also listed his occupation as beekeeper, died Jan 11, 2008, at Auckland.

ITALY: FEAST OF THE REDEEMER. July 20. Venice. Procession of gondolas and other craft commemorating the end of the epidemic of 1575. Annually, the third Sunday in July.

KARLFELDT, ERIK AXEL: 150th BIRTH ANNIVERSARY. July 20, 1864. Poet, born at Folkärna, Sweden, who was posthumously awarded the Nobel Prize in Literature in 1931. Karlfeldt's lyrical poems celebrated nature and the rustic roots of Swedish culture. He had turned down the Nobel in 1918 because he was also secretary at the Swedish Academy. But when he died Apr 8, 1931, at Stockholm, the Academy honored him despite seeming to go against the purpose of the prize (to aid living artists).

LAKE SUPERIOR DAY. July 20. Lake Superior, one of the world's largest lakes, is home to countless fish, birds, other animals and plants. And every day, each of the 600,000 human residents of the Lake Superior basin use water from the lake for drinking, home use, industrial use or recreation. The Lake Superior Binational Forum promotes this basin-wide special day to highlight the special connections people have to this unique world treasure. People, communities, businesses, tribes, First Nations, churches and other groups around the lake celebrate and organize events such as dragon boat races, beach cleanups, musical concerts, library displays and more. Annually, the third Sunday in July. For info: Lake Superior Binational Forum. Phone: (715) 682-1489. E-mail: lakesuperiorday@northland.edu. Web: www.lakesuperiorforum.org/outreach-2/lake-superior-day.

LOCUST PLAGUE OF 1874: ANNIVERSARY. July 20–30, 1874. The Rocky Mountain locust, long a pest in the American Midwest, became an even bigger threat in the summer of 1874. Beginning in late July, the largest recorded swarm of this insect descended on the Great Plains. It is estimated that 124 billion insects formed a swarm 1,800 miles long and 110 miles wide that ranged from Canada and the Dakotas down to Texas. Contemporary accounts said that the locusts blocked out the sun and devastated farms in mere minutes. The swarms continued in smaller size for the next several years and caused an estimated $200 million in crop destruction.

LUXEMBOURG: BEER FESTIVAL. July 20. At Diekirch an annual beer festival is held on the third Sunday in July.

NATIONAL ICE CREAM DAY. July 20. To promote America's favorite dessert, ice cream, on "Sundae Sunday." Annually, the third Sunday in July.

RAGBRAI®—THE *REGISTER*'S ANNUAL GREAT BICYCLE RIDE ACROSS IOWA™. July 20–26. A seven-day, leisurely tour from the western border of Iowa to the Mississippi River enjoying wonderful Iowa scenery and hospitality. RAGBRAI® is the largest, longest and oldest bicycle touring event in the world. The *Des Moines Register* is coordinator this ride, which attracts 10,000 riders from across the country (and around the world). Annually, the last full week in July. Est attendance: 10,000. For info: RAGBRAI, PO Box 622, Des Moines, IA 50306-0622. Phone: (800) 474-3342. E-mail: info@ragbrai.com. Web: www.ragbrai.com.

RIOT ACT: ANNIVERSARY. July 20, 1715. To "read the riot act" now usually means telling children to be quiet or less boisterous, but in 18th-century England reading the riot act was a more serious matter. On July 20, 1715, the Riot Act took effect. By law in England, if 12 or more persons were unlawfully assembled to the disturbance of the public peace, an authority was required "with a loud voice" to command silence and read the riot act proclamation: "Our sovereign lord the king chargeth and commandeth all persons, being assembled, immediately to disperse themselves, and peaceably to depart to their habitations, or to their lawful business, upon the pains contained in the act made in the first year of King George, for preventing tumults and riotous assemblies. God save the king." Any persons who failed to obey within one hour were to be seized, apprehended and carried before a justice of the peace.

SPACE MILESTONE: MOON DAY: 45th ANNIVERSARY. July 20, 1969. Anniversary of man's first landing on the moon. Two US astronauts (Neil Alden Armstrong and Edwin Eugene Aldrin, Jr) landed lunar module *Eagle* at 4:17 PM, EDT, and remained on the lunar surface 21 hours, 36 minutes and 16 seconds. The landing was made from the *Apollo XI*'s orbiting command-and-service module, code-named *Columbia*, whose pilot, Michael Collins, remained aboard. Armstrong was first to set foot on the moon. Armstrong and Aldrin were outside the spacecraft, walking on the moon's surface, approximately 2¼ hours. The astronauts returned to Earth July 24, bringing photographs and rock samples.

SPECIAL OLYMPICS: ANNIVERSARY. July 20, 1968. Official anniversary of the first ever International Special Olympics Competition, held at Soldier Field, Chicago, IL. Special Olympics is an international year-round program of sports training and competition for individuals with intellectual disabilities. More than 3.5 million athletes in more than 170 countries train and compete in 32 Olympic-style summer and winter sports. Founded in 1968 by Eunice Kennedy Shriver, Special Olympics provides people with intellectual disabilities continuing opportunities to develop fitness, demonstrate courage and experience joy as they participate in the sharing of gifts and friendship with other athletes, their families and the community. For info: Special Olympics, Inc. Web: www.specialolympics.org.

SWITZERLAND: DORNACH BATTLE COMMEMORATION. July 20. The victory at Dornach in 1499 is remembered on the battlefield and in the city of Solothurn on the Sunday nearest to July 22.

TURKEY: BOSPHORUS CROSS-CONTINENTAL SWIM. July 20. Istanbul. First held in 1989, this annual sporting event features 750 athletes swimming across the Bosphorus Strait from Asia to Europe. Annually, the third Sunday in July. For info: National Olympic Committee of Turkey. E-mail: info@olimpiyat.org.tr. Web: www.bosphorus.cc.

BIRTHDAYS TODAY

Ray Allen, 39, basketball player, born Merced, CA, July 20, 1975.

Kim Carnes, 68, singer, songwriter, born Hollywood, CA, July 20, 1946.

Judy Chicago, 75, artist, feminist, born Judy Cohen at Chicago, IL, July 20, 1939.

John Daley, 29, actor ("Freaks and Geeks"), born New York, NY, July 20, 1985.

Pavel Datsyuk, 36, hockey player, born Sverdlovsk, Russia, July 20, 1978.

Donna Dixon, 57, actress ("Bosom Buddies," *Dr. Detroit*), born Alexandria, VA, July 20, 1957.

Peter Forsberg, 41, hockey player, born Ornskoldvik, Sweden, July 20, 1973.

Josh Holloway, 45, actor ("Lost"), born San Jose, CA, July 20, 1969.

Sally Ann Howes, 84, actress (*Dead of Night, The History of Mr Polly*), singer, born London, England, July 20, 1930.

Michael Ilitch, 85, sports executive, former minor league baseball player, born Detroit, MI, July 20, 1929.

Cormac McCarthy, 81, author (*The Road, No Country for Old Men, All the Pretty Horses*), born Providence, RI, July 20, 1933.

Barbara Ann Mikulski, 78, US Senator (D, Maryland), born Baltimore, MD, July 20, 1936.

Enrique Peña Nieto, 48, President of Mexico, born Atlacomulco, State of Mexico, Mexico, July 20, 1966.

Claudio Reyna, 41, former soccer player, born Livingston, NJ, July 20, 1973.

Diana Rigg, 76, actress (Tony for *Medea*; *King Lear, Bleak House*, "The Avengers"), born Doncaster, Yorkshire, England, July 20, 1938.

Carlos Santana, 67, musician, born Autlan, Mexico, July 20, 1947.

July 2014	S	M	T	W	T	F	S
			1	2	3	4	5
	6	7	8	9	10	11	12
	13	14	15	16	17	18	19
	20	21	22	23	24	25	26
	27	28	29	30	31		

July 21 — Monday

DAY 202 — **163 REMAINING**

BATTLE OF BULL RUN: ANNIVERSARY. July 21, 1861. Union general Irvin McDowell was defeated by Confederate troops led by General Joseph E. Johnston at the first Battle of Bull Run at Manassas, VA. It was the first major engagement of the Civil War. It was during this battle that Confederate general T.J. Jackson won the nickname "Stonewall." In the second Battle of Bull Run, Aug 29–30, 1862, Union general John Pope was badly defeated by General Robert E. Lee.

BELGIUM: INDEPENDENCE DAY. July 21. Public holiday. Marks accession of first Belgian king, Leopold I, in 1831, after independence from Netherlands.

CLEVELAND, FRANCES FOLSOM: 150th BIRTH ANNIVERSARY. July 21, 1864. Wife of Grover Cleveland, 22nd and 24th president of the US, born at Buffalo, NY. She was the youngest first lady at age 21 and the first to marry a president in the White House (June 2, 1886). Cleveland was a popular first lady who championed higher education for women. Died at Baltimore, MD, Oct 29, 1947.

EVERS, JOHNNY: BIRTH ANNIVERSARY. July 21, 1881. John Joseph (Johnny) Evers, Baseball Hall of Fame second baseman, born at Troy, NY. Evers was a member of the Tinker-to-Evers-to-Chance double-play combination for the Chicago Cubs, which first took the field on Sept 13, 1902. Inducted into the Hall of Fame (with Tinker and Chance) in 1946. Evers died at Albany, NY, Mar 28, 1947.

FIRST ROBOT KILLING: 30th ANNIVERSARY. July 21, 1984. The first reported killing of a human by a robot occurred at Jackson, MI. A robot turned and caught a 34-year-old worker between it and a safety bar, crushing him. He died of the injuries July 26, 1984. According to the National Institute for Occupational Safety and Health, it was "the first documented case of a robot-related fatality in the US."

GUAM: LIBERATION DAY. July 21. National holiday. Commemorates US forces' return to Guam in 1944, freeing the island from the Japanese.

HEMINGWAY, ERNEST: BIRTH ANNIVERSARY. July 21, 1899. American author born at Oak Park, IL. Made his name with such works as *The Sun Also Rises* (1926), *A Farewell to Arms* (1929), *For Whom the Bell Tolls* (1940) and *The Old Man and the Sea* (1952). He was awarded the Nobel Prize in 1954 and wrote little thereafter. Hemingway shot himself July 2, 1961, at Ketchum, ID, having been seriously ill for some time.

HEMINGWAY BIRTHDAY CELEBRATION. July 21. Hemingway Museum, Oak Park, IL. Annual celebration of Ernest Hemingway's birth. Includes a lecture and reception. For info: The Ernest Hemingway Foundation of Oak Park, PO Box 2222, Oak Park, IL 60303-2222. Phone: (708) 848-2222. Fax: (708) 386-2952. E-mail: ehfop@sbcglobal.net. Web: www.ehfop.org.

JAPAN: MARINE DAY. July 21. National holiday. Observed on the third Monday in July.

LEBRIJA RAILWAY WRECK: ANNIVERSARY. July 21, 1972. A Madrid–Cadiz express train packed with more than 500 people crashed head-on into a local train—which had ignored a red light—outside the Spanish town of Lebrija. All 76 passengers on the local train were killed, and more than 100 passengers on board the express train were injured.

LOWEST RECORDED TEMPERATURE: ANNIVERSARY. July 21, 1983. At the USSR's Vostok Station in Antarctica, a temperature of 128.6 degrees below zero Fahrenheit (89.2 degrees below zero Celsius) was recorded on this date.

McLUHAN, MARSHALL: BIRTH ANNIVERSARY. July 21, 1911. Herbert Marshall McLuhan, university professor and author—called "the Canadian sage of the electronic age"—was born at Edmonton, AB, Canada. His *Understanding Media, The Medium Is the Massage* (not to be confused with his widely quoted aphorism: "The medium is the message") and other books were widely acclaimed for their fresh view of communication. McLuhan is reported to have said: "Most people are alive in an earlier time, but you must be alive in our own time." He died at Toronto, ON, Canada, Dec 31, 1980.

NATIONAL GET OUT OF THE DOGHOUSE DAY. July 21. In trouble with someone you know and care about? This is the day when anyone can "Get out of the doghouse!" Annually, the third Monday in July. For info: Heidi Richards Mooney, Success and Then Some, PO Box 550856, Fort Lauderdale, FL 33355. Phone: (954) 625-6606. E-mail: heidi@successandthensome.com.

NATIONAL WOMEN'S HALL OF FAME: 35th ANNIVERSARY. July 21, 1979. Seneca Falls, NY. Founded to honor American women whose contributions "have been of the greatest value in the development of their country" and located in the community known as the "birthplace of women's rights," where the first Women's Suffrage Movement convention was held in 1848, the Hall of Fame was dedicated with 23 inductees. An earlier National Women's Hall of Fame, honoring "Twenty Outstanding Women of the Twentieth Century," was dedicated at the New York World's Fair, on May 27, 1965.

NO PET STORE PUPPIES DAY. July 21. 3rd annual. Most pet shop puppies come from puppy mills, and so do most dogs sold over the Internet. The ASPCA's national "No Pet Store Puppies" campaign raises awareness about puppy mill cruelty and aims to reduce the demand for puppy mill puppies by urging consumers not to buy any items—including food, supplies or toys—if the store or website sells dogs. Help celebrate No Pet Store Puppies Day on July 21 by taking the pledge and refusing to shop in pet stores and on websites that sell puppies. Annually, July 21. For info: ASPCA, Media and Communications Dept, 520 8th Ave, 7th Fl, New York, NY 10018. Phone: (212) 876-7700. E-mail: press@aspca.org. Web: www.nopetstorepuppies.com.

US GIRLS' JUNIOR (GOLF) CHAMPIONSHIP. July 21–26. Forest Highlands Golf Club, Flagstaff, AZ. For info: USGA, Golf House, Championship Dept, PO Box 708, Far Hills, NJ 07931. Phone: (908) 234-2300. Fax: (908) 234-9687. Web: www.usga.org.

US JUNIOR AMATEUR (GOLF) CHAMPIONSHIP. July 21–26. The Club at Carlton Woods, The Woodlands, TX. For info: USGA, Golf House, Championship Dept, PO Box 708, Far Hills, NJ 07931. Phone: (908) 234-2300. Fax: (908) 234-9687. E-mail: usga@usga.org. Web: www.usga.org.

BIRTHDAYS TODAY

John Barrasso, 62, US Senator (R, Wyoming), born Casper, WY, July 21, 1952.

Justin Bartha, 36, actor (*National Treasure, The Hangover*), born West Bloomfield, MI, July 21, 1978.

Brandi Chastain, 46, sportscaster, former soccer player, born San Jose, CA, July 21, 1968.

Lance Guest, 54, actor ("Lou Grant," *The Last Starfighter*), born Saratoga, CA, July 21, 1960.

Josh Hartnett, 36, actor (*Pearl Harbor, Halloween H2O*), born San Francisco, CA, July 21, 1978.

Edward Herrmann, 71, actor (*The Paper Chase, Eleanor and Franklin*, "Gilmore Girls"), born Washington, DC, July 21, 1943.

Norman Jewison, 88, producer, director (*Moonstruck, Fiddler on the Roof*), born Toronto, ON, Canada, July 21, 1926.

Jon Lovitz, 57, actor (*A League of Their Own*, "NewsRadio"), born Tarzana, CA, July 21, 1957.

Dan Malloy, 59, Governor of Connecticut (D), born Stamford, CT, July 21, 1955.

Matt Mulhern, 54, actor ("Major Dad," *Biloxi Blues*), born Philadelphia, PA, July 21, 1960.

Janet Reno, 76, former US attorney general (Clinton administration), born Miami, FL, July 21, 1938.

C.C. Sabathia, 34, baseball player, born Vallejo, CA, July 21, 1980.

Cat Stevens, 66, singer, songwriter, chosen Muslim name is Yusuf Islam, born Stephen Demetri Georgiou at London, England, July 21, 1948.

Garry Trudeau, 65, political cartoonist ("Doonesbury"), born New York, NY, July 21, 1949.

Sarah Waters, 48, author (*Tipping the Velvet, The Night Watch*), born Neyland, Pembrokeshire, Wales, July 21, 1966.

Robin Williams, 62, comedian, actor ("Mork & Mindy," *Mrs Doubtfire, Dead Poets Society, Good Will Hunting*), born Chicago, IL, July 21, 1952.

July 22 — Tuesday

DAY 203 **162 REMAINING**

ALLIES TAKE PALERMO: ANNIVERSARY. July 22, 1943. Two weeks after the July 10 Allied invasion of Sicily, the principal northern town of Palermo was captured. Americans had cut off 50,000 Italian troops in the west, but Germans were escaping to the northeastern corner of the island. After 39 days, on Aug 17, 1943, the entire island of Sicily was under the control of Allied forces. The official total of Germans and Italians captured was put at 130,000. The Germans, however, managed to transfer 60,000 of their 90,000 men back to the Italian mainland.

CALDER, ALEXANDER: BIRTH ANNIVERSARY. July 22, 1898. Internationally acclaimed American abstract artist who invented the mobile. Born at Lawnton, PA, Calder took a degree in mechanical engineering but was drawn into art in the 1920s. By the 1930s he was the most famous American artist in the world. Calder created the mobile, a delicate hanging kinetic sculpture whose form changed continuously due to air currents or motors. His stationary abstract sculptures were termed "stabiles," and they influenced many generations of artists to turn to industrial materials and monumental scope for expression as he had (with works like *Flamingo* [1974]). Calder died Nov 11, 1976, at New York, NY.

DILLINGER, JOHN: 80th DEATH ANNIVERSARY. July 22, 1934. Bank robber, murderer, prison escapee and the first person to receive the FBI's appellation "Public Enemy Number 1" (July 1934). After nine years in prison (1924–33), Dillinger traveled through the Midwest, leaving a path of violent crimes. He was killed in Illinois by FBI agents led by Melvin Purvis as he left Chicago's Biograph movie theater (where he had watched *Manhattan Melodrama*, starring Clark Gable and Myrna Loy). He was born at Indianapolis, IN, June 28, 1902.

MENDEL, GREGOR JOHANN: BIRTH ANNIVERSARY. July 22, 1822. Botanist Gregor Mendel was born of peasant parents at Heinzendorf, Austria. His pioneering work in genetics became the basis for the modern science of genetics and heredity. Around 1856 Mendel began experiments in his small monastery garden, crossing different varieties of the garden pea. The import of Mendel's work was not seen until many years after his death, Jan 6, 1884, at Brünn, Austria. In 1900 other European botanists discovered his papers and confirmed and extended his theories.

NORWAY MASS MURDER: ANNIVERSARY. July 22, 2011. Anders Behring Breivik, an antigovernment extremist, was the sole perpetrator of two terrorist acts in Norway that ultimately killed 77 people and wounded more than 300. On the afternoon of July 22, 2011, a car bomb created by Breivik exploded at Oslo, near the offices of Prime Minister Jens Stoltenberg, killing 8 and wounding 209. Two hours later, Breivik, disguised as a police officer, appeared at Utoya Island, opening fire at a youth summer camp operated by the Norwegian Labor Party. He killed 69 teenagers and adults and wounded more than 100 before surrendering to authorities. At the resulting trial, Breivik acknowledged his involvement in the attacks but refused to plead guilty for them, citing his fierce nationalism and labeling the dead, his victims, as leftist traitors.

PIED PIPER OF HAMELIN: ANNIVERSARY—MAYBE. July 22, 1376. According to legend, the German town of Hamelin, plagued with rats, bargained with a piper who promised to, and did, pipe the rats out of town and into the Weser River. Refused payment for his work, the piper then piped the children out of town and into a hole in a hill, never to be seen again. More recent historians suggest that the event occurred in 1284 when young men of Hamelin left the city on colonizing adventures.

RAT-CATCHERS DAY. July 22. A day to recognize the rat-catchers who labor to exterminate members of the genus *Rattus*, disease-carrying rodents that infest most of the "civilized" world. Observed on the anniversary of the legendary feat of the Pied Piper of Hamelin on July 22, 1376 (according to 16th-century chronicler Richard Rowland Verstegen).

RILEY, JAMES WHITCOMB: DEATH ANNIVERSARY. July 22, 1916. American "Hoosier" poet, born at Greenfield, IN, Oct 7, probably in 1853, but possibly several years earlier. Riley died at Indianapolis, IN.

SPACE MILESTONE: *SOYUZ TM-3* (USSR). July 22, 1987. Two Soviet cosmonauts, Aleksandr Viktorenko and Aleksandr Aleksandrov, along with the first Syrian space traveler, Mohammed Faris, were launched on a projected 10-day mission. Launched from the Baikonur base in central Asia, the spacecraft orbited Earth for two days before linking with Soviet space station *Mir*. The *Soyuz TM-3* spacecraft was used as a shuttle to *Mir* into the 1990s.

SPOONER'S DAY (WILLIAM SPOONER BIRTH ANNIVERSARY). July 22. A day named for the Reverend William Archibald Spooner (born at London, England, July 22, 1844, warden of New College, Oxford, 1903–24, died at Oxford, England, Aug 29, 1930), whose frequent slips of the tongue led to coinage of the term *spoonerism* to describe them. A day to remember the scholarly man whose accidental transpositions gave us *blushing crow* (for crushing blow), *tons of soil* (for sons of toil), *queer old dean* (for dear old queen), *swell foop* (for fell swoop) and *half-warmed fish* (for half-formed wish).

VANDERBILT, AMY: BIRTH ANNIVERSARY. July 22, 1908. American journalist and etiquette expert, born at New York, NY. Her *Amy Vanderbilt's Complete Book of Etiquette* (1952) became the bible for manners of courtesy and society. Vanderbilt also hosted the television program "It's in Good Taste" from 1954 to 1960. She died at New York City on Dec 27, 1974.

BIRTHDAYS TODAY

Orson Bean, 86, actor ("To Tell the Truth," "Mary Hartman, Mary Hartman"), born Dallas Frederick Burroughs at Burlington, VT, July 22, 1928.

Irene Bedard, 47, actress ("Grand Avenue," "Crazy Horse"; voice of Pocahontas in the Disney film), born Anchorage, AK, July 22, 1967.

Albert Brooks, 67, comedian, director, actor (*Finding Nemo, Broadcast News, Mother*), born Albert Lawrence Einstein at Los Angeles, CA, July 22, 1947.

Willem Dafoe, 59, actor (*Spider-Man, Shadow of the Vampire, Platoon*), born Appleton, WI, July 22, 1955.

Oscar De La Renta, 82, fashion designer, born Santo Domingo, Dominican Republic, July 22, 1932.

Scott Dixon, 34, race car driver, born Brisbane, Australia, July 22, 1980.

Robert J. Dole, 91, former US senator (R, Kansas), born Russell, KS, July 22, 1923.

Rob Estes, 51, actor ("Melrose Place," "Silk Stalkings"), born Norfolk, VA, July 22, 1963.

Danny Glover, 67, actor (*Honeydripper, Beloved, Lethal Weapon, The Color Purple*), born San Francisco, CA, July 22, 1947.

Selena Gomez, 22, singer, actress ("Wizards of Waverly Place," *Spring Breakers, Ramona and Beezus*), born Grand Prairie, TX, July 22, 1992.

Don Henley, 67, musician (The Eagles), songwriter, born Linden, TX, July 22, 1947.

Rhys Ifans, 47, actor (*Notting Hill, Dancing at Lughnasa*), born Ruthin, Wales, July 22, 1967.

Keyshawn Johnson, 42, sportscaster, former football player, born Los Angeles, CA, July 22, 1972.

Josh Lawson, 33, actor (*The Wedding Party, The Campaign*, "House of Lies"), born Brisbane, Australia, July 22, 1981.

John Leguizamo, 50, actor, performer (stage: *Mambo Mouth, Freak, Ghetto Klown*; *Moulin Rouge!, Summer of Sam*), born Bogotá, Colombia, July 22, 1964.

Kristine Lilly, 43, former soccer player, born New York, NY, July 22, 1971.

Alan Menken, 65, film score composer (*Pocahontas, Aladdin*), born New Rochelle, NY, July 22, 1949.

Bobby Sherman, 69, singer, actor, born Santa Monica, CA, July 22, 1945.

David Spade, 49, actor ("Rules of Engagement," "Just Shoot Me," *Tommy Boy*), born Birmingham, MI, July 22, 1965.

Terence Stamp, 75, actor (*The Limey, Alien Nation, The Collector*), born London, England, July 22, 1939.

Keith Sweat, 53, R&B singer, born New York, NY, July 22, 1961.

Alex Trebek, 74, game show host ("Concentration," "Jeopardy!"), born Sudbury, ON, Canada, July 22, 1940.

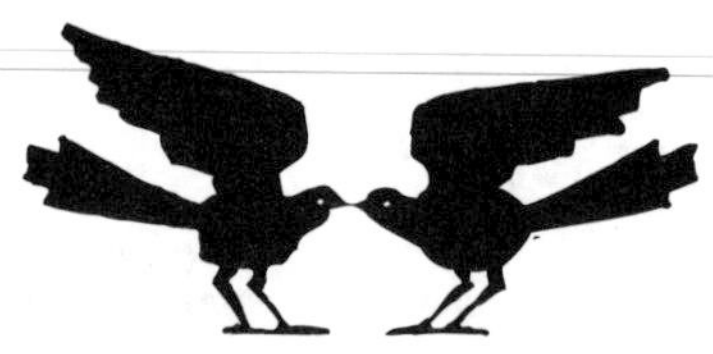

July 2014	S	M	T	W	T	F	S
			1	2	3	4	5
	6	7	8	9	10	11	12
	13	14	15	16	17	18	19
	20	21	22	23	24	25	26
	27	28	29	30	31		

July 23 — Wednesday

DAY 204 **161 REMAINING**

CHANDLER, RAYMOND: BIRTH ANNIVERSARY. July 23, 1888. The American master of postwar hard-boiled crime fiction didn't begin writing until he lost his management job at an oil company in 1933. After publishing short stories in *Black Mask* and other crime magazines, Chandler published his first novel, *The Big Sleep*, in 1939 to popular and critical acclaim. This and subsequent novels featured Philip Marlowe, a Los Angeles private eye who liked "liquor and women and chess and a few other things." Chandler was known for spare prose that featured gripping similes: "The wet air was as cold as the ashes of love" or "She had eyes like strange sins." Chandler also authored or coauthored three Hollywood screenplays, including the searing *Double Indemnity*. Born at Chicago, IL, Chandler died at La Jolla, CA, on Mar 26, 1959.

COMMONWEALTH GAMES. July 23–Aug 3. Glasgow, Scotland. The First British Empire Games were in Canada in 1930. The Commonwealth Games began with the Fifth British Empire Games in Vancouver, Canada, in 1954. Held every four years, this is the

20th Commonwealth Games. Athletes from nations and territories of the Commonwealth compete in 17 different disciplines. For info: Glasgow 2014 Limited, Commonwealth House, 32 Albion St, Glasgow G1 1LH, Scotland. Web: www.glasgow2014.com.

DRYSDALE, DON: BIRTH ANNIVERSARY. July 23, 1936. Elected to the Baseball Hall of Fame in 1984, Don Drysdale was a pitcher for the Brooklyn and Los Angeles Dodgers from 1956 to 1969, compiling a win-loss record of 209–166 with a career ERA of 2.95. Following his playing career he became a successful and popular broadcast announcer for the Chicago White Sox and then for the Los Angeles Dodgers. He was born at Van Nuys, CA, and died at Montreal, QC, Canada, July 3, 1993.

EGYPT: REVOLUTION DAY. July 23. National holiday. Anniversary of the Revolution in 1952, which was launched by army officers and changed Egypt from a monarchy to a republic led by Nasser.

FIRST US SWIMMING SCHOOL OPENS: ANNIVERSARY. July 23, 1827. The first swimming school in the US opened at Boston, MA. Its pupils included John Quincy Adams and James Audubon.

"THE GENE AUTRY SHOW" TV PREMIERE: ANNIVERSARY. July 23, 1950. Popular CBS Western starring movie actor Gene Autry ran for six years. Along with sidekick Pat Buttram, Autry helped bring criminals to justice.

HOOD RIVER COUNTY FAIR. July 23–26. Hood River, OR. From 4-H activities to the excitement of the carnival, this annual old-fashioned country fair is bustling with things to do! Est attendance: 25,000. For info: Hood River County Fair, Box 385, Odell, OR 97044. Phone: (541) 354-2865. Fax: (541) 354-2875. E-mail: hrfair@hrecn.net. Web: www.hoodriverfair.com.

HOT ENOUGH FOR YA DAY. July 23. We are permitted today to utter the words that suffice when nothing of intelligence comes to mind. "Is it hot enough for ya?" Annually, July 23. (©2006 by WH.) For info: Thomas & Ruth Roy, Wellcat Holidays, 2418 Long Ln, Lebanon, PA 17046-1708. Phone: (717) 279-0184. E-mail: info@wellcat.com. Web: www.wellcat.com.

JAPAN: SOMA NO UMAOI (WILD HORSE CHASING). July 23–25. Hibarigahara, Haramachi, Fukushima Prefecture. A thousand horsemen clad in ancient armor compete for possession of three shrine flags shot aloft on Hibarigahara Plain, and men in white costumes attempt to catch wild horses corralled by the horsemen.

LEO, THE LION. July 23–Aug 22. In the astronomical/astrological zodiac, which divides the sun's apparent orbit into 12 segments, the period July 23–Aug 22 is traditionally identified as the sun sign of Leo, the Lion. The ruling celestial body is the sun.

MAVERICK, SAMUEL: BIRTH ANNIVERSARY. July 23, 1803. The rancher, land baron and politician was born at Pendleton, SC, but spent most of his life in Texas. He was a key figure in the battle for Texas independence from Mexico. As a rancher, Maverick refused to brand his calves—claiming humanitarian reasons, but others saw that habit as a wily way to increase his herd by "adopting" unmarked cattle. Nevertheless, an unbranded or stray calf was remarked as being "Maverick's," and his last name became the synonym for a stubborn individual. Maverick died Sept 2, 1870, at San Antonio, TX, where he had twice been mayor.

OHIO STATE FAIR. July 23–Aug 3. Columbus, OH. Family fun, amusement rides, games, food booths, parades, entertainment, agriculture exhibits and educational displays. Est attendance: 850,000. For info: Ohio State Fair, 717 E 17th Ave, Columbus, OH 43211. Phone: (614) 644-3247 or (888) OHO-EXPO. Fax: (614) 644-4031. Web: www.ohiostatefair.com.

OREGON BREWERS FESTIVAL. July 23–27. Tom McCall Waterfront Park, Portland, OR. Here 81 microbreweries from across the country showcase their handcrafted brews to beer lovers. Annually, the last full weekend in July. Est attendance: 80,000. For info: Chris Crabb, Crabbsoup Public Relations. E-mail: chris@oregonbrewfest.com. Web: www.oregonbrewfest.com.

REESE, HAROLD HENRY "PEE WEE": BIRTH ANNIVERSARY. July 23, 1918. Hall of Fame shortstop, born at Ekron, KY. Died Aug 14, 1999, at Louisville, KY.

SAINT APOLLINARIS: FEAST DAY. July 23. First bishop of Ravenna, and a martyr, of unknown date. Observed July 23.

SHARM AL-SHEIKH BOMBINGS: ANNIVERSARY. July 23, 2005. In the worst act of terrorism in Egypt's recent history, the Red Sea resort city of Sharm al-Sheikh was the target of three bomb attacks that killed 88 people and injured more than 200. Various groups claimed responsibility for the attacks, which occurred on Egypt's Revolution Day.

SPACE MILESTONE: FIRST FEMALE COMMANDER: *COLUMBIA* (US): 15th ANNIVERSARY. July 23, 1999. Colonel Eileen Collins led a shuttle mission to deploy a $1.5 billion x-ray telescope, the Chandra observatory, into space. It is a sister satellite to the Hubble Space Telescope. The observatory is named after Nobel Prize–winner Subrahamyar Chandrasekhar.

BIRTHDAYS TODAY

Ronny Cox, 76, actor (*Deliverance, Bound for Glory, Total Recall*), born Cloudcroft, NM, July 23, 1938.

Gloria DeHaven, 89, actress (*Two Girls and a Sailor*, "Nakia"), born Los Angeles, CA, July 23, 1925.

Omar Epps, 41, actor ("House," *Love & Basketball*), born Brooklyn, NY, July 23, 1973.

Nicholas Gage, 75, journalist, film producer, writer (*Eleni*), born Lia, Greece, July 23, 1939.

Nomar Garciaparra, 41, sportscaster, former baseball player, born Whittier, CA, July 23, 1973.

Woody Harrelson, 53, actor (Emmy for "Cheers"; *Zombieland, The Messenger, Natural Born Killers*), born Midland, TX, July 23, 1961.

Philip Seymour Hoffman, 47, stage and screen actor (Oscar for *Capote*; *The Master, Boogie Nights, Doubt*), born Fairport, NY, July 23, 1967.

Don Imus, 74, radio personality, author, born Riverside, CA, July 23, 1940.

Arata Isozaki, 83, architect, born Oita, Japan, July 23, 1931.

Anthony M. Kennedy, 78, Associate Justice of the US, born Sacramento, CA, July 23, 1936.

Eriq La Salle, 52, actor ("ER," *Coming to America*), born Hartford, CT, July 23, 1962.

Edie McClurg, 63, actress ("WKRP in Cincinnati," *Eating Raoul, A River Runs Through It*), born Kansas City, MO, July 23, 1951.

Belinda Montgomery, 64, actress ("Miami Vice," "Doogie Howser, MD"), born Winnipeg, MB, Canada, July 23, 1950.

Gary Dwayne Payton, 46, former basketball player, born Oakland, CA, July 23, 1968.

Daniel Radcliffe, 25, actor (Harry Potter films, *The Woman in Black, My Boy Jack*), born London, England, July 23, 1989.

Brandon Roy, 30, baseball player, born Seattle, WA, July 23, 1984.

Marlon Wayans, 42, actor ("In Living Color," *Scary Movie*), born New York, NY, July 23, 1972.

July 24 — Thursday

DAY 205 **160 REMAINING**

BOLÍVAR, SIMON: BIRTH ANNIVERSARY. July 24, 1783. "The Liberator," born at Caracas, Venezuela. Commemorated in Venezuela and other Latin American countries. Died Dec 17, 1830, at Santa Marta, Colombia. Bolivia is named after him.

COUSINS DAY. July 24. A day to celebrate, honor and appreciate our cousins. For info: Claudia Evart, PO Box 85, New York, NY 10163. Phone: (646) 544-4780. E-mail: cevartl@earthlink.net.

DETROIT FOUNDED: ANNIVERSARY. July 24, 1701. Anniversary of the landing at the site of Detroit by Antoine de la Mothe Cadillac in the service of Louis XIV of France. Fort Pontchartrain du Detroit was the first settlement on site.

DUMAS, ALEXANDRE: BIRTH ANNIVERSARY. July 24, 1802. French playwright and novelist, born at Villers-Cotterets, France. He is said to have written more than 300 volumes, including *The Count of Monte Cristo* and *The Three Musketeers*. Father of Alexandre Dumas (Dumas fils), also a novelist and playwright (1824–95). Dumas died near Dieppe, France, Dec 5, 1870.

EARHART, AMELIA: BIRTH ANNIVERSARY. July 24, 1897. American aviatrix lost on flight from New Guinea to Howland Island, in the Pacific Ocean, July 2, 1937. First woman to cross the Atlantic solo, second person to cross the Atlantic solo and first person to fly solo across the Pacific from Hawaii to California. Born at Atchison, KS.

GREAT TEXAS MOSQUITO FESTIVAL. July 24–26. Clute, TX. A fun-filled, three-day family event. More than 85 arts and crafts and food booths, headline entertainment, novelty games, carnival and a variety of contests for all ages—including the Mr and Mrs Mosquito Legs Contest, Mosquito Calling Contest and Skeeter Beaters Baby Crawling Contest. Meet "Willie Man Chew," a 26-foot inflatable mosquito complete with cowboy boots and hat. Annually, the last Thursday, Friday and Saturday in July. Est attendance: 13,000. For info: Great Texas Mosquito Festival, City of Clute Parks and Recreation Dept, PO Box 997, Clute, TX 77531. Phone: (979) 265-8392 or (800) 371-2971. Fax: (979) 265-8767. E-mail: buzz@mosquitofestival.com. Web: www.mosquitofestival.com.

LUMBERJACK WORLD CHAMPIONSHIPS. July 24–26. Hayward, WI. The "Olympics of the Forest" welcomes the world's best lumberjacks facing off in a variety of competitions, including logrolling, tree climbing, cutting with saws and chain saws and pole climbing. Annually, the last weekend in July. For info: Lumberjack World Championships, PO Box 666, Hayward, WI 54843. Phone: (715) 634-2484. E-mail: contact@lumberjackworldchampionships.com. Web: www.lumberjackworldchampionships.com.

July 2014

S	M	T	W	T	F	S
		1	2	3	4	5
6	7	8	9	10	11	12
13	14	15	16	17	18	19
20	21	22	23	24	25	26
27	28	29	30	31		

NATIONAL DRIVE-THRU DAY. July 24. After WWII, California sunshine and a love affair with automobiles spurred the growth of roadside businesses in the Golden State catering specifically to motorists. As America's first major drive-through hamburger chain, Jack in the Box® restaurants (founded in 1951) helped pave the way for a delicious new dining experience. Annually, on July 24. For info: Brian Luscomb, Jack in the Box, 9330 Balboa Ave, San Diego, CA 92123. Phone: (858) 571-2121. Web: www.jackinthebox.com.

NATIONAL TELL AN OLD JOKE DAY. July 24. Keep traditional humor alive and well: tell someone an old joke! But keep it clean. Annually, July 24. For info (or old jokes): John Bohannon. Web: www.johnbohannon.com.

PIONEER DAY. July 24. Utah. State holiday. Commemorates the day in 1847 when Brigham Young and his followers entered the Salt Lake valley.

QUILT ODYSSEY 2014. July 24–27. Hershey Lodge and Convention Center, Hershey, PA. Judged national quilt competition; antique and special quilt exhibits. Large merchants' mall. Classes and lectures by nationally known professional quilters. Est attendance: 7,500. For info: Quilt Odyssey, 15004 Burnt Mill Rd, Shippensburg, PA 17257. Phone: (717) 423-5148. E-mail: quiltodyssey@embarqmail.com. Web: www.quiltodyssey.com.

RAF JAMS NAZI RADAR IN OPERATION GOMORRAH: ANNIVERSARY. July 24, 1943. On the first of the Royal Air Force Operation Gomorrah raids on Hamburg, Germany, "windows" (bales of 10½-inch strips of aluminum foil) were pushed out of the bombers, causing the German radar screens to display a snowstorm of false echo "aircraft." As a result, only 12 of the 791 bombers sent on the mission were shot down.

BIRTHDAYS TODAY

Barry Bonds, 50, former baseball player, born Riverside, CA, July 24, 1964.

Ruth Buzzi, 78, comedienne, actress ("Rowan & Martin's Laugh-In," "Sesame Street"), born Westerly, RI, July 24, 1936.

Rose Byrne, 35, actress ("Damages," *Bridesmaids, Sunshine*), born Balmain, Sydney, Australia, July 24, 1979.

Lynda Carter, 63, actress ("Wonder Woman," "Partners in Crime"), former Miss World–USA, singer, born Phoenix, AZ, July 24, 1951.

Kristin Chenoweth, 46, actress, singer (stage: *Wicked*; Tony for *You're a Good Man, Charlie Brown*; "The West Wing"), born Broken Arrow, OK, July 24, 1968.

Kadeem Hardison, 49, actor ("A Different World," "The Sixth Man"), born New York, NY, July 24, 1965.

Robert Hays, 67, actor (*Airplane!*, "Starman"), born Bethesda, MD, July 24, 1947.

Julie A. Krone, 51, former jockey, first woman in National Racing Hall of Fame, born Benton Harbor, MI, July 24, 1963.

Jennifer Lopez, 44, actress (*Maid in Manhattan, The Cell, Out of Sight*), singer, born the Bronx, NY, July 24, 1970.

Karl Malone, 51, Hall of Fame basketball player, born Summerfield, LA, July 24, 1963.

Claire McCaskill, 61, US Senator (D, Missouri), born Rolla, MO, July 24, 1953.

Eugene Mirman, 40, actor ("Bob's Burgers," "Flight of the Conchords"), born Moscow, USSR (now Russia), July 24, 1974.

Pat Oliphant, 79, cartoonist, born Adelaide, Australia, July 24, 1935.

Anna Paquin, 32, actress ("True Blood," the *X-Men* films, *The Piano, Fly Away Home*), born Winnipeg, MB, Canada, July 24, 1982.

Chris Sarandon, 72, actor (*Dog Day Afternoon, The Princess Bride*), born Beckley, WV, July 24, 1942.

Peter Serkin, 67, musician, born New York, NY, July 24, 1947.

July 25 — Friday

DAY 206 **159 REMAINING**

***ANDREA DORIA* SINKS: ANNIVERSARY.** July 25, 1956. The Italian luxury liner collided with the *Stockholm*, a Swedish liner, on its way to New York. Other ships in the area came to the aid of the *Andrea Doria*. During the ordeal 1,634 people were rescued, including the captain and the crew.

ANNIE OAKLEY DAYS. July 25–27. Greenville, OH. To keep alive the memory of Annie Oakley. Large antique and collectibles market. Annually, the last full weekend in July. Est attendance: 40,000. For info: Annie Oakley Days Committee, Inc, PO Box 129, Greenville, OH 45331. Phone: (937) 548-4249. E-mail: president@annieoakleyfestival.org. Web: www.AnnieOakleyFestival.org.

ARCADIA DAZE. July 25–27. Arcadia, MI. The scenic village of Arcadia is the setting for this midsummer event. Activities include a parade on Sunday at 1:30 PM on Lake Street. Art fair, steak fry, fishing contest, games for the children, pancake breakfast and 5k running race on Saturday, and a street dance on Friday and Saturday. Car show on Saturday. An old-fashioned good time for the whole family. Sponsor: Arcadia Lions Club. Est attendance: 2,500. For info: Wesley Hull, Arcadia Daze, 3269 Lake St, Arcadia, MI 49613. Phone: (231) 889-5555.

BANGOR STATE FAIR. July 25–Aug 3. Bass Park Complex, Bangor, ME. Fun for the whole family with Paul Bunyan Lumberjack Show, lobster roll eating championship, Grizzly Experience, free pony rides, EMRBA Rabbit Show, arm wrestling championship and more. Annually, beginning on the last Friday in July. For info: Bangor State Fair, 100 Dutton St, Bangor, ME 04401. Phone: (207) 947-5555. Fax: (207) 947-5105. E-mail: fair@bangormaine.gov. Web: www.bangorstatefair.com.

BERNE SWISS DAYS. July 25–26. Berne, IN. Discover Switzerland in Indiana with Alpine music, dancing, yodeling and a parade. Quilt show, "stein-toss" contest, polka bands, old-fashioned horse pull, factory tours and more. Est attendance: 25,000. For info: Berne Chamber of Commerce, 205 E Main St, Berne, IN 46711. Phone: (260) 589-8080. E-mail: chamber@bernein.com. Web: www.bernein.com.

COSTA RICA: GUANACASTE DAY. July 25. National holiday. Commemorates the 1814 transfer of the region of Guanacaste from Nicaragua to Costa Rica by Spain.

DODGE CITY DAYS. July 25–Aug 3. Dodge City, KS. Western heritage celebration with concerts, arts and crafts, parades, PRCA rodeo, street dances, cookouts and classic car show. Est attendance: 100,000. For info: Dodge City Days/Dodge City Area COC, 311 W Spruce, Dodge City, KS 67801. Phone: (620) 227-3119. Fax: (620) 227-2957. E-mail: dcdays@dodgechamber.com. Web: www.dodgecitydays.com.

FIRST AIRPLANE CROSSING OF ENGLISH CHANNEL: ANNIVERSARY. July 25, 1909. Louis Bleriot—after asking from the cockpit, "Where is England?"—took off from Les Baraques (near Calais), France, and landed on English soil at Northfall Meadow, near Dover, where he was greeted first by English police and customs officers. This, the world's first international overseas airplane flight, was accomplished in a 28-horsepower monoplane with a wingspan of 23 feet. See also: "Bleriot, Louis: Birth Anniversary" (July 1).

GERMANY: WAGNER FESTIVAL (BAYREUTHER FESTSPIELE). July 25–Aug 28. Bayreuth. Since 1876, the works of Richard Wagner are performed daily at the Festival Theatre, which Wagner had built in 1872–76. For info: Bayreuther Festspiele, Festspielhügel 1-2, D-95445 Bayreuth, Germany. Phone: (49) 921-78-78-0. Web: www.bayreuther-festspiele.de.

GILFORD, JACK: BIRTH ANNIVERSARY. July 25, 1907. American actor Jack Gilford was born Jacob Gellman at New York, NY. Though he was blacklisted for 10 years following refusal to answer questions before the House Un-American Activities Committee in the 1950s, he appeared in many films, stage productions and television programs including an Academy Award–nominated role opposite Jack Lemmon in *Save the Tiger* (1973) and his best-known role as Hysterium in the stage and film versions of *A Funny Thing Happened on the Way to the Forum*. He died June 4, 1990, at New York City.

GOLD DISCOVERY DAYS. July 25–27. Custer, SD. Parade, pancake breakfast, bed races, children's fair, fun run, arts and crafts festival, volleyball tournament and hot-air balloon rally. Est attendance: 9,000. For info: Gold Discovery Days Committee, PO Box 350, Custer, SD 57730. Phone: (605) 673-2244 or (800) 992-9818. E-mail: info@custersd.com. Web: www.golddiscoverydays.com.

HARRISON, ANNA SYMMES: BIRTH ANNIVERSARY. July 25, 1775. Wife of William Henry Harrison, ninth president of the US, born at Morristown, NJ. Died at North Bend, IN, Feb 25, 1864.

IOWA STORYTELLING FESTIVAL. July 25–26. City Park, Clear Lake, IA. This 26th annual storytelling event is held in a scenic lakeside setting. Friday evening "Stories After Dark." Two performances Saturday plus story exchange for novice tellers. Annually, the fourth Saturday in July with the preceding Friday. Est attendance: 800. For info: Jean Casey, Dir, Clear Lake Public Library, 200 N 4th St, Clear Lake, IA 50428. Phone: (641) 357-6133. Fax: (641) 357-4645. E-mail: clplib@netins.net.

MONTANA STATE FAIR. July 25–Aug 2. Great Falls, MT. Mighty Thomas Carnival, night shows, PRCA rodeo, free acts, food fair, 4-H exhibits and much more. Annually, beginning on the last Friday in July and ending on the first Saturday in August. Est attendance: 150,000. For info: Montana State Fair, 400 Third St NW, Great Falls, MT 59404. Phone: (406) 727-8900. Fax: (406) 452-8955. E-mail: info@goexpopark.com. Web: www.montanastatefair.com.

MUSSOLINI OUSTED: ANNIVERSARY. July 25, 1943. Two weeks after the Allied attack on Sicily began, the Fascist Grand Council met for the first time since December of 1939 and took a confidence vote resulting in Mussolini's being removed from office and placed under arrest. Italy's King Victor Emmanuel ordered Marshal Pietro Badoglio to form a new government.

NESHOBA COUNTY FAIR. July 25–Aug 1. Philadelphia, MS. Billed as "Mississippi's Giant Houseparty®," this is one of the nation's last Campground Fairs. At this 124th annual fair, harness racing, state and national political speaking, crafts, music and amusement are the order each day. Est attendance: 85,000. For info: Neshoba County Fair Assoc, 16800 Hwy 21 S, Philadelphia, MS 39350. Phone: (601) 656-8480. Fax: (601) 656-8461. Web: www.neshobacountyfair.org.

PUERTO RICO: CONSTITUTION DAY. July 25. Also called Commonwealth Day or Occupation Day. Commemorates proclamation of constitution in 1952.

PUERTO RICO: LOIZA ALDEA FIESTA. July 25–28. Loiza Aldea. Best known of Puerto Rico's patron saint festivities. Villagers of Loiza Aldea, 20 miles east of San Juan, don devil masks and colorful costumes for a variety of traditional activities.

SCOTLAND: ABERDEEN INTERNATIONAL YOUTH FESTIVAL. July 25–Aug 2. Aberdeen. Talented young people from all areas of the performing arts come from around the world to participate in this festival. Est attendance: 35,000. For info: Ruth Fisher, Custom House, 35 Regent Quay, Aberdeen, Scotland AB11 5BE. Phone: (44) (1224) 213-800. Fax: (44) (1224) 213-833. E-mail: info@aiyf.org. Web: www.aiyf.org.

SPAIN: SAINT JAMES DAY. July 25. Holy day of the patron saint of Spain. When this day falls on a Sunday, it is a Holy Year and pilgrims make the pilgrimage to Santiago de Compostela, the site of the saint's tomb. 2021 is the next Holy Year.

TEST-TUBE BABY: BIRTHDAY. July 25, 1978. Anniversary of the birth of Louise Brown at Oldham, England. First documented birth of a baby conceived outside the body of a woman. The attending physicians were Patrick Christopher Steptoe and Robert Geoffrey Edwards.

TUNISIA: REPUBLIC DAY. July 25. National holiday. Commemorates the proclamation of the republic in 1957.

BIRTHDAYS TODAY

Midge Decter, 87, journalist, born St. Paul, MN, July 25, 1927.

Illeana Douglas, 49, actress (*Message in a Bottle, Grace of My Heart*), born Boston, MA, July 25, 1965.

Iman, 59, model, actress (*Star Trek VI*), born Iman Mohamed Abdulmajid at Mogadishu, Somalia, July 25, 1955.

James Lafferty, 29, actor ("One Tree Hill," *A Season on the Brink*), born Hemet, CA, July 25, 1985.

Matt LeBlanc, 47, actor ("Episodes," "Friends"), born Newton, MA, July 25, 1967.

Evgeni Nabakov, 39, hockey player, born Ust-Kamenogorsk, USSR (now Osteman, Kazakhstan), July 25, 1975.

Nathaniel (Nate) Thurmond, 73, Hall of Fame basketball player, born Akron, OH, July 25, 1941.

July 26 — Saturday

DAY 207 **158 REMAINING**

ADMINISTRATIVE PROFESSIONALS EDUCATION FORUM AND ANNUAL MEETING (EFAM). July 26–30. Milwaukee Convention Center, Milwaukee, WI. Est attendance: 2,000. For info: Intl Assn for Administrative Professionals, 10502 N Ambassador Dr, Ste 100, Kansas City, MO 64153-1291. Phone: (816) 891-6600. Fax: (816) 891-9118. E-mail: efam@iaap-hq.org. Web: www.iaap-hq.org/efam.

AMERICANS WITH DISABILITIES ACT SIGNED: ANNIVERSARY. July 26, 1990. President George H.W. Bush signed the Americans with Disabilities Act, which went into effect two years later. It required that public facilities be made accessible to people with disabilities.

ANTIQUE AND CLASSIC BOAT RENDEZVOUS. July 26–27. Mystic Seaport, Mystic, CT. Pre-1970 power and sailing yachts on view for Mystic Seaport visitors. Mystic River parade on Sunday. Est attendance: 4,000. For info: Mystic Seaport, 75 Greenmanville Ave, Box 6000, Mystic, CT 06355. Phone: (860) 527-0711 or (888) 973-2767. Web: www.mysticseaport.org.

ARMED FORCES UNIFIED: ANNIVERSARY. July 26, 1947. President Truman signed legislation unifying the two branches of the armed forces into the Department of Defense. The branches merged were the War Department (Army) and the Navy. The Air Force was separated from the Army at the same time and made an independent force. Truman nominated James Forrestal to be the first secretary of defense. The legislation also provided for the National Security Council, the Central Intelligence Agency and the Joint Chiefs of Staff.

July 2014	S	M	T	W	T	F	S
			1	2	3	4	5
	6	7	8	9	10	11	12
	13	14	15	16	17	18	19
	20	21	22	23	24	25	26
	27	28	29	30	31		

CATLIN, GEORGE: BIRTH ANNIVERSARY. July 26, 1796. American artist famous for his paintings of Native American life, born at Wilkes-Barre, PA. In 1832 he toured North and South American tribes, recording their lives in his work. He died Dec 23, 1872, at Jersey City, NJ.

CLINTON, GEORGE: 275th BIRTH ANNIVERSARY. July 26, 1739. Fourth vice president of the US (1805–12), born at Little Britain, NY. Brigadier general under General George Washington during the American Revolution. Popular governor of New York (1777–95 and 1801–4). Vice president under Thomas Jefferson and James Madison. First vice president to die in office—at Washington, DC, Apr 20, 1812.

CUBA: NATIONAL DAY: ANNIVERSARY OF REVOLUTION. July 26. Anniversary of the 1953 beginning of Fidel Castro's revolutionary "26th of July Movement." He launched a failed attack on the Moncada army barracks, and most involved were killed or captured. He was captured and given a trial, during which he made his famous speech, "History will absolve me." Sentenced to 15 years, he was pardoned after just two.

CURAÇAO: CURAÇAO DAY. July 26. Traditional holiday commemorating Columbus companion Alonso de Ojeda's discovery of the island of Curaçao in 1499, when he sailed into Santa Ana Bay, the entrance of the harbor of Willemstad. Festivities on this day.

EDWARDS, BLAKE: BIRTH ANNIVERSARY. July 26, 1922. American film director, born William Blake Crump at Tulsa, OK. Best known as director of the successful Pink Panther comedies that starred actor Peter Sellers. Other notable films include *Breakfast at Tiffany's, Days of Wine and Roses, 10* and *Victor, Victoria.* He received an Honorary Academy Award in 2004 for his career achievements. He was married to actress and singer Julie Andrews for 41 years, and died Dec 15, 2010, at Santa Monica, CA.

GENEVA ARTS FAIR. July 26–27. Geneva, IL. More than 140 artist booths welcome visitors to an open-air Fine Art Show held amid shady trees surrounding the historic Kane County Courthouse. Annually, the fourth Saturday and Sunday in July. Est attendance: 22,000. For info: Geneva Chamber of Commerce, PO Box 481, 8 S Third St, Geneva, IL 60134. Phone: (630) 232-6060. Fax: (630) 232-6083. E-mail: chamberinfo@genevachamber.com. Web: www.genevachamber.com.

HANOVER DUTCH FESTIVAL. July 26. Hanover, PA. Handmade crafts, ethnic foods, music, entertainment, children's carnival, antique car show. Annually, the last Saturday in July. Est attendance: 10,000. For info: Hanover Area Chamber of Commerce, 146 Carlisle St, Hanover, PA 17331. Phone: (717) 637-6130. Web: www.hanoverchamber.com.

HUXLEY, ALDOUS: BIRTH ANNIVERSARY. July 26, 1894. English author, satirist, mystic and philosopher, Aldous Leonard Huxley was born at Godalming, Surrey, England. Best known of his works are *Brave New World* and *Point Counter Point.* Huxley died at Los Angeles, CA, Nov 22, 1963.

KUBRICK, STANLEY: BIRTH ANNIVERSARY. July 26, 1928. American filmmaker, born at the Bronx, NY. Kubrick started out in photography at the age of 16 with *Look* magazine. His first film, *Day of the Fight*, produced in 1950, was a documentary of his photo series about fighter Walter Cartier. His film credits include *Dr. Strangelove, Full Metal Jacket* and *2001: A Space Odyssey. Eyes Wide Shut,* Kubrick's final film, was released posthumously in the summer of 1999. He died at London, England, Mar 7, 1999.

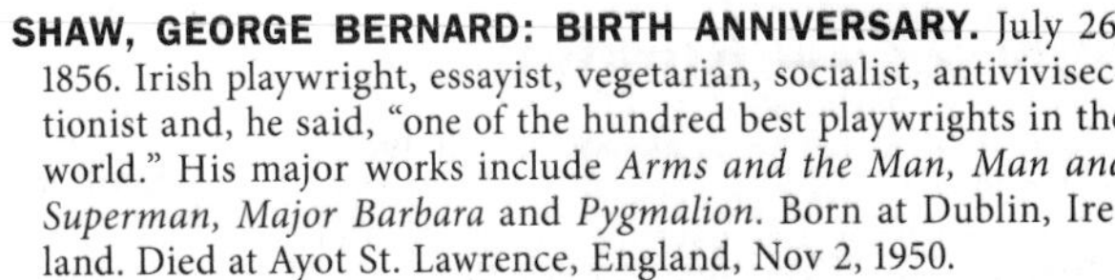

LIBERIA: INDEPENDENCE DAY. July 26. National holiday. Became republic in 1847, under aegis of the US societies for repatriating former slaves in Africa.

MALDIVES: INDEPENDENCE DAY. July 26. National holiday. Commemorates independence from Britain in 1965.

MOON PHASE: NEW MOON. July 26. Moon enters New Moon phase at 6:42 PM, EDT.

NATIONAL DAY OF THE COWBOY. July 26. Annually, the fourth Saturday in July is set aside as a day to pay homage to our cowboy and pioneer heritage, as well as to honor working cowboys and cowgirls, rodeo athletes, Western musicians, cowboy poets, Western artists, ranchers and all others who continue to contribute to the cowboy and pioneer culture. Proclaimed by the US Senate in Resolution 138 for the first time for July 23, 2005. For info: National Day of the Cowboy, PO Box 25298, Prescott Valley, AZ 86312. E-mail: info@nationaldayofthecowboy.com. Web: www.nationaldayofthecowboy.org.

NEW YORK RATIFICATION DAY. July 26, 1788. Became 11th state to ratify Constitution in 1788.

NORFOLK PUBLIC LIBRARY LITERATURE FESTIVAL. July 26. Lifelong Learning Center, Norfolk, NE. Presentations by award-winning, nationally known authors; book reviews; book displays and sales; and autograph sessions. Est attendance: 175. For info: Karen Drevo, Youth Services Librarian, Norfolk Public Library, 308 W Prospect Ave, Norfolk, NE 68701. Phone: (402) 844-2100. Fax: (402) 844-2102. E-mail: kdrevo@ci.norfolk.ne.us.

ONE VOICE. July 26. A synchronized reading of the Universal Peace Covenant by people on all continents at 1 PM, CDT. In conjunction with the new year of the natural-time calendar year, the School of Metaphysics invites people all around the world to create one voice of peace by reading this document, penned in 1996 by more than two dozen spiritual teachers aged 20 to 70, from varied cultures and walks of life. The Universal Peace Covenant is available in several languages at www.peacedome.org, or you can write to have a copy sent to you. For info: Mr Tad Messenger, School of Metaphysics World HQ, 163 Moon Valley Rd, Windyville, MO 65783. Phone: (417) 345-8411. E-mail: peace@som.org. Web: www.peacedome.org.

POTSDAM DECLARATION: ANNIVERSARY. July 26, 1945. As the Potsdam Conference came to a close in Germany, Churchill, Truman and China's representatives fashioned a communiqué to Japan offering it an opportunity to end the war. It demanded that Japan completely disarm; allowed it sovereignty to the four main islands and to minor islands to be determined by the Allies and insisted that all Japanese citizens be given immediate and complete freedom of speech, religion and thought. The Japanese would be allowed to continue enough industry to maintain their economy. The communiqué concluded with a demand for unconditional surrender. Unaware these demands were backed up by an atomic bomb, on July 28 Japanese prime minister Admiral Kantaro Suzuki rejected the Potsdam Declaration.

PUBLICATION OF FIRST ESPERANTO BOOK: ANNIVERSARY. July 26, 1887. On this date Dr. L.L. Zamenhof published *Lingvo internacia* (*International Language*), the first textbook about the universal language Esperanto. Zamenhof used the pen name Doktoro Esperanto (Doctor Hopeful) for the book, and this name was adopted for the language. See also: "Zamenhof, Ludwik Lejzer: Birth Anniversary" (Dec 15).

ROBARDS, JASON: BIRTH ANNIVERSARY. July 26, 1922. A staple on the American stage and screen for six decades, Robards was born at Chicago, IL, and was a decorated WWII veteran. He won the Oscar for Best Supporting Actor two years in a row, for 1976's *All the President's Men* and 1977's *Julia.* His most famous stage roles were in the plays of Eugene O'Neill, including *The Iceman Cometh* and *Long Day's Journey into Night.* He won the Tony Award in 1959 for his portrayal of a fictionalized F. Scott Fitzgerald in *The Disenchanted.* He died at Bridgeport, CT, Dec 26, 2000.

SHAW, GEORGE BERNARD: BIRTH ANNIVERSARY. July 26, 1856. Irish playwright, essayist, vegetarian, socialist, antivivisectionist and, he said, "one of the hundred best playwrights in the world." His major works include *Arms and the Man, Man and Superman, Major Barbara* and *Pygmalion.* Born at Dublin, Ireland. Died at Ayot St. Lawrence, England, Nov 2, 1950.

SPACE MILESTONE: *APOLLO 15* (US). July 26, 1971. Launched this date. Astronauts David R. Scott and James B. Irwin landed on moon (lunar module *Falcon*) while Alfred M. Worden piloted command module *Endeavor. Rover 1,* a four-wheel vehicle, was used for further exploration. Departed moon Aug 2, after nearly three days. Pacific landing Aug 7.

TAYLOR HORSEFEST. July 26–27. Taylor, ND. This 21st annual celebration is highlighted by a parade of horses and horse-drawn equipment, ethnic food fest, craft vendors, exhibits, demonstrations and music. Horse-drawn taxis provide transportation throughout the town during the day. Est attendance: 1,000. For info: Taylor Horsefest, PO Box 7, Taylor, ND 58656. Phone: (701) 974-4210 or (877) 757-7545. E-mail: eventinfo@taylorhorsefest.com. Web: www.taylorhorsefest.com.

US ARMY FIRST DESEGREGATION: 70th ANNIVERSARY. July 26, 1944. During WWII the US Army ordered desegregation of its training camp facilities. Later the same year black platoons were assigned to white companies in a tentative step toward integration of the battlefield. However, it was not until after the war—July 26, 1948—that President Harry Truman signed an order officially integrating the armed forces.

BIRTHDAYS TODAY

Kate Beckinsale, 41, actress (*Underworld, Pearl Harbor, Van Helsing*), born London, England, July 26, 1973.

Sandra Bullock, 50, actress (Oscar for *The Blind Side*; *Crash, Speed*), born Arlington, VA, July 26, 1964.

Susan George, 64, actress (*Straw Dogs*), born London, England, July 26, 1950.

Mick Jagger, 71, singer (Rolling Stones), born Michael Philip Jagger at Dartford, England, July 26, 1943.

Helen Mirren, 68, actress (Oscar for *The Queen*; *Gosford Park*, "Prime Suspect," "Elizabeth I"), born London, England, July 26, 1946.

Taylor Momsen, 21, actress (*How the Grinch Stole Christmas, Paranoid Park,* "Gossip Girl"), born St. Louis, MO, July 26, 1993.

Jeremy Piven, 50, actor ("Entourage," "Ellen," *Grosse Pointe Blank*), born New York, NY, July 26, 1964.

Kevin Spacey, 55, actor (Oscars for *American Beauty* and *The Usual Suspects*; Tony for *Lost in Yonkers*; *House of Cards*), born South Orange, NJ, July 26, 1959.

Cress Williams, 44, actor ("Hart of Dixie," "Friday Night Lights"), born Heidelberg, Germany, July 26, 1970.

July 27 — Sunday

DAY 208 **157 REMAINING**

ANNE HUTCHINSON MEMORIAL DAY. July 27. Anne Hutchinson Memorial, Founders' Brook Park, Portsmouth, RI (weather permitting—no rain day). An annual gathering to honor Anne Marbury Hutchinson (1591–1643), cofounder of Pocasset (Portsmouth), RI, in 1638. Wife, mother of 16, midwife, religious leader, she was a caretaker of and spiritual leader to women in Puritan Boston. Anne Hutchinson helped shape the tradition of free speech and religious tolerance that has become so important to modern Americans. Annually, on a Sunday before or after Anne Hutchinson's baptismal anniversary, July 20, 1591. For info: Valerie Debrule, Friends of Anne Hutchinson, 11 Cherry Creek Rd, Newport, RI 02840. Phone: (401) 846-8439. Fax: (401) 848-0373. E-mail: valeriedeb@gmail.com. Or Michael Ford. Phone: (401) 332-8279. E-mail: michaelstevenford@gmail.com.

ATLANTIC TELEGRAPH CABLE LAID: ANNIVERSARY. July 27, 1866. Cable laying successfully completed.

AUNTIES DAY. July 27. 6th annual. This day thanks, honors and celebrates the aunt in a child's life, whether she is an Auntie by Relation (ABR), Auntie by Choice (ABC) or godmother, for everything she does for a child not-her-own. The day is especially poignant for the 23 million American women who identify as PANKs, or Professional Aunts No Kids. Annually, the fourth Sunday in July. For info: Melanie Notkin, Savvy Auntie, 200 W 93rd St, Ste 6F, New York, NY 10025. Phone: (917) 449-2917. E-mail: Editor@Savvyauntie.com. Web: www.AuntiesDay.com.

BARBOSA, JOSÉ CELSO: BIRTH ANNIVERSARY. July 27, 1857. Puerto Rican physician and patriot, born at Bayamon, Puerto Rico. His birthday is a holiday in Puerto Rico. He died at San Juan, Puerto Rico, Sept 21, 1921.

CANADA: MINERAL CAPITAL ROCK SHOW. July 27. Bancroft, ON. Mineral specimens from central Ontario and Quebec dealers, mineral exhibits, lapidary demonstrations, silent auctions and grand live auction. Est attendance: 1,500. For info: Bancroft Gem and Mineral Club, PO Box 1749, Bancroft, ON, Canada K0L 1C0. Phone: (613) 332-1032. E-mail: wfmelanson@sympatico.ca.

DUMAS, ALEXANDRE (DUMAS FILS): BIRTH ANNIVERSARY. July 27, 1824. French novelist and playwright, as was his father. Author of *La Dame aux Camélias*. Dumas fils was born at Paris and died at Marly-le-Roi, France, Nov 27, 1895.

DUROCHER, LEO: BIRTH ANNIVERSARY. July 27, 1905. Leo Durocher was born at West Springfield, MA. He began his major league baseball career with the New York Yankees in 1925. He also played for the St. Louis Cardinals' "Gashouse Gang" and the Brooklyn Dodgers, where he first served as player-manager in 1939. On July 6, 1946, he used the phrase "Nice guys finish last," which would become his trademark. As a manager, he guided the New York Giants into two World Series. Following a five-year period away from baseball, he resurfaced as a coach with the Los Angeles Dodgers in 1961. In 1966 he signed with the Chicago Cubs as manager. After leaving the Cubs, he spent one season with the Houston Astros and then retired from baseball in 1973. He died Oct 7, 1991, at Palm Springs, CA.

INSULIN FIRST ISOLATED: ANNIVERSARY. July 27, 1921. Dr. Frederick Banting and his assistant at the University of Toronto Medical School, Charles Best, gave insulin to a dog whose pancreas had been removed. In 1922 insulin was first administered to a diabetic 14-year-old boy.

KOREAN WAR ARMISTICE: ANNIVERSARY. July 27, 1953. Armistice agreement ending war that had lasted three years and 32 days was signed at Panmunjom, Korea (July 26, US time), by US and North Korean delegates. Both sides claimed victory at conclusion of two years and 17 days of truce negotiations.

✦NATIONAL KOREAN WAR VETERANS ARMISTICE DAY. July 27. A special remembrance of the veterans of the Korean War, and especially those of the US and allied combatants who made the ultimate sacrifice in Korea. The display of the US flag is encouraged on this day.

✦PARENTS' DAY. July 27. To pay tribute to the men and women across our country whose devotion as parents strengthens our society and forms the foundation for a bright future for America. Public Law 103-362. Annually, the fourth Sunday in July.

TAKE YOUR HOUSEPLANTS FOR A WALK DAY. July 27. Walking your plants around the neighborhood enables them to become familiar with their environment, thereby providing them with a sense of knowing, bringing on wellness. (©2006 by WH.) For info: Thomas & Ruth Roy, Wellcat Holidays, 2418 Long Ln, Lebanon, PA 17046. Phone: (717) 279-0184. E-mail: info@wellcat.com. Web: www.wellcat.com.

TINKER, JOE: BIRTH ANNIVERSARY. July 27, 1880. Born at Muscotah, KS, shortstop Joseph Bert Tinker was part of the Chicago Cubs' famous Tinker-to-Evers-to-Chance double-play combination, which first took the field on Sept 13, 1902. For the next eight years this trio was the soul of the powerhouse Cubs—despite the fact that Tinker and Johnny Evers stopped speaking to each other in September 1905 (they continued the feud for 33 years). Tinker played with the Cincinnati Reds after the Cubs, played and managed in the Federal League and then managed the Cubs. Inducted into the Hall of Fame (with Evers and Chance) in 1946. Died at Orlando, FL, July 27, 1948. See also: "Tinker to Evers to Chance: First Double Play Anniversary" (Sept 15).

US DEPARTMENT OF STATE FOUNDED: 225th ANNIVERSARY. July 27, 1789. The first presidential cabinet department, called the Department of Foreign Affairs, was established by the Congress. Later the name was changed to Department of State.

WALK ON STILTS DAY. July 27. A day to walk on stilts, providing a chance to develop self-confidence through mastery of balance and coordination. A chance to enjoy the challenge of childhood no matter your age. A celebration of daring accomplishments at homes, circuses and theme parks everywhere. For info: Bill "Stretch" Coleman, 930 S Decatur St, Denver, CO 80219. Phone: (303) 922-4655. E-mail: stretch@stiltwalker.com. Web: www.stiltwalker.com.

BIRTHDAYS TODAY

Nikolaj Coster-Waldau, 44, actor ("Game of Thrones," *Mama, Black Hawk Down*), born at Denmark, July 27, 1970.

Peggy Gale Fleming, 66, sportscaster, Olympic figure skater, born San Jose, CA, July 27, 1948.

Bobbie Gentry, 72, singer, songwriter ("Ode to Billie Joe"), born Roberta Streeter at Chicasaw County, MS, July 27, 1942.

Courtney Kupets, 28, gymnast, born Bedford, TX, July 27, 1986.

July 2014

S	M	T	W	T	F	S
		1	2	3	4	5
6	7	8	9	10	11	12
13	14	15	16	17	18	19
20	21	22	23	24	25	26
27	28	29	30	31		

Norman Lear, 92, television scriptwriter, producer ("All in the Family," "Maude"), born New Haven, CT, July 27, 1922.

Maureen McGovern, 65, singer, actress, born Youngstown, OH, July 27, 1949.

Julian McMahon, 46, actor ("Charmed," "Nip/Tuck"), born Sydney, Australia, July 27, 1968.

Jonathan Rhys-Meyers, 37, actor ("The Tudors," *August Rush, Match Point, Elvis*), born County Dublin, Ireland, July 27, 1977.

Alex Rodriguez, 39, baseball player, born New York, NY, July 27, 1975.

Maya Rudolph, 42, actress (*Bridesmaids*), comedienne ("Saturday Night Live"), born Gainesville, FL, July 27, 1972.

Betty Thomas, 66, director, actress ("Hill Street Blues"), born St. Louis, MO, July 27, 1948.

Jerry Van Dyke, 83, actor ("Coach," "Teen Angel"), born Danville, IL, July 27, 1931.

James Victor, 75, actor (*Fuzz, Stand and Deliver*), born Santiago, Dominican Republic, July 27, 1939.

July 28 — Monday

DAY 209 **156 REMAINING**

CHAVEZ, HUGO: 60th BIRTH ANNIVERSARY. July 28, 1954. Born at rural Sabanetas, Venezuala, Chavez served as president of Venezuela from 1999 until his death at Caracas on Mar 5, 2013. While still serving in the army, Chavez began collaborating with leftist insurgents. Though an abortive coup landed him in prison, it afforded him national attention, which eventually brought him to an electoral victory. As president, Chavez instituted a program of economic centralization and increased military strength. He also became the principal antagonist of the United States in the Western Hemisphere, repeatedly taunting US leaders in his public statements.

EAA AIRVENTURE OSHKOSH. July 28–Aug 3. Wittman Regional Airport, Oshkosh, WI. World's largest sport aviation event. More than 10,000 airplanes annually fly in for this Experimental Aircraft Association gathering. Daily air shows; special programs; more than 500 forums, workshops and seminars. Est attendance: 500,000. For info: Dick Knapinski, Director of Communications, Experimental Aircraft Assn, PO Box 3086, Oshkosh, WI 54903-3086. Phone: (920) 426-4800. E-mail: communications@eaa.org. Web: www.eaa.org.

EID-AL-FITR: CELEBRATING THE FAST. July 28. Islamic calendar date: Shawwal 1, 1435. This feast/festival celebrates the completion of the Ramadan fasting and usually lasts for several days. Everyone wears new clothes; children receive gifts from parents and relatives; children are allowed to stay up late and participate in games, folktales, plays, puppet shows and trips to amusement parks. This holiday is known as Seker Bayram in Turkey and Hari Raya Puasa in Southeast Asia. Different methods for "anticipating" the visibility of the new moon crescent at Mecca are used by different Muslim groups. US date may vary. Began at sunset the preceding day.

FAROE ISLANDS: OLAI FESTIVAL. July 28–29. Torshavn. National festival held in honor of St. Olav, the patron saint of these small islands of the Norwegian Sea, which are part of the kingdom of Denmark. Begins the eve of St. Olav's Day (July 28) with a procession, sporting events, meetings and concerts. The festival continues on St. Olav's Day itself (July 29) with a ceremonial procession involving political, religious and community leaders to the parliament. After the prime minister's opening speech, the governmental year begins. Ceremonies end at midnight with community singing. Est attendance: 50,000.

FOX, TERRY: BIRTH ANNIVERSARY. July 28, 1958. With cancer requiring amputation of his right leg at age 18, Fox was determined to devote his life to a fight against the disease. His "Marathon of Hope," a planned 5,200-mile run westward across Canada, started Apr 12, 1980, at St. John's, NF, and continued 3,328 miles to Thunder Bay, ON, Sept 1, 1980, when he was forced to stop by spread of the disease. During the run (on an artificial leg) he raised $24 million for cancer research and inspired millions with his courage. Terry Fox was born at Winnipeg, MB, Canada, and died at New Westminster (near Vancouver), BC, Canada, June 28, 1981.

HAMBURG FIRESTORM: ANNIVERSARY. July 28, 1943. More than 42,000 civilians were killed when 2,326 tons of bombs, predominantly incendiaries, were dropped on Hamburg, Germany, by the Allies on this date. At the center of the firestorm the winds uprooted trees, and flames burned eight square miles in the eight hours the fire lasted. A firestorm occurs when the fires in a given area become so intense that they devour all the oxygen nearby and suck more into themselves, creating hurricane-force winds that feed the fires and move them at great speeds.

HEYWARD, THOMAS: BIRTH ANNIVERSARY. July 28, 1746. American Revolutionary soldier, signer of the Declaration of Independence. Died Mar 6, 1809.

ONASSIS, JACQUELINE LEE BOUVIER KENNEDY: 85th BIRTH ANNIVERSARY. July 28, 1929. Editor, widow of John Fitzgerald Kennedy (35th president of the US), born at Southampton, NY. Later married (Oct 20, 1968) Greek shipping magnate Aristotle Socrates Onassis, who died Mar 15, 1975. The widely admired and respected former first lady died May 19, 1994, at New York City.

PERU: INDEPENDENCE DAY. July 28. San Martin declared independence from Spain on this day in 1821. After the final defeat of Spanish troops by Simon Bolívar in 1824, Spanish rule ended.

PICCARD, JACQUES: BIRTH ANNIVERSARY. July 28, 1922. Oceanographer and explorer, born at Brussels, Belgium. The son of famed hot-air balloon adventurer Auguste Piccard, Jacques worked with his father to develop technology that enabled him to explore the deepest parts of the ocean. Using buoyancy techniques, he created a submersible called a bathyscaphe that he used in 1960 (in conjunction with the US Navy) to explore the Challenger Deep section of the Mariana Trench in the Pacific Ocean. This record-setting dive of nearly seven miles remains the deepest dive ever successfully attempted. He also built the first tourist submarine. He died at Lake Geneva, Switzerland, Nov 1, 2008.

POTTER, (HELEN) BEATRIX: BIRTH ANNIVERSARY. July 28, 1866. Author and illustrator of the Peter Rabbit stories for children, born at London, England. Died at Sawrey, Lancashire, England, Dec 22, 1943.

SINGING TELEGRAM: ANNIVERSARY. July 28, 1933. Anniversary of the first singing telegram, said to have been delivered to singer Rudy Vallee on his 32nd birthday. Early singing telegrams often were delivered in person by uniformed messengers on bicycle. Later they were usually sung over the telephone.

SPACE MILESTONE: *SKYLAB 3* (US). July 28, 1973. Alan L. Bean, Owen K. Garriott and Jack R. Lousma started 59-day mission in the space station to test human spaceflight endurance. Pacific splashdown Sept 25.

VALLEE, RUDY: BIRTH ANNIVERSARY. July 28, 1901. American singer, saxophone player and radio idol of millions during the 1930s. Born Hubert Prior Vallee, at Island Pond, VT, the crooner used a megaphone to amplify his voice and introduced his performances with the salutation "Heigh-ho-everybody!" Vallee appeared in a number of movies, including *How to Succeed in Business Without Really Trying.* Among his best-remembered songs are "I'm Just a Vagabond Lover," "Say It Isn't So" and his signature song, "My Time Is Your Time." Vallee died at age 84 at North Hollywood, CA, July 3, 1986.

VETERANS BONUS ARMY EVICTION: ANNIVERSARY. July 28, 1932. Some 15,000 unemployed veterans of WWI marched on Washington, DC, in the summer of 1932, demanding payment of a war bonus. After two months' encampment in Washington's Anacostia Flats, eviction of the bonus marchers by the US Army was ordered by President Herbert Hoover. Under the leadership of General Douglas MacArthur, Major Dwight D. Eisenhower and Major George S. Patton, Jr (among others), cavalry, tanks and infantry attacked. Fixed bayonets, tear gas and the burning of the veterans' tents hastened the end of the confrontation. One death was reported.

VIRGIN ISLANDS: HURRICANE SUPPLICATION DAY. July 28. Legal holiday. Population attends churches to pray for protection from hurricanes. Annually, the fourth Monday in July.

WORLD WAR I BEGINS: 100th ANNIVERSARY. July 28, 1914. Archduke Francis Ferdinand of Austria-Hungary and his wife were assassinated at Sarajevo, Bosnia, by a Serbian nationalist June 28, 1914, touching off the conflict that became WWI. Austria-Hungary declared war on Serbia July 28, the formal beginning of the war. Within weeks, Germany entered the war on the side of Austria-Hungary, and Russia, France and Great Britain entered on the side of Serbia.

BIRTHDAYS TODAY

William Warren (Bill) Bradley, 71, former US senator, Hall of Fame basketball player, born Crystal City, MO, July 28, 1943.

Jim Davis, 69, cartoonist ("Garfield"), born Marion, IN, July 28, 1945.

Manu Ginobili, 37, basketball player, born Bahai Blanca, Argentina, July 28, 1977.

Darryl Hickman, 83, actor ("The Americans," *The Tingler*), born Los Angeles, CA, July 28, 1931.

Linda Kelsey, 68, actress ("Lou Grant"), born Minneapolis, MN, July 28, 1946.

Lori Loughlin, 50, actress ("Full House," *Back to the Beach*), born Long Island, NY, July 28, 1964.

Scott Pelley, 57, journalist, broadcaster, born San Antonio, TX, July 28, 1957.

Sally Struthers, 66, actress ("All in the Family"), born Portland, OR, July 28, 1948.

July 2014	S	M	T	W	T	F	S
			1	2	3	4	5
	6	7	8	9	10	11	12
	13	14	15	16	17	18	19
	20	21	22	23	24	25	26
	27	28	29	30	31		

July 29 — Tuesday

DAY 210 **155 REMAINING**

HIMES, CHESTER: BIRTH ANNIVERSARY. July 29, 1909. Groundbreaking African-American author who accosted American racism in such novels as *If He Hollers Let Him Go* (1945). In the 1950s, after he relocated to a friendlier France, Himes created a series of hard-boiled mystery novels set in Harlem, NY, including *Cotton Comes to Harlem* (1965), that featured black detectives "Coffin Ed" Johnson and "Grave Digger" Jones. Born at Jefferson City, MO, Himes died Nov 12, 1984, at Moraira, Spain.

***INDIANAPOLIS* SUNK: ANNIVERSARY.** July 29, 1945. After delivering the atomic bomb to Tinian Island, the American cruiser *Indianapolis* was headed for Okinawa to train for the invasion of Japan when it was torpedoed by a Japanese submarine. Of 1,196 crew members, more than 350 were immediately killed in the explosion or went down with the ship. There were no rescue ships nearby, and those fortunate enough to survive endured the next 84 hours in ocean waters. By the time they were spotted by air on Aug 2, only 318 sailors remained alive, the others having either drowned or been eaten by sharks. This is the US Navy's worst loss at sea.

JENNINGS, PETER: BIRTH ANNIVERSARY. July 29, 1938. Television news anchor, born at Toronto, ON, Canada, who had immense success as a journalist despite never graduating from high school or college. Jennings was highly respected for his calm delivery and known for his travels around the world, reporting the news wherever it happened. He received 16 Emmy Awards as well as two George Foster Peabody Awards and served as chief anchor of ABC-TV's "World News Tonight" from 1983 until April 2005, when he announced during his broadcast that he had been diagnosed with lung cancer. He died on Aug 7, 2005, at New York, NY.

MUSSOLINI, BENITO: BIRTH ANNIVERSARY. July 29, 1883. Italian Fascist leader, born at Dovia, Italy. Self-styled "Il Duce" (the leader), Mussolini governed Italy, first as prime minister and later as absolute dictator during 1922–43. It was Mussolini who said: "War alone . . . puts the stamp of nobility upon the peoples who have the courage to face it." But military defeat of Italy in WWII was Mussolini's downfall. Repudiated and arrested by the Italian government, he was temporarily rescued by German paratroops in 1943. Later, while attempting to flee in disguise to Switzerland, he and his mistress, Clara Petacci, were killed by Italian partisans near Lake Como, Italy, Apr 28, 1945.

NASA ESTABLISHED: ANNIVERSARY. July 29, 1958. President Eisenhower signed a bill creating the National Aeronautics and Space Administration to direct US space policy.

NORWAY: OLSOK EVE. July 29. Commemorates Norway's Viking king St. Olav, who fell in battle at Stiklestad near Trondheim, Norway, July 29, 1030. Bonfires, historical pageants.

RAIN DAY AT WAYNESBURG, PENNSYLVANIA. July 29. Legend has it that rain will fall at Waynesburg, PA, on July 29 as it has most years for the last century, according to local records in this community, which was laid out in 1796 and incorporated in 1816.

ROOSEVELT, ALICE HATHAWAY LEE: BIRTH ANNIVERSARY. July 29, 1861. First wife of Theodore Roosevelt, 26th president of the US, whom she married in 1880. Born at Chestnut Hill, MA, she died at New York, NY, Feb 14, 1884.

SPAIN: FIESTA DE SANTA MARTA DE RIBARTEME (FESTIVAL OF NEAR DEATH EXPERIENCES). July 29. As Neves, Pontevedra, Galicia. Religious festival honoring Santa Marta. Those who have been near death and survived are carried in open coffins or march in shrouds to the local church. Est attendance: 5,000.

TARKINGTON, BOOTH: BIRTH ANNIVERSARY. July 29, 1869. American novelist (*The Magnificent Ambersons*), born at Indianapolis, IN. Died there May 19, 1946.

TOCQUEVILLE, ALEXIS DE: BIRTH ANNIVERSARY. July 29, 1805. French politician and author whose 1831 trip to the US inspired *Democracy in America*, one of the most insightful books written on the US. "America is a land of wonders," he wrote, "in which everything is in constant motion and every change seems an improvement." Born at Verneuil, France, Tocqueville died at Cannes, France, on Apr 16, 1859.

BIRTHDAYS TODAY

Ken Burns, 61, documentary filmmaker (*The Civil War, Baseball, Prohibition*), born New York, NY, July 29, 1953.

Danger Mouse, 37, musician, music producer, born Brian Joseph Burton at White Plains, NY, July 29, 1977.

Elizabeth Hanford Dole, 78, former US senator (R, North Carolina); former president, American Red Cross; former secretary of transportation and secretary of labor; born Salisbury, NC, July 29, 1936.

Fernando González, 34, tennis player, born Santiago, Chile, July 29, 1980.

Tim Gunn, 61, fashion consultant, television personality ("Project Runway"), born Washington, DC, July 29, 1953.

Martina McBride, 48, country singer, born Sharon, KS, July 29, 1966.

Alexandra Paul, 51, actress ("Baywatch," *Dragnet*), born New York, NY, July 29, 1963.

Josh Radnor, 40, actor ("How I Met Your Mother"), born Columbus, OH, July 29, 1974.

Patty Scialfa, 58, singer, born Deal, NJ, July 29, 1956.

Paul Taylor, 84, dancer, choreographer, born Allegheny, NY, July 29, 1930.

David Warner, 73, actor (Emmy for *Masada*; *The Omen, Tron, Titanic*), born Manchester, England, July 29, 1941.

Wil Wheaton, 42, actor ("Star Trek: The Next Generation," *Stand by Me*), born Burbank, CA, July 29, 1972.

July 30 — Wednesday

DAY 211 **154 REMAINING**

BRONTË, EMILY: BIRTH ANNIVERSARY. July 30, 1818. English novelist, one of the Brontë sisters, best known for *Wuthering Heights*. Born at Thornton, Yorkshire, England. Died Dec 19, 1848, at Haworth, Yorkshire.

CANADA: HALIFAX INTERNATIONAL BUSKER FESTIVAL. July 30–Aug 4. Halifax, NS. Street performers and artists from around the world: fire shows, acrobatics, dancing and more than 30 different shows. Est attendance: 450,000. For info: Halifax Intl Busker Fest, 1150 Belmont on the Arm, Halifax, NS, B3H 1J3, Canada. Web: www.buskers.ca.

CHINCOTEAGUE PONY PENNING. July 30–31. Chincoteague Island, VA. To round up the 150 wild ponies living on Assateague Island and swim them across the inlet to Chincoteague, where about 80–90 of them are sold. Annually, the last Wednesday and Thursday in July. Est attendance: 50,000. For info: Chincoteague Chamber of Commerce, 6733 Maddox Blvd, Chincoteague, VA 23336. Phone: (757) 336-6161. Fax: (757) 336-1242. E-mail: chincochamber@verizon.net. Web: www.chincoteaguechamber.com.

ELVIS PRESLEY'S FIRST CONCERT APPEARANCE: 60th ANNIVERSARY. July 30, 1954. Elvis Presley appeared in concert for the first time at Overton Park Orchestra Shell in Memphis, TN. He was billed third, and country crooner Slim Whitman was the headliner. Presley, only 19 years old, nervously began gyrating his leg and a legend was born. See also: "Elvis Presley's First Single Released: Anniversary" (July 19).

FATHER HIDALGO: EXECUTION ANNIVERSARY. July 30, 1811. Miguel Hidalgo y Costilla, fiery leader of revolutionary forces in Mexico seeking independence from Spain, was executed by firing squad in Chihuahua. His head and those of the other executed insurgent leaders were put on public display in Guanajuato, Mexico, for 10 years.

FORD, HENRY: BIRTH ANNIVERSARY. July 30, 1863. Industrialist Henry Ford, whose assembly-line method of automobile production revolutionized the industry, was born at Wayne County, MI, on the family farm. His Model T made up half of the world's output of cars during its years of production. Ford built racing cars until in 1903 he and his partners formed the Ford Motor Company. In 1908 the company presented the Model T, which was produced until 1927, and in 1913 Ford introduced the assembly line and mass production. This innovation reduced the time it took to build each car from 12½ hours to only 1½. This enabled Ford to sell cars for $500, making automobile ownership a possibility for an unprecedented percentage of the population. He is also remembered for introducing a $5-a-day wage for automotive workers and for his statement "History is bunk." Died Apr 7, 1947, at age 83 at Dearborn, MI, where his manufacturing complex was located.

HOFFA, JAMES: DISAPPEARANCE ANNIVERSARY. July 30, 1975. Former Teamsters Union leader, 62-year-old James Riddle Hoffa was last seen on this date outside a restaurant in Bloomfield Township, near Detroit, MI. His 13-year federal prison sentence had been commuted by President Richard M. Nixon in 1971. On Dec 8, 1982, seven years and 131 days after his disappearance, an Oakland County judge declared Hoffa officially dead as of July 30, 1982.

MOORE, HENRY: BIRTH ANNIVERSARY. July 30, 1898. English sculptor born at Castleford, Yorkshire, England. Died at Hertfordshire, England, Aug 31, 1986.

PAPERBACK BOOKS INTRODUCED: ANNIVERSARY. July 30, 1935. Although books bound in soft covers were first introduced in 1841 at Leipzig, Germany, by Christian Bernhard Tauchnitz, the modern paperback revolution dates to the publication of the first Penguin paperback by Sir Allen Lane at London, England, in 1935. Penguin Number 1 was *Ariel*, a life of Shelley by Andre Maurois.

SIEGE OF PETERSBURG: 150th ANNIVERSARY. July 30, 1864. After the Battle of Cold Harbor, Union general Ulysses S. Grant moved his troops across the James River toward Petersburg, VA. After initially failing to defeat the Confederate force around Petersburg, Grant prepared his army for a siege of the city. On this date an explosive charge planted in a tunnel under the Confederate defenses was detonated in one of the largest explosions ever seen on the American continent. Union forces stormed the breach in the defensive works but were pinned down by Confederate artillery. A Union command of black soldiers trained specially for the attack advanced through the breach and the pinned-down Northern forces and were cut to pieces by Rebel gunfire. The special force was initially held out of the attack because Grant feared such a disaster would lead to the Union's being accused of callously using black soldiers. The remaining Union troops were forced to retreat.

STENGEL, CHARLES DILLON (CASEY): BIRTH ANNIVERSARY. July 30, 1890. Baseball Hall of Fame outfielder and manager, born at Kansas City, MO. His success as manager of the New York Yankees (10 pennants and 7 World Series titles in 12 years) made him one of the game's enduring stars. Inducted into the Hall of Fame in 1966. Died at Glendale, CA, Sept 29, 1975.

VANUATU: INDEPENDENCE DAY. July 30. Vanuatu became an independent republic (from France and the United Kingdom) in 1980 and observes its national holiday.

VEBLEN, THORSTEIN: BIRTH ANNIVERSARY. July 30, 1857. American economist, born at Valders, WI, and died at Menlo Park, CA, Aug 3, 1929. "Conspicuous consumption," he wrote in *The Theory of the Leisure Class*, "of valuable goods is a means of reputability to the gentleman of leisure."

ZWORYKIN, VLADIMIR: 125th BIRTH ANNIVERSARY. July 30, 1889. Born at Mourom, Russia, scientist Zworykin held more than 120 patents during his life but is best remembered as the "father of television." His inventions of the iconoscope and kinescope laid the foundation for the picture tube television; he was also active in the field of electron microscopy and invented the electron microscope and infrared vision. In 1967 he was awarded the National Medal of Science by the National Academy of Sciences. When asked to comment on the content of American television in a 1981 interview, Zworykin replied, "Awful." Died July 29, 1982, at Princeton, NJ.

BIRTHDAYS TODAY

Paul Anka, 73, singer, songwriter, born Ottawa, ON, Canada, July 30, 1941.

William Atherton, 67, actor (*The Day of the Locust, Ghostbusters, Die Hard, Die Hard 2*), born New Haven, CT, July 30, 1947.

Simon Baker, 45, actor ("The Mentalist," "The Guardian," *Land of the Dead*), born Launceton, Tasmania, July 30, 1969.

Peter Bogdanovich, 75, producer, director (*The Last Picture Show, Paper Moon*), actor, born Kingston, NY, July 30, 1939.

Alton Brown, 52, chef, television personality ("Good Eats," "Iron Chef America"), born Los Angeles, CA, July 30, 1962.

Delta Burke, 58, actress ("Designing Women"), former Miss Florida, born Orlando, FL, July 30, 1956.

Kate Bush, 56, singer, songwriter, born Lewisham, England, July 30, 1958.

Edd Byrnes, 81, actor ("77 Sunset Strip," *Darby's Rangers*), born New York, NY, July 30, 1933.

James William (Bill) Cartwright, 57, basketball coach and former player, born Lodi, CA, July 30, 1957.

Laurence Fishburne, 53, actor (*Matrix* films, *Akeelah and the Bee, Boyz N the Hood, What's Love Got to Do with It?*; Tony for *Two Trains Running*; "CSI"), born Augusta, GA, July 30, 1961.

Anita Faye Hill, 58, law professor, born on an Oklahoma farm, July 30, 1956.

Lisa Kudrow, 51, actress ("Friends," *Romy and Michele's High School Reunion*), born Encino, CA, July 30, 1963.

Misty May-Treanor, 37, Olympic beach volleyball player, born Los Angeles, CA, July 30, 1977.

Christopher Paul (Chris) Mullin, 51, Hall of Fame basketball player, born New York, NY, July 30, 1963.

Ken Olin, 60, actor ("LA Doctors," "thirtysomething"), born Chicago, IL, July 30, 1954.

July 2014	S	M	T	W	T	F	S
			1	2	3	4	5
	6	7	8	9	10	11	12
	13	14	15	16	17	18	19
	20	21	22	23	24	25	26
	27	28	29	30	31		

Jaime Pressly, 37, actress ("My Name Is Earl," *Not Another Teen Movie*), born Kinston, NC, July 30, 1977.

David Sanborn, 69, saxophonist, composer, born Tampa, FL, July 30, 1945.

Arnold Schwarzenegger, 67, former governor of California (R), bodybuilder, actor (*The Terminator, True Lies*), born Graz, Austria, July 30, 1947.

Allan Huber "Bud" Selig, 80, Commissioner of Major League Baseball, born Milwaukee, WI, July 30, 1934.

Hope Solo, 33, soccer player, born Richland, WA, July 30, 1981.

Hilary Swank, 40, actress (Oscars for *Boys Don't Cry* and *Million Dollar Baby*), born Lincoln, NE, July 30, 1974.

July 31 — Thursday

DAY 212 **153 REMAINING**

BIX BEIDERBECKE MEMORIAL JAZZ FESTIVAL. July 31–Aug 3. Davenport, IA. 43rd annual. Four-day jazz festival honoring the memory and perpetuating the music of world-renowned cornetist, pianist and composer Bix Beiderbecke. Includes concerts in three venues, food, etc. Est attendance: 10,000. For info: Bix Beiderbecke Memorial Society, PO Box 3688, Davenport, IA 52808. Phone: (563) 324-7170. Fax: (563) 326-1732. E-mail: info@bixsociety.org. Web: www.bixsociety.org or www.visitquadcities.com.

CANADA: ROCKHOUND GEMBOREE. July 31–Aug 3. Bancroft, ON. 51st annual. Daily expeditions to prime mineral locations; dealers, demonstrations and displays; swapping gems, minerals, crystals, fossils; jewelry. Est attendance: 7,000. For info: Bancroft and District Chamber of Commerce, PO Box 539, Bancroft, ON, Canada K0L 1C0. Phone: (613) 332-1513. Fax: (613) 332-2119. E-mail: gemboree@bancroftdistrict.com. Web: www.bancroftdistrict.com.

FEAST OF SAINT IGNATIUS OF LOYOLA. July 31. 1491–1556. Founder of the Society of Jesus (Jesuits). Canonized in 1622.

FIRST INDIAN SAINT: ANNIVERSARY. July 31, 2002. In Mexico City, Mexico, Pope John Paul II canonized the Roman Catholic Church's first Indian saint, Juan Diego. In 1531 Diego claimed to have seen the Virgin of Guadalupe, whose rose-framed image later appeared on his cloak. See also: "Day of Our Lady of Guadalupe" (Dec 12).

FIRST US GOVERNMENT BUILDING: ANNIVERSARY. July 31, 1792. The cornerstone of the Philadelphia Mint, the first US government building, was laid on this day.

FRIEDMAN, MILTON: BIRTH ANNIVERSARY. July 31, 1912. A Nobel Prize–winning economist, teacher and author, Friedman was born at Brooklyn, NY. In 1946 he became a professor of economics at the University of Chicago, where he did some of his best-known work. The Chicago School, of which he was a member with like-minded scholars, promulgated influential free-market theories. Died at San Francisco, CA, Nov 16, 2006.

***MOBY-DICK* MARATHON.** July 31–Aug 1. Mystic Seaport, Mystic, CT. Marathon reading of the classic *Moby-Dick* in celebration of Herman Melville's birthday. Reading takes place on deck of the nation's last wooden whaler, the *Charles W. Morgan*. Annually, 24-hour reading from noon July 31 to noon Aug 1. Est attendance:

6,000. For info: Mystic Seaport, 75 Greenmanville Ave, PO Box 6000, Mystic, CT 06355-0990. Phone: (860) 572-0711 or (888) 973-2767. Web: www.mysticseaport.org.

NATIONAL CHILI DOG DAY. July 31. To celebrate the chili dog as one of America's favorite summertime foods. Annually, the last Thursday in July. For info: Doug Welsh, Hard Times Cafe Restaurants, 110 Surrey Ln, Locust Grove, VA 22508. Phone: (703) 608-7725. E-mail: dougwelsh101@gmail.com. Web: www.hardtimes.com.

QUANTRILL, WILLIAM: BIRTH ANNIVERSARY. July 31, 1837. Born at Canal Dover, OH, William Quantrill is one of the infamous characters of the American Civil War. He was leader of a guerrilla band ("Quantrill's Raiders") who conducted raids and harassed Union soldiers along the Kansas-Missouri border. Quantrill is most notorious for the violent Aug 21, 1863, raid he led on Lawrence, KS. More than 150 men and boys were killed, and homes and businesses were burned. Quantrill was killed in a Union ambush near Taylorsville, KY, June 6, 1865.

SALVADOR, FRANCIS: DEATH ANNIVERSARY. July 31, 1776. The first Jew to die in the American Revolution, Salvador was also the first Jew elected to office in colonial America. He was voted a member of the South Carolina Provincial Congress in January 1775.

SATCHMO SUMMERFEST. July 31–Aug 3. New Orleans, LA. The spirit of Louis "Satchmo" Armstrong lives with this annual birthday celebration of his music, legacy and cultural contributions. The free event includes a jazz-filled music festival, children's activities, seminars and panels, photo exhibits and cultural displays, a jazz mass and Satchmo-inspired New Orleans cuisine. It's all part of New Orleans's ongoing tribute to the "International Ambassador of Jazz" in the birthplace of jazz. Est attendance: 45,000. For info: French Quarter Festivals, Inc, 400 N Peters St, #205, New Orleans, LA 70130. Phone: (800) 673-5725 or (504) 522-5730. E-mail: info@fqfi.org. Web: www.fqfi.org.

"THE SHADOW" RADIO PREMIERE: ANNIVERSARY. July 31, 1930. "Who knows what evil lurks in the hearts of men? The Shadow knows!" This popular crime and suspense program premiered on CBS radio. Originally, the Shadow was just the narrator of the changing stories, but later he became a character with his own adventures—with the alter ego of Lamont Cranston. Orson Welles was the first Shadow.

US PATENT OFFICE OPENS: ANNIVERSARY. July 31, 1790. The first US Patent Office opened its doors, and the first US patent was issued to Samuel Hopkins of Vermont for a new method of making pearlash and potash. The patent was signed by George Washington and Thomas Jefferson.

WISCONSIN STATE FAIR. July 31–Aug 10. State Fair Park, West Allis, WI. The annual Wisconsin State Fair is the state's largest agricultural showcase, offering endless family entertainment at an exceptional value. The fair features the exciting SpinCity Amusement Ride and Game Area, 30 free stages of entertainment, numerous educational exhibits, plenty of shopping and hundreds of food and beverage options. Presented by US Cellular. (Call 24-hour recorded information line at (800) 884-FAIR for up-to-date information.) Est attendance: 920,000. For info: Wisconsin State Fair Park, 640 S 84th St, West Allis, WI 53214-0990. Phone: (414) 266-7000. Fax: (414) 266-7007. E-mail: wsfp@wisconsin.gov. Web: www.WiStateFair.com.

BIRTHDAYS TODAY

Dean Cain, 48, actor ("Lois & Clark: The New Adventures of Superman"), born Mount Clemens, MI, July 31, 1966.

Geraldine Chaplin, 70, actress (*Nashville, Roseland, Chaplin*), born Santa Monica, CA, July 31, 1944.

Susan Flannery, 71, actress ("The Bold and the Beautiful," "Dallas"), born Jersey City, NJ, July 31, 1943.

Evonne Goolagong, 63, Hall of Fame tennis player, born Griffith, Australia, July 31, 1951.

Gary Lewis, 68, singer, born New York, NY, July 31, 1946.

Evgeni Malkin, 28, hockey player, born Magnitogorsk, Russia, July 31, 1986.

Don Murray, 85, actor (*Bus Stop*, "Knots Landing"), born Hollywood, CA, July 31, 1929.

France Nuyen, 75, actress ("St. Elsewhere"), born Marseilles, France, July 31, 1939.

Jonathan Ogden, 40, football player, born Washington, DC, July 31, 1974.

Deval Patrick, 58, Governor of Massachusetts (D), born Chicago, IL, July 31, 1956.

Rico Rodriguez, 16, actor ("Modern Family"), born College Station, TX, July 31, 1998.

J.K. Rowling, 49, author (the Harry Potter series), born Joanne Rowling at Bristol, England, July 31, 1965.

Wesley Snipes, 52, actor (*Blade, US Marshals, Jungle Fever, White Men Can't Jump*), born Orlando, FL, July 31, 1962.

August

August 1 — Friday

DAY 213 **152 REMAINING**

AMERICAN ADVENTURES MONTH. Aug 1–31. This month celebrates vacationing in the Americas. Whether traveling in luxury or in primitive conditions, tourists are encouraged to explore South, Central and North America. Experiencing the Americas in a variety of ways unlocks new worlds for all travelers. Remember to keep adventure in every vacation. For info: Peter Kulkkula, American Adventurer, 381 Billings Rd, Fitchburg, MA 01420-1407. Phone: (978) 343-4009. E-mail: info@AmericanAdventures.info. Web: www.AmericanAdventures.info.

BENIN: INDEPENDENCE DAY. Aug 1. Public holiday. Commemorates independence from France in 1960. Benin at that time was known as Dahomey.

BLACK BUSINESS MONTH. Aug 1–31. Six months after Black History Month, the focus on and awareness of black-owned and operated enterprises needs a boost. This month is dedicated to starting, maintaining, growing, buying from and committing to black-owned businesses and entrepreneurs. For info: Sylvia Henderson, Springboard Training, PO Box 588, Olney, MD 20830-0588. Phone: (301) 260-1538. E-mail: sylvia@springboardtraining.com.

BLUEBERRY ARTS FESTIVAL. Aug 1–3. State Office Building, Methodist Church and Main Street Gallery, Ketchikan, AK. A street fair featuring arts and crafts, food, games and contests for all ages, performing arts events, and poetry and prose readings. Annually, the first weekend in August. Est attendance: 7,000. For info: Ketchikan Area Arts and Humanities Council, 330 Main St, Ketchikan, AK 99901. Phone: (907) 225-2211. E-mail: info@ketchikanarts.org. Web: www.ketchikanarts.org.

BLUEBERRY FESTIVAL. Aug 1–2. Library Lawn and Village Green, Montrose, PA. 35th annual fund-raiser for the Susquehanna County Library and Historical Society. Two days filled with food, fun and festivity. Raffles, book sale, children's games, silent auction, hand-stitched quilt, commemorative items and more. Annually, the first Friday and Saturday in August. Est attendance: 5,000. For info: Hilary Caws-Elwitt, Susquehanna County Library, 18 Monument St, Montrose, PA 18801. Phone: (570) 278-1881. Fax: (570) 278-9336. E-mail: info@susqcolibrary.org. Web: www.montrosepablueberryfestival.org.

BOOM DAYS. Aug 1–3. Leadville, CO. The city's oldest annual celebration features a large parade, street races, mining events, pack burro race and arts and crafts. Fun for the whole family. Est attendance: 3,000. For info: Chamber of Commerce, PO Box 861, Leadville, CO 80461. Phone: (719) 486-3900 or (888) 532-3845. Fax: (719) 486-8478. E-mail: info@leadvilleboomdays.com. Web: www.leadvilleboomdays.com.

BRAHAM PIE DAY. Aug 1. Freedom Park, Braham, MN. Celebrate Braham's status as "Homemade Pie Capital of Minnesota" during this one-day festival. Visitors will find homemade pies, craft displays, pie-eating contests, a pie auction, a pie art show, a pie trivia contest, the "Pie-alluia" chorus and performing artists in Braham's main street park. Est attendance: 4,000. For info: Braham Pie Day, PO Box 383, Braham, MN 55006. Phone: (320) 396-4956. Web: www.pieday.com.

BURK, MARTHA (CALAMITY JANE): DEATH ANNIVERSARY. Aug 1, 1903. Known as a frontierswoman and companion to Wild Bill Hickok, Calamity Jane Burk was born Martha Jane Cannary at Princeton, MO, in May 1852. As a young girl living in Montana, she became an excellent markswoman. She went to the Black Hills of South Dakota as a scout for a geologic expedition in 1875. Several opposing traditions account for her nickname, one springing from her kindness to people who were less fortunate, while another attributes it to the harsh warnings she would give men who offended her. She died at Terry, SD, and was buried at Deadwood, SD, next to Wild Bill Hickok.

BYSTANDER AWARENESS MONTH. Aug 1–31. The bystander effect is a social phenomenon within which an individual's likelihood of helping a person in need is directly tied to the number of people witnessing the person's need at the same time. Most people assume someone else will intervene, so they don't intervene themselves. Bystander Awareness Month hopes to change that phenomenon and to encourage individuals to become active bystanders when witnessing injustice, specifically domestic and sexual violence. During this month, youth will be engaged in schools, and adults will be in engaged in their communities and provided presentations, education and other tools to assist them as they transition from inactive to active bystanders. When people intervene for the good of others, it creates a safer community. For info: The Bridge Over Troubled Waters, Inc, 3811 Allen Genova Rd, Pasadena, TX 77504. Phone: (713) 472-0753. Fax: (713) 472-8759. E-mail: lanton@tbotw.org.

CANADA: AGRIFAIR. Aug 1–4. Abbotsford, BC. Affordable family fun, featuring attractions such as draft horses, dairy, beef and poultry; milking display; Pride of the Valley trade show; antique farm display bursting with antique toys; midway; local stage entertainment and a pro rodeo. Est attendance: 40,000. For info: Abbotsford Agrifair, PO Box 2334, Abbotsford, BC V2T 4X2, Canada. Phone: (604) 852-6674. Fax: (604) 852-6631. E-mail: agrifair@telus.net. Web: www.agrifair.ca.

CHILDREN'S EYE HEALTH AND SAFETY MONTH. Aug 1–31. Prevent Blindness America® provides information about amblyopia, a condition that can affect 2 to 3 percent of children and can cause permanent vision loss. Additional information includes tips about preventing eye injuries in children, signs of possible eye problems and general eye health. For info: Prevent Blindness America®, 211 W Wacker Dr, Ste 1700, Chicago, IL 60606. Phone: (800) 331-2020. E-mail: info@preventblindness.org. Web: www.preventblindness.org.

CHILDREN'S VISION AND LEARNING MONTH. Aug 1–31. Researchers estimate that one out of four children has an undiagnosed vision problem that is interfering with the ability to read and learn. Since 80 percent of learning is dependent upon vision, it is vital that parents and educators ensure they understand the signs of vision problems. With children getting ready to go back to school, August is the perfect month for education. For info: College of Optometrists in Vision Development, 215 W Garfield Rd, Ste 200, Aurora, OH 44202. Phone: (330) 995-0718 or (888) 268-3770. Fax: (330) 995-0719. E-mail: info@covd.org. Web: www.covd.org.

CLARK, WILLIAM: BIRTH ANNIVERSARY. Aug 1, 1770. The soldier, explorer and public servant was born at Caroline County, VA. He served seven years in the US Army and then gained his lasting fame when Meriwether Lewis asked him to join an expedition exploring the Louisiana Territory (1803–06). Clark was an able leader and contributed detailed maps and animal illustrations on the journey. A grateful President Thomas Jefferson made Clark brigadier general of militia for the Louisiana Territory (1807–13) and superintendent of Indian Affairs (1807–38). Clark was also governor of the Missouri Territory (1813–20) and surveyor general for Illinois, Missouri and Arkansas (1824–25). Clark foresaw the tension between US interests and the native peoples of the western US, and he urged that the US treat native tribes with respect. Clark died at St. Louis, MO, on Sept 1, 1838.

COLORADO: ADMISSION DAY: ANNIVERSARY. Aug 1, 1876. Colorado admitted to the Union as the 38th state. The first Monday in August is celebrated as Colorado Day.

CRAFTSMEN'S SUMMER CLASSIC ARTS & CRAFTS FESTIVAL. Aug 1–3. Myrtle Beach Convention Center, Myrtle Beach, SC. 32nd annual. Features work from more than 250 talented artists and craftspeople. All juried exhibitors' work has been handmade by the exhibitors and must be their own original design and creation. See the creative process in action with several exhibitors demonstrating throughout the weekend. Est attendance: 15,000. For info: Gilmore Enterprises, Inc, 3514-A Drawbridge Pkwy, Greensboro, NC 27410-8584. Phone: (336) 282-5550. E-mail: contact@gilmoreshows.com. Web: www.CraftShow.com or www.gilmoreshows.com.

DIARY OF ANNE FRANK: THE LAST ENTRY: 70th ANNIVERSARY. Aug 1, 1944. To escape deportation to concentration camps, the Jewish family of Otto Frank hid for two years in the warehouse of his food products business at Amsterdam, Netherlands. Gentile friends smuggled in food and other supplies during their confinement. Thirteen-year-old Anne Frank, who kept a journal during the time of their hiding, penned her last entry in the diary Aug 1, 1944: "[I] keep on trying to find a way of becoming what I would like to be, and what I could be, if . . . there weren't any other people living in the world." Three days later (Aug 4, 1944), Grüne Polizei raided the "Secret Annex" where the Frank family was hidden. Anne and her sister were sent to Bergen-Belsen concentration camp, where Anne died at age 15, two months before the liberation of Holland. Young Anne's diary, later found in the family's hiding place, has been translated into 30 languages and has become a symbol of the indomitable strength of the human spirit. See also: "Frank, Anne: Birth Anniversary" (June 12).

EMANCIPATION OF 500: ANNIVERSARY. Aug 1, 1791. Virginia planter Robert Carter III confounded his family and friends by filing a deed of emancipation for his 500 slaves. One of the wealthiest men in the state, Carter owned 60,000 acres over 18 plantations. The deed included the following words: "I have for some time past been convinced that to retain them in Slavery is contrary to the true principles of Religion and Justice and therefore it is my duty to manumit them." The document established a schedule by which 15 slaves would be freed each Jan 1, over a 21-year period, plus slave children would be freed at age 18 for females and 21 for males. It is believed this was the largest act of emancipation in US history and predated the Emancipation Proclamation by 70 years.

FIRST US CENSUS: ANNIVERSARY. Aug 1, 1790. The first census revealed that there were 3,939,326 citizens in the 16 states and the Ohio Territory. The US has taken a census every 10 years since 1790.

GARCIA, JERRY: BIRTH ANNIVERSARY. Aug 1, 1942. Jerome John Garcia was born at San Francisco, CA. Country, bluegrass and folk musician and a guitar player of remarkable ability, Garcia was the leading force behind the legendary Grateful Dead, the band that sustained a veritable industry for its legion of followers. He died Aug 9, 1995, at Forest Knolls, CA, ending a musical career that spanned more than three decades.

GIGGLEFEET DANCE FESTIVAL. Aug 1 and 3. Ketchikan, AK. Two evening performances celebrating dance in the community, including jazz, tap, ballet, modern, hip-hop, Native Alaskan, break-dance and more. Annually, the first Friday and Sunday in August, part of the Blueberry Arts Festival. Est attendance: 1,000. For info: Ketchikan Area Arts & Humanities Council, 330 Main St, Ketchikan, AK 99910. Phone: (907) 225-2211. E-mail: info@ketchikanarts.org. Web: www.ketchikanarts.org.

GIRLFRIEND'S DAY. Aug 1. Celebrate this special day by taking your girlfriend(s) shopping, to a play, to the movies, out to eat, to the spa and/or to the park. A fun slumber party is also recommended. Annually, Aug 1. For info: Thema Martin, 931 Monroe Dr NE, Ste A102, #226, Atlanta, GA 30308. Phone: (404) 939-3833. E-mail: tmartin@savionaire.com.

HAPPINESS HAPPENS MONTH. Aug 1–31. This 15th annual celebration is sponsored by the Secret Society of Happy People to encourage people to express happiness and discourage parade-raining. Visit our website to find out about activities, including Happython, a 24-hour social media event. For info: Secret Society of Happy People, 425 Busher Dr, Lewisville, TX 75067. Phone: (972) 459-7031. E-mail: pamelagail@sohp.com. Web: www.sohp.com.

HAWAII VOLCANOES NATIONAL PARK ESTABLISHED: ANNIVERSARY. Aug 1, 1916. Area of Hawaii's Hawaii Island, including active volcanoes Kilauea and Mauna Loa, was established as Hawaii National Park in 1916, but its name was changed to Hawaii Volcanoes National Park in 1961. For park info: Hawaii Volcanoes National Park, Hawaii National Park, HI 96718.

INDIANA STATE FAIR. Aug 1–17. Indiana State Fairgrounds, Indianapolis, IN. Top-rated livestock exhibition, top music and entertainment, giant midway and Pioneer Village's world-class harness racing. Est attendance: 900,000. For info: Andy Klotz, Public Relations Dir, Indiana State Fair, 1202 E 38th St, Indianapolis, IN 46205-2869. Phone: (317) 927-7577. Fax: (317) 927-7578. Web: www.indianastatefair.com.

INTERNATIONAL CLOWN WEEK. Aug 1–7. All over the world, clowns will be clowning around for a good cause this week. Originally proclaimed as a national week by President Richard Nixon in 1971, International Clown Week has blossomed in countries around the world—wherever there's a clown. Clowns have long been known as ambassadors of joy and goodwill, and this is the week we celebrate them and they give back by performing in the community. Annually, Aug 1–7.

JAMAICA: ABOLITION OF SLAVERY. Aug 1, 1834. National day. Spanish settlers introduced the slave trade into Jamaica in 1509 and sugarcane in 1640. Slavery continued until Aug 1, 1834, when it was abolished by the British.

KEY, FRANCIS SCOTT: BIRTH ANNIVERSARY. Aug 1, 1779. American attorney, social worker, poet and author of the US national anthem. While on a legal mission, Key was detained on a ship off Baltimore, MD, during the British bombardment of Fort McHenry on the night of Sept 13–14, 1814. Thrilled to see the American flag still flying over the fort at daybreak, Key wrote the poem "The Star-Spangled Banner." Printed in the *Baltimore American* Sept 21, 1814, it was soon popularly sung to the music of an old English tune, "Anacreon in Heaven." It did not become the official US national anthem until 117 years later when, on Mar 3, 1931, President Herbert Hoover signed into law an act for that purpose. Key was born at Frederick County, MD, and died at Baltimore, Jan 11, 1843.

LOLLAPALOOZA. Aug 1–3 (tentative). Grant Park, Chicago, IL. Music festival started in 1991 by Perry Farrell. Today's Lollapalooza spans more than 115 acres, a diverse array of more than 130 artists, multiple stages and lots more. Annually, the first weekend in August. For info: Lollapalooza. E-mail: info@lollapalooza.com. Web: www.lollapalooza.com.

LUGHNASADH. Aug 1. (Also called August Eve, Lammas Eve, Lady Day Eve and Feast of Bread.) One of the "Greater Sabbats" during the Wiccan year, Lughnasadh marks the first harvest. Annually, Aug 1.

MELVILLE, HERMAN: BIRTH ANNIVERSARY. Aug 1, 1819. American author and poet, best known for his epic novel, *Moby-Dick.* Its first sentence—"Call me Ishmael."—is one of the most famous in literature. In his Civil War poetry Melville wrote, "All wars are boyish, and are fought by boys." Born at New York, NY, Melville died there Sept 28, 1891.

MITCHELL, MARIA: BIRTH ANNIVERSARY. Aug 1, 1818. An interest in her father's hobby and an ability for mathematics resulted in Maria Mitchell becoming the first female professional astronomer. In 1847, while assisting her father in a survey of the sky for the US Coast Guard, Mitchell discovered a new comet and determined its orbit. She received many honors for this work, including being elected to the American Academy of Arts and Sciences—its first woman. Mitchell joined the staff at Vassar Female College in 1865—the first US female professor of astronomy—and in 1873 was a cofounder of the Association for the Advancement of Women. Born at Nantucket, MA, Mitchell died June 28, 1889, at Lynn, MA.

MTV PREMIERE: ANNIVERSARY. Aug 1, 1981. The all music video channel debuted on this date. VH1, another music channel owned by MTV Networks that is aimed at older pop music fans, premiered in 1985.

MUSIKFEST. Aug 1–10. Bethlehem, PA. Showcasing more than 500 musical performances on 14 indoor and outdoor stages throughout Bethlehem. The 10-day event also features delicious foods and desserts, children's activities, visual arts and fine crafts and a closing-night fireworks display. Est attendance: 1,000,000. For info: ArtsQuest, 25 W Third St, Bethlehem, PA 18015-1238. Phone: (610) 332-1300. Fax: (610) 332-1310. E-mail: info@artsquest.org. Web: www.musikfest.org.

NATIONAL CZECH FESTIVAL. Aug 1–3. Wilber, NE. 53rd annual. Festival to promote preservation of Czech culture, foods, traditions. With accordion, polka and Czech band music; three parades; national queen contest; art show; Czech dinners; programs; fellowship; reunions. Annually, the first weekend in August. Est attendance: 50,000. For info: Nebraska Czechs of Wilber, PO Box 652, Wilber, NE 68465. Web: www.nebraskaczechsofwilber.com.

NATIONAL IMMUNIZATION AWARENESS MONTH. Aug 1–31. Immunization is critical to maintaining health and preventing life-threatening diseases among people of all ages and cultures throughout the US. Each year in the US, tens of thousands of people die because of vaccine-preventable diseases or their complications, and even more experience pain, suffering and disability. This month calls attention to the importance of infant, child, adolescent and adult immunization and seeks to reduce disparities in vaccine use while maintaining public trust in its value and safety. Contact your health provider for more information.

August 2014	S	M	T	W	T	F	S
						1	2
	3	4	5	6	7	8	9
	10	11	12	13	14	15	16
	17	18	19	20	21	22	23
	24	25	26	27	28	29	30
	31						

NATIONAL MINORITY DONOR AWARENESS DAY. Aug 1. Intensive awareness campaign focuses on obstacles related to minorities and organ donation, promotes healthy living and disease prevention to decrease the need for transplantation and reaches out to all ethnic groups. Observances have included prayer breakfasts, health walks and donor drives. For info: US Dept of Health and Human Services, 200 Independence Ave SW, Washington, DC 20201. Phone: (877) 696-6775 or (202) 619-0257. Web: www.organdonor.gov.

NATIONAL SPINAL MUSCULAR ATROPHY AWARENESS MONTH. Aug 1–31. To promote awareness of this congenital disease. For info: Families of Spinal Muscular Atrophy, 925 Busse Rd, Elk Grove Village, IL 60007. Phone: (800) 886-1762. E-mail: info@fsma.org. Web: www.fsma.org.

NATIONAL TRAFFIC AWARENESS MONTH. Aug 1–31. To educate drivers of the serious repercussions of today's technology, distractions and issues, such as in-vehicle cell phone use, handsfree devices and GPS, as well as passenger interaction. The National Traffic Safety Institute's unique ideology: Values + Attitude = Behavior. For info: National Traffic Safety Institute, 618 E South St, Ste 556, Orlando, FL 32801. Phone: (407) 992-6238. E-mail: asmith@ntsi.com. Web: www.ntsi.com.

NEUROSURGERY OUTREACH MONTH. Aug 1–31. A month to help educate the public about the role of the neurosurgeon in treating a wide range of medical conditions and diseases. The American Association of Neurological Surgeons offers a large array of neurosurgical topics on its website under "Patient Information." For info: AANS, 5550 Meadowbrook Dr, Rolling Meadows, IL 60008. Phone: (847) 378-0500. Fax: (847) 378-0600. Web: www.AANS.org.

NEW JERSEY STATE FAIR®/SUSSEX COUNTY FARM AND HORSE SHOW. Aug 1–10. Sussex County Fairgrounds, Augusta, NJ. The state's largest agricultural fair also includes horse shows, educational exhibits, carnival, vendors, fair food, entertainment and much more. Est attendance: 175,000. For info: New Jersey State Fair, 37 Plains Rd, Augusta, NJ 07822. Phone: (973) 948-5500. Fax: (973) 948-0147. E-mail: thefair@njstatefair.org. Web: www.njstatefair.org.

OAK RIDGE ATOMIC PLANT BEGUN: ANNIVERSARY. Aug 1, 1943. Ground was broken at Oak Ridge, TN, for the first plant built to manufacture the uranium 235 needed to make an atomic bomb. The plant was largely completed by July 1944 at a final cost of $280 million. By August 1945 the total cost for development of the A-bomb ran to $1 billion.

QUILT EXHIBITION. Aug 1–Sept 21. Woodstock, VT. 27th annual. A juried showing of quilts made by Windsor County quilters. Daily quilting demonstrations and activities. Est attendance: 9,700. For info: Billings Farm and Museum, Rte 12 N, Woodstock, VT 05091. GPS address: 69 Old River Rd, Woodstock, VT 05091. Phone: (802) 457-2355. Fax: (802) 457-4663. E-mail: info@billingsfarm.org. Web: www.billingsfarm.org.

RESPECT FOR PARENTS DAY. Aug 1. A day set aside to think of the positive things parents contribute to society. Annually, Aug 1. For info: Marilyn Dalrymple. E-mail: marilyn160@verizon.net. Web: marilyn_93535.tripod.com.

ROUNDS RESOUNDING DAY. Aug 1. To sing rounds, catches and canons in folk contrapuntal tradition. Motto: "As rounds resound and resound, all the world's joined in a circle of harmony." Annually, Aug 1. For info: Gloria T. Delamar, Founder, Rounds Resounding Society. E-mail: glo@delamar.org. Web: www.delamar.org/roundsresoundingsociety.htm.

"THE RUSH LIMBAUGH SHOW" NATIONAL RADIO PREMIERE: ANNIVERSARY. Aug 1, 1988. Conservative political commentator and radio personality Rush Limbaugh began his nationally syndicated show on this date with 56 stations. It quickly became the nation's top-rated show and rejuvenated the radio talk format. Today, more than 645 stations carry the program to an estimated 20 million listeners.

SCOTLAND: EDINBURGH FESTIVAL FRINGE. Aug 1–25. Edinburgh. The largest arts festival in the world. Three weeks of nonstop entertainment with more than 2,500 different events in 250 venues around the city, including theater, comedy, dance, music and children's shows. Est attendance: 1,000,000. For info: Edinburgh Festival Fringe, 180 High St, Edinburgh, Scotland EH1 1QS. Phone: (44) (131) 226-0026. Fax: (44) (131) 226-0016. E-mail: admin@edfringe.com. Web: www.edfringe.com.

SCOTLAND: THE ROYAL EDINBURGH MILITARY TATTOO: THE MAIN EVENT. Aug 1–23. Edinburgh Castle, Edinburgh, Lothian. Display of military color and pageantry held at night on the floodlit esplanade of Edinburgh Castle. A unique blend of music, ceremony, entertainment and theater. Est attendance: 217,000. For info: The Royal Edinburgh Military Tattoo, The Tattoo Office, 32 Market St, Edinburgh, Scotland EH1 1QB. Phone: (44) (131) 225-1188. Fax: (44) (131) 225-8627. E-mail: tickets@edintattoo.co.uk. Web: www.edintattoo.co.uk.

SIOUX EMPIRE FAIR. Aug 1–10. W.H. Lyon Fairgrounds, Sioux Falls, SD. 75th annual. Grandstand concerts, free entertainment, livestock exhibits, 4-H activities, flower and vegetable displays and craft exhibits. Camping available, with full hook-ups. Est attendance: 300,000. For info: Sioux Empire Fair, W.H. Lyon Fairgrounds, 100 N Lyon Blvd, Sioux Falls, SD 57107. Phone: (605) 367-7178. Fax: (605) 367-7886. E-mail: info@siouxempirefair.com. Web: www.siouxempirefair.org.

SPIDER-MAN DEBUTS: ANNIVERSARY. Aug 1, 1962. Stan Lee and Steve Ditko introduced a new superhero for Marvel Comics in issue #15 of *Amazing Fantasy* that hit newsstands in August: Spider-Man. Nerdy teen Peter Parker is bitten by a radioactive spider and soon discovers that he has the proportionate strength and agility of the spider—as well as web-shooting talents and "spidey sense." The arachnid crime fighter got his own comic book in March 1963 and quickly became the center of a multimedia empire.

SWITZERLAND: CONFEDERATION DAY. Aug 1. National holiday. Anniversary of the founding of the Swiss Confederation. Commemorates a pact made in 1291. Parades, patriotic gatherings, bonfires and fireworks. Young citizens' coming-of-age ceremonies. Observed since 600th anniversary of Swiss Confederation was celebrated in 1891.

TALL TIMBER DAYS FESTIVAL. Aug 1–3. Grand Rapids, MN. Festival features the Sheer Brothers Lumberjack Show, chainsaw carvers, arts and crafts and competitions. Families welcome. Annually, the first full weekend in August. Est attendance: 10,000. For info: Tall Timber Days, PO Box 134, Grand Rapids, MN 55744. E-mail: talltimberdays@yahoo.com. Web: www.visitgrandrapids.com or www.talltimberdays.com.

TRINIDAD AND TOBAGO: EMANCIPATION DAY. Aug 1. Public holiday. Slavery was abolished in all British colonies on this day in 1834. Also called Discovery Day.

UNITED KINGDOM: MINDEN DAY. Aug 1. Day observed by several British Army units to commemorate the bravery shown by their regimental predecessors at the Battle of Minden on Aug 1, 1759. The battle, which was part of the Seven Years' War, saw outnumbered allied Anglo and German forces defeat French armies in northern Germany. According to legend, British soldiers picked roses as they advanced to battle, placing them on their uniforms. Today, regiments wear red, white or yellow roses in their caps to remember the men who fought and died.

US CUSTOMS: 225th ANNIVERSARY. Aug 1, 1789. "The first US customs officers began to collect the revenue and enforce the Tariff Act of July 4, 1789, on this date. Since then, the customhouse and the customs officer have stood as symbols of national pride and sovereignty at ports of entry along the land and sea borders of our country." (From Presidential Proclamation 4306.)

WALES: NATIONAL EISTEDDFOD OF WALES. Aug 1–9. Festival Fields, Millennium Coastal Park, Llanelli. In 1880 the National Eisteddfod association was formed and charged with the responsibility of staging an annual festival to be held in North and South Wales alternately, and with the exception of 1914 and 1940, this target has been successfully achieved. The National Eisteddfod of Wales is a cultural event with competitive festivals of music, drama, literature, art and crafts. All events conducted in Welsh with simultaneous translation into English available. Est attendance: 160,000. For info: Natl Eisteddfod of Wales, 40 Parc Ty Glas, Llanishen, Cardiff, Wales, UK CF14 5DU. Phone: (44) (845) 4090-300. Fax: (44) (29) 2076-3737. E-mail: gwyb@eisteddfod.org.uk. Web: www.eisteddfod.org.uk.

WARSAW UPRISING: 70th ANNIVERSARY. Aug 1, 1944. Having received radio reports from Moscow promising aid from Russia's Red Army, the Polish Home Army rose up against the Nazi oppressors. At 5 PM thousands of windows were thrown open and Polish patriots, 40,000 strong, began shooting at German soldiers in the streets. The Germans responded by throwing eight divisions into the battle. Despite appeals from the London-based Polish government-in-exile, no assistance was forthcoming from the Allies, and after two months of horrific fighting the rebellion was quashed.

WHAT WILL BE YOUR LEGACY MONTH. Aug 1–31. Many people do not realize how their actions affect others. They live their lives selfishly, not realizing the impact of their life choices on present and possibly future generations. What Will Be Your Legacy Month is a time for people to reflect on their past and present actions and vow to make positive changes that will affect generations. The seeds, whether positive or negative, that we plant in our children's lives will grow and reflect our teachings. For info: Martha J. Ross-Rodgers. Phone: (757) 543-9290. E-mail: Mrossrodge@aol.com. Web: www.jirehpublishers.com.

WORLD BREASTFEEDING WEEK. Aug 1–7. 21st annual. Breastfeeding advocates, healthcare professionals and social service agencies focus attention on the importance and benefits of breastfeeding. Fairs, picnics, fund-raising and government proclamations highlight the week. Also, commemorates signing of Innocenti Declaration. Annually, Aug 1–7. For info: World Alliance for Breastfeeding Action. E-mail: wbw@waba.org. Web: www.worldbreastfeedingweek.org.

WORLD LUNG CANCER DAY. Aug 1. 3rd annual. A day set aside to support, honor, encourage and commemmorate all those affected by lung cancer. Dedicated to the people affected by this disease. This is a nonpolitical and nonorganizational day of recognition and remembrance. In the US, it has been proclaimed in numerous states and cities, and worldwide, it has been recognized and celebrated. Annually, Aug 1. For info: Betty Thompson, Lung Cancer Survivors Foundation, PO Box 55041, Valencia, CA 91385. Web: www.facebook.com/LCSurvivors.

WORLD WIDE WEB: ANNIVERSARY. Aug 1, 1990. The creation of what would become the World Wide Web was suggested this month in 1990 by Tim Berners-Lee and Robert Cailliau at CERN, the European Laboratory for Particle Physics at Switzerland. By October they had designed a prototype Web browser. They also introduced HTML (hypertext markup language) and the URL (universal resource locator). Mosaic, the first graphical Web browser, was designed by Marc Andreessen and released in 1993. By early 1993 there were 50 Web servers worldwide.

ZODIAC KILLER NEWSPAPER LETTERS: 45th ANNIVERSARY. Aug 1, 1969. The California newspapers *San Francisco Chronicle, San Francisco Examiner* and the *Vallejo Times Herald* received letters on this date from a killer claiming credit for three area murders that had occurred Dec 20, 1968, and July 4, 1969. Until these letters arrived, police authorities had not tied the killings together. The letters included a cryptogram claiming (falsely) to reveal the killer's identity. This was the beginning of a public terror campaign from a man calling himself the Zodiac. The Zodiac killed two more people (perhaps more) and sent many letters threatening the school children of San Francisco, CA. He was never identified.

BIRTHDAYS TODAY

Demián Bechir, 51, actor ("Weeds," *A Better Life*), born Mexico City, Mexico, Aug 1, 1963.

Tempestt Bledsoe, 41, talk show host, actress ("Tempestt," "The Cosby Show"), born Chicago, IL, Aug 1, 1973.

Robert Cray, 61, singer, guitarist, songwriter, born Columbus, GA, Aug 1, 1953.

Giancarlo Giannini, 72, actor (*Swept Away . . . , Seven Beauties*), born La Spezia, Italy, Aug 1, 1942.

David James, 44, soccer player, born Welwyn Garden City, England, Aug 1, 1970.

Nwankwo Kanu, 38, former soccer player, born Owerri, Nigeria, Aug 1, 1976.

August 2 — Saturday

DAY 214 **151 REMAINING**

ALBERT EINSTEIN'S ATOMIC BOMB LETTER: 75th ANNIVERSARY. Aug 2, 1939. Albert Einstein, world-famous scientist, a refugee from Nazi Germany, wrote a letter to US president Franklin D. Roosevelt, first mentioning a possible "new phenomenon . . . chain reactions . . . vast amounts of power." "A single bomb of this type," he wrote, "carried by boat and exploded in a port, might very well destroy the whole port together with some of the surrounding territory." Six years and four days later, Aug 6, 1945, the Japanese port of Hiroshima was destroyed by the first atomic bombing of a populated place.

BALDWIN, JAMES: 90th BIRTH ANNIVERSARY. Aug 2, 1924. Black American author noted for descriptions of black life in the US. Born at New York, NY. His best-known work, *Go Tell It on the Mountain*, was published in 1953. Died at St. Paul-de-Vence, France, Nov 30, 1987.

BATTLE OF BUSHY RUN 251st ANNIVERSARY OBSERVANCE. Aug 2–3. Harrison City, PA. This reenactment commemorates the decisive battle of Pontiac's War on Aug 5 and 6, 1763. Event includes a guided tour through the battle's historic camps and demonstrations of military crafts. Annually, the first weekend in August. Est attendance: 4,000. For info: Bushy Run Battlefield, PO Box 468, Harrison City, PA 15636-0468. Phone: (724) 527-5584. E-mail: brbhs@winbeam.com.

CHINA: DOUBLE SEVEN FESTIVAL. Aug 2. Also called Chinese Valentine's Day. Observed on seventh day of seventh lunar month. From a folktale in which two lovers (a cowherd and a weaver) are separated by the Milky Way. They are able to meet once a year when all the world's magpies form a bridge for the lovers.

COSTA RICA: FEAST OF OUR LADY OF ANGELS. Aug 2. National holiday. Celebrates Costa Rica's patron saint, the Virgin of Los Angeles.

August 2014	S	M	T	W	T	F	S
						1	2
	3	4	5	6	7	8	9
	10	11	12	13	14	15	16
	17	18	19	20	21	22	23
	24	25	26	27	28	29	30
	31						

DECLARATION OF INDEPENDENCE: OFFICIAL SIGNING: ANNIVERSARY. Aug 2, 1776. Contrary to widespread misconceptions, the 56 signers did not sign as a group and did not do so July 4, 1776. John Hancock and Charles Thomson signed only draft copies that day, the official day the Declaration of Independence was adopted by Congress. The signing of the official declaration occurred Aug 2, 1776, when 50 men probably took part. Later that year, five more apparently signed separately, and one added his name in a subsequent year. (From "Signers of the Declaration . . ." US Department of the Interior, 1975.) See also: "Declaration of Independence Approval and Signing: Anniversary" (July 4).

ENGLAND: ABERDEEN ASSET MANAGEMENT COWES WEEK. Aug 2–9. Cowes, Isle of Wight. Cowes Week is the largest, longest-running (since 1826) and most prestigious international sailing regatta in the world, with more than 1,000 boats across almost 40 classes of yacht racing. The event is a spectacle to behold. Est attendance: 100,000. For info: Cowes Week Ltd, 18 Bath Rd, Cowes, Isle of Wight, England PO31 7QN. Phone: (44) (198) 3295744. E-mail: admin@aamcowesweek.co.uk. Web: www.aamcowesweek.co.uk.

FANCY FARM PICNIC. Aug 2. Downtown Fancy Farm, KY. Southern hospitality at its best. The small community volunteers its time to entertain with games, prizes and great fun. Raffle for a brand-new car. Bingo with wonderful prizes. Down-home country dinners including the famous Fancy Farm Picnic Barbecue. Annually, the first Saturday in August. Est attendance: 20,000. For info: Sharon Hayden, c/o Fancy Farm Picnic, 2759 Carrico Rd, Fancy Farm, KY 42039. Phone: (270) 623-6129. E-mail: toddhayden@wk.net.

HUNT, LAMAR: BIRTH ANNIVERSARY. Aug 2, 1932. A legend in American professional sports, executive Hunt innovated the NFL, nurtured the growth of professional soccer in the US and cofounded the World Championship Tennis circuit. Hunt cofounded the AFL, which merged with the NFL. The AFL-NFL championship game was coined the "Super Bowl" by Hunt. He owned the Kansas City Chiefs and several soccer teams. Hunt also cofounded the NASL and Major League Soccer, and in recognition for that, America's oldest sporting tournament, the US Open Cup, was renamed for him. Hunt was a Hall of Famer in football, soccer and tennis. Born in El Dorado, AR, Hunt died in his longtime home of Dallas, TX, on Dec 13, 2006.

IRAQ INVADES KUWAIT: ANNIVERSARY. Aug 2, 1990. On orders of President Saddam Hussein, the Iraqi army invaded Kuwait. Hussein claimed that Kuwait presented a serious threat to Iraq's economic existence by overproducing oil and driving prices down on the world market. After conquering the capital, Kuwait City, Hussein installed a military government in Kuwait, prior to annexing it to Iraq on the claim that Kuwait was historically part of Iraq. This led to the 100-hour war against Iraq, Operation Desert Storm.

LEAGUE OF NH CRAFTSMEN ANNUAL CRAFTSMEN'S FAIR. Aug 2–10. Mount Sunapee Resort, Newbury, NH. 81st annual. "America's oldest crafts fair." More than 200 crafts booths, Living with Crafts exhibit, CraftWear exhibit, sculpture garden, roving performers, children's activities and more. Est attendance: 30,000. For info: League of NH Craftsmen, 49 S Main St, Concord, NH 03301. Phone: (603) 224-3375. Fax: (603) 225-8452. Web: www.nhcrafts.org.

L'ENFANT, PIERRE CHARLES: BIRTH ANNIVERSARY. Aug 2, 1754. The architect, engineer and Revolutionary War officer who designed the plan for the city of Washington, DC, L'Enfant was born at Paris, France. He died at Prince Georges County, MD, June 14, 1825.

LOY, MYRNA: BIRTH ANNIVERSARY. Aug 2, 1905. America's favorite leading lady of the 1930s, Loy was born Myrna Adele Williams near Helena, MT. She soared to fame as the madcap New York sophisticate Nora Charles in the Thin Man movies with William Powell (Nick Charles). She also starred in the critically acclaimed *The Best Years of Our Lives* (1946). After a career spanning seven decades, she was awarded an honorary Oscar in 1991 and died at New York, NY, Dec 14, 1993.

MACEDONIA: NATIONAL DAY. Aug 2. Commemorates the nationalist uprising against the Ottoman Empire in 1903. Called Prophet

Elias Day or Illinden. (See also: "Saint Elias Day (Illinden): Macedonian Uprising: Anniversary" below.)

NATIONAL MUSTARD DAY. Aug 2. Middleton, WI. Mustard lovers across the nation pay tribute to the king of condiments by slathering their favorite mustard on hot dogs, pretzels, circus peanuts and all things edible. The National Mustard Museum holds the world's largest collection of mustards and mustard memorabilia. Activities include the mustard games, live music and lots of great food (with mustard, of course!). Ketchup is not allowed. Join in the mustard college fight song with the "POUPON U" marching band. Annually, the first Saturday in August. Est attendance: 6,000. For info: Barry M. Levenson, Curator, The National Mustard Museum, 7477 Hubbard Ave, Middleton, WI 53562. Phone: (800) 438-6878. E-mail: curator@mustardmuseum.com. Web: www.mustardmuseum.com.

O'CONNOR, CARROLL: 90th BIRTH ANNIVERSARY. Aug 2, 1924. Television, stage and screen actor born in New York, NY. He was best known for his portrayal of the bigoted, blue-collar Archie Bunker on "All in the Family." He played the role of Bunker from 1971 to 1979 and was nominated for eight Emmy Awards, winning four. He won a fifth Emmy in 1989 for "In the Heat of the Night." He was also inducted into the Television Hall of Fame in 1989. He died at Culver City, CA, on June 21, 2001.

REHOBOTH BEACH SANDCASTLE CONTEST. Aug 2. Fisherman's Beach, Rehoboth Beach, DE. 36th Annual. More than 100 teams and 800 participants are expected to express their artistic flair. Past creations have included swamp animals, mermaids, pyramids, crabs, dolphins, sharks and of course traditional sandcastles. Beachgoers who would rather watch than work are welcome to view the incredible creations free of charge. Registration begins at 8:30 AM and judging begins at 3:00 PM. Awards announced at approximately 5:00 PM. Annually, the first Saturday in August. For info: Rehoboth Beach-Dewey Beach Chamber of Commerce, PO Box 216, Rehoboth Beach, DE 19971. Phone: (800) 441-1329. Fax: (302) 227-8351. E-mail: rehoboth@beach-fun.com. Web: www.beach-fun.com.

SAINT ELIAS DAY (ILLINDEN): MACEDONIAN UPRISING: ANNIVERSARY. Aug 2, 1903. Most sacred, honored and celebrated day of the Macedonian people. Anniversary of the uprising of Macedonians against the Ottoman Empire. Turkish reprisals against the insurgents were ruthless, including the destruction of 105 villages and the execution of more than 1,700 noncombatants.

STRAIGHT, BEATRICE: 100th BIRTH ANNIVERSARY. Aug 2, 1914. Stage and screen actress born at Old Westbury, NY. She won a Best Supporting Actress Tony in the original stage production of *The Crucible* (1953) and a Best Supporting Actress Oscar for her role in *Network* (1977). She died Apr 7, 2001, at North Ridge, CA.

US VIRGIN ISLANDS NATIONAL PARK ESTABLISHED: ANNIVERSARY. Aug 2, 1956. The US Virgin Islands, including areas on St. John and St. Thomas, were established as a national park and preserve. On Oct 5, 1962, the Virgin Islands National Park was enlarged to encompass offshore areas, including coral reefs, shorelines and sea grass beds.

BIRTHDAYS TODAY

Joanna Cassidy, 70, actress ("Buffalo Bill," *Under Fire*), born Camden, NJ, Aug 2, 1944.

Wes Craven, 75, writer, director (*A Nightmare on Elm Street, Scream, Red Eye*), born Cleveland, OH, Aug 2, 1939.

James Fallows, 65, journalist, former editor (*US News & World Report*), born Philadelphia, PA, Aug 2, 1949.

David Ferrer, 32, tennis player, born Javea, Spain, Aug 2, 1982.

Edward Furlong, 37, actor (*American History X, Before and After, Terminator 2*), born Glendale, CA, Aug 2, 1977.

Kathryn Harrold, 64, actress ("I'll Fly Away," "The Larry Sanders Show," *Modern Romance*), born Tazewell, VA, Aug 2, 1950.

Victoria Jackson, 55, actress ("Saturday Night Live," *I Love You to Death*), born Miami, FL, Aug 2, 1959.

Peter O'Toole, 81, actor (*Venus, Lawrence of Arabia, Becket*), born Connemara, Ireland, Aug 2, 1933.

Mary-Louise Parker, 50, actress (Tony for *Proof*; "Weeds," *Fried Green Tomatoes*), born Fort Jackson, SC, Aug 2, 1964.

Huston Street, 31, baseball player, born Austin, TX, Aug 2, 1983.

Michael Weiss, 38, figure skater, born Washington, DC, Aug 2, 1976.

Sam Worthington, 38, actor (*Avatar, Clash of the Titans*), born Godalming, Surrey, England, Aug 2, 1976.

August 3 — Sunday

DAY 215 **150 REMAINING**

AMERICAN FAMILY DAY IN ARIZONA. Aug 3. Observed in Arizona on the first Sunday in August. The observance date is designated by statute.

ASSISTANCE DOG WEEK. Aug 3–9. Assistance dogs transform the lives of their human partners with debilitating physical and mental disabilities by serving as a companion, helper, aide, best friend and close member of the family. Assistance dogs include service dogs, guide dogs, hearing alert dogs and alert/seizure response dogs. They can be from a variety of breeds including, but not limited to, Labrador retrievers, golden retrievers and standard poodles, as well as shelter dogs. Please celebrate the selfless love and devotion these dogs so humbly provide to their disabled partners by observing Assistance Dog Week. For info: Marcie Davis, 59 Wildflower Way, Santa Fe, NM 87506. Phone: (505) 424-6631. Fax: (505) 424-6632. E-mail: mdavis@workinglikedogs.com. Web: www.workinglikedogs.com.

BURRO RACE. Aug 3. Leadville, CO. International Pack Burro Race leaves from Main Street up Mosquito Pass and back. Est attendance: 3,500. For info: Chamber of Commerce, Box 861, Leadville, CO 80461. Phone: (719) 486-3900 or (888) 532-3845. Fax: (719) 486-8478. E-mail: info@leadvilleboomdays.com. Web: www.leadvilleboomdays.com.

COLUMBUS SAILS FOR THE NEW WORLD: ANNIVERSARY. Aug 3, 1492. Christopher Columbus, "Admiral of the Ocean Sea," set sail half an hour before sunrise from Palos, Spain, on this date. With three ships, *Niña*, *Pinta* and *Santa Maria*, and a crew of 90, he sailed "for Cathay" but found instead a New World of the Americas, first landing at Guanahani (San Salvador Island in the Bahamas) on Oct 12. See also: "Columbus Day" (Oct 12).

EQUATORIAL GUINEA: ARMED FORCES DAY. Aug 3. National holiday.

GUINEA-BISSAU: COLONIZATION MARTYRS' DAY. Aug 3. National holiday. Also called Pidjiguiti Martyrs' Day. Commemorates the massacre of 50 striking workers at the Pidjiguiti Docks on Aug 3, 1959, by colonial police.

ITALY: JOUST OF THE QUINTANA. Aug 3. Ascoli/Piceno. The first Sunday in August is set aside for the Torneo della Quintana, a historical pageant with 15th-century costumes.

KUHN, MARGARET (MAGGIE): BIRTH ANNIVERSARY. Aug 3, 1905. When she was forced into retirement because she'd reached the age of 65, Maggie Kuhn founded the Gray Panthers organization to fight age discrimination. Subsequently she waged a battle that resulted in the banning of mandatory retirements. Born at Buffalo, NY, Kuhn died Apr 22, 1995, at Philadelphia, PA.

MOON PHASE: FIRST QUARTER. Aug 3. Moon enters First Quarter phase at 8:50 PM, EDT.

NATIONAL EXERCISE WITH YOUR CHILD WEEK. Aug 3–9. This week encourages parents and guardians to exercise with their children as part of a healthier lifestyle. Exercise enables children to improve their overall well-being, to maintain a healthier weight and to reduce the risk of hypertension and cardiovascular disease. For info: Sheila Madison, PO Box 2733, Washington, DC 20013. Phone: (281) 750-2767. E-mail: info@sheilamadison.com. Web: www.sheilamadison.com.

NIGER: INDEPENDENCE DAY. Aug 3. Niger gained its independence from France on this day in 1960.

"PRIMETIME LIVE" TV PREMIERE: 25th ANNIVERSARY. Aug 3, 1989. Sam Donaldson and Diane Sawyer were the first hosts of this magazine show featuring investigative and consumer reports as well as human-interest stories.

PYLE, ERNEST TAYLOR: BIRTH ANNIVERSARY. Aug 3, 1900. Ernie Pyle was born at Dana, IN, and began his career in journalism in 1923. After serving as managing editor of the *Washington Daily News*, in 1935 he returned to his first journalistic love of working as a roving reporter. His column was syndicated by nearly 200 newspapers and often focused on figures behind the news. His reports of the bombing of London in 1940 and subsequent reports from Africa, Sicily, Italy and France earned him a Pulitzer Prize in 1944. He was killed by machine-gun fire at the Pacific island of Ie Shima, Apr 18, 1945.

SCOPES, JOHN T.: BIRTH ANNIVERSARY. Aug 3, 1900. Central figure in a cause célèbre (the "Scopes Trial" or the "Monkey Trial"), John Thomas Scopes was born at Paducah, KY. An obscure, 24-year-old schoolteacher at the Dayton, TN, high school in 1925, he became the focus of world attention. Scopes never uttered a word at his trial, which was a contest between two of America's best-known lawyers, William Jennings Bryan and Clarence Darrow. The trial, July 10–21, 1925, resulted in Scopes's conviction. He was fined $100 "for teaching evolution" in Tennessee. The verdict was upset on a technicality, and the statute he was accused of breaching was repealed in 1967. Scopes died at Shreveport, LA, Oct 21, 1970.

SINGLE WORKING WOMEN'S WEEK. Aug 3–9. Single working women today do it all. They bring home the bacon, fry it—and do the dishes. They earn the money, buy the groceries—and take out the garbage. They feed, nurture and clean up after the pets. This week celebrates the single women who make the modern world a better place—and who find the money, time and energy to lovingly support others. Pick a day or two and buy your favorite single working woman a gift—or do a chore for her. Annually, the week that includes Aug 4, which is Single Working Women's Day. For info: Single Working Women's Affiliate Network (SWWAN), 942 N Wood St, Chicago, IL 60622. Phone: (773) 235-9363. E-mail: info@swwan.org. Web: www.swwan.org.

SISTERS' DAY®. Aug 3. Celebrating the spirit of sisterhood: sisters nationwide show appreciation and give recognition to one another for the special relationship they share. Send a card, make a phone call or share memories, photos, flowers and candy. Sisters may include biological sisters, sorority sisters, sisterly friends, etc. Annually, the first Sunday in August. Please call for a press kit. For info: Tricia Eleogram, 5112 Normandy Ave, Memphis, TN 38117. Phone: (901) 681-2145 or (901) 497-8362. Fax: (901) 754-9923. E-mail: triciaeleogram@gmail.com.

SWISS VOLKSFEST. Aug 3. New Glarus, WI. Celebration of Swiss Independence Day with a program of traditional Swiss entertainment, including choral folklore music, yodeling, flag throwing, thalerschwingen, alphorn playing and accordion music. Annually, the first Sunday in August. Est attendance: 2,000. For info: Volksfest, New Glarus Chamber of Commerce, PO Box 713, New Glarus, WI 53574. Phone: (608) 527-2095 or (800) 527-6838. E-mail: info@swisstown.com. Web: www.swisstown.com.

URIS, LEON: 90th BIRTH ANNIVERSARY. Aug 3, 1924. American novelist born to a family of Russian Jews at Baltimore, MD. His most successful novels were those that chronicled the Holocaust (1960's *Mila 18*) and the founding of Israel (1958's *Exodus*). His novels sold millions and were made into several feature films. Later titles included *QB VII*, a fictionalized account of his own trial for libel, and *Trinity*, which followed the life of three generations of an Irish family. Uris died June 21, 2003, at Shelter Island, NY.

	S	M	T	W	T	F	S
August 2014						1	2
	3	4	5	6	7	8	9
	10	11	12	13	14	15	16
	17	18	19	20	21	22	23
	24	25	26	27	28	29	30
	31						

BIRTHDAYS TODAY

Tony Bennett, 88, singer, born Anthony Dominick Benedetto at New York, NY, Aug 3, 1926.

Steven Berkoff, 77, actor, director, writer (*A Clockwork Orange, Beverly Hills Cop*), born London, England, Aug 3, 1937.

Tom Brady, 37, football player, born San Mateo, CA, Aug 3, 1977.

P.D. James, 94, mystery novelist, born Phyllis Dorothy James at Oxford, England, Aug 3, 1920.

Karlie Kloss, 22, model, born Chicago, IL, Aug 3, 1992.

Evangeline Lilly, 35, actress ("Lost"), born Fort Saskatchewan, AB, Canada, Aug 3, 1979.

Ryan Lochte, 30, Olympic swimmer, television personality ("What Would Ryan Lochte Do?"), born Rochester, NY, Aug 3, 1984.

John McGinley, 55, actor (*Platoon, Born on the Fourth of July*, "Scrubs"), born New York, NY, Aug 3, 1959.

Chris Murphy, 41, US Senator (D, Connecticut), born White Plains, NY, Aug 3, 1973.

Alejandro García Padilla, 43, Governor of Puerto Rico, born Coama, Puerto Rico, Aug 3, 1971.

Martin Sheen, 74, actor (*Apocalypse Now*, "The West Wing"), born Ramon Estevez at Dayton, OH, Aug 3, 1940.

Hannah Simone, 34, model, actress ("The New Girl"), born London, England, Aug 3, 1980.

Martha Stewart, 73, lifestyle consultant, television personality, writer, born Nutley, NJ, Aug 3, 1941.

Isaiah Washington, 51, actor ("Grey's Anatomy," *Romeo Must Die, Exit Wounds*), born Houston, TX, Aug 3, 1963.

Blaine Wilson, 40, former gymnast, born Columbus, OH, Aug 3, 1974.

August 4 — Monday

DAY 216 **149 REMAINING**

ANTIGUA AND BARBUDA: AUGUST MONDAY. Aug 4–5. The first Monday in August and the day following form the August Monday public holiday.

ARMSTRONG, LOUIS: BIRTH ANNIVERSARY. Aug 4, 1900 (or 1901). Jazz musician extraordinaire born at New Orleans, LA. Died at New York, NY, July 6, 1971. Armstrong often said he was born on the 4th of July, but documents in the Louis Armstrong Archives of Queens College, Flushing, NY, indicate that he was actually born Aug 4, 1900 or 1901. Asked to define jazz, Armstrong reportedly replied, "Man, if you gotta ask, you'll never know." The trumpet player was also known as Satchmo. He appeared in many films. Popular singles included "What a Wonderful World" and "Hello, Dolly" (with Barbra Streisand).

AUSTRALIA: PICNIC DAY. Aug 4. The first Monday in August is a bank holiday in New South Wales and Picnic Day in Northern Territory, Australia.

BAHAMAS: EMANCIPATION DAY. Aug 4. Public holiday in Bahamas. Annually, the first Monday in August. Commemorates the emancipation of slaves by the British in 1834.

BORDEN AX MURDERS: ANNIVERSARY. Aug 4, 1892. In a grisly scene, Andrew Jackson Borden, a wealthy area merchant, was found hacked to death in the parlor of his Fall River, MA, home. The body of his second wife, Abby Durfee Borden, lay upstairs. Lizzie Andrew Borden, home at the time, had discovered her father's lifeless form. She was arrested and tried for the murders, but the lack of solid evidence against her led to Borden's eventual acquittal. Debate over her guilt, innocence and motive has raged ever since. See also: "Lizzie Borden Verdict: Anniversary" (June 20).

BURKINA FASO: REVOLUTION DAY. Aug 4. National holiday. Commemorates 1983 coup.

CANADA: CIVIC HOLIDAY. Aug 4. The first Monday in August is observed as a holiday in seven of Canada's ten provinces. Civic holiday in Manitoba, New Brunswick, Northwest Territories, Ontario and Saskatchewan; British Columbia Day in British Columbia and Heritage Day in Alberta.

CIVIL RIGHTS WORKERS FOUND SLAIN: 50th ANNIVERSARY. Aug 4, 1964. After disappearing on June 21, three civil rights workers were found murdered and buried in an earthen dam outside Philadelphia, MS. The three young men were workers on the Mississippi Summer Project organized by the Student Nonviolent Coordinating Committee (SNCC) to increase black voter registration. Prior to their disappearance, James Chaney, Andrew Goodman and Michael Schwerner were detained by Neshoba County police on charges of speeding. When their car was found, burned, on June 23, President Lyndon Johnson ordered an FBI search for the men.

COAST GUARD DAY. Aug 4. Celebrates anniversary of founding of the Revenue Cutter Service in 1790, which merged with the Life Saving Service in 1915 to become the US Coast Guard.

COLORADO DAY. Aug 4. Colorado. Annually, the first Monday in August. Commemorates Admission Day, Aug 1, 1876, when Colorado became the 38th state.

CUNNINGHAM, GLENN: BIRTH ANNIVERSARY. Aug 4, 1909. "Kansas Ironman" Glenn Clarence Cunningham—American track athlete, 1934–37 world-record holder for the mile and member of the US Olympic teams in 1932 and 1936—was born at Atlanta, KS. On June 16, 1934, at Princeton, NJ, Cunningham set a world record for the mile (4:06.7) that stood for three years. After WWII, he and his wife opened a youth ranch and cared for more than 10,000 foster children plus 10 of their own. Cunningham died at Menifee, AR, Mar 10, 1988.

EXHIBITOR APPRECIATION WEEK. Aug 4–8. An opportunity for trade/consumer show organizers to recognize and appreciate the thousands of exhibitors who make their events possible. For info: Susan Friedmann, CSP, The Tradeshow Coach, 2301 Saranac Ave, Lake Placid, NY 12946. Phone: (518) 523-1320. E-mail: susan@thetradeshowcoach.com. Web: www.thetradeshowcoach.com.

GRENADA: EMANCIPATION DAY. Aug 4. Grenada observes a public holiday annually on the first Monday in August. Commemorates the emancipation of slaves by the British in 1834.

ICELAND: AUGUST HOLIDAY. Aug 4. National holiday. The first Monday in August. Commemorates Iceland's constitution of 1874.

JAMAICA: INDEPENDENCE DAY. Aug 4. National holiday observing Jamaica's independence from Britain Aug 6, 1962. Annually, the first Monday in August.

MANDELA ARREST: ANNIVERSARY. Aug 4, 1962. Nelson Rolihlahla Mandela, charismatic black South African lawyer and political activist, had been in conflict with the white government there much of his life. Acquitted of a treason charge after a trial that lasted from 1956 to 1961, he was apprehended again by security police Aug 4, 1962. The subsequent trial resulted in Mandela's being sentenced to five years in prison. In 1963 he was taken from the Pretoria prison to face a new trial—for sabotage, high treason and conspiracy to overthrow the government—and in June 1964 he was sentenced to life in prison. See also: "Mandela, Nelson: Prison Release Anniversary" (Feb 11).

NATIONAL BARGAIN HUNTING WEEK. Aug 4–10. A week encouraging shoppers and businesses to celebrate the thrill of the hunt—for bargains—and the triumph of their finds. Observed since 1996 on the first Monday through Sunday in August. For info: Debbie Keri-Brown, 652 Olde Towne Ave, #V, Columbus, OH 43214. Phone: (614) 226-1397. E-mail: bargainweek@yahoo.com. Web: http:\bargainhunting.webs.com.

OBAMA, BARACK H.: BIRTHDAY. Aug 4, 1961. 44th president of the US (2009–). Born at Honolulu, HI.

OLD FIDDLERS' CONVENTION. Aug 4–9. Galax, VA. 79th annual. Event features dance, folk songs and old-time and bluegrass music competition. Est attendance: 35,000. For info: Thomas L. Jones, Jr, Box 655, Galax, VA 24333. Phone: (276) 236-8541. Web: www.oldfiddlersconvention.com.

PATER, WALTER: 175th BIRTH ANNIVERSARY. Aug 4, 1839. Critic and essayist who, in such works as *The Renaissance* (1873) and *Marius the Epicurean* (1885), articulated the "arts for arts sake" philosophy that was key to the Pre-Raphaelite and Aestheticism movements. Such late 19th-century aesthetes as Oscar Wilde were influenced by Pater's writings. Pater was born at London, England, and died July 30, 1894, at Oxford.

PGA CHAMPIONSHIP. Aug 4–10. Valhalla Golf Club, Louisville, KY. The 96th championship conducted by the Professional Golfers' Association of America. Est attendance: 150,000. For info: PGA of America, 100 Ave of the Champions, Palm Beach Gardens, FL 33418. Phone: (561) 624-8495. Fax: (561) 624-8429. Web: www.pga.com.

PSYCHIC WEEK. Aug 4–8. To utilize the power of the psyche to bring peace, find lost individuals and concentrate "psychic power" on beneficial causes. Annually, the first week in August (Monday–Friday). (Created by the late Richard R. Falk.)

QUEEN ELIZABETH, THE QUEEN MOTHER: BIRTH ANNIVERSARY. Aug 4, 1900. A beloved member of the English royal family, the Queen "Mum" saw England through some of its most trying times in the 20th century. She was born Elizabeth Angela Marguerite Bowes-Lyon at London, England, and married the then Duke of York in 1923. When her husband was unexpectedly crowned King George VI in 1936 (after the abdication of Edward VIII), she became his strong and guiding support. She won the undying gratitude of her subjects, moreover, when she refused to move the royal family to the safety of the countryside during the German bombing of London in WWII. She died Mar 30, 2002.

RICHARD, MAURICE "ROCKET": BIRTH ANNIVERSARY. Aug 4, 1921. Hockey Hall of Fame right wing, born at Montreal, QC, Canada. Died May 27, 2000, at Montreal.

SCALIGER, JOSEPH JUSTUS: BIRTH ANNIVERSARY. Aug 4, 1540. (Old Style date.) French scholar who has been called the founder of scientific chronology. Born at Agen, France, the son of classical scholar Julius Caesar Scaliger. In 1582 he suggested a new system for measuring time and numbering years. His "Julian Period" (named for his father), which consisted of 7,980 consecutive years (beginning Jan 1, 4713 BC), is still in use by astronomers. He died at Leiden, Netherlands, Jan 21, 1609 (OS).

SCHUMAN, WILLIAM HOWARD: BIRTH ANNIVERSARY. Aug 4, 1910. American composer who won the first Pulitzer Prize for Composition and founded the Juilliard School of Music, born at New York City. His compositions include *American Festival Overture, New England Triptych*, the baseball opera *The Mighty Casey* and *On Freedom's Ground*, written for the centennial of the Statue of Liberty in 1986. He was instrumental in the conception of the Lincoln Center for the Performing Arts and served as its first president. In 1985 he was awarded a special Pulitzer Prize for his contributions. He also received a National Medal of Arts in 1985 and a Kennedy Center Honor in 1989. Schuman died at New York City, Feb 15, 1992.

SCOTLAND: SUMMER BANK HOLIDAY. Aug 4. Bank and public holiday in Scotland. The first Monday in August.

SHELLEY, PERCY BYSSHE: BIRTH ANNIVERSARY. Aug 4, 1792. Poet Percy Bysshe Shelley, one of the leading English Romantic poets and embodiment of a free spirit, was born at Warnham, Sussex. He lived abroad in Italy until his death at sea off the coast of Viareggio, just a month before his 30th birthday, July 8, 1822. Shelley's important works include "Ozymandias," published in 1818; "Ode to the West Wind," "The Cloud," "To a Skylark" and *Prometheus Unbound* in 1819; and *Adonais* (an elegy for John Keats) in 1821.

SINGLE WORKING WOMEN'S DAY. Aug 4. Honoring the many single working women who do it all. Part of Single Working Women's Week. For info: Single Working Women's Affiliate Network (SWWAN), 942 N Wood St, Chicago, IL 60622. Phone: (773) 571-4199. Fax: (312) 277-3722. E-mail: info@swwan.org. Web: www.swwan.org.

STURGIS RALLY. Aug 4–10. Sturgis, SD. 74th annual. The granddaddy of all motorcycle rallies and races. For almost seven decades the small community of Sturgis has welcomed motorcycle enthusiasts from around the world to a week of varied cycle racing, tours of the beautiful Black Hills, trade shows and thousands of bikes on display. Annually, beginning the Monday after the first full weekend in August. Est attendance: 350,000. For info: Sturgis.com, 511 W Jackson Blvd, Spearfish, SD 57783. Phone: (605) 642-8166. E-mail: info@blackhills.com. Web: www.sturgis.com.

August 2014	S	M	T	W	T	F	S
						1	2
	3	4	5	6	7	8	9
	10	11	12	13	14	15	16
	17	18	19	20	21	22	23
	24	25	26	27	28	29	30
	31						

UNITED KINGDOM AND BELGIUM: FIRST WORLD WAR CENTENARY OPENING DAY. Aug 4. Locations in Scotland, Belgium and England. The United Kingdom is commemorating the 100th anniversary of WWI with a four-year program, which is inaugurated by these opening day events. At Glasgow Cathedral, Glasgow, Scotland, there is a service for Commonwealth leaders, which is followed by a wreath laying at Glasgow's Cenotaph. At Mons, Belgium, there is a remembrance at the St. Symphorien Military Cemetery. A candlelit vigil of prayer and penitence takes place at Westminster Abbey, London, England, and finishes at 11 PM—the moment war was declared. For info: First World War Centenary. Web: www.gov.uk/ww1centenary.

US WOMEN'S AMATEUR (GOLF) CHAMPIONSHIP. Aug 4–10. Nassau Country Club, Glen Cove, NY. For info: USGA, Golf House, Championship Dept, PO Box 708, Far Hills, NJ 07931. Phone: (908) 234-2300. Fax: (908) 234-9687. E-mail: usga@usga.org. Web: www.usga.org.

ZAMBIA: YOUTH DAY. Aug 4. National holiday. Youth activities are the order of the day. The focal point is Lusaka's Independence Stadium. Annually, the first Monday in August.

BIRTHDAYS TODAY

Richard Belzer, 70, comedian, actor ("Law & Order: SVU," "Homicide: Life on the Street"), born Bridgeport, CT, Aug 4, 1944.

Roger Clemens, 52, former baseball player, born Dayton, OH, Aug 4, 1962.

Jeff Gordon, 43, race car driver, born Pittsboro, IN, Aug 4, 1971.

Daniel Dae Kim, 46, actor ("Lost," "24," "Hawaii Five-0"), born Pusan, South Korea, Aug 4, 1968.

Meghan Markle, 33, actress (*Horrible Bosses,* "Suits"), born Los Angeles, CA, Aug 4, 1981.

Barack Obama, 53, 44th President of the US, former US senator (D, Illinois), born Honolulu, HI, Aug 4, 1961.

Kristoffer Tabori, 62, actor ("Seventh Avenue," "Chicago Story"), born Los Angeles, CA, Aug 4, 1952.

Billy Bob Thornton, 59, actor (*Friday Night Lights, Bad Santa, Monster's Ball*), director, screenwriter (Oscar for *Sling Blade*), born Hot Springs, AR, Aug 4, 1955.

August 5 — Tuesday

DAY 217 | **148 REMAINING**

AIKEN, CONRAD: 125th BIRTH ANNIVERSARY. Aug 5, 1889. Poet, novelist, short-story writer and critic, born at Savannah, GA, and raised in New England. Winner of the Pulitzer Prize (1930), the National Book Award (1954), the Bollingen Prize (1956) and the National Medal for Literature (1969). He was also a consultant in poetry to the Library of Congress (1950–52)—now termed poet laureate. He believed, "In the evolution of man's consciousness, ever widening and deepening and subtilizing his awareness, and in his dedication of himself to this supreme task, man possesses all that he could possibly require in the way of a religious credo: when the half-gods go, the gods arrive; he can, if he only will, become divine." Aiken died at Savannhah, GA, Aug 17, 1973.

"AMERICAN BANDSTAND" TV PREMIERE: ANNIVERSARY. Aug 5, 1957. "American Bandstand" and Dick Clark are synonymous; he hosted the show for more than 30 years. "AB" started out as a local show at Philadelphia, PA, in 1952. Clark, then a disk jockey, took over as host at the age of 26. The format was simple: teens dancing, performers doing their latest hits and Clark introducing songs and listing the top 10 songs each week. This hour-long show was not only TV's longest-running musical series but also the first one devoted exclusively to rock and roll. The show was canceled six months after Clark turned over the hosting duties to David Hirsch in 1989.

ARMSTRONG, NEIL: BIRTH ANNIVERSARY. Aug 5, 1930. Astronaut and first man to walk on the moon, born at Wapakoneta, OH. Armstrong first flew in a Tin Goose aircraft at age 6 and could fly a plane before he could drive a car. He was a Navy fighter pilot during the Korean War, and later studied aeronautical engineering. An experimental test pilot for NASA in the 1950s, Armstrong became a candidate for the astronaut program due to his skill at piloting X-15 rocket planes. He flew *Gemini* spacecraft and trained on *Apollo* vehicles as well, and was ultimately chosen by NASA to command the mission to the moon. He took that "small step" on July 20, 1969. A quiet, humble man, he was startled by his own celebrity. He never returned to space but worked as an educator and businessman until his death at Cincinnati, OH, Aug 25, 2012.

BATTLE OF MOBILE BAY: 150th ANNIVERSARY. Aug 5, 1864. A Union fleet under Admiral David Farragut attempted to run past three Confederate forts into Mobile Bay, AL. After coming under fire, the Union fleet headed into a maze of underwater mines, known at that time as torpedoes. The ironclad *Tecumseh* was sunk by a torpedo, after which Farragut is said to have exclaimed, "Damn the torpedoes—full steam ahead!" The Union fleet was successful and Mobile Bay was secured.

BURKINA FASO: REPUBLIC DAY. Aug 5. Burkina Faso (formerly Upper Volta) gained autonomy from France in 1960.

CROATIA: HOMELAND THANKSGIVING DAY. Aug 5. National holiday.

ELIOT, JOHN: BIRTH ANNIVERSARY. Aug 5, 1604. (Old Style date.) American "Apostle to the Indians," translator of the Bible into an Indian tongue (the first Bible to be printed in America), was born at Hertfordshire, England. He died at Roxbury, MA, May 21, 1690 (OS).

FIRST ENGLISH COLONY IN NORTH AMERICA: ANNIVERSARY. Aug 5, 1583. Sir Humphrey Gilbert, English navigator and explorer, aboard his sailing ship, the *Squirrel*, sighted the Newfoundland coast and took possession of the area around St. John's harbor in the name of Queen Elizabeth I, thus establishing the first English colony in North America. Gilbert was lost at sea, in a storm off the Azores, on his return trip to England.

HUSTON, JOHN: BIRTH ANNIVERSARY. Aug 5, 1906. This larger-than-life Hollywood figure, son of the actor Walter Huston, spent his whole life before or behind the camera as an actor, writer and director. His first film, 1941's masterpiece of detective-noir, *The Maltese Falcon*, catapulted Humphrey Bogart away from gangster roles into dark heroic roles. Huston and Bogart collaborated on other great films: *The Treasure of the Sierra Madre* (which featured Huston's father in a Best Supporting Actor role), *Key Largo*, *The African Queen* and *Beat the Devil*. Born at Nevada, MO, Huston died Aug 28, 1987, at Middletown, RI, not long after completing his final film, *The Dead* (1987).

IRELAND: BANK HOLIDAY. Aug 5. Bank holiday in the Republic of Ireland.

LYNCH, THOMAS: BIRTH ANNIVERSARY. Aug 5, 1749. Signer, Declaration of Independence. Born Prince George's Parish, SC. Died 1779 (lost at sea, exact date of death unknown).

MERRICK, JOSEPH: BIRTH ANNIVERSARY. Aug 5, 1862. Born at Leicester, England, a young Merrick was forced into work as an itinerant sideshow attraction due to a severe case of what is now believed to have been Proteus Syndrome, a condition that causes head, bone and skin deformities. Known as "The Elephant Man," Merrick eventually took up residence at London Hospital in 1886. He died there Apr 11, 1890, of suffocation while he slept.

MONROE, MARILYN: DEATH ANNIVERSARY. Aug 5, 1962. The world fell in love with Monroe's unique combination of sensuality and approachability. She was the epitome of Hollywood glamour, making 29 films in her career. Her tragic death at age 36, at Los Angeles, CA, from an overdose of sleeping pills, is shrouded in controversy. She was born June 1, 1926, at Los Angeles.

NATIONAL NIGHT OUT. Aug 5. Designed to heighten crime prevention awareness and to promote police-community partnerships. Annually, the first Tuesday in August. For info: Matt A. Peskin, Dir, Natl Assn of Town Watch, PO Box 303, Wynnewood, PA 19096. Phone: (610) 649-7055 or (800) 648-3688. Fax: (610) 649-5456. E-mail: info@natw.org. Web: www.nationalnightout.org.

NATIONAL UNDERWEAR DAY. Aug 5. Each August, Freshpair.com celebrates all things underwear. From star-studded New York City parties and Times Square runway shows to 5,000 underwear online giveaways and specials promotions, the whole nation can celebrate underwear throughout the month. Since 80 percent of Americans are said to wear the same type of underwear their entire lives, Freshpair.com is on a mission to get people out of their boring tidy-whities and into something fun and new. For info: Freshpair Inc, 611 Broadway, Ste 523, New York, NY 10012. Phone: (212) 505-6900. Fax: (212) 202-4754. Web: www.nationalunderwearday.com or www.freshpair.com.

OMARR, SYDNEY: BIRTH ANNIVERSARY. Aug 5, 1926. Born Sidney Kimmelman at Philadelphia, PA, this world-famous astrologer became fascinated by numerology and astrology and changed his name to Sydney Omarr at age 15. He began contributing to astrology magazines and eventually became well known in Hollywood. He wrote dozens of books, an average of 13 per year, which sold more than 50 million copies. His newspaper astrology column was syndicated in more than 200 newspapers. He died Jan 16, 2003, at Santa Monica, CA.

TISHA B'AV OR FAST OF AB. Aug 5. Hebrew calendar date: Ab 9, 5774. Commemorates and mourns the destruction of the first and second Temples in Jerusalem (586 BC and AD 70). Began at sundown Aug 4.

WALLENBERG, RAOUL: BIRTH ANNIVERSARY. Aug 5, 1912. Swedish architect Raoul Gustaf Wallenberg was born at Stockholm, Sweden. He is credited with saving 100,000 Jews from almost certain death at the hands of the Nazis during WWII. Wallenberg was arrested by Soviet troops at Budapest, Hungary, Jan 17, 1945, and according to the official Soviet press agency, Tass, died in prison at Moscow, July 17, 1947 (although unconfirmed reports claim he died years later). He was the second person in history (Winston Churchill was the first) to be granted honorary American citizenship (US House of Representatives voted 396–2, Sept 22, 1981).

WORLD'S FAIR OF MONEY. Aug 5–9. Chicago, IL. See coins worth millions! Buy, sell and trade coins, paper money, medals and tokens. Numismatic education programs, exhibits and family activities. Web: www.worldsfairofmoney.com For info: American Numismatic Assn, 818 N Cascade Ave, Colorado Springs, CO 80903. Phone: (800) 367-9723. Fax: (719) 634-4085. E-mail: pr@money.org. Web: www.worldsfairofmoney.com.

BIRTHDAYS TODAY

Loni Anderson, 68, actress ("WKRP in Cincinnati," *The Jayne Mansfield Story*), born St. Paul, MN, Aug 5, 1946.

Ja'net DuBois, 76, actress ("Good Times," "Beverly Hills 90210"), born Philadelphia, PA, Aug 5, 1938.

Patrick Aloysius Ewing, 52, Hall of Fame basketball player, born Kingston, Jamaica, Aug 5, 1962.

Lorrie Fair, 36, former soccer player, born Los Altos, CA, Aug 5, 1978.

Eric Hinske, 37, baseball player, born Menasha, WI, Aug 5, 1977.

John Olerud, 46, former baseball player, born Seattle, WA, Aug 5, 1968.

Brian Sandoval, 51, Governor of Nevada (R), born Redding, CA, Aug 5, 1963.

John Saxon, 78, actor ("Falcon Crest," *Enter the Dragon, A Nightmare on Elm Street*), born Brooklyn, NY, Aug 5, 1936.

Jonathan Silverman, 48, actor ("The Single Guy," *Weekend at Bernie's*), born Los Angeles, CA, Aug 5, 1966.

Erika Slezak, 68, actress ("One Life to Live"), born Los Angeles, CA, Aug 5, 1946.

Jesse Williams, 33, actor ("Grey's Anatomy"), born Chicago, IL, Aug 5, 1981.

August 6 — Wednesday

DAY 218 **147 REMAINING**

ATOMIC BOMB DROPPED ON HIROSHIMA: ANNIVERSARY. Aug 6, 1945. At 8:15 AM, local time, an American B-29 bomber, the *Enola Gay*, dropped an atomic bomb named "Little Boy" over the center of the city of Hiroshima, Japan. The bomb exploded about 1,800 feet above the ground, killing more than 105,000 civilians and destroying the city. It is estimated that another 100,000 people were injured and died subsequently as a direct result of the bomb and the radiation it produced. This was the first time in history that such a devastating weapon had been used by any nation.

BALL, LUCILLE: BIRTH ANNIVERSARY. Aug 6, 1911. Film and television pioneer and comedienne born at Jamestown, NY. In addition to her many film and television credits, Lucille Ball will always be remembered for her role in the 1950's CBS sitcom "I Love Lucy." As Lucy Ricardo, the wife of bandleader Ricky Ricardo (her real-life husband, Desi Arnaz), she exhibited a comedic style that became a trademark of early television comedy. She died Apr 26, 1989, at Los Angeles, CA.

BOLIVIA: INDEPENDENCE DAY. Aug 6. National holiday. Gained freedom from Spain in 1825. Named after Simón Bolivar.

CANADA: CANADIAN OPEN OLD TIME FIDDLE CHAMPIONSHIP. Aug 6–10. Shelburne, ON. This event features Canada's top fiddlers in competition for more than $17,000 in prizes! Festivities begin with an evening concert; the contest proper starts with the playdowns on Friday and concludes with the finals on Saturday evening. Come and enjoy Canada's top fiddlers competing for the most prestigious prize, the Canadian Open Champion. Est attendance: 25,000. For info: Shelburne Rotary Club, PO Box 27, Shelburne, ON L0N 1S0, Canada. Phone: (519) 925-8620. E-mail: fiddleshelburne@yahoo.ca. Web: www.shelburnefiddlecontest.on.ca.

ELECTROCUTION FIRST USED TO CARRY OUT DEATH PENALTY: ANNIVERSARY. Aug 6, 1890. At Auburn Prison, Auburn, NY, William Kemmler of Buffalo, NY, became the first man to be executed by electrocution. He had been convicted of the hatchet murder of his common-law wife, Matilde Ziegler, on Mar 28, 1889. This first attempt at using electrocution to carry out the death penalty was a botched procedure. As reported by George Westinghouse, Jr, "It has been a brutal affair. They could have done better with an axe."

FIRST WOMAN SWIMS THE ENGLISH CHANNEL: ANNIVERSARY. Aug 6, 1926. The first woman to swim the English Channel was 19-year-old Gertrude Ederle of New York, NY. Her swim was completed in 14 hours, 31 minutes.

FLEMING, ALEXANDER: BIRTH ANNIVERSARY. Aug 6, 1881. Sir Alexander Fleming, Scottish bacteriologist, discoverer of penicillin and 1945 Nobel Prize recipient, was born at Lochfield, Scotland. He died at London, England, Mar 11, 1955.

HIROSHIMA DAY. Aug 6. Memorial observances in many places for victims of the first atomic bombing of a populated place, which occurred at Hiroshima, Japan, in 1945, when an American B-29 bomber dropped an atomic bomb over the center of the city. More than 205,000 civilians died either immediately in the explosion or subsequently of radiation.

JAMAICA: INDEPENDENCE ACHIEVED: ANNIVERSARY. Aug 6, 1962. Jamaica attained its independence after centuries of British rule. Sir Alexander Bustamante became the first Jamaican Prime Minister.

JAPAN: PEACE FESTIVAL. Aug 6. Hiroshima. The festival held annually at Peace Memorial Park is observed in memory of the victims of the Aug 6, 1945, atomic bomb explosion there.

JUDGE CRATER DISAPPEARANCE: ANNIVERSARY. Aug 6, 1930. Anniversary of mysterious disappearance at age 41 of Joseph Force Crater, justice of the New York State Supreme Court. Never seen or heard from after disappearance on this date. Declared legally dead in 1939.

MISS CRUSTACEAN USA BEAUTY PAGEANT AND OCEAN CITY CREEP. Aug 6. 6th St Beach, Ocean City, NJ. Participants are hermit tree crabs. To determine the most beautiful and fastest tree crab on Earth. Begins at 1 PM, EST. Est attendance: 500. For info: Mark Soifer, PR Dir, City of Ocean City, City Hall, Ocean City, NJ 08226. Phone: (609) 525-9300 or (609) 364-4010 (cell). Fax: (609) 525-0301. E-mail: msoifer@hotmail.com.

MITCHUM, ROBERT: BIRTH ANNIVERSARY. Aug 6, 1917. Film actor (*The Night of the Hunter, The Story of GI Joe*), born at Bridgeport, CT. Died July 1, 1997, at Santa Barbara County, CA.

O'CONNELL, DANIEL: BIRTH ANNIVERSARY. Aug 6, 1775. Irish Catholic political leader Daniel O'Connell, known as "the Liberator" for his role in achieving the right of Catholics to sit in parliament, was born near Cahirciveen, County Kerry. He died at age 81, May 15, 1847, at Genoa, Italy.

PARSONS, LOUELLA: BIRTH ANNIVERSARY. Aug 6, 1881. A legendary Hollywood gossip columnist, the first of her kind, Parsons was born at Freeport, IL. At the height of her popularity and power—from the 1930s to the 1950s—her column appeared in more than 400 newspapers and was read by approximately 20 million people. She gloried in her power and occasionally used her column in spite, making her a woman feared by many in Hollywood whose careers depended on their reputations and positive publicity. Parsons retired in 1965 and died Dec 9, 1972, at Santa Monica, CA.

ROOSEVELT, EDITH KERMIT CAROW: BIRTH ANNIVERSARY. Aug 6, 1861. Second wife of Theodore Roosevelt, 26th president of the US, whom she married in 1886. Born at Norwich, CT, she died at Long Island, NY, Sept 30, 1948.

August 2014

S	M	T	W	T	F	S
					1	2
3	4	5	6	7	8	9
10	11	12	13	14	15	16
17	18	19	20	21	22	23
24	25	26	27	28	29	30
31						

SPACE MILESTONE: *VOSTOK 2* (USSR). Aug 6, 1961. Launched on Aug 6, 1961, Gherman Titov orbited Earth 17 times over a period of 25 hours, 18 minutes. Titov broadcast messages in passage over countries and controlled spaceship manually for two hours.

TENNYSON, ALFRED, LORD: BIRTH ANNIVERSARY. Aug 6, 1809. English poet born at Somersby, Lincolnshire, England. His celebrated works include the poems "The Lady of Shalott" and "Ulysses" and the verse novelettes *Maud, Enoch Arden, In Memoriam, Locksley Hall Sixty Years After* and *The Idylls of the King.* Appointed English poet laureate in 1850 in succession to William Wordsworth and made a peer in 1884. Died at Aldworth, England, Oct 6, 1892.

VOTING RIGHTS ACT OF 1965 SIGNED: ANNIVERSARY. Aug 6, 1965. Signed into law by President Lyndon Johnson, the Voting Rights Act of 1965 was designed to thwart attempts to discriminate against minorities at the polls. The act suspended literacy and other disqualifying tests, authorized appointment of federal voting examiners and provided for judicial relief on the federal level to bar discriminatory poll taxes. Congress voted to extend the act in 1975, 1984 and 1991.

WARHOL, ANDY: BIRTH ANNIVERSARY. Aug 6, 1928. The artist, filmmaker and provocateur was born Andrew Warhola to Czech immigrant parents at Forest City, PA. (Some sources cite his birth year as 1927.) A leader of the Pop Art movement, Warhol challenged the definitions of art. After a stint as a commercial artist, Warhol gained attention in 1962 with paintings of ordinary commercial products—most famously, Campbell's Soup cans—and pop culture figures. He moved on to silk-screen portraits (of subjects such as Marilyn Monroe, Elvis Presley and Mao Tse-tung) and experimental film projects (*Empire* [1964] was a static depiction of the Empire State Building that ran more than eight hours). Warhol was the center of New York's celebrity scene, and in 1968 it was he who claimed, "In the future everyone will be world-famous for 15 minutes." Warhol died Feb 22, 1987, at New York, NY.

BIRTHDAYS TODAY

Peter Bonerz, 76, actor ("The Bob Newhart Show"), director, born Portsmouth, NH, Aug 6, 1938.

Soleil Moon Frye, 38, actress ("Punky Brewster"), born Glendora, CA, Aug 6, 1976.

Romola Garai, 32, actress (*I Capture the Castle, Atonement*), born Hong Kong, Aug 6, 1982.

Melissa George, 38, actress ("Alias"), born Perth, Australia, Aug 6, 1976.

Dorian Harewood, 64, actor (*The Falcon and the Snowman, Full Metal Jacket*), born Dayton, OH, Aug 6, 1950.

Catherine Hicks, 63, actress ("7th Heaven," *Peggy Sue Got Married*), born Scottsdale, AZ, Aug 6, 1951.

Shirley Ann Jackson, 68, physicist, born Washington, DC, Aug 6, 1946.

David Robinson, 49, Hall of Fame basketball player, born Key West, FL, Aug 6, 1965.

M. Night Shyamalan, 44, filmmaker (*Lady in the Water, Signs, The Sixth Sense*), born Pondicherry, India, Aug 6, 1970.

Robin van Persie, 31, soccer player, born Rotterdam, Netherlands, Aug 6, 1983.

Michelle Yeoh, 52, actress (*Crouching Tiger, Hidden Dragon*; *Tomorrow Never Dies*), born Yang Zi Chong at Ipoh, Perak, Malaysia, Aug 6, 1962.

August 7 — Thursday

DAY 219 **146 REMAINING**

AMERICAN PSYCHOLOGICAL ASSOCIATION CONVENTION. Aug 7–10. Washington, DC. 122nd annual. For info: Convention Office, American Psychological Assn, 750 First St NE, Washington, DC 20002-4242. Phone: (202) 336-6020. E-mail: convention@apa.org. Web: www.apa.org.

BIKILA, ABEBE: BIRTH ANNIVERSARY. Aug 7, 1932. Ethiopian marathoner and two-time Olympic gold medalist. Born at Jato, Ethiopia, Bikila became the first black African Olympic champion at the 1960 games in Rome. Four years later, he broke his own world record to win gold in the marathon again. In 1969, a car accident left Bikila paralyzed from the waist down. He died of a brain hemorrhage on Oct 25, 1973, in Ethiopia's capital, Addis Ababa. Tens of thousands attended Bikila's funeral, and Ethiopia declared a national day of mourning.

BONDS BREAKS AARON'S CAREER HOME RUN RECORD: ANNIVERSARY. Aug 7, 2007. Barry Bonds of the San Francisco Giants hit his 756th home run to pass Hank Aaron's career record of 755.

BUNCHE, RALPH JOHNSON: BIRTH ANNIVERSARY. Aug 7, 1904. American statesman, UN official, Nobel Peace Prize recipient (the first black to win the award), born at Detroit, MI. Died Dec 9, 1971, at New York, NY. See also: "Ralph Bunche Awarded Nobel Peace Prize: Anniversary" (Dec 10).

CANADA: EDMONTON FOLK MUSIC FESTIVAL. Aug 7–10. Gallagher Park, Edmonton, AB. Folk music and fun for the entire family highlighting blues, country, Celtic, traditional folk and bluegrass music, arts and crafts displays and a food fair. Est attendance: 85,000. For info: Edmonton Folk Music Festival Society, PO Box 4130, Edmonton, AB T6E 4T2, Canada. Phone: (780) 429-1899. E-mail: admin@efmf.ab.ca. Web: www.edmontonfolkfest.org.

COLOMBIA: BATTLE OF BOYACÁ DAY. Aug 7. National holiday. Commemorates victory over Spanish forces in 1819.

CONTIN-TAIL. Aug 7–10. Rodeo Grounds, Buena Vista, CO. Colorado's largest outdoor gem and mineral show. Dedicated to rock hounds all over the country since 1984. More than 100 vendors displaying anything related to rocks, minerals, fossils and the lapidary hobby. Annually, the second full weekend of August. Est attendance: 3,000. For info: Contin-Tail, 1130 Francis, #7010, Longmont, CO 80501. Phone: (720) 938-4194. E-mail: ctunnicliff@comcast.net. Web: www.coloradorocks.org.

CÔTE D'IVOIRE: NATIONAL DAY. Aug 7. Commemorates the independence of the Ivory Coast from France in 1960.

DESERT SHIELD: ANNIVERSARY. Aug 7, 1990. Five days after the Iraqi invasion of Kuwait, US President George H.W. Bush ordered the military buildup that would become known as Desert Shield to prevent further Iraqi advances.

FESTIVAL AT SANDPOINT. Aug 7–17. Sandpoint, ID. Summer concert series featuring classical, country, jazz, pop, world, blues and folk. Est attendance: 20,000. For info: Dyno Wahl, Exec Dir, Festival at Sandpoint, PO Box 695, Sandpoint, ID 83864. Phone: (888) 265-4554. Fax: (208) 263-6858. E-mail: festival@sandpoint.net. Web: www.festivalatsandpoint.com.

GREAT RIVER TUG FEST. Aug 7–9. Port Byron, IL, and LeClaire, IA. 28th annual. The Tug is the only tug-of-war across the mighty Mississippi River or any other moving body of water in the world. For two hours barge traffic, pleasure boats and gambling and paddle boats yield the right of way to a 400-foot, 680-pound rope that stretches between Illinois and Iowa. At 1 PM Saturday, the first team of 20 tuggers grip the rope, the crowd counts down and dirt starts flying! Festivals on both sides of the river Friday and Saturday. Fireworks Friday evening. Annually, the second weekend in August (including Thursday). For info: Great River Tug Fest. Phone: (563) 289-3946 or (309) 523-3734. Web: www.tugfest.com or www.visitquadcities.com.

GREENE, NATHANIEL: BIRTH ANNIVERSARY. Aug 7, 1742. (Old Style date.) Born at Patowomut, RI, American Revolutionary War general Nathaniel Greene was described as the "ablest military officer of the Revolution under Washington." Greene died at Savannah, GA, June 19, 1786.

GULF OF TONKIN RESOLUTION: 50th ANNIVERSARY. Aug 7, 1964. Congress approved the "Gulf of Tonkin Resolution," pertaining to the war in Vietnam, which gave President Lyndon Johnson authority "to take all necessary measures to repel any armed attack against the forces of the United States and to prevent further aggression."

HATFIELD-McCOY FEUD ERUPTS: ANNIVERSARY. Aug 7–9, 1882. The long-simmering tension between two Appalachian families who lived by Tug Fork on the Kentucky–West Virginia border erupted into full-scale violence on Election Day 1882. Brothers Tolbert, Pharmer and Randolph McCoy knifed and shot Ellison Hatfield. The Hatfield family captured the three McCoys. When Ellison Hatfield died on Aug 9, the Hatfields executed the brothers. The feud continued with much loss of life. In 1888, when Kentucky authorities sought to detain the feud murder suspects and West Virginia authorities complained, the dispute went all the way to the Supreme Court, which decided in Kentucky's favor. The feud sputtered out by the end of the century.

ILLINOIS STATE FAIR. Aug 7–17. Springfield, IL. Amusement rides, food booths, parade, various types of entertainment and tractor pulls. Est attendance: 700,000. For info: Illinois State Fair, PO Box 19427, Springfield, IL 62794. Phone: (217) 524-6858. Web: www.illinoisstatefair.info.

IOWA STATE FAIR. Aug 7–17. Iowa State Fairgrounds, Des Moines, IA. One of America's oldest and largest state fairs. A grand showcase of Iowa agriculture, talent and tradition. The fair features the largest foods department of any state fair and one of the largest livestock shows in the world. This annual August extravaganza inspired Phil Stong's acclaimed novel *State Fair,* three motion pictures and a Broadway musical. Est attendance: 1,000,000. For info: Iowa State Fair, PO Box 57130, Des Moines, IA 50317. Phone: 800-545-FAIR. E-mail: info@iowastatefair.org. Web: www.iowastatefair.org.

ISING, RUDOLF C.: BIRTH ANNIVERSARY. Aug 7, 1903. Rudolf C. Ising, cocreator with Hugh Harmon of "Looney Tunes" and "Merrie Melodies," was born at Kansas City, MO. Ising and Harmon's initial production, "Bosko the Talk-Ink Kid" (1929), was the first talkie cartoon synchronizing dialogue on the soundtrack with the action on screen. Ising received an Academy Award in 1940 for *Milky Way,* a cartoon about three kittens. During WWII he headed the animation division for the Army Air Corps movie unit developing training films. Ising died July 18, 1992, at Newport Beach, CA.

"LIL" MARGARET'S BLUEGRASS AND OLD-TIME MUSIC FESTIVAL. Aug 7–9. Leonardtown, MD. Bluegrass music, crafts, old-time cars and tractors, plenty of home-cooked meals and lots of fun. Annually, the second weekend in August. Est attendance: 1,000. For info: Joseph H. Goddard, Lil Margaret's Bluegrass, 20529 White Point Rd, Leonardtown, MD 20650. Phone: (301) 475-8191. Web: www.lilmargaretsbluegrass.com.

August 2014	S	M	T	W	T	F	S
						1	2
	3	4	5	6	7	8	9
	10	11	12	13	14	15	16
	17	18	19	20	21	22	23
	24	25	26	27	28	29	30
	31						

MATA HARI: BIRTH ANNIVERSARY. Aug 7, 1876. Mata Hari (child of the dawn) was born Margaret Gertrude Zelle at Leeuwarden, Netherlands. Her spectacular career as a dancer, courtesan and spy made her known around the world. Probably an ineffective double agent, she nevertheless fascinated royalty and high officials of several countries. Arrested as a German spy (Agent H-21) in a Paris hotel, Feb 13, 1917, she was tried, convicted and sentenced to death. The greatest of her many roles was the final one—when she refused a blindfold and threw a kiss to the firing squad at Vincennes, France, Oct 15, 1917.

McKECHNIE, BILL: BIRTH ANNIVERSARY. Aug 7, 1886. William Boyd (Bill) McKechnie, Baseball Hall of Fame manager, born at Wilkinsburg, PA. McKechnie is generally recognized as one of the greatest strategic managers in history. He took three National League teams to the pennant, the Pittsburgh Pirates in 1925, the St. Louis Cardinals in 1928 and the Cincinnati Reds in 1939 and 1940. Inducted into the Hall of Fame in 1962. Died at Bradenton, FL, Oct 29, 1965.

MISSOURI STATE FAIR. Aug 7–17. Sedalia, MO. Livestock shows, commercial and competitive exhibits, horse shows, motor sports, tractor pulls, carnival and headline musical entertainment. Economical family entertainment. Est attendance: 350,000. For info: Missouri State Fair, 2503 W 16th St, Sedalia, MO 65301. Phone: (660) 530-5600 or (800) 422-FAIR. Fax: (660) 827-8160. E-mail: mostatefair@mda.mo.gov. Web: www.mostatefair.com.

MOUNTAIN DANCE AND FOLK FESTIVAL. Aug 7–9. Asheville, NC. 87th annual festival. More than 400 performers in this three-day fest, which celebrates the cultural heritage of the southern Appalachian Mountains. Includes dance teams, mountain fiddlers, banjo pickers, old-time string bands, storytellers, bluegrass bands and dulcimer sweepers. Oldest of its kind, founded in 1928 by Bascom Lamar Lunsford. Est attendance: 1,500. For info: Asheville Area Chamber of Commerce, Folk Heritage, PO Box 1010, Asheville, NC 28802. Phone: (828) 258-6101. E-mail: info@folkheritage.org. Web: www.folkheritage.org.

NATIONAL HOBO CONVENTION. Aug 7–10. Britt, IA. Held since 1900, the National Hobo Convention celebrates current and retired hoboes and the independent lifestyle they lead. Events include the crowning of the Hobo King and Queen, parade, live entertainment, antique and classic car show and consumption of the traditional mulligan stew. Attractions include Hobo Museum, Hobo Cemetery, Queen's Gardens and Engraved Walkway. Est attendance: 21,000. For info: Hobo Foundation, PO Box 143, Britt, IA 50423. Phone: (641) 843-9104. E-mail: lindah@hobo.com. Web: www.hobo.com/convention.htm.

NATIONAL LIGHTHOUSE DAY. Aug 7. A day to honor and recognize America's historic lighthouses—on the anniversary of Congress signing into law on Aug 7, 1789, "An Act for the Establishment and Support of Lighthouse, Beacons, Buoys and Public Piers." On the 200th anniversary of this legislation, in 1989, Congress proclaimed National Lighthouse Day. Many historic US lighthouses still observe this day, opening their grounds to the public. For info: American Lighthouse Foundation, Inc, PO Box 565, Rockland, ME 04841. Phone: (207) 594-4174. E-mail: info@lighthousefoundation.org. Web: www.lighthousefoundation.org.

PARTICULARLY PREPOSTEROUS PACKAGING DAY. Aug 7. Buy anything lately? Did you succeed in getting the durn thing open? What do older people do when even younger adults can't open a simple bottle of aspirin, let alone a milk carton? Annually, Aug 7. (©2006 by WH.) For info: Thomas & Ruth Roy, Wellcat Holidays, 2418 Long Ln, Lebanon, PA 17046. Phone: (717) 279-0184. E-mail: info@wellcat.com. Web: www.wellcat.com.

PROFESSIONAL SPEAKERS DAY. Aug 7. A day celebrating the consummate professionals who through their oratorical skills help people. For info: Jim Barber, 1101 Marcano Blvd, Plantation, FL 33322. Phone: (954) 476-9252. E-mail: pro.speaker.day@thebarbershop.com. Web: www.professionalspeakersday.com.

PURPLE HEART: ANNIVERSARY. Aug 7, 1782. At Newburgh, NY, General George Washington ordered the creation of a Badge of Military Merit. The badge consisted of a purple cloth heart with silver braided edge. Only three are known to have been awarded during the Revolutionary War. The award was reinstituted on the bicentennial of Washington's birth, Feb 22, 1932, and recognizes those wounded in action.

RIBFEST. Aug 7–9. Kalamazoo, MI. Features the smell of sizzling ribs as rib-burners from throughout the US tantalize the taste buds. Festival features live entertainment, family-oriented events, food booths and the "Best Ribs in Kalamazoo" cook-off. Annually, the first full weekend in August (including Thursday). Est attendance: 30,000. For info: Deborah Droppers, The Arc Community Advocates, 814 S Westnedge St, Kalamazoo, MI 49008-1162. Phone: (269) 388-2830. E-mail: deb@eventkalamazoo.com. Web: www.ribfestkalamazoo.com.

SKOWHEGAN STATE FAIR. Aug 7–16. Skowhegan, ME. 196th annual. Huge fair with horse pulling, tractor pulls, harness racing, carnival midway, exhibits, flower show, grandstand shows, coliseum events, truck pulls, demolition derby and much more. Annually, beginning three weeks before Labor Day. Est attendance: 65,000. For info: Skowhegan State Fair Assn, PO Box 39, Skowhegan, ME 04976. Phone: (207) 474-2947. E-mail: skowfair@beeline-online.net. Web: www.skowheganstatefair.com.

SPACE MILESTONE: FIRST PICTURE OF EARTH FROM SPACE: 55th ANNIVERSARY. Aug 7, 1959. US satellite *Explorer VI* transmitted the first picture of Earth from space. For the first time we had a likeness of our planet based on more than projections and conjectures.

US WAR DEPARTMENT ESTABLISHED: 225th ANNIVERSARY. Aug 7, 1789. The second presidential cabinet department, the War Department, was established on this date by Congress.

WORLD TRADE CENTER TIGHTROPE WALK: 40th ANNIVERSARY. Aug 7, 1974. On this date, French juggler and street performer Philippe Petit made an illegal tightrope walk between the twin towers of the World Trade Center, 1,350 feet above the plaza. He and his crew spent months planning the "coup" and smuggling materials into the buildings. Petit crossed eight times in 45 minutes and faced charges of trespassing and disorderly conduct. The 2008 Oscar-winning documentary *Man on Wire* chronicled this "artistic crime of the century."

BIRTHDAYS TODAY

Sidney Crosby, 27, hockey player, born Cole Harbour, NS, Canada, Aug 7, 1987.

David Duchovny, 54, actor ("The X-Files," "Californication"), born New York, NY, Aug 7, 1960.

Stan Freberg, 88, satirist, born Pasadena, CA, Aug 7, 1926.

John Glover, 70, actor ("Smallville," *An Early Frost*), born Salisbury, MD, Aug 7, 1944.

Garrison Keillor, 72, humorist, producer, host ("A Prairie Home Companion"), author (*Lake Wobegon Days*), born Anoka, MN, Aug 7, 1942.

DeLane Matthews, 53, actress ("Dave's World"), born Rockledge, FL, Aug 7, 1961.

Harold Parrineau, 51, actor ("Lost," "Oz"), born Brooklyn, NY, Aug 7, 1963.

Alberto Salazar, 57, marathon runner, born Havana, Cuba, Aug 7, 1957.

Michael Shannon, 40, actor ("Boardwalk Empire," *Revolutionary Road*), born Lexington, KY, Aug 7, 1974.

Charlize Theron, 39, actress (Oscar for *Monster*; *Prometheus, Young Adult, Aeon Flux, The Italian Job*), born Benoni, South Africa, Aug 7, 1975.

Billy Joe (B.J.) Thomas, 72, singer ("Raindrops Keep Falling on My Head"), born Houston, TX, Aug 7, 1942.

August 8 — Friday

DAY 220 **145 REMAINING**

BONZA BOTTLER DAY™. Aug 8. To celebrate when the number of the day is the same as the number of the month. Bonza Bottler Day™ is an excuse to have a party at least once a month. For more information see Jan 1. For info: Gail Berger, 14 Fernwood Dr, Taylors, SC 29687. Phone: (864) 201-3988. E-mail: bonza@bonzabottlerday.com. Web: www.bonzabottlerday.com.

CANADA: ABBOTSFORD INTERNATIONAL AIRSHOW. Aug 8–10. Abbotsford Airport, Abbotsford, BC. "Canada's National Airshow." Leading air show in North America attracts the world's top aeronautical performers. Thrill to the grace of the Canadian Snowbirds, the raw power of the international air demonstration squadrons, daring performers and soloists. Ground displays include military and general aviation planes, concessions and trade booths. Airshow camping facilities. Est attendance: 100,000. For info: Abbotsford Intl Airshow, 1464 Tower St, Abbotsford, BC V2T 6H5, Canada. E-mail: info@abbotsfordairshow.com. Web: www.abbotsfordairshow.com.

CAPITOLFEST. Aug 8–10. Rome Capitol Theatre, Rome, NY. Central New York's 35mm rare silent and early talkie film festival attracts film buffs from around the country and world. Films are obtained from archives and shown in an authentic 1928 movie palace. Silent films are accompanied live on the theater's original-installation Möller theater organ. Annually, the second weekend in August (Friday–Sunday). Est attendance: 400. For info: Capitolfest, Rome Capitol Theatre, 220 W Dominick St, Rome, NY 13440. Phone/fax: (315) 337-6277. Web: www.romecapitol.com/capitolfest.html.

DE LAURENTIIS, DINO: 95th BIRTH ANNIVERSARY. Aug 8, 1919. Italian film producer, born at Torre Annunziata, Italy. After spending 30 years producing films in Europe, including several Fellini films, De Laurentiis came to the US in 1976. Over the next 35 years, he produced a diverse assortment of Hollywood projects, including *Serpico, Blue Velvet* and *Manhunter*, as well as several notably unsuccessful films such as *King Kong, Flash Gordon* and *Dune*. He died Nov 10, 2010, at Beverly Hills, CA.

GINZA HOLIDAY: JAPANESE CULTURAL FESTIVAL. Aug 8–10. Midwest Buddhist Temple, Chicago, IL. Experience the Waza (National Treasures tradition) by viewing 300 years of Edo craft tradition and seeing it come alive as master craftspeople from Tokyo demonstrate their arts. Japanese folk and classical dancing, martial arts, *taiko* (drums), flower arrangements and cultural displays. Chicken teriyaki, sushi, *udon*, shaved ice, corn on the cob and refreshments. Annually, the second weekend in August. Est attendance: 15,000. For info: Midwest Buddhist Temple, 435 W Menomonee St, Chicago, IL 60614. Phone: (312) 943-7801. Fax: (312) 943-8069. E-mail: office@midwestbuddhisttemple.org. Web: www.midwestbuddhisttemple.org.

HAPPINESS HAPPENS DAY. Aug 8. This day celebrates the 16th birthday of the Secret Society of Happy People by encouraging expressions of happiness and discouraging parade-raining. Suggested celebration activities (including Happython, a 24-hour social media event) are available on the website. For info: Secret Society of Happy People, 425 Busher Dr, Lewisville, TX 75067. Phone: (972) 459-7031. E-mail: pamelagail@sohp.com. Web: www.sohp.com.

HENSON, MATTHEW A.: BIRTH ANNIVERSARY. Aug 8, 1866. African-American explorer, born at Charles County, MD. He met Robert E. Peary while working in a Washington, DC, store in 1888 and was hired to be Peary's valet. He accompanied Peary on his seven subsequent Arctic expeditions. During the successful 1908–09 expedition to the North Pole, Henson and two of the four Eskimo guides reached their destination Apr 6, 1909. Peary arrived minutes later and verified the location. Henson's account of the expedition, *A Negro Explorer at the North Pole*, was published in 1912. In addition to the Congressional Medal awarded all members of the North Pole expedition, Henson received the Gold Medal of the Geographical Society of Chicago and, at 81, was made an honorary member of the Explorers Club at New York, NY. Died Mar 9, 1955, at New York.

INTERSTATE FAIR AND RODEO. Aug 8–16. Coffeyville, KS. "Largest outdoor fair and rodeo event in southeast Kansas and northeast Oklahoma." Includes concerts, demo derby, three thrilling nights of PRCA rodeo, livestock shows, carnival rides and more. Est attendance: 100,000. For info: Interstate Fair and Rodeo. E-mail: fairandrodeo@coffeyville.com. Web: www.fairandrodeo.com.

KOOL-AID DAYS. Aug 8–10. Hastings, NE. Family festival in the town where Kool-Aid was invented. Large inflatable games, cardboard and "Jammers" boat races, parade, rock tribute concert, live entertainment, festival foods, commemoratives, photos with the Kool-Aid Man, parade, sports tournaments, games for kids. Purchase a $2 mug and receive free Kool-Aid all day (14 flavors!) from the world's largest Kool-Aid stand. Free admission to Koncert Kool-Aid. Annually, the second weekend in August. Est attendance: 50,000. For info: Kool-Aid Days, Nebraska's Official Soft Drink Heritage Foundation, 301 S Burlington Ave, Ste 122, Hastings, NE 68901. Phone: (402) 461-8405. E-mail: koolaiddays@yahoo.com. Web: www.kool-aiddays.com.

LONG BEACH JAZZ FESTIVAL. Aug 8–10. Rainbow Lagoon, Long Beach, CA. 27th annual. The festival features some of the top artists in jazz. Incredible outdoor setting with a great selection of food, art works and much more. Est attendance: 20,000. For info: Rainbow Promotions, LLC, 3505 Long Beach Blvd, Ste 2G, Long Beach, CA 90807. Phone: (562) 424-0013. Web: www.LongBeachJazzFestival.com.

MARCH, FREDRIC: BIRTH ANNIVERSARY. Aug 8, 1897. Award-winning actor born Frederick McIntyre Bickel at Racine, WI. Over the course of his long and distinguished career, March performed on both the stage and screen. He made more than 65 movies and was nominated for five Academy Awards, winning in 1932 for his role in *Dr. Jekyll and Mr Hyde* and in 1947 for *The Best Years of Our Lives*. In 1956 he appeared on stage in the world premiere of Eugene O'Neill's *Long Day's Journey into Night*. He received the Tony Award for that performance. He died Apr 14, 1975, at Los Angeles, CA.

August 2014	S	M	T	W	T	F	S
						1	2
	3	4	5	6	7	8	9
	10	11	12	13	14	15	16
	17	18	19	20	21	22	23
	24	25	26	27	28	29	30
	31						

MARKERT, RUSSELL: BIRTH ANNIVERSARY. Aug 8, 1899. American choreographer Russell Markert was born at Jersey City, NJ. He founded the Radio City Music Hall Rockettes and directed them from 1932 to 1971. He died Dec 1, 1990, at Waterbury, CT.

MONTANAFAIR. Aug 8–16. MetraPark, Billings, MT. Montana's biggest event featuring exhibits, livestock events, carnival, rodeo and entertainment. Est attendance: 240,000. For info: MetraPark, PO Box 2514, Billings, MT 59103. Phone: (406) 256-2400. Web: www.metrapark.com or www.montanafair.com.

MORRIS, ESTHER HOBART McQUIGG: 200th BIRTH ANNIVERSARY. Aug 8, 1814. Esther Hobart McQuigg Morris was born at Tioga County, NY, but eventually moved to the Wyoming Territory, where she worked in the women's rights movement and had a key role in getting a women's suffrage bill passed. Morris became justice of the peace of South Pass City, WY, in 1870, one of the first times a woman held public office in the US. She represented Wyoming at the national suffrage convention in 1895. She died Apr 2, 1902, at Cheyenne, WY.

NATIONAL SCRABBLE CHAMPIONSHIP. Aug 8–13. Buffalo Niagara Convention Center, Buffalo, NY. Players compete for the national championship in the popular game invented by unemployed architect Alfred Butts in 1931. For info: North American Scrabble Players Association (NASPA), PO Box 12115, Dallas, TX 75225-0115. E-mail: info@scrabbleplayers.org. Web: www.scrabbleplayers.org.

ODIE: BIRTHDAY. Aug 8, 1978. Commemorates the birthday of Odie, Garfield's sidekick, who first appeared in the "Garfield" comic strip Aug 8, 1978. For info: Odie's Birthday. Web: www.garfield.com.

RAWLINGS, MARJORIE KINNAN: BIRTH ANNIVERSARY. Aug 8, 1896. American short-story writer and novelist (*The Yearling*), born at Washington, DC. Rawlings died at St. Augustine, FL, Dec 14, 1953.

"SÁBADO GIGANTE" TV PREMIERE: ANNIVERSARY. Aug 8, 1962. This popular variety show, originally seven hours long, premiered on Chilean television under the name "Sábados Gigantes." It is now broadcast from Miami, FL, and reaches 100 million viewers in 20 countries. The amiable Don Francisco has been the host from the beginning.

SCOTLAND: EDINBURGH INTERNATIONAL FESTIVAL. Aug 8–31. Edinburgh, Lothian. The festival is one of the most exciting places in the world to experience opera, dance, theater, classical music and visual arts. It offers the chance to see and hear some of the world's greatest companies and performers. Est attendance: 420,000. For info: Edinburgh Intl Festival, The Hub, Castlehill, Edinburgh, Scotland EH1 2NE. Phone: (44) (131) 473-2000. Fax: (44) (131) 473-2002. Web: www.eif.co.uk.

SECOND BATTLE OF AMIENS: ANNIVERSARY. Aug 8, 1918. Two days after the WWI Battle of Marne ended, the British Fourth Army mounted an offensive at Amiens with the objective of freeing the Amiens-Paris railway from bombardment by the German Second and Eighteenth Armies. More than 16,000 German prisoners were taken in two hours of fighting the first day. The German forces were forced back to the Hindenburg line by Sept 3. This battle is considered a turning point by many historians because of its impact on the psyche of Germany. Aug 8 was described by General Erich Ludendorff as a "Black Day" for Germany.

SHILTS, RANDY: BIRTH ANNIVERSARY. Aug 8, 1951. Journalist known for his reporting on the AIDS epidemic. One of the first openly homosexual journalists to work for a mainstream newspaper and the author of *And the Band Played On: Politics, People and the AIDS Epidemic*. Born at Davenport, IA, and died at Guerneville, CA, Feb 17, 1994.

SNEAK SOME ZUCCHINI ONTO YOUR NEIGHBORS' PORCH NIGHT. Aug 8. Due to overzealous planting of zucchini, citizens are asked to drop off baskets of the squash on neighbors' doorsteps. Annually, Aug 8. (©2006 by WH.) For info: Thomas & Ruth Roy, Wellcat Holidays, 2418 Long Ln, Lebanon, PA 17046. Phone: (717) 279-0184. E-mail: info@wellcat.com. Web: www.wellcat.com.

SPACE MILESTONE: *GENESIS* (US). Aug 8, 2001. The robotic explorer *Genesis* was launched on a mission to gather tiny particles of the sun. Its three-year, 20-million-mile round-trip mission was to shed light on the origin of the solar system. It traveled to a spot where the gravitational pulls of the sun and Earth are equal and gathered atoms from the solar wind hurtling by. But on Sept 8, 2004, the *Genesis* return capsule crashed in a western US desert and most of its solar samples were destroyed.

SPACE MILESTONE: *PIONEER VENUS* MULTIPROBE (US). Aug 8, 1978. Launch of second craft in Pioneer Venus program. Split into five and probed Venus' atmosphere Dec 9.

STATE FAIR OF WEST VIRGINIA. Aug 8–16. Lewisburg, WV. For info: The State Fair of West Virginia, PO Drawer 986, Lewisburg, WV 24901. Phone: (304) 645-1090. E-mail: events@statefairofwv.com. Web: www.wvstatefair.com.

TANZANIA: FARMERS' DAY. Aug 8. National holiday. Also called *Nane Nane* ("8–8").

TETONKAHA RENDEZVOUS. Aug 8–10. Hole in the Mountain County Park, Lake Benton, MN. Presents the fur-trading atmosphere of the 1840s. Muzzle-loader contest, tomahawk and knife throw, log sawing, canoe races and kids' games. Est attendance: 300. For info: Dave Huebner, Brookings Renegade Muzzle Loaders, 47826 Main St, Bushnell, SD 57276. Phone: (605) 693-4589.

ZAPATA, EMILIANO: BIRTH ANNIVERSARY. Aug 8, 1879. Hero of the Mexican Revolution (1910–20), commander of the Liberation Army of the South, who advocated agrarian reform and championed the cause of the peasant. Born at Anenecuilco, Mexico, Zapata was ambushed and assassinated at Morelos on Apr 10, 1919.

BIRTHDAYS TODAY

Keith Carradine, 64, actor (*Nashville, Will Rogers Follies*, "Dexter"), singer, born San Mateo, CA, Aug 8, 1950.

The Edge, 53, musician (U2), born David Evans at East London, England, Aug 8, 1961.

Roger Federer, 33, tennis player, born Basel, Switzerland, Aug 8, 1981.

Dustin Hoffman, 77, actor (Oscars for *Rain Man* and *Kramer vs Kramer*; *The Graduate, Midnight Cowboy*), born Los Angeles, CA, Aug 8, 1937.

Drew Lachey, 38, singer (98 Degrees), television personality ("Dancing with the Stars"), born Cincinnati, OH, Aug 8, 1976.

Deborah Norville, 56, television host ("Inside Edition"), born Dalton, GA, Aug 8, 1958.

Roberta Cooper Ramo, 72, first woman president of the American Bar Association, born Denver, CO, Aug 8, 1942.

Connie Stevens, 76, actress ("Hawaiian Eye"), born Brooklyn, NY, Aug 8, 1938.

Mel Tillis, 82, singer, songwriter, born Pahokee, FL, Aug 8, 1932.

Michael Urie, 34, actor ("Ugly Betty"), born Dallas, TX, Aug 8, 1980.

August 9 — Saturday

DAY 221 | **144 REMAINING**

ATOMIC BOMB DROPPED ON NAGASAKI: ANNIVERSARY. Aug 9, 1945. Three days after the atomic bombing of Hiroshima, an American B-29 bomber named *Bock's Car* left its base on Tinian Island carrying a plutonium bomb nicknamed "Fat Man." Its target was the Japanese city of Kokura, but because of clouds and poor visibility, the bomber headed for a secondary target, Nagasaki, where at 11:02 AM, local time, it dropped the bomb, killing an estimated 70,000 people and destroying about half the city. Memorial services are held annually at Nagasaki and also at Kokura, where those who were spared because of the bad weather also grieve for those at Nagasaki who suffered in their stead.

BUD BILLIKEN PARADE. Aug 9. Chicago, IL. 85th annual parade especially for children begun in 1929 by Robert S. Abbott. The second-largest parade in the US, it features bands, floats, drill teams and celebrities. There are 65,000 participants and 1.5 million spectators—plus another 25 million watching on TV. Annually, the second Saturday in August. Est attendance: 1,500,000. For info: Chicago Defender Charities. Phone: (773) 536-3710. E-mail: chicagodefendercharities@yahoo.com. Web: budbillikenparade.com.

COCHRAN, JACQUELINE: DEATH ANNIVERSARY. Aug 9, 1980. American pilot Jacqueline Cochran was born at Pensacola, FL, about 1910. She began flying in 1932, and by the time of her death, she had set more distance, speed and altitude records than any other pilot, male or female. She was founder and head of the WASPs (Women's Air Force Service Pilots) during WWII; she won the Distinguished Service Medal in 1945 and the US Air Force Distinguished Flying Cross in 1969. She died at Indio, CA.

CRATER LAKE RIM RUNS AND MARATHON. Aug 9. Crater Lake National Park, OR. 39th annual. One of the toughest and most spectacular races you'll ever run! Race routes are around Crater Lake, the deepest lake in the US. Included are a 6.7-mile walk and 6.7-mile run and a 13-mile (half marathon) and full marathon. The field is limited to 500 competitors. Annually, the second Saturday in August. For info: Crater Lake Rim Runs, 5830 Mack Ave, Klamath Falls, OR 97603. Phone: (541) 884-6939. E-mail: rimruns@aol.com or info@craterlakerimruns.com. Web: www.craterlakerimruns.com.

GAY GAMES 9. Aug 9–16. Cleveland and Akron, OH. First held in 1982. An eight-day sports and cultural festival. Includes sporting competitions, band and choral programs and an arts festival. 10,000 participants from more than 65 nations take part. For info: Federation of Gay Games. Web: www.gg9cle.com.

HOUSTON, WHITNEY: BIRTH ANNIVERSARY. Aug 9, 1963. Equally adept at danceable pop, stirring gospel and dramatic balladry, Whitney Houston, born at Newark, NJ, was one of the most influential recording artists in music history—and one of the most accomplished: she had a vocal range of three octaves. Early chart success was unprecedented: her 1985 debut, *Whitney Houston*, and *Whitney*, its 1987 follow-up, produced eight number one singles and went on to sell more than 50 million copies combined. "I Will Always Love You," her 1992 single from the film *The Bodyguard*, in which she also starred, topped the Billboard charts for a record 14 weeks and became her signature song. After Houston's accidental death on Feb 11, 2012, at Beverly Hills, CA, it was also the song that came to define her effusive singing style. It reentered the Billboard Hot 100 almost immediately, and peaked at number three.

JANSSON, TOVE: 100th BIRTH ANNIVERSARY. Aug 9, 1914. Finnish artist, cartoonist, novelist Jansson is best known as the creator of Moomintrolls, loosely based on the trolls of Swedish folklore, which began as children's books and later morphed into a syndicated cartoon strip "Moomins." Born at Helsinki, Finland, she died there June 27, 2001.

JAPAN: MOMENT OF SILENCE. Aug 9. Nagasaki. Memorial observance held at Peace Memorial Park for victims of second atomic bomb, which was dropped on Nagasaki by an American bomber Aug 9, 1945.

LASSEN VOLCANIC NATIONAL PARK ESTABLISHED: ANNIVERSARY. Aug 9, 1916. California's Lassen Peak and Cinder Cone National Monument, proclaimed May 6, 1907, and other wilderness lands were combined and established as a national park. For info: Lassen Volcanic Natl Park, Mineral, CA 96063.

LEADVILLE TRAIL 100. Aug 9. Leadville, CO. The race of all races: 100 miles across the high-altitude, extreme terrain of the Colorado Rockies. Created for only the most determined athletes. Starting at 10,152 feet and climbing to 12,424 feet, runners will be challenged to catch their breath—while the views try to take it away. Low point, 9,200 feet; high point is Columbine Mine, 12,424 feet. Majority is on forest trails with some mountain roads. Est attendance: 2,000. For info: Leadville Trail 100, 2902 Corporate Pl, Chanhassen, MN 55317. Phone: (240) 888-2952. E-mail: jsellinger@lifetimefitness.com. Web: www.leadvilleraceseries.com.

NATIONAL GARAGE SALE DAY. Aug 9. A day to turn the nation into a giant shopping mall! Annually, the second Saturday in August. (Copyright © 2001.) For info: C. Daniel Rhodes, 1900 Crossvine Rd, Hoover, AL 35244. Phone: (205) 908-6781. E-mail: rhodan@charter.net.

NIXON RESIGNS: 40th ANNIVERSARY. Aug 9, 1974. The resignation from the presidency of the US by Richard Milhous Nixon, which had been announced in a speech to the American people the night before, became effective at noon. Nixon, under threat of impeachment as a result of the Watergate scandal, became the first US president to resign.

PERSEID METEOR SHOWERS. Aug 9–13. Among the best-known and most spectacular meteor showers are the Perseids, peaking about Aug 10–12. As many as 50–100 may be seen in a single night. Wish upon a "falling star"!

ROBERT GRAY BECOMES FIRST AMERICAN TO CIRCUMNAVIGATE EARTH: ANNIVERSARY. Aug 9, 1790. When Robert Gray docked the *Columbia* at Boston Harbor, he became the first American to circumnavigate Earth. He sailed from Boston, MA, in September 1787, to trade with Indians of the Pacific Northwest. From there he sailed to China and then continued around the world. His 42,000-mile journey opened trade between New England and the Pacific Northwest and helped the US establish claims to the Oregon Territory.

SINGAPORE: NATIONAL DAY. Aug 9, 1965. Most festivals in Singapore are Chinese, Indian or Malay, but celebration of National Day is shared by all to commemorate the withdrawal of Singapore from Malaysia and its becoming an independent state in 1965. Music, parades and dancing.

SOMERSET ANTIQUE SHOW. Aug 9. Somerset, PA. 44th annual. More than 100 vendors dealing in quality antiques and collectibles. Est attendance: 5,000. For info: Sandy Berkebile, Somerset County Chamber of Commerce, 601 N Center Ave, Somerset, PA 15501. Phone: (814) 445-6431. E-mail: info@somersetcountychamber.com.

SOUTH AFRICA: NATIONAL WOMEN'S DAY. Aug 9. National holiday. Commemorates the march of women in Pretoria to protest the pass laws in 1956.

STREETSCENE. Aug 9. Covington, VA. Car show, open to all types of vehicles. Entertainment throughout the day. Annually, the second Saturday in August. Est attendance: 8,000. For info: Kars Unlimited, Inc, PO Box 851, Covington, VA 24426. Phone: (540) 962-3642. Web: www.commonwealtharms.com/karsunlimited.

TRAVIS, WILLIAM BARRET: BIRTH ANNIVERSARY. Aug 9, 1809. Born at Saluda County, SC, Travis was one of many young American men who sought fortune in the Mexican territory of Texas. Swept up in the burgeoning revolutionary activities by American settlers to secede from Mexico, Travis found himself at age 26 commander of a small band of volunteer troops at the Alamo at San Antonio, TX. Mexican troops, commanded by General Santa Anna, overwhelmed the small force on Mar 6, 1836, and all Texans were killed.

UNITED NATIONS: INTERNATIONAL DAY OF THE WORLD'S INDIGENOUS PEOPLE. Aug 9. On Dec 23, 1994, the General Assembly decided that the International Day of the World's Indigenous People be observed Aug 9 every year (Resolution 59/1740). For info: United Nations, Dept of Public Info, Public Inquiries Unit, Rm GA-57, New York, NY 10017. Phone: (212) 963-4475. E-mail: inquiries@un.org.

VEEP DAY. Aug 9. Commemorates the day in 1974 when Richard Nixon's resignation let Gerald Ford succeed to the presidency of the US. This was the first time the new constitutional provisions for presidential succession took effect. For info: Bob Birch, The Puns Corps, 3108 Dashiell Rd, Falls Church, VA 22042. Phone: (703) 533-3668.

WALTON, IZAAK: BIRTH ANNIVERSARY. Aug 9, 1593. (Old Style date.) English author of classic treatise on fishing, *The Compleat Angler*, published in 1653, was born at Stafford, England. Died at Winchester, England, Dec 15, 1683 (OS). "Angling," Walton wrote, "may be said to be so like the mathematics that it can never be fully learnt."

WEBSTER-ASHBURTON TREATY SIGNED: ANNIVERSARY. Aug 9, 1842. The treaty delimiting the eastern section of the Canadian-American border was negotiated by Daniel Webster, US secretary of state, and Alexander Baring, president of the British Board of Trade. Signed at Washington, DC, the treaty established the boundaries between the St. Croix and Connecticut rivers, between Lake Superior and the Lake of the Woods and between Lake Huron and Lake Superior.

WYOMING STATE FAIR AND RODEO. Aug 9–16. Douglas, WY. 102nd annual. Recognizing the products, achievements and cultural heritage of the people of Wyoming. Bringing together rural and urban citizens for an inexpensive, entertaining and educational experience. Features livestock shows for beef, goats, swine, sheep and horses; youth livestock shows for beef, swine, sheep, horses, goats, dogs, poultry and rabbits; competitions and displays for culinary arts, needlework, visual arts and floriculture; 4-H and FFA County/Chapters State qualification competitions; Demo Derby; live entertainment; carnival; PRCA rodeo and Ranch Rodeo and an antique tractor pull. Est attendance: 47,000. For info: Wyoming State Fair, PO Drawer 10, Douglas, WY 82633. Phone: (307) 358-2398. Fax: (307) 358-6030. E-mail: wsf@netcommander.com. Web: www.wystatefair.com.

BIRTHDAYS TODAY

Gillian Anderson, 46, actress ("The X-Files," *Bleak House, The House of Mirth*), born Chicago, IL, Aug 9, 1968.

Eric Bana, 46, actor (*Hulk, Munich*), born Melbourne, Australia, Aug 9, 1968.

Amanda Bearse, 56, actress ("Married . . . With Children"), born Winter Park, FL, Aug 9, 1958.

Jessica Capshaw, 38, actress ("Grey's Anatomy," "The Practice"), born Columbia, MO, Aug 9, 1976.

Robert Joseph (Bob) Cousy, 86, Hall of Fame basketball player, former coach, born New York, NY, Aug 9, 1928.

Sam Elliott, 70, actor ("Mission: Impossible," *Gettysburg*), born Sacramento, CA, Aug 9, 1944.

Derek Fisher, 40, basketball player, born Little Rock, AR, Aug 9, 1974.

Melanie Griffith, 57, actress (*Working Girl, Something Wild, Milk Money*), born New York, NY, Aug 9, 1957.

Brett Hull, 50, Hall of Fame hockey player, born Belleville, ON, Canada, Aug 9, 1964.

Michael Kors, 55, fashion designer, television personality ("Project Runway"), born Long Island, NY, Aug 9, 1959.

August 2014

S	M	T	W	T	F	S
					1	2
3	4	5	6	7	8	9
10	11	12	13	14	15	16
17	18	19	20	21	22	23
24	25	26	27	28	29	30
31						

Rodney George (Rod) Laver, 76, Hall of Fame tennis player, born Rockhampton, Australia, Aug 9, 1938.

Kevin McKidd, 41, actor ("Grey's Anatomy," "Rome"), born Elgin, Murray, Scotland, Aug 9, 1973.

Kenneth Howard (Ken) Norton, Sr, 69, former boxer, born Jacksonville, IL, Aug 9, 1945.

Deion Sanders, 47, Hall of Fame football player, former baseball player, born Fort Myers, FL, Aug 9, 1967.

David Steinberg, 72, comedian ("The David Steinberg Show"), born Winnipeg, MB, Canada, Aug 9, 1942.

Audrey Tautou, 38, actress (*Amélie, The Da Vinci Code*), born Beaumont, Puy-de-Dôme, France, Aug 9, 1976.

August 10 — Sunday

DAY 222 **143 REMAINING**

"CANDID CAMERA" TV PREMIERE: ANNIVERSARY. Aug 10, 1948. This show—which appeared at various times on the big three TV networks and in syndication—was created and hosted by Allen Funt. The show was initially an Armed Forces Radio program based on Funt's success in recording and broadcasting soldiers' gripes. The show's modus operandi was to catch people unawares on camera—either as part of a practical joke or just being themselves. It spawned numerous imitators.

CHINA: FESTIVAL OF HUNGRY GHOSTS. Aug 10. Important Chinese festival, also known as the Chung Yuan Festival. According to Chinese legend, during the seventh lunar month the souls of the dead are released from purgatory to roam the earth. Joss sticks are burned in homes; prayers, food and "ghost money" are offered to appease the ghosts. Market stallholders join together to hold celebrations to ensure that their businesses will prosper in the coming year. Wayang (Chinese street opera) and puppet shows are performed, and fruit and Chinese delicacies are offered to the spirits of the dead. Chung Yuan is observed on the 15th day of the seventh lunar month. Date in other countries will differ from China's.

ECUADOR: INDEPENDENCE DAY. Aug 10. National holiday. Celebrates declaration of independence in 1809. Freedom from Spain was attained May 24, 1822.

HERBERT HOOVER DAY. Aug 10. Iowa. Annually, the Sunday nearest Aug 10, the birthday of Herbert Hoover.

HOOVER, HERBERT CLARK: BIRTH ANNIVERSARY. Aug 10, 1874. The 31st president of the US (1929–33) was born at West Branch, IA. Hoover was the first president born west of the Mississippi River and the first to have a telephone on his desk (installed Mar 27, 1929). "Older men declare war. But it is youth that must fight and die," he said at Chicago, IL, at the Republican National Convention, June 27, 1944. Hoover died at New York, NY, Oct 20, 1964. In Iowa, the Sunday nearest Aug 10 is observed as Herbert Hoover Day.

ITALY: PALIO DEL GOLFO. Aug 10. La Spezia. A rowing contest over a 2,000-meter course is held on the second Sunday in August.

JAPAN'S UNCONDITIONAL SURRENDER: ANNIVERSARY. Aug 10, 1945. A gathering to discuss surrender terms took place in Emperor Hirohito's bomb shelter; the participants were stalemated. Hirohito settled the question, believing continuing the war would only result in further loss of Japanese lives. A message was transmitted to Japanese ambassadors in Switzerland and Sweden to accept the terms issued at Potsdam July 26, 1945, except that the Japanese emperor's sovereignty must be maintained. The Allies devised a plan in which the emperor and the Japanese government would administer under the rule of the Supreme Commander of the Allied Powers, and the Japanese surrendered.

MISSOURI: ADMISSION DAY: ANNIVERSARY. Aug 10. Became 24th state in 1821.

MOON PHASE: FULL MOON. Aug 10. Moon enters Full Moon phase at 2:09 PM, EDT.

NESTLÉ, HENRI: 200th BIRTH ANNIVERSARY. Aug 10, 1814. Inventor of infant formula and entrepreneur, Heinrich Nestlé was born at Frankfurt, Germany, but moved to Vevey, Switzerland, where he trained as a pharmacist. In 1867, perhaps spurred on by the high infant mortality among his siblings, he created farine lactée, a substitute breast milk for infants unable to nurse. By the 1870s he was distributing the formula worldwide. Nestlé sold the Nestlé company in 1875, but the company retained his name, which means "little nest" and only later expanded its business to include chocolate and condensed milk. Died July 7, 1890, at Glion, Switzerland.

SMITHSONIAN INSTITUTION FOUNDED: ANNIVERSARY. Aug 10, 1846. Founding of the Smithsonian Institution at Washington, DC. For info: Smithsonian Institution, 900 Jefferson Dr SW, Washington, DC 20560. Phone: (202) 357-2700.

STURGEON MOON. Aug 10. So called by Native American tribes of New England and the Great Lakes because at this time of year this important food fish was most abundant. The August Full Moon.

 BIRTHDAYS TODAY

Ian Anderson, 67, musician, lead singer (Jethro Tull), born Blackpool, England, Aug 10, 1947.

Rosanna Arquette, 55, actress (*Desperately Seeking Susan, New York Stories*), born New York, NY, Aug 10, 1959.

Antonio Banderas, 54, actor (*Spy Kids, The Mask of Zorro, Desperado*), born Malaga, Spain, Aug 10, 1960.

Riddick Bowe, 47, boxer, born Brooklyn, NY, Aug 10, 1967.

Angie Harmon, 42, actress ("Rizzoli & Isles," "Law & Order," "Baywatch Nights"), born Dallas, TX, Aug 10, 1972.

Betsey Johnson, 72, fashion designer, born Wethersfield, CT, Aug 10, 1942.

August 11 — Monday

DAY 223 **142 REMAINING**

ATCHISON, DAVID R.: BIRTH ANNIVERSARY. Aug 11, 1807. Missouri legislator who was president of the US for one day. Born at Frogtown, KY. Atchison's strong proslavery opinions made his name prominent in legislative debates. He served as president pro tempore of the Senate a number of times, and he became president of the US for one day—Sunday, Mar 4, 1849—pending the swearing in of President-elect Zachary Taylor on Monday, Mar 5, 1849. The city of Atchison, KS, and the county of Atchison, MO, are named for him. He died at Gower, MO, Jan 26, 1886.

BOND, CARRIE JACOBS: BIRTH ANNIVERSARY. Aug 11, 1862. American composer of well-known songs, including "I Love You Truly" and "A Perfect Day," and of scores for motion pictures, Carrie Jacobs Bond was born at Janesville, WI. She died at Hollywood, CA, at age 84, Dec 28, 1946.

CHAD: INDEPENDENCE DAY. Aug 11. National holiday. Commemorates independence from France in 1960.

DOUGLAS, MIKE: BIRTH ANNIVERSARY. Aug 11, 1925. This pioneer of daytime talk shows was born Michael Delaney Dowd, Jr, at Chicago, IL. Douglas hosted his first afternoon talk show in Cleveland in 1961 and within five years was a household name. His nationally syndicated show featured celebrity interviews and topics and remained on the air until 1981. The show received the first Emmy Award for Individual Achievement in Daytime Television, and memorable guests included first-time performances by Aretha Franklin, Barbra Streisand and Bill Cosby. Tiger Woods appeared at the age of two alongside avid golfer Bob Hope. Douglas died Aug 11, 2006, at North Palm Beach, FL.

ELVIS WEEK. Aug 11–17. Memphis, TN. Each year Elvis fans from around the world visit Memphis to celebrate the King of Rock and Roll® at his beloved home, Graceland Mansion. Events occur throughout the city with special events sponsored by Graceland. A commemoration of the music, magic and memories associated with the legacy of Elvis Presley. Est attendance: 75,000. For info: Graceland, 3734 Elvis Presley Blvd, Memphis, TN 38116. Phone: (800) 238-2000 or (901) 332-3322. Web: www.elvisweek.com.

HALEY, ALEX PALMER: BIRTH ANNIVERSARY. Aug 11, 1921. Born at Ithaca, NY, Alex Palmer Haley was raised by his grandmother at Henning, TN. In 1939 he entered the US Coast Guard and served as a cook, but eventually he became a writer and college professor. His interview with Malcolm X for *Playboy* led to his first book, *The Autobiography of Malcolm X*, which sold six million copies and was translated into eight languages. *Roots*, his Pulitzer Prize–winning novel published in 1976, sold millions, was translated into 37 languages and was made into an eight-part TV miniseries in 1977. The story generated an enormous interest in family ancestry. Haley died at Seattle, WA, Feb 13, 1992.

INGERSOLL DAY. Aug 11. Ingersoll Day is an annual celebration on or around Aug 11, the birthday of Robert Green Ingersoll, to celebrate the life and works of one of the most popular freethinkers in US history. For info: American Humanist Assn, 1777 T St NW, Washington, DC 20009. Phone: (202) 238-9088. Fax: (202) 238-9003. Web: www.secularseasons.org/August/ingersoll_day.html.

MAE WEST BIRTHDAY GALA. Aug 11–17. New York, NY. To commemorate the stage career of legendary Brooklyn-born entertainer Mae West, several Mae-themed events are scheduled in Manhattan. Events—including song recitals, exhibitions, readings, walking tours and archival installations—always kick off by or before Aug 17, the date of West's birth in 1893. The Mae West Gala has been featured on The Biography Channel, on Bloomberg Radio and in the print media. Est attendance: 5,000. For info: Conrad Bradford, 24 Fifth Ave, Box 611, New York, NY 10011. Phone: (917) 403-0980. E-mail: comeupseeMAE@aol.com. Web: MaeWest.blogspot.com.

PRESIDENTIAL JOKE DAY: 30th ANNIVERSARY. Aug 11, 1984. Anniversary of President Ronald Reagan's voice-test joke. In preparation for a radio broadcast, during a thought-to-be-off-the-record voice level test, instead of counting "one, two, three . . ." the president said: "My fellow Americans, I am pleased to tell you I just signed legislation which outlaws Russia forever. The bombing begins in five minutes." The statement was picked up by live television cameras and was heard by millions worldwide. The incident provoked national and international reactions, including a news network proposal of new ground rules concerning the use of "off-the-record" remarks.

SAINT CLARE OF ASSISI: FEAST DAY. Aug 11, 1253. Chiara Favorone di Offreduccio, a religious leader inspired by St. Francis of Assisi, was the first woman to write her own religious order rule. Born at Assisi, Italy, July 16, 1194, she died there Aug 11, 1253. A "Privilege of Poverty" freed her order from any constraint to accept material security, making the "Poor Clares" totally dependent on God.

♣ ♣ ♣

August 2014	S	M	T	W	T	F	S
						1	2
	3	4	5	6	7	8	9
	10	11	12	13	14	15	16
	17	18	19	20	21	22	23
	24	25	26	27	28	29	30
	31						

SPACE MILESTONE: *VOSTOK 3* (USSR). Aug 11, 1962. Launched on this date, Andrian Nikolayev orbited Earth 64 times over a period of 94 hours, 25 minutes, covering a distance of 1,242,500 miles. Achieved radio communication with *Vostok 4* and telecast from spacecraft.

US AMATEUR (GOLF) CHAMPIONSHIP. Aug 11–17. Atlanta Athletic Club, Atlanta, GA. For info: USGA, Golf House, Championship Dept, PO Box 708, Far Hills, NJ 07931. Phone: (908) 234-2300. Fax: (908) 234-9687. E-mail: usga@usga.org. Web: www.usga.org.

VICTORY DAY. Aug 11. Rhode Island. State holiday commemorating President Harry Truman's announcement of the surrender of the Japanese to the Allies on Aug 14, 1945. Annually, the second Monday in August.

WATTS RIOT: ANNIVERSARY. Aug 11, 1965. A minor clash between the California Highway Patrol and two young blacks set off six days of riots in the Watts area of Los Angeles. Thirty-four deaths were reported and more than 3,000 people were arrested. Damage to property was listed at $40 million. The less-immediate cause of the disturbance, and the others that followed, was racial tension between whites and blacks in American society.

WEIRD CONTEST WEEK. Aug 11–15. Music Pier, Ocean City, NJ. One contest daily. Contests include "That's the Way the Cookie Crumbles" (chewing something meaningful out of a huge cookie), saltwater taffy sculpting, french fry sculpting, paper clip sculpting, Little Miss and Little Mister Chaos and Miss and Mister Miscellaneous Contest. 11 AM. Annually, the third week in August. Est attendance: 4,500. For info: Mark Soifer, PR Dir, City of Ocean City, City Hall, 9th Asbury Ave, Ocean City, NJ 08226. Phone: (609) 525-9300 or (609) 364-4010. Fax: (609) 525-0301. E-mail: msoifer@hotmail.com.

ZIMBABWE: HEROES' DAY. Aug 11. National holiday. Followed by Defense Forces Day on Aug 12.

BIRTHDAYS TODAY

Joanna Coles, 70, children's author, born Newark, NJ, Aug 11, 1944.

Arlene Dahl, 86, actress ("One Life to Live," "Fantasy Island"), born Minneapolis, MN, Aug 11, 1928.

Viola Davis, 49, actress (*The Help, Doubt, Antwone Fisher*), born St. Matthews, SC, Aug 11, 1965.

Will Friedle, 38, actor ("Boy Meets World"), born Hartford, CT, Aug 11, 1976.

Chris Hemsworth, 31, actor (*Thor*, "Home and Away"), born Melbourne, Australia, Aug 11, 1983.

Hulk Hogan, 61, wrestler, actor, born Terry Gene Bollea at Augusta, GA, Aug 11, 1953.

Joe Jackson, 59, musician, songwriter, born Burton-on-Trent, England, Aug 11, 1955.

Ashley Jensen, 45, actress ("Ugly Betty," "Extras"), born Annan, Dumfries and Galloway, Scotland, Aug 11, 1969.

Chris Messina, 40, actor (*Argo*, "The Mindy Project," "The Newsroom"), born New York, NY, Aug 11, 1974.

Marilyn vos Savant, 68, columnist ("Ask Marilyn"), claims world's highest IQ, born St. Louis, MO, Aug 11, 1946.

Stephen Wozniak, 64, Apple computer cofounder, born Sunnyvale, CA, Aug 11, 1950.

August 12 — Tuesday

DAY 224 **141 REMAINING**

BAHAMAS: FOX HILL DAY. Aug 12. Nassau. Annually, the second Tuesday in August.

BEWICK, THOMAS: BIRTH ANNIVERSARY. Aug 12, 1753. English artist, wood engraver and author, remembered especially for his book illustrations in *General History of Quadrupeds, A History of British Birds* and *Aesop's Fables*. Born at Cherryburn, Northumberland, and died at Gateshead, Durham, England, Nov 8, 1828.

CANTINFLAS: BIRTH ANNIVERSARY. Aug 12, 1911. Mexico's most famous comic actor, Cantinflas, was born at Mexico City as Mario Moreno Reyes. Particularly popular with the poor people of Mexico because he most often portrayed the underdog, Cantinflas got his start in Mexico City *carpas*, the equivalent of vaudeville. He became internationally known for his starring role as Passepartout in *Around the World in 80 Days*. The name *Cantinflas* was invented by the comic to prevent his parents from learning he was in show business, which they considered a shameful endeavor. Died Apr 20, 1993, at Mexico City.

DeMILLE, CECIL B.: BIRTH ANNIVERSARY. Aug 12, 1881. Born at Ashfield, MA, Cecil Blount DeMille was a film showman extraordinaire known for lavish screen spectacles. He produced more than 70 major films, which were noted more for their large scale than for their subtle artistry, including *Cleopatra, The Plainsman, Reap the Wild Wind* and *The Ten Commandments* (in 1923 and 1956). DeMille was awarded an Oscar for *The Greatest Show on Earth* in 1953. He died Jan 21, 1959, at Hollywood, CA.

HOME SEWING MACHINE PATENTED: ANNIVERSARY. Aug 12, 1851. Isaac Singer developed the sewing machine for use in homes.

IBM PERSONAL COMPUTER INTRODUCED: ANNIVERSARY. Aug 12, 1981. IBM's first personal computer was released. The computer cost the equivalent of $3,000 in today's currency. Although IBM was one of the pioneers in making mainframe and other large computers, this was the company's first foray into the desktop computer market. Eventually, more IBM-compatible computers were manufactured by IBM's competitors than by IBM itself.

KIDD, MICHAEL: BIRTH ANNIVERSARY. Aug 12, 1915. Dancer and choreographer born Milton Greenwald at New York, NY. He was responsible for some of the most memorable Broadway productions of all time, including *Finian's Rainbow, Guys and Dolls* and *Can-Can*. His film choreography included *Seven Brides for Seven Brothers* and *Hello, Dolly!* He won five Tony Awards for his Broadway productions and an honorary Oscar for "service to the art of dance" in feature films. He died at Los Angeles, CA, Dec 23, 2007.

KING PHILIP ASSASSINATION: ANNIVERSARY. Aug 12, 1676. Philip, a son of Massasoit, chief of the Wampanog tribe, was killed near Mt Hope, RI, by a member of his own tribe, bringing to an end the first and bloodiest war between American Indians and white settlers of New England, a war that had raged for nearly two years and was known as King Philip's War.

MATHEWSON, CHRISTY: BIRTH ANNIVERSARY. Aug 12, 1880. Famed American baseball player Christopher (Christy) Mathewson, one of the first players named to Baseball's Hall of Fame, was born at Factoryville, PA. Died at Saranac Lake, NY, Oct 7, 1925. He pitched three complete games during the 1905 World Series without allowing opponents to score a run. In 17 years he won 372 games while losing 188 and striking out 2,499 players.

MOUNT OGURA PLANE CRASH: ANNIVERSARY. Aug 12, 1985. A Japan Airlines plane crashed into the side of Mount Ogura, Japan, claiming 520 lives. The worst air disaster involving a single plane. See also: "Canary Islands Plane Disaster: Anniversary" (Mar 27).

NIGHT OF THE MURDERED POETS: ANNIVERSARY. Aug 12, 1952. Thirteen prominent Jewish writers and leaders associated with the Jewish Anti-Fascist Committee were executed on the orders of Josef Stalin. After WWII, the JAC evolved into an organization promoting the revival of Jewish culture and identity in Russia. Stalin, a rabid anti-Semite, had fifteen of the committee's leaders arrested, tried and convicted on trumped up charges of treason.

OWENS, BUCK: 85th BIRTH ANNIVERSARY. Aug 12, 1929. Country-western star, creator of the "Bakersfield sound" in the 1960s, Alvis Edgar "Buck" Owens was born to a sharecropper outside Sherman, TX. His family moved west with Dust Bowl refugees during the Great Depression, and Owens became a honky-tonk performer in California. He had 19 consecutive No 1 singles from 1963 to 1967, and his success led him to a cohosting gig on the popular TV variety show "Hee Haw" (1969–86). Inducted into the Country Music Hall of Fame in 1996, Owens died at Bakersfield, CA, Mar 25, 2006.

SHARP, ZERNA ADDIS: 125th BIRTH ANNIVERSARY. Aug 12, 1889. Educator and originator of the "Dick and Jane" readers used for many years in American schools, Sharp collaborated with illustrator Eleanor B. Campbell and others to create the texts while a reading consultant for Scott Foresman. She selected easy-to-read words and patterned the plots from children's interests. Born at Hillisburg, IN, she died June 17, 1981, at Frankfort, IN.

SPACE MILESTONE: *ECHO I* (US). Aug 12, 1960. First successful communications satellite in Earth's orbit to relay voice and TV signals from one ground station to another was launched.

SPACE MILESTONE: *ENTERPRISE* (US). Aug 12, 1977. Reusable orbiting vehicle (space shuttle) makes first successful flight on its own within Earth's atmosphere. Launched from a Boeing 747 on Aug 12, 1977.

THAILAND: BIRTHDAY OF THE QUEEN. Aug 12. The entire kingdom of Thailand celebrates the birthday of Queen Sirikit.

UNITED NATIONS: INTERNATIONAL YOUTH DAY. Aug 12. Day to increase public awareness of the World Programme of Action for Youth to the Year 2000 and Beyond, which calls for action in 10 priority areas: education, employment, hunger and poverty, health, environment, drug abuse, juvenile delinquency, leisure-time activities, girls and young women, and full and effective participation of youths (15–24 years old) in the life of society and in decision making. For info: United Nations, Dept of Public Info, New York, NY 10017. Web: www.un.org.

VINYL RECORD DAY. Aug 12. We all need a reminder sometimes that life is good, regardless of national news and daily challenges. Favorite songs can bring back fond memories, and Vinyl Record Day encourages celebrating these musical memories with family and friends. The day also seeks to recognize the tremendous cultural influence that vinyl records and album covers have had for more than 60 years and the need to preserve that audio history. Annually, on Aug 12—the day Thomas Edison invented the phonograph in 1877. For info: Gary Freiberg, 1107 11th St, Los Osos, CA 93402. Phone: (888) 644-4567. E-mail: gary@VinylRecordDay.org. Web: www.VinylRecordDay.org.

WYATT, JANE: BIRTH ANNIVERSARY. Aug 12, 1910. Born at Bergen County, NJ, this Hollywood actress had her big break starring in Frank Capra's *Lost Horizon* in 1937. Other classic performances included her role opposite Gregory Peck in 1947's *Gentlemen's Agreement*. Wyatt's film career suffered when she criticized Senator Joseph McCarthy in the 1950s. She is best remembered for the television show "Father Knows Best," for which she won three consecutive Emmy Awards for her portrayal of Margaret Anderson (1958–61). Wyatt died Aug 20, 2006, at Bel Air, CA.

BIRTHDAYS TODAY

Casey Affleck, 39, actor (*The Assassination of Jesse James by the Coward Robert Ford, Gone Baby Gone*), born Falmouth, MA, Aug 12, 1975.

William Goldman, 83, writer (*The Princess Bride, Marathon Man*), born Chicago, IL, Aug 12, 1931.

George Hamilton, 75, actor (*Love at First Bite, Act One*, "The Survivors"), born Memphis, TN, Aug 12, 1939.

François Hollande, 60, President of France, born Rouen, France, Aug 12, 1954.

Sam J. Jones, 60, actor (*Flash Gordon, 10*), born Chicago, IL, Aug 12, 1954.

Peter Krause, 49, actor ("Parenthood," "Six Feet Under," "Sports Night"), born Minneapolis, MN, Aug 12, 1965.

Ann M. Martin, 59, author (The Baby-Sitters Club series, *A Corner of the Universe*), born Princeton, NJ, Aug 12, 1955.

Pat Metheny, 60, jazz guitarist, born Lee's Summit, MO, Aug 12, 1954.

Pete Sampras, 43, Hall of Fame tennis player, born Washington, DC, Aug 12, 1971.

George Soros, 84, billionaire, financier, philanthropist, born Budapest, Hungary, Aug 12, 1930.

Antoine Walker, 38, basketball player, born Chicago, IL, Aug 12, 1976.

August 13 — Wednesday

DAY 225 **140 REMAINING**

ANGSTROM, ANDERS JONAS: 200th BIRTH ANNIVERSARY. Aug 13, 1814. Astronomer born at Logdo, Sweden, Angstrom is noted for founding the science of spectroscopy—the study of light—and in particular, his spectral analyses of the sun and aurora borealis. His studies of the sun's spectra resulted in the discovery of hydrogen in its atmosphere in 1862. Angstrom deduced the principle of spectrum analysis, and the angstrom unit of length, which measures ten-billionth of a meter, was named in his honor. Died June 21, 1874, at Uppsala, Sweden.

ARTISTS IN THE PARK. Aug 13. Cate Park, Wolfeboro, NH. 35th annual. Juried exhibit and sale including 41 artists and craftspeople, demonstrations throughout the day and family entertainment. Held rain or shine, 10 AM–5 PM. Est attendance: 4,000. For info: Deborah Hopkins, Chair, Governor Wentworth Arts Council, PO Box 1322, Wolfeboro, NH 03894. Phone: (603) 569-4994. Web: www.wolfeboroarts.org.

BAIRD, JOHN LOGIE: BIRTH ANNIVERSARY. Aug 13, 1888. Born at Helensburgh, Scotland, Baird was the first person to demonstrate a working television. For decades scientists had been striving to realize the dream of transmitting images, yet it wasn't until 1924 that Baird first managed to produce a static image across a few feet using a crude mechanical appliance. In two short years he had fine-tuned his invention enough to offer the world a demonstration of moving images, and by 1928, his group, the Baird Television Development Company, achieved the first transatlantic transmission from London to New York. By 1937, however, Guglielmo Marconi's all-electronic television outshone Baird's invention, effectively making it obsolete. Baird died on June 14, 1946, at Bexhill-on-Sea, England.

August 2014	S	M	T	W	T	F	S
						1	2
	3	4	5	6	7	8	9
	10	11	12	13	14	15	16
	17	18	19	20	21	22	23
	24	25	26	27	28	29	30
	31						

BERLIN WALL ERECTED: ANNIVERSARY. Aug 13, 1961. Early in the morning, the East German government closed the border between the east and west sectors of Berlin with barbed wire to discourage further population movement to the West. Telephone and postal services were interrupted, and later in the week, a concrete wall was built to strengthen the barrier between official crossing points. The dismantling of the wall began Nov 9, 1989. See also: "Berlin Wall Opened: Anniversary" (Nov 9).

CAXTON, WILLIAM: BIRTH ANNIVERSARY. Aug 13, 1422. First English printer, born at Kent, England. Died at London, England, 1491. Caxton produced his first book printed in English (while he was at Bruges), the *Recuyell of the Histories of Troy*, in 1476, and in the autumn of that year set up a print shop at Westminster, becoming the first printer in England.

CENTRAL AFRICAN REPUBLIC: INDEPENDENCE DAY. Aug 13. Commemorates Proclamation of Independence from France in 1960.

HITCHCOCK, ALFRED (JOSEPH): BIRTH ANNIVERSARY. Aug 13, 1899. English film director and master of suspense born at London, England. Hitchcock's career as a filmmaker dates back to the silent film era when he made *The Lodger* in 1926, based on the tale of Jack the Ripper. American audiences were introduced to the Hitchcock style in 1935 with *The Thirty-Nine Steps* and *The Lady Vanishes* in 1938, after which he went to Hollywood. There he produced a string of classics including *Rebecca, Suspicion, Notorious, Rear Window, To Catch a Thief, The Birds, Psycho* and *Frenzy*, in addition to his TV series, "Alfred Hitchcock Presents." He died Apr 29, 1980, at Beverly Hills, CA.

HOGAN, BEN: BIRTH ANNIVERSARY. Aug 13, 1912. With Sam Snead and Byron Nelson (all born in 1912), one of the greatest golfers. Born at Stephenville, TX, but later moving to Fort Worth, Hogan caddied with friend and later rival Nelson at the Glen Garden Country Club. He struggled financially until 1938, when he began winning tournaments. His wins were interrupted by three years' military service during WWII. After almost dying in a Feb 2, 1949, auto accident, Hogan was able to recover and win the 1950 US Open. In 1953, Hogan won the Masters, US Open and British Open. New York City gave him a ticker-tape parade to celebrate his British Open win. He is one of only five players to win all four major professional championships, and his 64 career PGA victories rank him fourth after Sam Snead, Jack Nicklaus and Tiger Woods. Hogan died at Fort Worth, TX, July 25, 1997.

INTERNATIONAL CONGRESS OF MATHEMATICIANS 2014. Aug 13–21. Seoul, Republic of Korea. A major scientific event bringing together mathematicians from all over the world and demonstrating the vital role that mathematics play in our society. For info: International Congress of Mathematicians, International Math Union. E-mail: secretary@mathunion.org. Web: www.mathunion.org.

INTERNATIONAL LEFT-HANDERS DAY. Aug 13. Since 1992, an annual worldwide day when left-handers everywhere can celebrate their sinistrality and increase public awareness of the advantages and disadvantages of being left-handed. There are many ways to mark this day, including left versus right sports matches, a left-handed tea party or "Lefty Zones." Right-handers are encouraged to try out everyday left-handed objects to see just how awkward it can feel using the wrong equipment. Annually, Aug 13. For info: Left-Handers Club, Anything Left-Handed, PO Box 344, Tadworth, Surrey, KT20 9DL, England. Web: www.anythinglefthanded.co.uk.

KRUPP, ALFRIED von BOHLEN und HALBACH: BIRTH ANNIVERSARY. Aug 13, 1907. As sole owner of the massive Krupp industries, Alfried Krupp took over the factories of German-occupied countries and used them for the Nazi war machine. Sometimes he had complete facilities dismantled and reassembled inside Germany. He used prisoners of war, civilians from occupied countries and inmates of concentration camps as forced labor in his factories. Found guilty as a war criminal by the military court at Nuremberg in 1948, he regained his property after serving three years of a 12-year sentence. He was named Alfried von Bohlen und Halbach at birth, but the family was authorized by Emperor Wilhelm II to add the mother's maiden name of Krupp to their own. Born at Essen, Germany, he died there July 30, 1967.

OAKLEY, ANNIE: BIRTH ANNIVERSARY. Aug 13, 1860. Annie Oakley was born at Darke County, OH. She developed an eye as a markswoman early as a child, becoming so proficient that she was able to pay off the mortgage on her family farm by selling the game she killed. A few years after defeating vaudeville marksman Frank Butler in a shooting match, she married him and they toured as a team until joining Buffalo Bill's Wild West Show in 1885. She was one of the star attractions for 17 years. She died Nov 3, 1926, at Greenville, OH.

SPACE MILESTONE: *HELIOS* SOLAR WING. Aug 13, 2001. The solar-powered plane *Helios* broke the altitude records for propeller-driven aircraft and nonrocket planes on this date, soaring higher than 96,500 feet. The plane has a wingspan longer than a Boeing 747 and uses solar-powered motors to power 14 propellers, flying at speeds as high as 170 mph. NASA plans to develop similar craft for unmanned flights on Mars.

STONE, LUCY: BIRTH ANNIVERSARY. Aug 13, 1818. American women's rights pioneer, born near West Brookfield, MA, Lucy Stone dedicated her life to the abolition of slavery and the emancipation of women. Although she graduated from Oberlin College, she had to finance her education by teaching for nine years because her father did not favor college education for women. An eloquent speaker for her causes, she headed the list of 89 men and women who signed the call to the first national Woman's Rights Convention, held at Worcester, MA, October 1850. On May 1, 1855, she married Henry Blackwell. They aided in the founding of the American Suffrage Association, taking part in numerous referendum campaigns to win suffrage amendments to state constitutions. She died Oct 18, 1893, at Dorchester, MA.

SWEDEN: CRAYFISH PREMIERE. Aug 13. Crayfish may be sold and served in restaurants the day after the season opens. Annually, the second Wednesday in August.

TUNISIA: WOMEN'S DAY. Aug 13. General holiday. Celebration of independence of women.

BIRTHDAYS TODAY

Kathleen Battle, 66, opera singer, born Portsmouth, OH, Aug 13, 1948.

Danny Bonaduce, 55, radio personality, actor ("The Partridge Family"), born Broomall, PA, Aug 13, 1959.

Fidel Castro, 87, former president of Cuba (1959–2008), born Mayari, Oriente Province, Cuba, Aug 13, 1927.

Quinn Cummings, 47, actress (*The Goodbye Girl,* "Family"), born Los Angeles, CA, Aug 13, 1967.

Shani Davis, 32, Olympic speed skater, born Chicago, IL, Aug 13, 1982.

Pat Harrington, Jr, 85, actor, comedian ("The Jack Paar Show," "One Day at a Time"), born New York, NY, Aug 13, 1929.

Philippe Petit, 65, high-wire artist, juggler, author, born Nemours, France, Aug 13, 1949.

Kevin Tighe, 70, actor ("Emergency," *The Graduate, What's Eating Gilbert Grape?*), born Los Angeles, CA, Aug 13, 1944.

August 14 — Thursday

DAY 226 | **139 REMAINING**

ATLANTIC CHARTER SIGNING: ANNIVERSARY. Aug 14, 1941. The eight-point agreement was signed by US president Franklin D. Roosevelt and British prime minister Winston S. Churchill. The charter grew out of a three-day conference aboard ship in the Atlantic Ocean, off the Newfoundland coast, and stated policies and hopes for the future agreed to by the two nations.

CHANNEL ISLANDS: JERSEY BATTLE OF FLOWERS. Aug 14–15. Jersey, Channel Islands. Colorful parade of floats decorated with hundreds of flowers. First held in 1902 to mark the coronation of Edward VII and Queen Alexandra. Annually, the second Thursday and Friday in August. Est attendance: 27,500. For info: The Jersey Battle of Flowers Assn, Meadow Bank, St. Lawrence, Jersey, Channel Islands, England JE3 1EE. Phone: (44) (153) 463-9000. E-mail: battle@jerseymail.co.uk. Web: www.battleofflowers.com.

COLOGNE CATHEDRAL COMPLETION: ANNIVERSARY. Aug 14, 1880. The largest Gothic church in northern Europe, the Cologne Cathedral at Cologne, Germany, was completed on this date, 632 years after rebuilding began on Aug 14, 1248. In fact, there had been a church on its site since 873, but a fire in 1248 made rebuilding necessary. The cathedral was again damaged, by bombing, during WWII.

THE 59-MINUTE, 37-SECOND ANVIL MOUNTAIN CHALLENGE. Aug 14. Nome, AK. 19th annual running event that starts at the base of Anvil Mountain, where runners must run 834 feet up the face of the mountain and return in less than 59 minutes, 37 seconds or be disqualified from the competition. Trophies awarded for first–third finishers, first woman finisher and first finisher age 16 and younger. Record time is 25 minutes, 37 seconds. Est attendance: 1,000. For info: Rasmussen's Music Mart, PO Box 2, Nome, AK 99762-0002. Phone: (907) 443-2798 or (907) 443-2919. E-mail: leaknome@alaska.com.

JUST, ERNEST E.: BIRTH ANNIVERSARY. Aug 14, 1883. American marine biologist Ernest E. Just was born at Charleston, SC. He was the first recipient of the NAACP's Spingarn Medal and was a professor at Howard University from 1907 to 1941, where he was head of physiology at the medical school (1912–20) and head of zoology (1912–41). He died Oct 27, 1941, at Washington, DC.

KENTUCKY STATE FAIR (WITH WORLD'S CHAMPIONSHIP HORSE SHOW). Aug 14–25. Kentucky Fair and Expo Center, Louisville, KY. Midway, concerts by nationally known artists and the World's Championship Horse Show. Since 1904. Est attendance: 650,000. For info: Kentucky Fair and Expo Ctr, PO Box 37130, Louisville, KY 40233-7130. Phone: (502) 367-5000 or (502) 367-5180. Web: www.kyexpo.org or www.kystatefair.org.

LITTLE LEAGUE BASEBALL WORLD SERIES. Aug 14–24. South Williamsport, PA. Sixteen teams from the US and foreign countries compete for the World Championship. Est attendance: 300,000. For info: Little League International, Box 3485, Williamsport, PA 17701. Phone: (570) 326-1921. Web: www.LittleLeague.org.

MILWAUKEE IRISH FEST. Aug 14–17. Milwaukee, WI. 34th annual. World's largest Irish music and cultural event, with the best of Irish and Irish American music, dance and theater on 16 stages. Activities include a cultural village, sports, contests, parades, displays, food, marketplace and children's activities. Weeklong summer school (open to the public) precedes the festival. Annually, the third weekend in August. Est attendance: 130,000. For info: Milwaukee Irish Fest, 1532 Wauwatosa Ave, Milwaukee, WI 53213. Phone: (414) 476-3378. E-mail: info@irishfest.com. Web: www.irishfest.com.

NAVAJO NATION: NAVAJO CODE TALKERS DAY. Aug 14. The Navajo Nation Council has established Aug 14 of each year as a tribal holiday recognizing and honoring the distinguished record of the Code Talkers during WWII. The Code Talkers transmitted military messages in the Navajo language during the war, and Axis powers were unable to break the code. For info: Office of the

Speaker, Navajo Nation Council, PO Box 9000, Window Rock, AZ 86515. Phone: (928) 871-6386. Web: www.navajo-nsn.gov.

PAKISTAN: INDEPENDENCE DAY. Aug 14, 1947. Gained independence from Britain in 1947.

SOCIAL SECURITY ACT: ANNIVERSARY. Aug 14, 1935. President Franklin D. Roosevelt signed the Social Security Act, which contained provisions for the establishment of a Social Security Board to administer federal old-age and survivors' insurance in the US. By signing the bill into law, Roosevelt was fulfilling a 1932 campaign promise.

SUN PRAIRIE'S SWEET CORN FESTIVAL. Aug 14–17. Sun Prairie, WI. Family-oriented fun. Carnival, midget auto races, parade, beer, brats, food, exhibits, entertainment, craft fair and tons of hot, buttered sweet corn. Est attendance: 100,000. For info: Sun Prairie Chamber of Commerce, 109 E Main St, Sun Prairie, WI 53590. Phone: (608) 837-4547. Fax: (608) 837-8765. E-mail: spchamber@frontier.com. Web: www.sunprairiechamber.com.

THAYER, ERNEST LAWRENCE: BIRTH ANNIVERSARY. Aug 14, 1863. The man who wrote the famous comic baseball ballad "Casey at the Bat" was born at Lawrence, MA. He wrote a series of comic poems for the *San Francisco Examiner*, of which "Casey at the Bat" was the last. It was published Sunday, June 3, 1888, and Thayer received five dollars in payment for it. Thayer, who regarded the poem's fame as a nuisance and whose other writings are largely forgotten, died at Santa Barbara, CA, Aug 21, 1940.

365-INNING SOFTBALL GAME: ANNIVERSARY. Aug 14–15, 1976. The Gager's Diner softball team played the Bend'n Elbow Tavern in a 365-inning softball game. Starting at 10 AM Aug 14, the game was called because of rain and fog at 4 PM, Aug 15. The 70 players, including 20 women, raised $4,000 for construction of a new softball field and for the Monticello, NY, Community General Hospital. The Gagers beat the Elbows 491–467. To date, this remains the longest softball game on record.

V-J DAY: ANNIVERSARY. Aug 14, 1945. Anniversary of President Harry Truman's announcement that Japan had surrendered to the Allies, setting off celebrations across the US. Official ratification of surrender occurred aboard the USS *Missouri* at Tokyo Bay, Sept 2 (Far Eastern time).

BIRTHDAYS TODAY

Russell Baker, 89, journalist, author, television host ("Masterpiece Theatre"), born Loudoun County, VA, Aug 14, 1925.

Catherine Bell, 46, actress ("Army Wives," "JAG"), born London, England, Aug 14, 1968.

Halle Berry, 46, actress (*Die Another Day, X-Men*; Oscar for *Monster's Ball*), born Cleveland, OH, Aug 14, 1968.

Lynne Cheney, 73, wife of Dick Cheney, 46th vice president of the US, born Casper, WY, Aug 14, 1941.

David Crosby, 73, singer (Crosby, Stills & Nash), songwriter, born Los Angeles, CA, Aug 14, 1941.

Antonio Fargas, 68, actor (*Shaft, I'm Gonna Git You Sucka!, Car Wash*), born the Bronx, NY, Aug 14, 1946.

Buddy Greco, 88, singer, composer, musician, born Philadelphia, PA, Aug 14, 1926.

Marcia Gay Harden, 55, actress (Oscar for *Pollock; Into the Wild, Mystic River*), born La Jolla, CA, Aug 14, 1959.

Terin Humphrey, 28, gymnast, born St. Louis, MO, Aug 14, 1986.

Earvin "Magic" Johnson, Jr, 55, Hall of Fame basketball player, born Lansing, MI, Aug 14, 1959.

August 2014	S	M	T	W	T	F	S
						1	2
	3	4	5	6	7	8	9
	10	11	12	13	14	15	16
	17	18	19	20	21	22	23
	24	25	26	27	28	29	30
	31						

Mila Kunis, 31, actress (*Ted, Black Swan*, "That '70s Show"), born Kiev, Ukraine, Aug 14, 1983.

Arthur Betz Laffer, 74, economist (the Laffer curve), born Youngstown, OH, Aug 14, 1940.

Gary Larson, 64, cartoonist ("The Far Side"), born Tacoma, WA, Aug 14, 1950.

Jay Manuel, 42, photographer, makeup artist, television personality ("America's Next Top Model"), born Toronto, ON, Canada, Aug 14, 1972.

Steve Martin, 69, comedian, actor (*Shopgirl, LA Story, Roxanne, Parenthood*), novelist, born Waco, TX, Aug 14, 1945.

Spencer Pratt, 31, television personality, born Los Angeles, CA, Aug 14, 1983.

Susan Saint James, 68, actress ("McMillan and Wife," "Kate and Allie"), born Long Beach, CA, Aug 14, 1946.

Robin Soderling, 30, tennis player, born Tibro, Sweden, Aug 14, 1984.

Danielle Steel, 67, author (*Vanished, Wanderlust*), born New York, NY, Aug 14, 1947.

Tim Tebow, 27, football player, born Manila, Philippines, Aug 14, 1987.

Rusty Wallace, 58, auto racer, born St. Louis, MO, Aug 14, 1956.

August 15 — Friday

DAY 227 — **138 REMAINING**

ALLIED LANDINGS IN SOUTH OF FRANCE: 70th ANNIVERSARY. Aug 15, 1944. After several postponements, Allied forces began Operation Dragoon, the landing on the south coast of France during WWII. More than 2,000 transports and landing craft transported 94,000 men to an area between Toulon and Cannes, with only 183 Allied losses. They encountered minimal opposition, and by the end of August, the French coast from the mouth of the Rhône to Nice was in Allied hands.

ASSUMPTION OF THE VIRGIN MARY. Aug 15. Greek and Roman Catholic churches celebrate Mary's ascent to heaven. In Orthodox churches, called the Dormition of Theotokos and commemorated on Aug 15 or 28. A holiday in many Christian countries.

BARRYMORE, ETHEL: BIRTH ANNIVERSARY. Aug 15, 1879. Celebrated award-winning actress of stage, screen and television, born Ethel Blythe at Philadelphia, PA. Sister of John and Lionel Barrymore. Died at Beverly Hills, CA, June 18, 1959.

BEST FRIEND'S DAY. Aug 15. Celebrate this special day by doing something fun with your best friend. Go shopping, go to the movies, go to a park or restaurant, play a game or just hang out and be together. For info: Thema Martin, 931 Monroe Dr NE, Ste A102, #226, Atlanta, GA 30308. Phone: (404) 939-3833. E-mail: tmartin@savoinaire.com.

BOHEMIAN NIGHTS AT NEW WEST FEST. Aug 15–17. Fort Collins, CO. More than 250 artists showcase their creations during this music festival, which also features a children's carnival, family activities, food booths, beer gardens and eight stages of local bands, singers and dancers in Downtown Fort Collins. For info: Downtown Fort Collins Business Assn, 19 Old Town Square, #230, Fort Collins, CO 80524. Phone: (970) 484-6500. E-mail: info@DowntownFortCollins.com. Web: www.DowntownFortCollins.com.

BONAPARTE, NAPOLEON: BIRTH ANNIVERSARY. Aug 15, 1769. Anniversary of the birth of French emperor Napoleon Bonaparte on the island of Corsica (reigned as emperor 1804–15). He died in exile at 5:49 PM, May 5, 1821, on the island of St. Helena. Public holiday at Corsica, France.

CHAUVIN DAY. Aug 15. A day named for Nicholas Chauvin, French soldier from Rochefort, France, who idolized Napoleon and who eventually became a subject of ridicule because of his blind loyalty and dedication to anything French. Originally referring to bellicose patriotism, *chauvinism* has come to mean blind or absurdly intense attachment to any cause. Observed on Napoleon's birth anniversary because Chauvin's birth date is unknown.

CHECK THE CHIP DAY. Aug 15. 2nd annual. "Check the Chip Day" serves as a reminder to pet owners to have their pets microchipped and to keep their microchip registration information up-to-date. Annually, Aug 15. For info: American Veterinary Medical Association, 1931 N Meacham Rd, Ste 100, Schaumburg, IL 60173. Phone: (847) 285-6782. E-mail: dkirkpatrick@avma.org. Web: www.avma.org.

CHILD, JULIA: BIRTH ANNIVERSARY. Aug 15, 1912. America's beloved food authority, who didn't take a cooking lesson until she was in her 30s, was born at Pasadena, CA. Child's cookbooks and television shows (most famously, "The French Chef") encouraged Americans to cook and eat well and to be skeptical of food fads and diet strictures. "Cooking is not a chore; it is a joy," Child believed. She died at Santa Barbara, CA, Aug 13, 2004.

COEUR D'ALENE INDIAN PILGRIMAGE. Aug 15. Coeur d'Alene's Old Mission State Park, Cataldo, ID. The annual Feast of the Assumption pilgrimage by the Coeur d'Alene Indians. Annually, Aug 15. Est attendance: 1,800. For info: Coeur d'Alene's Old Mission State Park, PO Box 30, Cataldo, ID 83810-0030. Phone: (208) 682-3814. Fax: (208) 682-4032. E-mail: old@idpr.idaho.gov. Web: www.visitidaho.org or www.idahoparks.org.

COMISKEY, CHARLES: BIRTH ANNIVERSARY. Aug 15, 1859. Charles Albert Comiskey, Baseball Hall of Fame first baseman, manager and executive, born at Chicago, IL. Comiskey's career spanned 50 years, 30 of them as founding owner of the Chicago White Sox. But before that, he was an outstanding and innovative player and a tough, successful manager. Inducted into the Hall of Fame in 1939. Died at Eagle River, WI, Oct 26, 1931.

CONGO (BRAZZAVILLE): NATIONAL DAY. Aug 15. National day of the People's Republic of the Congo. Commemorates independence from France in 1960.

DORMITION OF THEOTOKOS. Aug 15. Orthodox observance. According to New Calendar (Gregorian), the Dormition Fast is observed Aug 1–14, followed by Dormition of Theotokos on this day.

ELWOOD GLASS FESTIVAL. Aug 15–17. Elwood, IN. Glass factory tours, parade, craft market, flea market, quilt show, entertainment, carnival, kids' activities and more. Est attendance: 20,000. For info: Chamber of Commerce, 108 S Anderson St, Elwood, IN 46036. Phone: (765) 552-0180. E-mail: elwoodchamber@sbcglobal.net. Web: www.elwoodchamber-in.org/chamber-home.

EQUATORIAL GUINEA: CONSTITUTION DAY. Aug 15. National holiday. Commemorates the 1982 revision of the original constitution of 1968.

FERBER, EDNA: BIRTH ANNIVERSARY. Aug 15, 1887. Edna Ferber was born at Kalamazoo, MI. She wrote her first novel, *Dawn O'Hara*, in 1911 and became a prolific writer, producing many popular magazine stories. Her novel *So Big* brought her commercial success in 1924 as well as a Pulitzer Prize. Her other novels include *Show Boat, Cimarron, Saratoga Trunk, Giant* and *Ice Palace*, all of which were made into successful films. Ferber collaborated with George Kaufman in writing for the stage on *The Royal Family, Dinner at Eight, Stage Door* and *Bravo*. Ferber died at New York, NY, Apr 16, 1968.

FESTIVAL OF THE LITTLE HILLS. Aug 15–17. Frontier Park and Historic Main, St. Charles, MO. The largest festival of the year. Includes more than 350 craft booths, live music and food and beverage booths. Annually, the weekend beginning on the third Friday in August. Est attendance: 300,000. For info: Festival of the Little Hills, PO Box 1323, St. Charles, MO 63302. Phone: (800) 366-2427 or (636) 940-0095. E-mail: info@festivalofthelittlehills.com. Web: www.festivalofthelittlehills.com.

FINLAND: HELSINKI FESTIVAL. Aug 15–31. Helsinki. Finland's largest arts festival provides a diverse program of events throughout the city, with experiences ranging from classical to world music and pop, from drama to contemporary dance, and from visual art to film and children's events. Lose yourself in the Night of the Arts or get carried away with our fringe program. This is a festival that brings the arts to everyone! Est attendance: 200,000. For info: Helsinki Festival. E-mail: info@helsinkifestival.fi. Web: www.helsinkifestival.fi.

HARDING, FLORENCE KLING DeWOLFE: BIRTH ANNIVERSARY. Aug 15, 1860. Wife of Warren Gamaliel Harding, 29th president of the US, born at Marion, OH. Died there Nov 21, 1924.

HAWAII ADMISSION DAY HOLIDAY. Aug 15. The third Friday in August is observed as a state holiday each year, recognizing the anniversary of Hawaii's statehood. Hawaii became the 50th state Aug 21, 1959.

HIROHITO'S RADIO ADDRESS: ANNIVERSARY. Aug 15, 1945. At noon Japanese radio broadcast the Japanese national anthem, followed by a prerecorded statement by Emperor Hirohito announcing Japan's decision to surrender, citing the devastating power of the new atomic bomb. This was the first time most Japanese citizens had heard the voice of their emperor.

INDIA: INDEPENDENCE DAY. Aug 15. National holiday. Anniversary of Indian independence from Britain in 1947.

KOREA: INDEPENDENCE DAY. Aug 15. National holiday commemorates acceptance by Japan of Allied terms of surrender in 1945, thereby freeing Korea from 36 years of Japanese domination. Also marks formal proclamation of Republic of Korea in 1948. Military parades and ceremonies throughout country.

LIECHTENSTEIN: NATIONAL DAY. Aug 15. Public holiday on Assumption Day.

MACHIAS WILD BLUEBERRY FESTIVAL. Aug 15–17. Machias, ME. 39th annual. Harvest festival includes crafts sale, lobster boil, five-mile race, entertainment, children's parade, blueberry foods and a wild blueberry pie-eating contest. Annually, the third weekend in August. Est attendance: 22,000. For info: Machias Wild Blueberry Festival, PO Box 265, Machias, ME 04654. Phone: (207) 255-6665. Web: www.machiasblueberry.com.

MUDDY FROGWATER COUNTRY CLASSIC FESTIVAL. Aug 15–17. Yantis Park, Milton-Freewater, OR. Art show, crafts, food, country music, book sale, fun run, square dancing, firefighters' water fight, barbecue chicken dinner, corn roast, watermelon feed, talent show and softball tournament. Annually, the third weekend in August. Est attendance: 5,000. For info: Milton-Freewater Area Chamber of Commerce, 157 S Columbia, Milton-Freewater, OR 97862. Phone: (541) 938-5563. Fax: (541) 938-5564. E-mail: mfmdfrog@mfchamber.com. Web: www.muddyfrogwatercountry.com.

NATIONAL AVIATION WEEK. Aug 15–21. A celebration of flight designed to increase public awareness, knowledge and appreciation of aviation. Annually, the week of Orville Wright's birthday, Aug 19.

NATIONAL RELAXATION DAY. Aug 15. Hold the phones, call in sick or just take a nap. Today is the perfect excuse to reduce stress and improve your lifestyle by relaxing. Spend a few minutes learning or sharing the art of relaxation with family, friends and coworkers. Annually, Aug 15. For info: Sean M. Moeller and A.C. Vierow, PO Box 71, Clio, MI 48420. E-mail: relax15@yahoo.com.

PANAMA CANAL OPENS: 100th ANNIVERSARY. Aug 15, 1914. After 10 years of construction and much multination diplomacy, the Panama Canal opened for operation. A self-propelled crane boat made the first passage through the canal, a 50-mile waterway connecting the Atlantic and Pacific oceans, on Jan 7, 1914. The first ocean steamer, the SS *Ancon*, passed through Aug 3, 1914, and the canal officially opened Aug 15, 1914.

PANAMA: PANAMA CITY FOUNDATION DAY. Aug 15. Traditional annual cultural observance recognizes foundation of Panama City.

PETERSON, OSCAR: BIRTH ANNIVERSARY. Aug 15, 1925. Jazz musician born at Montreal, QC, Canada. Also a composer and vocalist, he was considered one of the greatest pianists ever to perform and record in the genre. His recordings won seven Grammy Awards, and he is a member of several music halls of fame. He died at Mississauga, ON, Canada, Dec 23, 2007.

RAND, PAUL: 100th BIRTH ANNIVERSARY. Aug 15, 1914. Designer, considered the father of modern American graphic design, born Peretz Rosenbaum at New York, NY. Rand played an important role in introducing the visual language of cubism, constructivism, de Stijl and the Bauhaus into American design. He designed iconic logos for IBM, UPS, ABC and Westinghouse, among others. Died Nov 26, 1996 at Norwalk, CT.

SCOTT, SIR WALTER: BIRTH ANNIVERSARY. Aug 15, 1771. Born at Edinburgh, Scotland. Famed poet and novelist. "But no one shall find me rowing against the stream," he wrote in the introduction to *The Fortunes of Nigel*: "I care not who knows it—I write for the general amusement." Died at Abbotsford, Scotland, Sept 21, 1832.

TRANSCONTINENTAL US RAILWAY COMPLETION: ANNIVERSARY. Aug 15, 1870. The Golden Spike ceremony at Promontory Point, UT, May 10, 1869, was long regarded as the final link in a transcontinental railroad track reaching from an Atlantic port to a Pacific port. In fact, that link occurred unceremoniously on another date in another state. Diaries of engineers working at the site establish "the completion of a transcontinental track at a point 928 feet east of today's milepost 602, or 3,812 feet east of the present Union Pacific depot building at Strasburg (formerly Comanche)," CO. The final link was made at 2:53 PM, Aug 15, 1870. Annual celebration at Strasburg, CO, on a weekend in August. See also: "Golden Spike Driving: Anniversary" (May 10).

WESTERN IDAHO FAIR. Aug 15–24. Boise, ID. 117th annual. Largest fair in the state, including four stages of entertainment on the grounds with local and regional talent, three nights of grandstand concerts, carnival midway and 70 food booths. Annually, starting on the third Friday in August. Est attendance: 254,000. For info: Western Idaho Fair, 5610 Glenwood, Boise, ID 83714. Phone: (208) 287-5650. Fax: (208) 375-9972. E-mail: info@idahofair.com. Web: www.idahofair.com.

WOODSTOCK: 45th ANNIVERSARY. Aug 15, 1969. The Woodstock Music and Art Fair opened on this day in an alfalfa field on or near Yasgur's Farm at Bethel, NY. The three-day rock concert featured 24 bands and drew a crowd of more than 400,000 people.

August 2014	S	M	T	W	T	F	S
						1	2
	3	4	5	6	7	8	9
	10	11	12	13	14	15	16
	17	18	19	20	21	22	23
	24	25	26	27	28	29	30
	31						

BIRTHDAYS TODAY

Ben Affleck, 42, actor (*Argo, Hollywoodland, Pearl Harbor*), director (*Argo, Gone Baby Gone*), born Berkeley, CA, Aug 15, 1972.

Princess Anne, 64, Princess Royal of the UK, equestrian, born London, England, Aug 15, 1950.

Stephen G. Breyer, 76, Associate Justice of the US, born San Francisco, CA, Aug 15, 1938.

Mike Connors, 89, actor ("Mannix"), born Krekor Ohanian at Fresno, CA, Aug 15, 1925.

Linda Ellerbee, 70, journalist, born Bryan, TX, Aug 15, 1944.

Zeljko Ivanek, 57, actor ("Heroes," "Damages," "24," *Donnie Brasco*), born Ljubljana, Slovenia, Aug 15, 1957.

Joe Jonas, 25, singer (The Jonas Brothers), actor, born Casa Grande, AZ, Aug 15, 1989.

Vernon Jordan, Jr, 79, civil rights leader, born Atlanta, GA, Aug 15, 1935.

Jennifer Lawrence, 24, actress (Oscar for *Silver Linings Playbook*; *The Hunger Games, Winter's Bone, X-Men: First Class*), born Louisville, KY, Aug 15, 1990.

Debra Messing, 46, actress ("Will & Grace"), born Brooklyn, NY, Aug 15, 1968.

Phyllis Stewart Schlafly, 90, conservative spokeswoman, author, born St. Louis, MO, Aug 15, 1924.

Kerri Walsh, 36, Olympic beach volleyball player, born Santa Clara, CA, Aug 15, 1978.

Kathryn Whitmire, 68, first woman mayor of Houston, TX, born Houston, TX, Aug 15, 1946.

August 16 — Saturday

DAY 228 **137 REMAINING**

ANTIQUE MARINE ENGINE EXPOSITION. Aug 16–17. Mystic Seaport, Mystic, CT. Collectors from across the US and Canada gather for an annual exposition of pre-WWII marine engines and engine models. For info: Mystic Seaport, 75 Greenmanville Ave, PO Box 6000, Mystic, CT 06355-0990. Phone: (860) 572-0711 or (888) 973-2767. Web: www.mysticseaport.org.

BATTLE OF CAMDEN: ANNIVERSARY. Aug 16, 1780. Revolutionary War battle fought near Camden, SC. American troops led by General Horatio Gates suffered disastrous losses. Nearly 1,000 Americans killed and another 1,000 captured by the British. British losses about 325. One of America's worst defeats in the war.

BEGIN, MENACHEM: BIRTH ANNIVERSARY. Aug 16, 1913. Born at Brest Litovsk, Poland. A militant Zionist and anticommunist, he fled to Russia in 1939 ahead of the advancing Nazis; he was soon arrested and sent to Siberia. Freed in 1941, he went to Palestine and became a leader in the Jewish underground, fighting for Israel's independence; by 1943 he headed the national military organization. Elected prime minister of Israel in 1977, he signed the historic peace treaty between Israel and Egypt with President Anwar el Sadat of Egypt and US President Jimmy Carter at Camp David in 1979. Begin died Mar 9, 1992, at Tel Aviv, Israel.

BENNINGTON BATTLE DAY: ANNIVERSARY. Aug 16, 1777. Anniversary of battle is legal holiday in Vermont.

BIKE VAN BUREN. Aug 16–17. Van Buren County, IA. A leisurely two-day bicycle tour of the villages, landmarks and landscape of this rural Iowa county. The "red carpet of hospitality" is rolled out for the bikers as they pass through. Annually, the third weekend in August. Est attendance: 500. For info: Villages of Van Buren, Inc, PO Box 9, Keosauqua, IA 52565. Phone: (800) 868-7822. Fax: (319) 293-7116. E-mail: info@villagesofvanburen.com. Web: www.villagesofvanburen.com.

DOMINICAN REPUBLIC: RESTORATION OF THE REPUBLIC. Aug 16. The anniversary of the restoration of the Republic in 1863 is celebrated as an official public holiday.

FRANCE: INTERNATIONAL FEDERATION OF LIBRARY ASSOCIATIONS ANNUAL CONFERENCE. Aug 16–22. Lyon. 80th annual. Held in a country of avid readers and enthusiastic library patrons, the IFLA observes the theme: "Libraries, Citizens, Societies: Confluence of Knowledge." For info: Intl Federation of Library Assns. E-mail: ifla@ifla.org. Web: www.ifla.org.

INTERNATIONAL GEOCACHING DAY. Aug 16. A day to celebrate the sport of geocaching: a real-world outdoor treasure hunting game in which players search for hidden containers, called geocaches, using GPS-enabled devices. Geocaching is enjoyed by people of all ages, and the sport fosters a strong sense of community and support for the environment. Annually, the third Saturday in August. For info: Groundspeak, Inc, 837 N 34th St, Ste 300, Seattle, WA 98103. E-mail: contact@geocaching.com. Web: www.geocaching.com.

INTERNATIONAL HOMELESS ANIMALS DAY® AND CANDLELIGHT VIGILS. Aug 16. A day to call attention to the fact that millions of healthy dogs and cats are killed each year in US animal shelters because of overpopulation—a problem that has a solution: spaying/neutering. The vigils memorialize the animals killed in the preceding year and sympathize with the caring shelter personnel who must take the lives of the animals. Vigils will be held throughout the US and beyond. For info: Intl Society for Animal Rights, Inc, Susan Dapsis, Pres, PO Box F, Clarks Summit, PA 18411-0309. Phone: (570) 586-2200. Fax: (570) 586-9580. E-mail: contact@ISARonline.org.

JOE MILLER'S JOKE DAY. Aug 16. A day to tell a joke in honor of the English comic actor Joseph (or Josias) Miller, who was born in 1684 (exact date unknown). Miller acted at the Drury Lane Theatre at London, England, and was a popular favorite. He died at London, Aug 16, 1738. A book with which Miller had no direct connection, *Joe Miller's Jests*, was compiled by John Mottley and first published in 1739. It contained 247 jokes. Revised and expanded hundreds of times, it contained more than 1,500 jokes in the ensuing two centuries. From *Joe Miller's Jests*, London, 1739: "A melting Sermon being preached in a country Church, all fell a weeping but one Man, who being asked, why he did not weep with the rest? O! said he. I belong to another Parish."

KLONDIKE GOLD DISCOVERY: ANNIVERSARY. Aug 16, 1896. According to the oral tradition of the Tagish First Nations People, Skookum Jim, Dawson Charlie and George Carmack found gold in Rabbit Creek, a tributary of the Klondike River, lying "thick between the flaky slabs like cheese sandwiches." This event, which led to the great Klondike Gold Rush, is celebrated in the Yukon each year with a public holiday, Discovery Day, observed on the nearest Monday.

LAWRENCE, T.E.: BIRTH ANNIVERSARY. Aug 16, 1888. British soldier, archaeologist and writer, born at Tremadoc, North Wales. During WWI, Lawrence, as a British intelligence officer, led the Arab revolt against Turkey, a German ally that had ruled the Arab people for centuries. Lawrence, now hailed as "Lawrence of Arabia," organized successful guerilla attacks on the Turkish supply chain and captured the essential port of Aqaba. His book, *Seven Pillars of Wisdom*, is a personal account of the Arab revolt. Lawrence was killed in a motorcycle accident at Dorset, England, May 19, 1935.

MacFADDEN, BERNARR: BIRTH ANNIVERSARY. Aug 16, 1868. Physical culture enthusiast and publisher, born at Mill Springs, MO. He was publisher of *Physical Culture, True Story, True Romances, True Detective Mystery Magazine* and many others. MacFadden made parachute jumps on his 81st, 83rd and 84th birthdays. He died at Jersey City, NJ, of jaundice, following a three-day fast, Oct 12, 1955.

MEANY, GEORGE: BIRTH ANNIVERSARY. Aug 16, 1894. American labor leader George Meany was born at New York, NY. A plumber by trade, he became president of the American Federation of Labor (AFL) in 1952, and when he merged the AFL with the Congress of Industrial Organizations (CIO), he became the leading labor spokesperson in the US. In 1957 he expelled Jimmy Hoffa's Teamsters Union from the AFL-CIO, and he lost the United Auto Workers in 1967. His tenure as president lasted until 1979. He died Jan 10, 1980, at Washington, DC.

MINNESOTA RENAISSANCE FESTIVAL. Aug 16–Sept 28 (weekends; Labor Day; Sept 26). Shakopee, MN. A celebration of 16th-century Renaissance Europe with entertainment on 16 lively stages, food, arts and crafts, games and live jousting. Est attendance: 300,000. For info: Minnesota Renaissance Festival, 1244 S Canterbury Rd, Ste 306, Shakopee, MN 55379. Phone: (952) 445-7361. Fax: (952) 445-7380. E-mail: info@renaissancefest.com. Web: www.renaissancefest.com.

PARKER, FESS: 90th BIRTH ANNIVERSARY. Aug 16, 1924. American actor, renowned for his portrayals of Davy Crockett and Daniel Boone, born Aug 16, 1924, at Fort Worth, TX. His depiction of Crockett in the Disney television miniseries of 1955–1956 made him an overnight sensation. The program's accompanying merchandising blitz evidenced for the first time the power of television. A reported 10 million coonskin caps—the Crockett signature—were sold, along with various other proprietary items. Upon his retirement from acting, Parker spent the remainder of his life managing his real estate developments, which included the Fess Parker Winery and Vineyard. He died Mar 18, 2010, at Santa Ynez, CA.

PRESLEY, ELVIS: DEATH ANNIVERSARY. Aug 16, 1977. One of America's most popular singers, Elvis Presley was pronounced dead at the Memphis Baptist Hospital at 3:30 PM, Aug 16, 1977, at age 42. The anniversary of his death is an occasion for pilgrimages by admirers to Graceland, his home and gravesite, at Memphis, TN. See also: "Presley, Elvis: Birth Anniversary" (Jan 8).

RUTH, BABE: DEATH ANNIVERSARY. Aug 16, 1948. Baseball fans of all ages and all walks of life mourned when the great "Bambino" died of cancer at New York City at the age of 53. Born Feb 6, 1895, at Baltimore, MD, the left-handed pitcher and "Sultan of Swat" hit 714 home runs in 22 major league seasons of play and played in 10 World Series. His body lay in state at the main entrance of Yankee Stadium, where people waited in line for hours to march past the coffin. On Aug 19 countless people surrounded St. Patrick's Cathedral for the funeral mass and lined the streets along the route to the cemetery as America bade farewell to one of baseball's greatest legends.

STAGG, AMOS ALONZO: BIRTH ANNIVERSARY. Aug 16, 1862. Football player and coach born at West Orange, NJ. Stagg played baseball and football at Yale and then forsook the ministry for physical education. He built the football program at the University of Chicago as an integral part of William Rainey Harper's plan to build a great university. Over 40 years at Chicago, he became the game's greatest innovator and master strategist. When Chicago deemphasized football, he moved to the College of the Pacific, finishing his career with a record of 314–181–15. Died at Stockton, CA, Mar 17, 1965.

BIRTHDAYS TODAY

Angela Bassett, 56, actress (*Malcolm X, What's Love Got to Do with It, Waiting to Exhale*), born New York, NY, Aug 16, 1958.

James Cameron, 60, director (Oscar for *Titanic*; *Avatar, True Lies*), born Kapuskasing, ON, Canada, Aug 16, 1954.

Steve Carell, 51, actor, comedian ("The Office"; *Crazy, Stupid, Love; Get Smart; The 40-Year-Old Virgin*), born Acton, MA, Aug 16, 1963.

Frank Newton Gifford, 84, sportscaster, Hall of Fame football player, born Santa Monica, CA, Aug 16, 1930.

Kathie Lee Gifford, 61, television personality, singer, born Paris, France, Aug 16, 1953.

Timothy Hutton, 54, actor ("Leverage," *Sunshine State*; Oscar for *Ordinary People*), born Malibu, CA, Aug 16, 1960.

Laura Innes, 54, actress ("ER," "Wings"), born Pontiac, MI, Aug 16, 1960.

Madonna, 56, singer, actress (*Desperately Seeking Susan, Evita*), born Madonna Louise Veronica Ciccone at Bay City, MI, Aug 16, 1958.

Julie Newmar, 81, actress ("Batman," *Li'l Abner*), born Hollywood, CA, Aug 16, 1933.

Jeff Perry, 59, actor ("Scandal," "Nash Bridges"), founder of Chicago's Steppenwolf Theater, born Highland Park, IL, Aug 16, 1955.

Seth Peterson, 44, actor ("Providence"), born the Bronx, NY, Aug 16, 1970.

Reginald VelJohnson, 62, actor (*Ghostbusters, Die Hard, Die Hard 2*), born Queens, NY, Aug 16, 1952.

Lesley Ann Warren, 68, actress (*Victor/Victoria, Choose Me*, "Cinderella"), born New York, NY, Aug 16, 1946.

August 17 — Sunday

DAY 229 — **136 REMAINING**

ALLIES TAKE SICILY: ANNIVERSARY. Aug 17, 1943. After only 39 days, the entire island of Sicily was under the control of Allied forces. The official total of Germans and Italians captured was put at 130,000. The Germans, however, managed to transfer 60,000 of their 90,000 men back to the Italian mainland.

ARGENTINA: DEATH ANNIVERSARY OF SAN MARTÍN. Aug 17. National holiday. Commemorates the death in 1850 of the hero of Argentina's struggle for independence.

BALLOON CROSSING OF ATLANTIC OCEAN: ANNIVERSARY. Aug 17, 1978. Three Americans—Maxie Anderson, Ben Abruzzo and Larry Newman—all of Albuquerque, NM, became the first to complete a transatlantic trip in a balloon. Starting from Presque Isle, ME, Aug 11, they traveled some 3,200 miles in 137 hours, 18 minutes, landing at Miserey, France (about 60 miles west of Paris), in their craft, named the *Double Eagle II*.

CHASE, HARRISON V.: BIRTH ANNIVERSARY. Aug 17, 1913. Cofounder and coeditor of *Chase's Annual Events* from 1957 to 1970, Chase was a lifelong teacher. Born at Big Rapids, MI, he had several teaching stints and was a research analyst at the Office of Strategic Services (OSS) from 1943 to 1946 before joining the Department of Geography at Florida State University in 1947. Fondly remembered by colleagues and students (who called him Professor Quark) and awarded the Standard Oil Foundation outstanding teaching award in 1969, Chase retired in 1979. In the summer of 1957, he and brother William brainstormed and created a new reference book that would chronicle the important events and holidays of each year. From its origins as a pamphlet, painstakingly constructed by William and Harrison Chase using index cards, *Chase's Calendar of Events* is now a 752-page tome packed with more than 12,500 events. Harrison Chase died Feb 6, 2000, at Tallahassee, FL.

CLINTON'S "MEANING OF 'IS' IS": ANNIVERSARY. Aug 17, 1998. During grand jury hearings that sought to clarify President Bill Clinton's relationship with Monica Lewinsky, Clinton engaged in some semantic fine-tuning: "It depends on what your meaning of 'is' is. If 'is' means 'is and never has been,' that's one thing—if it means 'there is none,' that was a completely true statement." Clinton also parsed the meanings of "alone," "sexual relations" and "sex." His testimony was later televised to the nation on Sept 21.

CROCKETT, DAVID (DAVY): BIRTH ANNIVERSARY. Aug 17, 1786. American frontiersman, bear hunter, soldier and politician, born at Greene County, TN. After losing a reelection bid to represent Tennessee in Congress, Crockett moved to the colony of Texas and joined the settlers' effort to gain independence from Mexico. He died during the final heroic defense of the Alamo on Mar 6, 1836, at San Antonio, TX. The larger-than-life figure once boasted: "I can run faster, walk longer, leap higher, speak better and tell more and bigger lies."

FORT SUMTER SHELLED BY NORTHERN FORCES: ANNIVERSARY. Aug 17, 1863. In what would become a long siege, Union forces began shelling Fort Sumter at Charleston, SC. The site of the first shots fired during the Civil War on Apr 12, 1861, Sumter endured the siege for a year and a half before being returned to Union hands.

FULTON SAILS STEAMBOAT: ANNIVERSARY. Aug 17, 1807. Robert Fulton began the first American steamboat trip between Albany and New York, NY, on a boat later called the *Clermont*. After years of promoting submarine warfare, Fulton engaged in a partnership with Robert R. Livingston, the US minister to France, allowing Fulton to design and construct a steamboat. His first success came in August 1803 when he launched a steam-powered vessel on the Seine. That same year the US Congress granted Livingston and Fulton exclusive rights to operate steamboats on New York waters during the next 20 years. The first Albany–New York trip took 32 hours to travel the 150-mile course. Although his efforts were labeled "Fulton's Folly" by his detractors, his success allowed the partnership to begin commercial service the next year, Sept 4, 1808.

GABON: INDEPENDENCE DAY. Aug 17. National holiday. Commemorates independence from France in 1960.

GARVEY, MARCUS: BIRTH ANNIVERSARY. Aug 17, 1887. Born at St. Ann's Bay, Jamaica, Garvey founded the Universal Negro Improvement Association, through which he sought to organize Jamaicans (and after 1916, Americans) of African descent around principles of racial pride, racial separatism and economic empowerment through black business ownership. He died June 10, 1940, at London, England.

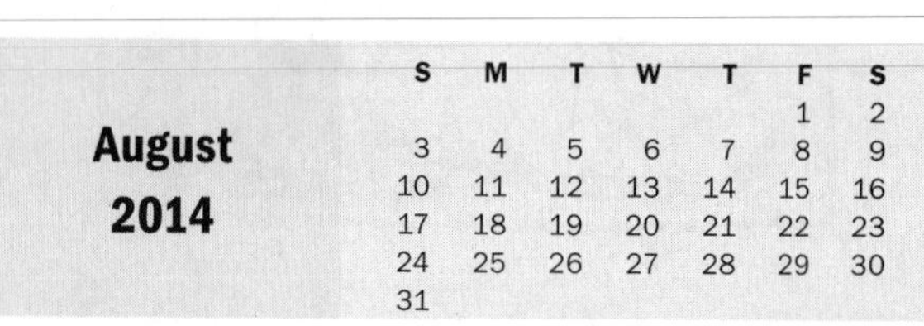

August 2014

S	M	T	W	T	F	S
					1	2
3	4	5	6	7	8	9
10	11	12	13	14	15	16
17	18	19	20	21	22	23
24	25	26	27	28	29	30
31						

INDIA: KRISHNA JANMASHTAMI. Aug 17. Hindu holiday. Birth anniversary of Lord Vishnu in his human incarnation as Krishna. Because there is no one universally accepted Hindu calendar, this holiday may be celebrated on a different date in some parts of India, but it always falls in August or September.

INDONESIA: INDEPENDENCE DAY: 65th ANNIVERSARY. Aug 17. National holiday. Republic proclaimed in 1945. It was only after several years of fighting, however, that Indonesia was formally granted its independence by the Netherlands, Dec 27, 1949.

MOON PHASE: LAST QUARTER. Aug 17. Moon enters Last Quarter phase at 8:26 AM, EDT.

POWERS, FRANCIS GARY: 85th BIRTH ANNIVERSARY. Aug 17, 1929. One of America's most famous aviators, Francis Gary Powers was born at Jenkins, KY. The CIA agent, pilot of a U-2 overflight across the Soviet Union, was shot down May 1, 1960, near Sverdlovsk, USSR. He was tried, convicted and sentenced to 10 years' imprisonment, at Moscow, USSR, in August 1960. Returned to the US in 1962, in exchange for an imprisoned Soviet spy (Colonel Rudolf Abel), he found an unwelcoming homeland. Powers died in a helicopter crash near Los Angeles, CA, Aug 2, 1977. On June 15, 2012, Powers was posthumously awarded a Silver Star—the military's third-highest decoration—by the US Air Force.

SMITH, ELINOR: BIRTH ANNIVERSARY. Aug 17, 1911. The pioneering aviatrix, who made her first solo flight at 15 years of age, was born at Long Island, NY. In 1930, after setting various flight records, Smith was voted best female pilot in America by her colleagues, beating out Amelia Earhart. The "Flying Flapper of Freeport" became the first woman to appear on a Wheaties cereal box in 1934—and she was the first female test pilot for an aircraft company. Smith died Mar 19, 2010, at Palo Alto, CA.

TURKISH EARTHQUAKE: 15th ANNIVERSARY. Aug 17, 1999. A quake with a magnitude of 7.4 struck northwestern Turkey where 45 percent of the population lives. More than 17,000 died and thousands more remained missing. Many of the deaths were due to the shoddy construction of apartment houses. Aftershocks in the region through September 1999 resulted in more deaths. On Nov 12, 1999, a magnitude 7.2 earthquake struck Turkey, killing more than 800 people. Also in 1999 there were earthquakes in Greece (139 dead) and Taiwan (2,200 dead and many missing).

WEST, MAE: BIRTH ANNIVERSARY. Aug 17, 1893 (some sources say 1892). The stage and screen siren, famous for her naughty wisecracks, was born Mary Jane West at Brooklyn, NY. She acted in vaudeville from age five and made her Hollywood debut in 1932. Unique among stars in that she wrote her own plays and film scripts—mostly concerning the joys of men and sex. Her Broadway play *Sex* resulted in her conviction for public obscenity in 1927 and she served time for eight days. Master of the risqué bon mot, West said in *I'm No Angel* (1933), "When I'm good, I'm very, very good, but when I'm bad, I'm better." She died Nov 22, 1980, at Los Angeles, CA.

BIRTHDAYS TODAY

Belinda Carlisle, 56, singer (Go-Go's), born Hollywood, CA, Aug 17, 1958.

Robert De Niro, 71, actor (Oscars for *Raging Bull, The Godfather Part II*; *Taxi Driver, The Deer Hunter*), born New York, NY, Aug 17, 1943.

Julian Fellowes, 65, producer, writer (*Gosford Park*, "Downton Abbey"), born Cairo, Egypt, Aug 17, 1949.

Jonathan Franzen, 55, author (*The Corrections, Freedom*), born Western Springs, IL, Aug 17, 1959.

Thierry Henry, 37, soccer player, born Paris, France, Aug 17, 1977.

Robert Joy, 63, actor ("CSI: NY," *Atlantic City, Longtime Companion*), born Montreal, QC, Canada, Aug 17, 1951.

Maureen O'Hara, 94, actress (*Miracle on 34th Street, The Hunchback of Notre Dame*), born Dublin, Ireland, Aug 17, 1920.

Sean Penn, 54, actor (Oscars for *Mystic River* and *Milk*; *Dead Man Walking*), born Santa Monica, CA, Aug 17, 1960.

Nelson Piquet, 62, former auto racer, born Brasilia, Brazil, Aug 17, 1952.

Mark Salling, 32, actor ("Glee"), born Dallas, TX, Aug 17, 1982.

Guillermo Vilas, 62, Hall of Fame tennis player, born Mar del Plata, Argentina, Aug 17, 1952.

Donnie Wahlberg, 45, actor ("Blue Bloods," "Band of Brothers"), singer (New Kids on the Block), born Boston, MA, Aug 17, 1969.

August 18 — Monday

DAY 230 — **135 REMAINING**

AMERICAN NEUTRALITY APPEAL: 100th ANNIVERSARY. Aug 18, 1914. President Woodrow Wilson followed his Aug 4 Proclamation of Neutrality with an appeal to the American people to remain impartial in thought and deed with respect to the war that was raging in Europe (WWI).

BAD POETRY DAY. Aug 18. After all the "good" poetry you were forced to study in school, here's a chance for a payback. Invite some friends over, compose some really rotten verse and send it to your old high school English teacher. (©2006 by WH.) For info: Thomas & Ruth Roy, Wellcat Holidays, 2418 Long Ln, Lebanon, PA 17046. Phone: (717) 279-0184. E-mail: info@wellcat.com. Web: www.wellcat.com.

BIRTH CONTROL PILLS SOLD: ANNIVERSARY. Aug 18, 1960. The first commercially produced oral contraceptives were marketed by the G.D. Searle Company of Illinois. The pill, developed by Gregory Pincus, had been undergoing clinical trials since 1954.

CANADA: YUKON DISCOVERY DAY. Aug 18. In the Klondike region of the Yukon, at Bonanza Creek (formerly known as Rabbit Creek), George Washington Carmack discovered gold Aug 16 or 17, 1896. During the following year, more than 30,000 people joined the gold rush to the area. Anniversary is celebrated as a holiday (Discovery Day) in the Yukon, on nearest Monday.

CLEMENTE, ROBERTO: 80th BIRTH ANNIVERSARY. Aug 18, 1934. National League baseball player, born at Carolina, Puerto Rico. Drafted by the Pittsburgh Pirates in 1954, he played his entire major league career with them. Clemente died in a plane crash Dec 31, 1972, while on a mission of mercy to Nicaragua to deliver supplies he had collected for survivors of an earthquake. He was elected to the Baseball Hall of Fame in 1973.

DARE, VIRGINIA: BIRTH ANNIVERSARY. Aug 18, 1587. (Old Style date.) Virginia Dare, the first child of English parents to be born in the New World, was born to Ellinor and Ananias Dare, at Roanoke Island, NC, on this date. When a ship arrived to replenish their supplies in 1591, the settlers (including Virginia Dare) had vanished without leaving a trace of the settlement.

LEWIS, MERIWETHER: BIRTH ANNIVERSARY. Aug 18, 1774. American explorer (Lewis and Clark expedition), born at Albemarle County, VA. Died Oct 11, 1809, near Nashville, TN.

MAIL-ORDER CATALOG: ANNIVERSARY. Aug 18, 1872. The first mail-order catalog was published by Montgomery Ward. It was only a single sheet of paper. By 1904 the Montgomery Ward catalog weighed four pounds. In 1985 Montgomery Ward closed its catalog operation; in 2000 it announced the closing of its retail stores.

✦MINORITY ENTERPRISE DEVELOPMENT WEEK. Aug 18–24 (tentative). Presidential Proclamation issued without request since 1983.

NINETEENTH AMENDMENT TO US CONSTITUTION RATIFIED: ANNIVERSARY. Aug 18, 1920. The 19th Amendment extended the right to vote to women.

SERENDIPITY DAY. Aug 18. 3rd annual. Serendipity is the faculty of making valuable and wonderful discoveries not sought for. This faculty is within us and this annual day encourages everyone to bring more serendipity into their lives and the lives of others. Make the world a happier place one person at a time. Annually, Aug 18. For info: Madeleine Kay. E-mail: mk@madeleinekay.com. Web: www.serendipitydayholiday.com.

BIRTHDAYS TODAY

Elayne Boosler, 62, comedienne, born Brooklyn, NY, Aug 18, 1952.

Felipe Calderón Hinojosa, 52, former president of Mexico (2006–12), born Morelia, Michoacán, Mexico, Aug 18, 1962.

Eleanor Rosalynn Smith Carter, 87, former first lady, wife of Jimmy Carter, 38th president of the US, born Plains, GA, Aug 18, 1927.

Bobby Higginson, 44, former baseball player, born Philadelphia, PA, Aug 18, 1970.

Mike Johanns, 64, US Senator (R, Nebraska), former US secretary of agriculture, former governor of Nebraska, born Osage, IA, Aug 18, 1950.

Luc Montagnier, 82, virologist, discovered the AIDS virus in 1983, born Chabris, France, Aug 18, 1932.

Martin Mull, 71, actor, comedian ("Sabrina, the Teenage Witch," "Roseanne"), born Chicago, IL, Aug 18, 1943.

Edward Norton, 45, actor (*The Incredible Hulk, 25th Hour, Primal Fear*), born Boston, MA, Aug 18, 1969.

Roman Polanski, 81, filmmaker (*The Ghost Writer, The Pianist, Rosemary's Baby, Chinatown*), born Paris, France, Aug 18, 1933.

Robert Redford, 77, actor (*Butch Cassidy and the Sundance Kid, The Sting, The Natural*), director (Oscar for *Ordinary People*), born Santa Monica, CA, Aug 18, 1937.

Andy Samberg, 36, comedian, actor ("Saturday Night Live"), born Mill Valley, CA, Aug 18, 1978.

Christian Slater, 45, actor (*Heathers, Broken Arrow, Pump Up the Volume*), born New York, NY, Aug 18, 1969.

Madeleine Stowe, 56, actress (*The Last of the Mohicans, Short Cuts*), born Los Angeles, CA, Aug 18, 1958.

Malcolm-Jamal Warner, 44, actor ("The Cosby Show"), born Jersey City, NJ, Aug 18, 1970.

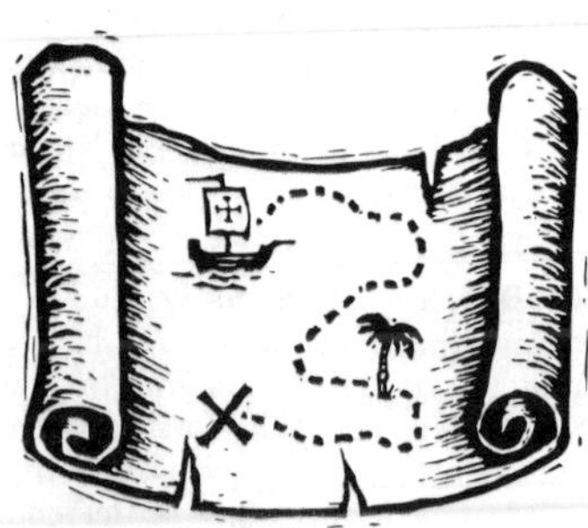

August 2014	S	M	T	W	T	F	S
						1	2
	3	4	5	6	7	8	9
	10	11	12	13	14	15	16
	17	18	19	20	21	22	23
	24	25	26	27	28	29	30
	31						

August 19 — Tuesday

DAY 231 **134 REMAINING**

AFGHANISTAN: INDEPENDENCE DAY: 95th ANNIVERSARY. Aug 19. National day. Gained independence from British control, Treaty of Rawalpindi in 1919.

"BLACK COW" ROOT BEER FLOAT CREATED: ANNIVERSARY. Aug 19, 1893. Frank J. Wisner, owner of Cripple Creek Brewing, served the first root beer float in Cripple Creek, CO. Inspired by the moonlit view of snowcapped Cow Mountain, he added a scoop of ice cream to his Myers Avenue Red root beer and began serving it as the "Black Cow Mountain." Kids loved it and shortened the name to "Black Cow." Cripple Creek Brewing still sells beverages based on the original formulas. For info: Michael Lynn, Cripple Creek Brewing, 23244 Rebecca Ct, Naperville, IL 60564. Phone: (630) 904-0022. E-mail: lbartl6415@aol.com. Web: www.cripplecreekbrewing.com.

CHANEL, COCO: BIRTH ANNIVERSARY. Aug 19, 1883. The most important fashion designer of the 20th century was born Gabrielle Chanel in rural Saumur, France. After starting out in a millinery shop, she began a fashion revolution when she moved on to couture fashion in the late teens: using men's clothing (pants) for women's wear; creating simple, comfortable clothing that was nonetheless elegant; making dramatic use of costume jewelry (especially ropes of pearls); and popularizing the "little black dress" and sportswear. She was the first couturier to put her name on a signature perfume: Chanel No. 5 (created in 1921, it was an immediate sensation and today sells every 30 seconds around the world). After closing her shop with the outbreak of WWII, Chanel reopened it in 1954 and introduced her signature suit of collarless, bias-trimmed jacket with skirt. "Elegance does not consist in putting on a new dress," she once stated. The fashion icon died on Jan 10, 1971, at Paris, France.

CLINTON, WILLIAM JEFFERSON (BILL): BIRTHDAY. Aug 19, 1946. The 42nd US president (1993–2001), born at Hope, AR.

FARNSWORTH, PHILO: BIRTH ANNIVERSARY. Aug 19, 1906. Farnsworth was a television pioneer who conceived of the idea of television broadcasting while still in high school and realized his dream at 21. His first transmitted image was of a dollar sign. Farnsworth was born at Beaver, UT, and died on Mar 11, 1971, at Salt Lake City, UT.

FEDERICO GARCÍA LORCA MURDER: ANNIVERSARY. Aug 19, 1936. Spanish poet and playwright Federico García Lorca was murdered along a rural road in Andalucia by Falangist militia and buried in a common grave with other political victims of the Spanish Civil War.

FORBES, MALCOLM: 95th BIRTH ANNIVERSARY. Aug 19, 1919. Publisher, born at New York, NY. Malcolm Forbes was an unabashed proponent of capitalism, and his beliefs led to his colorful and successful climb to the top of the magazine-publishing industry. Known as much for his lavish lifestyle as his publishing acumen, Forbes was also an avid motorcyclist and hot-air balloonist. He died Feb 24, 1990, at Far Hills, NJ.

GERMAN PLEBISCITE: 80th ANNIVERSARY. Aug 19, 1934. In a plebiscite, 89.9 percent of German voters approved giving Chancellor Adolf Hitler the additional office of president, placing the Führer in uncontestable supreme command of that country's destiny.

HO, DON: BIRTH ANNIVERSARY. Aug 19, 1930. The man who introduced Hawaiian music to the American public was born at Honolulu, HI. A Waikiki nightclub musician who began performing in Hollywood and Las Vegas, he had an unlikely Top 40 hit with "Tiny Bubbles" in 1966. In the 1970s he was a minor television celebrity, hosting his own variety show, but he was always most comfortable playing for the tourists at various nightclubs in Waikiki. Don Ho continued to entertain until his death at Honolulu on Apr 14, 2007.

LARDNER, RING, JR: BIRTH ANNIVERSARY. Aug 19, 1915. Born at Chicago, IL, son of fabled baseball writer and humorist Ring Lardner. Lardner, Jr, was an Academy Award–winning screenwriter (Oscar for *Woman of the Year*; *M*A*S*H*), and he also wrote for television. He was a member of the Hollywood Ten, a group of film industry executives sent to federal prison in 1950 for their refusal to tell the House Un-American Activities Committee if they were members of the Communist Party. He served nine months and was blacklisted for many years. Died at New York, NY, Oct 31, 2000.

NASH, OGDEN: BIRTH ANNIVERSARY. Aug 19, 1902. American writer, best remembered for his humorous verse. Born at Rye, NY; died May 19, 1971, at Baltimore, MD.

✦NATIONAL AVIATION DAY. Aug 19. Presidential Proclamation 2343, of July 25, 1939, covers all succeeding years. Always Aug 19 of each year since 1939. Observed annually on birth anniversary of Orville Wright, who piloted "first self-powered flight in history," Dec 17, 1903. First proclaimed by President Franklin D. Roosevelt.

RICHARDSON, SAMUEL: 325th BIRTH ANNIVERSARY. Aug 19, 1689. Born at Derbyshire, England, Richardson was an English novelist who founded a new school of writing focused on epistolary novels that juxtaposed inner thoughts and states of the individual with the tempo of outer life. His best-known novel is *Clarissa; or, The History of a Young Lady* (1748). He died July 4, 1761 at London, England.

RODDENBERRY, GENE: BIRTH ANNIVERSARY. Aug 19, 1921. The creator of the popular TV series "Star Trek," Gene Roddenberry was born at El Paso, TX. Turning from his first career as an airline pilot to writing, he created one of the most successful TV science fiction series ever. The original series, which ended its run in 1969, lives on in reruns and led to other popular spin-off series. Numerous films also have been spawned from the original concept. Roddenberry died Oct 24, 1991, at Santa Monica, CA.

SPACE MILESTONE: *SOYUZ T-7* (USSR). Aug 19, 1982. Launched from Tyuratam, USSR, with second woman in space (test pilot Svetlana Savitskaya) and two other cosmonauts. Docked at *Salyut 7* and visited the cosmonauts who had been in residence there for the three previous months before returning to Earth on Aug 27 in the *Soyuz T-5* vehicle, which had been docked there. The *Soyuz T-7* returned to Earth Dec 10.

SPACE MILESTONE: *SPUTNIK 5* (USSR). Aug 19, 1960. Space menagerie satellite with dogs Belka and Strelka, mice, rats, houseflies and plants launched. These passengers became the first living organisms recovered from orbit when the satellite returned safely to Earth the next day.

TRIAL OF SIXTEEN: ANNIVERSARY. Aug 19–24, 1936. The Trial of Sixteen began in the Soviet Union. This was the first of the Moscow show trials and the defendants included war heroes and longtime Communist functionaries accused of plotting to kill Joseph Stalin. The trial verdicts were predetermined ("guilty") and all were executed. This and later show trials marked the beginning of the Great Purge, which would take 8 to 10 million lives in the next two years.

UNITED NATIONS: WORLD HUMANITARIAN DAY. Aug 19. The General Assembly has designated Aug 19 each year as World Humanitarian Day (Resolution 63/139 of Dec 11, 2008). The Day is intended to increase public awareness about humanitarian assistance activities worldwide and the importance of international cooperation in that sphere. It also aims to honor all humanitarian and UN workers in the humanitarian cause, including those who have lost their lives in the cause of duty. For info: United Nations, Dept of Public Info, New York, NY 10017. Web: www.un.org.

WRIGHT, ORVILLE: BIRTH ANNIVERSARY. Aug 19, 1871. Aviation pioneer born at Dayton, OH, and died there Jan 30, 1948. See also: "Wright Brothers First Powered Flight: Anniversary" (Dec 17).

BIRTHDAYS TODAY

Adam Arkin, 58, actor ("Chicago Hope," "Northern Exposure"), born Brooklyn, NY, Aug 19, 1956.

Jim Carter, 66, actor ("Downton Abbey," "Cranford," *The Golden Compass*), born Harrogate, Yorkshire, England, Aug 19, 1948.

Erika Christensen, 32, actress (*Traffic, Swimfan,* "Parenthood"), born Seattle, WA, Aug 19, 1982.

William Jefferson Clinton, 68, 42nd president of the US, born Hope, AR, Aug 19, 1946.

Kevin Dillon, 49, actor ("Entourage"), born Mamaroneck, NY, Aug 19, 1965.

Peter Gallagher, 59, actor (*sex, lies and videotape*; *Short Cuts*, "The O.C."), born New York, NY, Aug 19, 1955.

Tipper Gore, 66, wife of Al Gore, 45th vice president of the US, advocate for the homeless, mental health and children's causes, born Mary Elizabeth Aitcheson at Washington, DC, Aug 19, 1948.

Gerald McRaney, 66, actor (*Red Tails*, "Deadwood," "Simon & Simon," "Major Dad"), born Collins, MS, Aug 19, 1948.

Jennifer Morrison, 35, actress ("Once Upon a Time," "House"), born Chicago, IL, Aug 19, 1979.

Diana Muldaur, 76, actress ("Star Trek: The Next Generation," "LA Law," *The Swimmer*), born New York, NY, Aug 19, 1938.

Franklin Story Musgrave, 79, former astronaut, born Boston, MA, Aug 19, 1935.

Cindy Nelson, 59, former alpine skier, born Lutsen, MN, Aug 19, 1955.

Matthew Perry, 45, actor ("Friends," *Fools Rush In*), born Williamstown, MA, Aug 19, 1969.

Jill St. John, 74, actress (*Diamonds Are Forever*), born Jill Oppenheim at Los Angeles, CA, Aug 19, 1940.

Kyra Sedgwick, 49, actress ("The Closer," *Phenomenon, Born on the Fourth of July*), born New York, NY, Aug 19, 1965.

Rick Snyder, 56, Governor of Michigan (R), born Battle Creek, MI, Aug 19, 1958.

John Stamos, 51, actor ("ER," "Full House"), born Los Angeles, CA, Aug 19, 1963.

Fred Thompson, 72, former US senator (R, Tennessee), actor ("Law & Order," *In the Line of Fire*), born Sheffield, AL, Aug 19, 1942.

August 20 — Wednesday

DAY 232 **133 REMAINING**

AMERICAN QUILTER'S SOCIETY QUILT SHOW—GRAND RAPIDS. Aug 20–23. DeVos Place Convention Center, Grand Rapids, MI. Features 500 quilts, special quilt exhibits, workshops and lectures. Est attendance: 20,000. For info: American Quilter's Society, PO Box 3290, Paducah, KY 42002. Phone: (270) 898-7903. E-mail: shows@AQSquilt.com. Web: www.americanquilter.com.

CORN PALACE FESTIVAL. Aug 20–24. Mitchell, SD. Celebration of the harvest and the annual redecoration of the world's only Corn Palace (with ears of corn). Midway and carnival rides, games, specialty vendors, food and top-name entertainment on the stage of the Corn Palace. Est attendance: 40,000. For info: Corn Palace, 612 N Main St, Mitchell, SD 57301. Phone: (605) 995-8427. Fax: (605) 995-8443. E-mail: mschilling@cornpalace.com. Web: www.cornpalace.com.

GUEST, EDGAR ALBERT: BIRTH ANNIVERSARY. Aug 20, 1881. Newspaperman and author of folksy, homespun verse that enjoyed great popularity and was syndicated in more than 100 newspapers. Born at Birmingham, England; died at Detroit, MI, Aug 5, 1959. "Eddie Guest Day" usually proclaimed on birth anniversary in Detroit.

HARRISON, BENJAMIN: BIRTH ANNIVERSARY. Aug 20, 1833. The 23rd president of the US, born at North Bend, OH. He was the grandson of William Henry Harrison, 9th president of the US. Benjamin Harrison's term of office, Mar 4, 1889–Mar 3, 1893, was preceded and followed by the presidential terms of Grover Cleveland (who thus became the 22nd president and 24th president of the US). Harrison died at Indianapolis, IN, Mar 13, 1901.

HUNGARY: SAINT STEPHEN'S DAY. Aug 20. National holiday. Commemorates the canonization of Saint Stephen, king and founder of the state, in 1083. Under the Communists, commemorated as Constitution Day.

LOVECRAFT, H.P.: BIRTH ANNIVERSARY. Aug 20, 1890. Howard Phillips Lovecraft, American author of horror tales of the supernatural, a pioneering science fiction writer and a notable epistoler, was born at Providence, RI, and died there Mar 15, 1937.

MOROCCO: REVOLUTION OF THE KING AND THE PEOPLE. Aug 20. National holiday. Commemorates the response of the people to Sultan (later King) Sidi Muhammed's being sent into exile in 1953 by the French.

O'HIGGINS, BERNARDO: BIRTH ANNIVERSARY. Aug 20, 1778. First ruler of Chile after its declaration of independence. Called the "Liberator of Chile." Born at Chillan, Chile. Died at Lima, Peru, Oct 24, 1842.

PLUTONIUM FIRST WEIGHED: ANNIVERSARY. Aug 20, 1942. University of Chicago scientist Glen Seaborg and his colleagues first weighed plutonium, the first man-made element.

PRESIDENT BENJAMIN HARRISON'S BIRTHDAY CELEBRATION. Aug 20. Benjamin Harrison Presidential Site, Indianapolis, IN. Celebrating the birthday of the 23rd president in his hometown. Includes free tours of his Victorian mansion. For info: Benjamin Harrison Presidential Site, 1230 N Delaware St, Indianapolis, IN 46202. Phone: (317) 631-1888. Fax: (317) 632-5488. E-mail: events@bhpsite.org. Web: www.bhpsite.org.

REEVES, JIM: 90th BIRTH ANNIVERSARY. Aug 20, 1924. Country music star Jim Reeves was born at Galloway, Panola County, TX, and died at Nashville, TN, July 31, 1964, when the single-engine plane in which he was traveling crashed in a dense fog. Reeves's biggest hit was "He'll Have to Go" (1959), and he was inducted into the Country Music Hall of Fame in 1967.

SAARINEN, EERO: BIRTH ANNIVERSARY. Aug 20, 1910. Born at Kirkkonummi, Finland, but raised in the United States by his architect father, Eliel, and sculptor mother. Eero Saarinen was a leading postwar architect and furniture designer whose sculptural designs were in contrast to the reigning International Style. He died Sept 1, 1961, at Ann Arbor, MI.

SAARINEN, ELIEL: BIRTH ANNIVERSARY. Aug 20, 1873. Famed architect. Born at Helsinki, Finland. Died at Bloomfield Hills, MI, July 1, 1950.

SPACE MILESTONE: *VIKING 1* AND *2* (US). Aug 20 and Sept 9, 1975. Sister ships launched toward Mars from Cape Canaveral, FL, on Aug 20 and Sept 9, 1975. *Viking 1*'s lander touched down on Mars July 20, 1976, and *Viking 2*'s lander on Sept 3, 1976. Sent back to Earth high-quality photographs, analysis of atmosphere, weather information and results of sophisticated experiments intended to determine whether life may be present on Mars.

SPACE MILESTONE: *VOYAGER 2* (US). Aug 20, 1977. This unmanned spacecraft journeyed past Jupiter in 1979, Saturn in 1981, Uranus in 1986 and Neptune in 1989, sending photographs and data back to scientists on Earth.

August 2014

S	M	T	W	T	F	S
					1	2
3	4	5	6	7	8	9
10	11	12	13	14	15	16
17	18	19	20	21	22	23
24	25	26	27	28	29	30
31						

BIRTHDAYS TODAY

Amy Adams, 39, actress (*The Master, The Fighter, Enchanted*), born Vicenza, Italy, Aug 20, 1975.

Joan Allen, 58, actress (The *Bourne* films, *Nixon, The Contender*; Tony for *Burn This*), born Rochelle, IL, Aug 20, 1956.

Andy Benes, 47, former baseball player, born Evansville, IN, Aug 20, 1967.

Connie Chung, 68, journalist, born Constance Yu-Hwa at Washington, DC, Aug 20, 1946.

Tara Dakides, 39, snowboarder, born Mission Viejo, CA, Aug 20, 1975.

Billy Gardell, 45, actor ("Mike & Molly," "My Name Is Earl"), born Pittsburgh, PA, Aug 20, 1969.

Todd Helton, 41, baseball player, born Knoxville, TN, Aug 20, 1973.

Donald (Don) King, 83, boxing promoter, born Cleveland, OH, Aug 20, 1931.

Mark Edward Langston, 54, former baseball player, born San Diego, CA, Aug 20, 1960.

Demi Lovato, 22, singer, actress (*Camp Rock*, "Sonny with a Chance"), born Dallas, TX, Aug 20, 1992.

Ron Paul, 79, politician, born Pittsburgh, PA, Aug 20, 1935.

Robert Plant, 66, singer, born Bromwich, England, Aug 20, 1948.

Al Roker, 60, television personality ("Today"), born Brooklyn, NY, Aug 20, 1954.

Theresa Saldana, 59, actress ("The Commish"), born Brooklyn, NY, Aug 20, 1955.

August 21 — Thursday

DAY 233 **132 REMAINING**

ACTON FAIR. Aug 21–24. Acton, ME. A country fair featuring horse and ox pulls; antique tractor pull; 4-H projects; flowers; arts and crafts; draft horse, pony and mule show; beef and dairy shows; woodman's carnival; 5k race; women's skillet toss; full midway; stage shows; and handicrafts. Vendors: contact Rick Burke Jr at (207) 457-1018. Est attendance: 10,000. For info: Lista C. Staples, Secy, 178 Nason Rd, Shapleigh, ME 04076. Phone: (207) 636-2026.

ALASKA STATE FAIR. Aug 21–Sept 1. Palmer, AK. Everybody's welcome at the Alaska State Fair, home of record-setting giant vegetables and beautiful flower gardens. Nestled in the heart of the Chugach Mountains, in the fertile Matanuska-Susitna Valley, the fairgrounds are just an hour north of Anchorage. The fair provides a setting for Alaska's last blast of summer, a showcase for Alaska's uniqueness and beauty. Visit the fair and enjoy year-round events and services, including horse shows, concerts, trade shows, facility rentals, winter RV and boat storage. Est attendance: 300,000. For info: Alaska State Fair, Inc, 2075 Glenn Hwy, Palmer, AK 99645. Phone: (907) 745-4827 or (800) 850-FAIR. Fax: (907) 746-2699. E-mail: info@alaskastatefair.org. Web: www.alaskastatefair.org.

AMERICAN BAR ASSOCIATION FOUNDING: ANNIVERSARY. Aug 21, 1878. Organized at Saratoga, NY.

AQUINO, BENIGNO: ASSASSINATION ANNIVERSARY. Aug 21, 1983. Filipino opposition leader Benigno S. Aquino, Jr, was shot and killed at the Manila airport on his return to the Philippines on this date. The killing precipitated greater anti-Marcos feeling and figured significantly in the Feb 7, 1986, election that brought about the collapse of the government administration of Ferdinand E. Marcos and the inauguration of Corazon C. Aquino, widow of the slain man, as president.

BEARDSLEY, AUBREY VINCENT: BIRTH ANNIVERSARY. Aug 21, 1872. English artist and illustrator born at Brighton, England. Died at Menton, France, Mar 16, 1898.

CHAMBERLAIN, WILT: BIRTH ANNIVERSARY. Aug 21, 1936. Basketball Hall of Fame center, born at Philadelphia, PA. Died Oct 12, 1999, at Los Angeles, CA.

HAWAII: ADMISSION DAY: 55th ANNIVERSARY. Aug 21, 1959. President Dwight Eisenhower signed a proclamation admitting Hawaii to the Union. The statehood bill had passed the previous March with a stipulation that statehood should be approved by a vote of Hawaiian residents. The referendum passed by a huge margin in June, and Eisenhower proclaimed Hawaii the 50th state on Aug 21.

HOTTER 'N HELL HUNDRED BIKE RACE. Aug 21–24. Wichita Falls, TX. 33rd annual. Cyclists of all ages participate in the largest sanctioned century ride in the US. Treks of 100, 50 or 25 miles. Est attendance: 15,000. For info: Hotter 'N Hell Hundred, PO Box 2096, Wichita Falls, TX 76307. Phone: (940) 322-3223. Fax: (940) 322-1118. E-mail: info@hh100.org. Web: www.hh100.org.

LINCOLN-DOUGLAS DEBATES: ANNIVERSARY. Aug 21–Oct 15, 1858. At Ottawa, IL, Abraham Lincoln began a series of debates throughout Illinois with Stephen A. Douglas that would propel Lincoln to national notoriety. Republican Lincoln was challenging Democrat Douglas's bid for reelection to the US Senate. The two men conducted seven spirited public debates that often wrestled with the question of slavery in US territories. Although Douglas won reelection, Lincoln's eloquence gained him acclaim and he was chosen to be the Republican Party's candidate for president in the 1860 elections. In 1860 Lincoln defeated Douglas to become president.

MINNESOTA STATE FAIR. Aug 21–Sept 1. St. Paul, MN. Twelve days of fun ending on Labor Day. Major entertainers, agricultural displays, arts, crafts, food, carnival rides, animal judging and performances. Est attendance: 1,700,000. For info: Minnesota State Fair, 1265 Snelling Ave N, St. Paul, MN 55108-3099. Phone: (651) 288-4400. E-mail: fairinfo@mnstatefair.org. Web: www.mnstatefair.org.

NEW YORK STATE FAIR. Aug 21–Sept 1. Syracuse, NY. Agricultural and livestock competitions, top-name entertainment, the International Horse Show, business and industrial exhibits, the midway and ethnic presentations. Est attendance: 1,000,000. For info: New York State Fair, 581 State Fair Blvd, Syracuse, NY 13209. Phone: (315) 487-7711. Fax: (315) 487-9260. Web: www.nysfair.org.

POET'S DAY. Aug 21. A day for all poets to celebrate their special talents and the vision that makes them so wonderful and dear. Poet's Day is a time to share special thoughts about poets and poetry. (©2001 C. Daniel Rhodes.) For info: C. Daniel Rhodes or Natalie Danielle Rhodes, 1900 Crossvine Rd, Hoover, AL 35244. Phone: (205) 908-6781. E-mail: rhodan@charter.net.

QUANTRILL'S RAID ON LAWRENCE, KANSAS: ANNIVERSARY. Aug 21, 1863. Confederate raider William Clarke Quantrill launched a predawn terrorist raid on Lawrence, KS, leaving 150 civilians dead and much of the town ruined. Quantrill had been denied a commission in the Southern army for his barbaric approach to war.

SEMINOLE TRIBE OF FLORIDA LEGALLY ESTABLISHED: ANNIVERSARY. Aug 21, 1957. In 1953 Congress adopted a proposal to terminate assistance to nonrecognized Indian tribes. Seminole leaders and tribal members began to fight the proposal by drafting a constitution and charter for the Seminole Tribe. These were later approved by the secretary of the interior. On this date a majority of tribal members voted to establish the Seminole Tribe of Florida. Today, 2,200 Seminoles live on five reservations in Florida.

SOLDIERS' REUNION CELEBRATION. Aug 21. Newton, NC. Parade climaxes the 125th annual soldiers' reunion celebration—"oldest patriotic event of its kind in the US, honoring all veterans." Annually, the third Thursday in August. Concerts, arts, crafts, food and games. Est attendance: 35,000. For info: Soldiers' Reunion Committee, Box 267, Newton, NC 28658. Phone: (828) 464-3930.

SPACE MILESTONE: *GEMINI 5* (US). Aug 21, 1965. Launched on this date, this craft, carrying astronauts Lieutenant Colonel Cooper and Lieutenant Commander Conrad, orbited Earth 128 times for a new international record of eight days.

SWEDEN: SOUR HERRING PREMIERE. Aug 21. By ordinance, the year's supply of sour (fermented) herring may begin to be sold on the third Thursday in August.

BIRTHDAYS TODAY

Usain Bolt, 28, Olympic track athlete, born Trelawny, Jamaica, Aug 21, 1986.

Steve Case, 56, founder of America Online (AOL), born Oahu, HI, Aug 21, 1958.

Kim Cattrall, 58, actress ("Sex and the City," *The Ghost Writer, Mannequin*), born Liverpool, England, Aug 21, 1956.

Jackie DeShannon, 70, singer, songwriter, born Hazel, KY, Aug 21, 1944.

Joanne Froggatt, 34, actress ("Downton Abbey," *In Our Name*), born Littlebeck, North Hampshire, England, Aug 21, 1980 (some sources say 1979).

Brody Jenner, 31, television personality, born Los Angeles, CA, Aug 21, 1983.

James Robert (Jim) McMahon, 55, former football player, born Jersey City, NJ, Aug 21, 1959.

Hayden Panettiere, 25, actress ("Nashville," "Heroes," "Guiding Light"), born Palisades, NY, Aug 21, 1989.

Kenny Rogers, 76, singer, born Houston, TX, Aug 21, 1938.

Jon Tester, 58, US Senator (D, Montana), born Havre, MT, Aug 21, 1956.

Melvin Van Peebles, 82, actor, director, playwright (*Ain't Supposed to Die a Natural Death*), born Chicago, IL, Aug 21, 1932.

Peter Weir, 70, director (*Dead Poets Society, Gallipoli, The Truman Show*), born Sydney, Australia, Aug 21, 1944.

Clarence Williams III, 75, actor ("The Mod Squad," *Purple Rain*), born New York, NY, Aug 21, 1939.

Alicia Witt, 39, actress ("Cybill"), born Worcester, MA, Aug 21, 1975.

August 22 — Friday

DAY 234 **131 REMAINING**

BATTLE OF STALINGRAD BEGINS: ANNIVERSARY. Aug 22, 1942. Having captured Sevastopol on the Crimea on July 2, after an eight-month seige, the Germans began an offensive to capture Stalingrad. During this five-month-long battle, the city of 500,000 people dwindled to a population of 1,515. In the fighting, Russia lost 750,000 troops, the Germans 400,000, the Romanians nearly 200,000 and the Italians 130,000—a total of 1,480,000. The last German strongholds at Stalingrad surrendered to the Russian army on Feb 2, 1943.

BE AN ANGEL DAY. Aug 22. A day to do "one small act of service for someone. Be a blessing in someone's life." Annually, Aug 22. For info: Angel Heights Healing Center, Rev Jayne M. Howard Feldman, PO Box 95, Upperco, MD 21155. Phone: (410) 833-6912. E-mail: earthangel4peace@aol.com.

BRADBURY, RAY: BIRTH ANNIVERSARY. Aug 22, 1920. Born at Waukegan, IL, Ray Bradbury was one of the preeminent science fiction/fantasy writers of the 20th century. His body of work, which critiqued social mores and depicted the consequences of unfettered technology, is considered timeless and transcends generations. Notable works include *Something Wicked This Way Comes, The Body Electric* and *Fahrenheit 451*, his most famous novel. Awarded a Special Citation by the Pulitzer Board (2007) for his oeuvre, Bradbury died June 5, 2012, at Los Angeles, CA. He once wrote, "Recreate the world in your own image and make it better for your having been here."

CAMEROON: VOLCANIC ERUPTION: ANNIVERSARY. Aug 22, 1986. Deadly fumes from a presumed volcanic eruption under Lake Nios at Cameroon killed more than 1,500 people. A similar occurrence two years earlier had killed 37 people.

CANADA: MORDEN CORN AND APPLE FESTIVAL. Aug 22–24. Morden, MB. It's fun and it's free! Find us on Facebook for more information. Est attendance: 70,000. For info: Morden Corn and Apple Festival, 200-379 Stephen St, Morden, MB R6M 1V1, Canada. Phone: (204) 823-2676. Fax: (204) 822-1625. E-mail: info@cornandapple.com. Web: www.cornandapple.com.

CARTIER-BRESSON, HENRI: BIRTH ANNIVERSARY. Aug 22, 1908. Pioneering photojournalist who cofounded the Magnum photo agency. Probably the most respected 20th-century photographer. Famous for looking for "the decisive moment." Born at Chanteloup, France, he died Aug 2, 2004, at I'lle-sur-Sorgue, France.

August 2014

S	M	T	W	T	F	S
					1	2
3	4	5	6	7	8	9
10	11	12	13	14	15	16
17	18	19	20	21	22	23
24	25	26	27	28	29	30
31						

COBBLESTONE FESTIVAL. Aug 22–24. Falls City, NE. Includes games, sporting events, contests, carnival rides, flea market, food concessions, fishing contest, parade, craft demos and more. Est attendance: 5,000. For info: Falls City Chamber of Commerce, 1705 Stone St, Falls City, NE 68355. Phone: (402) 245-4228. Fax: (402) 245-4228. E-mail: fcchamber@sentco.net.

COLORADO STATE FAIR. Aug 22–Sept 1. State Fairgrounds, Pueblo, CO. First held in 1869 as a horse exhibition, the Colorado State Fair is one of the nation's oldest western fairs; it is also Colorado's largest summer event. Family fun, top-name entertainment, lots of food and festivities. For info: Colorado State Fair, 1001 Beulah Ave, Pueblo, CO 81004. Phone: (800) 876-4567. E-mail: info@coloradostatefair.com. Web: www.coloradostatefair.com.

DEBUSSY, CLAUDE: BIRTH ANNIVERSARY. Aug 22, 1862. (Achille) Claude Debussy, French musician and composer, especially remembered for his impressionistic "tone poems," was born at St. Germain-en-Laye, France. He died at Paris, France, Mar 25, 1918.

HERRIMAN, GEORGE: BIRTH ANNIVERSARY. Aug 22, 1880. In 1910 when George Herriman introduced a cat and mouse as subplot characters to his comic strip "The Dingbat Family," their nonsequitur dialogue gained enough attention to result in a spin-off strip of their own. The superbly drafted "Krazy Kat and Ignatz" had as its central theme unrequited love. Kat loved Ignatz, but the malevolent mouse took every opportunity to throw bricks at the devoted cat. "Krazy Kat" was popular with a mass audience as well as artists and intellectuals, and it remained enormously popular after Herriman's death. Born at New Orleans, LA, he died at Hollywood, CA, Apr 25, 1944.

INTERNATIONAL YACHT RACE: ANNIVERSARY. Aug 22, 1851. A silver trophy (then known as the "Hundred Guinea Cup" and offered by the Royal Yacht Squadron) was won in a race around the Isle of Wight by the US yacht *America*, who defeated the United Kingdom's *Aurora*. The trophy, later turned over to the New York Yacht Club, became known as the America's Cup and was to be "a perpetual challenge cup for friendly competition between nations." The boat race is the oldest trophy in sports, predating the modern Olympic Games by 45 years.

LANGLEY, SAMUEL PIERPONT: BIRTH ANNIVERSARY. Aug 22, 1834. American astronomer, physicist and aviation pioneer for whom Langley Air Force Base, VA, is named. Born at Roxbury, MA, Langley died at Aiken, SC, Feb 27, 1906.

MARYLAND STATE FAIR. Aug 22–Sept 1. Timonium, MD. Home arts, agricultural and livestock presentations, midway rides, live entertainment and thoroughbred horse racing. Est attendance: 500,000. For info: Ms Edie Bernier, Maryland State Fair, PO Box 188, Timonium, MD 21094. Phone: (410) 252-0200, ext 227. E-mail: msfair@msn.com. Web: www.marylandstatefair.com.

MORMON CHOIR FIRST PERFORMANCE: ANNIVERSARY. Aug 22, 1847. What would later become the world-famous Mormon Tabernacle Choir gave its first public performance at Salt Lake City, UT, for an outdoor meeting of The Church of Jesus Christ of Latter-day Saints. Widely known for its concert tours, recordings and weekly radio and television broadcasts from Temple Square, the choir's radio program "Music and the Spoken Word" is the longest continuously running radio program in network history, dating back to 1929.

NEBRASKA STATE FAIR. Aug 22–Sept 1. Grand Island, NE. Showcasing Nebraska pride, people and products. Food booths, variety of entertainment, amusement rides, concerts, livestock shows and tractor pulls. Est attendance: 300,000. For info: Nebraska State Fair Coalition, PO Box 1387, Grand Island, NE 68802. Phone: (308) 382-1620. Web: www.statefair.org.

OREGON STATE FAIR. Aug 22–Sept 1. Salem, OR. Exhibits, products and displays illustrate Oregon's role as one of the nation's major agricultural and recreational states. Floral gardens, sports and recreation activities, sustainable energy displays, carnival, entertainment, horse show and food. Est attendance: 360,000. For info: Oregon State Fair, 2330 17th St NE, Salem, OR 97301-3201. Phone: (503) 947-3247. Web: www.oregonstatefair.org.

PARKER, DOROTHY: BIRTH ANNIVERSARY. Aug 22, 1893. Born Dorothy Rothschild at West End, NJ, the acclaimed poet, critic, author and wit was known as the "wittiest woman in America." She said, "I hate writing, I love having written." During her career, Parker wrote for *Vanity Fair, The New Yorker* (for whom she was an original contributor) and other top periodicals, and was one of the founding members of the elite literary group the Algonquin Round Table. Strong, albeit subtle, critiques of sexism were prevailing themes in her works, along with critiques of all other forms of social inequality. Parker was found dead in her New York City residential hotel on June 7, 1967.

RIEFENSTAHL, LENI: BIRTH ANNIVERSARY. Aug 22, 1902. Controversial actress and filmmaker who directed the infamous Nazi propaganda films *Triumph of the Will* (1935) and *Olympia* (1938). Both films are noted for innovative filming techniques. Born at Berlin, Germany, Riefenstahl died at Pöcking, Germany, Sept 8, 2003.

SOUTHERN HEMISPHERE HOODIE-HOO DAY. Aug 22. Long awaited by our "southern-half" friends, this is the day to go outdoors at high noon and yell "Hoodie-Hoo" to chase winter and make ready for spring, only one month away. (©2006 by WH.) For info: Thomas & Ruth Roy, Wellcat Holidays, 2418 Long Ln, Lebanon, PA 17046. Phone: (717) 279-0184. E-mail: info@wellcat.com. Web: www.wellcat.com.

VIETNAM CONFLICT BEGINS: ANNIVERSARY. Aug 22, 1945. Less than a week after the Japanese surrender ended WWII, a team of Free French parachuted into southern Indochina in response to a successful coup by a Communist guerrilla named Ho Chi Minh in the French colony.

 **BIRTHDAYS TODAY**

Adewale Akinnuoye-Agbaje, 47, actor ("Lost," "Oz"), born London, England, Aug 22, 1967.

Tori Amos, 51, musician, singer, songwriter, born Newton, NC, Aug 22, 1963.

Ty Burrell, 47, actor ("Modern Family," *Dawn of the Dead*), born Grants Pass, OR, Aug 22, 1967.

Gerald Paul Carr, 82, former astronaut, born Denver, CO, Aug 22, 1932.

Giada De Laurentiis, 44, chef, cookbook author, television personality ("Everyday Italian"), born Rome, Italy, Aug 22, 1970.

Valerie Harper, 73, actress ("The Mary Tyler Moore Show," "Rhoda"), born Suffern, NY, Aug 22, 1941.

Steve Kroft, 69, television journalist, editor ("60 Minutes"), born Kokomo, IN, Aug 22, 1945.

Paul Molitor, 58, Hall of Fame baseball player, born St. Paul, MN, Aug 22, 1956.

Duane Charles (Bill) Parcells, 73, former football coach, born Englewood, NJ, Aug 22, 1941.

E. Annie Proulx, 79, author (*The Shipping News, Accordion Crimes*, "Brokeback Mountain"), born Norwich, CT, Aug 22, 1935.

Kristin Wiig, 41, actress, screenwriter, comedienne ("Saturday Night Live," *Bridesmaids*), born Canandaigua, NY, Aug 22, 1973.

Cindy Williams, 66, actress (*American Graffiti*, "Laverne & Shirley"), born Van Nuys, CA, Aug 22, 1948.

Carl Michael Yastrzemski, 75, Hall of Fame baseball player, born Southampton, NY, Aug 22, 1939.

August 23 — Saturday

DAY 235 **130 REMAINING**

BELGIUM: WEDDING OF THE GIANTS. Aug 23–24. Ath. Traditional cultural event observed since Medieval times and now recognized by UNESCO as a unique cultural event. Goliath, King of the Festival, marries his fiancée at St. Juliens Church, then battles the shepherd David in the afternoon. A procession of Ath giants courses through the town. Annually, starting the Saturday before the fourth Sunday in August. For more info: City of Ath. Web: www.ath.be.

BUSHMILLER, ERNIE: BIRTH ANNIVERSARY. Aug 23, 1905. Comic strip artist famous for the "Nancy" strip featuring spiky haired Nancy, her pal Sluggo and glamorous Aunt Fritzi. Born at the Bronx, NY, Bushmiller died Aug 15, 1982, at Stamford, CT.

CORVETTE CROSSROADS AUTO SHOW. Aug 23. Mackinaw City, MI. Show and visitor viewing, awards and parade across the Mackinaw Bridge on Saturday at 7 PM. Est attendance: 4,000. For info: Corvette Show, PO Box 856, Mackinaw City, MI 49701. Phone: (231) 436-5574 or (888) 455-8100. Web: www.mackinawchamber.com.

FERRET BUCKEYE BASH. Aug 23. Columbus, OH. One of the largest ferret shows in the USA, with three championship rings, companion and all-specialty rings. Sanctioned by the American Ferret Association. The general public is welcome. For info: Ferret Buckeye Bash, Heart of Ohio Ferret Assn and Rescue, PO Box 298206, Columbus, OH 43229. Phone: (614) 428-0279. E-mail: president@hofarescue.org. Web: www.hofarescue.org.

FIRST MAN-POWERED FLIGHT: ANNIVERSARY. Aug 23, 1977. At Schafter, CA, Bryan Allen pedaled the 70-pound *Gossamer Condor* for a mile at a "minimal altitude of two pylons" in a flight certified by the Royal Aeronautical Society of Britain, winning a £50,000 prize offered by British industrialist Henry Kremer. See also: "First Man-Powered Flight Across English Channel: Anniversary" (June 12).

KELLY, GENE: BIRTH ANNIVERSARY. Aug 23, 1912. Actor, dancer, director, choreographer born at Pittsburgh, PA. His movies included the musicals *Singin' in the Rain* and *An American in Paris*. Kelly died at Beverly Hills, CA, Feb 2, 1996.

MACKINAC ISLAND FUDGE FESTIVAL. Aug 23–24. Mackinac Island, MI. 9th annual. Most people don't need an excuse to indulge in a piece or two of creamy, decadent fudge, but for those who do, the Mackinac Island Fudge Festival offers island dwellers and tourists a terrific reason to celebrate fudge—made fresh each day at Mackinac's 17 fudge shops. Music, ballet, culinary and other fun events occur all weekend—including fudge spa treatments. A Wonka-esque golden ticket search caps off the fun: tickets hidden in fudge boxes offer family vacations. For info: Mackinac Island Tourist Bureau, PO Box 451, Mackinac Island, MI 49757. Phone: (906) 847-3783. Web: www.mackinacislandfudgefestival.org.

MARYLAND RENAISSANCE FESTIVAL. Aug 23–Oct 19 (Saturdays, Sundays and Labor Day). Annapolis, MD. A 16th-century English festival with Henry VIII, sword swallowers, magicians, authentic jousting, juggling, music, theater, games, food and crafts. Est attendance: 298,000. For info: Jules Smith, Maryland Renaissance Festival, PO Box 315, Crownsville, MD 21032. Phone:

(410) 266-7304. Fax: (410) 573-1508. E-mail: info@rennfest.com. Web: www.MarylandRenaissanceFestival.com.

MASTERS, EDGAR LEE: BIRTH ANNIVERSARY. Aug 23, 1869. American poet and author of the *Spoon River Anthology.* He was born at Garnett, KS, and he died at Melrose Park, PA, Mar 5, 1950.

NATIONAL CHAMPIONSHIP CHUCKWAGON RACES. Aug 23–31. Clinton, AR. 29th annual. Five divisions of chuckwagon races, bronc fanning, Snowy River race, live entertainment, trail rides, barn dance, Western show, Western art, saddles, tack-clothing vendors. Est attendance: 25,000. For info: Dan Eoff, 2848 Shake Rag Rd, Clinton, AR 72031. Phone: (501) 745-8407. Fax: (501) 745-8473. E-mail: chuckwag@artelco.com. Web: www.chuckwagonraces.com.

PERRY, OLIVER HAZARD: BIRTH ANNIVERSARY. Aug 23, 1785. American naval hero, born at South Kingston, RI. Best remembered for his announcement of victory at the Battle of Lake Erie, Sept 10, 1813: "We have met the enemy, and they are ours." Died Aug 23, 1819, at sea.

PITTSBURGH RENAISSANCE FESTIVAL. Aug 23–Sept 28 (weekends; Labor Day). West Newton, PA. Re-creation of a 16th-century marketplace where the king and queen come on holiday. Featured are more than 100 craft shops, six themed stages, games, food and armored contact jousting. Est attendance: 60,000. For info: Lori Hughes, Pittsburgh Renaissance Festival, 112 Renaissance Ln, West Newton, PA 15089. Phone: (724) 872-1670. E-mail: info@pittsburghrenfest.com. Web: www.pittsburghrenfest.com.

ROMANIA SURRENDER TO USSR: 70th ANNIVERSARY. Aug 23, 1944. King Michael I of Romania removed pro-German Premier Jon Antonescue from his position, dismissed his entire government and broadcast to the people of Romania that all hostilities had ceased and that he had accepted all peace terms demanded by the Allies. Most important, the Ploesti oil fields would be secured by the Allies.

SACCO-VANZETTI EXECUTION: ANNIVERSARY. Aug 23, 1927. Nicola Sacco and Bartolomeo Vanzetti were electrocuted at the Charlestown, MA, prison on this date. Convicted of a shoe factory payroll robbery during which a guard had been killed, Sacco and Vanzetti maintained their innocence to the end. Six years of appeals marked this American cause célèbre during which substantial evidence was presented to show that both men were elsewhere at the time of the crime. On the 50th anniversary of their execution, Massachusetts Governor Michael S. Dukakis proclaimed Aug 23, 1977, a memorial day, noting that the 1921 trial had been "permeated by prejudice."

SPACE MILESTONE: *INTELSAT-4 F-7* (US). Aug 23, 1973. International Communications Satellite Consortium's *Intelsat* launched Aug 23, 1973, to relay communications from North and South America to Europe and Africa.

"STOCKHOLM SYNDROME" BANK ROBBERY: ANNIVERSARY. Aug 23–28, 1973. In a botched bank robbery at Stockholm, Sweden, Jan Erik Olsson took four hostages and barricaded himself with them and a friend, Clark Olofsson, in the vault. After a six-day siege, the police piped in gas and the hostages were freed. Afterward, it emerged that the hostages were more afraid of the police than of their captors, and Swedish professor Nils Bejerot coined the term "Stockholm syndrome" to explain the phenomenon of hostages identifying and sympathizing with their captors.

TASTE OF MONTGOMERY COUNTY. Aug 23. General Lew Wallace Study and Museum, Crawfordsville, IN. A panorama of sights, a symphony of sounds and a festival of flavors that represent all that's great about this little corner of the Midwest. Restaurants, caterers and food vendors from throughout Montgomery County gather on the shady, rolling hills of the General Lew Wallace Study and Museum to showcase a huge variety of their tastiest treats and most mouthwatering morsels. The Taste also features terrific live music to satisfy almost every palate. Annually, the fourth Saturday in August. Est attendance: 3,000. For info: Taste of Montgomery County, PO Box 662, Crawfordsville, IN 47933. Phone: (765) 362-5769. Fax: (765) 362-5768. E-mail: study@ben-hur.com. Web: www.tasteofmontgomerycounty.com.

UNITED NATIONS: INTERNATIONAL DAY FOR THE REMEMBRANCE OF THE SLAVE TRADE AND ITS ABOLITION. Aug 23. For info: United Nations, Dept of Public Info, New York, NY 10017. Web: www.un.org.

VALENTINO MEMORIAL SERVICE. Aug 23. Hollywood Cathedral Mausoleum, Hollywood Forever Cemetery, Los Angeles, CA. Since 1927 annual memorial service celebrating the life of the silent screen's biggest male star, Rudolph Valentino. Held each year on the anniversary of his 1926 death at 12:10 PM—the time he died (in New York City). Attendees include the "Lady in Black." For info: Hollywood Forever Cemetery, 6000 Santa Monica Blvd, Los Angeles, CA, 90038.

VIRGO, THE VIRGIN. Aug 23–Sept 22. In the astronomical/astrological zodiac, which divides the sun's apparent orbit into 12 segments, the period Aug 23–Sept 22 is traditionally identified as the sun sign of Virgo, the Virgin. The ruling planet is Mercury.

BIRTHDAYS TODAY

Tony Bill, 74, actor (*You're a Big Boy Now*), director (*My Bodyguard*), born San Diego, CA, Aug 23, 1940.

Kobe Bryant, 36, basketball player, born Philadelphia, PA, Aug 23, 1978.

Scott Caan, 38, actor ("Hawaii Five-0," "Entourage"), born Los Angeles, CA, Aug 23, 1976.

Barbara Eden, 80, actress ("I Dream of Jeannie," *Harper Valley P.T.A.*), born Barbara Huffman at Tucson, AZ, Aug 23, 1934.

Bill Haslam, 56, Governor of Tennessee (R), born Knoxville, TN, Aug 23, 1958.

Sonny Jurgensen, 80, Hall of Fame football player, born Wilmington, NC, Aug 23, 1934.

Jeremy Lin, 26, basketball player, born Los Angeles, CA, Aug 23, 1988.

Shelley Long, 65, actress ("Cheers," *Irreconcilable Differences*), born Fort Wayne, IN, Aug 23, 1949.

Patricia McBride, 72, former dancer, born Teaneck, NJ, Aug 23, 1942.

Vera Miles, 84, actress (*The Wrong Man, Psycho*), born Boise City, OK, Aug 23, 1930.

Jay Mohr, 44, actor (*Jerry Maguire, Picture Perfect*, "Action"), comedian, born Verona, NJ, Aug 23, 1970.

Antonia Novello, 70, first woman and first Hispanic US surgeon general (1990–93), born Fajardo, Puerto Rico, Aug 23, 1944.

Mark Russell, 82, political comedian, born Mark Ruslander at Buffalo, NY, Aug 23, 1932.

Richard Sanders, 74, actor ("WKRP in Cincinnati," "Berrenger's"), born Harrisburg, PA, Aug 23, 1940.

Rick Springfield, 65, singer, actor, born Sydney, Australia, Aug 23, 1949.

August 2014

S	M	T	W	T	F	S
					1	2
3	4	5	6	7	8	9
10	11	12	13	14	15	16
17	18	19	20	21	22	23
24	25	26	27	28	29	30
31						

August 24 — Sunday

DAY 236 **129 REMAINING**

ARAFAT, YASSER: 85th BIRTH ANNIVERSARY. Aug 24, 1929. Controversial Middle Eastern leader who for almost 50 years was the face of the Palestinian cause. Reviled by some as a terrorist (as leader of Al-Fatah and the PLO) and cheered by others as a freedom fighter, Arafat shared the 1994 Nobel Peace Prize with Shimon Peres and Yitzhak Rabin. Born Muhammad Abdul Raouf Arafat al-Qudwa al-Husseini at Cairo, Egypt (some sources say Jerusalem or Gaza), Arafat died Nov 11, 2004, in a hospital near Paris, France.

BORGES, JORGE LUIS: BIRTH ANNIVERSARY. Aug 24, 1899. Argentine author, critic and poet who created intellectually fantastical tales (collected in *Ficciones* and *The Aleph and Other Stories*). "There are so many futures," he said, "[all] quite different from each other." Born at Buenos Aires, Argentina, Borges died June 14, 1986, at Geneva, Switzerland.

ENGLAND: NOTTING HILL CARNIVAL. Aug 24–25. London. The biggest street carnival in Europe: annual Caribbean and multicultural celebration on the streets of West London. Three-mile route for spectacular costume bands, steel bands, calypsonians and soca-on-the-move. More than 35 sound systems, live stages featuring top national and international musicians, hundreds of street-trading stalls selling food from all over the world, and arts and crafts. Free event. Annually, the Sunday and Monday of the August bank holiday weekend. Est attendance: 2,000,000. For info: The Notting Hill Carnival. Web: www.thenottinghillcarnival.com.

"THE FACTS OF LIFE" TV PREMIERE: 35th ANNIVERSARY. Aug 24, 1979. This NBC sitcom was spun off from "Diff'rent Strokes" with Drummond family housekeeper Edna Garrett (Charlotte Rae) moving to Peekskill, NY, to take over as housemother at Eastland, a boarding school for girls. The cast included Lisa Whelchel, Mindy Cohn, Kim Fields, Molly Ringwald and Nancy McKeon. The last episode aired in 1986.

JARVIS, GREGORY B.: 70th BIRTH ANNIVERSARY. Aug 24, 1944. Gregory B. Jarvis, a civilian engineer with Hughes Aircraft Company, was born at Detroit, MI. He was the 41-year-old payload specialist who perished with other crew members and Christa McAuliffe in the space shuttle *Challenger* explosion on Jan 28, 1986. See also: "*Challenger* Space Shuttle Explosion: Anniversary" (Jan 28).

KAHANAMOKU, DUKE: BIRTH ANNIVERSARY. Aug 24, 1890. Duke Paoa Kahanamoku, Olympic gold medal swimmer and "father of international surfing," was born at Honolulu, HI. Kahanamoku won gold medals in the 100-meter freestyle at the 1912 Olympics and at the 1920 Olympics. In total, he won five medals in four Olympics. Credited with inventing the flutter kick, he enjoyed a long career, not retiring from competition until age 42. Kahanamoku was also Hawaii's ambassador of surfing, popularizing the sport around the world. In 1917, on a 16-foot, 114-pound board, he rode a wave off Waikiki for 1.75 miles. The "Duke" acted in movies and served as sheriff of Honolulu, running alternately on Republican and Democratic tickets. Died at Honolulu, Jan 22, 1968. Hawaii has honored him with a statue on Waikiki Beach, on which fans place leis.

LIBERIA: FLAG DAY. Aug 24. National holiday.

LUXEMBOURG: SCHUEBERMESS SHEPHERD'S FAIR. Aug 24–Sept 6. Fair dates from 1340. (Two weeks beginning on the next-to-last Sunday in August.)

PLUTO DEMOTED: ANNIVERSARY. Aug 24, 2006. On the last day of the annual International Astronomical Union meeting at Prague, Czech Republic, 424 astronomers voted to demote Pluto from planet status. They determined that Pluto is instead a dwarf planet.

SAINT BARTHOLOMEW'S DAY MASSACRE: ANNIVERSARY. Aug 24, 1572. Anniversary of the massacre in Paris and throughout France of thousands of Protestant Huguenots. The massacre began when the church bells tolled at dawn on Saint Bartholomew's Day, Aug 24, 1572, and continued for several days. Pope Gregory XIII ordered a medal struck to commemorate the event, but Protestant countries abhorred the killings, estimated at 5,000 to 30,000.

SOUTHERN CYCLONE: ANNIVERSARY. Aug 24, 1893. A hurricane hit Savannah, GA, and Charleston, SC, killing 1,000 to 2,000 people.

SPACE MILESTONE: *VOYAGER 2* (US) REACHES NEPTUNE: 25th ANNIVERSARY. Aug 24, 1989. Launched in 1977, *Voyager 2* had its first close encounter with Neptune.

UKRAINE: INDEPENDENCE DAY. Aug 24. National day. Commemorates independence from the former Soviet Union in 1991.

VESUVIUS DAY. Aug 24, AD 79. Anniversary of the eruption of Vesuvius, an active volcano in southern Italy, which destroyed the cities of Pompeii, Stabiae and Herculaneum. Pliny the Younger, who escaped the disaster, wrote of it to the historian Tacitus: "[B]lack and horrible clouds, broken by sinuous shapes of flaming winds, were opening with long tongues of fire."

WARNER WEATHER QUOTATION: ANNIVERSARY. Aug 24, 1897. Charles Dudley Warner, American newspaper editor for the *Hartford Courant*, published this now-famous and oft-quoted sentence: "Everybody talks about the weather, but nobody does anything about it." The quotation is often mistakenly attributed to his friend and colleague Mark Twain. Warner and Twain were part of the most notable American literary circle during the late 19th century. Warner was a journalist, essayist, novelist, biographer and author who collaborated with Twain in writing *The Gilded Age* in 1873.

WASHINGTON, DC: 200th INVASION ANNIVERSARY. Aug 24–25, 1814. British forces briefly invaded and raided Washington, DC, burning the Capitol, the president's house and most other public buildings. President James Madison and other high US government officials fled to safety until British troops (not knowing the strength of their position) departed the city two days later.

WILBERFORCE, WILLIAM: BIRTH ANNIVERSARY. Aug 24, 1759. British politician and abolitionist who, as a member in the House of Commons (1780–1825), sponsored legislation that eventually abolished the slave trade (1807) and then slavery (1833) in the British Dominions. Born at Hull, Wilberforce died July 29, 1833, at London, England—three days after passage of the Slavery Abolition Act.

WILLIAM WILBERFORCE DAY. Aug 24. Wilberforce University, Wilberforce, OH. 4th annual. A celebration of the life and legacy of William Wilberforce (1759–1833), inspirational abolitionist who, as a member of the British parliament, sponsored the first bills that helped end the slave trade. Est attendance: 2,500. For info: Dr. Rick Sheridan, Wilberforce University, PO Box 1001, Wilberforce, OH 45384-1001. Phone: (937) 708-5621. E-mail: rsheridanl@wilberforce.edu. Web: www.WilberforceYearbook.org.

BIRTHDAYS TODAY

Gerry Cooney, 58, former boxer, born New York, NY, Aug 24, 1956.

Bob Corker, 62, US Senator (R, Tennessee), born Orangeburg, SC, Aug 24, 1952.

Stephen Fry, 57, actor (*Gosford Park, Wilde,* "Jeeves and Wooster"), novelist, born Hampstead, London, England, Aug 24, 1957.

Rafael Furcal, 36, baseball player, born Loma de Cabrera, Dominican Republic, Aug 24, 1978.

John Green, 37, author (*The Fault Is in Our Stars, Looking for Alaska*), born Indianapolis, IN, Aug 24, 1977.

Rupert Grint, 26, actor (Harry Potter films), born Hertfordshire, England, Aug 24, 1988.

Steve Guttenberg, 56, actor ("Billy," *Three Men and a Baby*), born Brooklyn, NY, Aug 24, 1958.

Oscar Hijuelos, 63, author (*The Mambo Kings Play Songs of Love*), born New York, NY, Aug 24, 1951.

Mike Huckabee, 59, television host, former governor of Arkansas, born Hope, AR, Aug 24, 1955.

Craig Kilborn, 52, television personality, born Hastings, MN, Aug 24, 1962.

Joe Manchin III, 67, US Senator (D, West Virginia), born Farmington, WV, Aug 24, 1947.

Marlee Matlin, 49, actress (Oscar for *Children of a Lesser God*; *Walker*, "Reasonable Doubts"), born Morton Grove, IL, Aug 24, 1965.

Alexander McCall Smith, 66, author (*The No 1 Ladies' Detective Agency, The Sunday Philosophy Club*), professor, scholar, born Bulawayo, Southern Rhodesia (now Zimbabwe), Aug 24, 1948.

Reginald Wayne (Reggie) Miller, 49, former basketball player, born Riverside, CA, Aug 24, 1965.

Chad Michael Murray, 33, actor ("One Tree Hill," "Dawson's Creek," *House of Wax*), born Buffalo, NY, Aug 24, 1981.

Alex O'Loughlin, 38, actor ("Hawaii Five-0," "Moonlight"), born Canberra, Australia, Aug 24, 1976.

Michael Richards, 64, actor ("Seinfeld," *Trial and Error*), born Culver City, CA, Aug 24, 1950.

Calvin Edward (Cal) Ripken, Jr, 54, Hall of Fame baseball player, born Havre de Grace, MD, Aug 24, 1960.

Mason Williams, 76, composer, born Abilene, TX, Aug 24, 1938.

	S	M	T	W	T	F	S
August 2014						1	2
	3	4	5	6	7	8	9
	10	11	12	13	14	15	16
	17	18	19	20	21	22	23
	24	25	26	27	28	29	30
	31						

August 25 — Monday

DAY 237 **128 REMAINING**

BE KIND TO HUMANKIND WEEK. Aug 25–31. 26th annual. All of the negative news that you read and hear about in the media is disheartening—but the truth is the positive stories outweigh the negative stories by a long shot! We just don't hear about them as often. Take heart—most people are caring individuals. Show you care. Decide to be kind. Daily affirmations: Speak Kind Words Saturday, Sacrifice Our Wants for Others' Needs Sunday, Motorist Consideration Monday, Touch a Heart Tuesday, Willing to Lend a Hand Wednesday, Thoughtful Thursday, Forgive Your Foe Friday. For info: Lorraine Jara, 1 Mountain Stream Court, Barnegat, NJ 08005. E-mail: Lorraine@cjara.com. Web: www.bk2hk.org.

BERNSTEIN, LEONARD: BIRTH ANNIVERSARY. Aug 25, 1918. American conductor and composer Leonard Bernstein was born at Lawrence, MA. One of the greatest conductors in American music history, he first conducted the New York Philharmonic Orchestra at age 25 and was its director from 1959 to 1969. His musicals include *West Side Story* and *On the Town*, and his operas and operettas include *Candide*. He died five days after his retirement, Oct 14, 1990, at New York, NY.

BURNING MAN 2014. Aug 25–Sept 1 (tentative). Black Rock Desert, NV. A temporary art community in the desert. On the Saturday of this annual experiment in radical self-expression, a 50-foot statue will be burned. Participants must bring all necessities for survival, including food, water and shelter. Must have ticket to participate in this private event. Est attendance: 29,000. For info: Burning Man. Phone: (415) TO-FLAME. E-mail: press@burningman.com. Web: www.burningman.com.

FOUNDERS DAY. Aug 25. Celebrated within the National Park Service of the US to commemorate its founding on Aug 25, 1916. Founders Day is an opportunity for US parks to show pride, connect with visitors and reflect on the importance of the National Park Service mission. For info: National Park Service. Web: www.nps.gov.

GIBSON, ALTHEA: BIRTH ANNIVERSARY. Aug 25, 1927. Born at Silver, SC, Althea Gibson learned paddle tennis by chance as a child when her block of W 143rd St in New York was designated as a Police Athletic League play street. She overcame great financial and social adversity and eventually won 10 consecutive national titles in the American Tennis Association, a league for black players. On Aug 28, 1950, she became the first black player to compete in the national tennis championship at Forest Hills, NY. A few years later, she became the first black woman to win the singles championship at Wimbledon. In her prime, she was ranked as high as seventh in the US, winning titles at the French Open, Wimbledon and US Nationals at Forest Hills. She died at East Orange, NJ, Sept 28, 2003.

HARTE, BRET: BIRTH ANNIVERSARY. Aug 25, 1836. Francis Bret(t) Harte, journalist, poet, printer, teacher and novelist, especially remembered for his early stories of California ("The Luck of Roaring Camp," "The Outcasts of Poker Flat" and "How Santa Claus Came to Simpson's Bar"), was born at Albany, NY. He died at London, England, May 5, 1902.

HONG KONG: LIBERATION DAY. Aug 25. Public holiday to celebrate liberation from the Japanese in 1945. Annually, the last Monday in August.

KELLY, WALT: BIRTH ANNIVERSARY. Aug 25, 1913. Born at Philadelphia, PA, Kelly was one of the greatest "funny animal" artists of the postwar golden age in comics. He moved to California in 1935 to work in the animation studio of Walt Disney, but left in 1941 during a labor dispute. Kelly created Pogo Possum and Albert Alligator first for comic books and then in the hugely popular syndicated daily comic strip that ran from 1948 to 1973. The lovable and quirky denizens of Okefenokee Swamp had safe-for-all-ages adventures, but their creator was able nonetheless to inject some political satire during the run of the strip. It was Kelly's character Pogo who paraphrased Oliver Hazard Perry to say, "We has met the enemy, and it is us." Kelly died at Hollywood, CA, Oct 18, 1973.

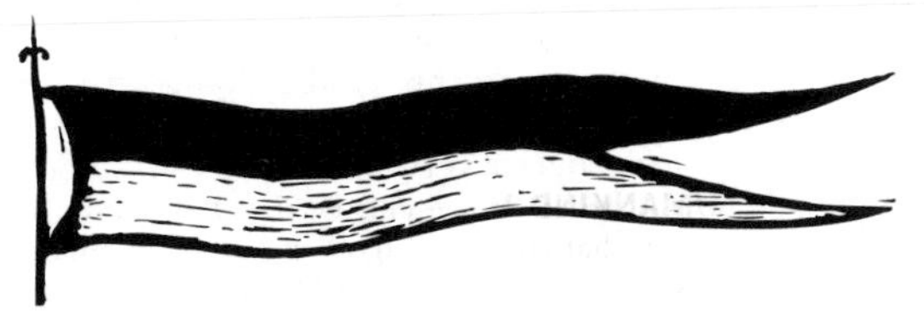

KISS-AND-MAKE-UP DAY. Aug 25. A day to make amends and for relationships that need mending. For info: Jacqueline V. Milgate, 121 Little Tree Ln, Hilton, NY 14468. E-mail: jacqueline825@yahoo.com.

MOON PHASE: NEW MOON. Aug 25. Moon enters New Moon phase at 10:13 AM, EDT.

NATIONAL OLD-TIME COUNTRY MUSIC CONTEST, FESTIVAL & EXPO. Aug 25–31. Plymouth County Fairgrounds, Le Mars, IA. Country music fans come from around the world to hear their favorites. Also many arts and crafts displays, other musical entertainment and food booths. Est attendance: 50,000. For info: Natl Old-Time Country Music Contest, Festival & Expo, PO Box 492, Anita, IA 50020. Phone: (712) 762-4363. E-mail: bobeverhart@yahoo.com. Web: www.ntcma.net.

NATIONAL PARK SERVICE FOUNDED: ANNIVERSARY. Aug 25, 1916. The Organic Act of 1916 established the National Park Service within the Department of the Interior. The act stated: "The service thus established shall promote and regulate the use of the Federal areas known as national parks, monuments, and reservations . . . , [as well as] to conserve the scenery and the natural and historic objects and the wild life therein and to provide for the enjoyment of the same in such manner and by such means as will leave them unimpaired for the enjoyment of future generations."

PARIS LIBERATED: 70th ANNIVERSARY. Aug 25, 1944. As dawn broke, the men of the Second French Armored Division entered Paris, France, ending the long German occupation of the City of Light. That afternoon General Charles de Gaulle led a parade down the Champs Elysées. Though Hitler had ordered the destruction of Paris, General Dietrich von Choltitz, the German occupying-officer, refused that order and instead surrendered to French Major General Jacques Le Clerc.

PHILIPPINES: NATIONAL HEROES' DAY. Aug 25. National holiday. The last Monday in August. Commemorates the Aug 26, 1896, beginning of the Philippine fight for independence from Spain.

PINKERTON, ALLAN: BIRTH ANNIVERSARY. Aug 25, 1819. Scottish-born American detective, founder of detective agency at Chicago, IL, in 1850, first chief of US Army's secret service, remembered now because of his strikebreaking and his lack of sympathy for working people. Pinkerton was born at Glasgow, Scotland, and died at Chicago, July 1, 1884.

RICHARD III'S REMAINS FOUND: ANNIVERSARY. Aug 25–Sept 5, 2012. Excavating a parking lot in Leicester, England, that stood over the ruins of Greyfriars Church, an archeological team from the University of Leicester found a medieval grave in the choir with the remains of a man—buried without shroud or coffin—who appeared to have scoliosis. During a press conference on Feb 4, 2013, scientists and archaeologists announced the results of a battery of tests—including DNA testing on a living descendant of Richard III's sister—confirming that the bones were the infamous king's. King Richard III, the last of the Plantagenets, died at the Battle of Bosworth Field on Aug 22, 1485. He was the last king of England to die in battle. The victor, Henry Tudor, ushered in a new dynasty of royalty as King Henry VII. The dig was conducted by the University of Leicester, with support from Leicester City Council and in association with the Richard III Society.

UNITED KINGDOM: SUMMER BANK HOLIDAY. Aug 25. Bank and public holiday in England, Wales and Northern Ireland. (Scotland not included.) Annually, the last Monday in August.

URUGUAY: INDEPENDENCE DAY. Aug 25. National holiday. Declared independence from Brazil in 1825. Independence granted in 1828.

US OPEN TENNIS CHAMPIONSHIP. Aug 25–Sept 8. Flushing Meadows, NY. Part of the Grand Slam of tennis tournaments. Est attendance: 720,000. For info: United States Tennis Assn, 70 W Red Oak Ln, White Plains, NY 10604. Phone: (914) 696-7000. Web: www.usopen.org or www.usta.com.

***THE WIZARD OF OZ* RELEASED: 75th ANNIVERSARY.** Aug 25, 1939. This motion-picture classic, directed by Victor Fleming, was a musical adaptation of the L. Frank Baum children's book with both black-and-white and color sequences. It starred Judy Garland as Dorothy as well as Frank Morgan as the Wizard (and four other characters), Ray Bolger as the Scarecrow, Bert Lahr as the Lion, Jack Haley as the Tin Man and Margaret Hamilton as the Wicked Witch of the West. Nominated for six Academy Awards, it won two for best original music score and best song, "Over the Rainbow" (Harold Arlen music and E.Y. Harburg lyrics).

BIRTHDAYS TODAY

Martin Amis, 65, author (*The Information, London Fields*), critic, born Oxford, England, Aug 25, 1949.

Anne Archer, 67, actress ("Falcon Crest"; stage: *A Couple of White Chicks Sitting Around Talking*), born Los Angeles, CA, Aug 25, 1947.

Albert Belle, 48, former baseball player, born Shreveport, LA, Aug 25, 1966.

Rachel Bilson, 33, actress ("Hart of Dixie," "The O.C."), born Los Angeles, CA, Aug 25, 1981.

Tim Burton, 56, director (*Alice in Wonderland, Sweeney Todd, Ed Wood, Edward Scissorhands*), born Burbank, CA, Aug 25, 1958.

Sean Connery, 84, actor (James Bond movies, *Entrapment, The Hunt for Red October, The Name of the Rose*), born Edinburgh, Scotland, Aug 25, 1930.

Elvis Costello, 60, singer, songwriter, born Declan McManus at Paddington, London, England, Aug 25, 1954.

Billy Ray Cyrus, 53, country singer, actor ("Hannah Montana"), born Flatwoods, KY, Aug 25, 1961.

Nathan Deal, 72, Governor of Georgia (R), born Millen, GA, Aug 25, 1942.

Frederick Forsyth, 76, author (*The Day of the Jackal*), born Ashford, Kent, England, Aug 25, 1938.

Monty Hall, 91, former game show host ("Let's Make a Deal"), born Winnipeg, MB, Canada, Aug 25, 1923.

Anthony Heald, 70, actor (*The Silence of the Lambs, Searching for Bobby Fischer*), born New Rochelle, NY, Aug 25, 1944.

Blake Lively, 27, actress (*Savages, Green Lantern, The Sisterhood of the Traveling Pants,* "Gossip Girl"), born Tarzana, CA, Aug 25, 1987.

Regis Philbin, 81, television personality ("Live with Regis & Kelly," "Who Wants to Be a Millionaire"), born New York, NY, Aug 25, 1933.

Rachael Ray, 46, chef, cookbook author, television personality ("30 Minute Meals," "$40 a Day"), born Cape Cod, MA, Aug 25, 1968.

John Savage, 65, actor (*The Deer Hunter, Hair*), born Long Island, NY, Aug 25, 1949.

Claudia Schiffer, 44, model, born Rheinberg, Germany, Aug 25, 1970.

Wayne Shorter, 81, jazz musician, born Newark, NJ, Aug 25, 1933.

Gene Simmons, 65, musician (KISS), actor, born Chaim Witz at Haifa, Israel, Aug 25, 1949.

Alexander Skarsgard, 38, actor ("True Blood"), born Stockholm, Sweden, Aug 25, 1976.

Tom Skerritt, 81, actor ("Picket Fences," *Steel Magnolias*), born Detroit, MI, Aug 25, 1933.

Blair Underwood, 50, actor ("One Life to Live," "LA Law"), born Tacoma, WA, Aug 25, 1964.

Ally Walker, 53, actress ("The Profiler"), born Tullahoma, TN, Aug 25, 1961.

Joanne Whalley, 50, actress ("The Singing Detective"; stage: *What the Butler Saw*), born Manchester, England, Aug 25, 1964.

August 26 — Tuesday

DAY 238 **127 REMAINING**

CORTÁZAR, JULIO: 100th BIRTH ANNIVERSARY. Aug 26, 1914. Argentine novelist, short-story writer, translator, born at Brussels, Belgium, most famous for *Hopscotch* (1963), a wildly inventive novel where readers can piece together their own narrative(s). Author of the short story that served as the basis for the 1966 film *Blow-up*. "For me, literature is a form of play," he explained in an interview, "It's a game, but it's a game one can put one's life into. One can do everything for that game." He died Feb 12, 1984, at Paris, France, where he had lived many years in exile from Argentina's military dictatorships.

De FOREST, LEE: BIRTH ANNIVERSARY. Aug 26, 1873. American inventor of the electron tube, the radio knife for surgery and the photoelectric cell; a pioneer in the creation of talking pictures and television. Born at Council Bluffs, IA, De Forest was holder of hundreds of patents but is perhaps best remembered by the moniker he gave himself in the title of his autobiography, *Father of Radio*, published in 1950. So unbelievable was the idea of wireless radio broadcasting that De Forest was accused of fraud and arrested for selling stock to underwrite the invention that later was to become an essential part of daily life. De Forest died at Hollywood, CA, June 30, 1961.

FIRST BASEBALL GAMES TELEVISED: 75th ANNIVERSARY. Aug 26, 1939. WXBS television, New York City, broadcast the first major league baseball games—a doubleheader between the Cincinnati Reds and the Brooklyn Dodgers at Ebbets Field. Announcer Red Barber interviewed Leo Durocher, manager of the Dodgers, and William McKechnie, manager of the Reds, between games.

ISHERWOOD, CHRISTOPHER: BIRTH ANNIVERSARY. Aug 26, 1904. Author of short stories, plays and novels, Christopher William Isherwood was born at High Lane, Cheshire, England. The play and motion picture *I Am a Camera* and the musical *Cabaret* were based on the short story "Sally Bowles" in his collection from the 1930s titled *Goodbye to Berlin*, which contained the line "I am a camera with its shutter open, quite passive, recording, not thinking." Isherwood died at Santa Monica, CA, Jan 4, 1986.

KRAKATOA ERUPTION: ANNIVERSARY. Aug 26, 1883. Anniversary of the biggest explosion in historic times. The eruption of the Indonesian volcanic island Krakatoa (Krakatau) was heard 3,000 miles away, created tidal waves 120 feet high (killing 36,000 people), hurled five cubic miles of earth fragments into the air (some to a height of 50 miles) and affected the oceans and the atmosphere for years.

August 2014

S	M	T	W	T	F	S
					1	2
3	4	5	6	7	8	9
10	11	12	13	14	15	16
17	18	19	20	21	22	23
24	25	26	27	28	29	30
31						

MONTGOLFIER, JOSEPH MICHEL: BIRTH ANNIVERSARY. Aug 26, 1740. French merchant and inventor, born at Vidalonlez-Annonay, France, who, with his brother Jacques Etienne in November 1782, conducted experiments with paper and fabric bags filled with smoke and hot air, which led to the invention of the hot-air balloon and man's first flight. Died at Balaruc-les-Bains, France, June 26, 1810. See also: "Montgolfier, Jacques Etienne: Birth Anniversary" (Jan 7), "First Balloon Flight: Anniversary" (June 5) and "Aviation History Month" (Nov 1).

NAMIBIA: HEROES' DAY. Aug 26. National holiday. Commemorates beginning of struggle for independence in 1966.

NATIONAL DOG DAY. Aug 26. More people in the US have dogs for pets than any other animal. Why? Because they are loving and loyal companions. They treat us better than we treat each other. Here is one day to recognize and honor them for their love, loyalty and lifesaving skills. Annually, Aug 26. For info: Colleen Paige, Animal Miracle Foundation, 4804 NW Bethany Blvd, Ste 12-197, Portland, OR 97229. Phone: (323) 552-9941. Web: www.nationaldogday.com.

SABIN, ALBERT BRUCE: BIRTH ANNIVERSARY. Aug 26, 1906. American medical researcher Albert Bruce Sabin was born at Bialystok, Poland. He is most noted for his oral vaccine for polio, which replaced Jonas Salk's injected vaccine because Sabin's provided lifetime protection. He was awarded the US National Medal of Science in 1971. Sabin died Mar 3, 1993, at Washington, DC.

SECOND BULL RUN CAMPAIGN: ANNIVERSARY. Aug 26, 1862. After various heavy and light skirmishes over previous weeks, the Second Bull Run Campaign of the Civil War intensified on this date when Stonewall Jackson's Confederate forces seized Manassas Junction and the railroad line there. Jackson divided his forces and encircled Northern general Pope's forces. Jackson succeeded in severing communication links between Pope and President Lincoln, forcing Pope to pull back from positions along the Rappahannock River.

SPACE MILESTONE: *SOYUZ 31* (USSR). Aug 26, 1978. Launched on Aug 26, Valery Bykovsky and Sigmund Jaehn docked at *Salyut 6* on Aug 27, stayed for a week, and then returned to Earth in *Soyuz 29*, leaving their *Soyuz 31* docked at the space station. Landed on Earth Sept 3.

✦WOMEN'S EQUALITY DAY. Aug 26. Presidential Proclamation issued in 1973 and 1974 at request and since 1975 without request.

WOMEN'S EQUALITY DAY. Aug 26. Anniversary of certification as part of US Constitution, in 1920, of the 19th Amendment, which prohibits discrimination on the basis of sex with regard to voting. Congresswoman Bella Abzug's bill to designate Aug 26 of each year as "Women's Equality Day" in August 1974 became Public Law 93–382.

BIRTHDAYS TODAY

Benjamin Crowninshield Bradlee, 93, journalist, editor, born Boston, MA, Aug 26, 1921.

Christopher Burke, 49, actor ("Life Goes On"), born New York, NY, Aug 26, 1965.

Macaulay Culkin, 34, actor (*Home Alone, My Girl*), born New York, NY, Aug 26, 1980.

Branford Marsalis, 54, musician, born Beaux Bridge, LA, Aug 26, 1960.

Melissa McCarthy, 44, actress (*Bridesmaids*, "Mike & Molly," "Gilmore Girls"), born Plainfield, IL, Aug 26, 1970.

Chris Pine, 34, actor (*Star Trek*), born Los Angeles, CA, Aug 26, 1980.

August 27 — Wednesday

DAY 239 **126 REMAINING**

COLUMBIA COUNTY FAIR. Aug 27–Sept 1. Chatham, NY. 174th annual fair. Midway and agricultural exhibits for the family to enjoy. For info: Columbia County Agricultural Society, PO Box 257, Chatham, NY 12037. Phone: (518) 392-2121. Web: www.columbiacountyny.org or www.columbiafair.com.

DAWES, CHARLES GATES: BIRTH ANNIVERSARY. Aug 27, 1865. 30th vice president of the US (1925–29), born at Marietta, OH. Won the Nobel Peace Prize in 1925 for the Dawes Plan for German reparations. Died at Evanston, IL, Apr 23, 1951.

DREISER, THEODORE: BIRTH ANNIVERSARY. Aug 27, 1871. American novelist Theodore Dreiser was born at Terre Haute, IN. He was an exponent of American naturalism in literature. His first novel, *Sister Carrie* (1900), was suppressed by his publisher on moral grounds. Dreiser's finest achievement is widely considered to be his novel *An American Tragedy* (1925). He died Dec 28, 1945, at Hollywood, CA.

"THE DUCHESS" WHO WASN'T DAY. Aug 27. At least once on this day repeat the following now-famous quotation from the novel *Molly Bawn*: "Beauty is in the eye of the beholder." Margaret Wolfe Hungerford often wrote under the pseudonym "The Duchess," which was the title of her most popular novel—hence the name of this event. A popular romance novelist with about 40 books published, Hungerford was born at Rosscarbery, County Cork, Ireland, on Aug 27, 1850; she died at Bandon, County Cork, in 1897. (Originated by the late Peggy Shirley.)

FIRST COMMERCIAL OIL WELL: ANNIVERSARY. Aug 27, 1859. W.A. "Uncle Billy" Smith discovered oil in a shaft being sunk by Colonel E.L. Drake at Titusville, in western Pennsylvania. Drilling had reached 69 feet 6 inches, when Smith saw a dark film floating on the water below the derrick floor. Soon 20 barrels of crude were being pumped each day. The first oil was refined to make kerosene for lighting, replacing whale oil. Later it was refined to make gasoline for cars. The first gas station opened in 1907.

"GOOD SEX! WITH DR. RUTH WESTHEIMER" TV PREMIERE: 30th ANNIVERSARY. Aug 27, 1984. This program premiered on the Lifetime Cable Channel with sex therapist Ruth Westheimer counseling actors appearing as her patients. The show's format later changed to include celebrity and physician interviews and call-ins.

HAMLIN, HANNIBAL: BIRTH ANNIVERSARY. Aug 27, 1809. 15th vice president of the US (1861–65), born at Paris, ME. Died at Bangor, ME, July 4, 1891.

JOHNSON, LYNDON BAINES: BIRTH ANNIVERSARY. Aug 27, 1908. The 36th president of the US succeeded to the presidency following the assassination of John F. Kennedy. Johnson's term of office: Nov 22, 1963–Jan 20, 1969. In 1964 he said: "The challenge of the next half century is whether we have the wisdom to use [our] wealth to enrich and elevate our national life—and to advance the quality of American civilization." Johnson was born near Stonewall, TX, and died at San Antonio, TX, Jan 22, 1973. His birthday is observed as a holiday in Texas.

MOLDOVA: INDEPENDENCE DAY. Aug 27. Republic of Moldova. Moldova declared its independence from the Soviet Union in 1991.

MOTHER TERESA: BIRTH ANNIVERSARY. Aug 27, 1910. Albanian Roman Catholic nun born Agnes Gonxha Bojaxhiu at Skopje, Macedonia. She founded the Order of the Missionaries of Charity, which cares for the destitute people of Calcutta, India, and other places. She won the Nobel Peace Prize in 1979. She died at Calcutta, Sept 5, 1997.

MOUNTBATTEN, LOUIS: 35th ASSASSINATION ANNIVERSARY. Aug 27, 1979. Lord Mountbatten (Louis Francis Albert Victor Nicholas Mountbatten), celebrated British war hero, cousin of Queen Elizabeth II, last viceroy of India, was killed by a bomb, along with his 14-year-old grandson and two others, while on his yacht in Donegal Bay off the coast of Ireland, on Aug 27, 1979. Provisional Irish Republican Army claimed responsibility for the explosion and for the killing of 18 British soldiers later the same day, deepening the crisis and conflict between Protestants and Catholics and between England and Ireland. Lord Mountbatten was born at Windsor, England, June 25, 1900.

RAYE, MARTHA: BIRTH ANNIVERSARY. Aug 27, 1916. Born at Butte, MT, Martha Raye began singing at age three. Raye performed for American servicemen during three wars and received the Jean Hersholt Humanitarian Award from the Academy of Motion Picture Arts and Sciences (1969) for that service. She appeared in her first film, *Rhythm on the Range*, in 1936. She had several TV shows, including "The Martha Raye Show" (1955–56). In 1993 Raye was awarded the Presidential Medal of Freedom. Martha Raye died Oct 19, 1994, at Los Angeles, CA.

SPAIN: LA TOMATINA. Aug 27. Buñol (near Valencia). The world's biggest food fight takes place today as 35,000 revelers hurl 120 tons of tomatoes at each other (and the town) for two hours. La Tomatina ("Tomato Festival") occurs annually the last Wednesday of August. Festivities kick off with a competition to see who can reach a ham at the top of a greased pole. With the ham secured, the trucks arrive with tomatoes.

BIRTHDAYS TODAY

Patrick J. Adams, 33, actor (*Old School*, "Suits," "Luck"), born Toronto, ON, Canada, Aug 27, 1981.

Sarah Chalke, 38, actress ("Roseanne," "Scrubs"), born Ottawa, ON, Canada, Aug 27, 1976.

Daryl Dragon, 72, musician (Captain & Tennille), songwriter, born Studio City, CA, Aug 27, 1942.

Carlos Moya, 38, tennis player, born Palma, Majorca, Spain, Aug 27, 1976.

Aaron Paul, 35, actor ("Big Love," Emmy for "Breaking Bad"), born Aaron Paul Sturtevant at Emmett, ID, Aug 27, 1979.

Paul Reubens, 62, actor, writer ("Pee-wee's Playhouse," *Pee-wee's Big Adventure*), born Peekskill, NY, Aug 27, 1952.

Tommy Sands, 77, singer, born Chicago, IL, Aug 27, 1937.

Jim Thome, 44, baseball player, born Peoria, IL, Aug 27, 1970.

Tuesday Weld, 71, actress ("The Many Loves of Dobie Gillis," *Looking for Mr Goodbar*), born Susan Kerr at New York, NY, Aug 27, 1943.

Chandra Wilson, 45, actress ("Grey's Anatomy"), born Houston, TX, Aug 27, 1969.

August 28 — Thursday

DAY 240 **125 REMAINING**

BLUE HILL FAIR. Aug 28–Sept 1. Blue Hill, ME. A "down-to-earth" country fair. Annually, Labor Day weekend. Est attendance: 35,000. For info: Blue Hill Fair, PO Box 390, Blue Hill, ME 04614. Phone: (207) 374-3701. Fax: (207) 374-3702. Web: www.bluehillfair.com.

BOYER, CHARLES: BIRTH ANNIVERSARY. Aug 28, 1897. Film star (*Mayerling, Gaslight*), born at Figeac, France. Died at Scottsdale, AZ, Aug 26, 1978.

FEAST OF SAINT AUGUSTINE. Aug 28. Bishop of Hippo, author of *Confessions* and *The City of God*, born Nov 13, 354, at Tagaste, in what is now Algeria. Died Aug 28, 430, at Hippo, also in North Africa.

GOETHE, JOHANN WOLFGANG von: BIRTH ANNIVERSARY. Aug 28, 1749. German author, poet, dramatist and philosopher, born at Frankfurt, Germany. Died Mar 22, 1832, at Weimar, Germany. Best known for the novels *The Sorrows of Young Werther* and *Wilheim Meister* and the play *Faust*.

HAYES, LUCY WARE WEBB: BIRTH ANNIVERSARY. Aug 28, 1831. Wife of Rutherford Birchard Hayes, 19th president of the US, born at Chillicothe, OH. Died at Fremont, OH, June 25, 1889. She was nicknamed "Lemonade Lucy" because she and the president, both abstainers, served no alcoholic beverages at White House receptions.

LE FANU, SHERIDAN: 200th BIRTH ANNIVERSARY. Aug 28, 1814. Popular Victorian author of the supernatural and macabre, born at Dublin, Ireland. Best known for the gothic novel *Uncle Silas* (1864) and the novella *Carmilla* (1872), about a female vampire. Le Fanu, who was also a journal editor, died at Dublin on Feb 7, 1873.

LOUISIANA SHRIMP AND PETROLEUM FESTIVAL AND FAIR. Aug 28–Sept 1. Morgan City, LA. Free admission to this event that recognizes and celebrates the importance of the shrimp and petroleum industries to the area. Arts, crafts, water and street parades, Cajun culinary classic, music in the park, unique children's village (a magical adventureland), gospel tent, coronation pageant and ball, carnival, blessing of the fleet. Chosen as the American Bus Association's "Festival of the Year" several times. Voted by the Southeastern Tourism Society as a Top 20 event for several years. Named Festival of the Year by the Louisiana Association of Fairs and Festivals several years. Est attendance: 150,000. For info: Louisiana Shrimp and Petroleum Festival and Fair Assn, PO Box 103, Morgan City, LA 70381. Phone: (985) 385-0703. Fax: (985) 384-4628. E-mail: info@shrimp-petrofest.org. Web: www.shrimp-petrofest.org.

❀ ❀ ❀

August 2014	S	M	T	W	T	F	S
						1	2
	3	4	5	6	7	8	9
	10	11	12	13	14	15	16
	17	18	19	20	21	22	23
	24	25	26	27	28	29	30
	31						

MARCH ON WASHINGTON: ANNIVERSARY. Aug 28, 1963. More than 250,000 people attended this civil rights rally at Washington, DC, at which Reverend Dr. Martin Luther King, Jr, made his famous "I have a dream" speech.

NORTHWEST MISSOURI STATE FAIR. Aug 28–Sept 1. Bethany, MO. Concerts, free shows, many exhibitors, youth activities, car races, Demo Derby, a wonderful carnival and many other activities for the entire family to enjoy! Annually, the Thursday through Monday of Labor Day weekend. For info: Northwest Missouri State Fair, PO Box 327, Bethany, MO 64424. Web: www.nwmostatefair.com.

O'CONNOR, DONALD: BIRTH ANNIVERSARY. Aug 28, 1925. Singer, dancer and vaudeville performer Donald O'Connor was born into a family of circus performers at Chicago, IL. He joined the family's vaudeville act at a very young age and was soon under contract with Universal Studios. He starred opposite Francis the Mule in a string of very successful film comedies throughout the 1950s but is best remembered for his role opposite Gene Kelly and Debbie Reynolds in *Singin' in the Rain* (1952). His solo number "Make 'Em Laugh" is considered one of Hollywood's finest moments. O'Connor died Sept 28, 2003, at Woodland Hills, CA.

OLD THRESHERS REUNION. Aug 28–Sept 1. McMillan Park, Mount Pleasant, IA. The reunion began in 1950. Old Threshers is a celebration of our rich agricultural heritage. Attractions range from displays of steam engines and agricultural exhibits to turn-of-the-century living and antique cars, tractors and gas engines. There are also steam trains, trolleys, crafts, museums, music and camping. Annually, five days ending on Labor Day. Est attendance: 40,000. For info: Midwest Old Threshers, 405 E Threshers Rd, Mt Pleasant, IA 52641. Phone: (319) 385-8937. Fax: (319) 385-0563. E-mail: info@oldthreshers.org. Web: www.oldthreshers.com.

ON THE WATERFRONT. Aug 28–31. Rockford, IL. Illinois's largest music festival. Five music stages, more than 80 performers, more than 40 specialty foods and dozens of special events. Annually, the Thursday through Sunday of Labor Day weekend. Est attendance: 300,000. For info: On the Waterfront, Inc, 308 W State St, Ste 115, Rockford, IL 61101. Phone: (815) 964-4388 or (815) 963-4FUN. E-mail: 4fun@onthewaterfront.com. Web: www.onthewaterfront.com.

PAYSON GOLDEN ONION DAYS. Aug 28–Sept 1. Payson, UT. This unique festival includes carnival and amusement rides, a grand parade, arts and crafts booth, entertainment, food booths and much more. Annually, Labor Day weekend. Est attendance: 20,000. For info: Payson Community Coordinator, 439 W Utah Ave, Payson, UT 84651. Phone: (801) 358-3357. E-mail: events@payson.org.

PETERSON, ROGER TORY: BIRTH ANNIVERSARY. Aug 28, 1908. Naturalist, author of *A Field Guide to Birds*, born at Jamestown, NY. Peterson died at Old Lyme, CT, July 28, 1996.

RACE YOUR MOUSE AROUND THE ICONS DAY. Aug 28. While you're waiting for any number of endless items to finally come up on your screen, don't just sit there. Race your mouse in and around the icons. You'll feel peppy for doing it. (©2006 by WH.) For info: Thomas & Ruth Roy, Wellcat Holidays, 2418 Long Ln, Lebanon, PA 17046. Phone: (717) 279-0184. E-mail: info@wellcat.com. Web: www.wellcat.com.

RADIO COMMERCIALS: ANNIVERSARY. Aug 28, 1922. Broadcasters realized radio could earn profits from the sale of advertising time. WEAF in New York ran a commercial "spot," which was sponsored by the Queensboro Realty Corporation of Jackson Heights to promote Hawthorne Court, a group of apartment buildings at Queens. The commercial rate was $100 for 10 minutes.

SOUTH DAKOTA STATE FAIR. Aug 28–Sept 1. Huron, SD. Grandstand entertainment nightly, six free stages with multiple shows daily, hundreds of commercial exhibits and thousands of livestock exhibits. One of the largest agricultural fairs in the US. Est attendance: 193,000. For info: South Dakota State Fair, 890 3rd St SW, Huron, SD 57350-1275. Phone: (605) 353-7340 or (800) 529-0900. Fax: (605) 353-7348. Web: www.sdstatefair.com.

TILL, EMMETT: DEATH ANNIVERSARY. Aug 28, 1955. Emmett Till, a 14-year-old African-American teenager from Chicago visiting relatives in Money, MS, was murdered on this date by a group of white men angry at Till's reported flirtation with a white woman. The Till murder and the acquittal of two of the men involved brought the nation's attention to racial tensions in the South and helped spark civil rights protests later—most famously, Rosa Parks's refusal to give up her seat to a white man on a municipal bus in Montgomery, AL, in December of that year.

BIRTHDAYS TODAY

Ronald Ames (Ron) Guidry, 64, former baseball player, born Lafayette, LA, Aug 28, 1950.

Scott Hamilton, 56, sportscaster, Olympic figure skater, born Toledo, OH, Aug 28, 1958.

Armie Hammer, 28, actor (*The Lone Ranger, Mirror Mirror, The Social Network*), born Los Angeles, CA, Aug 28, 1986.

Paul Martin, 76, 21st prime minister of Canada (2003–6), born Windsor, ON, Canada, Aug 28, 1938.

Lou Piniella, 71, former baseball manager, former player, born Tampa, FL, Aug 28, 1943.

Jason Priestley, 45, actor ("Beverly Hills 90210," *Tombstone*), born Vancouver, BC, Canada, Aug 28, 1969.

Carlos Quentin, 32, baseball player, born Bellflower, CA, Aug 28, 1982.

LeAnn Rimes, 32, singer, born Jackson, MS, Aug 28, 1982.

Rick Rossovich, 57, actor (*The Terminator, Roxanne*), born Palo Alto, CA, Aug 28, 1957.

Emma Samms, 54, actress ("General Hospital," "Dynasty"), born Emma Samuelson at London, England, Aug 28, 1960.

David Soul, 68, actor ("Starsky and Hutch," *Salem's Lot*), born Chicago, IL, Aug 28, 1946.

Daniel Stern, 57, actor (*City Slickers, Home Alone*), born Bethesda, MD, Aug 28, 1957.

Shania Twain, 49, country singer, born Eileen Twain at Windsor, ON, Canada, Aug 28, 1965.

Quvenzhané Wallis, 11, actress (*Beasts of the Southern Wild*), born Houma, LA, Aug 28, 2003.

August 29 — Friday

DAY 241 | **124 REMAINING**

"ACCORDING TO HOYLE" DAY (EDMOND HOYLE DEATH ANNIVERSARY). Aug 29, 1769. A day to remember Edmond Hoyle and a day for fun and games *according to the rules*. He is believed to have studied law. For many years he lived at London, England, and gave instructions in the playing of games. His "Short Treatise" on the game of whist (published in 1742) became a model guide to the rules of the game. Hoyle's name became synonymous with the idea of correct play according to the rules, and the phrase "according to Hoyle" became a part of the English language. Hoyle was born at London about 1672 and died there.

***AMISTAD* SEIZED: 175th ANNIVERSARY.** Aug 29, 1839. In January 1839, 53 Africans were abducted near modern-day Sierra Leone, taken to Cuba and sold as slaves. While being transferred to another part of the island on the ship *Amistad*, the Africans, led by Cinque, grabbed control of the ship, telling the surviving crew to take them back to Africa. However, the crew secretly changed course, and the ship sailed to Long Island, NY, where it and its "cargo" were seized as salvage. The *Amistad* was towed to New Haven, CT, where the Africans were imprisoned and a lengthy legal battle began to determine if they were property to be returned to Cuba, salvage for the US Coast Guard or free men. John Quincy Adams took their case all the way to the Supreme Court, where on Mar 9, 1841, it was determined that they were free and could return to Africa.

BENTON NEIGHBOR DAY. Aug 29–30. Benton, MO. Large festival that includes exhibits, greased pole climb, amusement park, Little Mr and Miss Contest, Queen Contest, Junior Miss Contest, live bands, antique car show, four-wheel drive mud racing, horseshoe tournament, parade and talent show, outdoor games for kids and adults. Annually, the Friday and Saturday before Labor Day. Est attendance: 3,000. For info: Benton Chamber of Commerce, PO Box 477, Benton, MO 63736. Phone: (573) 545-3125.

BERGMAN, INGRID: BIRTH ANNIVERSARY. Aug 29, 1915. One of cinema's greatest actresses. Bergman was born at Stockholm, Sweden, and died at London, England, on her 67th birthday, Aug 29, 1982. Three-time Academy Award winner for *Gaslight, Anastasia* and *Murder on the Orient Express*. Controversy over her personal life made her and her films unpopular to American audiences during an interval of several years between periods of awards and adulation.

BRITT DRAFT HORSE SHOW. Aug 29–31. Hancock County Fairgrounds, Britt, IA. One of the largest draft horse hitch shows in North America, featuring 18 six-horse hitches from the US and Canada representing the very best of the Belgian, Percheron and Clydesdale performance horses. Annually, Labor Day weekend. Est attendance: 10,000. For info: Randel or Melodie Hiscocks, Britt Draft Horse Assn, PO Box 312, Britt, IA 50423. Phone: (641) 843-4181.

COIN, JEWELRY & STAMP EXPO. Aug 29–31. Circus Circus Hotel, Las Vegas, NV. Est attendance: 4,000. For info: Israel Bick, Exec Dir, Intl Stamp & Coin Collectors Society, PO Box 854, Van Nuys, CA 91408. Phone: (818) 997-6496. Fax: (818) 988-4337. E-mail: iibick@sbcglobal.net. Web: www.bickinternational.com.

DANIEL BOONE PIONEER FESTIVAL. Aug 29–31. Winchester, KY. Take yourself back to the days of Daniel Boone and the pioneers. Features street dance, 5k run, walk with friends, talent contest, arts and crafts displays and food booths. A nationally known country music entertainer will perform in concert. Est attendance: 35,000. For info: Daniel Boone Pioneer Festival, 2 S Maple St, Winchester, KY 40391. Phone: (859) 744-0556 or (800) 298-9105. Fax: (859) 744-9229. E-mail: info@tourwinchester.com.

FORT BRIDGER RENDEZVOUS. Aug 29–Sept 1. Fort Bridger, WY. 42nd annual. A mountain man rendezvous in celebration of the Fur Trade Rendezvous Era that occurred in the Rocky Mountains between 1825–1840. It is one of the largest mountain man gatherings in the nation. Come and join in the family fun with entertainment, food booths, merchandise exhibits and much more. Est attendance: 30,000. For info: Fort Bridger Rendezvous Assn, 3989 N 2800 West, Farr West, UT 84404. Phone: (435) 213-5133. E-mail: fbrainc@fortbridgerrendezvous.net. Web: www.fortbridgerrendezvous.net.

HOG CAPITAL OF THE WORLD FESTIVAL. Aug 29–Sept 1. Kewanee, IL. World's largest outdoor pork BBQ. Also features professional entertainment, carnival, flea market, Model T races, parade and Hog Stampede (four-mile run). Annually, Labor Day weekend. Est attendance: 30,000. For info: Hog Festival Committee, 306 N Main St, Kewanee, IL 61443. Phone: (309) 852-4644. E-mail: info@kewaneehogdays.com. Web: www.kewaneehogdays.com.

HOISINGTON CELEBRATION. Aug 29–Sept 1. Bicentennial Park, Hoisington, KS. Annual event includes dances, demolition derby, parade, car show, carnival, kiddie events, baby contest, float contest. Annually, Labor Day weekend. Est attendance: 15,000. For info: Hoisington Labor Day Committee, 123 N Main, Hoisington, KS 67544. Phone: (620) 653-4311. E-mail: hoisingtoncofc@embarqmail.com. Web: www.hoisingtonkansas.com.

HOLMES, OLIVER WENDELL, SR: BIRTH ANNIVERSARY. Aug 29, 1809. Physician and author, father of Supreme Court Justice Oliver Wendell Holmes, Jr. The elder Holmes was born at Cambridge, MA. Died at Boston, MA, Oct 7, 1894. "A moment's insight," he wrote, "is sometimes worth a life's experience."

HURRICANE KATRINA STRIKES GULF COAST: ANNIVERSARY. Aug 29, 2005. After hitting the southern Florida coast on Aug 25, Hurricane Katrina moved into the Gulf of Mexico and grew into one of the most devastating hurricanes in US history. On this date, as a Category 3 storm, it struck Buras, LA, and surrounding areas, destroying communities up and down the Gulf Coast. Levees in New Orleans were breached, and within two days more than 80 percent of the city was underwater, stranding tens of thousands of people. The death toll in Louisiana, Mississippi, Alabama and Florida was more than 1,300, with more than 1,000 fatalities coming in Louisiana. Thousands remained missing at the end of 2005. The estimated one million people evacuated before and after the storm accounted for the largest movement of people in the US since the Great Depression and the Civil War. And with $100 billion to $200 billion in damage over 90,000 square miles, Hurricane Katrina was the most expensive natural disaster in US history.

INTERNATIONAL BAT NIGHT. Aug 29–31. 18th annual. Originally started by EUROBATS, this special day is now observed in more than 30 countries. Nature conservation agencies pass on information to the public about the way bats live and their needs with presentations, exhibitions and bat walks, often offering the opportunity to listen to bat sounds with the support of ultrasound technology. Annually, the last full weekend in August (although local organizers sometimes choose other dates). For info: EUROBATS, United Nations Campus, Hermann-Ehlers-Str 10, D-53113 Bonn, Switzerland. E-mail: eurobats@eurobats.org. Web: www.eurobats.org. Or Bat Conservation International, 500 N Capital of Texas Hwy, Bldg 1, Ste 200, Austin, TX 78746. Web: www.batcon.org.

JACKSON, MICHAEL: BIRTH ANNIVERSARY. Aug 29, 1958. The self-styled "King of Pop," born at Gary, IN. Rising from humble beginnings to become a child star at Motown with his older brothers as The Jackson 5, he later launched a solo career and achieved enormous success as both a singer and dancer/choreographer. He changed the face of music videos with his inventive dance sequences, and his albums *Off the Wall, Bad* and *Thriller* are among the bestselling of all time. His musical legacy was almost overshadowed by his frequent plastic surgeries, eccentric behavior and legal difficulties, but he remained one of the most popular artists in the world and his influence on the musical landscape of the 1970s and '80s was unsurpassed. He died at Los Angeles, CA, June 25, 2009.

JOHNSON CITY FIELD DAYS. Aug 29–Sept 1. Northside Park, Johnson City, NY. Amusement rides, game booths, live entertainment, food concessions, area's largest fireworks display. The annual celebration benefits many nonprofit organizations in Johnson City and the surrounding area. Annually, Labor Day weekend. For info: Johnson City Celebration Committee, 243 Main St, Johnson City, NY 13790. Phone: (607) 798-7861 or (607) 797-9098. Fax: (607) 798-7865. E-mail: jcplanning-secretary@stny.rr.com.

LIFELIGHT OUTDOOR MUSIC FESTIVAL. Aug 29–31. Worthing, SD. Outdoor Christian music festival, featuring more than 100 bands on six stages, plus children's activities, seminars, camping, extreme sports and much more. Annually, Labor Day weekend. Est attendance: 320,000. For info: LifeLight Communications, 2601 S Western Ave, Sioux Falls, SD 57105. Phone: (605) 338-2847. Fax: (605) 336-1056. E-mail: office@lifelight.org. Web: www.lifelight.org.

LOCKE, JOHN: BIRTH ANNIVERSARY. Aug 29, 1632. (Old Style date.) English philosopher, founder of philosophical liberalism, born at Wrington, England. His ideas influenced the American colonists and were enshrined in the Constitution. Locke died at Essex, England, Oct 28, 1704 (OS).

MORE HERBS, LESS SALT DAY. Aug 29. It's healthier, zestier and lustier! (©2006 by WH.) For info: Thomas & Ruth Roy, Wellcat Holidays, 2418 Long Ln, Lebanon, PA 17046. Phone: (717) 279-0184. E-mail: info@wellcat.com. Web: www.wellcat.com.

NATIONAL SWEETCORN FESTIVAL. Aug 29–Sept 1. McFerron Park, Hoopeston, IL. Annual festival includes 29 tons of free corn on the cob, nationally sanctioned beauty pageant, carnival, flea market, horse show, demolition derby, bands and talent shows. Est attendance: 50,000. For info: Danville Area CVB, 100 W Main St #146, Danville, IL 61832. Phone: (217) 442-2096. Fax: (217) 442-2137. E-mail: info@danvilleareainfo.com.

ODYSSEY—A GREEK FESTIVAL. Aug 29–Sept 1. Orange, CT. An indoor/outdoor festival celebrating Greek culture, featuring authentic Greek cuisine, live music and marketplace. Est attendance: 15,000. For info: St. Barbara Greek Orthodox Church, 480 Racebrook Rd, Orange, CT 06477. Phone: (203) 795-1347. Web: www.saintbarbara.org. Or: Greater New Haven Conv & Visitors Bureau, One Long Wharf Dr, New Haven, CT 06511. Phone: (203) 777-8550 or (800) 332-STAY. Fax: (203) 782-7755.

OREGON TRAIL RODEO. Aug 29–31. Hastings, NE. A PRCA-sponsored rodeo. Annually, Friday–Sunday of Labor Day weekend. Est attendance: 6,900. For info: Sandy Himmelberg, Gen Mgr, Oregon Trail Rodeo, 947 S Baltimore, Hastings, NE 68901. Phone: (402) 462-3247. Fax: (402) 462-4731. Web: www.adamscountyfairgrounds.com.

PARKER, CHARLIE: BIRTH ANNIVERSARY. Aug 29, 1920. Jazz saxophonist Charlie Parker was born at Kansas City, KS. He earned the nickname "Yardbird" (later "Bird") from his habit of sitting in the backyard of speakeasies, fingering his saxophone. His career as a jazz saxophonist took him from jam sessions in Kansas City to New York, where he met Dizzy Gillespie and others who were creating a style of music that would become known as bop or bebop. Although Parker's musical genius was unquestioned, his addiction to heroin haunted his life. He died at Rochester, NY, Mar 12, 1955, at age 34.

PENNSYLVANIA ARTS & CRAFTS COLONIAL FESTIVAL. Aug 29–Sept 1. Westmoreland Fairgrounds, Greensburg, PA. Step back to colonial times with more than 220 exhibits of handcrafted furniture, floral arrangements, ceramics, tole, decorative paintings and wrought iron. Historical encampment, fife and drum music and food booths. Est attendance: 16,000. For info: Debbie & Dave Stoner, Family Festivals Assn, Inc, PO Box 166, Irwin, PA 15642. Phone: (724) 863-4577. Fax: (724) 863-5427. E-mail: info@familyfestivals.com. Web: www.familyfestivals.com.

August 2014	S	M	T	W	T	F	S
						1	2
	3	4	5	6	7	8	9
	10	11	12	13	14	15	16
	17	18	19	20	21	22	23
	24	25	26	27	28	29	30
	31						

ROYAL GEORGE SINKS: ANNIVERSARY. Aug 29, 1782. Prized British battleship *Royal George* sank due to fatal human error in one of the worst maritime disasters in history. While the ship was being repaired at Spithead, the port side was tilted too close to the waterline. A gust of wind lowered the ship even farther, allowing tons of water to flood into its open gunports. The ship sank within minutes before many of the 1,300 people on board realized what was happening, and more than 900 drowned.

SANTA-CALI-GON DAYS FESTIVAL. Aug 29–Sept 1. Historic Square, Independence, MO. Regional celebration for the three trails—Santa Fe, California, Oregon—which all started in Independence. Huge arts and crafts show, live Nashville performers, large carnival midway, historical reenactments and free admission. Largest Labor Day weekend event in Kansas City metropolitan area. Est attendance: 250,000. For info: Santa-Cali-Gon Days, 210 W Truman Rd, Independence, MO 64050. Phone: (816) 252-4745. Web: www.santacaligon.com.

SHAYS'S REBELLION: ANNIVERSARY. Aug 29, 1786. Daniel Shays, veteran of the battles of Lexington, Bunker Hill, Ticonderoga and Saratoga, was one of the leaders of more than 1,000 rebels who sought redress of grievances during the depression days of 1786–87. They prevented general court sessions, and on Sept 26 they prevented Supreme Court sessions at Springfield, MA. On Jan 25, 1787, they attacked the federal arsenal at Springfield; Feb 2, Shays's troops were routed and fled. Shays was sentenced to death but pardoned June 13, 1788. Later he received a small pension for services in the American Revolution.

SLOVAKIA: NATIONAL UPRISING DAY. Aug 29. National holiday. Commemorates resistance to Nazi occupation in 1944.

SOVIET COMMUNIST PARTY SUSPENDED: ANNIVERSARY. Aug 29, 1991. The Supreme Soviet, the parliament of the USSR, suspended all activities of the Communist Party, seizing its property and bringing to an end the institution that ruled the Soviet Union for nearly 75 years. The action followed an unsuccessful coup Aug 19–21 that sought to overthrow the government of Soviet president Mikhail Gorbachev but instead prompted a sweeping wave of democratic change. Gorbachev quit as party leader Aug 24.

A TASTE OF COLORADO. Aug 29–Sept 1. Denver, CO. The Rocky Mountain region's largest free outdoor festival, this four-day food and entertainment extravaganza over Labor Day weekend features 50 Colorado area restaurants. Musical entertainment on six outdoor stages, gourmet cooking demonstrations, 280 arts and crafts vendors and children's music and activities. Annually, the Friday through Monday of Labor Day weekend. Est attendance: 500,000. For info: A Taste of Colorado, 511 16th St, Ste 200, Denver, CO 80202. Phone: (303) 295-6330. Web: www.atasteofcolorado.com.

UNITED NATIONS: INTERNATIONAL DAY AGAINST NUCLEAR TESTS. Aug 29. Convinced that every effort should be made to end nuclear tests in order to avert devastating and harmful effects on the lives and health of people and the environment, the General Assembly has declared this day to be observed annually on Aug 29 (Res 64/35, Dec 2, 2009). Devoted to enhancing public awareness and education about the effects of nuclear weapon test explosions or any other nuclear explosions and the need for their cessation as one means of achieving a nuclear-weapon-free world. For info: United Nations, Dept of Public Info, New York, NY 10017. Web: www.un.org.

VERMONT STATE FAIR. Aug 29–Sept 7. Fairgrounds, Rutland, VT. Est attendance: 100,000. For info: Vermont State Fair, 175 S Main St, Rutland, VT 05701. Phone: (802) 775-5200. E-mail: vtstfair@comcast.net. Web: www.vermontstatefair.net.

WEST VIRGINIA ITALIAN HERITAGE FESTIVAL. Aug 29–31. Clarksburg, WV. Includes pasta cook-off (participants cook a pasta dish to compete for prizes), homemade wine contest, live entertainment, parade and more. All free to the public. Annually, Labor Day weekend. The Pasta Cook-Off takes place the previous Saturday (Aug 23 in 2014). Est attendance: 150,000. For info: West Virginia Italian Heritage Festival Office, Box 1632, Clarksburg, WV 26302. Phone: (304) 622-7314. Fax: (304) 622-5727. E-mail: benvenuto79@wvihf.com. Web: www.wvihf.com.

WESTFEST. Aug 29–31. West, TX. West celebrates its Czech heritage with folk dances, Czech pastries, sausage, polka music, arts and crafts, children's area, 5k run, parade. Est attendance: 35,000. For info: Westfest, Box 65, West, TX 76691. Phone: (254) 826-5058. E-mail: info@westfest.com. Web: www.westfest.com.

WISCONSIN STATE COW-CHIP THROW. Aug 29–30. Prairie du Sac, WI. Cow-Chip Throw, 5k and 10k runs, arts and crafts fair, live music and parade. Annually, the Friday night and Saturday of Labor Day weekend. Est attendance: 50,000. For info: Wisconsin State Cow-Chip Throw, PO Box 3, Prairie du Sac, WI 53578. Phone: (608) 643-4317. Fax: (608) 643-5421. E-mail: marietta@toolsofmarketing.com.

WOODSTOCK FAIR. Aug 29–Sept 1. Woodstock, CT. Annually, Labor Day weekend. Est attendance: 185,000. For info: Woodstock Fair, PO Box 1, South Woodstock, CT 06267. Phone: (860) 928-3246. E-mail: info@woodstockfair.com. Web: www.woodstockfair.com.

WORLD CHAMPIONSHIP BARBECUE GOAT COOK-OFF AND ARTS AND CRAFTS FAIR. Aug 29–30. Richards Park, Brady, TX. 41st annual cook-off to promote Brady/McCulloch County and the goat industry. Arts and crafts fair featuring local and statewide artists. Annually, the Friday and Saturday of Labor Day weekend. Est attendance: 8,000. For info: Brady/McCulloch County Chamber of Commerce, 101 E First St, Brady, TX 76825. Phone: (325) 597-3491. Fax: (325) 792-9181. E-mail: info@bradytx.com. Web: www.bradytx.com.

BIRTHDAYS TODAY

Sir Richard Attenborough, 91, filmmaker (*In Which We Serve, The Great Escape*), born Cambridge, England, Aug 29, 1923.

Rebecca De Mornay, 52, actress (*Risky Business, The Hand That Rocks the Cradle*), born Santa Rosa, CA, Aug 29, 1962.

William Friedkin, 75, filmmaker (Oscar for *The French Connection*; *The Exorcist*), born Chicago, IL, Aug 29, 1939.

Richard Gere, 65, actor (*Chicago, An Officer and a Gentleman, Pretty Woman*), born Philadelphia, PA, Aug 29, 1949.

Elliott Gould, 76, actor (*M*A*S*H, The Long Goodbye*), born Elliott Goldstein at Brooklyn, NY, Aug 29, 1938.

Robin Leach, 73, television host ("Lifestyles of the Rich and Famous"), born London, England, Aug 29, 1941.

Jack Lew, 59, US Secretary of the Treasury, born New York, NY, Aug 29, 1955.

Pablo Mastroeni, 38, soccer player, born Mendoza, Argentina, Aug 29, 1976.

John Sidney McCain III, 78, US Senator (R, Arizona), 2008 presidential candidate, born Panama Canal Zone, Aug 29, 1936.

Lea Michele, 28, actress ("Glee"; stage: *Spring Awakening*), born the Bronx, NY, Aug 29, 1986.

Mark Morris, 58, choreographer, dancer, born Seattle, WA, Aug 29, 1956.

Roy Oswalt, 37, baseball player, born Kosciusko, MS, Aug 29, 1977.

William Edward (Will) Perdue III, 49, former basketball player, born Melbourne, FL, Aug 29, 1965.

Jay Ryan, 33, actor ("Beauty and the Beast"), born Auckland, New Zealand, Aug 29, 1981.

Pierre Turgeon, 45, hockey player, born Rouyn, QC, Canada, Aug 29, 1969.

August 30 — Saturday

DAY 242 **123 REMAINING**

ARTHUR, ELLEN LEWIS HERNDON: BIRTH ANNIVERSARY. Aug 30, 1837. Wife of Chester Alan Arthur, 21st president of the US, born at Fredericksburg, VA. Died at New York, Jan 12, 1880.

BOOTH, SHIRLEY: BIRTH ANNIVERSARY. Aug 30, 1898. American actress Shirley Booth was born Thelma Booth Ford at New York, NY. She won a Tony Award and an Oscar for her roles in the stage (1950) and film (1952) productions of *Come Back, Little Sheba*, but she is best known for her title role in the television program "Hazel" (1961–66). She died at Chatham, MS, Oct 16, 1992.

BUMBERSHOOT: SEATTLE'S MUSIC & ARTS FESTIVAL. Aug 30–Sept 1. Seattle Center, Seattle, WA. North America's largest urban arts festival takes place in the heart of the city at the 74-acre Seattle Center. Visitors from near and far spend the weekend reveling in the world of Bumbershoot, experiencing more than 225 scheduled performances and special installations in 20 unique venues. Come to Bumbershoot for the best in music, film, comedy, spoken word, dance, theater, performance, visual art, food and unique shopping experiences. Annually, Labor Day weekend. Est attendance: 100,000. For info: Bumbershoot. E-mail: info@onereel.org. Web: www.bumbershoot.org.

CAL FARLEY'S BOYS RANCH RODEO. Aug 30–31. Boys Ranch, TX. 70th annual. For everyone from young stick-horse riders to more experienced bull riders, this two-day event provides recognition and rewards for children living at Cal Farley's Boys Ranch and Cal Farley's Girlstown USA. Winners in each event are presented with rodeo belt buckles. Special awards are given to the All-Around Cowboy, All-Around Cowgirl and Junior All-Around Cowboy. Annually, Labor Day weekend. Est attendance: 10,000. For info: Cal Farley's, PO Box 1890, Amarillo, TX 79174. Phone: (806) 372-2341. Fax: (806) 372-6638. E-mail: info@calfarley.org. Web: www.calfarley.org.

CLEVELAND NATIONAL AIR SHOW. Aug 30–Sept 1. Burke Lakefront Airport, Cleveland, OH. Country's oldest air show, featuring extensive military and foreign aircraft participation. Annually, Labor Day weekend. Est attendance: 80,000. For info: Cleveland Natl Air Show, Burke Lakefront Airport, Cleveland, OH 44114. Phone: (216) 781-0747. Fax: (216) 781-7810. E-mail: info@clevelandairshow.com. Web: www.clevelandairshow.com.

COMMONWHEEL ARTISTS FESTIVAL. Aug 30–Sept 1. Memorial Park, Manitou Springs, CO. 40th annual juried arts and crafts festival, featuring 120 fine artists and craftsmen and a variety of foods with continuous live entertainment ranging from Celtic harp music to jazz, including original acoustic songwriters. Est attendance: 20,000. For info: Commonwheel Artists Fair, PO Box 42, Manitou Springs, CO 80829. Phone: (719) 577-7700. E-mail: festival@commonwheel.com. Web: www.commonwheel.com/festival.

DENMARK: HO SHEEP MARKET. Aug 30. The village of Ho, near Esbjerg, holds its annual sheep market on the last Saturday in August, when some 50,000 people visit the fair.

EASTERN IDAHO STATE FAIR. Aug 30–Sept 6. Blackfoot, ID. Family fun, amusement rides, food booths, entertainment, rodeo, demolition derby, tractor pulls and more. Est attendance: 224,000. For info: Eastern Idaho State Fair, PO Box 250, Blackfoot, ID 83221. Phone: (208) 785-2480. Fax: (208) 785-2483. Web: www.funatthefair.com.

August 2014

S	M	T	W	T	F	S
					1	2
3	4	5	6	7	8	9
10	11	12	13	14	15	16
17	18	19	20	21	22	23
24	25	26	27	28	29	30
31						

FIRST WHITE HOUSE PRESIDENTIAL BABY: BIRTH ANNIVERSARY. Aug 30, 1893. Frances Folsom Cleveland (Mrs Grover Cleveland) was the first presidential wife to have a baby at the White House when she gave birth to a baby girl (Esther). The first child ever born in the White House was a grandson to Thomas Jefferson in 1806.

HUEY P. LONG DAY. Aug 30. A legal holiday in Louisiana.

IROQUOIS ARTS FESTIVAL. Aug 30–31. Iroquois Indian Museum, Howes Cave, NY. 34th annual celebration of Iroquois arts. Demonstrations of Iroquois arts and crafts, including beadwork, cornhusk dolls, pottery and more. Many items for sale by the artists. Children's activities. Iroquois social dancing and nature walks. Annually, Labor Day weekend. Est attendance: 1,000. For info: Iroquois Indian Museum, PO Box 7, Howes Cave, NY 12092. Phone: (518) 296-8949. Fax: (518) 296-8955. E-mail: info@iroquoismuseum.org. Web: www.iroquoismuseum.org.

JUBILEE DAYS FESTIVAL. Aug 30–Sept 1. Zion, IL. 65th annual. Communitywide festival features arts and crafts, Queen's Pageant, Illinois' largest Labor Day parade and fireworks. Annually, Labor Day weekend. Est attendance: 10,000. For info: Richard Walker, Exec Dir, Jubilee Days Fest, Inc, PO Box 23, Zion, IL 60099. Phone: (847) 746-5500.

MacMURRAY, FRED: BIRTH ANNIVERSARY. Aug 30, 1908. Fred MacMurray was born at Kankakee, IL. His film and television career included a wide variety of roles, ranging from comedy (*The Absent-Minded Professor, Son of Flubber, The Shaggy Dog, The Happiest Millionaire*) to serious drama (*The Caine Mutiny, Fair Wind to Java, Double Indemnity*). During 1960–72 he portrayed the father on "My Three Sons," which is second only to "Ozzie and Harriet" as network TV's longest-running family sitcom. He died Nov 5, 1991, at Santa Monica, CA.

NATIONAL HOLISTIC PET DAY. Aug 30. A day to celebrate the growing interest in natural/holistic medicine and the animals that are treated holistically. For info: Shawn Messonnier, 2145 W Park, Plano, TX 75075. Phone: (972) 867-8800. Fax: (972) 985-9216. E-mail: shawnvet@sbcglobal.net.

PERU: SAINT ROSE OF LIMA DAY. Aug 30. Saint Rose of Lima was the first saint of the Western Hemisphere. She lived at the time of the colonization by Spain in the 16th century. Patron saint of the Americas and the Philippines. Public holiday in Peru.

RUTHERFORD, ERNEST: BIRTH ANNIVERSARY. Aug 30, 1871. Physicist, born at Nelson, New Zealand. He established the nuclear nature of the atom and the electrical structure of matter and achieved the transmutation of elements, research that later resulted in the atomic bomb. Rutherford died at Cambridge, England, Oct 19, 1937.

SHELLEY, MARY WOLLSTONECRAFT: BIRTH ANNIVERSARY. Aug 30, 1797. English novelist Mary Shelley, daughter of philosopher William Godwin and feminist Mary Wollstonecraft and wife of poet Percy Bysshe Shelley, was born at London, England, and died there Feb 1, 1851. In addition to being the author of the famous novel *Frankenstein*, Shelley is important in literary history for her work in the editing and publishing of her husband's unpublished work after his early death.

SPACE MILESTONE: *CHALLENGER STS-8* (US). Aug 30, 1983. Shuttle *Challenger* with five astronauts (Richard Truly, Daniel Brandenstein, Guion Bluford, Jr, Dale Garner and William Thornton) was launched from Kennedy Space Center, FL, on this date. Return landing six days later on Sept 5 at Edwards Air Force Base, CA.

SPAIN: VUELTA A ESPAÑA. Aug 30–Sept 21 (tentative). 69th edition. The third and last of the Grand Tours (along with the Giro d'Italia and the Tour de France) of world cycling. The Vuelta was organized in 1935 as a way to boost circulation of the newspaper *Informaciones*. The race is held over three weeks over an annually changing course and attracts the world's best professional riders. For info: Unipublic, SA, c/ Fuerteventura, 12, 28703 San Sebastian de los Reyes, Madrid, Spain. Phone: (34) (91) 623-27-31. Fax: (34) (91) 623-27-40. E-mail: info@unipublic.es. Web: www.lavuelta.com.

STRAITH, CLAIRE, MD: BIRTH ANNIVERSARY. Aug 30, 1891. Innovator in plastic and cosmetic surgery, born at Southfield, MI. After attending an international meeting at Paris, France, at the end of WWI to share information regarding reconstructive surgical techniques used on the battlefield, Straith dedicated his career to the new field of plastic surgery. He developed many of the techniques used in plastic and cosmetic surgery, designed new surgical instruments and led a campaign that persuaded automakers, in 1930, to use safety glass and remove dangerous projections from the interior of cars. Straith died July 13, 1958.

TASTE OF MADISON. Aug 30–31. Capitol Square, Madison, WI. Food and entertainment festival, including booths from more than 80 restaurants and three entertainment stages. Est attendance: 250,000. For info: Madison Festivals, Inc, 2981 Cahill Main, Ste 2, Madison, WI 53711. Phone: (608) 276-9797. Fax: (608) 276-9780. E-mail: events@madisonfestivals.com. Web: www.tasteofmadison.com.

TOTAH FESTIVAL. Aug 30–31. Farmington, NM. Native American arts and crafts show and marketplace—highlighted by a Navajo rug auction and pow-wow. Annually, the Saturday and Sunday of Labor Day weekend. Est attendance: 13,000. For info: Farmington CVB, 3041 E Main St, Farmington, NM 87402. Phone: (800) 448-1240 or (505) 326-7602. Fax: (505) 327-0577. E-mail: totahfestival@farmingtonnm.org. Web: www.farmingtonnm.org.

TURKEY: HELLESPONT SWIM. Aug 30. Eceabat and Canakkale. The Hellespont—a narrow channel between Asia and Europe—is undoubtedly one of the most significant open water swims in the world. In 1810, the English poet Lord Byron became the first known person to swim across the channel. He swam it in honor of Leander, who in Greek mythology would swim nightly across this stretch of water to his lover Hero. The swim, sponsored by the Canakkale Rotary Club, is about 3 miles long and takes place annually on Aug 30, which is Victory Day in Turkey.

TURKEY: VICTORY DAY. Aug 30. Commemorates victory in War of Independence in 1922. Military parades, performance by the Mehtar band (the world's oldest military band), fireworks.

WELLS, KITTY: 95th BIRTH ANNIVERSARY. Aug 30, 1919. Born Muriel Ellen Deason at Nashville, TN, this country singer was a pioneer in the music industry. One of the first commercially successful women ever signed to a major label, she was about to quit music to raise her family when she scored a surprise hit with 1952's "It Wasn't God Who Made Honky Tonk Angels." That song, the first by a woman to hit number one on the country charts, launched a career ranked the sixth-most-successful in the history of *Billboard*'s country charts. She died at Madison, TN, July 16, 2012.

WILKINS, ROY: BIRTH ANNIVERSARY. Aug 30, 1901. Civil rights leader Roy Wilkins, grandson of a Mississippi slave, was active in the National Association for the Advancement of Colored People (NAACP). He retired as its executive director in 1977. Born at St. Louis, MO. Died at New York, NY, Sept 8, 1981.

WILLIAMS, TED: BIRTH ANNIVERSARY. Aug 30, 1918. Born Theodore Samuel Williams at San Diego, CA, Ted Williams played his first major league baseball game for the Boston Red Sox on Apr 22, 1939. In the years that followed, he became known as perhaps the best hitter ever to play the game. His career batting average was .344, and his record average of .406 set during the 1941 season stands unsurpassed. He played 19 seasons for the Red Sox, but during the prime of his career, he missed three full seasons while serving as a navy pilot in WWII and most of two seasons serving as a marine pilot in the Korean War. He was elected to the Baseball Hall of Fame in 1966. He died July 5, 2002, at Inverness, FL.

BIRTHDAYS TODAY

Elizabeth Ashley, 75, actress (*Agnes of God, Cat on a Hot Tin Roof,* "Evening Shade"), born Elizabeth Ann Cole at Ocala, FL, Aug 30, 1939.

Lewis Black, 66, comedian ("The Daily Show"), born Silver Spring, MD, Aug 30, 1948.

Timothy Bottoms, 63, actor (*The Last Picture Show, The Paper Chase*), born Santa Barbara, CA, Aug 30, 1951.

Michael Chiklis, 51, actor (Emmy and Golden Globe for "The Shield"), born Lowell, MA, Aug 30, 1963.

Cameron Diaz, 42, actress (*Charlie's Angels, My Best Friend's Wedding, There's Something About Mary*), born San Diego, CA, Aug 30, 1972.

Jean-Claude Killy, 71, Olympic alpine skier, born Saint-Cloud, France, Aug 30, 1943.

Peggy Lipton, 67, actress ("The Mod Squad," "Twin Peaks"), born New York, NY, Aug 30, 1947.

Michael Michele, 48, actress ("Homicide: Life on the Street," "ER"), born Evansville, IN, Aug 30, 1966.

David Paymer, 60, actor (*City Slickers, Mr Saturday Night*), born Long Island, NY, Aug 30, 1954.

Andy Roddick, 32, tennis player, born Omaha, NE, Aug 30, 1982.

August 31 — Sunday

DAY 243 **122 REMAINING**

"ALICE" TV PREMIERE: ANNIVERSARY. Aug 31, 1976. Linda Lavin played the title role in this CBS comedy that was based on the 1975 film *Alice Doesn't Live Here Anymore*. Alice Hyatt had dreams of making it big as a singer—while trying to make ends meet by waitressing at a diner. Lavin's costars included Vic Tayback as diner owner Mel Sharples; Philip McKeon as Alice's son, Tommy; Beth Howland as waitress Vera Gorman; and Polly Holliday as sassy waitress Flo Castleberry. The last telecast aired on July 2, 1985.

BAGHDAD STAMPEDE: ANNIVERSARY. Aug 31, 2005. Close to 1,000 Shiite Muslims died when rumors of a suicide bomber sparked a panicked stampede among nearly one million participants in a religious procession in Baghdad, Iraq. Trapped on a bridge with one closed gate, most were trampled or suffocated. The bridge then collapsed into the Tigris River, drowning many. More than 800 were injured.

CHARLESTON EARTHQUAKE: ANNIVERSARY. Aug 31, 1886. Charleston, SC. The first major earthquake in the recorded history of the eastern US occurred on this date. It is believed that about

100 persons perished in the quake, centered near Charleston but felt up to 800 miles away. Though a number of smaller eastern US quakes had been described and recorded since 1638, this affected people living in an area of about two million square miles.

COBURN, JAMES: BIRTH ANNIVERSARY. Aug 31, 1928. Academy Award–winning actor born at Laurel, NE. He rose to fame as the knife thrower in *The Magnificent Seven* and became known for his tough-guy roles in films such as *The Great Escape* and *Our Man Flint.* He received an Oscar for his supporting role in *Affliction* (1999). He died at Los Angeles, CA, Nov 18, 2002.

"CRANKSHAFT": ANNIVERSARY. Aug 31, 1987. Celebrating the anniversary of the nationally syndicated comic strip that premiered Aug 31, 1987. For info: Tom Batiuk, 2750 Substation Rd, Medina, OH 44256. Phone: (330) 722-8755.

DIANA, PRINCESS OF WALES: DEATH ANNIVERSARY. Aug 31, 1997. Diana, Princess of Wales, died in a car crash with her companion, Dodi Fayed, on this date, at Paris, France. Although press photographers had been pursuing her car, French courts determined that the paparazzi were not responsible for the crash but rather a driver operating under the influence of alcohol. Diana, a very popular British royal who worked on behalf of many charities, was mourned the world over.

FAMILY DAY IN TENNESSEE. Aug 31. Observed annually on the last Sunday in August.

HARVEST WINE CELEBRATION. Aug 31–Sept 1. Livermore, CA. 33rd annual. An open-house event offering the public an opportunity to visit more than 43 wineries, sample wines, learn more about this historic wine region, enjoy entertainment and shop for arts and crafts. Shuttle bus service is available between the wineries. Annually, Labor Day weekend (Sunday and Monday). Est attendance: 10,000. For info: Livermore Valley Winegrowers Assn, 3585 Greenville Rd, Ste 4, Livermore, CA 94550. Phone: (925) 447-9463. Fax: (925) 447-0433. E-mail: events@lvwine.org. Web: www.lvwine.org.

KAZAKHSTAN: CONSTITUTION DAY. Aug 31. National holiday. Commemorates the constitution of 1995.

KLONDIKE ELDORADO GOLD DISCOVERY: ANNIVERSARY. Aug 31, 1896. Two weeks after the Rabbit/Bonanza Creek claim was filed, gold was discovered on Eldorado Creek, a tributary of Bonanza. More than $30 million worth of gold (worth $600–$700 million in today's dollars) was mined from the Eldorado Claim in 1896.

KYRGYZSTAN: INDEPENDENCE DAY. Aug 31. National holiday. Commemorates independence from the former Soviet Union in 1991.

LOVE LITIGATING LAWYERS DAY. Aug 31. Lawyer jokes abound, but when push comes to shove, these are the folks who can end up saving the day. (©2006 by WH.) For info: Thomas & Ruth Roy, Wellcat Holidays, 2418 Long Ln, Lebanon, PA 17046. Phone: (717) 279-0184. E-mail: info@wellcat.com. Web: www.wellcat.com.

MALAYSIA: FREEDOM DAY. Aug 31. National holiday. Commemorates independence from Britain in 1957.

MOLDOVA: NATIONAL LANGUAGE DAY. Aug 31. National holiday. Also called Mother Tongue Day. Commemorates the replacement of the Cyrillic alphabet with the Latin alphabet in 1991.

MONTESSORI, MARIA: BIRTH ANNIVERSARY. Aug 31, 1870. Italian physician and educator, born at Chiaraville, Italy. Founder of the Montessori method of teaching children. Montessori died at Noordwijk, Holland, May 6, 1952.

August 2014

S	M	T	W	T	F	S
					1	2
3	4	5	6	7	8	9
10	11	12	13	14	15	16
17	18	19	20	21	22	23
24	25	26	27	28	29	30
31						

MUSCULAR DYSTROPHY ASSOCIATION LABOR DAY TELETHON. Aug 31. The annual TV broadcast to raise money for 40 neuromuscular diseases. Annually, the Sunday of Labor Day weekend. For info: Muscular Dystrophy Assn—USA, 3300 E Sunrise Dr, Tucson, AZ 85718. Phone: (800) 572-1717. Web: www.mda.org.

POLAND: SOLIDARITY FOUNDED: ANNIVERSARY. Aug 31, 1980. The Polish trade union Solidarity was formed at the Baltic Sea port of Gdansk, Poland. It was outlawed by the government, and many of its leaders were arrested. Led by Lech Walesa, Solidarity persisted in its opposition to the Communist-controlled government, and Aug 19, 1989, Polish president Wojciech Jaruzelski astonished the world by nominating for the post of prime minister Tadeusz Mazowiecki, a deputy in the Polish Assembly, 1961–72, and editor in chief of Solidarity's weekly newspaper, bringing to an end 42 years of Communist Party domination.

PONY EXPRESS FESTIVAL. Aug 31 (tentative). Hollenberg Pony Express Station, State Historic Site, Hanover, KS. Reenactment of Pony Express ride with mochila exchange, pioneer living-history demonstrations, 1860s historic-dress group, circuit-rider church service and a noon meal on the grounds. Annually, the last Sunday in August. Sponsors: Kansas State Historical Society, Friends of Hollenberg Station. Est attendance: 2,000. For info: Hollenberg Pony Express Station, State Historic Site, RR1, 2889 23rd Rd, Hanover, KS 66945-9634. Phone: (785) 337-2635. Fax: (785) 337-2635. E-mail: hollenberg@kshs.org. Web: www.kshs.org/hollenberg.

SAROYAN, WILLIAM: BIRTH ANNIVERSARY. Aug 31, 1908. American writer of Armenian descent, author of *The Human Comedy* and of the Pulitzer Prize–winning play *The Time of Your Life*, was born at Fresno, CA, and died there May 18, 1981. In April 1981 he gave reporters a final statement for publication after his death: "Everybody has got to die, but I have always believed an exception would be made in my case. Now what?"

SCANDINAVIAN FEST. Aug 31. Vasa Park, Budd Lake, NJ. Celebrate and sample the cultures, traditions and contemporary life of the Nordic countries: Denmark, Estonia, Finland, Iceland, Norway and Sweden through food, entertainment, music, dancing, handicrafts and lectures. Annually, the Sunday before Labor Day. Est attendance: 6,000. For info: Carl Anderson, 5 Christopher Lee Dr, New Oxford, PA 17350. Phone: (610) 417-1483. E-mail: info@ScanFest.org. Web: www.ScanFest.org.

SHAWN, WILLIAM: BIRTH ANNIVERSARY. Aug 31, 1907. William Shawn, editor of the *New Yorker* for 35 years, was born at Chicago, IL. He was virtual dictator of editorial policy for the magazine, which in turn had an impact on the literary and reportorial styles of writers throughout the country. Nonfiction pieces in the *New Yorker* contributed to public opinion on important issues during Shawn's tenure. Shawn died Dec 8, 1992, at New York, NY.

TRINIDAD AND TOBAGO: INDEPENDENCE DAY. Aug 31. National holiday. Became an independent nation within the British Commonwealth on this day in 1962. Trinidad became a republic Sept 24, 1976.

WHITECHAPEL MURDERS BEGIN: ANNIVERSARY. Aug 31, 1888. At 3:40 AM, the body of Mary Ann Nichols was found in the impoverished Whitechapel district of London, England. This was (debatably) the first in a series of brutal murders that autumn that claimed the lives of at least five women, perhaps more, by a serial killer who has come to be known as "Jack the Ripper" because of the mutilations he inflicted on his victims. The ferocity of the Whitechapel killings created an "Autumn of Terror" in which the entire populace of London was terrified and where mobs frequently tried to mete out justice to suspects they picked. Mary Kelly, found Nov 9, is considered the last victim. No suspect was ever tried for the murders. See also: "'Jack the Ripper' Letter: Anniversary" (Sept 27).

BIRTHDAYS TODAY

Jennifer Azzi, 46, basketball coach and former player, born Oak Ridge, TN, Aug 31, 1968.

Larry Fitzgerald, 31, football player, born Minneapolis, MN, Aug 31, 1983.

Debbie Gibson, 44, singer, born Brooklyn, NY, Aug 31, 1970.

Van Morrison, 69, singer, songwriter, born Belfast, Northern Ireland, Aug 31, 1945.

Edwin Corley Moses, 59, Olympic track athlete, born Dayton, OH, Aug 31, 1955.

Hideo Nomo, 46, former baseball player, born Osaka, Japan, Aug 31, 1968.

Itzhak Perlman, 69, violinist, born Tel Aviv, Israel, Aug 31, 1945.

Sara Ramirez, 39, actress ("Grey's Anatomy"; stage: *Spamalot*), born Mazatlan, Mexico, Aug 31, 1975.

Pepe Reina, 32, soccer player, born Madrid, Spain, Aug 31, 1982.

Frank Robinson, 79, Hall of Fame baseball player, former baseball executive and manager, born Beaumont, TX, Aug 31, 1935.

Jack Thompson, 74, actor (*The Chant of Jimmie Blacksmith, Breaker Morant*), born Sydney, Australia, Aug 31, 1940.

Glenn Tilbrook, 57, singer, musician (Squeeze), born London, England, Aug 31, 1957.

Chris Tucker, 42, actor (*Silver Linings Playbook, Rush Hour*), born Decatur, GA, Aug 31, 1972.

September

September 1 — Monday

DAY 244 **121 REMAINING**

AKC RESPONSIBLE DOG OWNERSHIP MONTH. Sept 1–30. A month to celebrate the commitment it takes to have a canine companion, with a series of events that include educational and entertaining activities such as obedience/agility demonstrations, low-cost microchipping clinics, breed rescue information, therapy dog/service dog demonstrations, safety around dogs for kids presentations, giveaways and more! For info: American Kennel Club, 260 Madison Ave, 4th Fl, New York, NY 10016. Phone: (212) 696-8343. Fax: (212) 696-8345. E-mail: communications@akc.org. Web: www.akc.org/clubs/rdod/index.cfm.

"ART LINKLETTER'S HOUSE PARTY" TV PREMIERE: ANNIVERSARY. Sept 1, 1952. Television's longest-running daytime variety show was hosted by Art Linkletter. This blend of talk and audience participation started on radio. In 1968 the show was renamed "The Linkletter Show" and moved from the afternoon to a morning slot. The series was well known for its daily interview with four schoolchildren.

ATRIAL FIBRILLATION AWARENESS MONTH. Sept 1–30. To raise awareness of atrial fibrillation, the most common irregular heartbeat, and to wipe out afib-related strokes. For info: Mellanie True Hills, StopAfib.org, PO Box 541, Greenwood, TX 76246. Phone: (940) 466-9898. E-mail: mhills@stopafib.org. Web: www.StopAfib.org.

ATTENTION DEFICIT HYPERACTIVITY DISORDER MONTH. Sept 1–30. To educate healthcare groups, children and family organizations, teachers, parents and others interested in childhood health issues by providing information on effective treatments for ADHD. Some treatments have been scientifically validated, tested and proven to reduce the severity of ADHD symptoms and thereby reduce adverse consequences in the child's current and future life. For info: Fred S. Mayer, RPh, MPH, Pharmacists Planning Service, Inc (PPSI), PO Box 6760, San Rafael, CA 94903. Phone: (415) 479-8628 or (415) 302-7351. Fax: (415) 479-8608. E-mail: ppsi@aol.com. Web: www.ppsinc.org.

BABY SAFETY MONTH. Sept 1–30. Sponsored annually by the Juvenile Products Manufacturers Association (JPMA), this monthlong education campaign exists to increase consumer awareness of safety issues surrounding the safe use and selection of juvenile products. Observed since 1991. For info: JPMA, 15000 Commerce Pky, Ste C, Mount Laurel, NJ 08054. Phone: (856) 642-4420. Web: www.jpma.org.

BACKPACK SAFETY AMERICA MONTH. Sept 1–30. Millions of school-age children are straining in pain under backpacks that are too heavy for their growing bodies. This month is set aside to remind students, parents and teachers about the safe and proper ways to choose, pack, lift and carry a backpack. Annually, the month of September. For info: Backpack Safety Alliance, PO Box 2430, Mt Pleasant, SC 29465. Phone: (800) 672-4277. Fax: (843) 881-6746. E-mail: info@backpacksafe.com. Web: www.backpacksafe.com.

BE KIND TO EDITORS AND WRITERS MONTH. Sept 1–30. A time for editors and writers to show uncommon courtesy toward each other. For info: Lauren Barnett, Lone Star Publications of Humor, 8452 Fredericksburg Rd, PMB 103, San Antonio, TX 78229. E-mail: lspubs@aol.com.

BRAZIL: INDEPENDENCE WEEK. Sept 1–7. Brazil's independence from Portugal in 1822 is commemorated with civic and cultural ceremonies promoted by federal, state and municipal authorities. On Sept 7, a grand military parade takes place and the National Defense League organizes the Running Race in Honor of the Symbolic Torch of the Brazilian Nation.

BURROUGHS, EDGAR RICE: BIRTH ANNIVERSARY. Sept 1, 1875. US novelist (*Tarzan of the Apes*), born at Chicago, IL. Correspondent for the *Los Angeles Times*, died at Encino, CA, Mar 19, 1950.

CANADA: LABOR DAY. Sept 1. Annually, the first Monday in September.

CARTIER, JACQUES: DEATH ANNIVERSARY. Sept 1, 1557. French navigator and explorer who sailed from St. Malo, France, Apr 20, 1534, in search of a northwest passage to the Orient. Instead, he discovered the St. Lawrence River, explored Canada's coastal regions and took possession of the country for France. Cartier was born at St. Malo, about 1491 (exact date unknown) and died there.

CHICKEN BOY'S BIRTHDAY. Sept 1. Chicken Boy is a 22-foot statue of a boy with a chicken's head, holding a bucket of chicken. Formerly the mascot for the restaurant for which he is named, he was rescued from destruction by Future Studio of Los Angeles, a graphic design studio, when the restaurant went out of business. Chicken Boy has since become a pop culture icon and has been installed on a rooftop in Los Angeles along historic Route 66, so he once again can be seen by the public. For info: Amy Inouye, Future Studio, PO Box 292000, Los Angeles, CA 90029. Phone: (323) 254-4565. E-mail: amy@futurestudio.com. Web: www.chickenboy.com.

CHILDHOOD CANCER AWARENESS MONTH. Sept 1–30. Bear Necessities Pediatric Cancer Foundation is dedicated to eliminating pediatric cancer and to providing hope and support to those who are touched by it. Pediatric cancer is the number one cause of death by disease in children. For info: Bear Necessities Pediatric Cancer Foundation, 55 W Wacker Dr, Ste 1100, Chicago, IL 60601. Phone: (312) 214-1200. Fax: (312) 214-7797. E-mail: office@bearnecessities.org. Web: www.bearnecessities.org.

CHILE: NATIONAL MONTH. Sept 1–30. A month of special significance in Chile: arrival of spring, a Day of Unity on the first Monday in September, Independence of Chile anniversary (proclaimed Sept 18, 1810) and celebration of the 1980 Constitution and Army Day, Sept 19.

COLLEGE SAVINGS MONTH. Sept 1–30. Encourages families to plan ahead for the cost of college attendance. College savings programs make it easy and affordable for the average family to save and are available in most states. The programs offer affordable, flexible and tax-advantaged savings options that deliver the dream of education to our most precious resources—the children of America. Sponsored by the College Savings Plan Network of the National Association of State Treasurers. For info: National Association of State Treasurers, College Savings Plan Network, 2760 Research Park Dr, Lexington, KY 40578. Phone: (859) 244-8175. Fax: (859) 244-8053. E-mail: cspn@csg.org. Web: www.collegesavings.org.

EAT CHICKEN MONTH. Sept 1–30. Focuses food shoppers' and restaurant customers' attention on chicken as the most healthful, convenient, economical and versatile food available; in short, "America's favorite." For info: Bill Roenigk, Sr VP, Natl Chicken Council, 1152 15th St NW, Ste 430, Washington, DC 20005. Phone: (202) 296-2622. Fax: (202) 293-4005. E-mail: WRoenigk@chickenUSA.org. Web: www.nationalchickenmonth.com or www.eatchicken.com.

EMMA M. NUTT DAY. Sept 1. A day to honor the first woman telephone operator, Emma M. Nutt, who reportedly began her professional career at Boston, MA, Sept 1, 1878, and continued working as a telephone operator for 33 years.

FALL HAT MONTH. Sept 1–30. A month of celebration during which the straw hat is put aside by men and women in favor of the felt or fabric hat. Local businesses and the media are encouraged to plan hat-related activities. Widely observed in the fashion industry. Originally sponsored by the Headwear Information Bureau.

GERMANY: CAPITAL RETURNS TO BERLIN: 15th ANNIVERSARY. Sept 1, 1999. In July the monthlong process of moving the German government from Bonn to Berlin began, eight years after Parliament had voted to return to its prewar seat. Berlin officially became the capital of Germany on Sept 1, 1999, and Parliament reconvened at the newly restored Reichstag on Sept 7, 1999.

GREAT AMERICAN LOW-CHOLESTEROL, LOW-FAT PIZZA BAKE. Sept 1–30. Pizza parlors, restaurants and volunteer agencies nationwide create healthy pizza recipes to increase the public's awareness of the benefits of controlling high cholesterol levels through diet. For info: Fred S. Mayer, RPh, MPH, Pharmacists Planning Service, Inc (PPSI), PO Box 6760, San Rafael, CA 94903. Phone: (415) 479-8628 or (415) 302-7351. Fax: (415) 479-8608. E-mail: ppsi@aol.com. Web: www.ppsinc.org.

GREAT BATHTUB RACE. Sept 1. Nome, AK. 37th annual. Bathtubs mounted on wheels are raced down Front Street. Each team has five members, one in the tub, with bubbles apparent in the bathwater. Tub must be full of water at beginning and have at least 10 gallons at the finish line. The other four team members must wear large-brim hats and suspenders and carry either a bar of soap, washcloth, towel or bath mat for the entire race. Winning team claims trophy: a statue of Miss Piggy and Kermit taking a bath, which is handed down from year to year. Annually, at noon on Labor Day. Est attendance: 1,500. For info: Rasmussen's Music Mart, PO Box 2, Nome, AK 99762-0002. Phone: (907) 443-2798 or (907) 443-2919. E-mail: leaknome@alaska.com.

GYNECOLOGIC CANCER AWARENESS MONTH. Sept 1–30. During September, women are encouraged to learn more about gynecologic cancers—how they can be detected and prevented before they become fatal. For info: Foundation for Women's Cancer, 230 W Monroe, Ste 2528, Chicago, IL 60606. Phone: (312) 578-1439. Fax: (312) 578-9769. E-mail: info@foundationforwomenscancer.org. Web: www.foundationforwomenscancer.org.

HAPPY CAT MONTH. Sept 1–30. Cats are America's favorite pets. They outnumber dogs as domestic companions by more than 13 million yet they are half as likely to visit a veterinarian. And fewer lost or stray cats in animal shelters are reclaimed by their owners. Time to show some love: Happy Cat Month celebrates the joys of cat ownership. For info: The CATalyst Council, PO Box 3064, Annapolis, MD 21403. E-mail: info@catalystcouncil.org. Web: www.catalystcouncil.org.

HUNGER ACTION MONTH. Sept 1–30. Every September, Feeding America, the nation's leading domestic hunger relief organization, encourages people from all walks of life to raise awareness for hunger relief. Hunger Action Month is an effort to mobilize the public to raise awareness and take action in support of domestic hunger relief. For info: Feeding America. Web: www.hungeractionmonth.org

INTERNATIONAL ENTHUSIASM WEEK. Sept 1–7. Display genuine enthusiasm to every person, every project, every possibility that comes your way. It will change your week, your month, your year, your life. For info: Carolyn Stein. Phone: (877) 771-0772. Fax: (305) 682-1416. E-mail: carolynkstein@aol.com. Web: www.carolynstein.com.

INTERNATIONAL WOMEN'S FRIENDSHIP MONTH. Sept 1–30. Every woman has friends she can't live without; those women to whom she tells everything, friends who will always listen and who know just what to say. International Women's Friendship Month provides the perfect opportunity for women to acknowledge the amazing women in their lives and to create new friendships. For info: Heidi Roy, The Confidence Coalition, Kappa Delta Sorority, 3205 Players Ln, Memphis, TN 38123. Phone: (901) 748-1897. E-mail: heidi.roy@kappadelta.org. Web: www.womensfriendshipmonth.com.

JAPAN: KANTO EARTHQUAKE MEMORIAL DAY. Sept 1. A day to remember the 57,000 people who died during Japan's greatest earthquake in 1923.

KOREAN AIR LINES FLIGHT 007 DISASTER: ANNIVERSARY. Sept 1, 1983. Korean Air Lines Flight 007, en route from New York, NY, to Seoul, Korea, reportedly strayed more than 100 miles off course, flying over secret Soviet military installations on the Kamchatka Peninsula and Sakhalin Island. Two and one-half hours after it was said to have entered Soviet airspace, a Soviet interceptor plane destroyed the Boeing 747 with 269 persons on board, which then crashed into the Sea of Japan. There were no survivors. President Reagan, in Proclamation 5093, named Sunday, Sept 11, 1983, as a National Day of Mourning as "homage to the memory of those who died."

LABOR DAY. Sept 1. Legal public holiday. Public Law 90–363 sets Labor Day on the first Monday in September. Observed in all states. First observance was a parade on Tuesday, Sept 5, 1882, at New York, NY, probably organized by Peter McGuire, a Brotherhood of Carpenters and Joiners secretary. In 1883 a union resolution declared "the first Monday in September of each year a Labor Day." By 1893 more than half of the states were observing Labor Day on one or another day and a bill to establish Labor Day as a federal holiday was introduced in Congress. On June 28, 1894, President Grover Cleveland signed into law an act making the first Monday in September a legal holiday for federal employees and the District of Columbia. Canada also celebrates Labor Day on the first Monday in September. In most other countries, Labor Day is observed May 1. See also "First Labor Day Observance: Anniversary" (Sept 5).

LIBRARY CARD SIGN-UP MONTH. Sept 1–30. A month when the American Library Association and libraries across the country remind parents that a library card is the most important school supply of all. This observance was launched in 1987 to meet the challenge of then Secretary of Education William J. Bennett, who said, "Let's have a national campaign . . . every child should obtain a library card—and use it." Since then, thousands of public and school libraries join each fall in a national effort to ensure every child does just that. For info: American Library Assn, Public Information Office, 50 E Huron St, Chicago, IL 60611. Phone: (312) 280-4020 or (312) 280-2148. E-mail: pio@ala.org. Web: www.ala.org/librarycardsignup.

LIBYA: REVOLUTION DAY. Sept 1. Commemorates the revolution in 1969 when King Idris I was overthrown by Colonel Qaddafi. National holiday.

MACKINAC BRIDGE WALK. Sept 1. St. Ignace, MI. 57th annual event. This is the only day of the year pedestrians are permitted to walk across the five-mile-long span, one of the world's longest suspension bridges, connecting Michigan's two peninsulas. Walk is from St. Ignace to Mackinaw City. Est attendance: 50,000. For info: Mackinac Bridge Authority, N-415 Interstate 75, St. Ignace, MI 49781. Phone: (906) 643-7600. Fax: (906) 643-7668. Web: www.mackinacbridge.org.

MARCIANO, ROCKY: BIRTH ANNIVERSARY. Sept 1, 1923. Rocky Marciano, boxer born Rocco Francis Marchegiano at Brockton, MA. Marciano used superb conditioning to fashion an impressive record that propelled him to fight against Jersey Joe Walcott for the heavyweight title on Sept 23, 1952. Marciano knocked Walcott out, and in 1956 he retired as the only undefeated heavyweight champion. Died in a plane crash at Newton, IA, Aug 31, 1969. The film *Somebody Up There Likes Me* recounts his life story.

MEXICO: PRESIDENT'S STATE OF THE UNION ADDRESS. Sept 1. National holiday.

MILLION MINUTE FAMILY CHALLENGE™. Sept 1–Dec 31. 14th annual. A national effort to bring family, friends and neighbors together through nonelectronic games. Goal is one million minutes of game playing. Add your minutes to the running total at www.millionminute.com. Special organizer materials and media information available, including press kits, interviews, tips on hosting a game night, etc. Annually, September through December. For info: Beth Muehlenkamp, Million Minute Family Challenge, 1400 E Inman Pkwy, Beloit, WI 53511. Phone: (800) 524-4263. Fax: (608) 362-8178. E-mail: bethm@patchproducts.com. Web: www.millionminute.com.

MISSION SAN LUIS OBISPO DE TOLOSA: FOUNDING ANNIVERSARY. Sept 1, 1772. California mission to the Indians.

✦NATIONAL CHILDHOOD OBESITY AWARENESS MONTH. Sept 1–30. Since the 1970s, the rate of childhood obesity in our country has tripled, and today a third of American children are overweight or obese. This dramatic rise threatens to have far-reaching, long-term effects on our children's health, livelihoods and futures. This month is proclaimed annually to remind Americans that we must ensure the well-being of our children and stop this epidemic by discovering the fun in healthful eating and exercise.

NATIONAL COUPON MONTH. Sept 1–30. This month celebrates the nearly $4 billion savings American consumers receive each year by redeeming coupons for their favorite brands. Companies who offer and accept coupons plan activities on a national scale to raise the awareness of their coupons and the savings opportunities year-round. For info: NCH Marketing Services, Inc, 155 Pfingsten Rd, Ste 200, Deerfield, IL 60015. Phone: (847) 317-5500. E-mail: info@nchmarketing.com.

NATIONAL DNA, GENOMICS & STEM CELL EDUCATION AND AWARENESS MONTH. Sept 1–30. Pharmacists Planning Service, Inc (PPSI), along with the Pharmacy Council on Personalized Health Care (PCPHC), declare September as our education and awareness month. For posters, pamphlets, literature or any additional information, please contact us! For info: Fred S. Mayer, RPh, MPH, Pharmacists Planning Service, Inc (PPSI), PO Box 6760, San Rafael, CA 94903. Phone: (415) 479-8628 or (415) 302-7351. E-mail: ppsi@aol.com. Web: www.ppsinc.org.

NATIONAL HEAD LICE PREVENTION MONTH. Sept 1–30. To promote awareness of how to prevent pediculosis and protect against unnecessary and potentially harmful pesticide treatments for head lice. For info: Natl Pediculosis Assn, 1005 Boylston St, Ste 343, Newton Highlands, MA 02461. Phone: (617) 905-0176. E-mail: npa@headlice.org. Web: www.headlice.org or www.licemeister.org.

NATIONAL HONEY MONTH. Sept 1–30. To honor the US's 125,000 beekeepers and 2.49 million colonies of honeybees, which produce more than 148 million pounds of honey each year. For info: Natl Honey Board, 11409 Business Park Circle, Ste 210, Firestone, CO 80504-9200. Phone: (303) 776-2337. E-mail: honey@nhb.org. Web: www.honey.com.

September 2014

S	M	T	W	T	F	S
	1	2	3	4	5	6
7	8	9	10	11	12	13
14	15	16	17	18	19	20
21	22	23	24	25	26	27
28	29	30				

NATIONAL MUSHROOM MONTH. Sept 1–30. To promote the greater appreciation and use of fresh mushrooms. For info: The Mushroom Council, 2880 Zanker Rd, Ste 203, San Jose, CA 95134. E-mail: info@mushroominfo.com. Web: www.mushroominfo.com.

✦NATIONAL OVARIAN CANCER AWARENESS MONTH. Sept 1–30.

NATIONAL PAYROLL WEEK. Sept 1–5. Founded in 1996 by the American Payroll Association to recognize the important partnership of America's workers and the payroll professionals who pay them on time and accurately. Provides an annual opportunity to proudly proclaim "America Works Because We're Working for America!" For info: American Payroll Assn, 660 N Main Ave, Ste 100, San Antonio, TX 78205. Phone: (210) 226-4600. Fax: (210) 224-2028. E-mail: moreinfo@americanpayroll.org. Web: www.nationalpayrollweek.com.

✦NATIONAL PREPAREDNESS MONTH. Sept 1–30.

NATIONAL PREPAREDNESS MONTH. Sept 1–30. A nationwide coordinated effort held each September to promote emergency preparedness in the home, workplace, school and community. The US Department of Homeland Security and a wide variety of public and private sector organizations will participate in events and activities to highlight the importance of emergency preparedness. For info: Ready Campaign, FEMA/DHS. E-mail: ready@fema.gov. Web: www.ready.gov/pledge.

✦NATIONAL PROSTATE CANCER AWARENESS MONTH. Sept 1–30. Proclaimed annually to reaffirm support for prostate cancer patients and survivors, and to commend healthcare providers, advocates and researchers for their dedication and perseverance. Efforts to increase awareness of prostate cancer and bolster research will help save lives, and commitment to fathers, brothers and sons will contribute to a brighter tomorrow for future generations.

NATIONAL RECOVERY MONTH. Sept 1–30. 24th annual. A national observance sponsored by the US Department of Health and Human Services' Substance Abuse and Mental Health Services Administration. Celebrated each September throughout the country, this month highlights the benefits of addiction treatment and mental health services. National Recovery Month spreads the positive message that behavioral health is essential to overall health, that prevention works, that treatment is effective and that people can and do recover to live a healthy and rewarding life. This month also lauds the contributions of treatment and recovery service providers. (Previously observed as National Alcohol and Drug Addiction Recovery Month, this observance changed to its present title in 2011 to include all aspects of behavioral health.) For info: SAMHSA/CSAT, Consumer Affairs, Natl Recovery Month, 1 Choke Cherry Rd, 2nd Fl, Rockville, MD 20857. Phone: (240) 276-2750 or (800) 662-HELP. Fax: (240) 276-2710. Web: www.recoverymonth.gov.

NATIONAL RICE MONTH. Sept 1–30. To focus attention on the importance of rice to the American diet and to salute the US rice industry. For info: USA Rice Federation, 2101 Wilson Blvd, Ste 610, Arlington, VA 22201. Phone: (703) 236-2300. E-mail: riceinfo@usarice.com. Web: www.usarice.com.

NATIONAL SERVICE DOG MONTH. Sept 1–30. A month to honor guide dogs and military service dogs for the inspiring work they do that changes lives. Annually, the month of September. For info: National Service Dog Month, Petco Foundation. E-mail: mwest@west-pr.com. Web: www.nationalbalanceinc.com/national-service-dog-month.aspx.

NATIONAL SHAKE MONTH. Sept 1–30. For more than 100 years, Americans have craved the cold, creamy concoction made in a metal mixing cup. The milkshake has been used as a beverage, a meal, a dessert, a reward and an indulgence to cheat on some diets (now and then). Today, shakes are made of ice cream, custard, tofu and soy. They are flavored with cookies, candy, fruit and flavorings—including those with alcohol. They have become a mainstay of menus around the world. In fact, it is estimated that nearly 20 million milkshakes are sold around the world each year. To celebrate the end of summer and encompass National

Chocolate Shake Day (Sept 12), Johnny Rockets has celebrated September as National Shake Month since 2009. For info: Johnny Rockets. Phone: (949) 643-6100. E-mail: pr@johnnyrockets.com. Web: www.johnnyrockets.com.

NATIONAL SKIN CARE AWARENESS MONTH. Sept 1–30. A month to focus on achieving healthy, glowing beautiful skin. Take time to learn about protecting skin from the dangers of the sun, how diet and lifestyle affect skin, developing a proper skin care routine and myths and facts about skin care products. All important knowledge for great-looking skin. Throughout September, the event sponsor posts a *.pdf document with skin tips based on the latest research that anyone can download, copy and distribute. For info: Renee Rouleau Skin Care, 4025 Preston Rd, Ste 606, Plano, TX 75093. Phone: (972) 378-6655. Web: www.reneerouleau.com.

✦NATIONAL WILDERNESS MONTH. Sept 1–30. Protecting our wilderness areas and their riches—clean water, stretches of undisturbed land, thriving wildlife, and healthy ecosystems—is critical to the health of our environment and our communities. Today, wilderness areas serve as places to roam, hunt, fish, and find solitude. This month is declared annually to remind all Americans to visit and enjoy our wilderness areas, to learn about their vast history, and to aid in the protection of our precious national treasures.

ONE-ON-ONE MONTH. Sept 1–30. This is a month to get to know your coworkers, family members and friends better by meeting one on one. When people spend time together one on one, they are more likely to talk about their lives in a meaningful way. It is easier for them to express their hopes, dreams and ideas and share their interests in ways that they would never do in a group or even a threesome. Annually every September. For info: Harriet Meyerson. Phone: (214) 373-0080. Fax: (469) 854-2957. E-mail: Harriet@ConfidenceCenter.com.

ORTHODOX ECCLESIASTICAL NEW YEAR. Sept 1. This beginning of the Eastern Orthodox Church year has been observed on Sept 1 since the early days of Byzantine Christianity and long before the fall of Constantinople in 1453.

OVARIAN CANCER AWARENESS MONTH. Sept 1–30. For info: Natl Ovarian Cancer Coalition, 2501 Oak Lawn Ave, Ste 435, Dallas, TX 75219. Phone: (214) 273-4200 or (888) OVARIAN. E-mail: nocc@ovarian.org. Web: www.ovarian.org.

PHILLIS WHEATLEY'S POETRY COLLECTION PUBLISHED: ANNIVERSARY. Sept 1, 1773. On this date in 1773, the first book of poetry composed by an African American was published. Phillis Wheatley's *Poems on Various Subjects, Religious and Moral* was published at London, England, only 12 years after her arrival in America as a child slave from Senegal. In those 12 years, she learned to read and write English and studied literature in English and Latin. Feted in America and England, Wheatley eventually gained her freedom but died in poverty. See also: "Wheatley, Phillis: Death Anniversary" (Dec 5).

PLEASURE YOUR MATE MONTH. Sept 1–30. To promote love and show appreciation to your mate. Look for new ways to create happiness together. Use this event to establish a lifelong habit of sharing pleasure. Annually, the month of September. For info: Donald Etkes, PhD, 112 Harvard Ave #148, Claremont, CA 91711. Phone: (310) 405-9814. E-mail: drdonetkes@aol.com.

REUTHER, WALTER PHILIP: BIRTH ANNIVERSARY. Sept 1, 1907. American labor leader who began work in a steel factory at age 16 and later became president of the United Automobile Workers (UAW) and the Congress of Industrial Organizations (CIO). Born at Wheeling, WV, Reuther worked for two years in a Russian automobile factory. Often at the center of controversy, he was the target of an assassin in 1948. Reuther and his wife died in an airplane crash May 9, 1970, at Black Lake, MI. The UAW Family Education Center, a project that he had cherished, was later named for Walter and May Reuther.

ROY WEBSTER CROSS CHANNEL SWIM. Sept 1. Hood River, OR. 72nd annual. The annual swim across the mighty Columbia River draws 550 contestants each year to swim the approximately one-mile distance for fun. Annually, on Labor Day. Est attendance: 1,000. For info: Roy Webster Cross Channel Swim, Hood River County Chamber of Commerce, 720 E Port Marina Dr, Hood River, OR 97031. Phone: (800) 366-3530. E-mail: info@hoodriver.org. Web: www.hoodriver.org.

SEA CADET MONTH. Sept 1–30. Nationwide year-round youth program for boys and girls 11–17 teaches leadership and self-discipline with emphasis on nautically oriented training without military obligation. Various events will take place during each month, nationwide. Est attendance: 12,000. For info: US Naval Sea Cadet Corps, 2300 Wilson Blvd, Ste 200, Arlington, VA 22201. Phone: (703) 243-6910. Fax: (703) 243-3985. E-mail: jmonahan@NAVYLEAGUE.org. Web: www.seacadets.org.

SELF-UNIVERSITY WEEK. Sept 1–7. Since 1989. Reminds adults (in or out of school) that each of us has a responsibility to help shape the future by pursuing lifelong learning. Committed to self-education as the lifeblood of democracy and the key to living life to its fullest. Dedicated to furthering education not as something you get but as something you take. We assert that America's greatest treasures are found not in our shopping malls but in our libraries. Annually, the first seven days of September. For info: Charles Hayes, Publisher, Autodidactic Press, PO Box 872749, Wasilla, AK 99687. Phone: (907) 376-2932. Fax: (907) 376-2932. E-mail: info@autodidactic.com. Web: www.autodidactic.com.

SEPTEMBER IS HEALTHY AGING® MONTH. Sept 1–30. Annual health observance designed to focus national attention on the positive aspects of growing older. This month is part of the Healthy Aging® campaign, a national, ongoing health promotion designed to broaden awareness of the positive aspects of aging and to provide inspiration for adults, ages 50+, to improve their physical, mental, social and financial health. The campaign is developed and produced by Educational Television Network, Inc (ETNET), a nonprofit corporation based in Pennsylvania. For info: The Healthy Aging® Campaign, PO Box 442, Unionville, PA 19375. Phone: (610) 793-0979. E-mail: info@healthyaging.net. Web: www.healthyaging.net.

SHAMELESS PROMOTION MONTH. Sept 1–30. This is the month for you to go out and promote yourself, your business, your book or your product shamelessly. For outrageous tips, visit our website. For info: Marisa D'Vari, PO Box 2347, New York, NY 10163. E-mail: expert@deg.com.

SLOVAKIA: CONSTITUTION DAY. Sept 1. Anniversary of the adoption of the Constitution of the Slovak Republic in 1992.

SNAKE RIVER DUCK RACE. Sept 1. Nome, AK. Since 1992 thousands of plastic ducks have negotiated the historic Snake River to Nome's power plant. 2 PM. For info: Leo B. Rasmussen, Nome Rotary Club, PO Box 2, Nome, AK 99762. Phone: (907) 443-2798. E-mail: leaknome@alaska.com.

SPORTS EYE SAFETY MONTH. Sept 1–30. There are thousands of eye injuries each year related to sports and hazards around the house. Tips on how to protect yourself and your children from such eye injuries will be discussed. For info: Prevent Blindness America®, 211 W Wacker Dr, Ste 1700, Chicago, IL 60606. Phone: (800) 331-2020. E-mail: info@preventblindness.com. Web: www.preventblindness.org.

STOCK EXCHANGE HOLIDAY (LABOR DAY). Sept 1. The holiday schedules for the various exchanges are subject to change if relevant rules, regulations or exchange policies are revised. If you have questions, contact: CME Group (CME, CBOT, NYMEX, KCBT) (www.cmegroup.com), Chicago Board Options Exchange (www.cboe.com), NASDAQ (www.nasdaq.com), NYSE Euronext (www.nyse.com).

SUBLIMINAL COMMUNICATIONS MONTH. Sept 1–30. Not getting the results you want? Make a change for the positive and learn how to maximize your effectiveness. Learn how to put to use your entrepreneurial thinking to achieve your goals and increase your visibility socially or in the corporate world. Recognize and apply prosperity-building opportunities for increasing your networking, marketing and publicity goals through the use of color, scents and language. Finish the last quarter of the year successfully by using the powerful resources you already possess. It's your choice! For info: Lorrie Walters Marsiglio, Lorimar Communications, PO Box 284-CC, Wasco, IL 60183-0284. Phone: (630) 584-9368.

SUPERIOR RELATIONSHIPS MONTH. Sept 1–30. Superior relationships are the key to success in professional or personal life. Build superior relationships and get promoted, land a better job and have more influence on your coworkers and colleagues. Use this month to brush up on your people skills. For info: Karla Brandau, Workplace Power Institute, 4985 Chartley Circle, Ste 202, Lilburn, GA 30047. Phone: (770) 923-0883. Fax: (770) 931-2530. E-mail: karla@workplacepower.com.

***TITANIC* DISCOVERED: ANNIVERSARY.** Sept 1, 1985. Almost 75 years after the *Titanic* sank in the North Atlantic after striking an iceberg, a joint American-French expedition force led by marine geologist Dr. Robert Ballard located the wreck. The luxury liner was resting on the ocean floor 12,500 feet down—about 350 miles southeast from Newfoundland, Canada. In July 1986 Ballard returned in an expedition aboard the *Atlantis II* to explore the ship with underwater robots. Two memorial bronze plaques were left on the deck. See also: "Sinking of the *Titanic*: Anniversary" (Apr 15).

TOY TIPS EXECUTIVE TOY TEST. Sept 1. New York, NY. Annual event where senior corporate executives test toys and learn how to use creativity in the workplace. For info: Toy Tips, Inc. E-mail: marianne@toytips.com. Web: www.toytips.com.

TWITTY, CONWAY: BIRTH ANNIVERSARY. Sept 1, 1933. Country and western music star who began his career as a rock-and-roll performer in the style of Elvis Presley, born at Friars Point, MS. Died June 5, 1993, at Springfield, MO.

UPDATE YOUR RÉSUMÉ MONTH. Sept 1–30. This month encourages employed individuals to update and maintain their résumés. For info: Laura DeCarlo, Career Directors International, 1665 Clover Circle, Melbourne, FL 32935. Phone: (321) 752-0442. E-mail: info@careerdirectors.com.

UZBEKISTAN: INDEPENDENCE DAY. Sept 1. National holiday. Commemorates independence upon the dissolution of the Soviet Union in 1991.

WAIKIKI ROUGHWATER SWIM. Sept 1. Waikiki Beach, Honolulu, HI. The 45th annual swim is 2.4 miles from Sans Souci Beach to Duke Kahanamoku Beach. "The World's Most Prestigious Open Water Swimming Event." Preregistration is required. Online registration at www.pacificsportevents.com. Est attendance: 1,000. For info: Waikiki Roughwater Swim Committee, 6158 Summer, Honolulu, HI 96821. E-mail: kaiawrs@gmail.com. Web: www.wrswim.com.

☆ ☆ ☆

WHOLE GRAINS MONTH. Sept 1–30. Eating better is not an all-or-nothing choice; every little improvement you make in your food helps. This month is a great time for everyone to get on the whole grains bandwagon. Post a list of "baby steps" on the fridge and try as many as possible this month. For example, serve bulgur or brown rice instead of potatoes one night in the month, try a new cereal with at least 16 grams of whole grain per serving or try whole-wheat pasta for one meal. The Whole Grains Council offers education and promotions to consumers, retailers and health professionals. For info: The Whole Grains Council, 266 Beacon St, Boston, MA 02116. Phone: (617) 421-5500. Fax: (617) 421-5511. Web: www.wholegrainscouncil.org.

WORLD ANIMAL REMEMBRANCE MONTH. Sept 1–30. A worldwide observance to remember, respect and honor the memory of all animals—a month to pay tribute to companion animal family members; animal victims of abuse, cruelty and neglect; animals lost in natural disasters; and animals killed in the line of duty. Annually, the month of September. For info: PALS Foundation, PO Box 3631, San Luis Obispo, CA 93403. Phone: (805) 544-0984. Web: www.PALS.R8.org.

WORLD WAR II BEGINS: GERMANY INVADES POLAND: 75th ANNIVERSARY. Sept 1, 1939. After securing a nonagression pact with the USSR (that secretly allowed for the partition of Poland by the Soviet Union and Germany) on Aug 23, Germany invaded Poland without a declaration of war at 4:45 AM. Two days later, Britain and France declared war, with Canada, Australia, New Zealand and South Africa soon following with their own declarations. Poland, overwhelmed by German air and land power, was in German and Soviet hands before the month concluded.

BIRTHDAYS TODAY

Zendaya Coleman, 18, actress ("Shake It Up!"), television personality ("Dancing with the Stars"), born Oakland, CA, Sept 1, 1996.

Alan Dershowitz, 76, attorney, author, born Brooklyn, NY, Sept 1, 1938.

Gloria Estefan, 57, singer, born Havana, Cuba, Sept 1, 1957.

Barry Gibb, 68, singer (The Bee Gees), songwriter, born Manchester, England, Sept 1, 1946.

Timothy Duane (Tim) Hardaway, 48, former basketball player, born Chicago, IL, Sept 1, 1966.

Dr. Phil McGraw, 64, psychologist, author, television personality ("The Oprah Winfrey Show," "Dr. Phil"), born Vinita, OK, Sept 1, 1950.

Seiji Ozawa, 79, conductor, born Hoten, Japan, Sept 1, 1935.

Don Stroud, 77, actor ("Mike Hammer," *The Buddy Holly Story*, *License to Kill*), born Honolulu, HI, Sept 1, 1937.

Lily Tomlin, 75, actress, comedienne, born Detroit, MI, Sept 1, 1939.

September 2014

S	M	T	W	T	F	S
	1	2	3	4	5	6
7	8	9	10	11	12	13
14	15	16	17	18	19	20
21	22	23	24	25	26	27
28	29	30				

September 2 — Tuesday

DAY 245 **120 REMAINING**

BISON-TEN-YELL DAY. Sept 2. Honoring the "bicentennial" of the birth of Bison-Ten-Yell, imaginary inventor of a set of 10 battle yells as signals, based on the traditional memory aid system eventually adopted by football players. For info: Bob Birch, Grand Punscorpion, Puns Corps, 3108 Dashiell Rd, Falls Church, VA 22042. Phone: (703) 533-3668.

CALENDAR ADJUSTMENT DAY: ANNIVERSARY. Sept 2. Pursuant to the British Calendar Act of 1751, Britain (and the American colonies) made the "Gregorian Correction" in 1752. The act proclaimed that the day following Wednesday, Sept 2, should become Thursday, Sept 14, 1752. There was rioting in the streets by those who felt cheated and who demanded the 11 days back. The act also provided that New Year's Day (and the change of year number) should fall Jan 1 (instead of Mar 25) in 1752 and every year thereafter. As a result, 1751 only had 282 days. See also: "Gregorian Calendar Adjustment: Anniversary" (Feb 24, Oct 4).

FORTEN, JAMES: BIRTH ANNIVERSARY. Sept 2, 1766. James Forten was born of free black parents at Philadelphia, PA. As a powder boy on an American Revolutionary warship, he escaped being sold as a slave when his ship was captured due to the intervention of the son of the British commander. While in England he became involved with abolitionists. On his return to Philadelphia, he became an apprentice to a sailmaker and eventually purchased the company for which he worked. He was active in the abolition movement, and in 1816 his support was sought by the American Colonization Society for the plan to settle American blacks at Liberia. He rejected their ideas and their plans to make him the ruler of the colony. From the large profits of his successful sailmaking company, he contributed heavily to the abolitionist movement and was a supporter of William Lloyd Garrison's antislavery journal, *The Liberator*. Died at Philadelphia, PA, Mar 4, 1842.

GREAT FIRE OF LONDON: ANNIVERSARY. Sept 2–5, 1666. (Old Style date.) The fire generally credited with bringing about our system of fire insurance started Sept 2, 1666 (OS), in the wooden house of a baker named Farryner, at London's Pudding Lane, near the Tower. During the ensuing three days more than 13,000 houses were destroyed, though it is believed that only six lives were lost in the fire.

HISTORIC MARATHON RUNS: ANNIVERSARY. Sept 2–9, 490 BC. Anniversary of the event during the Persian Wars from which the marathon race is derived. Phidippides, "an Athenian and by profession and practice a trained runner," according to Herodotus, was dispatched from Marathon to Sparta (a distance of 26 miles) on Sept 2 to seek help in repelling the invading Persian army. Help being unavailable by religious law until after the next full moon, Phidippides ran the 26 miles back to Marathon Sept 4. Without Spartan aid, the Athenians defeated the Persians at the Battle of Marathon Sept 9. According to legend Phidippides carried the news of the battle to Athens and died as he spoke the words, "Rejoice, we are victorious." The marathon race was revived at the 1896 Olympic Games at Athens. Course distance, since 1924, is 26 miles, 385 yards. See also: "Battle of Marathon: Anniversary" (Sept 9).

LILIUOKALANI: BIRTH ANNIVERSARY. Sept 2, 1838. Born Liliu Kamakhea in Honolulu, the island of Hawaii, Liliuokalani was the Kingdom of Hawaii's only female sovereign and its last monarch. She was deposed in 1894 by a group led by Sanford Dole—first president of the Republic of Hawaii. Despite US President Grover Cleveland's insistence that Liliuokalani be restored to the throne, Dole refused. After a failed insurrection in 1895, she spent the remainder of her years leading the Oni pa'a movement, which opposed Hawaii's annexation by the US, until her death on Nov 11, 1917, at Honolulu.

McAULIFFE, CHRISTA: BIRTH ANNIVERSARY. Sept 2, 1948. Christa McAuliffe, a 37-year-old Concord, NH, high school teacher, was to have been the first "ordinary citizen" in space. Born Sharon Christa Corrigan at Boston, MA, she perished with six crew members in the Space Shuttle *Challenger* explosion Jan 28, 1986. See also: "Challenger Space Shuttle Explosion: Anniversary" (Jan 28).

MOON PHASE: FIRST QUARTER. Sept 2. Moon enters First Quarter phase at 7:11 AM, EDT.

NATIONAL STEARMAN FLY-IN. Sept 2–7. Galesburg, IL. The largest gathering of Stearman airplanes—the biplane trainers that gave wings to more military pilots than any other series of aircraft in the world. Est attendance: 7,500. For info: Galesburg Area CVB, 2163 E Main St, Galesburg, IL 61401. Phone: (309) 343-2485. Fax: (309) 343-2521. E-mail: visitors@visitgalesburg.com. Web: www.visitgalesburg.com.

PLAY DAYS. Sept 2–6. 37th annual. In a world filled with downsizing, rightsizing and shaftsizing, we need humor to reaffirm our humanity and sanity. In the week after Labor Day, the HUMOR Project will playfully spread the word on 1,001 ways to add humor to your life and work. Jest for success—humor works—the funny line and bottom line intersect! Annually, the Tuesday through Saturday after Labor Day. For info: The HUMOR Project, 10 Madison Ave, Saratoga Springs, NY 12866. Phone: (518) 587-8770. E-mail: chase@HumorProject.com. Web: www.HumorProject.com.

SHERMAN ENTERS ATLANTA: 150th ANNIVERSARY. Sept 2, 1864. After a four-week siege, Union General William Tecumseh Sherman entered Atlanta, GA. The city had been evacuated on the previous day by Confederate troops under General John B. Hood. Hood had mistakenly assumed Sherman was ending the siege Aug 27, when actually Sherman was beginning the final stages of his attack. Hood then sent troops to attack the Union forces at Jonesboro. Hood's troops were defeated, opening the way for the capture of Atlanta.

US TREASURY DEPARTMENT: 225th ANNIVERSARY. Sept 2, 1789. The third presidential cabinet department, the Treasury Department, was established by Congress.

VIETNAM: INDEPENDENCE DAY. Sept 2. Ho Chi Minh formally proclaimed the independence of Vietnam from France and the establishment of the Democratic Republic of Vietnam on this day in 1945. National holiday.

V-J DAY: ANNIVERSARY. Sept 2, 1945. Official ratification of Japanese surrender to the Allies occurred aboard the USS *Missouri* at Tokyo Bay Sept 2 (Far Eastern time) in 1945, thus prompting President Truman's declaration of this day as Victory-over-Japan Day. Japan's initial, informal agreement of surrender was announced by Truman and celebrated in the US Aug 14.

BIRTHDAYS TODAY

Nathaniel "Tiny" Archibald, 66, Hall of Fame basketball player, born New York, NY, Sept 2, 1948.

Terry Paxton Bradshaw, 66, sportscaster, Hall of Fame football player, born Shreveport, LA, Sept 2, 1948.

Marge Champion, 95, dancer, actress ("The Marge and Gower Champion Show," *Show Boat*), born Los Angeles, CA, Sept 2, 1919.

Jimmy Connors, 62, Hall of Fame tennis player, born East St. Louis, IL, Sept 2, 1952.

Eric Dickerson, 54, Hall of Fame football player, sportscaster, born Sealy, TX, Sept 2, 1960.

Mark Harmon, 63, actor ("NCIS," "St. Elsewhere," "Chicago Hope"), born Burbank, CA, Sept 2, 1951.

Salma Hayek, 48, actress (*Ask the Dust, Bandidas, Frida*), born Veracruz, Mexico, Sept 2, 1966.

Linda Purl, 59, actress ("Matlock"), born Greenwich, CT, Sept 2, 1955.

Keanu Reeves, 50, actor (*The Matrix, Speed*), born Beirut, Lebanon, Sept 2, 1964.

Peter Victor Ueberroth, 77, former commissioner of baseball and Olympic organizer, born Evanston, IL, Sept 2, 1937.

Carlos Valderrama, 53, former soccer player, born Santa Marta, Colombia, Sept 2, 1961.

Cynthia Watros, 46, actress ("Lost," "The Drew Carey Show," "Guiding Light"), born Lake Orion, MI, Sept 2, 1968.

September 3 — Wednesday

DAY 246 **119 REMAINING**

BEGINNING OF THE PENNY PRESS: ANNIVERSARY. Sept 3, 1833. Benjamin H. Day launched the *New York Sun*, the first truly successful penny newspaper in the US, on this date. The *Sun* was sold on sidewalks by newspaper boys. By 1836 the paper was the largest seller in the country with a circulation of 30,000. It was possibly Day's concentration on human interest stories and sensationalism that made his publication a success while efforts at penny papers at Philadelphia and Boston had failed.

BRITAIN DECLARES WAR ON GERMANY: 75th ANNIVERSARY. Sept 3, 1939. British ultimatum to Germany, demanding halt to invasion of Poland (which had started at dawn on Sept 1), expired at 11 AM, GMT, Sept 3, 1939. At 11:15 AM, in a radio broadcast, Prime Minister Neville Chamberlain announced the declaration of war against Germany. France, Canada, Australia, New Zealand and South Africa quickly issued separate declarations of war. Winston Churchill was named First Lord of the Admiralty. See also: "World War II Begins: Germany Invades Poland: 75th Anniversary" (Sept 1).

CRANDALL, PRUDENCE: BIRTH ANNIVERSARY. Sept 3, 1803. Born to a Quaker family at Hopkinton, RI, this American schoolteacher sparked controversy in the 1830s with her efforts to educate black girls. When her private academy for girls was boycotted because she admitted a black girl, she started a school for "young ladies and misses of colour." Died Jan 28, 1890, at Elk Falls, KS.

DEFEAT OF JESSE JAMES DAYS. Sept 3–7. Northfield, MN. Bank raid reenactment, 5k and 15k runs, arts, crafts, bike race, parade and professional rodeo. Annually, the Wednesday through Sunday after Labor Day. Est attendance: 100,000. For info: Defeat of Jesse James Days Committee, PO Box 23, Northfield, MN 55057. Phone: (507) 645-5604. Fax: (507) 663-7782. Web: www.djjd.org.

September 2014

S	M	T	W	T	F	S
	1	2	3	4	5	6
7	8	9	10	11	12	13
14	15	16	17	18	19	20
21	22	23	24	25	26	27
28	29	30				

DOUGLASS'S ESCAPE TO FREEDOM: ANNIVERSARY. Sept 3, 1838. Dressed as a sailor and carrying identification papers borrowed from a retired merchant seaman, Frederick Douglass boarded a train at Baltimore, MD, a slave state, and rode to Wilmington, DE, where he caught a steamboat to the free city of Philadelphia. He then transferred to a train headed for New York City, where he entered the protection of the Underground Railway network. Douglass later became a great orator and one of the leaders of the antislavery struggle.

FARMERS AND THRESHERMENS JUBILEE. Sept 3–7. New Centerville, PA. Held since 1953. Many steam engines; threshing demonstrations using manpower, horses and steam; quilt show and crafts; truck and tractor pulls. Live entertainment, good food. Est attendance: 25,000. For info: Farmers & Threshermens Jubilee, 1428 Casselman Rd, Rockwood, PA 15557. Phone: (814) 926-3142.

FILENE, EDWARD ALBERT: BIRTH ANNIVERSARY. Sept 3, 1860. American merchant and philanthropist, born at Salem, MA, to German immigrant parents. An innovative retailer and manager, he made the Filene family store into a retail powerhouse that featured the "bargain basement": here, merchandise was automatically discounted as time passed. His Employees Credit Union was the catalyst for the US credit union movement in 1921. Filene died at Paris, France, Sept 26, 1937.

FIRST SECRET SERVICE AGENT TO DIE IN THE LINE OF DUTY: ANNIVERSARY. Sept 3, 1902. While on duty protecting President Theodore Roosevelt, William Craig was killed when a streetcar collided with the carriage carrying the president (who suffered some cuts). The United States Secret Service was founded in 1865 as a branch of the Treasury Department entrusted with foiling counterfeiting but was given the additional role of protecting the US president upon the assassination of William McKinley. Craig, born in Glasgow, Scotland, in 1855, was also a bodyguard for Queen Victoria before moving to Chicago. Roosevelt affectionately called Craig his "shadow."

ITALY SURRENDERS: ANNIVERSARY. Sept 3, 1943. General Giuseppe Castellano signed three copies of the "short armistice," effectively surrendering "unconditionally" for the Italian government. That same day the British Eighth Army, commanded by General Bernard Montgomery, invaded the Italian mainland.

NOYES, JOHN HUMPHREY: BIRTH ANNIVERSARY. Sept 3, 1811. Born at Brattleboro, VT, Noyes was the founder of one of the most successful and long-lasting socialist communities in the US: the Oneida Community in New York (1848–79). He also coined the term "free love." Noyes died at Niagara Falls, ON, Canada, on Apr 13, 1886.

QATAR: INDEPENDENCE DAY. Sept 3. National holiday. Commemorates the severing in 1971 of treaty with Britain, which had handled Qatar's foreign relations.

SAN MARINO: NATIONAL DAY. Sept 3. Public holiday. Honors St. Marinus, the traditional founder of San Marino.

"SEARCH FOR TOMORROW" TV PREMIERE: ANNIVERSARY. Sept 3, 1951. This iconic soap lasted for 35 years. It began as a 15-minute program and expanded to 30 minutes in 1968, when performances began to be videotaped instead of airing live. "Search" was set in the town of Henderson, and its central character was Joanne Gardner Barron Tate Vincente Tourneur (played by Mary Stuart). Other notable cast members have included Don Knotts, Robert Mandan, Ken Kercheval, Jill Clayburgh, Natalie Schafer, Susan Sarandon, Robert Loggia, Hal Linden, Morgan Fairchild, Joe Morton, Robby Benson, Kevin Kline, Cynthia Gibb and Olympia Dukakis. The final episode aired on Dec 26, 1986.

SULLIVAN, LOUIS: BIRTH ANNIVERSARY. Sept 3, 1856. An American architect responsible for the modern, steel-framed skyscraper, his designs are characterized by rich ornamentation, plain outer surfaces and cubic forms. His famous motto was "form follows function." Frank Lloyd Wright was a student of Sullivan's before the two quarreled. Born at Boston, MA, Sullivan died Apr 14, 1924, at Chicago, IL.

TREATY OF PARIS ENDS AMERICAN REVOLUTION: ANNIVERSARY. Sept 3, 1783. Treaty between Britain and the US, ending the Revolutionary War, signed at Paris, France. American signatories: John Adams, Benjamin Franklin and John Jay.

BIRTHDAYS TODAY

Pauline Collins, 74, actress (Tony for *Shirley Valentine*; "Upstairs, Downstairs"), born Exmouth, England, Sept 3, 1940.

Paz de la Huerta, 30, actress ("Boardwalk Empire"), born New York, NY, Sept 3, 1984.

Kiran Desai, 43, author (*The Inheritance of Loss, Hullabaloo in the Guava Orchard*), born New Delhi, India, Sept 3, 1971.

Cristobal Huet, 39, hockey player, born Saint-Martin-d'Héres, France, Sept 3, 1975.

Anne Jackson, 88, actress (*Lovers and Other Strangers*), born Allegheny, PA, Sept 3, 1926.

Alison Lurie, 88, author (*Foreign Affairs, The War Between the Tates*), born Chicago, IL, Sept 3, 1926.

Valerie Perrine, 71, actress (*Lenny, W.C. Fields and Me*), born Galveston, TX, Sept 3, 1943.

Charlie Sheen, 49, actor ("Two and a Half Men," *Wall Street, Platoon*), born Carlos Irwin Estevez at New York, NY, Sept 3, 1965.

Mort Walker, 91, cartoonist ("Beetle Bailey"), born Addison Morton Walker at El Dorado, KS, Sept 3, 1923.

Shaun White, 28, Olympic snowboarder, born San Diego, CA, Sept 3, 1986.

September 4 — Thursday

DAY 247 **118 REMAINING**

BRUCKNER, ANTON: BIRTH ANNIVERSARY. Sept 4, 1824. Austrian composer born at Ansfelden, Austria. Died at Vienna, Austria, Oct 11, 1896.

BURNHAM, DANIEL: BIRTH ANNIVERSARY. Sept 4, 1846. American architect and city planner born at Henderson, NY. Daniel Hudson Burnham was an advocate of tall, fireproof buildings, probably the first to be called "sky-scrapers." In 1909 he proposed a long-range city plan for Chicago, IL, that was a key factor in the "forever open, clear and free" policy, which resulted in Chicago having the most beautiful lakefront of any major city in the US. Died June 1, 1912, at Heidelberg, Germany.

CANADA: OTTAWA FOLK FESTIVAL. Sept 4–7. Hog's Back Park, Ottawa, ON. 21st annual. Set amidst the natural beauty of Hog's Back Park, the Ottawa Folk Festival is a four-day celebration of music, dance, visual arts and community featuring an eclectic mix of musical performances on multiple stages, plus free participatory music workshops, special children's and family performances, wellness activities, beer gardens, artisan and craft vendors, and much, much more. We are family-friendly, community-focused, culturally diverse and committed to sustainability and eco-friendly initiatives. Est attendance: 17,000. For info: Ottawa Folk Festival, 265 Catherine St, 2nd Fl, Ottawa, ON, Canada K1R 7S5. Phone: (613) 230-8234, ext 302. Fax: (613) 247-2220. E-mail: officemanager@ottawafolk.com. Web: www.ottawafolk.com.

CANADA: TORONTO INTERNATIONAL FILM FESTIVAL. Sept 4–14 (tentative). Toronto, ON. 39th annual. A 10-day festival of contemporary Canadian and international cinema at various downtown theatres. Call or write for info or to be put on mailing list. Annually, beginning on the Thursday after Labor Day. Est attendance: 250,000. For info: Toronto Intl Film Festival, Reitman Square, 350 King St W, Toronto, ON, Canada M5V 3X5. Phone: (416) 968-FILM. Fax: (416) 967-9477. Web: www.tiff.net.

"CAPTAIN MIDNIGHT" TV PREMIERE: 60th ANNIVERSARY. Sept 4, 1954. A children's show starring Richard Webb as Captain Midnight, a WWI flying ace who battled crime as part of the Secret Squadron. Webb was joined by Sid Melton as Ichabod (Ikky) Mudd, his assistant, and Olan Soule as Tut, an eccentric scientist. "Captain Midnight" moved to TV from radio, where it was sponsored by Ovaltine. In reruns the name was changed to "Jet Jackson, Flying Commando" because Ovaltine owned the rights to the Captain Midnight name.

CHATEAUBRIAND, FRANCOIS RENE DE: BIRTH ANNIVERSARY. Sept 4, 1768. French poet, novelist, historian, explorer and statesman, witness to the French Revolution. Born at St. Malo, France, he died at Paris, France, July 4, 1848.

CURAÇAO: ANIMALS' DAY. Sept 4. In Curaçao the Association for the Protection of Animals organizes an animal show for this day and the best-kept animals are awarded prizes.

ENGLAND: THE LAND ROVER BURGHLEY HORSE TRIALS. Sept 4–7 (tentative). Burghley Park, Stamford, Lincolnshire, England. Major four-star event: dressage, cross country, show jumping, etc. Est attendance: 160,000. For info: Burghley Horse Trials, Stamford, Lincolnshire, PE9 2LH England. Phone: (44) (1780) 752-131. Fax: (44) (1780) 752-982. E-mail: info@burghley-horse.co.uk. Web: www.burghley-horse.co.uk.

FIRST ELECTRIC LIGHTING: ANNIVERSARY. Sept 4, 1882. Four hundred electric lights came on in offices on Spruce, Wall, Nassau and Pearl Streets in lower Manhattan as Thomas Edison hooked up lightbulbs to an underground cable carrying direct-current electrical power. Edison had demonstrated his first incandescent lightbulb in 1879. See also: "Incandescent Lamp Demonstrated: Anniversary" (Oct 21).

HARVEY, PAUL: BIRTH ANNIVERSARY. Sept 4, 1918. Legendary radio broadcaster and newsman, born at Tulsa, OK, he is best remembered for his syndicated features that ran twice per day on the ABC Radio Network. "The Rest of the Story" was a behind-the-scenes look at the rise to prominence of famous people from all walks of life, and his morning news program was opinionated, occasionally sarcastic and full of offbeat human interest stories. Harvey died at Phoenix, AZ, Feb 28, 2009.

LITTLE ROCK NINE: ANNIVERSARY. Sept 4–25, 1957. Governor Orval Faubus called out the Arkansas National Guard to turn away nine black students who had been trying to attend Central High School in Little Rock. President Eisenhower sent in the 101st Army Airborne to enforce the law allowing the students to integrate the school, and on Sept 25, national troops escorted the nine into the school.

LONGS PEAK SCOTTISH/IRISH HIGHLAND FESTIVAL. Sept 4–7. Estes Park, CO. 38th annual Scottish-Irish celebration festival with pipe bands, Highland and Irish dancing, jousting and gathering of the clans. Featuring professional Scottish and Irish entertainers, "Dogs of the British Isles" dog competition, professional Scottish athletes and vendors with imported and handcrafted merchandise. Annually, the first weekend after Labor Day. Est attendance: 70,000. For info: Longs Peak Scottish/Irish Highland Festival, Inc, PO Box 1820, Estes Park, CO 80517. Phone: (800) 903-7837. Fax: (970) 586-5328. E-mail: info@scotfest.com. Web: www.scotfest.com.

LOS ANGELES, CALIFORNIA, FOUNDED: ANNIVERSARY. Sept 4, 1781. Los Angeles founded by decree and called "El Pueblo de Nuestra Señora La Reina de Los Angeles de Porciuncula." The City of Los Angeles was incorporated on Apr 4, 1850.

MARION POPCORN FESTIVAL. Sept 4–6. Marion, OH. Performances by nationally known entertainers every evening; parade, athletic and popcorn-cooking competitions, arts and crafts. Annually, the first weekend after Labor Day. Est attendance: 350,000. For info: Marion Popcorn Festival, PO Box 1101, Marion, OH 43301-1101. Phone: (740) 387-3378. E-mail: marianpopcornfestival@gmail.com. Web: www.popcornfestival.com.

NEWSPAPER CARRIER DAY. Sept 4. Anniversary of the hiring of the first "newsboy" in the US, 10-year-old Barney Flaherty, who is said to have answered the following classified advertisement, which appeared in the *New York Sun* in 1833: "To the Unemployed—a number of steady men can find employment by vending this paper. A liberal discount is allowed to those who buy to sell again."

POLK, SARAH CHILDRESS: BIRTH ANNIVERSARY. Sept 4, 1803. Wife of James Knox Polk, 11th president of the US. Born at Murfreesboro, TN, and died at Nashville, TN, Aug 14, 1891.

UTAH STATE FAIR. Sept 4–14. Utah State FairPark, Salt Lake City, UT. Exhibits, livestock, family contests, cook-offs, concerts and entertainment. Annually, beginning the first Thursday after Labor Day. Est attendance: 314,000. For info: Utah State FairPark, 155 N 1000 W, Salt Lake City, UT 84116. Phone: (801) 538-8400. Fax: (801) 538-8455. E-mail: info@utahstatefair.com. Web: www.utahstatefair.com.

WRIGHT, RICHARD: BIRTH ANNIVERSARY. Sept 4, 1908. Novelist and short-story writer whose works include *Native Son, Uncle Tom's Children* and *Black Boy*, born at Natchez, MS. Wright died at Paris, France, Nov 28, 1960.

YELLOW DAISY FESTIVAL. Sept 4–7. Stone Mountain Park, Stone Mountain, GA. 46th annual. Arts and crafts festival with more than 400 exhibitors. Continuous entertainment and foods. Annually, the weekend after Labor Day. Est attendance: 200,000. For info: Special Events Office, Stone Mountain Park, PO Box 778, Stone Mountain, GA 30086. Phone: (770) 498-5633. Fax: (770) 413-5059. E-mail: ydf@stonemountainpark.com. Web: www.stonemountainpark.com.

BIRTHDAYS TODAY

Wes Bentley, 36, actor (*The Hunger Games, American Beauty*), born Jonesboro, AR, Sept 4, 1978.

Mitzi Gaynor, 83, singer, dancer, actress (*South Pacific*), born Francesca Mitzi Marlene de Charney von Gerber at Chicago, IL, Sept 4, 1931.

Max Greenfield, 34, actor ("New Girl," "Veronica Mars," "Ugly Betty"), born Dobbs Ferry, NY, Sept 4, 1980.

Judith Ivey, 63, actress (*Compromising Positions, Brighton Beach Memoirs*; stage: *Steaming*), born El Paso, TX, Sept 4, 1951.

Beyoncé Knowles, 33, singer, actress (*Dreamgirls*), born Houston, TX, Sept 4, 1981.

Michael Joseph (Mike) Piazza, 46, former baseball player, born Norristown, PA, Sept 4, 1968.

Jennifer Salt, 70, actress ("Soap"), born Los Angeles, CA, Sept 4, 1944.

Ione Skye, 44, actress (*Say Anything*), born Hertfordshire, England, Sept 4, 1970.

Thomas Sturges (Tom) Watson, 65, golfer, born Kansas City, MO, Sept 4, 1949.

Damon Wayans, 54, actor, comedian ("In Living Color"), born New York, NY, Sept 4, 1960.

September 2014

S	M	T	W	T	F	S
	1	2	3	4	5	6
7	8	9	10	11	12	13
14	15	16	17	18	19	20
21	22	23	24	25	26	27
28	29	30				

September 5 — Friday

DAY 248 **117 REMAINING**

BABE RUTH'S FIRST PRO HOMER: 100th ANNIVERSARY. Sept 5, 1914. Babe Ruth hit his first home run as a professional while playing for Providence in the International League, a type of minor league affiliate of the Boston Red Sox. He pitched a one-hit shutout against Toronto.

BE LATE FOR SOMETHING DAY. Sept 5. To create a release from the stresses and strains resulting from a consistent need to be on time. For info: Les Waas, Pres, Procrastinators' Club of America, Inc, Box 712, Bryn Athyn, PA 19009. Phone: (215) 947-0500. Fax: (215) 947-9010. E-mail: procrastinators_club_of_america@yahoo.com.

BRING YOUR MANNERS TO WORK DAY. Sept 5. A day to recognize the importance of minding your manners at work and treating others on the job with respect. Celebrated across all industries and professions, the day explores the dos and don'ts for good business behavior: every day, and every week, of the year. Annually, the first Friday in September. For info: The Protocol School of Washington, PO Box 676, Columbia, SC 29202. Phone: (877) 766-3757. E-mail: info@psow.edu. Web: www.psow.edu.

CAGE, JOHN: BIRTH ANNIVERSARY. Sept 5, 1912. Avant-garde American composer John Cage was born at Los Angeles, CA. He pioneered the experimental music and performance art schools. He used nontraditional instruments such as flowerpots and cowbells in innovative situations, such as performances governed by chance, in which the *I Ching* was consulted to determine the direction of the performance. In 1978 he was elected to the American Academy of Arts and Sciences and in 1982 was awarded France's highest honor for cultural contributions, *Commandeur de l'Ordre des Arts et des Lettres.* He died Aug 12, 1992, at New York, NY.

CARNOVSKY, MORRIS: BIRTH ANNIVERSARY. Sept 5, 1897. American actor Morris Carnovsky was born at St. Louis, MO. In 1931 with actor Lee Strasberg and others he founded the Group Theater at New York, NY. He was blacklisted in the 1950s by the House Un-American Activities Committee but was still asked by John Houseman to perform in the American Shakespeare Festival in 1956 and began a successful Shakespearean career. He was elected to the Theater Hall of Fame in 1979. Carnovsky died Sept 1, 1992, at Easton, CT.

CLINTON COUNTY CORN FESTIVAL. Sept 5–7. Clinton County Fairgrounds, Wilmington, OH. 37th annual. Help us celebrate our agricultural heritage as we honor one of the area's biggest industries. The festival features antique farm machinery, a parade (Saturday at 10 AM), games, all types of food made from corn, a quilt show, music, antiques, crafts and the Corn Olympics. This is an event not to miss in Clinton County! Est attendance: 10,500. For info: Clinton County CVB, 13 N South St, Wilmington, OH 45177. Phone: (877) 428-4748. E-mail: info@clintoncountyohio.com. Web: www.clintoncountyohio.com.

ENGLAND: BLACKPOOL ILLUMINATIONS. Sept 5–Nov 2. The Promenade, Blackpool, Lancashire. "A five-mile spectacle of lighting" since 1879. More than 400,000 lamps of various types and styles. Annually, from the first Friday in September through the first Sunday of November. Est attendance: 3,500,000. For info: Visit Blackpool. Web: www.visitblackpool.com.

FALL FAMILY DAYS. Sept 5–7. Gagetown, MI. Step back in time to see what life was like in the Roaring '20s up to WWII. Come and see the landmark Octagon Barn and enjoy the demonstrations and hands-on activities. Starts Friday with a fish dinner followed by music in the Octagon Barn. More than 200 vendors. Food on the grounds from breakfast through supper. Always the weekend after Labor Day. Est attendance: 15,000. For info: Fall Family Days, 6622 Kelly Rd, Cass City, MI 48726. Phone: (989) 872-3761. E-mail: hirnrjma@speednetllc.com.

FESTIVAL OF THE VINE. Sept 5–7. Geneva, IL. Flavors of fall are celebrated with music, wine tasting, antique carriage rides, arts and crafts, entertainment and specialties of Geneva's fine restaurants. Est attendance: 75,000. For info: Geneva Chamber of Commerce, 8 S Third St, PO Box 481, Geneva, IL 60134. Phone: (630) 232-6060. Fax: (630) 232-6083. E-mail: chamberinfo@genevachamber.com. Web: www.genevachamber.com.

FIRST CONTINENTAL CONGRESS ASSEMBLY: ANNIVERSARY. Sept 5, 1774. The first assembly of this forerunner of the US Congress took place at Philadelphia, PA. Peyton Randolph, delegate from Virginia, was elected president.

FIRST LABOR DAY OBSERVANCE: ANNIVERSARY. Sept 5, 1882. On this day in New York City, the first observance of Labor Day was held. It was organized by the Central Labor Union. Historians debate whether the inspiration came from Peter McGuire, general secretary of the Brotherhood of Carpenters and Joiners, or Matthew Maguire, secretary of the Central Labor Union. By 1884, other cities were honoring working people. In 1894, it became a federal holiday.

GERALD FORD: ASSASSINATION ATTEMPT: ANNIVERSARY. Sept 5, 1975. Lynette A. "Squeaky" Fromme, a follower of convicted murderer Charles Manson, attempted to shoot President Gerald Ford. On Sept 22 of the same year, another attempt on Ford's life occurred when Sara Jane Moore shot at him.

ISRAELI OLYMPIAD MASSACRE: ANNIVERSARY. Sept 5–6, 1972. Eleven members of the Israeli Olympic Team were killed in an attack on the Olympic Village at Munich and attempted kidnapping of team members. Four of seven guerrillas, members of the Black September faction of the Palestinian Liberation Army, were also killed. In retaliation, Israeli jets bombed Palestinian positions at Lebanon and Syria on Sept 8, 1972.

JAMES, JESSE: BIRTH ANNIVERSARY. Sept 5, 1847. Western legend and bandit Jesse Woodson James was born at Centerville (now Kearney), MO. His criminal exploits were glorified and romanticized by writers for Eastern readers looking for stories of Western adventure and heroism. After the Civil War, James and his brother, Frank, formed a group of eight outlaws who robbed banks, stagecoaches and stores. In 1873 the James gang began holding up trains. The original James gang was put out of business Sept 7, 1876, while attempting to rob a bank at Northfield, MN. Every member of the gang except for the James brothers was killed or captured. The brothers formed a new gang and resumed their criminal careers in 1879. Two years later, the governor of Missouri offered a $10,000 reward for their capture, dead or alive. On Apr 3, 1882, at St. Joseph, MO, Robert Ford, a member of the gang, shot 34-year-old Jesse in the back of the head and claimed the reward.

KANSAS STATE FAIR. Sept 5–14. Hutchinson, KS. Commercial and competitive exhibits, entertainment, carnival and other special attractions. Annually, beginning the first Friday after Labor Day. Est attendance: 350,000. For info: Kansas State Fair, 2000 N Poplar St, Hutchinson, KS 67502. Phone: (620) 669-3600. E-mail: info@kansasstatefair.com. Web: www.kansasstatefair.com.

KOESTLER, ARTHUR: BIRTH ANNIVERSARY. Sept 5, 1905. Born at Budapest, Hungary, Koestler is best known for his novel about his disillusionment with Communism, *Darkness at Noon*, and for *The God That Failed*. Died at London, England, Mar 3, 1983.

LOUIS XIV: BIRTH ANNIVERSARY. Sept 5, 1638. Born at Saint-Germain-en-Laye, France, Louis the Great or the Sun King centralized state power into his person, brilliantly directing able ministers and controlling the nobility. Abroad, he extended the borders of France in a series of wars, but his influence extended beyond politics into all spheres of life. He was a patron of writers, painters and architects, and his court at Versailles is a masterpiece of baroque architecture. He died Sept 1, 1715, at Versailles.

"THE MacNEIL-LEHRER NEWSHOUR" TV PREMIERE: ANNIVERSARY. Sept 5, 1983. Originally, this PBS news show was called "The MacNeil-Lehrer Report" and was on every weeknight for a half hour starting in 1976. Robert MacNeil and Jim Lehrer were joined by Charlayne Hunter-Gault and Judy Woodruff. In 1983 the show was expanded to an hour and became TV's first regularly scheduled daily hour news show. The show has been praised for its depth and objectivity. In 1995 Robert MacNeil retired and the show was retitled "The NewsHour with Jim Lehrer." Jim Lehrer retired in 2011.

MICHIGAN'S GREAT FIRE OF 1881: ANNIVERSARY. Sept 5, 1881. According to the Michigan Historical Commission, "Small fires were burning in the forests of the 'Thumb area of Michigan,' tinder-dry after a long, hot summer, when a gale swept in from the southwest on Sept 5, 1881. Fanned into an inferno, the fire raged for three days. A million acres were devastated in Sanilac and Huron counties alone. At least 125 persons died, and thousands more were left destitute. The new American Red Cross won support for its prompt aid to the fire victims. This was the first disaster relief furnished by this great organization."

MUSHROOM FESTIVAL. Sept 5–7. Downtown Kennett Square, PA. 29th annual weekend of fun, food and fungi in the Mushroom Capital of the World! Help taste and judge soup and wine at Wine Fest; attend cooking or growing demos. Also mushroom judging, parade (Sept 5), car show, carnival, Street Festival with entertainment and mushroom farm tours. Est attendance: 100,000. For info: The Mushroom Festival, PO Box 1000, 114 W State St, Kennett Square, PA 19348. Phone: (888) 440-9920. E-mail: info@mushroomfestival.org. Web: www.mushroomfestival.org.

NIELSEN, ARTHUR CHARLES: BIRTH ANNIVERSARY. Sept 5, 1897. Marketing research engineer, founder of AC Nielsen Company, in 1923, known for radio and TV audience surveys, was born at Chicago, IL, and died there June 1, 1980.

NORWALK SEAPORT OYSTER FESTIVAL. Sept 5–7. Norwalk, CT. 36th annual. Huge festival with vintage ships on display, 150 juried crafters, main-stage entertainment, oyster shucking and slurping contests and Kids' Cove (children's entertainment). Annually, the weekend following Labor Day. Est attendance: 55,000. For info: Norwalk Seaport Assn, 132 Water St, Norwalk, CT 06854. Phone: (203) 838-9444. Fax: (203) 855-1017. E-mail: info@seaport.org. Web: www.seaport.org.

OHIO RIVER STERNWHEEL FESTIVAL. Sept 5–7. Ohio River Levee, Marietta, OH. 39th annual. A three-day riverfront extravaganza. More than two dozen sternwheelers line the Ohio River shore at Marietta. Continuous musical entertainment for all ages, food concessions, queen coronation, sternwheel races, fireworks. Annually, the weekend following Labor Day. Est attendance: 85,000. For info: Ohio River Sternwheel Festival Committee, PO Box 2109, Marietta, OH 45750. Phone: (740) 373-5178 or (800) 288-2577. Fax: (740) 374-4959. E-mail: info@mariettaohio.org. Web: www.ohioriversternwheelfestival.org.

OKTOBERFEST. Sept 5–7. MainStrasse Village, Covington, KY. Celebration of the German "storybook wedding reception" kicks off with a beer-tapping ceremony. Features include German and American food, live music and entertainment on four stages, arts and crafts, children's rides and much more. Est attendance: 125,000. For info: MainStrasse Village, 406 W 6th St, Ste 201, Covington, KY 41011. Phone: (859) 491-0458. Fax: (859) 655-7932. E-mail: dkremer@mainstrasse.org. Web: www.mainstrasse.org.

ONE ARM DOVE HUNT. Sept 5–6. Olney, TX. 43rd annual. Held since 1972, the One Arm Dove Hunt is Texas's most unusual event and the only one of its kind on Earth. Every person with the loss of use of an arm or hand or who is an arm or hand amputee is invited to Olney for fellowship, for fun activities and to hunt doves. Events include Glove Swap, One Arm Jokes and Tales, One Arm Golf Tournament, Cow Chip Chunk'n (Amputee vs Politician), musical entertainment, auction and the famous 10 cents a finger breakfast. Annually, the Friday and Saturday after Labor Day. For info: Jack Northrup, One Arm Dove Hunt, PO Box 582, Olney, TX 76374. Web: www.onearmdovehunt.com.

POPEYE PICNIC. Sept 5–7. Chester, IL. 35th annual. A family festival celebrating America's favorite cartoon sailor and the man who created him, Chester native E.C. Segar. Features live music, Castor Oyl's Carnival Rides, Olive Oyl's Café, Wimpy's Wiener Dog Derby, exhibits of Popeye collectibles, Spinach Bowl and much more. Annually, the weekend after Labor Day. For info: Popeye Picnic Committee, 1001 State St, Chester, IL 62233. E-mail: sccl@popeyethesailor.com. Web: www.popeyepicnic.com or www.chesterill.com.

SPACE MILESTONE: *VOYAGER 1* (US). Sept 5, 1977. Twin of *Voyager 2*, which was launched Aug 20. On Feb 18, 1998, *Voyager 1* set a new distance record when after more than 20 years in space it reached 6.5 billion miles from Earth.

SWITZERLAND: SAINT GOTTHARD AUTOMOBILE TUNNEL OPENING: ANNIVERSARY. Sept 5, 1980. The longest underground motorway in the world, the St. Gotthard Auto Tunnel in Switzerland, was opened to traffic. More than 10 miles long, requiring $417 million and 10 years for construction, it became the most direct route from Switzerland to the southern regions of the continent. The St. Gotthard Pass, the main passage since the Middle Ages, was closed much of every year by massive snowdrifts.

TENNESSEE STATE FAIR. Sept 5–14. Nashville, TN. 108th annual. A huge variety of exhibits, carnival midway, animal and variety shows, live stage presentations, livestock, agricultural and craft competitions and food and game booths. Annually, beginning the first Friday after Labor Day. Est attendance: 240,000. For info: Tennessee State Fair Association, PO Box 24747, Nashville, TN 37202. Web: www.tnstatefair.org.

WASHINGTON STATE FAIR. Sept 5–21. Puyallup, WA. Since 1900. One of the top 10 fairs in attendance in the world. Entertainment, rodeo, animals, rides, displays and food. Est attendance: 1,100,000. For info: Washington State Fair, 110 Ninth Ave SW, Puyallup, WA 98371. Phone: (253) 845-1771. Fax: (253) 841-5390. E-mail: info@thefair.com. Web: www.thefair.com.

ZANUCK, DARRYL F.: BIRTH ANNIVERSARY. Sept 5, 1902. Born at Wahoo, NE, Darryl F. Zanuck became a celebrated—and controversial—movie producer. He was also a cofounder of Twentieth Century Studios, which later merged with Fox. His film credits include *The Jazz Singer* (the first full-length sound picture), *Forever Amber, The Snake Pit* and *The Grapes of Wrath.* He died Dec 21, 1979, at Palm Springs, CA.

BIRTHDAYS TODAY

Kristian Alfonso, 50, actress ("Days of Our Lives," "Melrose Place"), born Brockton, MA, Sept 5, 1964.

William Devane, 75, actor ("24," "Knots Landing"), born Albany, NY, Sept 5, 1939.

Dennis Dugan, 68, actor, director (*Big Daddy, Problem Child*), born Wheaton, IL, Sept 5, 1946.

Cathy Lee Guisewite, 64, cartoonist ("Cathy"), born Dayton, OH, Sept 5, 1950.

Kim Yu-Na, 24, Olympic figure skater, born Bucheon, Gyeonggi-do, South Korea, Sept 5, 1990.

Carol Lawrence, 79, singer, actress (*West Side Story*), born Carol Maria Laraia at Melrose Park, IL, Sept 5, 1935.

Rose McGowan, 41, actress (*Jawbreaker,* "Charmed"), born Florence, Italy, Sept 5, 1973.

Bob Newhart, 85, comedian (*Elf,* "The Bob Newhart Show," "Newhart"), born Chicago, IL, Sept 5, 1929.

Nicanor Parra, 100, poet, physicist, born San Fabián de Alico, Chillán, Chile, Sept 5, 1914.

Raquel Welch, 72, actress (*The Three Musketeers, Woman of the Year*), model, born Chicago, IL, Sept 5, 1942.

Dweezil Zappa, 45, singer, actor ("Normal Life"), born Hollywood, CA, Sept 5, 1969.

September 6 — Saturday

DAY 249 **116 REMAINING**

ADDAMS, JANE: BIRTH ANNIVERSARY. Sept 6, 1860. American worker for peace, social welfare, rights of women; founder of Hull House (Chicago); cowinner of Nobel Prize, 1931. Born at Cedarville, IL, she died May 21, 1935, at Chicago, IL.

BALTIC STATES' INDEPENDENCE RECOGNIZED: ANNIVERSARY. Sept 6, 1991. The Soviet government recognized the independence of the Baltic states—Latvia, Estonia and Lithuania. The action came 51 years after the Baltic states were annexed by the Soviet Union. All three Baltic states had earlier declared their independence, and many nations had already recognized them diplomatically, including the US, Sept 2, 1991.

BEECHER, CATHARINE ESTHER: BIRTH ANNIVERSARY. Sept 6, 1800. Catharine Esther Beecher was born at East Hampton, NY. In addition to teaching herself mathematics, philosophy and Latin, Beecher had been formally educated in art and music. An early advocate for equal education for women, she founded the Hartford Female Seminary, which was widely recognized for its advanced curriculum. She was also instrumental in the founding of women's colleges in Iowa, Illinois and Wisconsin. Beecher died May 12, 1878, at Elmira, NY.

BULGARIA: UNIFICATION DAY. Sept 6. National holiday. Commemorates the anniversary of the reunification of the southern part of Bulgaria with the rest of the country in 1885.

CHADDS FORD DAYS. Sept 6–7. Chadds Ford, PA. Open-air Brandywine celebration with 18th-century craft demonstrations, Brandywine Valley art, live music, kids korner, colonial and contemporary crafts for sale, Colonial Tavern with beverages and food by local restaurants. Est attendance: 8,000. For info: Chadds Ford Historical Society, 1736 Creek Rd, Chadds Ford, PA 19317. Phone: (610) 388-7376. Fax: (610) 388-7480. E-mail: info@chaddsfordhistory.org. Web: www.chaddsfordhistory.org.

September 2014

S	M	T	W	T	F	S
	1	2	3	4	5	6
7	8	9	10	11	12	13
14	15	16	17	18	19	20
21	22	23	24	25	26	27
28	29	30				

CLASSIC BOAT SHOW. Sept 6–7. Tuckerton, NJ. Join the Tuckerton Seaport and the Philadelphia Chapter of the Antique and Classic Boat Society for two splendid days of classic wood and glass boat exhibitors, demonstrations and entertainment. Watch the parent/child boat-building contest or take a cruise up Tuckerton Creek. The Classic Boat Show is fun for the whole family. Est attendance: 2,500. For info: Renee Kennedy, Tuckerton Seaport, 120 W Main St, PO Box 52, Tuckerton, NJ 08087. Phone: (609) 296-8868. Fax: (609) 296-5810. E-mail: info@tuckertonseaport.org. Web: www.tuckertonseaport.org.

DALTON, JOHN: BIRTH ANNIVERSARY. Sept 6, 1766. English chemist, physicist, teacher and developer of atomic theory, was born at Eaglesfield, near Cockermouth, England. Dalton died at Manchester, England, July 27, 1844.

FIRST RADIO BROADCAST OF A PRIZEFIGHT: ANNIVERSARY. Sept 6, 1920. In the first boxing match broadcast on radio, Jack Dempsey knocked out Billy Miske in the third round of a scheduled 10-round fight.

KENNEDY, JOSEPH P.: BIRTH ANNIVERSARY. Sept 6, 1888. Prominent businessman, government official and patriarch of the Kennedy dynasty born at Boston, MA. Harvard educated, Kennedy worked as a bank president, movie producer and shipbuilder before retiring as a multimillionaire in 1929. He was the first chairman of both the Security and Exchange Commission (1934–35) and the US Maritime Commission (1937); his appointment as first Irish-American US ambassador to the United Kingdom marked the pinnacle of his governmental career. Kennedy was instrumental in the advancement of his sons' political careers. He died at his home at Hyannis Port, MA, on Nov 18, 1969.

LAFAYETTE, MARQUIS DE: BIRTH ANNIVERSARY. Sept 6, 1757. The French general and aristocrat, whose full name was Marie-Joseph-Paul-Yves-Roch-Gilbert du Motier, came to America to assist in the revolutionary cause. Lafayette, who had convinced Louis XVI to send 6,000 French soldiers to assist the Americans, was given command of an army at Virginia and was instrumental in forcing the surrender of Lord Cornwallis at Yorktown. He was called "The Hero of Two Worlds" and was appointed a brigadier general on his return to France in 1782. He became a leader of the liberal aristocrats during the early days of the French revolution. As the commander of the newly formed national guard of Paris, he rescued Louis XVI and Marie-Antoinette from a crowd that stormed Versailles Oct 6, 1789. His popularity waned after his guards opened fire on angry demonstrators demanding abdication of the king in 1791. He fled to Austria with the overthrow of the monarchy in 1792, returning when Napoleon Bonaparte came to power. Born at Chavaniac, he died at Paris, May 20, 1834.

LITTLE FALLS ARTS AND CRAFTS FAIR. Sept 6–7. Little Falls, MN. 600 artists, craftspeople and hobbyists displaying and selling their items. Est attendance: 120,000. For info: Chamber of Commerce, 200 NW First St, Little Falls, MN 56345. Phone: (320) 632-5155. Fax: (320) 632-2122. E-mail: artsandcrafts@littlefallsmnchamber.com. Web: www.littlefallsmnchamber.com.

MUHLENBERG, HENRY MELCHIOR: BIRTH ANNIVERSARY. Sept 6, 1711. Born at Einbeck, Hanover, Germany, Muhlenberg was a Lutheran pastor who immigrated to the US in 1742 to help the nascent Lutheran congregations that needed experienced clergy. Beginning in Pennsylvania and working throughout the eastern seaboard, he organized churches and then convened the first Lutheran synod in the US in 1761. He is thus considered the founder of the US Lutheran church. Muhlenberg died on Oct 7, 1787, at Trappe, PA.

NANTICOKE INDIAN POWWOW. Sept 6–7. Millsboro, DE. Annual gathering of Native Americans during which Native American dances, music and storytelling are presented and Native American foods and arts and crafts are sold. Forty different tribes participate. Dance sessions: Saturday, noon–5 PM, Sunday, 2–5 PM. Sunday worship service, 10 AM. Annually, the weekend after Labor Day. Est attendance: 40,000. For info: Nanticoke Indian Assn, 27073 John J. William Hwy, Millsboro, DE 19966. Phone: (302) 945-3400. E-mail: nanticoke@verizon.net.

PAKISTAN: DEFENSE OF PAKISTAN DAY. Sept 6. National holiday. Commemorates the Indo-Pakistan War of 1965.

ROSE, BILLY: BIRTH ANNIVERSARY. Sept 6, 1899. The American theatrical producer, author, songwriter and husband of Fanny Brice was born William S. Rosenberg at New York, NY. His songs include "That Old Gang of Mine," "Me and My Shadow," "Without a Song," "It's Only a Paper Moon" and hundreds of others. Rose died at Montego Bay, Jamaica, Feb 10, 1966.

SAINT PETERSBURG NAME RESTORED: ANNIVERSARY. Sept 6, 1991. Russian legislators voted to restore the name Saint Petersburg to the nation's second-largest city. The city had been known as Leningrad for 67 years in honor of the Soviet Union's founder, Vladimir I. Lenin. The city, founded in 1703 by Peter the Great, had three names in the 20th century with Russian leaders changing its German-sounding name to Petrograd at the beginning of WWI in 1914 and Soviet Communist leaders changing its name to Leningrad in 1924 following their leader's death.

SCOTLAND: BRAEMAR ROYAL HIGHLAND GATHERING. Sept 6. Princess Royal and Duke of Fife Memorial Park, Braemar, Grampian. Kilted clansmen from all over the world gather. Traditional activities including tossing cabers, dancing and playing bagpipes. Est attendance: 18,000. For info: Mr W.A. Meston, Secretary, Coilacriech, Ballater, Aberdeenshire, Scotland AB35 5UH. Phone: (44) (1339) 755-377. E-mail: info@braemargathering.org.

SODBUSTER DAYS—THE HARVEST. Sept 6–7. Sunne Farm, Fort Ransom State Park, Fort Ransom, ND. Demonstrations of life on a small family farm of the 1920s during the fall harvest. Activities include threshing, fall fieldwork, gathering prairie hay, ladies' demonstrations, kids' games, food, music. Most farm machinery is horse drawn. Annually, the weekend after Labor Day. Located along the Sheyenne River Valley National Scenic Byway. Est attendance: 2,000. For info: Fort Ransom State Park, 5981 Walt Hjelle Pkwy, Fort Ransom, ND 58033-9712. Phone: (701) 973-4331. Fax: (701) 973-4151. E-mail: frsp@nd.gov. Web: www.parkrec.nd.gov.

SOUTHEAST MISSOURI DISTRICT FAIR. Sept 6–13. Arena Park Fairgrounds, Cape Girardeau, MO. Oldest outdoor fair in the state. Celebrating its 159th year with beauty pageants, livestock exhibition, horse show, entertainment, carnival, food and 4-H and FFA displays. Annually, starts the Saturday after Labor Day and continues to the next Saturday. Est attendance: 100,000. For info: SEMO District Fair Assn, 410 Kiwanis Dr, Ste 200, Cape Girardeau, MO 63701. Phone: (800) 455-FAIR or (573) 334-9250. E-mail: info@semofair.com. Web: www.semofair.com.

SWAZILAND: INDEPENDENCE DAY. Sept 6. National holiday. Commemorates attainment of independence from Britain in 1968. Also called Somhlolo Day in honor of the great 19th-century Swazi leader.

UNITED NATIONS: MILLENNIUM SUMMIT: ANNIVERSARY. Sept 6–8, 2000. More than 150 world leaders met at the United Nations in New York City, the largest gathering of such leaders in history. Among the kings, prime ministers, presidents and generals attending were US President Bill Clinton, Fidel Castro and Yasser Arafat. These leaders adopted a declaration that committed them to promote democracy, strengthen respect for human rights, reverse the spread of AIDS, cut poverty, protect the planet and improve the ability of the UN to keep the peace.

US MID-AMATEUR (GOLF) CHAMPIONSHIP. Sept 6–11. Saucon Valley Country Club, Bethlehem, PA. For info: USGA, Golf House, Championship Dept, PO Box 708, Far Hills, NJ 07931. Phone: (908) 234-2300. Fax: (908) 234-9687. Web: www.usga.org.

US WOMEN'S MID-AMATEUR (GOLF) CHAMPIONSHIP. Sept 6–11. Harbour Trees Golf Club, Noblesville, IN. For info: USGA, Golf House, Championship Dept, PO Box 708, Far Hills, NJ 07931. Phone: (908) 234-2300. E-mail: usga@usga.org. Web: www.usga.org.

VALPARAISO POPCORN FESTIVAL. Sept 6. Valparaiso, IN. 36th annual. Celebration of popcorn with a parade, the Popcorn Panic and Little Kernel Puff running races, arts, crafts, food booths, music and entertainment, kids' inflatables area and a hot-air balloon show. Annually, the first Saturday after Labor Day. Est attendance: 65,000. For info: Valparaiso Community Festivals and Events, 162 W Lincolnway, Valparaiso, IN 46383. Phone: (219) 464-8332. Fax: (219) 464-2343. E-mail: info@valparaisoevents.com. Web: www.valparaisoevents.com.

"WYATT EARP" TV PREMIERE: ANNIVERSARY. Sept 6, 1955. Officially titled "The Life and Legend of Wyatt Earp," this half-hour series marked the beginning of the trend toward "adult westerns." It was loosely based on fact, with Hugh O'Brian as Earp, marshall of Dodge City, KS, and later of Tombstone, AZ.

BIRTHDAYS TODAY

Chris Christie, 52, Governor of New Jersey (R), born Newark, NJ, Sept 6, 1962.

Jane Curtin, 67, actress ("Saturday Night Live," "3rd Rock from the Sun"), comedienne, born Cambridge, MA, Sept 6, 1947.

Jennifer Egan, 52, journalist, author (*A Visit from the Goon Squad*), born Chicago, IL, Sept 6, 1962.

Jeff Foxworthy, 56, comedian, actor ("The Jeff Foxworthy Show"), author (*No Shirt, No Shoes . . . No Problem*), born Atlanta, GA, Sept 6, 1958.

Tim Henman, 40, tennis player, born Oxford, England, Sept 6, 1974.

Swoosie Kurtz, 70, actress ("Sisters," *The World According to Garp*; Tony for *The House of Blue Leaves*), born Omaha, NE, Sept 6, 1944.

Rosie Perez, 50, actress (*King of the Jungle, White Men Can't Jump*), born Brooklyn, NY, Sept 6, 1964.

Sarah Strange, 40, actress ("Men in Trees," "Da Vinci's Inquest"), born Vancouver, BC, Canada, Sept 6, 1974.

Elizabeth Vargas, 52, television journalist, born Paterson, NJ, Sept 6, 1962.

Justin Whalin, 40, actor ("Charles in Charge," "Lois & Clark"), born San Francisco, CA, Sept 6, 1974.

Jo Anne Worley, 77, comedienne, actress ("Rowan & Martin's Laugh-In"), born Lowell, IA, Sept 6, 1937.

September 2014

S	M	T	W	T	F	S
	1	2	3	4	5	6
7	8	9	10	11	12	13
14	15	16	17	18	19	20
21	22	23	24	25	26	27
28	29	30				

September 7 — Sunday

DAY 250 **115 REMAINING**

ART IN THE GARDEN. Sept 7. Washington, PA. A unique blend of art, music and nature. Featuring more than 50 renowned artists working in all mediums. Annually, the Sunday after Labor Day. Est attendance: 600. For info: Washington County Historical Society, 49 E Maiden St, Washington, PA 15301. Phone: (724) 225-6740. Fax: (724) 225-8495. E-mail: wchspa@verizon.net. Web: www.wchspa.org.

BRAZIL: INDEPENDENCE DAY. Sept 7. Declared independence from Portugal in 1822. National holiday.

CORBETT-SULLIVAN PRIZEFIGHT: ANNIVERSARY. Sept 7, 1892. John L. Sullivan was knocked out by James J. Corbett in the 21st round of a prizefight at New Orleans, LA. It was the first major fight under the Marquess of Queensberry Rules.

DEBAKEY, MICHAEL E.: BIRTH ANNIVERSARY. Sept 7, 1908. Heart and vascular surgery pioneer, medical ambassador and inventor, born in Lake Charles, LA. DeBakey invented the roller pump, which helped make open-heart surgery a possibility, and he made the first connection between smoking and cancer. Performed more than 60,000 operations, and cited by the *American Journal of Medicine* as perhaps "the greatest surgeon ever." DeBakey died July 11, 2008, at Houston, TX.

"THE FLYING NUN" TV PREMIERE: ANNIVERSARY. Sept 7, 1967. This sitcom, about a nun at a convent in Puerto Rico who discovers that she can fly, starred Sally Field as Elsie Ethrington (Sister Bertrille) and featured Madeleine Sherwood, Marge Redmond, Shelley Morrison, Alejandro Rey and Vito Scotti.

GOOGLE FOUNDED: ANNIVERSARY. Sept 7, 1998. Sergey Brin and Larry Page incorporated the Internet search engine company Google on this date at Menlo Park, CA. Although still in beta, Google.com was receiving 10,000 queries a day at that time. Within a year, the company was doing 3 million searches a day. Before long, *Google* entered the pop culture zeitgeist by becoming a verb meaning "Internet searching."

GRANDMA MOSES DAY. Sept 7. Anna Mary Robertson Moses, modern primitive American painter born at Greenwich, NY, Sept 7, 1860. Started painting at the age of 78. Her 100th birthday was proclaimed Grandma Moses Day in New York state. Died at Hoosick Falls, NY, Dec 13, 1961.

HOLLY, BUDDY: BIRTH ANNIVERSARY. Sept 7, 1936. American music performer, composer and bandleader. Called one of the most innovative and influential musicians of his time, he was a pioneer of rock 'n' roll. His hits include "That'll Be the Day" and "Peggy Sue." Born Charles Harden Holley, at Lubbock, TX, he died at age 22 in an airplane crash near Mason City, IA, Feb 3, 1959.

ITALY: HISTORICAL REGATTA. Sept 7. Venice. Traditional competition among two-oar racing gondolas, preceded by a procession of Venetian ceremonial boats of the epoch of the Venetian Republic. Annually, the first Sunday in September.

ITALY: JOUST OF THE SARACEN. Sept 7. Arezzo. The first Sunday in September is set aside for the Giostra del Saracino, a tilting contest of the 13th century, with knights in armor.

KAZAN, ELIA: BIRTH ANNIVERSARY. Sept 7, 1909. Born Elia Kazanjoglou at Constantinople, Turkey, Elia Kazan was one of the most influential directors in the history of American stage and film. He directed the Broadway premieres of Arthur Miller's *Death of a Salesman* and Tennessee Williams's *A Streetcar Named Desire* as well as many other Williams plays. He won directing Oscars for the films *On the Waterfront* and *Gentleman's Agreement*. He discovered and promoted actors such as Marlon Brando, Warren Beatty and James Dean, whom he directed in *East of Eden*. In 1952 he angered much of Hollywood by testifying before the House Un-American Activities Committee, naming persons he thought to be members of the Communist Party. Kazan died at New York, NY, Sept 7, 2003.

LAWRENCE, JACOB: BIRTH ANNIVERSARY. Sept 7, 1917. African-American painter, born at Atlantic City, NJ. Lawrence was best known for his series of historical paintings on John Brown and on the migration of African Americans out of the South. A recipient of the NAACP's Spingarn Medal, he won many other awards during his lifetime. Lawrence died June 9, 2000, at Seattle, WA.

NATIONAL ASSISTED LIVING WEEK. Sept 7–13. A weeklong observance designed to raise awareness of the role assisted living plays in serving the nation's elderly. Planning guide available in June. Annually, Grandparents' Day through the following Saturday. For info: Natl Center for Assisted Living, 1201 L St NW, Washington, DC 20005. Phone: (202) 842-4444. Fax: (202) 842-3860. Web: www.ncal.org.

NATIONAL GRANDPARENTS' DAY. Sept 7. To honor grandparents, to give grandparents an opportunity to show love for their children's children and to help children become aware of the strength, information and guidance older people can offer. Annually, the first Sunday after Labor Day.

NATIONAL SUICIDE PREVENTION WEEK. Sept 7–13. 40th annual. Annually, the week that includes World Suicide Prevention Day on Sept 10. For info: American Assn of Suicidology, 5221 Wisconsin Ave NW, 2nd Fl, Washington, DC 20015. Phone: (202) 237-2280. Fax: (202) 237-2282. E-mail: info@suicidology.org. Web: www.suicidology.org.

"NEITHER SNOW NOR RAIN" DAY: 100th ANNIVERSARY. Sept 7, 1914. Anniversary of the opening to the public on Labor Day 1914 of the New York Post Office Building at Eighth Avenue between 31st and 33rd Streets. On the front of this building was an inscription supplied by William M. Kendall of the architectural firm that planned the building. The inscription, a free translation from Herodotus, reads: "Neither snow nor rain nor heat nor gloom of night stays these couriers from the swift completion of their appointed rounds." This has long been believed to be the motto of the US Post Office and Postal Service. They have, in fact, no motto—but the legend remains.

NORTHEAST MISSOURI TRIATHLON. Sept 7. Thousand Hills State Park, Kirksville, MO. Swim ¾ mile, bike 18 miles, run 5 miles. USA Triathlon sanctioned. Qualifier for International Course Nationals. Annually, the Sunday after Labor Day. Est attendance: 350. For info: ATSU-TCC, 210 S Osteopathy, Kirksville, MO 63501. Phone: (660) 626-2213. Fax: (660) 626-2071. E-mail: lcrossgrove@atsu.edu. Web: www.nemotriathlon.org.

PRO FOOTBALL HALL OF FAME CHARTER MEMBERS: ANNIVERSARY. Sept 7, 1963. The Pro Football Hall of Fame opened this day in Canton, OH, with the induction of 17 charter members: 11 players and six executives. The players selected were Sammy Baugh, Dutch Clark, Red Grange, Mel Hein, Pete Henry, Cal Hubbard, Don Hutson, Johnny McNally, Bronko Nagurski, Ernie Nevers and Jim Thorpe. They were joined by Bert Bell, Joe Carr, George Halas, Curly Lambeau, Tim Mara and George Preston Marshall.

QUEEN ELIZABETH I: BIRTH ANNIVERSARY. Sept 7, 1533. Queen of England, daughter of Henry VIII and Anne Boleyn, after whom the Elizabethan era was named, was born at Greenwich Palace. She ascended the throne in 1558 at the age of 25. During her reign, the British defeated the Spanish Armada in July 1588, the Anglican Church was essentially established and England became a world power. She died at Richmond, England, Mar 24, 1603.

SUBSTITUTE TEACHER APPRECIATION WEEK. Sept 7–12. Although substitute teachers get no sick days or respect, they teach when the regular teacher cannot and continually adjust to different classroom situations. For info: Dorothy Zjawin, 61 W Colfax Ave, Roselle Park, NJ 07204.

"TRUTH OR CONSEQUENCES" TV PREMIERE: ANNIVERSARY. Sept 7, 1950. This game show lasted for many years on both radio and TV. The half-hour show was based on a parlor game: contestants who failed to answer a question before the buzzer (nicknamed Beulah) went off had to perform stunts (i.e., pay the consequences). Ralph Edwards created and hosted the show until 1954, then it became a prime-time show hosted by Jack Bailey. Bob Barker succeeded him in 1966 and hosted it through its syndicated run. In 1977 the show was revived as "The New Truth or Consequences" with Bob Hilton as host.

VAN ALLEN, JAMES: 100th BIRTH ANNIVERSARY. Sept 7, 1914. Physicist born at Mt. Pleasant, IA, Van Allen studied Earth's magnetic field; cosmic rays; and Earth's radiation belts, now named the Van Allen belts. The position of these belts are now taken into consideration when planning spaceflights in order to plot courses that take spacecrafts through the weakest part of the radiation zones. Awarded the National Medal of Science in 1987, Van Allen died Aug 9, 2006, at Iowa City, IA.

BIRTHDAYS TODAY

Corbin Bernsen, 60, actor ("LA Law," "Ryan's Hope," *Major League*), born North Hollywood, CA, Sept 7, 1954.

Susan Blakely, 64, actress (*The Way We Were, The Lords of Flatbush, Shampoo*), born Frankfurt, Germany, Sept 7, 1950.

Michael Emerson, 60, actor ("Person of Interest," "Lost"), born Cedar Rapids, IA, Sept 7, 1954.

Michael Feinstein, 58, singer, pianist, born Columbus, OH, Sept 7, 1956.

Angela Gheorghiu, 49, opera singer, born Angela Burlacu at Adjud, Romania, Sept 7, 1965.

Chrissie Hynde, 63, singer, songwriter (Pretenders), born Akron, OH, Sept 7, 1951.

Julie Kavner, 63, actress (*Radio Days*, "Rhoda," Marge Simpson's voice on "The Simpsons"), born Los Angeles, CA, Sept 7, 1951.

Devon Sawa, 36, actor ("Nikita," *Final Destination, Wild America*), born Vancouver, BC, Canada, Sept 7, 1978.

Briana Scurry, 43, former soccer player, born Minneapolis, MN, Sept 7, 1971.

Evan Rachel Wood, 27, actress (*Thirteen, The Upside of Anger, Across the Universe*, "True Blood"), born Raleigh, NC, Sept 7, 1987.

Vera Zvonareva, 30, tennis player, born Moscow, Russia, Sept 7, 1984.

September 8 — Monday

DAY 251 **114 REMAINING**

AMERICA'S LARGEST RV SHOW. Sept 8–14. Hersheypark® Entertainment Complex, Hershey, PA. 46th annual. America's largest RV show, with more than 1,200 RVs on display. Sept 8–9 are for the trade only; show is open to the public Sept 10–14. Est attendance: 43,000. For info: PRVCA, 4000 Trindle Rd, Camp Hill, PA 17011. Phone: (888) 303-2887. Fax: (717) 303-0297. E-mail: rvcamping@prvca.org. Web: www.largestrvshow.com.

ANDORRA: NATIONAL HOLIDAY. Sept 8. Honors our Lady of Meritxell.

CHINA: MOON FESTIVAL (OR MID-AUTUMN FESTIVAL). Sept 8. According to folk legend this day is the birthday of the earth god T'u-ti Kung. The festival indicates that the year's hard work in the fields will soon end with the harvest. People express gratitude to heaven as represented by the moon and to the earth as symbolized by the earth god for all good things from the preceding year. Special harvest foods are eaten, especially "moon cakes." Observed on the 15th day of the eighth month of the Chinese lunar calendar, this festival is called by different names in different places but is widely recognized throughout the Far East, including Taiwan, Korea, Singapore and Hong Kong. Date here is for China; date in other countries will differ.

CLINE, PATSY: BIRTH ANNIVERSARY. Sept 8, 1932. Country and western singer, born Virginia Patterson Hensley at Winchester,

VA. Patsy Cline got her big break in 1957 when she won an Arthur Godfrey Talent Scout show, singing "Walking After Midnight." Her career took off, and she became a featured singer at the Grand Ole Opry, attaining the rank of top female country singer. She died in a plane crash Mar 5, 1963, at Camden, TN, along with singers Hawkshaw Hawkins and Cowboy Copas.

GALVESTON HURRICANE: ANNIVERSARY. Sept 8, 1900. The worst national disaster in US history in terms of lives lost. More than 6,000 people were killed when a hurricane struck Galveston, TX, with winds of more than 120 mph, followed by a huge tidal wave. More than 2,500 buildings were destroyed.

HARVEST MOON. Sept 8. So called because the full moon nearest the autumnal equinox extends the hours of light into the evening and helps the harvester with the long day's work.

HUEY P. LONG SHOT: ANNIVERSARY. Sept 8, 1935. Powerful US senator Huey P. Long was shot on this date at Baton Rouge, LA. The assassin was allegedly Carl Weiss, a political enemy who confronted Long and his bodyguards at the Louisiana State Capitol. The guards opened fire and Weiss was immediately killed. Long was wounded, either by Weiss or by a ricocheting bullet, and died two days later on Sept 10. See also: "Long, Huey Pierce: Birth Anniversary" (Aug 30).

KOREA: CHUSOK. Sept 8. Gala celebration by Koreans everywhere. Autumn harvest thanksgiving moon festival. Observed on 15th day of eighth lunar month (eighth full moon of lunar calendar) each year. Koreans pay homage to ancestors and express gratitude to guarding spirits for another year of rich crops. A time to visit tombs, leave food and prepare for the coming winter season. Traditional food is the "moon cake," made on the eve of Chusok, with rice, chestnuts and jujube fruits. Games, dancing and gift exchanges. Observed since Silla Dynasty (beginning of First Millennium).

MACEDONIA: INDEPENDENCE DAY. Sept 8. National holiday. Commemorates independence from the Yugoslav Union in 1991.

MALTA: SIEGE BROKEN: ANNIVERSARY. Sept 8. "Two Sieges and Regatta Day" festivities now commemorate victory over the Turks, Sept 8, 1565, when the siege that began in May 1565 was broken by the Maltese and the Knights of St. John after a loss of nearly 10,000 lives. Also commemorated is survival of the 1943 siege by the Axis Powers. Parades, fireworks, boat races, etc, especially at the capital, Valleta, and the Grand Harbour.

McGWIRE BREAKS HOME RUN RECORD: ANNIVERSARY. Sept 8, 1998. Mark McGwire of the St. Louis Cardinals hit his 62nd home run, breaking Roger Maris's 1961 record for the most home runs in a single season. McGwire hit his homer at Busch Stadium at St. Louis against pitcher Steve Trachsel of the Chicago Cubs as the Cardinals won, 6–3. McGwire finished the season with 70 home runs. On Oct 5, 2001, Barry Bonds hit his 71st home run, breaking McGwire's record. Bonds finished the season with 73 homers.

MISS AMERICA FIRST CROWNED: ANNIVERSARY. Sept 8, 1921. Margaret Gorman of Washington, DC, was crowned the first Miss America at the end of a two-day pageant at Atlantic City, NJ.

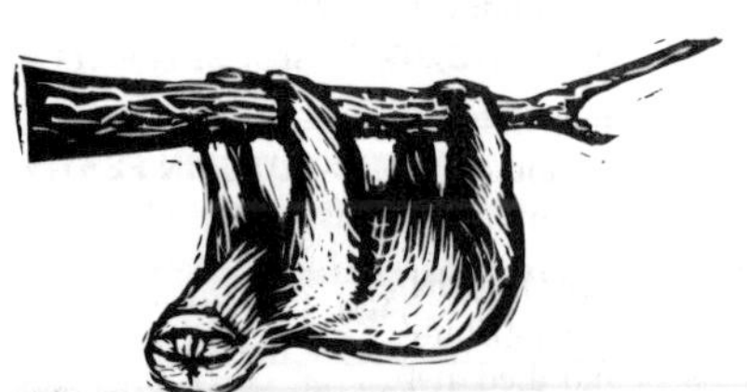

September 2014

S	M	T	W	T	F	S
	1	2	3	4	5	6
7	8	9	10	11	12	13
14	15	16	17	18	19	20
21	22	23	24	25	26	27
28	29	30				

MISSION SAN GABRIEL ARCHANGEL: FOUNDING ANNIVERSARY. Sept 8, 1771. California mission to the Indians founded on this date.

MOON PHASE: FULL MOON. Sept 8. Moon enters Full Moon phase at 9:38 PM, EDT.

NATIONAL BOSS/EMPLOYEE EXCHANGE DAY. Sept 8. To help bosses and employees appreciate each other by sharing each other's point of view for a day. Annually, the first Monday after Labor Day. For info: A.C. Vierow, Box 71, Clio, MI 48420-0071.

NATIONAL LINE DANCE WEEK. Sept 8–13. A week to celebrate the line dance! Line dance is a great way to exercise and to meet people. Annually, the second Monday in September through the following Saturday. For info: Shirley Mitchell, 19769 Murray Hill, Detroit, MI 48235. Phone: (313) 272-7618. E-mail: smitc87213@aol.com.

NIXON PARDONED: 40th ANNIVERSARY. Sept 8, 1974. Anniversary of the "full, free, and absolute pardon unto Richard Nixon, for all offenses against the United States which he, Richard Nixon, has committed or may have committed or taken part in during the period from January 20, 1969, through August 9, 1974." (Presidential Proclamation 4311, Sept 8, 1974, by Gerald R. Ford.)

NORTHERN PACIFIC RAILROAD COMPLETED: ANNIVERSARY. Sept 8, 1883. After 19 years of construction, the Northern Pacific Railroad became the second railroad to link the two coasts. The Union Pacific and Central Pacific lines met at Utah in 1869.

"THE OPRAH WINFREY SHOW" TV PREMIERE: ANNIVERSARY. Sept 8, 1986. This daytime talk show was the top-rated talk show for years and also has the distinction of being the first talk show hosted by an African-American woman, Oprah Winfrey. Her show was taped in front of a studio audience who were solicited for their questions and feedback. In the mid-1990s, fed up with the plethora of trashy talk shows that had sprung up everywhere, Winfrey decided to upgrade the quality of topics that her show presented. Her book club feature was a popular element of her show, and chosen books usually become bestsellers. The show finished its run on May 25, 2011.

PEDIATRIC HEMATOLOGY/ONCOLOGY NURSES DAY. Sept 8. Recognizes those nurses who care for the day-to-day needs of children with cancer and blood disorders, guiding families through the most difficult circumstances anyone can experience. For info: Elizabeth Sherman, Assn of Pediatric Hemotology/Oncology Nurses, PO Box 31756, Chicago, IL 60631. Phone: (855) 202-9760. E-mail: esherman@connect2amc.com. Web: www.aphon.org.

PEDDLER'S VILLAGE SCARECROW COMPETITION AND DISPLAY. Sept 8–Oct 26. Peddler's Village, Lahaska, PA. Contestants compete for $4,900 in cash prizes. Categories include: "A Traditional Scarecrow/Whirligig": a scarecrow that makes noise and moves with the wind, "An Extraordinary Contemporary Scarecrow": an imaginative piece created to give a good scare in the garden, Quite the Character, Keystone Krow, Group and Kids Only! Free registration. Est attendance: 650,000. For info: Peddler's Village, Routes 202 and 263, Lahaska, PA 18931. Phone: (215) 794-4000. Fax: (215) 794-4001. E-mail: info@peddlersvillage.com. Web: www.peddlersvillage.com.

PEPPER, CLAUDE DENSON: BIRTH ANNIVERSARY. Sept 8, 1900. US representative and senator, born near Dudleyville, AL. Pepper's career in politics spanned 53 years and 10 presidents, and he became the champion for America's senior citizens. He was elected to the US Senate in 1936, where he was a principal architect of many of the nation's "safety net" social programs including Social Security, the minimum wage and medical assistance for the elderly and for handicapped children. After a 14-year career in the Senate, he returned to Congress in the House of Representatives, where he served 14 terms. He served as chairman of the House Select Committee on Aging, drafted legislation banning forced retirement and fought against cutting Social Security benefits. Pepper died at Washington, DC, May 30, 1989.

SELLERS, PETER: BIRTH ANNIVERSARY. Sept 8, 1925. Award-winning British comedian and film star, born Richard Henry Sellers at Southsea, Hampshire, England. Sellers is remembered for his multiple roles in *Dr. Strangelove*, his Oscar-nominated role as Chance the Gardener in *Being There* and his role as the bumbling Inspector Clouseau in the Pink Panther films. Died at London, England, July 24, 1980.

"STAR TREK" TV PREMIERE: ANNIVERSARY. Sept 8, 1966. The first of 79 episodes of the TV series "Star Trek" was aired on the NBC network. Although the science fiction show set in the future only lasted a few seasons, it has remained enormously popular through syndication reruns. It has been given new life through many motion pictures, a cartoon TV series and popular spin-off TV series such as "Star Trek: The Next Generation," "Enterprise" and others. It has consistently ranked among the biggest titles in the motion picture, television, home video and licensing divisions of Paramount Pictures.

"TARZAN" TV PREMIERE: ANNIVERSARY. Sept 8, 1966. This hour adventure series was based on Edgar Rice Burroughs's character, who appeared for the first time on TV. Tarzan, an English lord who preferred the jungle, was played by Ron Ely. Manuel Padilla, Jr, was Jai, a jungle orphan; Alan Caillou was Jason Flood, Jai's tutor; and Rockne Tarkington was Rao, a veterinarian. There was no Jane.

"THAT GIRL" TV PREMIERE: ANNIVERSARY. Sept 8, 1966. "That Girl" was a half-hour sitcom starring Marlo Thomas as Ann Marie, an independent aspiring actress in New York City. Ted Bessell also starred as her boyfriend, Don Hollinger. They were finally engaged in 1970. Also featured were Lew Parker, Rosemary De Camp and Bonnie Scott. Well-known performers who appeared on the show include Dabney Coleman, George Carlin and Bernie Kopell.

UNITED NATIONS: INTERNATIONAL LITERACY DAY. Sept 8. An international day observed by the organizations of the United Nations system. For info: United Nations, Dept of Public Info, New York, NY 10017. Web: www.un.org.

BIRTHDAYS TODAY

David Arquette, 43, actor (*Scream, Muppets from Space*), born Winchester, VA, Sept 8, 1971.

Sid Caesar, 92, comedian, actor ("Your Show of Shows"), born Yonkers, NY, Sept 8, 1922.

Alan Feinstein, 73, actor ("The Edge of Night," "Love of Life," "Search for Tomorrow"), born New York, NY, Sept 8, 1941.

Martin Freeman, 43, actor ("Sherlock," *The Hobbit: An Unexpected Journey*, "The Office" [UK]), born Aldershot, Hampshire, England, Sept 8, 1971.

Pink, 35, singer, born Alecia Moore at Doylestown, PA, Sept 8, 1979.

Bernie Sanders, 73, US Senator (I, Vermont), born Brooklyn, NY, Sept 8, 1941.

Henry Thomas, 43, actor (*All the Pretty Horses, E.T. The Extra-Terrestrial*), born San Antonio, TX, Sept 8, 1971.

Jonathan Taylor Thomas, 33, actor ("Home Improvement"), born Bethlehem, PA, Sept 8, 1981.

Rogatien (Rogie) Vachon, 69, former hockey executive and player, born Palmarolle, QC, Canada, Sept 8, 1945.

September 9 — Tuesday

DAY 252 — **113 REMAINING**

BATTLE OF MARATHON: ANNIVERSARY. Sept 9. On the day of the ninth month's full moon in the year 490 BC, the numerically superior invading army of Persia was met and defeated on the Plain of Marathon by the Athenian army, led by Miltiades. More than 6,000 men died in the day's battle, which drove the Persians to the sea. The mound of earth covering the dead is still visible at the site. This date is in dispute. See also: "Historic Marathon Runs: Anniversary" (Sept 2) for the legendary running of Phidippides and the origin of the marathon race.

BATTLE OF SALERNO: ANNIVERSARY. Sept 9–16, 1943. US General Mark Clark's Fifth Army made an amphibious assault on Salerno, Italy (Operation Avalanche), at 3:30 AM. The British 1st Airborne Division seized the southern Italian port of Taranto (Operation Slapstick) without opposition. Initial gains along the western coast of Italy were checked by strong German forces by Sept 12. In some places the Allied forces were pushed back to within two miles of the coast. On Sept 15, the US 82nd Airborne and British 7th Armoured counterattacked, and on Sept 16 units of the American 5th Army and the British 8th Army joined up near Vallo di Lucania.

BONZA BOTTLER DAY™. Sept 9. To celebrate when the number of the day is the same as the number of the month. Bonza Bottler Day™ is an excuse to have a party at least once per month. For more information see Jan 1. For info: Gail Berger, 14 Fernwood Dr, Taylors, SC 29687. Phone: (864) 201-3988. E-mail: bonza@bonzabottlerday.com. Web: www.bonzabottlerday.com.

CALIFORNIA: ADMISSION DAY: ANNIVERSARY. Sept 9. Became the 31st state in 1850.

"FAT ALBERT AND THE COSBY KIDS" TV PREMIERE: ANNIVERSARY. Sept 9, 1972. This cartoon series was hosted by Bill Cosby, with characters based on his childhood friends at Philadelphia. Its central characters—Fat Albert, Weird Harold, Mush Mouth and Donald—were weird-looking but very human. The show sent messages of tolerance and harmony. In 1979 the show was renamed "The New Fat Albert Show."

HUSKER HARVEST DAYS. Sept 9–11. Grand Island, NE. The largest irrigated working agricultural show on a permanent site in the United States. 80 acres of exhibits, 700 acres of field demonstrations and more. Annually, the Tuesday–Thursday of the second full week of September. Est attendance: 50,000. For info: Renee Seifert, Grand Island/Hall County CVB, 2424 S Locust St, Ste C, Grand Island, NE 68801. Phone: (308) 382-4400. Fax: (308) 382-4908. E-mail: info@visitgrandisland.com. Web: www.huskerharvestdays.com.

JAPAN: CHRYSANTHEMUM DAY. Sept 9. Traditional chrysanthemum festival.

KOREA, DEMOCRATIC PEOPLE'S REPUBLIC OF: NATIONAL DAY. Sept 9. National holiday in the Democratic People's Republic of [North] Korea.

LUXEMBOURG: LIBERATION CEREMONY. Sept 9. Petange. Commemoration of liberation of Grand-Duchy by the Allied forces in 1944. Ceremony at monument of the American soldier.

MAO TSE-TUNG: DEATH ANNIVERSARY. Sept 9, 1976. People's Republic of China pays tribute to memory of the Chinese revolutionary leader, who died at Beijing. Memorial Hall, where his flag-draped body lies encased in crystal, was opened at Tiananmen Square at Beijing on the first anniversary of his death. Mao was born Dec 26, 1893, at Hunan Province, China.

"RHODA" TV PREMIERE: 40th ANNIVERSARY. Sept 9, 1974. This spin-off from "The Mary Tyler Moore Show" starred Valerie Harper as Rhoda Morgenstern, who returns to New York, finds a job and gets married (she also gets separated and divorced). The last episode aired in 1978.

SANDERS, COLONEL HARLAND DAVID: BIRTH ANNIVERSARY. Sept 9, 1890. Founder of Kentucky Fried Chicken, born near Henryville, IN. Died Dec 16, 1980, at Shelbyville, KY.

TAJIKISTAN: INDEPENDENCE DAY. Sept 9. National holiday commemorating independence from the Soviet Union in 1991.

TOLSTOY, LEO: BIRTH ANNIVERSARY. Sept 9, 1828. Russian novelist and moral philosopher, born at Tula Province, Russia. Best known for his novels (*War and Peace, Anna Karenina*), Tolstoy also wrote short stories, plays and essays. A member of the nobility, in his moral and religious writings he condemned private property and championed nonviolent protest. Died Nov 20, 1910, at Astapovo, Russia.

"WELCOME BACK, KOTTER" TV PREMIERE: ANNIVERSARY. Sept 9, 1975. In this half-hour sitcom, Gabe Kotter (Gabe Kaplan) returned to James Buchanan High School, his alma mater, to teach the "sweathogs," a group of hopeless underachievers. Other cast members included Marcia Strassman, John Travolta, Robert Hegyes, Ron Palillo, Lawrence Hilton-Jacobs and John Sylvester White. The theme song, "Welcome Back," was sung by John Sebastian. The last telecast was Aug 10, 1979.

WILLIAM, THE CONQUEROR: DEATH ANNIVERSARY. Sept 9, 1087. William I, The Conqueror, King of England and Duke of Normandy, whose image is portrayed in the Bayeux Tapestry, was born about 1028 at Falaise, Normandy. Victorious over Harold at the Battle of Hastings (the Norman Conquest) in 1066, William was crowned King of England at Westminster Abbey on Christmas Day of that year. Later, while waging war in France, William met his death at Rouen, Sept 9, 1087.

WONDERFUL WEIRDOS DAY. Sept 9. All of us are blessed with one or two wonderful weirdos in our lives. These are the folks who remind us to think outside the box, to be a little more true to ourselves. Today's the day to thank them. So give them a hug, and say, "I love you, you weirdo!" (©2006 by WH.) For info: Thomas & Ruth Roy, Wellcat Holidays, 2418 Long Lane, Lebanon, PA 17046. Phone: (717) 279-0184. E-mail: info@wellcat.com. Web: www.wellcat.com.

BIRTHDAYS TODAY

Mario Batali, 54, chef, author, television personality ("Molto Mario"), born Seattle, WA, Sept 9, 1960.

Shane Battier, 36, basketball player, born Birmingham, MI, Sept 9, 1978.

Michael Bublé, 39, singer, born Burnaby, BC, Canada, Sept 9, 1975.

Angela Cartwright, 62, actress ("Lost in Space," *The Sound of Music*), born Cheshire, England, Sept 9, 1952.

Christopher Coons, 51, US Senator (D, Delaware), born Greenwich, CT, Sept 9, 1963.

Charles Esten, 49, actor ("Nashville," "Big Love"), born Pittsburgh, PA, Sept 9, 1965.

Hugh Grant, 54, actor (*Notting Hill, About a Boy, Four Weddings and a Funeral*), born London, England, Sept 9, 1960.

Mike Hampton, 42, former baseball player, born Brooksville, FL, Sept 9, 1972.

Rachel Hunter, 45, model, born Glenfield, New Zealand, Sept 9, 1969.

Kazuhiro Ishii, 41, baseball player, born Chiba, Japan, Sept 9, 1973.

Michael Keaton, 63, actor (*Batman, Beetlejuice, My Life*), born Michael Douglas at Pittsburgh, PA, Sept 9, 1951.

Sylvia Miles, 80, actress (*Midnight Cowboy; Farewell, My Lovely*), born New York, NY, Sept 9, 1934.

Adam Sandler, 48, actor, comedian (*Happy Gilmore, The Wedding Singer*), born Brooklyn, NY, Sept 9, 1966.

Eric Stonestreet, 43, actor (Emmy for "Modern Family"), born Kansas City, KS, Sept 9, 1971.

Joseph Robert (Joe) Theisman, 65, sportscaster, Hall of Fame football player, born New Brunswick, NJ, Sept 9, 1949.

Goran Visnjic, 42, actor ("ER," *The Girl with the Dragon Tattoo, The Deep End*), born Sibenik, Croatia, Sept 9, 1972.

Michelle Williams, 34, actress (*Brokeback Mountain, Blue Valentine*, "Dawson's Creek"), born Kalispell, MT, Sept 9, 1980.

Tom Wopat, 63, actor ("The Dukes of Hazzard," "Cybill," *Annie Get Your Gun*), born Lodi, WI, Sept 9, 1951.

September 2014

S	M	T	W	T	F	S
	1	2	3	4	5	6
7	8	9	10	11	12	13
14	15	16	17	18	19	20
21	22	23	24	25	26	27
28	29	30				

September 10 — Wednesday

DAY 253 **112 REMAINING**

BELIZE: SAINT GEORGE'S CAYE DAY. Sept 10. Public holiday celebrated in honor of the 1798 battle between the European Baymen Settlers and the Spaniards for the territory of Belize.

BRAXTON, CARTER: BIRTH ANNIVERSARY. Sept 10, 1736. American revolutionary statesman and signer of the Declaration of Independence. Born at Newington, VA, he died Oct 10, 1797, at Richmond, VA.

CANADA: THE MASTERS. Sept 10–14. Spruce Meadows, Calgary, AB. International show jumping competition, along with Equi-Fair lifestyle marketplace and TELUS Battle of the Breeds. Featured events are the EnCana Cup, the ATCO Electric Circuit "Six-Bar," the BMO Nations' Cup and the CN International. Est attendance: 250,000. For info: Spruce Meadows, 18011 Spruce Meadows Way SW, Calgary, AB T2J 5G5, Canada. Phone: (403) 974-4200. Fax: (403) 974-4270. E-mail: information@sprucemeadows.com. Web: www.sprucemeadows.com.

GOULD, STEPHEN JAY: BIRTH ANNIVERSARY. Sept 10, 1941. Evolutionary biologist and influential writer for academic and lay audiences. With colleague Niles Eldredge, he proposed the theory of punctuated equilibrium to explain sudden changes (and lack of changes) in fossil records. He died in his birthplace city, New York, NY, on May 20, 2002.

"GUNSMOKE" TV PREMIERE: ANNIVERSARY. Sept 10, 1955. "Gunsmoke" was TV's longest-running western, moving from radio to TV. John Wayne turned down the role of Marshall Matt Dillon but recommended James Arness, who got the role. Other regulars included Amanda Blake as Kitty Russell, saloon-owner; Dennis Weaver as Chester B. Goode, Dillon's deputy; and Milburn Stone as Doc Adams. In 1962 Burt Reynolds joined the cast as Quint Asper, followed by Roger Ewing as Thad Greenwood and Buck Taylor as Newly O'Brien. In 1964 Ken Curtis was added as funnyman Festus Haggen, the new deputy. "Gunsmoke" was the number-one rated series for four seasons, and a top 10 hit for six seasons. The last telecast was Sept 1, 1975.

KURALT, CHARLES: 80th BIRTH ANNIVERSARY. Sept 10, 1934. TV journalist ("On the Road with Charles Kuralt") born at Wilmington, NC. Died at New York, NY, July 4, 1997.

MARIS, ROGER: 80th BIRTH ANNIVERSARY. Sept 10, 1934. Baseball player born Roger Eugene Maras at Hibbing, MN. In 1961 Maris surpassed the mark set by Babe Ruth in 1927, hitting

61 home runs, a record that wasn't broken until 1998. He won the American League MVP award in 1960 and 1961 and finished his career with the St. Louis Cardinals. Died at Houston, TX, Dec 14, 1985.

MORTON PUMPKIN FESTIVAL. Sept 10–13. Morton, IL. Carnival, parade, entertainment and fantastic food to celebrate the pumpkin in the "Pumpkin Capital of the World." Est attendance: 70,000. For info: Morton Chamber of Commerce, 415 W Jefferson St, Morton, IL 61550. Phone: (888) 765-6588. Fax: (309) 263-2401. E-mail: tstephens@mortonillinois.org. Web: www.mortonpumpkinfestival.org.

NATIONAL CHAMPIONSHIP AIR RACES. Sept 10–14. Reno, NV. 51st annual. Six classes of races—Unlimited, Sport, Jet, Formula One, T-6 and Biplane—compete. The event includes thrilling aerobatics and displays of military, vintage and contemporary aircraft. Est attendance: 223,000. For info: National Championship Air Races, Reno Air Racing Assn, 14501 Mt Anderson St, Reno, NV 89506. Phone: (775) 972-6663. Web: www.airrace.org.

NEW MEXICO STATE FAIR. Sept 10–21 (tentative). EXPO New Mexico, Albuquerque, NM. 76th annual. "The Biggest Show in New Mexico." Fair features nationally known recording artists on multiple stages, midway, parade, state fair queen contest, PRCA rodeo, exhibits and much more. For info: New Mexico State Fair, PO Box 8546, Albuquerque, NM 87198-8546. Phone: (505) 222-9700. Fax: (505) 266-7784. E-mail: expo.info@state.nm.us. Web: www.ExpoNM.com.

SCHIAPARELLI, ELSA: BIRTH ANNIVERSARY. Sept 10, 1890. Born in Rome, Italy, Elsa Schiaparelli was one of the world's leading fashion designers from the late 1920s through the 1950s. Based in Paris, France, Schiaparelli created striking, often surrealistic designs in collaboration with such artists as Salvador Dali and Jean Cocteau. She introduced the shoulder pad to women's fashion, named "shocking pink" (hot pink) and worked with man-made materials. A white evening dress bedecked with a lobster and a hat that appeared to be a giant shoe were some of her avant-garde looks. "If you define fashion as time moving," she wrote, "then you are not fully alive unless you are moving with it." Schiaparelli died at Paris on Nov 13, 1973.

SWAP IDEAS DAY. Sept 10. To encourage people to explore ways in which their ideas can be put to work for the benefit of humanity, and to encourage development of incentives that will encourage use of creative imagination. For info: Robert L. Birch, Puns Corps, 3108 Dashiell Rd, Falls Church, VA 22042. Phone: (703) 533-3668.

WERFEL, FRANZ: BIRTH ANNIVERSARY. Sept 10, 1890. Austrian author (*The Song of Bernadette, The Forty Days of Musa Dagh*), born at Prague, Czechoslovakia. Died at Hollywood, CA, Aug 26, 1945.

WISE, ROBERT: 100th BIRTH ANNIVERSARY. Sept 10, 1914. American film director, born at Winchester, IN. Wise's Hollywood career began in 1933 with a job in RKO Picture's shipping department. He later worked as a sound effects editor, but quickly moved on to directing, working proficiently in numerous genres throughout his career. His credits include the horror film *The Body Snatcher* (1945), a film noir classic, *Born to Kill* (1947), as well as science fiction, melodrama, westerns, and two musicals for which he won an Academy Award for Best Director: *West Side Story* (1961) and *The Sound of Music* (1965). Died Los Angeles, CA, Sept 14, 2005.

WORLD SUICIDE PREVENTION DAY. Sept 10. An opportunity for all sectors of the community—the public, charitable organizations, communities, researchers, clinicians, practitioners, politicians and policy makers, volunteers, those bereaved by suicide, other interested groups and individuals—to join with the International Association for Suicide Prevention and the WHO to focus on the unacceptable burden and costs of suicidal behaviors with diverse activities to promote understanding about suicide and highlight effective prevention activities. Annually, Sept 10. For info: International Association for Suicide Prevention, National Centre for Suicide Research and Prevention, Sognsvannsveien 21, Bygg 12, N-0372 Oslo, Norway. Web: www.iasp.info/wspd.

"THE X-FILES" TV PREMIERE: ANNIVERSARY. Sept 10, 1993. "The Truth Is Out There" was the mantra of FOX's scary and brainy sci-fi drama. Special FBI agents Fox Mulder (David Duchovny) and Dana Scully (Gillian Anderson) solved the cases too weird for the bureau and also uncovered a vast conspiracy involving aliens and human-alien hybrids. *TV Guide* named "The X-Files" one of the greatest TV shows of all time. Two feature-length films were created as well. The series ended in 2002.

BIRTHDAYS TODAY

José Feliciano, 69, singer, musician, born Lares, Puerto Rico, Sept 10, 1945.

Colin Firth, 54, actor ("Pride and Prejudice," *Bridget Jones's Diary*, Oscar for *The King's Speech*), born Grayshott, Hampshire, England, Sept 10, 1960.

Judy Geeson, 66, actress (*To Sir with Love, The Eagle Has Landed*), born Arundel, Sussex, England, Sept 10, 1948.

Amy Irving, 61, actress (*Carrie, Crossing Delancey*, "Alias"), born Palo Alto, CA, Sept 10, 1953.

Clark Johnson, 50, actor ("Homicide: Life on the Street," "The Wire"), born Philadelphia, PA, Sept 10, 1964.

Randy Johnson, 51, former baseball player, born Walnut Creek, CA, Sept 10, 1963.

Karl Lagerfeld, 76, fashion designer, born Hamburg, Germany, Sept 10, 1938.

Joe Nieuwendyk, 48, hockey player, born Oshawa, ON, Canada, Sept 10, 1966.

Arnold Palmer, 85, golfer, born Latrobe, PA, Sept 10, 1929.

September 11 — Thursday

DAY 254 **111 REMAINING**

ATTACK ON AMERICA: ANNIVERSARY. Sept 11, 2001. Terrorists hijacked four planes, piloting two of them into the World Trade Center's twin towers in New York City and one into the Pentagon in Washington, DC. Passengers on the fourth plane attempted to overcome the hijackers, causing the plane to crash in western Pennsylvania instead of reaching its target in Washington. The twin towers at the WTC collapsed about an hour after being hit. More than 3,000 people died as a result of the attacks. The hijackers were agents of the Al Qaeda terrorist group led by Islamic extremist Osama bin Laden, who was headquartered in Afghanistan. In response, the US began unprecedented internal security measures and launched a war on terrorism with the support of many nations. See also: "The Fall of Kabul: Anniversary" (Nov 13) and "World Trade Center Recovery and Cleanup Ends: Anniversary" (May 30).

BATTLE OF BRANDYWINE: ANNIVERSARY. Sept 11, 1777. The largest engagement of the American Revolution, between the Continental Army led by General George Washington and British troops led by General William Howe. General Howe was marching to take Philadelphia when Washington chose to try and stop the British advance at the Brandywine River near Chadds Ford, PA. The American forces were defeated and the British went on to take Philadelphia Sept 26. They spent the winter in the city while Washington's troops suffered at their encampment at Valley Forge, PA.

BRYANT, BEAR: BIRTH ANNIVERSARY. Sept 11, 1913. Paul William ("Bear") Bryant, college football player and legendary coach, born at Moro Bottoms, AR. Bryant earned his nickname by wrestling a bear for money as a young man. He played football at the University of Alabama and began coaching in 1940. After World War II, he was named head coach at Maryland. He later coached at Kentucky, Texas A&M and Alabama (1958–82). His Alabama teams appeared in bowl games 24 consecutive years and won six national championships. He won coach-of-the-year honors three times and finished his career with 325 wins, then a record. Died at Tuscaloosa, AL, Jan 26, 1983.

"THE CAROL BURNETT SHOW" TV PREMIERE: ANNIVERSARY. Sept 11, 1967. This popular comedy/variety show starred comedienne Carol Burnett, who started the show by taking questions from the audience and ended with an ear tug. Sketches and spoofs included recurring characters like "The Family" (later to be spun off as "Mama's Family") and "As the Stomach Turns." Regular cast members included Harvey Korman, Lyle Waggoner and Vicki Lawrence. Later, Tim Conway joined the cast. Dick Van Dyke briefly joined after Korman left in 1977.

ETHIOPIA: NEW YEAR'S DAY. Sept 11. In the year 2014, this day will start the year 2007 on the Ethiopian Orthodox calendar. On the Coptic Orthodox calendar, it begins the year 1730.

FOOD STAMPS AUTHORIZED: 55th ANNIVERSARY. Sept 11, 1959. Congress passed a bill authorizing food stamps for low-income Americans.

LAWRENCE, DAVID HERBERT: BIRTH ANNIVERSARY. Sept 11, 1885. English novelist, author of *Lady Chatterley's Lover*. Born at Eastwood, Nottinghamshire, England, D.H. Lawrence died Mar 2, 1930, at Vence, France.

LIND, JENNY: US PREMIERE: ANNIVERSARY. Sept 11, 1850. Jenny Lind, the "Swedish Nightingale," gave her first American performance in the Castle Garden Theatre, New York, NY, on this day.

"LITTLE HOUSE ON THE PRAIRIE" TV PREMIERE: 40th ANNIVERSARY. Sept 11, 1974. This hour-long family drama was based on books by Laura Ingalls Wilder. It focused on the Ingalls family and their neighbors living at Walnut Grove, MN: Michael Landon as Charles (Pa), Karen Grassle as Caroline (Ma), Melissa Sue Anderson as daughter Mary, Melissa Gilbert as daughter Laura (from whose point of view the stories were told), Lindsay and Sidney Greenbush as daughter Carrie and Wendi and Brenda Turnbaugh as daughter Grace. In its last season (1982), the show's name was changed to "Little House: A New Beginning." Landon appeared less often and the show centered around Laura and her husband.

September 2014

S	M	T	W	T	F	S
	1	2	3	4	5	6
7	8	9	10	11	12	13
14	15	16	17	18	19	20
21	22	23	24	25	26	27
28	29	30				

MARCOS, FERDINAND EDRALIN: BIRTH ANNIVERSARY. Sept 11, 1917. Former ruler of the Philippines, born at Sarrat, Philippines. Ferdinand Marcos served as head of state from 1966 until his ouster in 1986. His authoritarian regime was marred by widespread corruption and suppression of democratic processes. Marcos died in exile Sept 28, 1989, at Honolulu, HI.

MOUNTAIN MEADOWS MASSACRE: ANNIVERSARY. Sept 11, 1857. As tensions grew between the US government and Governor Brigham Young of the Utah Territory, a wagon train of 140 emigrants bound for California from Arkansas was attacked. On this date, the emigrants surrendered to local Mormon leader John Doyle Lee but were then massacred. Seventeen small children were parceled out to Mormon families. Despite the ensuing national uproar, federal prosecution didn't happen until 1875. Lee was executed in 1877.

NEWPORT INTERNATIONAL BOAT SHOW. Sept 11–14. Newport, RI. More than 650 new sailboats and powerboats in the water and displays of accessories, equipment and services. Newport for New Products program, seminars, etc. Est attendance: 42,000. For info: Newport Exhibition Group, PO Box 698, Newport, RI 02840. Phone: (401) 846-1115. Fax: (401) 848-0455. E-mail: info@newportexhibition.com. Web: www.newportboatshow.com.

O. HENRY (WILLIAM S. PORTER): BIRTH ANNIVERSARY. Sept 11, 1862. William Sydney Porter, American author, who wrote under the pen name O. Henry. Best known for his short stories, including "Gift of the Magi." Born at Greensboro, NC, he died at New York, NY, June 5, 1910.

OKLAHOMA STATE FAIR. Sept 11–21. State Fair Park, Oklahoma City, OK. One of the top state fairs in North America includes six buildings of commercial exhibits, 10 barns for livestock and horse competitions, Disney On Ice, PRCA championship rodeo, live entertainment and motor sports events. Est attendance: 1,000,000. For info: Oklahoma State Fair, PO Box 74943, Oklahoma City, OK 73147. Phone: (405) 948-6700. Fax: (405) 948-6828. E-mail: mail@okstatefair.com. Web: www.okstatefair.com.

PAKISTAN: FOUNDER'S DEATH ANNIVERSARY. Sept 11. Pakistan observes the death anniversary in 1948 of Qaid-e-Azam Mohammed Ali Jinnah (founder of Pakistan) as a national holiday. His birth date, Dec 25, is also a national holiday.

✦PATRIOT DAY AND NATIONAL DAY OF REMEMBRANCE. Sept 11. On Dec 18, 2001, a joint resolution of Congress amended Title 36, Chapter 1, Sec. 144 of the US Code to permit the president to declare Sept 11 of each year as Patriot Day, in commemoration of the terrorist attacks on the United States on Sept 11, 2001. The resolution requests that all state and local governments observe this day "with appropriate programs and activities," that the flag be displayed at half-staff from sunrise till sundown and that a moment of silence be observed in honor of those who lost their lives in the attacks.

1786 ANNAPOLIS CONVENTION: ANNIVERSARY. Sept 11–14, 1786. Twelve delegates from New York, New Jersey, Delaware, Pennsylvania and Virginia met at Annapolis, MD, to discuss commercial matters of mutual interest. The delegates voted, on Sept 14, to adopt a resolution prepared by Alexander Hamilton asking all states to send representatives to a convention at Philadelphia, PA, in May 1787 "to render the constitution of the Federal Government adequate to the exigencies of the Union."

SPACE MILESTONE: *MARS GLOBAL SURVEYOR* (US). Sept 11, 1997. Launched Nov 7, 1996, this unmanned vehicle was put into orbit around Mars. It was designed to compile global maps of Mars by taking high-resolution photos. This mission inaugurated a new series of Mars expeditions in which NASA launched pairs of orbiters and landers to Mars. *Mars Global Surveyor* was paired with the lander *Mars Pathfinder*. See also: "Space Milestone: *Mars Pathfinder*" (July 4).

TYLER'S CABINET RESIGNS: ANNIVERSARY. Sept 11, 1841. In protest of President John Tyler's veto of the Banking Bill, all of his cabinet except Secretary of State Daniel Webster resigned on this day.

BIRTHDAYS TODAY

Franz Beckenbauer, 69, soccer executive and Hall of Fame player, born Munich, Germany, Sept 11, 1945.

Harry Connick, Jr, 47, singer, pianist, stage and screen actor, born New Orleans, LA, Sept 11, 1967.

Brian De Palma, 74, filmmaker (*Mission: Impossible, The Untouchables, Carrie*), born Newark, NJ, Sept 11, 1940.

Lola Falana, 71, singer, dancer, actress (*The Liberation of L.B. Jones), born Camden, NJ, Sept 11, 1943.*

John Hawkes, 55, actor (*The Sessions, Winter's Bone*, "Deadwood"), born Alexandria, MN, Sept 11, 1959.

Donna Lopiano, 68, women's sports executive and former softball player, born Stamford, CT, Sept 11, 1946.

Ludacris, 37, rapper, actor (*Crash, Hustle & Flow*), born Christopher Bridges at Champaign, IL, Sept 11, 1977.

Amy Madigan, 63, actress (*Places in the Heart, Field of Dreams, Uncle Buck*), born Chicago, IL, Sept 11, 1951.

Virginia Madsen, 51, actress (*Sideways, Dune*), born Winnetka, IL, Sept 11, 1963.

Kristy McNichol, 52, actress ("Empty Nest," *Little Darlings, Summer of My German Soldier,* Emmys for "Family"), born Los Angeles, CA, Sept 11, 1962.

Moby, 49, rock singer, songwriter, born Richard Melville Hall at New York, NY, Sept 11, 1965.

September 12 — Friday

DAY 255 **110 REMAINING**

BATTLE OF SAINT-MIHIEL: ANNIVERSARY. Sept 12, 1918. Under the command of General John J. Pershing, the 1st US Army attacked the Germans at the Saint-Mihiel salient. This was the first major US offensive of WWI. Sixteen army divisions, coupled with French II Colonial Corps tanks and artillery support, forced back the Germans after 36 hours of heavy fighting and reclaimed 200 square miles of French territory that had been in the hands of the Germans since 1914. The 1st US Army lost about 7,000 soldiers in the Battle of Saint-Mihiel.

BENNINGTON CAR SHOW. Sept 12–14. Bennington, VT. Classic cars, Woodies and muscle cars. A display and demonstration of antique motorcycles, tractor and farm machinery are also featured. Live entertainment and flea market as well. Annually, the second weekend after Labor Day. Est attendance: 10,000. For info: Bennington Area Chamber of Commerce, 100 Veterans Memorial Dr, Bennington, VT 05201. Phone: (802) 447-3311 or (800) 229-0252. Fax: (802) 447-1163. E-mail: chamber@bennington.com. Web: www.bennington.com.

THE BIG E. Sept 12–28. West Springfield, MA. New England's autumn tradition and one of the nation's largest fairs. Each September, The Big E features top-name entertainment, a big-top circus and horse show. Also children's attractions, rides, daily parade with custom-built Mardi Gras floats, historic village, Avenue of States, Better Living Center and much more. Annually, beginning the second Friday after Labor Day. Est attendance: 1,250,000. For info: Eastern States Exposition, 1305 Memorial Ave, West Springfield, MA 01089. Phone: (413) 737-2443. Fax: (413) 787-0127. E-mail: info@thebige.com. Web: www.thebige.com.

BULLS SIGN MICHAEL JORDAN: 30th ANNIVERSARY. Sept 12, 1984. The Chicago Bulls signed their No. 1 draft choice, Michael Jordan, a guard from the University of North Carolina. Jordan was the No. 3 choice overall behind Akeem (later Hakeem) Olajuwon, taken by Houston, and Sam Bowie, selected by Portland.

CANYONLANDS NATIONAL PARK ESTABLISHED: 50th ANNIVERSARY. Sept 12, 1964. Area of southeastern Utah established as a national park. For info: Canyonlands Natl Park, 2282 SW Resource Blvd, Moab, UT 84532. Web: www.ups.gov/cany.

CHARLES LEROUX'S LAST JUMP: 125th ANNIVERSARY. Sept 12, 1889. American aeronaut of French extraction, born in New York, NY, about 1857, achieved world fame as a parachutist. After his first public performance (Philadelphia, PA, 1887) he toured European cities, where his parachute jumps attracted wide attention. Credited with 238 successful jumps. On Sept 12, 1889, he jumped from a balloon over Tallinn, Estonia, and perished in the Bay of Reval.

CHEVALIER, MAURICE: BIRTH ANNIVERSARY. Sept 12, 1888. Successful actor-singer born at Paris, France. Nominated for Academy Awards for his roles in *The Love Parade* (1929) and *The Big Pond* (1930), Chevalier was part of a wave of talented actor-singers who popularized the musical as a film genre. He was known for his suave style and signature straw boater, and his most well-known musicals include *Gigi* (1958), *Can-Can* (1960) and *Fanny* (1961). Chevalier won the Cecil B. DeMille Award at the Academy Awards in 1958 and died at Paris, Jan 1, 1972.

DEFENDERS DAY. Sept 12. Maryland. Public holiday. Annual reenactment of bombardment of Fort McHenry in 1814 that inspired Francis Scott Key to write "The Star-Spangled Banner."

ENGLAND: HARROGATE AUTUMN FLOWER SHOW. Sept 12–14. Great Yorkshire Showground, Harrogate, North Yorkshire. See Britain's finest blooms and talk to the experts. More than 90 nurseries plus plant societies and vegetable championships. Est attendance: 40,000. For info: Martin Fish, North of England Horticultural Society, Regional Agricultural Centre, Great Yorkshire Showground, Harrogate, North Yorkshire, England HG2 8NZ. Phone: (44) (1423) 546-158. E-mail: info@flowershow.org.uk. Web: www.flowershow.org.uk.

ENGLAND: JANE AUSTEN FESTIVAL. Sept 12–20. Bath. 14th annual. Festival celebrating the life and works of author Jane Austen (1775–1817) in the city where she lived briefly but which figures prominently in her novels. The festival opens with the spectacular Grand Regency Costumed Promenade and continues with hundreds of participants in authentic period dress and accompanied by a town crier. Other events include readings, film and theatrical presentations, dances, costume workshop, cookery demonstrations and "Undressing Mr Darcy." For info: The Jane Austen Centre, 40 Gay St, Bath BA1 2NT, England. E-mail: jafestival bath@gmail.com. Web: www.janeausten.co.uk.

GUINEA-BISSAU: NATIONAL HOLIDAY. Sept 12. Amilcar Cabral's birthday, Sept 12, is observed as a national holiday.

ISRAEL COMPLETES GAZA PULLOUT: ANNIVERSARY. Sept 12, 2005. In the early hours of Sept 12, the last of Israel's troops left Gaza, and the withdrawal of settlers and military begun in August 2005 was finished. Israel had occupied Gaza for 38 years. The Palestinian Authority assumed control of Gaza, but Hamas wrested control of the city in 2007.

KING TURKEY DAY (WITH TURKEY RACE). Sept 12–13. Worthington, MN. Community celebration that includes live turkey race between Paycheck, Worthington, MN, and Ruby Begonia, Cuero, TX. Also included are a grand parade, beer garden, free pancake breakfast and family activities. Est attendance: 10,000. For info: King Turkey Day, Inc, 1121 Third Ave, Worthington, MN 56187. Phone: (800) 279-2919 or (507) 372-2919. Fax: (507) 372-2827. E-mail: wcofc@frontiernet.net. Web: www.kingturkeyday.net.

"LASSIE" TV PREMIERE: 60th ANNIVERSARY. Sept 12, 1954. This long-running series was originally about a boy and his courageous and intelligent dog, Lassie (played by more than six different dogs, all male). For the first few seasons, Lassie lived on the Miller farm. The family included Jeff (Tommy Rettig); his widowed mother, Ellen (Jan Clayton); and George Cleveland as Gramps. Throughout the years there were many format and cast changes, as Lassie was exchanged from one family to another in order to have a variety of new perils and escapades. Other featured performers included Cloris Leachman, June Lockhart and Larry Wilcox.

"MAUDE" TV PREMIERE: ANNIVERSARY. Sept 12, 1972. Bea Arthur's character, Maude Findlay, was first introduced as Edith Bunker's cousin on "All in the Family." She was a loud, opinionated liberal, living with her fourth husband, Walter (Bill Macy). Other characters on the show were her divorced daughter by a previous marriage, Carol Trainer (Adrienne Barbeau); Conrad Bain as Dr. Arthur Harmon; Rue McClanahan as Arthur's wife, Vivian; Esther Rolle as Florida Evans, Maude's maid; and John Amos as her husband, Henry. This was one of the first shows to tackle the controversial issue of abortion.

MENCKEN, HENRY LOUIS: BIRTH ANNIVERSARY. Sept 12, 1880. American newspaperman, lexicographer and critic, the "Sage of Baltimore" was born at Baltimore, MD, and died there Jan 29, 1956. "If, after I depart this vale," he wrote in 1921 (Epitaph, *Smart Set*), "you ever remember me and have thought to please my ghost, forgive some sinner and wink your eye at some homely girl."

"THE MONKEES" TV PREMIERE: ANNIVERSARY. Sept 12, 1966. Featuring a rock group that was supposed to be an American version of the Beatles, this half-hour show featured a blend of comedy and music. Four young actors were chosen from more than 400 to play the group members: Micky Dolenz, Davy Jones, Mike Nesmith and Peter Tork. Dolenz and Jones had previous acting experience, and Tork and Nesmith had previous musical experience. The music that they performed on the show proved to be immensely popular; at first they sang with a studio band but later insisted on writing and performing their own music. They released several albums and toured several times. In 1986, the Monkees, except for Nesmith, were reunited for a 20th anniversary tour and the show was broadcast in reruns on MTV. The Monkees sans Nesmith also toured in 1996 for the 30th reunion celebration.

ON THE WATERFRONT SWAP MEET AND CAR SHOW. Sept 12–13. Downtown St. Ignace, MI. 23rd annual. Car show, toy show, truck display and swap meet. Est attendance: 8,000. For info: Nostalgia Prod, Inc, 268 Hillcrest Blvd, St. Ignace, MI 49781. Phone: (906) 643-8087. Fax: (906) 643-9784. E-mail: ereavie@nostalgia-prod.com. Web: www.nostalgia-prod.com or www.stignacecarshow.com.

OWENS, JESSE: BIRTH ANNIVERSARY. Sept 12, 1913. James Cleveland (Jesse) Owens, American athlete, winner of four gold medals at the 1936 Olympic Games at Berlin, Germany, was born at Oakville, AL. Owens set 11 world records in track and field. During one track meet, at Ann Arbor, MI, May 23, 1935, Owens, representing Ohio State University, broke three world records and tied a fourth in the space of 45 minutes. Died at Tucson, AZ, Mar 31, 1980.

RICHARD CRANE MEMORIAL TRUCK SHOW. Sept 12–14. St. Ignace, MI. 19th annual show featuring 18-wheeler competition. $2,000 cash Best of Show. Parade of Lights across the Mackinac Bridge. Est attendance: 10,000. For info: Nostalgia Productions, Inc, 268 Hillcrest Blvd, St. Ignace, MI 49781. Phone: (906) 643-8087. Fax: (906) 643-9784. E-mail: ereavie@nostalgia-prod.com. Web: www.nostalgia-prod.com or www.stignacecarshow.com.

September 2014	S	M	T	W	T	F	S
		1	2	3	4	5	6
	7	8	9	10	11	12	13
	14	15	16	17	18	19	20
	21	22	23	24	25	26	27
	28	29	30				

SPACE MILESTONE: *LUNA 2* (USSR): 55th ANNIVERSARY. Sept 12, 1959. First spacecraft to land on moon was launched.

SUMMERSET FESTIVAL. Sept 12–14. Clement Park, Littleton, CO. A family-oriented event, held for the purpose of saying good-bye to summer. There is something for everyone: car show, arts and crafts, business and nonprofit exhibitors, fishing derby, food concessions, kids' areas, softball tournament, entertainment and loads of family fun! Est attendance: 40,000. For info: Lora Knowlton, Summerset Festival, PO Box 621788, Littleton, CO 80162-1788. Phone: (303) 973-1209. Fax: (303) 948-5550. E-mail: summersetfest@aol.com. Web: www.summersetfest.com.

UNITED NATIONS: DAY FOR SOUTH-SOUTH COOPERATION. Sept 12. Formerly observed on Dec 19 (Res 58/220), marking the date when the General Assembly endorsed the Buenos Aires Plan of Action for Promoting and Implementing Technical Cooperation among Developing Countries. Changed on Dec 22, 2011, to be observed annually on Sept 12, to mark the date in 1978 when that same plan was actually adopted. For info: United Nations, Dept of Public Info, New York, NY 10017. Web: www.un.org.

WO-ZHA-WA DAYS FALL FESTIVAL. Sept 12–14. Wisconsin Dells, WI. Celebrates the beginning of the fall season. Arts, crafts, 100-unit parade, Maxwell Street Days, Wo-Zha-Wa Run and antique flea market. Est attendance: 100,000. For info: Wisconsin Dells Visitors Bureau, PO Box 390, Wisconsin Dells, WI 53965. Phone: (800) 223-3557. E-mail: info@wisdells.com. Web: www.wisdells.com/wozhawa.

BIRTHDAYS TODAY

Sam Brownback, 58, Governor of Kansas (R), former US senator (Kansas), born Garnett, KS, Sept 12, 1956.

Linda Gray, 73, actress ("Dallas," "Melrose Place"), born Santa Monica, CA, Sept 12, 1941.

Ian Holm, 83, actor (*The Sweet Hereafter*, Oscar for *Chariots of Fire*), born Goodmayes, England, Sept 12, 1931.

Jennifer Hudson, 33, singer, actress ("American Idol," Oscar for *Dreamgirls*; *The Secret Life of Bees*), born Chicago, IL, Sept 12, 1981.

Louis C.K., 47, comedian, actor ("Louie"), born Louis Szekely at Washington, DC, Sept 12, 1967.

Benjamin McKenzie, 36, actor ("Southland," "The O.C.," *Junebug*), born Austin, TX, Sept 12, 1978.

Yao Ming, 34, former basketball player, born Shanghai, China, Sept 12, 1980.

Maria Muldaur, 71, singer, born New York, NY, Sept 12, 1943.

Joe Pantoliano, 60, actor ("The Sopranos," *Risky Business, The Fugitive*; stage: *Orphans*), born Jersey City, NJ, Sept 12, 1954.

Emmy Rossum, 28, actress ("Shameless," *The Phantom of the Opera*), born New York, NY, Sept 12, 1986.

Peter Scolari, 60, actor ("Bosom Buddies," "Newhart"), born New Rochelle, NY, Sept 12, 1954.

Rachel Ward, 57, actress ("The Thorn Birds," *Against All Odds*), born London, England, Sept 12, 1957.

Amy Yasbeck, 51, actress (*The Mask*, "Wings"), born Cincinnati, OH, Sept 12, 1963.

September 13 — Saturday

DAY 256 **109 REMAINING**

ANDERSON, SHERWOOD: BIRTH ANNIVERSARY. Sept 13, 1876. American author and newspaper publisher, born at Camden, OH. His best remembered book is *Winesburg, Ohio.* Anderson died at Colon, Panama, Mar 8, 1941.

BARRY, JOHN: DEATH ANNIVERSARY. Sept 13, 1803. Revolutionary War hero John Barry, first American to hold the rank of commodore, died at Philadelphia, PA. He was born at Tacumshane, County Wexford, Ireland, in 1745. He has been called the "Father of the American Navy."

BIG MAC SHORELINE FALL SCENIC BIKE TOUR & RIDE ACROSS THE MACKINAC BRIDGE. Sept 13–14. Mackinaw City Recreation Complex, Mackinaw City, MI. A one-of-a-kind bike tour that has become a tradition for many bikers in Michigan and surrounding states. On Saturday, more than 600 participants ride 25-, 50-, 75- or 100-mile bike tours along the shores of Lake Michigan. The routes are clearly marked and a number of rest areas dot the course. SAG Safety Wagons also circle the route to ensure safety for riders. For those who participate on Saturday, there is a beautiful ride across Mackinac Bridge on Sunday at 7 AM. Est attendance: 600. For info: Mackinaw Chamber of Commerce, PO Box 856, Mackinaw City, MI 49701. Phone: (231) 436-5574. Fax: (231) 436-7989. E-mail: info@mackinawchamber.com. Web: www.mackinawchamber.com.

COLBERT, CLAUDETTE: BIRTH ANNIVERSARY. Sept 13, 1903. Actress and comedienne Colbert, born Lily Claudette Chauchoin at Paris, France, was a beloved movie star of the '30s. She was best known for her films *Midnight, Cleopatra* and *It Happened One Night,* for which she won an Oscar in 1934. In addition to more than 60 movies, she appeared in Broadway shows and won a Golden Globe Award for her role in the 1986 miniseries "The Two Mrs Grenvilles." She also received a Life Achievement Award from the Kennedy Center for Performing Arts in 1989. She died July 30, 1996, at Bridgetown, Barbados.

DAHL, ROALD: BIRTH ANNIVERSARY. Sept 13, 1916. Author (*Charlie and the Chocolate Factory, James and the Giant Peach*), born at Llandaff, South Wales, Great Britain. Died Nov 23, 1990, at Oxford, England.

FLAX SCUTCHING FESTIVAL. Sept 13–14. Stahlstown, PA. 107th annual. Demonstrations of the art of making linen from the flax plant. Second oldest continuous complete flax demonstration festival in the world. Annually, the second Saturday and Sunday in September. For info: Marilee Pletcher, Flax Scutching Festival, PO Box 77, Stahlstown, PA 15687. E-mail: flaxscutching@hotmail.com. Web: www.flaxscutching.org.

KIDS TAKE OVER THE KITCHEN DAY. Sept 13. Young Chefs Academy encourages kids and teens across the nation to take over their kitchen. The objective is to empower kids and teens to become more actively involved in the planning, preparation and cooking of meals. In turn, we foster family bonds and actively fight the battle against the many serious health and social issues related to our youth's eating habits in today's time. For info: Shelly Phipps, Young Chefs Academy, One Liberty Place, 100 N 6th St, Ste 100, Waco, TX 76701. Phone: (254) 751-1040. Fax: (254) 751-1875. E-mail: shellyp@ycintl.com. Web: www.youngchefsacademy.com/KTOKDay.

"LAW & ORDER" TV PREMIERE: ANNIVERSARY. Sept 13, 1990. Filmed on location at New York City, "Law & Order" showed the interaction between the police and the district attorney's office in dealing with a crime. Almost the entire cast changed over the life of this program and included Michael Moriarty (Assistant District Attorney Benjamin Stone), Sam Waterston (ADA Jack McCoy), Jerry Orbach (Detective Lennie Briscoe), Christopher Noth (Detective Mike Logan), Jesse L. Martin (Detective Edward Green) and many others. The acclaimed program's final episode aired May 24, 2010. "Law & Order" spun off two other successful series: "Law & Order: Special Victims Unit" and "Law & Order: Criminal Intent."

MONROE, BILL: BIRTH ANNIVERSARY. Sept 13, 1911. The father of bluegrass was born at Rosine, KY. The sound and style Monroe developed in the late 1930s—a furious alchemy of country, folk and blues influences, with four- and five-part harmonies delivered over that driving acoustic rhythm—with his band, the Blue Grass Boys, redefined the genre and made him a star. A true statesman of music, Bill Monroe's career spanned six decades and more than 50 releases. He died on Sept 9, 1996, at Springfield, TN.

"THE MUPPET SHOW" TV PREMIERE: ANNIVERSARY. Sept 13, 1976. This comedy-variety show was hosted by Kermit the Frog of "Sesame Street." The new Jim Henson puppet characters included Miss Piggy, Fozzie Bear and The Great Gonzo. Many celebrities appeared as guests on the show, which was broadcast in more than 100 countries. The show ran until 1981. *The Muppet Movie* (1979) was the first of many films based on "The Muppet Show."

NATIONAL CELIAC AWARENESS DAY. Sept 13. To raise awareness and to honor Dr. Samuel Gee, who first established the connection between celiac disease and diet. Dr. Gee was born Sept 13, 1839. Recognized by US Senate resolution. For info: Celiac Sprue Assn/USA, PO Box 31700, Omaha, NE 68131-0700. Phone: (877) CSA-4CSA. E-mail: celiacs@csaceliacs.org. Web: www.csaceliacs.org.

PERSHING, JOHN J.: BIRTH ANNIVERSARY. Sept 13, 1860. US Army general who commanded the American Expeditionary Force (AEF) during WWI, Pershing was born at Laclede, MO. The AEF, as part of the inter-Allied offensive, successfully assaulted the Saint-Mihiel salient in September 1918 and later that month quickly regrouped for the Meuse-Argonne operation that led to the Armistice of Nov 11, 1918. Pershing died July 15, 1948, at Washington, DC.

PRAIRIE DAY. Sept 13. George Washington Carver National Monument, Diamond, MO. Celebrating life on the Missouri prairie during the late 1880s when George Washington Carver was a child, this event includes basket weaving, candle-making, Dutch-oven cooking, spinning, weaving, storytelling, musical groups, quilting, a junior ranger station and more events. Annually, the second Saturday in September. For info: George Washington Carver National Monument, 5646 Carver Rd, Diamond, MO 64840. Phone: (417) 325-4151. E-mail: gwca_interpretation@nps.gov. Web: www.nps.gov/gwca.

REED, WALTER: BIRTH ANNIVERSARY. Sept 13, 1851. American army physician, especially known for his yellow fever research. Born at Gloucester County, VA, he served as an army surgeon for more than 20 years and as a professor at the Army Medical College. He died at Washington, DC, Nov 22, 1902. The US Army's general hospital at Washington, DC, is named in his honor.

ROALD DAHL DAY. Sept 13. The official Roald Dahl Day takes place every year on Sept 13—the birthday of the world's No. 1 storyteller. There are many scrumdiddlyumptious ways to celebrate: write a revolting rhyme; give someone a favorite book wrapped in newspaper and tied up in string just like Roald Dahl used to do; make a peach smoothie; read a Dahl book that you've never read before—and if you've read them all, read your favorite again; organize a Dahl quiz; drop "gobblefunk" convincingly into a conversation—and lots more. For info: Roald Dahl Day. E-mail: myday@roalddahlday.info. Web: www.roalddahlday.info or www.roalddahl.com.

"SCOOBY-DOO, WHERE ARE YOU?" TV PREMIERE: 45th ANNIVERSARY. Sept 13, 1969. A tremendously popular Saturday morning cartoon, Hanna-Barbera's show featured four wacky kids and lovable Great Dane Scooby-Doo solving spooky (and often hilarious) mysteries. Fred, Daphne and Velma usually do the work, while Shaggy (originally voiced by radio personality Casey Kasem) and Scooby-Doo look for something to eat. A live-action feature film was released in 2002 starring Freddie Prinze Jr, Sarah Michelle Gellar, Matthew Lillard, Linda Cardellini and a digital Scooby.

"SOAP" TV PREMIERE: ANNIVERSARY. Sept 13, 1977. "Soap" was a prime-time comedy that parodied soap operas. It had plots that were funny (e.g., Corinne's baby is possessed by the devil), controversial (e.g., Billy joins a cult) and downright bizarre (e.g., Burt is abducted by aliens). The show focused on two families, the wealthy Tates and the middle-class Campbells. It starred Katherine Helmond, Robert Mandan, Jennifer Salt, Diana Canova, Jimmy Baio, Robert Guillaume, Cathryn Damon, Richard Mulligan, Ted Wass, Billy Crystal, Richard Libertini, Kathryn Reynolds, Robert Urich, Arthur Peterson, Roscoe Lee Browne and Jay Johnson. Rod Roddy was the announcer who recapped what had happened on the previous episode.

STA-BIL NATIONALS CHAMPIONSHIP LAWN MOWER RACE. Sept 13. Delaware, OH. Five classes of races for winners of regional races held across the US. Mowers will travel at speeds ranging from 10 mph to more than 50 mph. Est attendance: 2,000. For info: US Lawn Mower Racing Assn, 1544 Shermer Rd, Ste F, Northbrook, IL 60062. Phone: (847) 272-2120. E-mail: letsmow@aol.com. Web: www.letsmow.com.

"THE STAR-SPANGLED BANNER" INSPIRED: 200th ANNIVERSARY. Sept 13–14, 1814. On the night of Sept 13, Francis Scott Key was aboard a ship that was delayed in Baltimore harbor by the British attack there on Fort McHenry. Key had no choice but to anxiously watch the battle. That experience and seeing the American flag still flying over the fort the next morning inspired him to pen the verses that, coupled with the tune of a popular drinking song, became our official national anthem in 1931, 117 years after the words were written.

SUMAC, YMA: BIRTH ANNIVERSARY. Sept 13, 1922. Peruvian singer ("The Nightingale of the Andes") who wowed audiences in the 1940s and '50s with her stunning four-octave vocal range. Born Zoila Augusta Emperatriz Chavarri del Castillo at Ichocan, Peru, Sumac claimed to be a descendent of Incan emperor Atahualpa—a claim the Peruvian government officially supported in 1946. Sumac's mysterious and exotic persona earned her international acclaim and helped her sell millions of records. She died Nov 1, 2008, at Los Angeles, CA.

UCI ROAD WORLD CHAMPIONSHIPS. Sept 13–21. Ponferrada, Spain. Road cycling's premier event, with expected worldwide television audience of 300 million. Sponsored by the International Cycling Union (UCI), a nonprofit organization founded on Apr 14, 1900. Est attendance: 250,000. For info: International Cycling Union (UCI), Ch de la Mêlée 12, 1860 Aigle, Switzerland. Phone: (41) (24) 468-58-11. Fax: (41) (24) 468-58-12. E-mail: admin@uci.ch. Web: www.uci.ch.

US CAPITAL ESTABLISHED AT NEW YORK CITY: ANNIVERSARY. Sept 13, 1788. Congress picked New York, NY, as the location of the new US government in place of Philadelphia, which had served as the capital up until this time. In 1790 the capital moved back to Philadelphia for 10 years, before moving permanently to Washington, DC.

USGA SENIOR AMATEUR (GOLF) CHAMPIONSHIP. Sept 13–18. Big Canyon Country Club, Newport Beach, CA. For info: USGA, Golf House, Championship Dept, PO Box 708, Far Hills, NJ 07931. Phone: (908) 234-2300. Fax: (908) 234-9687. E-mail: usga@usga.org. Web: www.usga.org.

US SENIOR WOMEN'S AMATEUR (GOLF) CHAMPIONSHIP. Sept 13–18. Hollywood Golf Club, Deal, NJ. For info: USGA, Golf House, Championship Dept, PO Box 708, Far Hills, NJ 07931. Phone: (908) 234-2300. Fax: (908) 234-9687. E-mail: usga@usga.org. Web: www.usga.org.

BIRTHDAYS TODAY

Fiona Apple, 37, singer, born New York, NY, Sept 13, 1977.

Jacqueline Bisset, 70, actress (*Rich and Famous, The Deep, Bullitt*, "Nip/Tuck"), born Weybridge, England, Sept 13, 1944.

Peter Cetera, 70, singer (former lead singer of Chicago), songwriter, born Chicago, IL, Sept 13, 1944.

Robert Indiana, 86, artist (*As I Opened Fire*), born New Castle, IA, Sept 13, 1928.

Michael Johnson, 47, track athlete, born Dallas, TX, Sept 13, 1967.

Richard Kiel, 75, actor (*The Longest Yard, Silver Streak, The Spy Who Loved Me*), born Detroit, MI, Sept 13, 1939.

Judith Martin, 76, author, journalist ("Miss Manners"), born Washington, DC, Sept 13, 1938.

Daisuke Matsuzake, 34, baseball player, born Tokyo, Japan, Sept 13, 1980.

Stella McCartney, 43, fashion designer, born London, England, Sept 13, 1971.

Thomas Müller, 25, soccer player, born Weilheim, Germany, Sept 13, 1989.

Tyler Perry, 45, actor (*Alex Cross, Diary of a Mad Black Woman, Madea's Family Reunion*), director, screenwriter, born Emmitt Perry, Jr, at New Orleans, LA, Sept 13, 1969.

Ben Savage, 34, actor ("Boy Meets World"), born Chicago, IL, Sept 13, 1980.

Fred Silverman, 77, television producer, born New York, NY, Sept 13, 1937.

Jean Smart, 55, stage and screen actress ("24," "Designing Women"), born Seattle, WA, Sept 13, 1959.

Bernabe (Bernie) Williams, 46, former baseball player, born San Juan, Puerto Rico, Sept 13, 1968.

September 2014

S	M	T	W	T	F	S
	1	2	3	4	5	6
7	8	9	10	11	12	13
14	15	16	17	18	19	20
21	22	23	24	25	26	27
28	29	30				

September 14 — Sunday

DAY 257 **108 REMAINING**

BELGIUM: GREAT PROCESSION OF TOURNAI. Sept 14. Tournai. Religious procession held since 1092 to honor the Virgin Mary delivering the city from the plague. Annually, the second Sunday of September. For more info: City of Tournai. Web: www.tournai.be/en.

DANTE ALIGHIERI: DEATH ANNIVERSARY. Sept 14, 1321. Italian poet, author of the *Divine Comedy*, died at Ravenna, Italy. He was born in May 1265 (exact date unknown) at Florence, Italy.

"THE GOLDEN GIRLS" TV PREMIERE: ANNIVERSARY. Sept 14, 1985. This comedy starred Bea Arthur, Betty White, Rue McClanahan and Estelle Getty as four divorced/widowed women sharing a house in Florida during their golden years. The last episode aired Sept 14, 1992, but the show remains popular in syndication.

"HAVE GUN WILL TRAVEL" TV PREMIERE: ANNIVERSARY. Sept 14, 1957. "Have Gun, Will Travel." So read the business card of Paladin (Richard Boone), a loner whose professional services were available for a price. This half-hour western also featured Kam Tong as his servant, Hey Boy. The show was extremely popular and ranked in the top five for most of its run.

"IRONSIDE" TV PREMIERE: ANNIVERSARY. Sept 14, 1967. This crime series starred Raymond Burr as Robert T. Ironside, Chief of Detectives for the San Francisco Police Department (he was in a wheelchair, paralyzed from an assassination attempt). Also featured were Don Galloway as his assistant, Detective Sergeant Ed Brown; Barbara Anderson as Officer Eve Whitfield; Don Mitchell as Mark Sanger, Ironside's personal assistant; Gene Lyons as Commissioner Dennis Randall; Elizabeth Baur as Officer Fran Belding; and Joan Pringle as Diana, Mark's wife.

ITALY: GIOSTRA DELLA QUINTANA. Sept 14. Foligno. A revival of a 17th-century joust of the Quintana, featuring 600 knights in full costume. Annually, the second Sunday in September.

McCLOSKEY, ROBERT: 100th BIRTH ANNIVERSARY. Sept 14, 1914. Beloved children's book author and illustrator. Won two Caldecott Awards, for *Make Way for Ducklings* (1941) and *Time of Wonder* (1957). Also wrote and illustrated *Blueberries for Sal* (1948). McCloskey was named a Living Legend by the Library of Congress in 2000. Born at Hamilton, OH, he died June 30, 2003, at Deer Isle, ME.

McKINLEY, WILLIAM: DEATH ANNIVERSARY. Sept 14, 1901. President William McKinley was shot at Buffalo, NY, Sept 6, 1901. He died eight days later. Assassin Leon Czolgosz was executed Oct 29, 1901.

MISS AMERICA PAGEANT. Sept 14 (tentative). Atlantic City, NJ. Developed by the Miss America Organization, the Miss America program exists to provide personal and professional opportunities for young women between the ages of 17 and 24 to promote their voices in culture, politics and the community. Almost all contestants either have received or are in the process of earning college or postgraduate degrees and use Miss America scholarship grants to further their educations. The Miss America Organization is the leading provider of scholarships for young women in the world. The Miss America Pageant has been held since 1921. For info: The Miss America Organization, 222 New Road, Ste 700, Linwood, NJ 08221. Phone: (609) 653-8700. Fax: (609) 653-8740. E-mail: info@MissAmerica.org. Web: www.MissAmerica.org.

MOORE, CLAYTON: 100th BIRTH ANNIVERSARY. Sept 14, 1914. Jack Carlton Moore, born at Chicago, IL, was a circus performer before going to Hollywood, where first he was a stuntman. Minor roles in film serials preceded his heroic role on televison's hit "The Lone Ranger." Moore, who played the West's masked righter-of-wrongs from 1949–52 and 1954–57, embraced the role and was comfortable with being identified as the Lone Ranger long after he retired from acting. With the backing of the public, he won the right to continue wearing the mask when legally challenged by the copyright owners. Inducted in the Hall of Great Western Performers and an honorary inductee to the Stuntman's Hall of Fame, Moore died Dec 28, 1999, at Los Angeles, CA.

MOTLEY, CONSTANCE BAKER: BIRTH ANNIVERSARY. Sept 14, 1921. New York's first black woman state senator and federal judge, and the first woman elected borough president of Manhattan, Constance Baker Motley became interested in law and civil rights when she was barred from a public beach at age 15. She went on to become one of the top civil rights lawyers of the '50s and '60s. She presented arguments before the US Supreme Court for seven cases and won them all. Motley was born at New Haven, CT, and died at New York, NY, Sept 28, 2005.

NATIONAL HUG YOUR HOUND DAY. Sept 14. A holiday dedicated to increasing awareness of the human-friendly and dog-friendly use of urban spaces and to encourage the inclusion of nature in all aspects of urban life. Annually, the second Sunday of September. For info: Ami Moore, National Hug Your Hound Day, 910 W Van Buren #242, Chicago, IL 60607. Phone: (847) 284-7760. E-mail: doggiedoright911@yahoo.com.

NICARAGUA: BATTLE OF SAN JACINTO DAY. Sept 14. National holiday. Commemorates the 1856 defeat of US invader William Walker.

PROSTATE CANCER AWARENESS WEEK. Sept 14–20. Free or low-cost prostate health assessment events for all men 35 years of age and older. Annually, the third full week in September. For info: Prostate Conditions Education Council, 7009 S Potomac St, Ste 125, Centennial, CO 80112. Phone: (303) 316-4685. Web: www.prostateconditions.org.

SANGER, MARGARET (HIGGINS): BIRTH ANNIVERSARY. Sept 14, 1879. Feminist, nurse and founder of the birth control movement in the US. Born at Corning, NY. (Note: Birth year not entirely certain because, apparently, Sanger often used a later date when obliged to divulge her birthday. Best evidence now points to Sept 14, 1879, rather than the frequently used 1883 date.) She died at Tucson, AZ, Sept 6, 1966.

SETON, ELIZABETH ANN: CANONIZATION: ANNIVERSARY. Sept 14, 1975. Elizabeth Ann Seton became the first native-born American to be canonized. She was a converted Catholic who founded the Sisters of Charity and several schools devoted to the Catholic education of young women. She was declared a saint in 1974 by Pope Paul VI.

SOLO TRANSATLANTIC BALLOON CROSSING: 30th ANNIVERSARY. Sept 14–18, 1984. Joe W. Kittinger, 56-year-old balloonist, left Caribou, ME, in a 10-story-tall, helium-filled balloon named *Rosie O'Grady's Balloon of Peace* Sept 14, 1984, crossed the Atlantic Ocean and reached the French coast, above the town of Capbreton, in bad weather Sept 17 at 4:29 PM, EDT. He crash-landed amid wind and rain near Savone, Italy, at 8:08 AM, EDT, Sept 18. Kittinger suffered a broken ankle when he was thrown from the balloon's gondola during the landing. His nearly 84-hour flight, covering about 3,535 miles, was the first solo balloon crossing of the Atlantic Ocean and a record distance for a solo balloon flight.

UNITED KINGDOM: BATTLE OF BRITAIN WEEK. Sept 14–20. Annually, the week of September containing Battle of Britain Day (Sept 15).

"THE WALTONS" TV PREMIERE: ANNIVERSARY. Sept 14, 1972. This epitome of the family drama spawned nearly a dozen knockoffs during its nine-year run on CBS. The drama was based on creator/writer Earl Hamner Jr's experiences growing up during the Depression in rural Virginia. It began as the TV movie "The Homecoming," which was turned into a weekly series covering the years 1933–43. The cast went through numerous changes through the years; the principals were Michael Learned and Ralph Waite as the parents of seven children living on the mountainside, and Richard Thomas, who portrayed John-Boy, the eldest son and narrator. The Walton grandparents were played by Ellen Corby and Will Geer. The last telecast aired Aug 20, 1981.

WILSON, JAMES: BIRTH ANNIVERSARY. Sept 14, 1742. Signer of the Declaration of Independence and one of the first associate justices of the US Supreme Court. Born at Fifeshire, Scotland, he died Aug 21, 1798, at Edenton, NC.

BIRTHDAYS TODAY

Jessica Brown Findlay, 25, actress ("Downton Abbey"), born Cookham, Berkshire, England, Sept 14, 1989.

Zoe Caldwell, 81, actress (*Medea, The Prime of Miss Jean Brodie*), born Melbourne, Australia, Sept 14, 1933.

Dan Cortese, 47, actor ("Veronica's Closet," *Public Enemies*), born Sewickley, PA, Sept 14, 1967.

Mary Crosby, 55, actress ("Dallas," *Tapeheads*), born Los Angeles, CA, Sept 14, 1959.

Faith Ford, 50, actress ("Hope and Faith," "Murphy Brown"), born Alexandria, LA, Sept 14, 1964.

Joey Heatherton, 70, actress (*Cry-Baby, Bluebeard*), born Rockville Centre, NY, Sept 14, 1944.

Walter Koenig, 78, actor, writer, director, producer ("Star Trek" and *Star Trek* movies), born Chicago, IL, Sept 14, 1936.

Melissa Leo, 54, actress ("Treme," *Frozen River*; Oscar for *The Fighter*), born New York, NY, Sept 14, 1960.

Andrew Lincoln, 41, actor ("The Walking Dead," *Love Actually*), born London, England, Sept 14, 1973.

Dmitry Medvedev, 49, Prime Minister of Russia, born Leningrad, USSR (now St. Petersburg, Russia), Sept 14, 1965.

Kate Millett, 80, feminist, writer (*Sexual Politics, Flying*), born St. Paul, MN, Sept 14, 1934.

Sam Neill, 67, actor (*My Brilliant Career, Jurassic Park, The Piano*), born Omagh, County Tyrone, Northern Ireland, Sept 14, 1947.

September 2014

S	M	T	W	T	F	S
	1	2	3	4	5	6
7	8	9	10	11	12	13
14	15	16	17	18	19	20
21	22	23	24	25	26	27
28	29	30				

September 15 — Monday

DAY 258 **107 REMAINING**

ACUFF, ROY: BIRTH ANNIVERSARY. Sept 15, 1903. Grand Ole Opry "King of Country Music" Roy Acuff was born at Maynardville, TN. Singer and fiddler Acuff (who was cofounder of Acuff-Rose Publishing Company, the leading publisher of country music) was a regular host on weekly Grand Ole Opry broadcasts. He frequently appeared at the Opry with his group, the Smoky Mountain Boys. In December 1991 Acuff became the first living member elected to the Country Music Hall of Fame. Some of his more famous songs were "The Wabash Cannonball" (his theme song), "Pins and Needles (in My Heart)" and "Night Train to Memphis." Roy Acuff died Nov 23, 1992, at Nashville, TN.

"BACHELOR FATHER" TV PREMIERE: ANNIVERSARY. Sept 15, 1957. John Forsythe (Bentley Gregg) and Noreen Corcoran (Kelly Gregg) starred in this sitcom about a bachelor attorney's life turning upside-down after his orphaned niece moves in with him. The last episode aired Sept 25, 1962. Supporting players included Sammee Tong as Peter Tong, the butler, and Jimmy Boyd as Kelly's boyfriend, Howard Meechim.

BALANCE AWARENESS WEEK. Sept 15–21. To develop public awareness of balance and disorders of the balance system (vestibular disorders); to unite professionals, educators, support groups and medical facilities in a weeklong effort to focus attention of the public and the media. Annually, the third week in September. For info: Vestibular Disorders Assn, 5018 NE 15th Ave, Portland, OR 97211. Phone: (800) 837-8428. Fax: (503) 229-8064. E-mail: info@vestibular.org. Web: www.vestibular.org.

BENCHLEY, ROBERT: 125th BIRTH ANNIVERSARY. Sept 15, 1889. Popular humorist and comedian of the 1920s and '30s, who, with Dorothy Parker and Robert Sherwood, formed the core of the Algonquin Round Table of wits in New York City. Benchley, born at Worcester, MA, was also an editor and drama critic at such magazines as *Vanity Fair* and the *New Yorker*. He began to present his comedy pieces on stage and eventually made many into short films, beginning a small acting career. His "How to Sleep" (1935) won the Academy Award for Best Short. Another popular piece was "The Treasurer's Report." Benchley died Nov 21, 1945, at New York, NY.

BIOY CASARES, ADOLFO: 100th BIRTH ANNIVERSARY. Sept 15, 1914. Born at Buenos Aires, Argentina, the writer Bioy created black comedies with a touch of menace or the surreal. His best-known work is the novella *The Invention of Morel* (1940), which was made into the film classic *Last Year at Marienbad* (1961). Bioy was a friend of fellow *porteño* Jorge Luis Borges, and they collaborated on several works together. A recipient of the Cervantes Prize in 1990, Bioy died Mar 8, 1999, at Buenos Aires.

"CHiPs" TV PREMIERE: ANNIVERSARY. Sept 15, 1977. A popular action-packed NBC police series depicting cases and chases of the motorcycle-riding California Highway Patrol. The show starred Erik Estrada as Francis "Ponch" Poncherello and Larry Wilcox as Jon Baker, two quick-witted cops. Wilcox left the show, and Estrada's new partner, Bobby "Hot Dog" Nelson, was played by Tom Reilly. The last telecast aired July 17, 1983.

CHRISTIE, AGATHA: BIRTH ANNIVERSARY. Sept 15, 1890. English author of nearly a hundred books (mysteries, drama, poetry and nonfiction), born at Torquay, England. Died at Wallingford, England, Jan 12, 1976. "Every murderer," she wrote in *The Mysterious Affair at Styles*, "is probably somebody's old friend."

"COLUMBO" TV PREMIERE: ANNIVERSARY. Sept 15, 1971. "Columbo," based on a 1968 made-for-TV movie, entered the lineup of NBC's "Mystery Movie" series on this date. Peter Falk starred as one of TV's great characters, Lieutenant Columbo, the crime-solving policeman dressed in rumpled raincoat and carrying a chewed-up cigar. In almost every episode, Columbo latches himself on to the main suspect, usually a polished sophisticate in comparison to Columbo's seeming simpleton, and nags him or her to death with questions and comments such as "But one thing bothers me, sir." The series ended in 1978 but reemerged in the form of periodic movies beginning in 1989.

COOPER, JAMES FENIMORE: 225th BIRTH ANNIVERSARY. Sept 15, 1789. American novelist, historian and social critic, born at Burlington, NJ, James Fenimore Cooper was one of the earliest American writers to develop a native American literary tradition. His most popular works are the five novels comprising *The Leatherstocking Tales,* featuring the exploits of one of the truly unique American fictional characters, Natty Bumppo. These novels, *The Deerslayer, The Last of the Mohicans, The Pathfinder, The Pioneers* and *The Prairie,* chronicle Natty Bumppo's continuing flight away from the rapid settlement of America. Other works, including *The Monikins* and *Satanstoe,* reveal Cooper as an astute critic of American life. He died Sept 14, 1851, at Cooperstown, NY, the town founded by his father.

COSTA RICA: INDEPENDENCE DAY. Sept 15. National holiday. Gained independence from Spain in 1821.

DATING AND LIFE COACH RECOGNITION WEEK. Sept 15–21. Coaches love to help people lead joyful, purposeful, successful lives. Whether the goals are to find love, pursue passions, embrace challenges, cultivate a career or achieve personal gratification, a coach's job is to empower, guide and inform. This week is a time to recognize the contributions dating and life coaches make to the well-being of society. For info: Robin Gorman Newman, 44 Somerset Dr N, Great Neck, NY 10020. Phone: (516) 773-0911. E-mail: rgnewman@optonline.net. Web: www.lovecoach.com.

EL SALVADOR: INDEPENDENCE DAY. Sept 15. National holiday. Gained independence from Spain in 1821.

FIRST NATIONAL CONVENTION FOR BLACKS: ANNIVERSARY. Sept 15, 1830. The first national convention for blacks was held at Bethel Church, Philadelphia, PA. The convention was called to find ways to better the condition of black people and was attended by delegates from seven states. Bishop Richard Allen was elected as the first convention president.

GREENPEACE FOUNDED: ANNIVERSARY. Sept 15, 1971. The environmental organization Greenpeace, committed to a green and peaceful world, was founded by 12 members of the Don't Make a Wave Committee of Vancouver, BC, Canada, when the boat *Phyllis Cormack* sailed to Amchitka, AK, to protest US nuclear testing. Greenpeace's basic principle is "that determined individuals can alter the actions and purposes of even the overwhelmingly powerful by 'bearing witness'—drawing attention to an environmental abuse through their mere unwavering presence, whatever the risk."

GUATEMALA: INDEPENDENCE DAY. Sept 15. National holiday. Gained independence from Spain in 1821.

HONDURAS: INDEPENDENCE DAY. Sept 15. National holiday. Gained independence from Spain in 1821.

"I SPY" TV PREMIERE: ANNIVERSARY. Sept 15, 1965. Bill Cosby made television history as the first African-American actor starring in a major dramatic role in this spy series. Cosby played Alexander "Scotty" Scott, an intellectual spy with a cover as a tennis trainer. Robert Culp played Kelly Robinson, the "tennis pro" and Scotty's partner in espionage. The series was notable for filming worldwide.

JAPAN: RESPECT FOR THE AGED DAY. Sept 15. National holiday to honor Japan's senior citizens—especially those who are centenarians. Annually, the third Monday in September.

LEHMAN BROTHERS COLLAPSES: ANNIVERSARY. Sept 15, 2008. On this date, venerable banking giant Lehman Brothers, with debt totaling more than $600 billion, filed for Chapter 11 bankruptcy protection. Prior to 2008, Lehman borrowed heavily to invest in the booming (and historically safe) housing market. However, when home prices plummeted as a result of 2008's "subprime mortgage crisis," Lehman, in its financially vulnerable position, suffered huge losses. The company's bankruptcy was by far the largest in US history, and its collapse caused a ripple effect throughout the global financial system.

LGBT CENTER AWARENESS DAY. Sept 15. A national day of action focused on awareness around the work of LGBT community centers everywhere. The day was planned to help bring national attention to the Community Center Movement within the LGBT movement, which serves more than 40,000 people weekly, and highlight the ways that people can get involved or utilize their local centers. Annually, Sept 15. For info: Denise Spivak, CenterLink: The Community of LGBT Centers, PO Box 24490, Fort Lauderdale, FL 33307. Phone: (954) 765-6024. Fax: (954) 765-6593. E-mail: denise@lgbtcenters.org. Web: www.lgbtcenters.org.

"THE LONE RANGER" TV PREMIERE: 65th ANNIVERSARY. Sept 15, 1949. This character was created for a radio serial in 1933 by George W. Trendle. The famous masked man was the alter ego of John Reid, a Texas Ranger who was the only survivor of an ambush. He was nursed back to health by his Native American friend, Tonto. Both men traveled around the West on their trusty steeds, Silver and Scout, fighting injustice. Clayton Moore played the Lone Ranger/John Reid and Jay Silverheels costarred as Tonto. The theme music was Rossini's "William Tell Overture." The last episode aired Sept 12, 1957.

MOON PHASE: LAST QUARTER. Sept 15. Moon enters Last Quarter phase at 10:05 PM, EDT.

✦NATIONAL HISPANIC HERITAGE MONTH. Sept 15–Oct 15. Presidential Proclamation. Beginning in 1989, always issued for Sept 15–Oct 15 of each year (PL 100–402 of Aug 17, 1988). Previously issued each year for the week including Sept 15 and 16 since 1968 at request (PL 90–498 of Sept 17, 1968).

NICARAGUA: INDEPENDENCE DAY. Sept 15. National holiday. Gained independence from Spain in 1821.

QUARTERLY ESTIMATED FEDERAL INCOME TAX PAYERS' DUE DATE. Sept 15. For those individuals whose fiscal year is the calendar year and who make quarterly estimated federal income tax payments, today is one of the due dates (Jan 15, Apr 15, June 16 and Sept 15, 2014).

16th STREET BAPTIST CHURCH BOMBING: ANNIVERSARY. Sept 15, 1963. In a horrific episode of the civil rights struggle, a bomb blast in the basement of the 16th Street Baptist Church in Birmingham, AL, killed four girls preparing for church: Denise McNair, Carole Robertson, Cynthia Wesley and Addie Mae Collins. Previously, the church had been the center for marches led by Dr. Martin Luther King, Jr. Three suspects were brought to trial in 1977, 2001 and 2002 and found guilty.

SPACE MILESTONE: *ARIANE-3* (ESA). Sept 15, 1987. European Space Agency rocket carrying two (Australian and European) communications satellites into Earth's orbit marked the re-entry of Western nations into commercial space projects. Launched this date from Kourou, French Guiana, with Arianespace, a private company, operating the rocket for the 13-nation European Space Agency.

TAFT, WILLIAM HOWARD: BIRTH ANNIVERSARY. Sept 15, 1857. The 27th president of the US was born at Cincinnati, OH. His term of office was Mar 4, 1909–Mar 3, 1913. Following his presidency he became a law professor at Yale University until his appointment as Chief Justice of the US Supreme Court in 1921. Died at Washington, DC, Mar 8, 1930, and buried at Arlington National Cemetery.

TINKER TO EVERS TO CHANCE: FIRST DOUBLE PLAY ANNIVERSARY. Sept 15, 1902. Chicago Cubs' shortstop Joe Tinker, second baseman Johnny Evers and first baseman Frank Chance recorded their first double play together on this date. This was two days after they took the field for the first time in this configuration, and the Cubs went on to beat the Cincinnati Reds, 6–3. The threesome were later immortalized in Franklin Adams's poem "Baseball's Sad Lexicon." Tinker, Evers and Chance were inducted together into the Baseball Hall of Fame in 1946. See also: "'Baseball's Sad Lexicon' Published: Anniversary" (July 10).

UNITED KINGDOM: BATTLE OF BRITAIN DAY. Sept 15. Commemorates end of biggest daylight bombing raid of Britain by German Luftwaffe, in 1940. Said to have been the turning point against Hitler's siege of Britain in WWII.

UNITED NATIONS: INTERNATIONAL DAY OF DEMOCRACY. Sept 15. The General Assembly has declared Sept 15 of each year as the International Day of Democracy (Res 62/7 of Nov 8, 2007) and encourages governments to strengthen national programs devoted to the promotion and consolidation of democracy, in an appropriate manner that contributes to raising public awareness. For info: United Nations, Dept of Public Info, New York, NY, 10017. Web: www.un.org.

US TROOPS ENTER GERMANY: 70th ANNIVERSARY. Sept 15, 1944. US troops of the VII and V Corps reached the southwestern frontier of Germany. The war had finally moved into the Third Reich's backyard.

***USA TODAY* FIRST PUBLISHED: ANNIVERSARY.** Sept 15, 1982. Media corporation Gannett published a new kind of daily—the "Nation's Newspaper"—that featured general-interest articles for a national audience on this date.

WRAY, FAY: BIRTH ANNIVERSARY. Sept 15, 1907. Hollywood's "Scream Queen" was born in Alberta, Canada, on this day. The star of numerous silent films (notably Erich von Stroheim's *The Wedding March*), Wray made her mark in 1930s thrillers—and then became a pop culture icon through her role as Ann Darrow, the giant ape's obsession in the 1933 film *King Kong*. Wray died at New York City, Aug 8, 2004. See also: "*King Kong* Film Premiere: Anniversary" (Mar 2).

BIRTHDAYS TODAY

Dave Annable, 35, actor ("Brothers & Sisters"), born Suffern, NY, Sept 15, 1979.

Josh Charles, 43, actor ("The Good Wife," "Sports Night"), born Baltimore, MD, Sept 15, 1971.

Norm Crosby, 87, comedian, born Boston, MA, Sept 15, 1927.

Tom Hardy, 37, actor (*The Dark Knight Rises, Inception*), born Hammersmith, London, England, Sept 15, 1977.

Prince Harry (Henry Charles Albert David), 30, second son of Prince Charles and Princess Diana, born London, England, Sept 15, 1984.

Tommy Lee Jones, 68, actor (Oscar for *The Fugitive*; *Coal Miner's Daughter, Men in Black, No Country for Old Men*), born San Saba, TX, Sept 15, 1946.

Mark Kirk, 55, US Senator (R, Illinois), born Champaign, IL, Sept 15, 1959.

Daniel Constantine (Dan) Marino, Jr, 53, former football player, born Pittsburgh, PA, Sept 15, 1961.

Carmen Maura, 69, actress (*Women on the Verge of a Nervous Breakdown*), born Madrid, Spain, Sept 15, 1945.

Heidi Montag, 28, television personality ("The Hills," "Laguna Beach"), born Crested Butte, CO, Sept 15, 1986.

Jessye Norman, 69, soprano, opera singer, born Augusta, GA, Sept 15, 1945.

Gaylord Jackson Perry, 76, Hall of Fame baseball player, born Williamston, NC, Sept 15, 1938.

Ben Schwartz, 33, actor ("House of Lies," "Parks and Recreation"), born New York, NY, Sept 15, 1981.

Oliver Stone, 68, director (*Platoon, JFK, Wall Street*), screenwriter, born New York, NY, Sept 15, 1946.

September 16 — Tuesday

DAY 259 **106 REMAINING**

ANNE BRADSTREET DAY. Sept 16. An official date proclaimed by the governor of the Commonwealth of Massachusetts to honor Anne Bradstreet, America's first poet, who is also recognized as the first published woman poet in the English language. Programs scheduled at Stevens Memorial Library and other locales. Anne Bradstreet was born in 1612 in England and came to America in 1630. Unbeknownst to Anne, her brother-in-law took some of her poetry back to England, where it was published in 1650 as *The Tenth Muse Lately Sprung Up in America*. Subsequent editions were also published in Boston. She died at Old Andover, MA, Sept 16, 1672. For info: Director, Stevens Memorial Library, 345 Main St, North Andover, MA 01845. Phone: (978) 688-9505. Fax: (978) 688-9507. E-mail: mquinn@mvlc.org.

CHEROKEE STRIP DAY: ANNIVERSARY. Sept 16, 1893. Optional school holiday, Oklahoma. Greatest "run" for Oklahoma land in 1893.

"FRASIER" TV PREMIERE: ANNIVERSARY. Sept 16, 1993. In this acclaimed spin-off of "Cheers," psychiatrist Dr. Frasier Crane (Kelsey Grammer) has moved to Seattle, where he dispenses advice on his radio show, produced by Roz Doyle (Peri Gilpin). He lives with his ex-cop father, Martin (John Mahoney) and Martin's physical therapist, Daphne Moon (Jane Leeves). His brother, Dr. Niles Crane (David Hyde Pierce), frequently asks for Frasier's advice about his love life. The show, which was a five-time Emmy winner for Outstanding Comedy Series (not to mention numerous Emmys for cast and crew), finished its run in 2004.

FUNT, ALLEN: 100th BIRTH ANNIVERSARY. Sept 16, 1914. Creator, producer and host of the first reality television show, Funt orchestrated elaborate hoaxes played on unsuspecting passersby and filmed by a hidden camera. With the catchphrase, "Smile, you're on Candid Camera," Funt would reveal he had captured the subjects "in the art of being themselves." Born at New York, NY, Funt worked with concealed wire recorders in the US Army Signal Corps during WWII. Premiering on radio as "Candid Microphone" in 1948, the show quickly moved to TV as "Candid Camera" and aired (later, hosted by Funt's son Peter) until 2004. Funt died Sept 5, 1999, at Pebble Beach, CA.

GENERAL MOTORS: FOUNDING ANNIVERSARY. Sept 16, 1908. The giant automobile manufacturing company was founded by William Crapo "Billy" Durant, a Flint, MI, entrepreneur.

GREAT SEAL OF THE US: ANNIVERSARY. Sept 16, 1782. On this date the Great Seal of the United States was, for the first time, impressed upon an official document. That document authorized

September 2014

S	M	T	W	T	F	S
	1	2	3	4	5	6
7	8	9	10	11	12	13
14	15	16	17	18	19	20
21	22	23	24	25	26	27
28	29	30				

George Washington to negotiate a prisoner of war agreement with the British. See also: "Great Seal of the United States: Anniversary" (Jan 28 and July 4).

KENTUCKY BOURBON FESTIVAL. Sept 16–21. Bardstown, KY. Visit the "Bourbon Capital of the World" and celebrate the history and making of Kentucky's finest product, Kentucky bourbon. Enjoy tours, displays, music, food, competitions and much more. Est attendance: 55,000. For info: Kentucky Bourbon Festival, One Court Square, Bardstown, KY 40004. Phone: (800) 638-4877. E-mail: info@kybourbonfestival.com. Web: www.kybourbonfestival.com.

"MANNIX" TV PREMIERE: ANNIVERSARY. Sept 16, 1967. Mike Connors starred as Joe Mannix, a Los Angeles private investigator working for the computer organization Intertect, in this long-running CBS crime series. Joseph Campanella played his boss, Lou Wickersham, during the first season. The show then changed format with Mannix setting up his own agency. The new cast members were Gail Fisher as Peggy Fair, his secretary; Robert Reed as Lieutenant Adam Tobias; and Ward Wood as Lieutenant Art Malcolm.

MAYFLOWER DAY: ANNIVERSARY. Sept 16, 1620. Anniversary of the departure of the *Mayflower* from Plymouth, England, with 102 passengers and a small crew. Vicious storms were encountered en route, which caused serious doubt about the wisdom of continuing, but the ship reached Provincetown, MA, Nov 21, and discharged the Pilgrims at Plymouth, MA, Dec 26, 1620.

MEXICO: INDEPENDENCE DAY. Sept 16. National Day. The official celebration begins at 11 PM, Sept 15 and continues through Sept 16. On the night of the 15th, the president of Mexico steps onto the balcony of the National Palace at Mexico City and voices the same "El Grito" (Cry for Freedom) that Father Hidalgo gave on the night of Sept 15, 1810, that began Mexico's rebellion from Spain.

MIDDLEMARK, MARVIN: 95th BIRTH ANNIVERSARY. Sept 16, 1919. Marvin Middlemark was born at Long Island, NY. His passion for inventing and tinkering led to many inventions, most of which enjoyed little commercial success, like the water-driven automatic potato peeler. But it was as the inventor of a device to improve TV reception, known as "rabbit ears," that he became successful. He died Sept 14, 1989, at Old Westbury, NY.

NETHERLANDS: PRINSJESDAG. Sept 16. Official opening of Parliament at The Hague. The reigning monarch, by tradition, rides in a golden coach to the hall of knights for the annual opening of Parliament. Annually, on the third Tuesday in September.

OLD IRONSIDES SAVED BY POEM: ANNIVERSARY. Sept 16, 1830. Alarmed by a newspaper report that Congress was to have the USS *Constitution* (popularly known as "Old Ironsides") sent to a scrap yard, law student Oliver Wendell Holmes dashed off a poem in protest. The poem began "Ay, tear her tattered ensign down!/Long has it waved on high,/And many an eye has danced to see/That banner in the sky." "Old Ironsides," published anonymously this day in the *Boston Daily Advertisor*, was to stir up national outrage as newspaper after newspaper reprinted it. Congress instead appropriated money for the frigate's reconstruction, and Old Ironsides still floats today. (Some historians think that Holmes never actually saw the ship he saved.) See also: "Old Ironsides Launched: Anniversary" (Oct 21).

PALESTINIAN MASSACRE: ANNIVERSARY. Sept 16, 1982. Christian militiamen (the Phalangists) entered Sabra and Shatila, two Palestinian refugee camps in West Beirut. They began shooting and by Sept 18 hundreds of Palestinians, including elderly men, women and children, were dead. Phalangists had demanded the blood of Palestinians since the assassination of their president, Bashir Gemayel, on Sept 14. Survivors of the massacre said they had not seen Israeli forces inside the camp; however, they claimed Israelis sealed off boundaries to the camps and allowed Christian militiamen to enter.

PANIZZI, ANTHONY: BIRTH ANNIVERSARY. Sept 16, 1797. Sir Anthony Panizzi, the only librarian ever hanged in effigy, was born Antonio Genesio Maria Panizzi at Brescello, Italy. As a young man he joined a forbidden Italian patriotic society that advocated the overthrow of the oppressive Austrians who then controlled most of northern Italy. Tried in absentia by an Austrian court in 1820, he was sentenced to death and all his property was confiscated. He fled to England in 1823, learned the language and by 1831 was employed in the British Museum where, in 1856, he was named principal librarian. Later described as the "prince of librarians," Panizzi died at London, England, Apr 8, 1879.

PAPUA NEW GUINEA: INDEPENDENCE DAY. Sept 16. National holiday. Commemorates independence from Australian administration in 1975.

PARKMAN, FRANCIS: BIRTH ANNIVERSARY. Sept 16, 1823. American historian, author of *The Oregon Trail*, was born at Boston, MA, and died there Nov 8, 1893.

TORQUEMADA, TOMAS DE: DEATH ANNIVERSARY. Sept 16, 1498. One of history's most malevolent persons, feared and hated by millions. As Inquisitor-General of Spain, he ordered burning at the stake for more than 10,000 persons and burning in effigy for another 7,000 (according to 18th-century estimates). Torquemada persuaded Ferdinand and Isabella to rid Spain of the Jews. More than a million families were driven from the country, and Spain suffered a commercial decline from which it never recovered. Torquemada was born at Valladolid, Spain, in 1420 (exact date unknown) and died at Avila, Spain.

UNITED NATIONS: INTERNATIONAL DAY FOR THE PRESERVATION OF THE OZONE LAYER. Sept 16. On Dec 19, 1994, the General Assembly proclaimed this day to commemorate the date in 1987 on which Montreal Protocol on Substances that Deplete the Ozone Layer was signed (Resolution 49/114). States are invited to devote the day to promote, at the national level, activities in accordance with the objectives of the protocol. The ozone layer filters sunlight and prevents the adverse effects of ultraviolet radiation from reaching the earth's surface, thereby preserving life on the planet. For info: United Nations, Dept of Public Info, Public Inquiries Unit, Rm GA-57, New York, NY 10017. Phone: (212) 963-4475. E-mail: inquiries@un.org. Web: www.un.org.

UNITED NATIONS: OPENING DAY OF GENERAL ASSEMBLY. Sept 16. The 69th session. Annually, the Tuesday of the third week in September, counting from the first week that contains at least one working day. For info: United Nations, Dept of Public Info, New York, NY 10017. Web: www.un.org.

BIRTHDAYS TODAY

Marc Anthony, 45, singer, actor (*Bringing Out the Dead*), born New York, NY, Sept 16, 1969.

Lauren Bacall, 90, actress (*Applause, Woman of the Year, Key Largo*), born Betty Joan Perske at New York, NY, Sept 16, 1924.

Elgin Gay Baylor, 80, Hall of Fame basketball player, former coach, born Washington, DC, Sept 16, 1934.

Ed Begley, Jr, 65, actor ("St. Elsewhere"), born Los Angeles, CA, Sept 16, 1949.

Alexis Bledel, 32, actress (*The Sisterhood of the Traveling Pants*, "Gilmore Girls"), born Houston, TX, Sept 16, 1982.

Sabrina Bryan, 30, singer, actress ("The Cheetah Girls," "Dancing with the Stars"), born Yorba Linda, CA, Sept 16, 1984.

David Copperfield, 58, illusionist, born David Kotkin at Metuchen, NJ, Sept 16, 1956.

Henry Louis Gates, Jr, 64, scholar of African-American studies, author, editor, born Keyser, WV, Sept 16, 1950.

Orel Leonard Hershiser IV, 56, former baseball player, born Buffalo, NY, Sept 16, 1958.

Nick Jonas, 22, singer (The Jonas Brothers), actor, born Dallas, TX, Sept 16, 1992.

B.B. King, 89, singer, born Itta Bena, MS, Sept 16, 1925.

Richard Marx, 51, singer, born Chicago, IL, Sept 16, 1963.

Mark McEwen, 60, weatherman, music editor, born San Antonio, TX, Sept 16, 1954.

Janis Paige, 92, singer, actress (stage: *The Pajama Game, Silk Stockings*), born Donna Mae Tjaden at Tacoma, WA, Sept 16, 1922.

Amy Poehler, 43, actress, comedienne (*Baby Mama*, "Parks and Recreation," "Saturday Night Live"), born Burlington, MA, Sept 16, 1971.

Tim Raines, 55, former baseball player, born Sanford, FL, Sept 16, 1959.

Mickey Rourke, 58, actor (*The Wrestler, Sin City, Diner*), born Schenectady, NY, Sept 16, 1956.

Susan Ruttan, 64, actress ("LA Law"), born Oregon City, OR, Sept 16, 1950.

Molly Shannon, 50, actress ("Saturday Night Live"), born Shaker Heights, OH, Sept 16, 1964.

Jennifer Tilly, 53, actress (*Johnny Be Good, Made in America*), born Los Angeles, CA, Sept 16, 1961.

Robin R. Yount, 59, Hall of Fame baseball player, born Danville, IL, Sept 16, 1955.

September 17 — Wednesday

DAY 260 **105 REMAINING**

AMERICAN MASSAGE THERAPY ASSOCIATION® NATIONAL CONVENTION. Sept 17–20. Colorado Convention Center, Denver, CO. Annual meeting and convention of the American Massage Therapy Association (AMTA). AMTA is a nonprofit professional association with 56,000 members from throughout the US. Includes continuing education classes, association governance and current massage research. Exhibit area of products and services pertinent to the profession. Est attendance: 1,400. For info: American Massage Therapy Assn, 500 Davis St, Ste 900, Evanston, IL 60201. Phone: (877) 905-2700. E-mail: convention@amtamassage.org. Web: www.amtamassage.org.

ANGOLA: DAY OF THE NATIONAL HERO. Sept 17. National holiday.

BATTLE OF ANTIETAM: ANNIVERSARY. Sept 17, 1862. This date has been called America's bloodiest day in recognition of the high casualties suffered in the Civil War battle between General Robert E. Lee's Confederate forces and General George McClellan's Union army. Estimates vary, but more than 25,000 Union and Confederate soldiers were killed or wounded in this battle on the banks of the Potomac River in Maryland.

"BEWITCHED" TV PREMIERE: 50th ANNIVERSARY. Sept 17, 1964. This sitcom centered around blonde-haired witch Samantha Stephens (Elizabeth Montgomery). Although she promises not to use her witchcraft in her daily life, Samantha finds herself twitching her nose in many situations. Her husband, Darrin Stephens, was played by Dick York and later Dick Sargent, and her daughter, Tabitha Stephens, was played by Erin and Diane Murphy. The last episode aired July 1, 1972. Other cast members included Agnes Moorehead, David White, Alice Ghostley, Bernard Fox and Paul Lynde.

BURGER, WARREN E.: BIRTH ANNIVERSARY. Sept 17, 1907. Former Chief Justice of the US Supreme Court, Warren E. Burger was born at St. Paul, MN. A conservative on criminal matters, but a progressive on social issues, he had the longest tenure (1969–86) of any chief justice in the 20th century. Appointed by President Nixon, he voted in the majority on *Roe v Wade* (1973), which upheld a woman's right to an abortion, and on *US v Nixon* (1974), which forced Nixon to surrender audiotapes to the Watergate special prosecutor. He died June 25, 1995, at Washington, DC.

✦CITIZENSHIP DAY. Sept 17. Presidential Proclamation always issued for Sept 17 at request (PL 82–261 of Feb 29, 1952). Customarily issued as "Citizenship Day and Constitution Week." Replaces Constitution Day.

CONNOLLY, MAUREEN: 80th BIRTH ANNIVERSARY. Sept 17, 1934. Maureen ("Little Mo") Catherine Connolly Brinker, tennis player born at San Diego, CA. Connolly became the second-youngest woman to win the US National championship at Forest Hills, NY, when she captured that title in 1951. She repeated in 1952 and won Wimbledon as well. In 1953 she became the first woman to win the Grand Slam, taking the US, French, Australian and Wimbledon championships. After winning a second straight French title and a third straight Wimbledon, she suffered a crushed leg in a horseback riding accident and never competed again. Died at Dallas, TX, June 21, 1969.

CONSTITUTION COMMEMORATION DAY IN ARIZONA. Sept 17. Arizona. This state holiday commemorates the signing of the US Constitution on Sept 17, 1787.

CONSTITUTION DAY/PLEDGE ACROSS AMERICA. Sept 17. Every school is invited to join a synchronized recitation of the Pledge of Allegiance coast to coast, 8 AM Hawaiian time to 2 PM Eastern time. This event enables our nation's youth to unite during regular school hours for a patriotic observance. Senator Robert Byrd drafted legislation—passed by Congress—requiring public schools to provide an exercise about the US Constitution on Constitution Day. Resources for schools available, including a free CD with musical renditions of the Pledge, Preamble, Constitution and Bill of Rights. Annually, Sept 17 (except when it falls on a weekend). For info: Paula Burton, President, Celebration USA, 18482 Valley Dr, Villa Park, CA 92861. Phone: (714) 974-3691. E-mail: pbcusa@sbcglobal.net. Web: www.celebrationusa.org.

CONSTITUTION OF THE US: ANNIVERSARY. Sept 17, 1787. Delegations from 12 states (Rhode Island did not send a delegate) at the Constitutional Convention at Philadelphia, PA, voted unanimously to approve the proposed document. Thirty-nine of the 42 delegates present signed it, and the Convention adjourned, after drafting a letter of transmittal to the Congress. The proposed constitution stipulated that it would take effect when ratified by nine states. This day is a legal holiday in Florida.

✦CONSTITUTION WEEK. Sept 17–23. Presidential Proclamation always issued for the period of Sept 17–23 each year since 1955 (PL 84–915 of Aug 2, 1956).

FOSTER, ANDREW (RUBE): BIRTH ANNIVERSARY. Sept 17, 1879. Rube Foster's efforts in baseball earned him the title of "The Father of Negro Baseball." He was a manager and star pitcher, pitching 51 victories in one year. In 1919, he called a meeting of black baseball owners and organized the first black baseball league, the Negro National League. He served as its president until his death in 1930. Foster was born at Calvert, TX, the son of a minister. He died Dec 9, 1930, at Kankakee, IL.

"THE FUGITIVE" TV PREMIERE: ANNIVERSARY. Sept 17, 1963. A nail-biting adventure series on ABC. Dr. Richard Kimble (David Janssen) was wrongly convicted and sentenced to death for his wife's murder but escaped from his captors in a train wreck. This popular program aired for four years detailing Kimble's search for

September 2014

S	M	T	W	T	F	S
	1	2	3	4	5	6
7	8	9	10	11	12	13
14	15	16	17	18	19	20
21	22	23	24	25	26	27
28	29	30				

the one-armed man (Bill Raisch) who had killed his wife, Helen (Diane Brewster). In the meantime Kimble himself was being pursued by Lieutenant Philip Gerard (Barry Morse). The final episode aired Aug 29, 1967, and featured Kimble extracting a confession from the one-armed man as they struggled from the heights of a water tower in a deserted amusement park. That single episode was the highest-rated show ever broadcast until 1976. The TV series generated a hit movie in 1993 with Harrison Ford as Kimble and Oscar-winner Tommy Lee Jones as Gerard.

GOLDEN ASPEN MOTORCYCLE RALLY. Sept 17–21. Ruidoso, NM. Trade show, bike shows, riding tours, skill events, parade, awards banquet, stunt shows and thousands in prizes. Est attendance: 35,000. For info: Golden Aspen Rally Assn, PO Box 1467, Ruidoso, NM 88355. Phone: (575) 973-4977. E-mail: info@motorcyclerally.com. Web: www.motorcyclerally.com.

HENDRICKS, THOMAS ANDREWS: BIRTH ANNIVERSARY. Sept 17, 1819. Twenty-first vice president of the US (1885) born at Muskingum County, OH. Died at Indianapolis, IN, Nov 25, 1885.

HERZOG, CHAIM: BIRTH ANNIVERSARY. Sept 17, 1918. President of Israel, an ex-general and chief delegate to the UN, author and lawyer, born at Belfast, Northern Ireland. He was a British army officer in WWII. Died at Tel Aviv, Israel, Apr 17, 1997.

"M*A*S*H" TV PREMIERE: ANNIVERSARY. Sept 17, 1972. This popular award-winning CBS series was based on the 1970 Robert Altman movie and a book by Richard Hooker. Set during the Korean War, the show aired for 11 years (lasting longer than the war). It followed the lives of doctors and nurses on the war front with both humor and pathos. The cast included Wayne Rogers, McLean Stevenson, Loretta Swit, Larry Linville, Gary Burghoff, William Christopher, Jamie Farr, Harry Morgan, Mike Farrell, David Ogden Stiers and Alan Alda as Captain "Hawkeye" Pierce. The final episode, "Goodbye, Farewell and Amen" was the highest-rated program of all time, topping the "Who Shot J.R.?" revelation on "Dallas." The show generated two spin-offs: "Trapper John, MD" and "After M*A*S*H." See also: "M*A*S*H: The Final Episode: Anniversary" (Feb 28).

"MISSION: IMPOSSIBLE" TV PREMIERE: ANNIVERSARY. Sept 17, 1966. This action-adventure espionage series, which appeared on CBS for seven years, had a simple premise: each week the IMF (Impossible Missions Force) leader would receive instructions on a super-secret mission to be carried out by the crew. Steven Hill played the first IMF leader, Dan Briggs. He was replaced by Peter Graves, who played Jim Phelps. Other cast members included Martin Landau as Rollin Hand, master of disguise; Barbara Bain, real-life wife of Landau, as Cinnamon Carter; Leonard Nimoy as Hand's replacement, Paris; Lesley Ann Warren as Dana Lambert; and Sam Elliott as Doug. The show was remade for ABC in 1988; it lasted two seasons. Tom Cruise resurrected the concept for several feature films, beginning in 1996.

NATIONAL CONSTITUTION CENTER CONSTITUTION DAY. Sept 17. To celebrate and commemorate the signing of the US Constitution Sept 17, 1787. The National Constitution Center hosts special events and activities. Est attendance: 50,000. For info: Natl Constitution Center, Independence Mall, 525 Arch St, Philadelphia, PA 19106. Phone: (215) 409-6600. Web: www.constitutioncenter.org.

NATIONAL FOOTBALL LEAGUE FORMED: ANNIVERSARY. Sept 17, 1920. The National Football League was formed at Canton, OH.

NATIONAL GUITAR FLAT-PICKING CHAMPIONSHIPS AND WALNUT VALLEY FESTIVAL. Sept 17–21. Cowley County Fairgrounds, Winfield, KS. The Walnut River is the site of this 43rd annual family event featuring four stages with eight contests, at least 14 workshops and many first-class concerts. The Walnut Valley Arts and Crafts Festival features handmade instruments and a large variety of arts and crafts items, both ornamental and functional. All-weather facilities. Est attendance: 45,000. For info: Walnut Valley Assn, Bob Redford, PO Box 245, Winfield, KS 67156. Phone: (620) 221-3250. Fax: (620) 221-3109. E-mail: hq@wvfest.com. Web: www.wvfest.com.

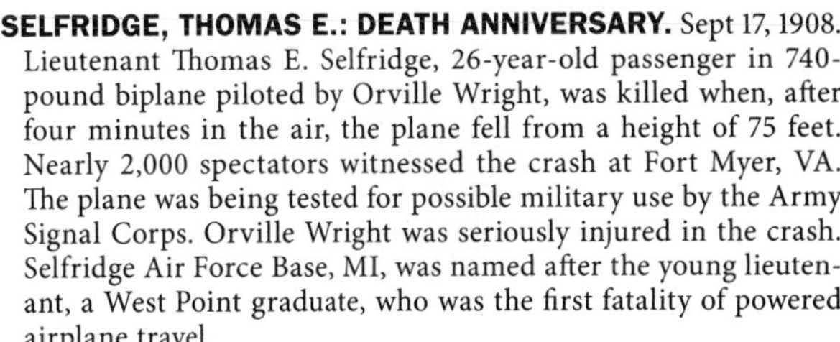

SELFRIDGE, THOMAS E.: DEATH ANNIVERSARY. Sept 17, 1908. Lieutenant Thomas E. Selfridge, 26-year-old passenger in 740-pound biplane piloted by Orville Wright, was killed when, after four minutes in the air, the plane fell from a height of 75 feet. Nearly 2,000 spectators witnessed the crash at Fort Myer, VA. The plane was being tested for possible military use by the Army Signal Corps. Orville Wright was seriously injured in the crash. Selfridge Air Force Base, MI, was named after the young lieutenant, a West Point graduate, who was the first fatality of powered airplane travel.

SPACE MILESTONE: *PEGASUS 1* (US). Sept 17, 1978. 23,000-pound research satellite broke up over Africa and fell to Earth. Major pieces are believed to have fallen into Atlantic Ocean off the coast of Angola. The satellite had been orbiting Earth for more than 13 years since being launched Feb 16, 1965.

VON STEUBEN, BARON FRIEDRICH: BIRTH ANNIVERSARY. Sept 17, 1730. Prussian-born general who volunteered to serve in the American Revolution. He died at Remsen, NY, Nov 28, 1794. Von Steuben Day is commemorated on this day, on the following Saturday or on the fourth Sunday in September.

WILLIAMS, HANK, SR: BIRTH ANNIVERSARY. Sept 17, 1923. Hiram King Williams, country and western singer, born at Georgia, AL. He achieved his first hit with "Lovesick Blues," which brought him a contract with the Grand Ole Opry. His string of hits include "Cold, Cold Heart," "Honky Tonk Blues," "Jambalaya," "Your Cheatin' Heart," "Take These Chains from My Heart" and "I'll Never Get Out of This World Alive," which was released prior to his death Jan 1, 1953, at Oak Hill, VA.

BIRTHDAYS TODAY

Tomas Berdych, 29, tennis player, born Valasske-Mezirici, Czech Republic, Sept 17, 1985.

Mark Brunell, 44, former football player, born Los Angeles, CA, Sept 17, 1970.

Kyle Chandler, 49, actor ("Friday Night Lights," "Homefront," *King Kong*), born Buffalo, NY, Sept 17, 1965.

Charles Grassley, 81, US Senator (R, Iowa), born New Hartford, IA, Sept 17, 1933.

Philip D. (Phil) Jackson, 69, former basketball coach, former player, born Deer Lodge, MT, Sept 17, 1945.

Chuck Liddell, 45, mixed martial artist, born Santa Barbara, CA, Sept 17, 1969.

Baz Luhrmann, 52, director (*The Great Gatsby, Moulin Rouge*), born Mark Anthony Luhrmann at Sydney, Australia, Sept 17, 1962.

Alexander Ovechkin, 29, hockey player, born Moscow, Russia, Sept 17, 1985.

Cassandra Peterson, 63, actress (movie hostess Elvira), born Manhattan, KS, Sept 17, 1951.

Rita Rudner, 58, comedienne, actress (*Peter's Friends*), born Miami, FL, Sept 17, 1956.

David H. Souter, 75, former associate justice of the US, born Melrose, MA, Sept 17, 1939.

Rasheed Wallace, 40, basketball player, born Philadelphia, PA, Sept 17, 1974.

September 18 — Thursday

DAY 261 **104 REMAINING**

"THE ADDAMS FAMILY" TV PREMIERE: 50th ANNIVERSARY. Sept 18, 1964. Charles Addams's quirky *New Yorker* cartoon creations were brought to life in this ABC sitcom about a family full of oddballs. John Astin played lawyer Gomez Addams; with Carolyn Jones as his morbid wife, Morticia; Ken Weatherwax as son Pugsley; Lisa Loring as daughter Wednesday; Jackie Coogan as Uncle Fester; Ted Cassidy as both Lurch, the butler, and Thing, a disembodied hand; Blossom Rock as Grandmama; and Felix Silla as Cousin Itt. The last episode aired Sept 2, 1966. In 1991, *The Addams Family* movie was released, followed by a sequel. Both starred Anjelica Huston as Morticia, Raul Julia as Gomez, Christopher Lloyd as Uncle Fester, Jimmy Workman as Pugsley and Christina Ricci as Wednesday.

BRAZZI, ROSSANO: BIRTH ANNIVERSARY. Sept 18, 1916. Hollywood actor Rossano Brazzi was born at Bologna, Italy. A leading romantic figure in the 1950s and 1960s, he appeared in more than 200 films (*South Pacific, Summertime*). He died Dec 24, 1994, at Rome, Italy.

CHILE: INDEPENDENCE DAY. Sept 18. National holiday. Declared independence from Spain in 1810. Sept 19 is commemorated as Armed Forces Day in Chile.

COLUMBUS'S LAST VOYAGE TO THE NEW WORLD: ANNIVERSARY. Sept 18, 1502. Columbus landed at Costa Rica on his fourth and last voyage to the New World. He returned to Spain in 1504 and died there in 1506.

DeMILLE, AGNES: BIRTH ANNIVERSARY. Sept 18, 1905. Dancer and choreographer for ballet and Broadway shows such as *Oklahoma*, born at New York, NY. DeMille died at New York, NY, Oct 7, 1993.

DIEFENBAKER, JOHN: BIRTH ANNIVERSARY. Sept 18, 1895. Canadian lawyer, statesman and Conservative prime minister (1957–63). Born at Normandy Township, ON, Canada, he died at Ottawa, ON, Aug 16, 1979. Diefenbaker was a member of the Canadian Parliament from 1940 until his death.

GARBO, GRETA: BIRTH ANNIVERSARY. Sept 18, 1905. International film actress Greta Garbo was born Greta Lovisa Gustafsson at Stockholm, Sweden. A famous recluse, she retired temporarily, then permanently, from films after 19 years and 27 films, which spanned the late silent era and beginning of sound movies. Her on-screen roles were characterized by an image of a seductress involved in tragic love affairs. She died Apr 15, 1990, at New York, NY.

September 2014

S	M	T	W	T	F	S
	1	2	3	4	5	6
7	8	9	10	11	12	13
14	15	16	17	18	19	20
21	22	23	24	25	26	27
28	29	30				

"GET SMART" TV PREMIERE: ANNIVERSARY. Sept 18, 1965. A spy-thriller spoof appearing on both NBC (1965–69) and CBS (1969–70). Don Adams starred as bumbling CONTROL Agent 86, Maxwell Smart. His mission was to thwart the evildoings of the KAOS organization. Agent Smart was usually successful with the help of his friends: Barbara Feldon as Agent 99 (whom Smart eventually married), Edward Platt as the Chief, Robert Karvelas as Agent Larrabee, Dick Gautier as Hymie the Robot and David Ketchum as Agent 13.

HUG A GREETING CARD WRITER DAY. Sept 18. Greeting card writers provide the words that we send at all life's most basic, personal moments whether everyday occasions or seasonal. They are the folks who furnish the sentiments that most people are unwilling or unable to say for themselves to someone dear. Greeting card writers are generally anonymous and often underappreciated, yet their words are present in every nook and cranny of America. As such, the least they deserve is a once-a-year hug! Annually, every Sept 18. For info: Sandra Miller-Louden, PO Box 485, Grantsville, MD 21536. Phone: (412) 477-4299. E-mail: sandra@greetingcardwriting.com. Web: www.greetingcardwriting.com.

HULL HOUSE OPENS: 125th ANNIVERSARY. Sept 18, 1889. This settlement house was founded in Chicago by Jane Addams and Ellen Gates Starr. It soon became the heart of one of the country's most influential social reform movements, offering a mix of cultural and education programs to new immigrants. See also: "Addams, Jane: Birth Anniversary" (Sept 6).

HUMMERBIRD CELEBRATION. Sept 18–21. Rockport and Fulton, TX. To celebrate the spectacular fall migration of the ruby-throated hummingbird and other birds from their summer nesting grounds in the north along the eastern Gulf Coast on the way to their winter grounds in Mexico and Central America and the hummerbirds' 500-mile journey across the Gulf. There are programs, workshops, booths, concessions and bus and boat tours. Est attendance: 6,000. For info: Rockport Fulton Area Chamber of Commerce, HummerBird Celebration, 319 Broadway, Rockport, TX 78382. Phone: (800) 242-0071 or (361) 729-6445. Fax: (361) 729-7681. E-mail: tourism@1rockport.org. Web: www.rockporthummingbird.com.

IRON HORSE OUTRACED BY HORSE: ANNIVERSARY. Sept 18, 1830. In a widely celebrated race, the first locomotive built in America, the Tom Thumb, lost to a horse. Mechanical difficulties plagued the steam engine over the nine-mile course between Riley's Tavern and Baltimore, MD, and a boiler leak prevented the locomotive from finishing the race. In the early days of trains, engines were nicknamed "Iron Horses."

JOHNSON, SAMUEL: BIRTH ANNIVERSARY. Sept 18, 1709. (Old Style date.) English lexicographer and literary lion, creator of the first great dictionary of the English language (1755) and author of poems, novels and essays. Johnson was born at Lichfield, Staffordshire, England, and died at London, England, Dec 13, 1784. Johnson, master of the quip, stated, "Patriotism is the last refuge of a scoundrel."

LITTLE BROWN JUG. Sept 18. Delaware County Fairgrounds, Delaware, OH. 69th annual. The most prestigious three-year-old pacing race in North America. Occurs during the Delaware County Fair (Sept 13–20). Est attendance: 50,000. For info: Little Brown Jug, Delaware County Fair, 236 Pennsylvania Ave, Delaware, OH 43015. E-mail: fair@delawarecountyfair.com. Web: www.delawarecountyfair.com.

"LOVE IS A MANY SPLENDORED THING" TV PREMIERE: ANNIVERSARY. Sept 18, 1967. A soap opera created by veteran writer Irna Phillips, airing on CBS for five years. It was based on the 1955 film starring William Holden and Jennifer Jones. Irna Phillips left the show after the network nixed interracial romance in favor of political story lines. David Birney, Bibi Besch and Donna Mills appeared on the show.

THE *NEW YORK TIMES* FIRST PUBLISHED: ANNIVERSARY. Sept 18, 1851. The *Times* debuted as the *New-York Daily Times*. The name was changed to the current one in 1857.

READ, GEORGE: BIRTH ANNIVERSARY. Sept 18, 1733. Lawyer and signer of the Declaration of Independence, born at Cecil County, MD. Died Sept 21, 1798, at New Castle, DE.

SCOTLAND: REFERENDUM ON INDEPENDENCE. Sept 18. The people of Scotland vote today in an independence referendum. They are asked the question: Should Scotland be an independent country? Yes or No. The Scottish Parliament has been granted the powers to organize the referendum and both UK and Scottish Governments have agreed they will respect the result. The main Scottish Independence Referendum Bill was introduced to the Scottish Parliament on Mar 21, 2013.

STORY, JOSEPH: BIRTH ANNIVERSARY. Sept 18, 1779. Associate justice of the US Supreme Court (1811–45), born at Marblehead, MA. "It is astonishing," he wrote a few months before his death, "how easily men satisfy themselves that the Constitution is exactly what they wish it to be." Story died Sept 10, 1845, at Cambridge, MA, having served 33 years on the Supreme Court.

US AIR FORCE ESTABLISHED: ANNIVERSARY. Sept 18, 1947. Although its heritage dates back to 1907 when the army first established military aviation, the US Air Force became a separate military service on this date. Responsible for providing an air force that is capable, in conjunction with the other armed forces, of preserving the peace and security of the US, the department is separately organized under the secretary of the air force and operates under the authority, direction and control of the secretary of defense.

US CAPITOL CORNERSTONE LAID: ANNIVERSARY. Sept 18, 1793. President George Washington laid the Capitol cornerstone at Washington, DC, in a Masonic ceremony. That event was the first and last recorded occasion at which the stone with its engraved silver plate was seen. In 1958, during the extension of the east front of the Capitol, an unsuccessful effort was made to find it.

US TAKES OUT ITS FIRST LOAN: 125th ANNIVERSARY. Sept 18, 1789. The first loan taken out by the US was negotiated and secured by Alexander Hamilton on Feb 17, 1790. After beginning negotiations with the Bank of New York and the Bank of North America on Sept 18, 1789, Hamilton obtained the sum of $191,608.81 from the two banks in what became known as the Temporary Loan of 1789. The loan was obtained without authority of law and was used to pay the salaries of the president, senators, representatives and officers of the first Congress. Repayment was completed on June 8, 1790.

"WAGON TRAIN" TV PREMIERE: ANNIVERSARY. Sept 18, 1957. "Wagon Train" was a popular western on NBC and ABC, airing for eight years with its last telecast Sept 5, 1965. Each week travelers on a journey along the wagon trail from Missouri to California encountered new surroundings and interacted with different guest stars. Ward Bond played wagonmaster Major Seth Adams until his death in 1960. He was replaced by John McIntire as Chris Hale. Other regulars were: Robert Horton (scout Flint McCullough), Frank McGrath (cook Charlie Wooster), Terry Wilson (Bill Hawks), Denny (Scott) Miller (scout Duke Shannon), Michael Burns (Barnaby West) and Robert Fuller as scout Cooper.

WHITE WOMAN MADE AMERICAN INDIAN CHIEF: ANNIVERSARY. Sept 18, 1891. Harriet Maxwell Converse was made a chief of the Six Nations Tribe at the Tonawanda Reservation, NY. She was given the name Ga-is-wa-noh, which means "The Watcher." She had been adopted as a member of the Seneca tribe in 1884 in appreciation of her efforts on behalf of the tribe.

WORLD WATER MONITORING DAY. Sept 18. An international education and outreach program that builds public awareness and involvement in protecting water resources around the world by engaging citizens to conduct basic monitoring of their local water bodies. In 2011 more than 300,000 people in 77 countries monitored their local waterways. Celebrate on Sept 18, and/or host your own World Water Monitoring Day anytime from Mar 22 (World Water Day) until Dec 31. Annually, Sept 18. For info: Water Environment Federation, 601 Wythe St, Alexandria, VA 22314. Phone: (703) 535-5264. E-mail: wwmd@wef.org. Web: www.worldwatermonitoringday.org.

BIRTHDAYS TODAY

Lance Armstrong, 43, retired cyclist, born Plano, TX, Sept 18, 1971.

Frankie Avalon, 75, singer, actor (*Beach Blanket Bingo*), born Philadelphia, PA, Sept 18, 1939.

Robert Blake, 76, actor ("Baretta," *In Cold Blood, Little Rascals*), born Michael Gubitosi at Nutley, NJ, Sept 18, 1938.

Scotty Bowman, 81, Hall of Fame hockey coach, born Montreal, QC, Canada, Sept 18, 1933.

Serge Ibaka, 25, basketball player, born Brazzaville, Zaire, Sept 18, 1989.

Ryne Sandberg, 55, baseball manager, Hall of Fame player, born Spokane, WA, Sept 18, 1959.

Jada Pinkett Smith, 43, actress (*The Nutty Professor, Menace II Society*), born Baltimore, MD, Sept 18, 1971.

Aisha Tyler, 44, television host, actress ("Talk Soup," "24," "CSI"), born San Francisco, CA, Sept 18, 1970.

September 19 — Friday

DAY 262 **103 REMAINING**

APPLEJACK FESTIVAL. Sept 19–21. Nebraska City, NE. Nebraska City is home to three apple orchards, which have expanded to include peaches, cherries, vineyards and more. Citywide events include All-You-Can-Eat Pancake Feed, Applejack Fun Run and Walk, Fire House Grill Lunch, annual parade and marching band competition, car show, Spaghetti Feed, AppleJam Carnival, craft fairs, specialty shopping deals, live music and much more. Est attendance: 45,000. For info: Nebraska City Tourism & Commerce, 806 1st Ave, Nebraska City, NE 68410. Phone: (402) 873-6654. Fax: (402) 873-6701. E-mail: tourism@nebraskacity.com. Web: www.nebraskacity.com.

ASIAN GAMES—INCHEON 2014. Sept 19–Oct 4. Incheon, South Korea. The 45 member nations of the Olympic Council of Asia will celebrate the 17th Asian Games. More than 13,000 athletes will participate in 36 events (28 Olympic events) in and around Incheon. Held every four years. For info: Asian Games—Incheon 2014. Web: www.incheon2014ag.org.

BROUGHAM, HENRY PETER: BIRTH ANNIVERSARY. Sept 19, 1778. Scottish jurist and orator born at Edinburgh, Scotland. Died at Cannes, France, May 7, 1868. The Brougham carriage was named after him. "Education," he said, "makes a people easy to lead, but difficult to drive; easy to govern, but impossible to enslave."

CARROLL, CHARLES: BIRTH ANNIVERSARY. Sept 19, 1737. (Old Style date.) American Revolutionary leader and signer of the Declaration of Independence, born at Annapolis, MD. The last surviving signer of the Declaration, he died Nov 14, 1832, at Baltimore, MD.

CRESTON/SOUTHWEST IOWA HOT AIR BALLOON DAYS. Sept 19–21. Creston, IA. Hare and hound races held at sunrise and sunset; parade and marching band contest; craft market; food and much more. Annually, the third weekend in September. Est attendance: 9,500. For info: Creston Chamber of Commerce, PO Box 471, Creston, IA 50801. Phone: (641) 782-7021. E-mail: chamber@crestoniowachamber.com. Web: www.crestoniowachamber.com.

DANGER RUN. Sept 19–Oct 25 (Friday and Saturday evenings). Louisville, KY, and Clarksville, IN. This Halloween-themed road rally (ghost run) features participants following a series of rhyming, limerick-style clues that lead to two premier haunted houses. Each of the clues, when solved correctly, will reveal the next turn that participants will make as they attempt to stay on the route. Prizes are awarded to the groups who follow the route most accurately as indicated by their vehicle odometer. A virtual version of the game is also available on the website. For info: Joe Bulleit, Danger Run, PO Box 2070, Clarksville, IN 47131. Phone: (800) 771-9750. Fax: (812) 280-7153. E-mail: joe@dangerrun.com. Web: www.dangerrun.com.

"ER" TV PREMIERE: 20th ANNIVERSARY. Sept 19, 1994. This medical drama took place in the emergency room of the fictional County General Hospital in Chicago. Doctors and nurses cared for life-and-death cases while experiencing their personal traumas as well. The cast included Anthony Edwards, George Clooney, Julianna Margulies, Sherry Stringfield, Noah Wyle, Laura Innes, Gloria Reuben, Eriq La Salle, Maura Tierney, Goran Visnjic, Alex Kingston, John Stamos and many others. On Dec 6, 2007, the 300th episode aired. The final episode aired on Apr 2, 2009.

FINLAND SIGNS ARMISTICE WITH ALLIES: 70th ANNIVERSARY. Sept 19, 1944. On the preceding Sept 2, Finland's new prime minister, Antti Hackzell, broke diplomatic relations with Germany. Two days later he declared a cease-fire on all fronts and began peace negotiations with Russia, signing an armistice with the Soviet Union on this date. For their part, the Soviets extended terms far more lenient than had been expected.

"FLIPPER" TV PREMIERE: 50th ANNIVERSARY. Sept 19, 1964. An adventure series starring Flipper, the intelligent, communicative and helpful dolphin. The human cast members included Brian Kelly as Chief Ranger Porter Ricks, Luke Halpin as his son Sandy, Tommy Norden as his son Bud and Ulla Strömstedt as biochemist Ulla Norstrand. The last telecast of this series was Sept 1, 1968. The series was briefly re-created under the same title in the '90s.

September 2014

S	M	T	W	T	F	S
	1	2	3	4	5	6
7	8	9	10	11	12	13
14	15	16	17	18	19	20
21	22	23	24	25	26	27
28	29	30				

GOLDING, SIR WILLIAM: BIRTH ANNIVERSARY. Sept 19, 1911. Born at Columb Minor at Cornwall, England, this celebrated author was recognized for his contributions to literature with a Nobel Prize in 1983. His first and most popular novel was *Lord of the Flies*. He died June 19, 1993, near Truro, Cornwall.

"ICEMAN" MUMMY DISCOVERED: ANNIVERSARY. Sept 19, 1991. At 10,531 feet in the Austrian-Italian Alps, two hikers discovered a 5,300-year-old frozen mummy from late Neolithic times. The man carried rough bow and arrows as well as a copper axe and wore a grass cloak for warmth. His shoes were made from bearskin, deer hide and tree bark. He now rests as a frozen exhibit at the South Tyrol Museum of Archaeology at Bolzano, Italy. The "Iceman" was gently thawed in September 2000 in order for scientists to conduct valuable DNA analysis and determine his last meal.

INTERNATIONAL TALK LIKE A PIRATE DAY. Sept 19. A day when people everywhere can swash their buckles and add a touch of larceny to their dialogue by talking like pirates: for example, "Arr, matey, it be a fine day." While it's inherently a guy thing, women have been known to enjoy the day because they have to be addressed as "me beauty." Celebrated by millions on all seven continents. Arr! Annually, Sept 19. For info: Mark "Cap'n Slappy" Summers, 925 First Ave E, Albany, OR 97321. Phone: (541) 619-9579. E-mail: capnslappy@talklikeapirate.com. Web: www.talklikeapirate.com.

JAMESTOWN BURNED BY BACON'S REBELLION: ANNIVERSARY. Sept 19, 1676. Virginia governor Sir William Berkeley, supporting Charles II's efforts to exploit the colony, adopted new laws allowing only property holders to vote, raising taxes and raising the cost of shipping while lowering the price for tobacco. The resulting discontent exploded when the frontier of the colony was attacked by local tribes and the governor refused to defend the settlers. Nathaniel Bacon, a colonist on the governor's council, led frontier farmers and successfully defeated the tribes. Denounced by Berkeley as rebels, Bacon and his men occupied Jamestown, forcing the governor to call an election, the first in 15 years. The Berkeley laws were repealed, and election and tax reforms were instituted. While Bacon and his troops were gone on a raiding party against the Indians, Berkeley again denounced them. They returned and attacked Berkeley's forces, defeating them and burning Jamestown on Sept 19, 1676. Berkeley fled and Bacon became ruler of Virginia. When he died suddenly a short time later, the rebellion collapsed. Berkeley returned to power, and Bacon's followers were hunted down; some were executed and their property confiscated. Berkeley was replaced the next year, and peace was restored.

LUYTS, JAN: BIRTH ANNIVERSARY. Sept 19, 1655. Dutch scholar, physicist, mathematician and astronomer, Jan Luyts was born at Hoorn in western Netherlands. Little remembered except for his books: *Astronomica Institutio . . .* (1689) and *Introductio ad Geographiam . . .* (1690).

"THE MARY TYLER MOORE SHOW" TV PREMIERE: ANNIVERSARY. Sept 19, 1970. This show—one of the most popular sitcoms of the '70s—combined good writing, an effective supporting cast and contemporary attitudes. The show centered around the two most important places in Mary Richards's (Mary Tyler Moore) life—the WJM-TV newsroom and her apartment at Minneapolis. At home she shared the ups and downs of life with her friend Rhoda Morgenstern (Valerie Harper) and the manager of her apartment building, Phyllis Lindstrom (Cloris Leachman). At work, as the associate producer (later producer) of "The Six O'Clock News," Mary struggled to function in a man's world. Figuring in her professional life were her irascible boss Lou Grant (Ed Asner), levelheaded and softhearted news writer Murray Slaughter (Gavin MacLeod) and narcissistic anchorman Ted Baxter (Ted Knight). In the last of 168 episodes (Mar 19, 1977), the unthinkable happened: everyone in the WJM newsroom except the inept Ted was fired.

MEXICO CITY EARTHQUAKE: ANNIVERSARY. Sept 19–20, 1985. Nearly 10,000 persons perished in the earthquakes (8.1 and 7.5, respectively, on the Richter scale) that devastated Mexico City. Damage to buildings was estimated at more than $1 billion, and 100,000 homes were destroyed or severely damaged.

MONTEREY JAZZ FESTIVAL. Sept 19–21. Monterey, CA. Celebrating its 57th year, the world's oldest continuous jazz festival features the sounds of some of the world's finest jazz musicians. Est attendance: 40,000. For info: Monterey Jazz Festival, PO Box JAZZ, Monterey, CA 93942. Phone: (831) 373-3366. E-mail: jazzinfo@montereyjazzfestival.org. Web: www.montereyjazzfestival.org.

✦NATIONAL POW/MIA RECOGNITION DAY. Sept 19. Annually, the third Friday of September.

NATIONAL TRADESMEN DAY. Sept 19. This day focuses on the "Hands that Build America and Keep It Running Strong" and includes celebrations, recognition events and activities throughout the country. IRWIN Tools sponsors this day with retailers and community groups and invites the nation to honor the men and women who work with their hands to contribute to our lives in so many meaningful ways. First observed in 2011. Annually, the third Friday in September. For info: Irwin Tools. Web: www.nationaltradesmenday.com or www.irwin.com.

NEW HAMPSHIRE HIGHLAND GAMES. Sept 19–21. Loon Mountain, Lincoln, NH. From the tossing of the caber to the lilting melodies of the clarsach plus massed pipe bands on parade, there's something for everyone at the New Hampshire Highland Games: a three-day Scottish festival crammed with music, dance, crafts, athletic events, Scottish food and more. For those of Scottish heritage, there's also a chance to look up one's clan connection, as more than 70 Scottish clans and societies have tents with displays. Admission charged. Est attendance: 21,000. For info: New Hampshire Highland Games, 17 Green St, Concord, NH 03301. Phone: (603) 229-1975. Fax: (603) 223-6678. E-mail: info@nhscot.org. Web: www.nhscot.org.

POWELL, LEWIS F., JR: BIRTH ANNIVERSARY. Sept 19, 1907. Former associate justice of the Supreme Court of the US, nominated by President Nixon Oct 21, 1971. (Powell took office Jan 7, 1972.) Justice Powell was born at Suffolk, VA. In 1987, he announced his retirement from the Court. He died Aug 25, 1998, at Richmond, VA.

RIVERFEST. Sept 19–20. Eden, NC. A celebration of Eden's art, history and river heritage, this two-day festival includes two stages of live entertainment, historical reenactments, antique engine display, an active Kids Zone, canoe and kayak excursions, handcrafted local and regional arts and crafts and lots of mouth-watering food. Come to beautiful and historic downtown Leaksville for a celebration on and around the rivers. Annually, the third weekend in September. Est attendance: 20,000. For info: City of Eden, PO Box 70, Eden, NC 27289. Phone: (336) 612-8049. E-mail: CAdams@EdenNc.us. Web: www.ExploreEdenNc.com.

ROYKO, MIKE: BIRTH ANNIVERSARY. Sept 19, 1932. Syndicated columnist to more than 600 newspapers nationwide, Pulitzer Prize–winner and author (*Boss, Slats Grobnick*). Born at Chicago, IL, Royko died there, Apr 29, 1997.

SAINT CHRISTOPHER (SAINT KITTS) AND NEVIS: INDEPENDENCE DAY. Sept 19. National holiday. Commemorates independence from Britain in 1983.

SAINT JANUARIUS (GENNARO): FEAST DAY. Sept 19. Fourth-century bishop of Benevento, martyred near Naples, Italy, whose relics in the Naples Cathedral are particularly famous because on his feast days the blood in a glass vial is said to liquefy in response to prayers of the faithful. In September 1979, the Associated Press reported that some 5,000 persons gathered at the cathedral at dawn, and that "the blood liquefied after 63 minutes of prayers." This phenomenon is said to occur also on the first Saturday in May.

TITAN II MISSILE EXPLOSION: ANNIVERSARY. Sept 19, 1980. The third major accident involving America's most powerful single weapon occurred near Damascus, AR. The explosion, at 3 AM, came nearly 11 hours after a fire had started in the missile silo. The multimegaton nuclear warhead (a hydrogen bomb) reportedly was briefly airborne but came to rest a few hundred feet away. One dead, 21 injured in accident. Previous major Titan Missile accidents: Aug 9, 1965, near Searcy, AR (53 dead); and Aug 24, 1978, near Rock, KS (2 dead, 29 injured).

"THE VIRGINIAN" TV PREMIERE: ANNIVERSARY. Sept 19, 1962. TV's first 90-minute western starred James Drury as the Virginian, a foreman trying to come to terms with the westward expansion of civilization. It was set on the Shiloh Ranch in Wyoming. Key players included Doug McClure (with Drury, the only cast member to stay for the entire run), Lee J. Cobb, Roberta Shore, Pippa Scott, Gary Clarke, David Hartman and Tim Matheson. In the last season, the title was changed to "The Men from Shiloh," and Stewart Granger and Lee Majors joined the cast.

BIRTHDAYS TODAY

James Anthony (Jim) Abbott, 47, former baseball player, born Flint, MI, Sept 19, 1967.

Jimmy Fallon, 40, talk show host, comedian, actor ("Saturday Night Live," *Fever Pitch*), born Brooklyn, NY, Sept 19, 1974.

Kevin Hooks, 56, actor, director ("The White Shadow," *Sounder*), born Philadelphia, PA, Sept 19, 1958.

Jeremy Irons, 66, actor (Oscar for *Reversal of Fortune*; *Lolita, Dead Ringers*, "The Borgias"), born Cowes, Isle of Wight, England, Sept 19, 1948.

Nick Johnson, 36, baseball player, born Sacramento, CA, Sept 19, 1978.

Joan Lunden, 63, broadcast journalist, born Sacramento, CA, Sept 19, 1951.

Randolph Mantooth, 69, actor ("Emergency"), born Sacramento, CA, Sept 19, 1945.

David McCallum, 81, actor ("NCIS," "The Man from U.N.C.L.E.," *The Great Escape*), born Glasgow, Scotland, Sept 19, 1933.

Joe Morgan, 71, sportscaster, Hall of Fame baseball player, born Bonham, TX, Sept 19, 1943.

Soledad O'Brien, 48, television journalist, born St. James, NY, Sept 19, 1966.

Tim Scott, 49, US Senator (R, South Carolina), born North Charleston, SC, Sept 19, 1965.

Columbus Short, 32, actor, dancer ("Scandal," *Stomp the Yard*), born Kansas City, MO, Sept 19, 1982.

Alison Sweeney, 38, actress ("Days of Our Lives"), television personality ("The Biggest Loser"), born Los Angeles, CA, Sept 19, 1976.

Twiggy, 65, actress (*The Boy Friend, The Blues Brothers*), model, born Leslie Hornby at London, England, Sept 19, 1949.

Adam West, 86, actor ("Batman," "The Last Precinct"), born Walla Walla, WA, Sept 19, 1928 (some sources say 1929 or 1930).

Paul Williams, 74, singer, composer (Oscar for "Evergreen"), actor, born Omaha, NE, Sept 19, 1940.

Trisha Yearwood, 50, singer, born Monticello, GA, Sept 19, 1964.

September 20 — Saturday

DAY 263 **102 REMAINING**

AKC RESPONSIBLE DOG OWNERSHIP DAY. Sept 20. NC State Fairgrounds, Raleigh, NC. This event celebrates the commitment it takes to have a canine companion with a day of educational and entertaining events such as obedience/agility demonstrations, low-cost microchipping clinics, breed rescue information, therapy dog/service dog demonstrations, safety around dogs for kids presentations, giveaways and more! Est attendance: 5,000. For info: American Kennel Club, 260 Madison Ave, New York, NY 10016. Phone: (212) 696-8343. Fax: (212) 696-8345. E-mail: communications@akc.org. Web: www.akc.org/clubs/rdod/index.cfm.

AUERBACH, RED: BIRTH ANNIVERSARY. Sept 20, 1917. Basketball coach Arnold Jacob Auerbach was born at Brooklyn, NY. As coach of the Boston Celtics from 1950 to 1966, he won nine NBA titles, including eight straight from 1959 to 1966. After retiring from coaching, Auerbach was either general manager or president of the Celtics from 1966 until 1997. He was team president from 2001 until his death at Washington, DC, on Oct 28, 2006. In 1980 he was named the greatest coach in NBA history by the Professional Basketball Writers Association and is widely considered to be the best sports executive in history.

BIG WHOPPER LIAR'S CONTEST. Sept 20. Murphy Auditorium, New Harmony, IN. Twenty "storytellers" compete to see who can tell the biggest whopper. Annually, the third Saturday in September. Est attendance: 250. For info: Jeff Fleming, PO Box 598, Olney, IL 62450. Phone: (618) 395-8491. Fax: (618) 392-3174.

BILLIE JEAN KING WINS THE "BATTLE OF THE SEXES": ANNIVERSARY. Sept 20, 1973. Billie Jean King defeated Bobby Riggs in the nationally televised "Battle of the Sexes" tennis match in three straight sets.

CHINA: BIRTHDAY OF CONFUCIUS. Sept 20. Observed on 27th day of eighth lunar month.

"THE COSBY SHOW" TV PREMIERE: 30th ANNIVERSARY. Sept 20, 1984. This Emmy Award–winning comedy set in New York City revolved around the members of the Huxtable family. Father Dr. Heathcliff Huxtable was played by Bill Cosby; his wife, Clair, an attorney, was played by Phylicia Rashad. Their four daughters were played by Sabrina Le Beauf (Sondra), Lisa Bonet (Denise), Tempestt Bledsoe (Vanessa) and Keshia Knight Pulliam (Rudy); Malcolm-Jamal Warner played son Theo. By the end of the series in 1992, the two oldest daughters had finished college and were married. "A Different World" was a spin-off set at historically black Hillman College where Denise was a student.

September 2014	S	M	T	W	T	F	S
		1	2	3	4	5	6
	7	8	9	10	11	12	13
	14	15	16	17	18	19	20
	21	22	23	24	25	26	27
	28	29	30				

COVERED BRIDGE FESTIVAL. Sept 20–21. Washington and Greene County, PA. Arts and crafts, entertainment and lots of homestyle food at each of 10 covered bridges. Annually, the third weekend in September. Est attendance: 110,000. For info: Washington County Tourism, 273 S Main St, Washington, PA 15301. Phone: (866) 927-4969 or (724) 228-5520. E-mail: info@visitwashingtoncountypa.com. Web: www.visitwashingtoncountypa.com.

EISENHOWER WORLD WAR II WEEKEND. Sept 20–21. Eisenhower National Historic Site, Gettysburg, PA. A living-history encampment featuring Allied soldiers, a German camp and military vehicles of that time. Annually, the third weekend in September. Est attendance: 3,500. For info: Eisenhower National Historic Site, 1195 Baltimore Pike, Ste 100, Gettysburg, PA 17325. Phone: (717) 338-9114. Fax: (717) 338-0821. E-mail: EISE_Site_Manager@nps.gov. Web: www.nps.gov/eise or www.gettysburg.travel.

EQUAL RIGHTS PARTY FOUNDING: ANNIVERSARY. Sept 20, 1884. The Equal Rights Party was formed at San Francisco, CA. Its candidate for president, nominated in convention, was Mrs Belva Lockwood. The vice presidential candidate was Marietta Stow.

FESTIVAL 2014: FESTIVAL OF FINE ARTS AND FINE CRAFTS. Sept 20–21. Dalton, GA. 51st annual. Fine arts and fine crafts festival includes outdoor artist booths, food vendors, children's activities, entertainment for adults and children, cash awards. Est attendance: 7,000. For info: Creative Arts Guild, 520 W Waugh St, Dalton, GA 30720. Phone: (706) 278-0168. E-mail: cagarts@creativeartsguild.org.

FINANCIAL PANIC OF 1873: ANNIVERSARY. Sept 20, 1873. For the first time in its history, the New York Stock Exchange was forced to close because of a banking crisis. Although the worst of the panic and crisis was over within a week, the psychological effect on businesspeople, investors and the nation at large was more lasting.

INTERNATIONAL COASTAL CLEANUP. Sept 20. 29th annual. Since 1985, 9 million volunteers have collected 145 million pounds of trash from beaches as well as below the water in 152 countries and locations. Annually, the third Saturday in September. For info: Ocean Conservancy, 1300 19th St NW, 8th Fl, Washington, DC 20036. Phone: (202) 429-5609. E-mail: cleanup@oceanconservancyva.org. Web: www.oceanconservancy.org.

LEVI COFFIN DAYS. Sept 20–21. Fountain City, IN. 47th annual gathering in which the community comes together for fun and fundraising. More than 400 booths, including all-local food vendors, free entertainment and a parade on Saturday morning. Levi Coffin (1798–1877) was an abolitionist who helped some 2,000 slaves to freedom. Annually, the third weekend in September. Est attendance: 10,000. For info: Fountain City Lions Club, PO Box 223, Fountain City, IN 47341. Phone: (765) 847-2691. E-mail: lc.gardner@comcast.net. Web: www.waynet.org/levicoffin/default.htm.

MORTON, FERDINAND "JELLY ROLL": BIRTH ANNIVERSARY. Sept 20, 1885. American jazz pianist, composer and orchestra leader was born at New Orleans, LA (some scholars believe in 1890). Morton, subject of a biography titled *Mr Jelly Roll* by Alan Lomax, died July 10, 1941, at Los Angeles, CA.

PEDDLER'S VILLAGE SCARECROW FESTIVAL. Sept 20–21. Peddler's Village, Lahaska, PA. Weekend festival includes scarecrow making, pumpkin-painting workshops, musical entertainment and scarecrow competition display. Free admission and free live entertainment, charge for workshops. Est attendance: 16,000. For info: Peddler's Village, Routes 202 and 263, Lahaska, PA 18931. Phone: (215) 794-4000. Fax: (215) 794-4001. E-mail: info@peddlersvillage.com. Web: www.peddlersvillage.com.

PERKINS, MAXWELL: BIRTH ANNIVERSARY. Sept 20, 1884. The most powerful and influential book editor of the early 20th century, Perkins discovered, nurtured, cajoled, guided and edited such authors as F. Scott Fitzgerald, Ernest Hemingway, Thomas Wolfe and others at Charles Scribners' Sons. Born at New York, NY, Perkins died June 17, 1947, at Stamford, CT.

"THE PHIL SILVERS SHOW" TV PREMIERE: ANNIVERSARY. Sept 20, 1955. This popular half-hour sitcom starred Phil Silvers as Sergeant Ernie Bilko, a scheming but good-natured con man whose schemes rarely worked out. Guest stars included Fred Gwynne, Margaret Hamilton, Dick Van Dyke and Alan Alda, in his first major TV role.

SINCLAIR, UPTON BEALL: BIRTH ANNIVERSARY. Sept 20, 1878. American novelist and politician born at Baltimore, MD. He worked for political and social reforms, and his best-known novel, *The Jungle*, prompted one of the nation's first pure-food laws. Died at Bound Brook, NJ, Nov 25, 1968.

TRAIL OF COURAGE LIVING-HISTORY FESTIVAL. Sept 20–21. Rochester, IN. Portrayal of life in frontier Indiana when it was Indian territory. Historic skits, two stages with music and dancing, historic encampments for Revolutionary War, French and Indian War, Voyageurs, War of 1812, Western Fur Trade and Plains Indians; re-created 1832 Chippeway Village, also Woodland Indian Village, pioneer foods and crafts, muzzle-loading and tomahawk contests, canoe rides. Museum, round barn and Living History Village on grounds. Special honored Potawatomi family from Indiana's history each year. Est attendance: 14,000. For info: Fulton County Historical Society, 37 E 375N, Rochester, IN 46975. Phone: (574) 223-4436. E-mail: fchs@rtcol.com. Web: www.fultoncounty history.org or www.potawatomi-tda.org.

BIRTHDAYS TODAY

Donald A. Hall, 86, former US poet laureate, born New Haven, CT, Sept 20, 1928.

Kristen Johnston, 47, actress ("3rd Rock from the Sun"), born Washington, DC, Sept 20, 1967.

Guy Damien LaFleur, 63, Hall of Fame hockey player, born Thurso, QC, Canada, Sept 20, 1951.

Sophia Loren, 80, actress (Oscar for *Two Women*; *Houseboat, El Cid, Marriage Italian Style, Grumpier Old Men*), born Sofia Scicolone at Rome, Italy, Sept 20, 1934.

George R.R. Martin, 66, author (*A Game of Thrones*), born Bayonne, NJ, Sept 20, 1948.

Anne Meara, 85, actress ("Fame"), comedienne (Stiller and Meara), born New York, NY, Sept 20, 1929.

September 21 — Sunday

DAY 264 **101 REMAINING**

ARMENIA: INDEPENDENCE DAY. Sept 21. Public holiday. Commemorates independence from Soviet Union in 1991.

BANNED BOOKS WEEK—CELEBRATING THE FREEDOM TO READ. Sept 21–27. Annual event celebrating the freedom to read and the importance of the First Amendment. Held during the last week of September, Banned Books Week highlights the benefits of free and open access to information while drawing attention to the harms of censorship by spotlighting actual or attempted bannings of books. Sponsors: American Library Association, American Booksellers Association, American Booksellers Foundation for Free Expression, American Society of Journalists and Authors, Association of American Publishers, National Association of College Stores. For info: American Library Assn, Office for Intellectual Freedom. E-mail: bbw@ala.org. Web: www.ala.org/bbooks.

BELIZE: INDEPENDENCE DAY. Sept 21. National holiday. Commemorates independence of the former British Honduras from Britain in 1981.

BUILD A BETTER IMAGE WEEK. Sept 21–27. In order to be a success, you need to look like one. This week is set aside for people to evaluate their professional image and take the steps necessary to improve on it. "10 Steps to a Better Image" tip sheet available. Annually, the third full week of September. For info: Marlys K. Arnold, ImageSpecialist, PO Box 901808, Kansas City, MO 64190-1808. Phone: (816) 746-7888. E-mail: marnold@imagespecialist .com. Web: www.imagespecialist.com.

HOPKINSON, FRANCIS: BIRTH ANNIVERSARY. Sept 21, 1737. Signer of the Declaration of Independence. Born at Philadelphia, PA, Hopkinson died there May 9, 1791.

HURRICANE HUGO HITS AMERICAN COAST: 25th ANNIVERSARY. Sept 21, 1989. After ravaging the Virgin Islands, Hurricane Hugo hit the American coast at Charleston, SC. In its wake, Hugo left destruction totaling at least $8 billion.

INTERNATIONAL CLEAN HANDS WEEK. Sept 21–27. Established by the Clean Hands Coalition, a unified alliance of public and private partners working together to create and support coordinated, sustained initiatives to significantly improve health and save lives through clean hands. Activities will be held around the world to raise awareness about the importance of good hand hygiene. Annually, the third full week in September. For info: Clean Hands Coalition. E-mail: info@cleaninginstitute.org. Web: www.facebook.com/cleanhandscoalition.

INTERNATIONAL WEEK OF THE DEAF. Sept 21–28. A week to draw the attention of politicians, authorities and the general public to the achievements of Deaf people and the concerns of the Deaf community. Organizations of Deaf people worldwide are encouraged to carry out information campaigns about their work and to publicize their demands and requests. This week also increases solidarity among Deaf people and their supporters and is used as a time to stimulate greater efforts to promote the rights of Deaf people throughout the world. The World Federation of the Deaf (WFD) first launched International Day of the Deaf in 1958; the day was later extended to a week. The International Week of the Deaf (IWD) is observed annually during the last full week of September. The week culminates with International Day of the Deaf on the last Sunday of the week. The first World Congress of the WFD took place in September 1951, and the choice of September to celebrate the International Week and Day of the Deaf is a commemoration of this historical event. For info: World Federation of the Deaf, PO Box 65, FIN-00401, Helsinki, Finland. E-mail: info@ wfdeaf.org. Web: www.wfdeaf.org.

JONES, CHUCK: BIRTH ANNIVERSARY. Sept 21, 1912. Born at Spokane, WA, Chuck Jones worked as a child extra in Hollywood in the 1920s. After attending art school, he landed a job washing animation cels for famed Disney animator Ub Iwerks. He learned the craft, and by 1962 he headed his own unit at Warner Bros. Animation. He created the characters Road Runner and Wile E. Coyote, Marvin the Martian and Pepe le Pew. He worked on the development of Bugs Bunny, Elmer Fudd, Daffy Duck and Porky Pig, and also produced, directed and wrote the screenplay for the animated 1966 television classic "Dr. Seuss' How the Grinch Stole Christmas." He won several Academy Awards for his work, and his cartoon "What's Opera, Doc?" is in the National Film Registry. He died on Feb 22, 2002, at Corona del Mar, CA.

JOSEPH, CHIEF: DEATH ANNIVERSARY. Sept 21, 1904. Admirable Nez Percé chief, whose Indian name was In-Mut-Too-Yah-Lat-Lat, was born about 1840 at Wallowa Valley, Oregon Territory, and died on the Colville Reservation at Washington. Faced with war or resettlement to a reservation, Chief Joseph led a dramatic attempt to escape to Canada. After three months and more than 1,000 miles, he and his people were surrounded 40 miles from Canada and sent to a reservation at Oklahoma. Though the few survivors were later allowed to relocate to another reservation at Washington, they never regained their ancestral lands.

MALTA: INDEPENDENCE DAY: 50th ANNIVERSARY. Sept 21. National Day. Commemorates independence from Britain in 1964.

"MONDAY NIGHT FOOTBALL" TV PREMIERE: ANNIVERSARY. Sept 21, 1970. Following the complete merger of the American Football League and the National Football League, ABC joined

CBS and NBC in televising weekly games with the debut of "Monday Night Football." The show began as an experiment but soon became an institution. Announcers Howard Cosell, Keith Jackson and Don Meredith called the first game, a 31–21 victory by the Cleveland Browns over the New York Jets. On Dec 26, 2005, "Monday Night Football" made its final telecast on ABC. In 2006, it moved to the cable channel ESPN.

✦**NATIONAL FARM SAFETY AND HEALTH WEEK.** Sept 21–27. Presidential Proclamation issued since 1982 for the third week in September. Previously, from 1944, for one of the last two weeks in July.

✦**NATIONAL HISTORICALLY BLACK COLLEGES AND UNIVERSITIES WEEK.** Sept 21–27 (tentative).

NATIONAL KEEP KIDS CREATIVE WEEK. Sept 21–27. More than ever before, kids today need encouragement to be imaginative. Their busy, task-oriented schedules in home and school give children little room for creative play. Set aside time this week to celebrate the inventive minds of kids. Encourage a child to make up a story, draw, even look for animals in cloud shapes—let their imaginations soar. Annually, the last week in September. For info: Bruce Van Patter, Let's Get Creative! Phone: (570) 524-9770. Web: www.brucevanpatter.com/keepkidscreative.html.

NATIONAL REHABILITATION AWARENESS CELEBRATION. Sept 21–27. The observance salutes the determination of the more than 50 million Americans with disabilities. It is a time to applaud the efforts of rehab professionals, provide a forum for education and offer an occasion to call upon our citizens to find new ways to fulfill needs that still exist. Annually, the third full week in Sept. For info: Natl Rehabilitation Awareness Foundation, 100 Abington Executive Park, Clarks Summit, PA 18411. Phone: (570) 341-4637 or (800) 943-6723. Fax: (570) 341-4331. Web: www.nraf-rehabnet.org.

NATIONAL SINGLES WEEK. Sept 21–27. To celebrate single life and to recognize singles and their contributions to society. For info: Rich Gosse, Chairman, American Singles, 205 Mark Twain Ave, San Rafael, CA 94903. Phone: (415) 479-3800. E-mail: rich@richgosse.com.

"NYPD BLUE" TV PREMIERE: ANNIVERSARY. Sept 21, 1993. This gritty New York City police drama had a large and changing cast. The central characters were partners Detective Bobby Simone (who later died), played by Jimmy Smits, and Detective Andy Sipowicz, played by Dennis Franz. Other cast members included Kim Delaney as Detective Diane Russell, James McDaniel as Lieutenant Arthur Fancy, Gordon Clapp as Detective Gregory Medavoy, Rick Schroder as Detective Danny Sorenson, Nicholas Turturro as Detective James Martinez, Mark-Paul Gosselaar as Detective John Clark and Esai Morales as Lieutenant Tony Rodriguez. The series ended in 2005.

"PERRY MASON" TV PREMIERE: ANNIVERSARY. Sept 21, 1957. Raymond Burr will forever be associated with the character of Perry Mason, a criminal lawyer who won the great majority of his cases. Episodes followed a similar format: the action took place in the first half, with the killer's identity unknown, and the courtroom drama took place in the latter half. Mason was particularly adept at eliciting confessions from the guilty parties. Regulars and semi-regulars included Barbara Hale, William Hopper, William Talman and Ray Collins. Following the series' end, with the last telecast on Jan 27, 1974, a number of successful "Perry Mason" TV movies aired, and the show remains popular in reruns.

TAYLOR, MARGARET SMITH: BIRTH ANNIVERSARY. Sept 21, 1788. Wife of Zachary Taylor, 12th president of the US, born at Calvert County, MD. Died Aug 18, 1852.

September 2014

S	M	T	W	T	F	S
	1	2	3	4	5	6
7	8	9	10	11	12	13
14	15	16	17	18	19	20
21	22	23	24	25	26	27
28	29	30				

"THE TEXACO STAR THEATER" TV PREMIERE: ANNIVERSARY. Sept 21, 1948. Also known as "The Milton Berle Show" and sponsored by Texaco until 1953, this popular variety show was a good sign for the fledgling TV industry. Milton Berle became a superstar. The show featured singing and comedy, especially sight gags and outrageous costumes, and guest stars. Changes were made in the fourth season: Berle cut back his appearances, new writers and a new director were added and the format was changed to a show-within-a-show. Ruth Gilbert, Fred Clark and Arnold Stang were featured, along with the new pitchman, ventriloquist Jimmy Nelson and his dummy, Danny O'Day.

TOLKIEN WEEK. Sept 21–27. To promote appreciation and enjoyment of the works of J.R.R. Tolkien. Annually, the week that includes Hobbit Day (Sept 22). For info: American Tolkien Society, PO Box 97, Highland, MI 48357-0097. E-mail: americantolkiensociety@yahoo.com. Web: www.americantolkiensociety.org.

UNITED NATIONS: INTERNATIONAL DAY OF PEACE. Sept 21. The General Assembly proclaimed the International Day of Peace in 1981, "devoted to commemorating and strengthening the ideals of peace both within and among all nations and peoples." In 2001, the assembly decided that, beginning in 2002, the International Day of Peace would be observed on Sept 21 each year (Resolution 55/282) as a day of global ceasefire and nonviolence, an invitation to all nations and people to honor a cessation of hostilities throughout the day. For info: United Nations, Dept of Public Info, New York, NY 10017. Web: www.un.org.

WELLS, HERBERT GEORGE: BIRTH ANNIVERSARY. Sept 21, 1866. English novelist and historian, born at Bromley, Kent, England. Among his books: *The Time Machine*, *The Invisible Man*, *The War of the Worlds* and *The Outline of History*. H.G. Wells died at London, Aug 13, 1946. "Human history," he wrote, "becomes more and more a race between education and catastrophe."

WORLD REFLEXOLOGY WEEK. Sept 21–27. A week to celebrate this form of therapy and to increase awareness of it. Reflexology is a scientific art based on the premise that there are reflex areas in the feet and hands that correspond to all the body parts. The physical act of applying specific pressure using thumb, finger and hand techniques results in stress reduction—and causes a physiological change in the body. Reflexology groups and associations around the world observe this week and reach out to their communities. Annually, the last full week in September. For info: Association of Reflexologists or International Council of Reflexologists. Web: www.aor.org.uk or www.icr-reflexology.org/wrw.htm.

XTERRA TRAIL RUNNING NATIONAL CHAMPIONSHIP. Sept 21. Ogden, UT. The XTERRA Trail Run Series boasts more than 80 events across the country with runs ranging from 5k to 50k. These extreme, off-road trail runs give runners the chance to prove their skills against a variety of terrain. From calf-burning hills to slippery, mud-covered paths, athletes will face the ultimate test of endurance. This race is the 2014 XTERRA Trail Run Series finale and features the main 21k championship along with 5k and 10k fun runs. For info: Emily McIlvaine, XTERRA/TEAM Unlimited, 720 Iwilei Road #290, Honolulu, HI 96817. Phone: 877-XTERRA-1. E-mail: emily@xterraplanet.com. Web: www.xterratrailrun.com.

BIRTHDAYS TODAY

Steve Beshear, 70, Governor of Kentucky (D), born Dawson Springs, KY, Sept 21, 1944.

Ethan Coen, 57, filmmaker (Oscars for *No Country for Old Men, Fargo*), born Minneapolis, MN, Sept 21, 1957.

Leonard Cohen, 80, singer, songwriter, born Montreal, QC, Canada, Sept 21, 1934.

David James Elliott, 54, actor ("JAG"), born Toronto, ON, Canada, Sept 21, 1960.

Cecil Grant Fielder, 51, former baseball player, born Los Angeles, CA, Sept 21, 1963.

Fannie Flagg, 70, actress, author (*Fried Green Tomatoes*), born Birmingham, AL, Sept 21, 1944.

Artis Gilmore, 65, Hall of Fame basketball player, born Chipley, FL, Sept 21, 1949.

Faith Hill, 47, country singer, born Jackson, MS, Sept 21, 1967.

Stephen King, 67, author (*Christine, Pet Sematary, The Shining, Misery, The Stand*), born Portland, ME, Sept 21, 1947.

Bill Kurtis, 74, television journalist, born Pensacola, FL, Sept 21, 1940.

Ricki Lake, 46, talk show host, actress (*Hairspray, Serial Mom*), born New York, NY, Sept 21, 1968.

Rob Morrow, 52, actor ("Numb3rs," "Northern Exposure," *Quiz Show*), born New Rochelle, NY, Sept 21, 1962.

Bill Murray, 64, comedian, actor (*Lost in Translation, Groundhog Day, Caddyshack*), born Evanston, IL, Sept 21, 1950.

Nicole Richie, 33, television personality ("The Simple Life"), born Berkeley, CA, Sept 21, 1981.

Kay Ryan, 69, poet, former US poet laureate (2008–10), born San Jose, CA, Sept 21, 1945.

Nancy Travis, 53, actress ("Becker," *Three Men and a Baby*), born New York, NY, Sept 21, 1961.

Luke Wilson, 43, actor (*Old School, The Royal Tenenbaums, Legally Blonde*), born Dallas, TX, Sept 21, 1971.

September 22 — Monday

DAY 265 — **100 REMAINING**

AMERICAN BUSINESS WOMEN'S DAY. Sept 22. A day set forth by Congress on which all Americans can recognize the important contributions more than 68 million American working women have made and are continuing to make to this nation. Annually, Sept 22. For info: American Business Women's Assn, 11050 Roe Ave, Ste 200, Overland Park, KS 66211. Phone: (800) 228-0007. Web: www.abwa.org.

AUTUMN. Sept 22–Dec 21. In the Northern Hemisphere, autumn begins today with the autumnal equinox, at 10:29 PM, EDT. Note that in the Southern Hemisphere today is the beginning of spring. Everywhere on Earth (except near the poles) the sun rises due east and sets due west and daylight length is nearly identical—about 12 hours, 8 minutes.

"CHARLIE'S ANGELS" TV PREMIERE: ANNIVERSARY. Sept 22, 1976. This extremely popular show of the '70s featured three attractive women solving crimes. Sabrina Duncan (Kate Jackson), Jill Munroe (Farrah Fawcett-Majors) and Kelly Garrett (Jaclyn Smith) signed on with detective agency Charles Townsend Associates. Their boss was never seen, only heard (the voice of John Forsythe); messages were communicated to the women by his associate, John Bosley (David Doyle). During the course of the series, Cheryl Ladd replaced Fawcett, and Shelley Hack and Tanya Roberts succeeded Kate Jackson. The show went off the air in 1981 but feature films were made in 2000 and 2003.

DEAR DIARY DAY. Sept 22. Put it on paper. You'll feel better. No need to be a professional writer. (©2006 by WH.) For info: Thomas & Ruth Roy, Wellcat Holidays, 2418 Long Ln, Lebanon, PA 17046. Phone: (717) 279-0184. E-mail: info@wellcat.com. Web: www.wellcat.com.

EMANCIPATION PROCLAMATION: ANNIVERSARY. Sept 22, 1862. One of the most important presidential proclamations of American history is that of Sept 22, 1862, in which Abraham Lincoln, by executive proclamation, freed the slaves in the rebelling states. "That on . . . [Jan 1, 1863] . . . all persons held as slaves within any state or designated part of a state, the people whereof shall then be in rebellion against the United States, shall be then, thenceforward, and forever, free." See also: "Thirteenth Amendment Anniversary" (Dec 18).

FAMILY DAY—BE INVOLVED. STAY INVOLVED™. Sept 22. A national initiative created by CASAColumbia™ to promote simple acts of parental engagement as key ways to prevent risky substance abuse in children and teens. Children with hands-on parents are far less likely to smoke, drink or use other drugs. Materials available on the power of parental engagement. Annually, the fourth Monday of September. For info: Family Day, The National Center on Addiction and Substance Abuse at Columbia University, 633 Third Ave, 19th Fl, New York, NY 10017. Phone: (212) 841-5200. Fax: (212) 956-8020. E-mail: familyday@casacolumbia.org. Web: www.casafamilyday.org.

"FAMILY TIES" TV PREMIERE: ANNIVERSARY. Sept 22, 1982. This popular '80s sitcom was set at Columbus, OH, and focused on the Keaton family: ex-hippies Elyse (Meredith Baxter-Birney), an architect, and Steven (Michael Gross), a station manager of the local public TV station; Alex (Michael J. Fox), their smart, conservative and financially driven son; Mallory (Justine Bateman), their materialistic, ditzy daughter and Jennifer (Tina Yothers), their tomboy youngest daughter. Later in the series Elyse gave birth to Andrew (Brian Bonsall). Marc Price played Irwin "Skippy" Handleman, the nerdy next-door neighbor who adored the Keatons, and Mallory in particular. The last episode aired Sept 17, 1989.

FARADAY, MICHAEL: BIRTH ANNIVERSARY. Sept 22, 1791. English scientist and early experimenter with electricity, born at Newington, Surrey, England. Died at Hampton Court, Aug 25, 1867.

FIRST ALL-WOMAN JURY EMPANELED IN COLONIES: ANNIVERSARY. Sept 22, 1656. The General Provincial Court at Patuxent, MD, empaneled the first all-woman jury in the colonies to hear the case of Judith Catchpole, accused of murdering her child. The defendant claimed she had never even been pregnant, and after all the evidence was heard, the jury acquitted her.

"FRIENDS" TV PREMIERE: 20th ANNIVERSARY. Sept 22, 1994. This hugely popular NBC comedy brought together six single friends and the issues in their personal lives, ranging from their jobs to their romances. The cast was Courteney Cox Arquette, Lisa Kudrow, Jennifer Aniston, Matthew Perry, David Schwimmer and Matt Le Blanc. The show concluded its run in 2004, with a finale in which 51.1 million viewers tuned in, making that episode the fourth most-watched TV program in history.

HOBBIT DAY. Sept 22. To commemorate the birthdays of Frodo and Bilbo Baggins and their creator J.R.R. Tolkien. For info: Secretary, American Tolkien Society, PO Box 97, Highland, MI 48357-0097. E-mail: americantolkiensociety@yahoo.com. Web: www.americantolkiensociety.org.

HOUSEMAN, JOHN: BIRTH ANNIVERSARY. Sept 22, 1902. American actor and producer John Houseman was born Jacques Haussmann at Bucharest. He is best known for his collaboration with Orson Welles on the 1938 radio production of *War of the Worlds* and for his role as Professor Kingsfield in the film and television version of *The Paper Chase*. He won an Oscar for that film role in 1974 and helped establish the Juilliard drama school and the Acting Company repertory group. He died Oct 30, 1988, at Malibu, CA.

ICE CREAM CONE: ANNIVERSARY. Sept 22, 1903. Italo Marchiony emigrated from Italy in the late 1800s and soon thereafter went into business at New York, NY, with a pushcart dispensing lemon ice. Success soon led to a small fleet of pushcarts, and the inventive Marchiony was inspired to develop a cone, first made of paper, later of pastry, to hold the tasty delicacy. On Sept 22, 1903, his application for a patent for his new mold was filed, and US Patent No 746971 was issued to him Dec 15, 1903.

INTERNATIONAL DAY OF RADIANT PEACE. Sept 22. Observed since 1999, this day celebrates and commemorates Radiant Peace. Commemorations of the International Day of Radiant Peace range from Walks for Radiant Peace to citywide and statewide proclamations recognizing the International Day of Radiant Peace, special Radiant Peace projects with children, ringing bells for Radiant Peace, and Radiant Peace Picnics. Observed annually on Sept 22. For info: The Radiant Peace Foundation Intl, Inc, PO Box 40822, St. Petersburg, FL 33743. Phone: (727) 343-8212. E-mail: RadiantPeaceIntl@gmail.com. Web: www.radiantpeace.org.

INTERNATIONAL WOMEN'S ECOMMERCE DAYS. Sept 22–29. This event will celebrate women around the globe and their economic impact and purchasing power. The schedule of events (subject to change) includes encouraging women around the world to make an online purchase today, sending information to the media on all continents, coordinating with more than 240 partnering organizations (made up of 250,000 members) to spread the word and culminating in a World Congress to be held in Miami, FL. For info: Heidi Richards, WECAI, PO Box 550856, Fort Lauderdale, FL 33355. Phone: (954) 625-6606. E-mail: heidi@wecai.org. Web: www.wecai.org.

IRAN-IRAQ WAR: ANNIVERSARY. Sept 22, 1980. Iraq invaded western Iran on this date, starting an eight-year war. This deadly war saw one million casualties, the use of chemical weapons and extensive damage to each nation's economy.

JAPAN: AUTUMNAL EQUINOX DAY. Sept 22. National holiday in Japan.

LONG COUNT DAY: ANNIVERSARY. Sept 22, 1927. Anniversary of world championship boxing match between Jack Dempsey and Gene Tunney, at Soldier Field, Chicago, IL. It was the largest fight purse ($990,446) in the history of boxing to that time. Nearly half the population of the US is believed to have listened to the radio broadcast of this fight. In the seventh round of the 10-round fight, Tunney was knocked down. Following the rules, Referee Dave Barry interrupted the count when Dempsey failed to go to the farthest corner. The count was resumed and Tunney got to his feet at the count of nine. Stopwatch records of those present claimed the total elapsed time from the beginning of the count until Tunney got to his feet at 12–15 seconds. Tunney, awarded 7 of the 10 rounds, won the fight and claimed the world championship. Dempsey's appeal was denied and he never fought again. Tunney retired the following year after one more (successful) fight.

September 2014	S	M	T	W	T	F	S
		1	2	3	4	5	6
	7	8	9	10	11	12	13
	14	15	16	17	18	19	20
	21	22	23	24	25	26	27
	28	29	30				

MABON. Sept 22. (Also called Alban Elfed.) One of the "Lesser Sabbats" during the Wiccan year, Mabon marks the second harvest as nature prepares for the coming of winter. Annually, on the autumnal equinox.

MALI: INDEPENDENCE DAY. Sept 22. National holiday commemorating independence from France in 1960. Mali, in West Africa, was known as the French Sudan while a colony.

"MAVERICK" TV PREMIERE: ANNIVERSARY. Sept 22, 1957. This popular western starred James Garner as Bret Maverick, a clever man who preferred card playing to fighting. A second Maverick was introduced when production was behind schedule—Jack Kelly played his brother Bart. Garner and Kelly played most episodes separately, and when Garner left in 1961, Kelly was in almost all the episodes. Other performers included Roger Moore, Robert Colbert and Diane Brewster. This western distinguished itself by its light touch and parody of other westerns.

NATIONAL CENTENARIAN'S DAY. Sept 22. A day to recognize and honor individuals who have lived a century or longer. A day not only to recognize these individuals but to listen to them discuss the memories—filled with historical information—they have of their rich lives. For info: Williamsport Retirement Village, 154 N Artizan St, Williamsport, MD 21795. Phone: (301) 223-7971. E-mail: mcliber@bgf.org.

NATIONAL WALK 'N' ROLL DOG DAY. Sept 22. 3rd annual. A day honoring and celebrating the dogs in wheelchairs who teach us to embrace each day with love, hope and joy. Annually, Sept 22. For info: Barbara Techel, 304 Kettleview Ct, Elkhart Lake, WI 53020. Phone: (920) 377-1749. E-mail: barb@joyfulpaws.com. Web: www.nationalwalknrolldogday.com.

NATIONAL WOMAN ROAD WARRIOR DAY. Sept 22. A day of recognition for the nation's traveling businesswomen. Like their male counterparts, Woman Road Warriors open and close deals, make sales, give presentations, attend or lead seminars and maintain that all-important in-person presence in the often impersonal corporate world. But simultaneously, many are often charged with keeping their families on track at home—especially their babies, toddlers and multitasking school-age children—and nurture them, even from a long distance. Annually, the fourth Monday in September. For info: Kathleen Ameche, 1341 W. Fullerton, Ste 157, Chicago, IL 60614. Phone: (312) 202-0034. Fax: (312) 642-6483. E-mail: kameche@womanroadwarrior.com. Web: www.womanroadwarrior.com.

STANHOPE, PHILIP DORMER: BIRTH ANNIVERSARY. Sept 22, 1694. (Old Style date.) Philip Dormer Stanhope, the 4th Earl of Chesterfield, born at London, England. He was a brilliant politician and orator. On Feb 20, 1751, he brought a bill into the House of Lords that caused the "New Style" Gregorian calendar to replace the "Old Style" Julian calendar in 1752. His influential political career was eclipsed by the fame of the letters he wrote to his son Philip, giving shrewd counsel on manners, morals and the ways of the world. Published less than a year after his own death at London, Mar 24, 1773, the *Letters* became immensely popular, were translated and republished in many editions. The Chesterfield, a kind of sofa, is said to be named for him.

US POSTMASTER GENERAL ESTABLISHED: 225th ANNIVERSARY. Sept 22, 1789. Congress established office of Postmaster General, following the Departments of State, War and Treasury.

BIRTHDAYS TODAY

Scott Baio, 53, actor ("Happy Days," "Diagnosis Murder," "Charles in Charge"), born Brooklyn, NY, Sept 22, 1961.

Shari Belafonte-Harper, 60, model, actress, born New York, NY, Sept 22, 1954.

Andrea Bocelli, 56, tenor, born Lajatico, Italy, Sept 22, 1958.

Debbie Boone, 58, singer ("You Light Up My Life"), born Hackensack, NJ, Sept 22, 1956.

Mireille Enos, 39, actress ("The Killing," "Big Love"), born Houston, TX, Sept 22, 1975.

Bonnie Hunt, 50, actress (*Jerry Maguire, Jumanji*), born Chicago, IL, Sept 22, 1964.

Joan Jett, 54, singer, born Philadelphia, PA, Sept 22, 1960.

Thomas Charles (Tommy) Lasorda, 87, Hall of Fame baseball manager and former player, born Norristown, PA, Sept 22, 1927.

Paul Le Mat, 69, actor (*American Graffiti, Melvin and Howard*), born Rahway, NY, Sept 22, 1945.

Catherine Oxenberg, 53, actress ("Dynasty"), born New York, NY, Sept 22, 1961.

Billie Piper, 32, actress ("Doctor Who," "Secret Diary of a Call Girl"), born Swindon, Wiltshire, England, Sept 22, 1982.

Mike Richter, 48, former hockey player, born Philadelphia, PA, Sept 22, 1966.

Ronaldo, 38, former soccer player, born Ronaldo Luiz Nazario de Lima at Rio de Janeiro, Brazil, Sept 22, 1976.

Junko Tabei, 75, mountaineer (first woman to climb Mount Everest), born Fukushima Prefecture, Japan, Sept 22, 1939.

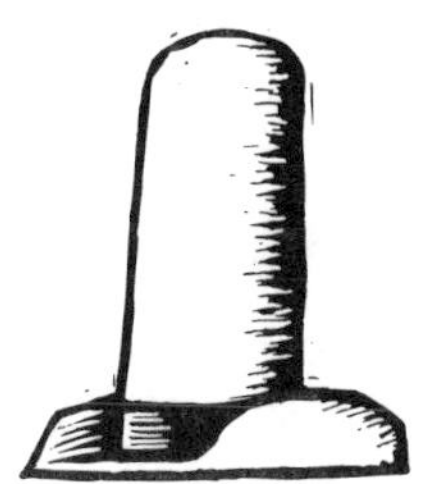

September 23 — Tuesday

DAY 266 — **99 REMAINING**

BASEBALL'S GREATEST DISPUTE: ANNIVERSARY. Sept 23, 1908. In the decisive game between the Chicago Cubs and the New York Giants, the National League pennant race erupted in controversy during the bottom of the ninth with the score tied 1–1, at the Polo Grounds, New York, NY. New York was at bat with two men on. The batter hit safely to center field, scoring the winning run. Chicago claimed that the runner on first, Fred Merkle, seeing the winning run scored, headed toward the dugout without advancing to second base, thus invalidating the play. The Chicago second baseman, Johnny Evers, attempted to get the ball and tag Merkle out, but was prevented by the fans streaming onto the field. Days later Harry C. Pulliam, head of the National Commission of Organized Baseball, decided to call the game a tie. The teams were forced to play a postseason play-off game, which the Cubs won 4–2. Fans invented the terms "boner" and "bonehead" in reference to the play, and it has gone down in baseball history as "Merkle's Boner."

CELEBRATE BISEXUALITY DAY. Sept 23. Observed internationally by the bisexual community and its supporters. Annually, Sept 23.

CHARLES, RAY: BIRTH ANNIVERSARY. Sept 23, 1930. Born at Albany, GA, Ray Charles Robinson began losing his sight at age 5. He began formal music training at the St. Augustine School for the Deaf and Blind, and by age 15 was earning a living as a musician. He went on to become one of the most influential performers of all time. As a pianist, singer, songwriter, bandleader and producer, he played country, jazz, rock, gospel and standards. His renditions of "Georgia on My Mind," "I Can't Stop Loving You" and "America the Beautiful" are considered true American classics. He died at Beverly Hills, CA, June 10, 2004.

CHECKERS DAY: ANNIVERSARY. Sept 23, 1952. Anniversary of the nationally televised "Checkers Speech" by then vice presidential candidate Richard M. Nixon. Nixon was found "clean as a hound's tooth" in connection with a private fund for political expenses, and he declared he would never give back the cocker spaniel, Checkers, which had been a gift to his daughters.

INNERGIZE DAY. Sept 23. A day set aside for anyone who has said, "I don't have time to do the personal things I want to do for myself." Today is the day to set time aside for yourself to do anything you want to do. Annually, the day after the autumnal equinox. For info: Michelle Porchia, inner dimensions LLC, 929 White Plains Rd, Trumbull, CT 06611. Phone: (203) 924-1012. E-mail: michelle@innerdimensionsllc.com. Web: www.innerdimensionsllc.com.

INTERNATIONAL INTERPRETERS AND TRANSLATORS WEEK. Sept 23–30. This week is an opportunity to celebrate pride in a profession that is becoming increasingly essential in everyday life. It is celebrated annually the last week of September, leading up to International Translation Day on Sept 30. Sept 30 is the Feast of St. Jerome, the Bible translator who is considered the patron saint of translators. The International Federation of Translators (FIT) has promoted International Translation Day since it was set up in 1953 to show solidarity with the worldwide translation community in an effort to promote the translation profession. For info: Lindsay McCarthy, University of Michigan Health System Interpreter Services, 2025 Traverwood Dr, Ste A4, Ann Arbor, MI 48105. Phone: (734) 998-2184. Fax: (734) 998-2161. E-mail: mccarthl@med.umich.edu. Web: www.med.umich.edu/interpreter.

"THE JETSONS" TV PREMIERE: ANNIVERSARY. Sept 23, 1962. "Meet George Jetson. His boy Elroy. Daughter Judy. Jane, his wife." These words introduced us to the Jetsons, a cartoon family living in the 21st century, the Flintstones of the Space Age. We followed the exploits of George and his family, as well as his work relationship with his greedy, ruthless boss, Cosmo Spacely. Voices were provided by George O'Hanlon as George, Penny Singleton as Jane, Janet Waldo as Judy, Daws Butler as Elroy, Don Messick as Astro, the family dog, and Mel Blanc as Spacely. New episodes were created in 1985, which also introduced a new pet, Orbity.

LEWIS & CLARK EXPEDITION RETURNS: ANNIVERSARY. Sept 23, 1806. After more than two years in the American West, the Corps of Discovery returned to St. Louis amid much fanfare. They had traveled—with the assistance of guides Toussaint Charbonneau and his wife, Sacagawea (a member of the Shoshone tribe)—to what is now North Dakota and Montana, over the Continental Divide and to the Columbia River, which took them to the Pacific (November 1805). They lost only one man from the 33-member group. Their valuable findings on Western tribes, geography, plants and animals dispelled many long-standing myths about the region.

LIBRA, THE BALANCE. Sept 23–Oct 22. In the astronomical/astrological zodiac that divides the sun's apparent orbit into 12 segments, the period Sept 23–Oct 22 is identified traditionally as the sun sign of Libra, the Balance. The ruling planet is Venus.

LIPPMANN, WALTER: 125th BIRTH ANNIVERSARY. Sept 23, 1889. American journalist, political philosopher and author. Born at New York, NY, he died there Dec 14, 1974. As a syndicated newspaper columnist he was the foremost and perhaps the most influential commentator in the nation. "Without criticism," he said in an address to the International Press Institute in 1965, "and reliable and intelligent reporting, the government cannot govern."

McGUFFEY, WILLIAM HOLMES: BIRTH ANNIVERSARY. Sept 23, 1800. American educator and author of the famous *McGuffey Readers*, born at Washington County, PA. Died at Charlottesville, VA, May 4, 1873.

PAULUS, FRIEDRICH: BIRTH ANNIVERSARY. Sept 23, 1890. The German commander of the Sixth Army who led the advance on Stalingrad in 1942, Friedrich von Paulus was born at Breitenau, Germany. Paulus's troops succeeded in taking most of Stalingrad in November 1942 but eventually became trapped within the city they had captured. Paulus surrendered to the Russians Jan 31, 1943, the same day that Hitler promoted him to field marshal. He appeared as a key witness for the Soviet prosecution at the Nuremberg trials. Paulus died Feb 1, 1957, at Dresden, East Germany.

PIDGEON, WALTER: BIRTH ANNIVERSARY. Sept 23, 1897. Actor Walter Pidgeon was born at East St. John, NB, Canada. He died at age 87, Sept 25, 1984, at Santa Monica, CA. He made his film debut in 1925 in *Mannequin*. Among his films are *Saratoga* and *Mrs Miniver*.

PLANET NEPTUNE DISCOVERY: ANNIVERSARY. Sept 23, 1846. Neptune is 2.796 billion miles from the sun (about 30 times as far from the sun as Earth). Eighth planet from the sun, Neptune takes 164.8 years to revolve around the sun. Diameter is about 31,000 miles compared to Earth at 7,927 miles. Discovered by German astronomer Johann Galle.

RYDER CUP 2014. Sept 23–28. Gleneagles, Scotland. Held every two years, this match pits American golfers against a European team. First held in 1927, this is the 39th match. For info: Ryder Cup, Professional Golfers' Association of America. Web: www.rydercup2014.com.

SAUDI ARABIA: KINGDOM UNIFICATION. Sept 23. National holiday. Commemorates unification in 1932.

WOODHULL, VICTORIA CLAFLIN: BIRTH ANNIVERSARY. Sept 23, 1838. American feminist, reformer and first female candidate (Equal Rights Party) for the presidency of the US born at Homer, OH. A feminist pioneer whose foremost cause was women's suffrage, she was also the first female head of a Wall Street brokerage firm as well as the first female weekly newspaper publisher. Her outspokenness about her beliefs resulted in her eventual rejection by society. She retired to England, where she died at Norton Park, Bremmons, Worcestershire, on June 10, 1927.

BIRTHDAYS TODAY

Jason Alexander, 55, actor ("Seinfeld," *Bye Bye Birdie*; Tony for *Jerome Robbins' Broadway*), born Jason Greenspan at Newark, NJ, Sept 23, 1959.

Ani DiFranco, 44, singer, songwriter, born Buffalo, NY, Sept 23, 1970.

Julio Iglesias, 71, singer, born Madrid, Spain, Sept 23, 1943.

Rob James-Collier, 38, actor ("Downton Abbey," "Coronation Street"), born Stockport, Greater Manchester, England, Sept 23, 1976.

Anthony Mackie, 35, actor (*The Hurt Locker, We Are Marshall*), born New Orleans, LA, Sept 23, 1979.

Larry Hogan Mize, 56, golfer, born Augusta, GA, Sept 23, 1958.

Elizabeth Peña, 53, actress (*Rush Hour, Lone Star, Jacob's Ladder*), born Elizabeth, NJ, Sept 23, 1961.

Paul Petersen, 69, actor ("The Donna Reed Show," *Houseboat*), born Glendale, CA, Sept 23, 1945.

Mary Kay Place, 67, writer, actress ("Mary Hartman, Mary Hartman," *The Big Chill*), born Tulsa, OK, Sept 23, 1947.

Mickey Rooney, 94, actor (*Andy Hardy* movies, *The Black Stallion*), born Joe Yule, Jr, at Brooklyn, NY, Sept 23, 1920.

Bruce Springsteen, 65, singer, songwriter, born Freehold, NJ, Sept 23, 1949.

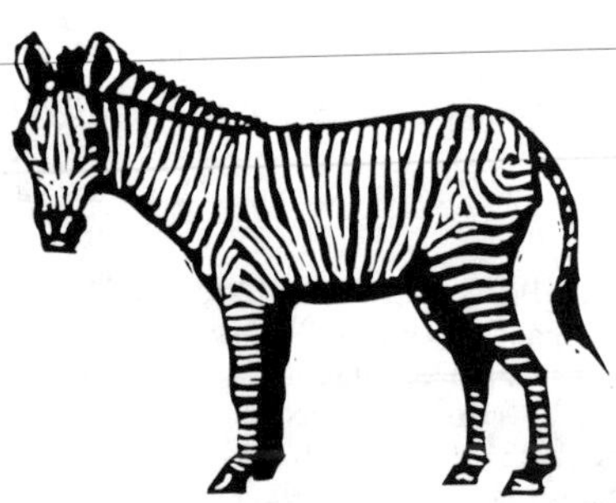

September 2014	S	M	T	W	T	F	S
		1	2	3	4	5	6
	7	8	9	10	11	12	13
	14	15	16	17	18	19	20
	21	22	23	24	25	26	27
	28	29	30				

September 24 — Wednesday

DAY 267 **98 REMAINING**

CAMBODIA: CONSTITUTIONAL DECLARATION DAY. Sept 24. National holiday. Commemorates the new constitution of 1993.

"DANIEL BOONE" TV PREMIERE: 50th ANNIVERSARY. Sept 24, 1964. A successful show based loosely on the life of pioneer Daniel Boone, who helped settle Kentucky in the 1770s. Fess Parker starred as the American hero. Ed Ames played Mingo, Boone's friend, an educated Cherokee, and Pat Blair played his wife, Rebecca. Also featured were Albert Salmi, Jimmy Dean, Roosevelt Grier, Darby Hinton, Veronica Cartwright and Dallas McKennon.

FANEUIL HALL OPENED TO THE PUBLIC: ANNIVERSARY. Sept 24, 1742. On this date Faneuil Hall at Boston, MA, opened to the public. Designed by painter John Smibiert, it was enlarged in 1805 according to plans by Charles Bulfinch. Today it is on the Freedom Trail, as part of the Boston Historical Park administered by the National Park Service.

FITZGERALD, F. SCOTT: BIRTH ANNIVERSARY. Sept 24, 1896. American short-story writer and novelist; author of *This Side of Paradise, The Great Gatsby* and *Tender Is the Night.* Born Francis Scott Key Fitzgerald, at St. Paul, MN, he died at Hollywood, CA, Dec 21, 1940.

GUINEA-BISSAU: INDEPENDENCE DAY. Sept 24. National holiday. Commemorates declaration of independence from Portugal in 1973.

HENSON, JIM: BIRTH ANNIVERSARY. Sept 24, 1936. Puppeteer, born at Greenville, MS. Jim Henson created a unique family of puppets known as the Muppets. Kermit the Frog, Big Bird, Rowlf, Bert and Ernie, Gonzo, Animal, Miss Piggy and Oscar the Grouch are a few of the puppets that captured the hearts of children and adults alike in television and film productions including "Sesame Street," "The Jimmy Dean Show," "The Muppet Show," *The Muppet Movie, The Muppets Take Manhattan, The Great Muppet Caper* and *The Dark Crystal.* Henson began his career in 1954 as producer of the TV show "Sam and Friends" at Washington, DC. He introduced the Muppets in 1956. His creativity was rewarded with 18 Emmy Awards, seven Grammy Awards, four Peabody Awards and five ACE Awards from the National Cable Television Association. Henson died unexpectedly May 16, 1990, at New York, NY.

"THE LOVE BOAT" TV PREMIERE: ANNIVERSARY. Sept 24, 1977. This one-hour comedy-drama featured guest stars aboard a cruise ship, the *Pacific Princess.* All stories had to do with finding or losing love. The ship's crew were the only regulars: Gavin MacLeod as Captain Merrill Stubing, Bernie Kopell as Doctor Adam Bricker, Fred Grandy as assistant purser Burl "Gopher" Smith, Ted Lange as bartender Isaac Washington and Lauren Tewes as cruise director Julie McCoy. The series ended with the last telecast on Sept 5, 1986, but special TV movies were broadcast in later years.

"LOVE OF LIFE" TV PREMIERE: ANNIVERSARY. Sept 24, 1951. This serial, which began as a 15-minute show, ran for 28 years. The story lines shifted from a focus on two sisters to a larger number of characters. The diverse cast included such notables as Christopher Reeve, Karen Grassle, Roy Scheider, Dana Delaney, John Aniston, Marsha Mason, Bert Convy, Warren Beatty and Barnard Hughes. The final airdate was Feb 1, 1980.

MARSHALL, JOHN: BIRTH ANNIVERSARY. Sept 24, 1755. Fourth Chief Justice of Supreme Court, born at Germantown, VA. Served in House of Representatives and as secretary of state under John Adams. Appointed by President Adams to the position of chief justice in January 1801, he became known as "The Great Chief Justice." Marshall's court was largely responsible for defining the role of the Supreme Court and basic organizing principles of government in the early years after adoption of the Constitution in such cases as *Marbury v Madison, McCulloch v Maryland, Cohens v Virginia* and *Gibbons v Ogden.* He died at Philadelphia, PA, July 6, 1835.

MOON PHASE: NEW MOON. Sept 24. Moon enters New Moon phase at 2:14 AM, EDT.

MOZAMBIQUE: ARMED FORCES DAY. Sept 24. National holiday. Commemorates the beginning of the war for independence in 1964.

"THE MUNSTERS" TV PREMIERE: 50th ANNIVERSARY. Sept 24, 1964. "The Munsters" was a half-hour sitcom about an unusual family who thought they were ordinary. Each family member resembled a different type of monster: Herman Munster (Fred Gwynne) was Frankenstein's monster; Lily, his wife (Yvonne DeCarlo), and Grandpa, her father (Al Lewis), were vampires; and his son, Eddie (Butch Patrick), was a werewolf. Only their niece, Marilyn (Beverly Owen and Pat Priest), looked normal, and they considered her the unattractive family member. Most of the show's laughs came from the family's interactions with outsiders. The last telecast was on Sept 1, 1966.

NATIONAL PUNCTUATION DAY. Sept 24. A celebration of the lowly comma, the correctly used quotation mark, and other proper uses of periods, semicolons, and the ever-mysterious ellipsis. For info: Jeff Rubin, Founder, 1517 Buckeye Court, Pinole, CA 94564. Phone: (510) 724-9507. Fax: (510) 741-8698. E-mail: jeff@nationalpunctuationday.com. Web: www.nationalpunctuationday.com.

NATIONAL WOMEN'S HEALTH AND FITNESS DAY. Sept 24. 13th annual event to promote the value of health and fitness for women of all ages. More than 1,000 local women's health events will be held across the country on the same day. Call the toll-free number for further info and how to participate. Annually, the last Wednesday in September. Est attendance: 100,000. For info: Patricia Henze, Executive Director, Health Information Resource Center, 328 W Lincoln Ave, Libertyville, IL 60048. Phone: (800) 828-8225. Fax: (847) 816-8662. E-mail: info@fitnessday.com. Web: www.fitnessday.com.

***NEVERMIND* RELEASED: ANNIVERSARY.** Sept 24, 1991. The grunge rock group Nirvana released this groundbreaking album—their second—on this date. Riding the popularity of its lead single, "Smells Like Teen Spirit," *Nevermind* became the first alternative rock album to break into mainstream success, unseating Michael Jackson's *Dangerous* as number-one album by January 1992. The album has sold more than 26 million copies.

PETIT JEAN FALL ANTIQUE AUTO SWAP MEET. Sept 24–27. Petit Jean Mountain, Morrilton, AR. 17th annual antique auto swap meet, flea market and open car show. Military vehicle show Friday and Saturday. More than 600 vendor spaces available. Est attendance: 7,500. For info: Alan Hoelzeman, Museum of Automobiles, 8 Jones Ln, Morrilton, AR 72110. Phone: (501) 727-5427. E-mail: info@museumofautos.com. Web: www.museumofautos.com.

ROSH HASHANAH BEGINS AT SUNDOWN. Sept 24. Jewish New Year. See also: "Rosh Hashanah" (Sept 25).

SCHWENKFELDER THANKSGIVING. Sept 24. On this day in 1734, members of the Schwenkfelder Society gave thanks for their deliverance from Old World persecution as they prepared to take up new lives in the Pennsylvania-Dutch counties of Pennsylvania. Still celebrated.

"60 MINUTES" TV PREMIERE: ANNIVERSARY. Sept 24, 1968. TV's longest-running prime-time program, and the first newsmagazine offering in-depth investigative reports and profiles, was originally hosted by Harry Reasoner and Mike Wallace. The show's correspondents have included Ed Bradley, Steve Kroft, Lesley Stahl, Morley Safer, Andy Rooney, Scott Pelley, Dan Rather, Diane Sawyer and Bob Simon. Tough interviewer Mike Wallace retired from the show in 2006.

SOUTH AFRICA: HERITAGE DAY. Sept 24. A celebration of South African nationhood, commemorating the multicultural heritage of this rainbow nation.

SPAIN: LA MERCÈ FESTIVAL. Sept 24. Barcelona, Catalonia. Since 1871, annual festival on the feast day of Our Lady of Mercy, which is Sept 24. Events and sights, which take place before and after the 24th, include papier-mâché giants, castells (human towers), fireworks, live music and more.

BIRTHDAYS TODAY

Gordon Clapp, 66, actor ("NYPD Blue"), born North Conway, NH, Sept 24, 1948.

Alan Colmes, 64, journalist, talk show host ("The Alan Colmes Show"), born New York, NY, Sept 24, 1950.

Morgan Hamm, 32, Olympic gymnast, born Ashland, WI, Sept 24, 1982.

Paul Hamm, 32, Olympic gymnast, born Ashland, WI, Sept 24, 1982.

Sheila MacRae, 91, singer, actress, born London, England, Sept 24, 1923.

Rafael Corrales Palmeiro, 50, former baseball player, born Havana, Cuba, Sept 24, 1964.

Kevin Sorbo, 56, actor ("Hercules"), born Mound, MN, Sept 24, 1958.

Nia Vardalos, 52, screenwriter, actress (*My Big Fat Greek Wedding*), born Winnipeg, MB, Canada, Sept 24, 1962.

September 25 — Thursday

DAY 268 **97 REMAINING**

BARNESVILLE PUMPKIN FESTIVAL. Sept 25–28. Downtown Barnesville, OH. This 51st annual festival features King Pumpkin contest, Queen Pageant, Giant Pumpkin Parade, classic car show, banjo and fiddle contest and more. Annually, the last full weekend of September. Est attendance: 100,000. For info: Tim Rockwell, President, Barnesville Pumpkin Festival, Inc, PO Box 5, Barnesville, OH 43713. Phone: (740) 425-1114. E-mail: trockwell.bpf09@yahoo.com. Web: www.barnesvillepumpkinfestival.com.

"BEAUTY AND THE BEAST" TV PREMIERE: ANNIVERSARY. Sept 25, 1987. This updated version of the fairy tale was a romantic hit and acquired a cult following. It followed the experiences of Catherine Chandler (Linda Hamilton), a Manhattan lawyer who is beaten and abandoned and subsequently found and cared for by Vincent (Ron Perlman), a man-beast living under the city. Other cast members included Roy Dotrice, Jay Acovone, Ren Woods, Cory Danziger and David Greenlee. Hamilton left the series at the beginning of the third season; the series ended shortly thereafter.

FAULKNER, WILLIAM CUTHBERT: BIRTH ANNIVERSARY. Sept 25, 1897. American novelist and short-story writer William Faulkner (born Falkner) was born at New Albany, MS. A Nobel Prize winner who changed the style and structure of the American novel, he died at Byhalia, MS, on July 6, 1962. Faulkner's first novel, *Soldiers' Pay*, was published in 1926. His best-known book, *The Sound and the Fury*, appeared in 1929. Shunning literary circles, Faulkner moved to a pre–Civil War house on the outskirts of Oxford, MS, in 1930. From 1930 until the onset of WWII, he published an incredible body of work. In June 1962 Faulkner published his last novel, *The Reivers*.

FIRST AMERICAN NEWSPAPER PUBLISHED: ANNIVERSARY. Sept 25, 1690. The first (and only) edition of *Publick Occurrences Both Foreign and Domestick* was published by Benjamin Harris, at the London-Coffee-House, Boston, MA. Authorities considered this first newspaper published in the US offensive and ordered immediate suppression.

FIRST WOMAN SUPREME COURT JUSTICE: ANNIVERSARY. Sept 25, 1981. Sandra Day O'Connor was sworn in as the first woman associate justice on the US Supreme Court on this date. She had been nominated by President Ronald Reagan in July 1981, and she retired from the court in 2006.

"FOUR STAR PLAYHOUSE" TV PREMIERE: ANNIVERSARY. Sept 25, 1952. The actors who founded Four Star Films—Dick Powell, Charles Boyer, Joel McCrea and Rosalind Russell—starred in this dramatic anthology series. David Niven and Ida Lupino replaced McCrea and Russell, who left shortly after the series began. Other guest actors included Ronald Colman in his first TV dramatic appearance (1952) and Joan Fontaine in her first major dramatic TV role (1953).

GREENWICH MEAN TIME BEGINS: ANNIVERSARY. Sept 25, 1676. (Old Style date.) Two very accurate clocks were set in motion at the Royal Observatory at Greenwich, England. Greenwich Mean Time (now known as Universal Time) became the standard for England; in 1884 it became the standard for the world.

MAJOR LEAGUE BASEBALL'S FIRST DOUBLEHEADER: ANNIVERSARY. Sept 25, 1882. The first major league baseball doubleheader was played between the Providence and Worcester teams.

NATIONAL ONE-HIT WONDER DAY. Sept 25. Honors the one-hit wonders of rock 'n' roll. Anyone who ever had a hit single deserves eternal remembrance. For info: Steven Rosen, 2906 Utopia Pl, Cincinnati, OH 45208. Phone: (513) 321-1018. E-mail: srosenone@aol.com.

PACIFIC OCEAN DISCOVERED: ANNIVERSARY. Sept 25, 1513. Vasco Núñez de Balboa, a Spanish conquistador, stood high atop a peak in the Darien, in present-day Panama, becoming the first European to look upon the Pacific Ocean, claiming it as the South Sea in the name of the King of Spain.

RAMEAU, JEAN PHILLIPPE: BAPTISM ANNIVERSARY. Sept 25, 1683. French composer Jean Phillippe Rameau was baptized today at Dijon, France (his birth date is unknown). Called by some the greatest French composer and musical theorist of the 18th century, Rameau died at Paris, France, Sept 12, 1764.

REEVE, CHRISTOPHER: BIRTH ANNIVERSARY. Sept 25, 1952. Born at New York, NY, this actor was best known for his portrayal of the title character in *Superman* (1978) and three sequels during the 1980s. After being paralyzed in a horseback riding accident, he was confined to a wheelchair and became an activist for spinal-cord research and awareness. He died at Mount Kisco, NY, Oct 10, 2004.

RIZZUTO, PHIL: BIRTH ANNIVERSARY. Sept 25, 1917. Hall of Fame baseball player who spent his entire career with the New York Yankees, born at Brooklyn, NY. He played shortstop 1941–56, winning the league MVP in 1950, and played in nine World Series, winning seven. After his playing career, he became the radio (and later television) broadcaster for the Yankees and remained on the air for more than 40 years. His home run call of "Holy Cow!" is considered legendary. He died at West Orange, NJ, Aug 13, 2007.

ROSH HASHANAH or JEWISH NEW YEAR. Sept 25–26. Jewish holy day observed on two consecutive days. Hebrew calendar date: Tishri 1–2, 5775. Rosh Hashanah (literally "Head of the Year") is the beginning of 10 days of repentance and spiritual renewal. (Began at sundown Sept 24.)

RWANDA: REPUBLIC DAY. Sept 25. National holiday. Marks the 1961 abolition of the monarchy.

★ ★ ★

September 2014

S	M	T	W	T	F	S
	1	2	3	4	5	6
7	8	9	10	11	12	13
14	15	16	17	18	19	20
21	22	23	24	25	26	27
28	29	30				

SEQUOIA AND KINGS CANYON NATIONAL PARK ESTABLISHED: ANNIVERSARY. Sept 25, 1890. Area in central California established as a national park. For further park info: Sequoia Natl Park, Three Rivers, CA 93271.

SHOSTAKOVICH, DMITRI: BIRTH ANNIVERSARY. Sept 25, 1906. Russian composer born at St. Petersburg, Russia. Died at Moscow, USSR, Aug 9, 1975.

SILVERSTEIN, SHEL: BIRTH ANNIVERSARY. Sept 25, 1930. Cartoonist and children's author, best remembered for his poetry that included *A Light in the Attic* and *The Giving Tree*. Silverstein won the Michigan Young Reader's Award for *Where the Sidewalk Ends*. Also a songwriter, he wrote "The Unicorn Song" and "A Boy Named Sue." Born at Chicago, IL, he died at Key West, FL, May 9, 1999.

SMITH, WALTER WESLEY "RED": BIRTH ANNIVERSARY. Sept 25, 1905. Pulitzer Prize–winning sports columnist and newspaperman for 54 years, Walter Wesley (Red) Smith was born at Green Bay, WI. Called the "nation's most respected sportswriter," Smith's columns appeared in almost 500 newspapers. He died at Stamford, CT, Jan 15, 1982.

VIRGINIA PEANUT FESTIVAL. Sept 25–28. Emporia, VA. Annual celebration promoting peanuts and harvesting. Features musical concerts, arts and crafts, parade, quilt show, carnival, car show and fireworks. Annually, the fourth weekend in September, including Thursday. For info: Kay Callahan, Chairman, Virginia Peanut Festival, 1509 Walnut Dr, Emporia, VA 23847. Phone: (434) 430-1023 or (434) 634-4744. E-mail: kcallahan@courts.state.va.us.

BIRTHDAYS TODAY

Chauncey Billups, 38, basketball player, born Denver, CO, Sept 25, 1976.

Tate Donovan, 51, actor ("Damages," *Argo, Love Potion No. 9*), born New York, NY, Sept 25, 1963.

Michael Douglas, 70, actor (Oscar for *Wall Street*; *Traffic, Wonder Boys, Fatal Attraction*), director, producer, born New York, NY, Sept 25, 1944.

Mark Hamill, 63, actor (*Star Wars*), born Oakland, CA, Sept 25, 1951.

Jamie Hyneman, 58, television personality, host ("MythBusters"), born Marshall, MI, Sept 25, 1956.

Heather Locklear, 53, actress ("Spin City," "Melrose Place," "Dynasty"), born Los Angeles, CA, Sept 25, 1961.

Michael Madsen, 55, actor (*Kill Bill* films, *Reservoir Dogs*), born Chicago, IL, Sept 25, 1959.

Lee Norris, 33, actor ("One Tree Hill," "Boy Meets World"), born Greenville, NC, Sept 25, 1981.

Scottie Pippen, 49, sportscaster, Hall of Fame basketball player, born Hamburg, AR, Sept 25, 1965.

Will Smith, 46, actor (*I Am Legend, Ali, Men in Black, Independence Day*), singer, born Philadelphia, PA, Sept 25, 1968.

Robert Walden, 71, actor ("Lou Grant," *All the King's Men*), born New York, NY, Sept 25, 1943.

Barbara Walters, 83, television journalist, interviewer, born Boston, MA, Sept 25, 1931.

Catherine Zeta-Jones, 45, actress (Oscar for *Chicago*; *Traffic, The Mask of Zorro*), born Swansea, Glamorgan, Wales, Sept 25, 1969.

September 26 — Friday

DAY 269 **96 REMAINING**

APPLESEED, JOHNNY: BIRTH ANNIVERSARY. Sept 26, 1774. John Chapman, better known as Johnny Appleseed, believed to have been born at Leominster, MA. Died at Allen County, IN, Mar 11, 1845. Planter of orchards and friend of wild animals, he was regarded as a great medicine man by the Indians.

BALTIMORE BOOK FESTIVAL. Sept 26–28 (tentative). Baltimore, MD. The mid-Atlantic's premier celebration of literary arts features authors, poetry readings, cooking demonstrations and more than 125 exhibitors and booksellers. Many special programs for children. For info: Baltimore Book Festival, 10 E Baltimore St, 10th Fl, Baltimore, MD 21202. Phone: (410) 752-8632. Web: www.baltimorebookfestival.org.

BATTLE OF MEUSE–ARGONNE FOREST: ANNIVERSARY. Sept 26, 1918. As part of four major efforts to break the Hindenburg line, a Franco-American offensive began on this date, with the US First Army striking between the Meuse River and the Argonne Forest and the French Fourth Army to their west. After four taxing weeks of attack, the Germans were gradually pushed back. By Oct 31, the Americans had advanced 10 miles, the French had reached the Aisne River 20 miles away and the Argonne Forest was rid of the Central Power forces. This was the final great battle of WWI.

"THE BEVERLY HILLBILLIES" TV PREMIERE: ANNIVERSARY. Sept 26, 1962. This half-hour comedy was one of the most successful "rural" comedies on TV; in addition, according to Nielsen, the eight most-watched half-hour shows are episodes of this series. "The Beverly Hillbillies" was about an Appalachian man, Jed Clampett (Buddy Ebsen), who found oil on his property, so he moved his family to a better life in Beverly Hills, CA. Most of its jokes were based on its fish-out-of-water premise. Also in the cast were Irene Ryan as Granny, Jed's mother-in-law; Donna Douglas as his daughter, Elly May; Max Baer Jr, as his nephew, Jethro Bodine; Raymond Bailey as neurotic Milburn Drysdale, Jed's neighbor and banker; Nancy Kulp as Jane Hathaway, Drysdale's secretary; and Harriet MacGibbon as Margaret Drysdale, Milburn's wife.

"THE BRADY BUNCH" TV PREMIERE: 45th ANNIVERSARY. Sept 26, 1969. This popular sitcom starred Robert Reed as widower Mike Brady, who has three sons and is married to Carol (played by Florence Henderson), who has three daughters. Housekeeper Alice was played by Ann B. Davis. Sons Greg (Barry Williams), Peter (Christopher Knight) and Bobby (Mike Lookinland) and daughters Marcia (Maureen McCormick), Jan (Eve Plumb) and Cindy (Susan Olsen) experienced the typical crises of youth. The program steered clear of social issues and portrayed childhood as a time of innocence. The last episode was telecast on Aug 30, 1974. The program continues to be popular in reruns, and there were also many spin-offs: a cartoon, a variety series, a sitcom, a short-lived dramatic series and films.

BUFFALO ROUNDUP. Sept 26. Custer, SD. 49th annual. To round up, brand and separate 1,300 buffalo before auction in November. Est attendance: 14,000. For info: Craig Pugsley, Custer State Park, 13329 US Highway 16A, Custer, SD 57730. Phone: (605) 255-4515. Fax: (605) 255-4460. E-mail: custerstatepark@state.sd.us. Web: www.custerstatepark.com.

CELTIC CLASSIC HIGHLAND GAMES & FESTIVAL. Sept 26–28. Bethlehem, PA. America's largest highland games and festival, celebrating Celtic culture with three free days of Celtic music, Irish dance, world-class Highland athletic competitions, Border Collie exhibitions, pipe band and drum major competitions, art and history workshops, foods, crafts, entertainment and much more. Annually, the last full weekend in September beginning on the last Friday. Est attendance: 250,000. For info: Celtic Cultural Alliance, Celtic Classic, 532 Main St, Bethlehem, PA 18018. Phone: (610) 868-9599. Fax: (610) 868-9730. E-mail: info@celticfest.org. Web: www.celticfest.org.

CHILI COOK-OFF AND FALL FESTIVAL OF THE ARTS AND CRAFTS. Sept 26–28. Washington, MO. Thirty teams compete for awards for best chili. Juried festival featuring the creative talents of two- and three-dimensional artists and crafters. Strassenfest, beer area, specialty foods, music and live entertainment. Admission includes a commemorative chili mug (Fall Festival is free). For info: Downtown Washington, Inc, PO Box 144, Washington, MO 63090. Phone: (636) 239-1743. Fax: (636) 239-4832. E-mail: events@downtownwashmo.org. Web: downtownwashmo.org.

DONIZETTI'S *LUCIA DI LAMMERMOOR* PREMIERE: ANNIVERSARY. Sept 26, 1835. *Lucia di Lammermoor*, one of opera's greatest tragic love stories, premiered in Naples, Italy. The opera was composed by Gaetano Donizetti with a libretto by Salvatore Cammarano. The plot was based on Sir Walter Scott's *The Bride of Lammermoor* and takes place in 17th-century Scotland.

ELIOT, THOMAS STEARNS: BIRTH ANNIVERSARY. Sept 26, 1888. Poet, literary critic, dramatist and editor born at St. Louis, MO. One of the 20th century's preeminent poets, Eliot—with friend and fellow poet Ezra Pound—worked to modernize contemporary poetic diction to one that reflected the rhythm of educated speech. Eliot's experiments in diction, versification and style are seen throughout the body of his works, which include *A Love Song for J. Alfred Prufrock* (1917), *Four Quartets* (1945) and *The Waste Land* (1922)—his most renowned poem. Awarded the Order of Merit and the Nobel Prize in Literature in 1948, Eliot died at London, England, Jan 24, 1965.

FABULOUS 1890s WEEKEND. Sept 26–27. Mansfield, PA. Night football in America began in 1892 with a game between Mansfield University and Wyoming Seminary. Annually, Mansfield celebrates a "Fabulous 1890s Weekend" to commemorate the event. Parade, period exhibits, crafts and other events, including the re-creation of the first night football game. Sponsors: Mansfield University of Pennsylvania and Mansfield Chamber of Commerce. Est attendance: 10,000. For info: Dennis Miller, Dir PR, Mansfield University, 516 North Hall, Mansfield, PA 16933. Phone: (570) 662-4293. E-mail: dmiller@mansfield.edu. Web: www.1890sweekend.com.

FAIRMOUNT MUSEUM DAYS/REMEMBERING JAMES DEAN FESTIVAL. Sept 26–28. Fairmount, IN. The town where James Dean grew up honors Dean and other celebrated former citizens such as Jim Davis, creator of Garfield, journalist Phil Jones and Robert Sheets, retired director of the National Hurricane Center. The Fairmount Museum boasts the Authentic James Dean Exhibit of memorabilia and personal items of Dean's, and it sponsors the festival that also includes a parade, James Dean Look-Alike Contest, custom car show featuring the James Dean Run for pre-1980 autos, Garfield Cat Photo and Art Contest, Garfield Great Run, carnival, booths, live '50s entertainment and more. James Dean Memorial Service is Sept 30. Annually, the last full weekend in September. Est attendance: 40,000. For info: Fairmount Historical Museum, Inc, 203 E Washington St, PO Box 92, Fairmount, IN 46928. Phone: (765) 948-4555. Web: www.jamesdeanartifacts.com.

FIRST TELEVISED PRESIDENTIAL DEBATE: ANNIVERSARY. Sept 26, 1960. The debate between presidential candidates John F. Kennedy and Richard Nixon was televised from WBBM-TV, a Chicago TV studio. Howard K. Smith was the moderator.

GERSHWIN, GEORGE: BIRTH ANNIVERSARY. Sept 26, 1898. American composer remembered for his many enduring songs and melodies, including: "The Man I Love," "Strike Up the Band," "Funny Face," "I Got Rhythm" and the opera *Porgy and Bess.* Many of his works were in collaboration with his brother, Ira. Born at

Brooklyn, NY, he died of a brain tumor at Beverly Hills, CA, July 11, 1937. See also: "Gershwin, Ira: Birth Anniversary" (Dec 6).

"GILLIGAN'S ISLAND" TV PREMIERE: 50th ANNIVERSARY. Sept 26, 1964. Seven people set sail aboard the *Minnow* for a three-hour tour and became stranded on an island. They used the resources on the island for food, shelter and entertainment. The cast included Bob Denver (Gilligan), Alan Hale, Jr (the Skipper), Jim Backus (Thurston Howell III), Natalie Schafer (Mrs "Lovey" Howell), Russell Johnson (the Professor), Dawn Wells (Mary Ann) and Tina Louise (Ginger Grant, the movie star). The last telecast aired on Sept 4, 1967.

"HAWAII FIVE-O" TV PREMIERE: ANNIVERSARY. Sept 26, 1968. "Book 'em, Dano" became a national catchphrase after this CBS crime series began airing. It starred the granite-jawed Jack Lord as Steve McGarrett, leader of a special Hawaiian state police force that only answered to the governor. His officers included Danny "Dano" Williams (James MacArthur), Chin Ho Kelly (Kam Fong), Duke Lukela (Herman Wedemeyer) and others. Filmed on location at Oahu, HI, and featuring a popular theme song by the Ventures, the show was a huge hit until it concluded in 1980. (CBS premiered a new version of the show in fall 2010.)

HEIDEGGER, MARTIN: 125th BIRTH ANNIVERSARY. Sept 26, 1889. Widely regarded the most original 20th-century philosopher, Heidegger focused on answering one fundamental question, the meaning of "being," which he explored in his seminal work *Being and Time* (1927), one of the 20th century's most influential books. His analysis revitalized the study of philosophy and strongly influenced Sartre and other existential philosophers. Born at Messkirch, Germany, Heidegger died May 26, 1976, at Freiburg, Germany.

HUG A VEGAN DAY. Sept 26. Hug all your vegan friends. If you are already vegan, make sure your friends and family show you some love! Annually, the last Friday in September. For info: peta2, 2154 W Sunset Blvd, Los Angeles, CA 90026. Phone: (323) 644-7382. E-mail: peta2@peta2.com. Web: www.peta2.com/hug.

"KNIGHT RIDER" TV PREMIERE: ANNIVERSARY. Sept 26, 1982. David Hasselhoff starred in this one-hour adventure series about a cop who was nearly killed but then brought back to life with a new identity (Michael Knight) by a mysterious millionaire. Together with a car that talked, a Pontiac Trans Am called KITT (Knight Industries Two Thousand), Knight had various adventures. William Daniels performed the voice of KITT.

LaLANNE, JACK: 100th BIRTH ANNIVERSARY. Sept 26, 1914. The son of French immigrants, born at San Francisco, CA, was to become America's fitness guru through his eponymous TV show and wacky stunts. "The Jack LaLanne Show" went national in 1959, and by the end of its run in the 1980s had 3,000 episodes. LaLanne, who kept a 30-inch waist, popularized the benefits of living heathfully with amazing stunts, such as swimming handcuffed from Alcatraz Island to Fisherman's Wharf while also towing a 1,000-pound boat (at age 60). LaLanne died Jan 23, 2011, at Morro Bay, CA, at age 96.

LIBERTY FALL FESTIVAL. Sept 26–28. Liberty, MO. Arts and crafts booth, food booths, children's activities, a carnival, a parade, entertainment provided throughout the three-day festival. Annually, the fourth weekend in September. Est attendance: 40,000. For info: Liberty Area Chamber of Commerce, 1170 W Kansas St, Ste H, Liberty, MO 64068. Phone: (816) 781-5200. Fax: (816) 781-4901. E-mail: info@libertyfallfest.com. Web: www.libertyfallfest.com.

LOVE NOTE DAY. Sept 26. Words of love—powerful and poignant—expressed on paper. Who doesn't like to receive a love note? When it is so easy to get caught up in the "busy-ness" of life, here's a day to remember what is truly important in our life: our love partner. Send a love note today. Annually, the fourth Friday in September. For info: Leona Hamel, Love Note Day, 2100 Keller Blvd, Apt 211, Ville St.-Laurent, QC, Canada H4K 1L4. Phone: (450) 578-6462. E-mail: leona@romanceunlimited.com.

MOUNT PLEASANT GLASS & ETHNIC FESTIVAL. Sept 26–28. Mount Pleasant, PA. The feel and sense of a "front porch neighborhood" festival in hometown America. Features glass demos, ethnic foods, arts and crafts, giant parade, national and regional entertainment, Old Town Mount Pleasant area and "Sparkle Spectacular," a nightly dancing light show to music. Free entertainment in three areas, fireworks, rides, games and Illumination Launch. Est attendance: 45,000. For info: Jeff Landy, Mount Pleasant Glass and Ethnic Festival, Municipal Bldg, 1 Etze Ave, Mount Pleasant, PA 15666. Phone: (724) 542-4711. Fax: (724) 547-0115. Web: www.mtpleasantglassandethnicfestival.com.

POPE PAUL VI: BIRTH ANNIVERSARY. Sept 26, 1897. Giovanni Battista Montini, 262nd pope of the Roman Catholic Church, born at Concesio, Italy. Elected pope June 21, 1963. Died at Castel Gandolfo, near Rome, Italy, Aug 6, 1978.

STATE FAIR OF TEXAS. Sept 26–Oct 19. Fair Park, Dallas, TX. Features a Broadway musical, college football games, new car show, concerts, livestock shows and traditional events and entertainment including exhibits, creative arts and parades. Est attendance: 3,000,000. For info: Public Relations, State Fair of Texas, PO Box 150009, Dallas, TX 75315. Phone: (214) 421-8715. Fax: (214) 421-8710. E-mail: pr@bigtex.com. Web: www.bigtex.com.

STATE FAIR OF VIRGINIA. Sept 26–Oct 5. Meadow Event Park, Doswell. It's the Big Red Barn, racing pigs, the State Fair Animal Nursery, the famous State Fair Duck Slide and more! Get up close and personal with more than 5,000 farm animals in Virginia's largest outdoor classroom. Enjoy 11 days of rides, thrills and fun for the whole family with blue-ribbon competitions, exhibits, midway rides and shows. It's a Virginia tradition and the only place to get that delicious State Fair food. Est attendance: 300,000. For info: State Fair of Virginia, PO Box 130, Doswell, VA 23047. Phone: (804) 994-2800. Fax: (804) 994-2927. Web: www.statefairva.org.

TACA FALL CRAFT FAIR. Sept 26–28. Centennial Park, Nashville, TN. 35th annual fair. The state's premier outdoor showcase for American fine crafts featuring more than 200 selected American craft artists from across the nation. TACA's Fall Craft Fair offers shoppers the opportunity to meet and talk with exhibiting artists, enjoy children's activities, visit special exhibits and demonstrations and purchase a wide variety of unique handcrafted works. Annually, the last weekend in September. Est attendance: 48,000. For info: Tennessee Assn of Craft Artists, PO Box 120066, Nashville, TN 37212. Phone: (615) 736-7600. Fax: (615) 736-2090. E-mail: taca@tennesseecrafts.org. Web: www.tennesseecrafts.org.

WARRENS CRANBERRY FESTIVAL. Sept 26–28. Warrens, WI. 42nd annual. A community celebration of the ruby-red fruit at the "Cranberry Capital of Wisconsin." During this "Cranfest," you can take a guided bus tour of a cranberry marsh to see how cranberries are raised and harvested. Also featured are more than 1,300 booths of arts, crafts, antiques and flea market items, and mouth-watering fall produce including flavored honey, candy, Amish noodles, apples and of course a variety of cranberry items. Est attendance: 110,000. For info: Warrens Cranberry Festival, Inc, PO Box 146, Warrens, WI 54666. Phone: (608) 378-4200. E-mail: cranfest@cranfest.com. Web: www.cranfest.com.

September 2014

S	M	T	W	T	F	S
	1	2	3	4	5	6
7	8	9	10	11	12	13
14	15	16	17	18	19	20
21	22	23	24	25	26	27
28	29	30				

***WEST SIDE STORY* PREMIERE: ANNIVERSARY.** Sept 26, 1957. Composer Leonard Bernstein's updated Romeo and Juliet musical premiered on Broadway and ran until 1960. Stephen Sondheim wrote the lyrics, Arthur Laurents wrote the book and Jerome Robbins created the choreography.

BIRTHDAYS TODAY

Lynn Anderson, 67, singer, born Grand Forks, ND, Sept 26, 1947.

Melissa Sue Anderson, 52, actress ("Little House on the Prairie"), born Berkeley, CA, Sept 26, 1962.

Michael Ballack, 38, former soccer player, born Gorlitz, Germany, Sept 26, 1976.

Jan Brewer, 70, Governor of Arizona (R), born Hollywood, CA, Sept 9, 1944.

Jim Caviezel, 46, actor ("Person of Interest," *The Passion of the Christ*), born Mount Vernon, WA, Sept 26, 1968.

Bryan Ferry, 69, singer, songwriter, born Durham, England, Sept 26, 1945.

Linda Hamilton, 57, actress (*The Terminator, Terminator 2*, "Beauty and the Beast"), born Salisbury, MD, Sept 26, 1957.

Mary Beth Hurt, 66, actress (*The World According to Garp, Six Degrees of Separation*), born Marshalltown, IA, Sept 26, 1948.

Olivia Newton-John, 66, singer, actress (*Grease*), born Cambridge, England, Sept 26, 1948.

Jane Smiley, 65, author (*A Thousand Acres, Moo*), born Los Angeles, CA, Sept 26, 1949.

Christine T. Whitman, 68, former administrator of the Environmental Protection Agency, former governor of New Jersey (R), born New York, NY, Sept 26, 1946.

Serena Williams, 33, tennis player, born Saginaw, MI, Sept 26, 1981.

September 27 — Saturday

DAY 270 — **95 REMAINING**

ADAMS, SAMUEL: BIRTH ANNIVERSARY. Sept 27, 1722. Revolutionary leader and Massachusetts state politician Samuel Adams, cousin to President John Adams (1797–1801), was born at Boston. He died there Oct 2, 1803. As a delegate to the First and Second Continental Congresses, Adams urged a vigorous stand against England. He signed the Declaration of Independence and the Articles of Confederation and supported the War for Independence. Adams served as lieutenant governor of Massachusetts under John Hancock from 1789 to 1793 and then as governor until 1797.

ANCESTOR APPRECIATION DAY. Sept 27. A day to learn about and appreciate one's forebears. For info: AAD Assn, 2460 Devonshire Rd, Ann Arbor, MI 48104-2706.

APPLE SATURDAYS. Sept 27 (also Oct 4 and 11). Sabbathday Lake Shaker Village, New Gloucester, ME. Free cider pressing, apple pie sale, Apple Art for kids, cider and donut sale. For info: United Society of Shakers, 707 Shaker Rd, New Gloucester, ME 04260. Phone: (207) 926-4597. E-mail: usshakers@aol.com. Web: www.shaker.lib.me.us.

BATTLE OF CAMBRAI–SAINT QUENTIN: ANNIVERSARY. Sept 27, 1918. British General Sir Douglas Haig moved his armies toward Cambrai and St. Quentin as part of four major efforts to break the Hindenburg line in the German salient that extended from Verdun to the sea. To the south the New Zealand and Canadian divisions smashed through the Hindenburg line on Oct 6. German General Erich Ludendorff resigned Oct 16, and the line was taken between Oct 18 and 20.

BUFFALO ROUNDUP ARTS FESTIVAL. Sept 27–28. Custer, SD. 21st annual. South Dakota artists and craftsmen display and sell their arts and crafts. Also Western and Native American entertainment, pancake feeds, chili cook-off and much more. Est attendance: 15,000. For info: Craig Pugsley, Visitor Services Coord, Custer State Park, 13329 US Highway 16A, Custer, SD 57730. Phone: (605) 255-4515. Fax: (605) 255-4460. E-mail: custerstatepark@state.sd.us. Web: www.custerstatepark.com.

CORNELIUS, DON: BIRTH ANNIVERSARY. Sept 27, 1936. Born at Chicago, IL, Cornelius was a pioneering and influential television producer and emcee. With his deep, resonant voice, creative drive and keen eye for talent, Don Cornelius created a hit musical variety show that brought black culture into American homes like no syndicated program before it. In 1970, Cornelius debuted "Soul Train" on WCIU-TV, a local Chicago television station. It went national a year later, and gave important exposure to now-legendary performers like James Brown, Michael Jackson and Marvin Gaye at a time when soul and R&B artists had few television outlets and scant access to white audiences. "Soul Train" also acted as a barometer for black youth culture, tracking and shaping the styles, slang and dances of the day. Cornelius remained in a production role on "Soul Train" until 2006. He died at Los Angeles, CA, on Feb 1, 2012.

CRUIKSHANK, GEORGE: BIRTH ANNIVERSARY. Sept 27, 1792. English artist, especially known for caricatures and illustrating of Charles Dickens's books. Born at London, England, and died there Feb 1, 1878.

ETHIOPIA: TRUE CROSS DAY. Sept 27. National holiday. Commemorates the finding of the true cross (*Maskal*). Also a holiday in Eritrea.

EVERYBODY'S DAY FESTIVAL. Sept 27. Thomasville, NC. A downtown street festival for everybody. Crafts, food vendors and live entertainment. Annually, the last Saturday in Sept. Est attendance: 80,000. For info: Thomasville Area Chamber of Commerce, Box 1400, Thomasville, NC 27361. Phone: (336) 475-6134. Fax: (336) 475-4802. E-mail: thomasvillechamber@thomasvillechamber.net. Web: www.everybodysday.com.

FAMILY HEALTH AND FITNESS DAY—USA. Sept 27. 18th annual national event promoting family health and fitness. Families across the country will be involved in locally organized health promotion activities at hundreds of locations all on the same day. Call the toll-free number for further info and how to participate. Always held the last Saturday in September. Est attendance: 50,000. For info: Patricia Henze, Executive Director, Health Info Resource Center, 328 W Lincoln Ave, Libertyville, IL 60048. Phone: (800) 828-8225. Fax: (847) 816-8662. E-mail: info@fitnessday.com. Web: www.fitnessday.com.

FISH AMNESTY DAY. Sept 27. Give animals a break by not fishing. Fish are intelligent animals who feel pain just like the dogs and cats who share our homes. Annually, the fourth Saturday in September. For info: PETA, 501 Front St, Norfolk, VA 23510. Phone: (757) 622-7382. E-mail: JennyW@peta.org. Web: www.peta.org.

GENEVA AREA GRAPE JAMBOREE. Sept 27–28. Geneva, OH. 51st annual celebration of grape harvest and products. Wine tasting, free entertainment, food and rides. Annually, the last full weekend in September. Est attendance: 200,000. For info: Geneva Grape Jamboree, Box 92, Geneva, OH 44041. Phone: (440) 466-5262. E-mail: info@grapejamboree.com. Web: www.grapejamboree.com.

GERMANY: BMW BERLIN MARATHON. Sept 27 (tentative—possibly Sept 28). Berlin. 41st annual. Awarded a road race Gold Label by the International Association of Athletics Federations. The Berlin Marathon—with 40,000 participants—offers fantastic atmosphere with the final meters of the course going through the Brandenburg Gate. Est attendance: 1,000,000. For info: Berlin Marathon, SCC Events GmbH. Phone: (49) 30-30-12-88-10. E-mail: office@berlin-marathon.com. Web: www.bmw-berlin-marathon.com.

GETTYSBURG OUTDOOR ANTIQUE SHOW. Sept 27. Gettysburg, PA. More than 150 dealers displaying their wares on the sidewalk. Est attendance: 25,000. For info: Gettysburg Area Retail Merchants Assn, PO Box 4070, Gettysburg, PA 17325. Phone: (717) 253-5750. E-mail: gettysburgantiqueshow@comcast.net. Web: gettysburgretailmerchants.com.

"JACK THE RIPPER" LETTER: ANNIVERSARY. Sept 27, 1888. In the midst of the "Autumn of Terror" in which London, England, was convulsed over the crimes of a brutal serial killer, the city's Central News Agency received a letter in red ink purportedly written by the killer. He dubbed himself "Jack the Ripper" and threatened more killings. Police at the time believed (and most historians today believe) the letter to be a hoax by an irresponsible journalist, but the name took hold in the public imagination and is forever associated with the Whitechapel murders of 1888. See also: "Whitechapel Murders Begin: Anniversary" (Aug 31).

MARION COUNTY COUNTRY HAM DAYS. Sept 27–28. Lebanon, KY. Country ham breakfast served under a tent in downtown Lebanon. Pokey pig 5k run, PIGasus parade, children's activities, car show, more than 100 arts and crafts booths and live entertainment. Annually, the last full weekend in September. Est attendance: 40,000. For info: Marion County Chamber of Commerce, 239 N Spalding Ave, Ste 201, Lebanon, KY 40033. Phone: (270) 692-9594. Fax: (270) 692-2661. E-mail: info@marioncountykychamber.com. Web: www.hamdays.com.

NAST, THOMAS: BIRTH ANNIVERSARY. Sept 27, 1840. American political cartoonist born at Landau, Germany, best known for his cartoons attacking New York's Tweed ring. Died Dec 7, 1902, at Guayaquil, Ecuador.

✦NATIONAL HUNTING AND FISHING DAY. Sept 27. Presidential Proclamation 4682, of Sept 11, 1979, covers all succeeding years. Annually, the fourth Saturday in September.

NATIONAL PUBLIC LANDS DAY. Sept 27. 21st annual. The nation's largest hands-on volunteer effort to improve and enhance the public lands that Americans enjoy. Each year, volunteers participate in National Public Lands day in all 50 states, the District of Columbia, Puerto Rico and other US territories. They build trails and bridges, plant trees and plants, remove trash and invasive species and restore historic sites. Sponsored by Toyota Motor Sales. Annually, the last Saturday in September. Est attendance: 175,000. For info: National Environmental Education Foundation, National Public Lands Day, 4301 Connecticut Ave NW, Ste 160, Washington, DC 20008. Phone: (202) 261-6479. Fax: (202) 261-6464. E-mail: npld@neefusa.org. Web: www.publiclandsday.org.

OCEAN COUNTY DECOY AND GUNNING SHOW. Sept 27–28. Tip Seaman County Park and Tuckerton Seaport, Tuckerton, NJ. Gathering to celebrate the local waterfowling heritage. Contests include decoy carving, working decoy rigs, sneakbox building, gunning, retrieving and goose- and duck-calling. Wildlife art, outdoor clothing and gear, hunting and fishing supplies. More than 400 vendors. Free. Rain or shine. Est attendance: 20,000. For info: Wells Mills Co Park. Phone: (609) 971-3085. Web: www.co.ocean.nj.us/OCparks.

OKLAHOMA STATE SUGAR ART SHOW AND GRAND NATIONAL WEDDING CAKE COMPETITION. Sept 27–28 (setup Sept 26). Tulsa, OK. 21st annual. The créme de la créme of cake designers vie for the Grand National title of "best of the best." Each year more than 80 competitors travel to Tulsa to compete in this contest as well as another 300 who compete in the companion event. There are approximately 600 showpieces entered at each event. This is the only contest of its kind in the US, which attracts food service professionals as well as the bridal market. This is a huge source of inspiration meant to push the envelope, educate and inspire. Est attendance: 80,000. For info: Kerry Vincent, Oklahoma State Sugar Art Show, 10530 S Urbana Ave, Tulsa, OK 74137. Phone: (918) 299-7125. Fax: (918) 745-0879. E-mail: kvsugarart@aol.com. Web: www.oklahomasugarartists.com.

R.E.A.D. IN AMERICA DAY. Sept 27. National Mall, Washington, DC. R.E.A.D. stands for "Reading helps Everyone Accomplish Dreams." An annual event, R.E.A.D. in America Day is sponsored by the CheeREADing program. The day's motto is "Anything is possible if you read." It is through the power of reading that goals are set and dreams are realized. The day's purpose is to raise awareness about youth literacy and to encourage the power of daily reading for our youth. The day's activities include a rally for reading (with local heroes and celebrities stopping by to read a book and share how reading has changed their lives), local bookstore "Power of One Hour" reading sessions and local school events. Annually, the fourth Saturday in September. For info: Ashley Anderson, CheeREADing, 5230 Norborne Ln, Houston, TX 77069. Phone: (713) 992-4334. E-mail: bkanderson1@sbcglobal.net.

SAINT VINCENT DE PAUL: FEAST DAY. Sept 27. French priest, patron of charitable organizations, and cofounder of the Sisters of Charity. Canonized 1737 (lived 1581?–1660).

SEMMES, RAPHAEL: BIRTH ANNIVERSARY. Sept 27, 1809. Born at St. Charles County, MD, and died Aug 30, 1877, at Mobile, AL. Daring Confederate naval officer, best known for his incredible raids on Union merchant ships during the middle two years of the Civil War. As commander of the *Alabama*, he captured, sank or burned 82 Union ships valued at more than $6 million.

SHEYENNE VALLEY ARTS & CRAFTS FESTIVAL. Sept 27–28. Fort Ransom, ND. This 47th annual festival is one of the oldest and best in the area. Artists and crafters from several states join local people in offering 150 displays, church bazaar and dinner, turkey barbecue—all in a rustic historic atmosphere. Annually, the last full weekend in September. Sponsor: Sheyenne Valley Arts and Crafts Assn, Inc, a nonprofit organization. Est attendance: 10,000. For info: SVACA, PO Box 21, Fort Ransom, ND 58033. Phone: (701) 973-4461. E-mail: svaca@drtel.net. Web: www.svaca.org.

SPACE MILESTONE: *SOYUZ 12* (USSR). Sept 27, 1973. Because of the death of the crew of *Soyuz 11* upon reentry, it was decided that cosmonauts must wear pressurized space suits on takeoff and landing. Thus there was no longer room for three cosmonauts on a flight. Two Soviet cosmonauts (V.G. Lazarev and O.G. Makarov) made the two-day flight launched on this date.

September 2014

S	M	T	W	T	F	S
	1	2	3	4	5	6
7	8	9	10	11	12	13
14	15	16	17	18	19	20
21	22	23	24	25	26	27
28	29	30				

"THE TONIGHT SHOW" TV PREMIERE: 60th ANNIVERSARY. Sept 27, 1954. "The Tonight Show" has gone through numerous changes over the years, yet it has remained a top-rated show that set the standards for all variety/talk shows to come. Steve Allen served as host 1954–57. He developed the show's format: an opening monologue, games or segments for the studio audience and then celebrity interviews. Jack Paar hosted 1957–62 and Johnny Carson reigned as the king of comedy 1962–92. Comedian Jay Leno was the popular host 1992–2009. After a brief period with Conan O'Brien taking over the desk, Leno returned in 2010.

TRI-STATE BAND FESTIVAL. Sept 27. Luverne, MN. 64th annual festival with more than 2,500 high school students from Minnesota, South Dakota and Iowa; trophies awarded in four classes. Annually, the last Saturday in September. For info: Jane Wildung Lanphere, Exec Dir, Luverne Area Chamber, 213 E Luverne St, Luverne, MN 56156. Phone: (507) 283-4061. Fax: (507) 283-4061. E-mail: luvernechamber@co.rock.mn.us. Web: www.luvernechamber.com.

WARREN COMMISSION REPORT: 50th ANNIVERSARY. Sept 27, 1964. On this day, the Warren Commission issued a report stating that Lee Harvey Oswald acted alone in the assassination of President John F. Kennedy on Nov 22, 1963. Congress reopened the investigation, and in 1979 the House Select Committee on Assassinations issued a report stating a conspiracy was most likely involved. See also: "Committee on Assassinations Report: Anniversary" (Mar 29).

WORLD TOURISM DAY. Sept 27. Observed on the anniversary of the adoption of the World Tourism Organization Statutes in 1970. Annually, Sept 27. For info: World Tourism Organization, Calle Capitán Haya 42, 28020 Madrid, Spain. Phone: (34) 91-567-81-00. Fax: (34) 91-571-37-33. Web: www.unwto.org.

BIRTHDAYS TODAY

Wilford Brimley, 80, actor (*Cocoon*, "Our House"), born Salt Lake City, UT, Sept 27, 1934.

Carrie Brownstein, 40, comedienne, actress ("Portlandia"), born Seattle, WA, Sept 27, 1974.

Shaun Cassidy, 55, television producer, singer, actor ("The Hardy Boys"), born Los Angeles, CA, Sept 27, 1959.

Claude Jarman, Jr, 80, actor (*The Yearling, Rio Grande*), born Nashville, TN, Sept 27, 1934.

Steve Kerr, 49, basketball executive, former player, born Beirut, Lebanon, Sept 27, 1965.

Avril Lavigne, 30, singer, born Belleville, ON, Canada, Sept 27, 1984.

Lil Wayne, 32, rapper, born Dwayne Michael Carter, Jr, at New Orleans, LA, Sept 27, 1982.

Jayne Meadows, 90, actress ("I've Got a Secret," "The Steve Allen Show," *Lady in the Lake*), born Chang, China, Sept 27, 1924.

Meat Loaf, 67, singer, musician (*The Rocky Horror Picture Show*), born Marvin Lee Aday at Dallas, TX, Sept 27, 1947.

Bello Nock, 46, circus clown, born Demetrius Nock at Sarasota, FL, Sept 27, 1968.

Michael Jack (Mike) Schmidt, 65, Hall of Fame baseball player, born Dayton, OH, Sept 27, 1949.

Delores Taylor, 75, actress, writer, producer (*Billy Jack, The Trial of Billy Jack*), born Winner, SD, Sept 27, 1939.

Francesco Totti, 38, soccer player, born Rome, Italy, Sept 27, 1976.

September 28 — Sunday

DAY 271 — **94 REMAINING**

CABRILLO DAY: ANNIVERSARY OF DISCOVERY OF CALIFORNIA. Sept 28, 1542. California. Commemorates discovery of California by Portuguese navigator Juan Rodríguez Cabrillo, who reached San Diego Bay. Cabrillo died at San Miguel Island, CA, Jan 3, 1543. His birth date is unknown. The Cabrillo National Monument marks his landfall, and Cabrillo Day is still observed in California (in some areas on the Saturday nearest Sept 28).

CAPP, AL: BIRTH ANNIVERSARY. Sept 28, 1909. The creator of the fictitious village of Dogpatch, KY, Al Capp was born Alfred Gerald Caplin at New Haven, CT. The comic strip "Li'l Abner" appeared in daily newspapers from 1934 until its final episode was published Nov 13, 1977. Along with the misadventures of Abner Yokum, Capp lampooned famous public figures. The minor American institution of "Sadie Hawkins Day" made its debut in "Li'l Abner." Al Capp died Nov 5, 1979, at Cambridge, MA.

FAST OF GEDALYA. Sept 28. Jewish holiday. Hebrew calendar date: Tishri 4, 5775. Tzom Gedalya begins at first light of day and commemorates the sixth-century BC assassination of Gedalya Ben Achikam.

FIRST NIGHT FOOTBALL GAME: ANNIVERSARY. Sept 28, 1892. The first night football game in America was played between Mansfield State Normal School (now Mansfield University) and Wyoming Seminary at Mansfield, PA.

✦GOLD STAR MOTHER'S DAY. Sept 28. Presidential Proclamation always for last Sunday of each September since 1936. Proclamation 2424 of Sept 14, 1940, covers all succeeding years.

"HAZEL" TV PREMIERE: ANNIVERSARY. Sept 28, 1961. "Hazel" was based on a comic strip of the same name about a maid working for the Baxter family who gets into everyone's business. Hazel was played by Shirley Booth, and the Baxters were played by Don DeFore, Whitney Blake and Bobby Buntrock. "Hazel" moved from NBC to CBS after the third season and Hazel switched families from George to younger brother Steve Baxter. These Baxters were played by Ray Fulmer, Lynn Borden and Julia Benjamin. This successful series also featured Mala Powers and Ann Jillian.

MASTROIANNI, MARCELLO: 90th BIRTH ANNIVERSARY. Sept 28, 1924. One of the great international stars of cinema, born at Fontana Liri, Italy. Mastroianni worked with the master directors of the mid-20th century, among them Federico Fellini and Luchino Visconti. Two of his most famous roles were the world-weary journalist of *La Dolce Vita* (1960) and the in-crisis movie director of *8½* (1963)—both films directed by Fellini. He was nominated for Oscars three times and twice won the Best Actor Award at the Cannes Film Festival. Died at Paris, France, Dec 19, 1996.

NATIONAL CHIMNEY SAFETY WEEK. Sept 28–Oct 4. Each year CSIA Certified Chimney Sweeps work to raise awareness of chimney safety. Annually, the week prior to National Fire Prevention Week. For a list of Certified Chimney Sweeps in your state, see our website. For info: CSIA, 2155 Commercial Dr, Plainfield, IN 46168. Phone: (317) 837-5362. Fax: (317) 837-5365. E-mail: office@csia.org. Web: www.csia.org.

SCHMELING, MAX: BIRTH ANNIVERSARY. Sept 28, 1905. First European boxer to hold the world heavyweight boxing title (1930–32). Best known for fighting American great Joe Louis twice: the first time defeating him, the second time losing. The Nazi government tried to use Schmeling—to his dismay—as a propaganda tool to demonstrate the superiority of the Aryan race. Schmeling rejected that role, never joined the Nazi party and was punished by being given dangerous WWII combat duties. Schmeling saved two Jewish boys during the November 1938 Kristallnacht terrors. Schmeling and Louis developed a strong friendship outside the ring, and Schmeling paid for Louis's funeral. Born at Klein Luckow, Germany, Schmeling died Feb 2, 2005, at Hollenstedt, Germany.

SULLIVAN, ED: BIRTH ANNIVERSARY. Sept 28, 1901. Known as the "King of TV Variety," born at New York, NY. Sullivan started his media career in 1932 as a sportswriter for the *Daily News* in New York. His popular variety show, "The Ed Sullivan Show" ("Toast of the Town"), ran from 1948 until 1971. It included such sensational acts as Elvis Presley and the Beatles. He died at New York, NY, Oct 13, 1974.

TAIWAN: CONFUCIUS'S BIRTHDAY AND TEACHERS' DAY. Sept 28. National holiday, designated as Teachers' Day. Confucius is the Latinized name of Kung-futzu, born at Shantung province on the 27th day of the tenth moon (lunar calendar) in the 22nd year of Kuke Hsiang of Lu (551 BC). He died at age 72, having spent 40 years as a teacher. Teachers' Day is observed annually on Sept 28.

WIGGIN, KATE DOUGLAS: BIRTH ANNIVERSARY. Sept 28, 1856. Kate Wiggin was born Kate Douglas Smith at Philadelphia, PA. She helped organize the first free kindergarten on the West Coast in 1878 at San Francisco, and in 1880 she and her sister established the California Kindergarten Training School. After moving back east she devoted herself to writing, producing a number of children's books including *The Birds' Christmas Carol, Polly Oliver's Problem* and *Rebecca of Sunnybrook Farm*. She died at Harrow, England, Aug 24, 1923.

WILLARD, FRANCES ELIZABETH CAROLINE: 175th BIRTH ANNIVERSARY. Sept 28, 1839. One of the best-known, most influential women of the late 19th century for her temperance and suffrage work, Willard was also influential in American education. One of the first female administrators of a major coeducational university when made dean of women for Northwestern University's Women's College, she left education to work with the Women's Christian Temperance Union, of which she was president 1879–98. Born at Churchville, NY, she died at New York, NY, Feb 18, 1898; more than 20,000 people paid their last respects at services in NYC and Chicago.

WORLD RABIES DAY. Sept 28. The mission of World Rabies Day is to raise awareness about the impact of human and animal rabies, how easy it is to prevent it, and how to eliminate the main global sources. Since the inaugural campaign in 2007, World Rabies Day events have been held in 150 countries, educating 182 million people and vaccinating 7.7 million animals. Stand united; end rabies. For info: Global Alliance for Rabies Control, 529 Humboldt St, Ste 1, Manhattan, KS 66502. Phone: (570) 899-4885. E-mail: info@rabiescontrol.net. Web: www.worldrabiesday.org.

BIRTHDAYS TODAY

Brigitte Bardot, 80, actress (*And God Created Woman, Viva Maria*), animal rights activist, born Camille Javal at Paris, France, Sept 28, 1934.

Hilary Duff, 27, actress (*A Cinderella Story,* "Lizzie McGuire"), born Houston, TX, Sept 28, 1987.

Janeane Garofalo, 50, actress (*Reality Bites, The Truth About Cats and Dogs*), born Newton, NJ, Sept 28, 1964.

Frankie Jonas, 14, actor ("Jonas LA"), born Wyckoff, NJ, Sept 28, 2000.

Jeffrey Jones, 67, actor (*Beetlejuice, Stay Tuned*), born Buffalo, NY, Sept 28, 1947.

Ben E. King, 76, singer, musician, born Henderson, NC, Sept 28, 1938.

Steve M. Largent, 60, Hall of Fame football player, born Tulsa, OK, Sept 28, 1954.

September 2014

S	M	T	W	T	F	S
	1	2	3	4	5	6
7	8	9	10	11	12	13
14	15	16	17	18	19	20
21	22	23	24	25	26	27
28	29	30				

Emeka Okafor, 32, basketball player, born Houston, TX, Sept 28, 1982.

Se Ri Pak, 37, golfer, born Daejeon, South Korea, Sept 28, 1977.

Gwyneth Paltrow, 41, actress (Oscar for *Shakespeare in Love; Proof, The Talented Mr Ripley*), born Los Angeles, CA, Sept 28, 1973.

Brian Rafalski, 41, hockey player, born Dearborn, MI, Sept 28, 1973.

Suzanne Whang, 52, comedian, television personality ("House Hunters"), actress ("Las Vegas"), born Arlington, VA, Sept 28, 1962.

September 29 — Monday

DAY 272 — **93 REMAINING**

ANTONIONI, MICHELANGELO: BIRTH ANNIVERSARY. Sept 29, 1912. Groundbreaking Italian filmmaker, born at Ferrara, Italy. His films are known for their experiments with color, cinematography, pacing and narrative structure. He was nominated for two Academy Awards for *Blow-up* (1966) and was granted a Lifetime Achievement Oscar in 1996. He died at Rome, Italy, July 30, 2007.

AUTRY, GENE: BIRTH ANNIVERSARY. Sept 29, 1907. Born at Tioga, TX, Autry was arguably America's favorite singing cowboy in a career that spanned almost seven decades. He began performing on local radio in his late teens before signing with Columbia Records in 1931 and appearing for a time on the "National Barn Dance" radio show. His film career began soon after, and he starred in nearly 100 films, almost all of which were B-westerns in which his singing featured prominently. After retiring from acting, Autry became a baseball sports executive. He died at Los Angeles, CA, on Oct 2, 1998.

DOW JONES BIGGEST DROP: ANNIVERSARY. Sept 29, 2008. The Dow Jones Industrial Average plunged 778 points during the worldwide financial crisis of autumn 2008—the biggest one-day drop in its history.

FERMI, ENRICO: BIRTH ANNIVERSARY. Sept 29, 1901. Nuclear physicist, born at Rome, Italy. Played a prominent role in the splitting of the atom and the construction of the first American nuclear reactor. Died at Chicago, IL, Nov 28, 1954.

HOWARD, TREVOR: BIRTH ANNIVERSARY. Sept 29, 1916. British actor Trevor Howard was born at Cliftonville, England. He appeared in more than 70 films including *The Third Man* (1950) and *Mutiny on the Bounty* (1962). He died Jan 7, 1988, at Bushey, England.

"MAKE ROOM FOR DADDY" TV PREMIERE: ANNIVERSARY. Sept 29, 1953. Danny Thomas starred as Danny Williams, a nightclub singer and comedian, in this popular family sitcom. The series was renamed "The Danny Thomas Show" in 1956 after Jean Hagen (who played his wife, Margaret) left the show.

MICHAELMAS. Sept 29. The feast of St. Michael and All Angels in the Greek and Roman Catholic churches.

NATIONAL ATTEND YOUR GRANDCHILD'S BIRTH DAY. Sept 29. Bonding with your grandchild should begin at birth. This day is set aside to encourage grandparents to participate in their grandchild's birth as well as his/her life. Annually, Sept 29. For info: Carolynn Zorn, PO Box 1424, Novi, MI 48376. E-mail: attendingthebirth@hotmail.com. Web: www.attendingthebirth.com.

NELSON, HORATIO: BIRTH ANNIVERSARY. Sept 29, 1758. English naval hero of the Battle of Trafalgar, born at Burnham Thorpe, Norfolk, England. Died during a battle at sea off Cape Trafalgar, Spain, Oct 21, 1805.

PARAGUAY: BOQUERÓN DAY. Sept 29. National holiday. Commemorates a victorious battle over Bolivia during the 1932 Chaco War.

SCOTLAND YARD FIRST APPEARANCE: ANNIVERSARY. Sept 29, 1829. The first public appearance of Greater London's Metropolitan Police occurred amid jeering and abuse from disapproving political opponents. Public sentiment turned to confidence and respect in the ensuing years. The Metropolitan Police had been established by an act of Parliament in June 1829, at the request of Home Secretary Sir Robert Peel, after whom the London police officers became more affectionately known as "bobbies." Scotland Yard, the site of their first headquarters near Charing Cross, soon became the official name of the force.

SPACE MILESTONE: *DISCOVERY* (US). Sept 29, 1988. Space shuttle *Discovery*, after numerous reschedulings, launched from Kennedy Space Center, FL, with a five-member crew on board, and landed Oct 3 at Edwards Air Force Base, CA. It marked the first American manned flight since the *Challenger* tragedy in 1986. See also: "*Challenger*, Space Shuttle Explosion: Anniversary" (Jan 28).

SPACE MILESTONE: *SALYUT 6* (USSR). Sept 29, 1977. Soviet space station launched this date. *Salyut* stayed in space for four years, during which 31 spacecraft docked with the space station. Burned up on July 29, 1982, when it reentered Earth's atmosphere after nearly five years.

"THIRTYSOMETHING" TV PREMIERE: ANNIVERSARY. Sept 29, 1987. This ABC drama series about a group of seven baby boomers was created by Ed Zwick and Marshall Herskovitz. It depicted the struggles of the show's characters—such as the death of a parent, illness, singlehood, marriage, divorce, career setbacks and the birth of a child. The cast featured Ken Olin as Michael Steadman; Mel Harris as his wife, Hope; Timothy Busfield as Michael's business partner, Elliot Weston; Patricia Wettig as Elliot's wife, Nancy; Polly Draper as Hope's friend Ellyn Warren; Melanie Mayron as Michael's cousin, Melissa Steadman; and Peter Horton as family friend Gary Shepherd. The last telecast was Sept 3, 1991.

UNAMUNO Y JUGO, MIGUEL DE: 150th BIRTH ANNIVERSARY. Sept 29, 1864. Born at Bilbao, Spain, Unamuno was a poet, novelist, essayist and philosophical leader of the "Generation of 98," those intellectuals who saw in Spain's defeat in the Spanish-American War both the end of Spain's colonial empire and the manifestation of its cultural and political decay. Existentialist in nature, Unamuno's writings sought a renewal of Spain's culture and politics, and earned him the title "the arouser of Spain." During an anti-Fascist rally, he stated, "Sometimes, to remain silent is to lie." He was placed under house arrest and died on Dec 31, 1936, at Salamanca.

UNITED NATIONS: WORLD MARITIME DAY. Sept 29. This date varies by nation, but always takes place during the last week in September. A day to stress the importance of shipping safety and the maritime environment. For info: United Nations, Dept of Public Info, New York, NY 10017. Web: www.un.org.

VETERANS OF FOREIGN WARS ESTABLISHED: ANNIVERSARY. Sept 29, 1899. This organization is loyal to the issues and actions affecting America's heroes. Its members offer assistance in addition to supporting veterans issues in Congress. Part of the organization's mission, according to its charter, is "to preserve and strengthen comradeship among its members; to foster true patriotism; and to preserve and defend the United States from all her enemies, whomsoever." For info: Veterans of Foreign Wars of the United States, 406 W 34th St, Kansas City, MO 64111. Phone: (816) 756-3390. Fax: (816) 968-1149. E-mail: info@vfw.org. Web: www.vfw.org.

BIRTHDAYS TODAY

Joe Donnelly, 59, US Senator (D, Indiana), born New York, NY, Sept 29, 1955.

Kevin Durant, 26, basketball player, born Washington, DC, Sept 29, 1988.

Anita Ekberg, 83, actress (*La Dolce Vita*), born Malmo, Sweden, Sept 29, 1931.

Bryant Gumbel, 66, television journalist, host, born New Orleans, LA, Sept 29, 1948.

Hersey R. Hawkins, Jr, 48, former basketball player, born Chicago, IL, Sept 29, 1966.

Patricia Hodge, 68, actress ("Rumpole of the Bailey," *The Elephant Man, Betrayal*), born Cleethorpes, Lincolnshire, England, Sept 29, 1946.

Jerry Lee Lewis, 79, singer, musician ("Great Balls of Fire"), born Ferriday, LA, Sept 29, 1935.

Emily Lloyd, 44, actress (*Wish You Were Here, In Country, A River Runs Through It*), born North London, England, Sept 29, 1970.

Ian McShane, 72, actor ("Deadwood," "Lovejoy," *Sexy Beast*; stage: *The Homecoming*), born Blackburn, England, Sept 29, 1942.

Bill Nelson, 72, US Senator (D, Florida), born Miami, FL, Sept 29, 1942.

John Paxson, 54, basketball executive, former player, born Dayton, OH, Sept 29, 1960.

Andriy Shevchenko, 38, former soccer player, born Kiev, Ukraine, Sept 29, 1976.

Lech Walesa, 71, Polish statesman, Solidarity founder, born Popowo, Poland, Sept 29, 1943.

Dave Wilcox, 72, Hall of Fame football player, born Ontario, OR, Sept 29, 1942.

September 30 — Tuesday

DAY 273 | **92 REMAINING**

BABE RUTH SETS HOME RUN RECORD: ANNIVERSARY. Sept 30, 1927. George Herman "Babe" Ruth hit his 60th home run of the season off Tom Zachary of the Washington Senators. Ruth's record for the most homers in a single season stood for 34 years—until Roger Maris hit 61 in 1961. Maris's record was broken in 1998 by Mark McGwire with 62 home runs. Barry Bonds broke McGwire's record on Oct 5, 2001.

BABE RUTH'S LAST GAME AS YANKEE: 80th ANNIVERSARY. Sept 30, 1934. On this date Babe Ruth played his last game for the New York Yankees. Soon after, while watching the fifth game of the World Series (between the St. Louis Cardinals and Detroit Tigers) and angry that he was not to be named Yankees manager, Ruth told Joe Williams, sports editor of the Scripp-Howard newspapers, that after 15 seasons he would no longer be playing for the Yankees.

BOLAN, MARC: BIRTH ANNIVERSARY. Sept 30, 1947. Influential, flamboyant glam rock star born Marc Feld at London, England. Founder of T. Rex, best known for the hit "Get It On" (1971). Died in a car crash, Sept 16, 1977, at London, England.

BOTSWANA: INDEPENDENCE DAY. Sept 30. National holiday. The former Bechuanaland Protectorate (British Colony) became the independent Republic of Botswana in 1966.

CAPOTE, TRUMAN: 90th BIRTH ANNIVERSARY. Sept 30, 1924. American novelist and literary celebrity, was born Truman Streckfus Persons at New Orleans, LA. He later took the name of his stepfather to become Truman Capote. Among his best-remembered books: *Other Voices, Other Rooms; Breakfast at Tiffany's* and *In Cold Blood*. He was working on a new novel, *Answered Prayers*, at the time of his death at Los Angeles, CA, Aug 25, 1984.

"CHEERS" TV PREMIERE: ANNIVERSARY. Sept 30, 1982. NBC sitcom revolving around the owner, employees and patrons of a Beacon Street bar at Boston. Original cast: Ted Danson as owner Sam Malone, Shelley Long and Rhea Perlman as waitresses Diane Chambers and Carla Tortelli, Nicholas Colasanto as bartender Ernie "Coach" Pantusso, John Ratzenberger as mailman Cliff Clavin and George Wendt as accountant Norm Peterson. Later cast members: Woody Harrelson as bartender Woody Boyd, Kelsey Grammer as Dr. Frasier Crane, Kirstie Alley as Rebecca Howe and Bebe Neuwirth as Dr. Lilith Sternin Crane. The theme song, "Where Everybody Knows Your Name," was sung by Gary Portnoy. The last episode aired Aug 19, 1993.

DEAN, JAMES: DEATH ANNIVERSARY. Sept 30, 1955. Rising young film star James Dean died in an auto accident near Cholame, CA, two hours after getting a speeding ticket. He was 24 years old. His final films, *Rebel Without a Cause* and *Giant*, were released posthumously in 1956. See also: "Dean, James: Birth Anniversary" (Feb 8).

FEAST OF SAINT JEROME. Sept 30. Patron saint of scholars and librarians.

FIRST ANNUAL FAIR IN AMERICA: ANNIVERSARY. Sept 30, 1641. According to the Laws and Ordinances of New Netherlands (now New York and New Jersey), on Sept 30, 1641, authorities declared that "henceforth there shall be held annually at Fort Amsterdam" a Cattle Fair (Oct 15) and a Hog Fair (Nov 1), and that "whosoever hath any things to sell or buy can regulate himself accordingly."

FIRST CRIMINAL EXECUTION IN AMERICAN COLONIES: ANNIVERSARY. Sept 30, 1630. John Billington, one of the first Pilgrims to land in America, was hanged for murder, becoming the first criminal to be executed in the American colonies.

"THE FLINTSTONES" TV PREMIERE: ANNIVERSARY. Sept 30, 1960. This Hanna Barbera cartoon comedy was set in prehistoric times. Characters included two Stone Age families, Fred and Wilma Flintstone and neighbors Barney and Betty Rubble.

GUADALUPE MOUNTAINS NATIONAL PARK ESTABLISHED: ANNIVERSARY. Sept 30, 1972. Area in western Texas along Texas–New Mexico border, originally authorized Oct 15, 1966, was established as a national park. For further park info: Guadalupe Mountains Natl Park, HC 60, Box 400, Salt Flat, TX 79847-9400.

GUTENBERG BIBLE PUBLISHED: ANNIVERSARY. Sept 30, 1452. The first section of the Gutenberg Bible, the first book printed from movable type, was published at Mainz, Germany. Johann Gutenberg was the printer. The book was completed by 1456.

HALEAKALA NATIONAL PARK ESTABLISHED: ANNIVERSARY. Sept 30, 1960. Summit of a volcano on Maui in the Hawaiian Islands was authorized as a part of Hawaii National Park on Aug 1, 1916. In 1960 Haleakala was established as a separate national park. The park was expanded in 1969 to include the Kipahulu Valley. For further park info: Haleakala Natl Park, PO Box 369, Makawao, HI 96768.

KERR, DEBORAH: BIRTH ANNIVERSARY. Sept 30, 1921. Film actress born at Helensburgh, Dunbartonshire, Scotland, she starred in such classics as *The King and I, From Here to Eternity* and *An Affair to Remember.* She was nominated for six Oscars, holding the record for most nominations without a win, but she did receive a Lifetime Achievement Award in 1994. She died at Suffolk, England, Oct 16, 2007.

***LITTLE WOMEN* PUBLISHED: ANNIVERSARY.** Sept 30, 1868. Louisa May Alcott's beloved Civil War–era novel of Jo, Meg, Beth and Amy was published on this date to great immediate success.

MEREDITH ENROLLS AT OLE MISS: ANNIVERSARY. Sept 30, 1962. Rioting broke out when James Meredith became the first African American to enroll in the all-white University of Mississippi. President Kennedy sent US troops to the area to force compliance with the law. Three people died in the fighting and 50 were injured. On June 6, 1966, Meredith was shot while participating in a civil rights march at Mississippi. On June 25, Meredith, barely recovered, rejoined the marchers near Jackson, MS.

"MURDER, SHE WROTE" TV PREMIERE: 30th ANNIVERSARY. Sept 30, 1984. Angela Lansbury starred as crime novelist Jessica Fletcher from Cabot Cove, Maine, who traveled the country solving murders. This top-rated detective show also featured Tom Bosley as Sheriff Amos Tupper and William Windom as Dr. Seth Hazlett. The program aired for 12 years and is still in syndication.

"THE RED SKELTON SHOW" TV PREMIERE: ANNIVERSARY. Sept 30, 1951. Vaudevillian and radio performer Red Skelton hosted several popular variety shows on NBC and CBS in a career that spanned 20 years. He was a gifted comedian, famous for his loony characters, sight gags, pantomimes and ad-libs. His show was also notable for introducing Johnny Carson and the Rolling Stones to a national audience.

September 2014	S	M	T	W	T	F	S
		1	2	3	4	5	6
	7	8	9	10	11	12	13
	14	15	16	17	18	19	20
	21	22	23	24	25	26	27
	28	29	30				

BIRTHDAYS TODAY

Deborah Allen, 61, singer, songwriter, born Memphis, TN, Sept 30, 1953.

Crystal Bernard, 50, actress ("Wings"), born Garland, TX, Sept 30, 1964.

Marion Cotillard, 39, actress (Oscar for *La Vie en Rose*; *Rust and Bone, Midnight in Paris*), born Paris, France, Sept 30, 1975.

Angie Dickinson, 83, actress (Emmy for "Police Woman"; *Dressed to Kill*), born Angeline Brown at Kulm, ND, Sept 30, 1931.

Fran Drescher, 57, actress ("The Nanny," *Jack*), born Flushing, NY, Sept 30, 1957.

Jenna Elfman, 43, actress ("Dharma & Greg," "Townies"), born Los Angeles, CA, Sept 30, 1971.

Martina Hingis, 34, former tennis player, born Kosice, Slovakia, Sept 30, 1980.

Johnny Mathis, 79, singer, born Gilmer, TX, Sept 30, 1935.

Marilyn McCoo, 71, singer (Fifth Dimension), actress, born Jersey City, NJ, Sept 30, 1943.

W.S. Merwin, 87, poet, former US poet laureate (2010–11), born New York, NY, Sept 30, 1927.

Dominique Moceanu, 33, Olympic gymnast, born Hollywood, CA, Sept 30, 1981.

Téa Obreht, 29, author (*The Tiger's Wife*), born Belgrade, Yugoslavia (now Serbia), Sept 30, 1985.

Eric Stoltz, 53, actor (*The House of Mirth, Memphis Belle, Fast Times at Ridgemont High*), born Los Angeles, CA, Sept 30, 1961.

Victoria Tennant, 61, actress ("Winds of War," *All of Me, LA Story*), born London, England, Sept 30, 1953.

Elie Wiesel, 86, author, human rights activist, Nobel Peace Prize recipient, founder of the Elie Wiesel Foundation for Humanity, born Sighet, Romania, Sept 30, 1928.

October 1 — Wednesday

DAY 274 **91 REMAINING**

ADOPT-A-SHELTER-DOG MONTH. Oct 1–31. To promote the adoption of dogs from local shelters, the ASPCA sponsors this important observance. "Make Pet Adoption Your First Option®" is a message the organization promotes throughout the year in an effort to end the euthanasia of all adoptable animals. For info: ASPCA, 520 8th Ave, 7th Fl, New York, NY 10018. Phone: (212) 876-7700, ext 4655. E-mail: press@aspca.org. Web: www.aspca.org.

AMERICAN CHEESE MONTH. Oct 1–31. 4th annual. American Cheese Month is a celebration of North American artisan, specialty and farmstead cheeses, held in communities throughout North America. From "Meet the Cheesemaker" and "Farmers Market"-style events, to special cheese tastings and classes at creameries and cheese shops, to cheese-centric menus featured in restaurants and cafés, American Cheese Month is celebrated by cheese lovers in communities large and small. For info on hosting or attending an event: American Cheese Society, 2696 S Colorado Blvd, Ste 570, Denver, CO 80222. Phone: (720) 328-2788. Fax: (720) 328-2786. E-mail: info@cheesesociety.org. Web: www.americancheesemonth.org.

ANTIDEPRESSANT DEATH AWARENESS MONTH. Oct 1–31. A month to remember those who have been injured or who have died as a result of taking antidepressants or at the hands of someone who was on antidepressants. Any adverse reactions or death while taking any drug should be reported to the Food and Drug Administration at www.fda.gov/Safety/Medwatch/default.htm or by calling (800) FDA-1088. For info: Ernest and Catherine Ryan, 9138 Legacy Ct, Temperance, MI 48182. Phone: (734) 847-2282.

BABE RUTH CALLS HIS SHOT?: ANNIVERSARY. Oct 1, 1932. In the fifth inning of game three of the 1932 World Series, with a count of two balls and two strikes and with hostile Cubs fans shouting epithets at him, Babe Ruth pointed to the center field bleachers in Chicago's Wrigley Field and followed up by hitting a soaring home run high above the very spot to which he had just gestured. With that homer Ruth squashed the Chicago Cubs' hopes of winning the game, and the Yankees went on to sweep the Series with four straight victories. Did Ruth actually call his shot that day? Even eyewitnesses disagree. Joe Williams of the *New York Times* wrote, "In no mistaken motions, the Babe notified the crowd that the nature of his retaliation would be a wallop right out of the confines of the park." But Cubs pitcher Charlie Root said, "Ruth did *not* point at the fence before he swung. If he'd made a gesture like that, I'd have put one in his ear and knocked him on his ass." Ruth's daughter has said that he denied it. But the Babe himself also claimed he did it.

BOORSTIN, DANIEL: 100th BIRTH ANNIVERSARY. Oct 1, 1914. Born at Atlanta, GA, Boorstin was an attorney and history professor who taught at Swarthmore College and the University of Chicago. Later a director of the Smithsonian Institution's National Museum of History and Technology from 1969 to 1975, he was appointed by President Gerald Ford to be 12th Librarian of Congress in 1975, serving until 1987. Also a prolific writer, Boorstin won a Pulitzer Prize in 1974 for *The Americans: The Democratic Experience*. Died Feb 28, 2004, at Washington, DC.

BRAZIL: FESTIVAL OF PENHA. Oct 1–31. Rio de Janeiro. Pilgrimages, especially on Saturdays during October, to the Church of Our Lady of Penha, which is built on top of a rock, requiring a climb of 365 steps (representing the days of the year), or a ride in a car on an inclined plane (for children, invalids and aged), for those troubled and sick who seek hope or cure.

BREAST CANCER AWARENESS MONTH. Oct 1–31. Established in 1985 to raise awareness of breast cancer and to encourage early detection practices. The third Friday in October (Oct 17 in 2014) is National Mammography Day. For info: American Cancer Society. Phone: (800) 227-2345. Web: www.cancer.org. Or National Cancer Institute. Phone: (800) 4-CANCER.

CARTER, JIMMY: 90th BIRTHDAY. Oct 1, 1924. 39th president of US (1977–81), Nobel Peace Prize recipient, born James Earl Carter, Jr, at Plains, GA.

CELEBRATING THE BILINGUAL CHILD MONTH. Oct 1–31. A month to recognize the many children who speak two or more languages and understand multiple cultures. These children connect our communities and can play a big part in improving global communications. For info: Anneke Forzani, Language Lizard, PO Box 421, Basking Ridge, NJ 07920. Phone: (888) 554-9273. Fax: (908) 613-3639. E-mail: info@LanguageLizard.com. Web: www.LanguageLizard.com.

CELIAC DISEASE AWARENESS MONTH. Oct 1–31. Observed since 1987, Celiac Disease Awareness Month is the perfect opportunity to get the word out: share something positive about the disease and the diet with friends and neighbors; meet with your local grocery store manager about the importance of the availability of gluten-free options; visit with clergy regarding the strict gluten-free diet, communion and church pot lucks; and many more ways. For info: Celiac Sprue Assn/USA, PO Box 31700, Omaha, NE 68131-0700. Phone: (877) CSA-4CSA. E-mail: celiacs@csaceliacs.org. Web: www.csaceliacs.org.

***CHASE'S CALENDAR OF EVENTS 2015* PUBLISHED.** Oct 1. The 2015 *Chase's* is now available. Buy a copy through your book retailer or on our website at www.chases.com.

CHINA, PEOPLE'S REPUBLIC OF: NATIONAL DAY: 65th ANNIVERSARY. Oct 1. Commemorates the founding of the People's Republic of China in 1949.

CHURCH LIBRARY MONTH. Oct 1–31. To encourage churches to begin and promote libraries/media centers and to encourage people of all ages to use their church libraries. For info: Evangelical Church Library Assn, PO Box 353, Glen Ellyn, IL 60138-0353. Phone: (630) 375-7865. E-mail: info@eclalibraries.org. Web: www.eclalibraries.org.

COLLINS, ALBERT: BIRTH ANNIVERSARY. Oct 1, 1932. Blues guitarist Albert Collins was born at Leona, TX. An exciting, improvisational musician, he won a Grammy for *Showdown!* (1985), which was recorded with blues guitarists Robert Cray and Johnny Copeland. He was inducted into the Blues Hall of Fame in 1989. He died Nov 24, 1993, at Las Vegas, NV.

CO-OP AWARENESS MONTH. Oct 1–31. Co-Op Awareness Month reminds advertisers to take advantage of the vast amounts of co-op funding made available by manufacturers to subsidize the cost of local advertising. Most funds are designed to expire on Dec 31, so advertisers not taking advantage could be throwing money away! For info: Christine Hunt, Sales Development Services, Inc, 600 N Cleveland Ave, Ste 260, Westerville, OH 43082. Phone: (800) 667-3237. Fax: (800) 548-4223. E-mail: christine@salesdevelopment.com. Web: www.admall.com.

COWBOY HALL OF FAME CEREMONY AND BANQUET. Oct 1. Willcox Community Center, Willcox, AZ. The Cowboy Hall of Fame events lead into the Rex Allen Days celebration. Open house 6 PM; dinner 7 PM. Includes Cowboy Hall of Fame induction ceremony, favorite son/daughter award. Est attendance: 280. For info: Willcox Chamber of Commerce. Phone: (520) 384-2272 or (800) 200-2272. Web: www.willcoxchamber.com.

CUT OUT DISSECTION MONTH. Oct 1–31. peta2 promotes each October as a special chance for students to discuss and promote alternatives to dissecting animals. For info: peta2, 2154 W Sunset Blvd, Los Angeles, CA 90026. Phone: (323) 644-7382. E-mail: peta2@peta2.com. Web: www.peta2.com or www.cutoutdissection.com.

"CYBERSPACE" COINED: *NEUROMANCER* PUBLISHED: 30th ANNIVERSARY. Oct 1, 1984. The groundbreaking science fiction novel *Neuromancer*, by William Gibson, was published on this day and featured a word now commonplace in popular culture: *cyberspace*. The novel won the Hugo, Nebula and Philip K. Dick awards.

CYPRUS: INDEPENDENCE DAY. Oct 1. National holiday. Commemorates independence from Britain in 1960.

DOMESTIC VIOLENCE AWARENESS MONTH. Oct 1–31. Commemorated since 1987, this month attempts to raise awareness of efforts to end violence against women and their children. The Domestic Violence Awareness Month Project is a collaborative effort of the National Resource Center on Domestic Violence, Futures Without Violence, National Coalition Against Domestic Violence, National Domestic Violence Hotline and National Network to End Domestic Violence. For info: NCADV, One Broadway, Ste B 210, Denver, CO 80203. Phone: (303) 839-1852. E-mail: main office@ncadv.org. Web: www.ncadv.org.

DYSLEXIA AWARENESS MONTH. Oct 1–31. This month's activities seek to raise public awareness of the signs of dyslexia in adults and children. For info: International Dyslexia Assn, 40 York Rd, Ste 400, Baltimore, MD 21204-5202. Phone: (410) 296-0232. Fax: (410) 321-5069. Web: www.interdys.org.

EMOTIONAL INTELLIGENCE AWARENESS MONTH. Oct 1–31. Since 2006, a month to increase public awareness and understanding of both the harmful and helpful effects of emotions. During this month the Emotional Intelligence Institute provides a variety of activities for youths and adults and disseminates important knowledge about emotions to local communities. Schools, religious organizations and the media are encouraged to make emotional intelligence a subject of discussion and productive study during October. For info: Emotional Intelligence Institute, 74-923 Hwy 111 #184, Indian Wells, CA 92210. Phone: (330) 550-1274. E-mail: guardianship@juno.com. Web: www.e-ii.org.

ENERGY MANAGEMENT IS A FAMILY AFFAIR—IMPROVE YOUR HOME. Oct 1–Mar 31, 2015. Replace energy-consuming units with new efficient home conveniences and remodel to prevent heating and cooling loss. Editorial package includes approximately 50 camera-ready stories and photos free to editors. Also available on website. For info: Carole C. Stewart, Home Improvement Time, Inc, PO Box 247, Oakdale, PA 15071-0247. Phone: (412) 787-2881. Fax: (412) 787-3233. Web: www.homeimprovementtime.com.

ENGLAND: NOTTINGHAM GOOSE FAIR. Oct 1–5. Forest Recreation Ground, Nottingham. A traditional fair with modern amusements. Held annually since 1284 (except during the Great Plague in 1665 and the two World Wars), the fair formerly lasted three weeks and boasted as many as 20,000 geese on display. The Nottingham Goose Fair always operates in early October—beginning on the Wednesday before the first Thursday of October and lasting through Sunday. Est attendance: 500,000. For info: Nottingham City, Markets and Fairs Department. E-mail: tourist.information@nottinghamcity.gov.uk. Web: www.nottinghamgoosefair.co.uk.

FIREPUP'S® BIRTHDAY. Oct 1. Firepup spends his time teaching fire and burn prevention and life safety awareness to children and their parents in a fun-filled and nonthreatening manner. Materials are available through local fire departments. For info: Natl Fire Safety Council, Inc, PO Box 378, Michigan Center, MI 49254-0378. Phone: (517) 764-2811. Web: www.nfsc.org.

GAY AND LESBIAN HISTORY MONTH. Oct 1–31. October was selected to commemorate the first two lesbian and gay marches on Washington in October 1979 and 1987.

GERMAN-AMERICAN HERITAGE MONTH. Oct 1–31. A month celebrating America's German heritage. Numerous historical programs, museum and library exhibits, cultural events, genealogical workshops and more planned. For info: Dr. Don Heinrich Tolzmann, German-American Citizens League, 6829 Westin Ridge, Cleves, OH 45002. Phone: (513) 574-1741. E-mail: dhtolzmann@yahoo.com. Web: www.gacl.org.

GLOBAL DIVERSITY AWARENESS MONTH. Oct 1–31. Celebrating, promoting and appreciating the global diversity of our society. Also, a month to foster and further our understanding of the inherent value of all races, genders, nationalities, age groups, religions, sexual orientations, classes and physical disabilities. Annually, in October. For info: Carole Copeland Thomas, 6 Azel Rd, Lakeville, MA 02347. Phone: (508) 947-5755. Fax: (508) 947-3903. E-mail: TellCarole@mac.com.

GO HOG WILD—EAT COUNTRY HAM MONTH. Oct 1–31. Suuu-eee! It's not just a word; it's a state of mind. For more than 200 years, Americans have been curing and eating country ham. This custom of curing ham, which began in the state of Virginia during the mid-1700s, continues today from Georgia to Missouri and points in between. Discover the difference between "city ham" and "country ham" and get some great recipes to boot during Eat Country Ham Month. For info: Natl Country Ham Assn, PO Box 948, Conover, NC 28613. Phone: (828) 466-2760. E-mail: eatham@countryham.org. Web: www.countryham.org.

HARRIS, RICHARD: BIRTH ANNIVERSARY. Oct 1, 1930. Born at Limerick, Ireland, Richard Harris became known as a stage actor on the London theater scene in the 1950s. Although his first love was the stage, it was in films that he earned his highest degree of success. He was unforgettable as King Arthur in the film version of *Camelot* (1967) and was twice nominated for a Best Actor Oscar: for 1963's *This Sporting Life* and 1991's *The Field*. He portrayed headmaster Albus Dumbledore in the first two Harry Potter films in 2001 and 2002. He died Oct 25, 2002, at London, England.

HARRISON, CAROLINE LAVINIA SCOTT: BIRTH ANNIVERSARY. Oct 1, 1832. First wife of Benjamin Harrison, 23rd president of the US, born at Oxford, OH. Died at Washington, DC, Oct 25, 1892. She was the second first lady to die in the White House.

HEALTH LITERACY MONTH. Oct 1–31. 16th annual. Health literacy is about communicating health information in ways others can understand. Join with health literacy advocates worldwide to raise awareness about the importance of understandable health information. For info: Health Literacy Consulting, 31 Highland St, Ste 201, Natick, MA 01760. Phone: (508) 653-1199. E-mail: helen@healthliteracy.com. Web: www.healthliteracymonth.org.

HOME EYE SAFETY MONTH. Oct 1–31. There are steps you can take to create a safe Halloween for children and teens. Information about the dangers of cosmetic contact lenses will be included, as the use of these lenses increases during this holiday. For info: Prevent Blindness America®, 211 W Wacker Dr, Ste 1700, Chicago, IL 60606. Phone: (800) 331-2020. E-mail: info@preventblindness.org. Web: www.preventblindness.org.

October 2014	S	M	T	W	T	F	S
				1	2	3	4
	5	6	7	8	9	10	11
	12	13	14	15	16	17	18
	19	20	21	22	23	24	25
	26	27	28	29	30	31	

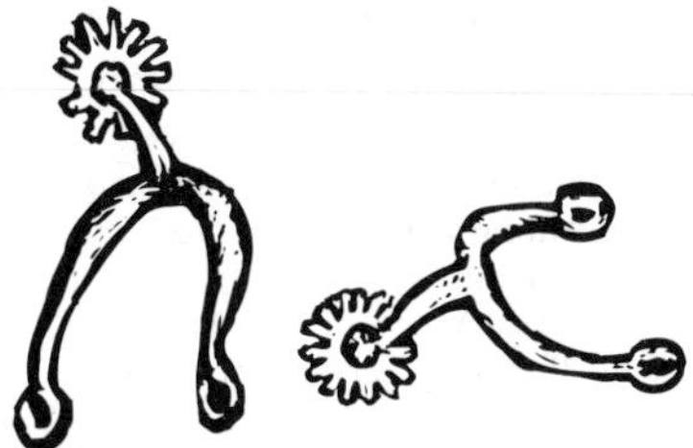

HOROWITZ, VLADIMIR: BIRTH ANNIVERSARY. Oct 1, 1904. Virtuoso pianist, born at Berdichev, Russia. Horowitz was widely hailed as one of the world's greatest pianists, renowned for his masterful technique. His debut was at Kiev in 1920, and at the age of 20 he played a series of 23 recitals at Leningrad, performing a total of more than 200 works with no duplications. He made his US debut in 1928 with the New York Philharmonic. He settled in the US in 1940 and became a citizen in 1944. His career swung full circle Apr 20, 1986, when he performed his first concert in his native Russia after a self-imposed absence of 60 years. He died Nov 5, 1989, at New York, NY.

INTERGENERATION MONTH. Oct 1–31. Connecting generations through communication, celebration and education. 42 states have endorsed this observance. Intergeneration Day/Week has now expanded to a month. For info: Intergeneration Foundation, 430 N Tejon St, Ste 300, Colorado Springs, CO 80903. Phone: (719) 471-3751. Web: www.intergenerationmonth.org.

***THE JOY OF SEX* PUBLISHED: ANNIVERSARY.** Oct 1, 1972. English publisher Mitchell Beazely released Dr. Alex Comfort's landmark book on this date. Published in the midst of the Western world's sexual revolution, *The Joy of Sex* was an immediate bestseller and to date has sold 12 million copies.

"KUNG FU" TV PREMIERE: ANNIVERSARY. Oct 1, 1972. David Carradine starred in this unusual ABC western as Kwai Chang Caine, a half-Chinese martial arts master and drifter who was exiled from China. Appearing in flashback were Keye Luke as Master Po, Philip Ahn as Master Kan and Radames Pera as the younger Caine. The show ran for three years.

LAWRENCE, JAMES: BIRTH ANNIVERSARY. Oct 1, 1781. Brilliant American naval officer, whose last battle was a defeat, but whose dying words became a most honored naval motto. Lawrence, born at Burlington, NJ, was captain of the *Chesapeake* when it engaged in a naval duel with HMS *Shannon* off Boston, June 1, 1813. The *Chesapeake* was captured and towed to Halifax as a British prize. Lawrence was mortally wounded by a musket ball during the engagement and uttered his famous last words, "Don't give up the ship," as he was being carried off the ship's deck.

LEVITTOWN OPENS: ANNIVERSARY. Oct 1, 1947. On this date the first residents moved into what would become Levittown at Long Island, NY. The community developed by William Levitt and his brother Alfred with their father, Abraham, started as affordable rental houses built for returning WWII veterans. In 1948 the Levitts began to sell the 800-square-foot homes for less than $8,000. By 1951, when this first community was finished, the Levitts had built 17,447 mass-produced Cape Cod and ranch homes. In 1952, they started construction on a new Levittown in Bucks County, PA, where they built another 17,000 houses, and beginning in 1958, they built 12,000 homes in Willingboro, NJ.

MARIS BREAKS RUTH'S HOME RUN RECORD: ANNIVERSARY. Oct 1, 1961. Roger Maris of the New York Yankees hit his 61st home run, breaking Babe Ruth's record for the most home runs in a season. Maris hit his homer against pitcher Tracy Stallard of the Boston Red Sox as the Yankees won, 1–0. Controversy over the record arose because the American League had adopted a 162-game schedule in 1961, and Maris played in 161 games. In 1927, when Ruth set his record, the schedule called for 154 games, and Ruth played in 151. On Sept 8, 1998, Mark McGwire of the St. Louis Cardinals hit his 62nd home run, breaking Maris's record. On Oct 5, 2001, Barry Bonds of the San Francisco Giants broke McGwire's record.

MATTHAU, WALTER: BIRTH ANNIVERSARY. Oct 1, 1920. Actor (*The Odd Couple, Grumpy Old Men*), born at New York, NY. Died July 1, 2000, at Santa Monica, CA.

"THE MERV GRIFFIN SHOW" TV PREMIERE: ANNIVERSARY. Oct 1, 1962. Singer and game show king Merv Griffin's first effort as an afternoon talk show host premiered on NBC but was later dropped for syndication. The afternoon show continued until 1969, when Griffin was tapped to host a late-night program on CBS to compete with "The Tonight Show with Johnny Carson."

MISSISSIPPI STATE FAIR. Oct 1–12. Jackson, MS. Features nightly professional entertainment, livestock show, midway carnival, domestic art exhibits. Annually, beginning on the first Wednesday of October. Est attendance: 620,000. For info: Mississippi Fair Commission, PO Box 892, Jackson, MS 39205. Phone: (601) 961-4000. Fax: (601) 354-6545.

MODEL T INTRODUCED: ANNIVERSARY. Oct 1, 1908. Ford introduced the Model T at a price of $850, but by 1924 the basic model sold for as little as $260. Between 1908 and 1927, Ford sold 15,007,033 Model Ts in the US. Although the first Model Ts were not built on an assembly line, the demand for the cars was so high that Ford developed a system in which workers remained at their stations and cars came to them. This enabled Ford to turn out a Model T every 10 seconds.

MONTH OF FREETHOUGHT. Oct 1–31. The Month of Freethought was inspired by the work done in Texas to commemorate the many German freethinkers who emigrated to that area, and several others across the US, during the 19th century. For info: American Humanist Assn, 1777 T St NW, Washington, DC 20009. Phone: (202) 238-9088. Fax: (202) 238-9003. E-mail: info@americanhumanist.org. Web: www.secularseasons.org/October/Freethought_month.html.

MOON PHASE: FIRST QUARTER. Oct 1. Moon enters First Quarter phase at 3:32 PM, EDT.

NATIONAL ANIMAL SAFETY AND PROTECTION MONTH. Oct 1–31. Observance to promote the appropriate ways to protect and care for domestic and wild animals and help people strengthen skills for staying safe around animals. For info: PALS Foundation, PO Box 3631, San Luis Obispo, CA 93403. Phone: (805) 544-0984. Web: www.PALS.R8.org.

✦NATIONAL ARTS AND HUMANITIES MONTH. Oct 1–31. Proclaimed annually to recognize the contributions of the arts and humanities not only by supporting the artists of today, but also by giving opportunities to the creative thinkers of tomorrow. Arts and humanities continue to break social and political barriers. Throughout our history, American hopes and aspirations have been captured in the arts, from the songs of enslaved Americans yearning for freedom to the films that grace our screens today. This month celebrates the enlightenment and insight gained from the arts and humanities, recommits to supporting expression that challenges our assumptions, sparks our curiosity and continues to drive us toward a more perfect union.

NATIONAL AUDIOLOGY AWARENESS MONTH. Oct 1–31. Nationwide celebration to promote audiology and the importance of hearing protection. Approximately 12 million Americans have hearing loss (and an additional 35 million Americans have some degree of loss) as a result of exposure to noise. You can permanently lose your hearing from prolonged exposure to noise, so make sure to follow these three tips to protect your hearing: turn down the volume, walk away from the noise, and wear hearing protection. For info: American Academy of Audiology, 11480 Commerce Park Dr, Ste 220, Reston, VA 20191. E-mail: info@audiology.org. Web: www.HowsYourHearing.org.

NATIONAL BAKE AND DECORATE MONTH. Oct 1–31. This month kicks off the fall and holiday baking season with baking and decorating tips and inspirational recipes for all types of sweet treats. Bring fall and holiday baking and decorating to life with color, sweetness and fun. For info: Vallory Farrasso, Wilton Enterprises, 2240 W 75th St, Woodridge, IL 60517. Phone: (630) 810-2221. E-mail: vfarrasso@wilton.com. Web: www.wilton.com.

NATIONAL BOOK IT! DAY. Oct 1. The Pizza Hut BOOK IT! Program kicks off in thousands of schools across the US today. Pizza Hut started BOOK IT! in 1985 to ignite kids' passion for reading. Pizza Hut is challenging young and old alike to "Read Your Heart Out." Annually, Oct 1. For info: The BOOK IT! Program. Web: www.pizzahut.com/bookit.

✦NATIONAL BREAST CANCER AWARENESS MONTH. Oct 1–31.

NATIONAL BULLYING PREVENTION AWARENESS MONTH. Oct 1–31. A month to observe bullying and cyber-bullying prevention awareness, with activities in schools and communities. Adults must empower the victims and help change the behavior of the bullies. Schools must react swiftly and redirect negative behaviors into positive and productive solutions. Bystanders who witness the assaults, harassment and threats must not remain silent. Parents must teach their kids and teens kindness, compassion and respect, and schools must do the same. Our kids and teens need to know they are valued and protected. For info: STOMP Out Bullying, 220 E 57th St, 9th Fl, Ste G, New York, NY 10022. Phone: (877) NO BULLY. E-mail: info@stompoutbullying.org. Web: www.stompoutbullying.org.

NATIONAL CHIROPRACTIC HEALTH MONTH. Oct 1–31. For info: American Chiropractic Assn, 1701 Clarendon Blvd, Arlington, VA 22209. Phone: (703) 276-8800. Web: www.acatoday.org.

NATIONAL CRIME PREVENTION MONTH. Oct 1–31. During Crime Prevention Month, individuals can commit to working on at least one of three levels—family, neighborhood or community—to drive violence and drugs from our world. It is also a time to honor individuals who have accepted personal responsibility for their neighborhoods and groups who work for the community's common good. Annually, every October. For info: Natl Crime Prevention Council, 2001 Jefferson Davis Highway, Ste 901, Arlington, VA 22202-4801. Phone: (202) 466-6272. Fax: (202) 296-1356. Web: www.ncpc.org.

NATIONAL CRITICAL ILLNESS AWARENESS MONTH. Oct 1–31. To create heightened awareness of the risks and financial consequences of the three leading critical illnesses (cancer, heart attack and stroke) and the importance of planning options available to Americans and their families. For info: Jesse Slome, Executive Director, Amer Assoc for Critical Illness Insurance, 3835 E Thousand Oaks Blvd, Ste 336, Westlake Village, CA 91362. Phone: (818) 597-3205. Web: www.AACII.org.

✦NATIONAL CYBER SECURITY AWARENESS MONTH. Oct 1–31. A month proclaimed annually to recognize the role we all play in ensuring our information and communications infrastructure is interoperable, secure, reliable and open to all. This month is observed with activities, events and training that enhance national security and resilience.

NATIONAL CYBER SECURITY AWARENESS MONTH. Oct 1–31. A national campaign focused on educating the American public, businesses, schools and government agencies about ways to secure their part of cyberspace, computers and our nation's critical infrastructure. The goal is to educate everyday Internet users on how to "Protect Yourself Before You Connect Yourself," by taking simple and effective steps to safeguard one's computer from the latest online threats, offer ways to respond to potential cyber-crime incidents and link how each person's cyber security affects securing our nation's critical infrastructure. For info: Natl Cyber Security Alliance. E-mail: info@staysafeonline.org. Web: www.staysafeonline.org.

NATIONAL DENTAL HYGIENE MONTH. Oct 1–31. To increase public awareness of the importance of preventive oral health care and the dental hygienist's role as the preventive professional. For info: American Dental Hygienists' Assn, 444 N Michigan Ave, Ste 3400, Chicago, IL 60611. Phone: (312) 440-8900 or (800) 243-ADHA. Fax: (312) 440-1702. E-mail: mail@adha.net. Web: www.adha.org.

NATIONAL DEPRESSION EDUCATION AND AWARENESS MONTH. Oct 1–31. A nonprofit campaign to educate patients, the elderly, consumers and professionals about depression disorders. Annually, the month of October. For info: Fred S. Mayer, RPh, MPH, Pharmacists Planning Service, Inc (PPSI), PO Box 6760, San Rafael, CA 94903. Phone: (415) 479-8628 or (415) 302-7351. Fax: (415) 479-8608. E-mail: ppsi@aol.com. Web: www.ppsinc.org.

✦NATIONAL DISABILITY EMPLOYMENT AWARENESS MONTH. Oct 1–31. Presidential Proclamation issued for the month of October (PL 100–630, Title III, Sec 301a, of Nov 7, 1988). Previously issued as "National Employ the Handicapped Week" for a week beginning during the first week in October since 1945.

NATIONAL DISABILITY EMPLOYMENT AWARENESS MONTH. Oct 1–31. To foster the full integration of people with disabilities into the workforce. For info: Office of Disability Employment Policy, US Dept of Labor, 200 Constitution Ave NW, Rm S1303, Washington, DC 20210-0002. Phone: (866) ODEP-DOL. TTY: (202) 693-7881. Fax: (202) 693-7888. E-mail: infoODEP@dol.gov. Web: www.dol.gov/odep.

✦NATIONAL DOMESTIC VIOLENCE AWARENESS MONTH. Oct 1–31.

NATIONAL DOWN SYNDROME AWARENESS MONTH. Oct 1–31. To promote better understanding of Down syndrome. For info: Natl Down Syndrome Congress, 30 Mansell Ct, Ste 108, Roswell, GA 30076. Phone: (800) 232-NDSC. E-mail: info@ndsccenter.org. Web: www.ndsccenter.org.

NATIONAL FIELD TRIP MONTH. Oct 1–31. A month to highlight the importance of the field trip as a way to help children learn. Studies show that children learn 85 percent more when a lesson is reinforced outside the classroom, and the field trip is a great way to teach valuable life skills and career education. For info: Field Trip Factory, 2211 N Elston Ave, Ste 304, Chicago, IL 60614. Phone: (800) 987-6409. Web: www.fieldtripfactory.com.

NATIONAL "GAIN THE INSIDE ADVANTAGE" MONTH. Oct 1–31. Gaining the "inside advantage" is how ordinary people accomplish extraordinary things. It refers to taking control of your life from the inside out. It means learning how to live deeply, joyfully and successfully. For info: Cathy W. Lauro. Phone: (813) 727-9859. E-mail: mind@CWLauro.com.

NATIONAL KITCHEN AND BATH MONTH. Oct 1–31. Established by the National Kitchen & Bath Association (NKBA) in 1982, this monthlong event raises awareness of and promotes excellence in kitchen and bath design by honoring the achievements of kitchen and bath professionals. During October, the NKBA provides home owners with guidance and assistance in adding value and livability to their homes, including free downloadable Kitchen and Bath Planners as well as a comprehensive list of NKBA professionals within their area. In addition, the NKBA and its members donate products to the Storehouse of World Vision, the official nonprofit partner of Kitchen & Bath Month. For info: National Kitchen and Bath Association. Web: www.nkba.org.

October 2014	S	M	T	W	T	F	S
				1	2	3	4
	5	6	7	8	9	10	11
	12	13	14	15	16	17	18
	19	20	21	22	23	24	25
	26	27	28	29	30	31	

NATIONAL LIVER AWARENESS MONTH. Oct 1–31. To increase understanding of the importance of liver functions, to promote healthful practices and to encourage research into the causes and cures of liver diseases, including hepatitis. For info: Marketing & Communications Dept, American Liver Foundation, 39 Broadway, Ste 2700, New York, NY 10006. E-mail: info@liverfoundation.org. Web: www.liverfoundation.org.

NATIONAL MEDICAL LIBRARIANS MONTH. Oct 1–31. Recognizes and celebrates the importance and the achievements of health sciences information professionals. Medical librarians offer efficient access to quality print and online medical and health-related information within a wide variety of healthcare settings. Librarians representing 23 specialty groups and 13 regional chapters of the Medical Library Association (MLA) sponsor several events and educational opportunities throughout the month of October. For info: Medical Library Assn, 65 E Wacker Pl, Ste 1900, Chicago, IL 60601. Phone: (312) 419-9094. Fax: (312) 419-8950. E-mail: info@mlahq.org. Web: www.mlanet.org.

NATIONAL ORTHODONTIC HEALTH MONTH. Oct 1–31. A beautiful, healthy smile is only the most obvious benefit of orthodontic treatment. Orthodontic care plays an important role in dental health, overall physical health and emotional well-being. National Orthodontic Health Month is sponsored by the American Association of Orthodontists (AAO), the oldest and largest dental specialty organization in the world, established in 1900. The AAO supports research and education leading to quality patient care, as well as increased public awareness of the need for and benefits of orthodontic treatment. For info: American Assn of Orthodontists, 401 N Lindbergh Blvd, St. Louis, MO 63141-7816. Phone: (314) 993-1700 or (800) STRAIGHT. E-mail: info@aaortho.org. Web: www.mylifemysmile.org.

NATIONAL PHYSICAL THERAPY MONTH. Oct 1–31. To increase awareness of the role of the physical therapist as the expert in restoring and improving motion in people's lives. Thousands of physical therapists, physical therapist assistants and physical therapy students nationwide celebrate by hosting special activities in their communities. For info: The American Physical Therapy Assn, 1111 N Fairfax St, Alexandria, VA 22314-1488. Phone: (800) 999-2782 or (703) 684-2782. Web: www.MoveForwardPT.com.

NATIONAL POPCORN POPPIN' MONTH. Oct 1–31. To celebrate the wholesome, economical, natural food value of popcorn, America's native snack. For info: The Popcorn Board, 330 N Wabash Ave, Ste 2000, Chicago, IL 60611. Phone: (312) 644-6610. Web: www.popcorn.org.

NATIONAL READING GROUP MONTH. Oct 1–31. Reading group members celebrate the joy of shared reading and inspire individuals who do not belong to a reading group to join one or start their own. Organizations, bookstores and libraries are encouraged to sponsor reading group events during this month. Signature event hosted by WNBA—Nashville chapter and the Southern Festival of Books. For info: Jill A. Tardiff, Women's National Book Association, 625 Madison St, Ste 2, Hoboken, NJ 07030. E-mail: jill.tardiff@gmail.com. Web: www.nationalreadinggroupmonth.org. Alternate contact: Valerie Tomaselli. E-mail: vtomaselli@mtmpublishing.com.

NATIONAL ROLLER SKATING MONTH. Oct 1–31. A monthlong celebration recognizing the health and fitness benefits as well as the recreational enjoyment of this long-loved pastime. For info: Roller Skating Assn International, 6905 Corporate Dr, Indianapolis, IN 46278. Phone: (317) 347-2626. Fax: (317) 347-2636. E-mail: rsa@rollerskating.com. Web: www.rollerskating.org.

NATIONAL SPINA BIFIDA AWARENESS MONTH. Oct 1–31. Promoting public awareness of current scientific, medical and educational issues related to spina bifida—the most frequently occurring permanently disabling birth defect. For info: Natl Resource Center, Spina Bifida Assn, 4590 MacArthur Blvd NW, Ste 250, Washington, DC 20007-4226. Phone: (202) 944-3285 or (800) 621-3141. E-mail: sbaa@sbaa.org. Web: www.spinabifidaassociation.org.

NATIONAL STAMP COLLECTING MONTH. Oct 1–31. Since 1981 the US Postal Service has designated the month of October as National Stamp Collecting Month (NSCM). Developed to introduce children aged 8–12 to this popular and educational hobby, the NSCM program is also intended to raise awareness about the recreational benefits of stamp collecting among all age groups. The Postal Service traditionally kicks off NSCM by issuing new commemorative stamps in late September or early October. For info and educational kits: US Postal Service. Web: www.usps.com.

NATIONAL STOP BULLYING MONTH. Oct 1–31. The self-esteem- and empathy-building international nonprofit organization Hey U.G.L.Y. (Unique Gifted Lovable You) has designated the month of October as a time for schools across America to conduct Stop Bullying classroom activities and school assembly presentations on how to eradicate bullying from schools and neighborhoods. For info: Hey U.G.L.Y., Inc, PO Box 345, Rolling Prairie, IN 46371. Phone: (219) 778-2011. E-mail: preventbullyingnow@heyugly.org. Web: www.heyugly.org and www.preventbullyingnow.org.

NATIONAL WORK AND FAMILY MONTH. Oct 1–31. On Sept 5, 2003, US Senate Resolution 210 was passed designating October as National Work and Family Month. The resolution expressed "the sense of the Senate that supporting a balance between work and personal life is in the best interest of national worker productivity" and that reducing any conflict between the two "should be a national priority."

NIGERIA: INDEPENDENCE DAY. Oct 1. National holiday. Became independent of Great Britain in 1960 and a republic in 1963.

***NIGHT OF THE LIVING DEAD* RELEASED: ANNIVERSARY.** Oct 1, 1968. George A. Romero's low-budget horror film of rampaging cannibalistic zombies was released on this date. It quickly became a cult favorite and influenced many other horror filmmakers.

NORWAY: PAGEANTRY IN OSLO. Oct 1. The Storting (Norway's parliament) convenes on the first weekday in October, when it decides the date for the ceremonial opening of the Storting—usually the following weekday—and the parliamentary session is then opened by King Harald V in the presence of Corps Diplomatique, preceded and followed by a military procession between the Royal Palace and the Storting.

ORGANIZE YOUR MEDICAL INFORMATION MONTH. Oct 1–31. This month is dedicated to learning how to acquire, understand, utilize and store pertinent medical information and knowledge, enabling each of us to become a more informed and active participant in our own medical care. This organization leads to fewer medical errors, shorter hospital stays, increased positive outcomes, the motivation to seek preventive care and the skills to negotiate the healthcare system. For info: Lynda Shrager. Phone: (518) 368-0322. E-mail: LShrager@otherwisehealthy.com.

PHOTOGRAPHER APPRECIATION MONTH. Oct 1–31. A month to acknowledge and appreciate the good work done by photographers everywhere to preserve family history, current events, the beauty of nature—in short, everything we all see yet tend to forget. Annually, the month of October. For info: Hud Andrews, 652 N Trezevant St, Memphis, TN 38112. Phone: (901) 452-4700. E-mail: canikeepit@comcast.net.

POLISH-AMERICAN HERITAGE MONTH. Oct 1–31. A national celebration of Polish history, culture and pride, in cooperation with the Polish-American Congress and Polonia Across America. For info: Michael Blichasz, Chair, Polish American Cultural Center, Natl HQ, 308 Walnut St, Philadelphia, PA 19106. Phone: (215) 922-1700. Fax: (215) 922-1518. E-mail: mail@polishamericancenter.com. Web: www.polishamericancenter.com.

POSITIVE ATTITUDE MONTH. Oct 1–31. Sometimes it just comes down to attitude! Zig Ziglar says that attitude, more than aptitude, affects altitude. Keith Harrell says attitude is everything. *Attatude* is a self-reflection of who you think you are. This month is dedicated to establishing, boosting or forcing ourselves to adopt positive attitudes and discovering and/or creating positive self-images. For info: Sylvia Henderson, Springboard Training, PO Box 588, Olney, MD 20830-0588. Phone: (301) 260-1538. E-mail: sylvia@springboardtraining.com.

REHNQUIST, WILLIAM HUBBS: BIRTH ANNIVERSARY. Oct 1, 1924. Born at Milwaukee, WI, William Hubbs Rehnquist earned master's degrees in political science and government before finishing Stanford Law School in 1952. He was serving as counsel in the Nixon White House when he was nominated to the US Supreme Court as associate justice in 1971. As the most conservative member of the court, he was a staunch supporter of states' rights and wrote a dissent to 1973's *Roe v Wade* decision. President Reagan nominated him as chief justice upon the retirement of Warren Burger, and he assumed that position on Sept 26, 1986. He presided over the impeachment hearing of President Clinton and ruled on *Bush v Gore* (2000), which awarded the presidential election to George W. Bush following controversial ballot miscounting in Florida. Rehnquist died Sept 3, 2005, at Arlington, VA.

"REMINGTON STEELE" TV PREMIERE: ANNIVERSARY. Oct 1, 1982. Laura Holt (Stephanie Zimbalist), an imaginative private detective, could not get a case of her own—until she made up a partner, Remington Steele, who was conveniently out of the office when clients came calling. Then she met the suave stranger (Pierce Brosnan) who called himself Remington Steele. They began a working partnership that ended in marriage. The show aired on NBC, with the last telecast on Mar 9, 1987, and costarred James Read, Janet DeMay and Doris Roberts. Henry Mancini composed the theme song.

RETT SYNDROME AWARENESS MONTH. Oct 1–31. To promote awareness of this neurological disease. For info: Intl Rett Syndrome Foundation, 4600 Devitt Dr, Cincinnati, OH 45246. Phone: (800) 818-RETT. E-mail: admin@rettsyndrome.org. Web: www.rettsyndrome.org.

RIGHT-BRAINERS RULE MONTH. Oct 1–31. Right-brainers are often ridiculed and reprimanded for their unorthodox and creative ways of doing things. The month of October is a chance to show how the right-brained person can survive and thrive in a very left-brained world. For info: Lee Silber, Creative Lee Speaking, 822 Redondo Ct, San Diego, CA 92109. Phone: (858) 735-4533. E-mail: leesilber@earthlink.net.

October 2014	S	M	T	W	T	F	S
				1	2	3	4
	5	6	7	8	9	10	11
	12	13	14	15	16	17	18
	19	20	21	22	23	24	25
	26	27	28	29	30	31	

SHAW, ROBERT GOULD: BIRTH ANNIVERSARY. Oct 1, 1837. Colonel in the Union army who led the country's first all-black regiment, the Massachusetts 54th. Born in Boston, MA, to prominent abolitionist parents, Shaw studied at Harvard before joining the fight against the Confederacy. He saw action with the 7th New York Infantry and the 2nd Massachusetts and was wounded at Antietam before being given command of the 54th and mustering its more than 600 soldiers from free blacks all over the North. Shaw was killed in action on July 18, 1863, during an assault on Confederate positions at Fort Wagner on Morris Island, SC.

SOUTH KOREA: ARMED FORCES DAY. Oct 1. Marked by many colorful military parades, aerial acrobatics and honor guard ceremonies, held around the reviewing plaza at Yoido, an island in the Han River.

SPINACH LOVERS MONTH. Oct 1–31. Spinach has finally become "the darling of vegetables": from its delectable taste to the breaking news on its lutein content for the prevention of macular degeneration. "Spinach—it's not just for breakfast anymore!" For info: Burgundy L. Olivier, "The Spinach Lady," 211 S Parkerson St, Rayne, LA 70578. Phone: (337) 334-6994. E-mail: email@ilovespinach.com.

SQUIRREL AWARENESS AND APPRECIATION MONTH. Oct 1–31. Set aside to honor one of our friendliest forms of wildlife: squirrels. Annually, the month of October. For info: Janet George, The Squirrel Lover's Club, PO Box 2701, Lower Burrell, PA 15068. Phone: (724) 335-2693. E-mail: jody@thesquirrelloversclub.com. Web: www.thesquirrelloversclub.com.

STOCKTON, RICHARD: BIRTH ANNIVERSARY. Oct 1, 1730. Lawyer and signer of the Declaration of Independence, born at Princeton, NJ. Died there, Feb 8, 1781.

TALK ABOUT PRESCRIPTIONS MONTH. Oct 1–31. 29th annual. This month serves as a means of ensuring that the safe and appropriate use of medicine remains part of the national public health dialogue. Given the estimated 4 billion prescriptions dispensed annually in the retail setting alone, the value of high-quality medicine communication, supported by the provision of useful written medicine information, cannot be overstated. For info: Natl Council on Patient Information and Education, 200-A Monroe St, Ste 212, Rockville, MD 20850-4448. Phone: (301) 340-3940. Fax: (301) 340-3944. E-mail: ncpie@ncpie.info. Web: www.talkaboutrx.org.

"THIS IS YOUR LIFE" TV PREMIERE: ANNIVERSARY. Oct 1, 1952. Ralph Edwards hosted this program that lured unsuspecting guests onto the show and surprised them by detailing their lives and achievements with their family and friends. It began as a radio show in 1948.

"TOM CORBETT, SPACE CADET" TV PREMIERE: ANNIVERSARY. Oct 1, 1950. This space show was set in the 2350s at the Space Academy and starred Frankie Thomas in the title role as an eager cadet. "Tom Corbett" was one of the few shows to be aired on all four major networks, including running on two networks (NBC and ABC) at the same time.

TUVALU: NATIONAL HOLIDAY. Oct 1. Gained independence from Britain on this day in 1978.

UNITED NATIONS: INTERNATIONAL DAY OF OLDER PERSONS. Oct 1. Designated by the General Assembly on Dec 14, 1990 (originally "International Day for the Elderly," the name was changed on Dec 21, 1995). A day to encourage all societies to better integrate aging issues into the larger context of development. States are encouraged to do everything in their power to enable all men and women to age with security and dignity. For info: United Nations, Dept of Public Info, Public Inquiries Unit, Rm GA-57, New York, NY 10017. Phone: (212) 963-4475. E-mail: inquiries@un.org. Web: www.un.org.

UNIVERSITY OF CHICAGO FIRST DAY OF CLASSES: ANNIVERSARY. Oct 1, 1892. The University of Chicago opened with an enrollment of 594 and a faculty of 103, including eight former college presidents.

US 2015 FEDERAL FISCAL YEAR BEGINS. Oct 1, 2014–Sept 30, 2015.

VEGETARIAN MONTH. Oct 1–31. This educational event advances awareness of the many surprising ethical, environmental, economic, health, humanitarian and other benefits of the increasingly popular vegetarian lifestyle. (Formerly Vegetarian Awareness Month.) For info: Vegetarian Awareness Network, PO Box 3545, Washington, DC 20027-0045. Phone: (800) 234-8343.

WOMEN WALKING IN THEIR OWN SHOES MONTH. Oct 1–31. Crystal City, VA. 3rd annual. Women Walking in Their Own Shoes (WWITOS) is a national movement that conducts an annual summit every October to empower and teach women how to make their life their business (become the CEO of their lives); and to live their life aligned to their purpose and passion. In addition to the summits, the movement will tour 10 major cities conducting mini-summits, with October being the major summit. For info: WWITOS, 16003 McKendree Rd, Ste B, Brandywine, MD 20613. Phone: (202) 497-0132. E-mail: tl@tawawnlowe.com. Web: www.walkinyourownshoes.com.

WORKPLACE POLITICS AWARENESS MONTH. Oct 1–31. Workplace politics may seem to be a moral morass and a colossal waste of time. Many of us try to avoid participating, but too often, we seem to be inevitably drawn in. This month is designed to increase awareness that trying to avoid workplace politics is futile—instead we can learn to deal with the situation. For info: Richard Brenner, Chaco Canyon Consulting, 700 Huron Ave, Ste 11J, Cambridge, MA 02138. Phone: (617) 491-6289. Fax: (617) 395-2628. E-mail: rbrenner@ChacoCanyon.com.

WORLD MENOPAUSE MONTH. Oct 1–31. The International Menopause Society, in collaboration with the World Health Organization, has designated Oct 18 as World Menopause Day. In observation of the Day, the IMS and the member national societies of the Council of Affiliated Menopause Societies distribute materials and organize activities to inform women about menopause, its management and the impact of estrogen loss. Since it is not always possible for local societies to arrange activities for this specific day, the IMS has also designated October as World Menopause Month. Local societies can also collaborate with other organizations working in the field of adult women's health, such as societies for osteoporosis and breast cancer, to organize joint events. For info: International Menopause Society. Web: www.imsociety.org.

WORLD VEGETARIAN DAY. Oct 1. Celebration of vegetarianism's benefits to humans, animals and our planet. In addition to individuals, participants include libraries, schools, colleges, restaurants, food service providers, healthcare centers, health food stores and workplaces. For info: North American Vegetarian Society, PO Box 72, Dolgeville, NY 13329. Phone: (518) 568-7970. Fax: (518) 568-7979. E-mail: navs@telenet.net. Web: www.worldvegetarianday.org.

YOSEMITE NATIONAL PARK ESTABLISHED: ANNIVERSARY. Oct 1, 1890. Yosemite Valley and Mariposa Big Tree Grove, granted to the state of California June 30, 1864, were combined and established as a national park. For info: Yosemite Natl Park, PO Box 577, Yosemite Natl Park, CA 95389.

BIRTHDAYS TODAY

Julie Andrews, 79, singer, actress (Emmy for "The Julie Andrews Hour"; Oscar for *Mary Poppins*), born Julia Wells at Walton-on-Thames, England, Oct 1, 1935.

Rodney Cline (Rod) Carew, 69, Hall of Fame baseball player, born Gatun, Panama Canal Zone, Oct 1, 1945.

Jimmy Carter, 90, 39th president of the US, born James Earl Carter, Jr, at Plains, GA, Oct 1, 1924.

Stephen Collins, 67, actor ("7th Heaven," *All the President's Men*), born Des Moines, IA, Oct 1, 1947.

Sarah Drew, 34, actress ("Grey's Anatomy," "Everwood"), born Charlottesville, VA, Oct 1, 1980.

Zach Galifianakis, 45, comedian, actor (*The Hangover,* "Bored to Death"), born Wilkesboro, NC, Oct 1, 1969.

Mark McGwire, 51, former baseball player, born Pomona, CA, Oct 1, 1963.

Esai Morales, 52, actor ("American Family," "NYPD Blue"), born Brooklyn, NY, Oct 1, 1962.

Tim O'Brien, 68, author (*In the Lake of the Woods, Going After Cacciato*), born Austin, MN, Oct 1, 1946.

Johnny Oduya, 33, hockey player, born Stockholm, Sweden, Oct 1, 1981.

Randy Quaid, 64, actor (*Brokeback Mountain, Independence Day, The Last Picture Show*), born Houston, TX, Oct 1, 1950.

Stella Stevens, 78, actress ("Ben Casey," "Flamingo Road"), born Hot Coffee, MS, Oct 1, 1936.

Grete Waitz, 61, marathoner, born Oslo, Norway, Oct 1, 1953.

October 2 — Thursday

DAY 275 **90 REMAINING**

"ALFRED HITCHCOCK PRESENTS" TV PREMIERE: ANNIVERSARY. Oct 2, 1955. Alfred Hitchcock was already an acclaimed director when he began hosting this mystery anthology series that aired on CBS and NBC for 10 years. Each episode began with an introduction by Hitchcock, the man with the world's most recognized profile. Hitchcock directed about 22 episodes of the series; Robert Altman also directed. Among the many stars who appeared on the show were Barbara Bel Geddes, Brian Keith, Gena Rowlands, Dick York, Cloris Leachman, Joanne Woodward, Steve McQueen, Peter Lorre, Dick Van Dyke, Robert Redford and Katherine Ross.

CHINA: CHUNG YEUNG FESTIVAL (OR DOUBLE NINE FESTIVAL). Oct 2. This festival relates to the old story of the Han dynasty, when a soothsayer advised a man to take his family to a high place on the ninth day of the ninth moon for 24 hours in order to avoid disaster. The man obeyed and found, on returning home, that all living things had died a sudden death in his absence. Part of the celebration is climbing to high places. Date in other countries will differ from China's.

DALTON DEFENDERS DAY. Oct 2–5. Coffeyville, KS. Event to honor citizens killed during the Dalton Gang's attempted robbery of two banks on Oct 5, 1892. Est attendance: 5,000. For info: Coffeyville CVB, PO Box 457, Coffeyville, KS 67337. Phone: (620) 251-2550 or (800) 626-3357. Fax: (620) 251-5448. E-mail: chamber@coffeyville.com. Web: www.coffeyvillechamber.org.

GANDHI, MOHANDAS KARAMCHAND (MAHATMA): BIRTH ANNIVERSARY. Oct 2, 1869. The Indian political and spiritual leader who achieved world honor and fame for his advocacy of nonviolent resistance as a weapon against tyranny was born at Porbandar, India. He was assassinated in the garden of his home at New Delhi, Jan 30, 1948. On the anniversary of Gandhi's birth (Gandhi Jayanti) thousands gather at the park on the Jumna River at Delhi where Gandhi's body was cremated. Hymns are sung; verses from the Gita, the Koran and the Bible are recited; and cotton thread is spun on small spinning wheels (one of Gandhi's favorite activities). Other observances are held at his birthplace and throughout India on this public holiday.

"THE GEORGE GOBEL SHOW" TV PREMIERE: 60th ANNIVERSARY. Oct 2, 1954. George Gobel hosted this comedy-variety show for five years on NBC. Chanteuse Peggy King and Jeff Donnell were also on the show, with Eddie Fisher as "permanent guest star." In 1959 Gobel switched networks to CBS and appeared for a year with Joe Flynn, Anita Bryant and Harry Von Zell.

GEORGIA NATIONAL FAIR. Oct 2–12. Georgia National Fairgrounds, Perry, GA. Traditional state agricultural fair features thousands of entries in horse, livestock, horticultural, youth, home and fine arts categories. Family entertainment, education, fun, concerts, fireworks. Sponsored by the State of Georgia. Est attendance: 465,000. For info: Georgia Natl Fair, 401 Larry Walker Pkwy, Perry, GA 31069. Phone: (478) 987-3247 or (800) 987-3247 (GA only). Fax: (478) 987-7218. E-mail: kkeuper@gnfa.com. Web: www.georgianationalfair.com.

GREAT AMERICAN BEER FESTIVAL. Oct 2–4. Denver, CO. Annual festival holds the Guinness World Record for most beers tapped in one location with 1,884 beers on tap. More than 408 US breweries will be found on the festival floor. In the cooking demonstration area you can learn to cook with beer and pair a beer style with a particular food. Est attendance: 46,000. For info: Brewers Assn, 736 Pearl St, Boulder, CO 80302. Phone: (303) 447-0816. Fax: (303) 447-2825. E-mail: info@brewersassociation.org. Web: www.GreatAmericanBeerFestival.com.

GREENE, GRAHAM: BIRTH ANNIVERSARY. Oct 2, 1904. British author Graham Greene was born at Berkhamsted, Hertfordshire, England. He centered his works around characters facing salvation and damnation in a world of chaos, often with complex Catholic settings. His works include *The Power and the Glory* (1940) and *The Third Man* (1950). He died Apr 3, 1991, at Vevey, Switzerland.

GUARDIAN ANGELS DAY. Oct 2. We all have guardian angels. Now's the time to give them recognition and thanks for being in our lives with their own day. Take the time today to find out how they've played a unique role in our lives, as well as in various cultures, religions and even foods. Celebrate today by doing something special to recognize their qualities. Annually, Oct 2. For info: Lorrie Walters Marsiglio, PO Box 284-CC, Wasco, IL 60183-0284.

GUINEA: INDEPENDENCE DAY. Oct 2. National Day. Guinea gained independence from France in 1958.

GUNN, MOSES: 85th BIRTH ANNIVERSARY. Oct 2, 1929. The 1981 winner of the NAACP Image Award for his performance as Booker T. Washington in the film *Ragtime* was born at St. Louis, MO. His appearances on stage ranged from the title role in *Othello* to Jean Genet's *The Blacks*. He received an Emmy nomination for his role in *Roots* and was awarded several Obies for off-Broadway performances. On film he appeared in *Shaft* and *The Great White Hope*. He died Dec 17, 1993, at Guilford, CT.

HULL, CORDELL: BIRTH ANNIVERSARY. Oct 2, 1871. American statesman who served in both houses of the Congress and as secretary of state, born at Pickett County, TN. Noted for his contributions to the "Good Neighbor" policies of the US with regard to countries of the Americas and to the establishment of the United Nations. Hull died at Bethesda, MD, July 23, 1955.

"THE JIMMY DURANTE SHOW" TV PREMIERE: 60th ANNIVERSARY. Oct 2, 1954. Affectionately known as "the Schnozz," Durante hosted a Saturday-night variety show with his former vaudeville partner, Eddie Jackson. It alternated with "The Donald O'Connor Show" on NBC and aired for two years.

MARSHALL, THURGOOD: SWORN IN TO SUPREME COURT: ANNIVERSARY. Oct 2, 1967. Thurgood Marshall was sworn in as the first black associate justice to the US Supreme Court. On June 27, 1991, he announced his resignation, effective upon the confirmation of his successor. See also: "Marshall, Thurgood: Birth Anniversary" (July 2).

October 2014	S	M	T	W	T	F	S
				1	2	3	4
	5	6	7	8	9	10	11
	12	13	14	15	16	17	18
	19	20	21	22	23	24	25
	26	27	28	29	30	31	

MARX, GROUCHO: BIRTH ANNIVERSARY. Oct 2, 1890. Born Julius Henry Marx at New York, NY. Comedian who along with his brothers constituted the famous Marx Brothers. The Marx Brothers began as a singing group and then acted in such movies as *Duck Soup* and *Animal Crackers*. During the '40s and '50s, Groucho was the host of the television and radio show "You Bet Your Life." Died at Los Angeles, CA, Aug 19, 1977.

McFARLAND, GEORGE (SPANKY): BIRTH ANNIVERSARY. Oct 2, 1928. Chubby child star of the "Our Gang" comedy film shorts. Born at Dallas, TX, and died at Grapevine, TX, June 30, 1993.

NATIONAL CUSTODIAL WORKERS DAY. Oct 2. A day to honor all janitorial and custodial workers—those who clean up after us. For info: Bette Tadajewski, Catholic Community of Alpena, 2425 Frederick, Alpena, MI 49707. Phone: (989) 354-3019.

"PEANUTS" DEBUTS: ANNIVERSARY. Oct 2, 1950. This comic strip by Charles Schulz featured Charlie Brown, Lucy, Linus, Sally and Charlie's dog, Snoopy. The last new "Peanuts" strip was published Feb 13, 2000.

PHILEAS FOGG'S WAGER DAY: ANNIVERSARY. Oct 2, 1872. Anniversary, from Jules Verne's *Around the World in Eighty Days*, of the famous wager upon which the book is based: "I will bet twenty thousand pounds against anyone who wishes, that I will make the tour of the world in eighty days or less." Then, consulting a pocket almanac, Phileas Fogg said: "As today is Wednesday, the second of October, I shall be due in London, in this very room of the Reform Club, on Saturday, the twenty-first of December, at a quarter before nine PM; or else the twenty thousand pounds . . . will belong to you." See also: "Phileas Fogg Wins a Wager Day" (Dec 21).

RAYMOND, ALEX: BIRTH ANNIVERSARY. Oct 2, 1909. This influential comic strip artist, born at New Rochelle, NY, created the science fiction strip "Flash Gordon" (1934). The strip's huge popularity led to Hollywood serials starring Buster Crabbe a few years later. Raymond also created "Secret Agent X-9" and "Rip Kirby," but his career was cut short by a fatal automobile accident on Sept 6, 1956, at Westport, CT.

STREETER, RUTH CHENEY: BIRTH ANNIVERSARY. Oct 2, 1895. Born at Brookline, MA, Ruth Cheney Streeter was the first director of the US Marine Corps Women's Reserve. She was active in unemployment relief, public health, welfare and old-age assistance in New Jersey during the 1930s. A student of aeronautics, she learned to fly while serving as an adjutant of a flight group in the Civil Air Patrol during the early years of WWII. She died Sept 30, 1990, at Morristown, NJ.

"THE TWILIGHT ZONE" TV PREMIERE: 55th ANNIVERSARY. Oct 2, 1959. "The Twilight Zone" went on the air with these now-familiar words: "There is a fifth dimension, beyond that which is known to man. It is a dimension as vast as space and as timeless as infinity. It is the middle ground between light and shadow, between science and superstition, and it lies between the pit of man's fear and the summit of his knowledge. This is the dimension of imagination. It is an area which we call The Twilight Zone." The anthology program ran five seasons for 154 installments, with a one-year hiatus between the third and fourth seasons. Created and hosted by Rod Serling, it is now considered to have been one of the best dramas to appear on television. The last original episode was telecast June 15, 1964.

UNITED NATIONS: INTERNATIONAL DAY OF NONVIOLENCE. Oct 2. Reaffirming the universal relevance of the principle of nonviolence, and desiring to secure a culture of peace, tolerance, understanding and nonviolence, on June 15, 2007, the General Assembly declared this day to be observed annually on Oct 2

(Resolution 61/271), the anniversary of Mahatma Gandhi's birth. For info: United Nations, Dept of Public Info, New York, NY, 10017. Web: www.un.org.

WORLD FARM ANIMALS DAY. Oct 2. Celebrated on Gandhi's birthday. To expose and memorialize the needless suffering and death of billions of innocent, sentient animals in factory farms and slaughterhouses. Local actions include memorial services, vigils, street theater, picketing, leafleting and information tables. For info: Farm Animal Rights Movement, 10101 Ashburton Ln, Bethesda, MD 20817. Phone: (888) ASK-FARM. E-mail: info@wfad.org. Web: www.wfad.org or www.farmusa.org.

BIRTHDAYS TODAY

Lorraine Bracco, 59, actress ("The Sopranos," *Goodfellas*), born Brooklyn, NY, Oct 2, 1955.

Donna Karan, 66, fashion designer, born Forest Hills, NY, Oct 2, 1948.

Don McLean, 69, singer, songwriter, born New Rochelle, NY, Oct 2, 1945.

Rex Reed, 75, movie critic, born Fort Worth, TX, Oct 2, 1939.

Kelly Ripa, 44, actress ("Hope and Faith," "All My Children"), television host ("Live with Regis and Kelly"), born Stratford, NJ, Oct 2, 1970.

Sting, 63, singer, songwriter, actor (*Dune*), born Gordon Sumner at London, England, Oct 2, 1951.

Paul Teutul, Jr, 40, motorcycle designer, television personality ("American Chopper"), born Oct 2, 1974.

October 3 — Friday

DAY 276 — **89 REMAINING**

"THE ANDY GRIFFITH SHOW" TV PREMIERE: ANNIVERSARY. Oct 3, 1960. The first of 249 episodes aired on this date. Set in rural Mayberry, NC, the show starred Griffith as Sheriff Andy Taylor; Ron Howard as his son, Opie; Frances Bavier as Aunt Bee Taylor and Don Knotts as Deputy Barney Fife. Although the last telecast aired Sept 16, 1968, more than 12,000 members of "The Andy Griffith Show" Rerun Watchers Club and others celebrate this day with festivities every year.

BANCROFT, GEORGE: BIRTH ANNIVERSARY. Oct 3, 1800. American historian, known as "the father of American History," born at Worcester, MA. Died at Washington, DC, Jan 27, 1891.

"CAPTAIN KANGAROO" TV PREMIERE: ANNIVERSARY. Oct 3, 1955. On the air until 1985, this was the longest-running children's TV show until it was surpassed by "Sesame Street." Starring Bob Keeshan as Captain Kangaroo, it was broadcast on CBS and PBS. Other characters included Mr Green Jeans, Grandfather Clock, Bunny Rabbit, Mr Moose and Dancing Bear. Keeshan was an advocate for excellence in children's programming and even supervised which commercials would appear on the program. In 1997 "The All New Captain Kangaroo" debuted, starring John McDonough.

COIN, JEWELRY & STAMP EXPO. Oct 3–5. Radisson Hotel, Anaheim, CA. Est attendance: 4,000. For info: Israel Bick, Exec Dir, Intl Stamp & Coin Collectors Society, PO Box 854, Van Nuys, CA 91408. Phone: (818) 997-6496. Fax: (818) 988-4337. E-mail: iibick@sbcglobal.net. Web: www.bickinternational.com.

COME AND TAKE IT FESTIVAL. Oct 3–5. Gonzales, TX. This celebration commemorating the first shot fired for Texas independence in 1835 is named for the defiant battle cry of the colonists when the Mexican military demanded the return of a cannon. Est attendance: 20,000. For info: Chamber of Commerce, 414 St. Lawrence, Gonzales, TX 78629. Phone: (830) 672-6532. Fax: (830) 672-6533. E-mail: info@gonzalestexas.com. Web: www.gonzalestexas.com.

"THE DICK VAN DYKE SHOW" TV PREMIERE: ANNIVERSARY. Oct 3, 1961. This Carl Reiner–created sitcom wasn't an immediate success but soon became a hit. It starred Dick Van Dyke as Rob Petrie, a TV show writer, and Mary Tyler Moore as his wife, Laura, a former dancer. This was one of the first shows revolving around the goings-on at a TV series. Other cast members included Morey Amsterdam, Rose Marie, Richard Deacon, Carl Reiner, Jerry Paris, Ann Morgan Guilbert and Larry Matthews. The last episode aired Sept 7, 1966, but the show remains popular in reruns.

FIRST WOMAN US SENATOR: ANNIVERSARY. Oct 3, 1922. On this date, Mrs W.H. (Rebecca) Felton, 87, of Cartersville, GA, was appointed by Governor Thomas Hardwick of Georgia to the Senate seat vacated by the death of Thomas E. Watson. It was a two-day ad interim appointment.

GERMAN REUNIFICATION: ANNIVERSARY. Oct 3, 1990. After 45 years of division, East and West Germany reunited just four days short of East Germany's 41st founding anniversary (Oct 7, 1949). The new united Germany took the name the Federal Republic of Germany, the formal name of the former West Germany, and adopted the constitution of the former West Germany. Today is a national holiday in Germany, Tag der Deutschen Einheit (Day of German Unity).

GORGAS, WILLIAM CRAWFORD: BIRTH ANNIVERSARY. Oct 3, 1854. Physician and sanitary engineer, born at Toulminville, AL. He eradicated yellow fever from Havana, Cuba, and the Panama Canal, allowing the completion of the canal. Gorgas died at London, England, July 4, 1920.

HERRIOT, JAMES: BIRTH ANNIVERSARY. Oct 3, 1916. Author and veterinarian, born James Alfred Wight at Glasgow, Scotland. Under the pen name Herriot he wrote more than 12 books chronicling his life as a veterinarian in northern England. His *All Creatures Great and Small* (1974) was made into a TV series that was an international hit. He was made a member of the Order of the British Empire in 1979. Herriot died Feb 23, 1995, at Yorkshire, England.

HONDURAS: FRANCISCO MORAZÁN HOLIDAY. Oct 3. Public holiday in honor of Francisco Morazán, national hero, who was born in 1799.

KENTUCKY APPLE FESTIVAL. Oct 3–4. Paintsville, KY. Apple blossom beauty pageants, country music show, arts and crafts, flea market, antique car show, Corvette show, Terrapin Trot, amusement rides, food booths, clogging and square dancing. Est attendance: 50,000. For info: Kentucky Apple Festival, Inc, PO Box 1245, Paintsville, KY 41240-5245. Phone: (606) 789-4355 or (800) 542-5790. Web: www.kyapplefest.org.

KOREA: NATIONAL FOUNDATION DAY. Oct 3. National holiday also called Tangun Day, as it commemorates day when legendary founder of the Korean nation, Tangun, established his kingdom of Chosun in 2333 BC.

KURTZMAN, HARVEY: BIRTH ANNIVERSARY. Oct 3, 1902. Cartoonist and founder of *Mad* magazine, Harvey Kurtzman was born at Brooklyn, NY. At 14 he had his first cartoon published, and he began his career in comic books in 1943. His career led him to EC (Educational Comics), and with the support of William Gaines, he created *Mad* magazine, which first appeared in 1952. He died Feb 21, 1993, at Mount Vernon, NY.

"LA LAW" TV PREMIERE: ANNIVERSARY. Oct 3, 1986. Set in the Los Angeles law firm of McKenzie, Brackman, Chaney and Kuzak, this drama had a large cast. Divorce lawyer Arnie Becker was played by Corbin Bernsen, public defender Victor Sifuentes by Jimmy Smits and managing partner Douglas Brackman by Alan Rachins. Other cast members included Harry Hamlin as Michael Kuzak, Richard Dysart as Leland McKenzie, Susan Dey as Grace Van Owen, Jill Eikenberry as Ann Kelsey, Michael Tucker as Stuart Markowitz and Susan Ruttan as Roxanne Melman. The last telecast was May 19, 1994.

LERMONTOV, MIKHAIL YUREVICH: 200th BIRTH ANNIVERSARY. Oct 3, 1814. (Old Style date; Oct 15, NS.) Influential Romantic author and poet as well as soldier, born at Moscow, Russia. A troublemaker in both his poetry and his personal life, Lermontov was transferred/exiled to posts in Georgia and the Caucasus (1836–40), which provided formative experiences for his great (and only) novel *A Hero of Our Time* (1840), featuring the antihero Pechorin. Like Pechorin, Lermontov died in a duel—at Pyatigorski, July 15, 1841, aged 26.

MANSON, PATRICK: BIRTH ANNIVERSARY. Oct 3, 1844. British parasitologist and surgeon sometimes called the father of tropical medicine. Manson's research into insects as carriers of parasites was instrumental in later understanding that mosquitoes transmit malaria. Born at Aberdeen, Scotland, Manson died Apr 9, 1922, at London, England.

"MICKEY MOUSE CLUB" TV PREMIERE: ANNIVERSARY. Oct 3, 1955. This afternoon show for children was on ABC. Among its young cast members were Mouseketeers Annette Funicello and Shelley Fabares. A later version, "The New Mickey Mouse Club," starred Keri Russell, Christina Aguilera and Britney Spears.

NATIONAL DIVERSITY DAY. Oct 3. A day to celebrate and embrace who we are, despite our differences, no matter what race, religion, gender, sexual orientation, age, nationality or disability. A day to reflect on and learn about different cultures and ideologies. A day to vow to uphold acceptance and tolerance. A day to consciously address these areas at educational and religious institutions, as well as in the workplace and at home. Our slogan: "Embrace diversity, embrace our world." Annually, the first Friday in October. For info: Leo Parvis. Phone: (612) 386-7102. E-mail: drparvis@gmail.com. Web: www.nationaldiversityday.com.

NATIONAL STORYTELLING FESTIVAL. Oct 3–5. Jonesborough, TN. Tennessee's oldest town plays host to the most dynamic storytelling event dedicated to the oral tradition. This three-day celebration showcases storytellers, stories and traditions from across America and around the world. Annually, the first full weekend in October. Est attendance: 10,000. For info: International Storytelling Center, 116 W Main, Jonesborough, TN 37659. Phone: (800) 952-8392. Fax: (423) 913-1320. E-mail: customerservice@storytellingcenter.net. Web: www.storytellingcenter.net.

NETHERLANDS: RELIEF OF LEIDEN DAY. Oct 3. Celebration of the liberation of Leiden in 1574.

OKTOBERFEST. Oct 3–4 (also Oct 10–11). New Ulm, MN. Celebrating New Ulm's German heritage, with musical entertainment, food and dancing. Annually, the first two weekends in October. Est attendance: 8,000. For info: Oktoberfest, c/o New Ulm Holiday Inn, 2101 South Broadway, New Ulm, MN 56073. Phone: (507) 359-2941 or (877) 359-2941. Web: www.newulmoktoberfest.com.

"OUR MISS BROOKS" TV PREMIERE: ANNIVERSARY. Oct 3, 1952. This half-hour sitcom began on the radio, and unlike the case with many other radio programs that moved to TV, most of the original radio cast members were retained. It was about a favorite high school English teacher named Connie Brooks (played by Eve Arden). Also featured were Gale Gordon, Richard Crenna, Gloria McMillan and Jane Morgan.

"OZZIE AND HARRIET" TV PREMIERE: ANNIVERSARY. Oct 3, 1952. "Ozzie and Harriet" was TV's longest-running sitcom. The successful radio-turned-TV show about the Nelson family starred the real-life Nelsons—Ozzie; his wife, Harriet; and their sons, David and Ricky. Officially titled "The Adventures of Ozzie and Harriet," this show was set in the family's home. The boys were one reason the show was successful, and Ricky used the advantage to become a pop star. David's and Rick's real-life wives—June Blair and Kris Nelson—also joined the cast. The show was canceled at the end of the 1965–66 season after 435 episodes, 409 of which were in black and white and 26 in color. The last episode aired Sept 3, 1966.

"THE PAT BOONE SHOW" TV PREMIERE: ANNIVERSARY. Oct 3, 1957. Clean-cut singer Pat Boone hosted three shows between 1957 and 1969. The first was a prime-time variety series with the McGuire Sisters and the Mort Lindsey Orchestra as regulars. The second show featured the Paul Smith Orchestra and was a daytime variety and talk show. "Pat Boone in Hollywood" was the title of the third, a 90-minute talk show.

"QUINCY" TV PREMIERE: ANNIVERSARY. Oct 3, 1976. This medically oriented crime show starred Jack Klugman as Dr. Raymond Quincy, a medical examiner for the Los Angeles coroner's office. Quincy's curiosity about his cases led to investigative work that often solved them. Later in the series, the show focused on social issues that were unrelated to forensic medicine. The last telecast aired on Sept 5, 1983.

"THE REAL McCOYS" TV PREMIERE: ANNIVERSARY. Oct 3, 1957. This first successful rural comedy program was one of the most popular, predating similar shows such as "The Beverly Hillbillies" by many seasons. It was set in rural California and featured the McCoys, played by Walter Brennan, Richard Crenna, Kathleen Nolan, Michael Winkelman and Lydia Reed.

ROBINSON NAMED BASEBALL'S FIRST BLACK MAJOR LEAGUE MANAGER: 40th ANNIVERSARY. Oct 3, 1974. The only major league player selected Most Valuable Player in both the American and National leagues, Frank Robinson was hired by the Cleveland Indians as baseball's first black major league manager. During his playing career Robinson represented the American League in four World Series playing for the Baltimore Orioles, led the Cincinnati Reds to a National League pennant and hit 586 home runs in 21 years of play.

SPRINGS FOLK FESTIVAL. Oct 3–4. Springs, PA. 57th annual festival during the peak of fall foliage in Amish country. Features 140 craftspeople, Dutch food and continuous live music. Est attendance: 12,000. For info: Springs Folk Festival, PO Box 293, Springs, PA 15562. Phone: (814) 442-4594. Web: www.springspa.org.

October 2014	S	M	T	W	T	F	S
				1	2	3	4
	5	6	7	8	9	10	11
	12	13	14	15	16	17	18
	19	20	21	22	23	24	25
	26	27	28	29	30	31	

TENNESSEE VALLEY OLD-TIME FIDDLERS CONVENTION. Oct 3–4. Athens State University, Athens, AL. This convention annually attracts thousands of old-time-music fans and brings some 200 contestants to the grounds of historic Athens State University. More than $11,000 in cash prizes is awarded, and the fiddle champion takes home $1,000 plus a trophy. There is competition in 18 categories at this, the "Granddaddy of Mid-South Fiddlers Conventions." Annually, the first full weekend in October. Est attendance: 20,000. For info: Rick Mould, Athens State University, 300 N Beaty St, Athens, AL 35611. Phone: (256) 233-8215. Fax: (256) 233-8189. E-mail: rick.mould@athens.edu. Web: www.athens.edu/fiddlers.

WORLD SMILE DAY. Oct 3. A day dedicated to good works and good cheer throughout the world. The official theme for the day is "Do an act of kindness. Help one person smile." The symbol for the day is the world-famous "smiley face" icon, created in 1963 by Harvey Ball of Worcester, MA. This icon is now the international symbol of happiness and goodwill. Annually, the first Friday in October. For info: Charles P. Ball, President, World Smile Corp, 22 Front St, PO Box 171, Worcester, MA 01614. Web: www.worldsmileday.com.

YAWM ARAFAT: THE STANDING AT ARAFAT. Oct 3. Islamic calendar date: Dhu-Hijjah 9, 1435. The day when people on the hajj (pilgrimage to Mecca) assemble for "the Standing" at the plain of Arafat at Mina, Saudi Arabia, near Mecca. This gathering is a foreshadowing of the Day of Judgment. Different methods for "anticipating" the visibility of the new moon crescent at Mecca are used by different Muslim groups. US date may vary. Began at sunset the preceding day.

YOM KIPPUR BEGINS AT SUNDOWN. Oct 3. Jewish Day of Atonement. See "Yom Kippur" (Oct 4).

BIRTHDAYS TODAY

Lindsey Buckingham, 67, singer, songwriter (Fleetwood Mac), born Palo Alto, CA, Oct 3, 1947.

Neve Campbell, 41, actress ("Party of Five," *Scream*), born Guelph, ON, Canada, Oct 3, 1973.

Chubby Checker, 73, musician, singer, born Ernest Evans at Philadelphia, PA, Oct 3, 1941.

Fred Couples, 55, golfer, born Seattle, WA, Oct 3, 1959.

Dennis Eckersley, 60, Hall of Fame baseball player, born Oakland, CA, Oct 3, 1954.

Lena Headey, 41, actress ("Game of Thrones," *300*), born Hamilton, Bermuda, Oct 3, 1973.

Zlatan Ibrahimovic, 33, soccer player, born Malmö, Sweden, Oct 3, 1981.

Janel Maloney, 45, actress ("From the Earth to the Moon," "The West Wing"), born Woodland Hills, CA, Oct 3, 1969.

Clive Owen, 50, actor (*Children of Men, Elizabeth: The Golden Age, Closer, Sin City*), born Keresley, Coventry, Warwickshire, England, Oct 3, 1964.

Gwen Stefani, 45, singer (No Doubt), born Anaheim, CA, Oct 3, 1969.

Jack P. Wagner, 55, actor ("Melrose Place," "General Hospital"), born Washington, MO, Oct 3, 1959.

Dave Winfield, 63, Hall of Fame baseball player, born St. Paul, MN, Oct 3, 1951.

October 4 — Saturday

DAY 277 **88 REMAINING**

ALBUQUERQUE INTERNATIONAL BALLOON FIESTA. Oct 4–12. Balloon Fiesta Park, Albuquerque, NM. Held since 1972, the largest hot-air balloon gathering in the world features more than 500 hot-air and gas balloons, mass ascensions, balloon glows and specially shaped balloons. The nine-day event includes entries from more than 20 countries. Annually, the first through second weekends in October. For info: Albuquerque International Balloon Fiesta, Inc, 4401 Alameda NE, Albuquerque, NM 87113. Phone: (505) 821-1000 or (888) 422-7277. Fax: (505) 828-2887. E-mail: balloons@balloonfiesta.com. Web: www.balloonfiesta.com.

"THE ALVIN SHOW" TV PREMIERE: ANNIVERSARY. Oct 4, 1961. This prime-time cartoon was based on Ross Bagdasarian's novelty group the Chipmunks, which began as recordings with speeded-up vocals. In the series, the three chipmunks, Alvin, Simon and Theodore, sang and had adventures along with their songwriter-manager, David Seville. Bagdasarian supplied the voices. "Alvin" was more successful as a Saturday-morning cartoon. It returned in reruns in 1979, prompted a sequel, "Alvin and the Chipmunks," in 1983 and inspired two feature films.

CHOWDERFEST. Oct 4–5. Bay Village, Beach Haven, NJ. Fans of Manhattan and New England chowders vote for their favorite recipes after sampling the entries of nearly 20 participating restaurants. The suspense is intense as each chef hopes to win and capture the trophy and bragging rights. Live music, a Merchants Mart featuring blowout bargains and an outdoor food court top off the festivities. For info: Southern Ocean County Chamber of Commerce, Chowderfest, 265 W 9th St, Ship Bottom, NJ 08008. Phone: (800) 292-6372. Web: www.chowderfest.com.

COHOCTON FALL FOLIAGE FESTIVAL. Oct 4–5. Cohocton, NY. 47th annual. Parade and more than 200 food, antiques and arts and crafts booths. Annually, the first full weekend in October. Est attendance: 50,000. For info: Tom Cox, PO Box 204, Cohocton, NY 14826-0204. Phone: (607) 382-1205. Web: www.fallfoliagefestival.com.

CORSICA LIBERATED: ANNIVERSARY. Oct 4, 1943. The island of Corsica became the first French territory in Europe freed from Nazi control when Free French troops entered the city of Bastia, the culmination of a French uprising that had begun on the island on Sept 19.

DICK TRACY DEBUTS: ANNIVERSARY. Oct 4, 1931. Square-jawed detective Dick Tracy made his comic strip debut in the *Detroit Daily Mirror* in "Plainclothes Tracy."

EID-AL-ADHA: FEAST OF THE SACRIFICE. Oct 4. Islamic calendar date: Dhu-Hijjah 10, 1435. Commemorates Abraham's willingness to sacrifice his son Ishmael in obedience to God. It is part of the hajj (pilgrimage to Mecca). The day begins with the sacrifice of an animal in remembrance of the Angel Gabriel's substitution of a lamb as Abraham's offering. One-third of the meat is given to poor people and the rest is shared with friends and family. Celebrated with gifts and general merrymaking, the festival usually continues for several days. It is celebrated as Tabaski in Benin, Burkina Faso, Guinea, Guinea-Bissau, Ivory Coast, Mali, Niger and Senegal; as Hari Raya Hajj in Southeast Asia and as Kurban Bayram in Turkey and Bosnia. Different methods for "anticipating" the visibility of the moon crescent at Mecca are used by different Muslim groups. US date may vary. Began at sunset the preceding day.

ELECTRA FALL CITYWIDE GARAGE SALE. Oct 4. Electra, TX. Sales throughout the Electra area. Chamber of Commerce will provide free coffee and maps at 7 AM. The Chamber of Commerce office will close at 8 AM so that staff, too, may enjoy all of the bargains. Est attendance: 2,000. For info: Sherry Strange, Electra Chamber of Commerce, 112 W Cleveland, Electra, TX 76360. Phone: (940) 495-3577. E-mail: electracoc@electratel.net. Web: www.electratexas.org.

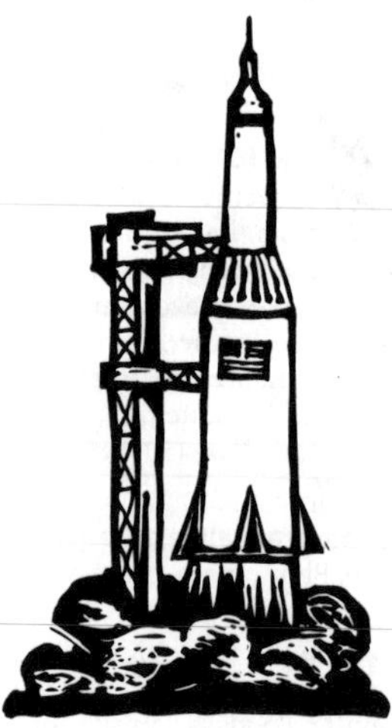

FALL ASTRONOMY DAY. Oct 4. To take astronomy to the people. International Fall Astronomy Day is observed on a Saturday near the first quarter moon between mid-September and mid-October. Cosponsored by 14 astronomical organizations. For info: Gary E. Tomlinson, Coord, Astronomy Day Headquarters, 30 Stargazer Ln, Comstock Park, MI 49321. Phone: (616) 784-9518. E-mail: gtomlins@sbcglobal.net. Web: www.astroleague.org.

GREGORIAN CALENDAR ADJUSTMENT: ANNIVERSARY. Oct 4, 1582. Pope Gregory XIII issued a bulletin that decreed that the day following Thursday, Oct 4, 1582, should be Friday, Oct 15, 1582, thus correcting the Julian calendar, then 10 days out of date relative to the seasons. This reform was effective in most Catholic countries; the Julian calendar continued in use in Britain and the American colonies until 1752, in Russia until 1918 and in Greece until 1923. See also: "Gregorian Calendar Day: Anniversary" (Feb 24) and "Calendar Adjustment Day: Anniversary" (Sept 2).

HAYES, RUTHERFORD BIRCHARD: BIRTH ANNIVERSARY. Oct 4, 1822. Rutherford Birchard Hayes, 19th president of the US (Mar 4, 1877–Mar 3, 1881), was born at Delaware, OH. In his inaugural address, Hayes said: "He serves his party best who serves the country best." He died at Fremont, OH, Jan 17, 1893.

HESTON, CHARLTON: BIRTH ANNIVERSARY. Oct 4, 1923. Born at Evanston, IL, the handsome, resolute Heston won the Best Actor Oscar for his role as Moses in the 1956 Hollywood epic *The Ten Commandments.* Over a career that spanned six decades, his credits include *Ben-Hur, Touch of Evil, Will Penny* and *Planet of the Apes.* Heston died Apr 5, 2008, at Beverly Hills, CA.

INDIA: DASARA (DUSSEHRA). Oct 4. Hindu holiday. Marks the triumph of Lord Rama over the demon king, Ravana, or the victory of good over evil. Effigies of Ravana are burned. Because there is no one universally accepted Hindu calendar, this holiday may be celebrated on a different date in some parts of India, but it always occurs in September or October.

ISSAQUAH SALMON DAYS FESTIVAL. Oct 4–5. Issaquah, WA. To celebrate the return of the spawning salmon to the hatchery, with more than 300 arts and crafts vendors, music, sporting events, food and more. Annually, the first full weekend in October. Est attendance: 180,000. For info: Issaquah Salmon Days Festival, 155 NW Gilman Blvd, Issaquah, WA 98027. Phone: (425) 392-0661. Fax: (425) 392-8101. E-mail: info@salmondays.org. Web: www.salmondays.org.

October 2014	S	M	T	W	T	F	S
				1	2	3	4
	5	6	7	8	9	10	11
	12	13	14	15	16	17	18
	19	20	21	22	23	24	25
	26	27	28	29	30	31	

JOHNNY APPLESEED FESTIVAL. Oct 4. Lake City, MN. Apple pie, arts and crafts fair, kid pedal tractor pull, scarecrow contest, pancake breakfast, live music and more. Annually, the first Saturday in October. Est attendance: 5,000. For info: Lake City Area Chamber of Commerce, 101 W Center St, Lake City, MN 55041. Phone: (800) 369-4123. E-mail: chamberevents@lakecity.org.

JOHNSON, ELIZA McCARDLE: BIRTH ANNIVERSARY. Oct 4, 1810. Wife of Andrew Johnson, 17th president of the US, born at Leesburg, TN. Died at Greeneville, TN, Jan 15, 1876.

KEATON, BUSTER: BIRTH ANNIVERSARY. Oct 4, 1895. Born Joseph Francis Keaton at Piqua, KS, Buster Keaton (supposedly nicknamed by Harry Houdini) was one of America's greatest filmmakers. He became a star on the vaudeville stage by age 6, in a family show with his parents, but moved on to films at age 21, costarring in several comic shorts with Roscoe "Fatty" Arbuckle and then starring in, writing, directing and producing his own shorts—which featured improbable stunts and physical gags along with Keaton's deadpan expression. His full-length silent films are regarded as masterpieces of American comedy, especially *Sherlock, Jr* (1924) and the Civil War epic *The General* (1927)—both of which are on the Library of Congress's National Film Registry. Alcoholism and troubled relations with the MGM studio sidelined his career in the 1930s and '40s, but he later began a quieter career writing gags, making comic cameos in such films as *Around the World in Eighty Days*, appearing on TV's "Candid Camera" and even performing as a clown in Paris's Cirque Medrano. Keaton died on Feb 1, 1966, at Los Angeles, CA.

"LEAVE IT TO BEAVER" TV PREMIERE: ANNIVERSARY. Oct 4, 1957. This family sitcom was a stereotypical portrayal of American family life. It focused on Theodore "Beaver" Cleaver (Jerry Mathers) and his family: his patient, understanding and all-knowing father, Ward (Hugh Beaumont); impeccably dressed housewife and mother, June (Barbara Billingsley); and Wally (Tony Dow), Beaver's good-natured, all-American older brother. The "perfectness" of the Cleaver family was balanced by other, less-than-perfect characters played by Ken Osmond, Frank Bank, Richard Deacon, Diane Brewster, Sue Randall, Rusty Stevens and Madge Blake. The last episode aired Sept 12, 1963. "Leave It to Beaver" remained popular in reruns.

LESOTHO: INDEPENDENCE DAY. Oct 4. National holiday. Commemorates independence from Britain in 1966. Formerly Basutoland.

MILLET, JEAN-FRANÇOIS: 200th BIRTH ANNIVERSARY. Oct 4, 1814. Painter of peasants and landscapes of rural France, born at Gruchy, France. Millet's famous works include *The Winnower* (1848), *The Gleaners* (1857), *The Angelus* (1859) and *Man with a Hoe* (1862). His paintings were admired for depicting their humble subjects with dignity and empathy. Van Gogh was one artist influenced by Millet, who died Jan 20, 1875, at Barbizon, France.

MORRO BAY HARBOR FESTIVAL. Oct 4–5. Morro Bay, CA. Celebrates a working waterfront at play. Showcases seafood, fishing industry and diversity of marine life and coastal lifestyles. Features California Seafood Faire, wine and premium beer tasting and a flotilla of family-oriented attractions. Annually, the first full weekend in October. Est attendance: 25,000. For info: Morro Bay Harbor Festival, Inc, 895 Napa St, Ste A-3, Morro Bay, CA 93442. Phone: (805) 772-1155. Phone in California: (800) 366-6043. Fax: (805) 772-2107. E-mail: info@mbhf.com. Web: www.mbhf.com.

NATIONAL APPLE HARVEST FESTIVAL. Oct 4–5 (also Oct 11–12). South Mountain Fairgrounds, Gettysburg, PA. 50th annual. Celebration includes tours of orchards, apple-butter boiling and antique cider press. Est attendance: 100,000. For info: National Apple Harvest Festival, 2880 Tablerock Rd, Biglerville, PA 17307. Phone: (717) 677-9413. E-mail: appleharvest@embarqmail.com. Web: www.appleharvest.com.

NATIONAL SHIPS-IN-BOTTLES DAY. Oct 4. A day commemorating the venerable art of building small ships and other objects to fit and be displayed in a bottle. Builders, who are often referred to as bottle shipwrights, are dedicated men and women who spend long hours researching the subject they wish to bottle and then equally long hours devising ways to place their creation securely and attractively inside a bottle. Annually, Oct 4. For info: Commander Don Hubbard, USN (Ret), Ships-in-Bottles Association of America, PO Box 180550, Coronado, CA 92178. Phone: (619) 435-3555. E-mail: dhubbardl@san.rr.com.

PROFESSIONAL FREIGHT RELOCATION SPECIALIST DAY. Oct 4. A day to celebrate the nation's truck drivers. They give up family time to ensure that freight is delivered all across this country. If you got it, it came by truck. Celebrated on 10-4 (the "okay" code used by truckers and others). For info: Thom Sisson, 14612 Harvey Oaks Ave, Omaha, NE 68144. E-mail: thom@thomsisson.com.

PUMPKIN AND APPLE CELEBRATION. Oct 4–5. Woodstock, VT. Hands-on activities and educational programs highlight these two versatile fall crops. Events include apple and pumpkin displays, apple tasting, trivia contest, cider pressing, apple peeling, pumpkin races and apples-on-a-string. Pumpkin and apple ice creams are made and apple butter is cooked in the farmhouse. For info: Billings Farm and Museum, Rte 12 N, Woodstock, VT 05091. GPS address: 69 Old River Rd, Woodstock, VT 05091. Phone: (802) 457-2355. Fax: (802) 457-4663. E-mail: info@billingsfarm.org. Web: www.billingsfarm.org.

REMINGTON, FREDERIC S.: BIRTH ANNIVERSARY. Oct 4, 1861. Born at Canton, NY. Artist and writer Frederic Remington was devoted to the outdoors of New York's North Country and the rugged characters and landscapes of the Old West. He began as an illustrator for popular magazines and worked to become a fine artist and sculptor, capturing images of Native Americans, buffalo soldiers, cowboys, horses and Western adventure. Died Dec 26, 1909, at age 48, at Ridgefield, CT, following an appendectomy. Illustrations, watercolors, oil paintings, sketches and bronzes on display at the Frederic Remington Art Museum. For info: Frederic Remington Art Museum, 303 Washington St, Ogdensburg, NY 13669. Phone: (315) 393-2425. E-mail: info@fredericremington.org. Web: www.fredericremington.org.

REVOLUTIONARY GERMANTOWN FESTIVAL. Oct 4. Philadelphia, PA. On Oct 4, 1777, Cliveden became a bloody battleground as General George Washington's colonial soldiers and British troops fought for Germantown. This significant moment in Philadelphia's history was first observed in 1877, and today's Revolutionary Germantown Festival keeps the tradition alive, energizing the community with a day of family entertainment and Battle of Germantown reenactments. Annually, the first Saturday in October. Est attendance: 4,000. For info: Cliveden of the National Trust, 6401 Germantown Ave, Philadelphia, PA 19144. Phone: (215) 848-1777. E-mail: info@cliveden.org. Web: www.cliveden.org.

RUNYAN, DAMON: BIRTH ANNIVERSARY. Oct 4, 1884. American newspaperman and author, born at Manhattan, KS, and died at New York, NY, Dec 10, 1946. The musical *Guys and Dolls* was based on one of his short stories. "Always try to rub up against money," he wrote, "for if you rub up against money long enough, some of it may rub off on you."

SAINT FRANCIS OF ASSISI: FEAST DAY. Oct 4. Giovanni Francesco Bernardone, religious leader, founder of the Friars Minor (Franciscan Order), born at Assisi, Umbria, Italy, in 1181. Died at Porziuncula, Italy, Oct 3, 1226.

SPACE MILESTONE: *LUNA 3* (USSR): 55th ANNIVERSARY. Oct 4, 1959. First satellite to photograph moon's distant side was launched on this date.

SPACE MILESTONE: *SPUTNIK* (USSR). Oct 4, 1957. Anniversary of launching of first successful man-made Earth satellite. *Sputnik I* ("satellite"), weighing 184 pounds, was fired into orbit from the USSR's Tyuratam launch site. Transmitted radio signal for 21 days; decayed Jan 4, 1958. Beginning of the Space Age and humankind's exploration beyond Earth. This first-in-space triumph by the Soviets resulted in a stepped-up emphasis on the teaching of science in American classrooms.

SPOON RIVER VALLEY SCENIC DRIVE. Oct 4–5 (also Oct 11–12). Fulton County, IL. 47th annual. Fall festival in 15 villages with fall foliage, arts and crafts, antiques and collectibles, demonstrations, exhibits, food and the beauty of the 140-mile-long Spoon River Valley. Annually, the first two weekends in October. Est attendance: 100,000. For info: Spoon River Valley Scenic Drive, PO Box 525, Canton, IL 61520. Phone: (309) 647-8980. E-mail: info@spoonriverdrive.org. Web: www.spoonriverdrive.org.

STRATEMEYER, EDWARD L.: BIRTH ANNIVERSARY. Oct 4, 1862. American author of children's books, Stratemeyer was born at Elizabeth, NJ. He created numerous series of popular children's books, including The Bobbsey Twins, The Hardy Boys, Nancy Drew and Tom Swift, hiring ghostwriters to work from his outlines. He and his "Stratemeyer Syndicate," using 60 or more pen names, produced more than 1,300 books, selling more than 200 million copies. Stratemeyer died at Newark, NJ, May 10, 1930, but his daughters continued his legacy of essentially mass-produced literature until 1982.

TEN-FOUR DAY. Oct 4. The fourth day of the tenth month is a day of recognition for radio operators, whose code words "Ten-Four" signal an affirmative reply.

UNITED NATIONS: WORLD SPACE WEEK. Oct 4–10. To celebrate the contributions of space science and technology to the betterment of the human condition. The dates recall the launch, on Oct 4, 1957, of the first artificial satellite, *Sputnik*, and the entry into force, on Oct 10, 1967, of the Treaty on Principles Governing the Activities of States in the Exploration and Use of Outer Space. For info: United Nations, Dept of Public Info, New York, NY 10017. Web: www.un.org.

WINFIELD ART-IN-THE-PARK FESTIVAL. Oct 4. Scenic Island Park, Winfield, KS. More than 75 artists and craftspersons display and sell their wares. Entertainment and food services available. Two-dollar contribution for those over age 12. Annually, the first Saturday in October. Est attendance: 4,000. For info: Winfield Arts and Humanities Council, 700 Gary, Ste A, Winfield, KS 67156-3731. Phone: (620) 221-2161. Fax: (620) 221-0587. E-mail: winfieldarts@gmail.com.

WOOFSTOCK. Oct 4. Wichita, KS. An annual celebration of peace, love and pets. Woofstock invites canines and their owners to participate in activities catered exclusively to them, including a one-mile walk, activities such as dog agility and water retrieval demonstrations, costume contests, doggie musical chairs, Ruff Races, a silent auction and more than 80 pet-friendly vendors. All proceeds benefit the Kansas Humane Society and the 16,000 animals it receives each year. Est attendance: 17,000. For info: Kansas Humane Society, 3313 N Hillside, Wichita, KS 67219. Phone: (316) 524-9196. Fax: (316) 554-0356. E-mail: jcampbell@kshumane.org. Web: www.kshumane.org.

YOM KIPPUR or DAY OF ATONEMENT. Oct 4. Holiest Jewish observance. A day for fasting, repentance and seeking forgiveness. Hebrew calendar date: Tishri 10, 5775. Began at sundown on Oct 3.

BIRTHDAYS TODAY

Armand Assante, 65, actor (*Belizaire the Cajun, The Mambo Kings, Fatal Instinct*), born New York, NY, Oct 4, 1949.

Abraham Benrubi, 45, actor ("ER," "Men in Trees"), born Indianapolis, IN, Oct 4, 1969.

Jackie Collins, 73, author (*Lucky*), born London, England, Oct 4, 1941.

Rachael Leigh Cook, 35, actress (*She's All That*, "The Baby-Sitters Club"), born Minneapolis, MN, Oct 4, 1979.

Clifton Davis, 69, singer, actor ("That's My Mama," "Amen"), composer, born Chicago, IL, Oct 4, 1945.

Anita L. DeFrantz, 62, Olympics executive and former rower, born Philadelphia, PA, Oct 4, 1952.

Charles (Chuck) Hagel, 68, US Secretary of Defense, former US senator (R, Nebraska), born North Platte, NE, Oct 4, 1946.

Tony La Russa, Jr, 70, former baseball manager and player, born Tampa, FL, Oct 4, 1944.

Anne Rice, 73, novelist (*Interview with the Vampire*), born New Orleans, LA, Oct 4, 1941.

Derrick Rose, 26, basketball player, born Chicago, IL, Oct 4, 1988.

Susan Sarandon, 68, actress (Oscar for *Dead Man Walking*; *Thelma and Louise*), born Susan Tomalin at New York, NY, Oct 4, 1946.

Alicia Silverstone, 38, actress (*Clueless, Batman & Robin*), born San Francisco, CA, Oct 4, 1976.

Alvin Toffler, 86, author (*Future Shock, Power Shift*), born New York, NY, Oct 4, 1928.

Christoph Waltz, 58, actor (Oscars for *Inglourious Basterds, Django Unchained*), born Vienna, Austria, Oct 4, 1956.

Jimy Williams, 71, baseball manager and former player, born Santa Maria, CA, Oct 4, 1943.

October 5 — Sunday

DAY 278 **87 REMAINING**

ARTHUR, CHESTER ALAN: BIRTH ANNIVERSARY. Oct 5, 1829. The 21st president of the US, Chester Alan Arthur, was born at Fairfield, VT, and succeeded to the presidency following the death of James A. Garfield. Term of office: Sept 20, 1881–Mar 3, 1885. Arthur was not successful in obtaining the Republican Party's nomination for the following term. He died at New York, NY, Nov 18, 1886.

BLESSING OF THE FISHING FLEET. Oct 5. Church of Saints Peter and Paul and Fisherman's Wharf, San Francisco, CA. Annually, the first Sunday in October.

BONDS BREAKS SEASON HOME RUN RECORD: ANNIVERSARY. Oct 5, 2001. Barry Bonds of the San Francisco Giants broke Mark McGwire's 1998 season home run record when he hit his 71st homer of the season in a game against the Los Angeles Dodgers at Pacific Bell Park. Later in the game he hit another homer. The Dodgers beat the Giants, 11–10, eliminating them from the playoffs. On Oct 7 Bonds hit one more homer, to finish the season with 73. He also broke Babe Ruth's slugging record of .847 with .863. On Aug 7, 2007, Bonds passed Hank Aaron on the all-time homer list by slugging number 756.

BYRD, RICHARD E.: BIRTH ANNIVERSARY. Oct 5, 1888. Pioneering American aviator and explorer who made the first flight over both polar axes, born to a prominent family at Winchester, VA. Educated at the University of Virginia and the US Naval Academy, Byrd's distinguished naval career included serving as its liaison officer to Congress (1919 to 1921), where he was responsible for the legislation that created the Navy's Bureau of Aeronautics. While also credited with the first flight over the North Pole on May 9, 1926, Byrd's primary polar explorations took place in Antarctica. He led the first flight over the South Pole on Nov 28–29, 1929, established the Little America exploration bases on the polar continent and in 1946 commanded Operation Highjump, which mapped 1.5 million square miles of Antarctica by aerial photography. Awarded the Medal of Honor, the Distinguished Service Medal, the Navy Cross, the National Geographic Hubbard Medal and the Department of Defense Medal of Freedom, Byrd died on Mar 11, 1957, at Boston, MA.

October 2014	S	M	T	W	T	F	S
				1	2	3	4
	5	6	7	8	9	10	11
	12	13	14	15	16	17	18
	19	20	21	22	23	24	25
	26	27	28	29	30	31	

CATTUS ISLAND NATURE FESTIVAL. Oct 5. Cattus Island County Park, Toms River, NJ. 34th annual environmental organizations fair with natural history programs throughout the day, including boat and van tours, kayak tours, children's games, nature walks and more. Est attendance: 1,500. For info: Cattus Island Park, 1170 Cattus Island Blvd, Toms River, NJ 08753. Phone: (732) 270-6960. E-mail: jkline@co.ocean.nj.us.

CHIEF JOSEPH SURRENDER: ANNIVERSARY. Oct 5, 1877. After a 1,700-mile retreat, Chief Joseph and the Nez Percé Indians surrendered to US Cavalry troops at Bear's Paw near Chinook, MT, Oct 5, 1877. Chief Joseph made his famous speech of surrender, "From where the sun now stands, I will fight no more forever."

CIVIL WAR "SUBMARINE" ATTACK: ANNIVERSARY. Oct 5, 1863. In an attempt to disrupt the Union blockade of Charleston Harbor, the Confederate semisubmersible *David* rammed the Union ironclad *New Ironsides* with a spar torpedo. This was the first successful Southern attack using a submersible craft. Although both sides experimented with submarine warfare during the Civil War, the results were far from encouraging as the submarines caused more fatalities to their own crews than to the opposing side.

COUNTRY INN, BED-AND-BREAKFAST DAY. Oct 5. Across America and Canada country inns and bed-and-breakfasts welcome visitors with information, special events and fellowship. The weekend also introduces people to the world of inns and B&Bs. Inns and their fans around the world are welcome to join the celebration. Annually, the first Sunday in October. For info: Tina Czarnota. Web: www.tinaczarnota.com.

EDWARDS, JONATHAN: BIRTH ANNIVERSARY. Oct 5, 1703. (Old Style date.) The famed theologian and leader of the "Great Awakening," the religious revival in the colonies, was born at East Windsor, CT. His "Sinners in the Hands of an Angry God" is the most famous sermon in American history. He later became president of the College of New Jersey (now Princeton University). Edwards died at Princeton, NJ, Mar 22, 1758, when he contracted smallpox from an inoculation.

EMERGENCY NURSES WEEK. Oct 5–11. Sponsored by the Emergency Nurses Association (ENA) since 1989, this is a weeklong celebration recognizing emergency nurses for their dedication, service and commitment to their patients and communities. Special focus is given on Wednesday, which is Emergency Nurses Day (Oct 8), to honor nursing professionals who provide care to those whose lives have been touched by life's tragedies. For info: Emergency Nurses Assn Headquarters, 915 Lee St, Des Plaines, IL 60016-6569. Phone: (800) 900-9659. E-mail: pr@ena.org. Web: www.ena.org.

ENRICO FERMI ATOMIC POWER PLANT ACCIDENT: ANNIVERSARY. Oct 5, 1966. A radiation alarm and Class I alert at 3:09 PM, EST, signaled a problem at the Enrico Fermi Atomic Power Plant, Lagoona Beach, near Monroe, MI. The accident was contained, but nearly a decade was required to complete the decommissioning and disassembly of the plant.

FINE, LARRY: BIRTH ANNIVERSARY. Oct 5, 1902. The fuzzy-haired Stooge, many times a victim of the mean-tempered Moe, was born Louis Feinberg at Philadelphia, PA. He started his show business career in vaudeville with a joke-and-violin act (he was an accomplished musician). Fine was an original member of the

Three Stooges, formed in 1925. Fine died Jan 24, 1975, at Woodland Hills, CA.

✦**FIRE PREVENTION WEEK.** Oct 5–11. Presidential Proclamation issued annually for the first or second week in October since 1925. For many years prior to 1925, National Fire Prevention Day was observed in October. Sponsored by the National Fire Protection Association. Annually, the Sunday–Saturday during which the Oct 9 anniversary date falls.

FIRE PREVENTION WEEK. Oct 5–11. To increase awareness of the dangers of fire and to educate the public on how to stay safe from fire. For info: Natl Fire Protection Assn, One Batterymarch Park, Quincy, MA 02169. Phone: (617) 770-3000 or (800) 344-3555. E-mail: publicaffairs@nfpa.org. Web: www.nfpa.org or www.firepreventionweek.org.

FRANCE: QATAR PRIX L'ARC DE TRIOMPHE. Oct 5. Longchamp Racecourse, Paris. One of the world's greatest horse races has been held on the first Sunday in October since 1920. Up to 20 of the best entire horses and fillies aged three and above line up each year for the mile-and-a-half contest. Since 2008 and the signature of a five-year partnership with the Qatar Racing and Equestrian Club, the "Arc" has become the richest thoroughbred race in the world, with a total purse of four million euros. More than one billion viewers in 30 countries. Est attendance: 60,000. For info: France Galop. E-mail: medias@france-galop.com. Web: www.prixarcdetriomphe.com.

GERMANY: ERNTEDANKFEST. Oct 5. A harvest thanksgiving festival, or potato harvest festival, Erntedankfest (or Erntedanktag) is generally observed on the first Sunday in October.

GODDARD, ROBERT HUTCHINGS: BIRTH ANNIVERSARY. Oct 5, 1882. "The father of the Space Age," born at Worcester, MA. Largely ignored or ridiculed during his lifetime because of his dreams of rocket travel, including travel to other planets. Launched a liquid-fuel-powered rocket Mar 16, 1926, at Auburn, MA. Died Aug 10, 1945, at Baltimore, MD. See also: "Goddard Day" (Mar 16).

HAVEL, VACLAV: BIRTH ANNIVERSARY. Oct 5, 1936. World-renowned poet, playwright, human rights activist and president of Czechoslovakia/Czech Republic, Vaclav Havel was born at Prague, Czechoslovakia (now Czech Republic). His literary works critiqued the dehumanizing effects of totalitarian political regimes, and he was imprisoned for four years (1979–1983) for his human rights activism in Communist-controlled Czechoslovakia. After the fall of communism, Havel was the first president of Czechoslovakia and then the Czech Republic (1989–2003); under his leadership, it was one of the first Eastern European countries invited to join NATO. One of the most respected figures of the 20th century, Havel died Dec 18, 2011, at Hradecek, Czech Republic.

JAMES BOND MOVIE SERIES LAUNCHED WITH *DR. NO*: ANNIVERSARY. Oct 5, 1962. Scottish actor Sean Connery played Ian Fleming's super secret agent James Bond, 007, in the first film of a blockbuster franchise.

LUMIÈRE, LOUIS: 150th BIRTH ANNIVERSARY. Oct 5, 1864. Born at Besançon, France, Louis Lumière with brother Auguste were film pioneers who created the first movie, *Workers Leaving the Lumière Factory (1895).* Lumière, considered the father of cinema in France, was inspired by Thomas Edison's Kinetoscope, and he created (with his brother's assistance) the Cinèmatographe, which could project and mechanically move a sprocketed strip of film images. This was patented on Feb 13, 1895. On Dec 28, 1895, the brothers projected short films for paying customers—the first time this had ever been done—at Paris's Grand Café. The Lumières directed or produced thousands of short films of both everyday life and news of the day in what were the first newsreels. The brothers retired from film production in 1901. Louis Lumière spent his later years working on photographic and film innovations, such as an early 3-D system. He died at Bandol, France, on June 6, 1948.

MENTAL ILLNESS AWARENESS WEEK. Oct 5–11. To increase public awareness of the causes of, symptoms of and treatments for mental illnesses. National Day of Prayer for Mental Illness Recovery and Understanding is Tuesday (Oct 7) and Bipolar Awareness Day is Thursday (Oct 9). Annually, the first full week in October. For info: National Alliance on Mental Illness, 3803 N Fairfax Dr, Ste 100, Arlington, VA 22203-1701. Phone: (800) 950-6264. E-mail: info@nami.org. Web: www.nami.org.

"MONTY PYTHON'S FLYING CIRCUS" TV PREMIERE: 45th ANNIVERSARY. Oct 5, 1969. This wacky comedy series debuted on BBC-1 in Great Britain and aired until 1974. The cast was made up of Graham Chapman, John Cleese, Eric Idle, Terry Jones, Michael Palin and American Terry Gilliam. John Philip Sousa's "Liberty Bell March" got the show started, and viewers were treated to surreal animation and such skits as "The Spanish Inquisition" and "The Ministry of Silly Walks." On Oct 6, 1974, "Monty Python's Flying Circus" began airing in the US. The cast members also made four films together.

MYSTERY SERIES WEEK. Oct 5–11. A celebration of continuing characters in mystery fiction. Two-thirds of all new mysteries each year feature a series detective. The series tradition has been alive and well for more than 100 years. Series readers today can choose from more than 20,000 adult mysteries featuring more than 4,000 continuing characters from living writers. Mystery Series Week celebrates fictional cops, private eyes and amateur sleuths from all walks of life—solving crimes from 55 BC to the 22nd century. Annually, the first full week in October. For info: Purple Moon Press, 3319 Greenfield Rd, #317, Dearborn, MI 48120-1212. Phone: (313) 593-1033. E-mail: mysteryseriesweek@willetta.com. Web: www.willetta.com.

NATIONAL CARRY A TUNE WEEK. Oct 5–11. This week calls for people to celebrate favorite tunes from the past by performing them in a concert, at school, at church or at home. The purpose is to remember tunes from America's past and keep them alive. Annually, the week nearest the birthday of William Billings (born Oct 7, 1746), America's first important tune composer ("Chester"). Sponsor: Tune Lovers Society. For info: Roger Hall, Pine Tree Productions, 235 Prospect St, Stoughton, MA 02072. Phone: (781) 344-6954. E-mail: pinetreemusic@aol.com. Web: www.americanmusicpreservation.com/carryatuneweek.htm.

NATIONAL WORK FROM HOME WEEK. Oct 5–11. A week to celebrate the trends, technology and tactics that allow millions of Americans to work from home as entrepreneurs, corporate telecommuters and heads of households handling family finances and affairs. For info: Jeff Zbar, PO Box 8263, Coral Springs, FL 33075-8263. Phone: (954) 346-4393. E-mail: jeff@chiefhomeofficer.com. Web: www.chiefhomeofficer.com.

NUCLEAR MEDICINE WEEK. Oct 5–11. Dedicated to recognizing the professionals devoted to using nuclear medicine as an integral part of patient care. This is the perfect time to promote the value and safety of nuclear medicine to patients, referring physicians and your community. Promotional items will be available through SNM. Annually, the first full week in October. For info: SNM, 1850 Samuel Morse Dr, Reston, VA 20190. Phone: (703) 708-9000. Fax: (703) 708-9015. Web: www.snm.org/nmw.

O'BRIEN, FLANN: BIRTH ANNIVERSARY. Oct 5, 1911. Pen name of Brian O'Nolan, born at Strabane, Ireland. O'Nolan, a career civil servant, was incognito a novelist, dramatist and journalist. Best known for *At Swim-Two-Birds* (1939) and *The Third Policeman* (1967). Under the name Myles na gCopaleen, he authored a popular satirical and humorous column for the *Irish Times.* O'Nolan died Apr 1, 1966, at Dublin, Ireland. In keeping with the mordant humor of his works, MylesDay is celebrated on his death day rather than his birthday. See "MylesDay" (Apr 1).

PORTUGAL: REPUBLIC DAY. Oct 5. National holiday. Commemorates establishment of the republic in 1910.

PULASKI DAY PARADE. Oct 5. Philadelphia, PA. Parade honoring the Polish patriot known as "the father of the American Cavalry." Begins at 20th and Benjamin Franklin Pkwy and ends at 19th and Benjamin Franklin Pkwy. For info: Polish American Congress, Eastern Pennsylvania District, 308 Walnut St, Philadelphia, PA 19106. Phone: (215) 739-3408. Fax: (215) 922-1518. Web: www.polishamericancongress.com.

SPACE MILESTONE: *CHALLENGER STS 41-G*: 30th ANNIVERSARY. Oct 5, 1984. Space shuttle *Challenger*'s sixth mission with crew of seven, including two women. Launched from Kennedy Space Center, FL, on this date and landed there on Oct 13, 1984. Kathryn D. Sullivan became the first American woman to walk in space.

STONE, THOMAS: DEATH ANNIVERSARY. Oct 5, 1787. Signer of the Declaration of Independence, born 1743 (exact date unknown) at Charles County, MD. Died at Alexandria, VA.

TECUMSEH: DEATH ANNIVERSARY. Oct 5, 1813. Shawnee Indian chief, born at Old Piqua near Springfield, OH, in March 1768. Tecumseh came to prominence between 1799 and 1804 as a powerful orator, defending his people against whites. He denounced as invalid all treaties by which tribes ceded their lands and condemned the chieftains who had entered into such agreements. With his brother Tenskwatawa, the Prophet, he established a town on the Tippecanoe River near Lafayette, IN, and then embarked on a mission to organize a confederation to stop white encroachment. Although he advocated peaceful methods and negotiation, he did not rule out war as a last resort as he visited tribes throughout the country. While he was away, William Henry Harrison defeated the Prophet at the Battle of Tippecanoe Nov 7, 1811, and burned the town. Tecumseh organized a large force of Indian warriors and assisted the British in the War of 1812. Tecumseh was defeated and killed at the Battle of the Thames.

UNITED NATIONS: WORLD TEACHERS' DAY. Oct 5. A day to honor teachers and their contributions to learning. For info: United Nations, Dept of Public Info, New York, NY 10017. Web: www.un.org.

WORLD COMMUNION SUNDAY. Oct 5. Communion is celebrated by Christians all over the world. Annually, the first Sunday in October.

"YOU BET YOUR LIFE" TV PREMIERE: ANNIVERSARY. Oct 5, 1950. This funny game show began on radio in 1947 and moved to TV with Groucho Marx as host and George Fenneman as announcer and scorekeeper. Players tried to answer questions in the category of their choice, but Groucho's improvised interviews stole the show. Many guests appeared who later became famous, including Phyllis Diller and Candice Bergen. Players could also win money by uttering the secret word, an everyday word suspended above the stage on a duck that dropped when the word was spoken. This was one of the few shows to be filmed, because the interviews needed to be edited. Two short-lived revivals of the series aired, with Buddy Hackett as host in 1980, and with Bill Cosby in 1992.

"ZANE GREY THEATER" TV PREMIERE: ANNIVERSARY. Oct 5, 1956. Officially titled "Dick Powell's Zane Grey Theater," this Western anthology series was hosted by Powell and featured both stories by Grey and original telecasts. Powell occasionally starred in an episode. Guest stars included Hedy Lamarr (in her only dramatic TV role), Ginger Rogers, Claudette Colbert and Esther Williams.

October 2014

S	M	T	W	T	F	S
			1	2	3	4
5	6	7	8	9	10	11
12	13	14	15	16	17	18
19	20	21	22	23	24	25
26	27	28	29	30	31	

BIRTHDAYS TODAY

Karen Allen, 63, actress (*The Wanderers, Raiders of the Lost Ark, Starman*), born Carrollton, IL, Oct 5, 1951.

Michael Andretti, 52, race car driver, son of Mario Andretti, born Bethlehem, PA, Oct 5, 1962.

Clive Barker, 62, author, born Liverpool, England, Oct 5, 1952.

Josie Bissett, 44, actress ("Melrose Place"), born Seattle, WA, Oct 5, 1970.

Ben Cardin, 71, US Senator (D, Maryland), born Baltimore, MD, Oct 5, 1943.

Bill Dana, 90, actor, comedian, born Quincy, MA, Oct 5, 1924.

Laura Davies, 51, golfer, born Coventry, England, Oct 5, 1963.

Jesse Eisenberg, 31, actor (*The Squid and the Whale, Adventureland, The Social Network*), born New York, NY, Oct 5, 1983.

Bob Geldof, 63, singer (Boomtown Rats), social activist, born Dublin, Ireland, Oct 5, 1951.

Grant Hill, 42, former basketball player, born Dallas, TX, Oct 5, 1972.

Glynis Johns, 91, actress (*Mary Poppins, The Ref, A Little Night Music*), born Pretoria, South Africa, Oct 5, 1923.

Mario Lemieux, 49, Hall of Fame hockey player, hockey executive, born Montreal, QC, Canada, Oct 5, 1965.

Steve Miller, 71, musician, singer (Steve Miller Band), born Dallas, TX, Oct 5, 1943.

Parminder K. Nagra, 39, actress (*Bend It like Beckham,* "ER"), born Leicester, Leicestershire, England, Oct 5, 1975.

Patrick Roy, 49, hockey manager and former player, born Quebec City, QC, Canada, Oct 5, 1965.

Neil deGrasse Tyson, 56, astrophysicist, television personality ("NOVA scienceNOW," "The Colbert Report"), born New York, NY, Oct 5, 1958.

Kate Winslet, 39, actress (Oscar for *The Reader*; *Revolutionary Road, Finding Neverland, Titanic*), born Reading, England, Oct 5, 1975.

October 6 — Monday

DAY 279 **86 REMAINING**

AMERICAN LIBRARY ASSOCIATION FOUNDING: ANNIVERSARY. Oct 6, 1876. Founded at Philadelphia, PA, by 103 librarians attending the Centennial Exposition.

BLUE SHIRT DAY™/WORLD DAY OF BULLYING PREVENTION. Oct 6. "Go Blue!" Kids and adults wear a blue shirt this day to show solidarity against bullying and cyber-bullying. Annually, the first Monday in October. For info: STOMP Out Bullying, 220 E 57th St, 9th Fl, Ste G, New York, NY 10022. Phone: (877) NO BULLY. E-mail: info@stompoutbullying.org. Web: www.stompoutbullying.org.

✦CHILD HEALTH DAY. Oct 6. Presidential Proclamation always issued for the first Monday in October. Proclamation has been issued since 1928. In 1959 Congress changed celebration day from May 1 to the present observance (Public Resolution No. 46 of May 18, 1928, and Public Law 86–352 of Sept 22, 1959).

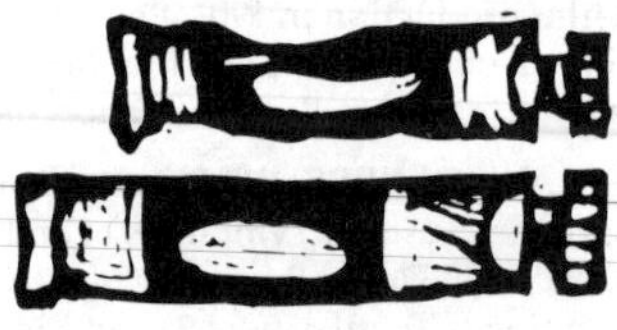

"CSI: CRIME SCENE INVESTIGATION" TV PREMIERE: ANNIVERARY. Oct 6, 2000. CBS's consistently top-rated mystery drama focuses on a crack Las Vegas police forensics team. "CSI" brings science to the foreground, with close-up looks at technology and lab techniques. The 200th episode aired Apr 2, 2009. The show spawned equally successful spin-offs: "CSI: Miami" and "CSI: New York."

EGYPT: ARMED FORCES DAY. Oct 6. The Egyptian army celebrates crossing into Sinai in 1973.

EL-SADAT, ANWAR: ASSASSINATION: ANNIVERSARY. Oct 6, 1981. Anwar el-Sadat, Egyptian president and Nobel Peace Prize recipient, was killed by assassins at Cairo while he was reviewing a military parade commemorating the 1973 Egyptian-Israeli War. At least eight other persons were reported killed in the attack on Sadat. Anwar el-Sadat was born Dec 25, 1918, at Mit Abu Al-Kom, a village near the Nile River delta.

FINANCIAL PLANNING WEEK. Oct 6–12. 13th annual. Everyone is entitled to objective advice from a competent, ethical financial planner to make smart financial decisions. This week is designed to help Americans discover the value of financial planning. For info: Ryanne Enyeart, Financial Planning Assn, 7535 E Hampden Ave, Ste 600, Denver, CO 80231. Phone: (800) 322-4237, ext 7151. Fax: (303) 759-0749. E-mail: PublicAwareness@fpanet.org. Web: www.FinancialPlanningWeek.org.

GAYNOR, JANET: BIRTH ANNIVERSARY. Oct 6, 1906. Born Laura Gainor at Philadelphia, PA, in 1929, she became the first winner of the Academy Award for Best Actress for her cumulative work in two 1927 films, *Sunrise* and *Seventh Heaven*, and for *Street Angel* (1928). Gaynor died Sept 14, 1984, at Palm Springs, CA.

HEYERDAHL, THOR: 100th BIRTH ANNIVERSARY. Oct 6, 1914. The anthropologist and explorer was born at Larvik, Norway. Seeking to prove the plausibility of South American peoples having settled Polynesia, he embarked on an epic raft ride with five companions in 1947. The *Kon-Tiki* made the 4,300-mile voyage from Peru to Raroia in 101 days. Heyerdahl's book chronicling the adventure became an international bestseller. He continued his travels (including a solo 1970 trip in a reed boat from North Africa to Barbados) and writing until his death. He died at Italy on Apr 18, 2002.

IRELAND: IVY DAY. Oct 6. The anniversary of the death of Irish nationalist leader and home-rule advocate Charles Stewart Parnell is observed, especially in Ireland, as Ivy Day. A sprig of ivy is worn on the lapel to remember Parnell. James Joyce's short story "Ivy Day in the Committee Room," published in the collection titled *Dubliners*, addresses this event. See also: "Parnell, Charles Stewart: Birth Anniversary" (June 27).

JACKIE MAYER REHAB DAY. Oct 6. Sandusky, OH. Known as Sandusky's "favorite daughter," Jacquelyn Jeanne Mayer, Miss America 1963 and stroke survivor since 1970, is honored on Oct 6, the anniversary of the 1997 renaming of Providence Hospital's rehab and nursing facility as the Jackie Mayer Rehab Center. After seven years of self-directed rehab to regain her speech and mobility, Jackie Mayer has been a motivational speaker and tireless advocate on behalf of stroke survivors across the US and Canada. For info: Dr. Nancy Linenkugel, OSF, 3334 Mowbray Ln, Cincinnati, OH 45226. Phone: (419) 322-1618. Web: www.jackiemayer.com.

KIDS' GOAL-SETTING WEEK. Oct 6–10. Encourages parents, teachers and coaches to foster goal-setting habits in children's lives so that the children can make their dreams come true. For info: Gary Ryan Blair, The GoalsGuy, 36181 E Lake Rd, Ste 139, Palm Harbor, FL 34685. Phone: (877) GOALS-GUY. Fax: (813) 435-2022. E-mail: info@goalsguy.com. Web: www.goalsguy.com.

LIND, JENNY: BIRTH ANNIVERSARY. Oct 6, 1820. Opera singer known as "the Swedish Nightingale," born at Stockholm, Sweden. She died at Malvern, England, Nov 2, 1887.

MOODY, HELEN WILLS: BIRTH ANNIVERSARY. Oct 6, 1905. One of the greatest tennis players of the 20th century was born at Centreville, CA. Moody, 1921's US national junior champion, had a phenomenal professional career with a .919 winning average. She won 52 out of 92 tournaments between 1919 and 1938. She won Wimbledon eight out of nine tries, the US Open seven times and the French Open four times. Amazingly, from 1927 to 1932, she did not lose one single set in any singles competition. A 1924 Olympic gold medal winner for singles and doubles, Moody also became the first player to win a grand slam (1928). "Little Miss Poker Face" (as she was nicknamed for her no-nonsense style) was inducted into the International Tennis Hall of Fame in 1969. She died Jan 1, 1998, at Carmel, CA.

✦NATIONAL GERMAN-AMERICAN DAY. Oct 6. Celebration of German heritage and the contributions German Americans have made to the building of the nation. A Presidential Proclamation has been issued each year since 1987. Annually, Oct 6.

NATIONAL GERMAN-AMERICAN DAY. Oct 6. Observed since the 19th century, this day honors the contributions of German immigrants to US culture and history. Celebrated on the date in 1683 when 13 Mennonite families disembarked near Philadelphia, PA, from Krefeld, Germany. These families later founded Germantown, PA. The day is celebrated by all those who are culturally German from all parts of Europe. This special day had a boost in popularity when President Ronald Reagan became the first US president to proclaim it in 1987.

NATIONAL METRIC WEEK. Oct 6–12. Since 1976, a week observing the importance of the metric system as the primary system of measurement for the US. Annually, the week of the 10th month containing the 10th day of the month. For info: US Metric Assn, 2032 Mendon Dr, Rancho Palos Verdes, CA 90275-1620. Phone: (310) 832-3763. Web: www.metric.org.

NATIONAL PHYSICIAN ASSISTANTS (PA) WEEK. Oct 6–12. To acknowledge the unique contribution of physician assistants in providing access to medical care on the anniversary of the graduation of the first class of PAs from Duke University (Oct 6, 1967). For info: American Academy of Physician Assistants, 2318 Mill Rd, Ste 1300, Alexandria, VA 22314-1552. Phone: (703) 836-2272. Fax: (703) 684-1924. E-mail: aapa@aapa.org. Web: www.aapa.org.

SEIBERT, FLORENCE: BIRTH ANNIVERSARY. Oct 6, 1897. American physician Florence B. Seibert was born at Easton, PA. She developed the test for tuberculosis that was adopted by the US and used worldwide by the World Health Organization. She died Aug 23, 1991, at St. Petersburg, FL.

SUPREME COURT 2014–2015 TERM BEGINS. Oct 6. Traditionally, the Supreme Court's annual term begins on the first Monday in October and continues with seven two-week sessions of oral arguments. Between the sessions are six recesses during which the opinions are written by the justices. Ordinarily, all cases are decided by the following June or July.

SZYMANOWSKI, KAROL: BIRTH ANNIVERSARY. Oct 6, 1882. Birthday of one of Poland's outstanding composers, whose art played a role in Polish 20th-century music. Born at Timoshovka, Ukraine. Died Mar 29, 1937, at Lausanne, Switzerland.

UNITED NATIONS: WORLD HABITAT DAY. Oct 6. The General Assembly, by a resolution of Dec 17, 1985, has designated the first Monday of October each year as World Habitat Day—a day to reflect on the living conditions of human beings and to take action to address the shortcomings of those conditions. The first observance of this day in 1986 marked the 10th anniversary of the first international conference on the subject. For info: United Nations,

Dept of Public Info, Public Inquiries Unit, Rm GA-57, New York, NY 10017. Phone: (212) 963-4475. E-mail: inquiries@un.org. Web: www.un.org.

WESTINGHOUSE, GEORGE: BIRTH ANNIVERSARY. Oct 6, 1846. Engineer and inventor of the air brake for trains, born at Central Bridge, NY. He was the first employer to give his employees paid vacations. Westinghouse died at New York, NY, Mar 12, 1914.

YOM KIPPUR WAR: ANNIVERSARY. Oct 6–25, 1973. A surprise attack by Egypt and Syria pushed Israeli forces several miles behind the 1967 cease-fire lines. Israel was caught off guard, partly because the attack came on the holiest Jewish religious day. After 18 days of fighting, hostilities were halted by the UN Oct 25. Israel partially recovered from the initial setback but failed to regain all the land lost in the fighting.

BIRTHDAYS TODAY

Britt Ekland, 72, actress (*The Night They Raided Minsky's*), born Stockholm, Sweden, Oct 6, 1942.

Rebecca Lobo, 41, sportscaster, former basketball player, born Southwick, MA, Oct 6, 1973.

Elisabeth Shue, 51, actress (*Adventures in Babysitting, Leaving Las Vegas*), born Wilmington, DE, Oct 6, 1963.

Jeremy Sisto, 40, actor ("Six Feet Under," "Law & Order"), born Green Valley, CA, Oct 6, 1974.

Stephanie Zimbalist, 58, actress ("Remington Steele"), born Encino, CA, Oct 6, 1956.

October 7 — Tuesday

DAY 280 **85 REMAINING**

***CATS* PREMIERE: ANNIVERSARY.** Oct 7, 1982. The second longest-running production in Broadway history (after *Phantom of the Opera*) opened this day. *Cats* was based on a book of poetry by T.S. Eliot and had a score by Andrew Lloyd Webber. More than 10 million theatergoers saw the New York City production, which closed Sept 10, 2000, after 7,485 performances. *Cats* was also produced in 30 other countries.

DOW JONES INDUSTRIAL AVERAGE: ANNIVERSARY. Oct 7, 1896. Dow Jones began reporting an average of the prices of 12 industrial stocks in the *Wall Street Journal* on this day. In the early years these were largely railroad stocks. In 1928 Mr Dow expanded the number of stocks to 30, where it currently remains. Today, the large, frequently traded stocks in the DJIA represent about a fifth of the market value of all US stocks.

NOBEL CONFERENCE 50. Oct 7–8. Gustavus Adolphus College, St. Peter, MN. Annual two-day scientific symposium (50th year), and the first one sanctioned by the Nobel Foundation, Stockholm. Annually, the first Tuesday and Wednesday in October. Est attendance: 6,000. For info: Dean Wahlund, Dir of Special Events, Gustavus Adolphus College, 800 W College Ave, St. Peter, MN 56082-1498. Phone: (507) 933-7520. E-mail: dwahlund@gustavus.edu. Web: www.gustavus.edu/nobelconference.

RODNEY, CAESAR: BIRTH ANNIVERSARY. Oct 7, 1728. (Old Style date.) Signer of the Declaration of Independence who cast a tie-breaking vote. Born near Dover, DE, he died June 26, 1784. Rodney is on the Delaware quarter issued by the US Mint in 1999, the first in a series of quarters that commemorate each of the 50 states.

WALLACE, HENRY AGARD: BIRTH ANNIVERSARY. Oct 7, 1888. 33rd vice president of the US (1941–45), born at Adair County, IA. Died at Danbury, CT, Nov 18, 1965.

WISE, THOMAS J.: BIRTH ANNIVERSARY. Oct 7, 1859. English bibliophile and literary forger, born at Gravesend, England. One of England's most distinguished bibliographic experts, he was revealed, in 1934, to have forged dozens of "first editions" and "unique" publications over a period of more than 20 years. Many of them had been sold at high prices to collectors and libraries. The forgeries in some cases purported to predate the real first editions. Wise died at Hampstead, England, May 13, 1937.

"YOUR HIT PARADE" TV PREMIERE: ANNIVERSARY. Oct 7, 1950. "Your Hit Parade" began as a radio show in 1935. When it finally made it to TV, the format was simple: the show's cast performed the week's top musical hits. To sustain interest, since many of the same songs appeared weekly, eye-catching production sequences were created. "YHP" was the starting point for many famous choreographers and dancers, including Peter Gennaro and Bob Fosse. Regulars included Dorothy Collins, Eileen Wilson, Snooky Lanson and Sue Bennett. The show was overhauled many times and switched networks before leaving the air in 1959. A summer revival in 1974 was short-lived. See also: "'Your Hit Parade' Radio Premiere: Anniversary" (Apr 12).

BIRTHDAYS TODAY

Shawn Ashmore, 35, actor (*X-Men: The Last Stand; X2*, "The Following"), born Richmond, BC, Canada, Oct 7, 1979.

Amiri Baraka, 80, poet, dramatist, born LeRoi Jones at Newark, NJ, Oct 7, 1934.

Joy Behar, 71, comedienne, television personality, born Brooklyn, NY, Oct 7, 1943.

Toni Braxton, 47, singer, born Severn, MD, Oct 7, 1967.

Simon Cowell, 55, television producer, personality ("American Idol"), born Brighton, East Sussex, England, Oct 7, 1959.

Charles Dutoit, 78, conductor, born Lausanne, Switzerland, Oct 7, 1936.

Thomas Keneally, 79, novelist (*Schindler's Ark, The Chant of Jimmie Blacksmith*), born New South Wales, Australia, Oct 7, 1935.

Yo-Yo Ma, 59, cellist, born Paris, France, Oct 7, 1955.

John Mellencamp, 63, singer, songwriter, born Seymour, IN, Oct 7, 1951.

Oliver Laurence North, 71, US Marine Corps lieutenant colonel (retired), born San Antonio, TX, Oct 7, 1943.

Vladimir Putin, 62, President of Russia, born Leningrad, USSR (now St. Petersburg, Russia), Oct 7, 1952.

Desmond Tutu, 83, South African archbishop, Nobel Peace Prize recipient, born Klerksdorp, South Africa, Oct 7, 1931.

October 2014

S	M	T	W	T	F	S
			1	2	3	4
5	6	7	8	9	10	11
12	13	14	15	16	17	18
19	20	21	22	23	24	25
26	27	28	29	30	31	

October 8 — Wednesday

DAY 281 **84 REMAINING**

ALVIN C. YORK DAY. Oct 8, 1918. While in the Argonne Forest, France, and separated from his patrol, Sergeant Alvin C. York killed 20 enemy soldiers and captured a hill, 132 enemy soldiers and 35 machine guns. He was awarded the US Medal of Honor and French Croix de Guerre. Ironically, York had petitioned for exemption from the draft as a conscientious objector but was turned down by his local draft board.

BATTLE OF PERRYVILLE: ANNIVERSARY. Oct 8, 1862. The most significant battle of the Civil War fought in Kentucky took place at Perryville on this date between Confederate forces led by General Braxton Bragg and Union forces under the command of General Don Carlos Bruell. Bruell's forces were victorious, and Bragg was forced to retreat southward. Casualties totaled more than 7,000 for both sides.

CROATIA: STATEHOOD DAY. Oct 8. Public holiday. Croatia's National Day.

EMERGENCY NURSES DAY. Oct 8. Sponsored by the Emergency Nurses Association (ENA) since 1989, this day serves to recognize emergency nurses for their dedication, service and commitment to their patients and communities. It honors nursing professionals who provide care to those whose lives have been touched by life's tragedies. Annually, the Wednesday of Emergency Nurses Week. For info: Emergency Nurses Assn Headquarters, 915 Lee St, Des Plaines, IL 60016-6569. Phone: (800) 900-9659. E-mail: pr@ena.org. Web: www.ena.org.

GERMANY: FRANKFURT BOOK FAIR. Oct 8–12. Fairgrounds, Frankfurt. World's largest international book fair; also important event for electronic media. Best place for international rights and licenses. Open to trade for three days and to the public for two. Est attendance: 280,000. For info: Frankfurt Book Fair, Braubachstr 16, 60311 Frankfurt am Main, Germany. Phone: (49) 69-2102-266. Fax: (49) 69-2102-227. E-mail: info@book-fair.com. Web: www.book-fair.com.

GREAT CHICAGO FIRE: ANNIVERSARY. Oct 8, 1871. Great fire of Chicago began, according to legend, when Mrs O'Leary's cow kicked over the lantern in her barn on DeKoven Street. The fire leveled 3½ square miles, destroying 17,450 buildings and leaving 98,500 people homeless and about 250 people dead. Financially, the loss was $200 million. On the same day a fire destroyed the entire town of Peshtigo, WI, killing more than 1,100 people.

HUNTER'S MOON. Oct 8. The full moon following Harvest Moon. So called because the moon's light in evening extends day's length for hunters. The October Full Moon.

INTERNATIONAL TOP SPINNING DAY. Oct 8. A free worldwide top celebration: The world is a large top, spinning on its axis. Spin a top or tops wherever you are in the world today to recognize this fun and scientific fact. Add your spins to the worldwide total and then e-mail the results to the sponsor, the Spinning Top & Yo-Yo Museum. Annually, the second Wednesday in October. For info: Spinning Top & Yo-Yo Museum, 533 Milwaukee Ave, Burlington, WI 53105. Phone: (262) 763-3946. E-mail: thetopmuseum@hotmail.com. Web: www.topmuseum.org.

LUNAR ECLIPSE. Oct 8. Total eclipse of the moon. Visible in Asia, Australia, the Pacific and the Americas.

MOON PHASE: FULL MOON. Oct 8. Moon enters Full Moon phase at 6:51 AM, EDT.

NATIONAL BRING YOUR TEDDY BEAR TO WORK DAY. Oct 8. A celebration and observation of the help and joy that teddy bears bring into the lives of people of all ages, at all stages. Annually, the second Wednesday in October. For info: Susan E. Schwartz, Teddies Are the Answer, 454 26th Ave, San Mateo, CA 94403. Phone: (650) 345-4944. E-mail: suwho@astound.net.

NATIONAL PIEROGY DAY. Oct 8. Celebration of the pierogy! Commemorates the day in 1952 that pierogies were first delivered to a grocery store in Shenandoah, PA—marking the emergence of the traditionally eastern European food as a mainstream American meal staple. Annually, Oct 8. For info: Mrs T's Pierogies, 600 E Center St, PO Box 606, Shenandoah, PA 17976. Phone: (570) 462-2745. Fax: (570) 462-3299. Web: www.pierogies.com.

NATIONAL STOP BULLYING DAY. Oct 8. Approximately 160,000 teens stay home from school every day because they fear for their safety. The self-esteem- and empathy-building international nonprofit organization Hey U.G.L.Y. (Unique Gifted Lovable You) has designated the second Wednesday in October (and the entire month of October) as a day and month for schools across America to conduct Stop Bullying classroom activities and school assembly presentations on how to eradicate bullying from schools and neighborhoods. For info and activity plans: Hey U.G.L.Y., Inc, PO Box 345, Rolling Prairie, IN 46371. Phone: (219) 778-2011. E-mail: preventbullyingnow@heyugly.org. Web: www.heyugly.org and preventbullyingnow.org.

OZZIE AND HARRIET RADIO DEBUT: 70th ANNIVERSARY. Oct 8, 1944. Ozzie and Harriet Nelson made their CBS Radio debut in "The Adventures of Ozzie and Harriet." Although their sons, David and Ricky, were referred to frequently on air and eventually played by others, it was not until Feb 20, 1949, that David (age 12) and Rick (age 8) first appeared playing themselves on the show. "The Adventures of Ozzie and Harriet" hit television airwaves Oct 3, 1952, on ABC.

PEKAR, HARVEY: 75th BIRTH ANNIVERSARY. Oct 8, 1939. Born at Cleveland, OH, this writer changed the face of American comic books with *American Splendor,* a semi-autobiographical look at the life of a cranky, depressed file clerk. The comics frankly depicted the mundane issues and irritations of life "off the streets of Cleveland." Pekar worked with many different artists on the series, including R. Crumb, and won an American Book Award in 1987 for his first anthology of collected strips. *American Splendor* was also adapted as a feature film in 2003. Pekar died at Cleveland Heights, OH, July 12, 2010.

PESHTIGO FOREST FIRE: ANNIVERSARY. Oct 8, 1871. One of the most disastrous forest fires in history began at Peshtigo, WI, the same day the Great Chicago Fire began. The Wisconsin fire burned across six counties, killing more than 1,100 people.

RICKENBACKER, EDWARD V.: BIRTH ANNIVERSARY. Oct 8, 1890. American auto racer, war hero and airline executive (Eastern Airlines). Dubbed "America's Ace of Aces" for his victories as a pilot in the 94th Aero Squadron during WWI. Recipient of the Congressional Medal of Honor, the Distinguished Service Medal and the French Croix de Guerre. Born at Columbus, OH, Rickenbacker died July 23, 1973, at Zurich, Switzerland.

SCHUTZ, HEINRICH: BIRTH ANNIVERSARY. Oct 8, 1585. German musician and composer sometimes called the father of German music. Born at Kostritz, Saxony, Schutz died at Dresden, Germany, Nov 6, 1672. His works enjoyed renewed attention on the occasions of the bicentennials (1885) and tricentennials (1985) of two of his most devoted followers: George Frederick Handel and Johann Sebastian Bach.

SOUTH CAROLINA STATE FAIR. Oct 8–19. Columbia, SC. North American Midway Entertainment (NAME), agricultural exhibits, rides, musical entertainment, food booths and children's activities. Est attendance: 500,000. For info: South Carolina State Fair, PO Box 393, Columbia, SC 29202. Phone: (803) 799-3387. Fax: (803) 799-1760. E-mail: geninfo@scstatefair.org. Web: www.scstatefair.org.

SUKKOT BEGINS AT SUNDOWN. Oct 8. Jewish Feast of Tabernacles. See "Sukkot" (Oct 9).

BIRTHDAYS TODAY

Rona Barrett, 78, gossip columnist, born New York, NY, Oct 8, 1936.

Chevy Chase, 71, comedian, actor ("Community," *Caddyshack*), born Cornelius Crane at New York, NY, Oct 8, 1943.

Clodagh, 77, designer, born Clodagh Aubry at Galway, Ireland, Oct 8, 1937.

Matt Damon, 44, actor (*The Departed, The Bourne Identity, Good Will Hunting*), born Cambridge, MA, Oct 8, 1970.

Bill Elliott, 59, race car driver, born Dawsonville, GA, Oct 8, 1955.

Darrell Hammond, 54, comedian, actor ("Saturday Night Live"), born Melbourne, FL, Oct 8, 1960.

Paul Hogan, 75, actor, writer (*Crocodile Dundee*), born Lightning Ridge, Australia, Oct 8, 1939.

Jesse Jackson, 73, clergyman, civil rights leader, born Greenville, NC, Oct 8, 1941.

Bruno Mars, 29, singer, born Peter Gene Hernandez at Honolulu, HI, Oct 8, 1985.

Michael "The Miz" Mizanin, 34, professional wrestler, born Parma, OH, Oct 8, 1980.

Sarah Purcell, 66, television personality ("Real People"), born Richmond, IN, Oct 8, 1948.

Faith Ringgold, 84, artist, writer (*Tar Beach, My Dream of Martin Luther King*), born New York, NY, Oct 8, 1930.

R.L. Stine, 71, author (Goosebumps series), born Columbus, OH, Oct 8, 1943.

Bella Thorne, 17, actress ("Shake It Up!"), born Pembroke Pines, FL, Oct 8, 1997.

Sigourney Weaver, 65, actress (*Ghostbusters, Gorillas in the Mist, Aliens*), born New York, NY, Oct 8, 1949.

October 2014	S	M	T	W	T	F	S
				1	2	3	4
	5	6	7	8	9	10	11
	12	13	14	15	16	17	18
	19	20	21	22	23	24	25
	26	27	28	29	30	31	

October 9 — Thursday

DAY 282 — **83 REMAINING**

AMERICAN DENTAL ASSOCIATION ANNUAL SESSION. Oct 9–14. Henry B. Gonzalez Convention Center, San Antonio, TX. 155th session. For info: American Dental Assn, 211 E Chicago Ave, Ste 200, Chicago, IL 60611. Phone: (847) 996-5876 or (800) 974-2925. E-mail: annualsession@ada.org. Web: www.ada.org.

BOK, EDWARD WILLIAM: BIRTH ANNIVERSARY. Oct 9, 1863. Influential magazine executive and editor, born at Den Helder, Netherlands. After immigrating with his family to Brooklyn, NY, Bok worked his way up in the magazine industry, eventually becoming editor of the *Ladies' Home Journal* from 1889 to 1919. He introduced journalistic innovations, championed social reforms (among them women's suffrage) and influenced contemporary culture. His position in society was such that by 1917 readers were sending his office one million letters a year. Bok died Jan 9, 1930, at Lake Wales, FL.

CHICAGO INTERNATIONAL FILM FESTIVAL. Oct 9–23. Chicago, IL. 50th annual. 175 films. 50 countries. 2 weeks. 1 city. North America's oldest competitive international film festival. Some of cinema's greatest filmmakers have been introduced at this festival. Gold and Silver Hugos awarded at its conclusion. For info: Chicago International Film Festival, 30 E Adams St, Ste 800, Chicago, IL 60603. Phone: (312) 683-0121. E-mail: info@chicagofilmfestival.com. Web: www.chicagofilmfestival.com.

DREYFUS, ALFRED: BIRTH ANNIVERSARY. Oct 9, 1859. This French army officer, born at Mulhouse, France, was the center of a military scandal from 1894 to 1906. From when he was accused of treason (forged documents were used to convict him) in 1894 and sentenced to life in 1895 at Devil's Island, the Dreyfus affair was a lightning rod for rival factions in France and exposed the virulent anti-Semitism in the country (Dreyfus was Jewish). The case was notable for the involvement of France's major literary figures in his defense, most famously Émile Zola, who published "J' Accuse" in 1898 in a periodical and accused the French army of a massive cover-up. Public outrage ensured two more trials for Dreyfus. He was still found guilty but was pardoned at his last trial in 1899. A 1906 civilian court finally cleared Dreyfus, who eventually returned to the military. He died July 12, 1935, at Paris, France.

ICELAND: LEIF ERIKSON DAY. Oct 9. Celebrates discovery of North America in the year 1000 by the Norse explorer.

KOREA: ALPHABET DAY (HANGUL). Oct 9. Celebrates anniversary of promulgation of Hangul (24-letter phonetic alphabet) by King Sejong of the Yi dynasty in 1446.

✦LEIF ERIKSON DAY. Oct 9. Presidential Proclamation always issued for Oct 9 since 1964 at request (PL 88–566 of Sept 2, 1964).

LENNON, JOHN: BIRTH ANNIVERSARY. Oct 9, 1940. John Winston Lennon, English composer, musician and member of The Beatles, the sensationally popular group of musical performers who captivated audiences first in England and Germany, and later throughout the world. A fervent activist for peace. Born at Liverpool, England, Lennon was murdered at New York City, Dec 8, 1980.

MISSION DELORES FOUNDING: ANNIVERSARY. Oct 9, 1776. The oldest building at San Francisco, CA. Formerly known as Mission San Francisco de Asis, the mission survived the great earthquake and fire of 1906.

PERU: DAY OF NATIONAL HONOR. Oct 9. Public holiday. Commemorates nationalization of the oil fields in 1968.

SPACE MILESTONE: NASA'S MOON CRASH: 5th ANNIVERSARY. Oct 9, 2009. On this date, NASA deliberately crashed two unmanned spacecrafts into the moon in an attempt to confirm the existence of water there. The impact sent a plume of debris more than a mile above the moon's surface, and water particles found in the plume confirmed NASA's suspicions.

SUKKOT, SUCCOTH or FEAST OF TABERNACLES. Oct 9–15. Hebrew calendar date: Tishri 15, 5775, begins seven-day festival in commemoration of Jewish people's 40 years of wandering in the desert and thanksgiving for the fall harvest. This High Holiday season closes with Shemini Atzeret (see entry on Oct 16) and Simchat Torah (see entry on Oct 17). Began at sundown Oct 8.

TATI, JACQUES: BIRTH ANNIVERSARY. Oct 9, 1908 (some sources say 1907). Born at Le Pecq, France, Tati was a filmmaker and performer who made internationally beloved comic masterpieces—often combining the best of silent comedy in films that depicted the Average Joe's misalliance with modern industrialized society. Tati's filmic alter ego was the pipe-smoking, rumpled hat-wearing Monsieur Hulot, who was always out of step wherever he was. Tati's six films include *Mr Hulot's Holiday* (1953), *Mon oncle* (*My Uncle,* 1958) and *Playtime* (1967). Tati died Nov 5, 1982, at Paris, France.

UGANDA: INDEPENDENCE DAY. Oct 9. National holiday commemorating achievement of autonomy from Britain in 1962.

UNITED NATIONS: WORLD POST DAY. Oct 9. An annual special observance of Postal Administrations of the Universal Postal Union (UPU). For info: United Nations, Dept of Public Info, Public Inquiries Unit, Rm GA-57, New York, NY 10017. Phone: (212) 963-4475. E-mail: inquiries@un.org. Web: www.un.org.

BIRTHDAYS TODAY

Scott Bakula, 60, actor ("Enterprise," "Quantum Leap"), born St. Louis, MO, Oct 9, 1954.

Jackson Browne, 64, singer, songwriter, born Heidelberg, Germany, Oct 9, 1950.

Zachery Ty Bryan, 33, actor ("Home Improvement"), born Aurora, CO, Oct 9, 1981.

David Cameron, 48, Prime Minister of Great Britain, born London, England, Oct 9, 1966.

Colin Donnell, 32, actor ("Arrow," "Pan Am"), born St. Louis, MO, Oct 9, 1982.

Paul LePage, 66, Governor of Maine (R), born Lewiston, ME, Oct 9, 1948.

Scotty McCreery, 21, country singer, television personality ("American Idol"), born Garner, NC, Oct 9, 1993.

Russell Myers, 76, cartoonist ("Broom Hilda"), born Pittsburg, KS, Oct 9, 1938.

Michael Pare, 55, actor (*Streets of Fire, The Philadelphia Experiment*), born Brooklyn, NY, Oct 9, 1959.

Joseph Anthony (Joe) Pepitone, 74, former baseball player, born New York, NY, Oct 9, 1940.

Brandon Routh, 35, actor ("One Life to Live," *Superman Returns*), born Des Moines, IA, Oct 9, 1979.

Tony Shalhoub, 61, actor (Emmys for "Monk"; "Wings," *Big Night*), born Green Bay, WI, Oct 9, 1953.

Donald Sinden, 91, actor (*The Day of the Jackal*), born Plymouth, England, Oct 9, 1923.

Michael (Mike) Singletary, 56, football coach and Hall of Fame player, born Houston, TX, Oct 9, 1958.

Annika Sorenstam, 44, former golfer, born Stockholm, Sweden, Oct 9, 1970.

Robert Wuhl, 63, writer, actor (*Bull Durham, Cobb*), born Union, NJ, Oct 9, 1951.

October 10 — Friday

DAY 283 **82 REMAINING**

AGNEW RESIGNATION: ANNIVERSARY. Oct 10, 1973. Spiro Theodore Agnew became the second person to resign the office of vice president of the US. Agnew entered a plea of no contest to a charge of income tax evasion (on contract kickbacks received while he was governor of Maryland and after he became vice president). He was sentenced to pay a $10,000 fine and serve three years' probation. Agnew was elected vice president twice, serving under President Richard M. Nixon. See also: "Agnew, Spiro: Birth Anniversary" (Nov 9).

ALGONQUIN MILL FALL FESTIVAL. Oct 10–12. Five miles south of Carrollton, OH. Presented by the Carroll County Historical Society. An 1800s pioneer festival featuring steam-powered gristmill and sawmill in operation. Also featured are antique tools and farm museum; antique cars and tractors; quilting, spinning, dyeing and weaving demonstrations; five log buildings (including a two-story home); musical entertainment and quality craftspeople selling their products. A one-room school and a railroad station are on exhibit. Est attendance: 20,000. For info: Carroll County CVB. Phone: (877) 727-0103. Web: www.carrollcountyohio.com/history.

APPLE BUTTER MAKIN' DAYS. Oct 10–12. Mount Vernon, MO. A large festival highlighting the making of apple butter in large copper kettles on the courthouse lawn. Also, 375 crafters displaying and selling handmade goods, free entertainment all three days, apple-pie-eating contest, hairy legs contest, log-sawing contest, bubble-gum-blowing contest, nail-driving contest, pet parade and terrapin race. Annually, the second full weekend in October. Est attendance: 60,000. For info: Mount Vernon Chamber of Commerce, PO Box 373, Mount Vernon, MO 65712. Phone: (417) 466-7654.

ARIZONA STATE FAIR. Oct 10–Nov 2 (tentative). Phoenix, AZ. Festival, concerts, entertainment and food. Closed Mondays and Tuesdays. For info: Arizona State Fair, 1826 W McDowell Rd, Phoenix, AZ 85007. Phone: (602) 252-6771. Fax: (602) 495-1302. E-mail: info@azstatefair.com. Web: www.azstatefair.com.

ARKANSAS STATE FAIR AND LIVESTOCK SHOW. Oct 10–19. Barton Coliseum and State Fairground, Little Rock, AR. Est attendance: 400,000. For info: Arkansas State Fair, 2600 Howard St, Little Rock, AR 72206. Phone: (501) 372-8341. Fax: (501) 372-4197. Web: www.arkansasstatefair.com.

"THE BOB NEWHART SHOW" TV PREMIERE: ANNIVERSARY. Oct 10, 1962. This half-hour variety series was hosted by Bob Newhart, a successful stand-up comedian famous for his trademark "telephone conversation" monologues. The show was critically acclaimed, winning both an Emmy and a Peabody in its short time on the air. Newhart later starred in situation comedies. In "The Bob Newhart Show," which aired 1972–78, he played a psychologist. See also: "'Newhart' TV Premiere: Anniversary" (Oct 25).

BONZA BOTTLER DAY™. Oct 10. To celebrate when the number of the day is the same as the number of the month. Bonza Bottler Day™ is an excuse to have a party at least once a month. For more information see Jan 1. For info: Gail Berger, 14 Fernwood Dr, Taylors, SC 29687. Phone: (864) 201-3988. E-mail: bonza@bonzabottlerday.com. Web: www.bonzabottlerday.com.

CANADA: KITCHENER-WATERLOO OKTOBERFEST. Oct 10–18. Kitchener and Waterloo, ON. The second-largest Oktoberfest in the world. More than 70 events and festhallen, including one of the premier parades in Canada on Canadian Thanksgiving morning. Est attendance: 700,000. For info: K-W Oktoberfest Inc, 17 Benton St, Kitchener, ON N2G 3G9, Canada. Phone: (519) 570-4267 or (888) 294-HANS. E-mail: info@oktoberfest.ca. Web: www.oktoberfest.ca.

COLUMBUS DAY FESTIVAL AND HOT-AIR BALLOON REGATTA. Oct 10–12. Columbus, KS. Regatta starts with Balloon Glow on Friday evening; prizes are awarded for both Saturday and Sunday races. Also, car show, arts and crafts fair, entertainment, children's festival and more. Est attendance: 15,000. For info: Columbus Chamber of Commerce, 320 E Maple, Columbus, KS 66725. Phone: (620) 429-1492. Fax: (620) 429-1492. E-mail: columbuschamber@columbus-ks.com. Web: www.columbus-kansas.com/chamber or www.columbusdayballoons.com.

CRAFTSMEN'S FALL CLASSIC ARTS & CRAFTS FESTIVAL. Oct 10–12. Roanoke Civic Center, Roanoke, VA. 27th annual. Features work from more than 250 talented artists and craftspeople. All juried exhibitors' work has been handmade by the exhibitors and must be their own original design and creation. See the creative process in action, with several exhibitors demonstrating throughout the weekend. Est attendance: 20,000. For info: Gilmore Enterprises, 3514-A Drawbridge Pkwy, Greensboro, NC 27410-8584. Phone: (336) 282-5550. E-mail: contact@gilmoreshows.com. Web: www.CraftShow.com or www.gilmoreshows.com.

CUBA: BEGINNING OF INDEPENDENCE WARS DAY. Oct 10. National holiday. Commemorates the beginning of Cuba's struggle against Spain in 1868.

DOUBLE TENTH DAY. Oct 10, 1911. Tenth day of 10th month, Double Tenth Day, is observed by many Chinese as the anniversary of the outbreak of the revolution against the imperial Manchu dynasty, Oct 10, 1911. Sun Yat-sen and Huan Hsing were among the revolutionary leaders. This is a holiday in Taiwan.

FALL VICTORIAN THEATRE. Oct 10–11 (also Oct 17–19). Benjamin Harrison Presidential Site, Indianapolis, IN. A progressive play through the rooms of the home of the 23rd president. Est attendance: 600. For info: Benjamin Harrison Presidential Site, 1230 N Delaware St, Indianapolis, IN 46202. Phone: (317) 631-1888. Fax: (317) 632-5488. E-mail: events@bhpsite.org. Web: www.bhpsite.org.

FORT LIGONIER DAYS. Oct 10–12. Ligonier, PA. Commemorates the Battle of Fort Ligonier (Oct 12, 1758). Reenactments, parade, outdoor entertainment, craft booths and food booths. Est attendance: 100,000. For info: Ligonier Chamber of Commerce, 120 E Main St, Ligonier, PA 15658. Phone: (724) 238-4200. Fax: (724) 238-4610. E-mail: office@ligonierchamber.com.

HAYES, HELEN: BIRTH ANNIVERSARY. Oct 10, 1900. Actress Helen Hayes, often called "the First Lady of the American Theater," was born at Washington, DC. Hayes's greatest stage triumph was her role as the long-lived British monarch Queen Victoria in the play *Victoria Regina*. Her first great success was in *Coquette* (1927). She won an Academy Award for Best Actress for her first major film role in *The Sin of Madelon Claudet* (1931) and won Best Supporting Actress for her role in *Airport* (1971). Helen Hayes died Mar 17, 1993, at Nyack, NY.

October 2014

S	M	T	W	T	F	S
			1	2	3	4
5	6	7	8	9	10	11
12	13	14	15	16	17	18
19	20	21	22	23	24	25
26	27	28	29	30	31	

MEDFORD JAZZ FESTIVAL. Oct 10–12. Medford, OR. Fourteen nationally known bands play in downtown Medford locations. More than 100 performances along with fun, food, dancing and music for all ages. Est attendance: 6,000. For info: Medford Jazz Festival, PMB 201, 221 N Central, Medford, OR 97501. Phone: (541) 770-6972 or (800) 599-0039. E-mail: info@medfordjazz.org. Web: www.medfordjazz.org.

MISSISSINEWA 1812. Oct 10–12. Marion, IN. Largest War of 1812 living-history event in US includes reenactment of battle. Military, trappers, woodland tribes, sutlers, artisans, food purveyors and musicians, living as they did 200 years ago. Est attendance: 30,000. For info: Mississinewa Battlefield Society, PO Box 1812, Marion, IN 46952. Phone: (800) 822-1812. Fax: (765) 662-1809. E-mail: info@mississinewa1812.com. Web: www.mississinewa1812.com.

NATIONAL HANDBAG DAY. Oct 10. 2nd annual. A day to celebrate the design, craftsmanship and fine materials that go into the thing we carry with us every day—the handbag. Everywhere you look, someone is carrying some kind of handbag—big, small, old, new, cheap or expensive. On the heels of New York Fashion Week, what better way to celebrate what you love to carry and why. Whether you have the newest "It Bag" like a Hermes Birkin or Celine Tote, or you carry your mother's vintage Louis Vuitton, or you have no idea what kind of bag you carry but you love it, use this day to share pictures and stories with other handbag fanatics. Annually, Oct 10. For info: Shannon Mahoney, PurseBlog, 261 Madison Ave, 9th Fl, New York, NY 10016. Phone: (614) 477-4397. E-mail: shannon@purseblog.com. Web: www.purseblog.com.

OCEAN COUNTY COLUMBUS DAY PARADE AND ITALIAN FESTIVAL. Oct 10–12. Seaside Heights, NJ. Parade features bands, floats, groups, organizations, antique cars and special performers from Italy. The festival features ethnic and traditional foods, entertainment, exhibits and performances from special guests. Est attendance: 80,000. For info: Ocean County Columbus Day Parade Committee, PO Box 1492, 500 Christopher Columbus Blvd, Seaside Heights, NJ 08751. Phone: (732) 477-6507. E-mail: info@ColumbusNJ.org. Web: www.ColumbusNJ.org.

OKLAHOMA HISTORICAL DAY. Oct 10. Oklahoma.

PEARL, DANIEL: BIRTH ANNIVERSARY. Oct 10, 1963. Born at Princeton, NJ, Pearl was a foreign correspondent for the *Wall Street Journal* when he was assassinated by a terrorist group in Pakistan. His body was found in Karachi, Pakistan, where he had been researching terrorist threats against America. British-born Islamic militant Ahmed Omar Sheikh, a leader of the National Movement for the Restoration of Pakistani Sovereignty, was convicted of Pearl's kidnapping and murder. Pearl was 38 at the time he was kidnapped, on Jan 23, 2002.

PINTER, HAROLD: BIRTH ANNIVERSARY. Oct 10, 1930. British playwright, actor and poet, born at East London, England, eponym of the dramatic term "Pinteresque." Known for such dark and absurd plays as *The Birthday Party, The Caretaker* and *The Homecoming*, described as "comedies of menace." The 2005 Nobel Prize for Literature went to Pinter, "who in his plays uncovers the precipice under everyday prattle and forces entry into oppression's closed rooms." In 2007 he received the French Legion of Honor. Pinter died Dec 24, 2008, at London.

ROCKPORT-FULTON SEAFAIR. Oct 10–12. Ski Basin area, Rockport and Fulton, TX. Features fresh-from-the-bay seafood, gumbo cook-off, ongoing live musical entertainment, crab races, arts and crafts booths and land parade on Saturday. Annually, Columbus Day weekend. Est attendance: 35,000. For info: Rockport-Fulton Seafair, 319 Broadway, Rockport, TX 78382. Phone: (800) 242-0071 or (361) 729-6445. E-mail: tourism@1rockport.org. Web: www.rockportseafair.com.

ST. CHARLES SCARECROW FEST. Oct 10–12. St. Charles, IL. More than 150 handcrafted scarecrows invade St. Charles along with live entertainment, carnival, children's activities, great food, huge craft show and much more. Annually, the weekend before Columbus Day. Est attendance: 150,000. For info: Greater St. Charles CVB, 311 N Second St, Ste 100, St. Charles, IL 60174. Phone: (800) 777-4373. Fax: (630) 513-0566. E-mail: info@scarecrowfest.com. Web: www.scarecrowfest.com.

SOUTHERN FESTIVAL OF BOOKS: A CELEBRATION OF THE WRITTEN WORD. Oct 10–12. War Memorial Plaza, Nashville, TN. The festival annually welcomes more than 200 authors from throughout the nation and in every genre for readings, panel discussions and book signings. The festival hosts popular book exhibitors and programs and features three performance stages throughout the event. Special events for children are planned throughout the weekend. Annually, the second full weekend in October. Est attendance: 20,000. For info: Southern Festival of Books, Humanities Tennessee, 306 Gay St, Ste 306, Nashville, TN 37201. Phone: (615) 770-0006. Fax: (615) 770-0007. E-mail: serenity@humanitiestennessee.org. Web: www.humanitiestennessee.org.

TAIWAN: DOUBLE TENTH DAY. Oct 10. Commemorates the proclamation of the Chinese Republic in 1911.

TAKE YOUR MEDICINE, AMERICANS WEEK. Oct 10–17. This campaign has been designed to help educate health professionals, patients and consumers about the problem of not taking prescription drugs or over-the-counter medicines. This is a $290 billion problem that needs a solution. For info: Fred S. Mayer, RPh, MPH, Pharmacists Planning Service, Inc (PPSI), PO Box 6760, San Rafael, CA 94903. Phone: (415) 479-8628 or (415) 302-7351. E-mail: ppsi@aol.com. Web: www.ppsinc.org.

TENNESSEE FALL HOMECOMING. Oct 10–12. Museum of Appalachia, Norris, TN. A celebration of the culture and heritage of Appalachian, pioneer, mountain and rural life. Five stages provide continuous musical performances by more than 400 old-time musicians and legendary greats. Scores of traditional mountain activities such as molasses making, rail splitting, soap making, basket making and sawmilling are demonstrated to help preserve the old ways in an interesting and educational manner. For info: Museum of Appalachia, 2819 Andersonville Hwy, Clinton, TN 37716. Phone: (865) 494-0514 or (865) 494-7680. E-mail: museum@museumofappalachia.org. Web: www.museumofappalachia.org.

TUXEDO CREATED: ANNIVERSARY. Oct 10, 1886. Griswold Lorillard of Tuxedo Park, NY, fashioned the first tuxedo for men by cutting the tails off a tailcoat.

UNITED NATIONS: WORLD MENTAL HEALTH DAY. Oct 10. For info: United Nations, Dept of Public Info, New York, NY 10017. Web: www.un.org.

"UPSTAIRS, DOWNSTAIRS" TV PREMIERE: ANNIVERSARY. Oct 10, 1971. The 52 episodes of this British series covered the years 1903–30 in the life of a wealthy London family ("Upstairs") and their many servants ("Downstairs"). Cast members included Angela Baddeley, Pauline Collins, Gordon Jackson and Jean Marsh. Won a Golden Globe for Best Drama TV Show in 1975 and an Emmy for Outstanding Limited Series in 1976. The last episode aired May 1, 1977. In 2010, the series was revived (without the comma in the title) for a few episodes set in 1936 with a new family occupying 165 Eaton Place but with Jean Marsh returning as Rose Buck.

US NAVAL ACADEMY FOUNDED: ANNIVERSARY. Oct 10, 1845. A college to train officers for the US Navy was established at Annapolis, MD. Women were admitted in 1976. The academy's motto is "Honor, Courage, Commitment." For info: www.usna.edu.

VERDI, GIUSEPPE: BIRTH ANNIVERSARY. Oct 10, 1813. Italian composer, born at Le Roncole, Italy. His 26 operas, including *Rigoletto, Il Trovatore, La Traviata* and *Aida*, are among the most popular of all operatic music today. Died at Milan, Italy, Jan 27, 1901.

BIRTHDAYS TODAY

Bob Burnquist, 38, skateboarder, born Rio de Janeiro, Brazil, Oct 10, 1976.

Charles Dance, 68, actor ("Game of Thrones," *The Jewel in the Crown, White Mischief*), born Worcestershire, England, Oct 10, 1946.

Dale Earnhardt, Jr, 40, race car driver, born Concord, NC, Oct 10, 1974.

Brett Favre, 45, former football player, born Gulfport, MS, Oct 10, 1969.

Jessica Harper, 65, actress (*Stardust Memories, Pennies from Heaven, My Favorite Year*), born Chicago, IL, Oct 10, 1949.

Mario Lopez, 41, talk show host, actor ("Saved by the Bell," "Pacific Blue"), born San Diego, CA, Oct 10, 1973.

Chris Pronger, 40, hockey player, born Dryden, ON, Canada, Oct 10, 1974.

Nora Roberts, 64, author (*Birthright, Hidden Riches, Rising Tides*), born Silver Spring, MD, Oct 10, 1950.

David Lee Roth, 59, singer (Van Halen), born Bloomington, IN, Oct 10, 1955.

Dan Stevens, 32, actor ("Downton Abbey," *Sense and Sensibility*), born Croydon, Surrey, England, Oct 10, 1982.

Tanya Tucker, 56, singer, born Seminole, TX, Oct 10, 1958.

Ben Vereen, 68, actor, singer, dancer (Tony for *Pippin*; *Roots, All That Jazz,* "Webster"), born Miami, FL, Oct 10, 1946.

October 11 — Saturday

DAY 284 | **81 REMAINING**

APPLE BUTTER FESTIVAL. Oct 11–12. Berkeley Springs, WV. Fall festival with spicy apple butter simmering in copper kettles in the town square. A parade, two days of mountain music and old-fashioned contests. Fine crafts, farmers market, down-home cooking and fall foliage. Annually, Columbus Day weekend. Est attendance: 40,000. For info: Apple Butter Festival, 127 Fairfax St, Berkeley Springs, WV 25411. Phone: (304) 258-9147. Web: www.berkeleysprings.com.

BLAKEY, ART: 95th BIRTH ANNIVERSARY. Oct 11, 1919. Born at Pittsburgh, PA, jazz musician Art Blakey recorded many albums with his group, the Jazz Messengers. Died at New York, NY, Oct 16, 1990.

CHINCOTEAGUE ISLAND OYSTER FESTIVAL. Oct 11. Maddox Family Campground, Chincoteague Island, VA. 42nd annual. An all-you-can-eat festival held to promote the seafood industry and mark the arrival of the oyster season. Oysters are prepared just about every way imaginable—and there are steamed crabs, clam fritters, clam chowder, hush puppies, potato salad, cole slaw, hot dogs and various beverages. Live entertainment for everyone's enjoyment. Held rain or shine. Tickets can be obtained in advance by contacting Chincoteague Chamber of Commerce. Tickets will sell out. Annually, Saturday of Columbus Day weekend. Est attendance: 2,700. For info: Chincoteague Chamber of Commerce, 6733 Maddox Blvd, Chincoteague Island, VA 23336. Phone: (757) 336-6161. Fax: (757) 336-1242. E-mail: chincochamber@verizon.net. Web: www.chincoteaguechamber.com.

CHOWDER DAYS. Oct 11–13. Mystic Seaport, Mystic, CT. A riverfront festival of New England chowders. Annually, Columbus Day weekend. Est attendance: 9,000. For info: Mystic Seaport, 75 Greenmanville Ave, PO Box 6000, Mystic, CT 06355-0990. Phone: (860) 572-0711 or (888) 973-2767. Web: www.mysticseaport.org.

✦GENERAL PULASKI MEMORIAL DAY. Oct 11. Presidential Proclamation always issued for Oct 11 since 1929. Requested by congressional resolution each year, 1929–1946. (Since 1947 has been issued by custom.) Note: Proclamation 4869, of Oct 5, 1981, covers all succeeding years.

HARVEST WEEKEND. Oct 11–12. Woodstock, VT. Traditional celebration of the harvest featuring a husking bee and barn dance. Also, farm harvest activities including food preservation, shelling corn and cider pressing. Est attendance: 1,600. For info: Billings Farm and Museum, Rte 12 N, Woodstock, VT 05091. GPS address: 69 Old River Rd, Woodstock, VT 05091. Phone: (802) 457-2355. Fax: (802) 457-4663. E-mail: info@billingsfarm.org. Web: www.billingsfarm.org.

LOUISIANA ART & FOLK FESTIVAL. Oct 11. Columbia, LA. Festival that centers on the rich folklife of Louisiana as well as on the fine arts. Wonderful music all day, craft booths, children's art and petting zoo as well as food to please everyone. Est attendance: 2,500. For info: Caldwell Parish Chamber of Commerce, PO Box 1808, Columbia, LA 71418. Phone: (318) 649-0726. E-mail: cpchamber60@yahoo.com.

MONSTER MYTHS BY MOONLIGHT. Oct 11. Milford State Park, Milford, KS. Learn the truth about spiders, snakes, bats, vultures, owls and other Halloween "monsters." Meet the real creatures as you walk the nature trail and learn the truth about them from witches, snake charmers and Little Red Riding Hood. Wear costumes. Cookies and cider served by Mother Nature. Sponsored by Friends of Milford Nature Center and State Park. Est attendance: 800. For info: Milford Nature Center, 3415 Hatchery Dr, Junction City, KS 66441. Phone: (785) 238-5323. Fax: (785) 238-5775. Web: www.kdwpt.state.ks.us.

MOUNTAIN GLORY FESTIVAL. Oct 11. Marion, NC. 31st annual. A celebration of mountain heritage in western North Carolina. Arts, crafts, children's area and continuous entertainment. Annually, the second Saturday in October. Est attendance: 20,000. For info: Mountain Glory Festival, PO Drawer 700, Marion, NC 28752. Phone: (828) 652-2215. Fax: (828) 652-1983. E-mail: info@mtngloryfestival.com. Web: www.mtngloryfestival.com.

NATIONAL COMING OUT DAY. Oct 11. A project of the Human Rights Campaign since 1988. Every Oct 11, thousands of lesbian, gay, bisexual and transgender (LGBT) individuals and their supportive allies celebrate National Coming Out Day, which encourages LGBT individuals to come out and be honest about themselves. Every year, workshops, speak-outs, rallies and other kinds of events are held—all aimed at showing the public that LGBT people are everywhere. For info: Human Rights Campaign, 1640 Rhode Island Ave NW, Washington, DC 20036. Phone: (800) 777-4723. E-mail: comingout@hrc.org. Web: www.hrc.org/comingout.

NORTHEAST MARBLE MEET. Oct 11–12. Marriott Courtyard, Marlborough, MA. Auction and exhibits; dealers and collectors buy, sell and trade marbles. Est attendance: 1,000. For info: Bert Cohen, 455 Clinton Rd, Brookline, MA 02467-1418. Phone: (617) 487-5808. E-mail: marblebert@aol.com.

PATENT ISSUED FOR FIRST ADDING MACHINE: ANNIVERSARY. Oct 11, 1887. A patent was granted to Dorr Eugene Felt for the Comptometer, which was the first adding machine known to be absolutely accurate at all times.

PINE BARRENS JAMBOREE. Oct 11. Wells Mills County Park, Waretown, NJ. Celebrate the culture and natural history of the New Jersey Pinelands. Live folk and country music, crafts, woodcarvers, live demonstrations, nature walks, canoeing, children's activities, animals, food and more. Includes exhibits featuring traditional industries of the Pinelands. Free; rain or shine. Est attendance: 2,000. For info: Wells Mills County Park, 905 Wells Mills Rd, Waretown, NJ 08758. Phone: (609) 971-3085. Fax: (609) 971-9540. Web: www.oceancountyparks.org.

★ ★ ★

October 2014

S	M	T	W	T	F	S
			1	2	3	4
5	6	7	8	9	10	11
12	13	14	15	16	17	18
19	20	21	22	23	24	25
26	27	28	29	30	31	

PRATER'S MILL COUNTRY FAIR. Oct 11–12. Dalton, GA. A Southern festival of artists, craftspeople, music and food. Est attendance: 10,000. For info: Prater's Mill Foundation, Inc, PO Drawer H, Varnell, GA 30756. Phone: (706) 694-MILL. Fax: (706) 694-8413. E-mail: PratersMill@PratersMill.org. Web: PratersMill.org.

PUNKIN CHUNKIN COLORADO. Oct 11. DeLaney Farm, Aurora, CO. Aurora's award-winning fall festival, featuring the Jack-o-Launch, family entertainment and practically every activity you can think of having to do with pumpkins. Annually, the second Saturday in October. Est attendance: 20,000. For info: City of Aurora, 15151 E Alameda Pkwy, Ste 4500, Aurora, CO 80012. Phone: (303) 739-7756. Fax: (303) 739-7191. Web: www.auroragov.org.

REVSON, CHARLES: BIRTH ANNIVERSARY. Oct 11, 1906. Revson, born at Boston, MA, was the colorful and hard-driving force behind Revlon cosmetics, a company he created in 1932. Revson was fond of saying, "Creative people are like a wet towel. You wring them out and pick up another one." By the time of his death, Aug 24, 1975, Revson had an estate valued at $100 million and a cosmetics empire.

ROBBINS, JEROME: BIRTH ANNIVERSARY. Oct 11, 1918. Choreographer and ballet dancer, born at New York, NY. Robbins choreographed several Broadway musicals including *Fiddler on the Roof, The King and I* and *On the Town.* He died at New York, NY, July 29, 1998.

ROBINSON, ROSCOE, JR: BIRTH ANNIVERSARY. Oct 11, 1928. The first black American to achieve the army rank of four-star general. Born at St. Louis, MO, and died at Washington, DC, July 22, 1993.

ROOSEVELT, ANNA ELEANOR: BIRTH ANNIVERSARY. Oct 11, 1884. Wife of Franklin Delano Roosevelt, 32nd president of the US, born at New York, NY. Eleanor Roosevelt led an active and independent life and was the first wife of a president to give her own news conference in the White House (1933). Widely known throughout the world, she was affectionately called "the first lady of the world." She served as US delegate to the United Nations General Assembly for a number of years before her death at New York, NY, Nov 7, 1962. A prolific writer, she wrote in *This Is My Story,* "No one can make you feel inferior without your consent."

"SATURDAY NIGHT LIVE" TV PREMIERE: ANNIVERSARY. Oct 11, 1975. Originally titled "NBC's Saturday Night," this live show features skits, commercial parodies and news satires, with a different guest host and musical guest performing weekly. Its first guest host was comedian George Carlin. Notable cast members have included Chevy Chase, Dan Aykroyd, John Belushi, Jane Curtin, Garrett Morris, Laraine Newman, Gilda Radner, Bill Murray, Joe Piscopo, Eddie Murphy, Billy Crystal, Martin Short, Christopher Guest, Harry Shearer, Joan Cusack, Robert Downey, Jr, Nora Dunn, Jon Lovitz, Dana Carvey, Phil Hartman, Jan Hooks, Dennis Miller, Chris Farley, Mike Myers, Adam Sandler, Will Ferrell, Molly Shannon, Tina Fey and Amy Poehler.

SCENIC DRIVE FESTIVAL. Oct 11–12. Van Buren County, IA. Scenic landscapes, historic architecture, flea market, arts festival, crafts and more. Annually, the second full weekend in October. Est attendance: 18,000. For info: Villages of Van Buren, Inc, PO Box 9, Keosauqua, IA 52565. Phone: (800) 868-7822. Fax: (319) 293-7116. E-mail: info@villagesofvanburen.com. Web: www.villagesofvanburen.com.

SIMON, JOE: BIRTH ANNIVERSARY. Oct 11, 1913. Artist Hymie "Joe" Simon was born Oct 11, 1913, at Rochester, NY. Working in New York City as comic books first flourished, Simon met artist Jack Kirby, and in 1941 the duo created superhero Captain America. Simon developed many other characters during this first comics Golden Age, and stayed active in the industry, serving as the first editor of the company that would become Marvel and creating notable additions to the romance and horror comic genres. In addition to his groundbreaking work in comics, Simon was also a talented commercial artist. He died Dec 14, 2011, at New York City.

SOUTHERN FOOD HERITAGE DAY. Oct 11. Join the Southern Food and Beverage Museum in celebrating Southern foods and drinks! Southern Food Heritage Day is the official day to pull out your cast iron pans and start up the smoker to enjoy your favorite Southern dishes, from cornbread to BBQ, from hoppin' john to shrimp and grits. Annually, Oct 11. For info: Southern Food and Beverage Museum. Phone: (504) 569-0405. Web: www.southernfood.org.

SPACE MILESTONE: *DISCOVERY STS-92*: 100th SHUTTLE FLIGHT. Oct 11, 2000. On this date, *Discovery* was launched on its 28th flight, marking the shuttle program's 100th mission. For this mission, the ship headed to the International Space Station, where it docked on Oct 13. On earlier flights, the shuttles *Columbia, Challenger, Endeavour, Atlantis* and *Discovery* had launched the Hubble Space Telescope and Chandra X-Ray Observatory, docked with the *Mir* space station and supported scientific research. The first shuttle flight took place in 1981. Since the first mission, space shuttles have carried 261 individuals and nearly three million pounds of payload, logging an estimated 350 million miles. See also: "Space Milestone: *Columbia STS-1*" (Apr 12).

STONE, HARLAN FISKE: BIRTH ANNIVERSARY. Oct 11, 1872. Former associate justice and later chief justice of the US who wrote more than 600 opinions and dissents for that court. Stone was born at Chesterfield, NH. He served on the Supreme Court from 1925 until his death, at Washington, DC, Apr 22, 1946.

UNIVERSAL MUSIC DAY. Oct 11. 8th annual. Music is our universal language; it's the bridge between head and heart—and from heart to heart. Celebrate music, musicians and music making from your heart. Annually, the second Saturday in October. For info: Susan Patricia Golden. E-mail: info@UniversalMusicDay.org. Web: www.UniversalMusicDay.org.

VATICAN COUNCIL II: ANNIVERSARY. Oct 11, 1962. The 21st ecumenical council of the Roman Catholic Church was convened by Pope John XXIII. It met in four annual sessions, concluding Dec 8, 1965. It dealt with the renewal of the Church and introduced sweeping changes, such as the use of the vernacular rather than Latin in the Mass.

WEEMS, PARSON (MASON LOCKE): BIRTH ANNIVERSARY. Oct 11, 1759. Mason Locke Weems was born at Anne Arundel County, MD. An Episcopal clergyman and traveling bookseller, Weems is remembered for the fictitious stories he presented as historical fact. Best known of his "fables" is the story describing George Washington cutting down his father's cherry tree with a hatchet. Weems's fictionalized histories, however, delighted many readers who accepted them as true. They became immensely popular and were bestsellers for many years. Weems died May 23, 1825, at Beaufort, SC.

WEST, DOTTIE: BIRTH ANNIVERSARY. Oct 11, 1932. American singer Dottie West was born at McMinnville, TN. In 1964 she won the first Grammy ever by a country vocalist for "Here Comes My Baby." She died Sept 4, 1991, at Nashville, TN.

BIRTHDAYS TODAY

Joan Cusack, 52, actress ("Shameless," *In & Out, Working Girl*), born Evanston, IL, Oct 11, 1962.

Emily Deschanel, 38, actress ("Bones"), born Los Angeles, CA, Oct 11, 1976.

Sean Patrick Flanery, 49, actor (*The Boondock Saints*, "Dexter"), born Lake Charles, LA, Oct 11, 1965.

Robert Gale, 69, physician, cofounder of the International Bone Marrow Registry, born Brooklyn Heights, NY, Oct 11, 1945.

Daryl Hall, 66, singer, musician (Hall and Oates), born Pottstown, PA, Oct 11, 1948.

Orlando "El Duque" Hernandez, 49, former baseball player, born Villa Clara, Cuba, Oct 11, 1965.

Jane Krakowski, 46, actress ("Ally McBeal," "30 Rock," Tony for *Nine*), born Parsippany, NJ, Oct 11, 1968.

Ron Leibman, 77, actor (*Norma Rae*; Tony for *Angels in America*), born New York, NY, Oct 11, 1937.

David Morse, 61, actor ("St. Elsewhere," *Proof of Life*), born Beverly, MA, Oct 11, 1953.

Stephen Moyer, 45, actor ("True Blood," "The Starter Wife"), born Brentwood, Essex, England, Oct 11, 1969.

Patty Murray, 64, US Senator (D, Washington), born Seattle, WA, Oct 11, 1950.

Luke Perry, 48, actor ("Beverly Hills 90210," *Buffy the Vampire Slayer*), born Fredericktown, MO, Oct 11, 1966.

Steve Young, 53, Hall of Fame football player, born Salt Lake City, UT, Oct 11, 1961.

October 12 — Sunday

DAY 285 **80 REMAINING**

BAHAMAS: DISCOVERY DAY. Oct 12. Commemorates the landing of Columbus in the Bahamas in 1492.

BALI TERRORIST BOMBING: ANNIVERSARY. Oct 12, 2002. Two bombs that were detonated in Kuta on the Indonesian island of Bali killed more than 200 people and injured hundreds. The bombs were placed at bars where vacationing tourists were known to gather. Although the terrorist group Al Qaeda claimed responsibility, suspects who later confessed to the crime stated that they were working independently.

BANK OF AMERICA CHICAGO MARATHON. Oct 12. Grant Park, Chicago, IL. Flat, fast 26.2-mile course attracts everyone from elite athletes to novice marathon runners from all 50 states and more than 120 foreign countries. Annually, the Sunday of Columbus Day weekend. Est attendance: 850,000. For info: Bank of America Chicago Marathon, 135 S LaSalle St, Ste 1160, MC: IL4-135-11-61, Chicago, IL 60603. Phone: (312) 904-9800. Fax: (312) 904-9820. E-mail: office@chicagomarathon.com. Web: www.chicagomarathon.com.

BELIZE: COLUMBUS DAY. Oct 12. Public holiday.

"THE BOB HOPE SHOW" TV PREMIERE: ANNIVERSARY. Oct 12, 1953. Premier funnyman, well-known and well-loved Bob Hope made monthly appearances on TV in the 1950s. During the first season, he hosted "The Colgate Comedy Hour," and during the later seasons, his show was seen replacing and then alternating with Milton Berle (and in 1955–56 with Martha Raye and Dinah Shore). Leo Robin and Ralph Rainger wrote Hope's trademark show-closing song, "Thanks for the Memory."

BOER WAR: ANNIVERSARY. Oct 12, 1899. The Boers of the Transvaal and Orange Free State in southern Africa declared war on the British. The Boer states were annexed by Britain in 1900, but guerrilla warfare on the part of the Boers caused the war to drag on. It finally ended May 31, 1902, by the Treaty of Vereeniging.

BRAZIL: CIRIO DE NAZARE. Oct 12–25. Belem, Para. Greatest festival of northern Brazil, the Feast of Cirio starts on the second Sunday in October in the city of Belem (St. Mary of Bethlehem), capital of the state of Para. Festival lasts two weeks.

BURGOO FESTIVAL. Oct 12. Downtown, North Utica, IL. Only the "Burgoomeister" knows the secret recipe for this pioneer stew, burgoo, served outdoors at this annual Utica festival. Other events include arts and crafts, antiques, food and music. Free admission. Annually, the Sunday of Columbus Day weekend. Est attendance: 30,000. For info: Burgoo Chairman, LaSalle County Historical Museum, 101 Canal St., Utica, IL 61373. Phone: (815) 667-4861. E-mail: office.lchs@gmail.com. Web: www.lasallecountymuseum.org.

"THE BURNS AND ALLEN SHOW" TV PREMIERE: ANNIVERSARY. Oct 12, 1950. The comedic husband-and-wife duo of George Burns and Gracie Allen starred as themselves in this comedy series in which Burns was the straight man and Allen was known for her ditziness. The show employed the technique of speaking directly to the camera ("breaking the fourth wall"); Burns often commented on the plot, told jokes or tried to make sense of Allen's actions and statements. Also on the show were their real-life son, Ronnie Burns; Bea Benaderet; Hal March; John Brown (until blacklisted by McCarthyites in the "red scare"); Fred Clark; Larry Keating; Bill Goodwin and Harry Von Zell. The show was done live for the first two seasons and included vaudeville scenes at the end of each episode.

COLUMBUS DAY (TRADITIONAL). Oct 12. Public holiday in most countries in the Americas and in most Spanish-speaking countries. Observed under different names (Dia de la Raza or Day of the Race) and on different dates (most often, as in US, on the second Monday in October). Anniversary of Christopher Columbus's arrival, Oct 12, 1492, after a voyage across "shoreless Seas," at the Bahamas (probably the island of Guanahani), which he renamed El Salvador and claimed in the name of the Spanish crown. See also: "Columbus Day Observance" (Oct 13).

DAY OF THE SIX BILLION: 15th ANNIVERSARY. Oct 12, 1999. According to the United Nations, the population of the world reached six billion on this date. More than one-third of the world's people live in China and India. It wasn't until 1804 that the world's population reached one billion; now a billion people are added to the population about every 12 years. See also: "Day of the Five Billion: Anniversary" (July 11).

EQUATORIAL GUINEA: INDEPENDENCE DAY. Oct 12. National holiday. Gained independence from Spain in 1968.

FREETHOUGHT DAY. Oct 12. During the Month of Freethought, Freethought "Coming Out" Day is an annual day of celebration that gives those freethinkers who have been unable to proudly declare themselves a platform from which to do so. On Oct 12, newly declared freethinkers can gain strength and support from fellow "open" freethinkers. For info: American Humanist Assn, 1777 T St NW, Washington, DC 20009. Phone: (202) 238-9088. Fax: (202) 238-9003. Web: www.secularseasons.org/October/Freethought_day.html.

GETTING THE WORLD TO BEAT A PATH TO YOUR DOOR WEEK. Oct 12–18. To focus attention on improving "public relationships" in order to create success for companies, products and individuals. Free self-evaluation available. For info: Gaughen Global Public Relations, 7456 Evergreen Dr, Santa Barbara, CA 93117. Phone: (805) 968-8567. E-mail: bgaughenmu@aol.com.

GORDONE, CHARLES: BIRTH ANNIVERSARY. Oct 12, 1925. First black playwright to win the Pulitzer Prize for Drama. He won it for his play *No Place to Be Somebody.* Born at Cleveland, OH. Died Nov 17, 1995, at College Station, TX.

GRANDMOTHER'S DAY IN FLORIDA. Oct 12. A ceremonial day on the second Sunday in October.

INTERNATIONAL MOMENT OF FRUSTRATION SCREAM DAY. Oct 12. To share any or all of our frustrations, all citizens of the world will go outdoors at 1200 hours Greenwich time and scream for 30 seconds. We will all feel better or Earth will go off its orbit. Annually, Oct 12. (©2006 by WH.) For info: Thomas & Ruth Roy, Wellcat Holidays, 2418 Long Ln, Lebanon, PA 17046. Phone: (717) 279-0184. E-mail: info@wellcat.com. Web: www.wellcat.com.

LEIF ERICSON DAY CELEBRATION. Oct 12. Statue of Thorfin Karlsefne, Philadelphia, PA. Celebration honoring the first European to set foot on the North American continent. Event also seeks to promote knowledge about and a realistic historic image of the Viking people as merchants, navigators, shipbuilders, artists, explorers and warriors. Sponsored by the Leif Ericson Viking Ship, Inc, and the Leif Ericson Society. Annually, the Sunday nearest Oct 9. For info: Leif Ericson Viking Ship, Inc, PO Box 393, Swarthmore, PA 19081-0393. Phone: (410) 275-8516. E-mail: info@vikingship.org or events@vikingship.org. Web: www.vikingship.org.

McNAIR, RONALD E.: BIRTH ANNIVERSARY. Oct 12, 1950. Ronald E. McNair, a 35-year-old physicist, was the second black American astronaut in space (February 1984). He was born at Lake City, SC. As mission specialist for the crew, he perished in the space shuttle *Challenger* explosion Jan 28, 1986. See also: "*Challenger* Space Shuttle Explosion: Anniversary" (Jan 28).

MEXICO: DIA DE LA RAZA. Oct 12. "Day of the Race" commemorates the discovery of America as well as the common interests and cultural heritage of the Spanish and Indian peoples and the Hispanic nations.

NATIONAL CHESTNUT WEEK. Oct 12–18. A celebration of the chestnut throughout the US. Events include farm visits, chestnut roasts, grower displays and more. Annually, the second full week in October. For info: Ray Young, PO Box 841, Ridgefield, WA 98642. Phone: (360) 887-3669. E-mail: Ray@ChestnutsOnLine.com. Web: www.wcga.net.

NATIONAL FOOD BANK WEEK. Oct 12–18. Educates and recognizes efforts of food banks, their donors and volunteers to alleviate hunger in the US. Observed at local food banks around the country. Annually, the week encompassing World Food Day (Oct 16). For information on activities in your area, go to Feeding America's website at www.feedingamerica.org and do a zip code search.

PAVAROTTI, LUCIANO: BIRTH ANNIVERSARY. Oct 12, 1935. Born at Modena, Italy, Pavarotti made opera accessible for a wide audience. The most popular tenor of his time, he was known for his perfect tone, especially in the highest ranges. A regular performer at the Metropolitan Opera House in New York City for decades, he brought his music to a wider audience in the 1980s and '90s by performing as one of the Three Tenors. He, along with Plácido Domingo and José Carreras, crossed into mainstream pop music with television appearances and nationwide tours and sold millions of records. A philanthropist, Pavarotti was active in raising funding and awareness for many humanitarian causes. Widely considered to be the best bel canto singer of the 20th century, he died at Modena Sept 6, 2007.

October 2014	S	M	T	W	T	F	S
				1	2	3	4
	5	6	7	8	9	10	11
	12	13	14	15	16	17	18
	19	20	21	22	23	24	25
	26	27	28	29	30	31	

SAMOA AND AMERICAN SAMOA: WHITE SUNDAY. Oct 12. The second Sunday in October. For the children of Samoa and American Samoa, this is the biggest day of the year. Traditional roles are reversed, as children lead church services, are served special foods and receive gifts of new church clothes and other special items. All the children dress in white. The following Monday is an official holiday.

SHAPING BLACK CULTURE IN THE DIASPORA. Oct 12. Leimert Park Village, Los Angeles, CA. A conference to address the urban culture core and its creative sector's "best practices" for the health and long-term sustainability of black cultural expression of the African diaspora locally, nationally and internationally. The conference, sponsored by Arts Culture Entertainment and African Diaspora Creative Industries, offers panels, speakers, conference planning sessions and closing-night festivities for participants and attendees. International African Diaspora Day is part of the observance. Est attendance: 1,500. For info: Ernest Dillihay, Arts Culture Entertainment. Phone: (626) 345-1864. E-mail: info@artscultureentertainment.com.

SPAIN: NATIONAL HOLIDAY. Oct 12. Called Hispanity Day or Day of Spanish Consciousness. Honors Christopher Columbus and the Spanish conquerors of Latin America.

TEEN READ WEEK™. Oct 12–18. The teen years are a time when many young adults reject reading as being just another dreary assignment. The goal of Teen Read Week is to encourage young adults to read for the fun of it and to remind parents, teachers, booksellers and others that reading for fun is important for teens. This week also seeks to increase awareness of the many library resources available. Thousands of school and public libraries across the US participate each year. For info: Young Adult Library Services Assn, American Library Assn, 50 E Huron St, Chicago, IL 60611. Phone: (800) 545-2433, ext 4390. E-mail: yalsa@ala.org. Web: www.ala.org/teenread.

TRUMBULL, JONATHAN: BIRTH ANNIVERSARY. Oct 12, 1710. American patriot, counselor and friend of George Washington, governor of Connecticut Colony, born at Lebanon, CT. Died there, Aug 17, 1785.

VAUGHAN WILLIAMS, RALPH: BIRTH ANNIVERSARY. Oct 12, 1872. Composer and conductor Ralph Vaughan Williams was born at Down Ampney, Gloucestershire, England. He is considered England's first great truly national composer, having rooted "modern" composition techniques in traditional English folk and Tudor music and themes to create a uniquely English style. Among his many works are nine symphonies, church and choral music, film and stage music and several operas. His major compositions include the *Mass in G Minor* and the opera *The Pilgrim's Progress*. He died Aug 26, 1958, at London.

WORLD RAINFOREST WEEK. Oct 12–18. Rain forest activists worldwide sponsor events to increase public awareness of rain forest destruction and motivate people to protect Earth's rain forests and support the rights of their inhabitants. The global rate of rain forest destruction is 2.4 acres per second—equivalent to two US football fields. For info: Rainforest Action Network, 425 Bush St, Ste 300, San Francisco, CA 94108. Phone: (415) 398-4404. E-mail: info@ran.org. Web: www.ran.org.

BIRTHDAYS TODAY

Susan Anton, 64, singer, actress (*Goldengirl*), born Yucaipa, CA, Oct 12, 1950.

Carlos Bernard, 52, actor ("24"), born Evanston, IL, Oct 12, 1962.

Kirk Cameron, 44, actor ("Growing Pains," "Kirk"), born Panorama City, CA, Oct 12, 1970.

Dick Gregory, 82, comedian, author, activist, born St. Louis, MO, Oct 12, 1932.

Josh Hutcherson, 22, actor (*The Hunger Games, The Kids Are All Right*), born Union, KY, Oct 12, 1992.

Hugh Jackman, 46, actor (*Les Misérables, The Prestige, X-Men, X2*), born Sydney, Australia, Oct 12, 1968.

Marion Jones, 39, former track athlete, born Los Angeles, CA, Oct 12, 1975.

Anthony Christopher (Tony) Kubek, 78, sportscaster, former baseball player, born Milwaukee, WI, Oct 12, 1936.

Jean Nidetch, 91, founder of Weight Watchers, born Brooklyn, NY, Oct 12, 1923.

Adam Rich, 46, actor ("Eight Is Enough"), born Brooklyn, NY, Oct 12, 1968.

Chris Wallace, 67, broadcaster ("Dateline"), White House correspondent, born Chicago, IL, Oct 12, 1947.

October 13 — Monday

DAY 286 **79 REMAINING**

AMERICAN INDIAN HERITAGE DAY (ALABAMA). Oct 13. First declared in 2000, this state holiday is also observed as Columbus Day in Alabama. Annually, the second Monday in October.

BROWN, JESSE LEROY: BIRTH ANNIVERSARY. Oct 13, 1926. Born at Hattiesburg, MS, Jesse Leroy Brown was the first black American naval aviator and also the first black naval officer to lose his life in combat when he was shot down over Korea, Dec 4, 1950. He was posthumously awarded the Distinguished Flying Cross. On Mar 18, 1972, USS *Jesse L. Brown* was launched as the first ship to be named in honor of a black naval officer (decommissioned in 1994).

BRUCE, LENNY: BIRTH ANNIVERSARY. Oct 13, 1925. Born Leonard Alfred Schneider at New York, NY, Lenny Bruce was an innovative, hip and searing stand-up comedian whose material touched on adult themes. His satiric and sometimes shocking routines gained him the wrath of public officials, and he was arrested multiple times on obscenity charges. His trials became celebrated calls to arms to protect First Amendment rights. By the time of his death by morphine overdose on Aug 3, 1966, at Hollywood Hills, CA, Bruce was banned in many US cities, Australia and England, and from comedy clubs that feared legal action.

BURUNDI: ASSASSINATION OF THE HERO OF THE NATION DAY. Oct 13. National holiday. Commemorates the assassination of Prince Louis Rwagasore in 1961.

CANADA: THANKSGIVING DAY. Oct 13. Observed on second Monday in October each year.

✦COLUMBUS DAY. Oct 13. Presidential Proclamation always the second Monday in October. Observed on Oct 12 from 1934 to 1970 (Pub Res No. 21 of Apr 30, 1934). Public Law 90–363 of June 28, 1968, required that beginning in 1971 it would be observed on the second Monday in October.

COLUMBUS DAY OBSERVANCE. Oct 13. Public Law 90–363 sets observance of Columbus Day on the second Monday in October. Applicable to federal employees and to the District of Columbia, but observed also in most states. Commemorates the landfall of Columbus in the New World, Oct 12, 1492. See also: "Columbus Day (Traditional)" (Oct 12).

DISCOVERERS' DAY IN HAWAII. Oct 13. Honors all discoverers, including Pacific and Polynesian navigators. Second Monday in October.

FIJI: INDEPENDENCE DAY. Oct 13. National holiday. Observed on the second Monday in October to commemorate Fiji's declaration of independence from Britain on Oct 10, 1970.

JAPAN: HEALTH-SPORTS DAY. Oct 13. National holiday to encourage physical activity for building a sound body and mind. Created in 1966 to commemorate the day of the opening of the 18th Olympic Games at Tokyo, Oct 10, 1964. Annually, the second Monday in October.

MONTAND, YVES: BIRTH ANNIVERSARY. Oct 13, 1921. French actor Yves Montand was born Ivo Livi at Monsummano Alto, Italy. His career was successful in both France and America, including more than 50 films. He died Nov 9, 1991, at Senlis, France.

NATIONAL KICK-BUTT DAY. Oct 13. On this day we commit to kicking ourselves in the butt to take action on goals we've set and not achieved, actions we've committed to and not taken, promises we've made and not kept, excuses we've created that have us stalled and difficulties we've faced and not overcome. This is the day we get our butts in gear and move forward in our lives. No butts about it! Annually, the second Monday in October. For info: Sylvia Henderson, Springboard Training, PO Box 588, Olney, MD 20830-0588. Phone: (301) 260-1538. E-mail: sylvia@springboardtraining.com.

✦NATIONAL SCHOOL LUNCH WEEK. Oct 13–17. Presidential Proclamation issued for the week beginning with the second Sunday in October since 1962 (PL 87–780 of Oct 9, 1962). Note: Not issued in 1981.

NATIONAL SCHOOL LUNCH WEEK. Oct 13–17. To celebrate good nutrition and healthy, safe school lunches. Created in 1962 by President John F. Kennedy. Annually, the second full week in October. For info: School Nutrition Assn, 120 Waterfront St, Ste 300, National Harbor, MD 20745. Phone: (301) 686-3100. Fax: (301) 686-3115. E-mail: servicecenter@schoolnutrition.org. Web: www.schoolnutrition.org.

NATIVE AMERICANS' DAY (SOUTH DAKOTA). Oct 13. Observed in the state of South Dakota as a legal holiday, dedicated to the remembrance of the great Native American leaders who contributed so much to the history of South Dakota. Annually, the second Monday in October.

NAVY BIRTHDAY. Oct 13. Since 1972 a navywide celebration (for members of the active forces and reserves, as well as retirees and dependents) recognizing the authorization of the Continental Navy on this date in 1775. The celebration is meant "to enhance a greater appreciation of [the] Navy heritage and to provide a positive influence toward pride and professionalism in the naval service." See also: "US Navy: Authorization Anniversary" (Oct 13). For info: www.history.navy.mil.

October 2014	S	M	T	W	T	F	S
				1	2	3	4
	5	6	7	8	9	10	11
	12	13	14	15	16	17	18
	19	20	21	22	23	24	25
	26	27	28	29	30	31	

PITCHER, MOLLY: BIRTH ANNIVERSARY. Oct 13, 1754. "Molly Pitcher," heroine of the American Revolution, was a water carrier at the Battle of Monmouth (June 28, 1778), where she distinguished herself by loading and firing a cannon after her husband, William Hays, was wounded. Affectionately known as "Sergeant Molly" after General Washington issued her a warrant as a noncommissioned officer. Her real name was Mary Hays McCauley (née Ludwig). Born near Trenton, NJ, she died at Carlisle, PA, Jan 22, 1832.

SAINT EDWARD, THE CONFESSOR: FEAST DAY. Oct 13. King of England, 1042–66, Edward was the son of King Ethelred the Unready. Born at Islip, England, in 1003, he died Jan 5, 1066, at London. On Oct 13, 1163, his remains were transported in a ceremony that was of national interest. Since then Oct 13 has been observed as his principal feast day.

THATCHER, MARGARET HILDA ROBERTS: BIRTH ANNIVERSARY. Oct 13, 1925. First woman prime minister in 700 years of English parliamentary history. Election of May 3, 1979, gave the Conservative Party victory, and Thatcher accepted Queen Elizabeth's appointment as prime minister on May 4. She held the office until forced to resign on Nov 22, 1990. She was given a life peerage as Baroness Thatcher of Kesteven, June 5, 1992, a position that entitled her to a seat in the House of Lords, where she remained an active Tory voice. Born Margaret Hilda Roberts at Grantham, Lincolnshire, England, Thatcher died Apr 8, 2013, at London, England.

UNITED NATIONS: INTERNATIONAL DAY FOR DISASTER REDUCTION. Oct 13. The General Assembly made this designation for Oct 13 each year as part of its efforts to foster international cooperation in reducing loss of life, property damage and social and economic disruption caused by natural disasters. For info: United Nations, Dept of Public Info, New York, NY 10017. Web: www.un.org.

US NAVY: AUTHORIZATION ANNIVERSARY. Oct 13, 1775. Commemorates legislation passed by Second Continental Congress authorizing the acquisition of ships and establishment of a navy.

VIRCHOW, RUDOLF: BIRTH ANNIVERSARY. Oct 13, 1821. German political leader, scientist, teacher and author. Called "the founder of cellular pathology." Born at Schivelbein, Prussia; died at Berlin, Germany, Sept 5, 1902.

VIRGIN ISLANDS–PUERTO RICO FRIENDSHIP DAY. Oct 13. Columbus Day (second Monday in October) also celebrates historical friendship between peoples of Virgin Islands and Puerto Rico.

WHITE HOUSE CORNERSTONE LAID: ANNIVERSARY. Oct 13, 1792. The presidential residence at 1600 Pennsylvania Avenue NW, Washington, DC, designed by James Hoban, observes its birthday Oct 13. The cornerstone was laid; the first presidential family to occupy the building was that of John Adams, in November 1800. With three stories and more than 100 rooms, the White House is the oldest building at Washington. First described as the "presidential palace," it acquired the name "White House" about 10 years after construction was completed. Burned by British troops in 1814, it was reconstructed, refurbished and reoccupied by 1817.

YORKTOWN VICTORY DAY. Oct 13. Observed as a holiday in Virginia. Annually, the second Monday in October. Commemorates the Revolutionary War battle fought in 1781.

BIRTHDAYS TODAY

Ashanti, 34, singer, actress (*The Muppets' Wizard of Oz*), born Ashanti Sequoiah Douglas at Long Island, NY, Oct 13, 1980.

Maria Cantwell, 56, US Senator (D, Washington), born Indianapolis, IN, Oct 13, 1958.

Chris Carter, 57, producer, screenwriter ("The X-Files"), born Bellflower, CA, Oct 13, 1957.

Sacha Baron Cohen, 43, comedian, actor ("Da Ali G Show," *Borat*), born London, England, Oct 13, 1971.

Melinda Dillon, 75, actress (*Close Encounters of the Third Kind, A Christmas Story*), born Hope, AR, Oct 13, 1939.

Sammy Hagar, 65, singer, musician, born Monterrey, CA, Oct 13, 1949.

Nancy Kerrigan, 45, former figure skater, born Woburn, MA, Oct 13, 1969.

Jermaine O'Neal, 36, basketball player, born Columbia, SC, Oct 13, 1978.

Marie Osmond, 55, actress, singer, born Ogden, UT, Oct 13, 1959.

Paul Pierce, 37, basketball player, born Oakland, CA, Oct 13, 1977.

Kelly Preston, 52, actress (*Christine, Twins*), born Honolulu, HI, Oct 13, 1962.

Jerry Rice, 52, Hall of Fame football player, born Starkville, MS, Oct 13, 1962.

Glenn Anton "Doc" Rivers, 53, basketball coach and former player, born Maywood, IL, Oct 13, 1961.

Paul Simon, 73, singer (Simon and Garfunkel), musician, born Newark, NJ, Oct 13, 1941.

Pamela Tiffin, 72, actress (*Harper*; stage: *Dinner at Eight*), born Oklahoma City, OK, Oct 13, 1942.

Kate Walsh, 47, actress ("Grey's Anatomy," "The Drew Carey Show"), born San Jose, CA, Oct 13, 1967.

October 14 — Tuesday

DAY 287 **78 REMAINING**

BATTLE OF HASTINGS: ANNIVERSARY. Oct 14, 1066. The Anglo-Saxon age came to an end with the death of King Harold Godwinson and the defeat of English forces by Norman invaders at Hastings on this day. William, Duke of Normandy, led the daring invasion and was crowned King of England on Dec 25, 1066.

BE BALD AND BE FREE DAY. Oct 14. For those who are bald and who either do wear or do not wear a wig or toupee, this is the day to go "shiny" and be proud. Annually, Oct 14. (©2006 by WH.) For info: Thomas & Ruth Roy, Wellcat Holidays, 2418 Long Ln, Lebanon, PA 17046. Phone: (717) 279-0184. E-mail: info@wellcat.com. Web: www.wellcat.com.

DE VALERA, EAMON: BIRTH ANNIVERSARY. Oct 14, 1882. Irish statesman, born at New York, NY. A revolutionary who survived the Easter Rising in 1916, De Valera went on to found the Fianna Fáil political party, which came to power in 1932 and by 1937 was successful in declaring the Free State of Ireland. As leader of Fianna Fáil, De Valera served as Ireland's prime minister three times and as president from 1959 to 1973. He died Aug 29, 1975, at Dublin, Ireland.

EISENHOWER, DWIGHT DAVID: BIRTH ANNIVERSARY. Oct 14, 1890. The 34th president of the US, Dwight David Eisenhower, was born at Denison, TX. Serving two terms as president, Jan 20, 1953–Jan 20, 1961, Eisenhower was the first president to be baptized after taking office (Sunday, Feb 1, 1953). Nicknamed "Ike," he held the rank of five-star general of the US Army (resigned in 1952, and restored by act of Congress in 1961). He served as supreme commander of the Allied forces in western Europe during WWII. In his Farewell Address (Jan 17, 1961), speaking about the "conjunction of an immense military establishment and a large arms industry," he warned: "In the councils of government, we must guard against the acquisition of unwarranted influence, whether sought or unsought, by the military-industrial complex. The potential for the disastrous rise of misplaced power exists and will persist." An American hero, Eisenhower died at Washington, DC, Mar 28, 1969.

FODOR, EUGENE: BIRTH ANNIVERSARY. Oct 14, 1905. Travel writer Eugene Fodor was born at Leva, Hungary. His first travel book was published in 1936, after which he published more than 140, bringing to them a human element previously lacking in travel books. He died Feb 18, 1991, at Torrington, CT.

GISH, LILLIAN: BIRTH ANNIVERSARY. Oct 14, 1893. American actress Lillian Diana Gish was born at Springfield, OH. Her film and stage career spanned more than 85 years, 100 films, the silent and sound eras of film and numerous stage productions. She was awarded an honorary Oscar in 1970 and made her last film appearance in *The Whales of August* (1987). She died Feb 27, 1993, at New York, NY.

JAPAN: MEGA KENKA MATSURI or ROUGHHOUSE FESTIVAL. Oct 14–15. Himeji. Palanquin bearers jostle one another to demonstrate their skill and balance in handling their burdens.

KING AWARDED NOBEL PEACE PRIZE: 50th ANNIVERSARY. Oct 14, 1964. Martin Luther King, Jr, became the youngest recipient of the Nobel Peace Prize on this date. King donated all of the prize money ($54,000) to furthering the causes of the civil rights movement.

LEE, FRANCIS LIGHTFOOT: BIRTH ANNIVERSARY. Oct 14, 1734. Signer of the Declaration of Independence. Born at Westmoreland County, VA, he died Jan 11, 1797, at Richmond County, VA.

MANSFIELD, KATHERINE: BIRTH ANNIVERSARY. Oct 14, 1888. Influential modernist author of short stories, born Katherine Mansfield Beauchamp at Wellington, New Zealand. Her collections include *Prelude* (1918), *Bliss* (1920) and *The Garden Party* (1922). Her life was cut short by tuberculosis, and she died at Fontainebleau, France, on Jan 9, 1923, while seeking treatment.

NATIONAL FACE YOUR FEARS DAY. Oct 14. This unique day celebrates people who face and overcome their fears—whether seeking a better job, flying on a plane or pursuing a new relationship. National Face Your Fears Day is all about going for it, and encouraging others to do the same. Annually, the second Tuesday in October. For info: Steve Hughes, 412 Luther Ct, St. Louis, MO 63122. Phone: (314) 821-8700. E-mail: info@hityourstride.com. Web: www.FaceYourFearsToday.com.

NATIONAL SCHOLARSHIP PROVIDERS ASSOCIATION ANNUAL CONFERENCE. Oct 14–17. Portland, OR. The NSPA Annual Conference is the convergence of our profession; the intersection between diverse funders, including institutions of higher education. For info: NSPA, 2222 14th St, Boulder, CO 80302. Phone: (303) 442-2524. Fax: (303) 443-5098. E-mail: info@scholarshipproviders.org. Web: www.scholarshipproviders.org.

NORTHERN INTERNATIONAL LIVESTOCK EXPOSITION. Oct 14–18. MetraPark, Billings, MT. PRCA rodeo, trade show exhibits, horse clinics and cattle, sheep, swine and horse sales. Est attendance: 25,000. For info: Justin Mills, Gen Mgr, NILE Office, PO Box 1981, Billings, MT 59103. Phone: (406) 256-2495. Fax: (406) 256-2494. E-mail: info@thenile.org. Web: www.thenile.org.

PENN, WILLIAM: BIRTH ANNIVERSARY. Oct 14, 1644. Founder of Pennsylvania, born at London, England. Penn died July 30, 1718, at Buckinghamshire, England. Presidential Proclamation 5284 of Nov 28, 1984, conferred honorary US citizenship on William Penn and his second wife, Hannah Callowhill Penn. They were the third and fourth persons to receive honorary US citizenship (following Winston Churchill and Raoul Wallenberg).

SOUND BARRIER BROKEN: ANNIVERSARY. Oct 14, 1947. Flying a Bell X-1 at Muroc Dry Lake Bed, CA, Air Force pilot Chuck Yeager broke the sound barrier, ushering in the era of supersonic flight.

SUPERSONIC SKYDIVE: ANNIVERSARY. Oct 14, 2012. Austrian daredevil Felix Baumgartner set several records in an incredible jump from a helium balloon in the stratosphere 24 miles above Earth: highest jump, fastest speed attained by a human not travelling in a powered craft and highest manned balloon flight. Baumgartner fell for nine minutes and reached a speed of 844 miles per hour (Mach 1.25) before triggering his parachute and landing safely in the desert near Roswell, NM.

WOODEN, JOHN: BIRTH ANNIVERSARY. Oct 14, 1910. One of the most successful basketball coaches in history, born at Hall, IN. Wooden led UCLA to a record-setting 10 NCAA championships in 12 years and is widely considered the most respected coach to ever take the court. His philosophies of leadership were adapted into the business world, and he was a successful author and motivational speaker in his later years. One of only three people inducted into both the collegiate and professional basketball halls of fame, Wooden died at Los Angeles, CA, June 4, 2010.

BIRTHDAYS TODAY

Harry Anderson, 62, actor ("Night Court," "Dave's World"), born Newport, RI, Oct 14, 1952.

Steve Coogan, 49, actor (*The Trip, Night at the Museum, 24 Hour Party People*), born Middleton, Lancashire, England, Oct 14, 1965.

Beth Daniel, 58, Hall of Fame golfer, born Charleston, SC, Oct 14, 1956.

John Dean, 76, lawyer (White House counsel during Watergate), born Akron, OH, Oct 14, 1938.

Greg Evigan, 61, actor ("B.J. and the Bear," "Masquerade"), born South Amboy, NJ, Oct 14, 1953.

Gary Graffman, 86, pianist, born New York, NY, Oct 14, 1928.

Ralph Lauren, 75, designer, born Ralph Lipschitz at the Bronx, NY, Oct 14, 1939.

Natalie Maines, 40, country singer (Dixie Chicks), born Lubbock, TX, Oct 14, 1974.

Roger Moore, 86, actor (James Bond movies, "The Saint"), born London, England, Oct 14, 1928.

David Oakes, 31, actor ("The Borgias," "The Pillars of the Earth"), born Hampshire, England, Oct 14, 1983.

Usher, 36, singer, actor ("Moesha"), television personality ("The Voice"), born Usher Raymond IV at Chattanooga, TN, Oct 14, 1978.

Mia Wasikowska, 25, actress (*Alice in Wonderland, The Kids Are All Right*), born Canberra, Australia, Oct 14, 1989.

October 2014

S	M	T	W	T	F	S
			1	2	3	4
5	6	7	8	9	10	11
12	13	14	15	16	17	18
19	20	21	22	23	24	25
26	27	28	29	30	31	

October 15 — Wednesday

DAY 288 — **77 REMAINING**

CHINA: CANTON AUTUMN TRADE FAIR. Oct 15–Nov 15. The Guangzhou (Canton) Autumn Trade Fair is held during the same dates each year.

CIRCLEVILLE PUMPKIN SHOW. Oct 15–18. Circleville, OH. More than 100,000 pounds of pumpkins, squash and gourds. Annually, starting the third Wednesday in October and running through the following Saturday. Est attendance: 400,000. For info: Pumpkin Show Inc, 159 E Franklin St, Circleville, OH 43113. Phone: (740) 474-7000. Fax: (740) 474-9216. Web: www.pumpkinshow.com.

CROW RESERVATION OPENED FOR SETTLEMENT: ANNIVERSARY. Oct 15, 1892. By presidential proclamation, 1.8 million acres of Crow reservation were opened to settlers. The government had induced the Crow to give up a portion of their land in the mountainous western area in the state of Montana, for which they received 50 cents per acre.

EAST TEXAS YAMBOREE. Oct 15–18. Gilmer, TX. 76th annual (since 1935, except during WWII). Great family festival with yam contest, yam pie contest, home canning contest, barn dances, coronation of the queen, livestock show, carnival, live music, exhibits and much more. Est attendance: 100,000. For info: Joan Small, Exec Dir, Gilmer Area Chamber of Commerce, Box 854, Gilmer, TX 75644. Phone: (903) 843-2413 or (903) 843-3981. Fax: (903) 843-3759. E-mail: upchamber@aol.com. Web: www.yamboree.com.

FIRST MANNED FLIGHT: ANNIVERSARY. Oct 15, 1783. Jean François Pilatre de Rozier and François Laurent, Marquis d'Arlandes, became the first people to fly when they ascended in a Montgolfier hot-air balloon at Paris, France, less than three months after the first public balloon flight demonstration (June 5, 1783), and only a year after the first experiments with small paper and fabric balloons by the Montgolfier brothers, Joseph and Jacques, in November 1782. The first manned free flight lasted about 4 minutes and carried the passengers at a height of about 84 feet. On Nov 21, 1783, they soared 3,000 feet over Paris for 25 minutes.

GALBRAITH, JOHN KENNETH: BIRTH ANNIVERSARY. Oct 15, 1908. Influential liberal economist, professor, author, diplomat and adviser to presidents Roosevelt, Kennedy and Johnson. Galbraith helped Lyndon Johnson create his Great Society programs. Galbraith's most famous book (out of 33 penned) is *The Affluent Society* (1958), in which he criticized a myopic US consumer culture that ignored community values. Born at Dunwich Township, ON, Canada, Galbraith died Apr 29, 2006, at Cambridge, MA.

HAGFISH DAY. Oct 15. Celebrate the beauty of ugly with Hagfish Day. This special day is a fun, somewhat tongue-in-cheek event with an important and serious goal: to raise awareness and understanding of the uniqueness and significance of all sea creatures—even the ugly, slimy, misunderstood or unusual (like the hagfish). Annually, the third Wednesday in October. For info: Whale Times, PO Box 2702, Tualatin, OR 97062. Phone: (503) 486-5298. E-mail: hagfishday@whaletimes.org. Web: www.whaletimes.org/hagfishday.htm.

"I LOVE LUCY" TV PREMIERE: ANNIVERSARY. Oct 15, 1951. This enormously popular sitcom, TV's first smash hit, starred the real-life husband-and-wife team of Cuban actor/bandleader Desi Arnaz and talented redheaded actress/comedienne Lucille Ball. They played Ricky and Lucy Ricardo, a New York bandleader and his aspiring actress/homemaker wife who was always scheming to get on stage. Costarring were William Frawley and Vivian Vance as Fred and Ethel Mertz, the Ricardos' landlords and good friends, who participated in the escapades and dealt with the consequences of Lucy's often well-intentioned plans. Famous actors guest-starred on the show, including Harpo Marx, Rock Hudson, William Holden, Hedda Hopper and John Wayne. This was the first sitcom to be filmed live before a studio audience, and it did extremely well in the ratings both the first time around and in reruns. The last telecast ran Sept 24, 1961.

JAPAN: NEWSPAPER WEEK. Oct 15–20. The Nihon Shinbun Kyokai (NSK), or The Japan Newspaper Publishers and Editors Association, sponsors this week to increase public awareness of the significance of "free and responsible newspapers" and, at the same time, to stimulate a sense of responsibility within the press. Originated in 1948. Annually, Oct 15–20. For info: NSK. Web: www.pressnet.or.jp.

MANN, MARTY: BIRTH ANNIVERSARY. Oct 15, 1904. The American social activist and author was born at Chicago, IL. She was founder in 1944 of the National Committee for Education on Alcoholism and author of *A New Primer on Alcoholism*. She died at Bridgeport, CT, July 22, 1980.

MATA HARI EXECUTION: ANNIVERSARY. Oct 15, 1917. Possibly history's most famous spy, Mata Hari refused a blindfold and threw a kiss to the firing squad at her execution. See also: "Mata Hari: Birth Anniversary" (Aug 7).

MISSOURI DAY. Oct 15. Observed by teachers and pupils in schools with appropriate exercises throughout state of Missouri. Annually, the third Wednesday in October.

MOON PHASE: LAST QUARTER. Oct 15. Moon enters Last Quarter phase at 3:12 PM, EDT.

NATIONAL CAKE DECORATING DAY. Oct 15. A day for everyone to celebrate and practice cake decorating. It is easy to create cakes with color, sweetness and fun. With the right tools, instruction and inspiration, anyone can achieve amazing results in cake decorating and sweet treat making. For info: Vallory Farrasso, Wilton Enterprises, 2240 W 75th St, Woodridge, IL 60517. Phone: (630) 810-2221. E-mail: vfarrasso@wilton.com. Web: www.wilton.com.

NATIONAL GROUCH DAY. Oct 15. Honor a grouch; all grouches deserve a day to be recognized. Created for and inspired by Alan Miller, retired teacher and Chairman of the Board, NAG (National Association of Grouches). Annually, Oct 15. For info: Alan R. Miller, NAG, 12281 Alexander St, Clio, MI 48420.

NATIONAL TAKE YOUR PARENTS TO LUNCH DAY. Oct 15. As part of National School Lunch Week, the School Nutrition Association encourages school cafeterias to reach out to parents for the Wednesday of NSLW (or a day of your choosing). Spread the word to parents (or guests like local policy makers) that healthy and tasty options are being served in school cafeterias every day. For info: School Nutrition Association. Web: www.schoolnutrition.org.

NIETZSCHE, FRIEDRICH WILHELM: BIRTH ANNIVERSARY. Oct 15, 1844. Influential, controversial and often misunderstood philosopher born at Rocken, Germany. Especially remembered for his declaration that "God is dead." Major works include *Thus Spake Zarathustra, Beyond Good and Evil* and *The Geneaology of Morals*. Nietzsche died at Weimar, Germany, Aug 25, 1900, a decade after suffering a mental breakdown.

SENATE CONFIRMS THOMAS TO SUPREME COURT: ANNIVERSARY. Oct 15, 1991. After three days of Senate Judiciary Committee hearings on charges of sexual harassment made against Judge Clarence Thomas by a former aide, Anita F. Hill, the Senate confirmed Thomas as the 106th US Supreme Court justice with a 52–48 vote on Oct 15, 1991. The vote was the closest for a 20th-century justice and made Thomas, who would replace retired Justice Thurgood Marshall, the second African American to sit on the Supreme Court.

SPACE MILESTONE: *CASSINI* (US). Oct 15, 1997. The plutonium-powered orbiter was launched on this day and passed between the rings of Saturn on June 30, 2004. It orbits the planet, sending back photographs and information on the planet and its 18 known moons. In 2004, it dispatched the *Huygens* probe to Titan, the largest of these moons.

SULLIVAN, JOHN L.: BIRTH ANNIVERSARY. Oct 15, 1858. Boxer, born at Roxbury, MA. "The Great John L." was one of America's first sports heroes. He captured the world's bare-knuckle heavyweight championship on Feb 7, 1882, and went six years without defending the title. He won the last bare-knuckle fight in 1889 and then lost the title to James J. Corbett in 1892. This was the first fight in which the boxers used gloves and were governed by the Marquess of Queensberry rules. Died at Abingdon, MA, Feb 2, 1918.

UNITED NATIONS: INTERNATIONAL DAY OF RURAL WOMEN. Oct 15. The General Assembly has declared Oct 15 of each year as a day to focus on improving the situation of rural women, including indigenous women, in their national, regional and global development strategies (Res 62/136, Dec 18, 2007). For info: United Nations, Dept of Public Info, New York, NY, 10017. Web: www.un.org.

✦WHITE CANE SAFETY DAY. Oct 15. Presidential Proclamation always issued for Oct 15 since 1964 (PL 88–628 of Oct 6, 1964).

WILSON, EDITH BOLLING GALT: BIRTH ANNIVERSARY. Oct 15, 1872. Second wife of Woodrow Wilson, 28th president of the US, born at Wytheville, VA. Died at Washington, DC, Dec 28, 1961.

WISHBONES FOR PETS. Oct 15–Nov 30. This is a voluntary program that asks professional pet sitters to host a pet goods or fund drive in their communities around Thanksgiving with all proceeds going to their favorite local pet-related charities. For info: Janet Depathy, Wishbones for Pets, 4 Charlotte Dr, Plymouth, MA 02360. Phone: (508) 747-4259. E-mail: icpets@comcast.net. Web: www.wishbonesforpets.com.

WODEHOUSE, PELHAM GRENVILLE: BIRTH ANNIVERSARY. Oct 15, 1881. English author, lyricist ("Bill") and humorist, creator of Bertie Wooster and Jeeves. Born at Guildford, Surrey, England, P.G. Wodehouse died at Southampton, Long Island, NY, Feb 14, 1975.

BIRTHDAYS TODAY

Victor Banerjee, 68, actor (*A Passage to India, The Home and the World*), born Calcutta, India, Oct 15, 1946.

Paige Davis, 45, actress, television personality ("Trading Spaces"), born Philadelphia, PA, Oct 15, 1969.

Sarah Ferguson, 55, Duchess of York (former wife of Prince Andrew), born London, England, Oct 15, 1959.

Lee Iacocca, 90, former automobile executive (Ford and Chrysler), born Allentown, PA, Oct 15, 1924.

Tito Jackson, 61, singer, musician (Jackson 5), born Toriano Adaryll Jackson at Gary, IN, Oct 15, 1953.

Linda Lavin, 75, actress (Tony for *Broadway Bound*; "Alice"), born Portland, ME, Oct 15, 1939.

Penny Marshall, 72, director (*Big, A League of Their Own*), actress ("Laverne & Shirley"), born New York, NY, Oct 15, 1942.

James Alvin (Jim) Palmer, 69, Hall of Fame baseball player, sportscaster, born New York, NY, Oct 15, 1945.

October 16 — Thursday

DAY 289 **76 REMAINING**

AMERICA'S FIRST DEPARTMENT STORE: ANNIVERSARY. Oct 16, 1868. Salt Lake City, UT. America's first department store, "ZCMI" (Zion's Co-Operative Mercantile Institution), is still operating at Salt Lake City (although under a new name and new ownership). It was founded under the direction of Brigham Young.

BEN-GURION, DAVID: BIRTH ANNIVERSARY. Oct 16, 1886. Born David Gruen at Plonsk, Poland, David Ben-Gurion was the first prime minister of Israel, a post he held for nearly two decades. He is widely credited with having willed Israel into being and setting the country's intellectual course. He died at Tel Aviv, Israel, Dec 1, 1973.

CANADA: TORONTO SKI, SNOWBOARD AND TRAVEL SHOW. Oct 16–19. International Centre, Mississauga, ON. Ski manufacturers (equipment, fashions, accessories), retailers, ski resorts, hotels, travel agencies, tourist bureaus, ski clinics and demonstrations, ski clubs, associations, movies and live entertainment. Catering to all ski disciplines—Alpine, cross-country and snowboarding. Est attendance: 35,000. For info: Canadian Natl Sportsmen's Shows, 30 Village Centre Pl, Mississauga, ON L4Z 1V9, Canada. Phone: (905) 361-2677. Fax: (905) 361-2679. Web: www.torontoskishow.com or www.snowboardshow.ca.

CRIMEAN WAR: ANNIVERSARY. Oct 16, 1853. The Ottoman Empire declared war on Russia on this day to stem Russian expansionist policies in the empire. Britain, France and parts of Italy allied themselves with the Turks against Russia. A battle in this war was immortalized in Tennyson's poem "The Charge of the Light Brigade." Health conditions for soldiers were scandalous, leading Florence Nightingale to work in the British hospital at Istanbul. This was the first war to be observed firsthand by newspaper reporters and photographers.

DICTIONARY DAY. Oct 16. The birthday of Noah Webster, American teacher and lexicographer, is an occasion to encourage every person to acquire at least one dictionary—and to use it regularly.

DOUGLAS, WILLIAM ORVILLE: BIRTH ANNIVERSARY. Oct 16, 1898. American jurist, world traveler, conservationist, outdoorsman and author. Born at Maine, MN, he served as justice of the US Supreme Court longer than any other (36 years). Died at Washington, DC, Jan 19, 1980.

FIRST BIRTH CONTROL CLINIC OPENED: ANNIVERSARY. Oct 16, 1916. Margaret Sanger, Fania Mindell and Ethel Burne opened the first birth control clinic in the US at 46 Amboy St, Brooklyn, NY. Sanger believed that the poor should be able to control the size of their families.

GET SMART ABOUT CREDIT DAY. Oct 16. Thousands of bankers visit high schools across America today to teach youth the importance of establishing and maintaining good credit. Annually, the third Thursday of October. For info: American Bankers Assn, 1120 Connecticut Ave NW, Washington, DC 20036. Phone: (800) BANKERS. E-mail: edufoun@aba.com. Web: www.aba.com or www.getsmartaboutcredit.com.

INTERNATIONAL CREDIT UNION DAY. Oct 16. On Jan 17, 1927, the Credit Union League of Massachusetts celebrated the first official holiday for credit union members and staff on the birthday of Benjamin Franklin, America's apostle of thrift. In 1948, the 100th anniversary of the credit union movement, the Credit Union National Association (CUNA) set aside the third Thursday in October as the day of observance. More than 51,000 credit unions, representing 196 million people in 100 countries, celebrate the credit union difference on this day. For info: ICU Day Coordinator, CUNA, PO Box 431, Madison, WI 53701. Phone: (800) 356-9655. E-mail: icuday@cuna.coop. Web: www.cuna.org.

JOHN BROWN'S RAID: ANNIVERSARY. Oct 16, 1859. White abolitionist John Brown, with a band of about 20 men, seized the US Arsenal at Harpers Ferry, WV. Brown was captured and the insurrection put down by Oct 19. Brown was hanged at Charles Town, WV, Dec 2, 1859.

MACKINAC ISLAND MUSIC FESTIVAL. Oct 16–18. Mackinac Island, MI. Mackinac Island has been a gathering place for centuries, and musicians from around the country will gather for this summer music festival. Performers in past years have included Mitch Ryder and the Detroit Wheels, Forbes Brothers, Johnny Bassett, Grand Hotel Jazz Quartet, Audra Kubat, Dick Seagal and the Brandos, Carolyn Striho and many others. The performances take place at the car-less island's quaint pubs, historic theaters and outdoor stages. For info: Mackinac Island Tourist Bureau, PO Box 451, Mackinac Island, MI 49757. Phone: (906) 847-3783. Web: www.mackinacislandmusicfestival.org.

MARIE ANTOINETTE: EXECUTION ANNIVERSARY. Oct 16, 1793. Queen Marie Antoinette, whose extravagance and "let them eat cake" attitude toward the starving French underclass made her a target of the French Revolution, was beheaded on this date.

MILLION MAN MARCH: ANNIVERSARY. Oct 16, 1995. Hundreds of thousands of black men met at Washington, DC, for a "holy day of atonement and reconciliation" organized by Louis Farrakhan, leader of the Nation of Islam. Marchers pledged to take responsibility for themselves, their families and their communities.

NATIONAL BOSS DAY. Oct 16. For all employees to honor their bosses. Annually, the weekday closest to Oct 16. Patricia Bays Haroski originated this event in 1958 in honor of her own boss, who also happened to be her father.

NORTH CAROLINA STATE FAIR. Oct 16–26. State Fairgrounds, Raleigh, NC. Agricultural fair with livestock, arts and crafts, home arts, entertainment and carnival. Est attendance: 775,000. For info: North Carolina State Fair, 1025 Blue Ridge Blvd, Raleigh, NC 27607. Phone: (919) 821-7400. Fax: (919) 733-5079. Web: www.ncstatefair.org.

O'NEILL, EUGENE GLADSTONE: BIRTH ANNIVERSARY. Oct 16, 1888. American playwright (*Long Day's Journey into Night, The Iceman Cometh, Ah! Wilderness*), recipient of four Pulitzer prizes as well as the Nobel Prize in Literature (1936). O'Neill's plays introduced the technique of realism through his portrayals of characters at society's periphery. Born at New York, NY, he died at Boston, MA, Nov 27, 1953. O'Neill is one of the most widely translated and produced playwrights in history, third only to William Shakespeare and George Bernard Shaw.

SHEMINI ATZERET. Oct 16. Hebrew calendar date: Tishri 22, 5775. The eighth day of Solemn Assembly, part of the Sukkot festival (see entry on Oct 9), with memorial services and cycle of biblical readings in the synagogue. Began at sundown on Oct 15.

UNITED NATIONS: WORLD FOOD DAY. Oct 16. Annual observance to heighten public awareness of the world food problem and to strengthen solidarity in the struggle against hunger, malnutrition and poverty. Date of observance is anniversary of founding of Food and Agriculture Organization (FAO), Oct 16, 1945, at Quebec, Canada. For info: United Nations, Dept of Public Info, New York, NY 10017. Web: www.un.org.

October 2014	S	M	T	W	T	F	S
				1	2	3	4
	5	6	7	8	9	10	11
	12	13	14	15	16	17	18
	19	20	21	22	23	24	25
	26	27	28	29	30	31	

WAR CRIMINALS (GERMAN) EXECUTION: ANNIVERSARY. Oct 16, 1946. The War Crimes Trials of Berlin and Nuremberg had sentenced 12 of the 22 defendants to death by hanging. They were: Hermann Goering, Joachim von Ribbentrop, Wilhelm Keitel, Ernst Kaltenbrunner, Alfred Rosenberg, Hans Frank, Wilhelm Frick, Julius Streicher, Fritz Sauckel, Alfred Jodl, Martin Bormann and Arthur von Seyss-Inquart. Goering committed suicide a few hours before his scheduled execution, and Martin Bormann had not been found (he was tried in absentia). The remaining 10 were hanged at Nuremberg Prison on this date.

WEBSTER, NOAH: BIRTH ANNIVERSARY. Oct 16, 1758. American teacher and journalist whose name became synonymous with the word *dictionary* after his compilations of the earliest American dictionaries of the English language. Born at West Hartford, CT, he died at New Haven, CT, May 28, 1843.

WILDE, OSCAR: BIRTH ANNIVERSARY. Oct 16, 1854. Irish wit, poet and playwright Oscar Fingal O'Flahertie Wills Wilde was born at Dublin, Ireland. At the height of his career he was imprisoned for two years on a morals offense, during which time he wrote "A Ballad of Reading Gaol." Best known of his plays is *The Importance of Being Earnest.* "We are all in the gutter," he wrote in *Lady Windermere's Fan*, "but some of us are looking at the stars." Wilde died at Paris, France, Nov 30, 1900.

WORLD FOOD DAY. Oct 16. To increase awareness, understanding and informed action on hunger. Annually, on the founding date of the UN Food and Agriculture Organization. For info: US Natl Committee for World Food Day, 2175 K St NW, Washington, DC 20437. Phone: (202) 653-2404. Web: www.worldfooddayusa.org.

YALE UNIVERSITY FOUNDED: ANNIVERSARY. Oct 16, 1701. (Old Style date.) The Collegiate School was founded at Branford, CT, by Congregationalists dissatisfied with the growing liberalism at Harvard. In 1716, the school was moved to New Haven, CT, where it became Yale College, named after Elihu Yale, a governor of the East India Company. The first degrees were awarded in 1716. Yale became a university in 1887. Founded as a school for men, Yale began admitting women undergraduates in 1969.

BIRTHDAYS TODAY

Melissa Louise Belote, 58, Olympic swimmer, born Washington, DC, Oct 16, 1956.

Barry Corbin, 74, actor ("Northern Exposure," *Stir Crazy, Any Which Way You Can*), born Dawson County, TX, Oct 16, 1940.

Jack Dalrymple, 66, Governor of North Dakota (R), born Minneapolis, MN, Oct 16, 1948.

Juan Gonzalez, 45, former baseball player, born Vaga Baja, Puerto Rico, Oct 16, 1969.

Günter Grass, 87, author (*The Tin Drum, Dog Years*), born Danzig, Germany, Oct 16, 1927.

Paul Kariya, 40, hockey player, born Vancouver, BC, Canada, Oct 16, 1974.

Angela Lansbury, 89, actress ("Murder, She Wrote;" *The Manchurian Candidate, Bedknobs and Broomsticks, Gaslight*; five Tony Awards), born London, England, Oct 16, 1925.

Kellie Martin, 39, actress ("Life Goes On," "ER"), born Riverside, CA, Oct 16, 1975.

John Mayer, 37, singer, born Bridgeport, CT, Oct 16, 1977.

Tim Robbins, 56, actor (Oscar for *Mystic River*; *The Player*), director, born West Covina, CA, Oct 16, 1958.

Suzanne Somers, 68, actress ("Three's Company," "Step by Step," *American Graffiti*), born San Bruno, CA, Oct 16, 1946.

Bob Weir, 67, musician (The Grateful Dead), born San Francisco, CA, Oct 16, 1947.

David Zucker, 67, writer, producer (*Naked Gun* movies, *Airplane!*), born Milwaukee, WI, Oct 16, 1947.

October 17 — Friday

DAY 290 **75 REMAINING**

AIDS WALK ATLANTA & 5K RUN. Oct 17. Piedmont Park, Atlanta, GA. AIDS Walk Atlanta is a 5K fundraising walk and run benefiting AID Atlanta and other AIDS service organizations and education providers around metro Atlanta. Est attendance: 10,000. For info: AIDS Walk Atlanta, 1605 Peachtree St NE, Atlanta, GA 30309. Phone: (404) 876-9255. Fax: (404) 870-7739. E-mail: walkinfo@aidatlanta.org. Web: www.aidswalkatlanta.com.

APPLE BUTTER STIRRIN'. Oct 17–19. Coshocton, OH. With more than 100 crafters, this invitational craft festival celebrates the sights, sounds and scents of autumn. Smell the fresh apple butter simmering over an open fire; listen to the tunes of bluegrass and old-time music. Living history, quilt raffle, canal boat rides, children's activities and more. Annually, the third weekend in October. Est attendance: 15,000. For info: Roscoe Village Foundation, 600 N Whitewoman St, Coshocton, OH 43812. Phone: (800) 877-1830 or (740) 622-7644. Fax: (740) 623-6555. E-mail: rvmarketing@roscoevillage.com. Web: www.roscoevillage.com.

ARTHUR, JEAN: BIRTH ANNIVERSARY. Oct 17, 1900. American actress Jean Arthur was born Gladys Georgianna Greene at Plattsburg, NY. Her films include *Mr Deeds Goes to Town* (1936), *Mr Smith Goes to Washington* (1939) and *Shane* (1953). She died June 19, 1991, at Carmel, CA.

CRAFTSMEN'S FALL CLASSIC ARTS & CRAFTS FESTIVAL. Oct 17–19. Dulles Expo and Convention Center, Chantilly, VA. 19th annual. Features work from more than 400 talented artists and craftspeople. All juried exhibitors' work has been handmade by the exhibitors and must be their own original design and creation. See the creative process in action, with several exhibitors demonstrating throughout the weekend. Something for every style, taste and budget with items from the most contemporary to the most traditional. Est attendance: 30,000. For info: Gilmore Enterprises, Inc, 3514-A Drawbridge Pkwy, Greensboro, NC 27410-8584. Phone: (336) 282-5550. E-mail: contact@gilmoreshows.com. Web: www.CraftShow.com or www.gilmoreshows.com.

EWING, BUCK: BIRTH ANNIVERSARY. Oct 17, 1859. William Buckingham (Buck) Ewing, Baseball Hall of Fame catcher, born at Hoagland, OH. Ewing was one of the best catchers of the 19th century and is credited by some with being the first to crouch immediately under the batter. Inducted into the Hall of Fame in 1939. Died at Cincinnati, OH, Oct 20, 1906.

FALL FESTIVAL OF LEAVES. Oct 17–19. Bainbridge, Ross County, OH. Celebrating the beauty of the season and region. Folk arts, crafts, music, antique car show, log-sawing contest, flea markets and parades. To obtain a map of self-guided scenic tours, send SASE. For info: Fall Festival of Leaves, Box 571, Bainbridge, Ross County, OH 45612. Phone: (740) 634-2997 or (740) 703-8833. Web: www.fallfestivalofleaves.com.

FOOD AND DRUG INTERACTION EDUCATION AND AWARENESS WEEK. Oct 17–24. This campaign has been designed to help educate health professionals, patients and consumers about the problems of certain foods mixed with prescription drugs, over-the-counter drugs and herbal/alternative medicines. For info: Fred S. Mayer, RPh, MPH, Pharmacists Planning Service, Inc (PPSI), PO Box 6760, San Rafael, CA 94903. Phone: (415) 479-8628 or (415) 302-7351. Fax: (415) 479-8608. E-mail: ppsi@aol.com. Web: www.ppsinc.org.

HAMMON, JUPITER: BIRTH ANNIVERSARY. Oct 17, 1711. America's first published black poet was born into slavery, probably at Long Island, NY. He was taught to read, however, and as a trusted servant was allowed to use his master's library. On Dec 25, 1760, Jupiter Hammon, then 49, published the 88-line broadside poem "An Evening Thought" and thus became the first black person in America to publish poetry. Hammon died around 1806 (exact date and place of death unknown).

"THE HOLLYWOOD SQUARES" TV PREMIERE: ANNIVERSARY. Oct 17, 1966. On this game show, nine celebrities sat in a giant grid. Two contestants played tic-tac-toe by determining if an answer given by a celebrity was correct. Peter Marshall hosted the show for many years with panelists Paul Lynde, Rose Marie, Cliff Arquette, Wally Cox, John Davidson and George Gobel, among others. John Davidson took over as host in 1986 for a new version of the game show with Joan Rivers and, later, Shadoe Stevens at center square. In 1998 "Hollywood Squares" appeared again with Tom Bergeron as host and Whoopi Goldberg as the center square.

JOHNSON, RICHARD MENTOR: BIRTH ANNIVERSARY. Oct 17, 1780. Ninth vice president of the US (1837–41). Born at Floyd's Station, KY. Died at Frankfort, KY, Nov 19, 1850.

KNIEVEL, ROBERT CRAIG, JR: BIRTH ANNIVERSARY. Oct 17, 1938. Known by his nickname, "Evel," Knievel gained worldwide fame as a stunt performer, conceiving of and executing a series of increasingly outlandish motorcycle jumps throughout the 1970s that often resulted in crashes and broken bones. Born at Butte, MT, he died Nov 30, 2007, at Clearwater, FL.

MILLER, ARTHUR: BIRTH ANNIVERSARY. Oct 17, 1915. Born at New York, NY, Miller began writing plays in college and also published several novels and collections of short stories. He won the Pulitzer Prize in 1949 for *Death of a Salesman*, one of the most significant works in American literature. The play won the Tony Award twice: once in 1949 and again in 1999 when it won for Best Revival. Miller also received a Tony for *The Crucible,* a drama about the Salem witch trials, and a lifetime achievement award in 1999. He was married to actress Marilyn Monroe in the 1950s and wrote the 1963 play *After the Fall* about their relationship. Miller died at Roxbury, CT, Feb 11, 2005.

MULLIGAN DAY. Oct 17. A day for giving yourself or another a second chance; a day for a "do-over." For info: C. Daniel Rhodes, 1900 Crossvine Rd, Hoover, AL 65244. Phone: (205) 908-6781. E-mail: rhodan@charter.net.

NATIONAL MAMMOGRAPHY DAY. Oct 17. On this day, or throughout the month of October, participating radiologists provide discounted or free screening mammograms. Annually, the third Friday in October. For info: NBCAM. Web: www.nbcam.org.

PENNSYLVANIA ARTS & CRAFTS CHRISTMAS FESTIVAL. Oct 17–19 (also Oct 25–26). Washington County Fairgrounds, Washington, PA. More than 220 exhibits of handcrafted furniture, gift items, children's toys, dolls, dried floral arrangements and clothing. Holiday food and entertainment. Est attendance: 18,000. For info: Debbie & Dave Stoner, Family Festivals Assn, Inc, PO Box 166, Irwin, PA 15642. Phone: (724) 863-4577. Fax: (724) 863-5427. E-mail: info@familyfestivals.com. Web: www.familyfestivals.com.

POPE JOHN PAUL I: BIRTH ANNIVERSARY. Oct 17, 1912. Albino Luciani, 263rd pope of the Roman Catholic Church. Born at Forno di Canale, Italy, he was elected pope Aug 26, 1978. Died at Rome, 34 days after his election, Sept 28, 1978. Shortest papacy since Pope Leo XI (Apr 1–27, 1605).

SAN FRANCISCO 1989 EARTHQUAKE: 25th ANNIVERSARY. Oct 17, 1989. The San Francisco Bay area was rocked by an earthquake registering 7.1 on the Richter scale at 5:04 PM, PDT, just as the nation's baseball fans settled in to watch the 1989 World Series at Candlestick Park. A large audience was tuned in to the pregame coverage when the quake hit and knocked the broadcast off the air. The quake caused damage estimated at $10 billion and killed 67 people, many of whom were caught in the collapse of the double-decked Interstate 80, at Oakland, CA.

SIEGEL, JERRY: 100th BIRTH ANNIVERSARY. Oct 17, 1914. Siegel, born at Cleveland, OH, was the writing half of a team that created comic book hero Superman, who debuted in *Action Comics* in June 1938. Siegel, the son of Jewish immigrants, worked with childhood friend Joe Shuster to create the powerful alien trying to find his way in a new world. Superman immediately exploded in popularity, but Siegel and Shuster never profited greatly, having sold the rights to the character in 1938 (although later legal action ensured a modest stipend and creative credit). Siegel died Jan 28, 1996, at Los Angeles, CA.

SIMCHAT TORAH. Oct 17. Hebrew calendar date: Tishri 23, 5775. Rejoicing in the Torah follows the seven-day Sukkot festival and Shemini Atzeret. Public reading of the Pentateuch is completed and begun again, symbolizing the need for ever-continuing study. Began at sundown on Oct 16.

STEPHEN FOSTER QUILT SHOW AND SALE. Oct 17–19. Stephen Foster Folk Culture Center State Park, White Springs, FL. As quilters gather to share their work, more than 200 quilts will be exhibited, including traditional bed quilts, art quilts and children's quilts. Workshops, keynote speakers and demonstrations are part of the fun. For info: Quilt Show, Stephen Foster Folk Culture Center State Park, PO Box G, White Springs, FL 32096. Phone: (877) 635-3655. Fax: (386) 397-4262. Web: www.floridastateparks.org/stephenfoster.

300 MILLIONTH AMERICAN BORN: ANNIVERSARY. Oct 17, 2006. The US Census Bureau reported that the 300 millionth American would be born in the early hours of Oct 17, 2006. A baby girl born at Chicago, IL, at 5:58 AM was probably that American—although there was a margin of error of a few hours. The US population now increases by one every 11 seconds. The 200 millionth American was born Nov 20, 1967.

UNITED NATIONS: INTERNATIONAL DAY FOR THE ERADICATION OF POVERTY. Oct 17. The General Assembly proclaimed this observance (Res 47/196) to promote public awareness of the need to eradicate poverty and destitution in all countries, particularly the developing nations. For info: United Nations, Dept of Public Info, New York, NY 10017. Web: www.un.org.

BIRTHDAYS TODAY

Ernie Els, 45, golfer, born Johannesburg, South Africa, Oct 17, 1969.

Eminem, 42, musician, rapper, actor, born Marshall Bruce Mathers III at Kansas City, MO, Oct 17, 1972.

Martin Heinrich, 43, US Senator (D, New Mexico), born Fallon, NV, Oct 17, 1971.

Mae Jemison, 58, scientist, astronaut, born Decatur, AL, Oct 17, 1956.

October 2014	S	M	T	W	T	F	S
				1	2	3	4
	5	6	7	8	9	10	11
	12	13	14	15	16	17	18
	19	20	21	22	23	24	25
	26	27	28	29	30	31	

Margot Kidder, 66, actress (*Superman* films, *The Amityville Horror*), born Yellowknife, NT, Canada, Oct 17, 1948.

Norm Macdonald, 51, comedian, actor ("Saturday Night Live," "Norm"), born Quebec City, QC, Canada, Oct 17, 1963.

Pat McCrory, 58, Governor of North Carolina (R), born Columbus, OH, Oct 17, 1956.

Michael McKean, 67, actor ("Laverne & Shirley," *This Is Spinal Tap*), born New York, NY, Oct 17, 1947.

Steve McMichael, 57, sportscaster, football coach, former football player, former professional wrestler, born Houston, TX, Oct 17, 1957.

Richard Roeper, 55, newspaper columnist, film reviewer ("Ebert & Roeper and the Movies"), born Chicago, IL, Oct 17, 1959.

George Wendt, 66, actor ("Cheers," "The Naked Truth"), born Chicago, IL, Oct 17, 1948.

October 18 — Saturday

DAY 291 **74 REMAINING**

ANDRÉE, SALOMON AUGUST: BIRTH ANNIVERSARY. Oct 18, 1854. Swedish explorer and balloonist, born at Grenna, Sweden. His North Pole expedition of 1897 attracted world attention but ended tragically. With two companions, Andrée left Spitzbergen, Norway, July 11, 1897, in a balloon, hoping to place the Swedish flag at the North Pole. The last message from Andrée, borne by carrier pigeons, was dated noon, July 13, 1897. The frozen bodies of the explorers were found 33 years later by another polar expedition in the summer of 1930. Diaries, maps and exposed photographic negatives also were found. The photos were developed successfully, providing a pictorial record of the ill-fated expedition.

AZERBAIJAN: INDEPENDENCE DAY. Oct 18. National holiday. Commemorates declaration of independence from the Soviet Union in 1991.

BERGSON, HENRI: BIRTH ANNIVERSARY. Oct 18, 1859. French philosopher, Nobel Prize winner and author of *Creative Evolution*, born at Paris, France. Died there Jan 4, 1941.

BRIDGE DAY. Oct 18. New River Gorge Bridge, Fayetteville, WV. 35th annual. World's biggest extreme sports event and West Virginia's largest festival. Up to 500 BASE jumpers leap off North America's longest single-span bridge at a height of 876 feet. Annually, the third Saturday in October. Est attendance: 80,000. For info: Official Bridge Day Festival, Fayette County Chamber of Commerce, 310 Oyler Av, Oak Hill, WV 25901. Phone: (800) 927-0263. E-mail: bridgeday@officialbridgeday.com. Web: www.officialbridgeday.com.

BROOKS, JAMES DAVID: BIRTH ANNIVERSARY. Oct 18, 1906. Born at St. Louis, MO. During the Depression Brooks worked as a muralist in the Federal Art Project of the Works Progress Administration. His best-known work of that period is *Flight*, a mural on the rotunda of the Marine Air Terminal at La Guardia National Airport in New York. It was painted over during the 1950s but restored in 1980. Brooks served with the US Army 1942–45. When he returned to New York, his interest shifted to abstract expressionism. His paintings were exhibited in the historic Ninth Street Exhibition as a part of the Museum of Modern Art's exhibits Twelve Americans and New American Painting, among others. He died Mar 8, 1992, at Brookhaven, NY.

CANADA: PERSONS DAY. Oct 18. A day to commemorate the anniversary of the 1929 ruling that declared women to be persons in Canada. Prior to this ruling English common law prevailed ("Women are persons in matters of pains and penalties, but are not persons in matters of rights and privileges"). The celebrated cause, popularly known as the "Persons Case," was brought by five women of Alberta, Canada; leader of the courageous "Famous Five" was Emily Murphy (1868–1933). This ruling by the Judicial Committee of England's Privy Council, Oct 18, 1929, overturned a 1928 decision of the Supreme Court of Canada. Fifty years after the Persons Case decision, in 1979, the Governor General's Awards in Commemoration of the Persons Case were established to recognize deserving persons who have made outstanding contributions to the quality of life of women in Canada.

CANALETTO, GIOVANNI ANTONIO: BIRTH ANNIVERSARY. Oct 18, 1697. Painter Giovanni Antonio Canaletto (born Canale), best known for his detailed landscapes of Venice and London, was born at Venice, Italy, and died there at age 70, Apr 20, 1768. He was known for his accurate use of perspective, shadow and light. He went to England in 1746 and expanded his range of subjects to include English landscapes and country homes.

A COMMUNITY AFFAIR. Oct 18. Menomonee Falls High School, Menomonee Falls, WI. Community League's 32nd annual fair features arts, crafts and collectibles and more than 80 exhibitors; country luncheon of homemade food and desserts; raffles; "Pastries 'n' More" and silent auction. Admission charged. Est attendance: 2,000. For info: Jeanne Verbsky, Community League, Inc, Publicity—ACA, PO Box 973, Menomonee Falls, WI 53052. Phone: (414) 581-0352. E-mail: cleague@communityleague.com. Web: www.communityleague.com.

DEUTSCH COUNTRY DAYS. Oct 18–19. Historic Luxenhaus Farm, Marthasville, MO. 33rd annual. An authentic re-creation of early German life in Missouri as 80 costumed artisans demonstrate log hewing, *kloppolei*, beekeeping, broom making, wood turning, natural dyeing and more. Period music, meals, a historic sorghum press demonstration and a steam-powered sawmill add to the festivities. Est attendance: 9,500. For info: Deutsch Country Days, Historic Luxenhaus Farm, 18055 State Hwy O, Marthasville, MO 63357. Phone: (636) 433-5669 or (636) 433-5611. E-mail: info@deutschcountrydays.org. Web: www.deutschcountrydays.org.

FIRST NEWSPAPER COMIC STRIP: ANNIVERSARY. Oct 18, 1896. Although cartoons had appeared in newspapers for many years, the comic strip—a narrative told in cartoons over several panels—took its main form with the appearance of "The Yellow Kid Takes a Hand at Golf" in the *New York Journal*'s weekly supplement, *American Humorist*. The creator was Richard Fenton Outcault. In March 1897 the *Yellow Kid Magazine* gathered the strips and became the first published collection of a comic strip—setting the stage for the first comic books in the late 1920s. See also: "Outcault, Richard Fenton: Birth Anniversary" (Jan 14).

FOOD AND NUTRITION CONFERENCE AND EXPO. Oct 18–21. Atlanta, GA. Est attendance: 8,000. For info: Academy of Nutrition and Dietetics, 120 S Riverside Plaza, Ste 2000, Chicago, IL 60606-6995. Phone: (312) 899-0040. Fax: (312) 899-0008. E-mail: media@eatright.org. Web: www.eatright.org.

INTERNATIONAL HOME FURNISHINGS MARKET (FALL). Oct 18–23. High Point and Thomasville, NC. The largest wholesale home furnishings market in the world. (Not open to the general public.) For info: High Point Market Authority, 164 S Main St, Ste 700, High Point, NC 27260. Phone: (336) 869-1000 or (800) 874-6492. Fax: (336) 869-6999. Web: www.highpointmarket.org.

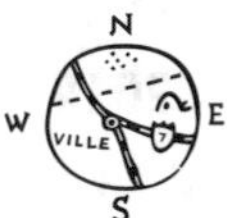

LIEBLING, A.J.: BIRTH ANNIVERSARY. Oct 18, 1904. American journalist and author who said, "Freedom of the press belongs to those who own one." Abbott Joseph Liebling was born at New York, NY, and died there Dec 28, 1963.

MERCOURI, MELINA: BIRTH ANNIVERSARY. Oct 18, 1920. Greek actress and politician Melina Mercouri was born Maria Amalia Mercouri at Athens, Greece, Oct 18, 1920 or 1925 (both reported). Of her more than 70 films and plays she is best known for her role in *Never on Sunday* (1960). In 1977 she was elected to Greece's parliament; she became the first woman in Greece's senior cabinet when appointed by Premier Andreas Papandreou to the position of minister of culture in 1981. She died Mar 6, 1994, at New York, NY.

MISSOURI DAY FESTIVAL. Oct 18–19. North Central Missouri Fairgrounds, Trenton, MO. Annual festival in conjunction with high school marching band competitions. Features a parade, craft booths, flea market, food vendors and entertainment of all kinds. Est attendance: 12,000. For info: Missouri Day Festival, Trenton Chamber of Commerce, 617 Main, Trenton, MO 64683. Phone: (660) 359-4324. E-mail: trentonchamber@grundyec.net.

MOSSY CREEK BARNYARD FESTIVAL. Oct 18–19. Warner Robins, GA. Arts and crafts chosen from best in the nation; heritage crafts, country and folk music and folktales in relaxed atmosphere. Annually, the third weekend in October. Est attendance: 25,000. For info: Carolyn Chester, Mossy Creek Barnyard Festival, Inc, 111 Nichole Ct, Perry, GA 31069. Phone: (478) 922-8265. E-mail: echester@bellsouth.net. Web: www.mossycreekfestival.com.

QUINCY PRESERVES FALL ARCHITECTURAL TOUR. Oct 18. Quincy, IL. Tour historic homes decked out in their finest. Homes range in size from Quincy's grandest mansions to quaint cottages. Inside each home, ticket holders are awed by the architectural splendors. 10 AM–4 PM. Annually, the third Saturday in October. Est attendance: 1,000. For info: Quincy Preserves, PO Box 1012, Quincy, IL 62306-1012. Phone: (217) 228-8696. E-mail: moreinfo@quincypreserves.org.

"ROSEANNE" TV PREMIERE: ANNIVERSARY. Oct 18, 1988. This comedy showed the blue-collar Conner family trying to make ends meet. Rosanne played wisecracking Roseanne Conner, John Goodman played her husband, Dan, and Laurie Metcalf played her sister, Jackie. The Conner children were played by Sara Gilbert (Darlene), Alicia Goranson and Sarah Chalke (Becky) and Michael Fishman (D.J.). The last episode aired Nov 14, 1997.

SAINT LUKE: FEAST DAY. Oct 18. Patron saint of doctors and artists, himself a physician and painter; authorship of the third Gospel and Acts of the Apostles is attributed to him. Died about AD 68. Legend says that he painted portraits of Mary and Jesus.

SAINT MARY'S COUNTY OYSTER FESTIVAL. Oct 18–19. Fairgrounds, Leonardtown, MD. Oysters served every style, national oyster-shucking contest and national oyster cook-off. Also featuring lots of other seafood and live entertainment! Est attendance: 18,000. For info: Karen Stone, Administrator, Oyster Fest Office, Box 766, California, MD 20619-0766. Phone: (301) 863-5015. E-mail: smcoysterfestival@gmail.com. Web: www.usoysterfest.com.

SWEETEST DAY. Oct 18. Around 1922, a candy company employee named Herbert Birch Kingston decided that it would be a wonderful thing to distribute candy to the sick, shut-ins and orphans of Cleveland, OH. Thus, Sweetest Day was born. Do something nice for someone today, something that will make him or her say, "Oh, that's so sweet!" Annually, the third Saturday in October.

TRUDEAU, PIERRE ELLIOTT: 95th BIRTH ANNIVERSARY. Oct 18, 1919. Prime minister of Canada 1968–79 and 1980–84. Born at Montreal, QC, Canada, he died there Sept 28, 2000.

October 2014	S	M	T	W	T	F	S
				1	2	3	4
	5	6	7	8	9	10	11
	12	13	14	15	16	17	18
	19	20	21	22	23	24	25
	26	27	28	29	30	31	

WATER POLLUTION CONTROL ACT: ANNIVERSARY. Oct 18, 1972. Overriding President Nixon's veto, Congress passed a $25 billion Water Pollution Control Act.

WISCONSIN DELLS AUTUMN HARVEST FEST. Oct 18–19. Wisconsin Dells, WI. Celebrate the 17th annual event with activities including scarecrow-stuffing contest, pumpkin decorating, an arts and crafts fair, hayrides and pony rides, live entertainment, microbrew tasting and more. Est attendance: 15,000. For info: Wisconsin Dells Visitor & Convention Bureau, PO Box 390, Wisconsin Dells, WI 53965. Phone: (800) 223-3557. E-mail: info@wisdells.com. Web: www.wisdells.com/ahf.

WORLD MENOPAUSE DAY. Oct 18. The World Menopause Day challenge calls on every nation to make menopausal health a principal issue in their research and public health agendas in order to help women prevent unpleasant symptoms that can affect productivity and quality of life, as well as reduce rates of osteoporosis, heart disease, colon cancer and other aging- and hormone-related diseases. For info: Intl Menopause Society, PO Box 98, Cambourne, Cornwall TR14 4BQ, United Kingdom. Web: www.imsociety.org.

YORKTOWN VICTORY CELEBRATION. Oct 18–19. Yorktown Victory Center, Yorktown, VA. Military life and artillery demonstrations mark the 233rd anniversary of America's climactic victory at Yorktown. To experience Continental Army life firsthand, visitors may enroll in "A School for the Soldier," where they can drill with wooden muskets and join in other hands-on military activities. Special programs also are held at Yorktown Battlefield, administered by the National Park Service. For info: Jamestown-Yorktown Foundation, PO Box 1607, Williamsburg, VA 23187. Phone: (757) 253-4838 or toll-free (888) 593-4682. Fax: (757) 253-5299. Web: www.historyisfun.org.

BIRTHDAYS TODAY

Chuck Berry, 88, singer, songwriter, musician, born Charles Edward Anderson at St. Louis, MO, Oct 18, 1926.

Pam Dawber, 63, actress ("Mork & Mindy," "My Sister Sam"), born Farmington, MI, Oct 18, 1951.

Mike Ditka, 75, sportscaster, Hall of Fame football player, former coach, born Carnegie, PA, Oct 18, 1939.

Zac Efron, 27, actor (*High School Musical, Hairspray*), born San Luis Obispo, CA, Oct 18, 1987.

Wynton Marsalis, 53, jazz musician, born New Orleans, LA, Oct 18, 1961.

Terry McMillan, 63, author (*How Stella Got Her Groove Back, Waiting to Exhale*), born Port Huron, MI, Oct 18, 1951.

Erin Moran, 53, actress ("Happy Days," "Joanie Loves Chachi"), born Burbank, CA, Oct 18, 1961.

Joe Morton, 67, actor (*The Brother from Another Planet, Trouble in Mind, City of Hope*), born New York, NY, Oct 18, 1947.

Martina Navratilova, 58, Hall of Fame tennis player, born Martina Subertova at Prague, Czechoslovakia (now the Czech Republic), Oct 18, 1956.

Ne-Yo, 35, singer, actor (*Stomp the Yard*), born Shaffer Chimere Smith, Jr, at Camden, AR, Oct 18, 1979.

Freida Pinto, 30, actress (*Slumdog Millionaire*), born Mumbai, India, Oct 18, 1984.

Ntozake Shange, 66, dramatist, poet, born Paulette L. Williams at Trenton, NJ, Oct 18, 1948.

Vincent Spano, 52, actor (*Baby, It's You*; *Rumblefish*), born New York, NY, Oct 18, 1962.

Jean-Claude Van Damme, 54, actor (*Kickboxer*), born Brussels, Belgium, Oct 18, 1960.

Lindsey Vonn, 30, Olympic skier, born St. Paul, MN, Oct 18, 1984.

October 19 — Sunday

DAY 292 **73 REMAINING**

BROWNE, THOMAS: BIRTH ANNIVERSARY. Oct 19, 1605. (Old Style date.) Physician, scholar and author, Browne was born at London, England. At age 55 he wrote: "The long habit of living indisposeth us for dying." His most famous work, *Religio Medici*, was published in 1642. Browne died at Norwich, England, Oct 19, 1682 (OS).

BULLYING BYSTANDERS UNITE WEEK. Oct 19–25. Bullying is a serious issue facing youth today. The missing link is the 85 percent who witness bullying. The self-esteem- and empathy-building international nonprofit organization Hey U.G.L.Y. (Unique Gifted Lovable You) has designated the third full week in October a time for schools and law enforcement agencies to launch a pledge drive to educate their communities on how to safely come to the aid of someone being bullied. For info and pledge forms: Hey U.G.L.Y., PO Box 345, Rolling Prairie, IN 46371. Phone: (219) 778-2011. E-mail: preventbullyingnow@heyugly.org. Web: www.preventbullyingnow.org and www.bullyingbystandersunite.org.

EVALUATE YOUR LIFE DAY. Oct 19. To encourage people to check and see if they're really headed where they want to be. (©2006 by WH.) For info: Thomas & Ruth Roy, Wellcat Holidays, 2418 Long Ln, Lebanon, PA 17042-0774. Phone: (717) 279-0184. E-mail: info@wellcat.com. Web: www.wellcat.com.

FREEDOM FROM BULLIES WEEK. Oct 19–25. A time for courage, support, inspiration and peace for people suffering health-endangering bullying and for others who witness the mistreatment. For info: Workplace Bullying Institute, PO Box 29915, Bellingham, WA 98228. Phone: (360) 656-6630. E-mail: info@workplacebullying.org. Web: www.workplacebullying.org or www.healthyworkplacebill.org.

JEFFERSON, MARTHA WAYLES SKELTON: BIRTH ANNIVERSARY. Oct 19, 1748. Wife of Thomas Jefferson, third president of the US. Born at Charles City County, VA, she died at Monticello, VA, Sept 6, 1782.

LUMIÈRE, AUGUSTE: BIRTH ANNIVERSARY. Oct 19, 1862. Born at Besançon, France, Auguste Lumière with brother Louis were film pioneers who created the first movie, *Workers Leaving the Lumière Factory* (1895). He died at Lyon, France, on Apr 10, 1954.

✦NATIONAL CHARACTER COUNTS WEEK. Oct 19–25. One of the greatest building blocks of character is citizen service. The future belongs to those who have the strength of character to live a life of service to others.

NATIONAL CHEMISTRY WEEK. Oct 19–25. To celebrate the contributions of chemistry to modern life and to help the public understand that chemistry affects every part of our lives. The American Chemical Society provides activities including open houses, contests, workshops, exhibits and classroom visits around the US and Puerto Rico. 2014 topic: "The Sweet Side of Chemistry: Candy!" 10 million participants nationwide. For info: Office of Volunteer Support, American Chemical Society, 1155 16th St NW, Washington, DC 20036. Phone: (800) 227-5558, ext 4458. Fax: (202) 872-4353. E-mail: ncw@acs.org. Web: www.acs.org/ncw.

✦NATIONAL FOREST PRODUCTS WEEK. Oct 19–25. Presidential Proclamation always issued for the week beginning with the third Sunday in October since 1960 (PL 86–753 of Sept 13, 1960).

NATIONAL FRIENDS OF LIBRARIES WEEK. Oct 19–25. 9th annual. The Association of Library Trustees, Advocates, Friends and Foundations (ALTAFF) sponsors this celebration to creatively promote library friends groups in the community, to raise awareness and to promote membership. Also an excellent opportunity for libraries and boards of trustees to recognize friends for their help and support of the library. Annually, the third full week in October. For info: American Library Assn, Public Info Office, 50 E Huron St, Chicago, IL 60611. Phone: (312) 280-5044. Fax: (312) 280-5274. E-mail: pio@ala.org. Web: www.ala.org.

NATIONAL MASSAGE THERAPY AWARENESS WEEK®. Oct 19–25. An annual educational program established in 1997 about the benefits of massage therapy, sponsored by the American Massage Therapy Association. Celebrated by association members and its chapters in all states, it attracts public attention to massage therapy and how it is an important element in health, and how to find a qualified massage therapist through www.findamassagetherapist.org. Annually, the last full week in October. For info: American Massage Therapy Assn, 500 Davis St, Ste 900, Evanston, IL 60201. Phone: (877) 905-2700. Fax: (847) 864-1279. E-mail: NMTAW@amtamassage.org. Web: www.amtamassage.org.

PASTORAL CARE WEEK. Oct 19–25. First observed in 1985. Honors clergy of all faiths who provide pastoral care in congregations and in such specialized settings as hospitals, correctional facilities, mental health systems, the military and counseling centers. For info: Pastoral Care Week, COMISS Network. E-mail: info@comissnetwork.org. Web: www.pastoralcareweek.org.

PECK, ANNIE S.: BIRTH ANNIVERSARY. Oct 19, 1850. World-renowned mountain climber Annie S. Peck also won an international following in 1895 when she climbed the Matterhorn in the Swiss Alps. Peck climbed the Peruvian peak Huascaran (21,812 feet), giving her the record for the highest peak climbed in the Western Hemisphere by an American man or woman, and at age 61 she climbed Mount Coropuna (21,250 feet) in Peru and placed a "Votes for Women" banner at its pinnacle. Peck died July 18, 1935, at New York City.

YORKTOWN DAY. Oct 19. Yorktown, VA. Representatives of the US, France and other nations involved in the American Revolution gather to celebrate the anniversary of the victory (Oct 19, 1781) that assured American independence. Parade and commemorative ceremonies. Annually, Oct 19. Est attendance: 5,000. For info: Public Affairs Officer, Colonial Natl Historical Park, PO Box 210, Yorktown, VA 23690. Phone: (757) 898-2410. Web: www.nps.gov/colo.

YORKTOWN DAY: ANNIVERSARY. Oct 19, 1781. More than 7,000 English and Hessian troops, led by British general Lord Charles Cornwallis, surrendered to General George Washington at Yorktown, VA, effectively ending the war between Britain and its American colonies. There were no more major battles, but the provisional treaty of peace was not signed until Nov 30, 1782, and the final Treaty of Paris, Sept 3, 1783.

BIRTHDAYS TODAY

Michael Gambon, 74, actor ("The Singing Detective," *The Cook, the Thief, His Wife & Her Lover*), born Dublin, Ireland, Oct 19, 1940.

Evander Holyfield, 52, boxer, born Atlanta, GA, Oct 19, 1962.

Patricia Ireland, 69, feminist, social activist, born Oak Park, IL, Oct 19, 1945.

John LeCarré, 83, author (*The Spy Who Came in from the Cold, The Constant Gardener*), born David John Moore Cornwell at Poole, Dorset, England, Oct 19, 1931.

John Lithgow, 69, actor (Tonys for *The Sweet Smell of Success, The Changing Room*; *Don Quixote*, "3rd Rock from the Sun"), author, born Rochester, NY, Oct 19, 1945.

Peter Max, 77, artist, designer, born Berlin, Germany, Oct 19, 1937.

Ty Pennington, 49, carpenter, television personality ("Trading Spaces," "Extreme Makeover: Home Edition"), born Atlanta, GA, Oct 19, 1965.

Jason Reitman, 37, writer, director (*Thank You for Smoking, Juno, Up in the Air*), born Montreal, QC, Canada, Oct 19, 1977.

Simon Ward, 73, actor (*The Three Musketeers, The Four Musketeers*), born London, England, Oct 19, 1941.

Michael Young, 38, baseball player, born Covina, CA, Oct 19, 1976.

October 20 — Monday

DAY 293 **72 REMAINING**

ALASKA DAY. Oct 20. Anniversary of transfer of Alaska on Oct 18, 1867, from Russia to the US. The transfer became official on Sitka's Castle Hill. This is a holiday in Alaska; when it falls on a weekend it is observed on the following Monday.

BIRTH OF THE BAB: ANNIVERSARY. Oct 20, 1819. Baha'i observance of anniversary of the birth in Shiraz, Persia, of Siyyid Ali Muhammad, who later took the title "the Bab"; the Bab was the prophet-herald of the Baha'i Faith. One of the nine days of the year when Baha'is suspend work. For info: Baha'is of the US, Office of Communications, 1233 Central St, Evanston, IL 60201. Phone: (847) 733-3559. Fax: (847) 733-3578. E-mail: ooc@usbnc.org. Web: www.bahai.us.

DEWEY, JOHN: BIRTH ANNIVERSARY. Oct 20, 1859. American psychologist, philosopher and educational reformer, born at Burlington, VT. His philosophical views of education have been termed pragmatism, instrumentalism and experimentalism. Died at New York, NY, June 1, 1952.

GUATEMALA: REVOLUTION DAY. Oct 20. Public holiday. Commemorates the overthrow of dictator Jorge Ubico Castañada in 1944.

JAMAICA: NATIONAL HEROES DAY. Oct 20. National holiday established in 1969. Always observed on third Monday in October.

KENYA: KENYATTA DAY. Oct 20. Public holiday.

LUGOSI, BELA: BIRTH ANNIVERSARY. Oct 20, 1882. Born Bela Ferenc Denzso Blasko at Lugos, Hungary. Known best for his role as Count Dracula in *Dracula*. Lugosi died of a heart attack at Los Angeles, CA, Aug 16, 1956.

MacARTHUR RETURNS: US LANDINGS ON LEYTE, PHILIPPINES: 70th ANNIVERSARY. Oct 20, 1944. In mid-September 1944 American military leaders made the decision to begin the invasion of the Philippines on Leyte, a small island north of the Surigao Strait. With General Douglas MacArthur in overall command, US aircraft dropped hundreds of tons of bombs in the area of Dulag. Four divisions were landed on the east coast, and after a few hours General MacArthur set foot on Philippine soil for the first time since he was ordered to Australia Mar 11, 1942, thus fulfilling his promise, "I shall return."

October 2014

S	M	T	W	T	F	S
			1	2	3	4
5	6	7	8	9	10	11
12	13	14	15	16	17	18
19	20	21	22	23	24	25
26	27	28	29	30	31	

MANN, JAMES ROBERT: BIRTH ANNIVERSARY. Oct 20, 1856. American lawyer and legislator, born near Bloomington, IL. Republican member of Congress from Illinois from 1896 until his death, Nov 30, 1922, at Washington, DC. Mann was the author and sponsor of the "White Slave Traffic Act," also known as the "Mann Act," passed by Congress on June 25, 1910. The act prohibited, under heavy penalties, the interstate transportation of women for immoral purposes.

MANTLE, MICKEY: BIRTH ANNIVERSARY. Oct 20, 1931. Baseball Hall of Famer, born at Spavinaw, OK. Died Aug 13, 1995, at Dallas, TX.

MISS AMERICAN ROSE DAY. Oct 20. Miss American Rose is a pageant devoted to high achievement and community service for girls and women of all ages. On this day, treat the women in your life like beautiful American roses, and/or perform a community service project. For info: Lynanne White, Miss American Rose Pageants, 25767 Norval Ln NW, Poulsbo, WA 98370. E-mail: miss@americanrose.com. Web: www.americanrose.com.

MOSCOW SOCCER TRAGEDY: ANNIVERSARY. Oct 20, 1982. The world's worst soccer disaster occurred at Moscow when 340 sports fans were killed during a game between Soviet and Dutch players. Details of the event, blaming police for the tragedy in which spectators were crushed to death in an open staircase, were not published until nearly seven years later (July 1989) in *Sovietsky Sport*.

NATIONAL NUCLEAR SCIENCE WEEK. Oct 20–24. Inaugurated in 2010, National Nuclear Science Week celebrates and educates about the nuclear advancements to the service of humankind including energy, medicine and scientific research efforts. For info: National Museum for Nuclear Science and History, 601 Eubank Blvd SE, Albuquerque, NM 87123. Phone: (505) 245-2137. Web: NuclearScienceWeek.org.

NATIONAL SCHOOL BUS SAFETY WEEK. Oct 20–24. This week is set aside to focus attention on school bus safety—from the standpoint of the bus drivers, students and the motoring public. Annually, Monday through Friday of the third full week in October. For info: Natl Assn for Pupil Transportation, 1840 Western Ave, Albany, NY 12203. Phone: (800) 989-6278. E-mail: info@napt.org. Web: www.napt.org.

ORBACH, JERRY: BIRTH ANNIVERSARY. Oct 20, 1935. Actor, born at the Bronx, NY, who starred in the original Broadway productions of *The Fantasticks, 42nd Street* and *Chicago*. He won a Best Actor Tony Award for *Promises, Promises* in 1969. Films include *Dirty Dancing* and the voice of Lumiere in Disney's *Beauty and the Beast*. His most popular role was that of wisecracking homicide detective Lennie Briscoe on television's "Law & Order," a role he played from 1992 until his death at New York, NY, on Dec 28, 2004.

SATURDAY NIGHT MASSACRE: ANNIVERSARY. Oct 20, 1973. Anniversary of dramatic turning point in the Watergate affair. On Oct 20, 1973, the White House announced at 8:24 PM, EDT, that President Richard M. Nixon had discharged Archibald Cox (special Watergate prosecutor) and William B. Ruckelshaus (deputy attorney general) and that Attorney General Elliot L. Richardson had resigned. Immediate and widespread demands for impeachment of the president ensued and were not stilled until President Nixon resigned, Aug 9, 1974.

"THE SIX MILLION DOLLAR MAN" TV PREMIERE: ANNIVERSARY. Oct 20, 1973. This action-adventure series based on the novel *Cyborg* was a monthly feature on "The ABC Suspense Movie" before becoming a regular series in 1974. Lee Majors starred as astronaut Steve Austin, who, after an accident, was "rebuilt" with bionic legs, arms and an eye. He worked for the Office of Strategic Information (OSI) carrying out sensitive missions. Also in the cast were Richard Anderson, Alan Oppenheimer and Martin E. Brooks. "The Bionic Woman," starring Lindsay Wagner, was a spin-off from this show, and the two main characters were paired for several made-for-TV sequels.

SYDNEY OPERA HOUSE OPENS: ANNIVERSARY. Oct 20, 1973. One of the most iconic and dramatic man-made structures of the 20th century, the Sydney Opera House, was opened by Queen Elizabeth II at Sydney, Australia, on this date. Designed by Danish architect Jørn Utzon, the theater is perched on Sydney Harbor and appears to be a ship in full sail. It took 14 years to build, and its roof is covered with more than one million tiles.

VIRGIN ISLANDS: HURRICANE THANKSGIVING DAY. Oct 20. Third Monday in October is a legal holiday celebrating the end of hurricane season.

WREN, CHRISTOPHER: BIRTH ANNIVERSARY. Oct 20, 1632. (Old Style date.) Sir Christopher Wren, English architect, astronomer and mathematician, was born at East Knoyle, Wiltshire, England. Died Feb 25, 1723 (OS), at London. His epitaph, written by his son, is inscribed over the interior of the north door at St. Paul's Cathedral, London: "Si monumentum requiris, circumspice." ("If you would see his monument, look about you.")

BIRTHDAYS TODAY

Danny Boyle, 58, filmmaker, director (Oscar for *Slumdog Millionaire*; *127 Hours, Trainspotting*), born Radcliffe, Lancashire, England, Oct 20, 1956.

William Christopher, 82, actor ("M*A*S*H," *With Six You Get Eggroll*), born Evanston, IL, Oct 20, 1932.

Snoop Dogg, 43, rapper, actor, record producer, born Calvin Cordozar Broadus, Jr, at Long Beach, CA, Oct 20, 1971.

Keith Hernandez, 61, former baseball player, born San Francisco, CA, Oct 20, 1953.

John Krasinski, 35, actor ("The Office," *Away We Go, Leatherheads*), born Newton, MA, Oct 20, 1979.

Melanie Mayron, 62, actress (Emmy for "thirtysomething"; *Car Wash, My Blue Heaven*), born Philadelphia, PA, Oct 20, 1952.

Viggo Mortensen, 56, actor (*The Road, Eastern Promises*, the Lord of the Rings trilogy), poet, born New York, NY, Oct 20, 1958.

Tom Petty, 61, singer, songwriter, born Gainesville, FL, Oct 20, 1953.

Brian Schatz, 42, US Senator (D, Hawaii), born Ann Arbor, MI, Oct 20, 1972.

Sheldon Whitehouse, 59, US Senator (D, Rhode Island), born New York, NY, Oct 20, 1955.

October 21 — Tuesday

DAY 294 **71 REMAINING**

ALDERSON, SAMUEL: 100th BIRTH ANNIVERSARY. Oct 21, 1914. Born at Cleveland, OH, Alderson was a physicist and engineer who invented the crash test dummy, an anthropomorphic, data-collecting human body substitute that revolutionized car safety. Alderson died Feb 11, 2005, at Los Angeles, CA.

BATTLE OF TRAFALGAR: ANNIVERSARY. Oct 21, 1805. This famous naval action between the British Royal Navy and the combined French and Spanish fleets removed the threat of Napoleon's invasion of England. The British victory, off Trafalgar on the coast of Spain, guaranteed the fame of Viscount Horatio Nelson, who died in the battle.

CARLETON, WILL: BIRTH ANNIVERSARY. Oct 21, 1845. Anniversary of the birth of poet Will Carleton, observed (by 1919 statute) in Michigan schools, where poems of Carleton must be read on this day. Best known of his poems: "Over the Hill to the Poorhouse." Carleton died in 1912.

COLERIDGE, SAMUEL TAYLOR: BIRTH ANNIVERSARY. Oct 21, 1772. English poet ("The Rime of the Ancient Mariner") and essayist born at Ottery St. Mary, Devonshire, England. Died at Highgate, England, July 25, 1834. In *Table Talk*, he wrote: "I wish our clever young poets would remember my homely definitions of prose and poetry; that is, prose = words in their best order; poetry = the *best* words in the best order."

CRUZ, CELIA: 90th BIRTH ANNIVERSARY. Oct 21, 1924. The Grammy Award–winning singer was dubbed "the Queen of Salsa" by her adoring fans. Born as Celia de la Caridad Cruz Alonso at Havana, Cuba (some sources cite her birth year as 1925 or 1929), Cruz had a career spanning six decades and recorded some 70 albums. Her energetic performances were punctuated by her call of "Azucar!" ("Sugar!") and flamboyant costumes. President Bill Clinton awarded her the National Medal of Arts in 1994. Cruz died at New York, NY, on July 16, 2003.

FILLMORE, CAROLINE CARMICHAEL McINTOSH: BIRTH ANNIVERSARY. Oct 21, 1813. Second wife of Millard Fillmore, 13th president of the US, born at Morristown, NJ. Died at New York, Aug 11, 1881.

GILLESPIE, JOHN BIRKS "DIZZY": BIRTH ANNIVERSARY. Oct 21, 1917. Dizzy Gillespie, trumpet player, composer, bandleader and one of the founding fathers of modern jazz, was born at Cheraw, SC. In the early 1940s Gillespie and alto saxophonist Charlie (Yardbird) Parker created bebop. In the late '40s he created a second music revolution by incorporating Afro-Cuban music into jazz. In 1953 someone fell on Gillespie's trumpet and bent it. Finding he could hear the sound better, he kept it that way; his puffed cheeks and bent trumpet became his trademarks. He won a Grammy in 1975 for *Oscar Peterson and Dizzy Gillespie* and again in 1991 for *Live at the Royal Festival Hall*. He died Jan 6, 1993, at Englewood, NJ.

INCANDESCENT LAMP DEMONSTRATED: ANNIVERSARY. Oct 21, 1879. Thomas A. Edison demonstrated the first incandescent lamp that could be used economically for domestic purposes. This prototype, developed at his Menlo Park, NJ, laboratory, could burn for 13½ hours.

NOBEL, ALFRED BERNHARD: BIRTH ANNIVERSARY. Oct 21, 1833. Chemist and engineer who invented dynamite, born at Stockholm, Sweden, and died at San Remo, Italy, Dec 10, 1896. His will established the Nobel Prize.

OLD IRONSIDES LAUNCHED: ANNIVERSARY. Oct 21, 1797. The USS *Constitution* was launched and christened by Captain James Sever on this date at Boston, MA, making this frigate the oldest commissioned warship afloat in the world. Congress had commissioned the *Constitution* and five other ships in 1794. The *Constitution* earned its nickname, "Old Ironsides," and place in America's heart through valiant service in the War of 1812. In a fight with Britain's HMS *Guerriere* on Aug 19, 1812, sailors reported a British shot repelled by the side of the ship and declared that its sides were made of iron. No enemy ever boarded the ship in its days of active service. It now rests at Boston Harbor. See also: "Old Ironsides Saved by Poem: Anniversary" (Sept 16).

SHAWN, TED: BIRTH ANNIVERSARY. Oct 21, 1891. Named Edwin Myers Shawn at birth, Ted Shawn was born at Kansas City, MO. Partially paralyzed by diphtheria, Shawn was introduced to ballet for therapeutic purposes and became a professional dancer by the age of 21. The Denishawn School of Dancing was established with the help of his wife, Ruth St. Denis, and became the epicenter of much innovation in 20th-century dance and choreography. Among his many achievements is Jacob's Pillow Dance Festival, which he inaugurated and directed for the remainder of his years, and such modern ballets as *Osage-Pawnee, Labor Symphony* and *John Brown*. He died Jan 9, 1972.

SOLTI, GEORG: BIRTH ANNIVERSARY. Oct 21, 1912. Conductor, born at Budapest, Hungary. Sir Georg conducted orchestras at London (for which he was knighted), Paris and Chicago. He died at Antibes, France, Sept 5, 1997.

TAIWAN: OVERSEAS CHINESE DAY. Oct 21. Thousands of overseas Chinese come to Taiwan for this and other occasions that make October a particularly memorable month.

VIETNAM WAR PROTESTERS STORM PENTAGON: ANNIVERSARY. Oct 21, 1967. Some 250 protesters were arrested when thousands of the 50,000 participants in a rally against the Vietnam War at Washington, DC, crossed the Potomac River and stormed the Pentagon. No shots were fired, but many demonstrators were struck with nightsticks and rifle butts.

BIRTHDAYS TODAY

Elvin Bishop, 72, musician, born Glendale, CA, Oct 21, 1942.

Carrie Fisher, 58, actress (*Star Wars, Shampoo*), novelist (*Postcards from the Edge*), born Beverly Hills, CA, Oct 21, 1956.

Frances Fitzgerald, 74, journalist, author (*The Fire in the Lake*), born New York, NY, Oct 21, 1940.

Edward Charles "Whitey" Ford, 86, Hall of Fame baseball player, born New York, NY, Oct 21, 1928.

Kim Kardashian, 34, television personality, born Los Angeles, CA, Oct 21, 1980.

Ursula K. LeGuin, 85, author (*The Wind's Twelve Quarters, A Wizard of Earthsea*), born Berkeley, CA, Oct 21, 1929.

Ken Watanabe, 55, actor (*The Last Samurai*), born Kansaku Watanabe at Koide, Niigata, Japan, Oct 21, 1959.

October 2014	S	M	T	W	T	F	S
				1	2	3	4
	5	6	7	8	9	10	11
	12	13	14	15	16	17	18
	19	20	21	22	23	24	25
	26	27	28	29	30	31	

October 22 — Wednesday

DAY 295 **70 REMAINING**

BEADLE, GEORGE: BIRTH ANNIVERSARY. Oct 22, 1903. Born on a farm near Wahoo, NE, Beadle began his professional career as a professor of genetics at Harvard, eventually becoming president of the University of Chicago. Dr. Beadle won many international honors, including the Nobel Prize in Medicine in 1958 for his work in genetic research, as well as the National Award of the American Cancer Society in 1959 and the Kimber Genetica Award of the National Academy of Science in 1960. Beadle demonstrated how the genes control the basic chemistry of the living cell. Because of his work, he has been described as "the man who did most to put modern genetics on its chemical basis." Beadle died June 9, 1989, at Pomona, CA.

CAPA, ROBERT: BIRTH ANNIVERSARY. Oct 22, 1913. Born Andrei Friedmann at Budapest, Hungary, Capa was one of the great photojournalists in the 20th century, best known for his gritty, close-up battle photography from the five wars he covered in his brief life—most notably the Spanish Civil War, WWII and the early Vietnam War. His handful of images from the midst of the D-Day invasion are legendary, as is his shot of a Spanish loyalist soldier who has just been killed in 1936. Cofounder of the elite Magnum Photos agency, Capa was killed by a land mine on May 25, 1954, at Thai Binh, Vietnam.

CUBAN MISSILE CRISIS: ANNIVERSARY. Oct 22, 1962. President John F. Kennedy, in a nationwide television address on this date, demanded the removal from Cuba of Soviet missiles, launched equipment and bombers and imposed a naval "quarantine" to prevent further weaponry from reaching Cuba. On Oct 28, the USSR announced it would remove the weapons in question. In return, the US removed missiles from Turkey that were aimed at the USSR.

FUNICELLO, ANNETTE: BIRTH ANNIVERSARY. Oct 22, 1942. "America's Sweetheart" was born at Utica, NY. Her first big break was as a Mouseketeer on Disney's "Mickey Mouse Show," a role she successfully transitioned into a career as a pop singer, scoring a string of hits in the 1950s. Funicello hit it big again in the early '60s with a series of "beach party" movies (*Bikini Beach, Pajama Party, Beach Blanket Bingo*), most alongside costar Frankie Avalon. Funicello was diagnosed with multiple sclerosis in 1987, and died from complications due to her condition Apr 8, 2013, at Bakersfield, CA.

HOWARD, CURLY: BIRTH ANNIVERSARY. Oct 22, 1903. Howard, born Jerome Lester Horwitz at Brooklyn, NY, was the brother of Stooges Moe and Shemp. The two older brothers groomed Curly for a life in show business, and he got his big break in 1932 when brother Shemp left the Stooges. Curly took his place, and his manic style of slapstick comedy (with trademark "n'yuk-n'yuks") quickly made him popular. On May 6, 1946, while shooting his 97th Three Stooges film, Howard suffered a stroke and subsequently retired. He died Jan 18, 1952, at San Gabriel, CA.

INTERNATIONAL STUTTERING AWARENESS DAY. Oct 22. For info: Jane Fraser, President, Stuttering Foundation of America, PO Box 11749, Memphis, TN 38111-0749. Phone: (800) 992-9392 or (901) 761-0343. E-mail: info@stutteringhelp.org. Web: www.stutteringhelp.org or www.tartamudez.org in Spanish.

LEARY, TIMOTHY: BIRTH ANNIVERSARY. Oct 22, 1920. Timothy Francis Leary was born at Springfield, MA. Prominent psychologist and professor at Harvard, Leary became an icon of the countercultural movement in the 1960s. He lost his professorship after giving a hallucinogenic drug, psilocybin, to students. Leary was arrested numerous times, and on one occasion, while being held at a California prison, he was forced to submit to a personality test that he had designed himself several years earlier. He continued to advocate the use of LSD in the pursuit of spiritual and political freedom and simply for the fun of it, until his death, of prostate cancer, May 31, 1996, at Beverly Hills, CA.

LISZT, FRANZ: BIRTH ANNIVERSARY. Oct 22, 1811. The Romantic composer Franz Liszt was born at Raiding, Hungary. He was the most celebrated pianist of the 19th century and taught most of the brilliant musicians of his time. In 1848, he moved to the German duchy of Weimar and began to write music. Liszt was a prolific composer best known for his piano music, but he wrote for many mediums, including a sonata, two orchestral symphonies and choral compositions. He died July 31, 1886, at Bayreuth, Germany.

METROPOLITAN OPERA HOUSE OPENING: ANNIVERSARY. Oct 22, 1883. Grand opening of the original New York Metropolitan Opera House was celebrated with a performance of Gounod's *Faust*.

RANDOLPH, PEYTON: DEATH ANNIVERSARY. Oct 22, 1775. First president of the Continental Congress, died at Philadelphia, PA. Born about 1721 (exact date unknown), at Williamsburg, VA.

REED, JOHN: BIRTH ANNIVERSARY. Oct 22, 1887. Journalist and Communist activist, born at Portland, OR. An in-demand reporter and war correspondent, Reed covered the Mexican Revolution and WWI. He married the feminist writer Louise Bryant and traveled with her to Russia in 1917, where they covered the October Revolution. As a supporter of Socialism and the rights of the worker, Reed was sympathetic to the Bolshevik cause. He died of typhus at Moscow on Oct 17, 1920. Reed was buried at the Kremlin Wall Necropolis at Red Square—reserved for heroes of the revolution. His chronicle of the Russian Revolution, *Ten Days That Shook the World* (1919), remains a vital eye-witness account.

SMART IS COOL DAY. Oct 22. A day to celebrate the wide range of abilities in young people and to increase appreciation for their unique areas of intelligence. First observed in West Hartford/Hartford, CT. Annually, Oct 22. For info: Signe Rogalski, Smart Is Cool, PO Box 370431, West Hartford, CT 06137. E-mail: sigrogalski@sbcglobal.net.

TACOMA HOLIDAY FOOD & GIFT FESTIVAL. Oct 22–26. Tacoma Dome, Tacoma, WA. Arts and crafts, gifts, gourmet foods, entertainment and dining, all under the Tacoma Dome. Come visit with artists in the Artists in Action area, bring the little ones down for a visit with Santa, learn culinary secrets from local chefs in the Cooking for the Holidays area and enjoy holiday entertainment by local schools and studios. Est attendance: 45,000. For info: Susie O'Brien Borer, Showcase Events, Inc, PO Box 2815, Kirkland, WA 98083. Phone: (425) 889-9494 or (800) 521-7469. Fax: (425) 889-8165. E-mail: tacoma@showcaseevents.org. Web: www.HolidayGiftShows.com and www.showcaseevents.org.

WORLD'S END DAY: ANNIVERSARY. Oct 22, 1844. Anniversary of the day set as the one on which the world would end by followers of William Miller, religious leader and creator of a movement known as Millerism. Stories about followers disposing of all earthly possessions and climbing to high places on that date are believed to be apocryphal. (Miller was born at Pittsfield, MA, Feb 15, 1782. Died at Low Hampton, NY, Dec 20, 1849.)

BIRTHDAYS TODAY

Brian Anthony Boitano, 51, Olympic figure skater, born Mountain View, CA, Oct 22, 1963.

Jan De Bont, 71, director (*Speed, Twister*), born Amsterdam, Netherlands, Oct 22, 1943.

Catherine Deneuve, 71, actress (*Repulsion, The Last Metro, Indochine*), born Catherine Dorleac at Paris, France, Oct 22, 1943.

Jesse Tyler Ferguson, 39, actor ("Modern Family," "The Class"), born Missoula, MT, Oct 22, 1975.

Jeff Goldblum, 62, actor (*The Big Chill, The Fly, Jurassic Park*), born Pittsburgh, PA, Oct 22, 1952.

Valeria Golino, 48, actress (*Big Top Pee-Wee, Hot Shots!*), born Naples, Italy, Oct 22, 1966.

Derek Jacobi, 76, actor (Tony for *Much Ado About Nothing*; "I, Claudius," "Cadfael," *Hamlet, Love Is the Devil*), born London, England, Oct 22, 1938.

Christopher Lloyd, 76, actor ("Taxi," *Back to the Future* films), born Stamford, CT, Oct 22, 1938.

Carlos Mencia, 47, comedian ("Mind of Mencia"), born San Pedro Sula, Honduras, Oct 22, 1967.

Tony Roberts, 75, actor (*Victor/Victoria, Annie Hall*), born New York, NY, Oct 22, 1939.

Ichiro Suzuki, 41, baseball player, born Kasugai, Japan, Oct 22, 1973.

Arsène Wenger, 65, soccer manager, born Strasbourg, France, Oct 22, 1949.

October 23 — Thursday

DAY 296 **69 REMAINING**

APPERT, NICOLAS: BIRTH ANNIVERSARY. Oct 23, 1752. Also known as "Canning Day," this is the anniversary of the birth of French chef, chemist, confectioner, inventor and author Nicolas Appert, at Chalons-sur-Marne, France. Appert, who also invented the bouillon tablet, is best remembered for devising a system of heating foods and sealing them in airtight containers. Known as "the father of canning," Appert won a prize of 12,000 francs from the French government in 1809 and the title "Benefactor of Humanity" in 1812, for his inventions, which revolutionized our previously seasonal diet. Appert died at Massy, France, June 3, 1841.

BATTLE OF LEYTE GULF: 70th ANNIVERSARY. Oct 23–26, 1944. In response to the Allied invasion of the Philippines at Leyte, the Japanese initiated Sho-Go ("Operation Victory"), an attempt to counter the Allies' next invasion by heavy air attacks. Four carriers were sent south from Japanese waters to lure the US aircraft carriers away from Leyte Gulf. At the same time, Japanese naval forces from Singapore were sent to Brunei Bay, split up into two groups and converged on Leyte Gulf from the north and southwest. The group in the north, under Vice Admiral Kurita Takeo, was to enter the Pacific through the San Bernardino Strait between the Philippine islands of Samar and Luzon. On Oct 23 Kurita lost two of his heavy cruisers to US submarine attack, and one of Japan's greatest battleships, the *Musashi*, was sunk in an aerial attack the next day, but Kurita made his way unopposed through the San Bernardino Strait on Oct 25. The southern group commanded by Vice Admiral Nishimura Teiji was detected on its way to the Surigao Strait and was practically annihilated by the US 7th Fleet as it entered the Leyte Gulf on Oct 25. Kurita, as a result, was forced to turn back from his planned rendezvous with Nishimura. Japan's Sho-Go, rather than inflicting damage on the Americans, resulted in serious losses for the Japanese.

BEIRUT TERRORIST ATTACK: ANNIVERSARY. Oct 23, 1983. A suicidal terrorist attack on American forces at Beirut, Lebanon, killed 240 US personnel when a truck loaded with TNT was driven into and exploded at US headquarters there. A similar attack on French forces killed scores more.

CAMBODIA: PEACE TREATY DAY. Oct 23. National holiday. Commemorates peace treaty of 1991.

CARSON, JOHNNY: BIRTH ANNIVERSARY. Oct 23, 1925. Television talk show host, born at Corning, IA. He worked for various radio and TV shows, including "Who Do You Trust?" He first appeared on "The Tonight Show" in 1958 and was named the permanent host in 1962 with the resignation of Jack Paar. He remained on the air for more than 30 years and, along with sidekick Ed McMahon and bandleader Doc Severinsen, basically invented the TV talk show format as we know it today. When he retired in 1992, he was regarded as a national institution. Carson died at Los Angeles, CA, Jan 23, 2005.

EDERLE, GERTRUDE: BIRTH ANNIVERSARY. Oct 23, 1906. American swimming champion, born at New York City, Gertrude Caroline Ederle was the first woman to swim the English Channel (from Cape Gris-Nez, France, to Dover, England). At age 19 she broke the previous world record by swimming the 35-mile distance in 14 hours, 31 minutes, on Aug 6, 1926. During her swimming career she broke many other records and was a gold medal winner at the 1924 Olympic Games. She died at Wyckoff, NJ, Nov 30, 2003.

FORT LAUDERDALE INTERNATIONAL BOAT SHOW. Oct 23–27. Fort Lauderdale, FL. Everything from small boats to mega-yachts to boating equipment. Visitors attend from all over the world. For info: Fort Lauderdale International Boat Show. Web: www.showmanagement.com or www.sunny.org.

HUNGARY: ANNIVERSARY OF 1956 REVOLUTION. Oct 23. National holiday. Also called Uprising Day of Remembrance. Commemorates revolt against Soviet domination, which was crushed on Nov 4, 1956.

HUNGARY DECLARES INDEPENDENCE: 25th ANNIVERSARY. Oct 23, 1989. Hungary declared itself an independent republic, 33 years after Russian troops crushed a popular revolt against Soviet rule. The announcement followed a weeklong purge by parliament of the Stalinist elements from Hungary's 1949 constitution, which defined the country as a socialist people's republic. Acting head of state Matyas Szuros made the declaration in front of tens of thousands of Hungarians at Parliament Square, speaking from the same balcony from which Imre Nagy addressed rebels 33 years earlier. Nagy was hanged for treason after Soviet intervention. Free elections held in March 1990 removed the Communist Party to the ranks of the opposition for the first time in four decades.

HUNGARY: REPUBLIC DAY. Oct 23. Public holiday observing Hungary's creation as an independent republic in 1989.

INDIA: DIWALI (DEEPAVALI). Oct 23–27. Diwali, the five-day festival of lights that begins today, is the prettiest of all Indian festivals. It celebrates the return of Lord Rama to Ayodhya after a 14-year exile. Thousands of flickering lights illuminate houses and transform urban landscapes while fireworks add color and noise. The goddess of wealth, Lakshmi, is worshipped in Hindu homes on Diwali. Houses are whitewashed and cleaned and elaborate designs drawn on thresholds with colored powder to welcome the fastidious goddess. Because there is no one universally accepted Hindu calendar, this holiday may be celebrated on a different date in some parts of India, but it always falls in the months of October or November.

IPOD UNVEILED: ANNIVERSARY. Oct 23, 2001. The Apple company unveiled its portable MP3 music player to the press on this date. The iPod officially went on sale on Nov 10, 2001, for $399. Critics at the time complained about the cost, but the iPod became incredibly popular. In January 2010, Apple announced that it had sold 250 million iPods.

MOON PHASE: NEW MOON. Oct 23. Moon enters New Moon phase at 5:57 PM, EDT.

NATIONAL MOLE DAY. Oct 23. Celebrated on Oct 23 each year from 6:02 AM to 6:02 PM in observance of the "mole." For 2014 the Mole Day theme is "MOLloween." The "mole" is a way of counting the Avogadro number, 6.02 × 10 to the 23rd power, of anything (just as a "dozen" is a way of counting 12 of anything). Mole Day owes its existence to an early 19th-century Italian physics professor named Amedeo Avogadro. He discovered that the number of molecules in a mole is the same for all substances. Because of this, chemists are able to precisely measure quantities of chemicals in the laboratory. Mole Day is celebrated to help all persons, especially chemistry students, become enthused about chemistry, which is the central science. For info: Rebecca Talik, Executive Director, National Mole Day Foundation, 3896 Leaman Ct, Freeland, MI 48623. E-mail: moleday@hotmail.com. Web: www.moleday.org.

October 2014	S	M	T	W	T	F	S
				1	2	3	4
	5	6	7	8	9	10	11
	12	13	14	15	16	17	18
	19	20	21	22	23	24	25
	26	27	28	29	30	31	

SAINT JOHN OF CAPISTRANO: DEATH ANNIVERSARY. Oct 23, 1456. Giovanni da Capistrano, Franciscan lawyer, educator and preacher, was born at Capistrano, Italy, in 1386, and died of the plague. Feast day is Mar 28.

SCORPIO, THE SCORPION. Oct 23–Nov 22. In the astronomical/astrological zodiac that divides the sun's apparent orbit into 12 segments, the period Oct 23–Nov 22 is traditionally identified as the sun sign of Scorpio, the Scorpion. The ruling planet is Pluto or Mars.

SOLAR ECLIPSE. Oct 23. Partial eclipse of the sun. Visible in the north Pacific, North America.

STATE FAIR OF LOUISIANA. Oct 23–Nov 9. Fairgrounds, Shreveport, LA. Educational, agricultural and commercial exhibits as well as entertainment. Est attendance: 450,000. For info: Chris Giordano, President, Louisiana State Fairgrounds, 3701 Hudson Ave, Shreveport, LA 71109. Phone: (318) 635-1361. Fax: (318) 631-4909. E-mail: info@statefairoflouisiana.com. Web: www.statefairoflouisiana.com.

STEVENSON, ADLAI EWING: BIRTH ANNIVERSARY. Oct 23, 1835. 23rd vice president of the US (1893–97), born at Christian County, KY. Died at Chicago, IL, June 14, 1914. He was grandfather of Adlai E. Stevenson, the Democratic candidate for president in 1952 and 1956. See also: "Stevenson, Adlai Ewing II: Birth Anniversary" (Feb 5).

SWALLOWS DEPART FROM SAN JUAN CAPISTRANO. Oct 23. Traditional date for swallows to depart for the winter from old mission of San Juan Capistrano, CA. See also: "Swallows Return to San Juan Capistrano" (Mar 19).

THAILAND: CHULALONGKORN DAY. Oct 23. Annual commemoration of the death of King Chulalongkorn the Great, who died Oct 23, 1910, after a 42-year reign. King Chulalongkorn abolished slavery in Thailand. Special ceremonies with floral tributes and incense at the foot of his equestrian statue in front of Bangkok's National Assembly Hall.

BIRTHDAYS TODAY

Douglas Richard (Doug) Flutie, 52, sportscaster, former football player, born Manchester, MD, Oct 23, 1962.

Nancy Grace, 56, talk show host, born Macon, GA, Oct 23, 1958.

Ang Lee, 60, director (Oscars for *Brokeback Mountain, Life of Pi* and *Crouching Tiger, Hidden Dragon*), born Taiwan, Oct 23, 1954.

Tiffeny Milbrett, 42, former soccer player, born Portland, OR, Oct 23, 1972.

Pelé, 74, former soccer player, born Edson Arantes do Nascimento at Tres Coracoes, Brazil, Oct 23, 1940.

Juan "Chi-Chi" Rodriguez, 80, former golfer, born Rio Piedras, Puerto Rico, Oct 23, 1934.

Keith Van Horn, 39, former basketball player, born Fullerton, CA, Oct 23, 1975.

Alfred Matthew "Weird Al" Yankovic, 55, singer, satirist, born Lynwood, CA, Oct 23, 1959.

Dwight Yoakam, 58, country singer, actor (*Sling Blade*), born Pikeville, KY, Oct 23, 1956.

October 24 — Friday

DAY 297 **68 REMAINING**

BATTLE OF VITTORIO VENETO: ANNIVERSARY. Oct 24–Nov 3, 1918. Italian forces, commanded by General Armando Diaz, began the last offensive against Austrian troops in upper Italy on this date. The battle began north of the Piave River, and on Oct 30 the Austrian headquarters at Vittorio Veneto was taken. By Nov 1 Austrian troops were breaking up into deserting mobs. A truce was signed at Villa Giusti on Nov 3, which provided for fighting to end the next day. This Allied victory led to the collapse of the Austro-Hungarian Empire.

FIRST BARREL JUMP OVER NIAGARA FALLS: ANNIVERSARY. Oct 24, 1901. The spectacle of Niagara Falls attracted no end of daredevils through the centuries, but the first one to go over the falls and survive in any kind of contraption was the unlikely Annie Edson Taylor, a 63-year-old former dance teacher who was down on her luck and hoping for fame and fortune. On this date, she accomplished this feat in a 160-pound barrel. No one repeated her stunt until 1911.

LOCKWOOD, BELVA A. BENNETT: BIRTH ANNIVERSARY. Oct 24, 1830. Belva Lockwood, an educator, lawyer and advocate for women's rights, was born at Royalton, NY. In 1879 she was admitted to practice before the US Supreme Court—the first woman to do so. While practicing law at Washington, DC, she secured equal property rights for women. By adding amendments to statehood bills, Lockwood helped to provide voting rights for women in Oklahoma, New Mexico and Arizona. In 1884 she was the first woman formally nominated for the US presidency. Died May 19, 1917, at Washington, DC.

NATIONAL PHARMACY BUYER DAY. Oct 24. A day recognizing the work done by the pharmacy buyer. These people perform the difficult job of making sure their pharmacies have needed medication and supplies so that pharmacists and technicians can provide quality health care to the public—all while keeping a watchful eye on the bottom line. It's an often thankless job, and we should take the time today to recognize their efforts. Annually, the Friday of the third full week in October. For info: Michael Thomas, National Pharmacy Purchasing Assn, 4747 Morena Blvd, Ste 340, San Diego, CA 92117. Phone: (858) 851-6373. Fax: (858) 851-6372. E-mail: mike@PharmacyPurchasing.com. Web: www.PharmacyPurchasing.com.

PRESCRIPTION ERRORS EDUCATION AND AWARENESS WEEK. Oct 24–31. According to a Harvard study, more than 107,000 Americans take their prescription medications incorrectly, resulting in hospitalization or death. This week focuses on educating patients and consumers about serious drug interactions, adverse drug events, allergies and the mixing of prescription drugs with herbals and over-the-counter medications. For info: Fred S. Mayer, RPh, MPH, Pharmacists Planning Service, Inc (PPSI), PO Box 6760, San Rafael, CA 94903. Phone: (415) 479-8628 or (415) 302-7351. Fax: (415) 479-8608. E-mail: ppsi@aol.com. Web: www.ppsinc.org.

PURVIS, MELVIN: BIRTH ANNIVERSARY. Oct 24, 1903. Born at Timmonsville, SC, Purvis was America's most famous FBI agent in the 1930s and an early protégé of J. Edgar Hoover, the bureau's influential director. On July 22, 1934, Purvis and his fellow agents cornered John Dillinger outside Chicago's Biograph Theater. The infamous bank robber was shot and killed, and the media hailed Purvis as "the Man Who Got Dillinger." This angered the mercurial and jealous Hoover, who forced him from the FBI for good. Purvis died Feb 29, 1960, at Florence, SC, of a self-inflicted gunshot wound.

SEA WITCH HALLOWEEN & FIDDLERS FESTIVAL. Oct 24–26. Rehoboth Beach/Dewey Beach, DE. Fiddlers Festival, costume parade and contest, Sea Witch Hunt, horse show on the beach, best-costumed pet contest, spook shows and entertainment. Annually, the last full weekend in October. Est attendance: 175,000. For info: Kate Bell, Festival Dir, PO Box 216, Rehoboth Beach, DE 19971. Phone: (800) 441-1329. Fax: (302) 227-8351. E-mail: rehoboth@beach-fun.com. Web: www.beach-fun.com.

SHERMAN, JAMES SCHOOLCRAFT: BIRTH ANNIVERSARY. Oct 24, 1855. 27th vice president of the US (1909–12), born at Utica, NY. Died there Oct 30, 1912.

SPACE MILESTONE: *CHANG'E-1* (PEOPLE'S REPUBLIC OF CHINA). Oct 24, 2007. China successfully launched its first lunar probe into space. Named *Chang'e-1*, the satellite orbited the moon thousands of times for 16 months before it was deliberately crashed onto the moon's surface in March 2009.

STOCK MARKET PANIC: 85th ANNIVERSARY. Oct 24, 1929. After several weeks of a downward trend in stock prices, investors began panic selling on Black Thursday, Oct 24, 1929. More than 13 million shares were dumped. Desperate attempts to support the market brought a brief rally. See also: "Stock Market Crash of 1929: Anniversary" (Oct 29).

✦UNITED NATIONS DAY. Oct 24. Presidential Proclamation. Always issued for Oct 24 since 1948. (By unanimous request of the UN General Assembly.)

UNITED NATIONS DAY: ANNIVERSARY OF FOUNDING. Oct 24, 1945. Official UN holiday commemorates founding of the United Nations and effective date of the UN Charter. In 1971 the General Assembly recommended this day be observed as a public holiday by UN member states (Resolution 2782/xxvi). For info: United Nations, Dept of Public Info, Public Inquiries Unit, Rm GA-57, New York, NY 10017. Phone: (212) 963-4475. Fax: (212) 963-0071. E-mail: inquiries@un.org. Web: www.un.org.

UNITED NATIONS: DISARMAMENT WEEK. Oct 24–30. In 1978 the General Assembly called on member states to highlight the danger of the arms race, propagate the need for its cessation and increase public understanding of the urgent task of disarmament. Observed annually, beginning on the anniversary of the founding of the UN. For info: United Nations, Dept of Public Info, New York, NY 10017. Web: www.un.org.

UNITED NATIONS: WORLD DEVELOPMENT INFORMATION DAY. Oct 24. Anniversary of 1970 adoption by General Assembly of the International Development Strategy for the Second United Nations Development Decade. Object is to "draw the attention of the world public opinion each year to development problems and the necessity of strengthening international cooperation to solve them." For info: United Nations, Dept of Public Info, New York, NY 10017. Web: www.un.org.

WORLD ORIGAMI DAYS. Oct 24–Nov 11. Let's get the world to fold! Celebrate origami by spreading the joy of paper folding during World Origami Days, a 2½-week celebration of the international community of origami. Make origami as visible as possible: teach a class, fold on the bus, give your friends origami, exhibit your models. The possibilities are limitless, just as with origami itself. Annually, Oct 24–Nov 11. For info: OrigamiUSA, 15 W 77th St, New York, NY 10024. Phone: (212) 769-5635. E-mail: admin@origamiusa.org. Web: origamiusa.org/wod.

BIRTHDAYS TODAY

F. Murray Abraham, 74, actor (Oscar for *Amadeus*), born El Paso, TX, Oct 24, 1940.

Drake, 28, singer, born Aubrey Drake Graham at Toronto, ON, Canada, Oct 24, 1986.

Kevin Kline, 67, actor (Oscar for *A Fish Called Wanda*; *Wild Wild West, Dave*), born St. Louis, MO, Oct 24, 1947.

Jeff Merkley, 58, US Senator (D, Oregon), born Myrtle Creek, OR, Oct 24, 1956.

Kweisi Mfume, 66, former NAACP president, born Baltimore, MD, Oct 24, 1948.

Monica, 34, singer, born Monica Arnold at Atlanta, GA, Oct 24, 1980.

Wayne Rooney, 29, soccer player, born Liverpool, England, Oct 24, 1985.

Kyla Ross, 18, Olympic gymnast, born Honolulu, HI, Oct 24, 1996.

Yelberton Abraham (Y.A.) Tittle, Jr, 88, Hall of Fame football player, born Marshall, TX, Oct 24, 1926.

Bill Wyman, 78, musician (Rolling Stones), born William Perks at London, England, Oct 24, 1936.

October 25 — Saturday

DAY 298 **67 REMAINING**

ALABAMA RENAISSANCE FAIRE. Oct 25–26. Florence, AL. Celebration in grand 16th-century style with music, arts and crafts, costumes, theater and dance. Listen to minstrels, dulcimers and autoharps, and watch as knights in shining armor transform Wilson Park into "Fountain-on-the-Green," the scene of a 16th-century faire. Annually, the fourth Saturday and Sunday of October. Est attendance: 30,000. For info: Florence/Lauderdale Tourism, One Hightower Pl, Florence, AL 35630. Phone: (256) 740-4141 or (800) 888-FLO-TOUR. Fax: (256) 740-4142. Web: www.visitflorenceal.com.

BERRYMAN, JOHN: 100th BIRTH ANNIVERSARY. Oct 25, 1914. Born at McAlester, OK, Berryman is considered one of the most innovative, important American poets of the 20th century and is best known for bringing idiomatic American English to poetry. Winner of the 1965 Pultizer Prize for *77 Dream Songs* and, later, the National Book Award for the entire *Dream Songs* collection, Berryman died Jan 7, 1972, at Minneapolis, MN.

BIZET: GEORGES: BIRTH ANNIVERSARY. Oct 25, 1838. Composer, christened Alexandre-César Léopold Bizet, born at Paris, France. His masterpiece *Carmen* (1875) presaged the work of the verismo school of opera that emphasized the realistic and gritty. Throughout his career, Bizet struggled to complete pieces and also to gain recognition for his achievements, which did not come until after his death. *Carmen* scandalized audiences when first performed by its representations of a sexually bold, unrepentant fallen woman and the gritty, immoral world she lives in and by its unconventional use of melodies and musical dissonances new to French opera at the time. Its apparent failure may have contributed to Bizet's early and sudden death on June 3, 1875, at Bougival, France.

October 2014	S	M	T	W	T	F	S
				1	2	3	4
	5	6	7	8	9	10	11
	12	13	14	15	16	17	18
	19	20	21	22	23	24	25
	26	27	28	29	30	31	

BLUE RIDGE FOLKLIFE FESTIVAL. Oct 25. Ferrum College/Blue Ridge Institute and Museum, Ferrum, VA. The largest celebration of authentic folkways in Virginia featuring food, crafts, music and exhibits. Annually, the fourth Saturday in October. Est attendance: 20,000. For info: Roddy Moore, BRI Dir, Ferrum College/BRI, PO Box 1000, Rte 40 W, Ferrum, VA 24088. Phone: (540) 365-4412. Fax: (540) 365-4419. E-mail: bri@ferrum.edu. Web: www.blueridgeinstitute.org.

CHAUCER, GEOFFREY: DEATH ANNIVERSARY. Oct 25, 1400. The best-known English writer and poet of the Middle Ages, Chaucer was born at London, England, probably about 1340. His greatest work, *Canterbury Tales*, consists of some 17,000 poetic lines. Unfinished at his death, it tells the stories of 23 pilgrims. Among his lesser-known prose writings is a treatise on the astrolabe titled *Brede and Milke for Children* (1387), written for "little Lewis, my son." Chaucer died at London and is buried at Westminster Abbey.

EMMA CRAWFORD FESTIVAL AND MEMORIAL COFFIN RACE. Oct 25. Manitou Springs, CO. Fun-filled day of artistically created coffins, Emma's costumes and coffin racing. Est attendance: 8,000. For info: Manitou Springs Chamber of Commerce, 354 Manitou Ave, Manitou Springs, CO 80829. Phone: (800) 642-2567. Fax: (719) 685-0355. Web: www.manitousprings.org.

FIRST FEMALE FBI AGENTS: ANNIVERSARY. Oct 25, 1972. The first women to become FBI agents completed training at Quantico, VA. The new agents, Susan Lynn Roley and Joanne E. Pierce, graduated from the 14-week course with a group of 45 men.

GRENADA INVADED BY US: ANNIVERSARY. Oct 25, 1983. Some 2,000 US Marines and Army Rangers invaded the Caribbean island of Grenada, taking control after a political coup the previous week had made the island a "Soviet-Cuban colony," according to President Reagan. Commemorated as Thanksgiving Day in Grenada, a public holiday.

HOGEYE FESTIVAL. Oct 25. Elgin, TX. Day's events include barbecue pork cook-off, crowning of King Hog or Queen Sowpreme, Cow Patty Bingo, car show, handmade arts and crafts, kids' activities and Elgin's famous hot sausage and live music. Annually, the fourth Saturday in October. Est attendance: 20,000. For info: Hogeye Festival, PO Box 591, Elgin, TX 78621. Phone: (512) 281-5724. Fax: (512) 285-3016. E-mail: hogeye@ci.elgin.tx.us. Web: www.elgintx.com.

INTERNATIONAL MAGIC WEEK. Oct 25–31. A week to celebrate the world of magic and the magicians who create it. Annually, culminates on Oct 31, the anniversary of Harry Houdini's death and Magic Day.

ISLAMIC NEW YEAR. Oct 25. Islamic calendar date: Muharram 1, 1436. The first day of the first month of the Islamic calendar. Different methods for "anticipating" the visibility of the new moon crescent at Mecca are used by different groups. US date may vary. Began at sunset the preceding day.

MACAULAY, THOMAS BABINGTON: BIRTH ANNIVERSARY. Oct 25, 1800. English essayist and historian, born at Rothley Temple, Leicestershire, England. "Nothing," he wrote, "is so useless as a general maxim." Died at Campden Hill, London, Dec 28, 1859.

MAKE A DIFFERENCE DAY. Oct 25. This national day of community service is sponsored by *USA Weekend Magazine*. Volunteer projects are judged by well-known celebrities. Selected projects receive $10,000 charitable awards to further their good work. Key projects are honored in April during National Volunteer Week. More than three million people nationwide participate. For info: Make a Difference Day, *USA Weekend Magazine*, 7950 Jones Branch Dr, McLean, VA 22107. Phone: (800) 416-3824. E-mail: diffday@usaweekend.com. Web: www.makeadifferenceday.com.

NATIONAL FORGIVENESS DAY. Oct 25. 9th annual. A celebration of unconditional love in which people take time to repair, restore, rebuild and revive damaged relationships using the process of unconditional love and forgiveness. Annually, the last Saturday in October. For info: Robert Moyers, 4203 County Rd U4, Liberty Center, OH 43532. Phone: (419) 533-4191. E-mail: bobmoy@wcnet.org. Web: www.unconditionallovelive.com/forgiveness.html.

"NEWHART" TV PREMIERE: ANNIVERSARY. Oct 25, 1982. Bob Newhart starred in this sitcom as Dick Loudon, an author of how-to books who moved with his wife, Joanna (Mary Frann), to Vermont to take over the Stratford Inn. Regulars included Tom Poston as George Utley, inn caretaker; Julia Duffy as Stephanie Vanderkellen, the reluctant maid; Peter Scolari as Michael Harris, producer of Dick's talk show and Stephanie's squeeze; and, as the owners of the Minute Man Café, William Sanderson as Larry and Tony Papenfuss and John Volstad as his silent brothers, both named Darryl. The last telecast was Sept 8, 1990.

PEARL, MINNIE: BIRTH ANNIVERSARY. Oct 25, 1912. Comedian, Grand Ole Opry star, born at Centerville, TN. Pearl died at Nashville, TN, Mar 4, 1996.

PICASSO, PABLO RUIZ: BIRTH ANNIVERSARY. Oct 25, 1881. Called by many the greatest artist of the 20th century, Pablo Picasso excelled as a painter, sculptor and engraver. He is said to have commented once: "I am only a public entertainer who has understood his time." Born at Málaga, Spain, he died Apr 8, 1973, at Mougins, France.

SAINT CRISPIN'S DAY. Oct 25. Martyr in the reign of Diocletian. Saint Crispin's Day is famous as the day in 1415 when King Henry V defeated the superior forces of France at the Battle of Agincourt. A passage in Shakespeare's *Henry V* notes this.

SASAKI, SADAKO: DEATH ANNIVERSARY. Oct 25, 1955. Born at Hiroshima, Japan, in 1943, Sadako Sasaki was two years old when her city was hit by an atomic bomb in the closing days of WWII. She was diagnosed with leukemia in January 1955, and, inspired by a folk tale in which the gods grant a wish to those who fold 1,000 paper cranes, began the task. She died on this date having folded 644 cranes, and her classmates finished the rest. Students across Japan, moved by her story, collected money to create a monument to her that was erected at Hiroshima Peace Park in 1958. Visitors continue to place folded cranes there.

SCARED SILLY: HALLOWEEN IN PROSPECT PARK. Oct 25. Prospect Park, Brooklyn, NY. Celebrate Halloween with a haunted walk through Lookout Hill and a full carnival on the Nethermead. Hear scary stories at Lefferts Historic House—even ride a haunted carousel. Meet creepy-crawly creatures at the Audubon Center. Est attendance: 10,000. For info: Marketing Office, Prospect Park Alliance, 95 Prospect Park W, Brooklyn, NY 11215. Phone: (718) 965-8999. Web: www.prospectpark.org.

TAIWAN EXPELLED FROM UN: ANNIVERSARY. Oct 25, 1971. The United Nations General Assembly voted to admit mainland China and expel Taiwan. This was after many years of debate about which government was the "official" government of China. In 1979 the US accorded diplomatic recognition to mainland China.

TAIWAN: RETROCESSION DAY. Oct 25. Commemorates restoration of Taiwan to Chinese rule in 1945, after a half century of Japanese occupation.

XTERRA KAPALUA TRAIL RUN. Oct 25. Kapalua, Maui, HI. The XTERRA Trail Run Series boasts more than 80 events across the country with runs ranging from 5k to 50k. These extreme, off-road trail runs give runners the chance to prove their skills against a variety of terrain. From calf-burning hills to slippery, mud-covered paths, athletes face the ultimate test of endurance. This race features off-road 5k and 10k trail runs. For info: Emily McIlvaine, XTERRA/TEAM Unlimited, 720 Iwilei Rd #290, Honolulu, HI 96817. Phone: (877) XTERRA-1. E-mail: emily@xterraplanet.com. Web: www.xterratrailrun.com.

BIRTHDAYS TODAY

Brian Kerwin, 65, actor ("Lobo," "The Blue and the Gray"), born Chicago, IL, Oct 25, 1949.

Robert Montgomery (Bobby) Knight, 74, former college basketball coach and player, born Orrville, OH, Oct 25, 1940.

Pedro Martinez, 43, baseball player, born Manoguyabo, Dominican Republic, Oct 25, 1971.

Midori, 43, violinist, born Osaka, Japan, Oct 25, 1971.

Katy Perry, 30, singer, born Santa Barbara, CA, Oct 25, 1984.

Helen Reddy, 72, singer, songwriter, born Melbourne, Australia, Oct 25, 1942.

Marion Ross, 78, actress ("Happy Days," *The Evening Star*), born Albert Lea, MN, Oct 25, 1936.

Anne Tyler, 73, author (*The Accidental Tourist, Breathing Lessons*), born Minneapolis, MN, Oct 25, 1941.

October 26 — Sunday

DAY 299 — **66 REMAINING**

AUSTRIA: NATIONAL DAY. Oct 26. National holiday. Commemorates the withdrawal of Soviet troops in 1955.

COOGAN, JACKIE: 100th BIRTH ANNIVERSARY. Oct 26, 1914. Born John Leslie Coogan at Los Angeles, CA, Coogan became a star after appearing as Charlie Chaplin's companion in *The Kid* (1921). Film earnings and merchandise associated with his name earned considerable income but was squandered by his mother and stepfather. Coogan sued them in 1938, and the legal battle resulted in the passage of the protective California Child Actor's Bill, often called the Coogan Act (1939). A glider pilot during WWII, Coogan later returned to film and television, most famously as Uncle Fester in "The Addams Family" (1964–66). He died Mar 1, 1984, at Santa Monica, CA.

DANTON, GEORGES: BIRTH ANNIVERSARY. Oct 26, 1759. Born at Arcis-sur-Aube, Danton was a lawyer who gradually emerged as a leader in the French Revolution. Despite his charisma, though, he was unable to rein in the murderous factions swirling in the movement. On Mar 29, 1794, Danton and his moderate followers were arrested. His last words before his execution by guillotine at Paris, France, on Apr 5 were: "Show my head to the people. It is worth the trouble."

ERIE CANAL: ANNIVERSARY. Oct 26, 1825. The Erie Canal, first US major man-made waterway, was opened, providing a water route from Lake Erie to the Hudson River. Construction started July 4, 1817, and the canal cost $7,602,000. Cannons fired and celebrations were held all along the route for the opening.

EUROPEAN UNION: DAYLIGHT SAVING TIME (SUMMER TIME) ENDS. Oct 26. Member countries of the European Union turn their clocks back one hour at 1 AM on the last Sunday in October.

A FAMILY HALLOWEEN. Oct 26. Billings Farm and Museum, Woodstock, VT. Mystery stories, doughnuts on a string, pumpkin carving and costume parades plus wagon rides. Children in costume accompanied by an adult admitted free. For info: Billings Farm and Museum, Rte 12 N, Woodstock, VT 05091. GPS address: 69 Old River Rd, Woodstock, VT 05091. Phone: (802) 457-2355. Fax: (802) 457-4663. E-mail: info@billingsfarm.org. Web: www.billingsfarm.org.

GUNFIGHT AT THE O.K. CORRAL: ANNIVERSARY. Oct 26, 1881. At 2:30 PM, the Earp brothers and gambler/dentist Doc Holliday confronted the Clanton and McLaury brothers at a vacant lot behind the O.K. Corral at Tombstone, AZ. After 30 seconds of gunfire, three deaths and decades of romanticizing, the incident would become the most notorious of the Old West. Marshal Virgil Earp and Deputy Marshals Wyatt and Morgan Earp attempted to disarm the Clanton faction, when gunfire erupted, although some witnesses claimed that the Clantons and McLaurys threw up their hands when ordered to. Billy Clanton and Frank and Thomas McLaury died. Virgil and Morgan Earp were wounded. After a 30-day murder trial, the presiding judge dismissed the charges, stating that the Earps and Holliday had acted in self-defense.

HANSOM, JOSEPH: BIRTH ANNIVERSARY. Oct 26, 1803. English architect and inventor Joseph Aloysius Hansom registered his "Patent Safety Cab" in 1834. The two-wheeled, one-horse, enclosed cab, with driver seated above and behind the passengers, quickly became a familiar and favorite vehicle for public transportation. Hansom was born at York, England, and died at London, June 29, 1882.

HAUTE DOG CHARITY HOWL'OWEEN PARADE. Oct 26. Belmont Shore, Long Beach, CA. Just about every breed from boxer to poodle will take over Belmont Shore for the annual Haute Dog Howl'oween Parade. The event has raised thousands of dollars for animal shelters, spay/neuter programs and rescue organizations. About 700 pooches—colorfully costumed for Halloween—are expected to pack Livingston Park for a Yappy Hour before beginning their parade down Second Street. Prizes awarded for the best canine costumes. Annually, the Sunday (on or) before Halloween. Est attendance: 3,000. For info: Justin Rudd. Phone: (562) 439-3316. E-mail: justin@justinrudd.com. Web: www.hautedogs.org.

JACKSON, MAHALIA: BIRTH ANNIVERSARY. Oct 26, 1911. Born at New Orleans, LA, Jackson was the most famous gospel singer of her time. After moving to Chicago, IL, in 1928, Jackson sang with the Johnson Gospel Singers. Thomas A. Dorsey, the father of gospel music, was her adviser and accompanist from 1937 to 1946. By the 1950s, Jackson could be heard in concert halls around the world. She sang at the inauguration of President John F. Kennedy and at the 1963 March on Washington rally. Dr. Martin Luther King, Jr, described her voice as "one heard once in a millennium." She died at Chicago, on Jan 27, 1972, and was buried at New Orleans, LA, where her funeral procession was thronged with mourners.

MOTHER-IN-LAW DAY. Oct 26. Traditionally, the fourth Sunday in October is occasion to honor mothers-in-law for their contributions to the success of families and for their good humor in enduring bad jokes.

MULE DAY. Oct 26. Anniversary of the first importation of Spanish jacks to the US, a gift from King Charles III of Spain. Mules are said to have been bred first in this country by George Washington from this pair of jacks delivered at Boston, MA, Oct 26, 1785.

REFORMATION SUNDAY. Oct 26. Many Protestant churches commemorate Reformation Day (Oct 31—anniversary of the day on which Martin Luther nailed his 95 theses to the door of Wittenberg's Palace church, protesting the sale of papal indulgences, in 1517) each year on the Sunday preceding Oct 31, or on the 31st, if a Sunday.

ROCKEFELLER, ABBY GREENE ALDRICH: BIRTH ANNIVERSARY. Oct 26, 1874. A philanthropist and art patron, Abby Rockefeller was one of the three founders of the New York Museum of Modern Art in 1929. Born at Providence, RI, she died Apr 5, 1948, at New York City.

October 2014	S	M	T	W	T	F	S
				1	2	3	4
	5	6	7	8	9	10	11
	12	13	14	15	16	17	18
	19	20	21	22	23	24	25
	26	27	28	29	30	31	

"ST. ELSEWHERE" TV PREMIERE: ANNIVERSARY. Oct 26, 1982. A popular one-hour medical drama set in St. Eligius Hospital at Boston. Among its large and changing cast were Ed Flanders; William Daniels; Ed Begley, Jr; David Morse; Howie Mandel; Christina Pickles; Denzel Washington; Norman Lloyd; David Birney; G.W. Bailey; Kavi Raz; Stephen Furst; Mark Harmon and Alfre Woodard. The last episode of the series aired on Aug 10, 1988.

SCARLATTI, DOMENICO: BIRTH ANNIVERSARY. Oct 26, 1685. Italian keyboard composer, born at Naples, Italy. Died July 23, 1757, at Madrid, Spain.

SPACE MILESTONE: *SOYUZ 3* (USSR). Oct 26, 1968. After the crash of *Soyuz 1* and the death of its cosmonaut, *Soyuz 3* was launched this date with Colonel Georgi Beregovoy. It orbited Earth 64 times, rendezvousing but not docking with unmanned *Soyuz 2*, which had been launched the day before. Both vehicles returned to Earth under ground control. *Soyuz* means "union."

XTERRA WORLD CHAMPIONSHIP. Oct 26. Kapalua, Maui, HI. The XTERRA World Championship is the culmination of more than 100 off-road triathlon events held across the globe. Includes 1.5k rough-water swim, 30k mountain bike race and 11k trail run. $105,000 pro purse. Est attendance: 10,000. For info: TEAM Unlimited, 720 Iwilei Rd #290, Honolulu, HI 96817. Phone: (808) 521-4322. Fax: (808) 538-0314. E-mail: info@xterraplanet.com. Web: www.xterramaui.com.

BIRTHDAYS TODAY

Phillip "CM Punk" Brooks, 36, professional wrestler, born Chicago, IL, Oct 26, 1978.

Tom Cavanagh, 46, actor ("Ed"), born Ottawa, ON, Canada, Oct 26, 1968.

Hillary Rodham Clinton, 67, former US secretary of state; former US senator (D, New York); former first lady, wife of Bill Clinton, 42nd president of the US; born Park Ridge, IL, Oct 26, 1947.

Sasha Cohen, 30, Olympic figure skater, born Westwood, CA, Oct 26, 1984.

Nick Collison, 34, basketball player, born Orange City, IA, Oct 26, 1980.

Pat Conroy, 69, author (*The Prince of Tides, The Lords of Discipline*), born Atlanta, GA, Oct 26, 1945.

Cary Elwes, 52, actor (*Saw, Glory, The Princess Bride*), born London, England, Oct 26, 1962.

Bob Hoskins, 72, actor (*Mona Lisa, Who Framed Roger Rabbit*), born Bury St. Edmonds, Suffolk, England, Oct 26, 1942.

Miikka Kiprusoff, 38, hockey player, born Turku, Finland, Oct 26, 1976.

Dylan McDermott, 52, actor ("The Practice"), born Waterbury, CT, Oct 26, 1962.

Natalie Merchant, 51, singer, born Jamestown, NY, Oct 26, 1963.

James Pickens, Jr, 60, actor ("Grey's Anatomy," "The X-Files," "The Practice"), born Cleveland, OH, Oct 26, 1954.

Jeff Probst, 52, television personality ("Survivor"), born Wichita, KS, Oct 26, 1962.

Ivan Reitman, 68, filmmaker (*Dave, Ghostbusters*), born Komarno, Czechoslovakia (now the Czech Republic), Oct 26, 1946.

Pat Sajak, 68, game show host ("Wheel of Fortune"), born Chicago, IL, Oct 26, 1946.

Jaclyn Smith, 67, actress ("Charlie's Angels"), former Breck Girl, born Houston, TX, Oct 26, 1947.

Keith Urban, 45, country singer, television personality ("American Idol"), born Whangarei, New Zealand, Oct 26, 1969.

October 27 — Monday

DAY 300 **65 REMAINING**

CHRISTOPHER, WARREN: BIRTH ANNIVERSARY. Oct 27, 1925. American public official and diplomat, born at Scranton, ND. As secretary of state in the first Clinton administration, Warren was an architect of the Oslo Peace Accords and the Israel–Jordan peace treaty, and also advocated for NATO expansion. Previously served as deputy attorney general in the Lyndon Johnson administration and the deputy secretary of state in the Jimmy Carter administration, where he oversaw the completion of the Panama Canal Treaty. Died Mar 18, 2011, at Los Angeles, CA.

COOK, JAMES: BIRTH ANNIVERSARY. Oct 27, 1728. (Old Style date.) English sea captain of the ship *Endeavour* and explorer who brought Australia and New Zealand into the British Empire. Born at Marton-in-Cleveland, Yorkshire, England, he was killed Feb 14, 1779, at the Hawaiian Islands, which he discovered.

CRANKY COWORKERS DAY. Oct 27. Because all of us have bad days (some more than others), here's a day when crankiness at work is actually encouraged. (©2006 by WH.) For info: Thomas & Ruth Roy, Wellcat Holidays, 2418 Long Ln, Lebanon, PA 17046. Phone: (717) 279-0184. E-mail: info@wellcat.com. Web: www.wellcat.com.

***FEDERALIST* PAPERS: ANNIVERSARY.** Oct 27, 1787. The first of the 85 *Federalist* papers appeared in print in a New York City newspaper. These essays, written by Alexander Hamilton, James Madison and John Jay, argued in favor of adoption of the new Constitution and the new form of federal government. The last of the essays was completed Apr 4, 1788.

HURRICANE MITCH: ANNIVERSARY. Oct 27, 1998. More than 7,000 people were killed at Honduras by flooding caused by Hurricane Mitch. Thousands more were killed in other Central American countries, especially Nicaragua.

IRELAND: OCTOBER BANK HOLIDAY. Oct 27. Bank holiday in the Republic of Ireland. Annually, the last Monday in October. Also called Halloween Holiday.

LICHTENSTEIN, ROY: BIRTH ANNIVERSARY. Oct 27, 1923. Pop artist who used comic strips and other elements of pop culture in his paintings. Born at New York City, he died there Sept 29, 1997.

NAVY DAY. Oct 27. Established in 1922 to honor the "past and present services" of the US Navy to the nation. Also honored Theodore Roosevelt, whose birth date is Oct 27 (and who had been assistant secretary of the Navy early in his public career). Not a national holiday, it was last observed in 1949.

NEW YORK CITY SUBWAY: ANNIVERSARY. Oct 27, 1904. Running from City Hall to W 145th St, the New York City subway began operation. It was privately operated by the Interborough Rapid Transit Company and later became part of the system operated by the New York City Transit Authority.

NEW ZEALAND: LABOR DAY. Oct 27. National holiday on the fourth Monday in October.

PAGANINI, NICOLO: BIRTH ANNIVERSARY. Oct 27, 1782. Hailed as the greatest violin virtuoso of all time, Paganini was born at Genoa, Italy. Unusually long arms contributed to his legendary Mephistophelian appearance—and probably to his unique skills as a performer. His immensely popular concerts brought him considerable wealth, but his compulsive gambling repeatedly humbled the genius. Paganini died at Nice, France, May 27, 1840.

ROOSEVELT, THEODORE: BIRTH ANNIVERSARY. Oct 27, 1858. 26th president of the US, succeeded to the presidency on the death of William McKinley. His term of office: Sept 14, 1901–Mar 3, 1909. Roosevelt was the first president to ride in an automobile (1902), to submerge in a submarine (1905) and to fly in an airplane (1910). Although his best-remembered quote was perhaps "Speak softly and carry a big stick," he also said: "The first requisite of a good citizen in this Republic of ours is that he shall be able and willing to pull his weight." Born at New York, NY, Roosevelt died at Oyster Bay, NY, Jan 6, 1919. His last words: "Put out the light."

SAINT VINCENT AND THE GRENADINES: INDEPENDENCE DAY: 35th ANNIVERSARY. Oct 27. National day commemorating independence from Britain in 1979.

THOMAS, DYLAN MARLAIS: 100th BIRTH ANNIVERSARY. Oct 27, 1914. Welsh poet, memoirist and playwright, born at Swansea, Wales. Thomas worked as a BBC broadcaster and poetry commentator in the 1940s and 1950s; his sonorous voice made him famous and contributed to the success of his US tours in the early 1950s. His famous poems include "Do Not Go Gentle into That Good Night" (1951). He died at New York, NY, Nov 9, 1953.

TURKMENISTAN: INDEPENDENCE DAY. Oct 27. National holiday. Commemorates independence from the Soviet Union in 1991.

"WALT DISNEY" TV PREMIERE: 60th ANNIVERSARY. Oct 27, 1954. This highly successful and long-running show appeared on different TV networks under different names but was essentially the same show. It was the first ABC series to break the Nielsen's top 20 and the first prime-time anthology series for kids. "Walt Disney" was originally titled "Disneyland" to promote the park and upcoming Disney releases. When it switched networks, it was called "Walt Disney's Wonderful World of Color" to highlight its being broadcast in color. Presentations featured edited versions of previously released Disney films and original productions (including natural history documentaries, behind-the-scenes peeks at Disney shows and dramatic shows, such as the popular Davy Crockett segments, which were the first TV miniseries). The show went off the air in December 1980 after 25 years, making it one of the longest-running series in prime-time TV history. In 1997 ABC revived the series as "Wonderful World of Disney."

ZAMBIA: INDEPENDENCE DAY. Oct 27. National holiday commemorates the independence of what was then Northern Rhodesia from Britain Oct 24, 1964. Celebrations in all cities, but main parades of military, labor and youth organizations are at the capital, Lusaka. Observed on the fourth Monday in October.

BIRTHDAYS TODAY

Roberto Benigni, 62, actor, director (Oscar for *Life Is Beautiful*), born Arezzo, Italy, Oct 27, 1952.

John Cleese, 75, actor, writer ("Monty Python's Flying Circus," "Fawlty Towers," *A Fish Called Wanda*), born Weston-Super-Mare, England, Oct 27, 1939.

Ruby Dee, 90, actress ("Ossie and Ruby," *Zora Is My Name, Do the Right Thing*), born Cleveland, OH, Oct 27, 1924.

Matt Drudge, 48, journalist ("The Drudge Report"), born Takoma Park, MD, Oct 27, 1966.

Nanette Fabray, 94, actress (Emmy for "Caesar's Hour"; "One Day at a Time," the Our Gang comedies), born San Diego, CA, Oct 27, 1920.

Simon LeBon, 56, singer (Duran Duran), born Bushey, England, Oct 27, 1958.

Fran Lebowitz, 64, essayist, humorist (*Social Studies*), born Morristown, NJ, Oct 27, 1950.

Marla Maples, 51, model, actress, born Dalton, GA, Oct 27, 1963.

Brandon Saad, 22, hockey player, born Pittsburgh, PA, Oct 27, 1992.

Zadie Smith, 39, author (*NW, On Beauty, White Teeth*), born Sadie Smith at Brent, London, England, Oct 27, 1975.

October 28 — Tuesday

DAY 301 **64 REMAINING**

BACON, FRANCIS: BIRTH ANNIVERSARY. Oct 28, 1909. Noted 20th-century artist whose work explored religion, social convention and the self with stark, often gruesome imagery. Born at Dublin, Ireland, Bacon spent much of his adult life in London, England. He died at Madrid, Spain, April 28, 1992.

CZECH REPUBLIC: INDEPENDENCE DAY. Oct 28. National Day. Anniversary of the bloodless revolution at Prague in 1918 resulting in independence from the Austro-Hungarian Empire, after which the Czechs and Slovaks united to form Czechoslovakia (a union they dissolved without bloodshed in 1993).

DONNER PARTY FAMINE: ANNIVERSARY. Oct 28, 1846–Apr 21, 1847. The pioneering Donner party, a group of 90 people consisting of immigrants, families and businessmen led by George and Jacob Donner and James F. Reed, headed toward California in 1846 from Springfield, IL, in hopes of beginning a new life. They experienced the normal travails of caravan travel until their trip took several sensational twists. Indian attacks and winter weather, which forced them to interrupt their journey, led to famine and outright cannibalism, which took their toll on members of the party, whose numbers dwindled to 48 by journey's end.

ERASMUS, DESIDERIUS: BIRTH ANNIVERSARY. Oct 28, 1467. Dutch author and scholar Desiderius Erasmus was born at Rotterdam, Netherlands, probably Oct 28, 1467. Best known of his writings is *Encomium Moriae* (*In Praise of Folly*). Erasmus died at Basel, Switzerland, July 12, 1536.

ESCOFFIER, GEORGES AUGUSTE: BIRTH ANNIVERSARY. Oct 28, 1846. Celebrated French chef and author, inventor of the pêche Melba (honoring the operatic singer Dame Nellie Melba), Escoffier became known as "the king of chefs and the chef of kings." Born at Villeneuve-Loubet, France. He was awarded the Legion d'Honneur in recognition of his contribution to the international reputation of French cuisine, and his service at the Savoy and Carlton hotels at London, England, brought him world fame. He died at Monte Carlo, Monaco, Feb 12, 1935.

FIRST WOMAN US AMBASSADOR APPOINTED: 65th ANNIVERSARY. Oct 28, 1949. Helen Eugenie Moore Anderson became the first woman to hold the post of US ambassador when she was sworn in by President Harry S Truman on this date. She served as ambassador to Denmark.

GERMAN REVOLUTION OF 1918: ANNIVERSARY. Oct 28, 1918. On this date in the final days of WWI, crews of six German battleships protested a series of planned cruiser raids. A mutiny broke out in the fleet at Kiel. All but one of the ships remaining in port ran up the red flag of revolution: 600 sailors were arrested and imprisoned on shore. The uprising spread to Hamburg, Bremen and Lubeck. On Nov 9 a general strike at Berlin brought the administration to a halt. The abdication of Kaiser Wilhelm began to be seen as the only way to avoid a full-scale revolution.

GREECE: OCHI DAY. Oct 28. National holiday. Commemorates Greek resistance and refusal to open its borders when Mussolini's Italian troops attacked Greece, Oct 28, 1940. *Ochi* means "no." Celebrated with military parades, especially at Athens and Thessaloniki.

HANSON, HOWARD: BIRTH ANNIVERSARY. Oct 28, 1896. Born at Wahoo, NE, Howard Hanson in 1921 became the first American to win the Prix de Rome. In 1924 he became head of the Eastman School of Music at the University of Rochester, NY, where he served for 40 years. Best known for the music he composed, Hanson was awarded the Pulitzer Prize as outstanding contemporary composer in 1944 for his composition *Symphony No. 4*, the George Foster Peabody Award in 1946, the Laurel Leaf of the American Composers Alliance in 1957 and the Huntington Hartford Foundation Award in 1959. He died at Rochester, Feb 26, 1981.

HARVARD UNIVERSITY FOUNDED: ANNIVERSARY. Oct 28, 1636. (Old Style date.) Harvard University was founded at Cambridge, MA, when the Massachusetts General Court voted to provide £400 for a "schoale or colledge."

"THE JACK BENNY PROGRAM" TV PREMIERE: ANNIVERSARY. Oct 28, 1950. One of radio's favorite comedians, Jack Benny made the transition to favorite TV personality with this situation comedy–variety show in 1950. Regulars included Eddie Anderson, Don Wilson, Dennis Day, Mel Blanc, Mary Livingstone (Benny's real-life wife) and Frank Nelson. Benny also had guest stars, including Ken Murray, Frank Sinatra, Claudette Colbert and Basil Rathbone as well as TV newcomers Johnny Carson, Marilyn Monroe and Humphrey Bogart. Famous for his cheapness, Benny had a guard for his vaults, which created many laughs.

SAINT JUDE'S DAY. Oct 28. St. Jude, the saint of hopeless causes, was martyred along with St. Simon at Persia, and their feast is celebrated jointly. St. Jude was supposedly the brother of Jesus and, like his brother, a carpenter by trade. He is most popular with those who attempt the impossible and with students, who often ask for his help on exams.

SALK, JONAS: 100th BIRTH ANNIVERSARY. Oct 28, 1914. Dr. Jonas Salk, developer of the Salk polio vaccine, was born at New York, NY. Salk announced his development of a successful vaccine in 1953, the year after a polio epidemic claimed some 3,300 lives in the US. Polio deaths were reduced by 95 percent after the introduction of the vaccine. Salk spent the last 10 years of his life doing AIDS research. He died June 23, 1995, at La Jolla, CA.

SPACE MILESTONE: INTERNATIONAL SPACE RESCUE AGREEMENT. Oct 28, 1970. US and USSR officials agreed upon space rescue cooperation.

STATUE OF LIBERTY DEDICATION: ANNIVERSARY. Oct 28, 1886. Frederic Auguste Bartholdi's famous sculpture, the statue of *Liberty Enlightening the World*, on Bedloe's Island at New York Harbor, was dedicated. Ground breaking for the structure was in April 1883. A sonnet by Emma Lazarus, inside the pedestal of the statue, contains the words "Give me your tired, your poor, your huddled masses yearning to breathe free, the wretched refuse of your teeming shore. Send these, the homeless, tempest-tossed, to me: I lift my lamp beside the golden door."

WILSON'S VOLSTEAD PROHIBITION ACT VETO OVERRIDDEN: 95th ANNIVERSARY. Oct 28, 1919. Woodrow Wilson's veto of the Volstead Prohibition Act was overridden by Congress.

October 2014

S	M	T	W	T	F	S
			1	2	3	4
5	6	7	8	9	10	11
12	13	14	15	16	17	18
19	20	21	22	23	24	25
26	27	28	29	30	31	

BIRTHDAYS TODAY

Jane Alexander, 75, actress (*The Great White Hope, Kramer vs Kramer*), former chair of the National Endowment for the Arts, born Jane Quigley at Boston, MA, Oct 28, 1939.

Charlie Daniels, 78, musician, singer, songwriter, born Wilmington, NC, Oct 28, 1936.

Jeremy Davies, 45, actor (*Saving Private Ryan*), born Rockford, IA, Oct 28, 1969.

Terrell Davis, 42, former football player, born San Diego, CA, Oct 28, 1972.

Dennis Franz, 70, actor ("Hill Street Blues," "NYPD Blue"), born Maywood, IL, Oct 28, 1944.

Bill Gates, 59, former computer software executive (Microsoft), philanthropist, born Seattle, WA, Oct 28, 1955.

Jami Gertz, 49, actress ("Still Standing," *Twister*), born Chicago, IL, Oct 28, 1965.

Lauren Holly, 51, actress (*Dumb and Dumber*, "Picket Fences"), born Geneva, NY, Oct 28, 1963.

Telma Hopkins, 66, singer, actress ("Family Matters"), born Louisville, KY, Oct 28, 1948.

Bruce Jenner, 65, television personality, Olympic decathlete, born Mount Kisco, NY, Oct 28, 1949.

Brad Paisley, 42, country singer, born Glen Dale, WV, Oct 28, 1972.

Annie Potts, 62, actress ("Designing Women," *Ghostbusters, Pretty in Pink*), born Nashville, TN, Oct 28, 1952.

Andy Richter, 48, actor, cohost ("Conan"), born Grand Rapids, MI, Oct 28, 1966.

Julia Roberts, 47, actress (Oscar for *Erin Brockovich*; *Ocean's Eleven, My Best Friend's Wedding*), born Smyrna, GA, Oct 28, 1967.

Matt Smith, 32, actor ("Doctor Who"), born Northampton, England, Oct 28, 1982.

October 29 — Wednesday

DAY 302 | **63 REMAINING**

BOSWELL, JAMES: BIRTH ANNIVERSARY. Oct 29, 1740. (Old Style date.) Scottish biographer, born at Edinburgh, Scotland. "I think," he wrote in his monumental biography, *Life of Samuel Johnson*, "no innocent species of wit or pleasantry should be suppressed: and that a good pun may be admitted among the smaller excellencies of lively conversation." Died at London, England, May 19, 1795.

DUNNE, DOMINICK: BIRTH ANNIVERSARY. Oct 29, 1925. Born at Hartford, CT, this writer and journalist enjoyed a long career in television production before writing fiction. It was following the brutal murder of his daughter in 1982 that he began chronicling true crime stories, mainly for *Vanity Fair* magazine. He is remembered for his diary-style coverage of assorted celebrity trials, notably those of O.J. Simpson and Claus von Bulow. Equally at home among the Hollywood jet set, he had a unique voice and talent for fictionalizing real-life events and scandals. Dunne died at New York, NY, Aug 26, 2009.

EBBETS, CHARLES: BIRTH ANNIVERSARY. Oct 29, 1859. Charles Hercules Ebbets, baseball executive, born at New York, NY. Ebbets bought into the Brooklyn baseball club in 1890 and became controlling owner in 1898. He sold 50 percent of the team to build Ebbets Field, the park whose enduring reputation has been the model for the new, old-fashioned parks constructed in recent years. Died at New York, Apr 18, 1925.

EMMETT, DANIEL DECATUR: BIRTH ANNIVERSARY. Oct 29, 1815. Creator of words and music for the song "Dixie's Land" ("Dixie"), which became a fighting song for Confederate troops and unofficial anthem of the South. Emmett was born at Mount Vernon, OH, and died there June 28, 1904.

GOEBBELS, PAUL JOSEF: BIRTH ANNIVERSARY. Oct 29, 1897. German Nazi leader, born at Rheydt, Germany, who became Hitler's minister of propaganda, having earlier been rejected by the military because of a limp caused by infantile paralysis. Killed himself, his wife and his children May 1, 1945, in Hitler's bunker in Berlin as Russian forces advanced into the city.

INTERNET CREATED: 45th ANNIVERSARY. Oct 29, 1969. The first connection on what would become the Internet was made on this day when bits of data flowed between computers at UCLA and the Stanford Research Institute. This was the beginning of ARPANET, the precursor to the Internet developed by the Department of Defense. By the end of 1969 four sites were connected: UCLA, the Stanford Research Institute, the University of California at Santa Barbara and the University of Utah. By the next year there were 10 sites, and soon there were applications like e-mail and file transfer utilities. The @ symbol was adopted in 1972, and a year later 75 percent of ARPANET traffic was e-mail. ARPANET was decommissioned in 1990, and the National Science Foundation's NSFnet took over the role of backbone of the Internet.

NATIONAL CAT DAY. Oct 29. Every year approximately 4 million cats enter shelters—and 1–2 million are euthanized. Often cats are overlooked and underappreciated because they don't usually have jobs like dogs. Yet cats still lower blood pressure, offer unconditional love and companionship and alert their owners of danger. Cats have so many purr-sonalities and there is so much to love about them! On National Cat Day, please visit a local shelter and offer love and life by adopting a cat. The goal of this day is to facilitate the adoption of 10,000 shelter cats nationwide. Even if you can't adopt a cat, offer to clean a cage or sit and play with a cat for a while. Who knows? You may just fall in love! Annually, Oct 29. For info: Colleen Paige, Animal Miracle Foundation, 4804 NW Bethany Blvd, Ste 12-197, Portland, OR 97229. Phone: (323) 552-9941. E-mail: info@animalmiraclefoundation.org. Web: www.nationalcatday.com.

SPACE MILESTONE: OLDEST MAN IN SPACE: *DISCOVERY* (US). Oct 29, 1998. Former astronaut and senator John Glenn became the oldest man in space when he traveled on the space shuttle *Discovery* at the age of 77. In 1962 on *Friendship 7* Glenn had been the first American to orbit Earth. See also: "Space Milestone: *Friendship 7*" (Feb 20).

STOCK MARKET CRASH OF 1929: 85th ANNIVERSARY. Oct 29, 1929. Prices on the New York Stock Exchange plummeted and virtually collapsed four days after President Herbert Hoover had declared, "The fundamental business of the country . . . is on a sound and prosperous basis." More than 16 million shares were dumped, and billions of dollars were lost. The boom was over, and the nation faced nearly a decade of depression. Some analysts had warned that the buying spree, with prices 15 to 150 times above earnings, had to stop at some point. Frightened investors ordered their brokers to sell at whatever price. The resulting Great Depression, which lasted until about 1939, involved North America, Europe and other industrialized countries. In 1932 one out of four US workers was unemployed.

SUPERSTORM SANDY SLAMS INTO US: ANNIVERSARY. Oct 29, 2012. The superstorm—almost 900 miles in diameter at landfall in the US—hit Atlantic City, NJ, on the evening of Oct 29, 2012, and wreaked havoc across the northeastern US. As a category 1 hurricane beginning on Oct 24, Sandy had swept through the Caribbean (causing 60 deaths in Haiti). By landfall on Oct 29, it was an extratropical cyclone. The loss in life in the US was more than 125 people; the damages were estimated at almost $50 billion. More than 8 million people were left without power. The storm affected the Mid-Atlantic states as well, causing three inches of snowfall in that region.

TURKEY: REPUBLIC DAY. Oct 29. Anniversary of the founding of the republic in 1923.

 BIRTHDAYS TODAY

Richard Dreyfuss, 67, actor (*Mr Holland's Opus, Jaws*; Oscar for *The Goodbye Girl*), born Brooklyn, NY, Oct 29, 1947.

Joely Fisher, 49, actress ("'Til Death," "Ellen"), born Los Angeles, CA, Oct 29, 1965.

Finola Hughes, 54, actress ("General Hospital," *Staying Alive*), born London, England, Oct 29, 1960.

Kate Jackson, 66, actress ("Charlie's Angels," "Scarecrow and Mrs King"), born Birmingham, AL, Oct 29, 1948.

Randy Jackson, 53, singer (Jackson 5), born Steven Randall Jackson at Gary, IN, Oct 29, 1961.

Melba Moore, 69, singer, actress, born New York, NY, Oct 29, 1945.

Winona Ryder, 43, actress (*Girl, Interrupted*; *Little Women*), born Winona Horowitz at Winona, MN, Oct 29, 1971.

Rufus Sewell, 47, actor (*Abraham Lincoln: Vampire Hunter, The Pillars of the Earth, Dark City*), born Twickenham, England, Oct 29, 1967.

Gabrielle Union, 42, actress (*Bring It On, The Honeymooners*), born Omaha, NE, Oct 29, 1972.

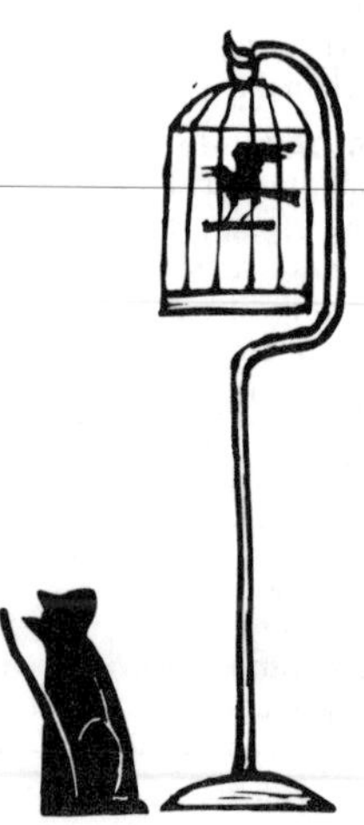

October 2014

S	M	T	W	T	F	S
			1	2	3	4
5	6	7	8	9	10	11
12	13	14	15	16	17	18
19	20	21	22	23	24	25
26	27	28	29	30	31	

October 30 — Thursday

DAY 303 **62 REMAINING**

ADAMS, JOHN: BIRTH ANNIVERSARY. Oct 30, 1735. Second president of the US (term of office: Mar 4, 1797–Mar 3, 1801). Adams had been George Washington's vice president and was the father of John Quincy Adams (sixth president of the US). Born at Braintree, MA, he once wrote in a letter to his wife, Abigail: "I must study politics and war that my sons may have liberty to study mathematics and philosophy." Adams and Thomas Jefferson died on the same day, July 4, 1826. Adams died at Quincy, MA. See also: "Adams, John, and Jefferson, Thomas: Death Anniversary" (July 4).

ATLAS, CHARLES: BIRTH ANNIVERSARY. Oct 30, 1893. Charles Atlas (former 97-pound weakling), whose original name was Angelo Siciliano, was born at Acri, Calabria, Italy. A bodybuilder and physical culturist, he created a popular mail-order bodybuilding course. The legendary sand-kicking episode used later in advertising for his course occurred at Coney Island, NY, when a lifeguard kicked sand in Atlas's face and stole his girlfriend. Three generations of comic book fans read his advertisements. He died Dec 24, 1972, at Long Beach, NY.

CHECKLISTS DAY. Oct 30. In recognition of the development of the first well-known checklist, following the crash of a B-17 Flying Fortress prototype caused by pilot error on this date in 1935. Use checklists to help avoid tragedy and disappointment and take advantage of opportunities. For info: Don Parcher, 580 Viridian Dr, #110, Lafayette, CO 80026. Phone: (619) 987-5434. E-mail: don@checklists.com. Web: checklists.com/checklists-day.

CLOSING OF COLUMBIAN EXPOSITION: ANNIVERSARY. Oct 30, 1893. After a rousing success, the Columbian Exposition at Chicago, IL, held "American Cities Day" Oct 28, and Chicago mayor Carter Harrison gave a speech before the visiting mayors. After he arrived home, Harrison was shot and killed by Patrick Eugene Prendergast. Instead of the elaborate ceremony that had been planned to close the exposition on Oct 30, a single speech was given and the flags were lowered to half-mast.

CREATE A GREAT FUNERAL DAY. Oct 30. A day to remind people of all the benefits of creating their own unique funerals or memorial services, regardless of age or state of health. For info: Stephanie West Allen, 1376 S Wyandot St, Denver, CO 80223. Phone: (303) 935-8866. E-mail: stephanie@westallen.com.

DEVIL'S NIGHT. Oct 30. Formerly a "Mischief Night" on the evening before Halloween and an occasion for harmless pranks, chiefly observed by children. However, in some areas of the US, the destruction of property and endangering of lives has led to the imposition of dusk-to-dawn curfews during the last two or three days in October. Not to be confused with "Trick or Treat," or "Beggar's Night," usually observed on Halloween. See also: "Hallowe'en" (Oct 31).

HALSEY, WILLIAM "BULL" FREDERICK: BIRTH ANNIVERSARY. Oct 30, 1882. American admiral and fleet commander who played a leading role in the defeat of the Japanese in the Pacific naval battles of WWII, William Halsey was born at Elizabeth, NJ. In April 1942, aircraft carriers under his command ferried Jimmy Doolittle's B-25s to within several hundred miles of Japan's coast. From that location the aircraft were launched from the decks of the carriers for a raid on Tokyo. In October 1942, as commander of all the South Pacific area, Halsey led naval forces in the defeat of Japan at Guadalcanal, and in November 1943 he directed the capture of Bougainville, both in the Solomon Islands. He supported the landings in the Philippines in June 1944. In the great naval battle of Leyte Gulf (Oct 23–26, 1944), he assisted in an overwhelming defeat of the Japanese. On Sept 2, 1945, Japan's final instrument of surrender was signed in Tokyo Bay aboard Halsey's flagship, the USS *Missouri*. Halsey died at Fishers Island, NY, Aug 16, 1959.

HAUNTED REFRIGERATOR NIGHT. Oct 30. Who knows what evil lurks in the refrigerators of men and women? It's time to be afraid, very afraid. Gather friends, open the refrigerator door and venture into the realm of the lower shelf, rear. That "thing" inside that container is much more horrifying than any haunted hayride. Annually, Oct 30. (©2006 by WH.) For info: Thomas & Ruth Roy, Wellcat Holidays, 2418 Long Ln, Lebanon, PA 17046. Phone: (717) 279-0184. E-mail: info@wellcat.com. Web: www.wellcat.com.

MALLE, LOUIS: BIRTH ANNIVERSARY. Oct 30, 1932. Born at Thumeries, France, film director Louis Malle was known for his experimental approach to filmmaking and his investigation of controversial topics. *La Souffle au Coeur* (1971), *Lacombe, Lucien* (1974) and *Pretty Baby* (1978), for instance, dealt with the issues of incest, the collaboration of France with its Nazi occupiers and child prostitution, respectively. Of all his films, Malle wished most to be remembered for *Au Revoir, Les Enfants* (1987). Died Nov 23, 1995, at Beverly Hills, CA.

MOON PHASE: FIRST QUARTER. Oct 30. Moon enters First Quarter phase at 10:48 PM, EDT.

POST, EMILY: BIRTH ANNIVERSARY. Oct 30, 1872. Emily Post was born at Baltimore, MD. Published in 1922, her book *Etiquette: The Blue Book of Social Usage* instantly became the American bible of manners and social behavior and established Post as a household name in matters of etiquette. It was in its 10th edition at the time of her death Sept 25, 1960, at New York, NY. *Etiquette* inspired a great many letters asking Post for advice on manners in specific situations. She used these letters as the basis for her radio show and her syndicated newspaper column, which eventually appeared in more than 200 papers.

POUND, EZRA LOOMIS: BIRTH ANNIVERSARY. Oct 30, 1885. Modernist poet, editor and critic, born at Hailey, ID. His success as a poet began in 1909 with the publication of *Personae*. In 1912 Pound initiated the Imagist movement; he edited its first anthology in 1914 and collaborated with James Joyce and T.S. Eliot. He moved to Italy in 1924. As a result of his pro-Fascist radio broadcasts from Italy, Pound was indicted for treason July 26, 1943, and arrested near Genoa by the US Army. He was confined to St. Elizabeth's Hospital, Washington, DC, from 1946 to 1958. Considered mentally unable to stand trial, he was never tried for treason. Pound died at Venice, Italy, Nov 1, 1972.

SHERIDAN, RICHARD BRINSLEY: BIRTH ANNIVERSARY. Oct 30, 1751. Dramatist, born at Dublin, Ireland. Died at London, England, July 7, 1816. Sheridan is said to have extended the following invitation to a young lady: "Won't you come into the garden? I would like my roses to see you."

SISLEY, ALFRED: 175th BIRTH ANNIVERSARY. Oct 30, 1839. English by background, but born at Paris, France, Sisley was one of the foremost landscape painters of the Impressionists. Preferring to work in the open air rather than in a studio, he completed over 900 landscapes. Never successful in his lifetime, Sisley's most well-known works, such as *Sands Heaps* and *The Bridge at Moret-sur-Loing*, demonstrate his mastery of the subtle interplay of light, color and brushstroke to evoke atmosphere. He died near Fontainbleau, Jan 29, 1899.

"WAR OF THE WORLDS": BROADCAST ANNIVERSARY. Oct 30, 1938. As part of a series of radio dramas based on famous novels, Orson Welles with the Mercury Players produced H.G. Wells's *War of the Worlds*. Near panic resulted when listeners believed the simulated news bulletins, which described a Martian invasion of New Jersey, to be real.

BIRTHDAYS TODAY

Robert A. Caro, 79, author (three-volume biography of Lyndon B. Johnson), born New York, NY, Oct 30, 1935.

Dick Gautier, 77, actor (*Bye Bye Birdie*, "Here We Go Again"), born Los Angeles, CA, Oct 30, 1937.

Harry Hamlin, 63, actor ("LA Law," "Studs Lonigan"), born Pasadena, CA, Oct 30, 1951.

Heidi Heitkamp, 59, US Senator (D, North Dakota), born Breckenridge, MN, Oct 30, 1955.

Ed Lauter, 74, actor (*The Longest Yard, Fat Man and Little Boy*), born Long Beach, NY, Oct 30, 1940.

Nastia Liukin, 25, Olympic gymnast, born Moscow, Russia, Oct 30, 1989.

Diego Armando Maradona, 54, soccer coach and former player, born Lanus, Argentina, Oct 30, 1960.

Andrea Mitchell, 68, news correspondent, born New York, NY, Oct 30, 1946.

Matthew Morrison, 36, actor ("Glee"), born Fort Ord, CA, Oct 30, 1978.

Kevin Pollak, 56, actor (*A Few Good Men, Grumpy Old Men*), born San Francisco, CA, Oct 30, 1958.

Grace Slick, 75, singer (Jefferson Airplane), born Chicago, IL, Oct 30, 1939.

Charles Martin Smith, 61, actor (*American Graffiti, The Untouchables*), director, born Los Angeles, CA, Oct 30, 1953.

Dick Vermeil, 78, former football coach, born Calistoga, CA, Oct 30, 1936.

Henry Winkler, 69, actor ("Happy Days"), director, children's author, born New York, NY, Oct 30, 1945.

October 31 — Friday

DAY 304 **61 REMAINING**

BAYOU BACCHANAL. Oct 31–Nov 2. New Orleans, LA. A Caribbean festival held every first weekend of November, featuring food, steelpan music and a masquarading parade. For info: Bayou Bacchanal, 147 Carondolet St, Box 1091, New Orleans, LA 70130. Phone: (504) 220-8441. E-mail: president@bayoubacchanal.org. Web: www.bayoubacchanal.org.

BOOKS FOR TREATS DAY. Oct 31. San Jose, CA. The Books for Treats cause gives gently read children's books at Halloween instead of candy. "Feed kids' minds, not their cavities. Give brain candy." Supported by the city of San Jose and numerous community institutions. For info: Rebecca Morgan, Books for Treats, 1440 Newport Ave, San Jose, CA 95125. Phone: (408) 998-7977. E-mail: rebecca@rebeccamorgan.com. Web: www.BooksForTreats.org.

"CAR TALK" NATIONAL RADIO PREMIERE: ANNIVERSARY. Oct 31, 1987. "Car Talk," the irreverent talk show that diagnoses auto ills, premiered nationally on National Public Radio on this date. Hosted by brothers Ray and Tom Magliozzi (also known as "Click and Clack, the Tappet Brothers"), "Car Talk" originally debuted in Boston, MA, in 1977. Almost 4.4 million listeners tune in to the Peabody Award–winning show on 588 NPR stations. In 2012, the brothers announced their retirement from the show, which would continue with re-airings of "best-of" moments.

CHIANG KAI-SHEK: BIRTH ANNIVERSARY. Oct 31, 1887. Chinese soldier and statesman, born at Chekiang, China. Educated at the Wampoa Military Academy, Chiang led the KMT (nationalist) forces in the struggle against the Communist army led by Mao Tse-tung and eventually had to flee mainland China. He died at Taipei, Taiwan, Apr 5, 1975.

FIRST BLACK PLAYS IN NBA GAME: ANNIVERSARY. Oct 31, 1950. Earl Lloyd became the first black ever to play in an NBA game when he took the floor for the Washington Capitols at Rochester, NY. Lloyd was actually one of three blacks to become NBA players in the 1950 season, the others being Nat "Sweetwater" Clifton, who was signed by the New York Knicks, and Chuck Cooper, who was drafted by the Boston Celtics (and debuted the night after Lloyd).

FRANKENSTEIN FRIDAY. Oct 31. This holiday honors and celebrates the "mother" and "father" of Frankenstein, Mary Shelley and Boris Karloff. Every year a different venue is used to celebrate this occasion. In years past it has included a torch-lighting ceremony, a film festival and the awarding of THE FRANKY. Annually, the last Friday in October. For info: Ron MacCloskey. E-mail: ronmac55@aol.com.

HALLOWE'EN or ALL HALLOWS' EVE. Oct 31. An ancient celebration combining Druid autumn festival and Christian customs. Hallowe'en (All Hallows' Eve) is the beginning of Hallowtide, a season that embraces the Feast of All Saints (Nov 1) and the Feast of All Souls (Nov 2). The observance, dating from the sixth or seventh century, has long been associated with thoughts of the dead, spirits, witches, ghosts and devils. In fact, the ancient Celtic Feast of Samhain, the festival that marked the beginning of winter and of the New Year, was observed Nov 1. See also: "Trick or Treat or Beggar's Night" (Oct 31).

HOUDINI, HARRY: DEATH ANNIVERSARY. Oct 31, 1926. Harry Houdini (whose real name was Ehrich Weisz), magician, illusionist and escape artist, died at Grace Hospital, Detroit, MI, of peritonitis following an Oct 19 blow to the abdomen. Houdini's death anniversary, on Halloween, is occasion for meetings of magicians. See also: "Houdini, Harry: Birth Anniversary" (Mar 24).

KEATS, JOHN: BIRTH ANNIVERSARY. Oct 31, 1795. One of England's greatest poets, born at London, England. Keats wrote to Fanny Brawne (in 1820): "If I should die . . . I have left no immortal work behind me—nothing to make my friends proud of my memory—but I have loved the principle of beauty in all things, and if I had had time I would have made myself remembered." Died at the age of 25 at Rome, Italy, Feb 23, 1821.

LANDON, MICHAEL: BIRTH ANNIVERSARY. Oct 31, 1936. American actor, born Eugene Maurice Orowitz, at Forest Hills, NY. He is best known for his roles in the television series "Bonanza" (1959–73), "Little House on the Prairie" (1974–83) and "Highway to Heaven" (1984–89). He died July 1, 1991, at Malibu, CA.

LOW, JULIETTE GORDON: BIRTH ANNIVERSARY. Oct 31, 1860. Founded Girl Scouts of the USA Mar 12, 1912, at Savannah, GA. Born at Savannah, Low died there Jan 17, 1927.

October 2014	S	M	T	W	T	F	S
				1	2	3	4
	5	6	7	8	9	10	11
	12	13	14	15	16	17	18
	19	20	21	22	23	24	25
	26	27	28	29	30	31	

MAGIC DAY. Oct 31. Traditionally observed on the anniversary of the death of Harry Houdini in 1926.

MOUNT RUSHMORE COMPLETION: ANNIVERSARY. Oct 31, 1941. The Mount Rushmore National Memorial was completed after 14 years of work. First suggested by Jonah Robinson of the South Dakota State Historical Society, the memorial was dedicated in 1925, and work began in 1927. The memorial contains sculptures of the heads of four US presidents—George Washington, Thomas Jefferson, Abraham Lincoln and Theodore Roosevelt. The 60-foot-tall sculptures represent, respectively, the nation's founding, political philosophy, preservation and expansion and conservation.

NATIONAL KNOCK-KNOCK DAY. Oct 31. Celebrated in tandem with Halloween, National Knock-Knock Day answers the age-old question "Who's there?" A day for kids of all ages to try out their best knock-knock jokes (Knock Knock/Who's there?/Weirdo/Weirdo who?/Weirdo you keep all your Halloween candy? I'm starving!). For a list of Halloween Knock-Knock Jokes, contact children's joke book authors Matt Rissinger and Philip Yates. Annually, Oct 31. For info: Matt Rissinger/Philip Yates. Phone: (610) 650-9136. E-mail: mrissinger@aol.com or laugharoni@msn.com.

✦NATIONAL UNICEF DAY. Oct 31. Presidential Proclamation 3817, of Oct 27, 1967, covers all succeeding years. Annually, Oct 31.

NEVADA: ADMISSION DAY: 150th ANNIVERSARY. Oct 31, 1864. Became 36th state in 1864. Observed as a holiday in Nevada.

NEVADA DAY CELEBRATION. Oct 31. The state of Nevada, which joined the Union on Oct 31, 1864, concludes its yearlong sesquicentennial celebrations today. Events kicked off Oct 31, 2013, as Nevadans shared their history, culture and future with each other and with people all over the world with both "Legacy Projects" and "Signature Events." The "Battle Born" state now begins its next chapter. For listings of statewide events and observances for the sesquicentennial, contact the Nevada 150 office in Reno, NV, and see the website at www.nevada150.org.

NEVADAPEX COIN AND STAMP EXPO. Oct 31–Nov 2. River Palms Casino, Laughlin, NV. Est attendance: 5,000. For info: Israel Bick, Exec Dir, Intl Stamp & Coin Collectors Society, PO Box 854, Van Nuys, CA 91408. Phone: (818) 997-6496. Fax: (818) 988-4337. E-mail: iibick@sbcglobal.net. Web: www.bickinternational.com.

PACA, WILLIAM: BIRTH ANNIVERSARY. Oct 31, 1740. Signer of the Declaration of Independence and governor of Maryland. Born near Abingdon, MD, he died Oct 13, 1799, at Talbot County, MD.

REFORMATION DAY: ANNIVERSARY. Oct 31, 1517. Anniversary of the day on which Martin Luther nailed his 95 theses to the door of Wittenberg's Palace church, denouncing the selling of papal indulgences—the beginning of the Reformation in Germany. Observed by many Protestant churches on Reformation Sunday, on this day if it is a Sunday or on the Sunday before Oct 31.

SAMHAIN. Oct 31. (Also called November Eve, Hallowmas, Hallowe'en, All Hallows' Eve, Feast of Souls, Feast of the Dead, Feast of Apples and Calan Gaeaf.) One of the "Greater Sabbats" during the Wiccan year, Samhain, or "Summer's end," marks the death of the Sun-God, who then awaits his rebirth from the Mother Goddess at Yule (Dec 21 in 2014). In the Celtic tradition, the feast of Samhain was also celebrated as New Year's Eve, as their new year began on Nov 1. Annually, Oct 31.

SLEIDANUS, JOHANNES: DEATH ANNIVERSARY. Oct 31, 1556. German historian, born at Schleiden in 1506. His *Famous Chronicle of Oure Time*, called *Sleidanes Comentaires*, was first translated into English in 1560. The translator spoke thus to the book: "Go forth my painful Boke, Thou art no longer mine. Eche man may on thee loke, The Shame or praise is thine." He died at Strasbourg.

TAIWAN: CHIANG KAI-SHEK DAY. Oct 31. National holiday to honor the memory of Generalissimo Chiang Kai-shek, the first constitutional president of the Republic of China, born Oct 31, 1887.

TRICK OR TREAT or BEGGAR'S NIGHT. Oct 31. A popular custom on Hallowe'en, in which children wearing costumes visit neighbors' homes, calling out "Trick or treat" and "begging" for candies or gifts to place in their beggars' bags. In recent years there has been increased participation by adults, often parading in elaborate or outrageous costumes and also requesting candy.

WATERS, ETHEL: BIRTH ANNIVERSARY. Oct 31, 1896. Married when she was 13, Ethel Waters began her singing career at the urging of friends. At age 17 she was singing at Baltimore, MD, billing herself as Sweet Mama Stringbean. Her career took her to New York, where she divided her work among the stage, nightclubs and films. She made her Broadway debut in 1927 in the revue *Africana*, and her other stage credits include *Blackbirds* and *Thousands Cheer*. Her memorable stage roles in *Cabin in the Sky* and *A Member of the Wedding* (for which she won the Drama Critics Award) were re-created for film. Born at Chester, PA, she died Sept 9, 1977, at Chatsworth, GA.

WORLD CHAMPIONSHIP PUNKIN CHUNKIN. Oct 31–Nov 2. Bridgeville, DE. 29th annual. "We're Gonna Hurl!" Adult and youth teams vie for the distinction of throwing an 8- to 10-pound pumpkin the farthest. The different classes include catapult, trebuchet, human power and theatrical, among others. Orange attire welcomed. Annually, the full weekend that includes the first Saturday in November. Est attendance: 35,000. For info: World Championship Punkin Chunkin Assn, PO Box 217, Nassau, DE 19969. E-mail: punkassoc@gmail.com. Web: www.punkinchunkin.com.

 BIRTHDAYS TODAY

Michael Collins, 83, former astronaut, born Rome, Italy, Oct 31, 1931.

Deidre Hall, 66, actress ("Our House," "Days of Our Lives"), born Lake Worth, FL, Oct 31, 1948.

Peter Jackson, 53, director (Lord of the Rings trilogy, *The Hobbit, King Kong*), born Pukerua Bay, North Island, New Zealand, Oct 31, 1961.

Frederick Stanley (Fred) McGriff, 51, former baseball player, born Tampa, FL, Oct 31, 1963.

Larry Mullen, 53, musician (U2), born Dublin, Ireland, Oct 31, 1961.

Dermot Mulroney, 51, actor (*About Schmidt, My Best Friend's Wedding*), born Alexandria, VA, Oct 31, 1963.

Jane Pauley, 64, journalist, television personality, born Indianapolis, IN, Oct 31, 1950.

Piper Perabo, 38, actress ("Covert Affairs"), born Dallas, TX, Oct 31, 1976.

Dan Rather, 83, journalist (former anchor of "CBS Evening News"), born Wharton, TX, Oct 31, 1931.

Stephen Rea, 68, actor (*The Crying Game, Michael Collins*), born Belfast, Northern Ireland, Oct 31, 1946.

Ron Rifkin, 75, stage and screen actor (Tony for *Cabaret*; *The Substance of Fire*, "Alias"), born New York, NY, Oct 31, 1939.

Rob Schneider, 51, actor (*Deuce Bigalow: Male Gigolo*, "Saturday Night Live"), born San Francisco, CA, Oct 31, 1963.

David Ogden Stiers, 72, actor ("M*A*S*H," *North and South*), born Peoria, IL, Oct 31, 1942.

Vanilla Ice, 47, rapper, actor, born Robert Van Winkle at Miami, FL, Oct 31, 1967.

✦ November ✦

November 1 — Saturday

DAY 305 **60 REMAINING**

ALGERIA: REVOLUTION DAY. Nov 1. National holiday. Commemorates beginning of revolt against France in 1954.

ALL HALLOWS or ALL SAINTS' DAY. Nov 1. Roman Catholic Holy Day of Obligation. Commemorates the blessed, especially those who have no special feast days. Observed on Nov 1 since Pope Gregory IV set the date of recognition in AD 835. All Saints' Day is a legal holiday in Louisiana. Halloween is the evening before All Hallows Day.

AMERICAN DIABETES MONTH. Nov 1–30. American Diabetes Month is designed to communicate the seriousness of diabetes and the importance of proper diabetes control and treatment to those diagnosed with the disease and their families. Throughout the month, the American Diabetes Association holds special events and programs on a variety of topics related to diabetes care and treatment. For info: American Diabetes Assn. Phone: (800) DIABETES. Web: www.diabetes.org.

ANTIGUA AND BARBUDA: INDEPENDENCE DAY. Nov 1. National holiday. Commemorates independence from Britain in 1981.

AVIATION HISTORY MONTH. Nov 1–30. Anniversary of aeronautical experiments in November 1782 (exact dates unknown) by Joseph Michel Montgolfier and Jacques Etienne Montgolfier, brothers living at Annonay, France. Inspired by Joseph Priestley's book *Experiments Relating to the Different Kinds of Air*, the brothers experimented with filling paper and fabric bags with smoke and hot air, leading to the invention of the hot-air balloon, man's first flight and the entire science of aviation and flight.

BANANA PUDDING LOVERS MONTH. Nov 1–30. What sweet memories we share of family sitting down together eating their banana pudding dessert. Banana Pudding Lovers Month is a time for families to re-create the memories of their happy childhood, or start creating memories for your own children! Let's pass the tradition from one generation to another. For info: Rodgers Banana Pudding, 1410 Poindexter St, Chesapeake, VA 23324. Phone: (757) 543-9290. E-mail: reggie@rodgersbananapudding.com. Web: www.rodgersbananapudding.com.

CRANE, STEPHEN: BIRTH ANNIVERSARY. Nov 1, 1871. American author (*The Red Badge of Courage*), born at Newark, NJ. Died June 5, 1900, at Badenweiler, Germany.

DIABETIC EYE DISEASE MONTH. Nov 1–30. Can people with diabetes prevent the onset of diabetic eye disease? During this observance, Prevent Blindness America® will offer information to help the 5.3 million Americans aged 18 and older who suffer from diabetic eye disease. For info: Prevent Blindness America®, 211 W Wacker Dr, Ste 1700, Chicago, IL 60606. Phone: (800) 331-2020. E-mail: info@preventblindness.org. Web: www.preventblindness.org.

***EBONY* MAGAZINE: ANNIVERSARY.** Nov 1, 1945. Black publishing entrepreneur John H. Johnson launched *Ebony* on this date—three years to the day after his first successful African-American lifestyle magazine, *Negro Digest* (1942). By 1946 *Ebony* had a circulation of more than 300,000 copies. On Nov 1, 1951, Johnson launched the equally successful publication *Jet*.

EUROPEAN UNION ESTABLISHED: ANNIVERSARY. Nov 1, 1993. The Maastricht Treaty went into effect on this day, formally establishing the European Union. The treaty was drafted in 1991. By 1993, 12 nations had ratified it. In 1995 three more nations ratified the treaty. The European Union grew out of the European Economic Community (also known as the Common Market), which was established in 1958.

EXTRA MILE DAY. Nov 1. Since 2009, a day recognizing the capacity we each have to create positive change in our families, organizations and communities when we go the extra mile. More than 400 cities participate in this event. Annually, Nov 1. For info: Extra Mile America, 13700 Marina Pointe Dr, Ste 606, Marina del Rey, CA 90292. Phone: (310) 402-4826. E-mail: info@ExtraMileAmerica.org. Web: www.ExtraMileAmerica.org.

GUATEMALA: KITE FESTIVAL OF SANTIAGO SACATEPEQUEZ. Nov 1. Long ago, when evil spirits disturbed the good spirits in the local cemetery, a magician told the townspeople a secret way to get rid of the evil spirits—by flying kites (because the evil spirits were frightened by the noise of wind against paper). Since then, the kite festival has been held at the cemetery each year on Nov 1 or Nov 2, and it is said that "to this day no one knows of bad spirits roaming the streets or the cemetery of Santiago Sacatepequez," a village about 20 miles from Guatemala City. Nowadays the youths of the village work for many weeks to make the giant, elaborate kites to fly on All Saints' Day (Nov 1) or All Souls' Day (Nov 2).

HOCKEY MASK INVENTED: 55th ANNIVERSARY. Nov 1, 1959. Tired of stopping hockey pucks with his face, Montreal Canadiens goalie Jacques Plante, having received another wound, reemerged from the locker room with seven new stitches—and a face mask he had made from fiberglass and resin. Cliff Benedict had tried a leather mask back in the '20s, but the idea didn't catch on until Plante wore his. Then goalies throughout the NHL began wearing protective plastic face shields.

LISBON EARTHQUAKE: ANNIVERSARY. Nov 1, 1755. A powerful earthquake struck Lisbon, Portugal, on this day. The earthquake probably had a Richter scale magnitude of 9 and caused a tsunami to sweep over the capital. In the resulting deluge and fires, more than 75 percent of Lisbon was destroyed. Some 90,000 people died in Portugal, and an additional 10,000 people died in other parts of the Mediterranean.

LUNG CANCER AWARENESS MONTH. Nov 1–30. LCAM is a national campaign dedicated to increasing attention to lung cancer issues—early detection, increased research funding and increased support for those living with lung cancer. The Lung Cancer Allliance is the leading organization dedicated to helping people at risk for and living with lung cancer. Support and education resources are available free of charge by phone, mail or Internet. For info: The Lung Cancer Alliance, 888 16th St NW, Ste 150, Washington, DC 20006. Phone: (202) 463-2080. E-mail: info@lungcanceralliance.org. Web: www.lungcanceralliance.org.

MEDICAL SCHOOL FOR WOMEN OPENED AT BOSTON: ANNIVERSARY. Nov 1, 1848. Founded in Boston, MA, by Samuel Gregory, a pioneer in medical education for women, the Boston Female Medical School opened as the first medical school exclusively for women. The original enrollment was 12 students. In 1874 the school merged with the Boston University School of Medicine and formed one of the first coed medical schools in the world.

MEXICO: DAY OF THE DEAD. Nov 1–2. Observance begins during last days of October when bakeries sell "dead men's bread"—round loaves decorated with sugar skulls. Departed souls are remembered not in mourning but with a spirit of friendliness and good humor. Cemeteries are visited, and graves are decorated.

MISSION SAN JUAN CAPISTRANO: FOUNDING ANNIVERSARY. Nov 1, 1776. California mission founded on this date, collapsed during the 1812 earthquake. The swallows of Capistrano nest in the ruins of the old mission church, departing each year on Oct 23 and returning the following year on or near St. Joseph's Day (Mar 19).

MOVEMBER. Nov 1–30. Every November, Movember is responsible for the sprouting of moustaches on thousands of men's faces around the world. These men raise vital funds and awareness for men's health, specifically prostate cancer and other cancers that affect men. Once registered at www.movember.com, men start Movember 1 clean shaven. For the rest of the month, these selfless and generous men, known as Mo Bros, groom, trim and wax their way into the annals of fine moustachery. Mo Bros raise funds by seeking out sponsorship for their Mo-growing efforts. For info: Movember, PO Box 2726, Venice, CA 90294-2726. Phone: (310) 450-3399. E-mail: info.us@movember.com. Web: www.us.movember.com.

✦NATIONAL ADOPTION MONTH. Nov 1–30.

NATIONAL ADOPTION MONTH. Nov 1–30. To raise awareness of the needs of children waiting to be adopted and to recognize those who have adopted or were adopted. A celebration of adoption! For info: Natl Council for Adoption, 225 N Washington St, Alexandria, VA 22314-2561. Phone: (703) 299-6633. Fax: (703) 299-6004. E-mail: ncfa@adoptioncouncil.org. Web: www.adoptioncouncil.org.

NATIONAL ALZHEIMER'S DISEASE AWARENESS MONTH. Nov 1–30. To increase awareness of Alzheimer's disease and what the Alzheimer's Association is doing to advance research and help patients, their families and their caregivers. For info: Alzheimer's Assn, 225 N Michigan Ave, Ste 1700, Chicago, IL 60601-7633. Phone: (312) 335-8700. E-mail: info@alz.org. Web: www.alz.org.

✦NATIONAL NATIVE AMERICAN HERITAGE MONTH. Nov 1–30.

NATIONAL AUTHORS' DAY. Nov 1. This observance was adopted by the General Federation of Women's Clubs in 1929 and in 1949 was given a place on the list of special days, weeks and months prepared by the US Department of Commerce. The resolution states in part: "By celebrating an Authors' Day as a nation, we would not only show patriotism, loyalty, and appreciation of the men and women who have made American literature possible, but would also encourage and inspire others to give of themselves in making a better America." It was also resolved "that we commemorate an Authors' Day to be observed on November First each year."

NATIONAL COOK FOR YOUR PETS DAY. Nov 1. This day focuses on pet nutrition and encourages people to make sure their pets are properly fed. Treat your pet to a nutritious home-cooked meal today! For info: Tennille Tejeda, PO Box 30422, Mesa, AZ 85275. Phone: (888) 220-2961. E-mail: contact@cookforyourpets.com. Web: www.cookforyourpets.com.

✦NATIONAL DIABETES MONTH. Nov 1–30.

NATIONAL EPILEPSY AWARENESS MONTH. Nov 1–30. To increase public awareness that despite dramatic gains in treatment, epilepsy is a serious and chronic health condition for which there is no cure. Annually, the month of November. For info: PR Dept, Epilepsy Foundation, 8301 Professional Pl, Landover, MD 20785. Phone: (800) 332-1000. Web: www.epilepsyfoundation.org.

✦NATIONAL FAMILY CAREGIVERS MONTH. Nov 1–30. To honor family members who care for aging relatives or those with disabilities.

NATIONAL FAMILY CAREGIVERS MONTH. Nov 1–30. A nationwide month of recognition for the 65 million family caregivers. For info: Natl Family Caregivers Assn, 10400 Connecticut Ave, Ste 500, Kensington, MD 20895-3944. Phone: (301) 942-6430. Fax: (301) 942-2302. E-mail: info@caregiveraction.org. Web: www.thefamilycaregiver.org.

NATIONAL FAMILY LITERACY DAY®. Nov 1. Celebrated all over the country with special activities and events that showcase the importance of family literacy programs. Family literacy programs bring parents and children together in the classroom to learn and support each other in efforts to further their education and improve their life skills. Annually, Nov 1. For info: Natl Center for Family Literacy, 325 W Main St, Ste 300, Louisville, KY 40202. Phone: (502) 584-1133. Fax: (502) 584-0172. E-mail: info@famlit.org. Web: www.famlit.org.

NATIONAL GEORGIA PECAN MONTH. Nov 1–30. To herald the Georgia pecan harvest and recognize Georgia's status as the nation's top pecan-producing state. For info: Marcia Crowley, Georgia Agricultural Commodity Commission for Pecans (GACCP), Commodities Promotion Div, Georgia Dept of Agriculture, 328 Agriculture Building, Capitol Sq, Atlanta, GA 30334. Phone: (404) 656-3678. Fax: (404) 656-9380. Web: www.antioxinut.org.

NATIONAL INSPIRATIONAL ROLE MODELS MONTH. Nov 1–30. To acknowledge the impact that contemporary and historic role models have on our lives. Individuals chosen for recognition may include celebrities, historic figures, relatives, friends, colleagues, associates, etc. Celebrate with creative projects and activities featuring historic role models and spend time with contemporary role models. Theme for 2014: "Celebrating the Inspiration of Art, Literature and Music—and Their Creators." For info: Darlene House, PO Box 23598, Detroit, MI 48223. Phone: (313) 778-1550. Web: www.nirmm.wordpress.com.

NATIONAL LONG-TERM CARE AWARENESS MONTH. Nov 1–30. Annual event organized by the American Association for Long-Term Care Insurance (AALTCI) and supported by association members and leading industry organizations. The goal is to create heightened awareness of the need for long-term care and the importance of planning options available to Americans and their families. For info: Jesse Slome, Exec Dir, American Assn for Long-Term Care Insurance, 3835 E Thousand Oaks Blvd, Ste 336, Westlake Village, CA 91362. Phone: (818) 597-3227. Web: www.AALTCI.org.

NATIONAL MARROW AWARENESS MONTH. Nov 1–30. A special nationwide effort to recruit volunteer marrow, blood stem cell and umbilical cord blood donors and to increase patient awareness of the option of unrelated transplantation. For info: US Dept of Health and Human Services, 200 Independence Ave SW, Washington, DC 20201. Phone: (877) 696-6775 or (202) 619-0257. Web: www.organdonor.gov.

NATIONAL MEMOIR WRITING MONTH. Nov 1–30. An opportunity to celebrate ourselves and our families by committing our life stories to writing. Preserving our autobiographies through memoir writing allows us to know ourselves better and to share our stories with future generations. As part of the monthlong celebration, free weekly memoir-writing teleclasses, memoir-writing prompts and community workshops are available. For info: The Memoir Network, 95 Gould Rd, #102, Lisbon Falls, ME 04252. Phone: (207) 353-5454. E-mail: memoirs@TheMemoirNetwork.com. Web: www.TheMemoirNetwork.com.

NATIONAL NOVEL WRITING MONTH. Nov 1–30. National Novel Writing Month, or NaNoWriMo, the world's largest writing challenge and nonprofit literary crusade—first observed in 1999. Participants pledge to write 50,000 words in a month, starting from scratch and reaching "The End" by Nov 30. There are no judges, no prizes, and entries are deleted from the server before anyone even reads them. More than 650 regional volunteers in more than 60 countries hold write-ins, hosting writers in coffee shops, bookstores and libraries. Write-ins offer a supportive environment and surprisingly effective peer pressure, turning the usually solitary act of writing into a community experience. For info: Office of Letters and Light. E-mail: info@nanowrimo.org. Web: www.nanowrimo.org or www.lettersandlight.org.

NATIONAL PATIENT ACCESSIBILITY WEEK. Nov 1–7. The purpose of this week is to increase awareness that physicians need, and are obligated to have, accessible healthcare facilities for patients who are older, obese or disabled in order to provide the requisite level of quality care. Annually, Nov 1–7. For info: Susan Kaiser, Public Relations, Midmark, 60 Vista Dr, Versailles, OH 45380. Phone: (937) 526-8785. Fax: (937) 526-7426. E-mail: skaiser@midmark.com. Web: www.midmark.com.

OZARK MOUNTAIN CHRISTMAS/BRANSON FESTIVAL OF LIGHTS. Nov 1–Dec 31. Branson, MO. More than 1.4 million visitors relish the opportunity to celebrate the season by combining a traditional Christmas ambience with a dash of dazzle as only Branson can offer. The area is illuminated in twinkling lights, with special holiday events and shows galore. For info: Branson Area CVB, PO Box 1897, Branson, MO 65615. Phone: (800) 296-0463. Fax: (417) 334-4139. E-mail: info@bransoncvb.com. Web: www.explorebranson.com.

PEANUT BUTTER LOVERS' MONTH. Nov 1–30. Celebration of America's favorite food and number one sandwich. For info: Southern Peanut Growers, 1025 Sugar Pike Way, Canton, GA 30115. Phone: (770) 998-7311. Fax: (770) 998-5962. Web: www.peanutbutterlovers.com.

PEDDLER'S VILLAGE APPLE FESTIVAL. Nov 1–2. Peddler's Village, Lahaska, PA. Craftspeople gather to show their wares and demonstrate their skills. Enjoy country apple butter, cider, fritters and dumplings. Live entertainment and pie-eating contests add to the festivities of this traditional fall celebration. Free admission. For info: Peddler's Village, Rtes 202 and 263, Lahaska, PA 18931. Phone: (215) 794-4000. Fax: (215) 794-4001. E-mail: info@peddlersvillage.com. Web: www.peddlersvillage.com.

PPSI AIDS AWARENESS MONTH. Nov 1–30. To educate consumers, patients, students and professionals on the prevention of AIDS and sexually transmitted diseases. Kit of materials available for $15. For info: Fred S. Mayer, Pres, Pharmacists Planning Service, Inc, PO Box 6760, San Rafael, CA 94903. Phone: (415) 479-8628. Fax: (415) 479-8608. E-mail: ppsi@aol.com. Web: www.ppsinc.org.

PRESIDENT OCCUPIES THE WHITE HOUSE: ANNIVERSARY. Nov 1, 1800. Philadelphia, PA, had served as the nation's capital from 1790 to 1800. On Nov 1, 1800, President John Adams and his family moved into the newly completed White House, as Washington, DC, became the new capital.

PRIME MERIDIAN SET: ANNIVERSARY. Nov 1, 1884. Delegates from 25 nations met in October at Washington, DC, at the International Meridian Conference to set up time zones for the world. On this day the treaty adopted by the conference took effect, making Greenwich, England, the Prime Meridian (i.e., 0° longitude) and setting the International Date Line at 180° longitude in the Pacific. Every 15° of longitude equals one hour, and there are 24 meridians. While some countries do not strictly observe this system (for example, while China stretches over five time zones, it is the same time everywhere in China), it has brought predictability and logic to time throughout the world.

SADIE HAWKINS DAY. Nov 1. Widely observed in US, usually on the first Saturday in November. Tradition established in "Li'l Abner" comic strip in 1930s by cartoonist Al Capp. A popular occasion when women and girls are encouraged to take the initiative in inviting the man or boy of their choice for a date. A similar tradition is associated with Feb 29 in leap years.

SEABISCUIT DEFEATS WAR ADMIRAL: ANNIVERSARY. Nov 1, 1938. In a special match race at Pimlico in Laurel, MD, Seabiscuit, ridden by George Wolff, defeated favored War Admiral before a crowd of 40,000. Seabiscuit captured the winner-take-all purse of $15,000.

November 2014	S	M	T	W	T	F	S
							1
	2	3	4	5	6	7	8
	9	10	11	12	13	14	15
	16	17	18	19	20	21	22
	23	24	25	26	27	28	29
	30						

STEEPLECHASE AT CALLAWAY GARDENS. Nov 1. Pine Mountain, GA. An eight-race steeplechase meet where riders match their horses for speed and split-second timing over brush jumps. Box seating and infield tailgating spaces available. Annually, the first Saturday in November. Est attendance: 10,000. For info: The Steeplechase at Callaway Gardens, PO Box 2311, Columbus, GA 31902. Phone: (706) 324-6252. Fax: (706) 324-3651. Web: www.steeplechaseatcallaway.org.

SWEDEN: ALL SAINTS' DAY. Nov 1. Honors the memory of deceased friends and relatives. Annually, the Saturday following Oct 30.

US VIRGIN ISLANDS: LIBERTY DAY. Nov 1. Officially "D. Hamilton Jackson Memorial Day," commemorating establishment of the first press in the Virgin Islands in 1915.

VEGAN MONTH. Nov 1–30. This outreach event encourages everyone to GO VEGAN! Vegans choose to neither eat nor use any animal products (meat, poultry, seafood, dairy products, eggs, gelatin, leather, fur). A growing number of caring, compassionate people are adopting this conscientious lifestyle. Primarily ethical reasons, but also health and environmental concerns, motivate them to GO VEGAN. For info: VEGANET, PO Box 3545, Washington, DC 20027-0045. Phone: (800) 234-8343.

VERBOORT SAUSAGE AND KRAUT DINNER. Nov 1. Visitation Parish, Forest Grove, OR. 80th annual event features crafts, bingo, raffles, beer garden, local produce, home-baked goods and, of course, famous Verboort sausage and kraut. Annually, the first Saturday in November. Est attendance: 8,000. For info: Visitation Parish, 4285 NW Visitation Rd, Forest Grove, OR 97116. Phone: (503) 357-3860. Web: www.verboort.org/dinner.

WILL ROGERS DAYS. Nov 1–4. Claremore and Oologah, OK. Festival celebrating the birth and life of the famed Oklahoma humorist with a variety of events and activities at the Will Rogers Birthplace Ranch at Oologah and at the Will Rogers Memorial Museum in Claremore. Includes a birthday party (at ranch), parade in downtown Claremore and wreath-laying ceremony at the museum. For info: Will Rogers Memorial Museum, 1720 W Will Rogers Blvd, Claremore, OK 74017. Phone: (800) 324-9455. Web: www.willrogers.com.

WORLDWIDE BEREAVED SIBLINGS MONTH. Nov 1–30. This month promotes support for bereaved siblings. Often people don't know what to say to or do for grieving siblings. So sometimes, they turn away and do nothing. We encourage people to turn back and begin to reach out to bereaved siblings by giving them a listener (not an adviser), a shoulder to cry on or a hug when appropriate and needed. For info: Peter and Deb Kulkkula, Bereavement Awareness, 381 Billings Rd, Fitchburg, MA 01420-1407. Phone: (978) 343-4009. E-mail: help@bereavementawareness.com. Web: www.bereavementawareness.com.

BIRTHDAYS TODAY

Penn Badgley, 28, actor ("The Bedford Diaries," "Gossip Girl"), born Baltimore, MD, Nov 1, 1986.

Toni Collette, 42, actress (*The Sixth Sense, About a Boy, Muriel's Wedding*), born Sidney, Australia, Nov 1, 1972.

Larry Claxton Flynt, 72, publisher, born Magoffin County, KY, Nov 1, 1942.

Lyle Lovett, 57, singer, born Klein, TX, Nov 1, 1957.

Jenny McCarthy, 42, model, actress (*Scary Movie 3*), born Chicago, IL, Nov 1, 1972.

Betsy Palmer, 88, actress ("I've Got a Secret," "Knots Landing," "The Today Show"), born Patricia Bromek at East Chicago, IN, Nov 1, 1926.

Gary Jim Player, 79, former golfer, born Johannesburg, South Africa, Nov 1, 1935.

Aishwarya Rai, 41, actress (*Enthiran, Bride and Prejudice, Devdas*), Goodwill Ambassador for UNAIDS, born Mangalore, India, Nov 1, 1973.

Rachel Ticotin, 56, actress (*Total Recall, Natural Born Killers*), born the Bronx, NY, Nov 1, 1958.

Fernando Anguamea Valenzuela, 54, former baseball player, born Navojoa, Sonora, Mexico, Nov 1, 1960.

November 2 — Sunday

DAY 306 **59 REMAINING**

ALL SOULS' DAY. Nov 2. Commemorates the faithful departed. Catholic observance.

BALFOUR DECLARATION: ANNIVERSARY. Nov 2, 1917. In a letter to the Zionist Federation of Great Britain and Ireland, British Foreign Secretary Arthur James Balfour expressed the support of the British government for the formation of a "national home for the Jewish people." Following World War I, the Ottoman Empire ceded Palestine to Britain, and both the peace treaty and the British Mandate for Palestine expressed the same goals, including the stipulation that the civil and religious rights of non-Jews living in Palestine be respected.

BOONE, DANIEL: BIRTH ANNIVERSARY. Nov 2, 1734. (New Style date.) American frontiersman, explorer and militia officer, born at Berks County, near Reading, PA. In February 1778 he was captured at Blue Licks, KY, by Shawnee Indians, under Chief Blackfish, who adopted Boone when he was inducted into the tribe as "Big Turtle." Boone escaped after five months and in 1781 was captured briefly by the British. He experienced a series of personal and financial disasters during his life but continued a rugged existence, hunting until his 80s. Boone died at St. Charles County, MO, Sept 26, 1820. The bodies of Daniel Boone and his wife, Rebecca, were moved to Frankfort, KY, in 1845.

DAYLIGHT SAVING TIME ENDS; STANDARD TIME RESUMES. Nov 2–Mar 8, 2015. Standard time resumes at 2 AM on the first Sunday in November in each time zone, as provided by the Uniform Time Act of 1966 (as amended in 1986 by Public Law 99-359). The Energy Policy Act of 2005 extended the period of daylight saving time beginning in 2007. Many people use the popular rule "spring forward, fall back" to remember which way to turn their clocks. See also: "Daylight Saving Time" (Mar 9).

ENGLAND: LONDON TO BRIGHTON VETERAN CAR RUN. Nov 2. London. A 60-mile run for approximately 500 veteran cars, along the A23 road from Hyde Park, London, to Madeira Drive, Brighton, starting at 6:58 AM. Only cars (three wheels or more) manufactured before Dec 31, 1904, are eligible to participate. Celebrates the November 1896 English law raising the speed limit of "light locomotives" from 4 mph to 14 mph. Annually, the first Sunday in November. (Saturday, Nov 1, is the concours display, Regent Street.) For info: Goose Communications Ltd, Sweetapple House, Catteshall Rd, Godalming, Surrey, GU7 3DJ England. Phone: (44) (1483) 524-433. E-mail: vcr@goose.co.uk. Web: www.veterancarrun.com.

FIRST SCHEDULED RADIO BROADCAST: ANNIVERSARY. Nov 2, 1920. Station KDKA at Pittsburgh, PA, broadcast the results of the presidential election. The station got its license to broadcast Nov 7, 1921. By 1922 there were about 400 licensed radio stations in the US.

HARDING, WARREN GAMALIEL: BIRTH ANNIVERSARY. Nov 2, 1865. The 29th president of the US was born at Corsica, OH. His term of office: Mar 4, 1921–Aug 2, 1923 (died in office). His undistinguished administration was tainted by the Teapot Dome scandal, and his sudden death in San Francisco, CA, while he was on a western speaking tour prompted many rumors.

THE ING NEW YORK CITY MARATHON. Nov 2. New York, NY. About 38,000 runners from all over the world gather to compete, with more than 2.5 million spectators watching from the sidelines. Annually, the first Sunday in November. Est attendance: 2,000,000. For info: NY Road Runners. Phone: (212) 423-2249. Web: www.ingnycmarathon.org.

LANCASTER, BURT: BIRTH ANNIVERSARY. Nov 2, 1913. Distinguished American actor, born Burton Stephen Lancaster, who began his career in show business as a circus acrobat. In a career spanning 45 years, he appeared in nearly 80 films. Some of his more memorable roles are in *From Here to Eternity* (1953), *The Bird Man of Alcatraz* (1962) and *The Leopard* (1963); he received an Academy Award for his performance in the title role of *Elmer Gantry* (1961). His later popular movies include *Atlantic City* (1981), *Local Hero* (1983) and *Field of Dreams* (1989). Born at New York City, he died Oct 20, 1994, at Los Angeles, CA.

NEW YORK SUBWAY ACCIDENT: ANNIVERSARY. Nov 2, 1918. The Brighton Beach Express, exceeding its speed limit five times over (going 30 mph) while approaching the station near the Malbone Street tunnel at Brooklyn, jumped the tracks, killing 97 people and injuring 100. The supervisor-engineer, taking the place of a striking motorman of the Brotherhood of Locomotive Engineers, was tried and acquitted of charges of negligence.

NORTH DAKOTA: ADMISSION DAY: 125th ANNIVERSARY. Nov 2. Became 39th state in 1889.

PLAN YOUR EPITAPH DAY. Nov 2. Dedicated to the proposition that a forgettable gravestone is a fate worse than death and that everyone can be in the same league with William Shakespeare and W.C. Fields. Annually, coincides with the Day of the Dead. For info: Lance Hardie, Dead or Alive, 3549 E St, Eureka, CA 95503. E-mail: headstone@hardiehouse.org. Web: www.hardiehouse.org/epitaph.

POLK, JAMES KNOX: BIRTH ANNIVERSARY. Nov 2, 1795. The 11th president of the US was born at Mecklenburg County, NC. His term of office: Mar 4, 1845–Mar 3, 1849. A compromise candidate at the 1844 Democratic Party convention, Polk was awarded the nomination on the ninth ballot. He declined to be a candidate for a second term and declared himself to be "exceedingly relieved" at the completion of his presidency. He died shortly thereafter at Nashville, TN, June 15, 1849.

SENECA FALLS CONVENTION ATTENDEE VOTES: ANNIVERSARY. Nov 2, 1920. The only woman who attended the historic Seneca Falls Women's Rights Convention in 1848 who lived long enough to exercise her right to vote under the 19th Amendment, Charlotte Woodward voted at Philadelphia, PA, in the general election on Nov 2, 1920.

SOUTH DAKOTA: ADMISSION DAY: 125th ANNIVERSARY. Nov 2. Became 40th state in 1889.

SPACE MILESTONE: INTERNATIONAL SPACE STATION INHABITED. Nov 2, 2000. On Oct 31, 2000, a *Soyuz* shuttle left with the first crew to live in the International Space Station, consisting of American commander Bill Shepherd and two Russian cosmonauts, Sergei Krikalev and Yuri Gidzenko. The flight left from the same site in central Asia where *Sputnik* was launched in 1957, beginning the Space Age. The astronauts stayed on board the International Space Station (ISS) until March 2001, when they were replaced by a crew that arrived on the shuttle *Discovery*. Currently, crew members rotate among astronauts of 16 nations; expanded to a crew of six in 2009.

SPRUCE GOOSE FLIGHT: ANNIVERSARY. Nov 2, 1947. The mammoth flying boat *Hercules*, then the world's largest airplane, was designed, built and flown (once) by Howard Hughes. Its first and only flight was about one mile and at an altitude of 70 feet over Long Beach Harbor, CA. The $25 million, 200-ton plywood craft was nicknamed the "Spruce Goose." It is now displayed at the Evergreen Aviation Museum in McMinnville, OR.

ZERO-TASKING DAY. Nov 2. Today is the day daylight saving time ends—when we turn our clocks back and "gain" an hour. Instead of filling that extra 60 minutes with more work and stress, use that hour to do nothing more than take a breath, relax, reenergize, refresh and deload (opposite of overload). For info: Nancy Christie. Phone: (330) 793-3675. E-mail: nancy@communityofchange.com.

BIRTHDAYS TODAY

Patrick Buchanan, 76, political commentator, born Washington, DC, Nov 2, 1938.

Shere Hite, 72, researcher on sexual behavior, author (*The Hite Report, Women and Love*), born St. Joseph, MO, Nov 2, 1942.

k.d. lang, 53, singer, born Kathryn Dawn Lang at Consort, AB, Canada, Nov 2, 1961.

Stefanie Powers, 72, actress ("Hart to Hart"), born Hollywood, CA, Nov 2, 1942.

David Knapp (Dave) Stockton, 73, golfer, born San Bernardino, CA, Nov 2, 1941.

Scott Walker, 47, Governor of Wisconsin (R), born Colorado Springs, CO, Nov 2, 1967.

November 2014	S	M	T	W	T	F	S
							1
	2	3	4	5	6	7	8
	9	10	11	12	13	14	15
	16	17	18	19	20	21	22
	23	24	25	26	27	28	29
	30						

November 3 — Monday

DAY 307 — **58 REMAINING**

ASHURA: TENTH DAY. Nov 3. Islamic calendar date: Muharram 10, 1436. For Shia Muslims, commemorates death of Muhammad's grandson at the Battle of Karbala. A time of fasting, reflection and meditation. Jews of Medina fasted on the 10th day in remembrance of their salvation from Pharoah. Different methods for "anticipating" the visibility of the new moon crescent at Mecca are used by different groups. US date may vary. Began at sunset the preceding day.

AUSTIN, STEPHEN FULLER: BIRTH ANNIVERSARY. Nov 3, 1793. A principal founder of Texas, for whom its capital city was named, Austin was born at Wythe County, VA. He first visited Texas in 1821 and established a settlement there the following year, continuing a colonization project started by his father, Moses Austin. Thrown in prison when he advocated formation of a separate state (Texas still belonged to Mexico), he was freed in 1835, lost a campaign for the presidency (of the Republic of Texas) to Sam Houston in 1836 and died (while serving as Texas secretary of state) at Austin, TX, Dec 27, 1836.

AUSTRALIA: RECREATION DAY. Nov 3. The first Monday in November is observed as Recreation Day at Northern Tasmania.

BRONSON, CHARLES: BIRTH ANNIVERSARY. Nov 3, 1921. Movie tough-guy Charles Bronson was born Charles Buchinsky at Ehrenfeld, PA. One of 15 children, he was raised in poverty and was working in the coal mines by age 16. He discovered acting after a stint in the army and was soon making low-budget films, usually violent. His best-known films include *The Magnificent Seven* (1960), *The Great Escape* (1963), *Death Wish* (1974) and four *Death Wish* sequels. He died at Los Angeles, CA, Sept 6, 2003.

BRYANT, WILLIAM CULLEN: BIRTH ANNIVERSARY. Nov 3, 1794. American poet ("Thanatopsis"), born at Cummington, MA. Died at New York, NY, June 12, 1878.

CANADA: NEW INUIT TERRITORY APPROVED: ANNIVERSARY. Nov 3, 1992. Canada's Inuit people voted to accept a federal land-claim package granting them control over a new territory, Nunavut, to be carved out of the existing Northwest Territories by 1999. The voting on Nov 3–5, 1992, indicated that 69 percent of the 9,648 eligible Inuit voters accepted the settlement. In exchange for the new territory, approximately 135,000 square miles, the Inuits gave up their rights to a territory of 775,000 square miles. See also: "Canada: Nunavut Independence: Anniversary" (Apr 1).

CLICHÉ DAY. Nov 3. Use clichés as much as possible today. Hey, why not? Give it a shot! Win some, lose some. You'll never know 'til you try it. Annually, Nov 3. (©2006 by WH.) For info: Thomas & Ruth Roy, Wellcat Holidays, 2418 Long Ln, Lebanon, PA 17046-1708. Phone: (717) 279-0184. E-mail: info@wellcat.com. Web: www.wellcat.com.

"DEWEY DEFEATS TRUMAN" HEADLINE: ANNIVERSARY. Nov 3, 1948. This headline in the *Chicago Tribune* notwithstanding, Harry Truman defeated Republican candidate Thomas E. Dewey for the US presidency.

DOMINICA: NATIONAL DAY. Nov 3. National holiday. Commemorates independence from Britain in 1978.

JAPAN: CULTURE DAY. Nov 3. National holiday.

JOB ACTION DAY. Nov 3. A day of empowerment for workers and job seekers—to put your career and job in the forefront, making plans, taking action steps. Annually, the first Monday in November. For info: Dr. Randall Hansen, Quintessential Careers, 520 Inchelium Hwy, Kettle Falls, WA 99141. Phone: (509) 738-9009. E-mail: randall@quintcareers.com. Web: www.jobactionday.com.

MICRONESIA, FEDERATED STATES OF: INDEPENDENCE DAY. Nov 3. National holiday commemorating independence from US in 1980.

NAGURSKI, BRONKO: BIRTH ANNIVERSARY. Nov 3, 1908. Bronislau ("Bronko") Nagurski, College Football Hall of Famer and charter member of the Pro Football Hall of Fame. Born at Rainy River, ON, Canada, he played football at the University of Minnesota, earning All-American honors at both tackle and fullback, and for the Chicago Bears. After retiring from football, Nagurski wrestled professionally. He died at International Falls, MN, Jan 7, 1990.

NATIONAL TRAFFIC DIRECTORS DAY. Nov 3. A day honoring radio and TV traffic departments, which schedule programs and announcements on the nation's broadcast stations. Annually, Nov 2 (observed on the following Monday if Nov 2 falls on a Saturday or Sunday). For info: Traffic Directors Guild of America, 26000 Avenida Aeropuerto, Ste 114, San Juan Capistrano, CA 92675. Phone: (949) 429-7063. Fax: (949) 429-7083. E-mail: tdga@cox.net. Web: www.tdga.org.

PANAMA: INDEPENDENCE DAY. Nov 3. Panama declared itself independent of Colombia in 1903.

PUBLIC TELEVISION DEBUTS: 45th ANNIVERSARY. Nov 3, 1969. A string of local educational TV channels united on this day under the Public Broadcasting System banner. Today there are more than 350 PBS stations.

SANDWICH DAY: BIRTH ANNIVERSARY OF JOHN MONTAGUE. Nov 3, 1718. A day to recognize the inventor of the sandwich, John Montague, Fourth Earl of Sandwich, born at London, England. England's first lord of the admiralty, secretary of state for the northern department, postmaster general and the man after whom Captain James Cook named the Sandwich Islands in 1778. A rake and a gambler, he is said to have invented the sandwich as a time-saving nourishment while engaged in a 24-hour-long gambling session in 1762. He died at London, Apr 30, 1792.

SOS ADOPTED: ANNIVERSARY. Nov 3, 1906. On this date the Second International Radio Telegraphic Conference at Berlin, Germany, proposed a new wireless distress signal: SOS. After its use during the sinking of the *Titanic* in 1912, SOS became the standard distress signal at sea. No longer used as a maritime distress signal since 1999, SOS is still a widely recognized code.

SPACE MILESTONE: *SPUTNIK 2* (USSR). Nov 3, 1957. A dog named Laika became the first animal sent into space. Total weight of craft and dog was 1,121 pounds. The satellite was not capable of returning the dog to Earth, and she died when her air supply was gone. Nicknamed "Muttnik" by the American press.

WHITE, EDWARD DOUGLASS: BIRTH ANNIVERSARY. Nov 3, 1845. Ninth chief justice of the US, born at Lafourche Parish, LA. During the Civil War he served in the Confederate army, after which he returned to New Orleans to practice law. Elected to the US Senate in 1891, he was appointed to the Supreme Court by President Grover Cleveland in 1894. He became chief justice under President William Taft in 1910 and served until 1921. He died at Washington, DC, May 19, 1921.

BIRTHDAYS TODAY

Adam Ant, 60, singer, born Stewart Goddard at London, England, Nov 3, 1954.

Ken Berry, 81, actor ("F Troop," "Mayberry RFD," "Mama's Family"), singer, dancer, born Moline, IL, Nov 3, 1933.

Kate Capshaw, 61, actress (*The Love Letter, How to Make an American Quilt, Indiana Jones and the Temple of Doom*), born Fort Worth, TX, Nov 3, 1953.

Michael S. Dukakis, 81, former governor of Massachusetts (D), 1988 presidential candidate, born Brookline, MA, Nov 3, 1933.

Mazie Hirono, 67, US Senator (D, Hawaii), born Fukushima, Japan, Nov 3, 1947.

Colin Kaepernick, 27, football player, born Milwaukee, WI, Nov 3, 1987.

Kathy Kinney, 60, actress ("The Drew Carey Show"), born Stevens Point, WI, Nov 3, 1954.

Dolph Lundgren, 55, actor (*A View to a Kill, Rocky IV*), born Stockholm, Sweden, Nov 3, 1959.

Dennis Miller, 61, comedian, actor ("Saturday Night Live," "The Dennis Miller Show"), born Pittsburgh, PA, Nov 3, 1953.

Evgeny Plushenko, 32, Olympic figure skater, born Vologograd, Russia, Nov 3, 1982.

Roseanne, 61, comedienne, actress ("Roseanne," *She-Devil*), born Roseanne Barr at Salt Lake City, UT, Nov 3, 1953.

Philip (Phil) Simms, 58, sportscaster, former football player, born Lebanon, KY, Nov 3, 1956.

Monica Vitti, 81, actress (*The Red Desert*), born Monica Luisa Ceciarelli at Rome, Italy, Nov 3, 1933.

November 4 — Tuesday

DAY 308 | **57 REMAINING**

AUSTRALIA: MELBOURNE CUP. Nov 4. Flemington Racecourse, Melbourne. First run in 1861, the Cup is one of the world's great horse races—celebrated throughout Australia and a public holiday in Melbourne. The handicapped race is 3,200 meters with prize money of AU$5.1 million. Famous winners include Phar Lap (1930) and Makybe Diva (2003, 2004, 2005). Annually, the first Tuesday in November. For info: Secretary, Victoria Racing Club, 448 Epsom Rd, Flemington Victoria 3031, Australia. E-mail: customerservice@vrc.net.au. Web: www.vrc.net.au.

BALSAM, MARTIN: 95th BIRTH ANNIVERSARY. Nov 4, 1919. Actor (*Twelve Angry Men*), born at New York, NY. Died at Rome, Italy, Feb 13, 1996.

CARNEY, ART: BIRTH ANNIVERSARY. Nov 4, 1918. Born at Mount Vernon, NY, this comedian and actor got his start on the vaudeville circuit. He appeared in dozens of Broadway shows and feature films, winning the Oscar for *Harry and Tonto* in 1974, but will always be best remembered for his role of sewer worker Ed Norton on the television classic "The Honeymooners." He played Jackie Gleason's upstairs neighbor on this show for many years, winning six Emmys. He died at Chester, CT, Nov 9, 2003.

CRONKITE, WALTER: BIRTH ANNIVERSARY. Nov 4, 1916. Legendary American broadcast journalist, Walter Leland Cronkite anchored the "CBS Evening News" from 1962 to 1981, covering such monumental events as President John Kennedy's assassination and the *Apollo 11* moon landing. A standard-bearer for exceptional television journalism. Cronkite's integrity earned him the nickname "the most trusted man in America." Born at St. Joseph, MO, Cronkite died at New York, NY, July 17, 2009.

GENERAL ELECTION DAY. Nov 4. Annually, the Tuesday after the first Monday in November. Many state and local government elections are held on this day, as well as presidential and congressional elections in the appropriate years. All US congressional seats and one-third of US senatorial seats are up for election in even-numbered years. Presidential elections are held in even-numbered years that can be divided equally by four. This day is a state holiday in 12 states.

ITALY: VICTORY DAY. Nov 4. Commemorates the signing of a WWI treaty by Austria in 1918, which resulted in the transfer of Trentino and Trieste from Austria to Italy.

KING TUT TOMB DISCOVERY: ANNIVERSARY. Nov 4, 1922. In 1922 one of the most important archaeological discoveries of modern times occurred at Luxor, Egypt. It was the tomb of Egypt's child-king, Tutankhamen, who became pharaoh at the age of nine and died, probably in the year 1352 BC, when he was 19. Perhaps the only ancient Egyptian royal tomb to have escaped plundering by grave robbers, it was discovered more than 3,000 years after Tutankhamen's death by English archaeologist Howard Carter, leader of an expedition financed by Lord Carnarvon. The priceless relics yielded by King Tut's tomb were placed in Egypt's National Museum at Cairo.

MAPPLETHORPE, ROBERT: BIRTH ANNIVERSARY. Nov 4, 1946. Born at Floral Park, NY, Mapplethorpe was one of photography's most controversial artists, known initially for his photographs of sadomasochistic rituals and later for his still lifes, nudes and portraits. Mapplethorpe died at Boston, MA, Mar 9, 1989. Exhibits of his work sparked controversy in 1989 and 1990, leading to intense political debate about the funding practices of the National Endowment for the Arts when its charter was up for renewal by Congress. An exhibition of his work in Cincinnati, OH, led to the arrest of the museum's curator, causing an additional uproar over First Amendment freedoms and obscenity issues.

MISCHIEF NIGHT. Nov 4. Observed in England, Australia and New Zealand. Nov 4, the eve of Guy Fawkes Day, is an occasion for bonfires and firecrackers to commemorate failure of the plot to blow up the Houses of Parliament Nov 5, 1605. See also: "England: Guy Fawkes Day" (Nov 5).

NATIONAL CHICKEN LADY DAY. Nov 4. Miami, FL. The Chicken Lady has helped thousands to learn the art of public speaking through her nonprofit organization The Professional Speakers Network, Inc. Each year as a thank-you, people come out and have a celebration to show their appreciation for what she has done to help them. More than 200 of them, thanks to the Chicken Lady, have published their own books. For info: Dr. Marthenia "Tina" Dupree, The Chicken Lady, PO Box 9906, Fort Lauderdale, FL 33310. Phone: (954) 485-5100. E-mail: chickenlady@prodigy.net.

PANAMA: FLAG DAY. Nov 4. Public holiday.

ROGERS, WILL: BIRTH ANNIVERSARY. Nov 4, 1879. William Penn Adair Rogers, American writer, actor, humorist and grassroots philosopher, born at Oologah, Indian Territory (now Oklahoma). With aviator Wiley Post, he was killed in an airplane crash near Point Barrow, AK, Aug 15, 1935. "My forefathers," he said, "didn't come over on the *Mayflower*, but they met the boat."

RUSSIA: UNITY DAY. Nov 4. Public holiday created in 2004 to commemorate the liberation of Moscow from occupying Polish troops in 1612. (Replaced Revolution Day, Nov 7, in the civic calendar.) Observed on following Monday when Nov 4 falls on a Saturday or Sunday.

SEIZURE OF US EMBASSY IN TEHRAN: 35th ANNIVERSARY. Nov 4, 1979. About 500 Iranians seized the US Embassy in Tehran, taking some 90 hostages, of whom 66 were Americans. They vowed to hold the hostages until the former shah, Mohammad Reza Pahlavi (in the US for medical treatments), was returned to Iran for trial. The shah died July 27, 1980, in an Egyptian military hospital near Cairo. Fourteen Americans were released in 1979 and 1980, but the remaining 52 hostages weren't released until Jan 20, 1981, after 444 days of captivity. The release occurred on America's Presidential Inauguration Day, during the hour in which the American presidency was transferred from Jimmy Carter to Ronald Reagan.

November 2014	S	M	T	W	T	F	S
							1
	2	3	4	5	6	7	8
	9	10	11	12	13	14	15
	16	17	18	19	20	21	22
	23	24	25	26	27	28	29
	30						

UNESCO: ANNIVERSARY. Nov 4, 1946. The United Nations Educational, Scientific and Cultural Organization was formed.

USE YOUR COMMON SENSE DAY. Nov 4. A day celebrating common sense in business and in life—on Will Rogers's birthday. Rogers said, "Common sense ain't all that common." On this day don't ignore your common sense—use it. Do at least one thing your common sense tells you to do: stop smoking for a day, have a talk with your children, begin an exercise program, etc. For info: Bud Bilanich, The Common Sense Guy, 191 University Blvd, #414, Denver, CO 80206. Phone: (303) 393-0446. Fax: (303) 393-0081. E-mail: Bud@BudBilanich.com.

WILL ROGERS DAY. Nov 4. Oklahoma.

BIRTHDAYS TODAY

Laura Bush, 68, former first lady, wife of George W. Bush, 43rd president of the US, born Midland, TX, Nov 4, 1946.

Sean "Diddy" Combs, 44, rapper, music and fashion executive, actor, born New York, NY, Nov 4, 1970.

Kathy Griffin, 48, comedienne, actress ("Kathy Griffin: My Life on the D List"), born Chicago, IL, Nov 4, 1966.

Devin Hester, 32, football player, born Riviera Beach, FL, Nov 4, 1982.

Ralph Macchio, 52, actor (*The Karate Kid*), born Huntington, NY, Nov 4, 1962.

Andrea McArdle, 51, singer, actress (Tony for *Annie*), born Philadelphia, PA, Nov 4, 1963.

Matthew McConaughey, 45, actor (*The Lincoln Lawyer, Sahara, A Time to Kill*), born Uvalde, TX, Nov 4, 1969.

Orlando Pace, 39, football player, born Sandusky, OH, Nov 4, 1975.

Markie Post, 64, actress ("Night Court," "Hearts Afire"), born Palo Alto, CA, Nov 4, 1950.

Doris Roberts, 84, actress ("Everybody Loves Raymond," "Remington Steele"), born St. Louis, MO, Nov 4, 1930.

Loretta Swit, 77, actress ("M*A*S*H"), born Passaic, NJ, Nov 4, 1937.

November 5 — Wednesday

DAY 309 **56 REMAINING**

BRANSON VETERANS HOMECOMING WEEK. Nov 5–11. Branson, MO. An areawide celebration honoring America's veterans. Annually, the seven days in November ending with the 11th. Est attendance: 50,000. For info: Branson Area CVB, PO Box 1897, Branson, MO 65615. Web: www.bransonveterans.com or www.explorebranson.com.

DEBS, EUGENE VICTOR: BIRTH ANNIVERSARY. Nov 5, 1855. American politician, first president of the American Railway Union, founder of the Social Democratic Party of America, and Socialist Party candidate for president of the US in 1904, 1908, 1912 and 1920; sentenced to 10-year prison term in 1918 (for sedition) and pardoned by President Warren Harding in 1921. Debs was born at Terre Haute, IN, and died at Elmhurst, IL, Oct 20, 1926.

DURANT, WILL: BIRTH ANNIVERSARY. Nov 5, 1885. American author and popularizer of history and philosophy. Among his books: *The Story of Philosophy* and *The Story of Civilization* (a 10-volume series of which the last four were coauthored by his wife, Ariel). Born at North Adams, MA, and died Nov 7, 1981, at Los Angeles, CA.

EL SALVADOR: DAY OF THE FIRST SHOUT FOR INDEPENDENCE. Nov 5. National holiday. Commemorates the first Central American battle for independence in 1811.

ENGLAND: GUY FAWKES DAY. Nov 5. United Kingdom. Anniversary of the "Gunpowder Plot." Conspirators planned to blow up the Houses of Parliament and King James I, Nov 5, 1605. Twenty barrels of gunpowder, which they had secreted in a cellar under Parliament, were discovered on the night of Nov 4, the very eve of the intended explosion, and the conspirators were arrested. They were tried and convicted, and Jan 31, 1606, eight (including Guy Fawkes) were beheaded and their heads displayed on pikes at London Bridge. Though there were at least 11 conspirators, Guy Fawkes is most remembered. In 1606 the Parliament, which was to have been annihilated, enacted a law establishing Nov 5 as a day of public thanksgiving. It is still observed, and on the night of Nov 5, the whole country lights up with bonfires and celebration. "Guys" are burned in effigy and the old verses repeated: "Remember, remember the fifth of November,/Gunpowder treason and plot;/I see no reason why Gunpowder Treason/Should ever be forgot."

FIRST SHATTERED BACKBOARD: ANNIVERSARY. Nov 5, 1946. Chuck Connors of the Boston Celtics became the first NBA player to shatter a backboard, doing so during the pregame warm-up in Boston Garden. Connors also played major league baseball with the Brooklyn Dodgers and the Chicago Cubs and gained fame as star of the television series "The Rifleman."

FORT HOOD KILLINGS: 5th ANNIVERSARY. Nov 5, 2009. A shooting rampage at Fort Hood, TX, left 13 dead and wounded 30 others. The accused gunman, Major Nidal Hasan, was a psychiatrist stationed at the army base. While initial reports speculated the shooting was rooted in radical Islamic beliefs, a clear motive for the attack is unknown.

LEIGH, VIVIEN: BIRTH ANNIVERSARY. Nov 5, 1913. Born Vivien Mary Hartley at Darjeeling, India, Leigh stunned Hollywood by her brilliant performance as Scarlett O'Hara in *Gone with the Wind* (1939). She received an Academy Award for that role and again for her portrayal of Blanche DuBois in *A Streetcar Named Desire* (1951). Midcareer, Leigh battled an extreme bipolar disorder that affected her ability to work and her marriage to fellow actor Lawrence Olivier; they divorced in 1960. Suffering from tuberculosis since the 1940s, she died from the disease on July 8, 1967, at London, England. George Cukor called her "a consummate actress, hampered by beauty."

LINCOLN REMOVES McCLELLAN FROM COMMAND: ANNIVERSARY. Nov 5, 1862. After months of increasing frustration with General George McClellan's reluctance to go on the offensive against Robert E. Lee's forces, President Abraham Lincoln issued orders removing McClellan from command and placing General Ambrose Burnside at the head of the Army of the Potomac.

LOEWY, RAYMOND: BIRTH ANNIVERSARY. Nov 5, 1893. Raymond Fernand Loewy, the "father of streamlining," an inventor, engineer and industrial designer whose ideas changed the look of 20th-century life, was born at Paris, France. His designs are evident in almost every area of modern life—the US Postal Service logo; the president's airplane, *Air Force One*; and streamlined automobiles, trains, refrigerators and pens. "Between two products equal in price, function and quality," he said, "the better looking will outsell the other." Loewy died at Monte Carlo, Monaco, July 14, 1986.

MAXWELL, ROBERT: DEATH ANNIVERSARY. Nov 5, 1991. Born Jan Ludwig Hoch in 1923 to a poor farm family in the Carpathian Mountains of Czechoslovakia, Maxwell became a billionaire with a media empire that included TV stations in France, the Macmillan Publishing Company in the US, newspapers in Hungary and the former East Germany, MTV Europe, the only official English-language newspaper in China and two of the biggest tabloids in the English-speaking world: New York's *Daily News* and London's *Daily Mirror*. After a brief career as a member of parliament, he began his rise as a media baron. Maxwell died after falling overboard from his yacht near the Canary Islands. After his death, his empire was found to be in significant financial disrepair.

McCREA, JOEL: BIRTH ANNIVERSARY. Nov 5, 1905. American actor Joel McCrea was born at South Pasadena, CA. His more than 80 films include *Wells Fargo* (1937), *Union Pacific* (1939), *Sullivan's Travels* (1941) and *Foreign Correspondent* (1940). He died Oct 20, 1990, at Los Angeles, CA.

"THE NAT KING COLE SHOW" TV PREMIERE: ANNIVERSARY. Nov 5, 1956. Popular African-American pianist and singer Cole hosted his own variety show for NBC. The Nelson Riddle Orchestra and the Randy Van Horne Singers also appeared as regulars on the show. It began as a 15-minute program, which was expanded to half an hour. Sponsors wouldn't back the show, however, and many affiliates declined to carry it. As a result, it was canceled.

***NEW YORK WEEKLY JOURNAL* FIRST ISSUE: ANNIVERSARY.** Nov 5, 1733. John Peter Zenger, colonial American printer and journalist, published the first issue of the *New York Weekly Journal* newspaper. He was arrested and imprisoned on Nov 17, 1734, for libel. The trial remains an important landmark in the history of the struggle for freedom of the press. See also: "Zenger, John Peter: Arrest Anniversary" (Nov 17).

ROGERS, ROY: BIRTH ANNIVERSARY. Nov 5, 1911. Known as the "King of the Cowboys," Rogers was born Leonard Slye at Cincinnati, OH. He made his acting debut in *Under Western Stars* in 1935 and later hosted his own TV series, "The Roy Rogers Show," in 1951; his wife, Dale Evans, was his leading lady. Sitting atop their horses, Trigger and Buttermilk, Rogers and Evans serenaded their audience at the conclusion of each show with "Happy Trails to You." Rogers died at Apple Valley, CA, on July 6, 1998. See also: "'The Roy Rogers Show' TV Premiere: Anniversary" (Dec 30).

TARBELL, IDA M.: BIRTH ANNIVERSARY. Nov 5, 1857. American writer born at Erie County, PA. She edited the muckraking journal *McClure's Magazine*, which exposed the political and industrial corruption of the day and emphasized the need for reform. Died at Bethel, CT, Jan 6, 1944.

BIRTHDAYS TODAY

Bryan Adams, 55, singer, songwriter, photographer, born Vancouver, BC, Canada, Nov 5, 1959.

Arthur (Art) Garfunkel, 73, singer (Simon and Garfunkel), actor (*Carnal Knowledge*), born Forest Hills, NY, Nov 5, 1941.

Kevin Jonas, 27, singer (The Jonas Brothers), actor, born Teaneck, NJ, Nov 5, 1987.

Javy Lopez, 44, former baseball player, born Ponce, Puerto Rico, Nov 5, 1970.

Corin Nemec, 43, actor ("Stargate SG-1," "Parker Lewis Can't Lose"), born Little Rock, AR, Nov 5, 1971.

Tatum O'Neal, 51, actress (Oscar for *Paper Moon*; *The Bad News Bears*), born Los Angeles, CA, Nov 5, 1963.

Sam Shepard, 71, dramatist, actor (*Buried Child*, *The Right Stuff*), born Samuel Shepard Rogers at Fort Sheridan, IL, Nov 5, 1943.

Elke Sommer, 73, actress (*A Shot in the Dark, The Prize*), born Elke Schletze at Berlin, Germany, Nov 5, 1941.

Jerry Stackhouse, 40, basketball player, born Kinston, NC, Nov 5, 1974.

Tilda Swinton, 54, actress (*Michael Clayton, The Deep End*), born London, England, Nov 5, 1960.

Bill Walton, 62, sportscaster, Hall of Fame basketball player, born Mesa, CA, Nov 5, 1952.

Gerry "Bubba" Watson, 36, golfer, born Bagdad, FL, Nov 5, 1978.

Geoffrey Wolff, 77, author (*The Duke of Deception, The Age of Consent*), born Los Angeles, CA, Nov 5, 1937.

November 6 — Thursday

DAY 310 **55 REMAINING**

BEAVER MOON. Nov 6. So called by Native American tribes of New England and the Great Lakes because at this time of year, beavers are industriously preparing themselves for the coming winter. The November Full Moon.

"GOOD MORNING AMERICA" TV PREMIERE: ANNIVERSARY. Nov 6, 1975. This ABC morning program, set in a living room, is a mixture of news reports, features and interviews with news makers and people of interest. It was the first program to compete with NBC's "The Today Show" and initially aired as "A.M. America." Hosts have included David Hartman, Nancy Dussault, Sandy Hill, Charles Gibson, Joan Lunden, Lisa McRee, Kevin Newman and Diane Sawyer.

INDIA: GURU NANAK'S BIRTH ANNIVERSARY. Nov 6. Celebrating the birth of Guru Nanak, the founder of Sikhism. Date can vary depending on whether lunar or solar calendar is used.

LOMBROSO, CESARE: BIRTH ANNIVERSARY. Nov 6, 1835. Italian founder of criminology, born at Verona, Italy. A professor of psychiatry, Lombroso believed that criminality could be identified with certain physical types of people. He died at Turin, Italy, Oct 19, 1909.

"MEET THE PRESS" TV PREMIERE: ANNIVERSARY. Nov 6, 1947. "Meet the Press" holds the distinction of being the oldest program on TV. It originally debuted on radio in 1945. The show has changed its format little since it began: a well-known guest (usually a politician) is questioned on current, relevant issues by a panel of journalists. The moderators have been Martha Rountree, Ned Brooks, Lawrence E. Spivak, Bill Monroe, Roger Mudd, Marvin Kalb, Chris Wallace, Garrick Utley, Tim Russert, Tom Brokaw and David Gregory.

MOON PHASE: FULL MOON. Nov 6. Moon enters Full Moon phase at 5:23 PM, EST.

November 2014	S	M	T	W	T	F	S
							1
	2	3	4	5	6	7	8
	9	10	11	12	13	14	15
	16	17	18	19	20	21	22
	23	24	25	26	27	28	29
	30						

MOROCCO: ANNIVERSARY OF THE GREEN MARCH. Nov 6. National holiday. Commemorates the march into the Spanish Sahara in 1975 to claim the land for Morocco.

NAISMITH, JAMES: BIRTH ANNIVERSARY. Nov 6, 1861. Born at Almonte, ON, Canada, Naismith was an athlete who became a physical education instructor and administrator. At a YMCA in Springfield, MA, he invented the game of "basket ball" out of the need for a safe and fun indoor winter sport. Naismith died on Nov 28, 1939, at Lawrence, KS, where he had been a physical education professor from 1917 until 1937. The Naismith Memorial Basketball Hall of Fame was established in Springfield in 1959, and James Naismith was the first inductee.

NATIONAL MEN MAKE DINNER DAY. Nov 6. One day set aside for "Non-Cooking Men Only" in the kitchen. Give wives a break, and let the men whip up some culinary delight with no help from family members. In the true spirit of Men Make Dinner Day, barbecues are not allowed. Annually, the first Thursday in November. For info: Sandy Sharkey. E-mail: sandy.sharkey@rocketmail.com. Web: www.menmakedinnerday.com.

PADEREWSKI, IGNACY JAN: BIRTH ANNIVERSARY. Nov 6, 1860. Polish composer, pianist, patriot born at Kurylowka, Podolia, Poland. He died at New York, NY, June 29, 1941. When Poland fell into the hands of the Soviets after WWII, his family decided he would remain buried in Arlington National Cemetery. In May 1963 President John F. Kennedy dedicated a plaque to Paderewski's memory and declared that the pianist would rest in Arlington until Poland was free. Paderewski's remains were returned to his native country on June 29, 1992, the 51st anniversary of his death, after Poland held its first parliamentary election following its independence from the Soviet Union.

"THE PHIL DONAHUE SHOW" TV PREMIERE: ANNIVERSARY. Nov 6, 1967. The first talk show with audience participation went on the air on this date at Dayton, OH. The first guest interviewed by host Phil Donahue was atheist Madalyn Murray O'Hair. In 1970 the program went national; it moved to Chicago in 1974 and to New York in 1985. In later years the program was titled "Donahue." After winning 19 Emmy Awards, the show left daytime TV in 1996. Phil Donahue briefly aired a show on the MSNBC cable network, but it was canceled after six months on Feb 25, 2003.

RETURN DAY. Nov 6. Georgetown, DE. The day when officially tabulated election returns are read from the balcony of Georgetown's redbrick, Greek Revival courthouse to the throngs of voters assembled below. Always the second day after a general election. An official "half-holiday" in Sussex County.

SAXOPHONE DAY (ADOLPHE SAX 200th BIRTH ANNIVERSARY). Nov 6. A day to recognize the birth anniversary of Adolphe Sax, Belgian musician and inventor of the saxophone and the saxotromba. Born at Dinant, Belgium, in 1814, Antoine Joseph Sax, later known as Adolphe, was the eldest of 11 children of a musical instrument builder. Sax contributed an entire family of brass wind instruments for band and orchestra use. He was accorded fame and great wealth, but business misfortunes led to bankruptcy. Sax died in poverty at Paris, France, Feb 7, 1894.

SOUSA, JOHN PHILIP: BIRTH ANNIVERSARY. Nov 6, 1854. American composer and band conductor, remembered for stirring marches such as "The Stars and Stripes Forever," "Semper Fidelis" and "El Capitan," born at Washington, DC. Died at Reading, PA, Mar 6, 1932. See also: "'The Stars and Stripes Forever' Day" (May 14).

SWEDEN: GUSTAVUS ADOLPHUS DAY. Nov 6. Honors Sweden's king and military leader killed in 1632.

UNITED NATIONS: INTERNATIONAL DAY FOR PREVENTING THE EXPLOITATION OF THE ENVIRONMENT IN WAR AND ARMED CONFLICT. Nov 6. A day calling attention to the irreparable damage to ecosystems and natural resources caused by armed conflict. For info: United Nations, Dept of Public Info, New York, NY 10017. Web: www.un.org.

BIRTHDAYS TODAY

Arne Duncan, 50, US Secretary of Education, born Chicago, IL, Nov 6, 1964.

Sally Field, 68, actress ("Brothers & Sisters," Oscars for *Norma Rae* and *Places in the Heart*; Emmy for *Sybil*), born Pasadena, CA, Nov 6, 1946.

Glenn Frey, 66, musician, songwriter, singer (The Eagles), born Detroit, MI, Nov 6, 1948.

Nigel Havers, 65, actor (*Chariots of Fire, Empire of the Sun*), born London, England, Nov 6, 1949.

Ethan Hawke, 44, actor (*Training Day, Gattaca, Before Sunrise, Dead Poets Society*), novelist, born Austin, TX, Nov 6, 1970.

Lance Kerwin, 54, actor ("James at 15"), born Newport Beach, CA, Nov 6, 1960.

Thandie Newton, 42, actress (*Crash, Mission: Impossible II, Beloved*), born London, England, Nov 6, 1972.

Mike Nichols, 83, film and stage director and producer (Oscar for *The Graduate*), born Michael Igor Peschkowsky at Berlin, Germany, Nov 6, 1931.

Rebecca Romijn, 42, model, actress (*X-Men, Femme Fatale,* "Ugly Betty"), born Berkeley, CA, Nov 6, 1972.

Kelly Rutherford, 46, actress ("Melrose Place," "Gossip Girl"), born Elizabethtown, KY, Nov 6, 1968.

Maria Owings Shriver, 59, broadcast journalist, former first lady of California, born Chicago, IL, Nov 6, 1955.

Emma Stone, 26, actress (*The Amazing Spider-Man, The Help, Easy A, Zombieland*), born Scottsdale, AZ, Nov 6, 1988.

November 7 — Friday

DAY 311 **54 REMAINING**

BANGLADESH: SOLIDARITY DAY. Nov 7. National holiday. Commemorates a coup in 1975.

BATTLE OF TIPPECANOE: ANNIVERSARY. Nov 7, 1811. William Henry Harrison, governor of the Indiana territory, defeated the Shawnee under Tecumseh at the Battle of Tippecanoe and burned their town. Harrison later ran for the presidency under the slogan "Tippecanoe and Tyler, Too." (John Tyler was his vice president.)

CAMUS, ALBERT: BIRTH ANNIVERSARY. Nov 7, 1913. The French writer and philosopher, winner of the Nobel Prize for Literature in 1957, was born at Mondavi, Algeria. Camus is renowned for his novels, particularly *The Stranger* (1942), which proffered themes—widely reflective of the feelings of the postwar intellectual—of the isolation of man and the estrangement of the individual from himself. With Jean-Paul Sartre, Camus is seen as the leading existential novelist of the era, although he rejected that or any other label. Camus was killed in an automobile accident at Paris, France, Jan 4, 1960.

CANADIAN PACIFIC RAILWAY: TRANSCONTINENTAL COMPLETION: ANNIVERSARY. Nov 7, 1885. At 9:30 AM the last spike was driven at Craigellachie, British Columbia, completing the Canadian Pacific Railway's 2,980-mile transcontinental railroad track between Montreal, QC, in the east and Port Moody, BC, in the west.

CHRISTKINDL MARKT. Nov 7–9. Cultural Center for the Arts, Canton, OH. 43rd annual. Fine arts and crafts show and sale. Sponsored by the Canton Fine Arts Associates to benefit the Canton Museum of Art. Est attendance: 5,000. For info: Christkindl Markt, 1001 Market Ave N, Canton, OH 44702. Phone: (330) 453-7666. Fax: (330) 453-1034. E-mail: carol@cantonart.org. Web: www.cantonchristkindl.org.

COIN, JEWELRY & STAMP EXPO: CALIFORNIA. Nov 7–9. Pasadena Convention Center, Pasadena, CA. Est attendance: 4,000. For info: Israel Bick, Exec Dir, Intl Stamp & Coin Collectors Society, PO Box 854, Van Nuys, CA 91408. Phone: (818) 997-6496. Fax: (818) 988-4337. E-mail: iibick@sbcglobal.net. Web: www.bickinternational.com.

COLORADO COUNTRY CHRISTMAS GIFT SHOW. Nov 7–9. Denver Merchandise Mart, Denver, CO. More than 400 booths of holiday gifts and specialty foods. Colorado Cookin' features local chefs performing cooking demonstrations. Bring the little ones to visit with Santa and have their pictures taken. Free parking. Est attendance: 25,000. For info: Susie O'Brien Borer or Kim Peck, Showcase Events, PO Box 2815, Kirkland, WA 98083. Phone: (800) 521-7469. Fax: (425) 889-8165. E-mail: denver@showcaseevents.org. Web: www.ColoradoCountryChristmas.com.

CRAFTSMEN'S CHRISTMAS CLASSIC ARTS & CRAFTS FESTIVAL. Nov 7–9. Richmond Raceway Complex, Richmond, VA. 35th annual. Features work from more than 450 talented artists and craftspeople. All juried exhibitors' work has been handmade by the exhibitors and must be their own original design and creation. See the creative process in action with several exhibitors demonstrating throughout the weekend. Visit Christmas Tree Village to view the uniquely decorated Christmas trees by some of the exhibitors. Est attendance: 35,000. For info: Gilmore Enterprises, Inc, 3514-A Drawbridge Pkwy, Greensboro, NC 27410-8584. Phone: (336) 282-5550. E-mail: contact@gilmoreshows.com. Web: www.ChristmasClassic.com or www.CraftShow.com.

CURIE, MARIE SKLODOWSKA: BIRTH ANNIVERSARY. Nov 7, 1867. Polish chemist and physicist, born at Warsaw, Poland. In 1903 she was awarded, with her husband, the Nobel Prize in Physics for their discovery of the element radium. Died near Sallanches, France, July 4, 1934.

DEAR SANTA LETTER WEEK. Nov 7–13. Consumer advocate Bob O'Brien answers "Dear Santa" letters for the holiday season. For info: Bob O'Brien, Consumer Advocate, 1061 Koelle Blvd, Secaucus, NJ 07094. Phone: (646) 233-6610. E-mail: robtfobrien@aol.com.

ESSENCE OF MOTOWN LITERARY JAM. Nov 7–8. Detroit, MI. Literary celebration for readers, writers, poets and authors. For info: Sylvia Hubbard, Essence of Motown, PO Box 43439, Detroit, MI 48243. Phone: (313) 289-8614. E-mail: sylviahubbard@gmail.com. Web: www.motownliteraryjam.com.

"FACE THE NATION" TV PREMIERE: 60th ANNIVERSARY. Nov 7, 1954. The CBS counterpart to NBC's "Meet the Press," this show employs a similar format: panelists interview a well-known guest. In 1983 the panel was changed to include experts in addition to journalists. Though usually produced at Washington, DC, the show occasionally interviews people elsewhere (such as Khrushchev in Moscow in 1957).

FIRST BLACK GOVERNOR ELECTED: 25th ANNIVERSARY. Nov 7, 1989. L. Douglas Wilder was elected governor of Virginia, becoming the first elected black governor in US history. Wilder had previously served as lieutenant governor of Virginia, becoming the first black elected to statewide office in the South since Reconstruction.

GREAT OCTOBER SOCIALIST REVOLUTION: ANNIVERSARY. Nov 7, 1917. The Bolshevik Revolution began at Petrograd, Russia, on the evening of Nov 6, 1917. A new government headed by Lenin took office the following day under the name Council of People's Commissars. Leon Trotsky was commissar for foreign affairs, and Joseph Stalin became commissar of national minorities. Formerly a holiday until canceled by the Russian Duma in 2004. According to the old Russian calendar, the revolution took place Oct 25, 1917. Soviet calendar reform caused the observance to fall on Nov 7 (Gregorian).

HOLIDAY MARKET. Nov 7–9. Greensboro Coliseum Complex Special Events Center, Greensboro, NC. 25th annual. Commercial holiday gift show that is a true feast for all the senses. Of course there is shopping with a capital SHOP! Features more than 360 specialty boutiques, shops and vendors offering holiday gifts for everyone on your list. Enjoy the singing of the Victorian-costumed strolling carolers, and let the children visit with Santa. You'll come away with recipes, samples, beauty makeovers and lots of holiday gifts and ideas. Est attendance: 30,000. For info: Gilmore Enterprises, 3514-A Drawbridge Pkwy, Greensboro, NC 27410. Phone: (336) 274-5550. E-mail: contact@gilmoreshows.com. Web: www.gilmoreshows.com or www.HolidayMarket.com.

JAGGER, DEAN: BIRTH ANNIVERSARY. Nov 7, 1903. American actor Dean Jagger was born at Columbus Grove, OH. Predominantly a character actor, he appeared in more than 120 films, including *Twelve O'Clock High* (1950), for which he won an Oscar for Best Supporting Actor. He died Feb 5, 1991, at Santa Monica, CA.

NATIONAL FARM TOY SHOW. Nov 7–9. Dyersville, IA. The "granddaddy" of farm toy shows, held since 1978. This slice of Americana features farm toys and farm collectibles as far as the eye can see—and much more. Annually, the first full weekend in November. Est attendance: 10,000. For info: National Farm Toy Museum, 1100 16th Ave Ct SE, Dyersville, IA 52040. Phone: (563) 875-2727. Web: www.toyfarmer.com.

NATIONAL MEDICAL SCIENCE LIAISON (MSL) AWARENESS AND APPRECIATION DAY. Nov 7. Created to educate the public on the role of medical science liaisons and what they do across the pharmaceutical, medical device and biotechnology industries. Annually, the first Friday in November. For info: Dr. Erin Albert, Pharm LLC, PO Box 335, Fishers, IN 46037. Phone: (317) 698-3202. E-mail: pharmllc@gmail.com.

NIXON'S "LAST" PRESS CONFERENCE: ANNIVERSARY. Nov 7, 1962. Richard M. Nixon, having been narrowly defeated in his bid for the presidency by John F. Kennedy in the 1960 election, returned to politics two years later as a candidate for governor of California in the election of Nov 6, 1962. Defeated again (this time by incumbent governor Edmund G. Brown), Nixon held his "last" press conference with assembled reporters in Los Angeles at midmorning the next day, at which he said: "Just think how much you're going to be missing. You won't have Nixon to kick around anymore, because, gentlemen, this is my last press conference."

REPUBLICAN SYMBOL: ANNIVERSARY. Nov 7, 1874. Thomas Nast used an elephant to represent the Republican Party in a satirical cartoon in *Harper's Weekly*. Today the elephant is still a well-recognized symbol for the Republican Party in political cartoons.

ROOSEVELT ELECTED TO FOURTH TERM: 70th ANNIVERSARY. Nov 7, 1944. Defeating Thomas Dewey, Franklin D. Roosevelt became the first, and only, person elected to four terms as president of the US. Roosevelt was inaugurated the following Jan 20 but died in office Apr 12, 1945, serving only 53 days of his fourth term.

RUSSIA: REVOLUTION DAY. Nov 7. Formerly a national holiday in Russia and Ukraine, it was canceled by the Russian Duma in 2004. Still observed unofficially by some of the population. Commemorates the Great Socialist Revolution, which occurred in October 1917 under the Old Style calendar.

SAMOA: ARBOR DAY. Nov 7. The first Friday in November is observed as Arbor Day in Samoa (formerly Western Samoa).

SUTHERLAND, DAME JOAN: BIRTH ANNIVERSARY. Nov 7, 1926. Born to Scottish parents at Sydney, Australia, Sutherland began her professional career as a singer at the age of 18. She rose through the ranks of the opera world, gaining a reputation as one of the greatest sopranos of all time, with a range able to reach coloratura with ease. She revitalized the bel canto repertory and style of opera in a career that spanned decades. Sutherland was dubbed "La Stupenda" by the Italian media, and Queen Elizabeth II made her a Dame Commander of the Order of the British Empire in 1978. She died Oct 11, 2010, at Les Avants, Switzerland.

USS *NEW YORK* COMMISSIONED: 5th ANNIVERSARY. Nov 7, 2009. On this date Navy Secretary Ray Mabus officially commissioned the state-of-the-art amphibious transport dock. Six thousand spectators turned out for the ceremony at New York City's Intrepid Sea-Air-Space Museum. The bow of the $1 billion warship contains 7¾ short tons of steel salvaged from the World Trade Center after its destruction in the terrorist attack of 9/11.

BIRTHDAYS TODAY

Rio Ferdinand, 36, soccer player, born Peckham, England, Nov 7, 1978.

William (Billy) Franklin Graham, 96, evangelist, born Charlotte, NC, Nov 7, 1918.

Keith Lockhart, 55, Boston Pops conductor, born Poughkeepsie, NY, Nov 7, 1959.

Jeremy London, 42, actor ("I'll Fly Away," "Party of Five"), born San Diego, CA, Nov 7, 1972.

Joni Mitchell, 71, singer, songwriter, born Roberta Joan Anderson at McLeod, AB, Canada, Nov 7, 1943.

Lucas Neff, 29, actor ("Raising Hope"), born Chicago, IL, Nov 7, 1985.

Barry Newman, 76, actor ("Petrocelli," *Vanishing Point*), born Boston, MA, Nov 7, 1938.

Johnny Rivers, 72, singer, born John Ramistella at New York, NY, Nov 7, 1942.

November 8 — Saturday

DAY 312 **53 REMAINING**

ABET AND AID PUNSTERS DAY. Nov 8. Laugh instead of groan at incredibly dreadful puns. All-time greatest triple pun: "Though he's not very humble, there's no police like Holmes," from the register of worst puns of Punsters Unlimited. (Originated by Earl Harris, retired, and the late William Rabe.)

BARNARD, CHRISTIAAN: BIRTH ANNIVERSARY. Nov 8, 1922. Pioneering heart surgeon, born at Beaufort West, South Africa. Barnard performed the first human heart transplant on Dec 3, 1967, after years of practicing the procedure, mainly on dogs. The patient, Louis Washkansky, lived for 18 days before dying from an infection. Today heart transplants are performed regularly and with good success. Barnard died at Paphos, Cyprus, Sept 2, 2001, of heart failure.

COOK SOMETHING BOLD AND PUNGENT DAY. Nov 8. Especially for those of us who have tightly closed up the house against chilly weather for the next six months. Now is the time to create the heavenly, homey odor of pungently bold cooking. Don't forget the sauerkraut and garlic! (©2006 by WH.) For info: Thomas & Ruth Roy, Wellcat Holidays, 2418 Long Ln, Lebanon, PA 17046. Phone: (717) 279-0184. E-mail: info@wellcat.com. Web: www.wellcat.com.

November 2014

S	M	T	W	T	F	S
						1
2	3	4	5	6	7	8
9	10	11	12	13	14	15
16	17	18	19	20	21	22
23	24	25	26	27	28	29
30						

CORTÉS CONQUERS MEXICO: ANNIVERSARY. Nov 8, 1519. After landing on the Yucatán peninsula in April, Spaniard Hernán Cortés and his troops marched into the interior of Mexico to the Aztec capital and took the Aztec emperor Montezuma hostage.

"DAYS OF OUR LIVES" TV PREMIERE: ANNIVERSARY. Nov 8, 1965. This popular daytime serial, like many others, has undergone many changes throughout its run. It expanded from 30 minutes to an hour; it went to number one in the ratings and slipped to 9 out of 12 in the 1980s; and it dropped or de-emphasized older characters, which angered its audience. The soap is set in Salem and centers around the Horton and Brady families. Notable cast members have included Mary Frann, Joan Van Ark, Susan Oliver, Mike Farrell, Kristian Alfonso, Garry Marshall, John Aniston, Josh Taylor, Wayne Northrop, John DeLancie, Andrea Barber, Deidre Hall, Thaao Penghlis, Jason Bernard, Marilyn McCoo, Charles Shaughnessy, Peter Reckell, Francis Reid, Patsy Pease and Genie Francis.

ENGLAND: LORD MAYOR'S SHOW. Nov 8. The City of London. Each year a colorful parade steps off at 11 AM from the Guildhall to the Royal Courts of Justice to mark the inauguration of the new Lord Mayor, who pledges allegiance to the Crown. Annually, the second Saturday in November. Est attendance: 500,000. For info: Pageantmaster, The Lord Mayor's Show, The Barge, Hindringham Rd, Great Walsingham, Norfolk, England NR22 6DR. Phone: (44) (1328) 824-420. Fax: (44) (1328) 824-422. E-mail: show@reidandreid.com. Web: www.lordmayorshow.org.

GELLHORN, MARTHA: BIRTH ANNIVERSARY. Nov 8, 1908. Pioneering female war correspondent who covered more than a dozen wars, from the Spanish Civil War to Vietnam. She was the author of numerous nonfiction and fiction works. She was married to Ernest Hemingway from 1940 to 1945 when both were covering WWII. Born at St. Louis, MO, Gellhorn died at London, England, Feb 15, 1998.

HALLEY, EDMUND: BIRTH ANNIVERSARY. Nov 8, 1656. (Old Style date.) Astronomer and mathematician born at London, England. Astronomer Royal, 1721–42. Died at Greenwich, England, Jan 14, 1742 (OS). He observed the great comet of 1682 (now named for him), first conceived its periodicity and wrote in his *Synopsis of Comet Astronomy*: "I may venture to foretell that this Comet will return again in the year 1758." It did, and Edmund Halley's memory is kept alive by the once-every-generation appearance of Halley's Comet. There have been 28 recorded appearances of this comet since 240 BC. Average time between appearances is 76 years. Halley's Comet is next expected to be visible in 2061.

MITCHELL, MARGARET: BIRTH ANNIVERSARY. Nov 8, 1900. American novelist who won a Pulitzer Prize (1937) for her only book, *Gone with the Wind*, a romantic novel about the Civil War and Reconstruction. *Gone with the Wind* sold about 10 million copies and was translated into 30 languages. Born at Atlanta, GA, Mitchell died there after being struck by an automobile Aug 16, 1949.

MONTANA: ADMISSION DAY: 125th ANNIVERSARY. Nov 8. Became 41st state in 1889.

MOUNT HOLYOKE COLLEGE FOUNDED: ANNIVERSARY. Nov 8, 1837. The first college for women in the US was founded as Mount Holyoke Seminary in 1837 at South Hadley, MA. While many colleges for women became coeducational institutions in the 1970s and 1980s, Mount Holyoke remains a women's college.

NATIONAL PARENTS AS TEACHERS DAY. Nov 8. To pay tribute to the thousands of organizations offering Parents as Teachers services across the country and around the world. These affiliates give all parents of young children support and information so all children will learn, grow and develop to realize their full potential. For info: Parents as Teachers, 2228 Ball Dr, St. Louis, MO 63146. Phone: (866) PAT-4YOU. Fax: (314) 432-8963. E-mail: info@ParentsAsTeachers.org. Web: www.ParentsAsTeachers.org.

PAGE, PATTI: BIRTH ANNIVERSARY. Nov 8, 1927. Singer Patti Page's sugary, adult pop sound danced effortlessly on the line between traditional vocal country and easy listening, and early hits like "The Tennessee Waltz" (1950) and "(How Much Is) That Doggie In the Window?" (1953) became standards of her lengthy career as a performer. Page sold millions of records in the 1950s—she was the top female singer of that decade—and while the explosion of rock and roll slowed her down, she continued to record and perform throughout the next several decades. Born Clara Ann Fowler at Claremore, OK, she died on Jan 1, 2013, at Encinitas, CA.

RORSCHACH, HERMANN: BIRTH ANNIVERSARY. Nov 8, 1884. Psychiatrist born at Zurich, Switzerland, who used his youthful interest in art and sketching to create the unusual and controversial inkblot test that now bears his name. In 1918 Rorschach began showing his patients inkblots on cards—created at random—and asked for their interpretations to gain insight into their unconscious. Rorschach, a psychoanalyst, continued his experimentation before publishing a comprehensive volume of his findings in 1921. He died Apr 2, 1922.

SHAKESPEARE'S FIRST FOLIO PUBLISHED: ANNIVERSARY. Nov 8, 1623. Printer Isaac Jaggard registered the first collected works of William Shakespeare (1564–1616) at Stationer's Hall, St. Paul's Churchyard, London, England. Entitled *Mr. William Shakespeares Comedies, Histories & Tragedies*, it was missing two plays, a problem corrected in subsequent editions. Two of Shakespeare's friends and fellow actors, John Heminge and Henry Condell, were the editors. The "First Folio" is now one of the most valuable books in the world.

X-RAY DISCOVERY DAY: ANNIVERSARY. Nov 8, 1895. On this day physicist Wilhelm Conrad Röntgen (1845–1923) discovered x-rays, beginning a new era in physics and medicine. Although x-rays had been observed previously, it was Röntgen, a professor at the University of Würzburg (Germany), who successfully repeated x-ray experimentation and who is credited with the discovery.

BIRTHDAYS TODAY

Edgardo Alfonzo, 41, baseball player, born St. Teresa, Venezuela, Nov 8, 1973.

Calvin Borel, 48, jockey, born St. Martin Parish, LA, Nov 8, 1966.

Sam Bradford, 27, football player, born Oklahoma City, OK, Nov 8, 1987.

Mary Hart, 63, television host, born Madison, SD, Nov 8, 1951.

Christie Hefner, 62, business executive (*Playboy*), born Chicago, IL, Nov 8, 1952.

Ricki Lee Jones, 60, singer, musician, born Chicago, IL, Nov 8, 1954.

Virna Lisi, 77, actress (*How to Murder Your Wife, The Secret of Santa Vittoria*), born Ancona, Italy, Nov 8, 1937.

Norman Lloyd, 100, actor (*Saboteur*, "St. Elsewhere"), director, producer, born Jersey City, NJ, Nov 8, 1914.

Parker Posey, 46, actress (*Personal Velocity, Best in Show, The House of Yes*), born Baltimore, MD, Nov 8, 1968.

Bonnie Raitt, 65, singer, born Los Angeles, CA, Nov 8, 1949.

Gordon Ramsay, 48, chef, television personality ("Hell's Kitchen," "The F Word"), born Glasgow, Scotland, Nov 8, 1966.

Tara Reid, 39, actress (*American Pie, Josie & the Pussycats*), born Wyckoff, NJ, Nov 8, 1975.

Morley Safer, 83, journalist ("60 Minutes"), born Toronto, ON, Canada, Nov 8, 1931.

Courtney Thorne-Smith, 47, actress ("According to Jim," "Ally McBeal"), born San Francisco, CA, Nov 8, 1967.

Alfre Woodard, 61, actress (*Cross Creek, Miss Evers' Boys, How to Make an American Quilt*), born Tulsa, OK, Nov 8, 1953.

November 9 — Sunday

DAY 313 **52 REMAINING**

AGNEW, SPIRO THEODORE: BIRTH ANNIVERSARY. Nov 9, 1918. The 39th vice president of the US, born at Baltimore, MD. Twice elected vice president (1968 and 1972), Agnew became the second person to resign that office, Oct 10, 1973. Agnew entered a plea of no contest to a charge of income tax evasion (on contract kickbacks received while he was governor of Maryland and after he became vice president). He died Sept 17, 1996, at Berlin, MD. See also: "Vice-Presidential Resignation: Anniversary" (Dec 28) and "Calhoun, John Caldwell: Birth Anniversary" (Mar 18).

BANNEKER, BENJAMIN: BIRTH ANNIVERSARY. Nov 9, 1731. American astronomer, mathematician, clock maker, surveyor and almanac author, called "first black man of science." Took part in original survey of Washington, DC. Banneker's *Almanac* was published during 1792–97. Born at Elliott's Mills, MD, he died at Baltimore, MD, Oct 9, 1806. A fire that started during his funeral destroyed his home, library, notebooks, almanac calculations, clocks and virtually all belongings and documents related to his life.

BERLIN WALL OPENED: 25th ANNIVERSARY. Nov 9, 1989. After 28 years as a symbol of the Cold War, the Berlin Wall was opened on this evening, and citizens of both sides walked freely through an opening in the barrier as others danced atop the structure to celebrate the end of a historic era. Coming amid the celebration of East Germany's 40-year anniversary, prodemocracy demonstrations led to the resignation of Erich Honecker, East Germany's head of state and party chief. It was Honecker who had supervised the construction of the 27.9-mile wall across the city during the night of Aug 13, 1961, because US president John F. Kennedy had ordered a troop buildup in response to the blockade of West Berlin by the Soviets.

BOSTON FIRE: ANNIVERSARY. Nov 9, 1872. Though Boston, MA, had experienced several damaging fires, the worst one started on this Saturday evening in a dry-goods warehouse. Spreading rapidly in windy weather, it devastated several blocks of the business district, destroying nearly 800 buildings. Damage was estimated at more than $75 million. It was said that the fire caused a bright red glare in the sky that could be seen from nearly 100 miles away. The Boston fire came one year, one month and one day after the Great Chicago Fire of Oct 8, 1871.

CAMBODIA: INDEPENDENCE DAY: 65th ANNIVERSARY. Nov 9. National Day. Declared independence from France in 1949.

DANDRIDGE, DOROTHY: BIRTH ANNIVERSARY. Nov 9, 1923. Actress and singer Dandridge was a child star, born at Cleveland, OH, who toured with her sisters, Vivian and Etta Jones, as the Dandridge Sisters. They played at the Cotton Club, sharing the stage with artists such as Cab Calloway and W.C. Handy. Dandridge went solo in 1941 to perform in Hollywood movies and on stage with the Desi Arnaz Band. Her big break came with the lead role in Otto Preminger's musical *Carmen Jones*. Dandridge received an Oscar nomination for her performance. Unfortunately, she could not overcome Hollywood's racism and tendency to typecast, and her career foundered. She died at West Hollywood, CA, Sept 8, 1965.

EAST COAST BLACKOUT: ANNIVERSARY. Nov 9, 1965. Massive electric power failure starting in western New York state at 5:16 PM cut electric power to much of northeastern US as well as Ontario and Quebec in Canada. More than 30 million people in an area of 80,000 square miles were affected. The experience provoked studies of the vulnerability of 20th-century technology.

ENGLAND: REMEMBRANCE SUNDAY. Nov 9. Cenotaph, Whitehall, London. Wreath-laying ceremony to commemorate the dead of both World Wars by Her Majesty the Queen, members of the royal family, government and service organizations. Annually, the Sunday closest to Nov 11. For info: Public Info Office, HQ London District Military, Horse Guards, Whitehall, London, England SW1A 2AX.

FULBRIGHT, J. WILLIAM: BIRTH ANNIVERSARY. Nov 9, 1905. US senator, born at Sumner, MO. He sponsored the legislation that created the Fulbright scholarships for international study for graduate students, faculty and researchers. Died Feb 9, 1995.

KRISTALLNACHT (CRYSTAL NIGHT): ANNIVERSARY. Nov 9–10, 1938. During the evening of Nov 9 and into the morning of Nov 10, 1938, mobs in Germany destroyed thousands of shops and homes, carrying out a pogrom against Jews. Synagogues were burned down or demolished. There were bonfires in every Jewish neighborhood, fueled by Jewish prayer books, Torah scrolls and volumes of philosophy, history and poetry. More than 30,000 Jews were arrested and 91 killed. The night got its name from the smashing of glass store windows.

LAMARR, HEDY: BIRTH ANNIVERSARY. Nov 9, 1913. Widely regarded as one of the most beautiful women of her era, actress and inventor Hedy Lamarr was born Hedwig Eva Maria Kiesler at Vienna, Austria. Starring alongside Hollywood legends like Clark Gable, Judy Garland and Spencer Tracy during a career that spanned nearly three decades, her most famous performance was in *Samson and Delilah* (1949). Insistent on being esteemed equally for her intelligence, in 1942 Lamarr, with composer George Antheil, patented a frequency hopping device that is now used in satellite and wireless technology. She died Jan 19, 2000, at Casselberry, FL.

THE LINKS, INC: ANNIVERSARY. Nov 9, 1946. In Philadelphia, PA, Margaret Roselle Hawkins and Sarah Strickland Scott founded a nonpartisan, volunteer organization called The Links, "linking" their friendship and resources in an effort to better the lives of disadvantaged African Americans after WWII. From a first group of nine, The Links grew to an incorporated organization of 8,000 women in 240 local chapters in 40 states plus the District of Columbia and two foreign countries. The Links promotes educational, cultural and community activities through a variety of projects here and in Africa. In May of 1985 The Links became an official nongovernmental organization of the UN.

LOVEJOY, ELIJAH P.: BIRTH ANNIVERSARY. Nov 9, 1802. American newspaper publisher and abolitionist born at Albion, ME. Died Nov 7, 1837, at Alton, IL, in a fire started by a mob angry about his antislavery views.

NATIONAL CHILD SAFETY COUNCIL FOUNDED: ANNIVERSARY. Nov 9, 1955. The National Child Safety Council (NCSC) at Jackson, MI, is the oldest and largest nonprofit organization in the US dedicated solely to child safety. Distributes comprehensive safety education materials to children, adults and seniors through local law enforcement and the Council's mascot, Safetypup®. For info: NCSC, Box 1368, Jackson, MI 49204-1368. Phone: (517) 764-6070. Web: www.nationalsafetycouncil.org.

November 2014	S	M	T	W	T	F	S
							1
	2	3	4	5	6	7	8
	9	10	11	12	13	14	15
	16	17	18	19	20	21	22
	23	24	25	26	27	28	29
	30						

"OMNIBUS" TV PREMIERE: ANNIVERSARY. Nov 9, 1952. This eclectic series deserved its name, offering a variety of presentations, including dramas, documentaries and musicals, for more than 10 years. Alistair Cooke hosted the program, which was the first major TV project to be underwritten by the Ford Foundation. Notable presentations included James Agee's "Mr Lincoln"; *Die Fledermaus*, with Eugene Ormandy conducting the Metropolitan Opera Orchestra; Agnes DeMille's ballet *Three Virgins and the Devil* (presented as *Three Maidens and the Devil*); and documentaries from underwater explorer Jacques Cousteau.

SAGAN, CARL: 80th BIRTH ANNIVERSARY. Nov 9, 1934. Astronomer, biologist, author (*Broca's Brain, Cosmos*), born at New York, NY. Died at Seattle, WA, Dec 20, 1996.

TUNISIA: TREE FESTIVAL. Nov 9. National agricultural festival. Annually, the second Sunday in November.

VIETNAM VETERANS MEMORIAL STATUE UNVEILING: 30th ANNIVERSARY. Nov 9, 1984. The Vietnam Veterans Memorial was completed by the addition of a statue, *Three Servicemen* (sculpted by Frederick Hart), which was unveiled on this date. The statue faces the black granite wall on which are inscribed the names of more than 58,000 Americans who were killed or missing in action in the Vietnam War.

WHITE, STANFORD: BIRTH ANNIVERSARY. Nov 9, 1853. American architect who designed the old Madison Square Garden, the Washington Square Arch, and the Players Club, Century and Metropolitan Club at New York City. Stanford White was born at New York City and was shot to death on the roof of Madison Square Garden by Harry Thaw, June 25, 1906.

WILHELM II ABDICATES: ANNIVERSARY. Nov 9, 1918. As WWI was coming to a close and it became clear their cause was lost, a revolt broke out in Germany. The kaiser was advised by his military staff that the loyalty of the army could not be guaranteed. On Nov 9, 1918, it was announced in Berlin that Kaiser Wilhelm II had abdicated his throne. The former leader then fled to Holland. Philipp Scheidemann, a Socialist leader, proclaimed a German Republic and became its first chancellor.

BIRTHDAYS TODAY

Nikki Blonsky, 26, actress (*Hairspray*), born Great Neck, NY, Nov 9, 1988.

Sherrod Brown, 62, US Senator (D, Ohio), born Mansfield, OH, Nov 9, 1952.

Eric Dane, 42, actor ("Grey's Anatomy," "Charmed," *Marley & Me*), born San Francisco, CA, Nov 9, 1972.

Adam Dunn, 35, baseball player, born Houston, TX, Nov 9, 1979.

David Duval, 43, golfer, born Jacksonville, FL, Nov 9, 1971.

Lou Ferrigno, 63, actor (*Pumping Iron*, "The Incredible Hulk"), former bodybuilder, born Brooklyn, NY, Nov 9, 1951.

Robert (Bob) Gibson, 79, Hall of Fame baseball player, born Omaha, NE, Nov 9, 1935.

Nick Lachey, 41, singer, television personality ("Newlyweds: Nick & Jessica"), born Harlan, KY, Nov 9, 1973.

Thomas Quasthoff, 55, opera singer, born Hanover, Germany, Nov 9, 1959.

Thomas Daniel (Tom) Weiskopf, 72, sportscaster, former golfer, golf course architect, born Massillon, OH, Nov 9, 1942.

November 10 — Monday

DAY 314 **51 REMAINING**

AREA CODES INTRODUCED: ANNIVERSARY. Nov 10, 1951. The 10-digit North American Numbering Plan, which provides area codes for Canada, the US and many Caribbean nations, was devised in 1947 by AT&T and Bell Labs. Eighty-four area codes were assigned. However, all long-distance calls at that time were operator-assisted. On this date in 1951, the mayor of Englewood, NJ (area code 201), direct-dialed the mayor of Alameda, CA. By 1960 all telephone customers could dial long-distance calls. The system is administered by the North American Numbering Plan Administration. For info: www.nanpa.com.

BURTON, RICHARD: BIRTH ANNIVERSARY. Nov 10, 1925. Welsh-born stage and film actor who led an intense and tempestuous personal life and career. Richard Burton was never knighted and never won an Oscar, but he was generally regarded as one of the great acting talents of his time. Born Richard Jenkins at Pontrhydyfen, South Wales, the son of a coal miner, he later took the name of his guardian, schoolmaster Philip Burton. Burton played King Arthur in the original production of *Camelot*. His films include *Cleopatra, Becket, Who's Afraid of Virginia Woolf?, Anne of the Thousand Days* and *Equus*. Burton died at Geneva, Switzerland, Aug 5, 1984.

***EDMUND FITZGERALD* MEMORIAL BEACON LIGHTING.** Nov 10. Noon–6 PM, Split Rock Lighthouse, Two Harbors, MN. Includes information on the *Edmund Fitzgerald* and other shipwrecks on Lake Superior; beacon lighting at dusk in memory of the 29 men lost on the *Edmund Fitzgerald* on Nov 10, 1975, and of all those who lost their lives in other Great Lakes shipwrecks. Lighthouse open. Est attendance: 500. For info: Lee Radzak, 3713 Split Rock Lighthouse Rd, Two Harbors, MN 55616. Phone: (218) 226-6372. E-mail: splitrock@mnhs.org. Web: www.mnhs.org/splitrock.

***EDMUND FITZGERALD* SINKING: ANNIVERSARY.** Nov 10, 1975. The ore carrier *Edmund Fitzgerald* broke in two during a heavy storm in Lake Superior (near Whitefish Point). There were no survivors of this, the worst Great Lakes ship disaster of the decade, which took the lives of 29 crew members.

GOLDSMITH, OLIVER: BIRTH ANNIVERSARY. Nov 10, 1728. Irish writer, author of the play *She Stoops to Conquer*. Born at Pallas, County Longford, Ireland, he died Apr 4, 1774, at London, England. "A book may be amusing with numerous errors," he wrote (Advertisement to *The Vicar of Wakefield*), "or it may be very dull without a single absurdity."

HOGARTH, WILLIAM: BIRTH ANNIVERSARY. Nov 10, 1697. English painter and engraver, famed for his satiric series of engravings (*A Harlot's Progress, A Rake's Progress, Four Stages of Cruelty*, etc). Born at London, England, he died there, Oct 26, 1764.

LUTHER, MARTIN: BIRTH ANNIVERSARY. Nov 10, 1483. The Augustinian monk who was a founder and leader of the Protestant Reformation was born at Eisleben, Saxony. Luther tacked his 95 Theses "On the Power of Indulgences" on the door of Wittenberg's castle church, on Oct 31, 1517, the eve of All Saints' Day. Luther asserted that the Bible was the sole authority of the church, called for reformation of abuses by the Roman Catholic Church and denied the supremacy of the pope. Tried for heresy by the Roman Church, threatened with excommunication and finally banned by a papal bull (Jan 2, 1521), he responded by burning the bull. In 1525 he married Katherine von Bora, one of nine nuns who had left the convent due to his teaching. Luther died near his birthplace, at Eisleben, Feb 18, 1546.

MARINE CORPS BIRTHDAY: ANNIVERSARY. Nov 10, 1775. Commemorates the Marine Corps's establishment in 1775. Originally part of the navy, it became a separate unit July 11, 1789.

NATIONAL YOUNG READER'S WEEK. Nov 10–14. Pizza Hut and the Center for the Book in the Library of Congress established National Young Reader's Week to remind Americans of the joys and importance of reading for kids. Schools, libraries, families and communities nationwide use this week to celebrate reading in a variety of creative and educational ways. Annually, the second week in November. For info: The BOOK IT! Program. Web: www.pizzahut.com/bookit.

PANAMA: FIRST SHOUT OF INDEPENDENCE. Nov 10. National holiday. Commemorates Panama's first battle for independence from Spain in 1821.

RAINS, CLAUDE: 125th BIRTH ANNIVERSARY. Nov 10, 1889. Stage, film and television actor, born at London, England. Rains trained at the Royal Academy of Dramatic Arts and overcame a speech impediment. Exposed to poison gas during WWI, his vocal chords were damaged, giving his deep voice a raspy quality that he used to great effect in *The Invisible Man* (1933), where he is only a voice until the film's final minutes, and as the corrupt Captain Louis Renault in *Casablanca* (1942). Rains's other notable films include *The Phantom of the Opera* (1943) and *Notorious* (1946). Died May 30, 1967, at Laconia, NH.

"SESAME STREET" TV PREMIERE: 45th ANNIVERSARY. Nov 10, 1969. An important, successful, long-running children's show, "Sesame Street" educates children while they have fun. It takes place along a city street, featuring a diverse cast of humans and puppets. Through singing, puppetry, film clips and skits, children are taught letters, numbers, concepts and other lessons. Shows are "sponsored" by letters and numbers. Human cast members have included Loretta Long, Matt Robinson, Roscoe Orman, Bob McGrath, Linda Bove, Buffy Sainte-Marie, Ruth Buzzi, Will Lee, Northern J. Calloway, Emilio Delgado and Sonia Manzano. Favorite Jim Henson Muppets include Ernie, Bert, Grover, Oscar the Grouch, the Cookie Monster, Big Bird and Mr Snuffleupagus.

STANLEY FINDS LIVINGSTONE: ANNIVERSARY. Nov 10, 1871. Having begun his search the previous March for the then two-years-missing explorer-missionary David Livingstone, explorer Henry M. Stanley found him on this day at Ujiji (Africa) and uttered those now immortal words, "Dr. Livingstone, I presume?"

VON SCHILLER, FRIEDRICH: BIRTH ANNIVERSARY. Nov 10, 1759. Born at Marbach, Württemberg, von Schiller was the leading German dramatist of his age. His works include *Don Carlos* (1787), the Wallenstein trilogy (1798–1801) and *Wilhelm Tell* (1804). His "An die Freude" ("Ode to Joy") was used by Beethoven in the choral finale to his Symphony No 9 in D Minor. Died May 9, 1805, at Weimar, Germany.

WORLD ORPHANS DAY. Nov 10. To facilitate public awareness of social issues surrounding orphans and displaced children, to highlight the current year's statistics on the AIDS orphans pandemic and to engage community support for the causes. Annually, the second Monday in November. For info: Cheryl Robeson, Chairman, The Stars Foundation. Phone: (704) 649-3132. E-mail: cheryl@worldorphansday.com. Web: www.thestarsfoundation.com or www.worldorphansday.com.

November 2014	S	M	T	W	T	F	S
							1
	2	3	4	5	6	7	8
	9	10	11	12	13	14	15
	16	17	18	19	20	21	22
	23	24	25	26	27	28	29
	30						

BIRTHDAYS TODAY

Vanessa Angel, 51, actress (*Spies like Us, Kingpin*), born London, England, Nov 10, 1963.

Hugh Bonneville, 51, actor ("Downton Abbey," *Notting Hill*), born London, England, Nov 10, 1963.

Isaac Bruce, 42, former football player, born Fort Lauderdale, FL, Nov 10, 1972.

Saxby Chambliss, 71, US Senator (R, Georgia), born Warrenton, NC, Nov 10, 1943.

Walton Coggins, 43, actor ("Justified," "The Shield"), born Birmingham, AL, Nov 10, 1971.

Roland Emmerich, 59, director, producer (*The Day After Tomorrow, Independence Day*), born Stuttgart, Germany, Nov 10, 1955.

Donna Fargo, 65, singer, songwriter, born Yvonne Vaughan at Mount Airy, NC, Nov 10, 1949.

Neil Gaiman, 54, author (*The Graveyard Book, American Gods*), comic book writer (*The Sandman*), born Porchester, England, Nov 10, 1960.

Miranda Lambert, 31, country singer, born Tyler, TX, Nov 10, 1983.

Tracy Morgan, 46, comedian, actor ("Saturday Night Live," "30 Rock"), born the Bronx, NY, Nov 10, 1968.

Mackenzie Phillips, 55, actress ("One Day at a Time," *American Graffiti*), born Alexandria, VA, Nov 10, 1959.

Ellen Pompeo, 45, actress ("Grey's Anatomy," *Moonlight Mile*), born Everett, MA, Nov 10, 1969.

Ann Reinking, 65, actress, director and choreographer (*Chicago*), born Seattle, WA, Nov 10, 1949.

Tim Rice, 70, writer, lyricist (Tonys for *Aida* and *Evita*; *Jesus Christ Superstar, The Lion King*), born Amersham, England, Nov 10, 1944.

Sinbad, 58, comedian, actor (*Jingle All the Way*, "A Different World"), born David Adkins at Benton Harbor, MI, Nov 10, 1956.

November 11 — Tuesday

DAY 315 — **50 REMAINING**

ANGOLA: INDEPENDENCE DAY. Nov 11. National holiday. Angola gained its independence from Portugal in 1975.

BONZA BOTTLER DAY™. Nov 11. To celebrate when the number of the day is the same as the number of the month. Bonza Bottler Day™ is an excuse to have a party at least once a month. For more information see Jan 1. For info: Gail Berger, 14 Fernwood Dr, Taylors, SC 29687. Phone: (864) 201-3988. E-mail: bonza@bonzabottlerday.com. Web: www.bonzabottlerday.com.

CANADA: REMEMBRANCE DAY. Nov 11. Honors those who died in WWI and WWII. Public holiday.

CHURCH OF ENGLAND VOTES TO ALLOW WOMEN PRIESTS: ANNIVERSARY. Nov 11, 1992. The Church of England, one of 28 national churches within the international Anglican Communion, voted Nov 11, 1992, to allow women to become priests.

COLOMBIA: CARTAGENA INDEPENDENCE DAY. Nov 11. National holiday. Commemorates declaration of independence from Spain of the city of Cartagena in 1811.

DEATH/DUTY DAY. Nov 11. Honoring soldiers on both sides who died on Nov 11, 1918, the day of the armistice that ended the fighting in WWI, 1914–18. The order was to stop fighting at 11 AM, rather than on receipt of the order. For info: Bob Birch, Punscorpion, The Puns Corps, 3108 Dashiell Rd, Falls Church, VA 22042. Phone: (703) 533-3668.

DOSTOYEVSKY, FYODOR MIKHAYLOVICH: BIRTH ANNIVERSARY. Nov 11, 1821. The Russian novelist, author of *The Brothers Karamazov, Crime and Punishment* and *The Idiot*, was born at Moscow, Russia, and died at St. Petersburg, Russia, Feb 9, 1881. A political revolutionary, he was arrested, tried, convicted and sentenced to death, but instead of execution he served a sentence in a Siberian prison and later served in the army there.

FAST, HOWARD: 100th BIRTH ANNIVERSARY. Nov 11, 1914. Prolific novelist, best known for *Spartacus* (1953), born at New York, NY. Was blacklisted in the 1950s for refusing to cooperate with HUAC and served three months in prison for contempt of Congress. Other key works are *Citizen Tom Paine* (1943), *Freedom Road* (1944) and *The Immigrants* (1977). He died Mar 12, 2003, at Old Greenwich, CT.

FUENTES, CARLOS: BIRTH ANNIVERSARY. Nov 11, 1928. World-renowned Mexican author, born Carlos Fuentes Macías at Panama City, Panama. Fuentes wrote across genres, penning a prolific oeuvre that includes political journalism, screenplays and novels. Combining realism, social protest and psychological insight, his postmodern works, which include *The Death of Artemio Cruz* (1962) and *Christopher Unborn* (1989), add depictions of Mexican identity previously ignored in the literary canon. He was the recipient of numerous prestigious awards, notably the Cervantes Prize (1987), the preeminent Spanish-language literary award. Fuentes died May 15, 2012, at Mexico City, Mexico. He wrote, "You start by writing to live. You end by writing so as not to die."

"GOD BLESS AMERICA" FIRST PERFORMED: ANNIVERSARY. Nov 11, 1938. Irving Berlin wrote this song especially for Kate Smith. She first sang it during her regular radio broadcast. It quickly became a great patriotic favorite of the nation and one of Smith's most requested songs.

JAPAN: ORIGAMI DAY. Nov 11. Sponsored by the Nippon Origami Association, an opportunity to learn and celebrate origami. Observed on World Peace Memorial Day/WWI Armistice Day. For info: Nippon Origami Assn, 2-064, Domir-Gobancho, 12 Gobancho Chiyoda-ku, Tokyo 102-0076, Japan. Web: www.origami-noa.com.

MALDIVES: REPUBLIC DAY. Nov 11. National holiday. Commemorates the abolition of the sultanate in 1968.

MARTINMAS. Nov 11. Feast day of St. Martin of Tours, who lived about AD 316–397. A bishop, he became one of the most popular saints of the Middle Ages. The period of warm weather often occurring about the time of his feast day is sometimes called St. Martin's Summer (especially in England).

PATTON, GEORGE S., JR: BIRTH ANNIVERSARY. Nov 11, 1885. American military officer, graduate of West Point (1909), George Smith Patton, Jr, was born at San Gabriel, CA. Ambitious and flamboyant, he lived for combat. He served in the punitive expedition into Mexico (1916), in Europe in WWI, and in North Africa and Europe in WWII. He received world attention and official censure in 1943 for slapping a hospitalized shell-shocked soldier. While a full general, owing to his critical public statements, he was relieved of his command in 1945. He died at Heidelberg, Germany, Dec 21, 1945, of injuries received in an automobile accident.

POLAND: INDEPENDENCE DAY. Nov 11. Poland regained independence in 1918, after having been partitioned among Austria, Prussia and Russia for more than 120 years.

SPACE MILESTONE: *COLUMBIA STS-5* (US). Nov 11, 1982. Shuttle *Columbia* launched from Kennedy Space Center, FL, with four astronauts: Vance Brand, Robert Overmyer, William Lenoir and Joseph Allen. "First operational mission" delivered two satellites into orbit for commercial customers. *Columbia* landed at Edwards Air Force Base, CA, Nov 16, 1982.

SPACE MILESTONE: *GEMINI 12* (US). Nov 11, 1966. Last Project Gemini manned Earth orbit launched. Buzz Aldrin spent five hours on a space walk, setting a new record.

SWEDEN: SAINT MARTIN'S DAY. Nov 11. Originally in memory of St. Martin of Tours; also associated with Martin Luther, who is celebrated the day before. Marks the end of the autumn's work and the beginning of winter activities.

SWITZERLAND: MARTINMAS GOOSE (MARTINIGIANS). Nov 11. Sursee, Canton Lucerne. At 3 PM on Martinmas, the "Gansabhauet" is staged in front of Town Hall. Blindfolded participants try to bring down, with a single sword stroke, a dead goose suspended on a wire.

✦VETERANS DAY. Nov 11. Presidential Proclamation. Formerly called Armistice Day and proclaimed each year since 1926 for Nov 11. PL 83-380 of June 1, 1954, changed the name to Veterans Day. PL 90-363 of June 28, 1968, required that, beginning in 1971, it would be observed the fourth Monday in October. PL 94-97 of Sept 18, 1975, required that, effective Jan 1, 1978, the observance would revert to Nov 11.

VETERANS DAY. Nov 11. Veterans Day was observed on Nov 11 from 1919 through 1970. Public Law 90-363, the "Monday Holiday Law," provided that, beginning in 1971, Veterans Day would be observed on the fourth Monday in October. This movable observance date, which separated Veterans Day from the Nov 11 anniversary of WWI armistice, proved unpopular. State after state moved its observance back to the traditional Nov 11 date, and finally Public Law 94-97 of Sept 18, 1975, required that, effective Jan 1, 1978, the observance of Veterans Day revert to Nov 11. As Armistice Day this is a holiday in Belgium, France and other European countries. At the 11th hour of the 11th day of the 11th month fighting ceased in WWI.

VICTOR EMMANUEL III: BIRTH ANNIVERSARY. Nov 11, 1869. Last king of Italy Victor Emmanuel III was born at Naples, Italy, and became king upon the assassination of his father in July 1900. For the first 20 years of his reign, Victor Emmanuel followed Italy's constitutional custom of selecting a prime minister based on the parliamentary majority, but with parliament in disarray after WWI, he named Benito Mussolini to form a cabinet and then failed to prevent Mussolini and the Fascists from seizing power. The king became little more than a figurehead. In 1946 Victor Emmanuel abdicated the throne, and he and the crown prince went into exile. He died at Alexandria, Egypt, Dec 28, 1947.

VIETNAM WOMEN'S MEMORIAL DEDICATION: ANNIVERSARY. Nov 11, 1993. In recognition of the 11,500 women who served in the Vietnam War, the bronze sculpture erected at Washington, DC, was dedicated this day.

VONNEGUT, KURT, JR: BIRTH ANNIVERSARY. Nov 11, 1922. Novelist and playwright, born at Indianapolis, IN. His idiosyncratic, semiautobiographical, blackly comic works were campus favorites in the Vietnam-roiled 1960s and '70s, especially *Cat's Cradle* (1963) and *Breakfast of Champions* (1973). *Slaughterhouse-Five* (1969), part of which was based on his WWII experience as a German prisoner of war, is frequently cited as one of the 100 best novels of the 20th century. Vonnegut died Apr 11, 2007, at New York, NY.

WASHINGTON: ADMISSION DAY: 125th ANNIVERSARY. Nov 11. Became 42nd state in 1889.

WORLD WAR I ARMISTICE: ANNIVERSARY. Nov 11, 1918. Anniversary of armistice between Allied and Central Powers ending WWI, signed at 5 AM, Nov 11, 1918, in Marshal Foch's railway car in the forest of Compiègne, France. Hostilities ceased at 11 AM. Recognized in many countries as Armistice Day, Remembrance Day, Veterans Day, Victory Day or WWI Memorial Day. Many places observe a silent memorial at the 11th hour of the 11th day of the 11th month each year. See also: "Veterans Day" (Nov 11).

BIRTHDAYS TODAY

Bibi Andersson, 79, actress (*Story of a Woman, Persona*), born Birgitta Anderson at Stockholm, Sweden, Nov 11, 1935.

Barbara Boxer, 74, US Senator (D, California), born Brooklyn, NY, Nov 11, 1940.

Leonardo DiCaprio, 40, actor (*The Great Gatsby, Django Unchained, The Departed, Titanic*), born Los Angeles, CA, Nov 11, 1974.

Calista Flockhart, 50, actress ("Ally McBeal," "Brothers & Sisters"), born Freeport, IL, Nov 11, 1964.

Demi Moore, 52, actress (*Charlie's Angels: Full Throttle, GI Jane, Ghost*), born Roswell, NM, Nov 11, 1962.

Reynaldo Ordonez, 42, former baseball player, born Havana, Cuba, Nov 11, 1972.

Frank Urban "Fuzzy" Zoeller, 63, golfer, born New Albany, IN, Nov 11, 1951.

November 12 — Wednesday

DAY 316 **49 REMAINING**

BIRTH OF BAHA'U'LLAH: ANNIVERSARY. Nov 12, 1817. Baha'i observance of the anniversary of the birth of Baha'u'llah (born Mirza Husayn Ali) at Nur, Persia. Baha'u'llah was prophet-founder of the Baha'i Faith. One of the nine days of the year when Baha'is suspend work. For info: Baha'is of the US, Office of Communications, 1233 Central St, Evanston, IL 60201. Phone: (847) 733-3559. Fax: (847) 733-3578. E-mail: ooc@usbnc.org. Web: www.bahai.us.

BLACKMUN, HARRY A.: BIRTH ANNIVERSARY. Nov 12, 1908. Former associate justice of the US, nominated by President Richard Nixon Apr 14, 1970. He retired from the Supreme Court Aug 3, 1994. Justice Blackmun was born at Nashville, IL, and died at Arlington, VA, Mar 4, 1999.

INTERNATIONAL DYSLEXIA ASSOCIATION READING, LITERACY AND LEARNING CONFERENCE. Nov 12–15. Hilton San Diego Bayfront, San Diego, CA. 65th annual. More than 2,000 teachers, administrators, speech-language pathologists, researchers and other professionals from across the US and around the world attend the premier professional development conference discussing dyslexia and related learning disabilities. The four-day program includes more than 125 educational sessions as well as four full-day symposia, keynote speakers, social events, networking opportunities and more. Est attendance: 2,000. For info: The International Dyslexia Assn, 40 York Rd, Ste 400, Baltimore, MD 21204. Phone: (410) 296-0232. Fax: (410) 321-5069. E-mail: lritchie@interdys.org. Web: www.interdys.org/AnnualConference.htm.

☆ ☆ ☆

November 2014	S	M	T	W	T	F	S
							1
	2	3	4	5	6	7	8
	9	10	11	12	13	14	15
	16	17	18	19	20	21	22
	23	24	25	26	27	28	29
	30						

KELLY, GRACE PATRICIA: 85th BIRTH ANNIVERSARY. Nov 12, 1929. American award-winning actress (Oscar for *The Country Girl*; *Rear Window, To Catch a Thief*) who became Princess Grace of Monaco when she married that country's ruler, Prince Rainier III, in 1956. Born at Philadelphia, PA, she died of injuries sustained in an automobile accident, Sept 14, 1982, at Monte Carlo, Monaco.

MEXICO: POSTMAN'S DAY. Nov 12. Every year on "Día del cartero," Mexicans show their appreciation for their postal carriers by leaving a little something in their mailboxes.

RODIN, AUGUSTE: BIRTH ANNIVERSARY. Nov 12, 1840. French sculptor (*The Kiss, The Thinker*), born at Paris, France. Died Nov 17, 1917, near Paris.

SPACE MILESTONE: *COLUMBIA STS-2* (US). Nov 12, 1981. Shuttle *Columbia*, launched from Kennedy Space Center, FL, with Joe Engle and Richard Truly on board, became the first spacecraft launched from Earth for a second orbiting mission. Landed at Edwards Air Force Base, CA, Nov 14, 1981.

STANTON, ELIZABETH CADY: BIRTH ANNIVERSARY. Nov 12, 1815. Women's suffragist and reformer, Elizabeth Cady Stanton was born at Johnstown, NY. "We hold these truths to be self-evident," she said at the first Women's Rights Convention, in 1848, "that all men and women are created equal." She died at New York, NY, Oct 26, 1902.

SUN YAT-SEN: BIRTH ANNIVERSARY (TRADITIONAL). Nov 12. Although his actual birth date in 1866 is not known, Dr. Sun Yat-sen's traditional birthday commemoration is held Nov 12. Heroic leader of China's 1911 revolution, he died at Beijing, China, Mar 12, 1925. A holiday in Taiwan. His death anniversary is also widely observed. See also: "Sun Yat-sen: Death Anniversary" (Mar 12).

TYLER, LETITIA CHRISTIAN: BIRTH ANNIVERSARY. Nov 12, 1790. First wife of John Tyler, 10th president of the US, born at New Kent County, VA. Died at Washington, DC, Sept 10, 1842.

VANS TRIPLE CROWN OF SURFING. Nov 12–Dec 20. Oahu, HI. 33rd annual. The Triple Crown includes three professional big-wave surf meets on Oahu's North Shore that mark the conclusion of the yearlong Association of Surfing Professionals (ASP) world tour. Following the Triple Crown, the ASP Men's and Women's Champions are crowned. Est attendance: 30,000. For info: Ocean Promotion, PO Box 223, Haleiwa, HI 96712. Phone: (808) 258-8533. E-mail: oceanpromotion@hawaii.rr.com. Web: www.triplecrownofsurfing.com.

BIRTHDAYS TODAY

Nadia Comaneci, 53, Olympic gymnast, born Onesti, Romania, Nov 12, 1961.

Ryan Gosling, 34, actor (*Drive, The Notebook, Lars and the Real Girl, Blue Valentine*), born London, ON, Canada, Nov 12, 1980.

Tonya Harding, 44, former figure skater, born Portland, OR, Nov 12, 1970.

Anne Hathaway, 32, actress (Oscar for *Les Misérables*; *The Dark Knight Rises, The Devil Wears Prada, The Princess Diaries*), born Brooklyn, NY, Nov 12, 1982.

Norman Mineta, 83, former US secretary of transportation, born San Jose, CA, Nov 12, 1931.

Megan Mullally, 56, actress ("Will & Grace"), born Los Angeles, CA, Nov 12, 1958.

Jack Reed, 65, US Senator (D, Rhode Island), born Providence, RI, Nov 12, 1949.

David Schwimmer, 48, actor ("Friends"), director, born Queens, NY, Nov 12, 1966.

Sammy Sosa, 46, former baseball player, born San Pedro de Macoris, Dominican Republic, Nov 12, 1968.

Russell Westbrook, 26, basketball player, born Long Beach, CA, Nov 12, 1988.

Neil Young, 69, singer (Buffalo Springfield and Crosby, Stills, Nash & Young), songwriter, born Toronto, ON, Canada, Nov 12, 1945.

November 13 — Thursday

DAY 317 **48 REMAINING**

BOOTH, EDWIN (THOMAS): BIRTH ANNIVERSARY. Nov 13, 1833. Famed American actor and founder of the Players Club, born near Bel Air, MD. His brother, John Wilkes Booth, assassinated President Abraham Lincoln. Died at New York, NY, June 7, 1893.

BRANDEIS, LOUIS DEMBITZ: BIRTH ANNIVERSARY. Nov 13, 1856. American jurist, associate justice of US (1916–39), born at Louisville, KY. Died at Washington, DC, Oct 5, 1941.

HOLLAND TUNNEL: ANNIVERSARY. Nov 13, 1927. The Holland Tunnel, running under the Hudson River between New York, NY, and Jersey City, NJ, was opened to traffic. The tunnel was built and operated by the New York–New Jersey Bridge and Tunnel Commission. Comprising two tubes, each large enough for two lanes of traffic, the Holland was the first underwater tunnel built in the US.

MAXWELL, JAMES CLERK: BIRTH ANNIVERSARY. Nov 13, 1831. British physicist noted for his work in the field of electricity and magnetism. Born at Edinburgh, Scotland, he died of cancer Nov 5, 1879, at Cambridge, England.

NATIONAL ASSOCIATION FOR GIFTED CHILDREN CONVENTION. Nov 13. Baltimore, MD. 61st annual. Educational sessions for administrators, counselors, coordinators, teachers and parents. Est attendance: 3,000. For info: Natl Assn for Gifted Children, 1331 H St NW, Ste 1001, Washington, DC 20005. Phone: (202) 785-4268. Fax: (202) 785-4248. E-mail: nagc@nagc.org. Web: www.nagc.org.

STEVENSON, ROBERT LOUIS: BIRTH ANNIVERSARY. Nov 13, 1850. Scottish author, born at Edinburgh, Scotland, known for his *Child's Garden of Verses* and novels such as *Treasure Island* and *Kidnapped*. Died at Samoa, Dec 3, 1894.

STOKES BECOMES FIRST BLACK MAYOR IN US: ANNIVERSARY. Nov 13, 1967. Carl Burton Stokes became the first black in the US elected mayor when he won the Cleveland, OH, mayoral election Nov 13, 1967. Died Apr 3, 1996.

WORLD KINDNESS DAY. Nov 13. As the name implies, World Kindness Day is about being kind to the world. The "Lonely Planet" not only refers to a travel guide but also is descriptive of Earth—the only planet in our solar system known to be teeming with life. It's all we have, and it's in everyone's best interest to make it the nicest place to live. There are many ways to share kindness on this day: Try to smile at 10 people today; leave something special on a neighbor's doorstep—flowers, a baked good, an invitation to share a meal; write a thank you or draw a picture for someone you love; pick up some trash; and lots more. For info: World Kindness Movement, Level 13 99 York St, Sydney 2000, NSW, Australia. E-mail: general.secretary@theworldkindnessmovement.org. Web: www.theworldkindnessmovement.org.

BIRTHDAYS TODAY

Gerard Butler, 45, actor (*P.S. I Love You, 300, The Phantom of the Opera*), born Glasgow, Scotland, Nov 13, 1969.

Monique Coleman, 24, actress (*High School Musical*), born Orangeburg, SC, Nov 13, 1980.

Sheila E. Frazier, 66, actress (*Super Fly*), born the Bronx, NY, Nov 13, 1948.

Whoopi Goldberg, 65, comedienne, actress (Oscar for *Ghost*; *Sister Act, The Color Purple*), born Caryn Elaine Johnson at New York, NY, Nov 13, 1949.

Jimmy Kimmel, 47, talk show host, comedian ("The Man Show," "Jimmy Kimmel Live"), born Brooklyn, NY, Nov 13, 1967.

Joe Mantegna, 67, actor (Tony for *Glengarry Glen Ross*; *House of Games, Things Change*, "Criminal Minds"), born Chicago, IL, Nov 13, 1947.

Garry Marshall, 80, producer, director (*Beaches, Pretty Woman*), actor ("Murphy Brown"), born New York, NY, Nov 13, 1934.

Chris Noth, 57, actor ("Sex and the City," "The Good Wife," "Law & Order"), born Madison, WI, Nov 13, 1957.

Tracy Scoggins, 55, actress ("Babylon 5"), born Galveston, TX, Nov 13, 1959.

Madeleine Sherwood, 92, actress ("The Flying Nun"), born Montreal, QC, Canada, Nov 13, 1922.

Vincent Frank (Vinny) Testaverde, 51, former football player, born New York, NY, Nov 13, 1963.

Dana Vollmer, 27, Olympic swimmer, born Syracuse, NY, Nov 13, 1987.

Steve Zahn, 46, actor (*Rescue Dawn, National Security, Sahara*), born Marshall, MN, Nov 13, 1968.

November 14 — Friday

DAY 318 **47 REMAINING**

BROOKS, LOUISE: BIRTH ANNIVERSARY. Nov 14, 1906. Born at Cherryvale, KS, Brooks started out as a dancer before finding fame as an actress in the 1920s' cinema. She is best known for her performances in two 1929 German films: *Pandora's Box* (as Lulu) and *Diary of a Lost Girl*. Would-be flappers the world over copied her trademark hairstyle: a sleek, helmetlike bob. Brooks wrote a well-received book of reminiscences, *Lulu in Hollywood* (1982), before her death on Aug 8, 1985, at Rochester, NY.

COIN, JEWELRY & STAMP EXPO: AMERICA. Nov 14–16. Radisson Hotel, Anaheim, CA. Est attendance: 4,000. For info: Israel Bick, Exec Dir, Intl Stamp & Coin Collectors Society, PO Box 854, Van Nuys, CA 91408. Phone: (818) 997-6496. Fax: (818) 988-4337. E-mail: iibick@sbcglobal.net. Web: www.bickinternational.com.

COPLAND, AARON: BIRTH ANNIVERSARY. Nov 14, 1900. American composer Aaron Copland was born at Brooklyn, NY. Incorporating American folk music and, later, the 12-tone system, he strove to create an American music style that was both popular and artistic. He composed ballets, film scores and orchestral works including *Fanfare for the Common Man* (1942), *Appalachian Spring* (1944; for which he won the Pulitzer Prize) and the score for *The Heiress* (1948; for which he won an Oscar). He died Dec 2, 1990, at North Tarrytown, NY.

CRAFTSMEN'S CHRISTMAS CLASSIC ART & CRAFT FESTIVAL. Nov 14–16 (tentative). South Carolina State Fairgrounds, Columbia, SC. 39th annual. Features original work and designs from hundreds of talented artists and craftspeople from across the nation. All juried exhibitors' work has been handmade by the exhibitors and must be their own original design and creation. Visit with the artisans as you browse the booths. Something for every style, taste and budget with thousands of choices from traditional to contemporary, functional to whimsical and decorative to fun and funky. Est attendance: 25,000. For info: Gilmore Enterprises, Inc, 3514-A Drawbridge Pkwy, Greensboro, NC 27410-8584. Phone: (336) 282-5550. E-mail: contact@gilmoreshows.com. Web: www.gilmoreshows.com.

DOW JONES TOPS 1,000: ANNIVERSARY. Nov 14, 1972. The Dow Jones Index of 30 major industrial stocks topped the 1,000 mark for the first time.

EISENHOWER, MAMIE DOUD: BIRTH ANNIVERSARY. Nov 14, 1896. Wife of Dwight David Eisenhower, 34th president of the US, born at Boone, IA. Died Nov 1, 1979, at Gettysburg, PA.

FOUR CORNER STATES BLUEGRASS FESTIVAL. Nov 14–16. Everett Bowman Rodeo Grounds, Wickenburg, AZ. 35th annual old-time fiddle, banjo, mandolin, flat-pick guitar championships. Includes gospel music. Special entertainment by nationally known bands as well as 13 competitive events. Est attendance: 5,000. For info: J. Brooks, Exec Dir, Chamber of Commerce, 216 N Frontier St, Wickenburg, AZ 85390. Phone: (928) 684-5479. Fax: (928) 684-5470. E-mail: events@wickenburgchamber.com. Web: www.wickenburgchamber.com.

FULTON, ROBERT: BIRTH ANNIVERSARY. Nov 14, 1765. Inventor of the steamboat, born at Little Britain, PA. Died Feb 24, 1815, at New York, NY.

GUINEA-BISSAU: READJUSTMENT MOVEMENT'S DAY. Nov 14. National holiday.

INDIA: CHILDREN'S DAY. Nov 14. Holiday observed throughout India.

INTERNATIONAL GIRLS DAY. Nov 14. A day to build confidence in girls and celebrate the power of girls to realize their dreams. Girls and their supporters across the country can plan celebrations with the theme "She Can Do Anything!" For info: Heidi Roy, International Girls Day, Kappa Delta Sorority, 3205 Players Ln, Memphis, TN 38125. Phone: (901) 748-1897. E-mail: heidi.roy@kappadelta.org. Web: www.celebrategirlsday.com.

LOOSEN UP, LIGHTEN UP DAY. Nov 14. A day to remind people of all the benefits of joy and laughter. For info: Stephanie West Allen, 1376 S Wyandot St, Denver, CO 80223. Phone: (303) 935-8866. E-mail: stephanie@westallen.com.

McCARTHY, JOSEPH: BIRTH ANNIVERSARY. Nov 14, 1908. Controversial politician born near Appleton, WI. As a Republican senator, McCarthy became a household name when he began making sweeping statements about the prevalence of secret Communists in the US. In this period of postwar uncertainty and distrust of the Soviets, Americans responded to his claims with fear and indignation. He soon spread his attacks, accusing politicians, State Department employees, journalists and members of the armed forces of being secret Communists. He held congressional hearings to uncover "traitors," using sensational methods that uncovered nothing of substance. After failing to prove any of his allegations, he soon fell out of favor and was censured by Congress for unbecoming conduct in December 1954. He died at Bethesda, MD, May 2, 1957.

MONET, CLAUDE: BIRTH ANNIVERSARY. Nov 14, 1840. French Impressionist painter (*Water Lilies*), born at Paris, France. Died at Giverny, France, Dec 5, 1926.

MOON PHASE: LAST QUARTER. Nov 14. Moon enters Last Quarter phase at 10:15 AM, EST.

"MURPHY BROWN" TV PREMIERE: ANNIVERSARY. Nov 14, 1988. This intelligent, often acerbic sitcom set in Washington, DC, starred Candice Bergen as an egotistical, seasoned journalist working for the fictitious TV news show "FYI." Featured were Grant Shaud as the show's high-strung producer, Miles Silverberg (later replaced by Lily Tomlin); Faith Ford as the former Miss America-turned-anchor, Corky Sherwood; Joe Regalbuto as neurotic reporter Frank Fontana; Charles Kimbrough as uptight anchorman Jim Dial; Pat Corley as Phil, owner of the local watering hole; and Robert Pastorelli as Eldin Bernecky, perfectionist housepainter and aspiring artist. The series ended with the May 31, 1998, episode.

NATIONAL DONOR SABBATH. Nov 14–16. To increase awareness about the dire need for organs and tissues for transplantation and to dispel fears that tissue and organ donation is incompatible with religion. Annually, the Friday, Saturday and Sunday two weekends before Thanksgiving. For info: US Dept of Health and Human Services,. Phone: (866) 99-DONATE. Web: www.organdonor.gov.

NEHRU, JAWAHARLAL: 125th BIRTH ANNIVERSARY. Nov 14, 1889. Indian leader who worked for independence and social reform, emphasizing economic welfare. First Indian prime minister after independence in 1947 and architect of India's foreign policy of nonalignment, he was greatly influenced by his friend Mohandas Gandhi. Born at Allahabad, India, Nehru died May 27, 1964, at New Delhi, India.

SALISBURY, HARRISON: BIRTH ANNIVERSARY. Nov 14, 1908. American journalist Harrison Evans Salisbury was born at Minneapolis, MN. *New York Times* Moscow correspondent from 1949 to 1954. Salisbury won the Pulitzer Prize in 1955 for a series of articles on the Soviet Union. He died July 5, 1993, at Providence, RI.

SALT LAKE'S FAMILY CHRISTMAS GIFT SHOW. Nov 14–16. Sandy, UT. A delightful holiday experience. Shoppers will find gifts, holiday decor, specialty foods and decorations from vendors across the nation. A festive shopping atmosphere with music, entertainment, Santa Claus and a holiday cooking demonstration area for all to enjoy. Est attendance: 25,000. For info: Showcase Events, Inc, PO Box 2815, Kirkland, WA 98083. Phone: (800) 521-7469. E-mail: saltlake@showcaseevents.org. Web: www.familychristmasgiftshow.com.

SPACE MILESTONE: *APOLLO 12* (US): 45th ANNIVERSARY. Nov 14, 1969. Launched this date. This was the second manned lunar landing—in Ocean of Storms. First pinpoint landing. Astronauts Pete Conrad, Alan Bean and Richard Gordon visited *Surveyor 3* and took samples. Earth splashdown Nov 24.

SPIRIT OF NSA DAY. Nov 14. The National Speakers Association (NSA) has designated today as a national day of advocacy encouraging professional speakers to support one another. NSA members are encouraged to focus on giving back, providing genuine support to speaking colleagues and taking time to connect, help, mentor or refer business to other members without any expectation of reciprocation. For info: NSA, 1500 S Priest Dr, Tempe, AZ 85281. Phone: (480) 968-2552. Fax: (480) 968-0911. Web: www.nsaspeaker.org.

STEIG, WILLIAM: BIRTH ANNIVERSARY. Nov 14, 1907. Prolific cartoonist, satirist and illustrator, William Steig was born at Brooklyn, NY. *The New Yorker* published more than 1,600 of his drawings, including 117 covers, and he wrote more than 25 books

November 2014

S	M	T	W	T	F	S
						1
2	3	4	5	6	7	8
9	10	11	12	13	14	15
16	17	18	19	20	21	22
23	24	25	26	27	28	29
30						

for children. He won the Caldecott Medal in 1970 for *Sylvester and the Magic Pebble* and received two Newbery Honors, for *Abel's Island* and *Dr. De Soto.* Other favorites include *The Amazing Bone, Brave Irene, CDB* and *Shrek*, the basis for a series of animated films. Steig died at Boston, MA, Oct 3, 2003.

STEVENSON, McLEAN: 85th BIRTH ANNIVERSARY. Nov 14, 1929. Actor, born at Bloomington, IL, Stevenson is perhaps best known for his role as the bumbling and womanizing Lieutenant Colonel Henry Blake in the long-running TV series "M*A*S*H." Stevenson died Feb 15, 1996, at Los Angeles, CA.

UNITED NATIONS: WORLD DIABETES DAY. Nov 14. Welcoming the fact that the International Diabetes Federation has been observing World Diabetes Day globally since 1991, with cosponsorship of the World Health Organization, the UN General Assembly on Dec 20, 2006, designated this day as a United Nations Day, to be observed every year beginning in 2007 (Resolution 61/225). For info: United Nations, Dept of Public Info, New York, NY 10017. Web: www.un.org.

BIRTHDAYS TODAY

Boutros Boutros-Ghali, 92, former secretary-general of the UN, born Cairo, Egypt, Nov 14, 1922.

Prince Charles, 66, Prince of Wales, heir to the British throne, born London, England, Nov 14, 1948.

Condoleezza Rice, 60, former US secretary of state, former US national security adviser, born Birmingham, AL, Nov 14, 1954.

Laura San Giacomo, 52, actress (*sex, lies and videotape*, "Just Shoot Me"), born Hoboken, NJ, Nov 14, 1962.

Curt Schilling, 48, former baseball player, born Anchorage, AK, Nov 14, 1966.

Joseph "Run" Simmons, 50, rapper (Run DMC), born Queens, NY, Nov 14, 1964.

D.B. Sweeney, 53, actor (*Spawn, The Cutting Edge*), born Shoreham, Long Island, NY, Nov 14, 1961.

Yanni, 60, New Age composer, born Yanni Chrysomalis at Kalamata, Greece, Nov 14, 1954.

November 15 — Saturday

DAY 319 — **46 REMAINING**

ALLEN, PHOG: BIRTH ANNIVERSARY. Nov 15, 1885. Forrest Clare ("Phog") Allen, basketball player and Basketball Hall of Fame coach, born at Jamesport, MO. Over 46 years, Allen's record as a coach (primarily at University of Kansas, his alma mater) was 771 games won, only 233 lost. He was instrumental in having basketball added to the Olympic program in 1936. Inducted into the Hall of Fame in 1959. Died at Lawrence, KS, Sept 16, 1974.

✦AMERICA RECYCLES DAY. Nov 15.

AMERICA RECYCLES DAY. Nov 15. To promote recycling and buying recycled products. Annually, Nov 15. For info: America Recycles Day. Web: www.americarecyclesday.org.

BELGIUM: DYNASTY DAY. Nov 15. National holiday in honor of Belgian monarchy.

BRAZIL: REPUBLIC DAY. Nov 15. Commemorates the proclamation of the republic in 1889. Celebrated on the Monday nearest Nov 15.

CUSTER STATE PARK BUFFALO AUCTION. Nov 15. Custer, SD. A live sale at 10 AM, MST, of 250–350 surplus buffalo (calves, yearlings, mature cows and two-year-old bulls). Est attendance: 400. For info: Gary Brundige, Custer State Park, 13329 US Hwy 16A, Custer, SD 57730. Phone: (605) 255-4515. Fax: (605) 255-4460. E-mail: gary.brundige@state.sd.us.

GEORGE SPELVIN DAY. Nov 15. Believed to be the anniversary of George Spelvin's theatrical birth—in Charles A. Gardiner's play *Karl the Peddler* on Nov 15, 1886, in a production at New York, NY. The name (or equivalent—Georgina, Georgetta, etc) is used in play programs to conceal the fact that an actor is performing in more than one role. The fictitious Spelvin is said to have appeared in more than 10,000 Broadway performances. See also: "England: Walter Plinge Day" (Dec 2) for British equivalent.

GYPSY CONDEMNATION ORDER: ANNIVERSARY. Nov 15, 1943. An order was issued by Heinrich Himmler for nomadic Gypsies and part-Gypsies to be placed in concentration camps. In cases of doubt, it was up to local heads of police to determine who was a Gypsy. Some estimates put the number of Gypsies killed in the Holocaust as high as half a million.

HERSCHEL, WILLIAM: BIRTH ANNIVERSARY. Nov 15, 1738. Sir Friedrich Wilhelm (William) Herschel, born at Hanover, Germany, was the most renowned astronomer of his time, discovering the planet Uranus, as well as its two moons, more than 2,000 nebulae and star clusters and Jupiter's moons. Named the "King's Astronomer" and knighted by King George III, Herschel built a 20-foot reflecting telescope with the king's grant money and systematically began to study the sky. He became the first to observe sunspots and confirm the gaseous nature of the sun, note the movement of the solar system through space and identify the infrared range of sunlight. A member of the Royal Society, he died at Slough, England, on Aug 25, 1822.

JAPAN: SHICHI-GO-SAN (7-5-3 FESTIVAL). Nov 15. Annual children's festival. The *Shichi-Go-San* (Seven-Five-Three) rite is "the most picturesque event in the autumn season." Parents take their three-year-old children of either sex, five-year-old boys and seven-year-old girls to the parish shrines dressed in their best clothes. There the guardian spirits are thanked for the healthy growth of the children, and prayers are offered for their further development.

MOORE, MARIANNE: BIRTH ANNIVERSARY. Nov 15, 1887. Acclaimed poet, critic and editor born at Kirkwood, MO. Her *Collected Poems* (1951) won the National Book Award, the Bollingen Prize and the Pulitzer Prize. She also received the National Medal for Literature—America's highest literary honor. Moore was frequently seen in a tricorn hat and cape—creating an indelible image that outlasted her death on Feb 5, 1972, at New York City.

NATIONAL BUNDT DAY. Nov 15. A day for everyone young and old to pull the Bundt pans from the cupboards and get ready for baking delicious masterpiece cakes during the upcoming holiday season. The Bundt pan has stood the test of time for more than 50 years and is a fixture in nearly every home in America. The Bundt is the quintessential kitchenware icon. Bake a cake in the traditional design or choose one of the more than 40 Bundt shapes for your own special creation to share with family and friends. For info: Dana Norsten, Nordicware, 5005 Hwy 7, Minneapolis, MN 55416. Phone: (952) 924-8601. Fax: (952) 924-9668. E-mail: dananorsten@nordicware.com. Web: www.nordicware.com.

O'KEEFFE, GEORGIA: BIRTH ANNIVERSARY. Nov 15, 1887. Described as one of the major American artists of the 20th century, Georgia O'Keeffe was born at Sun Prairie, WI. In 1924 she married the famous photographer Alfred Stieglitz. His more than 500 photographs of her have been called "the greatest love poem in the history of photography." She painted desert landscapes and flower studies. She died at Santa Fe, NM, Mar 6, 1986.

PCS AND HOMEPLACE FESTIVAL. Nov 15. Waretown, NJ. Featuring families playing country, bluegrass and traditional music. No alcoholic beverages or smoking allowed. For info: Albert Music Hall, PO Box 657, Waretown, NJ 08758. Web: www.alberthall.org.

REMEMBRANCE DAY PARADE AND CEREMONIES. Nov 15. Gettysburg, PA. An annual event held in conjunction with the Gettysburg Address Anniversary, with a parade of Civil War Living History to the Soldiers' National Cemetery. Remembrance Illumination is at the cemetery from 5:30 to 9:30 PM. Est attendance: 5,000. For info: Gettysburg CVB, 571 W Middle St, Gettysburg, PA 17325. Phone: (717) 334-6274. Fax: (717) 334-1166. E-mail: info@gettysburg.travel. Web: www.suvcw.org.

ROMMEL, ERWIN: BIRTH ANNIVERSARY. Nov 15, 1891. Field marshal and commander of the German Afrika Korps in WWII, Erwin Rommel was born at Heidenheim, in Württemberg, Germany. Rommel commanded the Seventh Panzer Division in the Battle of France. He was considered an excellent commander, and his early success in Africa made him a legend as the "Desert Fox," but in early 1943 he was outmaneuvered by Field Marshal Bernard Montgomery, and Germany surrendered Tunis in May of that year. Implicated in July 1944 in an attempted assassination of Hitler, he was given the choice of suicide or a trial and chose the former. Rommel died by his own hand at age 52, Oct 14, 1944, near Ulm, Germany.

SPACE MILESTONE: *BURAN* (USSR). Nov 15, 1988. The Soviet Union's first reusable space plane, *Buran*, landed on this date, completing a smooth, unmanned mission at approximately 1:25 AM, EST, after orbiting Earth twice in 3 hours, 25 minutes. Launched at Baikonur, Soviet central Asia. The importance of this mission was in its computer-controlled liftoff and return.

THAILAND: ELEPHANT ROUNDUP AT SURIN. Nov 15. Elephant demonstrations in morning, elephant races and tug-of-war between 100 men and one elephant. Observed since 1961 on third Saturday in November. Special trains from Bangkok on previous day.

BIRTHDAYS TODAY

Ed Asner, 85, actor ("The Mary Tyler Moore Show," "Lou Grant," *Roots*), born Kansas City, MO, Nov 15, 1929.

Daniel Barenboim, 72, musician, conductor, born Buenos Aires, Argentina, Nov 15, 1942.

Joanna Barnes, 80, actress (*The Parent Trap, Spartacus*), author, born Boston, MA, Nov 15, 1934.

Petula Clark, 82, singer, actress, born Ewell, Surrey, England, Nov 15, 1932.

November 2014	S	M	T	W	T	F	S
							1
	2	3	4	5	6	7	8
	9	10	11	12	13	14	15
	16	17	18	19	20	21	22
	23	24	25	26	27	28	29
	30						

Beverly D'Angelo, 60, actress (*Hair, Coal Miner's Daughter*), born Columbus, OH, Nov 15, 1954.

Kevin Eubanks, 57, musician, bandleader, born Philadelphia, PA, Nov 15, 1957.

Yaphet Kotto, 77, actor ("Homicide: Life on the Street," *Midnight Run, Blue Collar, Live and Let Die*), born New York, NY, Nov 15, 1937.

Jonny Lee Miller, 42, actor ("Elementary," "Eli Stone," *Trainspotting*), born Kingston-upon-Thames, Surrey, England, Nov 15, 1972.

Joseph Wapner, 95, television personality ("The People's Court"), retired judge, born Los Angeles, CA, Nov 15, 1919.

Sam Waterston, 74, actor ("Law & Order," "I'll Fly Away," *The Killing Fields, The Great Gatsby*), born Cambridge, MA, Nov 15, 1940.

Shailene Woodley, 23, actress (*The Descendants, Divergent,* "The Secret Life of the American Teenager"), born Simi Valley, CA, Nov 15, 1991.

November 16 — Sunday

DAY 320 — **45 REMAINING**

ESTONIA: DAY OF NATIONAL REBIRTH. Nov 16. National holiday. Commemorates the 1988 Declaration of Sovereignty. Became independent from the Soviet Union in 1991.

GERMANY: VOLKSTRAUERTAG. Nov 16. Memorial Day and national day of mourning in all German states for victims of National Socialism and the dead of both World Wars. Observed on the Sunday before Totensonntag. See also: "Germany: Totensonntag" (Nov 23).

HANDY, WILLIAM CHRISTOPHER: BIRTH ANNIVERSARY. Nov 16, 1873. American composer, bandleader, "father of the blues," W.C. Handy was born at Florence, AL. He died at New York, NY, Mar 28, 1958.

KAUFMAN, GEORGE S.: 125th BIRTH ANNIVERSARY. Nov 16, 1889. Playwright, director, producer and critic, born at Pittsburgh, PA. Working collaboratively on Broadway and in Hollywood from the 1920s through the 1950s, Kaufman was a theatrical rainmaker; his credits include *The Cocoanuts, Animal Crackers, You Can't Take It with You, The Royal Family* and *Guys and Dolls*. A drama critic for the *New York Times* (1917–30) and a member of the Algonquin Round Table, where his incisive wit and sharp one-liners were legendary: "I saw the play at a disadvantage," he wrote, "the curtain was up." Died June 2, 1961, at New York, NY.

LEWIS AND CLARK EXPEDITION REACHES PACIFIC OCEAN: ANNIVERSARY. Nov 16, 1805. Lewis and Clark's Corps of Discovery reached the Pacific Ocean on this date. They had glimpsed it on Nov 7, moving Clark to write in his journal: "Great joy in camp! We are in view of the Ocean, this great Pacific Ocean which we have been so anxious to see. And the roaring or noise of the waves breaking on the rocky shores . . . may be heard distinctly."

MEREDITH, BURGESS: BIRTH ANNIVERSARY. Nov 16, 1907. Actor (*Of Mice and Men, Rocky*) born at Cleveland, OH. Some sources give his year of birth as 1908 or 1909. Died at Malibu, CA, Sept 9, 1997.

OKLAHOMA: ADMISSION DAY: ANNIVERSARY. Nov 16. Became 46th state in 1907.

RIEL, LOUIS: HANGING: ANNIVERSARY. Nov 16, 1885. Born at St. Boniface, MB, Canada, Oct 23, 1844, Louis Riel, leader of the Metis (French/Indian mixed ancestry), was elected to Canada's House of Commons in 1873 and 1874 but never seated. Having been confined to asylums for madness (feigned or falsely charged, some said), Riel became a US citizen in 1883. In 1885 he returned to western Canada to lead the North West Rebellion. Defeated, he surrendered and was tried for treason, convicted and hanged, at Regina, SK, Canada. Seen as a patriot and protector of French culture in Canada, Riel became a legend and a symbol of the problems between French and English Canadians.

ROMAN CATHOLICS ISSUE NEW CATECHISM: ANNIVERSARY. Nov 16, 1992. For the first time since 1563, the Roman Catholic Church issued a new universal catechism, which addressed modern-day issues.

SAINT EUSTATIUS, WEST INDIES: STATIA AND AMERICA DAY. Nov 16, 1776. St. Eustatius, Leeward Islands. To commemorate the first salute to an American flag by a foreign government, from Fort Oranje in 1776. Festivities include sports events and dancing. During the American Revolution, St. Eustatius was an important trading center and a supply base for the colonies.

SPACE MILESTONE: *SKYLAB 4* (US). Nov 16, 1973. The 30th manned US spaceflight was launched with three astronauts, Gerald P. Carr, William R. Page and Edward G. Gibson, who spent 84 days on the space station. Space walks totaled 22 hours. Returned to Earth on Feb 8, 1974.

SPACE MILESTONE: *VENERA 3* (USSR). Nov 16, 1965. Launched this date, this unmanned space probe crashed into Venus, Mar 1, 1966. First man-made object on another planet.

UNITED NATIONS: INTERNATIONAL DAY FOR TOLERANCE. Nov 16. On Dec 12, 1996, the General Assembly established the International Day for Tolerance, to commemorate the adoption by UNESCO member states of the Declaration of Principles on Tolerance in 1995. For info: United Nations, Dept of Public Info, New York, NY 10017. Web: www.un.org.

UNITED NATIONS: WORLD DAY OF REMEMBRANCE FOR ROAD TRAFFIC VICTIMS. Nov 16. On Oct 26, 2005, the General Assembly invited member states and the international community to annually recognize the third Sunday in November as the World Day of Remembrance for Road Traffic Victims, as acknowledgment of victims of road traffic crashes and their families (Resolution 60/5). For info: United Nations, Dept of Public Info, New York, NY 10017. Web: www.un.org.

BIRTHDAYS TODAY

Oksana Baiul, 37, Olympic figure skater, born Dniepropetrovsk, Ukraine, Nov 16, 1977.

Lisa Bonet, 47, actress ("The Cosby Show," "A Different World," *Angel Heart*), born San Francisco, CA, Nov 16, 1967.

Susanna Clarke, 55, author (*Jonathan Strange & Mr Norrell*), born Nottingham, England, Nov 16, 1959.

Elizabeth Drew, 79, journalist, born Cincinnati, OH, Nov 16, 1935.

Dwight Eugene Gooden, 50, former baseball player, born Tampa, FL, Nov 16, 1964.

Maggie Gyllenhaal, 37, actress (*Crazy Heart, The Dark Knight, Secretary*), born New York, NY, Nov 16, 1977.

Marg Helgenberger, 56, actress ("CSI," "China Beach"), born Fremont, NE, Nov 16, 1958.

Diana Krall, 50, jazz singer, born Nanaimo, BC, Canada, Nov 16, 1964.

Martha Plimpton, 44, actress ("Raising Hope," *Top Girls, The Coast of Utopia*), born New York, NY, Nov 16, 1970.

Paul Scholes, 40, soccer player, born Salford, England, Nov 16, 1974.

Amare Stoudemire, 32, basketball player, born Lake Wales, FL, Nov 16, 1982.

November 17 — Monday

DAY 321 — **44 REMAINING**

AMERICAN EDUCATION WEEK. Nov 17–21. 93rd annual. This week, observed since 1921, spotlights the importance of providing every child in America with a quality public education from kindergarten through college and the need for everyone to do his or her part in making public schools great. Annually, the week preceding the week of Thanksgiving. For info: Natl Education Assn (NEA) Public Relations, 1201 16th St NW, Washington, DC 20036. Phone: (202) 833-4000. Web: www.nea.org.

HOMEMADE BREAD DAY. Nov 17. A day for the family to remember and enjoy the making, baking and eating of nutritious homemade bread. For info: Homemade Bread Day Committee, 2460 Devonshire Rd, Ann Arbor, MI 48104-2706.

HONDA, SOICHIRO: BIRTH ANNIVERSARY. Nov 17, 1906. Born at Hamamatsu, Japan, Honda was the enterprising auto racer turned businessman who founded the Honda Motor Company, a central part of Japan's postwar emergence as an economic power. Honda retired in 1973 and died Aug 5, 1991, at Tokyo, Japan.

MÖBIUS, AUGUST: BIRTH ANNIVERSARY. Nov 17, 1790. German astronomer, mathematician, teacher and author, August Ferdinand Möbius was born at Schulpforte, Germany. Möbius was a pioneer in the field of topology and first described the Möbius net and the Möbius strip. He died at Leipzig, Germany, Sept 26, 1868.

MONTGOMERY, BERNARD LAW: BIRTH ANNIVERSARY. Nov 17, 1887. Bernard Law Montgomery, who commanded the British Eighth Army to victory at El Alamein in North Africa in 1943, was born at St. Mark's Vicarage, Kennington Oval, London, England. He also led the Eighth Army in the Sicilian and Italian campaigns and commanded all ground forces in the 1944 Normandy landing. Montgomery died Mar 24, 1976, at Alton, Hampshire, England.

NATIONAL BOOK AWARDS WEEK. Nov 17–21. New York, NY. A week of festivities centered around the announcement of the winners for the National Book Awards, one of the nation's preeminent literary prizes. For info: Sherrie Young, National Book Foundation, 90 Broad St, Ste 604, New York, NY 10004. Phone: (212) 685-0261. E-mail: syoung@nationalbook.org. Web: www.nationalbook.org.

NATIONAL UNFRIEND DAY. Nov 17. Inspired by late-night talk show host Jimmy Kimmel, National Unfriend Day is the day in which Facebook users take an honest inventory of their friends list and eliminate all those who aren't true friends. By making cuts, they will be able to devote more time and energy to the people who really matter in their lives. Annually, Nov 17. For info: "Jimmy Kimmel Live," 6834 Hollywood Blvd, Hollywood, CA 90028. Phone: (323) 860-5918. Fax: (323) 860-5795. E-mail: trevor.x.duvall.-nd@abc.com. Web: www.abc.go.com/shows/jimmy-kimmel-live.

QUEEN ELIZABETH I: ACCESSION ANNIVERSARY. Nov 17, 1558. Anniversary of accession of Elizabeth I to English throne; celebrated as a holiday in England for more than a century after her death in 1603.

SUEZ CANAL: ANNIVERSARY. Nov 17, 1869. Formal opening of the Suez Canal. It had taken 1.5 million men a decade to dig the 100-mile canal. It shortened the sea route from Europe to India by 6,000 miles. An Anglo-French commission ran the canal until 1956, when Egypt's president, Gamal Abdel Nasser, seized it.

ZENGER, JOHN PETER: ARREST ANNIVERSARY. Nov 17, 1734. Colonial printer and journalist who established the *New York Weekly Journal* (first issue, Nov 5, 1733). Zenger was arrested Nov 17, 1734, for libel against the colonial governor but continued to edit his newspaper from jail. Trial was held during August 1735. Zenger's acquittal was an important early step toward freedom of the press in America. Zenger was born at Germany in 1697, came to the US in 1710 and died July 28, 1746, at New York, NY.

BIRTHDAYS TODAY

Terry Branstad, 68, Governor of Iowa (R), born Leland, IA, Nov 17, 1946.

Danny DeVito, 70, actor ("It's Always Sunny in Philadelphia," "Taxi," *Twins*), director (*Throw Momma from the Train*), born Neptune, NJ, Nov 17, 1944.

Daisy Fuentes, 48, actress, television personality, born Havana, Cuba, Nov 17, 1966.

Isaac Hanson, 34, singer (Hanson), born Tulsa, OK, Nov 17, 1980.

Lauren Hutton, 70, model, actress (*American Gigolo*), born Charleston, SC, Nov 17, 1944.

James M. Inhofe, 80, US Senator (R, Oklahoma), born Des Moines, IA, Nov 17, 1934.

Gordon Lightfoot, 76, singer, songwriter, born Orilla, ON, Canada, Nov 17, 1938.

Sophie Marceau, 48, actress (*The World Is Not Enough, Braveheart*), born Paris, France, Nov 17, 1966.

Mary Elizabeth Mastrantonio, 56, actress (*Robin Hood: Prince of Thieves, The Color of Money, Scarface*), born Oak Park, IL, Nov 17, 1958.

Lorne Michaels, 70, producer ("Saturday Night Live"), born Toronto, ON, Canada, Nov 17, 1944.

RuPaul, 54, model, actor, born RuPaul Andre Charles at San Diego, CA, Nov 17, 1960.

Martin Scorsese, 72, director (*Mean Streets, The Color of Money, Raging Bull, Goodfellas,* Oscar for *The Departed*), born Flushing, NY, Nov 17, 1942.

George Thomas (Tom) Seaver, 70, Hall of Fame baseball player, born Fresno, CA, Nov 17, 1944.

Matthew Settle, 45, actor ("Brothers & Sisters," "Gossip Girl"), born Hickory, NC, Nov 17, 1969.

Pat Toomey, 53, US Senator (R, Pennsylvania), born Providence, RI, Nov 17, 1961.

Dylan Walsh, 51, actor ("Nip/Tuck"), born Los Angeles, CA, Nov 17, 1963.

November 2014	S	M	T	W	T	F	S
							1
	2	3	4	5	6	7	8
	9	10	11	12	13	14	15
	16	17	18	19	20	21	22
	23	24	25	26	27	28	29
	30						

November 18 — Tuesday

DAY 322 **43 REMAINING**

DAGUERRE, LOUIS JACQUES MANDÉ: BIRTH ANNIVERSARY. Nov 18, 1787. French tax collector, theater scene-painter, physicist and inventor, born at Cormeilles-en-Paris, France. Remembered for his invention of the daguerreotype photographic process—one of the earliest to permit a photographic image to be chemically fixed to provide a permanent picture. It wasn't the first photographic process, but it was the most practically viable in that it dramatically reduced the time for an image to appear. The process was presented to the French Academy of Science Jan 7, 1839. In recognition of this accomplishment, Daguerre was admitted to France's Legion of Honour. He died near Paris, France, July 10, 1851.

GALLI-CURCI, AMELITA: BIRTH ANNIVERSARY. Nov 18, 1882. Acclaimed coloratura soprano and popular recording artist, a mainstay of New York City's Metropolitan Opera. Born at Milan, Italy, she made her American debut Nov 18, 1916, at Chicago, IL. Galli-Curci retired in 1937 and died at La Jolla, CA, Nov 26, 1963.

GATEWAY FARM EXPO. Nov 18–19. Buffalo County Fairgrounds, Kearney, NE. Est attendance: 8,000. For info: KAAPA, PO Box 1301, Kearney, NE 68848. Phone: (877) 720-4885. E-mail: farmexpo@kaapa.com. Web: www.gatewayfarmexpo.org.

GILBERT, SIR WILLIAM SCHWENCK: BIRTH ANNIVERSARY. Nov 18, 1836. English author of librettos for the famed Gilbert and Sullivan comic operas, born at London, England. Died May 29, 1911, at Harrow Weald, Middlesex, England, as a result of a heart attack experienced while saving a woman from drowning.

GRAY, ASA: BIRTH ANNIVERSARY. Nov 18, 1810. Botanist and natural history professor at Harvard, born at Paris, NY. Gray was known as a pioneer in the field of plant geography and a chief advocate of Darwin. Died at Cambridge, MA, Jan 30, 1888.

HAITI: ARMY DAY. Nov 18. Commemorates the Battle of Vertiéres, Nov 18, 1803, in which Haitians defeated the French.

"HOWARD STERN SHOW" RADIO PREMIERE: ANNIVERSARY. Nov 18, 1985. Radio's pioneering shock jock Howard Stern began broadcasting with sidekick Robin Quivers on New York radio station WXRK-FM. With outrageous humor and a gleeful disregard for taste, Stern quickly became popular nationally, but many remain outraged at his show elements. The FCC frequently fined his broadcasting company. Radio listeners at the show's peak of popularity were about 25 million. On Dec 16, 2005, Stern ended his show on regular radio and moved it to satellite radio in 2006.

JONESTOWN MASSACRE: ANNIVERSARY. Nov 18, 1978. On this date the Indiana-born, 47-year-old Reverend Jim Jones, leader of the "People's Temple," was reported to have directed the suicides of more than 900 persons at Jonestown, Guyana. US Representative Leo J. Ryan of California and four members of his party were killed in an ambush at Port Kaituma airstrip on Nov 18, 1978, when they attempted to leave after an investigative visit to the remote jungle location of the religious cult. On the following day Jones and his mistress killed themselves after watching the administration of Kool-Aid laced with the deadly poison cyanide to members of the cult. At least 912 persons died in the biggest murder-suicide in history.

LATVIA: INDEPENDENCE DAY. Nov 18. National holiday. Commemorates the declaration of an independent Latvia from Germany and Russia in 1918.

MARRIED TO A SCORPIO SUPPORT DAY. Nov 18. A worldwide day of remembrance to honor all those married to Scorpios and who suffer greatly. Assert yourself today! Hide their household flowcharts. Annually, Nov 18. (©2006 by WH.) For info: Thomas & Ruth Roy, Wellcat Holidays, 2418 Long Ln, Lebanon, PA 17046. Phone: (717) 279-0184. E-mail: info@wellcat.com. Web: www.wellcat.com.

MERCER, JOHN HERNDON (JOHNNY): BIRTH ANNIVERSARY. Nov 18, 1909. American songwriter, singer, radio performer and actor, born at Savannah, GA. Johnny Mercer wrote lyrics (and often the music) for some of the great American popular music from the 1930s through the 1960s, including "Autumn Leaves," "One for My Baby," "Satin Doll," "On the Achison, Topeka, and the Santa Fe," "You Must Have Been a Beautiful Baby," "Come Rain or Come Shine," "Hooray for Hollywood" and "Jeepers Creepers." Mercer died June 25, 1976, at Bel Air, CA.

MICKEY MOUSE'S BIRTHDAY. Nov 18. The comical activities of squeaky-voiced Mickey Mouse first appeared in 1928, on the screen of the Colony Theatre at New York City. The film, Walt Disney's "Steamboat Willie," was the first animated cartoon talking picture.

OMAN: NATIONAL HOLIDAY. Nov 18. Sultanate of Oman celebrates its national day, the birthday in 1942 of Sultan Qaboos bin Said.

"SEE IT NOW" TV PREMIERE: ANNIVERSARY. Nov 18, 1951. "See It Now" was a high-quality and significant public affairs show of the 1950s. Known for using its own film footage, unrehearsed interviews and no dubbing, "See It Now" covered many relevant and newsworthy stories of its time, including desegregation, lung cancer and anticommunist fervor. One of the most notable programs focused on Senator Joseph McCarthy, leading to McCarthy's appearance on the show—an appearance that damaged his credibility. "See It Now" was hosted by Edward R. Murrow, who also produced it jointly with Fred W. Friendly. Its premiere was the first live commercial coast-to-coast broadcast. The show had premiered on radio the year before as "Hear It Now."

SHEPARD, ALAN: BIRTH ANNIVERSARY. Nov 18, 1923. Former astronaut and the first American in space (in 1961), Shepard was born at East Derry, NH. He was one of only 12 Americans who have walked on the moon and was America's only lunar golfer, practicing his drive in space with a six iron. He was awarded the Congressional Medal of Honor in 1979. Shepard died near Monterey, CA, July 21, 1998.

SOUTH AFRICA ADOPTS NEW CONSTITUTION: ANNIVERSARY. Nov 18, 1993. After more than 300 years of white majority rule, basic civil rights were finally granted to blacks in South Africa. The constitution providing such rights was approved by representatives of the ruling party, as well as members of 20 other political parties.

SULLIVAN, JAMES: BIRTH ANNIVERSARY. Nov 18, 1860. James Edward Sullivan, amateur-sports promoter, born at New York, NY. Sullivan helped to establish the Amateur Athletic Union (AAU) in 1888 to preserve pure amateurism. He also worked as president of the American Sports Publishing Company and edited Spalding's Athletic Library series. The AAU Sullivan Award has been presented annually since 1930 in his honor to the best amateur athlete in the US. Died at New York, Sept 16, 1914.

US UNIFORM TIME ZONE PLAN: ANNIVERSARY. Nov 18, 1883. Charles Ferdinand Dowd, a college professor and one of the early advocates of uniform time, proposed a time zone plan of the US (four zones of 15 degrees), which he and others persuaded the railroads to adopt and place in operation on this date. Because it didn't involve the enactment of any law, some localities didn't change their clocks. A year later, an international conference applied the same procedure to create time zones for the entire world. US time zones weren't nationally legalized until 1918, with the passage of the Standard Time Act. See also: "Prime Meridian Set: Anniversary" (Nov 1) and "US Standard Time Act: Anniversary" (Mar 19).

BIRTHDAYS TODAY

Margaret Eleanor Atwood, 75, author (*Cat's Eye, The Handmaid's Tale*), born Ottawa, ON, Canada, Nov 18, 1939.

Dante Bichette, 51, former baseball player, born West Palm Beach, FL, Nov 18, 1963.

Linda Evans, 72, actress ("Dynasty," "The Big Valley"), born Hartford, CT, Nov 18, 1942.

Andrea Marcovicci, 66, actress ("Trapper John, MD"), singer, born New York, NY, Nov 18, 1948.

Harold Warren Moon, 58, Hall of Fame football player, born Los Angeles, CA, Nov 18, 1956.

Kevin Nealon, 61, comedian, actor ("Weeds," "Saturday Night Live"), born St. Louis, MO, Nov 18, 1953.

Jameson Parker, 67, actor ("Simon & Simon," *A Small Circle of Friends*), born Baltimore, MD, Nov 18, 1947.

Elizabeth Perkins, 54, actress ("Weeds," *Big, The Flintstones*), born Queens, NY, Nov 18, 1960.

Katey Sagal, 58, actress ("Married . . . With Children," "8 Simple Rules," "Futurama"), born Los Angeles, CA, Nov 18, 1956.

Chloë Sevigny, 40, actress ("Big Love," *Boys Don't Cry*), born Darien, CT, Nov 18, 1974.

Gary Sheffield, 46, former baseball player, born Tampa, FL, Nov 18, 1968.

Susan Sullivan, 70, actress ("Falcon Crest," "Dharma & Greg"), born New York, NY, Nov 18, 1944.

Brenda Vaccaro, 75, stage and film actress (*The Goodbye People*), born Brooklyn, NY, Nov 18, 1939.

Owen Wilson, 46, actor (*Midnight in Paris, Wedding Crashers, The Royal Tenenbaums*), screenwriter, born Dallas, TX, Nov 18, 1968.

November 19 — Wednesday

DAY 323 **42 REMAINING**

BELIZE: GARIFUNA DAY. Nov 19. Public holiday celebrating the first arrival of black Caribs from St. Vincent and Rotan at southern Belize in 1823.

CAMPANELLA, ROY: BIRTH ANNIVERSARY. Nov 19, 1921. Roy Campanella, one of the first black major leaguers and a star of one of baseball's greatest teams, the Brooklyn Dodgers' "Boys of Summer," was born at Philadelphia, PA. He was named the National League MVP three times in his 10 years of play, in 1951, 1953 and 1955. Campanella had his highest batting average in 1951 (.325), and in 1953 he established three single-season records for a catcher—most putouts (807), most home runs (41) and most runs batted in (142)—as well as having a batting average of .312. His career was cut short on Jan 28, 1958, when an automobile accident left him paralyzed. Campanella gained even more fame after his accident as an inspiration and spokesman for people with disabilities. He was named to the Baseball Hall of Fame in 1969. Roy Campanella died June 26, 1993, at Woodland Hills, CA.

COLD WAR FORMALLY ENDED: ANNIVERSARY. Nov 19–21, 1990. A summit was held at Paris, France, with the leaders of the Conference on Security and Cooperation in Europe (CSCE). The highlight of the summit was the signing of a treaty to dramatically reduce conventional weapons in Europe, thereby ending the Cold War.

DEDICATION DAY: 151st ANNIVERSARY OF THE GETTYSBURG ADDRESS. Nov 19. Gettysburg, PA. The anniversary of Lincoln's Gettysburg Address is celebrated with services at the Soldiers' National Monument in Gettysburg National Cemetery. Est attendance: 2,000. For info: Gettysburg Foundation, 1195 Baltimore Pike, Gettysburg, PA 17325. Phone: (717) 339-2148. E-mail: info@gettysburgfoundation.org. Web: www.gettysburgfoundation.org.

DRUCKER, PETER: BIRTH ANNIVERSARY. Nov 19, 1909. Born at Vienna, Austria, Drucker was an economist, theorist, consultant, journalist, professor and author. Arriving in America in 1937 (after leaving his Nazi-overrun homeland), Drucker grew to be one of the most important business thinkers of the century, practically inventing the idea of management as a profession. In 1954 he published his most famous work, *The Practice of Management*—one of almost 40 works. In his long career, he moved from thinking of the corporation as a community builder to being a critical gadfly in the wake of business scandals at the end of the century. He died Nov 11, 2005, at his home in Claremont, CA.

FIRST AUTOMATIC TOLL COLLECTION MACHINE: 60th ANNIVERSARY. Nov 19, 1954. At the Union Toll Plaza on New Jersey's Garden State Parkway, motorists dropped 25 cents into a wire mesh hopper and a green light would flash. The first modern toll road was the Pennsylvania Turnpike, which opened in 1940.

FIRST PRESIDENTIAL LIBRARY: 75th ANNIVERSARY. Nov 19, 1939. President Franklin D. Roosevelt laid the cornerstone for his presidential library at Hyde Park, NY. He donated the land, but public donations provided funds for the building, which was dedicated on June 30, 1941.

GARFIELD, JAMES ABRAM: BIRTH ANNIVERSARY. Nov 19, 1831. The 20th president of the US (and the first left-handed president) was born at Orange, OH. Term of office: Mar 4–Sept 19, 1881. While walking into the Washington, DC, railway station on the morning of July 2, 1881, Garfield was shot by disappointed office seeker Charles J. Guiteau. He survived, in very weak condition, until Sept 19, 1881, when he succumbed to blood poisoning at Elberon, NJ (where he had been taken for recuperation). Guiteau was tried, convicted and hanged at the jail at Washington, DC, June 30, 1882.

GERMANY: BUSS UND BETTAG. Nov 19. Buss und Bettag (Repentance Day) is observed on the Wednesday before the last Sunday of the church year. Formerly a national holiday, it remains a legal public holiday in the state of Saxony.

"HAVE A BAD DAY" DAY. Nov 19. For those who are filled with revulsion at being told endlessly to "have a nice day," this day is a brief respite. Store and business owners are to ask workers to tell customers to "have a bad day." Annually, Nov 19. (©2006 by WH.) For info: Thomas & Ruth Roy, Wellcat Holidays, 2418 Long Ln, Lebanon, PA 17046. Phone: (717) 279-0184. E-mail: info@wellcat.com. Web: www.wellcat.com.

LINCOLN'S GETTYSBURG ADDRESS: ANNIVERSARY. Nov 19, 1863. In 1863, 17 acres of the battlefield at Gettysburg, PA, were dedicated as a national cemetery. Noted orator Edward Everett spoke for two hours; the address that Lincoln delivered in less than two minutes was later recognized as one of the most eloquent of the English language. Five manuscript copies in Lincoln's hand survive, including the rough draft begun in ink at the executive mansion at Washington and concluded in pencil at Gettysburg on the morning of the dedication (kept at the Library of Congress).

MEXICO CITY EXPLOSION: 30th ANNIVERSARY. Nov 19, 1984. More than 300 people were killed when a gas truck explosion set off a series of explosions at a butane and liquefied gas storage facility in the Mexico City suburb Tlalnepantla. An area of approximately 60 acres was razed by the blasts and resulting fires. The four storage tanks involved held more than three million gallons of liquefied gas.

November 2014	S	M	T	W	T	F	S
							1
	2	3	4	5	6	7	8
	9	10	11	12	13	14	15
	16	17	18	19	20	21	22
	23	24	25	26	27	28	29
	30						

MONACO: NATIONAL HOLIDAY. Nov 19.

NATIONAL EDUCATIONAL SUPPORT PROFESSIONALS DAY. Nov 19. A mandate of the delegates to the 1987 National Education Association Representative Assembly called for a special day during American Education Week to honor the contributions of school support employees. Local associations and school districts salute support staff on this annual observance, the Wednesday of American Education Week. For info: Natl Education Assn (NEA), 1201 16th St NW, Washington, DC 20036. Phone: (202) 833-4000. Fax: (202) 822-7974. Web: www.nea.org.

PELÉ SCORES 1,000th GOAL: 45th ANNIVERSARY. Nov 19, 1969. Playing for the Santos team, legendary Brazilian soccer player Pelé scored his 1,000th goal in competition on a penalty kick against the team Vasco de Gama. Pelé dedicated this emotional and tremendous feat to Brazil's poor children and its elderly and suffering people. By the time Pelé retired in 1977, he had scored an astounding 1,281 goals in 1,363 matches—a world record that still stands.

PUERTO RICO: DISCOVERY DAY. Nov 19. Public holiday. Columbus discovered Puerto Rico in 1493 on his second voyage to the New World.

"ROCKY AND HIS FRIENDS" TV PREMIERE: 55th ANNIVERSARY. Nov 19, 1959. This popular cartoon featured the adventures of a talking squirrel, Rocky (Rocket J. Squirrel), and his friend Bullwinkle, a flaky moose. The tongue-in-cheek dialogue contrasted with the simple plots in which Rocky and Bullwinkle tangled with Russian bad guys Boris Badenov and Natasha (who worked for Mr Big). Other popular segments on the show included "Fractured Fairy Tales," "Bullwinkle's Corner" and the adventures of Sherman and Mr Peabody (an intelligent talking dog). In 1961 the show was renamed "The Bullwinkle Show," but the cast of characters remained the same.

SUFFRAGISTS' VOTING ATTEMPT: ANNIVERSARY. Nov 19, 1868. Testing the wording of the 14th Amendment stipulating that "no State shall make or enforce any law which shall abridge the privileges or immunities of citizens of the United States," 172 New Jersey suffragists, including four black women, attempted to vote in the presidential election. Denied, they cast their votes instead into a women's ballot box overseen by 84-year-old Quaker Margaret Pryer.

SUNDAY, BILLY: BIRTH ANNIVERSARY. Nov 19, 1862. Born William Ashley Sunday at Ames, IA, Sunday rose from poverty to become a professional baseball player with the Chicago White Stockings in 1883. He quit baseball in 1891 to devote himself to evangelism after hearing gospel singers at a Chicago mission. Sunday's fiery, athletic sermons—especially against demon rum—made him a star in the early 1900s, and at each revival he attracted about 100,000 listeners. At a typical revival in Detroit, MI, Sunday exhorted, "Help me, Jesus, help me save all in Detroit who are rushing to hell so fast that you can't see them for the dust." Sunday died Nov 6, 1935, at Chicago, IL.

WOMEN'S CHRISTIAN TEMPERANCE UNION ORGANIZED: ANNIVERSARY. Nov 19, 1874. Developed out of the Women's Temperance Crusade of 1873, the Women's Christian Temperance Union was organized at Cleveland, OH. The crusade had swept through 23 states with women going into saloons to sing hymns, pray and ask saloon keepers to stop selling liquor. Today the temperance group, headquartered at Evanston, IL, includes more than a million members with chapters in 72 countries and continues to be concerned with educating people on the potential dangers of the use of alcohol, narcotics and tobacco.

ZION NATIONAL PARK ESTABLISHED: 95th ANNIVERSARY. Nov 19, 1919. Utah's Mukuntuweap National Monument, proclaimed July 31, 1909, and later incorporated in Zion National Monument by proclamation on Mar 18, 1918, was established as Zion National Park in 1919.

BIRTHDAYS TODAY

Dick Cavett, 78, television pundit ("The Dick Cavett Show"), born Gibbon, NE, Nov 19, 1936.

Eileen Collins, 58, first female space shuttle commander; lieutenant colonel, USAF (retired), born Elmira, NY, Nov 19, 1956.

Ann Curry, 58, television journalist, born at Guam, Nov 19, 1956.

Gail Devers, 48, Olympic sprinter, born Seattle, WA, Nov 19, 1966.

Adam Driver, 31, actor (*Lincoln,* "Girls"), born San Diego, CA, Nov 19, 1983.

Terry Farrell, 51, actress ("Star Trek: Deep Space Nine," "Becker"), born Cedar Rapids, IA, Nov 19, 1963.

Jodie Foster, 52, actress (Oscars for *The Accused, The Silence of the Lambs; Taxi Driver*), director (*Home for the Holidays*), born Los Angeles, CA, Nov 19, 1962.

Savion Glover, 41, dancer, choreographer (*Bring in 'Da Noise, Bring in 'Da Funk*), born Newark, NJ, Nov 19, 1973.

Thomas R. Harkin, 75, US Senator (D, Iowa), born Cumming, IA, Nov 19, 1939.

Ryan Howard, 35, baseball player, born St. Louis, MO, Nov 19, 1979.

Scott Jacoby, 58, actor (*The Little Girl Who Lives Down the Lane, Return to Horror High*), born Chicago, IL, Nov 19, 1956.

Allison Janney, 54, actress (*American Beauty,* "The West Wing"), born Dayton, OH, Nov 19, 1960.

Patrick Kane, 26, hockey player, born Buffalo, NY, Nov 19, 1988.

Larry King, 81, talk show host ("Larry King Live"), born Lawrence Zeiger at Brooklyn, NY, Nov 19, 1933.

Calvin Klein, 72, fashion designer, born New York, NY, Nov 19, 1942.

Glynnis O'Connor, 59, actress (*Ode to Billy Joe*), born New York, NY, Nov 19, 1955.

Sean Parnell, 52, Governor of Alaska (R), born Hanford, CA, Nov 19, 1962.

Kathleen Quinlan, 60, actress (*Breakdown, Apollo 13*), born Pasadena, CA, Nov 19, 1954.

Ahmad Rashad, 65, sportscaster, former football player, born Bobby Moore at Portland, OR, Nov 19, 1949.

Meg Ryan, 53, actress (*When Harry Met Sally, Sleepless in Seattle*), born Fairfield, CT, Nov 19, 1961.

Kerri Strug, 37, Olympic gymnast, born Tucson, AZ, Nov 19, 1977.

Ted Turner, 76, baseball, basketball and television executive, born Cincinnati, OH, Nov 19, 1938.

Garrick Utley, 75, journalist, born Chicago, IL, Nov 19, 1939.

Jack Welch, 79, ex-chairman of GE, born Peabody, MA, Nov 19, 1935.

November 20 — Thursday

DAY 324 — **41 REMAINING**

AMERICAN SPEECH-LANGUAGE-HEARING ASSOCIATION CONVENTION. Nov 20–22. Orlando County Convention Center, Orlando, FL. Scientific sessions held on language, speech disorders, hearing science and hearing disorders and matters of professional interest to speech-language pathologists and audiologists. Est attendance: 12,000. For info: American Speech-Language-Hearing Assn, 2200 Research Blvd, Rockville, MD 20850. E-mail: convention@asha.org. Web: www.asha.org.

BATTLE OF TARAWA-MAKIN: ANNIVERSARY. Nov 20, 1943. The US began its offensive against Japan in the Central Pacific (Operation Galvanic) by attacking the Gilbert Islands, particularly the islets of Betio and Makin. The Japanese had heavily fortified the Tarawa chain of atolls, especially Tarawa, with pillboxes, blockhouses and ferroconcrete bombproofs. In the eight days it took the 5th Amphibious Corps, 2nd Marine Division and 27th Infantry Division to take the Tarawa and Makin Islands, 1,000 US soldiers were killed and 2,311 wounded. The Japanese loss was tallied at 4,700 men killed, 17 wounded and captured, and 129 Koreans surrendered. The US public, who through censorship previously had been kept in the dark about the human cost of the war, was appalled by casualty figures and photographs from this battle.

BILL OF RIGHTS: 225th ANNIVERSARY OF FIRST STATE RATIFICATION. Nov 20, 1789. New Jersey became the first state to ratify 10 of the 12 amendments to the US Constitution proposed by Congress Sept 25. These 10 amendments came to be known as the Bill of Rights.

BYRD, ROBERT: BIRTH ANNIVERSARY. Nov 20, 1917. The longest-serving senator in US history, born Cornelius Calvin Sale, Jr, at North Wilkesboro, NC. Coming from humble origins, including the early death of his mother and subsequent adoption by an aunt and uncle in coal mining country in West Virginia, he was elected to the West Virginia House of Delegates in 1946 and from there continued a 64-year political career in which he never lost an election. Byrd took night classes to earn his law degree while serving in the US House of Representatives and finally earned a bachelor's degree in 1994 at the age of 77. A crusader of liberal causes, his youthful affiliation with the Ku Klux Klan did create some scandal. He authored a four-volume history of the US Senate and was a staunch defender of its pomp, circumstance and traditions. He died at Fairfax, VA, June 28, 2010.

CHATTERTON, THOMAS: BIRTH ANNIVERSARY. Nov 20, 1752. English poet Thomas Chatterton was born at Bristol, England, and killed himself at age 17 by taking arsenic at his London garret, Aug 24, 1770. A gifted but lonely child, before he reached his teens Chatterton had created a fantasy poet-priest, Thomas Rowley, who lived in the 16th century. With his own pen, Chatterton created enough verses "by" Rowley to fill more than 600 printed pages. Chatterton's fantasy-forgery poems attracted little attention during his short life, but they were later admired by Wordsworth, Coleridge, Shelley, Keats and Byron. In addition, he became the subject of at least one play, an opera and a novel.

COOKE, ALISTAIR: BIRTH ANNIVERSARY. Nov 20, 1908. Broadcast journalist and author Alfred Alistair Cooke was born at Salford, England. He came to the US in the 1930s and eventually became an American citizen. His program "Letter from America" was broadcast in more than 50 countries by BBC Radio for an astonishing 58 years. He was the chief American correspondent for the *Guardian* for 26 years, and he hosted PBS's "Masterpiece Theatre" for more than 20 years. Highly regarded for his sophisticated grace and style in both writing and broadcasting, he continued to broadcast "Letter from America" until his death at New York, NY, Mar 30, 2004.

FRANCE: BEAUJOLAIS NOUVEAU RELEASE. Nov 20. By French law, Beaujolais Nouveau, a young red wine, can't be released for sale until the third Thursday of November. Once the third Thursday is reached, celebrations abound as the wine travels to markets all over the world.

GOULD, CHESTER: BIRTH ANNIVERSARY. Nov 20, 1900. In 1931 Chester Gould created comic strip character Dick Tracy, the clean-cut, square-jawed, plainclothed detective who represented the code that "crime doesn't pay." The strip first appeared Oct 4, 1931, in the *Detroit Daily Mirror* and later was syndicated in nearly 1,000 newspapers worldwide. "Dick Tracy" (originally called "Plainclothes Tracy") featured Tess Trueheart (later Mrs Tracy) and a host of bad guys with ugly names and faces to match their ugly ways—Mole, Pruneface, Flat Top, B-B Eyes, Mumbles and others. Closely following actual police methods of crime prevention, it included a "Crimestopper Notebook" with tips on self-protection. More violent than most comic strips, "Dick Tracy" was a combination of realism and science fiction. Chester Gould was born at Pawnee, OK, and died May 11, 1985, at Woodstock, IL.

GREAT AMERICAN SMOKEOUT. Nov 20. A day observed annually since 1977 to celebrate smoke-free environments. Annually, the third Thursday in November. For info: American Cancer Society. Phone: (800) ACS-2345. Web: www.cancer.org/smokeout.

HUBBLE, EDWIN POWELL: 125th BIRTH ANNIVERSARY. Nov 20, 1889. American astronomer Edwin Hubble was born at Marshfield, MO. His discovery and development of the concept of an expanding universe has been described as the "most spectacular astronomical discovery" of the 20th century. As a tribute, the Hubble Space Telescope, deployed Apr 25, 1990, from US space shuttle *Discovery*, was named for him. The Hubble Space Telescope, with a 240-centimeter mirror, was to allow astronomers to see farther into space than they had ever seen from telescopes on Earth. Hubble died at San Marino, CA, Sept 28, 1953.

KENNEDY, ROBERT FRANCIS: BIRTH ANNIVERSARY. Nov 20, 1925. US senator and younger brother of John F. Kennedy, 35th president of the US, was born at Brookline, MA. An assassin shot him at Los Angeles, CA, June 5, 1968, while he was campaigning for the presidential nomination. He died the next day. Sirhan Sirhan was convicted of his murder.

LAGERLOF, SELMA: BIRTH ANNIVERSARY. Nov 20, 1858. Swedish author, member of the Swedish Academy and the first woman to receive the Nobel Prize for Literature (1909) was born at Sweden's Varmland Province. She died there Mar 16, 1940.

LANDIS, KENESAW MOUNTAIN: BIRTH ANNIVERSARY. Nov 20, 1866. Baseball Hall of Fame executive born at Millville, OH. Landis, a federal judge, was named the first commissioner of baseball in 1920. He ruled with an absolutely firm hand and imposed his view of how baseball should operate upon owners and players alike. Inducted into the Hall of Fame in 1944. Died at Chicago, IL, Nov 25, 1944.

LAURIER, SIR WILFRED: BIRTH ANNIVERSARY. Nov 20, 1841. Canadian statesman (premier, 1896–1911), born at St. Lin, QC, Canada. Died Feb 17, 1919, at Ottawa, ON, Canada.

MANDELBROT, BENOIT: 90th BIRTH ANNIVERSARY. Nov 20, 1924. Influential mathematician and professor, born at Warsaw, Poland. Mandelbrot was "the father of fractals," and his theories affected economics and finance, computer science, astronomy and other fields of study. He died at Cambridge, MA, on Oct 14, 2010.

MARION, FRANCES: BIRTH ANNIVERSARY. Nov 20, 1888. Screenwriter, author, journalist born at San Francisco, CA. Widely regarded as one of Hollywood's foremost screenwriters, and at one point its highest paid, Marion broke down barriers for women in the film industry. Her screenplays for *The Big House* (1930) and *The Champ* (1931) received Academy Awards. She died at Hollywood, CA, May 12, 1973

November 2014	S	M	T	W	T	F	S
							1
	2	3	4	5	6	7	8
	9	10	11	12	13	14	15
	16	17	18	19	20	21	22
	23	24	25	26	27	28	29
	30						

MARRIAGE OF ELIZABETH AND PHILIP: ANNIVERSARY. Nov 20, 1947. The Princess Elizabeth Alexandra Mary was wed to Philip Mountbatten on Nov 20, 1947. Elizabeth was the first child of King George VI and Queen Elizabeth. Philip, the former Prince Philip of Greece, had become a British subject nine months earlier and the title Duke of Edinburgh was bestowed on him. The bride later became Elizabeth II, Queen of the United Kingdom of Great Britain and Northern Ireland and Head of the Commonwealth, upon the death of her father on Feb 6, 1952, her coronation taking place at Westminster Abbey on June 2, 1953.

MEXICO: REVOLUTION DAY. Nov 20. Anniversary of the social revolution launched by Francisco I. Madero in 1910. National holiday.

NAME YOUR PC DAY. Nov 20. Hey, why not? People name their boats! There are a lot more PCs than boats these days. "Binky" is already taken. Annually, Nov 20. (©2006 by WH.) For info: Thomas & Ruth Roy, Wellcat Holidays, 2418 Long Ln, Lebanon, PA 17046. Phone: (717) 279-0184. E-mail: info@wellcat.com. Web: www.wellcat.com.

NUREMBERG WAR CRIMES TRIALS: ANNIVERSARY. Nov 20, 1945. The first session of the German war crimes trials started at Berlin, Germany, with indictments against 24 former Nazi leaders. Later sessions were held at Nuremberg, Germany, starting Nov 20, 1945. One defendant committed suicide during his trial, and another was excused because of his physical and mental condition. The trials lasted more than 10 months, and delivery of the judgment was completed on Oct 1, 1946. Twelve were sentenced to death by hanging, three to life imprisonment, four to lesser prison terms, and three were acquitted.

***THE SHEIK* FILM RELEASE: ANNIVERSARY.** Nov 20, 1921. The silent film that catapulted Rudolph Valentino into stardom was given a general release on this date after premieres in New York, NY, and Los Angeles, CA. The romantic melodrama, about a prince of the desert's obsession with an Englishwoman, was a hit that actually had women fainting in theaters. The film was scandalously frank for the times about sexual desire. "Sheik" even became slang for a man whom women couldn't resist. While the film made Valentino a reluctant sex symbol, it also typecast him—to his frustration. A sequel, *The Son of the Sheik*, was released in September 1926 a few weeks after Valentino's sudden death.

TIERNEY, GENE: BIRTH ANNIVERSARY. Nov 20, 1920. Known best for the title role in the film *Laura*, actress Gene Tierney was born at Brooklyn, NY. Her other films include *Heaven Can Wait, A Bell for Adano, Advise and Consent* and her last film, *The Pleasure Seekers*. She died Nov 6, 1991, at Houston, TX.

TRANSGENDER DAY OF REMEMBRANCE. Nov 20. A day honoring the memory of those murdered because of anti-transgender prejudice. Initially observed to call attention to the murder of Rita Hester on Nov 28, 1998. Annually, Nov 20. For info: GLAAD, 5455 Wilshire Blvd, #1500, Los Angeles, CA 90036. Phone: (323) 933-2240. Fax: (323) 933-2241. Web: www.glaad.org/tdor or www.transgenderdor.org.

UNITED NATIONS: AFRICA INDUSTRIALIZATION DAY. Nov 20. The General Assembly proclaimed this day for the purpose of mobilizing the commitment of the international community to the industrialization of the continent (Resolution 44/237, Dec 22, 1989). For info: United Nations, Dept of Public Info, New York, NY 10017. Web: www.un.org.

UNITED NATIONS: UNIVERSAL CHILDREN'S DAY. Nov 20. Designated by the General Assembly as Universal Children's Day. First observance was in 1953. A time to honor children with special ceremonies and festivals and to make children's needs known to governments. Observed on different days and in different ways in more than 120 nations. For info: United Nations, Dept of Public Info, New York, NY 10017. Web: www.un.org.

VON FRISCH, KARL: BIRTH ANNIVERSARY. Nov 20, 1886. This Nobel Prize–winning ethologist, born at Vienna, Austria, gave the world astounding new knowledge about bees, his specialty. Von Frisch decoded the "dance" of the honeybee: actually a form of communication in which the dancer describes distance and location of pollen to its hive comrades. He also determined that bees use the sun as a compass and studied bees' sense of taste and smell. Von Frisch was jointly awarded the Nobel Prize in Physiology or Medicine in 1973 along with Konrad Lorenz and Nicholaas Tinbergen for their work on animal behavior. He died at Munich, Germany, on June 12, 1982.

WOLCOTT, OLIVER: BIRTH ANNIVERSARY. Nov 20, 1726. Signer of the Declaration of Independence, governor of Connecticut, born at Windsor, CT. Died Dec 1, 1797, at Litchfield, CT.

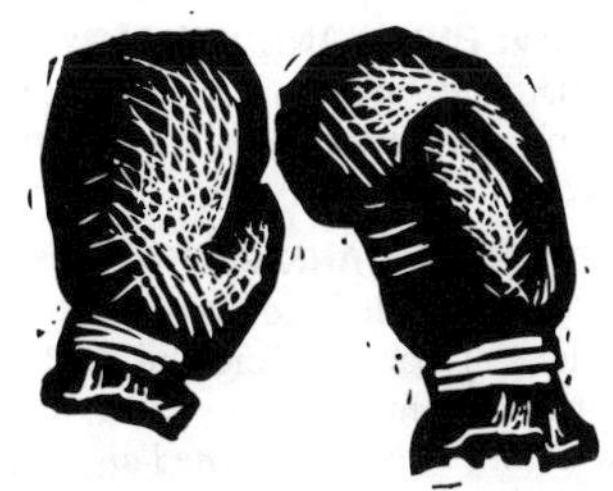

BIRTHDAYS TODAY

Dierks Bentley, 39, country singer, born Tempe, AZ, Nov 20, 1975.

Joseph (Joe) Robinette Biden, Jr, 72, 47th Vice President of the US, former US senator (D, Delaware), born Scranton, PA, Nov 20, 1942.

Carlos Boozer, 33, basketball player, born Juneau, AK, Nov 20, 1981.

Steve Dahl, 60, radio personality, born Pasadena, CA, Nov 20, 1954.

Don DeLillo, 78, author (*White Noise, Underworld*), born New York, NY, Nov 20, 1936.

Bo Derek, 58, actress (*10, Bolero, Tarzan, A Change of Seasons*), born Cathleen Collins at Long Beach, CA, Nov 20, 1956.

Nadine Gordimer, 91, Nobel laureate, author (*The Pickup, July's People*), born Springs, South Africa, Nov 20, 1923.

Veronica Hamel, 71, actress ("Hill Street Blues"), born Philadelphia, PA, Nov 20, 1943.

Sabrina Lloyd, 44, actress (*Sports Night, Sliders*), born Mount Dora, FL, Nov 20, 1970.

Richard Masur, 66, actor ("One Day at a Time," *Heartburn*), born New York, NY, Nov 20, 1948.

Estelle Parsons, 87, stage and screen actress (Oscar for *Bonnie and Clyde*; *August: Osage County*, "Roseanne"), born Marblehead, MA, Nov 20, 1927.

Dick Smothers, 75, comedian, folksinger (with brother Tom, "The Smothers Brothers Comedy Hour"), born New York, NY, Nov 20, 1939.

Ming-Na Wen, 47, actress ("ER," *One Night Stand*), born Macau, China, Nov 20, 1967.

Judy Woodruff, 68, journalist, author, born Tulsa, OK, Nov 20, 1946.

Sean Young, 55, actress (*Blade Runner, No Way Out*), born Louisville, KY, Nov 20, 1959.

November 21 — Friday

DAY 325 **40 REMAINING**

AMERICA'S HOMETOWN THANKSGIVING CELEBRATION. Nov 21–23. Plymouth Harbor and Waterfront, Plymouth, MA. 19th annual. Held at the birthplace of Thanksgiving, this festival has become a beloved holiday occasion as well as an important link to our nation's history and heritage. This celebration of Thanksgiving becomes history brought to life as pilgrims, Native Americans, soldiers, patriots and pioneers climb out of the history books and onto the streets of Plymouth. Includes Grand Parade, New England Food Festival, patriotic concerts, drum and bugle performances, tours of the *Mayflower*, Crafters Pavilion, kids' activities and much more. Annually, the weekend before Thanksgiving. Est attendance: 175,000. For info: Thanksgiving Celebration, Cordage Park Circle, Ste 230, Plymouth, MA 02360. Phone: (508) 746-1818. E-mail: info@usathanksgiving.com. Web: www.usathanksgiving.com.

BARTLETT, JOSIAH: BIRTH ANNIVERSARY. Nov 21, 1729. Signer of the Declaration of Independence. Born at Amesbury, MA, he died at Kingston, NH, May 19, 1795.

BEAUMONT, WILLIAM: BIRTH ANNIVERSARY. Nov 21, 1785. US Army surgeon whose contribution to classic medical literature and world fame resulted from another man's shotgun wound. When Canadian fur trapper Alexis St. Martin received a wound June 6, 1822—a nearly point-blank blast to the abdomen—Beaumont began observing his stomach and digestive processes through an opening in his abdominal wall. His findings were published in 1833 in *Experiments and Observations on the Gastric Juice and the Physiology of Digestion*. St. Martin returned to Canada in 1834 and resisted Beaumont's efforts to submit him to further study. He outlived his doctor by 20 years and was buried at a depth of eight feet to discourage any attempt at posthumous examination. Beaumont, born at Lebanon, CT, died Apr 25, 1853, at St. Louis, MO.

CHARLESTON'S HOLIDAY MARKET. Nov 21–23 (tentative). Charleston Coliseum and Convention Center, North Charleston, SC. 15th annual. Offering foods and fashions, gifts and glitter, music and magic—everything to make the holidays bright. This exciting Christmas extravaganza kicks off the season with specialty gift stores, fashion jewelry, clothing, gourmet foods, decorations and ideas, home accessories and decor, food and wine sampling, arts and crafts and, of course, Santa! Est attendance: 20,000. For info: Gilmore Enterprises, Inc, 3514-A Drawbridge Pkwy, Greensboro, NC 27410-8584. Phone: (336) 282-5550. E-mail: contact@gilmoreshows.com. Web: www.holidaymarket.com or www.gilmoreshows.com.

CONGRESS FIRST MEETS AT WASHINGTON: ANNIVERSARY. Nov 21, 1800. Congress met at Philadelphia, PA, from 1790 to 1800, when the north wing of the new Capitol at Washington, DC, was completed. The House and the Senate had been scheduled to meet in the new building Nov 17, 1800, but a quorum wasn't achieved until Nov 21.

CUNARD, SIR SAMUEL: BIRTH ANNIVERSARY. Nov 21, 1787. Born at Halifax, NS, Canada, Cunard was already a successful businessman when he contracted with the British government to deliver mail across the Atlantic Ocean on May 4, 1839. With a team of engineers and financiers, Cunard built the steamships necessary for fast, dependable transatlantic mail delivery in a venture called the British and North American Royal Mail Steam Packet Company—later called the Cunard Line. Cunard later expanded into passenger service. He died Apr 28, 1865, at London, England.

DOW JONES TOPS 5,000: ANNIVERSARY. Nov 21, 1995. The Dow Jones Index of 30 major industrial stocks topped the 5,000 mark for the first time.

ELLA FITZGERALD WINS APOLLO AMATEUR NIGHT: 80th ANNIVERSARY. Nov 21, 1934. A shy, impoverished teenager, dressed in borrowed clothes and men's shoes, stepped onto the stage of Harlem, NY's Apollo Theater for Amateur Night on this date. Ella Fitzgerald, in her stage debut, was so nervous that she fumbled her first song, but prompted to restart, she sang "Object of

My Affection" and "Judy" to a crowd that exploded with applause. She won the contest. Bandleader Benny Carter, whose orchestra was backing the amateurs that night, helped Fitzgerald make music industry connections, and in 1935 she began to find success as a singer.

FRENCHMAN ROWS ACROSS PACIFIC: ANNIVERSARY. Nov 21, 1991. Gerard d'Aboville completed a four-month solo journey across the Pacific Ocean on this date. D'Aboville began rowing across the Pacific on July 11 when he left Choshi, Japan. His journey ended at Ilwaco, WA.

GETTYSBURG HOLIDAY FESTIVAL. Nov 21–Dec 31 (weekends). Gettysburg, PA. Tours of decorated historic homes, live nativity scene, caroling and handbell choirs, Christmas parade, community concerts, tuba fest, candlelight walking tour and Adams County New Year's Eve Bash with fireworks. Annually, weekends in November–December and New Year's Eve. Est attendance: 10,000. For info: Gettysburg CVB, 571 W Middle St, Gettysburg, PA 17325. Phone: (717) 334-6274. Fax: (717) 334-1166. E-mail: info@gettysburg.travel. Web: www.gettysburg.travel.

GRAND ILLUMINATION CELEBRATION. Nov 21. Lahaska, PA. Santa switches on the village's outdoor light display on Friday at 6:15 PM to kick off the holiday season. Free cider and toasted marshmallows. Preview of new gift ideas in shops. Free admission. Est attendance: 5,000. For info: Peddler's Village, Rtes 202 and 263, Lahaska, PA 18931. Phone: (215) 794-4000. Fax: (215) 794-4001. E-mail: info@peddlersvillage.com. Web: www.peddlersvillage.com.

GREATER PITTSBURGH ARTS & CRAFTS HOLIDAY SPECTACULAR. Nov 21–23. Monroeville Convention Center, Monroeville, PA. Approximately 250 booths including pottery, jewelry, quilts, furniture, tole and decorative painting, toys and much more. Find that perfect gift for the holidays. Est attendance: 12,000. For info: Debbie & Dave Stoner, PO Box 166, Irwin, PA 15642. Phone: (724) 863-4577. E-mail: info@familyfestivals.com. Web: www.familyfestivals.com.

GREEN, HETTY: BIRTH ANNIVERSARY. Nov 21, 1834. Born at New Bedford, MA, Henrietta Howland Robinson Green was the richest woman in America during her lifetime. Although she hailed from a wealthy mercantile family, her spare Quaker upbringing taught her to live a simple, frugal life. In fact, her miserliness was legendary, and tales of her eccentric behavior were widely circulated at the time. She was a gifted financier, known as the "witch of Wall Street," who grew a substantial inheritance into a formidable fortune, which was estimated to have been in excess of $100 million. She died at New York, NY, July 3, 1916.

HOLIDAY FOLK FAIR INTERNATIONAL. Nov 21–23. Wisconsin State Fair Park, Milwaukee, WI. International festival featuring costumes, dancing, entertainment, exhibits, workshops, folk wares and cuisine from 65 cultures. Also children's activities. Annually, the weekend before Thanksgiving. Est attendance: 50,000. For info: Holiday Folk Fair International, Intl Institute of Wisconsin, 1110 N Old World Third St, Ste 420, Milwaukee, WI 53203. Phone: (414) 225-6220. Fax: (414) 225-6235. E-mail: HFF@iiwisconsin.org. Web: www.folkfair.org.

HOLIDAY LIGHTS ON THE LAKE. Nov 21–Jan 4, 2015. Lakemont Park, Altoona, PA. Drive-through displays of more than 51 acres of animated holiday lights, plus a holiday gift shop, food, model train displays and visits from Santa Claus. Annually, from the Friday before Thanksgiving Day through the Sunday after New Year's Day. Est attendance: 75,000. For info: Lakemont Park, 700 Park Ave, Altoona, PA 16602. Phone: (814) 949-7275 or (800) 434-8006. Fax: (814) 949-9207. E-mail: lakemontparkfun@hotmail.com. Web: www.lakemontparkfun.com.

✦NATIONAL FARM-CITY WEEK. Nov 21–27. Presidential Proclamation issued for a week in November since 1956, customarily for the week ending with Thanksgiving Day. Requested by congressional resolutions 1956–58; since 1959 issued annually without request.

NCAA DIVISION I FIELD HOCKEY CHAMPIONSHIP. Nov 21 and 23. Site TBD. 33rd annual. Est attendance: 1,000. For info: NCAA, PO Box 6222, Indianapolis, IN 46206-6222. Phone: (317) 917-6222. Web: www.NCAA.com.

NORTH CAROLINA: RATIFICATION DAY: 225th ANNIVERSARY. Nov 21. Became the 12th state to ratify the Constitution in 1789.

PEDDLER'S VILLAGE GINGERBREAD HOUSE COMPETITION & DISPLAY. Nov 21–Jan 3, 2015. Lahaska, PA. More than 100 gingerbread house entries compete for more than $3,400 in cash prizes in such categories as traditional, authentic reproduction of a significant building, amateur, incredibly unusual three-dimensional, Go Green, student and kids only! The creative masterpieces are displayed throughout the holiday season in the village gazebo. Free admission. Est attendance: 850,000. For info: Peddler's Village, Rtes 202 and 263, Lahaska, PA 18931. Phone: (215) 794-4000. Fax: (215) 794-4001. E-mail: info@peddlersvillage.com. Web: www.peddlersvillage.com.

POPE BENEDICT XV: BIRTH ANNIVERSARY. Nov 21, 1854. Giacomo della Chiesa, 258th pope of the Roman Catholic Church, born at Pegli, Italy, and elected pope Sept 3, 1914. Died at Rome, Italy, Jan 22, 1922.

PURCELL, HENRY: DEATH ANNIVERSARY. Nov 21, 1695. (Old Style date.) The great English composer of the early Baroque period, born in 1659 at London, England, had a tragically short life yet was a prolific composer. His fame rests on the proto-operas *Dido and Aeneas* (1689) and *The Fairy Queen* (1692, based on Shakespeare's *A Midsummer-Night's Dream*), ceremonial odes for the court of King Charles II and more than 100 songs. The holder of various court musical positions, Purcell died at London.

SILVER BELLS IN THE CITY. Nov 21. Lansing, MI. 30th annual. Michigan's capital city sparkles with hospitality and holiday cheer on the streets of downtown Lansing's business district for this celebration of lights, music and seasonal spirit. The festivities include an electric light parade, lighting of the official State of Michigan Christmas Tree and a fireworks display (weather permitting) over the state capitol dome. Annually, the Friday before Thankgiving. Est attendance: 120,000. For info: Downtown Lansing, Inc, 401 S Washington Sq, Ste 101, Lansing, MI 48933. Phone: (517) 487-3322. Web: www.silverbellsinthecity.org.

UNITED NATIONS: WORLD TELEVISION DAY. Nov 21. On Dec 17, 1996, the General Assembly proclaimed this day as World Television Day, commemorating the date in 1996 on which the first World Television Forum was held at the UN. For info: United Nations, Dept of Public Info, New York, NY 10017. Web: www.un.org.

VOLTAIRE, JEAN FRANÇOIS MARIE: BIRTH ANNIVERSARY. Nov 21, 1694. French author and philosopher to whom is attributed (perhaps erroneously) the statement: "I disapprove of what you say, but I will defend to the death your right to say it." His most famous work is the novel *Candide*. Born at Paris, France, he died there May 30, 1778.

November 2014	S	M	T	W	T	F	S
							1
	2	3	4	5	6	7	8
	9	10	11	12	13	14	15
	16	17	18	19	20	21	22
	23	24	25	26	27	28	29
	30						

WHO SHOT J.R.?: ANNIVERSARY. Nov 21, 1980. A record 86.6 million viewers watched CBS's hit drama, "Dallas," to see who shot villainous tycoon J.R. Ewing (Larry Hagman). An unseen assailant had gunned him down on the show's season finale Mar 21, 1980, and sparked international curiosity, a ubiquitous catchphrase ("Who shot J.R.?") and Las Vegas bets. (Sue Ellen Ewing's sister, Kristin Shephard, shot J.R.)

WORLD HELLO DAY. Nov 21. 42nd annual. Everyone who participates greets 10 people. People in 180 countries have participated in this annual activity for advancing peace through personal communication. Heads of state of 114 countries have expressed approval of the event. For info: The McCormacks, PO Box 15592, Beverly Hills, CA 90209. Web: www.worldhelloday.org.

YORK INTERNATIONAL POSTCARD FAIR. Nov 21–22. York Fairgrounds, York, PA. Est attendance: 1,000. For info: Mary Martin Ltd, PO Box 787, Perryville, MD 21903. Phone: (410) 939-0999. E-mail: marymartinpostcards@gmail.com.

BIRTHDAYS TODAY

Troy Aikman, 48, sportscaster, Hall of Fame football player, born West Covina, CA, Nov 21, 1966.

Bjork, 49, singer, actress, born Björk Godmundsdóttir at Reykjavik, Iceland, Nov 21, 1965.

Marcy Carsey, 70, television producer, born South Weymouth, MA, Nov 21, 1944.

James DePreist, 78, conductor, born Philadelphia, PA, Nov 21, 1936.

Richard J. Durbin, 70, US Senator (D, Illinois), born East St. Louis, IL, Nov 21, 1944.

George Kenneth (Ken) Griffey, Jr, 45, former baseball player, born Donora, PA, Nov 21, 1969.

Goldie Hawn, 69, actress (*The Banger Sisters, Private Benjamin*; Oscar for *Cactus Flower*), born Washington, DC, Nov 21, 1945.

Carly Rae Jepsen, 29, singer, born Mission, BC, Canada, Nov 21, 1985.

Laurence Luckinbill, 80, actor (*Star Trek V*), born Fort Smith, AR, Nov 21, 1934.

Lorna Luft, 62, singer, actress, born Los Angeles, CA, Nov 21, 1952.

Juliet Mills, 73, actress ("Nanny and the Professor," "Passions," *So Well Remembered*), born London, England, Nov 21, 1941.

Sam Palladio, 28, actor ("Nashville," "Episodes"), born Pembury, Kent, England, Nov 21, 1986.

Harold Ramis, 70, actor, director, writer, producer (*Groundhog Day, Ghostbusters*), born Chicago, IL, Nov 21, 1944.

Cynthia Rhodes, 58, actress, dancer (*Flashdance, Dirty Dancing*), born Nashville, TN, Nov 21, 1956.

Tasha Schwikert, 30, gymnast, born Las Vegas, NV, Nov 21, 1984.

Nicollette Sheridan, 51, actress ("Desperate Housewives," "Knots Landing"), born Worthing, Sussex, England, Nov 21, 1963.

Marlo Thomas, 76, actress ("That Girl"), author (*Free to Be . . . You and Me*), born Detroit, MI, Nov 21, 1938.

November 22 — Saturday

DAY 326 — **39 REMAINING**

ADAMS, ABIGAIL SMITH: BIRTH ANNIVERSARY. Nov 22, 1744. Wife of John Adams, second president of the US, and mother of John Quincy Adams, sixth president of the US. An intelligent woman interested in politics and current affairs, she was a prodigious letter writer and an influence on her husband. Abigail Adams argued to her husband that Congress "should remember the ladies" as the new American government took form. Born at Weymouth, MA, she died Oct 28, 1818, at Quincy, MA.

BRITTEN, EDWARD BENJAMIN: BIRTH ANNIVERSARY. Nov 22, 1913. One of the most important composers of the 20th century was born at Lowestoft, Suffolk, England. In addition to chamber and orchestral works, he was a composer of film scores, song cycles and experimental pieces in collaboration with poets such as W.H. Auden. His best-known and acclaimed works are the tragic opera *Peter Grimes* (1945)—its success made Britten a celebrity—and *War Requiem* (1962), a moving response to the horror of WWII that premiered in the newly rebuilt Coventry Cathedral. Britten's other operas include *Billy Budd, The Turn of the Screw* and *A Midsummer Night's Dream.* Lord Britten, Baron Britten of Aldeburgh, died at Aldeburgh, Dec 4, 1976.

CARMICHAEL, HOAGIE: BIRTH ANNIVERSARY. Nov 22, 1899. Hoagland Howard Carmichael, an attorney who gave up the practice of law to become an actor and songwriter, was born at Bloomington, IN. Among his many popular songs: "Stardust," "Lazybones," "Two Sleepy People" and "Skylark." Carmichael died at Rancho Mirage, CA, Dec 27, 1981.

***CHINA CLIPPER*: ANNIVERSARY.** Nov 22, 1935. A Pan American Martin 130 "flying boat" called the *China Clipper* began regular transpacific mail service on Nov 22, 1935. The plane, powered by four Pratt and Whitney Twin Wasp engines, took off from San Francisco, CA. It reached Manila, Philippines, 59 hours and 48 minutes later. About 20,000 persons watched the historic takeoff. Commercial passenger service was established the following year (Oct 21, 1936).

De GAULLE, CHARLES ANDRÉ MARIE: BIRTH ANNIVERSARY. Nov 22, 1890. President of France from December 1958 until his resignation in April 1969, Charles de Gaulle was born at Lille, France. A military leader, he wrote *The Army of the Future* (1934), in which he predicted just the type of armored warfare that was used against his country by Nazi Germany in WWII. After France's defeat at the hands of the Germans, he declared the existence of "Free France" and made himself head of that organization. When the French Vichy government began to collaborate openly with the Germans, the French citizenry looked to de Gaulle for leadership. His greatest moment of triumph was when he entered liberated Paris on Aug 26, 1944. De Gaulle died at Colombey-les-Deux-Eglises, France, Nov 19, 1970.

ELIOT, GEORGE: BIRTH ANNIVERSARY. Nov 22, 1819. English novelist George Eliot, whose real name was Mary Ann Evans, was born at Chilvers Coton, Warwickshire, England. Her works include *Silas Marner* and *Middlemarch.* She died at Chelsea, England, Dec 22, 1880.

GARNER, JOHN NANCE: BIRTH ANNIVERSARY. Nov 22, 1868. The 32nd vice president of the US (1933–41). Garner was a congressional representative from 1903 to 1933 and Speaker of the House for two years (1931–33). Garner worked closely with President Franklin D. Roosevelt on New Deal legislation but eventually split with the president over Roosevelt's plan to reorganize the Supreme Court. Garner was born at Red River County, TX; died at Uvalde, TX, Nov 7, 1967.

HOLIDAYS IN THE CITY GRAND ILLUMINATION PARADE. Nov 22. Norfolk, VA. A cherished tradition, the buildings of downtown Norfolk and Olde Towne Portsmouth illuminate their profiles to create a picture-postcard skyline. On the first evening of the illumination, a downtown lighted street parade kicks off the celebration of the season. All of the floats, bands and entries in this nighttime parade are lighted. Annually, the Saturday before

Thanksgiving. Est attendance: 100,000. For info: Parade Mgr, Downtown Norfolk Council, 201 Granby St, Ste 101, Norfolk, VA 23510. Phone: (757) 623-1757. Fax: (757) 623-1756. E-mail: hic@downtownnorfolk.org. Web: www.HolidaysintheCity.net.

THE HUMANE SOCIETY OF THE UNITED STATES: 60th ANNIVERSARY. Nov 22, 1954. When the Humane Society of the United States (HSUS) was founded by a handful of dedicated visionaries, the modern concept of "animal welfare" barely existed.

INTERNATIONAL AURA AWARENESS DAY. Nov 22. A day to increase awareness of the human energy body, or aura. Annually, the fourth Saturday in November. For info: Cynthia Larson, PO Box 7393, Berkeley, CA 94707. Phone: (510) 528-2044. E-mail: cynthia@realityshifters.com. Web: realityshifters.com/pages/auraday.html.

KENNEDY, JOHN F.: ASSASSINATION ANNIVERSARY. Nov 22, 1963. President John F. Kennedy was slain by a sniper while riding in an open automobile at Dallas, TX. Accused assassin Lee Harvey Oswald was killed by Jack Ruby while in police custody awaiting trial.

KING RANCH ANNUAL RANCH HAND BREAKFAST. Nov 22. King Ranch, Kingsville, TX. A breakfast cooked and served outdoors at the world-famous King Ranch. See longhorn cattle and real cowboys on horseback. Annually, the Saturday before Thanksgiving. Est attendance: 7,000. For info: Kingsville Convention & Visitors Bureau, 1501 N Hwy 77, Kingsville, TX 78363-1562. Phone: (361) 592-8516. Fax: (361) 592-3227. E-mail: howdy@kingsvilletexas.com. Web: www.king-ranch.com or www.kingsvilletexas.com.

LEBANON: INDEPENDENCE DAY. Nov 22. National Day. Gained independence from France in 1943.

MOON PHASE: NEW MOON. Nov 22. Moon enters New Moon phase at 7:32 AM, EST.

NAIA MEN'S AND WOMEN'S CROSS-COUNTRY NATIONAL CHAMPIONSHIPS. Nov 22. Rim Rock Farm, University of Kansas, Lawrence, KS. Men compete on an 8k course and women compete on a 5k course, with the top 30 individual finishers in each championship receiving All-America honors. 58th men's championship; 34th women's. For info: Natl Assn of Intercollegiate Athletics, 1200 Grand Blvd, Kansas City, MO 64106. E-mail: rstein@naia.org. Web: www.naia.org.

NATCHITOCHES FESTIVAL OF LIGHTS. Nov 22–Jan 4, 2015. Natchitoches, LA. A fairyland of multicolored lights, created by 350,000 Christmas bulbs strung along city streets and incorporated into 100 unique set pieces along Cane River Lake. Est attendance: 500,000. For info: Natchitoches Parish Tourist Commission, Calendar of Events, 780 Front St, Ste 100, Natchitoches, LA 71457. Phone: (318) 352-8072 or (800) 259-1714. Fax: (318) 352-2415. Web: www.natchitoches.net or www.christmasfestival.com.

NCAA DIVISION I CROSS COUNTRY CHAMPIONSHIP. Nov 22. Site TBD. For info: NCAA, PO Box 6222, Indianapolis, IN 46206-6222. Phone: (317) 917-6222. Web: www.NCAA.com.

***ON THE ORIGIN OF SPECIES* PUBLISHED: ANNIVERSARY.** Nov 22, 1859. Charles Darwin's monumental work, *On the Origin of Species by Means of Natural Selection, or the Preservation of Favoured Races in the Struggle for Life*, was published on this date by London publisher John Murray. The print run of 1,250 (priced at 15 shillings) sold out the same day. A second print run of 3,000 in December also sold quickly. The book immediately generated a firestorm of public and private discussion. The word *evolution* did not appear until the 1872 (last) edition of *Origin*.

POST, WILEY: BIRTH ANNIVERSARY. Nov 22, 1898. Barnstorming aviator, stunt parachutist and adventurer, Wiley Post was born at Grand Plain, TX. Post, who taught himself to fly, and his plane, the *Winnie Mae*, were the center of world attention in the 1930s. He was coauthor (with his navigator, Harold Gatty) of *Around the World in Eight Days*. In 1935 Post and friend Will Rogers started on a flight to Asia. Their plane crashed near Point Barrow, AK, Aug 15, 1935; both were killed.

PRIME MINISTER THATCHER RESIGNS: ANNIVERSARY. Nov 22, 1990. Margaret Thatcher announced that she would resign from her position as England's prime minister. She had been named prime minister in May 1979 and served until Nov 22, 1990. No other prime minister in the United Kingdom in the 20th century served the post as long as she.

SAGITTARIUS, THE ARCHER. Nov 22–Dec 21. In the astronomical/astrological zodiac that divides the sun's apparent orbit into 12 segments, the period Nov 22–Dec 21 is traditionally identified as the sun sign of Sagittarius, the Archer. The ruling planet is Jupiter.

SAINT CECILIA: FEAST DAY. Nov 22. The Roman virgin, Christian martyr and patron of music and musicians lived during the second or third century. Survived sentence of suffocation by steam but succumbed to sentence of beheading. Subject of poetry and musical compositions, and her feast day is still an occasion for musical events.

November 2014	S	M	T	W	T	F	S
							1
	2	3	4	5	6	7	8
	9	10	11	12	13	14	15
	16	17	18	19	20	21	22
	23	24	25	26	27	28	29
	30						

BIRTHDAYS TODAY

Boris Becker, 47, Hall of Fame tennis player, born Leimen, Germany, Nov 22, 1967.

Guion S. Bluford, Jr, 72, first black astronaut in space, born West Philadelphia, PA, Nov 22, 1942.

Tom Conti, 73, actor (Tony for *Whose Life Is It Anyway?*), born Paisley, Scotland, Nov 22, 1941.

Jamie Lee Curtis, 56, actress (*True Lies, Halloween, A Fish Called Wanda*), born Los Angeles, CA, Nov 22, 1958.

Harry Edwards, 72, sports sociologist, born St. Louis, MO, Nov 22, 1942.

Terry Gilliam, 74, actor, writer ("Monty Python's Flying Circus," *Life of Brian*), director (*Brazil*), born Minneapolis, MN, Nov 22, 1940.

Mariel Hemingway, 53, actress (*Manhattan, Personal Best, Superman IV*), born Ketchum, ID, Nov 22, 1961.

Scarlett Johansson, 30, actress (*The Avengers, Vicky Cristina Barcelona, Lost in Translation*), born New York, NY, Nov 22, 1984.

Richard Kind, 57, actor ("Spin City," "Mad About You"), born Trenton, NJ, Nov 22, 1957.

Billie Jean King, 71, Hall of Fame tennis player, born Long Beach, CA, Nov 22, 1943.

Mads Mikkelsen, 49, actor (*Casino Royale, The Hunt*, "Hannibal"), born Østerbro, Copenhagen, Denmark, Nov 22, 1965.

Mark Ruffalo, 47, actor (*The Kids Are All Right, Zodiac, You Can Count on Me*), born Kenosha, WI, Nov 22, 1967.

Robert Vaughn, 82, actor ("Hustle," "The Man from U.N.C.L.E.," *Bullitt, The Magnificent Seven*), born New York, NY, Nov 22, 1932.

November 23 — Sunday

DAY 327 **38 REMAINING**

ALASCATTALO DAY. Nov 23. Anchorage, AK. To honor humor in general and Alaskan humor in particular. Event is named after "alascattalo," said to be the genetic cross between a moose and a walrus. For info: Steven C. Levi, Parsnackle Press, PO Box 241467, Anchorage, AK 99524. Phone/fax: (907) 337-2021. E-mail: scl@parsnackle.com.

ASHFORD, EMMETT LITTLETON: 100th BIRTH ANNIVERSARY. Nov 23, 1914. Emmett Littleton Ashford, born at Los Angeles, CA, was the first black to officiate at a major league baseball game. Ashford began his pro career calling games in the minors in 1951 and went to the majors in 1966. He was noted for his flamboyant style when calling strikes and outs as well as for his dapper dress, which included cuff links with his uniform. He died Mar 1, 1980, at Marina del Rey, CA.

BILLY THE KID: BIRTH ANNIVERSARY. Nov 23, 1859. Legendary outlaw of western US. Probably named Henry McCarty at birth (New York, NY), he was better known as William H. Bonney. Ruthless killer, a failure at everything legal, he escaped from jail at age 21 while under sentence of hanging. Recaptured at Stinking Springs, NM, and returned to jail, he again escaped, only to be shot through the heart by pursuing Lincoln County sheriff Pat Garrett at Fort Sumner, NM, during the night of July 14, 1881. His last words, answered by two shots, reportedly were, "Who is there?"

CHURCH/STATE SEPARATION WEEK. Nov 23–29. A holiday inspired by the invaluable work of organizations such as Americans United for the Separation of Church and State, the Institute for First Amendment Studies and many others. Church/State Separation Week offers concerned and active citizens an opportunity to educate others about the importance of this subject. Annually, the week that includes the Thanksgiving holiday. For info: American Humanist Assn, 1777 T St NW, Washington, DC 20009. Phone: (202) 238-9088. Fax: (202) 238-9003. Web: www.secularseasons.org/November/separation_week.html.

"DOCTOR WHO" TV PREMIERE: ANNIVERSARY. Nov 23, 1963. The first episode of "Doctor Who" premiered on British TV with William Hartnell as the first Doctor. Traveling through time and space in the TARDIS (an acronym for Time and Relative Dimensions in Space), the Doctor and his companions found themselves in mortal combat with creatures such as the Daleks. The series aired until 1989, with a special film in 1996. "Doctor Who" didn't air in the US until Sept 29, 1975, but then attracted a huge cult following. A new version of the series began in 2005, with Christopher Eccleston and David Tennant as the ninth and tenth Doctors. Matt Smith made his debut as Doctor #11 in 2010, and Peter Capaldi began his reign as Doctor #12 on Dec 25, 2013.

FIRST PLAY-BY-PLAY FOOTBALL GAME BROADCAST: 95th ANNIVERSARY. Nov 23, 1919. The first play-by-play football game radio broadcast in the US took place on this day. Texas A&M blanked the University of Texas 7–0.

GERMANY: TOTENSONNTAG. Nov 23. In Germany, Totensonntag is the Protestant population's day for remembrance of the dead. It is celebrated on the last Sunday of the church year (the Sunday before Advent).

GILBERT ISLANDS TAKEN: ANNIVERSARY. Nov 23, 1943. The US Second Marine Division took control of the Gilbert Islands after fierce fighting on the heavily fortified Tarawa Atoll. In the 76-hour battle the Marines beat back a "death charge" in which the Japanese ran directly at the American guns. American troops sustained 3,500 killed and wounded. The Japanese suffered 5,000 killed and 17 wounded and captured. (The Gilbert Islands are the westernmost of the Polynesians, midway between Australia and Hawaii, and today are part of the nation of Kiribati.)

INTERNATIONAL IMAGE CONSULTANT DAY. Nov 23. Starting in 2013, the Association of Image Consultants International (AICI) board of directors formally recognizes Nov 23 as International Image Consultant Day. This day was first celebrated in 2012 by AICI's Mexico City chapter members. International Image Consultant Day celebrates the acumen and science of image consultants worldwide as they serve others in the disciplines of image consulting by promoting the highest professional standards in the fields of appearance, behavior and communication. The AICI board of directors held a formal reading and signing of the proclamation with an official declaration at the AICI International Conference in Glendale, AZ, on May 19, 2013. Annually, Nov 23. For info: Andy Shelp, AICI Executive Director, AICI, 1000 Westgate Dr, Ste 252, St. Paul, MN 55114. Phone: (651) 290-7468. E-mail: info@aici.org. Web: www.aici.org.

JAPAN: LABOR THANKSGIVING DAY. Nov 23. National holiday.

KARLOFF, BORIS: BIRTH ANNIVERSARY. Nov 23, 1887. Born William Henry Pratt at London, England. An actor known for his portrayal of ghoulish figures, his movies included *Frankenstein, The Body Snatcher* and *The Bride of Frankenstein.* Karloff died Feb 2, 1969, at Sussex, England.

***LIFE* MAGAZINE DEBUTS: ANNIVERSARY.** Nov 23, 1936. The illustrated magazine *Life* debuted on this day. The first cover featured a dramatic photograph by Margaret Bourke-White of Fort Peck Dam.

MARX, HARPO: BIRTH ANNIVERSARY. Nov 23, 1888. Harpo (Adolph Arthur) Marx was born at New York, NY. He was the second-born of the famed Marx Brothers, who were a popular comedy team of stage, screen and radio for 30 years. The silent brother, Harpo wore a red curly wig and communicated by honking a taxi horn at the most inopportune moments. He was a self-taught and expert player of the harp. Marx died Sept 28, 1964, at Hollywood, CA. Other family members who participated in the comedy team were Groucho (Julius), Chico (Leonard) and, briefly, Zeppo (Herbert) and Gummo (Milton).

MOTHER GOOSE PARADE. Nov 23. El Cajon, CA. 68th annual. "A celebration of children." Floats depict Mother Goose rhymes and fairy tales and/or annual theme. Bands, equestrians and clowns. Traditionally, the Sunday before Thanksgiving. Est attendance: 250,000. For info: Mother Goose Parade Assn, PO Box 1155, El Cajon, CA 92022. Phone: (619) 444-8712. Fax: (619) 442-2357. E-mail: info@themothergooseparade.com. Web: www.themothergooseparade.com.

NATIONAL BIBLE WEEK. Nov 23–30. Since 1941, an interfaith campaign to promote reading of the Bible. Free resources available. Governors and mayors across the country proclaim National Bible Week observance to their constituencies. Annually, from the Sunday preceding Thanksgiving to the following Sunday. For info: Natl Bible Assn, 405 Lexington Ave, 26th Fl, New York, NY 10174. Phone: (212) 907-6427. Fax: (212) 898-1147. E-mail: rbeni@nationalbible.org. Web: www.nationalbible.org.

✦NATIONAL FAMILY WEEK. Nov 23–29. To celebrate the inclusive spirit of American families and applaud the commitment of those family members who encourage us to reach new heights.

NATIONAL GAME & PUZZLE WEEK™. Nov 23–29. 20th annual event to increase appreciation of board games and puzzles while preserving the tradition of investing time with family and friends. Part of the Million Minute Family Challenge™, conducted Sept 1–Dec 31. Special organizer materials and media information available, including press kits, interviews, etc. Annually, the Sunday through Saturday of Thanksgiving week. For info: Beth Muehlenkamp, Natl Game & Puzzle Week, 1400 E Inman Pkwy, Beloit, WI 53511. Phone: (800) 524-4263. Fax: (608) 362-8178. E-mail: bethm@patchproducts.com. Web: www.millionminute.com.

PIERCE, FRANKLIN: BIRTH ANNIVERSARY. Nov 23, 1804. The 14th president of the US was born at Hillsboro, NH. Term of office: Mar 4, 1853–Mar 3, 1857. Not nominated until the 49th ballot at the Democratic Party convention in 1852, he was refused his party's nomination in 1856 for a second term. Pierce died at Concord, NH, Oct 8, 1869.

RUTLEDGE, EDWARD: BIRTH ANNIVERSARY. Nov 23, 1749. Signer of the Declaration of Independence, governor of South Carolina, born at Charleston, SC. Died there Jan 23, 1800.

BIRTHDAYS TODAY

Susan Anspach, 69, actress (*Five Easy Pieces; Play It Again, Sam; Montenegro*), born New York, NY, Nov 23, 1945.

Miley Cyrus, 22, actress, singer ("Hannah Montana"), born Destiny Hope Cyrus at Franklin, TN, Nov 23, 1992.

Lucas Grabeel, 30, actor (*High School Musical*), born Springfield, MO, Nov 23, 1984.

Chris Hardwick, 43, comedian, television personality ("The Nerdist"), born Louisville, KY, Nov 23, 1971.

Steve Harvey, 58, talk show host ("Steve Harvey"), comedian, actor ("The Steve Harvey Show"), born Welch, WV, Nov 23, 1956.

Mary L. Landrieu, 59, US Senator (D, Louisiana), born Arlington, VA, Nov 23, 1955.

Krzysztof Penderecki, 81, composer, born Debica, Poland, Nov 23, 1933.

Nicole "Snooki" Polizzi, 27, television personality ("Jersey Shore"), born Santiago, Chile, Nov 23, 1987.

Charles E. Schumer, 64, US Senator (D, New York), born Brooklyn, NY, Nov 23, 1950.

November 2014	S	M	T	W	T	F	S
							1
	2	3	4	5	6	7	8
	9	10	11	12	13	14	15
	16	17	18	19	20	21	22
	23	24	25	26	27	28	29
	30						

November 24 — Monday

DAY 328 **37 REMAINING**

BARKLEY, ALBEN WILLIAM: BIRTH ANNIVERSARY. Nov 24, 1877. The 35th vice president of the US (1949–53) was born at Graves County, KY. Died at Lexington, VA, Apr 30, 1956.

BATTLE OF CHATTANOOGA: ANNIVERSARY. Nov 24, 1863. After reinforcing the besieged Union army at Chattanooga, TN, General Ulysses S. Grant launched the Battle of Chattanooga on this date. Falsely secure in the belief that his troops were in an impregnable position on Lookout Mountain, Confederate general Braxton Bragg and his army were overrun by the Union forces, Bragg himself barely escaping capture. The battle is famous for the Union army's spectacular advance up a heavily fortified slope into the teeth of the enemy guns.

BETTER CONVERSATION WEEK. Nov 24–30. 14th annual. A time to have better conversations with friends, family and coworkers during Thanksgiving week. Strengthen personal bonds with meaningful, enjoyable talk. For info: Dr. Loren Ekroth, 9030 W Sahara Ave, Ste 430, Las Vegas, NV 89117. E-mail: loren@conversationmatters.com. Web: www.conversationmatters.com.

BUCKLEY, WILLIAM F., JR: BIRTH ANNIVERSARY. Nov 24, 1925. Entertaining and influential postwar conservative standard-bearer as well as author, editor, talk show host and master of polysyllabic parlance. Founded the *National Review* in 1955. Born at New York, NY, Buckley died Feb 24, 2008, at Stamford, CT.

CANADA: CANADIAN WESTERN AGRIBITION. Nov 24–29. Evraz Place, Regina, SK. Canada's premier agricultural show and marketplace featuring more than 4,200 head of livestock including 13 purebred cattle breeds, commercial cattle, light and heavy horses, bison, dairy cattle, sheep and goats, as well as specialized livestock displays. The show is also known for its extensive trade show, the Canadian Cowboy's Association Finals Rodeo and western entertainment and attractions. Est attendance: 140,000. For info: Canadian Western Agribition, PO Box 3535, Regina, SK, S4P 3J8, Canada. Phone: (306) 565-0565. Fax: (306) 757-9963. E-mail: info@agribition.com. Web: www.agribition.com.

CARNEGIE, DALE: BIRTH ANNIVERSARY. Nov 24, 1888. American inspirational lecturer and author Dale Carnegie was born at Maryville, MO. He was born into poverty and described himself as a "simple country boy." He began teaching public speaking in 1912 and parlayed his success there into his best-known book, *How to Win Friends and Influence People*, published in 1936. The perennial bestseller is still in print and has sold 15 million copies. Carnegie died at New York, NY, Nov 1, 1955.

CELEBRATE YOUR UNIQUE TALENT DAY. Nov 24. We all have at least one extraordinary—and many times weird—ability. Now's the time to get out there and indulge in yours. Sponsored by the record holder for the football-throwing game at ESPN Zone! For info: Shannon Hurd, 10556 Graymont Ln, #22C, Highlands Ranch, CO 80126. Phone: (720) 936-3326. Fax: (720) 920-9256. E-mail: uniquetalentday@yahoo.com. Web: www.youruniquetalent.com.

"D.B. COOPER" HIJACKING: ANNIVERSARY. Nov 24, 1971. A middle-aged man whose plane ticket was made out to "D.B. Cooper" parachuted from a Northwest Airlines 727 jetliner, carrying $200,000, which he had collected from the airline as ransom for the plane and passengers as a result of threats made during his earlier flight from Portland, OR, to Seattle, WA. He jumped from the plane over an area of wilderness south of Seattle and was never apprehended. Several thousand dollars of the marked ransom money turned up in February 1980, along the Columbia River, near Vancouver, WA.

DUFF, HOWARD: BIRTH ANNIVERSARY. Nov 24, 1913. American actor Howard Duff was born at Bremerton, WA. He played detective Sam Spade on radio in the 1940s and then went on to films and television ("Knots Landing"). He died July 8, 1990, at Santa Barbara, CA.

JOPLIN, SCOTT: BIRTH ANNIVERSARY. Nov 24, 1868. American musician and composer famed for his piano rags, born at Texarkana, TX. Died at New York, NY, Apr 1, 1917.

MANSTEIN, ERICH VON: BIRTH ANNIVERSARY. Nov 24, 1887. Considered by many to be the greatest strategist of WWII, Erich von Manstein was born at Berlin, Germany. His plan for Germany's invasion of France in 1940 was a complete success. He was dismissed by Hitler in March 1944. Manstein died at Irschenhausen, Germany, June 10, 1973.

SERRA, JUNIPERO: BIRTH ANNIVERSARY. Nov 24, 1713. Priest and pioneer, born Miguel Jose Serra at Petra, Majorca, Spain, whose missionary outposts introduced Catholicism to California and organized the California frontier for Spain's colonial aims. Serra entered the Franciscan order in 1730 and taught philosophy at Lullian University (Majorca) and also in Mexico City before beginning missionary work in 1750. When Spain began colonizing Alta California, he joined the expedition and founded Mission San Diego in 1769. He founded eight more California missions, converting many Native Americans to Christianity and also teaching them how to farm and raise livestock. Serra died at Mission San Carlos Borromeo on Aug 28, 1784.

SPINOZA, BARUCH: BIRTH ANNIVERSARY. Nov 24, 1632. (Old Style date.) Dutch philosopher, born at Amsterdam, Netherlands. Died at The Hague, Netherlands, Feb 21, 1677 (OS). "Peace is not an absence of war," wrote Spinoza, in 1670, "it is a virtue, a state of mind, a disposition for benevolence, confidence, justice."

STERNE, LAURENCE: BIRTH ANNIVERSARY. Nov 24, 1713. Renowned novelist and humorist, born at Clonmel, Ireland. Sterne's crowning achievement was the comic novel *Tristram Shandy*, published in installments from 1759 to 1767. The novel is notable for its use of unconventional narrative techniques, such as the nonlinear plotline and its demand of interactive participation on the part of the reader, as well as its references to Lockean philosophy. Sterne died of tuberculosis at London, England, Mar 18, 1768.

SWITZERLAND: ONION MARKET (ZIBELEMARIT). Nov 24. Berne. Best known and most popular of Switzerland's many autumn markets. Huge heaps of onions in front of Federal Palace. Fourth Monday in November commemorates granting of market right to people after great fire of Berne in 1405.

TAYLOR, ZACHARY: BIRTH ANNIVERSARY. Nov 24, 1784. The Mexican War hero and career soldier who became the 12th president of the US was born at Orange County, VA. Term of office: Mar 4, 1849–July 9, 1850. He was nominated at the Whig Party convention in 1848, but the story goes he did not accept the letter notifying him of his nomination because it had postage due. He had cast his first vote in 1846, when he was 62 years old. Becoming ill July 4, 1850, he died at the White House, July 9. His last words: "I am sorry that I am about to leave my friends."

TOULOUSE-LAUTREC, HENRI DE: 150th BIRTH ANNIVERSARY. Nov 24, 1864. French illustrator, lithographer, post-Impressionist painter. Born at Albi, France, Lautrec, deformed at an early age, found in the bohemian demimonde of Paris, especially the nightclubs and brothels of Montmartre, an outsider atmosphere that enticed him both personally and professionally. His drawings and posters in particular evoke the nightlife and habitués of that world. "Ugliness, everywhere and always, has its enchanting side," Lautrec said. "It is fascinating to discover it where no one else had noticed it." He died Sept 9, 1901, at Château Malromé, Gironde, France.

US MILITARY LEAVES PHILIPPINES: ANNIVERSARY. Nov 24, 1992. The Philippines became a US colony at the turn of the last century when it was taken over from Spain after the Spanish-American War. Though President Franklin D. Roosevelt signed a bill Mar 24, 1934, granting the Philippines independence to be effective July 4, 1946, before that date Manila and Washington signed a treaty allowing the US to lease military bases on the island. In 1991 the Philippine Senate voted to reject a renewal of that lease, and on Nov 24, 1992, after almost 100 years of military presence on the island, the last contingent of US Marines left Subic Base.

BIRTHDAYS TODAY

Garret Dillahunt, 50, actor ("Raising Hope," *Winter's Bone, No Country for Old Men*), born Castro Valley, CA, Nov 24, 1964.

Katherine Heigl, 36, actress ("Grey's Anatomy," *27 Dresses, Knocked Up*), born Washington, DC, Nov 24, 1978.

Sarah Hyland, 24, actress ("Modern Family," "Lipstick Jungle"), born New York, NY, Nov 24, 1990.

Stanley Livingston, 64, actor ("My Three Sons"), born Los Angeles, CA, Nov 24, 1950.

Keith Primeau, 43, hockey player, born Toronto, ON, Canada, Nov 24, 1971.

Oscar Palmer Robertson, 76, Hall of Fame basketball player, born Charlotte, TN, Nov 24, 1938.

Dwight Schultz, 67, actor ("Star Trek: The Next Generation," *Fat Man and Little Boy*), born Baltimore, MD, Nov 24, 1947.

Brad Sherwood, 50, comedian, actor ("Whose Line Is It Anyway?"), born Chicago, IL, Nov 24, 1964.

Rudolph (Rudy) Tomjanovich, 66, basketball coach and former player, born Hamtramck, MI, Nov 24, 1948.

November 25 — Tuesday

DAY 329 **36 REMAINING**

BOSNIA AND HERZEGOVINA: NATIONAL DAY. Nov 25. National holiday. Commemorates the declaration of statehood within the federation of Yugoslavia in 1943.

CARNEGIE, ANDREW: BIRTH ANNIVERSARY. Nov 25, 1835. American financier, philanthropist and benefactor of more than 2,500 libraries, born at Dunfermline, Scotland. Carnegie Hall, the Carnegie Foundation and the Carnegie Endowment for International Peace are among his gifts. Carnegie wrote in 1889, "Surplus wealth is a sacred trust which its possessor is bound to administer in his lifetime for the good of the community. . . . The man who dies . . . rich dies disgraced." Carnegie died at his summer estate, Shadowbrook, MA, Aug 11, 1919.

DiMAGGIO, JOSEPH PAUL (JOE): 100th BIRTH ANNIVERSARY. Nov 25, 1914. Baseball Hall of Fame outfielder, born at Martinez, CA. In 1941 he was on "the streak," getting a hit in 56 consecutive games. He was the American League MVP for three years, was the batting champion in 1939 and led the league in RBIs in both 1941 and 1948. DiMaggio was married to actress Marilyn Monroe in 1954, but they later divorced. He died at Harbour Island, FL, Mar 8, 1999.

GERMANY: FRANKFURT CHRISTMAS MARKET. Nov 25–Dec 23. "Weinachtsmarkt auf dem Romerberg," the Christmas market in Frankfurt, is one of Germany's best. Bells are rung simultaneously from nine downtown churches. Glockenspiels are sounded by hand and trumpets are blown from the old St. Nicolas Church.

KENNEDY, JOHN F., JR: BIRTH ANNIVERSARY. Nov 25, 1960. Lawyer, editor (*George* magazine), born at Washington, DC. Son of John F. Kennedy (35th president of the US) and Jacqueline Bouvier Kennedy. He died along with his wife, Carolyn, and his sister-in-law, Lauren Bessette, when the plane he was piloting crashed off of Cape Cod, MA, July 16, 1999.

MIRABEL SISTERS MURDERED: ANNIVERSARY. Nov 25, 1960. On this date Maria, Teresa and Minerva Mirabel, political activists in the Dominican Republic, were assassinated on orders of dictator Rafael Trujillo. The anniversary of their deaths is now observed by the United Nations as International Day for the Elimination of Violence Against Women.

NATION, CARRY AMELIA MOORE: BIRTH ANNIVERSARY. Nov 25, 1846. American temperance leader, famed as hatchet-wielding smasher of saloons, born at Garrard County, KY. Died at Leavenworth, KS, June 9, 1911.

POPE JOHN XXIII: BIRTH ANNIVERSARY. Nov 25, 1881. Angelo Roncalli, 261st pope of the Roman Catholic Church, born at Sotte il Monte, Italy. Elected pope on Oct 28, 1958. Died June 3, 1963, at Rome, Italy.

SAINT CATHERINE'S DAY. Nov 25. Patron saint of maidens, mechanics and philosophers, as well as of all who work with wheels.

SHOPPING REMINDER DAY. Nov 25. One month before Christmas, a reminder to shoppers that after today there are only 28 more shopping days (excluding Thanksgiving Day and Christmas Eve) until Christmas.

SURINAME: INDEPENDENCE DAY. Nov 25. Holiday. Gained independence from the Netherlands in 1975.

UNITED NATIONS: INTERNATIONAL DAY FOR THE ELIMINATION OF VIOLENCE AGAINST WOMEN. Nov 25. Observed by the United Nations since 1993 on the anniversary of the 1960 murders of the Mirabel sisters in the Dominican Republic. In 2004 UN Secretary-General Kofi Annan said, "Let us be encouraged that there is a growing understanding of the problem. But let us also pledge to do our utmost to protect women, banish such violence and build a world in which women enjoy their rights and freedoms on an equal basis with men." Annually, Nov 25. For info: www.un.org.

BIRTHDAYS TODAY

Christina Applegate, 43, actress (*Anchorman*, "Samantha Who?," "Married . . . With Children"), born Hollywood, CA, Nov 25, 1971.

Billy Burke, 48, actor ("Revolution," *Twilight Saga* films), born Bellingham, WA, Nov 25, 1966.

Cris Carter, 49, sportscaster, former football player, born Troy, OH, Nov 25, 1965.

Katie Cassidy, 28, actress ("Arrow," "Melrose Place," "Gossip Girl"), born Los Angeles, CA, Nov 25, 1986.

Bucky Dent, 63, former baseball player and manager, born Russell Earl O'Dey at Savannah, GA, Nov 25, 1951.

Jerry Ferrara, 35, actor ("Entourage"), born Brooklyn, NY, Nov 25, 1979.

Joe Jackson Gibbs, 74, Hall of Fame football coach, sportscaster, born Mocksville, NC, Nov 25, 1940.

Amy Grant, 54, singer, born Augusta, GA, Nov 25, 1960.

Jill Hennessy, 45, actress ("Crossing Jordan," "Law & Order"), born Edmonton, AB, Canada, Nov 25, 1969.

Joel Kinnaman, 35, actor ("The Killing," *The Girl with the Dragon Tattoo* [US]), born Stockholm, Sweden, Nov 25, 1979.

Bernie Joseph Kosar, Jr, 51, former football player, born Boardman, OH, Nov 25, 1963.

John Larroquette, 67, actor (Emmy for "Night Court"), born New Orleans, LA, Nov 25, 1947.

Lenny Moore, 81, Hall of Fame football player, born Reading, PA, Nov 25, 1933.

Eddie Steeples, 41, actor ("My Name Is Earl"), born at Texas, Nov 25, 1973.

Ben Stein, 70, actor, journalist, former speechwriter, born Washington, DC, Nov 25, 1944.

November 2014

S	M	T	W	T	F	S
						1
2	3	4	5	6	7	8
9	10	11	12	13	14	15
16	17	18	19	20	21	22
23	24	25	26	27	28	29
30						

November 26 — Wednesday

DAY 330 | **35 REMAINING**

***ALICE'S ADVENTURES IN WONDERLAND* PUBLISHED: ANNIVERSARY.** Nov 26, 1865. Lewis Carroll's fun-house novel was published on this date. *Through the Looking-Glass, and What Alice Found There* followed in 1871. Lewis Carroll was the pen name of Oxford lecturer in mathematics Charles L. Dodgson.

***CASABLANCA* PREMIERE: ANNIVERSARY.** Nov 26, 1942. Because of the landing of the Allies in North Africa on Nov 8, the premiere and release of the film were moved up from June 1943 to Nov 26, 1942, when it premiered at New York City on Thanksgiving Day. The general nationwide release followed on Jan 23, 1943, during the Roosevelt-Churchill conferences in Casablanca.

FIRST US HOLIDAY BY PRESIDENTIAL PROCLAMATION: 225th ANNIVERSARY. Nov 26, 1789. President George Washington proclaimed Nov 26, 1789, to be Thanksgiving Day. Both houses of Congress, by their joint committee, had requested him to recommend "a day of public thanksgiving and prayer, to be observed by acknowledging with grateful hearts the many and signal favors of Almighty God, especially by affording them an opportunity to peaceably establish a form of government for their safety and happiness." Proclamation issued Oct 3, 1789. Next proclaimed by President Abraham Lincoln in 1863 for the last Thursday in November. In 1939 President Franklin D. Roosevelt moved Thanksgiving to the fourth Thursday in November.

GOMEZ, LEFTY: BIRTH ANNIVERSARY. Nov 26, 1908. Vernon Louis ("Lefty") Gomez, Baseball Hall of Fame pitcher, born at Rodeo, CA. Gomez was a star pitcher with the New York Yankees from 1930 to 1942. He won six World Series games without a defeat and was the winning pitcher in the first All-Star game. Inducted into the Hall of Fame in 1972. Died at Greenbrae, CA, Feb 17, 1989.

HARVARD, JOHN: BIRTH ANNIVERSARY. Nov 26, 1607. English clergyman and scholar. Born at England, he died Sept 24, 1638, at the Massachusetts Bay Colony. Harvard bequeathed part of his estate to a local college, which renamed itself Harvard in his honor.

MONGOLIA: REPUBLIC DAY. Nov 26. National holiday. Commemorates the declaration of the republic in 1924.

MUMBAI TERROR ATTACKS: ANNIVERSARY. Nov 26–29, 2008. Over four days and three nights, 10 young, well-trained Pakistani nationals armed with AK-47s, hand grenades and timer bombs stalked and killed more than 160 people in Mumbai, the financial capital of India. Notable attacks took place in the historic Victoria Terminus train station, a Jewish community center, a hospital and two luxury hotels frequented by foreign dignitaries and tourists.

NATIONAL DEAL WEEK. Nov 26–Dec 3. Annual week organized by dealnews.com that celebrates the heaviest online spending period of the year, incorporating both Black Friday and Cyber Monday. This is a time when both brick-and-mortar stores and online retailers offer consumers great deals and deep discounts, and also marks the unofficial kickoff to the holiday shopping season. National Deal Week recognizes the progression of online shopping and e-commerce activity throughout the past decade and celebrates the growth in years to come. Annually, the week beginning the day before Thanksgiving. For info: Mark LoCastro, dealnews.com, 45 Main St, Ste 848, Brooklyn, NY 11201. Phone: (718) 618-4050. Fax: (256) 971-1867. E-mail: press@dealnews.com. Web: www.nationaldealweek.com.

"THE PRICE IS RIGHT" TV PREMIERE: ANNIVERSARY. Nov 26, 1956. This popular show is also TV's longest-running daily game show, surviving changes in format, networks, time slots and hosts. It began in 1956 with Bill Cullen as host and with Don Pardo as announcer; four contestants bid on an item, and the one who bid closest to the manufacturer's suggested price without going over won the item. In 1972, after a seven-year hiatus, "The Price Is Right" came back in two versions. Bob Barker was the host of the network version until 2007. Drew Carey is the current host.

QUEEN ELIZABETH II AGREES TO PAY TAXES: ANNIVERSARY. Nov 26, 1992. Prime Minister John Major announced that Britain's monarch, Queen Elizabeth, had decided to begin paying taxes on her personal income.

SCHULZ, CHARLES: BIRTH ANNIVERSARY. Nov 26, 1922. Cartoonist, born at Minneapolis, MN. Created the "Peanuts" comic strip, which debuted on Oct 2, 1950. The strip included Charlie Brown; his sister, Sally; his dog, Snoopy; friends Linus and Lucy and a variety of other characters. Schulz's last daily strip was published Jan 3, 2000, and his last Sunday strip was published Feb 13, 2000. The strip ran in more than 2,500 newspapers in many countries. Schulz won the Reuben Award in both 1955 and 1964 and was named International Cartoonist of the Year in 1978. Several TV specials were spin-offs of the strip, including "It's the Great Pumpkin, Charlie Brown" and "You're a Good Man, Charlie Brown." Schulz died at Santa Rosa, CA, Feb 12, 2000. See also: "'Peanuts' Debuts: Anniversary" (Oct 2).

SEVAREID, ERIC: BIRTH ANNIVERSARY. Nov 26, 1912. American journalist Eric (Arnold) Sevareid was born at Velva, ND. He worked for CBS News as a radio reporter during WWII, appeared regularly on "The CBS Evening News" from 1964 to 1977, won the Peabody Award for news interpretations (1950, 1964 and 1967) and earned two Emmys in 1973. He died July 9, 1992, at Washington, DC.

TIE ONE ON DAY. Nov 26. Give from the heart on Wednesday—then give thanks on Thursday. This Thanksgiving Eve, Tie One On (an apron of course!) and bring joy to the life of someone in need. Participation is easy and uplifting: simply wrap a loaf of bread or baked good in an apron and tuck an encouraging note or prayer into the pocket; then present your offering to a neighbor, friend or person in your community who could benefit from a gesture of kindness. Tie One On—and put the "give" back into Thanksgiving. Annually, the Wednesday before Thanksgiving. For info: EllynAnne Geisel, 605 W 17th St, Pueblo, CO 81003. Phone: (719) 545-5704. Fax: (719) 542-3947. E-mail: ellynanne@apronmemories.com. Web: www.apronmemories.com.

TRUTH, SOJOURNER: DEATH ANNIVERSARY. Nov 26, 1883. A former slave who had been sold four times, Sojourner Truth became an evangelist who argued for abolition and women's rights. After a troubled early life, she began her evangelical career in 1843, traveling through New England until she discovered the utopian colony called the Northampton Association of Education and Industry. It was there she was exposed to, and became an advocate for, the cause of abolition, working with Frederick Douglass, Wendell Phillips, William Lloyd Garrison and others. In 1850 she befriended Lucretia Mott, Elizabeth Cady Stanton and other feminist leaders and actively began supporting calls for women's rights. In 1870 she attempted to petition Congress to create a "Negro State" on public lands in the West. Born at Ulster County, NY, about 1790, with the name Isabella Van Wagener, she died Nov 26, 1883, at Battle Creek, MI.

"TWENTY QUESTIONS" TV PREMIERE: 65th ANNIVERSARY. Nov 26, 1949. This game show was based on the old guessing game. A celebrity panel had to guess the identity of an object (having been told only if it was animal, vegetable or mineral) by asking up to 20 questions. Bill Slater hosted two network versions of the show on NBC and DuMont. Jay Jackson took over when it switched from NBC to ABC. "Twenty Questions" began on radio. Regular panelists included Fred Van Deventer, Florence Rinard, Herb Polesie and Johnny McPhee.

WALKER, MARY EDWARDS: BIRTH ANNIVERSARY. Nov 26, 1832. American physician and women's rights leader, born at Oswego, NY. First female surgeon in US Army (Civil War). Spent four months in Confederate prison. First and only woman ever to receive Medal of Honor (Nov 11, 1865). Two years before her death, on June 3, 1916, a government review board asked that her award be revoked. She continued to wear it, in spite of official revocation, until her death, Feb 21, 1919, at Oswego. On June 11, 1977, the secretary of the army posthumously restored the Medal of Honor to Dr. Walker.

WONDERLAND OF LIGHTS. Nov 26–Dec 31. Marshall, TX. More than 10 million tiny white lights cover the city. Features lighted Christmas parade, outdoor ice-skating on the square, entertainment, carriage rides, bus tours and Santa Claus. Est attendance: 150,000. For info: Marshall CVB, 301 N Washington, Marshall, TX 75670. Phone: (903) 702-7777. E-mail: info@VisitMarshallTexas.org. Web: www.VisitMarshallTexas.org.

BIRTHDAYS TODAY

Garcelle Beauvais-Nilon, 48, actress ("NYPD Blue," *Bad Company*), born St. Marc, Haiti, Nov 26, 1966.

Shannon Dunn, 42, Olympic snowboarder, born Arlington Heights, IL, Nov 26, 1972.

Dale Jarrett, 58, race car driver, born Conover, NC, Nov 26, 1956.

Richard (Rich) Caruthers Little, 76, impressionist, born Ottawa, ON, Canada, Nov 26, 1938.

Jack A. Markell, 54, Governor of Delaware (D), born Newark, DE, Nov 26, 1960.

Tina Turner, 76, singer, born Anna Mae Bullock at Nutbush, TN, Nov 26, 1938.

November 27 — Thursday

DAY 331 **34 REMAINING**

AGEE, JAMES: BIRTH ANNIVERSARY. Nov 27, 1909. Poet, critic, novelist (*A Death in the Family*), social historian (*Let Us Now Praise Famous Men*), scriptwriter, born at Knoxville, TN. Died at New York, NY, May 16, 1955.

AMERICA'S THANKSGIVING PARADE®. Nov 27. Detroit, MI. One of Michigan's largest events, the parade has been a beloved Thanksgiving tradition since 1924. The streets of downtown Detroit come alive with bands, floats and more for all ages. Est attendance: 1,000,000. For info: The Parade Co, 9500 Mount Elliott, Studio A, Detroit, MI 48211. Phone: (313) 923-7400. Fax: (313) 923-2920. Web: www.theparade.org.

ATLANTA HALF MARATHON AND THANKSGIVING DAY 5K. Nov 27. Atlanta, GA. A Thanksgiving tradition: 13.1-mile race (USATF certified). Est attendance: 8,000. For info: Atlanta Track Club, 3097 E Shadowlawn Ave, Atlanta, GA 30305. Phone: (404) 231-9064. Fax: (404) 364-0708. E-mail: atc@atlantatrackclub.org. Web: www.atlantatrackclub.org.

DAYTONA FALL TURKEY RUN. Nov 27–30. Daytona International Speedway, Daytona Beach, FL. 41st annual car show of all makes of 1980 and older collector vehicles. Show includes display of classics, street rods, muscle cars, race cars, customs and special trucks on the speedway infield, with a large swap meet (2,200 vendors) of auto parts and accessories and car sales corral. Also a craft sale. Annually, Thanksgiving weekend. For info: Daytona Beach Car Shows, PO Box 1958, Daytona Beach, FL 32115-1958. Phone: (386) 255-7355. E-mail: kim@daytonabeachcarshows.com. Web: www.daytonabeachcarshows.com.

DUBCEK, ALEXANDER: BIRTH ANNIVERSARY. Nov 27, 1921. The man who attempted to give his country "socialism with a human face," Alexander Dubcek was born at Uhrocev, a village in western Slovakia. As first secretary of the Czechoslovak Communist Party during the "Prague Spring" of 1968, he moved to achieve the "widest possible democratization" and to loosen the dominant influence of the Soviet Union. As a result, Czechoslovakia was invaded by armed forces of the Warsaw Pact on Aug 21, 1968. Dubcek died Nov 7, 1992, at Prague.

FIRST FACE TRANSPLANT: ANNIVERSARY. Nov 27, 2005. In a five-hour operation, French surgeons transplanted the skin, muscles, veins, arteries, nerves and tissues of a brain-dead patient onto the face of a woman who had lost her nose and the bottom part of her face after a dog attack. Doctors said the partial transplant, the first of its kind, created a "hybrid" face—resembling neither the dead donor nor the original face of the recipient.

November 2014	S	M	T	W	T	F	S
							1
	2	3	4	5	6	7	8
	9	10	11	12	13	14	15
	16	17	18	19	20	21	22
	23	24	25	26	27	28	29
	30						

FOODS & FEASTS OF COLONIAL VIRGINIA. Nov 27–29. Jamestown Settlement, Williamsburg, VA; and Yorktown Victory Center, Yorktown, VA. Explore the 17th- and 18th-century culinary practices of Virginia at this three-day event starting on Thanksgiving Day. At Jamestown Settlement, learn how food was gathered, preserved and prepared on land and at sea by Virginia's English colonists and Powhatan Indians. At Yorktown Victory Center, learn about typical soldiers' fare during the American Revolution and trace the bounty of a 1780s farm from field to kitchen. For info: Jamestown-Yorktown Foundation, PO Box 1607, Williamsburg, VA 23187. Phone: (757) 253-4838 or (888) 593-4682. Fax: (757) 253-5299. Web: www.historyisfun.org.

HENDRIX, JIMI: BIRTH ANNIVERSARY. Nov 27, 1942. American musician and songwriter Jimi Hendrix was born at Seattle, WA. One of the greatest rock guitarists in history, he revolutionized the guitar sound with heavy use of feedback and incredible fretwork. His success first came in England, and then he achieved fame in the US after his appearance at the Monterey Pop Festival (1967). His albums included *Are You Experienced?*, *Electric Ladyland* and *Band of Gypsys*. He died Sept 18, 1970, at London, England.

LEE, BRUCE: BIRTH ANNIVERSARY. Nov 27, 1940. The actor and martial artist was born at San Francisco, CA, but raised in Hong Kong. In 1959 he returned to the US to teach martial arts, opening schools in Seattle, WA, and Oakland, CA. Spotted at a competition by a TV producer, Lee was cast as Kato in TV's *The Green Hornet* in 1966. He moved on to film, where he displayed an intense charisma that would make him a star. Before he could enjoy this new success, Lee died of a cerebral edema on July 20, 1973, at Hong Kong. His films include *Fists of Fury* (1972) and *Enter the Dragon* (1973).

LIVINGSTON, ROBERT R.: BIRTH ANNIVERSARY. Nov 27, 1746. (Old Style date.) Member of the Continental Congress, farmer, diplomat and jurist, born at New York, NY. It was Livingston who administered the oath of office to President George Washington in 1789. He died at Clermont, NY, Feb 26, 1813.

MACY'S THANKSGIVING DAY PARADE. Nov 27. New York, NY. 88th annual. Starts at 9 AM, EST, at Central Park West. A part of everyone's Thanksgiving, the parade grows bigger and better each year. Featuring floats, giant balloons, marching bands and famous stars, the parade is televised for the whole country. For info: New York CVB, 810 7th Ave, 3rd Fl, New York, NY 10019. Phone: (212) 484-1222. Web: www.nycvisit.com or macysparade.com.

MASTERSON, BAT: BIRTH ANNIVERSARY. Nov 27, 1853. Old American West gambler, saloon keeper, lawman and newswriter/editor. Born at Henryville, QC, Canada; died Oct 25, 1921, at New York, NY.

STOCK EXCHANGE HOLIDAY (THANKSGIVING DAY). Nov 27. Also early closures on Nov 26. The holiday schedules for the various exchanges are subject to change if relevant rules, regulations or exchange policies are revised. If you have questions, contact: CME Group (CME, CBOT, NYMEX, KCBT) (www.cmegroup.com), Chicago Board Options Exchange (www.cboe.com), NASDAQ (www.nasdaq.com), NYSE Euronext (www.nyse.com).

✦THANKSGIVING DAY. Nov 27. Presidential Proclamation. Always issued for the fourth Thursday in November. See also: "First US Holiday by Presidential Proclamation: Anniversary" (Nov 26).

THANKSGIVING DAY. Nov 27. Legal public holiday. (Public Law 90–363 sets Thanksgiving Day on the fourth Thursday in November.) Observed in all states. In most states, the Friday after Thanksgiving is also a holiday; in Nevada it is called Family Day.

TURKEY-FREE THANKSGIVING. Nov 27. This is a time for you to take turkey off your table, forgoing flesh foods "cold turkey" and having a harvest of health. Why not carve a compassionate celebration centerpiece—a tasty mock turkey made from tofu, tempeh or *seitan*? The turkeys will thank you for having a humane

holiday. For info: Vegetarian Awareness Network, PO Box 3545, Washington, DC 20027-0045. Phone: (800) 234-8343.

WEIZMANN, CHAIM: BIRTH ANNIVERSARY. Nov 27, 1874. Israeli statesman born near Pinsk, Byelorussia. He played an important role in bringing about the British government's Balfour Declaration, calling for the establishment of a national home for Jews at Palestine. He died at Tel Aviv, Israel, Nov 9, 1952.

BIRTHDAYS TODAY

Kathryn Bigelow, 63, director (Oscar for *The Hurt Locker*; *Zero Dark Thirty*, *Point Break*), born San Carlos, CA, Nov 27, 1951.

Robin Givens, 50, actress ("Head of the Class," *A Rage in Harlem*), born New York, NY, Nov 27, 1964.

Samantha Harris, 41, television personality ("Dancing with the Stars," "E! News"), born Hopkins, MN, Nov 27, 1973.

Jimmy Rollins, 36, baseball player, born Oakland, CA, Nov 27, 1978.

Gail Henion Sheehy, 77, author (*Passages*), born Mamaroneck, NY, Nov 27, 1937.

Fisher Stevens, 51, actor (*The Brother from Another Planet*, *Bob Roberts*), born Chicago, IL, Nov 27, 1963.

Nick Van Exel, 43, basketball coach and former player, born Kenosha, WI, Nov 27, 1971.

Jaleel White, 38, actor ("Family Matters"), born Los Angeles, CA, Nov 27, 1976.

November 28 — Friday

DAY 332 | **33 REMAINING**

ALBANIA: INDEPENDENCE DAY. Nov 28. Commemorates independence from the Ottoman Empire in 1912.

ALSTON, CHARLES H.: BIRTH ANNIVERSARY. Nov 28, 1907. African-American painter and sculptor born at Charlotte, NC, and died at New York, NY, Apr 27, 1977. Throughout his career, Alston experimented with styles ranging from realism to abstraction. His realistic WPA murals at Harlem Hospital depict a narrative in the style of Diego Rivera. The Cubist painting *The Family* (1955) is an excellent example of Alston's early work, influenced by Italian artist Amedeo Modigliani. *Black Man, Black Woman USA* has a decidedly Egyptian style of portraiture. *Walking* (1958), which depicts a silent crowd, almost prophesied the turmoil and social agitation of the Civil Rights movement.

AT&T HOLIDAY TREE LIGHTING AT ANCHORAGE. Nov 28. Town Square, Anchorage, AK. Join Santa and a live team of nine reindeer to celebrate the holiday season and the lighting of the Holiday Tree. Free cookies and cocoa. Annually, the Friday after Thanksgiving. Est attendance: 2,000. For info: Anchorage Downtown Partnership, Ltd, 333 W 4th Ave, Ste 317, Anchorage, AK 99501. Phone: (907) 279-5650. Fax: (907) 279-5651. E-mail: info@anchoragedowntown.org. Web: www.anchoragedowntown.org.

BELSNICKEL CRAFT SHOW. Nov 28–29. Boyertown High School, Boyertown, PA. Sale of juried fine crafts. Annually, the first Friday and Saturday after Thanksgiving. Est attendance: 3,000. For info: Lindsay Dieroff, Collection Dir, Boyertown Area Historical Society, 43 S Chestnut St, Boyertown, PA 19512. Phone: (610) 367-5255. E-mail: boyertownhistory@windstream.net or belsnickelcraft@aol.com. Web: www.boyertownhistory.org.

BLACK FRIDAY. Nov 28. The traditional beginning of the Christmas shopping season on the Friday after Thanksgiving. Called "Black Friday" because traditionally retailers were in the "black" by this day of the year.

BLAKE, WILLIAM: BIRTH ANNIVERSARY. Nov 28, 1757. English visionary poet and artist born at London, England. Composed "The Tyger," which begins memorably, "Tyger! Tyger! burning bright/In the forests of the night,/What immortal hand or eye/Could frame thy fearful symmetry?" Blake died in poverty at London on Aug 12, 1827.

BUNYAN, JOHN: BIRTH ANNIVERSARY. Nov 28, 1628. (Old Style date.) English cleric and author of *A Pilgrim's Progress*, born at Elstow, Bedfordshire, England. Died at London, England, Aug 31, 1688 (OS).

BUY NOTHING DAY. Nov 28–29. A 48-hour moratorium on consumer spending. A celebration of simplicity, about getting our runaway consumer culture back onto a sustainable path. Annually, beginning on the first shopping day after Thanksgiving. For info: Adbusters Media Foundation, 1243 W 7th Ave, Vancouver, BC V6H 1B7, Canada. Phone: (800) 663-1243 or (604) 736-9401. E-mail: bnd@adbusters.org. Web: www.adbusters.org.

CANADA: RALLY OF THE TALL PINES. Nov 28–29. Bancroft, ON. Combining winter road surfaces with the scenic, winding back roads of the Canadian Shield makes this event of the Canadian Rally Championship Circuit one of the most popular. For info: Rally of the Tall Pines, Box 301, Toronto, ON, M3J 0J2, Canada. Phone: (416) 606-5141. E-mail: ian@tallpinesrally.com. Web: www.tallpinesrally.com.

CHAD: REPUBLIC DAY. Nov 28. National holiday. Commemorates proclamation of the republic in 1958.

CHRISTMAS TRADITIONS. Nov 28–Dec 24. St. Charles, MO. Holiday festivities include caroling, chestnut roasting and authentically costumed Santas from around the world. Enjoy old-fashioned holiday shopping all day and night on Wednesdays, Fridays and Saturdays. Annually, from the day after Thanksgiving until Christmas. Est attendance: 50,000. For info: St. Charles CVB, 230 S Main St, St. Charles, MO 63301. Phone: (800) 366-2427. Web: www.stcharleschristmas.com.

CRAFTSMEN'S CHRISTMAS CLASSIC ARTS & CRAFTS FESTIVAL. Nov 28–30. Greensboro Coliseum Complex Special Events Center, Greensboro, NC. 41st annual. Features work from more than 450 talented artists and craftspeople. All juried exhibitors' work has been handmade by the exhibitors and must be their own original design and creation. See the creative process in action as many exhibitors demonstrate throughout the weekend. Visit Christmas Tree Village to view the uniquely decorated Christmas trees by some of our exhibitors. Est attendance: 25,000. For info: Gilmore Enterprises, 3514-A Drawbridge Pkwy, Greensboro, NC 27410. Phone: (336) 282-5550. E-mail: contact@gilmoreshows.com. Web: www.ChristmasClassic.com or www.CraftShow.com.

FAMILY DAY IN NEVADA. Nov 28. Observed annually on the Friday following the fourth Thursday in November.

LÉVI-STRAUSS, CLAUDE: BIRTH ANNIVERSARY. Nov 28, 1908. French anthropologist and philosopher best known for advocating the intellectual movement "structuralism." Born at Brussels, Belgium, Lévi-Strauss authored many books, including his acclaimed memoir *Tristes Tropiques*, which recounted his experiences among Brazilian tribes and challenged old ways of thinking about so-called "primitive" cultures. Lévi-Strauss died at Paris, France, Oct 30, 2009, at the age of 100.

LULLY, JEAN BAPTISTE: BIRTH ANNIVERSARY. Nov 28, 1632. Versatile musician and composer, born at Florence, Italy, who chose France for his homeland. Noted for his quick temper, it is said that he struck his own foot with a baton while in a rage. The resulting wound led to blood poisoning, from which he died, at Paris, France, Mar 22, 1687.

MAIZE DAY. Nov 28. Celebrating the First Nations of the Americas and the central role of corn in these cultures and cuisines. Almost every day, people throughout the Western Hemisphere enjoy foods cultivated by the indigenous people of North, Central and South America. On this day Americans celebrate living indigenous cultures, as well as cultures of the past. Families and friends gather to remember and talk about the cultures and to feast on the foods Native Americans have contributed to our amalgamated cultures. Annually, the Friday after Thanksgiving. For info: Corinne Lightweaver, 4020 Colonial Ave, Los Angeles, CA 90066. Phone: (310) 313-1848. E-mail: editor.corlight@verizon.net.

MAURITANIA: INDEPENDENCE DAY. Nov 28. National holiday. Attained sovereignty from France in 1960.

NATIONAL DAY OF LISTENING. Nov 28. First observed in 2008. On the day after Thanksgiving, StoryCorps asks all Americans to take an hour to record an interview with a loved one, using recording equipment that is readily available in most homes, such as computers, iPhones or tape recorders. This day provides a noncommercial alternative to "Black Friday" shopping sprees. Tens of thousands of Americans have participated in the National Day of Listening, and educators and community organizations have incorporated StoryCorps's interviewing techniques into their programs. For info: StoryCorps, 80 Hanson Pl, 2nd Fl, Brooklyn, NY 11217. Phone: (646) 723-7020. Web: www.storycorps.org or www.nationaldayoflistening.org.

NATIONAL FLOSSING DAY. Nov 28. Americans are encouraged to consider the role flossing has played in their lives and make plans to help spread "Peace of Mouth" in their own lives and the lives of others around them, in ways with and without floss. On this day children should also be made aware of the richness and health that flossing can bring to life. For info: Natl Flossing Council, 533 4th St SE, Washington, DC 20003. Phone: (202) 544-0711. E-mail: nfd@flossing.org. Web: www.flossing.org.

NATIVE AMERICAN HERITAGE DAY. Nov 28. The 111th Congress jointly approved this day June 26, 2009, to honor the achievements and contributions of Native Americans to the US (Public Law 111-33). This day encourages the people of the US, as well as federal, state and local governments and interested groups and organizations, to honor Native Americans with activities relating to (1) appropriate programs, ceremonies and events to observe Native American Heritage Day; (2) the historical status of Native American tribal governments as well as the present-day status of Native Americans; (3) the cultures, traditions and languages of Native Americans; and (4) the rich Native American cultural legacy that all Americans enjoy today. Annually, the Friday after Thanksgiving Day.

PANAMA: INDEPENDENCE FROM SPAIN. Nov 28. Public holiday. Commemorates the independence of Panama (which at the time was part of Colombia) from Spain in 1821.

ROYAL SOCIETY: ANNIVERSARY. Nov 28, 1660. One of the world's oldest scientific academies, the Royal Society, was founded on this date at Gresham College, London, with King Charles II as its patron. Scientists, engineers and technologists make up the membership (which has included women since 1945). Prominent fellows past and present include Christopher Wren, Robert Boyle, Isaac Newton, Joseph Banks, Charles Babbage, Charles Darwin, Albert Einstein, Stephen Hawking and Tim Berners-Lee. "If I have seen further," wrote Newton in tribute to his colleagues, "it is because I have stood upon the shoulders of giants."

November 2014	S	M	T	W	T	F	S
							1
	2	3	4	5	6	7	8
	9	10	11	12	13	14	15
	16	17	18	19	20	21	22
	23	24	25	26	27	28	29
	30						

SINKIE DAY. Nov 28. "Sinkies"—people who occasionally dine over the kitchen sink and elsewhere—are encouraged to celebrate this time-honored, casual-yet-tasteful cuisine culture. This is a particularly appropriate day to become acquainted with the sinkie style of dining. Christmas shopping and Thanksgiving leftovers provide the perfect reasons to enjoy a quick meal. Annually, the day after Thanksgiving. If it has anything to do with having a quick bite, it has everything to do with being a sinkie. For info: Norm Hankoff, Founder, Intl Assn of People Who Dine over the Kitchen Sink. E-mail: normh@sinkie.com. Web: www.sinkie.com.

SMITH, ANNA NICOLE: BIRTH ANNIVERSARY. Nov 28, 1967. Born Vickie Lynn Hogan at Houston, TX, this model and actress earned a certain degree of fame for appearing in *Playboy* and marrying an 89-year-old billionaire. Her life was one of publicity, scandal and drug abuse, and her death from a lethal drug interaction at Hollywood, FL, on Feb 8, 2007, sparked an unexpected media frenzy. The cause of her death, the paternity and custody of her infant daughter and the disposition of her estate were all subjects of intense interest by the tabloid and mainstream media.

SPACE MILESTONE: *MARINER 4* (US): 50th ANNIVERSARY. Nov 28, 1964. The first successful mission to Mars. Approached within 6,118 miles of Mars on July 14, 1965. Took photographs and instrument readings.

TEHRAN CONFERENCE: ANNIVERSARY. Nov 28–Dec 1, 1943. President Franklin D. Roosevelt, British prime minister Winston Churchill and Soviet premier Joseph Stalin met at Tehran, Iran, to formulate a plan for an Allied assault, a second front, in western Europe. The resulting plan was "Operation Overlord," which commenced with the landing on Normandy's beaches on June 6, 1944 ("D-day").

VICTORIAN CHRISTMAS CELEBRATION. Nov 28–Dec 31. Gordon-Roberts House, Cumberland, MD. Victorian Christmas tea and candlelight tours with musical entertainment. Various workshops and children's programs. Theme decorating in an 1867 Victorian mansion museum. Est attendance: 1,500. For info: Sharon Nealis, Admin, Gordon-Roberts House, 218 Washington St, Cumberland, MD 21502. Phone: (301) 777-8678. E-mail: info@gordon-robertshouse.com. Web: www.gordon-robertshouse.com.

WORLD FAMOUS FISH HOUSE PARADE. Nov 28. Aitkin, MN. 24th annual special parade of uniquely and humorously decorated fish houses used for ice fishing during the winter. Annually, the Friday after Thanksgiving. Est attendance: 6,000. For info: Aitkin Area Chamber of Commerce, PO Box 127, Aitkin, MN 56431. Phone: (800) 526-8342. E-mail: upnorth@aitkin.com. Web: www.aitkin.com.

BIRTHDAYS TODAY

Michael Bennet, 50, US Senator (D, Colorado), born New Delhi, India, Nov 28, 1964.

Berry Gordy, Jr, 85, record and motion picture executive (cofounder of Motown), born Detroit, MI, Nov 28, 1929.

Ed Harris, 64, actor (*The Hours, Pollock, The Right Stuff*), born Englewood, NJ, Nov 28, 1950.

Gary Hart, 76, former US senator, former presidential candidate, born Gary Hartpence at Ottawa, KS, Nov 28, 1938.

Ryan Kwanten, 38, actor ("True Blood," "Summerland"), born Sydney, New South Wales, Australia, Nov 28, 1976.

S. Epatha Merkerson, 62, actress ("Law & Order," *Lackawanna Blues*), born Detroit, MI, Nov 28, 1952.

Judd Nelson, 55, actor (*The Breakfast Club, St. Elmo's Fire*, "Suddenly Susan"), born Portland, ME, Nov 28, 1959.

Randy Newman, 71, singer, songwriter, composer (film scores for *Ragtime, The Natural*), born New Orleans, LA, Nov 28, 1943.

Paul Shaffer, 65, bandleader ("Late Show with David Letterman"), comedian, born Thunder Bay, ON, Canada, Nov 28, 1949.

Eric Shinseki, 72, US Secretary of Veterans Affairs, born Lihue, Kauai, HI, Nov 28, 1942.

Jon Stewart, 52, writer, comedian ("The Daily Show"), born Jonathan Stuart Leibowitz at New York, NY, Nov 28, 1962.

Matt Williams, 49, former baseball player, born Bishop, CA, Nov 28, 1965.

Mary Elizabeth Winstead, 30, actress (*Abraham Lincoln: Vampire Hunter; Scott Pilgrim vs the World*), born Rocky Mount, NC, Nov 28, 1984.

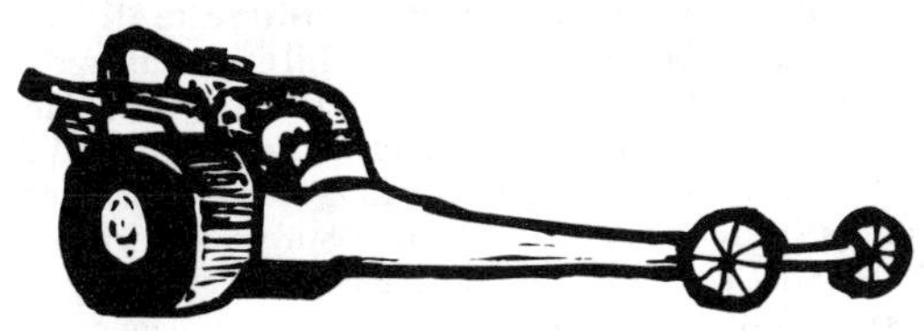

November 29 — Saturday

DAY 333 **32 REMAINING**

ALCOTT, LOUISA MAY: BIRTH ANNIVERSARY. Nov 29, 1832. American author, born at Philadelphia, PA. Died at Boston, MA, Mar 6, 1888. Her most famous novel is *Little Women*, the classic story of Meg, Jo, Beth and Amy.

BERKELEY, BUSBY: BIRTH ANNIVERSARY. Nov 29, 1895. William Berkeley Enos was born at Los Angeles, CA. After serving in WWI as an entertainment officer, he changed his name to Busby Berkeley and began a career as an actor. He turned to directing in 1921, and his lavish Broadway and Hollywood creations include *Forty-Second Street, Gold Diggers of 1933, Footlight Parade, Stage Struck, Babes in Arms, Strike Up the Band, Girl Crazy* and *Take Me Out to the Ball Game*. He retired in 1962 but returned to Broadway in 1970 to supervise a revival of *No, No, Nanette*. He died Mar 14, 1976, at Palm Springs, CA.

CZECHOSLOVAKIA ENDS COMMUNIST RULE: 25th ANNIVERSARY. Nov 29, 1989. Czechoslovakia ended 41 years of one-party Communist rule when the Czechoslovak parliament voted unanimously to repeal the constitutional clauses giving the Communist Party a guaranteed leading role in the country and promoting Marxism-Leninism as the state ideology. The vote came at the end of a 12-day revolution sparked by the beating of protestors Nov 17. Although the Communist Party remained in power, the tide of reform led to its ouster by the Civic Forum, headed by playwright Václav Havel. The Civic Forum demanded free elections with equal rights for all parties, a mixed economy and support for foreign investment. In the first free elections in Czechoslovakia since WWII, Václav Havel was elected president.

ELECTRONIC GREETINGS DAY. Nov 29. Save a letter carrier, save a tree, save a stamp! Today's the day to send your greetings the free, electronic way, via the Internet. (©2006 by WH.) For info: Thomas & Ruth Roy, Wellcat Holidays, 2418 Long Ln, Lebanon, PA 17046. Phone: (717) 279-0184. E-mail: info@wellcat.com. Web: www.wellcat.com.

FIRST ARMY-NAVY GAME: ANNIVERSARY. Nov 29, 1890. Army played Navy for the first time in football, and Navy won, 24–0. Red Emrich scored four touchdowns (worth four points each) and kicked two field goals (worth two points each), and Moulton Johnson added the other touchdown to account for all the scoring.

"KUKLA, FRAN AND OLLIE" TV PREMIERE: ANNIVERSARY. Nov 29, 1948. This popular children's show featured puppets created and handled by Burr Tillstrom and was equally popular with adults. Fran Allison was the only human on the show. Tillstrom's lively and eclectic cast of characters, called the "Kuklapolitans," included the bald, high-voiced Kukla, the big-toothed Oliver J. Dragon (Ollie), Fletcher Rabbit, Cecil Bill, Beulah the Witch, Colonel Crackie, Madame Ooglepuss and Dolores Dragon. Most shows were performed without scripts.

LEWIS, C.S. (CLIVE STAPLES): BIRTH ANNIVERSARY. Nov 29, 1898. British scholar, novelist and author (*The Screwtape Letters, Chronicles of Narnia*), born at Belfast, Ireland, died at Oxford, England, Nov 22, 1963.

MEXICO: GUADALAJARA INTERNATIONAL BOOK FAIR. Nov 29–Dec 7. Latin America's largest book fair with exhibitors from all over the Spanish-speaking world. Est attendance: 650,000. For info: David Unger, Guadalajara Book Fair—US Office, Div of Hum, NAC 5225, City College, New York, NY 10031. Phone: (212) 650-7925. Fax: (212) 650-7912. E-mail: filny@aol.com.

MOON PHASE: FIRST QUARTER. Nov 29. Moon enters First Quarter phase at 5:06 AM, EST.

ROSS, NELLIE TAYLOE: BIRTH ANNIVERSARY. Nov 29, 1876. Nellie Tayloe Ross became the first female governor in the US when she was chosen to serve out the last month and two days of her husband's term as governor of Wyoming after he died in office. She was elected in her own right in the Nov 4, 1924, election but lost the 1927 race. Ross was appointed vice chairman of the Democratic National Committee in 1926 and named director of the US Mint by President Franklin D. Roosevelt in 1933. She served in that capacity for 20 years. Born at St. Joseph, MO, she died Dec 20, 1977, at Washington, DC.

SMALL BUSINESS SATURDAY. Nov 29. A day to celebrate and support small businesses and all they do for their communities. Originated by American Express in 2010. For info: US Small Business Administration. Web: www.sba.gov/saturday.

SWITZERLAND: CLAUWAU—SANTA CLAUS WORLD CHAMPIONSHIP. Nov 29 (tentative). Samnaun. 14th annual. Santa Claus aspirants compete in nine disciplines in an effort to be world champion, including the Zipfybob Race, Sledge Race (with timed gift-giving), geography bee, Chimney Climb (with bag of gifts), Capricorn Sprint and more. For info: ClauWau. E-mail: samnaun@engadin.com. Web: www.clauwau.ch.

"TATORT" TV PREMIERE: ANNIVERSARY. Nov 29, 1970. This popular German detective drama ("Crime Scene" in English) is unique in that there are a dozen versions of it produced by regional TV stations. There are different world-weary detective teams for Hamburg, Berlin, Cologne, etc. "Tatort" focuses on characters rather than violence and has been praised for taking on controversial societal issues.

THOMSON, CHARLES: BIRTH ANNIVERSARY. Nov 29, 1729. America's first official record keeper. Chosen secretary of the First Continental Congress Sept 5, 1774, Thomson recorded proceedings for 15 years and delivered his journals together with tens of thousands of records to the federal government in 1789. Born at Ireland, he died Aug 16, 1824. It was Thomson who notified George Washington of his election as president.

UNITED NATIONS: INTERNATIONAL DAY OF SOLIDARITY WITH THE PALESTINIAN PEOPLE. Nov 29. Annual observance proclaimed by General Assembly in 1977. At request of the Assembly, observance is organized by secretary-general in consultation with Committee on the Exercise of the Inalienable Rights of the Palestinian People. Recommendations include a plan for return of the Palestinians to their homes and the establishment of an "independent Palestinian entity." For info: United Nations, Dept of Public Info, New York, NY 10017. Web: www.un.org.

WAITE, MORRISON R.: BIRTH ANNIVERSARY. Nov 29, 1816. Seventh chief justice of the US, born at Lyme, CT. Appointed chief justice by President Ulysses S. Grant Jan 19, 1874. The Waite Court is remembered for its controversial rulings that did much to rehabilitate the idea of states' rights after the Civil War and early Reconstruction years. Waite died at Washington, DC, Mar 23, 1888.

BIRTHDAYS TODAY

Don Cheadle, 50, actor ("House of Lies," *Talk to Me, Hotel Rwanda, Crash, Ocean's Eleven*), born Kansas City, MO, Nov 29, 1964.

Jacques Rene Chirac, 82, former president of France, born Paris, France, Nov 29, 1932.

Joel Coen, 60, filmmaker (Oscars for *No Country for Old Men, Fargo*), born Minneapolis, MN, Nov 29, 1954.

Kim Delaney, 53, actress ("NYPD Blue"), born Philadelphia, PA, Nov 29, 1961.

Rahm Emmanuel, 55, Mayor of Chicago, former White House chief of staff, born Chicago, IL, Nov 29, 1959.

Anna Faris, 38, actress (*The House Bunny,* "Entourage"), born Baltimore, MD, Nov 29, 1976.

Ryan Giggs, 41, soccer player, born Cardiff, Wales, Nov 29, 1973.

Kasey Keller, 45, former soccer player, born Olympia, WA, Nov 29, 1969.

Diane Ladd, 82, actress (*Alice Doesn't Live Here Anymore, Ramblin' Rose, The Cemetery Club*), born Rose Diane Ladner at Meridian, MS, Nov 29, 1932.

Howie Mandel, 59, comedian, game show host ("Deal or No Deal"), actor ("St. Elsewhere"), born Toronto, ON, Canada, Nov 29, 1955.

Chuck Mangione, 74, musician, composer (Grammy for "Bellavia"), born Rochester, NY, Nov 29, 1940.

John Mayall, 81, musician, bandleader (The Bluesbreakers), born Manchester, England, Nov 29, 1933.

Andrew McCarthy, 52, actor (*Pretty in Pink, Weekend at Bernie's*), author, born Westfield, NJ, Nov 29, 1962.

Cathy Moriarty, 54, actress (*Raging Bull, The Mambo Kings*), born the Bronx, NY, Nov 29, 1960.

Janet Napolitano, 57, US Secretary of Homeland Security, former governor of Arizona (D), born Pittsburgh, PA, Nov 29, 1957.

Mariano Rivera, 45, baseball player, born Panama City, Panama, Nov 29, 1969.

Vincent Edward (Vin) Scully, 87, sportscaster, born New York, NY, Nov 29, 1927.

Garry Shandling, 65, comedian ("The Larry Sanders Show"), born Chicago, IL, Nov 29, 1949.

November 2014	S	M	T	W	T	F	S
							1
	2	3	4	5	6	7	8
	9	10	11	12	13	14	15
	16	17	18	19	20	21	22
	23	24	25	26	27	28	29
	30						

November 30 — Sunday

DAY 334 **31 REMAINING**

ADVENT, FIRST SUNDAY. Nov 30. Advent includes the four Sundays before Christmas, Nov 30, Dec 7, Dec 14 and Dec 21 in 2014.

ARTICLES OF PEACE BETWEEN GREAT BRITAIN AND THE US: ANNIVERSARY. Nov 30, 1782. These provisional articles of peace, which were to end America's War of Independence, were signed at Paris, France. The refined and definitive treaty of peace between Great Britain and the US was signed at Paris on Sept 3, 1783. In it "His Britannic Majesty acknowledges the said United States . . . to be free, sovereign and independent states; that he treats them as such; and for himself, his heirs and successors, relinquishes all claims to the government, propriety and territorial rights of the same, and every part thereof. . . ."

BARBADOS: INDEPENDENCE DAY. Nov 30. National holiday. Gained independence from Great Britain in 1966.

CHISHOLM, SHIRLEY: 90th BIRTH ANNIVERSARY. Nov 30, 1924. Born at Brooklyn, NY, Shirley St. Hill Chisholm was an educator, author and politician who was the first African-American woman elected to the US House of Representatives. A liberal Democrat, she was known for her strong opinions and outspoken nature as she represented the Bedford-Stuyvesant neighborhood of New York City in Congress during 1974–82. She fought against poverty and discrimination and ran for the 1972 Democratic nomination for president just to prove that she could. She retired from politics in the 1980s and died at Ormond Beach, FL, Jan 1, 2005.

CHURCHILL, WINSTON: BIRTH ANNIVERSARY. Nov 30, 1874. Winston Leonard Spencer Churchill, British statesman and the first man to be made an honorary citizen of the US (by an act of Congress, Apr 9, 1963), was born at Blenheim Palace, Oxfordshire, England. Died Jan 24, 1965, at London, England. Dedicated to Britain and total victory over Germany, Churchill as minister of defense and prime minister was a strong leader during WWII. A stirring public speaker, Churchill said upon becoming prime minister in 1940, "I have nothing to offer but blood, toil, tears and sweat."

CLARK, DICK: 85th BIRTH ANNIVERSARY. Nov 30, 1929. As influential host of television's "American Bandstand" from 1957 to 1987, Dick Clark helped to promote and codify rock and roll and black rhythm and blues to mainstream audiences as those sounds wound their way into the country's psyche. Richard Wagstaff Clark was born at Bronxville, NY. After early stops in New York radio he moved to Philadelphia, PA, where he became the host of a local music show called "Bandstand." The show went national in 1957, and soon Clark was talking to every teenager in America. His easygoing style and youthful, clean-cut look became a constant in American popular culture. As the entrepreneur of a successful television production company and as the host of innumerable music shows, awards ceremonies and prime-time specials, Clark became the engaging emcee to four decades of entertainment culture. "America's Oldest Teenager" died Apr 18, 2012, at Santa Monica, CA.

CLEMENS, SAMUEL LANGHORNE (MARK TWAIN): BIRTH ANNIVERSARY. Nov 30, 1835. Celebrated American author, whose books include *The Adventures of Tom Sawyer, The Adventures of Huckleberry Finn* and *The Prince and the Pauper.* Born at Florida, MO, Twain is quoted as saying, "I came in with Halley's Comet in 1835. It is coming again next year, and I expect to go out with it." He did. Twain died at Redding, CT, Apr 21, 1910 (just one day after Halley's Comet perihelion).

COMPUTER SECURITY DAY. Nov 30. The use of computers and the concern for security increase daily. This annual observance, which began in 1988, reminds people to protect their computers, programs and data at home and at work. More than 1,500 companies participate worldwide. For info: Assn for Computer Security Day, 5014 Rodman Rd, Bethesda, MD 20816. Phone: (301) 229-2346. E-mail: computer_security_day@acm.org. Web: www.computersecurityday.com.

HANDEL'S MESSIAH SING-ALONG. Nov 30. Richard Nixon Library and Birthplace, Yorba Linda, CA. Audience members are invited to join in singing the choruses of this beloved oratorio in the beautiful East Room of the Nixon Library. Performers include a master choir, orchestra and soloists. Seventeenth-century costumes are encouraged. Free. Annually, the Sunday following Thanksgivng Day. Est attendance: 1,500. For info: Yorba Linda Arts Alliance, PO Box 1037, Yorba Linda, CA 92885. Phone: (714) 996-1960. E-mail: messiahsing@aol.com. Web: www.messiahsing.org.

HOFFMAN, ABBOT (ABBIE): BIRTH ANNIVERSARY. Nov 30, 1936. Political activist, born at Worcester, MA, Abbie Hoffman rose to prominence during the 1968 Democratic National Convention at Chicago, IL, and at his subsequent trial as a member of the Chicago Seven, a group of radicals accused of conspiring to disrupt the convention. Combining politics and street theater was a Hoffman trait. During the 1967 march on the Pentagon, he sought a permit to allow 1,200 demonstrators to encircle and levitate the military headquarters in an attempt to end the war in Vietnam. He, Jerry Rubin and Paul Krassner conceived the Yippie movement as a youth festival of life to run concurrently with the 1968 convention. Hoffman fled underground in 1974 to avoid trial on cocaine-possession charges and remained a fugitive for nearly seven years. Surrendering to authorities in 1980, he served his sentence in a work-release program. Hoffman died Apr 12, 1989, at New Hope, PA.

JOHN F. KENNEDY DAY IN MASSACHUSETTS. Nov 30. Annually, the last Sunday in November.

***THE JOY OF COOKING* PUBLISHED: ANNIVERSARY.** Nov 30, 1931. America's favorite all-purpose cookbook was self-published on this date by Irma Rombauer (1877–1962). Rombauer was a comforting voice for cooks during the Depression, and the book grew into an institution. The first commercial edition of the book appeared in 1936, and it offered a revolutionary "action format" (chronologically ordered ingredients followed by instructions) now commonplace in cookbooks. The numerous editions overseen by Rombauer and later her daughter and grandson sold more than 14 million copies.

NETHERLANDS: MIDWINTER HORN BLOWING. Nov 30–Jan 6, 2015. Twente and several other areas in the Netherlands. Midwinter horn blowing, folkloric custom of announcing the birth of Christ, begins with Advent and continues until Epiphany (Jan 6) of the following year.

NEWBORN HEART DEFECT SCREENING DAY. Nov 30. Each year, thousands of babies go home from the hospital with undetected congenital heart defects. This day seeks to increase awareness of congenital heart defect screening, also called pulse oximetry screening, of newborns. Annually, Nov 30. For info: Newborn Heart Defect Screening. Web: www.babyheartscreening.com.

PARKS, GORDON: BIRTH ANNIVERSARY. Nov 30, 1912. Award-winning and groundbreaking photojournalist and filmmaker, Parks was born the youngest of 15 children to a poor family at Fort Scott, KS. His photography career encompassed glamorous fashion shoots for *Vogue*, as well as portraits of world leaders and searing photo essays for *Life*, where he was that magazine's first black staff photographer. Parks became the first major black Hollywood film director, with such important works as *The Learning Tree* and *Shaft*. He died Mar 7, 2006, at New York, NY.

PHILIPPINES: BONIFACIO DAY. Nov 30. Also known as National Heroes' Day. Commemorates birth of Andres Bonifacio, leader of the 1896 revolt against Spain. Bonifacio was born in 1863.

RADIOLOGICAL SOCIETY OF NORTH AMERICA SCIENTIFIC ASSEMBLY AND ANNUAL MEETING. Nov 30–Dec 5. McCormick Place, Chicago, IL. 100th annual. Est attendance: 62,000. For info: Radiological Society of North America, 820 Jorie Blvd, Oak Brook, IL 60523-2251. Phone: (630) 571-2670. Fax: (630) 571-7837. Web: www.rsna.org.

SAINT ANDREW'S DAY. Nov 30. Feast day of the apostle and martyr Andrew, who died about AD 60. Patron saint of Scotland.

SIDNEY, PHILIP: BIRTH ANNIVERSARY. Nov 30, 1554. English poet, statesman and soldier born at Penshurst, Kent, England. Best known of his poems is *Arcadia* (1580). Mortally wounded as he led an English detachment aiding the Dutch near Zutphen, Netherlands, Sept 22, 1586, Sidney gave his water bottle to another dying soldier with the words, "Thy necessity is yet greater than mine." He died at Arnhem, Oct 17, 1586, and all England mourned his death.

STATUE OF RAMSES II UNEARTHED: ANNIVERSARY. Nov 30, 1991. Egyptian construction workers in the ancient provincial town of Akhimim, 300 miles south of Cairo, unearthed a statue of Ramses II. Akhimim was an important provincial district that included the city of Ipu, a mecca for worshippers of the fertility god Min. The statue was uncovered during an excavation to prepare a foundation for a post office. An additional statue was uncovered 33 feet away, but the identity of its subject was unknown.

STAY HOME BECAUSE YOU'RE WELL DAY. Nov 30. So we can call in "well," instead of faking illness, and stay home from work. (©2006 by WH.) For info: Thomas & Ruth Roy, Wellcat Holidays, 2418 Long Ln, Lebanon, PA 17046. Phone: (717) 279-0184. E-mail: info@wellcat.com. Web: www.wellcat.com.

SWIFT, JONATHAN: BIRTH ANNIVERSARY. Nov 30, 1667. (Old Style date.) Clergyman and satirist born at Dublin, Ireland. Died there Oct 19, 1745 (OS). Author of *Gulliver's Travels*. "I never saw, heard, nor read," Swift wrote in *Thoughts on Religion*, "that the clergy were beloved in any nation where Christianity was the religion of the country. Nothing can render them popular but some degree of persecution."

***THRILLER* RELEASED: ANNIVERSARY.** Nov 30, 1982. Michael Jackson's sixth studio album is one of the most popular and important albums of all time, charting seven songs in the Top Ten: "Wanna Be Startin' Somethin'," "The Girl Is Mine," "Thriller," "Beat It," "Billie Jean," "Human Nature" and "P.Y.T. (Pretty Young Thing)." It broke the pop charts wide open for black artists, who had often been relegated to R&B charts, and simultaneously gave musical forms like R&B and funk a wider audience while experimenting with bold genre crossovers in its songwriting and production. *Thriller* stayed on the charts for three years and has sold more than 110 million copies. On May 14, 2008, the album was added to the Library of Congress's National Recording Registry.

WINTER WAR: 75th ANNIVERSARY. Nov 30, 1939–Mar 13, 1940. The Soviet Union invaded Finland on Nov 30, 1939, but weakened and demoralized by Stalin's purges, the Red Army was unable to conquer Finland, despite massive numerical superiority. Throughout the bitterly cold winter, the Finns waged a guerrilla-style defense that included the use of Molotov cocktails. The Treaty of Moscow ended hostilities, with the Finns ceding 11 percent of their territory to the Soviets but retaining their sovereignty. The Soviet Union was expelled from the League of Nations over the invasion.

BIRTHDAYS TODAY

Richard Burr, 59, US Senator (R, North Carolina), born Charlottesville, VA, Nov 30, 1955.

Joan Ganz Cooney, 85, founder of the Children's Television Workshop and creator of "Sesame Street," born Phoenix, AZ, Nov 30, 1929.

Kaley Cuoco, 29, actress ("The Big Bang Theory," "8 Simple Rules"), born Camarillo, CA, Nov 30, 1985.

Elisha Cuthbert, 32, actress ("24," *The Girl Next Door*), born Calgary, AB, Canada, Nov 30, 1982.

Jessalyn Gilsig, 43, actress ("Glee," "Heroes," "Friday Night Lights"), born Montreal, QC, Canada, Nov 30, 1971.

Robert Guillaume, 87, actor ("Soap," "Benson"), born St. Louis, MO, Nov 30, 1927.

Billy Idol, 59, singer, songwriter, born William Michael Albert Broad at Surrey, England, Nov 30, 1955.

Vincent Edward "Bo" Jackson, 52, former baseball player, former football player, born Bessemer, AL, Nov 30, 1962.

G. Gordon Liddy, 84, convicted Watergate coconspirator, radio talk show host, born New York, NY, Nov 30, 1930.

David Mamet, 67, dramatist (*American Buffalo, Oleanna, Things Change*), born Chicago, IL, Nov 30, 1947.

Colin Mochrie, 57, comedian, actor ("Whose Line Is It Anyway?"), born Ayrshire, Scotland, Nov 30, 1957.

Sandra Oh, 44, actress (*Under the Tuscan Sun, Sideways*, "Grey's Anatomy"), born Nepean, ON, Canada, Nov 30, 1970.

Mandy Patinkin, 62, actor (Tony for *Evita*; *Sunday in the Park with George*, "Chicago Hope"), born Chicago, IL, Nov 30, 1952.

Ivan "Pudge" Rodriguez, 43, former baseball player, born Vega Baja, Puerto Rico, Nov 30, 1971.

Amy Ryan, 45, actress ("The Wire," *Gone Baby Gone*), born Queens, NY, Nov 30, 1969.

Ridley Scott, 77, director (*Prometheus, Alien, Blade Runner, Gladiator*), born Northumberland, England, Nov 30, 1937.

Ben Stiller, 49, actor, director (*Starsky & Hutch, Meet the Parents, Reality Bites*), born New York, NY, Nov 30, 1965.

Noel Paul Stookey, 77, singer, songwriter (Peter, Paul and Mary), born Baltimore, MD, Nov 30, 1937.

Allison Williams, 27, actress ("Girls," "The Mindy Project"), born New Canaan, CT, Nov 30, 1987.

Efrem Zimbalist, Jr, 91, actor ("The F.B.I.," *Airport*), born New York, NY, Nov 30, 1923.

✦ December ✦

December 1 — Monday

DAY 335 **30 REMAINING**

BASKETBALL CREATED: ANNIVERSARY. Dec 1, 1891. James Naismith was a teacher of physical education at the International YMCA Training School at Springfield, MA. To create an indoor sport that could be played during the winter months, he nailed up peach baskets at opposite ends of the gym and gave students soccer balls to toss into them. Thus was born the game of basketball.

BIFOCALS AT THE MONITOR LIBERATION DAY. Dec 1. Our hearts fill with compassion today for coworkers stuck wearing bifocals at the PC. Shed a tear as their heads bob up and down, in and out, trying to read the monitor, trying to decide which set of lenses to use. Annually, Dec 1. (©2006 by WH.) For info: Thomas & Ruth Roy, Wellcat Holidays, 2418 Long Ln, Lebanon, PA 17046. Phone: (717) 279-0184. E-mail: info@wellcat.com. Web: www.wellcat.com.

BINGO'S BIRTHDAY MONTH. Dec 1–31. To celebrate the innovation and manufacture of the game of Bingo in 1929 by Edwin S. Lowe. Bingo has grown into a five-billion-dollar-a-year charitable fund-raiser. For info: Tara Snowden, Pres, Bingo Bugle, Inc, Box 527, Vashon, WA 98070. Phone: (800) 327-6437 or (206) 463-5656. E-mail: tara@bingobugle.com.

CANADA: YUKON ORDER OF PIONEERS: ANNIVERSARY. Dec 1, 1894. The Yukon Order of Pioneers held its founding meeting on this date at Fortymile, Yukon. It began as a vigilante police force to deter claim jumping and later inaugurated Discovery Day (Aug 17), a statutory Yukon holiday commemorating the discovery of gold on Bonanza Creek in 1896.

CENTRAL AFRICAN REPUBLIC: NATIONAL DAY OBSERVED. Dec 1. Commemorates Proclamation of the Republic on Dec 1, 1958. Usually observed on the first Monday in December.

CHRISTMAS IN THE VILLAGES. Dec 1–31. Van Buren County, IA. Event features a tour of homes, Festival of Trees, bake sales, Santa visits, holiday dinners, lighting displays, soup suppers and the natural beauty of the season that is found throughout the county. Est attendance: 5,000. For info: Villages of Van Buren, Inc, PO Box 9, Keosauqua, IA 52565. Phone: (800) 868-7822. Fax: (319) 293-7116. E-mail: info@villagesofvanburen.com. Web: www.villagesofvanburen.com.

CHRISTMAS NEW ORLEANS STYLE. Dec 1–31. New Orleans, LA. Cathedral Christmas concerts, caroling in Jackson Square, holiday parades with Papa Noel, cooking demonstrations, Celebration in the Oaks, Christmas Day Concert, tours of 19th-century houses in holiday dress, Reveillon dinners and Papa Noel hotel rates. For info: French Quarter Festivals, Inc, 400 N Peters St, #205, New Orleans, LA 70130. Phone: (800) 673-5725 or (504) 522-5730. E-mail: info@fqfi.org. Web: www.fqfi.org.

CIVIL AIR PATROL FOUNDED: ANNIVERSARY. Dec 1, 1941. The Director of Civilian Defense, former New York Mayor Fiorello H. LaGuardia, signed a formal order creating the Civil Air Patrol (CAP), a US Air Force Auxiliary. The CAP has a three-part mission: to provide an aerospace education program, a CAP cadet program and an emergency services program. For info: Civil Air Patrol, 105 S Hansell St, Maxwell AFB, AL 36112-6332. Phone: (205) 953-5463.

COOKIE EXCHANGE WEEK. Dec 1–5. This week celebrates a delicious holiday tradition. Host a cookie exchange party this week and try new recipes or share personal favorites with others. Easy ideas, recipes, inspiration and instruction are availabe at the Wilton website. Other Wilton-sponsored activities include live web chats, photo exchanges and contests. Annually, the first week in December. For info: Wilton, 2240 W 75th St, Woodridge, IL 60517. Phone: (630) 810-2221. E-mail: Vfarrasso@wilton.com. Web: www.wilton.com.

CYBER MONDAY. Dec 1. Traditional beginning of the online Christmas shopping season—when consumers return to work and start ordering online. The Monday after Thanksgiving.

DAY WITH(OUT) ART. Dec 1. An international day of action and mourning in response to the AIDS crisis. Visual AIDS uses art to fight AIDS by provoking dialogue, supporting artists living with HIV/AIDS and preserving a legacy—because AIDS is not over. For info: Visual AIDS, 526 W 26th St, #510, New York, NY 10001. Phone: (212) 627-9855. Fax: (212) 627-9815. E-mail: info@visualAIDS.org. Web: www.visualAIDS.org.

ICELAND: UNIVERSITY STUDENTS' CELEBRATION: ANNIVERSARY. Dec 1, 1918. Marks the day in 1918 when Iceland became an independent state from Denmark (but still remained under the king of Denmark).

KIROV ASSASSINATION AND THE GREAT PURGE: 80th ANNIVERSARY. Dec 1, 1934. Sergei Mironovich Kirov, party boss and member of the Politburo, was shot dead at Communist Party headquarters in Leningrad by Leonid Nikolayev, a disgruntled junior party member. Some historians believe the assassination was ordered by Josef Stalin in order to eliminate the powerful and independent Kirov. Stalin publicly blamed the Kirov assassination on a larger anti-Stalinist conspiracy and used the assassination as a pretext to launch what became known as The Great Purge, in which Stalin eliminated virtually all of his political opponents. More than 700,000 people thought to be dangerous to the regime were executed, and hundreds of thousands more were sent to the gulags.

MARTIN, MARY: BIRTH ANNIVERSARY. Dec 1, 1913. Called "America's favorite leading lady of musical comedy," actress Mary Virginia Martin was born at Weatherford, TX. Discovered while singing at the Trocadero club in Los Angeles, CA, Martin immediately triumphed in her first appearance on Broadway in Cole Porter's *Leave It to Me* (1938). She is best known for her title role in the Broadway (1954–55) and television productions of *Peter Pan*. She won Tony Awards for her starring roles in the stage productions of *South Pacific*, *Peter Pan* and *The Sound of Music* (in which she originated the role of Maria von Trapp). She died Nov 3, 1990, at Rancho Mirage, CA.

MOORE, JULIA A. DAVIS: BIRTH ANNIVERSARY. Dec 1, 1847. Julia Moore, known as the "Sweet Singer of Michigan," was born in a log cabin at Plainfield, MI. A writer of homely verse and ballads, Moore enjoyed remarkable popularity and gave many public readings before realizing that her public appearances were occasions for laughter and ridicule. Her poems were said to be "so bad, her subjects so morbid and her naïveté so genuine" that they were actually gems of humorous genius. At her final public appearance she told her audience: "You people paid 50 cents to see a fool, but I got 50 dollars to look at a house full of fools." Moore died June 17, 1920, near Manton, MI.

NAIA MEN'S SOCCER NATIONAL CHAMPIONSHIP. Dec 1–6. Site TBD. 55th annual. A 32-team field competes for the national championship (after 16 opening round matches on Nov 22 at campus sites). For info: Natl Assn of Intercollegiate Athletics, 1200 Grand Blvd, Kansas City, MO 64106. E-mail: jford@naia.org. Web: www.naia.org.

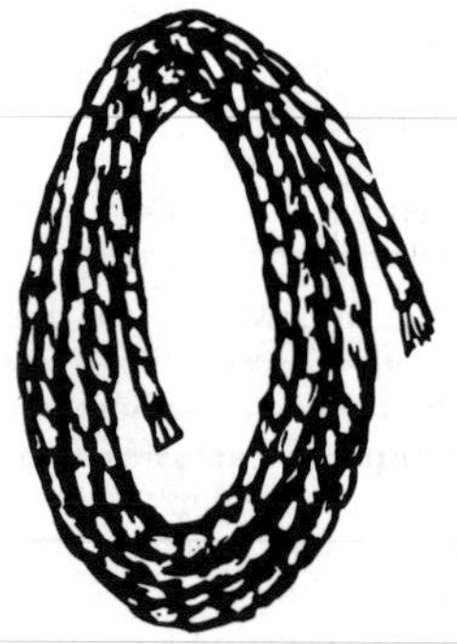

NAIA WOMEN'S SOCCER NATIONAL CHAMPIONSHIP. Dec 1–6. Site TBD. 31st annual. A 32-team field competes for the national championship at an opening round site—the final 16 go to the championship. For info: Natl Assn of Intercollegiate Athletics, 1200 Grand Blvd, Kansas City, MO 64106. E-mail: eolson@naia.org. Web: www.naia.org.

✦NATIONAL IMPAIRED DRIVING PREVENTION MONTH. Dec 1–31.

NATIONAL WRITE A BUSINESS PLAN MONTH. Dec 1–31. Time to get out of your cubicle and turn your business ideas into reality! Use the last month of the year to craft a business plan—and get a great start in the new year to come. For info: Nationwide Business Plans, LLC, 4898 S Fresno St, Chandler, AZ 85249. Fax: (866) 220-9542. E-mail: jocelynsaccuci@gmail.com.

OPERATION SANTA PAWS. Dec 1–19. During the holiday season extra help is needed for abused and abandoned animals in the care of local animal shelters. One grassroots organization, Operation Santa Paws, is helping by spearheading a canine/feline toy/treat drive to benefit less-fortunate pets this season. Animal lovers are encouraged to purchase a new dog or cat toy or treat or to supply food that will be delivered in time for Christmas to local shelters and rescue organizations. For info: Justin Rudd. Phone: (562) 439-3316. E-mail: justin@justinrudd.com. Web: www.santapaws.info.

***PLAYBOY* FIRST PUBLISHED: ANNIVERSARY.** Dec 1, 1953. *Playboy* magazine was launched at Chicago, IL, by publisher Hugh Hefner.

PORTUGAL: INDEPENDENCE DAY. Dec 1. Public holiday. Became independent of Spain in 1640.

PRYOR, RICHARD: BIRTH ANNIVERSARY. Dec 1, 1940. African-American comedian and actor, born at Peoria, IL, who began performing at age seven. He was known for his use of profanity, and his humor was frequently based on racial stereotypes. Extremely successful as a stand-up, Pryor won five Grammy Awards for his comedy albums, and he also wrote or starred in any number of classic comedy films, including *Stir Crazy, Silver Streak* and *Car Wash*. His drug problems were well documented in his comedy act, and he struggled with multiple sclerosis late in his life. He died at Encino, CA, Dec 10, 2005.

RAWLS, LOU: BIRTH ANNIVERSARY. Dec 1, 1933. Born at Chicago, IL, Rawls was the popular singer with the unmistakably smooth voice—"sweet as sugar, soft as velvet, strong as steel, smooth as butter"—at home equally in gospel, blues, jazz, soul and pop. The recipient of three Grammys (with 13 nominations) and the creator of 60 albums, later in life Rawls became an indefatigable supporter of humanitarian causes, most famously the United Negro College Fund. Rawls died Jan 6, 2006, at Los Angeles, CA.

December 2014

S	M	T	W	T	F	S
	1	2	3	4	5	6
7	8	9	10	11	12	13
14	15	16	17	18	19	20
21	22	23	24	25	26	27
28	29	30	31			

ROMANIA: NATIONAL DAY. Dec 1. National holiday. Marks unification of Romania and Transylvania in 1918 and the overthrow of the Communist regime in 1989.

ROSA PARKS DAY: ANNIVERSARY OF ARREST. Dec 1, 1955. Anniversary of the arrest of Rosa Parks, at Montgomery, AL, for refusing to give up her seat and move to the back of a municipal bus. Her arrest triggered a yearlong boycott of the city bus system and led to legal actions that ended racial segregation on municipal buses throughout the southern US. The event has been called the birth of the modern civil rights movement. Rosa McCauley Parks was born at Tuskegee, AL, Feb 4, 1913.

SAFE TOYS AND GIFTS MONTH. Dec 1–31. What are the most dangerous types of toys to children's eyesight? Tips on how to choose age-appropriate, safe toys will be distributed. For info: Prevent Blindness America®, 211 W Wacker Dr, Ste 1700, Chicago, IL 60606. Phone: (800) 331-2020. E-mail: info@preventblindness.org. Web: www.preventblindness.org.

STOUT, REX: BIRTH ANNIVERSARY. Dec 1, 1886. Mystery author Rex Todhunter Stout, born at Noblesville, IN, created two of the most enduring characters in the mystery genre: Nero Wolfe and his feisty sidekick Archie Goodwin. Stout received the highest honor of the mystery world when the Mystery Writers of America gave him their Grand Master Award in 1959. Stout died Oct 27, 1975, at Danbury, CT.

TUSSAUD, MARIE GROSHOLTZ: BIRTH ANNIVERSARY. Dec 1, 1761. Born Anna Maria Grosholtz at Strasbourg, France, Tussaud was a wax artist who created models of royalty and celebrities. When the French Revolution erupted, she survived by using her craft to satisfy the populace's desire to see likenesses of the executed: she made death masks using corpses as models. Married to François Tussaud in 1795, she went to England in 1802 with her waxworks and relics of the Revolution in a traveling show. In 1835, she established a permanent base at Baker Street, London. Tussaud was a savvy marketer, creating advertising campaigns and innovative exhibits such as the ghoulish Chamber of Horrors, which depicted famous killers. She died at London on Apr 15, 1850, but her wax museum empire—now in many cities around the globe—remains.

UNITED NATIONS: WORLD AIDS DAY. Dec 1. In 1988 the World Health Organization of the UN declared Dec 1 as World AIDS Day, an international day of awareness and education about AIDS. The WHO is the leader in global direction and coordination of AIDS prevention, control, research and education. A program called UN-AIDS was created to bring together the skills and expertise of the World Bank, UNDP, UNESCO, UNICEF, UNFPA and the WHO to strengthen and expand national capacities to respond to the pandemic. For info: United Nations, Dept of Public Info, New York, NY 10017. Web: www.un.org.

✦WORLD AIDS DAY. Dec 1.

WORLDWIDE FOOD SERVICE SAFETY MONTH. Dec 1–31. This month is geared toward professional food service safety. However, it also reminds cooks in homes all around the world to handle food safely. People working with food need to buy, store, prepare, serve and keep prepared food properly. Always remember to handle food safely both professionally and at home! For info: Harold LeBouf. Phone: (978) 632-8616 or (508) 243-3842. E-mail: info@SweetandSavoryFoodConcessions.com. Web: www.SweetandSavoryFoodConcessions.com.

YAMASAKI, MINORU: BIRTH ANNIVERSARY. Dec 1, 1912. American architect born at Seattle, WA. In 1951 he designed the St. Louis Airport and in 1955 the Pruitt-Igoe public housing project (also in St. Louis). Yamasaki's most famous buildings were the twin towers of the World Trade Center in New York City, which he designed along with Emery Roth starting in 1962. These buildings changed the Manhattan skyline. Yamasaki's original plan called for two 94-story buildings, but the developer insisted that they contain 10 million square feet of office space, so the buildings were expanded to 110 stories, which made them the tallest buildings in the world. These New York icons were destroyed by terrorists on Sept 11, 2001. Yamasaki died at Detroit, MI, Feb 7, 1986.

BIRTHDAYS TODAY

Woody Allen, 79, filmmaker (Oscar for *Annie Hall*; *Midnight in Paris, Manhattan, Hannah and Her Sisters*), actor, born Allen Stewart Konigsberg at Brooklyn, NY, Dec 1, 1935.

Carol Alt, 54, model, born New York, NY, Dec 1, 1960.

Nestor Carbonell, 47, actor (*The Dark Knight*, "Lost," "Suddenly Susan," "The Tick"), born New York, NY, Dec 1, 1967.

Bette Midler, 69, singer, actress (*Beaches, For the Boys, Down and Out in Beverly Hills*), born Paterson, NJ, Dec 1, 1945.

Reggie Sanders, 47, former baseball player, born Florence, SC, Dec 1, 1967.

Lee Buck Trevino, 75, golfer, born Dallas, TX, Dec 1, 1939.

Larry Walker, 48, former baseball player, born Maple Ridge, BC, Canada, Dec 1, 1966.

Treat Williams, 62, actor ("Everwood," *127 Hours, Hair*), born Rowayton, CT, Dec 1, 1952.

December 2 — Tuesday

DAY 336 **29 REMAINING**

ARTIFICIAL HEART TRANSPLANT: ANNIVERSARY. Dec 2, 1982. Barney C. Clark, 61, became the first recipient of a permanent artificial heart. The operation was performed at the University of Utah Medical Center at Salt Lake City. Near death at the time of the operation, Clark survived almost 112 days after the implantation. He died Mar 23, 1983.

BELL, JOSEPH: BIRTH ANNIVERSARY. Dec 2, 1837. Best known today as the inspiration for the fictional character Sherlock Holmes, Joseph Bell in his time was a well-respected physician and professor at the University of Edinburgh. Arthur Conan Doyle met Bell at the University of Edinburgh's medical school as a student and witnessed Bell's amazing ability to deduct facts about all aspects of a patient's life. Bell was also Queen Victoria's physician whenever she came to Scotland. Bell died in Edinburgh on Oct 4, 1911.

BROWN, JOHN: EXECUTION ANNIVERSARY. Dec 2, 1859. Abolitionist leader who is remembered for his raid on the US Arsenal at Harpers Ferry. Brown was hanged for treason at Charles Town, WV.

CALLAS, MARIA: BIRTH ANNIVERSARY. Dec 2, 1923. Soprano born Maria Anna Sofia Cecilia Kalogeropoulos to Greek immigrant parents at New York, NY. One of the most prominent artists of the 20th century, "La Divina" led the postwar revival of bel canto operas. A dramatic persona on and off stage, Callas epitomized the diva in popular culture. "To me, the art of music is magnificent, and I cannot bear to see it treated in a shabby way," she once stated. Callas died at Paris, France, Sept 16, 1977.

ENGLAND: WALTER PLINGE DAY. Dec 2. A day to recognize Walter Plinge, said to have been a London pub landlord in 1900. His generosity to actors led to the use of his name as an actor in play programs to conceal the fact that an actor was playing more than one role. See also: "George Spelvin Day" (Nov 15) for US equivalent.

ENRON FILES FOR BANKRUPTCY: ANNIVERSARY. Dec 2, 2001. The once high-flying Houston, TX, energy services company filed for bankruptcy on this date. Subsequent investigations revealed questionable accounting practices and unethical dealings, to the extent that "Enron" became the buzzword for corporate malfeasance of the late 1990s and into the 21st century. Many other corporations were found to have questionable financial statements after the Enron scandal (in which thousands of employees lost their jobs and retirement savings), and investor confidence in the US stock market was shaken. Federal Reserve chairman Alan Greenspan, in a July 16, 2002, report to the Senate Banking Committee, indicted such corporate misbehavior: "An infectious greed seemed to grip much of our business community [in the 1990s]."

FIRST SELF-SUSTAINING NUCLEAR CHAIN REACTION: ANNIVERSARY. Dec 2, 1942. Physicist Enrico Fermi led a team of scientists at the University of Chicago in producing the first controlled, self-sustaining nuclear chain reaction. Their first simple nuclear reactor was built under the stands of the university's football stadium.

GIVING TUESDAY. Dec 2. 3rd annual. A national day of giving to kick off the giving season on the Tuesday following Thanksgiving, Black Friday and Cyber Monday. It celebrates and encourages charitable activities that support nonprofit organizations. Created by 92Y in partnership with the United Nations Foundation. For info: 92Y, 1395 Lexington Ave, New York, NY 10128. Phone: (212) 415-5433. Web: www.givingtuesday.org.

"IMUS IN THE MORNING" RADIO PREMIERE: ANNIVERSARY. Dec 2, 1971. Award-winning radio broadcaster Don Imus signed on to New York City's WNBC on this date. The show offered cantankerous takes on current affairs. On Apr 12, 2007, CBS dropped the show due to racial slurs made by Imus. The show reemerged and is currently broadcast through Citadel Media and simulcast on TV on the Fox Business Network.

LAOS: NATIONAL DAY. Dec 2. National holiday commemorating declaration of the republic in 1975.

McCARTHY SILENCED BY SENATE: 60th ANNIVERSARY. Dec 2, 1954. On Feb 9, 1950, Joseph McCarthy, a relatively obscure senator from Wisconsin, announced during a speech in Wheeling, WV, that he had a list of Communists in the State Department. Over the next two years he made increasingly sensational charges and in 1953 McCarthyism reached its height as he held Senate hearings in which he bullied defendants. In 1954 McCarthy's tyranny was exposed in televised hearings during which he took on the Army, and on Dec 2, 1954, the Senate voted to censure him. McCarthy died May 2, 1957.

MONROE DOCTRINE: ANNIVERSARY. Dec 2, 1823. President James Monroe, in his annual message to Congress, enunciated the doctrine that bears his name and that was long hailed as a statement of US policy: "In the wars of the European powers in matters relating to themselves we have never taken any part. . . . We should consider any attempt on their part to extend their system to any portion of this hemisphere as dangerous to our peace and safety."

NAIA WOMEN'S NATIONAL VOLLEYBALL CHAMPIONSHIP. Dec 2–6. Sioux City, IA. 35th annual. 36 teams qualify. 24 teams play in opening-round pairings at campus sites. 12 winners join 12 byes at final site for 24-team pool-play tournament to determine the national champion. Est attendance: 3,000. For info: Natl Assn of Intercollegiate Athletics, 1200 Grand Blvd, Kansas City, MO 64106. E-mail: jadams@naia.org. Web: www.naia.org.

NATIONAL PARKS ESTABLISHED IN ALASKA: ANNIVERSARY. Dec 2, 1980. Eight national parks were established in Alaska on this date. Mount McKinley National Park, which was established Feb 26, 1917, and Denali National Monument, which was proclaimed Dec 1, 1978, were combined as Denali National Park and Preserve. Gates of the Arctic National Monument, proclaimed Dec 1, 1978; Glacier Bay National Monument, proclaimed Feb 25, 1925; and Katmai National Monument, proclaimed Sept 24, 1918, were established as national parks and preserves. Kenai Fjords National Monument, proclaimed Dec 1, 1978, and Kobuk Valley National Monument, proclaimed Dec 1, 1978, were established as national parks. Lake Clark National Monument, proclaimed Dec 1, 1978, and Wrangell–St. Elias National Monument, proclaimed Dec 1, 1978, were established as national parks and preserves. For info: www.nps.gov.

ROCKEFELLER CENTER CHRISTMAS TREE: ANNUAL LIGHTING. Dec 2 (tentative). New York, NY. Lighting of the huge Christmas tree in Rockefeller Center signals the opening of the holiday season at New York City. More than 30,000 lights are strung on five miles of electric wire. In 1933 the first formal tree lighting ceremony took place with 700 lights. Date is usually the Tuesday or Wednesday after Thanksgiving.

SAFETY RAZOR PATENTED: ANNIVERSARY. Dec 2, 1901. American King Camp Gillette designed the first razor with disposable blades. Up until this time, men shaved with a straight-edge razor that they sharpened on a leather strap.

SEURAT, GEORGES: BIRTH ANNIVERSARY. Dec 2, 1859. French Neo-Impressionist painter born at Paris, France. Died there Mar 29, 1891. Seurat is known for his style of painting with small spots of color, called *pointillism*, as in *Sunday Afternoon on the Island of Grand Jatte.*

SPECIAL EDUCATION DAY. Dec 2. Celebrate the anniversary of the first US special education law—Dec 2, 1975. A time to reflect and move forward. Where were we when President Ford signed the groundbreaking legislation? Where are we now? And where do we need to be tomorrow? A day to honor progress, dialogue about challenges we face and consider reforms for the future of educating all children. For info: Special Education Day Committee (SPEDCO). E-mail: info@specialeducationday.com. Web: www.specialeducationday.com.

UNITED ARAB EMIRATES: NATIONAL DAY. Dec 2. Anniversary of the day in 1971 when a federation of seven sheikdoms known as the Trucial States declared independence from the UK and became known as the United Arab Emirates.

UNITED NATIONS: INTERNATIONAL DAY FOR THE ABOLITION OF SLAVERY. Dec 2. Recalls the date of adoption by the General Assembly in 1949 of the Convention for the Suppression of the Traffic in Persons and the Exploitation of Others. For info: United Nations, Dept of Public Info, New York, NY 10017. Web: www.un.org.

WALSTON, RAY: 100th BIRTH ANNIVERSARY. Dec 2, 1914. Comic character actor, born at New Orleans, LA (some sources say in 1919), best known for playing Applegate (the Devil) in the orginal stage production and later film version of *Damn Yankees* and Uncle Martin O'Hara, the title character in the popular TV series "My Favorite Martian" (1963–66). Walston, who won a Tony Award for Best Actor in *Damn Yankees*, died Jan 1, 2001, at Beverly Hills, CA.

BIRTHDAYS TODAY

T. Coraghessan Boyle, 66, author (*Riven Rock, The Tortilla Curtain*), born Peekskill, NY, Dec 2, 1948.

Dan Butler, 60, actor ("Frasier"), born Huntington, IN, Dec 2, 1954.

Dennis Christopher, 59, actor (*Sweet Dreams, Breaking Away*), born Philadelphia, PA, Dec 2, 1955.

Brendan Coyle, 51, actor ("Downton Abbey," "Lark Rise to Candleford"), born Corby, Northamptonshire, England, Dec 2, 1963.

Cathy Lee Crosby, 66, actress ("That's Incredible," *Coach*), born Los Angeles, CA, Dec 2, 1948.

Nelly Furtado, 36, singer, born Victoria, BC, Canada, Dec 2, 1978.

Randy Gardner, 56, former figure skater, choreographer, born Marina del Rey, CA, Dec 2, 1958.

Julie Harris, 89, actress (*East of Eden, The Member of the Wedding*), born Grosse Pointe, MI, Dec 2, 1925.

December 2014	S	M	T	W	T	F	S
		1	2	3	4	5	6
	7	8	9	10	11	12	13
	14	15	16	17	18	19	20
	21	22	23	24	25	26	27
	28	29	30	31			

Lucy Liu, 47, actress ("Elementary," "Ally McBeal," *Charlie's Angels*), born Queens, NY, Dec 2, 1967.

Ann Patchett, 51, author (*Bel Canto, State of Wonder*), born Los Angeles, CA, Dec 2, 1963.

Stone Phillips, 60, anchor ("Dateline," "20/20"), born Texas City, TX, Dec 2, 1954.

Harry Reid, 75, US Senator (D, Nevada), born Searchlight, NV, Dec 2, 1939.

Aaron Rodgers, 31, football player, born Chico, CA, Dec 2, 1983.

Rick Scott, 62, Governor of Florida (R), born Bloomington, IL, Dec 2, 1952.

Monica Seles, 41, Hall of Fame tennis player, born Novi Sad, Yugoslavia (now Serbia), Dec 2, 1973.

Britney Spears, 33, singer, born Kentwood, LA, Dec 2, 1981.

William Wegman, 71, artist, photographer, born Holyoke, MA, Dec 2, 1943.

December 3 — Wednesday

DAY 337 **28 REMAINING**

BHOPAL POISON GAS DISASTER: 30th ANNIVERSARY. Dec 3, 1984. At Bhopal, India, a leak of deadly gas (methyl isocyanate) at a Union Carbide Corp plant killed more than 4,000 persons and injured more than 200,000 in the world's worst industrial accident.

CHRISTMAS ON THE RIVER. Dec 3–6. Demopolis, AL. Fun with arts and crafts, children's parade, Alabama State Barbecue Cook-Off and a riverboat parade. Est attendance: 40,000. For info: Demopolis Area Chamber of Commerce, PO Box 667, Demopolis, AL 36732. Phone: (334) 289-0270. Fax: (334) 289-0216. E-mail: demopchamber@yahoo.com. Web: www.demopolischamber.com.

CLERC-GALLAUDET WEEK. Dec 3–9. Week in which to celebrate the birth anniversaries of two pioneers of Deaf Education in America who were born in December: Laurent Clerc (Dec 26, 1785) and Thomas Hopkins Gallaudet (Dec 10, 1787). In 1816, Gallaudet met reknowned deaf teacher Clerc in Paris, France, and brought him to America. The week's celebrations begin Dec 3, a day that the United Nations annually proclaims (since 1992) as International Day of Persons with Disabilities. The White House has also proclaimed this day since 2009. For info: Library for Deaf Action, 2930 Craiglawn Rd, Silver Spring, MD 20904-1816. E-mail: ahagemeyer@gmail.com. Web: www.folda.net.

CONRAD, JOSEPH: BIRTH ANNIVERSARY. Dec 3, 1857. English novelist, born Józef Korzeniowski to Polish parents at Berdichev in the Ukraine. He learned English as a sailor on British ships. Author of *Lord Jim* and *Heart of Darkness*, among others. Died Aug 3, 1924, at Bishopsbourne, Kent, England.

FIRST HEART TRANSPLANT: ANNIVERSARY. Dec 3, 1967. Dr. Christiaan Barnard, a South African surgeon, performed the world's first successful heart transplantation at Cape Town, South Africa. See also: "Barnard, Christiaan Neethling: Birth Anniversary" (Nov 8).

HOLIDAY ALE FESTIVAL. Dec 3–7. Pioneer Courthouse Square, Portland, OR. The only beer festival in the Northwest to be held outdoors in the dark, cold and often wet month of December, the

Holiday Ale Festival is truly distinctive. Despite chilly temperatures and often-inclement weather outside, attendees stay warm and dry under a large clear tent that covers the venue while allowing for views of the city lights. More than 50 Northwest winter ales are featured at the event. Est attendance: 17,000. For info: Chris Crabb. Phone: (503) 314-7583. E-mail: holidayalefestival@gmail.com. Web: www.holidayale.com.

ILLINOIS: ADMISSION DAY: ANNIVERSARY. Dec 3. Became 21st state in 1818.

MONTOYA, CARLOS: BIRTH ANNIVERSARY. Dec 3, 1903. Guitarist and composer renowned for popularizing flamenco guitar music. His solo performances of the Spanish folk form lifted flamenco from its traditional accompaniment role. Montoya never learned to read music and relied on the traditional improvisational nature of flamenco rooted in the Andalusian Gypsy form of music that stressed rhythms and harmonic patterns. He was born at Madrid, Spain, and died Mar 3, 1993, at Wainscott, NY.

ROTA, NINO: BIRTH ANNIVERSARY. Dec 3, 1911. Born at Milan, Italy, Rota was a celebrated composer and conductor, famous for his work with Italian filmmaker Federico Fellini, which included the scores for such classics as *La Dolce Vita* (1960) and *8½* (1963). Other highlights of his lengthy list of opera and film score credits include his love theme for *Romeo & Juliet* (1969) and the theme to *The Godfather* (1972). Rota died at Rome, Italy, on Apr 10, 1979.

SPECIAL KIDS DAY. Dec 3. Wilder Mansion, Elmhurst, IL. A day to honor children of all ages with developmental or physical disabilities with an area-wide holiday celebration party. Now in its 25th year, this event builds on UN Resolution #47/3, which sets aside a day to promote the inclusion of those with disabilities into the community. This free, all-volunteer event features a photo session with Santa, gifts for all children with special needs and their siblings, face painters, music, craft projects and other activities. Est attendance: 550. For info: Rich Rosenberg, Special Kids Day, 111 Linden, Elmhurst, IL 60126. Fax: (630) 530-8800. E-mail: rich@specialkidsday.org. Web: www.SKD.org.

***A STREETCAR NAMED DESIRE* BROADWAY OPENING: ANNIVERSARY.** Dec 3, 1947. Tennessee Williams's drama opened on Broadway at the Ethel Barrymore Theatre with Jessica Tandy (as Blanche Du Bois) and newcomer Marlon Brando (as Stanley Kowalski). Williams was already a Broadway star with his first play, *Glass Menagerie*, and *Streetcar* was to be equally successful: it ran for two years and won the Pulitzer Prize for Drama. Marlon Brando's performance, using his Method style, was a sensation to audience members and critics. Tandy won the Tony Award for Best Actress in a Play.

STUART, GILBERT CHARLES: BIRTH ANNIVERSARY. Dec 3, 1755. American portrait painter whose most famous painting is that of George Washington. He also painted portraits of Madison, Monroe, Jefferson and other important Americans. Stuart was born near Narragansett, RI, and died July 9, 1828, at Boston, MA.

UNITED NATIONS: INTERNATIONAL DAY OF PERSONS WITH DISABILITIES. Dec 3. On Oct 14, 1992 (Res 47/3), at the end of the Decade of Disabled Persons, the General Assembly proclaimed Dec 3 to be an annual observance to promote the continuation of integrating the disabled into general society. Formerly called the International Day of Disabled Persons. For info: United Nations, Dept of Public Info, New York, NY 10017. Web: www.un.org.

WILLIAMS, ANDY: BIRTH ANNIVERSARY. Dec 3, 1927. The embodiment of "easy listening" as both a genre and way of life, Andy Williams made a career out of smooth balladry and clean-cut entertainment. Born at Wall Lake, IA, Williams sang with his brothers—the Williams Brothers—before going it alone and issuing a string of hits in the 1960s. His signature song was the Henry Mancini–Johnny Mercer composition "Moon River." Williams also hosted a popular Emmy Award–winning television variety show from 1962 to 1971, and was well known for his Christmas specials and holiday music showcases. Later in life, Williams had his own theater in the entertainment mecca of Branson, MO. He died there Sept 25, 2012.

BIRTHDAYS TODAY

Bruno Campos, 40, actor ("Nip/Tuck"), born Rio de Janeiro, Brazil, Dec 3, 1974.

Holly Marie Combs, 41, actress ("Picket Fences," "Charmed"), born San Diego, CA, Dec 3, 1973.

Michael Essien, 32, soccer player, born Accra, Ghana, Dec 3, 1982.

Brendan Fraser, 46, actor (*The Mummy, The Quiet American*), born Indianapolis, IN, Dec 3, 1968.

Jean Luc Godard, 84, filmmaker (*Breathless, Weekend*), born Paris, France, Dec 3, 1930.

Daryl Hannah, 53, actress (*Splash, Grumpy Old Men*), born Chicago, IL, Dec 3, 1961.

Bucky Lasek, 42, rally cross driver, skateboarder, born Baltimore, MD, Dec 3, 1972.

Rick Ravon Mears, 63, former auto racer, born Wichita, KS, Dec 3, 1951.

Julianne Moore, 53, actress (*Children of Men, The Hours, The Kids Are All Right*), born Fort Bragg, Fayetteville, NC, Dec 3, 1961.

Jaye P. Morgan, 82, singer, born Mancos, CO, Dec 3, 1932.

Ozzy Osbourne, 66, singer, songwriter (Black Sabbath), born Birmingham, England, Dec 3, 1948.

Alicia Sacramone, 27, Olympic gymnast, born Boston, MA, Dec 3, 1987.

Amanda Seyfried, 29, actress (*Les Misérables, Mamma Mia*, "Big Love"), born Allentown, PA, Dec 3, 1985.

David Villa, 33, soccer player, born David Villa Sánchez at Langreo, Spain, Dec 3, 1981.

Katarina Witt, 49, Olympic figure skater, born Karl-Marx-Stadt, East Germany (now Germany), Dec 3, 1965.

December 4 — Thursday

DAY 338 — **27 REMAINING**

BUTLER, SAMUEL: BIRTH ANNIVERSARY. Dec 4, 1835. English author (*Erewhon, The Way of All Flesh*), born at Bingham, Nottinghamshire, England. Died at London, June 18, 1902.

CARLYLE, THOMAS: BIRTH ANNIVERSARY. Dec 4, 1795. Scottish essayist and historian, born at Ecclefechan, Scotland. Died at London, Feb 4, 1881. "A well-written Life is almost as rare as a well-spent one," Carlyle wrote in his *Critical and Miscellaneous Essays*.

CHASE, HELEN M.: 90th BIRTH ANNIVERSARY. Dec 4, 1924. Longtime chronicler of contemporary civilization as coeditor of *Chase's Annual Events*. Born at Whitehall, MI, Chase died Feb 19, 2009, at Ann Arbor, MI.

CHASE'S CALENDAR OF EVENTS: BIRTHDAY. Dec 4, 1957. Today in 1957 the first copies of the first edition of *Chase's Calendar of Annual Events* (for the year 1958) were delivered by the printer at Flint, MI. Two thousand copies, consisting of 32 pages and listing 364 events, were printed. Now annual editions are more than 750 pages long and list more than 12,500 events.

"FALCON CREST" TV PREMIERE: ANNIVERSARY. Dec 4, 1981. This nighttime serial was set in California wine country and originally focused on Angela Channing's determined efforts to gain control of the Falcon Crest vineyard and winery; later in the nine-year run the emphasis turned to crime. Famous actors who were a part of the cast at one time or another include Jane Wyman, Lorenzo Lamas, Cliff Robertson, Lana Turner, Gina Lollobrigida, Parker Stevenson, Anne Archer, Apollonia, Cesar Romero, Morgan Fairchild, Ken Olin and Mary Ann Mobley. In the season finale, Angela received Falcon Crest and everyone was happy.

LAST AMERICAN HOSTAGE RELEASED IN LEBANON: ANNIVERSARY. Dec 4, 1991. A sad chapter of US history came to a close when Terry Anderson, an Associated Press correspondent, became the final American hostage held in Lebanon to be freed. Anderson had been held since Mar 16, 1985, one of 15 Americans who were held hostage for from two months to as long as six years and eight months. Three of the hostages, William Buckley, Peter Kilburn and Lieutenant Colonel William Higgins, were killed during their captivity. The other hostages, released previously one or two at a time, were Jeremy Levin, Benjamin Weir, the Reverend Lawrence Martin Jenco, David Jacobsen, Thomas Sutherland, Frank Herbert Reed, Joseph Cicippio, Edward Austin Tracy, Alan Steen, Jesse Turner and Robert Polhill.

***MARY CELESTE* DISCOVERED: ANNIVERSARY.** Dec 4, 1872. The English cargo ship *Dei Gratia* saw a ship under sail apparently out of control near the Azore Islands. After failing to get an answer from the vessel, the American brigantine *Mary Celeste*, members of the *Dei Gratia* boarded the ship and discovered a mystery: despite half a year's supply of food and water, all personal belongings—even pipes—still aboard and with the cargo intact, the ship's captain, his family and the crew had disappeared without a trace. The final entry in the ship's logbook was Nov 24 and recorded a position 700 miles away. Some minor damage and a missing lifeboat suggested a hasty abandonment, but for no clear reason. Numerous investigations and theories abounded, but the nautical mystery has never been solved. A young Scottish doctor, Arthur Conan Doyle, was intrigued enough to write the first (but not last) fictional story on the incident: "J. Habakuk Jephson's Statement" (1884).

MISSION SANTA BARBARA: FOUNDING ANNIVERSARY. Dec 4, 1786. Franciscan Mission to the Indians founded at Santa Barbara, CA. Present structure is the fourth to stand on same site. Last one destroyed by 1812 earthquake.

NATIONAL GRANGE FOUNDING: ANNIVERSARY. Dec 4, 1786. The anniversary of the National Grange, the first organized agricultural movement in the US.

RUSSELL, LILLIAN: BIRTH ANNIVERSARY. Dec 4, 1861. Born Helen Louise Leonard at Clinton, IA, Russell was the most popular female entertainer of the 19th century. The zaftig singer and actress specialized in operetta, appearing in several of Gilbert and Sullivan's works before turning to comedy. Considered a great beauty, Russell was also notorious for a wild personal life: four husbands and a long relationship with Diamond Jim Brady, with whom she shared a fondness for expensive baubles and fine food. Russell died on June 6, 1922, at Pittsburgh, PA.

SAINT BARBARA'S DAY. Dec 4. On this day, traditionally the feast day of St. Barbara, a young girl places a twig from a cherry tree in a glass of water. If it blooms by Christmas Eve, she is certain to marry the following year. Because the narratives of her life and martyrdom are legendary, St. Barbara was dropped from the Roman Catholic Calendar of Saints in 1970.

SAINT OLAF CHRISTMAS FESTIVAL. Dec 4–7. St. Olaf College, Northfield, MN. Annually since 1912. This celebration of the Christmas season brings together approximately 600 student musicians (a 90-piece symphony orchestra and 500 singers) to perform sacred and folk songs from around the world. Est attendance: 12,000. For info: Bob Johnson, St. Olaf College, 1520 St. Olaf Ave, Northfield, MN 55057-1098. Phone: (507) 786-3179. E-mail: musicman@stolaf.edu. Web: www.stolaf.edu.

December 2014	S	M	T	W	T	F	S
		1	2	3	4	5	6
	7	8	9	10	11	12	13
	14	15	16	17	18	19	20
	21	22	23	24	25	26	27
	28	29	30	31			

SPACE MILESTONE: INTERNATIONAL SPACE STATION LAUNCH (US). Dec 4, 1998. The shuttle *Endeavour* took a US component of the space station named *Unity* into orbit 220 miles from Earth where spacewalking astronauts fastened it to a component launched by the Russians Nov 20, 1998. On July 25, 2000, the Russian service module *Zvezda* docked with the station. On Oct 31, 2000, NASA launched the first expedition with a three-man crew to stay aloft for four months. Officially completed on May 27, 2011, the space station is 357 feet across and 240 feet long and supports a crew of up to six.

BIRTHDAYS TODAY

Fred Armisen, 48, comedian, actor ("Portlandia," "Saturday Night Live"), born Valley Stream, NY, Dec 4, 1966.

Max Baer, Jr, 77, actor ("The Beverly Hillbillies"), producer (*Ode to Billy Joe*), born Oakland, CA, Dec 4, 1937.

Tyra Banks, 41, model, actress, talk show host, born Los Angeles, CA, Dec 4, 1973.

Jeff Bridges, 65, actor (Oscar for *Crazy Heart*; *The Big Lebowski, Starman, The Last Picture Show*), born Los Angeles, CA, Dec 4, 1949.

Chris Hillman, 70, singer, musician (The Byrds, The Flying Burrito Brothers, Desert Rose Band), born Los Angeles, CA, Dec 4, 1944.

Jay-Z, 45, rapper, music executive, born Shawn Corey Carter at Brooklyn, NY, Dec 4, 1969.

Marisa Tomei, 50, actress (*In the Bedroom*; Oscar for *My Cousin Vinny*), born Brooklyn, NY, Dec 4, 1964.

Patricia Wettig, 63, actress ("St. Elsewhere," *City Slickers*; Emmys for "thirtysomething"), born Cincinnati, OH, Dec 4, 1951.

Cassandra Wilson, 59, jazz singer, born Jackson, MS, Dec 4, 1955.

December 5 — Friday

DAY 339 **26 REMAINING**

AFL-CIO FOUNDED: ANNIVERSARY. Dec 5, 1955. The American Federation of Labor and the Congress of Industrial Organizations joined together in 1955, following 20 years of rivalry, to become the nation's leading advocate for trade unions.

AUSTRIA: KRAMPUSLAUF. Dec 5. Salzburg region. On the eve of St. Nicholas's Day, Austrians celebrate the Krampuslauf (Krampus Run). In folklore, the Krampus is a devilish companion of St. Nicholas who punishes bad children just as St. Nicholas rewards good ones. The Krampus, represented by costumed revelers, is usually depicted as a dark, hairy, cloven-hooved beast with red horns, a leering mouth, chains and a switch. Children are invited to throw snowballs at the Krampus. Also known as Krampus Day.

BATHTUB PARTY DAY. Dec 5. Almost everyone nowadays takes showers, so here's a day to recall some of the warm-water luxury of days gone by. Invite a few friends. (©2006 by WH.) For info: Thomas & Ruth Roy, Wellcat Holidays, 2418 Long Ln, Lebanon, PA 17046. Phone: (717) 279-0184. E-mail: info@wellcat.com. Web: www.wellcat.com.

CHRISTMAS WALK AND HOUSE TOUR. Dec 5–6. Geneva, IL. A special holiday tradition emphasizing the warmth and hospitality of Geneva. Spend the day touring charming homes aglow with holiday decorations. In the evening Santa Lucia, the Swedish symbol of the season, arrives, and Santa Claus opens his house for children's visits. Merchants graciously serve traditional holiday refreshments, including roasted chestnuts, as carolers fill the air with the sounds of the season. Est attendance: 35,000. For info: Geneva Chamber of Commerce, PO Box 481, 8 S Third St, Geneva, IL 60134. Phone: (630) 232-6060. Fax: (630) 232-6083. E-mail: chamberinfo@genevachamber.com. Web: www.genevachamber.com.

CUSTER, GEORGE ARMSTRONG: 175th BIRTH ANNIVERSARY. Dec 5, 1839. Born at New Rumley, OH, Custer was a cavalry officer in the US Civil War whose courage and leadership brought him admiration and fame. He later spent ten years on the Great Plains fighting in the Indian Wars and leading a successful Black Hills expedition in 1874 to find gold. During a campaign to move the Lakota Sioux onto reservations to make way for the gold rush, Custer attacked an encampment of Sioux and Cheyenne on June 25, 1876. Outnumbered, he and about 215 of his men were quickly killed at the Battle of Little Bighorn—now considered one of the biggest military fiascoes in US history.

DISNEY, WALT: BIRTH ANNIVERSARY. Dec 5, 1901. Animator, filmmaker, theme park developer, born at Chicago, IL. Disney died at Los Angeles, CA, Dec 15, 1966.

GHANA: NATIONAL FARMERS' DAY. Dec 5. Public holiday. Honors and celebrates the farmers of Ghana. Observed the first Friday in December.

GRANT'S SPEECH OF APOLOGY: ANNIVERSARY. Dec 5, 1876. President Ulysses S. Grant delivered his speech of apology to Congress claiming mistakes he made while he was president were due to his inexperience. His errors, he said, were "errors of judgment, not intent." While Grant's personal integrity was never formally questioned, he was closely associated with many government scandals, which became public during his presidency. He unwittingly aided Jay Gould in an attempt to corner the gold market during his first term. During the second, the Credit Mobilier affair involving many of the president's friends aired, while significant fraud was discovered in the Treasury Department and Indian Service.

HAITI: DISCOVERY DAY. Dec 5. Commemorates the discovery of Haiti by Christopher Columbus in 1492. Public holiday.

"IRRATIONAL EXUBERANCE" ENTERS LEXICON: ANNIVERSARY. Dec 5, 1996. In a speech to the Washington, DC–based American Enterprise Institute for Policy Research, Federal Reserve Chairman Alan Greenspan uttered a new catchphrase that the media quickly saw as a warning about the high-flying 1990s stock market. He asked, "How do we know when irrational exuberance has unduly escalated asset values. . . . And how do we factor that assessment into monetary policy?" Those two words, buried in an academic speech, nonetheless sparked panic in markets fearing the Fed would raise interest rates. The Tokyo, Hong Kong, Frankfurt, London and US markets dropped 2–4 percent after his speech. Most economists thought Greenspan was simply suggesting that markets needed to slow down a bit. But "irrational exuberance" lives on as Greenspan's most famous quote.

MARTIN VAN BUREN WREATH-LAYING. Dec 5 (tentative). Martin Van Buren National Historic Site, Kinderhook, NY. Annual ceremony honoring Van Buren on his birth anniversary. Organized by the Village of Kinderhook. Participants include the mayor of Kinderhook, mayor of Valatie, a representative from the White House, the president of Friends of Lindenwald, the superintendent of Martin Van Buren NHS, local historians and local schoolchildren. Also on this day, the Winter Celebration by candlelight at the Van Buren homestead. For info: Chief Ranger, Martin Van Buren National Historic Site, 1013 Old Post Rd, Kinderhook, NY 12106-3605. Web: www.nps.gov/mava.

MONTGOMERY BUS BOYCOTT BEGINS: ANNIVERSARY. Dec 5, 1955. Rosa Parks was arrested at Montgomery, AL, for refusing to give up her seat on a bus to a white man. In support of Parks, and to protest the arrest, the black community of Montgomery organized a boycott of the bus system. The boycott lasted from Dec 5, 1955, to Dec 20, 1956, when a US Supreme Court ruling was implemented at Montgomery, integrating the public transportation system.

NATIONAL SALESPERSON'S DAY. Dec 5. Salespeople are essential resources for customers today. The talented salesperson filters the vast amount of information that is available to customers and helps businesspeople make the best purchasing decisions. Salespeople also help consumers make better, quicker decisions with the counsel they offer. With the impact of new technologies, the role of the salesperson continually evolves. Annually, the first Friday in December. For info: Maura Schreier-Fleming, Best@Selling, 7028 Judi, Dallas, TX 75252. Phone: (972) 380-0200. E-mail: Maura@BestAtSelling.com. Web: www.BestAtSelling.com.

PICKETT, BILL: BIRTH ANNIVERSARY. Dec 5, 1870. American rodeo cowboy, born at Williamson County, TX; died Apr 21, 1932, at Tulsa, OK. Inventor of bulldogging, the modern rodeo event that involves wrestling a running steer to the ground.

ROSSETTI, CHRISTINA: BIRTH ANNIVERSARY. Dec 5, 1830. English poet of beautiful yet melancholy verses who is best known for her lyrical fable "Goblin Market." Born at London, where she died on Dec 29, 1894.

THAILAND: KING'S BIRTHDAY AND NATIONAL DAY. Dec 5. Celebrated throughout the kingdom with colorful pageantry. Stores and houses decorated with spectacular illuminations at night. Public holiday.

THURMOND, STROM: BIRTH ANNIVERSARY. Dec 5, 1902. One of the longest-serving senators in American history, James Strom Thurmond was born at Edgefield, SC. The first senator ever elected by a write-in vote, he joined the US Senate in 1954. He was elected as both a Democrat and a Republican and is remembered for his record-breaking filibuster protesting pending civil rights legislation. He did not yield the floor for 24 hours, 18 minutes over Aug 28–29, 1957, although the legislation did pass less than two hours later. He served in the Senate until Nov 19, 2002, just a few weeks shy of his 100th birthday. He died at Edgefield on June 26, 2003.

TWENTY-FIRST AMENDMENT TO THE US CONSTITUTION RATIFIED: ANNIVERSARY. Dec 5, 1933. Prohibition ended with the repeal of the 18th Amendment, as the 21st Amendment was ratified. Congress proposed repeal of the 18th Amendment ("the manufacture, sale, or transportation of intoxicating liquors, within, the importation thereof into, or the exportation thereof from the United States and all territory subject to the jurisdiction thereof, for beverage purposes is hereby prohibited.") Feb 20, 1933. By Dec 5, 1933, the repeal amendment had been ratified by the required 36 states and went into effect immediately as the 21st Amendment to the US Constitution.

UNITED NATIONS: INTERNATIONAL VOLUNTEER DAY FOR ECONOMIC AND SOCIAL DEVELOPMENT. Dec 5. In a resolution of Dec 17, 1985, the United Nations General Assembly recognized the desirability of encouraging the work of all volunteers. It invited governments to observe annually on Dec 5 the "International Volunteer Day for Economic and Social Development, urging them to take measures to heighten awareness of the important contribution of volunteer service." A day commemorating the establishment in December 1970 of the UN Volunteers program and inviting world recognition of volunteerism in the international development movement. For info: United Nations, Dept of Public Info, Public Inquiries Unit, Rm GA-57, New York, NY 10017. Phone: (212) 963-4475. E-mail: inquiries@un.org. Web: www.un.org.

VAN BUREN, MARTIN: BIRTH ANNIVERSARY. Dec 5, 1782. The eighth president of the US (term of office: Mar 4, 1837–Mar 3, 1841) was the first to have been born a citizen of the US. He was a widower for nearly two decades before he entered the White House. His daughter-in-law, Angelica, served as White House hostess during an administration troubled by bank and business failures, depression and unemployment. Van Buren was born at Kinderhook, NY, and died there July 24, 1862.

WHEATLEY, PHILLIS: DEATH ANNIVERSARY. Dec 5, 1784. Born at Senegal, West Africa, about 1753 or 1754, Phillis Wheatley was brought to the US in 1761 and purchased as a slave by a Boston tailor named John Wheatley. She was allotted unusual privileges for a slave, including being allowed to learn to read and write. She wrote her first poetry at age 14, and her first work was published in 1770. Wheatley's fame as a poet spread throughout Europe as well as the US after her *Poems on Various Subjects, Religious and Moral* was published at England in 1773. She was invited to visit George Washington's army headquarters after he read a poem she had written about him in 1776. Phillis Wheatley died at about age 30, at Boston, MA.

WINTERFEST. Dec 5–7. Luverne, MN. Craft show, historical tours, entertainment and many other events. For info: Jane Wildung Lanphere, Exec Dir, Luverne Area Chamber, 213 E Luverne St, Luverne, MN 56156. Phone: (507) 283-4061. Fax: (507) 283-4061. E-mail: luvernechamber@co.rock.mn.us. Web: www.luvernechamber.com.

BIRTHDAYS TODAY

Morgan Brittany, 64, actress ("Dallas," "Glitter"), born Suzanne Cupito at Hollywood, CA, Dec 5, 1950.

José Carreras, 68, opera singer, one of the "Three Tenors," born Barcelona, Spain, Dec 5, 1946.

Margaret Cho, 46, actress, comedienne, born San Francisco, CA, Dec 5, 1968.

Joan Didion, 80, author, journalist (*The Year of Magical Thinking, The White Album*), born Sacramento, CA, Dec 5, 1934.

Jeroen Krabbe, 70, actor (*A World Apart, King of the Hill, The Fugitive*), born Amsterdam, Netherlands, Dec 5, 1944.

Little Richard, 79, singer, born Richard Penniman at Macon, GA, Dec 5, 1935.

Jim Messina, 67, singer, songwriter, born Maywood, CA, Dec 5, 1947.

Chad Mitchell, 78, singer, born Spokane, WA, Dec 5, 1936.

Art Monk, 57, Hall of Fame football player, born White Plains, NY, Dec 5, 1957.

Frankie Muniz, 29, actor ("Malcolm in the Middle," *My Dog Skip*), born Ridgewood, NJ, Dec 5, 1985.

Paula Patton, 39, actress (*Mission: Impossible—Ghost Protocol, Precious: Based on the Novel "Push" by Sapphire*), born Los Angeles, CA, Dec 5, 1975.

Calvin Trillin, 79, author (*American Stories, Remembering Denny*), born Kansas City, MO, Dec 5, 1935.

December 2014

S	M	T	W	T	F	S
	1	2	3	4	5	6
7	8	9	10	11	12	13
14	15	16	17	18	19	20
21	22	23	24	25	26	27
28	29	30	31			

December 6 — Saturday

DAY 340 **25 REMAINING**

ALTAMONT CONCERT: 45th ANNIVERSARY. Dec 6, 1969. A free concert featuring performances by the Rolling Stones; Jefferson Airplane; Santana; Crosby, Stills, Nash and Young and the Flying Burrito Brothers turned into tragedy. The "thank-you" concert for 300,000 fans was marred by overcrowding, drug overdoses and the fatal stabbing of a spectator by a member of the Hell's Angels motorcycle gang, who had been hired as security guards for the event. The concert was held at the Altamont Speedway, Livermore, CA.

BRUBECK, DAVE: BIRTH ANNIVERSARY. Dec 6, 1920. With his innovative and forever intuitive sound as both a pianist and composer, Dave Brubeck became one of the biggest stars of American jazz in the 1950s and '60s, at a time when rock and roll was the dominant force in popular music. Legendary records like his 1955 Columbia debut *Brubeck Time* and the ambitious *Time Out* (1959)—featuring the hit "Take Five" and the first million-selling jazz album—remain as hallmarks of jazz, and document how Brubeck and his collaborators defined the contours of American cool. A recipient of the National Medal of Arts, he was also the first modern jazz musician to be featured on the cover of *Time* magazine. Born at Concord, CA, Brubeck died Dec 5, 2012, at Norwalk, CT.

CALDWELL COUNTRY CHRISTMAS PARADE & FIREWORKS. Dec 6. Columbia, LA. Lighted nighttime parade will roll down Main St and through Historic Downtown Columbia. This parade is the highlight of the Christmas season with several bands from the area. Fireworks on the river follow the parade. Est attendance: 8,000. For info: Caldwell Parish Chamber of Commerce, PO Box 726, Columbia, LA 71418. Phone: (318) 649-0726. E-mail: cpchamber60@yahoo.com.

CHESTER GREENWOOD DAY PARADE. Dec 6. Farmington, ME. Celebration of Farmington's famous inventor of the earmuff. An earmuff-themed parade with flag raising. Annually, the first Saturday in December. Est attendance: 2,500. For info: Franklin County Chamber of Commerce, 615 Wilton Rd, Farmington, ME 04938. Phone: (207) 778-4215.

CHRISTMAS CANDLELIGHTINGS. Dec 6 (also Dec 13 and 20). Roscoe Village, Coshocton, OH. On the first three Saturdays of December, Roscoe Village cheers on the holiday season with its Christmas Candlelighting. Share in the tradition of lighting the Christmas tree and light your own candle as "Silent Night" is sung. Guests enjoy art with Santa Claus, strolling carolers, storytelling, roasted chestnuts, candlelight tours, complimentary hot mulled cider and cookies and many other holiday festivities. Est attendance: 3,000. For info: Roscoe Village Foundation, 600 N Whitewoman St, Coshocton, OH 43812. Phone: (740) 622-7644 or (800) 877-1830. Fax: (740) 623-6555. E-mail: rvmarketing@roscoevillage.com. Web: www.roscoevillage.com.

CHRISTMAS IN OLD APPALACHIA. Dec 6–24. Museum of Appalachia, Norris, TN. The spirit, memories and warmth of an old-time Christmas will be revived, recalling a time of simple gifts, handmade decorations and family gatherings. Pioneer cabins are decorated in austere frontier fashion. In the gaily decorated turn-of-the-century Homestead House, old-time musicians play and sing the songs of Christmas past; and the old log schoolhouse is decorated with ornaments made by local schoolchildren. For info: Museum of Appalachia, 2819 Andersonville Hwy, Clinton, TN 37716. Phone: (865) 494-7680. Fax: (865) 494-8957. E-mail:

museum@museumofappalachia.org. Web: www.museumofappalachia.org.

CHRISTMAS ON THE PRAIRIE. Dec 6–7. Saunders County Museum, Wahoo, NE. Old-fashioned Christmas featuring entertainment by local groups, special postal cancellation, children's activities common to the 1800s and demonstrations in the historical village decorated in the 1800s style. Annually, the first weekend of December. Sponsor: Christmas on the Prairie Steering Committee. Est attendance: 3,000. For info: Curator, Saunders County Museum, 240 N Walnut, Wahoo, NE 68066-1858. Phone: (402) 443-3090. E-mail: saunderscomuseum@hotmail.com. Web: www.saunderscountymuseum.org.

CHRISTMAS PARADE. Dec 6. El Centro, CA. 68th annual. Annually, the first Saturday in December. Est attendance: 5,000. For info: El Centro Chamber of Commerce, Box 3006, El Centro, CA 92244. Phone: (760) 352-3681. Fax: (760) 352-3246. Web: www.elcentrochamber.com.

COLD MOON. Dec 6. So called by Native American tribes of New England and the Great Lakes because the nights have become long at this time of year. Also called the Long Nights Moon. The December Full Moon.

DICKENS ON THE STRAND. Dec 6–7. Galveston, TX. Victorian Christmas celebration focuses on the 19th-century architecture of Galveston's Strand National Historic Landmark District and ties to Charles Dickens's 19th-century London. Annually, the first weekend in December. Est attendance: 35,000. For info: Galveston Historical Foundation, 502 20th St, Galveston, TX 77550. Phone: (409) 765-7834. Fax: (409) 765-3431. E-mail: angie.wierzbicki@galvestonhistory.org. Web: www.dickensonthestrand.org.

ECUADOR: DAY OF QUITO: FOUNDING ANNIVERSARY. Dec 6. Commemorates founding of city of Quito by Spaniards in 1534.

EISENSTAEDT, ALFRED: BIRTH ANNIVERSARY. Dec 6, 1898. American photojournalist Alfred Eisenstaedt was born at Dirschau, Prussia. One of the greatest photojournalists in US history, he is best known for his 86 photos that were used on covers of *Life* magazine, including the iconic image of a sailor kissing a nurse in New York's Times Square at the end of WWII. He died Aug 23, 1995, at Martha's Vineyard, MA.

EVERGLADES NATIONAL PARK ESTABLISHED: ANNIVERSARY. Dec 6, 1947. Part of vast marshland area on southern Florida peninsula, originally authorized May 30, 1934, was established as a national park.

FINLAND: INDEPENDENCE DAY. Dec 6. National holiday. Declaration of independence from Russia in 1917.

GERALD FORD SWEARING IN AS VICE PRESIDENT: ANNIVERSARY. Dec 6, 1973. Gerald Ford was sworn in as vice president under Richard Nixon, following the resignation of Spiro Agnew, who pled no contest to a charge of income tax evasion. See also "Agnew, Spiro Theodore: Birth Anniversary" (Nov 9) and "Ford, Gerald Rudolph: Birth Anniversary" (July 14).

GERSHWIN, IRA: BIRTH ANNIVERSARY. Dec 6, 1896. Pulitzer Prize–winning American lyricist and author who collaborated with his brother George and with many other composers. Among his Broadway successes: *Lady Be Good, Funny Face, Strike Up the Band* and such songs as "The Man I Love," "Someone to Watch Over Me" and "I Got Rhythm." Born at New York, NY, he died at Beverly Hills, CA, Aug 17, 1983.

HALIFAX, NOVA SCOTIA, DESTROYED: ANNIVERSARY. Dec 6, 1917. More than 1,650 people were killed at Halifax when the Norwegian ship *Imo* plowed into the French munitions ship *Mont Blanc*. *Mont Blanc* was loaded with 4,000 tons of TNT, 2,300 tons of picric acid, 61 tons of other explosives and a deck of highly flammable benzene, which ignited and touched off an explosion. In addition to those killed, 1,028 were injured. A tidal wave caused by the explosion washed much of the city out to sea.

HART, WILLIAM SURREY: 150th BIRTH ANNIVERSARY. Dec 6, 1864. American actor and film director best remembered as the first western movie star and a top box-office leading man in silent movies from 1914 to 1925. One of the rare movie cowboys who had actually worked on a cattle ranch, roles in *Hell's Hinges* (1916) and *The Narrow Trail* (1917) established Hart as the classic cowboy star whether he was playing the outlaw or the hero. Born in 1864 (or 1870) at Newburgh, NY, he closely identified with the Wild West, even serving as a pallbearer at Wyatt Earp's funeral on Jan 16, 1929. Hart died June 23, 1946, at Newhall, CA.

HOLLYWOOD BEACH CANDY CANE PARADE. Dec 6. Hollywood, FL. More than 75 floats and marching units line the Hollywood Beach Boardwalk during this popular evening event. Est attendance: 30,000. For info: Marketing, City of Hollywood, Dept of Parks, Recreation & Cultural Arts, 1405 S 28th Ave, Hollywood, FL 33020. Phone: (954) 921-3404.

KILMER, JOYCE (ALFRED): BIRTH ANNIVERSARY. Dec 6, 1886. American poet most famous for his poem "Trees," which was published in 1913, was born at New Brunswick, NJ. Kilmer was killed in action near Ourcy, France, in WWI, July 30, 1918. The Army's Camp Kilmer in New Jersey was named for him.

LEVINE, CHARLES A.: DEATH ANNIVERSARY. Dec 6, 1991. Charles A. Levine, whose efforts to beat Charles Lindbergh across the Atlantic by plane were stymied by a lawsuit, nevertheless became the first air passenger to cross the Atlantic Ocean. Levine's 225-horsepower plane, *The Columbia*, was grounded when one of his copilots filed a suit hours after Lindbergh took off from Roosevelt Field. Not to be overshadowed by Lindbergh's success, Levine announced that his flight, leaving June 4, 1927, would fly beyond Paris to Berlin, with himself as a passenger. Piloted by Clarence Chamberlin, the plane exhausted its fuel and landed at Eisleben, Germany, June 6, 100 miles short of his goal. The flight set a new record of 3,911 miles in 43 hours of nonstop flight, besting Lindbergh by approximately 300 miles. Levine was born at North Adams, MA, in 1897, and died at Washington, DC.

MISSOURI EARTHQUAKES: ANNIVERSARY. Dec 6, 1811. New Madrid, MO. Most prolonged series of earthquakes in US history occurred not in California, but in the Midwest. Lasted until Feb 12, 1812. There were few deaths because of the sparse population. These were the most severe earthquakes in the contiguous US; those higher on the Richter scale have all occurred in Alaska.

MOON PHASE: FULL MOON. Dec 6. Moon enters Full Moon phase at 7:27 AM, EST.

NATCHITOCHES CHRISTMAS FESTIVAL. Dec 6. Natchitoches, LA. 88th annual. Featuring a parade, fireworks, food, entertainment, a fun run/walk and Christmas lighting. Listed as one of the "Top 100 Events in North America" by the American Bus Association. Annually, the first Saturday in December. Est attendance: 150,000. For info: Natchitoches Parish Tourist Commission, 780 Front St, Ste 100, Natchitoches, LA 71457. Phone: (318) 352-8072 or (800) 259-1714. Fax: (318) 352-2415. Web: www.natchitoches.net or www.christmasfestival.com.

NATIONAL MINER'S DAY. Dec 6. In appreciation, honor and remembrance of the accomplishments and sacrifices of miners. To provide a sober reminder of the risks that miners are routinely exposed to in their work and to set aside some time on this day for quiet contemplation to honor those brave miners who have perished in our mines. A National Miner's Day resolution passed in the US Senate on Dec 3, 2009. Observed previously in West Virginia. For info: Creed Holden, 301 Nuzum Pl, Fairmont, WV 26554. Phone: (304) 366-0008. E-mail: creed.holden@gmail.com. Web: www.minersday.org.

NATIONAL PAWNBROKERS DAY. Dec 6. Celebrated on St. Nicholas Day, the patron saint of pawnbroking. Designed to acknowledge the valuable lending and retail services the pawnbroker provides his or her clientele. For info: Michael Goldstein, Empire Loan, 1130 Washington St, Boston, MA 02118. Phone: (617) 423-9366.

NORSKEDALEN'S OLD-FASHIONED CHRISTMAS. Dec 6–7. Coon Valley, WI. Celebrate an old-fashioned Christmas with decorated pioneer log homes to view, entertainment, à la carte ethnic foods, raffle, horse-drawn wagon/sleigh rides and outdoor activities. Fun for all ages. 10 AM–4 PM. Est attendance: 500. For info: Norskedalen Nature and Heritage Center, Inc, PO Box 235, Coon Valley, WI 54623. Phone: (608) 452-3424. Fax: (608) 452-3157. E-mail: info@norskedalen.org. Web: www.norskedalen.org.

RENOIR, CLAUDE: BIRTH ANNIVERSARY. Dec 6, 1914. French film cameraman Claude Renoir was born at Paris, France, a grandson of painter Pierre Renoir. His films include *The River* (1951) and *The Spy Who Loved Me* (1977). He died Sept 5, 1993, at Troyes, France.

ROBERT-HOUDIN, JEAN EUGÈNE: BIRTH ANNIVERSARY. Dec 6, 1805. The founder of modern magic who was the first to use electricity in his illusions. Robert-Houdin also popularized wearing evening attire (instead of wizard's robes) on stage. He inspired scores of younger magicians, including Harry Houdini, whose stage name saluted Robert-Houdin's name. Born at Blois, France, Robert-Houdin died at St. Gervais, France, on June 13, 1871.

SAINT NICHOLAS DAY. Dec 6. One of the most venerated saints of both Eastern and Western Christian churches, of whose life little is known, except that he was Bishop of Myra (in what is today's Turkey) in the fourth century, and that from early times he has been especially noted for his charity. Santa Claus and the presentation of gifts is said to derive from St. Nicholas.

SHAKER CHRISTMAS FAIR. Dec 6. Sabbathday Lake Shaker Village, New Gloucester, ME. Traditional holiday church fair featuring home-baked foods. Nine rooms of the 1816 Trustee's Office are filled with holiday items for all ages. For info: United Soceity of Shakers, 707 Shaker Rd, New Gloucester, ME 04260. Phone: (207) 926-4597. E-mail: usshakers@aol.com. Web: www.shaker.lib.me.us.

SPAIN: CONSTITUTION DAY. Dec 6. National holiday. Commemorates the voters' approval of a new constitution in 1978.

"TALENT SCOUTS" TV PREMIERE: ANNIVERSARY. Dec 6, 1948. Officially titled "Arthur Godfrey's Talent Scouts," this TV show was created when host Arthur Godfrey took his radio show to TV in 1948. On this talent show, celebrity guests introduced amateur and young professional acts. It was a weekly show until 1958. For several years beginning in 1960 it was a summer replacement series called "Celebrity Talent Scouts" and "Hollywood Talent Scouts." Hosts included Sam Levenson, Jim Backus, Merv Griffin and Art Linkletter. Pat Boone, Shari Lewis and the McGuire Sisters got their starts here.

December 2014

S	M	T	W	T	F	S
	1	2	3	4	5	6
7	8	9	10	11	12	13
14	15	16	17	18	19	20
21	22	23	24	25	26	27
28	29	30	31			

THIRTEENTH AMENDMENT TO THE US CONSTITUTION RATIFIED: ANNIVERSARY. Dec 6, 1865. The 13th Amendment to the Constitution was ratified, abolishing slavery in the US. "Neither slavery nor involuntary servitude, save as a punishment for crime whereof the party shall have been duly convicted, shall exist within the United States, or any place subject to their jurisdiction." This amendment was proclaimed Dec 18, 1865. The 13th, 14th and 15th amendments are considered the Civil War Amendments. See also: "Emancipation Proclamation: Anniversary" (Jan 1) for Lincoln's proclamation freeing slaves in the rebelling states.

BIRTHDAYS TODAY

Andrew Cuomo, 57, Governor of New York (D), born Queens, NY, Dec 6, 1957.

Macy Gray, 45, singer, born Canton, OH, Dec 6, 1969.

Thomas Hulce, 61, actor (*Amadeus, Parenthood*), born Plymouth, MI, Dec 6, 1953.

Ray LaHood, 69, US Secretary of Transportation, born Peoria, IL, Dec 6, 1945.

James Naughton, 69, actor (*The Paper Chase, The Good Mother*; stage: *Long Day's Journey into Night*), born Middletown, CT, Dec 6, 1945.

Craig Newmark, 62, founder of craigslist, born Morristown, NJ, Dec 6, 1952.

Sarah Rafferty, 42, actress ("Suits"), born Greenwich, CT, Dec 6, 1972.

Janine Turner, 52, actress ("Northern Exposure," *Cliffhanger*), born Lincoln, NE, Dec 6, 1962.

JoBeth Williams, 61, actress (*The Ponder Heart, The Big Chill*), born Houston, TX, Dec 6, 1953.

Steven Wright, 59, comedian, born New York, NY, Dec 6, 1955.

December 7 — Sunday

DAY 341 **24 REMAINING**

ADORATION PARADE. Dec 7. Branson, MO. The 66th annual Adoration Celebration Parade will present a celebration of Christmas—the traditional values of faith, family and friendliness. Annually, the first Sunday in December. For info: Branson/Lakes Area Chamber of Commerce and CVB, PO Box 1897, Branson, MO 65615. Phone: (800) 214-3661. Fax: (417) 334-4084. E-mail: info@bransoncvb.com. Web: www.explorebranson.com.

ARMENIAN EARTHQUAKE OF 1988: ANNIVERSARY. Dec 7, 1988. An earthquake measuring 6.9 on the Richter scale rocked the Soviet province of Armenia killing upward of 60,000 people. Many of the deaths were blamed on poor construction practices as many homes had been made of adobe, mud or stones; had unreinforced masonry or were prefabricated structures made of loosely connected concrete slabs. In the quake's aftermath, Soviet President Mikhail Gorbachev cut short his trip to the US to fly home and head the massive worldwide relief efforts.

CATHER, WILLA SIBERT: BIRTH ANNIVERSARY. Dec 7, 1873. American author born at Winchester, VA. Died at New York, NY, Apr 24, 1947. Best known for her novels about the development of early 20th-century American life, such as *O Pioneers!* and *My Ántonia*. She won a Pulitzer Prize in 1922 for her book *One of Ours*.

CHAPIN, HARRY: BIRTH ANNIVERSARY. Dec 7, 1942. Folksinger/songwriter Harry Chapin was one of only five songwriters to receive the Special Congressional Gold Medal for his devotion to the issue of hunger throughout the world. Born at New York, NY, he was killed in a car accident July 16, 1981, at Long Island, NY.

CHRISTMAS TO REMEMBER. Dec 7. Laurel, MT. 28th annual. To officially open the Christmas season in Laurel, this daylong celebration includes the arrival of Santa, live nativity, a community bazaar, tour of Christmas trees, children's craft activities, musical entertainment, lighting ceremony, parade and fireworks. Annually, the first Sunday of December. Est attendance: 5,000. For info: Christmas to Remember Committee, Jean Carroll Thompson, PO Box 463, Laurel, MT 59044. Phone: (406) 248-8557.

CÔTE D'IVOIRE: COMMEMORATION DAY. Dec 7. National holiday. Commemorates the death of the first president, Félix Houphouët-Boigny, in 1993.

DELAWARE RATIFIES CONSTITUTION: ANNIVERSARY. Dec 7, 1787. Delaware became the first state to ratify the proposed Constitution. It did so by unanimous vote.

1800s CHRISTMAS. Dec 7. North Port Library, North Port, FL. 9th Annual. Step back into a simpler time with reenactors, 19th-century crafts, entertainers and folks in 19th-century garb. Annually, the first Sunday in December. Est attendance: 400. For info: Carolann Palm-Abramoff, North Port Library, 13800 Tamiami Tr, North Port, FL 34287. Phone: (941) 861-1306. Fax: (941) 426-6564. E-mail: cpalmabram@scgov.net. Web: www.sclibs.net.

IRAN: STUDENTS DAY. Dec 7. Day commemorating the 1953 killing of three university students by the Shah's security forces. The students were among many protesting US Vice President Richard Nixon's visit to Iran after the Shah took power.

NATIONAL FIRE SAFETY COUNCIL: 35th FOUNDING ANNIVERSARY. Dec 7, 1979. Founded to promote fire and burn prevention and life safety awareness. Council distributes comprehensive material to children, adults and seniors through local fire departments and the Council's mascot, Firepup®. For info: Natl Fire Safety Council Inc, PO Box 378, Michigan Center, MI 49254-0378. Web: www.nfsc.org.

✦NATIONAL PEARL HARBOR REMEMBRANCE DAY. Dec 7.

PEARL HARBOR DAY: ANNIVERSARY. Dec 7, 1941. At 7:55 AM (local time) Dec 7, 1941, "a date that will live in infamy," nearly 200 Japanese aircraft attacked Pearl Harbor, Hawaii, long considered the US "Gibraltar of the Pacific." The raid, which lasted little more than one hour, left nearly 3,000 dead. Almost the entire US Pacific Fleet was at anchor there, and few ships escaped damage. Several were sunk or disabled, while 200 US aircraft on the ground were destroyed. The attack on Pearl Harbor brought about immediate US entry into WWII, a declaration of war being requested by President Franklin D. Roosevelt and approved by Congress Dec 8, 1941.

SEARS, RICHARD WARREN: BIRTH ANNIVERSARY. Dec 7, 1863. Founder, with Alvah C. Roebuck, and president of the huge retail and mail-order company Sears, Roebuck and Company. Born at Stewartville, MN, Sears died Sept 28, 1914, at Waukesha, WI.

SPACE MILESTONE: *APOLLO 17* (US). Dec 7, 1972. Launched this date with three-man crew—Eugene A. Cernan, Harrison H. Schmidt and Ronald E. Evans—who explored the moon, Dec 11–14. Lunar landing module named *Challenger*. Pacific splashdown, Dec 19. This was the last manned mission to the moon.

SPACE MILESTONE: *GALILEO* (US). Dec 7, 1995. Launched Oct 18, 1989, by the space shuttle *Atlantis*, the spacecraft *Galileo* entered the orbit of Jupiter after a six-year journey. It has been orbiting Jupiter ever since, sending out probes to study three of its moons. Organic compounds, the ingredients of life, were found on them. On May 25, 2001, it passed within 86 miles of Callisto, one of Jupiter's moons.

UNITED NATIONS: INTERNATIONAL CIVIL AVIATION DAY. Dec 7. On Dec 6, 1996, the General Assembly proclaimed Dec 7 as International Civil Aviation Day. On Dec 7, 1944, the Convention on International Civil Aviation, which established the International Civil Aviation Organization, was signed. For info: United Nations, Dept of Public Info, New York, NY 10017. Web: www.un.org.

XTERRA TRAIL RUNNING WORLD CHAMPIONSHIP. Dec 7. Kualoa Ranch, Oahu, HI. The XTERRA Trail Run Series boasts more than 80 events across the country with runs ranging from 5k to 50k. These extreme, off-road trail runs give runners the chance to prove their skills against a variety of terrains. From calf-burning hills to slippery, mud-covered paths athletes will face the ultimate test of endurance. This race features off-road 5k, 10k and half-marathon distance trail runs on the beautiful island of Oahu. For info: Emily McIlvaine, XTERRA/TEAM Unlimited, 720 Iwilei Rd #290, Honolulu, HI 96817. Phone: (877) XTERRA-1. E-mail: emily@xterraplanet.com. Web: www.xterratrailrun.com.

BIRTHDAYS TODAY

Johnny Lee Bench, 67, Hall of Fame baseball player, born Oklahoma City, OK, Dec 7, 1947.

Larry Joe Bird, 58, Hall of Fame basketball player, former coach, born West Baden, IN, Dec 7, 1956.

Ellen Burstyn, 82, actress (Tony for *Same Time, Next Year*; Oscar for *Alice Doesn't Live Here Anymore*), born Edna Rae Gilhooley at Detroit, MI, Dec 7, 1932.

Noam Chomsky, 86, philosopher, linguist, political activist, born Philadelphia, PA, Dec 7, 1928.

Thad Cochran, 77, US Senator (R, Mississippi), born Pontotoc, MS, Dec 7, 1937.

Susan M. Collins, 62, US Senator (R, Maine), born Caribou, ME, Dec 7, 1952.

Edd Hall, 56, announcer ("The Tonight Show with Jay Leno"), born Boston, MA, Dec 7, 1958.

C. Thomas Howell, 48, actor ("Two Marriages," *Soul Man, Tank*), born Los Angeles, CA, Dec 7, 1966.

Tino Martinez, 47, former baseball player, born Tampa, FL, Dec 7, 1967.

John Terry, 34, soccer player, born Barking, England, Dec 7, 1980.

Tom Waits, 65, singer, songwriter, actor (*Down by Law, Short Cuts*), born Pomona, CA, Dec 7, 1949.

Eli Wallach, 99, actor (Tony for *The Rose Tattoo*; *The Good, the Bad and the Ugly; The Magnificent Seven; Baby Doll*; Emmy for *Poppies Are Also Flowers*), born New York, NY, Dec 7, 1915.

December 8 — Monday

DAY 342 **23 REMAINING**

AMERICA ENTERS WORLD WAR II: ANNIVERSARY. Dec 8, 1941. One day after the surprise Japanese attack on Pearl Harbor, Congress declared war against Japan and the US entered WWII.

AMERICAN FEDERATION OF LABOR (AFL) FOUNDED: ANNIVERSARY. Dec 8, 1886. Originally founded at Pittsburgh, PA, as the Federation of Organized Trades and Labor Unions of the United States and Canada in 1881, the union was reorganized in 1886 under the name American Federation of Labor (AFL). The AFL was dissolved as a separate entity in 1955 when it merged with the Congress of Industrial Organizations to form the AFL-CIO. See also: "AFL-CIO Founded: Anniversary (Dec 5)."

CHINESE NATIONALISTS MOVE TO FORMOSA: 65th ANNIVERSARY. Dec 8, 1949. The government of Chiang Kai-Shek moved to Formosa (Taiwan) after being driven out of Mainland China by the Communists led by Mao Tse-Tung.

DAVIS, SAMMY, JR: BIRTH ANNIVERSARY. Dec 8, 1925. Born at New York, NY, Sammy Davis, Jr, was the son of vaudevillians and first appeared on the stage at the age of four. He made his first film appearance in *Rufus Jones for President* in 1931. He joined the Will Mastin Trio, a song-and-dance team popular on the nightclub circuit; as Davis matured, his singing, dancing and impersonations became the center of the act. Davis began performing on his own in the 1950s, headlining club engagements, appearing on television variety shows and making numerous records. His Broadway debut came in 1956 in the hit musical *Mr Wonderful*, and in the late '50s and early '60s he starred in a number of films, including a series with Frank Sinatra and the Rat Pack. Davis died at Los Angeles, CA, May 16, 1990.

DURANT, WILLIAM CRAPO: BIRTH ANNIVERSARY. Dec 8, 1861. "Billy" Durant, a leading producer of carriages at Flint, MI; promoter of the Buick car; cofounder of Chevrolet and founder, in 1908, of General Motors. He lost, regained and again lost control of GM, after which he founded Durant Motors, went bankrupt in the Depression and operated a Flint bowling alley in his last working years. Durant was born at Boston, MA, and died at New York, NY, Mar 18, 1947.

FEAST OF THE IMMACULATE CONCEPTION. Dec 8. Roman Catholic Holy Day of Obligation. A public holiday in Nicaragua.

INTERMEDIATE-RANGE NUCLEAR FORCES TREATY (INF) SIGNED: ANNIVERSARY. Dec 8, 1987. The USSR and the US signed a treaty at Washington eliminating medium-range and shorter-range missiles. This was the first treaty completely eliminating two entire classes of nuclear arms. These missiles, with a range of 500 to 5,500 kilometers, were to be scrapped under strict supervision within three years of the signing.

GUAM: LADY OF CAMARIN DAY. Dec 8. Declared a legal holiday by Guam legislature, Mar 2, 1971.

HOBAN, JAMES: DEATH ANNIVERSARY. Dec 8, 1831. Irish-born architect who designed the US President's Executive Mansion, later known as the White House. He was born at Callan, County Kilkenny, Ireland, in 1762 (exact date unknown) and died at Washington, DC. The cornerstone for the White House, Washington's oldest public building, was laid in 1792.

JOHN LENNON SHOT: ANNIVERSARY. Dec 8, 1980. On this date deranged gunman Mark David Chapman shot and killed rock star John Lennon outside his apartment building as he returned from a recording session. The death of the former Beatle, who was an international peace activist, shocked the world. His widow, Yoko Ono, asked for 10 minutes of silence at 2 PM EST on the following Sunday, Dec 14, and many US and international radio stations observed it. See also: "Lennon, John: Birth Anniversary" (Oct 9).

MORRISON, JIM: BIRTH ANNIVERSARY. Dec 8, 1943. Songwriter, poet, lead singer of The Doors, Jim Morrison is considered to be one of the fathers of contemporary rock. The bacchic Morrison, known as "The Lizard King," brought avant-garde theatrics to his musical performances and mystical influences to his songs. Born at Melbourne, FL, and died at Paris, France, July 3, 1971.

NAFTA SIGNED: ANNIVERSARY. Dec 8, 1993. President Clinton signed the North American Free Trade Agreement, which cut tariffs and eliminated other trade barriers among the US, Canada and Mexico. The agreement went into effect Jan 1, 1994.

RIVERA, DIEGO: BIRTH ANNIVERSARY. Dec 8, 1886. One of the greatest artists of Mexico, Rivera specialized in bold, colorful murals that depicted the struggle of the working classes and/or displayed the grandeur of Mexican history. A commissioned mural at the Rockefeller Center in New York City was famously destroyed in 1934 because it contained an image of Lenin. He was twice married to fellow artist Frida Kahlo. Born at Guanajuato, Mexico, Rivera died in his studio at San Angel, near Mexico City, Nov 25, 1957.

SEGAR, ELZIE CRISLER: BIRTH ANNIVERSARY. Dec 8, 1894. Popeye creator Elzie Crisler Segar was born at Chester, IL. Originally called *Thimble Theater*, the comic strip that came to be known as *Popeye* had the unusual format of a one-act play in cartoon form. Centered on the Oyl family, especially daughter Olive, the strip introduced a new central character in 1929. A one-eyed sailor with bulging muscles, Popeye became the strip's star attraction almost immediately. Popeye made it to the silver screen in animated form and in 1980 became a movie with Robin Williams playing the lead. Segar died Oct 13, 1938, at Santa Monica, CA.

SOVIET UNION DISSOLVED: ANNIVERSARY. Dec 8, 1991. The Union of Soviet Socialist Republics (USSR) ceased to exist, as the republics of Russia, Byelorussia and Ukraine signed an agreement at Minsk, Byelorussia, creating the Commonwealth of Independent States. The remaining republics, with the exception of Georgia, joined in the new commonwealth as it began the slow and arduous process of removing the yoke of Communism and dealing with strong separatist and nationalistic movements within the various republics.

THURBER, JAMES: BIRTH ANNIVERSARY. Dec 8, 1894. James Grover Thurber, American humorist and artist, longtime contributor to the *New Yorker*, born at Columbus, OH. Died at New York, NY, Nov 2, 1961.

UZBEKISTAN: CONSTITUTION DAY. Dec 8. National holiday. Commemorates the constitution of 1991.

WHITNEY, ELI: BIRTH ANNIVERSARY. Dec 8, 1765. Inventor of the cotton gin, born at Westboro, MA. Died at New Haven, CT, Jan 8, 1825.

December 2014

S	M	T	W	T	F	S
	1	2	3	4	5	6
7	8	9	10	11	12	13
14	15	16	17	18	19	20
21	22	23	24	25	26	27
28	29	30	31			

BIRTHDAYS TODAY

Gregg Allman, 67, singer (The Allman Brothers Band), actor (*Rush*), born Nashville, TN, Dec 8, 1947.

Kim Basinger, 61, actress (Oscar for *L.A. Confidential*; *Batman, The Natural*), born Athens, GA, Dec 8, 1953.

Gordon Arthur "Red" Berenson, 73, former hockey player and coach, born Regina, SK, Canada, Dec 8, 1941.

Ann Coulter, 53, political commentator, author (*Slander: Liberal Lies About the American Right*), born New Canaan, CT, Dec 8, 1961.

James Galway, 75, flutist, born Belfast, Northern Ireland, Dec 8, 1939.

Teri Hatcher, 50, actress ("Desperate Housewives," "Lois & Clark"), born Sunnyvale, CA, Dec 8, 1964.

Dwight Howard, 29, basketball player, born Atlanta, GA, Dec 8, 1985.

Nicki Minaj, 30, singer, rapper, born Onika Tanya Maraj at St. James, Port of Spain, Trinidad and Tobago, Dec 8, 1984.

Dominic Monaghan, 38, actor (Lord of the Rings trilogy, "Lost"), born Berlin, Germany, Dec 8, 1976.

Mike Mussina, 46, former baseball player, born Williamsport, PA, Dec 8, 1968.

Sinead O'Connor, 48, singer, songwriter, born Dublin, Ireland, Dec 8, 1966.

Maximilian Schell, 84, actor (*Deep Impact, Topkapi, Judgment at Nuremberg*), producer, born Vienna, Austria, Dec 8, 1930.

Ian Somerhalder, 36, actor ("Lost," "Smallville"), born Covington, LA, Dec 8, 1978.

Mary Woronov, 68, actress (*Rock 'n' Roll High School, Eating Raoul*), born Brooklyn, NY, Dec 8, 1946.

December 9 — Tuesday

DAY 343 — **22 REMAINING**

AMERICA'S FIRST FORMAL CREMATION: ANNIVERSARY. Dec 9, 1792. The first formal cremation of a human body in America took place near Charleston, SC. Henry Laurens, colonial statesman and signer of the Treaty of Paris ending the Revolutionary War, in his will provided: "I do solemnly enjoin it on my son, as an indispensable duty, that as soon as he conveniently can, after my decease, he cause my body to be wrapped in twelve yards of tow cloth and burned until it be entirely consumed, and then, collecting my bones, deposit them wherever he may think proper." Laurens died Dec 8, 1792, at his plantation and was cremated there.

BIRDSEYE, CLARENCE: BIRTH ANNIVERSARY. Dec 9, 1886. American industrialist who developed a way of deep-freezing foods. He was marketing frozen fish by 1925 and was one of the founders of General Foods Corporation. Born at Brooklyn, NY, he died at New York City, Oct 7, 1956.

"CORONATION STREET" TV PREMIERE: ANNIVERSARY. Dec 9, 1960. One of the UK's longest-running television series, "Coronation Street" depicts the working-class denizens of a neighborhood in Manchester, England. Created by Tony Warren, this soap is a cultural touchstone, and show story lines have been reported on the news. Its 7,000th episode aired Jan 28, 2009.

FOXX, REDD: BIRTH ANNIVERSARY. Dec 9, 1922. Born John Elroy Sanford at St. Louis, MO, Redd Foxx plied his comedic trade on vaudeville stages, in nightclubs, on television, in films and on record albums. His talents reached a national audience with the TV sitcom "Sanford and Son." He died after collapsing during a rehearsal for a new TV sitcom, "The Royal Family," at Los Angeles, CA, Oct 11, 1991.

GENOCIDE CONVENTION: ANNIVERSARY. Dec 9, 1948. The United Nations General Assembly unanimously approved the Convention on Prevention and Punishment of the Crime of Genocide on Dec 9, 1948. It took effect Jan 12, 1951, when ratification by 20 nations had been completed. President Truman sent it to the US Senate for approval on June 16, 1949; it was supported by presidents Kennedy, Johnson, Nixon, Ford, Carter and Reagan. Thirty-seven years after its submission, and after approval by more than 90 nations, the Senate approved it, Feb 19, 1986, by a vote of 83–11.

HARRIS, JOEL CHANDLER: BIRTH ANNIVERSARY. Dec 9, 1848. American author, creator of the "Uncle Remus" stories, born at Eatonton, GA. Died July 3, 1908, at Atlanta, GA.

HOPPER, GRACE: BIRTH ANNIVERSARY. Dec 9, 1906. Born at New York, NY. When she retired from the US Navy at the age of 79, she was the oldest naval officer ever on active duty. She attained the rank of rear admiral and was a leader in the computer revolution, having developed the computer language COBOL. Grace Hopper died Jan 1, 1992, at Arlington, WV.

KELLY, EMMETT: BIRTH ANNIVERSARY. Dec 9, 1898. American circus clown and entertainer, born at Sedan, KS. Kelly was best known for "Weary Willie," a clown dressed in tattered clothes, with a beard and large nose. Died at Sarasota, FL, Mar 28, 1979.

MILTON, JOHN: BIRTH ANNIVERSARY. Dec 9, 1608. English poet, historian, civil servant and defender of freedom of the press; born at Bread Street, Cheapside, London. Considered one of the greatest poets of the English language, second only to William Shakespeare. Author of the great verse epics *Paradise Lost* (1667) and *Paradise Regained* (1671). Died from gout, Nov 8, 1674, at London, England. "No man who knows aught," he wrote, "can be so stupid to deny that all men naturally were born free."

O'NEILL, THOMAS PHILIP, II (TIP): BIRTH ANNIVERSARY. Dec 9, 1912. Democratic congressman from Massachusetts 1953–87, Speaker of the House of Representatives 1977–87, Tip O'Neill was born at Cambridge, MA, and died Jan 5, 1994, at Boston, MA.

PETRIFIED FOREST NATIONAL PARK ESTABLISHED: ANNIVERSARY. Dec 9, 1962. Arizona's Petrified Forest National Monument, proclaimed Dec 8, 1906, was established as a national park. For further park info: Petrified Forest Natl Park, Petrified Forest Natl Park, AZ 86028.

SANDYS, EDWIN: BIRTH ANNIVERSARY. Dec 9, 1561. Sir Edwin Sandys, English statesman and one of the founders of the Virginia Colony (treasurer, the Virginia Company, 1619–20), born at Worcestershire, England. Died at Kent, England, in October 1629 (exact date unknown).

TANZANIA: INDEPENDENCE AND REPUBLIC DAY. Dec 9. Tanganyika became independent of Britain in 1961. The republics of Tanganyika and Zanzibar joined to become one state (Apr 27, 1964), renamed (Oct 29, 1964) the United Republic of Tanzania.

UNITED NATIONS: INTERNATIONAL ANTI-CORRUPTION DAY. Dec 9. On Oct 31, 2003, the General Assembly adopted the United Nations Convention against Corruption (Res 58/4) and designated Dec 9 as International Anti-Corruption Day, to raise awareness of corruption and of the role of the convention in combating and preventing it. The convention entered into force in December 2005. For info: United Nations, Dept of Public Info, New York, NY, 10017. Web: www.un.org.

BIRTHDAYS TODAY

Joan Armatrading, 64, singer, songwriter (*Me, Myself, I*), born St. Kitts, West Indies, Dec 9, 1950.

Reiko Aylesworth, 42, actress ("24," "One Life to Live"), born Chicago, IL, Dec 9, 1972.

Beau Bridges, 73, actor (Emmy for *Without Warning: The James Brady Story*; *The Descendants, The Fabulous Baker Boys*), born Los Angeles, CA, Dec 9, 1941.

Phil Bryant, 60, Governor of Mississippi (R), born Moorhead, MS, Dec 9, 1954.

Richard Marvin (Dick) Butkus, 72, Hall of Fame football player, sportscaster, actor, born Chicago, IL, Dec 9, 1942.

Thomas Daschle, 67, former US senator (D, South Dakota), born Aberdeen, SD, Dec 9, 1947.

Judi Dench, 80, actress (*Mrs Brown, Iris*; Oscar for *Shakespeare in Love*), born York, England, Dec 9, 1934.

Kara DioGuardi, 44, songwriter, record producer, television personality ("American Idol"), born Ossining, NY, Dec 9, 1970.

Kirk Douglas, 98, actor (*Champion, Lust for Life*), author, born Issur Danielovitch Demsky at Amsterdam, NY, Dec 9, 1916.

Mary Fallin, 60, Governor of Oklahoma (R), born Warrensburg, MO, Dec 9, 1954.

Kirsten Gillibrand, 48, US Senator (D, New York), born Albany, NY, Dec 9, 1966.

Simon Helberg, 34, actor ("The Big Bang Theory"), born Los Angeles, CA, Dec 9, 1980.

David Anthony Higgins, 53, actor ("Ellen," "Malcolm in the Middle"), born Des Moines, IA, Dec 9, 1961.

Felicity Huffman, 52, actress (*Transamerica*, "Desperate Housewives," "Sports Night"), born Bedford, NY, Dec 9, 1962.

Thomas O. Kite, Jr, 65, golfer, born Austin, TX, Dec 9, 1949.

Joe Lando, 53, actor ("Dr. Quinn, Medicine Woman"), born Chicago, IL, Dec 9, 1961.

John Malkovich, 61, actor (*Eragon, Ripley's Game, The Killing Fields*), filmmaker, born Christopher, IL, Dec 9, 1953.

McKayla Maroney, 19, Olympic gymnast, born Aliso Viejo, CA, Dec 9, 1995.

December 2014

S	M	T	W	T	F	S
	1	2	3	4	5	6
7	8	9	10	11	12	13
14	15	16	17	18	19	20
21	22	23	24	25	26	27
28	29	30	31			

Dina Merrill, 89, actress (*Desk Set, Operation Petticoat*), born New York, NY, Dec 9, 1925.

Jesse Metcalfe, 36, actor ("Desperate Housewives," "Passions"), born Waterford, CT, Dec 9, 1978.

Michael Nouri, 69, actor ("Search for Tomorrow," *Flashdance*), born Washington, DC, Dec 9, 1945.

Donny Osmond, 57, actor, singer, born Ogden, UT, Dec 9, 1957.

Dick Van Patten, 86, actor ("Eight Is Enough," "Mama"), born Richmond Hill, NY, Dec 9, 1928.

December 10 — Wednesday

DAY 344 **21 REMAINING**

DEWEY, MELVIL: BIRTH ANNIVERSARY. Dec 10, 1851. American librarian and inventor of the Dewey decimal book classification system was born at Adams Center, NY. Born Melville Louis Kossuth Dewey, he was an advocate of spelling reform, urged use of the metric system and was interested in many other education reforms. Dewey died at Highlands County, FL, Dec 26, 1931.

DICKINSON, EMILY: BIRTH ANNIVERSARY. Dec 10, 1830. One of America's greatest poets, Emily Dickinson was born at Amherst, MA. She was reclusive, mysterious and frail in health. Seven of her poems were published during her life, but after her death on May 15, 1886, at Amherst, MA, her sister, Lavinia, discovered almost 2,000 more poems written on the backs of envelopes and other scraps of paper locked in her bureau. They were published gradually, over 50 years, beginning in 1890. Dickinson now is recognized as one of the most original poets of the English-speaking world.

FIRST GRAND OLE OPRY BROADCAST: ANNIVERSARY. Dec 10, 1927. Grand Ole Opry made its first radio broadcast from Nashville, TN.

FIRST US HEAVYWEIGHT CHAMP DEFEATED IN ENGLAND: ANNIVERSARY. Dec 10, 1810. Tom Molineaux, the first unofficial heavyweight champion of the US, was a freed slave from Virginia. He was beaten in the 40th round by Tom Cribb, the English champion, in a boxing match at Copthall Common at London.

FIRST US SCIENTIST RECEIVES NOBEL PRIZE: ANNIVERSARY. Dec 10, 1907. University of Chicago professor Albert Michelson, eminent physicist known for his research on the speed of light and optics became the first US scientist to receive the Nobel Prize.

GALLAUDET, THOMAS HOPKINS: BIRTH ANNIVERSARY. Dec 10, 1787. A hearing educator who, with Laurent Clerc, founded the first public school for deaf people, the Connecticut Asylum for the Education and Instruction of Deaf and Dumb Persons (now named the American School for the Deaf), at Hartford, CT, Apr 15, 1817. Gallaudet was born at Philadelphia, PA, and died Sept 9, 1851, at Hartford, CT.

✦HUMAN RIGHTS DAY. Dec 10. Presidential Proclamation 2866, of Dec 6, 1949, covers all succeeding years. Customarily issued as "Bill of Rights Day, Human Rights Day and Week."

✦HUMAN RIGHTS WEEK. Dec 10–17. Presidential Proclamation issued since 1958 for the week of Dec 10–17, except in 1986. See also: "Human Rights Day" (Dec 10) and "Bill of Rights Day" (Dec 15).

JANE ADDAMS DAY. Dec 10. A day set aside to celebrate Jane Addams's life—on the anniversary of Addams receiving the first Nobel Peace Prize ever awarded to an American woman (1931). Illinois honors Jane Addams's memory with a commemorative holiday to observe her lifelong commitment to making the city of Chicago, the state of Illinois and the entire world a better place. First observed in 2007. Annually, Dec 10. For info: Jane Addams Hull-House Museum, 800 S Halsted St, Chicago, IL 60607. Phone: (312) 413-5353. Fax: (312) 413-2092. Web: www.hullhousemuseum.org.

LAMOUR, DOROTHY: 100th BIRTH ANNIVERSARY. Dec 10, 1914. Popular singer and actress of the 1930s and '40s. Best known for her appearances in the *Road* movies—*Road to Singapore* (1940) and many others—with Bing Crosby and Bob Hope, where she was often clad in a sarong. Other notable films include *The Hurricane* and *My Favorite Brunette*. Born Mary Leta Dorothy Kaumeyer at New Orleans, LA, she died Sept 22, 1996, at Los Angeles, CA.

"THE MIGHTY MOUSE PLAYHOUSE" TV PREMIERE: ANNIVERSARY. Dec 10, 1955. An all-time favorite of the Saturday-morning crowd (including adults). CBS had a hit with its pint-sized cartoon character Mighty Mouse, who was a tongue-in-cheek version of Superman. The show had other feature cartoons such as "The Adventures of Gandy Goose."

MISSISSIPPI: ADMISSION DAY: ANNIVERSARY. Dec 10. Became 20th state in 1817.

NOBEL PRIZE AWARDS CEREMONIES. Dec 10. Oslo, Norway, and Stockholm, Sweden. Alfred Nobel, Swedish chemist and inventor of dynamite who died in 1896, provided in his will that income from his $9 million estate should be used for annual prizes to be awarded to people who are judged to have made the most valuable contributions to the good of humanity. The Nobel Peace Prize is awarded by a committee of the Norwegian parliament and the presentation is made at the Oslo City Hall. Five other prizes, for physics, chemistry, medicine, literature and economics, are presented in a ceremony at Stockholm, Sweden. Both ceremonies traditionally are held on the anniversary of the death of Alfred Nobel. First awarded in 1901, the current value of each prize is about $1,000,000. See also "Nobel, Alfred Bernhard: Birth Anniversary" (Oct 21).

NORTON, MARY: BIRTH ANNIVERSARY. Dec 10, 1903. British author Mary Norton was born at London, England. An author of children's books, she is best known for *Bedknob and Broomstick* (1957). She died Aug 29, 1992, at Hartland, England.

PAN, HERMES: BIRTH ANNIVERSARY. Dec 10, 1909 (some sources say 1905 or 1910). American choreographer born Hermes Panagiotopolous at Memphis, TN. He is best known for choreographing nine of the ten films starring Fred Astaire and Ginger Rogers; he won the Academy Award in choreography for *A Damsel in Distress* (1937). Pan died at Beverly Hills, CA, on Sept 19, 1990.

RALPH BUNCHE AWARDED NOBEL PEACE PRIZE: ANNIVERSARY. Dec 10, 1950. Dr. Ralph Johnson Bunche became the first black man awarded the Nobel Peace Prize. Bunche was awarded the prize for his efforts in mediation between Israel and neighboring Arab states in 1949.

RED CLOUD: DEATH ANNIVERSARY. Dec 10, 1909. Sioux Indian chief Red Cloud was born in 1822 (exact date unknown), near North Platte, NE. A courageous leader and defender of Native American rights, Red Cloud was the son of Lone Man and Walks as She Thinks. His unrelenting determination caused US abandonment of the Bozeman trail and of three forts that interfered with Native American hunting grounds. Red Cloud died at Pine Ridge, SD.

SPACE MILESTONE: *SOYUZ 26* (USSR). Dec 10, 1977. Launched this date with cosmonauts Yuri Romanenko and Georgi Grechko who linked it with *Salyut 6* space station on Dec 11, after the unsuccessful attempt by *Soyuz 25* earlier that year. Returned to Earth in *Soyuz 27*, Mar 16, 1978, after record-setting 96 days in space.

THAILAND: CONSTITUTION DAY. Dec 10. National holiday. Commemorates the constitution of 1932, the nation's first.

TREATY OF PARIS ENDS SPANISH-AMERICAN WAR: ANNIVERSARY. Dec 10, 1898. Following the conclusion of the Spanish-American War in 1898, American and Spanish ambassadors met at Paris, France, to negotiate a treaty. Under the terms of this treaty, Spain granted the US the Philippine Islands and the islands of Guam and Puerto Rico and agreed to withdraw from Cuba. Senatorial debate over the treaty centered on the US's move toward imperialism by acquiring the Philippines. A vote was taken Feb 6, 1899, and the treaty passed by a one-vote margin. President William McKinley signed the treaty Feb 10, 1899.

UNITED NATIONS: HUMAN RIGHTS DAY. Dec 10. Official United Nations observance day. Date is the anniversary of adoption of the "Universal Declaration of Human Rights" in 1948. The declaration sets forth basic rights and fundamental freedoms to which all men and women in the world are entitled. For info: United Nations, Dept of Public Info, New York, NY 10017. E-mail: inquiries@un.org. Web: www.un.org.

BIRTHDAYS TODAY

Rod Blagojevich, 58, former governor of Illinois (D), born Chicago, IL, Dec 10, 1956.

John Boozman, 64, US Senator (R, Arkansas), born Fort Smith, AR, Dec 10, 1950.

Kenneth Branagh, 54, actor ("Wallander," *Shackleton*), director (*Hamlet*, *Henry V*), born Belfast, Northern Ireland, Dec 10, 1960.

Susan Dey, 62, model, actress ("The Partridge Family," "LA Law,"), born Pekin, IL, Dec 10, 1952.

Bobby Flay, 50, chef, television personality ("Boy Meets Grill," "Iron Chef America"), born New York, NY, Dec 10, 1964.

Gloria Loring, 68, singer, actress ("Days of Our Lives"), born New York, NY, Dec 10, 1946.

December 11 — Thursday

DAY 345 — **20 REMAINING**

BUELL, MARJORIE H.: BIRTH ANNIVERSARY. Dec 11, 1904. Cartoonist, creator of comic strip character Little Lulu, Marjorie Buell was considered a pioneer for creating a female character who outsmarted the neighborhood boys. She was born at Philadelphia, PA, and died May 30, 1993, at Elyria, OH.

BURKINA FASO: NATIONAL DAY. Dec 11. Gained independence within the French community, 1958.

CANNON, ANNIE JUMP: BIRTH ANNIVERSARY. Dec 11, 1863. American astronomer and discoverer of five stars, Annie Jump Cannon was born at Dover, DE, and educated at Wellseley College in physics and astronomy before becoming a "Pickering Woman" at the Harvard College Observatory in 1896. She later curated astronomical photographs at the observatory and was a professor of astronomy at Harvard. Cannon, renowned for her cataloging classification system of stars and awarded Oxford University's first honorary doctorate given to a woman (1925) and the National Academy of Science Draper Medal (1931), died at Cambridge, MA, Apr 13, 1941.

CLUTE'S CHRISTMAS IN THE PARK. Dec 11–13. Clute Municipal Park, Clute, TX. A Christmas event with nightly entertainment, Santa's Land, a beautifully decorated Christmas tree forest and a marshmallow roasting pit. Food and crafts. Great family fun for all ages; 6:00–8:30 PM. Est attendance: 1,500. For info: Clute Parks and Recreation, PO Box 997, Clute, TX 77531. Phone: (800) 371-2971 or (979) 265-8392. Fax: (979) 265-8767. E-mail: buzz@mosquitofestival.com.

EDWARD VIII ABDICATION: ANNIVERSARY. Dec 11, 1936. Christened Edward Albert Christian George Andrew Patrick David, King Edward VIII was born at Richmond Park, England, on June 12, 1894, and became Prince of Wales in July 1911. He ascended to the English throne upon the death of his father, George V, on Jan 20, 1936, but coronation never took place. He abdicated on Dec 11, 1936, in order to marry "the woman I love," twice-divorced American Wallis Warfield Simpson. They were married in France, June 3, 1937. Edward was named Duke of Windsor by his brother-successor, George VI. The duke died at Paris, May 28, 1972, but was buried in England, near Windsor Castle.

INDIANA: ADMISSION DAY: ANNIVERSARY. Dec 11. Became 19th state in 1816.

KOCH, ROBERT: BIRTH ANNIVERSARY. Dec 11, 1843. The great German physician and biologist, born Clausthal, Hannover (now Germany), discovered the bacilli that cause tuberculosis, cholera and anthrax. For his important work on tuberculosis, Koch received the 1905 Nobel Prize in Physiology and Medicine. He died May 27, 1910, at Baden-Baden, Germany.

LA GUARDIA, FIORELLO HENRY: BIRTH ANNIVERSARY. Dec 11, 1882. Popularly known as the "Little Flower," Fiorello H. La Guardia was not too busy as mayor of New York City to read the "funnies" to radio listeners during the New York newspaper strike. He said of himself: "When I make a mistake it's a beaut!" La Guardia was born at New York, NY, and died there Sept 20, 1947.

"MAGNUM, PI" TV PREMIERE: ANNIVERSARY. Dec 11, 1980. Premiered on CBS television network, starring Tom Selleck, John Hillerman, Roger E. Mosley and Larry Manetti. Each year on this anniversary, "Magnum" fans turn to the international fan organization Magnum Memorabilia by David Romas as the center of observances worldwide. For info: David Romas, Magnum Memorabilia, 438 Leroy St, Ferndale, MI 48220. E-mail: ac2942@wayne.edu.

MAHFOUZ, NAGUIB: BIRTH ANNIVERSARY. Dec 11, 1911. The only author from the Arab world to win the Nobel Prize in Literature (1988), Mahfouz was born at Old Cairo, Egypt. Mahfouz's work depicted a rapidly transforming Egypt. His masterwork is *The Cairo Trilogy* (1956–7), which chronicles three generations of an Egyptian family in the 1920s and 1930s. He wrote scores of novels, short stories and articles—and much of that work was made into films in the Arab world. In 1994, he survived a knife attack that damaged his nerves and slowed his output. Mahfouz died at Cairo on Aug 30, 2006.

SOLZHENITSYN, ALEKSANDR: BIRTH ANNIVERSARY. Dec 11, 1918. Russian author and dissident, born on this date in Kislovodsk, USSR (now Russia). Awarded the 1970 Nobel Prize in Literature in recognition of novels *One Day in the Life of Ivan Denisovich* and *The Gulag Archipelago* based on his experiences as a prisoner in Soviet forced labor camps (1945–53). Exiled from USSR in 1974; returned in 1994. By the time of his death on Aug 3, 2008, at Troitse-Lykovo, Russia, he had been embraced by his country as an elder statesman and honored author and humanitarian.

THOMASVILLE'S VICTORIAN CHRISTMAS. Dec 11–12. Thomasville, GA. Downtown Thomasville relives Christmas past as it celebrates the Victorian era of the late 1800s. Costumed strollers and carolers, horse-drawn carriages and colorful characters from the past fill the streets of downtown. Victorian-clad merchants welcome shoppers with hot cider and confections, and street vendors offer Christmas delicacies. Free admission. Est attendance: 30,000. For info: Thomasville Victorian Christmas, Thomasville Main Street, PO Box 1540, Thomasville, GA 31799. Phone: (229) 227-7020. E-mail: felicia@thomasville.org. Web: www.downtownthomasville.com.

December 2014	S	M	T	W	T	F	S
		1	2	3	4	5	6
	7	8	9	10	11	12	13
	14	15	16	17	18	19	20
	21	22	23	24	25	26	27
	28	29	30	31			

UNITED NATIONS: INTERNATIONAL MOUNTAIN DAY. Dec 11. With mountains covering one-quarter of the Earth's land surface and home to 12 percent of the world's population, mountain people are affected by conflict out of all proportion to their numbers and the land they occupy. The UN General Assembly declared Dec 11 International Mountain Day as a result of the successful observance of the UN International Year of Mountains in 2002, which increased global awareness of the importance of mountains, stimulated the establishment of national committees in 78 countries and strengthened alliances through promoting the creation of the Mountain Partnership. For info: United Nations, Dept of Public Info, New York, NY 10017. Web: www.un.org or www.mountainpartnership.org.

UNITED NATIONS: UNICEF ESTABLISHED: ANNIVERSARY. Dec 11, 1946. Anniversary of the establishment by the United Nations General Assembly of the United Nations International Children's Emergency Fund (UNICEF). For info: United Nations, Dept of Public Info, New York, NY 10017. Web: www.unicef.org.

BIRTHDAYS TODAY

Max Baucus, 73, US Senator (D, Montana), born Helena, MT, Dec 11, 1941.

Jay Bell, 49, former baseball player, born Pensacola, FL, Dec 11, 1965.

Mos Def, 41, rapper, actor (*16 Blocks, The Italian Job*), born Dante Terrell Smith at Brooklyn, NY, Dec 11, 1973.

Gary Dourdan, 48, actor ("CSI," *Alien: Resurrection*), born Philadelphia, PA, Dec 11, 1966.

Teri Garr, 65, actress (*Young Frankenstein, Tootsie, The Black Stallion*), born Lakewood, OH, Dec 11, 1949.

David Gates, 74, singer, songwriter, born Tulsa, OK, Dec 11, 1940.

Tom Hayden, 74, journalist, activist, politician, born Royal Oak, MI, Dec 11, 1940.

Jermaine Jackson, 60, singer, musician (Jackson 5), born Gary, IN, Dec 11, 1954.

John F. Kerry, 71, US Secretary of State, former US senator (D, Massachusetts), born Denver, CO, Dec 11, 1943.

Brenda Lee, 70, singer, born Brenda Mae Tarpley at Atlanta, GA, Dec 11, 1944.

Donna Mills, 71, actress ("Knots Landing," "Melrose Place"), born Chicago, IL, Dec 11, 1943.

Mo'Nique, 47, actress, talk show host (Oscar for *Precious: Based on the Novel "Push" by Sapphire*, "The Parkers"), born Monique Imes at Woodlawn, MD, Dec 11, 1967.

Rita Moreno, 83, singer, actress (Oscar for *West Side Story*; Tony for *The Ritz*), born Hunacao, Puerto Rico, Dec 11, 1931.

Susan Seidelman, 62, filmmaker (*Desperately Seeking Susan, Making Mr Right*), born Philadelphia, PA, Dec 11, 1952.

Hailee Steinfeld, 18, actress (*True Grit*), born Thousand Oaks, CA, Dec 11, 1996.

Mark Streit, 37, hockey player, born Englisberg, Switzerland, Dec 11, 1977.

Rider Strong, 35, actor ("Boy Meets World"), born San Francisco, CA, Dec 11, 1979.

Ken Wahl, 61, actor ("Wiseguy"; *The Wanderers; Fort Apache, The Bronx*), born Chicago, IL, Dec 11, 1953.

Curtis Williams, 52, musician, singer, born Buffalo, NY, Dec 11, 1962.

December 12 — Friday

DAY 346 **19 REMAINING**

BONZA BOTTLER DAY™. Dec 12. To celebrate when the number of the day is the same as the number of the month. Bonza Bottler Day™ is an excuse to have a party at least once a month. For more information see Jan 1. For info: Gail Berger, 14 Fernwood Dr, Taylors, SC 29687. Phone: (864) 201-3988. E-mail: bonza@bonzabottlerday.com. Web: www.bonzabottlerday.com.

DAY OF OUR LADY OF GUADALUPE. Dec 12. The legend of Guadalupe tells how in December 1531, an Indian, Juan Diego, saw the Virgin Mother on a hill near Mexico City. She instructed him to go to the bishop and have him build a shrine to her on the site of the vision. After his request was initially rebuffed, the Virgin Mother appeared to Juan Diego three days later. She instructed him to pick roses growing on a stony and barren hillside nearby and take them to the bishop as proof. Although flowers do not normally bloom in December, Juan Diego found the roses and took them to the bishop. As he opened his mantle to drop the roses on the floor, an image of the Virgin Mary appeared among them. The bishop built the sanctuary as instructed. Our Lady of Guadalupe became the patroness of Mexico City and by 1746 was the patron saint of all New Spain and by 1910 of all Latin America.

FIRST BLACK SERVES IN US HOUSE OF REPRESENTATIVES: ANNIVERSARY. Dec 12, 1870. Joseph Hayne Rainey of Georgetown, SC, was sworn in as the first black to serve in the US House of Representatives. Rainey filled the seat of Benjamin Franklin Whittemore, which had been declared vacant by the House. He served until Mar 3, 1879.

FLAUBERT, GUSTAVE: BIRTH ANNIVERSARY. Dec 12, 1821. French author whose works include one of the greatest French novels, *Madame Bovary*, was born at Rouen. Flaubert died at Croisset, France, May 8, 1880.

GARRISON, WILLIAM LLOYD: BIRTH ANNIVERSARY. Dec 12, 1805. American antislavery leader, poet and journalist, was born at Newburyport, MA. Garrison died at New York, NY, May 24, 1879.

INGALLS, CAROLINE LAKE QUINER: 175th BIRTH ANNIVERSARY. Dec 12, 1839. The first settler born at Brookfield, WI, Ingalls was a teacher before she married a restless Charles Ingalls, who moved his family from Wisconsin to Kansas to Iowa and Minnesota before finally landing at De Smet in the Dakota Territory. The mother of five children, including Laura Ingalls Wilder, who recorded her family's pioneer experience in the *Little House on the Prairie* novels. Ingalls died Apr 20, 1894, at De Smet, SD.

JAY, JOHN: BIRTH ANNIVERSARY. Dec 12, 1745. (Old Style date.) American statesman, diplomat and first chief justice of the US (1789–95), coauthor (with Alexander Hamilton and James Madison) of the influential *Federalist* papers, was born at New York, NY. Jay died at Bedford, NY, May 17, 1829.

KENYA: JAMHURI DAY. Dec 12. Jamhuri Day (Independence Day) is Kenya's official National Day, commemorating proclamation of the republic and independence from Britain in 1963.

KOCH, ED: BIRTH ANNIVERSARY. Dec 12, 1924. Politician born at New York, NY. A congressman from 1969–1977, Koch was elected mayor of New York City in 1977. A colorful figure who rode the subways, Koch reached out to his constituents for advice and commentary. His business acumen brought the city out of dire financial straits but he weathered many scandals and controversies during his tenure in office. After leaving office, he practiced law and taught at several universities, but was never far from the public eye. He wrote 17 books, including several mysteries, and made scores of cameo appearances in film and television, complete with a brief stint as a judge on "The People's Court." He died Feb 1, 2013, at New York, NY.

MEXICO: GUADALUPE DAY. Dec 12. One of Mexico's major celebrations. Honors the "Dark Virgin of Guadalupe," the republic's patron saint. Parties and pilgrimages, with special ceremonies at the Shrine of Our Lady of Guadalupe at Mexico City.

MUNCH, EDVARD: BIRTH ANNIVERSARY. Dec 12, 1863. Born at Löten, Norway, Munch was a painter and printmaker whose work influenced the development of German Expressionism. Munch's use of bold lines, violent imagery and blunt sexuality shocked conventional society, but he called it "soul painting." His most famous work, *The Scream* (1893), has become an icon of the anxiety inherent in modern consciousness. In 2012, at $120 million, it became the most expensive work of art ever sold at auction. Munch died at Ekely, Norway, on Jan 23, 1944.

NCAA DIVISION I MEN'S SOCCER CHAMPIONSHIP—THE COLLEGE CUP. Dec 12 and 14. Site TBD. For info: NCAA, PO Box 6222, Indianapolis, IN 46206-6222. Phone: (317) 917-6222. Web: www.NCAA.com.

O'BRIAN, PATRICK: 100th BIRTH ANNIVERSARY. Dec 12, 1914. Born Richard Patrick Russ at Chalfont St. Peter, England, O'Brian was a prolific novelist, biographer and translator. His most famous works are the maritime Aubrey-Maturin novels, a twenty-volume series set during the Napoleonic wars, which opened with *Master and Commander* (1969). O'Brian died Jan 2, 2000, at Dublin, Ireland.

OFFICIAL LOST AND FOUND DAY. Dec 12. 3rd annual. Today is a day for renewed hope and belief that lost items should never be forgotten or abandoned to lost and found limbo. Please take a moment on Official Lost and Found Day to make one more effort, one more leap of faith, that what you've lost isn't gone, it's just not conveniently handy. Reach out, make a call, stop by the office, retrace your steps. What was lost can be found. It's up to you. Annually, the second Friday in each December. For info: Lance Morgan, Official Lost and Found Day, Chautauqua Elementary, 9309 SW Cemetery Rd, Vashon, WA 98070. Phone: (206) 463-2882. Fax: (206) 463-0937. E-mail: lmorgan@vashonsd.org. Web: www.lostandfoundday.atspace.cc/.

PENNSYLVANIA RATIFIES CONSTITUTION: ANNIVERSARY. Dec 12, 1787. Pennsylvania became the second state to ratify the US Constitution, by a vote of 46 to 23, in 1787.

POINSETTIA DAY (JOEL ROBERTS POINSETT: DEATH ANNIVERSARY). Dec 12. A day to enjoy poinsettias and to honor Dr. Joel Roberts Poinsett, the American diplomat who introduced into the US the Central American plant that is named for him. Poinsett was born at Charleston, SC, Mar 2, 1799. He also served as a member of Congress and as secretary of war. He died near Statesburg, SC, Dec 12, 1851. The poinsettia has become a favorite Christmas season plant.

PUERTO RICO: LAS MAÑANITAS. Dec 12. Ponce, Puerto Rico. Procession at 5 AM honoring patron saint, Virgen de la Guadalupe. Mass with music from a mariachi band. Annually, on Dec 12.

SINATRA, FRANK: BIRTH ANNIVERSARY. Dec 12, 1915. Born at Hoboken, NJ, Frank Sinatra matured from a teen idol to the premier singer of American popular music. Known as the "Chairman of the Board" to his fans, he made more than 200 albums. His signature songs included "All the Way," "New York, New York" and "My Way." His film career included musicals (*On the Town* and *Pal Joey*) and two gritty films: *From Here to Eternity* (Oscar for Best Supporting Actor) and *The Man with the Golden Arm* (Oscar nomination). Died May 14, 1998, at Los Angeles, CA.

SUPREME COURT RULES FOR BUSH: ANNIVERSARY. Dec 12, 2000. The Supreme Court ruled by a vote of 5 to 4 that there could be no further counting of Florida's disputed presidential votes, ending deliberations over the 2000 presidential election. After five weeks of conflict over this pivotal vote count in Florida, Democratic candidate Al Gore conceded the election to George W. Bush. While Bush won the electoral vote to become the nation's 43rd president, Gore won the popular vote. Bush was only the fourth president in American history to be elected without winning the popular vote.

TURKMENISTAN: NEUTRALITY DAY. Dec 12. National holiday. Commemorates the UN's recognition of Turkmenistan's neutrality in 1995.

WATIE, STAND: BIRTH ANNIVERSARY. Dec 12, 1806. Born at Rome, GA, and died there Sept 9, 1871. Cherokee chief who, by signing the treaty of New Echota, surrendered his people's land in Georgia, forcing relocation to Oklahoma. Though the three other signers were murdered, Watie escaped and went on to initiate the first volunteer Cherokee regiment for the Confederates in the Civil War. Promoted to brigadier general, he was active in destroying the property of other Native Americans who supported the Union.

BIRTHDAYS TODAY

Tracy Ann Austin, 52, Hall of Fame tennis player, born Rolling Hills Estates, CA, Dec 12, 1962.

Bob Barker, 91, television personality, game show host (Emmy for "The Price Is Right"), born Darrington, WA, Dec 12, 1923.

Mayim Bialik, 39, actress ("Blossom," "The Big Bang Theory"), born San Diego, CA, Dec 12, 1975.

Jennifer Connelly, 44, actress (*Reservation Road, Blood Diamond,* Oscar for *A Beautiful Mind*), born Catskill Mountains, NY, Dec 12, 1970.

Sheila E, 55, singer, musician, born Sheila Escoveda at San Francisco, CA, Dec 12, 1959.

Connie Francis, 76, singer, born Constance Franconero at Newark, NJ, Dec 12, 1938.

Robert Lindsay, 65, actor (*Me and My Girl*), born Derbyshire, England, Dec 12, 1949.

Rey Mysterio, Jr, 40, professional wrestler, born Óscar Gutiérrez Rubio at Washington, DC, Dec 12, 1974.

Robert Lee (Bob) Pettit, Jr, 82, Hall of Fame basketball player, born Baton Rouge, LA, Dec 12, 1932.

Cathy Rigby, 62, Olympic gymnast, born Long Beach, CA, Dec 12, 1952.

Dionne Warwick, 73, singer, born East Orange, NJ, Dec 12, 1941.

Tom Wilkinson, 66, actor (*In the Bedroom, The Full Monty, Michael Clayton*), born Leeds, West Yorkshire, England, Dec 12, 1948.

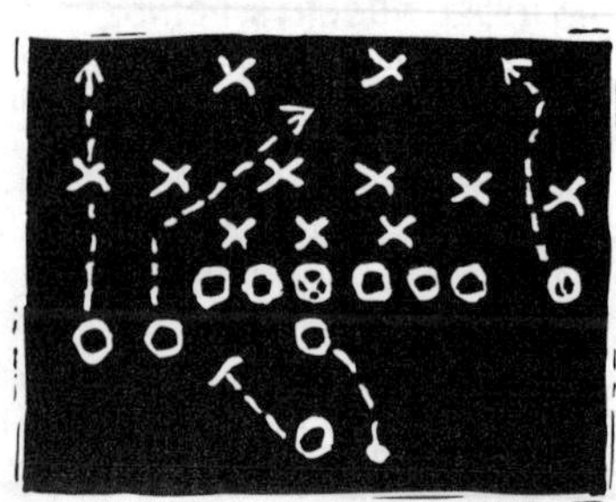

December 2014

S	M	T	W	T	F	S
	1	2	3	4	5	6
7	8	9	10	11	12	13
14	15	16	17	18	19	20
21	22	23	24	25	26	27
28	29	30	31			

December 13 — Saturday

DAY 347 **18 REMAINING**

AKC/EUKANUBA NATIONAL CHAMPIONSHIP. Dec 13–14. Orange County Convention Center, Orlando, FL. At the AKC/Eukanuba National Championship, the top dogs from around the globe compete for the biggest cash prizes offered in the sport. Intense competition, unique awards for breeders and special events for spectators make this the most exciting event in the dog world. For info: American Kennel Club, 260 Madison Ave, New York, NY 10016. Phone: (212) 696-8200. E-mail: invitational@akc.org. Web: www.akc.org.

BATTLE OF FREDERICKSBURG, VIRGINIA: ANNIVERSARY. Dec 13, 1862. Confederate forces were victorious at the Battle of Fredericksburg, VA. Total casualties on both sides estimated at more than 16,000 killed, injured or missing. General Ambrose E. Burnside led Union troops; General Robert E. Lee led the Confederates.

BELGIUM: NUTS FAIR (FOIRE AUX NOIX). Dec 13. Bastogne. Traditional cultural observance. Annually, the second Saturday in December. For more info: Commune de Bastogne. Web: www.bastogne.be.

GINGERBREAD DECORATING DAY. Dec 13. Gingerbread decorating is a classic holiday tradition for all ages: few things can serve as a more festive centerpiece than a gingerbread house. Decorating gingerbread houses is easy and brings the whole family together. Adults and kids can have a ball decorating with their favorite candies to create roof tiles, holly wreaths and playfully patterned window designs. The results and memories will be special. Ideas, instruction, recipes, trouble-shooting and more at the Wilton website. Annually, the second Saturday in December. For info:Wilton, 2240 W 75th St, Woodridge, IL 60517. Phone: (630) 810-2221. E-mail: Vfarrasso@wilton.com. Web: www.wilton.com.

HEINE, HEINRICH: BIRTH ANNIVERSARY. Dec 13, 1797. German poet and critic, born at Dusseldorf. Died at Paris, France, Feb 17, 1856.

INTERNATIONAL SHAREWARE DAY. Dec 13. A day to take the time to reward the efforts of thousands of computer programmers who trust that if we try their programs and like them, we will pay for them. Unfortunately, very few payments are received, thus stifling the programmers' efforts. This observance is meant to prompt each of us to inventory our PCs and Macs, see if we are using any shareware and then take the time in the holiday spirit to write payment checks to the authors. Hopefully this will keep shareware coming. Annually, the second Saturday in December. (Originated by David Lawrence.)

LINCOLN, MARY TODD: BIRTH ANNIVERSARY. Dec 13, 1818. Wife of Abraham Lincoln, 16th president of the US, born at Lexington, KY. Died at Springfield, IL, July 16, 1882.

LIVE: FAMILY CHRISTMAS AT THE BENJAMIN HARRISON HOME. Dec 13. Indianapolis, IN. Guided tour of the 23rd president's home decorated in seasonal Victorian style. For info: Benjamin Harrison Presidential Site, 1230 N Delaware St, Indianapolis, IN 46202-2531. Phone: (317) 631-1888. Fax: (317) 632-5488. E-mail: events@bhpsite.org. Web: www.bhpsite.org.

MALTA: REPUBLIC DAY. Dec 13. National holiday. Malta became a republic in 1974.

MOORE, ARCHIE: BIRTH ANNIVERSARY. Dec 13, 1913. Born Archibald Lee Wright at Benoit, MS. One of the most colorful fighters ever, Moore boxed from the mid-1930s to 1963, holding the light-heavyweight title for a record nine years. For much of his career, he fought an average of once a month. Moore let an aura of celebrity surround him: he lied about his age, ate an unusual diet, married five times and spoke out on a variety of political and social issues. Died at San Diego, CA, Dec 9, 1998.

NANKING MASSACRE: ANNIVERSARY. Dec 13–January 1938. "The Rape of Nanking" began after the Japanese took Nanking during the Sino-Japanese War. Hundreds of thousands of Chinese soldiers, civilians and women were murdered or raped.

NATIONAL DAY OF THE HORSE. Dec 13. The horse is a living link to the heritage and history of our nation and represents a common bond among all peoples who led the way in building our country. Today, the horse industry contributes more than $112 billion annually to the American economy. Therefore, the California State Legislature (as well as the US Senate) has declared the second Saturday of December to be the Day of the Horse in honor of these magnificent creatures.

NEW ZEALAND FIRST SIGHTED BY EUROPEANS: ANNIVERSARY. Dec 13, 1642. Captain Abel Tasman of the Dutch East India Company first sighted New Zealand but was kept from landing by Maori warriors. In 1769 Captain James Cook landed and claimed formal possession for Great Britain.

NORTH AND SOUTH KOREA END WAR: ANNIVERSARY. Dec 13, 1991. North and South Korea signed a treaty of reconciliation and nonaggression, formally ending the Korean War—38 years after fighting ceased in 1953. This agreement was not hailed as a peace treaty, and the armistice that was signed July 27, 1953, between the UN and North Korea, was to remain in effect until it could be transformed into a formal peace.

POLISH CHRISTMAS OPEN HOUSE. Dec 13. Polish American Cultural Center Museum, Philadelphia, PA. Sw. Mikolaj (Polish St. Nicholas) will greet everyone with gifts for the children. Polish Christmas tree and entertainment. Free admission. For info: Polish American Cultural Center Museum, 308 Walnut St, Philadelphia, PA 19106. Phone: (215) 922-1700. Fax: (215) 922-1518. E-mail: mail@polishamericancenter.com. Web: www.polishamericancenter.com.

SWEDEN: SANTA LUCIA DAY. Dec 13. Nationwide celebration of festival of light, honoring St. Lucia. Many hotels have their own Lucia, a young girl attired in a long, flowing white gown, who serves guests coffee and lussekatter (saffron buns) in the early morning.

BIRTHDAYS TODAY

Steve Buscemi, 56, actor ("Boardwalk Empire," *Ghost World, Fargo, Reservoir Dogs*), born Brooklyn, NY, Dec 13, 1958.

John Davidson, 73, singer, actor, former television host, born Pittsburgh, PA, Dec 13, 1941.

Richard Dent, 54, Hall of Fame football player, born Atlanta, GA, Dec 13, 1960.

Sergei Fedorov, 45, hockey manager and former player, born Pskov, Russia, Dec 13, 1969.

Jamie Foxx, 47, actor (Oscar for *Ray*; *Django Unchained, Jarhead, Collateral*), singer, musician, producer, born Eric Marlon Bishop at Terrell, TX, Dec 13, 1967.

Wendie Malick, 64, actress ("Just Shoot Me," "Hot in Cleveland"), born Buffalo, NY, Dec 13, 1950.

Ted Nugent, 65, singer, born Detroit, MI, Dec 13, 1949.

Christopher Plummer, 85, actor (Oscar for *Beginners*; *The Last Station, The Sound of Music*), born Toronto, ON, Canada, Dec 13, 1929.

Taylor Swift, 25, singer, born Reading, PA, Dec 13, 1989.

Dick Van Dyke, 89, comedian, actor (*Mary Poppins*, "The Dick Van Dyke Show," "Diagnosis Murder"), born West Plains, MO, Dec 13, 1925.

Tom Vilsack, 64, US Secretary of Agriculture, former governor of Iowa (D), born Pittsburgh, PA, Dec 13, 1950.

December 14 — Sunday

DAY 348 **17 REMAINING**

ALABAMA: ADMISSION DAY: ANNIVERSARY. Dec 14. Became 22nd state in 1819.

CHRISTMAS BIRD COUNT. Dec 14–Jan 5, 2015. In 1900, ornithologist Frank Chapman, an early officer in the then-budding Audubon Society, proposed a new holiday tradition—a "Christmas Bird Census"—that would count birds in the holidays rather than hunt them. Now, tens of thousands of volunteers throughout the Americas take part in an adventure that has become a family tradition among generations. Families and students, birders and scientists, armed with binoculars, bird guides and checklists go out on an annual mission—often before dawn. Each of the citizen scientists who annually braves snow, wind or rain to take part in the Christmas Bird Count makes an enormous contribution to conservation. Audubon and other organizations use data collected in this longest-running wildlife census to assess the health of bird populations—and to help guide conservation action. Annually, Dec 14 to Jan 5. For info: National Audubon Society, 225 Varick St, 7th Fl, New York, NY 10014. E-mail: cbcadmin@audubon.org. Web: www.audubon.org/bird/cbc/.

THE COMPASSIONATE FRIENDS WORLDWIDE CANDLE LIGHTING. Dec 14. A day to remember all children who have died. Annually, the second Sunday in December. For info: The Compassionate Friends, PO Box 3696, Oak Brook, IL 60522-3696. Phone: (877) 969-0010. E-mail: nationaloffice@compassionatefriends.org. Web: www.compassionatefriends.org.

DAVIS, ERNIE: 75th BIRTH ANNIVERSARY. Dec 14, 1939. The football running back was born in New Salem, PA, and grew up in Elmira, NY. Playing for Syracuse University, the "Elmira Express" became the first African American to win the Heisman Trophy in 1961. Drafted to the Cleveland Browns, he never played a game as he succumbed to leukemia at age 23. Davis died May 18, 1963, at Cleveland, OH.

DOOLITTLE, JAMES HAROLD: BIRTH ANNIVERSARY. Dec 14, 1896. American aviator and WWII hero General James Doolittle was born at Alameda, CA. A lieutenant general in the US Army Air Force, he was the first person to fly across North America in less than a day. On Apr 18, 1942, Doolittle led a squadron of 16 B-25 bombers, launched from aircraft carriers, on the first US aerial raid on Japan of WWII. He was awarded the Congressional Medal of Honor for this accomplishment. Doolittle also headed the Eighth Air Force during the Normandy invasion. He died Sept 27, 1993, at Pebble Beach, CA.

HALCYON DAYS. Dec 14–28. Traditionally, the seven days before and the seven days after the winter solstice. To the ancients, a time when fabled bird (called the halcyon—pronounced hal-cee-on) calmed the wind and waves—a time of calm and tranquility.

MOON PHASE: LAST QUARTER. Dec 14. Moon enters Last Quarter phase at 7:51 AM, EST.

NEWTOWN, CT, SCHOOL SHOOTINGS: ANNIVERSARY. Dec 14, 2012. Twenty-year-old Adam Lanza, a young man with a history of mental illness, fatally shot his mother in the home they shared. Then at approximately 9:30 AM, Lanza shot his way into Sandy Hook Elementary School, Newtown, CT. Carrying an AR-15 assault weapon and two pistols, he killed 20 children and 6 adults. As police moved in to apprehend him, Lanza turned one of the pistols on himself. The killings shocked the nation and spurred a new national debate over gun control.

NOSTRADAMUS: BIRTH ANNIVERSARY. Dec 14, 1503. French physician, best remembered for his astrological predictions (written in rhymed quatrains), was born Michel de Notredame, at St. Rémy, Provence, France. Many believed that his book of prophecies actually foretold the future. Nostradamus died at Salon, France, July 2, 1566.

SMITH, MARGARET CHASE: BIRTH ANNIVERSARY. Dec 14, 1897. American politician Margaret Madeline Chase Smith was born at Skowhegan, ME. As the first woman to be elected to both houses of Congress (1941 to the House and 1949 to the Senate), she was also one of seven Republican senators to issue a "declaration of conscience" to denounce Senator Joseph R. McCarthy's Communist witch hunt. She died May 29, 1995, at Skowhegan.

SOUTH POLE DISCOVERY: ANNIVERSARY. Dec 14, 1911. The elusive object of many expeditions dating from the 17th century, the South Pole was located and visited by Roald Amundsen with four companions and 52 sled dogs. All five men and 12 of the dogs returned to base camp safely. Next to visit the South Pole, Jan 17, 1912, was a party of five led by Captain Robert F. Scott, all of whom perished during the return trip. A search party found their frozen bodies 11 months later. See also: "Amundsen, Roald: Birth Anniversary" (July 16).

WASHINGTON, GEORGE: DEATH ANNIVERSARY. Dec 14, 1799. The first president of the US died at his home at Mount Vernon, VA, shortly before midnight. He had battled a sudden acute respiratory infection and been bled four times. "I die hard, but I am not afraid to go" were his famous near-dying words. After he confirmed his own burial plans, Washington's actual last words were, "'Tis well." He was mourned throughout the US and in Europe.

BIRTHDAYS TODAY

Craig Biggio, 49, former baseball player, born Smithtown, NY, Dec 14, 1965.

Jane Birkin, 68, actress (*Blow-Up, Death on the Nile, Evil Under the Sun*), born London, England, Dec 14, 1946.

Leonardo Boff, 76, Catholic theologian, born Concordia, Brazil, Dec 14, 1938.

William Joseph (Bill) Buckner, 65, former baseball player, born Vallejo, CA, Dec 14, 1949.

Patty Duke, 68, actress (Oscar for *The Miracle Worker*; Emmy for *My Sweet Charlie*), born New York, NY, Dec 14, 1946.

Vanessa Hudgens, 26, actress (*High School Musical*), born Salinas, CA, Dec 14, 1988.

Natascha McElhone, 45, actress ("Californication," *The Truman Show*), born Surrey, England, Dec 14, 1969.

Samantha Peszek, 23, Olympic gymnast, born McCordsville, IN, Dec 14, 1991.

Dee Wallace Stone, 66, actress (*10, E.T. The Extra-Terrestrial*), born Kansas City, MO, Dec 14, 1948.

December 2014

S	M	T	W	T	F	S
	1	2	3	4	5	6
7	8	9	10	11	12	13
14	15	16	17	18	19	20
21	22	23	24	25	26	27
28	29	30	31			

December 15 — Monday

DAY 349 **16 REMAINING**

BATTLE OF SAN PIETRO: ANNIVERSARY. Dec 15, 1943. A German panzer battalion inflicted heavy casualties on American forces trying to take the 700-year-old Italian village of San Pietro, before withdrawing from the town. San Pietro was reduced almost entirely to rubble. The American movie director John Huston, serving as an Army lieutenant, filmed the battle for the military. So graphic was the film that it was described as antiwar by the military brass at the War Department. The film was cut from five to three reels before censors allowed it to be released in 1944. It was later reedited for the television series "The Big Picture."

BILL OF RIGHTS: ANNIVERSARY. Dec 15, 1791. The first 10 amendments to the US Constitution, known as the Bill of Rights, became effective following ratification by Virginia. The anniversary of ratification and of effect is observed as Bill of Rights Day.

✦BILL OF RIGHTS DAY. Dec 15. Presidential Proclamation. Proclaimed each year since 1962, but omitted in 1967 and 1968. (Issued in 1941 and 1946 at Congressional request and in 1947 without request.) Since 1968 included in Human Rights Day and Week Proclamation.

CAT HERDERS DAY. Dec 15. If you can say that your job—or even your life—is like trying to herd cats, then this day is for you—with our sympathy. (©2006 by WH.) For info: Thomas & Ruth Roy, Wellcat Holidays, 2418 Long Ln, Lebanon, PA 17046. Phone: (717) 279-0184. E-mail: wellcat@comcast.net. Web: www.wellcat.com.

CURAÇAO: KINGDOM DAY AND ANTILLEAN FLAG DAY. Dec 15. This day commemorates the Charter of Kingdom, signed in 1954 at the Knight's Hall at The Hague, granting the Netherlands Antilles complete autonomy. The Antillean flag was hoisted for the first time on this day in 1959.

"DAVY CROCKETT" TV PREMIERE: 60th ANNIVERSARY. Dec 15, 1954. This show, a series of five segments, can be considered TV's first miniseries. Shown on Walt Disney's "Disneyland" show, it starred Fess Parker as American western hero Davy Crockett and was immensely popular. The show spawned Crockett paraphernalia, including the famous coonskin cap (although the real Crockett never wore one).

EAMES, RAY: BIRTH ANNIVERSARY. Dec 15, 1912. Born Ray Bernice Alexandria Kaiser at Sacramento, CA, designer known for attractive mass-producible furniture cocreated with her husband, Charles Eames. Their use of inexpensive but durable materials such as plywood allowed them to bring fashion into the living rooms of everyday Americans. The couple has also been credited with influencing other visual facets of American life, including architecture, textiles and photography. After Charles Eames died on Aug 21, 1978, Ray Eames continued their design firm's work until she died a decade later—to the day—on Aug 21, 1988, at Los Angeles, CA.

EIFFEL, ALEXANDRE GUSTAVE: BIRTH ANNIVERSARY. Dec 15, 1832. Eiffel, the French engineer who designed the 1,000-feet-high, million-dollar, open-lattice wrought-iron Eiffel Tower and who participated in designing the Statue of Liberty, was born at Dijon, France. The Eiffel Tower, weighing more than 7,000 tons, was built for the Paris International Exposition of 1889. Eiffel died at Paris, France, Dec 23, 1923.

GAL, UZI: BIRTH ANNIVERSARY. Dec 15, 1923. Inventor of the 9-millimeter submachine gun that bears his name, Uziel Gal was born in Germany but spent most of his life in Israel. A mechanical engineer, he fought in the 1948 Arab-Israeli war, to which he brought a homemade submachine gun. He went on to design the Uzi, and by 1956 it was being manufactured by Israeli Military Industries, whose management named it for him against his own wishes. The gun itself revolutionized automatic weaponry and is currently found in the arsenals of armies, secret-service organizations, bodyguards, etc, worldwide. Gal died at Philadelphia, PA, on Sept 2, 2002.

***GONE WITH THE WIND* FILM PREMIERE: 75th ANNIVERSARY.** Dec 15, 1939. One of the 20th century's biggest film blockbusters premiered on this date in Atlanta, GA. Based on Margaret Mitchell's bestselling and Pulitzer Prize–winning novel of Civil War passions, the film starred Vivian Leigh and Clark Gable and was produced by the dynamic David O. Selznick. It won an unprecedented eight Academy Awards, including best picture. Hattie McDaniel won a best supporting actress Oscar—the first time an African-American actor had won or been nominated. No film would touch its Oscar achievement or monetary grosses for decades. At the chilly Atlanta premiere, more than 300,000 people lined the streets to catch sight of the film's stars arriving at the Loew's Grand Theater. See also "*Gone with the Wind* Published: Anniversary" (May 19).

MILITARY DICTATORSHIP ENDED IN CHILE: 25th ANNIVERSARY. Dec 15, 1989. In an election on this date, Patricio Aylwin defeated General Augusto Pinochet's former finance minister, Hernan Buchi, bringing the military dictatorship of Pinochet to an end. Fourteen months previously, Pinochet had suffered defeat in a national plebiscite on eight more years of his rule. This defeat prompted democratic elections and crippled the Pinochet regime. Pinochet had come to power when the military overthrew the democratically elected government of Marxist president Salvador Allende in a 1973 coup. Patricio Aylwin avoided a two-candidate runoff by achieving 55.2 percent of the vote. He was inaugurated on Mar 11, 1990.

PUERTO RICO: NAVIDADES. Dec 15–Jan 6. Traditional Christmas season begins mid-December and ends on Three Kings Day. Elaborate nativity scenes, carolers, special Christmas foods and trees from Canada and US. Gifts on Christmas Day and on Three Kings Day.

SITTING BULL: DEATH ANNIVERSARY. Dec 15, 1890. Famous Sioux Indian leader, medicine man and warrior of the Hunkpapa Teton band. Known also by his native name, Tatanka-yatanka, Sitting Bull was born on the Grand River, SD. He first accompanied his father on the warpath at the age of 14 against the Crow and thereafter rapidly gained influence within his tribe. In 1866 he led a raid on Fort Buford. His steadfast refusal to go to a reservation led General Phillip Sheridan to initiate a campaign against him, which led to the massacre of Lieutenant Colonel George Custer's men at the Little Bighorn, after which Sitting Bull fled to Canada, remaining there until 1881. Although many in his tribe surrendered on their return, Sitting Bull remained hostile until his death in a skirmish with the US soldiers along the Grand River.

SPACE MILESTONE: *VEGA 1* (USSR): 30th ANNIVERSARY. Dec 15, 1984. Craft launched this date to rendezvous with Halley's Comet in March 1986. *Vega 2*, launched Dec 21, 1984, was part of same mission, which, in cooperation with the US, carried US-built "comet-dust" detection equipment.

US FORCES LAND IN MINDORO, PHILIPPINES: 70th ANNIVERSARY. Dec 15, 1944. After the usual barrage from naval guns, the US 24th Division landed on Mindoro, the largest of the islands immediately south of Luzon (the most important island of the Philippines). American soldiers easily advanced eight miles inland, took the perimeter of their beachhead and started construction of an airfield. Japanese kamikaze counterattacks, however, sank two motor torpedo boats and damaged the escort carrier *Marcus Island*, two destroyers and a third motor torpedo boat, making Mindoro a more costly conquest than the island of Leyte had been.

ZAMENHOF, LUDWIK LEJZER: BIRTH ANNIVERSARY. Dec 15, 1859. Born at Bialystok in what is now Poland, Zamenhof was an oculist who invented the language Esperanto (first published in 1887) in an effort to find a way to promote international tolerance and expanded communication. Zamenhof, who adopted the pen name Doktoro Esperanto (which means "Doctor Hopeful" in the language), created his vocabulary from the major Western languages—especially Latin. The popularity of the artificial language grew as Zamenhof translated major works of literature and spoke widely about it. The first Esperanto congress took place in 1905 in France. Zamenhof died Apr 14, 1917, at Warsaw, Poland.

BIRTHDAYS TODAY

Adam Brody, 35, actor ("The O.C.," *Growing Up Brady*), born San Diego, CA, Dec 15, 1979.

Dave Clark, 72, musician (Dave Clark Five), born London, England, Dec 15, 1942.

Tim Conway, 81, comedian, actor ("McHale's Navy," "The Carol Burnett Show"), born Willoughby, OH, Dec 15, 1933.

Michelle Dockery, 33, actress ("Downton Abbey," "Cranford," *Hanna*), born Essex, England, Dec 15, 1981.

Don Johnson, 65, actor ("Miami Vice," "Nash Bridges"), born Flatt Creek, MO, Dec 15, 1949.

Edna O'Brien, 83, author (*Country Girls Trilogy, Time and Tide*), born Tuamgraney, Ireland, Dec 15, 1931.

Helen Slater, 51, actress (*City Slickers, The Secret of My Success*), born Long Island, NY, Dec 15, 1963.

Alexandra Stevenson, 34, tennis player, born San Diego, CA, Dec 15, 1980.

Garrett Wang, 46, actor ("Star Trek: Voyager"), born Riverside, CA, Dec 15, 1968.

Mark Warner, 60, US Senator (D, Virginia), former governor of Virginia, born Indianapolis, IN, Dec 15, 1954.

December 16 — Tuesday

DAY 350 **15 REMAINING**

AUSTEN, JANE: BIRTH ANNIVERSARY. Dec 16, 1775. English novelist (*Pride and Prejudice, Sense and Sensibility*), born at Steventon, Hampshire, England. Died July 18, 1817, at Winchester, England.

BAHRAIN: INDEPENDENCE DAY. Dec 16. National holiday. Commemorates independence from British protection in 1971.

BANGLADESH: VICTORY DAY. Dec 16. National holiday. Commemorates victory over Pakistan in 1971. The former East Pakistan became Bangladesh.

BARBIE AND BARNEY BACKLASH DAY. Dec 16. If we have to explain this to you, you don't have kids. It's one day each year when Mom and Dad can tell the kids that Barbie and Barney don't exist. (©2006 by WH.) For info: Thomas & Ruth Roy, Wellcat Holidays, 2418 Long Ln, Lebanon, PA 17046. Phone: (717) 279-0184. E-mail: info@wellcat.com. Web: www.wellcat.com.

BATTLE OF THE BULGE: 70th ANNIVERSARY. Dec 16, 1944. A German offensive was launched in the Belgian Ardennes Forest, where Hitler had managed to concentrate 250,000 men. The Nazi commanders, hoping to minimize any aerial counterattack by the Allies, chose a time when foggy, rainy weather prevailed and the initial attack by eight armored divisions along a 75-mile front took the Allies by surprise, the Fifth Panzer Army penetrating to within 20 miles of crossings on the Meuse River. US troops were able to hold fast at bottlenecks in the Ardennes, but by the end of December the German push had penetrated 65 miles into the Allied lines (though their line had narrowed from the initial 75 miles to 20 miles). By that time the Allies began to respond, and the Germans were stopped by Montgomery on the Meuse and by Patton at Bastogne. The weather then cleared and Allied aircraft began to bomb the German forces and supply lines by Dec 26. The Allies reestablished their original line by Jan 21, 1945.

BATTLE OF NASHVILLE: 150th ANNIVERSARY. Dec 16, 1864. On the second day of battle at Nashville, Union troops defeated Confederate forces under General John B. Hood, essentially knocking the Confederate Army of Tennessee out of the war.

BEETHOVEN, LUDWIG VAN: BIRTH ANNIVERSARY. Dec 16, 1770. Regarded by many as the greatest orchestral composer of all time, Ludwig van Beethoven was born at Bonn, Germany. Impairment of his hearing began before he was 30, but even total deafness did not halt his composing and conducting. His last appearance on the concert stage was to conduct the premiere of his *Ninth Symphony*, at Vienna, May 7, 1824. He was unable to hear either the orchestra or the applause. Often in love, he never married. Of a stormy temperament, he is said to have died during a violent thunderstorm Mar 26, 1827, at Vienna.

BOSTON TEA PARTY: ANNIVERSARY. Dec 16, 1773. Anniversary of Boston patriots' boarding of British vessel at anchor at Boston Harbor. Contents of nearly 350 chests of tea were dumped into the harbor.

CALABRIA EARTHQUAKE: ANNIVERSARY. Dec 16, 1857. Calabria—an especially quake-prone region near Naples, Italy—experienced a devastating earthquake of great magnitude that left more than 10,000 people dead and entire villages destroyed. Between 1783 (the last big quake) and 1857, about 111,000 people lost their lives in the unstable region.

CLARKE, ARTHUR C.: BIRTH ANNIVERSARY. Dec 16, 1917. Born at Minehead, England, Clarke was a popular writer of science fiction in the 20th century. His short story "The Sentinel" (1951) was the inspiration for the successful film classic *2001: A Space Odyssey* (1968). Clarke, who was knighted in 2000, worked on sequels to the *2001* story and died Mar 19, 2008, at Colombo, Sri Lanka.

COWARD, NOËL: BIRTH ANNIVERSARY. Dec 16, 1899. English playwright, actor and wit known for his sophisticated comedies *Private Lives* (1930), *Design for Living* (1933), *Blithe Spirit* (1941) and others—many of which were later filmed. He is also known for such songs as "Mad Dogs and Englishmen." He advised actors: "Learn the lines and don't bump into the furniture." Born at Teddington, England, Coward died at St. Mary, Jamaica, on Mar 26, 1973.

"DRAGNET" TV PREMIERE: ANNIVERSARY. Dec 16, 1951. This famous crime show stressed authenticity, and episodes were supposedly based on real cases. It starred Jack Webb as stoic and determined Sergeant Joe Friday, a man whose life was his investigative police work and who was recognized by his recurring line, "Just the facts, ma'am." Friday had many partners: Barton Yarborough played Sergeant Ben Romero for three episodes; for the rest of the season Barney Phillips played Sergeant Ed Jacobs and Ben Alexander played his comedic sidekick, Officer Frank Smith. A new version appeared in 1967 with Webb and his new partner, Officer Bill Gannon (Harry Morgan). "Dragnet" is also known for its theme music and its narrative epilogue describing the fate of the bad guys.

☆ ☆ ☆

December 2014	S	M	T	W	T	F	S
		1	2	3	4	5	6
	7	8	9	10	11	12	13
	14	15	16	17	18	19	20
	21	22	23	24	25	26	27
	28	29	30	31			

KAZAKHSTAN: INDEPENDENCE DAY. Dec 16. National Day. Commemorates independence from the Soviet Union in 1991.

MEAD, MARGARET: BIRTH ANNIVERSARY. Dec 16, 1901. American anthropologist and author, especially known for her studies of peoples of the southwest Pacific area, and for her forthright manner in speaking and writing. Born at Philadelphia, PA, Mead died at New York, NY, Nov 15, 1978.

MEXICO: POSADAS. Dec 16–24. A nine-day annual celebration throughout Mexico. Processions of "pilgrims" knock at doors asking for posada (shelter), commemorating the search by Joseph and Mary for a shelter in which the infant Jesus might be born. Pilgrims are invited inside, and fun and merrymaking ensue with blindfolded guests trying to break a piñata filled with gifts and goodies suspended from the ceiling. Once the piñata is broken, the gifts are distributed and the celebration continues.

NEW WORLD SYMPHONY PREMIERE: ANNIVERSARY. Dec 16, 1893. Antonín Dvořák's *New World Symphony* premiered at the newly erected Carnegie Hall with the New York Philharmonic playing. The composer attended and enjoyed enthusiastic applause from the audience. The symphony contains snatches from black spirituals and American folk music. Dvořák, a Bohemian, had been in the US only a year when he composed it as a greeting to his friends in Europe.

"ONE DAY AT A TIME" TV PREMIERE: ANNIVERSARY. Dec 16, 1975. This sitcom about a divorced mother raising two girls in Indianapolis starred Bonnie Franklin as Ann Romano and Mackenzie Phillips and Valerie Bertinelli as daughters Julie and Barbara Cooper. Other regulars included Pat Harrington, Jr, as tool-belt-wearing maintenance man Dwayne Schneider; Richard Masur as David Kane, Ann's boyfriend; and Nanette Fabray as Ann's mother. All three female leads got married, and Ann opened her own ad agency before the series ended in 1984.

PHILIPPINES: PHILIPPINE CHRISTMAS OBSERVANCE. Dec 16–Jan 6. Philippine Islands. Said to be the world's longest Christmas celebration.

PHILIPPINES: SIMBANG GABI. Dec 16–25. Nationwide. A nine-day novena of predawn masses, also called "Misa de Gallo." One of the traditional Filipino celebrations of the holiday season.

SANTAYANA, GEORGE: BIRTH ANNIVERSARY. Dec 16, 1863. Philosopher and author born at Madrid, Spain. Santayana was educated and later tenured at Harvard where his foundational aesthetic philosophy of naturalism, for which he is most widely known, was first articulated. He left the US—and academia—in 1912 and returned to Europe, where he traveled widely and focused on his writing. In addition to his philosophical works, he was also an accomplished poet and is considered to be influential in the 20th century transformation of the literary canon. A survivor of both World Wars, Santayana died at Rome, Italy, on Sept 26, 1952. It was Santayana who first wrote, "Those who cannot remember the past are condemned to repeat it."

SOUTH AFRICA: RECONCILIATION DAY. Dec 16. National holiday. Celebrates the spirit of reconciliation, national unity and peace among all citizens.

UNITED NATIONS REVOKES RESOLUTION ON ZIONISM: ANNIVERSARY. Dec 16, 1991. The United Nations voted 111 to 25 to revoke Resolution 3379, which equated Zionism with racism. Resolution 3379 was approved Nov 10, 1975, with 72 countries voting in favor, 35 against and 32 abstentions. The largest block of changed votes came from the former Soviet Union and Eastern Europe.

BIRTHDAYS TODAY

Bruce N. Ames, 86, biochemist, cancer researcher, born New York, NY, Dec 16, 1928.

Steven Bochco, 71, television writer, producer ("Hill Street Blues," "NYPD Blue"), born New York, NY, Dec 16, 1943.

Benjamin Bratt, 51, actor (*Traffic, Miss Congeniality*, "Law & Order"), born San Francisco, CA, Dec 16, 1963.

Theo James, 30, actor (*Divergent*, "Golden Boy," "Downton Abbey"), born Oxford, England, Dec 16, 1984.

Alison La Placa, 55, actress ("The John Larroquette Show"), born Lincolnshire, IL, Dec 16, 1959.

William "The Refrigerator" Perry, 52, former football player, born Aiken, SC, Dec 16, 1962.

Pat Quinn, 66, Governor of Illinois (D), born Hinsdale, IL, Dec 16, 1948.

Lesley Stahl, 73, journalist ("60 Minutes," former White House correspondent), born Lynn, MA, Dec 16, 1941.

Jon Tenney, 53, actor ("Brooklyn South," "The Closer"), born Princeton, NJ, Dec 16, 1961.

Liv Johanne Ullmann, 75, actress (*Persona, Scenes from a Marriage*), born Tokyo, Japan, Dec 16, 1939.

December 17 — Wednesday

DAY 351 **14 REMAINING**

ARAB SPRING BEGINS/BOUAZIZI SELF-IMMOLATION: ANNIVERSARY. Dec 17, 2010. In the town of Sidi Bouzid, Tunisia, street vendor Mohamed Bouazizi, angry at a municipal official's confiscation of his wares and unable to get the local government to hear his case, set himself on fire in protest of the corruption he faced. Demonstrations began almost immediately and grew into the movement now known as the "Arab Spring"—a region wide revolution of street protests that caused regime change in Tunisia (President Ben Ali stepped down Jan 14, 2011), Egypt, Libya and Yemen; a violent civil war in Syria; and major social and political disruption in the rest of the Arab World. Bouazizi died of his burns Jan 4, 2011.

AZTEC CALENDAR STONE DISCOVERY: ANNIVERSARY. Dec 17, 1790. One of the wonders of the Western Hemisphere—the Aztec Calendar or Solar Stone—was found beneath the ground by workmen repairing Mexico City's Central Plaza. The centuries-old, intricately carved stone—11 feet, 8 inches in diameter and nearly 25 tons—proved to be a highly developed calendar monument to the sun. Believed to have been carved in the year 1479, this extraordinary time-counting basalt tablet originally stood in the Great Temple of the Aztecs. Buried along with other Aztec idols soon after the Spanish conquest in 1521, it remained hidden until 1790. Its 52-year cycle had regulated many Aztec ceremonies, including grisly human sacrifices, to save the world from destruction by the gods.

BOLÍVAR, SIMÓN: DEATH ANNIVERSARY. Dec 17, 1830. Commemorated in Venezuela and other Latin American countries. Bolívar, called "The Liberator," was born July 24, 1783, at Caracas, Venezuela, and died Dec 17, 1830, at Santa Marta, Colombia.

CHANUKAH. Dec 17–24. Feast of Lights or Feast of Dedication. Festival lasting eight days commemorates victory of Maccabees over Syrians (165 BC) and rededication of Temple of Jerusalem. Begins on Hebrew calendar date Kislev 25, 5775. Began at sundown on Dec 16.

***A CHRISTMAS CAROL* PUBLISHED: ANNIVERSARY.** Dec 17, 1843. This holiday classic by Charles Dickens was published in a print run of 6,000 copies that sold out in one week. By Jan 6, 1844, another 2,000 were sold. The reformation of Ebenezer Scrooge ("Bah humbug!") has remained immensely popular.

CLEAN AIR ACT PASSED BY CONGRESS: ANNIVERSARY. Dec 17, 1967. A sweeping set of laws passed to protect the nation from air pollution. This was the first legislation to place pollution controls on the automobile industry.

FIRST FLIGHT ANNIVERSARY CELEBRATION. Dec 17. Kill Devil Hills, NC. Each year since 1928, on the anniversary of the Wright brothers' first successful heavier-than-air flight at Kitty Hawk, NC, Dec 17, 1903, a celebration has been held at the Wright Brothers National Memorial, with wreaths, flyover and other observances—regardless of weather.

FLOYD, WILLIAM: BIRTH ANNIVERSARY. Dec 17, 1734. Signer of the Declaration of Independence, member of Congress, born at Brookhaven, Long Island. Died at Westernville, NY, Aug 4, 1821.

GUCCHIONE, BOB: BIRTH ANNIVERSARY. Dec 17, 1930. Founder and publisher of an adult magazine empire, the Brooklyn, NY, native launched his brainchild *Penthouse* magazine as a more explicit alternative to *Playboy* in 1965 with a bank loan of $1,170. When a marketing piece accidentally went to a mailing list that included children, preachers and housewives, the resulting controversy meant a sold-out first edition and a reputation for raunchiness that lasted for decades. Gucchione retained control of *Penthouse* until 2003; a series of financial reverses resulted in the loss of homes, art, investments and his beloved magazine empire. Once estimated to be worth $400 million, at the time of his death in Plano, TX, on Oct 20, 2010, Gucchione was virtually bankrupt.

HENRY, JOSEPH: BIRTH ANNIVERSARY. Dec 17, 1797. Scientist Joseph Henry was born at Albany, NY. One of his great discoveries was the principle of self-induction; the unit used in the measure of electrical inductance was named "the henry" in his honor. In 1831 Henry constructed the first model of an electric telegraph with an audible signal. This formed the basis of nearly all later work on commercial wire telegraphy. In 1832 Henry was named professor of natural philosophy at the College of New Jersey, now Princeton University. Henry was involved in the planning of the Smithsonian Institution and became its first secretary in 1846. President Lincoln named Henry as one of the original 50 scientists to make up the National Academy of Sciences in 1863. He served as that organization's president from 1868 until his death May 13, 1878, at Washington, DC.

KING, W.L. MACKENZIE: BIRTH ANNIVERSARY. Dec 17, 1874. Former Canadian prime minister, born at Berlin, ON. Served 21 years, the longest term of any prime minister in the English-speaking world. Died at Kingsmere, July 22, 1950.

LIBBY, WILLARD FRANK: BIRTH ANNIVERSARY. Dec 17, 1908. American educator, chemist, atomic scientist and Nobel Prize winner born at Grand Valley, CO. He was the inventor of the carbon-14 "atomic clock" method for dating ancient and prehistoric plant and animal remains and minerals. Died at Los Angeles, CA, Sept 8, 1980.

SAMPSON, DEBORAH: BIRTH ANNIVERSARY. Dec 17, 1760. Born at Plympton, MA, Deborah Sampson spent her childhood as an indentured servant. In 1782, wishing to participate in the Revolutionary War, she disguised herself as a man and enlisted in the Continental Army's Fourth Massachusetts Regiment under the name Robert Shurtleff. Her identity was unmasked, and she was dismissed from the army in 1783. In 1802 Sampson became perhaps the first woman to lecture professionally in the US when she began giving public speeches on her experiences. Deborah Sampson died Apr 29, 1827, at Sharon, MA. Full military pension was provided for her heirs by an act of Congress in 1838.

SATURNALIA. Dec 17–23. Ancient Roman festival honoring Saturnus, the god of agriculture. It was a time of merriment at the end of harvesting and wine making. Presents were exchanged, sacrifices offered, and masters served their slaves. Approximates the winter solstice. Some say that the date for the observance of the nativity of Jesus was selected by the early Christian church leaders to fall on Dec 25 partly to counteract the popular but disapproved-of pre-Christian Roman festival of Saturnalia.

"THE SIMPSONS" TV PREMIERE: 25th ANNIVERSARY. Dec 17, 1989. TV's hottest animated family, "The Simpsons," premiered on this date. The originator of Homer, Marge, Bart, Lisa and Maggie is cartoonist Matt Groening. The show's 300th episode, "Barting Over," aired Feb 16, 2003. The 400th episode, "You Kent Always Say What You Want," aired May 20, 2007. The 500th episode, "At Long Last Leave," aired Feb 19, 2012.

TAKE A NEW YEAR'S RESOLUTION TO STOP SMOKING (TANYRSS). Dec 17–Feb 1, 2015. To educate consumers/patients and health care professionals to take a New Year's resolution to stop smoking. Final day of observance is on Super Bowl Sunday. For info: Fred S. Mayer, Pres, Pharmacists Planning Service, Inc, c/o Pharmacy Council on Tobacco Dependence (PCTD), PO Box 6760, San Rafael, CA 94903. E-mail: ppsi@aol.com. Web: www.ppsinc.org.

TBS DEBUT: ANNIVERSARY. Dec 17, 1976. Media entrepreneur Ted Turner launched Turner Broadcasting System—transforming a local Atlanta, GA, UHF station that he had purchased in 1970 into an influential national cable television network that came to be known as the "Superstation."

TINY TIM WEDS MISS VICKI ON "THE TONIGHT SHOW": 45th ANNIVERSARY. Dec 17, 1969. In the highest-rated show in "The Tonight Show" history, 45 million viewers saw ukulele-playing eccentric Tiny Tim marry Miss Vicki (née Budinger), his 17-year-old girlfriend. The live ceremony was accented by thousands of tulips, since Tiny Tim's claim to fame was his falsetto revival of the song "Tiptoe through the Tulips."

WHITTIER, JOHN GREENLEAF: BIRTH ANNIVERSARY. Dec 17, 1807. Poet and abolitionist, born at Haverhill, Essex County, MA. Whittier's books of poetry include *Legends of New England* and *Snowbound*. Died at Hampton Falls, NH, Sept 7, 1892.

✦WRIGHT BROTHERS DAY. Dec 17. Presidential Proclamation always issued for Dec 17 since 1963 (PL 88–209 of Dec 17, 1963). Issued twice earlier at Congressional request in 1959 and 1961.

WRIGHT BROTHERS FIRST POWERED FLIGHT: ANNIVERSARY. Dec 17, 1903. Orville and Wilbur Wright, brothers, bicycle-shop operators, inventors and aviation pioneers, after three years of experimentation with kites and gliders, achieved the first documented successful powered and controlled flights of an airplane. The flights, near Kitty Hawk, NC, piloted first by Orville and then by Wilbur Wright, were sustained for less than one minute but represented man's first powered airplane flight and the beginning of a new form of transportation. Orville Wright was born at Dayton, OH, Aug 19, 1871, and died there Jan 30, 1948. Wilbur Wright was born at Millville, IN, Apr 16, 1867, and died at Dayton, OH, May 30, 1912.

BIRTHDAYS TODAY

Pope Francis, 78, leader of the Roman Catholic Church, born Jorge Mario Bergoglio at Buenos Aires, Argentina, Dec 17, 1936.

Bernard Hill, 70, actor (*Great Expectations, Titanic*), born Manchester, England, Dec 17, 1944.

Laurie Holden, 45, actress ("The Walking Dead," "The Shield"), born Los Angeles, CA, Dec 17, 1969.

Ernie Hudson, 69, actor (*Ghostbusters, The Hand That Rocks the Cradle*), born Benton Harbor, MI, Dec 17, 1945.

Eugene Levy, 68, comedian, actor (*American Pie, Best in Show*, "SCTV"), born Hamilton, ON, Canada, Dec 17, 1946.

Bill Pullman, 60, actor (*Independence Day, While You Were Sleeping*), born Delphi, NY, Dec 17, 1954.

Tommy Steele, 78, actor (*The Happiest Millionaire, Half a Sixpence*), born London, England, Dec 17, 1936.

Sean Patrick Thomas, 44, actor (*Save the Last Dance*, "The District"), born Wilmington, DE, Dec 17, 1970.

Chase Utley, 36, baseball player, born Pasadena, CA, Dec 17, 1978.

Shannon Woodward, 30, actress ("Raising Hope," "The Riches"), born Phoenix, AZ, Dec 17, 1984.

December 18 — Thursday

DAY 352 **13 REMAINING**

BRANDT, WILLY: BIRTH ANNIVERSARY. Dec 18, 1913. Former West German chancellor Willy Brandt was born Herbert Ernst Karl Frahm at Lubeck, Germany. An anti-Nazi exile during WWII, he won the Nobel Peace Prize in 1971 for seeking better East-West relations. While in exile in Norway and Sweden he worked as a journalist, during which time he assumed the name Willy Brandt. He returned to Germany at the end of WWII and reestablished German citizenship upon deciding to return to politics. One of the cornerstones of his political career was Ostpolitik, a policy that promoted the recognition of and commercial interaction with East Germany and other Soviet Bloc countries. He died Oct 8, 1992, at Unkel, Germany.

COBB, TYRUS RAYMOND "TY": BIRTH ANNIVERSARY. Dec 18, 1886. One of the all-time-great baseball players. Born at Narrows, GA, Cobb had a lifetime batting average of .367 compiled over 24 years, during which he played in more than 3,000 games—mostly for the Detroit Tigers. His runs scored record was not broken until 2001, and his stolen bases record stood until 1979. Cobb was among the first five players inducted into the National Baseball Hall of

December 2014

S	M	T	W	T	F	S
	1	2	3	4	5	6
7	8	9	10	11	12	13
14	15	16	17	18	19	20
21	22	23	24	25	26	27
28	29	30	31			

Fame in 1936. A savvy businessman who quickly realized the value of using his celebrity for marketing, Cobb died at Atlanta, GA, on July 17, 1961.

DAVIS, BENJAMIN O., JR: BIRTH ANNIVERSARY. Dec 18, 1912. The WWII hero was born at Washington, DC, to the Army's first black general. Davis had a distinguished career serving the US: he was the first African American to graduate from West Point in the 20th century; he led the first all-black air unit, the 99th Pursuit Squadron (the Tuskegee Airmen), in WWII; he helped plan the integration of the US Air Force in 1948–49 and he was the Air Force's first black general (1954). He died at Washington, DC, on July 4, 2002. See also "Tuskegee Airmen Activated: Anniversary" (Mar 22).

DAVIS, OSSIE: BIRTH ANNIVERSARY. Dec 18, 1917. Born at Cogdell, GA, Davis began his career as an actor with the Rose McClendon Players in Harlem, NY, in the 1940s. He became involved with civil rights, counting among his friends W.E.B. DuBois, Richard Wright and Langston Hughes, and worked to promote African Americans in the entertainment industry throughout his life. Often sharing the stage or screen with wife Ruby Dee, he was featured in dozens of stage productions and feature films. He died at Miami Beach, FL, Feb 4, 2005.

GRIMALDI, JOSEPH: BIRTH ANNIVERSARY. Dec 18, 1778. Known as the "greatest clown in history" and the "king of pantomime," Joseph Grimaldi began his stage career at age two. He was an accomplished singer, dancer and acrobat. Born at London, England, he is best remembered as the original "Joey the Clown" and for the innovative humor he brought to the clown's role in theater. Illness forced his early retirement in 1823, and he died at London, May 31, 1837.

MEXICO: FEAST OF OUR LADY OF SOLITUDE. Dec 18. Oaxaca. Pilgrims venerate the patron of the lonely.

NCAA DIVISION I WOMEN'S VOLLEYBALL CHAMPIONSHIP. Dec 18 and 20. Chesapeake Energy Arena, Oklahoma City, OK. For info: NCAA, PO Box 6222, Indianapolis, IN 46206-6222. Phone: (317) 917-6222. Web: www.NCAA.com.

NEW JERSEY RATIFICATION DAY: ANNIVERSARY. Dec 18, 1787. New Jersey became the third state to ratify the Constitution (following Delaware and Pennsylvania). It did so unanimously.

NIGER: REPUBLIC DAY. Dec 18. National holiday. Gained autonomy within the French community in 1958.

STRADIVARI, ANTONIO: DEATH ANNIVERSARY. Dec 18, 1737. Celebrated Italian violin maker was born probably in the year 1644 and died at Cremona, at about age 93.

"TO TELL THE TRUTH" TV PREMIERE: ANNIVERSARY. Dec 18, 1956. This long-running, popular game show was a production of the Mark Goodson–Bill Todman team. A celebrity panel (and the home audience) tried to guess which of three guests claiming to be the same person was telling the truth. Panelists took turns questioning the guests, and, at the conclusion, the identity of the person was revealed. Hosts have included Bud Collyer, Garry Moore, Joe Garagiola, Robin Ward, Gordon Elliott and Alex Trebek. Celebrity panelists included Dick Van Dyke, Tom Poston, Peggy Cass, Kitty Carlisle and Bill Cullen.

UNITED NATIONS: INTERNATIONAL MIGRANTS DAY. Dec 18. Recognizes the contributions that millions of migrant workers make to the global economy and seeks to draw attention to the precarious state of their rights. For info: United Nations, Dept of Public Info, New York, NY 10017. Web: www.un.org.

BIRTHDAYS TODAY

Christina Aguilera, 34, singer, born Staten Island, NY, Dec 18, 1980.

Josh Dallas, 33, actor ("Once Upon a Time," *Thor*), born Louisville, KY, Dec 18, 1981.

Rachel Griffiths, 46, actress (*Hilary and Jackie*, "Six Feet Under," "Brothers & Sisters"), born Melbourne, Australia, Dec 18, 1968.

Katie Holmes, 36, actress (*Batman Begins, Pieces of April*, "Dawson's Creek"), born Toledo, OH, Dec 18, 1978.

Ray Liotta, 59, actor (*Unforgettable, Goodfellas, Field of Dreams, Something Wild*), born Newark, NJ, Dec 18, 1955.

Leonard Maltin, 64, movie critic, author (*Maltin's Guide*), born New York, NY, Dec 18, 1950.

Charles Oakley, 51, former basketball player, born Cleveland, OH, Dec 18, 1963.

Brad Pitt, 50, actor (*Moneyball, Babel, Ocean's Eleven*), born Shawnee, OK, Dec 18, 1964.

Keith Richards, 71, musician, singer (Rolling Stones), born Dartford, England, Dec 18, 1943.

Steven Spielberg, 67, filmmaker (Oscars for *Schindler's List, Saving Private Ryan*; *War Horse, Jurassic Park, Jaws*), born Cincinnati, OH, Dec 18, 1947.

December 19 — Friday

DAY 353 **12 REMAINING**

BREZHNEV, LEONID: BIRTH ANNIVERSARY. Dec 19, 1906. Leader of the Soviet Union after the overthrow of Nikita Khrushchev in 1964 (which he had a part in). He expanded and modernized Soviet military and nuclear power at the cost of the country's economic health. Born at Kamenskoye, Ukraine, Brezhnev died at Moscow, Russia, Nov 10, 1982.

FISKE, MINNIE MADDERN: BIRTH ANNIVERSARY. Dec 19, 1865. American theater actress with a long, distinguished career. First stage appearance at the age of three as "Little Minnie Maddern." Born at New Orleans, LA, she died Feb 15, 1932, at Hollis, NY.

LIVERMORE, MARY ASHTON: BIRTH ANNIVERSARY. Dec 19, 1821. American reformer and women's suffrage leader, born at Boston, MA. Died May 23, 1905, at Melrose, MA.

***THE MUSIC MAN* PREMIERE: ANNIVERSARY.** Dec 19, 1957. Meredith Willson's musical premiered on Broadway today and ran until 1961. It received five Tony Awards, including Best Musical (beating out *West Side Story*) and Best Actor for star Robert Preston.

PARRY, WILLIAM: BIRTH ANNIVERSARY. Dec 19, 1790. British explorer Sir William Edward Parry was born at Bath, England. Remembered for his Arctic expeditions and for his search for a Northwest Passage, Parry died at Ems, Germany, July 8, 1855.

SHERMAN, ROBERT B.: BIRTH ANNIVERSARY. Dec 19, 1925. With his brother Richard, Robert B. Sherman formed a successful songwriting partnership that created memorable, enduring classics like the Disney anthem "It's a Small World (After All)" as well as "Chim Chim Cheree" and "Supercalifragilisticexpialidocious," both from the film *Mary Poppins* (1964). The Shermans' work for *Mary Poppins* netted them an Academy Award (for "Chim Chim Cheree"), while as staff songwriters at Disney they scored films and shorts like *The Jungle Book*, *The Parent Trap* and "Winnie the Pooh." An expressive writer and thinker, Sherman said that his combat experience in World War II influenced his later songwriting work, which often explored themes of joy, happiness and a generally hopeful outlook for society. Born at Brooklyn, NY, Sherman died in London, England, on Mar 6, 2012.

SPACE MILESTONE: FIRST RADIO BROADCAST FROM SPACE. Dec 19, 1958. At 3:15 PM, EST, the US Earth satellite *Atlas* transmitted the first radio voice broadcast from space, a 58-word recorded Christmas greeting from President Dwight D. Eisenhower: "to all mankind America's wish for peace on earth and goodwill toward men everywhere." The satellite had been launched from Cape Canaveral Dec 18.

SPACE MILESTONE: *INTELSAT 4 F-3* (US). Dec 19, 1971. Communications satellite launched by NASA on contract with COMSAT. Mission involved intercontinental relay phone and TV communications.

***TITANIC* RELEASED: ANNIVERSARY.** Dec 19, 1997. The most expensive film made (up to that time) at $200 million was released in theaters on this date. *Titanic*, written and directed by James Cameron, featured the drama of star-crossed lovers (Leonardo DiCaprio and Kate Winslet) paired with the amazing special effects re-creation of the doomed 1912 ocean liner's first and last voyage. The film won 11 Academy Awards, including best picture, which tied it with 1959's *Ben-Hur*.

UNDERDOG DAY. Dec 19. To salute, before the year's end, all of the underdogs and unsung heroes—the Number Two people who contribute so much to the Number One people we read about. (Sherlock Holmes's Dr. Watson and Robinson Crusoe's Friday are examples.) Observed annually on the third Friday in December since its founding in 1976 by the late Peter Moeller, THE Chief Underdog. For info: A.C. Vierow, Underdogs Intl, Box 71, Clio, MI 48420-0071.

WOODSON, CARTER GODWIN: BIRTH ANNIVERSARY. Dec 19, 1875. Historian who introduced black studies to colleges and universities, born at New Canton, VA. His scholarly works included *The Negro in Our History, The Education of the Negro Prior to 1861*. Known as the father of Black history, he inaugurated Negro History Week. Woodson was working on a six-volume *Encyclopaedia Africana* when he died at Washington, DC, Apr 3, 1950.

BIRTHDAYS TODAY

Jennifer Beals, 51, actress ("The L Word," *Flashdance*), born Chicago, IL, Dec 19, 1963.

Janie Fricke, 62, country singer, born Whitney, IN, Dec 19, 1952.

Jake Gyllenhaal, 34, actor (*Brokeback Mountain, Jarhead, Donnie Darko*), born Los Angeles, CA, Dec 19, 1980.

Richard Hammond, 45, television personality ("Top Gear"), born Solihull, West Midlands, England, Dec 19, 1969.

Richard E. Leakey, 70, anthropologist, born Nairobi, Kenya, Dec 19, 1944.

Kevin Edward McHale, 57, Hall of Fame basketball player, born Hibbing, MN, Dec 19, 1957.

Alyssa Milano, 42, actress ("Charmed," "Melrose Place"), born Brooklyn, NY, Dec 19, 1972.

Rob Portman, 59, US Senator (R, Ohio), born Cincinnati, OH, Dec 19, 1955.

Tim Reid, 70, actor ("Frank's Place," "WKRP in Cincinnati"), born Norfolk, VA, Dec 19, 1944.

Kristy Swanson, 45, actress (*Buffy the Vampire Slayer*), born Mission Viejo, CA, Dec 19, 1969.

Cicely Tyson, 81, actress (Emmy for *The Autobiography of Miss Jane Pittman; Sounder*), born New York, NY, Dec 19, 1933.

December 2014	S	M	T	W	T	F	S
		1	2	3	4	5	6
	7	8	9	10	11	12	13
	14	15	16	17	18	19	20
	21	22	23	24	25	26	27
	28	29	30	31			

December 20 — Saturday

DAY 354 **11 REMAINING**

AMERICAN POET LAUREATE ESTABLISHMENT: ANNIVERSARY. Dec 20, 1985. A bill empowering the Librarian of Congress to name, annually, a poet laureate/consultant in poetry was signed into law by President Ronald Reagan. In return for a stipend as poet laureate and a salary as the consultant in poetry, the person named will present at least one major work of poetry and will appear at selected national ceremonies. The first poet laureate of the US was Robert Penn Warren, appointed to that position by the Librarian of Congress Feb 26, 1986. Other poet laureates have included Robert Frost, Donald Hall and Billy Collins.

CATHODE-RAY TUBE PATENTED: ANNIVERSARY. Dec 20, 1938. The kinescope, today known as the cathode-ray tube, was patented by Russian immigrant Vladimir Zworykin. It is still used today in computer monitors and television sets.

CLINTON IMPEACHMENT PROCEEDINGS: ANNIVERSARY. Dec 20, 1998. President William Clinton was impeached by a House of Representatives that was divided along party lines. He was convicted of perjury and obstruction of justice stemming from a sexual relationship with a White House intern. He was then tried by the Senate in January 1999. On Feb 12, 1999, the Senate acquitted him on both charges. Clinton was only the second US president to undergo impeachment proceedings. Andrew Johnson was impeached by the House in 1868, but the Senate voted against impeachment and he finished his term of office. See also: "Johnson Impeachment Proceedings" (Feb 24).

"THE DATING GAME" TV PREMIERE: ANNIVERSARY. Dec 20, 1965. Another game show developed by Chuck Barris, it typically featured a "bachelorette" who questioned three men who were hidden from her view and decided, based on their answers, which guy appealed to her the most. The couple was then sent on a date, courtesy of the show. Occasionally, a bachelor would question three women. Jim Lange was the host of the network series and two syndicated ones. Elaine Joyce and Jeff MacGregor hosted one season each on the retitled "The New Dating Game."

FIRESTONE, HARVEY S.: BIRTH ANNIVERSARY. Dec 20, 1868. American industrialist, businessman and founder of the Firestone Tire and Rubber Company, Harvey Samuel Firestone was born at Columbiana County, OH. A close friend of Henry Ford, Thomas Edison and John Burroughs, Firestone died at Miami Beach, FL, Feb 7, 1938.

IT'S A WONDERFUL LIFE FILM PREMIERE: ANNIVERSARY. Dec 20, 1946. America's favorite Christmas drama premiered on this date at New York, NY. Directed by Frank Capra and starring James Stewart (George Bailey), Donna Reed (Mary Bailey), Henry Travers (as Clarence Oddbody, trying to earn his angel wings) and Lionel Barrymore (as villainous Mr Potter), the film was nominated for five Academy Awards.

LANGER, SUSANNE K.: BIRTH ANNIVERSARY. Dec 20, 1895. Susanne Langer, a leading American philosopher, author of *Philosophy in a New Key: A Study in the Symbolism of Reason, Rite, and Art*, was born at New York, NY. Her studies of aesthetics and art exerted a profound influence on thinking in the fields of psychology, philosophy and the social sciences. She died at Old Lyme, CT, July 17, 1985.

MACAU REVERTS TO CHINESE CONTROL: 15th ANNIVERSARY. Dec 20, 1999. Macau, a tiny province on the southeast coast of China, reverted to Chinese rule. It had been a Portuguese colony since 1557.

MENZIES, ROBERT GORDON: BIRTH ANNIVERSARY. Dec 20, 1894. Australian statesman and conservative leader, born at Jeparit, Victoria, Australia, Sir Robert died at Melbourne, Australia, May 14, 1978, at age 83.

MERKLE, FRED: BIRTH ANNIVERSARY. Dec 20, 1888. Frederick Charles Merkle, born at Watertown, WI, will forever occupy a place in baseball history for his part in the events of Sept 23, 1908, when his team, the New York Giants, played the Chicago Cubs in a crucial game. Merkle was on first in the bottom of the ninth when the winning run apparently scored on a single. As was customary, he did not touch second base. Cubs second baseman Johnny Evers set off baseball's greatest dispute by demanding that Merkle be called out, which he was, in a play dubbed "Merkle's Boner" by baseball historians. Died at Daytona Beach, FL, Mar 2, 1956.

MONTGOMERY BUS BOYCOTT ENDS: ANNIVERSARY. Dec 20, 1956. The US Supreme Court ruling of Nov 13, 1956, calling for integration of the Montgomery, AL, public bus system was implemented. Since Dec 5, 1955, the black community of Montgomery had refused to ride on the segregated buses. The boycott was in reaction to the Dec 1, 1955, arrest of Rosa Parks for refusing to relinquish her seat on a Montgomery bus to a white man.

MUDD DAY: ANNIVERSARY. Dec 20, 1833. A day to remember Dr. Samuel A. Mudd (born near Bryantown, MD, Dec 20, 1833), sentenced to life imprisonment for giving medical aid to disguised John Wilkes Booth, fleeing assassin of Abraham Lincoln. Imprisoned four years before being pardoned by President Andrew Johnson. Died on Jan 10, 1883.

NAIA FOOTBALL NATIONAL CHAMPIONSHIP GAME. Dec 20. Site TBA. 59th annual. Sixteen-team field competes, ending with the final two teams vying for the national championship. For info: Natl Assn of Intercollegiate Athletics, 1200 Grand Blvd, Kansas City, MO 64106. E-mail: dgreen@naia.org. Web: www.naia.org.

RICKEY, BRANCH: BIRTH ANNIVERSARY. Dec 20, 1881. Wesley Branch Rickey, Baseball Hall of Fame player, manager and executive born at Lucasville, OH. Rickey was baseball's most innovative general manager. He invented the farm system, instituted unique training and teaching methods and, most prominently, signed Jackie Robinson to play major league baseball with the Brooklyn Dodgers. Inducted into the Hall of Fame in 1967. Died at Columbia, MO, Dec 9, 1965.

SACAGAWEA: DEATH ANNIVERSARY. Dec 20, 1812. As a young Shoshone Indian woman, Sacagawea in 1805 (with her two-month-old son strapped to her back) traveled with the Lewis and Clark expedition, serving as an interpreter. It is said that the expedition could not have succeeded without her aid. She was born about 1787 and died at Fort Manuel on the Missouri River, Dec 20, 1812. Few other women have been so often honored. There are statues, fountains and memorials of her, and her name has been given to a mountain peak. In 2000 the US Mint issued a $1 coin honoring her.

SOUTH CAROLINA SECESSION: ANNIVERSARY. Dec 20, 1860. South Carolina's legislature voted to secede from the US, the first state to do so. Within six weeks, five more states seceded. On Feb 4, 1861, representatives from the six states met at Montgomery, AL, to establish a government and on Feb 9 Jefferson Davis was elected president of the Confederate States of America. By June 1861, 11 states had seceded.

UNITED NATIONS: INTERNATIONAL HUMAN SOLIDARITY DAY. Dec 20. In connection with its observance of first UN Decade for the Eradication of Poverty (1997–2006), the UN General Assembly, on Dec 22, 2005, declared this date each year as International Human Solidarity Day (Resolution 60/209). In taking that action, it recalled that the Millennium Declaration identified solidarity as one of the fundamental and universal values that should underlie relations between peoples in the 21st century. For info: United Nations, Dept of Public Info, New York, NY 10017. Web: www.un.org.

US INVASION OF PANAMA: 25th ANNIVERSARY. Dec 20, 1989. The US launched operation "Just Cause," invading Panama in an attempt to seize Manuel Noriega and bring him to justice for narcotics trafficking. Seven months after Noriega had ruled unfavorable election results null and void, the US toppled the Noriega government and oversaw the installation of Guillermo Endara as president. Although the initial military action was declared a success, Noriega eluded capture. He surrendered to US troops on Jan 4, 1990, and was tried, convicted and imprisoned in the US.

VIRGINIA COMPANY EXPEDITION TO AMERICA: ANNIVERSARY. Dec 20, 1606. Three small ships, the *Susan Constant*, *Godspeed* and *Discovery*, commanded by Captain Christopher Newport, departed London, England, bound for America, where the royally chartered Virginia Company's approximately 120 persons established the first permanent English settlement in what is now the United States at Jamestown, VA, May 14, 1607.

WIGHTMAN, HAZEL: BIRTH ANNIVERSARY. Dec 20, 1886. Hazel Virginia Hotchkiss Wightman, tennis player, born at Healdsburg, CA. Known as the "Queen Mother of Tennis," Wightman was a championship player, an instructor, a benefactor and the donor of the Wightman Cup, a trophy offered for competition between teams of women players from the US and England. Died at Chestnut Hill, MA, Dec 5, 1974.

BIRTHDAYS TODAY

Jenny Agutter, 62, actress (Emmy for *The Snow Goose*; *Walkabout, Logan's Run, Equus*), born London, England, Dec 20, 1952.

David Cook, 32, singer, television personality ("American Idol"), born Houston, TX, Dec 20, 1982.

Uri Geller, 68, psychic, clairvoyant, born Tel Aviv, Israel, Dec 20, 1946.

Jonah Hill, 31, actor (*Moneyball, Superbad*), born Los Angeles, CA, Dec 20, 1983.

John Hillerman, 82, actor ("Magnum, PI"), born Denison, TX, Dec 20, 1932.

David Levine, 88, artist, caricaturist (*New York Review of Books*), born Brooklyn, NY, Dec 20, 1926.

William Julius Wilson, 79, sociologist, educator, writer (*When Work Disappears*), born Derry Township, PA, Dec 20, 1935.

December 21 — Sunday

DAY 355 **10 REMAINING**

BÖLL, HEINRICH: BIRTH ANNIVERSARY. Dec 21, 1917. German novelist, winner of the 1972 Nobel Prize in Literature, author of some 20 books including *Billiards at Half-Past Nine, The Clown* and *Group Portrait with Lady*, born at Cologne, Germany. He died near Bonn, Germany, July 16, 1985.

DISRAELI, BENJAMIN: BIRTH ANNIVERSARY. Dec 21, 1804. British novelist and statesman, born at London and died there Apr 19, 1881. "No government," he wrote, "can be long secure without a formidable opposition."

ELVIS PRESLEY MEETS PRESIDENT NIXON: ANNIVERSARY. Dec 21, 1970. After writing President Richard M. Nixon offering to be a "Federal Agent-at-Large" to fight drug abuse and the drug culture, Elvis Presley met with Nixon at the White House on this date. Presley was not made a federal agent, but the two men had a cordial meeting. The photograph of them shaking hands is the most requested reproduction from the National Archives (more than the Bill of Rights or the US Constitution).

FIRST CROSSWORD PUZZLE: ANNIVERSARY. Dec 21, 1913. The first crossword puzzle was compiled by Arthur Wynne and published in a supplement to the *New York World*.

FOREFATHERS' DAY. Dec 21. Observed mainly in New England in commemoration of landing at Plymouth Rock on this day in 1620.

GIBSON, JOSH: BIRTH ANNIVERSARY. Dec 21, 1911. Joshua (Josh) Gibson, Baseball Hall of Fame catcher born at Buena Vista, GA, is regarded as the greatest slugger to play in the Negro Leagues and perhaps the greatest ballplayer ever. Gibson starred with the Pittsburgh Crawfords. His long home runs are the stuff of legend. Inducted into the Hall of Fame in 1972. Died at Pittsburgh, PA, Jan 20, 1947.

HUMBUG DAY. Dec 21. Allows all those preparing for Christmas to vent their frustrations. Twelve "humbugs" allowed. (©2006 by WH.) For info: Thomas & Ruth Roy, Wellcat Holidays, 2418 Long Ln, Lebanon, PA 17046. Phone: (717) 279-0184. E-mail: info@wellcat.com. Web: www.wellcat.com.

MOON PHASE: NEW MOON. Dec 21. Moon enters New Moon phase at 8:36 PM, EST.

PAN AMERICAN FLIGHT 103 EXPLOSION: ANNIVERSARY. Dec 21, 1988. Pan Am World Airways Flight 103 exploded in midair and crashed into the heart of Lockerbie, Scotland, the result of a terrorist bombing. The 259 passengers and crew members and 11 persons on the ground were killed in the disaster. The tragedy raised questions about security and the notification of passengers in the event of threatened flights. In the resultant investigation it was revealed that government agencies and the airline had known that the flight was possibly the target of a terrorist attack.

December 2014

S	M	T	W	T	F	S
	1	2	3	4	5	6
7	8	9	10	11	12	13
14	15	16	17	18	19	20
21	22	23	24	25	26	27
28	29	30	31			

PARKINSON, JAMES: DEATH ANNIVERSARY. Dec 21, 1824. The remarkable English physician and paleontologist first described the "shaking palsy" and later had it named for him—Parkinson's disease. He was the author of numerous books and articles on a variety of subjects. His *Organic Remains of a Former World* is called the first attempt to give a scientific account of fossils. Under oath, Parkinson declared that he was a member of the group that hatched the "Pop-gun Plot" to assassinate King George III in a theater, using a poisoned dart for the deed. Parkinson was born at London about 1755, and died there, Dec 21, 1824.

PHILEAS FOGG WINS A WAGER DAY. Dec 21. Anniversary, from Jules Verne's *Around the World in Eighty Days*, of the winning of Phileas Fogg's wager, on Dec 21, 1872, when Fogg walked into the saloon of the Reform Club at London, announcing, "Here I am, gentlemen!" exactly 79 days, 23 hours, 59 minutes and 59 seconds after starting his trip "around the world in 80 days," to win his £20,000 wager. See also: "Phileas Fogg's Wager Day" (Oct 2).

PILGRIM LANDING: ANNIVERSARY. Dec 21, 1620. According to Governor William Bradford's *History of Plymouth Plantation*, "On Munday," [Dec 21, 1620, New Style] the Pilgrims, aboard the *Mayflower*, reached Plymouth, MA, "sounded ye harbor, and founde it fitt for shipping; and marched into ye land, & founde diverse cornfields, and ye best they could find, and ye season & their presente necessitie made them glad to accepte of it. . . . And after wards tooke better view of ye place, and resolved wher to pitch their dwelling; and them and their goods." Plymouth Rock, the legendary place of landing since it first was "identified" in 1769, nearly 150 years after the landing, has been a historic shrine since. The landing anniversary is observed in much of New England as Forefathers' Day. See also: "Forefathers' Day" (above).

SHERMAN TAKES SAVANNAH: 150th ANNIVERSARY. Dec 21, 1864. Despite efforts by Confederate General William Hardee to defend the city of Savannah, GA, Southern troops were forced to pull out of the city, and on this date Union forces under William Tecumseh Sherman captured the town. By marching from Atlanta to the coast at Savannah, Sherman had cut the lower South off from the center.

***SNOW WHITE AND THE SEVEN DWARFS* FILM PREMIERE: ANNIVERSARY.** Dec 21, 1937. America's first full-length animated feature film (and also the first Technicolor feature) premiered on this date at the Carthay Circle Theater, Hollywood, CA. The labor of love from Walt Disney—who for years wanted to create a feature-length cartoon—involved more than 750 artists and 1,500 colors in four years of development. The film features the classic songs "Some Day My Prince Will Come" and "Whistle While You Work." Walt Disney received a special Oscar for *Snow White*—along with seven miniature Oscars.

SPACE MILESTONE: *APOLLO 8* (US). Dec 21, 1968. First moon voyage launched, manned by Colonel Frank Borman, Captain James A. Lovell Jr and Major William A. Anders. Orbited moon Dec 24, returned to Earth Dec 27. First men to orbit the moon and see the side of the moon away from Earth.

STALIN, JOSEPH: BIRTH ANNIVERSARY. Dec 21, 1879. Soviet dictator whose family name was Dzhugashvili, was born at Gori, Georgia. One of the most powerful and most feared men of the 20th century, Stalin died (of a stroke) at the Kremlin, at Moscow, Mar 5, 1953.

SZOLD, HENRIETTA: BIRTH ANNIVERSARY. Dec 21, 1860. Teacher, writer, social worker, organizer and pioneer Zionist, Henrietta Szold is best remembered as founder and first president of Hadassah, the Women's Zionist Organization of America. Born at Baltimore, MD, she was influenced by her father Rabbi Benjamin Szold, an active and vocal abolitionist. She established the first "night school" at Baltimore, focused on teaching English and job skills to immigrants. Her trip to Palestine in 1910 sparked the genesis of Hadassah. While there, Szold was alarmed by the lack of social, medical and educational services and returned with the idea that a national women's Zionist organization must be formed to carry out practical projects. The "Mother of Social Service in Palestine," Szold died at Jerusalem, Feb 13, 1945. See also: "Hadassah: Anniversary" (Feb 24).

UNITED KINGDOM ALLOWS SAME-SEX CIVIL PARTNERSHIPS: ANNIVERSARY. Dec 21, 2005. On this date a new law took effect legally recognizing same-sex civil unions in the United Kingdom. The law took effect on Dec 19 in Northern Ireland, but on Dec 20 in Scotland and then Dec 21 in England and Wales. Pop star Elton John and his partner filmmaker David Furnish were among the first celebrities to wed on the 21st.

WINTER. Dec 21–Mar 20, 2015. In the Northern Hemisphere winter begins today with the winter solstice, at 6:03 PM, EST. Note that in the Southern Hemisphere today is the beginning of summer. Between the equator and Arctic Circle the sunrise and sunset points on the horizon are farthest south for the year and daylight length is minimum (ranging from 12 hours, 8 minutes, at the equator to zero at the Arctic Circle).

YALDA. Dec 21. Yalda, the longest night of the year, is celebrated by Iranians. The ceremony has an Indo-Iranian origin, where Light and Good were considered to struggle against Darkness and Evil. With fires burning and lights lit, family and friends gather to stay up through the night helping the sun in its battle against darkness. They recite poetry, tell stories and eat special fruits and nuts until the sun, triumphant, reappears in the morning.

YULE. Dec 21. (Also called Alban Arthan.) One of the "Lesser Sabbats" during the Wiccan year, Yule marks the death of the Sun-God and his rebirth from the Earth Goddess. Annually, on the winter solstice.

ZAPPA, FRANK: BIRTH ANNIVERSARY. Dec 21, 1940. Rock musician and composer, Zappa was noted for his satire and for being a leading advocate against censorship of contemporary music. He formed the group Mothers of Invention. Born at Baltimore, MD, he died Dec 4, 1993, at Los Angeles, CA, at age 52.

BIRTHDAYS TODAY

Tina Brown, 61, journalist, editor (*The Daily Beast*), author, born London, England, Dec 21, 1953.

Andy Dick, 49, actor ("NewsRadio"), born Charleston, SC, Dec 21, 1965.

Phil Donahue, 79, former television talk show host ("Donahue"), born Cleveland, OH, Dec 21, 1935.

Christine Marie (Chris) Evert, 60, sportscaster, Hall of Fame tennis player, born Fort Lauderdale, FL, Dec 21, 1954.

Jane Fonda, 77, actress (Oscars for *Klute*, *Coming Home*; *Julia*, *On Golden Pond*), born New York, NY, Dec 21, 1937.

Samuel L. Jackson, 66, actor (*SWAT*, *Shaft*, *Pulp Fiction*), born Washington, DC, Dec 21, 1948.

Jane Kaczmarek, 59, actress ("Malcolm in the Middle"), born Milwaukee, WI, Dec 21, 1955.

Jackson Rathbone, 30, actor (*Twilight*), born at Singapore, Dec 21, 1984.

Ray Romano, 57, comedian, actor ("Everybody Loves Raymond"), born Queens, NY, Dec 21, 1957.

Kiefer Sutherland, 48, actor ("24," *Flatliners*, *A Few Good Men*), born London, England, Dec 21, 1966.

Michael Tilson Thomas, 70, conductor, pianist, organist, born Hollywood, CA, Dec 21, 1944.

Andrew James (Andy) Van Slyke, 54, former baseball player, born Utica, NY, Dec 21, 1960.

Karrie Webb, 40, golfer, born Ayr, Queensland, Australia, Dec 21, 1974.

Steven Yeun, 31, actor ("The Walking Dead"), born Seoul, South Korea, Dec 21, 1983.

December 22 — Monday

DAY 356 — **9 REMAINING**

ASHCROFT, PEGGY: BIRTH ANNIVERSARY. Dec 22, 1907. British actress Dame Edith Margaret Emily Ashcroft was born at Croydon, England. In addition to her many accolades on the British stage, she won an Oscar for her supporting role in *Passage to India* (1985) and a special British Olivier Award for lifetime achievement in 1991. She died June 14, 1991, at London, England.

CAPRICORN, THE GOAT. Dec 22–Jan 19. In the astronomical and astrological zodiac that divides the sun's apparent orbit into 12 segments, the period Dec 22–Jan 19 is traditionally identified as the sun sign of Capricorn, the goat. The ruling planet is Saturn.

"DING DONG SCHOOL" TV PREMIERE: ANNIVERSARY. Dec 22, 1952. Named by a three-year-old after watching a test broadcast of the opening sequence (a hand ringing a bell), "Ding Dong School" was one of the first children's educational series. Miss Frances (Dr. Frances Horwich, head of Roosevelt College's education department at Chicago) was the host of this weekday show.

ELLERY, WILLIAM: BIRTH ANNIVERSARY. Dec 22, 1727. Signer of the Declaration of Independence, born at Newport, RI, and died there Feb 15, 1820.

FIRST GORILLA BORN IN CAPTIVITY: ANNIVERSARY. Dec 22, 1956. "Colo" was born at the Columbus, OH, zoo, weighing in at 3¼ pounds, the first gorilla born in captivity.

JOHNSON, CLAUDIA TAYLOR (LADY BIRD): BIRTH ANNIVERSARY. Dec 22, 1912. Former First Lady, born Claudia Alta Taylor at Karnack, TX, this daughter of an East Texas cotton grower married young politician Lyndon Baines Johnson in 1934. She ran his congressional office during his navy stint in WWII and was at his side as his career ran its course from Texas congressman to 36th president of the US. Her personal causes included highway beautification, and she founded the National Wildflower Research Center in Austin, TX, in 1995 (later renamed for her). She died at Austin, July 11, 2007.

OGLETHORPE, JAMES EDWARD: BIRTH ANNIVERSARY. Dec 22, 1696. English general, author and colonizer of Georgia. Founder of the city of Savannah. Oglethorpe was born at London. He died June 30, 1785, at Cranham Hall, Essex, England.

PUCCINI, GIACOMO: BIRTH ANNIVERSARY. Dec 22, 1858. Italian composer of such operas as *La Boheme*, *Tosca* and *Madama Butterfly*. Born at Lucca, Tuscany, Italy, he died Nov 29, 1924, at Brussels, Belgium.

RACINE: JEAN-BAPTISTE: 375th BIRTH ANNIVERSARY. Dec 22, 1639. French dramatist and playwright. Working during the reign of Louis XIV, Racine was a contemporary of Molière and ultimately a rival of Corneille. His works include *Andromaque* (1667), *Iphegénie* (1674) and *Phèdre* (1677). He brought to the classical tradition a sublimely refined style, and his plays introduced a new focus—the passions overruling tragic figures—rather than the presentation of a complicated chain of events. Born at La Ferté-Milon, he died Apr 22, 1699, at Paris.

ROBINSON, EDWIN ARLINGTON: BIRTH ANNIVERSARY. Dec 22, 1869. Three-time Pulitzer Prize winner best known for his short dramatic poems, including "Richard Cory" and "Miniver Cheevy." Born at Head Tide, ME, and died at Los Angeles, CA, Apr 6, 1935.

BIRTHDAYS TODAY

Steven Norman (Steve) Carlton, 70, Hall of Fame baseball player, born Miami, FL, Dec 22, 1944.

Ted Cruz, 44, US Senator (R, Texas), born Calgary, AB, Canada, Dec 22, 1970.

Hector Elizondo, 78, actor (*Pretty Woman, Frankie and Johnny*, "Chicago Hope"), born New York, NY, Dec 22, 1936.

Ralph Fiennes, 52, actor (Harry Potter films, *Schindler's List, The English Patient*), born Suffolk, England, Dec 22, 1962.

Steve Garvey, 66, former baseball player, born Tampa, FL, Dec 22, 1948.

Diane K. Sawyer, 68, journalist, anchor ("ABC World News"), born Glasgow, KY, Dec 22, 1946.

Jan Stephenson, 63, golfer, born Sydney, Australia, Dec 22, 1951.

December 23 — Tuesday

DAY 357 **8 REMAINING**

FEDERAL RESERVE SYSTEM: ANNIVERSARY. Dec 23, 1913. Established pursuant to authority contained in the Federal Reserve Act of Dec 23, 1913, the system serves as the nation's central bank, with the responsibility for execution of monetary policy. It is called on to contribute to the strength and vitality of the US economy, in part by influencing the lending and investing activities of commercial banks and the cost and availability of money and credit.

FIRST NONSTOP FLIGHT AROUND THE WORLD WITHOUT REFUELING: ANNIVERSARY. Dec 23, 1987. Dick Rutan and Jeana Yeager set a new world record of 216 hours of continuous flight, breaking their own record of 111 hours set July 15, 1986. The aircraft *Voyager* departed from Edwards Air Force Base in California, Dec 14, 1987, and landed Dec 23, 1987. The journey covered 24,986 miles at an official speed of 115 miles per hour.

HUMANLIGHT CELEBRATION. Dec 23. HumanLight is a celebration of humanist values: tolerance, compassion, empathy, honesty, free inquiry, reason, rationality and more. The event began in New Jersey by the New Jersey Humanist Network in 2001. The event provides an excellent alternative to Christmas celebrations. For info: American Humanist Assn, 1777 T St NW, Washington, DC 20009. Phone: (202) 238-9088. Fax: (202) 238-9003. Web: www.humanlight.org.

JAPAN: BIRTHDAY OF THE EMPEROR. Dec 23. National Day. Holiday honoring Emperor Akihito, born in 1933.

METRIC CONVERSION ACT: ANNIVERSARY. Dec 23, 1975. The Congress of the US passed Public Law 94–168, known as the Metric Conversion Act of 1975. This act declares that the SI (International System of Units) will be this country's basic system of measurement and establishes the United States Metric Board, which is responsible for the planning, coordination and implementation of the nation's voluntary conversion to SI. (Congress had authorized the metric system as a legal system of measurement in the US by an act passed July 28, 1866. In 1875, the US became one of the original signers of the Treaty of the Metre, which established an international metric system.)

MEXICO: FEAST OF THE RADISHES. Dec 23. Oaxaca. Figurines of people and animals cleverly carved out of radishes are sold during festivities.

MONROE, HARRIET: BIRTH ANNIVERSARY. Dec 23, 1860. American poet, editor and founder of *Poetry* magazine. Born at Chicago, IL. Died Sept 26, 1936, at Arequipa, Peru.

RABI'I: THE MONTH OF THE MIGRATION. Dec 23. Begins on Islamic calendar date Rabi al-AwaI 1, 1436. The third month of the Islamic calendar, the month of the migration of the Prophet Muhammad from Mecca to Medina in AD 622, the event that was used as the starting year of the Islamic lunar calendar. Different methods for "anticipating" the visibility of the new moon crescent at Mecca are used by different Muslim groups. US date may vary. Began at sunset the preceding day. Due to the differences in the lunar and Gregorian calendars, Rabi'i falls twice in calendar 2014.

SMITH, JOSEPH, JR: BIRTH ANNIVERSARY. Dec 23, 1805. The founding prophet of The Church of Jesus Christ of Latter-day Saints was born at Sharon, VT. He was assassinated by an armed mob on June 27, 1844, at Carthage, IL. See also: "Smith, Joseph, Jr, and Hyrum: Death Anniversary" (June 27).

TOJO HIDEKI EXECUTION: ANNIVERSARY. Dec 23, 1948. Tojo Hideki, prime minister of Japan from Oct 16, 1941, until his resignation July 19, 1944. After Japan's surrender in August 1945, Tojo was arrested as a war criminal, tried by a military tribunal and sentenced to death Nov 12, 1948. Born at Tokyo, Japan, Dec 30, 1884, Tojo was hanged (with six other Japanese wartime military leaders) at Sugamo Prison, Tokyo, Dec 23, 1948, the sentence being carried out by the US 8th Army.

TRANSISTOR UNVEILED: ANNIVERSARY. Dec 23, 1947. John Bardeen, Walter Brattain and William Shockley of Bell Laboratories shared the 1956 Nobel Prize for their invention of the transistor, which led to a revolution in communications and electronics. It was smaller, lighter, more durable and more reliable and generated less heat than the vacuum tube that had been used up to that time.

BIRTHDAYS TODAY

Akihito, 81, Emperor of Japan, born Tokyo, Japan, Dec 23, 1933.

Robert Bly, 88, poet, author (*Iron John, What Have I Ever Lost by Dying?*), born Madison, MN, Dec 23, 1926.

Carol Ann Duffy, 59, Poet Laureate of the United Kingdom (2009–), born Glasgow, Scotland, Dec 23, 1955.

Scott Gomez, 35, hockey player, born Anchorage, AK, Dec 23, 1979.

James Joseph (Jim) Harbaugh, 51, football coach and former player, born Toledo, OH, Dec 23, 1963.

Susan Lucci, 65, actress ("All My Children," *Mafia Princess*), born Westchester, NY, Dec 23, 1949.

Gerald O'Loughlin, 93, actor ("The Rookies," "Our House"), born New York, NY, Dec 23, 1921.

Hanley Ramirez, 31, baseball player, born Samana, Dominican Republic, Dec 23, 1983.

December 2014

S	M	T	W	T	F	S
	1	2	3	4	5	6
7	8	9	10	11	12	13
14	15	16	17	18	19	20
21	22	23	24	25	26	27
28	29	30	31			

December 24 — Wednesday

DAY 358 **7 REMAINING**

***AIDA* PREMIERE: ANNIVERSARY.** Dec 24, 1871. Giuseppe Verdi's opera *Aida* premiered at Cairo. It was commissioned by the Khedive of Egypt to celebrate the opening of the Suez Canal.

ARNOLD, MATTHEW: BIRTH ANNIVERSARY. Dec 24, 1822. English poet and essayist, born at Laleham, England. Died Apr 15, 1888, at Liverpool, England. "One has often wondered," he wrote in *Culture and Anarchy*, "whether upon the whole earth there is anything so unintelligent, so unapt to perceive how the world is really going, as an ordinary young Englishman of our upper class."

AUSTRIA: "SILENT NIGHT, HOLY NIGHT" CELEBRATIONS. Dec 24. Oberndorf, Hallein and Wagrain, Salzburg, Austria. Commemorating the creation of the Christmas carol here in 1818.

CARSON, CHRISTOPHER "KIT": BIRTH ANNIVERSARY. Dec 24, 1809. American frontiersman, soldier, trapper, guide and Indian agent best known as Kit Carson. Born at Madison County, KY, he died at Fort Lyon, CO, May 23, 1868.

CHRISTMAS BELLS RING AGAIN IN ST. BASIL'S: ANNIVERSARY. Dec 24, 1990. For the first time since the death of Lenin in 1924, the bells of St. Basil's Cathedral, on Red Square in Moscow, rang to celebrate Christmas.

CHRISTMAS EVE. Dec 24. Family gift-giving occasion in many Christian countries.

ENGLAND: FESTIVAL OF NINE LESSONS AND CAROLS. Dec 24. King's College Chapel, Cambridge University, Cambridge. Since 1918, a Christmas Eve service of carols and readings from the Bible performed by the Choir of King's College. The carols and readings vary from year to year with the exception of the opening carol, which is always "Once in Royal David's City." Each year the service also includes a new, specially commissioned carol. The service has been broadcast on radio since 1928 and is now broadcast to millions of people around the world. Members of the public who wish to attend must join a queue on the college grounds via the Front Gate from 7:30 AM. For info: King's College, Cambridge University. Web: www.kings.cam.ac.uk.

FIRST SURFACE-TO-SURFACE GUIDED MISSILE: ANNIVERSARY. Dec 24, 1942. German rocket engineer Wernher von Braun launched the first surface-to-surface guided missile. Buzz bombs, a form of guided missile, were used by Germany against Great Britain starting Sept 8, 1944. On Feb 24, 1949, the first rocket to reach outer space (an altitude of 25 miles) was fired. The two-stage rocket, a Wac Corporal set in the nose of a German V-2, was launched from the White Sands Proving Grounds, NM, by a team of scientists headed by von Braun.

GARDNER, AVA: BIRTH ANNIVERSARY. Dec 24, 1922. Actress and leading sex symbol of the 1940s and '50s, Ava Lavinnia Gardner was born at Smithfield, NC. Among Gardner's numerous movies are *The Barefoot Contessa, Bhowani Junction, The Sun Also Rises* and *The Life and Times of Judge Roy Bean*. Gardner was married to Mickey Rooney (1942–43), Artie Shaw (1945–46) and Frank Sinatra (1951–57). Died at London, England, Jan 25, 1990.

HUGHES, HOWARD ROBARD: BIRTH ANNIVERSARY. Dec 24, 1905. Wealthy American industrialist, aviator and movie producer who spent his latter years as a recluse. Born at Houston, TX, he died in an airplane en route from Acapulco, Mexico, to Houston, Apr 5, 1976.

JOULE, JAMES PRESCOTT: BIRTH ANNIVERSARY. Dec 24, 1818. English physicist and inventor after whom Joule's Law (the first law of thermodynamics) was named. Born at Salford, Lancashire, England. The unit of measurement of the mechanical equivalent of heat is known as the joule. He died at Cheshire, England, Oct 11, 1889.

LIBYA: INDEPENDENCE DAY. Dec 24. Libya gained its independence from Italy in 1951.

"THE PERRY COMO SHOW" TV PREMIERE: ANNIVERSARY. Dec 24, 1948. Singer Perry Como hosted "The Chesterfield Supper Club" when it came to TV from radio. Also featured were the Mitchell Ayres Orchestra and the Fontane Sisters. The show was retitled "The Perry Como Show" during 1955–59 and then "The Kraft Music Hall" during 1959–63. The Ray Charles Singers and the Louis DaPron Dancers were featured. Como's theme song was "Dream Along with Me."

BIRTHDAYS TODAY

Diedrich Bader, 48, actor ("The Drew Carey Show"), born Alexandria, VA, Dec 24, 1966.

Mary Higgins Clark, 83, author (*Where Are the Children?, Silent Night*), born New York, NY, Dec 24, 1931.

Lee Daniels, 55, producer, director (*Precious: Based on the Novel "Push" by Sapphire, Monster's Ball*), born Philadelphia, PA, Dec 24, 1959.

Anil Kapoor, 55, actor (*Slumdog Millionaire, Pukar*), born Mumbai, India, Dec 24, 1959.

Ricky Martin, 43, singer, actor ("General Hospital"), born Enrique José Martín at San Juan, Puerto Rico, Dec 24, 1971.

Stephenie Meyer, 41, author (*Twilight* series), born Hartford, CT, Dec 24, 1973.

Ryan Seacrest, 40, television host ("American Idol"), radio personality ("America's Top 40"), born Atlanta, GA, Dec 24, 1974.

Jeff Sessions, 68, US Senator (R, Alabama), born Hybart, AL, Dec 24, 1946.

December 25 — Thursday

DAY 359 **6 REMAINING**

A'PHABET DAY. Dec 25. Also known as "No-L" Day, this celebration is for people who do not want to send Christmas cards but who want to greet their friends; so they send out cards listing the letters of the alphabet in order, but with a gap where L would be. For info: Bob Birch, The Puns Corps, 3108 Dashiell Rd, Falls Church, VA 22042. Phone: (703) 533-3668.

BARTON, CLARA: BIRTH ANNIVERSARY. Dec 25, 1821. Clarissa Harlowe Barton, American nurse and philanthropist, founder of the American Red Cross, was born at Oxford, MA. In 1881, she became first president of the American Red Cross (founded May 21, 1881). She died at Glen Echo, MD, Apr 12, 1912.

BOGART, HUMPHREY: BIRTH ANNIVERSARY. Dec 25, 1899. American stage and screen actor, Humphrey DeForest Bogart was born at New York, NY. Among his best-remembered films are *The African Queen, The Maltese Falcon, Casablanca* and *To Have and Have Not*. Bogart died Jan 14, 1957, at Hollywood, CA.

BOOTH, EVANGELINE CORY: BIRTH ANNIVERSARY. Dec 25, 1865. Salvation Army general, active in England, Canada and the US. Author and composer of songs, Booth was born at London, England. She died at Hartsdale, NY, July 17, 1950.

CALLOWAY, CAB: BIRTH ANNIVERSARY. Dec 25, 1907. American singer and bandleader Cabell Calloway was born at Rochester, NY. George Gershwin modeled the part of Sportin' Life in *Porgy and*

Bess (1935) after this jazz singer who also played the role across the US until 1956. He is best known for his song "Minnie the Moocher" (1931). He died Nov 18, 1994, at Hockessin, DE.

CEAUSESCU, NICOLAE: 25th DEATH ANNIVERSARY. Dec 25, 1989. On Christmas evening a broadcast of a Christmas symphony on state-run television was interrupted with the report that Romanian president Nicolae Ceausescu and his wife had been executed, bringing to an end the last hard-line regime in the Soviet bloc. Ceausescu's downfall began when he ordered members of his black-shirted state police, the Securitate, to use force to quell a disturbance in the town of Timisorara. The brutal crackdown led to estimates of as many as 4,500 killed. Ceausescu's rule was marked by corruption, deprivation and terror.

CHRISTMAS. Dec 25. Christian festival commemorating the birth of Jesus of Nazareth. Most popular of Christian observances, Christmas as a Feast of the Nativity dates from the fourth century. Although Jesus's birth date is not known, the Western church selected Dec 25 for the feast, possibly to counteract the non-Christian festivals of that approximate date. Many customs from non-Christian festivals (Roman Saturnalia, Mithraic sun's birthday, Teutonic yule, Druidic and other winter solstice rites) have been adopted as part of the Christmas celebration (lights, mistletoe, holly and ivy, holiday tree, wassailing and gift giving, for example). Some Orthodox churches celebrate Christmas Jan 7 based on the "old calendar" (Julian). Theophany (recognition of the divinity of Jesus) is observed on this date and also on Jan 6, especially by the Eastern Orthodox Church.

CUBA: CHRISTMAS RETURNS: ANNIVERSARY. Dec 25, 1998. Christmas was celebrated in Cuba after Fidel Castro's government announced that it was again a regular holiday in the Cuban calendar. In 1997 the government had granted a Christmas holiday in deference to Pope John Paul II who was visiting the island the next month. Christmas had been abolished as a holiday in Cuba in 1969.

FARLEY, CAL: BIRTH ANNIVERSARY. Dec 25, 1895. Cal Farley, known as "America's Greatest Foster Father," started Cal Farley's Boys Ranch in 1939 with nine boys. The ranch has grown into a modern community of 441 boys (and girls since 1992), which has housed and educated more than 4,000 boys and girls over the years. Cal Farley was born at Saxton, IA; he died Feb 19, 1967, at Boys Ranch, TX.

FIRST INDOOR BASEBALL GAME: ANNIVERSARY. Dec 25, 1888. Long before the domed stadiums of the late 20th century, a large building at the state fairgrounds in Philadelphia, PA, was the site of the first indoor baseball game. Two thousand spectators watched the Downtowners beat the Uptowners, 6–1.

IT'S ABOUT TIME WEEK! Dec 25–31. Innovative week encourages creativity and honors ideas and pilot programs. For info: The Art House, 1307 Hillyer Ave, Macon, GA 31204.

JINNAH, MOHAMMED ALI (QAID-E-AZAM): BIRTH ANNIVERSARY. Dec 25, 1876. The founder of the Islamic Republic of Pakistan, Mohammed Ali Jinnah was born at Karachi, then part of India. When Pakistan became an independent political entity (Aug 15, 1947), Jinnah became its first governor general. He was given the title Qaid-e-Azam (Great Leader) in 1947. He died at Karachi, Sept 11, 1948. Jinnah's birth anniversary is a holiday in Pakistan.

"METROPOLITAN OPERA RADIO BROADCASTS" PREMIERE: ANNIVERSARY. Dec 25, 1931. On Christmas Day 1931, the Metropolitan Opera of New York City broadcast an entire opera, *Hansel and Gretel*, on the NBC radio network—the first time this had ever been done. This broadcast was the first of an ongoing radio series of Saturday matinees. On Dec 7, 1940, Texaco (now ChevronTexaco) became a sponsor and began the longest continuous sponsorship in broadcast history—a sponsorship that ended after the 2003–2004 season. For decades, the Metropolitan Opera radio broadcasts have introduced opera to new fans far from New York. Today, the broadcasts are heard internationally in 42 countries and are currently sponsored by Toll Brothers.

PATHÉ, CHARLES: BIRTH ANNIVERSARY. Dec 25, 1863. Born at Paris, France, Pathé, with his three brothers, founded the innovative film company Pathé Freres (Pathé Brothers) in 1896. A vertically integrated business, Pathé Freres made film stock, cameras and projectors; produced films and exhibited their works in their own theaters. In 1909, Pathé released its first feature-length film—*Les Misérables*—as well its first newsreel. Soon Pathé Freres had worldwide production facilities and a distribution network that made them dominant in the industry. Charles Pathé retired in 1929 and died Dec 26, 1957, at Monte-Carlo, Monaco.

"THE STEVE ALLEN SHOW" TV PREMIERE: ANNIVERSARY. Dec 25, 1950. Talented actor, comedian, singer and musician, Steve Allen hosted a number of variety shows from 1950 to 1969 (with a few breaks in between to host specials and "The Tonight Show"). For two years, his television show was similar to his radio show and featured singer Peggy Lee, announcer Bern Bennett and Llemuel the llama. His next show competed with Ed Sullivan's show, though Allen's stressed comedy. Some of his "funnymen" were Don Knots; Tom Poston; Louis Nye; Gabe Dell; Pat Harrington, Jr; Dayton Allen and Bill Dana. His other shows included a talk show, a game show, a comedy show, an educational music show and a flashback-comedy show.

STOCK EXCHANGE HOLIDAY (CHRISTMAS DAY). Dec 25. Also early closures Dec 24. The holiday schedules for the various exchanges are subject to change if relevant rules, regulations or exchange policies are revised. If you have questions, contact: CME Group (CME, CBOT, NYMEX, KCBT) (www.cmegroup.com), Chicago Board Options Exchange (www.cboe.com), NASDAQ (www.nasdaq.com), NYSE Euronext (www.nyse.com).

TAIWAN: CONSTITUTION DAY. Dec 25. National holiday. Commemorates the adoption of the 1946 constitution.

UNITED KINGDOM: CHRISTMAS HOLIDAY. Dec 25. Bank and public holiday in England, Wales, Scotland and Northern Ireland.

WASHINGTON CROSSES THE DELAWARE: ANNIVERSARY. Dec 25, 1776. One of the most famous events of the American Revolution happened on a bleak Christmas night, during driving snow. General George Washington led 2,400 men across the Delaware River at McConkey's Ferry, Bucks County, PA, to conduct a surprise attack on Hessian troops at Trenton, NJ. Local fishermen conducted the troops across the river, finally assembling at 3:00 AM on the other side. Washington achieved victory at Trenton, a key event that changed the course of the war to the rebelling colonists' favor.

WEST, REBECCA: BIRTH ANNIVERSARY. Dec 25, 1892. English author, literary critic, prizewinning journalist and noted feminist, Dame Rebecca West was born Cicily Isabel Fairfield at London, England. She died there Mar 15, 1983.

December 2014

S	M	T	W	T	F	S
	1	2	3	4	5	6
7	8	9	10	11	12	13
14	15	16	17	18	19	20
21	22	23	24	25	26	27
28	29	30	31			

BIRTHDAYS TODAY

Jimmy Buffett, 68, singer ("Margaritaville"), songwriter, born Pascagoula, MS, Dec 25, 1946.

Lawrence Richard (Larry) Csonka, 68, Hall of Fame football player, born Stow, OH, Dec 25, 1946.

Rickey Henderson, 56, Hall of Fame baseball player, born Chicago, IL, Dec 25, 1958.

Annie Lennox, 60, singer, born Aberdeen, Scotland, Dec 25, 1954.

Barbara Mandrell, 66, singer, born Houston, TX, Dec 25, 1948.

Karl Rove, 64, political consultant, former presidential adviser, born Denver, CO, Dec 25, 1950.

Gary Sandy, 69, actor ("All That Glitters," "WKRP in Cincinnati"), born Dayton, OH, Dec 25, 1945.

Hanna Schygulla, 71, actress (*The Marriage of Maria Braun, Berlin Alexanderplatz*), born Kattowitz, Germany, Dec 25, 1943.

Mary Elizabeth (Sissy) Spacek, 65, actress (*In the Bedroom, Crimes of the Heart, Carrie*; Oscar for *Coal Miner's Daughter*), born Quitman, TX, Dec 25, 1949.

December 26 — Friday

DAY 360 **5 REMAINING**

ALLEN, STEVE: BIRTH ANNIVERSARY. Dec 26, 1921. American entertainer and TV pioneer, Steve Allen created the original "Tonight Show" for NBC in 1953. Also known as a composer and the author of more than 40 books, he was born at New York, NY, Dec 26, 1921. He died at Encino, CA, Oct 30, 2000.

BABBAGE, CHARLES: BIRTH ANNIVERSARY. Dec 26, 1792. English mathematician, born at Teignmouth, England. He developed the principles on which modern computers are designed. Babbage died at London, England, Oct 18, 1871.

BAHAMAS: JUNKANOO. Dec 26. Kaleidoscope of sound and spectacle combining a bit of Mardi Gras, mummers' parade and ancient African tribal rituals. Revelers in colorful costumes parade through the streets to sounds of cowbells, goatskin drums and many other homemade instruments. Always on Boxing Day.

BOXING DAY. Dec 26. Ordinarily observed on the first day after Christmas. A legal holiday in Canada, the United Kingdom and many other countries. Formerly (according to Robert Chambers) a day when Christmas gift boxes were "regularly expected by a postman, the lamplighter, the dustman and generally by all those functionaries who render services to the public at large, without receiving payment therefore from any individual." When Boxing Day falls on a Saturday or Sunday, the Monday or Tuesday immediately following may be proclaimed or observed as a bank or public holiday.

BOXING DAY AT THE HEMINGWAY BIRTHPLACE. Dec 26. Hemingway Birthplace, Oak Park, IL. The Hemingway family celebrated Boxing Day with extended family, eating special foods and sharing literary works and poetry. The Ernest Hemingway Foundation of Oak Park will re-create this holiday celebration with English tea, music and dramatic readings of Christmas tales. For info: The Ernest Hemingway Foundation, PO Box 2222, Oak Park, IL 60303-2222. Phone: (708) 848-2222. Fax: (708) 386-2952. E-mail: ehfop@sbcglobal.net. Web: www.ehfop.org.

CLERC, LAURENT: BIRTH ANNIVERSARY. Dec 26, 1785. The first deaf teacher in America, Laurent Clerc assisted Thomas Hopkins Gallaudet in establishing the first public school for the deaf, Connecticut Asylum for the Education and Instruction of Deaf and Dumb Persons (now the American School for the Deaf), at Hartford, CT, in 1817. For 41 years Clerc trained new teachers in the use of sign language and in methods of teaching the deaf. Clerc was born at LaBalme, France, and died July 18, 1869.

DECEMBRIST REVOLT: ANNIVERSARY. Dec 26, 1825–Jan 15, 1826. (Dates New Style.) Following the death of Tsar Alexander I, Russian military officers with 3,000 men occupied the Senate Square in St. Petersburg, demanding reforms, including the abolition of serfdom and the advent of a constitutional monarchy. Once the crowd was dispersed, the leaders were arrested and hanged in Russia's last public executions, but the revolt spurred reform and inspired revolutionaries in Russia.

FIRST BLACK HEAVYWEIGHT CHAMPION: ANNIVERSARY. Dec 26, 1908. Jack Johnson became the first black man to win the heavyweight boxing championship when he knocked out Tommy Burns in the 14th round of a fight at Sydney, Australia.

IRELAND: DAY OF THE WREN. Dec 26. Dingle Peninsula. Masked revelers and musicians go from door to door asking for money. Traditional day and night of public merrymaking.

KWANZAA. Dec 26–Jan 1, 2015. African-American family observance created in 1966 by Dr. Maulana Karenga in recognition of traditional African harvest festivals. This seven-day festival stresses unity of the black family, with a harvest feast (karamu) on the first day and a day of meditation on the final one. *Kwanzaa* means "first fruit" in Swahili.

LUXEMBOURG: BLESSING OF THE WINE. Dec 26. Greiveldange, Luxembourg. Winemakers parade to the church, where a barrel of wine is blessed.

MAO TSE-TUNG: BIRTH ANNIVERSARY. Dec 26, 1893. Chinese librarian, teacher, communist revolutionist and "founding father" of the People's Republic of China, born at Hunan Province, China. Died at Beijing, Sept 9, 1976.

MILLER, HENRY (VALENTINE): BIRTH ANNIVERSARY. Dec 26, 1891. Controversial American novelist (*Tropic of Cancer*), born at New York, NY. Died at Pacific Palisades, CA, June 7, 1980.

NATIONAL WHINER'S DAY™. Dec 26. A day dedicated to whiners, especially those who return Christmas gifts and need lots of attention. People are encouraged to be happy about what they do have, rather than unhappy about what they don't have. The most famous whiner(s) of the year will be announced. Nominations accepted through Dec 15. For more info, please send SASE to: Kevin C. Zaborney, 2023 Vickory Rd, Caro, MI 48723. Phone: (989) 673-6696. E-mail: kevin@nationalhuggingday.com. Web: www.nationalhuggingday.com.

NELSON, THOMAS: BIRTH ANNIVERSARY. Dec 26, 1738. Merchant and signer of the Declaration of Independence. Fourth governor of Virginia (after Thomas Jefferson). Born at Yorktown, VA, he died at Hanover County, VA, Jan 4, 1789.

RADIUM DISCOVERED: ANNIVERSARY. Dec 26, 1898. French scientists Pierre and Marie Curie discovered the element radium, for which they later won the Nobel Prize in Physics.

SAINT STEPHEN'S DAY. Dec 26. One of the seven deacons named by the apostles to distribute alms. Died during first century. Feast Day is Dec 26 and is observed as a public holiday in Austria and the Republic of Ireland.

SECOND DAY OF CHRISTMAS. Dec 26. Observed as a holiday in many countries.

SHENANDOAH NATIONAL PARK ESTABLISHED: ANNIVERSARY. Dec 26, 1935. Area of Blue Ridge Mountains of Virginia, originally authorized May 22, 1926, was established as a national park. For further park info: Shenandoah Natl Park. Web: www.nps.gov/shen.

SLOVENIA: INDEPENDENCE DAY. Dec 26. National holiday. Commemorates 1990 announcement of separation from the Yugoslav Union.

SOUTH AFRICA: DAY OF GOODWILL. Dec 26. National holiday. Replaces Boxing Day.

SUMATRAN-ANDAMAN EARTHQUAKE AND TSUNAMIS: 10th ANNIVERSARY. Dec 26, 2004. One of the strongest and most lethal earthquakes of modern history unleashed tsunami waves that devastated coasts all around the Indian Ocean, where it was centered. An estimated 250,000 people died, with thousands missing and millions displaced. With a magnitude in the range of 9.3, this was the second-strongest earthquake of all time. The power was the equivalent of a 100 gigaton bomb, and its action vibrated the entire planet. The earth spun faster and the day was fractionally shortened as a result. This was also the longest-lasting earthquake recorded, with a length of about 10 minutes as opposed to the more typical few seconds.

UNITED KINGDOM: BOXING DAY BANK HOLIDAY. Dec 26. Bank and public holiday in England, Wales, Scotland and Northern Ireland.

WIDMARK, RICHARD: 100th BIRTH ANNIVERSARY. Dec 26, 1914. Charismatic actor, born at Sunrise, MN, whose screen debut in 1947 as the giggling psychopathic killer in the film noir *Kiss of Death* made him an instant star. Other notable films were *Panic in the Streets* (1950), *No Way Out* (1950), *Night and the City* (1950), *Judgment at Nuremberg* (1961) and *Madigan* (1968). Widmark died Mar 24, 2008, at Roxbury, CT.

BIRTHDAYS TODAY

Beth Behrs, 29, actress ("Two Broke Girls"), born Lancaster, PA, Dec 26, 1985.

Chris Daughtry, 35, singer, television personality ("American Idol"), born Roanoke Rapids, NC, Dec 26, 1979.

Carlton Ernest Fisk, 67, Hall of Fame baseball player, born Bellows Falls, VT, Dec 26, 1947.

Kit Harington, 28, actor ("Game of Thrones"; stage: *War Horse*), born Christopher Catesby Harington at London, England, Dec 26, 1986.

Marcelo Rios, 39, former tennis player, born Santiago, Chile, Dec 26, 1975.

Osborne Earl (Ozzie) Smith, 60, Hall of Fame baseball player, born Mobile, AL, Dec 26, 1954.

Phil Spector, 74, music producer, born New York, NY, Dec 26, 1940.

December 2014

S	M	T	W	T	F	S
	1	2	3	4	5	6
7	8	9	10	11	12	13
14	15	16	17	18	19	20
21	22	23	24	25	26	27
28	29	30	31			

December 27 — Saturday

DAY 361 — **4 REMAINING**

CAYLEY, GEORGE: BIRTH ANNIVERSARY. Dec 27, 1773. Aviation pioneer Sir George Cayley, English scientist and inventor, a theoretician who designed airplanes, helicopters and gliders. He is credited as the father of aerodynamics, and he was the pilot of the world's first manned glider flight. Born at Scarborough, Yorkshire, England, he died at Brompton Hall, Yorkshire, Dec 15, 1857.

DIETRICH, MARLENE: BIRTH ANNIVERSARY. Dec 27, 1901. Born at Berlin, Germany, Dietrich enrolled in Max Reinhardt's drama school. Her first big break was in 1930 when Josef Von Sternberg cast her in *The Blue Angel*, the first talkie made in Germany. A year later, she and Sternberg moved to Hollywood and began a string of six films together with *Morocco*, the only film for which she received an Academy Award nomination. Some of her other films were *Destry Rides Again, Around the World in 80 Days, Touch of Evil, Judgment at Nuremberg* and *Witness for the Prosecution*. During the 1950s she was a cabaret singer in a stage revue that toured the globe. Dietrich died May 6, 1992, at Paris, France.

"HOWDY DOODY" TV PREMIERE: ANNIVERSARY. Dec 27, 1947. The first popular children's show was brought to TV by Bob Smith and was one of the first regular NBC shows to be shown in color. It was set in the circus town of Doodyville. Children sat in the bleachers' "Peanut Gallery" and participated in activities such as songs and stories. Human characters were Buffalo Bob (Bob Smith), the silent clown Clarabell (Bob Keeshan, Bobby Nicholson and Lew Anderson), storekeeper Cornelius Cobb (Nicholson), Chief Thunderthud (Bill LeCornec), Princess Summerfall Winterspring (Judy Tyler and Linda Marsh), Bison Bill (Ted Brown) and wrestler Ugly Sam (Dayton Allen). Puppet costars included Howdy Doody, Phineas T. Bluster, Dilly Dally, Flub-a-Dub, Captain Scuttlebutt, Double Doody and Heidi Doody. The filmed adventures of Gumby were also featured. In the final episode, Clarabell broke his long silence to say, "Goodbye, kids."

KEPLER, JOHANNES: BIRTH ANNIVERSARY. Dec 27, 1571. One of the world's greatest astronomers, called "the father of modern astronomy," German mathematician Johannes Kepler was born at Württemberg, Germany; he died at Regensburg, Germany, Nov 15, 1630.

PASTEUR, LOUIS: BIRTH ANNIVERSARY. Dec 27, 1822. French chemist-bacteriologist born at Dole, Jura, France. Died at Villeneuve l'Etang, France, Sept 28, 1895. Discoverer of prophylactic inoculation against rabies. Pasteurization process named for him.

RADIO CITY MUSIC HALL: ANNIVERSARY. Dec 27, 1932. Radio City Music Hall, at New York City, opened on this date. Among the opening-night performers were the "Radio Roxyettes."

SAINT JOHN, APOSTLE-EVANGELIST: FEAST DAY. Dec 27. Son of Zebedee, Galilean fisherman, and Salome. Died about AD 100. Roman Rite Feast Day is Dec 27. (Observed May 8 by Byzantine Rite.)

SALK, LEE: BIRTH ANNIVERSARY. Dec 27, 1926. American child psychologist Lee Salk was born at New York, NY. He became well known for proving the calming effect of a mother's heartbeat on a newborn infant. Salk's warning during the 1970s that women should not abandon full-time child rearing was met with wide opposition, especially from working mothers. He died May 2, 1992, at New York, NY.

BIRTHDAYS TODAY

Gerard Depardieu, 66, actor (*The Return of Martin Guerre, Cyrano de Bergerac*), born Chateauroux, France, Dec 27, 1948.

Tovah Feldshuh, 62, actress (*Holocaust*), born New York, NY, Dec 27, 1952.

Masi Oka, 40, actor ("Heroes," "Hawaii Five-0"), born Tokyo, Japan, Dec 27, 1974.

Carson Palmer, 35, football player, born Fresno, CA, Dec 27, 1979.

Cokie Roberts, 71, news correspondent, born New Orleans, LA, Dec 27, 1943.

Sarah Vowell, 45, journalist, author (*The Wordy Shipmates*), social commentator ("The Daily Show," "This American Life"), born Muskogee, OK, Dec 27, 1969.

December 28 — Sunday

DAY 362 **3 REMAINING**

AUSTRALIA: PROCLAMATION DAY. Dec 28. Observed in South Australia.

ENDANGERED SPECIES ACT: ANNIVERSARY. Dec 28, 1973. President Richard Nixon signed the Endangered Species Act into law.

FIRST CINEMA: ANNIVERSARY. Dec 28, 1895. The Lumière brothers—Louis and Auguste—projected short films for paying customers on this date at the Grand Café in Paris, France. This was the first time this had ever been done and is considered a key moment in film history.

HOLY INNOCENTS DAY (CHILDERMAS). Dec 28. Commemoration of the massacre of children at Bethlehem, ordered by King Herod who wanted to destroy, among them, the infant Savior. Early and medieval accounts claimed as many as 144,000 victims, but more recent writers, noting that Bethlehem was a very small town, have revised the estimates of the number of children killed to between 6 and 20.

IOWA: ADMISSION DAY: ANNIVERSARY. Dec 28. Became 29th state in 1846.

MESSINA EARTHQUAKE: ANNIVERSARY. Dec 28, 1908. Messina, Sicily. The ancient town of Messina was struck by an earthquake. Nearly 80,000 persons died in the disaster, and half of the town's buildings were destroyed.

MOON PHASE: FIRST QUARTER. Dec 28. Moon enters First Quarter phase at 1:31 PM, EST.

PLEDGE OF ALLEGIANCE RECOGNIZED: ANNIVERSARY. Dec 28, 1945. The US Congress officially recognized the Pledge of Allegiance and urged its frequent recitation in America's schools. The pledge was composed in 1892 by Francis Bellamy, a Baptist minister. At the time, Bellamy was chairman of a committee of state school superintendents of education, and several public schools adopted his pledge as part of the Columbus Day quadricentennial celebration that year. In 1954 the Knights of Columbus persuaded Congress to add the words "under God" to the pledge. In 2002 a federal appeals court found the pledge unconstitutional for use in public schools due to the "under God" phrase, but the Supreme Court reversed the case for procedural reasons and did not comment on the issue of constitutionality.

***POOR RICHARD'S ALMANACK*: ANNIVERSARY.** Dec 28, 1732. The *Pennsylvania Gazette* carried the first known advertisement for the first issue of *Poor Richard's Almanack* by Richard Saunders (Benjamin Franklin) for the year 1733. The advertisement promised "many pleasant and witty verses, jests and sayings . . . new fashions, games for kisses . . . men and melons . . . breakfast in bed, &c." America's most famous almanac, *Poor Richard's* was published through the year 1758 and has been imitated many times since.

VICE PRESIDENTIAL RESIGNATION: ANNIVERSARY. Dec 28, 1832. John C. Calhoun, who had served as vice president of the US under two presidents (John Quincy Adams and Andrew Jackson), Mar 4, 1825–Dec 28, 1832, finding himself in growing disagreement with President Jackson, resigned the office of vice president, the first to do so. He spent most of his subsequent political life as a US senator from South Carolina.

WILSON, WOODROW: BIRTH ANNIVERSARY. Dec 28, 1856. The 28th president of the US was born Thomas Woodrow Wilson at Staunton, VA. Twice elected president (1912 and 1916), it was Wilson who said, "The world must be made safe for democracy," as he asked the Congress to declare war on Germany, Apr 2, 1917. His first wife, Ellen, died Aug 6, 1914, and he married Edith Bolling Galt, Dec 18, 1915. He suffered a paralytic stroke, Sept 16, 1919, never regaining his health. There were many speculations about who (possibly Mrs Wilson?) was running the government during his illness. His second term of office ended Mar 3, 1921, and he died at Washington, DC, Feb 3, 1924.

BIRTHDAYS TODAY

David Archuleta, 24, singer, television personality ("American Idol"), born Miami, FL, Dec 28, 1990.

Michael Beebe, 68, Governor of Arkansas (D), born Amagon, AR, Dec 28, 1946.

James Blake, 35, tennis player, born Yonkers, NY, Dec 28, 1979.

Ray Bourque, 54, former hockey player, born Montreal, QC, Canada, Dec 28, 1960.

Malcolm Gets, 50, actor ("Caroline in the City"), born near Gainesville, FL, Dec 28, 1964.

Hubert Myatt (Hubie) Green III, 68, golfer, born Birmingham, AL, Dec 28, 1946.

Johnny Isakson, 70, US Senator (R, Georgia), born Atlanta, GA, Dec 28, 1944.

Tim Johnson, 68, US Senator (D, South Dakota), born Canton, SD, Dec 28, 1946.

John Legend, 36, R&B singer, born John Stephens at Springfield, OH, Dec 28, 1978.

Joe Manganiello, 38, actor ("True Blood," "One Tree Hill," *Magic Mike*), born Pittsburgh, PA, Dec 28, 1976.

Sienna Miller, 33, actress (*Factory Girl, Interview*), born New York, NY, Dec 28, 1981.

Patrick Rafter, 42, Hall of Fame tennis player, born Mount Isa, Queensland, Australia, Dec 28, 1972.

Todd Richards, 45, Olympic snowboarder, born Worchester, MA, Dec 28, 1969.

Maggie Smith, 80, actress (Oscars for *The Prime of Miss Jean Brodie* and *California Suite*; Harry Potter films; Tony for *Lettice & Lovage*; "Downton Abbey"), born Ilford, England, Dec 28, 1934.

Denzel Washington, 60, actor (*The Hurricane, Malcolm X*; Oscars for *Training Day* and *Glory*), born Mount Vernon, NY, Dec 28, 1954.

Edgar Winter, 68, singer, musician, born Beaumont, TX, Dec 28, 1946.

December 29 — Monday

DAY 363 **2 REMAINING**

ANDREW JOHNSON WREATH-LAYING. Dec 29. Monument Hill, The National Cemetery, Andrew Johnson National Historic Site, Greeneville, TN. Wreath-laying at the president's grave on Monument Hill. For info: Andrew Johnson National Historic Site, 121 Monument Ave, Greeneville, TN 37743. Phone: (423) 638-3551. Fax: (423) 798-0754. Web: www.nps.gov/anjo.

CASALS, PABLO: BIRTH ANNIVERSARY. Dec 29, 1876. Famed cellist Pablo Carlos Salvador Defillio de Casals was born at Venrell, Spain. He died at Rio Pedros, Puerto Rico, Oct 22, 1973.

GLADSTONE, WILLIAM EWART: BIRTH ANNIVERSARY. Dec 29, 1809. English statesman and author for whom the Gladstone (luggage) bag was named. Inspiring orator, eccentric individual, intensely loved or hated by all who knew him (cheered from the streets and jeered from the balconies), Gladstone is said to have left more writings (letters, diaries, journals, books) than any other major English politician. However, his preoccupation with the charitable rehabilitation of prostitutes was perhaps easily misunderstood. Born at Liverpool, England, he was four times Britain's prime minister. Gladstone died at Hawarden, Wales, May 19, 1898.

JOHNSON, ANDREW: BIRTH ANNIVERSARY. Dec 29, 1808. Seventeenth president of the US, Andrew Johnson, proprietor of a tailor shop at Laurens, SC, before he entered politics, born at Raleigh, NC. Upon Abraham Lincoln's assassination Johnson became president. He was the first president to be impeached by the House and was acquitted Mar 26, 1868, by the Senate. After his term of office as president (Apr 15, 1865–Mar 3, 1869) he made several unsuccessful attempts to win public office. Finally he was elected to the US Senate from Tennessee and served in the Senate from Mar 4, 1875, until his death at Carter's Station, TN, July 31, 1875.

RASPUTIN, GRIGORY YEFIMOVICH: ASSASSINATION ANNIVERSARY. Dec 29, 1916. Russian monk and mystic, born Grigory Yefimovich Novjkh, about 1871, at Siberia. Rasputin gained great influence with Russian emperor Nicholas II and the empress Alexandra, urging severe measures in dealing with the peasant masses, virtually dictating government policy. Notoriously dissolute and corrupt, Rasputin was said to have possessed hypnotic powers. He claimed divine inspiration and the ability to perform miracles. His name became synonymous with corruption and evil, and he was called the "plague pot" of Russia. In fact, Rasputin was a nickname from the Russian word *rasputny*, meaning "debauched, profligate, licentious." When an attempt to poison him failed, he was shot to death and his body dropped through a hole in the ice into the Neva River. It was recovered three days later and buried in a silver casket at Tsarkoe Selo. The imperial government was crushed by the 1917 Revolution within a year of his death.

SAINT THOMAS OF CANTERBURY: FEAST DAY. Dec 29. Thomas, Archbishop of Canterbury, was born at London in 1118 and was murdered at the Canterbury Cathedral on this date in 1170.

TEXAS: ADMISSION DAY: ANNIVERSARY. Dec 29. Became 28th state in 1845.

TICK TOCK DAY. Dec 29. Time runs out! All those dreams you've had, all those fantasies? It's time, friend. Do it! Annually, Dec 29. (©2006 by WH.) For info: Thomas & Ruth Roy, Wellcat Holidays, 2418 Long Ln, Lebanon, PA 17046. Phone: (717) 279-0184. E-mail: info@wellcat.com. Web: www.wellcat.com.

WOUNDED KNEE MASSACRE: ANNIVERSARY. Dec 29, 1890. Anniversary of the massacre of more than 200 Native American men, women and children by the US Seventh Cavalry at Wounded Knee Creek, SD. Government efforts to suppress a ceremonial religious practice, the Ghost Dance (which called for a messiah who would restore the bison to the plains, make the white men disappear and bring back the old Native American way of life), had resulted in the death of Sitting Bull, Dec 15, 1890, which further inflamed the disgruntled Native Americans and culminated in the slaughter at Wounded Knee, Dec 29.

YMCA ORGANIZED: ANNIVERSARY. Dec 29, 1851. The first US branch of the Young Men's Christian Association was organized at Boston. It was modeled on an organization begun at London in 1844.

BIRTHDAYS TODAY

Patricia Clarkson, 55, actress (*Married Life, Lars and the Real Girl, The Station Agent, Far from Heaven*), born New Orleans, LA, Dec 29, 1959.

Ted Danson, 67, actor ("CSI," "Cheers," "Becker," *Three Men and a Baby*), born San Diego, CA, Dec 29, 1947.

Marianne Faithfull, 68, singer, actress, born London, England, Dec 29, 1946.

Thomas Edwin Jarriel, 80, broadcast journalist, born LaGrange, GA, Dec 29, 1934.

Jason Kreis, 42, soccer coach and former player, born Omaha, NE, Dec 29, 1972.

Jude Law, 42, actor (*Sherlock Holmes, Closer, Cold Mountain, The Talented Mr Ripley*), born London, England, Dec 29, 1972.

Mary Tyler Moore, 78, actress (two Emmys for "The Dick Van Dyke Show"; three Emmys for "The Mary Tyler Moore Show"; *Ordinary People*), born Brooklyn, NY, Dec 29, 1936.

Jon Polito, 64, actor ("Homicide: Life on the Street"), born Philadelphia, PA, Dec 29, 1950.

Paula Poundstone, 55, comedienne, born Sudbury, MA, Dec 29, 1959.

Jon Voight, 76, actor (*Midnight Cowboy, Deliverance*), born Yonkers, NY, Dec 29, 1938.

Andy Wachowski, 47, filmmaker (*The Matrix* with sibling Lana Wachowski), born Chicago, IL, Dec 29, 1967.

December 2014

S	M	T	W	T	F	S
	1	2	3	4	5	6
7	8	9	10	11	12	13
14	15	16	17	18	19	20
21	22	23	24	25	26	27
28	29	30	31			

December 30 — Tuesday

DAY 364 **1 REMAINING**

FALLING NEEDLES FAMILY FEST. Dec 30. Now that the yuletide tree's been up for weeks and hasn't been watered since a couple of days before Christmas, gather the gang around and watch the needles gently fall one by one. Live it up! Dance barefoot! (©2006 by WH.) For info: Thomas & Ruth Roy, Wellcat Holidays, 2418 Long Ln, Lebanon, PA 17046. Phone: (717) 279-0184. E-mail: info@wellcat.com. Web: www.wellcat.com.

GUGGENHEIM, SIMON: BIRTH ANNIVERSARY. Dec 30, 1867. American capitalist and philanthropist, born at Philadelphia, PA. He established, in memory of his son, the John Simon Guggenheim Memorial Foundation, in 1925. Died Nov 2, 1941, at New York, NY.

JONES, DAVY: BIRTH ANNIVERSARY. Dec 30, 1945. Well known as a member of 1960s pop group The Monkees, Davy Jones was born Dec 30, 1945, at Manchester, England. After his big break as the Artful Dodger in a West End, London, production of *Oliver!*, Jones was cast as a member of the fun-loving made-for-TV combo, singing lead on such hits as "Daydream Believer." Originally airing from 1966 to 1971, "The Monkees" show was also a hit in syndication, and its ubiquity allowed for numerous band reunions and nostalgia tours that kept Jones in the public eye until his death from a heart attack Feb 29, 2012, at Stuart, FL.

KIPLING, RUDYARD: BIRTH ANNIVERSARY. Dec 30, 1865. English poet, novelist and short story writer, Nobel Prize laureate, Kipling was born at Bombay, India. After working as a journalist at India, he traveled around the world. He married an American and lived in Vermont for several years. Kipling is best known for his children's stories, such as *The Jungle Book* and *Just So Stories* and poems such as "The Ballad of East and West" and "If." He died at London, England, Jan 18, 1936.

LEACOCK, STEPHEN: BIRTH ANNIVERSARY. Dec 30, 1869. Canadian economist and humorist, born at Swanmore, Hampshire, England. Died Mar 28, 1944, at Toronto, Canada. "Lord Ronald," he wrote in *Nonsense Novels*, "flung himself upon his horse and rode madly off in all directions."

"LET'S MAKE A DEAL" TV PREMIERE: ANNIVERSARY. Dec 30, 1963. Monty Hall hosted this outrageous and no-skill-required game show. Audience members, many of whom wore costumes, were selected to sit in the trading area, and some were picked to "make a deal" with Hall by trading something of their own for something they were offered. Sometimes prizes were worthless ("zonks"). At the end of the show, the two people who had won the most were given the option to trade their winnings for a chance at the "Big Deal," hidden behind one of three doors. A 21st-century revival is hosted by Wayne Brady.

***MONITOR* SINKS: ANNIVERSARY.** Dec 30, 1862. The Union ironclad ship USS *Monitor* (which achieved fame after its battle with the *Virginia*) sank off Cape Hatteras during a storm. Sixteen of its crew were lost. See also: "Battle of Hampton Roads: Anniversary" (Mar 9).

PARKS, BERT: 100th BIRTH ANNIVERSARY. Dec 30, 1914. Bert Parks was born at Atlanta, GA. An actor whose career spanned radio, film, television and Broadway, his name became synonymous with the Miss America pageant, which he emceed for 25 years. He was fired from the Miss America post in 1980 when pageant officials wanted to acquire a younger look. Parks made a special return appearance for the 1990 pageant, once again singing his signature song "There She Is." He got his big break in show business in 1945 as the emcee for the radio quiz show "Break the Bank" and later as the host of "Stop the Music." When both shows moved to television they did so with Parks at the microphone, launching a television career that included hosting a variety of quiz shows and guest appearances on dramatic series. He died Feb 2, 1992, at La Jolla, CA.

PHILIPPINES: RIZAL DAY. Dec 30. National holiday. Commemorates martyrdom of Dr. Jose Rizal in 1896.

"THE ROY ROGERS SHOW" TV PREMIERE: ANNIVERSARY. Dec 30, 1951. This very popular TV Western starred Roy Rogers and his wife, Dale Evans, as themselves. It also featured Pat Brady as Rogers's sidekick who rode a jeep named Nellybelle, the singing group Sons of the Pioneers, Rogers's horse Trigger, Evans's horse Buttermilk and a German shepherd named Bullet. This half-hour show was especially popular with young viewers.

USSR ESTABLISHED: ANNIVERSARY. Dec 30, 1922. After the Russian revolution of 1917 and the subsequent three-year civil war, the Union of Soviet Socialist Republics (or Soviet Union) was founded, a confederation of Russia, Byelorussia, the Ukraine and the Transcaucasian Federation. It was the first state in the world to be based on Marxist communism. The Soviet Union was dissolved Dec 8, 1991. See also: "Soviet Union Dissolved: Anniversary" (Dec 8).

BIRTHDAYS TODAY

Joseph Bologna, 76, actor, writer (*The Big Bus, My Favorite Year, Blame It on Rio*), born Brooklyn, NY, Dec 30, 1938.

James Burrows, 74, director ("Cheers," "Taxi"), born Los Angeles, CA, Dec 30, 1940.

Eliza Dushku, 34, actress ("Dollhouse," "Buffy the Vampire Slayer," "Angel"), born Boston, MA, Dec 30, 1980.

Sean Hannity, 53, journalist, radio and television talk show host ("Hannity," "The Sean Hannity Show"), born New York, NY, Dec 30, 1981.

LeBron James, 30, basketball player, born Akron, OH, Dec 30, 1984.

Sanford (Sandy) Koufax, 79, Hall of Fame baseball player, former sportscaster, born Brooklyn, NY, Dec 30, 1935.

Kristin Kreuk, 32, actress ("Beauty and the Beast," "Smallville"), born Vancouver, BC, Canada, Dec 30, 1982.

Matt Lauer, 57, anchor ("The Today Show"), born New York, NY, Dec 30, 1957.

Kenyon Martin, 37, basketball player, born Saginaw, MI, Dec 30, 1977.

Michael Nesmith, 72, singer, songwriter (The Monkees), director, born Houston, TX, Dec 30, 1942.

Patti Smith, 68, singer, born Chicago, IL, Dec 30, 1946.

Russ Tamblyn, 79, actor ("Twin Peaks," *Peyton Place, West Side Story*), born Los Angeles, CA, Dec 30, 1935.

Concetta Tomei, 69, actress ("Providence," "China Beach"), born Kenosha, WI, Dec 30, 1945.

Tracey Ullman, 55, actress, singer ("The Tracey Ullman Show," *I Love You to Death*), born Buckinghamshire, England, Dec 30, 1959.

Meredith Vieira, 63, television journalist and personality, born Providence, RI, Dec 30, 1951.

Eldrick "Tiger" Woods, 39, golfer, born Cypress, CA, Dec 30, 1975.

December 31 — Wednesday

DAY 365 **0 REMAINING**

DENVER, JOHN: BIRTH ANNIVERSARY. Dec 31, 1943. Born Henry John Deutschendorf at Roswell, NM, this singer-songwriter ("Rocky Mountain High," "Sunshine on My Shoulders") died in a plane crash off the coast of California, Oct 12, 1997.

FIRE AND ICE NEW YEAR'S EVE CELEBRATION. Dec 31. Town Square, Downtown Anchorage, AK. Celebrate the New Year Alaska style—outdoors in the cold! Event features live outdoor music, light show, ice skating, fire jugglers, ice carving demonstrations and fabulous fireworks. Est attendance: 4,000. For info: Anchorage Downtown Partnership, Ltd, 333 W 4th Ave, Ste 317, Anchorage, AK 99501. Phone: (907) 279-5655. Fax: (907) 279-5651. E-mail: info@anchoragedowntown.org. Web: www.anchoragedowntown.org.

FIRST BANK OPENS IN US: ANNIVERSARY. Dec 31, 1781. The first modern bank in the US, the Bank of North America, was organized by Robert Morris and received its charter from the Confederation Congress. It began operations Jan 7, 1782, at Philadelphia, PA.

FIRST NIGHT BOSTON. Dec 31. Boston, MA. The largest New Year's arts festival in North America, First Night Boston has grown to be a highly anticipated tradition. The festival features more than 1,000 artists in 200 performances and exhibitions in 40 venues throughout downtown Boston, a Mardi Gras–style Grand Procession, large-scale ice sculptures, music, dance, theater, family entertainment, fireworks at midnight and much more! Boston was the site of the first First Night in 1976. Est attendance: 1,000,000. For info: First Night, Inc, 36 Bromfield St, Ste 204, Boston, MA 02108. Phone: (617) 542-1399. Fax: (617) 426-9531. E-mail: info@firstnight.org. Web: www.firstnight.org.

FIRST NIGHTS. Dec 31. Family-oriented, nonalcoholic community celebrations of the New Year—first observed in Boston, MA, in 1976. Observed in scores of American and Canadian cities and communities.

HYUNDAI SUN BOWL. Dec 31. Sun Bowl Stadium, El Paso, TX. 81st annual. First held on Jan 1, 1935, the Sun Bowl is the second oldest college football bowl after the Rose Bowl. Sponsored by Hyundai. For info: Sun Bowl Assn, 4150 Pinnacle St, Ste 100, El Paso, TX 79902-1019. Phone: (800) 915-BOWL or (915) 533-4416. Fax: (915) 533-0661. Web: www.sunbowl.org.

JAPAN: NAMAHAGE. Dec 31. Oga Peninsula, Akita Prefecture, Japan. In the evening, groups of "Namahage" men disguised as devils make door-to-door visits, growling, "Any good-for-nothing fellow hereabout?" The object of this annual event is to give sluggards an opportunity to change their minds and become diligent. Otherwise, according to legend, they will be punished by devils.

KALAMAZOO NEW YEAR'S FEST. Dec 31. Bronson Park, Kalamazoo, MI. Kalamazoo comes alive as families, teens and seniors come downtown to welcome the New Year. Featuring more than 28 different artists, performances are hosted in nine different indoor sites throughout downtown Kalamazoo. The cultural celebration offers music, theater, puppetry, dance, mime and storytelling. Artists come from throughout the Midwest to join in this nonalcoholic celebration. Est attendance: 6,500. For info: New Year's Fest, Inc, 141 E Michigan Ave, Ste 100, Kalamazoo, MI 49007. Phone: (269) 388-2830. E-mail: deb@eventkalamazoo.com. Web: www.newyearsfest.com.

December 2014	S	M	T	W	T	F	S
		1	2	3	4	5	6
	7	8	9	10	11	12	13
	14	15	16	17	18	19	20
	21	22	23	24	25	26	27
	28	29	30	31			

LEAP SECOND ADJUSTMENT TIME. Dec 31. One of the times that have been favored for the addition or subtraction of a second from clock time (to coordinate atomic and astronomical time). The determination to adjust is made by the International Earth Rotation Service of the International Bureau of Weights and Measures, at Paris, France. See also: "Leap Seconds" (see Contents).

MAKE UP YOUR MIND DAY. Dec 31. A day for all those people who have a hard time making up their minds. Make a decision today and follow through with it! Annually, Dec 31. For info: A.C. Vierow and M.A. Dufour, Box 71, Clio, MI 48420-0071.

MARSHALL, GEORGE CATLETT: BIRTH ANNIVERSARY. Dec 31, 1880. Chairman of the newly formed Joint Chiefs of Staff Committee throughout the US's involvement in WWII, General George Marshall was born at Uniontown, PA. He accompanied Roosevelt or represented the US at most Allied war conferences. He served as secretary of state and was designer of the Marshall Plan after the war. Died Oct 16, 1959, at Washington, DC.

MATISSE, HENRI: BIRTH ANNIVERSARY. Dec 31, 1869. Painter born at Le Cateau, France. Matisse also designed textiles and stained-glass windows. Died at Nice, France, Nov 3, 1954.

NEW YEAR'S EVE. Dec 31. The last evening of the Gregorian calendar year, traditionally a night for merrymaking to welcome in the new year.

NIXON, JOHN: DEATH ANNIVERSARY. Dec 31, 1808. Revolutionary patriot and businessman, Commander of the Philadelphia City Guard, born 1733 (exact date unknown). Appointed to conduct the first public reading of the Declaration of Independence, July 8, 1776. Died at Philadelphia, PA.

NO INTERRUPTIONS DAY. Dec 31. On this day—the last business day of the year—there shall be no interruptions! At work we will minimize or eliminate interruptions to our thought processes or tasks we are performing. At home we will silence and shut down all devices that interrupt us so we can devote ourselves to our families or to ourselves. This is a day for quiet and/or focus. It is a day to renew our energies to prepare ourselves for the new calendar year ahead. For info: Sylvia Henderson, Springboard Training, PO Box 588, Olney, MD 20830-0588. Phone: (301) 260-1538. E-mail: sylvia@springboardtraining.com.

PANAMA: ASSUMES CONTROL OF CANAL: 15th ANNIVERSARY. Dec 31, 1999. With the expiration of the Panama Canal Treaty of 1979 at noon, the Republic of Panama assumed full responsibility for the canal and the US Panama Canal Commission ceased to exist.

SAINT SYLVESTER'S DAY. Dec 31. Observed in Belgium, Germany, France and Switzerland. Commemorates death of Pope Sylvester I in AD 335. Feasting, particularly upon "St. Sylvester's Carp."

SAMOA: SAMOAN FIRE DANCE. Dec 31. New Year's Eve is occasion for Samoan bamboo fireworks, singing and traditional performances such as the Samoan Fire Dance.

SCOTLAND: HOGMANAY. Dec 31. The Scottish New Year celebrations date from ancient pagan times. Hogmanay (no one is sure the origin of the name) traditions include fireworks and torch-lit processions in the cities and bonfires in the rural areas. "First footing" is still observed: it is believed to be good luck for the first foot over the threshold to be that of a dark-haired stranger bearing a piece of coal, shortbread or whiskey. After the midnight chimes, everyone sings "Auld Lang Syne."

SUMMER, DONNA: BIRTH ANNIVERSARY. Dec 31, 1948. Born LaDonna Adrian Gaines at Boston, MA, Summer started her singing career as a child in the church choir. She eventually moved to New York City before joining the Munich production of *Hair* in 1967. Summer's career thrived in Germany, but by 1974 she had returned to the US, where a collaboration with producer Giorgio Moroder led to a string of smash disco singles: "Love to Love You," "I Feel Love" and "Hot Stuff." The "Queen of Disco" continued recording and performing in America and Europe throughout the 1980s and '90s. A recipient of five Grammy Awards, she died May 17, 2012, at Englewood, FL.

UNIVERSAL HOUR OF PEACE. Dec 31. Begins at 11:30 PM on Dec 31, 2014, and ends at 12:30 AM on Jan 1, 2015. An hour dedicated to creating peace throughout our planet. Every man, woman and child is asked to spend the hour in meditation, prayer, conversation, listening to beautiful music or whatever helps them concentrate on peace. The simple truth is "living peaceably begins by thinking peacefully." To add your name to the "Millions for Peace" list, e-mail your name, city, state/country to peace@som.org. A recording of the Universal Peace Covenant voiced in seven languages is available at no charge by contacting SOM. One hour of peace, a world of difference. For info: Mr Tad Messenger, School of Metaphysics World HQ, 163 Moon Valley Rd, Windyville, MO 65783. Phone: (417) 345-8411. Fax: (417) 345-6668. E-mail: peace@som.org. Web: www.peacedome.org.

VESALIUS, ANDREAS: 500th BIRTH ANNIVERSARY. Dec 31, 1514. Born at Brussels, Belgium, anatomist Vesalius contributed to medicine's inclusion as an empirical science and wrote one of the most important books in medical history, *De Humani Corporis Fabrica* (*On the Fabric of the Human Body*). He broke with medical conventions and dissected cadavers with his students; his subsequent anatomical discoveries overturned the fourteen-centuries-old Galenic canon and founded modern scientific anatomy. *Fabrica* continues to be renowned for its anatomical accuracy, beauty and aestheticism. He died Oct 15, 1564, in a shipwreck at Zenta, Greece.

WIESENTHAL, SIMON: BIRTH ANNIVERSARY. Dec 31, 1908. Born at Buczacz, Austria-Hungary (now the Ukraine), Wiesenthal was a Holocaust survivor who dedicated his postwar life to fighting anti-Semitism and speaking out against racism. For more than 50 years, his Jewish Documentation Center in Vienna compiled data about war criminals not yet apprehended as well as information about the 6 million victims of Nazi persecution. In all, he helped to bring almost 1,100 Nazi war criminals to trial—most famously Adolf Eichmann. In 1977, The Simon Wiesenthal Center, an internationally renowned organization dedicated to remembering the Holocaust, was established in Los Angeles, CA. Wiesenthal died at Vienna, Sept 20, 2005.

WORLD PEACE MEDITATION. Dec 31. An opportunity for people around the world to focus their thoughts and energy on peace. The event is observed internationally, beginning at noon Greenwich Mean Time (GMT) and lasting one hour (7 AM–8 AM, EST). For info: Quartus Foundation, PO Box 1768, Boerne, TX 78006. Phone: (830) 249-3985. E-mail: quartus@quartus.org. Web: www.quartus.org.

BIRTHDAYS TODAY

Gabrielle Douglas, 19, Olympic gymnast, born Virginia Beach, VA, Dec 31, 1995.

Alex Ferguson, 73, soccer executive, former manager, born Glasgow, Scotland, Dec 31, 1941.

Jeff Flake, 52, US Senator (R, Arizona), born Snowflake, AZ, Dec 31, 1962.

Sir Anthony Hopkins, 77, actor (Oscar for *The Silence of the Lambs*; *Nixon, The Remains of the Day*), born Port Talbot, Wales, Dec 31, 1937.

Val Kilmer, 55, actor (*Batman Forever, The Doors, Heat*), born Los Angeles, CA, Dec 31, 1959.

Ben Kingsley, 71, actor (Oscar for *Gandhi*; *Sexy Beast, Schindler's List*), born Krishna Bhanji at Yorkshire, England, Dec 31, 1943.

Tim Matheson, 66, actor (*Animal House*, "The Virginian," "Bonanza"), born Los Angeles, CA, Dec 31, 1948.

Sarah Miles, 73, actress (*The Servant, Blow-Up, Hope and Glory*), born Ingatestone, England, Dec 31, 1941.

Bebe Neuwirth, 56, actress ("Cheers," "Frasier"; stage: *Chicago*), born Newark, NJ, Dec 31, 1958.

Psy, 37, singer ("Gangnam Style"), born Park Jae-sang at Seoul, South Korea, Dec 31, 1977.

James Remar, 61, actor (*48 Hrs, Drugstore Cowboy*), born Boston, MA, Dec 31, 1953.

Nicholas Sparks, 49, author (*A Walk to Remember, The Notebook, Message in a Bottle*), born Omaha, NE, Dec 31, 1965.

Andy Summers, 72, musician (The Police), born Poulton-le-Fylde, England, Dec 31, 1942.

Diane Halfin von Furstenberg, 69, fashion designer, author, born Brussels, Belgium, Dec 31, 1945.

Calendar Information for the Year 2014

Time shown is Eastern Standard Time. All dates are given in terms of the Gregorian calendar.

(Based in part on information prepared by the Nautical Almanac Office, US Naval Observatory.)

ERAS	YEAR	BEGINS
Byzantine	7523	Sept 14
Jewish*	5775	Sept 25
Chinese (Year of the Horse)	4712	Jan 31
Roman (AUC)	2767	Jan 14
Nabonassar	2763	Apr 23
Japanese (Heisei)	26	Jan 1
Grecian (Seleucidae)	2326	Sept 14 (or Oct 14)
Indian (Saka)	1936	Mar 22
Diocletian	1731	Sept 11
Islamic (Hegira)**	1436	Oct 25

**Year begins the previous day at sunset.*

***Year begins the previous evening at moon crescent.*

RELIGIOUS CALENDARS

Epiphany .... Jan 6
Shrove Tuesday .... Mar 4
Ash Wednesday .... Mar 5
Lent .... Mar 5–Apr 19
Palm Sunday .... Apr 13
Good Friday .... Apr 18
Easter Day .... Apr 20
Ascension Day .... May 29
Whit Sunday (Pentecost) .... June 8
Trinity Sunday .... June 15
First Sunday in Advent .... Nov 30
Christmas Day (Thursday) .... Dec 25

Eastern Orthodox Church Observances

Great Lent begins .... Mar 3
Pascha (Easter) .... Apr 20
Ascension .... May 29
Pentecost .... June 8

Jewish Holy Days*

Purim .... Mar 16
Passover (1st day) .... Apr 15
Shavuot .... June 4–5
Tisha B'av .... Aug 5
Rosh Hashanah (New Year) .... Sept 25–26
Yom Kippur .... Oct 4
Succoth .... Oct 9–15
Chanukah .... Dec 17–24

**All Jewish holy days begin the previous day at sundown.*

Islamic Holy Days**

First Day of Ramadan (1435) .... June 28
Eid-Al-Fitr (1435) .... July 28
Islamic New Year (1436) .... Oct 25

***All Islamic holy days begin the previous evening at moon crescent.*

CIVIL CALENDAR—USA—2014

New Year's Day .... Jan 1
Martin Luther King's Birthday (obsvd) .... Jan 20
Lincoln's Birthday .... Feb 12
Washington's Birthday (obsvd)/Presidents' Day .... Feb 17
Memorial Day (obsvd) .... May 26
Independence Day .... July 4
Labor Day .... Sept 1
Columbus Day (obsvd) .... Oct 13
General Election Day .... Nov 4
Veterans Day .... Nov 11
Thanksgiving Day .... Nov 27

Other Days Widely Observed in US—2014

Groundhog Day (Candlemas) .... Feb 2
St. Valentine's Day .... Feb 14
St. Patrick's Day .... Mar 17
Mother's Day .... May 11
Flag Day .... June 14
Father's Day .... June 15
National Grandparents Day .... Sept 7
Hallowe'en .... Oct 31

CIVIL CALENDAR—CANADA—2014

Victoria Day .... May 19
Canada Day .... July 1
Labor Day .... Sept 1
Thanksgiving Day .... Oct 13
Remembrance Day .... Nov 11
Boxing Day .... Dec 26

CIVIL CALENDAR—MEXICO—2014

New Year's Day .... Jan 1
Constitution Day .... Feb 5
Benito Juarez Birthday .... Mar 21
Labor Day .... May 1
Battle of Puebla Day (Cinco de Mayo) .... May 5
Independence Day* .... Sept 16
Dia de La Raza .... Oct 12
Mexican Revolution Day .... Nov 20
Guadalupe Day .... Dec 12

**Celebration begins Sept 15 at 11:00 P.M.*

CIVIL CALENDAR—UNITED KINGDOM—2014

Accession of Queen Elizabeth II .... Feb 6
St. David (Wales) .... Mar 1
Commonwealth Day .... Mar 10
St. Patrick (Ireland) .... Mar 17
Birthday of Queen Elizabeth II .... Apr 21
St. George (England) .... Apr 23
Coronation Day .... June 2
The Queen's Official Birthday (tentative) .... June 14
Birthday of Prince Philip, Duke of Edinburgh .... June 10
Remembrance Sunday .... Nov 9
Birthday of the Prince of Wales .... Nov 14
St. Andrew (Scotland) .... Nov 30

BANK AND PUBLIC HOLIDAYS—UNITED KINGDOM—2014

Observed during 2014 in England and Wales, Scotland and Northern Ireland unless otherwise indicated.

New Year .... Jan 1
Bank Holiday (Scotland) .... Jan 2
St. Patrick's Day (Northern Ireland) .... Mar 17
Good Friday .... Apr 18
Easter Monday (except Scotland) .... Apr 21
May Day Bank Holiday .... May 5
Spring Bank Holiday .... May 26
Orangeman's Day (Battle of the Boyne) (Northern Ireland)* .... July 12
Bank Holiday (Scotland) .... Aug 4
Summer Bank Holiday (except Scotland) .... Aug 25
Christmas Day Holiday .... Dec 25
Boxing Day Holiday .... Dec 26

**Observed on July 14 in 2014.*

SEASONS

Spring (Vernal Equinox) .... Mar 20, 12:57 PM, EDT
Summer (Summer Solstice) .... June 21, 6:51 AM, EDT
Autumn (Autumnal Equinox) .... Sept 22, 10:29 PM, EDT
Winter (Winter Solstice) .... Dec 21, 6:03 PM, EST

DAYLIGHT SAVING TIME SCHEDULE—2014

Sunday, Mar 9, 2:00 AM–Sunday, Nov 2, 2:00 AM—in all time zones.

CHRONOLOGICAL CYCLES

Dominical Letter .... E
Epact 29
Golden Number (Lunar Cycle) I
Julian Period (year of) 6727
Roman Indiction 7
Solar Cycle 7

Calendar Information for the Year 2015

Time shown is Eastern Standard Time. All dates are given in terms of the Gregorian calendar.

(Based in part on information prepared by the Nautical Almanac Office, US Naval Observatory.)

ERAS	YEAR	BEGINS
Byzantine	7524	Sept 14
Jewish*	5776	Sept 14
Chinese (Year of the Sheep)	4713	Feb 19
Roman (AUC)	2768	Jan 14
Nabonassar	2764	Apr 23
Japanese (Heisei)	27	Jan 1
Grecian (Seleucidae)	2327	Sept 14 (or Oct 14)
Indian (Saka)	1937	Mar 22
Diocletian	1732	Sept 11
Islamic (Hegira)**	1437	Oct 14

**Year begins the previous day at sunset.*
***Year begins the previous evening at moon crescent.*

RELIGIOUS CALENDARS

Epiphany .... Jan 6
Shrove Tuesday .... Feb 17
Ash Wednesday .... Feb 18
Lent .... Feb 18–Apr 4
Palm Sunday .... Mar 29
Good Friday .... Apr 3
Easter Day .... Apr 5
Ascension Day .... May 14
Whit Sunday (Pentecost) .... May 24
Trinity Sunday .... May 31
First Sunday in Advent .... Nov 29
Christmas Day (Friday) .... Dec 25

Eastern Orthodox Church Observances

Great Lent begins .... Feb 23
Pascha (Easter) .... Apr 12
Ascension .... May 21
Pentecost .... May 31

Jewish Holy Days*

Purim .... Mar 5
Passover (1st day) .... Apr 4
Shavuot .... May 24–25
Tisha B'av .... July 26
Rosh Hashanah (New Year) .... Sept 14–15
Yom Kippur .... Sept 23
Succoth .... Sept 28–Oct 4
Chanukah .... Dec 7–14

**All Jewish holy days begin the previous day at sundown.*

Islamic Holy Days**

First Day of Ramadan (1436) .... June 18
Eid-Al-Fitr (1436) .... July 17
Islamic New Year (1437) .... Oct 14

***All Islamic holy days begin the previous evening at moon crescent.*

CIVIL CALENDAR—USA—2015

New Year's Day .... Jan 1
Martin Luther King's Birthday (obsvd) .... Jan 19
Lincoln's Birthday .... Feb 12
Washington's Birthday (obsvd)/Presidents' Day .... Feb 16
Memorial Day (obsvd) .... May 25
Independence Day .... July 4
Labor Day .... Sept 7
Columbus Day (obsvd) .... Oct 12
General Election Day .... Nov 3
Veterans Day .... Nov 11
Thanksgiving Day .... Nov 26

Other Days Widely Observed in US—2015

Groundhog Day (Candlemas) .... Feb 2
St. Valentine's Day .... Feb 14
St. Patrick's Day .... Mar 17
Mother's Day .... May 10
Flag Day .... June 14
Father's Day .... June 21
National Grandparents Day .... Sept 13
Hallowe'en .... Oct 31

CIVIL CALENDAR—CANADA—2015

Victoria Day .... May 25
Canada Day .... July 1
Labor Day .... Sept 7
Thanksgiving Day .... Oct 12
Remembrance Day .... Nov 11
Boxing Day .... Dec 26

CIVIL CALENDAR—MEXICO—2015

New Year's Day .... Jan 1
Constitution Day .... Feb 5
Benito Juarez Birthday .... Mar 21
Labor Day .... May 1
Battle of Puebla Day (Cinco de Mayo) .... May 5
Independence Day* .... Sept 16
Dia de La Raza .... Oct 12
Mexican Revolution Day .... Nov 20
Guadalupe Day .... Dec 12

**Celebration begins Sept 15 at 11:00 P.M.*

CIVIL CALENDAR—UNITED KINGDOM—2015

Accession of Queen Elizabeth II .... Feb 6
St. David (Wales) .... Mar 1
Commonwealth Day .... Mar 9
St. Patrick (Ireland) .... Mar 17
Birthday of Queen Elizabeth II .... Apr 21
St. George (England) .... Apr 23
Coronation Day .... June 2
The Queen's Official Birthday (tentative) .... June 13
Birthday of Prince Philip, Duke of Edinburgh .... June 10
Remembrance Sunday .... Nov 8
Birthday of the Prince of Wales .... Nov 14
St. Andrew (Scotland) .... Nov 30

BANK AND PUBLIC HOLIDAYS—UNITED KINGDOM—2015

Observed during 2015 in England and Wales, Scotland and Northern Ireland unless otherwise indicated.

New Year .... Jan 1
Bank Holiday (Scotland) .... Jan 2
St. Patrick's Day (Northern Ireland) .... Mar 17
Good Friday .... Apr 3
Easter Monday (except Scotland) .... Apr 6
May Day Bank Holiday .... May 4
Spring Bank Holiday .... May 25
Orangeman's Day (Battle of the Boyne) (Northern Ireland)* .... July 12
Bank Holiday (Scotland) .... Aug 3
Summer Bank Holiday (except Scotland) .... Aug 31
Christmas Day Holiday .... Dec 25
Boxing Day Holiday .... Dec 26

**Observed on July 13 in 2015.*

SEASONS

Spring (Vernal Equinox) .... Mar 20, 6:45 PM, EDT
Summer (Summer Solstice) .... June 21, 12:38 PM, EDT
Autumn (Autumnal Equinox) .... Sept 23, 4:21 AM, EDT
Winter (Winter Solstice) .... Dec 21, 11:48 PM, EST

DAYLIGHT SAVING TIME SCHEDULE—2015

Sunday, Mar 8, 2:00 AM–Sunday, Nov 1, 2:00 AM—in all time zones.

CHRONOLOGICAL CYCLES

Dominical Letter .... D
Epact 10
Golden Number (Lunar Cycle) II
Julian Period (year of) 6728
Roman Indiction 8
Solar Cycle 8

Calendar Information for the Year 2016

Time shown is Eastern Standard Time. All dates are given in terms of the Gregorian calendar.

(Based in part on information prepared by the Nautical Almanac Office, US Naval Observatory.)

ERAS	YEAR	BEGINS
Byzantine	7525	Sept 14
Jewish*	5777	Oct 3
Chinese (Year of the Monkey)	4714	Feb 8
Roman (AUC)	2769	Jan 14
Nabonassar	2765	Apr 23
Japanese (Heisei)	28	Jan 1
Grecian (Seleucidae)	2328	Sept 14 (or Oct 14)
Indian (Saka)	1938	Mar 22
Diocletian	1733	Sept 11
Islamic (Hegira)**	1438	Oct 2

**Year begins the previous day at sunset.*

***Year begins the previous evening at moon crescent.*

RELIGIOUS CALENDARS

Epiphany . . . Jan 6
Shrove Tuesday . . . Feb 9
Ash Wednesday . . . Feb 10
Lent . . . Feb 10–Mar 26
Palm Sunday . . . Mar 20
Good Friday . . . Mar 25
Easter Day . . . Mar 27
Ascension Day . . . May 5
Whit Sunday (Pentecost) . . . May 15
Trinity Sunday . . . May 22
First Sunday in Advent . . . Nov 27
Christmas Day (Sunday) . . . Dec 25

Eastern Orthodox Church Observances

Great Lent begins . . . Mar 14
Pascha (Easter) . . . May 1
Ascension . . . June 9
Pentecost . . . June 19

Jewish Holy Days*

Purim . . . Mar 24
Passover (1st day) . . . Apr 23
Shavuot . . . June 12–13
Tisha B'av . . . Aug 14
Rosh Hashanah (New Year) . . . Oct 3–4
Yom Kippur . . . Oct 12
Succoth . . . Oct 17–23
Chanukah . . . Dec 25–Jan 1, 2017

**All Jewish holy days begin the previous day at sundown.*

Islamic Holy Days**

First Day of Ramadan (1437) . . . June 6
Eid-Al-Fitr (1437) . . . July 6
Islamic New Year (1438) . . . Oct 2

***All Islamic holy days begin the previous evening at moon crescent.*

CIVIL CALENDAR—USA—2016

New Year's Day . . . Jan 1
Martin Luther King's Birthday (obsvd) . . . Jan 18
Lincoln's Birthday . . . Feb 12
Washington's Birthday (obsvd)/Presidents' Day . . . Feb 15
Memorial Day (obsvd) . . . May 30
Independence Day . . . July 4
Labor Day . . . Sept 5
Columbus Day (obsvd) . . . Oct 10
General Election Day . . . Nov 8
Veterans Day . . . Nov 11
Thanksgiving Day . . . Nov 24

Other Days Widely Observed in US—2016

Groundhog Day (Candlemas) . . . Feb 2
St. Valentine's Day . . . Feb 14
St. Patrick's Day . . . Mar 17
Mother's Day . . . May 8
Flag Day . . . June 14
Father's Day . . . June 19
National Grandparents Day . . . Sept 11
Hallowe'en . . . Oct 31

CIVIL CALENDAR—CANADA—2016

Victoria Day . . . May 23
Canada Day . . . July 1
Labor Day . . . Sept 5
Thanksgiving Day . . . Oct 10
Remembrance Day . . . Nov 11
Boxing Day . . . Dec 26

CIVIL CALENDAR—MEXICO—2016

New Year's Day . . . Jan 1
Constitution Day . . . Feb 5
Benito Juarez Birthday . . . Mar 21
Labor Day . . . May 1
Battle of Puebla Day (Cinco de Mayo) . . . May 5
Independence Day* . . . Sept 16
Dia de La Raza . . . Oct 12
Mexican Revolution Day . . . Nov 20
Guadalupe Day . . . Dec 12

**Celebration begins Sept 15 at 11:00 P.M.*

CIVIL CALENDAR—UNITED KINGDOM—2016

Accession of Queen Elizabeth II . . . Feb 6
St. David (Wales) . . . Mar 1
Commonwealth Day . . . Mar 14
St. Patrick (Ireland) . . . Mar 17
Birthday of Queen Elizabeth II . . . Apr 21
St. George (England) . . . Apr 23
Coronation Day . . . June 2
The Queen's Official Birthday (tentative) . . . June 11
Birthday of Prince Philip, Duke of Edinburgh . . . June 10
Remembrance Sunday . . . Nov 13
Birthday of the Prince of Wales . . . Nov 14
St. Andrew (Scotland) . . . Nov 30

BANK AND PUBLIC HOLIDAYS—UNITED KINGDOM—2016

Observed during 2016 in England and Wales, Scotland and Northern Ireland unless otherwise indicated.

New Year . . . Jan 1
Bank Holiday (Scotland) . . . Jan 2
St. Patrick's Day (Northern Ireland) . . . Mar 17
Good Friday . . . Mar 25
Easter Monday (except Scotland) . . . Mar 28
May Day Bank Holiday . . . May 2
Spring Bank Holiday . . . May 30
Orangeman's Day (Battle of the Boyne) (Northern Ireland) . . . July 12
Bank Holiday (Scotland) . . . Aug 1
Summer Bank Holiday (except Scotland) . . . Aug 29
Christmas Day Holiday . . . Dec 25
Boxing Day Holiday . . . Dec 26

SEASONS

Spring (Vernal Equinox) . . . Mar 20, 12:30 AM, EDT
Summer (Summer Solstice) . . . June 20, 6:34 PM, EDT
Autumn (Autumnal Equinox) . . . Sept 22, 10:21 AM, EDT
Winter (Winter Solstice) . . . Dec 21, 5:44 AM, EST

DAYLIGHT SAVING TIME SCHEDULE—2016

Sunday, Mar 13, 2:00 AM–Sunday, Nov 6, 2:00 AM—in all time zones.

CHRONOLOGICAL CYCLES

Dominical Letter . . . CB
Epact . . . 21
Golden Number (Lunar Cycle) . . . III
Julian Period (year of) . . . 6729
Roman Indiction . . . 9
Solar Cycle . . . 9

Looking Forward

2015

Special Olympics World Summer Games, Los Angeles, CA
Rugby World Cup, England
Cricket World Cup, Australia and New Zealand
Magna Carta, 800th anniversary
St. Augustine, FL, settled, 450th anniversary
Battle of Waterloo, 200th anniversary
Civil War ends, 150th anniversary
Abraham Lincoln assassinated, 150th anniversary
13th Amendment ratified, abolishing slavery in the US, 150th anniversary
W.B. Yeats's birth, 150th anniversary
Yosemite National Park established, 125th anniversary
Lusitania sinking, 100th anniversary
Billie Holiday's birth, 100th anniversary
Frank Sinatra's birth, 100th anniversary

2016

Transit of Mercury
Leap Year
Games of the XXXI Olympiad, Rio de Janeiro, Brazil
US presidential election
Miguel de Cervantes's death, 400th anniversary
William Shakespeare's death, 400th anniversary
Charlotte Brontë's birth, 200th anniversary
Indiana Statehood Bicentennial
National Park Service established, 100th anniversary
First birth control clinic opened, 100th anniversary
James Herriot's birth, 100th anniversary

2017

Russian Revolution, 100th anniversary
Mexican Constitution, 100th anniversary
Ernest Rutherford splits the atom, 100th anniversary
Mississippi Statehood Bicentennial
John Quincy Adams's birth, 250th anniversary
Andrew Jackson's birth, 250th anniversary
Frank Lloyd Wright's birth, 150th anniversary
John F. Kennedy's birth, 100th anniversary

2018

FIFA World Cup, Russia
XXIII Olympic Winter Games, PyeongChang, South Korea
Commonwealth Games, Australia
Karl Marx's birth, 200th anniversary
Illinois Statehood Bicentennial
Flu Pandemic, 100th anniversary
World War I armistice, 100th anniversary
US Standard Time Act, 100th anniversary
Czar Nicholas II executed, 100th anniversary

2019

Alabama Statehood Bicentennial
Eighteenth Amendment (Prohibition) passed, 100th anniversary
Grand Canyon National Park established, 100th anniversary
Apollo 11 astronauts walk on the moon, 50th anniversary

2020

Leap Year
Games of the XXIV Olympiad
US presidential election
Maine Statehood Bicentennial
Nineteenth Amendment (Women's Suffrage) passed, 100th anniversary

2050

World population predicted to be 9 billion

2061

Halley's Comet returns

Perpetual Calendar, 1753–2100

A perpetual calendar lets you find the day of the week for any date in any year. Because January 1 may fall on any of the seven days of the week and may be a leap or nonleap year, 14 different calendars are possible. The number next to each year corresponds to one of the 14 calendars. Calendar 4 will be used in 2014; calendar 5 will be used in 2015; calendar 13 will be used in 2016; calendar 1 will be used in 2017.

YEAR	NO	YEAR	NO	YEAR	NO	YEAR	NO	YEAR	NO	YEAR	NO	YEAR	NO	YEAR	NO	YEAR	NO	YEAR	NO	YEAR	NO	YEAR	NO
1753	2	1782	3	1811	3	1840	11	1869	6	1898	7	1927	7	1956	8	1985	3	2014	4	2043	5	2072	13
1754	3	1783	4	1812	11	1841	6	1870	7	1899	1	1928	8	1957	3	1986	4	2015	5	2044	13	2073	1
1755	4	1784	12	1813	6	1842	7	1871	1	1900	2	1929	3	1958	4	1987	5	2016	13	2045	1	2074	2
1756	12	1785	7	1814	7	1843	1	1872	9	1901	3	1930	4	1959	5	1988	13	2017	1	2046	2	2075	3
1757	7	1786	1	1815	1	1844	9	1873	4	1902	4	1931	5	1960	13	1989	1	2018	2	2047	3	2076	11
1758	1	1787	2	1816	9	1845	4	1874	5	1903	5	1932	13	1961	1	1990	2	2019	3	2048	11	2077	6
1759	2	1788	10	1817	4	1846	5	1875	6	1904	13	1933	1	1962	2	1991	3	2020	11	2049	6	2078	7
1760	10	1789	5	1818	5	1847	6	1876	14	1905	1	1934	2	1963	3	1992	11	2021	6	2050	7	2079	1
1761	5	1790	6	1819	6	1848	14	1877	2	1906	2	1935	3	1964	11	1993	6	2022	7	2051	1	2080	9
1762	6	1791	7	1820	14	1849	2	1878	3	1907	3	1936	11	1965	6	1994	7	2023	1	2052	9	2081	4
1763	7	1792	8	1821	2	1850	3	1879	4	1908	11	1937	6	1966	7	1995	1	2024	9	2053	4	2082	5
1764	8	1793	3	1822	3	1851	4	1880	12	1909	6	1938	7	1967	1	1996	9	2025	4	2054	5	2083	6
1765	3	1794	4	1823	4	1852	12	1881	7	1910	7	1939	1	1968	9	1997	4	2026	5	2055	6	2084	14
1766	4	1795	5	1824	12	1853	7	1882	1	1911	1	1940	9	1969	4	1998	5	2027	6	2056	14	2085	2
1767	5	1796	13	1825	7	1854	1	1883	2	1912	9	1941	4	1970	5	1999	6	2028	14	2057	2	2086	3
1768	13	1797	1	1826	1	1855	2	1884	10	1913	4	1942	5	1971	6	2000	14	2029	2	2058	3	2087	4
1769	1	1798	2	1827	2	1856	10	1885	5	1914	5	1943	6	1972	14	2001	2	2030	3	2059	4	2088	12
1770	2	1799	3	1828	10	1857	5	1886	6	1915	6	1944	14	1973	2	2002	3	2031	4	2060	12	2089	7
1771	3	1800	4	1829	5	1858	6	1887	7	1916	14	1945	2	1974	3	2003	4	2032	12	2061	7	2090	1
1772	11	1801	5	1830	6	1859	7	1888	8	1917	2	1946	3	1975	4	2004	12	2033	7	2062	1	2091	2
1773	6	1802	6	1831	7	1860	8	1889	3	1918	3	1947	4	1976	12	2005	7	2034	1	2063	2	2092	10
1774	7	1803	7	1832	8	1861	3	1890	4	1919	4	1948	12	1977	7	2006	1	2035	2	2064	10	2093	5
1775	1	1804	8	1833	3	1862	4	1891	5	1920	12	1949	7	1978	1	2007	2	2036	10	2065	5	2094	6
1776	9	1805	3	1834	4	1863	5	1892	13	1921	7	1950	1	1979	2	2008	10	2037	5	2066	6	2095	7
1777	4	1806	4	1835	5	1864	13	1893	1	1922	1	1951	2	1980	10	2009	5	2038	6	2067	7	2096	8
1778	5	1807	5	1836	13	1865	1	1894	2	1923	2	1952	10	1981	5	2010	6	2039	7	2068	8	2097	3
1779	6	1808	13	1837	1	1866	2	1895	3	1924	10	1953	5	1982	6	2011	7	2040	8	2069	3	2098	4
1780	14	1809	1	1838	2	1867	3	1896	11	1925	5	1954	6	1983	7	2012	8	2041	3	2070	4	2099	5
1781	2	1810	2	1839	3	1868	11	1897	6	1926	6	1955	7	1984	8	2013	3	2042	4	2071	5	2100	6

1

2017

JAN	S	M	T	W	T	F	S
	1	2	3	4	5	6	7
	8	9	10	11	12	13	14
	15	16	17	18	19	20	21
	22	23	24	25	26	27	28
	29	30	31				

FEB	S	M	T	W	T	F	S
				1	2	3	4
	5	6	7	8	9	10	11
	12	13	14	15	16	17	18
	19	20	21	22	23	24	25
	26	27	28				

MAR	S	M	T	W	T	F	S
				1	2	3	4
	5	6	7	8	9	10	11
	12	13	14	15	16	17	18
	19	20	21	22	23	24	25
	26	27	28	29	30	31	

APR	S	M	T	W	T	F	S
							1
	2	3	4	5	6	7	8
	9	10	11	12	13	14	15
	16	17	18	19	20	21	22
	23	24	25	26	27	28	29
	30						

MAY	S	M	T	W	T	F	S
		1	2	3	4	5	6
	7	8	9	10	11	12	13
	14	15	16	17	18	19	20
	21	22	23	24	25	26	27
	28	29	30	31			

JUNE	S	M	T	W	T	F	S
					1	2	3
	4	5	6	7	8	9	10
	11	12	13	14	15	16	17
	18	19	20	21	22	23	24
	25	26	27	28	29	30	

JULY	S	M	T	W	T	F	S
							1
	2	3	4	5	6	7	8
	9	10	11	12	13	14	15
	16	17	18	19	20	21	22
	23	24	25	26	27	28	29
	30	31					

AUG	S	M	T	W	T	F	S
			1	2	3	4	5
	6	7	8	9	10	11	12
	13	14	15	16	17	18	19
	20	21	22	23	24	25	26
	27	28	29	30	31		

SEPT	S	M	T	W	T	F	S
						1	2
	3	4	5	6	7	8	9
	10	11	12	13	14	15	16
	17	18	19	20	21	22	23
	24	25	26	27	28	29	30

OCT	S	M	T	W	T	F	S
	1	2	3	4	5	6	7
	8	9	10	11	12	13	14
	15	16	17	18	19	20	21
	22	23	24	25	26	27	28
	29	30	31				

NOV	S	M	T	W	T	F	S
				1	2	3	4
	5	6	7	8	9	10	11
	12	13	14	15	16	17	18
	19	20	21	22	23	24	25
	26	27	28	29	30		

DEC	S	M	T	W	T	F	S
						1	2
	3	4	5	6	7	8	9
	10	11	12	13	14	15	16
	17	18	19	20	21	22	23
	24	25	26	27	28	29	30
	31						

2

JAN	S	M	T	W	T	F	S
		1	2	3	4	5	6
	7	8	9	10	11	12	13
	14	15	16	17	18	19	20
	21	22	23	24	25	26	27
	28	29	30	31			

FEB	S	M	T	W	T	F	S
					1	2	3
	4	5	6	7	8	9	10
	11	12	13	14	15	16	17
	18	19	20	21	22	23	24
	25	26	27	28			

MAR	S	M	T	W	T	F	S
					1	2	3
	4	5	6	7	8	9	10
	11	12	13	14	15	16	17
	18	19	20	21	22	23	24
	25	26	27	28	29	30	31

APR	S	M	T	W	T	F	S
	1	2	3	4	5	6	7
	8	9	10	11	12	13	14
	15	16	17	18	19	20	21
	22	23	24	25	26	27	28
	29	30					

MAY	S	M	T	W	T	F	S
			1	2	3	4	5
	6	7	8	9	10	11	12
	13	14	15	16	17	18	19
	20	21	22	23	24	25	26
	27	28	29	30	31		

JUNE	S	M	T	W	T	F	S
						1	2
	3	4	5	6	7	8	9
	10	11	12	13	14	15	16
	17	18	19	20	21	22	23
	24	25	26	27	28	29	30

JULY	S	M	T	W	T	F	S
	1	2	3	4	5	6	7
	8	9	10	11	12	13	14
	15	16	17	18	19	20	21
	22	23	24	25	26	27	28
	29	30	31				

AUG	S	M	T	W	T	F	S
				1	2	3	4
	5	6	7	8	9	10	11
	12	13	14	15	16	17	18
	19	20	21	22	23	24	25
	26	27	28	29	30	31	

SEPT	S	M	T	W	T	F	S
							1
	2	3	4	5	6	7	8
	9	10	11	12	13	14	15
	16	17	18	19	20	21	22
	23	24	25	26	27	28	29
	30						

OCT	S	M	T	W	T	F	S
		1	2	3	4	5	6
	7	8	9	10	11	12	13
	14	15	16	17	18	19	20
	21	22	23	24	25	26	27
	28	29	30	31			

NOV	S	M	T	W	T	F	S
					1	2	3
	4	5	6	7	8	9	10
	11	12	13	14	15	16	17
	18	19	20	21	22	23	24
	25	26	27	28	29	30	

DEC	S	M	T	W	T	F	S
							1
	2	3	4	5	6	7	8
	9	10	11	12	13	14	15
	16	17	18	19	20	21	22
	23	24	25	26	27	28	29
	30	31					

3

JAN	S	M	T	W	T	F	S
			1	2	3	4	5
	6	7	8	9	10	11	12
	13	14	15	16	17	18	19
	20	21	22	23	24	25	26
	27	28	29	30	31		

FEB	S	M	T	W	T	F	S
						1	2
	3	4	5	6	7	8	9
	10	11	12	13	14	15	16
	17	18	19	20	21	22	23
	24	25	26	27	28		

MAR	S	M	T	W	T	F	S
						1	2
	3	4	5	6	7	8	9
	10	11	12	13	14	15	16
	17	18	19	20	21	22	23
	24	25	26	27	28	29	30
	31						

APR	S	M	T	W	T	F	S
		1	2	3	4	5	6
	7	8	9	10	11	12	13
	14	15	16	17	18	19	20
	21	22	23	24	25	26	27
	28	29	30				

MAY	S	M	T	W	T	F	S
				1	2	3	4
	5	6	7	8	9	10	11
	12	13	14	15	16	17	18
	19	20	21	22	23	24	25
	26	27	28	29	30	31	

JUNE	S	M	T	W	T	F	S
							1
	2	3	4	5	6	7	8
	9	10	11	12	13	14	15
	16	17	18	19	20	21	22
	23	24	25	26	27	28	29
	30						

JULY	S	M	T	W	T	F	S
		1	2	3	4	5	6
	7	8	9	10	11	12	13
	14	15	16	17	18	19	20
	21	22	23	24	25	26	27
	28	29	30	31			

AUG	S	M	T	W	T	F	S
					1	2	3
	4	5	6	7	8	9	10
	11	12	13	14	15	16	17
	18	19	20	21	22	23	24
	25	26	27	28	29	30	31

SEPT	S	M	T	W	T	F	S
	1	2	3	4	5	6	7
	8	9	10	11	12	13	14
	15	16	17	18	19	20	21
	22	23	24	25	26	27	28
	29	30					

OCT	S	M	T	W	T	F	S
			1	2	3	4	5
	6	7	8	9	10	11	12
	13	14	15	16	17	18	19
	20	21	22	23	24	25	26
	27	28	29	30	31		

NOV	S	M	T	W	T	F	S
						1	2
	3	4	5	6	7	8	9
	10	11	12	13	14	15	16
	17	18	19	20	21	22	23
	24	25	26	27	28	29	30

DEC	S	M	T	W	T	F	S
	1	2	3	4	5	6	7
	8	9	10	11	12	13	14
	15	16	17	18	19	20	21
	22	23	24	25	26	27	28
	29	30	31				

4 2014

JAN	S	M	T	W	T	F	S
				1	2	3	4
	5	6	7	8	9	10	11
	12	13	14	15	16	17	18
	19	20	21	22	23	24	25
	26	27	28	29	30	31	

FEB	S	M	T	W	T	F	S
							1
	2	3	4	5	6	7	8
	9	10	11	12	13	14	15
	16	17	18	19	20	21	22
	23	24	25	26	27	28	

MAR	S	M	T	W	T	F	S
							1
	2	3	4	5	6	7	8
	9	10	11	12	13	14	15
	16	17	18	19	20	21	22
	23	24	25	26	27	28	29
	30	31					

APR	S	M	T	W	T	F	S
			1	2	3	4	5
	6	7	8	9	10	11	12
	13	14	15	16	17	18	19
	20	21	22	23	24	25	26
	27	28	29	30			

MAY	S	M	T	W	T	F	S
					1	2	3
	4	5	6	7	8	9	10
	11	12	13	14	15	16	17
	18	19	20	21	22	23	24
	25	26	27	28	29	30	31

JUNE	S	M	T	W	T	F	S
	1	2	3	4	5	6	7
	8	9	10	11	12	13	14
	15	16	17	18	19	20	21
	22	23	24	25	26	27	28
	29	30					

JULY	S	M	T	W	T	F	S
			1	2	3	4	5
	6	7	8	9	10	11	12
	13	14	15	16	17	18	19
	20	21	22	23	24	25	26
	27	28	29	30	31		

AUG	S	M	T	W	T	F	S
						1	2
	3	4	5	6	7	8	9
	10	11	12	13	14	15	16
	17	18	19	20	21	22	23
	24	25	26	27	28	29	30
	31						

SEPT	S	M	T	W	T	F	S
		1	2	3	4	5	6
	7	8	9	10	11	12	13
	14	15	16	17	18	19	20
	21	22	23	24	25	26	27
	28	29	30				

OCT	S	M	T	W	T	F	S
				1	2	3	4
	5	6	7	8	9	10	11
	12	13	14	15	16	17	18
	19	20	21	22	23	24	25
	26	27	28	29	30	31	

NOV	S	M	T	W	T	F	S
							1
	2	3	4	5	6	7	8
	9	10	11	12	13	14	15
	16	17	18	19	20	21	22
	23	24	25	26	27	28	29
	30						

DEC	S	M	T	W	T	F	S
		1	2	3	4	5	6
	7	8	9	10	11	12	13
	14	15	16	17	18	19	20
	21	22	23	24	25	26	27
	28	29	30	31			

5 2015

JAN	S	M	T	W	T	F	S
					1	2	3
	4	5	6	7	8	9	10
	11	12	13	14	15	16	17
	18	19	20	21	22	23	24
	25	26	27	28	29	30	31

FEB	S	M	T	W	T	F	S
	1	2	3	4	5	6	7
	8	9	10	11	12	13	14
	15	16	17	18	19	20	21
	22	23	24	25	26	27	28

MAR	S	M	T	W	T	F	S
	1	2	3	4	5	6	7
	8	9	10	11	12	13	14
	15	16	17	18	19	20	21
	22	23	24	25	26	27	28
	29	30	31				

APR	S	M	T	W	T	F	S
				1	2	3	4
	5	6	7	8	9	10	11
	12	13	14	15	16	17	18
	19	20	21	22	23	24	25
	26	27	28	29	30		

MAY	S	M	T	W	T	F	S
						1	2
	3	4	5	6	7	8	9
	10	11	12	13	14	15	16
	17	18	19	20	21	22	23
	24	25	26	27	28	29	30
	31						

JUNE	S	M	T	W	T	F	S
		1	2	3	4	5	6
	7	8	9	10	11	12	13
	14	15	16	17	18	19	20
	21	22	23	24	25	26	27
	28	29	30				

JULY	S	M	T	W	T	F	S
				1	2	3	4
	5	6	7	8	9	10	11
	12	13	14	15	16	17	18
	19	20	21	22	23	24	25
	26	27	28	29	30	31	

AUG	S	M	T	W	T	F	S
							1
	2	3	4	5	6	7	8
	9	10	11	12	13	14	15
	16	17	18	19	20	21	22
	23	24	25	26	27	28	29
	30	31					

SEPT	S	M	T	W	T	F	S
			1	2	3	4	5
	6	7	8	9	10	11	12
	13	14	15	16	17	18	19
	20	21	22	23	24	25	26
	27	28	29	30			

OCT	S	M	T	W	T	F	S
					1	2	3
	4	5	6	7	8	9	10
	11	12	13	14	15	16	17
	18	19	20	21	22	23	24
	25	26	27	28	29	30	31

NOV	S	M	T	W	T	F	S
	1	2	3	4	5	6	7
	8	9	10	11	12	13	14
	15	16	17	18	19	20	21
	22	23	24	25	26	27	28
	29	30					

DEC	S	M	T	W	T	F	S
			1	2	3	4	5
	6	7	8	9	10	11	12
	13	14	15	16	17	18	19
	20	21	22	23	24	25	26
	27	28	29	30	31		

6

JAN	S	M	T	W	T	F	S
						1	2
	3	4	5	6	7	8	9
	10	11	12	13	14	15	16
	17	18	19	20	21	22	23
	24	25	26	27	28	29	30
	31						

FEB	S	M	T	W	T	F	S
		1	2	3	4	5	6
	7	8	9	10	11	12	13
	14	15	16	17	18	19	20
	21	22	23	24	25	26	27
	28						

MAR	S	M	T	W	T	F	S
		1	2	3	4	5	6
	7	8	9	10	11	12	13
	14	15	16	17	18	19	20
	21	22	23	24	25	26	27
	28	29	30	31			

APR	S	M	T	W	T	F	S
					1	2	3
	4	5	6	7	8	9	10
	11	12	13	14	15	16	17
	18	19	20	21	22	23	24
	25	26	27	28	29	30	

MAY	S	M	T	W	T	F	S
							1
	2	3	4	5	6	7	8
	9	10	11	12	13	14	15
	16	17	18	19	20	21	22
	23	24	25	26	27	28	29
	30	31					

JUNE	S	M	T	W	T	F	S
			1	2	3	4	5
	6	7	8	9	10	11	12
	13	14	15	16	17	18	19
	20	21	22	23	24	25	26
	27	28	29	30			

JULY	S	M	T	W	T	F	S
					1	2	3
	4	5	6	7	8	9	10
	11	12	13	14	15	16	17
	18	19	20	21	22	23	24
	25	26	27	28	29	30	31

AUG	S	M	T	W	T	F	S
	1	2	3	4	5	6	7
	8	9	10	11	12	13	14
	15	16	17	18	19	20	21
	22	23	24	25	26	27	28
	29	30	31				

SEPT	S	M	T	W	T	F	S
				1	2	3	4
	5	6	7	8	9	10	11
	12	13	14	15	16	17	18
	19	20	21	22	23	24	25
	26	27	28	29	30		

OCT	S	M	T	W	T	F	S
						1	2
	3	4	5	6	7	8	9
	10	11	12	13	14	15	16
	17	18	19	20	21	22	23
	24	25	26	27	28	29	30
	31						

NOV	S	M	T	W	T	F	S
		1	2	3	4	5	6
	7	8	9	10	11	12	13
	14	15	16	17	18	19	20
	21	22	23	24	25	26	27
	28	29	30				

DEC	S	M	T	W	T	F	S
				1	2	3	4
	5	6	7	8	9	10	11
	12	13	14	15	16	17	18
	19	20	21	22	23	24	25
	26	27	28	29	30	31	

7

JAN	S	M	T	W	T	F	S
							1
	2	3	4	5	6	7	8
	9	10	11	12	13	14	15
	16	17	18	19	20	21	22
	23	24	25	26	27	28	29
	30	31					

FEB	S	M	T	W	T	F	S
			1	2	3	4	5
	6	7	8	9	10	11	12
	13	14	15	16	17	18	19
	20	21	22	23	24	25	26
	27	28					

MAR	S	M	T	W	T	F	S
			1	2	3	4	5
	6	7	8	9	10	11	12
	13	14	15	16	17	18	19
	20	21	22	23	24	25	26
	27	28	29	30	31		

APR	S	M	T	W	T	F	S
						1	2
	3	4	5	6	7	8	9
	10	11	12	13	14	15	16
	17	18	19	20	21	22	23
	24	25	26	27	28	29	30

MAY	S	M	T	W	T	F	S
	1	2	3	4	5	6	7
	8	9	10	11	12	13	14
	15	16	17	18	19	20	21
	22	23	24	25	26	27	28
	29	30	31				

JUNE	S	M	T	W	T	F	S
				1	2	3	4
	5	6	7	8	9	10	11
	12	13	14	15	16	17	18
	19	20	21	22	23	24	25
	26	27	28	29	30		

JULY	S	M	T	W	T	F	S
						1	2
	3	4	5	6	7	8	9
	10	11	12	13	14	15	16
	17	18	19	20	21	22	23
	24	25	26	27	28	29	30
	31						

AUG	S	M	T	W	T	F	S
		1	2	3	4	5	6
	7	8	9	10	11	12	13
	14	15	16	17	18	19	20
	21	22	23	24	25	26	27
	28	29	30	31			

SEPT	S	M	T	W	T	F	S
					1	2	3
	4	5	6	7	8	9	10
	11	12	13	14	15	16	17
	18	19	20	21	22	23	24
	25	26	27	28	29	30	

OCT	S	M	T	W	T	F	S
							1
	2	3	4	5	6	7	8
	9	10	11	12	13	14	15
	16	17	18	19	20	21	22
	23	24	25	26	27	28	29
	30	31					

NOV	S	M	T	W	T	F	S
			1	2	3	4	5
	6	7	8	9	10	11	12
	13	14	15	16	17	18	19
	20	21	22	23	24	25	26
	27	28	29	30			

DEC	S	M	T	W	T	F	S
					1	2	3
	4	5	6	7	8	9	10
	11	12	13	14	15	16	17
	18	19	20	21	22	23	24
	25	26	27	28	29	30	31

8

JAN	S	M	T	W	T	F	S
	1	2	3	4	5	6	7
	8	9	10	11	12	13	14
	15	16	17	18	19	20	21
	22	23	24	25	26	27	28
	29	30	31				

FEB	S	M	T	W	T	F	S
				1	2	3	4
	5	6	7	8	9	10	11
	12	13	14	15	16	17	18
	19	20	21	22	23	24	25
	26	27	28	29			

MAR	S	M	T	W	T	F	S
					1	2	3
	4	5	6	7	8	9	10
	11	12	13	14	15	16	17
	18	19	20	21	22	23	24
	25	26	27	28	29	30	31

APR	S	M	T	W	T	F	S
	1	2	3	4	5	6	7
	8	9	10	11	12	13	14
	15	16	17	18	19	20	21
	22	23	24	25	26	27	28
	29	30					

MAY	S	M	T	W	T	F	S
			1	2	3	4	5
	6	7	8	9	10	11	12
	13	14	15	16	17	18	19
	20	21	22	23	24	25	26
	27	28	29	30	31		

JUNE	S	M	T	W	T	F	S
						1	2
	3	4	5	6	7	8	9
	10	11	12	13	14	15	16
	17	18	19	20	21	22	23
	24	25	26	27	28	29	30

JULY	S	M	T	W	T	F	S
	1	2	3	4	5	6	7
	8	9	10	11	12	13	14
	15	16	17	18	19	20	21
	22	23	24	25	26	27	28
	29	30	31				

AUG	S	M	T	W	T	F	S
				1	2	3	4
	5	6	7	8	9	10	11
	12	13	14	15	16	17	18
	19	20	21	22	23	24	25
	26	27	28	29	30	31	

SEPT	S	M	T	W	T	F	S
							1
	2	3	4	5	6	7	8
	9	10	11	12	13	14	15
	16	17	18	19	20	21	22
	23	24	25	26	27	28	29
	30						

OCT	S	M	T	W	T	F	S
		1	2	3	4	5	6
	7	8	9	10	11	12	13
	14	15	16	17	18	19	20
	21	22	23	24	25	26	27
	28	29	30	31			

NOV	S	M	T	W	T	F	S
					1	2	3
	4	5	6	7	8	9	10
	11	12	13	14	15	16	17
	18	19	20	21	22	23	24
	25	26	27	28	29	30	

DEC	S	M	T	W	T	F	S
							1
	2	3	4	5	6	7	8
	9	10	11	12	13	14	15
	16	17	18	19	20	21	22
	23	24	25	26	27	28	29
	30	31					

9

JAN	S	M	T	W	T	F	S
		1	2	3	4	5	6
	7	8	9	10	11	12	13
	14	15	16	17	18	19	20
	21	22	23	24	25	26	27
	28	29	30	31			

FEB	S	M	T	W	T	F	S
					1	2	3
	4	5	6	7	8	9	10
	11	12	13	14	15	16	17
	18	19	20	21	22	23	24
	25	26	27	28	29		

MAR	S	M	T	W	T	F	S
						1	2
	3	4	5	6	7	8	9
	10	11	12	13	14	15	16
	17	18	19	20	21	22	23
	24	25	26	27	28	29	30
	31						

APR	S	M	T	W	T	F	S
		1	2	3	4	5	6
	7	8	9	10	11	12	13
	14	15	16	17	18	19	20
	21	22	23	24	25	26	27
	28	29	30				

MAY	S	M	T	W	T	F	S
				1	2	3	4
	5	6	7	8	9	10	11
	12	13	14	15	16	17	18
	19	20	21	22	23	24	25
	26	27	28	29	30	31	

JUNE	S	M	T	W	T	F	S
							1
	2	3	4	5	6	7	8
	9	10	11	12	13	14	15
	16	17	18	19	20	21	22
	23	24	25	26	27	28	29
	30						

JULY	S	M	T	W	T	F	S
		1	2	3	4	5	6
	7	8	9	10	11	12	13
	14	15	16	17	18	19	20
	21	22	23	24	25	26	27
	28	29	30	31			

AUG	S	M	T	W	T	F	S
					1	2	3
	4	5	6	7	8	9	10
	11	12	13	14	15	16	17
	18	19	20	21	22	23	24
	25	26	27	28	29	30	31

SEPT	S	M	T	W	T	F	S
	1	2	3	4	5	6	7
	8	9	10	11	12	13	14
	15	16	17	18	19	20	21
	22	23	24	25	26	27	28
	29	30					

OCT	S	M	T	W	T	F	S
			1	2	3	4	5
	6	7	8	9	10	11	12
	13	14	15	16	17	18	19
	20	21	22	23	24	25	26
	27	28	29	30	31		

NOV	S	M	T	W	T	F	S
						1	2
	3	4	5	6	7	8	9
	10	11	12	13	14	15	16
	17	18	19	20	21	22	23
	24	25	26	27	28	29	30

DEC	S	M	T	W	T	F	S
	1	2	3	4	5	6	7
	8	9	10	11	12	13	14
	15	16	17	18	19	20	21
	22	23	24	25	26	27	28
	29	30	31				

10

JAN	S	M	T	W	T	F	S
			1	2	3	4	5
	6	7	8	9	10	11	12
	13	14	15	16	17	18	19
	20	21	22	23	24	25	26
	27	28	29	30	31		

FEB	S	M	T	W	T	F	S
						1	2
	3	4	5	6	7	8	9
	10	11	12	13	14	15	16
	17	18	19	20	21	22	23
	24	25	26	27	28	29	

MAR	S	M	T	W	T	F	S
							1
	2	3	4	5	6	7	8
	9	10	11	12	13	14	15
	16	17	18	19	20	21	22
	23	24	25	26	27	28	29
	30	31					

APR	S	M	T	W	T	F	S
			1	2	3	4	5
	6	7	8	9	10	11	12
	13	14	15	16	17	18	19
	20	21	22	23	24	25	26
	27	28	29	30			

MAY	S	M	T	W	T	F	S
					1	2	3
	4	5	6	7	8	9	10
	11	12	13	14	15	16	17
	18	19	20	21	22	23	24
	25	26	27	28	29	30	31

JUNE	S	M	T	W	T	F	S
	1	2	3	4	5	6	7
	8	9	10	11	12	13	14
	15	16	17	18	19	20	21
	22	23	24	25	26	27	28
	29	30					

JULY	S	M	T	W	T	F	S
			1	2	3	4	5
	6	7	8	9	10	11	12
	13	14	15	16	17	18	19
	20	21	22	23	24	25	26
	27	28	29	30	31		

AUG	S	M	T	W	T	F	S
						1	2
	3	4	5	6	7	8	9
	10	11	12	13	14	15	16
	17	18	19	20	21	22	23
	24	25	26	27	28	29	30
	31						

SEPT	S	M	T	W	T	F	S
		1	2	3	4	5	6
	7	8	9	10	11	12	13
	14	15	16	17	18	19	20
	21	22	23	24	25	26	27
	28	29	30				

OCT	S	M	T	W	T	F	S
				1	2	3	4
	5	6	7	8	9	10	11
	12	13	14	15	16	17	18
	19	20	21	22	23	24	25
	26	27	28	29	30	31	

NOV	S	M	T	W	T	F	S
							1
	2	3	4	5	6	7	8
	9	10	11	12	13	14	15
	16	17	18	19	20	21	22
	23	24	25	26	27	28	29
	30						

DEC	S	M	T	W	T	F	S
		1	2	3	4	5	6
	7	8	9	10	11	12	13
	14	15	16	17	18	19	20
	21	22	23	24	25	26	27
	28	29	30	31			

11

JAN	S	M	T	W	T	F	S
				1	2	3	4
	5	6	7	8	9	10	11
	12	13	14	15	16	17	18
	19	20	21	22	23	24	25
	26	27	28	29	30	31	

FEB	S	M	T	W	T	F	S
							1
	2	3	4	5	6	7	8
	9	10	11	12	13	14	15
	16	17	18	19	20	21	22
	23	24	25	26	27	28	29

MAR	S	M	T	W	T	F	S
	1	2	3	4	5	6	7
	8	9	10	11	12	13	14
	15	16	17	18	19	20	21
	22	23	24	25	26	27	28
	29	30	31				

APR	S	M	T	W	T	F	S
				1	2	3	4
	5	6	7	8	9	10	11
	12	13	14	15	16	17	18
	19	20	21	22	23	24	25
	26	27	28	29	30		

MAY	S	M	T	W	T	F	S
						1	2
	3	4	5	6	7	8	9
	10	11	12	13	14	15	16
	17	18	19	20	21	22	23
	24	25	26	27	28	29	30
	31						

JUNE	S	M	T	W	T	F	S
		1	2	3	4	5	6
	7	8	9	10	11	12	13
	14	15	16	17	18	19	20
	21	22	23	24	25	26	27
	28	29	30				

JULY	S	M	T	W	T	F	S
				1	2	3	4
	5	6	7	8	9	10	11
	12	13	14	15	16	17	18
	19	20	21	22	23	24	25
	26	27	28	29	30	31	

AUG	S	M	T	W	T	F	S
							1
	2	3	4	5	6	7	8
	9	10	11	12	13	14	15
	16	17	18	19	20	21	22
	23	24	25	26	27	28	29
	30	31					

SEPT	S	M	T	W	T	F	S
			1	2	3	4	5
	6	7	8	9	10	11	12
	13	14	15	16	17	18	19
	20	21	22	23	24	25	26
	27	28	29	30			

OCT	S	M	T	W	T	F	S
					1	2	3
	4	5	6	7	8	9	10
	11	12	13	14	15	16	17
	18	19	20	21	22	23	24
	25	26	27	28	29	30	31

NOV	S	M	T	W	T	F	S
	1	2	3	4	5	6	7
	8	9	10	11	12	13	14
	15	16	17	18	19	20	21
	22	23	24	25	26	27	28
	29	30					

DEC	S	M	T	W	T	F	S
			1	2	3	4	5
	6	7	8	9	10	11	12
	13	14	15	16	17	18	19
	20	21	22	23	24	25	26
	27	28	29	30	31		

12

JAN	S	M	T	W	T	F	S
					1	2	3
	4	5	6	7	8	9	10
	11	12	13	14	15	16	17
	18	19	20	21	22	23	24
	25	26	27	28	29	30	31

FEB	S	M	T	W	T	F	S
	1	2	3	4	5	6	7
	8	9	10	11	12	13	14
	15	16	17	18	19	20	21
	22	23	24	25	26	27	28
	29						

MAR	S	M	T	W	T	F	S
		1	2	3	4	5	6
	7	8	9	10	11	12	13
	14	15	16	17	18	19	20
	21	22	23	24	25	26	27
	28	29	30	31			

APR	S	M	T	W	T	F	S
					1	2	3
	4	5	6	7	8	9	10
	11	12	13	14	15	16	17
	18	19	20	21	22	23	24
	25	26	27	28	29	30	

MAY	S	M	T	W	T	F	S
							1
	2	3	4	5	6	7	8
	9	10	11	12	13	14	15
	16	17	18	19	20	21	22
	23	24	25	26	27	28	29
	30	31					

JUNE	S	M	T	W	T	F	S
			1	2	3	4	5
	6	7	8	9	10	11	12
	13	14	15	16	17	18	19
	20	21	22	23	24	25	26
	27	28	29	30			

JULY	S	M	T	W	T	F	S
					1	2	3
	4	5	6	7	8	9	10
	11	12	13	14	15	16	17
	18	19	20	21	22	23	24
	25	26	27	28	29	30	31

AUG	S	M	T	W	T	F	S
	1	2	3	4	5	6	7
	8	9	10	11	12	13	14
	15	16	17	18	19	20	21
	22	23	24	25	26	27	28
	29	30	31				

SEPT	S	M	T	W	T	F	S
				1	2	3	4
	5	6	7	8	9	10	11
	12	13	14	15	16	17	18
	19	20	21	22	23	24	25
	26	27	28	29	30		

OCT	S	M	T	W	T	F	S
						1	2
	3	4	5	6	7	8	9
	10	11	12	13	14	15	16
	17	18	19	20	21	22	23
	24	25	26	27	28	29	30
	31						

NOV	S	M	T	W	T	F	S
		1	2	3	4	5	6
	7	8	9	10	11	12	13
	14	15	16	17	18	19	20
	21	22	23	24	25	26	27
	28	29	30				

DEC	S	M	T	W	T	F	S
				1	2	3	4
	5	6	7	8	9	10	11
	12	13	14	15	16	17	18
	19	20	21	22	23	24	25
	26	27	28	29	30	31	

13

2016

JAN	S	M	T	W	T	F	S
						1	2
	3	4	5	6	7	8	9
	10	11	12	13	14	15	16
	17	18	19	20	21	22	23
	24	25	26	27	28	29	30
	31						

FEB	S	M	T	W	T	F	S
		1	2	3	4	5	6
	7	8	9	10	11	12	13
	14	15	16	17	18	19	20
	21	22	23	24	25	26	27
	28	29					

MAR	S	M	T	W	T	F	S
			1	2	3	4	5
	6	7	8	9	10	11	12
	13	14	15	16	17	18	19
	20	21	22	23	24	25	26
	27	28	29	30	31		

APR	S	M	T	W	T	F	S
						1	2
	3	4	5	6	7	8	9
	10	11	12	13	14	15	16
	17	18	19	20	21	22	23
	24	25	26	27	28	29	30

MAY	S	M	T	W	T	F	S
	1	2	3	4	5	6	7
	8	9	10	11	12	13	14
	15	16	17	18	19	20	21
	22	23	24	25	26	27	28
	29	30	31				

JUNE	S	M	T	W	T	F	S
				1	2	3	4
	5	6	7	8	9	10	11
	12	13	14	15	16	17	18
	19	20	21	22	23	24	25
	26	27	28	29	30		

JULY	S	M	T	W	T	F	S
						1	2
	3	4	5	6	7	8	9
	10	11	12	13	14	15	16
	17	18	19	20	21	22	23
	24	25	26	27	28	29	30
	31						

AUG	S	M	T	W	T	F	S
		1	2	3	4	5	6
	7	8	9	10	11	12	13
	14	15	16	17	18	19	20
	21	22	23	24	25	26	27
	28	29	30	31			

SEPT	S	M	T	W	T	F	S
					1	2	3
	4	5	6	7	8	9	10
	11	12	13	14	15	16	17
	18	19	20	21	22	23	24
	25	26	27	28	29	30	

OCT	S	M	T	W	T	F	S
							1
	2	3	4	5	6	7	8
	9	10	11	12	13	14	15
	16	17	18	19	20	21	22
	23	24	25	26	27	28	29
	30	31					

NOV	S	M	T	W	T	F	S
			1	2	3	4	5
	6	7	8	9	10	11	12
	13	14	15	16	17	18	19
	20	21	22	23	24	25	26
	27	28	29	30			

DEC	S	M	T	W	T	F	S
					1	2	3
	4	5	6	7	8	9	10
	11	12	13	14	15	16	17
	18	19	20	21	22	23	24
	25	26	27	28	29	30	31

14

JAN	S	M	T	W	T	F	S
							1
	2	3	4	5	6	7	8
	9	10	11	12	13	14	15
	16	17	18	19	20	21	22
	23	24	25	26	27	28	29
	30	31					

FEB	S	M	T	W	T	F	S
			1	2	3	4	5
	6	7	8	9	10	11	12
	13	14	15	16	17	18	19
	20	21	22	23	24	25	26
	27	28	29				

MAR	S	M	T	W	T	F	S
				1	2	3	4
	5	6	7	8	9	10	11
	12	13	14	15	16	17	18
	19	20	21	22	23	24	25
	26	27	28	29	30	31	

APR	S	M	T	W	T	F	S
							1
	2	3	4	5	6	7	8
	9	10	11	12	13	14	15
	16	17	18	19	20	21	22
	23	24	25	26	27	28	29
	30						

MAY	S	M	T	W	T	F	S
		1	2	3	4	5	6
	7	8	9	10	11	12	13
	14	15	16	17	18	19	20
	21	22	23	24	25	26	27
	28	29	30	31			

JUNE	S	M	T	W	T	F	S
					1	2	3
	4	5	6	7	8	9	10
	11	12	13	14	15	16	17
	18	19	20	21	22	23	24
	25	26	27	28	29	30	

JULY	S	M	T	W	T	F	S
							1
	2	3	4	5	6	7	8
	9	10	11	12	13	14	15
	16	17	18	19	20	21	22
	23	24	25	26	27	28	29
	30	31					

AUG	S	M	T	W	T	F	S
			1	2	3	4	5
	6	7	8	9	10	11	12
	13	14	15	16	17	18	19
	20	21	22	23	24	25	26
	27	28	29	30	31		

SEPT	S	M	T	W	T	F	S
						1	2
	3	4	5	6	7	8	9
	10	11	12	13	14	15	16
	17	18	19	20	21	22	23
	24	25	26	27	28	29	30

OCT	S	M	T	W	T	F	S
	1	2	3	4	5	6	7
	8	9	10	11	12	13	14
	15	16	17	18	19	20	21
	22	23	24	25	26	27	28
	29	30	31				

NOV	S	M	T	W	T	F	S
				1	2	3	4
	5	6	7	8	9	10	11
	12	13	14	15	16	17	18
	19	20	21	22	23	24	25
	26	27	28	29	30		

DEC	S	M	T	W	T	F	S
						1	2
	3	4	5	6	7	8	9
	10	11	12	13	14	15	16
	17	18	19	20	21	22	23
	24	25	26	27	28	29	30
	31						

National Days of the World for 2014

(Compiled from publications of the U.S. Department of State, the United Nations and from information received from the countries listed.)

Most nations set aside one or more days each year as national public holidays, often recognizing the anniversary of the attainment of independence or the birthday of the country's ruler. Below, the national days are listed alphabetically. It should be noted that in some countries the Gregorian Calendar date of observance varies from year to year. See the Index and the main chronology for further details of observance and for numerous holidays in addition to the national days listed here.

Afghanistan .... Aug 19
Albania .... Nov 28
Algeria .... Nov 1
Andorra .... Sept 8
Angola .... Nov 11
Antigua and Barbuda .... Nov 1
Argentina .... May 25
Armenia .... Sept 21
Australia .... Jan 26
Austria .... Oct 26
Azerbaijan .... May 28
Bahamas .... July 10
Bahrain .... Dec 16
Bangladesh .... Mar 26
Barbados .... Nov 30
Belarus .... July 3
Belgium .... July 21
Belize .... Sept 21
Benin .... Aug 1
Bhutan .... Dec 17
Bolivia .... Aug 6
Bosnia and Herzegovina .... Mar 1
Botswana .... Sept 30
Brazil .... Sept 7
Brunei Darussalam .... Feb 23
Bulgaria .... Mar 3
Burkina Faso .... Dec 11
Burundi .... July 1
Cambodia .... Nov 9
Cameroon .... May 20
Canada .... July 1
Cape Verde .... July 5
Central African Republic .... Dec 1
Chad .... Aug 11
Chile .... Sept 18
China .... Oct 1
Colombia .... July 20
Comoros .... July 6
Congo .... Aug 15
Congo, Democratic Republic of .... June 30
Costa Rica .... Sept 15
Cote D'Ivoire .... Aug 7
Croatia .... Oct 8
Cuba .... Jan 1
Cyprus .... Oct 1
Czech Republic .... Oct 28
Denmark .... June 5
Djibouti .... June 27
Dominica .... Nov 3
Dominican Republic .... Feb 27
Ecuador .... Aug 10
Egypt .... July 23
El Salvador .... Sept 15
Equatorial Guinea .... Oct 12
Eritrea .... May 24
Estonia .... Feb 24
Ethiopia .... May 28
Fiji .... Oct 10
Finland .... Dec 6
France .... July 14
Gabon .... Aug 17
Gambia .... Feb 18
Georgia .... May 26
Germany .... Oct 3
Ghana .... Mar 6
Greece .... Mar 25
Grenada .... Feb 7
Guatemala .... Sept 15
Guinea .... Oct 2
Guinea-Bissau .... Sept 24
Guyana .... Feb 23
Haiti .... Jan 1
Holy See .... Mar 13
Honduras .... Sept 15
Hungary .... Aug 20
Iceland .... June 17
India .... Jan 26
Indonesia .... Aug 17
Iran .... Apr 1
Iraq .... †
Ireland .... Mar 17
Israel .... May 6
Italy .... June 2
Jamaica .... Aug 4
Japan .... Dec 23
Jordan .... May 25
Kazakhstan .... Dec 16
Kenya .... Dec 12
Kiribati .... July 12
Korea, Democratic People's Republic of .... Sept 9
Korea, Republic of .... Aug 15
Kosovo, Republic of .... Feb 17
Kuwait .... Feb 25
Kyrgyzstan .... Aug 31
Lao People's Democratic Republic .... Dec 2
Latvia .... Nov 18
Lebanon .... Nov 22
Lesotho .... Oct 4
Liberia .... July 26
Libya .... Oct 23
Liechtenstein .... Aug 15
Lithuania .... Feb 16
Luxembourg .... June 23
Macedonia .... Sept 8
Madagascar .... June 26
Malawi .... July 6
Malaysia .... Aug 31
Maldives .... July 26
Mali .... Sept 22
Malta .... Sept 21
Marshall Islands .... May 1
Mauritania .... Nov 28
Mauritius .... Mar 12
Mexico .... Sept 16
Micronesia (Federated States of) .... May 10
Moldova, Republic of .... Aug 27
Monaco .... Nov 19
Mongolia .... July 11
Montenegro, Republic of .... July 13
Morocco .... July 30
Mozambique .... June 25
Myanmar .... Jan 4
Namibia, Republic of .... Mar 21
Nauru .... Jan 31
Nepal .... May 29
Netherlands .... Apr 27
New Zealand .... Feb 6
Nicaragua .... Sept 15
Niger .... Dec 18
Nigeria .... Oct 1
Norway .... May 17
Oman .... Nov 18
Pakistan .... Mar 23
Palau, Republic of .... July 9
Panama .... Nov 3
Papua New Guinea .... Sept 16
Paraguay .... May 15
Peru .... July 28
Philippines .... June 12
Poland .... May 3
Portugal .... June 10
Qatar .... Sept 3
Romania .... Dec 1
Russian Federation .... June 12
Rwanda .... July 1
Saint Christopher (St Kitts) and Nevis .... Sept 19
Saint Lucia .... Feb 22
Saint Vincent and the Grenadines .... Oct 27
Samoa .... June 1
San Marino .... Sept 3
Sao Tome and Principe .... July 12
Saudi Arabia .... Sept 23
Senegal .... Apr 4
Serbia .... Feb 15
Seychelles .... June 18
Sierra Leone .... Apr 27
Singapore .... Aug 9
Slovakia .... Sept 1
Slovenia .... June 25
Solomon Islands .... July 7
Somalia .... July 1
South Africa .... Apr 27
South Sudan .... July 9
Spain .... Oct 12
Sri Lanka .... Feb 4
Sudan .... Jan 1
Suriname .... Nov 25
Swaziland .... Sept 6
Sweden .... June 6
Switzerland .... Aug 1
Syria .... Apr 17
Taiwan .... Oct 10
Tajikistan .... Sept 9
Tanzania, United Republic of .... Apr 26
Thailand .... Dec 5
Timor-Leste .... Nov 28
Togo .... Apr 27
Tonga .... June 4
Trinidad and Tobago .... Aug 31
Tunisia .... Mar 20
Turkey .... Oct 29
Turkmenistan .... Oct 27
Tuvalu .... Oct 1
Uganda .... Oct 9
Ukraine .... Aug 24
United Arab Emirates .... Dec 2
United Kingdom .... ††
United States of America .... July 4
Uruguay .... Aug 25
Uzbekistan .... Sept 1
Vanuatu .... July 30
Venezuela .... July 5
Vietnam .... Sept 2
Yemen .... May 22
Zambia .... Oct 27
Zimbabwe .... Apr 18

† Iraq has yet to declare a new national day.
†† United Kingdom does not observe a national day.

Selected Special Years: 1995–2014

As sponsored by the United Nations

Year for Tolerance: 1995
Intl Year for Eradication of Poverty: 1996
Intl Year of the Ocean: 1998
Intl Year of Older Persons: 1999
Intl Year for the Culture of Peace: 2000
Intl Year of Thanksgiving: 2000
Intl Year of Volunteers: 2001
Year of Dialogue Among Civilizations: 2001
Intl Year of Mobilization Against Racism: 2001
Intl Year of Mountains: 2002
Intl Year of Ecotourism: 2002
Intl Year of Freshwater: 2003
Intl Year of Microcredit: 2005
Intl Year of Human Rights Learning: 2008–2009
Intl Year of Languages: 2008
Intl Year of the Potato: 2008
Intl Year of Planet Earth: 2008
Intl Year of Sanitation: 2008
Intl Year of Astronomy: 2009
Intl Year of Natural Fibers: 2009
Intl Year of Reconciliation: 2009
Intl Year for the Rapproachment of Cultures: 2010
Intl Year of Biodiversity: 2010
Intl Year of the Seafarer: 2010
Intl Year of Youth: Aug 12, 2010–Aug 11, 2011
Intl Year of Forests: 2011
Intl Year of Chemistry: 2011
Intl Year for People of African Descent: 2011
Intl Year of Cooperatives: 2013
Intl Year of Sustainable Energy for All: 2013
Intl Year of Water Cooperation: 2013
Intl Year of Quinoa
Intl Year of Crystallography: 2014
Intl Year of Family Farming: 2014
Intl Year of Small Island Developing States: 2014

Chinese Calendar

The Chinese lunar year is divided into 12 months of 29 or 30 days. The calendar is adjusted to the length of the solar year by the addition of extra months at regular intervals. The years are arranged in major cycles of 60 years. Each successive year is named after one of 12 animals. These 12-year cycles are continuously repeated.

2009 .... Ox
2010 .... Tiger
2011 .... Hare
2012 .... Dragon
2013 .... Snake
2014 .... Horse
2015 .... Sheep (Goat)
2016 .... Monkey
2017 .... Rooster
2018 .... Dog
2019 .... Boar (Pig)
2020 .... Rat

Wedding Anniversary Gifts

1st .... paper, plastics, clocks
2nd .... cotton, china, calico
3rd .... leather, crystal, glass
4th .... books, electrical appliances, silk, fruit, flowers
5th .... wood, silverware
6th .... sugar, candy, wood, iron
7th .... wool, copper, desk sets
8th .... bronze, pottery, linens, laces, electrical appliances
9th .... pottery, willow, leather
10th .... tin, aluminum, diamond jewelry
11th .... steel, fashion jewelry, accessories
12th .... silk, linen, pearls, colored gems
13th .... lace, textiles, furs
14th .... ivory, gold jewelry
15th .... crystal, watches, glass
16th .... silver hollowware
17th .... furniture
18th .... porcelain
19th .... bronze
20th .... china, platinum
21st .... brass, nickel
22nd .... copper
23rd .... silver plate
24th .... musical instruments
25th .... silver
26th .... original pictures
27th .... sculpture
28th .... orchids
29th .... new furniture
30th .... pearl, diamond
31st .... timepieces
32nd .... conveyances (including automobiles)
33rd .... amethyst
34th .... opal
35th .... coral, jade
36th .... bone china
37th .... alabaster
38th .... beryl, tourmaline
39th .... lace
40th .... ruby
41st .... land
42nd .... improved real estate
43rd .... trips
44th .... groceries
45th .... sapphire
46th .... original poetry tributes
47th .... books
48th .... optical (spectacles, microscopes, telescopes)
49th .... luxuries of any kind
50th .... gold
55th .... emerald
60th .... diamond
75th .... diamond

World Map of Time Zones

Reprinted courtesy of Her Majesty's Nautical Almanac Office and the UK Hydrographic Office.

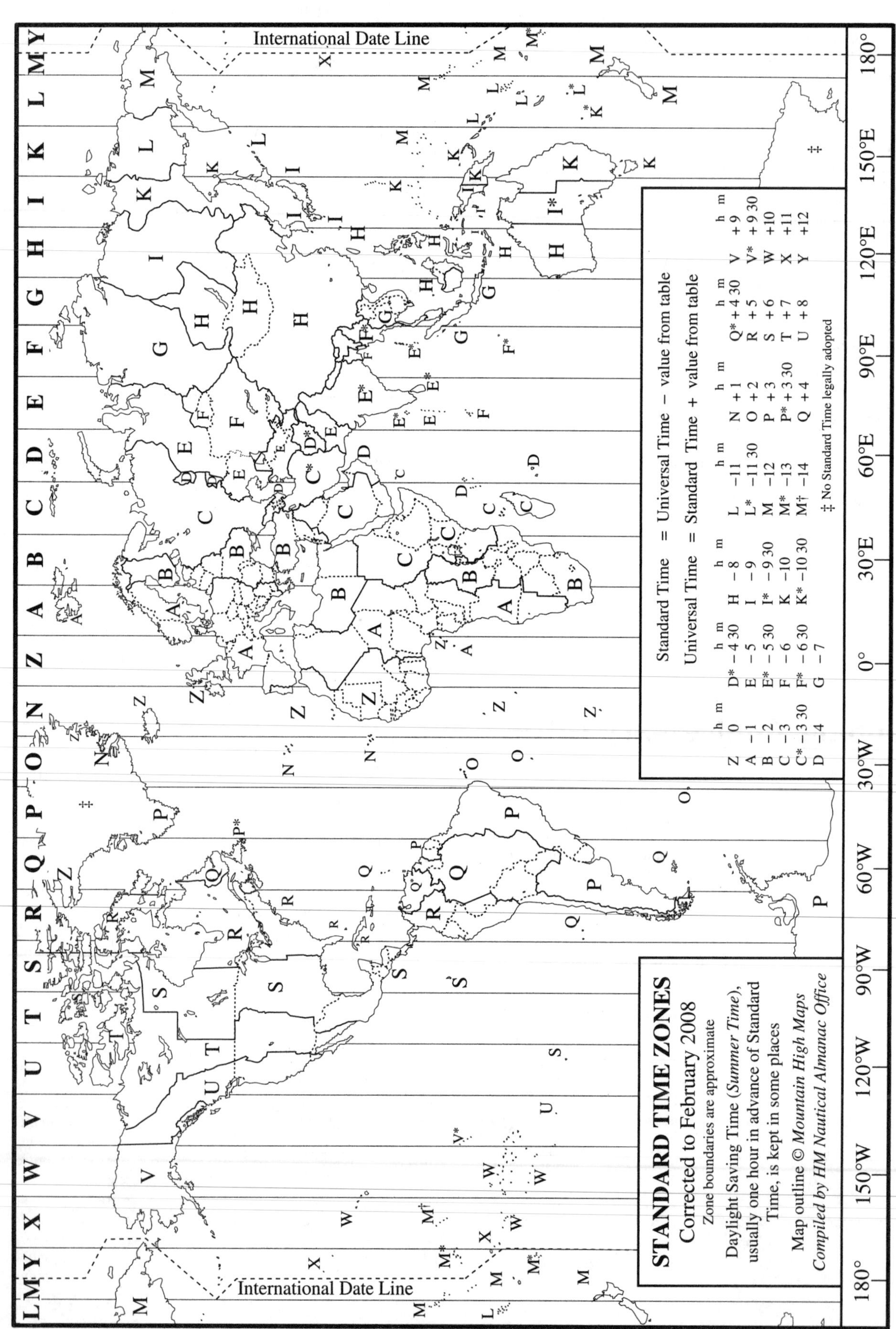

Universal, Standard and Daylight Times

Universal Time (UT) is also known as Greenwich Mean Time (GMT) and is the standard time of the Greenwich meridian (longitude 0°). A time given in UT may be converted to local mean time by the addition of east longitude (or the subtraction of west longitude), where the longitude of the place is expressed in time-measure at the rate of one hour for every 15°. Local clock times may differ from standard times, especially in summer when clocks are often advanced by one hour ("daylight saving" or "summer" time).

The time used in this book is Eastern Standard Time. The following table provides conversion between Universal Time and all time zones in the United States. An asterisk denotes that the time is on the preceding day.

UNIVERSAL TIME	EASTERN DAYLIGHT TIME	EASTERN STANDARD TIME AND CENTRAL DAYLIGHT TIME	CENTRAL STANDARD TIME MOUNTAIN DAYLIGHT TIME	MOUNTAIN STANDARD TIME PACIFIC DAYLIGHT TIME	PACIFIC STANDARD TIME
0^h	*8 PM	*7 PM	*6 PM	*5 PM	*4 PM
1	*9	*8	*7	*6	*5
2	*10	*9	*8	*7	*6
3	*11 PM	*10	*9	*8	*7
4	0 MIDNIGHT	*11 PM	*10	*9	*8
5	1 AM	0 MIDNIGHT	*11 PM	*10	*9
6	2	1 AM	0 MIDNIGHT	*11 PM	*10
7	3	2	1 AM	0 MIDNIGHT	*11 PM
8	4	3	2	1 AM	0 MIDNIGHT
9	5	4	3	2	1 AM
10	6	5	4	3	2
11	7	6	5	4	3
12	8	7	6	5	4
13	9	8	7	6	5
14	10	9	8	7	6
15	11 AM	10	9	8	7
16	12 NOON	11 AM	10	9	8
17	1 PM	12 NOON	11 AM	10	9
18	2	1 PM	12 NOON	11 AM	10
19	3	2	1 PM	12 NOON	11 AM
20	4	3	2	1 PM	12 NOON
21	5	4	3	2	1 PM
22	6	5	4	3	2
23	7 PM	6 PM	5 PM	4 PM	3 PM

The longitudes of the standard meridians for the standard time zones are:
Eastern . . . . . 75° West Central . . . . . 90° West Mountain . . . . . 105° West Pacific . . . . . 120° West

Leap Seconds

The information below is developed by the editors from data supplied by the US Naval Observatory.

Because of Earth's slightly erratic rotation and the need for greater precision in time measurement, it has become necessary to add a "leap second" from time to time to man's clocks to coordinate them with astronomical time. Rotation of the Earth has been slowing since 1900, making an astronomical second longer than an atomic second. Since 1972, by international agreement, adjustments have been made to keep astronomical and atomic clocks within 0.9 second of each other. The determination to add (or subtract) seconds is made by the Central Bureau of the International Earth Rotation Service, in Paris. Preferred times for adjustment have been June 30 and December 31, but any time may be designated by the International Earth Rotation Service. The first such adjustment was made in 1972, and as of July 2013, a total of 25 leap seconds had been added. The additions have been made at 23:59:60 UTC (Coordinated Universal Time) = 6:59:60 EST (Eastern Standard Time). Leap seconds have been inserted into the UTC time scale on the following dates:

June 30, 1972
Dec 31, 1972
Dec 31, 1973
Dec 31, 1974
Dec 31, 1975
Dec 31, 1976
Dec 31, 1977
Dec 31, 1978
Dec 31, 1979
June 30, 1981
June 30, 1982
June 30, 1983
June 30, 1985
Dec 31, 1987
Dec 31, 1989
Dec 31, 1990
June 30, 1992
June 30, 1993
June 30, 1994
Dec 31, 1995
June 30, 1997
Dec 31, 1998
Dec 31, 2005
Dec 31, 2008
June 30, 2012

Astronomical Phenomena for the Years 2014–2016

All dates are given in terms of Eastern Standard or Daylight Time and the Gregorian calendar.

(Based in part on information prepared by the Nautical Almanac Office, US Naval Observatory.)

2014

PRINCIPAL PHENOMENA, EARTH

Perihelion	Jan 4
Aphelion	July 3
Equinoxes	Mar 20, Sept 22
Solstices	June 21, Dec 21

PHASES OF THE MOON

● New Moon	☽ First Quarter	○ Full Moon	☾ Last Quarter
Jan 1	Jan 7	Jan 15	Jan 24
Jan 30	Feb 6	Feb 14	Feb 22
Mar 1	Mar 8	Mar 16	Mar 23
Mar 30	Apr 7	Apr 15	Apr 22
Apr 29	May 6	May 14	May 21
May 28	June 5	June 13	June 19
June 27	July 5	July 12	July 18
July 26	Aug 3	Aug 10	Aug 17
Aug 25	Sept 2	Sept 8	Sept 15
Sept 24	Oct 1	Oct 8	Oct 15
Oct 23	Oct 30	Nov 6	Nov 14
Nov 22	Nov 29	Dec 6	Dec 14
Dec 21	Dec 28		

ECLIPSES

Total eclipse of the Moon	Apr 15
Annular eclipse of the Sun	Apr 29
Total eclipse of the Moon	Oct 8
Partial eclipse of the Sun	Oct 23

2015

PRINCIPAL PHENOMENA, EARTH

Perihelion	Jan 4
Aphelion	July 6
Equinoxes	Mar 20, Sept 23
Solstices	June 21, Dec 21

PHASES OF THE MOON

● New Moon	☽ First Quarter	○ Full Moon	☾ Last Quarter
		Jan 4	Jan 13
Jan 20	Jan 26	Feb 3	Feb 11
Feb 18	Feb 25	Mar 5	Mar 13
Mar 20	Mar 27	Apr 4	Apr 11
Apr 18	Apr 25	May 3	May 11
May 18	May 25	June 2	June 9
June 16	June 24	July 1	July 8
July 15	July 24	July 31	Aug 6
Aug 14	Aug 22	Aug 29	Sept 5
Sept 13	Sept 21	Sept 27	Oct 4
Oct 12	Oct 20	Oct 27	Nov 3
Nov 11	Nov 19	Nov 25	Dec 3
Dec 11	Dec 18	Dec 25	

ECLIPSES

Total eclipse of the Sun	Mar 20
Total eclipse of the Moon	Apr 4
Partial eclipse of the Sun	Sept 13
Total eclipse of the Moon	Sept 27

2016

PRINCIPAL PHENOMENA, EARTH

Perihelion	Jan 2
Aphelion	July 4
Equinoxes	Mar 20, Sept 22
Solstices	June 20, Dec 21

PHASES OF THE MOON

● New Moon	☽ First Quarter	○ Full Moon	☾ Last Quarter
			Jan 2
Jan 9	Jan 16	Jan 23	Jan 31
Feb 8	Feb 15	Feb 22	Mar 1
Mar 8	Mar 15	Mar 23	Mar 31
Apr 7	Apr 13	Apr 22	Apr 29
May 6	May 13	May 21	May 29
June 4	June 12	June 20	June 27
July 4	July 11	July 19	July 26
Aug 2	Aug 10	Aug 18	Aug 24
Sept 1	Sept 9	Sept 16	Sept 23
Sept 30	Oct 9	Oct 16	Oct 22
Oct 30	Nov 7	Nov 14	Nov 21
Nov 29	Dec 7	Dec 13	Dec 20
Dec 29			

ECLIPSES

Total eclipse of the Sun	Mar 9
Penumbral eclipse of the Moon	Mar 23
Penumbral eclipse of the Moon	Aug 18
Annular eclipse of the Sun	Sept 1
Penumbral eclipse of the Moon	Sept 16

The Naming of Hurricanes

Why are hurricanes named? Experience shows that the use of short, distinctive names greatly reduces confusion when two or more tropical storms occur at the same time. The use of easily remembered names in written and spoken communication is quicker and less subject to error than the older, more cumbersome latitude-longitude identification methods, advantages which are especially important in exchanging detailed storm information between hundreds of widely scattered stations, airports, coastal bases and ships at sea.

During World War II forecasters and meteorologists began using female names for storms in weather map discussions, and in 1953 the US weather services adopted the practice, creating a new international phonetic alphabet of women's names from A–W to name hurricanes. In 1978 men's names were also introduced into the storm lists.

Because hurricanes affect other nations and are tracked by their weather services, the lists have an international flavor. Names are agreed upon during international meetings of the World Meteorological Organization by the nations involved, and can be retired and replaced with new names in the event of particularly severe storms. For example, Iniki—the name of the hurricane that devastated Hawaii—has been replaced with Iolana on List 2.

The National Hurricane Center near Miami, FL, keeps a constant watch on oceanic storm-breeding areas for tropical disturbances that may herald the formation of a hurricane. If a disturbance intensifies into a tropical storm—with rotary circulation and wind speeds above 39 miles per hour—the Center will give the storm a name from one of six lists. The Atlantic and Eastern Pacific lists are rotated year by year so that the 2014 set, for example, will be used again to name storms in 2020.

The lists of names for Central Pacific and Western Pacific hurricanes (tropical cyclones) are not rotated on a yearly basis. Meteorologists follow each list until all those names have been used, then go on to the next list.

ATLANTIC HURRICANE NAMES

2014	2015	2016
Arthur	Ana	Alex
Bertha	Bill	Bonnie
Cristobal	Claudette	Colin
Dolly	Danny	Danielle
Edouard	Erika	Earl
Fay	Fred	Fiona
Gonzalo	Grace	Gaston
Hanna	Henri	Hermine
Isaias	Ida	Ian
Josephine	Joaquin	Julia
Kyle	Kate	Karl
Laura	Larry	Lisa
Marco	Mindy	Matthew
Nana	Nicholas	Nicole
Omar	Odette	Otto
Paulette	Peter	Paula
Rene	Rose	Richard
Sally	Sam	Shary
Teddy	Teresa	Tobias
Vicky	Victor	Virginie
Wilfred	Wanda	Walter

EASTERN PACIFIC HURRICANE NAMES

2014	2015	2016
Amanda	Andres	Agatha
Boris	Blanca	Blas
Cristina	Carlos	Celia
Douglas	Dolores	Darby
Elida	Enrique	Estelle
Fausto	Felicia	Frank
Genevieve	Guillermo	Georgette
Hernan	Hilda	Howard
Iselle	Ignacio	Isis
Julio	Jimena	Javier
Karina	Kevin	Kay
Lowell	Linda	Lester
Marie	Marty	Madeline
Norbert	Nora	Newton
Odile	Olaf	Orlene
Polo	Patricia	Paine
Rachel	Rick	Roslyn
Simon	Sandra	Seymour
Trudy	Terry	Tina
Vance	Vivian	Virgil
Winnie	Waldo	Winifred
Xavier	Xina	Xavier
Yolanda	York	Yolanda
Zeke	Zelda	Zeke

If more than 24 tropical cyclones occur in a year, then the Greek alphabet will be used following Zelda or Zeke.

CENTRAL PACIFIC TROPICAL CYCLONE NAMES

LIST 1	LIST 2	LIST 3	LIST 4
Akoni	Aka	Alika	Ana
Ema	Ekeka	Ele	Ela
Hone	Hene	Huko	Halola
Iona	Iolana	Iopa	Iune
Keli	Keoni	Kika	Kilo
Lala	Lino	Lana	Loke
Moke	Mele	Maka	Malia
Nolo	Nona	Neki	Niala
Olana	Oliwa	Omeka	Oho
Pena	Pama	Pewa	Pali
Ulana	Upana	Unala	Ulika
Wale	Wene	Wali	Walaka

WESTERN PACIFIC TROPICAL CYCLONE NAMES

LIST 1	LIST 2	LIST 3	LIST 4	LIST 5
Damrey	Kong-rey	Nakri	Krovanh	Sarika
Haikui	Yutu	Fengshen	Dujuan	Haima
Kirogi	Toraji	Kalmaegi	Mujigae	Meari
Kai-Tak	Man-yi	Fung-wong	Choi-wan	Ma-on
Tembin	Usagi	Kanmuri	Koppu	Tokage
Bolaven	Pabuk	Phanfone	Ketsana	Nock-ten
Sanba	Wutip	Vongfong	Parma	Muifa
Jelawat	Sepat	Nuri	Melor	Merbok
Ewiniar	Fitow	Sinlaku	Nepartak	Nanmadol
Malaksi	Danas	Hagupit	Lupit	Talas
Gaemi	Nari	Jangmi	Mirinae	Noru
Prapiroon	Wipha	Mekkhala	Nida	Kulap
Maria	Francisco	Higos	Omais	Roke
Son-Tinh	Lekima	Bavi	Conson	Sonca
Bopha	Krosa	Maysak	Chanthu	Nesat
Wukong	Haiyan	Haishen	Dianmu	Haitang
Sonamu	Podul	Noul	Mindulle	Nalgae
Shanshan	Lingling	Dolphin	Lionrock	Banyan
Yagi	Kaziki	Kujira	Kompasu	Washi
Leepi	Faxai	Chan-hom	Namtheun	Pakhar
Bebinca	Peipah	Linfa	Malou	Sanvu
Rumbia	Tapah	Nangka	Meranti	Mawar
Soulik	Mitag	Soudelor	Fanapi	Guchol
Cimaron	Hagibis	Molave	Malakas	Talim
Jebi	Neoguri	Goni	Megi	Doksuri
Mangkhut	Rammasun	Morakot	Chaba	Khanun
Utor	Matmo	Etau	Aere	Vicente
Trami	Halong	Vamco	Songda	Saola

Some Facts About the US Presidents

	NAME	BIRTHDATE, PLACE	PARTY	TENURE	DIED	FIRST LADY	VICE PRESIDENT
1.	**George Washington**	2/22/1732, Westmoreland Cnty, VA	Federalist	1789–1797	12/14/1799	Martha Dandridge Custis	John Adams
2.	**John Adams**	10/30/1735, Braintree (Quincy), MA	Federalist	1797–1801	7/4/1826	Abigail Smith	Thomas Jefferson
3.	**Thomas Jefferson**	4/13/1743, Shadwell, VA	Democratic-Republican	1801–1809	7/4/1826	Martha Wayles Skelton	Aaron Burr, 1801–05 George Clinton, 1805–09
4.	**James Madison**	3/16/1751, Port Conway, VA	Democratic-Republican	1809–1817	6/28/1836	Dolley Payne Todd	George Clinton, 1809–12 Elbridge Gerry, 1813–14
5.	**James Monroe**	4/28/1758, Westmoreland Cnty, VA	Democratic-Republican	1817–1825	7/4/1831	Elizabeth Kortright	Daniel D. Tompkins
6.	**John Q. Adams**	7/11/1767, Braintree (Quincy), MA	Democratic-Republican	1825–1829	2/23/1848	Louisa Catherine Johnson	John C. Calhoun
7.	**Andrew Jackson**	3/15/1767, Waxhaw Settlement, SC	Democrat	1829–1837	6/8/1845	Mrs. Rachel Donelson Robards	John C. Calhoun, 1829–32 Martin Van Buren, 1833–37
8.	**Martin Van Buren**	12/5/1782, Kinderhook, NY	Democrat	1837–1841	7/24/1862	Hannah Hoes	Richard M. Johnson
9.	**William H. Harrison**	2/9/1773, Charles City Cnty, VA	Whig	1841	4/4/1841†	Anna Symmes	John Tyler
10.	**John Tyler**	3/29/1790, Charles City Cnty, VA	Whig	1841–1845	1/18/1862	Letitia Christian Julia Gardiner	
11.	**James K. Polk**	11/2/1795, near Pineville, NC	Democrat	1845–1849	6/15/1849	Sarah Childress	George M. Dallas
12.	**Zachary Taylor**	11/24/1784, Barboursville, VA	Whig	1849–1850	7/9/1850†	Margaret Mackall Smith	Millard Fillmore
13.	**Millard Fillmore**	1/7/1800, Locke, NY	Whig	1850–1853	3/8/1874	Abigail Powers Mrs. Caroline Carmichael McIntosh	
14.	**Franklin Pierce**	11/23/1804, Hillsboro, NH	Democrat	1853–1857	10/8/1869	Jane Means Appleton	William R. D. King
15.	**James Buchanan**	4/23/1791, near Mercersburg, PA	Democrat	1857–1861	6/1/1868		John C. Breckinridge
16.	**Abraham Lincoln**	2/12/1809, near Hodgenville, KY	Republican	1861–1865	4/15/1865*	Mary Todd	Hannibal Hamlin, 1861–65 Andrew Johnson, 1865
17.	**Andrew Johnson**	12/29/1808, Raleigh, NC	Democrat	1865–1869	7/31/1875	Eliza McCardle	
18.	**Ulysses S. Grant**	4/27/1822, Point Pleasant, OH	Republican	1869–1877	7/23/1885	Julia Boggs Dent	Schuyler Colfax, 1869–73 Henry Wilson, 1873–75
19.	**Rutherford B. Hayes**	10/4/1822, Delaware, OH	Republican	1877–1881	1/17/1893	Lucy Ware Webb	William A. Wheeler
20.	**James A. Garfield**	11/19/1831, Orange, OH	Republican	1881	9/19/1881*	Lucretia Rudolph	Chester A. Arthur

	NAME	BIRTHDATE, PLACE	PARTY	TENURE	DIED	FIRST LADY	VICE PRESIDENT
21.	**Chester A. Arthur**	10/5/1829, Fairfield, VT	Republican	1881–1885	11/18/1886	Ellen Lewis Herndon	
22.	**Grover Cleveland**	3/18/1837, Caldwell, NJ	Democrat	1885–1889	6/24/1908	Frances Folsom	Thomas A. Hendricks, 1885
23.	**Benjamin Harrison**	8/20/1833, North Bend, OH	Republican	1889–1893	3/13/1901	Caroline Lavinia Scott Mrs. Mary Dimmick	Levi P. Morton
24.	**Grover Cleveland**	3/18/1837, Caldwell, NJ	Democrat	1893–1897	6/24/1908	Frances Folsom	Adlai Stevenson, 1893–97
25.	**William McKinley**	1/29/1843, Niles, OH	Republican	1897–1901	9/14/1901*	Ida Saxton	Garret A. Hobart, 1897–99 Theodore Roosevelt, 1901
26.	**Theodore Roosevelt**	10/27/1858, New York, NY	Republican	1901–1909	1/6/1919	Alice Hathaway Lee Edith Kermit Carow	Charles W. Fairbanks
27.	**William H. Taft**	9/15/1857, Cincinnati, OH	Republican	1909–1913	3/8/1930	Helen Herron	James S. Sherman
28.	**Woodrow Wilson**	12/28/1856, Staunton, VA	Democrat	1913–1921	2/3/1924	Ellen Louise Axson Edith Bolling Galt	Thomas R. Marshall
29.	**Warren G. Harding**	11/2/1865, near Corsica, OH	Republican	1921–1923	8/2/1923†	Florence Kling DeWolfe	Calvin Coolidge
30.	**Calvin Coolidge**	7/4/1872, Plymouth Notch, VT	Republican	1923–1929	1/5/1933	Grace Anna Goodhue	Charles G. Dawes
31.	**Herbert C. Hoover**	8/10/1874, West Branch, IA	Republican	1929–1933	10/20/1964	Lou Henry	Charles Curtis
32.	**Franklin D. Roosevelt**	1/30/1882, Hyde Park, NY	Democrat	1933–1945	4/12/1945†	Eleanor Roosevelt	John N. Garner, 1933–41 Henry A. Wallace, 1941–45 Harry S. Truman, 1945
33.	**Harry S. Truman**	5/8/1884, Lamar, MO	Democrat	1945–1953	12/26/1972	Elizabeth Virginia (Bess) Wallace	Alben W. Barkley
34.	**Dwight D. Eisenhower**	10/14/1890, Denison, TX	Republican	1953–1961	3/28/1969	Mamie Geneva Doud	Richard M. Nixon
35.	**John F. Kennedy**	5/29/1917, Brookline, MA	Democrat	1961–1963	11/22/1963*	Jacqueline Lee Bouvier	Lyndon B. Johnson
36.	**Lyndon B. Johnson**	8/27/1908, near Stonewall, TX	Democrat	1963–1969	1/22/1973	Claudia Alta (Lady Bird) Taylor	Hubert H. Humphrey
37.	**Richard M. Nixon**	1/9/1913, Yorba Linda, CA	Republican	1969–1974**	4/22/1994	Thelma Catherine (Pat) Ryan	Spiro T. Agnew, 1969–73 Gerald R. Ford, 1973–74
38.	**Gerald R. Ford**	7/14/1913, Omaha, NE	Republican	1974–1977	12/26/2006	Elizabeth (Betty) Bloomer	Nelson A. Rockefeller
39.	**James E. Carter, Jr**	10/1/1924, Plains, GA	Democrat	1977–1981		Rosalynn Smith	Walter F. Mondale
40.	**Ronald W. Reagan**	2/6/1911, Tampico, IL	Republican	1981–1989	6/5/2004	Nancy Davis	George H. W. Bush
41.	**George H. W. Bush**	6/12/1924, Milton, MA	Republican	1989–1993		Barbara Pierce	J. Danforth Quayle
42.	**William J. Clinton**	8/19/1946, Hope, AR	Democrat	1993–2001		Hillary Rodham	Albert Gore Jr.
43.	**George W. Bush**	7/6/1946, New Haven, CT	Republican	2001–2009		Laura Welch	Richard Cheney
44.	**Barack H. Obama**	8/4/1961, Honolulu, HI	Democrat	2009–		Michelle Robinson	Joe Biden

** assassinated while in office*
*** resigned Aug 9, 1974*
† died while in office—nonviolently

Some Facts About the United States

STATE	CAPITAL	POPULAR NAME	AREA (SQ. MI.)	STATE BIRD	STATE FLOWER	STATE TREE	ADMITTED TO THE UNION	ORDER OF ADMISSION
Alabama	Montgomery	Cotton or Yellowhammer State; or Heart of Dixie	51,609	Yellowhammer	Camellia	Southern pine (Longleaf pine)	1819	22
Alaska	Juneau	Last Frontier	591,004	Willow ptarmigan	Forget-me-not	Sitka spruce	1959	49
Arizona	Phoenix	Grand Canyon State	114,000	Cactus wren	Saguaro (giant cactus)	Palo Verde	1912	48
Arkansas	Little Rock	The Natural State	53,187	Mockingbird	Apple blossom	Pine	1836	25
California	Sacramento	Golden State	158,706	California valley quail	Golden poppy	California redwood	1850	31
Colorado	Denver	Centennial State	104,091	Lark bunting	Rocky Mountain columbine	Blue spruce	1876	38
Connecticut	Hartford	Constitution State	5,018	Robin	Mountain laurel	White oak	1788	5
Delaware	Dover	First State	2,044	Blue hen chicken	Peach blossom	American holly	1787	1
Florida	Tallahassee	Sunshine State	58,664	Mockingbird	Orange blossom	Cabbage (sabal) palm	1845	27
Georgia	Atlanta	Empire State of the South	58,910	Brown thrasher	Cherokee rose	Live oak	1788	4
Hawaii	Honolulu	Aloha State	6,471	Nene (Hawaiian goose)	Hibiscus	Kukui	1959	50
Idaho	Boise	Gem State	83,564	Mountain bluebird	Syringa (mock orange)	Western white pine	1890	43
Illinois	Springfield	Prairie State	56,345	Cardinal	Native violet	White oak	1818	21
Indiana	Indianapolis	Hoosier State	36,185	Cardinal	Peony	Tulip tree or yellow poplar	1816	19
Iowa	Des Moines	Hawkeye State	56,275	Eastern goldfinch	Wild rose	Oak	1846	29
Kansas	Topeka	Sunflower State	82,277	Western meadowlark	Sunflower	Cottonwood	1861	34
Kentucky	Frankfort	Bluegrass State	40,409	Kentucky cardinal	Goldenrod	Kentucky coffeetree	1792	15
Louisiana	Baton Rouge	Pelican State	47,752	Pelican	Magnolia	Bald cypress	1812	18
Maine	Augusta	Pine Tree State	33,265	Chickadee	White pine cone and tassel	White pine	1820	23
Maryland	Annapolis	Old Line State	10,577	Baltimore oriole	Black-eyed Susan	White oak	1788	7
Massachusetts	Boston	Bay State	8,284	Chickadee	Mayflower	American elm	1788	6
Michigan	Lansing	Wolverine State	58,527	Robin	Apple blossom	White pine	1837	26
Minnesota	St. Paul	North Star State	84,402	Common loon	Pink and white lady's-slipper	Norway, or red, pine	1858	32
Mississippi	Jackson	Magnolia State	47,689	Mockingbird	Magnolia	Magnolia	1817	20
Missouri	Jefferson City	Show Me State	69,697	Bluebird	Hawthorn	Flowering dogwood	1821	24
Montana	Helena	Treasure State	147,046	Western meadowlark	Bitterroot	Ponderosa pine	1889	41

STATE	CAPITAL	POPULAR NAME	AREA (SQ. MI.)	STATE BIRD	STATE FLOWER	STATE TREE	ADMITTED TO THE UNION	ORDER OF ADMISSION
Nebraska	Lincoln	Cornhusker State	77,355	Western meadowlark	Goldenrod	Cottonwood	1867	37
Nevada	Carson City	Silver State	110,540	Mountain bluebird	Sagebrush	Single-leaf piñon	1864	36
New Hampshire	Concord	Granite State	9,304	Purple finch	Purple lilac	White birch	1788	9
New Jersey	Trenton	Garden State	7,787	Eastern goldfinch	Purple violet	Red oak	1787	3
New Mexico	Santa Fe	Land of Enchantment	121,593	Roadrunner	Yucca flower	Piñon, or nut pine	1912	47
New York	Albany	Empire State	49,108	Bluebird	Rose	Sugar maple	1788	11
North Carolina	Raleigh	Tar Heel State or Old North State	52,669	Cardinal	Dogwood	Pine	1789	12
North Dakota	Bismarck	Peace Garden State	70,702	Western meadowlark	Wild prairie rose	American elm	1889	39
Ohio	Columbus	Buckeye State	41,330	Cardinal	Scarlet carnation	Buckeye	1803	17
Oklahoma	Oklahoma City	Sooner State	69,956	Scissortail flycatcher	Mistletoe	Redbud	1907	46
Oregon	Salem	Beaver State	97,073	Western meadowlark	Oregon grape	Douglas fir	1859	33
Pennsylvania	Harrisburg	Keystone State	45,308	Ruffed grouse	Mountain laurel	Hemlock	1787	2
Rhode Island	Providence	Ocean State	1,212	Rhode Island Red	Violet	Red maple	1790	13
South Carolina	Columbia	Palmetto State	31,113	Carolina wren	Carolina jessamine	Palmetto	1788	8
South Dakota	Pierre	Sunshine State	77,116	Ring-necked pheasant	American pasqueflower	Black Hills spruce	1889	40
Tennessee	Nashville	Volunteer State	42,114	Mockingbird	Iris	Tulip poplar	1796	16
Texas	Austin	Lone Star State	266,807	Mockingbird	Bluebonnet	Pecan	1845	28
Utah	Salt Lake City	Beehive State	84,899	Seagull	Sego lily	Blue spruce	1896	45
Vermont	Montpelier	Green Mountain State	9,614	Hermit thrush	Red clover	Sugar maple	1791	14
Virginia	Richmond	Old Dominion	40,767	Cardinal	Dogwood	Dogwood	1788	10
Washington	Olympia	Evergreen State	68,139	Willow goldfinch	Coast rhododendron	Western hemlock	1889	42
West Virginia	Charleston	Mountain State	24,231	Cardinal	Rhododendron	Sugar maple	1863	35
Wisconsin	Madison	Badger State	56,153	Robin	Wood violet	Sugar maple	1848	30
Wyoming	Cheyenne	Equality State	97,809	Meadowlark	Indian paintbrush	Cottonwood	1890	44

State & Territory Abbreviations: United States

Alabama........AL
Alaska........AK
Arizona........AZ
Arkansas........AR
American Samoa........AS
California........CA
Colorado........CO
Connecticut........CT
Delaware........DE
District of Columbia........DC
Florida........FL
Georgia........GA
Guam........GU
Hawaii........HI
Idaho........ID
Illinois........IL
Indiana........IN
Iowa........IA
Kansas........KS
Kentucky........KY
Louisiana........LA
Maine........ME
Maryland........MD
Massachusetts........MA
Michigan........MI
Minnesota........MN
Mississippi........MS
Missouri........MO
Montana........MT
Nebraska........NE
Nevada........NV
New Hampshire........NH
New Jersey........NJ
New Mexico........NM
New York........NY
North Carolina........NC
North Dakota........ND
Ohio........OH
Oklahoma........OK
Oregon........OR
Pennsylvania........PA
Puerto Rico........PR
Rhode Island........RI
South Carolina........SC
South Dakota........SD
Tennessee........TN
Texas........TX
Utah........UT
Vermont........VT
Virginia........VA
Virgin Islands........VI
Washington........WA
West Virginia........WV
Wisconsin........WI
Wyoming........WY

State Governors/US Senators/US Supreme Court

GOVERNORS
Name (Party, State)

Robert Bentley (R, AL)
Sean Parnell (R, AK)
Jan Brewer (R, AZ)
Michael Beebe (D, AR)
Jerry Brown (D, CA)
John Hickenlooper (D, CO)
Dan Malloy (D, CT)
Jack A. Markell (D, DE)
Rick Scott (R, FL)
Nathan Deal (R, GA)
Neil Abercrombie (D, HI)
Butch Otter (R, ID)
Pat Quinn (D, IL)
Mike Pence (R, IN)
Terry Branstad (D, IA)
Sam Brownback (D, KS)
Steve Beshear (D, KY)
Bobby Jindal (R, LA)
Paul LePage (R, ME)
Martin O'Malley (D, MD)
Deval Patrick (D, MA)
Rick Snyder (R, MI)
Mark Dayton (D, MN)
Phil Bryant (R, MS)
Jay Nixon (D, MO)
Steve Bullock (D, MT)
David Heineman (R, NE)
Brian Sandoval (R, NV)
Maggie Hassan (D, NH)
Chris Christie (R, NJ)*
Susana Martinez (R, NM)
Andrew M. Cuomo (D, NY)
Pat McCrory (R, NC)
Jack Dalrymple (R, ND)
John Kasich (R, OH)
Mary Fallin (R, OK)
John Kitzhaber (D, OR)
Tom Corbett (R, PA)
Lincoln Chafee (I, RI)
Nikki Haley (R, SC)
Dennis Daugaard (R, SD)
Bill Haslam (R, TN)
Rick Perry (R, TX)
Gary R. Herbert (R, UT)
Peter Shumlin (R, VT)
Bob McDonnell (R, VA)*
Jay Inslee (D, WA)
Earl Ray Tomblin (R, WV)
Scott Walker (R, WI)
Matt Mead (D, WY)

Office holders were current as of July 2013.

*Elections take place in November 2013 for those seats marked with a *.*

SENATORS
Name (Party, State)

Richard Shelby (R, AL)
Jeff Sessions (R, AL)
Mark Begich (D, AK)
Lisa Murkowski (R, AK)
John McCain (R, AZ)
Jeff Flake (R, AZ)
John Boozman (R, AR)
Mark Pryor (D, AR)
Dianne Feinstein (D, CA)
Barbara Boxer (D, CA)
Mark Udall (D, CO)
Michael Bennet (D, CO)
Richard Blumenthal (D, CT)
Chris Murphy (D, CT)
Christopher Coons (D, DE)
Thomas R. Carper (D, DE)
Bill Nelson (D, FL)
Marco Rubio (R, FL)
Saxby Chambliss (R, GA)
Johnny Isakson (R, GA)
Mazie Hirono (D, HI)
Brian Schatz (D, HI)*
Jim Risch (R, ID)
Michael Crapo (R, ID)
Richard J. Durbin (D, IL)
Mark Kirk (R, IL)
Joe Donnelly (D, IN)
Daniel R. Coats (R, IN)
Charles E. Grassley (R, IA)
Tom Harkin (D, IA)
Jerry Moran (R, KS)
Pat Roberts (R, KS)
Mitch McConnell (R, KY)
Rand Paul (R, KY)
Mary L. Landrieu (D, LA)
David Vitter (R, LA)
Angus King (I, ME)
Susan M. Collins (R, ME)
Barbara A. Mikulski (D, MD)
Benjamin Cardin (D, MD)
Ed Markey (D, MA)*
Elizabeth Warren (D, MA)
Carl Levin (D, MI)
Debbie A. Stabenow (D, MI)
Al Franken (D, MN)
Amy Klobuchar (D, MN)
Thad Cochran (R, MS)
Roger Wicker (R, MS)
Roy Blunt (R, MO)
Claire McCaskill (D, MO)
Max Baucus (D, MT)
Jon Tester (D, MT)
Mike Johanns (R, NE)
Deb Fischer (R, NE)
Harry Reid (D, NV)
Dean Heller (R, NV)
Kelly Ayotte (R, NH)
Jeanne Shaheen (D, NH)
Jeffrey Chiesa (R, NJ)†
Robert Menendez (D, NJ)
Tom Udall (D, NM)
Martin Heinrich (D, NM)
Charles E. Schumer (D, NY)
Kirsten Gillibrand (D, NY)
Kay Hagan (D, NC)
Richard Burr (R, NC)
Heidi Heitkamp (D, ND)
John Hoeven (R, ND)
Rob Portman (R, OH)
Sherrod Brown (D, OH)
James N. Inhofe (R, OK)
Tom Coburn (R, OK)
Ron Wyden (D, OR)
Jeff Merkley (D, OR)
Pat Toomey (R, PA)
Robert P. Casey Jr (D, PA)
Jack Reed (D, RI)
Sheldon Whitehouse (D, RI)
Lindsey Graham (R, SC)
Tim Scott (R, SC)
Tim Johnson (D, SD)
John R. Thune (R, SD)
Lamar Alexander (R, TN)
Bob Corker (R, TN)
Ted Cruz (R, TX)
John Cornyn (R, TX)
Orrin G. Hatch (R, UT)
Mike Lee (R, UT)
Patrick J. Leahy (D, VT)
Bernard Sanders (I, VT)
Mark Warner (D, VA)
Tim Kaine (D, VA)
Patty Murray (D, WA)
Maria Cantwell (D, WA)
Joe Manchin III (D, WV)
Jay Rockefeller (D, WV)
Tammy Baldwin (D, WI)
Ron Johnson (R, WI)
John Barrasso (R, WY)
Michael B. Enzi (R, WY)

SUPREME COURT JUSTICES
Name (Appointed by, Year)

John G. Roberts Jr, Chief Justice (G.W. Bush, 2005)
Antonin Scalia (Reagan, 1986)
Anthony M. Kennedy (Reagan, 1988)
Clarence Thomas (G.H.W. Bush, 1991)
Ruth Bader Ginsburg (Clinton, 1993)
Stephen G. Breyer (Clinton, 1994)
Samuel A. Alito Jr (G.W. Bush, 2006)
Sonia Sotomayor (Obama, 2009)
Elena Kagan (Obama, 2010)

† Jeffrey Chiesa was appointed to serve as acting senator upon the death of Frank Lautenberg. A special election occurs October 2013 for a permanent replacement.

Some Facts About Canada

PROVINCE/TERRITORY	CAPITAL	POPULATION*	FLOWER	LAND/FRESH WATER (SQ. MI.)	TOTAL AREA
Alberta	Edmonton	3,645,257	Wild Rose	248,000/7,541	255,541
British Columbia	Victoria	4,400,057	Pacific dogwood	357,216/7,548	364,764
Manitoba	Winnipeg	1,208,268	Prairie crocus	213,729/36,387	250,116
New Brunswick	Fredericton	751,171	Purple violet	27,587/563	28,150
Newfoundland & Labrador	St. John's	514,536	Pitcher plant	144,343/12,100	156,543
Northwest Territories	Yellowknife	41,462	Mountain avens	456,791/62,943	519,734
Nova Scotia	Halifax	921,727	Mayflower	20,593/752	21,345
Nunavut	Iqaluit	31,906	Purple saxifrage	747,537/60,648	808,185
Ontario	Toronto	12,851,821	White trillium	354,341/61,256	415,599
Prince Edward Island	Charlottetown	140,204	Lady's-slipper	2,185/0	2,185
Quebec	Quebec City	7,903,001	White garden lily	527,079/68,313	595,391
Saskatchewan	Regina	1,033,381	Western red lily	228,445/22,921	251,366
Yukon Territory	Whitehorse	33,897	Fireweed	183,163/3,109	186,272

**Based on the 2011 Canadian Census*

Province & Territory Abbreviations: Canada

Alberta . . . . AB
British Columbia . . . . BC
Manitoba . . . . MB
New Brunswick . . . . NB
Newfoundland & Labrador . . . . NF
Northwest Territories . . . . NT
Nova Scotia . . . . NS
Nunavut . . . . NU
Ontario . . . . ON
Prince Edward Island . . . . PE
Quebec . . . . QC
Saskatchewan . . . . SK
Yukon Territory . . . . YT

Some Facts About Mexico

STATE	ABBREVIATION	CAPITAL	POPULATION*	AREA (SQ. MI.)
Aguascalientes	Ags.	Aguascalientes	1,184,924	2,156
Baja California	B.C.	Mexicali	3,154,174	27,655
Baja California Sur	B.C.S.	La Paz	637,065	27,979
Campeche	Camp.	Campeche	822,001	19,672
Chiapas	Chis.	Tuxtla Gutiérrez	4,793,406	28,732
Chihuahua	Chih.	Chihuahua	3,401,140	94,831
Coahuila	Coah.	Saltillo	2,748,366	58,067
Colima	Col.	Colima	650,129	2,010
Distrito Federal	D.F.	Mexico City	8,873,017	573
Durango	Dgo.	Durango	1,632,860	47,691
Guanajuato	Gto.	Guanajuato	5,485,971	11,805
Guerrero	Gro.	Chilpancingo	3,386,706	24,887
Hidalgo	Hgo.	Pachuca	2,664,969	8,058
Jalisco	Jal.	Guadalajara	7,350,355	31,152
México	Mex.	Toluca	15,174,272	8,268
Michoacán	Mich.	Morelia	4,348,485	23,202
Morelos	Mor.	Cuernavaca	1,776,727	1,917
Nayarit	Nay.	Tepic	1,084,957	10,547
Nuevo León	N.L.	Monterrey	4,643,321	25,136
Oaxaca	Oax.	Oaxaca	3,801,871	36,375
Puebla	Pue.	Puebla	5,779,007	13,126
Querétaro	Qro.	Querétaro	1,827,985	4,432
Quintana Roo	Q.R.	Chetumal	1,324,257	19,630
San Luis Potosí	S.L.P.	San Luis Potosí	2,585,942	24,417
Sinaloa	Sin.	Culiacán	2,767,552	22,582
Sonora	Son.	Hermosillo	2,662,432	70,484
Tabasco	Tab.	Villahermosa	2,238,818	9,783
Tamaulipas	Tamps.	Ciudad Victoria	3,270,268	30,734
Tlaxcala	Tlax.	Tlaxcala	1,169,825	1,555
Veracruz	Ver.	Jalapa	7,638,378	27,759
Yucatán	Yuc.	Mérida	1,953,027	14,868
Zacatecas	Zac.	Zacatecas	1,490,550	28,125

**Based on the 2010 Mexican Census*

2014 Special Months

For more information on these special months, see the listing on the first day of the month (unless specified otherwise).

January

Be Kind to Food Servers Month
Be On-Purpose Month, Natl
Book Blitz Month
Brain Teaser Month, Intl
Celebration of Life Month
Child-Centered Divorce Awareness Month, Intl
Clean Up Your Computer Month, Natl
Creativity Month, Intl
Get a Life Balanced Month
Get Organized Month
Glaucoma Awareness Month, Natl
Hot Tea Month, Natl
Mentoring Month, Natl
New Year's Resolutions Month for Businesses, Intl
Oatmeal Month
Personal Self-Defense Awareness Month, Natl
Poverty in America Awareness Month, Natl
Radon Action Month, Natl
Rising Star Month, Worldwide
Self-Help Group Awareness Month
Self-Love Month
Shape Up US Month
Skating Month, Natl
Slavery and Human Trafficking Awareness Month, Natl
Stalking Awareness Month, Natl
Teen Driving Awareness Month
Volunteer Blood Donor Month, Natl
Wayfinding Month, Intl

February

AMD/Low Vision Awareness Month
American Heart Month
Bake for Family Fun Month
Beat the Heat Month
Bird-Feeding Month, Natl
Black History Month, Natl
Boost Self-Esteem Month, Intl
Cherry Month, Natl
Condom Month, Natl
Expect Success Month, Intl
February Is Fabulous Florida Strawberry Month
"From Africa to Virginia" Month
Library Lovers' Month
Marfan Syndrome Awareness Month
Mend a Broken Heart Month, Natl
Parent Leadership Month, Natl
Pet Dental Health Month, Natl
Plant the Seeds of Greatness Month
Renaissance of the Heart Month, Worldwide
Return Shopping Carts to the Supermarket Month
Spay/Neuter Awareness Month
Spunky Old Broads Month
Teen Dating Violence Awareness and Prevention Month, Natl
Time Management Month, Natl
Wise Health Care Consumer Month
Women Inventors Month, Natl
Youth Leadership Month

March

Caffeine Awareness Month, Natl
Clean Up Your IRS Act Month, Natl
Colic Awareness Month
Colorectal Cancer Education and Awareness Month, Natl
Craft Month, Natl
Credit Education Month
Employee Spirit Month
Expanding Girls' Horizons in Science and Engineering Month
Eye Donor Month, Natl
Frozen Food Month, Natl
Humorists Are Artists Month
Ideas Month, Intl
Irish-American Heritage Month
Kidney Month, Natl
Listening Awareness Month, Intl
Malignant Hyperthermia Awareness and Training Month
Mirth Month, Intl
Multiple Sclerosis Education and Awareness Month, Natl
Music in Our Schools Month
Nutrition Month, Natl
Optimism Month
Peanut Month, Natl
Play-the-Recorder Month
Poison Prevention Awareness Month
Red Cross Month
Save Your Vision Month
Sing with Your Child Month
Social Work Month, Natl
Umbrella Month, Natl
Women's History Month, Natl
Workplace Eye Wellness Month
Youth Art Month

March–April–May

Deaf History Month (Mar 13–Apr 15)
Kite Month, Natl (Mar 29–May 3)

April

African-American Women's Fitness Month, Natl
Alcohol Awareness Month
Autism Awareness Month, Natl
Bereaved Spouses Awareness Month, Worldwide
Cancer Control Month
Car Care Month (April)
Card and Letter Writing Month, Natl
Child Abuse Prevention Month, Natl
Confederate History Month
Couple Appreciation Month
Customer Loyalty Month, Intl
Decorating Month, Natl
Defeat Diabetes Month
Distracted Driving Awareness Month
Donate Life Month, Natl
Emotional Overeating Awareness Month
Fresh Florida Tomato Month
Grange Month
Holy Humor Month
Humor Month, Natl
Informed Woman Month
Jazz Appreciation Month
Knuckles Down Month, Natl
Landscape Architecture Month, Natl
Month of the Young Child
Occupational Therapy Month, Natl
Pecan Month, Natl
Pest Management Month, Natl
Pet First Aid Awareness Month
Pharmacists' War on Diabetes
Poetry Month, Natl
Prevention of Animal Cruelty Month
Rebuilding Month, Natl
Rosacea Awareness Month
School Library Month
Sexual Assault Awareness and Prevention Month, Natl
Sexually Transmitted Diseases (STDs) Education and Awareness Month, Natl
Soyfoods Month, Natl
Straw Hat Month
Stress Awareness Month
Twit Award Month, Intl
Women's Eye Health and Safety Month
Workplace Conflict Awareness Month
World Habitat Awareness Month
Youth Sports Safety Month, Natl

May

Allergy/Asthma Awareness Month, Natl
Arthritis Awareness Month
Asian American and Pacific Islander Heritage Month
Barbecue Month, Natl
Better Hearing and Speech Month
Bike Month, Natl
Civility Awareness Month, Global
Fibromyalgia Education and Awareness Month
Foster Care Month, Natl
Gardening for Wildlife Month
Get Caught Reading Month
Gifts From the Garden Month
Good Car-Keeping Month, Natl
Haitian Heritage Month
Hamburger Month, Natl
Heal the Children Month
Healthy Vision Month
Hepatitis Awareness Month, Natl
Home Schooling Awareness Month
Huntington's Disease Awareness Month
Jewish American Heritage Month
Latino Books Month
Meditation Month, Natl
Mediterranean Diet Month, Intl
Melanoma/Skin Cancer Detection and Prevention Month
Mental Health Month, Natl
Military Appreciation Month, Natl
Motorcycle Safety Month
Moving Month, Natl
Older Americans Month
Osteoporosis Month, Natl
Photo Month, Natl
Physical Fitness and Sports Month, Natl
Preservation Month, Natl
REACT Month
Salad Month, Natl
Salsa Month, Natl
Social Security Education Month
Spiritual Literacy Month
Strike Out Strokes Month
Stroke Awareness Month, Natl
Sweet Vidalia Onion Month, Natl
Teen CEO Month
Tennis Month
Ultraviolet Awareness Month
Victorious Woman Month, Intl
Vinegar Month, Natl
Women's Health Care Month
Young Achievers/Leaders of Tomorrow Month

May–June

Prepare Tomorrow's Parents Month (May 11–June 15)

June

Accordion Awareness Month, Natl
Adopt-A-Shelter-Cat Month
African-American Music Appreciation Month
Aphasia Awareness Month, Natl
Audiobook Appreciation Month
Bathroom Reading Month, Natl
Cancer from the Sun Month
Caribbean-American Heritage Month, Natl
Cataract Awareness Month
Child Vision Awareness Month
Childhood Cancer Awareness Month, Intl
Children's Awareness Month
Dairy Alternatives Month
Effective Communications Month
Entrepreneurs "Do It Yourself" Marketing Month
Georgia Blueberry Month
GLBT Book Month, Natl
Great Outdoors Month
Iced Tea Month, Natl
June Dairy Month
June Is Perennial Gardening Month
Lesbian, Gay, Bisexual and Transgender Pride Month
Men's Health Education and Awareness Month
Men's Month, Intl
Migraine Awareness Month
Pharmacists Declare War on Alcoholism
Rebuild Your Life Month
Rivers Month, Natl
Safety Month, Natl
Skyscraper Month
Soul Food Month, Natl
Sports America Kids Month
Student Safety Month
Surf Music Month, Intl

June–July

Fireworks Safety Months (June 1–July 31)

July

Alopecia Month for Women, Intl
Bereaved Parents Awareness Month, Worldwide
Bioterrorism/Disaster Education and Awareness Month
Blondie and Deborah Harry Month, Intl
Blueberries Month, Natl
Cell Phone Courtesy Month
"Doghouse Repairs" Month, Natl
Grilling Month, Natl
Herbal/Prescription Interaction Awareness Month
Horseradish Month, Natl
Hot Dog Month, Natl
Ice Cream Month, Natl
Make a Difference to Children Month, Natl
Park and Recreation Month, Natl
Smart Irrigation Month
Women's Motorcycle Month
Zine Month, Intl

August

American Adventures Month
Black Business Month
Bystander Awareness Month
Children's Eye Health and Safety Month
Children's Vision and Learning Month
Happiness Happens Month
Immunization Awareness Month, Natl
Neurosurgery Outreach Month
Spinal Muscular Atrophy Awareness Month, Natl
Traffic Awareness Month, Natl
What Will Be Your Legacy Month

September

AKC Responsible Dog Ownership Month
Animal Remembrance Month, World
Atrial Fibrillation Awareness Month
Attention Deficit Hyperactivity Disorder Month
Baby Safety Month
Backpack Safety America Month
Be Kind to Editors and Writers Month
Childhood Cancer Awareness Month
Childhood Obesity Awareness Month, Natl
College Savings Month
Coupon Month, Natl
DNA, Genomics and Stem Cell Education and Awareness Month, Natl
Eat Chicken Month
Fall Hat Month
Gynecologic Cancer Awareness Month
Happy Cat Month
Head Lice Prevention Month, Natl
Honey Month, Natl
Hunger Action Month
Library Card Sign-Up Month
Mushroom Month, Natl
One-on-One Month
Ovarian Cancer Awareness Month, Natl
Pleasure Your Mate Month
Preparedness Month, Natl
Prostate Cancer Awareness Month, Natl
Recovery Month, Natl
Rice Month, Natl
Sea Cadet Month
September Is Healthy Aging Month
Service Dog Month, Natl
Shake Month, Natl
Shameless Promotion Month
Skin Care Awareness Month, Natl
Sports Eye Safety Month
Subliminal Communications Month
Superior Relationships Month
Update Your Resume Month
Whole Grains Month
Wilderness Month, Natl
Women's Friendship Month, Intl

September–October

Hispanic Heritage Month, Natl (Sept 15–Oct 15)

October

Adopt-a-Shelter-Dog Month
American Cheese Month
Animal Safety and Protection Month, Natl
Antidepressant Death Awareness Month
Arts and Humanities Month, Natl
Audiology Awareness Month, Natl
Bake and Decorate Month, Natl
Breast Cancer Awareness Month, Natl
Bullying Prevention Awareness Month, Natl
Car Care Month (October)
Celebrating the Bilingual Child Month
Celiac Disease Awareness Month
Chiropractic Health Month, Natl
Church Library Month
Co-op Awareness Month
Crime Prevention Month, Natl
Critical Illness Awareness Month, Natl
Cut Out Dissection Month
Cyber Security Awareness Month, Natl
Dental Hygiene Month, Natl
Depression Education and Awareness Month, Natl
Disability Employment Awareness Month, Natl
Domestic Violence Awareness Month
Down Syndrome Awareness Month, Natl
Dyslexia Awareness Month
Emotional Intelligence Awareness Month
Field Trip Month, Natl
"Gain the Inside Advantage" Month, Natl
Gay and Lesbian History Month
German-American Heritage Month
Global Diversity Awareness Month
Go Hog Wild–Eat Country Ham Month
Health Literacy Month
Home Eye Safety Month
Intergeneration Month
Kitchen and Bath Month, Natl
Liver Awareness Month, Natl
Medical Librarians Month, Natl
Menopause Month, World
Month of Freethought
Organize Your Medical Information Month
Orthodontic Health Month, Natl
Photographer Appreciation Month
Physical Therapy Month, Natl
Polish-American Heritage Month
Popcorn Poppin' Month, Natl
Positive Attitude Month
Reading Group Month, Natl
Rett Syndrome Awareness Month
Right-Brainers Rule Month
Roller Skating Month, Natl
Spina Bifida Awareness Month, Natl
Spinach Lovers Month
Squirrel Awareness and Appreciation Month
Stamp Collecting Month, Natl
Stop Bullying Month, Natl
Talk About Prescriptions Month
Vegetarian Month
Women Walking in Their Own Shoes Month
Work and Family Month, Natl
Workplace Politics Awareness Month

November

Adoption Month, Natl
AIDS Awareness Month, PPSI
Alzheimer's Disease Awareness Month, Natl
American Diabetes Month
Aviation History Month
Banana Pudding Lovers Month
Bereaved Siblings Month, Worldwide
Diabetes Month, Natl
Diabetic Eye Disease Month
Epilepsy Awareness Month, Natl
Family Caregivers Month, Natl
Georgia Pecan Month, Natl
Inspirational Role Models Month, Natl
Long-Term Care Awareness Month, Natl
Lung Cancer Awareness Month
Marrow Awareness Month, Natl
Movember
Memoir Writing Month, Natl
Native American Heritage Month, Natl
Novel Writing Month, Natl
Peanut Butter Lovers' Month
Vegan Month

December

Bingo's Birthday Month
Food Service Safety Month, Worldwide
Impaired Driving Prevention Month, Natl
Safe Toys and Gifts Month
Write a Business Plan Month, Natl

Presidental Proclamations Issued, January 1, 2012–June 30, 2013

NO.	TITLE, OBSERVANCE DATES (DATE OF SIGNING)
2012	
8773	Martin Luther King, Jr., Federal Holiday, 2012: Jan 16, 2012 (Jan 13, 2012)
8774	Religious Freedom Day, 2012: Jan 16, 2012 (Jan 13, 2012)
8775	American Heart Month, 2012: February (Jan 31, 2012)
8776	National African American History Month, 2012: February (Jan 31, 2012)
8777	National Teen Dating Violence Awareness and Prevention Month, 2012: February (Jan 31, 2012)
8778	American Red Cross Month, 2012: March (Mar 1, 2012)
8779	Irish-American Heritage Month, 2012: March (Mar 1, 2012)
8780	Women's History Month, 2012: March (Mar 1, 2012)
8781	Read Across America Day, 2012: Mar 2, 2012 (Mar 2, 2012)
8782	National Consumer Protection Week, 2012: Mar 4–10, 2012 (Mar 5, 2012)
8783	To Implement the United States–Korea Free Trade Agreement (Mar 6, 2012)
8784	National Poison Prevention Week, 2012: Mar 18–24, 2012 (Mar 16, 2012)
8785	National Day of Honor: Mar 19, 2012 (Mar 19, 2012)
8786	Cesar Chavez Day, 2012: Mar 31, 2012 (Mar 23, 2012)
8787	Greek Independence Day: A National Day of Celebration of Greek and American Democracy, 2012: Mar 25, 2012 (Mar 23, 2012)
8788	To Modify Duty-Free Treatment Under the Generalized System of Preferences and for Other Purposes (Mar 26, 2012)
8789	Vietnam Veterans Day: Mar 29, 2012 (Mar 29, 2012)
8790	National Cancer Control Month, 2012: April (Apr 2, 2012)
8791	National Child Abuse Prevention Month, 2012: April (Apr 2, 2012)
8792	National Donate Life Month, 2012: April (Apr 2, 2012)
8793	National Financial Capability Month, 2012: April (Apr 2, 2012)
8794	National Sexual Assault Awareness and Prevention Month, 2012: April (Apr 2, 2012)
8795	World Autism Awareness Day, 2012: Apr 2, 2012 (Apr 2, 2012)
8796	Education and Sharing Day, U.S.A., 2012: Apr 3, 2012 (Apr 3, 2012)
8797	National Volunteer Week, 2012: Apr 15–21, 2012 (Apr 9, 2012)
8798	Pan American Day and Pan American Week, 2012: Apr 14 and Apr 8–14, 2012 (Apr 9, 2012)
8799	National Former Prisoner of War Recognition Day, 2012: Apr 9, 2012 (Apr 9, 2012)
8800	National Equal Pay Day, 2012: Apr 17, 2012 (Apr 17, 2012)
8801	National Park Week, 2012: Apr 21–29, 2012 (Apr 20, 2012)
8802	Earth Day, 2012: Apr 22, 2012 (Apr 20, 2012)
8803	Establishment of the Fort Ord National Monument (Apr 20, 2012)
8804	National Crime Victims' Rights Week, 2012: Apr 22–28, 2012 (Apr 23, 2012)
8805	Workers Memorial Day, 2012: Apr 28, 2012 (Apr 27, 2012)
8806	Asian American and Pacific Islander Heritage Month, 2012: May (May 1, 2012)
8807	National Building Safety Month, 2012: May (May 1, 2012)
8808	National Physical Fitness and Sports Month, 2012: May (May 1, 2012)
8809	Older Americans Month, 2012: May (May 1, 2012)
8810	Law Day, U.S.A., 2012: May 1, 2012 (May 1, 2012)
8811	Loyalty Day, 2012: May 1, 2012 (May 1, 2012)
8812	National Day of Prayer, 2012: May 3, 2012 (May 1, 2012)
8813	Jewish American Heritage Month, 2012: May (May 2, 2012)
8814	National Foster Care Month, 2012: May (May 2, 2012)
8815	National Charter Schools Week, 2012: May 6–12, 2012 (May 7, 2012)
8816	Military Spouse Appreciation Day, 2012: May 11, 2012 (May 11, 2012)
8817	Mother's Day, 2012: May 13, 2012 (May 11, 2012)
8818	To Implement the United States–Colombia Trade Promotion Agreement and for Other Purposes (May 14, 2012)
8819	National Defense Transportation Day and National Transportation Week, 2012: May 18 and May 13–19, 2012 (May 14, 2012)
8820	National Women's Health Week, 2012: May 13–19, 2012 (May 14, 2012)
8821	Peace Officers Memorial Day and Police Week, 2012: May 15 and May 13–19, 2012 (May 14, 2012)
8822	150th Anniversary of the United States Department of Agriculture (May 14, 2012)
8823	Armed Forces Day, 2012: May 19, 2012 (May 18, 2012)
8824	Emergency Medical Services Week, 2012: May 20–26, 2012 (May 21, 2012)
8825	National Safe Boating Week, 2012: May 19–25, 2012 (May 21, 2012)
8826	National Small Business Week, 2012: May 20–26, 2012 (May 21, 2012)
8827	World Trade Week, 2012: May 20–26, 2012 (May 21, 2012)
8828	National Maritime Day, 2012: May 22, 2012 (May 22, 2012)
8829	Commemoration of the 50th Anniversary of the Vietnam War (May 25, 2012)

NO.	TITLE, OBSERVANCE DATES (DATE OF SIGNING)
8830	National Hurricane Preparedness Week, 2012: May 27–June 2, 2012 (May 25, 2012)
8831	Prayer for Peace, Memorial Day, 2012: May 28, 2012 (May 25, 2012)
8832	African-American Music Appreciation Month, 2012: June (June 1, 2012)
8833	Great Outdoors Month, 2012: June (June 1, 2012)
8834	Lesbian, Gay, Bisexual and Transgender Pride Month, 2012: June (June 1, 2012)
8835	National Caribbean-American Heritage Month, 2012: June (June 1, 2012)
8836	National Oceans Month, 2012: June (June 1, 2012)
8837	Flag Day and National Flag Week, 2012: June 14 and June 10–16, 2012 (June 11, 2012)
8838	World Elder Abuse Awareness Day, 2012: June 15, 2012 (June 14, 2012)
8839	Father's Day, 2012: June 17, 2012 (June 15, 2012)
8840	To Modify Duty-Free Treatment Under the Generalized System of Preferences, and for Other Purposes (June 29, 2012)
8841	Captive Nations Week, 2012: July 15–21, 2012 (July 16, 2012)
8842	Honoring the Victims of the Tragedy in Aurora, Colorado (July 20, 2012)
8843	Anniversary of the Americans with Disabilities Act, 2012: July 26, 2012 (July 26, 2012)
8844	National Korean War Veterans Armistice Day, 2012: July 27, 2012 (July 27, 2012)
8845	World Hepatitis Day, 2012: July 28, 2018 (July 27, 2012)
8846	Honoring the Victims of the Tragedy in Oak Creek, Wisconsin (Aug 6, 2012)
8847	National Health Center Week, 2012: Aug 5–11, 2012 (Aug 6, 2012)
8848	Women's Equality Day, 2012: Aug 29, 2012 (Aug 24, 2012)
8849	Death of Neil A. Armstrong (Aug 27, 2012)
8850	National Alcohol and Drug Addiction Recovery Month, 2012: September (Aug 31, 2012)
8851	National Childhood Cancer Awareness Month, 2012: September (Aug 31, 2012)
8852	National Childhood Obesity Awareness Month, 2012: September (Aug 31, 2012)
8853	National Ovarian Cancer Awareness Month, 2012: September (Aug 31, 2012)
8854	National Preparedness Month, 2012: September (Aug 31, 2012)
8855	National Prostate Cancer Awareness Month, 2012: September (Aug 31, 2012)
8856	National Wilderness Month, 2012: September (Aug 31, 2012)
8857	Labor Day, 2012: Sept 3, 2012 (Aug 31, 2012)
8858	National Grandparents Day, 2012: Sept 9, 2012 (Sept 7, 2012)
8859	National Days of Prayer and Remembrance, 2012: Sept 7–9, 2012 (Sept 7, 2012)
8860	Patriot Day and National Day of Service and Remembrance, 2012: Sept 11, 2012 (Sept 10, 2012)
8861	Honoring the Victims of the Attack in Benghazi, Libya (Sept 12, 2012)
8862	Constitution Day and Citizenship Day, Constitution Week, 2012: Sept 17, 2012 and Sept 17–23, 2012 (Sept 13, 2012)
8863	National Hispanic Heritage Month, 2012: Sept 15–Oct 15, 2012 (Sept 14, 2012)
8864	National Employer Support of the Guard and Reserve Week, 2012: Sept 16–22, 2012 (Sept 14, 2012)
8865	National Farm Safety and Health Week, 2012: Sept 16–22, 2012 (Sept 14, 2012)
8866	National Hispanic-Serving Institutions Week, 2012 : Sept 16–22, 2012 (Sept 14, 2012)
8867	National POW/MIA Recognition Day, 2012: Sept 21, 2012 (Sept 20, 2012)
8868	Establishment of the Chimney Rock National Monument (Sept 21, 2012)
8869	National Historically Black Colleges and Universities Week, 2012: Sept 23–29, 2012 (Sept 21, 2012)
8870	National Hunting and Fishing Day, 2012: Sept 22, 2012 (Sept 21, 2012)
8871	National Public Lands Day, 2012: Sept 29, 2012 (Sept 28, 2012)
8872	Gold Star Mother's and Family's Day, 2012: Sept 30, 2012 (Sept 28, 2012)
8873	National Arts and Humanities Month, 2012: October (Oct 1, 2012)
8874	National Breast Cancer Awareness Month, 2012: October (Oct 1, 2012)
8875	National Cybersecurity Awareness Month, 2012: October (Oct 1, 2012)
8876	National Disability Employment Awareness Month, 2012: October (Oct 1, 2012)
8877	National Domestic Violence Awareness Month, 2012: October (Oct 1, 2012)
8878	National Energy Action Month, 2012: October (Oct 1, 2012)
8879	National Substance Abuse Prevention Month, 2012: October (Oct 1, 2012)
8880	Child Health Day, 2012: Oct 1, 2012 (Oct 1, 2012)
8881	Fire Prevention Week, 2012: Oct 7–13, 2012 (Oct 5, 2012)

NO.	TITLE, OBSERVANCE DATES (DATE OF SIGNING)
8882	Columbus Day, 2012: Oct 8, 2012 (Oct 5, 2012)
8883	German-American Day, 2012: Oct 6, 2012 (Oct 5, 2012)
8884	Establishment of the Cesar E. Chavez National Monument (Oct 8, 2012)
8885	Leif Erikson Day, 2012: Oct 9, 2012 (Oct 9, 2012)
8886	50th Anniversary of the Office of the United States Trade Representative: Oct 11, 2012 (Oct 9, 2012)
8887	General Pulaski Memorial Day, 2012: Oct 11, 2012 (Oct 11, 2012)
8888	National School Lunch Week, 2012: Oct 14–20, 2012 (Oct 12, 2012)
8889	Blind Americans Equality Day, 2012: Oct 15, 2012 (Oct 15, 2012)
8890	Death of Arlen Specter (Oct 15, 2012)
8891	National Character Counts Week, 2012: Oct 21–27, 2012 (Oct 19, 2012)
8892	National Forest Products Week, 2012: Oct 21–27, 2012 (Oct 19, 2012)
8893	United Nations Day, 2012: Oct 24, 2012 (Oct 24, 2012)
8894	Implementation of the United States–Panama Trade Promotion Agreement (Oct 29, 2012)
8895	Military Family Month, 2012: November (Nov 1, 2012)
8896	National Adoption Month, 2012: November (Nov 1, 2012)
8897	National Alzheimer's Disease Awareness Month, 2012: November (Nov 1, 2012)
8898	National Diabetes Month, 2012: November (Nov 1, 2012)
8899	National Entrepreneurship Month, 2012: November (Nov 1, 2012)
8900	National Family Caregivers Month, 2012: November (Nov 1, 2012)
8901	National Native American Heritage Month, 2012: November (Nov 1, 2012)
8902	Veterans Day, 2012: Nov 11, 2012 (Nov 7, 2012)
8903	World Freedom Day, 2012: Nov 9, 2012 (Nov 9, 2012)
8904	American Education Week, 2012: Nov 11–17, 2012 (Nov 9, 2012)
8905	America Recycles Day, 2012: Nov 15, 2012 (Nov 15, 2012)
8906	National Family Week, 2012: Nov 18–24, 2012 (Nov 16, 2012)
8907	National Child's Day, 2012: Nov 20, 2012 (Nov 20, 2012)
8908	Thanksgiving Day, 2012: Nov 22, 2012 (Nov 20, 2012)
8909	World AIDS Day, 2012: Dec 1, 2012 (Nov 29, 2012)
8910	Critical Infrastructure Protection and Resilience Month, 2012: December (Nov 30, 2012)
8911	National Impaired Driving Prevention Month, 2012: December (Nov 30, 2012)
8912	Minority Enterprise Development Week, 2012: Dec 2–8, 2012 (Nov 30, 2012)
8913	International Day of Persons With Disabilities, 2012: Dec 3, 2012 (Dec 3, 2012)
8914	National Pearl Harbor Remembrance Day, 2012: Dec 7, 2012 (Dec 6, 2012)
8915	Human Rights Day and Human Rights Week, 2012: Dec 10, 2012 and Dec 10–17, 2012 (Dec 10, 2012)
8916	Bill of Rights Day, 2012: Dec 15, 2012 (Dec 14, 2012)
8917	Honoring the Victims of the Tragedy in Newtown, Connecticut (Dec 14, 2012)
8918	Wright Brothers Day, 2012: Dec 17, 2012 (Dec 17, 2012)
8919	Death of Senator Daniel K. Inouye, President Pro Tempore of the Senate (Dec 18, 2012)
8920	To Extend Nondiscriminatory Treatment (Normal Trade Relations Treatment) to the Products of the Russian Federation and the Republic of Moldova (Dec 20, 2012)
8921	To Take Certain Actions Under the African Growth and Opportunity Act and for Other Purposes (Dec 20, 2012)
8922	National Mentoring Month, 2013: January (Dec 31, 2012)
8923	150th Anniversary of the Emancipation Proclamation: Jan 1, 2013 (Dec 31, 2012)
8924	National Slavery and Human Trafficking Prevention Month, 2013: January (Dec 31, 2012)
8925	National Stalking Awareness Month, 2013: January (Dec 31, 2012)

2013

NO.	TITLE, OBSERVANCE DATES (DATE OF SIGNING)
8926	Religious Freedom Day, 2013: Jan 16, 2013 (Jan 16, 2013)
8927	Martin Luther King, Jr., Federal Holiday, 2013: Jan 21, 2013 (Jan 18, 2013)
8928	National Day of Hope and Resolve, 2013: Jan 21, 2013 (Jan 21, 2013)
8929	American Heart Month, 2013: February (Jan 31, 2013)
8930	National African American History Month, 2013: February (Jan 31, 2013)
8931	National Teen Dating Violence Awareness and Prevention Month, 2013: February (Jan 31, 2013)
8932	100th Anniversary of the Birth of Rosa Parks: Feb 4, 2013 (Feb 1, 2013)
8933	American Red Cross Month, 2013: March (Feb 28, 2013)
8934	Irish-American Heritage Month, 2013: March (Feb 28, 2013)
8935	Women's History Month, 2013: March (Feb 28, 2013)
8936	Read Across America Day, 2013: Mar 2, 2013 (Feb 28, 2013)
8937	National Consumer Protection Week, 2013: Mar 3–9, 2013 (Mar 1, 2013)
8938	10th Anniversary of the Department of Homeland Security: Mar 1, 2013 (Mar 1, 2013)
8939	100th Anniversary of the Department of Labor: Mar 4, 2013 (Mar 1, 2013)
8940	National Poison Prevention Week, 2013: Mar 17–23, 2013 (Mar 15, 2013)
8941	Education and Sharing Day, U.S.A., 2013: Mar 22, 2013 (Mar 21, 2013)
8942	Greek Independence Day: A National Day of Celebration of Greek and American Democracy: Mar 25, 2013 (Mar 22, 2013)
8943	Establishment of the Harriet Tubman Underground Railroad National Monument (Mar 25, 2013)
8944	Establishment of the First State National Monument (Mar 25, 2013)
8945	Establishment of the Charles Young Buffalo Soldiers National Monument (Mar 25, 2013)
8946	Establishment of the Rio Grande del Norte National Monument (Mar 25, 2013)
8947	Establishment of the San Juan Islands National Monument (Mar 25, 2013)
8948	National Cancer Control Month, 2013: April (Mar 29, 2013)
8949	National Child Abuse Prevention Month, 2013: April (Mar 29, 2013)
8950	National Donate Life Month, 2013: April (Mar 29, 2013)
8951	National Financial Capability Month, 2013: April (Mar 29, 2013)
8952	National Sexual Assault Awareness and Prevention Month, 2013: April (Mar 29, 2013)
8953	Cesar Chavez Day, 2013: Mar 31, 2012 (Mar 29, 2013)
8954	World Autism Awareness Day, 2013: Apr 2, 2013 (Apr 1, 2013)
8955	National Equal Pay Day, 2013: Apr 9, 2013 (Apr 8, 2013)
8956	National Former Prisoner of War Recognition Day, 2013: Apr 9, 2013 (Apr 8, 2013)
8957	Pan American Day and Pan American Week, 2013: Apr 14 and Apr 14–20, 2013 (Apr 12, 2013)
8958	Honoring the Victims of the Tragedy in Boston, Massachusetts (Apr 16, 2013)
8959	National Crime Victims' Rights Week, 2013: Apr 21–27, 2013 (Apr 19, 2013)
8960	National Volunteer Week, 2013: Apr 21–27, 2013 (Apr 19, 2013)
8961	National Park Week, 2013: Apr 20–28, 2013 (Apr 19, 2013)
8962	Earth Day, 2013: Apr 22, 2013 (Apr 19, 2013)
8963	Honoring the Victims of the Explosion in West, Texas (Apr 24, 2013)
8964	Workers Memorial Day, 2013: Apr 28, 2013 (Apr 26, 2013)
8965	Asian American and Pacific Islander Heritage Month, 2013: May (Apr 30, 2013)
8966	Jewish American Heritage Month, 2013: May (Apr 30, 2013)
8967	National Building Safety Month, 2013: May (Apr 30, 2013)
8968	National Foster Care Month, 2013: May (Apr 30, 2013)
8969	National Mental Health Awareness Month, 2013: May (Apr 30, 2013)
8970	National Physical Fitness and Sports Month, 2013: May (Apr 30, 2013)
8971	Older Americans Month, 2013: May (Apr 30, 2013)
8972	Law Day, 2013: May 1, 2013 (Apr 30, 2013)
8973	Loyalty Day, 2013: May 1, 2013 (Apr 30, 2013)
8974	National Day of Prayer, 2013: May 2, 2013 (May 1, 2013)
8975	National Charter Schools Week, 2013: May 5–11, 2013 (May 3, 2013)
8976	Military Spouse Appreciation Day, 2013: May 10, 2013 (May 9, 2013)
8977	National Defense Transportation Day and National Transportation Week, 2013: May 17, 2013 and May 12–18, 2013 (May 10, 2013)
8978	National Women's Health Week, 2013: May 12–18, 2013 (May 10, 2013)
8979	Peace Officers Memorial Day and Police Week, 2013: May 15, 2013 and May 12–18, 2013 (May 10, 2013)
8980	Mother's Day, 2013: May 12, 2013 (May 10, 2013)
8981	National Safe Boating Week, 2013: May 18–24, 2013 (May 17, 2013)
8982	Emergency Medical Services Week, 2013: May 19–25, 2013 (May 17, 2013)
8983	World Trade Week, 2013: May 19–25, 2013 (May 17, 2013)
8984	Armed Forces Day, 2013: May 18, 2013 (May 17, 2013)
8985	National Maritime Day, 2013: May 22, 2013 (May 21, 2013)
8986	National Hurricane Preparedness Week, 2013: May 26–June 1, 2013 (May 24, 2013)
8987	Memorial Day, Prayer for Peace: May 27, 2013 (May 24, 2013)
8988	Great Outdoors Month, 2013: June (May 31, 2013)
8989	Lesbian, Gay, Bisexual and Transgender Pride Month, 2013: June (May 31, 2013)
8990	National Caribbean-American Heritage Month, 2013: June (May 31, 2013)
8991	National Oceans Month, 2013: June (May 31, 2013)
8992	African-American Music Appreciation Month, 2013: June (May 31, 2013)
8993	Flag Day and National Flag Week, 2013: June 14, 2013 and June 9–15, 2013 (June 7, 2013)
8994	National Small Business Week, 2013: June 16–22, 2013 (June 14, 2013)
8995	World Elder Abuse Awareness Day, 2013: June 15, 2013 (June 14, 2013)
8996	Father's Day, 2013: June 16, 2013 (June 14, 2013)
8997	To Modify Duty-Free Treatment Under the Generalized System of Preferences and for Other Purposes (June 27, 2013)

Major Awards Presented in 2012–2013

AWARDS FOR STAGE, FILM AND TELEVISON

TONY AWARDS

67th Annual, for 2012–2013 Achievement

Play: *Vanya and Sonia and Masha and Spike*
Musical: *Kinky Boots*
Book of a Musical: Dennis Kelly, *Matilda the Musical*
Original Musical Score: Cyndi Lauper, *Kinky Boots*
Revival of a Play: *Who's Afraid of Virginia Woolf?*
Revival of a Musical: *Pippin*
Director of a Play: Pam MacKinnon, *Who's Afraid of Virginia Woolf?*
Director of a Musical: Diane Paulus, *Pippin*
Leading Actor in a Play: Tracy Letts, *Who's Afraid of Virginia Woolf?*
Leading Actress in a Play: Cicely Tyson, *The Trip to Bountiful*
Leading Actor in a Musical: Billy Porter, *Kinky Boots*
Leading Actress in a Musical: Patina Miller, *Pippin*
Featured Actor in a Play: Courtney B. Vance, *Lucky Guy*
Featured Actress in a Play: Judith Light, *The Assembled Parties*
Featured Actor in a Musical: Gabriel Ebert, *Matilda the Musical*
Featured Actress in a Musical: Andrea Martin, *Pippin*
Scenic Design of a Play: John Lee Beatty, *The Nance*
Scenic Design of a Musical: Rob Howell, *Matilda the Musical*
Costume Design of a Play: Ann Roth, *The Nance*
Costume Design of a Musical: William Ivey Long, *Rodgers & Hammerstein's Cinderella*
Lighting Design of a Play: Jules Fisher and Peggy Eisenhauer, *Lucky Guy*
Lighting Design of a Musical: Hugh Vanstone, *Matilda the Musical*
Sound Design of a Play: Leon Rothenberg, *The Nance*
Sound Design of a Musical: John Shivers, *Kinky Boots*
Choreography: Jerry Mitchell, *Kinky Boots*
Orchestrations: Stephen Oremus, *Kinky Boots*

2013 ACADEMY AWARDS

85th Annual, for 2012 Achievement

Picture: *Argo*
Director: Ang Lee, *Life of Pi*
Actor: Daniel Day-Lewis, *Lincoln*
Actress: Jennifer Lawrence, *Silver Linings Playbook*
Supporting Actor: Christoph Waltz, *Django Unchained*
Supporting Actress: Anne Hathaway, *Les Misérables*
Original Screenplay: Quentin Tarantino, *Django Unchained*
Adapted Screenplay: Chris Terrio, *Argo*
Foreign Language Film: *Amour* (Austria)
Animated Feature: *Brave*
Animated Short Film: "Paperman"
Live Action Short Film: "Curfew"
Documentary Feature: *Searching for Sugar Man*
Documentary Short Subject: "Inocente"
Film Editing: *Argo*
Production Design: Rick Carter and Jim Erickson, *Lincoln*
Costume Design: Jacqueline Durran, *Anna Karenina*
Cinematography: Claudio Miranda, *Life of Pi*
Visual Effects: Bill Westenhofer, *Life of Pi*
Makeup: Lisa Westcott and Julie Dartnell, *Les Misérables*
Sound Mixing: Andy Nelson, Mark Paterson and Simon Hayes, *Les Misérables*
Sound Editing: tie: Per Hallberg and Karen Baker Landers, *Skyfall*, and Paul N.J. Ottosson, *Zero Dark Thirty*
Original Score: Mychael Danna, *Life of Pi*
Original Song: Adele Adkins and Paul Epworth, "Skyfall" from *Skyfall*

2013 SUNDANCE FILM FESTIVAL AWARDS

32nd Annual

Dramatic Grand Jury Prize: *Fruitvale* (retitled *Fruitvale Station*)
Documentary Grand Jury Prize: *Blood Brother*
Dramatic Audience Award: *Fruitvale* (retitled *Fruitvale Station*)
Documentary Audience Award: *Blood Brother*
World Cinema Dramatic Jury Prize: *Jiseul*
World Cinema Documentary Jury Prize: *A River Changes Course*
World Cinema Audience Award, Dramatic: *Metro Manila*
World Cinema Audience Award, Documentary: *The Square*
Directing Award, Dramatic: Jill Soloway, *Afternoon Delight*
Directing Award, Documentary: Zachary Heinzerling, *Cutie and the Boxer*
World Cinema Directing Award, Dramatic: Sebastián Silva, *Crystal Fairy*
World Cinema Directing Award, Documentary: Tinatin Gurchiani, *The Machine Which Makes Everything Disappear*
Cinematography Award, Dramatic: David Lowery, *Ain't Them Bodies Saints*, and Andrew Dosunmu, *Mother of George*
Cinematography Award, Documentary: Richard Rowley, *Dirty Wars: The World Is a Battlefield*
World Cinematography Award, Dramatic: Jacek Borcuch, *Lasting*
World Cinematography Award, Documentary: Marc Silver, *Who Is Dayani Cristal?*
Editing Award, Documentary: Dawn Porter, *Gideon's Army*
World Cinema Editing Award, Documentary: Nick Ryan, *The Summit*
Waldo Salt Screenwriting Award: Lake Bell, *In a World . . .*
World Cinema Screenwriting Award: Barmak Akram, *Wajma (An Afghan Love Story)*
Best of NEXT Audience Award: *This Is Martin Bonner*
Alfred P. Sloan Feature Film Prize: *Computer Chess*
Dramatic Special Jury Award for Sound Design: Shane Carruth and Johnny Marshall, *Upstream Color*
Dramatic Special Jury Award for Acting: Miles Teller and Shailene Woodley, *The Spectacular Now*
World Cinema Dramatic Special Jury Award: *Circles*
World Cinema Documentary Special Jury Award for Punk Spirit: *Pussy Riot—A Punk Prayer*
Short Film Grand Jury Prize: *The Whistle*
Short Film Jury Award: US Fiction: *Whiplash*
Short Film Jury Award: International Fiction: *The Date*
Short Film Jury Award: Nonfiction: *Skinningrove*
Short Film Jury Award: Animation: *Irish Folk Furniture*
Short Film Special Jury Award for Acting: Joel Nagle, *Palimpsest*
Short Film Special Jury Award: Kahlil Joseph, *Until the Quiet Comes*
Short Film Audience Award: *Catnip: Egress to Oblivion?*

2013 CANNES FILM FESTIVAL

66th Annual

Palme d'Or (Golden Palm): *La Vie d'Adele—Chapitre 1 & 2 (Blue Is the Warmest Colour)*
Grand Prix: *Inside Llewyn Davis*
Jury Prize: *Soshite Chichi Ni Naru ("Like Father, Like Son")*
Best Actress: Bérénice Bejo, *Le Passé ("The Past")*
Best Actor: Bruce Dern, *Nebraska*
Best Director: Amat Escalante, *Heli*
Best Screenplay: Jia Zhangke, *Tian Zhu Ding (A Touch of Sin)*
Best Short Film: Moon Byoung-Gon, *Safe*
Camera d'Or (Best First-Time Director): Anthony Chen, *Ilo Ilo*

2013 GOLDEN GLOBE AWARDS
70th Annual, for 2012 Achievement

MOVIES

Drama: *Argo*
Musical or Comedy: *Les Misérables*
Director: Ben Affleck, *Argo*
Actor, Drama: Daniel Day-Lewis, *Lincoln*
Actress, Drama: Jessica Chastain, *Zero Dark Thirty*
Actor, Musical or Comedy: Hugh Jackman, *Les Misérables*
Actress, Musical or Comedy: Jennifer Lawrence, *Silver Linings Playbook*
Supporting Actor: Christoph Waltz, *Django Unchained*
Supporting Actress: Anne Hathaway, *Les Misérables*
Screenplay: Quentin Tarantino, *Django Unchained*
Animated Film: *Brave*
Foreign Language Film: *Amour,* Austria
Original Score: Mychael Danna, *Life of Pi*
Original Song: Adele, Paul Epworth, "Skyfall," *Skyfall*

TELEVISION

Series, Drama: "Homeland"
Series, Musical or Comedy: "Girls"
Miniseries or TV Movie: *Game Change*
Actor, Series, Drama: Damian Lewis, "Homeland"
Actress, Series, Drama: Claire Danes, "Homeland"
Actor, Series, Musical or Comedy: Don Cheadle, "House of Lies"
Actress, Series, Musical or Comedy: Lena Dunham, "Girls"
Actor, Miniseries or TV Movie: Kevin Costner, *Hatfields & McCoys*
Actress, Miniseries or TV Movie: Julianne Moore, *Game Change*
Actor, Supporting Role: Ed Harris, *Game Change*
Actress, Supporting Role: Maggie Smith, "Downton Abbey: Season 2"

2012 PRIME TIME EMMY AWARDS
Major Categories—64th Annual

Drama: "Homeland," Showtime
Comedy: "Modern Family," ABC
Miniseries: *Game Change,* HBO
Variety, Music or Comedy Series: "The Daily Show with Jon Stewart," Comedy Central
Variety, Music or Comedy Special: "The Kennedy Center Honors," CBS
Children's Program: "Wizards of Waverly Place," Disney Channel
Children's Nonfiction Program: "Sesame Street: Growing Hope Against Hunger," PBS
Animated Program (One Hour or More): "The Penguins of Madagascar: The Return of the Revenge of Dr. Blowhole," Nickelodeon
Animated Program (Less Than One Hour): "Regular Show: Eggscellent," Cartoon Network
Reality Program: "Undercover Boss," CBS
Reality/Competition Program: "The Amazing Race," CBS
Nonfiction Series: "Frozen Planet," Discovery Channel
Nonfiction Special: "George Harrison: Living in the Material World," HBO
Special Class Program: *65th Annual Tony Awards,* CBS
Lead Actress in a Drama Series: Claire Danes, "Homeland," Showtime
Lead Actor in a Drama Series: Damian Lewis, "Homeland," Showtime
Lead Actress in a Comedy Series: Julia Louis-Dreyfus, "Veep," HBO
Lead Actor in a Comedy Series: Jon Cryer, "Two and a Half Men," CBS
Lead Actress in a Miniseries or TV Movie: Julianne Moore, *Game Change,* HBO
Lead Actor in a Miniseries or TV Movie: Kevin Costner, *Hatfields & McCoys,* History
Supporting Actress in a Drama Series: Maggie Smith, "Downton Abbey," PBS
Supporting Actor in a Drama Series: Aaron Paul, "Breaking Bad," AMC
Supporting Actress in a Comedy Series: Julie Bowen, "Modern Family," ABC
Supporting Actor in a Comedy Series: Eric Stonestreet, "Modern Family," ABC
Supporting Actress in a Miniseries or TV Movie: Jessica Lange, *American Horror Story,* FX Networks
Supporting Actor in a Miniseries or TV Movie: Tom Berenger, *Hatfields & McCoys,* History
Guest Actor in a Drama Series: Jeremy Davies, "Justified," FX Networks
Guest Actress in a Drama Series: Martha Plimpton, "The Good Wife," CBS
Guest Actor in a Comedy Series: Jimmy Fallon, "Saturday Night Live," NBC
Guest Actress in a Comedy Series: Kathy Bates, "Two and a Half Men," CBS
Voice-over Performance: Maurice Lamarche, "Futurama: The Silence of the Clamps," Comedy Central
Host for a Reality or Reality/Competition Program: Tom Bergeron, "Dancing with the Stars," ABC
Drama Series Directing: Tim Van Patten, "Boardwalk Empire: To the Lost," HBO
Comedy Series Directing: Steven Levitan, "Modern Family: Baby on Board," ABC
Variety, Music or Comedy Series Directing: Don Roy King, "Saturday Night Live," NBC
Variety, Music or Comedy Special Directing: Glenn Weiss, *65th Annual Tony Awards,* CBS
Miniseries, TV Movie or Dramatic Special Directing: Jay Roach, *Game Change,* HBO
Nonfiction Directing: Martin Scorsese, "George Harrison: Living in the Material World," HBO
Drama Series Writing: Alex Gansa, Howard Gordon and Gideon Raff, "Homeland: Pilot," Showtime
Comedy Series Writing: Louis C.K., "Louie: Pregnant," FX Networks
Variety, Music or Comedy Series Writing: Steve Bodow, Jon Stewart et al, "The Daily Show with Jon Stewart," Comedy Central
Variety, Music or Comedy Special Writing: Louis C.K., "Louis C.K. Live at the Beacon Theatre," FX Networks
Miniseries, TV Movie or Dramatic Special Writing: Danny Strong, *Game Change,* HBO
Nonfiction Writing: Geoffrey C. Ward, "Prohibition," PBS

2013 DAYTIME EMMY AWARDS
40th Annual

Drama: "Days of Our Lives," NBC
Lead Actress in a Drama Series: Heather Tom, "The Bold and the Beautiful," CBS
Lead Actor in a Drama Series: Doug Davidson, "The Young and the Restless," CBS
Supporting Actress in a Drama Series: Julie Marie Berman, "General Hospital," ABC

Supporting Actor in a Drama Series: tie: Scott Clifton, "The Bold and the Beautiful," CBS, and Billy Miller, "The Young and the Restless," CBS
Younger Actress in a Drama Series: Kristen Alderson, "General Hospital," ABC
Younger Actor in a Drama Series: Chandler Massey, "Days of Our Lives," NBC
Drama Series Writing Team: "The Bold and the Beautiful," CBS
Drama Series Directing Team: "The Bold and the Beautiful," CBS
Preschool Children's Series: "Sesame Street," PBS
Preschool Animated Program: "Bubble Guppies," Nickelodeon
Children's Series: "R.L. Stine's The Haunting Hour: The Series," HUB Network
Performer in a Children's Series: Kevin Clash, "Sesame Street," PBS
Children's Series Writing Team: "Sesame Street," PBS
Children's Series Directing Team: "Sesame Street," PBS
Children's Animated Program: "Kung Fu Panda: Legends of Awesomeness," Nickelodeon
Performer in an Animated Program: David Tennant, "Star Wars: The Clone Wars," Cartoon Network
Special Class Animated Program: "Star Wars: The Clone Wars," Cartoon Network
Special Class Series: "Made," MTV
Special Class Special: "Guy's Family Reunion," Food Network
Special Class Writing Team: "The Ellen DeGeneres Show," syndicated
Special Class Directing: "Disney Parks Christmas Day Parade," ABC
Morning Program: "CBS Sunday Morning," CBS
Talk Show/Entertainment: "The Ellen DeGeneres Show," syndicated
Talk Show/Informative: "The Dr. Oz Show," syndicated
Talk Show Host: Ricki Lake, "The Ricki Lake Show," syndicated
Talk Show/Morning Program Directing: tie: "Today Show," NBC, and "The Ellen DeGeneres Show," syndicated
Game Show: "The Price Is Right," CBS
Game Show Host: Ben Bailey, "Cash Cab"
Legal/Courtroom Program: "Judge Judy," syndicated
Lifestyle Program: "The Martha Stewart Show," Hallmark
Lifestyle/Travel Program Host: Leeza Gibbons, "My Generation," PBS
Culinary Program: tie: "Best Thing I Ever Made," Food Network, and "Trisha's Southern Kitchen," Food Network
Culinary Program Host: Lidia Bastianich, "Lidia's Italy," PBS
Travel Program: "Jack Hanna's Into the Wild," syndicated
Lifestyle/Culinary/Travel Program Directing: "Joseph Rosendo's Travelscope," PBS
Lifetime Achievement Awards: Monty Hall and Bob Stewart

AWARDS FOR ARTS, HUMANITIES AND JOURNALISM

NOBEL PRIZES

Highly prestigious international awards given yearly since 1901. Details can be found at www.nobel.se.

2012 Recipients:
Peace: European Union
Physics: Serge Haroche and David J. Wineland
Chemistry: Robert J. Lefkowitz and Brian K. Kobilka
Physiology or Medicine: Sir John B. Gurdon and Shinya Yamanaka
Literature: Mo Yan
Economic Sciences: Alvin E. Roth and Lloyd S. Shapley

2013 PULITZER PRIZES

THE ARTS

Fiction: *The Orphan Master's Son,* Adam Johnson
Drama: *Disgraced,* Ayad Akhtar
History: *Embers of War: The Fall of an Empire and the Making of America's Vietnam,* Fredrik Logevall
Biography: *The Black Count: Glory, Revolution, Betrayal and the Real Count of Monte Cristo,* Tom Reiss
Poetry: *Stag's Leap,* Sharon Olds
General Nonfiction: *Devil in the Grove: Thurgood Marshall, the Groveland Boys and the Dawn of a New America,* Gilbert King
Music: *Partita for 8 Voices,* Caroline Shaw

JOURNALISM

Public Service: *Sun Sentinel* (Fort Lauderdale, FL)
Breaking News Reporting: *The Denver Post* staff
Investigative Reporting: David Barstow and Alejandra Xanic von Bertrab, *The New York Times*
Explanatory Reporting: *The New York Times* staff
Local Reporting: Brad Schrade, Jeremy Olson and Glen Howatt, *Star Tribune,* (Minneapolis, MN)
National Reporting: Lisa Song, Elizabeth McGowan and David Hasemyer, *InsideClimate News* (Brooklyn, NY)
International Reporting: David Barboza, *The New York Times*
Feature Writing: Josh Branch, *The New York Times*
Commentary: Bret Stephens, *The Wall Street Journal*
Criticism: Philip Kennicott, *The Washington Post*
Editorial Writing: Tim Nickens and Daniel Ruth, *Tampa Bay Times*
Editorial Cartooning: Steve Sack, *Star Tribune* (Minneapolis, MN)
Breaking News Photography: Rodrigo Abd, Manu Brabo, Narciso Contreras, Khalil Hamra and Muhammed Muheisen, The Associated Press
Feature Photography: Javier Manzano, freelance photographer, Agence France–Presse

2012 GEORGE POLK AWARDS

Awarded for special achievement in journalism.

Political Reporting: David Corn, *Mother Jones: 47% Story*
Foreign Reporting: David Barboza and *Bloomberg News* staff, *The New York Times*: "The Princelings," and *Bloomberg News* staff: "China Betrayed"
War Reporting: David Enders, Austin Tice and correspondent team, McClatchy Newspapers: "Inside Syria" series
Local Reporting: Gina Barton, *Milwaukee Journal Sentinel*: "A Death in Police Custody"
Magazine Reporting: Sarah Stillman, *The New Yorker*: "The Throwaways"
Medical Reporting: Peter Whoriskey, *The Washington Post*: "Biased Research, Big Profits"
Video Reporting: Tracey Shelton, *GlobalPost:* "Inside Syria"
Justice Reporting: Sam Dolnick, *The New York Times*: "Unlocked"
National Reporting: John Hechinger and Janet Lorin, *Bloomberg News*: "Indentured Students"
Education Reporting: Colin Woodard, *Maine Sunday Telegram*: "The Profit Motive"
State Reporting: Ryan Gabrielson, *California Watch*: "Broken Shield"
Television News Reporting: Holly Williams, Andrew Portch, CBS News: coverage of Chinese human rights campaigner (1), coverage of Chinese human rights campaigner (2)
Television Documentary: Martin Smith, Michael Kirk, Marcela Gaviria, Jim Gilmore and Mike Wiser, *Frontline*: "Money, Power and Wall Street"
Business Reporting: David Barstow, Alejandra Xanic von Bertrab, *The New York Times*: "Walmart Abroad"

2012 PEABODY AWARDS

72ND ANNUAL

"Under Fire: Journalists in Combat" (Documentary Channel)
"Why Poverty?" (PBS/Steps International)
"MLK: The Assassination Tapes" (Smithsonian Channel)
"Reel Time: Salat (Bone Dry)" (GMA News TV)
"Sheikh Jarrah, My Neighborhood" (Al Jazeera)
"The Loving Story" (HBO)
"Marina Abramović: The Artist Is Present" (HBO)
"Sri Lanka's Killing Fields: War Crimes Unpunished" (Channel 4, UK)

"Exposure: The Other Side of Jimmy Savile" (ITV1) and "Exposure: Banaz: An Honour Killing" (ITV)
"Putin, Russia and the West" (BBC2, UK)
"Independent Lens: Summer Pasture" (PBS)
"Ford Escape: Exposing a Deadly Defect" (KNXV-TV, Phoenix)
"Deception at Duke" (CBS)
"Superstorm Sandy" (ABC)
"Investigating the IRS" (WTHR-TV)
"Joy in the Congo" (CBS)
"Investigating the Fire" (KMGH-TV)
"Rapido y Furioso (Fast and Furious)" (Univision)
"Breaking News: Tragedy at Sandy Hook Elementary School" (WVIT-TV)
CNN's coverage inside Syria and Homs 2012 (CNN)
"Southland" (TNT)
"Switched at Birth" (ABC Family)
"D.L. Hughley: The Endangered List" (Comedy Central)
"Real Sports with Bryant Gumbel" (HBO)
"Louie" (FX)
"Girls" (HBO)
"Syria 2012" (NPR)
"Teen Contender" (NPR)
"This American Life: What Happened at Dos Erres" (WBEZ Radio)
"Inside the National Recording Registry" (WNYC/Public Radio International)
"The Leonard Lopate Show" (WNYC-FM)
SCOTUSblog (SCOTUSblog.com)
"Snow Fall: The Avalanche at Tunnel Creek" (www.nytimes.com)
"Design Ah!" (NHK Educational Channel)
Rare individual Peabody awarded to Lorne Michaels
"Doctor Who" (BBC America)
Michael Apted's "Up" Series (ITV 1)
"Robin's Journey" (ABC)

AWARDS FOR LITERATURE

NATIONAL BOOK AWARDS 2012

Given annually by the National Book Foundation.

Fiction: *The Round House*, Louise Erdrich
Nonfiction: *Behind the Beautiful Forevers: Life, Death and Hope in a Mumbai Undercity*, Katherine Boo
Poetry: *Bewilderment: New Poems and Translations*, David Ferry
Young People's Literature: *Goblin Secrets*, William Alexander

THE NATIONAL BOOK CRITICS CIRCLE AWARDS 2012

Fiction: *Billy Lynn's Long Halftime Walk*, Ben Fountain
General Nonfiction: *Far from the Tree: Parents, Children and the Search for Identity*, Andrew Solomon
Biography: *The Passage of Power: The Years of Lyndon Johnson*, Robert Caro
Autobiography: *Swimming Studies*, Leanne Shapton
Poetry: *Useless Landscape, or a Guide for Boys*, D.A. Powell
Criticism: *Stranger Magic: Charmed States and the Arabian Nights*, Marina Warner

PEN/FAULKNER AWARD FOR FICTION 2013

An award given by an organization of writers to honor their peers.

Benjamin Alire Sáenz, *Everything Begins and Ends at the Kentucky Club*
Finalists
Amelia Gray, *Threats*
Laird Hunt, *Kind One*
T. Geronimo Johnson, *Hold it 'Til It Hurts*
Thomas Mallon, *Watergate*

THE INDIES CHOICE BOOK AWARD WINNERS 2013

Given annually by the American Booksellers Association, formerly known as the Book Sense Books of the Year.

Adult Fiction: *The Round House: A Novel*, Louise Erdrich
Adult Nonfiction: *Wild: From Lost to Found on the Pacific Crest Trail*, Cheryl Strayed
Adult Debut: *The Snow Child: A Novel*, Eowyn Ivey
Young Adult: *The Fault in Our Stars*, John Green
Middle Reader: *Wonder*, R.J. Palacio
New Picture Book: *Extra Yarn*, Mac Barnett and Jon Klassen (illustrator)

2013 AMERICAN LIBRARY ASSOCIATION AWARDS FOR CHILDREN'S BOOKS

NEWBERY MEDAL

For most distinguished contribution to American literature for children published in 2012:

Katherine Applegate, author, *The One and Only Ivan*
Honor Books
Laura Amy Schlitz, author, *Splendors and Glooms*
Steve Sheinkin, author, *Bomb: The Race to Build—and Steal—the World's Most Dangerous Weapon*
Sheila Turnage, author, *Three Times Lucky*

CALDECOTT MEDAL

For most distinguished American picture book for children published in 2012:

Jon Klassen, illustrator and author, *This Is Not My Hat*
Honor Books
Aaron Reynolds, author; Peter Brown, illustrator; *Creepy Carrots!*
Mac Barnett, author; Jon Klassen, illustrator; *Extra Yarn*
Laura Vaccaro Seeger, illustrator and author, *Green*
Toni Buzzeo, author; David Small, illustrator; *One Cool Friend*
Mary Logue, author; Pamela Zagarenski, illustrator; *Sleep Like a Tiger*

CORETTA SCOTT KING AWARD

For outstanding books by African-American authors and illustrators:

Andrea Davis Pinkney, author and illustrator, *Hand in Hand: Ten Black Men Who Changed America*
Bryan Collier, illustrator, *I, Too, Am America*
Honor Book—Authors
Jacqueline Woodson, *Each Kindness*
Vaunda Micheaux Nelson, *No Crystal Stair: A Documentary Novel of the Life and Work of Lewis Micheaux, Harlem Bookseller*
Honor Books—Illustrators
Daniel Minter, *Ellen's Broom*
Christopher Myers, illustrator and author, *H. O. R. S. E.*
Kadir Nelson, illustrator, *I Have a Dream: Martin Luther King, Jr.*

CORETTA SCOTT KING–VIRGINIA HAMILTON AWARD FOR LIFETIME ACHIEVEMENT

Demetria Tucker, recipient

MICHAEL L. PRINTZ AWARD

For excellence in writing literature for young adults:

Nick Lake, author, *In Darkness*
Honor Books
Benjamin Alire Sáenz, author, *Aristotle and Dante Discover the Secrets of the Universe*
Elizabeth Weinn, author, *Code Name Verity*
Terry Pratchett, author, *Dodger*
Beverley Brenna, author, *The White Bicycle*

SCHNEIDER FAMILY BOOK AWARD

For books that embody an artistic expression of the disability experience:

Harry Mazer and Peter Lerangis, authors, *Somebody, Please Tell Me Who I Am*
Sarah Lean, author, *A Dog Called Homeless*
Claire Alexander, author, *Back to Front and Upside Down!*

ROBERT F. SIBERT AWARD
For most distinguished informational book for children published in 2012:

Steve Sheinkin, author, *Bomb: The Race to Build—and Steal—the World's Most Dangerous Weapon*
Honor Books
Robert Byrd, author and illustrator, *Electric Ben: The Amazing Life and Times of Benjamin Franklin*
Phillip M. Hoose, author and illustrator, *Moonbird: A Year on the Wind with the Great Survivor B95*
Deborah Hopkinson, author, *Titanic: Voices from the Disaster*

PURA BELPRÉ AWARDS
For the Latino author whose work best portrays, celebrates and affirms Latino culture in a children's book:

Benjamin Alire Sáenz, author award, *Aristotle and Dante Discover the Secrets of the Universe*
David Diaz, illustrator award, *Martín de Porres: The Rose in the Desert*
Honor Books—Authors
Sonia Manzano, *The Revolution of Evelyn Serrano*
Honor Books—Illustrators
No honor books named.

THEODOR SEUSS GEISEL MEDAL
For the author and illustrator of the most distinguished contribution to the body of American children's literature known as beginning reader books published in 2012:

Ethan Long, author, *Up, Tall and High!*
Honor Books can be found at www.ala.org

MILDRED L. BATCHELDER AWARD
For the best children's book in English translation (first published in a foreign country) published in the US:

Dial Books, an imprint of Penguin Group (USA) Inc., publisher, *My Family for the War*, written by Anne C. Voorhoeve, translated by Tammi Reichel
Honor Books can be found at www.ala.org

ANDREW CARNEGIE MEDAL FOR EXCELLENCE IN CHILDREN'S VIDEO

Katja Torneman, producer, *Anna, Emma and the Condors*

MAY HILL ARBUTHNOT LECTURE AWARD

Andrea Davis Pinckney, recipient

MARGARET A. EDWARDS AWARD
For lifetime achievement in writing books for young adults:

Tamora Pierce, recipient

WILLIAM C. MORRIS AWARD
For a debut book published by a first-time author writing for teens:

Rachel Hartman, author, *Seraphina*

YALSA AWARD FOR EXCELLENCE IN NONFICTION FOR YOUNG ADULTS

Steve Sheinkin, author, *Bomb: The Race to Build—and Steal—the World's Most Dangerous Weapon*

ODYSSEY AWARD
For the best audiobook produced for children and/or young adults:

Brilliance Audio, producer, *The Fault in Our Stars,* written by John Green, narrated by Kate Rudd

STONEWALL BOOK AWARD
Mike Morgan & Larry Romans Children's & Young Adult Literature Award given annually to English language children's and young adult books of exceptional merit relating to the gay, lesbian, bisexual and transgender experience:

Benjamin Alire Sáenz, author, *Aristotle and Dante Discover the Secrets of the Universe*

THE NATIONAL JEWISH BOOK AWARDS 2012
Given annually to the most outstanding books on aspects of Jewish life. 62nd annual.

Jewish Book of the Year: *City of Promises: A History of the Jews of New York, with a Visual Essay by Diana L. Linden,* Howard B. Rock, Annie Polland, Daniel Soyer and Jeffrey S. Gurock (Deborah Dash Moore, ed.)
Lifetime Achievement: Eric R. Kandel
American Jewish Studies: *Messianism, Secrecy and Mysticism*, Laura Arnold Leibman
Education and Jewish Identity: *Development, Learning and Community*, Jeffrey S. Kress
Anthologies and Collections: *Jewish Jocks: An Unorthodox Hall of Fame*, Franklin Foer and Marc Tracy, editors
Biography, Autobiography and Memoir: *Howard Fast: Life and Literature in the Left Lane*, Gerald Sorin
Children's and Young Adult Literature: *Meet at the Ark at Eight*, Ulrich Hub, illustrated by Jörg Mühle
Contemporary Jewish Life and Practice: *Davening: A Guide to Meaningful Jewish Prayer*, Rabbi Zalman M. Schachter-Shalomi with Joel Segel
Fiction: *The Innocents*, Francesca Segal
History: *Israel: A History*, Anita Shapira
Holocaust: *Collect and Record: Jewish Holocaust Documentation in Early Postwar Europe*, Laura Jockusch
Illustrated Children's Books: *The Shema in the Mezuzah: Listening to Each Other*, Rabbi Sandy Eisenberg Sasso, illustrated by Joani Keller Rothenberg
Modern Jewish Thought and Experience: *Koren Talmud Bavli*, Rabbi Adin Even-Israel Steinsaltz
Debut Fiction: *The Sensualist: A Novella*, Daniel Torday
Scholarship: *The Chosen Few: How Education Shaped Jewish History, 70–1492*, Maristella Botticini and Zvi Eckstein
Sephardic Culture: *Poverty and Welfare Among the Portuguese Jews of Early Modern Amsterdam*, Tirtsah Levie Bernfeld
Women's Studies: *The Men's Section: Orthodox Jewish Men in an Egalitarian World*, Elana Maryles Sztokman
Writing Based on Archival Material: *The History of the Holocaust in Romania*, Jean Ancel, author, Yaffah Murciano, translator, Leon Volovici, editor

THE MAN BOOKER PRIZE 2012
Given annually to the best full-length novel written in English by a citizen of the UK, the Commonwealth, Eire, Pakistan or South Africa.

Bring Up the Bodies, Hilary Mantel
Shortlisted titles
Narcopolis, Jeet Thayil
Swimming Home, Deborah Levy
The Garden of Evening Mists, Tan Twan Eng
The Lighthouse, Alison Moore
Umbrella, Will Self

COSTA BOOK AWARDS 2012
An award given to celebrate the most enjoyable British writing of the year.

Novel: *Bring Up the Bodies*, Hilary Mantel
First Novel: *The Innocents*, Francesca Segal
Poetry: *The Overhaul*, Kathleen Jamie
Biography: *Dotter of Her Father's Eyes*, Mary and Bryan Talbot
Children's Book: *Maggot Moon*, Sally Gardner
Book of the Year: *Bring Up the Bodies*, Hilary Mantel

2013 WOMEN'S PRIZE FOR FICTION
A British award celebrating the excellence of women's writing.
May We Be Forgiven, A.M. Homes
Shortlisted titles
Where'd You Go, Bernadette, Maria Semple
Bring Up the Bodies, Hilary Mantel
Life After Life, Kate Atkinson
Flight Behaviour, Barbara Kingsolver
NW, Zadie Smith

THE EDGAR AWARDS 2013
The Mystery Writers of America honor the best in mystery writing produced in the previous year. Named in honor of Edgar Allan Poe.
Best Novel: *Live by Night*, Dennis Lehane
Best First Novel by an American Author: *The Expats*, Chris Pavone
Best Paperback Original: *The Last Policeman: A Novel*, Ben H. Winters
Best Fact Crime: *Midnight in Peking: How the Murder of a Young Englishwoman Haunted the Last Days of Old China*, Paul French
Best Critical/Biographical Work: *The Scientific Sherlock Holmes: Cracking the Case with Science and Forensics*, James O'Brien
Best Short Story: "The Unremarkable Heart," Karin Slaughter, in *Mystery Writers of America Presents: Vengeance*
Best Juvenile: *The Quick Fix*, Jack D. Ferraiolo
Best Young Adult: *Code Name Verity*, Elizabeth Wein
Best Television Episode Teleplay: "A Scandal in Belgravia" ("Sherlock"), Steven Moffat
Robert L. Fish Award: "When They Are Done with Us," Patricia Smith
Grand Master: Ken Follett and Margaret Maron
Raven Award: Mysterious Galaxy Bookstore, San Diego and Redondo Beach, CA; Oline Cogdill
Ellery Queen Award: Akashic Books
Simon & Schuster–Mary Higgins Clark Award: *The Other Woman*, Hank Phillippi Ryan

THE HUGO AWARDS 2012
Also known as the Science Fiction Achievement Award, given annually by the World Science Fiction Society. 57th annual.
Best Novel: *Among Others*, Jo Walton
Best Novella: "The Man Who Bridged the Mist," Kij Johnson
Best Novelette: "Six Months, Three Days," Charlie Jane Anders
Best Related Work: *The Encyclopedia of Science Fiction, Third Edition*, John Clute, David Langford, Peter Nicholls and Graham Sleight, editors
Best Short Story: "The Paper Menagerie," Ken Liu
Best Graphic Story: *Digger*, Ursula Vernon

Best Dramatic Presentation, Long Form: "Game of Thrones (Season 1)," created by David Benioff and D.B. Weiss; written by David Benioff, D.B. Weiss, Bryan Cogman, Jane Espenson and George R.R. Martin; directed by Brian Kirk, Daniel Minahan, Tim van Patten and Alan Taylor
Best Dramatic Presentation, Short Form: "The Doctor's Wife" ("Doctor Who"), written by Neil Gaiman, directed by Richard Clark
Best Editor, Short Form: Sheila Williams
Best Editor, Long Form: Betsy Wollheim
Best Professional Artist: John Picacio
Best Semiprozine: *Locus*, edited by Liza Groen Trombi, Kirsten Gong-Wong et al.
Best Fanzine: *SF Signal*, John DeNardo
Best Fan Writer: Jim C. Hines
Best Fan Artist: Maurine Starkey
John W. Campbell Award for Best New Writer: E. Lily Yu

THE NEBULA AWARDS 2012
48th annual awards given by Science Fiction and Fantasy Writers of America, Inc.
Novel: *2312*, Kim Stanley Robinson
Novella: "After the Fall, Before the Fall, During the Fall," Nancy Kress
Novelette: "Close Encounters," Andy Duncan
Short Story: "Immersion," Aliette de Bodard
Dramatic Production: *Beasts of the Southern Wild*, Lucy Alibar and Benh Zeitlin, writers; Benh Zeitlin, director
Andre Norton Award: *Fair Coin*, E.C. Myers
Damon Knight Grand Master Award: Gene Wolfe
Solstice Award: Carl Sagan and Ginjer Buchanan
Service to SFWA Award: Michael H. Payne

THE LAMBDA LITERARY AWARDS 2013
25th annual, to recognize excellence in lesbian/gay/bisexual/transgender (LGBT) literature, for works published in 2012.
Bisexual Literature: tie: *In One Person*, John Irving, and *My Awesome Place: The Autobiography of Cheryl B*, Cheryl Burke
Transgender Fiction: *The Collection: Short Fiction from the Transgender Vanguard*, Tom Léger and Riley MacLeod, editors
Transgender Nonfiction: *Transfeminist Perspectives in and Beyond Transgender and Gender Studies*, Anne Enke
LGBT Anthology: *No Straight Lines: Four Decades of Queer Comics*, Justin Hall
LGBT Children/Young Adult: *Aristotle and Dante Discover the Secrets of the Universe*, Benjamin Alire Sáenz
LGBT Drama/Theater: *The Myopia and Other Plays*, David Greenspan
LGBT Nonfiction: *Flagrant Conduct: The Story of Lawrence v. Texas*, Dale Carpenter
LGBT Science Fiction/Fantasy/Horror: *Green Thumb*, Tom Cardamone
LGBT Studies: *Performing Queer Latinidad: Dance, Sexuality, Politics*, Ramón H. Rivera-Servera
LGBT Debut Fiction: *The Summer We Got Free*, Mia McKenzie
Lesbian Erotica: *The Harder She Comes: Butch/Femme Erotica*, D.L. King
Lesbian Fiction: *The World We Found: A Novel*, Thrity Umrigar
Lesbian Memoir/Biography: *Why Be Happy When You Could Be Normal?*, Jeanette Winterson
Lesbian Mystery: *Ill Will*, J. M. Redmann
Lesbian Poetry: *Sea and Fog*, Etel Adnan
Lesbian Romance: *Month of Sundays*, Yolanda Wallace
Gay Erotica: *The Facialist*, Mykola Dementiuk
Gay Fiction: *Everything Begins and Ends at the Kentucky Club*, Benjamin Alire Sáenz
Gay Memoir/Biography: *Fire in the Belly: The Life and Times of David Wojnarowicz*, Cynthia Carr
Gay Mystery: *Lake in the Mountain*, Jeffrey Round
Gay Poetry: *He Do the Gay Man in Different Voices*, Stephen S. Mills
Gay Romance: *Kamikaze Boys*, Jay Bell

THE JAMES BEARD FOUNDATION/KITCHENAID BOOK AWARDS 2013

Given annually to the best original, English-language books on culinary topics published in the previous year.

American Cooking: *Mastering the Art of Southern Cooking,* Nathalie Dupree and Cynthia Graubart
Baking: *Flour Water Salt Yeast: The Fundamentals of Artisan Bread and Pizza,* Ken Forkish
Beverage: *Wine Grapes: A Complete Guide to 1,368 Vine Varieties, Including Their Origins and Flavours,* Jancis Robinson, Julia Harding and José Vouillamoz
Cooking from a Professional Point of View: *Toqué! Creators of a New Quebec Gastronomy,* Normand Laprise
General: *Canal House Cooks Every Day,* Melissa Hamilton and Christopher Hirsheimer
Focus on Health: *Cooking Light The New Way to Cook Light: Fresh Food & Bold Flavors for Today's Home Cook,* Scott Mowbray and Ann Taylor Pittman
International: *Jerusalem: A Cookbook,* Yotam Ottolenghi and Sami Tamimi
Photography: *What Katie Ate: Recipes and Other Bits & Pieces,* Katie Quinn Davies
Reference and Scholarship: *The Art of Fermentation: An In-Depth Exploration of Essential Concepts and Processes from Around the World,* Sandor Ellix Katz
Single Subject: *Ripe: A Cook in the Orchard,* Nigel Slater
Focus on Vegetables: *Roots,* Diane Morgan
Writing and Literature: *Yes, Chef: A Memoir,* Marcus Samuelsson
Cookbook Hall of Fame: Anne Willan
Cookbook of the Year: *Gran Cocina Latina: The Food of Latin America,* Maricel E. Presilla

AWARDS FOR MUSIC

2012 AMERICAN MUSIC AWARDS
40th Annual Awards

Artist of the Year Justin Bieber

POP/ROCK

Male Artist: Justin Bieber
Female Artist: Katy Perry
Band, Duo or Group: Maroon 5
Album: *Believe,* Justin Bieber

SOUL/RHYTHM & BLUES

Male Artist: Usher
Female Artist: Beyoncé
Album: *Talk That Talk,* Rihanna

ALTERNATIVE ROCK MUSIC

Artist: Linkin Park

ADULT CONTEMPORARY MUSIC

Artist: Adele

SPRINT NEW ARTIST OF THE YEAR

Carly Rae Jepsen

COUNTRY

Male Artist: Luke Bryan
Female Artist: Taylor Swift
Band, Duo or Group: Lady Antebellum
Album: *Blown Away,* Carrie Underwood

RAP/HIP-HOP

Artist: Nicki Minaj
Album: *Pink Friday: Roman Reloaded,* Nicki Minaj

LATIN

Artist: Shakira

2012 COUNTRY MUSIC AWARDS
46th Annual Awards

Entertainer of the Year: Blake Shelton
Male Vocalist of the Year: Blake Shelton
Female Vocalist of the Year: Miranda Lambert
Vocal Group of the Year: Little Big Town
Vocal Duo of the Year: Thompson Square
New Artist of the Year: Hunter Hayes
Single of the Year: "Pontoon," Little Big Town
Album of the Year: *Chief,* Eric Church
Song of the Year: "Over You," Miranda Lambert and Blake Shelton
Musician of the Year: Mac McAnally
Musical Event of the Year: "Feel Like a Rock Star," Kenny Chesney and Tim McGraw
Video of the Year: "Red Solo Cup," Toby Keith

2013 ACADEMY OF COUNTRY MUSIC AWARDS
48th Annual Awards

Entertainer of the Year: Luke Bryan
Male Vocalist of the Year: Jason Aldean
Female Vocalist of the Year: Miranda Lambert
Vocal Group of the Year: Little Big Town
Vocal Duo of the Year: Thompson Square
Songwriter of the Year: Dallas Davidson
New Artist of the Year: Florida Georgia Line
Single Record of the Year: "Over You," Miranda Lambert
Album of the Year: *Chief,* Eric Church
Song of the Year: "Over You," Miranda Lambert (Miranda Lambert, Blake Shelton, songwriters)
Video of the Year: "Tornado," Little Big Town (Producer: Iris Baker, Director: Shane Drake)
Vocal Event of the Year: "The Only Way I Know," Jason Aldean with Luke Bryan and Eric Church

2013 GRAMMY AWARDS

Record of the Year: "Somebody That I Used to Know," Gotye featuring Kimbra
Album of the Year: *Babel,* Mumford & Sons
Song of the Year: "We Are Young," Jack Antonoff, Jeff Bhasker, Andrew Dost and Nate Ruess, songwriters (fun. featuring Janelle Monáe)
Best New Artist: fun.
Best Pop Solo Performance: "Set Fire to the Rain [Live]," Adele
Best Pop Duo/Group Performance: "Somebody That I Used to Know," Gotye featuring Kimbra
Best Pop Instrumental Album: *Impressions,* Chris Botti
Best Pop Vocal Album: *Stronger,* Kelly Clarkson
Best Dance Recording: "Bangarang," Skrillex featuring Sirah
Best Dance/Electronica Album: *Bangarang,* Skrillex
Best Traditional Pop Vocal Album: *Kisses on the Bottom,* Paul McCartney
Best Rock Performance: "Lonely Boy," The Black Keys
Best Hard Rock/Metal Performance: "Love Bites (So Do I)," Halestorm
Best Rock Song: "Lonely Boy," Dan Auerbach, Brian Burton and Patrick Carney, songwriters (The Black Keys)
Best Rock Album: *El Camino,* The Black Keys
Best Alternative Music Album: *Making Mirrors,* Gotye
Best R&B Performance: "Climax," Usher
Best Traditional R&B Performance: "Love on Top," Beyoncé
Best R&B Song: "Adorn," Miguel Pimentel, songwriter (Miguel)
Best Urban Contemporary Album: *Channel Orange,* Frank Ocean
Best R&B Album: *Black Radio,* Robert Glasper Experiment
Best Rap Performance: "N****s in Paris," Jay-Z and Kanye West
Best Rap/Sung Collaboration: "No Church in the Wild," Jay-Z and Kanye West featuring Frank Ocean and The-Dream

Best Rap Song: "N****s in Paris," Shawn Carter, Mike Dean, Chauncey Hollis and Kanye West, songwriters (W.A. Donaldson, songwriter) (Jay-Z and Kanye West)
Best Rap Album: *Take Care,* Drake
Best Country Solo Performance: "Blown Away," Carrie Underwood
Best Country Duo/Group Performance: "Pontoon," Little Big Town
Best Country Song: "Blown Away," Josh Kear and Chris Tompkins, songwriters (Carrie Underwood)
Best Country Album: *Uncaged,* Zac Brown Band
Best New Age Album: *Echoes of Love,* Omar Akram
Best Jazz Vocal Album: *Radio Music Society,* Esperanza Spalding
Best Improvised Jazz Solo: "Hot House," Gary Burton and Chick Corea, soloists
Best Jazz Instrumental Album, Individual or Group: *Unity Band,* Pat Metheny Unity Band
Best Large Jazz Ensemble Album: *Dear Diz (Every Day I Think of You),* Arturo Sandoval
Best Latin Jazz Album: *¡Ritimo!,* The Clare Fischer Latin Jazz Big Band
Best Gospel/Contemporary Christian Music Performance: "10,000 Reasons (Bless the Lord)," Matt Redman
Best Gospel Song: "Go Get It," Erica Campbell, Tina Campbell and Warryn Campbell, songwriters (Mary Mary)
Best Contemporary Christian Music Song: tie: "10,000 Reasons (Bless the Lord)," Jonas Myrin and Matt Redman, songwriters (Matt Redman), and "Your Presence Is Heaven," Israel Houghton and Micah Massey, songwriters (Israel & New Breed)
Best Gospel Album: *Gravity,* Lecrae
Best Contemporary Christian Music Album: *Eye on It,* TobyMac
Best Latin Pop Album: *MTV Unplugged Deluxe Edition,* Juanes
Best Latin, Rock, Urban or Alternative Album: *Imaginaries,* Quetzal
Best Tropical Latin Album: *Retro,* Marlow Rosado y La Riqueña
Best Regional Mexican Music Album (Including Tejano): *Pecados y Milagros,* Lila Downs
Best Americana Album: *Slipstream,* Bonnie Raitt
Best Bluegrass Album: *Nobody Knows You,* Steep Canyon Rangers
Best Blues Album: *Locked Down,* Dr. John
Best Folk Album: *The Goat Rodeo Sessions,* Yo-Yo Ma, Stuart Duncan, Edgar Meyer and Chris Thile
Best Regional Roots Music Album: *The Band Courtbouillon,* Wayne Toups, Steve Riley and Wilson Savoy
Best Reggae Album: *Rebirth,* Jimmy Cliff
Best World Music Album: *The Living Room Sessions Part 1,* Ravi Shankar
Best Children's Album: *Can You Canoe?,* The Okee Dokee Brothers
Best Spoken Word Album: *Society's Child: My Autobiography,* Janis Ian
Best Comedy Album: *Blow Your Pants Off,* Jimmy Fallon
Best Musical Theater Album: *Once: A New Musical*
Best Compilation Soundtrack Album for Visual Media: *Midnight in Paris,* various artists
Best Score Soundtrack Album for Visual Media: *The Girl with the Dragon Tattoo,* Trent Reznor and Atticus Ross, composers
Best Song Written for Visual Media: "Safe & Sound" (from *The Hunger Games*), T Bone Burnett, Taylor Swift, John Paul White and Joy Williams, songwriters (Taylor Swift and The Civil Wars)
Best Instrumental Composition: "Mozart Goes Dancing," Chick Corea, composer (Chick Corea and Gary Burton)
Best Instrumental Arrangement: "How About You," Gil Evans, arranger (Gil Evans Project)
Best Instrumental Arrangement Accompanying Vocalist(s): "City of Roses," Thara Memory and Esperanza Spalding, arrangers (Esperanza Spalding)
Best Recording Package: *Biophilia,* Michael Amzalag and Mathias Augustyniak, art directors (Björk)
Best Boxed or Special Limited Edition Package: *Woody at 100: The Woody Guthrie Centennial Collection,* Fritz Klaetke, art director (Woody Guthrie)
Best Album Notes: *Singular Genius: The Complete ABC singles,* Billy Vera, album notes writer (Ray Charles)
Best Historical Album: *The Smile Sessions (Deluxe Box Set),* Alan Boyd, Mark Linett, Brian Wilson and Dennis Wolfe, compilation producers; Sam Okell and Mark Linett, mastering engineers (The Beach Boys)
Best Engineered Album, Non-Classical: *The Goat Rodeo Sessions,* Richard King, mastering engineer; (Yo-Yo Ma, Stuart Duncan, Edgar Meyer and Chris Thile)
Producer of the Year, Non-Classical: Dan Auerbach
Best Remixed Recording, Non-Classical: "Promises (Skrillex and Nero Remix)," Skrillex, remixer (Nero)
Best Surround Sound Album: *Modern Cool,* Jim Anderson, surround mix engineer; Darcy Proper, surround mastering engineer; Michael Friedman, surround producer (Patricia Barber)
Best Engineered Album, Classical: *Life and Breath—Choral Works By René Clausen,* Tom Caulfield and John Newton, engineers; Mark Donahue, mastering engineer (Charles Bruffy and Kansas City Chorale)
Producer of the Year, Classical: Blanton Alspaugh
Best Orchestral Performance: *Adams: Harmonielehre and Short Ride in a Fast Machine,* Michael Tilsen Thomas, conductor (San Francisco Symphony)
Best Opera Recording: *Wagner: Der Ring Des Nibelungen,* James Levine and Fabio Luisi, conductors; Hans-Peter König, Jay Hunter Morris, Bryn Terfel and Deborah Voigt; Jay David Saks, producer (The Metropolitan Opera Orchestra; The Metropolitan Opera Chorus)
Best Choral Performance: *Life and Breath—Choral Works by René Clausen,* Charles Bruffy, conductor (Matthew Gladden, Lindsey Lang, Rebecca Lloyd, Sarah Tannehill and Pamela Williamson; Kansas City Chorale)
Best Classical Compendium: *Penderecki: Fonogrammi; Horn Concerto; Partita; The Awakening of Jacob; Anaklasis* Antoni Wit, conductor; Aleksandra Nagórko and Andrzej Sasin, producers
Best Chamber Music/Small Ensemble Performance: *Meanwhile,* Eighth Blackbird
Best Classical Instrumental Solo: *Kurtág and Ligeti: Music for Viola,* Kim Kashkashian, conductor
Best Classical Vocal Solo: *Poèmes,* Renée Fleming (Alan Gilbert and Seiji Ozawa; Orchestre National de France and Orchestre Philharmonique de Radio France)
Best Contemporary Classical Composition: *Meanwhile: Incidental Music to Imaginary Puppet Plays,* Stephen Hartke, composer (Eighth Blackbird)
Best Short Form Music Video: "We Found Love," Rihanna featuring Calvin Harris
Best Long Form Music Video: *Big Easy Express,* Mumford & Sons, Edward Sharpe and The Magnetic Zeros and Old Crow Medicine Show

Index